September 7–11, 2015
Paris, France

Association for Computing Machinery

Advancing Computing as a Science & Profession

MobiCom '15

Proceedings of the 21st Annual International Conference on Mobile Computing and Networking

Sponsored by:

ACM SIGMOBILE

Supported by:

Atos Worldline, NSF, CISCO, Google, HP, Alcatel-Lucent, Huawei, Inria, Microsoft Research, NEC Laboratories America, Orange, Technicolor, LIP6, and UPMC

Association for
Computing Machinery

Advancing Computing as a Science & Profession

The Association for Computing Machinery
2 Penn Plaza, Suite 701
New York, New York 10121-0701

Notice to Past Authors of ACM-Published Articles
ACM intends to create a complete electronic archive of all articles and/or other material previously published by ACM. If you have written a work that has been previously published by ACM in any journal or conference proceedings prior to 1978, or any SIG Newsletter at any time, and you do NOT want this work to appear in the ACM Digital Library, please inform permissions@acm.org, stating the title of the work, the author(s), and where and when published.

ISBN: 978-1-4503-3619-2 (Digital)

ISBN: 978-1-4503-4027-4 (Print)

Additional copies may be ordered prepaid from:

ACM Order Department
PO Box 30777
New York, NY 10087-0777, USA

Phone: 1-800-342-6626 (USA and Canada)
+1-212-626-0500 (Global)
Fax: +1-212-944-1318
E-mail: acmhelp@acm.org
Hours of Operation: 8:30 am – 4:30 pm ET

Printed in the USA

General Chairs' Welcome

MobiCom 2015 represents a unique experience, bringing together a premier forum on Mobile Computing and Networking with the land of *savoir-vivre* and the amazing city of Paris.

This year's MobiCom continues its tradition of excellence and diversity to illustrate cutting-edge developments within the field. The research and innovation presented at the MobiCom`15 conference play an integral role in all sectors of our economy and society; both by strengthening their foundation as well as advancing towards the future. Paris, the City of Lights, provides an ideal balance between intellectual work and the numerous pleasures that the city can offer — be it museums, gastronomy or simply enjoying the beauty of its surroundings. Paris is not only a hot spot for tourism, but also a high-tech corridor with its universities, large company headquarters and myriads of SMEs. We are very pleased to welcome you to various locations around the city, such as the Jussieu Campus of UPMC Sorbonne University in the vibrant heart of Paris, the Pasteur Institute facility where the main event is hosted, and of course, the Eiffel Tower landmark of our capital city.

A dedicated team of individuals has devoted their time and expertise to make MobiCom 2015 enjoyable for you in all dimensions.

This weeklong event is articulated around the main conference and its strong program that was put together by Sneha Kumar Kasera and Heather Zheng, along with the support of their solid program committee.

We have enriched the technical program with high profile keynotes and invited talk presentations. We hope that they will inspire and influence your thoughts and vision for the future.

- *Agility and Fragility in a Real-Time World,* Gilles Grapinet (Atos SEVP & Worldline CEO)
- *Research Challenges and Opportunities in a Mobility Centric World,* Jim Kurose (Umass and NSF)
- *European Research Towards 5G,* Rémy Bayou (European Commission, DG Connect)

In addition, participants will view and discuss state of the art demo and poster presentations in a session organized by Thanasis Korakis, Nathalie Mitton and Aki Nakao for the demos; and Fan Ye, Gustavo Marfia and Gaogang Xie for posters. Our student research competition co-chairs, Mehmet Can Vuran and Andrzej Duda, have selected the best student poster from a highly talented pool. Wenjun Hu, Rui Aguiar and Hirsohi Esaki have put together a panel on a hotly debated topic "Big data, IoT, ... buzz words for academia or reality for industry." Lars Wolf, Dae Young Kim, and Xia Zhou have done an excellent job as publicity co-chairs, as has Hubert Tardieu acting in the role of corporate liaison chair.

Marco Leverato, Marcelo Dias de Amorim and Jorg Wilmer have selected 9 informative workshops that nicely complement the conference on core topical subjects. Finally, we will bring together the MobiCom community for a celebratory banquet organized at the historic Maison des Polytechniciens.

MobiCom has a longstanding dedication to promoting student participation. Our student travel grant chairs, Mario Gerla, Jiannong Cao and Martin May, have used the generous support from our government agency supporters and corporate sponsors to allow grant awardees the opportunity to attend this event.

MobiCom 2015 also materializes into proceedings. Aline Viana deserves our special thanks in supporting the authors and orchestrating the conference's content, also working with Lisa M. Tolles and the Sheridan Communications team.

We knew that organizing MobiCom would require a huge effort. This comes true as the result of a dynamic, motivated and friendly team composed of Manuella Portier, Frederic Vaissade, Nina Kurose and Marguerite Sos, supported by PhD candidates, Post-Docs and faculties of the Networking research group at LIP6/UPMC, the LINCS laboratory, and our other supporting institutions. Our sincere gratitude for your time and effort to master all issues and challenge the unpredictable. The web site was designed and managed by our preferred team composed of Rita Tse and Yubin Xiao. Our gratitude also goes to the Steering Committee for their trust, support and guidance.

We would especially like to commend our two award winners this year. Romit Roy Choudhury, recipient of the 2015 SIGMOBILE RockStar Award, is recognized for outstanding research made early on in his career; and Prof. Mario Gerla, who is awarded this year's SIGMOBILE Outstanding Contribution Award, for his significant contributions to the field of mobile computing, communications and wireless networking.

We are very grateful to our sponsors for their financial support and confidence that has enabled us to organize a high-level event in a beautiful venue. Thanks to Atos Worldline and NSF (Platinum sponsors); SIGMOBILE (Gold sponsor); CISCO, Google, and HP (Silver sponsors); Alcatel-Lucent, Huawei, Inria, LIP6, Microsoft, NEC laboratories, Orange, Technicolor, and UPMC (Bronze sponsors).

Our objective is to provide you with a memorable MobiCom 2015 conference. We hope that you take advantage of this enriched and busy week in Paris to discuss and share your *savoir-faire,* as well as to enjoy our unique art of living.

Serge Fdida
MobiCom 2015 General Chair
UPMC Sorbonne University, France

Giovanni Pau
MobiCom 2015 General Chair
UPMC Sorbonne University, France

Technical Program Committee Chairs' Message

Welcome to ACM MobiCom 2015, the 21st Annual International Conference on Mobile Computing and Networking. MobiCom is the premier forum for publishing and presenting cutting-edge research in mobile systems and wireless networks. The technical program this year features 38 outstanding papers that cover a wide variety of topics including energy, sensing, security, wireless access, applications, localization, Internet of things, mobile cloud, measurement and analysis. We created a new *Experience* track this year to encourage authors to present extensive experiences with implementation, deployment, and operations of mobile computing and wireless networks. One of the accepted papers is an Experience paper on cellular networks.

This year's call for papers attracted 207 qualified submissions from across the globe that were carefully reviewed by 46 Technical Program Committee (TPC) members (+2 TPC chairs) along with a selected group of external experts. The TPC was formed with the goal of covering diverse research expertise as well as diverse perspectives and approaches. The TPC included researchers from 12 countries including China, France, Germany, India, Italy, Singapore, South Korea, Spain, Sweden, Switzerland, UK, and USA. 25% of the members were female, the highest ever in the history of MobiCom. We also had broad industry participation with TPC members from Alcatel-Lucent, Google, HP, IBM, Microsoft, NEC, and Telefonica.

The paper review process was double-blinded and carried out in three phases. In the first phase, each paper was reviewed by at least three TPC members, and the top 112 papers were selected for the second phase. In addition to reviewer scores, reviewer confidence and normalization with respect to other papers in a reviewer's pile, were also considered in selecting papers. In the second phase, each paper was reviewed by at least two more reviewers followed by an online, often intense, discussion, producing 68 papers for the final phase. The final TPC meeting was held on May 28th and 29th in Salt Lake City, Utah. These 68 papers were organized by their topic areas, and discussed at length at the meeting. Eventually, 38 papers were shortlisted for inclusion in the program and a shepherd from the TPC was assigned to each of these papers. As the last step, each of the shortlisted papers was shepherded through a "blind" process where the authors interacted with all the reviewers and the shepherd to address the review comments without knowing the reviewers' or the shepherds' identities. The end result is an exciting technical program composed of 38 very high quality papers.

During the review process, Prof. Robin Kravets, the TPC co-chair of MobiCom 2013, handled the papers that were co-authored by TPC chairs, and those that had conflict-of-interest with both TPC chairs. To ensure fairness and preserve the anonymity of all authors and reviewers, the assignment of reviewers, the reviews and discussions of these papers were done out of band without any exposure to the TPC chairs.

As TPC co-chairs, we would like to express our sincere gratitude to many for their hard work and contributions. First, we thank all the authors who submitted their great research to the conference. We are very grateful to all the TPC members and external reviewers – their dedication and enthusiasm were instrumental in constructing the strong technical program. We also thank the entire MobiCom 2015 team, especially General chairs Giovanni Pau and Serge Fdida, Publication chairs Aline Viana and Nina Kurose, and Lisa Tolles at Sheridan Communications, for their tremendous support and behind-the-scenes effort. Finally, we extend our thanks and appreciation to the MobiCom Steering Committee for their guidance and wisdom.

Again, welcome to MobiCom 2015 in the beautiful city of Paris. We hope that you will enjoy the program!

Heather Zheng
Technical Program Co-Chair
University of California at Santa Barbara, USA

Sneha Kumar Kasera
Technical Program Co-Chair
University of Utah, USA

Table of Contents

ACM MobiCom 2015 Conference Organization xiii

MobiCom 2015 Sponsor & Supporters xvi

Keynote Address 1

- **Agility and Fragility in a Real-Time World** 1
  Gilles Grapinet *(ATOS & Chief Executive Officer Worldline)*

Session 1: Energy Energy Energy

- **Wireless Power Hotspot that Charges All of Your Devices** 2
  Lixin Shi, Zachary Kabelac, Dina Katabi, David Perreault *(Massachusetts Institute of Technology)*
- **Rethinking Energy-Performance Trade-Off in Mobile Web Page Loading** 14
  Duc Hoang Bui *(Korea Advanced Institute of Science and Technology)*, Yunxin Liu *(Microsoft Research)*,
  Hyosu Kim, Insik Shin *(Korea Advanced Institute of Science and Technology)*, Feng Zhao *(Microsoft Research)*
- **Optimizing Smartphone Power Consumption through Dynamic Resolution Scaling** 27
  Songtao He *(University of Science and Technology of China & Microsoft Research)*,
  Yunxin Liu, Hucheng Zhou *(Microsoft Research)*
- **Smartphone Background Activities in the Wild: Origin, Energy Drain, and Optimization** 40
  Xiaomeng Chen, Abhilash Jindal, Ning Ding, Yu Charlie Hu *(Purdue University, Mobile Enerlytics)*,
  Maruti Gupta, Rath Vannithamby *(Intel Corporation)*
- **Precise Power Delay Profiling with Commodity WiFi** 53
  Yaxiong Xie, Zhenjiang Li, Mo Li *(Nanyang Technological University)*

Session 2: RF can Sense

- **Understanding and Modeling of WiFi Signal Based Human Activity Recognition** 65
  Wei Wang *(Nanjing University)*, Alex X. Liu *(Nanjing University & Michigan State University)*,
  Muhammad Shahzad *(Michigan State University)*, Kang Ling, Sanglu Lu *(Nanjing University)*
- **WiDraw: Enabling Hands-Free Drawing in the Air on Commodity WiFGi Devices** 77
  Li Sun *(University at Buffalo, SUNY)*, Souvik Sen *(HP Labs)*,
  Dimitrios Koutsonikolas *(University at Buffalo, SUNY)*, Kyu-Han Kim *(HP Labs)*
- **Keystroke Recognition Using WiFi Signals** 90
  Kamran Ali *(Michigan State University)*, Alex X. Liu *(Michigan State University & Nanjing University)*,
  Wei Wang *(Nanjing University)*, Muhammad Shahzad *(Michigan State University)*
- **Reusing 60GHz Radios for Mobile Radar Imaging** 103
  Yanzi Zhu, Yibo Zhu, Ben Y. Zhao, Haitao Zheng *(University of California, Santa Barbara)*
- **mTrack: High-Precision Passive Tracking Using Millimeter Wave Radios** 117
  Teng Wei, Xinyu Zhang *(University of Wisconsin - Madison)*

Session 3: New Security Threats

- **Acoustic Eavesdropping Through Wireless Vibrometry** 130
  Teng Wei, Shu Wang *(University of Wisconsin - Madison)*,
  Anfu Zhou *(ICT, Chinese Academy of Sciences & University of Wisconsin - Madison)*,
  Xinyu Zhang *(University of Wisconsin - Madison)*
- **Snooping Keystrokes with mm-Level Audio Ranging on a Single Phone** 142
  Jian Liu, Yan Wang *(Stevens Institute of Technology)*, Gorkem Kar *(Rutgers University)*,
  Yingying Chen *(Stevens Institute of Technology)*, Jie Yang *(Florida State University)*,
  Marco Gruteser *(Rutgers University)*
- **Mole: Motion Leaks Through Smartwatch Sensors** 155
  He Wang, Ted Tsung-Te Lai, Romit Roy Choudhury *(University of Illinois at Urbana-Champaign)*

Demonstrations

- **Demo: Platform for Collecting Data from Urban Sensors Using Vehicular Networking** ... 168
  Pedro M. Santos, Tania Calcada, Diogo Guimarães *(Universidade do Porto)*, Tiago Condeixa *(VENIAM)*, Susana Sargento *(Universidade de Aveiro)*, Ana Aguiar *(Universidade do Porto)*, João Barros *(Universidade do Porto & VENIAM)*
- **Demo: AntMonitor – A System for Mobile Traffic Monitoring and Real-Time Prevention of Privacy Leaks** ... 170
  Anastasia Shuba, Anh Le *(CalIT2 & UC Irvine)*, Minas Gjoka *(CalIT2 & UC Irvine)*, Janus Varmarken, Simon Langhoff *(IT University of Copenhagen)*, Athina Markopoulou *(CalIT2 & University of California, Irvine)*
- **Demo – Car-Fi: Opportunistic V2I by Exploiting Dual-Access Wi-Fi Networks** ... 173
  Davide Pesavento, Giulio Grassi, Giovanni Pau *(UPMC Sorbonne Universités)*, Paramvir Bahl *(Microsoft Research)*, Serge Fdida *(UPMC Sorbonne Universités)*
- **Demo – FIT IoT-LAB: A Large Scale Open Experimental IoT Testbed** ... 176
  Gaetan Harter, Roger Pissard-Gibollet, Frederic Saint-Marcel, Guillaume Schreiner, Julien Vandaele *(Inria)*
- **Demo: OpenVLC1.0 Platform for Research in Visible Light Communication Networks** ... 180
  Qing Wang *(IMDEA Networks Institute & UC3M)*, Shengrong Yin, Omprakash Gnawali *(University of Houston)*, Domenico Giustiniano *(IMDEA Networks Institute)*
- **Demo: An Open-source Software Defined Platform for Collaborative and Energy-aware WiFi Offloading** ... 182
  Aaron Yi Ding, Yanhe Liu, Sasu Tarkoma *(University of Helsinki)*, Hannu Flinck *(Nokia)*, Jon Crowcroft *(University of Cambridge)*
- **Demo: Optimizing Smartphone Power Consumption through Dynamic Resolution Scaling** ... 185
  Songtao He *(Microsoft Research & University of Science and Technology of China)*, Yunxin Liu, Hucheng Zhou *(Microsoft Research)*
- **Demo: Modular Multi-Radio Wireless Sensor Platform for IoT Trials with Plug&Play Module Connection** ... 188
  Konstantin Mikhaylov, Juha Petäjäjärvi, Marko Mäkeläinen, Anton Paatelma, Tuomo Hänninen *(University of Oulu)*
- **Demo: Wireless Link Selection on Smartphone: Throughput vs Battery Drain** ... 190
  Krzysztof Grochla, Paweł Foremski *(ITIS PAN)*
- **Demo – Closer to Cloud-Ran: Ran as a Service** ... 193
  Navid Nikaein, Raymond Knopp, Lionel Gauthier *(Eurecom)*, Eryk Schiller, Torsten Braun *(University of Bern)*, Dominique Pichon *(Orange Labs)*, Christian Bonnet, Florian Kaltenberger, Dominique Nussbaum *(Eurecom)*
- **Demo: Witals, AP-Centric Health Diagnosis of WiFi Networks** ... 196
  Mukulika Maity, Avinash Chaurasia *(IIT Bombay)*, Rachit Srivastava *(AirTight Networks)*, Bhaskaran Raman, Mythili Vutukuru *(IIT Bombay)*
- **Demo – OneLab: Major Computer Networking Testbeds for IoT and Wireless Experimentation** ... 199
  Loïc Baron, Fadwa Boubekeur, Radomir Klacza, Mohammed Yasin Rahman, Ciro Scognamiglio, Nina Kurose, Timur Friedman, Serge Fdida *(UPMC Sorbonne Universités)*
- **Demo: Molecular MIMO with Drift** ... 201
  Changmin Lee, Bonhong Koo, Na-Rae Kim, H. Birkan Yilmaz *(Yonsei University)*, Nariman Farsad, Andrew Eckford *(York University)*, Chan-Byoung Chae *(Yonsei University)*
- **Demo: Exploring Autoregressive Integrated Models for Time Synchronization in Wireless Sensor Networks** ... 204
  Wasif Masood, Jorge F. Schmidt *(Institute of Networked and Embedded Systems)*
- **Demo Abstract: Live Adaptations of Low-power MAC Protocols** ... 207
  Georgios Z. Papadopoulos, Antoine Gallais, Guillaume Schreiner, Thomas Noël *(University of Strasbourg)*
- **Demo: Implementation of Real-Time WiFi Receiver in Ziria, Language for Rapid Prototyping of Wireless PHY** ... 210
  Gordon Stewart *(Ohio University)*, Mahanth Gowda *(University of Illinois at Urbana-Champaign)*, Geoffrey Mainland *(Drexel University)*, Božidar Radunović, Dimitrios Vytiniotis *(Microsoft Research)*

Posters

- **Poster: Mobile Data Offloading Testbed** 212
  Matteo Pozza, Claudio Enrico Palazzi, Armir Bujari *(University of Padua)*
- **Poster: Can Smart Devices Protect Us from Violent Crime?** 215
  Alan Ferrari, Daniele Puccinelli, Silvia Giordano
  (University of Applied Sciences of Southern Switzerland (SUPSI))
- **Poster: Privacy-Preserving Server-Driven Dynamic Spectrum Access System** 218
  Yanzhi Dou, Kexiong (Curtis) Zeng, Yaling Yang *(Virginia Tech)*
- **Poster: On the Low-Cost and Distance-Adaptive Device-free Localization** 221
  Chen Liu, Dingyi Fang *(Northwest University)*, Hongbo Jiang *(Huazhong University)*,
  Xiaojiang Chen, Zhany Tang, Ju Wang, Weike Nie *(Northwest University)*
- **Poster: NLOS-aware Localization Based on Phase Shift Measurements** 224
  Yannic Schröder, Georg von Zengen, Lars Wolf *(Technische Universität Braunschweig)*
- **Poster: 3D Printing Your Wireless Coverage** 227
  Justin Chan *(Dartmouth College)*, Changxi Zheng *(Columbia University)*, Xia Zhou *(Dartmouth College)*
- **Poster: Evaluating Android Applications with Multipath TCP** 230
  Quentin De Coninck, Matthieu Baerts, Benjamin Hesmans, Olivier Bonaventure
  (Université catholique de Louvain)
- **Poster: Network-Based UE Mobility Estimation in Mobile Networks** 233
  Dalia-Georgiana Herculea *(Alcatel-Lucent Bell Labs)*, Majed Haddad *(University of Avignon)*,
  Veronique Capdevielle *(Alcatel-Lucent)*, Chung Shue Chen *(Alcatel-Lucent Bell Labs)*
- **Poster: Extremely Parallel Resource Pre-Fetching for Energy Optimized Mobile Web Browsing** 236
  Mohammad A. Hoque, Sasu Tarkoma *(University of Helsinki)*, Tuikku Anttila *(Aalto University)*
- **Poster: VPN Tunnels for Energy Efficient Multimedia Streaming** 239
  Mohammad A. Hoque, Kasperi Saarikoski, Eemil Lagerspetz, Julien Mineraud,
  Sasu Tarkoma *(University of Helsinki)*
- **Poster: A Low Cost People Flow Monitoring System for Sensing the Potential Danger** 242
  Ju Wang, Dingyi Fang, Xiaojiang Chen, Liqiong Chang, Zhanyong Tang,
  Tianzhang Xing, Chen Liu *(Northwest University)*
- **Poster: Unified RemoteU$_i$ for Mobile Environments** 245
  Miguel Almeida Carvalho, João Nuno Silva *(Universidade de Lisboa, Portugal)*
- **Poster – Use Your Senses: A Smooth Multipath TCP WiFi/Mobile Handover** 248
  Alexander Frömmgen, Sreeram Sadasivam, Sabrina Müller, Anja Klein, Alejandro Buchmann *(TU Darmstadt)*
- **Poster: Towards Encrypted Query Processing for the Internet of Things** 251
  Hossein Shafagh, Anwar Hithnawi, Andreas Droescher *(ETH Zurich)*,
  Simon Duquennoy *(SICS Swedish ICT AB)*,Wen Hu *(UNSW)*
- **Poster: Regression-Based Characterization of 802.11ac Indoor Performance** 254
  Edgar Costa Molero *(ETH Zürich)*, Lito Kriara *(Disney Research Zürich)*, Thomas Gross *(ETH Zürich)*
- **Poster: ParkMaster – Leveraging Edge Computing in Visual Analytics** 257
  Giulio Grassi, Matteo Sammarco *(Sorbonne Universitès, UPMC Univ Paris 06)*,
  Paramvir Bahl *(Microsoft Research)*, Kyle Jamieson *(University College London)*,
  Giovanni Pau *(Sorbonne Universitès, UPMC Univ Paris 06)*
- **Poster: User Location Fingerprinting at Scale** 260
  Puneet Jain *(Duke University)*, Justin Manweiler *(IBM Research)*, Romit Roy Choudhury *(University of Illinois)*
- **Poster: Understanding YouTube QoE in Cellular Networks with YoMoApp - A QoE Monitoring Tool for YouTube Mobile** 263
  Florian Wamser, Michael Seufert *(University of Würzburg)*,
  Pedro Casas *(The Telecommunications Research Center - FTW Vienna)*,
  Ralf Irmer *(Vodafone Research and Development)*, Phuoc Tran-Gia *(University of Würzburg)*,
  Raimund Schatz *(The Telecommunications Research Center - FTW Vienna)*

- **Poster: Continuous and Fine-Grained Respiration Volume Monitoring Using Continuous Wave Radar** 266
  Phuc Nguyen *(University of Colorado, Denver)*, Xinyu Zhang *(University of Wisconsin-Madison)*, Ann C. Halbower *(University of Colorado School of Medicine & Children's Hospital Colorado)*, Tam Vu *(University of Colorado, Denver)*
- **Poster: Distributed Voronoi-Based Acoustic Source Localization with Wireless Sensor Networks** 269
  Xueshu Zheng, Naigao Jin, Lei Wang *(Dalian University of Technology)*, Mathew L. Wymore, Daji Qiao *(Iowa State University)*
- **Poster – TRIM: A Truthful Incentive Mechanism for Dynamic and Heterogeneous Tasks in Mobile Crowdsensing** 272
  Yue Fan, Hailong Sun, Xudong Liu *(Beihang University)*
- **Poster: A Multi-Drone Platform for Empowering Drones' Teamwork** 275
  Seungho Yoo, Kangho Kim, Jongtack Jung, Albert Y. Chung, Jiyeon Lee, Suk Kyu Lee, Hyung Kyu Lee, Hwangnam Kim *(Korea University)*
- **Poster: Visible Light Communication in the Dark** 278
  Zhao Tian, Andrew T. Campbell, Xia Zhou *(Dartmouth College)*
- **Poster: Scoping Environment to Assist 60 GHz Link Deployment** 281
  Sanjib Sur, Xinyu Zhang *(University of Wisconsin - Madison)*
- **Poster: Crowdsourced Location Aware Wi-Fi Access Control** 284
  Bingxian Lu, Zhicheng Zeng, Lei Wang *(Dalian University of Technology)*, Brian Peck, Daji Qiao *(Iowa State University)*
- **Poster: An Insomnia Therapy for Clock Synchronization in Wireless Sensor Networks** 287
  Meng Jin, Dingyi Fang, Xiaojiang Chen *(Northwest University)*, Lin Cai *(University of Victoria)*, Zhe Yang *(Northwestern Polytechnical University)*, Zhanyong Tang *(Northwest University)*

Keynote Address 2

- **Research Challenges and Opportunities in a Mobility-centric World** 290
  James Kurose *(University of Massachusetts)*

Session 4: New Access Techniques I

- **Recitation: Rehearsing Wireless Packet Reception in Software** 291
  Zhenjiang Li, Yaxiong Xie, Mo Li *(Nanyang Technological University)*, Kyle Jamieson *(University College London)*
- **Hekaton: Efficient and Practical Large-Scale MIMO** 304
  Xiufeng Xie *(University of Wisconsin-Madison)*, Eugene Chai *(NEC Labs America)*, Xinyu Zhang *(University of Wisconsin-Madison)*, Karthikeyan Sundaresan, Amir Khojastepour, Sampath Rangarajan *(NEC Labs America)*
- **FreeBee: Cross-technology Communication via Free Side-channel** 317
  Song Min Kim, Tian He *(University of Minnesota)*

Session 5: Emerging Sensing Methods

- **Human Sensing Using Visible Light Communication** 331
  Tianxing Li, Chuankai An, Zhao Tian, Andrew T. Campbell, Xia Zhou *(Dartmouth College)*
- **Extending Mobile Interaction Through Near-Field Visible Light Sensing** 345
  Chi Zhang, Joshua Tabor, Jialiang Zhang, Xinyu Zhang *(University of Wisconsin-Madison)*
- **EcoDrive: A Mobile Sensing and Control System for Fuel Efficient Driving** 358
  Lei Kang, Bozhao Qi, Dan Janecek, Suman Banerjee *(University of Wisconsin-Madison)*

Session 6: Applications

- **Kaleido: You Can Watch It But Cannot Record It** 372
  Lan Zhang *(Tsinghua University)*, Cheng Bo *(University of North Carolina at Charlotte)*,
  Jiahui Hou *(Illinois Institute of Technology & University of Science and Technology of China)*,
  Xiang-Yang Li *(Tsinghua University & Illinois Institute of Technology)*,
  Yu Wang *(University of North Carolina at Charlotte)*, Kebin Liu, Yunhao Liu *(Tsinghua University)*
- **CAreDroid: Adaptation Framework for Android Context-Aware Applications** 386
  Salma Elmalaki *(University of California, Los Angeles)*, Lucas Wanner *(Federal University of Santa Catarina)*,
  Mani Srivastava *(University of California, Los Angeles)*
- **CIDER: Enabling Robustness-Power Tradeoffs on a Computational Eyeglass** 400
  Addison Mayberry, Yamin Tun, Pan Hu *(University of Massachusetts)*,
  Duncan Smith-Freedman, Deepak Ganesan, Benjamin M. Marlin,
  Christopher Salthouse *(University of Massachusetts, Amherst)*
- **piStream: Physical Layer Informed Adaptive Video Streaming over LTE** 413
  Xiufeng Xie, Xinyu Zhang *(University of Wisconsin-Madison)*,
  Swarun Kumar *(Massachusetts Institute of Technology)*, Li Erran Li *(Fudan University)*
- **The Design and Implementation of a Wireless Video Surveillance System** 426
  Tan Zhang *(University of Wisconsin, Madison)*,
  Aakanksha Chowdhery, Paramvir (Victor) Bahl *(Microsoft Research)*,
  Kyle Jamieson *(University College London)*, Suman Banerjee *(University of Wisconsin Madison)*

Session 7: Measurement, Reliability and Experience

- **SAMPLES: Self Adaptive Mining of Persistent LExical Snippets for Classifying Mobile Application Traffic** 439
  Hongyi Yao *(University of Michigan)*, Gyan Ranjan, Alok Tongaonkar, Yong Liao *(Symantec Corp.)*,
  Z. Morley Mao *(University of Michigan)*
- **Performance Characterization and Call Reliability Diagnosis Support for Voice over LTE** 452
  Yunhan Jack Jia, Qi Alfred Chen, Z. Morley Mao *(University of Michigan)*,
  Jie Hui, Kranthi Sontinei, Alex Yoon, Samson Kwong, Kevin Lau *(T-Mobile USA Inc.)*
- **ABSENCE: Usage-based Failure Detection in Mobile Networks** 464
  Binh Nguyen *(University of Utah)*, Zihui Ge *(AT&T Labs - Research)*,
  Jacobus Van der Merwe *(University of Utah)*, He Yan, Jennifer Yates *(AT&T Labs - Research)*
- **Experience: Rethinking RRC State Machine Optimization in Light of Recent Advancements** 477
  Theodore Stoner, Xuetao Wei, Joseph Knight *(University of Cincinnati)*, Lei Guo *(Northeastern University)*

Keynote Address 3

- **European Research towards 5G** 486
  Rémy Bayou *(European Commission)*

Session 8: Localization and RFID

- **See Through Walls with COTS RFID System!** 487
  Lei Yang, Qiongzheng Lin *(Tsinghua University)*,
  Xiangyang Li *(Tsinghua University & Illinois Institute of Technology)*,
  Tianci Liu, Yunhao Liu *(Tsinghua University)*
- **Come and Be Served: Parallel Decoding for COTS RFID Tags** 500
  Jiajue Ou, Mo Li *(Nanyang Technological University)*,
  Yuanqing Zheng *(The Hong Kong Polytechnic University)*
- **Last-Mile Navigation Using Smartphones** 512
  Yuanchao Shu *(Zhejiang University & The University of Michigan)*, Kang G. Shin *(The University of Michigan)*,
  Tian He *(University of Minnesota)*, Jiming Chen *(Zhejiang University)*

- **EchoTag: Accurate Infrastructure-Free Indoor Location Tagging with Smartphones**....... 525
  Yu-Chih Tung, Kang G. Shin *(The University of Michigan)*
- **ToneTrack: Leveraging Frequency-Agile Radios for Time-Based Indoor Wireless Localization**....... 537
  Jie Xiong *(University College London)*, Karthikeyan Sundaresan *(NEC Laboratories America)*, Kyle Jamieson *(University College London)*

Panel Session

- **Big Data, IoT, ... Buzz Words for Academia or Reality for Industry?**....... 550
  Rui Aguiar *(Universidade de Aveiro)*, Nora Benhabiles *(CEA)*, Tobias Pfeiffer *(Preferred Networks)*, Pablo Rodriguez *(Telefonica)*, Harish Viswanathan *(Alcatel Lucent Bell Labs)*, Jia Wang *(AT&T Labs - Research)*, Hui Zang *(Huawei)*

Session 9: New Access Techniques II

- **MZIG: Enabling Multi-Packet Reception in ZigBee**....... 552
  Linghe Kong, Xue Liu *(McGill University)*
- **AirExpress: Enabling Seamless In-band Wireless Multi-hop Transmission**....... 566
  Bo Chen, Yue Qiao, Ouyang Zhang, Kannan Srinivasan *(The Ohio State University)*
- **Control Channel Design for Many-Antenna MU-MIMO**....... 578
  Clayton Shepard, Abeer Javed, Lin Zhong *(Rice University)*

Session 10: Mobile Cloud

- **QuickSync: Improving Synchronization Efficiency for Mobile Cloud Storage Services**....... 592
  Yong Cui, Zeqi Lai *(Tsinghua University)*, Xin Wang *(Stony Brook University)*, Ningwei Dai, Congcong Miao *(Tsinghua University)*
- **FlexiWeb: Network-Aware Compaction for Accelerating Mobile Web Transfers**....... 604
  Shailendra Singh *(University of California, Riverside)*, Harsha V. Madhyastha *(University of Michigan)*, Srikanth V. Krishnamurthy *(University of California, Riverside)*, Ramesh Govindan *(University of Southern California)*

Author Index....... 617

ACM MobiCom 2015 Conference Organization

General Co-Chairs:	Serge Fdida *(UPMC/LIP6, France)* Giovanni Pau *(UPMC/LIP6, France)*
Program Co-Chairs:	Sneha Kumar Kasera *(University of Utah, USA)* Heather Zheng *(University of California, Santa Barbara, USA)*
Workshop Co-Chairs:	Marco Leverato *(University of California, Irvine, USA)* Marcelo Dias de Amorim *(UPMC/LIP6, France)* Jorg Widmer *(IMDEA Networks Institute, Spain)*
Panels Co-Chairs:	Wenjun Hu *(Yale University, USA)* Rui Aguiar *(Universidade de Aveiro, Portugal)* Hiroshi Esaki *(University of Tokyo, Japan)*
Demo Co-Chairs:	Thanasis Korakis *(NYU Polytechnic School of Engineering, USA)* Nathalie Mitton *(Inria, France)* Aki Nakao *(University of Tokyo, Japan)*
Posters Co-Chairs:	Fan Ye *(Stony Brook University, USA)* Gustavo Marfia *(University of Bologna, Italy)* Gaogang Xie *(Institute of Computing Technology, Chinese Academy of Science, China)*
SRC Co-Chairs:	Mehmet Can Vuran *(University of Nebraska-Lincoln, Lincoln, USA)* Andrzej Duda *(Grenoble INP-Ensimag, France)*
Publication Co-Chairs:	Aline Carneiro Viana *(Inria, France)* Nina Kurose *(UPMC/LIP6, France)*
Finance Chair	Marguerite Sos *(UPMC/LIP6, France)*
Web Chair:	Rita Tse *(Macao Polytechnic Institute, Macao)*
Web Master:	Yubin Xiao *(Macao Polytechnic Institute, Macao)*
Local Arrangements Co-Chairs:	Manuella Portier *(UPMC/LIP6, France)* Frederic Vaissade *(UPMC/LIP6, France)*
Publicity Co-Chair:	Lars Wolf *(Technische Universität Braunschweig, Germany)* Dae Young Kim *(Chungnam University, Korea)* Xia Zhou *(Dartmouth College, New Hampshire, USA)*
Registration Chair:	Marguerite Sos *(UPMC/LIP6, France)*

Student Travel Grants Co-Chairs: Mario Gerla *(University of California, Los Angeles, USA)*
Jiannong Cao *(The Hong Kong Polytechnic University, Hong Kong)*
Martin May *(Technicolor, France)*

Corporate Liasion Chair: Hubert Tardieu *(Atos, France)*

Steering Committee: Victor Bahl (Chair) *(Microsoft Research, USA)*
Suman Banerjee *(University of Wisconsin-Madison, USA)*
Ramesh Govindan *(University of Southern California, USA)*
David B. Johnson *(Rice University, USA)*
Kang Shin *(University of Michigan, USA)*

Program Committee: Victor Bahl *(Microsoft Research Redmond, USA)*
Aruna Balasubramanian *(Stony Brook University, USA)*
Sujata Banerjee *(HP Labs, USA)*
Suman Banerjee *(University of Wisconsin-Madison, USA)*
Milind Buddhikot *(Bell Labs, Alcatel Lucent, USA)*
Srdjan Capkun *(ETH Zurich, Switzerland)*
Yingying Chen *(Stevens Institute of Technology, USA)*
Ranveer Chandra *(Microsoft Research Redmond, USA)*
Sabrina Gaito *(Università degli Studi di Milano, Italy)*
Ben Greenstein *(Google, USA)*
Shyamnath Gollakota *(University of Washington, USA)*
Marco Gruteser *(Rutgers University, USA)*
Y. Charlie Hu *(Purdue University, USA)*
Wenjun Hu *(Yale University, USA)*
Robin Kravets *(University of Illinois, USA)*
Srikanth Krishnamurthy *(University of California, Riverside, USA)*
Sung-Ju Lee *(KAIST, Korea)*
Ilias Leontiadis *(Telefonica, Spain)*
Li Erran Li *(Bell-labs, Alcatel Lucent, USA)*
Mo Li *(Nanyang Technological University, Singapore)*
Xiangyang Li *(Illinois Institute of Technology, USA)*
Yunhao Liu *(Tsinghua University, China)*
Chenyang Lu *(Washington University in St. Louis, USA)*
Songwu Lu *(University of California, Los Angeles, USA)*
Petri Mähönen *(RWTH Aachen University, Germany)*
Z. Morley Mao *(University of Michigan, Ann Arbor, USA)*
Thyagarajan Nandagopal *(National Science Foundation, USA)*
Panos Papadimitratos *(KTH Royal Institute of Technology, Sweden)*
Guevara Noubir *(Northeastern University, USA)*
Neal Patwari *(University of Utah, USA)*
Giovanni Pau *(UPMC/LIP6, France)*
Chunyi Peng *(Ohio State University, USA)*

Program Committee (continued):

Chiara Petriolli *(University of Rome "La Sapienza", Italy)*
Lili Qiu *(University of Texas, Austin, USA)*
Bozidar Radunovic *(Microsoft Research Cambridge, UK)*
Ramachandran Ramjee *(Microsoft Research India, India)*
Eric Rozner *(IBM Research, USA)*
Jacky Shen *(Microsoft Research Asia, China)*
Alex Snoeren *(University of California, San Diego, USA)*
Kannan Srinivasan *(Ohio State University, USA)*
Lakshmi Subramanian *(New York University, USA)*
Karthik Sundaresan *(NEC, USA)*
Matt Welsh *(Google, USA)*
Xinyu Zhang *(University of Wisconsin-Madison, USA)*
Lin Zhong *(Rice University, USA)*
Xia Zhou *(Dartmouth College, USA)*

Additional reviewer: Yasutaka Furukawa

MobiCom 2015 Sponsors & Supporters

Sponsor:

Platinum Supporters:

Silver Supporters:

Bronze Supporters:

Agility and Fragility in a Real-time World

Gilles Grapinet
Senior Executive Vice President, ATOS &
Chief Executive Officer Worldline

ABSTRACT

Connected mobile devices have now reached the age of being perceived as a commodity. Users expect to be able to enjoy the same level of service and performance both on the go and at home. A new wave of cloud-supported services brought about by the integration of machine learning in consumer electronics –such as Smart watches, NEST sensors, and Self-Driving cars –is entering the market with a disruptive power. The Internet of Everything is already on our wrists, cars, buildings, and pockets, and is pushing through new economic models (such as Shared Economy or Data Economy). Current technology is struggling to meet the demands posed by new applications and services; specifically, it lacks the agility needed to adapt to fast-changing business models and technical requirements; it also comes with fragilities as most of our current infrastructures, systems and solutions were not designed to allow massive usage of real-time applications at personal level. Security, connectivity, mobility, latency, and scalability are just some of the many challenges that pave the way towards a seamless user experience. Device-to-device communications along with new business and trust models will dominate the Internet. It is essential for the Internet of Everything to succeed, and that industry, government and academia join forces to build brand new protocol architectures, computing paradigms, and regulatory frameworks designed to support mobility, high performance services, strong security and a fine user privacy granularity adapted to an expanding level of personal data dissemination.

Categories and Subject Descriptors
C.2.1 [Computer-Communication Networks]: Network Architecture and Design— Network communications; Wireless communication. H.0 [Information System]: General

Keywords
Mobile networks; Internet of Things; Security Models; Trust Models; Privacy; Regulation

MobiCom '15, September 7–11, 2015, Paris, France.
ACM 978-1-4503-3619-2/15/09.
DOI: http://dx.doi.org/10.1145/2789168.2790090

BIO

A graduate of the French "Ecole Nationale d'Administration", Grapinet joined the French "Inspection Générale des Finances" in 1992, where he worked for four years on numerous financial audits and assessment assignments for both the French Government and international organizations (International Monetary Fund, World Bank, etc.). In 1996, he moved to the French tax department as the Head of Strategy and Controlling, before being appointed Director of Information Systems and Strategy. Between 2000 and 2002, he was appointed CIO, heading of the nation-wide "Copernic program" that was aimed at entirely rebuilding the French tax information system in order to create a multi-channel, service-oriented e-tax administration. Between 2003 and end 2004, he joined the private office of the French Prime Minister as Senior Advisor for Economic and Financial Affairs. And between 2005 and 2007, he acted as director and chief of staff of the French Economy, Finance and Industry in the Minister's private office.

In 2007, Gilles Grapinet joined the Executive Committee of the international banking group, Credit Agricole SA, where he was Head of Strategy before being appointed director of the Payment Systems & Services business division.

In December 2008, as Senior Executive Vice President in charge of Global functions, Grapinet joined Atos Origin (since July 2011, the name of the company has been changed to Atos, following the Siemens IT acquisition), as one of the two SEVP of the Company. In July 2013, in addition of his position in Atos, he is appointed CEO of Worldline, a listed subsidiary of the Atos Group specialized in e-Payment services.

Wireless Power Hotspot that Charges All of Your Devices

Lixin Shi, Zachary Kabelac, Dina Katabi, David Perreault
Massachusetts Institute of Technology
Cambridge, MA, USA
{lixin, zek, dina}@csail.mit.edu, djperrea@mit.edu

ABSTRACT

Each year, consumers carry an increasing number of gadgets on their person: mobile phones, tablets, smartwatches, etc. As a result, users must remember to recharge each device, every day. Wireless charging promises to free users from this burden, allowing devices to remain permanently unplugged. Today's wireless charging, however, is either limited to a single device, or is highly cumbersome, requiring the user to remove all of her wearable and handheld gadgets and place them on a charging pad.

This paper introduces MultiSpot, a new wireless charging technology that can charge multiple devices, even as the user is wearing them or carrying them in her pocket. A MultiSpot charger acts as an access point for wireless power. When a user enters the vicinity of the MultiSpot charger, all of her gadgets start to charge automatically. We have prototyped MultiSpot and evaluated it using off-the-shelf mobile phones, smartwatches, and tablets. Our results show that MultiSpot can charge 6 devices at distances of up to 50 cm.

CATEGORIES AND SUBJECT DESCRIPTORS

C.2.2 [**Computer Systems Organization**]: Computer-Communications Networks

KEYWORDS

Wireless Power Transfer; MIMO; Magnetic Resonance; Energy; Beamforming; Mobile and Wearable Devices

1. INTRODUCTION

Our daily lives rely on a multitude of personal mobile devices, such as phones, tablets, and wearables. While every new device has made our lives easier in many respects, having to remember and manage to charge all of our mobile devices is a recurring and increasingly significant burden. If we could wirelessly charge our devices, it would alleviate this daily anxiety, and may even allow such devices to be permanently unplugged. While previous work has taken initial steps towards this goal, it remains limited to a single device at a time [1, 2, 3], or is highly cumbersome requiring the user to remove all of her wearable and handheld gadgets and place them on a charging pad [4, 5], as in Fig. 1a.

Imagine, however, if one had a single wireless charger that was able to charge all of its surrounding devices simultaneously, even if they were on the user's body or in her purse. In some sense, this would emulate a miniature WiFi hotspot –i.e., the wireless charger would act as a power access point; once the user is in the vicinity of the charger, her devices start receiving power as needed, and if she moves away the charging stops. One could use such a charger as a desk mat. Whenever the user sits at her desk, the iPhone in her pocket, the tablet in her purse, and the smartwatch on her wrist would charge automatically without even thinking of them, as shown in Fig. 1b.

But how can one deliver a wireless power hotspot? As we investigate the answer to this question, we focus on charging via magnetic coupling because it is the approach adopted by the wireless charging standards [6, 7] and all consumer wireless charging products, and is deemed safe and compliant with FCC rules [8].[1] In magnetic coupling, the power transmitter uses one or more coils. When an AC current traverses the transmitter's coil, it creates a variable magnetic field. If this magnetic field traverses a nearby coil, it generates an electric current, hence delivering power to that device. The stronger the magnetic field is at the receiver, the more power is delivered. The challenge, however, is that the magnetic field dies very quickly with distance, and hence typical wireless charging devices operate at a very short distance of a couple of centimeters [6, 15].

Last year however, a MobiCom paper proposed a solution called MagMIMO [1], where multiple coils on the transmitter act as a multi-antenna system, shaping the magnetic field in a beam and focusing it on the receiver, in a manner similar to beamforming in MIMO systems.[2] The paper demonstrated that for *a single receiver*, beamforming of the magnetic field can increase the charging range up to 40 cm and allow for a flexible phone orientation. Motivated by this recent development, we investigate whether one can charge multiple receivers at distance by shaping the magnetic field in multiple beams focused on the various receivers.

At first blush, it might seem that one can beamform the magnetic field to multiple receivers by directly borrowing from multi-user MIMO. Unfortunately, there is an intrinsic difference between multi-user MIMO in RF communications and the physics of wireless charging. Specifically, consider the effect of introducing mul-

[1] In particular, we use magnetic resonance [7]. Some start-ups have advocated the use of RF radiation [9, 10], ultrasound [11], or lasers [12] for wireless power transfer. None of those approaches have made it into the standards for consumer electronics. Further, charging consumer electronics, e.g., phones, using RF or lasers raises safety concerns [13, 14] (for further details see §2).

[2] The term "magnetic beamforming" in [1] and this paper refers to shaping the magnetic flux in the near field in the form of a beam (or multiple beams). In contrast, traditional beamforming in wireless communication systems operates over radiated waves in the far field.

MobiCom'15, September 07–11, 2015, Paris, France.
© 2015 ACM. ISBN 978-1-4503-3619-2/15/09 ...$15.00.
DOI: http://dx.doi.org/10.1145/2789168.2790092.

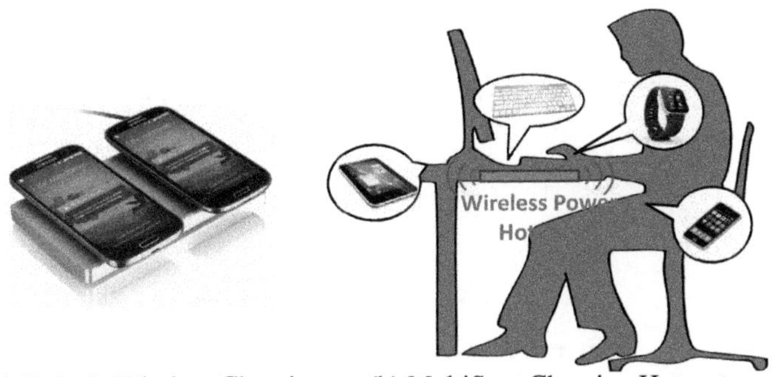

(a) Today's Wireless Charging (b) MultiSpot Charging Hotspot

Figure 1: (a): Today's wireless chargers require careful placement of each device on the charging pad. (b) MultiSpot acts as a wireless power hotspot. Mounted as a desk mat, it charges all surrounding personal electronics, including cellphones, tablets, smartwatches, wireless keyboards and touchpads.

tiple receivers. In a conventional wireless communication system, each receiver is a passive listener that only receives signals. In contrast, in a wireless charging system, receivers interact with each other. A receiver not only accepts power, but also reflects power back to the transmitters and other receivers. The presence of a receiver affects the magnetic field observed by other receivers and transmitters. As a result, adding, removing, or moving just a single receiver in the system affects all of the other receivers, which is not the case in RF communication systems. In fact not accounting for these interactions can lead to large errors in shaping the magnetic field and consequent charging failures, as we show in §7.2. One therefore needs to account for these fundamental differences between the models of multi-user RF channels and multi-receiver magnetic channels, while formulating and solving the magnetic charging problem.

This paper introduces MultiSpot, a multi-coil power transmitter that can beam its magnetic field toward multiple power receivers simultaneously. MultiSpot formulates the multi-receiver magnetic charging problem and derives a solution whose equations account for inter-receiver interactions. By shaping the magnetic field into beams and focusing them towards the receivers, MultiSpot can significantly increase the range of multi-receiver wireless charging. Further, by steering the beams with receiver motion and orientation, MultiSpot can accommodate a flexible charging pattern capable of charging a smartwatch on the user's wrist, a phone in her hand, and a tablet in her purse.

MultiSpot has three key features:

1. MultiSpot is analytically proven to maximize the power delivered to the receivers. Said differently, given an input power and a particular topology of the transmit and receive coils (and hence their resulting magnetic couplings), MultiSpot delivers a closed-form solution that sets the charging parameters to guarantee maximum power delivery to the receivers' coils.
2. MultiSpot's solution is adaptive. It adjusts to movements of the receivers and re-converges to the optimal solution. In our implementation, MultiSpot adapts to receivers' movements in just a few milliseconds.
3. A MultiSpot charger can beamform without any communication or coordination of the receivers, despite the fact that MultiSpot's beamforming is impacted by the interactions between the receivers (i.e., their inter-receiver magnetic couplings). The MultiSpot transmitter passively infers all needed information based on the reflected power it observes at the Tx coils.

Implementation and Results: We built a prototype of MultiSpot and evaluated it with smart phones, a smartwatch, and a tablet. We also compared MultiSpot to multiple baselines: Duracell Powermat [4], Energizer Qi [5] and LUXA2 [16], and a reference design by WiTricity called WiT-5000 [15]. Our results show the following:

- MultiSpot can charge 6 devices at distances up to 50 cm, whereas the baselines are limited to 2 devices at 5cm.
- MultiSpot charges different types of devices simultaneously. When attached to an office desk, and with the user sitting at the desk, MultiSpot simultaneously charged a smartwatch on the user's wrist, an iPhone in her pocket, and a nearby tablet, keyboard, and touchpad.
- MultiSpot's charging time is lower than all wireless charging baselines, for the same distance. The charging time depends on distance. For distances less than 20 cm, MultiSpot charges two phones from dead batteries to full charge in less than 1.5x of the time taken for wired charging. The charging time increases to 3x when the phones are 35cm away from the charger, and 5x when they are 50cm away.
- Interestingly, the presence of multiple receivers can increase the range of power transfer. We show that the maximal range is 10cm larger with two phones than it is with one phone, and 17cm larger with 4 phones.
- Finally, we compare MagMIMO [1] to MultiSpot in the presence of two phones. Our results show that MagMIMO's charging time is comparable to MultiSpot *only* when the two phones are co-located and hence can be considered as one device. Otherwise, MagMIMO takes an order of magnitude longer time or might fail to charge one of the phones altogether. This is because MagMIMO has no mechanism to disentangle the magnetic couplings of different receivers, and hence in the presence of multiple receivers it can fail to compute the correct beamforming solution.

Contributions: 1) A provably optimal solution to maximize power transfer to multiple receivers by shaping the magnetic field of a multi-coil power transmitter. 2) An implementation and empirical evaluation with off-the-shelf devices including smart phones, a smart watch, and a tablet. 3) Empirical results showing that MultiSpot's magnetic coupling can charge mobile phones and wearables up to 50 cm and in flexible orientations.

2. RELATED WORK

Wireless power transfer has spread across a vast array of fields expanding the capabilities of devices such as phones [4, 17], wearables [18], medical implants [19, 20], electric vehicles [21], sensors [22, 23], etc.

The standard approach for wireless charging of consumer devices is based on magnetic coupling. In fact, magnetic coupling is used in all commercial wireless chargers for phones and smartwatches [3, 24], as well as current industry standards [6, 7]. Earlier products have used inductive magnetic coupling [17], but recent ones are moving to magnetic resonance, which yields higher efficiency [25]. Commercial chargers however are highly limited in both range and flexibility. They require the user to carefully place her charged devices on the charging pad and have them perfectly aligned with the pad [4, 5, 16], as in Fig.1a.

Academic research has taken important steps towards wirelessly delivering power to multiple receivers using magnetic coupling. We distinguish between two classes of work: The first class can deal with a small receiver coil that fits in the back of a phone or the strap of a smartwatch and achieve a maximum distance of 10 cm [26, 27, 28, 29]. The second class can deliver power at larger ranges up to 30cm [30, 31, 32], but they require large receiver coils that could not possibly fit on the back of a phone or wearable. In addition, both classes assume the receiver coil is aligned with the transmitter coil, and do not deal with different receiver orientations with respect to the transmitter. In practice, however, the user cannot benefit from an increase in charging distance if she has to hold her device on top of the charging pad and maintain a perfect alignment with the charger. MultiSpot is unique in that it adapts the shape of the magnetic field according to the location and orientation of the receivers by constructively combining the magnetic fields of multiple Tx coils. This allows MultiSpot to reduce the size of the receiver coil to fit on phones and wearables, while supporting larger ranges and flexible receiver orientations.

Researchers have also explored using multiple transmit coils to beamform the magnetic field to receivers. In fact, MultiSpot is inspired by MagMIMO's techniques [1]. However, as described earlier in Sec. §1, MagMIMO does not work in the presence of more than one receiver, while MultiSpot is designed to work with any number of receivers. We show in experiments (Sec.§7) that when two receivers are separated from each other, MagMIMO cannot charge them.

Very recently, another work was accepted for publication, which also uses multiple transmit coils, and examines the possibility of combining their fields at up to 2 receivers [33]. While the work demonstrates the potential of multi-user charging, it presents an optimal solution only for a single receiver, and uses brute force exploration to determine the optimal solution for two receivers. Further, the work presents an implementation only for the single receiver case, and uses simulation for the two-receiver case. In contrast, MultiSpot presents an optimal solution for any number of receivers. Further, MultiSpot is implemented and empirically evaluated for up to 6 receivers.

We also note that there have been recent proposals of wireless charging using physical phenomena other than magnetic coupling. Ultrasound [11], lasers [12], and power delivery via RF radiation [9, 10] have been proposed by startup companies. However, none of these companies have published their technologies nor offered a product. Furthermore, ultrasound charging is limited to line-of-sight scenarios and will be disrupted if the phone is not directly in front of the charger [34]. It can also negatively affect pets who hear some types of ultrasound [35]. Lasers can cause damage to one's eyesight [13], and delivering power to mobile devices via RF radiation at hundreds of MHz to GHz heats up water which composes most of a human body, similarly to how a microwave oven cooks food [14].[3] Beyond the safety problems, it is also unclear how these technologies can be compliant with FCC regulations.

3. PRIMER

In this section, we explain how magnetic coupling works at a high level. In this approach, the transmitter coil is driven by an AC current to generate an oscillating magnetic field. When another conductive coil is placed within range of the transmitter, some of the magnetic field passes through the center of its coil. This field induces an AC current on the receiver, which can be used to power the device.

To boost the efficiency of power transfer, state-of-the-art systems and industrial standards [6, 7], use a technique called *magnetic resonance* [25], in which they add a capacitor to the transmitter and receiver circuits and make them resonate at the same frequency. The oscillations cause the circuits to resonate back and forth without consuming much energy. Magnetic resonance is the underlying power transfer mechanism used in MultiSpot.

[3]To see how delivering power via RF radiation to a phone might be dangerous, let us do a rough calculation. Say that a standard phone requires at least 1W to turn on charging, and it has an area of 5cm×10cm, i.e., the power density is 20mW/cm^2. As a comparison, FDA (Food and Drug Administration) enforces microwave oven leakage to be below 5mW/cm^2 in order to be considered safe [36].

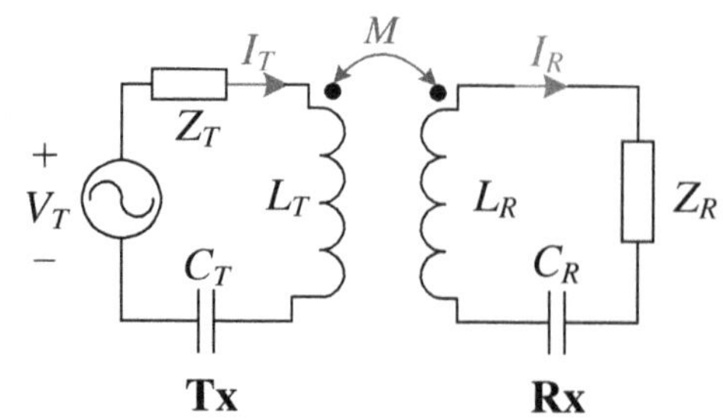

Figure 2: **Single-Coil Tx, Single Rx Schematic**

3.1 Circuit Equations

Magnetic coupling and the resulting power transfer can be mathematically described via basic circuit equations [37].

Single Coil System: Consider the system in Fig. 2, which shows a single coil transmitter and a single receiver. Let us write the equations that describe this system. As we do so, we will take into account that in magnetic resonance, the inductance and capacitor are chosen so that their impacts cancel each other at the resonant frequency (i.e., $j\omega L + \frac{1}{j\omega C} = 0$). Thus, we can ignore those terms.

We can describe the system in Fig. 2 using two equations. The first equation determines how a current in the transmit coil, I_T, induces a current in the receive coil, I_R, i.e.:

$$Z_R I_R = j\omega M I_T \qquad (1)$$

where M is the magnetic coupling between the transmit and receive coils, Z_R is the impedance of the receiver and ω is the resonant frequency.

The above equation would have been sufficient to describe the system if one could directly apply a current to the transmit coil. Unfortunately, in practice, one has to use a voltage source instead. Thus, we need a second equation that determines the relationship between the voltage one applies to the transmitter, V_T and the resulting transmitter current, I_T.

For the circuit in Fig. 2, we have: $V_T = Z_T I_T - j\omega M I_R$, where Z_T represents the impedance in the transmitter. Note in this equation how the current in the receiver induces a voltage back on the transmitter via the same magnetic coupling M. We can further substitute I_R from Eq. (1) to obtain:

$$V_T = \left(Z_T + \omega^2 M^2 / Z_R\right) I_T. \qquad (2)$$

Together Eq. (1) and Eq. (2) describe the single-coil charging system.

Multi-Coil System: The above two equations can be generalized to the case of multiple transmitter coils and multiple receiver coils, shown in Fig. 3a. The difference is that now every pair of coils has magnetic coupling between them. Specifically, there are three types of couplings: M_{Tik} between transmitter i and k, M_{iu} between transmitter i and receiver u, and M_{Ruv} between receiver u and v.

We can update Eq. (1) and Eq. (2) to account for the additional coupling between transmitter coils, and between receiver coils. Re-

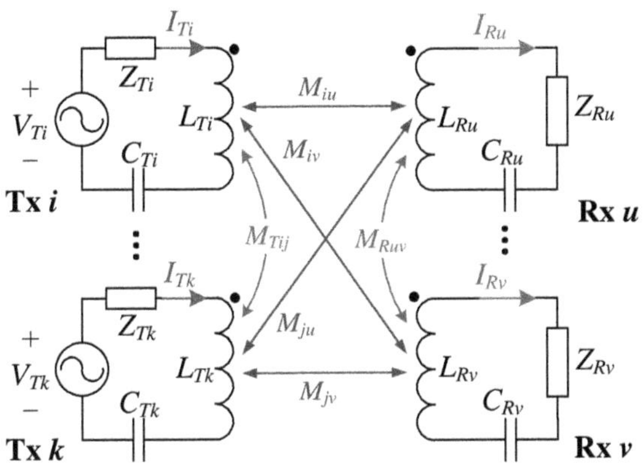

(a) Multi-coil Tx, Multiple Rx Schematic

Term	Definition	Explanation
n	Number of Tx coils	
m	Number of Rx coils	
$\vec{v}_T$	$[V_{T1}, V_{T2}, \cdots, V_{Tn}]^\top_{n\times 1}$	Tx voltages
$\vec{i}_T$	$[I_{T1}, I_{T2}, \cdots, I_{Tn}]^\top_{n\times 1}$	Tx currents
$\vec{i}_R$	$[I_{R1}, I_{R2}, \cdots, I_{Rm}]^\top_{n\times 1}$	Rx currents
Z_R	$\begin{bmatrix} Z_{R1} & j\omega M_{R12} & \cdots & j\omega M_{R1m} \\ j\omega M_{R21} & Z_{R2} & \cdots & j\omega M_{R2m} \\ \vdots & \vdots & \ddots & \vdots \\ j\omega M_{Rm1} & j\omega M_{Rm2} & \cdots & Z_{Rm} \end{bmatrix}_{m\times m}$	Rx impedance and inter-Rx magnetic couplings
Z_T	$\begin{bmatrix} Z_{T1} & j\omega M_{T12} & \cdots & j\omega M_{T1n} \\ j\omega M_{T21} & Z_{T2} & \cdots & j\omega M_{T2n} \\ \vdots & \vdots & \ddots & \vdots \\ j\omega M_{Tn1} & j\omega M_{Tn2} & \cdots & Z_{Tn} \end{bmatrix}_{n\times n}$	Tx impedance and inter-Tx magnetic couplings
M	$\begin{bmatrix} M_{11} & M_{21} & \cdots & M_{n1} \\ \vdots & \vdots & \ddots & \vdots \\ M_{1m} & M_{2m} & \cdots & M_{nm} \end{bmatrix}_{m\times n}$	Tx-Rx magnetic couplings

(b) Matrix & Vector Denotations

Figure 3: **Circuit Schematic and Denotations of a Multi-Coil Tx, Multiple Rx Wireless Power Delivery System**

ceiver u's circuit equation becomes:

$$Z_{Ru}I_{Ru} + \underbrace{\sum_{v\neq u} j\omega M_{Ruv}I_{Rv}}_{\text{from the other receivers}} = \underbrace{\sum_{i} j\omega M_{iu}I_{Ti}}_{\text{from the transmitters}} \tag{3}$$

while the transmitter voltage at coil i is:

$$V_{Ti} = Z_{Ti}I_{Ti} + \underbrace{\sum_{k\neq i} j\omega M_{Tik}I_{Tk}}_{\text{from the other transmitters}} - \underbrace{\sum_{u} j\omega M_{iu}I_{Ru}}_{\text{from the receivers}} \tag{4}$$

For convenience, we rewrite Eq. (3) and (4) in matrix form:

$$\text{Rx Equation:} \quad \vec{i}_R = j\omega Z_R^{-1} M \vec{i}_T \tag{5}$$

$$\text{Tx Equation:} \quad \vec{v}_T = \left(Z_T + \omega^2 M^\top Z_R^{-1} M\right) \vec{i}_T \tag{6}$$

where the matrix and vector denotations are defined in Table 3b.[4]

Eq. (5) and Eq. (6) are sufficient to describe the multi-coil system in Fig. 3a. Specifically, Eq. (5) describes what receiver current $\vec{i}_R$ we will get if a transmitter current $\vec{i}_T$ is applied, thus we call it the *Receiver Equation*. Eq. (6), on the other hand, shows what voltage $\vec{v}_T$ we need to apply in order to obtain transmitter currents $\vec{i}_T$, so we name it the *Transmit Equation*. These two equations describe the most fundamental relationships in our multi-Tx multi-Rx system, and are the basis of *all* of the following conclusions of MultiSpot.

4. MULTISPOT

MultiSpot is a new technology for charging multiple devices wirelessly via magnetic resonance. It uses multiple transmit coils, which could be built into a desk mat to deliver a user experience analogous to a mini hotspot –i.e., when the user sits at her desk, all of her electronic gadgets start receiving power automatically. MultiSpot's design is mainly focused on the transmitter side. The receiver design follows that of standard wireless charging circuits, which can be built into the sleeve of a phone or the strap of a smartwatch.

[4]Note that similar to the single-Tx single-Rx case, Eq. (6) is obtained by first rewriting Eq. (4) into $\vec{v}_T = Z_T\vec{i}_T - j\omega M^\top \vec{i}_R$ and then substituting $\vec{i}_R$ using Eq. (5).

At first blush, it might seem that one can build a wireless power hotspot by beamforming the magnetic field to one receiver at a time using MagMIMO [1], and iterating between receivers using a TDMA style MAC. Unfortunately MagMIMO intrinsically assumes only one receiver. If multiple receivers are nearby, they all couple with each other and the transmitter coils. As a result, MagMIMO cannot discover the coupling due to each receiver (i.e., the magnetic channel to the receiver [1]) and hence cannot compute the beamforming parameters correctly. In fact MagMIMO would not know whether there is a single or multiple receivers. One could also try to add out-of-band communication (via WiFi or Bluetooth) to coordinate receivers, turn some receivers off so that at any point in time there is coupling only from one receiver, synchronize the receivers as they turn on and off, and have receivers detect any motion and inform each other so that they may re-estimate coupling. Such an approach is excessively complex and high overhead, and is not even clear how one can extend this idea into a full system.

Below we describe a design that requires neither receiver coordination nor out-of-band communication. It operates entirely on the transmitter allowing it to shape the magnetic field in multiple beams focused on the receivers, in a manner that is analytically proven to maximize power delivery.

4.1 Optimizing Power Delivery to Receivers

In wireless communication systems, such as MU-MIMO, beamforming effectively combines the signals constructively at the receivers so that the received signal gets maximized. This is achieved by carefully setting the transmitter signal according to the wireless channels. Similar concepts can be applied to wireless power delivery systems. However, to beamform in MultiSpot, we need to answer two questions. What exactly are the "signals" and "channels"? And how do we maximize the power of the received signal?

(a) Magnetic Channel: The Receiver Eq. (5) provides us a way to analogously define magnetic channels. Specifically, if we analogize currents to signals, the transmitted and received signals will be $\vec{i}_T$ and $\vec{i}_R$. Therefore, the coefficient between them is the magnetic channel, i.e.:

$$\vec{i}_R = H\vec{i}_T, \quad \text{where } H = j\omega Z_R^{-1} M \tag{7}$$

Note that the magnetic channel H is different from the channel matrix in MU-MIMO, where it is simply a concatenation of individual channels between every pair of transmitter and receiver. Rather, in MultiSpot, it is the multiplication of two parts: $\boldsymbol{H} = \boldsymbol{H}_{Rx-Rx}\boldsymbol{H}_{Rx-Tx}$ where $\boldsymbol{H}_{Rx-Rx} = \boldsymbol{Z}_R^{-1}$ contains receiver-receiver couplings and $\boldsymbol{H}_{Rx-Tx} = j\omega\boldsymbol{M}$ contains transmitter-receiver couplings. Physically, these two sub-channel matrices describe two processes that occur in multi-TX-coil multi-receiver power transfer system: $\boldsymbol{H}_{Rx-Tx}$ characterizes the induced power on the receivers from transmitters, while $\boldsymbol{H}_{Rx-Rx}$ captures the redistribution of transmitted power among receivers due to receiver-receiver coupling.

(b) Maximizing Received Power: The challenge becomes how to set the transmitter signals, (i.e., $\vec{\boldsymbol{i}}_T$), so that the received power is maximized. This question can be formulated as an optimization problem that maximizes the received power P_R, under the constraint of a total input power P.

The received power P_R can be written as the summation of the power delivered to each receiver, i.e.:

$$P_R = \vec{\boldsymbol{i}}_R^*\boldsymbol{R}_R\vec{\boldsymbol{i}}_R, \tag{8}$$

where $\vec{\boldsymbol{i}}_R$ is a vector of the receiver currents. The superscript (*) denotes conjugate transpose, and $\boldsymbol{R}_R$ is a diagonal matrix whose entries are the resistances of each receiver.[5]

The input power can be written as the total power dissipated on the transmitter and receivers, i.e., $P = P_R + P_T$. This is because power does not disappear, and hence must either be delivered to the receivers, or be consumed on the transmitters. Thus:

$$P = P_R + P_T = \vec{\boldsymbol{i}}_R^*\boldsymbol{R}_R\vec{\boldsymbol{i}}_R + \vec{\boldsymbol{i}}_T^*\boldsymbol{R}_T\vec{\boldsymbol{i}}_T, \tag{9}$$

where $\boldsymbol{R}_R$ and $\boldsymbol{R}_T$ are diagonal matrices of transmitter and receiver resistances.

Now, we can re-write the optimization problem that maximizes power transfer by substituting the received power and the input power by their values from Eq. (8) and Eq. (9). We also substitute the received currents from Eq. (7), $\vec{\boldsymbol{i}}_R = \boldsymbol{H}\vec{\boldsymbol{i}}_T$. Thus, our optimization problem becomes: Find the transmit currents that satisfy:

$$\begin{aligned} \vec{\boldsymbol{i}}_T^{\text{bf}} &= \arg\max \left\{\vec{\boldsymbol{i}}_T^*\boldsymbol{H}^*\boldsymbol{R}_R\boldsymbol{H}\vec{\boldsymbol{i}}_T\right\} \\ \text{conditioned on: } & \vec{\boldsymbol{i}}_T^*\boldsymbol{R}_T\vec{\boldsymbol{i}}_T + \vec{\boldsymbol{i}}_T^*\boldsymbol{H}^*\boldsymbol{R}_R\boldsymbol{H}\vec{\boldsymbol{i}}_T = P, \end{aligned} \tag{10}$$

where $\vec{\boldsymbol{i}}_T^{\text{bf}}$ denotes the set of currents that beamforms.

In Appendix A, we prove that the solution to this optimization is:

THEOREM 4.1. *The following transmitter current vector will maximize the received power:*

$$\vec{\boldsymbol{i}}_T^{bf} = c \cdot maxeig(\boldsymbol{H}^*\boldsymbol{R}_R\boldsymbol{H}) \tag{11}$$

where maxeig $(\boldsymbol{H}^*\boldsymbol{R}_R\boldsymbol{H})$ is the eigenvector of $\boldsymbol{H}^*\boldsymbol{R}_R\boldsymbol{H}$ that corresponds to the largest real eigenvalue λ, and c is a normalization scalar defined in App. A. Specifically, the maximal delivered power is equal to $\frac{\lambda}{\lambda+1}P$.

This theorem guarantees that MultiSpot maximizes the power delivered from the transmitter coils to the receiver coils. This means that for the same hardware and any given relative locations of transmitter and receiver coils, no other algorithm can deliver more power than what is specified by the theorem.

(c) Applying the Beamforming Solution: The solution from Thm. 4.1 would be sufficient if one could directly apply the currents to the coil. However, in practice, one has to use a voltage source instead. Therefore, we need to convert these currents to their corresponding voltages so that they are directly applicable to the Tx coils via standard voltage sources.

Fortunately, the Transmitter Eq. (6) that relates transmitter currents to voltages was derived in §3.1. Specifically, the set of voltages that we need to apply to the Tx coils is:

$$\vec{\boldsymbol{v}}_T^{\text{bf}} = \left(\boldsymbol{Z}_T + \omega^2\boldsymbol{M}^\top\boldsymbol{Z}_R^{-1}\boldsymbol{M}\right)\vec{\boldsymbol{i}}_T^{\text{bf}}. \tag{12}$$

In summary, maximizing power delivery requires two steps:

1. Calculate the beamforming currents, $\vec{\boldsymbol{i}}_T^{\text{bf}}$.
2. Convert the currents to voltages by $\vec{\boldsymbol{v}}_T^{\text{bf}}$, and apply the voltages to the transmitter coils.

4.2 Eliminating Need for Receivers' Communication

In the previous section, we showed how a MultiSpot charger could beamform. However, two steps are needed to beamform, both of which require information that resides on the receivers, and is unavailable at the transmitter.

- In the first step, the beamforming currents, $\vec{\boldsymbol{i}}_T^{\text{bf}}$, are calculated via Thm. 4.1, which is strictly dependent on knowing $\boldsymbol{H}^*\boldsymbol{R}_R\boldsymbol{H}$. Recall, however, that the channel contains receiver-receiver couplings, unknown to the transmitter.
- In the second step, the beamforming voltages, $\vec{\boldsymbol{v}}_T^{\text{bf}}$, are computed using Eq. (12), which depends on knowing $(\boldsymbol{Z}_T + \omega^2\boldsymbol{M}^\top\boldsymbol{Z}_R^{-1}\boldsymbol{M})$. $\boldsymbol{Z}_T$ contains only transmitter specific parameters (i.e., transmitter to transmitter couplings and impedances) and hence can be estimated a priori in a factory setting (for details, see Appendix D). However, the matrix $(\omega^2\boldsymbol{M}^\top\boldsymbol{Z}_R^{-1}\boldsymbol{M})$ contains receiver-receiver couplings and receiver impedances. This matrix which we denote $\boldsymbol{Y} = \omega^2\boldsymbol{M}^\top\boldsymbol{Z}_R^{-1}\boldsymbol{M}$ is unknown a priori to the transmitter (and changes with time because the coupling depends on receiver position).

Thus, beamforming requires estimating $\boldsymbol{H}^*\boldsymbol{R}_R\boldsymbol{H}$ and $\boldsymbol{Y}$, both of which involve receiver dependent information. So, how can a MultiSpot transmitter estimate these matrices without explicit information from the receivers?

Estimating $\boldsymbol{Y}$: Let us first consider estimating $\boldsymbol{Y}$. The Transmitter Eq. (6) can be rewritten as $\vec{\boldsymbol{v}}_T = (\boldsymbol{Z}_T + \boldsymbol{Y})\vec{\boldsymbol{i}}_T$, where the only unknown coefficient is $\boldsymbol{Y}$ because $\boldsymbol{Z}_T$ is measured during pre-calibration. By applying voltages and measuring the resulting currents on the Tx coils, we can estimate the coefficient between them. Since both $\vec{\boldsymbol{v}}_T$ and $\vec{\boldsymbol{i}}_T$ are vectors of length n, we need to repeat the measurement process n times before applying matrix inversion, where n is the number of Tx coils. More formally, if one applies n different sets of voltages $\vec{\boldsymbol{v}}_T^{(1)}, \cdots, \vec{\boldsymbol{v}}_T^{(n)}$ and measures the corresponding currents $\vec{\boldsymbol{i}}_T^{(1)}, \cdots, \vec{\boldsymbol{i}}_T^{(n)}$, one can estimate $\boldsymbol{Y}$ by:

$$\boldsymbol{Y} = \left[\vec{\boldsymbol{v}}_T^{(1)} \ \cdots \ \vec{\boldsymbol{v}}_T^{(n)}\right] \cdot \left[\vec{\boldsymbol{i}}_T^{(1)} \ \cdots \ \vec{\boldsymbol{i}}_T^{(n)}\right]^{-1} - \boldsymbol{Z}_T \tag{13}$$

Estimating $\boldsymbol{H}^*\boldsymbol{R}_R\boldsymbol{H}$: After obtaining $\boldsymbol{Y}$, we are still left with the problem of estimating $\boldsymbol{H}^*\boldsymbol{R}_R\boldsymbol{H}$. Recall that $\boldsymbol{H} = j\omega\boldsymbol{Z}_R^{-1}\boldsymbol{M}$, which means both transmitter-receiver couplings and receiver-receiver couplings need to be estimated. Unlike the matrix $\boldsymbol{Y}$ however, which can be estimated at the transmitter using measurements of $\vec{\boldsymbol{v}}_t$ and $\vec{\boldsymbol{i}}_T$, there is no way to measure $\boldsymbol{H}$ at the transmitter.

Fortunately, MultiSpot does not need to estimate $\boldsymbol{H}$. Instead, we show that a MultiSpot transmitter can estimate the matrix product

[5] If a receiver is not fully resistive, i.e., its impedance Z_{Ru} has an imaginary component, then $R_{Ru} = Real(Z_{Ru})$.

1 MultiSpot Algorithm

1: $\widetilde{\boldsymbol{Y}} \leftarrow \text{rand}(n \times n)$ ▷ $\widetilde{Y}$ can be initialized to any matrix
2: **while** true **do**
3: $\vec{\boldsymbol{i}}_T^{\text{bf}} = c \cdot \text{maxeig}(\text{Real}(\widetilde{\boldsymbol{Y}}))$ ▷compute beamforming currents
4: Apply $\vec{\boldsymbol{v}}_T^{\text{bf}} = \left(\boldsymbol{Z}_T + \widetilde{\boldsymbol{Y}}\right) \vec{\boldsymbol{i}}_T^{\text{bf}}$ ▷beamform
5: Measure $\vec{\boldsymbol{i}}_T$ on the transmitter
6: $\Delta\vec{\boldsymbol{i}}_T \leftarrow \vec{\boldsymbol{i}}_T^{\text{bf}} - \vec{\boldsymbol{i}}_T$
7: **if** $\Delta\vec{\boldsymbol{i}}_T \neq \vec{0}$ **then** ▷ if the channel changes
8: $\widetilde{\boldsymbol{Y}} \leftarrow \widetilde{\boldsymbol{Y}} + \frac{\Delta\vec{\boldsymbol{v}}_T \Delta\vec{\boldsymbol{v}}_T^\top}{\Delta\vec{\boldsymbol{v}}_T^\top \vec{\boldsymbol{i}}_T}$, where $\Delta\vec{\boldsymbol{v}}_T = (\boldsymbol{Z}_T + \widetilde{\boldsymbol{Y}})\Delta\vec{\boldsymbol{i}}_T$ ▷ update $\widetilde{Y}$
9: **end if**
10: **end while**

$\boldsymbol{H}^*\boldsymbol{R}_R\boldsymbol{H}$ as a whole; and it can do so completely passively. Further, we can relate $\boldsymbol{H}^*\boldsymbol{R}_R\boldsymbol{H}$ to something we have already measured, namely $\boldsymbol{Y}$. Specifically, we prove in Appendix B the following theorem:

THEOREM 4.2. *Define Real(·) as the real part of a matrix, then*

$$\boldsymbol{H}^*\boldsymbol{R}_R\boldsymbol{H} = \textit{Real}(\boldsymbol{Y}) \tag{14}$$

where $\boldsymbol{H} = j\omega\boldsymbol{Z}_R^{-1}\boldsymbol{M}$ *and* $\boldsymbol{Y} = \omega^2\boldsymbol{M}^\top\boldsymbol{Z}_R^{-1}\boldsymbol{M}$.

Since we have already shown how to compute $\boldsymbol{Y}$, the above theorem allows us to compute $\boldsymbol{H}^*\boldsymbol{R}_R\boldsymbol{H}$ by taking its real part.

Therefore, we have developed a method to estimate all needed parameters solely on the transmitter, without any communication or feedback from the receivers.

4.3 Adaptive Beamforming

Next, we would like to ensure that MultiSpot can smoothly adapt to receiver motion and receivers entering and leaving the system. This is particularly important for wearable receivers which tend to be highly dynamic, e.g., a smartwatch on a user's wrist.

When receivers move (or are added/removed), the magnetic couplings change across all devices, leading to new values for $\boldsymbol{H}$ and $\boldsymbol{Y}$. One could address this problem by repeatedly estimating $\boldsymbol{Y}$ and $\boldsymbol{H}^*\boldsymbol{R}_R\boldsymbol{H}$, as explained in §4.2. This, however, would be suboptimal since estimating $\boldsymbol{Y}$ from scratch requires the MultiSpot charger to stop beamforming and apply other voltages in order to obtain enough measurements as required by Eq. (13). Furthermore, since the transmitter does not know when receivers move, it is left with a difficult choice: Either it can repeat the estimation infrequently, which would be inefficient in scenarios with lots of motion, or it can repeat the estimation, often leading to frequent and unnecessary interruptions in beamforming when the receivers are static.

In this section, we propose an adaptive algorithm, which we call *adaptive beamforming*, that addresses the conflict: It uninterruptedly beamforms whenever the receivers remain static, and seamlessly and quickly adapts when any receiver moves.

The key idea is that instead of estimating $\boldsymbol{Y}$ from scratch, which would interrupt beamforming, the adaptive algorithm iteratively computes the new $\boldsymbol{Y}$. In each iteration, the algorithm computes an incremental update to $\boldsymbol{Y}$ that satisfies the following two constraints: 1) If no receiver moves, the update is zero; and 2) If any receiver moves, the update rule is guaranteed to move $\boldsymbol{Y}$ toward its true value and converge to the true value within a small number of steps.

Alg. 1 outlines MultiSpot's adaptive beamforming. For clarity, we use $\widetilde{\boldsymbol{Y}}$ to denote the algorithm's estimate of the true $\boldsymbol{Y}$ matrix. To start the algorithm randomly assigns an initial matrix to $\widetilde{\boldsymbol{Y}}$. In each iteration, the algorithm calculates the beamforming currents and converts them to beamforming voltages, which it applies to the transmitter coils.

Next (Line 5), the algorithm measures the currents on the transmit coils. If $\widetilde{\boldsymbol{Y}}$ is accurate, the measured currents should be equal to the currents that beamform ($\vec{\boldsymbol{i}}_T^{\text{bf}}$). Otherwise the algorithm uses the mismatch between the measured and expected currents and the resulting mismatch in voltages to update its estimate of $\widetilde{\boldsymbol{Y}}$ (Line 7).

It should be clear from the update rule in Line 7 that if nothing changes (e.g., no receiver moves), no update will occur and the beamforming is unmodified. Further, the theorem below guarantees that when a change occurs, the algorithm quickly converges to the optimal beamforming solution.

THEOREM 4.3. *If* $\widetilde{\boldsymbol{Y}} \neq \boldsymbol{Y}$, *then Alg. 1 is guaranteed to update* $\widetilde{\boldsymbol{Y}}$ *to* $\boldsymbol{Y}$ *in less than* n *iterations, where* n *is the number of transmitters.*

Thm. 4.3 is formally proven in Appendix C. Thm. 4.3 not only proves convergence but it puts an upper bound on the time to convergence. The convergence time is bounded only by the number of transmit coils, and is independent of the number of receivers. [6] In our implementation where the transmitter uses a standard microcontroller, each iteration in Alg. 1 can be finished in less than 1ms. When there is any movement, the algorithm takes about 5ms to converge to the new set of channels. This speed is more than sufficient for our application.

4.4 Power Distribution Among Receivers

The previous section presents an algorithm that adaptively delivers maximal power to the receivers. But how does the solution distribute this power among the various receivers? In order to gain insight into power distribution, we discuss three representative cases.

- In the first scenario, we consider identical receivers from the perspective of wireless charging – i.e., receivers with the same battery level, distance, and orientation with respect to the transmitter, and hence the same magnetic coupling. In this case, all receivers are allocated equal amounts of power. This is because the system is symmetric with respect to the receivers and hence an even power distribution yields the optimal solution.
- In the second scenario, we consider receivers that have the same battery level (i.e., the same demands for charging), but different magnetic couplings. Physically, this can be caused by some receivers being placed closer to the transmitter than others, with more favorable orientations, or simply having a larger coil. Either way, the receivers with stronger magnetic coupling will receive more power. This property is similar in spirit to resource allocation in typical networking systems. For example, TCP flows with shorter RTTs and WiFi clients with higher SNRs receive higher data rates.
- In the final case, we consider what happens as some receivers approach a fully charged battery while others are still in need for charging. We argue that in this case the MultiSpot charger naturally reduces the power allocated to the more charged receivers, diverting that power to those receivers who are still in need for wireless power. Specifically, consider two receivers with the same magnetic coupling, one of which is fully charged while the other has a low battery level.

[6] It is worth noting that a MultiSpot charger does not need to know the number of receivers to run Alg. 1. The charger has enough information to infer the number of receivers, which is equal to the rank of $\boldsymbol{Y}$.

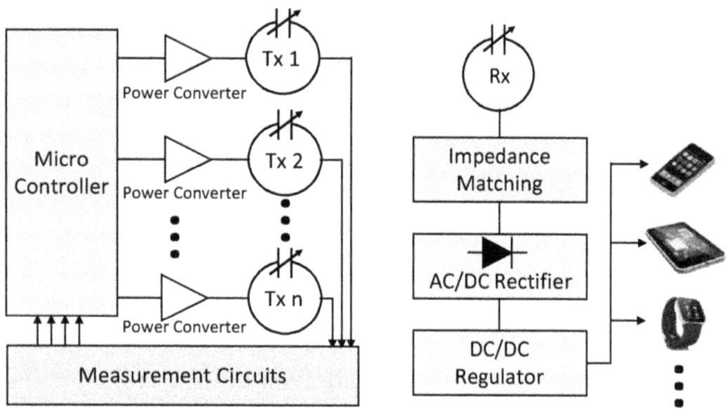

(a) Tx Diagram (b) Rx Diagram

Figure 4: **Circuit Diagram of MultiSpot's Tx and Rx**

When the battery is charged, the device needs very little power so it does not accept current. In this case the receiver circuit can be approximated by an open circuit, i.e., $I_R \approx 0$ for that receiver [38]. As a result, the receiver does not reflect power toward the transmitter. Therefore, the MultiSpot transmitter will not sense this receiver or beamform to it. In general, the progression from accepting current when the receiver has low battery levels to not accepting current when it is fully charged is gradual. Therefore, the algorithm gradually allocates less power to devices that are more charged.

To validate this intuition, we test each of the above situations experimentally in §7.

5. IMPLEMENTATION

We have built a prototype of MultiSpot to charge electronics in an office scenario. Our setup is similar to past work [1]. Specifically, the transmitter is composed of 6 copper coils and is mounted to the bottom of an office desk. Each transmit coil covers an area of 0.05m^2, which collectively cover an area of 0.38m^2. The transmitter can be attached to a regular office desk with metallic, plastic and wood contents. The only restriction of the system is that the desk surface must not be conductive.[7] Each phone receiver contains a single copper coil, of area 0.005m^2, that is embedded into a sleeve that attaches to the back of the device. As for the smartwatch, we embed the coil into the band of the watch.

In our implementation, the transmitter and receivers resonate at 1MHz, as in [1], which is within the frequency range of common wireless charging systems [15, 6, 7]. In addition, the setup is compatible with FCC regulations including part 15 and part 18.

The transmitter's architecture is shown in Fig. 4(a). MultiSpot drives 6 transmit coils to beamform a magnetic field towards the receivers. The output voltage and current of each coil are measured by the measurement circuit. This circuit employs quadrature mixers, AD8333 [40], to acquire the phase and amplitude of each signal and output them to the microcontroller. The microcontroller platform, Zynq 7Z010 [41], takes as input these amplitudes and phases and runs MultiSpot's algorithm. Every time Alg. 1 receives new measurements, it updates its estimates accordingly, and calculates the new voltages needed to beamform. It then sends the new set of voltages to the controller circuits which apply them to the transmit coils using a Class D Full Bridge Power Converter [42]. This converter allows the controller circuit to flexibly control both the amplitudes and phases of the voltages applied to the transmit coils.

The receiver circuit is shown in Fig. 4(b). It has an impedance matching network designed to maximize the power that gets delivered to the device. This is followed by a full bridge rectifier which converts the AC signal into a DC voltage. This DC voltage passes through a DC-DC voltage regulator that converts the input voltage to a constant 5V. This allows the power to be distributed across a USB port so that the receiver can support a large variety of unmodified devices that can be charged via USB, including most phones, tablets and wearables.

6. EVALUATION ENVIRONMENT

Metrics: We define *distance* as the distance between the nearest point on the receiver coil and the transmitter coils. For example, if a receiver is in the same plane of the transmitter but outside the area that the transmitter coils cover, then the distance is from the edge of the receiver to the edge of the nearest transmitter coil.

We define *charging time ratio* as the ratio between the time taken to wirelessly charge a phone from dead to full battery, to the time it takes a wall plug to do the same. For multiple phones, the charging time ratio reported is the largest time ratio of all involved phones, i.e., it is the charging time of the phone that takes longest to charge.

We define *orientation* as the angle between the plane of the receiver coil and the plane of the transmitter coils.

Baselines: We compare the following systems:

- Commercially available multi-device wireless chargers: Duracell Powermat [4], Energizer Qi [5] and LUXA2 [16]. Each of them requires a proprietary receiving case, which we attach to the phone during the experiments.
- State-of-the-art Prototype. Specifically, we choose the WiTricity WiT-5000 prototype [15] that charges multiple devices. Since the prototype is not publicly available, we extract the data from their technical sheet [15].
- *Idealized* Selective Coil: This baseline uses the same 6 Tx coils as MultiSpot, but given a set of receivers, it identifies the best Tx coil for each receiver, and divides the input power equally between the set of best Tx coils. For example, given two receivers, it identifies the best Tx coil for the first receiver, and the best Tx coil for the second receiver, and divides the power between those two Tx coils.
  We note that this baseline requires an oracle to decide which Tx coil would deliver the maximum power to each receiver. Specifically, one cannot identify the Tx coil that has the best magnetic coupling to a receiver in the presence of other receivers. Hence, to implement this system, for each receiver, we physically remove the other receivers and measure the receiver coupling to the transmitter. While this is hard to do in a real-world setup, the baseline provides insights about how well one can do by distributing the input power between the best performing Tx coils.
- Our MultiSpot prototype described in §5.
- MagMIMO [1] using the same Tx coils as MultiSpot.

We note that the input powers of Duracell Powermat [4], Energizer Qi [5], LUXA2 [16], and WiTricity WiT-500 [15] are 15W, 18W, 22W, and 24W, respectively. Since these baselines have different input powers, we set the input power of MultiSpot, selective coil, and MagMIMO to the mean of those values, i.e., 20W.

Setup: All experiments are performed in an office environment. The charger is placed on a standard office desk. Unless specified otherwise, the charged devices (e.g., phones) are held using config-

[7]Conductive materials as large as the desk surface might negatively affect MultiSpot's performance. This is a standard assumption required by magnetic wireless power delivery and can be found in research papers [1] and commercial systems [39].

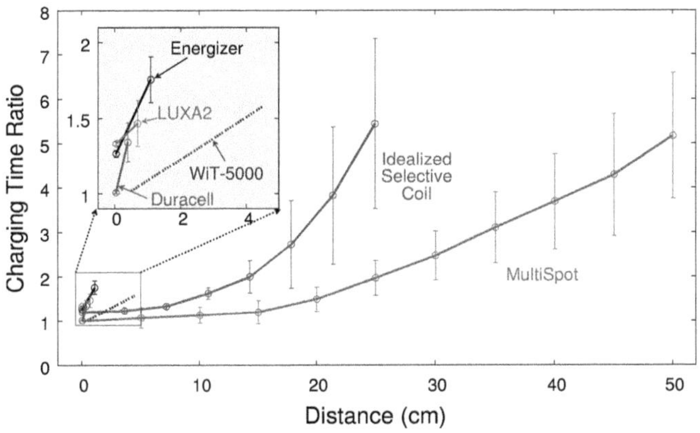

Figure 5: **Charging Time Ratio vs. Distance from Charger.** Each run uses 2 phones at equal distance, but in different locations.

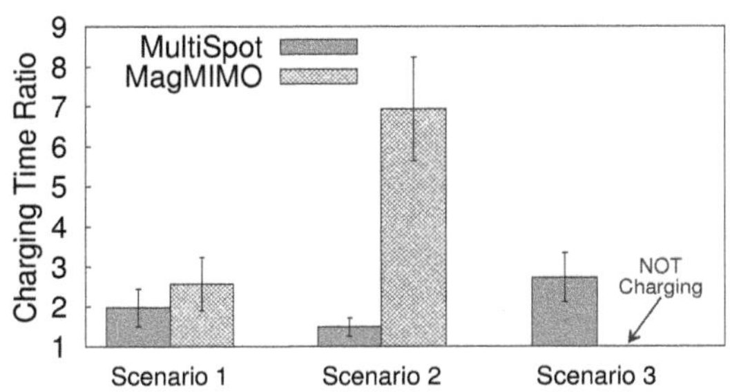

Figure 6: **Comparison with MagMIMO:** Scenario 1: two receivers 5cm apart and both 25cm away from the transmitter; Scenario 2: two receivers 60cm apart and both 10cm away from the transmitter; Scenario 3: two receivers 60cm apart and both 20cm away. The figure shows that MagMIMO works well for co-located receivers, but can completely fail if the receivers are far apart.

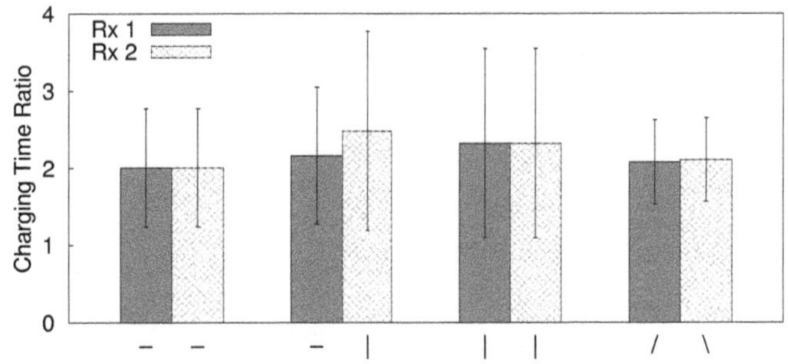

Figure 7: **Charging Time vs. Orientation.** We plot the charging time ratio versus different orientations. Each group of two bars represent a combination of orientations, where "—" denotes horizontal, "|" denotes vertical, while "/" and "\" denote 45°. All receivers are 25cm away from the charger.

urable arms which allows us to test different charging distances and orientations.

7. RESULTS

7.1 Charging Time vs. Distance

We evaluate MultiSpot's ability to charge multiple phones at various distances from the transmitter. We run each experiment with 2 phones because the commercial baselines are constrained to charging 2 receivers. The distance of both receivers is increased from 2cm to 50cm together. At each distance, multiple experiments are run with different receiver positions and orientations.

Fig. 5 shows the charging time ratio of MultiSpot and the baselines as a function of the distance from the charger. At near distances (0-10cm), MultiSpot's charging time is comparable to a wired charger. It starts to increase at mid-range to far-range. MultiSpot reaches as far as 50cm. Comparing with the baselines, MultiSpot has much larger range, and shorter charging time at the same range. The commercial baselines (Energizer, LUXA2, Duracell) and development prototype (WiT-5000) are constrained to less than 5cm. Even when compared to the idealized selective-coil, MultiSpot reaches much larger range. And even within the same range, MultiSpot's charging time is on average 3x smaller than that of idealized selective coil.

7.2 Comparison with MagMIMO

MultiSpot is inspired by MagMIMO [1], which proposes magnetic beamforming to a single device. Thus, in this experiment we compare MagMIMO with MultiSpot. We separate this experiment from the other baselines since MagMIMO is not intended for charging multiple devices. Still one might wonder how MagMIMO would perform when there are multiple devices around, and how does it compare to MultiSpot.

We use the same hardware to run MultiSpot and MagMIMO. We use two receivers and run both MagMIMO and MultiSpot in three different scenarios. In the first scenario, the two receivers are co-located within 5cm from each other, and both are 25cm away from the transmitter. In the second scenario, the receivers are 60cm apart, and both 10cm away from the transmitter. In the third scenario, the two receivers are 60cm apart and both 20cm away from the transmitter.

Fig. 6 shows that MagMIMO is comparable to MultiSpot only when the two phones are co-located and hence can be considered as one device. Otherwise, MagMIMO's charging time becomes an order of magnitude longer than MultiSpot, or it fails to charge one of the phones all together. The reason is that MagMIMO has no mechanism for separating the magnetic couplings of the two receivers, and hence interprets the magnetic channels of both receivers as one channel and tries to create one beam to charge both phones. When the phones are adjacent, this technique works because one beam can charge both receivers, but as this distance increases, the charging time ratio inevitably goes up. MultiSpot on the other hand, creates two beams for both receivers and is able to power both phones regardless of the distance between them.

7.3 Charging Time vs. Orientation

We investigate MultiSpot's performance with different receiver orientations. For all experiments, the distances of both receivers is fixed to be 25cm, while their orientations are varied. We test four scenarios: both phones horizontal, one horizontal and one vertical, both vertical, and both at 45° tilt.

The results in Fig. 7 show that the time that MultiSpot's performance is almost orientation agnostic. Although there are some variations in the charging time ratio between different orientation scenarios, but the difference remain relatively small. For example, charging two horizontal phones take about 2x wired charging time, while two vertical phones take 2.3x wired charging time.

7.4 Performance vs. Number of Receivers

Next, we evaluate MultiSpot's performance along a few dimensions as the number of receivers increases.

Charging Time vs. Number of Receivers: We evaluate MultiSpot's ability to charge different numbers of receivers. We run

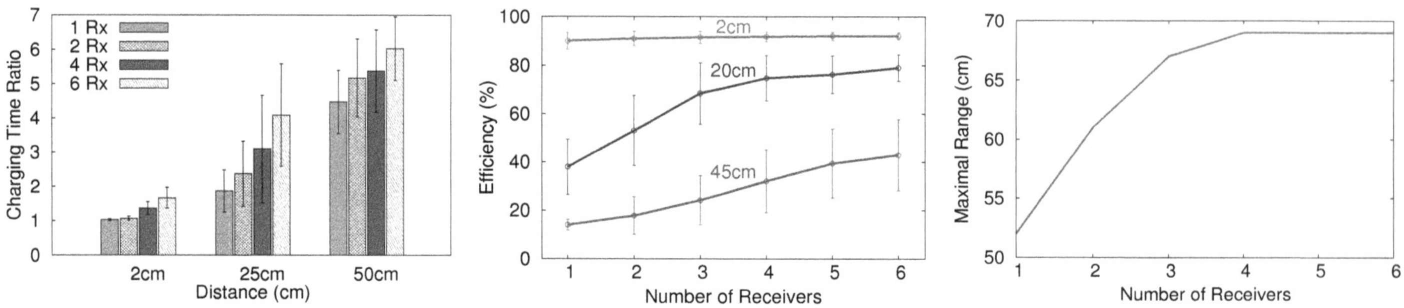

(a) Charging Time Ratio vs. Number of Rx (b) Efficiency vs. Number of Rx (c) Maximal Range vs. Number of Rx

Figure 8: **MultiSpot's Performance with Number of Receivers.** (a) MultiSpot's charging time ratio with up to 6 receivers; (b) MultiSpot's efficiency as a function of receiver number and distance to the charger. (c) MultiSpot's maximal charging range increases with receivers.

experiments with 1, 2, 4, and 6 receivers. In each experiment, all of the receivers are placed at the same distance from the charger, but at random positions and orientations. To show the results we pick three representative distances, 2cm (near range), 25cm (mid range) and 50cm (far range). Fig. 8a shows the charging time ratio versus number of receivers. In all cases MultiSpot is able to charge all of the phones. However, the charging time increases with distance and number of receivers. This is because MultiSpot needs to split more beams when there are more receivers, so the power that is carried in each beam will go down with more receivers.

Efficiency vs. Number of Receivers: We test MultiSpot's efficiency with different locations and number of receivers. The distance of all receivers to the transmitter is fixed while the number of receivers is increased. For a given distance and number of receivers, the positions and orientations are varied across runs. We evaluate MultiSpot's efficiency. Similar to past work [1], we define efficiency as the ratio between the total received power at all receiving coils divided by the total input power at the transmitting coils. The experiment is repeated with 3 different distances: near range (2cm), mid range (25cm) and far range (45cm). For each range we repeat the experiments for different number of receivers.

Based on Fig. 8b, we make a few observations:

- For a single device, MultiSpot has similar or better efficiency compared with state-of-the-art systems. For example, MagMIMO [1] reports 89% and 34% efficiency with single device at 2cm and 20cm, while MultiSpot's efficiencies are 90% and 38% at 2cm and 20cm, At near range, MultiSpot's efficiency is better than commercial systems. For example, WiTricity WiT-5000 [15] reaches its best efficiency (90%) at 0.6cm, while MultiSpot has 90% efficiency at a larger distance (2cm).
- We also find it interesting that the system efficiency increases with the number of receivers. For example, at 45cm the efficiency increases from 14% with single device to 43% with 6 receivers. This effect is more apparent when the receivers are at mid-range and far-range. The reason is that the more receivers are around, the more magnetic flux can be picked up by the receivers. This happens because the beams are relatively wide, and hence when there are more receivers, they can collectively pick up more energy.

Maximal Range vs. Number of Receivers: As the number of receivers increases, the efficiency of MultiSpot increases. With this increased efficiency, it may be possible to charge a receiver at a larger distance when more receivers are in the system. Therefore, this experiment is aimed to find the maximum distance from the transmitter a phone can still charge from, given a number of receivers. To get a feel of how the range increases with number of devices, we put all phones horizontally above the coils and find the maximal z distance. Different phones are aligned and spaced vertically.

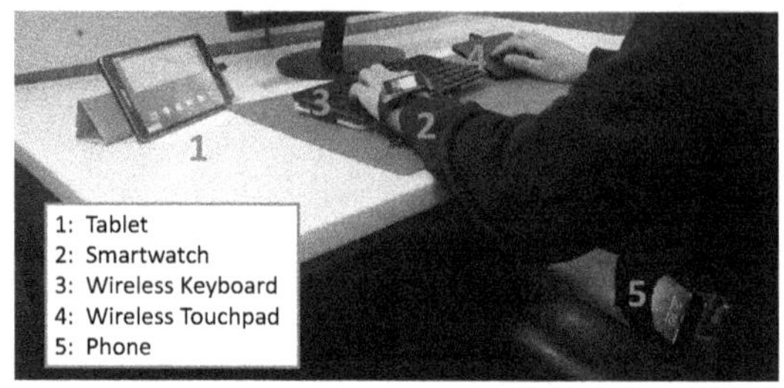

(a) The Experimental Setup

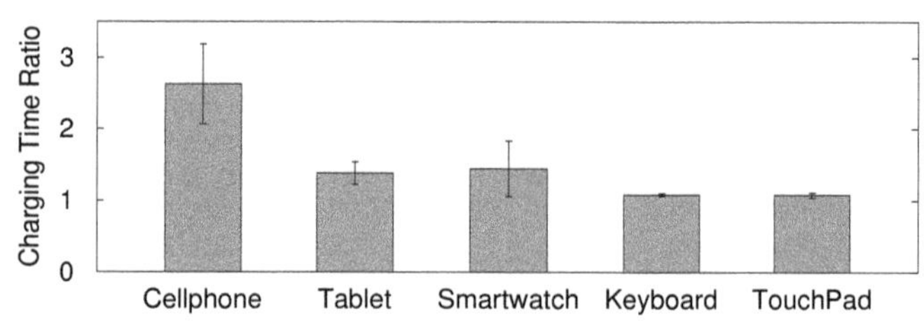

(b) Charging Time Result

Figure 9: **User Experiment:** MultiSpot can charge multiple types of devices concurrently in an office desk scenario as shown in (a).

Fig. 8c shows the maximal charging range vs. the number of receivers. The maximum range does indeed increase with the number of receivers. From one receiver to two receivers, the distance increases by 10cm. With 4 phones, the extension of range is 17cm.

In particular, because of the magnetic coupling between the receivers, one receiver might induce power on another receiver. In this case the receiver acts as a power relay, extending the maximal range of power delivery.

7.5 User Experiment

The goal of this experiment is two-fold: first, we want to ensure that MultiSpot works with a diversity of devices; second, we want to show that MultiSpot could charge all devices while the user is interacting with them or moving them.

We use the same setup as used by other experiments. However, we involve a variety of receiver devices. Specifically, we have tested cellphones (iPhone 4s/5s/6, Nexus 4, Samsung Galaxy S4/S5, HTC Evo and Motorola Droid X2), tablets (Samsung Glaxy Tab 4 and Kindle Paper White), smartwatch (Samsung Gear Live Smartwatch), wireless keyboard (Logitech K810) and wireless touchpad

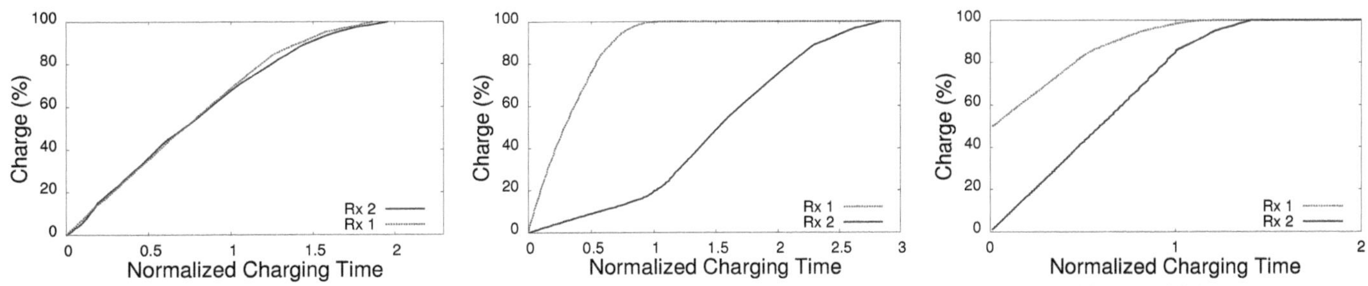

Figure 10: **Charging Curves of Two Phones For Three Scenarios:** The x-axis is charge time normalized by charge time of a wall plug to charge from dead battery to full. The scenarios are: (a): Charging two phones from dead batteries, with the same distance (25cm); (b): Same as (a), but with different distances (Rx1: 10cm, Rx2: 40cm). (c): Same as (a) but the two phones start with different battery levels (0%, 50%).

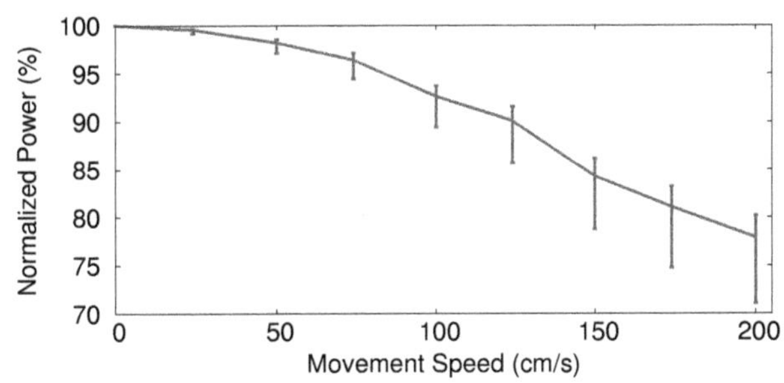

Figure 11: **Normalized Power vs. Motion Speed.** We plot the normalized received power versus different movement speed of the receiver. The reduction of received power is less than 3% when the speed is less than 50cm/s; it goes up to 20%-30% when the receiver moves at 200m/s.

(Logitech T650). In each experiment, we place the keyboard and touchpad flatly on the desk, and place the tablet against a stand. We then ask the user to sit in front of the desk and type on the keyboard, with a cellphone in her pocket and a smartwatch on her wrist (see Fig. 9a for a photo while the experiment is running). We measure the charging time ratio for each type of devices. We repeat the experiment with 3 users.

Fig. 9b shows the charging time ratio of the various device types. MultiSpot can charge all of the devices, however the charging time ratio of each of them is different. The cellphone and smartwatch have relatively higher charging time ratios and standard deviations. This is because they are carried by the user, while the other devices are static on the desk. Also, according to Fig. 9b, the cellphone takes longer than the smartwatch to charge. This is because as the user works, their wrist is moving above the desk while the phone is in their pocket, so naturally the phone is on average farther away from the coils.

Finally, we have used a temperature gun infrared thermometer [43] to monitor the temperature of the devices during the experiment. The maximal temperature increase we have measured is 4°C over a duration of 5 hours.

7.6 Power Distribution among Receivers

In this section, we select three representative scenarios to show how MultiSpot distributes power among receivers. We charge two iPhones 5s, in different scenarios:

- *Same Distance and Initial Battery*: We put each of the two phones 25cm away from the charger and let them charge from a dead battery. Fig. 10a shows their charging curve, i.e., battery percentage vs. time. Since all factors of these two phones are almost exactly the same, the phones charge at the same rate, as shown in the figure.
- *Different Distances*: We charge two phones with dead batteries but with different distances from the transmitter (10cm and 40cm). Fig. 10b shows the charging rate of the two phones. The figure shows that initially, the phone closer to the transmitter (i.e., Rx1) charges faster since it has a stronger magnetic coupling with the charger. However, once this phone is fully charged, MultiSpot transfers the power to the second receiver (Rx2), increasing its charging rate. Said differently, when one phone is fully charged and has no demand for power, MultiSpot automatically re-allocates the power to serve the other receiver which still has demands.
- *Different Initial Batteries*: We repeat the previous experiment, with different battery levels (0% and 50%). The results presented in Fig. 10c show that the phone with a lower battery level charges faster. Thus, when all other factors are the same, MultiSpot allocates more power to the device that has a lower battery level, i.e., the device with higher demands for power.

7.7 Performance vs. Motion

In this experiment, we aim to evaluate MultiSpot's performance with regard to the motion of the receiver. We use the same setup as other experiments, but add controlled movements to the receiver. Specifically, we attach the receiver to a motor which moves across the table where the charger is mounted, and vary the speeds across different experiments. During the experiments, the receiver is always 15cm above the table.

To measure MultiSpot's performance, we pick 5 evenly distanced locations in the motion's path, measure the received power at each location, and average them. We then normalize it by the power when there is no motion. Fig. 11 shows the normalized power versus motion speed. We can see that MultiSpot works well with mild receiver motion, and degrades if the speed increases. Various surveys [44, 45, 46] have suggested that the average speed of natural human arm movements is under 50cm/s, in which case the received power is almost unaffected (<3% degradation). If the speed reaches 200cm/s, the reduction of power is around 20%-30%.

8. CONCLUSION

This paper presents MultiSpot, a power hotspot that can charge multiple devices wirelessly and simultaneously, at distances up to 50cm. MultiSpot can be attached to an office desk, and used to charge surrounding electronic devices. It can also charge devices carried by the user once she is in the vicinity of a MultiSpot charger. This allows MultiSpot to be used in more practical scenarios, where the area of movement by the user is relatively constrained, such as bed-stands, car seats, coffee shops, airports waiting seats, etc. We believe MultiSpot pushes the state-of-the-art of wireless charging and significantly improves the user experience. Important tasks for future work include evaluating our system for a wider range of mobile devices and applications, and allowing the system to explicitly specify how much power is delivered to each receiver.

9. ACKNOWLEDGEMENTS

We thank the anonymous reviewers and shepherd for their constructive comments. We are grateful to Omid Abari, Fadel Adib, Haitham Hassanieh, Swarun Kumar, John MacDonald, Deepak Vasisht, for their constructive feedbacks. We also thank the NETMIT group for their support. This research is funded by NSF. We thank members of the MIT Wireless Center: Amazon, Cisco, Google, Intel, Mediatek, Microsoft and Telefonica for their interest and general support.

APPENDIX

A. PROOF OF THEOREM 4.1

Proof: We start with converting the optimization problem to another equivalent one. Specifically, if we define $\vec{x} = \sqrt{\boldsymbol{R}_T}\vec{i}_T$, [8] then the problem becomes that we want to find $\vec{i}_T^{\text{bf}} = \sqrt{\boldsymbol{R}_T^{-1}}\vec{x}_T^{\text{bf}}$, where $\vec{x}_T^{\text{bf}}$ is the solution to the following:

$$\vec{x}_T^{\text{bf}} = \arg\max_{\vec{x}} \{\vec{x}^*\boldsymbol{A}\vec{x}\}, \text{ where } \boldsymbol{A} \triangleq \sqrt{\boldsymbol{R}_T^{-1}}\boldsymbol{H}^*\boldsymbol{R}_R\boldsymbol{H}\sqrt{\boldsymbol{R}_T^{-1}}$$

The constraint correspondingly becomes $\vec{x}^*\vec{x} + \vec{x}^*\boldsymbol{A}\vec{x} = P$. Now, since $\boldsymbol{A}$ is a positive semi-definite Hermitian matrix (recall both $\boldsymbol{R}_R$ and $\boldsymbol{R}_T$ are real positive diagonal matrices), it can be eigen-decomposed to $\boldsymbol{A} = \boldsymbol{Q}\boldsymbol{\Lambda}\boldsymbol{Q}^*$, where $\boldsymbol{Q}$ is a unitary matrix and $\boldsymbol{\Lambda}$ is a diagonal matrix of the eigenvalues of $\boldsymbol{A}$. Furthermore, all eigenvalues, $\lambda_1, \cdots, \lambda_n$, are real and non-negative. If we define $\vec{x}' = \boldsymbol{Q}^*\vec{x}$, then the objective function $\vec{x}^*\boldsymbol{A}\vec{x}$ can be written as $(\vec{x}')^*\boldsymbol{\Lambda}\vec{x}' = \sum_i \lambda_i|x_i'|^2$. Similarly, the constraint becomes: $\vec{x}^*\vec{x} + \vec{x}^*\boldsymbol{A}\vec{x} = (\vec{x}')^*\vec{x}' + (\vec{x}')^*\boldsymbol{\Lambda}\vec{x}' = \sum_i(\lambda_i + 1)|x_i'|^2$. Therefore, we have converted our optimization problem to:

$$\begin{array}{ll} \max & \sum_i \lambda_i|x_i'|^2 \\ \text{s.t.} & \sum_i(\lambda_i + 1)|x_i'|^2 = P \end{array}$$

Since all λ_i's are real non-negative, the optimal solution $\vec{x}'$ is zero in every entry except the one that λ_i is maximal. More formally, say that $\lambda_k = \arg\max\{\lambda_1, \cdots, \lambda_n\}$, then $\vec{x}'$ is zero on entries except the k-th one. In this case, the maximal value that is achieved is $\frac{\lambda_k}{\lambda_k+1}P$. Recall that $\vec{x}' = \boldsymbol{Q}^*\vec{x}$, or equivalently, $\vec{x} = \boldsymbol{Q}\vec{x}'$. Therefore, the optimal solution $\vec{x}_T^{\text{bf}}$ is proportional to k-th column of $\boldsymbol{Q}$ (i.e., the k-th eigenvector of $\boldsymbol{A}$). Substituting back $\vec{x} = \sqrt{\boldsymbol{R}_T}\vec{i}_T$, we get the optimal $\vec{i}_T^{\text{bf}}$:

$$\vec{i}_T^{\text{bf}} = c \cdot \sqrt{\boldsymbol{R}_T^{-1}} \cdot \text{maxeig}\left(\sqrt{\boldsymbol{R}_T^{-1}}\boldsymbol{H}^*\boldsymbol{R}_R\boldsymbol{H}\sqrt{\boldsymbol{R}_T^{-1}}\right)$$

In this paper, to simplify the equations, we assume the transmitter coils are identical, i.e., $R_{T1} = \cdots = R_{Tn} = R_T$. In this case, $\boldsymbol{R}_T$ is proportional to an identity matrix, thus when multiplied with another matrix, will not change it eigenvectors. Therefore, in this case, the solution is $\vec{i}_T^{\text{bf}} = c \cdot \text{maxeig}(\boldsymbol{H}^*\boldsymbol{R}_R\boldsymbol{H})$. c is a scalar that captures R_T and other terms. It can be solved by substituting $\vec{i}_T$ by $\vec{i}_T^{\text{bf}}$ to the constraint $\vec{i}_T^*\boldsymbol{R}_T\vec{i}_T + \vec{i}_T^*\boldsymbol{H}^*\boldsymbol{R}_R\boldsymbol{H}\vec{i}_T = P$. Note that this does not substantially change any of the conclusions in this paper; plugging back $\boldsymbol{R}_T$ into them is straightforward.

[8] $\sqrt{\boldsymbol{R}_T}$ is a diagonal matrix whose diagonal entries are square root of those of $\boldsymbol{R}_T$. Similarly, $\sqrt{\boldsymbol{R}_R}$ can be defined.

B. PROOF OF THEOREM 4.2

Let's first expand $\boldsymbol{H}^*\boldsymbol{R}_R\boldsymbol{H}$ and $\boldsymbol{Y}$: $\boldsymbol{H}^*\boldsymbol{R}_R\boldsymbol{H} = \omega^2\boldsymbol{M}^\top\left(\boldsymbol{Z}_R^{-1}\right)^*\boldsymbol{R}_R\boldsymbol{Z}_R^{-1}\boldsymbol{M}$, and $\boldsymbol{Y} = \omega^2\boldsymbol{M}^\top\boldsymbol{Z}_R^{-1}\boldsymbol{M}$. Recall that $\boldsymbol{M}$ is a real matrix, therefore in order to prove $\boldsymbol{H}^*\boldsymbol{R}_R\boldsymbol{H} = \text{Real}(\boldsymbol{Y})$, what we need to prove is

$$\left(\boldsymbol{Z}_R^{-1}\right)^*\boldsymbol{R}_R\boldsymbol{Z}_R^{-1} = \text{Real}\left(\boldsymbol{Z}_R^{-1}\right)$$

which is proved as follows:

Proof: Note that: 1) $\boldsymbol{R}_R$ is the real part of $\boldsymbol{Z}_R$, therefore,

$$\boldsymbol{R}_R = \frac{1}{2}\left(\boldsymbol{Z}_R + \overline{\boldsymbol{Z}_R}\right) \tag{15}$$

where $\overline{\boldsymbol{Z}_R}$ means entry-wise conjugate of $\boldsymbol{Z}_R$; 2) $\boldsymbol{Z}_R$ is symmetric, i.e., $\boldsymbol{Z}_R = \boldsymbol{Z}_R^\top$, thus by conjugating both sides, we get $\overline{\boldsymbol{Z}_R} = \boldsymbol{Z}_R^*$. Inverting both sides yields

$$\left(\overline{\boldsymbol{Z}_R}\right)^{-1} = \left(\boldsymbol{Z}_R^{-1}\right)^* \tag{16}$$

Substituting them, we get:

$$\begin{aligned}\left(\boldsymbol{Z}_R^{-1}\right)^*\boldsymbol{R}_R\boldsymbol{Z}_R^{-1} &\overset{\text{Eq. (15)}}{\Longrightarrow} \tfrac{1}{2}\left(\boldsymbol{Z}_R^{-1}\right)^*\left(\boldsymbol{Z}_R + \overline{\boldsymbol{Z}_R}\right)\boldsymbol{Z}_R^{-1} \\ &\overset{\text{Eq. (16)}}{\Longrightarrow} \tfrac{1}{2}\left(\boldsymbol{Z}_R^{-1}\right)^* + \tfrac{1}{2}\left(\overline{\boldsymbol{Z}_R}\right)^{-1}\overline{\boldsymbol{Z}_R}\boldsymbol{Z}_R^{-1} \\ &\overset{\text{Eq. (16)}}{\Longrightarrow} \tfrac{1}{2}\left(\overline{\boldsymbol{Z}_R^{-1}} + \boldsymbol{Z}_R^{-1}\right) = \text{Real}\left(\boldsymbol{Z}_R^{-1}\right)\end{aligned}$$

Thus, $\left(\boldsymbol{Z}_R^{-1}\right)^*\boldsymbol{R}_R\boldsymbol{Z}_R^{-1} = \text{Real}\left(\boldsymbol{Z}_R^{-1}\right)$. □

C. PROOF OF THEOREM 4.3

We prove the theorem by showing that the rank of $\boldsymbol{Y} - \widetilde{\boldsymbol{Y}}$ gets reduced in every iteration, by the following lemma:

LEMMA C.1. *For any complex symmetric matrix $\boldsymbol{A}$ (i.e., $\boldsymbol{A} = \boldsymbol{A}^\top$), any vector $\vec{\eta}$ such that $\vec{\eta}^\top\boldsymbol{A}\vec{\eta} \neq 0$, define $\vec{\xi} = \boldsymbol{A}\vec{\eta}$, then rank $\left(\boldsymbol{A} - \frac{\vec{\xi}\vec{\xi}^\top}{\vec{\xi}^\top\vec{\eta}}\right) \leq$ rank$(\boldsymbol{A}) - 1$.*

Proof: Since $\boldsymbol{A}$ is a complex symmetric matrix, there exists an Autonne-Takagi factorization [47] such that

$$\boldsymbol{A} = \boldsymbol{Q}\boldsymbol{\Lambda}\boldsymbol{Q}^\top, \text{ where } \boldsymbol{\Lambda} = \begin{bmatrix} \boldsymbol{\Lambda}_0 & \boldsymbol{O} \\ \boldsymbol{O} & \boldsymbol{O} \end{bmatrix}$$

where $\boldsymbol{Q}$ is a $n \times n$ unitary matrix, and $\boldsymbol{\Lambda}_0$ is a $r \times r$ diagonal matrix, where r is the rank of $\boldsymbol{A}$. Now substitute this as well as $\vec{\xi} = \boldsymbol{A}\vec{\eta}$, we get:

$$\boldsymbol{A} - \frac{\vec{\xi}\vec{\xi}^\top}{\vec{\xi}^\top\vec{\eta}} = \boldsymbol{Q}\left(\boldsymbol{\Lambda} - \frac{\boldsymbol{\Lambda}\boldsymbol{Q}^\top\vec{\eta}\vec{\eta}^\top\boldsymbol{Q}\boldsymbol{\Lambda}}{\vec{\eta}^\top\boldsymbol{Q}\boldsymbol{\Lambda}\boldsymbol{Q}^\top\vec{\eta}}\right)\boldsymbol{Q}^\top \tag{17}$$

Define $\vec{\zeta} = \boldsymbol{Q}^\top\vec{\eta}$, and substitute it into Eq. (17), we get

$$\boldsymbol{A} - \frac{\vec{\xi}\vec{\xi}^\top}{\vec{\xi}^\top\vec{\eta}} = \boldsymbol{Q}\begin{bmatrix} \boldsymbol{\Lambda}_0 - \frac{\boldsymbol{\Lambda}_0\vec{\zeta}_0\vec{\zeta}_0^\top\boldsymbol{\Lambda}_0}{\vec{\zeta}_0^\top\boldsymbol{\Lambda}_0\vec{\zeta}_0} & \vec{0} \\ \vec{0}^\top & \boldsymbol{O} \end{bmatrix}\boldsymbol{Q}^\top$$

Since $\boldsymbol{Q}$ is unitary, the rank of $\boldsymbol{A} - \frac{\vec{\xi}\vec{\xi}^\top}{\vec{\xi}^\top\vec{\eta}}$ is equal to the rank of $\boldsymbol{\Lambda}_0 - \frac{\boldsymbol{\Lambda}_0\vec{\zeta}_0\vec{\zeta}_0^\top\boldsymbol{\Lambda}_0}{\vec{\zeta}_0^\top\boldsymbol{\Lambda}_0\vec{\zeta}_0}$, which we define as matrix $\boldsymbol{B}$. If we define $\vec{\zeta}_0$ to be the first r entries of $\vec{\zeta}$, we observe that:

$$\boldsymbol{B}\vec{\zeta}_0 = \boldsymbol{\Lambda}_0\vec{\zeta}_0 - \frac{\boldsymbol{\Lambda}_0\vec{\zeta}_0\vec{\zeta}_0^\top\boldsymbol{\Lambda}_0}{\vec{\zeta}_0^\top\boldsymbol{\Lambda}_0\vec{\zeta}_0}\vec{\zeta}_0 = \boldsymbol{\Lambda}_0\vec{\zeta}_0 - \boldsymbol{\Lambda}_0\vec{\zeta}_0 = \vec{0}$$

i.e., $\boldsymbol{B}$ is not full rank, such that rank$(\boldsymbol{B}) \leq$ rank$(\boldsymbol{A}) - 1$. Therefore, rank $\left(\boldsymbol{A} - \frac{\vec{\xi}\vec{\xi}^\top}{\vec{\xi}^\top\vec{\eta}}\right) \leq$ rank$(\boldsymbol{A}) - 1$. □

Since $\boldsymbol{Y}$ is a complex symmetric matrix, we can set $\boldsymbol{A} = \boldsymbol{Y} - \tilde{\boldsymbol{Y}}$, $\vec{\boldsymbol{\eta}} = \vec{\boldsymbol{i}}_T$, thus $\vec{\boldsymbol{\xi}} = (\boldsymbol{Y} - \tilde{\boldsymbol{Y}})\vec{\boldsymbol{i}}_T = \Delta\vec{\boldsymbol{v}}_T$. Therefore, applying the lemma, we get: rank $\left(\boldsymbol{Y} - \tilde{\boldsymbol{Y}} - \frac{\Delta\vec{\boldsymbol{v}}_T \Delta\vec{\boldsymbol{v}}_T^\top}{\Delta\vec{\boldsymbol{v}}_T^\top \vec{\boldsymbol{i}}_T}\right) \leq \text{rank}(\boldsymbol{Y} - \tilde{\boldsymbol{Y}}) - 1$. This means that the rank of $\boldsymbol{Y} - \tilde{\boldsymbol{Y}}$ gets reduced by at least 1 in each iteration. Since the initial rank cannot be larger than n, which is the size of the matrix, then the number of iterations that is needed cannot exceed n.

D. PRE-CALIBRATION

The goal of pre-calibration is to estimate $\boldsymbol{Z}_T$. It can be done immediately after manufacturing the transmitter coils where their relative positions are hardcoded. During pre-calibration, there is no receiver around, so the Transmitter Eq. (6) is reduced to $\vec{\boldsymbol{v}}_T = \boldsymbol{Z}_T \vec{\boldsymbol{i}}_T$. Now, in order to estimate $\boldsymbol{Z}_T$, we need to apply n different sets of $\vec{\boldsymbol{v}}_T$ and measure the corresponding $\vec{\boldsymbol{i}}_T$. $\boldsymbol{Z}_T$ can be consequently obtained by matrix inversion, i.e., similar to how we estimate $\boldsymbol{Y}$ in Sec. §4.2.

10. REFERENCES

[1] J. Jadidian and D. Katabi. Magnetic MIMO: How to charge your phone in your pocket. In *ACM MobiCom*, 2014.
[2] A. Sample, B. Waters, S. Wisdom, and J. Smith. Enabling seamless wireless power delivery in dynamic environments. *Proceedings of the IEEE*, 101(6), 2013.
[3] Datasheet for Qi-enabled charger. RAV Power.
[4] Duracell powermat for 2 devices. Duracell Corp.
[5] Energizer dual inductive charger. Energizer.
[6] Qi specification 1.1.2, 2014. Wireless Power Consortium.
[7] Rezence specification. Alliance for Wireless Power.
[8] Highly resonant wireless power transfer: Safe, efficient, and over distance. Technical report, WiTricity Corp, 2012.
[9] Wattup. Energous Corp.
[10] Cota wireless power. Ossia Inc.
[11] Wireless charging, at a distance, moves forward for ubeam, 2014. The New York Times.
[12] Wi-charge. http://www.wi-charge.com/about.php.
[13] F. C. Delori, R. H. Webb, and D. H. Sliney. Maximum permissible exposures for ocular safety (ansi 2000), with emphasis on ophthalmic devices. 2007.
[14] M. Zahn. *Electromagnetic Field Theory: A Problem Solving Approach*. Krieger Pub Co, 2003.
[15] WiT-5000 development kit data sheet. WiTricity Corporation.
[16] TX-200 dual wireless charging pad. LUXA2.
[17] Nokia wireless charging plate. Nokia Corp.
[18] J. Cassell. http://press.ihs.com/press-release/technology/apple-watch-spurs-rapid-growth-market-wireless-charging-wearable-technology.
[19] P. Li and R. Bashirullah. A wireless power interface for rechargeable battery operated medical implants. *Circuits and Systems II, IEEE Transactions on*, 2007.
[20] S. Kim, J. S. Ho, and A. S. Poon. Wireless power transfer to miniature implants: Transmitter optimization. *Antennas and Propagation, IEEE Transactions on*, 2012.
[21] U. K. Madawala and D. J. Thrimawithana. A bidirectional inductive power interface for electric vehicles in V2G systems. *Industrial Electronics, IEEE Transactions on*, 2011.
[22] B. Tong, Z. Li, G. Wang, and W. Zhang. How wireless power charging technology affects sensor network deployment and routing. In *Distributed Computing Systems, IEEE*, 2010.
[23] L. Xie, Y. Shi, Y. T. Hou, and A. Lou. Wireless power transfer and applications to sensor networks. *Wireless Communications, IEEE*, 2013.
[24] Proxi-point transmitter for the LTC4120. PowerByProxi.
[25] A. Kurs, A. Karalis, R. Moffatt, J. D. Joannopoulos, P. Fisher, and M. Soljačić. Wireless power transfer via strongly coupled magnetic resonances. 317(5834), 2007.
[26] B. L. Cannon, J. F. Hoburg, D. D. Stancil, and S. C. Goldstein. Magnetic resonant coupling as a potential means for wireless power transfer to multiple small receivers. *Power Electronics, IEEE Transactions on*, 2009.
[27] J. Casanova, Z. N. Low, and J. Lin. A loosely coupled planar wireless power system for multiple receivers. *Industrial Electronics, IEEE Transactions on*, 56(8), 2009.
[28] J. Kim, D. Kim, and Y. Park. Analysis of capacitive impedance matching networks for simultaneous wireless power transfer to multiple devices. *Industrial Electronics, IEEE Transactions on*, 2014.
[29] J.-W. Kim, H.-C. Son, D.-H. Kim, K.-H. Kim, and Y.-J. Park. Analysis of wireless energy transfer to multiple devices using cmt. In *Microwave Conference Proceedings, IEEE*, 2010.
[30] D. Ahn and S. Hong. Effect of coupling between multiple transmitters or multiple receivers on wireless power transfer. *Industrial Electronics, IEEE Transactions on*, 60(7), 2013.
[31] A. Kurs, R. Moffatt, and M. Soljacić. Simultaneous mid-range power transfer to multiple devices. *Applied Physics Letters*, 2010.
[32] D. Ahn and S. Hong. A study on magnetic field repeater in wireless power transfer. *Industrial Electronics, IEEE Transactions on*, 2013.
[33] B. Waters, B. Mahoney, V. Ranganathan, and J. Smith. Power delivery and leakage field control using an adaptive phased-array wireless power system. *(Accepted and Pre-Published) IEEE Transactions on Power Electronics.*
[34] M. Moon. uBeam demo video. http://www.engadget.com/2014/08/07/ubeam-wireless-charger-ultrasound/.
[35] S. Budiansky. *Truth about Dogs*. 2000.
[36] Performance standards for microwave and radio frequency emitting products. Title 21, Part 1030, U.S. Food and Drug Administration.
[37] W. H. Paul Horowitz. *The Art of Electronics*. Cambridge University Press, 1989.
[38] Understanding li+ battery operation lessens charging safety concerns. Technical Report APP 4169, Maxim Integrated Products, Inc., 2008.
[39] Can witricity technology transfer power through walls or obstructions? http://witricity.com/technology/witricity-faqs/.
[40] AD8333: DC to 50 MHz, dual I/Q demodulator and phase shifter data sheet (Rev. E). Analog Devices.
[41] Zynq-7000 all programmable soc (z-7010, z-7015, and z-7020): Technical reference manual. Xlin.
[42] M. K. Kazimierczuk. Class d voltage-switching mosfet power amplifier. In *Electric Power Applications, IEEE*, 1991.
[43] Temperature gun infrared thermometers. Omega Inc.
[44] P. Morasso. Spatial control of arm movements. *Experimental Brain Research*, 42(2), 1981.
[45] C. Atkeson and J. Hollerbach. Kinematic features of unrestrained vertical arm movements. *The Journal of Neuroscience*, 5(9), 1985.
[46] W. Abend, E. Bizzi, and P. Morasso. Human arm trajectory formation. *Brain*, 1982.
[47] T. Takagi. On an algebraic problem related to an analytic theorem of Carathéodory and Fejér and on an allied theorem of landau. *Japan. J. Math*, 1, 1924.

Rethinking Energy-Performance Trade-Off in Mobile Web Page Loading

Duc Hoang Bui†, Yunxin Liu*, Hyosu Kim†, Insik Shin†, Feng Zhao*
†KAIST, Daejeon, South Korea, *Microsoft Research, Beijing, China
{ducbuihoang, hyosu.kim, ishin}@kaist.ac.kr, {yunliu, zhao}@microsoft.com

ABSTRACT

Web browsing is a key application on mobile devices. However, mobile browsers are largely optimized for performance, imposing a significant burden on power-hungry mobile devices. In this work, we aim to reduce the energy consumed to load web pages on smartphones, preferably without increasing page load time and compromising user experience. To this end, we first study the internals of web page loading on smartphones and identify its energy-inefficient behaviors. Based on our findings, we then derive general design principles for energy-efficient web page loading, and apply these principles to the open-source Chromium browser and implement our techniques on commercial smartphones. Experimental results show that our techniques are able to achieve a 24.4% average system energy saving for Chromium on a latest-generation big.LITTLE smartphone using WiFi (a 22.5% saving when using 3G), while not increasing average page load time. We also show that our proposed techniques can bring a 10.5% system energy saving on average with a small 1.69% increase in page load time for mobile Firefox web browser. User study results indicate that such a small increase in page load time is hardly perceivable.

Categories and Subject Descriptors

H.4.3 [**Information Systems Applications**]: Communications Applications—*Information Browser*

General Terms

Design; Measurement; Performance

Keywords

Smartphones; Mobile Web Browser; Web Page Loading; Energy Efficiency

1. INTRODUCTION

Web browsing is one of the core applications on smartphones and other mobile devices such as tablets. However, web browsing, particularly web page loading, is of high energy consumption. As energy is a paramount concern on smartphones, it is desirable to improve the energy efficiency of web browsing, particularly web page loading. In this paper, we seek to reduce the energy consumption of web page loading on smartphones without compromising user experience. In particular, we aim to not increase page load time.

To achieve this goal, we study browser internals and system behaviors to understand how the energy is spent in loading web pages, and to identify opportunities to improve the energy efficiency. Although many browser manufacturers have made an effort on improving energy efficiency for mobile devices, our findings indicate that the current mobile browsers are not yet fully energy optimized for web page loading. First, the web resource processing is aggressively conducted regardless of network conditions at the risk of energy inefficiency. Second, the content painting rate is unnecessarily high, consuming a lot energy without bringing user-perceivable benefits. Finally, the power-saving capability of modern CPUs with the emerging ARM big.LITTLE architecture [3] is under-utilized. Fundamentally, the web page loading is overly optimized for performance but not for energy cost.

We argue that the energy-performance trade off must be reconsidered for web page loading on mobile devices. Based on our findings, we formulate new design principles for energy-efficient web page loading. Based on these principles, we develop three new techniques, each one addressing one of the above energy-inefficiency issues. First, we propose to use the *network-aware resource processing* (NRP) technique to effectively trade off performance for energy reduction adapting to changing network conditions. We use adaptive resource buffering to control the speed of web resource processing dynamically with regard to the speed of resource download, in order to become energy efficient without increasing page load time. Second, we propose the *adaptive content painting* (ACP) technique to avoid unnecessary content paints to reduce the energy overhead. We study the trade off between energy saving and page load time increase to ensure the user experience is not compromised. Finally, to better leverage the big.LITTLE architecture, we propose the *application-assisted scheduling* (AAS) technique to leverage internal knowledge of the browser to make better scheduling decisions. Specifically, we employ adaptive thread scheduling based on QoS feedback in a way that the browser keeps threads running on *little* cores to save energy, as long as their related QoS requirements are being satisfied.

We have implemented all the three techniques on commercial smartphones, by revising the Chromium browser. Collectively, these techniques achieve significant reductions in the energy cost of web page loading. Experimental evaluations using the Alexa top 100 websites in the U.S. [2] show that, on a big.LITTLE smartphone using WiFi, our revised Chromium browser is able to achieve 24.4%

MobiCom'15, September 7–11, 2015, Paris, France.
© 2015 ACM. ISBN 978-1-4503-3619-2/15/09 ...$15.00.
DOI: http://dx.doi.org/10.1145/2789168.2790103.

average system energy saving while decreasing 0.38% page load time, compared to the default Chromium browser. When using 3G, the average system energy saving is 22.5% and the average page load time increase is 0.41%. On another smartphone without big.LITTLE supported, our techniques can still reduce the energy consumption by 11.7% on average when using WiFi. We have also conducted a user study to confirm that our techniques do not affect user perceived experience. Moreover, all participants show their intention (or interest) to use our techniques either all the time (72%) or when the battery level is low (28%).

Although our implementation is based on Chromium, our proposed techniques can be also be applied to other mobile browsers. The first two energy-inefficiency issues of Chromium are related to the general procedure of web content downloading, processing, and painting. Thus, other mobile browsers are generally subject to the same issues, though with different levels of significance. Besides Chromium, we also have applied our ACP and AAS techniques to Firefox, even without a deep understanding of Firefox internals, and it resulted in a significant energy saving (10.5%) on average with a marginal increase (1.69%) in page load time, compared to the default Firefox.

The main contributions of this paper are:

1. We show that web page loading on popular mobile web browsers, including Chrome, Firefox, Opera Mobile, and UC Browser, is overly optimized for performance but not for energy-efficiency, and identify the opportunities to reduce the energy cost.
2. We derive design principles and propose techniques to improve the energy efficiency of web page loading on smartphones.
3. We implement our techniques by revising the Chromium browser, demonstrating the applicability of our techniques in real-world mobile browsers. We also implement the proposed ACP and AAS in the Firefox browser, showing that our findings can be applied to other mobile browsers.
4. We conduct comprehensive experiments and a user study to show that our techniques effectively reduce energy consumption of mobile web page loading without compromising the user experience.

The rest of this paper is organized as follows. Section 2 introduces the Chromium browser and the big.LITTLE architecture as the background. Section 3 reports the energy-inefficiency issues and derive general guidelines to reduce the energy cost. Section 4 describes our novel techniques. Section 5 shows the implementation details and Section 6 presents the evaluation results. Section 7 discusses more aspects on the energy-saving techniques and the future work, Section 8 surveys the related work, and Section 9 concludes.

2. BACKGROUND

In this section, we introduce the Chromium browser and the big.LITTLE architecture as the background.

2.1 Chromium Browser Architecture

Figure 1 shows the architecture of the Chromium web browser. Chromium uses a multi-process architecture of a single *Browser* process and multiple *Renderer* processes. Each Renderer process runs an instance of the rendering engine (previously WebKit [14] and now Blink [4]) and the JavaScript engine that parse and execute web content. Each Renderer process typically corresponds to one tab in the web browser UI. The Browser process runs the network stack and fetches web resources from the network for all Renderer processes, allowing efficient network resource sharing among all Renderer processes. Renderer processes run in a sandboxed environment with limited access to the client device and the network, preventing exploits in rendering engine from compromising the whole web browser.

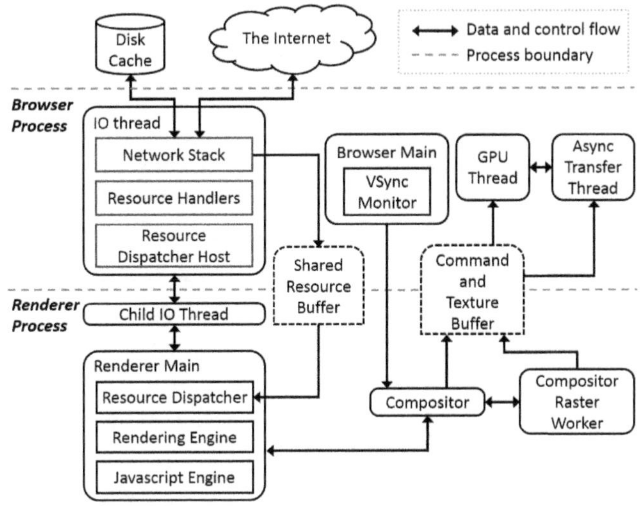

Figure 1: Architecture of the Chromium web browser

Each process in Chromium has multiple threads. Table 1 provides a brief description of the main threads. Processes and threads are designed to work asynchronously. The Browser process and a Renderer process communicate with each other through IPC mechanisms (e.g., named pipes) and exchange data using shared memory. The Browser process puts the fetched web resources into the Shared Resource Buffer from which the Renderer process reads the data to create graphic layers for the corresponding web page. The Compositor thread then saves the generated graphic data into the Command and Texture Buffer for GPU processing in the Browser process, because the sandboxed Renderer process does not have the privilege to access the GPU directly. The GPU thread generates the final screen image into the display frame buffer to be displayed on the device screen.

The graphic composition and GPU processing are driven by a callback from Android framework called vertical synchronization (VSync). Each VSync signal indicates the beginning of a display frame, so that graphic data should be generated and moved to the display frame buffer for drawing on the screen before the next VSync. VSync signals are generated at 60 times per second. In the Browser process, the VSync Monitor of the Browser Main thread monitors VSync signals and forwards them to the Compositor thread in a Renderer process.

The architecture shown in Figure 1 also applies to Google Chrome, Opera Mobile and Android stock browser which are built on top of Chromium source code [6, 19]. The browsers share the same rendering engine, JavaScript engine, and underlying core modules.

2.2 big.LITTLE Architecture and Scheduling

The ARM big.LITTLE architecture [3] combines high performance and high power *"big"* cores together with power efficient but low performance *"little"* cores in a single ARM CPU. By running lightweight tasks on the little cores and heavy tasks on big cores, a big.LITTLE CPU is able to meet both the need for higher performance and the desire for longer battery life on mobile devices. For example, the Samsung Galaxy S5 SM-G900H smartphone uses a Samsung Exynos 5422 System-on-Chip (SoC) with 4 Cortex-A15 (big) cores and 4 Cortex-A7 (little) cores. The Exynos 5422 SoC

Thread name	Description
CrBrowserMain	Starts and initializes the browser, monitor VSync callbacks, and renders the user interface
CrRendererMain	Runs the rendering engine and the Javascript engine
Chrome_IOThread	Communicates with other processes (such as Renderer and GPU processes), and the environment (such as the network and the disk cache)
Chrome_ChildIOThread*	Communicates with other processes using the IPC mechanism
Compositor	Generates platform-independent GPU commands to composite the web page layers into the final screen image
CompositorRasterWorker*	Rasterizes the web page layers into graphic textures
Chrome_InProcGpuThread	Executes GPU commands issued by the Compositor thread to draw textures of each layer into the frame buffer for displaying the final web page image on the screen
AsyncTransferThread	Uploads textures provided by Compositor to the GPU memory
SimpleCacheWorker*	Reads and writes web resources on the browser disk cache

∗ possible multiple thread instances

Table 1: Main threads in the Chromium web browser

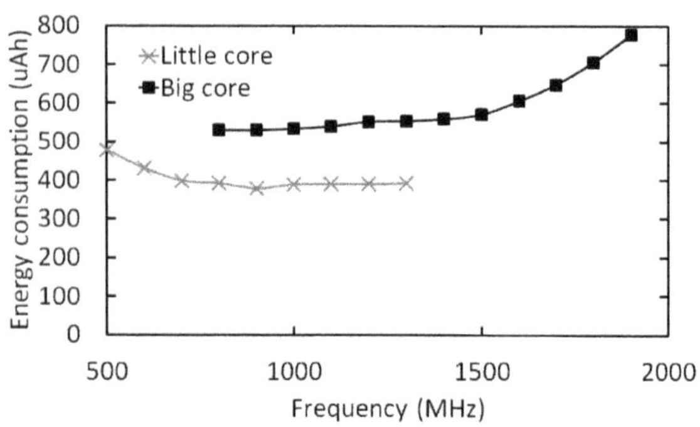

Figure 2: Total energy consumption of a little core and a big core on a Samsung S5 SM-G900H smartphone in running the same workload with a fixed number of operations

uses Heterogeneous Multi-Processing (HMP) [18], so it can utilize all the 8 cores simultaneously. The little and big cores can operate in a frequency range from 500 MHz to 1.3 GHz and from 800 MHz to 1.9 GHz, respectively. Figure 2 shows our measured total energy consumption of a little core and a big core of the Galaxy S5 smartphone in running the same workload, at different frequencies with 100% core utilization. The workload is a busy loop for a fixed number of iterations which emulates the characteristics of CPU-bound workloads with no periods of idleness. At its highest frequency of 1.3 GHz, a little core can reduce the energy consumption by a factor of 2 (392 uAh vs. 777 uAh), compared to a big core at its own highest frequency of 1.9 GHz. The measurement result is consistent with a previous study [17] and demonstrates the big potential of big.LITTLE architecture in saving energy.

In the Linux kernel, the task scheduler divides all the cores into two scheduling domains: one for the little cores and the other for the big cores [37]. The scheduler may migrate a thread from the big core cluster to the little core cluster or vice versa, by tracking the loads of all the threads. Basically, the scheduler will move a thread from a little core to a big core if the load contribution of a thread is larger than an *up threshold* and vice versa with a *down threshold*.

Commercial big.LITTLE smartphones have become increasingly popular. Beside Samsung, other mobile processor makers including Qualcomm, LG, Huawei and MTK have also shipped or announced their big.LITTLE products.

3. UNDERSTANDING ENERGY COST OF PAGE LOADING

In this section, we study Chromium browser internals and the system-scheduling behaviors and identify three energy-inefficient issues in loading web pages: inefficient web resource processing, unnecessary content painting, and underutilized little cores. We also study the behaviors of other mobile browsers and show that they also have the same energy-inefficient issues. Based on the findings, we derive general design guidelines for energy-efficient web page loading.

Unless otherwise specified, all the numbers presented in this section are the average experiment results obtained on a Samsung Galaxy S5 SM-G900H big.LITTLE smartphone, using the Alexa top 10 websites in the US [2], including Google, Facebook, Youtube, Yahoo, Amazon, Wikipedia, Linkedin, Ebay, Twitter, and Pinterest. The websites were loaded on an emulated 3G network (Download 2 Mbps, Upload 1 Mbps, RTT 120 ms) for repeatable experiments. The total system energy consumption of the smartphone was measured using a Monsoon power monitor [29].

3.1 Inefficient Web Resource Processing

Web resource processing is one of the main components of browsing, along with resource downloading and content painting. Web resource processing typically includes HTML and CSS parsing, image decoding, Javascript execution, and updating DOM tree and graphic layers. In Chromium, the Renderer process conducts the above processing whenever it is notified of the data available from the Browser process. As shown in Figure 1, those two processes exchange data using a shared resource buffer. The Browser process uses the *read* system call on a socket handler to receive the resources of a web page from the network. Each *read* system call directly writes received data into the resource buffer with a maximum data size of 32 KB by default. Upon each *read* system call, the Browser process immediately notifies the Renderer process to start to process the received data, no matter how much data is received.

Although immediately processing the received data is natural and minimizes the page load time, it is not energy efficient. The reason is that many *read* system calls return a small amount of data and thus lead to a large number of IPCs between the Browser process and the Renderer process. In loading the 10 websites, 99% of the *read* calls return a data chunk less than 3 KB and the average data size returned per *read* is only 1.3 KB. On average there are 319 *read* calls (62 per second) in loading one web page. Each *read* may cause multiple IPCs between the Browser process and the Renderer process. On average the total number of IPCs per web page is 871 (176 per second). Each IPC has a fixed overhead. Moreover, there are also other overheads in web resource processing. Each time when processing a data chunk, even if the data chunk is small, the Renderer process has to go through the whole data rendering pipeline. In particular, for image data, many graphic

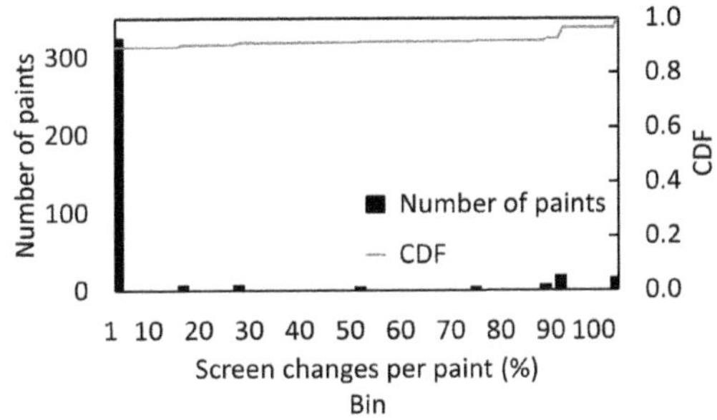

Figure 3: Visible screen update in loading instagram.com

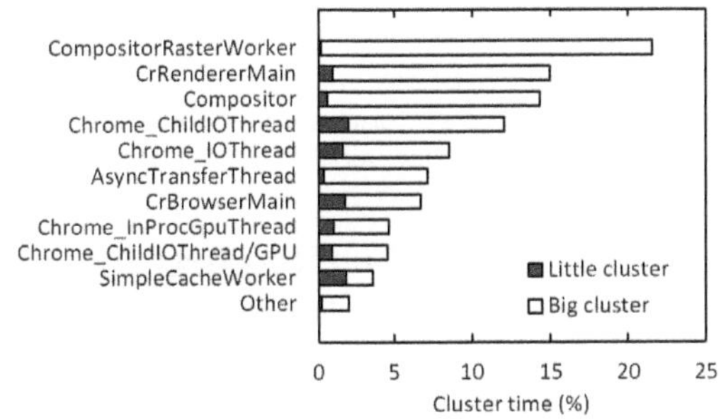

Figure 4: Execution time of Chromium threads on the big and little cores in loading instagram.com

activities are involved in the Compositor, Raster Worker and Async Transfer threads. As a result, the accumulated overheads are high and thus waste much energy, more than 10% of the total system energy cost as we will show in Section 6.

3.2 Unnecessary Content Painting

When loading a web page, Chromium processes the web resources progressively and keeps updating the partially rendered display results onto the screen. As shown in Figure 1, the screen updates are driven by VSync signals. Upon receiving a VSync signal, the Compositor thread ships the current rendered graphic data to the GPU thread of the Browser process through the shared command and texture buffer. The GPU thread then executes platform-specific graphic commands on the GPU to composite all the textures into the final graphic result to be displayed on the screen. This graphic pipeline of data rendering and screen updating is called *content painting*. Many content paints may occur in loading a web page. For example, in loading *instagram.com*, a popular photo-sharing website, the browser does 359 paints (23.1 per second) even the web page does not have any animation.

However, we have observed that most of the times, content painting generates a very small or even zero visible change on the screen. To demonstrate this observation, we log the visual progress of each content painting using Telemetry [11], the performance testing framework of Google Chrome. The tool collects the *Paint* events from the rendering engine and calculates how many visible pixels of the screen are changed by each *Paint* event. Figure 3 shows the results in loading *instagram.com*, including both the histogram and the CDF. Among all the 359 paints, 321 (89%) of them generate a zero visible change on the screen. For the top 10 websites, there are also many paints with a zero or very small visible screen change: 56% of the paints do not generate any visible screen change, and 62% of the paints generate a visible screen change of less than 5%. These paints with a zero or very small visible screen change do not help improve the user experience. However, they cause overheads in the whole graphic processing pipeline and the IPCs between the two processes, and thus lead to unnecessary energy cost. This design of high-rate content painting is overly optimized for performance, not energy efficient, and must be re-considered on mobile devices.

3.3 Underutilized Little Cores

Although big.LITTLE is designed to save energy, we find that the energy-saving potential of big.LITTLE is not fully exploited in the case of Chromium. Specifically, we find that the little cores are underutilized. For example, Figure 4 shows the average execution time of Chromium threads in loading *instagram.com*. Most of the times, the threads are executed on the big cores. 89% of the total execution time is on the big cores but only 11% of the total execution time is on the little cores. Some threads, such as the Compositor Raster Worker and Async Transfer thread, are almost completely (more than 95%) executed on the big cores.

The reason of low little-core utilization is that the OS schedules threads based on a load-driven approach that favors performance more than energy saving. The scheduler tries to finish a thread sooner rather than saving more energy. On symmetric multi-core architectures, since all the CPU cores are equal, this load-driven approach is energy efficient. If a thread can finish its task faster, the CPU can go to sleep sooner to save energy [16]. However, on heterogeneous multi-core architectures like big.LITTLE, finishing a thread sooner may not reduce the energy cost. As shown in Figure 2, a little core has a lower energy per instruction cost than a big core. As a result, it takes longer but consumes less energy to run a thread on a little core than on a big core. Thus, a thread should run on a little core as long as it can tolerate a resulting delay. However, the OS cannot know how much delay a thread can tolerate, and thus cannot decide whether to run the thread on a little core for better energy efficiency or not.

3.4 Guidelines for Improvements

The above energy-inefficient issues are not Chromium-specific. Even without analyzing source codes, we observe the behaviors of several other mobile browsers when they load the same set of web pages. After monitoring the number of screen updates and thread scheduling behaviors, we conclude that those mobile browsers basically share the same energy-inefficiency issues with Chromium: they also do aggressive content processing and screen updating, and rely on the OS for passive thread-scheduling.

We monitor the screen update by dumping information from Android SurfaceFlinger. For example, when loading *instagram.com*, Firefox updates its SurfaceView 614 times in 17.1 sec or 35.9 frames/s. Similar behavior is also observed on Opera Mobile web browser which is based upon Chromium. Another popular web browser, UC Browser, even keeps updating at a fixed 60 times per second even there is no change on the content. Thereby, even when the content does not change, UC Browser has 1755 mW average power consumption while other browsers (Chromium, Firefox and Opera) have only 475-542 mW average power consumption. Moreover, Firefox for Android puts its major threads onto big cores: 84% of its Gecko rendering engine thread and 60% of its Compositor thread on big cores.

Based on these findings, we make the following guidelines for reducing the energy cost in web page loading: 1) the web resource processing should adapt to download speed to become energy efficient; 2) the content painting should adapt to visible changes on the screen to save energy; and 3) the OS scheduler should be aware of QoS of threads to make energy-friendly scheduling decisions. Next we show how we develop techniques for energy-efficient web page loading according to these design guidelines.

4. ENERGY-EFFICIENT PAGE LOADING

In this section, we describe the three techniques aiming to better balance the energy cost and performance in mobile web page loading. We carefully design the techniques to control their impact on the page loading time.

4.1 Network-Aware Web Resource Processing

The choice of how often to conduct web resource processing influences performance and energy efficiency. Frequent resource processing may come with energy inefficiency, since it can yield marginal progress while consuming a significant amount of energy. As shown in 3.1, the Renderer process may conduct the web resource processing over each small amount of data (e.g., less than 3 KB in 2 Mbps download speed). This entails the need to perform batch processing of web resources to become more cost-effective. However, this may delay the processing of web resources and increase the page loading time. For example, an HTML resource typically contains links to other web resources such as images and JavaScript libraries. While the Renderer process delays the processing of the HTML resource, the Browser process cannot proceed to download the embedded resources from the network. So it calls for a good strategy to coalesce resources for energy-efficient resource processing yet without increasing the page loading time.

To this end, we propose to design the web resource processing adaptive to the speed of downloading web resources, which we refer to as *Network-aware Resource Processing* (NRP). A basic underlying principle is that the faster downloading, the larger batch size for better energy-efficiency should be. That is, we have a smaller batch size for slower downloading so as not to introduce excessive delays in web resource processing. We enforce the Browser process to buffer the data received from the network and notify the Renderer process only if the buffered data amount is larger than a threshold. This way, we can reduce the times of web resource processing as well as the number of IPCs involved, and thus can reduce the energy cost.

To balance the trade-off between resource processing delay and energy efficiency, we design the buffer threshold `buf_threshold` and the total buffer size `buf_size` to adapt to the resource downloading speed `net_goodput` as follows.

$$\begin{aligned} \texttt{buf\_threshold} &= \alpha * \texttt{net\_goodput} \\ \texttt{buf\_size} &= \beta * \texttt{buf\_threshold}, \end{aligned}$$

where `net_goodput` is estimated using the exponentially weighted moving average (EWMA), a linear history-based estimator, with a smoothing factor of 0.3, as described in [25, 32]. The parameter α indicates the maximum latency that a piece of data can experience in the buffer and is set to 0.5 second, at which we find a balance between energy saving and resource processing delay. The parameter β controls the total buffer size. It is increased when the buffer is overused and decreased when underused. When the buffer is full, it is increased linearly and decreased when average buffer usage of the last 20 samples is less than 50%. We cap the maximum buffer size to 2 MB.

The additional parameter `buf_size` is designed to minimize the total memory usage. To process each web resource, it requires allocating a dedicated buffer of size `buf_size`. As there may be many web resources in loading a web page, the total memory usage may be high if the buffer size is large. With our approach, we design the `buf_size` to be small while big enough to allow the downloading to keep up with the processing of resources.

Ideally, NRP should adapt directly to the user-perceived content changes on the screen. That is, the buffering should be adaptive to how fast the web content is displayed on the screen. However, detecting the changes of the displayed content from the received data is difficult and imposes high overhead because of dynamic content like JavaScript. Therefore, we choose the network throughput (the rate of receiving data) as an indirect but low-overhead indicator of the changes of the displayed content. By controlling the buffer threshold according to the throughput, we balance the energy cost and the latency of the web-resource processing.

To further reduce the impact of NRP on page loading time, we do not apply the buffering to critical resources that may delay the downloading of other resources. Such critical resources include the top level HTML resources (called *main resources* in Chromium) of the main frame and the sub-frames or iframes of a web page. Those resources are processed immediately after they are received from the network. Furthermore, we do not buffer the last chunk of a web resource even if the chunk size is smaller than `buf_threshold`, to prevent a small last data chunk from staying in the resource buffer for a long time. This is achieved by detecting if the response completed or not, which is performed by a network stream parser in the browser. Therefore, it is applicable to dynamic content as well. If the response completed, we notify the Renderer process starts to process all the received data immediately instead of waiting for reaching `buf_threshold`.

4.2 Adaptive Content Painting

Content painting comes with a trade-off between user experience and energy overhead. Although a high frame rate can provide very smooth user experience, it can incur a high overhead to GPU and CPU to render web pages and, when combined with high resolution, consume a lot of energy [33]. As shown in Section 3.2, each individual content paint may introduce a different degree of change on the screen. As the majority of content paints generate a zero or very small visible screen change, multiple content paints can be aggregated together to save energy without compromising user experience. Motivated by this, we design the content painting to be adaptive to the visible changes on the screen, which we refer to as *Adaptive Content Painting* (ACP), as follows.

We introduce a new parameter, called `paint_rate`, that limits the rate of content painting and dynamically adapts to the content changing speed so that we can aggregate content painting to save energy while preserving user experience. For a given value of `paint_rate`, ACP enforces that the actual content painting rate will never exceed the value of `paint_rate` (the actual rate can be lower than `paint_rate`). The `paint_rate` parameter ranges from a minimum painting rate to a maximum one. The initial value of `paint_rate` is set to the minimum value. The `paint_rate` parameter increases when the content changes fast and vice versa. After the Compositor thread paints the changed content to the screen, if the web page continues changing and needs to update the screen to reflect the change, we increase the parameter linearly by one to the maximum value. On the other hand, we decrease the parameter to the minimum value when the content of web page display stops changing after the Compositor delivers all the changes to the screen. In Section 5 we describe how we detect the speed of the content changes in Chromium.

We cap the maximum painting rate to 10 frames/s to balance the energy cost and the smoothness of content display. We argue that 10 frames/s should be smooth enough because 1) during page loading time, the web content is only partially displayed and thus the impact on user experience is small (especially on smartphones with small screens); and 2) the rate of content changes on the screen is often low as shown in Section 3.2. Furthermore, existing research [39] shows that a delay of up to 100 ms is typically not perceivable. Therefore, we believe that 10 frames/s (i.e., 100 ms per frame) provides a good trade-off between user experience and energy saving. We set the minimum painting rate to 2 frames/s to save more energy when the content changes slowly.

Ideally, ACP technique should quantify the visual changes between painted frames to adapt with the degree of changes of content. However, doing so requires comparing consecutive frames pixel by pixel, which imposes heavy computation and thus a high energy cost. Therefore, we use a light-weight approach of linearly increasing the `paint_rate` parameter, without any extra computation cost.

Furthermore, the content painting should be aware of user interactions. A high painting rate should be used when the user touches the screen, to ensure smooth user experience. Therefore, in our implementation, we also detect user inputs and stop rate throttling when the user touches the screen.

The two techniques of NRP and ACP are not completely independent. NRP batches the processing of resources and thus also slows down the content painting. Similar to NRP, ACP also reduces the number of IPCs between the Browser process and a Renderer process to save energy.

4.3 Application-Assisted Scheduling

To better leverage big.LITTLE architecture to save energy, we propose to leverage internal knowledge of browsers for energy-efficient scheduling. Instead of letting the OS task scheduler make all the scheduling decisions by passively observing the load of threads, we allow browsers to decide whether a thread should run on a big or little core. Browsers know much more information about their threads than the OS scheduler, e.g., what type of tasks the threads do, how important the threads are, how long finishing time a thread can tolerate, the semantics of the threads, and the relationship among them. Therefore, browsers may make better decisions on assigning threads to big or little cores. We call this kind of technique *Application-Assisted Scheduling* (AAS).

We design the AAS technique adaptive to Quality of Service (QoS), as QoS is important to user experience. The QoS is estimated by the frame rate of the browser. The QoS requirement is dynamically adjusted to the changing value of `paint_rate`. If ACP is not working, then the requirement is fixed as the maximum limit on painting rate (i.e., 10 frames/s). AAS first allocates a set of threads related to the QoS on little cores and monitors the current frame rate. When the current frame rate is lagging behind the QoS requirement, AAS considers it the violation of QoS. For example, if the value of `paint_rate` is 5, the QoS is defined as painting each frame within 200 ms. If the browser fails to paint each frame within 200 ms, AAS decides that the QoS is violated and thus migrates the threads related on big cores. When the current frame rate becomes exceeding the QoS requirement in a stable manner, AAS brings those threads back to little cores. AAS makes such a decision when it finds the cumulative gap between the current frame rate and the QoS requirement over a window is no less than a threshold. Thus, while the QoS is being satisfied, its corresponding threads keep remaining on the little cores to save energy without compromising user experience.

To better utilize little cores to save more energy, we design AAS to move a thread from a little core to a big core in a conservative way of using a time window of three seconds, and move a thread from a big core back to a little core using a smaller time window of one second.

ACP adjusts `paint_rate` limit while AAS only monitors the actual frame rate (frame painting time) and schedules threads to satisfy the limit. Since the `paint_rate` sets only the maximum painting rate rather than a fixed painting rate, there is no strict circular dependency between the AAS technique and the frame rate.

Thread migration between little cores and big cores in AAS is generic to all applications. The AAS technique dynamically changes the affinity of the QoS-related threads, and thus does not require hard assignments of specific threads to cores. However, which threads should be managed by AAS and how to define the QoS are application specific. In Section 5 we show to which threads of Chromium we apply the AAS technique.

5. IMPLEMENTATION

We have implemented the three techniques on Android by modifying the source code of Chromium version 38, the latest stable version of Chromium when we conducted the work of this paper. We use the Content module (ContentShell.apk build target) that has the core code upon which Android Google Chrome browser is built [5]. Compared to Content Shell, Chrome has additional features such as auto fill, translation, and account setting synchronization.

In total, we add about 1,200 lines of code into various modules of the Chromium web browser. No rooting or modification to websites and OS kernel are needed. As we focus on page load time, we enable the techniques only during loading a web page, we disable the techniques after the web page loading is finished.

Network-aware Resource Processing. We implemented adaptive resource buffering by modifying the *BufferedResourceHandler* class in the Resource Handler chain in the Browser process. We revise the resource handler so that it keeps buffering until the received data size reaches the buffer threshold or the web-resource fetching has completed. In addition, the revised handler decides the resource type embedded in the HTTP requests. For top-level HTML resources and nested frames, it does not perform resource buffering to avoid delaying the loading of the web resources embedded in the HTML pages.

The Buffered Resource Handler can be paused when the rendering engine has not finished processing the resource and there is no space left in the resource buffer. When it resumes, it continues receiving data.

Adaptive Content Painting. We control content painting rate by controlling the rate of VSync callbacks. To do it, we wrote a shim layer on the *WindowAndroid* class which represents an Android activity window and holds a VSync monitor. This shim layer intercepts actual VSync callback from the VSync monitor and delays them by multiple of VSync periods before sending to the Compositor thread.

The content changing speed is determined by looking at the VSync request from the Compositor thread. If the rendering engine needs to update the layer tree and thus the Compositor thread still needs a VSync to perform a paint after all the changes have been painted, it indicates that the content have been changed since the last time. On the other hand, when the Compositor thread stops needing VSyncs to perform another paint, this indicates that the content does not change further. At this point, we stops requesting VSync from Android and decrease the frame rate limit to the minimum value.

Throttling the content painting rate may cause apparent lags when the user touches the screen. To solve this problem, we detect the user inputs to enable and disable content painting rate dynamically. We do this by instrumenting the *ContentViewCore* class which represents the view of a web page. Thereby, user will not feel any animation lagging when he interacts with the screen during page loading.

Application-Assisted Scheduling. We implement AAS by extending current Chromium threading management module to support changing thread CPU affinity dynamically and systematically.

On Android OS, thread CPU affinity is altered by system call *sched_setaffinity*, which does not require root privilege. Since default bionic C library level 19 on Android 4.4 does not provide native *sched_setaffinity* API, we directly invokes its assembly language interface by using *syscall* function together with its system call number and a CPU core list. We monitor the frame rate by using the layer tree debugging feature in Chromium which provides frame rate counter and paint time.

According to the analysis of the web browser architecture in Section 2, AAS schedules the Compositor Raster Worker and Async Transfer Thread. These threads affect the rate of frames painted to the screen by the graphic pipeline so directly relate to the user experience. They also have high CPU workload so scheduling them to little core will have high reduction to energy consumption of the browser.

6. EVALUATION

In this section, we evaluate our implementation by answering the following questions: 1) how much total energy we can save; 2) how much energy is saved by each of the three techniques; and 3) how much the techniques affect page load time and user experience.

6.1 Experiment Setup

Devices. We conduct experiments on two variants of the Samsung Galaxy S5 smartphones: S5-E and S5-S. S5-E is the SM-G900H model that uses Samsung Exynos 5422 SoC with 4 Cortex-A15 big cores and 4 Cortex-A7 little cores and Linux kernel 3.10. S5-S is the SM-G900K model that uses a quad-core Qualcomm Snapdragon 801 SoC and Linux kernel 3.4. Both smartphones run Android Kitkat 4.4.2 and Chromium version 38. We use a Monsoon Power Monitor tool [29] to measure the total system energy consumption of the smartphones.

To minimize measurement noise, we remove all unnecessary applications and background services, disable irrelevant hardware components such as camera, GPS and other sensors, and turn off all wireless network interfaces except WiFi. The screen brightness is set to the lowest level.

Testbed and network conditions. For repeatable experiments and to avoid the noises of unstable cellular network and unpredictable response of web servers, we build a testbed to load websites from a local emulated server. The Linux server records and replays responses of websites using the *Web Page Replay* [13] tool. The smartphones load the web pages from the server through a local WiFi network. The server emulates a 3G cellular network using the *dummynet* network emulator [7]. Based on previous measurement studies [40, 26, 1, 27] on 3G cellular networks, we use the following parameters to emulate typical cellular network conditions: 2 Mbps downlink bandwidth, 1 Mbps uplink bandwidth, and a 120 ms round-trip time (RTT).

Data set. We evaluate our techniques using the top 100 websites in the U.S. according to Alexa [2] in May 2014. The 100 websites include diverse websites including sophisticated ones with many images and simple ones with mostly textual contents. Among them, 88 websites have a mobile-friendly design. By default, we use the homepage of the websites in our experiments. For the websites requiring a user login, we record and replay the response of the website after logging in, or choose a representative public web page from the website. For the websites with a so trivial homepage (such as search engine *ask.com*), we choose a non-trivial, representative, second-level web page.

Automation tool. We develop a tool to automate the experiments and data collection. The tool has two modules, one running on a smartphone and the other running on a Windows PC that runs the Monsoon Power Monitor software to collect energy consumption data. On the smartphone, the tool is a module on the content shell layer (e.g., ShellManager class) of Chromium. It takes a list of URLs and controls Chromium to visit the URLs one by one. Before visiting each URL, it clears the cache of Chromium. During loading a web page, it collects the data about the page loading such as the page load time. After the experiments are finished, it transfers all the collected data to the PC. On the PC, the tool controls the Monsoon software to record the energy consumption data. The tool also precisely synchronizes the time of the smartphone and the PC using a synthetic falling edge on the power trace. Therefore, we can align the power trace data collected on the PC to the page loading data on the smartphone.

Page load time. Page Load Time (PLT) measures the time since a web page starts loading, i.e., the Navigation Start event, until the page finishes loading, i.e., the Load Event End event [24, 23, 22]. We revise Chromium to record the timestamps of the Navigation Start event and Load Event End event, and thus our automation tool can calculate the PLT of each single web page. We measure cold page loading time with the browser cache and DNS cache cleared.

Unless otherwise stated, we repeat each experiment for at least 5 times. Measurement outliers are detected and removed by applying the modified Z-score [28] on page load time values of each configuration combination. We add more experiments if the number of remaining samples after removing outliers is too small. Each point on the cumulative distribution function (CDF) graphs on this section presents the average for each website. For estimating variation, we calculated 95% confidence intervals for each average but do not present here because most of the confidence intervals are less than 5% of the average values.

6.2 Energy Saving

Total energy saving. We first evaluate how much total energy saving can be achieved by all the three techniques together. Figure 5 shows the result. On S5-E, the average total energy saving in loading the 100 websites is 24.4%, ranging from 0.02% to 66.5%. 62 websites have an energy saving of 15%-45%, and 7 websites have an energy saving of more than 50%. These results demonstrate that our techniques are able to significantly reduce the energy cost of web page loading. We should also be able to achieve this high energy saving on Chromium-based web browsers such as Google Chrome and Opera Mobile. The most energy saving (66.5%) website is *infusionsoft.com* that has a heavy slide show of high resolution images with a fading transition effect. The least energy saving websites are the ones with simple text content such as *usps.com*.

The S5-S smartphone has a smaller energy saving than the S5-E smartphone. On S5-S, the average energy saving is 11.7%, ranging from 0.21% to 57.1%. 66 websites have an energy saving of 5%-30% and only two websites have an energy saving more than 50%. The reason is that S5-S does not support big.LITTLE and thus cannot benefit from application-assisted scheduling which is the most energy saving technique as we will show later in this section.

The above energy savings are measured in terms of the total system energy consumption, *including the energy cost of the screen*, because the web browser does not load web pages with screen off. Therefore, in order to evaluate the impact of power of the screen, we use a separate experiment. We run the experiment twice with the screen turned on and off. The screen power is then measured as the system power difference between the two different types of experiments. The two smartphones use the same type of screen and the screen power is 186 mW at the lowest brightness level. Exclud-

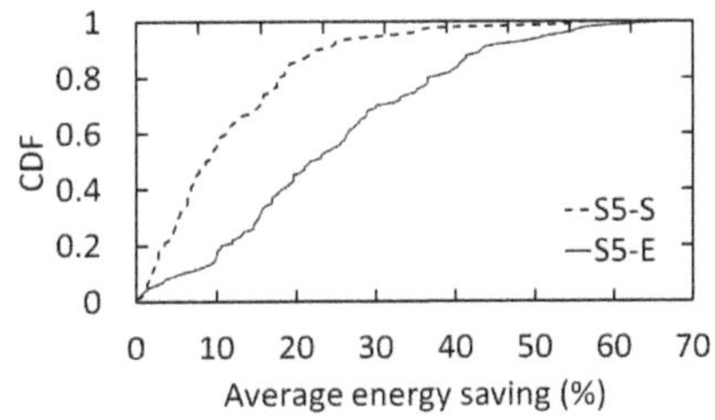

Figure 5: Total energy saving

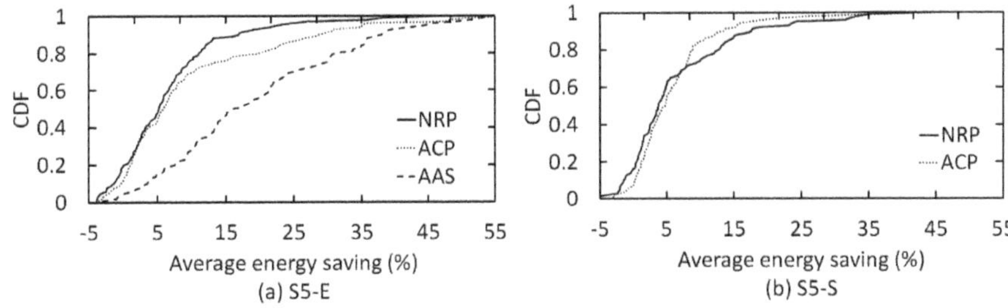

Figure 6: Energy saving of individual techniques

ing the energy cost of screen, the average energy saving increases from 24.4% to 26.6% on S5-E and from 11.7% to 13.0% on S5-S.

Energy saving of individual techniques. We next evaluate to what extent each technique can save energy consumption. Figure 6 shows the results when only one of the three techniques is enabled. NRP, ACP, and AAS stand for energy-aware resource buffering, aggregated content painting, and application-assisted scheduling, respectively.

On S5-E, the most energy saving technique is AAS, reducing the average energy consumption by 19.5%. The other two techniques are also useful, with an average energy saving of 10.2% for NRP and 6.8% for ACP, respectively. Only NRP and ACP can be used on S5-S and have average energy savings of 6.8% and 6.3%, respectively. If we exclude the energy cost of screen, on S5-E, the average energy savings for NRP, ACP and AAS are 11.1%, 7.4% and 21.1%, respectively; and on S5-S, the average energy savings of NRP and ACP are 7.6% and 6.9%, respectively. These results demonstrate that all the three techniques are effective in reducing the energy consumption of web page loading.

It is worth to note that, for some websites, enabling only one of the techniques may slightly increase the system energy cost. For example, on S5-E, if only the AAS technique is enabled, four websites have increased energy costs, ranging from 0.28% to 3.0%. The maximum energy cost increases on S5-E and S5-S are 3.8% and 5.6%, respectively. However, with all the three techniques (two on S5-S), it never increased the energy consumption for all the 100 websites.

6.3 Page Load Time and User Experience

Next we evaluate how much PLT is increased by the combination of the three techniques and by each individual technique, and study the impact of the techniques on user perceived experience using Speed Index [10] and a user study.

Total page load time increase. Our techniques impose minimal extra PLT. Figure 7 shows the results on the two smartphones (all the three techniques are enabled on S5-E and only two techniques are enabled on S5-S). On S5-E, the average PLT is decreased by 0.38% (or decrease 29 ms in terms of the absolute PLT), ranging from -8.11% to 6.38%. In fact, 55 websites have a decreased PLT and 93 websites have PLT increases less than 3%. In terms of the absolute PLT, 94 websites have PLT increases less than 0.2 seconds. On S5-S, the average PLT increase is almost zero, 0.01%, ranging from -4.1% to 4.5%. 51 websites have a decreased PLT, and 94 websites have a PLT increase less than 3%. In terms of the absolute PLT, the average PLT is increased by 6.7 ms, and 93 websites have a PLT increase less than 0.2 seconds. We argue that it is worth to trade this small PLT increase for the significant energy saving. In particular, we are indeed able to decrease the PLT of about half of the 100 websites.

Page load time increase of individual techniques. We also measure the PLT increase caused by each individual technique. Figure 8 shows the results. As one may expect, each technique alone also introduces minimal extra PLT. On S5-E, AAS introduces the highest average PLT increase but the increase is only 0.23% and it even decreases 22.8 ms in terms of absolute PLT. The PLT increase for NRP and ACP are 0.04% (-2.6 ms) and -0.45% (-49.9 ms), respectively. On S5-S, the PLT increase is 0.76% (56.2 ms) for NRP and -0.25% (-24.5 ms) for ACP, respectively. Compared to the other two techniques, ACP has the smallest impact on PLT as it decreases PLT on both phones.

Configuration	Average PLT increase		Average energy saving (%)	
	Relative (%)	Absolute (ms)	With screen	No screen
All	-0.38	-29.0	24.4	26.6
NRP	0.04	-2.6	10.2	11.1
ACP	-0.45	-49.9	6.8	7.4
AAS	0.23	-22.8	19.5	21.1

Table 2: Energy saving and PLT increase on S5-E

Configuration	Average PLT increase		Average energy saving (%)	
	Relative (%)	Absolute (ms)	With screen	No screen
All	0.01	6.7	11.7	13.0
NRP	0.76	56.2	6.8	7.6
ACP	-0.25	-24.5	6.3	6.9

Table 3: Energy saving and PLT increase on S5-S

Table 2 and Table 3 summarize the average energy savings and PLT increase on S5-E and S5-S, respectively. It is worth noting that the three techniques are not completely independent, and thus the total energy saving is not equal to the sum of the energy savings of individual techniques.

Impact on visually complete progress. In order to evaluate the impact of the techniques on the visual loading progress of web pages, we measure the Speed Index [10] in addition to the page load time. The metric measures how quickly the page content is visually populated, and is calculated as in the following formula:

$$SpeedIndex = \int_0^{end} (1 - \frac{VC}{100}),$$

where end is the end time in milliseconds and VC is the percentage of visually complete. Lower Speed Index is better because the user will see the web page content painted earlier and thus faster visual loading progress.

We use Telemetry tool to get visual progress from paint events exposed by Blink through the DevTools timeline. Compared to getting visual progress from video capture, this method deals with pages that update and change better [10, 12]. Moreover, it worked more reliably on the websites in our dataset specially ones with animations.

Our techniques increase the metric by 1.8% on average, so they delay the page loading progress only slightly. Figure 9 shows the increase of Speed Index of the All configuration compared to the

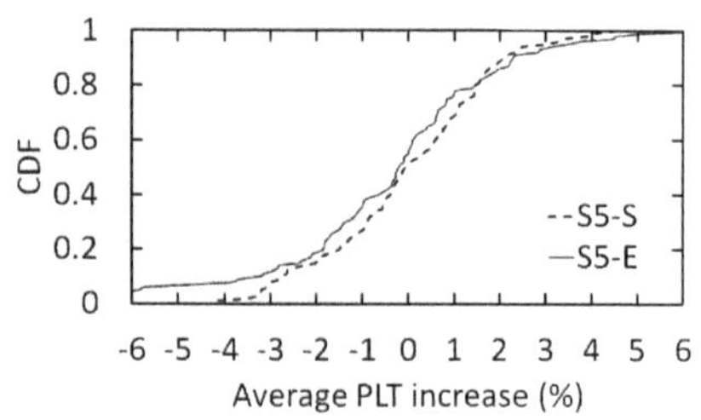

Figure 7: Total PLT increase

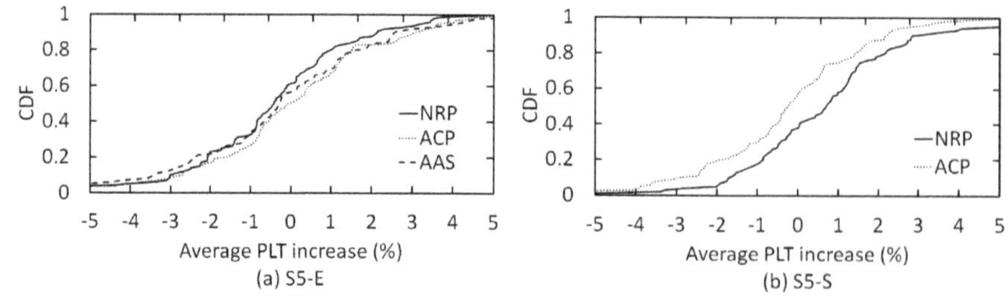

Figure 8: PLT increase of individual techniques

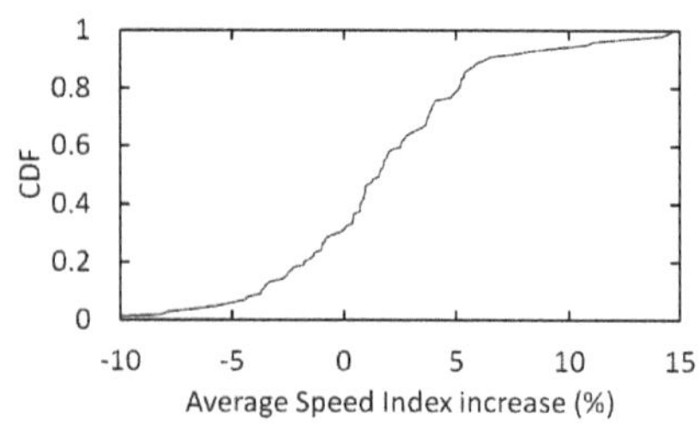

Figure 9: Impact of All configuration on Speed Index metric

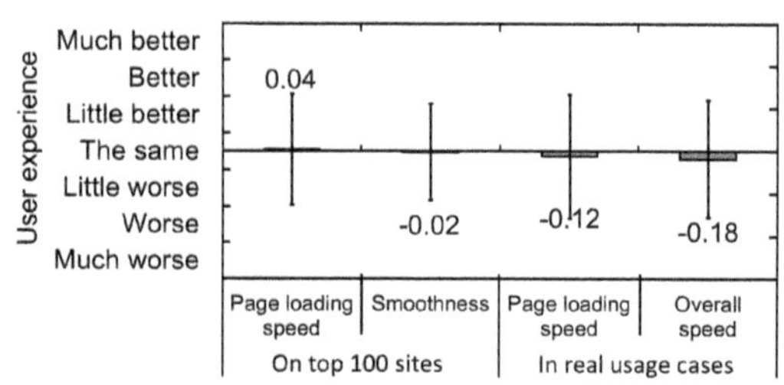

Figure 10: User perceived experience on our revised Chromium compared to the default Chromium

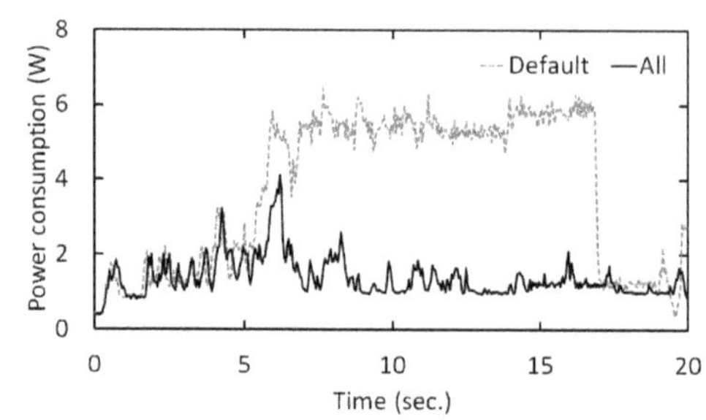

Figure 11: Power consumption in loading infusionsoft.com with All configuration

Default. We report the results for 99 websites, except *conduit.com* which contains a continuously rotating image and for which the Telemetry tool reported an abnormal decrease of 42% by our techniques.

User perceived experience To further evaluate the impact of the increased PLT on user perceived experience, we conduct a user study to collect real user feedback on our techniques on real-world environments. Therefore, we recruited 18 undergraduate students in our university, 11 males and 7 females and performed two tests using the S5-E smartphone on a real-world WiFi network. In the first test, we use the default Chromium and our revised Chromium to load 10 web pages randomly selected from the top 100 websites. Each website is loaded using either the default Chromium or our revised Chromium browser. We show the web page loading to the users but do not let them know which Chromium version is used. User can ask to repeat loading any web page as many times as he/she wants. We then ask them whether our revised Chromium is better or worse than the default Chromium in terms of page loading speed and smoothness, using a seven-level scale (from 3 to -3 for much better, better, little better, the same, little worse, worse, and much worse, respectively). In the second test, we let the users do web browsing in their favorite way, using each version of the browser for 5 minutes, respectively. The users also do not know which Chromium version being used. This test includes not only page loading but also page reading and users interactions (e.g., scrolling). Then we ask them to compare the two browsers again using the same seven-level scale, in terms of page loading speed and the overall speed.

Figure 10 shows the results. For the first test, 4 of 18 (22%) users told that it is difficult to tell which browser is faster. 10 (55%) users even gave a higher score on our revised browser. For smoothness, most of the users could not tell the difference. The average scores of page loading speed and smoothness are almost zero: 0.04 (standard deviation(stdev) 1.30) and -0.02 (stdev 1.14), respectively. In the second test of real usage, we get similar results: 7 (39%) users told that our revised browser is faster in page loading, and 5 (28%) users told that our revised browser is faster in overall speed. The average scores of page loading speed and the overall speed are also near zero: -0.12 (stdev 1.45) and -0.18 (stdev 1.38), respectively. These results demonstrate that our techniques impose a minimal impact on user experience and such a small impact is hardly perceivable by the users. After the tests, we asked the users how they would like to use our techniques. 13 (72%) of them would always use our techniques and 5 (28%) of them would use when the battery level is low.

6.4 Energy Saving Analysis: Case Study

To investigate further how our proposed techniques reduce energy consumption, we present a detailed analysis for *infusionsoft.com* as a case study since it is the most energy saving website for each technique. In essence, our techniques decrease the total energy consumption by reducing system power and CPU utilization. We examine the results obtained on the S5-E smartphone.

System power reduction. As our techniques introduce a minimal increase of PLT while reducing total consumed energy, what we actually reduce is system power consumption. Figure 11 shows the power traces in loading *infusionsoft.com*, the website that has the highest energy saving (66.5%). Our techniques are able to significantly reduce the system power. For the time period of 5.0 sec - 17.0 sec in the figure, the average system power in using the default Chromium is 5.28 W; with our techniques enabled, the aver-

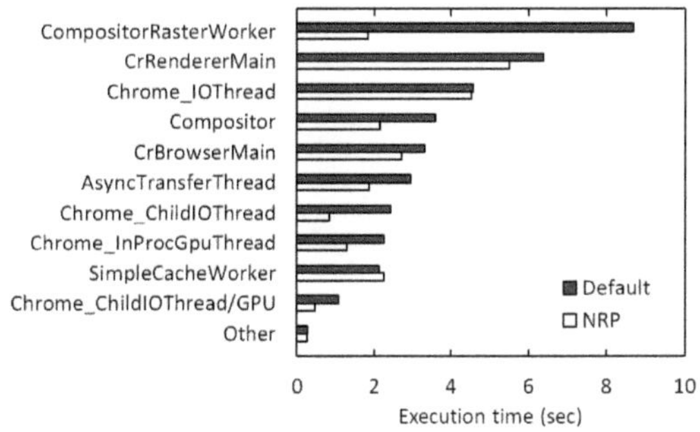

Figure 12: Thread CPU time in loading infusionsoft.com with NRP configuration

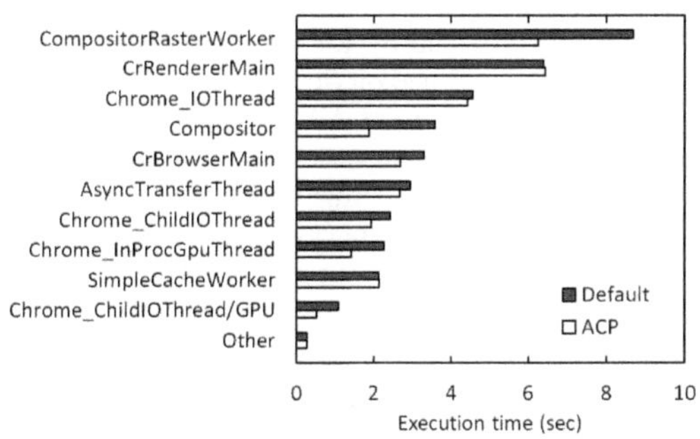

Figure 13: Thread CPU time in loading infusionsoft.com with ACP configuration

age system power is reduced to 1.44 W. This significant reduction of system power comes from the reduced CPU utilization, as shown below.

CPU utilization reduction of NRP. Figure 12 shows the CPU time of the main threads in loading *infusionsoft.com*, using the default Chromium and using our revised Chromium with only the NRP technique enabled. When NRP is enabled, the CPU time of the *Chrome_ChildIOThread* thread is significantly reduced, from 2.42 seconds to 0.84 seconds, or a reduction of 65.3%. This is because NRP is designed to the reduce IPCs between the Browser process and the Renderer process. NRP also reduces the CPU time of the *CompositorRasterWorker* thread (from 8.68 seconds 1.83 to seconds, or 78.9%), *Compositor* thread (from 3.58 seconds to 2.14 seconds, or 40.2%), *Chrome_InProcGpuThread* thread (from 2.26 seconds to 1.29 seconds, or 42.9%), and *AsyncTransferThread* thread (from 2.94 seconds to 1.86 seconds, or 36.7%). This is because increasing data size for each processing reduces the number of changes to layers of a web page and thereby the number of content rendering. This way, it significantly reduces the CPU processing time of the rendering engine and graphic processing.

CPU utilization reduction of ACP. Figure 13 shows the results with only the ACP technique enabled. When ACP is enabled, the CPU time of the following four threads are significantly reduced: for *Compositor* thread, from 3.58 seconds to 1.87 seconds (47.8%), for *Chrome_InProcGpuThread* thread, from 2.26 seconds to 1.41 seconds (37.5%), and for *CompositorRasterWorker* thread, from 8.68 seconds to 6.25 seconds (28.0%). These results demonstrate the effectiveness of ACP in reducing the processing cost of the graphic processing pipeline.

CPU utilization reduction of AAS. AAS reduces big cores workload significantly while increasing utilization of little cores for energy efficient processing. Figure 14 shows the utilization of little and big clusters when loading *infusionsoft.com*. In default

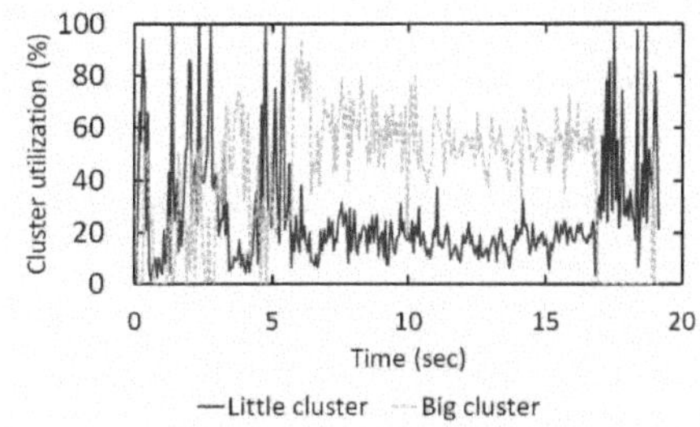

(a) Default configuration

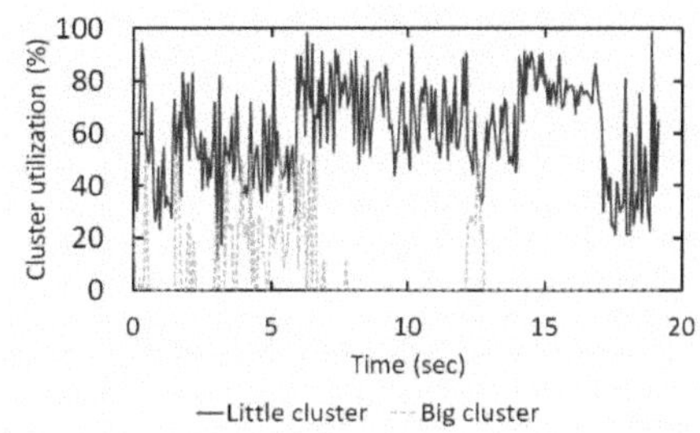

(b) AAS configuration

Figure 14: Utilization on clusters of application-assisted scheduling

Configuration	Average PLT increase		Average energy saving (%)	
	Relative (%)	Absolute (ms)	With screen	No screen
All	1.69	180	10.5	11.9
ACP	-0.46	-36	9.5	10.5
AAS	2.00	195	3.3	3.9

Table 4: Energy saving and PLT increase on Firefox

Chromium, the average utilization of little and big cores are 25.2% and 40.9%, respectively. Using AAS, the average utilization of little cores increases to 60.1% while the average utilization of big cores decreases to only 6.1%.

6.5 Energy Saving on Other Web Browser

In order to demonstrate applicability of techniques on other web browsers, we implement the ACP and AAS techniques on Firefox for Android open source web browser. Among the top 100 websites, our experiments were performed on 72 websites that use HTTP protocol. This is because it is problematic for Firefox to establish HTTPS connections to the Web Page Replay server which uses a self-signed encryption certificate. We use Firefox version 38, the latest version at the time of writing this paper. For ACP, the implementation is only 50 lines of code in the CompositorParent class which is responsible for graphical composition in Firefox. The implementation of AAS involves changes to thread management module. Because the NRP technique requires considerable implementation of a whole new buffer layer in the network stack of Firefox, we leave it as future work.

With the ACP and AAS techniques, the revised Firefox web browser saves a non-trivial amount of energy while affect page load time minimally. On S5-E, both techniques save 10.5% average system energy saving while increasing 1.69% (180 ms) PLT. For each technique, average system energy saving is 9.5% for ACP and 3.3% for AAS. The PLT increase is -0.46% for ACP and 0.2% for AAS. The results are shown in Table 4. The reason the AAS technique does not save much energy on Firefox is that the AAS technique attempts to put Compositor thread to little cores. However, although the thread has higher CPU utilization than other threads, it still has light CPU load. Therefore, putting Compositor thread onto a lit-

Device	Average PLT increase		Average energy saving (%)	
	Relative (%)	Absolute (ms)	With screen	No screen
S5-E	-0.06	-3.5	21.8	23.4
S5-S	-0.92	-47.3	6.0	6.5

Table 5: Energy saving and PLT increase on a fast network

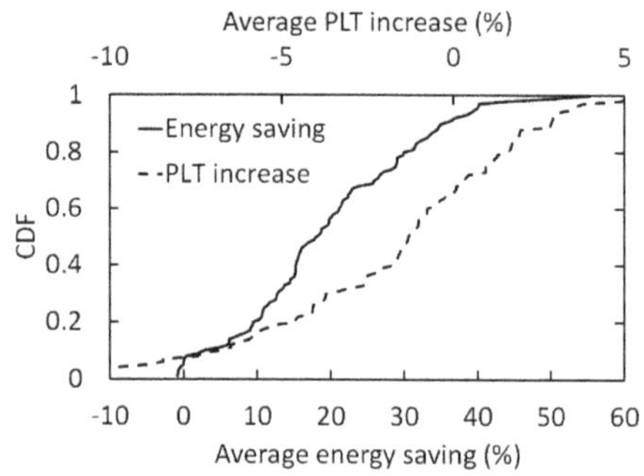

Figure 15: Energy saving and PLT increase in hot loading

tle core does not save much energy compared with the case where the Compositor thread is running on a big core at the least possible frequency.

6.6 Energy Saving on Fast Networks

We also evaluate how much energy our techniques can save on fast networks such 4G cellular and WiFi. We emulated a fast network with 20 Mbps downlink bandwidth, 10 Mbps uplink bandwidth, and 50 ms RTT. Table 5 shows that our techniques still save 21.8% and 6.0% of system energy on S5-E and S5-S, respectively. Excluding screen energy, our techniques save 23.4% and 6.5% on S5-E and S5-S, respectively. The PLT is even decreased by 0.06% (S5-E) and 0.92% (S5-S). This decrease of PLT may come from two reasons: 1) when the network is faster, the extra latency introduced by NRP becomes smaller; 2) as AAS makes better use of little cores, it leaves more capacity of big cores to the rendering engine and thus makes content rendering faster.

6.7 Energy Saving in Hot Loading

We evaluate the performance of our techniques in case of web page loading with cached content. We test on the hot web page loading in which the web browser loads the web pages again immediately after a cold load. Thereby, many resources are still in the web browser cache and DNS lookup results are also still in the local DNS cache of the OS. We use the emulated WiFi network with 2 Mbps downlink, 1 Mbps uplink bandwidth and a 120 ms RTT.

Our techniques are still effective in reducing the system energy consumption in hot loading. The results of the All configuration on S5-E are shown in Figure 15. The average system energy is reduced by 19.6% and average page load time is decreased by 1.73% (or 67 ms in terms of absolute page load time). The decrease of page load time can be explained similarly as on fast networks.

6.8 Energy Saving on 3G Network

We evaluate the energy saving of our techniques when running on a 3G network, given that the power consumption profile of a cellular network interface is different from WiFi [36]. For repeatable experiments, web pages are loaded from our Web Page Replay server. The server throttles bandwidth by 2 Mbps download and 1 Mbps upload while not adding any delay. Given the 3G (HSPA+) network is fast enough, the bandwidth is limited at the server side. The delay is not controlled and determined by the 3G network. We

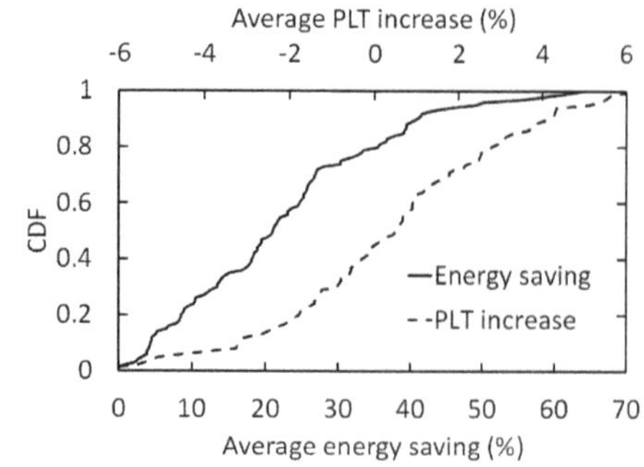

Figure 16: Effectiveness of All configuration on a 3G network

use the 3G network provided by KT Corporation, and the phone has only its 3G interface turned on (its WiFi interface is off).

Figure 16 shows the results of All configuration on S5-E. Our techniques have average system energy saving of 22.5% and average PLT increase of 0.41% (27 ms in absolute page load time). Average system energy saving when using a cellular network interface is still high although it is about 2% lower than when using a WiFi network interface (24.4%). Given the amount of downloaded data for each web page is not large (e.g., 1.1 MB on average in our dataset), the processing on the CPU generally dominates the power consumption of the whole system. The measured energy is the total system energy which includes the 3G tail energy during web page load time but does not include the tail energy after the page loading finishes.

7. DISCUSSION AND FUTURE WORK

Apply the proposed techniques to other applications. Other browsers and applications may use the three proposed techniques to improve their energy efficiency. Two techniques, NRP and ACP, are about general processing of web contents and thus may benefit other browsers. In particular, the Chromium-based web browsers such as Opera Mobile and WebKit-based web browser such as Safari may directly benefit from the techniques.

Furthermore, many mobile apps are designed to access web contents (e.g., a native app of a news website) and some of them are even directly built on top a browser control (e.g., the Chromium-based WebView class on Android). They are essentially customized browsers and thus may also benefit from our techniques. Furthermore, AAS is not specifically designed for browsers. The idea of leveraging application internals to make better scheduling decisions is general enough to be used by more applications. In particular, on big.LITTLE platforms, we see big potential of this technique and plan to investigate more on how to apply this technique to more applications. Furthermore, AAS technique is applicable to non-rooted Android since setting thread cpu affinity does not require the root priviledge. Also, current Android 5.0 also uses the same kernel version 3.10 on big.LITTLE architecture phones as on Android 4.4 so this technique will be also effective.

Reduce energy consumption after page loading. Although we focus on the energy consumption of page loading in this paper, it is possible to save more energy after page loading, i.e., when a user reads and interacts with a web page. In fact, the AAS technique may be applied to user reading time as well. We have measured the energy consumption of the top 100 websites with 10 seconds of non-interactive user reading time, and found that AAS is able to reduce the system energy consumption in the user reading time by 4.6% (5.6% excluding screen energy) with minimal user experience degradation. Furthermore, after page loading, the web contents have been processed and thus we may apply more aggressive CPU power saving policies to save more energy. We plan to investigate more energy saving techniques for the time period after page loading.

Offload more graphic processing to GPU. As we have shown, the graphic-processing pipeline has heavy workload and is energy consuming, especially the rasterization. As GPU is more efficient in doing graphic tasks, it is possible to move the graphic processing currently done on CPU (such as Raster Worker) to GPU to save energy. In fact, recent experimental features of Chrome have demonstrated big improvement in reducing frame generation time [38], and thus has potential to reduce energy consumption. However, this technique is orthogonal to our techniques. We focus on optimizing IPCs overhead, granularity of content processing and painting, and task scheduling on big.LITTLE architecture.

Real deployment and field study. Although our in-lab experiments and user study have demonstrated the effectiveness of our techniques, they show few insights on how our techniques could perform in real usage. It is desirable to deploy our revised Chromium browser to end users and further evaluate its performance in more realistic and diverse network conditions and settings. We plan to conduct a long-term field study to collect real user feedback from daily use.

Re-design mobile browser architecture. Ideally, the architecture of mobile web browsers should be re-designed to have energy consumption as the first-class consideration at the very beginning. The web browser should be aware of the energy cost of each stage of the content fetching and processing pipeline, adapt to the user-perceived experience, and reduce the interaction overhead of different components. It should also better utilize new hardware capabilities such as big.LITTLE cores to save energy. We plan to investigate more on how systematic architecture re-design may help us further balance the energy consumption and user experience of mobile web browsing.

8. RELATED WORK

Energy-efficient mobile web browsing has been explored through various approaches. Thiagarajan *et al.* [41] examined the energy consumed to render individual web page primitives, such as HTML, images, JavaScript, and Cascade Style Sheets (CSS), and suggested guidelines for designing energy-efficient web pages, such as diminishing complex JavaScript and CSS and using JPEG images. Zhu *et al.* [46] introduced energy-efficient, latency-sensitive scheduling of web pages for mobile browsing over heterogeneous cores, according to statistical inference models that estimate page load time and energy consumption through the characteristics of web page primitives, HTML and CSS. Butkiewicz *et al.* [15] presented a linear regression model that predicts page load times according to the characteristics of web pages (e.g., number and size of images) and web servers (e.g., number of servers/origins). Chameleon [20, 21] renders web pages with energy-efficient color schemes on OLED mobile systems under user-supplied constraints. Qian *et al.* [35] provided a deep analysis of how mobile web browsing uses wireless network resources and offered guidelines for energy-efficient browsing, such as decomposing a tall web page into several smaller subpages and reducing JavaScript-triggered delayed or periodic data transfers in cellular networks. Zhao et al. [45] reorganized computation stages in web browsers and predicted user reading time in order to quickly put the radio interface into the power-saving IDLE state on 3G based phones. Our work can be differentiated from the above approaches in that we leverage browser internals (e.g., process/thread structure, resource fetching/processing pipelines) for energy-efficient browsing, while the others focus on the characteristics of web pages (e.g., primitives, colors, network accesses). Thereby, we believe our work can be integrated with others to improve energy efficiency further.

Mobile browsing performance optimization. Many techniques have been developed to reduce page load time without taking energy concerns into account. New web protocols such as SPDY [9] and HTTP 2.0 [8] are now under development to improve the performance of current HTTP protocol. Their key features include (i) multiplexing HTTP transactions into a single TCP connection and (ii) prioritizing some object loads over others (e.g., JavaScript over images). A recent study [42] found that SPDY can improve page load time significantly over HTTP 1.1 by largely benefiting from the use of a single TCP connection. However, they also showed that such a benefit can be overwhelmed by dependencies in web pages and browser computation, and suggested to restructure the page load process to reduce page load time. In addition to such infrastructure-related approaches, client-only approaches were developed with the benefit of easy deployment without infrastructure support. Wang *et al.* [43] showed that two popular client-only schemes, caching and prefetching, can be ineffective for mobile browsing, while speculative loading can be helpful to overcome their limitation. Ma *et al.* [30] first proposed and used a proactive approach for a comprehensive study on mobile web cache performance to identify the problems of unsatisfactory cache performance and revealed the root causes. Meyerovich *et al.* [31] introduced algorithms to parallelize web page layout and rendering engines to speedup browser computation.

Energy saving for mobile apps. Pathak *et al.* [34] examined the energy consumption of smartphone apps in a fine-grained manner, reporting some interesting findings such as third-party advertisement modules consume about two-thirds of energy spent in free apps. Xu *et al.* [44] studied energy saving on email client through various techniques, including reducing 3G tail time and decoupling data transmission from data processing. Some researchers focus on effectiveness of DVFS on mobile CPU. A recent study [17] considered energy saving on big.LITTLE architecture with a focus on integrating core offlining with frequency scaling, while paying no attention to determining on which type of cores (big or little) apps run for energy efficiency.

9. CONCLUSION

This paper presented three effective techniques to optimize the energy consumption of web page loading on smartphones. Two of the techniques, network-aware resource processing and adaptive content painting, are designed to address energy-inefficiency issues of the current mobile web browsers in its content processing and graphic processing pipelines. The third one, application-assisted scheduling, is designed to balance the trade-off between the energy saving and the QoS big.LITTLE platforms. We have implemented the proposed techniques on Chromium and Firefox, and conducted comprehensive evaluations using real-world websites and latest-generation smartphones. Experimental results and user study show that the techniques are able to significantly reduce the energy cost of web page loading and introduce hardly perceivable page load time increase.

ACKNOWLEDGEMENTS

This work was supported in part by ICT/SW Creative research program (2014-H0510-14-1008) of MSIP/NIPA, Korea, and Microsoft Research and by SW Computing R&D Program (2011-10041313) of MSIP/KEIT, Korea. We also thank our anonymous reviewers and shepherd for their insightful and constructive comments that helped us improve this paper.

10. REFERENCES

[1] 3G/4G wireless network latency: Comparing Verizon, AT&T, Sprint and T-Mobile in February 2014.

[2] Alexa, Top Sites in United States. http://www.alexa.com/topsites/countries/US.

[3] ARM big.LITTLE technology. http://www.thinkbiglittle.com.

[4] Blink. http://www.chromium.org/blink.

[5] Content module. http://www.chromium.org/developers/content-module.

[6] Differences between Google Chrome and Linux distro Chromium. http://code.google.com/p/chromium/wiki/ChromiumBrowserVsGoogleChrome.

[7] The dummynet project. http://info.iet.unipi.it/~luigi/dummynet.

[8] Hypertext transfer protocol version 2.0, draft-ietf-httpbis-http2-07. http://tools.ietf.org/html/draft-ietf-httpbis-http2-07.

[9] SPDY. http://www.chromium.org/spdy.

[10] Speed index. http://sites.google.com/a/webpagetest.org/docs/using-webpagetest/metrics/speed-index.

[11] Telemetry. http://www.chromium.org/developers/telemetry.

[12] Visual progress - dev tools. http://www.webpagetest.org/forums/showthread.php?tid=12216.

[13] Web Page Replay. http://www.github.com/chromium/web-page-replay.

[14] WebKit. http://www.webkit.org.

[15] M. Butkiewicz, H. V. Madhyastha, and V. Sekar. Understanding Website Complexity: Measurements, Metrics, and Implications. In *Proc. ACM IMC*, 2011.

[16] A. Carroll and G. Heiser. Mobile multicores: Use them or waste them. In *Proc. USENIX HotPower*, 2013.

[17] A. Carroll and G. Heiser. Unifying DVFS and offlining in mobile multicores. In *Proc. IEEE RTAS*, 2014.

[18] H. Chung, M. Kang, and H. D. Cho. Heterogeneous Multi-Processing Solution of Exynos 5 Octa with ARM big.LITTLE Technology, 2012.

[19] A. Cunningham. New Opera for Android looks like Opera, tastes like Chrome. http://arstechnica.com/information-technology/2013/05/new-opera-for-android-looks-like-opera-tastes-like-chrome.

[20] M. Dong and L. Zhong. Chameleon: A Color-adaptive Web Browser for Mobile OLED Displays. In *Proc. ACM MobiSys*, 2011.

[21] M. Dong and L. Zhong. Chameleon: A Color-Adaptive Web Browser for Mobile OLED Displays. *IEEE Transactions on Mobile Computing (TMC)*, 2012.

[22] S. Dutton. Measuring Page Load Speed with Navigation Timing. http://www.html5rocks.com/en/tutorials/webperformance/basics, 2011.

[23] J. Glauner. Analyzing Website Performance at a Glance. http://www.stratigent.com/community/analytics-insights-blog/analyzing-website-performance-glance, 2013.

[24] U. Gundecha. *Selenium Testing Tools Cookbook*. Packt Publishing, 2012.

[25] Q. He, C. Dovrolis, and M. Ammar. On the predictability of large transfer TCP throughput. In *Proc. ACM SIGCOMM*, 2005.

[26] J. Huang. *Performance and Power Characterization of Cellular Networks and Mobile Application Optimizations*. PhD thesis, The University of Michigan, 2013.

[27] J. Huang, Q. Xu, B. Tiwana, Z. M. Mao, M. Zhang, and P. Bahl. Anatomizing application performance differences on smartphones. In *Proc. ACM MobiSys*, 2010.

[28] B. Iglewicz and D. Hoaglin. *Volume 16: How to Detect and Handle Outliers*. 1993.

[29] Monsoon Solutions Inc. Monsoon power monitor. http://www.msoon.com/LabEquipment/PowerMonitor.

[30] Y. Ma, X. Liu, S. Zhang, R. Xiang, Y. Liu, and T. Xie. Measurement and Analysis of Mobile Web Cache Performance. In *Proc. WWW*, 2015.

[31] L. A. Meyerovich and R. Bodik. Fast and parallel webpage layout. In *Proc. WWW*, 2010.

[32] M. Mirza, J. Sommers, P. Barford, and Xiaojin Zhu. A machine learning approach to TCP throughput prediction. *Networking, IEEE/ACM Transactions on*, 18(4):1026–1039, 2010.

[33] K. W. Nixon, X. Chen, H. Zhou, Y. Liu, and Y. Chen. Mobile gpu power consumption reduction via dynamic resolution and frame rate scaling. In *HotPower*, 2014.

[34] A. Pathak, Y. C. Hu, and M. Zhang. Where is the Energy Spent Inside My App?: Fine Grained Energy Accounting on Smartphones with Eprof. In *Proc. ACM EuroSys*, 2012.

[35] F. Qian, S. Sen, and O. Spatscheck. Characterizing Resource Usage for Mobile Web Browsing. In *Proc. ACM MobiSys*, 2014.

[36] F. Qian, Z. Wang, A. Gerber, Z. M. Mao, S. Sen, and O. Spatscheck. Characterizing Radio Resource Allocation for 3G Networks. In *Proc. ACM IMC*, 2010.

[37] M. Rasmussen. sched: Task placement for heterogeneous MP systems. http://www.lwn.net/Articles/517250, 2012.

[38] R. Schoen. Wicked Fast (Performance investments). In *Chrome Dev Summit*, 2014.

[39] B. Shneiderman, C. Plaisant, M. Cohen, and S. Jacobs. *Designing the User Interface: Strategies for Effective Human-Computer Interaction*. Fifth edition, 2009.

[40] J. Sommers and P. Barford. Cell vs. wifi: On the performance of metro area mobile connections. In *Proc. ACM IMC*, 2012.

[41] N. Thiagarajan, G. Aggarwal, A. Nicoara, D. Boneh, and J. P. Singh. Who Killed My Battery?: Analyzing Mobile Browser Energy Consumption. In *Proc. WWW*, 2012.

[42] X. S. Wang, A. Balasubramanian, A. Krishnamurthy, and D. Wetherall. How Speedy is SPDY? In *Proc. USENIX NSDI*, 2014.

[43] Z. Wang, F. X. Lin, L. Zhong, and M. Chishtie. How Far Can Client-only Solutions Go for Mobile Browser Speed? In *Proc. WWW*, 2012.

[44] F. Xu, Y. Liu, T. Moscibroda, R. Chandra, L. Jin, Y. Zhang, and Q. Li. Optimizing Background Email Sync on Smartphones. In *Proc. ACM MobiSys*, 2013.

[45] B. Zhao, Q. Zheng, G. Cao, and S. Addepalli. Energy-Aware Web Browsing in 3G Based Smartphones. In *Proc. IEEE ICDCS*, 2013.

[46] Y. Zhu and V. J. Reddi. High-performance and Energy-efficient Mobile Web Browsing on Big/Little Systems. In *Proc. IEEE HPCA*, 2013.

Optimizing Smartphone Power Consumption through Dynamic Resolution Scaling

Songtao He[1,2], Yunxin Liu[1], Hucheng Zhou[1]

[1]Microsoft Research, Beijing, China
[2]University of Science and Technology of China, Hefei, China

hst@mail.ustc.edu.cn, {yunliu, huzho}@microsoft.com

ABSTRACT

The extremely-high display density of modern smartphones imposes a significant burden on power consumption, yet does not always provide an improved user experience and may even lead to a compromised user experience. As human visually-perceivable ability highly depends on the user-screen distance, a reduced display resolution may still achieve the same user experience when the user-screen distance is large. This provides new power-saving opportunities. In this paper, we present a flexible dynamic resolution scaling system for smartphones. The system adopts an ultrasonic-based approach to accurately detect the user-screen distance at low-power cost and makes scaling decisions automatically for maximum user experience and power saving. App developers or users can also adjust the resolution manually as their needs. Our system is able to work on existing commercial smartphones and support legacy apps, without requiring re-building the ROM or any changes of apps. An end-to-end dynamic resolution scaling system is implemented on the Galaxy S5 LTE-A and Nexus 6 smartphones, and the correctness and effectiveness are evaluated against 30 games and benchmarks. Experimental results show that all the 30 apps can run successfully with per-frame, real-time dynamic resolution scaling. The energy per frame can be reduced by 30.1% on average and up to 60.5% at most when the resolution is halved, for 15 apps. A user study with 10 users indicates that our system remains good user experience, as none of the 10 users could perceive the resolution changes in the user study.

Categories and Subject Descriptors

I.3.4 [**Computer Graphics**]: Graphics Utilities—*Software support*

General Terms

Experiments; Measurement; Performance

MobiCom'15, September 07–11, 2015, Paris, France.

DOI: http://dx.doi.org/10.1145/2789168.2790117.

Keywords

Smartphone; GPU; Power Consumption; Display Resolution; Dynamic Resolution Scaling

1. INTRODUCTION

The display resolution of smartphones has become increasingly high. Since the "Retina display" of the iPhone 4 released in 2010 [18], display resolution of smartphones has continued to rise, from 960x640 pixels of the iPhone 4 to 1920x1080 pixels (Full HD) and recently to 2560x1440 pixels (2K). As a result, latest smartphones have an extremely-high display density. For example, the LG G3 [16] has a display of 538 pixels per inch (ppi), while the Samsung Galaxy S5 LTE-A [17] has a display of 577 ppi.

However, this extremely-high display density does not always help bring an improved user experience. The Retina display of the iPhone 4 has a display density of only 326 ppi. The high display density of the LG G3 and the Samsung Galaxy S5 LTE-A is far beyond the human ability of visual acuity, and thus does not lead to visibly-sharper content and interfaces displayed on the screen. Nevertheless, a high-resolution display consumes a large amount of system resources, especially the GPU computation, and thus results in high system power consumption (see Section 2). As energy is a paramount concern on smartphones, it is desirable to study the tradeoff between display density and power consumption.

In this paper, we propose to optimize the high power consumption caused by high-density displays through Dynamic Resolution Scaling (DRS). Based on the viewing distance (i.e., the screen-user distance), DRS dynamically adjusts the user-interface resolution displayed on the screen but ensures that the pixels are always small enough to be individually unobservable by human eyes. The philosophy of DRS is that the system should render the interface with exactly as many details as it is perceptible to a user, in order to maximize both user experience and battery life. When a resolution is too high for a viewing distance, DRS reduces the resolution to save power.

Enabling DRS imposes several requirements. First, DRS must seamlessly adjust the resolution in real-time as the viewing distance changes, without compromising the user experience. Second, DRS must be done systematically and is transparent from applications. Third, DRS must be able to accurately determine the viewing distance of a user in real-time and with minimal energy cost.

To meet the requirements, we develop per-frame DRS technique for seamless and real-time resolution adjusting. We intercept the system graphics pipeline to enable system-wide DRS, without requiring any changes or recompiling from applications, or re-building a new smartphone ROM. We further propose to use ultrasonic sensors to detect the viewing distance of a user, which is accurate and low-power. Based on the detected viewing distance, we utilize existing knowledge of the human visual system to define the required display-pixel density for optimal user experience, and adjust the extravagant resolution accordingly.

We have implemented a DRS system that works on existing commercial smartphones including the Galaxy S5 LTE-A and the Nexus 6. We conduct comprehensive experiments and a user study to evaluate the DRS implementation against 30 real gaming and benchmark applications. Experimental results show that all the 30 applications can run successfully with per-frame, real-time dynamic resolution scaling. The energy per frame can be reduced by 30.1% in average and up to 60.5% at most when the resolution is halved, for 15 applications. Even for other less GPU-intensive applications such as Adobe Reader and web browser, we still reduce the energy per frame for about 10%. A user study with 10 users indicates that our system remains good user experience: none of the 10 users could perceive the resolution changes in the user study although the resolution changed for more than 100 times for each user.

To the best of our knowledge, we are the first to design and implement a DRS system for smartphones. The main contributions of this paper are as the following:

1. We present a per-frame and application-transparent system-level DRS design and implementation.
2. We adopt an ultrasonic-based approach that detects the user-screen distance in real-time and with low power.
3. We conduct experiments and a user study to confirm the effectiveness of our system for maximum user experience and power saving.

The rest of this paper is organized as follows. Section 2 motivates the need of DRS and set our goals. Section 3 introduces how the graphics pipeline works on Android platform as background. Section 4 overviews the architecture design and the key components of DRS. Section 5 and Section 6 presents how to enable DRS and how to determine the viewing distance of users, respectively. Section 7 describes more implementation details and Section 8 reports the evaluation results. Section 9 discusses the limitations and future work, Section 10 surveys the related work and Section 11 concludes.

2. MOTIVATION AND GOALS

In this section, we describe three problems caused by high-resolution displays on smartphones, to motivate our work and set our goals of this paper.

2.1 Motivation

High-resolution displays can be only justified if they can improve the user experience, e.g., allowing sharper images or more content to be legibly displayed. However, they fail to provide an improved user experience on smartphones because the physical size of display is small and thus the

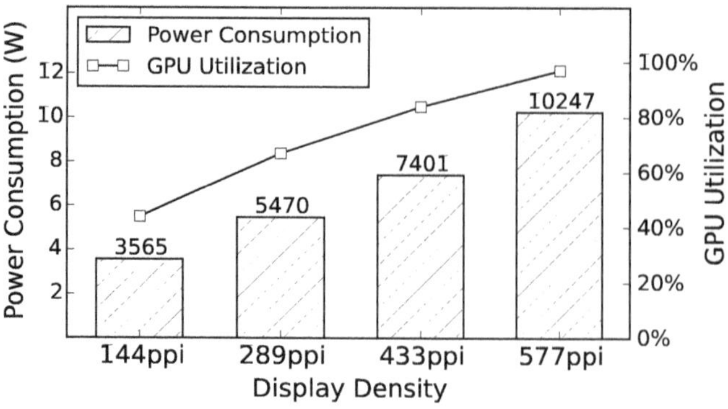

Figure 1: System power and GPU utilization of Galaxy S5 LTE-A in different display resolutions.

extremely-high display density surpasses the human ability of visual acuity. Instead, high-resolution displays consume a large amount of system resources and cause the following three issues on smartphones.

High power consumption. High-resolution displays significantly increase the system power mainly because rendering extra pixels imposes very high GPU workload and memory usage. To verify this, we wrote a test program to render a 3D scene with a fixed number of vertexes/triangles at 60 frames per second (fps). The program was specially designed to generate independent arithmetic, special function and memory access workload on GPU. So, the GPU can reach its peak power consumption while processing those workload concurrently. We ran the program on Galaxy S5 LTE-A with different display resolutions and measured the system power (with the screen turned off) and the GPU utilization. The result is shown in Figure 1. The system power increases almost linearly when the display density increases and a higher display resolution consumes significantly more power than a lower display resolution. For example, when the display resolution is 2560x1440 pixels (577 ppi), the system power is 10247 mW, 87.3% higher than the system power when the display resolution is 1280x720 pixels (289 ppi). This power increase is mainly caused by the increased GPU workload. Indeed, to support a high-resolution display, smartphones have to utilize a high-performance and thus power-hungry GPU. For example, the Galaxy S5 LTE-A utilizes an Adreno 420 GPU that dominates the system power of more than 10 W in Figure 1.

Compromised user experience. The high GPU workload imposed by a high-resolution setting may saturate the GPU and thus lead to a reduced frame rate. For example, we ran the GFX Benchmark [1] on the Galaxy S5 LTE-A with the native resolution (2560x1440 pixels), the frame rate of the Manhattan scene is only 11.5 fps, far lower than the default frame rate of 60 fps on Android. As shown in Figure 2, even if we reduce the resolution to 1280x720 pixels, the frame rate only increases to 30.2 fps. When the frame rate is too low (e.g., less than 30 fps), users may perceive visible delay on the display. Thus, this high overhead of display may significantly impact apps performance and harm the user experience.

Overheating. The high power consumption caused by a high-resolution display also generates more heat energy. To prevent overheating, smartphone systems will force to re-

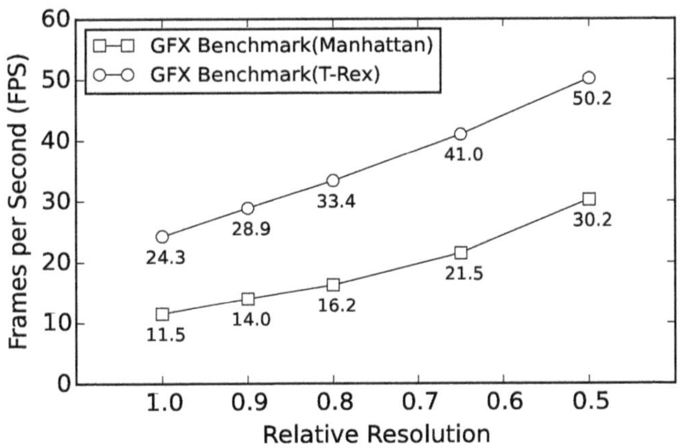

Figure 2: GFX benchmark frame rate in different display resolutions.

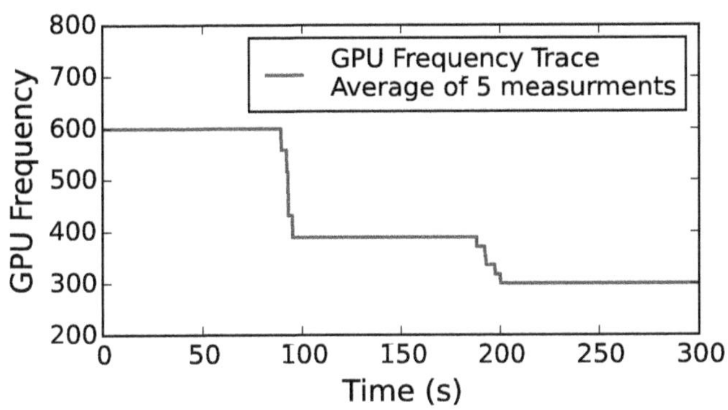

Figure 3: GPU frequency in running the Ridge Racer Slipstream game on Galaxy S5 LTE-A.

duce the operating frequencies of the CPU and GPU when their temperatures exceed predefined thresholds. Such frequency throttling would happen aggressively. Figure 3 shows the GPU frequency in running the *Ridge Racer Slipstream* game [4] on the Galaxy S5 LTE-A. Within 5 minutes, the GPU frequency were quickly throttled from 600 MHz to 300 MHz. As a consequence, the gaming performance is significantly downgraded resulting in an unacceptable user experience.

To alleviate or eliminate these issues caused by extravagant display resolutions, it is desirable for users to flexibly change the display resolution of their smartphones when needed. However, existing commercial smartphones including iPhones, Windows Phones, and Android phones, always run at the native display resolution and provide no way for app developers or users to change the display resolution.

2.2 Goals

In this paper, we seek to enable users to change the display resolution of their smartphones on-the-fly. The proposed DRS system should work on existing commercial smartphones and support all legacy applications without requiring any changes or recompiling from applications, or re-building a new ROM. The system should also be flexible enough for various usage scenarios, and we below describe three example scenarios.

Automatic power optimization. The DRS system runs transparently in the background, automatically infers the viewing distance, and decides the best display density for maximum user experience but with minimal system power consumption.

Run high-performance applications. Sometimes users may want to run a high-performance application, e.g., the latest version of a 3D game, but their last-generation old phones cannot afford. With the DRS system, users can force to reduce the rendering resolution and run it smoothly.

Extend battery life aggressively. Users may also use our system to reduce the display resolution of their phones in a proactive way. This would be particularly useful when the battery is low but the user still wants to use the phone for a longer time, e.g., to continue enjoying the game or composing a long email. In this case, the user could tolerate the compromised user experience to save power and extend the battery life.

It is worth to note that we do not change the physical resolution of smartphone displays. As a software solution, we cannot change the number of hardware pixels of a smartphone display. What we change is the resolution of the user interface (i.e., the final image generated to the system frame buffer) to be displayed on the screen. After we reduce the resolution, one pixel of the user-interface image is displayed by multiple physical pixels of the display hardware. As the physical pixels are very small, the users may still perceive a smooth user experience. Consequently, we save power by reducing the GPU computations in rendering the user interface at a lower resolution, rather than by reducing the power consumption of the display hardware. Unless otherwise stated, in this paper, we refer "display resolution" as the resolution of the content to be displayed on the screen.

On smartphones, GPU is mainly used for 3D and 2D graphics acceleration. It is not only heavily used by high-end 3D games but also widely used for rendering 2D user interfaces in non-gaming apps and system UI. With the support of OpenCL [11] on smartphones, GPU can also be used for general-purpose computing (GPGPU) such as accelerating various machine-learning algorithms. In this paper, we mainly focus on GPU-intensive gaming apps but we will show that non-gaming apps can also benefit from our DRS system to reduce their power consumption.

3. ANDROID GRAPHICS FUNDAMENTALS

In this section, we describe the background information on Android graphics architecture and pipeline on top of which we design our DRS system.

3.1 Android Graphics Overview

Figure 4 shows an overview of Android graphics architecture focusing on the data flow. On Android, OpenGL ES/EGL[1] is used for GPU-accelerated graphics. Applications call the OpenGL ES API [31] to use the GPU for graphics processing and to draw their User Interface (UI). The processing result is put into a graphics buffer in a structure

[1]OpenGL ES (Open Graphics Library for Embedded Systems) is the standard for embedded accelerated graphics [29]. OpenGL ES relies on the EGL (Embedded-System Graphics Library) API [28].

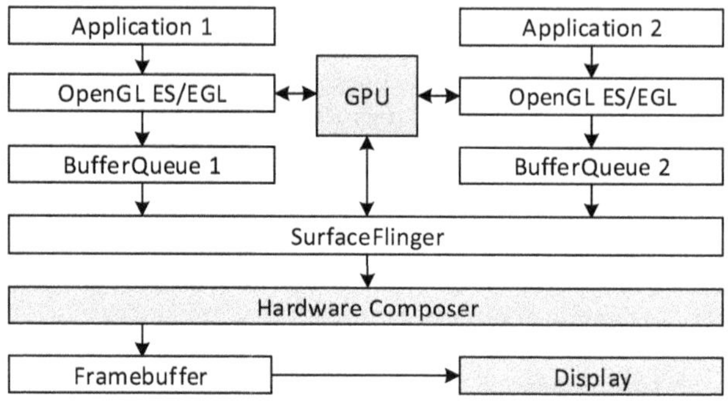

Figure 4: Android Graphics Overview.

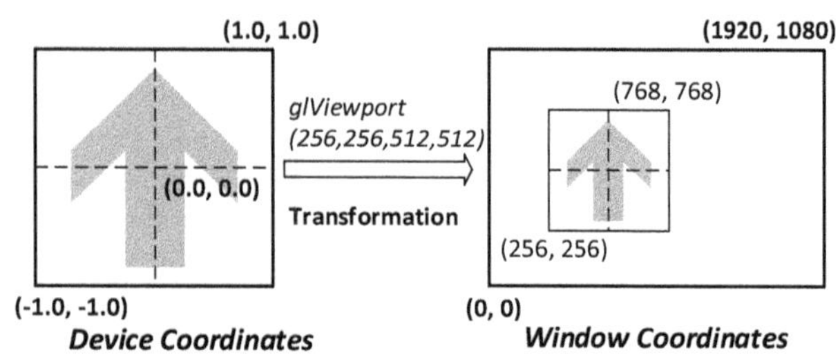

Figure 5: Transformation from normalized device coordinates to window coordinates.

called *BufferQueue*. Each application has its own BufferQueue that has three graphics buffers by default. The system UI process also has a dedicated BufferQueue for drawing the system UI elements such as the "navigation bar" at the bottom of the screen and the "status bar" at the top of the screen.

Android uses a system service called *SurfaceFlinger* to coordinate all the graphics layers from the running applications and the system UI process. SurfaceFlinger knows the layout of all the UI windows in the system by working with the *WindowManager* service. Smartphone displays typically refresh at a rate of 60 fps and for each frame period the system generates a VSYNC signal. When a VSYNC signal arrives, SurfaceFlinger collects all the graphics buffers for visible layers and asks the *Hardware Composer* to composite all visible layers together. Usually the Hardware Composer will do the composition itself and generates the final graphics data into the system *Framebuffer* for displaying on the screen. Sometimes the Hardware Composer may determine that the most efficient way to composite the buffers is using the GPU and thus asks SurfaceFlinger to call OpenGL ES API to use the GPU for buffer composition. In this case, SurfaceFlinger also generates GPU workload. After SurfaceFlinger consumes a graphics buffer in a BufferQueue, the corresponding application is notified for drawing a new frame.

3.2 Graphics Pipeline and Coordinates

Graphics processing consists of a sequence of steps called graphics pipeline. A modern graphics pipeline may be very complex and usually has more than ten stages. These stages may be grouped into three high-level stages: vertex processing, rasterization, and pixel processing.

In OpenGL ES, complex geometry scenes are represented by basic vertexes and the relationships among them. For example, three vertexes form a triangle face. The vertex-processing stage processes vertices, typically performing operations such as transformations and skinning [26]. Vertex processing is done in a square, uniform coordinate system called *normalized device coordinate space*. In this space, the lower left corner corresponds to (-1, -1) and the upper right corner corresponds to (1, 1), as shown on the left side in Figure 5. After the vertex-processing stage, each vertex has its own normalized device coordinates.

Then, the rasterization stage solves the relationships (lines, triangles etc.) among these vertexes and maps these lines and triangles from the continuous device-coordinate space to a discrete window-pixel space as shown on the right side in Figure 5. In OpenGL ES, this coordinate mapping is configured by calling the *glViewport()* function that takes four parameters to determine the affine transformation. As an example shown in Figure 5, *glViewport(256, 256, 512, 512)* maps the points (-1, -1) and (1, 1) in the normalized device coordinates to the points (256, 256) and (256+512, 256+512) in the window coordinates.

Finally, the pixel-processing stage generates per-pixel data such as colors and depths for each pixel. This is done in the window-coordinate space. Since OpenGL ES 2.0, vertex-processing and pixel-processing become programmable. Developers can define the functions of these two stages by using shader programs. Typically, shader programs are written using a specific programming language, *OpenGL ES Shader Language* [30]. The source code can be compiled and linked at runtime through OpenGL ES API calls.

For a given scene, if the display resolution increases, there will be more pixels to compute, and thus the GPU workload of the two pixel-based stages of rasterization and pixel-processing will increase accordingly. The GPU workload of the vertex-processing stage will remain unchanged because vertex-processing is done in the device-coordinate space which is independent from the display resolution. Consequently, DRS saves power by reducing the GPU workload generated in the rasterization stage and the pixel-processing stage.

According to Figure 4, to reduce the resolution of display content, a simple approach is to let SurfaceFlinger scale down the pixel resolution of the graphics buffers in the BufferQueues. However, this approach cannot save power because the GPU workload required to generate those graphics buffers remains the same and thus consumes the same amount of power. Therefore, we have to seek for a new approach and next we describe how our approach works.

4. SYSTEM ARCHITECTURE

Enabling DRS on existing smartphones imposes a couple of challenges. First, we must reduce the number of pixels in all the pixel-related computations from the complex procedures of rasterization and pixel-processing involving many OpenGL function calls. Second, OpenGL libraries are close source and thus we cannot revise and re-compile the source code to add new functionalities. And we cannot require rebuilding a smartphone ROM or making application-specific modifications. Third, we must design a lightweight approach to decide the user-screen distance for automatic resolution scaling.

To address the above challenges, we employ binary-rewriting techniques that are able to hook and intercept the function

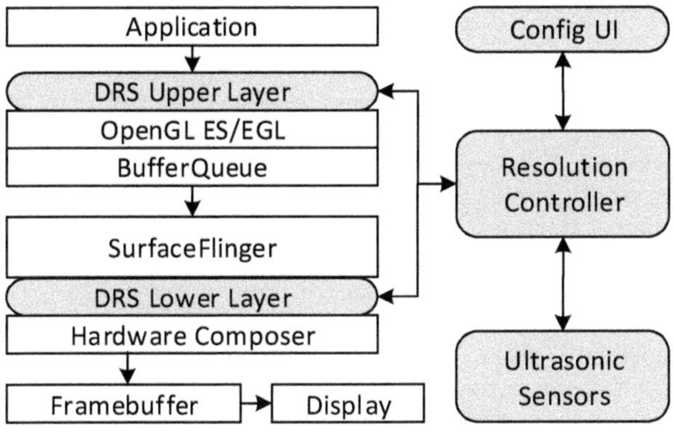

Figure 6: DRS System Architecture.

calls in existing binaries and add new functionalities. As a result, we can enable DRS on commercial smartphones without requiring any source-code level changes. Due to the complexity of OpenGL rendering context, it is non-trivial to intercept the right function calls to make DRS work correctly. In Section 5 we describe the details. To detect the user-screen distance, we design a lower-power ultrasonic based approach and we provide more details in Section 6.

Figure 6 shows the architecture of our DRS system. To enable resolution scaling, we add two new layers into the existing system. The first layer is the *DRS Upper Layer* that sits between the application layer and the OpenGL ES/EGL layer. It intercepts the necessary OpenGL ES function calls and EGL function calls to ensure that the graphics rendering is done with a proper display resolution. It applies a scaling factor to the parameters of the necessary OpenGL ES/EGL function calls to transform the default display resolution to a targeted one.

The second layer is the *DRS Lower Layer* that locates between the SurfaceFlinger layer and the Hardware Composer. This layer intercepts the function calls passed to the Hardware Composer to ensure that the composition is done with a proper display resolution. This second layer is needed because after the DRS Upper Layer scales down the resolution, we must scale the resolution up so that the rendered content can be correctly displayed on the screen in the native display resolution. These two DRS layers synchronize with each other to make sure they use the same targeted display resolution for the same graphics buffer in the BufferQueue. This is necessary because if a user changes the targeted display resolution to a new value, the DRS Upper Layer will start to use a new scaling factor to generate graphics buffers into the BufferQueue. The DRS Lower Layer needs to make sure that the older scaling factor is used for previously-generated graphics buffers and the new scaling factor is applied only to newly-generated graphics buffer during the composition.

To decide a proper targeted display resolution, we add ultrasonic sensors into the system for instant and accurate viewing-distance detection. Based on the measured viewing-distance, the *Resolution Controller* calculates the best display resolution for maximum user experience and maximum power optimization, and indicates the two DRS layers to do scaling transformation for the calculated display resolution. In addition, our DRS system also provide a UI for users to configure the system behaviors, e.g., enabling automatic resolution scaling based on the viewing-distance or setting to a fixed display resolution.

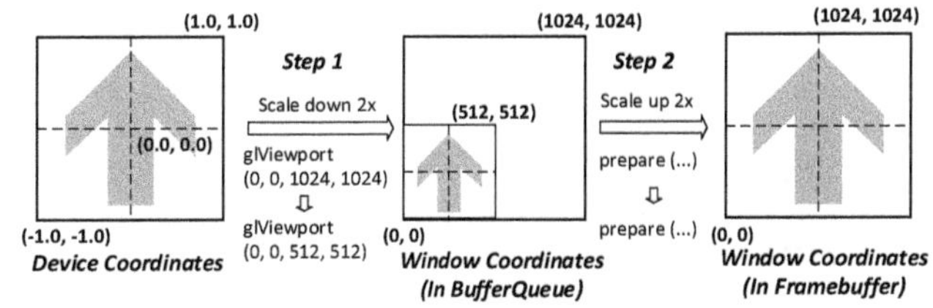

Figure 7: Scaling process for a default render target.

5. DYNAMIC RESOLUTION SCALING

The key of DRS is to control the pixel-resolution of the graphics results rendered by the GPU. In OpenGL ES, the GPU-rendered graphics results are stored in a memory buffer called *render target*. There are two types of render targets: default render target and user-defined render target. A default render target is a graphics buffer in a BufferQueue as shown in Figure 4. The size of a default render target is typically equal to the native display resolution of the device screen, as its content will be drawn on the device screen. In applications that cannot support the native display resolution, they may use a smaller default render target. In this case, the graphics buffers will be scaled up, e.g., by 2x, in the composition stage of SurfaceFlinger, to fill up the whole device screen.

User-defined render targets are usually used for off-screen content rendering, to calculate the intermediate graphics results that will not be directly drawn on the device screen. Instead, the content of a user-defined render target may be used as the input to other render targets, e.g., to a default render target for displaying on the device screen. User-defined render targets are widely used in many graphics algorithms such as high dynamic range [20], shadows [21] and depth of field [47].

To achieve maximum power saving, our system support DRS for both default render targets and user-defined render targets. For a given render target, we intercept all the OpenGL ES/EGL API calls that manipulate the render target for correct resolution scaling. Next we describe the details.

5.1 DRS for Default Render Target

We design a two-step DRS scheme for default render targets, each step running in one of the two DRS layers, respectively. Assume that the native display resolution of a smartphone is 1024x1024 pixels and we want to scale down the resolution by 2x to 512x512 pixels (i.e., the scaling factor is 0.5), Figure 7 shows the scaling process for a default render target. In Step 1, we intercept all the *glViewport()* function calls on the default render target and apply the scaling factor of 0.5 to their parameters. That is, we convert the function calls of *glViewport(0, 0, 1024, 1024)* to *glViewport(0, 0, 512, 512)*. As a result, the content of the default render target is scaled down to 512x512 pixels as shown in the middle of Figure 7. Then the GPU will do rasterization and pixel processing using this small pixel block rather than

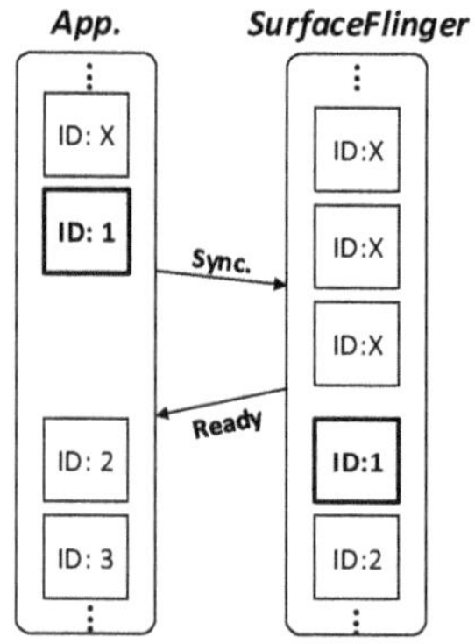

(a) Sync. of frame ID

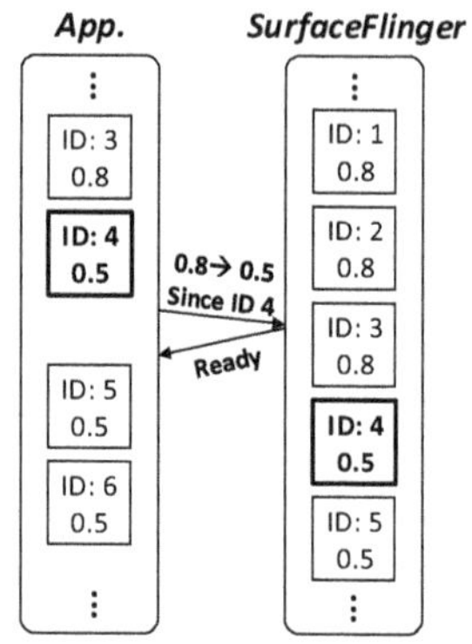

(b) Sync. of scaling factor

Figure 8: Synchronizing frame ID and scaling factor between application and SurfaceFlinger.

the original big one of 1024x1024. Consequently, the GPU workload and thus its power consumption are reduced.

In Step 2, we intercept the *prepare()* function calls during the composition stage in SurfaceFlinger. For each frame, SurfaceFlinger uses the *prepare()* function to tell the Hardware Composer how to do the composition. By changing the parameters of the *prepare()* function call, we tell the Hardware Composer to scale up the reduced pixel block back to the original size so that it can be correctly displayed on the device screen.

The scaling process in Figure 7 is simplified for easy illustration. More functions must be intercepted to ensure that all the function calls have a consistent OpenGL ES rendering context. In Section 7, we list the functions that we intercepted in our implementation.

Synchronization. The two steps must agree on the same scaling factor to ensure that the final graphics UI is correctly displayed on the device screen. As they run in different processes, Step 1 in the application process and Step 2 in the SurfaceFlinger process, a synchronization scheme is needed. A simple approach is to extend the data structure of graphics buffers in BufferQueue to add a new field for the scaling factor. However, this approach is not feasible without changing and recompiling the source code of the Android graphics system, because the graphics buffers are totally managed by the Android graphics system and transparent from applications. Thus, we design a new synchronization scheme as shown in Figure 8.

The key idea of our scheme is to assign a unique ID to each graphics buffer in a BufferQueue. We call it *frame ID.* As we cannot change the data structure of a graphics buffer to add a frame ID, the application and SurfaceFlinger maintain their own frame IDs separately. For a graphics buffer, the same frame ID must be used by both the application and SurfaceFlinger. To achieve it, the application initiates a process to synchronize frame ID with SurfaceFlinger, as shown in Figure 8a. The application holds its current graphics buffer (dequeued from the BufferQueue) without adding it back into the BufferQueue. The application assigns a frame ID of 1 to the graphics buffer and sends a message to SurfaceFlinger and waits for a response. SurfaceFlinger continues to consume the graphics buffers in the BufferQueue of the application as normal. After all the graphics buffers in the BufferQueue are consumed, SurfaceFlinger sends a *ready* message back to the application. Then the application resumes to enqueue its graphics buffer into the BufferQueue as normal and SurfaceFlinger assigns the same frame ID of 1 to the first graphics buffer in the BufferQueue after the ready message. Consequently, the application and SurfaceFlinger are able to assign the same frame ID to all the graphics buffers afterwards. As three graphics buffers are used in a BufferQueue, with a frame rate of 60 fps, the application waits for SurfaceFlinger to consume at most two graphics buffers, i.e., up to 33 ms. Such a small latency is hardly invisible to users, and we only need to do this synchronization process once for each application launch. Therefore, this frame-ID synchronization introduces negligible impact on the user experience.

Figure 8b shows what happens when the scaling factor is changed. The application simply applies the new scaling factor to its current graphics buffer and sends a message to tell SurfaceFlinger from which frame the scaling factor is changes, and waits for a response. For the example in Figure 8b, the scaling factor is changed from 0.8 to 0.5 starting from frame 4. As SurfaceFlinger uses the same frame ID, it can reply a ready message immediately and use the new scaling factor starting from frame 4. This process introduces less than 1 ms extra latency. Thus, we are able to enable per-frame, real-time resolution scaling.

5.2 DRS for User-Defined Render Target

Enabling DRS for a user-defined render target is more complex than the case of a default render target. Similar to a default graphics buffer in a BufferQueue that is managed by the Android graphics system, a user-defined graphics buffer is completely managed by OpenGL ES libraries and we cannot directly change its content. Different from a default graphics buffer, a user-define graphics buffer is used in a much more complex way. User-defined render targets are typically used to create a variety of texture effects that can be reused later, known as *render to texture* technique [46]. However, we cannot change the texture parameters such as the texture size for resolution scaling without re-allocating the memory of the graphics buffer. Furthermore, when a user-defined render target is used as the input of another rendering process, OpenGL ES system uses the relative coordinates to locate points in a texture, which causes another transformation from the relative coordinate to the absolute-pixel coordinate. Maintaining those coordinate transformations in all the involved function calls can be very complex.

Therefore, we take a different approach to make DRS for user-defined render targets easy. Instead of using the graphics buffer managed by OpenGL ES system, we allocate a new graphic buffer for a user-defined render target and use the new buffer for the whole graphics-rendering pipeline. As we can totally control the new buffer, we can easily set the size and other necessary parameters for correct resolution scaling. When the content of the render target is used by other render targets, we replace the original graphics buffer managed by OpenGL ES system with our new buffer. This approach causes extra memory overhead. However, allocating a new buffer happens only when resolution scaling is needed and the buffer is smaller than the default one for the lower display resolution. Furthermore, latest smartphones

Original Exp.	→	New Exp.
gl_FragCoord.x	→	(gl_FragCoord.x * ScalingFactor_Rec)
gl_FragCoord.y	→	(gl_FragCoord.y * ScaleFactor_Rec)
gl_FragCoord.xy	→	(gl_FragCoord.xy * ScalingFactor_Rec)

Table 1: Expression replacement in pixel-shader programs.

have a large memory size and thus this memory overhead may not be significant.

As user-defined render targets are for off-screen rendering, Step 2 in Figure 7 and thus the synchronization scheme in Figure 8 are not required in DRS for user-defined render targets.

5.3 Shader Program Issue

As aforementioned in Section 3, developers may use shader programs that are compiled and shipped to the GPU by OpenGL ES system at runtime. A shader program may obtain the position of a point and use the returned position values for further graphics processing. If the position of the point is returned in relative values to the render target size, it does not cause any problem. This is true for vertex processing. However, for pixel processing, the returned values are in the absolute-pixel coordinates. If we do resolution scaling, the returned values will be wrong, making the rendering result incorrect. This happens for both default render targets and user-defined render targets.

To address this issue, we scan all the pixel-shader programs at the initialization stage. In OpenGL ES system, the position of a point in window-pixel coordinates are stored in a built-in variable *gl_FragCoord*. We replace all the *gl_FragCoord* expressions in a pixel-shader program by multiplying the reciprocal of the scaling factor (*ScaleFactor_Rec*) used in our resolution scaling, as shown in Table 1. We set *ScaleFactor_Rec* as an input variable of the shader program, thus we can change its value on the fly, without re-compiling the shader program. Consequently, we can guarantee the correctness of the pixel processing stage by assigning proper values to the *ScaleFactor_Rec*, while display resolution changing.

6. DETERMINE DISPLAY RESOLUTION

In this section, we describe how to determine the best display resolution for maximum user experience and maximum power saving. We utilize existing knowledge of the human visual system to define the maximum observable display density based on the user-screen distance.

6.1 Human Visual Acuity and Display Density

Human visual acuity is typically measured by utilizing a Snellen or Landolt C chart, on which multiple, similar characters of set sizes are printed. Users are then asked to stand a set distance from the chart and identify the smallest characters that are legible to them. In both cases, a human adult is considered to have normal vision when they are able to separate contours that are approximately 1.75 mm apart on the chart when standing 20 feet away [42]. In order to connect the vision ability and resolvable pixels conveniently, we use angular resolving acuity to define the visual acuity. The angular size of an object can be described using the equation

$$\delta = 2\ tan^{-1}\Big(\frac{d}{2D}\Big) \tag{1}$$

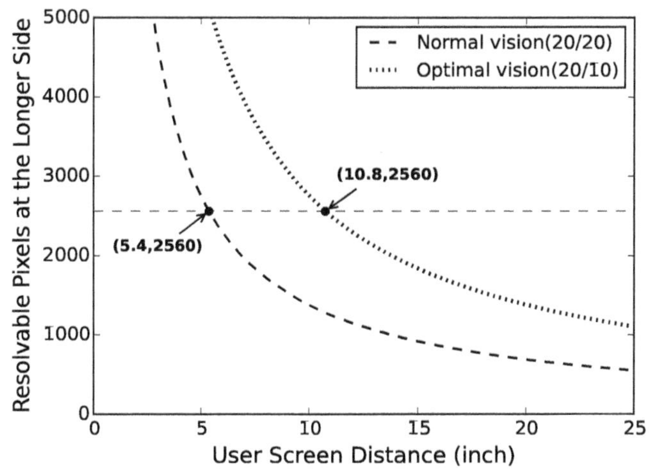

Figure 9: Relationship among resolvable pixel number, user-screen distance and user visual acuity.

where d is the actual size of an object, D is its distance from the observer(both measured with the same unit), and δ is the angular size of the object in radians. Based on Equation 1, normal vision[2] can be represented with an angular resolving acuity of $\delta_{normal} = 2.9 \times 10^{-4}$ radians, and $\delta_{optimal} = 1.45 \times 10^{-4}$ radians for optimal vision[3].

For a specific device, we consider the number of pixels at the longer side of the display as resolvable pixel number when the pixel density of it can just meet the users' visual acuity. Obviously, resolvable pixel number will changed due to different user-screen distance and different user visual acuity. The relationship among resolvable pixel number, user-screen distance and user visual acuity can be approximately described using equation

$$N = \frac{L}{2D\ tan\Big(\frac{\delta}{2}\Big)} \tag{2}$$

where N is the resolvable pixel number, L is the length of the longer side of the display, D is the user screen distance and δ is the angular resolving acuity of the user. For example, Figure 9 illustrates the variation of resolvable pixels number with user screen distance for users with normal vision and optimal vision on the Galaxy S5 LTE-A.

The Galaxy S5 LTE-A utilizes a 5.1-inch display with a resolution of 2560x1440 pixels. It has 2560 pixels on the longer side (4.44 inches). As shown in Figure 9, this high display density surpasses the visual acuity of users with normal vision when the user-screen distance beyond 5.4 inches, and 10.8 inches for users with optimal vision.

6.2 User-Screen Distance Detection

We adopt an ultrasonic-based approach for low-power user-screen distance detection. We utilize an ultrasonic ranging module HC-SR04 [5] that has an ultrasonic transmitter and an ultrasonic receiver. The module measures the distance by

[2]Normal vision is commonly referred as 20/20 vision (vulgar fraction expression) or 1.0 (decimal number expression).

[3]Optimal vision is commonly referred as 20/10 vision (vulgar fraction expression) or 2.0 (decimal number expression).

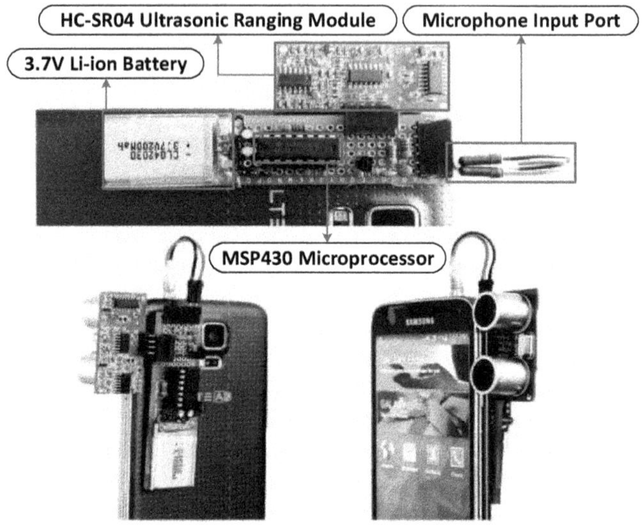

Figure 10: Ultrasonic-based hardware prototype for user-screen distance detection.

sending a 40 KHz ultrasonic signal and measures the waiting time until a reflected signal is detected by the ultrasonic receiver. The measured distances are very accurate, with a small error of only 3 mm, which is enough for our system.

Figure 10 shows our hardware prototype. We utilize an ultra-low-power microprocessor (MSP430G2231) to control the HC-SR04 module. The microprocessor simply encodes and sends the distance values measured by the HC-SR04 module to the smartphone through the microphone input headset port of the smartphone. At the smartphone side, the Resolution Controller in Figure 6 samples and records the microphone input data at 44.1 KHz rate, and then decodes the input data to get a measured distance value. Based on the distance value, the Resolution Controller can determine the desirable display resolution according to Equation 2.

This ultrasonic-based approach consumes a very low power less than 6 mW. For comparison, a camera-based approach needs more than 100 mW [37], even without considering the extra power consumption of the distance-estimation algorithm. Furthermore, this ultrasonic based approach is conservative: its measured distance is never larger than the real distance. This feature is desirable for our DRS system as we want to do conservative resolution scaling for maximum user experience.

7. IMPLEMENTATION

We have implemented our DRS prototype system on the Galaxy S5 LTE-A [17] running a Samsung-customized OS based Android 4.4.2. Like many other Android-based smartphones, the OS is not fully open source. In particular, the OpenGL ES libraries are vendor specific and not open source. Thus, we cannot modify the source code and re-build the ROM. Instead, we utilize binary-rewriting techniques to intercept the API calls.

API interception. As shown in Figure 11, there are three different ways for an application to call an OpenGL ES API function: link to the wrapper library and thus directly call the function (*path 1*); use the *eglGetProcAddress* function in EGL library to get a pointer to the function (*path 2*); and use the system *dlopen* and *dlsym* functions to dynamically load the OpenGL ES library (*path 3*). We handle all these three cases. For *path 1*, we modify the system *linker* program that is used to start application. In launching an application, our new linker program scans all the intercepted API calls and replaces the original functions using our own functions. We implement all our interception functions in a separate library. For *path 2* and *path 3*, we intercept the *eglGetProcAddress*, *dlopen*, and *dlsym* functions and change the function address returned by them to re-direct to our own interception function.

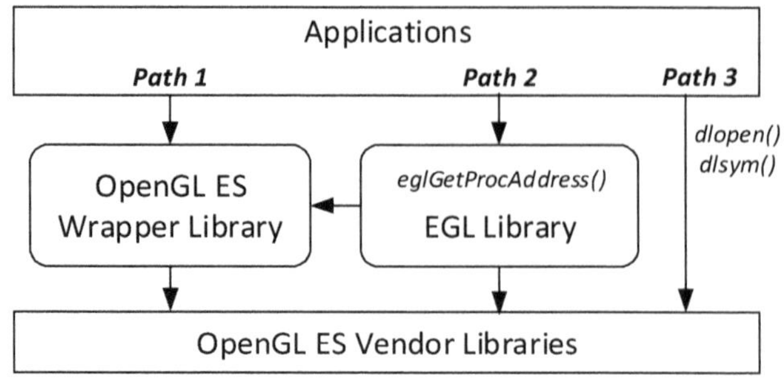

Figure 11: Three paths for applications to call OpenGL ES API functions.

EGL Library	
eglSwapBuffer	eglGetProcAddress
OpenGL ES Library	
glViewport	glScissor
glClear	glBindFramebuffer
glTexStorage2D	glTexImage2D
glBindTexture	glFramebufferTexture2D
glShaderSource	glAttachShader
glUseProgram	
HW Composer Driver Library and HAL Interface	
prepare	hw_get_module_by_class

Table 2: Intercepted functions.

SurfaceFlinger call the *prepare* function in the hardware composer driver through Android's hardware abstract layer (HAL) interface, which is packaged in the *libhardware.so* shared library. Thus, we first intercept the interface function (*hw_get_module_by_class*) in that library. Then, based on the intercepted interface function, we intercept the *prepare* function in the hardware composer driver (hwcomposer.apq8084.so).

To implement the two DRS layers, in total we intercept 15 functions in the libraries of OpenGL ES/EGL, hardware composer driver and HAL interface, as shown in Table 2. The two DRS layers use *Unix Domain Socket* for inter process communication (IPC), to implement the frame synchronization.

Determine display resolution. We use a predefined lookup table to determine the display resolution according to the user-screen distance. For minimizing the overhead, we use a set of discrete scaling factors rather than doing continuous scaling. Table 3 shows the scaling factors used in our implementation. When the distance is larger than 30 inches, we resume to the native display resolution for conservative scaling. Such a large distance may indicate that

Scaling Factors		1.0	0.9	0.8	0.65	0.5	1.0
PPI		577	519	462	375	289	577
Range(inch) Optimal Vision	Start	0.0	12.0	13.5	16.6	21.5	30.0
	End	12.0	13.5	16.6	21.5	30.0	$+\infty$
Range(inch) Normal Vision	Start	0.0	6.0	6.7	8.3	10.8	30.0
	End	6.0	6.7	8.3	10.8	30.0	$+\infty$

Table 3: Scaling factors vs. distance range.

the user is out of the sensor's detection range (±15 degrees), which rarely happens in practice though.

We configure the ultrasonic sensor to detect the distance for three times per second (3 Hz) and the Resolution Controller reads the distance value from the sensor at a 2x sampling rate of 6Hz. We smooth the detected distance values using a one-second time window for stable resolution scaling.

Lines of code. In total our implementation consists of 4,280 lines of code, including the DRS Upper Layer and Lower Layer, the Resolution Controller and its UI, the new linker program, and the code running on the MSP430 microprocessor.

Implementation on the Nexus 6. To study whether our implementation can work on other smartphones, we have experimented on a Nexus 6 smartphone that uses the same Adreno 420 GPU as the Galaxy S5 LTE-A but runs Android 5.0. Our implementation developed for the Galaxy S5 LTE-A can seamlessly run on the Nexus 6, without requiring any source-code changes, thanks to the common API layer of OpenGL. We expect that our implementation may easily work on more other Android smartphones.

8. EVALUATION

We evaluate our prototype system using a Galaxy S5 LTE-A smartphone, in terms of the application coverage, power savings in different display resolutions, system overhead, and user feedback from a user study.

8.1 Application Coverage

To study how many OpenGL ES applications our DRS system can support, we install 30 GPU-intensive applications (apps) on the S5 phone, including various 3D games and graphics benchmarks. We choose these apps for their large size and complex graphics computations. Thus, they are supposed to be the hardest apps to support. 12 out of the 30 apps have an installation package size larger than 500 MB. Two of them are extremely large, with an installation package size larger than 1,500 MB. Our DRS system is able to support all these 30 apps. That is, they run as normal with our DRS system enabled, demonstrating that our system has a very good app coverage.

8.2 Power Saving

From the 30 apps in the coverage test, we use 15 apps including 14 games and a benchmark (names listed in Table 4) to evaluate how much power can be saved in different display resolutions. We select at least one game from each game category and thus we think the games we use are representative for various gaming behaviors. For each game, we adopt a specific repeatable scene as the test case. For the *GFXBench* benchmark, we test two different scenes: *Manhattan* and *T-Rex*. Thus, in total we have 16 test cases.

We run the test cases on the S5 phone and use a Monsoon Power Monitor [3] to measure the system power. We turn

Application(Scene) Name	Scale Factor			
	0.9	0.8	0.65	0.5
Games				
Badland	95.1%	91.2%	86.7%	83.5%
Hitman Sniper	94.0%	85.5%	80.6%	73.0%
Iron man 3	94.5%	90.1%	83.4%	75.9%
Leo's Fotune	95.4%	92.8%	88.7%	84.3%
Minecraft PE	94.5%	90.4%	82.6%	76.1%
NFS Most Wanted	94.3%	89.6%	79.7%	72.3%
Over Kill 3	95.7%	92.0%	88.3%	82.5%
Ridge Racer Slipstream	94.5%	85.0%	76.8%	65.9%
Riptide GP2	95.3%	89.0%	77.5%	68.7%
Shine Runner	95.9%	90.1%	81.2%	74.2%
Smash Hit	93.9%	89.5%	81.1%	72.8%
Temple Run Brave	93.7%	85.6%	78.9%	71.2%
Tiny Troopers 2	94.4%	90.0%	82.7%	76.1%
Warships	95.3%	90.7%	84.3%	76.4%
Graphics Benchmark				
GFX Bench Manhattan	84.2%	70.4%	56.7%	39.5%
GFX Bench T-Rex	85.9%	73.1%	57.6%	48.0%

Table 4: Normalized energy per frame of games and benchmarks in different scaling factors.

the phone into airplane mode, disable unnecessary hardware components such as GPS and camera, and set the backlight brightness to 50%. We lock the GPU frequency to 500 MHz to avoid the inference of DVFS of GPU. We cool down the phone before each test to make sure that the GPU can keep working at 500 MHz for at least 60 seconds. We repeat each test for three times and report the average results.

We adopt the total system energy per frame (EPF) as the metric to evaluate the power saving of our prototype system. In order to conveniently compare the different results, we normalize the results to the case of the native display resolution. Table 4 shows the normalized EPF in different scaling factors. The scaling factors are normalized to the native display resolution, i.e., the scaling factor is 1.0 for the full resolution. When we reduce the display resolution by half (i.e., the scaling factor is 0.5, reducing the display resolution from 2560x1440 pixels to 1280x720 pixels), on average for the 16 test cases, we can reduce the EPF by 30.1%, ranging from 15.7% (in *Leo's Fortune*) to 60.5% (in *GFX-Manhattan*). For the 14 games, they always run at a fixed frame rate no matter what value the scaling factor is. Thus, the same amount of saving on power consumption can be achieved in practice (24.9% if we only count the 14 games).

For the two GFXBench cases, as the benchmark always tries to use up all the GPU processing capability, their power consumptions remain almost the same in all the scaling factors. However, as we mentioned in Section 2, the resolution can extremely influence the frame rate. For a smaller scaling factor, they may run at a higher frame rate and thus provide a better user experience.

Indeed, the display resolution of 1280x720 pixels (a.k.a 720p) is still pretty high and widely used on many mainstream smartphones. If we reduce the display resolution further, we may save more power. Furthermore, as smartphone makers are continuing the arms race on even higher display resolutions (e.g., 4K, or 3840x2160 pixels), more power-optimization opportunities can be provided by our DRS system.

Benefits from DRS for user-defined render targets. Figure 12 shows how much extra benefit can be achieved by applying DRS to user-defined graphics buffers, for the two

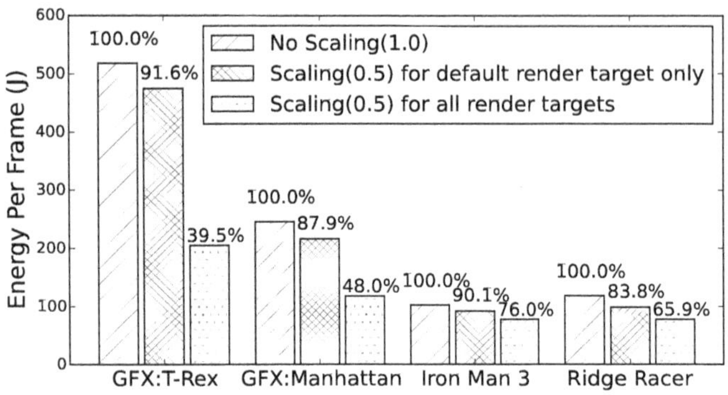

Figure 12: Benefit from scaling for user-defined render target.

Application Name	Scale Factor = 0.5
Adobe PDF Reader	90.6%
Dolphin Browser	92.4%
The Weather Channel	86.3%

Table 5: Normalized energy per frame of three non-gaming applications with halved resolution.

benchmark cases and two games (*Iron Man 3* and *Ridge Racer Slipstream*), when the scaling factor is 0.5. On average, it improves the power/energy optimization room by an extra 31.0%. The extra improvement for GFX-Manhattan is as high as 52.1% as it extensively utilize user-defined graphics buffers as the render targets. The extra saving for the two apps are relatively small but still more than 14.1%. Thus, user-defined render targets must be considered in scaling the display resolution.

Power saving of DRS for non-gaming apps. Although in this paper we focus on GPU-intensive apps, we also evaluate how much power DRS can save for non-gaming apps that are less GPU intensive than games. To this end, we measure the power consumption of three popular non-gaming apps, including *Adobe PDF Reader*, *Dolphin Browser*, and *The Weather Channel*. We use monkeyrunner[2] to generate the same sets of touch events for repeatable experiments including browsing a opened PDF file, scrolling the web page of www.yahoo.com, and updating the weather information.

Table 5 shows the results when the resolution is halved, compared to the full-resolution case. As expected, the savings are much smaller than the ones of games, only 10.2% on average. This is because that these apps generate much less GPU workload, compared to the games and graphics benchmarks. However, 10.2% of saving is still valuable, given that energy is a very scarce resource on smartphones.

In all the experiments we have conducted, we take a conservative approach, assuming that the user has the optimal vision (i.e., 2.0 in decimal number expression). If a user has the normal vision (i.e., 1.0 in decimal number expression), our DRS system may further save more power.

8.3 System Overhead

Synchronization latency. As shown in Section 5, when the scaling factor is changed, the DRS Upper Layer needs to notify the DRS Lower Layer and block the graphics rendering for a while due to the communication delay. To quantify the delay, we manually generate a large number of resolution-scaling signals into our DRS system and measure the synchronization latency. We run the test for 100 seconds. The extra latency caused by each resolution-scaling ranges from 0.41 ms to 0.94 ms. It is small, compared to the frame duration of 16.7 ms. Furthermore, in our implementation, we change the screen resolution at most for three times per second. Thus, such a small latency is negligible.

Memory overhead. Our system allocate extra memory for handling user-defined render targets. To quantify the memory overhead, we measure the extra memory used in the four games/benchmarks in Figure 12. The memory overhead depends on how many user-defined render targets are used. The *GFX:Manhattan* test has a high memory overhead of 238.8 MB because it is a benchmark program using user-defined render targets extensively. However, the memory overheads of the two real games are not large: 59.7 MB for *Iron Man 3* and 33.6 MB for *Ridge Racer Slipstream*, respectively. The *GFX:T-Rex* test also has a small memory overhead of 59.7 MB.

Energy overhead. The extra hardware we used for user-screen distance detection consumes extra energy. However, the energy overhead is small. We use the Monsoon Power Monitor [3] to measure the additional hardware's power consumption. Due to the power consumption of the additional hardware is relatively stable and repeatable, we simply regard the average power consumption of a long time (e.g., 60 seconds) as the power consumption of the additional hardware. For a distance-detecting rate of 3 Hz, we measure that the total power consumption of the ultrasonic sensor and the MSP430 microprocessor is only 5-6 mW, depending on how large the user-screen distance is. We imagine that in the future, smartphones may integrate an internal ultrasonic sensor to further reduce the power consumption of user-screen detection, as the MSP430 is not needed anymore.

8.4 User Study

To study the impact of DRS on user experience, we conducted a user study with 10 users. They are all young students and all of them have at least normal vision.

In the study, we let each user play two games, one is *Smash Hit* and the other is *Temple Run Brave*. For each game, the users play it for 10 minutes. During the 10 minutes, we randomly select the first 5 minutes or the last 5 minutes to enable our DRS system without notifying the users. We encourage the users to play the games in any way they want, changing their postures freely and trying different user-screen distances during the test. After the test, we ask the users whether they felt any differences between the first 5 minutes and the last 5 minutes. None of the 10 users could tell the difference when our DRS system was turned on or off, even though the resolution has been changed for 136 times on average for each user. This result demonstrates that our DRS system is able to remain good user experience.

9. DISCUSSION

In this section, we discuss the limitations of our current implementation and further work.

9.1 Limitations

Our implementation is limited in several aspects. First, it only supports one app for resolution scaling. While for the most of the time, smartphones typically runs only one front-ground app, some latest smartphones such as the LG G3 [16] allow running two apps simultaneously and show their UIs side-by-side on the screen. Resolution scaling for multiple apps can be supported by extending our current implementation so that SurfaceFlinger can connect to multiple apps and do the frame synchronization with all of them. Consider that multiple apps share the display simultaneously is a rare case, the current system is already useful for many users.

Our implementation is also limited that it is only developed and tested on the Galaxy S5 LTE-A and the Nexus 6. It is not clear whether it works for other types of Android smartphones. Despite our API-interception based design is general, more efforts are needed to study how to implement the design and test it on more Android smartphones. Furthermore, it may be worthy to study how to enable DRS for other mobile OSes such as iOS and Windows Phone. It may not be hard to implement DRS in iOS, since iOS uses the same OpenGL ES as Android that is mostly platform neutral. However, Windows Phone utilizes the Direct X [9] as the graphic API, which needs extra engineering efforts.

Another limitation is that we only test the performance of our DRS prototype on Adreno 420 GPU. It is not clear how much energy we can save on other types of GPUs, without porting our implementation on them. Mobile GPU's architectures vary significantly from vendors to vendors. In terms of the graphic pipelines, ARM's Mali GPU [7] adopts TBR (Tiled Based Render) pipeline, PowerVR GPU [12] and Nvidia's Tegra series GPUs [13] adopt TBDR (Tailed Based Deferred Render) pipeline, and Qualcomm's Adreno GPU [6] adopts a flex render pipeline that can support both TBR and TBDR. In terms of the shader organization form, PowerVR GPU, Mali GPU, and Adreno GPU adopt unified shader [14], while Tegra series GPUs adopt non-unified shader. Luckily, although the architectures of different GPUs are very different, they all share the same character that the GPU workload is proportional to the number of pixels. Meanwhile, several power models for mobile GPU [34, 33, 45] have already pointed out that the GPU power consumption and GPU workload approximately have the linear relationship. Thus we believe our DRS system can achieve similar performance on other GPUs as well as it does on Adreno 420.

In addition, we add extra hardware for user-instance detection and the ultrasonic sensor is not very small. It may be an issue how to integrate an ultrasonic sensor into a smartphone. Fortunately, the emerging miniaturization techniques have already brought micrometer-level ultrasonic emitters [22] and detectors [36] into reality. It is even possible to put an ultrasonic detector into human body [39] for medical treatment. Therefore, we expect that it is not hard to integrate an ultrasonic sensor into new-generation smartphones, due to the small size and low power.

9.2 Future Work

We plan to extend our current implementation to support resolution scaling for multiple apps, and port our implementation onto more Android smartphones for more testing. In addition, we also plan to consider other opportunities to further reduce the power consumption of the GPU. Below we describe some ideas.

Scene moving speed. Existing studies and our own user study show that human visual-perceivable ability depends on the moving speed of objects. If the objects in a scene move fast, users are not as sensitive on the display resolution as they are for a slowly-changing scene. This suggests another angle besides user-screen distance for resolution scaling without compromising the user experience. We may detect the moving speed of a scene and apply more aggressive resolution scaling to save more power without compromising the user experience.

Frame rate. Another factor tightly related to GPU workload is frame rate [25, 45, 43]. The higher frame rate, the more GPU workload and thus the more power consumption. Thus, we may consider frame rate scaling for more power saving. The frame rate scaling also depends on the user-screen distance. It would be interesting to see how the right dynamic frame rate scaling strategy is designed given that we have already a costless approach to detect user-screen distance.

GPU frequency. We only qualitatively conclude that resolution down-scaling can reduce the GPU workload, but do not consider how it may affect GPU frequency. As a lower workload may trigger the GPU frequency down-scaling, it may be interesting to study how our DRS can work together with GPU DVFS for more power saving.

10. RELATED WORK

Dynamic Resolution Scaling. Dynamic resolution scaling is not a new technique, which has been already discussed and recommended to application developers to achieve better image quality and performance optimization [8]. Also this technique has already been used in real games, e.g., Witcher 3 [15], to achieve the tradeoff between resolution and framerate. However, these techniques are implemented by application developers or implemented as plugin for specific applications [10]. In this paper, we reuse the term of dynamic resolution scaling but our work is different from previous application-specific approaches. Specifically, we design a system-level dynamic resolution scaling to optimize the power consumption of smartphones. Our DRS system can achieve per-frame resolution scaling for legacy applications without any modifications of their source code and introduce minimal system overhead.

Dalton *et al.* [24] proposed to use camera to detect the presence of users to turn on or off the display to save power. This work can be considered as an extreme case of DRS but it does not provide a full DRS system and the camera-based approach is less useful for smartphones due to the high power consumption.

GPU power optimization. There have been related works on GPU power modeling [32, 35, 33], power consumption characters [38] and optimization mainly for desktop/server, which mainly resort to dynamic frequency scaling [41, 35, 19, 27, 48]. These techniques are generally applicable to smartphones. Usually, GPU frequency scaling is controlled in the vendor-provided drivers, and it is hard to be configured by applications even at the operating system level. In this paper, we optimize GPU power from another angle via dynamic resolution scaling.

Analysis on the PC gaming experience is presented [23, 40] when display resolution and refresh rate is changed. It is reported that lower frame rates may lead to system power reduction [25, 45, 43]. In this paper, we further give the detailed quantitative analysis among GPU power and display resolution, and present specific techniques on dynamic resolution scaling without changing the app source code.

Tradeoff between power saving and user experience. Techniques such as frequency scaling usually do not consider the user experience, either poor user experience with aggressive frequency scaling or poor power saving with conservative frequency scaling. Huge opportunities exist if we take into consideration the tradeoff between power saving and user experience. Previous analysis only discusses the relationship between power saving and display resolution scaling [23, 40] or frame rate scaling [25, 45, 43], however, they did not discuss the relationship between user experience and resolution or frame rate scaling. In this paper, quantitative analysis between resolution and user-screen distance is presented with user experience preserved, and the analysis framework can also guide app developers or users to decide the right tradeoff if they tolerate certain degree of downgraded user experience.

Nixon *et al.* [44] reported that the display on some modern devices already exceeds human perceptive capabilities and studied the relationship between GPU power and display resolution on the Nexus 4 and 5. They share the same motivation with us. However, they did not provide any end-to-end implementation and evaluation.

11. CONCLUSION

In this paper, we have built the first end-to-end DRS system for smartphones. By intercepting the function calls of OpenGL ES/EGL, our system requires no changes from applications and is able to work on existing smartphones without re-building a new ROM. We design an ultrasonic-based, low-power approach for user-screen distance detection. Based on the measured user-screen distance, our system can enable automatic resolution scaling for maximum user experience and power saving. Experimental results and user feedback demonstrate that our system is able to support a large set of real applications, provide per-frame and real-time resolution scaling with low system overhead, and retain good user experience.

ACKNOWLEDGEMENTS

We thank our anonymous reviewers and shepherd for their insightful and constructive comments that helped us improve this paper. We also thank Kent W. Nixon for his help on the early investigations and experiments of this work.

12. REFERENCES

[1] GFXBench 3.0, Unified cross-platform 3D graphics benchmark . http://gfxbench.com/.

[2] Monkeyrunner. http://developer.android.com/tools/help/monkeyrunner_concepts.html.

[3] Monsoon Power Monitor. https://www.msoon.com/LabEquipment/PowerMonitor/.

[4] RidgeRacerSlipstream. http://www.ign.com/prime/promo/ridge-racer-slipstream-free.

[5] Ultrasonic Ranging Module HC - SR04. http://www.micropik.com/PDF/HCSR04.pdf.

[6] Adreno GPU. https://developer.qualcomm.com/software/adreno-gpu-sdk/gpu, 2015.

[7] ARM Mali Graphics. http://www.arm.com/products/multimedia/mali-graphics-hardware/, 2015.

[8] Dynamic Resolution Rendering. https://software.intel.com/en-us/articles/dynamic-resolution-rendering-article, 2015.

[9] Graphics and Gaming. https://msdn.microsoft.com/en-us/library/windows/desktop/ee663279(v=vs.85).aspx, 2015.

[10] Hialgo Boost. http://www.hialgo.com/TechnologyBOOST.html, 2015.

[11] OpenCL - the open standard for parallel programming of heterogeneous systems. https://www.khronos.org/opencl/, 2015.

[12] PowerVR GPU. http://www.imgtec.com/powervr/graphics.asp, 2015.

[13] Tegra GPU. http://www.nvidia.com/object/tegra-4-processor.html, 2015.

[14] Unified Shader Model. https://en.wikipedia.org/wiki/Unified_shader_model, 2015.

[15] Witcher 3 uses dynamic resolution scaling on Xbox One to hit 1080p. http://www.extremetech.com/gaming/205487-witcher-3-uses-dynamic-resolution-scaling-on-xbox-one-to-hit-1080p, 2015.

[16] LG G3. http://www.lg.com/us/mobile-phones/g3, Feb. 2015.

[17] Samsung Galaxy S5 LTE-A. http://www.samsung.com/us/news/23327, Feb. 2015.

[18] Apple iPhone. http://www.apple.com/iphone/features/retina-display.html, Jun. 2010.

[19] Y. Abe, H. Sasaki, M. Peres, K. Inoue, K. Murakami, and S. Kato. Power and performance analysis of gpu-accelerated systems. In *Proceedings of the 2012 USENIX conference on Power-Aware Computing and Systems, ser. HotPower*, volume 12, pages 10–10, 2012.

[20] A. O. Akyüz. High dynamic range imaging pipeline on the gpu. *Journal of Real-Time Image Processing*, 10(2):273–287, 2012.

[21] L. Bavoil. Advanced soft shadow mapping techniques. In *Presentation at the game developers conference*, volume 2008, page 11, 2008.

[22] L. Belsito, E. Vannacci, F. Mancarella, M. Ferri, G. P. Veronese, E. Biagi, and A. Roncaglia. Fabrication of fiber-optic broadband ultrasound emitters by micro-opto-mechanical technology. *Journal of Micromechanics and Microengineering*, 24(8):085003, 2014.

[23] M. Claypool and K. Claypool. Perspectives, frame rates and resolutions: it's all in the game. In *Proceedings of the 4th International Conference on Foundations of Digital Games*, pages 42–49. ACM, 2009.

[24] A. B. Dalton and C. S. Ellis. Sensing user intention and context for energy management. In *HotOS*, pages 151–156, 2003.

[25] M. Dong and L. Zhong. Power modeling and optimization for oled displays. *Mobile Computing, IEEE Transactions on*, 11(9):1587–1599, 2012.

[26] R. Fernando. Chapter 3 and 4. In *GPU gems*. Addison-Wesley Professional, 2004.

[27] R. Ge, R. Vogt, J. Majumder, A. Alam, M. Burtscher, and Z. Zong. Effects of dynamic voltage and frequency scaling on a k20 gpu. In *Parallel Processing (ICPP), 2013 42nd International Conference on*, pages 826–833. IEEE, 2013.

[28] K. Group. Khronos Native Platform Graphics Interface (EGL Version 1.4 - February 11, 2013). `https://www.khronos.org/registry/egl/specs/eglspec.1.4.20130211.pdf`, Feb. 2013.

[29] K. Group. OpenGL ES – The Standard for Embedded Accelerated 3D Graphics. https://www.khronos.org/opengles/, Jan. 2013.

[30] K. Group. The OpenGL ES Shading Language (Specification). `https://www.khronos.org/files/opengles_shading_language.pdf`, May. 2009.

[31] K. Group. OpenGL ES Common Profile Specification Version 2.0.25 (Full Specification). `https://www.khronos.org/registry/gles/specs/2.0/es_full_spec_2.0.25.pdf`, Nov. 2010.

[32] S. Hong and H. Kim. An integrated gpu power and performance model. In *ACM SIGARCH Computer Architecture News*, volume 38, pages 280–289. ACM, 2010.

[33] T. Jin, S. He, and Y. Liu. Towards accurate gpu power modeling for smartphones. In *Proceedings of the 2nd Workshop on Mobile Gaming*, pages 7–11. ACM, 2015.

[34] Y. G. Kim, M. Kim, J. M. Kim, M. Sung, and S. W. Chung. A novel gpu power model for accurate smartphone power breakdown. *ETRI Journal*, 37(1):157–164, 2015.

[35] J. Leng, T. Hetherington, A. ElTantawy, S. Gilani, N. S. Kim, T. M. Aamodt, and V. J. Reddi. Gpuwattch: enabling energy optimizations in gpgpus. *ACM SIGARCH Computer Architecture News*, 41(3):487–498, 2013.

[36] H. Li, B. Dong, Z. Zhang, H. F. Zhang, and C. Sun. A transparent broadband ultrasonic detector based on an optical micro-ring resonator for photoacoustic microscopy. *Scientific reports*, 4, 2014.

[37] R. LiKamWa, B. Priyantha, M. Philipose, L. Zhong, and P. Bahl. Energy characterization and optimization of image sensing toward continuous mobile vision. In *Proceeding of the 11th annual international conference on Mobile systems, applications, and services*, pages 69–82. ACM, 2013.

[38] X. Ma, Z. Deng, M. Dong, and L. Zhong. Characterizing the performance and power consumption of 3d mobile games. *Computer*, (4):76–82, 2013.

[39] T. Maleki, N. Cao, S. H. Song, C. Kao, S.-C. A. Ko, and B. Ziaie. An ultrasonically powered implantable micro-oxygen generator (imog). *Biomedical Engineering, IEEE Transactions on*, 58(11):3104–3111, 2011.

[40] J. D. McCarthy, M. A. Sasse, and D. Miras. Sharp or smooth?: comparing the effects of quantization vs. frame rate for streamed video. In *Proceedings of the SIGCHI conference on Human factors in computing systems*, pages 535–542. ACM, 2004.

[41] X. Mei, L. S. Yung, K. Zhao, and X. Chu. A measurement study of gpu dvfs on energy conservation. In *Proceedings of the Workshop on Power-Aware Computing and Systems*, page 10. ACM, 2013.

[42] E. Messina. Standards for visual acuity. *National Institute for Standards and Technology*, 2006.

[43] B. Mochocki, K. Lahiri, and S. Cadambi. Power analysis of mobile 3d graphics. In *Proceedings of the conference on Design, automation and test in Europe: Proceedings*, pages 502–507. European Design and Automation Association, 2006.

[44] K. W. Nixon, X. Chen, H. Zhou, Y. Liu, and Y. Chen. Mobile gpu power consumption reduction via dynamic resolution and frame rate scaling. In *Proceedings of the 6th USENIX conference on Power-Aware Computing and Systems*, pages 5–5. USENIX Association, 2014.

[45] A. Pathania, Q. Jiao, A. Prakash, and T. Mitra. Integrated cpu-gpu power management for 3d mobile games. In *Design Automation Conference (DAC), 2014 51st ACM/EDAC/IEEE*, pages 1–6. IEEE, 2014.

[46] C. Wynn. Opengl render-to-texture. *GDC. NVIDIA Corporation*, 2002.

[47] T.-T. Yu. Depth of field implementation with opengl. *Journal of Computing Sciences in Colleges*, 20(1):136–146, 2004.

[48] Y. Zhu, A. Srikanth, J. Leng, and V. J. Reddi. Exploiting webpage characteristics for energy-efficient mobile web browsing. *Computer Architecture Letters*, 13(1):33–36, 2014.

Smartphone Background Activities in the Wild: Origin, Energy Drain, and Optimization

Xiaomeng Chen[†^] Abhilash Jindal[†^] Ning Ding[†^] Y. Charlie Hu[†^] Maruti Gupta[*]
Rath Vannithamby[*]
[†]Purdue University [^]Mobile Enerlytics [*]Intel Corporation

ABSTRACT

As new iterations of more powerful and better connected smartphones emerge, their limited battery life remains a leading factor adversely affecting the mobile experience of millions of smartphone users. While it is well-known that many apps can drain battery even while running in background, there has not been any study that quantifies the extent and severity of such background energy drain for users in the wild. To extend battery life, various new features are being incorporated within the phone, one of them being preventing applications from running in background, *i.e.*, when the screen is off, but their impact is largely unknown.

This paper makes several contributions. First, we present a large-scale measurement study that performs an in-depth analysis of the activities of various apps running in background on thousands of phones in the wild. Second, we quantify the amount of battery drain by all such background activities and possible energy saving. Third, we develop a metric to measure the usefulness of background activities that is personalized to each user. Finally, we present a system called HUSH (screen-off optimizer) that monitors the metric online and automatically identifies and suppresses background activities during screen-off periods that are not useful to the user experience. In doing so, our proposed HUSH saves screen-off energy of smartphones by 15.7% on average while incurring minimal impact on the user experience with the apps.

Categories and Subject Descriptors

C.4 [**Computer System Organization**]: Performance of Systems—*Modeling techniques*; D.2.8 [**Metrics**]: Performance measures

General Terms

Experimentation, Measurement, Performance

Keywords

Smartphones, background activities, screen-off energy drain

1. INTRODUCTION

It is well known that many apps on smartphones wake up periodically to run when users are not actively interacting with them. This happens predominantly during screen-off periods but can also happen when other apps are running in the foreground during screen-on periods. The reasons for such periodic wakeups are severalfold: (1) to perform a refresh of the app state, *e.g.*, in apps that provide updates for news, financial stocks, weather or twitter feed updates, (2) to sync with cloud services and get status updates or notifications, *e.g.*, in social networking apps such as Facebook, WeChat, and Google+, (3) to support non-touch based user interactions such as in audio apps Pandora and Spotify which periodically download files to play songs, or apps used for location tracking or navigation which allow a user to listen to directions without screen interactions. Additionally, many system services may run in the background due to either direct invocations by apps (*e.g.*, MediaPlaybackService) or the registration and callback mechanism where an app during initiation registers for future events monitored by the system services (*e.g.*, LocationManagerService).

More generally, many mobile apps are designed to run in background to enable a model of always-on connectivity and to provide fast response time. This means that once installed and initiated by the user, apps can register themselves with the services provided by the OS framework for background activities, regardless of the user's actual usage of the app. This is true of both iOS and Android OS [2, 7]. This leads one to the conjecture that the apps running in background and the system services they invoke may be consuming a significant amount of energy. Despite such general perception, there has not been any quantitative measurement of the background activities and energy drain by apps running on user phones in the wild. To quantify such app background activities and energy drain on real users' phones, we conducted a large-scale measurement of 2000 Samsung Galaxy phones in the wild. Our analysis shows that background activities of apps and services are prevalent and on average 28.9% of the daily energy drain is due to apps and services running during screen-off intervals.

Given the perception of the effects of app background activities on the phone's battery, it is not surprising that smartphones now come with features to turn off background activities, *e.g.*, iOS provides a feature called "Disable Background Refresh" [6] which basically prevents the apps from running in the background altogether. Android has a similar feature called "Restrict Background Data" [1] which prevents the user from running up charges on their mobile data usage due to background data activities by switching background data refresh to using WiFi only. Such blanket solutions disable background activities of all apps and hence do not distinguish background activities of apps that are potentially more useful to the user from the rest, which can adversely affect user experience. Some apps provide the user with the option of disabling background activities. However, it is very cumbersome for a user to manually change the settings for every installed app on the phone.

MobiCom'15, September 07–11, 2015, Paris, France.

ACM 978-1-4503-3619-2/15/09 ...$15.00 .
DOI: http://dx.doi.org/10.1145/2789168.2790107 .

In this paper, we explore effective ways of optimizing background activities of apps and services. Our exploration is motivated by two hypotheses: (1) background activities of apps are meant to improve user app experience but they are only useful if the user interacts with those apps in foreground sometime during the next screen-on interval; (2) the usefulness of background activities of an app is likely to be user-dependent and thus their occurrences should be personalized.

First, we propose a metric to measure this usefulness of app background activities called Background to Foreground Correlation (BFC). Second, we experimentally confirm the hypotheses using our 2000-user trace. The confirmation suggests the level of background activities of an app should be *personalized* to individual users. We then design a screen-off energy optimizer on Android called HUSH that monitors the BFC of all apps on a phone online and automatically identifies and suppresses app background activities during screen-off intervals that are not useful to the user experience. In doing so, HUSH saves screen-off energy of smartphones by 15.7% on average with minimal impact on the user experience with the apps.

2. RELATED WORK

There have been recently a lot of interests in measurement studies of smartphone app traffic and their impact on power consumption. In [13], Falaki *et al.* characterized smartphone traffic based on traffic traces collected from 43 users and showed how power consumption could be reduced. In [16, 14], Huang *et al.* studied 3G and LTE network performance and described the impact of the RRC radio power states on radio energy consumption. In [26], Xu *et al.* studied the smartphone usage patterns via network measurement from a tier-1 cellular network provider. AppInsight [23] monitors the performance of mobile apps in the wild by instrumenting app binary. In [25], Sommers and Barford studied the WiFi and cellular performance using the Speedtest.net data. None of the work above, however, provided a thorough analysis of how energy is consumed on the smartphones in the wild.

In [15], Huang *et al.* collected traffic from 20 users and studied screen-off radio energy consumption due to cellular network and proposed to provide savings by shifting this traffic load over WiFi instead, on an opportunistic basis. In [26], Xu *et al.* studied the energy drain of email sync operations of two email apps when the phone is in standby mode (*i.e.,* during screen-off) using a powermeter and proposed ways to optimize the email sync operations.

In summary, while there have been many studies recently that characterize the traffic seen on smartphones, only a few have looked at the impact of background traffic activities on the power consumption, *e.g.,* on network components such as WiFi and cellular radios, using small-scale measurement or in the lab setting.

Most recently, Chen *et al.* performed the first large-scale measurement study of energy drain on Android phones in the wild. Their focus is on a holistic analysis that comprehensively breaks down the total daily energy drain into different phone components as well as apps and services running on the phones and further draws implications to the designers of different components of smartphone and app developers.

The first part of this paper also presents a large-scale measurement study of Android phones in the wild, but the focus is on a detailed analysis of the activity, origin, and energy drain of background apps and services. Second, we introduce a new metric that characterizes the usefulness of background activities in a way that is customized to each app and each user. Finally, we present a novel technique called HUSH with implementation on Android phones that reduces the energy consumption due to background activities and show its energy impact on actual phones.

Table 1: Trace statistics.

Devices ($\geq$ 7 days trace)	2000
Aggregate trace duration	55759 days
Median trace duration	27.9 days
Countries of origin	61
Mobile operators	191
Unique phone types	2 (Galaxy S3 and S4)
Rate of mobile RSSI reading	when signal changes, effective: 1/min
Rate of network usage reading	screen-on: every 1 second, screen-off: every 5 seconds

3. CHARACTERIZING BACKGROUND ACTIVITIES IN THE WILD

In this section, we study the background activities on the 2000 phones in the wild.

3.1 Trace Collection

To perform the measurement study, we designed a free Android app called eStar [4] that when installed on a user's phone, performs periodic logging of the usage of various phone components by apps and system services. As discussed in Section 4, the logged information is also sufficient to drive a carefully designed power model to estimate the energy drain of the apps and services and various phone components in each logging interval. Since the app does not require any modifications to the Android framework or the kernel, its logging can be performed on smartphones in the wild. All the information collected (summarized below) are anonymized before uploaded to our server.

In principle, the shorter the logging interval, the more fine-grained the collected information, which leads to better accuracy in estimating energy drain, but also the higher the logging overhead. In designing the app, we carefully chose logging intervals to strike a balance between these two objectives.

Coarse-grained logging. Coarse-grained logging happens every 5 minutes, where the app logs app-wise CPU usage (from */proc/[pid]/stat*), and the per-core CPU usage (from */proc/stat*) and the time duration spent in different frequencies (from */sys/devices/system/cpu/cpu[id]/*).

Fine-grained logging. Fine-grained logging happens every 5 seconds during screen-off when CPU is on and every 1 second during screen-on, where the app logs the network usage (in bytes) of all apps that had data transfer during the interval, by reading */proc/uid_stat/[uid]/*.

On-demand event logging. Finally, dynamic events are logged on demand. These include WiFi, mobile data, and screen being switched on and off, WiFi being associated and scanning, WiFi and cellular signal strength change, battery level change (1% granularity), and the time each app starts and stops.

Trace collection. We released the eStar app in Google Play on September 1, 2014 which was downloaded by thousands of users worldwide [1]. The trace we used in this study contains logs from 2000 Galaxy S3 and S4 devices. Each user trace ranges from 7 to 40 days in length, with an average of 27.9 days (median 30 days). The detailed characteristics of the trace are shown in Table 1.

Logging overhead. The logging was shown in [11] to incur very low overhead: the average overhead per day across the devices in the trace were 2.4% of the total CPU time, 0.3% of the total network bytes, and 0.6% of the total energy drain.

[1]eStar received exemption from the full requirement of 45 CFR 46 or 21 CFR 56 by the IRB of our organization.

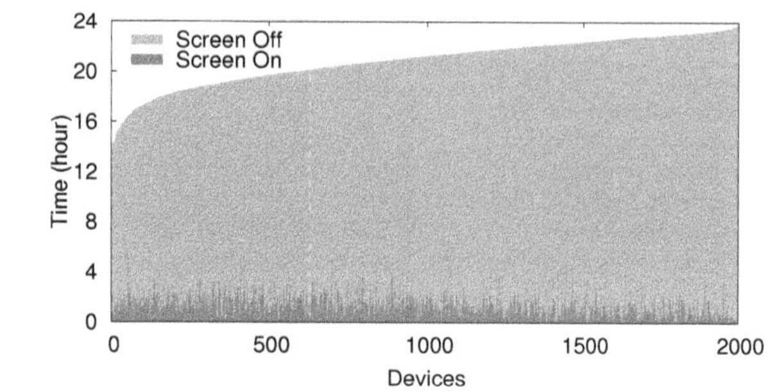

Figure 1: Daily screen-on vs screen-off time across users.

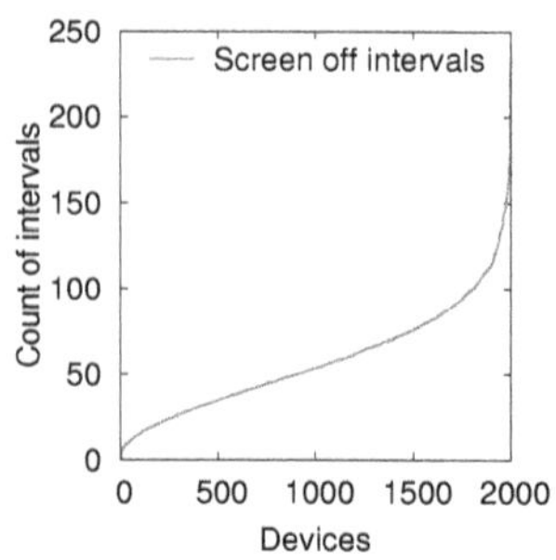

Figure 2: Average number of screen-on (and hence screen-off) intervals per day across users.

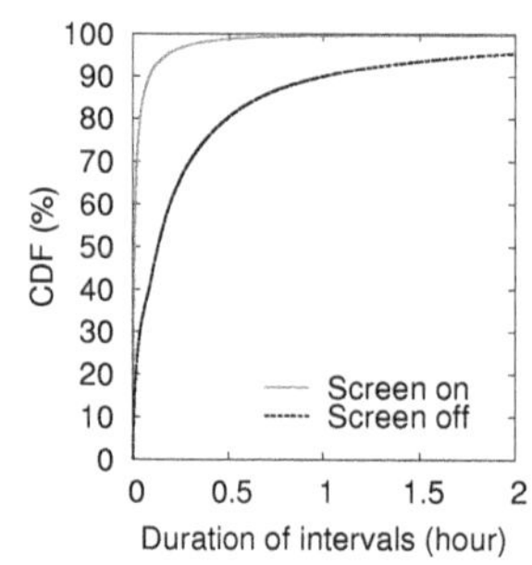

Figure 3: CDF of screen-on and screen-off interval durations across users for all days.

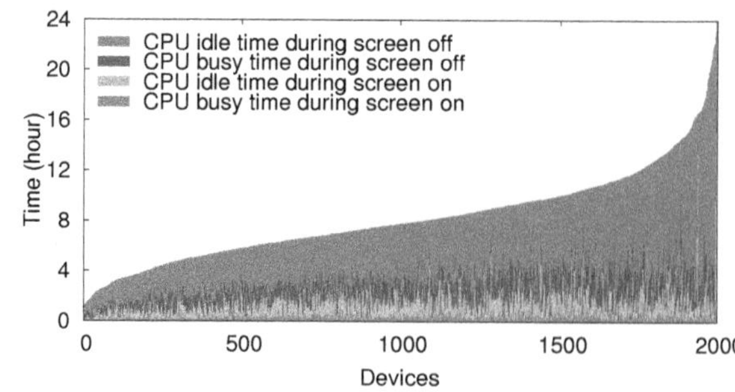

(a) Percentage CPU time breakdown of all devices.

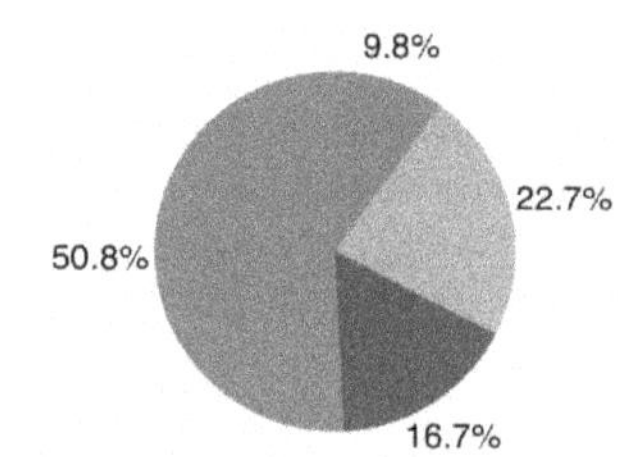

(b) Average of percentage breakdown of CPU time across all devices.

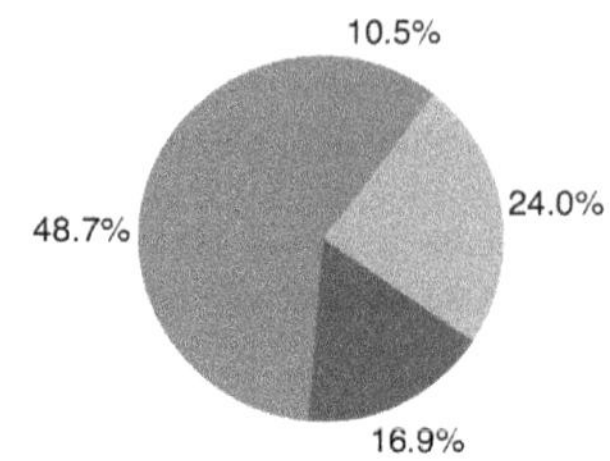

(c) After removing USB charging intervals and CPU lingering time.

Figure 4: Distribution of daily CPU busy and idle time during screen-on and screen-off periods.

3.2 Screen-off Intervals

We start with an overview of the smartphone foreground and background usage across the 2000 devices. Figure 1 shows the distribution of the average daily total time spent in screen-off and screen-on intervals across the 2000 devices sorted by the total time. The reason the screen-off and screen-on time do not add up to 24 hours is that a phone can be turned off. On average, the users spend around 2.56 hours per day actively interacting with their phones; the 10th percentile, and 90th percentile screen-on time are 0.84 and 4.62 hours, respectively.

Next, we study the frequency and duration of screen-on and screen-off intervals. Figure 2 shows other than the 9.3% users who on average turn their phones on over 100 times a day, the usage by the rest of the users is spread almost uniformly between 2 to 100 times a day. Overall, the average, 10th percentile, and 90th percentile numbers of screen-on/screen-off intervals per day are 58.3, 21.4, 99.0, respectively. The last user (the rightmost) on average turned the device on 237 times a day for a total average daily screen-on time of 4.2 hours, to mainly check two apps – Whatsapp and Instagram.

The roughly similar total screen-on time (Figure 1) but diverse numbers of screen-on intervals suggest the screen-on and screen-off intervals (Figure 2) differ significantly in duration. Figure 3 plots the CDF of the duration of individual screen-on/off intervals for all users across all days, truncated at 2 hours. We observe that as expected, (1) the duration of screen-on/off intervals differ significantly, and (2) the screen-off intervals tend to last much longer than screen-on intervals. The average, 10th percentile, and 90th percentile durations are 2.9 minutes, 4.9 seconds, and 5.2 minutes for screen-on intervals, and 26.8 minutes, 18.0 seconds, and 60.0 minutes for screen-off intervals, respectively.

3.3 Background Activities in Screen-off

A longer screen-off interval does not necessarily imply more background activities and more energy drain. To understand background activities and energy drain, we first measure the CPU time spent to perform background activities. To this end, we break down the total CPU time of a device, *e.g.,* in a day, into the following components:

- CPU idle time during screen-off;
- CPU busy time (background apps and services) during screen-off;
- CPU idle time during screen-on;
- CPU busy time (for all apps and services) during screen-on.

Note the rest of the time where the CPU is neither busy nor idle is when the CPU is in suspended state or the phone is powered off.

Figure 4(a) shows the average percentage breakdown of daily CPU time across the 2000 devices, sorted in the increasing order of the total CPU time, and Figure 4(b) shows the average of the percentage CPU time breakdowns of the 2000 devices. We make the following observations. (1) Out of the total CPU time in a day, on average, the total CPU busy time during screen-on and screen-off intervals are 9.8% and 16.7%, respectively, suggesting a significant portion of the total CPU busy time is spent during screen-off intervals running apps and services in the background. (2) On average, the fractions of the total CPU time spent in CPU idle during screen-off and screen-on intervals are 50.8% and 22.7%, respectively. The large fraction of CPU idle time compared to CPU busy time during screen-on is intuitive because the OS is often waiting for screen input but the user is idle most of the time when interacting with many apps, *e.g.,* reading web pages or emails. But the large fraction of CPU idle time during screen-off intervals is surprising, as the phone is expected to go back to sleep (*i.e.,* CPU suspended) right after waking up to perform any background activities. (3) Across the devices, while the CPU busy and idle time during screen-on and CPU busy time during screen-off stay more or less similar, the average absolute CPU idle time during screen-off increases significantly,

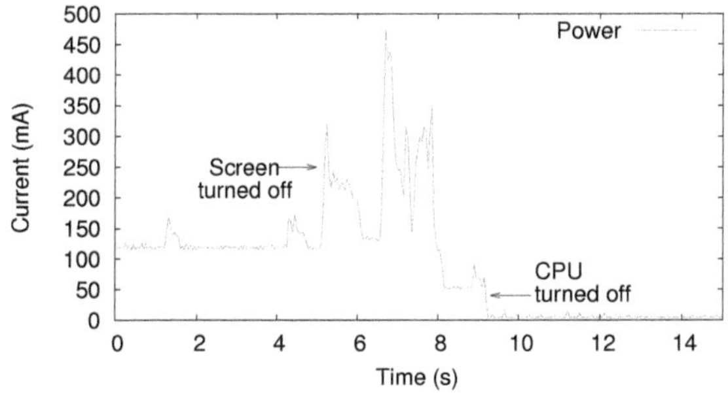

Figure 5: CPU lingers for 2-6 seconds after screen is turned off.

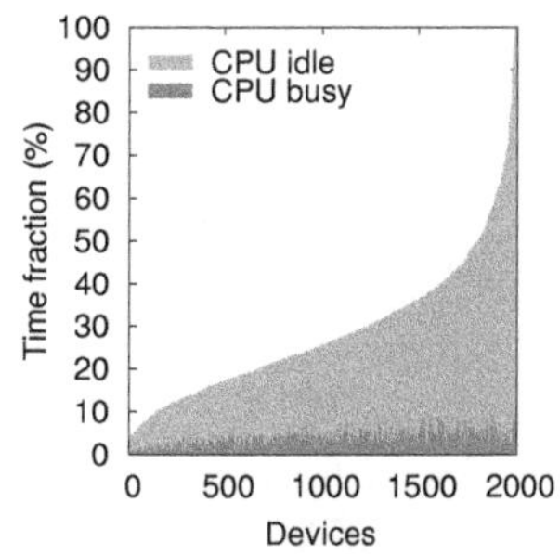

Figure 6: Total CPU busy and idle time as fractions of total interval duration of all screen-off intervals per device, after removing USB charging intervals and CPU lingering time.

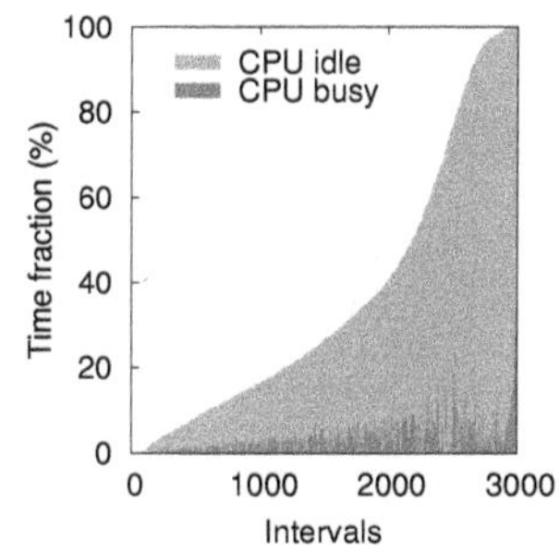

Figure 7: CPU busy and idle time as fractions of each interval duration, for 3000 sampled intervals, after removing CPU lingering time and excluding USB charging intervals.

from 1.4 hours on average among the least active 10% devices (on the left of Figure 4(a)) all the way up to 9.7 hours among the most active 10% devices (on the right)!

USB charging. Our quick examination of the trace revealed that the CPU was always fully awake in screen-off intervals when the phones were being charged via USB. We then verified using our own S3 and S4 phones running Android versions 4.3 and 4.3.1 that indeed when during USB charging, the CPU/SOC was never suspended.

Lingering CPU time after screen-on interval. In processing the trace, we discovered a persistent lingering CPU-on period upon entering each screen-off interval (*i.e.,* right after a screen-on interval). In our lab experiment using a powermeter as the energy source for a Galaxy S3 phone, we confirmed that the CPU stays on right after entering a screen-off interval for 2-6 seconds, as indicated by the powermeter reading shown in Figure 5. The Linux /proc shows the second lingering duration is broken down into 940 ms, 740 ms, and 4180 ms of user time, system time, and idle time, respectively. Most of the user time, 750 ms out of 940 ms, is spent in the Android's framework services, while the rest is waiting for the foreground app to pause its activities and for the other apps listening on *Intent.ACTION_SCREEN_OFF* broadcast messages. Similarly, most of the system time is also spent in various shutdown activities.

In the rest of the section, we removed all the USB charging intervals and the 6-second CPU linger time (2 seconds of busy time and 4 seconds of idle time) from all the rest screen-off intervals. Figure 4(c) re-plots the CPU time breakdown. We see that the average fraction of daily CPU time spent in CPU idle during screen-off intervals remains high at 48.7%.

3.4 Background App Activities

To understand the high CPU idle time during screen-off intervals, we plot the total CPU busy and idle time of all screen-off intervals as fractions of the total screen-off interval durations for each device in Figure 6. We see that the fractions are high – out of the 2000 devices, over 200 devices have the CPU staying up (busy or idle) for over 50% of the screen-off interval durations.

Since ultimately it is the apps and system services they depend on that wake up the device during screen-off intervals, we next zoom into the apps running on the 100 devices with the highest total fractions of CPU idle and busy time in Figure 6, *i.e.,* the rightmost 100 devices in the figure, and analyze the app activities during screen-off intervals.

(1) App busy/idle time per device. We first try to understand if there is any correlation between app busy time and app idle time in screen-off intervals. We plot in Figure 8 both quantities for the selected 100 devices. We see that there is no significant correlation between the total app busy time and the total CPU idle time across the 100 devices – on average, the CPU busy time per device in a day due to the apps in screen-off intervals is only 2.0 hours, while

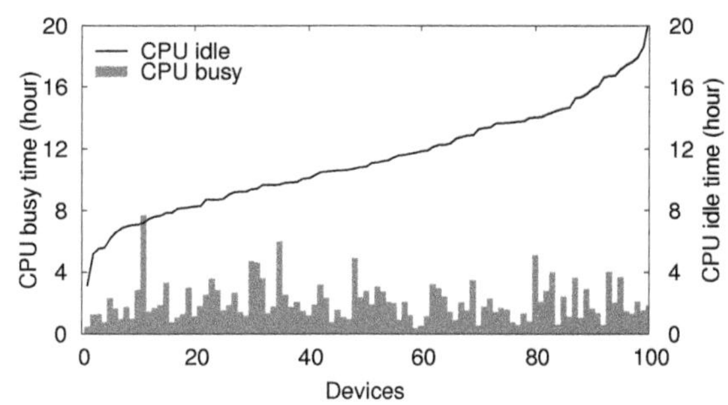

Figure 8: Cumulative daily app busy time in screen-off intervals across 100 heavily used devices, sorted by daily CPU idle time in screen-off.

the corresponding CPU idle time varies from 3.1 hours all the way to 20.5 hours.

(2) App busy/idle time per interval. Next, we analyze the CPU busy and idle time in individual screen-off intervals. We uniformly sampled 3000 screen-off intervals from all 2000 devices and plotted the distribution of CPU busy and idle time in each screen-off interval as fractions of the interval duration in Figure 7. We see that the CPU busy+idle time is over 50% of the interval duration for over 27.1% of the intervals, and over 95% for 9.4% of the intervals. Further, the CPU idle time alone is over 50% of the interval duration for over 18.0% of the intervals (not directly shown).

(3) App holding wakelocks for long durations. Our investigation suggests the primary suspect for causing the large fractions of CPU idle time during screen-off intervals is inefficient or incorrect use of wakelocks in apps. Specifically, we suspect there are apps that when running in the background hold wakelocks for unnecessarily long durations causing the CPU to remain in idle for extended periods of time. To verify our hypothesis, for each device, we flag the apps that appear in more than half of the screen-off intervals when CPU hardly suspends, *i.e.,* the intervals with over 95% CPU busy+idle time, which include 9.4% all screen-off intervals as shown in Figure 7, as *suspicious apps* for that device. If one app is installed on at least 2 devices and there are more devices that have this app as suspicious than the devices that have this app but do not mark it as suspicious, then the app is marked as a "no-sleep" app [21]. Among the apps on all devices, we found 76 no-sleep apps, and 56 of them contain wakelock permissions in their manifest file. We installed 22 of them on an S4 phone running

Table 2: **Summary of the hybrid power model.**

Hardware component	Model type	Logged data
CPU	utilization	CPU time + CPU frequency
GPU	utilization	GPU time + GPU frequency
Screen	utilization	screen on time + brightness
WiFi	non-utilization	bytes + signal strength
3G/LTE	non-utilization	bytes + signal strength
WiFi beacon	constant	WiFi status
WiFi scan	constant	WiFi status
Cellular Paging	constant	cellular status
SOC Suspension	constant	phone status

Samsung's Android version 4.3 (Jelly Bean) in the lab for 9 hours and found that the CPU was never suspended. On further investigation, we found that one of the suspicious apps installed, Hi [5], held a wakelock, **sync*_com.android.contacts_Account*, for the entire time; indeed for the entire 9-hour duration of the screen-off interval, the CPU was busy for 1.5 hours and in the rest of the time it was in the CPU idle state. In summary, while we cannot directly confirm the reason for the large fractions of CPU idle time during screen-off intervals on the phones in the wild, we believe the likely cause is that certain apps hold wakelocks for unnecessarily long periods of time.

4. ENERGY DRAIN

In this section, we characterize the energy drain of the background activities on the 2000 devices.

4.1 Methodology

We adopt the methodology used in [11] for measuring and analyzing energy drain on unmodified user phones. In a nut shell, the measurement is performed in three steps: (1) developing a power model that uses triggers that can be collected without any modifications to the Android framework or the kernel or rooting the phones; (2) developing and deploying an app that collects all the triggers for the power model; (3) post-processing the trace to estimate the energy drain on the phones.

A hybrid power model. To accurately capture the power behavior of all the identified components, a hybrid utilization-based and FSM-based power model was developed in [11] which does not require modifying the Android framework or the kernel yet achieves good modeling accuracy. The model uses utilization-based modeling (*e.g.*, [24, 27]) to capture the power behavior of CPU, GPU, and screen whose power draw has linear correlation with utilization (it estimates the average screen power draw as a function of the brightness level), and FSM-based modeling (*e.g.*, [10, 17, 22, 18, 19, 12]) for wireless interfaces such as WiFi/3G/LTE. The model collects network usage in each logging interval and then estimates the send and receive system calls as triggers to drive the FSM models [20]. It further models cellular paging, WiFi beacon, and WiFi scanning as constant power draws by averaging their power spikes over time, and SOC suspension power (base power) as a constant power draw. Table 2 summarizes the power model type and triggers collected for the set of components modeled, which are selected as those that show significant power draw. As in [11], we further confirmed the component power draw are largely independent, and hence the total power draw can be approximated by summing the power draw of individual components.

We focus on Galaxy S3 and S4 phones in our measurement study, which are the most popular Android phones [3]. The details of the power models for Galaxy S3 and S4 can be found in [11].

Model validation. The hybrid model was validated in [11] using both micro-benchmarks and real apps. Using micro-benchmarks, the measured error in estimating the energy drain by individual components is within 11% of the powermeter output. On a phone with 25 popular apps installed, the measured error in estimating the energy drain of the whole phone during both screen-on and screen-off intervals is within 10% of the powermeter output.

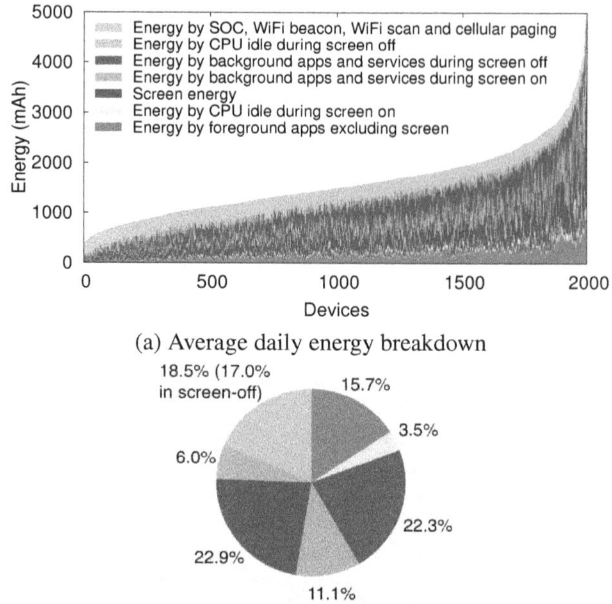

(a) Average daily energy breakdown

(b) Daily energy percentage breakdown, average over all devices.

Figure 9: Daily energy breakdown.

4.2 Background Energy Analysis

We break down the total energy per day per device among different activities as follows:

- Energy by WiFi beacon, WiFi scanning, cellular paging, and SOC base power during screen-off;
- Energy by CPU idle during screen-off;
- Energy by background services and apps during screen-off;
- Energy by background services and apps during screen-on;
- Screen energy during screen-on.
- Energy by CPU idle during screen-on;
- Energy by foreground apps excluding screen.

We note each app and service energy component includes both CPU and networking energy.

Figure 9 shows the energy breakdown across the 2000 devices. We make the following observations. (1) **Overall screen-on vs. screen-off:** Across the 2000 devices, on average 45.9% of the total energy drain in a day occurs during screen-off periods, including 17.0% due to SOC, WiFi beacon, WiFi scan and cellular paging. This is rather surprising, debunking the perception that when a phone is turned off, it should consume little energy. (2) **Background app/service energy in screen-off:** The background apps and services during screen-off including the induced CPU idle together contribute to 28.9% of the total energy drain[2], in contrast to the 11.1% by background apps and services during screen-on. The 28.9% gives an upper bound on how much daily energy can be saved from suppressing background activities of apps and services during screen-off intervals. (3) **CPU idle energy in screen-off:**

[2]This number is slightly higher than in [11], since the average logged screen-off duration per day in this trace (Figure 1), 18.3 hours, is longer than in that trace.

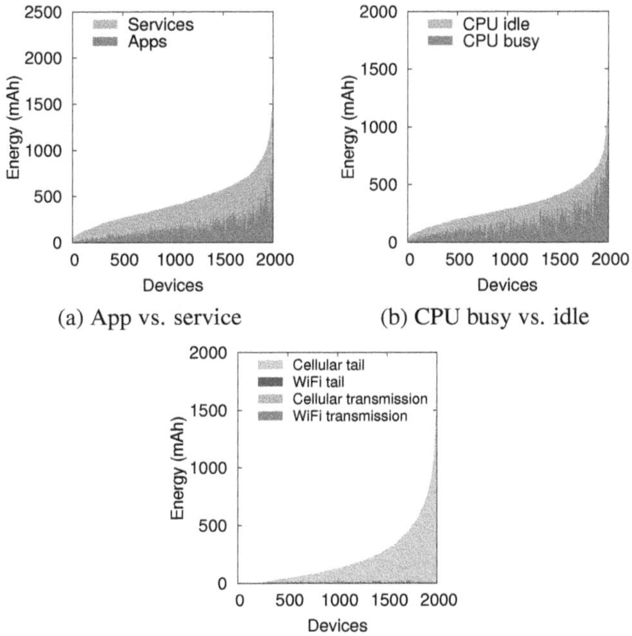

(a) App vs. service (b) CPU busy vs. idle

(c) WiFi vs. cellular, transmission vs. tail energy

Figure 10: Breakdown of background energy between apps and services, CPU busy and idle, and wireless radios.

Although on average the CPU spends 50.8% of the total CPU time in idle in screen-off (Figure 4(b)), it only drains on average 6.0% of the total energy, primarily due to the effectiveness of frequency scaling – in entering the idle state, the CPU quickly drops to the lowest frequency, *e.g.,* 384MHz on Galaxy S3, and then further into a power-saving C state which draws minimum power.

Next, we zoom into the background app and service activities during screen-off intervals, and break down the energy drain due to apps versus services, CPU busy versus CPU idle, and network energy among different radios and states. The results, shown in Figure 10, show that across the 2000 devices, on average the energy drain of background activities is roughly split 55.4% to 44.6% between apps and services, and 70.8% to 29.2% between CPU busy and CPU idle, and the vast majority of the network energy by background apps and services is spent in 3G/LTE tail energy.

5. KEY IDEA

Our analysis of energy drain of 2000 devices in the wild shows that on average 28.9% of the daily energy drain is due to apps and services running during screen-off intervals. The current solutions to curtailing this energy drain are limited. For example, iOS provides a feature called "Disable Background Refresh" [6] which prevents the apps from running in background altogether, while Android provides a similar feature called "Restrict Background Data" [1] which switches background data refresh to using WiFi links only.

In this paper, we propose HUSH, a simple yet effective screen-off energy optimizer that reduces smartphone battery drain due to background activities. The two premises behind HUSH are that (1) *background activities of apps are meant to improve user app experience but they are only useful if the user interacts with those apps in foreground some time during the next screen-on interval; and (2) the usefulness of background activities of an app is likely to be user-dependent and thus their occurrences should be personalized.*

The basic idea behind HUSH is to extract the correlation between an app's background activities, *i.e.,* whether it runs during a screen-off interval, and its foreground activities, *i.e.,* whether it would run in the foreground during the next screen-on interval. If there is a strong correlation, the background activities of the app during screen-off intervals are likely to be *useful* to the user experience. For example, for a user who checks her Facebook feeds frequently, the periodic synchronization of the Facebook app with the server during a screen-off interval reduces the response time when the user checks her Facebook during the next screen-on interval and thus enhances the user experience. On the other hand, if a user rarely checks her Facebook feeds, the background activities are likely *not useful* to the user, and disabling such periodic synchronization with the server in screen-off intervals is unlikely to affect the user experience.

Once HUSH learns the usefulness of apps' background activities during screen-off intervals, it instructs the Android scheduler to selectively avoid scheduling the execution of certain apps during screen-off intervals to save the screen-off energy.

6. BFC ANALYSIS

To validate the premise behind HUSH, in this section, we propose a metric to measure the correlation between background-foreground app activities called Background-Foreground Correlation (BFC). We then perform an extensive analysis of the BFC of all background and foreground activities on the 2000 devices. Our analysis shows that (1) the usefulness of the background activities of different apps for the same user can differ significantly; (2) the usefulness of the same app differs significantly for different users, and thus background activities of apps should be personalized to individual users. We then propose and evaluate an online algorithm that disables app background activities during screen-off intervals judiciously.

6.1 BFC Analysis

The motivation for the BFC metric is to capture the likelihood that a user will interact with an app during a screen-on interval after it had any background activities during the preceding screen-off interval. Formally, for a given app k, let B_k denote a given sequence of all screen-off intervals in time order during which app k was active. For each interval b in B_k, we define binary function $X_k(b) = 1$, if app k ran in foreground during the screen-on interval following b, and $X_k(b) = 0$, otherwise. The BFC metric of app k for B_k is calculated as

$$\text{BFC}_k(B_k) = \sum_{b \in B_k} X_k(b)/|B_k| \tag{6.1.1}$$

The BFC of an app is thus a value between 0 and 1. The lower the BFC value, the weaker the correlation between the app's background activities during screen-off intervals and its foreground activities during subsequent screen-on intervals, and hence suppressing the app's background activities during screen-off intervals will most likely not affect the user experience with the app.

Limitations. The BFC metric does not capture well the usefulness of the class of apps that primarily run in the background, such as file-syncing apps or health monitoring apps. For example, Dropbox is used by users to upload files to the Dropbox site and this may happen on a scheduled frequency which may occur during screen-off intervals only, and the user may only infrequently access the Dropbox app itself during screen-on. In this case, the BFC metric will be low yet the background upload activities are considered useful to the user. For such apps, HUSH provides a feature that allows users to whitelist them to bypass the suppressing procedure.

BFC of the apps of the same user varies. We first measure the BFC of different apps on the same device. We randomly picked

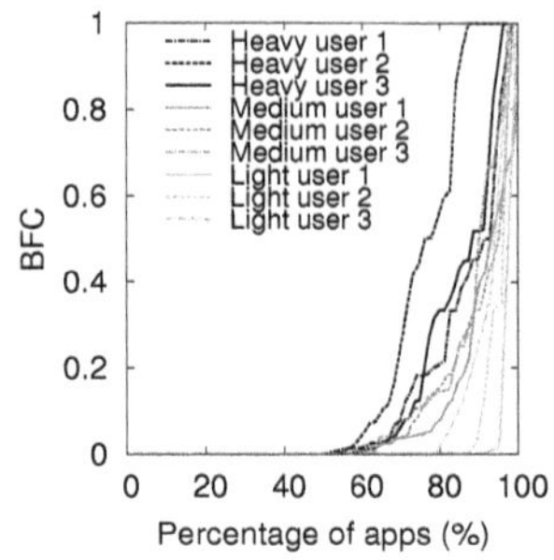

Figure 11: BFC of all apps across 3 light users, 3 median users, and 3 heavy users.

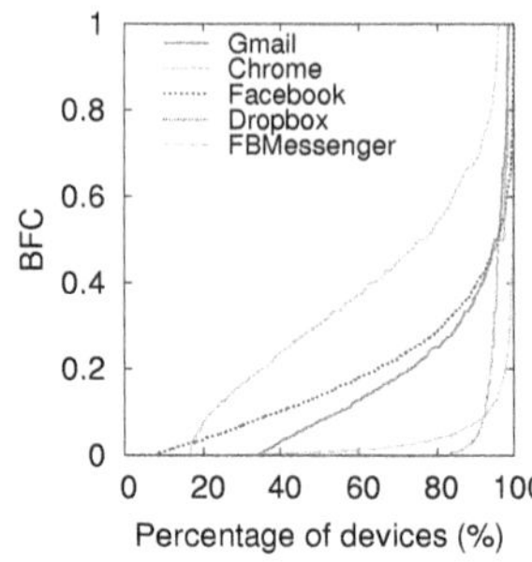

Figure 12: BFC of top 5 most popular apps across users

Table 3: Top 5 popular apps in the 2000-user trace.

App	Popularity
Gmail	1718
Chrome	1601
Facebook	1462
Dropbox	1259
FB Messenger	1257

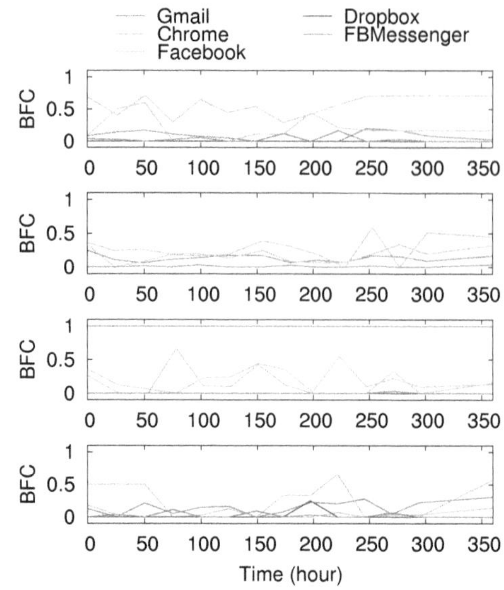

Figure 13: Stability of the BFC of 5 apps on 4 selected devices.

3 light users, 3 median users and 3 heavy users according to daily screen-on time of Figure 1. Figure 11 shows the BFC for all the apps during the trace period, 27.9-day long on average, for each of the 9 users. We make several observations. First, the heavy users have the highest BFC, followed by the median users and by light users. This is intuitive as heavy users spend more time playing apps in foreground, making more background app updates useful. Second, for all 9 users, nearly 60% of the apps have a BFC value of 0, suggesting that many apps are not accessed at all by users after they performed some background activities. This is often the case where the user used an app for a short while, and then lost interest and stopped using it. In other cases, an app's background activities may not be a driving factor (*e.g.,* the app did not generate any notifications) for the user to access it, and thus the user experience is likely unaffected if its background activities are suppressed. Third, for the remaining 30%–40% of the apps on each device, their BFC values vary significantly, all the way from 0 to 1, suggesting the BFC is highly app-dependent.

BFC of an app varies with users. Next, we measure the BFC of an app across different users. We pick the top 5 most popular apps in our 2000-user trace, shown in Table 3, and calculate the BFC for each of them on the 2000 devices. The results are shown in Figure 12. We make several observations. First, the BFC of all 5 apps indeed vary significantly, ranging between 0 to 1, suggesting it is highly user-dependent. Second, even for popular apps such as Gmail, the BFC is zero for 35% of the users, who will benefit from HUSH which would suppress the app from running during screen-off intervals and save battery, without experiencing any adverse user experience. Third, interestingly, while Dropbox indeed has a BFC of zero for about 80% of the users, its BFC is large for the remaining 20% users, reaching 1 for 1.1% of the users. The detailed trace shows for those devices, the user checks Dropbox in foreground every time after it synchronizes with its server in a screen-off interval.

Stability of BFC. Next, we measure whether the BFC of a given app on a given user's phone is stable over time. For each user trace, we divide the trace duration into non-overlapping windows of 24 hours each, and calculate the BFC for each window for each app that has at least 24 daily background activities (on average one per hour). Figure 13 plots the BFC values across all the windows for the same 5 apps studied in Figure 12 and 4 out of the 9 devices in Figure 11 (the second user has no Dropbox). Further, we pick top 25 apps across the devices, calculate the standard deviation of the BFC values for all the windows for each app on each device that has it, and plot in Figure 14 the distribution of standard deviation values per app across all the devices. We observe that (1) the BFC for the same app on the same device is fairly steady (*e.g.,* FBMessenger) or changes slowly (*e.g.,* Facebook), and (2) while the BFC for the same app may vary sharply across users, it is fairly stable for individual users.

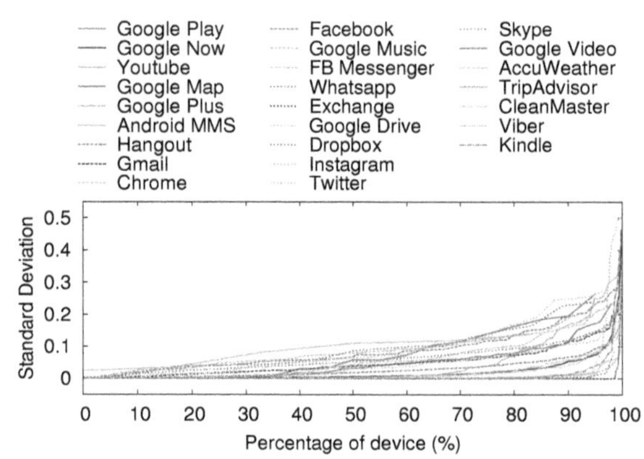

Figure 14: Standard deviation of the BFC of top 25 apps on all devices.

In summary, the results from the above three measurements suggest that the BFC value is both user-dependent and app-dependent but is fairly steady for the same app and same user, and therefore should be and can be learned on a per-app and per-user basis.

6.2 Prediction-based Online Algorithm

The BFC analysis above motivated us to develop a prediction-based online algorithm for suppressing app background activities to reduce the background energy drain. The algorithm uses an exponential moving average to continuously update the BFC for each

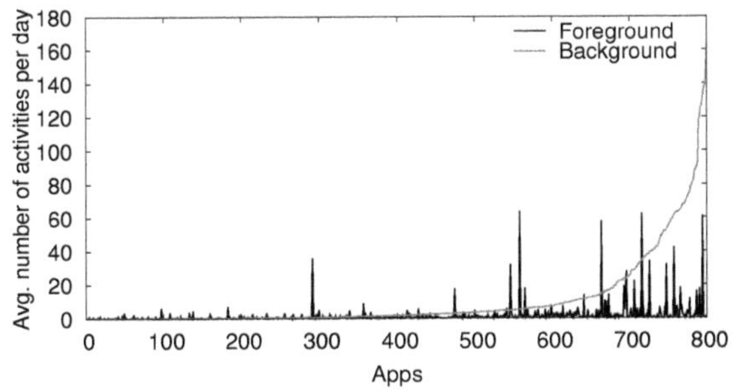

Figure 15: Average numbers of foreground and background activities per day of top 800 apps on the 2000 devices.

app on each device, as follows:

$$\text{BFC}_k(i) = \beta \cdot \text{BFC}_k(i-1) + (1-\beta) \cdot X_k(i) \qquad (6.2.1)$$

where $\text{BFC}_k(i)$ denotes the BFC updated at the end of the screen-on interval after screen-off interval i which had background activities of app k, and $X_k(i)$ records if app k ran in that screen-on interval.

In the following screen-off interval $i+1$ when app k attempts to wake up to perform background activities, the algorithm compares the app's current BFC(i) to a predetermined cutoff value α: the background activity is suppressed if $\text{BFC}_k(i) \leq \alpha$. However, $\text{BFC}_k(i+1)$ is updated as usual regardless if the background activities during interval $i+1$ were suppressed or not.

6.3 Choosing Parameters

The online algorithm above has two key parameters: coefficient β in the exponential moving average calculation and cutoff α for suppressing app background activities. Both parameters directly affect the suppression operations of the algorithm.

To gain insight into how to choose the parameters, we first show the average numbers of foreground and background activities per day of the top 800 apps on the 2000 devices (*i.e.,* with over 15 users) in Figure 15. We find 22% apps have more than 10 background activities per day, 10% apps have more than 36 background activities per day, and 77% of apps have more daily background activities than daily foreground activities. We further study the 300-hour long background and foreground activity sequences of 10 popular apps running on a dozen devices, and calculated their BFC under β values of 0.1, 0.5, and 0.9. Figure 16 shows the results for 6 representative app-device combinations. Based on these background activity patterns, we can group apps into three cases:

- Case 1: there are few foreground activities and hence many background activities per foreground activity (*e.g.,* Google Now, and Gmail);
- Case 2: there are many foreground activities and hence few background activities per foreground activity (*e.g.,* Facebook-User 2, Whatsapp-User 2);
- Case 3: the app contains alternating phases with few and many foreground activities (*e.g.,* Facebook-User 1, Whatsapp-User 1).

Notice the same app (*e.g.,* Whatsapp) can fall into different cases on different devices because of different user behavior.

The above categorization of app background activities can be intuitively explained as follows. All the background activities that we see are push-based. Pushed information are either *time-sensitive* or *time-insensitive*. If the information is time-sensitive, the app typically notifies the user to use the app and the user is likely to open the app. For example, chats and certain types of posts (*e.g.,* a friend directly interacts with a user by sending messages or writing to her timeline) are generally considered time-sensitive and produce notifications, and hence Whatsapp and Facebook (User 2) fall into Case 2. In contrast, the information fetched by Google Now in background, *e.g.,* recommended news and weather forecast, seldom are time-sensitive or generate notifications, and rarely prompt the user to use the app. Hence Google Now falls into Case 1. The information fetched by Facebook may consist of a mix of general friend's posts which are not time-sensitive, and time-sensitive posts mentioned above. Thus, Facebook can also fall into Case 3, *e.g.,* Facebook - User 1.

Picking the β value. In Case 1, since the app has few foreground activities, the app's BFC should stay low, and hence a large β value is preferred as it favors the steady-state (low) BFC; with a small β, transient foreground activities would cause the BFC to jump up significantly, as shown in Figure 16(c)(d).

In Case 2, there are many foreground activities and also background activities, and hence $X_k(i)$ oscillates between 0 and 1 frequently. Since many background activities are useful, background activities should not be suppressed and hence BFC should not go too low. In this case, a larger β is preferred as using a small β value would give too much weight to the most recent $X_k(i)$ which can cause the BFC to fluctuate between close-to-0 and close-to-1 values, as seen in Figure 16(b)(f).

Finally, in Case 3, the app transitions between strong and weak correlation phases, a small β is preferred since it allows the BFC to quickly adjust to the steady-state value in the new phase, as shown in Figure 16(a)(e).

In summary, the three cases prefer different values of β. We pick β=0.5 to strike a balance between the difference preferences. As shown in Figure 16, using β=0.5 keeps the BFC sufficient low for Case 1 and sufficiently high for Case 2, and adapts the BFC quickly for Case 3. The BFC curves using β=0.5 in the figure also suggest that using a low value of α in the range of 0.1-0.2 will suppress most background activities appropriately.

6.4 Trace-driven Evaluation

We now evaluate the effectiveness of our online BFC-based algorithm for suppressing background activities to save screen-off energy using trace-driven simulation, using our 2000-user trace. The *energy saving* is defined as $\frac{E_b - E_a}{E_b}$, where E_b and E_a are the total energy on each device before and after our suppression algorithm is turned on.

Methodology. When we suppress background activities in screen-off, we assume their networking is completely avoided, *i.e.,* not delayed to be performed during the next screen-on activity of the app, which potentially can increase the screen-on part of the app energy. Since we do not know the causality between app and system service activities, we break down the total energy drain due to system services in each logging interval and attribute them to the apps that ran in that interval proportionally to their CPU busy time. Similarly, we break down the CPU idle time and hence energy in each interval and attribute them to the apps that ran in that interval proportionally to their CPU busy time. When an app background activity is suppressed, the associated service and CPU idle energy drain are also avoided.

Since we have networking statistics per 5-second logging interval, the total network energy calculation in Section 4 already took into account app background networking activities in the same 5-second interval would share network tail energy. Similarly, when an app background activity in a screen-off interval is suppressed, its share of network energy is deducted appropriately, *i.e.,* if other apps and services had networking activities in the same 5-second interval, the tail energy is not deducted.

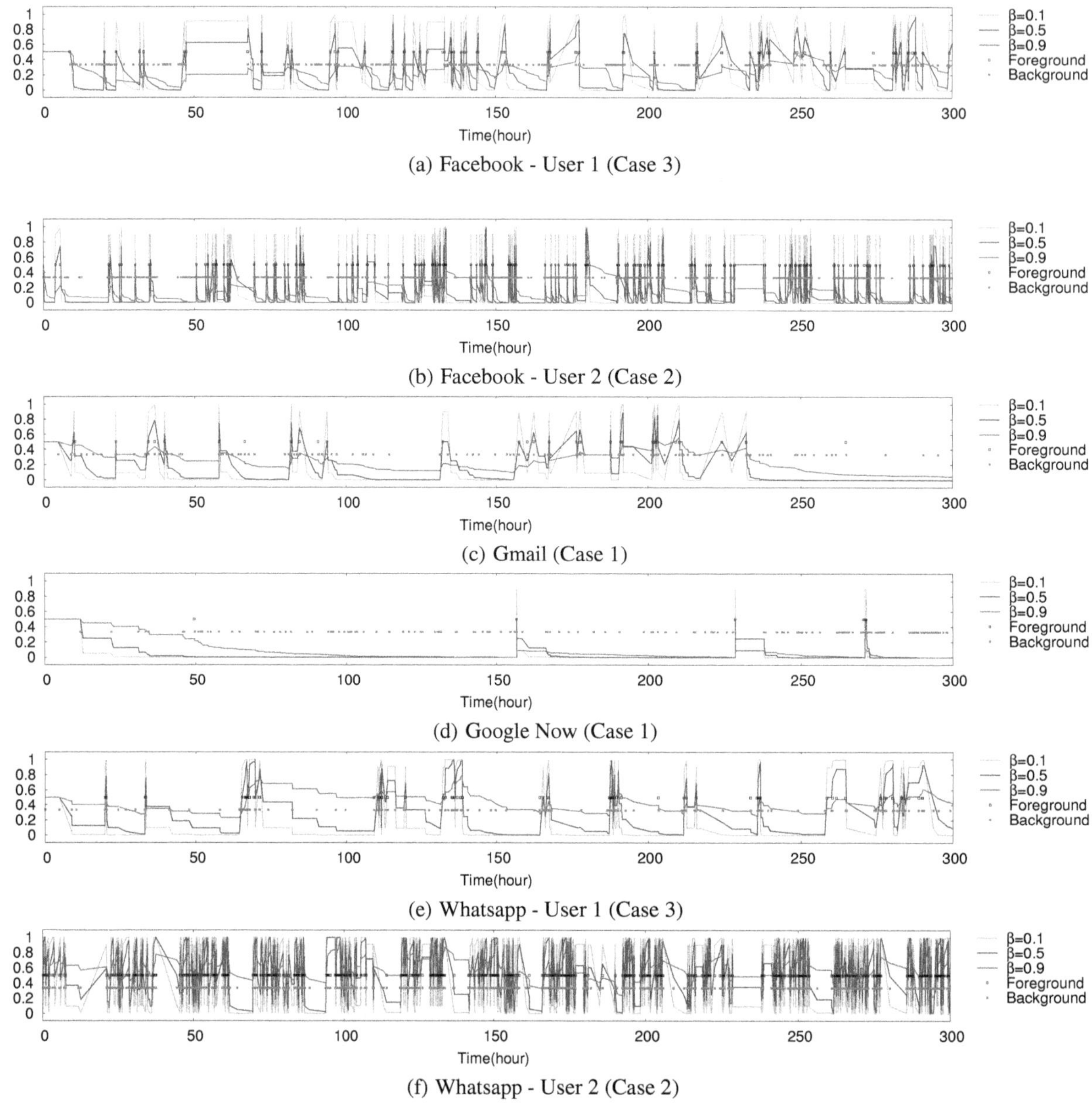

Figure 16: Background/foreground activities and online BFC calculation under three β values. BFC is initialized to 0.5.

Staleness. Since our practical algorithm uses an app's past BFC to predict its future BFC, it can mispredict and suppress background activities that turned out to be useful, *i.e.,* the next screen-on interval had foreground activities of the app. To quantify such mispredictions, we define the *staleness* for each app foreground activity as the elapsed time since the last background activity, or the last foreground activity of the app, whichever is closer in time. The *staleness of an app* on a device is then defined as the average staleness of all its foreground activities on that device. We note under this definition, even without any suppression, the staleness of an app is not zero, but an incorrect suppression increases the staleness.

Optimal energy saving. Before presenting the results for our online prediction-based algorithm, we calculate the *optimal energy saving*, the energy saving of an optimal suppression algorithm that knows the future and disables all background activities of any app that ran in screen-off interval b but did not run in the screen-on interval immediately following screen-off interval b. In doing so, the screen-off energy would be reduced by 14.1%–90.0% across the 2000 devices, with an average of 55.6%, which translates into 0.2%–63.1% total daily energy saving, with an average of 17.1% and a median of 15.7%, as shown in Figure 17(b).

Energy saving. We evaluate the algorithm with different threshold α values, which control the trade-off between screen-off energy reduction with app staleness. For example, an α value of 0 is the most conservative – an app's background activities are suppressed only if its current BFC metric is 0, which also leads to the least amount of energy saving.

Figures 17(a)(b) show the percentage of background activities suppressed and the total energy saving across the 2000 devices as α varies between 0 and 0.8 and $\beta = 0.5$. We observe that using a small α value of 0.1, significant amount of background energy can already be reduced across the 2000 devices, with the average, the 10th, 50th, and 90th percentile total energy saving being 16.4%, 6.0%, 14.9% and 29.4%, respectively. Additional energy saving with more aggressive suppression, *i.e.,* by relaxing α all the way to 0.8, is small, with the average, the 10th, 50th, and 90th percentile

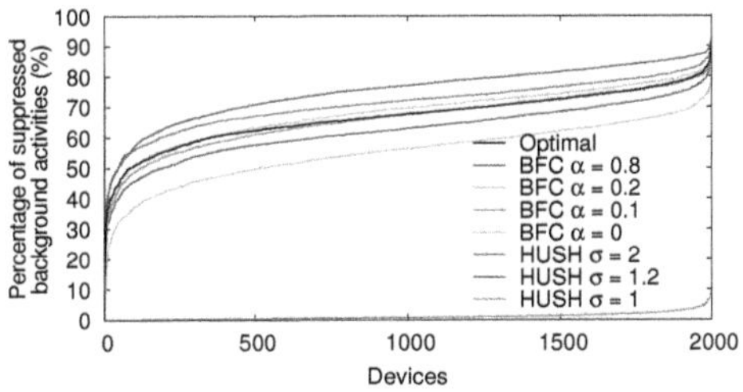

(a) Percentage of suppressed background activities

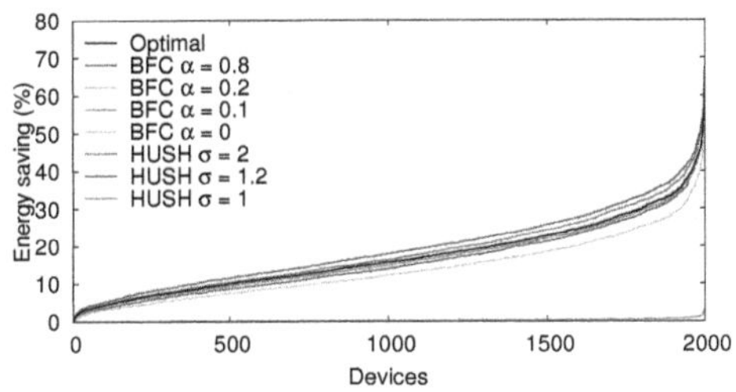

(b) Energy saving

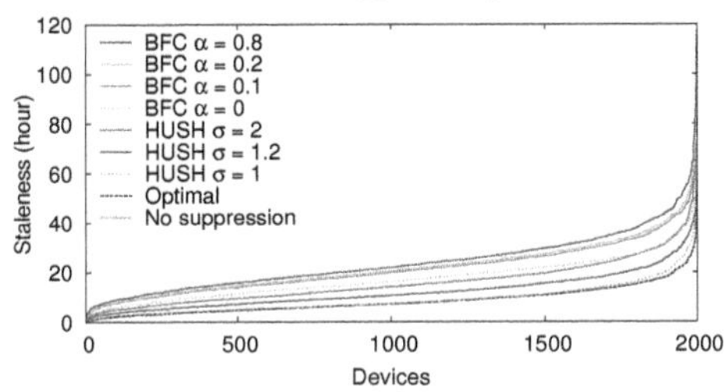

(c) Average staleness of apps

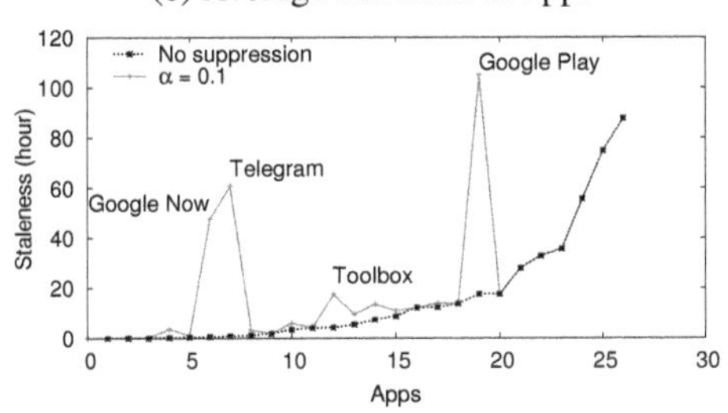

(d) Staleness per app on one device from BFC-based algorithm (with 2.5x staleness for α=0.1)

Figure 17: Results from running the BFC-based algorithm and the HUSH algorithm across the devices, β=0.5.

total energy saving being 19.3%, 7.3%, 17.9%, and 33.2%, respectively. This is because most of the energy saving comes from Case 1 apps, whose BFC will almost always stay below 0.1.

Figure 17(c) shows the corresponding app staleness under the different α values. We see that suppressing background activities increases the app staleness from on average 2.5x with $\alpha = 0.1$ to 3.1x with $\alpha = 0.8$. The above trade-off between energy saving and app staleness suggests choosing an α value of 0.1 strikes a good balance between the two metrics. To understand the seemingly large staleness increase, we picked the device that corresponds to 2.5x increase under α=0.1 in Figure 17(c), device 1400, and plot the staleness of the individual apps on it before and after running the suppression algorithm, in Figure 17(d), sorted by staleness without suppression. We see that for most apps, the staleness stays the same, suggesting the suppression of their background activities was accurate; only 4 out of 27 apps have significantly increased staleness, which contributes to the 2.5x average staleness of the device.

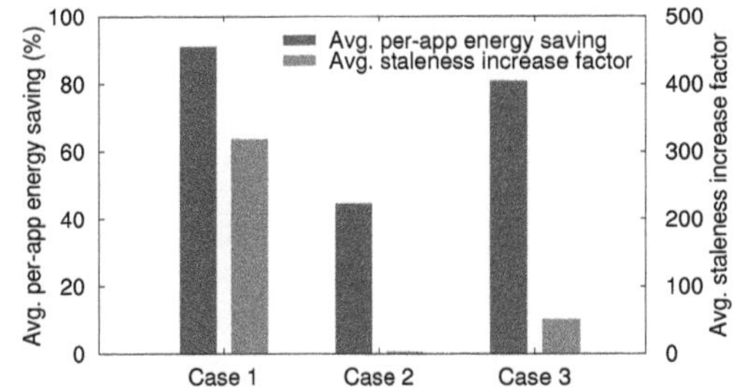

Figure 19: Average energy saving and staleness increase factors of apps in the 3 cases on the 2000 devices.

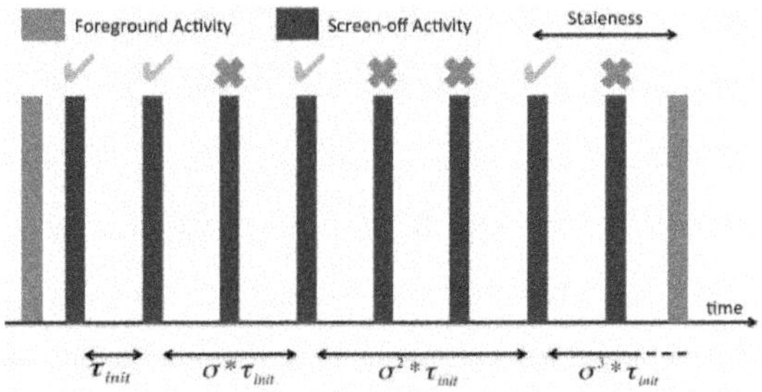

Figure 20: The HUSH suppression algorithm.

Algorithm refinement. We dig deeper into the 4 apps (Google Now, Telegram, All-In-One Toolbox, Google Play) with large staleness and plot their 300-hour long background and foreground activity sequences in Figure 18 (with Google Play omitted due to page limit). We observe these apps are all Case 1 apps; they rarely run in foreground, and hence when background activities in between two adjacent foreground activities are suppressed, the screen-off energy is reduced significantly but the staleness also skyrockets.

To generalize this finding, we classify the user-app combinations into each case using a simple algorithm as follows. We assign a user-app combination as Case 1 (Case 2) if for 80% of the foreground activities there are more (less) than 5 background activities until the next foreground activity, and Case 3 otherwise. We draw the average per-app energy saving and the ratio of staleness (after and before suppression) in Figure 19 under α=0.1 for the three Cases of apps and observe that Case 1 apps indeed have the most energy savings as well as the highest staleness increase.

The BFC-based suppression algorithm strictly follows an all-or-none policy; once the BFC decays below α, it suppresses *all* background activities in the subsequent screen-off intervals leaving the staleness grow boundlessly until the next foreground activity. We observe that the staleness of Case 1 apps can be significantly reduced while retaining their energy saving, by relaxing the strictness of the suppressing policy to include an exponential backoff and omitting the need to maintain BFC calculation, as shown in Figure 20. We denote this new algorithm as HUSH.

HUSH does not maintain the BFC calculation since for Case 1 apps the BFC between two foreground activities will be very low that it cannot predict the next foreground activity anyway. Instead, it simply maintains and tunes a single threshold time parameter (τ) for each app; an app's next screen-off activity is allowed only if its previous background activity happened τ earlier, and is otherwise suppressed. Whenever HUSH allows a screen-off activity, τ is multiplied by a scaling factor σ (>1), making screen-off activities less and less frequent. However, when an app comes to foreground, its τ is reset back to τ_{init}. Figure 18 shows how HUSH suppresses the background activities for the 3 apps for different values of σ.

Compared to the BFC algorithm, HUSH just allows $O(log_{\sigma}(K))$ screen-off activities where K is the total screen-off activities be-

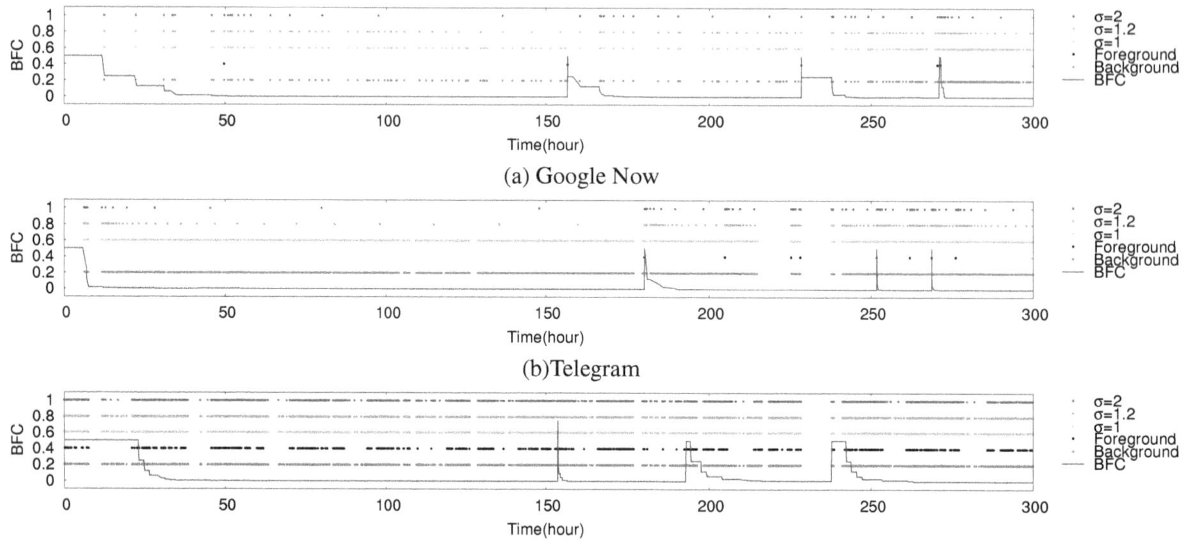

(a) Google Now

(b)Telegram

(c) All-in-one Toolbox

Figure 18: Original background/foreground activities, and background activities after suppression by the BFC algorithm and by the HUSH algorithm, for 3 apps with large staleness.

tween two foreground activities with interval D, while bounding app staleness to be about $\frac{\sigma-1}{\sigma} \cdot D$, assuming the background activities are equally spaced. Thus, it turns out HUSH works well not only for Case 1 apps, but also for Case 2 (and hence Case 3 apps), for which the background activities will be barely suppressed as desired, if τ_{init} is set to an appropriate value – we set it to 1 minute.

We also plot the average energy savings and staleness of apps across 2000 devices in Figure 17 for HUSH with different values of σ. We see the HUSH algorithm does not incur large staleness and yet is able to achieve similar energy savings as the BFC algorithm. With $\sigma = 1.2$, the average energy saving across the 2000 devices is 15.7% compared to 16.4% for BFC with $\alpha = 0.1$, and the staleness increase is 1.3x on average compared to 2.5x in BFC with $\alpha = 0.1$.

7. HUSH SCREEN-OFF ENERGY OPTIMIZER

The Android framework exposes to apps several services such as Location Manager, Alarm Manager, and Power Manager, which run with higher privilege than apps in a separate process, *system_-server*. Android services typically use the publish-subscribe pattern where apps subscribe to updates (*e.g.*, location updates) from the services (*e.g.*, Location Manager), and services then *invoke* app callbacks upon the subscribed event (*e.g.*, user location changed), via either the synchronous RPC mechanism *Binder*, or the asynchronous IPC message passing mechanism *Intent*.

Thus, to suppress the default app background activities, HUSH tracks app foreground and background activities and intercepts app invocations by framework services during screen-off intervals by either allowing or rejecting them.

7.1 HUSH Design

Figure 21 shows the architecture of HUSH design. The main algorithm of HUSH is implemented inside *BatteryStatsImpl*, where Android maintains runtime statistics of the whole system and for each individual app such as the total screen-on time, total number of wakeups caused by each app, and total time a wakelock was held by each app. Other HUSH components directly interact with the *BatteryStatsImpl* module. *ActivityManagerService* and *BatteryStatsImpl.Uid.Pkg.Serv* notify the central components of any foreground and background app activities, respectively.

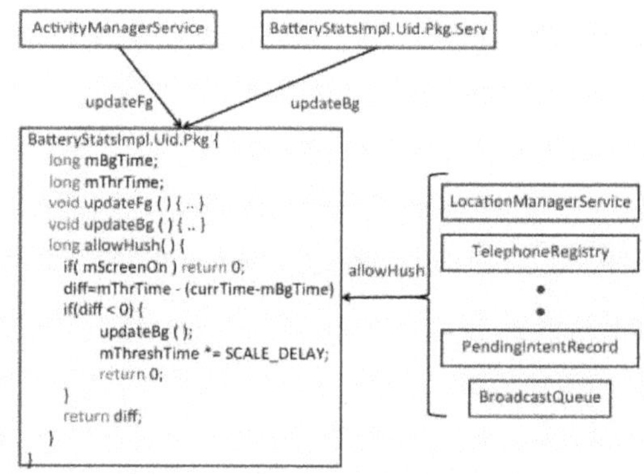

Figure 21: Architecture of HUSH.

Most framework services including *AlarmManagerService* [9] and *GoogleCloudMessaging* [8] send data to apps or simply wake up apps' *BroadcastReceiver* via lightweight asynchronous IPC mechanism – *Intent. BroadcastQueue* now only sends broadcasts when *allowHush* returns true.

Other framework services such as *LocationManagerService* use Android's synchronous RPC mechanism– *Binder*. We directly edit such framework services to only make the remote call if *allowHush* returns true. HUSH does not intercept *Binder* remote calls since upon *allowHush* failure, HUSH cannot (1) throw an exception, since any remote exceptions are not sent back to the caller and hence a caller generally does not expect an exception, or (2) return a garbage value as it can break the caller's code logic.

We note that none of these changes harm user-facing app components. *allowHush* allows all requests when the screen is on and when an app is perceptible to the user in screen-off, such as music streaming apps and navigation apps. Users can also whitelist apps and vary the aggressiveness of HUSH by changing the decay parameter σ in Android settings, as shown in Figure 22.

In total, HUSH adds and modifies 450 and 272 lines of code, respectively. The HUSH source code was released in March 2015 and can be downloaded at *github.com/hushnymous*.

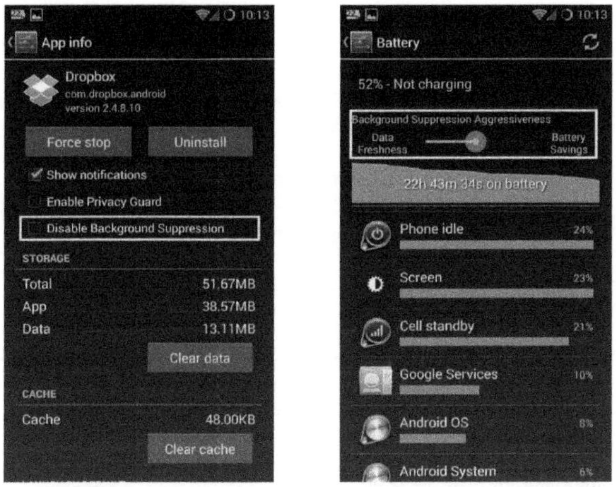

(a) Disable background suppression for selected apps.

(b) Control background suppression aggressiveness.

Figure 22: Hush allows users to control its behavior.

Table 4: Statistics of HUSH running on two Samsung Galaxy S3 phones with Android Jelly Bean for 6 days.

	User-1		User-2	
Number of installed apps	73		52	
Daily screen-on intervals	85		29	
Daily screen-on time (min)	82.35		49.95	
Daily suppressions by HUSH	4400		5543	
	Android	HUSH	Android	HUSH
Daily CPU busy time (min)	164.2	97.04	60.81	27.24
Maintenance power (mA)	12.76	12.76	12.12	12.12
Avg. screen-off power (mA)	15.57	5.27	3.19	2.18
Avg. screen-on power (mA)	316.8	323.5	271.4	273.0
Overall avg. power (mA)	45.50	36.34	27.32	18.99

7.2 Evaluation

We evaluate HUSH on two Samsung Galaxy S3 phones. Both phones ran Android with HUSH for 3 days and unmodified Android for the other 3 days. We installed and whitelisted eStar in HUSH so we can use it to monitor the usage pattern and energy drain rate of the phones.

Table 4 shows the usage pattern for the two users. User-1 uses his phone heavily having 73 apps installed on the phone and keeps the screen on for an average of 82 minutes daily. While User-2 has 52 apps and turns on the screen for 50 minutes daily. On average, HUSH suppressed 4400 and 5543 app background activities on the two phones daily, which reduced the daily CPU busy time by 1.69x and 2.23x. The maintenance power, which includes the normalized power draw by cellular paging, WiFi beacon, WiFi scanning, and SOC in suspension, differ slightly between the two phones which were connected to WiFi for different durations. HUSH significantly reduced the average screen-off power, *i.e.*, screen-off energy normalized by screen-off duration, by 2.95x and 1.46x, while the average screen-on power is slightly increased, leading to an overall average power reduction of 1.25x and 1.44x for the two users, respectively.

Next, we sort all the apps by the ratio of the number of times they were allowed to perform screen-off activity to the number of times they were suppressed by HUSH. We only consider apps that tried to perform screen-off activities at least 5 times.

Table 5 shows the top 5 most allowed and most suppressed apps by HUSH on the two phones. The majority of apps in both allowed and suppressed tables are from the Communication Google Play category which comprises of IM clients, email clients and browsers. The top most allowed app for User-2 is Sogou input which is a keyboard app for typing Chinese characters and hence comes to foreground often. Sogou input syncs with its server during screen-off to get the current popular words and phrases.

Table 5: Most allowed/suppressed apps by HUSH.

User-1		User-2	
App	Allow-deny ratio	App	Allow-deny ratio
Most allowed			
Whatsapp	0.338	Sogou input	2.000
Google Hangout	0.333	iReader	0.473
Google Plus	0.182	Chrome	0.403
Meditation Helper	0.182	Skype	0.354
Gmail	0.142	Gmail	0.235
Most suppressed			
Hydro Coach	0.041	Evernote	0.000
Cover Screen	0.042	Zaker	0.020
Email	0.048	QQ	0.035
Chrome	0.059	Wechat	0.091
Aviate	0.065	Weibo	0.097

We found that both users keep more than one app that perform the same function, *e.g.*, messaging. However, out of these, the users typically use one app to perform one function. Hence exactly one app performing similar functionalities appears in the most allowed app list; the alternates are in the most suppressed list, because they hardly ran in foreground, with the sole exception of Whatsapp and Google Hangout. For User-1, Gmail is in the most allowed app list, but Email is the most suppressed list. In IM apps for User-2, Skype is in the most allowed list but Wechat and QQ are in the most suppressed list. Similarly, in news & magazines category, iReader is among the most allowed but Zaker is among the most suppressed.

Limitations. Although we released the source code of HUSH in March 2015, we have had limited experience with evaluating HUSH on real users' phones so far. The challenge stems from the difficulty in performing controlled experiments, *i.e.*, to subject a user's phone with and without running HUSH to the same user app usage and external conditions. A related limitation is that we have not performed any human subject study, *i.e.*, to measure whether running HUSH on a user's phone affects the user experience. We plan to study ways of overcoming these challenges in our future work.

8. CONCLUSIONS

In this paper, we performed to our knowledge the first in-depth large-scale measurement study of background activities on smartphones in the wild and their impact on battery drain. Our analysis shows that across the 2000 Galaxy S3 and S4 devices, on average 45.9% of the total energy drain in a day occurs during screen-off intervals, and the background apps and services and induced CPU idle time during screen-off together contribute to 28.9% of the total energy drain. We then proposed the BFC metric to measure the usefulness of background activities and showed the usefulness of background activities is highly app-dependent and user-dependent. Finally, we presented a screen-off energy optimizer called HUSH that automatically identifies and suppresses background activities of individual apps during screen-off periods that are not useful to the experience of the user. We show HUSH can save the screen-off energy across the 2000 smartphones by 15.7% on average.

Acknowledgment. We thank the anonymous reviewers and our shepherd for their constructive comments which helped to improve this paper. This work was supported in part by NSF grant CCF-1320764 and by Intel.

9. REFERENCES

[1] Android background app usage restriction.

[2] Android service. http://developer.android.com/reference/android/app/Service.html.

[3] AppBrain, top android phones. www.appbrain.com/stats/top-android-phones.

[4] estar energy saver. https://play.google.com/store/apps/details?id=com.mobileenerlytics.estar.

[5] Hi. https://play.google.com/store/apps/details?id=com.didirelease.view.

[6] ios background app refresh.

[7] ios background execution.

[8] Receive a message. developer.android.com/google/gcm/client.html#sample-receive.

[9] Using pending intent. developer.android.com/reference/android/app/AlarmManager.html#set(int, long, android.app.PendingIntent).

[10] N. Balasubramanian, A. Balasubramanian, and A. Venkataramani. Energy consumption in mobile phones: a measurement study and implications for network applications. In *Proc of IMC*, 2009.

[11] X. Chen, N. Ding, A. Jindal, Y. C. Hu, M. Gupta, and R. Vannithamby. Smartphone energy drain in the wild: Analysis and implications. In *ACM SIGMETRICS*, 2015.

[12] N. Ding, D. Wagner, X. Chen, A. Pathak, Y. C. Hu, and A. Rice. Characterizing and modeling the impact of wireless signal strength on smartphone battery drain. In *ACM SIGMETRICS*, 2013.

[13] H. Falaki, D. Lymberopoulos, R. Mahajan, S. Kandula, and D. Estrin. A first look at traffic on smartphones. In *Proc. of IMC*, 2010.

[14] J. Huang, F. Qian, A. Gerber, Z. M. Mao, S. Sen, and O. Spatscheck. A close examination of performance and power characteristics of 4g lte networks. In *Proc. of Mobisys*, 2012.

[15] J. Huang, F. Qian, Z. M. Mao, S. Sen, and O. Spatscheck. Screen-off traffic characterization and optimization in 3g/4g networks. In *IMC*, 2012.

[16] J. Huang, Q. Xu, B. Tiwana, Z. M. Mao, M. Zhang, and P. Bahl. Anatomizing application performance difference on smartphones. In *Proc. of Mobisys*, 2010.

[17] C.-Y. Li, C. Peng, S. Lu, and X. Wang. Energy-based rate adaptation for 802.11n. In *Proc. of ACM MobiCom*, 2012.

[18] R. Mittal, A. Kansal, and R. Chandra. Empowering developers to estimate app energy consumption. In *Proc. of ACM MobiCom*, 2012.

[19] A. Pathak, Y. C. Hu, and M. Zhang. Where is the energy spent inside my app? fine grained energy accounting on smartphones with eprof. In *Proc. of EuroSys*, 2012.

[20] A. Pathak, Y. C. Hu, M. Zhang, P. Bahl, and Y.-M. Wang. Fine-grained power modeling for smartphones using system-call tracing. In *Proc. of EuroSys*, 2011.

[21] A. Pathak, A. Jindal, Y. C. Hu, and S. Midkiff. What is keeping my phone awake? characterizing and detecting no-sleep energy bugs in smartphone apps. In *Proc. of Mobisys*, 2012.

[22] F. Qian, Z. Wang, A. Gerber, Z. Mao, S. Sen, and O. Spatscheck. Profiling resource usage for mobile applications: a cross-layer approach. In *Proc. of Mobisys*, 2011.

[23] L. Ravindranath, J. Padhye, S. Agarwal, R. Mahajan, I. Obermiller, and S. Shayandeh. Appinsight: Mobile app performance monitoring in the wild. In *OSDI*, 2012.

[24] A. Shye, B. Scholbrock, and G. Memik. Into the wild: studying real user activity patterns to guide power optimizations for mobile architectures. In *MICRO*, 2009.

[25] J. Sommers and P. Barford. Cell vs. wifi: On the performance of metro area mobile connections. In *IMC*, 2012.

[26] Q. Xu, J. Erman, A. Gerber, Z. Mao, J. Pang, and S. Venkataraman. Identifying diverse usage behaviors of smartphone apps. In *Proc. of IMC*, 2011.

[27] L. Zhang, B. Tiwana, Z. Qian, Z. Wang, R. Dick, Z. Mao, and L. Yang. Accurate Online Power Estimation and Automatic Battery Behavior Based Power Model Generation for Smartphones. In *Proc. of CODES+ISSS*, 2010.

Precise Power Delay Profiling with Commodity WiFi

Yaxiong Xie, Zhenjiang Li, Mo Li
School of Computer Engineering, Nanyang Technological University, Singapore
{yxie005, lzjiang, limo}@ntu.edu.sg

ABSTRACT

Power delay profiles characterize multipath channel features, which are widely used in motion- or localization-based applications. Recent studies show that the power delay profile may be derived from the CSI traces collected from commodity WiFi devices, but the performance is limited by two dominating factors. The resolution of the derived power delay profile is determined by the channel bandwidth, which is however limited on commodity WiFi. The collected CSI reflects the signal distortions due to both the channel attenuation and the hardware imperfection. A direct derivation of power delay profiles using raw CSI measures, as has been done in the literature, results in significant inaccuracy. In this paper, we present Splicer, a software-based system that derives high-resolution power delay profiles by splicing the CSI measurements from multiple WiFi frequency bands. We propose a set of key techniques to separate the mixed hardware errors from the collected CSI measurements. Splicer adapts its computations within stringent channel coherence time and thus can perform well in presence of mobility. Our experiments with commodity WiFi NICs show that Splicer substantially improves the accuracy in profiling multipath characteristics, reducing the errors of multipath distance estimation to be less than $2m$. Splicer can immediately benefit upper-layer applications. Our case study with recent single-AP localization achieves a median localization error of $0.95m$.

Categories and Subject Descriptors

B.2.1 [**Computer-Communication networks**]: Wireless Communication

Keywords

Wireless; channel state information (CSI); power delay profile; resolution; bandwidth; channel combination; phase; localization

1. INTRODUCTION

Motivation. The power delay profile gives the power strength of a signal received through a multipath channel as a function of propagation delay, that profiles the multipath arrivals of the signal.

MobiCom'15, September 7–11, 2015, Paris, France.
© 2015 ACM. ISBN 978-1-4503-3619-2/15/09...$15.00.
DOI: http://dx.doi.org/10.1145/2789168.2790124.

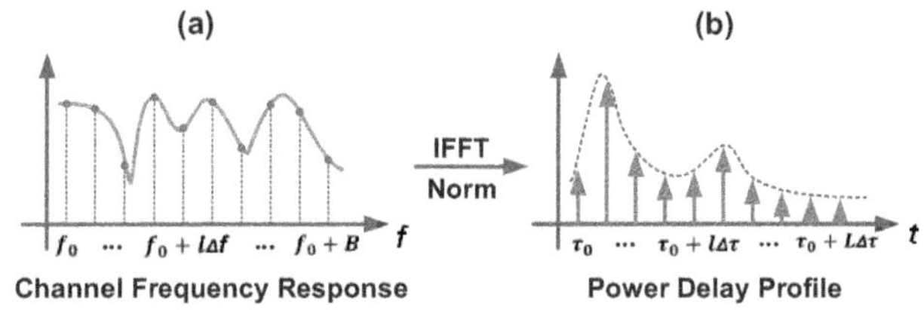

Figure 1: Transformation from a channel frequency response to the power delay profile. (a) A channel frequency response, where f_0, Δf, and B represent starting frequency, frequency sampling resolution, and bandwidth, respectively; (b) Derived power delay profile, where τ_0 and $\Delta\tau$ represent the propagation delay of LoS path and the power delay profile resolution, respectively.

A power delay profile fully characterizes a multipath channel, and has been recently used in various motion- or location-based applications [9, 17, 27, 28, 35, 37, 38, 46] — multipath channel dynamics can be unveiled from consecutive measures of the power delay profile, *e.g.*, tracking the power delay profile changes in a multipath channel can detect an object's movement [9, 10, 34, 35, 38], like a person's walking, falling, talking, or gestures, etc. In addition, the exact power level measured from each signal path can also be used to estimate the path length, *i.e.*, ranging between a pair of transmitters [28, 37].

A power delay profile can be measured by directly detecting multipath signals with different arrival times in the time domain, which however requires dedicated hardware of high signal sampling frequency [23, 26]. An alternative way to describe the channel is using the Channel State Information (CSI) which can be obtained from commodity WiFi network interface cards (NICs), *e.g.*, Intel 5300, Atheors 9580, etc. Theoretically, the frequency domain CSI can be transformed lossless to the time domain power delay profile through IFFT (Inverse Fast Fourier Transform). Figure 1 illustrates the process (which will be detailed in §2).

The time resolution of the derived power delay profile from CSI, *e.g.*, $\Delta\tau$ in Figure 1(b), is limited by the bandwidth of the transmitted signal [7, 26], *e.g.*, B in Figure 1(a), and $\Delta\tau = 1/B$. A high resolution power delay profile can differentiate subtle multipath channel changes, and consequently detect tiny activities. For the widely used 20MHz bandwidth in 802.11n [12], the power delay profile resolution is up to $50ns$, which leads to a $15m$ resolution in measuring the multipath lengths. Such a resolution imposes inevitable uncertainty in mobility detection [9, 35, 38, 45, 46], gesture recognition [33], or localization [28, 37]. For a finer grained motion detection, *e.g.*, less than $1.5m$ uncertainty to differentiate slight human body movements, at least 200MHz bandwidth is needed, which is impossible for current commodity WiFi NICs. Some re-

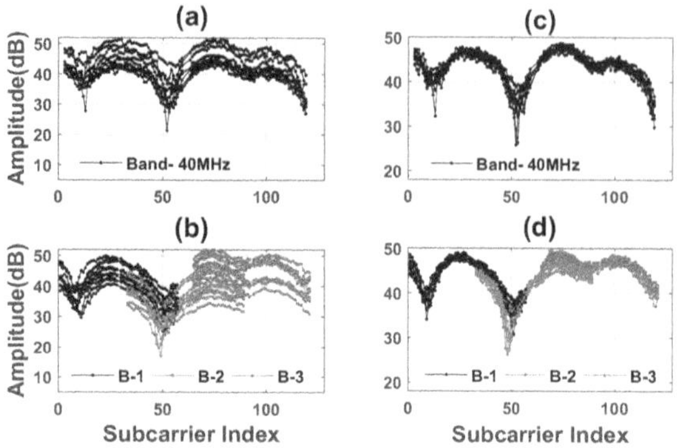

Figure 2: CSI amplitude measurements. Raw CSI amplitudes from (a) one 40MHz 802.11n band and (b) three 20MHz bands; Amplitudes after the offset removal from (c) the 40MHz band and (d) three 20MHz bands.

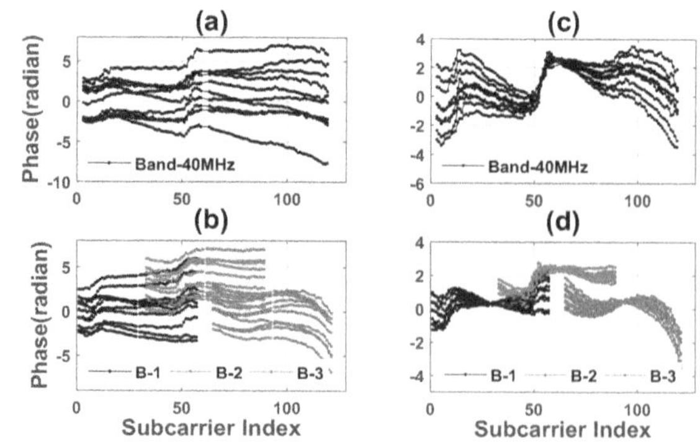

Figure 3: CSI phase measurements. Raw CSI phases from (a) the 40MHz band and (b) three 20MHz bands; Phases after the offset removal from (c) the 40MHz band and (d) three 20MHz bands. The CSI traces in this Figure are the same with Figure 2.

cent works directly use CSI in replacement of power delay profile to learn the channel dynamics. The CSI description of the channel is, however, essentially limited by the bandwidth. In addition, CSI description is indirect and dependent of hardware uncertainty.

In this paper, we observe that although the width of each individual WiFi band is limited, *e.g.*, 20MHz/40MHz, the total bandwidth allocated to 802.11 WiFi is wide, *e.g.*, more than 200MHz at 5GHz frequency band in 802.11n, which covers 10/5 different 20/40MHz channels. Furthermore, the CSIs measured from these individual WiFi channels can be spliced to derive a finer power delay profile with much higher time resolution. Figure 2 reports the results of our initial measurement study in 802.11n (detailed experiment settings reported in §3.1). The CSI measurements are complex values and hence contain two parts, the amplitude and the phase. Figure 2 (a) presents the CSI amplitude measurements (multiple times) from one 802.11n 40MHz band and Figure 2 (b) presents the CSI amplitude measurements from three 802.11n 20MHz bands that together cover the same 40MHz band in Figure 2 (a). From Figure 2 (a) and (b), we can observe obvious offsets between the measured CSI amplitudes at different times. After removing the amplitude offsets among all measurements, we see that the spliced CSI from 20MHz bands can be very similar in its shape to the one measured from the 40MHz band (Figure 2 (c) and (d)).

Compared with the amplitude splicing, the phase splicing may result much severer errors. Figure 3 depicts the phases of the same CSI traces in Figure 2. The raw CSI phases[1] measured at different times have offsets as well (Figure 3 (a) and (b)). However, even we remove their mutual offsets when splice the traces, the residual phases do not have a common shape, demonstrating diverse phase shifts in different sub-carriers. Consequently, the multiple instances of the 40MHz CSI phase measurements as depicted in Figure 3 (c) do not match each other. The CSI traces from 20MHz bands cannot match the 40MHz measurement neither. To derive an accurate power delay profile, such phase shifts must be precisely compensated because the phase value falls in a small range of $[-\pi, \pi)$, and a slight phase error will result in significant inaccuracy in the power delay profile (as we will demonstrate in §3.1).

Challenges. Removing the CSI measurement error, however, is challenging. The CSI calculated by the commodity WiFi NICs contains the signal distortions due to both channel propagation and imperfect signal processing on the hardware, *e.g.*, imprecise sampling frequencies at the sender and receiver, shift of the central frequencies, and power control uncertainties. WiFi communication systems do not have to explicitly separate the two sources of signal distortions, because only end-to-end distortion needs to be captured and compensated as a whole in the equalization stage. To derive a precise power delay profile for the channel, however, it requires to precisely separate the channel attenuation part from the mixed signal distortions due to hardware imperfection, which is non-trivial. The sampling clock frequency uncertainty causes frequency-relevant CSI phase measurement errors in each individual channel. The central clock frequency shift and the power control uncertainty further introduce notable phase and amplitude offsets cross different channels, respectively. Based on the raw CSI measures, it is unknown how to compensate those errors for CSI splicing without the knowledge of ground-truth CSI. In addition to above challenges, wireless channels are time-varying, especially in the mobile environment. Few CSI measurements are allowed for scanning the whole WiFi band during a short coherence time. To deal with such a practical limit, we have to devise an effective method to correct and splice CSI measurements with insufficient samples and affordable computation cost.

Contributions. This paper presents a set of key techniques to address above challenges. At the high level, we exercise the observation that the CSIs collected from different frequency bands should lead to the same power delay profile that characterizes the communication channel itself. We propose an efficient method that searches for a CSI manipulation that maximizes the matching between the power delay profiles derived from CSIs obtained at different frequency bands, based on which we can perform a preliminary CSI splicing. However, the power delay profiles used for matching are derived from narrow WiFi bands with limited bandwidth, so the spliced CSI is still of low quality. We devise a wider frequency window and perform a rolling-based calibration on the spliced CSI, based on which we refine the error correction to achieve a precisely spliced CSI. To accommodate the computations in the limited coherence time, we further develop a lightweight scheduler that is able to determine the optimal number of CSIs to measure from each individual WiFI band to strike a trade-off between the error compensation and the total bandwidth that can be afforded for the CSI splicing.

We develop a system, called Splicer, to incorporate above techniques on commodity Atheors 9580 NICs. Our benchmark exper-

[1] A raw CSI phase is in the range of $[-\pi, \pi)$. For a clear representation, we expand the measured CSI phases θ, using $\theta = \theta \pm 2k\pi$, to the range of $[-\infty, +\infty]$ across different channels.

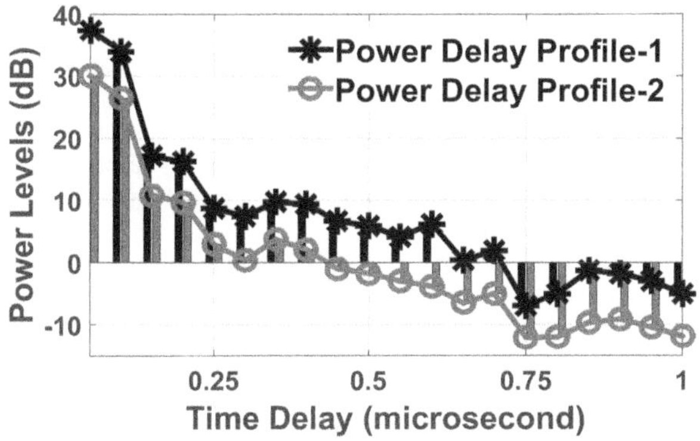

Figure 4: Power delay profiles derived using two CSI with an amplitude offset of 7dB.

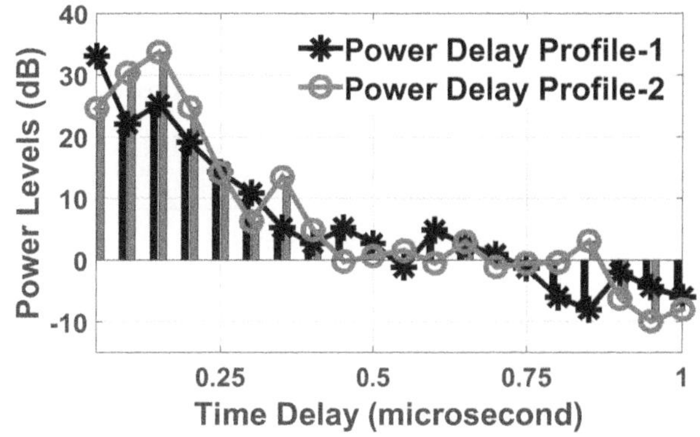

Figure 5: Power delay profiles derived using two CSIs with raw phases and average amplitude of the CSI traces in Figure 4.

iments show that Splicer can derive high resolution power delay profiles from spliced CSI. We evaluate the derived power delay profile by estimating the distance between the sender and the receiver. According to our experiments, Splicer can reduce the median ranging error from $7.1m$ to $1.63m$ compared with using raw CSI traces from NICs. In light of such a high resolution, Splicer can immediately enhance the performance of a plethora of upper-layer applications, *e.g.*, object tracking, gesture recognition, localization, etc., without additional modification to the original application design. We demonstrate this benefit with a case study. We build the recent single-AP localization CUPID [28] on top of Splicer. Our evaluations show that the localization accuracy can be substantially improved. In particular, Splicer improves the CUPID localization accuracy by 71%, with median localization errors about $0.95m$.

The rest of the paper is organized as follows. The design principle is stated in §2 and the Splicer design is detailed in §3. We investigate the accuracy of the derived power delay profile using spliced CSIs and evaluate a case study atop Splicer in §4. Related works are reviewed in §5. We conclude in §6.

2. PRINCIPLE OF CSI SPLICING

In this section, we give the theoretical foundation for CSI splicing. According to [7, 26], the channel frequency response $h(f)$ can be expressed by Eq. (1):

$$h(f) = \sum_{l=0}^{L} \alpha_l \cdot e^{-j \cdot 2\pi \cdot f \cdot \tau_l}, \tag{1}$$

where L is the total number of multipaths, α_l and τ_l stand for the attenuation and the propagation delay of the signal through path l, respectively. Figure 1 (a) depicts a channel frequency response when the channel bandwidth is B, *e.g.*, $f_0 \leq f \leq f_0 + B$. Channel frequency response is reported in the form of CSI in 802.11 WiFi, which is a set of discrete channel frequency response samples. With the sampling rate $F_f = \frac{1}{\Delta f}$, where Δf is the sampling resolution in the frequency domain, a receiver can obtain $M = \frac{B}{\Delta f}$ channel frequency response samples, and each sample contains amplitude and phase information.

To obtain the power delay profile, the CSI can be transformed to the channel impulse response $f(t)$ by IFFT:

$$f(t) = \sum_{l=0}^{L} \alpha_l \cdot \delta(t - \tau_l), \tag{2}$$

where $\delta(\cdot)$ is the delta function, and L, α_l, and τ_l have the same definitions as they are in Eq. (1). Figure 1 (b) illustrates the channel impulse response transformed from Figure 1 (a). The norm of $f(t)$, $||f(t)||_2$, then gives the power delay profile, which describes the power levels of each multipath with different propagation delays.

Feasibility of CSI splicing. According to Eq (1), given one multipath channel, *i.e.*, given each α_n, τ_n, and N in Eq (1), and channel bandwidth B, the channel state information is *deterministic* at each frequency f. We can thus obtain all M CSI samples from either a single measurement covering the entire bandwidth or multiple measurements where each measurement covers a subset of M samples. With the M samples, we can derive a unique power delay profile using Eq. (2) and the norm operation.

Resolution of power delay profile. After the IFFT transformation, we obtain a series of signal samples in the time domain with various delays τ_l in Eq. (2). The norm of each multipath component, $||\alpha_l \cdot \delta(t - \tau_l)||_2$, indicates its power level as shown in Figure 1 (b), where the first impulse corresponds to the Line-of-Sight (LoS) path. According to the IFFT theory, the time resolution $\Delta\tau$ of power delay profile is connected to the sampling resolution Δf of the channel impulse response, *i.e.*, $\Delta\tau = 1/(N \cdot \Delta f)$, where N is the IFFT length. As $N \cdot \Delta f = 1/B$, we have $\Delta\tau = 1/B$, where B is the bandwidth. Such a connection indicates that a wider bandwidth CSI leads to a higher resolution of power delay profile.

Given channel bandwidth B, two multipaths of propagation delays τ_1 and τ_2 are not distinguishable if $|\tau_1 - \tau_2| < 1/B$. Hence, all multipaths whose propagation delays differences are less than $1/B$ are viewed as one multipath component in the power delay profile, and the corresponding power level indicates the aggregated power level of those multipaths. As a result, the time resolution $\Delta\tau$ leads to $\frac{c}{B}$ uncertainty in terms of the length difference between non-distinguishable paths, where c is the speed of the signal propagation. In 802.11 WiFi in a 20MHz or 40MHz channel, the path length uncertainty is $15m$ or $7.5m$, respectively, which can merely support coarse mobility tracking and activity recognition.

3. DESIGN

3.1 CSI splicing in practice

We first locate the error sources of CSI splicing in the 802.11 physical layer in §3.1 and then present the design details to address each of them from §3.2 to §3.5.

CSI measurement errors. We perform preliminary CSI measurements to investigate how CSI measurement errors will affect the derived power delay profiles. We use Atheros 9580 NICs that support 802.11n with 20MHz/40MHz channels at the 2.4G/5G frequency band, and modify the driver to extract CSI from the physical

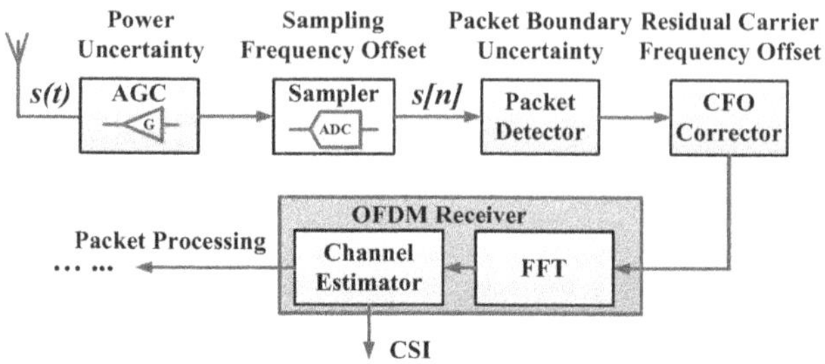

Figure 6: Illustration of signal processing in 802.11.

layer. We configure Atheros nodes to transmit packets with minimum payload to ensure a short transmission delay, *i.e.*, about $0.2ms$ in our experiment. We collect the CSI traces from one 802.11n 40MHz band as well as three 20MHz bands. The measurement results are reported in Figures 2 and 3, which have been discussed in §1. In this section, we further derive the power delay profiles from the CSI traces and investigate how the CSI amplitude and phase errors may impact the final power delay profiles.

CSI amplitude. In Figure 4, we select two arbitrary CSI traces from the same WiFi band (20MHz-2 in Figure 2) with an amplitude offset of 7dB, and derive two power delay profiles[2]. Figure 4 shows that although two derived power delay profiles have different power levels, *e.g.* the average difference is 7.05 dB, they follow similar shapes. We compute the variance of the power difference for each path to quantify the similarity of two power delay profiles, which is less than 1.0 dB. We observe similar results from other CSI combinations. All of these results indicate that the derived power delay profiles approximately characterize the same multipath channel environment except that their power levels are scaled due to amplitude offsets of the CSI measurements.

CSI phases. In Figure 5, we use the raw phases of two CSI traces in Figure 4 to derive two power delay profiles[3]. The two profiles in Figure 5 demonstrate opposite results. One power delay profile indicates the existence of the LoS between the transmission pair (*i.e.*, the first multipath component has the strongest power level), however another one indicates that there is no LoS (NLoS) path (*i.e.*, the first arrived signal is much weaker in strength than later arrived signals). In addition, the power levels of each multipath component in these two profiles are very different, *e.g.*, the power difference of the LoS path is more than 10 dB and the variance of the power level differences is up to 4.7 dB. Figure 5 indicates that the CSI phase errors will significantly impact the derived power delay profiles, which completely change both the power loss and the multipath channel features.

As our initial experiment results suggest, the CSIs collected from WiFi NICs are mixed with rich hardware distortions. The raw CSIs cannot derive accurate power delay profiles. We identify the measurement error sources in 802.11 physical layer process and propose solutions to compensate each of them.

Sources of CSI measurement errors. Figure 6 illustrates the wireless signal processing in the 802.11 NICs. An incoming signal from the antenna is down converted to the base band signal $s(t)$ and sampled by Analog-to-Digital (ADC) to derive the digital $s[n]$. The packet boundary detector (PBD) performs correlation between $s[n]$ and a pre-defined 802.11 preamble pattern to confirm an incoming packet. Once the preamble of a packet is detected, the signal central frequency is calibrated by the central frequency offset (CFO) corrector. The OFDM receiver estimates the CSI based on the calibrated $s[n]$ and the CSI is passed to the subsequent equalization module (not shown) to compensate errors prior to the packet decoding. Due to the hardware imperfection, the CSIs measured by NICs introduce the following errors.

Power control uncertainty. Limited by the hardware resolution, Automatic Gain Controller (AGC) cannot perfectly compensate the signal amplitude attenuation to the transmitted power level. The measured CSI amplitude equals to the compensated power level, which is mixed with the power control uncertainty error. According to [14], the CSI amplitude offsets in individual bands can be removed by averaging. However, if the number of CSI measurements on each channel is not sufficient, which may be the usual case due to the stringent delay constraint (§3.5), the averaging cannot perfectly eliminate the power uncertainty. The residual offset between different WiFi bands disallows a direct CSI amplitude splicing.

Sampling frequency offset (SFO). The sampling frequencies of a transmission pair exhibit an offset due to non-synchronized clocks, which can cause $s[n]$ after ADC a time shift τ_o with respect to the transmitted signal. Because clock offsets are relatively stable within a short time, τ_o will introduce near constant errors λ_o to the CSI phases measured from different sub-carriers.

Packet boundary detection (PBD) error. Due to correlator sensitivity of packet detector, the packet detection introduces another time shift τ_b, with respect to the transmitted signal [6, 31]. The timing shift τ_b causes random errors λ_b to the measured CSI phases.

Central frequency offset (CFO). The central frequencies of the transceiver cannot be perfectly synchronized. The central frequency offset is compensated by the CFO corrector, but due to the hardware imperfection, the compensation is incomplete. Signal $s[n]$ still carries residual errors, which can cause the CSI phase offsets β.

The last three error sources cause CSI phase measurement errors. Due to the diverse phase shifts from SFO and PBD, the phases of the overlapped sub-carriers measured from two consecutive bands are inconsistent (different), which impairs the CSI phase splicing. The CSI phases measured from different bands also suffer from notable offsets. In the next section, we introduce our solutions to compensate above CSI errors.

3.2 Phase error correction

We denote S as the number of sub-carriers in one WiFi band. Based on [31, 32], the reported CSI phase value ϕ_k from any sub-carrier k by WiFi NICs can be expressed:

$$\phi_k = \theta_k + k \cdot (\lambda_b + \lambda_o) + \beta, \quad (3)$$

where θ_k is the phase rotation of subcarrier k which is caused by the channel propagation, λ_b and λ_o are phase errors introduced by the packet boundary detection uncertainty and the sampling frequency offset, respectively, β is the phase error caused by the central frequency offset, and $k = 1, 2, \ldots, S$. As $\lambda_b + \lambda_o$ is multiplied by the sub-carrier index k in Eq. (3), the phase errors cross different sub-carriers are diverse among different CSI measures as shown in Figure 3. Our target is to obtain the phase value θ_k by eliminating the impact of other parameters, *i.e.*, the λ_b, the λ_o and the β. We focus on the removal of λ_b and λ_o from ϕ_k in the rest of this subsection, and introduce the removal of β when we splice the CSI phases in §3.3.

PBD phase error λ_b removal. Phase error λ_b is caused by the time shift τ_b from the packet boundary detection uncertainty. To investigate the effect of τ_b, we examine the discrete Fourier

[2] To isolate the impact of the CSI phases, we use the average phases of the two CSI traces such that the derived power delay profiles only differ in the amplitude.

[3] Similar to the experiment in Figure 4, we use the average amplitude of the two CSI traces to derive power delay profiles to avoid the impact from the amplitude.

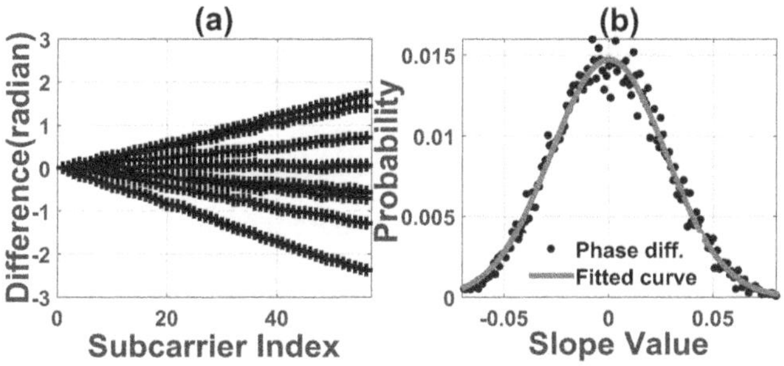

Figure 7: Phase differences cross sub-carriers and the distribution of $\Delta\lambda_b$. (a) The phase differences $k \cdot \Delta\lambda_b$ of 8 randomly CSI pairs; (b) Distribution of slope $\Delta\lambda_b$ calculated from 180 CSIs.

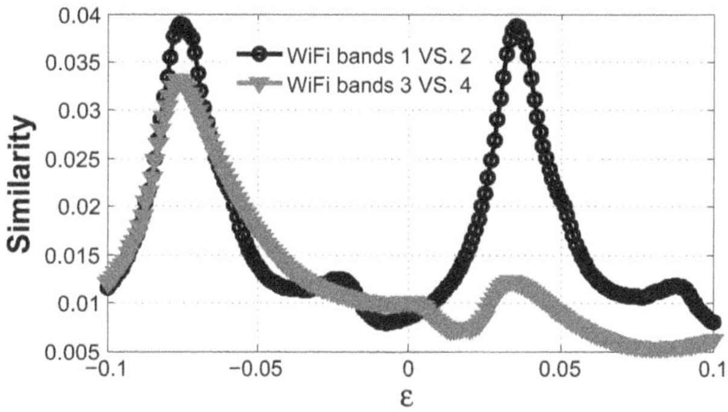

Figure 8: The power delay profile similarities for two pairs of WiFi bands when ϵ varies from -0.1 to 0.1.

transform of the channel frequency response in Eq. (4):

$$h[k] = \sum_{n=0}^{N-1} f[n] \cdot e^{-j \cdot 2\pi \cdot k \cdot n / N}, \quad (4)$$

where $h[k]$ and $f[n]$ are the discrete versions of $h(f)$ in Eq. (1) and $f(t)$ in Eq. (2), respectively, and N is the IFFT length. With a time shift τ_b in $f[n]$, Eq. (4) can be rephrased as:

$$h[k] \cdot e^{-j \cdot 2\pi \cdot k \cdot \tau_b / N} = \sum_{n=0}^{N-1} f[(n - \tau_b)_N] \cdot e^{-j \cdot 2\pi \cdot k \cdot n / N},$$

where the term $e^{-j \cdot 2\pi \cdot k \cdot \tau_b / N}$ indicates that the time shift τ_b can introduce a phase error, $2\pi \cdot k \cdot \tau_b / N$, in each sub-carrier k. Therefore, $\lambda_b = 2\pi \cdot \tau_b / N$.

To remove λ_b from each ϕ_k, we leverage an observation that the time shift τ_b varies in each packet reception but follows a Gaussian distribution with the zero mean [31]. The error λ_b thus changes accordingly in different CSI measurements and $\lambda_b \sim N(0,\sigma^2)$, where σ is the standard deviation. According to the weak law of large numbers, λ_b can be removed by averaging over the measured CSI phases ϕ_k.

To validate this observation, we perform a trial of experiments in Figure 7. In Eq. (3), λ_b is mixed with λ_o, β, and θ_k in the CSI phase ϕ_k, and we cannot directly investigate its distribution. Therefore, for the collected CSIs from the same WiFi band, we calculate the mutual phase differences of those CSIs and obtain a set of $\Delta\theta_k + k \cdot (\Delta\lambda_b + \Delta\lambda_o) + \Delta\beta = k \cdot \Delta\lambda_b + a$ for each sub-carrier k[4], where a is a constant. We thus examine the distribution of $\Delta\lambda_b$, because if $\lambda_b \sim N(0,\sigma^2)$, $\Delta\lambda_b$ should be a Gaussian with the zero mean as well. We collect 180 CSIs from a 20MHz channel within a short time interval when the environment is stable. Figure 7 (a) plots the $k \cdot \Delta\lambda_b$ value versus the sub-carrier index k for 8 randomly selected CSI pairs (we omit the constant a for the presentation clarity). Figure 7 (a) shows each line is a straight line and the slopes of those lines are different. The result indicates that λ_b is a constant to each sub-carrier in each individual measure, but varies cross different measures. To further examine its distribution, in Figure 7 (b), we divide the range $[-0.075, 0.075]$ into 100 bins on the x-axis and plot the frequency of $\Delta\lambda_o$ falling into each bin on the y-axis. After the curve fitting, we find that $\Delta\lambda_b$ indeed follows a Gaussian distribution with the zero mean.

According to the λ_b distribution, we can remove it by averaging over the measured CSI phases ϕ_ks. In principle, more measurements lead to a better error removal, but it will prolong the latency to scan each single band. In §3.5, we will determine an optimal number of CSIs collected from each band to balance this trade-off subjected to the stringent channel coherence time. Given the optimal amount $\dot{n}_i$ for any band i, we calculate:

$$\overline{\phi}_k^i = \sum_{i=1}^{\dot{n}_i} \phi_k^i(j) / \dot{n}_i, \quad (5)$$

where $\phi_k^i(j)$ stands for the j-th CSI measure from band i. After λ_b is removed, $\overline{\phi}_k^i = \theta_k^i + k \cdot \lambda_o + \beta$. In the next subsection, we introduce how to remove λ_o from $\overline{\phi}_k^i$.

SFO phase error λ_o removal. Phase error λ_o is caused by the offset of the sampling frequencies of the sender and the receiver, f_s and f_r. We denote $\zeta = \frac{f_s}{f_r} - 1$ as the fractional difference in sampling frequency, and the effect of the sampling frequency offset is to introduce a term, $e^{j \cdot \zeta' \cdot k}$, to the channel frequency response: $h'[k] = h[k] \cdot e^{j \cdot \zeta' \cdot k}$, where ζ' stands for ζ multiplied with a constant and $h[k]$ is the channel frequency response without the sampling frequency offset (Eq. (4)). Hence, $\lambda_o = \zeta'$. As the fractional frequency difference keeps stable in the order of minutes [13], λ_o is a constant during the process of the CSI splicing.

To remove λ_o from $\overline{\phi}_k^i = \theta_k^i + k \cdot \lambda_o + \beta$, obtained from Eq. (5), we leverage an observation that the power delay profiles derived from different WiFi bands should be the same after λ_o is removed (we will show in §3.3 that the phase offest β has no impact on the derived power delay profile), since they characterize the same multipath channel. For any WiFi band i, the CSI phases $\overline{\phi}_k^i$s from all S sub-carriers form a vector $\overline{\Phi}^i = [\overline{\phi}_1^i, \overline{\phi}_2^i, \ldots, \overline{\phi}_S^i]^T$. Therefore, we propose to gradually "rotate" two distinct $\overline{\Phi}^i$ and $\overline{\Phi}^j$ in the frequency domain[5] and stop when the two derived power delay profiles best match each other. We repeat this process for different pairs of WiFi bands to improve the accuracy. To quantify the likelihood of two power delay profiles, *e.g.*, P_1 and P_2, we define their similarity as:

$$\rho(P_1, P_2) = \frac{1}{||P_1 - P_2||_2}, \quad (6)$$

where the dominator essentially measures the power level differences of each multipath component in the two power delay profiles. A large $\rho(P_1, P_2)$ value indicates that P_1 and P_2 are more similar.

To illustrate this solution, we measure four different 20MHz WiFi bands, and compute the similarities for two channel pairs in Figure 8. We compensate λ_o by $\lambda_o - \epsilon$ and search for the optimal

[4] λ_o is a constant that can be removed by the deduction, which is detailed in the SFO phase error removal.

[5] We multiply $\overline{\Phi}^i$ and $\overline{\Phi}^j$ with $e^{j \cdot \epsilon \cdot k}$, and gradually vary ϵ.

Algorithm 1: SFO Phase Error Compensation

1 **for** *each WiFi band pair c* **do**
2 Record the top-two local maximal similarity values and the corresponding ϵ: $< \epsilon_1^c, \rho_1^c >$ and $< \epsilon_2^c, \rho_2^c >$.
3 Clustering on ϵ and find the cluster with the maximal similarity sum.
4 Return the cluster center as the final ϵ value.

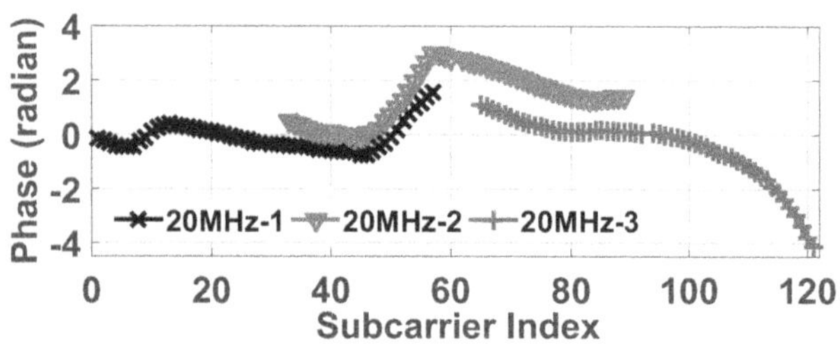

Figure 9: CSI phases after the removal of λ_s and λ_o.

ϵ for both positive and negative directions. For the first pair, we observe four local maximum points, and for the second pair, we observe three local maximum points when ϵ varies in $[-0.1, 0.1]$. According to Algorithm 1, we can determine the final ϵ as the average of ϵ_1 and ϵ_2 in Figure 8. With the optimal ϵ obtained from Algorithm 1, for each $\overline{\Phi}^i$ after the PBD phase error λ_b removal, we can further remove λ_o by $\widetilde{\Phi}^i = \overline{\Phi}^i - [\epsilon, 2\epsilon, \ldots, S\epsilon]^T$, where S is the number of subcarriers.

Although the ϵ searching introduces extra computational delays, Algorithm 1 does not need to be executed parallel to the CSI sampling in real-time. As a matter of fact, once sufficient CSIs can be obtained subjected to the stringent channel coherence time (§3.5), the latency of Algorithm 1 only impacts the frequency to generate power delay profiles to the upper-layer applications. We evaluate the computational efficiency in §4.

3.3 CSI phase splicing

Figure 9 plots the corrected CSI phases at this stage for the three 20MHz channels in Figure 3 (b). From the result, we observe that after the phase error removals of λ_b and λ_o, the shapes of the overlapped sub-carrier phases from different WiFi bands now become similar and consistent. The only barrier that remains is the offsets. In this subsection, we target to removing offsets to finally enable the phase splicing.

CSI phase offset β removal. Phase offset β is caused by the central frequency offset of the transmission pair. Through our study, we find that for individual WiFi bands, phase offset β has no impact on the derived power delay profile, *i.e.*, given a pair of CSI amplitude (ω) and phase (θ), the power delay profile derived by ω and θ is identical to the one derived by ω and $\theta + \beta$. The reason is that offsets are frequency independent. After IFFT, the error will result in a constant phase rotation term in each α_l of Eq. (2), which will not change the norm operation result. Hence the power level of each multipath component keeps unchanged. According to this observation, we can use the phase measured from any band as a reference and compensate β by calibrating the phases measured from other bands with respect to the reference.

Spliced CSI phase refinement. So far, the CSI phases measured from different channels can be spliced already. However, we find that the CSI phase accuracy can be further improved by leveraging

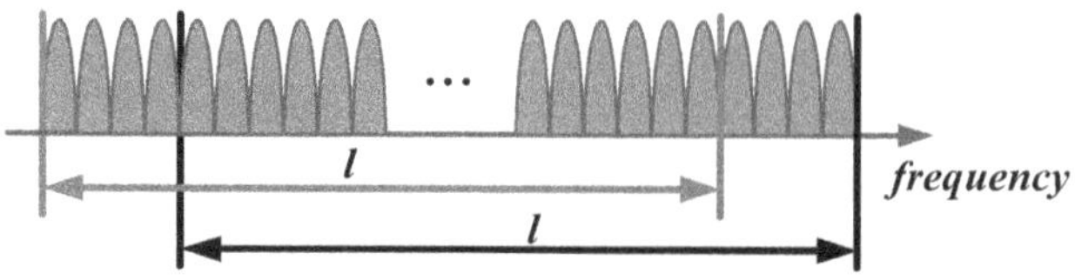

Figure 10: Spliced CSI phase refinement.

the primarily spliced result. In the SFO phase error λ_o removal, we rely on the similarity of the derived power delay profile to compensate λ_o, but the derived power delay profiles are based on the CSI from single WiFi bands with limited bandwidth. The phase error λ_o thus cannot get fully corrected using low-resolution power delay profiles. To refine the phase information, in the phase splicer, we further manually divide the spliced channel bandwidth into multiple windows illustrated in Figure 10. Each window has a much wider bandwidth, denoted as l, than each single WiFi band. We slide the window and obtain a set of l-wide phase pieces. For each phase pair, we call Algorithm 1 to estimate the SFO phase error compensator ϵ, and use their average value to further compensate the spliced CSI phase.

In Figure 10, the window size l balances a trade-off. A larger l will lead to a higher-resolution power delay profile, which potentially can better compensate the phase error λ_o. However, with a large l, the channel information carried by each divided CSI piece will be highly redundant (more overlapped sub-carriers). Two such power delay profiles will produce a large body of local maximal points in Figure 8, which are dominated by the channel information redundancy, instead of the removal of the phase error λ_o. It thus prevents to find the optimal ϵ to compensate λ_o. Therefore, the length l needs to be carefully selected. In Figure 11, we investigate this trade-off. The experimental setting is detailed in §4, where we use ranging accuracy as the metric for the evaluation. We set the window size l as a fraction of the total bandwidth that the spliced CSI covers. Initially, when we increase the window size, the ranging accuracy improves because λ_o is better compensated by higher-resolution power delay profiles. However, when l is excessive large, *e.g.*, close to 0.95, the accuracy decreases due to the unreliability in the optimal ϵ search. According to Figure 11, we set l to be $\frac{3}{4}$ of the total bandwidth that the spliced CSI covers as default in Splicer.

3.4 CSI amplitude splicing

In Figure 2, we have shown that the amplitudes of raw CSIs also exhibit significant offsets. The reason is that the power control uncertainty [8, 14], which also follow a Gaussian distribution. However, different from the CSI phases, the power uncertainty is frequency band independent, *i.e.*, the amplitudes measured from different bands follow the same distribution. Thus, for CSI amplitudes, there is no need to average them for individual WiFi bands. Instead, we can average the amplitudes after we collect all CSIs for the splicing. The total number of CSIs to collect for splicing is determined by the channel coherence time, which will be discussed and given in the next subsection.

So far, both the CSI amplitudes and phases both can be spliced. Figure 12 depicts the splicing result covering the entire 802.11n WiFi band, 200MHz, obtained from our experiments in §4.

3.5 Battle the coherence time constraint

Wireless channels are time-varying, which enforce a stringent time budget for each round of CSI splicing, since the spliced CSI

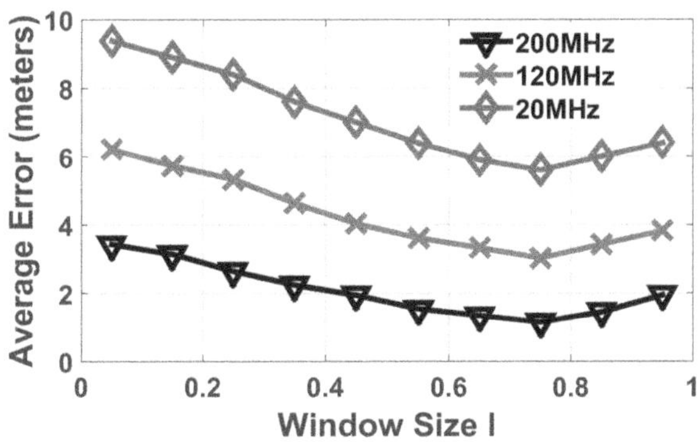

Figure 11: Empirical investigation of window size l.

is valid only when the channel condition is relatively stable. In this subsection, we first estimate the minimum number of CSIs to collect from each individual band that can fully compensate phase errors, and then propose an efficient CSI sampling scheduler to balance the trade-off between the error compensation quality in each individual band and the total bandwidth that can be afforded for the CSI splicing within the time budget.

Stringent time budget. The channel coherence time T_c can be expressed as $T_c \approx \frac{1}{2 \cdot f_d}$, where f_d stands for the Doppler shift. Previous works [7] have studied the Doppler shifts caused in typical mobile environments. For instance, when people are walking, the Doppler shifts are usually less than 12Hz, which can be translated into $T_c = 40ms$ with 2.4GHz WiFi. In Splicer, the transmission delay of each packet (without minimum payload) is around $0.2ms$, *e.g.*, approximately 200 CSIs can be collected within the time budget. In our current design, we reply on the empirical results from the literature to set T_c. We leave the cooperation with advanced channel coherence time measurement schemes [16] in Splicer as the future work of this study.

CSI measurements for each band. As aforementioned in §3.2, for each WiFi band, we need to collect sufficient CSI measures to fully compensate phase error λ_b, which is caused by the signal boundary detection uncertainty and follows a Gaussian distribution. According to the weak law of large numbers, more CSIs lead to a better compensation. However, we have a stringent time budget T_c to scan the entire WiFi band, which on the other hand limits the number of CSI collected from each WiFi band. To deal with this trade-off, we first investigate the minimum number of CSIs for each band that can achieve a given confidence level.

When we collect n CSIs from one band, for any sub-carrier k, we can calculate the average phase value $\overline{\phi}_k$ by Eq. (5). According to [2], we can define a confidence range $(\overline{\phi}_k - \frac{\sigma}{\sqrt{n}} z_{\alpha/2}, \overline{\phi}_k + \frac{\sigma}{\sqrt{n}} z_{\alpha/2})$, where σ is the standard deviation of λ_b, α is an error rate, and z_j is a normal distribution related parameter that can be obtained from a table [2]. When n increases, the range shrinks, *i.e.*, the confidence increases. The theory in [2] proves that the probability that $E[\phi_k]$ falls into this range is greater than $1 - \alpha$. Therefore, given α and the confidence range length r, the minimal number of CSIs to collect, $\dot{n}$, can be determined when $\frac{\sigma}{\sqrt{\dot{n}}} z_{\alpha/2} \leq r/2$.

To cover the entire WiFi band, we need to scan multiple (*e.g.*, C) individual WiFi bands, *e.g.*, $C = 5$ for 802.11n at 2.4GHz. However, due to the stringent time budget, it could be infeasible to collect all $C \times \dot{n}$ CSIs within T_c. Therefore, we propose to balance the trade-off between the error compensation quality in each individual

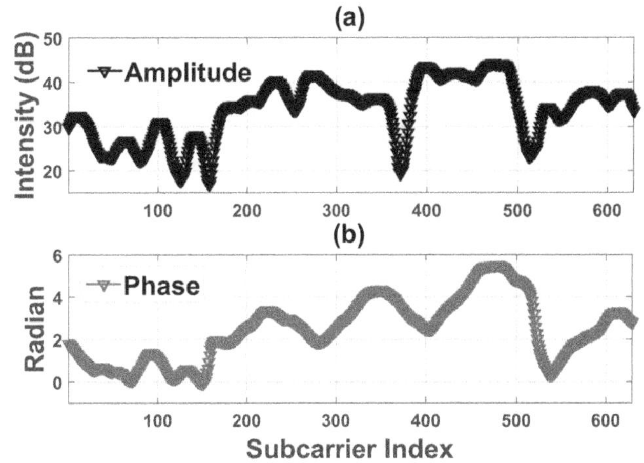

Figure 12: CSI splicing result. (a) The spliced CSI amplitude; (b) The spliced CSI phase.

band and the total bandwidth that can be afforded for the CSI splicing. Through our study, we observe that for any three consecutive WiFi bands, if the CSI phases in the first and the third channels are well compensated, they can serve as two anchors to further calibrate the CSI phase from the second band if its phase error is not fully corrected. In particular, we can rotate the CSI phase from the second band and stop when its phase differences for the overlapped sub-carriers with other two bands are minimized. With this observation, the scheduling of the CSI measurement for each band is as follows. We have three constraints:

- Collecting $\dot{n}$ CSIs from a set of WiFi bands whose indices are odd. They form anchors.
- For each even-indexed band in between, we set a lower bound that the number of CSIs collected from those even-indexed bands is greater than this bound.
- All CSIs are collected within the time budget T_c.

The scheduling objective is to maximize the total number of bands, both odd and even, that can be used for the CSI splicing. After solving this optimization problem, we can determine the optimal CSI collection assignment. When enough CSIs are collected from each band, the time delay handler informs the physical layer to send an ACK such that the sender and the receiver switch to the next band synchronously. As a contingency plan, the sender and receiver will switch back to the first channel if no packets received for a given time-out duration.

Early termination. Due to the wireless channel dynamics, the time budget we adopt from the literature may not always precisely capture the channel coherence time. It is possible that the wireless channel changes dramatically in the middle of CSI collection so that the CSIs from rest WiFi bands will become useless for splicing. To address this issue, we propose an early termination strategy to detect such a case in real time, which leverages the following observation. If the channel is stable, θ_k for any sub-carrier k of a WiFi band in Eq. (3) keeps unchanged. When we collect multiple CSIs from this band and compute their phase differences, we can obtain a set of straight lines as shown in Figure 7. Later, when the channel condition is changed, if we collect another CSI trace from the new channel and compare the phase difference with the CSI from the previous channel, the result demonstrates not a straight line. Therefore, we can apply the linear regression on the phase difference and use the regression error to indicate the level of the channel condition change.

In light of this, after receiving all CSIs for each round of CSI splicing, the receiver will not directly use them. Instead, for each individual WiFi band involved in the splicing, the receiver will compute the phase difference between the first and the last CSIs collected from this band, and apply linear regression to check the regression error. If the error is greater than a threshold, the receiver will discard all CSIs from this band, as well as all subsequent bands (we will evaluate its effectiveness in §4). CSI splicing only utilizes non-discarded bands.

4. EVALUATION

In this section, we conduct testbed-based experiments to evaluate the performance of Splicer. We introduce our experimental setting in §4.1, evaluate the efficacy of Splicer in §4.2, and report the end-to-end system performance of Splicer-enhanced CUPID in §4.3, which is one of the state-of-the-art indoor localization designs [28].

4.1 Experimental setup

We conduct experiments in a laboratory, which is a typical indoor office environment. We install five APs at five known locations. Each AP is a laptop connected to an Atheors 9580 NIC. The five APs are configured in the monitoring mode as receivers. We select 500 different locations in the laboratory and place another AP, which is set to the RootAP mode as sender, at each of these locations sequentially. At each location, the AP sender conducts multiple rounds of CSI splicing to each of the five AP receivers. To examine the accuracy of the power delay profiles derived by Splicer, we first evaluate the accuracy of the power level measured from the Line-of-Sight (LoS) path. To this end, we measure the distance between the sender and each of the receivers at all 500 different locations as the ground truth. At each location, we compare the derived distance from the power delay profile with the ground truth for evaluation. In addition to the LoS path, we also evaluate the quality of the derived power delay profiles using the power level stability for Non-Line-of-Sight (NLoS) paths.

We first provides a detailed performance analysis of Splicer in §4.2, we disable the sampling scheduler (described in §3.5), and manually control the number of scanned channels. From each channel, we collect 30 CSI traces. After that, in §4.3, we enable the sampling scheduler and evaluate the end-to-end performance with the full-version Splicer in a localization application.

4.2 Results

Phase error correction. To investigate the effectiveness of the CSI error correction designs in Splicer, we first evaluate the ranging performance to estimate the LoS path length d in each single 20MHz WiFi band without using CSI splicing. We evaluate Splicer for three different versions to investigate where the performance gains Splicer achieves come from: the full version with both λ_b and λ_o compensations, as well as two degraded versions — without λ_b compensation and without any phase error compensation. We compare the three versions against the measured ground truth to one randomly selected receiver in Figure 13. In the figure, the x-axis presents different locations and the y-axis illustrates the ranging results of each Splicer version (as well as the ground truth). Each reported accuracy value is the average from 10 measurements. From the result, we observe that without any phase error correction, the ranging performance is highly unreliable. After the phase error λ_b removal, the ranging accuracy Splicer achieves has been dramatically improved, but it is still far away from the ground truth. After the compensations of λ_b and λ_o, we find that the accuracy

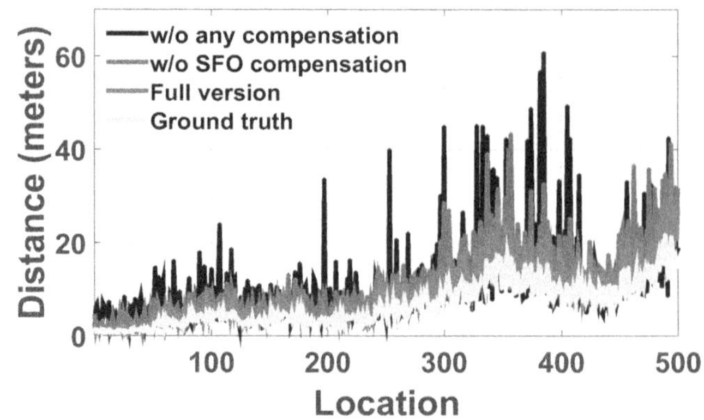

Figure 13: Ranging results at 500 different locations by different versions of Splicer in a single WiFi band.

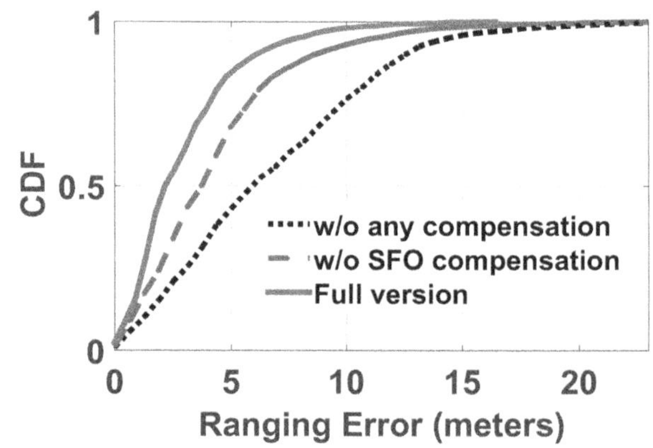

Figure 14: CDF of ranging errors from a single band.

is very close to the true distance value between the sender and the receiver at different locations.

In Figure 14, we provide detailed statistical results for the performance achieved by different Splicer versions in Figure 13. From the result, we see that when the raw CSI phases are used, the ranging error is 10.7m for 80% of the measurements. The median and the maximum errors are 6.1m and 24m, respectively, compared with the ground truth. After the compensation of phase error λ_b, the ranging error is reduced to 6.3m for 80% measurements. After the removal of both λ_b and λ_o, the ranging error is less than 4.3m for 80% of cases. The improvement is as high as 4.8m on average compared with the traditional ranging performance using the raw phase information.

CSI splicing. In Figure 15, we evaluate the ranging performance of Splicer after we enable CSI splicing from different WiFi bands. As the power delay profile resolution is determined by the channel bandwidth, we select two representative bandwidths after splicing, 200MHz that is the total bandwidth allocated to 802.11n and 120MHz that is in between the entire WiFi band and each single WiFi band. We select all spliced CSIs with these two selected bandwidths to report the the performance. As a benchmark, we also include the performance of the full version Splicer in 20MHz for comparison.

Figure 15 plots CDF of the ranging errors from those three approaches. From the result, we find that the performance of Splicer

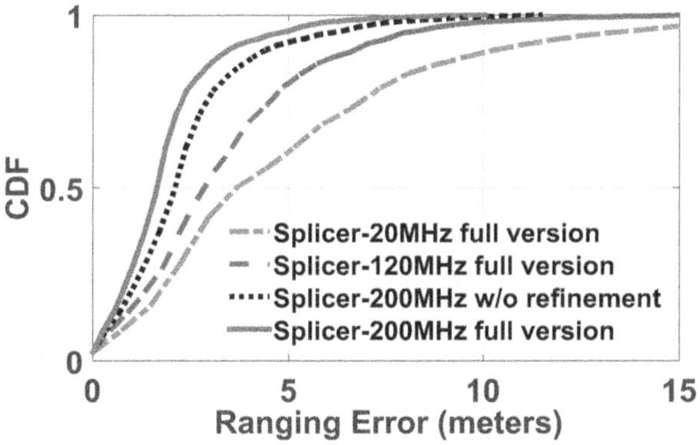

Figure 15: CDF of ranging errors with CSI splicing.

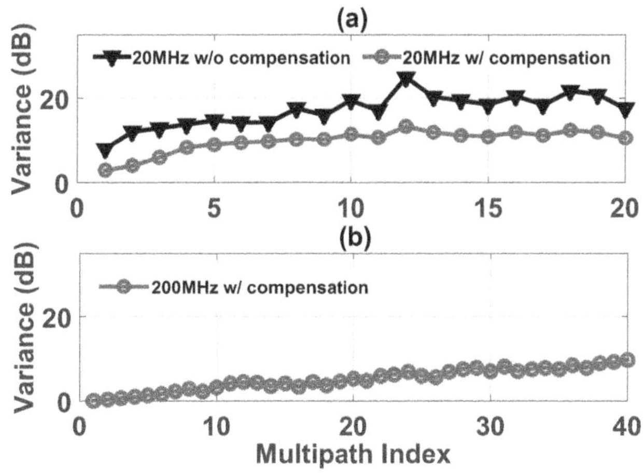

Figure 16: Measured power level variance for NLoS path components in the derived power delay profiles. (a) In 20MHz WiFi band; (b) In 200MHz WiFi band.

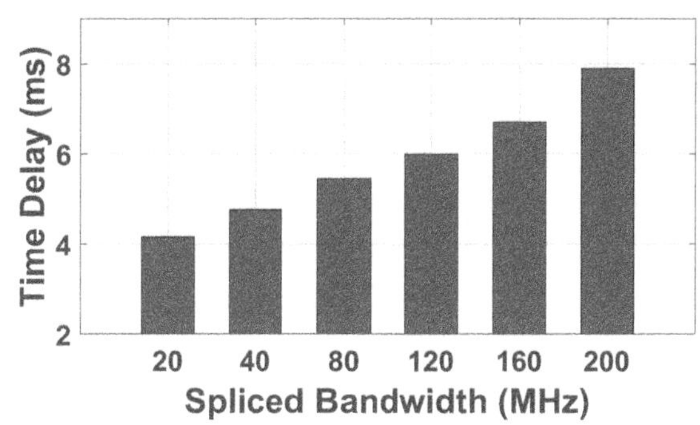

Figure 17: Computation delay of Splicer.

using merely a single WiFi band is still limited, even with the CSI error correction. In general, the wider the bandwidth Splicer uses, the smaller error the ranging can achieve. The performance gain stems from more accurate power level measurement of the LoS path. According to the statistics, on average Splicer-120MHz and Splicer-200MHz can outperform Splicer-20MHz by 22.7% and 55.5%, respectively. The performance gain of Splicer stems from both the CSI splicing as well as the CSI phase refinement (§3.2). In Figure 15, we also show the performance gain the phase refinement provides. From the result, we see that the CSI phase refinement can reduce the ranging error by $0.42m$ approximately.

Non-line-of-sight paths. In Figures 13 to 15, we have evaluated the LoS power accuracy in the derived power delay profiles. In this experiment, we investigate the quality of the derived power delay profiles for all other NLoS paths. In practice, the absolute power level of a NLoS path is not directly useful in applications. Instead, the relative change of the power level of each NLoS path indicates the multipath channel dynamics, which has been used for activity or gesture recognitions [24, 33, 35]. To this end, we randomly select 10 locations in the laboratory. At each location, the transmission pair performs multiple rounds of CSI splicing. We evaluate the stability of the measured power levels for NLoS paths.

Figure 16 depicts the results. In Figure 16 (a), we examine the NLoS path power level stability using a single 20MHz WiFi channel. However, we observe that without the phase error compensation, the power variance is high, *e.g.*, around 16 dB, even the pair of transmitters are static at their locations. Our CSI error compensation designs can reduce the variance to be less than 10 dB on average for single WiFi bands. In Figure 16 (b), due to the CSI splicing, we can derive higher-resolution power delay profiles. Hence, the measured power level for each multipath component is aggregated from fewer non-distinguishable multipaths (§2), which should suffer from even less uncertainty. The result in Figure 16 (b) is consistent to our analysis, which shows that the power level variance for NLos paths in the derived power delay profiles using 200MHz spliced bandwidth is less than 5.2dB in our experiment.

Computational delay. We evaluate the computational delay of Splicer on commodity WiFi APs to investigate its frequency to generate new power delay profiles to upper-layer applications. We examine the absolute computation delays for Splicer to complete one round of CSI splicing with different aggregated bandwidths in Figure 17. Overall, the computation delay increases when more bands are spliced, since we need to compare more pairs of single bands for the phase error λ_o removal. From Figure 17, we find that the delays increase from $4.1ms$ to $7.9ms$ when the total bandwidth varies from 20MHz to 200MHz. We suppose the channel coherence time budget is $50ms$. With the maximum bandwidth, one round of CSI splicing can be finished within $60ms$. Therefore, Splicer can generate 16 new power delay profiles in one second, which fits the needs of most mobile applications [5, 11, 18, 19, 28].

4.3 Case study: indoor localization

In §4.2, we have evaluated the accuracy of the derived power delay profiles by Splicer. With high resolution power delay profiles, the performance of a plethora of upper-layer applications, *e.g.*, localization, object tracking, gesture recognition, etc., can be significantly improved. In this subsection, we take localization as a vehicle to demonstrate this capability of Splicer.

4.3.1 Case study overview

We integrate Splicer into the recent single-AP location approach CUPID [28]. In CUPID, a mobile user can locate its location as follows. The mobile device of the user transmits a packet to an AP with known location. The AP extracts the CSI upon receiving this packet and derives the power delay profile. According to the power level of the LoS path, the AP can estimate this path length. On the other hand, the AP further apply the MUSIC algorithm on the CSI to compute its pseudo spectrum, which can approximate the signal arrival direction from the LoS path. According to the path length

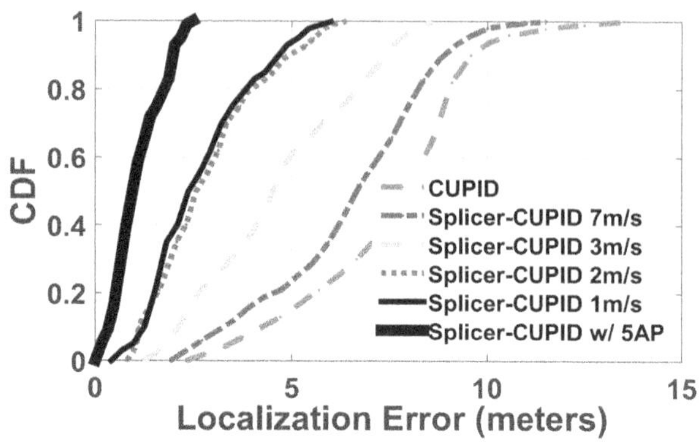

Figure 18: CDF of localization errors using the original CUPID and the enhanced CUPID by Splicer.

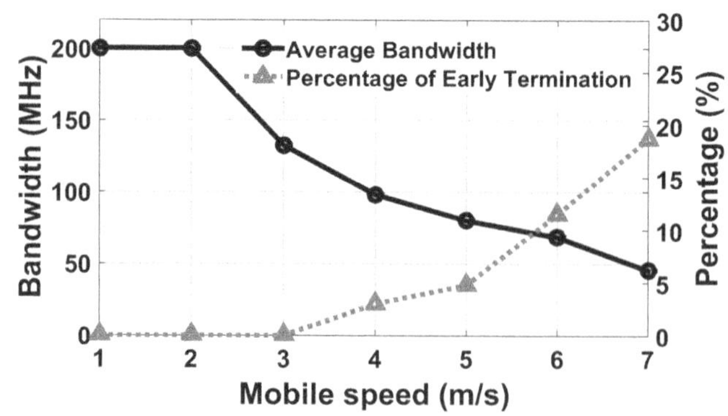

Figure 19: Bandwidth used for localization under different moving speeds. (Left) Spliced bandwidth; (right) Percentages of early terminations.

and the signal arrival direction, the AP can locate the mobile user and send the localization result back to the user.

To enhance CUPID, we use the spliced CSI as the system input and keep the rest of the CUPID design unchanged. To evaluate the performance, we install one AP in the laboratory with known location and deploy one AP on a robot. The robot is programmed to move along a predefined trajectory with a known speed. According to the time stamp contained in each packet, we can calculate the instant location of the robot when the mobile AP transmits this packet. To evaluate the end-to-end system performance, we enable the sampling scheduler in Splicer.

4.3.2 *Results*

Localization accuracy. In Figure 18 (a), we compare the performance of the original CUPID and the enhanced CUPID by Splicer, denoted as Splicer-CUPID. We vary the moving speeds of the robot in the experiment. Since the localization in the original CUPID depends on a single CSI measurement, the localization performance of CUPID is not impacted by the moving speed of the robot. For Splicer-CUPID, a higher moving speed leads to a shorter channel coherence time. As a consequence, fewer WiFi bands can be included in each round of CSI splicing and the localization accuracy will decrease. From Figure 18, we find that in general, the localization accuracy of CUPID is not quite accurate, *e.g.*, around $8m$ for 80% of localizations, which is consistent to the performance reported in [28]. For Splicer-CUPID, with a normal moving speed of a person ($< 2m/s$), the accuracy can be dramatically improved, *e.g.*, the median localization error is $2.3m$ and $2.5m$ when the speed is $1m/s$ and $2m/s$, respectively. The localization error is less than $6.4m$ throughout the experiment. With an even higher moving speed, *e.g.*, $7m/s$, Splicer-CUPID still outperforms CUPID.

In [28], the authors propose an AP selection scheme to further improve the localization accuracy by harnessing a dense AP deployment. According to the experiment results in [28], the localization accuracy of Splicer-CUPID using a single AP achieves comparable performance to CUPID with 5 APs, which can significantly improve the usefulness of indoor localizations. In Figure 18, we also leverage such an improvement opportunity. The result shows that the gain from Splicer-CUPID is significant. Localization errors are reduced to $1.75m$ for 80% cases and the median error is $0.95m$ when 5 APs are used. Although more APs may improve the localization performance, if the ranging accuracy is not high at the first place, improvement with more APs is limited.

Impact of moving speeds. In Figure 19 (left y-axis), we investigate the total bandwidth that can be spliced using Splicer with respect to different moving speeds of transmitters. In general, a higher speed leads to a shorter channel coherence time. As a result, CSI traces are spliced from fewer WiFi channels and the power delay profile resolution is lower. From Figure 19, we see that Splicer can make full use of the 200MHz available WiFi frequency band, when the speed is smaller than $2m/s$. The small localization errors observed in this case in Figure 18 is compatible with such an observation. When we accelerate the moving speed from $3m/s$ to $6m/s$, the utilized bandwidth drops from 130MHz to 60MHz, which, however, is still wider than a single WiFi channel, *i.e.* 20MHz or 40MHz. Further more, the bandwidth will drop to 45.5MHz when the speed increases to $7m/s$, which is comparable to one single 40MHz channel. Nevertheless, Splicer-CUPID still improve the localization performance since Splicer compensates the CSI measurement errors.

In Figure 18, we further examine the percentages of early terminations (§3.5) occurred in our experiment, in Figure 19 (right y-axis). From the result, we see that the early termination strategy can discover 4.8% to 18.7% rapid channel varying within the channel coherence time budget.

Performance in different environments. In addition to the evaluation in the laboratory environment, we further conduct experiments in other representative environments for localization, including a corridor, a car park, and a lecture hall. Figure 20 plots the median localization error for Splicer-CUPID in comparison with the original CUPID with normal walking speed ($1m/s$). From the results, we see that the localization error of the original CUPID design can be largely reduced by Splicer-CUPID, *e.g.*, 70.9% in laboratory, 74.0% in corridor, 74.2% in car park, and 76% in the lecture hall. In summary, Splicer achieves general performance gains with different environments.

5. RELATED WORK

Channel sounding. Measuring the wideband channel frequency response requires high-end hardware with high sampling frequencies [4, 20]. The authors in [21, 22] develop systems to measure channel frequency responses from a group of narrow bands to approximate a wideband channel. In [15], the receiver only listens to a few harmonics of a wideband signal each time and then can reconstruct the wideband frequency response. Such a design does not require the modification at the sender. In addition, CSI-SF proposed in [3] can estimate the channel state information for multi-streams using the single stream measurement result. Some ToA-based localization approaches [41, 42] also propose to increase the resolu-

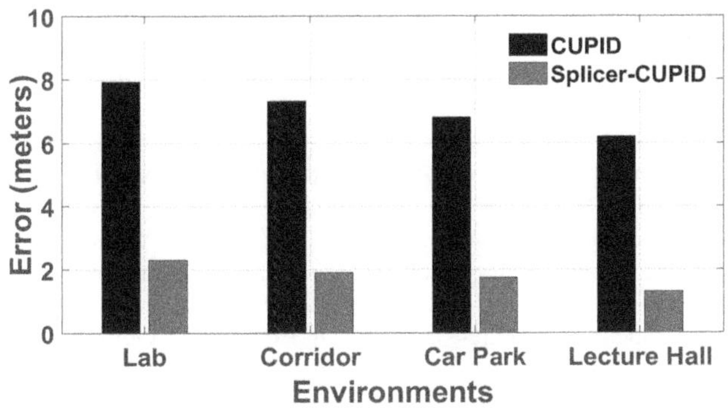

Figure 20: Localization errors in different environments using the original CUPID and the enhanced CUPID by Splicer.

tion using the channel combination, however, only with Software-Defined-Radio. Although Splicer shares a similar principle with those existing works, most of them require tight synchronization between the sender and receiver, *e.g.* devices are connected by the same clock or use GPS and atomic clocks. In this work, however, we meet and address particular challenges due to the hardware imperfection and stringent channel coherence delay constraint, which do not exist in any of existing works. In addition, Splicer can be integrated into commodity NICs without any hardware modification.

CSI phase calibration. Prior works also notice that the CSI traces reported by WiFi NICs contain phase errors introduced by hardware [40, 43, 44]. ArrayPhaser [6] enables the phased array signal processing on commodity WiFi devices. However, ArrayPhaser does not correct any of those phase errors, instead they just treat the phase values measured from one NIC as the reference to calibrate the phase values of other NICs. Hence, they cannot truthfully remove the phase values to derive precise power delay profiles. Prior works [28, 36] try to synchronize the phases from two consecutive received CSIs via a linear transform. After the transformation, if the two measurements are from the same multipath channel, even the collected CSIs are different due to hardware noises, the transformation on these two CSIs leads to the same result, which could be used as fingerprint for localization. Some recent works aim to explicitly correct CSI phase errors, *e.g.*, MegaMIMO [25]. However, MegaMIMO requires both nanosecond-level synchronization and the access to the raw signal at PHY layer, which are not available on commodity NICs. In summary, existing works cannot directly remove measurement errors from CSIs reported by commodity WiFi NICs, and hence cannot address the challenges we met in Splicer.

Power delay profile based applications. At different locations, the received power delay profiles will be different, which can makes them a good choice for the fingerprint-based localization design [29, 39]. On the other hand, the Line-of-Sight information can be directly inferred from the power delay profile [36]. The power level of the LoS path can also be used to ranging between a pair of transmitters [28, 37]. Indoor localization based on the ranging results requires no dense AP deployments, no manual fingerprinting site survey, and no sophisticated AP hardware [28, 37]. For activity recognition, although the detailed relation between the multipath channel variance and the different activities is unknown, recent works propose to learn the inner relation. For example, to detect the existence of human beings [46], to count the number of people moving around [38], to detect human falling down in [9], and recognize different types of human activities [1, 30, 35]. Splicer can benefit all above applications since we can obtain a wider CSI containing more frequency band information to derive a higher-resolution power delay profile, which more precisely describes the multipath channel.

6. CONCLUSION

This paper presents Splicer to derive precise power delay profiles on commodity WiFi devices. The Splicer design leverages the CSIs measured from individual WiFi bands to obtain the CSI of an equivalent wider WiFi band after the CSI splicing, based on which Splicer can derive high-resolution power delay profiles. The major design challenge is that the CSIs collected from commodity NICs do not merely contain the channel information. They are mixed with rich hardware errors. We propose a series of techniques to address the challenge and also battle the stringent channel coherence time constraint. Our experiments on commodity WiFi NICs report high accuracy of the power delay profiles derived by Splicer. The CSI measurement errors stem from several signal-processing modules in the physical layer of standard 802.11 NICs, including the AGC, signal sampler, and packet detector, so Splicer is general for different WiFi chipsets and independent to the hardware. Due to the channel hopping by Splicer, the normal communication of other users to an AP may be interrupted, which is a limitation of the current design. We believe that such a limitation can be mitigated by employing less-active or dedicated APs for Splicer. In the paper, we use thet indoor localization application to showcase that Splicer can immediately benefit existing motion- or location-based systems. In the future work, we will study how the high-resolution power delay profile derived from Splicer can be utilized to support more interesting applications like, object tracking, gesture recognition, and so on.

Acknowledgement

We would like to thank the anonymous reviewers and shepherd for their valuable comments and suggestions that improve the quality of this paper. This work is supported by Singapore MOE AcRF Tier 2 Grant MOE2012-T2-1-070 and NTU Nanyang Assistant Professorship (NAP) Grant M4080738.020.

References

[1] F. Adib, Z. Kabelac, D. Katabi, and R. C. Miller. 3d tracking via body radio reflections. In *Proc. of USENIX NSDI*, 2014.

[2] A. Azzalini. A class of distributions which includes the normal ones. *Scandinavian journal of statistics*, 1985.

[3] R. Crepaldi, J. Lee, R. Etkin, S.-J. Lee, and R. Kravets. CSI-SF: Estimating wireless channel state using CSI sampling and fusion. In *Proc. of IEEE INFOCOM*, 2012.

[4] T. Felhauer, P. Baier, W. Konig, and W. Mohr. Optimum spread spectrum signals for wideband channel sounding. *Electronics Letters*, 1993.

[5] Y. Gao, W. Dong, C. Chen, J. Bu, T. Chen, M. Xia, X. Liu, and X. Xu. Domo: passive per-packet delay tomography in wireless ad-hoc networks. In *Proc. of IEEE ICDCS*, 2014.

[6] J. Gjengset, G. McPhillips, and K. Jamieson. Arrayphaser: Enabling signal processing on WiFi access points. *Proc. of ACM MobiCom*, 2014.

[7] A. Goldsmith. *Wireless communications*. Cambridge university press, 2005.

[8] D. Halperin, W. Hu, A. Sheth, and D. Wetherall. Predictable 802.11 packet delivery from wireless channel measurements. In *Proc. of ACM SIGCOMM*, 2010.

[9] C. Han, K. Wu, Y. Wang, and L. Ni. WiFall: Device-free fall detection by wireless networks. In *Proc. of IEEE INFOCOM*, 2014.

[10] J. Han, C. Qian, X. Wang, D. Ma, J. Zhao, P. Zhang, W. Xi, and Z. Jiang. Twins: Device-free object tracking using passive tags. In *Proc. of IEEE INFOCOM*, 2014.

[11] L. He, L. Fu, L. Zheng, Y. Gu, P. Cheng, J. Chen, and J. Pan. Esync: An energy synchronized charging protocol for rechargeable wireless sensor networks. In *Proc. of ACM MobiHoc*, 2014.

[12] IEEE Standard for Information Technology—Part 11: Wireless LAN Medium Access Control (MAC) and Physical Layer Specifications, Mar. 2012.

[13] S. Jana and S. K. Kasera. On fast and accurate detection of unauthorized wireless access points using clock skews. In *Proc. of ACM MobiCom*, 2008.

[14] V. Jimenez, M. Fernandez-Getino Garcia, F. Serrano, and A. Armada. Design and implementation of synchronization and agc for ofdm-based wlan receivers. *IEEE Transactions on Consumer Electronics*, 2004.

[15] B. Kempke, P. Pannuto, and P. Dutta. Harmonia: Wideband spreading for accurate indoor rf localization. In *Proc. of ACM HotWireless*, 2014.

[16] M. Khalid, Y. Wang, I. Butun, H.-j. Kim, I.-h. Ra, and R. Sankar. Coherence time-based cooperative mac protocol 1 for wireless ad hoc networks. In *EURASIP Journal on Wireless Communications and Networking*, 2011.

[17] H. Liu, Y. Gan, J. Yang, S. Sidhom, Y. Wang, Y. Chen, and F. Ye. Push the limit of wifi based localization for smartphones. In *Proc. of ACM MobiCom*, 2012.

[18] Q. Ma, K. Liu, X. Xiao, Z. Cao, and Y. Liu. Link scanner: Faulty link detection for wireless sensor networks. In *Proc. of IEEE INFOCOM*, 2013.

[19] A. T. Mariakakis, S. Sen, J. Lee, and K.-H. Kim. SAIL: Single access point-based indoor localization. In *Proc. of ACM MobiSys*, 2014.

[20] A. Molina, P. Fannin, and J. Timoney. Generation of optimum excitation waveforms for mobile radio channel sounding. *IEEE Transactions on Vehicular Technology*, 1995.

[21] D. Molkdar and P. Matthews. Measurements and characterization of the UHF mobile radio channel. part 1: Measurements over the band 853-885 MHz. *Electronic and Radio Engineers, Journal of the Institution of*, 1988.

[22] K. Pahlavan and A. H. Levesque. *Wireless information networks*. John Wiley & Sons, 2005.

[23] J. Parsons, D. Demery, and A. Turkmani. Sounding techniques for wideband mobile radio channels: a review. *Communications, Speech and Vision, IEE Proceedings I*, 1991.

[24] Q. Pu, S. Gupta, S. Gollakota, and S. Patel. Whole-home gesture recognition using wireless signals. In *Proc. of ACM MobiCom*, 2013.

[25] H. S. Rahul, S. Kumar, and D. Katabi. Jmb: Scaling wireless capacity with user demands. In *Proc. of ACM SIGCOMM*, 2014.

[26] T. S. Rappaport et al. *Wireless communications: principles and practice*. prentice hall PTR New Jersey, 1996.

[27] S. Sen, R. R. Choudhury, and S. Nelakuditi. Spinloc: Spin once to know your location. In *Proc. of ACM HotMobile*, 2012.

[28] S. Sen, J. Lee, K.-H. Kim, and P. Congdon. Avoiding multipath to revive inbuilding WiFi localization. In *Proc. of ACM MobiSys*, 2013.

[29] S. Sen, B. Radunovic, R. R. Choudhury, and T. Minka. You are facing the mona lisa: Spot localization using PHY layer information. In *Proc. of ACM MobiSys*, 2012.

[30] L. Shangguan, Z. Yang, A. X. Liu, Z. Zhou, and Y. Liu. Relative localization of rfid tags using spatial-temporal phase profiling. In *Proc. of USENIX NSDI*, 2015.

[31] M. Speth, S. Fechtel, G. Fock, and H. Meyr. Optimum receiver design for wireless broad-band systems using OFDM. i. *IEEE Transactions on Communications*, 1999.

[32] J. K. Tan. An adaptive orthogonal frequency division multiplexing baseband modem for wideband wireless channels. Master's thesis, Massachusetts Institute of Technology, 2006.

[33] G. Wang, Y. Zou, Z. Zhou, K. Wu, and L. M. Ni. We can hear you with Wi-Fi! In *Proc. of ACM MobiCom*, 2014.

[34] L. Wang, Y. He, Y. Liu, W. Liu, J. Wang, and N. Jing. It is not just a matter of time: oscillation-free emergency navigation with sensor networks. In *Proc. of IEEE RTSS*, 2012.

[35] Y. Wang, J. Liu, Y. Chen, M. Gruteser, J. Yang, and H. Liu. E-eyes: Device-free location-oriented activity identification using fine-grained WiFi signatures. In *Proc. of ACM MobiCom*, 2014.

[36] C. Wu, Z. Yang, Z. Zhou, K. Qian, Y. Liu, and M. Liu. Phaseu: Real-time LOS identification with wifi. In *Proc. of IEEE INFOCOM*, 2014.

[37] K. Wu, J. Xiao, Y. Yi, M. Gao, and L. Ni. FILA: Fine-grained indoor localization. In *Proc. of IEEE INFOCOM*, 2012.

[38] W. Xi, J. Zhao, X.-Y. Li, K. Zhao, S. Tang, X. Liu, and Z. Jiang. Electronic frog eye: Counting crowd using WiFi. In *Proc. of IEEE INFOCOM*, 2014.

[39] J. Xiao, K. Wu, Y. Yi, and L. Ni. FIFS: Fine-grained indoor fingerprinting system. In *Proc. of IEEE ICCCN*, 2012.

[40] J. Xiong and K. Jamieson. Arraytrack: A fine-grained indoor location system. In *Proc. of USENIX NSDI*, 2013.

[41] J. Xiong, K. Jamieson, and K. Sundaresan. Synchronicity: Pushing the envelope of fine-grained localization with distributed mimo. In *Proc. of ACM HotWireless*, 2014.

[42] J. Xiong, K. Sundaresan, and K. Jamieson. Tonetrack: Overcoming bandwidth constraints for indoor wireless localization. In *Proc. of ACM MobiCom*, 2015.

[43] L. Yang, Y. Chen, X.-Y. Li, C. Xiao, M. Li, and Y. Liu. Tagoram: Real-time tracking of mobile rfid tags to high precision using cots devices. In *Proc. of ACM MobiCom*, 2014.

[44] L. Yang, J. Han, Y. Qi, C. Wang, T. Gu, and Y. Liu. Season: Shelving interference and joint identification in large-scale rfid systems. In *Proc. of IEEE INFOCOM*, 2011.

[45] L. Zhang, K. Liu, Y. Jiang, X.-Y. Li, Y. Liu, and P. Yang. Montage: Combine frames with movement continuity for realtime multi-user tracking. In *Proc. of IEEE INFOCOM*, 2014.

[46] Z. Zhou, Z. Yang, C. Wu, L. Shangguan, and Y. Liu. Omnidirectional coverage for device-free passive human detection. *IEEE Transactions on Parallel and Distributed Systems*, 2014.

Understanding and Modeling of WiFi Signal Based Human Activity Recognition

Wei Wang† Alex X. Liu†‡ Muhammad Shahzad‡ Kang Ling† Sanglu Lu†
†State Key Laboratory for Novel Software Technology, Nanjing University, China
‡Dept. of Computer Science and Engineering, Michigan State University, USA
ww@nju.edu.cn, {alexliu,shahzadm}@cse.msu.edu, lingkang@smail.nju.edu.cn, sanglu@nju.edu.cn

Abstract

Some pioneer WiFi signal based human activity recognition systems have been proposed. Their key limitation lies in the lack of a model that can quantitatively correlate CSI dynamics and human activities. In this paper, we propose CARM, a CSI based human Activity Recognition and Monitoring system. CARM has two theoretical underpinnings: a CSI-speed model, which quantifies the correlation between CSI value dynamics and human movement speeds, and a CSI-activity model, which quantifies the correlation between the movement speeds of different human body parts and a specific human activity. By these two models, we quantitatively build the correlation between CSI value dynamics and a specific human activity. CARM uses this correlation as the profiling mechanism and recognizes a given activity by matching it to the best-fit profile. We implemented CARM using commercial WiFi devices and evaluated it in several different environments. Our results show that CARM achieves an average accuracy of greater than 96%.

Categories and Subject Descriptors

C2.1 [**Network Architecture and Design**]: Wireless communication

General Terms

Experimentation,Measurement

Keywords

Channel State Information (CSI);WiFi; Activity Recognition;

1. INTRODUCTION

1.1 Motivation

Human activity recognition is the core technology that enables a wide variety of applications such as health care, smart homes, fitness tracking, and building surveillance. Traditional approaches use cameras [6], radars [2], or wearable sensors [7, 33]. However, camera based approaches have the fundamental limitations of requiring line of sight with enough lighting and breaching human privacy potentially. Low cost 60 GHz radar solutions have limited operation range of just tens of centimeters [2]. Wearable sensors based approaches are inconvenient sometimes because of the sensors that users have to wear. Recently, WiFi signal based human activity recognition systems, such as WiSee [17], E-eyes [27], and WiHear [26], have been proposed based on the observation that different human activities introduce different multi-path distortions in WiFi signals. WiSee uses USRP to capture the OFDM signals and measures the Doppler shift in signals reflected by human bodies to recognize nine gestures. E-eyes uses Channel State Information (CSI) histograms as fingerprints for recognizing daily human activities such as brushing teeth. WiHear uses specialized directional antennas to obtains CSI variations caused by lip movement for recognizing spoken words. Their key advantages over camera and sensor based approaches are that they do not require lighting, provide better coverage as they can operate through walls, preserve user privacy, and do not require users to carry any devices as they rely on the WiFi signals reflected by humans.

MobiCom'15, September 7–11, 2015, Paris, France.
 ISBN 978-1-4503-3619-2/15/09 ...$15.00.
DOI: http://dx.doi.org/10.1145/2789168.2790093.

1.2 Limitations of Prior Art

The key limitation of these pioneer WiFi based human activity recognition systems is the lack of a model that can quantitatively correlate CSI dynamics and human activities. As such, these systems mostly rely on the statistical characteristics of WiFi signals, such as Doppler movement directions and distributions of signal strength, to distinguish different human activities. The lack of such a model limits the further development of WiFi based human activity recognition technologies. Without such a model, it is difficult to understand the correlation between WiFi signal dynamics and human activities. Furthermore, without such a model, it is difficult to optimize the performance of such systems due to the lack of adjustable parameters, and we have to resort to trial-and-error for performance optimization.

1.3 Proposed Approach

In this paper, we propose CARM, a CSI based human Activity Recognition and Monitoring system. CARM consists of two Commercial Off-The-Shelf (COTS) WiFi devices as shown in Figure 1, one for continuously sending signals, which can be a router, and one for continuously receiving signals, which can be a laptop. When a human activity is performed in the range of these two devices, on the WiFi signal receiver end, CARM recognizes the human activity based on how the CSI value changes. CARM has two theoretical underpinnings that we propose in this paper: a *CSI-speed model* and a *CSI-activity model*. Our CSI-speed model quantifies the correlation between CSI value dynamics and human movement speeds. Our CSI-activity model quantifies the correlation between the movement speeds of different human body parts and a specific human activity. By these two models, we quantitatively build the correlation between CSI value dynamics and a specific human activity. CARM uses this quantitative correlation as the profiling mechanism and recognizes a given activity by matching it to the best-fit profile.

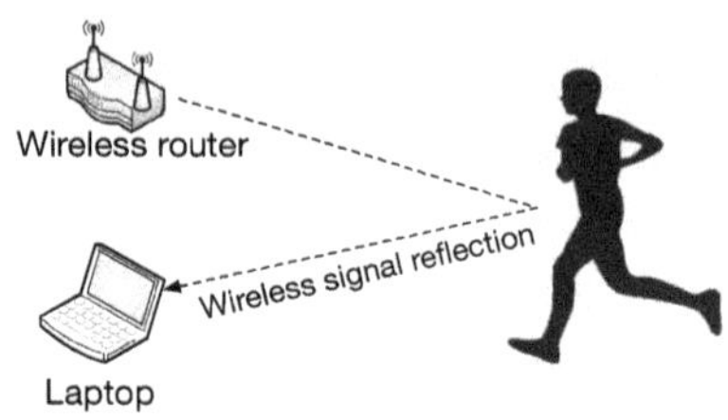

Figure 1: CARM System

Our CSI-speed model and CSI-activity model advance the state-of-the-art on WiFi signal based human activity recognition from two fronts. First, they provide us the theoretical basis to understand, even quantitatively, the relationship between CSI value dynamics and human movement speeds, and the relationship between the movement speeds of different human body parts and human activities. Regarding the relationship between CSI value dynamics and human movement speeds, for example, our model shows that high-speed body part movement generates high-frequency changes in CSI values. Regarding the relationship between the movement speeds of different human body parts and human activities, taking the activity of falling down as an example, our model shows that it can be characterized as a sudden increase in body movement speed in less than one second. Second, these two models provide us the tunable parameters to optimize the performance of WiFi signal based human activity recognition. For example, according to our models, the CSI sampling rate should be chosen as 800 samples per second because the typical human movement speed corresponds to CSI components of lower than 300 Hz.

1.4 Technical Challenges and Our Solutions

The first technical challenge is to estimate human movement speeds from CSI values based on our CSI-speed model. This is challenging because the CSI measurements at the receiver are mixed WiFi signals arrived from multiple paths, which changes as human moves. Furthermore, different human body parts move at different speeds for a given activity and the WiFi signals reflected by different body parts are also mixed at the receiver. Our key observation is that these signals are linearly combined so that their frequencies are preserved when they are mixed together. Therefore, we use Discrete Wavelet Transform (DWT) to separate the frequency components that represent different movement speeds. The advantage of DWT is that it provides a proper tradeoff between time and frequency resolution and enables the measurement of both fast and slow activities.

The second challenge is to build the CSI-activity model that is robust for different humans. For the same activity, to a certain degree, different people perform it differently and even the same person performs it differently at different times. To address this challenge, we propose a Hidden Markov Model (HMM) based human activity recognition approach. We use the patterns of movement speeds for different activities to build their corresponding HMM based models. The features that we extract to infer the speed patterns are only affected by movement speeds of the body and are relatively agonistic to environmental changes. This enables us to recognize activities even when the environment changes. We choose HMM because of its inherent capability to recognize the same activities that are done at different speeds. To recognize a sample of an unknown activity, we evaluate the unknown samples against HMMs of all activities and find the model that gives the highest likelihood.

The third challenge is that CSI values are too noisy to be directly used for human activity recognition. Even in a static environment without any human activity, CSI values fluctuate because WiFi devices are susceptible to surrounding electromagnetic noises. Moreover, the internal state changes in WiFi devices, *e.g.*, transmission rate adaptation and transmission power adaptation often introduce impulse and burst noises in CSI values. General purpose denoising methods, such as low-pass filters or median filters, do not perform well in removing these impulse and bursty noises for two reasons: First, the sampling rates that these methods require are much higher than the frequency of the WiFi signal. Second, the noise density in CSI values is too high for traditional filters, which only work well for low density noise. In this paper, we propose a principal component analysis (PCA) based CSI denoising scheme. This scheme is based on our observation that the signal fluctuations caused by body movements in all subcarriers of the CSI values are correlated.

The fourth challenge is to capture body movements in the presence of carrier frequency offset (CFO). CFO is the dynamically changing difference in carrier frequencies between a pair of WiFi devices, which occurs due to the minor physical differences in hardware and other factors such as temperature changes [8]. CFO causes the phase values of the received signal to change, making it hard to distinguish whether the phase value changed is due to CFO or due to human movement. To address this challenge, we use the CSI signal power to infer the body movement. We show that CSI signal power is not affected by CFO, but retains information about the movement speeds of the body.

The fifth challenge is to automatically detect the start and end of a human activity. To address this challenge, we use the eigenvectors obtained from PCA. The key idea is that in the absence of any activity, the time-series of CSI values contain random noise and consequently, the signal eigenvector varies randomly. During a human activity, the signals in subcarriers become correlated and the signal eigenvector becomes smooth. We capture the smoothness of the eigenvector by calculating its high-frequency energy and compare it to a dynamically adapting threshold to detect start and end.

1.5 Key Technical Novelty and Results

The key technical novelty of this paper is two fold. First, we propose the CSI-speed model and the CSI-activity model to quantify the correlation between CSI value dynamics and a specific human activity. Second, we propose a set of signal processing techniques, such as PCA based denoising and DWT based feature extraction, for human activity recognition based on the CSI-speed model and the CSI-activity model. The key technical depth of this paper lies in the signal processing aspect such as the theoretical analysis of the correlation between CSI values of subcarriers and the relationship between multi-path speeds and CFR power. We implemented CARM on commercial WiFi devices and evaluated it in multiple environments. Our results show that CARM achieves an average activity recognition accuracy of 96%. For a new environment and a new person that the system has never been trained on, CARM can still achieve a recognition accuracy for more than 80%.

2. RELATED WORK

Existing work on device-free human activity recognition and localization can be divided into four categories: Received Signal Strength Indicator (RSSI) based, specialized hardware based, radar based, and CSI based.

RSSI Based: RSSI based human activity recognition systems leverage the signal strength changes caused by human activities [3,22,23]. This approach can only do coarse grained human activity recognition with low accuracy because the RSSI values provided by the commercial devices have very low resolution [23]. For RSSI based gesture recognition, the accuracy is 56% over 7 different gestures [21]. Sigg *et al.* use software radio to improve the granularity of RSSI values and consequently improve the accuracy of activity recognition to 72% for 4 activities [22]. In comparison, CARM uses CSI values and achieves an accuracy of 96%.

Specialized Hardware Based: Fine-grained radio signal measurements can be collected by software defined radio or specially designed hardware [11, 12, 14, 17]. WiSee uses USRP to capture the WiFi OFDM signals and measures the Doppler shift in signals reflected by human bodies to recognize a set of nine different gestures with an accuracy of 95% [17]. AllSee uses a specially designed analog circuit to extract the amplitude of the received signals and uses their envelopes to recognize gestures within a short distance of 2.5 feet [14]. Wision uses multi-path reflections to build an image for nearby objects [11]. In comparison, CARM requires no specialized hardware and at the same time achieves high activity recognition accuracy at longer distances.

Radar Based: Device-free human activity recognition has also been studied using radar technology [4, 5, 16, 25]. Using the micro Doppler information, radars can measure the movement speeds of different parts of human body [25]. WiTrack uses specially designed Frequency Modulated Carrier Wave (FMCW) signals to track human movements behind the wall with a resolution of approximately 20cm [4,5]. Compared to the specially designed radar signals such as FMCW or Ultra-wideband (UWB) signals, WiFi signals have much narrower bandwidth. For example, 802.11a/b/g usually use a bandwidth of 20 MHz, while FMCW uses bandwidth of up to 1.79 GHz [4]. Compared to prior work in radar technology, CARM designed a new set of signal processing methods that are suitable for the OFDM signal used in WiFi.

CSI Based: CSI values are available in many commercial devices such as Intel 5300 [9] and Atheros 9390 network interface cards (NICs) [19]. Recently CSI has been used for human activity recognition [10,26,27,30,35] as well as indoor localization [19,32]. Han *et al.* proposed to use CSI to detect a single human activity of falling [10]. Zhou *et al.* proposed to use CSI to detect the presence of a person in an environment [35]. Xi *et al.* proposed to use CSI to count the number of people in a crowd [30]. WiHear uses specialized directional antennas to obtain CSI variations caused by lip movement for recognizing spoken words [26]. E-eyes recognizes a set of nine daily human activities using CSI. Note that WiHear and E-eyes use CSI in quite different ways than CARM. WiHear does not effectively denoise CSI values; thus, it has to use directional antennas to reduce the noise in CSI values to achieve acceptable accuracy. In comparison, we denoise CSI values and use commercial WiFi devices with built-in omnidirectional antennas. E-eyes uses CSI histograms as fingerprints for recognizing human daily activities, such as brushing teeth, taking showers, and washing dishes, which are relatively location dependent. In comparison, CARM uses CSI values based on our CSI-speed and CSI-activity models.

3. UNDERSTANDING WIFI MULTI-PATH

3.1 Overview of CSI

WiFi NICs continuously monitor variations in the wireless channel using CSI, which characterizes the frequency response of the wireless channel [1]. Let $X(f,t)$ and $Y(f,t)$ be the frequency domain representations of transmitted and received signals, respectively, with carrier frequency f. The two signals are related by the expression $Y(f,t) = H(f,t) \times X(f,t)$, where $H(f,t)$ is the complex valued channel frequency response (CFR) for carrier frequency f measured at time t. CSI measurements basically contains these CFR values. Let N_{Tx} and N_{Rx} represent the number of transmitting and receiving antennas, respectively. As CSI is measured on 30 selected OFDM subcarriers for a received 802.11 frame, each CSI measurement contains 30 matrices with dimensions $N_{Tx} \times N_{Rx}$. Each entry in any matrix is a CFR value between an antenna pair at a certain OFDM subcarrier frequency at a particular time. Onwards, we call the time-series of CFR values for a given antenna pair and OFDM subcarrier as *CSI stream*. Thus, there are $30 \times N_{Tx} \times N_{Rx}$ CSI streams in a time-series of CSI values.

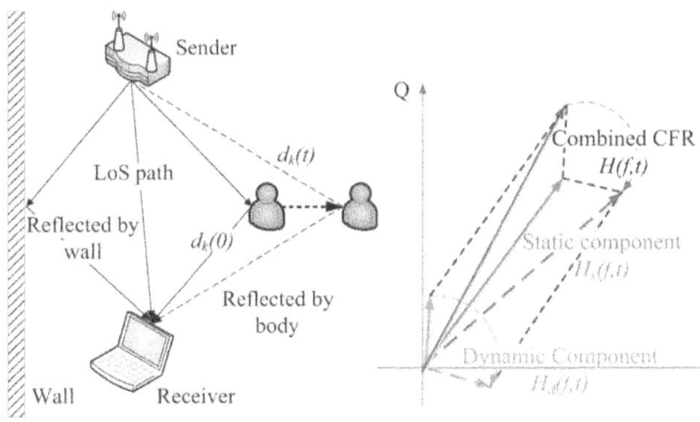

(a) Visual representation (b) Phasor representation

Figure 2: Multi-paths caused by human movements

3.2 Phase Changes for Paths

Surrounding objects reflect wireless signals due to which a transmitted signal arrives at the receiver through multiple paths. If a radio signal arrives at the receiver through N different paths, then $H(f,t)$ is given by the following equation [24]:

$$H(f,t) = e^{-j2\pi\Delta f t} \sum_{k=1}^{N} a_k(f,t) e^{-j2\pi f \tau_k(t)} \quad (1)$$

where $a_k(f,t)$ is the complex valued representation of attenuation and initial phase offset of the kth path , $e^{-j2\pi f \tau_k(t)}$ is the phase shift on the kth path that has a propagation delay of $\tau_k(t)$, and $e^{-j2\pi\Delta f t}$ is phase shift caused by the carrier frequency difference Δf between the sender and the receiver.

The changes in the length of a path lead to the changes in the phase of the WiFi signal on the corresponding path. Consider the scenario in Figure 2(a), where the WiFi signal is reflected by the human body through the kth path. When the human body moves by a small distance between time 0 and time t, the length of the kth path changes from $d_k(0)$ to $d_k(t)$. Since wireless signals travel at the speed of light, denoted as c, the delay of the kth path, denoted as $\tau_k(t)$ can be written as $\tau_k(t) = d_k(t)/c$. Let f and λ represents the carrier frequency and the wavelength, where $\lambda = c/f$. Thus, the phase shift $e^{-j2\pi f \tau_k(t)}$ on this path can be written as $e^{-j2\pi d_k(t)/\lambda}$, which means that when the path length changes by one wavelength, the receiver experiences a phase shift of 2π in the received subcarrier.

3.3 Practical Limitations

Theoretically, it is possible to precisely measure the phase of the path in systems where sender and receiver are perfectly synchronized, *e.g.*, as in RFID systems [31]. But, unfortunately, commercial WiFi devices have non-negligible carrier frequency offsets (CFO) due to hardware imperfections and environmental variations [8]. IEEE 802.11n standard allows the carrier frequency of a device to drift by up to 100 kHz from the central frequency of the channel for 5 GHz band [1]. Such frequency drift leads to rapid phase changes in CSI values. Commercial WiFi NICs take one set of CSI measurements per frame. With a transmission rate of 4,000 frames per second, which is around the maximum number of frames that the commercial device can continuously transmit due to the frame aggregation mechanism in 802.11n [1], the phase shift caused by the term $e^{-j2\pi\Delta ft}$ in Equation (1) cloud be as large as 50π between consecutive CSI values.

Our measurements on commercial devices show that phases of CFR are too noisy to be used for activity recognition due to CFO. Figure 3 shows the CSI phase differences for consecutive frames sent through a WiFi link between two commercial devices. Due to the randomness of the packet sending process, the interval Δt between two consecutive frames is randomly distributed in the range of 300~550 microseconds (μs). This gives us a chance to measure the fine grained phase differences for different Δt. Each dot in Figure 3 gives the phase difference for a pair of frame separated by the given Δt, thus we can obtain the relationship between Δt and the phase shift. As shown by Figure 3, the phase difference $2\pi\Delta f\Delta t$ changes by 8π (four vertical strips) when Δt increase from 350 μs to 400 μs. Thus, the CFO can be calculated as $\Delta f = \frac{8\pi}{2\pi(400-350)\mu s}$ = 80 kHz. There are two causes that lead to the imprecision of CFR phase. First, from the width of the vertical strips in Figure 3, we observe that CFR phase has measurement error as large as 0.5π. In most cases, the phase changes caused by human reflection are much smaller than 0.5π. Thus, phase changes caused by movements are often buried in phase nosies. Second, our measurements on commercial devices show that the central frequency often drifts by tens of Hz per second, making it hard to predict CFR phase and separate the phase change caused by clock drifts from the small phase shifts caused by body movements. Furthermore, the phase sanitization method introduced in [20] could not work for our case because the phase sanitization process also removes the phase shifts caused by body movements.

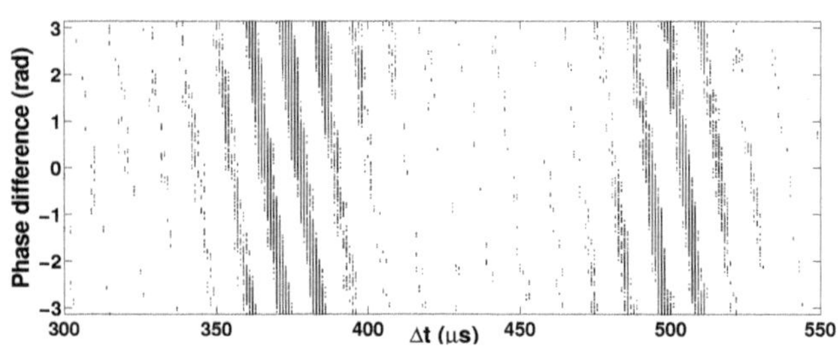

Figure 3: Phase differences for consecutive frames

3.4 CSI-Speed Model

While it is hard to directly measure the phase of a path, it is possible to infer the phase of a path using the CFR power *i.e.*, $|H(f,t)|^2$. The principle behind our method is that when the lengths of multi-paths change, the CFR power varies according to the path length change.

To understand the relationship between CFR power and the length change of a path, we first express CFR as a sum of dynamic CFR and static CFR and then calculate the power. Dynamic CFR, represented by $H_d(f,t)$, is the sum of CFRs for paths whose lengths change with the human movement, and is given by $H_d(f,t) = \sum_{k\in P_d} a_k(f,t)e^{-j2\pi d_k(t)/\lambda}$, where P_d is the set of dynamic paths whose lengths change. Static CFR, represented by $H_s(f)$, is the sum of CFRs for static paths. Thus, the total CFR is given by the following equation.

$$H(f,t) = e^{-j2\pi\Delta ft}\Big(H_s(f) + \sum_{k\in P_d} a_k(f,t)e^{-j\frac{2\pi d_k(t)}{\lambda}}\Big) \quad (2)$$

The total CFR has time-varying power because in complex plane, the static component $H_s(f)$ is a constant vector while the dynamic component $H_d(f,t)$ is superposition of vectors with time varying phases and amplitudes, as shown in Figure 2(b). When the phase of the dynamic component changes, the magnitude of the combined CFR changes accordingly.

Now, consider how CFR power changes with an object moving around. Let an object move at a constant speed such that the length of the kth path changes at a constant speed v_k for a short time period, *e.g.*, 100 milliseconds. Let $d_k(t)$ be the length of the kth path at time t. Thus, $d_k(t) = d_k(0) + v_k t$. The instantaneous CFR power at time t can be derived as follows (detailed derivations are omitted due to space constraints).

$$\begin{aligned}|H(f,t)|^2 &= \sum_{k\in P_d} 2|H_s(f)a_k(f,t)|\cos\left(\frac{2\pi v_k t}{\lambda} + \frac{2\pi d_k(0)}{\lambda} + \phi_{sk}\right)\\ &+ \sum_{\substack{k,l\in P_d\\ k\neq l}} 2|a_k(f,t)a_l(f,t)|\cos\left(\frac{2\pi(v_k - v_l)t}{\lambda} + \frac{2\pi\,(d_k(0) - d_l(0))}{\lambda} + \phi_{kl}\right)\\ &+ \sum_{k\in P_d} |a_k(f,t)|^2 + |H_s(f)|^2 \end{aligned} \quad (3)$$

where $\frac{2\pi d_k(0)}{\lambda} + \phi_{sk}$ and $\frac{2\pi(d_k(0)-d_l(0))}{\lambda} + \phi_{kl}$ are constant values representing initial phase offsets.

Equation (3) provides a key insight: *the total CFR power is the sum of a constant offset and a set of sinusoids, where the frequencies of the sinusoids are functions of the speeds of path length changes.* By measuring the frequencies of these sinusoids and multiplying them with the carrier wavelength, we can obtain the speeds of path length change. In this way, we can build a CSI-speed model which relates the variations in CSI power to the movement speeds.

3.5 Model Verification

We use a simple moving object to verify our CSI-speed model in Equation (3). We move a steel plate with diameter of 30 cm along the perpendicular bisector of the sender/receiver, similar to the scenario shown in Figure 2(a). Flat steel objects can serve as mirrors for radio waves [34]. Thus, there is only one path dominating the signal reflected by the steel plate and Equation (3) reduces to one sinusoid wave plus a constant offset. The frequency of the sinusoid changes according to the instantaneous moving speed. This can be verified by Figure 4(a), which shows the CSI waveform caused by steel plate movements. When there is only one dominating sinusoid wave, the movement distance can be calculated by measuring the phase change of the signal, which is the integral of the signal frequency over time.

We use Hilbert Transform to calculate the phase change of the waveform as follows. We first remove the DC component that accounts for the static paths. We then use Hilbert Transform to derive the analytic signal from the waveform. The unwrapped instantaneous phase of the analytic signal keeps track of the phase change of the waveform. We can then multiply the phase change with the wavelength to get the path length change. Since the reflected signal goes through a round-trip from the reflector, the path length change is approximately two times of the movement distance of the reflector in this case [29].

The Hilbert Transform based distance measurement has average accuracy of 2.86 cm, as showing in Figure 4(b) and 4(c) . In the experiments, we move the steel plate for a random distance in the

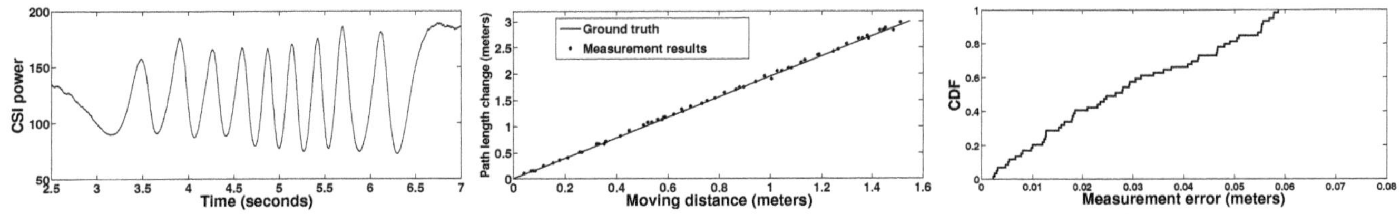

(a) CSI waveform for a movement with 0.8m pathlength change (b) Measurements of path length change (c) CDF of measurement error

Figure 4: Experiments with steel plates moving along a straight line.

range of 0∼1.6 m which incurs 0∼3.2 m path length change. The ground truth path length change is measured by a laser rangefinder, which provides distance measurement accuracy of 0.1 cm. Under carrier frequency of 5.825 GHz, which has wavelength of 5.15cm, our path length measurement has maximal error of 5.87 cm and mean error of 2.86 cm. The major error sources are errors in deciding the phase of the starting and ending cycle. Therefore, the measurement error does not increase with the movement distance and is uniformly distributed in the range of 0∼6 cm, see Figure 4(c).

4. MODELING OF HUMAN ACTIVITIES

4.1 Human Activity Characteristics

Modeling CFR power change caused by human activity is challenging. Unlike the simple object used in section 3.5, human bodies have complex shapes and different body parts can move at different speeds. Moreover, the reflections from body parts may go through different paths in complex indoor environments. From Equation (3), we see that the CFR power is a linear combination of all the reflected paths and the speeds of path length change are preserved in the combination process. Therefore, we can use Time-Frequency analysis tools, such as Short-Time Fourier Transform (STFT) or Discrete Wavelet Transform (DWT) to separate these components in the frequency domain. Human activity can be modeled by profiling the energy of each frequency component derived from Time-Frequency analysis tools. As an example, Figure 5 illustrates the waveform and the corresponding spectrogram for three human activities: walking, falling and sitting down. The spectrogram shows how the energy of each frequency component evolves with time, where high-energy components are colored in red. In the spectrogram for the walking activity, there is a high-energy band around 35∼40Hz frequency, as shown in Figure 5(d). With a wavelength of 5.15 cm, these frequency components represent 0.9∼1.0 m/s movement speed after considering the round-trip path length change. This coincides the normal movement speed of human torso while walking [25]. Figure 5(e) shows the spectrogram of falling, which has an energy increase in the frequency range of 40∼80 Hz between 1∼1.5 seconds. This indicates a fast speed-up from below 0.5 m/s speed to 2 m/s, during a short time period of 0.5 seconds, which is a clear sign of falling. The activity of sitting down shown in Figure 5(f) is different from falling, as the speed for sitting down is much slower. Using the energy profile of different frequencies, we can build CSI-activity model, which quantifies the correlation between the movement speeds of different human body parts and a specific human activity.

4.2 Robustness of Activity Speeds

We next study whether the speed based CSI-activity model are robust across different scenarios. It is well known that the path length change is determined by both the position of the sender/receiver and the movement directions [29]. Movements with the same speed may introduce different path length change speeds when movement directions are different. Furthermore, different people may perform the same activity with different speeds and the multi-path conditions may change under different environments.

Our experiments show that different human activities actually incur path length change speed with significant difference, so that the minor measurement differences caused by movement direction and the different ways to perform the same activity can be safely ignored. To study the robustness of the movement speeds, we collect more than 780 activity samples for three activities, walking, running and sitting down, performed by 25 volunteers with different ages and genders. The activities are performed at different locations with different directions, *e.g.*, we ask the volunteer to walk around a large table so that four different walking directions are captured. Figure 6 shows the estimated torso speed distribution for the three different activities. Note that we estimate the torso speed by dividing the speed of path length change by two. This usually gives a smaller estimation than the actual speed because depending on the movement direction, moving by 1 cm usually cause less than 2 cm path length change [29]. Even with different movement directions, we observe that the three activities have different speeds in Figure 6. Such speed difference can be used for activity classification. As an example, we can achieve a classification accuracy of 88% for all three activities, when we divide the samples to three types with estimated speed of 0∼0.61 m/s, 0.61∼1.0 m/s and above 1.0 m/s. By looking at various different activities, we found that most human activities contains speed components ranging from 0∼2.5 m/s and the frequency components for a given activity are stable across different scenarios, including apartments, offices, and large open area, see our evaluations in Section 8. Therefore, the strength of the frequency components can serve as a robust feature for human activities.

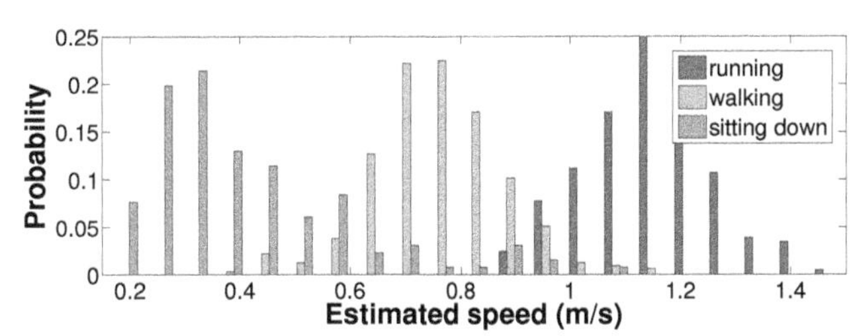

Figure 6: Histogram of speeds for different activities

4.3 CSI-Activity Model

We propose to use Hidden Markov Model (HMM) to build CSI-activity models that consist of mutiple movement states. As an example, we observe that the action of falling comprises several states from Figure 5(e). The person first moves slowly, with most CSI energy on the low frequency (slow movement) components. Then, there is a fast transition to very high speed movement where sub-

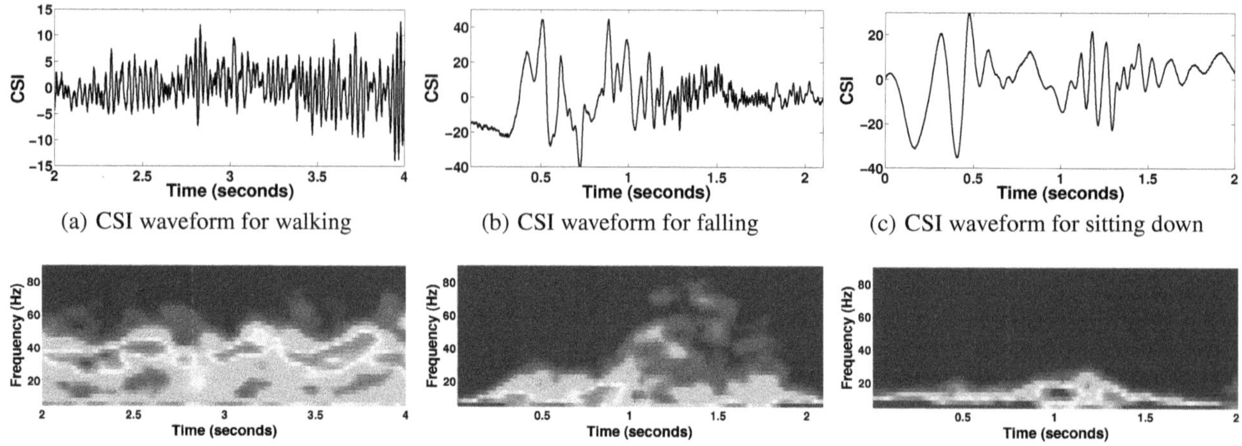

(a) CSI waveform for walking (b) CSI waveform for falling (c) CSI waveform for sitting down

(d) Sepctrogram for walking (e) Sepctrogram for falling (f) Sepctrogram for sitting down

Figure 5: Waveforms and spectrograms for different activities.

stantial energy are on high frequency components. After that, there is a quick transition to the silent state, where the movement energy reduces to nearly zero. By looking at these transitions between different states, we can infer that the person is possibly falling. Similarly, other human activities also contain states with can be characterized by their movement speeds.

Hidden Markov Model (HMM) is a suitable tool to build state transition models using time-dependent features. It has been extensively used in several recognition applications such as speech recognition [18], handwriting recognition, and gesture recognition in videos [6]. Use of HMMs for activity recognition is based on the assumption that the sequence of observed feature vectors corresponding to an activity is generated by a Markov model, which is a finite state machine that changes state once every time unit. Each time a state is entered, a feature vector is generated from a probability density called *output probability density*. Furthermore, the transition from one state to another or back to itself is also probabilistic and is governed by a discrete probability called *transition probability*. Hidden Markov Models are called hidden because in practice, the sequence of feature vectors is known but the underlying sequence of states that generated those feature vectors is hidden.

HMM can capture information from all training samples and thus works very well even when there is high within-class variance. Provided that a sufficient number of representative training samples of an activity are available, an HMM can be constructed that implicitly models all of the many sources of variability inherent in the activity. Compared to existing works which uses statistical features along a long period [10, 27], HMM based models utilizes the transitions within the activity that provide more details about the activity. For details related to HMM model training and classification, please refer to Section 7.

4.4 Discussion

Detection of high-speed and low-speed movements: CARM can reliably detect both high-speed movement and low-speed movements. Commercial WiFi devices provide CSI values with sampling rates high enough to accurately obtain the values of these frequencies. From our extensive activity dataset, we have observed that indoor human movements introduce frequency components of no more than 300Hz in the CFR power, which corresponds to a top human movement speed of about $300 \times 0.0515/2 = 7.7$m/s, when the wavelength is 5.15 cm. Note that 7.7 m/s is already too fast a speed for a human to move with. Commercial WiFi NICs can easily sample CSI values at a rate of up to 2500 samples/second, which is far greater than the sampling rate required by the Nyquist criteria for a 300Hz signal. Thus, we can apply signal processing techniques on the denoised CSI values and get the frequency components in CFR power and infer the speed. For slow movements that only move a few centimeters per second, CARM utilizes wavelet transforms to extract low frequency components below 1 Hz to capture slow movements such as brushing teeth, see Section 6.

Movement of different body parts: Time-frequency analysis tools can separate the movement of different body parts when they move at different speeds. For example, the weak energy bands in frequency components between 50$\sim$70 Hz in Figure 5(d) are actually caused by swing of legs when walking [25]. In general, CFR power changes caused by the movements of arms/legs have smaller in energy compared to torso movements as the reflection areas for arms/legs are smaller. Our feature extraction process captures both the body movement and arms/legs movements. Therefore, CARM can distinguish whether the activity involves the whole body or just arms/legs. For example, CARM can recognize falling, running and boxing, which are all high speed movements but involve different body parts.

Scenarios with multiple persons: When there are multiple persons within the same room, CARM can recognize the activity when only one person is moving, see details in Section 8. When both persons are actively moving, we need multiple sender/receivers to capture the actions. Activities that are closer to the given sender/receiver introduce higher distortions in CFR power. Therefore, we can use blind signal separation methods [15] to extract CFR power distortions caused by different person. However, this is out of the scope of this paper and will be studied in our future works.

5. PCA BASED CSI DENOISING SCHEME

CARM builds the HMM model in following three steps as described in Sections 5, 6, and 7, respectively. First, CARM collects CSI values and removes the noises in the measurements. Second, CARM extracts human movement features from the denoised CSI values using DWT. Third, CARM trains an HMM model for each activity and uses the CSI-activity models to recognize activities in real time.

5.1 Sources of Noise in CSI

The CSI streams provided by commercial WiFi devices are extremely noisy. Figure 7 plots a noisy CSI stream that we collected from an Intel 5300 NIC at a sampling rate of 2.5 kHz for a period of 1.75 seconds. One major sources of noise in CSI streams are the internal state transitions in sender and receiver WiFi NICs such as transmission power changes, transmission rate adaptation, and internal CSI reference level changes. These internal state transitions result in high amplitude impulse and burst noises in CSI streams. An interesting feature of these impulse and burst noises is that their effect is highly correlated across all CSI streams, *i.e.*, they affect samples in all streams at the same time. For example, if sender WiFi NIC increases the transmission power by 0.5dB, all streams see a power increase of 0.5dB.

5.2 Traditional Filter based Denoising

Traditional filters such as low-pass filters or median filters do not perform well in removing the impulse and burst noises. Theoretically, a low-pass filter, such as a Butterworth filter, should be able to remove such noise. However, due to the high energy and high bandwidth of impulse noises in CSI, the pass band for the low-pass filters usually need to be less than one-twentieth of the sampling rate so that the energy of residual noise in the pass band becomes negligible compared to the signal energy [26]. When the sampling rate is not high enough, the residual noises can still distort the filtered stream. Figure 7(b) shows the output of a low-pass filter with a cutoff frequency of 100 Hz when applied to the CSI stream in Figure 7(a), which has sampling rate of 2,500 samples per second. We observe that the filtered stream is still severely distorted and the low-pass filter could not effectively denoise it. Another type of filters, called median filters, is specifically designed to remove impulse noise, but they do not work well on CSI streams because the density of the noises is very high. Figure 7(c) shows the output of a 5-point median filter when applied to the CSI stream in Figure 7(a). We again observe that the filtered stream is still severely distorted.

5.3 Correlation in CSI Streams

Our denoising method leverages the fact that the changes introduced in all CSI streams by body movement are correlated. CSI streams of different subcarriers are linear combinations of the same set of time-varying signals and thus they are highly correlated. To show this, consider an object that moves by a small distance between time 0 and time t. Let the length of the path changes by $\Delta_k(t)$ between time 0 and time t when the object moves. Thus, $d_k(t) = \Delta_k(t) + d_k(0)$, where $d_k(0)$ is the initial length of the path. When the initial phase offset of the subcarrier is ϕ_k, the phase of the subcarrier s in Equation (3) seen by the receiver at time t is given by the following equation.

$$\begin{aligned}\cos\left(\frac{2\pi d_k(t)}{\lambda_s}+\phi_k\right) &= \cos\left(\frac{2\pi \Delta_k(t)}{\lambda_s}+\frac{2\pi d_k(0)}{\lambda_s}+\phi_k\right)\\ &= \cos\left(\frac{2\pi d_k(0)}{\lambda_s}+\phi_k\right)\cos\left(\frac{2\pi\Delta_k(t)}{\lambda_s}\right)\\ &\quad -\sin\left(\frac{2\pi d_k(0)}{\lambda_s}+\phi_k\right)\sin\left(\frac{2\pi\Delta_k(t)}{\lambda_s}\right)\end{aligned} \quad (4)$$

Consider two subcarriers with wavelengths λ_1 and λ_2 that traverse the kth multipath. The difference between wavelengths of subcarriers in a WiFi channel is small. For example, in a 20MHz WiFi channel, the lowest and highest frequency subcarriers are separated by about 17MHz. Thus, in 5GHz band, wavelengths λ of subcarriers differ by at most 0.34%. This slight difference in wavelengths usually does not change the number of multipaths across subcarriers. We make two observations from Equation (4). First, the time-varying terms in the equation above are approximately equal, *i.e.*, $\cos\left(\frac{2\pi\Delta_k(t)}{\lambda_1}\right) \approx \cos\left(\frac{2\pi\Delta_k(t)}{\lambda_2}\right)$ and $\sin\left(\frac{2\pi\Delta_k(t)}{\lambda_1}\right) \approx \sin\left(\frac{2\pi\Delta_k(t)}{\lambda_2}\right)$ because $\Delta_k(t)$ is small and λ_1 and λ_2 differ only slightly. Second, the constant terms in Equation (4) are unequal for the two subcarriers because initial path length $d_k(0)$ is much greater than $\Delta_k(t)$ and thus, results in a non-negligible initial phase difference between the two subcarriers even though the wavelengths differ only slightly. For example, for a path length of 10 meters, a radio signal with wavelength of 5.150 cm traverses distance equal to 194.1 full wavelengths on this path, where as a radio signal with wavelength of 5.168 cm ($= 5.15 \times 1.0034$) traverses distance equal to 193.5 wavelengths. Thus, there is an initial phase difference of $(194.1 - 193.5) \times 2\pi = 1.2\pi$ between these two signals at the receiver.

These two observations show that CFR for different subcarriers is a linear combination of the same set of time-varying waveforms with different initial phases, *i.e.*, $\cos\left(\frac{2\pi\Delta_k(t)}{\lambda_s}\right)$ and $\sin\left(\frac{2\pi\Delta_k(t)}{\lambda_s}\right)$. Therefore, the CSI streams are correlated. Similar results can be obtained for CSI streams between different antenna pairs because the difference in positions of antennas only causes initial phases and attenuations for each multipath to be different.

Our measurements confirm the observation that CSI streams are correlated. Figure 8 plots the 180 CSI streams for a link with $N_{Tx} = 2$ and $N_{Rx} = 3$ when a human is walking around. We group the CSI streams in their transmission/receiving antenna pairs, *e.g.*, streams 1∼30 are the 30 subcarriers for transmitting antenna 1 and receiving antenna 1. Each CSI stream is a curve that is similar to the one in Figure 5(a), where the amplitudes for CSI values are represented by the color, *i.e.*, red colors are "peaks" and blue colors are "valleys" in the curve. We have following observation in the CSI streams. First, CSI streams are correlated. The "peaks" and "valleys" have similar shapes in all CSI streams across different antenna pairs and different subcarriers. Moreover, the phases of CSI streams changes smoothly across different subcarriers in the same antenna pair, *e.g.*, streams 1∼30 and 151∼180, because the subcarriers on the same antenna pair only differs slightly in their frequencies. Second, there is no single "good" CSI stream. Although we can see clear "peaks" and "valleys" in stream 151∼180 at time between 2.5∼2.6 and 2.8∼2.9 seconds, the changes in measurements are vague during the time 2.9∼3 seconds for the same set of streams. However, we observe streams 1∼30 give clear CSI fluctuations during time 2.9∼3 seconds. This implies that we need to combine different streams to get optimal observations in the movements. Third, simply using weighted average over CSI streams [13] cannot provide good results. We see that the phase of different CSI streams are different so that if we simply add them up, they can cancel each other as the time point for the "peak" of a stream may be the "valleys" of other streams. Therefore, it is important to find a good way to combine CSI streams.

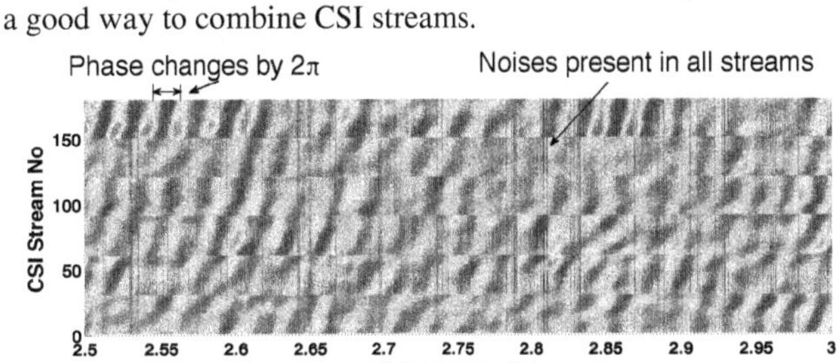

Figure 8: Correlation in CSI streams

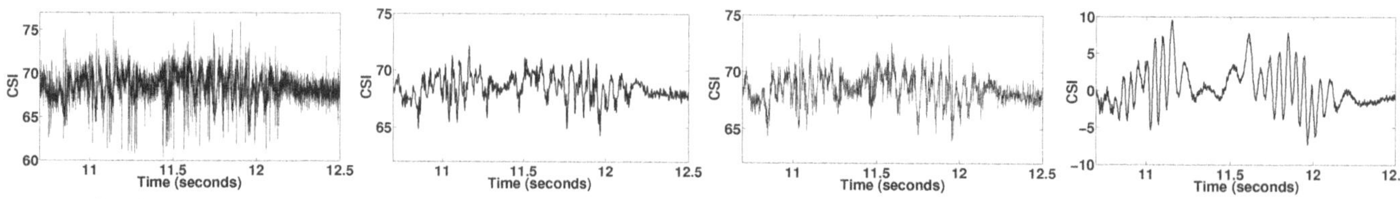

(a) Original CSI Stream (b) Butterworth low-pass filter (c) 5-point median filter (d) PCA based denoising

Figure 7: Denoising the time-series of CSI values

5.4 Principal Component Analysis

To address the challenges in combining CSI streams, we apply PCA to discover the correlations between CSI streams. With PCA, we can track the time-varying correlations between CSI streams, and optimally combine them to extract principal components of CSI streams. CARM applies PCA to CSI streams using the following four steps.

(1) *Preprocessing:* In this step, CARM first removes the static path components from each CSI stream by subtracting the corresponding constant offsets from the streams. It calculates the constant offset for each stream through long-term averaging over that stream, *i.e.*, average CSI amplitude for 4 seconds. After that, it cut CSI streams into chunks that contain samples obtained in 1-second interval and arrange chunks of different CSI streams in columns to form a matrix of $\mathbf{H}$. We choose interval size to be 1 second so that the distance moved by the object is short and at the same time the number of samples is large enough to ensure accurate correlation estimation, which is the next step.

(2) *Correlation estimation:* CARM calculates the correlation matrix as $\mathbf{H}^T \times \mathbf{H}$. The correlation matrix has dimension of $N \times N$, where N is the number of CSI streams. For the example in Figure 8, we have $N = 180$.

(3) *Eigendecomposition:* CARM performs Eigendecomposition of the correlation matrix to calculate the eigenvectors.

(4) *Movement Signal Reconstruction:* In this step, CARM constructs the principal components using the equation $\mathbf{h}_i = \mathbf{H} \times \mathbf{q}_i$, where $\mathbf{q}_i$ and $\mathbf{h}_i$ are the ith eigenvector and the ith principal components, respectively.

CARM discards the first principal component $\mathbf{h}_1$ and retains the next five principal components to be used for feature extraction. As discussed in 5.1, noises caused by internal state changes present in all CSI streams, which are the vertical lines appear in Figure 8. Due to the high correlation, these noises are captured in $\mathbf{h}_1$ along with the human movement signal. However, an interesting result is that all the information about the human movement signal captured in $\mathbf{h}_1$ is also captured in other principal components, because by Equation (4), the phase of a subcarrier is a linear combination of two orthogonal components: $\cos\left(\frac{2\pi\Delta_k(t)}{\lambda}\right)$ and $\sin\left(\frac{2\pi\Delta_k(t)}{\lambda}\right)$. Since the PCA components are uncorrelated, the first principal component only contains one of these orthogonal components and the other component is retained in the rest PCA components. Therefore, we can safely discard the first principal component without losing any information. The number of PCA components used for feature extraction is empirically selected to achieve a good tradeoff between classification performance and computational complexity. Figure 7(d) shows the second PCA component of our denoising scheme. We observe that our proposed method outperforms traditional filtering methods and does not contain the high frequency noise.

6. FEATURE EXTRACTION

6.1 Extracting Features from CSI

To obtain activity features from CSI, CARM needs to extract frequency components from different activities at different time scales. This is because human activities have two aspects associated with them, duration and frequency. Duration represents the time a person takes to perform an activity and frequency represents the speed of multi-paths due to body movements during the activity. Different activities may have similar durations but different frequencies. For example, sitting down and falling both have short durations but the speeds of paths are significantly higher in falling than in sitting down. Consequently, the frequencies in CFR power for falling are greater than the frequencies for sitting down. Similarly, different activities may have similar frequencies but different durations. For example, running and falling both have similar frequencies but the duration of falling is shorter than running. Thus, to analyze CFR power for human activities, we need to extract frequencies from it at multiple resolutions on multiple time scales.

The most relevant signal processing tool that can enable us to extract frequencies at multiple resolutions on multiple time scales is discrete wavelet transform (DWT). DWT provides high time resolution for activities with high frequencies in CFR signals and high frequency resolution for activities with slow speeds. DWT calculates the energies in different levels at any given time in the CFR signals, where each level corresponds to a frequency range. The frequency ranges of adjacent DWT levels decrease exponentially. For example, if level 1 DWT represents a frequency range of 150$\sim$300Hz, which corresponds to 3.85$\sim$7.7 m/s movement speed in 5GHz band, then level 2 DWT represents a frequency range that is half of the frequency range for level 1, *i.e.*, 75$\sim$150Hz, which corresponds to 1.925$\sim$3.85 m/s. The higher the energy in a DWT level is, the more likely it is that the speed of the path is in a range associated with the frequency range of that level. Figure 9(a) shows the wavelet transform for a falling action, where higher brightness represents higher energy level. Although DWT has lower resolution compared to spectrogram in Figure 5(e), we can see the high energy region moves from level 6 to level 2 from 1 to 1.5 seconds. The advantage of DWT compared to STFT is as follows: First, DWT has nice tradeoffs in time and frequency resolutions. DWT naturally groups frequencies that differ by several orders of magnitude into a few levels so that both high speed movements and low speed movements can be captured. Second, DWT reduces the size of data so that the classification algorithm can run in real time.

To extract features for classification from a sample of an activity, CARM applies DWT to decompose the PCA components into 12 levels that span the frequency range from 0.15Hz to 300Hz. The DWT results of the five PCA components are averaged to capture the movement information present in different PCA components. From the output of DWT on each 200ms interval, CARM extracts a 27 dimensional feature vector that includes three types of features. 1). The energy in each level, which represents the intensity of movement in each speed range. 2). Difference in the energy of each level between consecutive 200ms intervals, which represents the rate of change of speed of a multi-path for the activity. 3). Estimated torso and leg speeds using the percentile method introduced in Doppler radar [25].

6.2 Resilience to Environmental Changes

Environmental changes such as adding an extra chair in a room change the number of multi-paths arriving at the receiver. However, even when the number of multi-paths changes due to environmental changes, the speed of change in lengths of multi-paths does not change because it depends on the movement of human body and not on the number of multi-paths in an environment. Consequently, the frequency components in the CFR power stay the same as long as the person performs the same activity, and DWT gives higher energy in the same levels regardless of how many multi-paths have appeared or disappeared. Figures 10(a) and 10(b) plot the time-series of denoised CSI values for the activity of falling. To emulate the change in environment, our volunteer performed the action at two different locations. Figures 9(a) and 9(b) plot the DWTs of these two waveforms. We observe from these figures that even though the time-series of denoised CSI values look very different for the same activity in different environments, the features that CARM extracts look very similar. Compared to directly using the CSI waveform, the features that CARM uses are resilient to environmental changes, see detailed evaluations in Section 8.

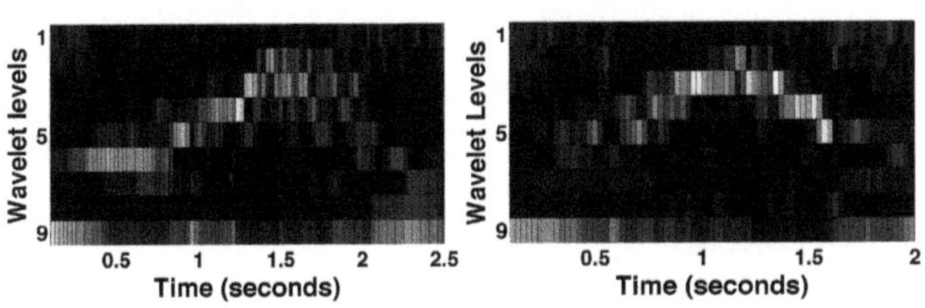

(a) Environment 1 (b) Environment 2

Figure 9: DWT of time-series for falling

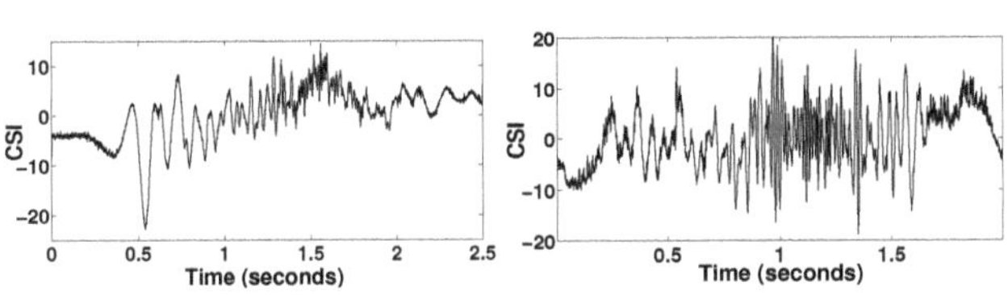

(a) Environment 1 (b) Environment 2

Figure 10: Denoised CSI time-series for falling

7. CLASSIFICATION & RECOGNITION

7.1 Building Activity Models

CARM constructs an HMM for each activity using the training samples of that activity. It also constructs an activity model for the situation when there is no activity in the room. To estimate mean vector and covariance matrix corresponding to each state and the transition probabilities for the HMM, CARM uses the well-known Baum-Welch algorithm [28]. Baum-Welch algorithm needs a rough guess of these probabilities to start with. To guess the initial values, CARM first divides the sequence of feature vectors from each training sample equally amongst the states and then calculates the initial values for the mean vector and covariance matrix of each state using the feature vectors assigned to that state. CARM also calculates the initial transition probabilities by first counting the number of transitions between every pair of states from the sequence of feature vectors of all training samples divided equally amongst states and then dividing the counts by total number of transitions in all training samples. To decide the number of states, CARM iterates through various number of states and selects the number that provides highest cross validation accuracy. To avoid overfitting of Baum-Welch algorithm to a particular person or moving direction, in generating the model of an activity, we include samples of that activity from different people and different movement directions. Furthermore, we evaluate the models using both 10-fold cross validation and separated testing samples collected in different environments to ensure that the models do not overfit on samples from specific scenarios.

7.2 Real Time Activity Recognition

Once CARM generates HMMs for all activities, it can recognize activities in real-time. We will first explain how CARM detects the start and end of the activity and then explain how it recognizes the unknown activity.

Activity Detection: To detect the start and end of an activity, CARM monitors the second eigenvector $\mathbf{q}_2$ and the corresponding principal component $\mathbf{h}_2$. Our activity detection method is based on two key observations. First, in the absence of an activity, the eigenvector $\mathbf{q}_2$ varies randomly over neighboring subcarriers because CSI streams contain uncorrelated values; whereas, in the presence of an activity, the CSI streams become correlated and $\mathbf{q}_2$ varies smoothly over neighboring subcarriers. Second, in the absence of an activity, the principal component $\mathbf{h}_2$ has smaller variance; whereas in the presence of an activity, it has higher variance.

CARM empirically calculates the variance, $\mathbb{E}\{\mathbf{h}_2^2\}$, of the time series $\mathbf{h}_2$ and the mean of first difference of the eigenvector $\mathbf{q}_2$ given by $\delta_{\mathbf{q}_2} = \frac{1}{S-1}\sum_{l=2}^{S}|\mathbf{q}_2(l) - \mathbf{q}_2(l-1)|$, where S is the number of CSI streams and $|\mathbf{q}_2(l) - \mathbf{q}_2(l-1)|$ is the difference in coefficients for neighboring subcarriers. In the presence of an activity, $\mathbb{E}\{\mathbf{h}_2^2\}$ has a higher value because the time-series for human movement signal varies more frequently, whereas $\delta_{\mathbf{q}_2}$ has a smaller value because the eigenvector becomes more smooth. Therefore, we define the *activity indicator* as $\mathbb{E}\{\mathbf{h}_2^2\}/\delta_{\mathbf{q}_2}$. Figure 11 plots $\mathbb{E}\{\mathbf{h}_2^2\}$, $\delta_{\mathbf{q}_2}$, and the activity indicator over a period of about 10 seconds. We observe that activity indicator increase at 1.4 second and decreases at 9 seconds, which is the start and end times of the action, respectively. The activity indicator $\mathbb{E}\{\mathbf{h}_2^2\}/\delta_{\mathbf{q}_2}$ has better detection performance because it has sharper edges than the metrics of $\mathbb{E}\{\mathbf{h}_2^2\}$ and $\delta_{\mathbf{q}_2}$.

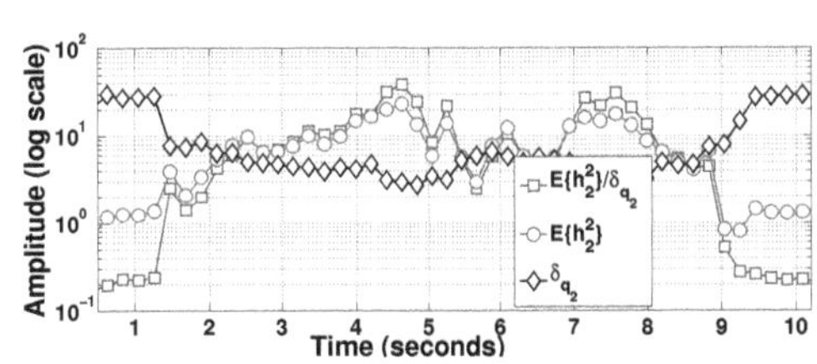

Figure 11: Activity detection indicators

To automatically detect the start or end of an activity, CARM compares the activity indicator with a threshold that it adjusts dynamically based on the background noise level. To dynamically adjust the threshold, we use an Exponential Moving Average (EMA) algorithm to update the detection threshold. In case of a sudden increase in noise level, CARM can incorrectly detect the start of an activity. To handle this, when CARM builds activity models, it also collects some samples for the situation when there is no activity and builds a model for "no activity" using these samples. CARM classifies a detected activity using all activity models and decides whether a detected activity indeed had an activity in it or not. If it finds that there was no activity, it adjusts the detection threshold accordingly.

Activity Recognition: CARM identifies the activity in following four steps. First, it takes all CSI values between the start and end times and denoises them using the PCA based denoising method described in Section 5.4. Second, from every 200ms interval between the start and end times, it extracts a 27 dimensional feature vector as described in Section 6.1. Third, it uses dynamic programming to calculate the likelihood of each HMM generating this sequence of feature vectors [18]. Finally, the model with the highest likelihood identifies the activity.

8. IMPLEMENTATION & EVALUATION

8.1 Implementation

CARM consists of two components: a laptop with a WiFi card and a commercially available WiFi access point (AP). We implemented CARM on a Think-pad X200 laptop equipped with Intel 5300 WiFi card and tested it using two commercially available 802.11ac APs: NETGEAR JR6100 and TP-Link TL-WDR7500. To obtain CSI values from regular data frames transmitted by the access point, we installed the CSI tool developed by Halperin *et al.* on the laptop [9].

All the experiments that we report in this paper were performed in the 5GHz frequency band with 20MHz bandwidth channels. We choose 5GHz band for shorter wavelength, which lead to better movement speed resolution. We also tested CARM in 2.4GHz. Due to the longer wavelength, frequencies of the CSI waveforms in 2.4GHz are lower for the same activity compared to those in 5GHz. CARM acquires CSI measurements from the CSI tool and processes it in real-time using MATLAB. CARM is computationally efficient. For example, on a Think-pad laptop with Intel i5-3320 CPU and 4GB RAM, CARM takes 85.6ms to process 200ms CSI values sampled at a rate of 2,500 samples/second. Note that it is possible to further improve the computational efficiency of CARM by implementing it in C or using DSP to accelerate the signal processing.

8.2 Evaluation Setup

We collected training samples for eight different activities in our lab, which is 7.7m in length and 6.5m in width, as shown in Figure 12(a). We collected a total of 1,400 samples for the testing activities from 25 volunteers. The volunteers included 20 male and 5 female graduate/undergraduate students with ages in the range of 19–22.

We evaluated the recognition accuracy of CAMR through two sets of experiments, one is in the trained environments and the other is in the untrained environments. We use the lab where we collected the training dataset as the trained environments. For the untrained environments, we evaluate on three typical indoor scenarios, including: 1) a large open lobby area, which has a length, width, and height of 45m, 5.3m, and 4m, respectively; 2) a small apartment, which has area of $70m^2$ as shown in Figure 12(b); 3) a small office, which has a length, width, and height of 5.6m, 3.4m, and 2.7m, respectively.

The activities for which we collected training samples are listed in Table 1, along with their abbreviations and number of training samples for each activity. We collected training samples for each activity except walking and running at the location marked with star in Figure 12(a). For walking and running, our volunteers followed

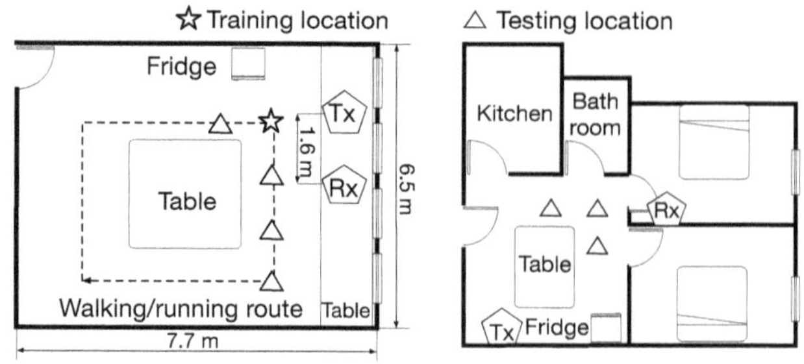

(a) Lab (b) Apartment

Figure 12: Floor plans

the path marked with a dashed line around the table in the center of the lab. Tx and Rx represent the locations of the transmitter AP and receiver laptop. While collecting the training data, we requested the volunteers to change their orientation to ensure the generality of the collected data. Triangles in Figures 12(a) and 12(b) represent the locations where our volunteers performed activities when evaluating accuracy of CARM. The total training time for our activity data set with 1,400 samples was 100.55 seconds on a laptop with Intel i5-4285 CPU, as shown in Table 1. Note that our activities have no location dependency. Furthermore, once CARM is trained on the given training set, it can be directly applied to environments and persons that have not been included in the training set. Thus, CARM does not need the on-site training data collection as for E-eyes [27]. Consequently, the one-time training can be done on a large training set using a data center.

Activity	Samples	Training Time
(R) Running	205	16.38s
(W) Walking	315	26.84s
(S) Sitting down	266	14.49s
(O) Opening refrigerator	213	13.49s
(F) Falling	98	5.02s
(B) Boxing	75	4.88s
(P) Pushing one hand	72	7.00s
(T) Brushing teeth	96	7.35s
(E) Empty (*i.e.*, no activity)	60	5.10s

Table 1: Summary of activity dataset

8.3 Activity Detection

Now we present the accuracy CARM achieves in detecting the presence of an activity. We evaluate the accuracy using two metrics: true positive rate (TPR) and false alarm rate (FAR). TPR is the ratio of the number of times CARM correctly detects the presence of an activity to the total number of times the activity is performed. FAR is the ratio of the number of times that CARM incorrectly detects the presence of an activity when actually there is no activity.

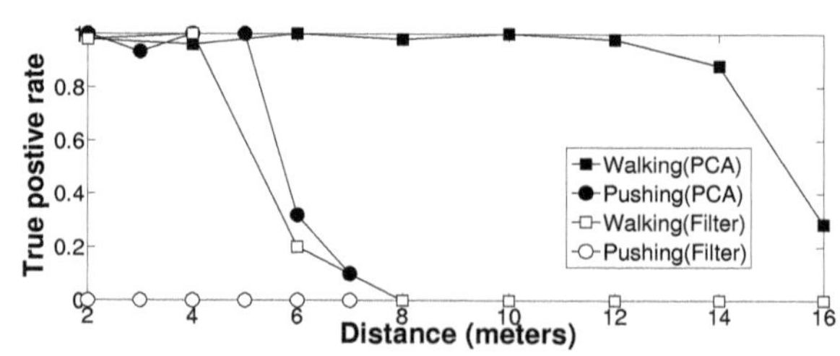

Figure 13: Detection range of CARM

CARM detects small movements such as pushing one hand and large movements such as walking with a TPR larger than 98% at distances of up to 5 meters and 12 meters, respectively. Figure 13 plots CARM's TPR for two different activities in the open lobby area as described in section 8.2, where the sender and receiver were separated by 3.5 meters. Each TPR for an activity was calculated from 20 samples of that activity collected at three different locations while ensuring that the distance of each point from the receiver was the same. Our PCA denoising method has a much longer detection range for walking compared to the range of 4 meters achieved by the low-pass filtering approach. Furthermore, without PCA, low-pass filtering cannot reliably detect small movements such as pushing at a distance of 2 meters. This shows that compared to the conventional low-pass filtering approach, PCA is more efficient in extracting small changes in CSI values caused by human movements. Using PCA denoising, CARM achieves a large coverage area: with a single Tx/Rx pair, it reliably detects the presence of activities in a $450m^2$ open region.

CARM has a low FAR of 1.4 false alarms per hour. To measure CARM's FAR, we record the activity log for 14 hours from 6:00pm to 8:00am on a certain day when no one was around the sender and receiver. During these 14 hours, we saw only 20 false alarms, which were primarily caused by sudden increase in noise levels.

8.4 Activity Recognition

CARM achieves an average cross validation accuracy of 96.5% across all activities. Figure 14 shows the recognition accuracy of 10-fold cross validation using the training data set collected in the "lab". Except for "sitting down", "opening fridge" and "falling", CARM achieves close to 100% accuracy, when the sampling rate is 2,500 samples per second. The accuracy for "empty" is 100%, which means that if CARM incorrectly detects the presence of an activity when in reality there was no activity, it can correctly find out that there was no activity as soon as it evaluates the detected sample against the activity models.

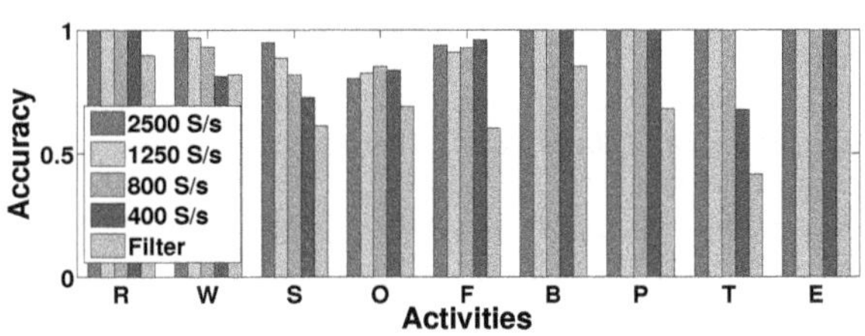

Figure 14: Impact of sampling rates on accuracy

Accuracy of CARM improves when CSI values are sampled at a higher sampling rate, but the increase is not significant beyond the sampling rate of 800 samples/second. Figure 14 plots CARM's recognition accuracy for each activity under four different sampling rates. From this figure, we observe that with sampling rates of 800 samples/second and higher, the average cross validation accuracy is over 94.8%, which is only a slight drop compared to 96.5% achieved for a sampling rate of 2,500 samples/second. Sampling rate of 800 samples/second is very close to the Nyquist sampling rate because the frequency components in CFR power go up to 300Hz due to human movements, as discussed in Section 5.2. When sampling rate further reduces to 400 samples/second, the average accuracy reduces significantly to 87%. In comparison, the average recognition accuracy for low-pass filtering approach is only 73% with the sampling rate of 2,500 samples/second. In the low-pass filtering approach, the accuracies for activities of "falling" and small activities such as "brushing teeth" drop significantly because filtering cannot reliably preserve the high frequency components and small fluctuations in CSI values. In our real-time experiments, CARM tolerates wireless interference caused by other devices that are using the same channel. When facing a high packet loss rate, CARM interpolates the missing CSI values and uses a lower sampling rate to achieve an acceptable recognition accuracy.

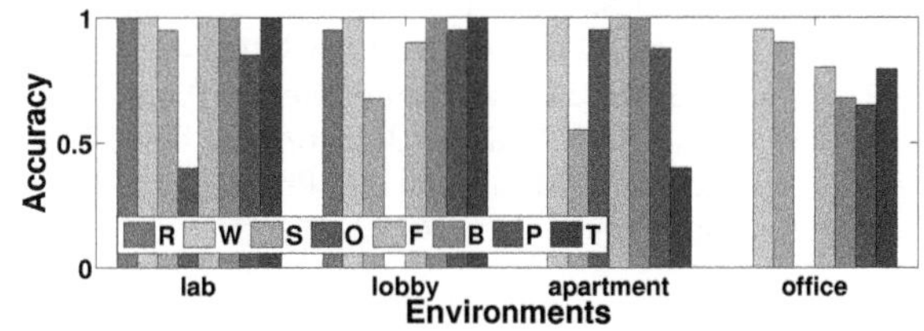

Figure 15: Accuracy in different environments

CARM achieves an accuracy of more than 80% for environments and persons that it has not been trained on. Figure 15 shows the accuracy CARM achieves in different environments for each activity. In each environment, we randomly picked 3 to 6 locations and performed each activity for three times in each location to calculate the recognition accuracy. Two volunteers who were not in the training set performed these activities. Note that this figure does not have results for "opening refrigerator" in the lobby and office, "running" in the apartment and office due to equipment and space constraints. In the lab, lobby, office and apartment, CARM achieves average accuracy of 90%, 93%, 83% and 80%, respectively. For the environment that is the same as the training environment, *i.e.*, "lab", the average accuracy reduces moderately to 90% with lower accuracy for a single activity, "opening refrigerator", due to the different ways of performing the activity. For the more challenging case where CARM is applied to a new environment that it have no training data, the average accuracy drops to around 80%. Most of the recognition errors are in a few activities, *e.g.*, "sitting down" for the lobby and apartment case and "brushing teeth" for the apartment case. The major causes for the errors are due to the drastic change in multi-path conditions. For example, there are no LOS path between the sender and the receiver in the apartment case as shown in Figure 12(b), while our training data are all collected in the lab with LOS path. The performance of CARM can be improved by including more scenarios in the training set. During the experiments, there are other persons sitting or using computers in the same room. CARM is robust to multiple persons coexisting in the same room given that they do not move at the same time. Recognizing simultaneous activities of multiple persons is left as future work of this paper. Currently, CARM uses a single Tx/Rx pair. The performance of CARM can be improved by simultaneously using multiple Tx/Rx pairs located at different positions in the environment. We will explore this direction in our future work.

9. CONCLUSION

In this paper, we make the following three key contributions. First, we propose the CSI-speed model, which quantifies the correlation between CSI value dynamics and the movement speeds of different human body parts, and the CSI-activity model, which quantifies the correlation between the movement speeds of different human body parts and a specific human activity. Second, we propose several signal processing techniques, such as PCA based denoising and DWT based feature extraction, for human activity recognition based on the two models. Third, we implemented CARM using commercial WiFi devices and evaluated it in several different environments. Our results show that CARM achieves an average accuracy of greater than 96%.

Acknowledgments

We would like to thank the anonymous reviewers and the shepherd for their valuable comments for improving the quality of the paper. We thank the students and volunteers in our lab who helped us in collecting the activity dataset. This work is partially supported by the National Natural Science Foundation of China under Grant Numbers 61373129, 61472184, 61321491, 61272546, 91218302, 61321491, 61472185, the Jiangsu Future Internet Program under Grant Number BY2013095-4-08, the Jiangsu High-level Innovation and Entrepreneurship (Shuangchuang) Program and EU FP7 IRSES Mobile-Cloud Project Grant (612212).

10. REFERENCES

[1] Enhancements for higher throughput. IEEE Standard 802.11n, 2009.

[2] Google project Soli. https://www.youtube.com/watch?v=0QNiZfSsPc0.

[3] H. Abdelnasser, M. Youssef, and K. A. Harras. WiGest: A ubiquitous wifi-based gesture recognition system. In *Proceedings of IEEE INFOCOM*, 2015.

[4] F. Adib, Z. Kabelac, and D. Katabi. Multi-person motion tracking via RF body reflections. In *Proceedings of Usenix NSDI*, 2015.

[5] F. Adib, Z. Kabelac, D. Katabi, and R. C. Miller. 3D tracking via body radio reflections. In *Proceedings of Usenix NSDI*, 2013.

[6] J. K. Aggarwal and S. R. Michael. Human activity analysis: A review. *ACM Computing Surveys*, 43(3), 2011.

[7] E. Ertin, N. Stohs, S. Kumar, A. Raij, M. al'Absi, and S. Shah. AutoSense: unobtrusively wearable sensor suite for inferring the onset, causality, and consequences of stress in the field. In *Proceedings of ACM Sensys*, 2011.

[8] J. Gjengset, J. Xiong, G. McPhillips, and K. Jamieson. Phaser: Enabling phased array signal processing on commodity WiFi access points. In *Proceedings of ACM MobiCom*, 2014.

[9] D. Halperin, W. Hu, A. Sheth, and D. Wetherall. Tool release: Gathering 802.11n traces with channel state information. *ACM SIGCOMM CCR*, 41(1):53, 2011.

[10] C. Han, K. Wu, Y. Wang, and L. M. Ni. Wifall: Device-free fall detection by wireless networks. In *Proceedings of IEEE INFOCOM*, pages 271–279, 2014.

[11] D. Huang, R. Nandakumar, and S. Gollakota. Feasibility and limits of Wi-Fi imaging. In *Proceedings of ACM SenSys*, pages 266–279, 2014.

[12] K. R. Joshi, S. S. Hong, and S. Katti. Pinpoint: Localizing interfering radios. In *Proceedings of Usenix NSDI*, pages 241–253, 2013.

[13] B. Kellogg, A. Parks, S. Gollakota, J. R. Smith, and D. Wetherall. Wi-Fi backscatter: Internet connectivity for RF-powered devices. In *ACM SIGCOMM*, 2014.

[14] B. Kellogg, V. Talla, and S. Gollakota. Bringing gesture recognition to all devices. In *Proceedings of Usenix NSDI*, 2014.

[15] T. Kim, H. T. Attias, S.-Y. Lee, and T.-W. Lee. Blind source separation exploiting higher-order frequency dependencies. *IEEE Transactions on Audio, Speech, and Language Processing*, 15(1):70–79, 2007.

[16] B. Lyonnet, C. Ioana, and M. G. Amin. Human gait classification using microdoppler time-frequency signal representations. In *Proceedings of IEEE Radar Conference*, pages 915–919, 2010.

[17] Q. Pu, S. Gupta, S. Gollakota, and S. Patel. Whole-home gesture recognition using wireless signals. In *Proceedings of ACM MobiCom*, 2013.

[18] L. R. Rabiner and B.-H. Juang. *Fundamentals of speech recognition*. Prentice Hall, 1993.

[19] S. Sen, J. Lee, K.-H. Kim, and P. Congdon. Avoiding multipath to revive inbuilding WiFi localization. In *Proceeding of ACM MobiSys*, pages 249–262, 2013.

[20] S. Sen, B. Radunovic, R. R. Choudhury, and T. Minka. You are facing the mona lisa: spot localization using phy layer information. In *Proceedings of ACM MobiSys*, pages 183–196, 2012.

[21] S. Sigg, U. Blanke, and G. Troster. The telepathic phone: Frictionless activity recognition from WiFi-RSSI. In *IEEE PerCom*, pages 148–155, 2014.

[22] S. Sigg, M. Scholz, S. Shi, Y. Ji, and M. Beigl. RF-sensing of activities from non-cooperative subjects in device-free recognition systems using ambient and local signals. *IEEE Transactions on Mobile Computing*, 13(4):907–920, 2014.

[23] S. Sigg, S. Shi, F. Buesching, Y. Ji, and L. Wolf. Leveraging RF-channel fluctuation for activity recognition: Active and passive systems, continuous and rssi-based signal features. In *Proceedings of ACM MoMM*, 2013.

[24] D. Tse and P. Viswanath. *Fundamentals of wireless communication*. Cambridge university press, 2005.

[25] P. Van Dorp and F. Groen. Feature-based human motion parameter estimation with radar. *IET Radar, Sonar & Navigation*, 2(2):135–145, 2008.

[26] G. Wang, Y. Zou, Z. Zhou, K. Wu, and L. M. Ni. We can hear you with Wi-Fi! In *Proceedings of ACM MobiCom*, 2014.

[27] Y. Wang, J. Liu, Y. Chen, M. Gruteser, J. Yang, and H. Liu. E-eyes: In-home device-free activity identification using fine-grained WiFi signatures. In *Proceedings of ACM MobiCom*, 2014.

[28] L. R. Welch. Hidden markov models and the baum-welch algorithm. *IEEE Information Theory Society Newsletter*, 53(4):10–13, 2003.

[29] N. J. Willis. *Bistatic Radar*. SciTech Publishing Inc., 2005.

[30] W. Xi, J. Zhao, X.-Y. Li, K. Zhao, S. Tang, X. Liu, and Z. Jiang. Electronic frog eye: Counting crowd using WiFi. In *Proceedings of IEEE INFOCOM*, 2014.

[31] L. Yang, Y. Chen, X.-Y. Li, C. Xiao, M. Li, and Y. Liu. Tagoram: real-time tracking of mobile RFID tags to high precision using cots devices. In *ACM MobiCom*, pages 237–248, 2014.

[32] Z. Yang, Z. Zhou, and Y. Liu. From RSSI to CSI: Indoor localization via channel response. *ACM Computing Surveys*, 46(2):25, 2013.

[33] K. Yatani and K. N. Truong. Bodyscope: a wearable acoustic sensor for activity recognition. In *Proceedings of ACM UbiComp*, pages 341–350, 2012.

[34] X. Zhou, Z. Zhang, Y. Zhu, Y. Li, S. Kumar, A. Vahdat, B. Y. Zhao, and H. Zheng. Mirror mirror on the ceiling: flexible wireless links for data centers. In *Proceedings of ACM SIGCOMM*, pages 443–454, 2012.

[35] Z. Zhou, Z. Yang, C. Wu, L. Shangguan, and Y. Liu. Towards omnidirectional passive human detection. In *Proceedings of IEEE INFOCOM*, pages 3057–3065, 2013.

WiDraw: Enabling Hands-free Drawing in the Air on Commodity WiFi Devices

Li Sun
University at Buffalo, SUNY
lsun3@buffalo.edu

Souvik Sen
HP Labs
souvik.sen@hp.com

Dimitrios Koutsonikolas
University at Buffalo, SUNY
dimitrio@buffalo.edu

Kyu-Han Kim
HP Labs
kyu-han.kim@hp.com

ABSTRACT

This paper demonstrates that it is possible to leverage WiFi signals from commodity mobile devices to enable hands-free drawing in the air. While prior solutions require the user to hold a wireless transmitter, or require custom wireless hardware, or can only determine a pre-defined set of hand gestures, this paper introduces *WiDraw*, the first hand motion tracking system using commodity WiFi cards, and without any user wearables. *WiDraw* harnesses the Angle-of-Arrival values of incoming wireless signals at the mobile device to track the user's hand trajectory. We utilize the intuition that whenever the user's hand occludes a signal coming from a certain direction, the signal strength of the angle representing the same direction will experience a drop. Our software prototype using commodity wireless cards can track the user's hand with a median error lower than 5 cm. We use *WiDraw* to implement an in-air handwriting application that allows the user to draw letters, words, and sentences, and achieves a mean word recognition accuracy of 91%.

Categories and Subject Descriptors

C.2.1 [**Network Architecture and Design**]: Wireless communication; H.5.2 [**User Interfaces**]: Input devices and strategies

General Terms

Design, Experimentation, Performance

Keywords

Wireless; Motion Tracking; Gesture Recognition; Channel State Information; Angle-of-Arrival

1. INTRODUCTION

Today, a user can write, scroll, swipe, or draw on a touch screen of a smart phone, tablet, or laptop. Users can even interact hands-free with a computing device using commercial hardware systems such as Kinect [1] and Leap Motion [2]. While these systems are highly popular, they require a dedicated hardware setup or line-of-sight (LOS) to the user. Recently, researchers have made progress in detecting human hand gestures using wireless signals [3–8], enabling gesture recognition in non-line-of-sight (NLOS) scenarios. However, prior solutions are limited because they either require the user to hold a wireless transmitter [7], or require a custom wireless hardware to track the user's hand motions [3–6, 8]. More importantly, most of the current solutions [3–5, 8] require a priori learning of wireless signal patterns, which limits them to recognize only a fixed set of pre-defined hand gestures. We believe that, if we can leverage wireless signals to automatically track the detailed trajectory of the human hand in the air, we can greatly simplify interaction of the user with today's computing devices including laptops, smart TVs, tablets, and even devices that do not have a dedicated user input (e.g., sensors and IoT devices). Since WiFi signals do not require LOS and can traverse through material (e.g., cloth), hands-free drawing can also be used by the user to interact with the mobile device in a pocket or a bag - e.g., to control volume or answer a call, or simply draw the name of the callee in the air to start a conversation.

MobiCom'15, September 7–11, 2015, Paris, France.
© 2015 ACM. ISBN 978-1-4503-3619-2/15/09...$15.00.
DOI: http://dx.doi.org/10.1145/2789168.2790129.

This paper demonstrates that it is possible to leverage WiFi signals from commodity mobile devices to enable hands-free drawing in the air. We introduce *WiDraw*, the first hand motion tracking solution that can be enabled on existing mobile devices using only a software patch. *WiDraw* leverages physical layer information and multiple antennas on commodity devices to track the detailed trajectory of the user's hand in both LOS and NLOS scenarios, without requiring the user to touch the device or hold any hardware. As shown in Figure 1(a), using *WiDraw*, a user can draw arbitrary lines, curves, or even alphabetical characters, simply by using hand motions in the air.

WiDraw utilizes the Angle-of-Arrival (AoA) values of incoming wireless signals at the mobile device to track the user's hand trajectory. Existing techniques such as MUSIC [9] can utilize the *Channel State Information* (CSI) from multiple antennas to estimate the angles at which a wireless signal from a transmitter arrives at the receiver. MUSIC also reports the signal strength of the incoming signal component arriving from a given angle. We utilize the intuition that whenever the user's hand blocks a signal coming from a certain direction, the signal strength of the AoA representing the same direction will

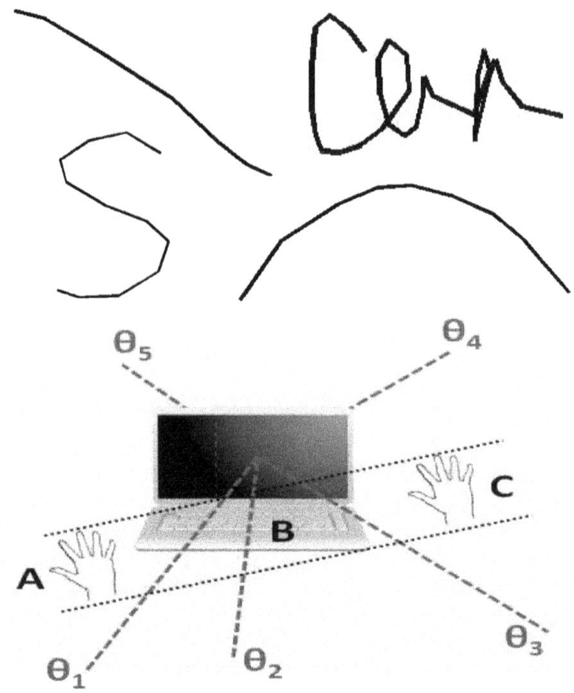

Figure 1: (a) *WiDraw*'s estimated trajectory when the user drew a straight line, a circular curve, the letter "S", and the word "can". (b) The user's hand perturbs the signal strength of several AoAs along its trajectory.

experience a sharp drop. E.g., in Figure 1(b), if the hand passes through the trajectory ABC, it will occlude the AoAs θ_1, θ_2, and θ_3 in sequence. By tracking the signal strength of the AoAs, it is possible to determine when such occlusions happen. Thereafter, by utilizing the azimuth and elevation of the affected AoAs, it is possible to determine a set of horizontal and vertical coordinates along the hand's trajectory. The depth of the user's hand can also be approximated using the drop in the overall signal strength. E.g., if the hand is close to the receiver, it will occlude a larger number of AoAs in comparison to when the hand is farther away from it. By estimating the hand's depth, along with horizontal and vertical coordinates, *WiDraw* tracks the hand's trajectory w.r.t. the WiFi antennas of the receiver.

We demonstrate the feasibility of *WiDraw* by building a software prototype on HP Envy laptops, using Atheros AR9590 chipsets and 3 antennas. The tracking granularity of *WiDraw* depends on the number of AoAs along the hand's trajectory. While periodic access point beacons can contribute several angles, the tracking granularity can be further increased by employing lightweight probing mechanisms to obtain AoAs from neighboring client devices as well. We show that by utilizing the AoAs from up to 25 WiFi transmitters, the *WiDraw*-enabled laptop can track the user's hand with a median error lower than 5 cm. *WiDraw*'s rate of false positives - motion detection in the absence of one - is less than 0.04 events per minute over a 360 minute period in a busy office environment. Experiments across 10 different users also demonstrate that *WiDraw* can be used to write words and sentences in the air, achieving a mean word recognition accuracy of 91%.

Our main contributions are summarized as follows:

- ***WiDraw* is the first hand motion tracking system using commodity WiFi cards:** Existing systems can only track a few gestures, require special hardware, or require the user to hold a device.
- **We identify the opportunity to utilize the AoA information to enable hands-free drawing in the air:** Our solution harnesses the effect of hand occlusions on the signal strength of incoming signal directions.
- **We implement and demonstrate our solution using commodity wireless cards:** We exploit the CSI information from the three antennas of the Atheros AR9590 chipset and evaluate our system using more than 90,000 trajectories drawn by 10 users.
- **We design and implement a virtual handwriting application using WiDraw:** Our system achieves an average letter and word recognition accuracy of 95% and 91%, respectively.

The subsequent sections expand on each of these contributions, including experimental observations, followed by algorithms, design, and evaluation.

2. BACKGROUND AND OBSERVATIONS

This section presents the relevant background on AoA estimation followed by our observations that suggest that AoAs can be used to estimate the motion of the human hand in a 3D space. For our measurements, we use HP laptops running Linux OS. We note that AoA estimation is possible from commodity chipsets if they can report per packet *Channel State Information (CSI)* [10,11]. Next we briefly describe the mechanism to obtain AoAs from the CSI.

2.1 AoA estimation from CSI

A wireless signal from a transmitter arrives at several angles at the receiver. The AoA at the receiver can be computed by comparing the phase of the CSI values acquired from multiple antennas, a quantity which changes linearly by 2π for every wavelength λ along the path from the transmitter to the receiver. E.g., if the receiver has only two antennas placed at a distance of $\lambda/2$ and a measured phase difference of the CSI acquired from the two antennas is $\Delta\phi$, we can estimate the angle-of-arrival θ as:

$$\theta = \arcsin(\Delta\phi/\pi)$$

Rather than analyzing the phase differences between every pair of antennas individually, the receiver can employ AoA estimation algorithms such as MUSIC [9]. MUSIC utilizes the phase difference values and yields a pseudospectrum (Figure 2(a)). Each peak in the pseudospectrum is an estimated *AoA*. Multiple peaks in Figure 2(a) imply incoming signals along different directions from the transmitter.

Since wireless signals propagate in a 3-D space, the angle of an incoming signal at the receiver has both azimuth and elevation components (Figure 2(b)). MUSIC can compute both the azimuth and elevation of an AoA if the receiver's antennas are arranged in a special pattern [12]. However, when applied to linear antenna arrays such as those within a laptop or tablet screen, MUSIC can only compute a one-dimensional representation of the AoA (θ in Figure 2(b)). The 1-D AoA value θ, as reported by MUSIC, is related to the azimuth (az) and elevation (el) values of the AoA:

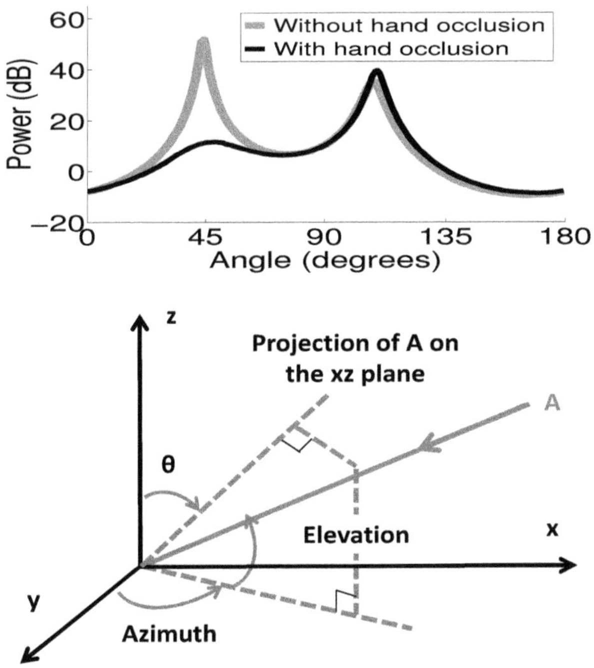

Figure 2: (a) MUSIC's pseudospectrum output with and without occlusion by human hand. (b) MUSIC yields the 1-D angle-of-arrival (AoA) which is related to the azimuth and elevation of the AoA.

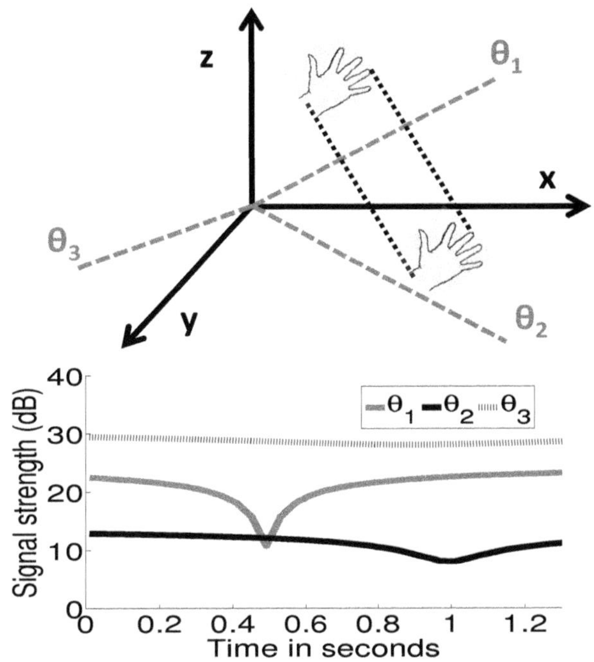

Figure 3: (a) Trajectory of human hand through 3 AoA values. (b) Change in amplitude of the AoAs as the human hand passes through them.

$$\theta = \frac{\pi}{2} - \tan^{-1}\left(\frac{\tan(el)}{\sin(az)}\right) \qquad (1)$$

Observe that θ is upper bounded by $(\frac{\pi}{2} - el)$, which occurs when the azimuth angle is $\frac{\pi}{2}$. In section 3.1, we will use these observations to compute both the azimuth and elevation values of the AoA from the existing linear antenna array of the laptop.

2.2 Effect of human hand on the AoA

To track the motion of a human hand near the wireless receiver, we observe that if the user's hand blocks the signal arriving along a specific AoA, the AoA's signal strength will experience a sharp drop (as shown in Figure 2(a)). On the other hand, if the trajectory of the user's hand does not occlude the signal arriving on a specific AoA, its signal strength will not demonstrate any drop. To illustrate the above, consider 3 different AoA values as observed by the receiver in Figure 3(a). The trajectory of the user's hand blocks θ_1 completely and θ_2 partially but does not pass through θ_3. Figure 3(b) shows the change in signal strength values of the 3 angles over time. The time instant when the signal strength of a given AoA attains its minimum value corresponds to the moment when the user's hand arrives at a location that is closest to that angle on its moving trajectory. We find that the drop in the signal strength of a given AoA value is proportional to proximity of the hand to the AoA trajectory, which is why θ_1 demonstrates a larger drop than θ_2 in Figure 3(b).

The set of AoAs whose signal strength values attain a minimum provides a mechanism to determine the hand's position and motion. If the user's hand is y_i units away from receiver and it causes an AoA with azimuth (az) and elevation (el) to attain a minimum, the horizontal (x_i) and vertical (z_i) coordinates of the user's hand can be computed as:

$$x_i = \frac{y_i}{\cot(az)} \qquad z_i = \frac{y_i * \tan(el)}{\cos(az)} \qquad (2)$$

The trajectory of the human hand can be estimated by using the sequence of coordinates, as obtained from the AoAs whose signal strength drops. Of course the tracking accuracy depends on the number of angles along the hand's trajectory. A large number of angles placed close to each other along the hand's trajectory can allow tracing the trajectory with fine granularity. On the other hand, a small number of angles far apart from each other, along the hand's trajectory, will result in low accuracy. Therefore, the feasibility and limitations of hand tracking depend on the distribution of AoA values in real environments. Next, we study these requirements in detail.

2.3 AoA density for hand motion tracking

As shown in Figure 4(a), due to their radial nature, the spatial distance between incoming signal directions increases with larger distance from the WiFi antennas. Near the receiver, the density of the AoAs is quite high implying that the user's hand can be tracked with high granularity. However, farther the user's hand is from the receiver, lower will be the granularity of trajectory tracking. The density of the AoAs in a given environment in turn depends on the number of transmitters within the range of the *WiDraw*-enabled receiver. Figure 4(b) plots the average number of access points (APs) and WiFi-enabled devices across 50 different locations in different environments - apartment, office, cafeteria. To track the movement of the user's hand, *WiDraw* needs to periodically obtain

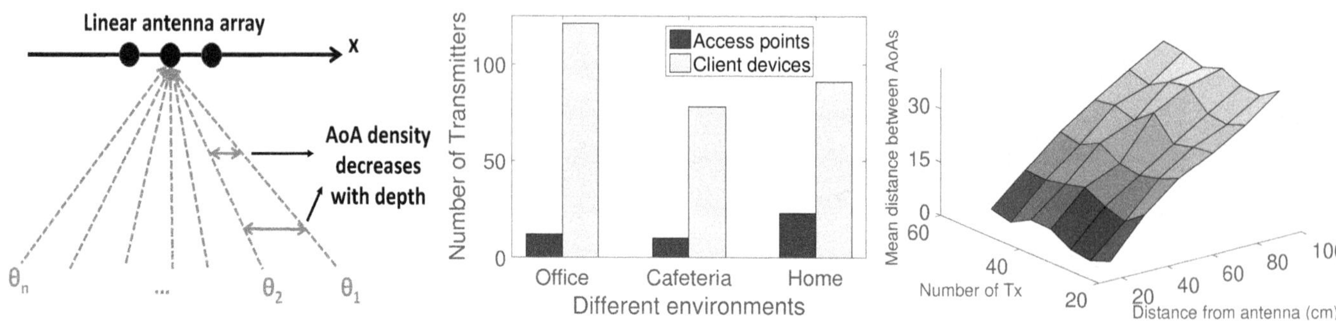

Figure 4: (a) Distance between nearby angles increases with greater distance from the receiver. (b) Average number of APs and WiFi-enabled devices across 50 different locations in different environments. (c) The average distance between neighboring AoAs increases with lower number of WiFi transmitters and increasing depth of the hand from the receiver.

and analyze the incoming signal directions of each transmitter. If the transmitter is an AP, *WiDraw* can obtain the CSI and AoA of its transmitted signal by leveraging periodic beacons. However, if the transmitter is a client device, the *WiDraw*-enabled receiver may have to periodically probe the device to obtain its AoA values. Therefore, *WiDraw* may only be able to leverage a few neighboring clients.

To estimate the tracking granularity using angles, we estimated the AoA values from neighboring transmitters whose signals are incident on the receiver at the frontside, using the data from the same 50 locations as in Figure 4(b). We consider the AoAs only at the front side of the receiver because the user will likely draw in front of the receiver. Figure 4(c) plots the average distance between nearby AoAs as a function of the number of transmitters and increasing distance from the laptop. We observe that for a modest number of transmitters (e.g., 30), the inter-AoA distance values are reasonably low (12.75 cm) for a distance of 1 foot but increases to greater than 24.65 cm for distances more than 2 feet. This suggests that at a larger distance from the receiving antennas, we will only be able to track coarse hand motion trajectories. However, as long as the human hand is within 2 feet from the receiver, the density of the AoAs may be reasonable enough to allow us to track finer hand motions.

2.4 Effect of environmental changes on AoA

AoA values need to be reasonably stable at least during the motion of the user's hand. The AoA values can change rapidly if the transmitter is mobile, making it difficult to use it for motion detection [11]. On the other hand, if the transmitter is static, an AoA will change only if a dominant propagation path between the transmitter and the receiver is affected. We find that the changes in signal strength of the AoAs due to environmental changes are structurally different from those because of the user's hand near the receiver. First, as shown in Figure 5(a), unlike hand occlusions, signal strength variations due to environmental fluctuations are often random and therefore can be removed using a low pass filter. Second, after filtering, the drop in signal strength due to environmental changes is significantly lower than when a human hand occludes the AoA (Figure 5(b)). Third, while hand occlusions result into a large drop in signal strength within a few seconds, such large changes occur much more slowly due to environmental fading. Therefore, it may be possible to increase robustness by estimating the hand's trajectory from the AoAs

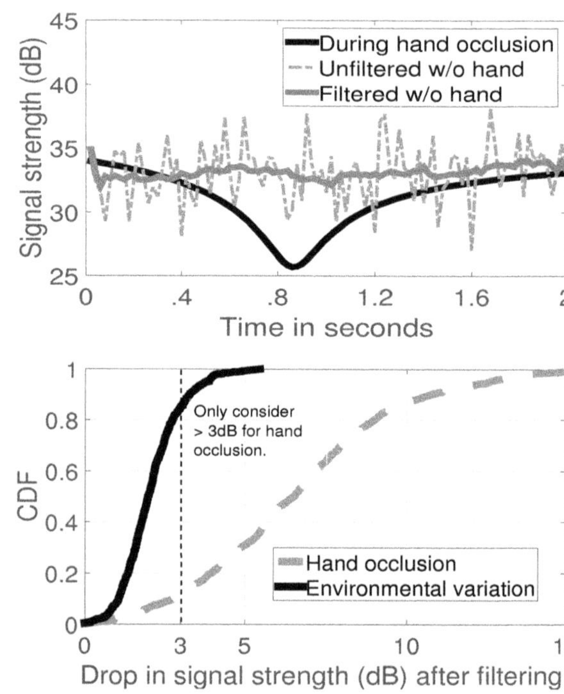

Figure 5: Signal strength fluctuations in a busy cafeteria: (a) Drop in signal strength over time is significantly lower than that due to occlusion from human hand. (b) Distribution of signal strength fluctuations at 50 different locations with and without hand occlusions.

whose signal strength demonstrates a large drop. Of course, our system requires more robust mechanisms if any particular AoA's signal strength changes significantly.

In conclusion, we observed that human hand causes significant drop in the signal strength of the AoAs along its trajectory. We found that the occlusion due to human hand causes deeper perturbations than random environment related fluctuation. Therefore, by tracking the azimuth and elevation of the AoAs which undergo significant changes in signal strength, it may be possible to determine the trajectory of the human hand. However, as observed in our measurements, several challenges remain: (1) How will we determine the azimuth and elevation angle from the 1-D angle reported by MUSIC? (2) How can we ensure fine-grained tracking by using the incoming signals from a modest number of transmitters? (3) While 2D hand position may be obtained by considering the azimuth and elevation of an AoA, how can we track the hand's depth to enable 3D motion tracking? (4) The incoming signal from a transmitter can change if the transmitter is mobile or the wireless environment is changing quickly. How can we enable robust motion tracking under such AoA changes? The next section answers these questions and presents our system called *WiDraw* that enables fine-grained hand trajectory tracking using AoA values of wireless signals.

3. HAND TRACKING ALGORITHMS

This section presents our solutions that enable tracking the user's hand near the WiFi receiver. We begin by explaining how the azimuth and elevation of an AoA can be computed. Thereafter, we explain how we track the hand's motion using the azimuth and elevation values.

3.1 Azimuth and elevation estimation

To calculate the azimuth and elevation values from MUSIC's 1-D AoA output, we refer to Equation 1. Observe in Figure 2(b) that, if the user rotates the linear antenna array over the Z axis (as shown in Figure 6), the azimuth of a given AoA will gradually increase until the signal incidents the laptop along its antenna array, when the azimuth becomes 90°. At that moment, the 1-D AoA value reported by MUSIC (θ in Figure 2(b)) will attain its maximum value and according to Equation 1 it will essentially be equal to the (90° - elevation angle). Therefore we ask the user to turn the laptop around its Z-axis as shown in Figure 6 and collect MUSIC's pseudospectrum outputs. From the pseudospectrums, for each 1-D AoA, we compute the maximum value it attains and use it to compute the elevation. Once we know the elevation, the azimuth of the AoA is estimated using Equation 1.

A pertinent question is how frequently will the user have to turn the laptop for motion tracking? Observe that a recalibration is only required when the direction of incoming signals from a given transmitter changes completely. This happens when an existing dominant incoming signal direction is blocked and thus, another incoming signal appears with a different AoA value. We will explain in Section 4.3 how we determine such changes and automatically calculate the new azimuth and elevation values, without any user initiated calibration.

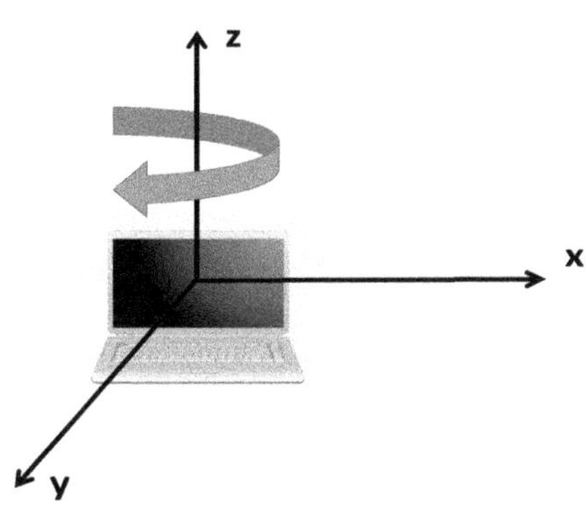

Figure 6: User turns the laptop around its Z-axis to help *WiDraw* compute the per AoA azimuth and elevation.

3.2 Hand trajectory tracking

During the hand's motion, if an AoA's signal strength attains a minimum, we can calculate the instantaneous spatial coordinates of the hand by applying the AoA's azimuth and elevation values in Equation 2. However, Equation 2 can compute the horizontal and vertical coordinates of the hand only if the hand's depth from the receiver is known. Therefore, we begin by discussing how the hand's depth can be estimated.

Determining hand's depth

To determine the hand's initial depth, we track the average of the RSSI values of all incoming signals from the neighboring transmitters. Figure 7(a) plots the drop in the average RSSI value when the user's hand is placed at varying depths from the receiver. We find that, on average, the drop in the average RSSI is higher if the user's hand is placed closer to the receiver. This happens because, when the hand is closer to the receiver's antenna, a larger number of incoming signals from different transmitters are blocked. Therefore, we calculate the drop in the average RSSI value when the user's hand first appears near the receiver. Thereafter, we calculate the approximate initial depth of the hand using the relationship established in Figure 7(a).

The depth of the user's hand will not change in case the user is drawing on a plane parallel to the receiver's antenna. However, if the user's hand moves in all 3 dimensions, the depth value will not remain constant. By tracking the changes in the average RSSI value across all transmitters, it is possible to approximately determine the depth changes as well. We try to further improve the accuracy of depth estimation by analyzing the time difference between consecutive AoA minima. Our intuition is that, if the hand is moving towards the receiver, the time difference value between consecutive AoAs will be smaller than if the hand is moving away from the receiver. By analyzing the time difference values, it is possible to geometrically find the change in the hand's depth. E.g., in Figure 7(b) let the user's hand pass through 3 consecutive AoAs - AoA_0, AoA_1, and AoA_2 at times t_0, t_1, and t_2, respectively. The depth of the hand changes by h_1 units between t_0 and t_1 and by h_2 units between t_0 and t_2. Since we know the initial depth of the hand at time t_0, we can compute the coordinates of the points A, B, C, which capture the trajectory of the hand if its depth remained constant. If d_1, d_2 are the distances between these coordinates (as shown in 7(b)), geometrically we can obtain the change in depth h_2 at time t_2 as:

$$h_2 = \frac{(d_1 + d_2) * \alpha - d_1}{(\tan{\theta_2}^{-1} - \tan{\theta_1}^{-1}) * \alpha} \tag{3}$$

in which $\alpha = (t_1 - t_0)/(t_2 - t_0)$. By utilizing the above equation, we can determine the change in depth of the hand's trajectory. This, when combined with the hand's initial depth, allows us to track the hand's absolute depth.

Determining horizontal and vertical coordinates

The spatial coordinates computed from an AoA when it attains a minimum may not represent the exact coordinates of the user's hand. This is because, if the user's hand does not occlude the AoA completely but is placed near its trajectory, the AoA's signal strength will still drop. Figure 7(c) shows the drop in signal strength with increasing proximity of the hand

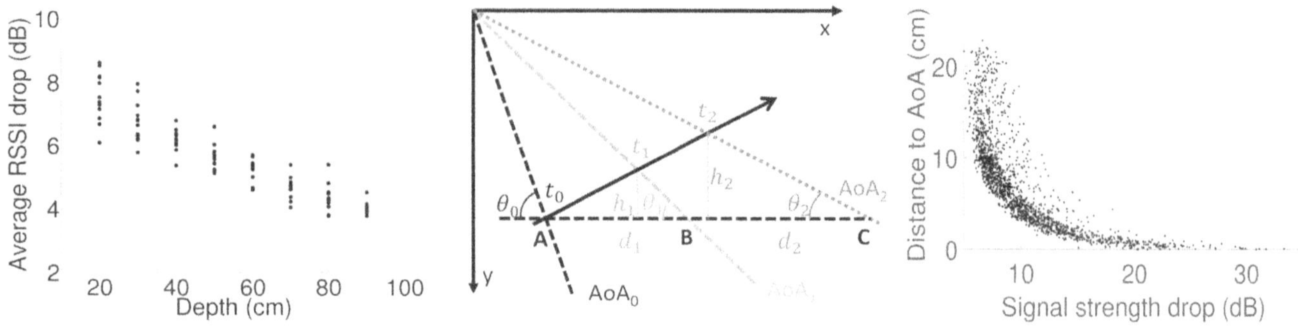

Figure 7: (a) Average RSSI drop across all AoAs vs. depth of the hand from the *WiDraw* receiver. 25 locations in the same 2x2 square feet area were picked uniformly at each depth value. (b) Estimating depth changes by utilizing the time duration between AoA minima. The user's hand crossed 3 AoAs (AoA_0, AoA_1, and AoA_2) in a 3D movement. The trajectories of the hand movement and 3 AoAs were projected to the 2D X-Y plane. (c) The drop in signal strength of an AoA is proportional to the hand's distance from the AoA.

to the AoA's trajectory. The drop in signal strength can therefore suggest the approximate distance of the hand from the coordinates computed from the AoA's azimuth and elevation values. E.g., consider AoA_0 in Figure 8. If the drop in signal strength the moment it attains its minimum value is 8.5 dB, the hand's actual location can be anywhere on the perimeter of a circle with a radius of 5 cm. Further, the trajectory of the user's hand at that moment is also tangential to the same circle.

We determine the location of the user's hand on the circle by analyzing the trend (increasing or decreasing) of the neighboring angles' signal strength values at the moment when AoA_0 attains a minimum. If the signal strength of a neighboring angle is increasing, then the hand's direction is away from it and vice versa. E.g., in Figure 8, the hand is moving towards AoA_1 and AoA_3 but is moving away from AoA_2. Consider the unit vectors along the tangents in Figure 8 which pass through the coordinates obtained from the neighboring angles. The direction of a particular unit vector is towards the angle if the angle's signal strength is decreasing, and away from the angle if it is increasing. The hand's direction is closer to the direction of a unit vector if the corresponding angle's signal strength is decreasing faster. Therefore, we aggregate these unit vectors by computing their weighted average based on the rate of change of the corresponding angle's signal strength. Mathematically, if the rate of change in the signal strength of the neighboring angle AoA_i is v_i, and the corresponding unit vector is $\hat{u}_i$, the weighted average ($\hat{U}$) is

$$\hat{U} = \frac{\sum_{i=1}^{n} |v_i| * \hat{u}_i}{\sum_{i=1}^{n} |v_i|} \quad (4)$$

The direction of the aggregate vector $\hat{U}$ provides us the estimate of the hand's direction. Observe in Figure 8, there can be only 2 tangents to the circle whose direction matches with that of $\hat{U}$. The hand's coordinate can be either of the points where these two tangents meet the circle (A and B in Figure 8). To select one of the two points, we (i) use the coordinates of A or B to estimate signal strength drop for each AoA based on the relationship established in Figure 7(c) and (ii) calculate the actual signal strength drop for each AoA by

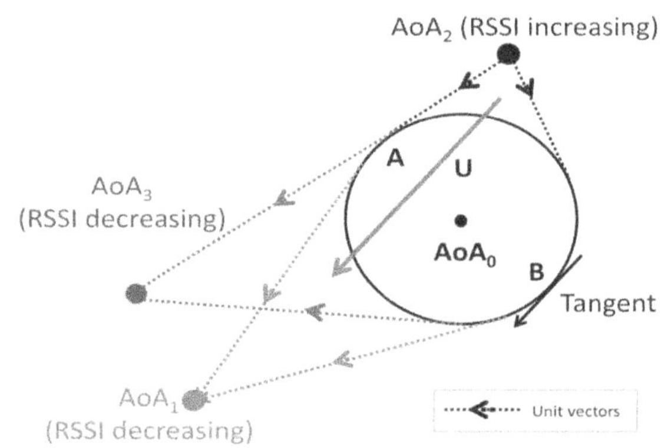

Figure 8: Determining spatial coordinates for the user's hand when AoA_0 attains a minimum, using the signal strength trend of neighboring angles.

comparing the currently measured signal strength value with the initial one. Then, we can break the tie between A and B by choosing the point which yields a more accurate estimate of signal strength drop for most AoAs.

3.3 Dealing with large environmental variations

We found in Section 2.4 that the changes in signal strength due to random environmental related fluctuations have a different structure than the changes due to the user's hand movement. Such random fluctuations can be ignored by applying filtering and by ignoring any signal strength drop which is smaller than 3dB (Figure 5(b)). Large and gradual drop in the signal strength of an AoA due to environmental variations can still occur. If large environmental variations affect an AoA near the hand's trajectory, this will reflect in our trajectory tracking error. However, if such an AoA is far away from the hand's trajectory, it needs to be detected as an outlier. Further if the time interval between consecutive AoA minima is too long, then they were probably a result of random environmental fluctuation and not due to the hand's motion. Formally, if θ_{i-1} and θ_i are two consecutive AoAs which demonstrated a large drop in signal strengths at time t_{i-1} and t_i, and resulting into 2D coordinates C_{i-1} and C_i respectively, we declare θ_i as an outlier if

$$\frac{|\hat{C_i} - \hat{C_{i-1}}|}{t_i - t_{i-1}} > \tau_m \quad (5)$$

where τ_m is the maximum expected speed of the user's hand, which is fixed at 3 feet/second in our implementation. We also declare both θ_{i-1} and θ_i as outliers if the time duration between them is more than a threshold (T):

$$t_i - t_{i-1} > T \quad (6)$$

To determine the accuracy of identifying the AoAs whose signal strengths change due to the hand's motion and not because of large environmental fluctuations, we collected 2 sets of traces over a duration of 6 hours. The first trace consists of AoA data when the user draws in front of the receiver's antenna, while in the second trace she is sitting idle in front of the receiver. Table 1 shows the accuracy and false positives of identifying the relevant AoAs computed from the above 2 sets of traces. If we consider AoAs that undergo a significant drop in signal strength within a considerably long duration (T in Equation 6) as valid, false positives expectedly increase, and so does accuracy. However, as long as we reject AoAs that undergo minima beyond 1.5 seconds, it is possible to maintain low false positive rate with a slight decrease in accuracy. We further note that while using a threshold of 1.5 seconds, 13 short trajectories were falsely recorded within a duration of 6 hours, implying that our false positive rate is less than 0.04 events/minute.

4. DESIGN AND IMPLEMENTATION

In this section, we present *WiDraw*'s detailed design.

4.1 Setup and implementation details

In our solution, we equip the laptop with a wireless network card equipped with Atheros 9590 chipset. The network card is attached to 3 antennas and is able to extract the Channel State Information (CSI) from all antennas on receiving a wireless frame. The reported CSI is a matrix containing one complex number per subcarrier and per receive antenna at the receiver. During the calibration period, the Atheros card is set in monitor mode to capture the MAC addresses of neighboring 802.11 devices – both APs and clients. If the neighboring device is a client, *WiDraw* may need to probe it to obtain the CSI information from the received ACK. To keep the probing overhead low, the *WiDraw* receiver uses link layer NULL frames to probe a client device. Note that neighboring devices will respond to the NULL frame with an ACK, irrespective of their connection state. Thereafter, *WiDraw* uses the CSI values from the ACK to compute and analyze the AoA values.

Time duration threshold (sec)	Accuracy	False positives
0.5	84.8%	0.02%
1.0	87.8%	0.03%
1.5	89.5%	0.06%
2.0	91%	0.11%

Table 1: Accuracy & false positive rate of identifying the relevant AoAs whose signal strength changes due to hand occlusions and not due to environmental fluctuations.

Implementation details *WiDraw* is implemented as a combination of driver modifications and user-space programs. The WiFi driver collects CSI and RSSI values of incoming signals and sends it to a userspace program written in C. The userspace program calculates the 1-D AoAs using MUSIC. It also calculates the azimuth and elevation values for each AoA and reports these values along with the signal strength changes over time to another module written in MATLAB, which uses this information to track the hand's trajectory.

4.2 Transmitter selection

Apart from APs, *WiDraw* should only utilize stationary client devices for AoA estimation since, if the device is mobile, its AoA values will not be stable. To determine if a device is actually static, we adopt the algorithm as studied in [13]. Briefly, we compute the correlation of the CSI values over time, which captures the similarity between a current and a past CSI value. Low correlation values imply rapid changes in the wireless channel between the client device and the *WiDraw* receiver, due to mobility or environmental variations. Therefore, in our implementation, we avoid clients whose CSI correlation values are lower than 0.9. Further, we observe that the user will mostly draw in front of the laptop's screen. Therefore, we optimize by selecting only those transmitters whose AoAs fall within the same region.

4.3 Azimuth and elevation estimation after user initiated calibration

The transmitter selection procedure runs during the user initiated calibration phase when the azimuth and elevation of the AoAs are identified. After the calibration is completed, the AoA value of a chosen client device may change. Further, new client devices whose AoAs can be suitably used for trajectory tracking may appear in the neighborhood. It is impractical to ask the user to calibrate whenever such changes happen. To detect the azimuth and elevation values of these unknown AoAs without calibration, we track their signal strength while a user is drawing in the air. If an unknown AoA's signal strength demonstrates a minimum at a given moment, we choose the coordinates obtained by the AoAs whose minima occurred right before and after the unknown AoA. Thereafter, we compute the coordinates of the user's hand during the unknown AoA's minimum as a weighted average of the two chosen coordinates. Once the coordinates are known we use Equation 2 to compute the azimuth and elevation of the unknown AoA. Thereafter, the new AoA can be used to track the user's hand.

4.4 System architecture

Figure 9 shows the overall architecture of *WiDraw*. During the calibration phase, the laptop's WiFi card is set in monitor mode to capture MAC addresses of nearby 802.11 devices and select the initial set of transmitters (Section 4.1). During the same phase, the receiver uses the CSI of incoming signals and MUSIC to estimate their 1-D AoA values (Section 2.1). Then, the user is asked to rotate the laptop and the system calculates the azimuth and elevation of each AoA (Section 3.1).

During normal operation, the *WiDraw* receiver periodically collects RSSI and CSI from incoming signals. Then, it uses CSI correlation values over time (Section 4.2) and filtering (Section 3.3) to filter out signals from mobile clients or those affected by large environmental variations. For stable AoAs, *WiDraw* processes the RSSI value and obtains an estimate of the hand's depth (Section 3.2). If a minimum signal strength value of an AoA is detected, the depth estimation is refined using Equation 3. If the azimuth and elevation of the AoA are known, we use the algorithm in Section 3.2 to estimate the hand's coordinates. Otherwise, for unknown AoAs, the hand's coordinates are estimated as the weighted average of the coordinates of two known neighboring AoAs (Section 4.3).

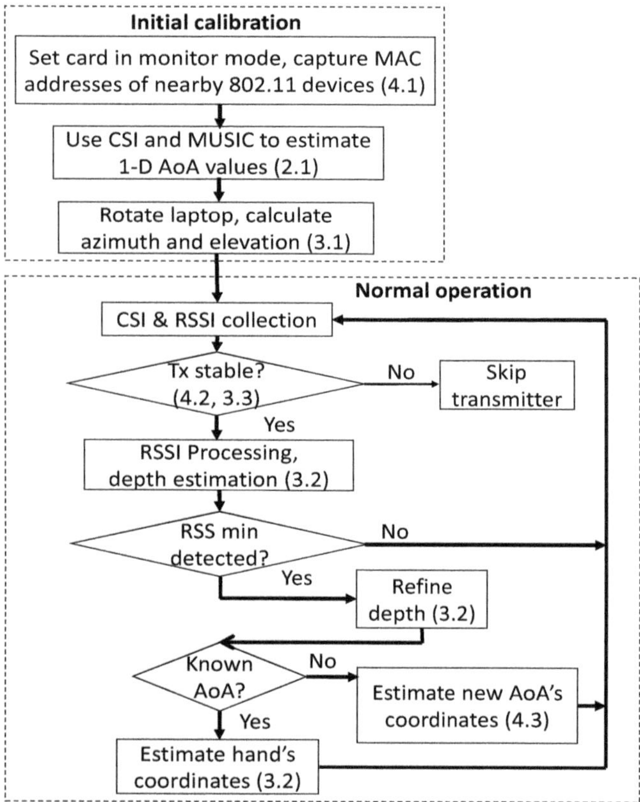

Figure 9: *WiDraw* Architecture.

5. EVALUATION

In this section, we evaluate *WiDraw*'s trajectory tracking accuracy when the user draws 2D and 3D lines, curves, and English alphabetical characters. Unless otherwise stated, the user sits in front of the laptop and starts drawing at a location within 2 feet distance from the laptop's antenna, at an approximate speed of 1.5 feet/second. We evaluate *WiDraw* in a typical office building during normal business hours as well as a busy cafeteria. In the default case, the laptop computes AoA values from 30 neighboring transmitters, including both APs and client devices. For each transmitter, *WiDraw* computes the AoA values 20 times/second.

Ground truth collection: We compute the ground truth of the hand's trajectory by collocating a Leap Motion controller [2] with the laptop's WiFi antenna. Leap Motion reports the 3D location of the palm in millimeters w.r.t. the Leap Motion controller as the origin, which we use as the ground truth coordinates of the user's hand. *WiDraw*'s tracking error is computed by calculating the point-by-point position difference between the ground truth trajectory and *WiDraw*'s estimated trajectory.

5.1 2D Tracking Evaluation

We begin by evaluating the accuracy of tracking a total number of 8448 2D movements including line segments and circular curves on a 2D plane parallel to the laptop's screen. Figure 10(a) shows the distribution of tracking errors for both lines and curves. The error increases with increasing depth from the laptop's antenna (Figure 10(b)). The impact of increasing depth is twofold: first, the distance between consecutive coordinates obtained from the AoAs becomes larger; second, the drop in signal strength at a particular AoA due to hand occlusion becomes weaker and may be mistakenly attributed to environmental noise. Nonetheless, at a depth of 2 feet (60 cm) from the laptop, *WiDraw*'s median tracking error is 5.4 cm. The median tracking error does not reduce significantly if the neighboring APs or client devices are probed with a greater number of probe packets every second (Table 2). *WiDraw*'s tracking error also does not accumulate over time. Table 2 shows that *WiDraw* can track reasonably long trajectories (up to 300 seconds) with only a slight increase in estimation error. *WiDraw*'s tracking error however depends on the number of neighboring transmitters used for AoA estimation (Figure 10(c)). Nonetheless, even by using only the 12 neighboring transmitters, *WiDraw* can track the user's hand with a median error lower than 6.4 cm.

Packets/sec	Drawing time (seconds)				
	10	30	60	120	300
100	4.41	4.76	4.77	4.81	4.82
50	4.42	5.01	5.05	5.06	5.05
25	4.83	5.01	5.11	5.09	5.09
10	5.22	5.34	5.71	5.76	5.76

Table 2: Median tracking error (cm) for varying probing frequency and drawing time.

5.2 3D Tracking Evaluation

We evaluate the accuracy of *WiDraw* in distinguishing between 2D and 3D movements and tracking the 3D movements. The user draws a total of 1560 straight lines or curves while moving the hand either towards or away from the laptop. Table 3 shows the accuracy and false positives of distinguishing between 2D and 3D movements by utilizing the change in the average RSSI value, as described in Section 3.2. Once we determine that the user is drawing in all 3 dimensions, we start tracking the changes in the hand's depth by using the algorithm specified in section 3.2. Figure 11(a) shows that while *WiDraw* can often estimate the depth change with less than 10% error, there are occasions when the estimated depth change does not conform with the actual depth change, resulting into tracking errors. Figure 11(b) shows the distribution of the 3D trajectory estimation errors. The median tracking error (8.6 cm) is higher than in the case of 2D trajectories because of an additional error introduced by changing depth values. Therefore, we find that the 3D tracking error is proportional to the depth estimation error (Figure 11(c)).

5.3 Tracking English Characters

Next, we evaluate if *WiDraw* can effectively track the trajectory of English characters drawn by the user. English characters are more difficult to track than simple drawings because they consist of multiple sharp turns, segments, etc. In our study, we used 75,880 characters drawn by a total of 3 users.

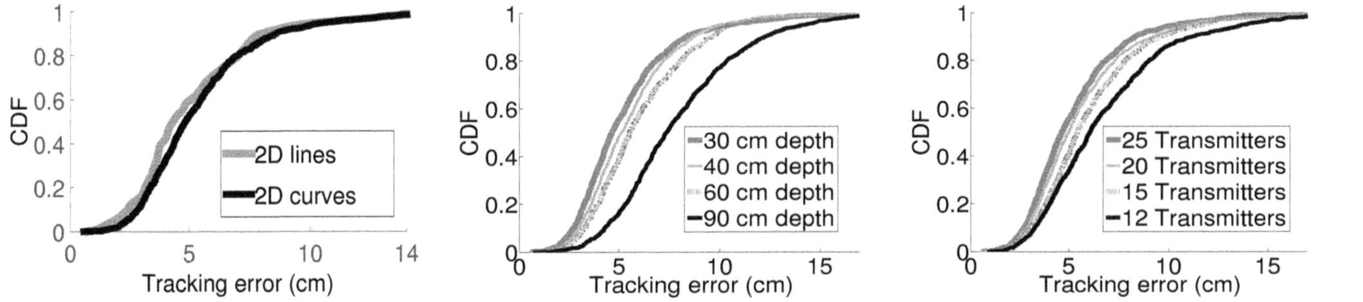

Figure 10: (a) CDF of tracking error for 2D lines and curves drawn by the user. Tracking error increases with (b) depth of the user's hand from the receiver, (c) decreasing number of neighboring transmitters.

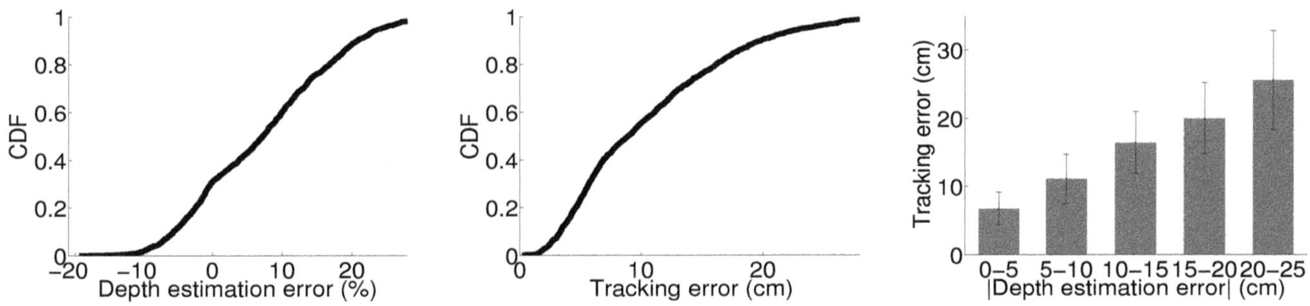

Figure 11: (a) CDF of depth change estimation error for 3D trajectories. Percentage of error calculated as (ground truth depth change - estimated depth change)/(ground truth depth change). Ground truth depth change varies between 1 and 3 feet. (b) CDF of tracking error for 3D lines. (c) Tracking error increases with increasing error in depth estimation.

Ground Truth	Detection result(%)	
	2D	3D
2D	98.36	1.64
3D	2.81	97.19

Table 3: Distinguishing between 2D and 3D trajectories.

We designed experiments to determine the dimensions of the 3D area, near the receiver, within which *WiDraw* can effectively identify the letters drawn by the user. We asked the users to draw letters of different sizes naturally, at varying distance from the receiver. Figures 12(a) and 12(b) show the distribution of trajectory tracking error when the users draw characters at increasing depth and horizontal distance from the receiver respectively. We observe that, for a depth and horizontal distance smaller than 2 feet, the median tracking error remains lower than 5.2 cm.

Figure 12(c) shows that the tracking error increases with the letter size, since, for large sizes, some segments of the trajectory will be farther away from the receiver's antenna. However, notice that the tracking error does not fully capture the *WiDraw*'s capability of identifying letters. Even with large tracking errors, *WiDraw*'s estimated trajectory can be successfully recognized by a simple handwriting recognition app if there are enough AoA minima, as we evaluate in the next section. This happens because *WiDraw*'s errors are not independent random errors. Most of the errors are due to depth estimation errors or lack of motion information between two AoA minima. Therefore, although the tracking error is a few centimeters, the estimated trajectory is either an enlarged or squeezed version of the original letter. Similarly, a very small tracking error may not yield high recognition accuracy if there are not enough AoA minima to capture every segment of the trajectory. As an example, from the results in Figure 12(c) we find that for a reasonable letter size of 30 cm, *WiDraw*'s median tracking accuracy is approximately 4.1 cm. In the next section, we show that even with such errors, a simple handwriting recognition app can successfully identify the letters in up to 98% of the cases.

5.4 Evaluation in different environments

The above results demonstrate *WiDraw*'s performance in an office environment. In this section, we evaluate *WiDraw*'s performance in a busy cafeteria and in NLOS environments where the user's hand is not visible to the receiver. In the cafeteria experiment, a user draws several curves and letters at a distance of 1 foot from the laptop screen. Figure 13(a) plots *WiDraw*'s tracking error when dealing with environmental noise and automatically adjusting for changes in AoA values. The error is higher than in the experiments in the office building because of the environmental noise. Recall that *WiDraw* computes the azimuth and elevation values of the AoA by asking the user to turn the receiver around its Z-axis. Figure 13(b) shows the median tracking error over time after a user calibration. Figure 13(b) also shows the tracking error over time in an NLOS scenario when the *WiDraw* receiver is placed in a bag, while the user is drawing lines in the air at a distance of 1 foot from it. We find that after 1 hour since calibration, the median tracking error in both the LOS and the NLOS scenario is within 6 cm.

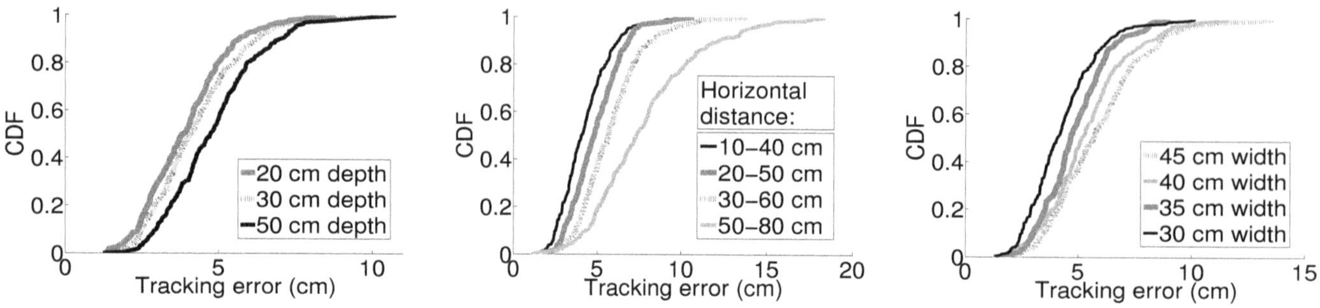

Figure 12: CDF of trajectory estimation error for upper and lower case English letters with (a) increasing depth (horizontal distance: 10-40 cm, letter width: 30 cm) and (b) horizontal distance from the receiver's antenna (depth: 30 cm, letter width: 30 cm). (c) Tracking error increases with increasing width of the letters (depth: 30 cm, horizontal distance: 10-40 cm).

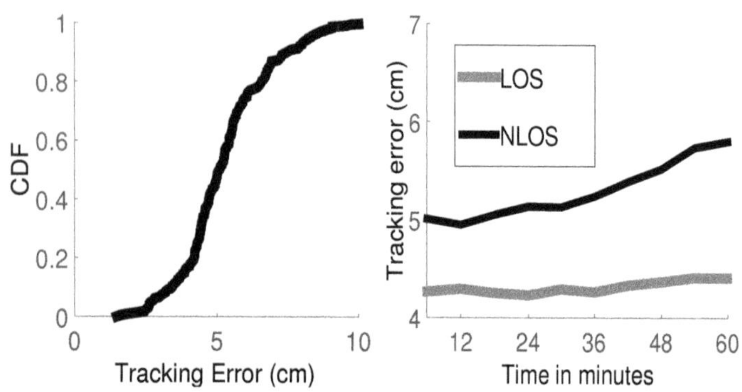

Figure 13: (a) CDF of trajectory estimation error in a busy cafeteria. (b) Estimation error over time in both LOS and NLOS environments.

6. USING *WiDraw* FOR TEXT INPUTS

In this section, we show how *WiDraw* can be used to allow the user to reliably input texts to a computer by writing in the air. Similar to the approach in [7], we interface *WiDraw* with the MyScript Stylus app on Android [14]. As the user writes in the air, we feed *WiDraw*'s estimated trajectory into MyScript and we use its handwriting recognition functionality to interpret the text written by the user. Using MyScript's output, we evaluate the character and word recognition accuracy of *WiDraw*. We begin by studying the effect of various constraints on letter recognition accuracy.

6.1 Letter Recognition Accuracy

Table 4 shows *WiDraw*'s letter recognition accuracy for both capital and small letters drawn by the user. The accuracy drops with increasing depth and horizontal distance of the user's hand from the receiver's antenna. *WiDraw*'s letter recognition accuracy is less than 80% beyond 2 feet from the receiver. The above results suggest that for good results the user should draw the characters within a $3.3 \times 2 \times 2$ cubic feet area in front of the laptop's antenna. The letter recognition accuracy also decreases with decreasing character sizes (Figure 14), but the accuracy is quite high for sizes greater than 30 cm. We find that even if the median trajectory tracking error for letters is around 5 cm (as demonstrated in section 5.3), characters of reasonable sizes can still be recognized because most of the errors are due to transformation and distortion in the shape of the trajectory rather than independent positioning errors.

Horizontal range (cm)	Depth (cm) 30	40	50	60
0-30	0.98/0.97	0.95/0.87	0.95/0.82	0.91/0.80
10-40	0.98/0.96	0.96/0.94	0.92/0.87	0.89/0.79
20-50	0.96/0.92	0.90/0.83	0.89/0.80	0.87/0.77
30-60	0.88/0.89	0.85/0.78	0.85/0.79	0.76/0.73

Table 4: Letter recognition accuracy for uppercase/lowercase English letters (letter width 30 cm).

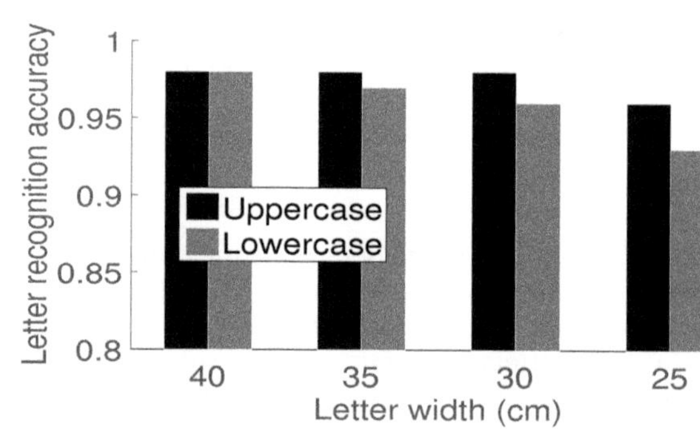

Figure 14: Letter recognition accuracy decreases with decreasing width of the letters. Distance from Rx: 1 foot.

6.2 Writing Words using *WiDraw*

WiDraw allows users to write cursive words in the air. The average size of a user's handwritten letter that is supported by *WiDraw* is around 30 cm. Further, the width of the horizontal plane on which the user can write is limited to 100 cm. Therefore, while writing words, we allow the users to write up to 3 characters contiguously. If a word consists of more than 3 characters, the user needs to start drawing the 4th character from the beginning of the line. Figure 15(a) shows *WiDraw*'s estimated trajectory when the user writes "*widraw*" in the air. Notice that the estimated trajectory overlaps "wid" with "raw" and includes a horizontal line between the 3rd ("d") and the 4th ("r") character and hence it is hard to recognize. *WiDraw*

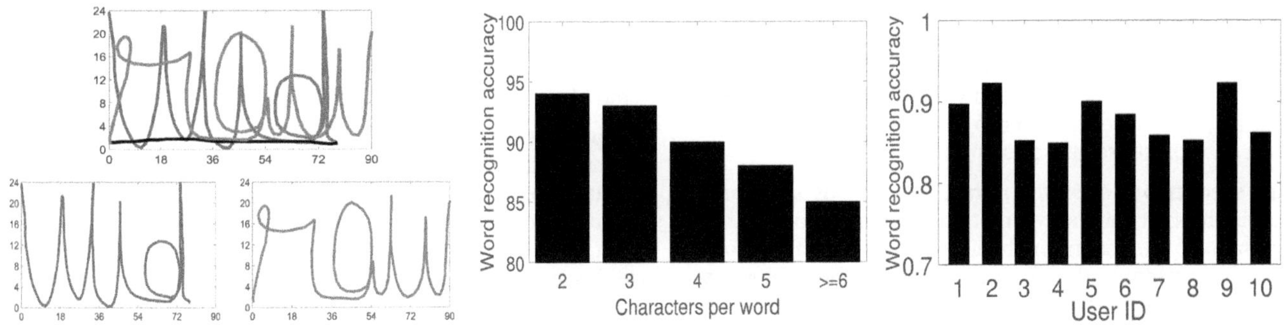

Figure 15: (a) User starts every 4th character in a newline, *WiDraw* segments the drawing to make the letters contiguous. (b) Word recognition accuracy reduces with increasing number of letters per word. (c) Word recognition accuracy for 10 different users when the users write continuous sentences.

determines this horizontal line, removes it from the trace, and then places every 3 letters in sequence (Figure 15(a)). The horizontal line separating two groups of 3 letters will be close to 90 cm since each letter's approximate width is 30 cm. Therefore, if the user is drawing words, *WiDraw* determines any horizontal straight line which is more than 2 letters wide ($>$ 60 cm) and then segments the trace into separate halves based on the starting and ending coordinates of the straight line.

We evaluate *WiDraw*'s word recognition accuracy by estimating the trajectories of 1000 words drawn by 3 users at a distance of 1 foot from the receiver, and thereafter feeding these trajectories into the MyScript Stylus app. Figure 15(b) shows *WiDraw*'s word recognition accuracy as a function of the number of letters in the word. Expectedly, as the word gets longer, it is more difficult to recognize it correctly. However, even by using a simple handwriting recognition software such as MyScript, the average word recognition accuracy is more than 91%. Of course the accuracy can be improved by using advanced techniques in natural language processing [15].

6.3 Writing Sentences using *WiDraw*

To enable the user to write sentences using *WiDraw* we ask the users to pause for a moment (typically 1 second) between consecutive words. Since the user pauses between words, there will be a little change in the signal strength of different AoAs in between two words. Therefore, to segment words in a sentence, we track the rate of change in signal strength of different AoAs. If the signal strength of a threshold percentage of AoAs does not change for more than 500ms, we classify it as a pause and segment the words accordingly. The accuracy of pause detection reduces slightly if we increase the threshold of the percentage of AoAs. However, false positives may imply wrongly breaking up a single word into multiple words. In our implementation, we chose a threshold of 92% since it results into no false positives and achieves a high word segmentation accuracy of 96%.

An undetected pause may not necessarily mean an error in word recognition. This is because MyScript can sometimes detect if a sequence of characters actually consist of multiple words. To evaluate the accuracy of writing multiple words we asked 10 users to write a passage of 100 words continuously in the air, with 3 characters per line and a pause between two words. Figure 15(c) shows that even with a simple Android handwriting recognition software such as MyScript, *WiDraw*'s word recognition accuracy for continuous writing is higher than 85% across all users. Note that, for the evaluation of RF-IDraw [7], the system closest to ours, the authors manually segmented the user's writing into words. As pointed out in [7], standard segmentation methods from natural language processing [16] can be used to further improve the word segmentation accuracy. Overall, the result in this section implies that *WiDraw* can be used to input different kind of texts to the mobile device.

7. RELATED WORK

Gesture recognition and hand motion tracking related research can be classified in three types.

Camera-based Vision-based gesture recognition has been a well-researched topic for over two decades [17, 18]. Recent works use depth cameras (e.g., [1]) or infrared cameras (e.g., [2, 19]) to enable in-air 3D human computer interactions. Despite their popularity, these approaches require a dedicated hardware setup and LOS to the user.

Motion sensor-based Some recent works rely on motion sensors available in today's smartphones to perform gesture recognition, or allow the user to write in the air (e.g., [20, 21]). Others make use of such sensors on wearables such as smartwatches [22], armbands [23], wristbands [24], and rings [25, 26]. In contrast to *WiDraw*, all motion-based systems require an external device such as a smartphone or a wearable. Moreover, most of these approaches rely on machine learning to achieve fine-grained gesture recognition.

RF-based *WiDraw* belongs to a recent class of systems which employ RF signals to enable a user to interact with their environment in both LOS and NLOS scenarios [3–8, 27, 28]. Most of these works [3–6, 8, 27] require the use of custom wireless hardware and/or signal processing capabilities unavailable on off-the-shelf devices. In addition, several solutions [3–5, 8] require a priori learning of the effect of hand motions on wireless signal patterns, which allows them to recognize only a pre-defined set of gestures; others [6, 27] focus on human motion tracking rather than fine-grained gesture recognition and can only identify coarse-grained gestures (e.g., a pointing gesture).

Wi-Fi Gestures [28] and WiGest [29] are the only two works to our best knowledge that perform WiFi-based gesture recognition using RSSI and CSI information from off-the-shelf devices. However, they also rely on a priori learning, and as a result, they can only classify a few simple gestures. Lastly, RF-IDraw [7] is the first RF-based system that can accurately track the trajectory of the hand, enabling a virtual touch screen based on RF signals. While RF-IDraw can achieve good tracking accuracy, it requires the user to hold an RFID transmitter, similar to motion sensor-based solutions.

WiDraw's contribution: In contrast to previous solutions, *WiDraw* is the first hands-free motion tracking solution that can be enabled on existing mobile devices using only a software patch, combining the desired features of the above two approaches. Similar to Wi-Fi Gestures and WiGest, it uses information readily available from commodity devices, without requiring the user to hold any device; and similar to RF-IDraw, it can identify an arbitrary number of fine-grained gestures without any requirements of a priori learning.

8. DISCUSSION AND LIMITATIONS

Gesture recognition vs. hand motion tracking: In-the-air user interfaces can be divided into two classes. The first class is based on defining a limited set of gestures and using machine learning to learn patterns and classify gestures into the learned categories [3–5, 8, 28]. The second class includes interfaces enabled by systems such as RF-IDraw [7] and *WiDraw*. These interfaces require no priori learning and can track an arbitrary set of hand motions, enabling a much richer set of applications.

Distance from the receiver's antenna: Our prototype achieves satisfactory tracking accuracy if the hand is within 2 feet from the receiver's antenna. The error at larger distances can be reduced if the receiver is equipped with a larger number of antennas. One way to achieve this is to equip the receiver with multiple wireless cards [10]. Future mobile devices may also be equipped with more antennas – the 802.11ac standard [30] provides support for up to 4 antennas on client devices.

Number of transmitters: *WiDraw* requires at least a dozen of transmitters in order to track the user's hand with high accuracy. We believe this number is not a challenge in today's enterprise and home environments in urban areas. A recent study [31] reports a median number of 17 and a maximum number of 78 neighboring APs in dense urban environments. This number can be further reduced if the receiver is equipped with a larger number of antennas, which is the current trend as mentioned above. Alternatively, if the number of APs is not sufficient, WiDraw may also use nearby clients. We further emphasize that, similar to other RF-based motion tracking systems, *WiDraw* does not require LOS between the transmitter and the receiver.

Probing overhead: If the number of neighboring APs is not sufficient, or if we need a higher frequency of CSI sampling, WiDraw may also probe APs or nearby clients. We believe that this probing overhead can be kept low. For example, Table 2 shows that the tracking error does not increase significantly when the probing frequency is reduced from 25 packets/second to 10 packets/second (a typical beacon transmission rate). We leave a detailed study of the impact of probing on the performance of other ongoing WiFi transmissions as future work.

Calibration: *WiDraw* asks the user to turn the laptop for azimuth and elevation computation during setup. An alternative approach we plan to investigate as part of our future work is to ask the user to perform a set of pre-defined gestures (similar to Leap Motion [2]) and compute the azimuth and elevation by observing the angle minima.

Depth estimation error: The 3D tracking error of *WiDraw* is larger than the 2D error primarily due to the difficulty in accurately tracking depth changes; improving the depth estimation error is part of our future work. However, note that, while accurate 2D motion tracking is required for enabling a virtual touch screen, several applications often need only a very small set of 3D gestures (e.g., push, pull in gaming), where distinguishing between 2D and 3D motion (which *WiDraw* achieves with 97% accuracy) is more critical than accurately tracking the depth change.

9. CONCLUSION

This paper introduced *WiDraw*, the first hand motion tracking system in both LOS and NLOS scenarios using commodity WiFi cards. *WiDraw* harnesses the AoA values of incoming wireless signals utilizing the intuition that whenever the user's hand occludes a signal coming from a certain direction, the signal strength along that direction will experience a drop. Unlike prior solutions, *WiDraw* can be enabled on today's mobile devices using only a software patch, without requiring the use of any wearable or any dedicated hardware setup. Our prototype using commodity wireless cards can track the user's hand with less than 5 cm error on average. We also use WiDraw to implement an in-air handwriting application that achieves an average word recognition accuracy of 91%. We believe that *WiDraw* can open up a whole new class of applications in human-computer interaction.

10. ACKNOWLEDGMENT

We sincerely thank the anonymous shepherd and MobiCom reviewers for their insightful feedback.

11. REFERENCES

[1] Microsoft kinect. http://www.microsoft.com/en-us/kinectforwindows/.

[2] Leap motion, inc. leap motion: Mac & pc gesture controller for game, design and more. https://www.leapmotion.com/.

[3] Qifan Pu, Sidhant Gupta, Shyamnath Gollakota, and Shwetak Patel. Whole-home gesture recognition using wireless signals. In *Proceedings of ACM Mobicom*, 2013.

[4] Fadel Adib and Dina Katabi. See through walls with WiFi! In *Proceedings of ACM SIGCOMM*, 2013.

[5] Bryce Kellogg, Vamsi Talla, and Shyam Gollakota. Bringing gesture recognition to all devices. In *Proceedings of USENIX NSDI*, 2014.

[6] Fadel Adib, Zach Kabelac, Dina Katabi, and Robert C Miller. 3D tracking via body radio reflections. In *Proceedings of USENIX NSDI*, 2014.

[7] Jue Wang, Deepak Vasisht, and Dina Katabi. RF-IDraw: Virtual Touch Screen in the Air Using RF Signals. In *Proceedings of ACM SIGCOMM*, 2014.

[8] Pedro Melgarejo, Xinyu Zhang, Parameswaran Ramanathan, and David Chu. Leveraging directional antenna capabilities for fine-grained gesture recognition. In *Proceedings of ACM Ubicomp*, 2014.

[9] Ralph O Schmidt. Multiple emitter location and signal parameter estimation. *IEEE Transactions on Antennas and Propagation*, AP-34(3):276–280, 1986.
[10] Jon Gjengset, Jie Xiong, Graeme McPhillips, and Kyle Jamieson. Phaser: enabling phased array signal processing on commodity wifi access points. In *Proceedings of ACM Mobicom*, 2014.
[11] Souvik Sen, Jeongkeun Lee, Kyu-Han Kim, and Paul Congdon. Avoiding multipath to revive inbuilding wifi localization. In *Proceeding of ACM MobiSys*, 2013.
[12] Kainam Thomas Wong and Michael D Zoltowski. Root-music-based azimuth-elevation angle-of-arrival estimation with uniformly spaced but arbitrarily oriented velocity hydrophones. *Signal Processing, IEEE Transactions on*, 47(12):3250–3260, 1999.
[13] Li Sun, Souvik Sen, and Dimitrios Koutsonikolas. Bringing mobility-awareness to WLANs using PHY layer information. In *Proceedings of the ACM CoNEXT*, 2014.
[14] Myscript. Myscript stylus app. http://myscript.com/.
[15] Wenwei Wang, Anja Brakensiek, and Gerhard Rigoll. Combination of multiple classifiers for handwritten word recognition. In *Frontiers in Handwriting Recognition, 2002. Proceedings. Eighth International Workshop on*, pages 117–122. IEEE, 2002.
[16] Réjean Plamondon and Sargur N Srihari. On-line and off-line handwriting recognition: A comprehensive survey. *IEEE Transactions on Pattern Analysis and Machine Intelligence*, 22(1):63–84, 2000.
[17] James M Rehg and Takeo Kanade. Visual tracking of high DOF articulated structures: an application to human hand tracking. In *Proceedings of the European Conference on Computer Vision*, 1994.
[18] Thad Starner and Alex Pentland. Real-time american sign language recognition from video using hidden markov models. In *Proceedings of the International Symposium on Computer Vision*, 1995.
[19] Nintendo wii. http://www.nintendo.com/wiiu.
[20] Sandip Agrawal, Ionut Constandache, Shravan Gaonkar, Romit Roy Choudhury, Kevin Caves, and Frank DeRuyter. Using mobile phones to write in air. In *Proceedings of ACM MobiSys*, 2011.
[21] Taiwoo Park, Jinwon Lee, Inseok Hwang, Chungkuk Yoo, Lama Nachman, and Junehwa Song. E-Gesture: A Collaborative Architecture for Energy-efficient Gesture Recognition with Hand-worn Sensor and Mobile Devices. In *Proceedings of ACM SenSys*, 2011.
[22] Chao Xu, Parth H. Pathak, and Prasant Mohapatra. Finger-writing with smartwatch: A case for finger and hand gesture recognition using smartwatch. In *Proceedings of ACM HotMobile*, 2015.
[23] Myo: Gesture control armband. https://www.thalmic.com/en/myo/.
[24] Abhinav Parate, Meng-Chieh Chiu, Chaniel Chadowitz, Deepak Ganesan, and Evangelos Kalogerakis. RisQ: recognizing smoking gestures with inertial sensors on a wristband. In *Proceedings of ACM MobiSys*, 2014.
[25] Jeremy Gummeson, Bodhi Priyantha, and Jie Liu. An energy harvesting wearable ring platform for gestureinput on surfaces. In *Proceedings of ACM MobiSys*, 2014.
[26] Shahriar Nirjon, Jeremy Gummeson, Dan Gelb, and Kyu-Han Kim. TypingRing: A Wearable Ring Platform for Text Input. In *Proceedings of ACM MobiSys*, 2015.
[27] Fadel Adib, Zach Kabelac, and Dina Katabi. Multi-Person Localization via RF Body Reflections. In *Proceedings of USENIX NSDI*, 2015.
[28] Rajalakshmi Nandakumar, Bryce Kellogg, and Shyamnath Gollakota. Wi-fi gesture recognition on existing devices. http://arxiv.org/ftp/arxiv/papers/1411/1411.5394.pdf.
[29] Heba Abdelnasser, Moustafa Youssef, and Khaled Harras. Wigest: A ubiquitous wifi-based gesture recognition system. In *Proceedings of IEEE INFOCOM*, 2015.
[30] IEEE 802.11ac – Amendment 4: Enhancements for Very High Throughput for Operation in Bands below 6 GHz. IEEE P802.11ac/D5.0, 2013.
[31] Ioannis Pefkianakis, Henrik Lundgren, Augustin Soule, Jaideep Chandrashekar, Pascal Le Guyadec, Christophe Diot, Martin May, Karel Van Doorselaer, and Koen Van Oost. Characterizing Home Wireless Performance: The Gateway View. In *Proceedings of IEEE INFOCOM*, 2015.

Keystroke Recognition Using WiFi Signals

Kamran Ali† Alex X. Liu†‡ Wei Wang‡ Muhammad Shahzad†

†Dept. of Computer Science and Engineering, Michigan State University, USA

‡State Key Laboratory for Novel Software Technology, Nanjing University, China

†{alikamr3,alexliu,shahzadm}@cse.msu.edu, ‡ww@nju.edu.cn

ABSTRACT

Keystroke privacy is critical for ensuring the security of computer systems and the privacy of human users as what being typed could be passwords or privacy sensitive information. In this paper, we show for the first time that WiFi signals can also be exploited to recognize keystrokes. The intuition is that while typing a certain key, the hands and fingers of a user move in a unique formation and direction and thus generate a unique pattern in the time-series of Channel State Information (CSI) values, which we call CSI-waveform for that key. In this paper, we propose a WiFi signal based keystroke recognition system called WiKey. WiKey consists of two Commercial Off-The-Shelf (COTS) WiFi devices, a sender (such as a router) and a receiver (such as a laptop). The sender continuously emits signals and the receiver continuously receives signals. When a human subject types on a keyboard, WiKey recognizes the typed keys based on how the CSI values at the WiFi signal receiver end. We implemented the WiKey system using a TP-Link TL-WR1043ND WiFi router and a Lenovo X200 laptop. WiKey achieves more than 97.5% detection rate for detecting the keystroke and 96.4% recognition accuracy for classifying single keys. In real-world experiments, WiKey can recognize keystrokes in a continuously typed sentence with an accuracy of 93.5%.

Categories and Subject Descriptors

C.2.1 [**Network Architecture**]: Wireless Communications; D.4.6 [**Security and Protectione**]: Keystroke recovery

Keywords

Gesture recognition; Wireless security; Keystroke recovery; Channel State Information; COTS WiFi devices

1. INTRODUCTION

Keystroke privacy is critical for ensuring the security of computer systems and the privacy of human users as what being types could be passwords or privacy sensitive information. The research community has studied various ways to recognize keystrokes, which can be classified into three categories: acoustic emission based approaches, electromagnetic emission based approaches, and vision based approaches. Acoustic emission based approaches recognize keystrokes based on either the observation that different keys in a keyboard produce different typing sounds [1, 2] or the observation that the acoustic emanations from different keys arrive at different surrounding smartphones at different time as the keys are located at different places in a keyboard [3]. Electromagnetic emission based approaches recognize keystrokes based on the observation that the electromagnetic emanations from the electrical circuit underneath different keys in a keyboard are different [4]. Vision based approaches recognizes keystrokes using vision technologies [5].

In this paper, we show for the first time that WiFi signals can also be exploited to recognize keystrokes. WiFi signals are pervasive in our daily life at home, offices, and even shopping centers. The key intuition is that while typing a certain key, the hands and fingers of a user move in a unique formation and direction and thus generate a unique pattern in the time-series of Channel State Information (CSI) values, which we call *CSI-waveform*, for that key. The keystrokes of each key introduce relative unique multi-path distortions in WiFi signals and this uniqueness can be exploited to recognize keystrokes. Due to the high data rates supported by modern WiFi devices, WiFi cards provide enough CSI values within the duration of a keystroke to construct a high resolution CSI-waveform for each keystroke.

We propose a WiFi signal based keystroke recognition system called WiKey. WiKey consists of two Commercial Off-The-Shelf (COTS) WiFi devices, a sender (such as a router) and a receiver (such as a laptop), as shown in Figure 1. The sender continuously emits signals and the receiver continuously receives signals. When a human subject types in a keyboard, on the WiFi signal receiver end, WiKey recognizes the typed keys based on how the CSI value changes. CSI values quantify the aggregate effect of wireless phenomena such as fading, multi-paths, and Doppler shift on the wireless signals in a given environment. When the environment changes, such as a key is being pressed, the impact of these wireless phenomena on the wireless signals change, resulting in unique changes in the CSI values. There are three key technical challenges. The first technical challenge is to segment the CSI time series to identify the start time and end time of each keystroke. We studied the characteristics of typical CSI-waveforms of different keystrokes and observed that the waveforms of different keys show a similar rising and falling trends in the changing rate of CSI values.

MobiCom'15, September 7–11, 2015, Paris, France.

© 2015 ACM. ISBN 978-1-4503-3619-2/15/09 ...$15.00.

DOI: http://dx.doi.org/10.1145/2789168.2790109.

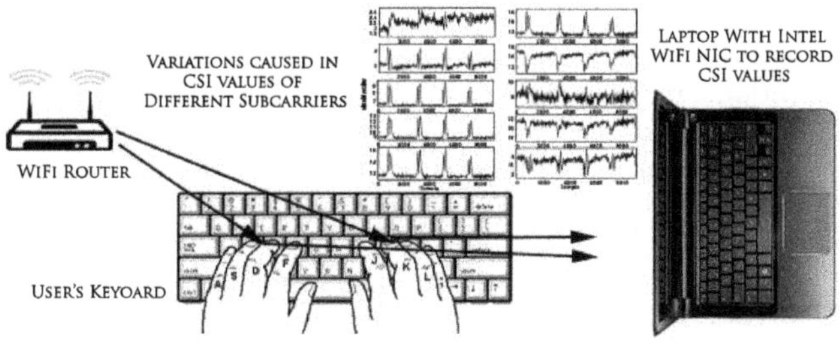

Figure 1: WiKey System

Based on this observation, we design a keystroke extraction algorithm that utilizes CSI streams of all transmit-receive antenna (TX-RX) pair pairs to determine the approximate start and end points of individual keystrokes in a given CSI-waveform by continuously matching the trends in CSI time series with the experimentally observed trends using a sliding window approach.

The second technical challenge is to extract distinguishing features for generating classification models for each of the 37 keys (10 digits, 26 alphabets and 1 space-bar). As the keys on a keyboard are closely placed, conventional features such as maximum peak power, mean amplitude, root mean square deviation of signal amplitude, second/third central moment, rate of change, signal energy or entropy, and number of zero crossings cannot be used because the values of these features for adjacent keys are almost identical. To address this challenge, we use the CSI-waveform shapes of each key from each TX-RX antenna pair as features. As the waveforms for each key contain a large number of samples, we apply the Discrete Wavelet Transform (DWT) technique on these waveforms to reduce the number of samples while keeping the shape preserving time and frequency domain information intact. We use the waveforms resulting from the DWT of individual keystrokes as their shape features.

The third technical challenge is to compare shape features of any two keystrokes. The midpoints of extracted CSI-wavforms of different keystrokes rarely align with each other because the start and end points determined by extraction algorithm are never exact. Moreover, the lengths of different keystroke waveforms also differ because the duration of pressing any key is often different. Consequently, the midpoints and lengths of shape features do not match either. Another issue is that the shape of different keystroke waveforms of the same key are often distorted versions of each other because of slightly different formation and direction of motion of hands and fingers while pressing that key. Thus, two shape features cannot be compared using standard measures like correlation coefficient or Euclidean distance. To address this challenge, we use the Dynamic Time Warping (DTW) technique to quantify the distance between the two shape features. DTW can find the minimum distance alignment between two waveforms of different lengths.

The key novelty of this paper is on proposing the first WiFi signal based keystroke recognition approach. Some recent work uses CSI values to recognize various *macro* aspects of human movements such as falling down [6], household activities [7], detection of human presence [8], and estimating the number of people in a crowd [9]. These schemes extract coarse grained information from the CSI values to recognize the macro-movements such as falling down or recognizing fullbody/limb gestures. They cannot be directly adapted to recognize keystrokes because such coarse grained information does not capture the minor variations in the CSI values caused by human *micro*-movements such as those of hands and fingers while typing. Some recent work, namely WiHear, uses CSI values to extract the micro-movements of mouth to recognize 9 syllables in the spoken words [10]. However, WiHear uses special hardware including directional antennas and stepper motors to direct WiFi beams towards speaker's mouth and extract the micro-movements. We implemented the WiKey system using COTS devices, i.e. a TP-Link TL-WR1043ND WiFi router and a Lenovo X200 laptop with Intel 5300 WiFi NIC. In the evaluation process, we build a keystroke database of 10 human subjects with IRB approval. WiKey achieves more than 97.5% detection rate for detecting the keystroke and 96.4% recognition accuracy for classifying single keys. In real-world experiments, WiKey can recognize keystrokes in a continuously typed sentence with an accuracy of 93.5%.

In this paper, we have shown that fine grained activity recognition is possible by using COTS WiFi devices. Thus, the techniques proposed in this paper can be used for several HCI applications. Examples include zoom-in, zoom-out, scrolling, sliding, and rotating gestures for operating personal computers, gesture recognition for gaming consoles, in-home gesture recognition for operating various household devices, and applications such as writing and drawing in the air. Other than being a potential attack, our WiKey technology can be potentially used to build virtual keyboards where human users type on a printed keyboard.

2. RELATED WORK

2.1 Device Free Activity Recognition

Device-free activity recognition solutions use the variations in wireless channel to recognize human activities in a given environment. Existing solutions can be grouped into three categories: (1) Received Signal Strength (RSS) based, (2) CSI based, and (3) Software Defined Radio (SDR) based.

RSS Based: Sigg *et al.* proposed activity recognition schemes that utilize RSS values of WiFi signals to recognize four activities including crawling, lying down, standing up, and walking [11, 12]. They achieved activity recognition rates of over 80% for these four activities. To obtain the RSS values from WiFi signals, they used USRPs, which are specialized hardware devices compared to the COTS WiFi devices that we used in our work. While RSS values can be used for recognizing macro-movements, they are not suitable to recognize the micro-movements such as those of fingers and hands in keyboard typing because RSS values only provide coarse-grained information about the channel variations and do not contain fine-grained information about small scale fading and multi-path effects caused by these micro-movements.

CSI Based: CSI values obtained from COTS WiFI network interface cards (NICs) (such as Intel 5300 and Atheros 9390) have been recently proposed for activity recognition [6–10, 13] and localization [14–16]. Han *et al.* proposed WiFall that detects fall of a human subject in an indoor environment using CSI values [6]. Zhou *et al.* proposed a passive human detection scheme which exploits multi-path variations for detecting human presence in an indoor environment using CSI values [8]. Zou *et al.* proposed Electronic Frog Eye that counts the number of people in a crowd using

CSI values by treating the people reflecting the WiFi signals as "virtual antennas" [9]. Wang *et al.* proposed E-eyes that exploits CSI values for recognizing household activities such as washing dishes and taking a shower [7]. Nandakumar *et al.* leverage the CSI and RSS information from off-the-shelf WiFi devices to classify four arm gestures - push, pull, lever, and punch [13]. The fundamental difference between these schemes and our scheme is that these schemes extract coarse grained features from the CSI values provided by the COTS WiFi NIC to perform these tasks while our proposed scheme refines these CSI to capture fine grained variations in the wireless channel for recognizing keystrokes. Wang *et al.* propose WiHear that uses CSI values recognizes the shape of mouth while speaking to detect whether a person is uttering one of a set of nine predefined nine syllables [10]. While WiHear can capture the micro-movements of lips, it uses special purpose directional antennas with stepper motors for directing the antenna beams towards a person's mouth to obtain a clean signal for recognizing mouth movements. In contrast, our proposed scheme does not use any special purpose equipment and recognizes the micro-movements of fingers and hands using COTS WiFi NIC.

SDR Based: Researchers have proposed schemes that utilize SRDs and special purpose hardware to transmit and receive custom modulated signals for activity recognition [17–20]. Pu *et al.* proposed WiSee that uses a special purpose receiver design on USRPs to extract small Doppler shifts from OFDM WiFi transmissions to recognize human gestures [17]. Kellogg *et al.* proposed to use a special purpose analog envelop detector circuit for recognizing gestures within a distance of up to 2.5 feet using backscatter signals from RFID or TV transmissions [18] . Lyonnet *et al.* use micro Doppler signatures to classify gaits of human subjects into multiple categories using specialized Doppler radars [19]. Adib *et al.* proposed WiTrack that uses a specially designed frequency modulated carrier wave radio frontend to track human movements behind a wall [20]. Recently, Chen *et al.* proposed an SDR based custom receiver design which can be used to track keystrokes using wireless signals [21]. In contrast to all these schemes, our scheme does not use any specialized hardware or SDRs rather utilizes COTS WiFi NICs to recognize keystrokes.

2.2 Keystrokes Recognition

To the best of our knowledge, there is no prior work on recognizing keystrokes by leveraging variations in wireless signals using commodity WiFi devices. Other than the SDRs based keystroke tracking approach proposed in [21] which uses wireless signals to track keystrokes, researchers have proposed several keystrokes recognition schemes that are based on other sensing modalities such as acoustics [1–3,22], electromagnetic emissions [4], and video cameras [5]. Next, we give a brief overview of the other existing schemes that utilize these sensing modalities to recognize keystrokes.

Acoustics Based: Asonov *et al.* proposed a scheme to recognize keystrokes by leveraging the observation that different keys of a given keyboard produce slightly different sounds during regular typing [1]. They used backpropagation neural network for keystroke recognition and fast fourier transform (FFT) of the time window of every keystroke peak as features for training the classifiers. Zhuang *et al.* proposed another scheme that recognizes keystrokes based on the sounds generated during key presses [2]. They used cepstrum features [22] instead of FFT as keystroke features and used unsupervised learning with language model correction on the collected features before using them for supervised training and recognition of different keystrokes. Zhu *et al.* proposed a context-free geometry-based approach for recognizing keystrokes that leverage the acoustic emanations from keystrokes to first calculate the time difference of keystroke arrival and then estimate the physical locations of the keystrokes to identify which keys are pressed [3].

Electromagnetic Emissions Based Vuagnoux *et al.* used a USRP to capture the electromagnetic emanations while pressing the keys [4]. These electromagnetic emanations originated from the electrical circuit underneath each key in conventional keyboards. The authors proposed to capture the entire raw electromagnetic spectrum and process it to recognize the keystrokes. Unfortunately, this scheme is highly susceptible to background electromagnetic noise that exists in almost all environments these days such as due to microwave ovens, refrigerators, and televisions.

Video Camera Based Balzarotti *et al.* proposed ClearShot that processes the video of a person typing to reconstruct the sentences (s)he types [5]. The authors propose to use context and language sensitive analysis for reconstructing the sentences.

3. CHANNEL STATE INFORMATION

Modern WiFi devices that support IEEE 802.11n/ac standard typically consist of multiple transmit and multiple receive antennas and thus support MIMO. Each MIMO channel between each transmit-receive (TX-RX) antenna pair of a transmitter and receiver comprises of multiple subcarriers. These WiFi devices continuously monitor the state of the wireless channel to effectively perform transmit power allocations and rate adaptations for each individual MIMO stream such that the available capacity of the wireless channel is maximally utilized [23]. These devices quantify the state of the channel in terms of CSI values. The CSI values essentially characterize the *Channel Frequency Response* (CFR) for each subcarrier between each transmit-receive (TX-RX) antenna pair. As the received signal is the resultant of constructive and destructive interference of several multipath signals scattered from the walls and surrounding objects, the disturbances caused by movement of hands and fingers while typing on a keyboard near the WiFi receiver not only lead to changes in previously existing multipaths but also to the creation of new multipaths. These changes are captured in the CSI values for all subcarriers between every TX-RX antenna pair and can then be used to recognize keystrokes.

Let M_T denote the number of transmit antennas, M_R denote the number of receive antennas and S_c denote the number of OFDM sub-carriers. Let $\mathbf{X}_i$ and $\mathbf{Y}_i$ represent the M_T dimensional transmitted signal vector and M_R dimensional received signal vector, respectively, for subcarrier i and let $\mathcal{N}_i$ represent an M_R dimensional noise vector. An $M_R \times M_T$ MIMO system at any time instant can be represented by the following equation.

$$\mathbf{Y}_i = \mathsf{H}_i\mathbf{X}_i + \mathcal{N}_i \quad i \in [1, S_c] \tag{1}$$

In the equation above, the $M_R \times M_T$ dimensional channel matrix H_i represents the Channel State Information (CSI) for the sub-carrier i. Any two communicating WiFi devices estimate this channel matrix H_i for every subcarrier by regularly transmitting a known preamble of OFDM symbols between each other. For each Tx-Rx antenna pair, the driver of our Intel 5300 WiFi NIC reports CSI values for $S_c = 30$ OFDM subcarriers of the 20 MHz WiFi Channel [24]. This leads to 30 matrices with dimensions $M_R \times M_T$ per CSI sample.

4. NOISE REMOVAL

The CSI values provided by commodity WiFi NICs are inherently noisy because of the frequent changes in internal CSI reference levels, transmit power levels, and transmission rates. To use CSI values for recognizing keystrokes, such noise must first be removed from the CSI time series. For this, WiKey first passes the CSI time series from a low-pass filter to remove high frequency noises. Unfortunately, a simple low pass filter does not denoise the CSI values very efficiently. Although strict low-pass filtering can remove noise further, it causes loss of useful information from the signal as well. To extract useful signal from the noisy CSI time series, WiKey leverages our observation that the variations in the CSI time series of all subcarriers due to the movements of hands and fingers are correlated. Therefore, it applies Principal Component Analysis (PCA) on the filtered subcarriers to extract the signals that only contain variations caused by movements of hands. Next, we first describe the process of applying the low-pass filter on the CSI time series and then explain how WiKey extracts hand and finger movement signal using our PCA based approach.

4.1 Low Pass Filtering

The frequency of variations caused due to the movements of hands and fingers lie at the low end of the spectrum while the frequency of the noise lies at the high end of the spectrum. To remove noise in such a situation, *Butterworth* low-pass filter is a natural choice which does not significantly distort the phase information in the signal and has a maximally flat amplitude response in the passband and thus does not distort the hand and finger movement signal much. WiKey applies the Butterworth filter on the CSI time series of all subcarriers in each TX-RX antenna pair so that every stream experiences similar effects of phase distortion and group delay introduced by the filter. Although this process helps in removing some high frequency noise, the noise is not completely eliminated because Butterworth filter has slightly slow fall off gain in the stopband.

We observed experimentally that the frequencies of the variations in CSI time series due to hand and finger movements while typing approximately lie anywhere between 3Hz to 80 Hz. As we sample CSI values at a rate of $F_s = 2500$ samples/s, we set the cut-off frequency ω_c of the Butterworth filter at $\omega_c = \frac{2\pi * f}{F_s} = \frac{2\pi * 80}{2500} \approx 0.2$ rad/s. Figure 2(a) shows the amplitudes of the unfiltered CSI waveform of a keystroke and Figure 2(b) shows the resultant from the Butterworth filter. We observe that Butterworth filter successfully removes most of the bursty noises from the CSI waveforms.

4.2 PCA Based Filtering

We observed experimentally that the movements of hands and fingers results in correlated changes in the CSI time series for each subcarrier in every transmit-receive antenna pair. Figure 3 plots the amplitudes of CSI time series of 10 different subcarriers for one transmit-receive antenna pair

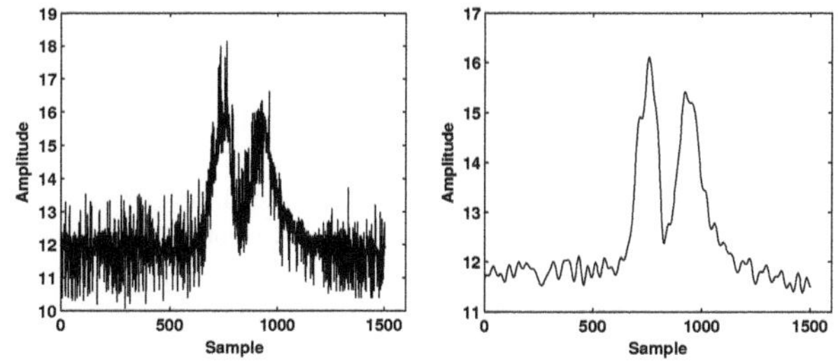

(a) Original time series (b) Filtered time series

Figure 2: Original and filtered CSI time series

while a user was repeatedly pressing a key. We observe from this figure that all subcarriers show correlated variations in their time series when the user presses the keys. The subcarriers that are closely spaced in frequency show identical variations whereas the subcarriers that farther away in frequency show non-identical changes. Despite non-identical changes, a strong correlation still exists even across the subcarriers that are far apart in frequency. WiKey leverages this correlation and calculates the principal components from all CSI time series. It then chooses those principal components that represent the most common variations among all CSI time series.

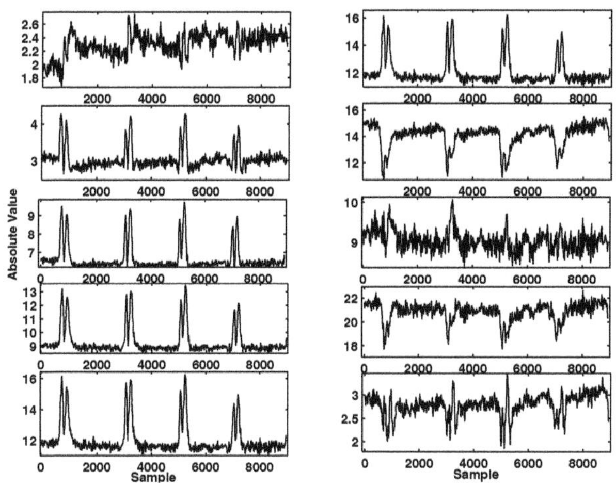

(a) # 1,2,3,4,5 (b) # 5,10,15,20,25

Figure 3: Correlated variations in subcarriers

There are two main advantages of using PCA. First, PCA reduces the dimensionality of the CSI information obtained from the 30 subcarriers in each TX-RX stream, which is useful because using information from all subcarriers for keystroke extraction and recognition significantly increases the computational complexity of the scheme. Consequently, PCA automatically enables WiKey to obtain the signals that are representative of hand and finger movements, without having to devise new techniques and define new parameters for selecting appropriate subcarriers for further processing. Second, PCA helps in removing noise from the signals by taking advantage of correlated varations in CSI time series of different subcarriers. It removes the uncorrelated noisy components, which can not be removed through traditional low pass filtering. This PCA based noise reduction is one of the major reasons behind high keystroke extraction and recognition accuracies of our scheme.

5. KEYSTROKE EXTRACTION

WiKey segments the CSI time series to extract the CSI waveforms for individual keystrokes. For this, WiKey operates on the CSI time series resulting from the butterworth filtering. Let $\mathsf{H}_{t,r}(i)$ be an $S_c \times 1$ dimensional vector containing the CSI values of the S_c subcarriers between an arbitrary TX-RX antenna pair $t-r$ for the ith CSI sample. Let $\mathbf{H}_{t,r}$ be an $N \times S_c$ dimensional matrix containing the CSI values of the S_c subcarriers between an arbitrary TX-RX antenna pair $t-r$ for N consecutive CSI samples. This matrix is given by the following equation.

$$\mathbf{H}_{t,r} = [\mathsf{H}_{t,r}(1)|\mathsf{H}_{t,r}(2)|\mathsf{H}_{t,r}(3)|...|\mathsf{H}_{t,r}(N)]^T \quad (2)$$

The columns of the matrix $\mathbf{H}_{t,r}$ represent the CSI time series for each OFDM subcarrier. To detect the starting and ending points of any arbitrary key, WiKey first normalizes the $\mathbf{H}_{t,r}$ matrix such that every CSI stream has zero mean and unit variance. We denote the normalized version of $\mathbf{H}_{t,r}$ by $\mathbf{Z}_{t,r}$. WiKey then performs the PCA based dimensionality reduction and denoising (as described in Section 4.2) on $\mathbf{Z}_{t,r}$ and the resultant waveforms are further processed to detect the starting and ending points of the keystrokes from this particular TX-RX antenna pair. WiKey repeats this process on the CSI time series for all antenna pairs and obtains values for starting and ending points for keys based on the CSI time series from each antenna pair one by one. Finally, WiKey combines the starting and ending points obtained from all TX-RX antenna pairs to calculate a robust estimate of starting and ending points of the time windows containing those keystrokes. Next we explain these steps in more detail.

5.1 PCA on Normalized Stream

Let $\Phi_Z^{\{1:p\}}$ be an $S_c \times p$ dimensional matrix that contains the top p principal components obtained from PCA on $\mathbf{Z}_{t,r}$. We remove the first component from those top p principal components based on our observation that the first component captures majority of the noise, while subsequent components contain information about movements of hands and fingers while typing. This happens because PCA ranks principal components in descending order of their variance, due to which the noisy components with higher variance gets ranked among top principal components. Due to correlated nature of variations in multiple CSI time series, the removal of this PCA component does not lead to any significant information loss as remaining PCA components still contain enough information required for successfully detecting starting and ending points of the keystrokes.

If we exclude the first component, the projection of the CSI stream $\mathbf{Z}_{t,r}$ of t-r transmit-receive antenna pair onto the remaining principal components $\Phi_Z^{\{2:p\}}$ can then be written as:

$$\mathbf{Z}_{t,r}^{\{2:p\}} = \mathbf{Z}_{t,r} \times \Phi_Z^{\{2:p\}} \quad (3)$$

where $\mathbf{Z}_{t,r}^{\{2:p\}}$ is an $N \times (p-1)$ dimensional matrix containing the projected CSI streams in its columns. We choose the $p = 4$ in our implementation based on our observation that only top 4 principal components contained most significant variations in CSI values caused by different keystrokes. Figure 4(a) shows the result of projecting normalized CSI time series $\mathbf{Z}_{t,r}$ onto its top 4 principal components. We observe from Figure 4(b) that by removing the first principle component, we essentially remove the most noisy projection among the all 4 projections of $\mathbf{Z}_{t,r}$.

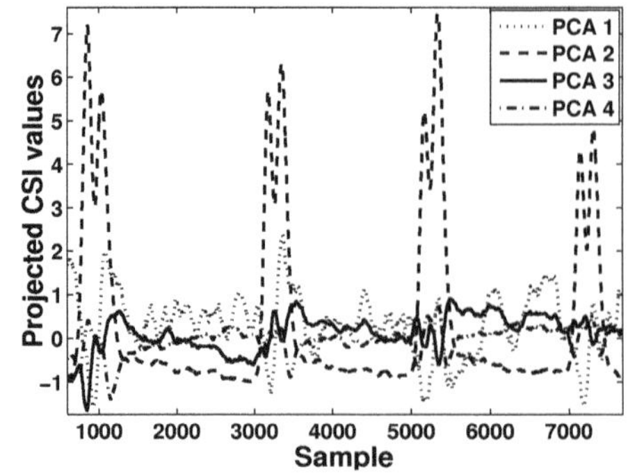

(a) Top 4 projections

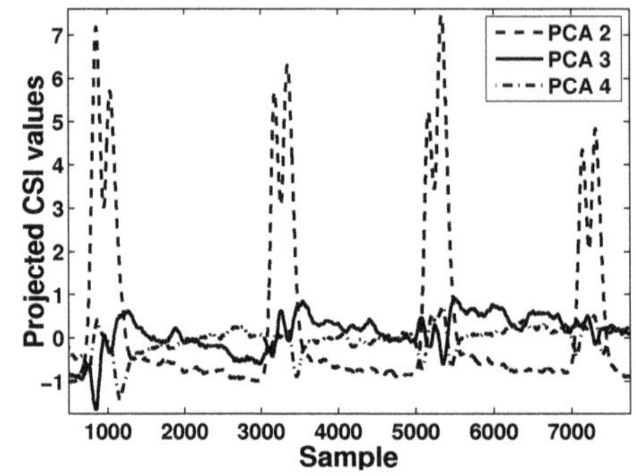

(b) Projections 2, 3 & 4

Figure 4: PCA of Z-normalized CSI stream $\mathbf{Z}_{t,r}$

5.2 Keystroke Detection

Although existing DFAR schemes propose techniques to automatically detect the start and end of activities, they can not be directly adapted for use in detecting the start and end of keystrokes. Existing schemes use simple threshold based algorithms for detecting the start and end of activities. While, threshold based schemes work well for macro-movements, they are not well suited for micro-movements such as those of hands and fingers while typing, where we need to precisely segment time series of keystrokes that are closely spaced in time. Unlike general purpose threshold based algorithms, we propose a keystroke detection algorithm that provides better detection accuracy, since it is strictly based on the experimentally observed shapes of different keystroke waveforms. The intuition behind our algorithm is that the CSI time series of every keystroke shows a typical increasing and decreasing trend in rates of change in CSI time series, similar to the one shown in Figure 2. To detect such increase and decrease in rates of change in CSI time series, our algorithm uses a moving window approach to detect the increasing and decreasing trends in rates of change in all $p-1$ time series for each transmit-receive antenna pair *i.e.*, on each column of $\mathbf{Z}_{t,r}^{2:p}$. Our algorithm detects the starting and ending points of keystrokes in following six steps.

First, the algorithm calculates the mean absolute deviation (MAD) for each of the $p-1$ time series for each window of size W at j-th iteration. This is done primarily to detect the extent of variations in the values of a given time series. The main reason behind choosing MAD instead of variance is that in calculating, the deviations from the mean are squared which gives more weight to extreme values. In cases where a time series contains outliers, this results in undue weight given to those outlying values and that significantly corrupts the measure of deviation. The MAD is calculated using following equation.

$$\triangle m_j[k] = \frac{\sum_{i=j}^{j+W} |\mathbf{Z}_{t,r}^{\{k\}}(i) - \overline{\mathbf{Z}}_{t,r}^{\{k\}}(j:j+W)|}{W} \quad (4)$$

where $\overline{\mathbf{Z}}_{t,r}^{\{k\}}(j:j+W)$ represents the vector of means of the kth projected CSI stream in j-th window. It calculates the value of $\triangle m_j$ for each sample point j and for the principle components $2 \leq k \leq p$.

Second, the algorithm adds the mean absolute deviations in each waveform to calculate a combined measure $\triangle M_j$ of MAD in all $p-1$ waveforms, which is calculated in the following equation.

$$\triangle M_j = \sum_{k=2}^{p} \triangle m_j[k] \quad (5)$$

Third, the algorithm compares $\triangle M_j$ to a heuristically set threshold $Thresh$. Let $\delta_j = \triangle M_j - Thresh$, then $\delta_j > 0$ shows that the current window j contains significant variations in CSI amplitudes.

Fourth, the algorithm compares δ_j to its value in last window δ_{j-1} to detect increasing or decreasing trend in detected variations. When $\delta_j - \delta_{j-1} > 0$, there is an increasing trend in the rate of change in combined MAD ($\triangle M_j$) of CSI time series and vice versa. These increasing and decreasing trends are captured in variables i_u and d_u, respectively. The algorithm increments the value of i_u by 1 whenever $\delta_j - \delta_{j-1} > 0$ and d_u by 1 whenever $\delta_j - \delta_{j-1} < 0$. Let σ represent *forgetting factor*, which is used to "forget" the variations caused by noise to avoid false positives. To forget such variations, the algorithm decrements both i_u and d_u by 1 if $\triangle M_j < Thresh$ for a duration of σW.

Fifth, as soon as the values of i_u and d_u exceed empirically determined thresholds I_u and D_u, respectively, the algorithm detects the start of the keystroke. As soon as the algorithm detects a keystroke, it estimates the starting point s_m and ending point e_m of the keystroke waveforms using following equations.

$$s_m = j - \beta W - B_{left} \quad (6)$$

$$e_m = j - \beta W + \mathfrak{t}_{avg} + B_{right} \quad (7)$$

where $\mathfrak{t}_{avg}$ is the average number of data points spanned by waveforms of different keystrokes, β is the *span factor* which determines the estimated starting point of the keystroke and B_{left} and B_{right} are *guard* intervals on both sides of the estimated keystroke interval. The guard intervals ensure that the detected keystroke waveforms are complete.

Last, our algorithm calculates the sum of powers in all waveforms lying within those starting and ending points and then compares this combined power with a *sum power threshold* (P_{avg}) to confirm the presence of a complete keystroke within that interval. This ensures that the training models are built using only those waveforms which contain complete shapes of the keystrokes. Once keystroke detection is confirmed, the algorithm finally returns the starting point (s_m) of the detected keystroke and jumps $\triangle\mathfrak{t}_{avg}$ data points ahead of s_m to look for next keystroke, where $\triangle\mathfrak{t}_{avg}$ is the average number of data points between arrival of two consecutive keystrokes. From the CSI data set we collected from our volunteers, we observed that on average the waveforms of a keystroke spanned $\mathfrak{t}_{avg} \approx 650$ data points and average number of data points between arrival of two consecutive keystrokes was $\triangle\mathfrak{t}_{avg} \approx 1250$ data points at the CSI sampling rate of $F_s = 2500$ samples/s. We empirically determined appropriate values for the remaining constants including W, D_u, I_u, σ, β, B_{left}, B_{right}, $Thresh$ and P_{avg}.

5.3 Combining Results from Antenna Pairs

As mentioned earlier, we obtain the starting points of keystrokes independently from each TX-RX antenna pair. Let $\mathbf{S}_{t,r}$ represent the set containing the starting points of all keystrokes obtained from the keystroke detection algorithm applied on the antenna pair $t-r$. First, we obtain the set $\mathbf{S}_{t,r}$ for each $t-r$ pair. Second, we take the average of all the starting points that are within $\triangle\mathfrak{t}_{avg}$ of each other in all sets $S_{t,r}$ to obtain a robust estimate of starting points of keystrokes. Third, based on experimentally measured average span $\mathfrak{t}_{avg}$ of different keystrokes, we calculate the ending points of all keystrokes by simply adding $\mathfrak{t}_{avg}$ to the corresponding starting point.

5.4 Extracting Keystroke Waveforms

Once the algorithm calculates the set of starting and corresponding ending points for keystrokes, we use those points to extract the waveforms from CSI matrix $\mathbf{H}_{t,r}$. Let $\mathbf{K}_{m,t,r}$ represent the CSI waveform of mth keystroke extracted from the antenna pair *t-r*. Let $\overline{s}_m$ represent the average of the starting points for the mth keystroke from all antenna pairs. We can express $\mathbf{K}_{m,t,r}$ in terms of $\mathbf{H}_{t,r}$ follows.

$$\mathbf{K}_{m,t,r} = \mathbf{H}_{t,r}(\overline{s}_m : \overline{s}_m + \mathfrak{t}_{avg}) \quad (8)$$

After extracting the CSI waveforms $\mathbf{K}_{m,t,r}$ from all subcarriers of the *t-r* antenna pair, we apply PCA on those CSI waveforms to remove the noisy components and obtain the components that represent the variations caused by movements of hands and fingers.

Unlike principle components derived from normalized streams, it is difficult to decide which PCA component represents noise and should be removed from the top p principal components for the case of $\mathbf{K}_{m,t,r}$. The difficulty arises because $\mathbf{K}_{m,t,r}$ contains the set of waveforms for a specific keystroke instead of the whole CSI stream, due to which the variance of noisy component often becomes small. We observe that the noisy PCA component keeps changing positions between 1st and 2nd place among the sorted PCA components for different extracted keystroke waveforms. In order to get rid of this problem, we first project $\mathbf{K}_{m,t,r}$ onto all top q principal components. Let $\Phi_K^{\{1:q\}}$ be an $S_c \times q$ dimensional matrix that represent the top q principal components in $\mathbf{K}_{m,t,r}$ obtained after applying PCA and $\mathbf{K}_{m,t,r}^{\{1:q\}}$ be an $L \times q$ dimensional matrix containing the projected CSI streams in its columns, where L is the length of segmented keystroke waveform. Thus, $\mathbf{K}_{m,t,r}^{\{1:q\}}$ is given by the following equation.

$$\mathbf{K}_{m,t,r}^{\{1:q\}} = \mathbf{K}_{m,t,r} \times \Phi_K^{\{1:q\}} \quad (9)$$

In our implementation, we choose $q = 4$. This choice is again based on the observation that the top 4 principal components contain enough information about keystrokes required to achieve high accuracy during classification.

To detect which waveform in $\mathbf{K}_{m,t,r}^{\{1:q\}}$ represents the noisy projection, we chose the top 2 projected waveforms and divide each of them into R bins and calculate the variances in those bins. We then compare the variances calculated for different bins of one waveform with the corresponding bins of the other waveform. The waveform that has larger number of higher variance bins is considered to be the noisy projection, which we remove from $\mathbf{K}_{m,t,r}^{\{1:q\}}$ to finally get $q-1$ waveforms. Here we leverage the fact that although overall variance of a noisy projection may be smaller than the variance of other waveforms, but if the waveform is divided into appropriate number of smaller bins then the number of bins in which the variance of the noisy projection is higher than the corresponding bins of other waveforms is always larger. This is because the impact of noise is more dominant in smaller time windows compared to larger time windows. We used R=10 in our implementation of WiKey.

PCA can lead to different ordering of principal components in waveforms of different keystrokes of the same key, because the ordering of waveforms done by PCA is based solely on the value of their variance, which can change even if a key is pressed in a slightly different way. This is problematic because to recognize the keystrokes, we need to compare the projections of an unseen key with the corresponding projections of the keys in the training data. In order to minimize the possibility of reordering, we order the projected keystroke waveforms in descending order of their peak to peak values before using the waveforms for feature extraction and classifier training.

6. FEATURE EXTRACTION

To differentiate between keystrokes, we need to extract features that can uniquely represent those keystrokes. As different keys on a keyboard are closely placed, standard features such as maximum peak power, mean amplitude, root mean square deviation of signal amplitude, second/third central moments, rate of change, signal energy or entropy, and number of zero crossings cannot be used because adjacent keys give almost the same values for these features. Tables 1 and 2 show means and variances of some of these features calculated for 2nd waveform in the extracted CSI-waveforms for keystrokes of alphabetic keys pressed by a users. It can be observed that the values of these features for different keys (for example 'c' and 'd') come out to be very similar. Looking at the means calculated for features like energy and number of zero crossings in Table 1, it seems that they have different values for different keys. But as we observe from Table 2, the variance of those features is high. Due to the reasons above, it becomes infeasible to use these features for keystroke classification. Frequency analysis is also not feasible because the frequency components in keystrokes of many different keys are similar. Another reason behind inapplicability of frequency domain analysis is that they lead to complete loss of time domain information.

From our data set, we have observed that although the frequency components in most keys are similar, they occur at different time instants for different keys. Therefore, we use shapes of the extracted keystroke waveforms as their features because the shapes retain both time and frequency domain information of the waveforms and are thus more suited for use in classification. We observed experimentally that the shapes of different keystroke waveforms were quite different from each other, as shown by Figure 5(a) and 5(b).

Directly using the extracted keystroke waveforms as keystroke features leads to high computational costs in the classification process because waveforms contain hundreds of data points per keystroke. Therefore, we apply Discrete Wavelet Transform (DWT) to compress the extracted keystroke waveforms while preserving most of the time and frequency domain information.

The DWT of a discrete signal $y[n]$ can be written in terms of wavelet basis functions as:

$$y[n] = \frac{1}{\sqrt{L}} \sum_{k} \lambda(j_0, k)\varphi_{j_0,k}(n) + \frac{1}{\sqrt{L}} \sum_{j=j_0}^{\infty} \sum_{k} \gamma(j,k)\psi_{j,k}(n)$$

where L represents the length of signal $y[n]$. The functions $\varphi_{j,k}(n)$ are called *scaling functions*, where as the corresponding coefficients $\lambda(j,k)$ are known as *scaling* or *approximation coefficients*. Similarly, the functions $\psi_{j,k}(n)$ are known as *wavelet functions* and the corresponding coefficients $\gamma(j,k)$ are known as *wavelet* or *detail coefficients*. To calculate approximation and detail coefficients, the scaling and wavelet functions are chosen such that they are orthonormal to each other. Thus, the following condition holds.

$$\langle \psi_{j,k}(n), \varphi_{j_0,m}(n) \rangle = \delta_{j,j_0}\delta_{k,m}$$

Based on the condition above, the approximation and detail coefficients calculated for j-th scale can then be written as:

$$\lambda(j,k) = \langle y[n], \varphi_{j+1,k}(n) \rangle = \frac{1}{\sqrt{L}} \sum_{n} y[n]\varphi_{j+1,k}(n)$$

$$\gamma(j,k) = \langle y[n], \psi_{j+1,k}(n) \rangle = \frac{1}{\sqrt{L}} \sum_{n} y[n]\psi_{j+1,k}(n)$$

To achieve desired compression using DWT, we need to select appropriate wavelet and scaling filters. We tested the accuracy of our classifier using two different wavelet filters: Daubechies and Symlets. We choose Daubechies D4 (four coefficients per filter) wavelet and scaling filters because the models trained with the DWT features extracted using these filters achieved higher classification accuracy. For each keystroke, we perform DWT 3 times on each one of its $(q-1) = 3$ waveforms, which is achieved by applying DWT on the approximation coefficients obtained from the previous steps. We choose to apply DWT 3 times because this preserves enough details of those waveforms required for successful classification while achieving maximum compression. WiKey uses only the approximation coefficients as keystroke features and discards the detail coefficients because approximation coefficients alone result in good classification accuracy. Therefore, we have $3 \times M_T \times M_R$ keystroke shapes for every keystroke, *i.e.* the approximation coefficients of all 3 waveforms extracted from the CSI time series in each TX-RX antenna pair, where M_T is the number of transmitting antennas and M_R is the number of receiving antennas. Figures 5(a) through 5(d) show feature extraction procedure performed on the 2nd keystroke waveforms for keys 'i' and 'o', extracted from TX-1, RX-1 antenna pair.

7. CLASSIFICATION

After obtaining DWT based shape features of keystrokes, WiKey builds training models for classification using them. As WiKey needs to compare shape features of different keystrokes, we need a comparison metric that provides an effective measure of similarity between shape features of two keystrokes. WiKey uses a well-known method called *dynamic time warping* (DTW) that calculates the distance between

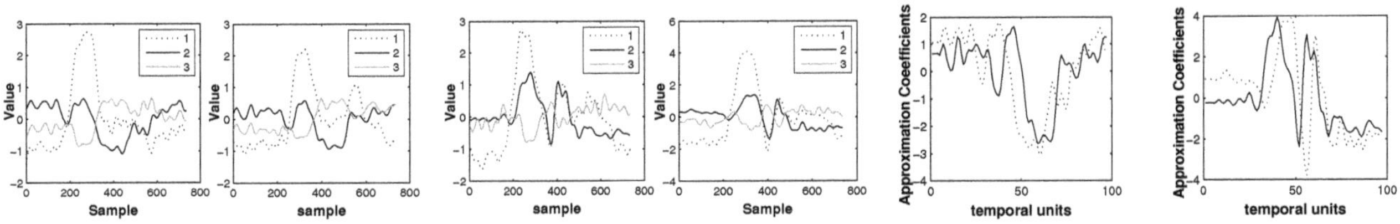

(a) Keystroke waveforms for key **i** (b) Keystroke waveforms for key **o** (c) DWT features of **i** from 2nd waveforms (d) DWT features of **o** from 2nd waveforms

Figure 5: Feature extraction from 2nd keystroke waveforms extracted from TX-1, RX-1 for I and O

Table 1: Average values of features extracted from keystrokes of keys a-z collected from user 10

Features	a	b	c	d	e	f	g	h	i	j	k	l	m	n	o	p	q	r	s	t	u	v	w	x	y	z
Mean amplitude	-0	-0.04	0.0124	-0.03	0.045	-0.043	-0.076	-0.06	0.014	-0.03	0.03	-0.01	-0	0.032	0.02	0.03	-0.012	0.008	0.054	7E-04	-0.013	-0.02	-0	-0.1	-0.02	0.06
Second central moment	0.08	0.133	0.0801	0.083	0.156	0.1818	0.6523	0.263	0.12	0.231	0.33	0.11	0.1	0.108	0.09	0.19	0.1022	0.051	0.245	0.192	0.062	0.12	0.097	0.26	0.09	0.21
Third central moment	0.02	-0.03	0.0036	-0.01	0.029	-0.06	-0.919	-0.05	-0.01	-0.1	0.05	0.02	-0	0.01	0.01	0.04	-0.006	0.003	0.098	-0.101	-0.01	0.029	0.023	-0	-0.02	0.04
RMS deviation	0.27	0.359	0.2782	0.285	0.385	0.4244	0.7899	0.506	0.332	0.472	0.57	0.32	0.3	0.323	0.29	0.43	0.3137	0.222	0.472	0.434	0.242	0.335	0.306	0.5	0.3	0.45
Energy	71.5	116.6	69.788	73.34	137.5	159.43	570.8	232.1	104.8	201.4	288	95.2	83.7	94.98	75.6	167	88.928	44.22	215.5	167.1	54.56	104.4	84.48	227	81.5	182
Entropy	9.76	9.762	9.7616	9.762	9.762	9.7616	9.7616	9.762	9.762	9.762	9.76	9.76	9.76	9.762	9.76	9.76	9.7616	9.762	9.762	9.762	9.762	9.762	9.762	9.76	9.76	9.76
Zero Crossings	11.8	6.913	12.363	6.225	6.4	4.375	4.075	3.4	12.08	9.088	6.05	13.7	10	9.063	13.8	12.9	11.85	15.41	6.35	12.85	16.75	11.88	14.3	6.48	10.1	7.55

waveforms by performing optimal alignment between them. Using DTW distance as the comparison metric between keystroke shape features, WiKey trains an ensemble of *k-nearest neighbour* (kNN) classifiers using those features from all TX-RX antenna pairs. WiKey obtains decisions from each classifier in the ensemble and uses majority voting to obtain final result. Next, we first explain how we apply DTW on the keystroke shape features and then explain how we train the ensemble of classifiers.

7.1 Dynamic Time Warping

DTW is a dynamic programming based solution for obtaining minimum distance alignment between any two waveforms. DTW can handle waveforms of different lengths and allows a non-linear mapping of one waveform to another by minimizing the distance between the two. In contrast to Euclidean distance, DTW gives us intuitive distance between two waveforms by determining minimum distance warping path between them even if they are distorted or shifted versions of each other. *DTW distance* is the Euclidean distance of the optimal warping path between two waveforms calculated under boundary conditions and local path constraints [25]. In our experiments, DTW distance proves to be very effective metric for comparing two shape features of different keystrokes. WiKey uses the open source implementation of DTW in the Machine Learning Toolbox (MLT) by Jang [26]. WiKey uses local path constraints of 27, 45, and 63 degrees while determining minimum cost warping path between two waveforms. For the features extracted for keys 'i' and 'o' shown in figures 5(a) and 5(b), the DTW distance among features of key 'i' was 18.79 and the DTW distance among features of key 'o' was 19.44. However, the average DTW distance between features of these keys was 44.2.

7.2 Classifier Training

To maximize the advantage of having multiple shape features per keystroke obtained from multiple transmit-receive antenna pairs, we build separate classifiers for each of those shape features. We build an ensemble of $3 \times M_T \times M_R$ classifiers using kNN classification scheme. WiKey requires the user to provide training data for the keystrokes to be recognized and each classifier is trained using the corresponding features extracted from CSI time series from all TX-RX antenna pairs. To classify a detected keystroke, WiKey feeds the shape features of that keystroke to their corresponding kNN classifiers and obtains a decision from each classifier in the ensemble. Each kNN classifier searches for the majority class label among k nearest neighbors of the corresponding shape feature using DTW distance metric. WiKey calculates the final result through majority voting on the decisions of all kNN classifiers in the ensemble.

8. IMPLEMENTATION & EVALUATION

8.1 Hardware Setup

We implemented our scheme using off-the-shelf hardware devices. Specifically, we use a Lenovo X200 laptop with Intel Link 5300 WiFi NIC as the receiver that connects to the three antennas of the X200 laptop. The X200 laptop has 2.26GHz Intel Core 2 Duo processor with 4GB of RAM and Ubuntu 14.04 as its operating system. We used TP-Link TL-WR1043ND WiFi router as transmitter operating in 802.11n AP mode at 2.4GHz. We collect the CSI values from the Intel 5300 NIC using a modified driver developed by Halperin *et al.* [24]. The transmitter has 2 antennas and the receiver has 3 antennas, *i.e.*, $M_T = 2$ and $M_R = 3$. This gives $3 \times 2 \times 3 = 18$ classification models for each key in our evaluations.

We place the X200 laptop at a distance of 30 cm from the keyboard such that the back side of its screen faces the keyboard on which the users type and its screen is within the line-of-sight (LOS) of the WiFi router it is connected to. The distance of WiFi router from the target keyboard is 4 meters. The CSI values are measured on ICMP *ping* packets sent from the WiFi router, *i.e.*, the TP-Link TL-WR1043ND, to the laptop at high data rate of about 2500 packets/s. Setting a higher *ping* frequency leads to higher sampling rate of CSI, which ensures that the time resolution of the CSI values is high enough for capturing maximum details of different type of keystrokes.

8.2 Data Collection

To evaluate the accuracy of WiKey, we collected training and testing dataset from 10 users. These 10 users were general university students who volunteered for the experiments and only 2 out of them had some know how of wireless communication. Users 1–9 first provided 30 samples for

Table 2: Variance of different features extracted from keystrokes of keys a-z collected from user 10

Features	a	b	c	d	e	f	g	h	i	j	k	l	m	n	o	p	q	r	s	t	u	v	w	x	y	z
Mean amplitude	0.00029	4E-04	0.0003	1E-04	4E-04	0.0002	0.0003	8E-04	5E-04	5E-04	5E-04	2E-04	5E-04	3E-04	3E-04	5E-04	0.0003	0.00018	6E-04	4E-04	3E-04	1E-04	3E-04	4E-04	6E-04	4E-04
Second central moment	0.00513	0.003	0.0011	0.001	0.007	0.0028	0.1008	0.012	0.005	0.009	0.016	0.006	0.002	0.003	0.002	0.007	0.0017	0.00041	0.03	0.003	0.001	0.006	0.002	0.007	0.003	0.005
Third central moment	0.00155	9E-04	0.0001	2E-04	0.002	0.0033	0.7021	0.002	0.001	0.007	0.009	0.017	5E-04	3E-04	5E-04	0.003	0.0003	7.70E-05	0.024	0.003	1E-04	0.015	9E-04	0.001	6E-04	0.003
RMS deviation	0.0108	0.006	0.0031	0.004	0.011	0.0038	0.0348	0.011	0.011	0.01	0.012	0.009	0.006	0.005	0.004	0.008	0.0042	0.00196	0.026	0.004	0.004	0.008	0.004	0.007	0.007	0.007
Energy	3874.59	2283	816.91	912.4	5204	2160	76863	9315	3925	6846	12094	4883	1679	2153	1150	5048	1296.2	308.95	23201	2181	886.9	4714	1403	5166	2100	4147
Entropy	0	0	0	0	0	0	0	0	0	0	0	0	0	0	0	0	0	0	0	0	0	0	0	0	0	0
Zero Crossings	26.3859	12.36	33.196	12.94	9.433	6.2627	3.9943	3.585	44.91	13.14	12.58	31.14	28.51	15.25	29.24	24.09	21.673	17.3847	12.21	17.7	36.85	21.63	27.71	13.67	31.49	6.529

each of the 37 keys (26 alphabets, 10 digits and 1 space bar) by pressing that key multiple times. After this, these users typed the sentence S_1 = "the quick brown fox jumped over the lazy dog" two times, without spaces.

To evaluate how the number of training samples impact the accuracy, we collected 80 samples for each of the 37 keys from User 10. Afterwards, this user typed each of the following sentences 5 times, without spaces: S_1 ="the quick brown fox jumps over the lazy dog", S_2 = "nobody knew why the candles blew out", S_3 = "the autumn leaves look like golden snow", S_4 = "nothing is as profound as the imagination" and S_5 = "my small pet mouse escaped from his cage". We asked users to type naturally with multiple fingers but only press one key at a time while keeping the average keystroke inter-arrival time at 1 second. After recording the CSI time series for each of the above experiments, we first applied our keystroke extraction algorithm on those recorded CSI time series to extract the CSI waveforms for individual keys and then extracted the DWT based shape features from each of the extracted keystroke waveforms.

8.3 Keystroke Extraction Accuracy

We evaluate the accuracy of our keystroke extraction algorithm in terms of the detection ratio, which is defined as the total number of correctly detected keystrokes in a CSI time series divided by the total number of actual keystrokes. *The detection ratio of our proposed algorithm is more than 97.5%.* Figure 6(a) shows the color map showing the percentage of the missed keystrokes of all 37 keys for all 10 users.

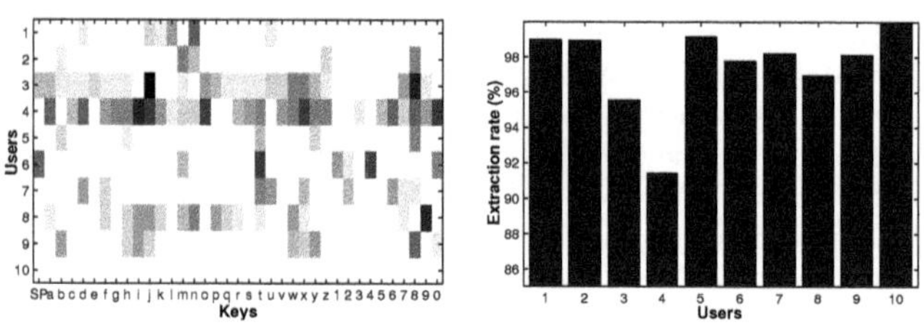

(a) Colormap for missed keys (b) Keystroke extraction rates per user averaged over all keys

Figure 6: Keystroke extraction results

The darker areas represent higher rate of missed keystrokes. We can observe from this figure that the number of missed keystrokes vary for different individuals depending upon their typing behaviors. For example we observed that the keystrokes of user 4 were missed in higher percentage with average detection ratio of 91.8% whereas the keystrokes of user 10 were not missed at all with average detection ratio of 100% calculated over all 37 keys. The lower extraction accuracy for user 4 shows that more keystrokes were missed, which is due to the significant difference in his typing behavior compared to other users. The accuracy of our scheme for such a user can be increased significantly by tuning the parameters of our algorithm for the given user.

We also observe from this figure that the keystrokes that are missed are usually those for which fingers move very little when typing. For example, in pressing keys 'a', 'd', 'f', 'i', 'j' and 'x' the hands and fingers move very little, and thus the variations in the CSI values sometimes go undetected. Figure 6(b) shows the keystroke extraction rate for each user averaged over all 37 keys. The experimental results show that our keystroke extraction algorithm is robust because it consistently achieves high performance over different users without requiring any user specific tuning of system parameters.

8.4 Classification Accuracy

We evaluate the classification accuracy of WiKey through two sets of experiments. In the first set of experiments, we build classifiers for each of the 10 users using 30 samples and measure the 10-fold cross validation accuracy of those classifiers. In the second set of experiments, we build classifier for user 10 while increasing the number of samples from 30 to 80 in order to observe the impact of increase in the number of training samples on the classification accuracy. Cross validation automatically picks a part of data for training and remaining for testing and does not use any data in testing that was used in training. Recall that the WiKey uses kNN classifiers for recognizing keys. In all of following experiments, we set $k = 15$.

8.4.1 Accuracy with 30 Samples per Key

We evaluate the classification accuracy of WiKey in terms of average accuracy per key and average accuracy on all keys of any given user. We also present confusion matrices resulting from our experiments. A confusion matrix tells us which key was recognized by WiKey as which key with what percentage. We calculate the average accuracy per key by taking the average of confusion matrices obtained from all users and average accuracy on all keys of any given user by averaging the accuracy on all keys within the confusion matrix of that user. For each user, we trained each classifier using features from 30 samples of each key. We conducted our experiments on all 37 keys as well as on only 26 alphabet keys and performed 10-fold cross validation to obtain the confusion matrices.

WiKey achieves an overall keystroke recognition accuracy of 82.87% in case of 37 keys and 83.46% in case of 26 alphabetic keys when averaged over all keys and users. Figure 7 shows the recognition accuracy for each key across all users for the 26 alphabetic keys. Similarly, Figure 8 shows the recognition accuracy for each key across all users for all 37 keys. Figure 9 shows the average recognition accuracy achieved by each user for both 26 keys and 37 keys. We observe that the recognition accuracy for 26 alphabetic keys is on average greater than the recognition accuracy for the all 37 keys. This is because the keystroke waveforms of the digit keys (0-9) often show similarity with keystroke waveforms of alphabet keys in the keyboard row staring with QWE, which leads to slightly greater number of misclassifications.

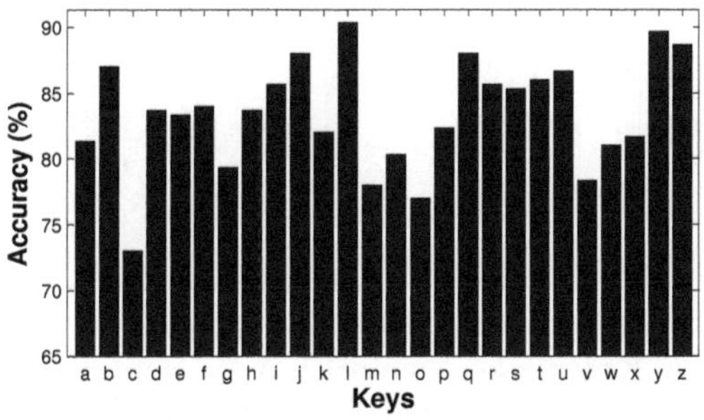

Figure 7: Mean accuracy for keys A-Z (Users 1-10)

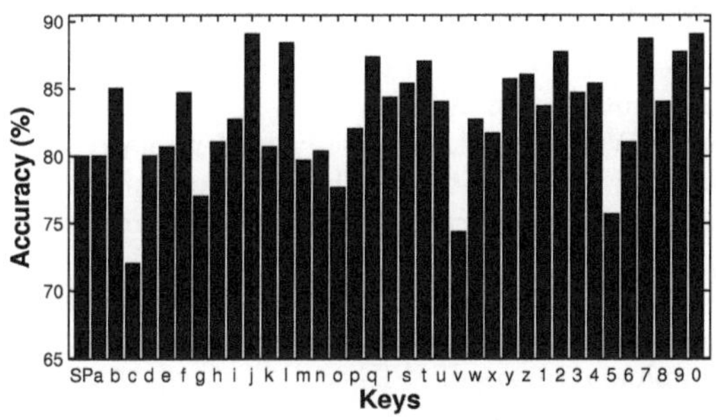

Figure 8: Mean accuracy for all 37 keys (Users 1-10)

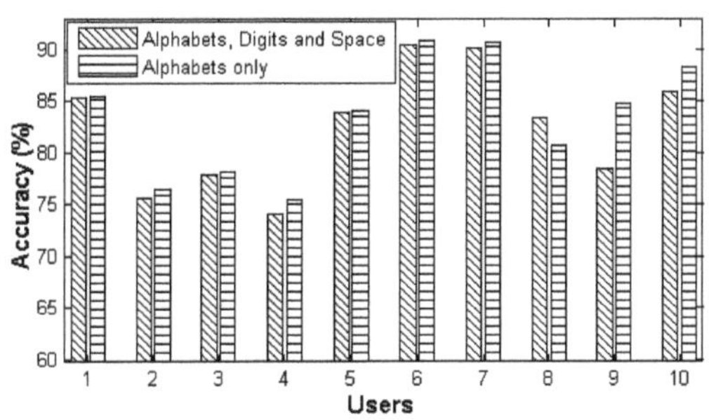

Figure 9: Per user average classifier accuracies

8.4.2 Accuracy vs. the Size for Training Set

To determine the impact of the number for training samples on the accuracy of WiKey, we again perform two sets of experiments: one for 26 alphabetic keys and other for all 37 keys.

The accuracy of WiKey increases when the number of training samples per key are increased from 30 to 80. Figure 10 shows the results from 10-fold cross validation for the 26 alphabetic keys when 80 training samples are used per key. We observe from this figure that the recognition accuracy increased from 88.3% (as seen in Figure 9) to 96.4% when the number of training samples are increased from 30 to 80. Figure 11 shows the results from 10-fold cross validation for all 37 keys when 80 training samples are used per key. We again observe that the recognition accuracy increased from 85.95% (as seen in Figure 9) to 89.7% when the number of training samples are increased from 30 to 80. The gray-scale maps of the confusion matrix obtained after 10-fold cross-validation on 80 training samples of User 10 is shown in Figure 12.

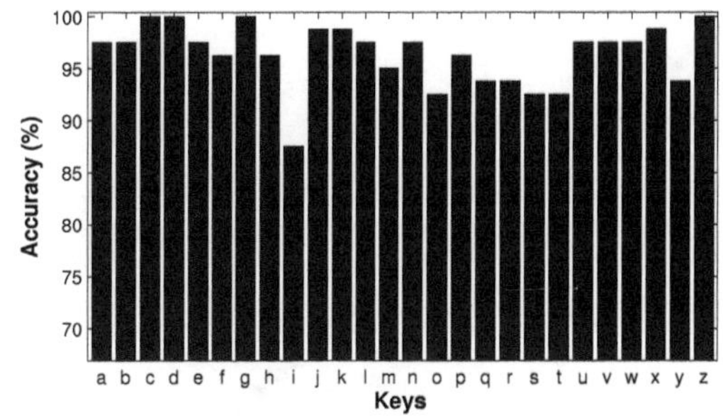

Figure 10: Accuracy for keys A-Z from user 10

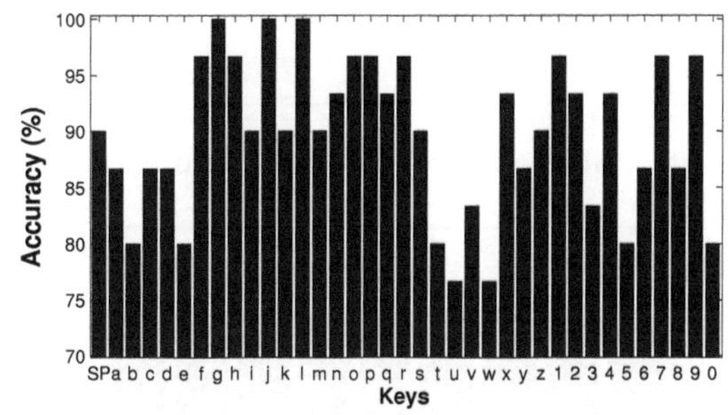

Figure 11: Accuracy for all 37 keys from user 10

8.4.3 Effects of CSI Sampling Rate and Number of Training Samples

In previous experiments, we used high CSI sampling rate of 2500 samples/s. Furthermore, the 10-fold cross validation automatically chose 10% of the data for testing and remaining 90% for training. Next, we evaluate the effect of changing the CSI sampling rate and the percentage of data used for training on accuracy. To extract keystrokes, we halved the values used for W, D_u, I_u, B_{left}, and B_{right}. We performed $X-$fold cross validation ($2 \leq X \leq 10$) on the data obtained for alphabetic keys from user 10. Figure 13 plots the accuracies for number of folds varying from 2 to 10, where each plotted value if the average over all alphabet keys. We observe from Figure 13 that the accuracies dropped compared to previously achieved accuracy because of the drop in resolution of keystroke shapes due to reduced sampling rate. We also observe that recognition accuracies of the keys for which hands and fingers move little were affected the most. When 50% of data was used for training, *i.e.*, for 2-fold cross validation, the accuracies for keys 'j','x','v' and 'p' dropped below 60%. However, the average accuracy remained approximately 80% for all folds.

8.5 Real-world Evaluation on Sentences

To evaluate WiKey in real world scenarios, we collected CSI data for different sentences typed by users 1-10 as mentioned earlier in Section 8.2. For recognition of keystrokes in sentences, we performed training using the dataset of individual keystrokes and the keystrokes extracted from datasets obtained from typing the sentences were used as test data.

WiKey achieves an average keystroke recognition accuracy of 77.43% for typed sentences when 30 training samples per key were used. For each user, we trained classifiers using 30 samples for each of the 26 alphabetic keys. We then applied our keystroke extraction algorithm to first extract waveforms of individual keys, applied PCA on them to denoise the waveforms and then extracted the shape features for each extracted key and feeded them to the classifiers to

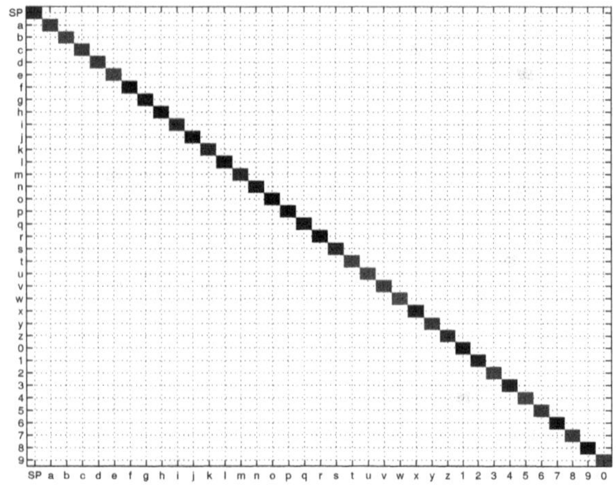

Figure 12: Color map of user 10's confusion matrix

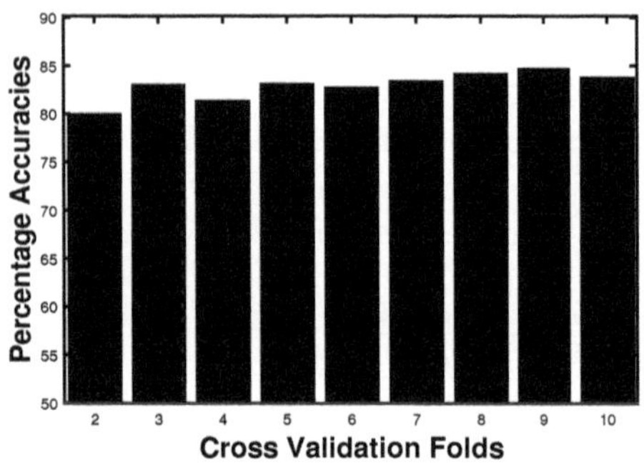

Figure 13: Multifold cross-validated average accuracies for user 10's lower resolution keystrokes

recognize the keystrokes in the sentence. Figure 14 shows the keystroke recognition accuracy for the sentences typed by each user.

WiKey achieves an average keystroke recognition accuracy is 93.47% in continuously typed sentences with 80 training samples per key. We first trained classifiers using 80 samples for each of the 26 alphabetic keys and then fed them with keystrokes from typed sentences. Figure 15 shows the keystroke recognition accuracy for all the sentences (S_1 to S_5) typed by user 10. The average keystroke recognition accuracy rate for user 10 in previous experiment, which used 30 samples for training classifiers was just 80%. Thus, we can conclude that increasing the number of training samples increases the accuracy of WiKey.

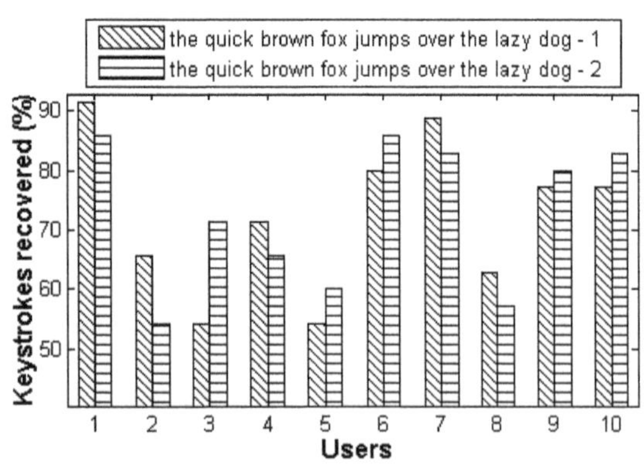

Figure 14: Keystroke recognition for sentences collected from all users using 30 samples per key

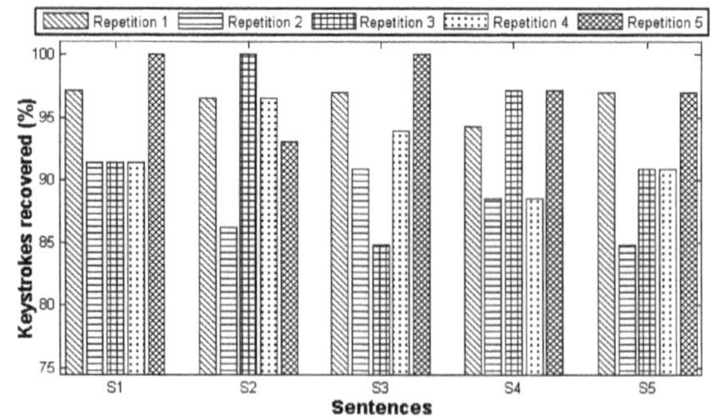

Figure 15: Keystroke recognition for sentences collected from user 10 using 80 samples per key

9. LIMITATIONS

In this section, we discuss the key limitations of the current implementation of WiKey.

Currently WiKey works well only under relatively stable and controlled environments. The accuracy of our current scheme is affected by variations in the environment such as human motion in surrounding areas, changes in orientation and distance of transceivers, typing speeds, and keyboard layout and size. Next, we elaborate some limitations of our current implementation of WiKey.

Interference Free Surroundings. During our experiments, we assumed that the major motion is due to keystrokes of the target user only and no other major motion such as walking occurs in the room where CSI data is collected. WiKey is currently designed for and tested with only two persons in a room i.e. the person guiding the user during data collection and the user himself. WiKey may be extended to allow small movement in the environment e.g. having multiple persons walking in a library, however this would require training WiKey with the profiles of those activities and adding the capability to subtract the waveforms of those activities to extract the waveforms of keystrokes. Furthermore, most of the parameters used in our keystroke extraction algorithm are scenario dependent and need to be changed if CSI sampling rates or physical environment changes such as change in distance or orientation of transceivers. In future, we plan to develop schemes for automatic tuning of system parameters.

Devices Positioning. We tested the accuracy of WiKey using the same keyboard for all users while keeping the transceivers at the same distance and in same direction with respect to the keyboard. Furthermore, we took all samples from any given user on the same day because it took around 2 hours to get complete data from each user. It was difficult for the users to spare time to provide data for different orientations and distances and on multiple days. Therefore, we put the laptop at a fixed distance and direction from the user and used maximum sampling rate to get maximum information from CSI time series. Figures 16 and 17 show the shapes of the waveforms for key '5' when distance and orientation of receiver is changed with respect to the target keyboard, while WiFi AP is at 2 meters distance from the keyboard. We increased the distance linearly, while remaining in LOS of the transmitter. We observe from these figures that not only the shapes of the waveforms change but the measured variations (e.g. peak to peak values) due to keystrokes also attenuate. Similarly, when changing ori-

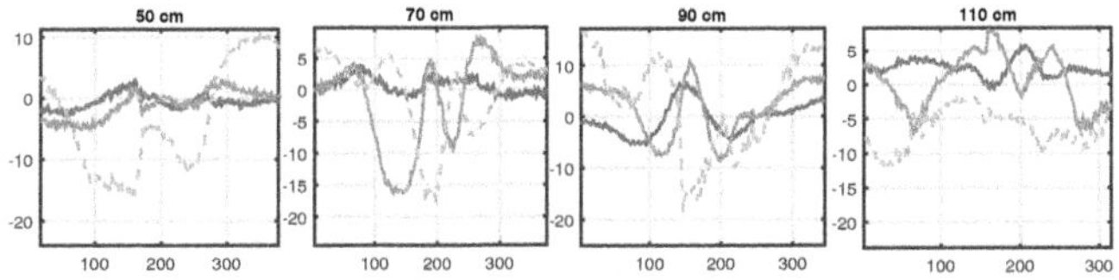

Figure 16: Change in shape with RX distance

entation, we observed that as we orient away from LOS of transmitter, the variations attenuate progressively. Similar trends were observed when AP was placed at different distances from keyboard, while keeping the receiver 30cm from keyboard, as shown in figure 19. These observations are consistent with the results of previous studies [27] [28] that also show that CSI values tend to be different at different locations in an area. Figure 18 shows how CSI waveforms of the key look on different days. The dissimilarities in CSI waveforms can be attributed to inconsistencies in user's typing behavior on different days. As the shapes of waveforms tend to differ on different days or when distance and orientation of transceivers change, in its current form, WiKey needs to be trained in each given scenario.

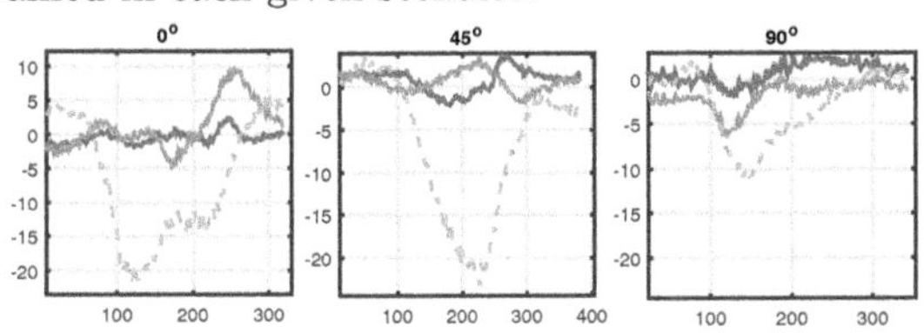

Figure 17: Change in shape of with angle

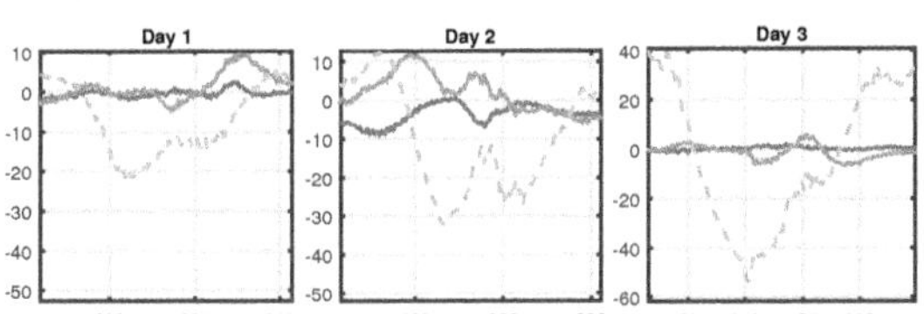

Figure 18: Change in shape with days

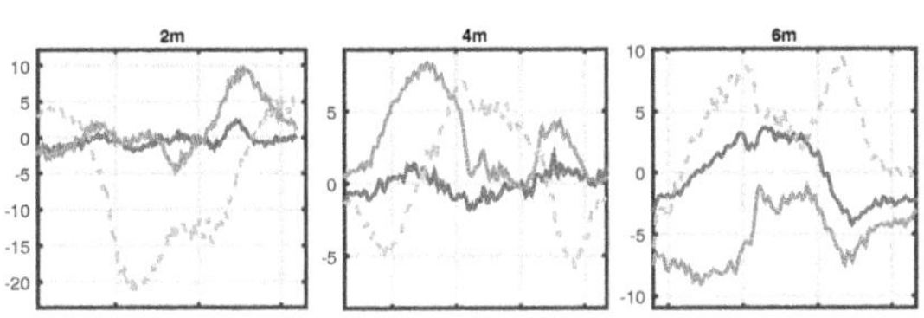

Figure 19: Change in shape with AP distance

Controlled Typing. During data collection, we instructed the users not to move their heads or other body parts significantly while typing. However, we allowed natural motions which occur commonly when a person types, such as eye winking and movements in the arm, shoulder and fingers on the side of the hand being used for typing. We also instructed the users to type one key at a time while keeping the inter arrival time of keystrokes between 0.5 to 1 second to facilitate correct identification of start and end times of keystrokes. However, we did allow users to use multiple fingers for typing so that they use whichever finger they naturally use to press any given key.

CSI Sampling Rate. The sampling rate of CSI is directly related to allowable inter-arrival times of keystrokes *i.e.*, how fast a user can be allowed to type. Both keystroke extraction and keystroke recognition accuracies depend on the time resolution of CSI values. The time resolution is high, there are more samples between two keystrokes, which increases the keystroke extraction accuracy. Similarly, when the time resolution is high, there are more samples for each keystroke; consequently, there is more information in the CSI waveform, which increases the keystroke recognition accuracy. We used highest possible sampling rate of 2500 samples/second, which translates to 2500 packets/second. Although real-world WiFi APs may not transmit at such high rates, an attacker can use his own AP to transmit ping packets at such a high rate to launch the attack.

Training Requirements. When collecting data from users, we did not bind the users to be consistent in their typing behavior. Consequently, waveforms for different keystrokes for a specific key were sometimes inconsistent even though we collected data from the users in the same sitting. To get high recognition accuracies with such a data, WiKey requires many samples per key from each user which may be difficult to obtain in real life attack scenarios. Still, there exist ways through which an attacker can obtain the training data. For example, an attacker can start an online chat session with a person sitting near him and record CSI values while chatting with him.

User Specific Training. In our current implementation of WiKey, we train the classifiers using one user and test the classifier using the test samples from the same user. However, we hypothesize that if we train our classifier using a large number of users, the trained classifier will be able to capture commonalities between users and will then be able to recognize the keystrokes of any unknown user. At the same time, we also acknowledge that it is extremely challenging to build such a universal classifier that works for almost every user because WiFi signals are susceptible to various factors such as finger length/width, typing styles, and environmental noise.

10. CONCLUSION

In this paper, we make the following key contributions. First, we propose the first WiFi based keystroke recognition approach, which exploits the variations in CSI values caused by the micro-movements of hands and fingers in typing. The key intuition is that while typing a certain key, the hands and fingers of a user move in a unique formation and direction and thus generate a unique pattern in the time-series of CSI values for that key. Second, we propose a keystroke extraction algorithm that automatically detects and segments the recorded CSI time series to extract the waveforms for individual keystrokes. Third, we implemented and evaluated the WiKey system using a TP-Link TL-WR1043ND WiFi router and a Lenovo X200 laptop. Our experimental results show that WiKey achieves more than 97.5% detection rate for detecting the keystroke and 96.4% recognition accuracy for classifying single keys. In real-world experiments, WiKey can recognize keystrokes in a continuously typed sentence with an accuracy of 93.5%. The key scientific value of this work is in demonstrating the possibility of recognizing micro-gestures such as keystrokes using commodity WiFi devices. We have shown that our technique works in controlled environments, and in future we plan to address the problem of mitigating the effects of more harsh wireless environments by building on our micro-gesture extraction and recognition techniques proposed in this paper.

11. REFERENCES

[1] Dmitri Asonov and Rakesh Agrawal. Keyboard acoustic emanations. In *2012 IEEE Symposium on Security and Privacy*, pages 3–3. IEEE Computer Society, 2004.

[2] Li Zhuang, Feng Zhou, and J Doug Tygar. Keyboard acoustic emanations revisited. *ACM Transactions on Information and System Security (TISSEC)*, 13(1):3, 2009.

[3] Tong Zhu, Qiang Ma, Shanfeng Zhang, and Yunhao Liu. Context-free attacks using keyboard acoustic emanations. In *Proceedings of the 2014 ACM SIGSAC Conference on Computer and Communications Security*, pages 453–464. ACM, 2014.

[4] Martin Vuagnoux and Sylvain Pasini. Compromising electromagnetic emanations of wired and wireless keyboards. In *USENIX Security Symposium*, pages 1–16, 2009.

[5] Davide Balzarotti, Marco Cova, and Giovanni Vigna. Clearshot: Eavesdropping on keyboard input from video. In *Security and Privacy, 2008. SP 2008. IEEE Symposium on*, pages 170–183. IEEE, 2008.

[6] Chunmei Han, Kaishun Wu, Yuxi Wang, and Lionel M Ni. Wifall: Device-free fall detection by wireless networks. In *INFOCOM, 2014 Proceedings IEEE*, pages 271–279. IEEE, 2014.

[7] Yan Wang, Jian Liu, Yingying Chen, Marco Gruteser, Jie Yang, and Hongbo Liu. E-eyes: device-free location-oriented activity identification using fine-grained wifi signatures. In *Proceedings of the 20th annual international conference on Mobile computing and networking*, pages 617–628. ACM, 2014.

[8] Zimu Zhou, Zheng Yang, Chenshu Wu, Longfei Shangguan, and Yunhao Liu. Towards omnidirectional passive human detection. In *INFOCOM, 2013 Proceedings IEEE*, pages 3057–3065. IEEE, 2013.

[9] Wei Xi, Jizhong Zhao, Xiang-Yang Li, Kun Zhao, Shaojie Tang, Xue Liu, and Zhiping Jiang. Electronic frog eye: Counting crowd using wifi. In *INFOCOM, 2014 Proceedings IEEE*, pages 361–369, April 2014.

[10] Guanhua Wang, Yongpan Zou, Zimu Zhou, Kaishun Wu, and Lionel M Ni. We can hear you with wi-fi! In *Proceedings of the 20th annual international conference on Mobile computing and networking*, pages 593–604. ACM, 2014.

[11] Stephan Sigg, Shuyu Shi, Felix Buesching, Yusheng Ji, and Lars Wolf. Leveraging rf-channel fluctuation for activity recognition: Active and passive systems, continuous and rssi-based signal features. In *Proceedings of International Conference on Advances in Mobile Computing & Multimedia*, page 43. ACM, 2013.

[12] Stephan Sigg, Markus Scholz, Shuyu Shi, Yusheng Ji, and Michael Beigl. Rf-sensing of activities from non-cooperative subjects in device-free recognition systems using ambient and local signals. *Mobile Computing, IEEE Transactions on*, 13(4):907–920, 2014.

[13] Rajalakshmi Nandakumar, Bryce Kellogg, and Shyamnath Gollakota. Wi-fi gesture recognition on existing devices. *arXiv preprint arXiv:1411.5394*, 2014.

[14] Souvik Sen, Jeongkeun Lee, Kyu-Han Kim, and Paul Congdon. Avoiding multipath to revive inbuilding wifi localization. In *Proceeding of the 11th annual international conference on Mobile systems, applications, and services*, pages 249–262. ACM, 2013.

[15] Jiang Xiao, Kaishun Wu, Youwen Yi, and Lionel M Ni. Fifs: Fine-grained indoor fingerprinting system. In *Computer Communications and Networks (ICCCN), 2012 21st International Conference on*, pages 1–7. IEEE, 2012.

[16] Zheng Yang, Zimu Zhou, and Yunhao Liu. From rssi to csi: Indoor localization via channel response. *ACM Computing Surveys (CSUR)*, 46(2):25, 2013.

[17] Qifan Pu, Sidhant Gupta, Shyamnath Gollakota, and Shwetak Patel. Whole-home gesture recognition using wireless signals. In *Proceedings of the 19th annual international conference on Mobile computing & networking*, pages 27–38. ACM, 2013.

[18] Bryce Kellogg, Vamsi Talla, and Shyamnath Gollakota. Bringing gesture recognition to all devices. In *Usenix NSDI*, volume 14, 2014.

[19] Bastien Lyonnet, Cornel Ioana, and Moeness G Amin. Human gait classification using microdoppler time-frequency signal representations. In *Radar Conference, 2010 IEEE*, pages 915–919. IEEE, 2010.

[20] Fadel Adib, Zach Kabelac, Dina Katabi, and Robert C Miller. 3d tracking via body radio reflections. In *Usenix NSDI*, volume 14, 2013.

[21] Bo Chen, Vivek Yenamandra, and Kannan Srinivasan. Tracking keystrokes using wireless signals. In *Proceedings of the 13th Annual International Conference on Mobile Systems, Applications, and Services*, pages 31–44. ACM, 2015.

[22] Donald G Childers, David P Skinner, and Robert C Kemerait. The cepstrum: A guide to processing. *Proceedings of the IEEE*, 65(10):1428–1443, 1977.

[23] Daniel Halperin, Wenjun Hu, Anmol Sheth, and David Wetherall. 802.11 with multiple antennas for dummies. *ACM SIGCOMM Computer Communication Review*, 40(1):19–25, 2010.

[24] Daniel Halperin, Wenjun Hu, Anmol Sheth, and David Wetherall. Tool release: gathering 802.11 n traces with channel state information. *ACM SIGCOMM Computer Communication Review*, 41(1):53–53, 2011.

[25] Meinard Müller. Dynamic time warping. *Information retrieval for music and motion*, pages 69–84, 2007.

[26] Jyh-Shing Roger Jang. Machine learning toolbox, available at http://mirlab.org/jang/matlab/toolbox/machinelearning, accessed on december 23, 2014.

[27] Neal Patwari and Sneha K Kasera. Robust location distinction using temporal link signatures. In *Proceedings of the 13th annual ACM international conference on Mobile computing and networking*, pages 111–122. ACM, 2007.

[28] Neal Patwari and Sneha K Kasera. Temporal link signature measurements for location distinction. *Mobile Computing, IEEE Transactions on*, 10(3):449–462, 2011.

Reusing 60GHz Radios for Mobile Radar Imaging

Yanzi Zhu, Yibo Zhu, Ben Y. Zhao and Haitao Zheng
Department of Computer Science, UC Santa Barbara, CA 93106, USA
{yanzi, yibo, ravenben, htzheng}@cs.ucsb.edu

ABSTRACT

The future of mobile computing involves autonomous drones, robots and vehicles. To accurately sense their surroundings in a variety of scenarios, these mobile computers require a robust environmental mapping system. One attractive approach is to reuse millimeter-wave communication hardware in these devices, *e.g.* 60GHz networking chipset, and capture signals reflected by the target surface. The devices can also move while collecting reflection signals, creating a large synthetic aperture radar (SAR) for high-precision RF imaging. Our experimental measurements, however, show that this approach provides poor precision in practice, as imaging results are highly sensitive to device positioning errors that translate into phase errors. We address this challenge by proposing a new 60GHz imaging algorithm, *RSS Series Analysis*, which images an object using only RSS measurements recorded along the device's trajectory. In addition to object location, our algorithm can discover a rich set of object surface properties at high precision, including object surface orientation, curvature, boundaries, and surface material. We tested our system on a variety of common household objects (between 5cm–30cm in width). Results show that it achieves high accuracy (cm level) in a variety of dimensions, and is highly robust against noises in device position and trajectory tracking. We believe that this is the first practical mobile imaging system (re)using 60GHz networking devices, and provides a basic primitive towards the construction of detailed environmental mapping systems.

Categories and Subject Descriptors

C.2.2 [**Computer Systems Organization**]: Computer-Communications Networks

Keywords

60GHz; RF imaging; environmental mapping; mobile radar

1. INTRODUCTION

Mobile computing is evolving. For decades, mobile computing centered around the user and her movements, whether it was on foot, or on vehicles such as buses or cars. However, the next generation of mobile computing and its challenges will likely be defined in the context of a variety of autonomous mobile agents, including drones, self-driving cars, or semi-autonomous robots. Today, autonomous drones are scanning large crop fields and farm livestock, unmanned helicopters are delivering supplies to soldiers in the field, while water-proof drones patrol the underground sewer system in Barcelona [3]. In the near future, flying drones will deliver our mail, packages and groceries, self-driving cars will drop us off at work, and first responder robots will be first on scene to rescue victims of disasters [31].

A key challenge for the widespread deployment of these autonomous devices is the environmental sensing system, *e.g.* a mobile imaging radar system that captures the position, shape and surface material of nearby objects. These systems must provide accurate and robust information about the device's surrounding at night or in dark areas (*e.g.* tunnels), while moving at moderate speeds. Highly accurate results are critical, and errors can produce dire consequences. For example, Google's self-driving cars use maps with inch-level precisions [35], while devices that assist the visually impaired must have errors smaller than 10cm [9, 22]. Finally, to be placed on a variety of autonomous devices, the imaging system should be compact, lightweight and cost-effective.

None of the existing solutions meet these needs. Traditional visible light imaging systems (*e.g.* cameras) perform poorly in dark or low-light conditions, and lack the precision desired by these applications. Acoustic solutions have been used successfully for ranging over short distances [39, 49], but are easily disrupted by background noise and fail over longer distances. Prior works on RF imaging use WiFi bands to track human motion and activity [7, 8, 15, 12], detect metal objects [12], and map large obstacles [36]. But they require costly specialized hardware or large antennas unsuitable for mobile devices. A recent project reuses WiFi communication devices with multiple antennas to image objects, but its precision is fundamentally limited by WiFi's large wavelength [25]. Finally, while today's millimeterwave imaging systems can offer accurate object imaging [6, 10, 34, 42], they all require specialized hardware, *e.g.* large lens radars and FMCW circuits, and do not fit the size or cost constraints of commodity mobile devices.

RF Imaging via 60GHz Networking Radios. One attractive approach is RF imaging radar that reuses commodity 60GHz networking radios to "image" the environment by capturing 60GHz transmissions reflected by nearby objects. Such a high frequency RF radar system has several key advantages over alternatives. *First*, 60GHz links are highly directional, making them relatively immune to interference from environmental factors such as ambient sound or wireless interference. *Second*, 60GHz beams exhibit good reflective properties, and work reliably in a wide range of lighting conditions in both indoor and outdoor locations. *Finally*, 60GHz ra-

MobiCom'15, September 7–11, 2015, Paris, France.
© 2015 ACM. ISBN 978-1-4503-3619-2/15/09 ...$15.00.
DOI: http://dx.doi.org/10.1145/2789168.2790112.

dios are relatively inexpensive ($<$ \$40 [45, 51]), and small enough to be included in today's smartphones and tablets.

The real challenge of building accurate mobile RF imaging is achieving high accuracy within a small device. A simple rule from imaging radar theory [13], defined by eq.(1), holds for antenna size (aperture) and the optimal accuracy (radar resolution):

$$Resolution = \frac{wavelength \cdot distance}{aperture}. \quad (1)$$

For smartphone-sized antennas, even the most high frequency radios (5-120GHz) can produce resolutions no better than 1 meter, clearly inadequate!

Our initial work in this space explored the possibility of using device mobility to emulate a *virtual antenna array* with large aperture [52]. This design uses the mobile device as a receiver, with a decoupled transmitter either embedded in the infrastructure or "deployed" on-demand by the user, (*e.g.*, mounted on a nearby drone). By taking measurements of the same reflected signal at multiple locations and applying the *Synthetic Array Radar (SAR)* algorithm [14], the system emulates the signals received by different elements of a large antenna array. Using 60GHz beams is especially advantageous here. Since 60GHz has a carrier wavelength of 5mm (12x shorter than WiFi/cellular), a user using 60GHz links can obtain fine-grain resolution with just small movements in the measurement area [52].

Practical Limitations of SAR. The goal of our work is to design, build, and deploy an accurate mobile imaging system for practical applications. Through experiments on an experimental testbed, we quickly identified *two* fundamental limitations with the SAR approach to imaging radar in real-world mobile settings. *First*, SAR is highly sensitive to receiver trajectory tracking noise. Any deviation from the path produces significant error in the predicted points on the reflection surface. This impact becomes particularly notable when the deviation is greater than λ, the RF wavelength. Whether the receiver is a handheld device, a robot, or a flying drone, its movement is likely to deviate from the targeted straight line trajectory, and deviations are likely much greater than λ for 60GHz links, which is 5mm. *Second*, high resolution imaging via SAR requires knowledge of the beam's phase information (ϕ). But any mm-level error in the receiver's position or trajectory introduces large errors in computing ϕ, and thus using phase information actually adds large errors into the SAR imaging result.

Ensuring accurate positioning and movement tracking to the level of millimeters is difficult using commodity hardware. Thus, accurate mobile 60GHz imaging requires a new imaging approach robust to device positioning and trajectory errors.

60GHz Imaging via RSS Series Analysis. Our observation is that the SAR algorithm is sensitive to positioning errors because each error propagates when computing positions on each object's surface. As a more robust alternative, we propose an approach that identifies the location, overall shape, size and material of the target object, by comparing the measured distribution of 60GHz received signal strength (RSS) values against RSS value distributions predicted from our general surface-reflection model. Since key surface properties (*e.g.* width and curvature) are strongly correlated with reflected RSS distributions, we can accurately determine the overall surface shape of the target object. We call this approach *RSS Series Analysis*, or RSA for short. Finally, our work leverages a unique advantage of 60GHz radios – as the receiver moves and (re)aligns its beam, it reports the (strongest) receive beam direction and the corresponding RSS value [2]. Such directional RSS measurements carry ample information of the reflection surface to enable high precision imaging.

RSA is robust against small device positioning and tracking errors because unlike SAR, it does not image an object by locating the individual points on the reflected surface. Instead, RSA focuses on how the collection of these points creates a distribution of RSS values at different observation locations. Such a distribution not only captures the overall shape of the target object, but also tolerates local deviations and errors in device positioning and tracking. Using testbed experiments, we find that an RSA-based 60GHz system can achieve accurate imaging results in the presence of positioning errors as large as 10cm.

In the remainder of this paper, we present our 60GHz-based mobile imaging system. We describe techniques for automatically estimating object location, orientation, surface curvature, surface boundaries, and even the surface material of nearby objects. We also present a detailed workflow of a practical implementation of our 60GHz imaging, including techniques for detecting the presence of objects and planning the receiver movement. Finally, we use detailed experimental measurements on a local 60GHz wireless testbed to validate the utility and accuracy of our techniques. Our testbed results on 12 common household objects (of 5cm-30cm in width) show that our proposed imaging system can image these objects at a high precision (*e.g.* ~5cm in object location and surface boundaries) with just small movement (~1m) by the receiver.

Limitations. Our work provides a first step in the development of high precision RF imaging (re)using 60GHz networking chipsets. Our current design has several limitations; some fundamental to the choice of 60GHz radios, while others can potentially be reduced via a better design.

First, to stay robust against device positioning/tracking errors, our RSA imaging does not use any phase information from the radio[1]. As a result, we are unable to recognize fine-grained details on an object, *e.g.* the individual keys on a computer keyboard. Instead we can identify the overall rectangular shape of the keyboard. Similarly we were unable to identify very small objects like keyrings. Improving imaging precision in the presence of device positioning errors is an area of open research. *Second*, the working range of our imaging system is determined by the underlying 60GHz radios and the object surface material[2]. While our solution does not need actual high speed transmissions, accurate RSS measurements require signals to be sufficiently stable. Using an off-the-shelf, low-cost mobile 60GHz chipset (from Wilocity), we found that the imaging range[3] is at least 10m for metal objects, and 5m for cardboard boxes (like those found in Amazon packaging). *Finally*, because 60GHz signals cannot penetrate walls or most objects, our imaging system works when both transmitter and receiver have line-of-sight to the target object. Thus to perform effective imaging, especially in 3D, mobile devices must have a way to intelligently navigate across complex spaces. This is another active research problem.

2. MOBILE 60GHZ RADAR

In this section, we set the context for mobile imaging using 60GHz transmissions. First, we begin by identifying key challenges facing mobile imaging systems, and explain why 60GHz radios provide an attractive solution. We then describe initial designs on 60GHz

[1]In some cases, not requiring phase can be an advantage of our system, since most COTS radios do not report phase but only RSS.

[2]Objects of different materials introduce different degree of signal loss. Metal objects in general introduce no loss while wood objects introduce 12dB loss in signal strength.

[3]Here the imaging range defines the distance between the object and the receiver, assuming the transmitter and receiver are of equal distance to the object.

imaging radar using synthetic array radar (SAR) algorithms, and the limitations they face in real deployment settings.

2.1 Mobile Imaging Radar and 60GHz

Mobile imaging radar systems face additional technical challenges compared to their traditional counterparts. Traditional imaging radars detect the position and shape of an object by emitting RF signals and analyzing the reflected signal [7, 8, 15, 12, 36, 6, 10, 34, 42]. They typically make use of specialized hardware such as FM circuits and highly directional, large dish antennas, and thus are not suitable for mobile devices. Instead, to be placed on a variety of autonomous devices from smartphones to drones, the imaging system should be severely constrained in size in both the processing hardware and the antenna, which severely limits the maximum imaging resolution (see Eq. 1). For smartphone-sized antennas ($2.5cm$ aperture), maximum imaging resolution for an object of $10m$ away is $1m$ using 120GHz transmissions or $24m$ at 5GHz. Furthermore, mobile radar systems target commodity devices, which rules out costly FM pulse circuits. Similarly, cost constraints prevent the use of fine accuracy positioning devices, or dispersion analysis for material detection (specialized transmitters).

Instead, mobile imaging radar can (re)use existing wireless networking chipsets on mobile devices, but leverage human or device mobility to greatly extend antenna aperture. This can provide resolution better than the limit defined by Eq. (1). Next, we describe key components of such a system.

Leveraging 60GHz Radios. Today's mobile devices are equipped with multiple wireless interfaces, *e.g.* cellular, WiFi, Bluetooth, and 60GHz radio[4]. Among them, 60GHz is ideal for mobile imaging for three reasons.

- Carrier wavelength of 60GHz is 5mm, over 12x shorter than WiFi/cellular. This translates into 12x smaller required antenna aperture than WiFi/cellular under the same imaging resolution.
- 60GHz's short wavelength leads to more predictable propagation, *i.e.* minimal multi-path effects and signal strength is strongly correlated to propagation distance. The system can easily detect the presence of objects by distinguishing between line-of-sight (LoS) and reflected signals.
- The object reflection profile is more stable at 60GHz. Since reflection loss is strongly correlated to object material [30], the radar system can determine the material type of the reflection surface using signal strength measurements.

Emulating virtual antenna arrays with mobility. A mobile device can emulate a large aperture virtual antenna array by moving and taking signal measurements at different positions along its trajectory[5]. This allows a small mobile device to produce high-resolution imaging results despite its small aperture antenna. For example, a device can take signal measurements along a 1 meter trajectory and achieve an (optimal) resolution at 60GHz of 15mm, from a distance of 3 meters away. Finally, user mobility also increases the system's ability to detect surface curvature of objects, as reflected signals at different locations help capture the curvature of each of the object's multiple faces.

Decoupling transmitter and receiver. Given the small size of mobile devices, the power of a radar system is limited. Under the limited power, decoupling the transmitter and receiver, a.k.a *bistatic radar system*, can significantly improve radar range over a single transceiver (monostatic) [40]. We consider a mobile radar system including the primary mobile device acting as a receiver and a decoupled transmitter. For example, a system to assist the visually impaired may include an app on the user's smartphone, and transmitters embedded in the walls or ceiling. The transmitter/receivers duties can also be split across multiple mobile devices, *e.g.* multiple drones scanning underground tunnels.

[4]Qualcomm is producing low-cost 60GHz chipsets at or below previous prices of \$37.5, with a range of $23m$ or more [45, 51]. HP recently released a laptop equipped with the Intel 60GHz chipset [1].

[5]Aperture of a virtual antenna array is equal to the distance traveled by the device.

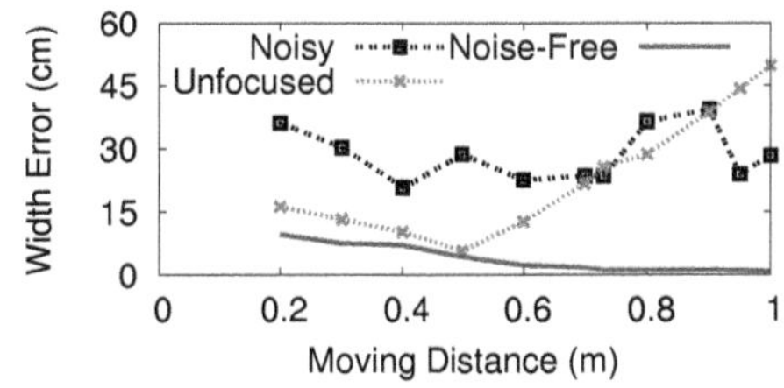

Figure 1: Experimental results demonstrate the limitations of SAR.

The transmitter (TX) sends 60GHz beacons that reflect off of nearby objects. Each beacon includes the angle of transmission, and if possible the transmitter's relative location to the receiver. Each RX moves and periodically scans and records signal strengths for beacons, and processes these data on the fly to identify, locate and image nearby objects.

2.2 A Synthetic Array Radar (SAR) System

Our earlier work proposed a 60GHz imaging system [52], where the receiver estimates object location and surface boundary using the Synthetic Array Radar (SAR) algorithm [14]. Applying SAR on measurements along a trajectory emulates the process where a large array focuses its narrow beam on different points of the object surface. Controlled testbed measurements achieve centimeter level accuracy in detecting object location and surface boundaries.

The SAR Algorithm. The imaging process is driven by the traditional SAR algorithm for bistatic radar [41]. TX transmits a simple sine wave, which is reflected by the object towards RX. RX measures the reflected signal at different locations as it moves. To understand SAR, consider a simple case where the object is a point. Let N represent the number of signal measurements taken by RX. The complex signal $r_i(t)$ measured at RX location i is $r_i = A_i e^{-j\phi_i}$ where A_i is the product of the transmit and receive antenna field radiation pattern and total propagation/reflection loss at i, and ϕ_i is the change in phase. Assuming signal reflection does not introduce any phase change, $\phi_i = \frac{2\pi}{\lambda} d_i$ where d_i is the total propagation distance. SAR computes the relative power $\mathcal{P}(p)$ at any point p in space using the RSS $|r_i|$ and phase shift ϕ_i at different locations: $\mathcal{P}(p) = \left|\sum_i r_i e^{j\frac{2\pi}{\lambda}\hat{d}_i}\right|$, where $\hat{d}_i$ is the distance from TX to each RX location i through the point p. If this point is a point on the object surface, *i.e.* $\hat{d}_i = d_i$, then the summation is constructive and $\mathcal{P}(p)$ is large. Otherwise because of destructive interference, the relative power becomes small. Thus SAR determines the object location and shape by searching for the strongest $\mathcal{P}(p)$ values across space.

2.3 Limitations of SAR

Existing design [52] makes two "idealistic" assumptions on device positioning: (1) TX and RX have perfect knowledge of their relative position; (2) RX moves in a perfect trajectory *e.g.* a straight line. However, in practice these two assumptions do not hold, and the imaging performance degrades significantly.

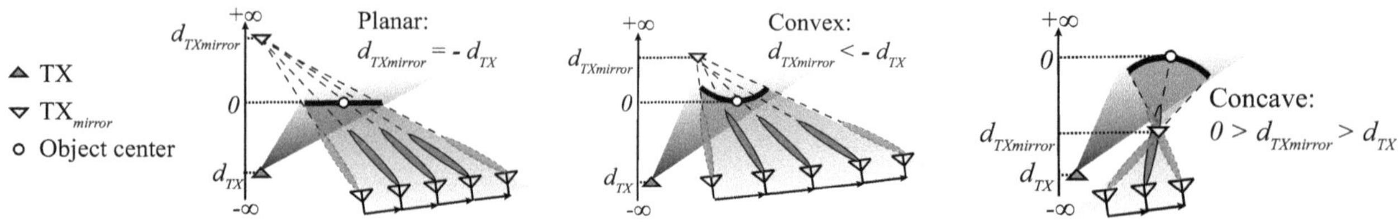

(a) Planar surface (b) Convex surface (c) Concave surface

Figure 2: An abstract view of the 60GHz signal reflection and RX's signal measurements as it moves.

Limitation 1: Sensitivity to trajectory noise. It is well-known that SAR is highly sensitive to trajectory noise – when moving, RX often deviates from the targeted path, and its trajectory cannot be tracked accurately. Such noise translates into errors in computing $\hat{d}_i$ and thus affects $\mathcal{P}(p)$. The impact becomes highly visible when the error is comparable to or larger than RF wavelength λ. For 60GHz, $\lambda = 5$mm. Thus even a few millimeter deviation in trajectory can largely affect the imaging result.

We perform experiments to examine this artifact. Figure 1 plots the imaging performance in terms of the error in derived surface boundary, for different object-to-RX distances. We compare two systems: "noise-free SAR" where the RX moves in a straight line and "noisy SAR" where we introduce random deviations (up to 5mm) to the actual RX trajectory. We see that in the presence of noise, the imaging error magnifies by at least 4 folds to 40cm! We also observe that errors in TX-RX positioning have similar effect (results omitted due to space limits). SAR cannot tolerate such small errors, let alone the 10cm error typically seen from the trajectory of mobile devices like drones.

To address this problem, one may consider using motion sensors to record the trajectory precisely. But commercial sensors cannot achieve millimeter-level accuracy. For example, accelerometer reports only the acceleration of device, and the translation information can only be obtained by integrating the result twice, resulting in poor performance [38]. GPS is known to have meter-level errors. Another approach by traditional SAR is to estimate the movement noise [27]. This can be effective for aircraft radars because the movement noise comes from air turbulence and can be approximated to the level of their operating wavelength (more than 10m). But for our targeted 60GHz mobile scenarios, the movement noise is much more random and harder to predict at the millimeter level.

Limitation 2: Dependency on phase information. To achieve high resolution, SAR requires the knowledge of the phase information ϕ_i. However, since the positioning/trajectory errors will corrupt the phase transition process, using the phase information actually introduces large errors in imaging. An alternative solution is to use "unfocused" SAR which assumes $\{\phi_i\}_{i=1}^{N}$ are all identical, *i.e.* $\phi_i = 0$, and only uses RSS to compute $\mathcal{P}(p)$ [52]. This reduces the impact of trajectory errors, but sacrifices imaging resolution: the longer the receiver trajectory, the more the "uniform phase approximation" error amplifies and degrades imaging accuracy. Figure 1 shows that unfocused SAR performs slightly better than noisy SAR but far worse than noise-free SAR. Note that while (noise-free) SAR always benefits from longer moving distance (larger antenna aperture), unfocused SAR is highly sensitive to this parameter. After the trajectory distance exceeds some threshold, compounded error from the "uniform phase approximation" overcomes the gain of larger apertures, and imaging performance deteriorates quickly. This threshold is object dependent and hard to identify *a priori*[6], making the performance of unfocused SAR unpredictable. Similarly, existing work reported that unfocused SAR can be 10 times worse than SAR [28].

[6]Our measurements show that the threshold scales linearly with the object width and RX-object distance, thus hard to identify *a priori*.

Summary. These results highlight the fact that SAR-based systems are highly sensitive to device positioning errors. Because of 60GHz's small wavelength (5mm), even small deviations in position translate into large distortions in phase transition results, and significant errors in imaging quality. Given these fundamental limitations, we must explore SAR alternatives to achieve the high accuracy demanded by next generation autonomous devices.

3. RSS SERIES ANALYSIS (RSA)

Our proposal to address these limitations is *RSS Series Analysis* (RSA), a new 60GHz imaging algorithm. Unlike SAR, RSA images an object using *only* RSS measurements recorded along the receiver's trajectory. We summarize RSA here and present the detailed algorithm in §4. RSA offers two advantages over prior work on RF imaging [25, 29, 52]:

- RSA can discover a rich set of object surface properties at high resolution (cm level). These include object surface location, orientation, curvature, boundary and material.
- RSA is highly robust against device positioning and trajectory tracking noise. Testbed results show that it can tolerate deviations as large as 10cm without degrading imaging quality.

3.1 Core Concept

RSA achieves high-precision imaging by combining receiver mobility with the high directionality of 60GHz beamforming. Specifically, RSA treats each object surface as a continuous medium that reflects a directional 60GHz signal towards the directional receiver RX. As RX moves and continually (re)aligns its beam to maximize received signal strength, the measured RSS value and its receive beam direction (angle of arrival (AoA)) carry information of the object surface. By analyzing these *directional* RSS measurements across multiple RX locations, RSA recovers important properties of the object surface, including position, curvature, boundary and material. At a high level, RSA works in 3 sequential steps.

1. Surface curvature & center position. Consider a scenario in Figure 2(a) where TX points towards and reflects its beam off a flat object surface. As it moves, the directional receiver RX maximizes RSS by pointing the receive beam towards the mirror point of TX respect to the object surface, *i.e.*, TX_{mirror}. This is a hypothetical point that would have originated the signals if there was no reflection, which can be computed as the intersection of AoAs, *i.e.*, the strongest RSS direction, for different points on the RX trajectory. While in practice the AoA reported by RX might deviate slightly due to non-ideal antenna patterns, imperfect reflection and measurement artifacts, one can still locate TX_{mirror} by intersecting the series of (noisy) AoAs collected as RX moves.

Now consider the scenario where the object surface is curved, either convex (Figure 2(b)) or concave (Figure 2(c)). We can still

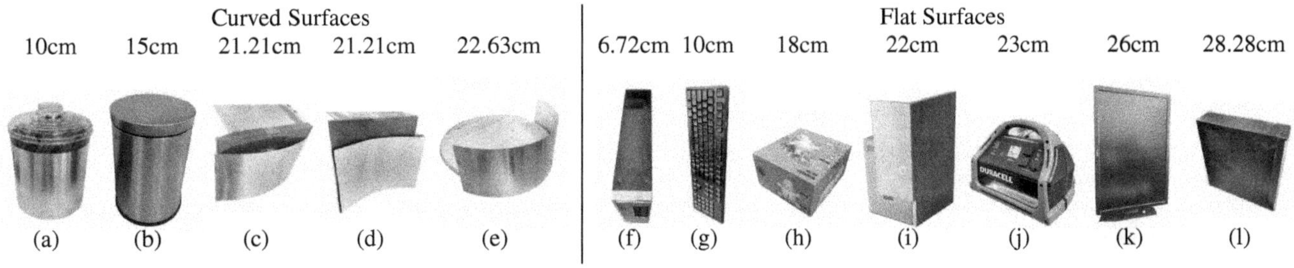

Figure 3: Objects used in our experiments. The number on top of each object is the width of the object. The left five objects (a)-(e) have curved surfaces and the right seven objects (f)-(l) have flat surfaces.

locate TX_{mirror} by intersecting the reported AoAs. Following the mirror and lens equation [24], a surface's curvature type is determined by its focal length f:

$$\frac{1}{f} = \frac{1}{d_{TX}} + \frac{1}{d_{TX_{mirror}}} \tag{2}$$

where d_{TX} and $d_{TX_{mirror}}$ are defined in Figure 2. Both values are under sign convention, *i.e.*, positive if behind the object, and negative when in front of the object. The surface is convex if $f > 0$, concave if $f < 0$, plane if $f \to \infty$, and $|f|$ is half of the curvature radius. Therefore, we can identify surface curvature by computing d_{TX} and $d_{TX_{mirror}}$. This requires information of the position and surface orientation of the object center, which can be estimated by intersecting the TX center beam direction with the reported AoAs.

2. Surface boundary. Once curvature is determined, RSA detects surface boundary by exploiting the unique effect of 60GHz directionality on signal reflection. When RX is within the area of "object coverage area" (Figure 2(a)), the corresponding RSS is strong because RX can align its beam to capture the (strong) reflected signals. But when RX moves outside of this area, the quality of its beam alignment (and RSS) degrades quickly. Thus shape of observed RSS values across different RX locations is strongly correlated to the object surface boundary. Using the estimated surface curvature, center location and orientation, we can model this correlation to enable reliable detection of surface boundary.

3. Material. When a signal hits a surface, parts of it may be "absorbed," leading to a *reflection loss*. At 60GHz, this reflection loss has a strong correlation of the surface material and the incident angle [30]. In particular, the RSS of a reflected signal is the RSS of a LoS signal (of the same propagation distance) minus the reflection loss (all in dB). Once we know surface location and curvature, we can derive the reflection loss and incident angle, and thus identify the likely surface material(s).

3.2 Quantifying Correlation via Measurements

Our intuition is that RSS measurements along a trajectory are highly correlated to a number of properties of a reflection surface. We use a commodity 60GHz radio testbed (details in §6) to better understand these correlations. We experimented with twelve objects (listed in Figure 3) of different width (5cm–30cm), curvature, material (wood, metal, plastic) and surface roughness (smooth vs. rough)[7]. We varied the TX and RX locations to examine the impact of object placement.

We experimented with four movement patterns involving a 1-meter straight line trajectory in space: a drone flying[8], a user moving a mobile phone over a line, an arc, and a perfect straight line. All four trajectories use the same start and end positions, and take the same amount of time to finish. RSS measurements are taken every 1cm, leading to a total of $N = 100$ measurements per trajectory. Each experiment collects $\{RSS_i, AoA_i\}_{i=1}^N$, where RSS_i is the strongest RSS value as RX rotates its beam at location i and AoA_i is the corresponding receive beam direction.

Our experiments led to two key observations.

1. Strong correlation with object surface properties. Our experiments confirm a strong correlation between RSS measurements and object surface properties. We show in Figure 4 that the RSS patterns, either as RSS values or AoAs, can be used to distinguish objects of different surface curvature, surface boundary (*i.e.* width), and material. The groundtruth of focal length in Figure 4(a) is 0.6m, 0.6m, and infinity, respectively.

2. Robustness against trajectory noise. The RSS series (both RSS and AoA) are highly robust against trajectory noise. Figure 5 illustrates different views of the four trajectories, and the RSS values along the trajectories when imaging an object of 6.7cm wide. While the trajectories deviate from each other by as far as 10cm, their spatial RSS patterns align well. We experimented with other movement patterns and objects, and arrived at similar conclusions. A closer look shows that RSS values correlate most strongly with propagation distance d. But in practice, d is at least multiple meters, and trajectory errors are in centimeters. Thus trajectory errors have little impact on RSS.

While these results may not be representative, they validate our intuition that much about properties of the reflection surface can be found in RSS measurements along the movement trajectory. Next we present techniques to extract these properties from RSS data.

4. RSA IMAGING ALGORITHM

Our RSA algorithm provides highly accurate imaging results on distance, curvature, boundary, and material detection, all while tolerating positioning and trajectory errors. It takes three inputs: a sequence of RSS measurements in RSS and Angle of Arrival tuples $\{RSS_i, AoA_i\}_{i=1}^N$, RX's trajectory (*i.e.* RX location i) and its relative position to TX, and TX's transmit beam direction and pattern. We will discuss in §5 the procedure to obtain these inputs and the sensing process for TX to focus its beam on the object.

Imaging an object takes four processing steps on the RSS data. We estimate location and orientation of the object center, then compute surface curvature, and boundaries, and finally identify a set of potential surface materials. We first describe these key components

[7] A surface is considered smooth if $h < \frac{\lambda}{8cos\theta}$ and rough if $h > \frac{\lambda}{8cos\theta}$ [48]. Here h is the min to max surface protuberance, $\lambda = 5mm$ and θ is the incident angle. For our objects, the plastic keyboard is "rough" and a monitor surface is "smooth."

[8] Using a high-end IRIS+ drone by 3D Robotics Inc., we captured its movement trajectory when configured to fly straight.

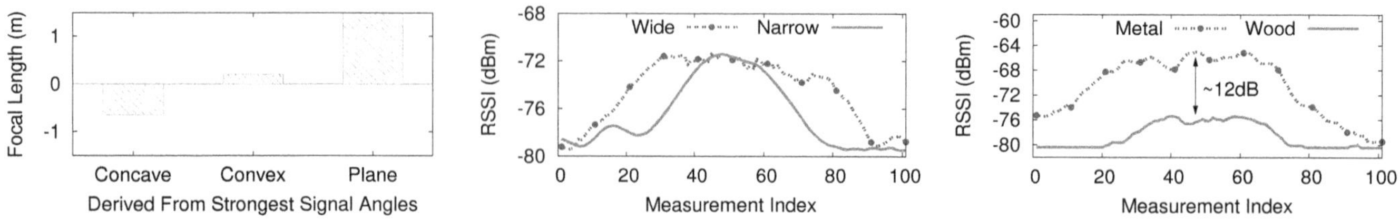

(a) Plane vs Convex (b) Narrow vs Wide (c) Metal vs Wood

Figure 4: The observed RSS seires are strongly correlated with the object surface properties.

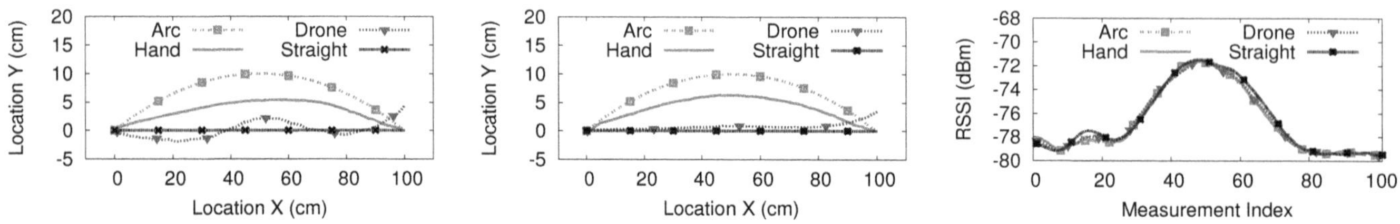

(a) Noisy trajectory (top view) (b) Noisy trajectory (front view) (c) Stable RSS pattern for 6.7cm wide object

Figure 5: The measured RSS series remains stable across all four (noisy) 3D trajectories.

to image a single surface, and then the process to image multiple surfaces/objects. Finally, we describe how RSA mitigates noise from device localization, interference and RSS measurements.

4.1 Estimating Object Center & Orientation

RSA starts by computing an initial estimate of the location and surface orientation of the object center, since it is input for subsequent steps. The intuition is simple: when TX's beam covers the object evenly and TX/RX are perfectly aligned, we can locate the object surface center at the intersection of the TX beam direction and each AoA. While the TX/RX alignment is imperfect (since TX fixes its beam), the intersection with each AoA_i is still a good approximation of the reflection surface.

Like [52], RSA estimates the object center by performing a "majority vote" on the set of intersection points. Given K ($K < N$) intersection points, RX identifies a cluster of $\lfloor \frac{K}{2} \rfloor + 1$ points with the minimum mean square error (MSE) among themselves. It approximates the object center as the center of the cluster, *i.e.* the position with minimum MSE to all other points in the cluster. To generate the K intersections, RSA picks a subset of AoAs from $\{AoA_i\}_i^N$ whose RSS_i is among the strongest (and above the noise level) and intersects them with the center direction of TX beam.

Since the incident and reflected angles are equal, we can compute the (candidate) direction of the object surface's principal axis with respect to each of the K AoAs. We derive the object center's orientation by computing the principal axis using majority vote over K candidates, then computing its perpendicular direction.

A key difference from [52] is that RSA iterates to improve its estimate of object center and orientation, using as input the curvature and boundary results from later steps. This helps to mitigate the impact of TX/RX positioning errors and other artifacts (§4.6).

4.2 Characterizing Surface Curvature

After object position comes surface curvature. We characterize an object's surface curvature based on the mirror and lens equation defined by eq. (2). We first compute the "TX mirror point" and then compute the focal length f from d_{TX} and $d_{TX_{mirror}}$. We compute it as the intersection of angle of arrivals for different points on the RX trajectory (Figure 2). To mitigate noise/artifacts in AoA measurements, RSA first smoothens the AoAs using a moving window, *e.g.*, of size 3 in our current design, then performs a majority vote on pair-wise AoA intersections to derive the mirror point.

Given the estimate of object center point and orientation, we calculate d_{TX} and $d_{TX_{mirror}}$ by projecting the TX and the TX mirror point to the principal axis (see Figure 2). If we set the object center as position 0, d_{TX} is negative and $d_{TX_{mirror}}$ is positive. RX then computes f based on eq. (2). The surface is convex if $f > 0$, and concave if $f < 0$, and $2f$ is the curvature radius. In theory, a flat/planar surface should have $f = \infty$. Yet in practical scenarios, $f >$1 meter is sufficient to identify most objects with a flat surface.

4.3 Computing Surface Boundary

The next step is to compute the surface boundary, *i.e.*, the width of the surface if the object was projected to the plane of RX's movement trajectory. We exploit the strong correlation between the RSS sequence $\{RSS_i\}_{i=1}^N$ and the object surface, and propose a simple RSS model for surface reflection. After adding surface curvature and center location as parameters, this model generates a direct one-to-one mapping between a specific surface boundary and the sequence of RSS values captured by RX. Thus we can estimate the surface boundary by searching for a surface profile whose model-predicted RSS sequence matches those observed by RX.

A RSS model for surface reflection. We develop a new surface reflection model, which takes into account the reflection property of a "fixed-size" reflection surface. Consider the TX transmission towards the object as a collection of sharp rays, each reaching a point p on the object is reflected towards RX. Here we consider a general scattering reflection scenario where the point p uniformly scatters signals in space according to the Lambertian reflection model [26, 53]. We also consider a far-field scenario where the propagation distance is much larger than wavelength (*i.e.*, > 100 times larger). In our case, the wavelength of 60GHz is $5mm$, and the overall propagation distance in our system should be at least $0.5m$. Using the complex baseband representation under far-field approximation, the 60GHz received signal at RX location i is

$$r_i(t) = \int_{\mathbb{P}} \underbrace{\frac{\lambda\sqrt{G_p(i)}e^{-j\frac{2\pi}{\lambda}d_p(i)}}{4\pi d_p(i)}}_{\text{overall propagation}} \underbrace{\Gamma_p(i)e^{-j\phi_p(i)}}_{\text{reflection}} u(t)dp \quad (3)$$

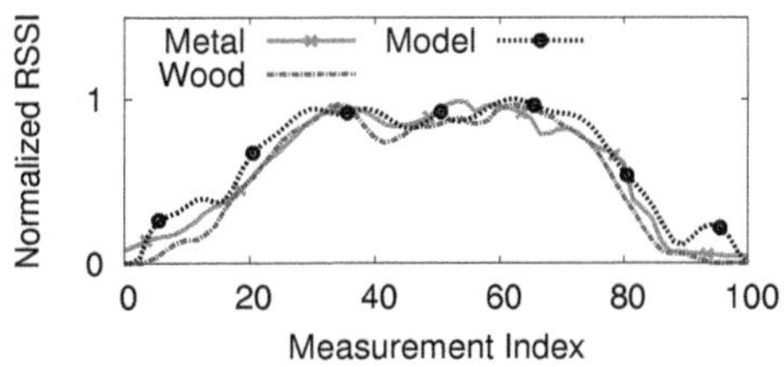

Figure 6: Comparing measured and predicted RSS patterns.

where for the pth reflected path arriving at location i, $G_p(i)$ is the product of the corresponding transmit and receive antenna field radiation pattern, $d_p(i)$ is the total propagation length, $\Gamma_p(i)$ is the amplitude reflection coefficient, $\phi_p(i)$ is the corresponding change in phase, $u(t)$ is the complex baseband transmitted signal, and $\mathbb{P}$ represents the object surface in 3D space. The key to this model is the constraint of the fixed size reflection surface, captured by the integral over $\mathbb{P}$.

Because our design targets the overall shape of the object, we simplify Eq.(3) by assuming the surface is relatively smooth, *i.e.* ignoring the fine-grained details. Therefore we consider a uniform reflection pattern: *i.e.*, $\Gamma_p(i) = \Gamma, \phi_p(i) = \phi, \forall p \in \mathbb{P}, i = 1..N$. Then we can pull out the $\Gamma_p(i)$ term, and derive RSS as:

$$RSS_i = P_t \cdot \Gamma^2 \left| \int_{\mathbb{P}} R_p(i) dp \right|^2 \tag{4}$$

where $R_p(i) = \frac{\lambda \sqrt{G_p(i)} e^{-j\frac{2\pi}{\lambda} d_p(i)}}{4\pi d_p(i)}$. Given the object curvature and center location, and locations of TX and RX(i), we can calculate $R_p(i)$. Given the object surface boundary or width, we can construct $\mathbb{P}$ and then derive RSS_i[9]. To remove the contribution of Γ which is unknown, we can normalize RSS_i across i.

We verified this model using testbed experiments on objects in Figure 3. Example results in Figure 6 show that normalization effectively separates the contribution of materials from that of the surface boundary, *i.e.* two objects of the same width but different materials have the same normalized RSS series. The measured RSS series closely matches the series predicted by our model.

Fitting Measurements to Model. We determine the surface boundary by matching the observed RSS values to a range of RSS series produced by the model. In this process, we consider a range of possible surface width values. For each candidate width w, we construct the physical surface $\mathbb{P}$, use the model to predict the (normalized) RSS series, and compare it with our (normalized) measured RSS series. To compute "similarity" between two series (or curves), we experimented with multiple metrics, including MSE, MSE of the derivatives, and MSE of the dynamic time warping algorithm [37]. Among these, MSE of the derivatives is the best:

$$\eta = 1 / \sum_{i=1}^{N} \left(\Delta_i^{model} - \Delta_i^{real} \right)^2 \tag{5}$$

where Δ_i^{real} and Δ_i^{model} are the derivatives of the normalized RSS at i using the measured values and the modeled values, respectively. This metric works well because computing surface width means detecting the two edges, which lead to fast RSS degradation at the corresponding RX locations. The RSS derivatives effectively capture such RSS variation. We leave the task of finding the optimal metric to future work.

[9]For efficiency, we approximate $\mathbb{P}$ as a collection of points whose interspacing $\leq$ 5mm.

Minimizing Search Space. We can significantly reduce the search space for the surface boundary size, by looking at only widths that can exist within the triangle formed by the start and end points of the RX trajectory, and the TX mirror point (see Figure 2(a)). RX can detect if the width w is large enough for the triangle to bound the reflection surface (steep dropoff in RSS before and after the surface boundaries). For very large surfaces, RX might need to extend its trajectory to detect the surface boundary. Assuming the surface is bounded by the triangle, we can estimate the maximum value of w using geometry. We then search for the true value of w starting from the max down to $1cm$ in the unit of $0.1cm$. These settings are sufficient for the target imaging precision. Going for a higher granularity adds extra computation complexity but little improvement of imaging quality. Currently our search takes less than $3s$ for all our twelve test objects using a matlab implementation on a standard MacbookPro. As future work, we can further prune the search space using sophisticated methods such as cutting planes.

Measuring Curved Surfaces. For curved surfaces, the reflected RSS series display a different pattern: a convex surface will *scatter* signals to a wider area while a concave will *gather* signals towards a smaller area (Figure 2). Thus using the above method, we will likely image a narrow, convex object as a wide object.

To address this, we apply a slightly different algorithm. Upon determining that the object surface is non flat, RSA computes the surface boundary using $\{R\hat{SS}(\theta)_i\}_{i=1}^N$, *i.e.* the RSS measured at a *fixed* receive beam direction θ across all positions along the RX trajectory. Here $\theta = AoA_j$, $j = \text{argmax}_{i=1..N} RSS_i$, *i.e.* the AoA of the strongest RSS across all the RX locations. Intuitively, this direction θ is parallel to the surface's principal axis, thus $R\hat{SS}(\theta)_i$ includes less contribution of surface scattering (or gathering) but more impact of surface boundary. This way, we can apply the same surface reflection model by using the curvature detection result to construct $\mathbb{P}$. In §6, we show that this method is accurate and also robust against errors in the estimated curvature radius.

4.4 Identifying Potential Surface Materials

Finally, we seek to estimate the surface material based on the reflection loss Γ^2. Existing measurement studies on 60GHz propagation and reflection have built a table of Γ^2 values as a function of the surface material and the angle of incident [30]. We can estimate the angle of incidence given the estimated surface orientation and curvature. From Eq. (4), $\Gamma^2 = RSS_i^{real} / \left(P_t \left(\frac{\lambda}{4\pi}\right)^2 \left|\int_{\mathbb{P}} R_p(i) dp\right|^2 \right)$. With Γ^2 and the angle of incidence, we can *narrow down* the material type using the reflection loss table. For example, we can distinguish metal objects (0.3dB loss) from wood (12dB loss) or plastic objects (8dB loss).

To obtain a reliable estimate of Γ^2 for flat surfaces, we select a group of the strongest RSS measurement locations, and calculate the Γ^2 as above for each location. We then compute Γ^2 as their average. This helps to mitigate noise contributed by reflection artifacts near object boundaries.

Estimating Γ^2 for curved surfaces is more challenging because as signals scatter or gather, the above calculation becomes less reliable. Our current solution is to introduce a compensation factor that approximates the impact of signal scattering or gathering. Specifically, we input the already derived object curvature and width into the RSS model, use it to generate the RSS series (ignoring Γ^2), and record the maximum RSS value, γ_{curve}. We then input the width into the RSS model but treat the surface as flat, generate the RSS series and record the max, γ_{flat}. The final reflection loss estimate is $\Gamma^2 \cdot \gamma_{flat}/\gamma_{curve}$ where $\gamma_{flat}/\gamma_{curve}$ reflects the impact of signal scattering/gathering.

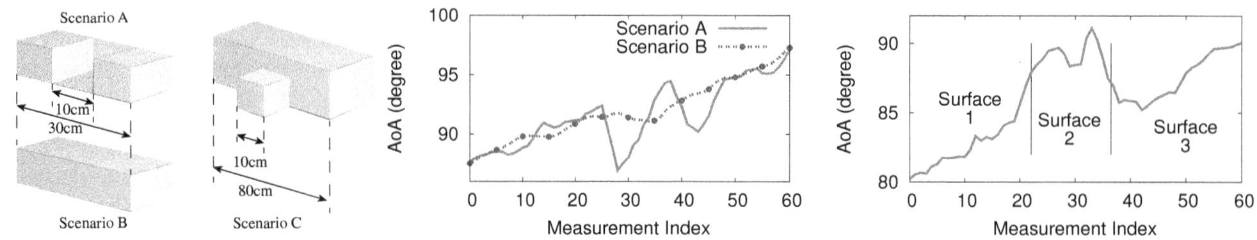

(a) Three Surface Scenarios (b) AoA Patterns for Scenario A and B (c) AoA Patterns for Scenario C

Figure 7: Detecting and imaging multiple objects. (a) The three scenarios considered: two surfaces separated by a gap, a single continuous surface, and one small surface in front of a big one. (b) The AoA pattern changes abruptly when two surfaces are separated. (c) The AoA pattern displays three segments when a small surface is in front of a big one.

4.5 Imaging Multiple Surfaces/Objects

So far our discussion targets scenarios with a single object surface. We now discuss the feasibility of RSA for detecting and imaging multiple objects/surfaces. We consider two representative scenarios: (1) two nearby objects separated by some space; and (2) a smaller object in front of a larger one (see Figure 7(a)).

Intuitively, a key difference between single and multiple surface reflection should be the reflection angle, *i.e.*, the AoAs. Using testbed measurements, we verified that for the above two multi-surface scenarios the AoA pattern is significantly different from a single surface of the same width. For example, Figure 7(b) plots the reported AoAs as a function of the measurement location (1-60) over a 60cm RX trajectory. For an even surface of 30cm in width, the AoA pattern grows smoothly as the RX moves. But when this object is replaced by two 10cm objects separated by 10cm (same overall width), the AoA pattern changes abruptly (by $3-5°$). Similarly, Figure 7(c) plots the AoA pattern when one 10cm-wide object is placed in front of a 80cm-wide one. It is segmented into three regions, corresponding to the uncovered portions of the larger object surface on each side and the small object in the middle.

These significant changes in AoA patterns suggest that multiple objects can be detected using AoA derivatives along the trajectory. For all object scenarios we tested[10], a threshold of $3°$ can reliably detect and extract multiple objects. We can then apply the single-object based RSA to each segment to image individual surfaces of moderate sizes. The key limitation here is that our imaging system lacks the precision to image small objects and fine-grained surface details, *e.g.* individual keys on a computer keyboard. Instead, it should detect and image an Amazon package on the floor.

Above results also suggest that RSA can handle interference due to reflection from other objects. We treat the 80cm-width surface in scenario C as the background object, where our system can still identify and image the 10cm-wide object (surface 2) in the middle.

4.6 Handling Noise & Interference

We design RSA to stay robust to three types of noise or errors: *positioning error* for locating TX and RX, *trajectory noise* when RX's trajectory deviates from the ideal line, and *RSS measurement noise* caused by RF interference or background reflection.

TX/RX positioning errors. Errors in TX/RX positions can propagate to errors in locating object center point and TX mirror point. We address this by exploiting the fact that the measured RSS series is stable and strongly correlated with the object surface. After one round of imaging, RSA introduces *controlled perturbations* to explore possible small shifts in center location and surface boundary values that lead to a better match between the model predicted RSS profile and measured RSS data. Specifically, it shifts the TX/RX locations by up to $10cm$ and repeats the imaging process. This iterative search stops when the similarity metric (defined by eq. (5)) exceeds some threshold, or the boundary results of two consecutive iterations differ by 1cm or less, *e.g.* convergence.

RX trajectory errors. The basic imaging algorithm assumes precise data on RX's trajectory. In practice, the movement itself is noisy – a high-end drone configured to fly a straight line can deviate by 4cm. Motion-tracking (via accelerometers or other sensors) can easily generate 10cm errors in less than a second [4, 38].

Trajectory errors can translate into errors in locating the object center and TX mirror point, and errors in RSS model. For the former, RSA denoises by applying "majority vote" across multiple RX AoA measurements (§4). For the latter, we found the impact on imaging quality to be minimal, and both RSS model and measurements are insensitive to trajectory errors $< 10cm$. In our scenarios, we configure RX to move in a line and rely on external trajectory control to keep the trajectory error less than $10cm$. In practice, any errors that do propagate will add to noise in estimates of object center and TX mirror point. These will be addressed together with any resulting noise from TX/RX positioning errors (see above).

Interference. Background reflection from other objects can be handled via the multi-surface detection and imaging process described in §4.5. The bigger challenge comes from possible corruption of RSS measurement values by RF interference from other 60GHz transmissions, *e.g.*, strong signals from a LoS transmitter to RX will distort the AoA values.

If angular separation between the interfering signal and reflected TX signals is sufficiently large, RSA can eliminate interference using 60GHz directionality. As RX scans across directions, it detects and decodes signals from different sources and only uses those from TX to construct the RSS series. In rare cases where the signals are closely aligned, the interference will likely affect data transmission between TX and RX during imaging, *e.g.* high RSS but recurring packet errors. When this is detected, TX and RX can switch to another 60GHz channel or change physical location.

5. IMPLEMENTATION

We now present the detailed workflow of a practical implementation of RSA imaging. First, TX and RX determine each other's position. They scan for any objects, and once found, TX focuses its beam on the object and computes the RX movement direction and distance. RX moves, collects RSS measurements and images the object. The process does not require tight synchronization between TX and RX, only that TX signals remain consistent during imaging,

[10] In our scenarios, when two objects are separated, the gap $\geq$ 10cm. The ability to detect 10cm gaps between objects is sufficient for most mobile applications like drones.

e.g., a simple sine wave, so that RSS is stable over time. In particular, for 802.11ad [2], our sine wave based design can directly use single carrier (SC) to send consistent 0s or 1s and generate a regular sine wave, or use one of the OFDM subcarriers for imaging.

TX/RX positioning. To determine each other's location, TX and RX can exchange their locations (if known), or apply existing mobile localization/ranging techniques based on RF or acoustic signals [11, 29, 39, 49]. We can also apply 60GHz localization in addition to improve localization accuracy to centimeter-level (if TX and RX have line of sight).

60GHz localization leverages the 802.11ad bootstrapping procedure and includes two steps. First, TX (in directional mode) steers its beam in different directions and embeds its beam direction in the signal. RX (in omni-directional mode) receives signals over time and identifies the strongest signal strength r and TX beam direction α. If a LoS path exists between them, then RX can compute its distance to TX d from r (using the 60GHz Friis propagation model [19]). To detect whether LoS exists, TX compares α and r with those estimated by the external localization technique. If the discrepancy is large, especially if d is larger, the path is reflected. Otherwise, LoS exists and TX locates RX via α and d. Next, TX transmits in α direction. RX enters directional mode and scans for the strongest signal. RX can locate TX using the strongest receive direction at RX and d.

Object Sensing & RX Movement Planning. TX and RX use the above two steps of 60GHz localization to sense nearby objects and compute the appropriate RX trajectory. There are two modifications from the sequence above. In step one, instead of reporting only the strongest RSS, RX reports a list of TX beam directions where the RSS exceeds the noise level. After pruning the list by removing the LoS directions, the remaining represent reflected signals. From these directions, RX identifies a set of TX beam directions $\{\alpha^k\}_{k=1}^{T}$ that TX should focus on based on their beam radiation patterns and steering granularity. If an object is too wide to be covered by a single TX beam, RSA can image the object by having TX steering sequentially in multiple segments and stitching the image results, or by TX modifying its antenna radiation pattern to form a wider beam (if possible).

In the second step, TX slowly steers its beam in each of these directions while RX measures AoA for each α^k direction. Ideally, for each α^k, RX should move perpendicularly to the corresponding AoA to detect object width. Furthermore, RSA uses the intersection of α^k and AoA to approximate the object location and thus the total propagation distance d_p. The projected RX movement distance is then the width of the TX beam pattern at distance d_p, which is sufficient to discover the object surface shape. Together the recommended path and distance allow RX to create a virtual antenna array large enough to discover the object's surface while minimizing the travel distance.

Object Imaging. TX focuses its transmission on each specific direction (while embedding the beam direction in its signal). As RX moves, it collects RSS measurements using the 802.11ad *antenna alignment* procedure. Collecting the (RSS, AoA) tuple across multiple directions (§4.3 and §4.6) does not require extra measurements, and is done by modifying 802.11ad to report additional data. Since for phased array, full-scope beam steering takes less than 1ms[11], RX can perform real-time measurements as it moves, even when TX rotates its beam across multiple directions to image multiple objects. Finally, RX analyzes the data to image the object(s).

[11]Phased array beam steering delay is as low as 50ns [47]. Scanning 360° in the steps of 1° takes 18μs.

Latency. We expect the imaging delay is dominated by those of RX movement and RSA data analysis. For latter, our current implementation finishes in less than 3s and can easily be further optimized, *e.g.*, using convex optimization during iterative search (§4.6).

6. EVALUATION

We evaluate RSA in practical settings using off-the-shelf 60GHz radios. We study its utility and imaging quality in the presence of device localization and trajectory errors and background reflections. We also examine its error tolerance, and its sensitivity to different system/hardware configurations. Finally, we compare RSA with SAR and unfocused SAR, and perform a multi-object case study by emulating drones locating a target object using RSA.

6.1 Testbed and Experimental Setup

We consider two types of 60GHz beamforming radios. The first uses a pair of Dell D5000 dock (as transmitter) and 6430u laptop (as receiver), both equipped with a low-cost Wilocity 60GHz chipset designed for indoor mobile communications. The chipset uses a 2×8 rectangular antenna array, and operates under the IEEE 802.11ad standard [2]. Unfortunately, the chipset does not expose RSS values and the corresponding beam directions. Thus we use it only for understanding the range of our 60GHz imaging design when implemented on 802.11ad networking radios (§6.2).

The second and our main imaging testbed uses two HXI Gigalink 6451 60GHz radios, designed for outdoor communications. Since there are no suitable 60GHz steerable antenna arrays on the market, we emulate beam steering by setting a horn antenna (of 10° 3dB beamwidth) on an electronic controlled mechanical rotator. The horn antenna's main lobe pattern closely align with that of a 10×10 array with 1dBi elements and 21dBi gain, and the rotator physically adjusts the beam direction in units of 0.15°. The HXI radios use the On-Off-Keying modulation to generate sine waves in random on-off periods and reports RSS every 50ms. We note that under the same environment, the RSS of the HXI link is actually 17dB[12] weaker than that of the Wilocity chipset. This is because our HXI radio transmits at 0dBm and the cable that connects the horn antenna to the radio introduces 23dB loss (in order to enable mechanical antenna rotation).

The results of HXI radios with horn antennas should generalize to phased arrays, because our emulation matches phased arrays in three key aspects. *First*, 60GHz signal strength is largely determined by directionality and signal patterns of the main beam lobe (the side lobe is 13.26 dB weaker), and our horn antenna's main lobe pattern closely aligns with that of a 10x10 array [51]. *Second*, because 60GHz propagation is stable over time (verified by others [23, 50] and our own measurements), at each location RX can accurately measure RSS along different directions despite its slow beam steering speed. *Third*, the fine granularity of our rotator allows us to emulate beam steering of phased arrays, *e.g.* in units of $1-3°$ required by the 802.11ad standard [5].

Experiment Setup. Our experiments take place in a classroom of size 8m×12m with concrete walls. We place an object in the middle of the room with LoS to both TX and RX. We move both TX and RX to study imaging range and angle. By default, TX is 2m away from the object and RX is 3.5m away. We tried other distances with little impact on results as long as the total propagation path (from TX to object and then to RX) does not exceed the radio range. By default, the testbed steers beam at a 1° granularity.

[12]The HXI radios have 0dBm transmit power, 25dBi antenna gain per radio and 23dB cable loss due to the use of rotator. To compare with, the Wilocity chipset has 10dBm transmit power and 17dBi antenna gain per radio.

We consider two types of RX movement: human waving smartphone and drone flying. The mechanical beamsteering means we cannot perform imaging in real time. Instead, we record five trajectories per type (by marking on paper) from actual movement of human users and our Iris drone, and use them to drive RSS measurements on our mechanical beamsteered radio. We align the trajectories so that the start and end points are 1 meter apart. Whether it's a user waving the device or a flying drone path, the maximum trajectory errors against a straight line are roughly $10cm$. To follow a specific moving trajectory, we mark the trajectory on the floor and pinpoint the receiver to each trajectory point using a plumb-bob.

We implemented the 60GHz localization mechanism (discussed in §5) for TX and RX. Across multiple scenarios, the measured TX/RX localization error is consistently between 2 and 6cm. We broaden our tests by adding random 2-6cm TX/RX position errors to our data analysis. In total, we have 60 noise instances per object/scenario to obtain statistically significant results.

Test Objects. Like existing works on radar imaging [25, 36, 21, 20], we evaluate the utility and accuracy of our proposed design by imaging real objects of different size, curvature, and material. In addition to the objects listed in Figure 3 which are of 5cm-30cm in width, we also test smaller objects including a keyring and a small wrench (2.5cm in width). From these we seek to identify objects that our system can accurately image and those that it cannot.

6.2 Imaging Range & Angle

We first use the Wilocity radios to verify the working range of our 60GHz imaging system when implemented using today's 802.11ad mobile devices. For a pair of TX and RX, we block the LoS path between them, forcing the link to search and use NLoS paths, *i.e.* the reflection path. Using objects of different materials as the reflector, we measure the maximum propagation path length (TX to object to RX) such as TX can successfully transmit a 100MB file to RX. The path length is 20m for strong reflection material like metal, and 10m for weak reflection material like cardboard boxes (used for Amazon packaging). Assuming that TX and RX are of the same distance to the object, the corresponding imaging range (from object to RX) are 10m and 5m, respectively. We note that in our measurements the RSS is sufficient to support high speed communication (385Mbps) at these distances. When it comes to imaging, the RSS requirement can be much lower as long as the resulting RSS measurement is accurate. This means that the actual imaging range can be much longer.

As discussed earlier, due to extra cabling loss, our HXI link is 17dB weaker despite its stronger antenna gain. As a result, the imaging range is less than half of the Wilocity link, and we have to move the devices closer than we expect. Again this is due to artifacts of our testbed configuration.

Impact of Imaging Angle. Like [25], we found that the imaging quality depends on the imaging angle, defined by the relative location of TX to the object and the trajectory of RX. Specifically, to identify the object, TX's beam should cover the object and the reflected signal should reach RX along its trajectory. Our system addresses this issue by performing object sensing and RX movement planning before running actual imaging (as discussed in §5). This also helps to reduce the amount of movement required to detect the overall object shape. For example, we have tested our algorithm by varying the object orientation relative to TX, *i.e.* the angle of incident, between 30° and 45°, and found that it always provides an ideal RX movement trajectory, and the subsequent imaging results remain consistent across these experiments. We also found that RX's actual movement can deviate from the ideal trajectory by at least 7° without noticeable impact on imaging quality.

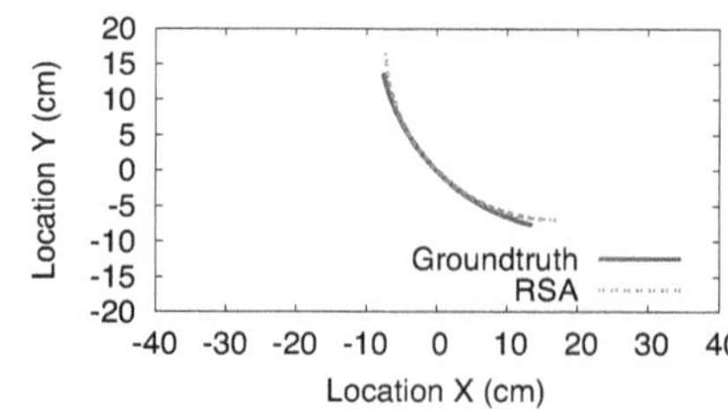

Figure 8: Result of imaging a curved surface.

6.3 Imaging Precision

Position/Curvature/Width. Table 1 lists RSA's overall imaging results in terms of errors in object center position and orientation, detected curvature type, shape deviation[13], and errors in surface boundary (width) estimation. We list the median and max values across all experiments while varying TX/RX position errors (60 instances) and RX trajectories (10 instances, 5 user-waving, 5 drones). The results for human waving and drone flying are consistent, so we did not isolate them.

We see that in the presence of position/trajectory noises, RSA achieves centimeter-level accuracy across all the objects, flat or curved. In terms of center locations, the max error is below 4cm for metal flat surfaces, and slightly larger (6-9cm) for curved surfaces and other materials (due to weaker reflection). Note that the depth of the object can be calculated based on the estimated object center position and the location of RX, which we found has a max error of $6cm$. The orientation error is always $< 1°$. RSA detects the curvature type accurately, and characterizes the shape of the surface within $0.68cm$ deviation for flat surfaces and $< 6cm$ for curved surfaces. The maximum error in surface width estimation is bounded $4.5cm$. Figure 8 plots the imaging result of a curved surface which captures the overall curved shape while being a slightly wider than the actual object.

Material. Using existing measurements on 60GHz reflection [18, 30], we built a reflection database of 39 materials. We added the profile of cardboxes using our own measurements. Using RSA estimated reflection loss and incident angle, we identify from the database the top three material candidates. Table 2 lists the result for four flat objects of different types (metal, plastic, wood and cardboard) and two curved objects, where RSA can successfully narrow down the material type.

Observed Limitations. We also make the following key observations from our experiments. *First*, RSA reuses COTS 60GHz radios to image objects in the presence of device movement and tracking noises. To be robust to such noises (which existing designs like SAR fail to address), RSA has to sacrifice some degree of imaging precision without using the phase information[14]. As a result, our design seeks to identify the overall shape of an object surface (location, orientation, surface boundaries, material), rather than fine-grained details such as individual keys on a computer keyboard. *Second*, our design is unable to accurately image small objects. It can detect and locate a wrench handle (of 2.5cm width), but the detected width varies between 1cm to 5cm. It cannot locate a keyring because the reflection is too weak to be captured by our HXI radios. To recognize these small objects, one could

[13]Shape deviation is defined by the maximum difference between the actual object surface and the imaged object surface projected onto the object surface's principal axis.

[14]In practice, not requiring phase information can be an advantage, since most COTS radios do not report phase but only RSS values.

Ground truth				Detected Position			Detected Shape				
				Center location error		Orientation	Detected	Shape deviation		Width error	
Objects in Figure 3	Shape	Radius	Width	Median	Max	error (Max)	curvature	Median	Max	Median	Max
(a) Aluminum Jar	Convex	$+10.0$	10.00	4.55	8.11	$0.29°$	Convex	1.59	2.22	1.00	2.33
(b) Steel cylinder	Convex	$+15.0$	15.00	4.43	4.98	$0.51°$	Convex	1.46	1.78	1.03	1.88
(c) Curved steel surface	Convex	$+29.0$	21.21	7.26	9.47	$0.69°$	Convex	1.47	1.93	2.67	4.22
(d) Curved steel surface	Concave	-29.0	21.21	6.64	7.65	$0.90°$	Concave	-1.64	-1.59	1.21	1.79
(e) Curved steel surface	Convex	$+23.0$	22.63	5.51	7.37	$1.05°$	Convex	4.46	6.35	0.91	3.59
(f) Metal desktop front	Flat	$+\infty$	06.72	2.82	3.64	$0.49°$	Flat	0.13	0.62	0.82	1.02
(g) Plastic keyboard	Flat	$+\infty$	10.00	4.44	7.31	$0.81°$	Flat	0.16	0.36	2.69	4.16
(h) Cardboard box	Flat	$+\infty$	18.00	4.31	5.13	$0.72°$	Flat	0.15	0.28	2.41	3.00
(i) Wood board	Flat	$+\infty$	22.00	3.83	8.73	$0.44°$	Flat	0.43	0.68	3.09	4.17
(j) Plastic battery case	Flat	$+\infty$	23.00	2.06	3.17	$0.47°$	Flat	0.28	0.48	1.70	3.51
(k) Plastic monitor	Flat	$+\infty$	26.00	4.07	6.29	$0.45°$	Flat	0.10	0.11	0.64	1.06
(l) Metal desktop side	Flat	$+\infty$	28.28	2.69	2.95	$0.58°$	Flat	0.12	0.12	1.78	3.16

Table 1: RSA imaging performance in terms of error in object center position and orientation, detected curvature type, deviation of overall shape, and error in object width (surface boundary). All the numbers are in the unit of *centimeter* except for the orientation error and curvature type.

Object (Material)	Estimated Reflection Loss	Top 3 Matches (out of 39)
Desktop (Metal)	0.3dB	**Metal**, Quartzite, Glass
Box (Cardboard)	6.1dB	**Cardboard**, Pertinax, Acrylic glass
Monitor (Plastic)	7.9dB	Chipboard, Fiberboard, **Plastic**
Board (Wood)	12.7dB	**Wood**, Brick, Breeze block
Cylinder (Metal)	0.3dB	**Metal**, Quartzite, Glass

Table 2: Results of RSA material detection.

use a stronger radio, or move TX and RX much closer to the object, *e.g.* <0.5m which becomes a near-field scenario and requires a new imaging design. *Third*, the accuracy of width estimation depends heavily on the RX movement distance. The amount of RX movement distance required to maintain high precision increases linearly with the sensing range and object size. We found that for our HXI testbed and all the test objects, 1 meter RX movement is sufficient. Our RX movement planning also predicts the same trajectory length (see §5).

6.4 Robustness to Noise

While Table 1 lists the imaging result when the TX/RX positioning error is bounded by $6cm$, we expand our noise model to explore RSA's noise tolerance. We found that RSA's performance is insensitive to trajectory errors when the deviation is bounded by $10cm$. Thus we focus on the TX/RX position errors. Specifically, we pick X as the maximum location error (deviation from the ground truth), draw a circle of radius X around the ground truth and randomly pick a point on the circle as TX's relative location to RX. We repeat this 20 times per X and report the maximum imaging errors. Using object (g) as an example, Figure 9 plots the maximum error in center location and width estimation for X between 0 and 20cm. We see that both errors grow gracefully with X, indicating that RSA is robust against TX/RX positioning errors. We observe this same trend for all objects.

6.5 RSA vs. SAR and unfocused SAR

We also compare RSA with SAR and unfocused SAR (as described by existing work [52]). Since both SAR algorithms do not offer curvature and material information, we only evaluate object center location error and width error. Specifically, for each scenario defined by TX/RX positioning error, RX trajectory, and the object, we compute the amount of error reduction achieved by RSA, *e.g.* $\frac{\text{width error (SAR)}}{\text{width error (RSA)}}$ or $\frac{\text{center location error (SAR)}}{\text{center location error (RSA)}}$. We report the min, median, and max values across the eleven objects, 10 trajectories and 20 instances of position errors for a given range X. Because unfocused SAR is highly sensitive to the choice of RX movement distance, we use 0.5 meter for unfocused SAR (which provides the best overall performance across all the objects), and 1 meter for RSA and SAR.

Figure 10 lists the error reduction factor of RSA. For center point estimation, SAR and unfocused SAR have very similar performance [52], so we only report one. We see that RSA can effectively reduce the imaging error. This is particularly true for width estimation – the median reduction factor is 2-6.7 (over unfocused SAR) and 2.9-8.2 (over SAR); while the maximum value can reach 18 and 38 respectively. Also, width error reduction peaks at zero TX/RX position error, confirming RSA is highly robust against trajectory errors. Finally, RSA reduces errors in center point estimation by a factor of 1.2-2.32 (median). This is mostly due to the iterative search process (§4.6).

6.6 Microbenchmarks

RX Movement Distance. Figure 11 compares the object width error at different RX movement distances. We see that RSA follows the same trend as noise-free SAR: imaging error reduces with moving distance and gradually converges to a stable value. This aligns with the theoretical limit in Eq. (1) where increasing aperture (via RX movement) leads to higher imaging precision. Unfocused SAR, however, is highly sensitive to this parameter.

RSS Measurement Frequency. This factor translates into the choice of N, the number of measurements for a given movement distance. In practice, we want to minimize measurement frequency to save energy. Yet insufficient number of measurements reduces the accuracy of our model fitting. Our results in the above perform one measurement per 1cm. At a slow movement speed of 0.5m/s (1.1mph), the measurement frequency is once per 20ms. We found that the results remain the same even at a lower frequency of once per 80ms (*i.e.* once per 4cm).

Beam Steering Granularity. Using an electronically controlled mechanical rotator, our testbed can steer antenna beam in increments of $0.15°$. While our experiments above use data from $1°$ steering, we also perform imaging under $0.15°$, $3°$ and $5°$ steering to examine the impact of antenna hardware (steerable phased arrays). To separate its impact on localization, we use the same TX/RX localization result of $1°$ across all the experiments. Our results show that $1° - 3°$ steering is an efficient choice – increasing granularity to $0.15°$ reduces width error by $< 0.5cm$ while relaxing to $5°$ doubles the width error.

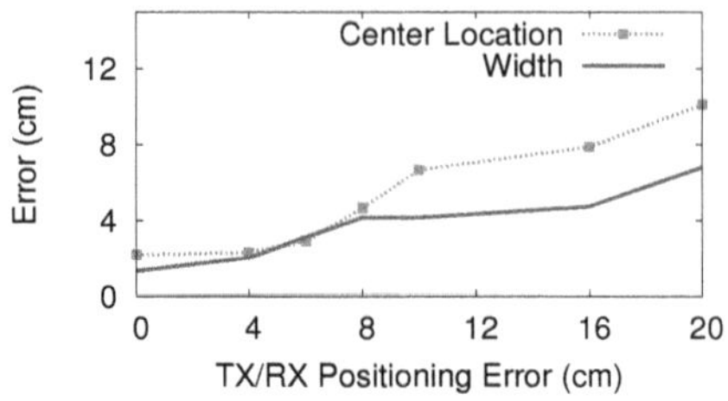

Figure 9: RSA's imaging errors scale gracefully with TX/RX position errors. RX trajectory noises are present for all the experiments.

TX/RX Positioning Error (cm)	center location error (SAR) / center location error (RSA)			width error (unfocused SAR) / width error (RSA)			width error (SAR) / width error (RSA)		
	Median	Min	Max	Median	Min	Max	Median	Min	Max
0	1.20	1.00	2.07	6.71	3.88	17.95	6.92	3.16	19.09
4	1.72	1.24	2.77	4.44	2.59	11.44	8.20	4.59	38.33
8	1.72	1.44	2.63	3.23	1.27	6.67	5.06	3.34	10.39
16	1.85	1.62	3.83	2.32	1.11	5.29	2.90	1.84	6.89
20	2.32	1.47	2.78	2.18	1.01	3.82	3.05	1.44	6.09

Figure 10: Comparing RSA to SAR and unfocused SAR in terms of the ratio of error under SAR (or unfocused SAR) and error under RAS. The RX trajectory errors are present in all the experiments. Since the performance of unfocused SAR is sensitive to RX moving distance, we configure it as 0.5 meter while SAR and RAS use 1 meter.

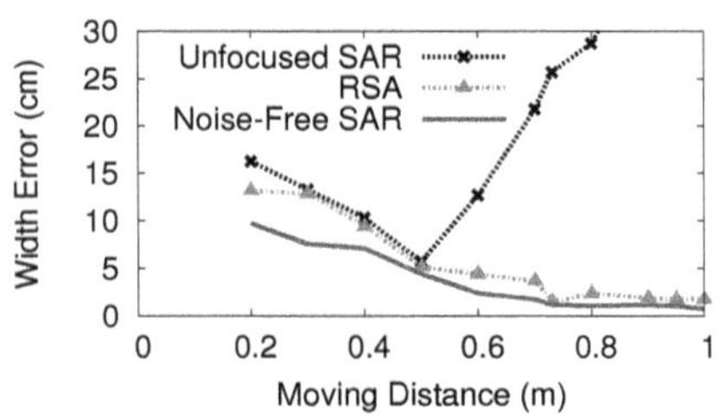

Figure 11: Impact of measurement configurations on RSA imaging performance, in terms of width error.

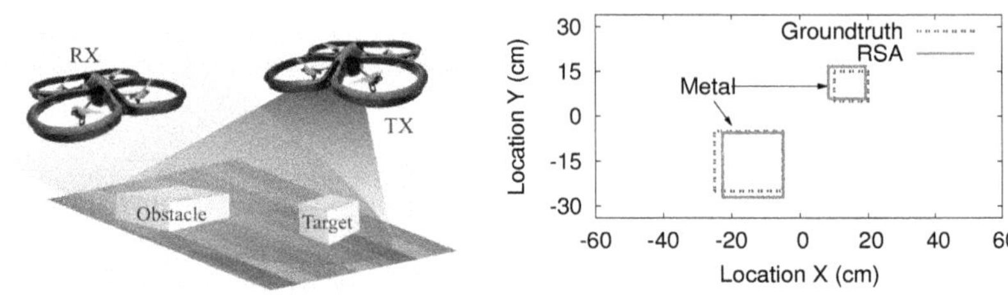

(a) Scenario setup

(b) Imaging result (top view)

Figure 12: "Realistic" case study of RSA imaging: a drone seeks to locate the small metal object while avoiding a nearby obstacle.

6.7 Case Study: Multiple Objects Detection

Consider a scenario in Figure 12(a), where a drone uses RSA imaging to locate an object, *i.e.* a square metal box of size 8cm×8cm. The target rests on a wood floor with a nearby larger (metal) object (size 18cm×18cm) as the obstacle. To locate (and pick up) the object, a drone needs to recognize both objects, with the help of another drone as TX.

With two testbed radios emulating drones, they first perform 60GHz localization to locate each other. They then coordinate to sense the objects. Since the two objects are in proximity they can be covered by a single TX beam. After TX focuses its beam on the two objects (and sends beacon signals), RX moves in two directions sequentially to determine location, curvature, width and height, and material. The visual imaging result and the ground truth are shown in Figure 12(b) where RSA recognizes two flat metal objects, their overall shape/size, and the wood floor in between.

7. RELATED WORK

Camera-based Imaging. Camera is widely used for object recognition [16, 32, 33]. Detecting object position and shape, however, requires bulky, high-end cameras (*e.g.* Google's Project Tango requires an infrared depth camera and a fish-eye lens). These mechanisms require good visibility and cannot reliably identify object material. RSA takes a low-cost RF-based approach leveraging mobile networking chipsets, and its 60GHz reflected signals reveal key properties of the object surface without any light.

Sonar and Radar Systems. These systems have been applied to many fields [43], from mapping terrain contour, tracking moving targets, to detecting concealed weapons at security checkpoints [17, 6, 10, 34, 42, 46]. They use special hardware like X-Ray or bulky lenses to achieve high precision, which are too large/expensive for mobile devices. RSA differs by using commodity 60GHz networking chipsets that are being integrated into today's mobile devices.

RF-based Systems. Researchers have explored WiFi-band solutions to detect human motion, activity and gestures, and to detect (metal) objects [8, 7, 15, 36, 29, 40, 12]. A recent work built WiFi imaging using OFDM and large phased arrays (available on APs) and discussed the resolution limitation due to its large wavelength [25]. Our work considers 60GHz (mmwave) communications because it offers several desirable qualities for mobile imaging when compared with WiFi: tiny wavelength, high directionality, stable and predictable signal propagation. In addition to providing high-resolution (∼1-5cm), our imaging algorithm is also different by using just RSS measurements (rather than phase [25]) without requiring specialized hardware (*e.g.* [8, 7]). Our work was inspired by recent 60GHz radar designs [52, 44] that apply SAR to detect object surface location and boundary in absence of noise. Our work develops a new imaging solution that is robust against noise and also detects surface curvature and materials.

8. LIMITATIONS AND FUTURE WORK

Our proposed 60GHz mobile radar detects the location, orientation, curvature and surface boundaries of nearby objects using only signal strength measurements, and achieves cm-level precision.

Several limitations remain before we can realize a high precision, environmental mapping system using RF reflections. *First*, our imaging works when both TX and RX have line-of-sight to the target object because 60GHz signals cannot penetrate walls or most objects. To perform environmental mapping in 3D, TX and RX (*e.g.*, mobile devices) must have a way to intelligently navigate across space while coordinating their positions. *Second*, so far we only consider the general shape of static and regular object surfaces where reflected RSS is stable over time and predictable via a model. For moving or irregular objects, *e.g.*, humans, and detailed shape, *e.g.*, keys on keyboard, we need new models to define the correlation between object shape and reflected signal patterns. *Finally*, we need to develop an algorithm for TX and RX to reliably and iteratively scan individual surfaces while moving in unknown environments. Such schemes must be robust and work reliably in large environments with complex objects (*e.g.* caves, collapsed tunnels).

ACKNOWLEDGEMENT

We thank our anonymous shepherd and reviewers for their constructive feedback. This work is supported in part by NSF grants IIS-1321083, CNS-1224100, and CNS-1317153.

9. REFERENCES

[1] HP Elite x2 1011 G1 Datasheet. http://www8.hp.com/us/en/ads/elite-products/elitex2-1011.html.

[2] IEEE 802.11 Task Group AD. http://www.ieee802.org/11/Reports/tgad_update.htm.

[3] Meet the drones patrolling Barcelona's sewers. http://www.cnet.com/news/meet-the-drones-patrolling-the-pipes-of-barcelonas-sewers/.

[4] Sensor fusion on android devices: A revolution in motion processing. http://davidcrowley.me/?p=370.

[5] Draft standard - part 11: Wireless lan medium access control (mac) and physical layer (phy) specifications - amendment 4: Enhancements for very high throughput in the 60ghz band. IEEE P802.11adTM/D9.0, July 2012.

[6] ADAMS, C., HOLBROOK, D., AND SENGSTEN, R. A handheld active millimeter wave camera. In *Technologies for Homeland Security (HST), 2010 IEEE International Conference on* (2010).

[7] ADIB, F., KABELAC, Z., KATABI, D., AND MILLER, R. C. 3d tracking via body radio reflections. In *Proc. of NSDI* (2014).

[8] ADIB, F., AND KATABI, D. See through walls with wi-fi! In *Proc. of SIGCOMM* (2013).

[9] AL-SALIHI, N. Precise positioning in real-time for visually impaired people using navigation satellites. *International Journal of Engineering and Technology 12*, 2 (2010), 83–89.

[10] APPLEBY, R., AND ANDERTON, R. Millimeter-wave and submillimeter-wave imaging for security and surveillance. *Proceedings of the IEEE* (2007), 1683–1690.

[11] BAHL, P., AND PADMANABHAN, V. N. Radar: An in-building rf-based user location and tracking system. In *Proc. of INFOCOM* (2000).

[12] BHARADIA, D., JOSHI, K. R., AND KATTI, S. Full duplex backscatter. In *Proc. of HotNets* (2013).

[13] CHAN, Y. K., AND KOO, V. C. An introduction to synthetic aperture radar (sar). *Progress in Electromagnetics Research B* (2008), 27–60.

[14] CHENEY, M., AND BORDEN, B. *Fundamentals of Radar Imaging*, vol. 79. SIAM, 2009.

[15] CHETTY, K., SMITH, G. E., AND WOODBRIDGE, K. Through-the-wall sensing of personnel using passive bistatic wifi radar at standoff distances. *Trans. on Geoscience and Remote Sensing 50*, 4 (2012), 1218–1226.

[16] DAVISON, A. J., REID, I. D., MOLTON, N. D., AND STASSE, O. Monoslam: Real-time single camera slam. *Trans. on Pattern Analysis and Machine Intelligence* (2007).

[17] FEDERICI, J. F., GARY, D., BARAT, R., AND ZIMDARS, D. Thz standoff detection and imaging of explosives and weapons. In *Proc. of Defense and Security* (2005).

[18] FRICKE, A., REY, S., ACHIR, M., LE BARS, P., KLEINE-OSTMANN, T., AND KURNER, T. Reflection and transmission properties of plastic materials at thz frequencies. In *Proc. of IRMMW-THz* (2013).

[19] FRIIS, H. T. A note on a simple transmission formula. *In Proc. of IRE 34*, 5 (1946), 254–256.

[20] GRAJAL, J., BADOLATO, A., RUBIO-CIDRE, G., UBEDA-MEDINA, L., MENCIA-OLIVA, B., GARCIA-PINO, A., GONZALEZ-VALDES, B., AND RUBINOS, O. 3-d high-resolution imaging radar at 300 ghz with enhanced fov. *Microwave Theory and Techniques, IEEE Transactions on 63*, 3 (March 2015).

[21] GU, F., ZHANG, Q., LOU, H., LI, Z., AND LUO, Y. Two-dimensional sparse synthetic aperture radar imaging method with stepped-frequency waveform. *Journal of Applied Remote Sensing 9*, 1 (2015).

[22] GUERRERO, L. A., VASQUEZ, F., AND OCHOA, S. F. An indoor navigation system for the visually impaired. In *Proc. of Sensors* (2012).

[23] HALPERIN, D., KANDULA, S., PADHYE, J., BAHL, P., AND WETHERALL, D. Augmenting data center networks with multi-gigabit wireless links. In *Proc. of SIGCOMM* (2011).

[24] HECHT, E. *Optics*. Addison-Wesley, 2002.

[25] HUANG, D., NANDAKUMAR, R., AND GOLLAKOTA, S. Feasibility and limits of wi-fi imaging. In *Proc. of SenSys* (2014).

[26] JUDS, S. *Photoelectric Sensors and Controls: Selection and Application, First Edition*. Taylor & Francis, 1988.

[27] KOO, V. C., LIM, T. S., AND CHUAH, H. T. A comparison of autofocus algorithms for sar imagery. In *Proc. of PIERS* (2005).

[28] KULPA, K., PURCHLA-MALANOWSKA, M., AND MALANOWSKI, M. P. Improvement of resolution in real-time unfocused sar algorithm. In *Proc. of EuSAR* (2004).

[29] KUMAR, S., GIL, S., KATABI, D., AND RUS, D. Accurate indoor localization with zero start-up cost. In *Proc. of MobiCom* (2014).

[30] LANGEN, B., LOBER, G., AND HERZIG, W. Reflection and transmission behavior of building materials at 60ghz. In *Proc. of PIMRC* (1994).

[31] LINE, M. Robot rescue: First-responders of the future. FoxNews.com, June 2014.

[32] LOWE, D. G. Object recognition from local scale-invariant features. In *Proc. of ICCV* (1999).

[33] LOWE, D. G. Distinctive image features from scale-invariant keypoints. *International journal of computer vision 60*, 2 (2004).

[34] MACKENZIE, J., AND BROWN-KENYON, E. Wide-bandwidth mobile radar for isar/sar radar imaging. In *IEE Colloquium on Radar and Microwave Imaging* (1994).

[35] MADRIGAL, A. C. The trick that makes google's self-driving cars work. The Atlantic, May 2014.

[36] MOSTOFI, Y. Cooperative wireless-based obstacle/object mapping and see-through capabilities in robotic networks. *IEEE TMC 12*, 5 (2013), 817–829.

[37] MÜLLER, M. *Information Retrieval for Music and Motion*. Springer Berlin Heidelberg, 2007.

[38] NIESSNER, M., DAI, A., AND FISHER, M. Combining inertial navigation and icp for real-time 3d surface reconstruction. In *Proc. of Eurographics* (2014).

[39] PENG, C., SHEN, G., ZHANG, Y., LI, Y., AND TAN, K. Beepbeep: a high accuracy acoustic ranging system using cots mobile devices. In *Proc. of SenSys* (2007).

[40] PU, Q., GUPTA, S., GOLLAKOTA, S., AND PATEL, S. Whole-home gesture recognition using wireless signals. In *Proc. of MobiCom* (2013).

[41] QIU, X., DING, C., AND HU, D. *Bistatic SAR Data Processing Algorithms*. Wiley, 2013.

[42] SATO, M., AND MIZUNO, K. *Millimeter-wave imaging sensor*. InTech, 2010.

[43] SCHEER, J. A., AND MELVIN, W. L. *Principles of modern radar*. The Institution of Engineering and Technology, 2013.

[44] SEO, M., ANANTHASUBRAMANIAM, B., MADHOW, U., AND RODWELL, M. J. Millimeterwave (60 ghz) imaging wireless sensor network: Recent progress. In *Proc. of ACSSC* (2007).

[45] SHANKLAND, S. Wilocity: 2015 phones getting extra-fast 802.11ad networking. CNet, February 2014.

[46] TSENG, T.-F., WUN, J.-M., CHEN, W., PENG, S.-W., SHI, J.-W., AND SUN, C.-K. High-resolution 3-dimensional radar imaging based on a few-cycle w-band photonic millimeter-wave pulse generator. In *Proc. of OFC* (2013).

[47] VALDES-GARCIA, ET AL. Single-element and phased-array transceiver chipsets for 60-GHz Gb/s communications. *IEEE Communications Magazine 49*, 4 (April 2011), 120 –131.

[48] ZHANG, H., VENKATESWARAN, S., AND MADHOW, U. Channel modeling and mimo capacity for outdoor millimeter wave links. In *Proc. of WCNC* (2010).

[49] ZHANG, Z., CHU, D., CHEN, X., AND MOSCIBRODA, T. Swordfight: Enabling a new class of phone-to-phone action games on commodity phones. In *Proc. of MobiSys* (2012).

[50] ZHOU, X., ZHANG, Z., ZHU, Y., LI, Y., KUMAR, S., VAHDAT, A., ZHAO, B. Y., AND ZHENG, H. Mirror mirror on the ceiling: Flexible wireless links for data centers. In *Proc. of SIGCOMM* (2012).

[51] ZHU, Y., ZHANG, Z., MARZI, Z., NELSON, C., MADHOW, U., ZHAO, B. Y., AND ZHENG, H. Demystifying 60GHz outdoor picocells. In *Proc. of MobiCom* (2014).

[52] ZHU, Y., ZHU, Y., ZHANG, Z., ZHAO, B. Y., AND ZHENG, H. 60GHz mobile imaging radar. In *Proc. of HotMobile* (2015).

[53] ZHURBENKO, V. *Electromagnetic Waves*. InTech, 2011.

mTrack: High-Precision Passive Tracking Using Millimeter Wave Radios

Teng Wei and Xinyu Zhang
Department of Electrical and Computer Engineering
University of Wisconsin - Madison
twei7@wisc.edu, xyzhang@ece.wisc.edu

ABSTRACT

Radio-based passive-object sensing can enable a new form of pervasive user-computer interface. Prior work has employed various wireless signal features to sense objects under a set of predefined, coarse motion patterns. But an operational UI, like a trackpad, often needs to identify fine-grained, arbitrary motion. This paper explores the feasibility of tracking a passive writing object (*e.g.*, pen) at sub-centimeter precision. We approach this goal through a practical design, *mTrack*, which uses highly-directional 60 GHz millimeter-wave radios as key enabling technology. mTrack runs a discrete beam scanning mechanism to pinpoint the object's initial location, and tracks its trajectory using a signal-phase based model. In addition, mTrack incorporates novel mechanisms to suppress interference from background reflections, taking advantage of the short wavelength of 60 GHz signals. We prototype mTrack and evaluate its performance on a 60 GHz reconfigurable radio platform. Experimental results demonstrate that mTrack can locate/track a pen with 90-percentile error below 8 *mm*, enabling new applications such as wireless transcription and virtual trackpad.

Categories and Subject Descriptors

C.3 [**Special-Purpose and Application-Based Systems**]: *Signal processing systems*; H.5.2 [**Information Interfaces and Presentation**]: User Interfaces—*Input devices and strategies*

Keywords

60 GHz; Millimeter-wave; Tracking; Phase Shift; Background Cancellation

1. INTRODUCTION

Radio-based passive object sensing is a rapidly developing technology that detects the motion of human body parts or associated objects through wireless signals. Compared with conventional vision-based approaches [1], e.g., LeapMotion [2] and Kinect [3], it is less intrusive and unaffected by ambient light conditions or the sunlight interference. Catalyzed by the proliferation of mobile devices, this technology holds potential to enable new ubiquitous user-mobile interfaces and spur a wide range of applications. The lastest passive sensing technology can already accurately distinguish a prescribed set of body/limb movement [4] based on Doppler patterns or signal strength variation. Hand gesture sensing [5] is also achievable by training a pattern-matching model. To satisfy a broader range of applications, however, two design challenges remain open: fine resolution and unsupervised motion tracking.

We envision one such application scenario: tracking a writing object (*e.g.*, a stylus pen or marker) wirelessly. Conceptually, empowered by multiple wireless devices, we can create an interactive trackpad on any conventional surface, *e.g.*, whiteboard or desktop. This way, we can deploy large touch screens in a more flexible and ecomonic way than traditional graphic tablets. This vision entails tracking a small writing object with at least sub-centimeter precision. Such precision has proven feasible in certain active RF sensing systems like Tagoram [6]. However, they are applicable only to objects instrumented with an RFID tag or radio receiver.

In this paper, we design mTrack, which leverages 60 GHz millimeter wave (mmWave) radios to track the trajectory of a writing object at high precision. 60 GHz radios are standardized in IEEE 802.11ad [7], and anticipated to penetrate one third of wireless links by 2018 [8]. Commercial 802.11ad-capable smartphones have already been demonstrated [9]. Adopting mmWave instead of conventional microwave band (2.4 GHz or 5 GHz) brings multifold advantages. A shorter wavelength can create stronger reflections from small objects (*e.g.*, a pen), since wireless signals cannot easily bypass objects larger than wavelength. More importantly, mmWave devices like 802.11ad allow for miniaturized phase-array with dozens of antenna elements, which together create highly-directional "pencil-beams". Such directional beams are electronically steerable, thereby creating a new dimension for object localization/tracking.

mTrack's design harnesses these unique advantages of mmWave. It uses one transmitter (Tx) to emit 60 GHz signals and illuminate a handhold object that roams on a trackpad area. Part of the signals are diffused by the object's surface and captured by two directional receivers (Rx). mTrack leverages the received signal strength (RSS) and phase (relative to Tx) to localize and track the object. Simply put, by measuring the arriving direction of reflected signals, each Rx can estimate the object's relative angle, and pinpoint its initial *location* on the trackpad. We refer to this as *anchor point acquisition* (APA). When the object moves, the reflected signals' path length varies, which alters the phase, providing salient hints for *tracking* the object with sub-wavelength resolution. Our feasibility study using a 60 GHz software-radio (Section 3) verifies these principles, and unveils the unique advantage of mmWave passive tracking over its microwave counterpart, in terms of potential precision, sensitivity to target size, *etc.* Yet in practical environ-

MobiCom'15, September 7–11, 2015, Paris, France.

ACM 978-1-4503-3619-2/15/09 ...$15.00.
http://dx.doi.org/10.1145/2789168.2790113.

Properties	Tagoram [6]	RF-IDraw [10]	Tomography [11, 12]	WiVi [13]	WiTrack [14]	mTrack
Object Type	Active	Active	Passive	Passive	Passive	Passive
Signal Feature	Phase	Phase	RSS	Phase	RSS	Phase/RSS
Methodology	Hologram	Interferometry	FP/AoA	ISAR	FMCW radar	PS/BS
Track static object	Yes	Yes	Yes	No	No	Yes
# of Tx&Rx	≥ 2	8	$10 \sim 100$	≥ 4	4	≥ 3
Tracking Range	$1 \sim 10m$	$2 \sim 5m$	$3m \sim 20m$	$2 \sim 7m$	$3 \sim 9m$	$1m$
Granularity	$14mm$	$49mm$	$80cm \sim 3m$	$1m$	$30cm$	$8mm$

Table 1: Comparison of different RF-based tracking systems. FP, PS and BS stand for fingerprint, phase shift and beam-steering. Data are from reported figures of cited works.

ment, these principles entail unique challenges, which we propose to solve in mTrack.

First, reflected signals from irrelevant background objects can severely distort the target-reflected signal and affect phase-tracking accuracy. Prior passive tracking techniques use ultra-wideband [14], or measure and subtract static background reflection directly [15]. In contrast, mTrack's mmWave uses single-carrier phase-tracking, and needs to handle background dynamics. To meet this challenge, we develop two algorithms: *dual-differential background removal*, and *phase counting and regeneration*, to recover the legitimate phase change induced by target movement only. These two techniques take unique advantage of short wavelength of mmWave signals, and stay at different vantage points when considering a tradeoff between tracking precision and resilience to the inherent phase noise in 60 GHz radios.

Second, although 60 GHz signals are commonly simplified as pseudo-optical [16], our measurement shows that they can be widely diffused after hitting a small object. Thus, one cannot migrate the specular reflection effect in laser/infrared tracking systems [17] for 60 GHz tracking. In mTrack, we observe that 60 GHz antenna response bears a roll-off response pattern, and reflected RSS is strongest when the object direction matches the peak response. mTrack's APA mechanism thus leverages steerable 60 GHz Rx antenna to find the matching point, and identify the object's relative angle. Since practical 60 GHz phase-array antennas can only switch between a discrete set of directions, mTrack reconstructs the ideal continuous scanning results from discrete sampling. Consequently, it can work even if the switching angle is much larger than beamwidth.

We have implemented mTrack on a custom-built 60 GHz software-radio platform. We evaluate mTrack's APA and phase-tracking performance when user is navigating a pen over a $50cm \times 50cm$ virtual trackpad region. Experimental results show that mTrack can localize the pen's angular position with error less than $1°$, and track its motion trajectory with only 6 mm of median error and 8 mm of 90-percentile error. We also found that mTrack can be readily used to enable touch event detection (*i.e.*, pen clicking/leaving the trackpad), owing to the constrained beam pattern of mmWave antennas. Using a simple feature-based detection algorithm, it achieves a detection accuracy of around 94%.

The main contributions of mTrack include the following:

(i) A feasibility study of fine-grained, sub-centimeter scale object localization/tracking using mmWave radios with steerable antennas, in contrast to microwave radios (Sec. 3).

(ii) A phase-based approach to track small objects like pens to high precision, thus realizing trackpad applications. The tracking scheme builds on two novel algorithms to counteract the impact of background interference (Sec. 5).

(iii) A localization mechanism that leverages 60 GHz antennas to pinpoint the object's initial location and complement phase-tracking via opportunistic calibration (Sec. 6).

(iv) Implementing mTrack on a reconfigurable 60 GHz radio testbed, and validating its localization/tracking performance in a practical wireless trackpad setup (Sec. 8).

2. RELATED WORK

RF-based Active Tracking. Localization of radio-equipped objects has been explored extensively. RSS alone [18], or combined with phase [19], can serve as location signatures. But mapping channel information to location usually requires site survey and the accuracy is time and environment dependent [20]. In short-range, static environment, it is possible to locate a radio using a path-loss model (4cm error in an $1m^2$ area) [21]. However, for passive tracking, RSS-model becomes inaccurate due to multipath effects. Thus, mTrack only resorts to the variation of phase to realize passive tracking, which does not rely on any RSS-distance model.

Centimeter-scale RFID localization was achieved recently in RF-IDraw [10], which uses an interferometry technique to measure the relative phase between multiple RFID readers. Tagoram [6] generates a phase hologram that statistically maps measured phase to a potential position, and computes moving trajectory through phase shifting. These tracking schemes require an RFID tag on the object, which is not readily available for writing objects in daily use. To enable high precision passive tracking, mTrack faces two new technical challenges unseen in [6, 10]. First, reflected signal from irrelevant background objects can severely distort the target-reflected signal and affect phase-tracking accuracy (more details in Section 5.2.2). Second, current 60 GHz radio hardware still has non-negligible phase noise, which contaminates the phase shifting. To meet these challenges, mTrack incorporates two novel processing techniques that recover legitimate phase change (Section 5). In addition, mTrack leverages the unique feature of beam steerability in 60 GHz radios to realize precise localization.

RF-based Passive Tracking. Passive object tracking is reminiscent of the vast literature in radar systems [14, 22]. Conventional radar, however, mainly focused on tracking large moving objects using Doppler methods, and pushing the granularity *using wideband radios with GHz of sampling rate*. mTrack, in contrast, leverages single-carrier phased-based approach, taking advantage of electronically steerable 60 GHz antennas to track small objects with sub-centimeter precision, thus enabling near-field interactive applications like a trackpad. On the other hand, typical ranging radars require dedicated hardware, which is not readily available in 60 GHz communication system. Pulse radar [23] needs high-speed pulse generator while frequency-modulation continuous wave (FMCW) radar [14] requires a swiping carrier frequency controlled by VCO. On the contrary, mTrack's single-carrier design can be easily realized using 60 GHz communication hardware. Radar object tracking also faces interferences from background reflection. However, mTrack's mmWave phase-tracking method en-

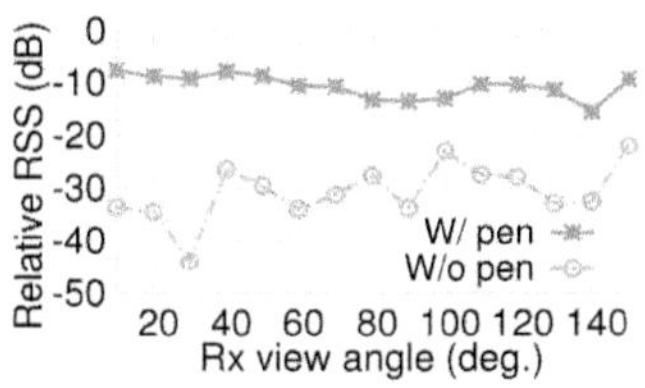

Figure 1: Small object (pen) causes diffusive 60 GHz signals that can be captured over different view angles.

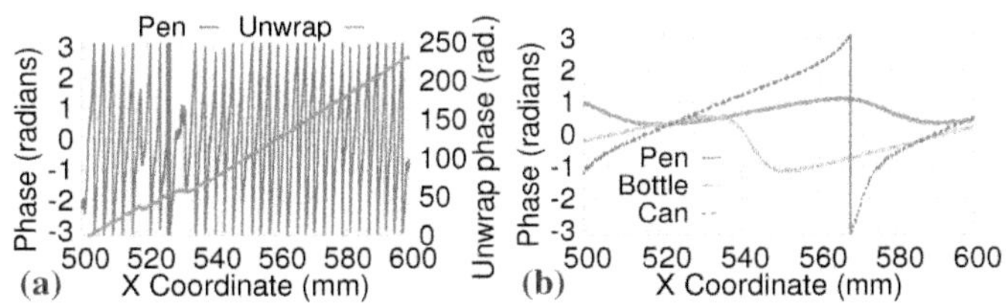

Figure 2: Tracking under same 30° beamwidth (diameter: pen 1.2cm, bottle 5.8cm and can 10.3cm). (a) Small object (pen) can cause [$-\pi$,π] phase variation in **mmWave. (b) Microwave** needs an object (*e.g.* can) of size 9× larger.

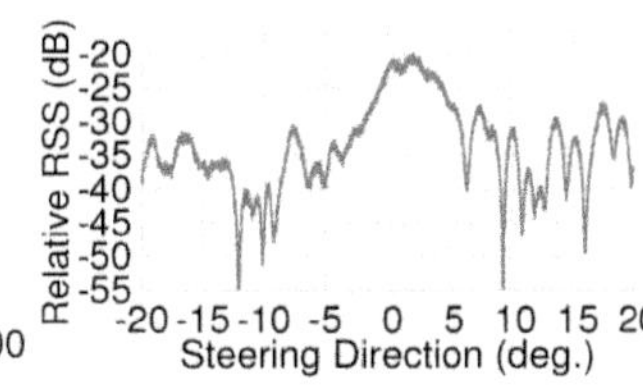

Figure 3: Beam steering to locate target direction. Receiver gets strong RSS when steering toward the target.

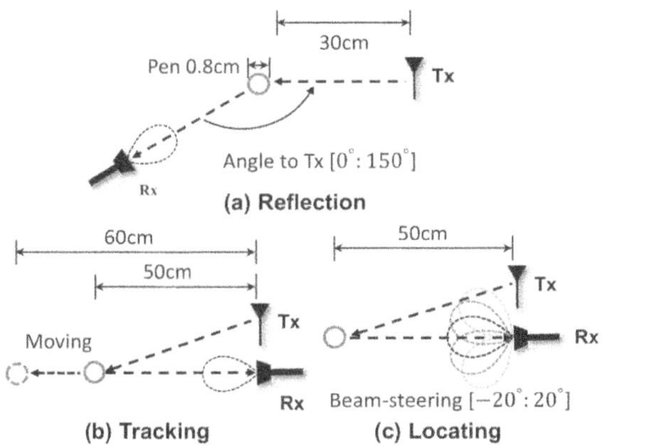

Figure 4: Setup of feasibility test. (a) Reflection test (Sec. 3.1): Rx centrally rotates around the target. **(b) Tracking test (Sec. 3.2):** Rx points to a moving target. **(c) Locating test (Sec. 3.3):** Rx steers its beam toward various directions.

counters unique challenges that have not been addressed in existing radar tracking algorithms [12, 14, 15, 24] (more details in Sec. 5.2.2).

Radio tomography and imaging techniques [11,25] deploy a mesh of sensors around sensing area and locate a person by identifying shadowed area that shows weak RSS or outstanding variation. mTrack is based on object reflection instead of blockage effect, and achieves a fine-grained tracking with much fewer sensing nodes. WiFi imaging (*e.g.*, [26]) creates an image of sensing area through an antenna array, though with a low resolution. WiFi RSS and Doppler metric have also been leveraged in gesture recognition [4, 5], but the identification algorithm needs to be trained with known patterns. Besides tracking, millimeter wave has been used to infer object's surface curvature and material [27], which can be applied to identify the target of interest.

To our knowledge, mTrack represents the first work that achieves sub-centimeter scale passive object tracking, taking advantage of the small wavelength and steerable antennas of mmWave radios. Table 1 compares mTrack with other recent RF-based active and passive tracking systems.

3. UNDERSTANDING MMWAVE PASSIVE TRACKING

We first use our 60 GHz testbed to explore mmWave characteristics pertaining to high-precision passive object localization/tracking. Our experiments examine whether small writing objects can effectively reflect mmWave signals, and whether the reflected RSS/phase can serve as subtle location/motion hints. The experiments also reveal unique advantages of mmWave over 2.4 GHz microwave-band signals.

For a feasibility test, we create a simplified setup illustrated in Figure 4. Our testbed implementation is detailed in Section 8. By default, the receiver antenna is placed at view angle 0° co-located with the transmitter. Irrelevant reflections from background objects are reduced by placing RF absorbers [28] (with approximately 35 dB attenuation) near the boundary of testing region.

3.1 Reflection/Diffusion of Signals by Objects

To enable mmWave passive tracking, receiver must receive reflection signal from the target despite the view angle *w.r.t.* target. However, 60 GHz signals are often deemed to possess a pseudo-optical property. So, will they create mirror-like specular reflections when hitting glossy objects? We examine the reflective property by rotating the receiver's view angle around the location of the target – a stylus pen (0.4 cm radius) with a metal surface.

Figure 1 plots the average RSS of 100 measured values at each view angle (*with* and *without* are abbreviated as w and w/). In the presence of the pen, the RSS remains consistently high from view angle 0° to 150°, indicating that *when reflecting 60 GHz signals, the target acts like a quasi-omni-directional antenna, rather than a mirror. Thus, even a highly directional 60 GHz receiver can capture the reflection from a wide range of view angles, as long as the target is illuminated by the transmitter.*

We also make two other observations. First, the transmitter's beamwidth determines the illumination coverage. 90° to 180° beamwidth can ensure the target is illuminated as it moves across a wide region in front of the transmitter. Second, even without target, the RSS varies, partly due to residual reflections from background, and partly due to leakage signal from the transmitter especially at a wide view angle.

3.2 Phase Variation Enables Fine-Grained Motion Tracking

Moving distance. Under ideal propagation/reflection, the phase offset between transmitter and receiver should only depend on the signal path length (illumination plus reflection). Figure 2(a) shows the phase variation as the target moves at 24 mm/second away from the transmitter/receiver. Owing to extremely short wavelength, *i.e.*, around 5 mm, even a small change of total signal path length can vary the phase significantly. By unwrapping [29] the phase value, we observe an increasing trend, indicating increasing path length, a consequence of the target's actual movement pattern. In addition, we see that the unwrapped phase value increases by 230 radians, translating to a distance $\frac{230}{2\pi} \times 0.25cm \approx 9.15cm$, roughly matching the actual moving distance of 10 cm (Note that each phase cycle corresponds to both illuminating and reflecting paths). In effect, when zooming in one phase cycle, we can see that even sub-wavelength movement resolution is feasible.

These two observations hint that *phase change of reflected signals can indicate whether the target is moving towards/against the Tx/Rx, and the relative moving distance. Small wavelength of 60 GHz signals enables fine-grained distance resolution.* However, two challenges remain open: *(i)* A single receiver cannot resolve the target's moving angle within a 2D plane. *(ii)* Phase has an inherent aliasing effect, and cannot indicate the absolute location of target. This can be clearly observed from Figure 2(a), where phase exhibits cyclic behavior, with many locations sharing the same phase value.

It is worthy to note that the phase value experiences a jump between 520ms and 540ms in Figure 2(a). This is caused by the signals from background reflection — the RF absorber in our feasibility test is not large enough to isolate all background objects. Our phase processing techniques (Section 5) will remove such abnormality and guarantee the correctness of accumulated phase.

Target size. Electromagnetic waves can easily bypass around obstacles whose size is smaller than the wavelength, and will be blocked/reflected otherwise. Thus, we hypothesize that *passive tracking of small targets is a unique advantage of mmWave signals over microwave.* To verify the hypothesis, we place a pair of 2.4 GHz software radios following the same setup as above. Figure 2(b) plots the resulting phase variation as the target moves. For the stylus pen, the signal phase can hardly reach a full cycle of $-\pi$ to π, and shows no clear correlation with wavelength. This is because the majority of the microwave signals bypass around the pen, with a radius much smaller than the wavelength (12.5 cm). Hence, background reflections from afar tend to dominate and distort the phase. Only when the target (*e.g.*, a can) size is sufficiently large can the reflected signals dominate and manifest full cyclic behavior as in the mmWave case. This result confirms our hypothesis.

It is worth noting that mmWave signals may still suffer from distortion under strong background reflection. This is a unique challenge in comparison to tracking active objects (*e.g.*, those instrumented with RFID tags [6,10]), and will be investigated in mTrack.

3.3 Beam Steering Enables Localizing Absolute Position

Despite the wide diffusion angle of the object (Figure 1), a 60 GHz receiver can have highly narrow beamwidth and will be able to capture the diffused signals only when it is pointing to the target. Figure 3 verifies this property. We steer the receiver's pointing angle between -20° to 20°, at 1° granularity. The measured RSS peaks at around 0° when the receiver points towards the target. This indicates that *we can take advantage of 60 GHz beams' steerability to fix the target's absolute angle relative to the Tx/Rx.*

In practice, a 60 GHz antenna may not be steered continuously as in our experiment. In addition, the RSS may also suffer from background reflection effect, which causes multipath effect and RSS variation as shown in Figure 1. mTrack is designed to meet these challenges.

4. AN OVERVIEW OF mTrack

mTrack builds on the foregoing measurement observations to realize a high-precision mmWave trackpad. Figure 5 shows a typical mTrack setup. One quasi-omni Tx and two directional Rx antennas are placed to form a right angle, and track an object within a rectangular trackpad region ($0 < x < 2a$, $0 < y < 2b$). a and b are set to 50 *cm* by default.

Both the quasi-omni and directional beam patterns can be readily generated via 802.11ad devices' phased-array antennas [7,30]. The quasi-omni transmitter beam in mTrack is used to illuminate the trackpad area. Typical quasi-omni beamwidth in 60 GHz ranges from 20° to 180°. The transmit signal is able to cover the tracking

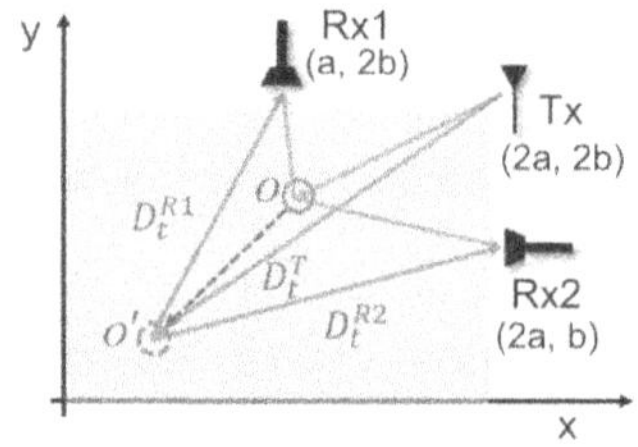

Figure 5: mTrack setup. Gray area denotes tracking region.

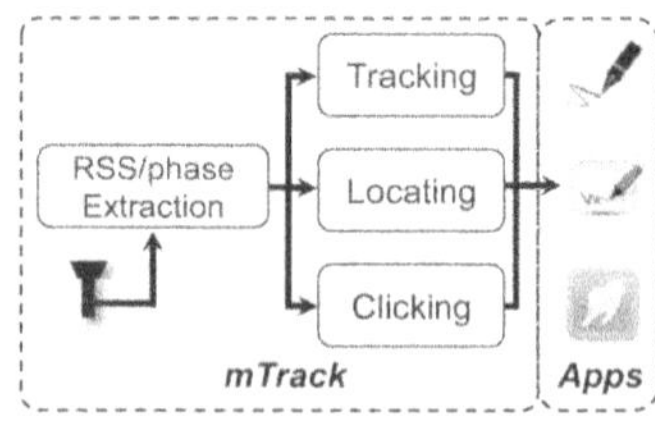

Figure 6: mTrack system components and functionalities.

region, without the need to adjust the transmitter's beam direction for scanning target. On the other hand, the Rx adopts highly directional antennas, for two reasons. First, with a high antenna gain, it can substantially boost signal quality, enabling mTrack to capture the weak reflections from target. Second, a directional receiver can help isolate the leakage interference from the Tx, which may otherwise overwhelm the target-reflected signals. Using highly directional antennas reduces the beams' intersecting area. The receiver keeps track of the target by adaptively steering the beam direction. The system detects target's entrance and exit through the touch detection module (detailed in Section 7). It also knows when the target starts to move and the moving tendency by measuring the trend and amount of phase shifting (detailed in Section 5).

Figure 6 illustrates mTrack's design components and their interaction. The *phase tracking* module continuously tracks the target's location by measuring and manipulating phase incremental at each Rx. It resolves the grand challenge from background reflections and achieves *mm*-scale tracking accuracy. The *anchor point acquisition* (APA) module estimates the target's initial position through beam searching, leveraging our observation in Section 3.3. APA has lower location resolution than phase-tracking. Hence, it is only opportunistically called on to provide absolute location value for phase tracking and prevent its error accumulation. The *touch detection* module detects user lifting the writing object or reposition it on the trackpad. Finally, the tracking/locating/touching output can serve a variety of applications, including not only trackpad, but also handwriting transcription, gesture recording, *etc.*

5. PHASE TRACKING IN mTrack

5.1 Basic Successive Tracking Algorithm

Translating phase change into path-length change. We first model the relation between target's moving distance and relative phase change between a pair of transmitter and receiver. The model formalizes our empirical observations in Section 3.2 and builds the foundation for phase-tracking.

Suppose the transmitter sends a single-tone signal of frequency f_c, represented as: $T_b(t) = Ae^{j(2\pi f_c t)}$, where A is the transmit signal magnitude. After target reflection and propagation, the receiver-captured signal becomes:

$$R_b(t) = \eta A e^{j[2\pi f_c(t-\tau)+\Phi_1]},$$

where η is the attenuation factor. Signal propagation time $\tau = \frac{D_t^T + D_t^R}{c}$, where c is the light velocity, and D_t^T and D_t^R are the distance from target to the transmitter and receiver, respectively. Φ_1 denotes the phase change caused by the reflection on the target's surface, which is a constant for the same material. Then the *phase shift*, defined as the received signal's phase change from time $t-1$ to t, and labeled as $\Delta \arg(R_b)_{t-1}^{t}$, is proportional to the change of total path length due to movement:

Algorithm 1 Basic Phase Tracking Algorithm

Input: phase shift $\Delta\arg(R1)^t_{t-1}$ and $\Delta\arg(R2)^t_{t-1}$,
Output: new location $o'(x_t, y_t)$
if $isempty(D^T_{t-1}, D^{R1}_{t-1}, D^{R2}_{t-1})$
  $o'(x_t, y_t) \leftarrow APA()$ /*Locating module*/
  $\{D^T_{t-1}, D^{R1}_{t-1}, D^{R2}_{t-1}\} \leftarrow \{|\overrightarrow{o'} - \overrightarrow{o(Tx)}|, |\overrightarrow{o'} - \overrightarrow{o(Rx1)}|, |\overrightarrow{o'} - \overrightarrow{o(Rx2)}|\}$ /*Acquire initial path length*/
else /*Successive tracking*/
  $\{D^T_t, D^{R1}_t, D^{R2}_t\} \leftarrow path(D^T_{t-1}, D^{R1}_{t-1}, D^{R2}_{t-1}, \Delta\arg(R1)^t_{t-1}, \Delta\arg(R2)^t_{t-1})$ /*Find new path lengths*/
  /*Find new location and Update path lengths*/
  $o'(x_t, y_t) \leftarrow (\frac{D^{R1\,2}_t - D^{T\,2}_t + 3a^2}{2a}, \frac{D^{R2\,2}_t - D^{T\,2}_t + 3b^2}{2b})$
  $\{D^T_{t-1}, D^{R1}_{t-1}, D^{R2}_{t-1}\} \leftarrow \{D^T_t, D^{R1}_t, D^{R2}_t\}$
return $o'(x_t, y_t)$

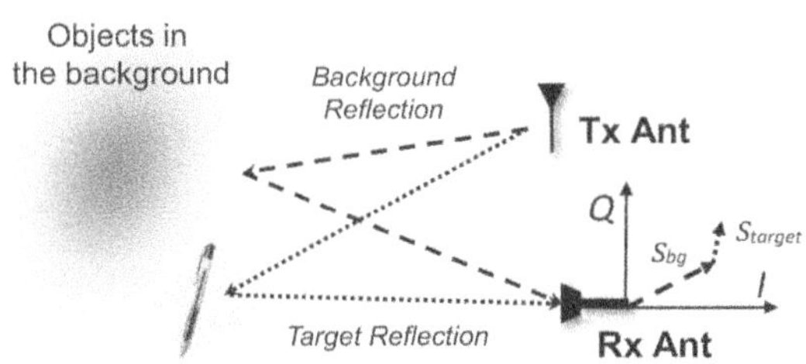

Figure 7: Multipath Reflection. We model the multipath reflections into two types: background reflection and target reflection. The sum of two reflection components is illustrated in phasor space.

$$\Delta\arg(R)^t_{t-1} = \frac{2\pi(D^T_t + D^R_t - D^T_{t-1} - D^R_{t-1})}{\lambda_c}, \tag{1}$$

where λ_c is the wavelength corresponding to carrier frequency f_c.

From distance tracking to 2D tracking. Figure 5 illustrates mTrack's basic model setup. When deploying mTrack, the Tx and two Rxs are placed at $(2a, 2b)$, $(a, 2b)$ and $(2a, b)$, respectively. Both a and b are known.

Consider two consecutive signal samples $t-1$ and t, while the target is moving. Based on Eq. (1), we have:

$$(D^T_t + D^{R1}_t) = (D^T_{t-1} + D^{R1}_{t-1}) + \frac{\lambda_c \Delta\arg(R1)^t_{t-1}}{2\pi}$$
$$(D^T_t + D^{R2}_t) = (D^T_{t-1} + D^{R2}_{t-1}) + \frac{\lambda_c \Delta\arg(R2)^t_{t-1}}{2\pi}.$$

In addition with an inherent geometrical constraint of those signal path lengths (Figure 5), we can solve for three unknown path lengths D^T_t, D^{R1}_t and D^{R2}_t with three sets of equations, given that the corresponding path-lengths at $t-1$ have already been obtained. This computation runs in a successive manner, with initial values D^T_0, D^{R1}_0 and D^{R2}_0 given by mTrack's anchor point acquisition (APA) module (to be discussed in Section 6). Finally, the target's absolute coordinate at time t is computed using the triangulation method, given the path length to the transmitter and both receivers' locations. Algorithm 1 summarizes the successive phase-tracking in mTrack.

This successive tracking is promising for real-time tracking because the solutions of path length and new location can be expressed in closed-form formulas and computed efficiently by single-step operations.

Notably, using highly directional receive antennas may result in a relatively small detection region. For example, with two Rx antennas of beamwidth $4.5°$ and 0.5m away from the tracking region, the intersection area of two beams is only $5cm \times 5cm$. mTrack expands the detection region by adaptively steering the beam, whenever it gauges that the target may fall out of the Rx's beam coverage in the next 0.5 second, assuming its speed is consistent within this short period.

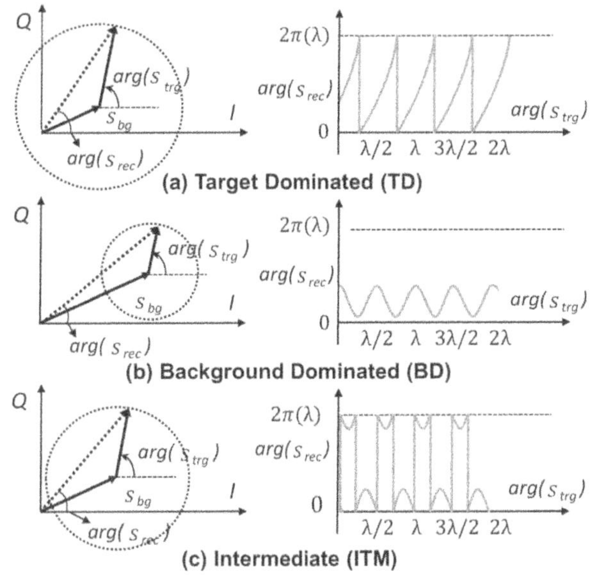

Figure 8: Impact of (static) background reflection on phase shift. (a) Target reflection dominates background. **(b)** Target reflection is much weaker than background. **(c)** Intermediate case.

5.2 Tracking under Background Reflection

5.2.1 *Impact of background reflection on phase shift*

Though directional antennas can alleviate multipath effect, antenna beamwidth still needs to be broad enough to cover a reasonably large detection region. Thus, background reflection is unavoidable. We model how background reflection affects mTrack's successive tracking and derive insights that help disentangle target reflection from background reflection. We use vector form on the I-Q plane to represent a signal sample (Figure 7). Since baseband signal is a single-carrier, background reflections can aggregate into a single signal sample $\overrightarrow{S}_{bg}$. Similarly, target-reflected signal sample is modeled as $\overrightarrow{S}_{trg}$. The demodulated signal at the receiver $\overrightarrow{S}_{rec}$ at any time is the sum of two reflected components:

$$\overrightarrow{S}_{rec} = \overrightarrow{S}_{trg} + \overrightarrow{S}_{bg}. \tag{2}$$

Phase shift of $\overrightarrow{S}_{trg}$ *carriers information about the moving distance of target, but the receiver can only measure the mixed signal* $\overrightarrow{S}_{rec}$. So, can this mixed signal's phase still translate into target's moving distance? We answer the question by analyzing how the phase of $\overrightarrow{S}_{rec}$ cycles as the target moves over half-wavelength (*i.e.*, the phase of $\overrightarrow{S}_{trg}$ cycles from 0 to 2π). The phase cycling pattern in turn depends on the magnitude of target reflection $|\overrightarrow{S}_{trg}|$, which we classify into three ranges, as shown in Figure 8.

(a) Target dominating (TD): Suppose background reflection is stationary as the target moves across half-wavelength. Accordingly, as $\overrightarrow{S}_{trg}$ rotates its phase through one cycle, $\overrightarrow{S}_{rec}$ crosses the I-plane once, resulting in phase shift of 2π. Thus, phase shift can still reveal the moving distance when target travels integer multiples of half-wavelength $\lambda_{0.5}$.

(b) Background dominating (BD): As the phase of $\overrightarrow{S}_{trg}$ goes through a 2π cycle, the measured phase of $\overrightarrow{S}_{rec}$ does not cross the

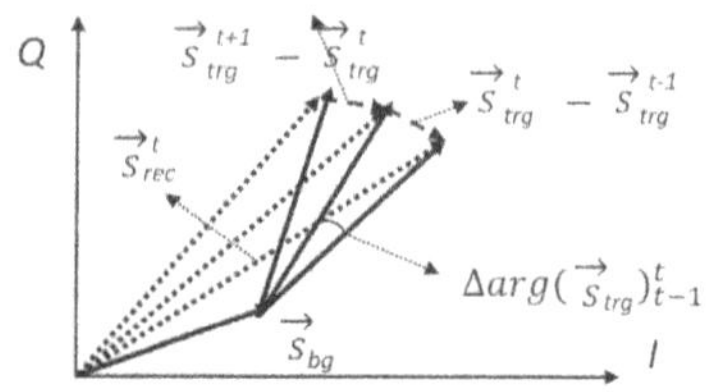

Figure 9: Illustration of signal vectors relation for differential background removal algorithm.

I-plane, and phase shift is smaller than 2π. The stronger the background reflection, the smaller it will be. Accordingly, the moving distance estimated from the phase shift of $\vec{S}_{rec}$ is always shorter than actual value.

(c) Intermediate (ITM) case between above two: As shown in Figure 8(c), $\vec{S}_{rec}$ crosses the I-plane twice, causing phase jump at each crossing point. Due to phase ambiguity of measured signal $\vec{S}_{rec}$, the measured phase shift also will not reveal the correct moving distance.

5.2.2 Dealing with Background Reflection

Why is it challenging? Multipath reflection from background is a unique challenge for mTrack which aims to track small passive objects at high precision. Unlike radar-like systems that track large targets (*e.g.*, human body [12, 14]), reflections from small objects tend to be weaker or comparable to background reflections. Due to the high sensitivity of mmWave, background reflection can disturb the signal phase even as the target moves over a short distance. Radar systems can use ultra-wideband signals to resolve the time-of-arrival of reflected signal paths, thus separating the foreground and background [31]. In contrast, mTrack relies on a narrow-band (single-tone) continuous wave that mixes background and target reflection.

Unlike active tracking systems [6, 10] where reflected paths originate coherently from the same radio transmitter, in passive tracking, only parts of the reflected signals contain desired information and need to be extrapolated. Background suppression in active tracking systems is much simpler, since the signal phase changes are caused by baseband modulation, which operates at much higher rate (*e.g.*, multiple kHz in RFID [6]) than background variation. Hence, any background reflection can be considered as relatively static and filtered out by a DC filter [32]. This approach is not applicable to passive tracking systems where phase changes at slow rate due to target movement.

Dual-differential Background Removal. Since the phase shift directly from the received signal $\vec{S}_{rec}$ is contaminated by background reflection, mTrack employs a *Dual-differential Background Removal* (DDBR) algorithm to remove such impact, thus limiting the tracking error.

Underlying background removal are two assumptions: *(i)* Background reflection remains stationary across at least 3 consecutive signal samples. This holds in general because 60 GHz radios take RSS/phase samples (assuming one sample per packet) much more frequently than the change of background. *(ii)* Target reflection has the same decreasing or increasing trend of phase shift, and approximate RSS, across 3 consecutive samples. This holds again because of the high sampling rate relative to the writing object's slow motion.

Under these assumptions, the idea behind background cancellation is intuitive — we leverage the invariant behind signal differential:

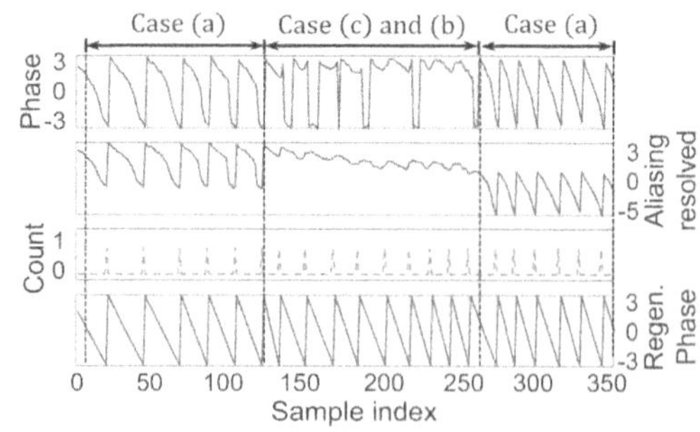

Figure 10: An example snapshot of using PCR to remove background reflection.

$$\vec{S}^{\,t}_{rec} - \vec{S}^{\,t-1}_{rec} = (\vec{S}^{\,t}_{trg} + \vec{S}^{\,t}_{bg}) - (\vec{S}^{\,t-1}_{trg} + \vec{S}^{\,t-1}_{bg}) \approx \vec{S}^{\,t}_{trg} - \vec{S}^{\,t-1}_{trg}. \quad (3)$$

The average phase shift among three consecutive samples can be computed as:

$$\frac{1}{2}[\Delta \arg(\vec{S}_{trg})^t_{t-1} + \Delta \arg(\vec{S}_{trg})^{t+1}_t] = \arg(\vec{S}^{\,t+1}_{trg} - \vec{S}^{\,t}_{trg}) - \arg(\vec{S}^{\,t}_{trg} - \vec{S}^{\,t-1}_{trg}). \quad (4)$$

The proof for the above equation directly follows the geometrical relation shown in Figure 9, which is detailed in Appendix A.

From Eqs. (3) and (4), we get the phase shift with background reflection canceled by differentiating the phase of differential received signal:

$$\Delta \arg(\vec{S}_{trg})^{t+1}_{t-1} = \Delta \arg(\vec{S}_{trg})^t_{t-1} + \Delta \arg(\vec{S}_{trg})^{t+1}_t \approx 2[\arg(\vec{S}^{\,t+1}_{rec} - \vec{S}^{\,t}_{rec}) - \arg(\vec{S}^{\,t}_{rec} - \vec{S}^{\,t-1}_{rec})]. \quad (5)$$

The resulting $\Delta \arg(\vec{S}_{trg})^{t+1}_{t-1}$ is deemed as a single phase shift sample (with background canceled) to replace the one in the basic successive tracking Algorithm 1 to improve tracking accuracy.

Millimeter-wave radios typically have non-negligible phase noise which is inherent to its ultra-high frequency synthesizer. To prevent phase noise from contaminating the phase shift measurement, mTrack adapts its phase sampling rate (by dropping intermediate samples), to ensure the phase shift between consecutive samples is not dominated by phase noise. We retain a phase sample only if its shift (relative to the previous sample) is above variance of the phase noise (available from hardware specifications).

5.3 Phase Counting and Regeneration

One limitation of the above DDBR algorithm is that it attempts to average out phase noise at the cost of lowering sampling rate. Consequently, between 3 consecutive sampling period, the background reflection may have already changed, thus violating DDBR's assumption.

To overcome this limitation, we design a complementary algorithm called *phase counting and regeneration* (PCR). PCR maintains a high sampling rate, but collects a sufficient number of samples (instead of 3) to recover the target-reflected signal from noise and background reflection. Under background reflection, although the absolute phase change of measured signal is no longer linear *w.r.t.* target's moving distance, its phase still exhibits a periodic pattern (Section 5.2.1). PCR harnesses this phenomenon to *identify/count the phase cycles* of measured signal, based on which it *regenerates* the phase change caused purely by target reflection. Then, it can simply run the basic phase-tracking Algorithm 1 to translate phase change into moving distance.

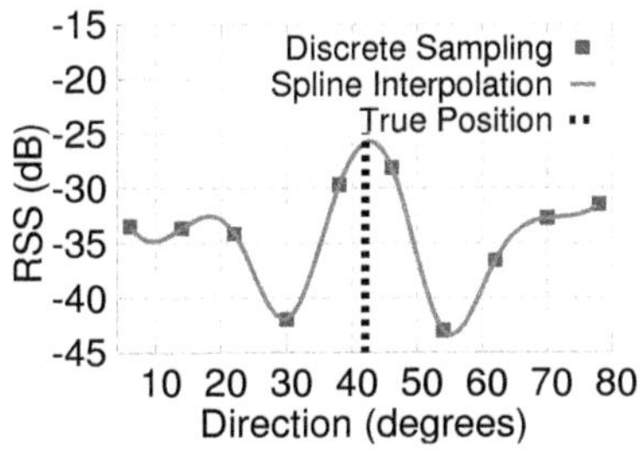

Figure 11: Spline interpolation improves granularity of direction estimation from discrete steering.

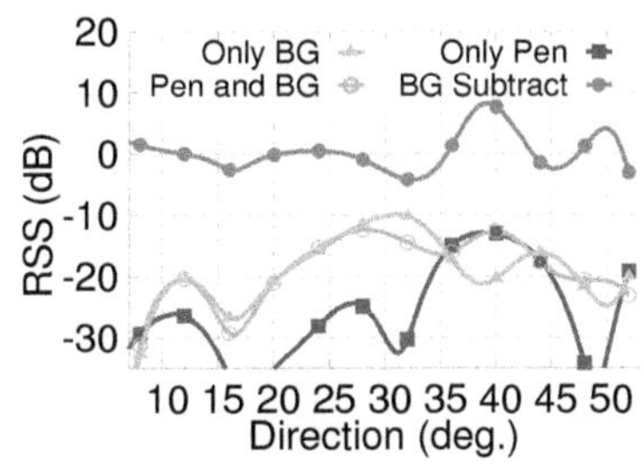

Figure 12: APA improves locating accuracy that is disturbed by background reflection.

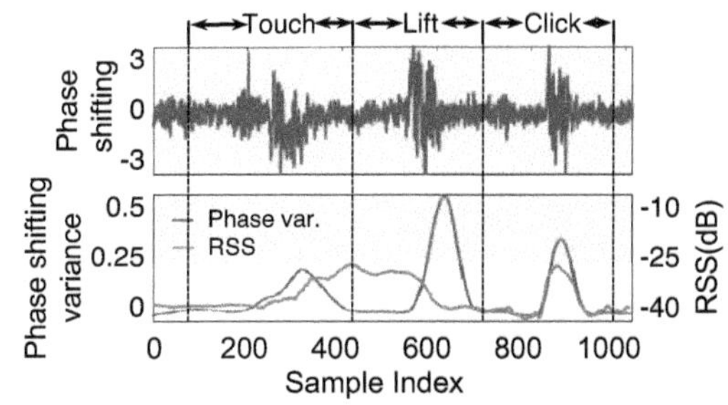

Figure 13: Example snapshot of three type events. Phase shift variance and RSS are for event detection and classification.

Params	Basic	DDBR	PCR
Complexity	Low	Low	High
Latency	Small	Small	Large
BG Resilient	No	Yes	Yes
Error w/ BG	≈30mm	≈5mm	≈8mm
Noise Resilient	Yes	No	Yes
Error w/ Noise	≈8mm	≈20mm	≈8mm

Table 2: Performance profiles of mTrack's phase tracking algorithms. Error statistics from Section 8.

The three different patterns of background contamination (Section 5.2.1) impose significant challenges to this approach. First, the three cases may be mixed together, and the ITM case has severe phase aliasing effects. Second, we need to identify the periodicity based only on a few phase cycles to maintain the timeliness of tracking. Both challenges deter simple periodicity identification algorithms like Fast Fourier Transform. PCR addresses these challenges through three key steps (Figure 10 shows an example).

Reducing ITM to BD. We address the first issue by detecting the ITM case, and convert it to the BD case which has no phase aliasing effect. For detection, PCR leverages the unique phase "jumps" in the ITM case caused by aliasing, *i.e.*, neighboring two jumps are in opposite directions (Figure 8). Formally, given a time series of N phase samples $x[1], x[2], \cdots, x[N]$, it sequentially searches for a point m_i with phase jump:

$$m_i = \arg\min_{2 \le i \le N} \mathit{find}(|x[i] - x[i-1]| > \pi). \quad (6)$$

It then checks if there exists a follow-on point that together constitutes the feature in ITM:

$$m_j = \arg\min_{m_i \le j \le N} \mathit{find}(|x[j] - x[j-1]| > \pi) \quad (7)$$

$$s.t.\ m_j - m_i < T_h \quad (8)$$

$$|x[m_i] - x[m_j]| > \pi, \quad (9)$$

where T_h is the largest periodicity that PCR can detect. Eq. (9) ensures the phase jumps at m_i and m_j are opposite.

Once an ITM case is detected, we can reduce it to the BD case by compensating the difference between discontinuous series:

$$x[i] = x[i] - (x[m_i] - x[m_i - 1]), \forall i \in [m_i, m_j). \quad (10)$$

Periodicity Counting. To reliably detect the periodicity T of the time series of samples after alias removal, we adopt the phase coherence analysis in [33]. Let sequence $\mathbf{L}[i,d] = \{x[i + jd] \mid \forall\, 0 \le j < \lfloor N/d \rfloor\}$, where $\{\}$ denotes concatenation of samples. Since $\mathbf{L}[i,d]$ are samples that are separated by d points in the given time series, by the periodicity definition, variance of $\mathbf{L}[i,d]$ will be minimized, *i.e.* 0, when $d = T$. Hence, we find the periodicity T by iterating possible values in range $[T_l, T_h]$ for all sequence i:

$$T = \arg\min_t var(\{\overline{\mathbf{L}[i,t]} \mid \forall 1 \le i \le t\}), \forall t \in [T_l, T_h],$$

where $\overline{\mathbf{L}[i,t]}$ is $\mathbf{L}[i,t]$ with its mean value subtracted.

Regeneration. PCR will generate the counting sequence (red curve in Figure 10) based on the periodicity detected in the time series samples. The correct phase pattern is regenerated by creating 2π phase shift between any two neighboring counts. The trend of phase shift, either increasing or decreasing, is available from the basic successive tracking or DDBR algorithm.

We emphasize that *PCR* is uniquely designed for passive tracking using small-wavelength mmWave signals. It assumes the background reflection does not change as the target moves over $\lambda_{0.5}$, which may not hold when using microwave signals. In addition, its resolution is around $\lambda_{0.5}$, hence PCR's precision worsens to multiple centimeters when using microwave signals.

Table 2 summarizes and compares three processing algorithms. Since PCR algorithm works on time-series of samples spanning multiple phase cycles, it incurs proportionally higher complexity and tracking latency than Basic (successive tracking) and DDBR, which work on 2 and 3 samples, respectively. However, it is more resilient to the phase noise, as will be verified in experiments.

6. ANCHOR POINT ACQUISITION

APA complements phase tracking in two aspects: *(i)* estimating initial location, which serves as an anchor point to bootstrap the successive tracking; *(ii)* opportunistically calibrating the tracking results to prevent error accumulation.

Locating through discrete beam steering. Our feasibility study in Section 3 reveals a key challenge in locating the target: practical 60 GHz antennas can only be steered at discrete angles. We resolve this challenge by leveraging the roll-off pattern of the antenna gain. The gain of a 60 GHz directional Rx antenna (either horn antenna or phased-array [30]) decreases continuously near its beam edge. Accordingly, as a signal source moves from the beam center towards beam edge RSS falls off smoothly. The fall-off trend is preserved even if Rx steers itself in discrete steps.

Built on this observation, mTrack realizes discrete spatial sampling of the target's direction, thereby relaxing the beam resolution requirement. In analog-to-digital signal conversion, a continuous signal can be preserved by interpolating it across discrete samples, using sinc as the basis function. Similarly for mTrack, the continuous spatial RSS variation can be reconstructed by interpolating the discrete samples, using antenna gain pattern (over angles) as basis function. Yet, since the exact gain pattern is unavailable, we choose to use *spline interpolation* instead. Spline interpolation performs

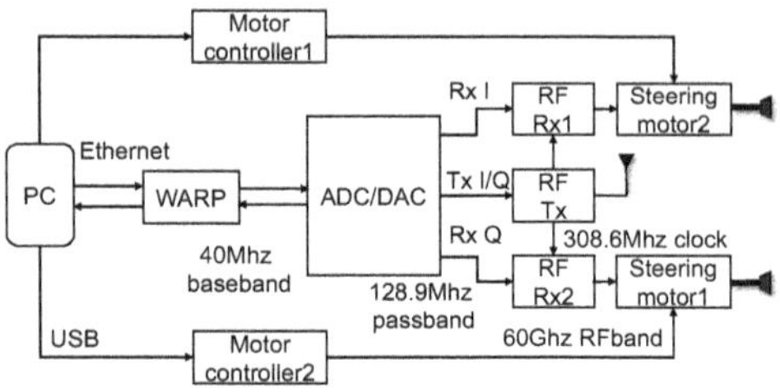

Figure 14: Hardware architecture of mTrack.

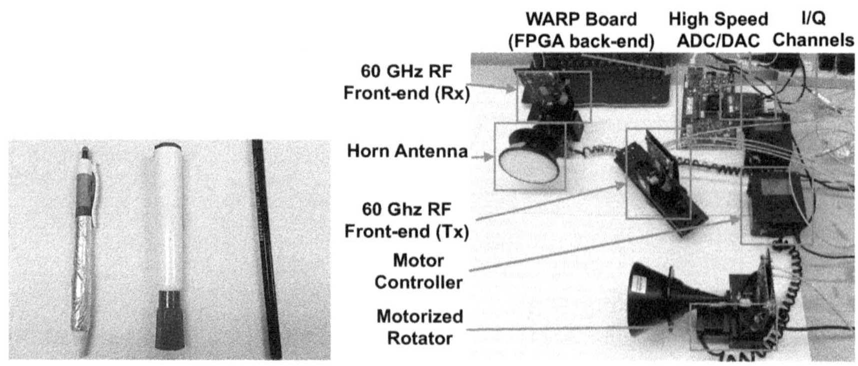

Figure 15: mmWave testbed. Testing metal-surfaced pen, plastic marker, wood pencil. Radios are placed 10cm beside 50cm×50cm writing region.

piecewise polynomial approximation to the discrete samples with an objective that minimizes curve bending. It can thus recover the peak RSS position. To perfectly reconstruct continuous variation, angle of beam-steering for each step is required to be smaller than 2× the beamwidth.

Figure 11 shows one example test result, with discrete RSS samples (blue dots) at 8° beam-steering steps, along with the interpolated curve. We can see that the interpolated maximum RSS position is very close to the ground truth.

Following mTrack's setup (Figure 5), the target's angle relative to each Rx antenna can be translated into its absolute location via simple geometrical manipulation. We omit the details for the sake of space.

Background RSS Subtraction. Similar to the successive phase tracking, the RSS values captured during APA may be contaminated by background reflection. However, RSS is much less sensitive than phase because the locating result will be affected *only if* the background change alters the peak in the RSS scanning. Thus, mTrack employs a simple iterative background RSS subtraction method in APA. Before use, each Rx collects the RSS of background reflection for each steering angle. When a new APA is invoked, the background RSS at each steering direction is subtracted from the measured RSS. During the writing process, it knows the precise angular location of the target by combining phase tracking and initial APA. Hence, it periodically rescans the background RSS by steering off the target position.

During APA, the tracking module has to be temporarily blocked. However, since mmWave phase-array antenna can instantaneously switch its beam (at *ns* level latency as specified in 802.11ad [34]), the impact on tracking is negligible.

Figure 12 illustrates one test experiment, where a metal-surface cup is placed $25cm$ behind the detection region and a pen is used as tracking target. When there is only pen (blue curve) or only background (yellow curve) in the environment, mTrack can locate the direction of target accurately (in $40°$ and $30°$ respectively). When the tracking target is mixed with background object, the system is misled to take the later as locating result (in green curve) due to its stronger reflected signal strength. In the red curve, background subtraction cancels the background reflection from cup, and thus the target position can be accurately located.

Opportunistic Calibration. To curtail the error accumulation from successive phase tracking, APA is invoked opportunistically to recalibrate the absolute target position.

mTrack adopts a k/θ *test* to determine when to invoke a calibration. APA module periodically estimates anchor points. If past k anchor points all fall in a sector of angle θ originating from current position, the deviation of tracking trajectory can be considered as sufficiently large. In this case, the calibration will be applied by updating current position to the latest anchor point. In practice, mTrack empirically chooses $k = 3$ and $\theta = 120°$.

7. TOUCH EVENT DETECTION

Besides tracking, mTrack detects touch-related gestures including: *(i)* "touch" – pen landing on writing region, *(ii)* "lift" – pen lifting above the region, and *(iii)* "click" – essentially a sequential combination of "touch" and "lift" event. The touch gestures can serve as commands, *e.g.*, start/pause of tracking and segmentation of writing trajectory.

The key principle in mTrack's gesture detection algorithm is to identify signal features that discriminate each gesture, and distinguish them from normal writing. Given the ultra-narrow beam, one may consider the touch gestures as "beam cutting" events, and use RSS variation patterns to detect them [5]. However, we find that RSS fluctuates significantly during writing, which incurs frequent false alarms. To address this problem, we resort to the *phase variance* as an additional feature along with RSS. Since phase shift reveals the target's movement, its variance will characterize the abruptness of change in the pen's moving speed, which is suitable for gesture detection.

Figure 13 illustrates a snapshot of signal features for the three types of gestures. A sliding window of duration $0.1s$ is used to smooth the phase variance. We can see that all gestures will create large phase variance, which is amenable for flagging a valid gesture event. To discriminate different types of gestures, we can resort to the RSS pattern, which tends to have higher value when the pen is in the tracking region. Based on above observations, mTrack identifies and classifies the gesture using a simple decision tree (Alg. 2).

Algorithm 2 Decision Tree for Touch Gesture Detection

Input: phase variance $\mathbf{P}[n]$ and RSS $\mathbf{R}[n]$
$\{V, m\} \leftarrow max(\mathbf{P})$ /*max value and index*/
if $V > H$
  if $\mathbf{R}[m] > mean(\mathbf{R}[m : m + s])$ and $\mathbf{R}[m] > mean(\mathbf{R}[m - s : m])$ /*Check RSS*/
    return "Click" /*Click generates RSS peak*/
  else if $mean(\mathbf{R}[m : m + s]) > mean(\mathbf{R}[m - s : m])$
    return "Touch" /*Touch increases RSS*/
  else
    return "Lift" /*Lift decreases RSS*/
return "NULL" /*Event not detected*/

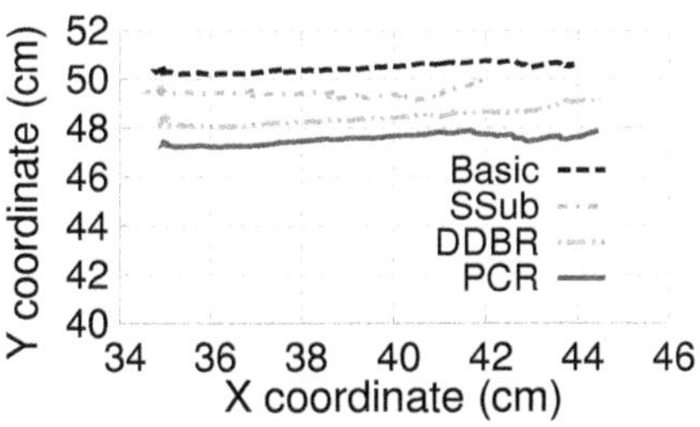

Figure 16: Tracking along an example linear trajectory(10 *cm*) without BG.

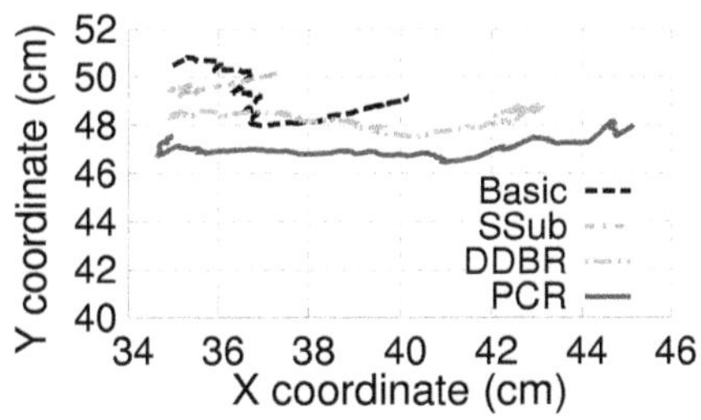

Figure 17: Tracking example with background reflection.

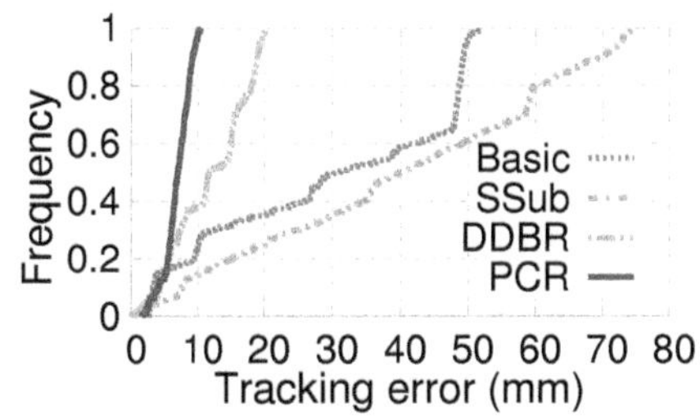

Figure 18: Error CDF of tracking methods under background reflection.

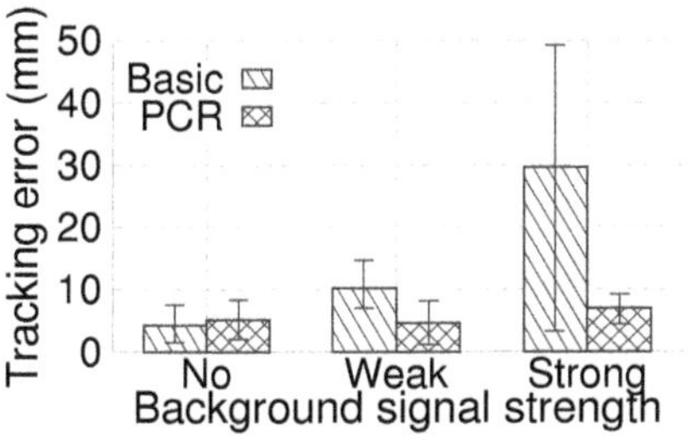

Figure 19: PCR performance under different background strength.

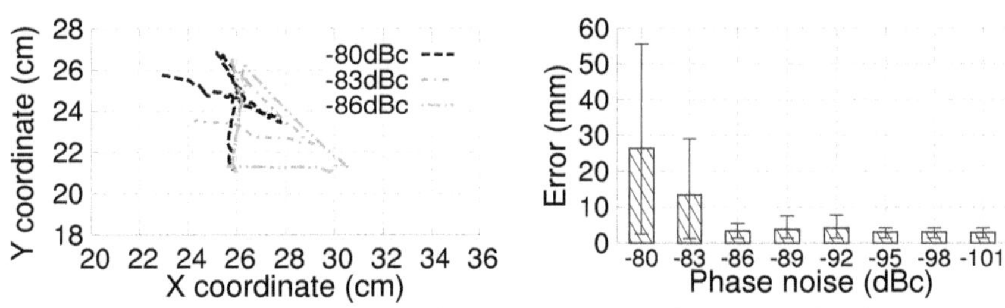

Figure 20: Tracking trajectory and tracking error of the DDBR algorithm under different levels of phase noise.

In Algorithm 2, there are two parameters. s is the number of samples that are used to compute average RSS, which is empirically chosen as 0.1s. H denotes the threshold for a valid peak of phase variance. Since different users' gesture styles (*e.g.*, touching speed) may differ, mTrack requests the user to provide a 10-sample training set before using the gesture detector. It then selects an H that minimizes the difference (computed using standardized Euclidean distance [35]) between the widths of the 10 peaks.

8. IMPLEMENTATION AND EVALUATION

We use a custom-built 60 GHz software-radio testbed (Figure 14) to evaluate the viability and performance of mTrack. The testbed uses WARP [36] as baseband processing unit, but extends its carrier frequency to 60 GHz. Baseband digital waveforms are generated in a host PC, forwarded to WARP, and converted to analog using a high-speed DAC. Resulting analog signals are carrier-modulated and transmitted by the Vubiq 60 GHz RF front-end [37]. Two receivers are synchronized by a 308.6 MHz external clock signal sourcing from transmitter oscillator. Received signals will be decoded following reverse path, and eventually reach the PC host which runs mTrack's algorithms.

Tx and Rx RF front-end each has a waveguide module as interface to 60 GHz antennas (Figure 15). Transmitter uses its original waveguide module PEM-001 as antenna, which is quasi-omni-directional (180° beamwidth). Tx sends 5 MHz single-carrier baseband signals modulated by 60 GHz carrier waves. Regarding receiver, we are unaware of any programmable 60 GHz phased-array antenna. Thus, in our prototype, signals are captured by a directional receiver with horn antenna PE9881-34 of 3.4° beamwidth. To emulate the effect of beam steering, the Rx antenna is mounted on a motion control system [38] that is connected to the PC host and allows programmable azimuth rotation at 1° granularity.

We also implement the RSS/phase extraction module on the 60 GHz testbed. It generates and sends single-tone frames (3000 samples each) through Tx, and estimates a pair of RSS and phase values from each received frame. To avoid phase ambiguity, the change between any two phase values cannot exceed π. By default, the extraction module samples RSS/phase at 300 Hz. Thus, the highest tracking speed that our prototype can support is 2.5mm$\times$300 Hz/2 = 37.5cm/s. The speed is sufficiently fast to capture normal hand writing. Note that 300 Hz phase sampling rate is far below our hardware limit. With 40 MHz bandwidth, the phase sampling rate can be up to 40 MHz/3000 = 13 KHz, equivalently translated to a tracking speed of 26 m/s.

On top of the RSS/phase extraction, we implement mTrack's major modules, *i.e.*, tracking, locating and touch detection. Core processing algorithms DDBR, PCR and APA are designed as middleware plugins that work transparently between RSS/phase extraction and these modules. Algorithms operate on samples that are loaded sequentially into a data buffer.

8.1 Micro Benchmark

8.1.1 *Passive Tracking Performance*

The experiments are conducted in an office environment with natural background: one Rx antenna faces a human and a metal cabinet 1.5 *m* away; the other one faces a drywall 2 *m* away. For a micro-benchmark test, a pen is first attached to the motion track and moves linearly under the control of the PC host. This setup allows us to obtain the pen's location over time, and use it as ground truth to evaluate mTrack. Unless noted otherwise, we use the PCR algorithm in mTrack (Section 5.3) to combat background reflection.

Combating background reflection. We compare mTrack with the ground-truth (Oracle) and two alternative techniques: *(i) Basic*, which directly employs the phase-tracking algorithm in Section 5 without handling background reflection. *(ii) Static subtraction* (SSub), which surveys the background reflection offline when the target is out of tracking region. Then, it subtracts the measured background directly from baseband signals, assuming the background is static and remains the same w/ or w/o target present. This is typically used in scenario where background signals have long coherent time, *e.g.*, radar-based object identification [13, 31].

Figure 16 and 17 depict example trajectory outputs of these schemes when the pen moves linearly across 10 *cm* w/ and w/o background reflection. Figure 18 plots the CDF of tracking errors across the trajectory and over 10 trials. When there is no background, all

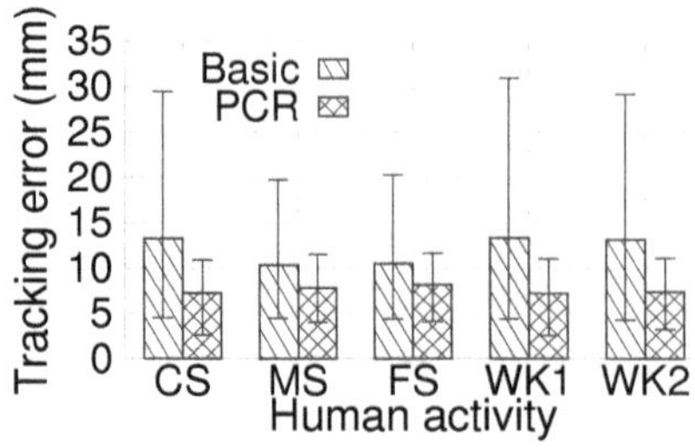

Figure 21: PCR performance under human as dynamic background.

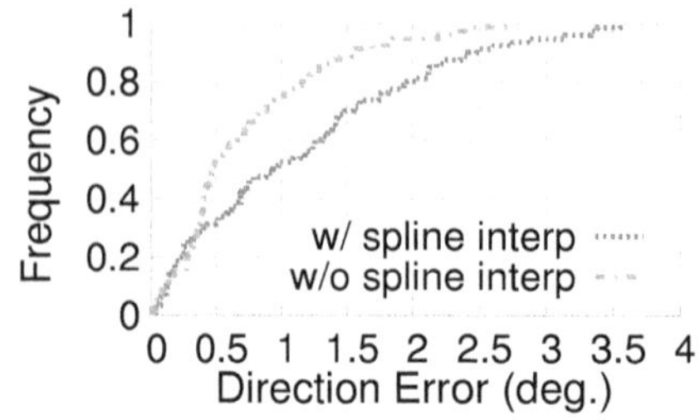

Figure 22: APA performance with spline interpolation.

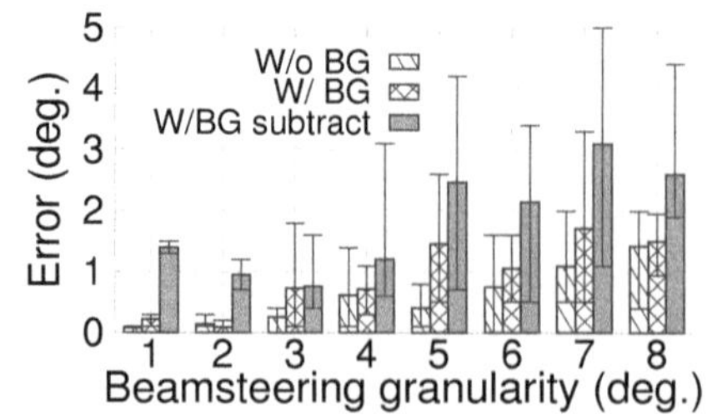

Figure 23: Effectiveness of background subtraction in APA.

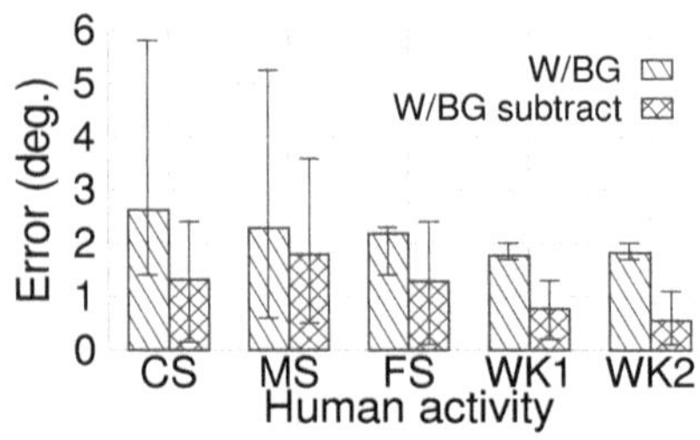

Figure 24: APA under dynamic background. Step of antenna steer 4°.

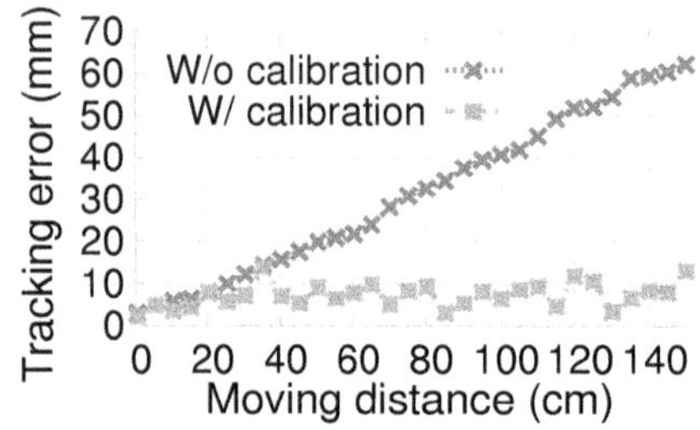

Figure 25: Error w/ and w/o opportunistic calibration.

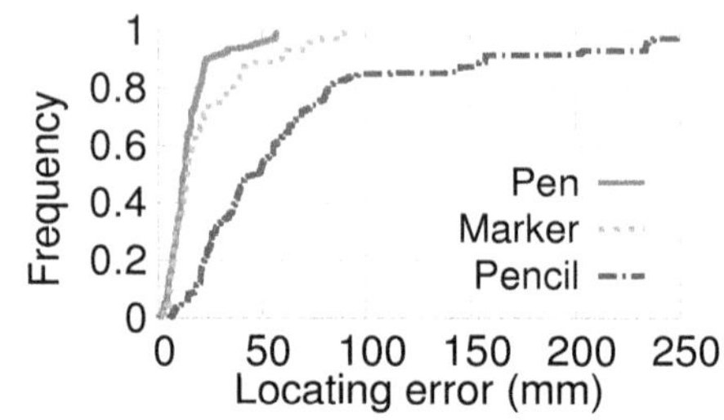

Figure 26: Locating error of different materials.

methods have little deviation. When background is present, the basic method exhibits large deviation (median error of 30 *mm* and 90-percentile 5 *mm*). Static subtraction leads to even larger error (median 40 *mm* and 90-percentile 70 *mm*), because mmWave's phase is highly sensitive to environment. The background signals hardly remain static and subtracting an incorrect estimation incurs large penalty because of equivalently introducing an artificial background.

In contrast, mTrack's DDBR and PCR algorithms both demonstrate *mm*-scale precision, with median (90-percentile) error of 11 (18) *mm* and 6.5 (9) *mm*, respectively. PCR achieves higher accuracy than DDBR mainly because our 60 GHz software defined radio platform has relatively high phase noise (-80dBc at 5Mhz offset from carrier according to our measurement). It can lead to maximum deviation of up to 0.2 radian within one phase cycle. COTS 60 GHz radios have much lower phase noise (typically <110dBc at 5Mhz) [39]. Our trace-based simulation shows that DDBR can outperform PCR significantly under such noise level.

Impact of phase noise on DDBR performance. We evaluate DDBR's performance under different levels of phase noise through trace-based simulation. The phase shift of target reflection is generated by simulating the target moving along a triangle of size 5cm×5cm following the setup in Figure 5. Meanwhile, there is background reflection from a static reflector, whose reflectivity is 1/3 of the target. The simulated phase shift is contaminated by the trace of phase noise collected from our platform.

Figure 20 shows the impact of phase noise. DDBR's tracking error decreases by more than 80% when the phase noise is reduced from -80dBc to -86dBc, and after background removal, the trajectory is close to the oracle shape (triangle). Further reducing the phase noise (to <-86dBc) will not significantly improve tracking performance since phase noise is sufficiently small for DDBR to function correctly.

Different types of background. We now evaluate the performance of *Basic* and mTrack (using PCR) under 3 different background types: *(i)* Strong background: a metal cabinet is placed near the tracking region, facing one Rx antenna. *(ii)* Weak background: a 60 GHz RF absorber is placed at the end of tracking region to isolate the impact of cabinet on one Rx antenna, leaving background reflection from drywall to the other antenna. *(iii)* No background: RF absorbers are placed along both the x- and y-axis, protecting both Rx antennas from background reflection.

We also evaluate mTrack with human as dynamic background: *(i)* CS, MS, and FS: A human stands 1m, 2m and 3m facing one Rx antenna. Human breathing changes background reflection signals. *(ii)* WK1 and WK2: The human randomly walks in parallel or perpendicular at 2∼3m to Rx antenna.

Figure 19 shows that mTrack maintains *mm*-scale precision across all background types. Its PCR algorithm effectively eliminates the impact of background reflection, leaving median (90-percentile) residual error of only around 8 (12) *mm* compared with the perfect case (no background). In contrast, the basic phase tracking deviates by up to 30 (50) *mm*. Figure 21 shows that PCR can still effectively reduce tracking error under human walking as dynamic background, since human body will not strongly reflect mmWave signals.

8.1.2 Performance of APA

We proceed to verify mTrack's APA algorithm with similar experiment setup as above. The target pen is randomly placed over 30 positions 40 to 50 *cm* away from the receivers. We evaluate mTrack's error in locating the target's angle relative to the transmitter/receiver (Section 6).

Benchmarking APA with discrete-step beam-steering. To emulate practical behavior of 60 GHz switched-beam antenna, we steer the antenna at discrete steps of 8° ($2\times$ the beamwidth). Figure 22 shows that the spline interpolation does play a crucial role in mitigating the effect of discrete switching between beam directions. Compared with the basic method that directly takes the RSS-maximizing direction (Section 6), it reduces the 90-percentile error from 2.5° to 1.5°, translating to positioning error of 10.5 *mm*.

Background subtraction for APA. In this experiment, in addition to the default background (cabinet and drywall), we intentionally place a metal cup near the end of writing region. Unlike large background like cabinet or drywall, small reflective object as such

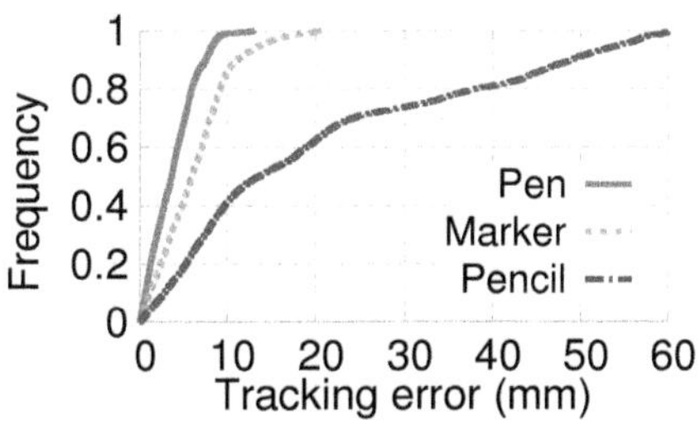

Figure 27: Tracking error of different materials.

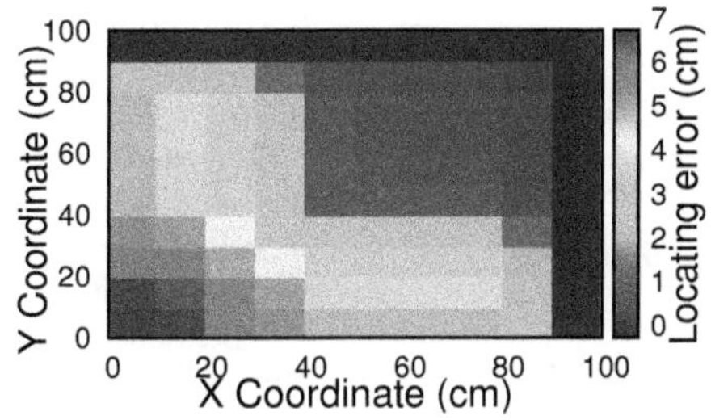

Figure 28: Error map of APA

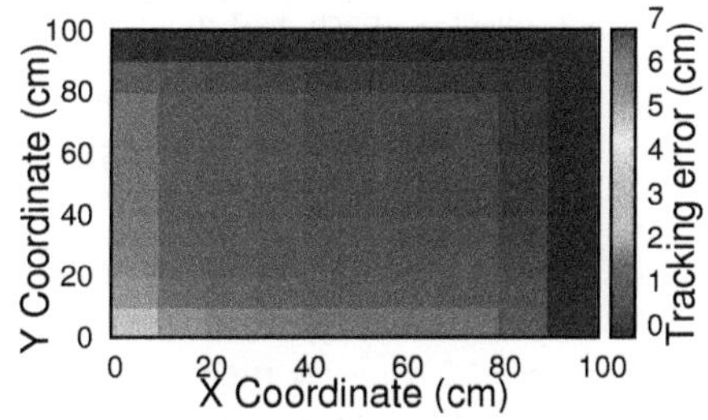

Figure 29: Error map of Phase-tracking.

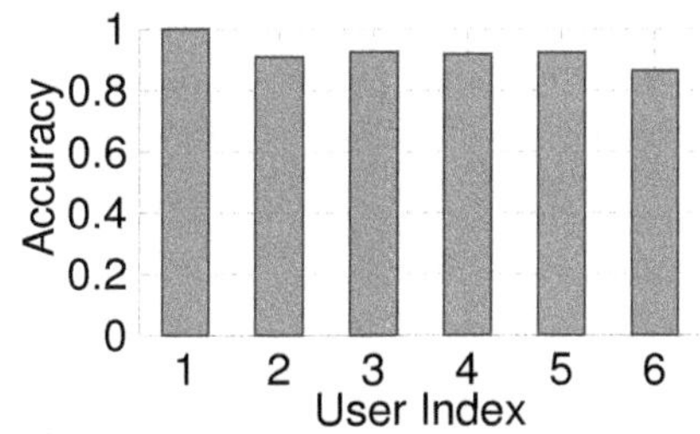

Figure 30: Detection accuracy for different users.

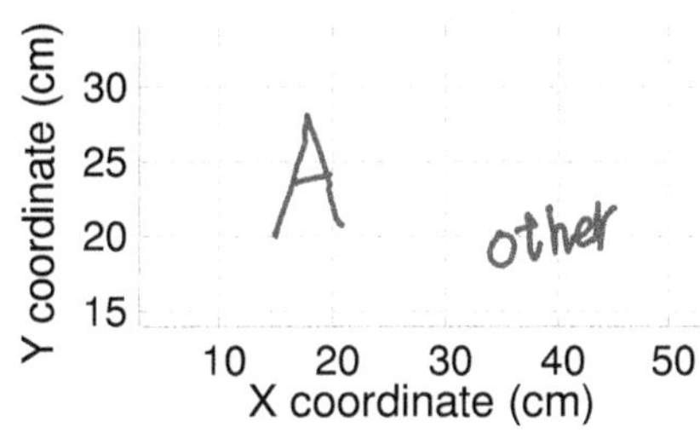

Figure 31: mTrack example of letter and word.

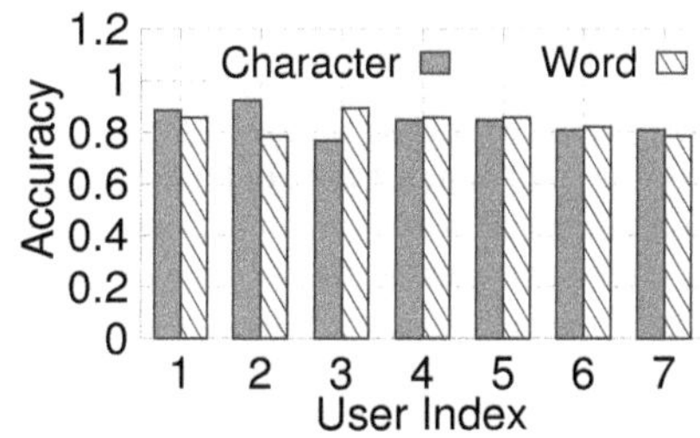

Figure 32: Character and word recognition accuracy.

is more likely to create sharp peak along certain direction, thus disturbing APA.

Figure 23 shows the anchor positioning performance. When beam steering granularity is high (*e.g.*, $\leq 4°$), mTrack has a small direction estimation error (around $1°$) even without background subtraction. This is because the pen is closer to the antennas and generates stronger reflection than the background cup. Their reflection peaks can thus be reliably distinguished through fine-grained scanning. However, with coarser steering granularity, their peaks tend to merge, leading to an increasing error. Fortunately, background subtraction effectively mitigates the impact of background reflection, hence reducing the estimation error by 50%.

Figure 24 shows the APA performance under human movement as dynamic background. Human movement at 2m away from receiver does not affect positioning error, since reflecting RSS from human body is much weaker than pen. Estimation error without background subtraction increases to $2.8°$ when human stands close to receive antenna. However, background subtraction can still consistently reduce positioning error even under human movement.

8.1.3 Joint Performance of Tracking and APA.

Recall APA facilitates phase tracking through opportunistic calibration. In this experiment, we verify the effectiveness of this joint execution. The target pen moves along a *circular* trajectory of radius 7 cm. mTrack continuously runs phase tracking, and performs the k/θ-test (Section 6) every 2 seconds. It invokes APA calibration if the test dictates so. Figure 25 shows the tracking error at every 2-second check point. Without APA calibration, the phase tracking error steadily accumulates over time and reaches 46 *cm* when moving 150 cm continuously along the circle. In contrast, APA calibration caps the phase tracking error below 10 *mm* across 90% of the trajectory.

8.2 Performance on a Trackpad

We now evaluate mTrack's performance in a real trackpad application. The experiments are conducted in an office environment with natural background (drywall, metal cabinet, a user, and occasional human walking by). A $50cm \times 50cm$ writing region is created on a wood table. To test the precision of APA in locating anchoring points, the user rests the pen tip on 40 random locations, ensuring the bottom part of the pen is exposed to the antennas. mTrack steers the antennas with granularity of $8°$. To test phase tracking, the user draws 10 circles and 10 triangles (with 20 *cm* perimeter) following printed trajectories in the normal hand-writing speed. Since human-hand deformation will affect phase tracking, testers hold the middle portion of pen, while directional antennas point to the bottom portion. Due to lack of timing-synchronization between user writing trajectory and tracking estimation, we approximate the tracking error as the minimum projection distance from mTrack's location estimation to the trajectory.

Types of writing objects. We evaluate APA for 3 writing objects of different reflectivity: metal-surfaced pen, plastic marker, and wood pencil (Figure 15(b)). Our benchmark measurement shows that, at 40 away from the transmit/receive antenna, the SNR of signals reflected by these objects are 12.3 dB, 10.1 dB and 4.7 dB, respectively. Figure 26 plots the APA error distribution, which shows 90-percentile error of 2 *cm*, 4 *cm* and 16 *cm*, respectively. Obviously, *object with strong reflectivity enables APA to easily combat noise, thus achieving higher precision.* Note that the APA precision for pen is lower than the benchmark test in Section 8.1.2, mainly because the presence of user's hand creates more uncertainties.

Remarkably, mTrack's phase-tracking algorithm demonstrates the high accuracy in this trackpad application (Figure 27). The 90-percentile errors for pen, marker and pencil are 8 *mm*, 11 *mm* and 4.8 *cm* respectively.

Localization/tracking error across a large region. Distance between the target and the receiver determines the reflected signal strength and hence may affect mTrack's accuracy. The transmitter and receivers are placed at coordinates (100, 100) *cm*, (50, 100)*cm* and (100, 50)*cm*, respectively. To quantify such location-dependent error, we partition the writing area into $10cm \times 10cm$ squares, and repeat the previous precision test on each square. Figure 28 and 29 plot the APA and phase-tracking error across all squares within a $90cm \times 90cm$ region.

When the pen is close to both receivers (distance $< 60cm$), mTrack can achieve high accuracy with APA/tracking error of <1.5 *cm* and <8 *mm*, respectively. Accuracy starts degrading when the tar-

Event	Touch	Lift	Click	ND
Touch	94.0%	0	0	6.0%
Lift	0	93.5%	0	6.5%
Click	0	0	94.8%	5.2%

Table 3: Classification accuracy. ND is not detected.

get moves over 70 *cm* away from receiver, and hence SNR drops. Nonetheless, the tracking error is still within 1.5 *cm* even when the target is 90 *cm* from the receiver. mmWave attenuates to almost noise floor at 100 cm owing to high pathloss of mmWave signals. We expect at least two ways of scaling the writing region: increasing the transmit power, and placing more receivers along the x- and y-axis. We leave such exploration for future work.

Accuracy of touch event detection. To verify mTrack's event detection algorithm, we recruit 7 users to perform the "touch", "lift" and "click" gestures on the writing region using a pen. Each user first provides a 10-sample training set to find the best threshold H (Sec. 7), and then repeat each gesture for 50 times to test the detection algorithm. Table 3 shows the confusion matrix of gesture detection among all users, and Figure 30 plots the detection accuracy of each users over all events. The detection accuracy of all three types of events is around 94% and does not vary noticeably across users. Notably, the event misclassification rate is 0, indicating that the RSS based approach can reliably discriminate different gesture events owing to the highly directional beams. The miss detection of events is mainly due to the variation of users' touching speed, which may not always be consistent with the training set.

8.3 Application of mTrack

We integrate mTrack with a word recognition application to showcase its potential in computer-human interaction. In specific, we record the writing trace from mTrack word by word, and then export the trace to control the mouse on a PC that runs the MyScript Stylus [40] word recognition software. mTrack's event detector is used to segment the connections between characters in a word. Figure 31 shows two examples when we use mTrack to track the character/word trajectory, which exhibit high fidelity even if each character spans only 1 or 2 *cm*.

We further recruit 7 users to each write 100 random characters and 50 words using metal-surfaced pen on a 15 cm× 15cm writing region. The words are randomly picked from the standard MacKenzie set [41], which well represents the usage frequency of English words. Figure 32 plots the recognition accuracy across users. The accuracy for both character and word ranges from 81 to 89% across users. Users also perform the same test on a real trackpad, and the recognition accuracy is from 88 to 92%, which shows that mTrack's performance is close to the trackpad. Considering the potential penetration of portable millimeter-wave radios [8, 9], we believe mTrack holds potential as a new form of "in-situ" transcription system.

9. DISCUSSION

Object shape and size. mTrack is designed to track writing objects of small size, like pen or marker, which can be approximated as a point reflector, because their dimension (with diameter $\approx 1cm$) is much smaller than its distance to the antennas ($> 20cm$). Objects with deformable shape or large size, *e.g.* human hand and body, do not possess these properties, and hence cannot use mTrack's model-driven tracking algorithm. Similarly, mTrack can not differentiate phase change due to large hand-shape deformation. Thus, users need to keep a relatively consistent hand shape when writing to avoid confusing the tracking algorithm. They also need to ensure a sizable part of the pen is exposed to the Tx/Rx to reflect the mmWave signals.

Phased-Array Antennas. Due to hardware limitation, we are only able to evaluate our concept with directional antennas. Beam pattern of a horn antenna differs slightly from that of an 802.11ad phase-array in two aspects: *(i)* The beamwidth of a phased-array is dependent on steering direction. For example, for a linear antenna array, beamwidth along 0° direction can be twice of that along 90° [30]. However, since beamforming codebook is predefined and known, we can still compensate the gain distortion of discrete sampling. The systematic solution to this problem will be left for our future work. *(ii)* Sidelobes of a phased array may be relatively large compared with that of a directional horn antenna. Sidelobes may capture signals from undesired directions. However, since they usually have much smaller gain compared to the main lobe, as long as there is a RSS peak when pointing to the target, mTrack's beam-steering based APA mechanism can still work.

Tracking multiple objects. mTrack can be potentially extended to track multiple targets simultaneously. When the objects are sufficiently separated, and not falling in the same beam direction, the receiver radios can steer the beam towards different objects in a time-interleaving manner and update their tracking trajectories sequentially. Further exploration of this idea is left for our future work.

10. CONCLUSION

We have presented mTrack, a high precision passive object tracking system that uses 60 GHz signals as sensing medium. mTrack takes advantage of the short wavelength and steerable directional beams of 802.11ad-like 60 GHz radio devices, and uses subtle RSS/phase variation to track passive writing objects on a trackpad-like area. It can track a pen at sub-centimeter level accuracy, which even outperforms existing systems that use radio-instrumented objects. Considering the growing popularity of 60 GHz devices, we believe mTrack can potentially open up a wide range of mobile sensing applications.

Acknowledgement

We appreciate the constructive comments from anonymous reviewers. The work reported in this paper was supported in part by the NSF under Grant CNS-1318292, CNS-1343363, CNS-1350039 and CNS-1404613.

11. REFERENCES

[1] J. P. Wachs, M. Kölsch, H. Stern, and Y. Edan, "Vision-based Hand-gesture Applications," *Communications of the ACM*, vol. 54, no. 2, 2011.

[2] K. McElhearn, "Leap motion controller fails in normal conditions," http://www.mcelhearn.com/not-a-review-leap-motioncontroller-fails-in-normal-conditions/, 2014.

[3] "RoboRealm: Microsoft Kinect." http://www.roborealm.com/help/Microsoft Kinect.php, 2013.

[4] Q. Pu, S. Gupta, S. Gollakota, and S. Patel, "Whole-home Gesture Recognition using Wireless Signals," in *ACM MobiCom*, 2013.

[5] P. Melgarejo, X. Zhang, P. Ramanathan, and D. Chu, "Leveraging Directional Antenna Capabilities for Fine-grained Gesture Recognition," in *ACM UbiComp*, 2014.

[6] L. Yang, Y. Chen, X.-Y. Li, C. Xiao, M. Li, and Y. Liu, "Tagoram: Real-time Tracking of Mobile RFID Tags to High Precision using COTS Devices," in *ACM MobiCom*, 2014.

[7] "IEEE 802.11ad PHY Specifications: Enhancements for Very High Throughput in the 60 GHz Band," 2012.

[8] Dailywireless, "60 GHz Backhaul for Small Cells," 2013. [Online]. Available: http://www.dailywireless.org/2014/01/03/60ghz-backhaul-for-small-cells/

[9] PC Magazine, "Wilocity Unveils Blazing Fast 802.11ad Smartphone Wi-Fi Chip," 2014. [Online]. Available: http://www.pcmag.com/article2/0,2817,2454187,00.asp

[10] J. Wang, D. Vasisht, and D. Katabi, "RF-IDraw: Virtual Touch Screen in the Air using RF Signals," in *ACM SIGCOMM*, 2014.

[11] N. Patwari, L. Brewer, Q. Tate, O. Kaltiokallio, and M. Bocca, "Breathfinding: A Wireless Network That Monitors and Locates Breathing in a Home," *JSAC*, vol. 8, no. 1, 2014.

[12] C. Xu, B. Firner, R. S. Moore, Y. Zhang, W. Trappe, R. Howard, F. Zhang, and N. An, "SCPL: Indoor Device-free Multi-subject Counting and Localization Using Radio Signal Strength," in *Proc. of ACM/IEEE IPSN*, 2013.

[13] F. Adib and D. Katabi, "See Through Walls with WiFi!" in *Proc. of ACM SIGCOMM*, 2013.

[14] F. Adib, Z. Kabelac, D. Katabi, and R. C. Miller, "3D Tracking via Body Radio Reflections," in *Proc. of USENIX NSDI*, 2014.

[15] A. Edelstein and M. Rabbat, "Background Subtraction for Online Calibration of Baseline RSS in RF Sensing Networks," *CoRR*, vol. abs/1207.1137, 2012.

[16] A. Maltsev and R. Maslennikov and A. Sevastyanov and A. Lomayev and A. Khoryaev, "Statistical Channel Model for 60 GHz WLAN Systems in Conference Room Environment," in *Proc. of European Conference on Antennas and Propagation*, 2010.

[17] "VICON." http://www.vicon.com/.

[18] H. Wang, S. Sen, A. Elgohary, M. Farid, M. Youssef, and R. R. Choudhury, "No Need to War-drive: Unsupervised Indoor Localization," ser. ACM MobiSys, 2012.

[19] S. Sen, B. Radunovic, and et al, "Spot Localization using PHY Layer Information," in *ACM MobiSys*, 2012.

[20] H. Liu, Y. Gan, J. Yang, S. Sidhom, Y. Wang, Y. Chen, and F. Ye, "Push the Limit of WiFi Based Localization for Smartphones," in *ACM MobiCom*, 2012.

[21] H. Fang, "60 GHz RSS Localization with Omni-directional and Horn Antennas," Ph.D. dissertation, 2010.

[22] J. Nanzer, *Microwave and millimeter-wave remote sensing for security applications.* Artech House, 2012.

[23] G. Ossberger, T. Buchegger, E. Schimback, A. Stelzer, and R. Weigel, "Non-invasive respiratory movement detection and monitoring of hidden humans using ultra wideband pulse radar," in *Conference on Ultrawideband Systems and Technologies*, 2004.

[24] M. Youssef, M. Mah, and A. Agrawala, "Challenges: Device-free Passive Localization for Wireless Environments," in *Proc. of ACM MobiCom*, 2007.

[25] B. Wei, A. Varshney, W. Hu, N. Patwari, and C. T. Chou, "dRTI: Directional RadioTomographic Imaging," *CoRR*, vol. abs/1402.2744, 2014.

[26] Huang, Donny and Nandakumar, Rajalakshmi and Gollakota, Shyamnath, "Feasibility and Limits of Wi-Fi Imaging," in *ACM SenSys*, 2014.

[27] Y. Zhu, Y. Zhu, Z. Zhang, B. Y. Zhao, and H. Zheng, "60ghz mobile imaging radar," ser. HotMobile '15, 2015.

[28] "TDK IS-005A RF Absorber," http://www.tdk.com/.

[29] K. Abbas, "A new recurrent approach for phase unwrapping," *International Journal of Applied Science and Engineering*, 2005.

[30] J. Wang, Z. Lan, C.-S. Sum, and et al, "Beamforming Codebook Design and Performance Evaluation for 60GHz Wideband WPANs," in *IEEE Vehicular Technology Conference*, 2009.

[31] J. Nanzer, *Microwave and Millimeter-Wave Remote Sensing for Security Applications.* Artech House, 2012.

[32] P. V. Nikitin, R. Martinez, S. Ramamurthy, H. Leland, G. Spiess, and K. Rao, "Phase based spatial identification of UHF RFID tags," in *IEEE International Conference on RFID*, 2010.

[33] J. LindstrÃűm, H. Kokko, and E. Ranta, "Detecting Periodicity in Short and Noisy Time Series Data," *Oikos*, vol. 78, no. 2, 1997.

[34] A. Valdes-Garcia, S. Reynolds, A. Natarajan, D. Kam, D. Liu, J.-W. Lai, Y.-L. Huang, P.-Y. Chen, M.-D. Tsai, J.-H. Zhan *et al.*, "Single-element and phased-array transceiver chipsets for 60-GHz Gb/s communications," *Communications Magazine, IEEE*, 2011.

[35] I. H. Witten and E. Frank, *Data Mining: Practical Machine Learning Tools and Techniques.* Morgan Kaufmann Publishers, 2005.

[36] Rice University, "Wireless Open-Access Research Platform," http://warp.rice.edu/trac/wiki, 2013.

[37] "Vubiq 60GHz System," http://vubiq.com/v60wgd03/, 2014.

[38] "Axis360 Motion Control System," http://cinetics.com/two-axis360/.

[39] A. Waheed and A. Ashik, "Mitigation of Phase Noise at Millimeter-Wave Frequencies for Wireless Personal Area Network Applications," *Masters Theses*, 2008.

[40] "MyScript technology," http://myscript.com/technology/, 2015.

[41] I. S. MacKenzie and R. W. Soukoreff, "Phrase Sets for Evaluating Text Entry Techniques," in *ACM CHI Extended Abstracts*, 2003.

APPENDIX

A. PROOF OF EQUATION (4)

In this section, we derive the rationale behind background removal as stated in Equation (4). For clarity, we introduce the following notations: $\theta_1 = \Delta \arg(\overrightarrow{S}_{trg})_{t-1}^{t}$, $\theta_2 = \Delta \arg(\overrightarrow{S}_{trg})_{t}^{t+1}$, and $\theta_3 = \arg(\overrightarrow{S}_{trg}^{t+1} - \overrightarrow{S}_{trg}^{t}) - \arg(\overrightarrow{S}_{trg}^{t} - \overrightarrow{S}_{trg}^{t-1})$. Since the target's reflection signal strength remains similar among three consecutive samples, the two triangles in solid line of Figure 9 can be considered as isosceles triangles. Following the geometrical relation, we have:

$$\frac{\pi - \theta_1}{2} + \frac{\pi - \theta_2}{2} + \theta_3 = \pi,$$

or equivalently $\theta_3 = \frac{\theta_1 + \theta_2}{2}$, which proves Equation (4). □

Acoustic Eavesdropping through Wireless Vibrometry

Teng Wei[†], Shu Wang[†], Anfu Zhou[*†] and Xinyu Zhang[†]
[†]University of Wisconsin - Madison, [*]Institute of Computing Technology, Chinese Academy of Sciences
{twei7, swang367, azhou9}@wisc.edu, xyzhang@ece.wisc.edu

ABSTRACT

Loudspeakers are widely used in conferencing and infotainment systems. Private information leakage from loudspeaker sound is often assumed to be preventable using sound-proof isolators like walls. In this paper, we explore a new acoustic eavesdropping attack that can subvert such protectors using radio devices. Our basic idea lies in an acoustic-radio transformation (ART) algorithm, which recovers loudspeaker sound by inspecting the subtle disturbance it causes to the radio signals generated by an adversary or by its co-located WiFi transmitter. ART builds on a modeling framework that distills key factors to determine the recovered audio quality. It incorporates diversity mechanisms and noise suppression algorithms that can boost the eavesdropping quality. We implement the ART eavesdropper on a software-radio platform and conduct experiments to verify its feasibility and threat level. When targeted at vanilla PC or smartphone loudspeakers, the attacker can successfully recover high-quality audio even when blocked by sound-proof walls. On the other hand, we propose several pragmatic countermeasures that can effectively reduce the attacker's audio recovery quality by orders of magnitude.

Categories and Subject Descriptors

C.3 [**Special-Purpose and Application-Based Systems**]: [Signal processing systems]

Keywords

Acoustic Eavesdropping; Acoustic-radio Transformation; WiFi Sensing; Vibration Sensing

1. INTRODUCTION

Despite powerful security-proof measures in this digital communication age, sound – the primitive medium of unencrypted human communication and side-product of many private activities – remains a vulnerable source of information leakage. The pursuit for high-fidelity sound capturing has motivated more powerful acoustic hardware on consumer devices. Meanwhile, it creates a looming threat of acoustic eavesdropping that impinges on people's everyday privacy [1]. Even subtle acoustic emanation from keystrokes [2], printers [3], and PC electronic components [4], can be exploited to decode sensitive information. However, such acoustic attacks all require a tampered microphone in the vicinity of the victim sound source which, to some extent, thwarts eavesdroppers who cannot approach the target's physical space.

We explore a new eavesdropping mechanism that uses wireless transceivers to decode loudspeaker sounds from afar. Our basic idea lies in a translation between acoustic vibration and radio signal fluctuation. Audio emission causes small vibration of the loudspeaker body. Such minute motion pattern is invisible to human eyes. But it can resonance with radio waves reflected by the loudspeaker, or originating from a wireless transmitter co-located with the loudspeaker. The contaminated radio waves can be captured by a tampered receiver and processed to recover the original audio played by the loudspeaker. We refer to such a remote sound acquisition/recovery system as *wireless vibrometry*.

Built on commonly available radio devices, and harnessing the better penetration of radio signals, such an acoustic eavesdropping system raises alarming issues in security and privacy. Today, loudspeakers are widely used in communication and infotainment systems, *e.g.*, tele-conference call, VoIP hangout and home theater. In such usage scenarios, we envision two categories of threats, categorized according to how the target loudspeaker modulates the radio waves: *(i) Reflective vibrometry:* The adversary is a pair of radio transmitter and receiver. The transmitter continuously sends radio signals, while the receiver decodes sound vibration from the signals reflected and disturbed by the loudspeaker vibration. *(ii) Emissive vibrometry:* The adversary is a radio receiver. The target loudspeaker is co-located with a WiFi radio on the same platform, *e.g.*, a smartphone, smart TV, or speaker dock. The loudspeaker's minute motion causes tiny variation in the WiFi radio's outgoing signals, which can be overheard and leveraged by the adversary to recover the sound.

The concept underlying wireless vibrometry resembles laser radar (LADAR) [5], which is commonly used to test the stability of building structures. A LADAR projects laser beams towards vibrating objects and discerns the vibration patterns based on the shaking reflective beams. In contrast, the unique advantage of wireless vibrometry lies in its ability to penetrate opaque obstacles. This advantage comes with more challenges. The narrow field-of-view of LADAR enables them to measure even micron movements very accurately, because tiny motion can alter the reflecting angle. In contrast, radio devices are far less directive and suffer from severe reflection/diffusive loss. More importantly, under the aforementioned threat scenarios, adversary's radios may not even fall in the line-of-sight (LOS) of the victim loudspeaker and cannot "point" towards the vibrating loudspeaker.

In lieu of such challenges, we explore a new set of mechanisms to extract and boost the acoustic signals from radio channel dynamics.

(i) Basic acoustic-radio transformation (ART) algorithm, which harnesses the received signal strength (RSS) and phase information, readily available on typical radio transceivers [6], to "demodulate" acoustic signals from the target loudspeaker. Our basic idea is to model the procedure of audio vibration disturbing radio waves as a procedure of low-rate amplitude/phase modulation. With this model, we design a frequency-domain demodulator to isolate irrele-

MobiCom'15, September 7–11, 2015, Paris, France.

ACM 978-1-4503-3619-2/15/09 ...$15.00.
http://dx.doi.org/10.1145/2789168.2790119.

vant radio signal components, extrapolate the audio signals, project them to the time-domain, which eventually become perceptible by human.

(ii) Diversity mechanisms to enhance reflective vibrometry. Whereas LADAR essentially discriminates the displacement of vibrating surface, we found that wireless vibrometry is mostly sensitive to the multipath overlapping patterns, with both analytical and experimental evidence. We design two diversity mechanisms to take advantage of this effect, so as to amplify the loudspeaker vibration.

First, we design a simple frequency selection mechanism to foster the case where multiple signal paths involving loudspeaker reflection can strengthen each other. *Second*, we adapt multi-antenna beamforming to amplify the signal paths reflected by the loudspeaker. Since loudspeaker cannot provide any location or anchoring signals to facilitate the MIMO beamforming, we adopt the strategy of *blind beamforming* that coherently combines the signals on multiple antennas, without prior knowledge of target. In addition to receiving beamforming similar to [7,8], we take advantage of transmit beamforming gain through a role-switching mechanism.

(iii) RSS sampling and amplification mechanisms for emissive vibrometry. We design packet processing algorithms to extrapolate RSS values from legacy WiFi packets emitted by uncontrolled wireless devices. Consequently, we can reduce the RSS noise by orders of magnitude, thereby substantially amplifying the tiny radio RSS disturbance caused by the target's audio vibration.

The feasibility and effectiveness of the above approaches is verified through a software-radio based eavesdropper implementation, for both the reflective and emissive vibrometry. Through comprehensive experiments, we identify various practical factors, such as spatial separation, obstacle blockage, loudspeaker model, and environment dynamics, that determine the threat level. The results demonstrate that a basic wireless vibrometry setup, with eavesdropper placed close to the loudspeaker, can easily transform acoustic vibration into quality sounds. Using a combination of the diversity mechanisms, the eavesdropper can decode the loudspeaker's sound from 5 *m* apart, even with a sound-proof wall in between. In emissive vibrometry, the eavesdropper can decode the audio from unmodified WiFi devices with loudspeakers, at a much higher level of fidelity owing to high radio signal power emitted (instead of reflected) by the target.

These results pose alarming challenges to securing acoustic information. Using sound-proof walls is no longer effective, and even a radio shield may not work because the eavesdropper can attack from a wide range of radio frequencies. However, we show that several pragmatic counter-measures may make the eavesdropping significantly hard and thwart adversaries. In particular, we analytically provide a guideline of safety distance for a reflective victim and propose PHY-layer power randomization mechanisms for an emissive victim, which can reduce the eavesdropper's recovered audio quality by orders of magnitude. The impact of nearby human movement is also quatitatively evaluated through experiments. Slow and minor movement, *e.g.*, breathing, has negligible influence on the ART attack; Rapid larger-scale body movement, *e.g.*, walking, will considerably undermine the eavesdropping quality.

Contributions. In contrast to prior laser or vision based approaches [5,9] to remote acoustic sensing, this work is the first to thoroughly investigate vibrometry on wireless devices, from both theoretical and experimental perspectives. We design a simple ART algorithm to decode remote acoustic vibration on loudspeakers by monitoring the reflective/emissive radio signals disturbed by the loudspeakers. Through an analytical framework and extensive experiments, we distill the key factors that enable highly sensitive WiFi vibrometry, and empower the vibrometry with a blind beamforming and frequency selection framework. The enhancement techniques share similar spirit with diversity mechanisms in wireless communications, but a wireless link can use known preambles to synchronize/train the transmitter/receiver channel. From a security/privacy perspective, we are the first to examine the factors that determine how threatening wireless vibrometry can be when applied in acoustic eavesdropping in practice, and to propose countermeasures.

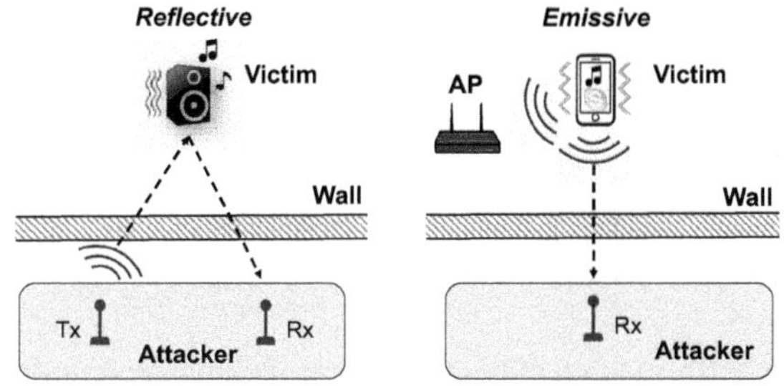

Figure 1: Two threat models based on wireless vibrometry: *Reflective and Emissive.*

2. WIRELESS VIBROMETRY: AN OVERVIEW

In this section, we brief the basic assumptions behind wireless vibrometry, given its two targeted scenarios (Figure 1). In general, both scenarios involve an eavesdropper (also referred to as attacker or adversary) and a target (or victim) loudspeaker. The target is assumed to be static. The eavesdropper controls radio transceivers that can run at a specific frequency band, with a practical transmit power level. The eavesdropping radios can be compromised devices within LOS of the target, or unfettered devices that are separated from the target by *sound-proof* obstacles (walls, windows, *etc.*). In any case, the eavesdropper can transmit/capture radio signals, but has no direct control over the target. However, as long as the eavesdropper's radio signals can reach the target, wireless vibrometry is feasible. Specifically, we explore a set of solutions, colloquially referred to as *audio-radio transformation* (ART), to enable wireless vibrometry.

(i) Basic ART (Sec. 3) directly decodes audio by processing the RSS/phase of radio signals disturbed by the loudspeaker. It is the basic decoding mechanism for both reflective and emissive vibrometry.

(ii) Enhanced reflective ART (Sec. 4) works in the reflective vibrometry scenario, where the adversary sends single-tone radio signals, and captures the signals reflected by the loudspeaker body. This enhanced mechanism harnesses diversity mechanisms, including multi-antenna blind beamforming and frequency selection to maximize the threat.

(iii) Enhanced emissive ART (Sec. 5) works in the emissive vibrometry scenario, where the target loudspeaker and a WiFi radio are co-located in the same device. The adversary captures the target's outgoing WiFi packets, extrapolates the RSS, and executes a set of amplification algorithms to enhance the decoded audio quality. Here the adversary has no knowledge about the target's WiFi radio identity and does not need to decode the actual content of the packets.

We will further propose countermeasures against ART in Sec. 6.

3. BASIC ART

In this section, we model wireless vibrometry as a process where audio vibrations modulate the radio signal magnitude/phase. Then we describe the basic acoustic-radio transformation (ART) algo-

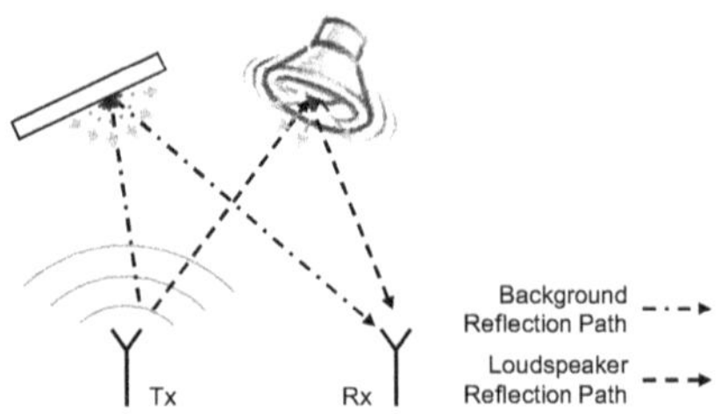

Figure 2: Illustration of loudspeaker modulation and multipath effects of reflective radio vibrometry.

rithm as the reverse demodulation process. We focus on reflective vibrometry, since the emissive vibrometry is a simplified special case. We further conduct experiments to evaluate the feasibility of ART, and identify the potential design knobs that warrant an enhanced ART.

3.1 Modeling Audio-Radio Frequency Translation

Let's consider a simple Line-of-Sight (LOS) scenario illustrated in Figure 2, where an adversary's radio Tx broadcasts wireless signals. Some of the signals undergo multipath reflections on the loudspeaker's surface. Part of the reflected signals will eventually be captured by the Rx. When the loudspeaker surface is vibrating, it will modulate the RSS and phase of reflected signal accordingly.

We first assume the loudspeaker is playing a mono sound with single frequency ω. The loudspeaker membrane and surface resonates and vibrates at the same frequency ω. Suppose the vibration displaces its surface by $d(t)$ at time t:

$$d(t) = k \sin(\omega t + \theta), \tag{1}$$

where k is the vibration magnitude, determined by the sound volume, and θ is the initial phase of sound. For simplicity, we omit the time index t of functions in later notations. Hence, $d \equiv d(t)$.

(a) Impact of vibration on radio RSS: We model the RSS of signals reflected from loudspeaker as:

$$RSS_L = \sigma A^2(d_O + \hat{d}), \tag{2}$$

where $\hat{d} = d \cos \beta$, β being the angle between vibration direction and reflection direction. d_O denotes the distance between antenna and loudspeaker. σ is the reflectivity (reflection gain) of loudspeaker surface ($0 < \sigma < 1$). $A(\cdot)$ is the channel gain function (equivalent to $1/pathloss$). The square operation over $A(\cdot)$ models the attenuation of signals due to round-trip propagation: one for path from Tx to loudspeaker and the other for path from loudspeaker to Rx. The loudspeaker surface is considered as a virtual transmitter that emits reflected signals.

For clarity, here we only consider the direct reflection path from loudspeaker. The analysis can easily incorporate the secondary-order reflection signals. The function $A(\cdot)$ can be assumed to follow any classical pathloss models in communications theory, *e.g.* free-space or log-normal [10]. Owing to continuity of the pathloss, we can expand Eq. (2) following Taylor's theorem:

$$RSS_L = \sigma[A^2(d_O) + 2A(d_O)A'(d_O)\hat{d} + \cdots + o(d_O)\hat{d}^k], \tag{3}$$

in which $A'(\cdot)$ is the first order derivative, and $o(d_O)$ is the Peano form of remainder.

The first term $A^2(d_O)$ is the DC component (carrier signals sent by the radio) and can be filtered out by a DC filter. The second term $2A(d_O)A'(d_O)\hat{d}$ carries the sound frequency components, and $2A(d_O)A'(d_O)$ can be considered as the *sensitivity*, or *gain* of audio-to-radio transformation. All remaining terms are the harmonic components of audio frequency. Eq. (3) implies that *the magnitude of harmonic frequencies is determined by the linearity of path loss function $A(\cdot)$ w.r.t. to distance.* The larger the path loss exponent, the more non-linear $A(\cdot)$ will be, and thus the stronger the harmonic becomes.

(b) Impact of vibration on radio signal phase: Assuming the adversary's Tx transmits a mono tone signal with frequency f_r, and up-modulated to carrier frequency f_O (with wavelength λ_O). Then, the phase can be expressed as signal path length divided by wavelength:

$$Phase_L = \frac{2\pi(d_O + 2\hat{d})}{\lambda_O} + \gamma \tag{4}$$

where γ is the initial phase of reflection path. The $\frac{4\pi\hat{d}}{\lambda_O}$ term contains the audio frequency from loudspeaker.

The above two sets of analysis imply that the *sensitivity of vibrometry is determined by the following factors*: *(i)* The vibration direction β relative to the reflection signal direction. The closer β is to 0, the stronger the vibrometry effect will be. *(ii)* The volume of the sound that determines the magnitude of displacement d, and hence the strength of vibrometry. *(iii)* The radio's carrier frequency f_O or wavelength λ_O. In addition, for RSS based vibrometry, the strength is proportional to the reflectivity of the loudspeaker surface σ, and inversely proportional to the distance d_O between radio adversary and the loudspeaker victim.

The emissive vibrometry model is similar, except that the signal source comes directly from the radio antenna vibrating together with the loudspeaker. We thus omit the details.

3.2 Demodulating the Transformed Audio

We proceed to design a basic ART that can demodulate the loudspeaker's audio out of the reflected radio waves. We focus on demodulation using the radio RSS (Eq. (2)), but the technique can be easily extended to phase based recovery.

Several challenges emerge here. First, the reflected signals become extremely weak as attacker-victim distance d_O increases beyond a few meters. Second, the vibration magnitude d of the loudspeaker surface falls within sub-millimeter scale [11]. The variation it causes to the radio signal is orders of magnitude lower than the signal power itself. Third, the leakage signal directly coming from the adversary's Tx to Rx, and reflections from irrelevant background objects, can overwhelm the signals modulated by the loudspeaker alone.

Algorithm 1 Decoding the audio that is modulated by ART

INPUT: received radio samples $y[t]$
OUTPUT: recovered audio samples $d^*[s]$
/*Get one audio sample from every m radio samples*/
foreach segment s in set $[0{:}S)$
  $y_s \leftarrow y[sm+1, (s+1)m]$ /*Segment radio signals*/
  $z(v) \leftarrow \sum_{u=1}^{m} y_s(u) e^{\frac{-i2\pi vu}{m}}$ /*FFT analysis*/
  $g(s) \leftarrow |\frac{z(\lfloor \frac{f_r}{f_b} \times m \rfloor)}{m}|^2$ /*Pick RSS of CW's freq.*/
endforeach
$d^* \leftarrow filter_{bandpass}(g)$ /*Filter out the DC component*/

To address the challenges, we exploit a unique feature inside the audio-modulated radio signals, *i.e.*, the radio sampling rate is far beyond the audio frequency. Thus, we can enforce an averaging on the oversampled signals so as to amplify and promote the audio out of noise. In addition, we observe that the leakage and background signals are typically quasi-stationary compared to the audio vibration, and thus can be isolated from the ART signals through proper filtering. Algorithm 1 formalizes our basic decoder that incorporates these solutions. Below we detail the key steps.

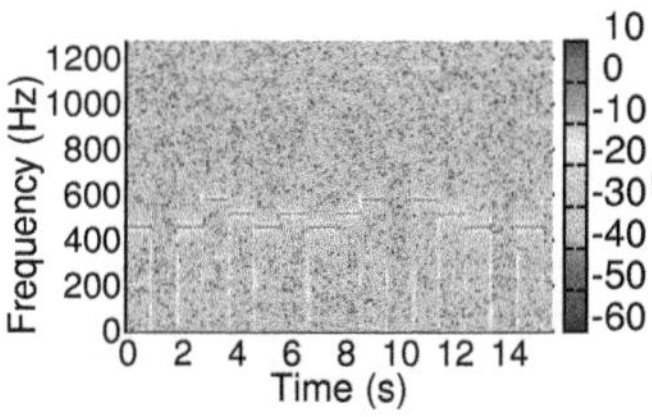

Figure 3: Decoding a sequence of piano sounds.

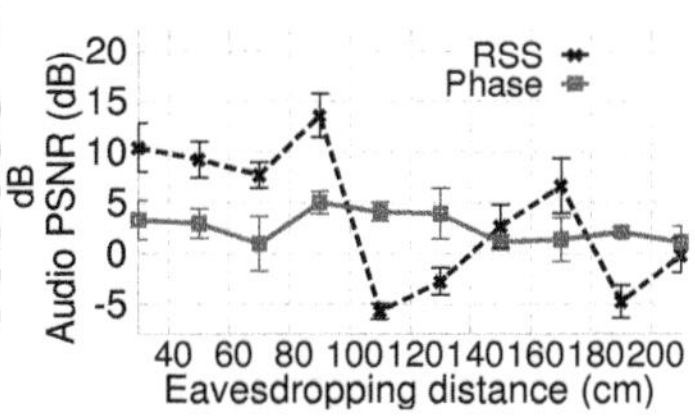

Figure 4: Audio PSNR over various distances to loudspeaker.

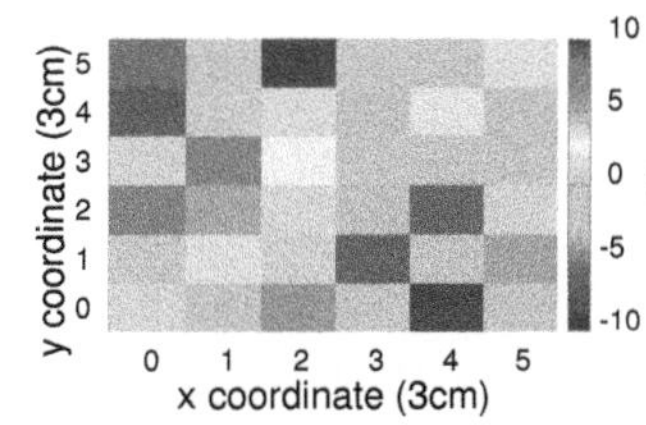

Figure 5: Audio PSNR over various locations of antenna.

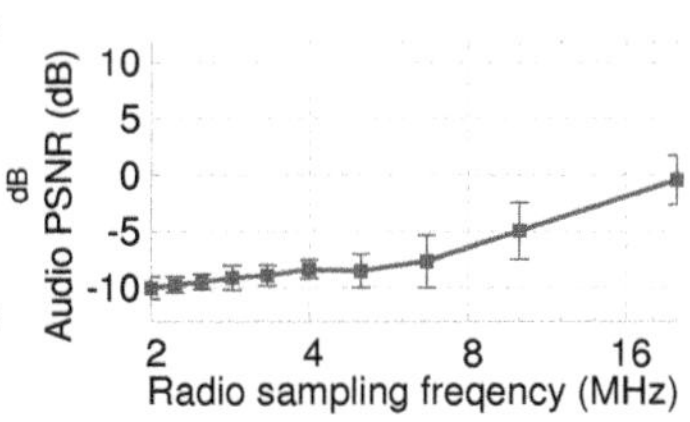

Figure 6: PSNR over different radio sampling frequencies.

Capturing audio-modulated radio samples: The eavesdropper transmits a baseband continuous wave (CW) with frequency f_r, comprised of T samples:

$$x(t) = \sin(2\pi f_r t), \quad t \in [0, T). \tag{5}$$

Meanwhile, the loudspeaker vibrates following Eq. (1). Based on the RSS modulation model in Eq. (3), we approximate the received radio samples as follows,

$$y(t) = \sqrt{RSS_L(t) + RSS_e}\, x(t) + n(t), t \in [0, T) \tag{6}$$

where $RSS_L(t)$ and RSS_e are signal strengths reflected from loudspeaker and relatively stationary objects in the environment. $n(t)$ is the noise. For clarity, we have omitted the phase term of signal components from multipaths.

Segmenting the samples: We divide all T radio samples into S segments, each containing m samples. Since audio vibrates at a much lower rate, audio signals within any small segment of radio samples can be considered stationary. Thus, we have $RSS_L(sm) \approx RSS_L(sm+u), \forall u \in [0, m)$ and $s \in [0, S)$. For the sth segment y_s, we can approximate the *u-th* sample inside as:

$$y_s(u) \approx \sqrt{RSS_L(s) + RSS_e}\, x(sm+u) + n_s(u), \tag{7}$$

where $n_s(u) \triangleq n(sm+u)$. Samples in each segment are regarded as single-tone radio signals modulated by an audio of constant amplitude, plus a stationary component and noise.

Signal processing – time-frequency domain translation: To extract the amplitude modulated on top of radio signal, we apply the discrete Fourier transform (DFT) on each segment y_s. The resulting sequence of DFT coefficients is given by:

$$z(v) = \sum_{u=1}^{m} y_s(u) e^{-i2\pi vu/m}, \qquad v \in [0, m). \tag{8}$$

Since the transmitted signals is a single-tone of frequency f_r, we only need to inspect the coefficient of that frequency bin, and extrapolate the audio signal strength within this radio segment:

$$g(s) = |\frac{z(v^*)}{m}|^2 = RSS_L(s) + RSS_e \tag{9}$$

where $v^* = \left\lfloor \frac{f_r}{f_b} \times m \right\rfloor$ denotes the frequency-bin index of f_r, and f_b is the radio receiver's sampling rate.

Repeating the procedure above on all radio samples produces audio signals sampled at rate $\frac{f_b}{m}$. Clearly, a higher radio sampling frequency means a lager audio sampling frequency, which will lead to higher recovered audio quality.

Bandpass filter: The series of $g(s), s \in [0, S)$ still contains the DC component, which originates from background reflections, *e.g.*, the term RSS_e (Eq. (9)), and the term $\sigma A^2(d_0)$ in RSS_L (Eq. (3)). DC component can be eliminated via a bandpass filter. We empirically choose the lower and upper stopping frequencies as 20 Hz and 1500 Hz, which correspond to the range of human voice.

3.3 Feasibility of Basic ART

We have implemented the basic ART demodulator on a software-radio testbed with a custom-built FPGA core (see Sec. 7 for details). In this section, we conduct testbed experiments to verify the key factors that govern the performance of ART, and explore opportunities that warrant improvement.

Our basic experimental setup complies with the foregoing model assumptions. The adversary radio emits a single tone with 5 MHz baseband frequency, carrier-modulated to 2.485 GHz (WiFi channel 14). The target is a PC loudspeaker 2 *m* away. Figure 3 showcases a time-frequency plot of a piano sound decoded using the basic ART. The piano sound has three piano notes of frequencies 440Hz, 493.88Hz and 554.365Hz. We observe a close-to-perfect recovery and the decoded audio is clearly audible. In addition, the result also shows weaker harmonics of audio frequencies (*e.g.*, 880Hz), as predicted by our model.

Audio quality vs. distance: We now vary the distance between the eavesdropper and loudspeaker at steps of 20 *cm*. Peak-Signal-to-Noise-Ratio (PSNR) is a commonly used metric to quantify the decoded audio quality [9]. Note that for single-frequency audio, PSNR above -13dB is typically audible to human, while for multi-frequency audio like human speech, PSNR above 0dB is audible [12]. Here the loudspeaker is forced to play a 400 Hz tone, without loss of generality. For each location, we repeat the experiment 10 times, and plot the mean PSNR in Figure 4.

We make the following observations: *(i)* Either phase or RSS can be used to decode the audio. Moreover, performance of the RSS and phase based decoders does not show clear correlation. However, the highest audio PSNR from RSS is higher than that from phase. *(ii)* There does not exist a monotonic trend between PSNR and range. We suspect this is due to multi-path effects, which deserves a more in-depth investigation.

Audio quality variation over space: We highlight the multipath effect by varying the adversary radio location within a small 15*cm* × 15*cm* region, sampled at 3 cm granularity. Figure 5 shows that *the decoded audio quality is highly sensitive to adversary location*: even with a minor location change of 3 *cm*, the PSNR can differ by up to 10 dB. We will model the root cause and propose an enhanced ART algorithm that exploit this effect in Sec. 4.

Audio quality vs. radio sampling rate: Figure 6 shows that the audio PSNR improves proportionally with radio sampling frequency f_b. Hence, *a wideband eavesdropper presents a higher level of threat.* The frequency of human speech sounds typically falls below 500Hz [13]. To recover human speech, the audio sampling frequency should be at least twofold of the audio's frequency , according to Nyquist sampling theorem. A common WiFi device with 20Mbps bandwidth is good enough for eavesdropping human speech, since $f_a = \frac{20e6}{1024} \approx 19.5$KHz $\gg$ 1KHz, when we use a typical segment length $m = 1024$.

4. ENHANCING REFLECTIVE AUDIO EAVESDROPPING

The above analysis/experiments hint that the performance of ART is closely related with radio signal/channel diversity, which we now explore to enable a more powerful ART for reflective vibrometry.

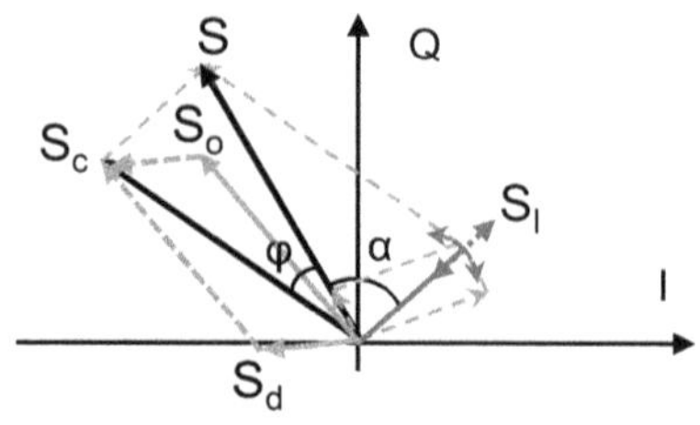

Figure 7: Model of multipath effects in baseband received signals. S_l denotes reflection path from loudspeaker. S_o and S_d represents signal from other objects and LOS path.

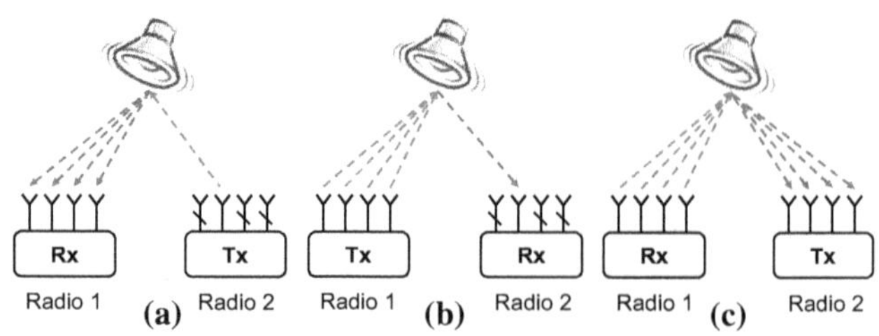

Figure 8: Three stages of role-switching beamforming algorithm. (a) Rx beam-searching (b) Rx-guided Tx beamforming (c) Tx-Rx beamforming.

4.1 Modeling Multipath Effects in ART

We first extend the analysis of basic ART to incorporate multipath reflection, which will become the foundation for the enhanced ART. As illustrated in Figure 2, the received signals S contain LOS component S_d between adversary Tx and Rx, reflection components S_l from loudspeaker and irrelevant component S_o from other objects. Since the transmitted signal is a single-frequency tone, these components can be analyzed on an I-Q plane (Figure 7):

$$\vec{S} = \vec{S_c} + \vec{S_l}, \text{ and } \vec{S_c} = \vec{S_o} + \vec{S_d}. \quad (10)$$

Note that reflection component S_l is a time-varying vector due to the modulation effect from audio vibration, thus the magnitude of S_l vibrates. We represent this strength vibration using the arrow along S_l in the figure. Similarly, the tangent arrow represents the phase vibration of S_l caused by audio vibration.

We again focus on signal magnitude without loss of generality. From wireless channel prospective, reflected signal from loudspeaker and other n paths can be formalized as:

$$S_l = h_0 x + n_1, \text{ and } S_c = \sum_{i=1}^{n} h_i x + n_2 = \boldsymbol{h}x + n_2, \quad (11)$$

where $|h_0|^2 = \sigma A^2$, σ and A are the material reflectivity and path loss model discussed in Section 3.1. x is the transmitted symbol. h_i is the channel coefficient factor, and n_i denotes the noise in channel. In classical channel models [10], $\boldsymbol{h}$ and n_i can be modeled as complex Gaussian, *i.e.*, $\boldsymbol{h} \sim CN(0, N_h)$ and $n_i \sim CN(0, N_0)$.

From Figure 7, we can derive the radio RSS by simple geometry:

$$|S| = |S_l| \cos\alpha + |S_c| \cos\varphi, \quad (12)$$

where α (φ) is the angle between S and S_l (S_c). In our ART decoder (Section 3.2), m radio samples are used to extrapolate one audio sample, and audio samples pass through a DC filter. Hence, the recovered audio PSNR is determined by the ratio of non-DC part of S_l over S_c, *i.e.*:

$$PSNR = \frac{mpE[|S_l|^2]\cos^2\alpha}{E[|S_c|^2]\cos^2\varphi + N_0} \approx \frac{2mp\sigma A(d_0)A'(d_0)k\cos\beta|x|^2\cos^2\alpha}{N_h|x|^2\cos^2\varphi + N_0}, \quad (13)$$

where the approximation omits high-order harmonic terms. p denotes factor of energy loss due to NLOS eavesdropping, *e.g.* penetrating the wall.

The analysis unveils the following insights:

(i) The PSNR is determined by α and φ, which depend on the relative arriving angle between signals reflected by loudspeaker and other objects, which in turn depend on the adversary's location and frequency (wavelength). Thus, the PSNR can be improved by judiciously selecting position or radio frequency. This insight also corroborates the foregoing feasibility study: *the PSNR fluctuation is mainly attributed to the multipath coherence combining effect, rather than the minor distance changes between adversary and loudspeaker.*

(ii) The transmit symbol term x appears in both nominator and denominator, implying that *the adversary cannot achieve an arbitrarily high PSNR by increasing its radio signal power.* However, it can improve by reducing the term $N_h|x|^2\cos^2\varphi$. More specifically, this can be achieved by adopting wireless beamforming technology, which can focus the energy on a certain spot, *e.g.*, the loudspeaker surface.

4.2 Harnessing Diversity

We now exploit diversity techniques to enhance the reflective ART. Diversity has been well studied in communications theory [10]. However, we will show that it takes new facets in ART, particularly because the adversary has no control over the target loudspeaker.

4.2.1 *Blind Beamforming to Amplify Reflective ART*

Based on the prior analytical insights, we explore multi-antenna beamforming to enhance the reflective ART. Unlike traditional beamforming in wireless communications [10], which enforces channel training between active Tx/Rx radios using known preambles, here we need to *amplify signals from a passive loudspeaker with unknown channel signature.* One may consider existing blind beamforming algorithms [7, 10] that search and assign different weights to the Tx/Rx antennas to maximize SNR. However, due to slow time scale of audio playback, the accumulated time of such trials is formidable and thwarts any in situ eavesdropping attack. Moreover, previous algorithms [7] can have a cooperative target (*i.e.*, a target human performs special gestures) to estimate channel preamble, but in eavesdropping case the eavesdropper doesn't have any control on the loudspeaker.

We propose a *role-switching beamforming* (RSBF) algorithm to address these challenges. From a high level, RSBF comprises three steps, as illustrated in Figure 8: *(i)* One-time test transmission (lasting for a few seconds, just enough to obtain one audio segment). Any one antenna, *e.g.*, 2nd, of radio 2 acts as transmitter. All antennas in radio 1 receive the data and run an *Rx beamforming* (RXBF) algorithm to compute their beamforming weights. *(ii)* Rx-guided Tx beamforming. Antennas of radio 1 act as transmitter and beamform to one antenna of radio 2. The Tx beamforming weights are directly derived from their Rx weights, with no extra runtime overhead. *(iii)* Tx-Rx beamforming, where antennas of radio 2 compute new Rx beamforming weights under Tx beamforming from radio 1. Algorithm 2 summarizes the RSBF procedure. Below we elaborate on the design.

Calibrating RF Heterogeneity. Due to hardware imperfection, antennas and RF chains may have different initial phase offsets and gains. Heterogeneity calibration first measures the normalized distortion of different RF ports *w.r.t.* the first one. All calibrating an-

Algorithm 2 Role-switching Beamforming

/*RF Heterogeneity Calibration*/
$\Gamma_r[n] = y_r[n]/y_r[1]$
$\Gamma_t[n] = y_t[n]/y_t[1]$
$\mathbf{W} = Rx\_BF(\mathbf{D}[1:N])$ /*Rx beamforming*/
$\mathbf{W_t} = \frac{\mathbf{W}\Gamma_\mathbf{r}}{\Gamma_\mathbf{t}}$ /*Rx-guided Tx weights*/
/*New Rx weights under Tx beamforming*/
$\mathbf{W_r} = Rx\_BF(\mathbf{D_T}[1:N])$

tennas can be placed on a circle around one transmit antenna. Since they have the same distance to transmit antenna, their received signals $\mathbf{Y}$ will experience similar distortion H. The difference of received signals are mainly caused by antenna heterogeneity $\Gamma_\mathbf{r}$:

$$\mathbf{Y} = H\Gamma_\mathbf{r}X,$$

where $\mathbf{Y} = [y_1, y_2, \ldots, y_N]$ and $\Gamma_\mathbf{r} = [f_{r1}, f_{r2}, \ldots, f_{rN}]$ are 1×N matrixs, and X is the transmit symbol. The normalized distortion $\overline{\Gamma_\mathbf{r}}$ is then:

$$\overline{\Gamma_\mathbf{r}} = [1, \frac{f_{r2}}{f_{r1}}, \ldots, \frac{f_{rn}}{f_{r1}}] = [1, \frac{y_2}{y_1}, \ldots, \frac{y_n}{y_1}] = \overline{\mathbf{Y}},$$

where $\overline{\mathbf{Y}}$ is the normalized received signals *w.r.t.* to the first antenna. In a similar way, we can estimate the transmit RF heterogeneity. $\overline{\Gamma_\mathbf{t}}$

Rx Beamforming without Channel Training. The objective of the Rx beamforming algorithm is to find the weights $\mathbf{W} = \{w[i] | 1 \leq i \leq N\}$ for radio signals arriving at different antennas, in order to maximize the audio PSNR:

$$\arg\max_{\mathbf{W}} \ \textit{PSNR}(\sum_{i=1}^{N} w[i]\mathbf{D}[\mathbf{i}]), \tag{14}$$

where $\mathbf{D}[\mathbf{i}]$ is the signals at i^{th} antenna. Directly searching for the optimal weights is computationally inefficient as the search space lies in the continuous complex domain. We thus propose the following approximation. First, the amplitude and phase are discretized into range $[A_l : A_h]$ and $[P_l : P_h]$ with step A_s and P_s respectively. We choose $A_l = 0.5$ and $A_h = 2$, which cover $\pm 3dB$ magnitude range, and $P_l = 0$ $P_h = 2\pi$ to cover the whole phase range. Empirically, $A_s = 0.05$ and $P_s = 0.1$ is sufficient in terms of granularity.

Our Rx beamforming algorithm recursively computes the optimal complex weight for the ith antenna *w.r.t.* to previous $i - 1$ antennas. It ensures the weight for a new antenna will not degrade the audio PSNR when co-working with existing antennas. To avoid trapping into local maxima, we randomize the antenna ordering. Our algorithm differs from existing beamforming weight searching [7] that computes the weights for $N-1$ antennas *independently w.r.t.* to the first one, which cannot prevent audio PSNR from degrading when antennas are co-working.

Note that computation of the optimal complex weights is an offline procedure. In other words, we assess the beamforming weights by collecting and then processing a single short time series of radio signals, rather than real-time over-the-air transmission and processing. To compare the effects of different weight selections, we first use existing voice detection methods to identify if there is sound of interest in the decoded audio. Then we recurse on the weight selection with higher PSNR.

Rx-guided Tx Beamforming. The basic idea behind Rx-guided Tx beamforming is to leverage the channel reciprocity, *i.e.*, wireless link will distort signals in a similar way by reversing the role of Tx and Rx. Hence, Rx beamforming weights which focus on signals coming from certain position can also concentrate the energy onto

Algorithm 3 Rx_BF – "Offline"Rx Beamforming

INPUT: received data stream $\mathbf{D}[i]$
OUTPUT: weights $\mathbf{W}$
$\mathbf{cur}_D \leftarrow \mathbf{D}[1], m\_PSNR \leftarrow 0$ /*Initialize*/
foreach antenna i in set [2:N]
  $m_\psi \leftarrow 0, m\_\rho \leftarrow 0$
  foreach ψ in range $[P_l{:}P_s{:}P_h]$ /*Search phase*/
    $\mathbf{T}_D \leftarrow \mathbf{cur}_D + \exp(1i * \psi)\mathbf{D}[i]$
    if $PSNR(\mathbf{T}_D) > m\_PSNR$
      $m\_PSNR \leftarrow PSNR(\mathbf{T}_D), m\_\psi \leftarrow \psi$
  foreach ρ in range $[A_l{:}A_s{:}A_h]$ /*Search amplitude*/
    $\mathbf{T}_D \leftarrow \mathbf{cur}_D + \rho * \exp(1i * m\_\psi)\mathbf{D}[i]$
    if $PSNR(\mathbf{T}_D) > m\_PSNR$
      $m\_PSNR \leftarrow PSNR(\mathbf{T}_D), m\_\rho \leftarrow \rho$
  $W[i] \leftarrow m\_\rho * \exp(1i * m\_\psi)$
  $\mathbf{cur}_D \leftarrow \mathbf{cur}_D + W[i]\mathbf{D}[i]$
return W

the same spot when used as Tx weights. Mathematically, the rationale can be expressed by: $\mathbf{W_r}H = (H^T\mathbf{W_r}^T)^T$, where $(.)^T$ denotes the transpose of matrix. Left (right) part of the equation show the case when weights are used at receiver (transmitter) side. However, RF heterogeneity must be compensated before applying the weights:

$$\mathbf{W_t} = \mathbf{W_r}^T\Gamma_\mathbf{r}/\Gamma_\mathbf{t}, \tag{15}$$

where $\mathbf{W_r}$ represents Rx weights. The guided Tx (radio 1) beamforms to one of antennas at Rx (radio 2). To fully leverage the beamforming power, Rx runs another round of RXBF algorithm to maximize the audio PSNR.

4.2.2 *Amplifying Multipath Effect via Frequency Selection*

Besides leveraging spatial diversity of beamforming, we can also harness the *frequency diversity* — a radio signal and its reflected version may either strengthen or weaken each other, depending on its frequency (or wavelength). This in turn affects the audio quality of ART decoding.

Typical wireless systems (*e.g.*, WiFi) adopt a two-level channelization: a transceiver first selects a residential band at a certain carrier frequency, and then splits the band into multiple bins called *subcarriers*. We examine the channelization impact on ART by fixing the adversary location. Figure 9 plots the PSNR of recovered audio when adversary sends an 1 MHz baseband sine-tone through WiFi channel 1 to 14 (corresponding to carrier frequency from 2.412 GHz to 2.485 GHz). Figure 10 further plots the PSNR when the sine-tone is sent through different subcarriers within one WiFi channel.

The figures show that, owing to wider frequency separation, *channel-level frequency diversity has much more significant impact than subcarrier-level diversity*. The former typically creates 20 dB of PSNR discrepancy among channels, versus 10 dB in the latter. Another observation is that higher radio channel gain does not always mean higher audio quality, which is consistent with our theoretical prediction.

Based on these findings, we design a two-level channel selection mechanism to foster the multipath strengthening effect. Specifically, when initiating eavesdropping, the adversary spies on each channel for a few seconds, and fixes on the one with highest PSNR. Then, within that channel it transmit the single-tone through the subcarrier with highest channel gain. Note that the adversary can estimate the channel gain of all subcarriers simultaneously by sending a single OFDM packet with a training preamble.

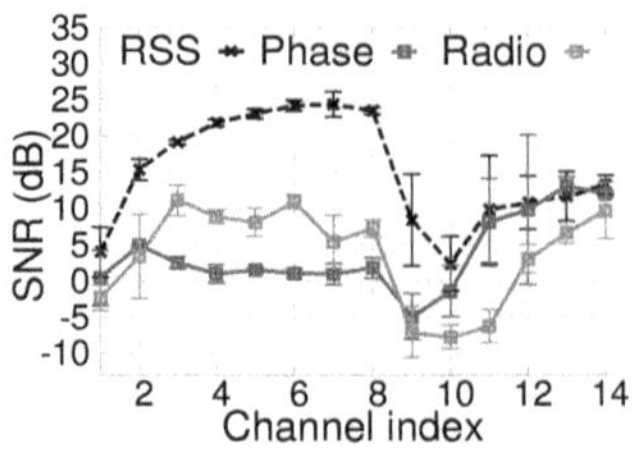

Figure 9: Audio and radio SNR over channel.

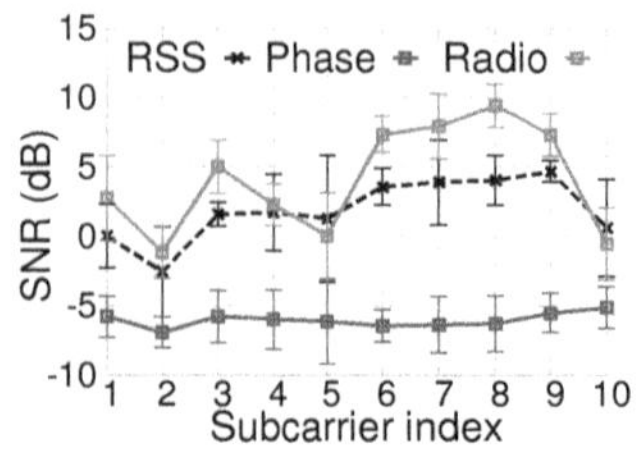

Figure 10: Audio and radio SNR over subcarrier.

5. EMISSIVE AUDIO EAVESDROPPING

Unlike the reflective case, an adversary in emissive vibrometry needs to decode audio by monitoring the RSS vibration of WiFi packets from the target. These packets are modulated across a wide spectrum, arrive randomly, and are beyond the control of the adversary. Our basic solution follows the same principle as the basic RSS-based ART (Sec. 3), but incorporates mechanisms to extract and amplify RSS values from the legacy WiFi packets.

Packet Detection: Following the 802.11 standard, each WiFi packet starts with a known preamble called Short Training Field (STF), which has a repetitive pattern in time domain. Hence, we follow the typical approach in [14], which can detect such periodic preambles using a self-correlation algorithm. We further use an 802.11 OFDM demodulator [15] to decode the unencrypted MAC header which conveys the data symbol modulation scheme (*e.g.*, BPSK).

RSS Estimation and Amplification: Suppose the target's MAC address is known to the adversary (we will discuss about how to relax this assumption). The simplest way to extract RSS is to single out target's WiFi packets, and extrapolate the time-domain signal power level across each packet to obtain one RSS value. However, we found this approach only leads to around -8 dB of PSNR even if the eavesdropper is 5 *cm* away from the target. The underlying reason is the high peak-to-average power ratio (PAPR) in 802.11's OFDM modulated packets, which renders a simple RSS averaging highly inaccurate.

To solve this problem, we first demodulate the OFDM-modulated packet into low-level data symbols. Let's first consider a simple case with BPSK or QPSK modulated data symbols, which all have the same magnitude in the constellation diagram. We can estimate the RSS by simply computing the average power over all N data symbols inside the packet:

$$RSS = \frac{\sum_{i=1}^{N} |s[i]|^2}{N}, \tag{16}$$

which circumvents the high PAPR. In general, data symbols may not have the same magnitude when using higher modulation order, *i.e.* 16QAM and 64QAM. We need to normalized the received symbols according to their constellation magnitude before computing the average power.

A typical WiFi packet has an N-value of thousand scale (*e.g.*, $N = 2048$ for a 512-byte QPSK modulated packet). Our RSS averaging method essentially reduces the noise level by N, thus potentially boosting the PSNR of ART by orders of magnitude. We thus refer to this approach as *RSS amplification.*

Reinterpolation of Non-uniform Packet Arrival: Since 802.11 MAC adopts CSMA, the timing gap between two consecutive packets is highly random. Thus, the RSS directly obtained through the above approach has non-uniform intervals. However, basic ART only works under uniform RSS samples. Our solution is to reinterpolate the audio signals based on non-uniform sampling theory [16], which essentially remaps the RSS samples to a grid of uniform intervals.

Under non-uniform sampling, the effective sampling rate is determined by the maximum gap between samples. To sample the audio from the target with frequency of 500Hz (for human speech), we thus need a packet arrival rate of 1000 pkt/s. This rate can be easily achieved in modern WiFi protocols and applications.

Three points are worth further discussion regarding emissive ART. *(i)* We have assumed the adversary knows the target's MAC address. In practice, the adversary can simply attempt to overhear packets from each MAC address nearby and run ART over it. The one resulting in a high PSNR and meaningful speech can be identified as the target.

(ii) Beamforming is still applicable as an amplification mechanism. However, in contrary to the reflective case, where beamforming aims to amplify one of the multipaths, in the emissive case, the beamforming objective is to amplify all signals sent from the target device. Hence, this problem can be reduced to traditional receiver beamforming [10]. We omit more details for the sake of space.

(iii) The emissive eavesdropping quality depends on the packet rate of the victim's smartphone. A very slow packet rate *e.g.*, 200 pkt/s as evaluated in Section 8, cannot provide sufficient sampling rate to recover the audio. However, this problem can be alleviated by applying techniques such as ARP attack [17] and RTS injection [18] that force "silent" idling WiFi device to "talk". We leave more exploration of such approaches as future work

6. COUNTER MEASURES

In this section, we propose counter measures that can thwart reflective/emissive eavesdropping in practice.

6.1 Combating Reflective ART

Params	Value	Params	Value	Params	Value
p	-8dB	N_0	-90dBm	β	0
m	4096	d	1mm	α	0
σ	1	$\|x\|^2$	100dBm	φ	90

Table 1: Parameters of counter measures for reflective eavesdropping.

Distance between adversary and victim is a critical factor that determines the capability of reflective ART. Following an empirical analysis, we can derive the *safety distance* d_{safe}, *i.e.*, the upper-bound distance that an adversary can sustain to launch an attack.

Our analysis extends the model in Sec. 3.1. We use free-space propagation [10] as our pathloss model: $A(d_0)^2 = \frac{\lambda^2}{(4\pi)^2 d_0^2 L}$. Real world wireless signals typically undergo stronger attenuation than free-space model, and thus have a shorter d_{safe}. λ is the wavelength, *i.e.* 12.5cm for 2.4 GHz. $L (L \geq 1)$ is the system loss, which is set as 1, *i.e.* no loss, in our analysis. Transmit/receive antenna gains G_t and G_r are set to typical values for high-gain WiFi antennas [19]: $G_t = G_r = 12dB$. We assume the adversary needs to penetrate through drywall, with 8 dB of round-trip loss: p = -8dB [20]. Other parameters are optimistic values for the adversary and summarized in Table 1.

Based on above settings and our model in Eq. (13), we can derive the relation between d_{safe} and audio PSNR, which is plotted in Figure 11. Free-space model (pathloss exponent = 2) requires d_{safe} to be larger than 26.5m so that audio PSNR drops below -13 dB, *i.e.* the PSNR level below which even a single frequency becomes inaudible (page 5 of [12]). For practical multipath channels with higher pathloss (*e.g.* office environment with path loss exponent

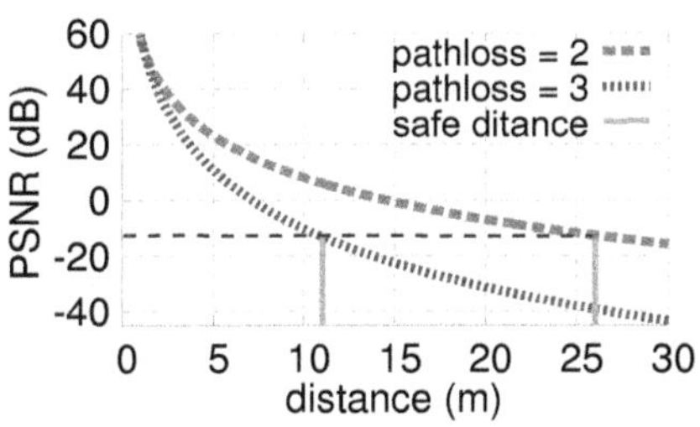

Figure 11: Safety distance vs. Audio PSNR. (Audios with PSNR lower than -13 dB cannot be detected).

3 [10]), safety distance can be reduced to 11m. It is worthy noting that the derived d_{safe} is conservative, which assumes optimistic parameters for adversary. In practice, the distance an adversary needs to recover recognizable audio has to be much smaller than d_{safe}.

Besides the safety distance, many other mechanical vibrations, *e.g.*, human activity, that have overlapping vibration frequencies with human sound can act as *interfering signals* to reduce the eavesdropping PSNR. However, it is worth noting that human movement does not *guarantee* keeping the victim from being eavesdropped. Part of the audio may still be recovered if victim temporarily slows down the movement. For minor human movements, *e.g.*, breathing, audio can still be recovered because they mainly cause low-frequency vibrations, and thus can be filtered by a bandpass filter. On the contrary, it is hard to recover audio signals when rapid movements, such as walking, is taking place nearby. We quantitatively evaluate the impact of human movement in Section 8. Overall, although human activity cannot completely thwart the ART attack, it is still a good approach to undermine the eavesdropping quality.

6.2 Combating Emissive ART

For the emissive case, the victim has a better control of the source of information leakage, and they can combat ART using more active mechanisms. Given this advantage, we propose a PHY layer countermeasure mechanism called *Transmission Power Randomization (TPR)*, which randomizes the transmission power across different radio packets transmitted by itself, so as to disturbs the RSS variation from acoustic vibration. Specifically, suppose the t-th packet has a legitimate transmit power of $P(t)$ (typically remaining as a constant in WiFi [21]). We randomize its power as $f(t) \cdot P(t)$, where $f(t)$ follows a normal distribution $N(1, \delta^2)$. The randomization intensity depends on the standard deviation δ, and determines the effectiveness of this countermeasure. δ should be kept small, so as not to affect the normal MAC/PHY protocol. However, we find that even a small value of $\delta = 0.05$ can already reduce the eavesdropper's PSNR by several orders of magnitude, as will be shown in our experiments (Sec. 8.3),

Similar rationale may be applied to thwart phase-based emissive ART. However, practical radio front-end already has a random initial phase offset for each packet, which naturally thwarts phased-based emissive ART.

7. IMPLEMENTATION

We prototype the eavesdropper based on the WARP software defined radio (SDR) [22]. The WARP radios are controlled by a laptop PC which implements the signal processing mechanisms that constitute basic/reflective/emissive ART (Sec. 3, 4 and 5). The radio transmitter directly takes baseband signals from the PC in the format of discrete I/Q samples, and then sends them through any WiFi channel. The receiver captures signals, converts them to baseband, and passes to the PC for processing. In addition, each WARP radio uses up to 4 antennas to run the RSBF algorithm in Sec. 4.2.

Our implementation of reflective ART sends/receives customized single-tone signals at 2.485 GHz, following the algorithms in Sec. 3 and Sec. 4. To realize the emissive ART, we have implemented an 802.11g/n-compliant OFDM communication library. Its receiver module consists of packet detection, synchronization, frequency offset compensation, and OFDM/symbol demodulation functions. It can directly decode OFDM symbols from legacy 802.11 packets, and then process the symbols using the RSS extraction and amplification module (Section 5).

Besides the 2.4 GHz WiFi channels, we also pair each WARP radio with WURC [23], a third-party RF front-end that enables transmitting/receiving signals over the UHF band. The UHF band experiments are conducted under an FCC experimental license, which allows us to use the vacant TV channels 40 and 41 (626 – 638 MHz) in our area.

Due to the interface latency between the PC and WARP [24], current WARP driver only allows transmitting/receiving bursts of I/Q samples at 3000 bursts/second, each burst containing 2^{10} samples. This translates to only up to 3 KHz of audio sampling rate (Sec. 5), and further reduces by 4 folds when using 4 beamforming antennas. We overcome the limitation by retrofitting the WARP FPGA kernel, and implementing a continuous streaming mode, which leverages WARP's internal memory to store extra data samples. This enables continuously writing/reading of up to 2^{28} I/Q samples, and the audio sampling rate can be as high as $\frac{20e6}{2^{10}} \approx 19.5$ KHz. The maximum time duration of a single recording can be $\frac{2^{28}}{20e6} \approx 13.4s$.

8. EXPERIMENTAL VALIDATION

Based on the prototype implementation, we evaluate reflective and emissive vibrometry, each following two steps. First, we conduct micro-benchmark validation of different enhancement mechanisms, separately. Second, we combine these mechanisms and perform blind-tests to demonstrate the overall eavesdropping threats under various practical scenarios. Finally, we validate the proposed countermeasures. Unless noted otherwise, there are working people inside the room, sitting roughly 2m away from the antennas and loudspeaker.

8.1 Validating Reflective Eavesdropping

8.1.1 Micro-benchmark of Diversity Mechanisms

We first verify the effectiveness of the diversity mechanisms in Sec. 4.2. By default, the loudspeaker plays a single-tone 400 Hz audio. Besides LOS, we create NLOS test case by separating the adversary and loudspeaker using an office partition. For each test case, we try 10 different eavesdropper locations 1 *m* away from the loudspeaker, and then measure the decoded PSNR.

Impact of blind beamforming: Recall the blind beamforming comprises 3 steps (Sec. 4.2.1): *(i)* Rx beamforming; *(ii)* Tx beamforming guided by Rx weights; *(iii)* TxRx beamforming. We first investigate the Rx beamforming performance as the number of antennas increases. From the experiments (Figure 12), we observe obvious improvement when the number of antennas increases from 1 to 2, but the gain saturates quickly. This is consistent with the log scale beamforming gain in traditional communications [10]. It also implies that the adversary can harness the majority of beamforming gain even with a small number of antennas.

Figure 13 depicts the eventual PSNR after the 3-step beamforming described in Sec. 4.2.1. we have two observations. First, the effect of beamforming is location-dependent: the beamforming gain ranges from 3 to 13.5 dB across the 10 locations. This is a direct

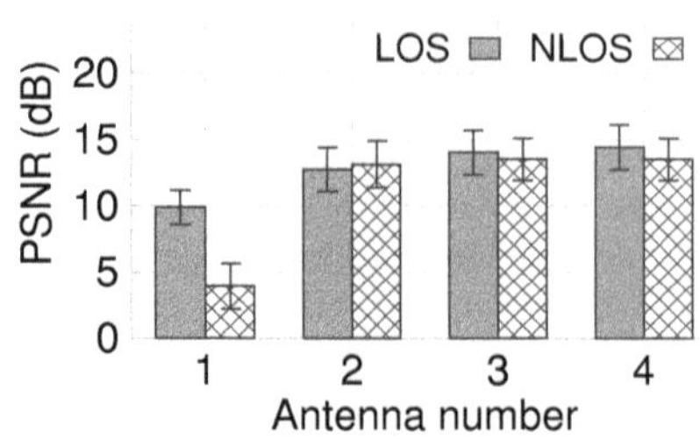

Figure 12: Audio quality gain vs. number of Rx beamforming antennas.

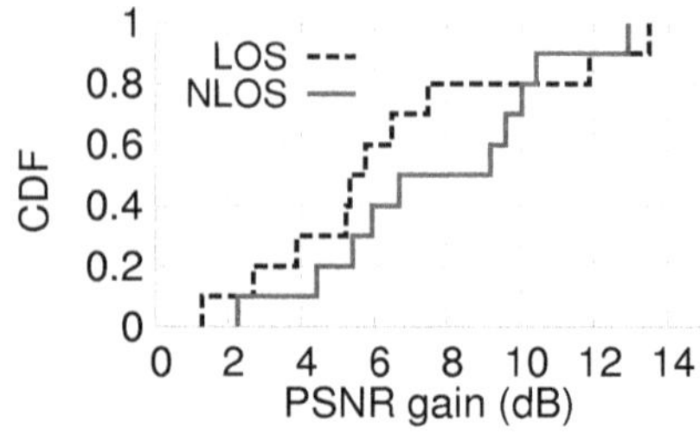

Figure 13: CDF of PSNR improvement of 4Tx-to-4Rx beamforming.

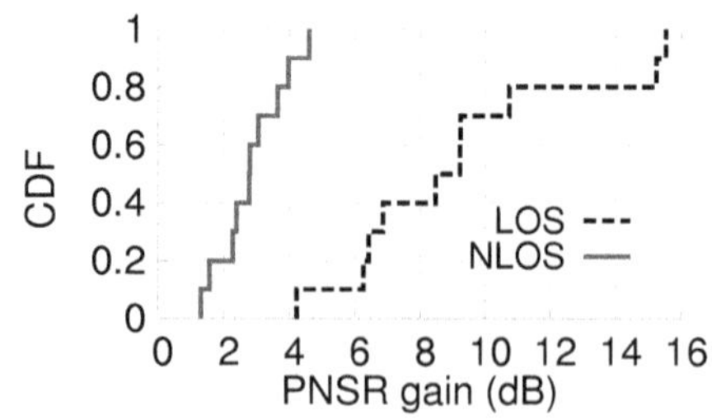

Figure 14: CDF of improvement by channel selection.

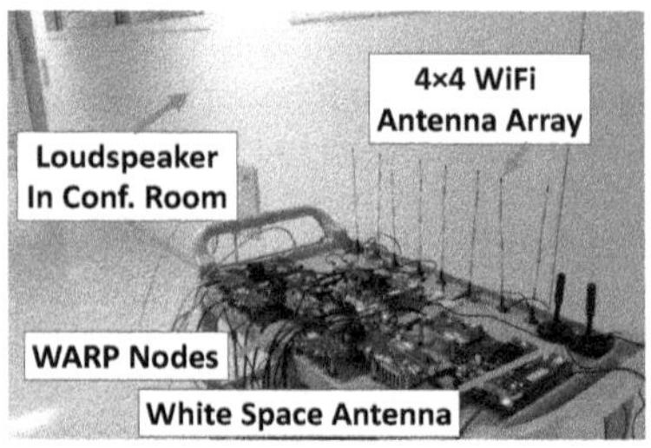

Figure 15: ART hardware platform. Testing ART outside a conference room.

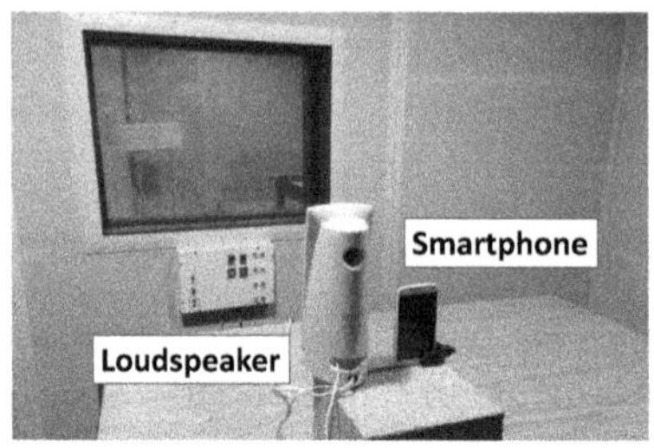

Figure 16: Testing ART performance. Loudspeaker is inside a soundproof room.

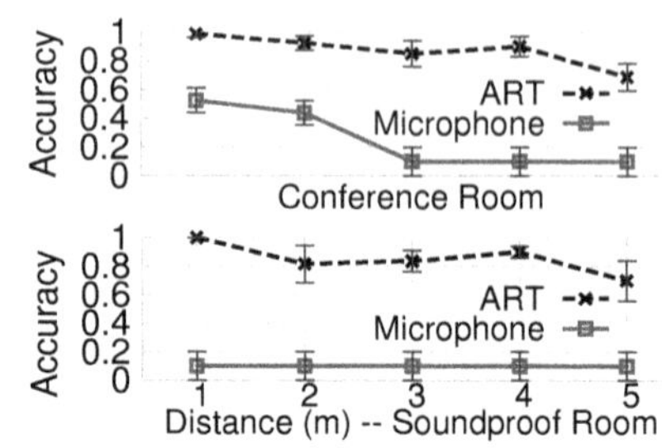

Figure 17: Through-wall recognition accuracy of ART compared with a microphone.

consequence of the location-dependent property in single-antenna ART (Sec. 3.3): when the multiple antennas all have strong PSNR and are uncorrelated, beamforming leads to highest amplification.

Secondly, there are more substantial benefits of beamforming at NLOS scenarios. On average, the NLOS beamforming gain is 8 dB across 10 locations, in contrast to 5.6 dB in LOS. This is because in NLOS, multipath diversity becomes dominant, leading to highly uncorrelated channel across antennas, which boosts beamforming gain.

Impact of channel selection: We run the two-level channel selection mechanism (Sec. 4.2) for each of the adversary location and plot the CDF of PSNR gain in Figure 14. As expected, channel selection plays a significant role in improving eavesdropping performance. We also observe that the average improvement ratio under LOS (*i.e.*, 60% and 9.5dB) is larger than that under NLOS (*i.e.*, 40% and 2.9dB), which is different from the beamforming case. Still, the reason is that when multipath diversity becomes dominant in NLOS, all channels degrade significantly. Moreover, the better channels under LOS have a larger deterioration since their dominating LOS paths with stronger signal are blocked. In consequence, channel selection yields a lower gain in NLOS.

8.1.2 Overall Eavesdropping Threat Analysis.

We now combine all the diversity mechanisms, and evaluate the overall eavesdropping threat under realistic settings.

Through-wall eavesdropping threats: We perform experiments in two closed rooms. The first is a typical conference room with drywalls all around, located in our office building (Figure 15). The second is a specialized soundproof room for conducting children behavior research (Figure 16). In both scenarios, we place a loudspeaker (for the reflective cases) and a smartphone (for the emissive cases) inside the room. The eavesdropper Tx/Rx are deployed outside.

To quantify the eavesdropping threat, we set up a blind test to evaluate the quality of recovered audio in comparison to a iPhone microphone. Specifically, the loudspeaker plays human speech sounds that pronounce random numbers between "zero" to "nine". Meanwhile, the microphone is placed at the same location as the eavesdropper and records the sound. We permute the numbers in each experiment, and invite 6 users to listen and transcribe the numbers recorded by the microphone and diversity-enhanced ART, respectively. We use the percentage of correctly-transcribed numbers as evaluation metric, referred to as *recognition accuracy*.

Figure 17 plots the recognition accuracy as we increase the distance between eavesdropper radios and the loudspeaker (with wall in between). Human ear can recognize the sound recovered by ART with almost 100% accuracy when the distance is less than 1 *m* outside conference room. Moreover, ART can keep a high recognition accuracy of more than 80% for up to 4 *m*. In contrast, the microphone recorder can only recover around 50% even below 2 *m* distance. Beyond that, the microphone cannot record any sound from the loudspeaker. For the purpose of experimental contrast, we cap the accuracy to 10% by assuming all testers randomly guess one out of ten numbers. For the sound-proof room, the experiment results are more interesting: while the microphone cannot capture any sound at all, ART can easily penetrate the sound-proof obstruction and still achieve high recognition accuracy.

To sum up, *an ART-enabled eavesdropper can indeed penetrate conventional sound isolators like walls and sound-proof windows.* Naturally, the attack may fail if the isolator (*e.g.*, metal walls) blocks radio signals completely. However, the above experiment already demonstrates alarming threat in the real-world.

From our extensive experiments, we also establish empirical relation between PSNR and recognition accuracy. When PSNR is above 15dB, testers typically can recognize words with close to 100% accuracy. When PSNR> 10dB, most words can be recognized (>60% accuracy). The testers fail to recognize any words when PSNR falls below 6dB. In what follows, we continue with a more microscopic examination of other factors that may affect the threat level.

Eavesdropping using different carrier frequencies: It is known that lower-frequency radio signals experience less propagation loss and penetration loss through obstacles. We now run the basic ART algorithm over the 626-638 MHz UHF band and compare it with the 2.4 GHz WiFi band. For a fair comparison, the transmit power and RF gains of corresponding radios are calibrated such that, for

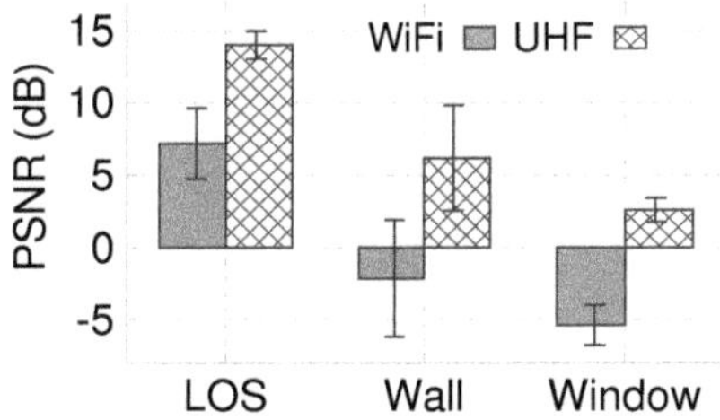

Figure 18: Eavesdropping quality using UHF and WiFi band signals, respectively.

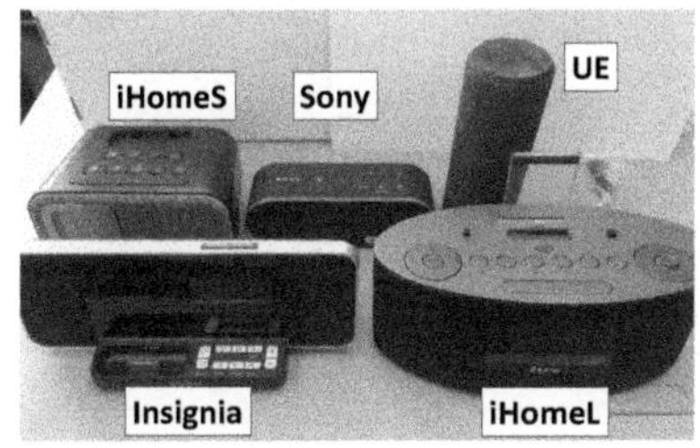

Figure 19: Testing 5 loudspeakers of different size and shape.

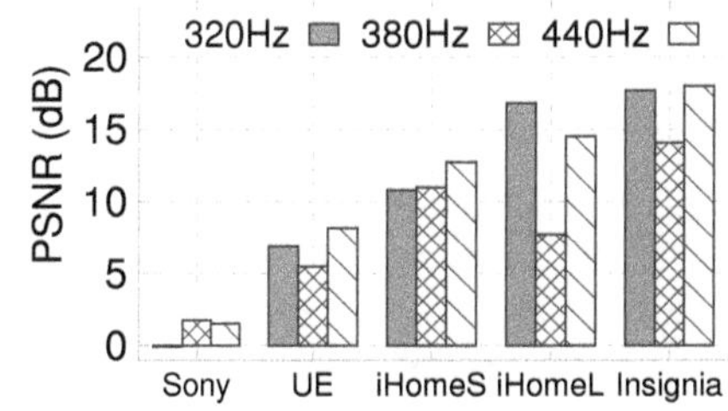

Figure 20: PSNR of different loudspeakers, with increasing size from left to right.

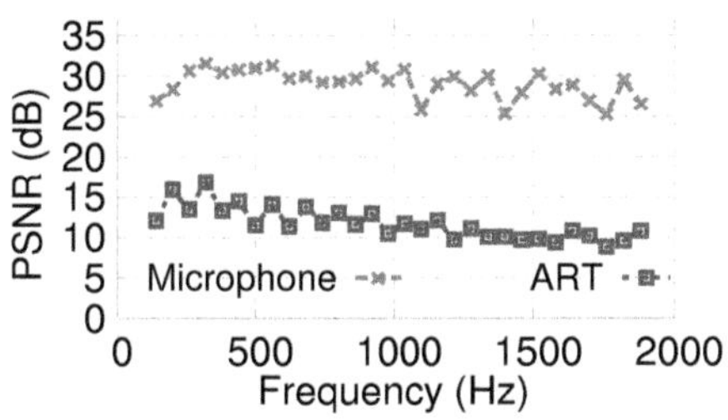

Figure 21: Frequency selectivity of ART compared to microphone.

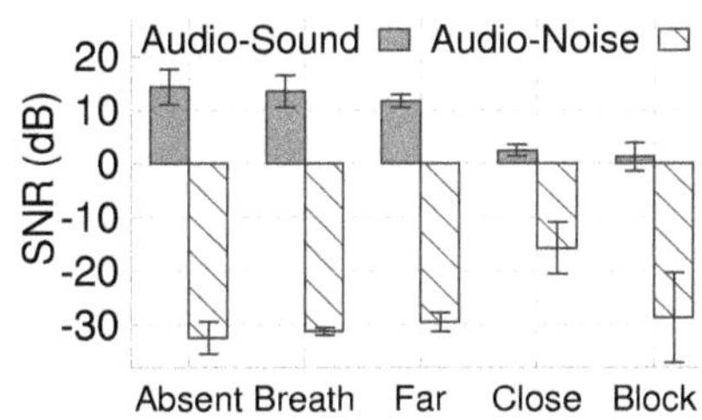

Figure 22: Impact of human present and activity on recovered audio quality.

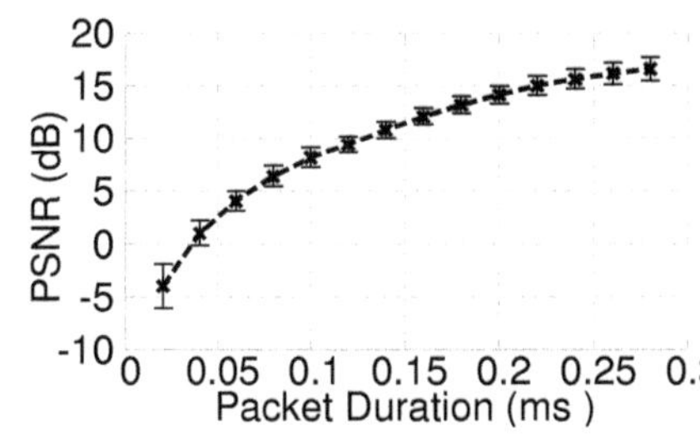

Figure 23: Audio PSNR under different packet lengths.

the same link distance, the received signal power levels' difference follows the free-space model. The results in Figure 18 show that *low-frequency UHF band presents a much higher level of PSNR in sound recovery*. The gain ranges from 7.5dB in LOS and 7 to 9 dB with wall or sound-proof window in between.

Impact of physical properties of loudspeaker: We have also evaluated ART's performance among 5 different commodity loudspeakers (Figure 19): Insignia, iHomeL, iHomeS, Sony and UE. The loudspeakers' volume is set to their largest level. Figure 20 shows that ART has high PSNR of recovered sound across all loudspeakers, and those with larger size tend to have higher PSNR due to stronger vibration.

Frequency fidelity of recovered audio: A common metric for evaluating the fidelity of sound acquisition system is the frequency response. We now test ART against this metric, in comparison with the microphone of a smartphone. The eavesdropper and microphone are both placed 1 *m* away, and within LOS of the loudspeaker. Figure 21 plots the PSNR across 140 Hz to 1900 Hz, covering the frequency range of human voice. ART's frequency response is relatively flat (*std.* 1.96 dB) and comparable to the microphone recorder (*std.* 1.77dB), which shows that the ART can achieve high-fidelity sound recovery, and does not distort audio differently across different frequencies.

Impact of environment dynamics: We next evaluate how nearby human activities affect ART. We test 5 different cases: *(i) Human Absence*: no human activity. *(ii) Nearby Breath*: a human stands 40*cm* away from the Tx (without blocking) and breaths normally. *(iii) Walk Far and (iv) Close*: a human randomly walks at a distance around 4*m* and 40*cm* to the Tx. *(v) Human Block*: a human blocks the LOS path between Tx and the loudspeaker. In all cases, the Tx is 1*m* away from the loudspeaker which plays a 400Hz sound. Figure 22 plots the recovered sound PSNR and audio noise floor.

We see that Human Breath and Walk Far almost have no impact on the PSNR or audio noise floor. Walk Close and Human Block decrease the audio PSNR by around 10dB. However, the root causes for the decrease differ in the two cases. For Walk Close case, human motion acts like a strong noise source to loudspeaker vibration, thus lowering the PSNR. In the Human Block case, the noise floor remains similar to the Human Absence, but the human body blockage significantly reduces the reflection signal strength.

From the test result, we conclude that ART can tolerate minor human movement, like breathing, or large motion, but not being too close to the loudspeaker or eavesdropper.

8.2 Validating Emissive Eavesdropping

8.2.1 Micro-benchmark Test

In the following experiments, the target is a smartphone (Moto X XT1053) with internal loudspeaker playing audio. Meanwhile, it sends packets through its WiFi interface to a nearby commercial access point Belkin N150. We do not modify any hardware or software on either the smartphone or the access point. Thus, their communication completely follows the IEEE 802.11g protocol. The adversary SDR works on the sniffer mode, which only captures raw signal samples overheard from the smartphone. We decode the WiFi packets on a PC using our software 802.11g decoder and then reconstruct the audio signals. Since the adversary has no control of the target smartphone, we evaluate the eavesdropping performance when the smartphone generates different traffic patterns. Note that due to 802.11's CSMA contention mechanism, the transmission time of packets is non-uniform, and we handle this problem using the re-interpolation designed in Sec. 5.

First, the smartphone initiates a TCP file transfer at 10 Mbps traffic rate, but with different packet lengths. Meanwhile, it plays a 400 Hz audio. Figure 23 shows that the decoded audio PSNR is logarithmically proportional to packet length. This is consistent with our asymptotic analysis in Sec. 5, which showed that the *RSS amplification algorithm can effectively improve PSNR by accumulating energy across each packet duration.*

We have a similar observation for the impact of packet rate (Figure 24): the PSNR improves by about 8dB as the packet rate increases from 1100 pkt/s to 1900 pkt/s.

The experiments clearly reveal alarming threats in today's wireless communications systems that strive for speed. Modern wireless

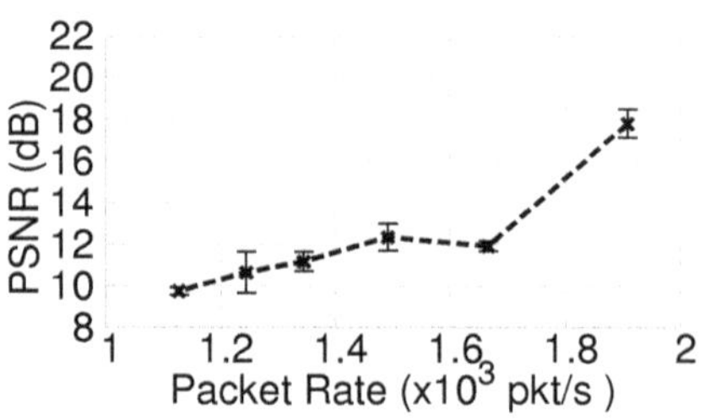

Figure 24: PSNR over different Packet Rate.

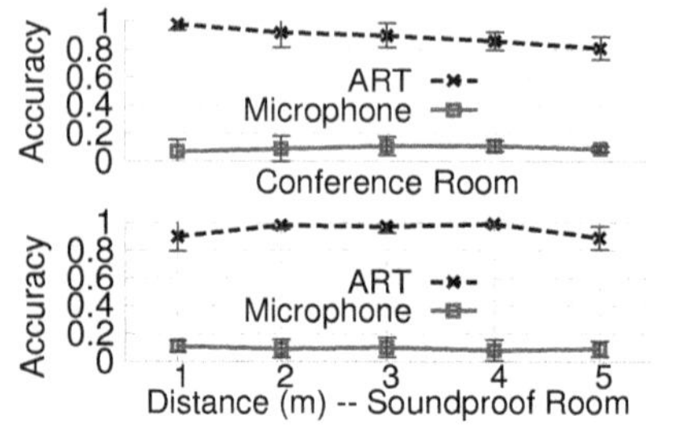

Figure 25: Accuracy of ART compared with a microphone.

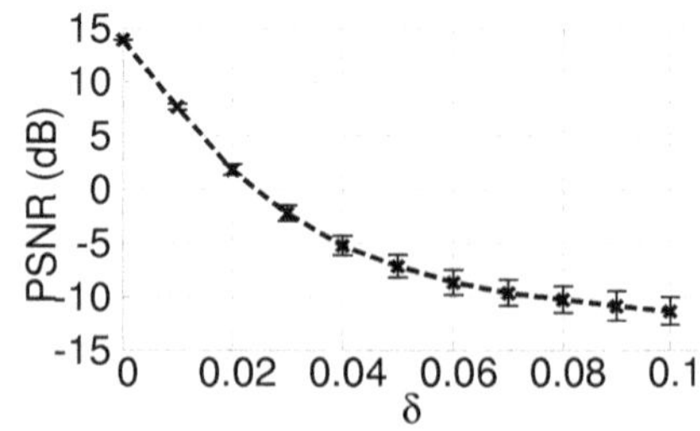

Figure 26: TPR's effect on Audio PSNR.

standards like 802.11n/ac widely adopt packet aggregation to improve transmission efficiency (*e.g.*, 802.11ac allows for up to 5.5ms of packet duration). Meanwhile, packet rate is escalating owing to high PHY-layer bit-rate (*e.g.*, 802.11ad enables up to hundred-Mega per second of packet rate). Riding on these trends, an adversary with wireless vibrometry can easily launch eavesdropping with ultra-high PSNR.

8.2.2 *Overall Threat Analysis*

Threats from through-wall emissive eavesdropping: To evaluate the practical threat, we use a similar blind-test setup as in the reflective vibrometry, except that the target is a smartphone playing the number sounds while running a file uploading application (with a mean packet duration of 0.25 ms and 1900 pkt/s). Figure 25 plots the blind-test results. We can see that emissive ART achieves almost 100% accuracy when eavesdropper is less than than 3 *m* away from the target with drywall or sound-proof window in between. In contrast, a microphone can barely recognize anything at all distances. Interestingly, the eavesdropping has good performance in spite of the low volume. The is attributed to the more "pure" vibration in the emissive case, where the radio signals come exclusively from the smartphone, whereas the irrelevant reflections in the reflective case contaminate radio signals.

To sum up, *emissive vibrometry constitutes a higher level of threat due to strong signals directly emitted by the target.* Considering the wide penetration of mobile devices that co-locate loudspeaker with radios, emissive ART can easily impinge on private communications over such devices.

Threats under real traffic patterns: Above we have tested emissive ART when the target is running file-uploading applications through WiFi. We have also tested other upload-traffic-dominated applications including FTP and Skype video call. We found FTP results in similar eavesdropping audio quality as above. Yet Skype call has a packet rate below 200 pkts/second, which is insufficient to provide usable audio sampling rate (Sec. 5). However, as camera resolution on smartphone increases along with WiFi bit-rate, we expect the packet rate of such applications will eventually reach the threat level. Besides, we also tested the emissive ART under environment dynamics, with similar observations as the reflective ART. We thus omit the details for the sake of space.

8.3 Validating TPR as a Counter Measure

In this section, we validate the TPR approach against emissive eavesdropping (Sec. 6). Since off-the-shelf smartphone's WiFi chipset cannot be modified to vary transmit power on a fine-grained way, we conduct trace-driven simulation instead. We collect the packet RSS traces following similar setup as in the micro-benchmark test, with default packet length 400 bytes and rate around 1900 pkt/s. Then, we enforce the RSS randomization mechanism on each of the collected packet, and inject the resulting packet trace into ART decoder. Figure 26 plots the decoded audio PSNR. We observe that PSNR is logarithmically proportional to randomization intensity δ, *i.e.*, it drops quickly as δ increases. Even with a small value $\delta = 0.05$, TPR reduces the PSNR from 14 dB to -7 dB (more than 2 orders of magnitude reduction), rendering the decoded sound inaudible. This δ value translates into a variation of transmit power by only 5%, which is unlikely to affect normal wireless communications. Therefore, once TPR is deployed on WiFi firmware, it can effectively counteract the emissive ART.

9. RELATED WORK

Our work is most closely related with prior art in the following domains:

Remote vibration detection. Microwave-based sound recovery was reported early in [25]. We differ from [25] in multiple aspects. First, our system builds on closed-from analysis, together with testbed experiments to demonstrate that both RSS and phase can be effectively used for audio-radio transformation. Second, whereas [25] works in LOS with directional antennas, we leverage the widely available MIMO radios for NLOS sound recovery. Third, we propose a novel emissive attack model that imposes emergent threats on ubiquitous WiFi devices.

Our work has also been inspired by the LADAR concept [5], conventionally used for inspecting structure safety (*e.g.*, bridge shaking under strong wind) and verifying rotational speed of mechanical vibration systems. A LADAR based laser microphone [26] can "hear" sound by measuring the vibration of a window. Recently, Davis *et al.* [9] showed that LADAR can be realized by directly monitoring and computing the vibrating spectrum of target using a high-speed camera. Limitations of such laser or vision based vibrometry systems are discussed in Section 1. WiFi-based vibrometry is less likely to be suspected by a victim, compared with laser or high-speed camera. It can exist in a tampered WiFi device near the victim, or even outside the sight. It is, however, more challenging, as WiFi signals are much less sensitive due to longer wavelength, omni-directional nature, and vulnerability to fading effects.

Radar based activity sensing. The reflective vibrometry follows a similar paradigm in radar sensing. Conventional military radar systems are used for ranging and moving target tracking [27]. Periodic human body activities, such as heart-beat, breathing, and walking, can cause an outstanding Doppler shift in the reflected signal [28, 29], which can be discerned by a radar receiver. But such detection systems require high frequency resolution, with multiple GHz of receiver sampling rate. Recently, substantial work has focused on realizing radar-like functions for mobile applications simply using WiFi signals. WiSee [7] can discriminate the fine Doppler patterns of 9 gestures by transforming WiFi signals into ultra-narrow-band pulses with high frequency resolution. WiVi [30] tracks human walking and gestures by creating a virtual antenna array, and improving spatial resolution using the inverse synthetic aperture radar (ISAR) technology. WiHear [8] aims to detect human speech by analyzing radio reflections from mouth movements. It builds on a supervised learning framework, requires individual user to train the system extensively, and can recognize only a limited number of words (6 words) with high accuracy.

Acoustic eavesdropping. Auditory surveillance on human conversations is a common practice in espionage, mostly realized in practice using high-sensitivity microphones with wireless transmission capability. Modern acoustic eavesdropping techniques begin targeting electronic apparatus. For example, it is well established that keys on a keyboard can be distinguished by their sound, due to minute differences in mechanical properties such as their position on a slightly vibrating circuit board [2, 31]. Vibrations from key presses can also leak keystroke identities [32]. Remarkably, human speech can also disturb a nearby gyroscope's readings [33], which can in turn infer coarse information about the speaker (*e.g.*, gender).

10. CONCLUSION

We have presented ART, a new acoustic eavesdropping method that penetrates conventional sound-proof isolators using reflective or emissive wireless signals. The key principle and challenge lies in recovering and strengthening the loudspeaker's subtle vibration from the radio signal strength variation. Through an analytical framework and extensive experiments, we distill the key factors that enable highly sensitive ART, and enhance it with diversity-harnessing mechanisms that requires no training preambles from the information source (*i.e.*, the loudspeaker). We implement the ART eavesdropper on a software-radio platform and demonstrate its effectiveness in decoding high-quality audio even through sound-proof walls, showing its severe threat in practice. We have also introduced pragmatic countermeasures in response to this new threat.

Acknowledgement

The work reported in this paper was supported in part by the NSF under Grant CNS-1318292, CNS-1343363, CNS-1350039 and CNS-1404613. It was also partly supported by National Natural Science Foundation of China No. 61202410.

11. REFERENCES

[1] Z. C. Taysi, M. A. Guvensan, and T. Melodia, "TinyEARS: Spying on House Appliances with Audio Sensor Nodes," in *Proc. of ACM BuildSys*, 2010.

[2] L. Zhuang, F. Zhou, and J. D. Tygar, "Keyboard Acoustic Emanations Revisited," *ACM Transactions on Information System Security*, vol. 13, no. 1, 2009.

[3] M. Backes, M. Dürmuth, S. Gerling, M. Pinkal, and C. Sporleder, "Acoustic Side-channel Attacks on Printers," in *Proc. of USENIX Security*, 2010.

[4] D. Genkin, A. Shamir, and E. Tromer, "RSA Key Extraction via Low-Bandwidth Acoustic Cryptanalysis," 2014.

[5] P. Castellini, M. Martarelli, and E. Tomasini, "Laser Doppler Vibrometry: Development of Advanced Solutions Answering to Technology's Needs," *Mechanical Systems and Signal Processing*, vol. 20, no. 6, 2006.

[6] S. Sen, B. Radunovic, R. R. Choudhury, and T. Minka, "You Are Facing the Mona Lisa: Spot Localization Using PHY Layer Information," in *Proc. of ACM MobiSys*, 2012.

[7] Q. Pu, S. Gupta, S. Gollakota, and S. Patel, "Whole-home Gesture Recognition using Wireless Signals," in *ACM MobiCom*, 2013.

[8] G. Wang, Y. Zou, Z. Zhou, K. Wu, and L. M. Ni, "We Can Hear You with Wi-Fi!" in *Proc. of ACM MobiCom*, 2014.

[9] A. Davis, M. Rubinstein, N. Wadhwa, G. J. Mysore, F. Durand, and W. T. Freeman, "The Visual Microphone: Passive Recovery of Sound from Video," *ACM Trans. Graph.*, vol. 33, no. 4, 2014.

[10] D. Tse and P. Viswanath, *Fundamentals of Wireless Communication*. Cambridge University Press, 2005.

[11] W. Klippel and J. Schlechter, "Measurement and Visualization of Loudspeaker Cone Vibration," 2006. [Online]. Available: http://www.aes.org/e-lib/browse.cfm?elib=13716

[12] J. R. Stuart, "Noise: methods for estimating detectability and threshold," *Journal of the Audio Engineering Society*, 1994.

[13] M. Vorlander, *Auralization: Fundamentals of Acoustics, Modelling, Simulation, Algorithms and Acoustic Virtual Reality*. Springer, 2008.

[14] X. Zhang and K. G. Shin, "E-Mili: Energy-Minimizing Idle Listening in Wireless Networks," *Proc. of ACM MobiCom*, 2011.

[15] S. Sur, T. Wei, and X. Zhang, "Bringing Multi-Antenna Gain to Energy-Constrained Wireless Devices," in *Proc. of ACM/IEEE IPSN*, 2015.

[16] J. Selva, "Functionally weighted Lagrange interpolation of band-limited signals from nonuniform samples," *IEEE Transactions on Signal Processing*, 2009.

[17] "ARP Request Replay Attack," http://www.aircrack-ng.org/doku.php?id=arp-request_reinjection, 2010.

[18] A. Musa and J. Eriksson, "Tracking Unmodified Smartphones Using Wi-Fi Monitors." Proc. of ACM SenSys, 2012.

[19] "Introduction to Wi-Fi Wireless Antennas," http://compnetworking.about.com/od/homenetworkhardware/a/introduction-to-wifi-wireless-antennas.htm, 2015.

[20] "WiFi Signal Attenuation," http://www.liveport.com/wifi-signal-attenuation, 2015.

[21] V. Shrivastava, D. Agrawal, A. Mishra, S. Banerjee, and T. Nadeem, "On the (in)feasibility of Fine Grained Power Control," *Mobile Computing and Communications Review*, vol. 11, no. 2, 2007.

[22] Rice University, "Wireless Open-Access Research Platform," http://warp.rice.edu/trac/wiki, 2013.

[23] Volo Wireless LLC., "Wideband UHF Daughter Card (WURC)," 2014.

[24] "WARPLab 7_3_0 Benchmarks," http://warpproject.org/trac/wiki/WARPLab/Benchmarks/WARPLAB_7_3_0, 2014.

[25] W. McGrath, "Technique and Device for Through-the-Wall Audio Surveillance," 2005, US Patent App. 11/095,122.

[26] R. P. Muscatell, "Laser Microphone," 1984, US Patent 4,479,265.

[27] J. Nanzer, *Microwave and Millimeter-wave Remote Sensing for Security Applications*. Artech House, 2012.

[28] V. Chen, F. Li, S.-S. Ho, and H. Wechsler, "Analysis of Micro-Doppler Signatures," *IEE Proceedings on Radar, Sonar and Navigation*, vol. 150, no. 4, 2003.

[29] F. Adib, Z. Kabelac, D. Katabi, and R. C. Miller, "3D Tracking via Body Radio Reflections," in *Proc. of USENIX NSDI*, 2014.

[30] F. Adib and D. Katabi, "See Through Walls with WiFi!" in *Proc. of ACM SIGCOMM*, 2013.

[31] S. Narain, A. Sanatinia, and G. Noubir, "Single-stroke Language-agnostic Keylogging Using Stereo-microphones and Domain Specific Machine Learning," in *Proc. of ACM WiSec*, 2014.

[32] P. Marquardt, A. Verma, H. Carter, and P. Traynor, "(Sp)iPhone: Decoding Vibrations from Nearby Keyboards Using Mobile Phone Accelerometers," in *Proc. of ACM CCS*, 2011.

[33] Y. Michalevsky, D. Boneh, and G. Nakibly, "Gyrophone: Recognizing Speech From Gyroscope Signals," in *Proc. of USENIX Security Symposium*, 2014.

Snooping Keystrokes with mm-level Audio Ranging on a Single Phone

Jian Liu†, Yan Wang†, Gorkem Kar*, Yingying Chen†, Jie Yang§, Marco Gruteser*
†Stevens Institute of Technology, Hoboken, NJ 07030, USA
*Rutgers University, North Brunswick, NJ 08902, USA
§Florida State University, Tallahassee, FL 32306, USA
†{jliu28, ywang48, yingying.chen}@stevens.edu, *{gkar87, gruteser}@winlab.rutgers.edu,
§jyang5@fsu.edu

ABSTRACT

This paper explores the limits of audio ranging on mobile devices in the context of a keystroke snooping scenario. Acoustic keystroke snooping is challenging because it requires distinguishing and labeling sounds generated by tens of keys in very close proximity. Existing work on acoustic keystroke recognition relies on training with labeled data, linguistic context, or multiple phones placed around a keyboard — requirements that limit usefulness in an adversarial context.

In this work, we show that mobile audio hardware advances can be exploited to discriminate mm-level position differences and that this makes it feasible to locate the origin of keystrokes from only a single phone behind the keyboard. The technique clusters keystrokes using time-difference of arrival measurements as well as acoustic features to identify multiple strokes of the same key. It then computes the origin of these sounds precise enough to identify and label each key. By locating keystrokes this technique avoids the need for labeled training data or linguistic context. Experiments with three types of keyboards and off-the-shelf smartphones demonstrate scenarios where our system can recover 94% of keystrokes, which to our knowledge, is the first single-device technique that enables acoustic snooping of passwords.

Categories and Subject Descriptors

K.6.5 [**Security and Protection**]: Unauthorized access

Keywords

Keystroke Snooping, Time Difference of Arrival (TDoA), Audio Ranging, Single Phone

1. INTRODUCTION

Mobile device hardware is increasingly supporting high definition audio capabilities targeted at audiophiles. In particular, this includes microphone arrays for stereo recording and noise cancellation as well as 4x improvement in audio sampling rates.

MobiCom'15, September 7-11, 2015, Paris, France.
© 2015 ACM. ISBN 978-1-4503-3619-2/15/09...$15.00.
DOI: http://dx.doi.org/10.1145/2789168.2790122.

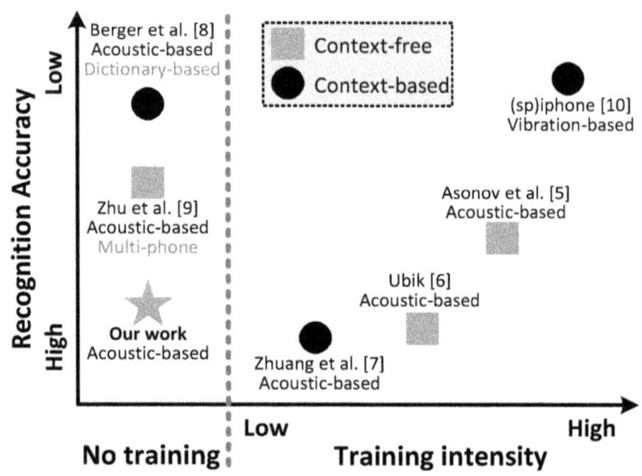

Figure 1: Design Space: comparing to related work.

For example, the Samsung Galaxy Note 3 includes three microphones and its audio chips are capable of 192kHz playback and recording. One can debate whether all these advances actually lead to improvements in music playback and audio recording quality that are perceivable by the human auditory system and not all these hardware capabilities are currently made available by drivers and operating system software. Such advances, however, could have a significant impact on the accuracy of audio ranging and localization.

Audio localization has been explored with mobile devices to achieve centimeter level accuracy in various applications, such as phone-to-phone ranging and 3D localization [1, 2], mobile motion games [3], and driver phone use detection [4]. Will advanced mobile audio hardware capabilities lead to order of magnitude improvements and let us achieve mm-level accuracy or do the limiting factors lie in multipath distortions and the accuracy of signal detection techniques?

We explore these questions in the context of keystroke snooping, a particularly challenging localization technique and one with important security implications. To eavesdrop on keystrokes, an adversary can inconspicuously leave a phone near a keyboard of the target user. Or, an adversary can co-opt the target users own phone, for example by adding malware into an app with microphone access. Keystroke snooping is particularly challenging because of the large number of different keys to distinguish and the small cm-level separation between individual keys. It has important security implications because using keyboard is still an important way of entering sensitive information into computing systems and crucially, passwords remain the primary means to authenticate with remote systems, including financial- and health-related services. Besides these security and privacy breaches there is also potential to create improved input methods for mobile devices that do not directly require typing on the confined mobile screens. Additionally, the proposed solution also has the capacity to facilitate other applications that benefit from fine-grained localization, such as extending interactions with the touch screen of a mobile device to its adjacent surfaces for controlling music players or video games; tracking speakers in multiparty conversations in a meeting room; and locating trapped disaster victims. The proposed audio ranging solution leveraging geometry based information (i.e., time difference of arrival) and unique acoustic characteristics extracted from potential sound sources could deal with many limitations of mobile devices, such as only two stereo recording microphones, limited sampling rate, and restrained distance between two microphones.

Prior work. Existing research has already recognized the significance of this question and found limited potential to recover keystrokes from audio recordings. In particular, Asonov *et al.* [5] conducted an initial study that observed that each key produces unique acoustic emanations and designed a supervised learning method to recognize individual keys. UbiK [6] improves accuracy for keystrokes on solid surfaces (i.e., a paper keyboard on a table) fingerprinting acoustic differences due to multi-path fading. These approaches require extensive labeled training data from the exact keyboard setting to learn the acoustic profiles for each key, which can be challenging to obtain in adversarial scenarios. Later, Zhuang *et al.* [7] propose to add language constraints to improve recognition accuracy. Berger *et al.* [8] further trades off training requirements for accuracy through a dictionary-based approach that leverages the similarity of acoustic signals from nearby keys. Such methods, however, improve keystroke recognition only for natural language and fail for strong passwords composed of random characters. Zhu *et al.* [9] proposes to utilize microphones on three phones to identify keystrokes of a nearby keyboard based on time difference of arrival (TDoA) measurements. The requirements of three collaborating phones and the achieved moderate accuracy make their approach less feasible for real attack scenarios. There is also a related line of work that has explored vibrations sensing of keystrokes using accelerometers such as (e.g., [10]). The accuracy of such approaches generally remains lower than that of audio sensing. Figure 1 illustrates the design space and the results offered by existing work. Due to the limited accuracy, the use of multiple recording devices, the need for linguistic context, or training with extensive labeled data, none of these techniques can easily be applied to snoop on passwords.

Approach. This paper demonstrates that the mobile audio hardware advances can indeed be exploited for high accuracy mm-level ranging and that practical scenarios exist where it is possible to localize keystroke sounds with an accuracy sufficient to snoop on passwords. It explores a novel point in the keystroke recognition design space by showing the feasibility of keystroke snooping that is (i) training-free, (ii) context-free, (iii) based on single phone. The approach is training-free because it does not require a-priori labeled training data, which is often difficult to obtain for an adversary. Comparing to the training-based keystroke recovering solutions, e.g., using labeled keystroke data to train a neural network to recognize subsequent keystrokes [5], our work develops unsupervised algorithms without any labeled data to cluster a set of keystrokes. The approach is context-free because it does not require on any linguistic models such as letter, letter sequence (n-gram), or word likelihoods and can therefore be applied to random key sequences such as passwords. And the approach is based on a single phone because it does not require multiple phones or recording devices to be placed around the keyboard; it only relies on two microphones in a single phone.

Our work achieves this by discriminating keystrokes based on the time-difference-of-arrival (TDoA) of the keystroke sound at the two phone microphones and by refining such estimates using acoustic differences in the sound emitted by each key. For certain placements of the phone, relative to the keyboard, there exist measurable differences in TDoA value between most keys. Different from general acoustic TDoA localization approaches which require at least three distributed microphones, our work only uses two microphones with highly constrained distances on a single phone, which produce a limited range of single-dimensional TDoA measurements for locating the keystroke. While a single TDoA measurement will not allow determining a unique 2D location for the keystroke, it does restrict the possible locations for this keystroke to a hyperbola. Given multiple keystrokes of the same key and information about the keyboard geometry, this hyperbola can be placed with mm-level precision so that it uniquely identifies a key. To obtain multiple audio samples of the same key, even under random typing, the approach clusters keystrokes based on the observed TDoA and mel-frequency cepstral coefficients (MFCCs), which capture (slightly) different acoustic signatures of each keystroke such as those due to physical imperfections across keys. Since the acoustic signatures are only used for improving clustering, there is no need for training of acoustic signatures. Further, since the final TDoA values describe relative locations, they can be directly used to label keystrokes if the keyboard geometry and phone position is known (e.g., keyboard with phone/tablet stand) or if it can be inferred (i.e., enough keystrokes can be observed to derive the key layout). The labeling process only requires finding a best match between the measured TDoA and the expected TDoA for each key, given the geometry and placement.

The contributions of our work are summarized as follows:

- We demonstrate that a single off-the-shelf phone can recover keystrokes by exploiting mm-level acoustic ranging and fine-grained acoustic features. We develop a training-free approach on a smartphone that does not require a linguistic model, allowing it to recover random keystrokes (e.g., random passwords).
- We exploit recent mobile audio hardware advances to stretch the limits towards mm-level audio localization accuracy.
- We develop a keystroke snooping framework, which leverages hardware advances (i.e., stereo recording with high sampling rate) of off-the-shelf mobile devices to narrow down possible positions of a keystroke. The framework further exploits the geometry-based information (i.e., TDoA) and unique acoustic signatures of keystrokes to ping-point their positions on a keyboard.
- We conduct extensive experiments with three kinds of keyboards to show that an off-the-shelf phone with $48kHz$ microphone sampling rate can accurately identify a set of keystrokes with over 85% accuracy. With higher sampling rate (e.g., $192kHz$), the accuracy could be increased to over 94% accuracy. Even for a single keystroke input, our system can achieve 97% accuracy of identifying keystrokes in the top-3 candidate keys with $48kHz$ sampling rate. We believe that these are the first results to raise serious concerns about acoustic password snooping.

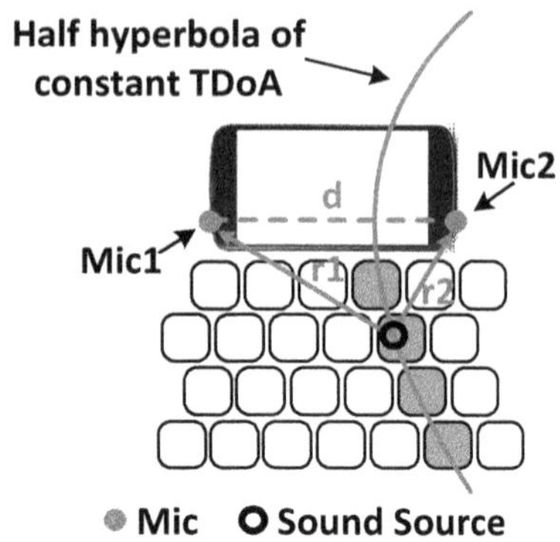

(a) Geometrical TDoA measured by a pair of microphones.

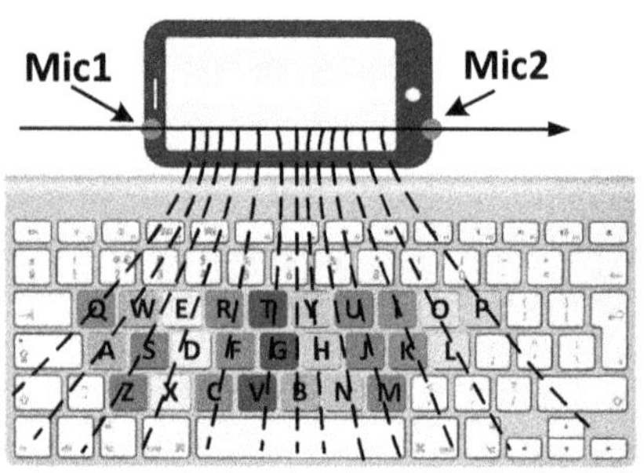

(b) Theoretical key groups and corresponding half hyperbolas.

Figure 2: Illustration of the geometrical TDoA on a single-phone and theoretical key groups.

2. ATTACK MODEL & LIMITS OF TDOA WITH A SINGLE PHONE

In this section, we introduce the attack scenarios and the rationale for their selection. We also analyze key factors affecting the accuracy of keystroke snooping when using a single phone and define basic concepts.

2.1 Attack Model

We consider a scenario where an adversary seeks to identify each entered character in a sequence of keystrokes from the acoustic signal generated by depressing a key ("typing sound"). We assume that adversaries have the access to stereo audio recordings from a single mobile device (e.g., smartphone or tablet) that is placed close to a victim's keyboard. Two representative scenarios where this is plausible are: (1) the adversary inconspicuously leaves a prepared recording device next to the victim's keyboard, perhaps in a confined setting such as library seats where physical proximity is not suspicious; (2) the adversary gains software access to the microphones of the victim's phone, perhaps through a malicious app, and waits until the victim places the phone next to a keyboard. We note that it is not uncommon for users to place their phone on the desk while working on a laptop keyboard. Moreover, tablets and large phones are frequently used with external Bluetooth keyboards, where the device is placed directly behind the keyboard. We believe that this latter scenario is particularly likely and use it as the primary example in this paper.

We do not assume any particular structure in the typed information. This means that adversary seeks to identify not only text input matching a known linguistic model but also seeks to identify random input strings such as strong passwords. We also explicitly do not assume that the adversary has access to labeled training data (i.e., audio recordings for each key, where it is known which key was pressed). Such training data is specific to a particular phone-keyboard combination, the exact placement, and the exact acoustic environment. It would therefore be challenging to obtain in many adversarial settings.

2.2 Basic Concepts of Single Phone TDoA Localization

The selection of the attack model is rooted in an understanding of the fundamental limits of acoustic localization. To avoid the need for labeled training data we disregard fingerprinting techniques and focus on time-of-flight measurements, which are attractive given the relatively low propagation speeds of audio signals. Since we do not know when a particular keystroke sound is emitted, we rely on measuring the time-difference-of-arrival (TDoA) of this sound across the two microphones of the device.

A TDoA measurement reveals information about the direction of the incoming sound. Determining an exact position of origin for the sound normally requires triangulation, that is at least two direction measurements from different locations. In the keyboard snooping scenario, however, there is a discrete and relatively small set of candidate positions from which the sound can emanate: the center of each key. If the relative phone position and keyboard geometry is known, it is therefore possible to locate the sound even with a single TDoA measurement by finding the best match between the direction estimate and the expected direction for each key.

This process, however, requires mm-level accuracy, which is an order of magnitude beyond the cm-level accuracies that have been previously demonstrated in audio localization. Operating at this level of accuracy involves estimating precise hyberbolas instead of coarse direction estimates. Consider our primary scenario as illustrated in Figure 2(a). Let's denote the distance between two microphones as d, and the distance between the sound source (i.e., the keystroke made on the keyboard) to that of two microphones as $r1$ and $r2$, respectively. Suppose Δt is the TDoA measured at two microphones, the derived distance difference Δr from the pressed key to two microphones can be represented as:

$$\Delta r = r1 - r2 = \Delta t \cdot s_0, \tag{1}$$

where s_0 is the velocity of sound. All possible locations that satisfy Δr lie on a hyperbola as illustrated by the red curve in Figure 2(a). This hyperbola typically crosses several keys on the keyboard as indicated by the darker keys in the figure (and one key may also be crossed by more than one hyperbola). Narrowing this to a single key therefore involves determining the closest key center to this hyperbola. As can be seen in the figure, shifting the hyperbola by only a few mm would bring it closer to the center of a different key. For this reason, the process require mm-level precision and accuracy.

2.3 Factors Affecting Accuracy

The achievable accuracy and precision with TDoA measurements depend on several key factors.

Sampling Rate. When recording the keystroke sound, the sound is digitized by an Analog to Digital Converter (ADC) with a fixed sampling rate before it becomes accessible to applications. This therefore limits the resolution with which the time difference of arrival can be measured by application software. While signal processing techniques exist that promise sub-sample accuracy, this time resolution serves as a useful guideline.

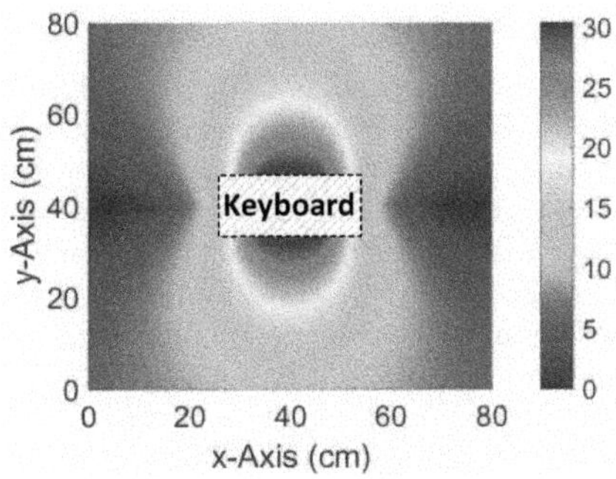

(a) Horizontally placed.

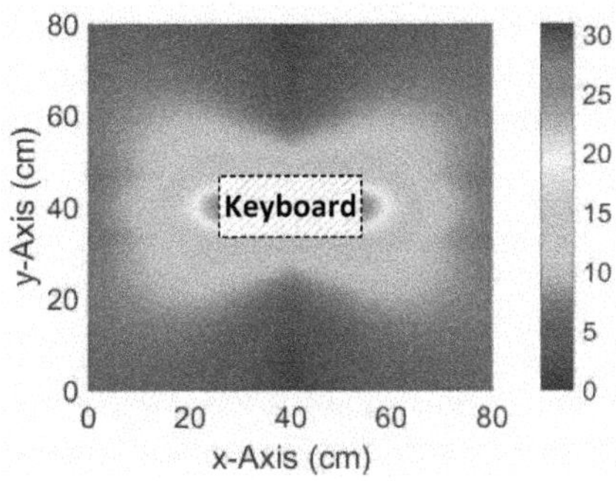

(b) Vertically placed.

Figure 3: Good phone locations for keystroke snooping. Warmer color indicates locations from which a higher range of TDOA values can be observed over different keys.

Current state-of-the-art audio hardware on mobile devices supports up to $192kHz$ sampling rate but drivers and or operating system usually still limit this to $48kHz$. At a speed of sound of 343m/s, this results in a resolution for the distance difference Δr of $\approx 1.8mm$ and $\approx 7.15mm$ for the two sampling rates, respectively.

Distance between Two Mics. The number of distinguishable hyberbolas also depends on the range of possible TDoA measurements. The range is bounded by the distance between two microphones on the phone. It can be calculated based on the triangle inequality theorem. As can be inferred from Figure 2(a), the range of Δr is $[-d, +d]$. The TDoA value Δt then falls into the range of $[-d/s_0, +d/s_0]$, which corresponds to the number of distinguishable hyberbolas N at the sample level as expressed below:

$$N = \lceil \frac{2d \cdot f_s}{s_0} \rceil. \quad (2)$$

For example, the distance between the two microphones of the Samsung Galaxy Note 3 smartphone is $d = 15.3cm$. With a sampling rate $f_s = 48kHz$, this yields 42 hyperbolas that can be discriminated at the sample level.

Placement of the Mobile Device. In practice, only a subset of these N hyperbolas may actually cross the keyboard and be useful for distinguishing keystrokes. The size of this subset depends on the size of the keyboard and the relative location of the recording device. Figure 3 shows the size of this subset depending on the phone position around the keyboard, for two different phone orientations. Warm colors indicate good phone positions relative to the keyboard. Horizontal phone orientation means that a line connecting the two microphones would be parallel to the long side of the keyboard (as also the case in Figure 2(a)). Vertical

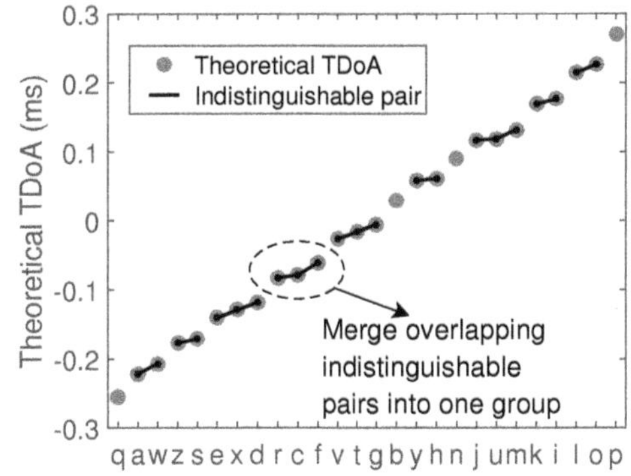

Figure 4: Illustration of sorted TDoAs for theoretical key groups construction.

orientation means that the phone is rotated 90 degrees to the left, so that the line is parallel to the short side of the keyboard. This analysis assumes a sampling rate of $48kHz$, a keyboard size of $28cm \times 13cm$ (as for the Apple wireless keyboard MC184LL/A) and microphone distance of $d = 15.3cm$ (as on the Samsung Galaxy Note 3). The results show that a vertically placed phone on the side needs to be in very close proximity but a horizontally placed phone behind the keyboard offers a bit more flexibility. Such placements are consistent, however, with the attack scenarios that we have identified earlier. In our primary scenario (e.g., a Samsung Galaxy Note 3 is placed behind an apple keyboard as illustrated in Figure 2(a)), in particular, this leaves us with 31 hyperbolas crossing the 26 alphabetic keys.

2.4 Theoretical TDoA and Key Groups

Given known keyboard geometry and phone placement, keystroke snooping can be simplified as a matching process between measured TDoA values and expected TDoA values for each key. By solving for Δt in Equation (1), it is possible to compute an expected TDoA value for each key, which we also refer to as the theoretical TDoA value for a key.

In addition to the limiting measurement factors discussed earlier, measurements will be affected by noise. This further limits the distinguishability of keys and leads us to introduce the notion of theoretical key groups, which are groups of keys whose expected TDoA values are so close that we would expect them to be difficult to distinguish. For instance, the 26 alphabetic keys in our primary scenario are grouped into 13 theoretical key groups, each illustrated through a separate color in Figure 2(b).

These key groups are established as follows. We first sort the keys based on their theoretical TDoAs. We then link any pair of keys whose difference in theoretical TDoA is less than a threshold τ. Based on our experiments with different keyboards and sampling rates, we empirically determine τ as $\frac{1}{480}ms$ (which corresponds to $1, 2, 4$ TDoA samples corresponding to $48kHz$, $96kHz$ and $192kHz$). Each connected set of keys is then considered as one theoretical key group, as illustrated in Figure 4.

We will explain how to use these concepts and how to achieve accuracy below the level of a theoretical key group next.

3. SYSTEM OVERVIEW

To accurately recover keystrokes using a single mobile device, we design an approach that leverages TDoA measurements and

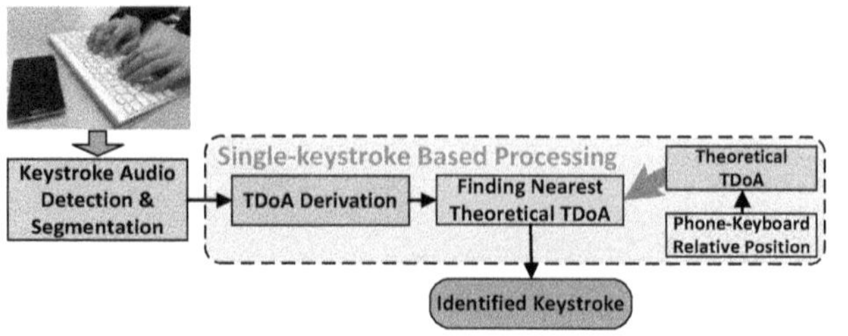

Figure 5: System architecture: single-keystroke based processing.

fine-grained acoustic signatures of keystrokes. In this section, we discuss the challenges and architecture of our system design.

3.1 Challenges

To achieve the goal of accurately recognizing keystrokes by utilizing a single mobile device without relying on training and contextual information, the design and implementation of our system involve a number of challenges:

Sensing with Single Mobile Device. Using one single mobile device to recover keystrokes is challenging as most commercial mobile devices only support stereo recording with two microphones, while general acoustic TDoA localization approaches require at least three microphones to create multiple half-hyperbolas to locate a sound source. Moreover, the distance between two microphones in a phone is highly constrained, which limits the range of possible TDoA values. Although some mobile devices have three microphones, for example iPhone $5s$ and Samsung Galaxy Note 3, neither Apple nor Google provides API to record 3-channel audio with three microphones. Therefore, our system must be designed in a way that it can accurately identify keystrokes based on the stereo recording of two microphones.

Imperfect measurement of TDoA. Different from some recent TDoA localization studies [1–4] that utilize customized acoustic signals, such as a high frequency narrow band signal, our work locates more challenging sound sources, i.e., keystrokes, which cannot be controlled and contain rich frequency components. Meanwhile, the range of possible TDoA values is limited by the distance between two microphones and is affected by the placement of the mobile device. Also, the sampling frequency limits the resolution with which the time difference of arrival can be measured. Moreover, the measured TDoA may also be affected by multipath effects and environmental noises. These factors result in imperfect measurements of TDoA which make it hard to uniquely locate each keystroke.

Training-free Keystroke Recognition. Without the cooperation of the targeted user, developing training-free keystroke recognition is critical when performing keystroke snooping, especially when an adversary seeks to derive the user's sensitive typing information. Our system aims to recognize keystrokes without training efforts that involve target users (e.g., requiring the target user to type each key repeatedly to label the data beforehand).

Recovering Keystrokes without Linguistic Model. Users may type not only sentences following English language constraints (e.g., emails and articles), but also random letters or numbers (e.g., passwords and credit card numbers). Our developed method should have the ability to recover sensitive information consisting of random combination of letters and numbers. This requires our system to recognize keystrokes without relying on linguistic models or dictionaries.

3.2 System Architecture

The basic idea of our system is to perform keystroke snooping leveraging the dual-microphone on a single smartphone through studying the fine-grained acoustic signatures inherent from key typing sounds. In particular, we consider two processing approaches, namely *Single-keystroke Based Processing* and *Set-keystroke Based Processing*. These two approaches seek to cover various practical scenarios that have different requirements on the accuracy and response time. The *Single-keystroke Based Processing* can be applied to even a small set of recovered keystrokes, since it can process each keystroke individually. The *Set-keystroke Based Processing* exploits a larger set of keystroke samples to improve the recognition accuracy. It reduces the effect of imperfect measurement of TDoA by combining multiple keystroke samples from the same key. It can identify strokes of the same key by extracting the acoustic cepstral features of keystrokes as well as by using coarse TDoA matching.

In our proposed system, we assume the relative position of the mobile device to the keyboard is known. This information can be obtained if an adversary intentionally places the mobile device close to the keyboard, or when the external keyboard is attached to the mobile device (e.g., Microsoft Surface). There are also other means to obtain such information. For example, the adversary may take a picture of the setting of the keyboard and mobile device. The adversary may also estimate the setting using a bunch of collected keystrokes of multiple keys. It is important to note that such process does not need the participation of the target user as in the traditional training phase. Additionally, we discuss how to derive such information when the relative position the mobile device is unknown in Section 5.3.

Single-keystroke Based Processing. A quick way to recover each individual keystroke is to leverage the theoretical calculated TDoAs based on the relative position between the mobile device and keyboard. The Single-keystroke Based Processing method compares the measured TDoA derived from the input keystroke to the computed theoretical values and determine which key has been pressed. The main steps of this method are depicted in Figure 5 and described as follows: For each captured keystroke sound, this method first perform *Keystroke Audio Detection & Segmentation* to extract the audio signals corresponding to the press and release phases of the keystroke. It then derives the TDoA based on the extracted keystroke acoustic signal using signal processing techniques. Next, it determines which key has been pressed by finding the top-w keys that have the theoretical TDoAs closest to that of the input keystroke (i.e., *Finding the Nearest Theoretical TDoA*).

Set-keystroke Based Processing. This method aims to reduce the impact of the imperfect TDoA measurement by examining a set of input keystrokes and study the statistics of the fine-grained acoustic features in addition to pure TDoA computation. Figure 6 illustrates the steps of the Set-keystroke Processing approach. This method first takes as input a set of different keystroke sounds recorded by a nearby mobile device. It then extracts the audio signals corresponding to the keystrokes and derives the TDoAs. Next, it performs *Pre-grouping of Keystrokes Using TDoA* to categorize the input keystrokes to multiple key groups based on the pre-calculated theoretical key groups in Section 2. To overcome the limited accuracy, this method then extracts the cepstral features (e.g., Mel Frequency Cepstral Coefficients (MFCCs)) from the keystroke sounds through the *Keystroke Acoustic Features (MFCCs) Extraction* component. The MFCC features are utilized to further cluster the keystrokes in the same key group so that each cluster only contains strokes of the same key. This allows calculation

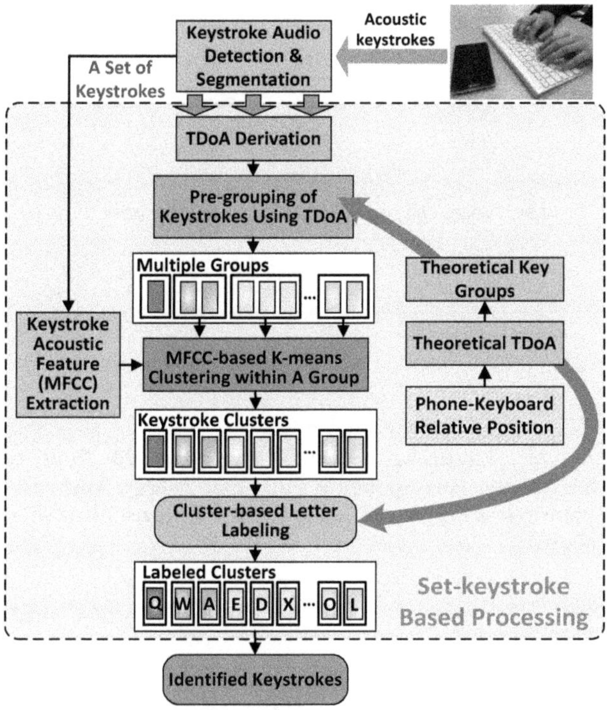

Figure 6: System architecture: set-keystroke based processing.

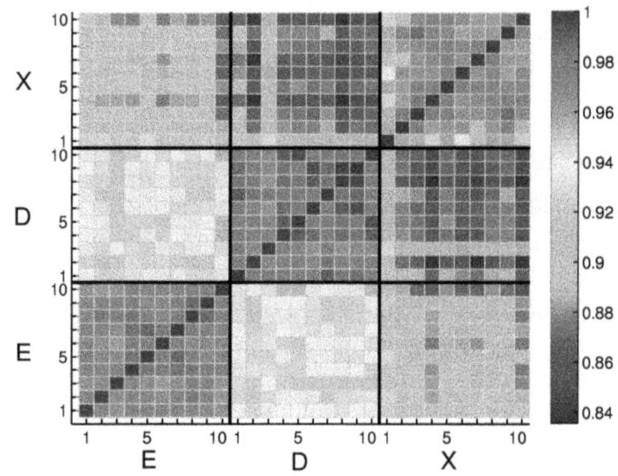

Figure 7: Pearson Correlation between MFCC features of three keys within a group: same key shows higher correlation, while different keys present lower correlation.

of mean TDoA values over several strokes of the key, which helps reduce measurement noise. Finally, the system performs key labeling of each cluster to recover each keystroke by examining the distance difference between the mean TDoA of each cluster to that of the theoretical TDoAs. We discuss the details of this approach in Section 4.

4. SET-KEYSTROKE BASED PROCESSING

4.1 Pre-grouping Keystrokes Into Theoretical Key Groups

After a set of keystrokes are collected, the Set-keystroke Based Processing approach first obtains the TDoA of each keystroke based on the techniques described in Section 5. It then utilizes these derived TDoA values to assign each keystroke into a theoretical key group based on the discussion in Section 2. We denote each key as K_i^n, where i is the key ID and n is the corresponding theoretical key group ID (e.g., K_1^1 is the key "Q" and K_{19}^{12} is the key "L"). We further denote the theoretical TDoAs of keys with the theoretical key group ID n as $D_n = \{\Delta t_i^n\}$, where i is the key ID and Δt_i^n is the theoretical TDoA of the key K_i^n. We then put each input keystroke into one of the theoretical key group by comparing its measured TDoA Δt with the theoretical TDoAs Δt_i^n. The input keystroke will be assigned to the theoretical key group n, if the differential TDoA between Δt and Δt_i^n is the minimum as shown below:

$$G = \arg\min_{n} |\Delta t - \forall \Delta t_i^n \in D_n|. \quad (3)$$

At the end, each input keystroke is assigned with a theoretical key group ID.

4.2 MFCC Based K-means Clustering

We next explore the acoustic features of keystroke sound to further separate the keystrokes within the same key group.

MFCC Feature Extraction. In our experiments, we find that the Mel-Frequency Cepstral Coefficients (MFCCs) [11, 12] of keystroke sounds capture acoustic signatures of different keys within the same theoretical key group. MFCC utilizes the magnitude of the Fourier Transform of the time-domain speech frames to analyze acoustic signals. The rationale of using MFCC to distinguish different keystrokes in the same theoretical key group is that physical uniqueness of each key component results in slightly different keystroke sounds for different keys. In addition, the keystroke sounds of keys at different locations experience different multipath effects. In particular, we extract the MFCC features from the entire duration of a keystroke sound. The number of filterbank channels is set to 32, and 16th-order cepstral coefficients are computed in each $10ms$ Hanning window, shifting $2.5ms$ each time. To exclude the frequency range of ambient noise, we only consider acoustic signal from $400Hz$ to $14kHz$ for MFCC extraction.

To illustrate the effectiveness of using the MFCC features to distinguish different keystrokes within a key group, we repeatedly type "E","D", and "X" keys (which are within the same theoretical key group) 10 times respectively and examine the correlation between the MFCC features extracted from the keystrokes. Figure 7 shows the Pearson correlation coefficient [13] between any two MFCC features derived from those keystrokes. We observe that the MFCC features of the same key present higher correlation than that of different keys. It thus appears promising to use MFCC features to distinguish keystrokes within a group. We note only one channel of the keystroke sound is used to extract MFCC features. If dual-microphones have different characteristics, we could combine parallel features to improve the clustering performance [14].

In-group K-means based Clustering. To reduce the effect of the imperfect measurement of TDoA and minimize the impact of environmental noise, we further cluster keystrokes within a group into different clusters based on the MFCC features (if the corresponding theoretical key group contains multiple keys). In particular, we use the *cityblock* distance to measure the distance between MFCC features of different keystrokes using K-means clustering [15]. In order to obtain the optimal clustering results, we minimize the variances of the MFCC features of keystrokes in each cluster by satisfying:

$$\arg\min_{C} \sum_{k=1}^{K} \sum_{n=1}^{N_k} |m_i^k - \mu_k|^2, \quad (4)$$

where N_k represents the number of keystrokes in the kth cluster, m_n^k denotes the MFCC features of the nth keystroke in the kth cluster, and μ_k is the mean value of the MFCC features in the kth cluster.

4.3 Cluster Based Letter Labeling

Finally we label each cluster. We leverage the statistical information of TDoAs in each cluster to determine which key the cluster belongs to. In practice, the TDoA measured from multiple keystrokes for the same key may have slightly different values as the touch point may change slightly each time. In our experiments, we find that keystroke sounds emitted from different keys within group have different distributions of TDoAs which result in slightly different mean TDoA. Moreover, the mean TDoA of the keystroke sounds emitted by the same key is very close to the corresponding theoretical TDoA. Thus, we compare the mean values of the measured TDoAs of each cluster to the theoretical TDoAs. The keystrokes in the cluster will be labeled as the key whose theoretical TDoA has the minimum distance to the mean TDoA of that cluster.

5. IMPLEMENTATION

5.1 Keystroke Segmentation

A typical keystroke acoustic signal can be divided into three parts [5, 7]: *touch peak*, *hit peak* and *release peak*. These peaks correspond to touch, hit and release the key respectively. Figure 8 shows an example of these three peaks from two different keyboards (i.e., Apple wireless keyboard and Razer Black Widow keyboard).

In order to extract the acoustic sound of a keystroke, we first examine the energy levels of the acoustic signal to determine the starting point of the keystroke sound [6, 7, 9]. Particularly, we calculate the energy levels of a keystroke sound by accumulating the square of the signal amplitude in a sliding time window as shown below:

$$A(t) = \sum_{n=t}^{t+W} r^2(n), \quad (5)$$

where W is the length of the time window and $r(n)$ is the amplitude of the sound signal within the time window. We empirically determine the length of the sliding window as $W = 2ms$ (i.e., 96 samples with $48kHz$ sampling rate). Figure 8 illustrates the energy levels of the keystroke signals from two keyboards.

We identify the starting point of the keystroke sound when the energy level exceeds a threshold. An empirical threshold of 0.05 is used in our work to determine the starting point p_s. We find the length of keystrokes is typically about 100 milliseconds. We thus extract the keystroke sound as the acoustic signal between $[p_s - 5ms, p_s + 100ms]$. Note that our system uses the entire keystroke sound to generate MFCC features, whereas the system only uses about first $20ms$ segment roughly corresponding to *touch peak* and *hit peak* to calculate the TDoA as these two peaks result in more accurate TDoA estimation than using the whole keystroke sound.

5.2 TDoA Derivation

Once we have input keystroke segment, we could find out how many delayed samples between two digital audio signals recorded at two microphones at a mobile device to obtain the time delay between two microphones when receiving keystroke sound. Suppose the acoustic signal of a keystroke is recorded at the two microphones as $r_1(n)$ and $r_2(n)$ with length L respectively, where $n = 1, \ldots, L$. We use cross-correlation between the two recorded signals to derive the TDoA. Cross-correlation is a standard signal

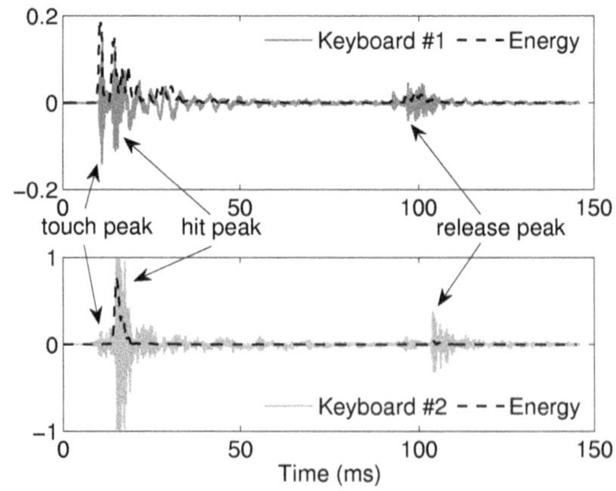

Figure 8: Keystroke acoustic signals emitted from two keyboards and corresponding short-time energy, keyboard-1 (Apple wireless keyboard) and keyboard-2 (Razer Blackwidow keyboard).

processing technique to measure the similarity between two signals and is calculated as:

$$cc(d) = \frac{\sum_n [(r_1(n) - \mu_{r_1}) \cdot (r_2(n-d) - \mu_{r_2})]}{\sqrt{\sum_n (r_1(n) - \mu_{r_1})^2 \cdot \sum_n (r_2(n-d) - \mu_{r_2})^2}}, \quad (6)$$

where μ_{r_1} and μ_{r_2} are the means of the corresponding signals. $cc(d)$ provides the similarity between $r_1(n)$ and shifted (delayed) copies of $r_2(n-d)$. If the Equation 6 is computed for all delays $d = 0, 1, \ldots, L-1$ then it results in a cross correlation series of the original $r_1(n)$ or $r_2(n)$. Then, the TDoA Δt (i.e., time delay) between $r_1(n)$ and $r_2(n)$ can be obtained as:

$$\Delta t = \frac{1}{f_s} \cdot (\arg\max_d cc(d) - L). \quad (7)$$

5.3 Relative Position Estimation

The relative position of the phone to the keyboard is needed in our method to calculate the ground truth of TDoA (i.e., theoretical TDoA values). This information could be obtained if the adversary intentionally places the phone at a pre-identified location or if the phone/tablet is used in a tablet stand. If the adversary plants a malware into the victim's smartphone, such information could be inferred based on the keyboard layout and the measured TDoA of keystrokes.

Keyboard layout can be obtained offline as long as the keyboard model is known. The keyboard model could be detected by capturing Bluetooth identifiers or through manual visual identification. With the keyboard layout, we then can define the coordinates of keys. For the sake of simplicity, we assume there are m keys K_i with known coordinate or location loc_i, where $i = 1, 2, ..., m$. Given the measured TDoA of a collection of keystrokes, we have the TDoA value of each key to that of two microphones with certain measurement error. We assume the measured TODA of each key to that of two microphones is $\hat{\Delta t_i}$, and the sorted one is $\hat{\Delta t_j}$, with $j = 1, 2, ..., m$.

With the above information, we can estimate the locations of two microphones M_1 and M_2, with the constraint $\|M_1 - M_2\| = d$, where d is the known distance between two microphones. With the arbitrary locations of microphones and known location of the key loc_i, we can calculate the theoretical TDoA of each key to that of two microphones as Δt_i, with the sorted one Δt_j. The optimal location of the two microphones thus can be estimated as follow:

$$\arg\min_{M_1,M_2} \sum_{j=1}^{j=m} \|\hat{\Delta t_j} - \Delta t_j\|, \quad (8)$$

where $\|\hat{\Delta t_j} - \Delta t_j\|$ represents squared distance between $\hat{\Delta t_j}$ and Δt_j.

Note that we may not get the measured TDoA of each key in practice. Even so we can calculate the location of two microphones as long as we obtain several measured TDoA values. Moreover, the measured TDoA of different keystrokes for the same key may be different slightly. Empirical study shows that the difference is small (i.e., about one or two samples). We could then group similar TDoA values together and use the averaged value to represent the TDoA of one key.

6. SYSTEM EVALUATION

In this section, we first present the experimental methodology, and then evaluate the performance of both set-keystroke based and single-keystroke based approaches. We also discuss the impact of multipath propagation on the keystroke snooping.

6.1 Experimental Methodology

6.1.1 Keyboard & Phone

Keyboard. Although we do not study the sound intensity level of each key, we evaluate our system with three different kinds of keyboards (i.e., an Apple wireless keyboard MC184LL/A, a Microsoft surface keyboard and a mechanical keyboard Razer Black Widow Ultimate) that produce different keystroke sound intensity levels. In particular, the keystroke sound from the mechanical keyboard is much louder than that from the Apple keyboard. And the keystroke sound from the Microsoft surface keyboard is the weakest. These keyboards have different designs and dimensions resulting in different layout of keyboards and different characteristics of keystroke sounds. Specifically, the Apple wireless keyboard and Microsoft surface keyboard have comparable dimension (i.e., $\sim 28mm \times 13mm$), whereas Razer keyboard is much larger (i.e., $\sim 47mm \times 17mm$). Moreover, the depth of key caps on the Apple and Microsoft keyboards (i.e., $\sim 2mm$) is much smaller than that of the Razer keyboard (i.e., $\sim 6mm$).

Mobile Phone. In our experiments, we utilize the Samsung Galaxy Note 3 as the mobile device to launch attacks. The operating system of the phone is Android 4.4.2. Although the Samsung Galaxy Note 3 has equipped with three microphones on the top, bottom and right bottom, the microphone on the right bottom edge is only used for noise cancelation. We thus use the top and bottom microphones to record the keystroke sound. The distance between these two microphones is about $15.3cm$.

6.1.2 Sampling Rate

The audio chipset on smartphone (i.e., Samsung Galaxy Note 3) is Qualcomm Snapdragon 800 MSM8974 [16], which supports $24bit$ nominal quantization at $192kHz$ sampling rate. Although the Android 4.4.2 system only supports up to $48kHz$ sampling rate, Smartphone Operating Systems are increasingly supporting higher sampling rate, for example recently released Android 5.0 claims it could support up to $96kHz$ sampling rate [17]. We thus envision that the software restriction on the sampling rate will be loosed and the smartphone could use $192kHz$ for audio recording in a near future. In the evaluation, we study the impact of different sampling rates on the performance of keystroke snooping. We simulate the

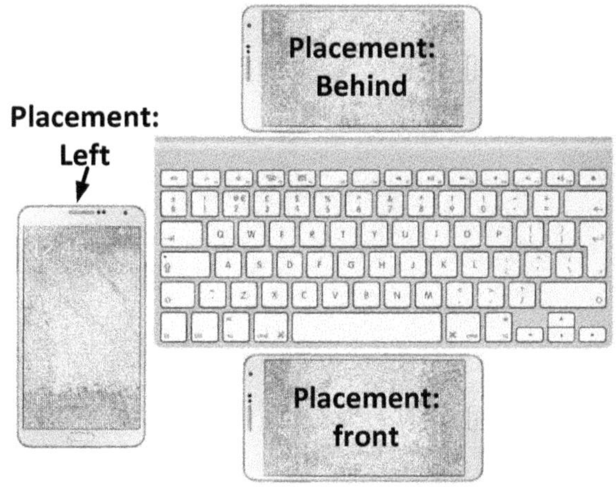

Figure 9: Three typical placements of the phone to the keyboard in the experiments.

high sampling rate (i.g., $96kHz$ and $192kHz$) by utilizing a pair of omni-directional microphones connected to a laptop through a USB adapter (i.e., Diamond Tube). We place the two microphones $15.3cm$ apart from each other to simulate the Samsung Galaxy Note 3 with $96kHz$ and $192kHz$ sampling rates.

6.1.3 Placement

We concentrate on the primary usage scenario, where the mobile device is placed behind the keyboard. We further study two more placement scenarios, where the mobile device is typically placed by the user when using the keyboards: in front of the keyboard and left side of the keyboard. These three placements are shown in Figure 9.

6.1.4 Data Collection

We focus on experiment on the 26 alphabet letters, but our method also applies to the whole keyboard. Three participants are involved to randomly type the 26 keys *a-z* on keyboards in typical office environments (i.e., two laboratory rooms with ambient noise (e.g., HVAC noise)). For each experimental setup (i.e., a specific type of keyboard, placement, and sampling rate), 520 keystrokes are collected. In total there are $3,640$ keystrokes from three participants for our experimental evaluation.

6.1.5 Metrics

We use the following three metrics to evaluate the performance of keystroke snooping:

Precision. Given N_k keystrokes of a key k, precision of recognizing the key k is defined as $P_k = \frac{N_k^T}{N_k^T + M_k^F}$, where N_k^T is number of keystrokes correctly recognized as the key k, M_k^F is the number of keystrokes corresponding to other keys mistakenly recognized as the key k.

Recall. Recall of the key k is defined as the percentage of the keystrokes that are correctly recognized as the key k among all keystrokes of the key k, which is $R_k = \frac{N_k^T}{N_k}$.

Top-w Accuracy. Given w identified key candidates, we want to know whether the pressed key is among these w candidates. The *top-w* accuracy measures overall performance of the keystroke recognition. Assuming the number of keys on keyboard is K, the *top-w* accuracy is defined as $A = \frac{\sum_{k=1}^{K} P_k^{T,w}}{\sum_{k=1}^{K} N_k}$, where P_k^T is the number of the keystrokes that are correctly identified as one of

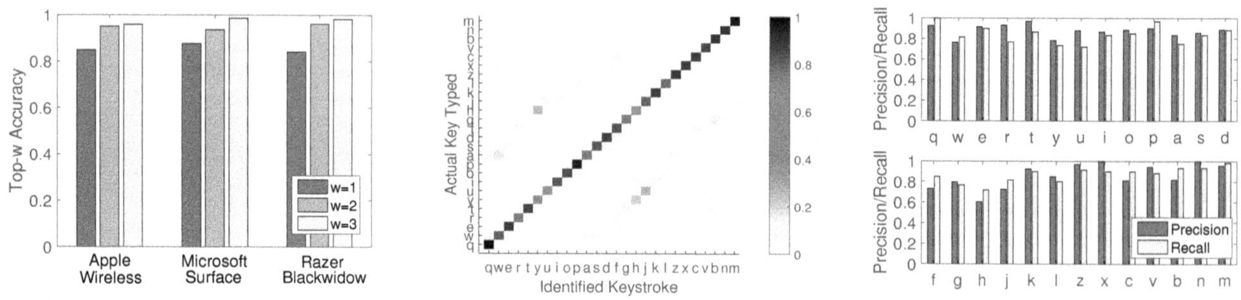

(a) Top-w accuracy with different keyboards.

(b) Confusion matrix.

(c) Precision and recall.

Figure 10: Performance of set-keystroke based processing using three keyboards and off-the-shelf phone (48kHz).

the keys among the *top-w* candidates, N_k is the total number of keystrokes for key k.

6.2 Performance of Set-keystroke Based Processing

6.2.1 *Overall Performance*

We evaluate the overall performance of the set-keystroke based processing with the primary attack scenario (i.e, the phone is placed behind the keyboard). The sampling rate is set as $48kHz$. Figure 10(a) shows the overall accuracy for keystroke identification with three different keyboards. We find that the phone can capture different levels of keystroke sound intensity from all three keyboards when the mobile phone is placed close to the keyboard. We observe that all three keyboards have comparable high accuracies. In particular, the top-1 accuracy is about 85.5%, whereas the top-2 and top-3 accuracy increase to 94.9% and 97.6%, respectively. These results show that our training-free and context-free approach provides sufficient accuracy to snoop on passwords composed of random characters.

Figure 10(b) plots the confusion matrix for the keystroke recognition after combining the results from three keyboards. We find that there are only few keystrokes are mistakenly identified as incorrect keys. These mistakenly recognized keystrokes usually correspond to the neighboring keys that have the same TDoA value. For example, a few keystrokes of the key w are mistakenly recognized as the key a which is crossed by the same hyperbola as that of the key w, as shown in Figure 2(b). Moreover, two neighboring keys may produce similar keystroke sounds resulting in high similarity of MFCC features. This could also lead to a few keystrokes mistakenly recognized as different keys.

The precision and recall of recognizing each alphabetic key is shown in Figure 10(c). It combines the results for all three keyboards. Overall, the average precision is about 87% and the average recall is about 85%. This result shows that our system could recognize each individual alphabetic letter without linguistic model. Thus, our system could recover passwords consisting of random combination of letters.

6.2.2 *TDoA Ranging*

We next study how accurately we can measure TDoAs with the phone's microphone capability of $192kHz$ sampling rate. We compare the measured distance difference (i.e., measured TDoA multiplies velocity of sound) of the keystroke sound to the true distance difference of the key at the two phone microphones. We use Apple wireless keyboard and each alphabet key is typed ten times in the experiment. Figure 11 illustrates mean and standard deviation of error for each key. We observe that the average ranging error is about $2mm$ indicating that mm-level accuracy could be achieved at $192kHz$ which is the frequency supported by the smartphone audio hardware.

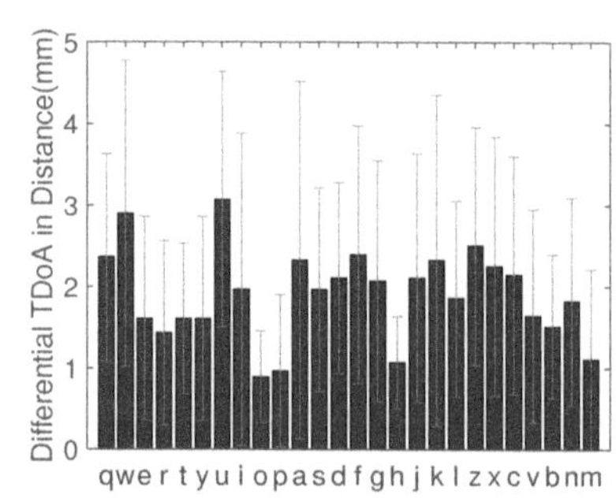

Figure 11: Differential between measured TDoA and theoretical TDoA with 192kHz sampling rate.

6.2.3 *Effect of Sampling Rate*

The impact of the sampling rate on the recognition accuracy is shown in Figure 12(a). The Microsoft surface keyboard is used in the experiment with the sampling rates of $48kHz$, $96kHz$ and $192kHz$. From Figure 12(a), we observe that higher sampling rate indeed improves the recognition accuracy as it provides higher TDoA resolution to discriminate the close by keys. In particular, the accuracy is improved from about 84.8% to 94.2% for top-1 candidate when increases the sampling rate from $48kHz$ to $192kHz$. However, the improvement on the top-3 candidates is marginal since these top-3 candidates usually covers these keys are spaced closely with the similar TDoA. The improved sampling frequency thus has limited improvement for the top-3 candidates.

Figure 12(b) and Figure 12(c) show the precision and recall for each key, respectively. We find higher sampling frequency in general improves the precision and recall, especially for the keys that hard to be distinguished at lower sampling frequency. For example, the keys w and a are physically close and the corresponding recalls and precisions are very low (at around 50%) when the sampling frequency is $48kHz$. They are improved to over 90% for both w and a at the sampling frequency of $192kHz$. This is also because higher sampling rate provides better TDoA resolution to distinguish close by keys.

6.2.4 *Effect of Phone's Placement*

Next, we study the performance under different phone placements. As shown in Figure 9, the phone is placed at three different

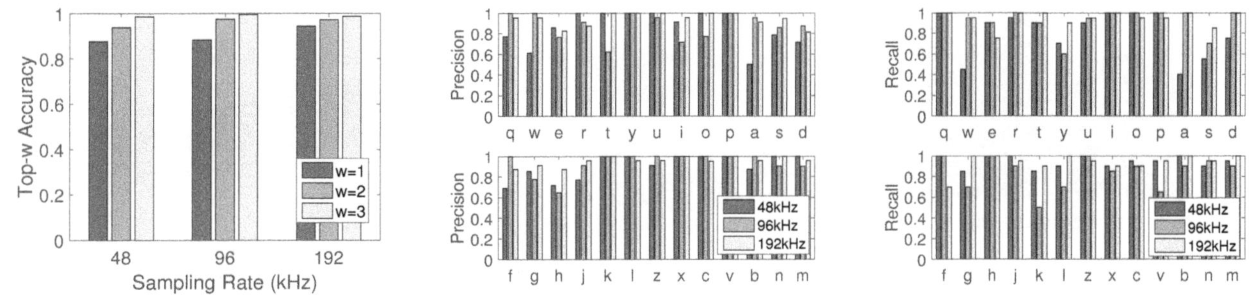

(a) Top-w accuracy with different sampling rates.

(b) Precision.

(c) Recall.

Figure 12: Performance of set-keystroke based processing using different sampling rates.

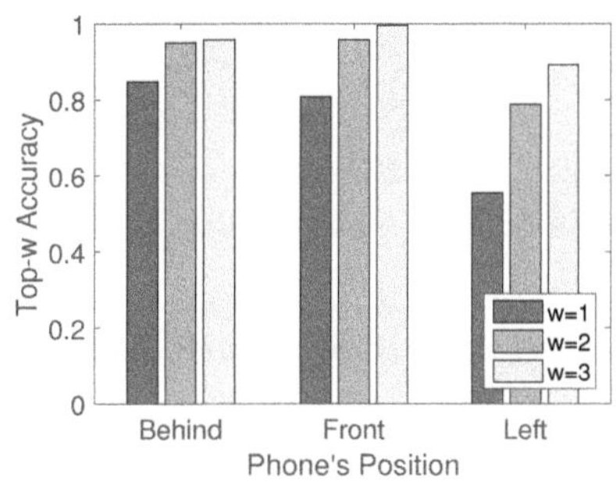

Figure 13: Top-w accuracy of set-keystroke processing with different placements of the phone to the keyboard.

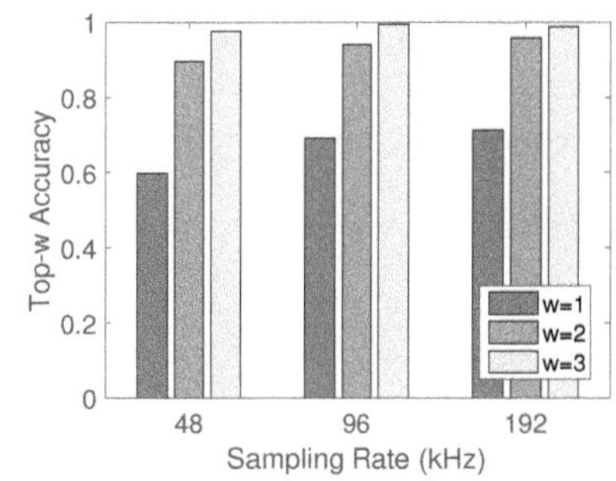

Figure 14: Top-w accuracy of single-keystroke processing with different sampling rates.

positions (i.e.,*behind*, $front$ and $left$) close to the Apple wireless keyboard. Figure 13 depicts the top-w accuracy for three phone placements. We observe that the placements of $front$ and *behind* result in higher accuracy than that of $left$. This is inline with our analysis on phone placement shown in Figure 3(a). This also shows that the primary placement of phone-keyboard (i.e., *behind*) when the users use external keyboard is more vulnerable to keystroke snooping. In particular, top-1 2 and 3 accuracies are about 84.8%, 95%, and 95.7% for the primary placement respectively, whereas they are about 80.1%, 95.7%, and 99% for $front$ placement respectively.

6.3 Performance of Single-keystroke Based Processing

We evaluate the naive approach, the single-keystroke based processing, by using the same dataset as we used for the set-keystroke based processing. Figure 14 shows the overall accuracy under different sampling rates. As expected, the naive approach has worse performance for top-1 accuracy when comparing to the set-keystroke based processing. This is because the single-keystroke based processing identifies keys based on a single TDoA value without exploiting acoustic features and statistic information of keystrokes of the same key. In particular, the top-1 accuracy of the single-keystroke based processing is about 60% at $48kHz$. The accuracy however increases dramatically to 89.6% for the top-2 accuracy and to 97.7% for the top-3 accuracy. This is due to that the top-2 and top-3 candidates usually cover the close-by keys that are hard to distinguish with one single TDoA.

In addition, the accuracy can be further improved by increasing the sampling rate to $96kHz$ or $192kHz$. With $192kHz$, the single-keystroke based processing can achieve 95% and 98% accuracy for top-2 and 3 candidates respectively. Figure 15 further shows the precision and recall of each key at $48kHz$ sampling rate. Since the single-keystroke based processing is hard to distinguish two keys with theoretical TDoAs within one sample, several keys are mistakenly recognized as others, such as keys *w,g,h,c* and *m* shown in Figure 15.

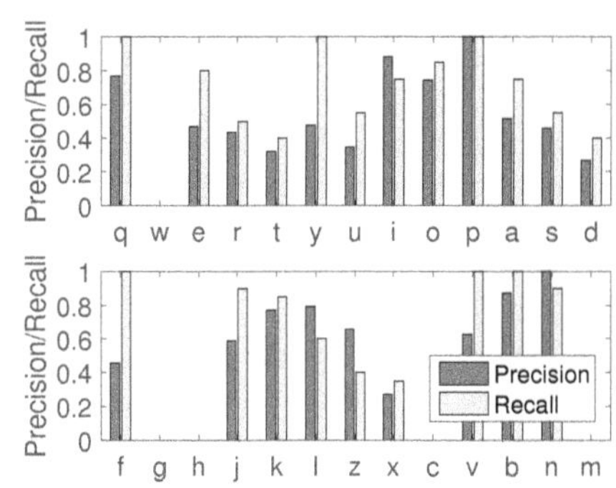

Figure 15: Precision and recall of single-keystroke processing with $48kHz$ sampling rate.

6.4 Multi-path Investigation

Multi-path Effects through Keys . Like many other wireless signals, multi-path effects may change the characteristics of acoustic signal. For keystrokes, because the sound sources are mostly inside each key and always below neighboring keys, it is important to understand the impact of multipath on the TDoA estimation in

(a) Keyboard with keycaps.

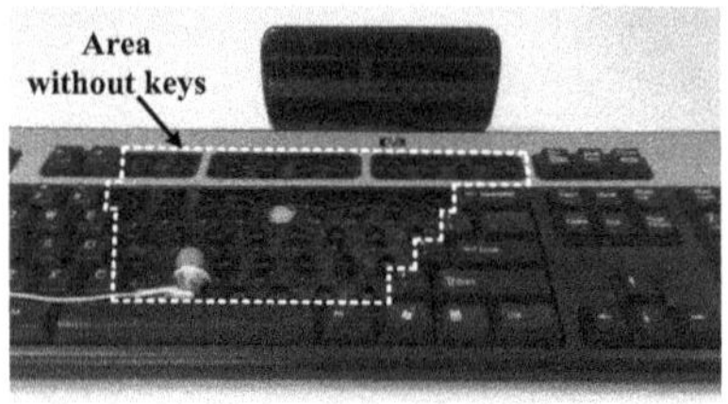

(b) Keyboard without keycaps.

Figure 16: Experimental Setups for multi-path investigation.

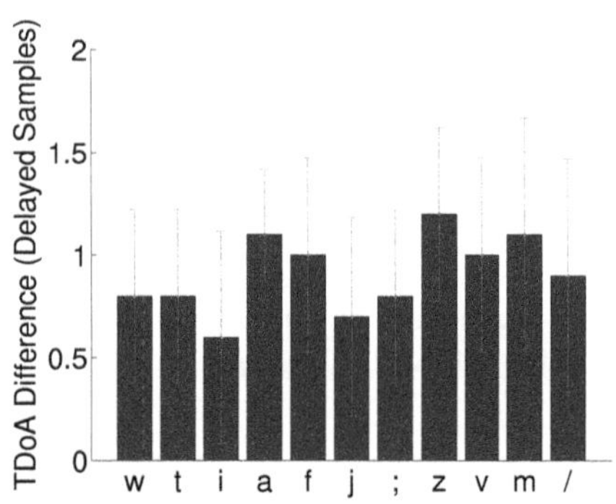

Figure 17: Differential TDoA between higher multi-path keyboard and lower multi-path keyboard (removed keys).

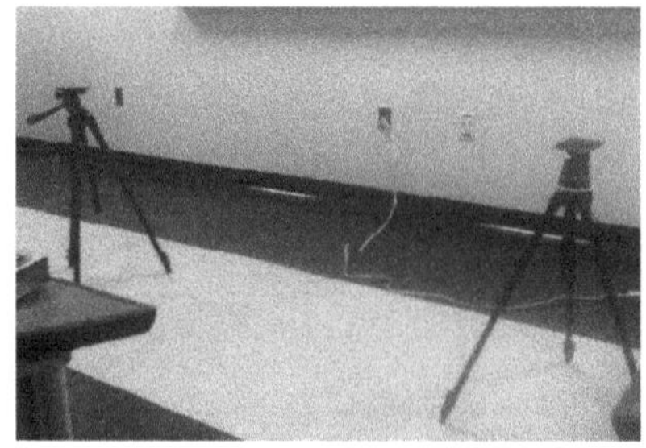

(a) Line-of-sight(LOS) environment.

(b) Non-line-of-sight(NLOS) environment.

Figure 18: Experimental Setups for multi-path investigation.

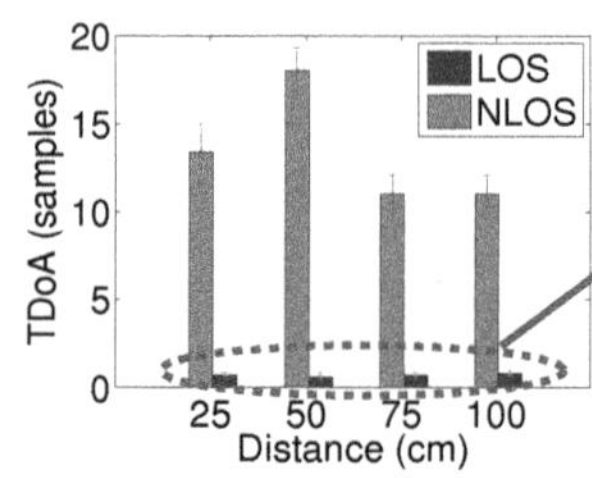

(a) LOS and NLOS TDoA estimation.

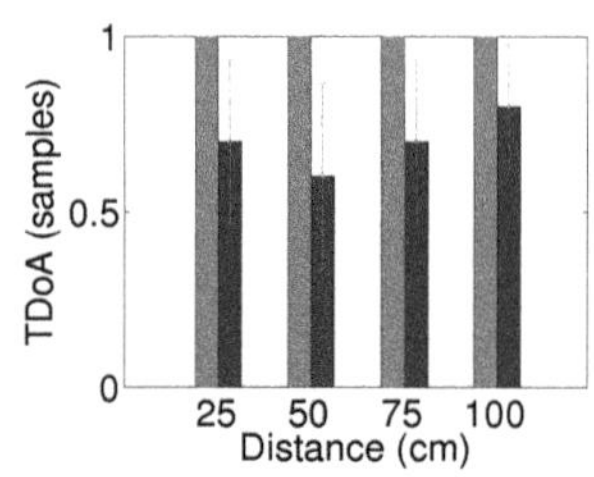

(b) Zoomed LOS and NLOS TDoA estimation.

Figure 19: TDoA estimation for LOS and NLOS environment.

our system. Particularly, we conduct following experiments: as shown in Figure 16(a), we first use the Samsung Galaxy Note 3 to play a pre-recorded chirp sound signal via a earbud, which is to make sure the sound comes below neighboring key caps and thus has multipath effects, for 20 times at each target key's position on a regular keyboard. Next, we repeat the same experiment, but remove the neighboring key caps as shown in Figure 16(b). Note that the phone is placed at 90 degree angle with the keyboard and the microphones are at a higher level than the keys on the keyboard to better study the multipath effects through keys. We remove all the keys between the earbud and the phone in order to simulate a lower multi-path environment. Figure 17 shows the difference of measured TDoA between such keyboards with different levels of multi-path effects. The average difference is only about 1 sample, and we thus conclude that the impact of multi-path (key caps on keyboard) does not have much influence on the TDoA estimation.

Non Line of Sight Effects. In the experiment, we use two mobile phones(i.e., Samsung Galaxy Note 3 and HTC Evo 4G) on two tripod at heights 1 meter above the ground as shown in Figure18(a). Similarly, we use the Samsung phone to record the chirp sound played by the HTC phone for 20 times. We align two phones to make sure the measured TDoA is close to 0 in the line-of-sight scenario. Next, we repeat the experiment, but with a thick card board separator placed in between the two phones to simulate the non-line-of-sight scenario as shown in Figure 18(b). Figure 19(a) shows the overall statistics of TDoAs in both the line-of-sight(LOS) scenario and non-line-of-sight(NLOS) scenario. Figure 19(b) is the enlarged part within the circle in Figure 19(a). Compared to the LOS scenario, the measured TDoAs increase dramatically in the NLOS scenario.

7. DISCUSSION

Environmental Accuracy. There are several factors that have an important effect on accuracy including phone placement, multi-path, and noise. Our system has been evaluated with different phone placements close to the keyboard. Accuracy would significantly degrade for recordings taken at larger distances and meter-level distances would require much larger microphone separation, for example by using multiple cooperating devices. We believe, however, that close proximity is possible even in adversarial settings, for example if the adversary co-opts the users own phone or if the attack takes place in relatively confined space (e.g., airplane). As any time-of-arrival related localization technique, our system relies on a detectable signal arriving on the line-of-sight path. If this path is significantly attenuated by an obstacle, our system will measure a reflected signal which leads to errors too large to allow for recovery of keystrokes (as illustrated in section 6.4). Phone placement close to the keyboard makes such an obstacle unlikely, however. We evaluate our system in typical office environments (i.e., two laboratory rooms with ambient noises (e.g., HVAC noise)), and our results show little impact under such ambient noises. Although we observe that loud noises (e.g., people talking) could impact the detection accuracy, we believe that additional filtering or context-based word correction could further improve the accuracy.

Security Concerns. To our knowledge, this is the first demonstration of acoustic keystroke recovery that raises more serious concerns regarding password snooping. It appears practical that malicious background apps with microphone access could recover passwords entered from a nearby keyboard (either an associated Bluetooth keyboard or a keyboard used for another device). If high definition stereo audio trickles down from professional video conference systems, to voice over ip and video calling apps, keys typed during a call could potentially be recovered by the remote party. It may also be possible for an adversary to inconspicuously place a phone near a victim's keyboard, particularly in tight settings such as an airplane. That said, the attack is currently only possible with select phone models that expose stereo recording and have large microphone separation and even at future expected sampling rates of 192kHz there is only a moderate chance of accurately capturing a long random password on first attempt. Still, this significantly reduces the password entropy to a small set of candidates that can be brute-forced and the accuracies would be sufficiently higher for the many weaker passwords in use, when combining the keystroke recognition results with knowledge about common password patterns.

While there is already considerable awareness of privacy risks associated with microphones, this awareness usually extends only to spoken words and not necessarily to keystrokes. Users might therefore type sensitive information even if they know that recording devices are present. Overall, these results indicate that microphone access on mobile device should be tightly controlled and we hope to raise awareness to that the recoverable information from mobile device audio recordings extends far beyond spoken conversations.

Localization Implications. More generally, the results show that low-multipath scenarios exist where mobile audio enable mm-level ranging and localization. Such high accuracies could be exploited for numerous applications from motion tracking [3], over driver phone use detection [4], to user interface improvements [18]. Currently, app-level access to these audio capabilities is still very limited; the capabilities are primarily used for specific functions such as noise cancellation during calls or high definition audio playback. In light of these localization results, we argue that app-level software access to multiple microphones and high sampling rates for localization purposes should become a higher priority.

8. RELATED WORK

There have been active research efforts in keystroke recognition based on the acoustic emanation or vibration of the keystroke [5–10, 19–21]. Acoustic emanation based approaches [5, 7–9] mainly rely on the observation that each key produces unique acoustic signal when typed, whereas the vibration based methods [10, 19–21] capture the correlation between the vibration of the keystroke and the location of the keystroke occurred. Vibration based methods all require training efforts to label the keystrokes and usually have less recognition accuracy than that of acoustic emanation based approaches.

In particular, Asonov *et al.* [5] observe that the sound of keystrokes differs slightly from key to key and build a supervised learning based approach to recognize keystrokes. This problem is then revisited by Zhuang *et al.* [7] through adding the language modeling to boost the English text recognition. Berger *et al.* [8] propose a dictionary-based approach leveraging the observation the keystroke sounds correlate to their physical positions on the keyboard. UbiK [6] proposes to locate the location of keystrokes made on solid surfaces leveraging multi-path fading with moderate training efforts. More recently, Zhu *et al.* [9] proposes to utilize microphones on three phones to identify the keystroke of nearby keyboard. The requirements of three phones and the achieved accuracy (i.e., 72.2%) make their approach less feasible for real attack scenarios. Comparing to the above research efforts, our approach is able to achieve high keystroke recognition accuracy by using a single phone without any training.

Another body of related work is smartphone based localization or ranging using acoustic signals [1–4, 22–29]. Beepbeep [1] and SwordFight [3] propose phone-to-phone ranging systems that can achieve centimeter level accuracy. Qiu *et al.* [2] develops a 3D continuous localization system for phone-to-phone scenarios with about 10 cm accuracy. The above work however requires application-level communication between two involved phones. Yang *et al.* [4] introduces an acoustic relative-ranging system that classifies phone's position inside the car. This approach relies on customized beep sound for acoustic signal detection. Tarzia *et al.* [22] introduces a technique based on ambient sound fingerprint achieve room-level accuracy. Constandache *et al.* [23] deploys extra acoustic infrastructure inside the building for correcting users' movement traces captured by the accelerometer and compass. In our work, we exploit dual microphones on smartphone to locate the keystroke with high accuracy without customized beep sound or phone-to-phone communication.

9. CONCLUSION

In this paper, we show that microphones on a single off-the-shelf phone can be used to discriminate mm-level position differences, which not only creates potential security and privacy concerns related to recovering keystrokes being typed on a nearby keyboard, but could also benefits a broad range of applications relying on fine-grained localization (e.g., sensing touch interaction on surfaces around mobile devices and tracking speakers in multiparty conversations in a meeting room). The implemented system does not require any training or linguistic model, which makes it applicable in real-world adversarial context and has the capability to recover random typing (e.g., passwords). In particular, our system exploits digital acoustic signals received at the microphones from an off-the-shelf phone and leverages the integration of geometry-based TDoA and fine-grained acoustic signatures to exceed the resolution limit of TDoA and accurately identify keystrokes. Extensive experiments involving three types of keyboards demonstrate that, with $48kHz$ sampling rate, our proposed system can accurately identify a set of keystrokes with over 85% accuracy. The accuracy of our system can achieve as high as 94% with the higher sampling rate (i.e., $192kHz$). Additionally, our system can snoop even a single keystroke input at the accuracy of 97% among the top-3 candidate keys with $48kHz$ sampling rate.

10. ACKNOWLEDGEMENT

We thank our anonymous shepherd and reviewers for their insightful comments. This work was partially supported by the National Science Foundation Grants CNS-0954020, CNS-1409767, SES-1450091, CNS-1505175, CNS-1223977, CNS-1409811 and Army Research Office W911NF-13-1-0288.

11. REFERENCES

[1] C. Peng, G. Shen, Y. Zhang, Y. Li, and K. Tan, "Beepbeep: A high accuracy acoustic ranging system using cots mobile devices," in *Proceedings of the 5th International Conference on Embedded Networked Sensor Systems (ACM SenSys)*, 2007.

[2] J. Qiu, D. Chu, X. Meng, and T. Moscibroda, "On the feasibility of real-time phone-to-phone 3d localization," in *Proceedings of the 9th ACM Conference on Embedded Networked Sensor Systems (ACM SenSys)*, 2011.

[3] Z. Zhang, D. Chu, X. Chen, and T. Moscibroda, "Swordfight: enabling a new class of phone-to-phone action games on commodity phones," in *Proceedings of the 10th Annual International Conference on Mobile Systems, Applications, and Services (ACM MobiSys)*, pp. 1–14, 2012.

[4] J. Yang, S. Sidhom, G. Chandrasekaran, T. Vu, H. Liu, N. Cecan, Y. Chen, M. Gruteser, and R. P. Martin, "Detecting driver phone use leveraging car speakers," in *Proceedings of the ACM International Conference on Mobile Computing and Networking (ACM MobiCom)*, 2011.

[5] D. Asonov and R. Agrawal, "Keyboard acoustic emanations," in *2012 IEEE Symposium on Security and Privacy*, 2004.

[6] J. Wang, K. Zhao, X. Zhang, and C. Peng, "Ubiquitous keyboard for small mobile devices: harnessing multipath fading for fine-grained keystroke localization," in *Proceedings of the 12th Annual International Conference on Mobile Systems, Applications, and Services (ACM MobiSys)*, pp. 14–27, 2014.

[7] L. Zhuang, F. Zhou, and J. Tygar, "Keyboard acoustic emanations revisited," in *Proceedings of the 12th ACM Conference on Computer and Communications Security*, pp. 373–382, 2005.

[8] Y. Berger, A. Wool, and A. Yeredor, "Dictionary attacks using keyboard acoustic emanations," in *Proceedings of the 13th ACM Conference on Computer and Communications Security*, pp. 245–254, 2006.

[9] T. Zhu, Q. Ma, S. Zhang, and Y. Liu, "Context-free attacks using keyboard acoustic emanations," in *Proceedings of the 2014 ACM SIGSAC Conference on Computer and Communications Security*, pp. 453–464, 2014.

[10] P. Marquardt, A. Verma, H. Carter, and P. Traynor, "(sp) iphone: decoding vibrations from nearby keyboards using mobile phone accelerometers," in *Proceedings of the 18th ACM Conference on Computer and Communications Security*, pp. 551–562, 2011.

[11] K. S. R. Murty and B. Yegnanarayana, "Combining evidence from residual phase and mfcc features for speaker recognition," *IEEE Signal Processing Letters*, vol. 13, no. 1, pp. 52–55, 2006.

[12] T. Kinnunen and H. Li, "An overview of text-independent speaker recognition: From features to supervectors," *Speech Communication*, vol. 52, no. 1, pp. 12–40, 2010.

[13] "Pearson product-moment correlation coefficient." http://en.wikipedia.org/wiki/Pearson-product-moment-correlation-coefficient,2015.

[14] Y. Obuchi, "Mixture weight optimization for dual-microphone mfcc combination," in *IEEE Workshop on Automatic Speech Recognition and Understanding*, pp. 325–330, IEEE, 2005.

[15] D. J. MacKay, *"Information theory, inference, and learning algorithms"*. Cambridge University Press, 2003.

[16] "Snapdragon 800 processors." https://www.qualcomm .com/products/snapdragon/processors/800, 2015.

[17] A. KJ, "Android l update to bring sound quality that will please audiophiles." http://www.ibtimes.co.uk /android-l-update-bring-sound-quality-that-will-please-audiophiles-1454695,2014.

[18] J. Schwarz, D. Klionsky, C. Harrison, P. Dietz, and A. Wilson, "Phone as a pixel: enabling ad-hoc, large-scale displays using mobile devices," in *Proceedings of the SIGCHI Conference on Human Factors in Computing Systems*, pp. 2235–2238, 2012.

[19] E. Miluzzo, A. Varshavsky, S. Balakrishnan, and R. R. Choudhury, "Tapprints: your finger taps have fingerprints," in *Proceedings of the 10th International Conference on Mobile Systems, Applications, and Services (ACM MobiSys)*, pp. 323–336, 2012.

[20] E. Owusu, J. Han, S. Das, A. Perrig, and J. Zhang, "Accessory: password inference using accelerometers on smartphones," in *Proceedings of the 12th Workshop on Mobile Computing Systems & Applications*, p. 9, 2012.

[21] Z. Xu, K. Bai, and S. Zhu, "Taplogger: Inferring user inputs on smartphone touchscreens using on-board motion sensors," in *Proceedings of the 5th ACM Conference on Security and Privacy in Wireless and Mobile Networks*, pp. 113–124, 2012.

[22] S. P. Tarzia, P. A. Dinda, R. P. Dick, and G. Memik, "Indoor localization without infrastructure using the acoustic background spectrum," in *Proceedings of the 9th International Conference on Mobile Systems, Applications, and Services (ACM MobiSys)*, 2011.

[23] I. Constandache, X. Bao, M. Azizyan, and R. R. Choudhury, "Did you see bob?: human localization using mobile phones," in *Proceedings of the 16th Annual International Conference on Mobile Computing and Networking (ACM MobiCom)*, 2010.

[24] H. Liu, Y. Gan, J. Yang, S. Sidhom, Y. Wang, Y. Chen, and F. Ye, "Push the limit of wifi based localization for smartphones," in *Proceedings of the 18th Annual International Conference on Mobile Computing and Networking (ACM MobiCom)*, pp. 305–316, 2012.

[25] C. Jiang, M. Fahad, Y. Guo, J. Yang, and Y. Chen, "Robot-assisted human indoor localization using the kinect sensor and smartphones," in *Proceedings of the IEEE/RSJ International Conference on Intelligent Robots and Systems (IROS)*, 2014.

[26] K. Liu, X. Liu, and X. Li, "Guoguo: Enabling fine-grained indoor localization via smartphone," in *Proceeding of the 11th Annual International Conference on Mobile Systems, Applications, and Services (ACM MobiSys)*, pp. 235–248, 2013.

[27] W. Huang, Y. Xiong, X.-Y. Li, H. Lin, X. Mao, P. Yang, and Y. Liu, "Shake and walk: Acoustic direction finding and fine-grained indoor localization using smartphones," in *Proceedings IEEE INFOCOM*, pp. 370–378, 2014.

[28] B. Xu, G. Sun, R. Yu, and Z. Yang, "High-accuracy tdoa-based localization without time synchronization," *IEEE Transactions on Parallel and Distributed Systems*, vol. 24, no. 8, pp. 1567–1576, 2013.

[29] M. Uddin and T. Nadeem, "Rf-beep: A light ranging scheme for smart devices," in *2013 IEEE International Conference on Pervasive Computing and Communications (PerCom)*, pp. 114–122, 2013.

MoLe: Motion Leaks through Smartwatch Sensors

He Wang
University of Illinois at Urbana-Champaign
Champaign, IL, USA
hewang5@illinois.edu

Ted Tsung-Te Lai
University of Illinois at Urbana-Champaign
Champaign, IL, USA
tedlai@illinois.edu

Romit Roy Choudhury
University of Illinois at Urbana-Champaign
Champaign, IL, USA
croy@illinois.edu

ABSTRACT

Imagine a user typing on a laptop keyboard while wearing a smart watch. This paper asks whether motion sensors from the watch can leak information about what the user is typing. While its not surprising that some information will be leaked, the question is *how much?* We find that when motion signal processing is combined with patterns in English language, the leakage is substantial. Reported results show that when a user types a word W, it is possible to shortlist a median of 24 words, such that W is in this shortlist. When the word is longer than 6 characters, the median shortlist drops to 10. Of course, such leaks happen without requiring any training from the user, and also under the (obvious) condition that the watch is only on the left hand. We believe this is surprising and merits awareness, especially in light of various continuous sensing apps that are emerging in the app market. Moreover, we discover additional "leaks" that can further reduce the shortlist – we leave these exploitations to future work.

Categories and Subject Descriptors

K.6.5 [**Management of Computing and Information Systems**]: Security and Protection — Invasive software; C.3 [**Special-purpose and Application-based Systems**]: Real-time and embedded systems

Keywords

motion leaks; smartwatch; side-channel attacks; accelerometer; gyroscope; security; malware; Bayesian inference; gesture

1. INTRODUCTION

Rich sensors on wearable devices are offering valuable data, enabling important applications in mobile health, user-interfaces, context-awareness, activity tracking, gaming, etc. Of course, such data are often "double edged swords" since they leak information about aspects of lives that are considered private. In our struggle to define what level of data exposure is appropriate, the core question often comes to: *what can be inferred from a given sensor data?* Every so often, we find that highly surprising inferences can be made from an apparently harmless data, forcing us to push back on information exposure. While this is a broad area of research, and immense work has been performed in this direction, new platforms and applications warrant a continuous vigil on information leakage. This paper looks into a narrow piece of this general problem. We ask: *can accelerometer and gyroscope data from smart watches be mined to infer the words that a user is typing.* In other words, given that a user's wrist moves in the granularity of few centimeters while typing, can the corresponding motion data be used to derive the keys that the user has typed? If so, the ramifications are serious – a smart watch app can be disguised as an activity tracker to heavily leak a user's emails, search queries, and other keyboard-typed documents. Unlike keystroke loggers that need to find loopholes in the operating system, the activity tracker malware can obtain the user's permission and easily launch a side channel attack.

Of course, this is not the first work that combines motion data processing with language structure to infer higher level semantics. Recent research have explored various systems and applications, including writing in the air [1], remote control [2], gesture-based signing and authentication [3, 4], smoking gestures [5], etc. While all these systems bear similarity in abstraction, unique challenges (and opportunities) emerge when a particular application is addressed end to end. In our case, we find that the absence of data from the right hand is a unique constraint, and so is the issue of inferring which finger executed the key-press. For a given position of the wrist watch, any one of 3 or 4 different keys could have been pressed, which could be further interspersed by unknown number of keys pressed by the right hand. Moreover, not all users type with equal dexterity – some use their little finger far less efficiently while others use specific fingers when it comes to digits or corner keys. Finally, detecting the typed key is also a function of where the finger was previously, injecting a notion of dependency between consecutive inferences. With these and more application-specific issues, global typing or motion models do not apply. While fundamentally new signal processing or learning algorithms may not be needed, modifying existing techniques and systematically integrating them into a whole is the crux of our contribution.

Importantly, the application of typing also offers a number of opportunities that should be leveraged to improve the inference capability of the watch. For instance, the watch motion is mostly confined to the 2D keyboard plane, in contrast to 3D gestures in air in other applications [3, 6]. The orientation of the watch is relatively uniform across various users and, in many users, moves

MobiCom'15, September 7–11, 2015, Paris, France.
 ISBN 978-1-4503-3619-2/15/09 ...$15.00.
DOI: http://dx.doi.org/10.1145/2789168.2790121.

back to a reference position while typing (the "F" and "J" keys). Finally, knowing spelling priors from English dictionary further helps in developing Bayesian decisions. The combination of these challenges and opportunities motivates the research, with the aim of quantifying the degree of information leakage.

This paper develops *Motion Leaks* (*MoLe*), a completely functional system on Samsung Gear Live smart watches. Briefly, two of the authors pretend to be attackers and type 500 words each wearing the smart watch on their left wrist. The accelerometer and gyroscope data is used as training data, and processed through a sequence of steps, including key-press detection, hand-motion tracking, character point cloud computation, and Bayesian modeling and inference. Then, 8 different volunteers are recruited, and each asked to type 300 different English words from a dictionary. The smart-watch sensor data from the volunteers are transferred to our server, which then short-lists K words, ranked in the decreasing order of probability (i.e., the first ranked word is considered the most probable guess). The actual words typed by volunteers are then revealed and each word's rank computed from the short-list.

We plot the distribution of rank across all the typed words. With this being the core of the evaluation methodology, we obviously test for various parameters and conditions, including different word lengths, sensor sampling rate, different keyboards, etc. Current limitations of this work include: (1) inability to infer non-valid English words, such as passwords; (2) scalability across different watch models; (3) inability to parse sentences due to difficulties in detecting the "space bar". We have also not tested with other wearable devices, such as *Fitbits* – we believe with some customization, the attacks can be launched on those platforms as well.

In light of these, the main contributions in the paper may be summarized as:

- *Identifying the possibility of leakage when users type while wearing a smart watch.* Developing the required building blocks through techniques in key-press detection, hand-motion tracking, cross-user data matching, and Bayesian inference.

- *Developing the system on Samsung Gear Live smart watches and experimenting with real users.* Performing experiments across 8 users and revealing how typed words can be inferred with reasonable accuracy. Individuals who came to know about our results expressed a sense of alarm and suggested that the findings be disseminated publicly.

The rest of the paper expands on these contributions, beginning with some groundwork and measurements, followed by system overview, assumptions, design detail, and evaluation.

2. SMART WATCH DATA: A FIRST LOOK

To understand the problem landscape, we take a first look into the data from smart watches. Basic questions pertain to the amount of wrist displacement for typed keys, whether displacements for nearby keys are even visually discernible, whether the displacements are consistent over time, etc. To this end, two of the authors wore a smart watch and recorded the accelerometer and gyroscope data as they typed each character one by one. The positive X axis of the watch is parallel to the arm and pointed towards the fingers, the positive Y axis is perpendicular and upward, and the positive Z axis pointed upwards from the plane of the arm. To capture ground truth, we placed a phone camera right on top of the keyboard and recorded video at 30 fps (Figure 1). A green and a yellow sticker placed on the watch helps with tracking the watch movement by using computer vision techniques. The watch, the phone camera, and the keyboard logger were all time-synchronized via the network time protocol (NTP). The synchronization offers precise correspondence between the sensor and visual data, extending semantic meaning to the motion signals.

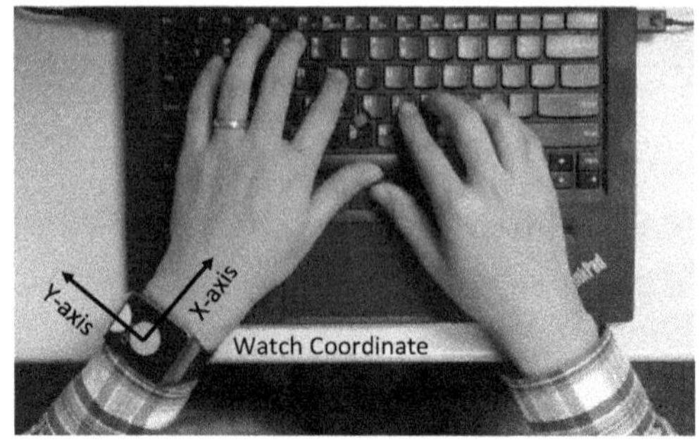

Figure 1: Watch coordinate system and ground truth measurement by recording hand typing with a smartphone camera view.

Figure 2 shows an example sequence of video frames capturing the process of typing the character "T". The left hand starts from a home position (i.e., the key "F"), moves along the +X direction to press "T", hits the key, and returns back to the home position. The yellow arrow on the arm shows the displacement of the green marker on the watch.

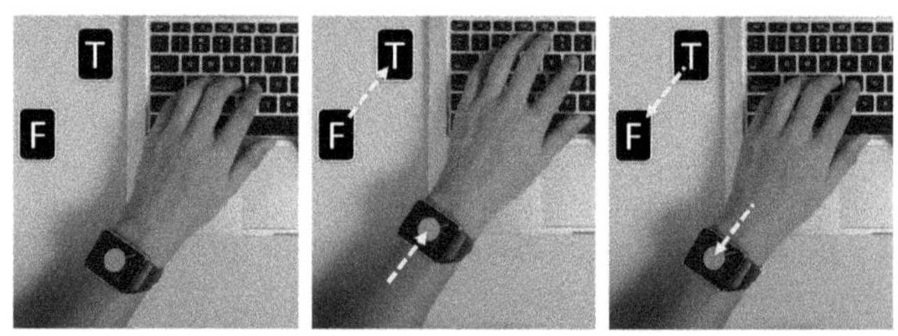

Figure 2: 3 **video frames show the process of typing "T" from "F".**

Figure 3 plots motion data from 20 different characters located on the left side of the keyboard. For each graph, the X axis is time and the Y axis is the displacement of the watch computed from the accelerometer's X axis data (the accelerometer's Y and Z axes are not shown). The light gray vertical bar in each graph marks the time of the key-press, obtained from the keyboard logger. Observe that the displacements align well with the keyboard's layout. The first row (12345) generates the largest positive displacement and the last row (zxcvb) produces negative displacement. The left fingers are initially placed on the third row (asdf), so nearly no displacement is detected for these characters. Although preliminary, these signals offer first indication of information leakage through watches.

Figure 4 shows the watch displacement for the same 20 keys, but in 2D space (i.e., using the combined X and Y axes data from the accelerometer). Each color represents one row on the keyboard. While some keys (e.g., 1, t, r, 4, 5) are quite isolated, others overlap strongly – in particular, "asdf", "zxcv" and "q23" exhibit the strongest overlaps. This is not surprising. Cluster "asdf" is an

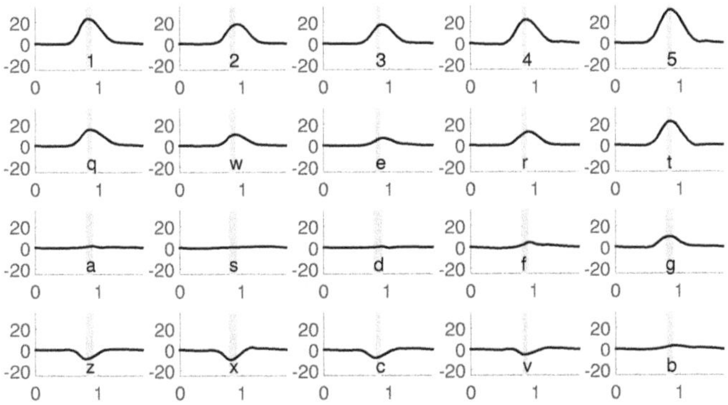

Figure 3: The watch X axis displacements while a human types 20 characters. In the figures, X axis is time in seconds and Y axis is watch X axis displacement in millimeter. The gray bar shows the keystroke press and release time interval.

outcome of the fingers being on these keys in the home position – the wrist hardly needs to move when typing these keys. Similarly, the fingers move uniformly downward for "zxcv" resulting in similarity between the keys. Finally, the hand movement for "q" is similar to "2" and "3" even though they are all not on the same row. This is because the little finger is shorter, and to type the character "q", it must move as much as the ring finger must move to type "2".

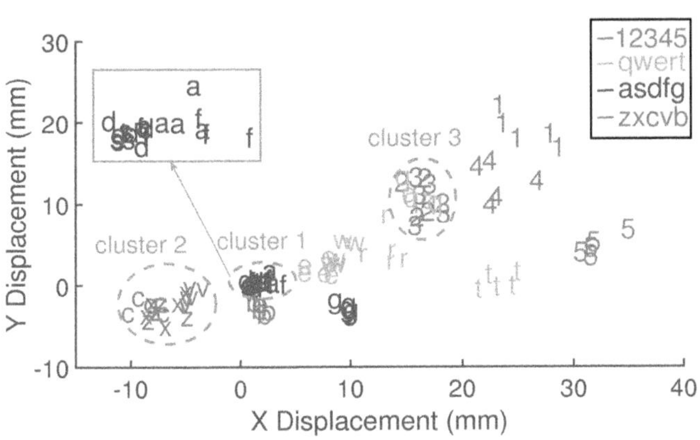

Figure 4: Watch 2D displacements while a human types 20 characters with her left hand. Each character is typed repeatedly 5 times. (0,0) is the initial location when left hand fingers are placed on home position ("asdf"). Note that X and Y axes in the graph are in the watch's coordinate system.

Decoding characters gets more complicated when the user types a word rather than just a single character. Figure 5 shows the sequence of hand displacements where the word "teacher" is typed. Obvious issues emerge: The wrist motion for each character is no longer aligned with the earlier observations since the motion is relative to the previous position of the key. Observe that "e", "a" and "c" are all far away from their respective clusters detected earlier in Figure 4. Moreover, we did not record "h" (pressed by the right hand), rather a small random motion of the left hand during this time. Finally, real world environments do not have cameras, and hence the data is completely unlabeled – a wrong decision about any of the keys can derail all subsequent decisions. In sum, while sensor data from smart watches indeed encode the human-typed information, decoding them reliably in real world conditions presents non-trivial challenges.

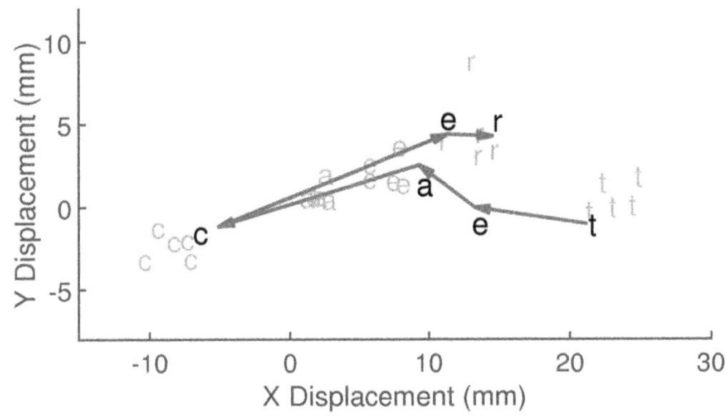

Figure 5: Comparison of typing "teacher" continuously (in black) against each character separately (in gray). Note that the positions of "e", "a" and "c" are away from their original points due to sequential typing. Also, "h" is not captured due to right hand typing.

3. SYSTEM OVERVIEW

This section presents a functional overview of *MoLe*; details of the technical building blocks will follow in Section 4. In the scenario of interest, we assume that the attacker has successfully installed the *MoLe* app in the user's smart watch and is receiving accelerometer and gyroscope data at the *MoLe* cloud server.

Figure 6 illustrates the flow of operations in the end to end *MoLe* system. At the backend server, the attacker types each character on a computer keyboard multiple times and computes a *character point cloud (CPC)* similar to the one in Figure 4. The operation is performed offline, and is stored separately for use later. The cloud can also be computed from multiple people (e.g., accomplices of the attacker) strengthening the robustness of the attack.

Now, when the raw sensor data from the user arrives, it is passed through a "Keystroke Detection" module, responsible for two tasks. (1) It detects the timing of each key stroke by analyzing the *Z* axis of the sensor data – every time a user presses a key, the watch exhibits a discernible dip in the negative Z axis. (2) It computes the net 2D displacement of the watch by processing the signal through multiple steps, including gravity removal, mean removal, double integration, and Kalman Filtering. The output of the keystroke detection module is a set of $< location_i, time_i >$ tuples, where $location_i$ denotes the estimated location of the watch at $time_i$ when the key was pressed. When all the locations are plotted on the 2D plane, an *unlabeled point cloud (UPC)* emerges (note that the characters corresponding to each point in this cloud is not known). Figure 7 shows a comparison of the character point cloud developed offline by the attacker and an unlabeled point cloud computed from the attackee's data.

The UPC is forwarded to the "Cloud Fitting" module whose task is to assign approximate labels to the points in UPC. For this, the cloud fitting module obtains the CPC that was computed earlier, and scales and rotates the convex hull of the CPC to best fit the convex hull of the UPC. The output is a rotated and scaled CPC which serves as the *reference template* for decoding the unlabeled points in UPC.

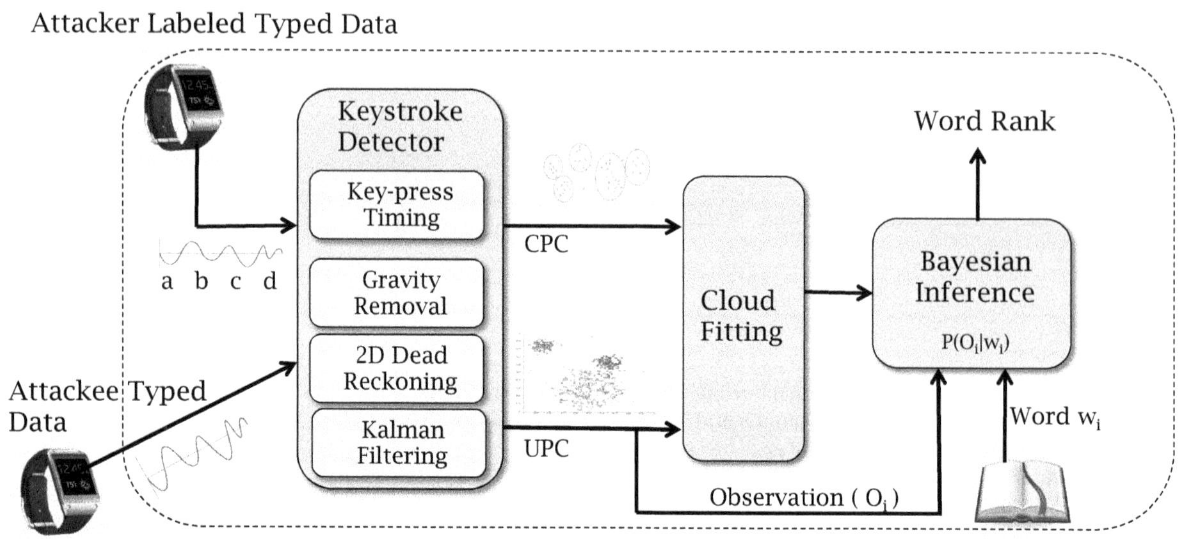

Figure 6: System Overview: The typed data from users are pre-processed through gravity removal and timing analysis blocks, superimposed on the refitted typing templates, and passed through a Bayesian inference model that leverages the patterns and structures in English words to ultimately decode the typed words. Note, training is only required from the attacker's end; no training needed for the user.

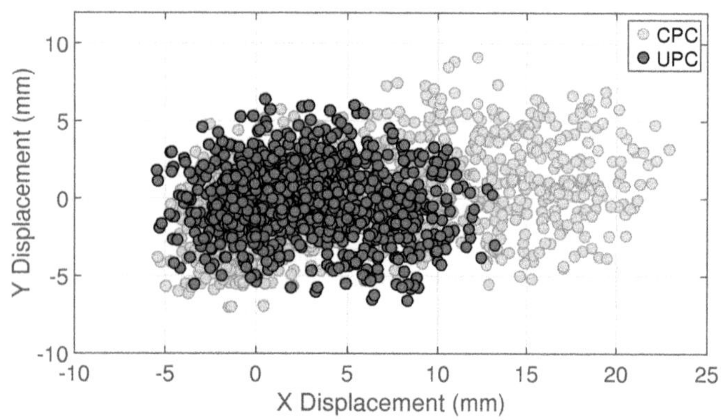

Figure 7: (a) Character point cloud computed from attackers data; (b) Unlabeled point cloud computed from user's data.

A "Bayesian Inference" module now accepts three items as input: (1) the template output from Cloud Fitting, (2) the unlabeled points from the UPC, and (3) a dictionary W of valid English words, w_i[1]. Briefly, for each valid word w_i, the Bayesian Inference module (BIM) computes the *a posteriori* probability that the unlabeled points form w_i. For instance, if w_i is the word "dear", BIM computes the probability that the first unlabeled point is "d", the second unlabeled point is "e", and so on. The product of the probabilities is the final probability that the unlabeled points is the word "dear". BIM computes this probability for each word w_i, and outputs a ranked list of $< word, probability >$ tuples as a guess of the user-typed word. If its a password, the attacker can now try out all the guesses above some probability threshold; if its an email or a search query, the attacker could manually try to decode the text from the possible sets of words. Even though *MoLe* does not offer a single suggestion, the probability estimate associated to each guess dramatically reduces the search space for the attacker. Results in Section 5.2 will quantify this reduction from the attacker's point of view.

[1]For practical purposes, W contains the 5000 most frequently used English words, available from [7].

3.1 Assumptions

Before moving forward, we intend to enumerate a number of assumptions we make. These assumptions make *MoLe* inadequate for launching a real life attack, however, we believe that the assumptions are not fundamental and can be relaxed with some more work.

- The evaluation is performed in a controlled environment where volunteers type one word at a time (as opposed to free-flowing sentences).
- We assume valid English words – passwords that contain interspersed digits, or non-English character-sequences, are not decodable as of now.
- We have used the same Samsung smart watch model for both the attacker and the user – in reality the attacker can generate the CPC for different watch models and use the appropriate one based on the user's model.
- We assume the user is seasoned in typing in that he/she roughly uses the appropriate fingers – novice typists who do not abide by basic typing rules may not be subject to our proposed attacks.

Under these assumptions, the design details and evaluation of *MoLe* are presented next.

4. DESIGN DETAILS

We describe the main techniques executed by each module in Figure 6.

4.1 Keystroke Detector

Given sensor signals as input, this module is responsible for computing the time and location of each key-press present in the signal. The location is essentially a 2D vector with the origin as the "F" key on the keyboard. Aggregating all the key-press locations will yield the point cloud as discussed earlier.

Key-press Timing

The intuition to detect key presses is rooted in the hand's motion in the vertical direction. When the finger dips while typing a key, the wrist also undergoes a partial dipping motion, expected to reflect in the Z axis of the watch. Figure 8 shows an example of the Z axis motion when the user types the word "administrative". Using ground truth, we observe that the actual key presses generally produce prominent peaks, however, false positives and false negatives occur. False positive occur mainly during transition from one key to another – the hand moves up slightly to make the movement, which manifests in Z-axis motion. False negatives typically arise due to subtle Z axis motion for keys like "asdf" that can go undetected.

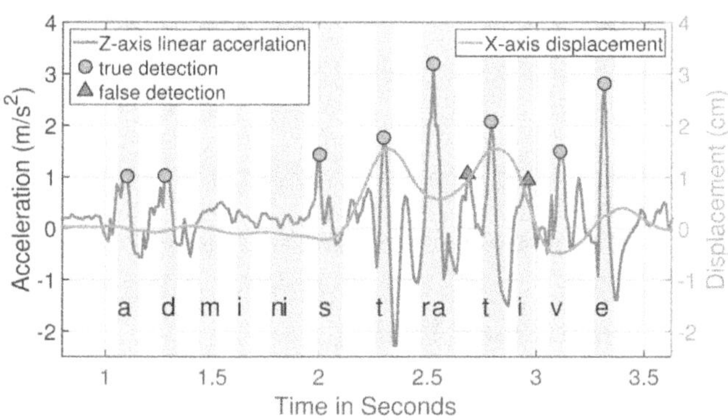

Figure 8: A simple peak detection scheme to detect keystrokes. The left Y-axis represents acceleration and the right Y-axis indicates displacement. Note that, for "a","d","s" keystrokes, lower Z-axis acceleration is generated because of left hand's initial position. At time 2.7 and 3 seconds, there are two false detections due to the left hand moving from "a" to "t" and from "t" to "v".

To cope with these issues, we use *bagged decision trees* to classify keystrokes. A bagged decision tree is a ensemble classifier that trains multiple decision trees by selecting different subsets of feature and training examples. The classifier improves the stability and accuracy by letting each subtree learn on the attacker's labeled data, apply the learning to the unlabeled data, and then compute the final results via voting. To obtain the labeled data, we first apply a simple threshold-based peak detection method [8] on the Z axis acceleration, and label true/false detection on the attacker's template. We purposely set the peak detection threshold to be low so that we do not miss true keystrokes. Then we extract features within a time window around the labels and train the classifier.

The feature set includes: the width, height, prominence of the Z axis peak; the mean, variance, max, min, skewness, and kurtosis for each of the 3-axis displacement, velocity, acceleration, and gyroscope rotation; the magnitude of acceleration/gyroscope; and finally the correlation of each pair between acceleration and gyroscope vectors. When the attackee's sensor data arrives, we apply the same peak detection scheme and obtain many candidate keystrokes and their features. Then the classifier identifies the validity of the keystroke and selects the max value of Z axis acceleration to denote the timing of the key-press. Figure 9 shows an example of the classification result of the word "administrative".

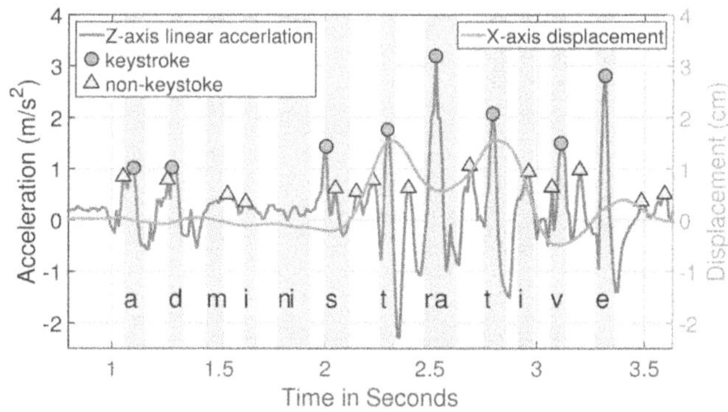

Figure 9: Bagged decision classification results: A peak detection tool with low thresholds is first applied to the Z-axis acceleration data and marks potential keystrokes (both yellow triangles and green circles). The classifier then identifies whether the peaks are keystrokes or not. Note that for the first "a" and "d", since two peaks are too close, the classifier would identify only one peak with highest Z-axis acceleration within a time window.

Figure 10 shows the detection rate for each key press when using one author's template model to test on 8 different volunteer recruited in section 5.1 (and ground truth recorded by the keyboard logger software). Expectedly, the keys pressed by the right hand are largely undetected.

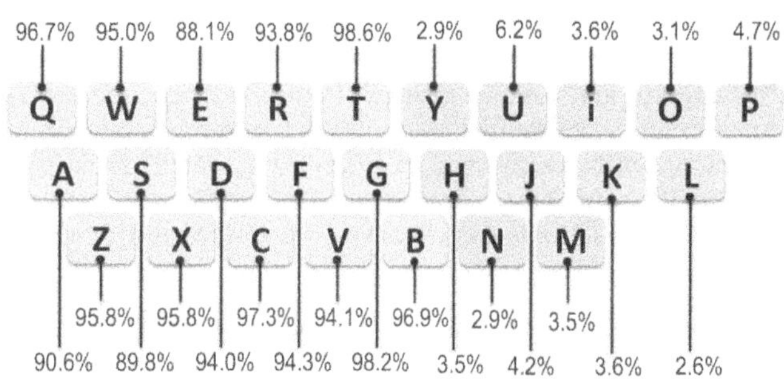

Figure 10: Keystroke detection rate for each character.

Key-Press Location Estimation

The core challenge here pertains to tracking the hand motion as it moves from one key to another, and therefrom, infer the location of each key-press. Tracking over time is non-trivial since the required accuracy is high (in the granularity of key sizes); moreover, incorrect detection of one key will affect subsequent results. The hope we have is that the the left index finger periodically moves back to the home key "F", and hence, its an opportunity to recalibrate the tracking process at the start and end of a sequence of typed characters.

As a first cut, we used the linear acceleration (offered by the native Android API) to compute displacement – we applied established double integration and mean removal techniques. Figure 11 compares the X displacement computed by Android API and *MoLe*, against ground truth (available from the camera). The errors proved inadequate for our purposes. Hence, we developed an improved tracking technique tailored to the *MoLe* application. We define each of the steps below.

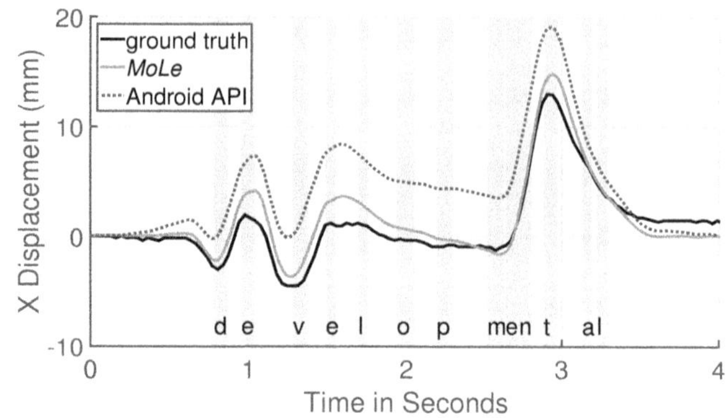

Figure 11: Comparison of *MoLe* and Android API x-axis displacement results. Y-axis has similar results but is omitted due to space.

(1) Find gravity to define an absolute coordinate system. Before the attacker (or attackee) starts to type, his/her hand is stable – we use this opportunity to estimate the direction of gravity in the watch's coordinate system; we can then estimate the orthogonal plane, which is the absolute horizontal plane. We then project the watch's X axis to the absolute horizontal plane to get the absolute X axis. Since the absolute Z axis is essentially along the direction of gravity, the cross product of Z and X axes yields the absolute Y axis. $C = (X, Y, Z)$ is the absolute coordinate system (represented by the watch's coordinate system). Of course, since the wrist orientation changes during typing, this representation changes as well. Thus, at the starting point, we represent the absolute coordinates as $C(0) = (X(0), Y(0), Z(0))$.

(2) Estimate and remove gravity. From the gyroscope, we estimate the rotation matrix over time $R(t)$ and use it to estimate the variation in watch's gravity $g(t)$, in the watch's coordinate system. We sample acceleration $a(t)$ in watch's coordinate system and it is polluted by gravity. Now we remove gravity and get $a_{rg}(t) = a(t) - g(t)$.

(3) Estimate $C(t)$ and calculate projected acceleration. Note that directly integrating $a_{rg}(t)$ has no physical meaning even if gravity has already been removed. This is because $a_{rg}(t)$ is along the watch's axes and watch rotates overtime. Ideally, we want to integrate along fixed directions of the absolute coordinate system. Those directions are $X(t)$, $Y(t)$ and $Z(t)$ mentioned before in $C(t)$ – we can get $C(t)$ with the help of the rotation matrix $R(t)$. Thus, $a'_{rg}(t)$ can be obtained by projecting $a_{rg}(t)$ to $X(t)$, $Y(t)$ and $Z(t)$. Integrating $a'_{rg}(t)$ now yields the speed $v'(t)$, and integrating $v'(t)$ ultimately returns the displacement $s'(t)$.

(4) Calibrate by mean removal (speed and displacement). Of course, this is erroneous, however, if we know that at time T, $v'(T) = 0$ and $s'(T) = 0$ (i.e., the watch has come to a stop), we can refine the estimates of speed and displacement by mean removal.

(5) Kalman smoothing. The displacement estimation is still not stable – occasionally the result becomes poor. We carefully checked the data and detected that gravity estimation is not entirely reliable. Thus, we apply a Kalman smoothing to $a'_{rg}(t)$ to estimate the gravity estimation error $g'_e(t)$. The idea is to think about $a'_{rg}(t)$ as $g'_e(t)$ plus noise, where noise is generated due to the act of typing. We set a large noise parameter in Kalman smoothing such that Kalman smoothing output does not closely follow $a'_{rg}(t)$, but it shows the underlying shifting trend hidden in $a'_{rg}(t)$. Now, we refine $a'_{rg}(t)$ to $a'_{rg}(t) - g'_e(t)$. The performance improves consistently.

Figure 12 plots the final result comparison between *MoLe* and original Android API method. It is clear that *MoLe* provides better watch displacement estimation.

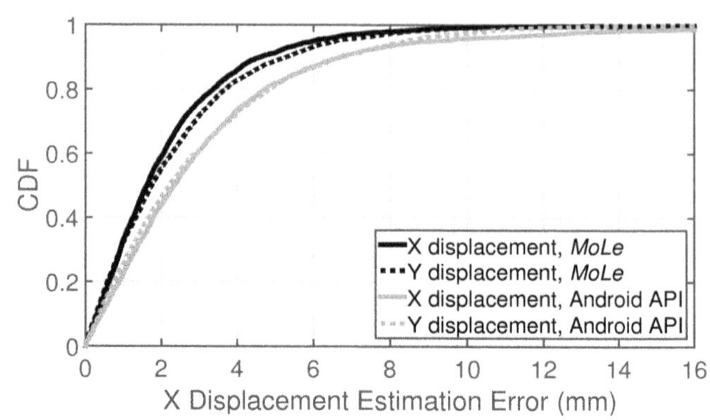

Figure 12: Comparison of *MoLe* and Android API displacement result.

4.2 Point Cloud Fitting

From the estimated displacements for each key, *MoLe* generates a *unlabeled point cloud (UPC)* for the attackee. Since the points in this UPC are not labeled, we fit the attacker's *character point cloud (CPC)* to the UPC. The key intuition is that the relative motions between keys (reflected in the relative locations of the point clouds) should bear similarity across all users. To achieve this fitting, we compute the convex hulls for the CPC and the UPC.

Observing that the fitting parameters for up and down hand displacements can be different, we compute 2 convex hulls for the CPC – one for all the positive X displacements (denoted by H^{CPC}_{pos}) and the other for all the negative X displacements (denoted by H^{CPC}_{neg}). Similarly, we compute 2 convex hulls for the UPC – H^{UPC}_{pos} and H^{UPC}_{neg}. We fit H^{CPC}_{pos} to H^{UPC}_{pos} and H^{CPC}_{neg} to H^{UPC}_{neg} respectively.

To fit a convex hull H_1 to another convex hull H_2, we first calculate their cords C_1 and C_2 which originate from the origin and pass through their centroids. Then, we (1) rotate H_1 such that C_1 aligns with C_2, (2) scale H_1 in the direction of C_1 such that C_1 equals to C_2, (3) scale H_1 in the orthogonal direction of C_1 such that the area of H_1 equals to that of H_2. Figure 13 shows an example of point cloud fitting.

The metric for fitting is defined by the degree of overlap between the CPC and UPC's convex hulls. More precisely, we compute the ratio of the intersection and union of the convex hulls.

An attacker might be able to generate multiple CPCs, perhaps from her accomplices. *MoLe* performs the fitting for each of these CPCs and selects the one that maximizes the intersection/union ratio. The rotated and scaled CPC is now superimposed on the UPC and a framework is ready to estimate labels for each point in the UPC.

4.3 Bayesian Inference

Even if the keystroke detection and point cloud fitting are perfect, *MoLe* still does not know the characters typed by the right

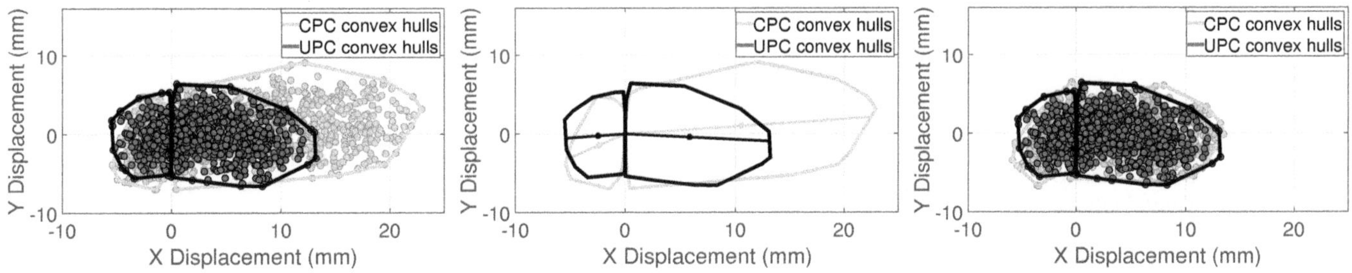

Figure 13: Point Cloud Fitting. Black points are the CPC attacker template and gray points are UPC from attackee. (a) Finding each convex hull (b) Calculate the centroids and perform rotate and scale. (c) Point cloud fitting result.

hand. Thus, as a first step, we attempt to fill in these "holes" to infer the complete word. The rather obvious step is to calculate the *posterior probability* of each word in the English dictionary, given the motion inferences from the left hand. The words corresponding to the top-K highest probabilities can be enumerated as candidates. We apply Bayes' theorem formulated as:

$$P(W \mid O) = \frac{P(O \mid W)P(W)}{P(O)} \tag{1}$$

where

- W is a candidate word from the dictionary and O is the observation motion data
- $P(W|O)$ is the posterior probability of the word given the observed motion data
- $P(O|W)$ is the likelihood function that estimates the probability of the word W based on the observed motion data
- $P(W)$ is the prior probability which captures the word's occurrence frequency
- $P(O)$ is the probability of the observation

Since $P(O)$ is the same for all possible words, we are only interested in calculating $P(O|W)$ and $P(W)$. That is,

$$P(W \mid O) \quad \propto \quad P(O \mid W) \quad \times \quad P(W) \tag{2}$$

$P(W)$ can be obtained from a contemporary English corpus. In the current experiment, we assume $P(W)$ is equal among words, meaning each word has same occurrence frequency. The key goal translates to obtaining the maximum (or high) values of the likelihood $P(O|W)$. In the following, we present a few opportunities to refine the likelihood function and the posterior probability.

Step I: Using the Number of Keystrokes

Our first intuition is simply to employ the number of detected keystrokes as observations to match the word. The keystroke detector gives us the number of keys typed by the left hand and this number is used to match each word. For example, when two keys detected, matching the word "the" produces higher likelihood than the word "teacher", because the number of peaks generated while typing "the" is much closer to 2 than "teacher". Now, for each of the detected keystroke, we would like to match them with the characters in the word. Since the keystroke could be caused by any characters in the word, we need to consider all possible assignments.

To calculate P(O | W), we can write

$$P(O \mid W) = P(N \mid W) = \sum_{(\alpha_1,\dots,\alpha_N)} P((c_{\alpha_1},\dots,c_{\alpha_N}) \mid W) \tag{3}$$

where N is the number of keystrokes and $(\alpha_1,\dots,\alpha_N)$ represents one possible N-element combination from $\{1,2,\dots,L\}$ and L is the word length. The summation adds up all possible combinations. c_i is the i_{th} character in W; $P((c_{\alpha_1},\dots,c_{\alpha_N}) \mid W)$ is probability that N peaks are generated by $c_{\alpha_1},\dots,c_{\alpha_N}$.

For instance, let's assume two keystrokes are detected and we want to calculate the likelihood of the word "the" by using the keystroke detector result in Figure 10.

$$\begin{aligned} P(O=2 \mid W=\text{"}the\text{"}) &= 0.986 * 0.035 * 0.119 \; (c_{\alpha_1}=t; c_{\alpha_2}=h) \\ &+ 0.986 * 0.965 * 0.881 \; (c_{\alpha_1}=t; c_{\alpha_2}=e) \\ &+ 0.014 * 0.035 * 0.881 \; (c_{\alpha_1}=h; c_{\alpha_2}=e) \\ &= 0.84 \end{aligned}$$

In above equation, 0.119 means the probability that "e" is not detected and equals to $(1-0.881)$. In a similar way, we calculate the probability that "t" is not detected (0.014) and "h" is detected (0.035).

Thus, by iterating over all words in the dictionary, we can obtain the likelihood for each word. Of course, further refinements are possible.

Step II: Consecutive Characters

In some cases, our key-press timing module detects only one keystroke for two consecutive characters such as "er", "sa" or "re". These keys are adjacent on the keyboard and the watch dips in so close succession that they are not separable. Therefore, we treat these character pairs as one key. Figure 14 shows the experimental results that these common character–pairs are detected as zero, one, or two key-presses. Evidently, treating them as a single key-press should be appropriate in a majority of the cases.

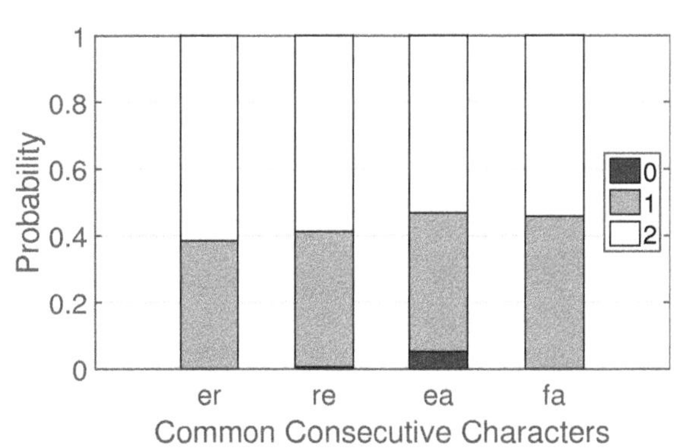

Figure 14: The probability of number of keystroke detections for consecutive characters.

Step III: Adding Watch Displacement

MoLe is now ready to leverage the actual watch displacement. Assuming fingers are placed over the home position ("F" and "J"), recall that the key-press location estimation module computes the location of each key press (Figure 4). Of course, the estimated location is not accurate due to the noise in the hardware, minute differences in the hand motions, minute differences in hand's 2D orientation, etc. However, given that the CPC has been fitted to the user's UPC, it is now possible to better predict the word by taking displacement into consideration. Thus, equation 3 can be rewritten as:

$$\begin{aligned} &P(O \mid W) \\ &= P(N \cap d_i, i = 1,2,...,N \mid W) \\ &= \sum_{(\alpha_1,...,\alpha_N)} P((c_{\alpha_i},...,c_{\alpha_N}) \mid W) p((d_1,...,d_N) \mid (c_{\alpha_i},...,c_{\alpha_N}), W) \end{aligned} \quad (4)$$

where $p((d_1,...,d_N) \mid (c_{\alpha_i},...,c_{\alpha_N}), W)$ is probability density of typing $c_{\alpha_1},...,c_{\alpha_N}$ of W at character displacements $d_1,...,d_N$, and d_i is the i_{th} character displacement in W.

MoLe models each character's location as a Gaussian distribution. Assuming the distribution of displacement d_i only depends on current character c_{α_i}, we simplify Equation 4 as:

$$P(O \mid W) = \sum_{(\alpha_1,...,\alpha_N)} P((c_{\alpha_1},...,c_{\alpha_N}) \mid W) \prod_{i=1}^{N} p(d_i \mid c_{\alpha_i}) \quad (5)$$

where $p(d_i \mid c_{\alpha_i})$ is probability density of d_i given character c_{α_i}.

Step IV: Character Transitions

We assumed above that each character displacement is independent. However, typing a word consists of sequential movements and the current displacement is indeed influenced by the location of the previous character. Figure 15 illustrates an example – we compare the displacement of "a" when previous char is "v" versus "r". Clearly, the distributions are different. For "ra", the displacement of typing "a" is shifted towards the position of character "r" because the little finger types "a" right after "r", before returning to home position. For "va", the displacement of "a" is clear close to "v", because of the same reason.

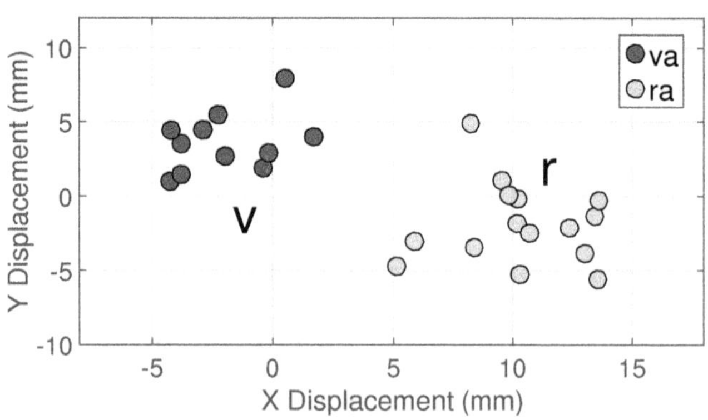

Figure 15: Comparison of "a" displacement while previous character is "v" or "r". The key locations of v and r are marked in the figure.

Given this observation, we extend the likelihood function to the following:

$$P(O \mid W) \approx \sum_{(\alpha_1,...,\alpha_N)} P((c_{\alpha_1},...,c_{\alpha_N}) \mid W) \prod_{i=1}^{N} p(d_i \mid c_{\alpha_i}, c_{\alpha_{i-1}}) \quad (6)$$

Now the displacement probability density $p(d_i \mid c_{\alpha_i}, c_{\alpha_{i-1}})$ not only consider c_{α_i} but also the previous char $c_{\alpha_{i-1}}$.

Step V: Keystroke Interval

Timing of the key-presses on the left hand should also encode information about missing keys. We ask, given the time detected interval between consecutive keystrokes, what is the probability that there are N right hand characters between them? Correct guesses of N can obviously help. For example, when typing the word "t h a n k s" (characters typed on the left hand are underlined), the observed interval between "t" and "a" may be expectedly shorter than between "a" and "s".

Figure 16 plots the distribution of time intervals for increasing lengths of character sequences. These sequences consists of right hand characters in the middle and are surrounded by two left characters. Unsurprisingly, the time interval generally increases with the number of keystrokes. However, we observe high variance. For example, even though the segment "-b i l i t-" and "-t i o n a-" both have three right hand characters in the middle, the average interval of "-t i o n a-" is shorter than "-b i l i t-" due to hand geometry and typing familiarity.

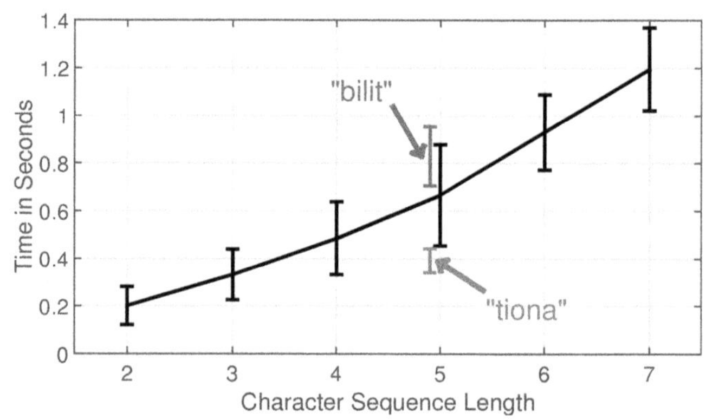

Figure 16: Y-axis is the time interval between two detected keystrokes and X-axis is the number of sequence length.

Therefore, for better timing observation, we should obtain the time interval distribution of every possible character-sequence that is preceded and followed by two left-hand characters, and use this distribution in the Bayesian model.
The observation can be written into

$$\begin{aligned} &P(O \mid W) \\ &= P(N \cap d_i, i = 1,2,...,N \cap t_j, j = 1,2,...,N-1 \mid W) \\ &\approx \sum_{(\alpha_1,...,\alpha_N)} P((c_{\alpha_1},...,c_{\alpha_N}) \mid W) \prod_{i=1}^{N} p(d_i \mid c_{\alpha_i}, c_{\alpha_{i-1}}) p((t_1,...,t_{N-1}) \\ &\mid (c_{\alpha_1},...,c_{\alpha_N}), (d_1,...,d_N), W) \end{aligned} \quad (7)$$

where $N-1$ interval distributions, t_j with $j = 1,2,...,N-1$, are added into the observation. Note that the attacker and attackee are typing at slightly different speeds. *MoLe* compensates this speed bias with a factor k, calculated from the ratio of attacker to attackee's average typing interval.

5. EVALUATION

5.1 Data Collection and Methodology

MoLe has been implemented on the Galaxy Gear Live smart watch, which runs the latest Android Wear platform. When activated, the *MoLe* client on the watch continuously logs accelerometer and gyroscope readings at 200Hz, along with timestamps. The sensor data is stored locally during data collection and transferred to the backend (MATLAB) server for analysis.

MoLe is evaluated with 8 subjects, recruited by advertising about these experiments in the university campus. The subjects were offered an incentive of $10 per hour, and each subject invited to our lab for a 2 hour session. All subjects were familiar with English typing (5 of them are native English speakers, 3 of them were females). Each subject was asked to type 300 English words randomly selected from 5000 most frequently used words [7]. The word-length ranged from 1 to 14, and was equally distributed. In total, we test 2400 words across all users.

Each subject was seated at a desk in front of a Lenovo laptop. Our experiment GUI popped up one word at a time on the laptop screen – the volunteer's task was to type the same word in a text box on the screen. If any of the character is incorrectly typed, we discard the data and let the subject re-enter the word. Between each word recording, we ask the subject to initialize their hand position on "F" and "J". During the typing, the laptop was also programmed to record the timing of the keystroke – this will later serve as ground truth. To collect the offline training data, two of the authors (pretending to be attackers) performed the same procedure, but with Top-500 longest words in the dictionary. Long words help capture the diversity of the typing patterns. The whole data collection is done a Lenovo ThinkPad equipped with a regular full-sized keyboard.

For full ground truth recording, we mount an Android Samsung Galaxy S4 phone on top of the keyboard and use the front camera to capture the video of hand movement. We apply the camera calibration toolbox in Matlab [9] to calibrate the camera pixel, and measure the watch distance and location from each frame (Figure 1).

5.2 Performance Results

The following questions are of interest in this section:

- How well can *MoLe* guess each word (i.e., in an ordered list of guesses by *MoLe*, what is the rank of the actual word?)
- What factors affect this rank?
- How different opportunities contribute towards overall performance.
- How can we prevent the threat introduced by *MoLe*?
- Does keyboard matter?
- Can humans guess better by looking at a sequence of candidate guesses?

(1) How well can *MoLe* guess each word?

Figure 17 plots the CDF of rank, computed from each of the 2400 words typed by the subjects of the experiments. The average across all 8 subjects is shown in black, while *MoLe*'s performance for each individual subject shown in gray. We observe that the median rank of a word is 24, while for 30 percentile, the rank is 5. Put differently, when a user types a word, there is a 30% chance that *MoLe* would narrow down the typed word to only 5 possibilities, and a 50% chance to only 24 possibilities. Given that 5000 words are possible, this is an appreciable reduction of the search space, and makes it amenable to brute-force attacks.

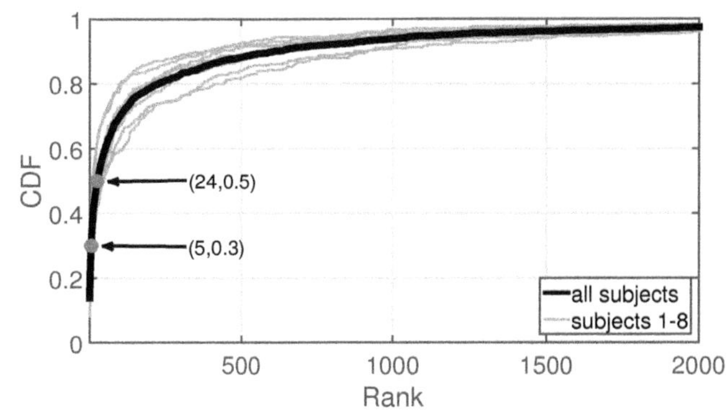

Figure 17: CDF of rank computed for each of the 2400 words typed by 8 subjects.

Figure 18 plots the ranks of typed words for each test subject. The ranks are generally higher (i.e., *MoLe*'s guesses are better) for subjects S2, S5, and S8. On examining the video and sensor traces for these subjects, we find that they have lower variance in their hand movements, probably because they type as per the prescribed guidelines. We also test the case with perfect key-press detection (i.e., using the actual number and timing of keystrokes only from the left hand, gathered from the ground truth timing information recorded during the experiments). Surprisingly, the 30th percentile drops sharply to 1, meaning that *MoLe* can exactly guess the word; the 50th percentile drops to 6. Clearly, further improvements in key-press detection is the key to improving *MoLe*.

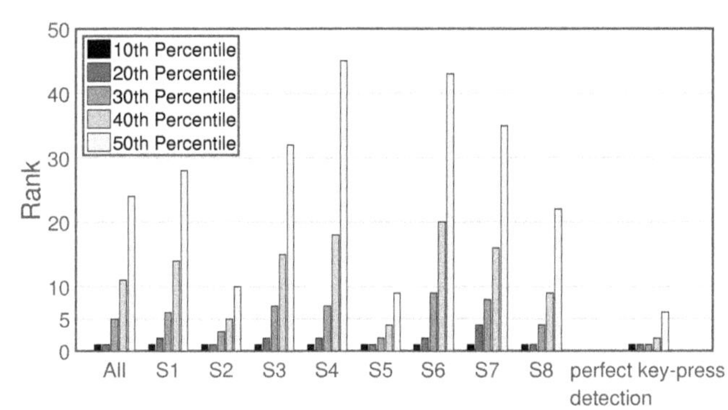

Figure 18: Rank of average, across users and with perfect key-press detection

(2) What factors affect the rank?

Figure 19 plots the median rank of words for increasing word-lengths. The rank generally decreases with word length greater than 6, primarily because (1) there are greater number of keystrokes that get detected in a longer word, and (2) because the number of words of that length reduces, in turn reducing the number of words to be confused with. Words of length 4 – 7 on the other hand, have less keystrokes; also, there are many more words of such lengths, adding to the difficulty of detection.

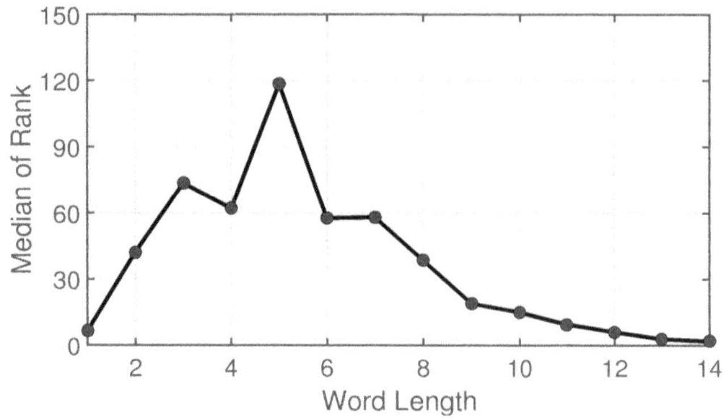

Figure 19: Median rank plotted against increasing word length – 4 – 7 length words show worse performance due to fewer keys to be detected while such words occur in large numbers.

Figure 20 shows the number of left hand characters in a word. With increasing number of left characters, *MoLe* naturally gains richer information about the word, ultimately improving its ability to guess. When a word contains more than 5 left characters, *MoLe* is able to bring down the rank below 20. When left character are 2 to 4, performance degrades because a large number of words have the same 2 – 4 left hand characters in them.

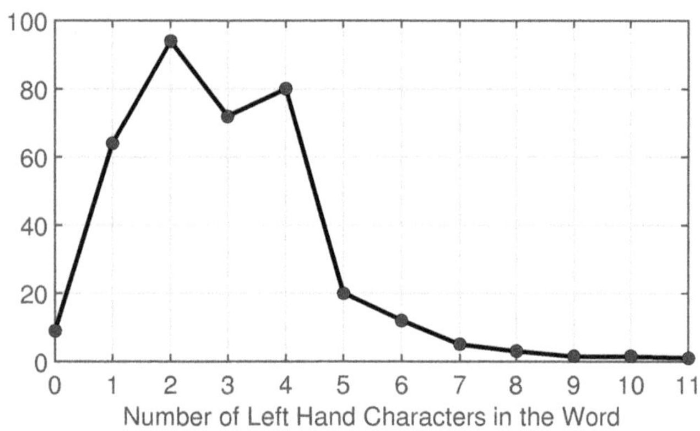

Figure 20: Variation of rank against the number of characters typed by the left hand.

(3) Impact of Each Bayesian Opportunity

Section 4.3 leveraged a number of opportunities under the Bayesian model. Figure 21 shows the break-down of contributions from each of them. Using only the number of detected keystrokes (step 1 and 2 in section 4.3), *MoLe* performs rather poorly on the dataset. When the displacement information is added (step 3 and 4), *MoLe* improves the rank from 340 to 49 at 50th percentile. Finally, when time interval is incorporated (step 5), the median rank improves from 49 to 24.

(4) Impact of Sampling Rate

Figure 22 characterizes the impact of sensor sampling rate (200Hz, 100Hz, 50Hz, 20Hz) on the median rank of words for all of the subjects. Evidently, *MoLe*'s ability to guess degrades drastically with lower sampling rates – median ranking falls as 64, 141 and 1218. Perhaps this could be a way to mitigate the attack through smart-watches. A typing classifier could first

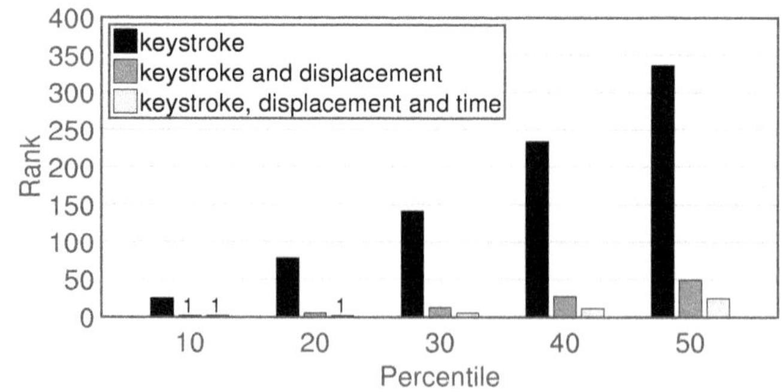

Figure 21: Contribution of different opportunities towards the overall performance of *MoLe*.

detect whether the user is typing, and if so, the sampling rate of the sensor data can be diminished to less than 50Hz.

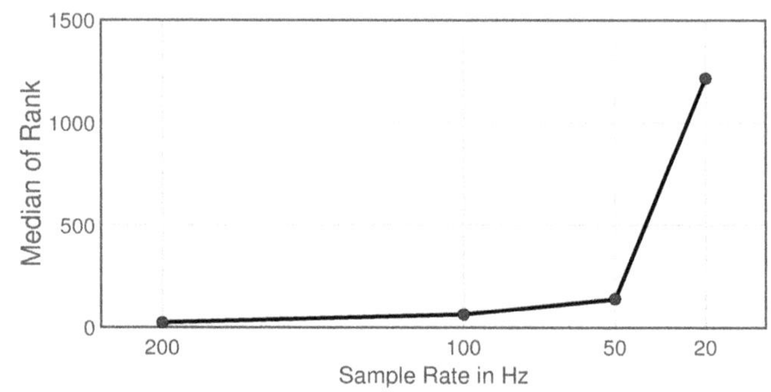

Figure 22: Lower sensor sampling rate rapidly reduces the ability to guess the word, perhaps indicating a way to thwart *MoLe*'s attack.

(5) Keyboard Variant

The difference in the shape of desktop and laptop keyboards may translate to decoding errors with *MoLe*. To test this, subject S5 was asked to repeat the same data collection process on a desktop keyboard. Figure 23 plots a histogram of the rank differences of each word, when decoded from the two keyboards. We notice that 45.2% of rank differences are less than 10. More specifically, the laptop keyboard presents a median rank of 10 and 30 percentile rank of 4. The computer keyboard's median rank is 14 and 30 percentile rank is still at 4. The results show that the system performance is close between two keyboards, *even though the attackers used the laptop keyboard for training the system.* If the attackers generated models from various keyboards, and applied the best one during the keystroke detector and cloud fitting process, the results can be even better.

(6) Recovery via Human Observation

Although *MoLe* is not able to detect spaces and separate the words at this moment, we are interested to know how the threat would become even worse if this limitation is relaxed. To this end, we ask subject *S5* to enter (one-by-one) the words from an actual sentence. Table 1 shows *MoLe*'s end-to-end prediction result for each of the words in the sentence (which contains 8 words). For each word, the *Top-5* guesses are listed from top to down. As would be expected, the words in each column bear similarity in the character sequences embedded in them. For example, W_6 typically starts with "t" or "th" and W_8 contains many left hand characters. We present this table to colleagues in

Rank	W_1	W_2	W_3	W_4	W_5	W_6	W_7	W_8
1.	motor	pistol	profound	technology	angel	those	that	disappear
2.	monitor	list	journalism	remaining	spray	today	tight	discourse
3.	them	but	originally	telephone	super	third	tightly	secondary
4.	the	lost	original	meanwhile	fire	through	thirty	adviser
5.	then	most	profile	headline	shore	towel	truth	discover

Table 1: *Can you guess the correct sentence?* The words in each column are ranked in decreasing order of probability; also note that some words may not feature in the $top-5$ words presented in each column. The answer is made available at end of the paper[2].

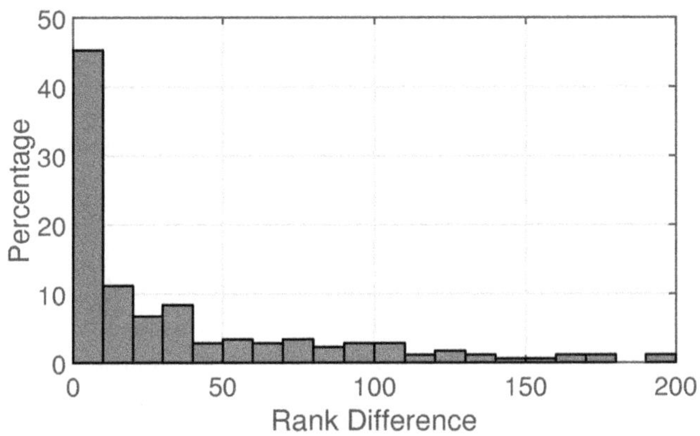

Figure 23: A histogram shows the rank difference of each word between 2 keyboards. The trend indicates that most words have similar rank, so the difference is low.

our department and most of them could recover the sentence in a few minutes. We encourage the readers to reconstruct sentence on their own – the answer is made available at end of the paper[2].

6. POINTS OF DISCUSSION

We discuss a few limitations and opportunities for improvement.

(1) Confined to separate words. *MoLe* is not yet a real-world attack since it is not able to detect the space bar and separate out words from a sentence. Also, without any priors on digit sequences, it is difficult to detect what digits users are typing. Additional work is necessary to further separate out these keystrokes. However, we believe there is opportunity. We have found early evidence that the magnetic field on the keyboard is quite telling of the position of the wrist. With some signal processing, the magnetic field may offer valuable hints on how the wrist is moving and when it is coming back to its original position. We leave this to future work.

(2) Applying nature language processing. To recover the whole sentence, techniques from nature language processing (NLP) may also apply. For example, we can apply N-gram language models which predict the Nth word given a previous $N-1$ word sequence. Thus, even if a few words have low accuracy in the sentence, it may still be possible to infer the sentence, or even the broad semantic content.

(3) Typing activity classifier. In a real world attack, we would first need to subject the sensor data to a classifier which will output whether the user is typing or not. Only when the user is known to be typing, should *MoLe* be applied on the data. We have not developed a "typing or not" detector in this paper, but believe that it can be developed (perhaps from the orientation of the watch and the slight back and forth movement). Also, we need to be able to identify whether the watch is worn on the left or right hand, left to future work.

7. RELATED WORK

We categorize this section into inferring keystrokes on traditional computer keyboards and sensor information leaks on smart devices.

Inferring keystrokes on computer keyboards

Many researches have attempted to infer keystrokes on computer keyboards. Various modalities have been leveraged, such as acoustics signal [10, 11], input timing analysis [12–14], RF radio [15], and electromagnetic emanations [16]. These researches have successfully delivered high accuracy results. However, none of them use motion sensor data; also, to intercept physical signals and decode the data, these methods are typically required to install additional hardware or software, which make them somewhat difficult to widely deploy the attacks. In contrast, *MoLe* can be launched with ease on top of commericially available wearable devices. Marquardt et al. demonstrated the (Sp)iPhone [17] and show that it is possible to use the accelerometer on iPhone to recover text entered on a keyboard when the phone is placed nearby, on the same table surface. Both (Sp)iPhone and *MoLe* exploit side channels, however, *MoLe* uses the wrist motion data in 3D, different from the surface vibrations in (Sp)iPhone.

Sensor Information leaks on smart devices

Researchers have studied side channel attacks to infer keystrokes on smartphones and tablets [18] [19] [20] [21]. The core idea behind these works is that when typing on different locations on a virtual keyboard, the keystrokes cause distinct vibrations/rotations. The motion data on smartphones can thus be used to infer the tapped location. TouchLogger [19] and accessory [18] are the early works, and use accelerometer only to infer tap location on screen. Cai et al. [20] and Miluzzo et al. [21] advance the technique to infer keystrokes and show that gyroscope has better accuracy than accelerometer based inference. *MoLe* bears similarity in that it is also a side channel attack. However, there are two main differences. Firstly, above works are feature-based. They design features to capture distinct screen motions caused by the touches and train models with these features to infer the touch positions. In contrast, since smartwatch is on the user's wrist, we track the movement of the wrist to infer what the user has typed. Secondly, we are only able to sense partial keystrokes with one hand, as well as indirect data of the wrist. To recover the whole input word, *MoLe* must rely much more strongly on the Bayesian models. GyroPhone [22] presents a new type of threat to intercept human speech by using gyroscope on smartphone. The authors found that the MEMS gyro sensors are able to pick up air vibrations from sound at low frequency. *MoLe* is still different since it attempts to extract semantic understanding of the human's hand motions.

8. CONCLUSION

This paper demonstrates that sensor data from smart watches can leak information about what the user is typing on a regular (laptop or desktop) keyboard. By processing the accelerometer and gyroscope signals, tracking the wrist micro-motions, and combining them with the structure of valid English words, reasonable guesses can be made about typed words. Given the excitement around a smart-watch app store, such an attack can be severely penetrating into the private lives of humans. While we find that diminishing the sampling rate of the accelerometer and gyroscope can alleviate the attack, we believe additional side channels like magnetic field variations need to be carefully investigated. Otherwise, wearable devices could soon become a "double edged sword" slowing down future innovations on this platform.

9. ACKNOWLEDGMENTS

We sincerely thank our shepherd and the anonymous reviewers for their valuable comments and suggestions. This research is partially funded by NSF research grant CNS-1430064, and by a fellowship by the Ministry of Science and Technology of Taiwan. We are also grateful to Google, Qualcomm, Samsung and Huawei for partially funding this research.

10. REFERENCES

[1] Sandip Agrawal, Ionut Constandache, Shravan Gaonkar, Romit Roy Choudhury, Kevin Caves, and Frank DeRuyter, "Using mobile phones to write in air," in *Proceedings of the 9th International Conference on Mobile Systems, Applications, and Services*. 2011, MobiSys '11, pp. 15–28, ACM.

[2] Shahriar Nirjon, Jeremy Gummeson, Dan Gelb, and Kyu-Han Kim, "TypingRing: A wearable ring platform for text input," in *Proceedings of the 13th Annual International Conference on Mobile Systems, Applications, and Services*. 2015, MobiSys '15, pp. 227–239, ACM.

[3] Jiayang Liu, Zhen Wang, Lin Zhong, J. Wickramasuriya, and V. Vasudevan, "uWave: Accelerometer-based personalized gesture recognition and its applications," in *Pervasive Computing and Communications, 2009. PerCom 2009. IEEE International Conference on*, March 2009, pp. 1–9.

[4] Chao Xu, Parth H. Pathak, and Prasant Mohapatra, "Finger-writing with smartwatch: A case for finger and hand gesture recognition using smartwatch," in *Proceedings of the 16th International Workshop on Mobile Computing Systems and Applications*. 2015, HotMobile '15, pp. 9–14, ACM.

[5] Abhinav Parate, Meng-Chieh Chiu, Chaniel Chadowitz, Deepak Ganesan, and Evangelos Kalogerakis, "Risq: Recognizing smoking gestures with inertial sensors on a wristband," in *Proceedings of the 12th Annual International Conference on Mobile Systems, Applications, and Services*. 2014, MobiSys '14, pp. 149–161, ACM.

[6] Sangki Yun, Yi-Chao Chen, and Lili Qiu, "Turning a mobile device into a mouse in the air," in *Proceedings of the 13th Annual International Conference on Mobile Systems, Applications, and Services*. 2015, MobiSys '15, pp. 15–29, ACM.

[7] "Word Frequency Data Set," `http://www.wordfrequency.info/`.

[2] "The most profound technologies are those that disappear" - Mark Weiser, 1991

[8] "MATLAB Peak Analysis Library," `http://www.mathworks.com/help/signal/examples/peak-analysis.html`.

[9] "Camera Calibration Toolbox for Matlab," `http://www.vision.caltech.edu/bouguetj/calib_doc/`.

[10] Li Zhuang, Feng Zhou, and J. D. Tygar, "Keyboard acoustic emanations revisited," *ACM Trans. Inf. Syst. Secur.*, vol. 13, no. 1, pp. 3:1–3:26, Nov. 2009.

[11] Dmitri Asonov and Rakesh Agrawal, "Keyboard acoustic emanations," in *Security and Privacy, 2004. Proceedings. 2004 IEEE Symposium on*, May 2004, pp. 3–11.

[12] Denis Foo Kune and Yongdae Kim, "Timing attacks on pin input devices," in *Proceedings of the 17th ACM Conference on Computer and Communications Security*. 2010, CCS '10, pp. 678–680, ACM.

[13] Dawn Xiaodong Song, David Wagner, and Xuqing Tian, "Timing analysis of keystrokes and timing attacks on SSH," in *Proceedings of the 10th Conference on USENIX Security Symposium - Volume 10*. 2001, SSYM'01, USENIX Association.

[14] Kevin S. Killourhy and Roy A. Maxion, "Comparing anomaly-detection algorithms for keystroke dynamics," in *Dependable Systems Networks, 2009. DSN '09. IEEE/IFIP International Conference on*, June 2009, pp. 125–134.

[15] "Key Sweeper," `http://samy.pl/keysweeper/`.

[16] Martin Vuagnoux and Sylvain Pasini, "Compromising electromagnetic emanations of wired and wireless keyboards," in *Proceedings of the 18th Conference on USENIX Security Symposium*. 2009, SSYM'09, pp. 1–16, USENIX Association.

[17] Philip Marquardt, Arunabh Verma, Henry Carter, and Patrick Traynor, "(sp)iphone: Decoding vibrations from nearby keyboards using mobile phone accelerometers," in *Proceedings of the 18th ACM Conference on Computer and Communications Security*. 2011, CCS '11, pp. 551–562, ACM.

[18] Emmanuel Owusu, Jun Han, Sauvik Das, Adrian Perrig, and Joy Zhang, "Accessory: Password inference using accelerometers on smartphones," in *Proceedings of the Twelfth Workshop on Mobile Computing Systems and Applications*. 2012, HotMobile '12, pp. 9:1–9:6, ACM.

[19] Liang Cai and Hao Chen, "TouchLogger: Inferring keystrokes on touch screen from smartphone motion," in *Proceedings of the 6th USENIX Conference on Hot Topics in Security*. 2011, HotSec'11, pp. 9–9, USENIX Association.

[20] Liang Cai and Hao Chen, "On the practicality of motion based keystroke inference attack," in *Proceedings of the 5th International Conference on Trust and Trustworthy Computing*. 2012, TRUST'12, pp. 273–290, Springer-Verlag.

[21] Emiliano Miluzzo, Alexander Varshavsky, Suhrid Balakrishnan, and Romit Roy Choudhury, "Tapprints: Your finger taps have fingerprints," in *Proceedings of the 10th International Conference on Mobile Systems, Applications, and Services*. 2012, MobiSys '12, pp. 323–336, ACM.

[22] Yan Michalevsky, Dan Boneh, and Gabi Nakibly, "Gyrophone: Recognizing speech from gyroscope signals," in *23rd USENIX Security Symposium (USENIX Security 14)*. Aug. 2014, pp. 1053–1067, USENIX Association.

Demo: Platform for Collecting Data From Urban Sensors Using Vehicular Networking

Pedro M. Santos[*†], Tania Calcada[*†], Diogo Guimarães[†], Tiago Condeixa[‡], Susana Sargento[*§], Ana Aguiar[*†], João Barros[*†‡]

[*] Instituto de Telecomunicações
[†] DEEC, Faculdade de Engenharia, Universidade do Porto
[‡] VENIAM
[§] Departamento de Electrónica, Telecomunicações e Informática, Universidade de Aveiro

{pedro.salgueiro,tcalcada,ee10158}@fe.up.pt, tcondeixa@veniamworks.com, susana@ua.pt, {anaa,jbarros}@fe.up.pt

ABSTRACT

A large-scale urban sensing platform, composed of multiple Data Collection Units (DCUs) equipped with sensor hardware scattered accross the city, allows pervasive monitoring of environmental parameters. Gathering sensor data from a number of disparate locations at a backend server can be supported by delay-tolerant services provided by existing vehicular networks. Our real-world sensing platform takes advantage of an existing vehicular network with more than 400 vehicles equipped with On-Board Units (OBUs). A purposely-developed implementation of a delay tolerant service is installed in all elements involved in the communication flow, from DCUs to the backend server. In this demo, we showcase the full end-to-end data flow with the actual equipment being used in our real-world deployment. Data produced at a DCU is collected by an OBU installed in a vehicle and delivered to a Road-Side Unit (RSU), which then forwards the data to the backend server.

Categories and Subject Descriptors

C.2.1 [**Network Architecture and Designs**]: Store and forward networks

Keywords

urban sensors, delay-tolerant, vehicular network

1. INTRODUCTION

In recent years, pervasive monitoring became possible by the development of small sensing devices with communication capabilities. The UrbanSense project aims to perform pervasive sensing in the city of Porto, Portugal. A number of processing devices equipped with environmental sensors

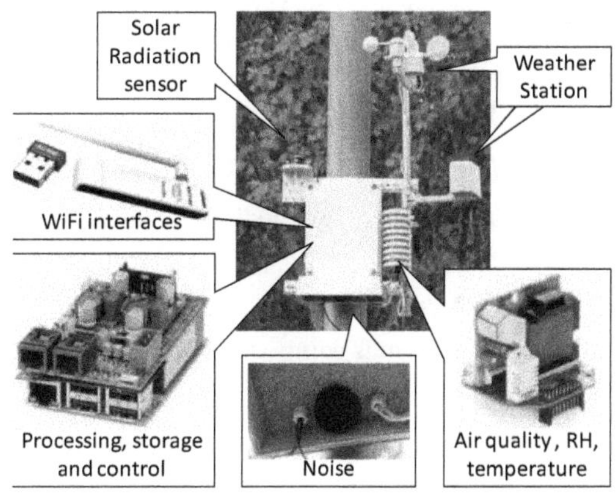

Figure 1: Data Collection Unit (DCU) deployed in R. Damião de Góis, Porto, Portugal. DCUs are composed of processing devices (Raspberry Pi) that gather data from environmental sensors and communicate via a IEEE 802.11b/g/n interface.

and a WiFi interface, called Data Collection Units (DCUs), are being deployed at several strategic locations of the city of Porto. Figure 1 shows a DCU deployed at an important artery of the city. One of the major challenges in such large-scale sensing platform is to perform low-cost aggregation of the collected data at a central database. Solutions such as cellular networks, dedicated M2M systems ([5, 3]) or physical wiring to all sensors may be impractical or costly when compared with data benefits.

Data collection via vehicular networks provides an alternative cost-efficient solution, as it takes advantage of an already deployed, cost-free infrastructure. In Porto, the public transportation and municipal services vehicles are equipped with wireless On-Board Units (OBUs), creating a vehicular network that provides WiFi access points to passengers and utilizes DSRC for V2X communication. This set of vehicles covers a significant area of the city on a daily basis, creating opportunities to collect data from the various DCUs. To cope with the opportunistic and disruption-prone nature of communications in this scenario, we use Delay Tolerant Networking (DTN) [2]. A purposely-developed DTN service exists in all physical elements of the architecture.

MobiCom'15, September 7–11, 2015, Paris, France.
ACM 978-1-4503-3619-2/15/09.
DOI: http://dx.doi.org/10.1145/2789168.2789169.

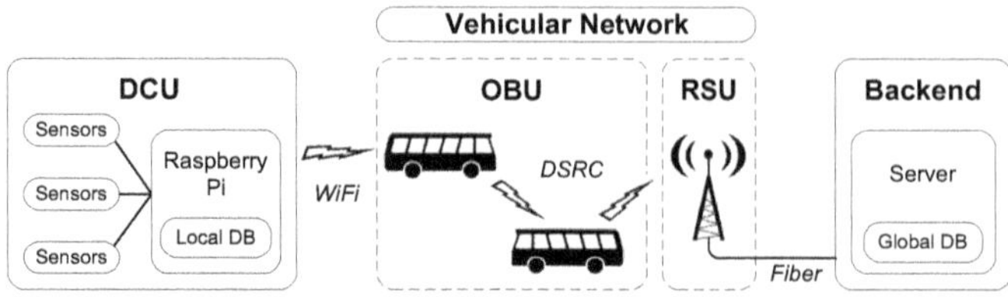

Figure 2: Physical architecture of the collection platform. Sensor data is gathered at the DCUs, transmitted through the vehicular network, and delivered to a backend server.

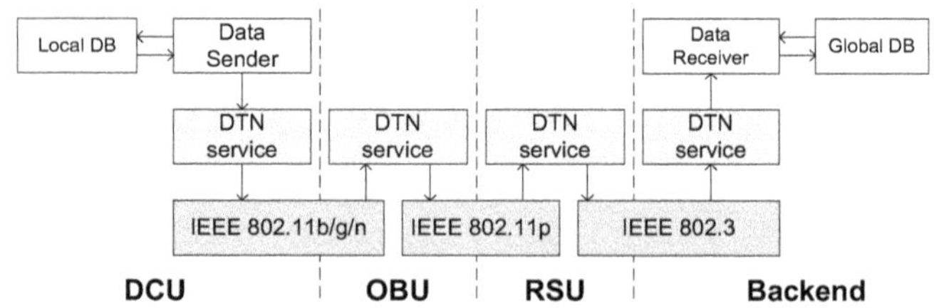

Figure 3: Logical architecture of the collection platform and data collection flow (indicated by arrows). ***DataSender*** **and** ***DataReceiver*** **modules reside at communication end-points.**

This demo showcases a proof-of-concept of the data collection platform using the actual equipment deployed on site. It is composed of one DCU, one OBU installed on a vehicle (a scooter), one Road-Side Unit (RSU) that interfaces the mobile node and the backend server, and a laptop representing the backend server. Communication between the DCU and the mobile OBUs uses WiFi, whereas the OBU and the RSU communicate with DSRC.

2. COLLECTION INFRASTRUCTURE

We present the physical and logical architecture of the data collection platform.

2.1 Physical Architecture

Our collection platform is composed of three main physical elements: (i) the Data Collection Units, (ii) the vehicular network, and (iii) the backend server. Fig.2 presents the physical architecture and the wireless technologies used.

The core of the DCUs are off-the-shelf Raspberry Pi devices, equipped with a number of environmental sensors and a IEEE 802.11b/g/n interface. Sensors monitor wind direction and speed, rain, solar radiation, luminosity, humidity, temperature, and noise. All hardware is encapsulated in hermetic casing and deployed at sites of interest. Collected data is stored in a local database.

The vehicular network is composed of On-Board Units, installed in mobile nodes, and static Road-Side Units. OBUs have IEEE 802.11b/g/n and 802.11p interfaces [1] and provide a WiFi Access Point (AP) service for the bus passengers. The Road Side Units are infrastructural devices, located at strategic locations of the city, that interface the vehicular network and the Internet. RSUs are equipped with 802.11p hardware to communicate with the mobile nodes, and an optical fiber-based connection to the Internet. The backend server receives, acknowledges and stores the data collected by all sensing devices in a global database.

2.2 Logical Architecture

We created a software DTN implementation that supports delay-tolerant communication over all elements of the architecture, and application software modules at the end-points (the DCUs and the backend server) to manage the end-to-end data flow, named communication modules. Fig.3 presents the logical architecture and depicts the collection data flow.

The DTN implementation used in our collection platform is based on the end-to-end architecture of the *bundle protocol*, described in RFC 5050 [4]. The bundle protocol defines the bundle layer, that sits between the application and data-link layers; corresponding datagrams are called *bundles*. Our version of the bundle protocol implements a subset of functionalities defined in RFC 5050 to support store-and-forward operation: (i) *neighboring* – keep track of current neighbors in the multiple interfaces/networks; (ii) *routing* – decide which bundles to send to which neighbors; (iii) *storage* – keep bundles in storage and provide easy access.

The communication modules are named *DataSender* and *DataReceiver*, and are deployed at the DCU and server respectively. The DCU constantly searches for opportunistic connections to passing OBUs. When a connection is initiated, the *DataSender* module fetches sensor data from the local database and stores it into a bundle, which delivers to the bundle layer. The information about which data was sent is locally stored. Upon reception of an acknowledgement of the previously sent data, the DCU deletes that data from the local database. The *DataReceiver* module, the communication module at the backend server, is in charge of receiving and processing the bundles delivered by the bundle layer and storing them in the global database, and sends acknowledgements to the sensing device that originated the data via the bundle layer.

3. DEMONSTRATION

We now present the elements and operation of our demonstration. Fig. 4 depicts the overall setup. A demostrative video can be found in https://www.youtube.com/watch?v=Hqjx28hpuT8.

This demonstration is composed of four elements: a static Data Collection Unit, a scooter equipped with an On-Board Unit, a static Road-Side Unit, and a laptop acting as backend server. The DCU has a IEEE 802.11b/g/n interface, whereas the RSU is DSRC-capable due to a IEEE 802.11p interface. Given that they do not share a common wireless technology, the DCU and the RSU are not able to communicate wirelessly. The OBU mounted on the scooter has both technologies, and also runs a WiFi Access Point (AP) service. The RSU and the laptop are connected by a standard ethernet cable.

The demonstration operates as follows. The DCU collects data from sensor hardware (temperature / humidity / luminosity, etc.) and constantly scans the wireless medium in search of an WiFi AP client. When the OBU becomes in range of the DCU, collected data is off-loaded to the OBU. The scooter then physically heads to the RSU and, when the OBU and RSU come into communication range, collected data is transfered to the RSU. A TCP connection is established between RSU and laptop to transmit the sensor

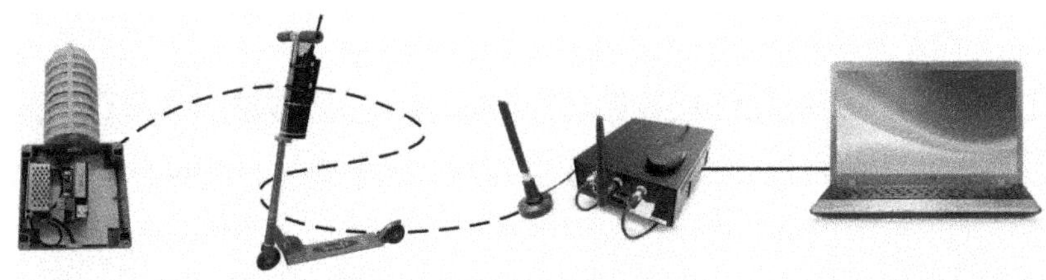

Figure 4: Diagram of demonstration setup. DCU and RSU cannot communicate wirelessly; scooter with OBU transports delay tolerant data.

data to the server, which then stores received data in the database. New data arrival is shown by means of a graph depiction updated in real-time.

4. CONCLUSIONS

We present a practical use case for delay-tolerant networking, that of sensor data collection from disparate urban location and aggregation at a backend server. A data collection platform based on vehicular networking has been developed for this purpose and successfully deployed in a real-world platform. The demonstration aims to showcase the end-to-end operation of this collection platform.

Acknowledgments

This work was supported by projects and grants SenseBusNet (PEst-OE/EEI/LA0008/2013), I-City for Future Mobility (NORTE-07-0124-FEDER-000064), FP7 – Future Cities (FP7-REGPOT-2012-2013-1, 316296), Vital Responder 2 (PTDC/EEI-ELC/2760/2012), IT (UID/EEA/50008/2013), FCT individual grant (SFRH/BD/67178/2009), and by applicable financial framework of R&D Unit 50008 (FCT/MEC through national funds and when applicable co-funded by FEDER – PT2020 partnership agreement).

5. REFERENCES

[1] C. Ameixieira, J. Matos, R. Moreira, A. Cardote, A. Oliveira, and S. Sargento. An IEEE 802.11p/WAVE implementation with synchronous channel switching for seamless dual-channel access (poster). In *Vehicular Networking Conference (VNC), 2011 IEEE*, pages 214–221, Nov 2011.

[2] V. Cerf, S. Burleigh, A. Hooke, L. Torgeson, R. Durst, K. Scott, K. Fall, and H. Weiss. Delay-Tolerant Networking Architecture. RFC 4838 (Experimental). April 2007.

[3] M2M Spectrum Networks. http://www.m2mspectrum.com.

[4] K. Scott and S. Burleigh. Bundle Protocol Specification. RFC 5050. November 2007.

[5] SIGFOX. http://www.sigfox.com.

Demo: AntMonitor - a System for Mobile Traffic Monitoring and Real-Time Prevention of Privacy Leaks

Anastasia Shuba
CalIT2, EECS, CPCC
UC Irvine
ashuba@uci.edu

Anh Le
CalIT2, UC Irvine
anh.le@uci.edu

Minas Gjoka
CalIT2, UC Irvine
mgjoka@uci.edu

Janus Varmarken
IT Univ. of Copenhagen
janv@itu.dk

Simon Langhoff
IT Univ. of Copenhagen
siml@itu.dk

Athina Markopoulou
CalIT2, EECS, CPCC
UC Irvine
athina@uci.edu

ABSTRACT

Mobile devices play an essential role in the Internet today, and there is an increasing interest in using them as a vantage point for network measurement from the edge. At the same time, these devices store personal, sensitive information, and there is a growing number of applications that leak it. We propose AntMonitor – the first system of its kind that supports (i) collection of large-scale, semantic-rich network traffic in a way that respects users' privacy preferences and (ii) detection and prevention of leakage of private information in real time. The first property makes AntMonitor a powerful tool for network researchers who want to collect and analyze large-scale yet fine-grained mobile measurements. The second property can work as an incentive for using AntMonitor and contributing data for analysis. As a proof-of-concept, we have developed a prototype of AntMonitor, deployed it to monitor 9 users for 2 months, and collected and analyzed 20 GB of mobile data from 151 applications. Preliminary results show that fine-grained data collected from AntMonitor could enable application classification with higher accuracy than state-of-the-art approaches. In addition, we demonstrated that AntMonitor could help prevent several apps from leaking private information over unencrypted traffic, including phone numbers, emails, and device identifiers.

Categories and Subject Descriptors

C.2.3 [**Computer-Communication Networks**]: Network Operations—*network monitoring*; D.4.6 [**Operating Systems**]: Security and Protection—*access controls*

Keywords

Mobile Network Monitoring; Android Security; Privacy Leakage Detection

This work has been supported by NSF Awards 1228995 and 1028394. Varmarken and Langhoff were visiting UCI when this work was conducted.

MobiCom'15, September 7–11, 2015, Paris, France.
ACM. ISBN 978-1-4503-3619-2/15/09
http://dx.doi.org/10.1145/2789168.2789170.

1. INTRODUCTION

Mobile devices, such as smart phones and tablets, have become ubiquitous. With multiple wireless interfaces, including Wi-Fi and 3G/4G, these devices have persistent Internet connectivity throughout the day. As a result, the amount of traffic generated by these devices has grown rapidly in recent years and is expected to grow 10 times in the next 5 years [1]. Consequently, collecting and studying mobile network traffic has become a critical task in network infrastructure planning and Internet measurement research.

The growth of these mobile devices has been accompanied by an increasing number of personal information leakage [2, 3]. Examples of such information include personally identifiable information (PII) that can be used to uniquely identify an individual in a specific context (IMEI, email), data associated with the user (contacts, SMS messages), and demographic information (age, location).

We present a novel system, called AntMonitor, to address the needs of researchers for mobile traffic data and the needs of users for enhanced privacy, as outlined below.

Objective 1: Large Scale, Semantic-Rich Data Collection. First, AntMonitor is compatible with Android OS versions 4.0+, which makes it work with more than 94% of Android devices today [6]. Second, AntMonitor is carefully designed to scale and supports tens of thousands of users [5]. Third, AntMonitor collects packet traces in PCAP Next Generation format [7], which allows the system to collect arbitrary information alongside with the raw packets, such as the names of applications that are associated with packets. Such information is only available at the client side, and yet it plays a critical role in subsequent analyses by providing ground truth for application classification. Last, AntMonitor is designed to provide maximum user comfort: it has a simple interface with minimal configuration, runs seamlessly in the background, does not require the user to root the phone, and most importantly, has modest CPU and battery usage while maintaining high network performance [5].

Objective 2: Enhanced User Privacy. First, to address privacy concerns in data collection, AntMonitor is designed to provide users with complete control over what data they may want to contribute. In particular, they can choose specific applications, and either full packets or just packet headers to contribute. Second, AntMonitor is able to search unencrypted outgoing packets for sensitive information. Moreover, it can prevent this information from leaking on-the-fly, by blocking the current communication or replacing the sensitive strings with randomly generated ones, depending on the user's decision.

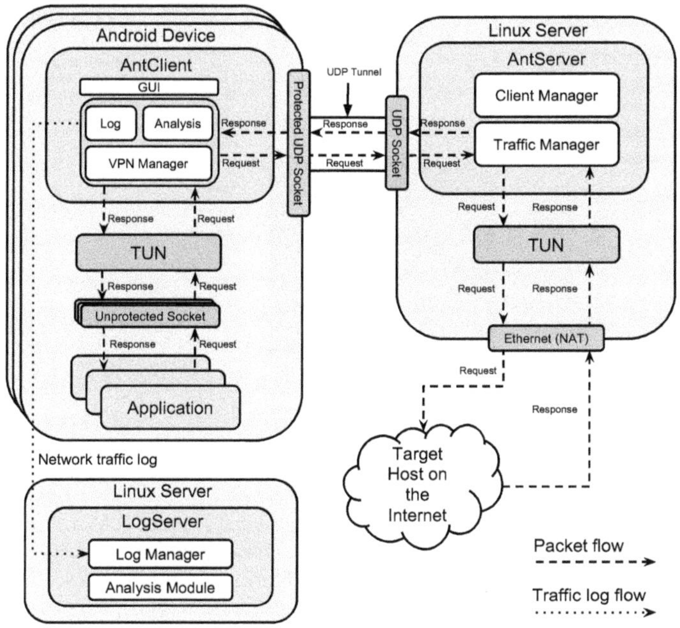

Figure 1: AntMonitor System Overview

The rest of this paper is organized as follows. Section 2 discusses related work. Section 3 describes the design and implementation of AntMonitor. Section 4 describes the demo.

2. RELATED WORK

Data Collection. There is a large body of work on collecting and analyzing network traffic data. Depending on the vantage point of data collection, there are the following approaches: (i) applications installed on the device [8], (ii) traffic collection inside the network [9], (iii) custom operating systems or rooted phones [10, 11], and (iv) the Virtual Private Network (VPN) based approach, which AntMonitor takes. (i) provides fine-grained but small-scale traces from a limited set of users; (ii) suffers from coarse-grained traces; and (iii) inconveniences the user. Although the VPN approach (iv) alters the path of the packets and introduces additional processing per packet, it allows for interception of all network traffic, and thus can enable useful features, *e.g.*, privacy leakage prevention. Most importantly, the VPN approach works on almost all mobile devices today without significantly impacting the user experience.

Privacy Leakage Detection. Detecting leakage of privacy sensitive data has also been extensively studied in the literature. TaintDroid [2] was one of the early tools built to identify privacy leaks in realtime using taint tracking, and it was used to identify a variety of privacy leaks on 30 popular Android apps. Similar work [3] automatically explores the GUI of Android apps and uses Taintdroid to detect privacy leaks. These approaches, however, are not suitable for large-scale deployment as they require a rooted phone. Another approach is to use static analysis of binary code [12]; yet, this method can be fooled by obfuscated code. Meddle [4] also adopted the VPN-based approach and supports detection of leakage of sensitive information; however, this detection is carried out at the VPN server, when the sensitive information already leaked out of the device.

AntMonitor. The description of the prototype appears in the SIGCOMM Workshop [5]. A video demonstrating the capabilities of AntMonitor can be found on the project website [13].

3. SYSTEM OVERVIEW

The AntMonitor system consists of three components: a client-side Android application, called AntClient, and two server applications, called AntServer and LogServer for routing and collecting packets, respectively. Fig. 1 shows how the three work together. Each component is described in detail elsewhere [5]. Here, we provide the overview of the functionalities of AntMonitor.

Traffic Interception and Routing. AntClient establishes a VPN service on the device. This VPN service creates a virtual (layer-3) TUN interface that intercepts all outgoing traffic. Once a packet arrives at the TUN interface, AntMonitor sends it through a UDP socket to AntServer. AntServer routes the packets to the intended Internet host and delivers responses back to AntClient using another TUN interface and IP Masquerading (packet forwarding with Network Address Translation).

Data Collection. AntClient saves packets in log files and uploads them to LogServer at a later time, *e.g.*, when the device is charging and has Wi-Fi or when explicitly requested by the user. LogServer extracts features from the log files and inserts them into a database to support various types of analysis. LogServer receives crowd-sourced data from a large number of devices, which enables global large-scale analysis. In our pilot deployment to volunteering students at UC Irvine, we collected and analyzed 20 GB of data from 151 applications, and were able to classify network flows to a specific app with F1-score of 70.1% using a Linear SVM [5]. To put this result in context, Meddle [4] reports a 64.1% precision score in classifying flows for the 92 most popular Android applications by using the Host and User-Agent payload features.

Enhanced Privacy Control. When designing AntMonitor, we made an explicit decision to decouple the routing and logging functionalities: they are provided by two separate servers. This separation is to provide transparency, fine-grained data collection, and enhanced privacy control. Our design choices for privacy are as follows: First, AntServer only routes traffic and must not log any traffic. This is in line with privacy protection provided by some of the most popular VPN services [14]. Second, the LogServer, which logs and analyzes traffic, must only have access to the information explicitly allowed by the user. In other words, the user must be able to choose which applications to log, as shown in Fig. 2(c).

Privacy Leakage Prevention. AntClient allows users to configure which private information they want to prevent from leaking, as shown in Fig. 2(d). The information can be of two types: (i) sensitive information that is readily available to applications on the phone, such as, IMEI, email, and phone number, or (ii) custom strings that the user wants to protect. Examples of custom strings include a user's home address, ethnicity, gender, age, *etc.* This type of information is typically not stored on the phone; however, a user may input and send them to a friend in a previous communication, and the user wants to make sure that no other apps can sniff (*e.g.*, keyboard apps) and send this information elsewhere.

If the user selects one or more strings to protect (as shown in Fig. 2(d)), then AntClient inspects every outgoing packet for any of the protected strings, before sending it out. The search is currently implemented with the widely used Aho-Corasick algorithm [15]. If a string is found within the packet, AntClient notifies the user, as shown in Fig.2(e). The user is then able to either allow the packet to continue on its way, replace the sensitive string, or block it. As deep packet inspection is costly, we have implemented this part of AntClient in native C so as not to significantly impact CPU usage and battery life. It has been shown that the Aho-Corasick algorithm is able to reach gigabits per second throughput [16], which is sufficient for mobile devices whose wireless networks typically reach several megabits per second. Although the current version

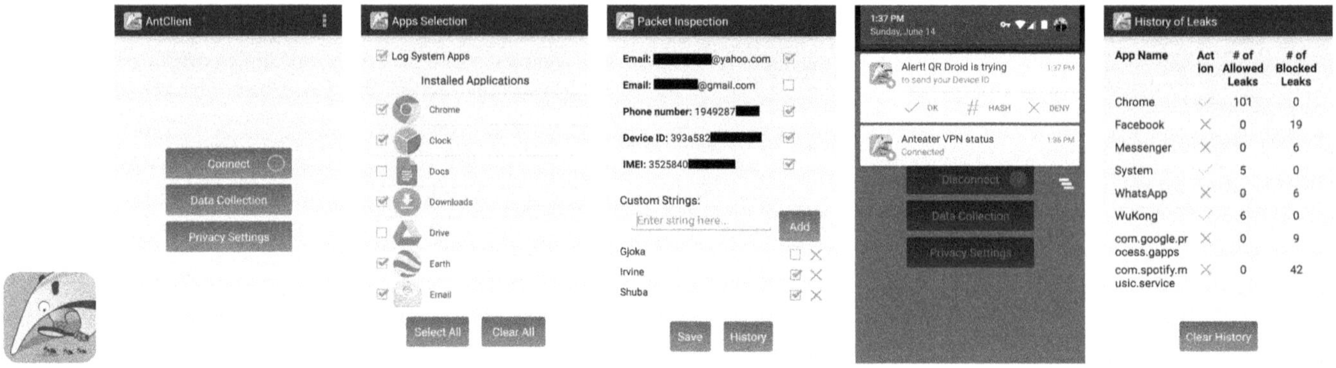

(a) Icon (b) Home Screen (c) Selecting Apps for Data Collection (d) Selecting Strings for Inspection (e) Privacy Leak Notification (f) History of Leaks

Figure 2: Screenshots of AntClient. A video demo can be found on the project website [13].

of AntClient can only search through unencrypted traffic, we are working on an improved version that can inspect encrypted traffic, leveraging the SSL Bumping technique [17, 4].

4. DEMONSTRATION

4.1 Description

Our demo will consist of two parts: the first one will show how users can contribute data, and the second will demonstrate how AntMonitor detects and prevents privacy leaks in real time.

In the first demo, we will start by opening AntClient on an Android phone and connecting it to the AntServer, as shown in Fig. 2(b). Then we will select some apps whose traffic will be logged, as shown in Fig. 2(c). Next, we will continue to use the phone as usual, *e.g.* check weather, email, and play a game. Afterward, we will ask AntClient to upload data to LogServer. We will observe the log files arriving at LogServer by showing the LogServer's database on a laptop screen. We will also demonstrate real-time measurements that show the high performance (throughput and delay) and low cost (battery consumption) of AntClient.

In the second demo, we will navigate to AntClient's privacy screen, as shown in Fig. 2(d). We will then select IMEI, device ID, email, and phone number to monitor and use several apps known to leak them. When a leak occurs, AntClient will generate a notification, as shown in Fig. 2(e). We can then either allow the leak, replace the leaking string, or block the leak (packet) completely. Lastly, we will navigate to AntClient's leak history screen to review the number of leaks from the apps we used and the actions (allow, replace, block) we took, as shown in Fig. 2(f).

4.2 Setup Requirement

Our demo requires one Android phone (or several phones to demo to more than one users at the booth at the same time) and one laptop that we will provide on our own (a screen would be nice to have, but optional). We need Internet connectivity for both the phones and the laptop, preferably Wi-Fi. (We will try to get 4G for the phones at the venue but from our past experience, this can be difficult.) A small table with a close-by power outlet will suffice. The setup requires preparing the phones and the laptop and will take about 10 minutes.

5. REFERENCES

[1] Cisco Visual Networking Index: Global Mobile Data Traffic Forecast Update 2014-2019. `http://goo.gl/Zu8f2r`.

[2] W. Enck, P. Gilbert, B. Chun, L. P. Cox, J. Jung, P. McDaniel, and A. N. Sheth. Taintdroid: an information-flow tracking system for realtime privacy monitoring on smartphones. *ACM Transactions on Computer Systems (TOCS)*, 2014.

[3] Vaibhav Rastogi, Yan Chen, and William Enck. Appsplayground: automatic security analysis of smartphone applications. In *Proc. of the 3rd ACM conference on Data and application security and privacy (CODASPY)*, 2013.

[4] A. Rao, A. M. Kakhki, A. Razaghpanah, A. Tang, S. Wang, J. Sherry, P. Gill, A. Krishnamurthy, A. Legout, A. Mislove, and D. Choffnes. Using the Middle to Meddle with Mobile. Technical report, Northeastern University, Dec. 2013.

[5] Anh Le, Janus Varmarken, Simon Langhoff, Anastasia Shuba, Minas Gjoka, and Markopoulou Athina. AntMonitor: A System for Monitoring from Mobile Devices. In *(to appear) Proc. of ACM SIGCOMM Workshop on Crowdsourcing and Crowdsharing of Big Data*, 2015.

[6] Android Versions. `developer.android.com/about/dashboards`.

[7] PCAPNG File Format. `http://goo.gl/y89d9U`.

[8] J. Sommers and P. Barford. Cell vs. WiFi: On the Performance of Metro Area Mobile Connections. In *Proc. of IMC*, 2012.

[9] Q. Xu, J. Erman, A. Gerber, Z. Mao, J. Pang, and S. Venkataraman. Identifying Diverse Usage Behaviors of Smartphone Apps. In *Proc. of IMC*, 2011.

[10] PhoneLab, University at Buffalo. `https://www.phone-lab.org/`.

[11] H. Falaki, D. Lymberopoulos, R. Mahajan, S. Kandula, and D. Estrin. A First Look at Traffic on Smartphones. *IMC'10*.

[12] Clint Gibler, Jonathan Crussell, Jeremy Erickson, and Hao Chen. Androidleaks: Automatically detecting potential privacy leaks in android applications on a large scale. In *Proc. of the International Conf. on Trust and Trustworthy Computing*, 2012.

[13] AntMonitor: Project Webpage and Demo. `http://antmonitor.calit2.uci.edu/`.

[14] Private Internet Access Privacy Policy. `http://goo.gl/Yt8jNx`.

[15] Multifast. `http://multifast.sourceforge.net/`.

[16] Nathan Tuck, Timothy Sherwood, Brad Calder, and George Varghese. Deterministic memory-efficient string matching algorithms for intrusion detection. In *Proc. of INFOCOM'04*.

[17] Squid Proxy. Squid-in-the-middle SSL Bump.

Demo: Car-Fi: Opportunistic V2I by Exploiting Dual-Access Wi-Fi Networks

Davide Pesavento
Sorbonne Universités, UPMC
Univ Paris 06, CNRS, LIP6
davide.pesavento@lip6.fr

Giulio Grassi
Sorbonne Universités, UPMC
Univ Paris 06, CNRS, LIP6
giulio.grassi@lip6.fr

Giovanni Pau
Sorbonne Universités, UPMC
Univ Paris 06, CNRS, LIP6
giovanni.pau@lip6.fr

Paramvir Bahl*
Microsoft Research, USA
bahl@microsoft.com

Serge Fdida
Sorbonne Universités, UPMC
Univ Paris 06, CNRS, LIP6
serge.fdida@lip6.fr

ABSTRACT

The need for Internet access from moving vehicles has been steadily increasing in the past few years. Solutions that rely on cellular connectivity are becoming impractical to deploy due to technical and economic reasons. Car-Fi proposes an approach that leverages existing home Wi-Fi access points configured in dual-access mode, in order to offload all data traffic from the congested and expensive cellular infrastructure to whatever Wi-Fi network is available. Thanks to an improved scanning algorithm and numerous optimizations to the connection setup, Car-Fi makes downloading large amounts of data from a moving car feasible.

Categories and Subject Descriptors

C.2.1 [**Computer-communication Networks**]: Network Architecture and Design—*Wireless communication*

General Terms

Design, Experimentation, Measurement, Performance

Keywords

802.11; fast roaming; scanning; V2I; vehicular networks

1. MOTIVATION

In the past few years the mobile data traffic requirements of our cars have been growing at a tremendous rate: the on-board computer software must be updated regularly, especially in the first months of life of the vehicle; applications can be downloaded and run on the car; the digital maps of the GPS navigator must also be updated to account for changes in road topology; quasi real-time traffic information on the chosen route can be fetched and displayed to the driver; diagnostic data gathered by the on-board unit is sent to the car manufacturer for analysis. These are only few examples, the number and variety of use cases for vehicle-to-infrastructure communication increases every day.

The following table shows the approximate amount of data transferred by several applications that are already deployed by car manufacturers. Note that, in addition to the data usage and frequency, different latency requirements should also be considered.

Activity	Data usage	Frequency
Car software update	300 MB	1/quarter
Application download	5~20 MB	1~2/week
Local map update	100~500 MB	6~8/year
Regional map update	2.5 GB	1~2/year
Real-time road traffic	50~100 KB	10/hour
Telemetry data upload	0.1~1 MB	1/day

In most cases it is the car manufacturer that pays the mobile network operator for the amount of data traffic generated by each vehicle. However, with more and more Internet-enabled cars entering the market, providing cellular connectivity to all of them will soon become prohibitively expensive for the manufacturer.

Therefore, we set out to investigate a viable alternative that does *not* rely on costly cellular networks. Our solution leverages existing *dual access* Wi-Fi networks (sometimes called clustered wireless community network) to satisfy the cars' data needs.

2. DUAL ACCESS WIRELESS NETWORKS

In recent years, a growing number of mobile network operators started to offer free Wi-Fi connectivity to their customers, in an effort to reduce the load on the cellular infrastructure. There are two main directions in which operators are working in order to achieve the desired wireless coverage.

The first possibility is to leverage existing wireless access points (APs) that are nowadays installed in almost every home, office, or café. In particular, this means sharing the physical capacity of the 802.11 radio channel(s) and the available bandwidth of the Internet connection between a "private" and a "public" Wi-Fi network. The former is usually password-protected via WPA/WPA2-PSK and only accessible to the AP owner, while the latter can be either open

*Paramvir Bahl contributed to this work while on sabbatical at UPMC/LIP6 between December 2014 and January 2015.

MobiCom'15, September 7–11, 2015, Paris, France.
ACM 978-1-4503-3619-2/15/09.
DOI: http://dx.doi.org/10.1145/2789168.2789171.

with browser-based authentication, or encrypted using the so-called WPA-Enterprise mode[3]. This approach is especially common for mobile operators that are also Internet service providers, and it guarantees widespread Wi-Fi coverage at a very low cost, since little or no new infrastructure needs to be deployed.

The second approach consists in installing dedicated outdoor Wi-Fi access points in carefully chosen spots, such as 4-way road intersections, in order to maximize the wireless range of the AP and minimize interference. This obviously has higher costs than the previous solution, but it might be the only possibility in those areas where the density of home APs is not sufficient, or where the buildings are too far from the street. On the other hand, operators can use hardware of better quality for these dedicated APs, thereby providing increased throughput and extended coverage to their users.

2.1 Challenges

Connecting to indoor access points from a moving car is a difficult task. Cabernet[1] attempted in the past to connect to Wi-Fi APs while on the go, however it:

- requires the wireless card on the client to operate in monitor mode;
- makes use of low-level features such as *radiotap*;
- employs a custom transport protocol;
- does not work at all if the AP has any kind of encryption or authentication enabled.

The last point is of particular importance since there are virtually no open access points anymore. Nowadays the great majority of networks are protected using either a Web-based authentication scheme (captive portal), or the WPA/WPA2 standards with PSK or EAP[3].

Virgil[2] proposed an improved AP discovery and selection system, but it needs to run a battery of tests for each access point in range, which is unfeasible in the short time we have driving by. Moreover, we conjecture that the signal strength by itself is not a sufficiently reliable indicator, and may result in an uneven load distribution on the available APs.

In order to gain more insights on the problem space, we performed an extensive measurement campaign in Paris (France) and Los Angeles (CA) in February 2015, aimed at characterizing the *link duration* and the *inter-AP time* in a variety of scenarios.

Figures 1 and 2 show the CDF for these two metrics in a urban area of Paris. We can see that the median values are respectively 9.5 and 4.5 seconds, while the 90th percentile of the inter-AP time is 29 seconds.

The data collected in Los Angeles is plotted in Figures 3 and 4, again as a CDF. Here we notice that the median link duration is much longer than Paris, at about 23 seconds. The inter-AP time median value is about 7 seconds, and the 90th percentile is 15 seconds.

3. CAR-FI SYSTEM DESIGN

Car-Fi is composed of two main actors: a *car agent*, that runs in every participating vehicle, and a *coordinator*, that runs on one or more servers anywhere on the Internet. The car agent includes a few different components:

- a WPA and IEEE 802.1X supplicant;

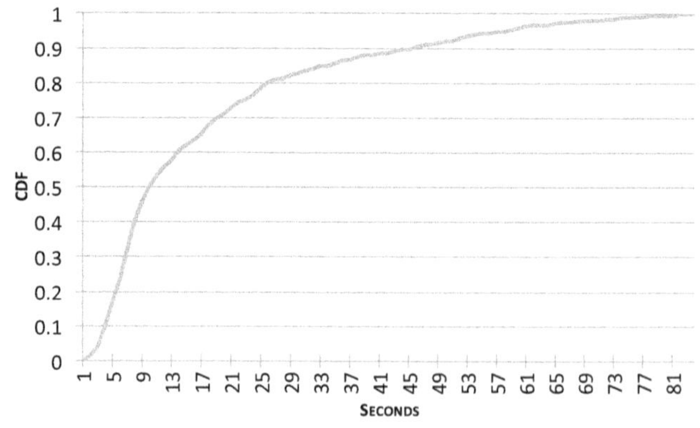

Figure 1: CDF of the link duration in Paris.

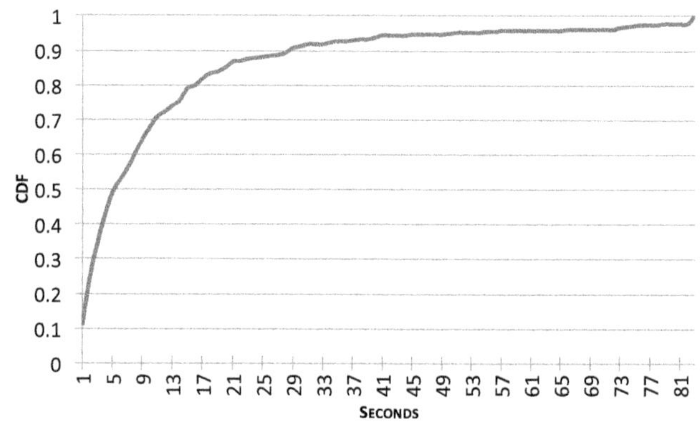

Figure 2: CDF of the inter-AP time in Paris.

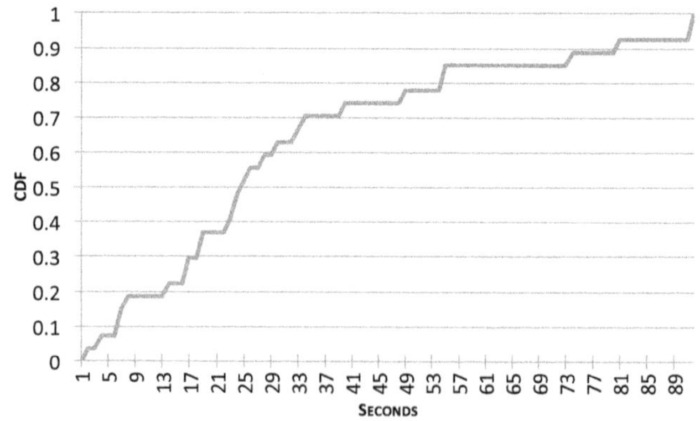

Figure 3: CDF of the link duration in Los Angeles.

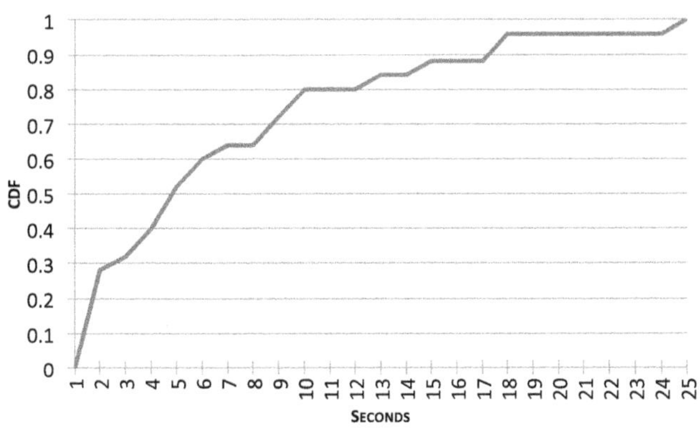

Figure 4: CDF of the inter-AP time in Los Angeles.

- sophisticated heuristics for scanning, roaming, and access point selection;
- an upload/download manager;
- a GPS receiver.

The car agent is able to communicate with the coordinator in order to obtain a database of APs to which it can potentially connect along the route. For each AP, the database includes its approximate area of coverage, in GPS coordinates, its operating channel, and a rough estimate of its performance characteristics, to aid in the selection process. Since APs are often rebooted, change channel, and their performance can change at any time, the database is very dynamic and the car agent must periodically request updates from the coordinator.

Every time a vehicle successfully connects to an access point, it learns the performance characteristics of that network and, if possible, it submits the newly acquired information back to the server, which then updates the AP database for future client requests. This is basically the same idea as *crowdsourcing*.

When the car agent has no connectivity to the Internet, and thus cannot reach the coordinator, it falls back to a *disconnected* mode. In this mode of operation, the agent still scans and tries to connect to Wi-Fi networks, but its roaming decision will solely be based on information available locally, such as the RSSI and a few other parameters. Moreover, the agent keeps collecting all the data about the APs it encounters during this time, and as soon as Internet connectivity is reestablished, it will synchronize its local AP database with the database of the coordinator.

4. DEMO SETUP

The purpose of the demo is to demonstrate that Car-Fi is able to download a (small) file from a server on the Internet in a matter of minutes, depending on wireless coverage along the chosen route.

The idea is to drive around the conference venue with a car (provided by us), showing the running system to the passengers. Since only 2 or 3 people at a time can be accommodated in the car, a camera mounted inside the cabin will stream a video feed back to the demo room, where it will be displayed on a screen, so that more people can see what is happening in the car.

Figure 5: The node that runs the car agent.

Figure 6: Various antennas mounted on the roof of the test car.

To summarize, in the demo room we will need just a screen, power for one laptop and the screen itself, and Internet access to be able to stream a standard resolution video from the camera situated in the car.

5. REFERENCES

[1] J. Eriksson, H. Balakrishnan, and S. Madden. Cabernet: vehicular content delivery using WiFi. In *Proceedings of the 14th ACM international conference on Mobile computing and networking*, pages 199–210. ACM, 2008.

[2] A. J. Nicholson, Y. Chawathe, M. Y. Chen, B. D. Noble, and D. Wetherall. Improved access point selection. In *Proceedings of the 4th international conference on Mobile systems, applications and services*, pages 233–245. ACM, 2006.

[3] D. Stanley, J. Walker, and B. Aboba. Extensible authentication protocol (EAP) method requirements for wireless LANs. *Request for Comments*, 4017, 2005.

Demo: FIT IoT-LAB
A Large Scale Open Experimental IoT Testbed

Gaetan Harter[1]
gaetan.harter@inria.fr

Roger Pissard-Gibollet[1]
roger.pissard@inria.fr

Frederic Saint-Marcel[1]
frederic.saint-marcel@inria.fr

Guillaume Schreiner[2]
schreiner@unistra.fr

[1]Inria, France
[2]University of Strasbourg, France

Julien Vandaele[1]
julien.vandaele@inria.fr

ABSTRACT

FIT IoT-LAB's goal is to provide a very large scale open experimental testbed for the Internet of Things, by deploying more than 2700 experimentation nodes over 6 sites in France. Our demonstration purpose is to illustrate what the IoT-LAB platform offers through small applications involving radio communications and mobile nodes. Thanks to these examples, we will show how to run an experiment in the testbed and some of the tools it provides to help in developing, tuning and monitoring such large-scale applications.

Categories and Subject Descriptors

C.2.1 [**Computer-Communication Networks**]: Network Architecture and Design—*Wireless communication*

Keywords

wireless sensor network, internet of things, testbed

1. INTRODUCTION

The Internet of Things (IoT) is a reality today. Millions of devices are deployed in cities, industries and houses. But before hitting the market, IoT solutions need to be tested and fine-tuned. Verifying the performance of a technology, of an operating system or of an application is more effective when done under real-world conditions. Conducting large-scale experiments on real hardware yields more accurate results than using simulation tools, which suffer from several imperfections as it is based on artificial assumptions on radio propagation, traffic failure patterns and topologies. Due to the massively distributed nature of IoT applications, their design, implementation and evaluation are complex and tend to be daunting and consuming tasks.

To overcome these obstacles, FIT IoT-LAB[1] offers a large-scale experimental platform offering: a heterogeneous and rich environment (from hardware and software point of views); the ability to manage, interact and monitor running experiments; the ability to instrument an experiment, through visualization and reproductibility tools.

Details on the implementation of the platform are presented in Section 2. Section 3 details the demonstrations illustrating how to use the IoT-LAB through small applications involving radio communications and mobile nodes, respectively detailed in Section 3.1 and Section 3.2. Finally, Section 4 gather the needs to run this demonstration.

2. TESTBED OVERVIEW

IoT-LAB is part of the "Future Internet of Things" (FIT[2]) experimental platform, a set of complementary components that enable experimentation on innovative services for academic and industrial users.

With over 2700 wireless sensor nodes deployed across six sites in France, IoT-LAB is the largest open low-power wireless remote testbed in the world today. Deployed in 3D grids, 2D plans or more irregulars manner, nodes can be allocated in various topologies through all sites.A variety of wireless sensors are available, with different processor architectures – ranging from the low-power TI MSP430 to the powerful ARM Cortex-A8 and including the representative of today's IoT devices ARM Cortex-M3 – and wireless chips – intended for 868MHz or 2.54GHz frequencies. Also, a number of generic host nodes, designed to welcome the own boards of a user, starts to be deployed over two sites, taking advantage of the back-end management solution of the IoT-LAB. The nodes are fully programmable; meaning that a user has a full "bare-metal" access to the nodes. IoT-LAB does not impose any constraint on the binary image loaded onto the nodes; the user is free to deploy code written in any programming language, using any library and with any operating system. In addition to static nodes, mobile robots embedding a sensor node are under deployment in the IoT-LAB, to handle experiment scenarios involving mobility. Today, 6 robots are in production, and we plan to reach a total of more than an hundred. For the moment, the user has a possibility to choose between several path on which the robot will loop during the experiment. In near future, the user will have also the choice to choose between several mobility patterns (random way point, Manhattan) or the possibility to set navigation goals at running.

The IoT-LAB is an open access platform. Once register, the user can use his credentials to log in to the IoT-LAB web

[1]`https://www.iot-lab.info`

[2]`https://www.fit-equipex.fr`

MobiCom'15, September 7–11, 2015, Paris, France.
ACM. ISBN 978-1-4503-3619-2/15/09
DOI: http://dx.doi.org/10.1145/2789168.2789172.

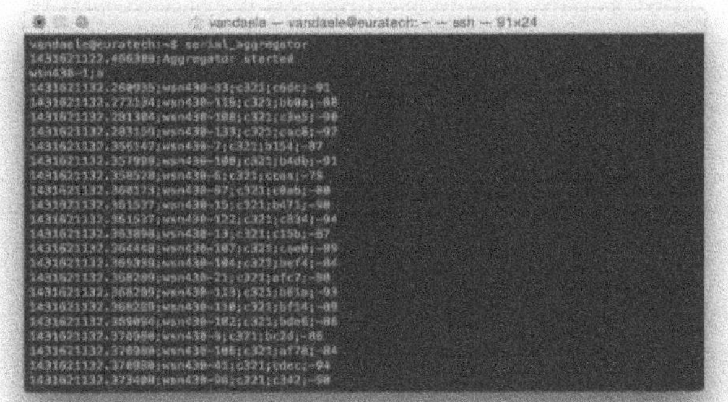

Figure 1: Serial-aggregator running on ssh-frontend of euratechno site.

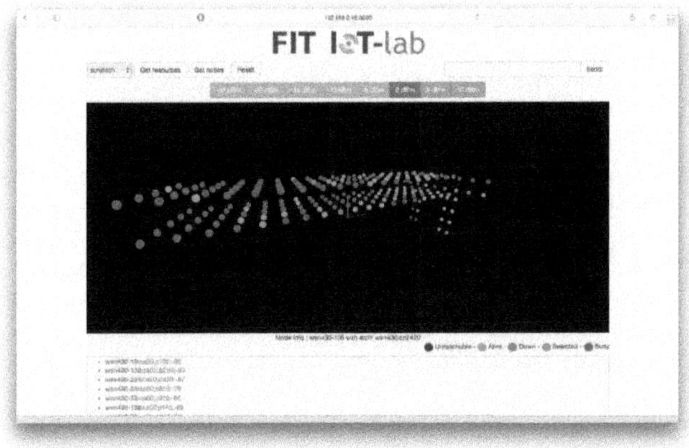

Figure 2: Web view of the radio collision demo.

portal. Its key functionality is the submission of new experiment: through a web form, the user specifies resources, date, duration, firmware(s) and nodes configuration for the experiment. Once it is submitted, a batch scheduler plans the experiment in accordance with requested resources and their availability. During the running of the experiment, the user can interact with nodes and access to nodes serial links redirected on TCP ports.

3. DEMONSTRATION OVERVIEW

Here we are not going to propose one application demo, but rather to demonstrate the usage of the IoT-LAB testbed through several small applications. Involving radio communications at a large scale, we will present interaction and visualization tools provided as open source[3]. Involving mobile nodes, we will show the specific features and the exploitation of the results when using robots.

3.1 Radio Communications

Experimenting radio communications in wireless sensor networks, and particularly on a remote testbed, could be a pretty hard task. User needs a concrete feedback on the behaviour of its application. Since one of the easiest way to log information is to print on the serial link, the need of reading and writing on nodes serial links are essential. On the IoT-LAB, nodes serial link are redirected on TCP sockets reachable from the site SSH front-end; asking potentially to the user to open a socket for each node. To ease the use and improve efficiency in the management of these sockets, a python tool named **`serial-aggregator`** has been created and shared to the user community[4]. For example, users can have read and write access of all serial links in a unique console, like shown in Figure 1.

Data from serial links can give an idea of radio activity on the network, but graphical representation is much easier to understand. Linked to the serial-aggregator, we chose to use web technologies to display activities of the sensor network. They are well-known and easy-to-learn technologies for developers, who will be able to modify or extend the open source code distributed on the IoT-LAB's github repository for their own needs. For a real-time interpretation of events, we chose to use web-sockets, implementing the web application with the node.js[5] platform. For a better understanding of radio propagation, it is important to have a realistic representation. That's why we implemented a 3D view of nodes topology, using the three.js[6] javascript library.

3.1.1 Radio Propagation

In this first simple application, the firmware flashed on the node is:

- reading characters on its serial link, interpreting characters from 'a' to 'h' into sending of a broadcast message at radio power between -30dBm and 5dBm;
- listening on its radio interface, and writing a report when receiving a broadcast message.

We use the web interface to interact with the nodes. First, we select a node in the 3D view. Then, we use one of the *radio power* buttons, which matches with the sending of a character to the selected node. The web application will read messages from nodes reached by the broadcast message and change the color of the node represented in the 3D view. We are then able to see which nodes have received the broadcast message on the whole testbed site. Playing with different powers helps in understanding the radio propagation on a testbed site.

3.1.2 Radio Collision

In this second application, the firmware flashed on nodes is:

- reading character on its serial link, waiting for a 'b' character to broadcast a 'ping' radio message;
- listening on its radio interface, writing a report if a broadcast message is received before answering to the source node with a 'pong' unicast message.

Like in the previous application, we use the web interface to select the source of the broadcast by clicking on a *broadcast* button, and observe the automatic color change of the nodes which received this radio message. Additionally, they will

[3]Source code and documentation available at `http://github.com/iot-lab`
[4]`https://github.com/iot-lab/aggregation-tools`
[5]`https://nodejs.org`
[6]`http://threejs.org/`

change color a second time if the source node has received the unicast response. In this last step we compare two versions of the firmware: the first one without MAC layer, the second using a CSMA MAC layer. Comparing the response rates produced by these two firmwares eases the understanding of the radio collision problem at large scale and a solution given by the MAC layer.

3.2 Mobile Nodes Tracking Demonstration

Supporting mobility with mobile nodes carried by robots is a significant feature of the IoT-LAB testbed. Experiments with mobile nodes fully automatize and available 24/7 is a real challenge. Currently few mobile nodes using Turtlebot2 are in production in three sites : Grenoble, Lille and Strasbourg. Figure 3 shows an example of robot in Grenoble.

Turtlebot2[7] is an open-source robot using ROS framework [8], it is composed by a mobile robot Kobuki, a laptop running on Linux and a Microsoft Kinect. Thanks to the automatic docking driven by an infrared beam, the robot automatically and autonomously recharges using its docking station.

Figure 3: A Turtlebot2 mobile node in the lab corridor

The user interaction with a mobile open node is similar to that of a fixed node. The laptop communicates with the IoT-LAB infrastructure through a dedicated wifi link and it controls the physical robot using ROS. The IoT-LAB node is carried around by the robot and is accessible like a fixed node.

The behavior of the mobile node is predefined. It moves along a predefined circuit trajectory, as chosen on the configuration panel. During its motion, the mobile node can avoid obstacles autonomously. When the experiment is terminated, the mobile node goes back to the docking station. During the experiment, the user can retrieve the position of the robot in real time through a programmatic interface.

The main objective of this demonstration is to show a use-case of an experimentation using mobility features of the IoT-LAB testbed. The use case scenario is a mobile node tracking using physical sensors or RF. On the Grenoble site, most of the sensor nodes are located in the corridors of the lab building in the ceiling and under the floor tiles (see Figure 4). They embed physical sensors as a tri-axis accelerometer/magnetometer (STMicroelectronics LSM303DLHC). In this ambient intelligence use case, we use magnetometers to detect the passage of a Turtlebot2 through the magnetic perturbations its electrical motors generate. In addition to using this physical detection, we implement a basic RF localization: periodically, the mobile node sends packets which are received by nearby fixed nodes. Detection events are collected and displayed on a web interface using JavaScript (see Fig. 5). This demonstration provides a starting point for more elaborate scenarios with mobiles nodes.

A tutorial on how to run this demo on your computer and a video of the demo are available on the IoT-LAB's github wiki[9].

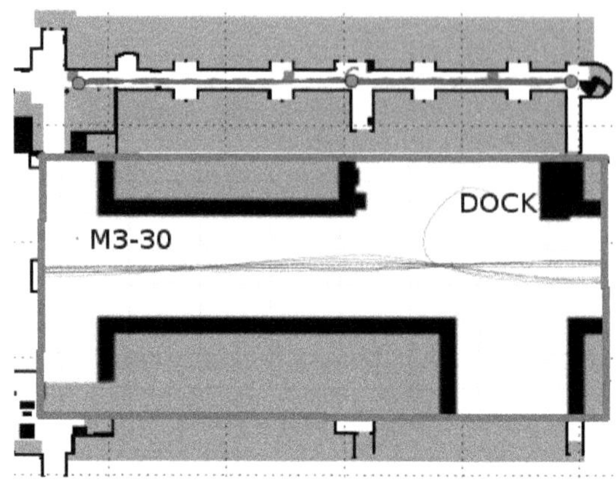

Figure 4: 2D mobile node trajectory visualization

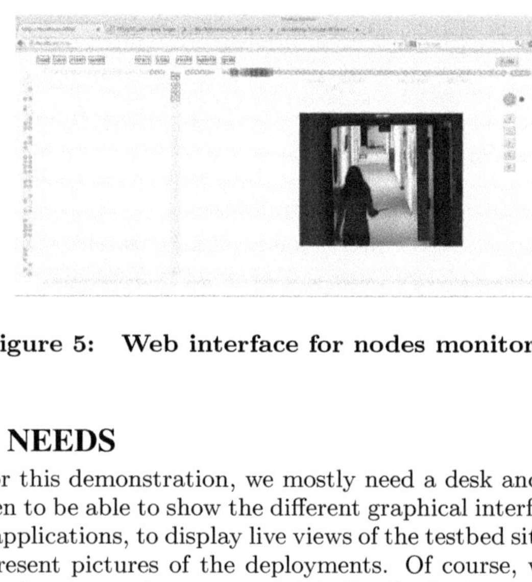

Figure 5: Web interface for nodes monitoring

4. NEEDS

For this demonstration, we mostly need a desk and a big screen to be able to show the different graphical interfaces of the applications, to display live views of the testbed sites and to present pictures of the deployments. Of course, we will need also one or two power points for the laptops running the demonstrations.

As we are interacting with a remote platform, it is imperative that we have a stable and efficient internet connection, with ports HTTP(80), HTTPS(443) and SSH(22) opened.

Required space is limited to the desk. If we have a little more space we may bring and expose hardware nodes and robots deployed in the testbed.

Required setup time is about 30 minutes.

[7] `http://www.turtlebot.com/`

[8] `http://www.ros.com/`

[9] Running the Smart Tiles Demo: `https://github.com/iot-lab/iot-lab/wiki/Running-the-Smart-Tiles-Demo`

Demo: OpenVLC1.0 Platform for Research in Visible Light Communication Networks

Qing Wang
IMDEA Networks Institute & UC3M
Madrid, Spain
qing.wang@imdea.org

Shengrong Yin
University of Houston
Houston, USA
syin@cs.uh.edu

Omprakash Gnawali
University of Houston
Houston, USA
gnawali@cs.uh.edu

Domenico Giustiniano
IMDEA Networks Institute
Madrid, Spain
domenico.giustiniano@imdea.org

ABSTRACT

Built around a cost-effective embedded Linux platform, OpenVLC is an open source project (`www.openvlc.org`) for research in Visible Light Communication (VLC) Networks. In this work, we introduce and demonstrate the OpenVLC1.0 platform, a flexible, software-defined, and low-cost research platform. OpenVLC1.0 consists of a simple electronic design, and a new driver of the Linux operating system that implements the MAC, part of the PHY layers and it offers an interface to Internet protocols. The electronics of OpenVLC implement a flexible optical front-end consisting of commodity low- and high-power Light Emitting Diodes (LEDs), photodiodes (PDs), and ancillary electronic circuitry. In order to quickly start playing with VLC Networks, we have designed and developed a printed circuit board (OpenVLC1.0 cape). The cape can be plugged into the main embedded Beaglebone board. Researchers can then swiftly build PHY and MAC protocols using the software implementation (OpenVLC1.0 driver), and prototype innovative solutions in realistic network setups. In this demo, we show that OpenVLC1.0 can switch between different MAC protocols, it can choose different optical channel for data transmission and reception, and it can be employed jointly with standard TCP/IP diagnostic tools.

Categories and Subject Descriptors

C.2.1 [**Computer-Communication Networks**]: Network Architecture and Design—*Wireless Communication*

Keywords

Visible light communication networks; OpenVLC; Open-source; Low-cost; Research platform

MobiCom'15, September 07–11, 2015, Paris, France.
ACM 978-1-4503-3619-2/15/09.
DOI: http://dx.doi.org/10.1145/2789168.2789173.

Figure 1: On the top: The OpenVLC1.0 cape. On the bottom: the cape plugged into an embedded board, that runs a Debian Linux and the OpenVLC1.0 driver to interface the OpenVLC1.0 cape to the Internet. The optical components are: (1) high-power LED; (2) low-power LED; (3) Photodiode (PD).

1. INTRODUCTION

Visible Light Communication (VLC) is emerging as a complementary technology to traditional Radio Frequency (RF) technologies. VLC is believed to be a proper candidate for the next-generation cellular networks [11, 3], accurate indoor localization [8, 2] and the Internet of Things [7, 14, 9]. Recent attempts for "softwarization" of VLC networks [14, 10, 4] show the need to speed up the research progress in this new field. Among these former works, only our low-cost OpenVLC project is open-source from the very beginning and it is designed to provide real-time functionalities for rapid prototyping of networked VLC systems [13].

In this demo, we introduce the OpenVLC1.0 platform, that interfaces an optical front-end consisting of a high-power LED, a low-power LED and a Photodiode (PD) to a cost-effective and powerful embedded board. In order to ease the exploration of the optical front-end, we have designed and implemented a printed circuit board (OpenVLC1.0 cape) that can be easily attached to the main embedded board. This plug-and-play approach allows researchers to focus on the software design of communication network protocols, without the hassle of wiring the optical components and the electronics in a breadboard. The cape is controlled using the OpenVLC1.0 driver, that implements key primitives at MAC and PHY layer such as signal sampling, symbol detection, coding/decoding, channel contention, carrier sensing and Internet protocol interoperability [14]. Among its many benefits, OpenVLC1.0 provides the basic tools to implement various protocols and prototype them in real-world VLC network setups.

2. SYSTEM DESIGN

OpenVLC1.0 is a software-defined platform built upon a BeagleBone Black (BBB) board [1] and a front-end transceiver that adopts a high-power LED, a low-power LED and a PD to transmit and receive light signals. A block diagram of the front-end transceiver and the software stack of the implementation are shown in Fig. 2 and Fig. 3, respectively. Several communication links are possible: OpenVLC1.0 can choose between high- and low-power LEDs as the optical transmitter, and between low-power LED and PD as the optical receiver. Each configuration comes with its own unique features in terms of channel propagation, receiver sensitivity, Field-of-View (FoV), etc. Flexible protocols can be designed that can dynamically choose the most desired configuration based on the current circumstance.

For instance, the high-power LED can be used to emulate the scenarios of communication under typical indoor illumination from the ceiling, while low-power LED can be enabled for those applications where the primary goal is communication, and the illumination is used as visual feedback. The LED as a receiver can be used to increase the resilience to ambient noise (e.g., sunlight and indoor illumination [7]) with no need for additional optical filters [5]. However, it comes with a smaller FoV than PDs. In our design, a software-defined optical selector allows to choose either the low-power or the high-power LED as the transmitter. Similarly, we can choose the low-power LED or the PD as the receiver.

Low-/high-power LED-to-PD communication: OpenVLC supports the communications between a low-/high-power LED and a PD. Low-power LED-to-PD can be used in scenarios where a more directional communication (e.g. secure communication) is perceived of interest, while a high-power LED can be used as an access point that serves a number of users.

Low-power LED-to-LED communication: while photodiodes are normally used as receivers, a reverse-biased LED (rather than a photodiode) may be used as a receiver to implement bidirectional LED-to-LED communication [6]. This principle has been exploited to introduce the concept of LED-to-LED communication networks [7] and to design an open-source platform for VLC research [13, 14]. In our

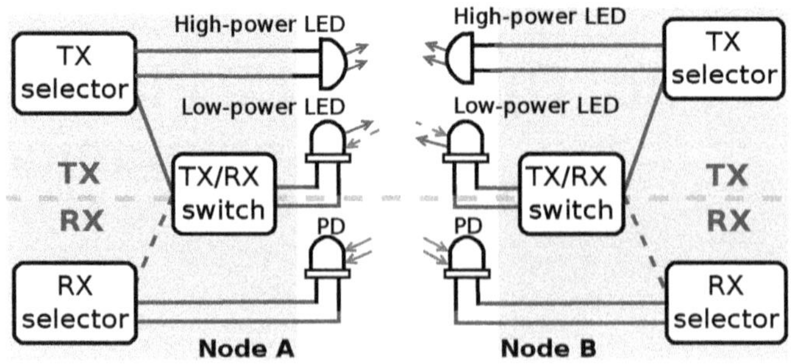

Figure 2: Block diagram of the OpenVLC1.0 cape.

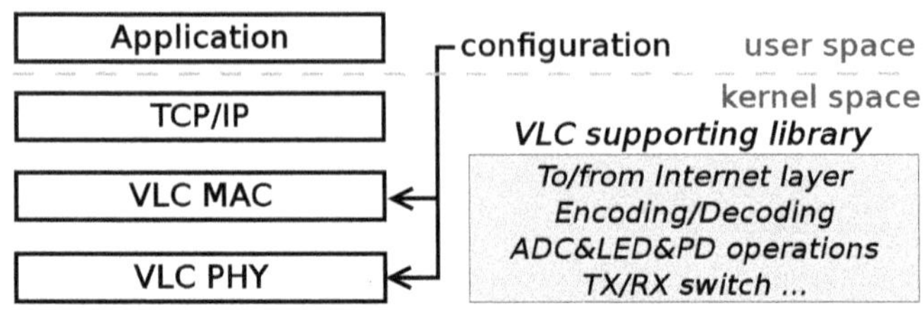

Figure 3: OpenVLC1.0 driver implementation in the software stack of an embedded Linux operating system.

design, a software-defined Transmitter/Receiver switch allows to control the operation mode of the low-power LED. This approach enables the implementation of time-division duplex protocols in the visible light spectrum [12].

High-power LED to low-power LED communication: the communications between high- and low-power LEDs are also supported by OpenVLC1.0. Under this case, a pair of high-power LED and a PD can form a transceiver that acts as an access point with wide FoV; while a single LED can be a transceiver residing into embedded size-limited devices.

3. DEMONSTRATION SETUP

The Linux operating system running on the BBB board is the Debian Linux Distribution (with kernel version 3.8.13) with the Xenomai patch. Off-the-shelf electronic components are used in the OpenVLC1.0 cape. To ensure fair channel access among nodes and reduce collisions, we implement three contention-based MAC protocols in the OpenVLC1.0 driver:

- listen-before-talk CSMA/CA (Carrier Sensing Multiple Access with Collision Avoidance) protocol for any configuration of the transceiver;
- listen-before&while-talk CSMA/CD (CSMA with Collision Detection) protocol for the low-power LED-to-LED communication [7];
- listen-before&while-talk CSMA/CD-HA (CSMA with Collision Detection&Hidden Avoidance) for the low-power LED-to-LED communication networks [12].

We implement the On-Off-Keying (OOK) with Manchester run-length line code and Reed-Solomon correction code as part of the PHY layer of the OpenVLC1.0 driver.

We demonstrate some functionality of OpenVLC1.0 through the following scenarios:

Scenario 1: Optical transceivers. We select on the fly the optical components for communication, such as choosing low-/high-power LED as the transmitter, and selecting the PD or low-power LED as the receiver.

Scenario 2: MAC protocols. We demonstrate the MAC protocols CSMA/CD, CSMA/CA, and CSMA/CD-HA using two to three OpenVLC1.0 nodes. We first show the interaction between two communicating nodes with a focus on the backoff mechanism. After that, we demonstrate the collision and hidden-node detection mechanism, i.e., as a node detects a collision, it interrupts the ongoing frame transmission or will not start a transmission. Since visible light is the communication medium, the attendees will be able to observe visually how the protocols are affected by collisions and hidden-nodes.

Scenario 3: Networking diagnostic tools. We demonstrate the network layer performance through the well-known networking diagnostic tools `ping` and `iperf` using two OpenVLC1.0 nodes. We demonstrate the results in a terminal when one node pings the other, and in another experiment where we test the UDP performance with `iperf`.

Demo setup. We need a table to hold one to two laptop(s) and two to three VLC nodes (a normal office table is enough) and a power socket extension. Additionally, we need a poster holder to introduce the demonstrator.

4. CONCLUSION

The goal of this demonstration is to introduce the OpenVLC1.0 platform, prove its flexibility for selecting different optical components for the communication, and showcase several prototyped network protocols. OpenVLC1.0 adopts a plug-and-play electronic approach, it relies on a customizable software implementation and it aims to be a starter kit for VLC networks research.

Acknowledgement

This research work has been partially supported by the Madrid Regional Government through the TIGRE5-CM program (S2013/ICE-2919), and partially supported by the National Science Foundation of the United States under grant no. IIS-1111507.

5. REFERENCES

[1] BeagleBone Black. *http://beagleboard.org/Products/BeagleBone+Black.*

[2] ByteLight. *http://bytelight.com/.*

[3] PureLiFi. *http://purelifi.com/.*

[4] J. Baranda, P. Henarejos, and C. G. Gavrincea. An SDR implementation of a visible light communication system based on the IEEE 802.15.7 standard. In *Proceedings of the International Conference on Telecommunications*, pages 1–5, 2013.

[5] H. Chun, S. Rajbhandari, G. Faulkner, D. Tsonev, H. Haas, and D. O'Brien. Demonstration of a Bi-directional visible light communication with an overall sum-rate of 110 Mb/s using LEDs as emitter and detector. In *Proceedings of the IEEE Photonics Conference*, pages 132–133, 2014.

[6] P. Dietz, W. Yerazunis, and D. Leigh. Very low-cost sensing and communication using bidirectional LEDs. In *TR2003-35*, 2003.

[7] D. Giustiniano, N. Tippenhauer, and S. Mangold. Low-complexity visible light networking with LED-to-LED communication. In *Proceedings of the IFIP Wireless Days (WD)*, pages 1–8, 2012.

[8] Y.-S. Kuo, P. Pannuto, K.-J. Hsiao, and P. Dutta. Luxapose: Indoor positioning with mobile phones and visible light. In *Proceedings of the ACM MobiCom*, pages 447–458, 2014.

[9] J. Li, A. Liu, G. Shen, L. Li, C. Sun, and F. Zhao. Retro-VLC: Enabling Battery-free Duplex Visible Light Communication for Mobile and IoT Applications. In *Proceedings of the ACM HotMobile*, pages 21–26, 2015.

[10] Y. Qiao, H. Haas, and K. Edward. Demo: A Software-defined Visible Light Communications System with WARP. *Demo at the ACM Workshop on Visible Light Communication Systems*, 2014.

[11] D. Tsonev, S. Videv, and H. Haas. Towards a 100 Gb/s visible light wireless access network. *Optics Express*, 23(2):1627–1637, 2015.

[12] Q. Wang and D. Giustiniano. Communication networks of visible light emitting diodes with intra-frame bidirectional transmission. In *Proceedings of the ACM CoNEXT*, pages 21–28, 2014.

[13] Q. Wang, D. Giustiniano, and D. Puccinelli. OpenVLC: Software-defined Visible Light Embedded Networks. In *Proceedings of the 1st ACM MobiCom Workshop on Visible Light Communication Systems*, pages 15–20, 2014.

[14] Q. Wang, D. Giustiniano, and D. Puccinelli. An open-source research platform for embedded visible light networking. *IEEE Wireless Communication*, 22(2):94–100, 2015.

Demo: An Open-source Software Defined Platform for Collaborative and Energy-aware WiFi Offloading

Aaron Yi Ding[†], Yanhe Liu[†], Sasu Tarkoma[†], Hannu Flinck[‡], Jon Crowcroft[*]
[†]University of Helsinki, [‡]Nokia, [*]University of Cambridge
{aaron.ding, yanhe.liu, sasu.tarkoma}@cs.helsinki.fi hannu.flinck@nokia.com
jon.crowcroft@cl.cam.ac.uk

ABSTRACT

This demonstration presents a novel software defined platform for achieving collaborative and energy-aware WiFi offloading. The platform consists of an extensible central controller, programmable offloading agents, and offloading extensions on mobile devices. Driven by our extensive measurements of energy consumption on smartphones, we propose an effective energy-aware offloading algorithm and integrate it to our platform. By enabling collaboration between wireless networks and mobile users, our solution can make optimal offloading decisions that improve offloading efficiency for network operators and achieve energy saving for mobile users. To enhance deployability, we have released our platform under open-source licenses on GitHub.

Categories and Subject Descriptors

C.2.1 [**Network Architecture and Design**]: Network communications

Keywords

Software-defined Networking; Mobile Data Offloading

1. INTRODUCTION

Cellular networks are experiencing a data explosion posed by the increasing bandwidth demands from current mobile applications and services. Although operators are continuously promoting new-generation wireless technologies (e.g., 4G/LTE) to upgrade their networks, the growth in bandwidth capacity is still behind the notable demands [1]. Therefore, operators are resorting to leverage auxiliary networks (e.g., deploying WiFi networks) and offload mobile traffic for additional capacity. However, traffic offloading without comprehensive controlling may result in poor network utilization and undesirable user experience [2]. In this demonstration, we show how the proposed solution achieves optimal traffic offloading by considering different real factors and thus avoiding naive decisions. Supported by a novel energy-aware offloading algorithm, our platform can guide mobile devices to select the most beneficial WiFi access point for traffic offloading. The highlights of our solution include:

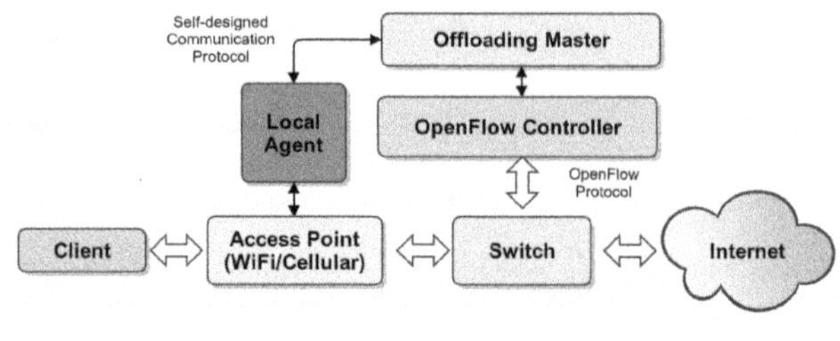

Figure 1: System Architecture

- Collaborative and efficient management - Based on a hierarchical design, our platform can efficiently control cellular and WiFi networks in a collaborative manner. By splitting offloading functionality between central controller and offloading agents deployed on access points, our solution strikes a balance between responsiveness and global control for WiFi offloading.

- Optimal offloading decision - Energy awareness is a key feature of our solution. To benefit both network operators and end users, our platform extracts essential context information from wireless networks and mobile devices and utilizes our offloading algorithm to achieve optimal decision in terms of offloading efficiency and energy saving.

- Openness and extensibility - Our platform builds on open standard protocols (e.g., OpenFlow) and benefits from the programmability of SDN. We aim at a lightweight overlay design for wireless networks without adding extra modifications or requirements towards existing standards. The integration of our energy-aware offloading algorithm is a good example to demonstrate how do we add new applications on top of this open and extensible platform.

- Deployability - To encourage future collaboration with networking research communities, we have released our platform under open-source license. The source codes can be found via:
`https://github.com/TKTL-SDN/SoftOffload`

MobiCom'15, September 7–11, 2015, Paris, France.
ACM. ISBN 978-1-4503-3619-2/15/09
DOI: http://dx.doi.org/10.1145/2789168.2789174.

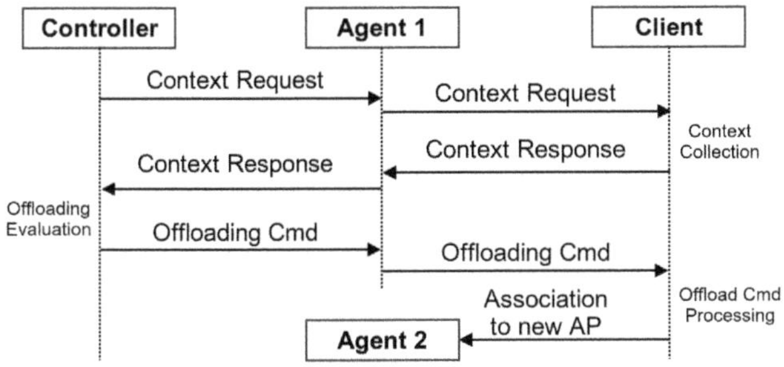

Figure 2: Operation Sequence

2. SYSTEM DESIGN

Our platform is designed to enable collaboration in wireless networks where one or several WiFi APs are deployed within the coverage of mobile network cells. Through a unified and collaborative management, our platform can guide mobile devices to offload traffic from cellular access to WiFi access, and also across neighboring WiFi APs. Inspired by the work of Odin [3], we develop our solution based on software-defined networking (SDN) paradigm. Figure 1 illustrates the overall architecture of our platform, which consists of three major components: a central controller, local agents deployed on access points, and an extension module for mobile devices. We use OpenFlow-enabled switches for monitoring and managing traffic flows.

In our solution, the central controller manages the entire network. It is responsible for tracking all the clients and agents in the managed network, collecting traffic information from network devices, and further making offloading decisions based on inputs from various sources. In addition to obtain flow information, our local agents monitor the association status of mobile devices and serve as an information channel between mobile devices and central controller. The extension deployed on mobile devices collects context information from the devices and access environment, including user movement and signal strength of neighboring WiFi APs. Central controller collects such information from local agents and end devices to perform optimal offloading management.

Figure 2 illustrates the operation sequence of WiFi offloading in a typical scenario across two access points. To initiate traffic offloading, a central controller monitors its managed network by collecting network statistics from OpenFlow switches. If it detects unbalanced or congested traffic patterns in a specific access network (WiFi or cellular), the controller triggers the offloading and follows the steps shown in Figure 2.

By observing the importance of a balanced decision that can benefit both network operators and end users [2], we propose an energy-aware offloading decision algorithm to assist the central controller to make optimal decisions. Our approach is based on extensive measurements of multiple smartphones regarding their energy consumptions and communication performance under different signal levels. The measurement results are shown in Figure 3.

The core of our offloading algorithm, which produces an offloading metric value to guide central controller for selecting optimal offloading targets, is shown below:

$$\mu \cdot (1-P) \cdot \frac{estimatedBw}{\arg\max estimatedBw} \cdot \frac{restBw}{totalBw} - c \cdot O \quad (1)$$

We use μ to evaluate mobility effects on potential throughput, and O as an indicator function for offloading overhead. c is a weight factor to adjust the effect overhead and we use an empirical value 0.2 for c in experiments. The throughput penalty $P = e^{-k_0(S-k_1)}$ is an exponential coefficient to reflect the impact of signal strength. The $\frac{estimatedBw}{\arg\max estimatedBw} \cdot \frac{restBw}{totalBw}$ measures bandwidth capacity and utilization.

According to our measurement data on several smartphones shown in Figure 3a and 3b, we observe a steep drop of performance together with high energy consumption when the signal level is decreasing down to -73 dBm in 802.11n. Since the energy consumption is proportional to the transmission performance, we utilize this feature to reflect the impact of signal level and integrate energy awareness into our solution. We derive a penalty factor $e^{-k_0(S-k_1)}$ based on the observation and assign $k_0 = \frac{1}{3}$, and $k_1 = -73$. As shown in Figure 3c, this penalty coefficient on signal level S matches coherently to the performance and energy consumption in Figure 3a and Figure 3b, respectively.

3. IMPLEMENTATION AND EXPERIMENT

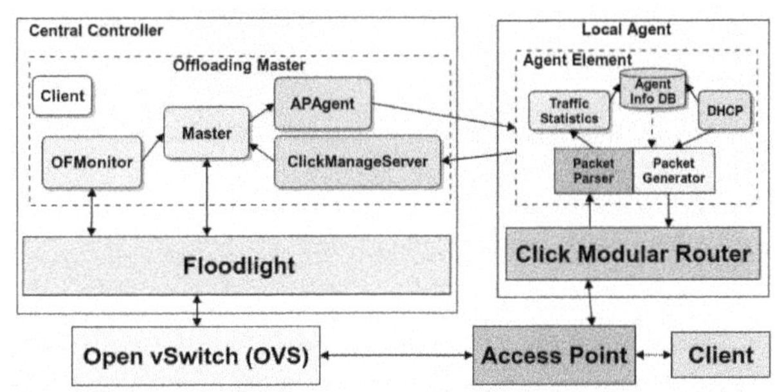

Figure 4: System Implementation

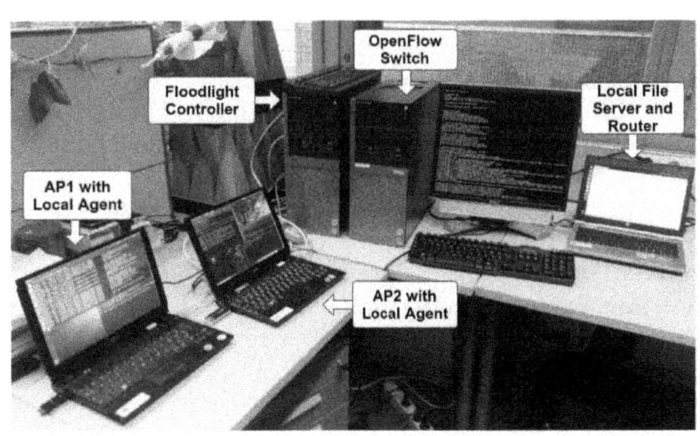

Figure 5: Experiment Testbed

We have developed a prototype system based on our design. Figure 4 illustrates the key components and schematics of our platform. The central controller is implemented on the Floodlight OpenFlow controller [4] and works as an independent application on top of the Floodlight. The local agent is developed based on Click modular router [5]

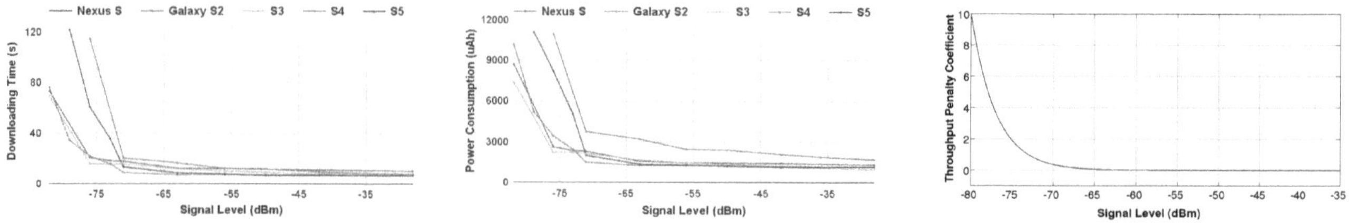

(a) Downloading Time (b) Energy Consumption (c) Offloading Penalty

Figure 3: Signal Level and Penalty Coefficient $e^{-\frac{1}{3}(S-(-73))}$

Table 1: Offloading Metric Values For Different Test Cases

Signal Strength and Available Bandwidth	-34 dBm 16 Mbps	-66 dBm 16 Mbps	-31 dBm 8 Mbps	-65 dBm 8 Mbps	-75 dBm 16 Mbps	-78 dBm 16 Mbps
Throughput (Mbps)	15.12	15.04	7.84	7.52	3.68	**3.04**
Offloading Metric	1	0.903	0.5	0.465	-0.947	**-4.294**

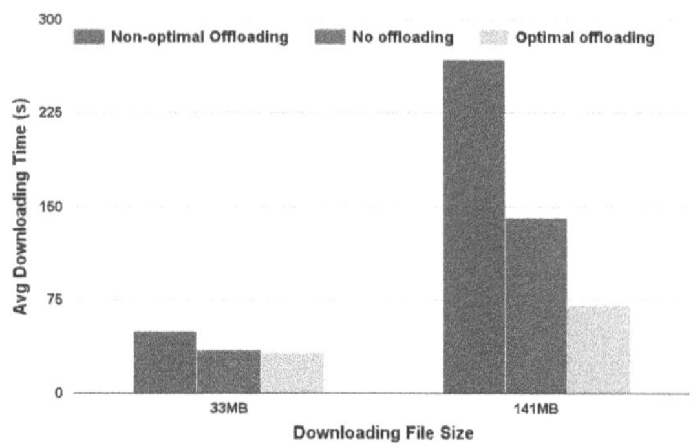

Figure 6: Static Offloading Experiments

and deployed on each AP. It monitors the wireless interfaces and reports association events to the central controller. The client extension is implemented as an Android application, which listens on a specific port for controlling messages from the controller and local agents, and reacts to the requests. In addition, we run Open vSwitch which provides the OpenFlow supports for our platform.

Regarding the effectiveness of our solution, Figure 6 shows the experimental results for a series of static offloading tests conducted in our testbed. The testbed layout is depicted in Figure 5. The "Non-optimal Offloading" bars represent the results when a mobile device is connected to a congested AP for offloading, which has only half of the bandwidth compared to the previously associated AP. The "Optimal Offloading" bars show the results by using our offloading solution, which can guide the devices to select an AP with better bandwidth (3x in our case). As revealed in Figure 6, when the download file size is large, there is a clear advantage to adopt our offloading guidance. Meanwhile, when the file size is relatively small, the improvement is less visible due to the overhead of switching between APs.

To show the efficacy of energy-aware offloading algorithm, Table 1 presents the "Offloading Metric" values when matching against measurement results obtained in our testbed. The metric values are essential for central controller to make the offloading decision (e.g., selecting the optimal AP for WiFi offloading). The trend is clear in the table: when the signal strength and bandwidth decreases, our offloading algorithm yields the values in accordance with the trend. For example, when an AP is of weak signal strength -78 dBm (e.g., far away from the end user), even if its available bandwidth is good (16 Mbps in this case), the overall performance is still poor, which matches to our offloading metric value -4.294. This indicates that the central controller in our platform will not select this AP as the offloading target, thereby avoiding the potential poor performance and energy cost.

4. DEMONSTRATION REQUIREMENTS

In this demonstration, we present a typical use case of our platform to offload traffic from one access network to another in a seamless way. Figure 5 depicts our prototype system, which consists of two laptops functioning as wireless access points, one laptop as the file server, and one desktop machine installed with our central controller. All entities are connected through a virtual switch (Open vSwitch version 2.3.0) installed on a desktop machine. To present this system in Paris, we have integrated both the central controller and virtual switch on a single fanless compact fit-PC. Although we only showcase traffic offloading across WiFi APs in this setup due to the limitation of accessing cellular resources, our platform is designed for general scenarios and can be applied to offload traffic across cellular and WiFi networks.

For demonstration, we require one table (preferably 120x90 cm). We need an extension cord supporting 5 plugs (EU standard), a USB keyboard, and an LCD display supporting HDMI interface with HDMI cable. Our prototype system requires approximately 30 minutes to setup. We will bring three laptops and one fit-PC machine on site.

5. REFERENCES

[1] Cisco visual networking index: Global mobile data traffic forecast update, 2013-2018, 5 February 2014.

[2] Aaron Yi Ding and et al. Enabling energy-aware collaborative mobile data offloading for smartphones. IEEE SECON '13, 2013.

[3] Lalith Suresh and et al. Towards programmable enterprise wlans with odin. HotSDN '12, 2012.

[4] Floodlight. `http://www.projectfloodlight.org/`.

[5] Eddie Kohler and et al. The click modular router. *ACM Trans. Comput. Syst.*, Vol. 18(No. 3), August 2000.

Demo: Optimizing Smartphone Power Consumption through Dynamic Resolution Scaling

Songtao He[1,2], Yunxin Liu[1], Hucheng Zhou[1]

[1]Microsoft Research, Beijing, China
[2]University of Science and Technology of China, Hefei, China

hst@mail.ustc.edu.cn, {yunliu, huzho}@microsoft.com

ABSTRACT

The extremely-high display density of modern smartphones imposes a significant burden on power consumption, yet does not always provide an improved user experience and may even lead to a compromised user experience. As human visually-perceivable ability highly depends on the user-screen distance, a reduced display resolution may still achieve the same user experience when the user-screen distance is large. This provides new power-saving opportunities.

We present a flexible dynamic resolution scaling system for smartphones. The system adopts an ultrasonic-based approach to detect the user-screen distance at low-power cost and makes scaling decisions automatically for maximum user experience and power saving. App developers or users can also adjust the resolution manually and dynamically as their needs. Our system is able to work on the existing commercial smartphones and support the legacy apps, without requiring re-building the ROM or any changes from apps.

Categories and Subject Descriptors

I.3.4 [**Computer Graphics**]: Graphics Utilities—*Software support*

General Terms

Experiments; Measurement; Performance

Keywords

Smartphone; GPU; Power Consumption; Display Resolution; Dynamic Resolution Scaling

1. INTRODUCTION

The display resolution of smartphones has become increasingly high. Since the "Retina display" of the iPhone 4 released in 2010 [5], display resolution of smartphones has continued to rise, from 960x640 pixels of the iPhone 4 to 1920x1080 pixels (Full HD) and recently to 2560x1440 pixels (2K). As a result, latest smartphones have an extremely-high display density. For example, the LG G3 [3] has a display of 538 pixels per inch (ppi), while the Samsung Galaxy S5 LTE-A [4] has a display of 577 ppi.

However, this extremely-high display density does not always help bring an improved user experience. The Retina display of the iPhone 4 has a display density of only 326 ppi. The high display density of the LG G3 and the Samsung Galaxy S5 LTE-A is far beyond the human ability of visual acuity, and thus does not always lead to visibly-sharper content and interfaces displayed on the screen. Nevertheless, a high-resolution display consumes a large amount of system resources, especially the GPU computation, and thus results in high system power consumption. As energy is a paramount concern on smartphones, it is desirable to study the tradeoff between display density and power consumption.

In this demo, we propose to optimize the power consumption of high-density displays through Dynamic Resolution Scaling (DRS). DRS dynamically adjusts the display resolution based on the viewing distance (i.e., the screen-user distance) but ensures that the pixels are always small enough to be individually unobservable by human eye. The philosophy of DRS is that the system should render the interface with exactly as much detail as is perceptible to a user, in order to maximize both user experience and battery life. When a display resolution is too high for a viewing distance, DRS reduces the display resolution to save power.

Enabling DRS imposes several requirements. First, DRS must seamlessly adjust display resolution in real-time as the viewing distance changes, without compromising the user experience. Second, DRS must be done systematically and is transparent from applications. Third, DRS must be able to determine the viewing distance of a user in real-time and with minimal energy cost.

To meet the requirements, we develop per-frame DRS technique for seamless and real-time display-resolution adjusting. We intercept the system graphics pipeline to enable system-wide DRS, without requiring any changes or recompiling from applications, or re-building a new smartphone ROM. And we propose to use ultrasonic sensors to detect the viewing distance of a user, which is accurate and low-power. Based on the detected viewing distance, we utilize existing knowledge of the human visual system to define the required display-pixel density for optimal user experience, and adjust the extravagant display resolution accordingly.

We have implemented a DRS system that works on existing commercial smartphones including the Galaxy S5 LTE-A and the Nexus 6. We conduct comprehensive experi-

MobiCom'15, September 7–11, 2015, Paris, France.
ACM ISBN 978-1-4503-3619-2/15/09.
DOI: http://dx.doi.org/10.1145/2789168.2789175.

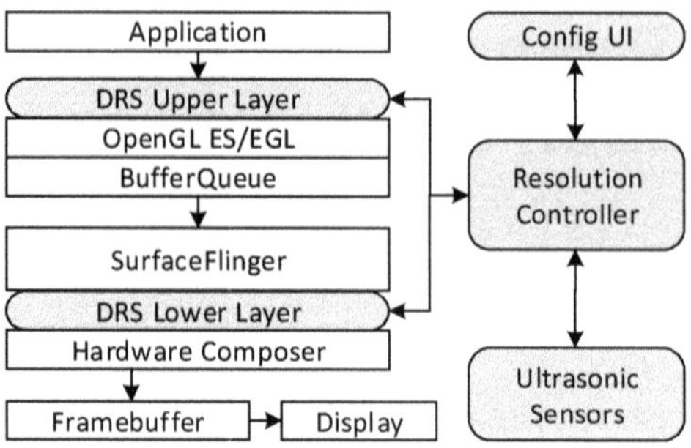

Figure 1: DRS System Architecture.

ments and a user study to evaluate the DRS implementation against 30 real gaming and benchmark applications. Experimental results show that all the 30 applications can run successfully with per-frame, real-time dynamic resolution scaling. The energy per frame can be reduced by 30.1% in average and up to 60.5% at most when the resolution is halved, for 15 applications. Even for other less GPU-intensive applications such as Adobe Reader and web browser, we still reduce the energy per frame for about 10%. A user study with 10 users indicates that our system remains good user experience: none of the 10 users could perceive the resolution changes in the user study although the resolution changed for more than 100 times for each user.

2. SYSTEM OVERVIEW

Enabling DRS on existing smartphones imposes a couple of challenges. First, we must reduce the number of pixels in all the pixel-related computations from the complex procedures of rasterization and pixel-processing involving many OpenGL function calls. Second, OpenGL libraries are close source and thus we cannot revise and re-compile the source code to add new functionalities. And we cannot require rebuilding a smartphone ROM or making application-specfic modifications. Third, we must design a lightweight approach to decide the user-screen distance for automatic resolution scaling.

To address the above challenges, we employ binary-rewriting techniques that are able to hook and intercept the function calls in existing binaries and add new functionalities. As a result, we can enable DRS on commercial smartphones without requiring any source-code level changes. Meanwhile, to detect the user-screen distance, we design a lower-power ultrasonic based approach to minimize the overhead.

Figure 1 shows the architecture of our DRS system. To enable resolution scaling, we add two new layers into the existing android graphic system[1].

The first layer is the *DRS Upper Layer* that sits between the application layer and and the OpenGL ES/EGL layer. It intercepts the necessary OpenGL ES function calls and EGL function calls and applies a scaling factor to the parameters of the those function calls to transform the default display region to a targeted smaller one, which locates at the bottom-left corner of the original graphic buffer.

The second layer is the *DRS Lower Layer* that locates between the SurfaceFlinger layer and the Hardware Composer. This layer intercepts the function call passed to the Hardware Composer, and let the Hardware Composer scale up the bottom-left region of the passed in graphic buffer to the original size using the same scaling factor.

By using this approach, we can reduce the energy cost of generating the high resolution image, and still make the image appear at the original region of the screen with a smaller virtual resolution.

In fact, the detailed parameter interception strategy is carefully designed to ensure the correctness of the scaling transformation. Meanwhile, a synchronization mechanism is also designed to synchronize the DRS upper layer and DRS lower layer. Due to the BufferQueue locates between these two layers, we need this synchronization mechanism to make sure that they use the same target display resolution for the same graphics buffer, while the resolution is changing for each frame.

To decide a proper targeted display resolution, we need to know the viewing-distance of a user. We add ultrasonic sensors[2] into the system for instant and accurate viewing-distance detection. Based on the measured viewing-distance, the *Resolution Controller* calculates the best display resolution for maximum user experience and maximum power optimization, and indicates the two DRS layers to do scaling transformation for the calculated display resolution.

In order to connect the user-screen distance and resolvable pixels, we use angular resolving acuity to define the visual acuity of human. According to the standards for visual acuity[6], Normal vision[1] can be represented with a angular resolving acuity of $\delta_{normal} = 2.9 \times 10^{-4}$ radians, and $\delta_{optimal} = 1.45 \times 10^{-4}$ radians for optimal vision[2].

For a specific device, we consider the number of pixels at the longer side of the display as resolvable pixel number when the pixel density of it can just meet the users' visual acuity. Resolvable pixel number varies with different user-screen distance and different user visual acuity. The relationship among resolvable pixel number, user-screen distance and user visual acuity can be approximately described using equation

$$N = \frac{L}{2D\,tan\left(\frac{\delta}{2}\right)} \tag{1}$$

where N is the resolvable pixel number, L is the length of the longer side of the display, D is the user screen distance and δ is the angular resolving acuity of the user.

Figure 2 demonstrates the variation of resolvable pixels number with user screen distance for users with normal vision and optimal vision on the Galaxy S5 LTE-A, the high display density of which can surpass the visual acuity of users with normal vision when the user-screen distance is beyond 5.4 inches, and 10.8 inches for users with optimal vision. After the user-screen distance reach these thresholds, our DRS system will dynamically reduce the display resolution based on equation(1) for maximum power optimization without compromising user experience.

As shown in Table 1, we evaluate the potential power optimization room for 15 apps (16 scenes) on the Galaxy S5 LTE-A. When locking the GPU Frequency to 500MHz, the energy per frame (whole system) can be reduced by 30.1% in average and up to 60.5% at most when the resolution is halved.

[1]Normal vision is commonly referred as 20/20 vision (vulgar fraction expression) or 1.0 (decimal number expression).
[2]Optimal vision is commonly referred as 20/10 vision (vulgar fraction expression) or 2.0 (decimal number expression).

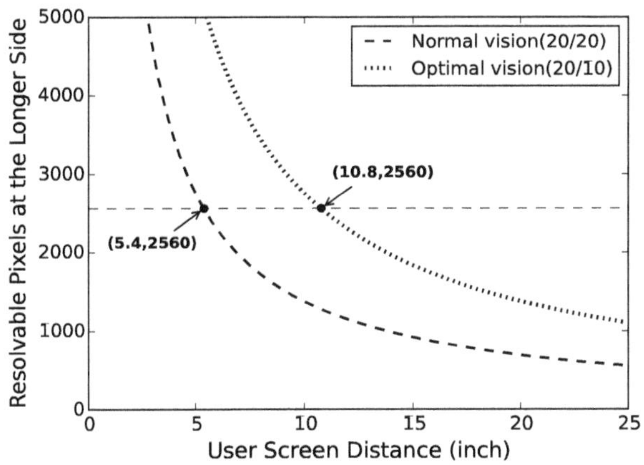

Figure 2: Relationship among resolvable pixel number, user-screen distance and user visual acuity.

Application(Scene) Name	Scale Factor 0.9	0.8	0.65	0.5
Games				
Badland	95.1%	91.2%	86.7%	83.5%
Hitman Sniper	94.0%	85.5%	80.6%	73.0%
Iron man 3	94.5%	90.1%	83.4%	75.9%
Leo's Fotune	95.4%	92.8%	88.7%	84.3%
Minecraft PE	94.5%	90.4%	82.6%	76.1%
NFS Most Wanted	94.3%	89.6%	79.7%	72.3%
Over Kill 3	95.7%	92.0%	88.3%	82.5%
Ridge Racer Slipstream	94.5%	85.0%	76.8%	65.9%
Riptide GP2	95.3%	89.0%	77.5%	68.7%
Shine Runner	95.9%	90.1%	81.2%	74.2%
Smash Hit	93.9%	89.5%	81.1%	72.8%
Temple Run Brave	93.7%	85.6%	78.9%	71.2%
Tiny Troopers 2	94.4%	90.0%	82.7%	76.1%
Warships	95.3%	90.7%	84.3%	76.4%
Graphics Benchmark				
GFX Bench Manhattan	84.2%	70.4%	56.7%	39.5%
GFX Bench T-Rex	85.9%	73.1%	57.6%	48.0%

Table 1: Normalized energy per frame of games and benchmarks in different scaling factors.

3. DEMONSTRATION

In this demo, we will show the power consumption optimizing opportunity by using our dynamic resolution scaling (DRS) system. We have implemented our prototype system on two smartphones, a Galaxy S5 LTE-A and a Nexus 6. Figure 3(a) shows a prototype system based on Galaxy S5 LTE-A. In the demo, we will provide each participant with our prototype system, and let them have a video game or watching a game scene. Meanwhile, they are encouraged to moving the prototype freely, so that the user-screen distance can vary and the display resolution will change properly.

As shown in Figure 3(b), we put a floating window at the top-right corner of the screen. In that window, we show the feedback information in the past 60 seconds of our prototype system, including the display resolution, GPU information and power consumption measured by smartphone's internal sensor. Thus, the power consumption's variation and other variations caused by DRS can be easily observed by participants.

Equipments and Setup. Our demo equipments are simple. We will bring our prototype system and a laptop by ourselves. And the setup time of our demo is within 5 minutes.

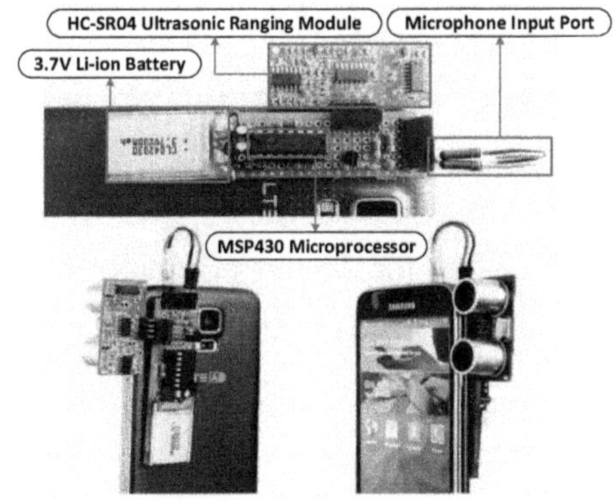

(a) Demo System Based on Galaxy S5 LTE-A

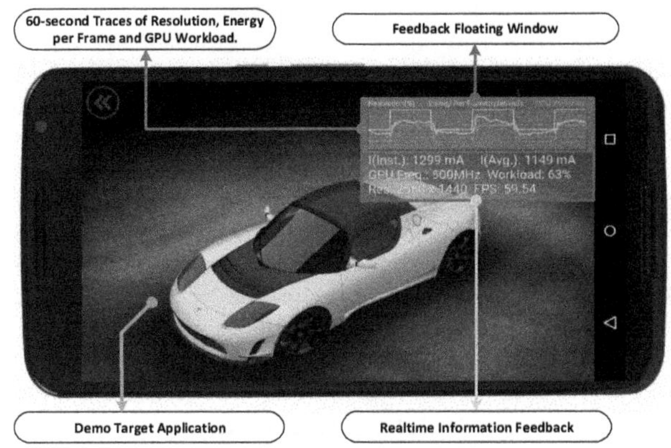

(b) Demo Realtime Feedback UI

Figure 3: Demonstration System

4. DISCUSSION

To the best of our knowledge, we are the first to design and implement a DRS system for smartphones. Based on the measured user-screen distance, our system can enable automatic resolution scaling for maximum user experience and power saving. Besides the user-distance driven resolution scaling, our DRS system can also be used as an infrastructure to support a series of use cases which are remained to be studied in the future work toward alleviating performance, energy and over heating issue on smartphones and improving user experience.

5. REFERENCES

[1] Android Graphics Architecture. `https://source.android.com/devices/graphics/architecture.html`.

[2] Ultrasonic Ranging Module HC - SR04. `http://www.micropik.com/PDF/HCSR04.pdf`.

[3] LG G3. `http://www.lg.com/us/mobile-phones/g3`, Feb. 2015.

[4] Samsung Galaxy S5 LTE-A. http://www.samsung.com/us/news/23327, Feb. 2015.

[5] Apple iPhone. `http://www.apple.com/iphone/features/retina-display.html`, Jun. 2010.

[6] E. Messina. Standards for visual acuity. *National Institute for Standards and Technology*, 2006.

Demo: Modular Multi-radio Wireless Sensor Platform for IoT Trials with Plug&Play Module Connection

Konstantin Mikhaylov, Juha Petäjäjärvi, Marko Mäkeläinen, Anton Paatelma and Tuomo Hänninen
Centre for Wireless Communications (CWC), P.O.Box 4500, FI-90014, University of Oulu
{konstantin.mikhaylov, juha.petajajarvi, marko.makelainen, anton.paatelma, tuomo.hanninen}@ee.oulu.fi

ABSTRACT
In the paper we present and demonstrate the modular prototyping platform designed for trialing the Internet of Things (IoT) applications. The new devices are constructed by stacking together the various hardware modules encapsulating power sources, processing units, wired and wireless transceivers, sensors and actuators, or sets of those. The main processing unit automatically identifies all the attached modules and adjusts own operation accordingly. The demo will showcase how the platform can be used for building up multi-radio technology enabled wireless devices which will automatically form a heterogeneous wireless sensor and actuator network (WSAN). The possible use case scenarios and the ongoing research activities around the platform will be highlighted as well.

Categories and Subject Descriptors
C.3 [**Special-Purpose and Application-Based Systems**]: Microprocessor/Microcomputer Applications, Real-Time and Embedded Systems
C.2.1 [**Computer-communication networks**]: Network Architecture and Design - *wireless communication*
B.4 [**Input/Output and Data Communications**]: Input/Output Devices, Data Communications Devices

General Terms
Design, Experimentation, Measurement, Verification, Algorithms

Keywords
Wireless Sensor Actuator Networks; WSN; Internet of Things; IoT; Architecture; Platform; Module; Plug-and-Play; Node; Experimentation

1. INTRODUCTION
The recent years have been characterized by significant progress in IoT related technologies. The pure theoretic concept a while ago became almost a reality today. Nonetheless, effective utilization of myriads devices with highly diversified requirements, communication interfaces, capabilities and tasks within one and the same network still has many unsolved research challenges. Despite this, in the current work we approach the problem from the engineering perspective and present a solution and architecture enabling easy and effective construction of the new IoT and WSAN devices. The proposed platform enables easy, time and cost effective trialing the new scenarios and technologies, and can serve as the basis for wide range of real-life applications.

MobiCom'15, September 07-11, 2015, Paris, France
ACM 978-1-4503-3619-2/15/09.
http://dx.doi.org/10.1145/2789168.2789176.

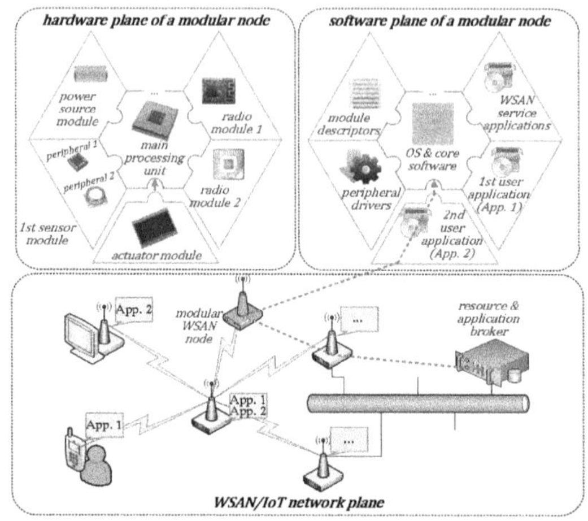

Figure 1. Illustration of the proposed concept

In the demo we present the proof of concept prototype of our platform. According to our vision (see Figure 1), the new nodes can be built by stacking together the hardware (HW) modules encapsulating various peripherals, like e.g. power supply sources, processing units, wireless transceivers, etc. Once a node is built, its *main processing unit* (MPU) automatically detects the attached modules, identifies the peripherals available on each module, and maps their data communication interfaces to the available pins of MPU. If the MPU does not possess the software (SW) modules necessary for working with a peripheral – these can be either obtained from a module or downloaded from WSAN. The same applies for the application-level SW. Since each module contains the data describing the hosted peripherals, an MPU always has complete information on its structure and can use these data to optimize own operation or to enable network-level optimizations and task distribution between the nodes.

2. TECHNOLOGY

Plug-and-Play (P&P) connection of modules is enabled by employing the developed *Intelligent Modular Periphery Interface* (IMPI) and the special module architecture. Unlike the existing platforms (e.g., [1-2]), our modules (see Figure 2) are addressed based on their order of connection. This eliminates address collisions and enables connection of multiple identical modules. The availability of numerous parallel communication interfaces enables an MPU to communicate with multiple peripherals simultaneously. The further details about IMPI, the details of technical solutions and parameters of the platform are available in [3-4].

To enable exploitation of HW dynamism and connection of multitude various HW modules the embedded SW featuring novel architecture has been designed and implemented. The core component of our SW is the *resource manager*, which identifies the connected modules, choses the communication technologies to be used, and decides which applications and services can be launched.

The server and a web-based graphical user interface (GUI) are used in the demo to obtain and display the data from the nodes and control their operation in real time.

3. DEMO SETUP

The demo setup is illustrated in Figure 3. In the demo we will show how the nodes of various structures can be assembled out of modules. Once ready and powered on, a node will automatically identify connected modules and use available wireless communication interfaces for connecting to the network and reporting its data to the server running on a laptop. The GUI will display the topology of the network, the set of modules composing selected node and the information about particular module (e.g., measurements from sensors, configuration of radio transceivers or status of actuators). Also the GUI can be used to give orders to the nodes and control their operation.

In the demo we will especially emphasize the wireless communication capabilities of the proposed platform. Namely, we will demonstrate how the platform can be used for building the nodes hosting multiple radio modules for the same (e.g., two or three IEEE 802.15.4 radio modules) or even different radio technologies (e.g., IEEE 802.15.4 and an ultra-wideband transceiver). In both cases, the nodes will automatically join the heterogeneous network.

4. RESEARCH ACTIVITIES

The proposed platform is currently widely used in the research activities of CWC. Namely, the platform is employed in experiments related to:

- studies of performance of ultra-wideband radios,
- wireless localization for robots,
- wide-area IoT technologies and
- heterogeneous WSAN and IoT.

Some preliminary results of these studies and the lessons learned will be presented during the demo as well.

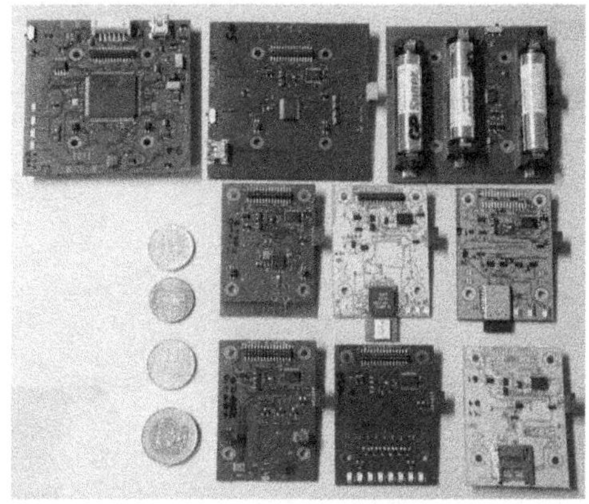

Figure 2. Module boards to be used in the demo (top row: main board and power boards, middle row – radio options, bottom row – sensors, actuators & memory)

Figure 3. Demo setup: radio nodes featuring different structure and communication interfaces and the laptop-based graphical user interface displaying the network topology, structure of a node and the received module

5. REFERENCES

[1] Martinez-Catala, R.V. and Barrett, J. 2009. A Modular Wireless Sensor Platform With Fully Integrated Battery, *IEEE Trans. Compon. Packag. Technol.* 32, 3 (Sept. 2009), 617-626. DOI=TCAPT.2009.2014875

[2] Ouwerkerk, M., Pasveer, F. and Engin, N. 2006. SAND: a modular application development platform for miniature wireless sensors. In *Proceedings of the 2006 International Workshop on Wearable and Implantable Body Sensor Networks* (Cambridge, MA, USA, 3-5 April 2006). BSN'06. IEEE, III/35-III/38. DOI=BSN.2006.47

[3] Mikhaylov, K. and Huttunen, M. 2014. Modular wireless sensor and Actuator Network Nodes with Plug-and-Play module connection. In *Proceedings of the 2014 IEEE SENSORS conference* (Valencia, Spain, 2-5 November 2014). SENSORS'14. IEEE, 470-473. DOI=ICSENS.2014.6985037

[4] Mikhaylov, K., Petäjäjärvi, J. and Hämäläinen, M. 2015. Modular Wireless Sensor and Actuator Network Nodes with Plug-and-Play Module Connection. In press.

Demo: Wireless Link Selection on Smartphone: Throughput vs Battery Drain

Krzysztof Grochla
IITIS PAN
Bałtycka 5
Gliwice, Poland
+48 32 2317319
kgrochla@iitis.pl

Paweł Foremski
IITIS PAN
Bałtycka 5
Gliwice, Poland
+48 32 2317319
pjf@iitis.pl

ABSTRACT
The method for automatic selection of wireless interface on smart phones is presented. We consider the selection between WiFi and LTE / 3G radios to maximize the throughput of the data transmission and minimize the amount of energy used to scan and measure the throughput of the network. The proposed selection algorithm defines when to measure and how to estimate the network throughput to balance between the accuracy of the selection and the battery drain caused by the measurements. The link speed estimation method optimized for LTE and WiFi networks is also demonstrated.

Categories and Subject Descriptors
C.2.1 [**Network Architecture and Design**]: Wireless communication

General Terms
Measurement, Performance

Keywords
LTE, WiFi, link selection, throughput estimation

1. INTRODUCTION
The mobile phones are typically equipped with two wireless interfaces used for data transmission: IEEE 802.11 and cellular (3G or LTE). Most of the currently used devices implement a simple priority selection which uses WiFi interface when it is possible, and fall back to cellular when the device is outside of the range of WiFi AP. This method is based on the assumption that WiFi is faster and more efficient than cellular transmission, what is not always true. Although according to [1] 2/3 of users prefer WiFi to Cellular, because WiFi is free in most cases, while the cellular data plan requires a monthly fee and WiFi is often perceived as more efficient than cellular. The IEEE 802.11 standard offers very high transmission rates of up to 300Mbps in local networks, but the actual bandwidth is often limited by an ADSL link to which the WiFi access point is connected, typically between 2 and 25Mbps. In crowded locations, where many users share the same backhaul connection or where many interfering APs are deployed, the WiFi performance is heavily degraded [1]. On the other hand, the average throughput offered by LTE networks varies between 9Mbps [2] and 13Mbps [3], which is higher than the throughput of a low-cost ADSL link. The performance of a LTE connection depends on the distance to the base station and on the number of users transmitting data through it, so it can significantly change in space and time. The measurement presented in [3] shows that it may change between 0.6Mbps per 5 percentile to 24Mbps for the 95 percentile. Thus, deciding which of the two: WiFi or LTE offers a faster transmission is not an easy task.

From the user perspective, the ubiquitous of wireless interface selection is crucial. The mobile device should simply use the interface that offers the fastest data transfer in the current location. Users may manually enable or disable the WiFi interface, but this consumes time and causes nuisance. There are applications available which automate this process and disable the WiFi interface in locations where the user configured the phone to do so, such as e.g. Smart WiFi Toggler [4]. But it requires manual configuration per location and may introduce errors when the performance of WiFi or Cellular changes in time. We believe that the optimal selection of the link in specific location should estimate the available bandwidth on both WiFi and LTE interfaces, and realize the selection quickly and in an energy efficient way. This can be achieved by measuring on the client side which of the two interfaces provides faster access to the Internet. The throughput estimation should minimize the amount of data transferred, to minimize the cost of its use and minimize the energy utilization. To the best of our knowledge, there is no such tool currently available.

MobiCom'15, September 7-11, 2015, Paris, France.
ACM 978-1-4503-3619-2/15/09.
http://dx.doi.org/10.1145/2789168.2789177

2. SELECTION OF LINK WITH HIGHER THROUGHPUT

To select the link which provides higher throughput the mobile phone must be able to measure, whichever of the two available connections is faster. The basic idea is to make periodic and lightweight measurements of the instantaneous download speeds in locations where the user has active WiFi connection.

Multiple measurement methods for estimation of available end-to-end bandwidth (called ABE) have been proposed in the literature. A review paper [5] gives an experimental assessment of 9 ABE methods in the same networking environment, comparing response time, intrusiveness, and exactness in presence of cross-traffic data transfer. All except 3 evaluated methods (Spruce, pathChirp and Assolo) required more than 500KB per measurement. Authors of [6] show that currently known ABE tools are not accurate in large-scale distributed network. They report a significant under-estimation of the available network throughput. We have repeated those measurements, to confirm that the popular ABE algorithms show significant deviation between the result of the algorithm and the throughput achieved during a large file download through a TCP connection [7]. However we aim in choosing the better performing link on mobile devices, not to estimate the actual bandwidth. Thus the direct application of ABE methods may not always be a best solution, as instead of throughput estimation we need a stable algorithm that selects which of the two links provides higher throughput.

In our previous work we have developed a custom method for selection of better performing wireless interface, called *pik* [7]. The algorithm sends a short burst of UDP packets and measures the reception time, as the difference between the time at which the last packet and the time at which first packet were received. Additionally we measure the round trip time (RTT) using by sending ICMP echo requests. The measurement process is executed as follows. The client, who is the receiver part wanting to know its available bandwidth, registers at the server and obtains a random password used for further authentication. Next, the client sends a PING request, to which the server replies with a 50B response. This step is repeated by default 5 times with a 1-second timeout, and the average time between sending the request and receiving the response is treated as the link RTT. Finally, the client sends a START request, to which the server replies with a peak of data, by default 100 packets of 1KB length. The server sends the data to the network as fast as possible, in a single loop without any pauses. The client assumes reception of the first packet at the time of the START request plus RTT, but the time of the last packet is measured. The duration of the peak at the receiver side is calculated, and finally the available bandwidth is the amount of data received divided by the peak duration. This final stage has a time limit of 3 seconds by default.

The network throughput available to the user changes in time and space as a function of the number of users sharing the same radio resources (hosts in a WLAN network or clients serviced by a single base station), interferences or configuration of the wireless point of access. To provide the credible selection decision the proposed algorithm periodically repeats the measurements. The decision is based on the aggregated statistic. Hence, we present a heuristic approach, instead of comparing the bandwidths directly.

3. ENERGY USAGE MINIMIZATION

The energy required to execute the proposed method is proportional to the frequency of measurements of the available bandwidth. To minimize the energy usage the link selection system can schedule bandwidth measurements each few hours, provided that the screen is off and a configured WiFi network is available. New data should replace old measurements. However, there is a trade-off between frequent updates and the amount of transferred data, hence the update rate should be chosen wisely. Finally, we believe the estimated bandwidth without active measurements, e.g. by observing the interface byte counters, is prone to errors. One could not assume that current transmissions are not band-limited at the sender side (e.g. video streams). Mobile devices allow for only one active connection, so it would be cumbersome to passively profile two links at the same time.

To minimize the energy usage we have developed a set of functions disabling the wireless interface when it is not used and scheduling the measurement to find a balance between its accuracy and the energy used. We have implemented a function detecting the movement of the mobile device by monitoring the accelerometer measurements. The algorithm decides to start the scan when the mobile device is enabled and it was moved. Additionally the measurement is repeated every pre-defined period of time (by default few times a day) even when the device is not moved. It allows detecting the time variability of transmission speed within the particular location.

4. LINK SELECTION APPLICATION

The link selection algorithm described about has been implemented on the Android platform as ``BX Network" application [8]. The application implements the *pik* which is executed according to a predefined schedule. The application works in the background and monitors the behavior of the user detecting the device movement and the activation of the screen. When the screen is turned on the BX Network runs the link selection algorithm. The decision of the algorithm is implemented by enabling or disabling the WiFi interface and the data transfer over cellular network. The Android API is used to execute the algorithm choice, basing on previous measurement for particular location. When the screen is turned off all links are switched off, but the application periodically enables one of the links for a short period of time, letting the Android synchronization to run and to executed the *pik* measurements. The scheduling to have a minimum of a configured number of measurements per particular location is executed to select the moments at which the *pik* measurement is started. The results are stored within a tiny SQLlite database, tagged with geolocation, timestamp and information about the ESSID used (for WiFi). The scheduler runs *pik* at most every 3 hours in the same location. If there are less than 5 measurements in the last 7 days for the current location, the scheduler allows more frequent updates, to collect the data as fast as possible. If there are no credentials for a WiFi network in range, the measurements are not started.

The *pik* measurements have been implemented using Android native API (NDK) to increase the accuracy of timestamp measurements. Whenever the application executes the best link selection procedure, the location information is read from the operating system, and measurements from previous 7 days for the specified location are fetched from the database. Thus the decision is very quick, as it bases only on calculation and does not require additional measurements. The application of the selection of a link is done within less than 1s in most of the cases.

The final effect of running BX Network on a smartphone is that it automatically switches to the best available Internet connection ubiquitously after unlocking the screen.

5. DEMONSTRATION PROCEDURE

The demonstration of *BX Network* is shown on a using a PC, a WiFi AP and an Android smartphone. A wired or wireless internet connection is required for the PC. The PC is configured as the HTTP server, providing data to the mobile device via a WiFi or LTE interface. It is connected to the WiFI AP and to the internet via an Ethernet port. The WiFi AP is used as a point of network access for the smartphone. The AP has the bandwidth throttling functionality, which is used to limit the available throughput for the client (to force the application on the mobile phone to select LTE connectivity) or to increase the available bandwidth (to force the switching to WiFi). To visualize the method of the connection the PC visualizes the graph of data rate transmitted to the mobile phone and the interface, which is used (by detecting whenever data are routed through the WiFi AP or through the Internet and LTE network). The mobile phone runs the demonstrated application, which automatically selects the optimal wireless interface basing on the measured throughput.

The demonstration is carried on by showing how the algorithm measures and selects best link depending on the bandwidth limitation applied on the WiFi AP. The functionality of automatic selection of the link within few seconds after turning on the phone is also presented. The *BX Network* mobile application allows also to manually triggering the interface selection, as well as automatic detection of link degradation. The energy saving functions are demonstrated by presenting how the application turns off the WiFi interface when it is more effective to use LTE or how the data transmission over cellular interface is disabled when WiFi network is performing better.

6. ACKNOWLEDGMENTS

This work was funded by the Polish National Centre for Research and Development, under research grant nr LIDER/10/194/L-3/11: project ``Optimization and load balancing in next generation wireless networks'', http://projekty.iitis.pl/zosb .

7. REFERENCES

[1] Abinader, F.M. et al., Performance Evaluation of IEEE 802.11n WLAN in Dense Deployment Scenarios, In: Vehicular Technology Conference (VTC Fall), 2014 IEEE 80th, IEEE (2014) 1—5

[2] Huang, J., Qian, F., Guo, Y., Zhou, Y., Xu, Q., Mao, Z.M., Sen, S., Spatscheck, O.: An in-depth study of LTE: effect of network protocol and application behavior on performance, In: ACM SIGCOMM 2013 Proceedings, ACM (2013) 363—374

[3] Huang, J., Qian, F., Gerber, A., Mao, Z.M., Sen, S., Spatscheck, O.: A close examination of performance and power characteristics of 4G LTE networks, In: ACM MobiSys 2012 Proceedings, ACM (2012) 225--238

[4] Aguehian, S.: Smart WiFi Toggler, https://play.google.com/store/apps/details?id=com.sebouh00.smartwifitoggler&hl=en, Accessed: 2015-01-29.

[5] Goldoni, E., Schivi, M.: End-to-end available bandwidth estimation tools, an experimental comparison. In: Traffic Monitoring and Analysis, Springer (2010) 171--182

[6] Croce, D., Mellia, M., Leonardi, E.: The quest for bandwidth estimation techniques for large-scale distributed systems, ACM SIGMETRICS Performance Evaluation Review 37 (3) (2010), 20--25

[7] Foremski P., Grochla K.: LTE or WiFi? Client-side Internet link selection for smartphones, In: Computer Networks 2015 Proceedings, Springer

[8] BX Network application, https://play.google.com/store/apps/details?id=com.bxlabs.network, Accessed: May 15th 2015.

Demo – Closer to Cloud-RAN: RAN as a Service

Navid Nikaein†, Raymond Knopp†, Lionel Gauthier†
Eryk Schiller*, Torsten Braun*, Dominique Pichon§,
Christian Bonnet†, Florian Kaltenberger†, and Dominique Nussbaum†
† Eurecom 06410 Biot Sophia-Antipolis, France firstname.name@eurecom.fr
* University of Bern lastname@iam.unibe.ch
§ Orange Labs dominique.pichon@orange.com

ABSTRACT

Commoditization and virtualization of wireless networks are changing the economics of mobile networks to help network providers (e.g., MNO, MVNO) move from proprietary and bespoke hardware and software platforms toward an open, cost-effective, and flexible cellular ecosystem. In addition, rich and innovative local services can be efficiently created through cloudification by leveraging the existing infrastructure. In this work, we present RANaaS, which is a cloudified radio access network delivered as a service. RANaaS provides the service life-cycle of an on-demand, elastic, and pay as you go 3GPP RAN instantiated on top of the cloud infrastructure. We demonstrate an example of real-time cloudified LTE network deployment using the OpenAirInterface LTE implementation and OpenStack running on commodity hardware as well as the flexibility and performance of the platform developed.

Categories and Subject Descriptors

C.2.1 [**Computer-Communication Networks**]: Network Architecture and Design - Wireless Communication System.

Keywords

OpenAirInterface, LTE/LTE-A, Cloud Computing, Cloud-RAN, Virtualization, RANaaS.

1. INTRODUCTION

In the last few decades, radio access networks (RANs) have significantly evolved from analog to digital signal processing units, where hardware components are often replaced with flexible and reusable software-defined functions. In a pure software-defined radio (SDR) system, the entire radio function runs on a general-propose processor (GPP) and only requires analog-to-digital and digital-to-analog conversions, power amplifiers, and antennas, whereas in typical cases, the system is based upon a programmable dedicated hardware (e.g. ASIC, ASIP, or DSP) and associated control software. Thus, the flexibility offered by a pure SDR improves service life-cycle and cross-platform portability at the cost of lower power and computational efficiency (i.e. ASIC: 1x, DSP: 10x, GPP: 100x).

Virtual RAN extends this flexibility through abstraction (or virtualization) of the execution environment. Consequently, radio functions become a general-purpose application that operates on top of a virtualized environment and interacts with physical resources either directly or through a full or partial hardware emulation layer. The resulted virtualized software radio application can be delivered as a service and managed through a cloud controller [1]. This changes the economics of mobile networks towards a cheap and easy to manage software platforms. Furthermore, cloud environment enables the creation of new services, such as RAN as a service (RANaaS) [2, 3], and more generally, network as a service (NaaS), such as LTEaaS, associated with the cloud RAN (C-RAN) [4–6]. C-RAN systems replace traditional base stations with distributed (passive) radio elements connected to a centralized baseband processing pool. Decoupling of the radio elements from the processing serves two main purposes. Centralized processing has the benefit of cost reduction due to fewer number of sites, easy software upgrade, performance improvement with coordinated multi-cell signal processing. Also, the remote radio heads have a much smaller footprint than a base station with on site processing, allowing for simpler and cost-effective network densification. C-RAN can be realized in two main steps, namely:

- **Commoditization and Softwarization:** refers to a software implementation of network functions on top of GPPs with no or little dependency on a dedicated hardware (e.g. DSP, FPGA, or ASIC). In addition, the programmability in RF domain can be achieved with the Field Programmable Radio Frequency (FPRF) technology.
- **Virtualization and Cloudification:** refers to execution of network functions on top of virtualized (and shared) computing, storage, and networking resources controlled by a cloud OS. I/O resources can be shared among multiple physical servers, and in particular that of radio front-end through multi root I/O virtualization (MR-IOV).

Many architectures have been proposed to support RANaaS ranging from a partially accelerated to a fully software-defined RAN. Recent efforts have shown the feasibility and efficiency of a full software implementation of the LTE RAN functions over GPPs. Two software implementations of the fully functional LTE/LTE-A already exist, namely Amarisoft[1] and OpenAirInterface[2] delivered as open-source. A full GPP approach to RAN brings the cloud and virtualization even closer to the wireless world allowing us to build a cloud-native RANaaS along with the following principles [1, 7]:

[1] www.amarisoft.com
[2] www.openairinterface.org

MobiCom'15, September 07-11, 2015, Paris, France.
ACM 978-1-4503-3619-2/15/09.
http://dx.doi.org/10.1145/2789168.2789178.

- **Mircoservice Architecture:** breaks down the network into a set of horizontal functions that can be combined together, assigned with target performance parameters, mapped onto the infrastructure resources (physical or virtual), and finally delivered as a service.[3]
- **Scalability:** monitors the RAN events (e.g. workload variations, optimization, relocation, or upgrade) and automatically adds/removes resources without any degradations in the required network performance (scale out/in).
- **Reliability:** shares the RAN contexts across multiple RAN services while keeping the required redundancy (making RAN stateless), and distributes the loads among them.
- **Placement:** optimizes the cost and/or performance by locating the RAN services at the specific geographic area subjected to performance, cost, and availability of the RF front-end and cloud resources.
- **Real-time Service:** offers a direct access to real-time radio information (e.g. radio status, statistics) for low-latency and high-bandwidth service deployed at the network edge [9].

In this work, we present RANaaS describing the service life-cycle of an on-demand, elastic, and pay as you go 3GPP RAN instantiated on top of the cloud infrastructure. The RANaaS service life-cycle management is a process of network design, deployment, resource provisioning, runtime management, and disposal that allows to rapidly architect, instantiate, and reconfigure the network components and their associated services. The proof-of-concept demonstrator is built upon the OpenAirInterface LTE software implementation, low latency Linux kernel, Linux containers, OpenStack, Heat orchestrater, and Open vSwitch as well as commodity PCs and National Instrument/Ettus USRP B210 RF front-end. It proves the feasibility of a real-time cloudified LTE network deployment using commodity hardware by providing a multimedia service to a commercial LTE-compatible user equipment.

2. FEASIBILITY STUDY OF CLOUD-RAN

To demonstrate the feasibility of C-RAN, we rely on the OpenAirInterface (OAI) LTE implementation upon which different C-RAN testbeds can be built [10]. In this section, we present the profiling results of OAI base band unit under various physical resource block (PRB) allocations, modulation and coding schemes (MCS), and for different virtualization technologies [11]. The experiments are performed using a single user with no mobility, in FDD SISO mode with AWGN channel, and full buffer traffic.

Fig. 1 compares the baseband processing time for a GPP platform with different virtualized environments, namely Linux Containers (LXC), Docker, and KVM, on the SandyBridge architecture (3.2 GHz). It can be observed that processing load is mainly dominated by the uplink and increases with growing PRBs and MCSs. Furthermore, the ratio and variation of downlink processing load to that of uplink also grows with the increase of PRB and MCS. While on average processing times are very close for all the considered virtualization environments, both GPP and LXC have slightly lower variations than that of DOCKER and KVM, especially when PRB and MCS increase. The results also reveals how the computing resources have to be provisioned to meet the real-time requirements.

[3]Microservice architecture is in opposition to the so-called "monolithic" architecture, where all functionality is offered by a single logical executable, see http://martinfowler.com/articles/microservices.html. It has to be noted that the micorservice architecture supports the ETSI NFV architecture [8], in which each VNF can be seen as a service.

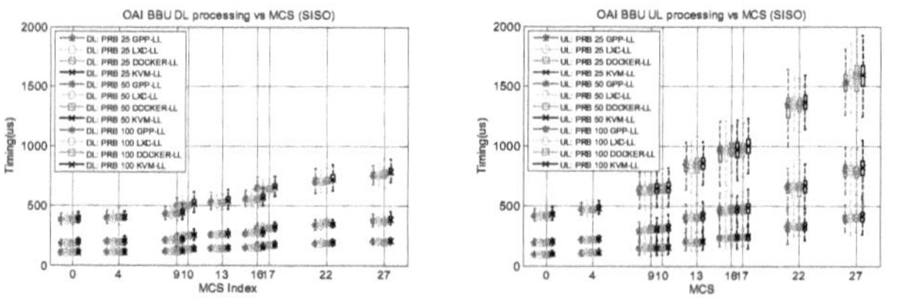

Figure 1: BBU processing time in downlink (left) and uplink(right) for different virtualized environments.

By analyzing processing time for a 1 ms LTE sub-frame, the main conclusion for the considered reference setup (FDD, 20 MHz, SISO, AWGN) is that 2 cores at 3 GHz are needed to handle the total processing of an eNB. One processor core for the receiver processing assuming 16-QAM on the uplink and approximately 1 core for the transmitter processing assuming 64-QAM on the downlink are required to meet the HARQ deadlines for a fully loaded system. With the AVX2 optimizations, the computational efficiency is expected to double and thus a full software solution would fit with an average of 1 x86 core per eNB.

Comparing results for different virtualization environments, we can conclude that containers (LXC and Docker) offer near bare metal runtime performance, while preserving the benefits of virtual machines in terms of flexibility, fast deployment, and migration. Due to the fact that containers are built upon modern kernel features such as `cgroups`, `namespace`, `chroot`, they share the host kernel and can benefit from the host scheduler, which is a key to meet real-time deadlines. This makes containers a cost-effective solution without compromising the performance.

3. C-RAN PROTOTYPE

Fig. 2 presents a proof-of-concept prototype of the RANaaS including the evolved packet core (EPC) and home subscriber server (HSS) services. The prototype has three top-level components, namely a web service, OpenStack, and a Heat stack. The web service features a user interface (UI) for network providers (e.g. MNO, MVNO) to manage their services. A service manager (SO) provides supporting services for the UI and requests the creation of the service from the service orchestrater (SO). SO is in charge of end-to-end life-cycle management of the RANaaS instance through an interaction with Heat. Typically, the OpenStack cloud manages large pools of computing, storage, and networking resources throughout a local *nano data-center*. Our OpenStack worker is deployed on top of Ubuntu 14.04 with the low latency kernel (3.17). To meet the strict timing requirements of RAN, the newly introduced SCHED_DEADLINE scheduler is used, which preempts the kernel to allocate the requested runtime (i.e. CPU time) at each period to meet requested deadlines. The OpenStack installation includes Heat orchestrater whose mission is to create a human- and machine-accessible service for managing the entire life-cycle of the virtual infrastructure and applications within OpenStack. Heat implements an orchestration engine to manage multiple composite cloud applications described in a form of text-based templates, called Heat Orchestration Templates (HoTs) and organized as the Heat stack, which is a stack of virtualized entities (e.g. network, LXCs). The Heat Template specifies LTE network elements with required networking wrapped up for a particular (business) domain. Thus, HoT manages the service instantiation of each LTE network function provided by OAI with desired granularity. The LTE network functions such as eNB, EPC, HSS are automatically programmed through the image flavor and meta-data provided to the LXC-based VMs.

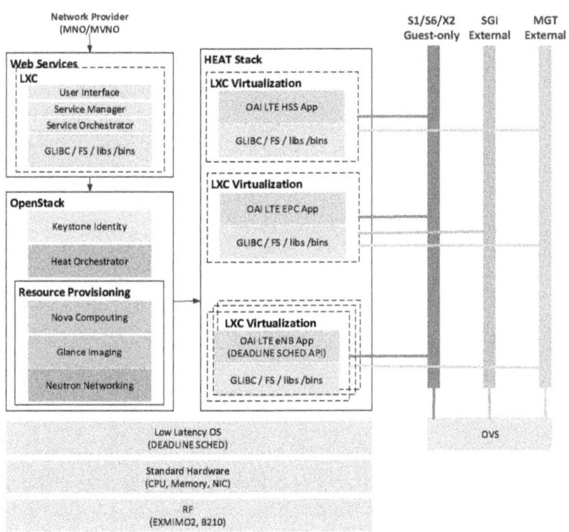

Figure 2: RANaaS prototype.

4. DEMO DESCRIPTION

The considered demonstration scenario is depicted in Fig. 3, and consists of 1 commercial LTE-enabled smart-phone (Samsung Galaxy S5), 1 Intel-based mini-PC (Intel i7 at 3.2 GHz, 8 GB RAM, 250 GB SSD) running 1 OAI soft eNB, 1 OAI soft EPC, and 1 OAI HSS as a Heat stack under the control of OpenStack, National Instrument/Ettus USRP B210 RF front-end, and 1 Faraday cage. Various setups are possible ranging from an all-in-one to all in a physically separated entities, which are deployment-specific. For the demo, we plan to demonstrate an all-in-one setup, in which the LTE eNB, EPC, and HSS functions are performed inside the same cloud infrastructure.

The demonstration will be deployed in FDD 2x2 MIMO mode with 5 MHz channel bandwidth. The target frequencies will be band 7 (Europe) in a controlled indoor radio environment. In the proposed demonstration, we will assess the following objectives

- feasibility of real-time C-RAN under different conditions,
- ease of deployment and service life cycle management,
- rapid service provisioning at the network edge.

The demonstration will be presented live and obtained results will be gathered on-the-fly. We will discuss the critical issues of C-RAN, show the life-cycle management procedure, and assess the performance of the network.

5. LESSON LEARNT

The experiments allowed us to closely observe and evaluate the behavior of a cloudified LTE network under different conditions. Therefore, based on the analysis of the results, a set of high level conclusions can be drawn. FDD LTE HARQ requires a round trip time (RTT) of 8 ms that imposes an upper-bound of less than 3 ms for the eNB TX/RX processing. Failing to meet such a deadline has a serious impact on the user performance. A virtualized execution environment of the BBU pool must provide the required runtime within the requested deadline. Containers proved to be more adequate for GPP RAN as they offer near-bare metal performance and provide direct access to the RF hardware. Virtual machines, in particular KVM, also provide very good performance, but require low latency mechanisms to access (virtualized) I/O resources (passthrough). In the case of containers, real-time or low latency kernels are required on the host. In the case of full virtualization

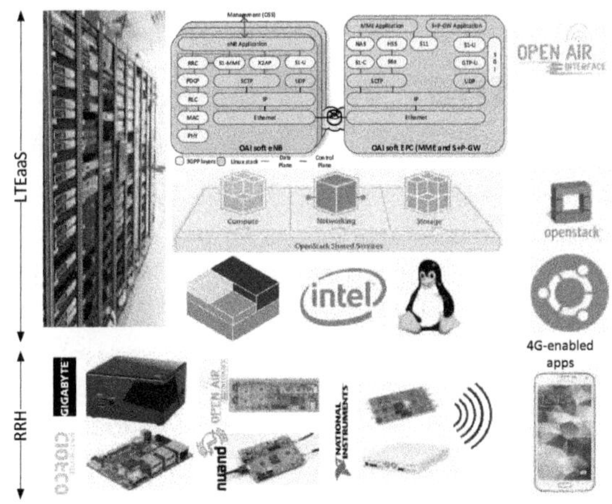

Figure 3: Hardware and software components

(e.g., KVM), both the hypervisor and the guest OS must support real time/low latency tasks (different techniques are required for hypervisors type 1 and 2).

In addition, the cloudified network has to natively support scale in/out for resource provisioning and sharing across multiple instances as well as load balancing to deal with cell load variations. For this purpose, the network, when instructed by the service orchestrator, has to adjust the number of attached terminals (e.g. trigger handover or detach users) and/or to limit the maximum throughput (e.g., MCS, transmission mode) to align with the available resources (processing, storage, and networking). In terms of reliability, the terminal and network contexts have to be shared among different replicated network instances.

Acknowledgement

The research and development leading to these results has received funding from the European Research Council under the European Community Seventh Framework Programme (FP7/2014- 2017) grant agreement 318109 MCN and 612050 FLEX project.

6. REFERENCES

[1] Bill Wilder. *Cloud Architecture Patterns*. O'Reilly, 2012.

[2] MCN. Mobile cloud networking project, `http://www.mobile-cloud-networking.eu`.

[3] iJoin. Interworking and joint design of an open access and backhaul network architecture for small cells based on cloud networks, `http://www.ict-ijoin.eu/`.

[4] Y. Lin, L. Shao, Z. Zhu, Q. Wang, and R. K. Sabhikhi. Wireless network cloud: Architecture and system requirements. *IBM Journal of Research and Development*, 2010.

[5] China Mobile Research Institute. C-RAN the road towards green RAN, 2013. White paper, v3.0.

[6] A. Checko, H. L. Christiansen, Y. Yan, L. Scolari, G. Kardaras, M. S. Berger, and L. Dittmann. Cloud RAN for mobile networks - a technology overview. *Communications Surveys Tutorials, IEEE*, 2014.

[7] MCN D2.5. Final overall architecture definition. Technical report, 2015.

[8] ETSI. Network Functions Virtualisation (NFV), white paper, 2014.

[9] Milan Patel, Jerome Joubert, Julian Roldan Ramos, Nurit Sprecher, Sadayuki Abeta, and Adrian Neal. Mobile-edge computing. *ETSI*, 2014.

[10] N. Nikaein, R. Knopp, F. Kaltenberger, L. Gauthier, C. Bonnet, D. Nussbaum, and R. Gaddab. Demo: OpenAirInterface: an open LTE network in a PC. In *Mobicom*, 2014.

[11] I. Alyafawi, E. Schiller, T. Braun, D. Dimitrova, A. Gomes, and N. Nikaein. Critical issues of centralized and cloudified LTE FDD radio access networks. In *ICC*, 2015.

Demo: Witals, AP-centric Health Diagnosis of WiFi Networks

Mukulika Maity
IIT Bombay
mukulika@cse.iitb.ac.in

Avinash Chaurasia
IIT Bombay
avinashk@cse.iitb.ac.in

Rachit Srivastava
AirTight Networks
rachit.srivastava@airtightnetworks.com

Bhaskaran Raman
IIT Bombay
br@cse.iitb.ac.in

Mythili Vutukuru
IIT Bombay
mythili@cse.iitb.ac.in

ABSTRACT

We present *Witals*, a system for WiFi performance diagnosis. In Witals, a live access point diagnoses the health of the WiFi network by examining the health of the air around it. Such diagnosis is critical functionality for sysads, and is an important addition to the state of the art. In the demo we will show WiFi performance diagnosis by Witals live at MobiCom venue and also from past collected traces in other settings & for controlled experiments.

1. INTRODUCTION & MOTIVATION

[1] Although the raw capacity of WiFi has seen tremendous growth, the real world WiFi deployments have become more troublesome for the system administrators (sysads). Diagnosing WiFi performance problem is a non trivial problem due to complex interdependence of different factors in the network stack. Witals aims to provide a sanitized view of WiFi network's health to the sysads. Prior approaches of WiFi performance diagnosis is not complete and they use heavy weight infrastructures. Witals runs at the operating AP and provides live diagnosis. We have carefully designed Witals to be low overhead, so that the AP can manage such analysis even when operating at the high data rates of 802.11n. Witals diagnoses performance problem from the perspective of downlink traffic which is a common case.

For such diagnosis, we first come up with a causal diagnosis graph which relates causes to different WiFi performance problems. Next, we identify a set of metrics corresponding to the nodes in this causal graph. Witals measures those metrics in real-time in an operational AP. The metrics quantify the impact of the performance problem. Finally using the metrics and causal relationships we design diagnosis algorithm. This ultimately presents a sanitized view of WiFi network's health to the sysad. We have implemented a prototype of Witals on an enterprise grade 802.11n AP platform. Using a variety of controlled as well as real-life measurements, we have verified that our diagnosis framework follows ground truth accurately.

[1]This work was supported in part by AirTight Networks.

MobiCom'15, September 7–11, 2015, Paris, France.
ACM. ISBN 978-1-4503-3619-2/15/09
DOI: http://dx.doi.org/10.1145/2789168.2789179.

2. CAUSAL DIAGNOSIS GRAPH

We first discuss our causal diagnosis graph shown in Fig 1. The graph relates various causes to different kinds of performance problems. The graph is designed to be complete, as it identifies all possibilities of any WiFi performance problem. The nodes in the graph are possible WiFi performance problems. The edges in the graph are causal relationships between the nodes. The underlined nodes are the various conditions Witals can diagnose. We denote AP_W to refer the access point on which Witals runs.

If the downlink throughput of AP_W is low, there are only three possible reasons. (A) Low offered load: AP_W does not have enough data to transmit, (B) Not enough airtime: AP_W has data to transmit but does not get enough opportunities to transmit, (C) Inefficient utilization of provided airtime: AP_W has data to transmit and it gets enough opportunities to transmit as well but it is not able to utilize airtime efficiently.

(A) Low offered load: marked as "A" in Fig 1. This could be caused by variety of non-wireless related reasons such as DHCP server issues, client issues etc. Witals does not distinguish between the different reasons causing low offered load.

(B) Not enough airtime: marked as "B" in Fig 1. If AP_W has data but does not get enough airtime to transmit the possible reasons are i) *Wasted non decodable energy*: The air is occupied by non decodable energy. This comprises of *non-WiFi energy* and *WiFi non-frame energy*. ii) *Control, management overheads*: Even when the energy is decodable, it could be occupied by control and management overheads. iii) *Other BSS*: Now when the airtime is taken up by data, it might belong to other BSS operating on same/nearby channel of AP_W. iv) *Upload*: Even within AP_W's BSS, airtime could be taken up by uplink transmissions. v) *MAC unfairness*: Now when above factors are not affecting AP_W's airtime, DCF MAC can result in unfairness in transmission opportunities (txop) and/or airtime. vi) Finally, even when DCF MAC is overall fair, the number of radios N on the channel might be high, although AP_W gets its fair share i.e. $\frac{1}{N}$ airtime, but due to high value of N, downlink throughput suffers.

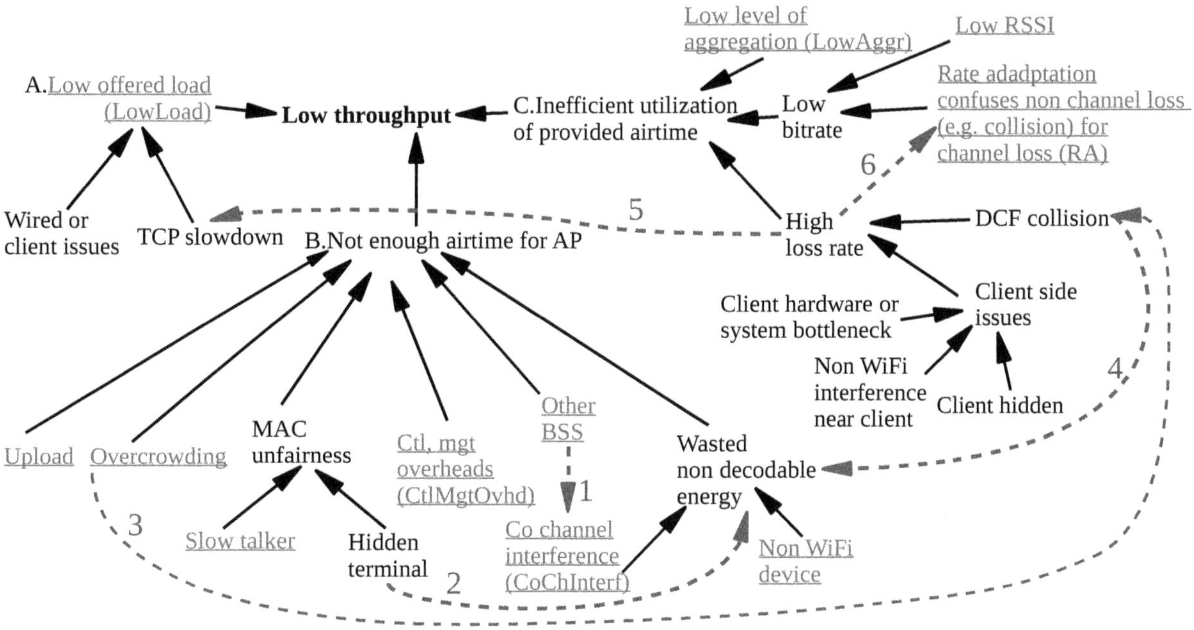

Figure 1: Witals Diagnosis: Causal Graph

(C) Inefficient utilization of provided airtime: marked as "C" in Fig 1. Finally, AP_W has data and gets enough airtime as well, but AP_W cannot utilize that efficiently. The possible reasons are i) *Low bitrate*: AP_W might be operating at a low bitrate either due to poor RSSI or rate adaptation algorithm makes wrong decisions and picks a suboptimal bitrate unnecessarily. ii) *High loss rate*: Now, even when AP_W is operating at optimal bitrate, the airtime utilization could be inefficient if link layer loss rate is high. High loss rate could be caused by DCF collision and/or client side issues. iii) *Low aggregation*: In case of 802.11n, even if bitrate is optimal and loss rate is low, still airtime utilization could be inefficient if AP_W uses lower level of frame aggregation.

While the above dependencies are from a certain perspective, for completeness, we also need several "cross-links" in the causal graph as shown in Fig 1. For instance *cross-link 1* captures the fact that if other BSS operate on same/near by channel of AP_W, some of energy might not be decodable to AP_W, this causes co channel interference.

3. WITALS FOR DIAGNOSIS

Corresponding to different nodes of the causal diagnosis graph, we come up with a suitable metric which quantifies the impact of the problem. The metrics are *comparable* with one another. We can identify and quantify multiple simultaneous causes of WiFi performance problems. We use hardware supported registers and per frame information for measurement of the metrics. We calculate these in windows of time, of duration denoted as T_W. Table 1 lists the various possible diagnoses of Witals and the corresponding metrics to diagnose those & also how we measure the metrics.

4. DIAGNOSIS ALGORITHM

Using the causal diagnosis graph and the corresponding metrics we develop the diagnosis algorithm. The algorithms gives a refined view to the sysad representing the health of the network. The algorithm runs at the end of every T_W. It gives diagnosis as one or more as listed in Table 1. In our implementation we choose $T_W = 2s$.

Diagnosis	Metric
Healthy	-
LowLoad	I (idle airtime)
NonWiFi	W (airtime lost due to wasted non-decodable energy)
CoChInterf	W, OB (airtime occupied by frames of other BSS)
CtlMgtOvhd	O (airtime occupied by control and management frames)
OtherBSS	OB
Upload	Ul (airtime occupied by uplink transmissions)
SlowTalker	S_{redn} (how much more airtime AP_W could have achieved if all radios were at least as fast as AP_W)
Overcrowding	W, N (number of radios)
LowRSSI	$RSSI_{redn}$ (throughput reduction for operating at lower than ideal bitrate due to poor RSSI)
RA	RA_{redn} (throughput reduction due to operating at lower rate as opposed to operating at ideal RSSI bitrate), N
LowAggr	$Aggr_{redn}$ (throughput reduction for operating at lower than ideal level of frame aggregation)

Table 1: Diagnosis Table

Algorithm is summarized in Algorithm 1. At each T_W we pick three major throughput reduction metrics call this set as $\mathbb{M}$. We apply a minimum threshold percentage (here 10%) for any metric to have an impact on performance. If $\mathbb{M}$ is empty we diagnose *Healthy*. Given $\mathbb{M}$ is nonempty, if idle percentage is more than a threshold (here 50%), i.e. mostly idle, then we diagnose *LowLoad* and *Healthy*. The diagnosis of *CtlMgtOvhd*, *OtherBSS*, *Upload*, *SlowTalker*, *LowRSSI*,

Algorithm 1 Diagnosis algo, runs every T_W

$\mathbb{M}$ = Set of up to 3 major witals metrics > (10%)
if $\mathbb{M}$ *is* $\emptyset$ **output** Healthy
if $I > 50$ **then** ▷ Channel more idle than busy
  output LowLoad, Healthy
else ▷ Channel more busy than idle
  if $O \in \mathbb{M}$ **output** CtlMgtOvhd
  if $OB \in \mathbb{M}$ **output** OtherBSS
  if $Ul \in \mathbb{M}$ **output** Upload
  if $S_{redn} \in \mathbb{M}$ **output** SlowTalker
  if $RSSI_{redn} \in \mathbb{M}$ **output** LowRSSI
  if $RA_{redn} \in \mathbb{M}$ **output** RA
  if $Aggr_{redn} \in \mathbb{M}$ **output** LowAggr
  if $W \in \mathbb{M}$ **then**
    if $N > 5$ **output** Overcrowding
    if $OB > 10$ **output** CoChInterf
    if neither of the above **output** NonWiFi
  end if
end if

RA, *LowAggr* is straightforward, we simply check if the corresponding metric is in $\mathbb{M}$. Some problems are trickier to diagnose because their impact cannot be captured in any one metric. Overcrowding, non WiFi device and co-channel interference all cause increase of W. So, we use other metrics to distinguish between these. If N is more than a threshold (here 5, empirically observed) we diagnose *Overcrowding*. The presence of significant interference from other BSS is used to flag *CoChInterf*. But if neither of the above is true we conclude diagnosis as *NonWiFi* device.

Diagnosing at every T_W might be too fine grained as many transient problems could be shown up. So if the sysad is more interested in diagnosing persistent performance problems, the framework allows to run the algorithm for long term by taking the output of previous T_W algorithm over multiple such windows as input.

5. WITALS DEMO

At the demo we will show the performance diagnosis by Witals for controlled experiments and for the WiFi deployment at MobiCom venue & also from past collected traces in other settings. While Witals is designed to run on an operational AP, it can equivalently run from a nearby sensor in the same channel as the AP. Also note that the diagnosis is passive: no extra traffic is generated.

Controlled experiments: For controlled experiments, we will set up our access point in 5Ghz band, so that it does not interfere with existing WiFi network there. We will perform experiment for diagnosis of *OtherBSS* , *SlowTalker* and *LowRSSI* by artificially creating each problem.

Live demo: We will also show live performance diagnosis at the venue. Witals will diagnose presence of any performance problem in the network. Thus we can examine the health of the WiFi network at the venue and diagnose the persistent problems (if any) for better deployment of WiFi for such conferences in future.

Now to better understand what the demo will show, we illustrate using examples. From our real life experiments we take two real life scenarios, classroom and conference.

Classroom: We ran Witals in a classroom where 80 clients were associated with AP_W. The class activity was online quiz using tablet devices. Fig. 2 shows Witals' diagnosis plotted over time. We can see here that *Overcrowding*, *OtherBSS* and *CoChInterf* are the major performance problems for this network.

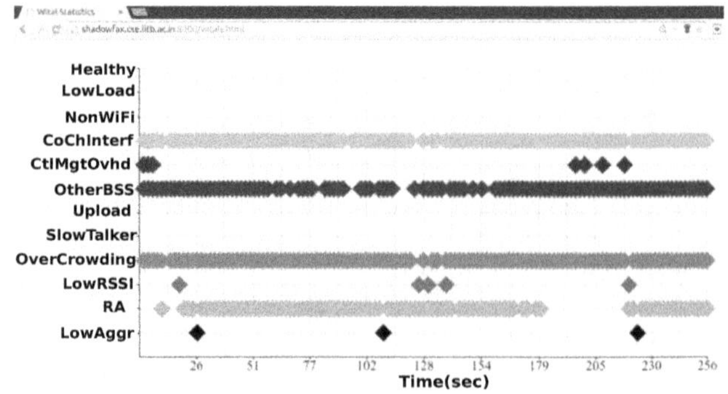

Figure 2: Diagnosis screenshot: classroom

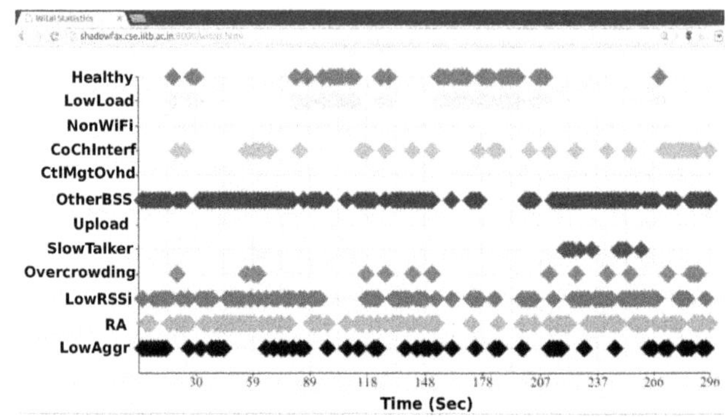

Figure 3: Diagnosis screenshot: conference

Conference: We ran Witals at a research conference. Here AP_W acted like a sniffer, collected metrics of operating AP. We did analysis from the saved metrics. There were many access points on same and nearby channel of operating AP. Fig. 3 shows Witals' diagnosis plotted over time. Unlike classroom, *Overcrowding* is not a major problem here. This is expected, as unlike classroom users do not use the network simultaneously. In several time windows the network is healthy and lightly loaded. As pointed out by diagnosis, *OtherBSS*, *LowRSSI*, *RA* and *LowAggr* are major performance problems in this network. *LowRSSI* problem might have been caused as the conference venue was across two floors.

6. SETUP

Equipment: we will bring our own Witals enabled APs (2-3).

Space needed: one table is sufficient, set up time is around 5min.

Addition facilities: power is needed, Internet is not required.

7. ACKNOWLEDGEMENT

This work was supported in part by AirTight Networks.

Demo: OneLab: Major Computer Networking Testbeds for IoT and Wireless Experimentation

Loïc Baron, Fadwa Boubekeur, Radomir Klacza, Mohammed Yasin Rahman, Ciro Scognamiglio, Nina Kurose, Timur Friedman, Serge Fdida
LIP6 Laboratory
UPMC Sorbonne Universités
firstname.lastname@lip6.fr

ABSTRACT[1]

Gathering the required measurements to produce accurate results for mobile communications and wireless networking protocols, technologies and applications, relies on the use of expensive experimental computer networking facilities. Until very recently, large-scale testbed facilities have existed in separate silos, each with its own authentication mechanisms and experiment support tools. There lacked a viable federation model that reconciled the challenges posed by how to provide a single entry point to access heterogeneous and distributed resources, and how to federate these resources that are under the control of multiple authorities. The OneLab experimental facility, which came online in 2014, realizes this model, making a set of world-class testbeds freely available to researchers through a unique credential for each user and a common set of tools. We allow users to deploy innovative experiments across our federated platforms that include the embedded object testbeds of FIT IoT-Lab, the cognitive radio testbed of FIT CorteXlab, the wireless testbeds of NITOS-Lab, and the internet overlay testbed PlanetLab Europe (PLE), which together provide thousands of nodes for experimentation. Also federated under OneLab are the FUSECO Playground, which includes cloud, M2M, SDN, and mobile broadband; w-iLab.t wireless facilities; and the Virtual Wall testbed of wired networks and applications. Our demo describes the resources offered by the OneLab platforms, and illustrates how any member of the MobiCom community can create an account and start using these platforms today to deploy experiments for mobile and wireless testing.

General Terms

Measurement, Performance, Reliability, Experimentation, Verification

Keywords

Experimental facility, heterogeneous testbed federation, unique credential, Slice-based Federation Architecture, MySlice

1. RESEARCH TO BE PRESENTED

The OneLab[2] federation of testbeds fills a unique niche: we allow users to deploy innovative experiments across heterogeneous testbeds; and we provide users with the access to these resources with the minimum possible requirements. MySlice,[3] the portal technology that we have developed, provides a tool for easy access to these testbeds. New users sign up and, in a matter of minutes start browsing and reserving resources. Our portal provides a path for users to transition to becoming power users, able to access the same testbeds via a simple and powerful API.

Our demonstration at MobiCom 2015 will present the software behind the OneLab portal and will show users how they may deploy experiments across our heterogeneous IoT and wireless platforms from a single access point. It will also illustrate the characteristics and testing environments that our platforms offer to experimenters.

1.1 The OneLab portal and MySlice

In creating OneLab, we faced with the technical challenges of how to (i) federate distributed resources that are under the control of multiple authorities; (ii) federate heterogeneous resources; and (iii) provide a single access portal to distributed and heterogeneous resources.

Challenge (i) is handled through OneLab's adoption of the Slice-based Federation Architecture (SFA), an API for authentication and authorization that we helped pioneer through the first working SFA-based federation, between PlanetLab Europe and PlanetLab Central in the United States. SFA allows for a distributed web of trust to be constructed around a hierarchy of independent authorities.

MySlice addresses challenge (ii), how to federate heterogeneous resources. Different testbed resources are

MobiCom'15, September 07-11, 2015, Paris, France
ACM 978-1-4503-3619-2/15/09.
http://dx.doi.org/10.1145/2789168.2789180

[2] https://onelab.eu

[3] http://www.myslice.info

described in XML files called resource specifications (RSpecs). MySlice exposes diverse RSpecs to users through a common table view, as well as through a set of plug-ins that enable testbed-specific characteristics, such as the geographic location of nodes, to be shown.

The OneLab portal's single access point reconciles challenge (iii), allowing for use of testbeds with the minimum possible requirements: internet access and a web browser; making the portal resources accessible to all users. From our demo, users will easily understand how to use the portal to browse the federated resources and reserve nodes from any of our platforms.

1.2 OneLab platforms

The OneLab federation is made up of the following platforms, encompassing wireless, sensor and mobility testbeds; Internet overlaid testbeds; and broadband access and core testbeds. Our MobiCom demo will educate participants on the characteristics of all of our testbeds, while the experiment will focus on our IoT platforms.

- **FIT IoT-Lab**[4] is made up of six platforms spread across France, boasting a total of 2728 wireless sensor nodes for testing small wireless sensor devices and heterogeneous communicating objects. IoT-Lab platforms have two generations of nodes: SensLAB nodes operating WSN340 open nodes; and IoT-LAB nodes operating M3 and A8 open nodes
- **CorteXlab**[5] is a cognitive radio testbed with WSN, IoT-Lab and SDR radio nodes, and allows for the operating frequency, bandwidth, emitted power and waveform to be adjusted so as to customize the testing environment
- **NITLab**[6] and **FIT NITOS-Lab**[7] platforms provide wireless nodes based on commercial Wi-Fi cards and Linux open source drivers. These NITOS platforms allow for reproducibility of experimentation and evaluation of protocols and applications in real world settings
- **PlanetLab Europe**[8] provides users access to over one thousand nodes on 530 sites worldwide, allowing for large-scale, extensive, and remote testing
- **FUSECO Playground**[9] provides core network technologies such as multi-access network environments, M2M and IoT, sensor networks and mobile broadband, and SDN and openflow cloud environments.
- **w-iLab.t**[10] testbeds allows for wireless networks and solutions testing activities by providing multiple wireless interfaces such as sensor nodes, Bluetooth and Wi-Fi nodes, and offers both fixed and mobile nodes.
- **Virtual Wall**[11] testbeds provide an environment for wired networks and solutions experimentation

2. EXPERIMENT DEMONSTRATION

For the experimentation aspect of our demonstration, we will deploy a basic experiment on the IoT-Lab platform via the OneLab portal. We step users through the process of obtaining an account on OneLab, creating a slice, reserving the IoT-Lab WSN430 nodes, and deploying the experiment. The nodes will send UDP messages to the root over a tree build by the routing protocol RPL; for example: each of the reserved nodes will send to the root a UDP message every second. This rate of traffic is higher than classical surveillance radio traffic but has been considered for practical reasons. Nodes closer to the root have to forward traffic coming from downstream nodes in addition to their own traffic. The root node acknowledges each received data packet. Experiments will run for 200 seconds. Through deployment on IoT-Lab's WSN430 nodes, we will be able to measure the energy consumption of nodes and real time delay and the packet reception rate.

Engineers from the OneLab team and PhD student Fadwa Boubekeur, who works extensively on FIT IoT-Lab for her research, will carry out the demo to show students, researchers and industrial representatives how they can use the OneLab portal and its testbeds to easily deploy their experiments. This demonstration will show to users the ability to have very fine control over what can be done on a node.

3. REQUIREMENTS

3.1 Equipment to be used

For this demonstration, we will need a wired Ethernet connection and a power outlet. Ideally, we would also need a monitor (with HDMI/VGA cables) to connect to the laptop and show the demo on a large screen. Accompanying the experiment will be poster on OneLab's federated testbeds and the MySlice software, which will also require use of an easel to mount the poster.

3.2 Set up and space

As the demonstration is done remotely and through the web, there is minimal setup and space required. We will need one table upon which to set our laptop (plus the monitor, if available) and a poster easel. Most of the demo can be set up ahead of time, so on-site set-up will only be to connect to the various cables and set up the poster.

---

[4] https://www.iot-lab.info/
[5] http://www.cortexlab.fr/
[6] http://nitlab.inf.uth.gr/
[7] http://fit-nitos.fr/
[8] http://planet-lab.eu/
[9] http://fuseco-playground.org
[10] http://ilabt.iminds.be/wilabt
[11] http://ilabt.iminds.be/virtualwall

Demo: Molecular MIMO with Drift

Changmin Lee, Bonhong Koo, Na-Rae Kim, H. Birkan Yilmaz, Nariman Farsard†, Andrew Eckford†, and Chan-Byoung Chae
Yonsei Institute of Convergence Technology, School of Integrated Technology, Yonsei University, Korea.
†Dept. of Electrical Engineering and Computer Science, York University, Toronto, Canada
cbchae@yonsei.ac.kr

ABSTRACT

In molecular communication information is transferred with the use of molecules. Molecular multiple-input multiple-output (MIMO) system with drift (positive velocity) at macro-scale will be presented and the improvement against single-input single-output (SISO) molecular communication systems will be verified via our testbed. Until now it was unclear whether MIMO techniques, which are extensively used in modern radio frequency (RF) communications, could be applied to molecular communication. In the demonstration, using our MIMO testbed we will show that we can achieve nearly 1.7 times higher data rate than SISO molecular communication systems. Moreover, signal-to-inter-link-interference metric for one-shot signal will be depicted for a given symbol duration.

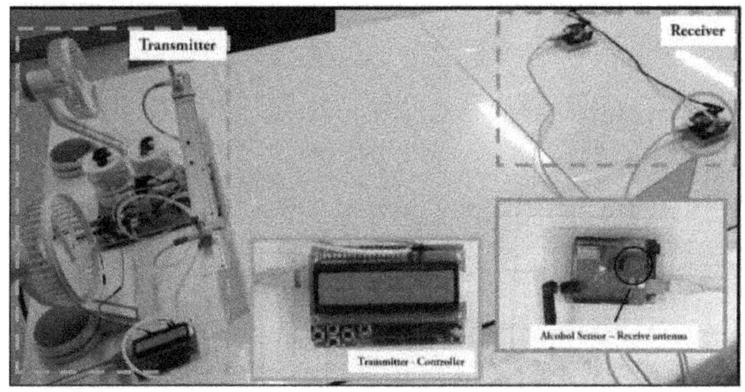

Figure 1: The tabletop molecular MIMO communication platform.

1. BACKGROUND

With the development of nanobots and micro machines, a new research domain, which focuses on communication requirements and techniques for these scales has emerged [10]. In small scales, electromagnetic communication is challenging because of constraints such as the ratio of the antenna size to the wavelength of the electromagnetic signal [1, 10]. Inspired by nature, one possible solution is to use chemical signals as carriers of information, which is called molecular communication [6]. It can be utilized where radio based communication fails or is inefficient: for example, city infrastructure monitoring in smart cities at macro-scale [11], and body area nanonetworks for health monitoring and targeted drug delivery at micro-scale [2].

Mostly, literature on molecular communication has focused on micro-scale systems such as diffusion-based communications [2, 7, 9]. Most of these works have been theoretical, and only recently some experimental implementations of molecular communication systems are proposed at macro-scale [3]. More recently, nonlinearity in diffusion channel at macro-scale is modeled as noise [5].

MobiCom'15, September 7–11, 2015, Paris, France.
ACM 978-1-4503-3619-2/15/09 .
http://dx.doi.org/10.1145/2789168.2789181 .

In prior work, a pioneering single-input single-output (SISO) macro-scale molecular communication link was demonstrated [3, 4]. We also demonstrated a simple molecular MIMO (without drift) at IEEE INFOCOM 2015 [8] and got the Best Demo Award for this work. In this demonstration, we will show the world's first molecular multiple-input multiple-output (MIMO) communication link with drift, where an artificial flow exists in the environment. MIMO is a technique, which is used in modern radio communication to increase transmission data rate. The feasibility of using MIMO technique in macro-scale molecular communication will be demonstrated.

2. TESTBED

Our testbed is a macro-scale version of the molecular MIMO communication system at micro-scales. The transmitter and the receiver are equipped with multiple sprays and sensors to further increase the data rate. The system is inexpensive, and the platform is available as a modifiable and re-programmable research testbed.

2.1 Hardware Layout

In Fig. 1, the main components of the testbed are shown and consist of molecular MIMO transmitter and receiver. The propagation channel in between is several meters of free-space. With using standard fan, the environment may have flow that assists the propagation. The transmitter consists of: 1) a simple user interface for text entry, 2) a microcontroller for executing transmitter algorithms, 3) two reservoir for chemicals, and 4) two chemical release mechanism (i.e.

Figure 2: Sample text message entered at the transmitter.

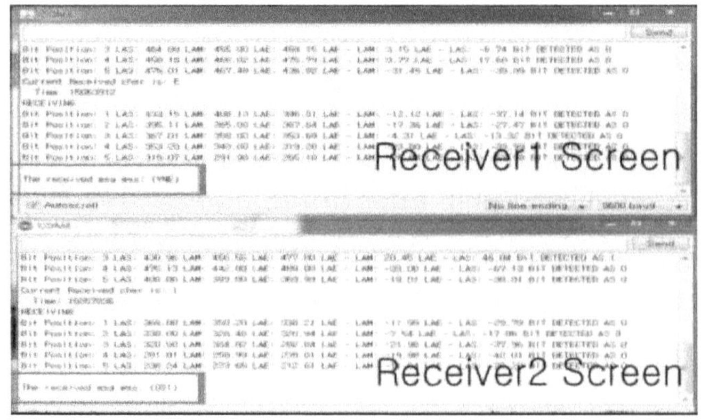

Figure 3: On the receiver screens the decoded characters are seen.

two sprays with adjustable separation). At the receiver, the hardware consists of: 1) two chemical sensors for MIMO operation, 2) two microcontrollers that forward electrical signal that originated from chemical sensors to computer, and 3) a computer for demodulating, decoding the signal, and visualizing results.

2.2 System Operation

Basically, the transmitter separates the strings into two parts and converts them to bit sequences via using international telegraph alphabet no. 2 (ITA2). The molecular MIMO system feeds the coded bits to the transmitter antennas (sprays) one and two independently. Which can be considered as utilizing spatial domain for increasing the transmission data rate. At the receiver site, molecule concentrations at two antennas are recorded as voltage readings from sensors and demodulator detects the intended symbol at each symbol duration. Unlike prior work in RF communication, non-coherent detection is required since the coherent time of the molecular channel is zero.

2.3 Setup

Setup time for the molecular MIMO testbed is nearly 40 minutes and the testbed requires a table with size (at least) 76×260 centimeters. We also need at least 6 power plugs for the equipments and a big monitor to visualize the demonstration output.

2.4 Health and Safety

As part of the demonstration low volumes of alcohol will be diffused in open air. There will not be any chemical risks since the alcohol used will be safe for humans and of a small quantity. Moreover, we will put the testbed equipment behind a transparent shielded screen to respect religious sensitivities and avoid any unwanted alcohol odors at the demo hall.

3. DEMONSTRATION

There will be mainly two types of demonstrations: one is text message (any number of characters) transmission and the other is visualizing the signal and interference for one shot signal.

3.1 Text Message Transmission

The main goal of the demonstration is to show that text messages can be continuously and reliably carried via molecular MIMO system. In Fig. 2, the sample text is depicted at the transmitter and Fig. 3 illustrates the receiver screen. Molecular MIMO system divides the sample text into two and sends independently. As can be seen from the figure, three character strings are decoded independently at the receivers. Table 1 compares the transmission time and the data rate of SISO and MIMO systems, from which we observe that the MIMO system show 1.7 times higher data rate than the SISO system.

Table 1: Experiment results of the macro-scale SISO and MIMO molecular communication testbed.

Type	TX time (s)	Data rate (bps)
SISO w/ Drift	74	0.41
MIMO w/ Drift	44	0.68

Most mathematical models developed for molecular communication have relied on Fick's diffusion equation and been validated via Monte-Carlo simulations [12]. Moreover, most prior work has assumed perfect transmission, propagation, and reception [7]. These assumptions, however, do not hold in practice, and more realistic models based on experimental data are necessary [5]. Measurement data, which are obtained from our MIMO platform, may play a crucial role in developing more accurate molecular MIMO channel models.

3.2 Interference Measurements

In molecular MIMO setup inter link interference (ILI) is an important metric to measure and it depends on the separation distance between the antennas. We denote the separation between the transmitter antenna-1 (Tx1) and Tx2 by h. In Table 2, signal-to-ILI (S-ILI) ratios are measured and given for distance of $90\,cm$, different symbol durations, and antenna separation distances.

During the demonstration, we will visualize the signal and the S-ILI ratio metric for one shot signal without demodulation. S-ILI ratio is evaluated by sending bit-1 at Tx1 and bit-0 (silence) at Tx2 and evaluating

$$\text{S-ILI Ratio} = \sum_{t=0}^{t=t_s} s_{\text{Rx1}}(t) \;/\; \sum_{t=0}^{t=t_s} s_{\text{Rx2}}(t) \qquad (1)$$

where t_s and $s_{\text{Rxi}}(t)$ denote the symbol duration and received signal at receiver i (Rxi), respectively. As can be

Table 2: Measurement data of S-ILI Ratios (without drift).

Symbol Duration	$h = 30\,cm$	$h = 40\,cm$
$t_s = 1\,s$	10.18	11.03
$t_s = 2\,s$	24.09	26.70
$t_s = 3\,s$	39.78	59.31

seen from Table 2, increasing the symbol duration and the antenna separation increase S-ILI ratio, which makes the signal easier to detect.

4. CONCLUSION

In this demonstration, we present the first macro-scale molecular MIMO communication system with drift that can reliably transmit short text messages. We also demonstrate the interference measurements due to independent Tx1 and Tx2 antenna (spray) transmissions. Our goal is to show that molecular communication can be used as an alternative to radio communication in challenging environments. To improve the low transmission rate of molecular communication, we implement novel molecular MIMO detection algorithms. The main challenge in our design was implementing a signal separation algorithm for the molecular MIMO channel, since MIMO detection algorithms for classical RF communications could not be directly applied. We hope to motivate researchers, and fill a gap between theory and practice of molecular communication.

5. DEMO VIDEO

The demo video is available at http://www.cbchae.org.

6. ACKNOWLEDGEMENT

This research is funded by the MSIP (Ministry of Science, ICT & Future Planning), under the "IT Consilience Creative Program" (IITP-2015-R0346-15-1008) and by the Basic Science Research Program (2014R1A1A1002186) funded by the MSIP, through the National Research Foundation of Korea. The authors would like to thank C. Kim for his help in implementing the hardware.

7. REFERENCES

[1] I. F. Akyildiz, F. Brunetti, and C. Blazquez. Nanonetworks: A new communication paradigm. *Elsevier Comput. Netw.*, 52(12):2260–2279, Aug. 2008.

[2] B. Atakan, O. Akan, and S. Balasubramaniam. Body area nanonetworks with molecular communications in nanomedicine. *IEEE Commun. Mag.*, 50(1):28–34, January 2012.

[3] N. Farsad, W. Guo, and A. Eckford. Tabletop molecular communication: Text messages through chemical signals. *PLoS One*, 2013.

[4] N. Farsad, W. Guo, and A. Eckford. Molecular communication link. In *Proc. IEEE Int. Conf. on Comput. Commun. (INFOCOM)*, 2014.

[5] N. Farsad, N.-R. Kim, A. Eckford, and C.-B. Chae. Channel and noise models for nonlinear molecular communication systems. *IEEE J. Sel. Areas Commun.*, 32(12):1–10, Dec. 2014.

[6] N. Farsad, H. B. Yilmaz, A. Eckford, C.-B. Chae, and W. Guo. A comprehensive survey of recent advancements in molecular communication. *arXiv:1410.4258*, Oct. 2014.

[7] N.-R. Kim and C.-B. Chae. Novel modulation techniques using isomers as messenger molecules for nano communication networks via diffusion. *IEEE J. Sel. Areas Commun.*, 31(12):847–856, Dec. 2013.

[8] C. Lee, B. Koo, N.-R. Kim, H. B. Yilmaz, N. Farsad, A. Eckford, and C.-B. Chae. Molecular MIMO communication link. In *Proc. IEEE Int. Conf. on Comput. Commun. (INFOCOM)*, 2015.

[9] I. Llatser, A. Cabellos-Aparicio, and E. Alarcon. Networking challenges and principles in diffusion-based molecular communication. *IEEE Wireless Commun.*, 19(5):36–41, Oct 2012.

[10] T. Nakano, A. W. Eckford, and T. Haraguchi. *Molecular communication.* Cambridge University Press, first edition, 2013.

[11] F. Stajano, N. Hoult, I. Wassell, P. Bennett, C. Middleton, and K. Soga. Smart bridges, smart tunnels: Transforming wireless sensor networks from research prototypes into robust engineering infrastructure. *Elsevier Ad Hoc Netw.*, 8:872–888, Nov. 2010.

[12] H. B. Yilmaz and C.-B. Chae. Simulation study of molecular communication systems with an absorbing receiver. *Elsevier Simul. Model. Pract. Theory*, 49:136–150, Dec. 2014.

Demo: Exploring Autoregressive Integrated Models for Time Synchronization in Wireless Sensor Networks

Extended Abstract

Wasif Masood
Wasif.Masood@aau.at

Jorge F. Schmidt
Jorge.Schmidt@aau.at

Institute of Networked and Embedded Systems,
University of Klagenfurt, Austria.

ABSTRACT

Time synchronization provides the basis for several applications in wireless sensor networks but the limited memory and computational power, and the use of low precision oscillators make the task of time synchronization non-trivial. In this demonstration, we present a novel time synchronization scheme that is based on time series analysis. To provide a general model for the practical behavior of low precision oscillators, autoregressive integrated moving average models are explored. Based on the analysis of experimental data, an autoregressive integrated model (ARI (1,1)) is derived. Unlike the resource hungry Kalman filter based formulations, the proposed scheme is resource efficient as it results in simple linear regression processing. Experiments are performed on real sensor devices including Zolertia and TelosB, where an accuracy below 1 clock tick[1] is achieved.

1. INTRODUCTION

Several applications of Wireless Sensor Networks (WSN) [10, 11, 13] require a stable and accurate time synchronization solution. But the limited memory and computational power, and the use of low-precision oscillators make time synchronization a challenging task [7]. Specifically, a time synchronization solution has to be computationally efficient and compact in memory size so that it can sit under the application layer without depleting the resources. The use of low-precision oscillators further curtails the efficiency of time synchronization solutions. An oscillator is characterized by its nominal frequency which generates the *local time* of the device. Due to slight variations in manufacturing processes, supply voltage and aging of an oscillator, variations in the nominal frequency are evident. Such variations create *phase noise* and *frequency offset* between the oscillators. Frequency offset causes the clocks to *drift* from the actual time while phase noise further adds *jitter* in the drift. In addition to that, harsh environmental conditions concerning temperature and humidity add further uncertainty in oscillator behavior.

Taking into account the aforementioned limitations of sensor nodes, several solutions have been proposed. The pioneering work in [12] proposed a linear programming approach to estimate clock offset, but the results are limited in terms of synchronization accuracy. A convex hull optimization approach is proposed in [14], but due to the computational complexity, it is not practical for resource-constrained sensor nodes. There exist also several solutions based on Kalman filter formulation [1, 2, 8, 9], but the analysis is only based on simulations without assessing their implementation feasibility for sensor nodes. On the other hand, the solution proposed in [6] is simple enough to be implemented on sensor nodes but lacks the accuracy to meet the ever increasing synchronization demands of WSN applications.

In this demonstration, we present the actual implementation of our Autoregressive Integrated (ARI (1,1)) model for time synchronization in wireless sensor networks. This approach significantly outperforms existing low-complexity solutions as it effectively handles the non-stationarity in the sensor data. ARI (1,1) is derived using the well established building process of ARIMA models by performing experiments on Zolertia (Z1) [15] and TelosB platforms. Parameter estimation does not involve any matrix inversion operations as required by online recursion in Kalman filter based approaches and hence the overall complexity is low. Experiments show that 10 packets for parameter estimation are enough to achieve an accuracy below 1 clock tick.

2. SYNCHRONIZATION MODEL

Time synchronization is concerned with the estimation of the clock offset between nodes. Clock offsets exist because of the different bootup times of the devices and varies over time due to offset between their frequencies. Therefore, a model has to be identified to trace the varying behavior of clocks.

Let the local time of a node be $c(t)$. The relative clock offset between nodes A and B, at time instance t can be written as $\Delta_{A,B}(t) = c_A(t) - c_B(t)$. Using the instantaneous sampling period $\tau(t)$, the instantaneous clock drift $\alpha(t)$ is given by

$$\alpha_{A,B}(t) = \frac{d\Delta_{A,B}(t)}{dt} \approx \frac{\Delta_{A,B}(t) - \Delta_{A,B}(t - \tau(t))}{\tau(t)}. \quad (1)$$

[1]With a 32 kHz crystal oscillator of Z1/TelosB, 1 tick=30.52 µs.

MobiCom'15, September 7–11, 2015, Paris, France.
ACM 978-1-4503-3619-2/15/09.
DOI: http://dx.doi.org/10.1145/2789168.2789182.

For practical purposes, a discrete clock model is desirable. The local time, $c(t)$ can be discretized by the exchange of timestamped messages that represent discrete samples of a continuous clock. Using uniform sampling $\tau(t) = \tau$, the discretized offset and drift become

$$\Delta_{A,B}[k] = c_{A,B}[k], \quad (2)$$
$$\alpha_{A,B}[k] = \Delta_{A,B}[k] - \Delta_{A,B}[k-1], \quad (3)$$

where $c_n = \{c[1], c[2], c[3], \cdots, c[n]\}$ with $n \in \mathbb{N}$, is the univariate discrete time series representation of $c(t)$ and $c_{A,B}[k]$ is the time of reception of the kth packet from A at B. c_n represents the local time of a node and hence is a non-stationary time series. Using (3), the clock offset can be written as

$$\Delta_{A,B}[k] = \Delta_{A,B}[k-1] + \alpha_{A,B}[k]. \quad (4)$$

To model (4), we exploit the well known ARIMA models [3] that are able to extract the local level (offset) and trend information (clock drift) from a non-stationary time series [5]. The integrate part removes the non-stationarity from the time series so that it can be modeled as an autoregressive moving average (ARMA) process. The AR terms capture the Markov-like behavior in the resulting time series while the MA part combines the randomness from past samples using a moving window.

The general form of ARIMA (p, d, q) model of autoregressive (AR), difference and moving average (MA) orders p, d and q respectively, for the discrete time series representation of a clock is given as

$$\phi(B)\nabla^d c[k] = \alpha_0 + \theta(B)\epsilon[k], \quad (5)$$

where B is the back-shift operator ($B^m c[k] = c[k-m]$), and α_0 and ϵ are the deterministic linear trend and white noise respectively. $\nabla = c[k] - c[k-1]$ is the difference operator, where d represents the difference required to achieve stationarity. Finally, the polynomials representing the AR and MA terms of (5) are respectively

$$\phi(B) = 1 - \phi_1 B - \phi_2 B^2 - \cdots - \phi_p B^p, \quad (6)$$

$$\theta(B) = 1 - \theta_1 B - \theta_2 B^2 - \cdots - \theta_q B^q. \quad (7)$$

The first step in ARIMA (p, d, q) modeling is about identifying the orders of p, d and q. These orders are determined by visualizing the patterns appearing in autocorrelation (ACF) and partial-autocorrelation (PACF) analysis of c_n. Following the detailed steps explained in [4, Chp. 6], $p = 1$, $d = 1$, and $q = 0$ are obtained. Writing (4) in ARI (1,1) form (ARI because of the absence of MA terms), we have

$$w[k] = \phi\, w[k-1] + \alpha_0 + \epsilon[k], \quad (8)$$

where $w[k] = \nabla^{d=1} c[k] = c[k] - c[k-1]$ represents the stationary form of $c[k]$, α_0 is the constant linear drift and ϕ is the AR (1) coefficient. Since $\epsilon[k]$ is mainly caused by observation and measurement noise, it is reasonable to assume $\epsilon[k]$'s are independent with variance σ_ϵ^2. Alternatively,

$$c[k] = c[k-1] + \phi\, c[k-1] - \phi\, c[k-2] + \alpha_0 + \epsilon[k]. \quad (9)$$

Instead of measuring $\alpha(t)$ in (1), α_0 is modeled as a constant while the jitters in clock drift are compensated using the autoregressive term in (9).

Preliminary results concerning the synchronization accuracy of ARI (1,1) are given in figure 1. The results are averaged over 900 time series generated experimentally from 25 real Z1 devices. Parameter estimation is performed on increasing number of samples, N. It can be seen from figure 1 that as few as 10 samples are sufficient for parameter estimation, which is a very practical feature considering memory limited sensor nodes.

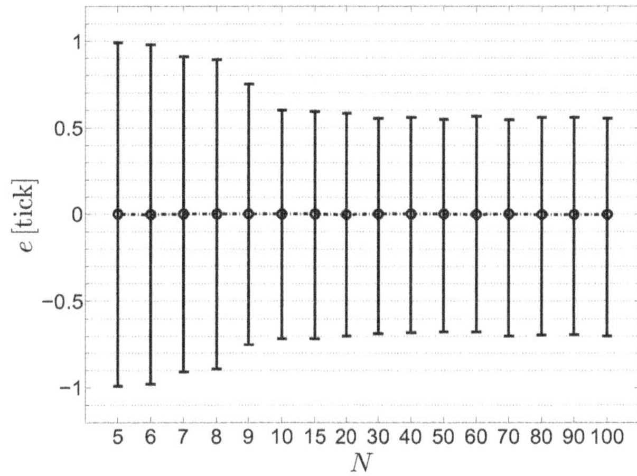

Figure 1: Accuracy of ARI (1,1) for increasing sample sizes. Each bar represents 5% and 95%-quantiles of the results.

3. DEMONSTRATIONS

In this demonstration, we will show the authenticity of our synchronization scheme by implementing it on real sensor nodes. By demonstrating the individual adjustments of each entity an observer gets an intuitive picture of how the synchronization strategy works. By appending wooden pendula to the microcontrollers, the step-wise synchronization processes of the technical devices is visualized by the corresponding gradual movement of the pendula arms.

In this demonstration, we intend to do the following:

Blinking LEDs.

We will use blinking lights on sensor nodes (we have 100 pieces of Z1 nodes but we will use them as per the feasibility of the space) to show the synchronization among them. The Z1 are one among the many low-cost off-the-shelf sensor nodes that are based on a 32 kHz low-precision crystal oscillator. Attendees will be allowed to randomly reset the nodes and experience the emergence of synchronization.

Wooden Pendula.

We will further use wooden pendula to better visualize the synchronization process. The pendula are custom designed wooden devices operated via servo motors, which we will operate using our Z1/TelosB nodes. The nodes will communicate over the wireless channel and will project the current state of synchronization by adjusting the to-and-fro motion of the pendulum attached. The steady convergence of their to-and-fro motion will give a more refine pictorial view to the attendees.

4. ACKNOWLEDGMENTS

This work was partly supported by Lakeside Labs GmbH, Klagenfurt, Austria, and funding from the ERDF, KWF, and BABEG under grant 20214/23794/35530.

5. REFERENCES

[1] L. Auler and R. d'Amore. Adaptive Kalman Filter for Time Synchronization over Packet-Switched Networks: An Heuristic Approach. In *ACM Proc. on Communication Systems Software and Middleware (COMSWARE)*, pages 1–7, 2007.

[2] A. Bletsas. Evaluation of Kalman filtering for network time keeping. *IEEE Trans. on Ultrasonics, Ferroelectrics, and Frequency Control*, 52(9):1452–1460, 2005.

[3] G. E. Box and G. M. Jenkins. Times series analysis. *Forecasting and Control, Holda-Day*, 1970.

[4] G. E. P. Box, G. Jenkins, and G. C. Reinsel. *Time Series Analysis: Forecasting and Control*. Probability and Statistics. Wiley, July 2008.

[5] J. Contreras, R. Espinola, F. J. Nogales, and A. J. Conejo. ARIMA models to predict next-day electricity prices. *IEEE Trans. on Power Systems*, 18(3):1014–1020, 2003.

[6] J. Elson, L. Girod, and D. Estrin. Fine-grained network time synchronization using reference broadcasts. *ACM SIGOPS Operating Systems Review*, 36(SI):147–163, 2002.

[7] N. M. Freris and P. Kumar. Fundamental limits on synchronization of affine clocks in networks. In *IEEE Proc. on Decision and Control (CDC)*, pages 921–926, 2007.

[8] B. R. Hamilton, X. Ma, Q. Zhao, and J. Xu. ACES: adaptive clock estimation and synchronization using Kalman filtering. In *ACM Proc. on Mobile Computing and Networking (MobiCom)*, pages 152–162, 2008.

[9] Q. Liu, X. Liu, J. L. Zhou, G. Zhou, G. Jin, Q. Sun, and M. Xi. Adasynch: A general adaptive clock synchronization scheme based on Kalman filter for wsns. *Wireless Personal Communications*, 63(1):217–239, 2012.

[10] G. Lu, N. Sadagopan, B. Krishnamachari, and A. Goel. Delay efficient sleep scheduling in wireless sensor networks. In *IEEE Proc. on Computer and Communications Societies (INFOCOM)*, pages 2470–2481, 2005.

[11] A. Mainwaring, D. Culler, J. Polastre, R. Szewczyk, and J. Anderson. Wireless sensor networks for habitat monitoring. In *ACM Workshop on Wireless Sensor Networks and Applications (WSNA)*, pages 88–97, 2002.

[12] S. B. Moon, P. Skelly, and D. Towsley. Estimation and removal of clock skew from network delay measurements. In *IEEE Proc. on Computer and Communications Societies (INFOCOM)*, volume 1, pages 227–234, 1999.

[13] L. Paladina, M. Scarpa, and A. Puliafito. Advantages in synchronization for wireless sensor networks. In *IEEE Symp. on Wireless Pervasive Computing (ISWPC)*, pages 160–164, 2008.

[14] L. Zhang, Z. Liu, and C. Honghui Xia. Clock synchronization algorithms for network measurements. In *IEEE Proc. on Computer and Communications Societies (INFOCOM)*, volume 1, pages 160–169, 2002.

[15] Zolertia WSN platform, Z1 Datasheet. `http://zolertia.com/sites/default/files/Zolertia-Z1-Datasheet.pdf`.

Demo Abstract:
Live Adaptations of Low-power MAC Protocols

Georgios Z. Papadopoulos, Antoine Gallais, Guillaume Schreiner and Thomas Noël
ICube Laboratory, University of Strasbourg, France
[gpapadopoulos, gallais, schreiner, noel]@unistra.fr

ABSTRACT

This demonstration aims at observing in an interactive manner the impact of modification of preamble and sampling periods at the low-power family of MAC protocols, and thus, illustrating in real-time the energy consumption and delay performance of each node accordingly. To do so, we implemented the ability for users to generate traffic at some remote nodes that are involved in two distinct deployed topologies. Those deployed networks operate with either a statically configured network, by employing X-MAC on top of the Contiki OS, or T-AAD, a lightweight traffic auto-adaptive protocol that allows live and automatic modifications of duty-cycle configurations.

Categories and Subject Descriptors

C.2.1 [**Network Architecture and Design**]: Wireless Communication; C.2.2 [**Network Protocols**]: *MAC protocols*

Keywords

Wireless Sensor Network, MAC, Low-power Protocols, Bursty Traffic, Traffic Adaptivity

1. MOTIVATION

For more than a decade there has been significant interest in designing and deploying WSNs, with deployments ranging from monitoring of patients to animals. In such applications, contrary to the traditional a priori known time-driven traffic patterns, event-driven networks face occasional, bursty and unanticipated multi-hop data transmissions. In wildlife monitoring for instance, the nodes (usually with limited-memory devices) operate under limited internet access for the majority of the time. When a network connection is detected, the mobile nodes should immediately upload their stored data (bursts) at the sink station before losing again the connection. Such sudden dynamic and bursty traffic cause certain anomalies in the network and fuel the research community to find appropriate solutions.

MobiCom'15, September 7–11, 2015, Paris, France.
ACM ISBN 978-1-4503-3619-2/15/09.
DOI: http://dx.doi.org/10.1145/2789168.2789184.

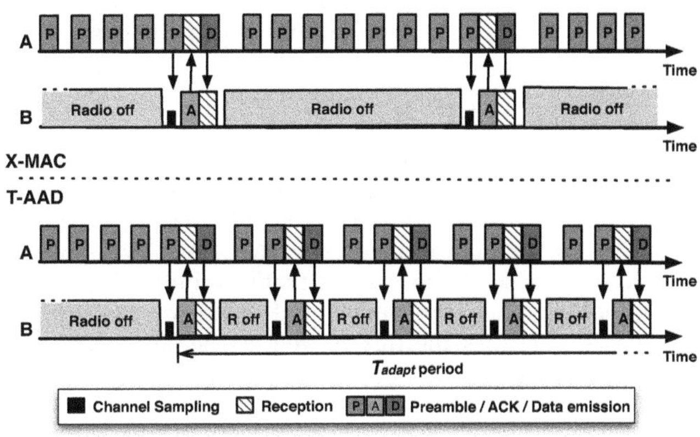

Figure 1: Enhancements introduced by the T-AAD protocol over the statically configured X-MAC protocol.

The Medium Access Control (MAC) layer manages the communications between two nodes. In WSN, it is also responsible for switching the radio device *ON* and *OFF* at regular intervals. This duty-cycling functionality results in a fundamental trade-off between energy consumption and network performance (e.g. latency). Numerous MAC protocols have been devised [2], but to the best of our knowledge very few of them address the needs implied by the presence of variable traffic in the network. Hence, no successful runtime auto-adaptation to the traffic load has ever been experienced in any WSN deployment.

In this demonstration, we consider preamble-sampling family of MAC protocols [2] mainly because they are scalable (e.g. local decisions) and robust to network changes (e.g. mobility). In these protocols, nodes in the network asynchronously check the radio channel for incoming packets at regular intervals. In between, they turn *OFF* their radio to save energy. The period between two channel samplings is referred to as the Sleeping Time (i.e. ST). Then, a node expecting to transmit a data packet will have to send beforehand strobe packets for a preamble period longer than the ST, to ensure that its target is awakened. While a longer ST allows nodes to save energy, it reduces the amount of traffic they can handle. Conversely, a shorter ST allows nodes to handle more traffic, at the cost of increased energy consumption. Figure 1 (upper chronogramme) illustrates the functionality of the well-known X-MAC protocol [1].

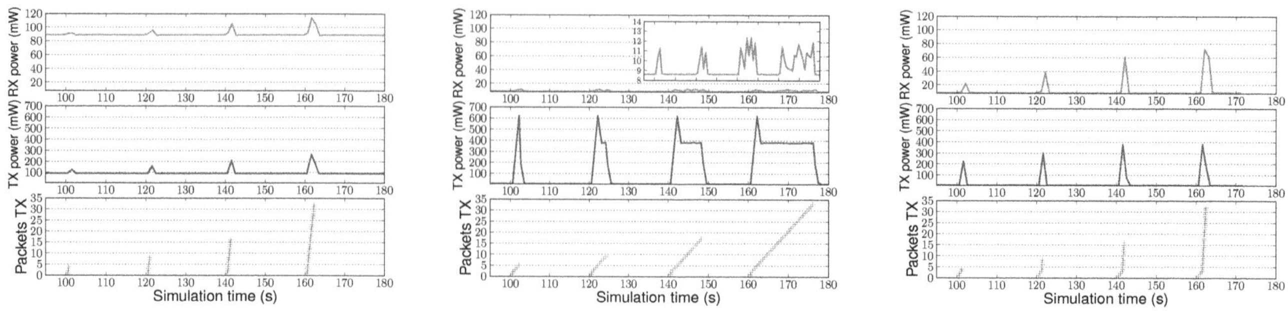

(a) X-MAC with 32 ms duty-cycle. (b) X-MAC with 500 ms duty-cycle. (c) T-AAD.

Figure 2: The energy consumption (both at sender and receiver sides) and delay performance for two TelosB motes testbed for T-AAD and X-MAC with 32 ms and 500 ms duty cycle respectively.

2. T-AAD DESIGN

In this paper we briefly describe T-AAD, a lightweight traffic auto-adaptive mechanism for WSNs addressing dynamic and bursty traffic [4]. T-AAD anticipates traffic load variations by tuning automatically the MAC layer parameters according to the upcoming traffic volume of the concerned nodes. Thus, by employing T-AAD, we can observe the increase network lifetime as well as the decrease of the end-to-end latency.

2.1 T-AAD in a Nutshell

In T-AAD a receiving node switches from long to short ST mode for the period of traffic variation, and then back to the long mode. Thus, the node adopts a short ST configuration for a certain time in order to quickly handle a high traffic load, and then it switches back to long ST during periods of sporadic traffic, thus maintaining a low-power MAC configuration. In order to achieve it, one piece of information is included in each packet. This allows the indication of the number of packets that a node expects to transmit in a row. This value is used to calculate the period of time (here referred as T_{adapt}) during which the receiving node stays in short ST mode.

Two nodes (A and B) are to handle a bursty traffic. Node B is receiving from A and should be allowed to sample the medium more often in order to cope with incoming bursty traffic. This way, both the A and B nodes will be able to handle the traffic variation quickly (i.e. decreasing the delay while increasing the throughput) and in an energy efficient fashion (i.e. extending the battery lifetime). Figure 1 illustrates X-MAC protocol, without and with the T-AAD enhancements.

2.2 Implementation of T-AAD & initial results

Note that the mechanism presented in this demonstration can be applied on top of various asynchronous preamble-sampling protocols. Our initial scenario involves two nodes, where a transmitter node periodically sends from 4, 8, 16 to 32 packets in burst to a single receiver in order to avoid contention and competition for the radio medium. This way, we aim at obtaining accurate results both for senders and receivers behavior. Regarding the MAC settings, we kept the standard format with ST of 32 and 500 ms (i.e. X-MAC32 and X-MAC500 respectively). We run number of experiments with TelosB motes for pre-configured X-MAC32 and X-MAC500, and we compared them with T-AAD.

Figure 3: A view of ICube's platform.

Figure 2 illustrates the evaluation for energy consumption and latency, for each case of study. The two upper subplots of each figure represent the energy consumption for receiver and transmitter node respectively while bottom subplot represents the delay performance (i.e. packet transmission on time). As can be observed, the transmitter operating with X-MAC500 consumes the most energy (see Figure 2b), since long preamble of half second has to be transmitted first before sending the actual data packet. On the opposite, at the receiver side, a node configured to sample the medium more frequently (i.e. every 32 ms), will consume more. Conversely, T-AAD allows to consume less energy, and both at receiver and transmitter side, since both nodes consume less than any X-MAC setup, (c.f. very short peaks, see Figure 2c). Furthermore, T-AAD achieves to reduce the delay performance significantly, similar to X-MAC32. This phenomenon is due to both a better handling of messages during periods of high traffic load, and to lower sampling frequencies during calm periods in the network.

Based on these promising results of two nodes, we expect attendees to experience the functionality and consequently the gain of T-AAD protocol over a large scale network (i.e. several dozen of nodes) and in multi-hop manner.

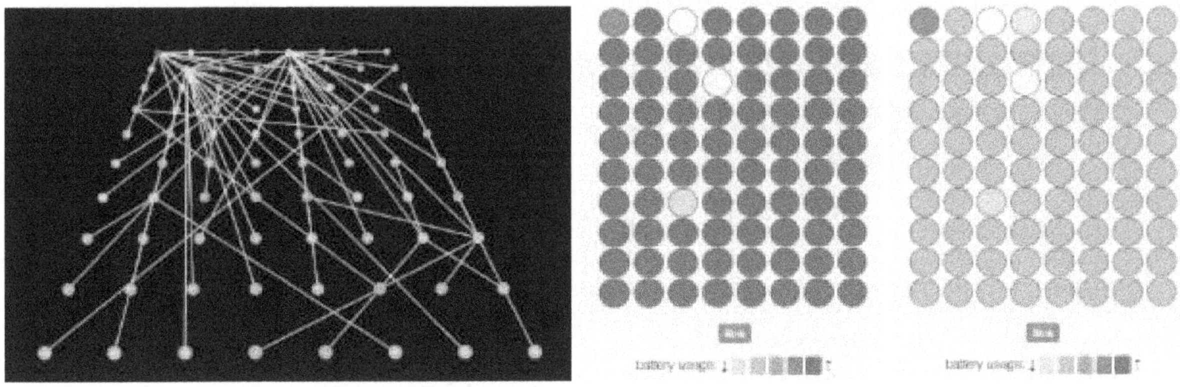

(a) Routing construction (i.e. gradient).

(b) X-MAC: statically configured network.

(c) T-AAD: runtime auto-adaptive network.

Figure 4: Real-time gradient construction (a) and induced energy consumption (b, c).

3. PLATFORM ARCHITECTURE

In our demonstration, we utilized the platform installed in the University of Strasbourg (i.e. ICube's platform). The platform contains 256 WSN430, 120 M3 and 24 A8 nodes, and is structured in a 3D grid. The nodes are distributed in 3 layers (see Figure 3). ICube's platform is part of the open and large scale FIT IoT-LAB [5] testbed which is composed of 2728 wireless sensor nodes distributed over six different sites in France, Inria Grenoble (928), Inria Lille (640), ICube Strasbourg (400), Inria Rocquencourt (344), Inria Rennes (256) and Mines-Telecom Paris (160).

4. DEMO DESCRIPTION

At MobiCom, we will allow attendees to generate events and traffic on 160 remote nodes in two distinct layers (80 nodes each) deployed in Strasbourg's platform. In the upper layer, nodes will be configured with static X-MAC protocol while T-AAD will be employed in the second one. More specifically, the X-MAC we be configured with the standard settings (i.e. ST of 32 and 500 *ms*), while T-AAD topology will allow live adaptations according to the traffic load changes induced by attendees. Furthermore, viewers will also be able to have a live video feedback from the platform, thus getting a realtime overview of the deployed running nodes. They will also observe the resulting configurations after their events and will be able to compare live energy consumption and delays that are induced. The demonstration scenario is shown in Figure 4. In particular, at first, we will present the routing construction among the sensor nodes (Figure 4a), and later we will focus on live visualization of traffic auto-adaptations and significant gains in terms of latency and energy consumption, when compared against statically configured network.

5. FACILITY REQUIREMENTS

Our facility requirements can be listed as follows.

- **Equipment requirement:** A large screen is needed to display the remotely connected demonstration. Moreover, two stands for background posters will be appreciated.
- **Internet requirement and power supply:** For the demonstration, Wi-Fi connection with SSH access will be required. The power plug is needed for the laptop and screen.
- **Space requirement:** There is no special requirements for the exhibition space. A typical desk or table will work, where the screen and a laptop will be placed.

6. REFERENCES

[1] M. Buettner, G. V. Yee, E. Anderson, and R. Han. X-MAC: A Short Preamble MAC Protocol for Duty-Cycled Wireless Sensor Networks. In *Proceedings of the 4th ACM Conference on Embedded Networked Sensor Systems (Sensys)*, pages 307–320, 2006.

[2] C. Cano, B. Bellalta, A. Sfairopoulou, and M. Oliver. Low energy operation in WSNs: A survey of preamble sampling MAC protocols. *Computer Networks*, 55(15):3351–3363, 2011.

[3] C. Merlin and W. Heinzelman. Duty Cycle Control for Low-Power-Listening MAC Protocols. *IEEE Transactions on Mobile Computing*, 9(11):1508 –1521, 2010.

[4] G. Z. Papadopoulos, J. Beaudaux, A. Gallais, and T. Noel. T-AAD: Lightweight Traffic Auto-ADaptations for Low-power MAC Protocols. In *Proceedings of the 13th IEEE IFIP Annual Mediterranean Ad Hoc Networking Workshop (MED-HOC-NET)*, pages 79–86, 2014.

[5] G. Z. Papadopoulos, J. Beaudaux, A. Gallais, T. Noel, and G. Schreiner. Adding value to WSN simulation using the IoT-LAB experimental platform. In *Proceedings of the 9th IEEE International Conference on Wireless and Mobile Computing, Networking and Communications (WiMob)*, pages 485–490, 2013.

Demo: Implementation of Real-time WiFi Receiver in Ziria, Language for Rapid Prototyping of Wireless PHY

Gordon Stewart [1]
Ohio University
gstewart@ohio.edu

Mahanth Gowda [1]
UIUC
gowda2@illinois.edu

Geoffrey Mainland [2]
Drexel
mainland@cs.drexel.edu

Božidar Radunović
Microsoft Research
bozidar@microsoft.com

Dimitrios Vytiniotis
Microsoft Research
dimitris@microsoft.com

ABSTRACT

Software-defined radios (SDR) have the potential to bring major innovation in wireless networking design. However, their impact so far has been limited due to complex programming tools. Most of the existing tools are either too slow to achieve the full line speeds of contemporary wireless PHYs or are too complex to master. In this demo we present our novel SDR programming environment called Ziria. Ziria consists of a novel programming language and an optimizing compiler. The compiler is able to synthesize very efficient SDR code from high-level PHY descriptions written in Ziria language. To illustrate its potential, we present the design of an LTE-like PHY layer in Ziria. We run it on the Sora SDR platform and demonstrate on a test-bed that it is able to operate in real-time.

1. INTRODUCTION

The past few years have witnessed tremendous innovation in the design and implementation of wireless protocols, both in industry and academia ([8, 5, 3]). Much of the work has occurred at the physical (PHY) layer of the protocol stack, which manages the translation between radio hardware signals and protocol packets. The numerous new signal processing algorithms and novel coding schemes that have resulted—many of which were first implemented using software-defined radio (SDR) platforms—have greatly increased the efficiency of existing radio communication channels.

However, SDRs have not yet reached the mainstream of wireless research. The main impediment is implementation complexity. Wireless PHY algorithms have to be very fast and efficient to meet line rate requirements. Software has to process tens of millions of complex samples per second, which is equivalent to a processing rate of close to a gigabit per second. To cope with these speeds a programmer has to have a good understanding of the underlying SDR hardware architecture and the effects of her design choices on performance.

[1]This work was done during an internship with Microsoft Research.

[2]Part of the work was done while the author was with Microsoft Research.

MobiCom'15, September 7–11, 2015, Paris, France.
ACM. ISBN 978-1-4503-3619-2/15/09
DOI: http://dx.doi.org/10.1145/2789168.2789185.

In order to design wireless algorithms, an SDR programmer has to have a profound understanding of signal processing and wireless networking, and in order to efficiently implement them she has to be an expert in computer architecture and system design. An average graduate student finds it quite hard to master all these areas, which is why only very few research groups have found enough resources to pursue this line of research.

To illustrate this complexity we consider two popular SDR designs. The first example is FPGA-based platforms, such as Warp [6] and Lyrtech [7]. A typical state-of-the-art SDR programming tool for FPGA platforms is based on Matlab, Simulink and an FPGA compiler. One of the main benefits of this environment is a rich set of DSP bulding blocks (such as basic fixed-point arithmetics, FFT, encoders, decoders, etc.). Further, being integrated in Matlab, this environment provides a programmer with powerful tools for debugging input and output signals, and for simulating different real-world effects using readily available libraries. However, the programming model is essentially the same as hardware design in VHDL or Verilog. A programmer has to have a fundamental understanding of how FPGAs operate. She has to be aware of different propagation delays and their effects on the system performance. One misplaced delay element can easily lead to a week of debugging!

Recently, several SDR platforms, such as GnuRadio [4] and Sora [10], allow programmers to design SDR code on general-purpose CPU processors. The hardware part of the platform performs analog-to-digital and digital-to-analog conversion of the baseband signals and supplies these signals to a CPU, where a programmer can further process it as desired.

Signal processing on a CPU provides great flexibility and permits rapid experimentation, but often at the price of decreased performance. Writing fast, real-time PHY code on a CPU can be equally, if not more complex than programming FPGAs. In fact, most of the recent academic works on SDR do not even attempt to process signals in real-time. They only use SDR platforms to capture signals. Post-processing is later done offline at much smaller processing rates than required by PHY. This approach clearly precludes any real-world networking experiments on SDR platforms.

One of the first CPU-based SDR platforms that has managed to process wireless baseband signals at a line rate is Sora [10]. It has demonstrated interoperability with commodity WiFi cards. But this performance comes with increased complexity. The code for Sora has to be written in C/C++ and a programmer needs to manually optimize the code to achieve the required speeds. The Sora project has put substantial effort into designing a C++ template library that eases the programming pain. However, the use of templates imposes several limitations, in particular on state sharing and dynamic reconfigurability of the dataflow graphs. It is worth noting that GnuRadio has a similar architecture based on C++ templates and similar limitations. We next overview the architecture of Ziria and we explain how it addresses these issues.

2. ZIRIA

Ziria is a new wireless programming platform [9]. It consists of the Ziria language and an optimizing compiler. Ziria has a 2-layer design. The lower layer is an imperative language. It can be seen as a mix of C and Matlab code, with features of the two selectively choosen to guarantee efficient compilation. The higher layer is the language used to specify and stage stream processors.

The Ziria optimizing compiler consists of two parts. It has a front-end which parses a Ziria program and stores it in an abstract representation, and then performs several optimization passes on it. It also has a back-end which compiles the optimized abstract representation into a low-level execution model optimized for a target architecture. Our current back-end targets a low-level execution model in C for the Sora SDR platform, but it can easily be extended to other platforms, such as GnuRadio.

There are several benefits of this approach when compared to the existing approaches:

- *Dynamic staging of the control graph:* Ziria language for staging data flows allows for a dynamic reconfiguration of the control graph. This reconfiguration is very flexible, so for example a downstream component can reconfigure an upstream component or any other part of the graphs (for example using parameter passing and the repeat construct). This is in contrast with Sora and GnuRadio C++ templates that allow limited downstream reconfigurability using the multiplexing block.

- *No need for shared state:* Ziria dynamic reconfigurability and parameter passing between blocks eliminate the need for share states. Instead, a state is passed explicitly between components and all the dependencies are checked at the compile time. This is in contrast with Sora and GnuRadio which heavily rely on shared states. One example of a negative consequence is that an unitialized state cannot be detected by the compiler and causes program misbehaviour.

- *Code optimization:* Ziria compiler's optimization phase can optimize jointly the imperative part of the language and the data-flow graph. It can merge data-flow blocks, change input and output widths, inline expressions and unroll loops. One example of a useful code optimization are look-up tables. Ziria compiler can automatically identify blocks of code that operate on small bit inputs (e.g. scrambler and encoder) and convert them into lookup tables, which execute much faster on a CPU than bit operations. All this is in contrast to Sora and GnuRadio C++ template libraries where C compiler does not have an explicit understanding of the control flow graph and can perform far fewer optimizations. Lookup tables have to be implemented and tuned manually.

Overall, Ziria code is much more concise. For example, an implementation of a WiFi scrambler in Sora takes 90 lines of C++ code. The same code can be implemented in Ziria in 13 lines. It is easier to understand and has very similar performance to the hand-tuned Sora code.

3. DEMO DESCRIPTION

In the demo we present a Ziria implementation of standard compliant 802.11g packet sniffer. We will connect a bladeRF [1], a $400 small-form-factor USB board to a laptop. We will set up an off-the-shelf 802.11g access point and we will use another commodity device to connect to that access point. We will display packets being transmitted to establish this connection in real-time on the laptop with bladeRF running the sniffer. All sniffer code is developed entirely in Ziria and a real-time WiFi packet reception is a proof-of-concept of the real-time performance of Ziria.

Ziria is released as an open-source project. Further information about the project as well as a link to the code, examples and documentation can be found on [2].

4. REFERENCES

[1] bladerf. `https://www.nuand.com/`.

[2] Ziria. `http://research.microsoft.com/en-us/projects/ziria/`.

[3] T. Bansal et al. Symphony: Cooperative packet recovery over the wired backbone in enterprise WLANs. In *MOBICOM*, 2013.

[4] E. Blossom. GNURadio: tools for exploring the radio frequency spectrum. *Linux Journal*, 2004(122):4, 2004.

[5] T. Li et al. CRMA: Collision-resistant multiple access. In *MOBICOM*, 2011.

[6] P. Murphy, A. Sabharwal, and B. Aazhang. Design of WARP: a wireless open-access research platform. In *ESPC*, 2006.

[7] Nutaq. Zeptosdr. `http://nutaq.com/en/products/zeptosdr`.

[8] S. Sen, R. R. Choudhury, and S. Nelakuditi. No time to countdown: Migrating backoff to the frequency domain. In *MOBICOM*, 2011.

[9] G. e. a. Stewart. Ziria: A dsl for wireless systems programming. In *ASPLOS*, 2015.

[10] K. Tan et al. Sora: High performance software radio using general purpose multi-core processors, 2009.

Poster: Mobile Data Offloading Testbed

Matteo Pozza
Department of Mathematics
University of Padua
Padua, Italy
matteo.pozza
@studenti.unipd.it

Claudio Enrico Palazzi
Department of Mathematics
University of Padua
Padua, Italy
cpalazzi
@math.unipd.it

Armir Bujari
Department of Mathematics
University of Padua
Padua, Italy
abujari
@math.unipd.it

ABSTRACT

Recent research has proposed swarming protocols as a possible approach to offload the Internet infrastructure when some content can be shared by several users. However, simulations have been generally used as experimental means. Instead, we present an application platform that allows a rapid development and testing of swarming protocols using off-the-shelf smartphones.

Categories and Subject Descriptors

C.2.1 [**Computer-Communication Networks**]: Network Architecture—*wireless communication*

Keywords

Data offload; mobile; testbed; wireless

1. INTRODUCTION

Mobile data traffic is exponentially growing, thus posing a major burden on network providers, causing traffic overload problems and a degraded network service [1, 2, 3]. In-network solutions addressing this phenomenon have been proposed, spanning from the deployment of specialized infrastructure to intelligent software solutions [4, 5, 6]. However, evidence shows this is not sufficient and additional means are required.

In this context, swarming protocols represent a promising approach addressing the issue by engaging a lower number of direct connections with the network hosted server(s), while the requesters share the content among them. Unfortunately, simulations have been the sole means of study so far [7, 8]; instead, while they embody a simple and useful first step, nothing beats real experiments with protocols and devices in showing the actual outcome of a new technology.

Filling this gap, we propose and discuss here a mobile application that allows a rapid development and testing of mobile data offloading techniques, such as swarming protocols, using off-the-shelf smartphones. We consider a general scenario with a network hosted server and a set of clients requesting a certain content from it. A single client downloads a certain content directly from the server, while applying a swarming approach to spread it among the other clients, thus reducing the the need for Internet connectivity.

MobiCom'15, September 07-11, 2015, Paris, France
ACM 978-1-4503-3619-2/15/09.
http://dx.doi.org/10.1145/2789168.2795159

2. OUR SOLUTION

Our solution allows to test classic swarming approaches, considering both a *star* (or centralized) sharing scheme (Figure 1a) and a *waterfall* (or distributed) sharing scheme (Figure 1b). Through the former, the single client retrieving the content from the server (A) also acts as resource provider for all the other clients (B, C, D and E). In the second approach, the single client downloading the content from the server (A) forwards it only to one other client (B), which does the same in turn for another client (C), and so on till the last node in the "chain" (E).

The main aim of our solution is measuring the performance of networks based on swarming protocols; to do so, it handles two distinct flows of data, the incoming flow and the outgoing one. The first one consists in the data flow going from a certain source (i.e., the server or another client) to the considered device, while the second one is the data flow departing from the considered device and reaching one or more destinations. Several measurements are performed on each of these flows; they include the instantaneous data rate, the average data rate, the standard deviation of the data rate and the total transfer time. These measurements are both shown on screen and stored into log files.

Our solution runs on Android 4.0 (API level 14) or later versions. Even if some previous version of Android may not support the Wi-Fi Direct protocol, the Android Developer wiki reports that our choice includes more than 90% of active Android devices. The Android framework is sufficient to provide for all the needs of the application, including the communication through Bluetooth and Wi-Fi Direct.

3. EXPERIMENTAL ASSESSMENT

We have tested our application on Samsung Galaxy Nexus GT-i9250 devices and consider 4 combinations of the following configuration parameters:

- Sharing schemes: {star, waterfall}.
- Wireless technologies: {Bluetooth v3.0, Wi-Fi Direct}.

All the configurations have been tested using 5 smartphones, as a representative case, as shown in Figure 1a and 1b.

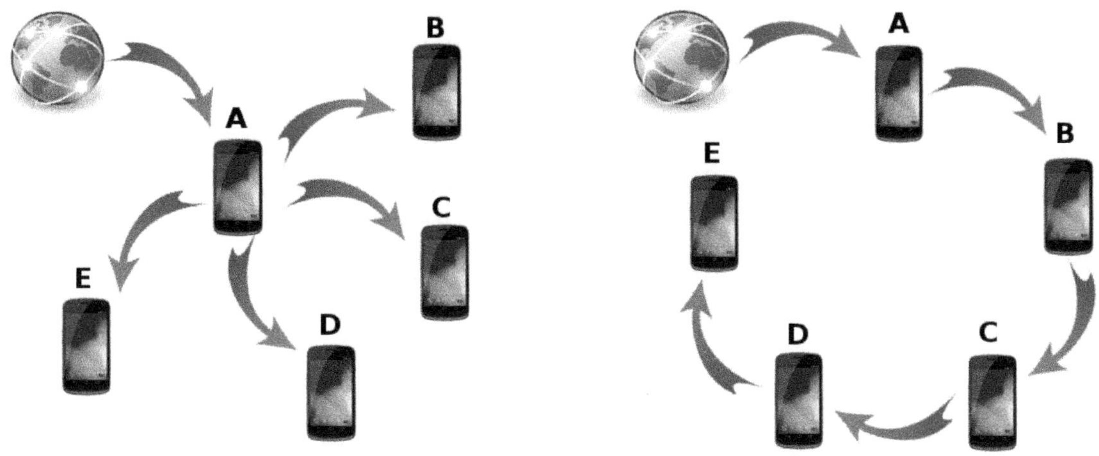

(a) Star

(b) Waterfall

Figure 1: Classic swarming approaches

For each configuration, we have considered the averaged outcome of 20 tests where a 10 MB file had to be distributed to all the considered devices. In each test we periodically gathered samples of the download progression by each device. In summary, we gathered 10 samples for each download, the first one when 10% of the resource has been received, the second one at 20%, and so on. Each sample includes the following data:

- the instantaneous data rate;
- the total average data rate;
- the standard deviation of the data rate;
- the time elapsed from the beginning of the sharing.

We have tested representative energetic profiles corresponding to a combination of different energy consumption sources, like the usage of the Wi-Fi connection and the number of communications performed with other devices. In particular, we have focused on the device which downloads the resource from the server: in fact it is the device which has to perform the most energy-consuming tasks since it has both to download the resource and transmit it toward a certain number of other devices. Therefore, it is important to understand how much these tasks impact on the battery life of the device involved.

To measure the battery consumption, we have used *PowerMonitor*, a tool for precise measurements on energy consumption [9].

In order to better understand the measured energy consumption, a baseline profile value is needed. Our baseline configuration consists in the following elements:

- the brightness of the screen has been set to the maximum value;
- the background of the device has been set with a custom defined image [1];
- all the communication devices (Wi-Fi, 3G/HSDPA, Bluetooth, NFC) have been switched off;
- no application is active in background;
- the energy consumption is considered as the power consumption after 10 minutes of inactivity.

The average power consumption value obtained has been compared with the results obtained from the analysis of the energetic profiles in order to understand how much the energy consumption required deviates from the one requested by a phone in stand-by.

4. EXPERIMENTAL RESULTS

Looking at Figure 2, we can see that there is no great difference between the performances of the two sharing schemes

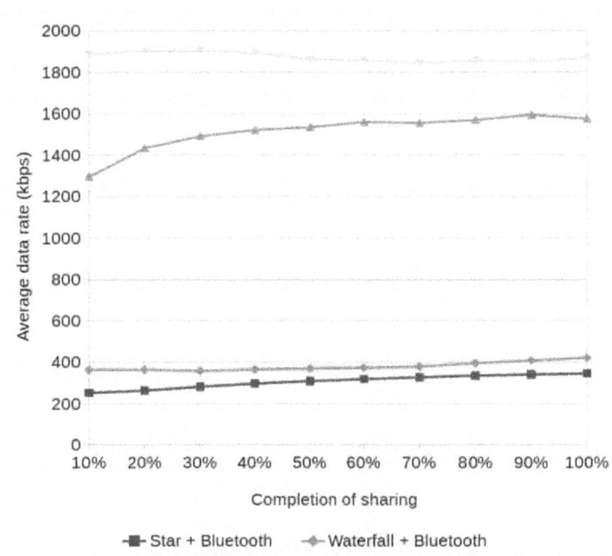

Figure 2: Data rate comparison

[1]Solid color background, Hue: 0, Saturation: 5, Value: 33, Red: 85, Green: 81, Blue: 81, HTML code: 555151.

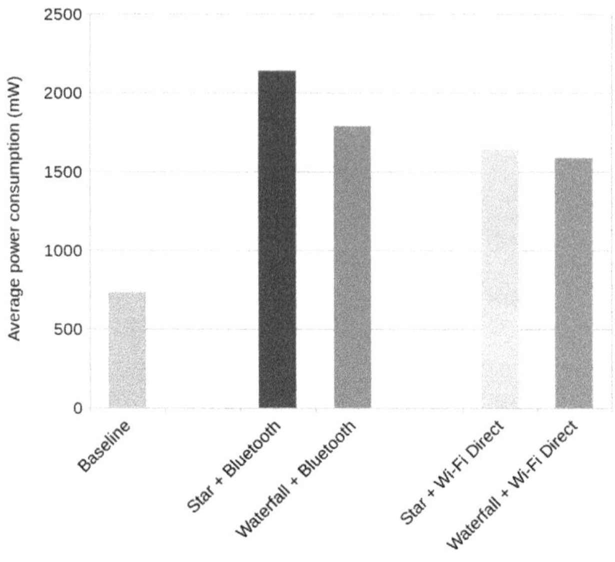

Figure 3: Energetic measurements regarding the device retrieving the resource from the Internet

using Bluetooth technology, even if the waterfall scheme behaves slightly better than the competitor. Instead, the star sharing scheme outperforms the waterfall one when using Wi-Fi Direct technology to spread the file among the involved devices.

This is because Wi-Fi Direct relies on IEEE 802.11 MAC, which uses CSMA/CA to regulate the access to the medium. With a star sharing scheme, it is easier to avoid interferences among devices' transmissions as there is only a single device (node A in Figure 1a) transmitting data to all the others. Instead, in a waterfall configuration, the attempt of each device to communicate forwarding data to other nodes can lead to frequent collisions/retransmissions, as well as be subject to the channel capture phenomenon, thus impeding an efficient transmission pipeline.

It is also worth mentioning that Bluetooth uses time division multiplexing to efficiently avoid interferences. This works even in a scatternet such as the network configuration corresponding to the waterfall sharing scheme, thus allowing actual pipelining. Instead, in a star configuration the client acting as the server simply transmits data in a specific order to the connected clients.

The charts in Figure 3 show the energy measurements collected on the "resource provider" node, which corresponds to the device A in both Figure 1a and 1b. The leftmost (cyan) column represents the baseline profile, while the other columns correspond to the same configurations previously analyzed from the data rate point of view.

As it is evident, Bluetooth configurations present significant differences in energy consumption, whereas Wi-Fi Direct ones are more homogeneous. Furthermore, nodes with less destinations to serve experience less energy consumption: in fact, the star sharing scheme requires more energy than the waterfall one regardless the employed transmission technology.

Unexpectedly, Wi-Fi Direct profiles show lower battery consumptions than Bluetooth ones in all comparisons. This interesting result is due to the Bluetooth design as a cable replacement conceived for short and relatively rare transmissions of a few bytes, while Wi-Fi Direct inherits the Wi-Fi standard properties devoted to big and relatively fast data transmissions. Therefore, the experiment did not use Bluetooth in its classic, designed-for way but rather intensively and for long periods.

5. CONCLUSION

We have analyzed different swarming techniques combined with wireless technologies available on off-the-shelf smartphones in order to partially offload Internet traffic on the clients. We have shown that the two proposed sharing schemes behaves differently depending on the wireless technology adopted. Finally, we have seen how in the considered scenario Wi-Fi Direct offers a higher data rate at a lower energy cost than Bluetooth: for these motivations, it seems the most suitable technology for swarming protocols enforcement.

6. REFERENCES

[1] Cisco VNI - Cisco Visual Networking Index: Global Mobile Data Traffic Forecast Update, 2013–2018.

[2] M. Pozza, C.E. Palazzi, A. Bujari, BlueFall: Testing Swarming Protocols through Mobile Phones. In Proc. of *International Conference on Computing, Networking and Communications (ICNC)*. February 2015.

[3] C.E. Palazzi, S. Ferretti, M. Roccetti, G. Pau, M. Gerla, What's in that magic box? The home entertainment center's special protocol potion, revealed IEEE Transactions on Consumer Electronics, vol.52, no.4, pp.1280-1288, Novemeber 2006.

[4] C.E. Palazzi, A. Bujari, G. Marfia, M. Roccetti An Overview of Opportunistic Ad Hoc Communication in Urban Scenarios. In Proc. of the *Annual Mediterranean Ad Hoc Networking Workshop (MED-HOC-NET)*. June 2014.

[5] D. Calin, H. Claussen, H. Uzunalioglu, On femto deployment architectures and macrocell offloading benefits in joint macro-femto deployments. IEEE Communications Magazine, vol.48, no.1, pp.26,32, January 2010.

[6] M. Anas, C. Rosa, F.D. Calabrese, K.I. Pedersen, P.E. Mogensen. Combined Admission Control and Scheduling for QoS Differentiation in LTE Uplink. in Proc. of *IEEE Vehicular Technology Conference (VTC 2008-Fall)*. September 2008.

[7] A. Nandan, S. Das, G. Pau, M.Y. Sanadidi, M. Gerla, Cooperative Downloading in Vehicular Ad Hoc Wireless Networks. In Proc. of *IEEE/IFIP International Conference on Wireless On demand Network Systems and Services (WONS '05)*. January 2005.

[8] U. Lee, J.S. Park, J. Yeh, G. Pau, M. Gerla, Code Torrent: Content Distribution Using Network Coding in VANET. In Proc. of *International Workshop on Decentralized Resource Sharing in Mobile Computing and Networking (MobiShare '06)*. September 2006.

[9] Monsoon Solutions Inc - PowerMonitor: https://www.msoon.com/LabEquipment/PowerMonitor/.

Poster: Can Smart Devices Protect Us from Violent Crime?

Alan Ferrari, Daniele Puccinelli, and Silvia Giordano
Networking Laboratory
University of Applied Sciences of Southern Switzerland
(SUPSI)
Manno, Switzerland
firstName.lastName@supsi.ch

ABSTRACT

To explore the applicability of mobile smart devices to personal protection against violent crime, we propose a system that can detect the onset of hazardous situations involving violent crime by leveraging standard activity recognition strategies on smartphones and sensory inputs from wearable devices, as well as send help requests to alert the authorities.

Keywords

activity recognition; smartwatch; personal security.

1. INTRODUCTION

In 2013, over a million violent crimes were reported in the United States [1], including murder and non-negligent manslaughter, rape, robbery, and aggravated assault. At the time of writing, no off-the-shelf solution can automatically detect the onset of such crimes and automatically send alerts to the authorities. A rich body of work exists in the activity recognition space. We argue that existing activity recognition solutions can be used to detect hazardous situations with wearable devices such as smartwatches.

The goal of the following paper is to leverage the current state of the art in activity recognition to detect the onset of hazardous situations with personal mobile devices (smartphones and wearables) and automatically ask for help. After reviewing the related work, we will delve into the system details and we will conclude with an overview of the future work that we are currently developing.

2. RELATED WORK

Activity recognition is a widely studied research area in the field of ubiquitous computing. Recently, the emergence of mobile and wearable devices have paved the way to a set of new applications that exploit context-awareness in order to gain a more dynamic and less intrusive interaction with their users.

MobiCom'15, September 7–11, 2015, Paris, France.
ACM. ISBN 978-1-4503-3619-2/15/09
DOI: http://dx.doi.org/10.1145/2789168.2795160.

Dey and Abowd [2] define a system as **context-aware** if it uses context to provide relevant information and/or services to the user, where relevancy depends on the user's task. Activity recognition can be viewed as a subset of context information. An early notable contribution in this space was provided by Ravi et. al. [2], who used a homemade board and an iPAQ Palm device to collect information. They recorded a dataset that contains seven different activities (ranging from walking to brushing teeth) and on two subjects on multiple days. The authors use a set of different classifiers (from NaïveBayes to Hidden Markov Model) to estimate the corresponding activity and they achieved a reasonably high accuracy using a single triaxial accelerometer; however, they noted that it is hard to recognize activities involving hand movements (i.e. brushing teeth).

Today's personal smart devices offer a set of internal sensors (such as accelerometers, gyroscopes, and even pressure sensors) that have been utlized in a large body of work in recent years. One of the first activity recognition efforts with personal smart devices was proposed by Kwapisz et. al. [3]; the authors use a gyroscope on an Android-based smartphone and recorded a set of six activities (walking, jogging, ascending stairs, descending stairs, sitting, and standing) carried out by 29 participants. They used decision trees (J48), logistic regression, and multilayer neural networks to classify human activities with over 90% accuracy. Various recent efforts use Hidden Markov Model as their main classification method [4]. Others are experimenting with different kind of sensors; for instance, Vanini et. al. [5] present a technique based on barometric pressures mixed with Long Short Term Memory neural networks [6] and studied a dataset of six different activities, achieving over 95% accuracy.

Despite the huge amount of academic literature, activity recognition is still far from a mainstream commodity. We are now witnessing the uptake of wearable devices, such as smartwatches [7], which are also sensor-rich; currently available models, for istance, can measure acceleration and heartbeat and feature microphones. Recently, there have been efforts to device activity recognition applications for smartwatches, such as the work of Bernaerts et al. [8]) on using smartwatches to streamline human interaction in office settings.

The following propose proposes to leverage the uptake of wearables and the rich body of work on activity recognition to detect when a user is in danger and, if applicable, to ask for help automatically.

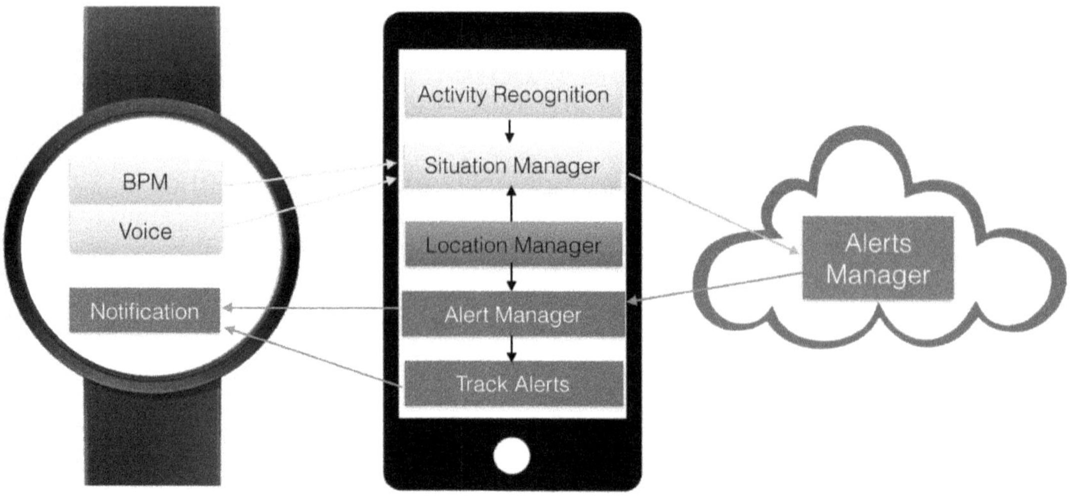

Figure 1: Rational of the system where gray boxes and arrows indicate the detect of the situation the red arrows and boxes indicate the alerting system.

3. SYSTEM ARCHITECTURE

The system includes three components: a wearable device (typically, a smartwatch), a smartphone, and a cloud server; a dedicated application runs on each component. In this section, we outline our experimental implementation of the system. As illustrated in Figure 1, the system performs two main activities:

- it detects the *onset of a danger situation*;
- it sends out a *help request* with the user's location to a cloud server, which can forward it to a predefined list of addressees (such as the local law enforcement authorities).

3.1 Danger onset detection

Different sources of information are combined to detect the onset of a danger situation:

- a location manager, implemented in the smartphone;
- an activity recognition engine, implemented in the smartphone;
- a heart rate estimate provided by the wearable device;
- a voice recognition engine, implemented in the wearable device.

The location manager is based on Android's LocationManager component. If desired, the system can leverage the location manager to dynamically self-configure (or be pre-configured by the user) to be active only when the user is in sensitive locations and/or at certain times of day, based on crime statistics. The user may also elect to disable the system over a desired time frame. Otherwise, the system starts off in the *armed* state.

When the system is in the *armed* state, the activity recognition engine employs a combination of strategies to infer the activity performed by the user, with the goal of determining whether the user is walking. At the same time the Location Manager starts detecting the current location such that the data are immediately available in the *alarm* state.

If the user is determined not to be walking, a heart rate estimate is obtained from the wearable device. A heart rate estimate is also obtained periodically from the wearable device to establish a baseline for the user. If the current heart rate estimate is found to differ significantly from the baseline, the system transitions into a *pre-alarm* state.

The system minimizes the communication between the smartphone and smartwatch to preserve the battery lifetime of both devices. Therefore, the heartbeat baseline is only stored locally on the smartwatch, and a message signaling an abormal heart rate is only transmitted by the smartwatch to the smartphone in the *pre-alarm* state.

The system transitions from the *pre-alarm* state to the *alarm* state if a confirmation message spoken by the user is detected by the voice recognition engine (turned on as the *pre-alarm* state is entered). The confirmation message must match a passphrase chosen and pre-recorded by the user.

This approach is designed to minimize the false alarm rate; as part of our future work, we plan to test our system in real-world settings to verify whether this approach is viable; alternative approaches will be designed based on our real-world experiments (which we plan to carry out in collaboration with a local law enforcement agency).

3.2 Help requests

There are several possible ways to send out help requests. In our current implementation, we use a push service running in a cloud server (we use SWITCHEn- gines[9], which provides provides computing and storage services to Swiss academic institutions). Help requests are automatically geotagged and forwarded to a pre-defined contact list (including law enforcement agencies) as well as to any personal mobile device running our application located within a certain distance. It is also possible to send e-mails and/or SMSs to a predefined contact list.

4. IMPLEMENTATION DETAILS

We have implemented the system ind Android [10] and Android Wear [10]. We used Long Short Term Memory (LSTM)[6] neural network as inference mechanism. LSTM is a recurrent neural network that can remember an arbitrary value for a length of time. The LSTM has been compared to traditional RNN and Hidden Markov Model and outperforms them in numerous applications (e.g. unsegmented connected handwriting recognition, speech recognition, ...). We train the system offline using a set of different activities following the set provided in Android's Activity Recognition service (in vehicle, on bicycle, on foot, tilting, still, running, walking).

We test the system in two devices. Moto X[1] as smartphone and Moto 360 [2]as smartwatch, which estimates the user's hear trate based on photoplethysmography (PPG). Because we cannot physically recreate an authentic danger situation, we use mocking techniques [11] to send fake data to the smartwatch and to the smartphone to simulate an act of violence.

5. CONCLUSION AND FUTURE WORK

This work has described the architecture of a system able to to detect the onset of dangerous situations. We are currently working on testing the system. We will compare LSTM with other strategies for activity recognition (namely back-propagation neural network, Hidden Markov model, and the Android's Activity Recognition service). As part of our future work, we plan to collaborate with a local law enforcement agency to run real-world experiments and collect a credible dataset to iteratively refine and evaluate our system design. Moreover, to augment the accuracy and reduce the energy consumption of the localization process we plan to study and implement new solutions (e.g. ELS from Papandrea et. al[12]).

Acknowledgements

This work was supported by the EU FP7 ERANET program under grant CHIST-ERA-2012 MACACO.

6. REFERENCES

[1] FBI Violent Crime stats. http://www.fbi.gov, March 2015.

[2] Gregory D Abowd, Anind K Dey, Peter J Brown, Nigel Davies, Mark Smith, and Pete Steggles. Towards a better understanding of context and context-awareness. In *Handheld and ubiquitous computing*, pages 304–307. Springer, 1999.

[3] Jennifer R Kwapisz, Gary M Weiss, and Samuel A Moore. Activity recognition using cell phone accelerometers. *ACM SigKDD Explorations Newsletter*, 12(2):74–82, 2011.

[4] Zhen Li, Zhiqiang Wei, Yaofeng Yue, Hao Wang, Wenyan Jia, Lora E Burke, Thomas Baranowski, and Mingui Sun. An adaptive hidden markov model for activity recognition based on a wearable multi-sensor device. *Journal of medical systems*, 39(5):1–10, 2015.

[5] Silvia Giordano Salvatore Vanini, Alan Ferrari. Using Barometric Pressure Data for Activity Recognition on Smartphones. In *Under Submission*, 2015.

[6] Sepp Hochreiter and Jürgen Schmidhuber. Long short-term memory. *Neural computation*, 9(8):1735–1780, 1997.

[7] Silvia Giordano and Daniele Puccinelli. When sensing goes pervasive. *Pervasive and Mobile Computing*, 2014.

[8] Yannick Bernaerts, Matthias Druwé, Sebastiaan Steensels, Jo Vermeulen, and Johannes Schöning. The office smartwatch: development and design of a smartwatch app to digitally augment interactions in an office environment. In *Proceedings of the 2014 companion publication on Designing interactive systems*, pages 41–44. ACM, 2014.

[9] SWITCHengines: Dynamic Compute and Storage services for research and education. http://www.switch.ch/engines/, May 2015.

[10] Android Operating System. http://www.android.com, May 2015.

[11] Alan Ferrari, Daniele Puccinelli, and Silvia Giordano. Managing your privacy in mobile applications with mockingbird. In *2015 IEEE International Conference on Pervasive Computing and Communications Work in Progress (WiP?15)*, pages 148–150. IEEE, 2015.

[12] Michela Papandrea and Silvia Giordano. Location prediction and mobility modelling for enhanced localization solution. *Journal of Ambient Intelligence and Humanized Computing*, 5(3):279–295, 2014.

[1]https://www.motorola.com/us/motomaker?pid=FLEXR2
[2]https://moto360.motorola.com

Poster: Privacy-Preserving Server-Driven Dynamic Spectrum Access System

Yanzhi Dou, Kexiong (Curtis) Zeng, and Yaling Yang
Department of Electrical and Computer Engineering
Virginia Tech, Blacksburg, VA, USA
{yzdou, kexiong6, yyang8}@vt.edu

ABSTRACT

Dynamic spectrum access (DSA) technique has been widely accepted as a crucial solution to mitigate the potential spectrum scarcity problem. As a key form of DSA, government is proposing to release more federal spectrum for sharing with commercial wireless users. However, the flourish of federal-commercial sharing hinges upon how privacy issues are managed. In current DSA proposals, the sensitive operation parameters of both federal incumbent users (IUs) and commercial secondary users (SUs) need to be shared with the dynamic spectrum access system (SAS) to realize efficient spectrum allocation. Since SAS is not necessarily operated by a trusted third party, the current proposals dissatisfy the privacy requirement of both IUs and SUs. To address the privacy issues, this paper presents a privacy-preserving SAS design, which realizes the complex spectrum allocation decision process of DSA through secure computation over ciphertext based on homomorphic encryption, thus none of the IU or SU operation parameters are exposed to SAS.

Categories and Subject Descriptors

C.2.1 [**Computer-Communication Networks**]: Network Architecture and Design—*Wireless communication*; K.4.1 [**Computer and Society**]: Public Policy Issues—*Privacy*

Keywords

server-driven DSA; privacy; homomorphic encryption

1. INTRODUCTION

The depletion of wireless spectrum has greatly promoted the advances in DSA. In DSA, unlicensed secondary users can opportunistically access licensed spectrum under the constraint that they do not impose harmful interference to incumbent users. Sharing between the government incumbents (i.e. federal or non-federal agencies) and commercial wireless broadband operators/users is one of the key forms of DSA that is recommended by the NTIA and FCC. Recommendations in the President's Council of Advisors on Science and Technology (PCAST) report has recommended to set up a spectrum access system (SAS) database to govern the spectrum sharing between federal incumbent users (IUs) and commercial secondary users (SUs) [5]. In a typical scenario in these SAS-driven systems, both IUs and SUs need to send their operation data to SAS to realize DSA.

One of the critical concerns in light of the increasing prospects of the SAS-driven spectrum sharing between federal government incumbent systems and non-government systems is the privacy issue. For national security reasons, operation information of government incumbent users is often classified data. For example, the IUs in 3.5 GHz DSA band include military and fixed satellite service licensees, whose operation data is highly sensitive. Similarly, secondary users' operation parameters may also be sensitive commercial secrets for their operators. Yet, to realize efficient spectrum access, current server-driven designs require IUs and SUs to send their operation data to SAS for spectrum allocation, which exposes the IUs and SUs to potentially severe privacy violation.

In this paper, we aim to solve the privacy issues of SUs and IUs for SAS by designing a privacy-preserving SAS system that realizes the spectrum allocation decision process of DSA while preserving users' privacy. The main challenge is that the spectrum allocation process needs to consider many factors and use complex signal propagation models. To solve the challenge, (1) we separate the parameters in a radio propagation model that need privacy protection from those that are open knowledge, and only the part of radio propagation model that involves private parameters need to be carried out securely over ciphertext. (2) We strategically disintegrate the spectrum allocation computation related to private operation parameters into a small set of primitives like addition, substraction and scalar multiplication that can be homomorphically evaluated by Paillier cryptosystem [4] efficiently. Under our design, SUs and IUs's interactions with the SAS follow the typical database interaction pattern (e.g. update, query, response and confirmation) and do not need to stay connected with the SAS system beyond the most basic handshakes. To the best of our knowledge, we are the first to be able to successfully realize practical secure spectrum allocation. Preliminary evaluation results are given, which show the performance of our secure SAS design is reasonable on real world data.

MobiCom'15, September 7–11, 2015, Paris, France.
ACM. ISBN 978-1-4503-3619-2/15/09
http://dx.doi.org/10.1145/2789168.2795161.

2. PRELIMINARIES

2.1 Paillier Cryptosystem

The design of our secure SAS system is based on Paillier cryptosystem [4], which is a public-key encryption scheme that efficiently supports additive, subtractive and scalar multiplicative homomorphic operations as follows:

$$\begin{cases} Dec(\widehat{m_1} \oplus \widehat{m_2}) = m_1 + m_2 \\ Dec(\widehat{m_1} \ominus \widehat{m_2}) = m_1 - m_2 \\ Dec(c \otimes \widehat{m_1}) = c \times m_1 \end{cases},$$

where m_1, m_2 are arbitrary messages, $\widehat{m}$ is the ciphertexts of message m after encryption, $\oplus, \ominus, \otimes$ are used to represent the homomorphic version of addition, substraction, and scalar multiplication operation respectively, c is a constant value in plaintext, and $Dec()$ denotes the decryption operation.

2.2 Reference Model of Traditional SAS

In this section, we describe a reference model of the traditional server-driven SAS, which serves as the basis for understanding our design henceforth. In the typical scenario, there are three parties involved, including IUs, SUs and SAS Server. SAS Server refers to a cloud-based spectrum management infrastructure that allocates spectrum resources while considering incumbent protection. SAS Server receives SUs' spectrum access request, calculates the availability of the spectrum requested by SUs, and returns the corresponding request response to SUs. To accurately determine the spectrum availability requested by SUs, SAS Server predicts the aggregate SU interference on all IUs using some radio propagation model based on the operation parameters provided by IUs and SUs. If the predicted interference on any IU exceeds a desirable threshold when the requesting SU is allowed to transmit, SAS Server will respond the requesting SU with a denial of access right. Otherwise, the requesting operation is permitted. Upon receiving a permission, an SU may transmit a confirmation to SAS, confirming its reception of the license.

3. SECURE SAS SYSTEM DESIGN

Assume that the SAS is semi-honest, and the goal of our scure SAS is to realize the same computation task as the traditional SAS while protecting the data privacy of both IUs and SUs from the semi-honest SAS.

3.1 Design Overview

As shown in Figure 1, our design includes four different parties: (1) a SAS Server for computing spectrum allocation, (2) an IU Aggregator that is responsible for keeping track of IUs and is operated by a trusted party of the IUs, (3) SUs in the service area of SAS Server, (4) Key Distributor. Key Distributor creates a group Paillier public/private key pair (pk_G, sk_G) and is trusted for keeping sk_G a secret only known to itself. In addition, each SU b has his own pair of Paillier public/private keys (pk_b, sk_b) and uploads pk_b to Key Distributor. Using pk_b and sk_G, Key Distributor can provide ciphertext conversion service to SAS Server, where it converts a ciphertext encrypted by pk_G to a ciphertext encrypted by pk_b so that the ciphertext can be decrypted by SU b. Note that Key Distributor is not fully trusted, instead it is only trusted in keeping sk_G secret. So messages

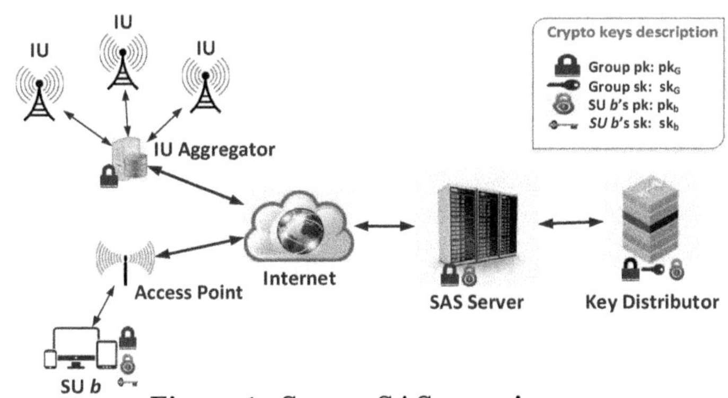

Figure 1: Secure SAS overview

sent to Key Distributor will be hidden by adding some blind factors first.

3.2 Private Input Information to SAS

The core step in our SAS design is the secure computation of the aggregate of SU interference on IUs. In essence, this means that the aggregate RSS of all SUs on all IUs must be derived based on a certain radio propogation model and its required radio operation information. To compute the RSS, we adopt the highly-sophisticated and accurate Longley-Rice (L-R) model. L-R model is a complex model which takes as many as thirteen parameters as input, but in our problem, the only five parameter values that need to be considered are distance, the transmitter and receiver antenna heights, transmit power, and the terrain elevation profiles (frequency is a constant in single channel case). Observe that among the five parameters that we consider, only the transmitter and receiver configurations (e.g. locations, antenna heights, transmit power) are privacy related. The remaining factor – terrain information – is public knowledge that can be easily found on government terrain database like [1]. Thus, to use L-R model to compute if SU interference exceeds IU tolerance, the following private operation information needs to be transmitted to SAS Server:

(1) Private IU information transmitted from IU Aggregator to SAS: Interference threshold of each IU, location of each IU, and antenna height of each IU. The interference threshold represents the maximum amount of aggregate SU interference that an IU can tolerate.

To reduce computation overhead, we quantize all the possible values of location and antenna height into limited choices. Specifically, we divide the service area of a SAS Server into L small grids of equal size and express an IU's location using its grid number. In addition, we quantize IU receiver antenna height into H_I levels. Using the above quantization, a two-dimensional matrix $\mathbf{T} := \{T(l, h_I)\}_{L \times H_I}$ is used to represent the IU operation information that is transmitted to SAS. When an IU of antenna height h_I is located in geographic grid l, $T(l, h_I)$ equals the interference threshold of the IU. Otherwise, $T(l, h_I)$ is set to an extremely large number (e.g. 100W) that cannot be exceeded in realistic radio propagation scenarios, representing an infinite tolerance to interference. $\mathbf{T}$ is encrypted by pk_G before sending to SAS Server, and the generated ciphertexts is denoted as $\widehat{\mathbf{T}}$.

(2) Private SU information transmitted from an SU b to SAS: Maximum transmit power, location, and antenna height of SU b.

Similar to the IU case, a two-dimensional matrix $\mathbf{R}_b := \{R_b(j, h_S)\}_{L \times H_S}$ is used to represents the above SU operation parameters, where the SU transmitter antenna height is quantized into H_S levels. $R_b(j, h_S)$ equals SU b's maximum transmit power if SU b is located in grid j and has an antenna height of h_S. Otherwise, $R_b(j, h_S)$ equals 0, indicating no active transmission in such a configuration. $\mathbf{R}_b$ is encrypted by pk_G before sending to SAS Server, and the generated ciphertexts is denoted as $\widehat{\mathbf{R}_b}$.

3.3 Secure Dynamic Spectrum Allocation

With the up-to-date ciphertext of IU operation information (i.e. $\widehat{\mathbf{T}}$) from IU Aggregator, SAS Server can securely compute whether SU Interference exceeds IU tolerance level. SAS Server first precomputes a plaintext attenuation map $\mathbf{I} := \{I(l, j, h_I, h_S)\}_{L^2 \times H_I \times H_S}$ based on the public terrain information. Here the entry $I(l, j, h_I, h_S)$ represents the precomputed path attenuation from a transmitter with h_S antenna height in grid j to a receiver with h_I antenna height in grid l. Given $\mathbf{I}$, after SU b uploads $\widehat{\mathbf{R}_b}$ to SAS Server in its request for spectrum access, the interference that SU b imposes on an IU in grid l with antenna height h_I can be derived as:

$$\widehat{F_b}(l, h_I) := \oplus_{j,h_S} \left[I(l, j, h_I, h_S) \otimes \widehat{R_b}(j, h_S) \right], \quad (1)$$

where $\oplus_{j,h_S}$ and $\otimes$ are the homomorphic version of the summation symbol $\sum_{j,h_S}$ and the scalar multiplication symbol respectively, and $\widehat{F_b}(l, h_I)$ is the ciphertext of the SU interference.

SAS Server then can compute if adding SU b will exceed the interference threshold of some IU. First, SAS Server maintains an interference budget matrix $\widehat{\mathbf{N}} := \{\widehat{N}(l, h_I)\}_{L \times H_I}$ of IUs. Each entry $\widehat{N}(l, h_I)$ holds the ciphertext of the amount of additional SU interference that can be tolerated at every grid. The initial value of the interference budget matrix $\widehat{\mathbf{N}}$ is set to be the same as the interference threshold matrix $\widehat{\mathbf{T}}$, which is provided by IU Aggregator. In essence, this means that if an IU with antenna height of h_I exist in grid l, the initial value of $\widehat{N}(l, h_I)$ equals the ciphertext of the interference threshold of the IU. If no such IU exists, $\widehat{N}(l, h_I)$ is a ciphertext of an extremely large power value.

Then, using (1), SAS Server can create an interference indicator matrix $\widehat{\mathbf{G}_b} := \{\widehat{G_b}(l, h_I)\}_{L \times H_I}$ as follows:

$$\widehat{G_b}(l, h_I) := \widehat{N}(l, h_I) \ominus \widehat{F_b}(l, h_I). \quad (2)$$

The signs of all $\widehat{G_b}(l, h_I)$'s plaintexts indicate whether SU b should be allowed to operate. If there exists a $\widehat{G_b}(l, h_I)$ that holds the ciphertext of a non-positive value, it means that an IU with antenna height h_I exists in grid l and this IU runs out of its interference budget if SU b operates. In such a case, SU b is not allowed to operate and SAS does not compute a valid spectrum access license for SU b. Only when all $\widehat{\mathbf{G}_b}$ entries are ciphertext of positive values, SU b is safe to operate. In this case, SAS generates a valid license to give SU b spectrum access right. Such license computation is made by employing ciphertext conversion service provided by Key Distributor. On a high level, Key Distributor transfers the sign information contained in $\widehat{\mathbf{G}_b}$ (encrypted by pk_G) to a license (encrypted by pk_b). If there exists one $\widehat{\mathbf{G}_b}$ entry whose plaintext is non-positive value, an invalid license is generated. Otherwise, a valid license is generated.

SAS Server then sends a response back to SU b. The response includes the encrypted license and $\widehat{\mathbf{F}_b}$. Upon receiving the response, SU b finds out the availability of the spectrum by checking the validity of the license after decrypting using his own private key sk_b. Then SU b creates a matrix $\widehat{\mathbf{U}_b} := \{\widehat{U_b}(l, h_I)\}_{L \times H_I}$ by:

$$\widehat{U_b}(l, h_I) := \begin{cases} \widehat{F_b}(l, h_I) \oplus \widehat{0}(l, h_I), & \text{SU } b \text{ gets the valid license} \\ \widehat{0}(l, h_I), & \text{SU } b \text{ gets no valid license} \end{cases}, \quad (3)$$

$\widehat{\mathbf{U}_b}$ is then sent to SAS Server along with SU b's confirmation message. SAS Server then updates the interference budget matrix by substracting $\widehat{\mathbf{U}_b}$ from $\widehat{\mathbf{N}}$ as follows:

$$\widehat{N}(l, h_I) \leftarrow \widehat{N}(l, h_I) \ominus \widehat{U_b}(l, h_I). \quad (4)$$

Combining (3) and (4), we can see that, when SU b receives the license, the interference budgets (i.e. the plaintexts of $\widehat{\mathbf{N}}$ entries) are reduced by SU b's interference. When SU b does not get the license, interference budgets stay the same. In such a manner, $\widehat{\mathbf{N}}$ is gradually reduced as more SUs obtain their operation licenses. In addition, the homomorphic addition of $\widehat{0}(l, h_I)$ to $\widehat{F_b}(l, h_I)$ in (3) ensures that the ciphertext $\widehat{U_b}(l, h_I)$ stays different from the ciphertext $\widehat{F_b}(l, h_I)$ even when their plaintexts are the same. Thus, SAS Server cannot guess the spectrum allocation results by comparing $\widehat{U_b}(l, h_I)$ with $\widehat{F_b}(l, h_I)$.

4. PRELIMINARY EVALUATION RESULTS

To evaluate our SAS system, we set the service area to be a large 154.82 km^2 area in Washington DC. We employ L-R model provided by SPLAT! [2] to calculate the attenuation map $\mathbf{I}$ in this area. We feed high resolution SRTM3 [1] terrain elevation data to SPLAT!. We construct the Paillier cryptosystem in C programming language based on GMP library [3]. Notably, The length of security parameter n is set to be 2048 bits, so the Paillier cryptosystem we build has an equivalent security level of 112 bits. The SAS system is built based on the Paillier cryptosystem implementation. For parallelization implementation, we employ the POSIX Threads in C programming and we divide the computation in SAS into 16 concurrent threads, and each of two desktops runs 8 threads. Evaluation results show that the total time to process a request in SAS Server is around 3 minutes, and the total communication bandwidth overhead between SU and SAS Server in one handshake is 6.68 MB.

5. CONCLUSIONS

In this paper, we build a secure SAS system which performs DSA while preserving users' privacy. Our design coverts complex DSA process into limited computation types provided by Paillier homomorphic crypotosystem. The computation and communication overhead is both moderate for practical SAS service.

6. REFERENCES

[1] `http://dds.cr.usgs.gov/srtm/version2_1/SRTM3/`.

[2] `http://www.qsl.net/kd2bd/splat.html`.

[3] `https://gmplib.org/`.

[4] P. Paillier. Public-key cryptosystems based on composite degree residuosity classes. In *EUROCRYPT'99*, pages 223–238. Springer, 1999.

[5] PCAST. Report to the president realizing the full potential of government-held spectrum to spur economic growth. 2012.

Poster: On the Low-Cost and Distance-Adaptive Device-free Localization

Chen Liu[1],Dingyi Fang[1],Hongbo Jiang[2],Xiaojiang Chen* [1],Zhany Tang[1],Ju Wang[1],Weike Nie[1]
[1]Northwest University, Xi'an, China
[2]Huazhong University of Science and Technology, Wuhan, China
{liuchen,dyf}@nwu.edu.cn, hongbojiang2004@gmail.com,
{xjchen,zytang,jvwang}@nwu.edu.cn, onetwo3817@sohu.com

ABSTRACT

This poster introduces JRD, a novel device-free localization system which can achieve high accuracy with low cost and little human effort, and is even robust to different scenarios. Unlike the previous Radio Signal Strength (RSS)-based systems which depend on the dense deployment to provide high accuracy, JRD extracts the fine-grained RSS distributions of a single link and presents a voting algorithm based on multi-link to identify the object location accurately while maintaining a low-cost deployment. Furthermore, JRD is flexible to different scenarios by using the transferring technique with less time-consuming and human effort. Experimental results show that JRD can improve the localization accuracy by up to 50% with less cost as compared with the existing RSS approaches.

Categories and Subject Descriptors

C.2.1 [**Network Architecture and Design**]: Wireless Communication

Keywords

Device-free Localization; Low-cost; Transferring Learning

1. INTRODUCTION

Localization [1] has been playing a key role over years in many applications, such as intrusion detection and wildlife monitoring. Recently, there has been a growing interest in device-free techniques, since they do not rely on the carry-on devices. Compared with other device-free localization techniques, such as GPS, camera [2] or CSI (Channel State Information), which need some special devices, localization through RSS is widely used because of its low cost of both infrastructure and technology in many common applications.

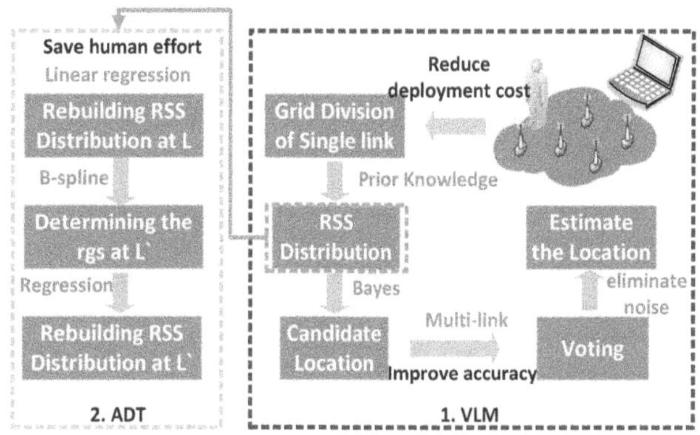

Figure 1: Framework of JRD System.

Current RSS-based localization systems [3, 4, 5] have already obtained multiple advances. However, in order to achieve high accuracy, these systems depend on the dense deployment, which is impossible in practice and is exacerbated in large monitoring scenarios. That is because a large number of nodes will cause more hardware costs and result in congestion, even lead to a low localization accuracy. Besides, the calibration phase in existing localization approaches requires a lot of effort. It is difficult and costly in practice when require the RSS fingerprints when changing area for different scenarios. Being able to reuse RSS measurements elsewhere would be extremely useful in practice.

This poster presents JRD, a novel device-free Localization system that provides sufficient accuracy even with low cost of deployment and little human effort, and is robust when changing area for different scenarios. JRD addresses the following challenges:

(1) How to reduce the deployment cost while achieve high accuracy? We investigate this problem by dividing the covered area of a single link into grids and extracting its fine-gained corresponding RSS distributions (as shown in Fig.2). By doing so, we can achieve high accuracy without dense deployment. For each disturbed link, we use Bayes classifier to obtain the candidate locations based on its RSS distribution. Then we propose a voted localization algorithm using multi-link to identify the object location.

(2) How to reduce the human effort when apply JRD to different scenarios? To solve this problem, we propose an adaptive dynamic transferring algorithm which can reuse RSS measurements without requiring a calibration phase of collecting RSS fingerprints when changing area for different scenarios.

*corresponding author.

MobiCom'15, September 7–11, 2015, Paris, France.
ACM. ISBN 978-1-4503-3619-2/15/09
DOI: http://dx.doi.org/10.1145/2789168.2795162.

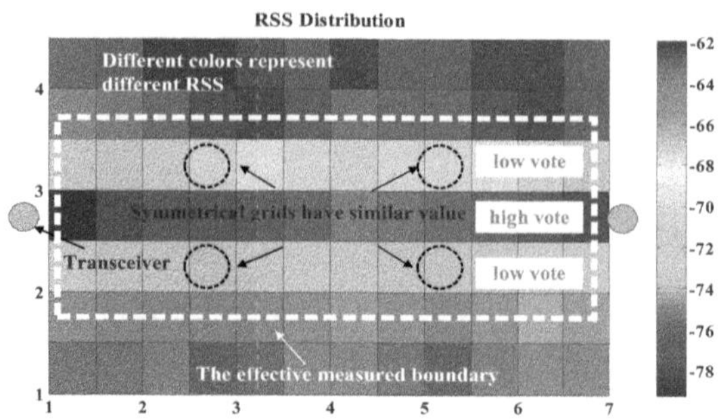

Figure 2: Grid division and its RSS distribution of a singe link.

2. SYSTEM DESIGN

In this section, we introduce the architecture of the JRD system, as shown in Fig. 1. Its infrastructure includes a database which stores the IDs and 2-D positions of the nodes. JRD contains two algorithms: the VLM Algorithm and the ADT Algorithm. When an object moves into the monitoring area, its location can be estimated by VLM in a computing center going through the following steps: 1) Compute the candidate locations of the object according to each disturbed link; 2) Vote for candidate based on multi-link and estimate the object location. Furthermore, when the area or transceiver distance changing, we use ADT to reduce the cost and human effort.

2.1 Voted Localization Algorithm

(1) How to Decide the Candidate Locations?

For each pair of the transmitter and receiver, we divide its covered area into several grids. In an offline phase, a priori probability of the RSS distribution is learned from a large amount of location-labeled RSS, e.g., $[Po^L, R^L]$. When the object is passing by the link, its RSS fluctuates and we denote this disturbed link as *Voter Link*. For each Voter Link vp_i, we can use the Bayes classifier to obtain the candidate locations of the object. In an online phase, let $r^{\hat{L}}_{object}$ be the RSS vector of the Voter Link. The posterior probability that the object is at candidate location $po^L \in Po^L$ can be calculated by:

$$\arg\max_{po^L} P(l|r^{\hat{L}}_{object}) = \arg\max_{po^L} P(r^{\hat{L}}_{object}|po^L). \quad (1)$$

(2) How to vote for the Candidate Locations?

In order to facilitate the communication and the calculation, VLM operates in two stages (Fig. 3). In the first stage, each Voter Link with long distance casts one vote on each candidate location to form the Candidate Region. In the second stage, each Voter Link with short distance votes within the Candidate Region. Then the location with the highest total votes will be considered as the object location.

We suppose that the vote is designed to be equal or more than 0. When the RSS fluctuation is zero or slight, the vote is 0, otherwise, the vote becomes higher as it gets large (as shown in Fig. 2). We define the RSS fluctuation degree for each Voter Link vp_i as $\Delta r^{p_i} = |r^{p_i} - r^{p_i}_{state}|/|r^{p_i}_{state}|$. Thus, the Voter Link vp_i's vote on location po_k is calculated by: $Vote_{vp_i}(po_k) = \parallel \Delta r^{p_i} \parallel^2$.

Furthermore, the RSS is often affected by the interference due to the different environment. Fig. 4 shows a RSS sequence of one link and we observe that there are two obvious fluctuations. Case 1 is resulted from the environmental noise, which is a quick peak. Case 2 is caused by the object, which continues a period of time. It indicates that the RSS changing is correlated with time (we define this as "RSS cooling procedure"), thus, we can update the vote at time ti by time $ti-1$ to eliminate the environment noise and provide the high localization accuracy. According to Newton's law of cooling , $Vote_{vp_i}(ti)' = -\lambda \times (Vote_{vp_i}(ti) - Vote^I_{vp_i})$, where λ is the cooling coefficient and $Vote^I_{vp_i}$ is the vote when where is no object. In our experiment, we set λ as 0.025. To solve this equation, we obtain: $Vote_{vp_i}(ti) = Vote_{vp_i}(ti-1)e^{-\lambda(ti-(ti-1))}$. The final Vote is calculated by $Vote_{vp_i}(po_k, ti) = (Vote_{vp_i}(po_k) - Vote_{vp_i}(ti)) \times p + Vote_{vp_i}(ti))$. where p is the ratio of the RSS fluctuation, which is related to the object's moving speed, the distance between two nodes and the sampling frequency of nodes. The higher total vote $Vote(po_k, ti) = \sum_i Vote_{vp_i}(po_k, ti)$ is, the more likely po_k is the actual location of the object.

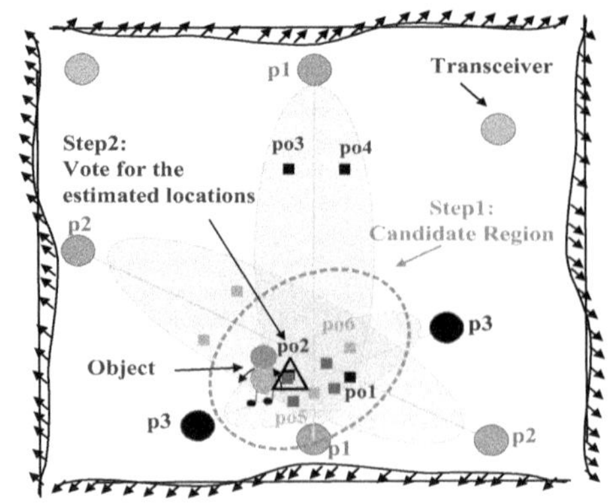

Figure 3: An example of VLM.

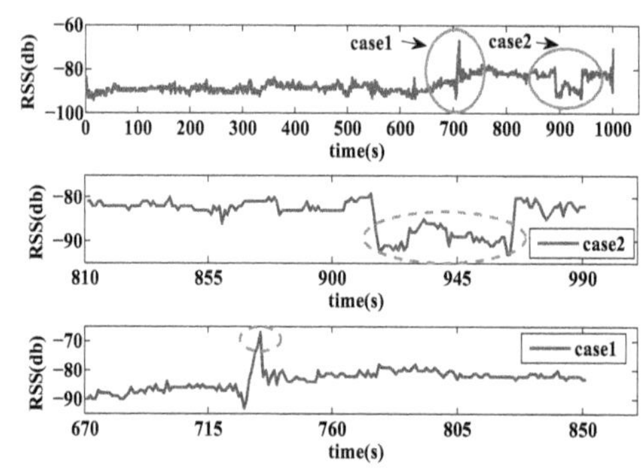

Figure 4: An example of RSS fluctuation.

2.2 Adaptive Dynamic Transferring Algorithm

To reduce the time-consuming and human effort, we present ADT algorithm which can reuse the RSS distribution at distance L to learn that at L'. ADT contains the following steps:

(1) Rebuilding the RSS distribution at distance L: According to the previous experiment, we observe that the RSS values over different grids are correlated for a given pair of the transmitter and receiver. For a pair of the transmitter and receiver at distance L, we denote the grids along the parallel lines (PL) and the vertical line (VL) as the Reference Grids (rg), while other grids are non-Reference Grids (nrg). Mo-

Figure 5: Deployment of JRD System.

tivated by this observation, we can apply a multiple linear regression model to learn the RSS correlations between rgs and a nrg. More specifically, let $Ra^k = \{\alpha_u^k, 1 \le u \le n_1\}$ be the regression coefficient matrix of one nrg k. Thus, the RSS distribution $r_{nrg_k}^L$ of one nrg can be expressed by other rgs as $r_{nrg_k}^L = Ra^k R_{rg}^L$.

(2) Determining the Reference Grids at distance L': Due to the grid division, it is obviously that different transceiver distance has different number of grids, since each grid has the same length. In order to use the regression coefficient matrix Ra into distance L', we should aline the rgs of different distances. We set the distance L as the baseline. Let the sequence $\{1, 2, ..., i, ..., n_3\}$ be the raw index of rgs of L' and its normalizing index sequence can be calculated by $Index^{L'} = \{1 + j \times \lceil n_3/n_1 \rceil, 0 \le j < n_1\}$, where n_1 and n_3 are the number of rgs of L and L', respectively. Similarly, we can normalize the index sequences along PL and VL.

(3) Building the RSS Distribution at L' using Regression Coefficient Matrix: We can obtain the regression RSS distribution $r_{nrg_k}^{L'REG}$ of one nrg k using regression coefficient matrix Ra^k: $r_{nrg_k}^{L'REG} = \alpha_0^k + \alpha_1^k r_{rg_1}^{L'} + ... + \alpha_u^k r_{rg_u}^{L'} + ... + \alpha_{n_1}^k r_{rg_{n_1}}^{L'} + \xi_k$, where $k \in po[Index^{L'}]$. However, the $R_{nrg}^{L'REG} = \{r_{nrg_k}^{L'REG}\}$ is just a part of the RSS distribution at distance L', since L is shorter than L' and the number of grids at L is also less than that of L'. We observe that the RSS distribution along each PL and VL is piecewise smooth and each junction is smoothness. Thus, for each row and column, we use B-spline to obtain the unknown RSS values, respectively. After the rebuilding procedure, we can derive the whole RSS distribution $R^{L'REG}$ at distance L'.

3. PRELIMINARY RESULTS

We implement the prototype by MICAZ nodes with Chipcon CC2420 and the radio frequency 2.4GHz. All nodes are put on the height of 0.95 m on the playground as shown in Fig.5. The monitoring region is $28m \times 25m$, where 14 nodes are randomly deployed and we set the node distance ranging from 4m to 8m, resulting in a relatively sparse deployment compared with the previous works. We compare JRD with three state-of-the-art algorithms in locating the object based on RSS, i.e., midpoint algorithm, intersection algorithm in [3], and RASS algorithm in [4].

(1)Localization Accuracy and Deployment Cost: In order to keep the fairness, we fix the number of nodes and set the node distance as 4m. Fig. 6(a) illustrates the results of 200 samples. We can observe that in terms of the localization accuracy, JRD outperforms the other three algorithms whatever the error tolerance is. (Given the error tolerance, we can calculate the percentage of the estimations that have

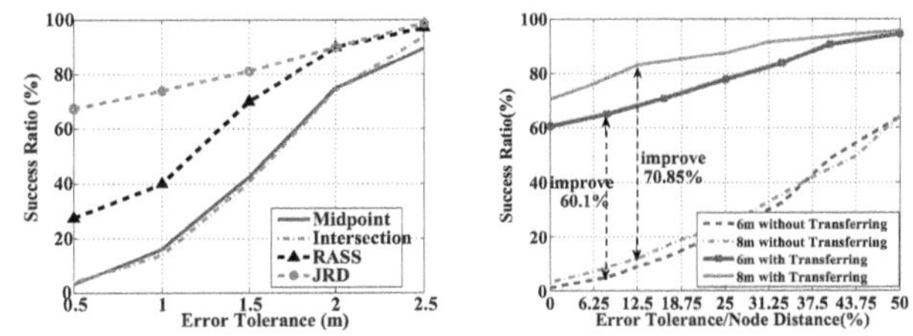

(a) (b)

Figure 6: (a)Localization accuracy. (b)Transferring comparison.

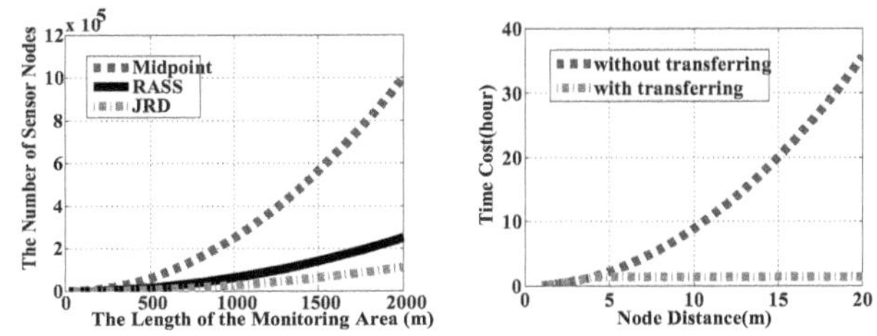

(a) (b)

Figure 7: (a)Deployment cost. (b)Time-cost (Human effort).

errors below the error tolerance, named *success ratio.*) These results indicate that JRD can obtain a higher accuracy compared with existing algorithms when using the same number of nodes under a sparse deployment. Furthermore, we change the size of monitoring area and evaluate the number of nodes that needed to fully cover the area. As shown in Fig. 7(a), the deployment cost of JRD grows slowly as compared with the other two algorithms.

(2)Localization with Transferring: As shown in Fig. 6(b), taking 6m and 8m for example, it is obviously that the success ratio of localization has improved a lot compared to the one without transferring.

(3)Reducing the Human Efforts with Transferring: We compare the time-cost of collecting the RSS distribution in the conditions with and without transferring, respectively. Fig. 7(b) shows the results. It is clearly that the time-cost generally increases as the node distance becomes longer. In contrast, the time-cost is very small with transferring.

4. ACKNOWLEDGMENTS

This work was supported by NSFC (61170218, 61272461, 61202393, 61373177), Project of National Key Technology R&D Program (2013BAK01B02, 2013BAK01B05), Department of Education research project of Shaanxi province, China (2013JK1126, 2013JK1127).

5. REFERENCES

[1] G. Tan, H. Jiang, S. Zhang, Z. Yin, and A. Kermarrec. Connectivity-based and anchor-free localization in large-scale 2d/3d sensor networks. *ACM TOSN*, 10(1):6, 2013.

[2] L. Liu, X. Zhang, and H. Ma. Localization-oriented coverage in wireless camera sensor networks. *Wireless Communications, IEEE Transactions on*, 10(2):484–494, 2011.

[3] D. Zhang, J. Ma, Q. Chen, and L.M. Ni. An rf-based system for tracking transceiver-free objects. In *Proceedings of IEEE PerCom'07*, pages 135–144, 2007.

[4] D. Zhang, Y.H. Liu, and L.M. Ni. Rass: A real-time, accurate and scalable system for tracking transceiver-free objects. In *Proceedings of IEEE PerCom*, pages 197–204, 2011.

[5] Y. Wen, X. Tian, X. Wang, and S. Lu. Fundamental limits of rss fingerprinting based indoor localization. In *Proceedings of the of IEEE INFOCOM*, 2015.

Poster: NLOS-aware Localization Based on Phase Shift Measurements

Yannic Schröder
TU Braunschweig, IBR
Mühlenpfordtstr. 23
38106 Braunschweig, Germany
schroeder@ibr.cs.tu-bs.de

Georg von Zengen
TU Braunschweig, IBR
Mühlenpfordtstr. 23
38106 Braunschweig, Germany
vonzengen@ibr.cs.tu-bs.de

Lars Wolf
TU Braunschweig, IBR
Mühlenpfordtstr. 23
38106 Braunschweig, Germany
wolf@ibr.cs.tu-bs.de

ABSTRACT

Modern cars are already able to park in parking spaces adjacent to streets. Soon autonomous cars will be able to navigate themselves through parking garages to find a parking lot assigned to them. Indoor localization is essential to qualify cars and parking garages to perform this operation. Currently the reliability of many indoor localization schemes suffers from non-line-of-sight propagation paths. We present a position estimation algorithm for indoor localization systems based on phase measurements of electromagnetic signals. Our algorithm is designed to detect and exclude measurements originating from these non-line-of-sight paths to reduce their harmful influence on the localization.

1. INTRODUCTION

In future parking garages cars will drive autonomously from a drop-off point to their designated parking lot and back. During parking times electric cars may drive to special lots with charging capabilities and back to normal lots when fully charged to allow other autonomous cars to charge their batteries as well [9, 5]. For autonomous driving operations inside the parking garage the car needs to know its own position for navigation. Further, the parking garage must be aware of the position of all cars present to distinguish empty from occupied lots. In parking garages Global Positioning System (GPS) is not accurate enough to serve the needs of the described application. Also it can be unavailable due to attenuation of the signal by structural elements.

Further, indoor localization can be useful when guiding customers through a shopping mall. In this scenario small shops connected to a big hallway will result in many Non-Line-Of-Sight (NLOS) connections between fixed reference nodes with known positions (anchors) and mobile nodes (tags) carried by customers.

Therefore, we present an indoor localization system to overcome the disadvantages of GPS. Unlike other indoor localization solutions our system is optimized to detect and handle often challenging NLOS measurements.

Our system utilizes phase difference measurements to determine the distance between nodes [2]. In this work we concentrate on how to estimate the position of a tag after measuring its distance to multiple anchors.

Other systems include NLOS measurements in their calculations by accounting for possible distance offsets and higher errors [6]. Phase measurements of NLOS connections cannot be included into distance estimations due to unpredictable reflections and refractions in different materials.

The proposed algorithm was tested in the Microsoft Indoor Localization Competition 2015 [1]. The system ranked 9th out of 23 competitors with an average distance error of 1.63 meters over 20 tested locations.

After giving a short overview of related work in Section 2 we present our map based approach to detect and mitigate NLOS measurements in Section 3. Afterwards, we describe the evaluation at the competition in Section 4.

2. RELATED WORK

Many indoor localization systems are prone to harmful influences of NLOS conditions. Especially in radio-based approaches the exact propagation path is often unknown resulting in wrong distance measurements and ultimately in wrong position estimates [8, 4].

Jung et al. detect NLOS conditions by using a known map of the environment for Time of Arrival (ToA) measurements in Ultra Wide Band (UWB) networks [6]. In ToA approaches the propagation path is critical as reflections prolong the time of flight and therefore the measured distance.

The algorithm proposed by Sathyan et al. returns multiple solutions from a ToA measurement [7]. Thereby the probability of the Line-Of-Sight (LOS) measurement being among the results increases. However, this approach fails when no LOS is available and all results are based on NLOS paths.

3. NLOS-AWARE APPROACH

The proposed algorithm is designed to localize a mobile node even in challenging environments like parking garages. It is based on measured distances to deployed anchor nodes.

Distances are calculated from phase shift measurements of a radio signal. The measurement is done by the Atmel Ranging Toolbox (RTB) [2]. This software is designed

MobiCom'15, September 7–11, 2015, Paris, France.
ACM. ISBN 978-1-4503-3619-2/15/09
DOI: http://dx.doi.org/10.1145/2789168.2795163.

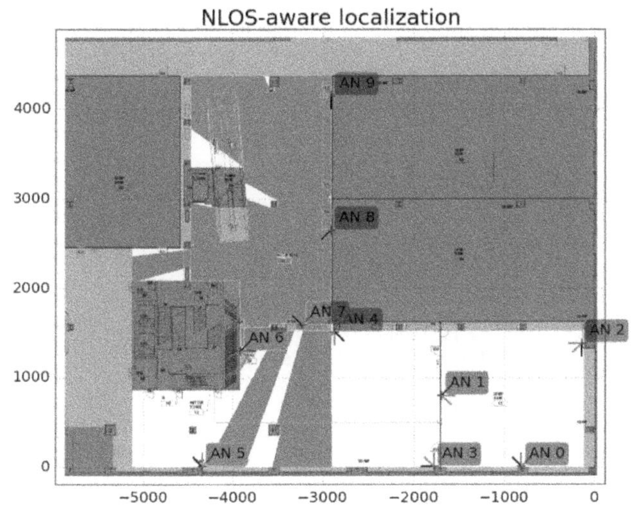

Figure 1: Output of our software with shadow map of anchor AN 8 (gray area). Both axes in cm

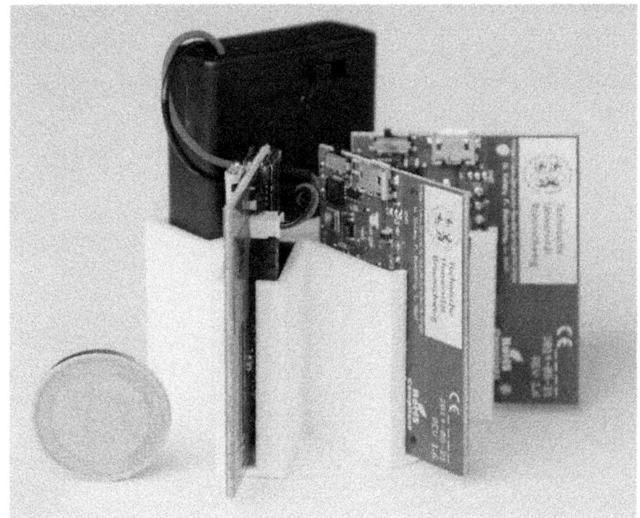

Figure 2: Anchor node consisting of three INGA sensor nodes with a coin for scale

to use the Phase Difference Measurement Unit (PMU) of the IEEE 802.15.4 radio transceiver AT86RF233. The RTB reports a measured distance and a Distance Quality Factor (DQF). The DQF indicates the quality of the measurement and can be used to classify good and bad measurements by applying a cut-off value. Measurements may be bad if the radio channel is disturbed by other services like IEEE 802.11. Phase measurements are prone to errors due to NLOS-conditions. If the electromagnetic wave is reflected at a surface or refracted while passing through an object its phase is shifted. A reflection results in a phase shift of 180° while a refraction results in an unknown phase shift that depends on the refractive index of the object. Both phenomena can occur simultaneously resulting in unpredictable phase shifts.

Our localization algorithm uses a known 2D map of the deployment area to detect NLOS-conditions and impossible locations for the mobile node. We use a grid based approach comparable to a particle filter with particles aligned on a fixed grid. The grid can be represented as a matrix M enabling the use of optimized math libraries for computing the solution. Each element in this matrix represents a square cell in the deployment area. The size of M can be configured based on the needed accuracy and available computational capabilities. The 2D map of the environment is represented by a second matrix E of the same size as M. Each element of E indicates one of two special conditions for this cell of the environment:

NLOS obstacle: No LOS is possible through this cell and the mobile node cannot be located here (red areas in Figure 1). This condition is used to indicate walls.

Positioning blocked: A LOS is possible but the mobile node cannot be positioned here (green areas in Figure 1). This condition is used for restricted areas like atriums. In a parking garage this would indicate sidewalks or staircases as these are invalid locations for a car.

Shadow maps S_i are computed for each anchor a_i. Each shadow map is a boolean matrix that indicates LOS of all cells to the anchor node. Figure 1 shows the shadow map as an overlay (gray area) over the deployment area.

Our battery powered anchor nodes consist of three INGA sensor nodes [3] and therefore feature three directional antennas, see Figure 2. The predominant directions of the antennas are 22.5° apart. Thus we can divide the area covered by each anchor node into three sectors. A distance value is measured for every sector individually.

The algorithm computes a probability for each cell that the mobile node is located in it. To do this, for each anchor a temporary matrix T_i is allocated. For each antenna sector an arc is drawn at the measured distance between the anchor and the mobile node. By using arcs and sectors we can reduce ambiguities that would arise when using full circles to mark possible locations. Drawn arcs can be configured to represent a specific probability distribution of distance measurements in the deployment area. Each arc is further weighted with the reported DQF of the measurement as a higher value indicates a better measurement result. The shadow map S_i is now used to remove impossible measurements for anchor a_i. The probability of every cell in T_i marked as NLOS in S_i is set to 0. T_i now contains the probabilities for the mobile node being in each cell based on the measurements from anchor a_i. The results in T_i are now added to the overall probabilities in M.

To find the most probable position for the mobile node the environment map E is taken into account. The probability of every cell in M not marked as normal cell in E is set to 0. By finding the maximum value in M the most probable location of the tag is computed. The indices of this cell in M correspond to the coordinates of the tags position in the deployment area. Figure 3 shows the final values of M color mapped as an overlay of the deployment area. In this example the tag is most likely located at the point (-3500, 2400) which translates to 35 and 24 meters, respectively.

4. EVALUATION

Our algorithm was tested in the Microsoft Indoor Localization Competition [1]. The evaluation area had a size of roughly $2000\,m^2$ (50 x 40 m) and consisted of an empty room and a big hallway with features like structural columns, beams, escalators and a staircase resulting in many NLOS

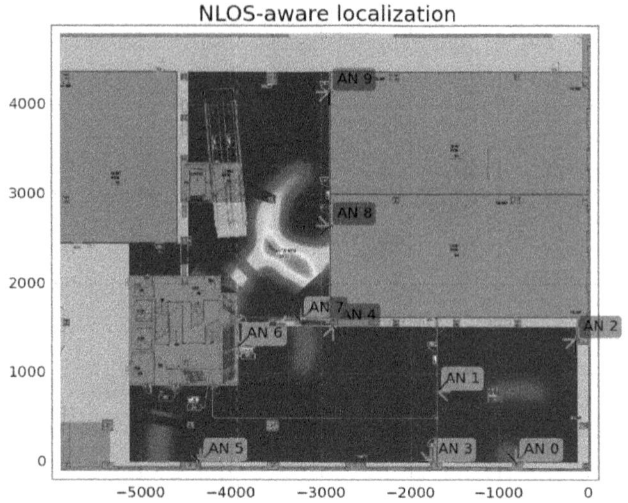

Figure 3: Relative probabilities of a tag's position in the deployment area. Both axes in cm

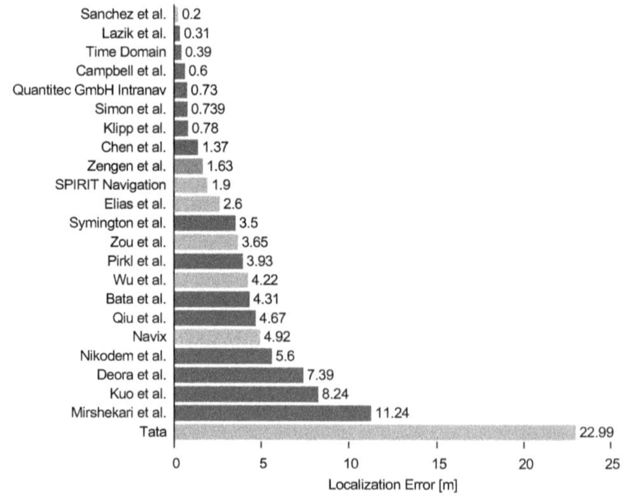

Figure 4: Official results of the Microsoft Indoor Localization Competition 2015, reproduced from [1].

connections (see Figure 1). The area was not empty during measurements, but conference attendees and other competing teams were using the space as well. However, other system were turned off during the evaluation.

The competing systems were categorized by their need for additional infrastructure. Every contestant that deployed extra hardware was categorized as infrastructure-based and was allowed to deploy 10 units. As we deployed anchor nodes our system was infrastructure-based. All other systems were infrastructure-free and were only allowed to use a mobile device for localization. However, the supplied conference WLAN could to be used as reference.

As a CAD file of the evaluation area was available prior to the event we were able to generate the needed map of the environment E beforehand. Only small adjustments were needed at the venue due to inaccuracies in the provided file.

The evaluation consisted of two days. On the first day all teams were allowed to set up their systems during a 7 hour time window. On the second day 20 previously unknown positions were marked down in the area. Each team had to locate every point and report its measured position to the referee. From these measurements the average distance error was calculated for each team.

Figure 4 shows the official results of the competition with infrastructure-free submissions marked in green. Our system (red) achieved an average distance error of 1.63 meters.

5. REFERENCES

[1] Microsoft indoor localization competition - IPSN 2015. http://research.microsoft.com/en-us/events/indoorloccompetition2015/. Accessed: 2015-05-12.

[2] Atmel Corporation, San Jose. *Atmel AVR2152: RTB Evaluation Application Software User's Guide User's Guide*, 8443a-avr-02/2013 edition, Feb. 2013.

[3] F. Büsching, U. Kulau, and L. Wolf. Architecture and evaluation of INGA - an inexpensive node for general applications. In *Sensors, 2012 IEEE*, pages 842–845, Taipei, Taiwan, oct. 2012. IEEE.

[4] D. Dardari, A. Conti, U. Ferner, A. Giorgetti, and M. Win. Ranging with ultrawide bandwidth signals in multipath environments. *Proceedings of the IEEE*, 97(2):404–426, Feb 2009.

[5] P. Furgale, U. Schwesinger, M. Rufli, W. Derendarz, H. Grimmett, P. Muhlfellner, S. Wonneberger, J. Timpner, S. Rottmann, B. Li, B. Schmidt, T. Nguyen, E. Cardarelli, S. Cattani, S. Bruning, S. Horstmann, M. Stellmacher, H. Mielenz, K. Koser, M. Beermann, C. Hane, L. Heng, G. H. Lee, F. Fraundorfer, R. Iser, R. Triebel, I. Posner, P. Newman, L. Wolf, M. Pollefeys, S. Brosig, J. Effertz, C. Pradalier, and R. Siegwart. Toward automated driving in cities using close-to-market sensors: An overview of the v-charge project. In *Intelligent Vehicles Symposium (IV), 2013 IEEE*, pages 809–816, June 2013.

[6] J. Jung and H. Myung. Indoor localization using particle filter and map-based nlos ranging model. In *Robotics and Automation (ICRA), 2011 IEEE International Conference on*, pages 5185–5190, May 2011.

[7] T. Sathyan and M. Hedley. Range-only tracking in multipath environments - an algorithm based on particle filtering. In *Global Telecommunications Conference, 2009. GLOBECOM 2009. IEEE*, pages 1–6, Nov 2009.

[8] H. Soganci, S. Gezici, and H. Poor. Accurate positioning in ultra-wideband systems. *Wireless Communications, IEEE*, 18(2):19–27, April 2011.

[9] J. Timpner and L. Wolf. A Back-end System for an Autonomous Parking and Charging System for Electric Vehicles. In *Proceedings of the IEEE International Electric Vehicle Conference (IEVC '12)*, pages 693–700, Greenville, SC, Mar. 2012. IEEE.

Poster: 3D Printing Your Wireless Coverage

Justin Chan*, Changxi Zheng†, Xia Zhou*
Dartmouth College*, Columbia University†
{justin.k.l.chan, xia.zhou}@dartmouth.edu, cxz@cs.columbia.edu

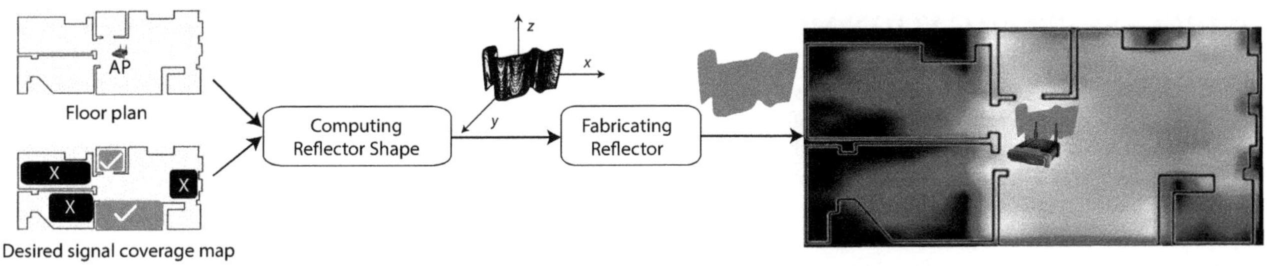

Figure 1: Overview of WiPrint system. User can input a floor plan, location of an AP and a desired signal map to the system. The desired signal pattern is marked with red and black regions indicating areas which should have strong and weak signals respectively. WiPrint uses an optimization algorithm to produce a reflector shape. This reflector is then fabricated and applied to an AP to achieve this desired signal pattern.

Categories and Subject Descriptors

C.2.1 [**Computer-Communication Networks**]: Network Architecture and Design—*Wireless communication*

Keywords

Wireless networking; 3D printing; Signal map; Design

1. INTRODUCTION

Today most Wi-Fi access points (APs) are omnidirectional sources of electromagnetic waves. Since the wireless channel is a broadcast medium, wireless transmissions suffer two well-known concerns. *First*, wireless signals are emitted in all directions, causing energy waste in undesired directions. Consider a Wi-Fi AP placed near the window at home, a large amount of wireless signals leak outside the window. *Second*, wireless transmissions are vulnerable to traffic eavesdropping and other security and privacy attacks. Even if we encrypt the data transmission or secure the wireless network with a password, the attacker can still leverage wireless signal strength to physically locate the transmitter.

Addressing both concerns requires judicious control over how wireless signals propagate in the air. It is an inherently challenging task given the complex nature of electromagnetic wave propagation and its interaction with the environment [1]. The common solution today is to use directional antennas, which concentrate wireless signals in a desired direction using either horn-shaped antennas or an array of antenna elements with phases electronically configurable. However, directional antennas dictate rather limited working scenarios. They can be made in a small form-factor for high-frequency band (e.g., 60GHz) transmissions because of the short signal wavelength. Unfortunately, for lower frequency bands such as Wi-Fi bands (2.4 or 5GHz), directional antennas are typically bulky, expensive, do not come with ordinary routers by default, and have very limited granularity and flexibility in controlling signal propagation in the practical environment. It is hard, if not impossible, to control wireless signal coverage in a fine granularity while taking into account a specific wireless propagation environment.

In this poster, we propose WiPrint. The key idea is to place a 3D-printed glossy reflector surrounding a wireless AP. The reflector shape is computationally optimized such that it steers the wireless signals to form a desired strength distribution. In fact, anecdotal experiments [14] have demonstrated substantial bandwidth gain by simply placing a soda can behind a Wi-Fi AP. WiPrint generalizes the idea of reflecting wireless signals in two aspects: (i) WiPrint aims to achieve *any* user-specified target signal distribution by optimizing the details of the reflector shape, and (ii) our optimization considers wireless signals' interaction with a specific environment and thus can adapt to different environmental settings.

Specifically, as shown in Figure 1, WiPrint takes the following input: (i) a digitzed environmental setting (e.g., furniture, floor plan) obtained using 3D geometry reconstruction techniques [3, 6], which have been well developed in computer vision and graphics; and (ii) the desired wireless coverage, which can be a user-specified Wi-Fi signal heatmap, or even simply a set of small coverage regions picked by the user, or an ideal Wi-Fi signal distribution automatically learned based on the mobility pattern and density of users. The core of our approach is a computational algorithm that optimizes reflector shape to form the desired signal distribution. Finally we use commodity 3D printers to fabricate the optimized reflector and mount it near the wireless router to physically realize the desired signal distribution. WiPrint is low-cost, easy-to-use by ordinary users, requires no modifications on existing wireless APs, and adapts to varying physical environments and a wide range of frequency bands.

MobiCom'15, September 7–11, 2015, Paris, France.
ACM. ISBN 978-1-4503-3619-2/15/09
DOI: http://dx.doi.org/10.1145/2789168.2795164.

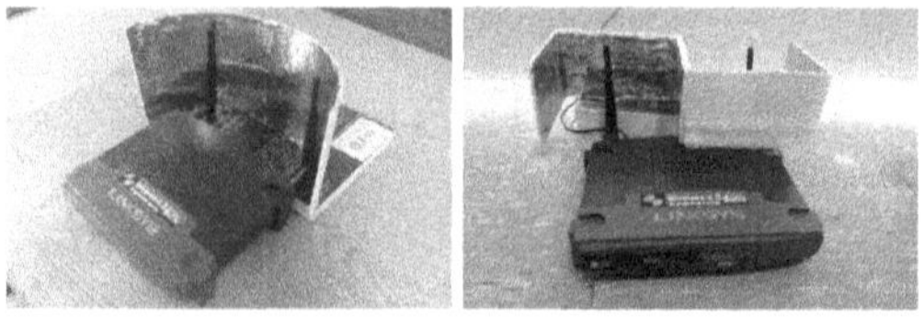

(a) Concave reflector (b) Square-wave reflector w/ metal layer

Figure 2: Reflectors in experiments.

2. WIRELESS PROPAGATION MODEL

The first core component of WiPrint is a model of wireless signal propagation, which predicts the wireless signal distribution in a given environment and in turn helps to design the reflector shape. We chose ray tracing with a partition model [2, 7], which achieves the best accuracy for typical indoor environments. We extend the conventional ray tracing using the Uniform Theory of Diffraction (UTD) [12] in acoustics to capture the signal diffraction.

Ray Tracing. Ray tracing [13] captures the wave behavior of wireless radio waves using rays exhibiting particle-like behavior. It has been widely used by prior studies [4, 5, 7] as one of the most accurate propagation models with tractable complexity. Wireless signals are represented by rays launched from the transmitter. Rays are attenuated around the room until they reach a receiver. The received signal strength (RSS) of a ray at the receiver is determined by the the distance traveled by the ray, the ray's frequency and the number of reflections and transmissions it encountered before reaching the receiver.

We consider the *reflection* and *diffraction* of the radio rays when they propagate in an environment with surrounding objects (e.g, walls, furniture). Inspired by the fast-wave acoustics simulations in computer graphics, we leverage the Uniform Theory of Diffraction (UTD) [12] in acoustics simulations to capture the diffraction of wireless signals.

3. COMPUTING THE REFLECTOR SHAPE

The second core component of WiPrint is to compute the reflector shape in detail to achieve a desired signal strength distribution. The computational algorithm takes the following input: 1) the user's desired signal map M_D that is either *low-resolution* or *high-resolution*. A low-resolution signal map means that the user broadly specifies regions where they want stronger or weaker wireless signals. Figure 5(a) shows an example of the low-resolution desired signal map, where red and black regions represent areas where users desire stronger or weaker (or no) signals respectively. A high-resolution signal map divides the environment into small cells and marks a target RSS value for each cell; 2) the environment layout E; 3) the AP location L_{AP}; and 4) the initial reflector shape R represented as a polynomial.

Our algorithm iteratively mutates the initial reflector shape, estimates the resulting signal strength distribution map M_R for the mutated shape R, calculates the difference between desired and estimated signal maps, and searches for the optimal shape $R^\star$ that minimizes the difference.

Defining the Reflector Shape. We define the reflector shape as a contiguous series of lines. We explore reflectors that can be represented as a polynomial function. The polynomial is defined by its degree and the location of its control points relative to the AP. The reflector shape R is a feature vector denoting the properties of a polynomial function.

Searching for the Optimal Reflector Shape. Our searching algorithm initializes the reflector shape R as a straight horizontal line above the AP. It then mutates the shape over iterations. To evaluate the effectiveness of a mutated shape R, we calculate the difference $\delta(M_D, M_R)$ between the desired signal map M_D and the signal map M_R generated by placing the reflector R. For high-resolution input signal maps, $\delta(M_D, M_R)$ is calculated as below:

$$\delta(M_D, M_R) = -\sum_{i=0}^{n} |M_D(i) - M_R(i)|,$$

where n denotes the number of cells in the signal maps, $M_D(i)$ and $M_R(i)$ are the signal strength values in dB at cell i in the desired and estimated map respectively. For low-resolution maps, M_D consists of a set of good regions A_{good}, where users desire strong wireless signals, and bad regions A_{bad}, where users desire no or weak signals. Then $\delta(M_D, M_R)$ is calculated as below:

$$\delta(M_D, M_R) = \sum_{i \in A_{good}} (M_R(i) - S_{min}) + \sum_{i \in A_{bad}} (S_{max} - M_R(i)),$$

where S_{min} and S_{max} are the signal value thresholds for good or bad signal regions.

Given the objective function, we apply simulated annealing, a randomized optimization algorithm, to search for $R^\star$:

$$R^\star = \operatorname*{argmax}_R \delta(M_D, M_R).$$

Simulated annealing combines hill-climbing and exploration to search for $R^\star$. Hill-climbing greedily maximizes the objective function, i.e., accepts a candidate shape only if it is strictly better than the previous solution. The exploration part of the algorithm accepts candidate solutions that have lower objective function values than the previous solution, with an acceptance probability of p, to avoid being stuck at local optimums [7].

Fabricating the Reflector. The final step of WiPrint is to fabricate the reflector in the optimized shape. The ideal materials for the reflectors are glossy metals (e.g., aluminum), since they absorb less electromagnetic waves and better reflect wireless signals. To maintain a low cost, we first 3D print a plastic reflector substrate and then wrap it tightly with aluminum sheets (Figure 2).

4. FEASIBILITY RESULTS

Accuracy of Signal Propagation Modeling. Figure 3 shows how accurately our signal propagation model can match the actual signal propagation. We start with the baseline scenario where no reflector is placed around the transmitter. We measure the signal maps when placing the AP in the center or in the corner of the room, and examine how close they are to the signal maps estimated by the propagation model.

Impact of Reflector Shape. Next we examine the impact of reflector shape on the resulting signal distribution. We test two types of reflector shapes: concave and square-wave reflector. Both reflectors are printed using a Stratasys Mojo 3D printer. For both reflectors, we apply foil tape on the reflector surface. Figure 4(a)(b) show their final looks and their sizes with respect to the router.

Effectiveness of Optimized Reflector Shape. Figure 5 shows an example of a low-resolution desired signal map, the optimized reflector shape calculated by WiPrint algorithm, and the estimated signal map before and after placing the reflector behind the AP. The user desires stronger signals in region 2 and 3 and weaker or no signals in region 1 and 4. Using the optimized reflector shape

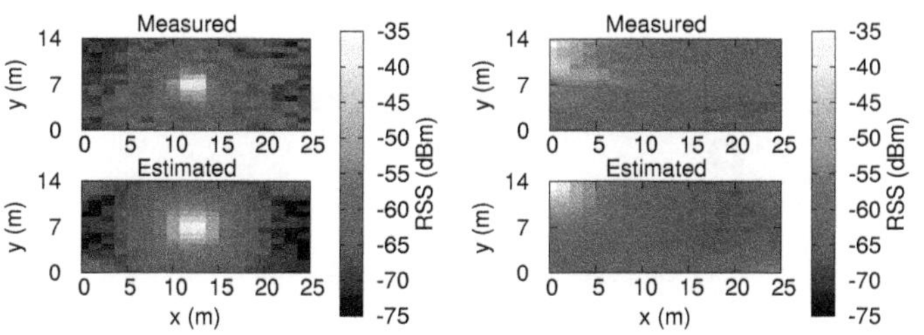

(a) TX in the center (b) TX in the corner

Figure 3: When no reflector is placed around the transmitter.

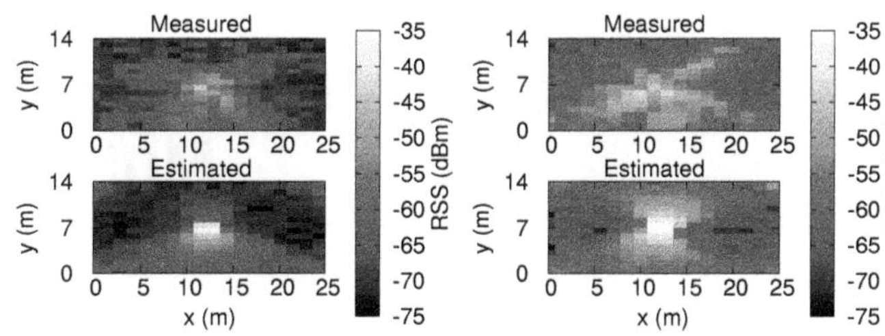

(a) Concave reflector (b) Square-wave reflector

Figure 4: Impact of the reflector shape on the signal distribution.

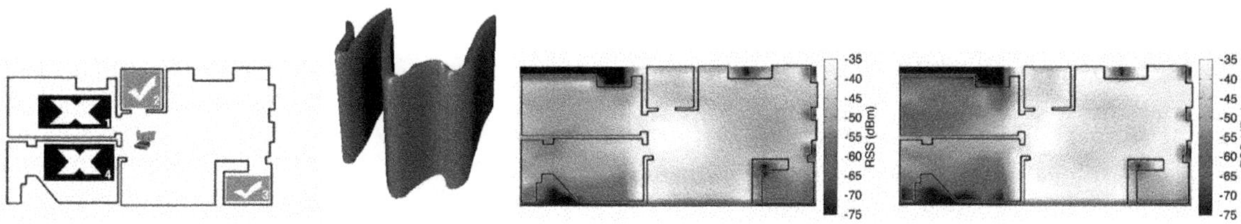

(a) Low-resolution desired signal map (b) Optimized reflector shape (c) Propagation without reflector (d) Propagation with reflector

Figure 5: Effectiveness of optimized reflector shape in steering wireless signal propagation.

(Figure 5(b)) generated by WiPrint, we effectively steer the signals away from region 1 and 4 and strengthen the signal in region 2 and 3, where the signal was originally weakened by the wall blockage. The resulting signal maps match the target signal maps, demonstrating the efficacy of WiPrint's preliminary algorithm design.

Cost Analysis. Printing the reflector took roughly 17 hours and consumed 6 in^3 of material for the model and 3 in^3 of material for support purposes. The material used by the printer was ABS-P430 thermoplastic and the material of the reflector costs around \$45. This is significantly cheaper than directional antennas (e.g., the Phocus Array used in [8, 10] costs \$9000 [11]). Less advanced directional antennas cost around \$100 [9]. Users can easily use online 3D printing services to manufacture the reflector, even if they do not have physical access to a 3D printer.

5. FUTURE WORK

We plan to evaluate desired signal maps (both in low and high resolution) more extensively, 3D fabricate the optimized reflector shape, and measure the actual signal maps. We also intend to more rigorously quantify the granularity our reflectors can provide and the resolution in the resulting signal coverage map. We also plan to compare our results to ones produced by antenna arrays.

Multiple Reflectors. Our current algorithm focuses on generating a single reflector in the optimized shape. An interesting extension is to consider multiple reflectors that can relay wireless signals to regions unreachable due to severe occlusion.

Higher Frequency Bands. We plan to extend WiPrint to higher electromagnetic wave frequency bands such as millimeter-wave band and visible light spectrum band. EM waves at higher frequency have better reflection properties and hence can be more effectively directed by fabricated reflectors.

6. ACKNOWLEDGEMENTS

This work is supported in part by the Dartmouth Burke Research Initiation Award and the the Class of 1993 Alumni Fund at Dartmouth College. Any opinions, findings, and conclusions or recommendations expressed in this material are those of the authors and do not necessarily reflect those of the funding agencies or others.

7. REFERENCES

[1] ANDERSEN, J. B., RAPPAPORT, T. S., AND YOSHIDA, S. Propagation measurements and models for wireless communications channels. *Communications Magazine, IEEE 33*, 1 (1995), 42–49.

[2] BAHL, P., AND PADMANABHAN, V. N. RADAR: An in-building RF-based user location and tracking system. In *Proc. of INFOCOM* (2000).

[3] CHEN, J., BAUTEMBACH, D., AND IZADI, S. Scalable real-time volumetric surface reconstruction. In *Proc. of SIGGRAPH* (2013).

[4] GERMAN, G., ET AL. Wireless indoor channel modeling: statistical agreement of ray tracing simulations and channel sounding measurements. In *Proc. of ICASSP* (2001).

[5] ISKANDER, M. F., AND YUN, Z. Propagation prediction models for wireless communication systems. *Microwave Theory and Techniques, IEEE Transactions on 50*, 3 (2002), 662–673.

[6] IZADI, S., ET AL. KinectFusion: Real-time 3D Reconstruction and Interaction Using a Moving Depth Camera. In *Proc. of UIST* (2011).

[7] JI, Y., BIAZ, S., PANDEY, S., AND AGRAWAL, P. ARIADNE: a dynamic indoor signal map construction and localization system. In *Proc. of MobiSys* (2006).

[8] NAVDA, V., ET AL. MobiSteer: using steerable beam directional antenna for vehicular network access. In *Proc. of MobiSys* (2007).

[9] Directional WiFi Antennas. `http://www.radiolabs.com/products/wireless/directional-wireless-antenna.php`.

[10] SHETH, A., SESHAN, S., AND WETHERALL, D. Geo-fencing: Confining Wi-Fi coverage to physical boundaries. In *Pervasive Computing*. Springer, 2009, pp. 274–290.

[11] Fidelity Comtech Introduces New Commercial Phocus Array(TM) System. `http://www.tmcnet.com/usubmit/2008/01/24/3227843.htm`.

[12] TSINGOS, N., FUNKHOUSER, T., NGAN, A., AND CARLBOM, I. Modeling acoustics in virtual environments using the uniform theory of diffraction. In *Proc. of SIGGRAPH* (2001).

[13] VALENZUELA, R. A. A ray tracing approach to predicting indoor wireless transmission. In *Proc. of VTC* (1993).

[14] Dramatically Improve WIFI Speed With a Soda Can! https://youtu.be/yz4aPaebe-k.

Poster: Evaluating Android Applications with Multipath TCP

Quentin De Coninck*, Matthieu Baerts*, Benjamin Hesmans†, Olivier Bonaventure†
Université catholique de Louvain, Louvain-la-Neuve, Belgium
*first.last@student.uclouvain.be
†first.last@uclouvain.be

Categories and Subject Descriptors

C.2.1 [**Computer-Communication Networks**]: Network Architecture and Design—Wireless Communication; C.2.3 [**Computer-Communication Networks**]: Network Operations—Network Management; C.4 [**Performance of System**]: Measurement techniques, Performance attributes

Keywords

Multipath TCP; smartphones; measurement; automation; Android

1. INTRODUCTION

Smartphones are the most popular mobile multihomed devices. End-user expects that thanks to their WiFi and cellular interfaces, they are able to seamlessly use all available networks. Unfortunately, reality tells us that seamless coexistence between cellular and WiFi is not as simple as what the user expect.

Several cellular/WiFi coexistence technologies have been proposed during the last years [4]. Some of them have been deployed. Recently, Multipath TCP [3] received a lot of attention when it was selected by Apple to support its voice recognition (Siri) application. As of this writing, Siri is the only deployed smartphone application that uses Multipath TCP. and there is no public information about the benefits of using Multipath TCP with it.

Multipath TCP is a TCP extension that allows to send data from one end-to-end connection over different paths. On a smartphone, Multipath TCP allows the applications to simultaneously send and receive data over both WiFi and cellular interfaces. It achieves this objective by establishing one TCP connection, called subflow in [3], over each interface. Once the subflows have been established, data can be sent over any of the subflows. Researchers have analyzed the performance of Multipath TCP in such hybrid networks [7, 1, 5, 2]. However, these analyses have been performed with bulk transfers between laptops and servers. As of this writing, no detailed analysis of the performance of real smartphone applications with Multipath TCP has been published.

We fill this gap in this paper by proposing a framework that automates user actions on Android smartphone applications to perform network measurements. We use it to analyze how eight popular smartphone applications interact with Multipath TCP.

MobiCom'15, September 7–11, 2015, Paris, France.
ACM. ISBN 978-1-4503-3619-2/15/09
DOI: http://dx.doi.org/10.1145/2789168.2795165.

2. AUTOMATING MEASUREMENTS

In order to collect a large number of measurements, we developed an automated tests framework that automates the interactions with these applications[1]. It contains more than 4000 lines of code and is divided into two distinct parts: one to control the smartphone and one to mimic user interactions in a reproducible way. It was designed to be reusable, modular using parameters and to cope with unexpected situations caused by the limited reliability of this kind of device.

2.1 Test scenarios

Our test scenarios can be divided into two categories: *upload intensive* and *download intensive* scenarios. Each test takes less than 120 seconds.

Upload intensive We first consider two interactive applications: Facebook and Messenger. With the Facebook application, our test first updates the news feed, then writes a new status, takes and shares a new photo with a description and finally performs a new check out status. With Messenger, it sends a text message, then puts a smiley and finally sends a new photo. Then we consider two cloud storage applications: Dropbox and Google Drive. For both, we create a fresh file containing 20 MB of purely random data and upload it.

Download intensive First, we use Firefox to browse the main page of the top 12 Alexa web sites with an empty cache. Our second application is Spotify. This is a music delivery application. The test plays a new music (shuffle play feature) for 75 seconds. Finally, we consider two popular video streaming applications: Dailymotion and Youtube. For both applications, we play three different videos in the same order and watch them for 25 seconds. Those videos are available in HD and we fetch the best possible quality even when using cellular networks.

2.2 Using Multipath TCP on smartphones

Several backports of the Multipath TCP kernel on Android smartphones have been released in the last years. However, these ports were often based on older versions of the

[1]See: `github.com/MPTCP-smartphone-thesis/uitests`

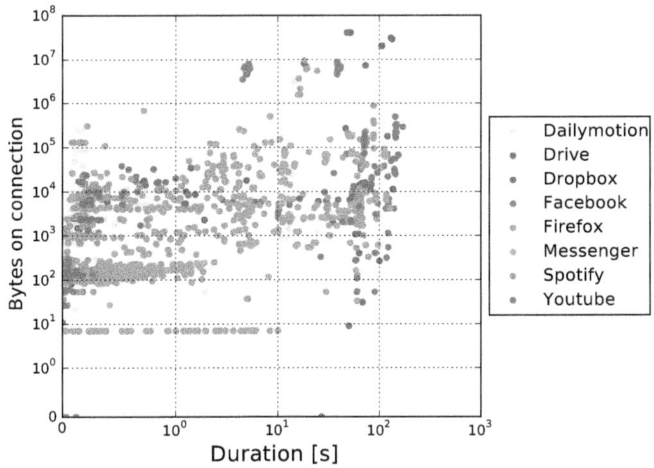

Figure 1: The smartphone applications, each point correspond to a connection for both upload and download traffic.

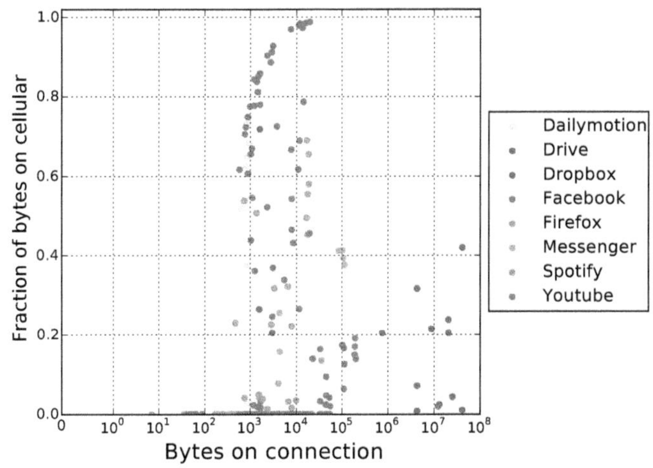

Figure 2: When the default route points to the WiFi interface, Multipath TCP mainly uses WiFi in upload for the short connections

Multipath TCP kernel. Measurements with such ports are not always representative of the current state of the implementation. For this work, we use the latest version 0.89v5 of the Multipath TCP Linux kernel that was backported on a Nexus 5 running Android 4.4.4. We also modified Android to enable the smartphone to use both interfaces simultaneously.

All the popular smartphone applications use TCP to interact with servers managed by the application developers. As of this writing, it is impossible to convince them to install Multipath TCP on their servers. To overcome this issue, we configured the smartphone to use a Multipath TCP capable SOCKS proxy server for all its connections. Each connection initiated by the smartphone is thus redirected to, and terminated at, the proxy server. The proxy server then establishes a regular TCP connection to the server. Thanks to this setup, the smartphone can use Multipath TCP over the cellular and WiFi interfaces while interacting with legacy servers. The SOCKS server itself is ShadowSocks and is configured to use the simplest encryption scheme to reduce the overhead. On the smartphone, we use the standard ShadowSocks client.

This setup allows us to capture all the packets sent by both the smartphone and the SOCKS server. We captured more than 85,000 connections over about 1200 tests conducted in February and March 2015 carrying more than 15 GBytes of data. The entire dataset is publicly available[2].

3. MEASUREMENTS

We first analyze the characteristics of the TCP connections that are used by smartphone applications. Figure 1 plots the TCP connections created by our studied applications when the smartphone uses only its WiFi interface. Each point on this figure represents one captured TCP connection. The x-axis (in logarithmic scale) is the connection duration in seconds while the y-axis is the number of bytes exchanged on the connection. Firefox is clearly the application that uses the largest number of connections (63.9 % of all connections) which is not surprising given that our Firefox scenario contacts the 12 top Alexa web sites. Dropbox (31.75%), Youtube (29.7%), Drive (19.9%), Dailymotion (9.6 %) and Spotify (4.96 %) are the applications that exchange the largest volume. On the other hand, our Facebook scenario generates long TCP connections that do not exchange too many bytes.

Some of the connections that we observed are caused by the utilization of a SOCKS proxy. We observe hundreds connections that last up to tens of seconds but only transfer seven bytes of data. After investigation, Firefox preventively opens new TCP connections but sometimes never uses them. The seven exchanged bytes correspond to the command sent by the SOCKS client. Most of the short connections that only transfer about 100 bytes are the DNS requests that are sent over TCP by the SOCKS client.

In our experiments, the connections can be categorized in 3 types: *(i)* the short ones with around 75% of all connections that last less than 1 second, *(ii)* the long ones that carry 98.5% of the overall volume, and *(iii)* long-lived ones with around 18% of all connections that do not carry a lot data (less than 10 KB).

Another important factor for TCP is the measured round-trip-time. In the upstream direction, we measured a median round-trip-time of 42.6 msec (50 msec for the mean). In the downstream direction, the median RTT is only 38.1 msec. On WiFi, 60% of the connections have a RTT shorter than 15.4 msec. There is some bufferbloat on the cellular network, mainly in the upstream direction, but bufferbloat remains reasonable compared to other networks.

3.1 Multipath measurements

We now enable Multipath TCP on our smartphone and perform the same measurements to understand how our eight applications interact with Multipath TCP. The first, but important, point to be noted is that we did not observe any incompatibility between the applications and Multipath TCP.

When a cellular and a WiFi interface are pooled together it is interesting to analyze how the smartphone balances its sending traffic over which interface. With the Multipath TCP implementation in the Linux kernel [6], this balancing

[2]See: `multipath-tcp.org/data/Mobicom15`

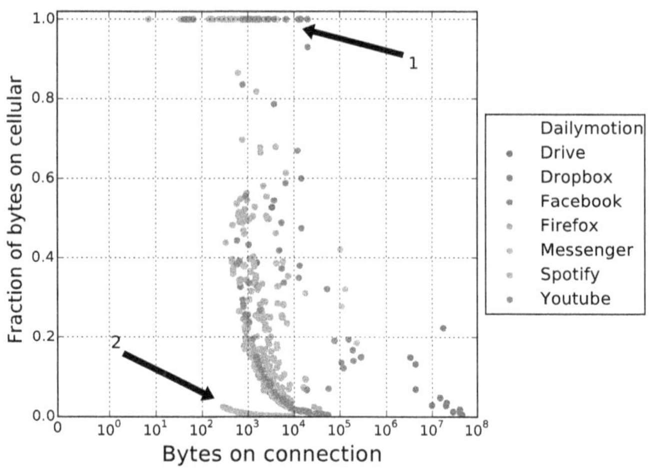

Figure 3: When the default route points to the cellular interface, lot of connections are aspired by Wifi in upload traffic.

depends on the interactions between the congestion control scheme, the packet scheduler, the underlying networks and the application.

On figure 2, we observe that 92.4% of all the connections only use the WiFi interface, but these connections only carry 1.1% of all data bytes. There are several factors that explain why Multipath TCP does not use the cellular network for these connections. The first one is the configured `default` route. When an application initiates a connection, Multipath TCP sends the `SYN` over the interface with the `default` route, in our case over WiFi. Preferring WiFi is the standard configuration of Android smartphones. If the Multipath TCP connection is short and only transfers a few KB, then most of the data fits inside the initial congestion window and can be sent over the WiFi interface while the second subflow is established over the cellular interface. Furthermore, the RTT over the WiFi interface is shorter than over the cellular interface. Thus, as long as the congestion window is open over the WiFi interface, Multipath TCP's RTT-based scheduler [8] prefers to send packets over WiFi. Indeed, 94.88% of connections in that case have a better average RTT on WiFi than 4G (this percentage is 75.44% if the maximal RTT seen is considered).

When setting the default route via the cellular interface, Figure 3 shows that most of short connections still use this one (as annotated as 1), but it concerns only 53.22% of all connections. It seems that even if the cellular interface is the default one, connections still mainly use WiFi, even for connections exchanging less than 1 KB. This occurs for connections that do not push data as fast as possible data. If the connection lasts more than two RTT, Multipath TCP has enough time to establish the second subflow. The packet scheduler will select the flow with the lowest RTT — 82.74% of all connections have a WiFi flow with a lower maximal RTT than the cellular one.

This explains the bottom of figure 3 (annotated as 2): a set of Firefox connections transferring fewer than 10 KB uses nearly exclusively the WiFi interface. A closer look at the packet trace reveals that these connections are part of the connection pool managed by Firefox. This behavior does not happen with other applications. When Firefox creates a connection in the pool, the initial handshake and the SOCKS command to our SOCKS server are sent. These packets are exchanged over the cellular interface and Firefox does not immediately send data over these established connections. This leaves enough time to Multipath TCP to create the subflow over the WiFi interface and measure its RTT. When Firefox starts to transmit data over such a connection, the RTT-based scheduler used by Multipath TCP prefers the WiFi subflow and no data (except the initial SOCKS command) is sent over the cellular one.

When the applications push more data over the Multipath TCP connection, the distribution of the traffic between the cellular and the WiFi interface also depends on the evolution of the congestion windows over the two subflows. If the application pushes data at a low rate, then the packet scheduler will send it over the lowest-RTT interface (WiFi in our case). However, this can be fragile. If one packet is lost, then the congestion window is reduced and the next data might be sent over the other interface. If the application pushes data at a higher rate, then the congestion window over the lowest-RTT interface is not large enough and the packet scheduler will send data over the second subflow.

4. DISCUSSION

In this paper, we have proposed and implemented[3] a measurement testing framework that enables researchers to conduct reproducible experiments with traffic generated by real applications. We have used it to evaluate how these applications interact with Multipath TCP. Our initial results show that smartphone applications work well with Multipath TCP. However, they also show that Multipath TCP uses too many subflows for short connections and that the default route has an impact on the traffic distribution. Our measurement framework will enable researchers to assess the impact of proposed modifications to Multipath TCP on real applications.

5. REFERENCES

[1] Chen, Y.-C., et al. A Measurement-based Study of Multipath TCP Performance over Wireless Networks. In *IMC'13* (2013).

[2] Deng, S., et al. WiFi, LTE, or both?: Measuring multi-homed wireless internet performance. In *IMC '14* (2014), ACM, pp. 181–194.

[3] Ford, A., et al. TCP Extensions for Multipath Operation with Multiple Addresses. RFC 6824, January 2013.

[4] Lee, K., et al. Mobile data offloading: How much can wifi deliver? In *SIGCOMM '10* (2010).

[5] Lim, Y.-s., et al. How green is Multipath TCP for mobile devices? In *AllThingsCellular '14* (2014), ACM.

[6] Paasch, C., Barre, S., et al. Multipath TCP in the Linux kernel. `http://www.multipath-tcp.org`.

[7] Paasch, C., et al. Exploring Mobile/WiFi Handover with Multipath TCP. In *ACM SIGCOMM CellNet workshop* (2012), pp. 31–36.

[8] Paasch, C., et al. Experimental evaluation of Multipath TCP schedulers. In *CSWS '14* (2014).

[3]All our code has been released on `multipath-tcp.org`

Poster: Network-Based UE Mobility Estimation in Mobile Networks

Dalia-Georgiana Herculea[1], Majed Haddad[2], Veronique Capdevielle[3], and Chung Shue Chen[1]

[1] Alcatel-Lucent Bell Labs, [2] University of Avignon, [3] Alcatel-Lucent

[1,3] Centre de Villarceaux, Route de Villejust, 91620 Nozay, France

[2] Rue Louis Pasteur, 84000 Avignon, France

INRIA-Alcatel-Lucent Bell Labs Joint Research Center, France

{dalia-gerogiana.herculea, veronique.capdevielle, cs.chen}@alcatel-lucent.com

majed.haddad@univ-avignon.fr

ABSTRACT

The co-existence of small cells and macro cells is a key feature of 4G and future networks. This heterogeneity, together with the increased mobility of user devices can generate a high handover frequency that could lead to unreasonably high call drop probability or poor user experience. By performing smart mobility management, the network can pro-actively adapt to the user and guarantee seamless and smooth cell transitions. In this work, we introduce an algorithm that takes as input sounding reference signal (SRS) measurements available at the base station (eNodeB in 4G systems) to estimate with a low computational requirement the mobility level of the user and with no modification at the user device/equipment (UE) side. The performance of the algorithm is showcased using realistic data and mobility traces. Results show that the classification of UE speed to three mobility classes can be achieved with accuracy of 87% for low mobility, 93% for medium mobility, and 94% for high mobility, respectively.

Categories and Subject Descriptors

C.2.3 [**Computer-Communication Networks**]: Network Operations - *network monitoring, network management.*

General Terms

Algorithms, Management, Measurement, Performance, Design.

Keywords

Mobile networks; Heterogeneous cellular networks; User mobility estimation; Time-based spectral spreading method.

1. INTRODUCTION

Future cellular networks will consist of dense small cells overlaid by macro cells. With the deployment of heterogeneous networks (HetNets), a mobile user will switch from one cell to another whereas the network must ensure continuous service and high quality user experience. Supporting service continuity is especially challenging due to potentially high handover frequency and the future requirement of ultra low latency. However, if the UE mobility information is available, then the network can pro-actively adapt to the user and guarantee seamless and smooth UE handover with optimal cell selection such that a UE could always experience maximum throughput [1].

For example, if the UE is classified as having low mobility, it may be more appropriate to attach him/her to a small cell so he/she can benefit from higher link capacity. Also, the network can decide to use such a UE for device-to-device (D2D) communications, multiple-input-multiple-output (MIMO) or other techniques that require a certain network topology for relatively long period. On the other hand, if the UE is classified as having a high mobility, the network may attach him/her to a macro cell to minimize the handover rate and maintain service continuity.

Several methods have been proposed in the literature to estimate the UE speed in specific use cases, e.g., crossing level based methods [2], covariance based methods [3-4], maximum likelihood (ML) based methods [5], and power spectrum based methods. The main drawback of these methods is that they do not cope with the large periodicity of SRS measurements as they aim at analyzing the speed dependent fast fading and Doppler characteristics of the signals. Due to large sampling period of sounding reference signal (SRS), the Nyquist frequency for avoiding spectrum aliasing will be reduced, which limits the maximum observable Doppler frequency and thus decreases the maximum observable speed. Furthermore, it is known that crossing level based methods are less efficient than covariance methods for small observation windows. Both techniques are sensitive to noise for small Doppler spreads. The ML based methods could provide near optimal performance but would need to know the signal-to-noise-ratio (SNR) and the Gaussian noise and have high implementation complexity.

In this paper, we propose a new method by defining a novel metric that is a function of the auto-correlation of the SRS measurements. This metric depends on the ratio of the UE speed to the decorrelation distance. Given this dependency, we can estimate the UE mobility by lookup in a reference data basis providing a one-to-one mapping between the metric and the UE speed, for a given decorrelation distance. The algorithm has low complexity. Meanwhile, simulation results using realistic data and mobility traces from the city of Cologne [6] show that the proposed method can determine the user mobility with high accuracy.

2. TIME-BASED SPECTRAL SPREADING METHOD (TSSM)

Shadowing is a spatial correlated process. The correlation between shadow fading at two points separated by a distance will decrease with the increase of their distance. This property is

MobiCom'15, September 07-11, 2015, Paris, France

ACM 978-1-4503-3619-2/15/09.

http://dx.doi.org/10.1145/2789168.2795166

notably captured by Gudmundson's correlation model for shadowing [7]:

$$\mathcal{R}_{\psi}(\tau) = \mathbb{E}[(\psi(t-\tau)-\mu_{\psi})(\psi(t)-\mu_{\psi})]$$
$$= \sigma_{\psi}{}^{2} e^{-\frac{v\,\tau}{D}} \qquad (1)$$

where $\psi(t)$ is a Gaussian random process, μ_{ψ} and σ_{ψ} in decibel are its shadowing fading mean and standard deviation values, v is the UE's speed while τ is the time variable, and D is the decorrelation distance at which the signal autocorrelation equals to $1/e$ of its maximum value [8].

Since $D = vt$, where v and t are the speed and time, our purpose is to find a metric that would vary proportionally with the speed. By applying the Fourier transform of the auto-correlation function [9], the power spectral density of the shadowing process gives a Lorentzian function with frequency

$$f = v/D \qquad (2)$$

which is to say that there exists a spread in spectrum under the effect of velocity. However, the Fourier transform is computationally expensive. Therefore, we will derive in time-domain a method to capture this behavior.

It is of interest to observe that when computing the second derivative of the autocorrelation function of the shadowing:

$$\left.\frac{\partial^2 R_{rr}(\tau)}{\partial^2 \tau}\right|_{\tau=0} = R_{r'r'}(0) = \mathbb{E}[(r'(t))^2], \qquad (3)$$

where $r(t)$ is the received signal amplitude. The relationship between the speed and the derivative of the SRS measurement can be thus expressed as:

$$\mathbb{E}\left[\left(r'(t)\right)^2\right] \sim \frac{\sigma_{\psi}{}^2 v^2}{D^2}. \qquad (4)$$

This implies that the standard deviation of the derivative of the measurements is a linear function of v/D.

Now, we define the TSSM metric as:

$$\sqrt{\mathbb{E}\left[\left(r'(t)\right)^2\right]} \qquad (5)$$

which is equal to v/D and corresponds to the spectrum spreading of the received signal amplitude. This leads to the following estimate approximation of the speed as a function of the received signal amplitude:

$$v \sim D\sqrt{\mathbb{E}\left[\left(r'(t)\right)^2\right]}. \qquad (6)$$

3. ALGORITHM AND SYSTEM MODEL

The speed dependent spread of the power spectral density is detected in time by exploiting the variance of the temporal derivative of the SRS signal. Figure 1 shows the TSSM metric as a function of the speed and decorrelation distance. As expected, the metric is increasing with the increase of speed and with the decrease of the decorrelation distance.

Given this observation, we build a database that maps the TSSM metric function of user speed for different values of the decorrelation distance. This database is stored at the eNodeB. The only prior knowledge necessary for the algorithm is the decorrelation distance corresponding to the environment. Its value can be determined through an initial learning phase. Once the database is built offline, the speed estimation is done online, for UE. The algorithm consists of the following steps illustrated in Figure 2.

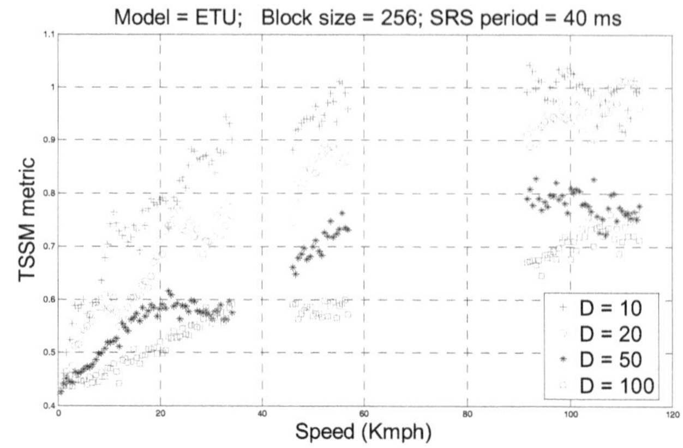

Figure 1. TSSM metric as a function of UE speed for different decorrelation distance *D*.

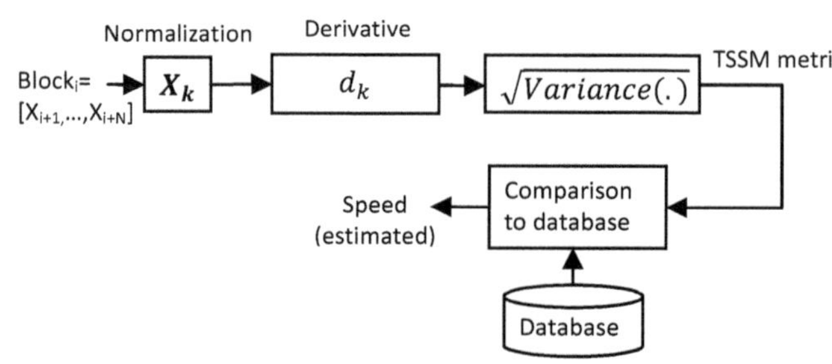

Figure 2. Per block implementation of the TSSM algorithm.

Taking blocks of N samples of SRS measurements, denoted by $[X_{i+1}, \ldots, X_{i+N}]$, the signal is first normalized:

$$X_k = X_k/\sqrt{norm(X_i)}. \qquad (7)$$

Next, derivatives are computed over the temporal blocks. This operation enables to smooth the signal, thus reduces fast fading and Doppler variations, for capturing only the slow variations of shadowing. Here,

$$d_k = (\mathbb{E}[X_k] - \mathbb{E}[X_{k-n}])/(n * T) \qquad (8)$$

where n is the delay between two points of derivatives and T is the measurements sampling period.

Then, the TSSM metric is computed per block i from the set of all derivatives d_k as follows:

$$\mathrm{TSSM}_i = \sqrt{\frac{1}{K}\sum_{k=1}^{K}(d_k - m)^2} \qquad (9)$$

where K is the number of derivatives computed on block i and m is the mean value over these K derivatives.

The above estimated metric in (9) is compared to the database that provides a one-to-one mapping between the speed and the TSSM metric, given shadowing decorrelation distance D. The speed that corresponds to the closest dispersion from this database is outputted as the estimated UE speed.

For 4G (3GPP-LTE) cellular networks, we consider three classes of UE mobility: low mobility class for speeds below 40 Kmph, medium mobility class for speeds between 40 and 90 Kmph, and high mobility class for speeds above 90 Kmph. The estimated speed will be compared to the above thresholds and then classified accordingly.

4. EXPERIMENTAL EVALUATION

We use signal measurements provided by Alcatel-Lucent eNodeB to test our algorithm. The SRS signals are sampled with a period of 80 ms, proving a proper resolution. For the mobility, we use real world vehicular traces provided by Kolontrace project that comprise recordings of user speeds in the city Cologne [6]. 3GPP extended typical urban (ETU) channel model is considered with 4G (3GPP-LTE) carrier frequency of 1.9 GHz. We build 160 minutes of signal measurements.

The normalization of the SRS signals is performed on blocks of size $N = 125$ signal samples. After taking derivatives, we compute the TSSM metric. By searching the nearest value to our TSSM metric in the database, the estimated speed is found by performing the one-to-one mapping. Figure 3 shows an example of the real trace of the speed of one user in the experiment in comparison to the estimated speed by the proposed algorithm.

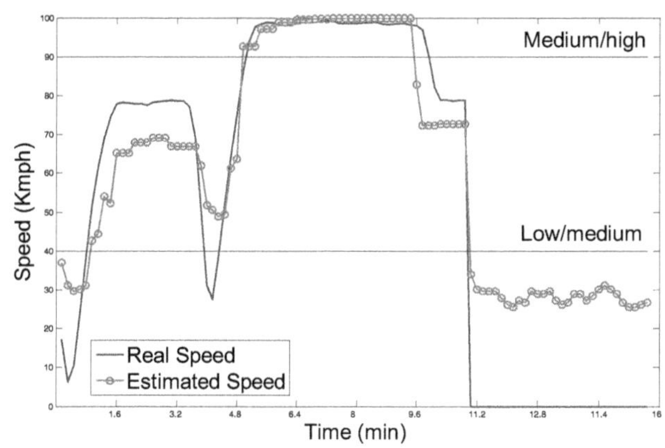

Figure 3. Example of real speed versus the estimated speed.

The above result is then classified into different classes by comparing to previously defined thresholds. These operations can be done in an adaptive manner. The estimation can be done not by blocks of samples but by using a moving time window. The percentages of correct classification in our experiment of 160 minutes are summarized in Table 1. These percentages offer a good accuracy in determining the speeds of mobile users in today's 4G (3GPP-LTE) networks.

Table 1. The percentages of correct classification of UE speed

	Low mobility class	Medium mobility class	High mobility class
Probability of correct classification	87%	93%	94%

For implementation and practical considerations, in Table 2, we list the key operations and computation requirements due to the proposed TSSM method in order to highlight its possible impacts to the eNodeB CPU and memory.

Table 2. Key operation and characteristics in TSSM

Main Functional Elements	• Normalization operation • Derivative computation • Variance computation
To eNodeB CPU	Around 10 operations per UE speed estimation
To eNodeB Memory	Circular buffer of 15 samples

5. CONCLUSION

In this paper, we have presented a new method to estimate the user mobility for LTE and future networks. TSSM method exploits shadow fading effects, taking advantage of the existence of SRS measurements at the network side, and provides a method of low (CPU) computation and memory requirement. Our evaluation studies based on real data and mobility traces show success rates of 87% for low mobility class, 93% for medium mobility class, and 94% for high mobility class, and indicate a high-accuracy implementable solution with low complexity.

6. ACKNOWLEDGMENTS

This work was partially supported by ANR project IDEFIX under grant number ANR-13-INFR. A part of the work was carried out at LINCS (www.lincs.fr). We would like to thank Frederic Ratovelomanana and Nidham Ben Rached of Alcatel-Lucent and Eitan Altman of INRIA for their valuable discussion and continuous supports in this work.

7. REFERENCES

[1] Nguyen, V. M., Chen, C. S., and Thomas, L. 2013. A unified stochastic model of handover measurement in mobile networks. *IEEE/ACM Transactions on Networking.*

[2] Zhang, H. and Abdi, A. 2004. Mobile speed estimation using diversity combining in fading channels. *IEEE Globecom.*

[3] Holtzman, J. M. and Sampath, A. 1995. Adaptive averaging methodology for handoffs in cellular systems. *IEEE Trans. on Vehicular Technology.*

[4] Zheng, R. Y. and Xiao, C. 2009. Mobile speed estimation for broadband wireless communications over Rician fading channels. *IEEE Trans. on Wireless Communications.*

[5] Braun, M., Sturm, C., and Jondral, F. K. 2010. Maximum likelihood speed and distance estimation for OFDM radar. *IEEE Radar Conference.*

[6] http://kolntrace.project.fr

[7] Gudmundson, M. 1991. Correlation model for shadow fading in mobile radio systems. *Electronics Letters.*

[8] Marsan, M., Hess, G. C., and Gilbert, S. S. 1990. Shadow variability in an urban land mobile radio environment. *Electronics Letters.*

[9] Haddad, M., Capdevielle, V., Altman, E., and Feki, A., Method and system for user speed estimation in wireless networks. *Filed patent 813871-EP-EPA*

Poster: Extremely Parallel Resource Pre-Fetching for Energy Optimized Mobile Web Browsing

Mohammad A. Hoque, Sasu Tarkoma
University of Helsinki, Finland
firstname.lastname@cs.helsinki.fi

Tuikku Anttila
Aalto University, Finland
firstname.lastname@aalto.fi

ABSTRACT

Mobile web browsing is experienced slow because of the limited rendering capability of the mobile devices, wireless latency, and incremental rendering of the page or resource loading. The browser renders resources in between two consecutive resource downloads. However, during this period, the wireless interfaces consume energy doing nothing useful. In this work, we measure the performance of SPDY for mobile web browsing. We demonstrate that mobile devices waste energy by keeping the wireless network interface idle between consecutive resource downloads. We next show that by identifying the embedded resources in a web page and downloading those resources in parallel at the very beginning can reduce the small idle periods and thus energy consumption by 20-50%, depending on the wireless network type.

Categories and Subject Descriptors

H.3.4 [**Systems and Software**]: Performance evaluation (efficiency and effectiveness); C.4 [**Performance of Systems**]: Measurement techniques

Keywords

web browsing, parallel connection, energy consumption, SPDY.

1. INTRODUCTION

Web browsers are among the important applications in mobile devices. Upon submitting an URL, the browser downloads the landing page. However, the landing pages are designed to be more interactive and resource oriented [5]. A typical such page can have ten to hundred resources from diverse domains, depending on the characteristics of the websites [1]. Therefore, the amount of total downloaded content may range few megabytes. The types of resources are mainly the Cascaded Style Sheets (CSS), JavaScripts, html files, and images.

MobiCom'15, September 07-11, 2015, Paris, France.
ACM 978-1-4503-3619-2/15/09.
http://dx.doi.org/10.1145/2789168.2795167.

Energy consumption for a web page loading comprises energy for downloading resources and for rendering the page. SPDY is a networking protocol that aims to reduce the networking latency by multiplexing a number of connections and compressing the headers [3]. On a mobile browser, network round-trip and resource loading times are the major causes of delay [8]. Therefore, multiplexing of connections results fewer round-trips that have a positive impact on the page load time. Modern browsers, such as Chrome and Firefox, already support this protocol. Google has additional infrastructure support, i.e. SPDY proxy which compresses web elements, specifically images [10]. Therefore, SPDY proxies are part of the web infrastructure [7]. The limitation of SPDY is head of line blocking. Problem with one connection will degrade the performance of the other multiplexed connections and thus overall performance degradation. Consequently, an UDP version of the protocol, called QUIC [2], is also in action in Android Lollipop devices. However, since the page rendering is a sequential process, SPDY and other protocols inherit the delay between two consecutive resource requests while rendering.

In this work, we first study how SPDY performs on Android platform. We measured the page download time on Samsung Galaxy S3 4G when SPDY enabled and disabled in Chrome browser, and the energy consumption of the mobile device using WiFi, 3G (HSPA) and 4G (LTE) networks. We found that wireless interfaces can waste energy by remaining idle in between two consecutive resource downloads. To remedy this, we developed a local proxy in a smartphone, which downloads all the resources at the very beginning in parallel connections. Therefore, there is no head of line blocking issue. We show that such approach can optimize wireless network resource utilization and energy consumption significantly.

2. MOBILE WEB BROWSING WITH SPDY

We selected six websites from the SPDY supported website list [4], and measured the page downloading time and energy consumption of Samsung Galaxy S3 4G when browsing with Chrome Beta via Wi-Fi, HSPA, and LTE. Fast Dormancy and CELL_PCH was supported by the HSPA network and DRX was enabled in the LTE network. We accessed the desktop version of the websites in the smartphone.

2.1 Page Downloading Speed

Table 1 summarizes the download times for different website connections. The total number of resources for a page

Site	3G SPDY	WiFi SPDY	LTE SPDY	3G SPDY Proxy	WiFi SPDY Proxy	LTE SPDY Proxy
wordpress	6.5	4.0	4.3	4.8	2.0	3.2
webtide	7.5	3.9	4.3			
cloudflare	7.8	3.8	5.5			
twitter	6.1	3.3	3.5			
facebook	6.8	3.9	3.4	4.4	3.2	3.2
youtube	7.2	3.8	4.2	4.0	3.4	3.5

Table 1: Average total time (S) required for downloading the front page and resources of websites with Chrome (SPDY and SPDY Proxy).

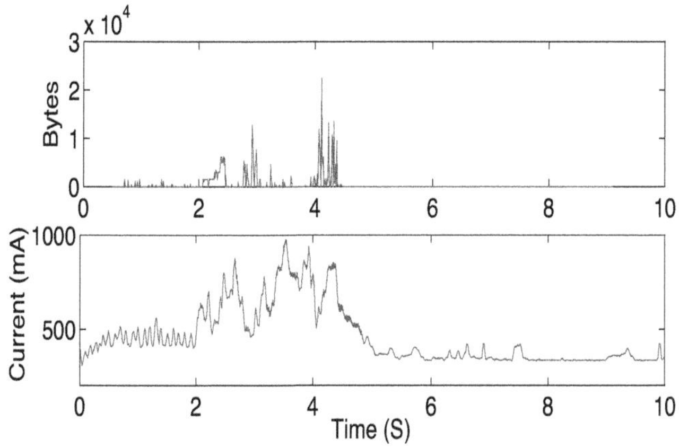

Figure 1: Traffic pattern and current consumption for accessing the YouTube page via HSPA with SPDY proxy.

varied from 20 to 80. The downloading time varied greatly over a 3G connection, and also somewhat on the Wi-Fi and LTE connectivity. However, according to the measurements SPDY seems to have a positive effect on download time, especially in 3G network conditions. We measured that SPDY improves by a maximum of 20% for HSPA access compared with browsing without SPDY. With Wi-Fi, SPDY was observed to slow down and in a LTE network SPDY has a small effect in half of the cases, 5% at best. One reason for SPDY being slower on a Wi-Fi connection might be that on a faster network, multiple concurrent connections get data faster than a single one. This was also observed in [1]. Table 1 also reflects the combined effect of SPDY and compression to the images in the SPDY proxy on download times.

2.2 Energy Consumption

While browsing the web pages, we captured traffic at the phone and measured the current consumption with the Monsoon Power Monitor. Figure 1 shows one such session. We can see that traffic is sporadic in nature and current consumption is high. Such sporadic download of the resources was also observed by Qian et al. [5]. Therefore, even though the actual data transfer for an individual resource takes a small amount of time, the interface remains active for a longer period. After the data transmission is over, current consumption reduces as the HSPA interface changes state from CELL_DCH to IDLE or CELL_PCH and DRX acts for LTE.

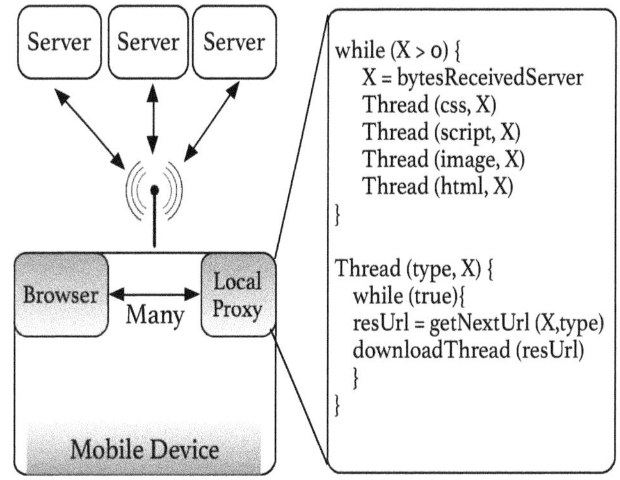

Figure 2: Pre-fetching web page resources at the local proxy in a mobile device.

3. RESOURCES PRE-FETCHING

We noticed that SPDY reduces total number of TCP connections, improves page load times, specially in slower network conditions. In addition, compression at the proxy can reduce the downloading time. Although rendering JavaScripts and CSSs can be equally expensive as an image [6], the nature of traffic still is a challenge. In order to alleviate the effect of sporadic traffic on the energy consumption, we suggest to pre-fetch all the resources embedded in a web page, while downloading the page itself.

Site	3G	Wi-Fi	LTE
wordpress	3.8	1.8	2.5
cloudflare	3.5	1.9	2.5
twitter	3.3	1.7	2.3
facebook	3.3	1.8	2.7

Table 2: Average total time (S) required for downloading the front page of the websites with resources using local proxy.

We developed a proxy for the Android phone and the mechanism is illustrated in Figure 2. The browser sends a request to the local proxy and the proxy retrieves the page on behalf of the browser. While receiving data for the page, the proxy scans the embedded URLs of four kinds of resources (CSS, JavaScript, image, and HTML page). It employs four separate threads; each for one type of resource. Each of these thread in turn generates multiple threads to download the actual resources depending on the number of resource URLs available of a particular type in the received data of the page. As a result, whenever the browser requests any resource while rendering, the proxy can serve locally. The downloading threads create separate TCP connections to retrieve the resources. Therefore, the idle period between two consecutive resource downloads is reduced. We accessed the HTTP version of the websites via this local proxy. Table 2 shows the required downloading time for all the resources and the webpage itself for four websites. We can see that such aggressive pre-fetching can reduce the downloading time significantly. We have also observed improvements in energy consumption with this strategy of aggressive pre-fetching.

4. DISCUSSION AND CONCLUSION

Some browsers may request and receive critical resources (CSS and JavaScript) at the very beginning of a page loading for fast rendering and keep the remaining resources in the queue. On the contrary, we aim to reduce the idle time between two consecutive resource downloads and DNS pre-lookup or caching can complement our mechanism. However, there are a number of challenges still required to be addressed. There can be hidden resources which are downloaded while rendering a downloaded resource and thus can jeopardize the pre-fetching effort. In addition, it is not guaranteed that all the downloaded resources will be utilized by the browser. Therefore, energy consumption or downloading could be further optimized if there would be a preprocessed list of resources for a webpage. HTML5 offers a mechanism namely AppCache with a cache manifest file for every page at the server in order to provide offline browsing support. Wang et al. [9] proposed a similar approach by constructing and caching a resource graph. However, these approaches face the above challenges for rapidly changing web sites and a solution is needed.

5. REFERENCES

[1] J. Erman, V. Gopalakrishnan, R. Jana, and K. K. Ramakrishnan. Towards a spdy'ier mobile web? In *Proceedings of the Ninth ACM Conference on Emerging Networking Experiments and Technologies*, CoNEXT '13, pages 303–314, New York, NY, USA, 2013. ACM.

[2] Google and Chromium. Quick UDP Internet Connections. `http://www.ietf.org/proceedings/88/slides/slides-88-tsvarea-10.pdf`.

[3] Google and Chromium. Spdy: An experimental protocol for a faster web, white paper, June 2013.

[4] Netcraft. Web server survey, May 2012.

[5] F. Qian, S. Sen, and O. Spatscheck. Characterizing resource usage for mobile web browsing. In *Proceedings of the 12th Annual International Conference on Mobile Systems, Applications, and Services*, MobiSys '14, pages 218–231, New York, NY, USA, 2014. ACM.

[6] N. Thiagarajan, G. Aggarwal, A. Nicoara, D. Boneh, and J. P. Singh. Who killed my battery?: analyzing mobile browser energy consumption. In *Proceedings of the 21st international conference on World Wide Web*, WWW '12, pages 41–50, New York, NY, USA, 2012. ACM.

[7] B. Thomas, R. Jurdak, and I. Atkinson. SPDYing up the web. *Commun. ACM*, 55(12):64–73, Dec. 2012.

[8] Z. Wang, F. X. Lin, L. Zhong, and M. Chishtie. Why are web browsers slow on smartphones? In *Proceedings of the 12th Workshop on Mobile Computing Systems and Applications*, HotMobile '11, pages 91–96, New York, NY, USA, 2011. ACM.

[9] Z. Wang, F. X. Lin, L. Zhong, and M. Chishtie. How far can client-only solutions go for mobile browser speed? In *Proceedings of the 21st International Conference on World Wide Web*, WWW '12, pages 31–40, New York, NY, USA, 2012. ACM.

[10] M. Welsh and I. Grigorik. Data compression proxy, Mar 2013.

Poster: VPN Tunnels for Energy Efficient Multimedia Streaming

Mohammad A. Hoque, Kasperi Saarikoski,
Eemil Lagerspetz, Julien Mineraud, Sasu Tarkoma
University of Helsinki, Finland
firstname.lastname@cs.helsinki.fi

ABSTRACT

Minimizing the energy consumption of mobile devices for wireless network access is important. In this article, we analyze the energy efficiency of a new set of applications which use Virtual Private Network (VPN) tunnels for secure communication. First, we discuss the energy efficiency of a number of VPN applications from a large scale deployment of 500 K devices. We next measure the energy consumption of some of these applications with different use cases. Finally, we demonstrate that a VPN tunnel can be instrumented for enhanced energy efficiency with multimedia streaming applications. Our results indicate energy savings of 40% for this class of applications.

Categories and Subject Descriptors

C.4 [**Performance of Systems**]: Measurement techniques; H.3.4 [**Systems and Software**]: Performance evaluation (efficiency and effectiveness)

Keywords

Virtual Private Network, traffic scheduling, energy consumption, multimedia streaming.

1. INTRODUCTION

Typically VPN applications are used for secure Internet, remote access to workplace, or making secure online transactions, for example. They are also useful to bypass the geo restrictions for different applications. Although the VPN applications cannot make users Internet access completely anonymous, they enhance privacy and security by using an encrypted secure tunnel, such as the SSH tunnel. Therefore, an attacker will see only the encrypted packets.

There are two kinds of tunneling; layer two and layer three. Layer 3 provides the underlying structure to set a VPN connection at the application layer. Modern mobile devices are powered with layer 3 tunneling protocol, such as IPSec, for exchanging IP packets. On the other hand, layer 2 protocols use frames. Figure 1 illustrates the path of a packet flow from a server to a mobile VPN client via a VPN server. At the OpenVPN server, the packet travels from kernel to the user space through the *tun*0 interface. The VPN server then encrypts the packet, fragments it if required, encapsulates with UDP/IP header, and again pushes the packet back to the kernel. As soon as the packet arrives at the client, the VPN application pulls the packet to the user space by reading the *tun*0 interface. The packet is decapsulated and the fragments are aggregated before being decrypted. In other words, the packet follows the reverse path, i.e. kernel→VPN user space→kernel→Application. In the case of an outgoing packet from the application at the mobile, the reverse process will be applied on the packet.

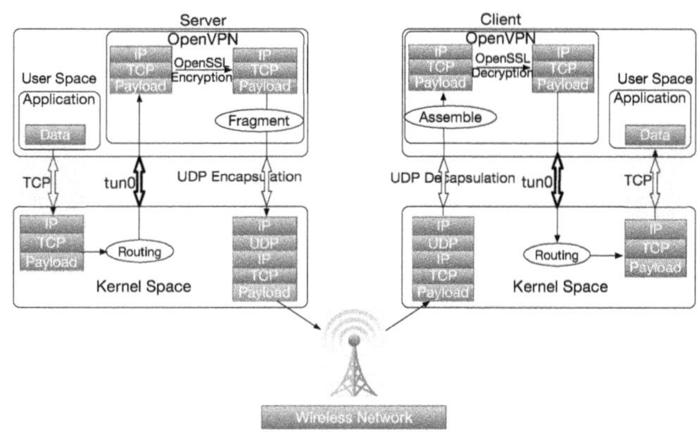

Figure 1: The flow of a packet in a VPN client-server communication with layer 3 tunneling.

If a TCP/UDP flow or the tunnel is idle for a while, the server pings the client. This ping interval is configured at the server and there is no standard procedure to configure the interval. However, frequent pings for mobile devices are not energy efficient and therefore, the ping interval can be increased to a higher value. At the same time, the traveling of the packets multiple times at the application layer may cause additional delay and energy consumption due to encryption/decryption. In this work, we take the first step to understand the energy consumption of some VPN applications available in the Android Play Store, such as Hola, Freedome, etc. First, we discuss the energy consumption of the VPN clients from the Carat energy ratings point view [6]

MobiCom'15, September 07-11, 2015, Paris, France.
ACM 978-1-4503-3619-2/15/09.
http://dx.doi.org/10.1145/2789168.2795168.

VPN App	Carat Users	Android Users	Avg. Battery Life (Hr)
Freedome	304	500-1000K	13.24
SurfEasy	62	1-5M	11.48
TunnelBear	258	1-5M	8.09
Hola	733	1-5M	8.38
CyberGhost	51	100-500K	7.75
VyprVpn	99	100-500K	7.97
Secureline	21	1-5M	7.68
HidemyAssprovpn	29	100-500 K	7.74

Table 1: Carat ratings of the VPN applications.

(see Section 2.1). We next measure the energy consumption of the VPN clients and our measurement results indicate that these clients create energy overhead for mobile devices (see Section 2.2). Finally, we demonstrate that a VPN tunnel can be instrumented for better energy efficiency with the multimedia streaming applications [3] (see Section 3).

2. ENERGY CONSUMPTION

In this section, we analyze the energy consumption of some popular VPN clients. First, we discuss their Carat energy ratings. Next, we present our measurement results.

2.1 Carat Energy Rating

Carat is a large scale collaborative data analysis framework for mobile application energy efficiency. It has both Android and iOS applications for collecting information from mobile devices and providing feedback to the users. The applications collect the battery and application information as samples from mobile devices. A sample collection event is triggered whenever there is a change in the battery level. In order to compute the rate distribution of the applications, Carat depends on the samples while discharging. In the cloud, Carat converts a set of samples from a client to a set of discharge rates. First, the samples are sorted according to time and then only those consecutive samples are considered over a period of time during which the device was not restarted, or not plugged with the charger. Then the discharging rates are computed from two adjacent samples. The higher the discharging rate, the lower is the battery life. Since, a sample also contains information about the running applications, we can correlate the rate with the application, when two adjacent samples indicate that application X is running. For more detail, the readers can follow [6].

Table 1 shows the energy consumption of a set of VPN tunneling applications, the number of users installed these applications, and the energy ratings of the applications. We notice that Freedome and SurfEasy offer better battery life than the others. In the next section, we measure the energy consumption of first four VPN applications from the list presented in Table 1 and compare with the Carat findings.

2.2 Measurements

We measured the energy consumption of Samsung Galaxy S5 in presence of the VPN applications presented in Table 2. We used the Monsoon power monitor [2] to measure the power consumption. The measurement scenarios were the following; energy consumption in airplane mode, only Wi-Fi enabled, only a VPN application was active, and an application traffic was tunneled through the VPN tunnel. We measured the power consumption while using three multimedia applications with four VPN clients. The duration of an application usage was 3-5 minutes and each usage scenario was repeated 3-4 times. The volume of the phone was lowest during the experiments.

VPN App	Avg. Power Consumption	Testing App	VPN Server Location
TunnelBear	206 mW		USA
	1638 mW	YouTube(4:31)	
	920 mW	TuneIn(3min)	
	491 mW	Skype (4 min)	
Hola	112 mW		USA
	1562 mW	YouTube(4:31)	
	720 mW	TuneIn(3min)	
	405 mW	Skype (4 min)	
SurfEasy	115 mW		USA
	1594 mW	YouTube(4:31)	
	700 mW	TuneIn(3min)	
	414 mW	Skype (4 min)	
Freedome	85 mW		Finland
	1521 mW	YouTube(4:31)	
	716 mW	TuneIn(3min)	
	390 mW	Skype (4 min)	

Table 2: Average Power Consumption of Galaxy S5 in presence of different VPN client with different usage scenarios via Wi-Fi.

The average power consumption of Galaxy S5 in airplane Mode is 15 mW. Then with Wi-Fi enabled, the device consumes 56 mW. The power consumption of the VPN applications was measured for two usage conditions. First, only the VPN application is running without any other active application. This would allow us to understand the power consumption of the VPN application when the device is not being actively used. Second, we investigated the energy consumption when both the target and the VPN application is running. Table 2 describes these four scenarios for each VPN application. We notice that Freedome consumes the lowest energy without any active application. Consequently, the energy consumed in presence of YouTube and other applications are also the smallest. On the other hand, in presence of Hola, TunnelBear, and SurfEasy, the mobile device consumes the highest energy. These results demonstrate that Carat ratings of the target applications follow the measurement.

3. ENERGY EFFICIENT TUNNEL

We can estimate the actual energy consumption of our target applications by subtracting the standalone VPN power consumption from the total power consumption. From the measurement results, it is obvious that a VPN application introduces energy overhead. The underlying factors can be the VPN configuration, the encryption mechanism, or the implementation of other application specific features, such as Hola uses P2P routing for better privacy.

In Figure 1, we can see that a VPN tunnel enables the access and control over all the packets coming from different applications. Hence, it is possible to manipulate the packets inside the tunnel for making the communication energy efficient at least for some multimedia streaming applications. The packets can be buffered for few seconds at the OpenVPN sever before being encrypted. This buffering makes the traffic bursty and saves energy at the client [4]. However, buffering is not applicable to the realtime traffic of Skype-like applications.

We configured the OpenVPN server for the ping interval of 1800 s and modified both endpoints of the VPN tunnel. First we modified the server-side of the tunnel to buffer the incoming audio streaming packets for the TuneIn Internet radio application. The buffering periods and the corresponding power consumption tuples are the following; (0s, 730mW), (1s, 550mW), and (2s, 490mW). We notice that a small amount of delay of the packets at the VPN server enables the smartphone to save a significant amount of energy and the power consumption decreases further as the amount of delay increases. However, we observed that coalescing the packets beyond 2 seconds triggers TCP retransmission and increases the periodicity of the packets. Consequently, the smooth playback at the client suffers and there is an increase in the energy consumption of the smartphone.

The VPN server can delay the packets even for longer periods by generating acknowledgements for both the streaming client and server. However, such a mechanism requires complex re-implementation of TCP at the VPN-server application. We rather apply a different approach at the client-side of the VPN tunnel. We modified the ICS OpenVPN client [1] to alternate the receive window size between zero and a higher value periodically. Setting the windows size zero forces the streaming server to buffer the data at it's TCP sending buffer until the VPN client generates an acknowledgment packet with higher window size. We preliminary investigated with the TCP window size resetting interval of 10 seconds and estimated that average power consumption was reduced by 40% from 730 mW to 443 mW.

4. CONCLUSIONS

Setting window size zero triggers TCP flow control and the streaming server sends window probe message according to the TCP persist timer. Therefore, the server-side of the tunnel can block the window probe by generating the zero window advertisements, which enables the smartphone sleep completely until it updates the window size.

Instrumenting a VPN tunnel would allow to schedule the traffic of multimedia streaming applications in general and in addition such a mechanism does not require any changes to the operating system or the application. However, the applications may have their own scheduling for energy efficient multimedia streaming [3,5], and overriding application flow control may not be always energy efficient. Therefore, a system-wide scheduling solution requires recognizing the traffic pattern of an application on the fly and then apply the appropriate scheduling of the streaming traffic without affecting the smooth playback. Our future work includes instrumenting the VPN tunnel for learning the traffic pattern.

5. REFERENCES

[1] ICS OpenVPN, https://github.com/schwabe/ics-openvpn.

[2] Power Monitor, www.msoon.com.

[3] M. A. Hoque, M. Siekkinen, and J. K. Nurminen. Using crowd-sourced viewing statistics to save energy in wireless video streaming. In *Proceedings of the 19th Annual International Conference on Mobile Computing & Networking*, MobiCom '13, pages 377–388, New York, NY, USA, 2013. ACM.

[4] M. A. Hoque, M. Siekkinen, J. K. Nurminen, S. Tarkoma, and M. Aalto. Saving energy in mobile devices for on-demand multimedia streaming – a cross-layer approach. *ACM Trans. Multimedia Comput. Commun. Appl.*, 10(3):25:1–25:23, Apr. 2014.

[5] X. Li, M. Dong, Z. Ma, and F. Fernandes. GreenTube: Power Optimization for Mobile Video Streaming via Dynamic Cache Management. In *Proceedings of the ACM Multimedia*, acmmm'12, New York, NY, USA, 2012. ACM.

[6] A. J. Oliner, A. P. Iyer, I. Stoica, E. Lagerspetz, and S. Tarkoma. Carat: Collaborative energy diagnosis for mobile devices. In *Proceedings of the 11th ACM Conference on Embedded Networked Sensor Systems*, SenSys '13, pages 10:1–10:14, New York, NY, USA, 2013. ACM.

Poster: A Low Cost People Flow Monitoring System For Sensing The Potential Danger

Ju Wang, Dingyi Fang, Xiaojiang Chen*, Liqiong Chang,
Zhanyong Tang, Tianzhang Xing, Chen Liu
Northwest University, Xi'an, China
{wangju,dyf,xjchen,lqc,zytang,xtz,lc}@nwu.edu.cn

ABSTRACT

For a long history, stampede is one of the high potential disaster when thousands of people gathered. Current monitoring systems, however, can only detect the presence of a small number of sparsely located targets, rather than to monitor the change of people flow where there are large number of dense crowd in the environment. This paper presents DanSen, a low-cost people flow monitoring system for sensing the potential danger using the existing wifi infrastructures. Inspired by the dynamic light scattering theory, the designed DanSen calculates the correlations between the initial channel state information (CSI) data and all the history CSI data to monitor the changes of people flow and also estimates the sharpness of the changes. By doing so, DanSen can be utilised to perceive the potential danger. Real-world experimental results illustrate the advantage of DanSen.

Categories and Subject Descriptors

C.2.1 [**Network Architecture and Design**]: Wireless communication

Keywords

People Flow; Device-free; DLS; CSI

1. INTRODUCTION

Recently, many people have been killed in the stampede, such as the Shanghai Bund stampede deaths up to 36 in 2014 [4]. One of the major factors that leading to such a tragedy is the lack of an effective approach to monitor the change of people flow. Many disasters however would be avoided if we can know the changes in the people flow. For example, Indian media reported that if they can learn the change of people flow, then a reasonable crowd control can be implemented and the 115 deaths in stampede could have been avoided [4].

There are two major related technologies can be utilised to monitor the change of people flow, i.e., the device-based method [7] and the device-free method [3]. By attaching devices (such as RFID tags or cellphones) to people , the device-based method can monitor the change of people flow. However, it is impossible to bind devices to all the people. It also may cause leakage of privacy. Unlike device-based method, device-free solutions are promising to monitor the change of people flow while keeping people unattached any devices and unaware of monitoring [1, 3].

Many RF based device-free monitoring approaches have been proposed [5, 2, 1]. However, these approaches have fundamental limitations that render them impractical for real-world environments. Specifically, they either require dedicated hardware (such as special RFID reader in [1]) or covering the mornitoring area with a dense, surveyed grid of sensors [5]. Those methods are not cost-efficient for large scale systems, such as retailing, warehouse, cargo transportation. Additionally, these past proposals are also limited in their ability to monitor the changes of people flow. In particular, they assume that the number of people is small and the human objects are located very sparsely. For example, R# [1] can only count the number of people at most 10 and do not work well when the region is densely distributed by many people. Indeed, a large number of dense crowd is a natural environment that we are facing when we monitor the change of people flow.

This paper introduces DanSen[1], **a low-cost people flow monitoring system that can be utilised to perceive the potential danger**. Compared with deploying many dedicated devices, DanSen use existing WiFi access points and WiFi devices (e.g., desktops, thermostats, refrigerators, smartTVs, laptops) for sensing the people flow, which has two main advantages: low cost and reusing of existing WiFi infrastructure. In its traditional form, DanSen needs the initial RF signal (such as the channel state information (CSI)[2] in this paper) measurements at the beginning of monitoring. Unlike past approaches [1, 5], which simply utilize the difference of initial data and online data to detect the presence of targets, resulting in less sensitive to the changes of people flow when many people densely gathered. DanSen leverages the DLS theory [6] to calculate the correlations between the initial data and the historical data over all time series. The advantages of leveraging DLS are (i) the change of correlations is sensitive to the change of people flow (or target density), which can be used to perceive the potential

*corresponding author.

MobiCom'15, September 07-11, 2015, Paris, France.
ACM ISBN 978-1-4503-3619-2/15/09.
DOI: http://dx.doi.org/10.1145/2789168.2795169.

[1]DanSen stands for Danger Sensing.

[2]CSI is a commonly used signal feature, which is a fine-grained value from the PHY layer.

danger when many people gathered; (ii) the characteristic decay time introduced by DLS, can be utilised to monitor the sharpness of changes, which is important for emergency rescue.

2. DESIGN OF DANSEN

In designing DanSen's method for monitoring the change of people flow, we are inspired by the DLS theory in statistical physics. Consider a glass of water, it is understandable that the pressure of the glass wall, which is caused by the molecular movement, is fluctuation over time. DLS describes the changes of the molecular movement based on a set of correlations. It has been verified that the movement of people would distort the signal fluctuation over time [1, 5]. When many people are gathered, if we consider each person as a molecule and the pressure of the glass as the signal distortion caused by the people, then, we can borrow the well-established DLS theory to monitor the change of people flow.

Design: We deploy some transceivers in the monitoring area. Each pair of transceivers measure a set of CSI amplitude time series. For a given CSI series $\{A(k)\}$, $1 \leq k \leq N$, where N is the number of sampled data. DanSen first calculates the correlation $f_{cor}[(A(1), A(k)]$ between the initial value $A(1)$ and the kth value $A(k)$ over all the N time series. Based on the DLS theory [6], the correlation $f_{cor}[(A(1), A(k)]$ is given by,

$$f_{cor}[A(1), A(k)] \cong \frac{1}{N}\sum_{j=1}^{N} A(j)A(j+k), \qquad (1)$$

where, $A(j)$ is the jth CSI amplitude data. Usually, the initial state of the people flow is safe. For example, all the people are in an orderly admission before the start of assembly. We suppose that the corresponding initial value $A(1)$ is known. Based on (1), we can get a set of correlations $G = \{f_{cor}[A(1), A(k)]\}$, where $1 \leq k \leq N$. DanSen utilises the trends in G to quantify and monitor the change of people flow.

Safety situation. If the elements of set G, keep a constant value over time, then it indicates that the people flow has not changed and all the people are safe.

Dangerous situation. If the elements of set G start with an exponential decay, then it indicates that the people flow has been changed and the potentially dangerous event, such as the stampede, may happen.

Now we will show how to estimate the sharpness of the changes in a potentially dangerous situation, which is important for emergency rescue. The sharpness of the changes can be described based on the characteristic decay time τ, which is introduced by the DLS theory. According to DLS [6], the elements of set G are an exponential decay function of k, which should satisfy the follows exponential expression,

$$G(k) = a + (b-a)e^{-k/\tau}, \qquad (2)$$

where, $a \cong [\frac{1}{N}\sum_{j=1}^{N} \mathrm{A}(1)A(j)]^2$, $b = [A(1)]^2$. Note that, (i) the set G is known as we mentioned before, i.e., G has been calculated based on (1); (ii) the the value of a and b also can be be easily calculated. Thus, there is only one unknown, i.e., the characteristic decay time τ, which can be acquired by the non-linear least squares,

$$\hat{\tau} = \arg\{\min_{\tau} \frac{1}{N}\sum_{k=1}^{N} \left\| G(k) - a - (b-a)e^{-k/\tau} \right\|^2\}. \qquad (3)$$

Based on DLS, the smaller the τ is, the more the sharpness of the changes are. Let's examine (2) closely. As we can see that, the smaller the τ is, the more rapidly the correlation decreased. Note that the correlation describes the similarity between the initial situation (safety situation) and the current situation. If the current situation changes to the dangerous situation quickly, then the correlation would decrease rapidly, i.e., the τ also would decrease rapidly. Thus, the characteristic decay time τ can be used to describe the sharpness of the people flow changes.

3. PERFORMANCE EVALUATION

We conduct real-world experiments on campus. Two pairs of transceivers are deployed on both sides of the road, as shown in Fig. 1. The transmitter (Tx) is an access point (TP WR740N) and the receiver (Rx) is an embedded notebook with the Intel WiFi Link 5300 NICs. We collect a set of CSI time series from 11:30 to 12:30 with the sample interval of 0.1s. The data is divided into three sets based on three time slots, i.e., "Time 1" from 11:30 to 11:50, "Time 2" from 11:50 to 12:10, and "Time 3" from 12:10 to 12:30. During the time slot "Time 1" and "Time 3", there is only a few people pass the road, which can be regarded as the safety situation, as shown in Fig. 1(a). While, there are lots of students pass the road to the canteen during the "Time 2", which can be regarded as the potentially dangerous situation, as shown in Fig. 1(b).

Comparison: In order to examine the performance of DanSen, we implement the state-of-the-art method, i.e., Ichnaea [5], for comparison. If the mean and standard deviation of CSI data show large distortions, then Ichnaea regards that the targets present.

Results: Fig. 2 shows the normalized correlations of "Time 1" (up) and "Time 3" (down), respectively. As we can see that the correlations almost keep a constant. Based on the previous analysis, such a constant suggests that the people flow has not changed and all the people are safe, which meets the real situation. Fig. 3 shows the normalized correlations of "Time 1" and "Time 2", i.e., the correlation results from 11:30 to 12:10. As we can see that the normalized correlations shows an exponential decay. Such a decay indicates that the people flow has been changed and the students in the potential danger, which also meets the real situation. As comparison, Fig. 4 shows the mean and standard deviation of the measured CSI time series. As we can see that the values of mean and standard deviation show some fluctuations (or distortions) in all the three time series. However, the distortions between "Time 2" and "Time 1" (or "Time 3") show a similar trend, and the distortions do not reflect the change of people. For example, there are large distortions even when there are a few people in the "Time 1" and "Time 3". The reason is that Ichnaea, including most of current methods [1], is designed to detect the present of a small number of sparsely located targets, rather than to monitor the change of people flow where large number of dense crowd in the environment. While DanSen leverages the correlations between the initial data and the historical data to monitor the change of people flow, which shows a better performance.

(a) Scenario with a few people. (b) Scenario with lots of people.

Figure 1: Experiment scene. In (a), a few people pass the road, which can be regarded as the safety situation. In (b), a large number of students pass the road, which can be regarded as the potentially dangerous situation.

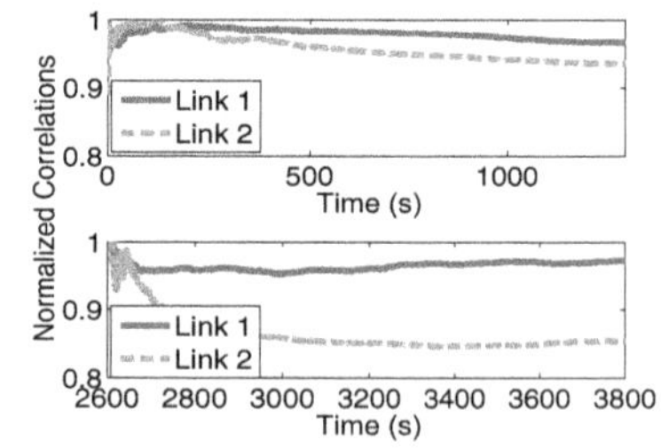

Figure 2: Normalized correlations under safety situation.

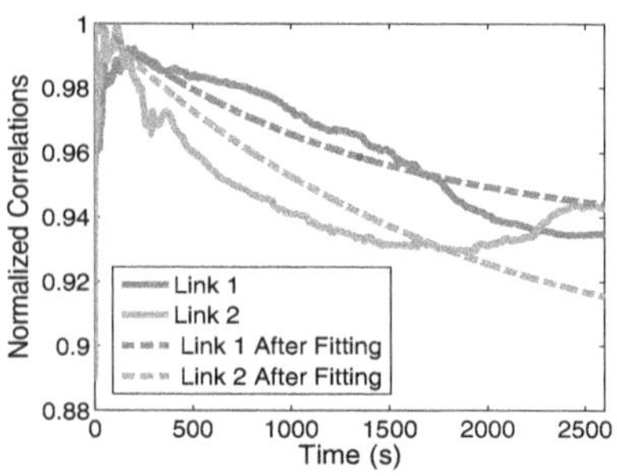

Figure 3: Normalized correlations under potential dangerous situation.

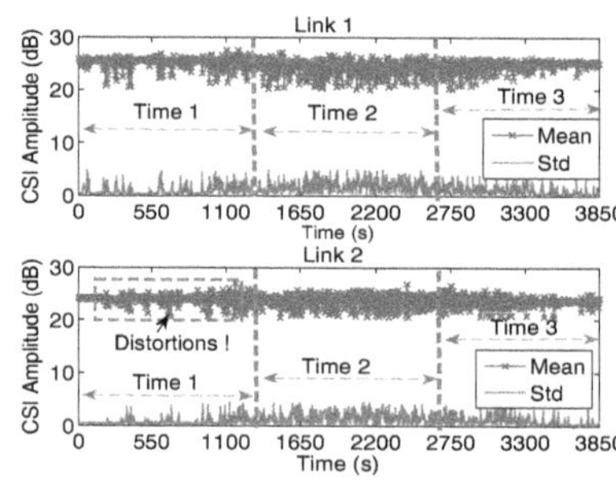

Figure 4: Morning results based on mean value and standard deviation.

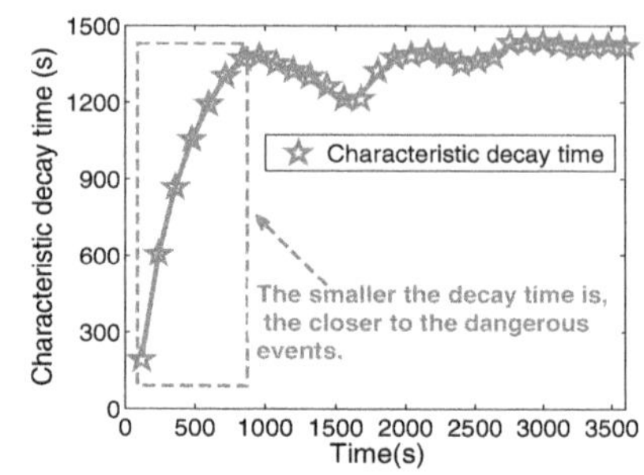

Figure 5: Sharpness of the changes.

In the last experimental results, we shall show how characteristic decay time τ reflects the sharpness of the changes. Let 12:00 be the time point when the potentially dangerous taken place. We choose different time that earlier than 12:00 as the initial monitoring time. For each time interval, which starts from an initial time and ends to 12:00, we calculate the characteristic decay time τ. Fig. 5 shows the relationship between time interval and normalized correlations. As we can see that, the closer to the accident event, the smaller the τ is. Thus, characteristic decay time is a rule that measures the distance from the danger to you!

Acknowledgments

This work was supported by Project NSFC (61170218, 61272461, 61373177), Project National Key Technology R&D Program (2013BAK01B02, 2013BAK01B05), and Graduate Innovative Education Project of Northwest University YZZ14002.

4. REFERENCES

[1] H. Ding, J. Han, A. Liu, J. Zhao, W. Xi, Z. Jiang, and P. Yang. Human object estimation via backscattered radio frequency signal. In *IEEE INFOCOM*, pages 361–369, 2015.

[2] H. Jiang, T. Yu, C. Tian, G. Tan, and C. Wang. Connectivity-based segmentation in large-scale 2-d/3-d sensor networks: Algorithm and applications. *IEEE/ACM Transactions on Networking*, 23(1):15 – 27, 2015.

[3] H. Ma, C. Zeng, and C. X. Ling. A reliable people counting system via multiple cameras. *ACM Transactions on Intelligent Systems and Technology*, 3(2):31, 2012.

[4] B. NEWS. `http://www.bbc.com/news/world/asia`.

[5] A. Saeed, A. E. Kosba, and M. Youssef. Ichnaea: A low-overhead robust wlan device-free passive localization system. *IEEE Journal of Selected Topics in Signal Processing*, 8(1):5–15, 2014.

[6] K. Schmitz. *Introduction to dynamic light scattering by macromolecules.* Elsevier, 2012.

[7] Y. Wen, X. Tian, X. Wang, and S. Lu. Fundamental limits of rss fingerprinting based indoor localization. In *IEEE INFOCOM*, pages 485–483, 2015.

Poster: Unified RemoteU¡ for Mobile Environments

Miguel Almeida Carvalho João Nuno Silva
INESC-ID Lisboa – Instituto Superior Técnico Portugal – Universidade de Lisboa, Portugal
miguel.d.carvalho@tecnico.ulisboa.pt joao.n.silva@inesc-id.pt

ABSTRACT
In our daily lives we assist to an exponential growth of mobile and fixed devices that surround us, though many of them having limited resources, and not even providing an interface screen. In this paper, we present remoteU¡, a middleware that allows the interaction of those devices with users, resorting to simple but expressive programming mechanisms, and providing efficient implementation and communication.

Categories and Subject Descriptors
C.2.4 [**Computer-Communication Networks**]: Distributed Systems – Distributed applications

H.5.2 [**Information Interfaces and Presentation**]: User Interfaces – Graphical user interfaces (GUI)

Keywords
Mobile user interface; Mobile computing; IoT; Middleware

1. INTRODUCTION
In the past few years there has been a popularization of mobile devices, especially smartphones, and nowadays many accessories are being developed to interact with them, expanding their capabilities. This has motivated developers to design applications that can improve the communication between them.

Ambient intelligence is another area where this type of applications are relevant, since one of the main goals is that the technology disappears and only the user interface is perceived by users. Also Internet of Things aims to interconnect any kind of objects and requires user interaction so that users can access and control them.

Developing applications that interact with users is demanding. In many cases programmers need to develop a whole server-client architecture application, and it's from greater importance to provide them with tools that can ease this process. Good examples of these devices are "Chromecast" from "Google" and the smartwatches, devices that interact with or are controlled by mobile phones, but require the development of both client and server applications.

In this work we present a middleware that allows complex interaction between devices (with limited resources and no screen) and users, resorting to local connectivity and mobile devices (such as smartphones or tablets), also relieving the programmer from the communication and interaction programming burden.

MobiCom'15, September 07-11, 2015, Paris, France
ACM 978-1-4503-3619-2/15/09.
http://dx.doi.org/10.1145/2789168.2795170

2. RELATED WORK
In current mobile environments the presentation of information on remote devices resort to remote screen protocols, Distributed UI infrastructures or to web based architectures. These systems allow the interaction between the user and the scattered devices, but require the existence of external infrastructures, complex programming or demand high computational resources. In order to reduce the programming of explicit client/server interaction between the devices and the screens, several approaches exist.

Several mobile UI systems (such as MoCHA [**5**]) are web-based systems and allow for rich interactions between pervasive displays and users with mobile devices, in which both interact through a web page available at a certain address. MoCHA assumes that there is an Internet connection, and only a prototype is presented, not providing any kind of API.

PuReWidgets [**2**] is a toolkit for developing interactive public display applications, composed by a widget library and web service that handles interaction events, providing programmers with high-level interaction abstractions. It was developed using a cloud platform that implies the dependency of Internet connection.

A web-based toolkit for remote direct manipulation interaction with public displays via smartphones [**3**] is being developed to help programmers in the creation of applications with less effort. The toolkit provides controls such as joystick, text input, and multi-touch cursor events. The work is still in development, and it is a browser-based architecture.

The DireWolf [**4**] is a framework for distributed web applications based on widgets. It helps managing of a set of devices providing easy distribution of widgets among them, and guaranteed the preservation of the state. This work is more targeted for designing collaborative and multi-user applications.

The concept of remote screen isn't new in computation as many systems based on this idea started being developed long time ago, though we only mention the most relevant. One of the most interesting systems with the same client-server approach we present is the X Window System (X11) [**1**]. X11 uses a client-server model where the users terminal is the server and the applications the clients. It provides a framework for a GUI environment, though it doesn't implement the user interface, as each application is responsible for that, resulting in many different types.

Virtual Network Computing (VNC) [**6**] is an application originated in the late nineties that allows sharing a screen remotely. It is particularly useful for remote technical support and accessing files on remote computers, like accessing a work computer from home. One of the most interesting features of VNC is that is platform-independent and the code is open source thus is has generated a vast number of implementations.

2.1 Current limitations
Most of the mobile UI systems are implemented in a browser-based architecture, and in most cases require Internet access so they aren't able to operate in a closed environment. Moreover

many of them are prototype architectures that don't provide any API for third-party developers.

Regarding to X11 and VNC, both of these systems present many disadvantages when implementing in small devices, the most relevant being the fact that, as they aren't designed for this purpose, they will consume too many resources. Also they add too much network overhead when transmitting the necessary information to generate interactions. The fact that they don't provide the same UI to the user when dealing with different applications is another negative aspect.

3. ARCHITECTURE

The main requirements of our system are: i) it should be generalizable to avoid the duplication of implementations; ii) provide the presentation of the usual interactions so that the interface matches the appearance of the most popular applications; iii) hide the client/server architecture from the programmer making it possible to develop without worrying with the underlying interaction methods; and iv) be interoperable with the majority of the available devices.

3.1 Solution

Figure 1 depicts the proposed solution architecture. Both the headless and mobile devices are represented and divided by layers.

The first layer (L1) represents the network, which consists in any kind of connection, such as Wi-Fi or Bluetooth, or even a wired connection such as USB. We assume that there is a communication socket established where the middleware application operates. Thus we don't implement discovery mechanisms, how devices recognize each other and establish the communication process is out of the scope of this work.

The second layer (L2) is the core of the middleware system, and it's represented both in the headless device, where the main application runs, and in the mobile device by the remoteU¡ library. The system will be responsible for providing interaction mechanisms between them and this will be made through the generation and management of defined messages.

The programming API represents the third level (L3) of the architecture, as it's one of the distinctive features of the remoteU¡ system. It provides a set of methods that can be invoked in the application that will automatically generate the widgets that will be displayed in the user mobile device. At present it is available in Java and C++ languages.

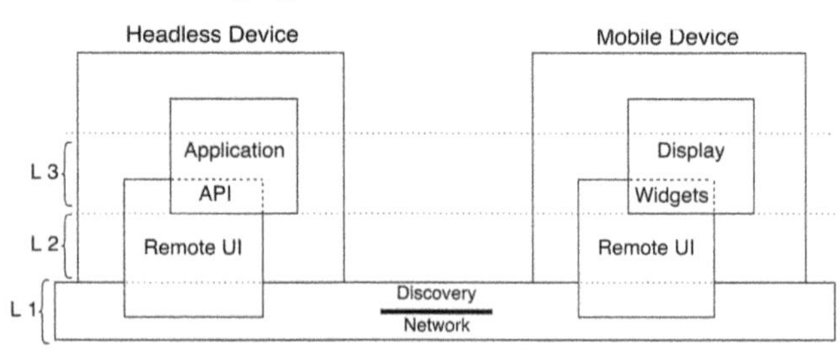

Figure 1 - System Architecture.

RemoteU¡ is communication agnostic. It operates over any kind of socket connection that is available. In order to exchange the messages between the client and server, instead of the traditional languages such as XML or JSON we use "Protocol Buffers", which are an efficient mechanism for serializing structured data, and are simpler and faster then the others. Resources and service discovery mechanisms are also independent of our solution. The application logic is programmed with the regular language structures, and the user interaction is done through the remoteU¡ API.

3.2 Widgets

Widgets are one of the most useful resources programmers have nowadays for implementing interaction features in their applications, as they represent interface components with clear functionality dedicated to small tasks. Widgets are reusable for multiple purposes in different applications so their use in the design of mobile applications is very common. It reduces the overhead in the development and also provides users with a common language for interacting with the applications.

RemoteU¡ allows the creation of screens containing instances of the more common classes of widgets: Button; Textbox; Checkbox; Radio Button; Slider; Range Slider; Date Picker. It is also possible to display text or images on the screen, or send files to open in the appropriate application. "jQuery Mobile" is used for the widgets implementation, offering wide compatibility and availability and allowing the presentation using a consistent design and layout.

3.3 Interaction

RemoteU¡ allows atomic interaction implementing request-response transactions, much like an RPC call in "command line interfaces". The main difference is that the interaction process is programmed on the client and presented in the mobile device. It is also possible to implement an asynchronous behavior, so that the system may send results whenever there are changes on the widgets input. It is also possible to update fields like images or text fields of an already presented screen. The interaction flow is defined by the structure of the source code (not event driven) and is programmed using the developed API that provides methods to generate each type of widget mention in section 3.3.

As use case scenario, we present an example in the context of IoT, in home automation domain. Imagine you want to use the mobile phone to control the lighting system of a room. Instead of the programmer having to implement the interfaces according to each light device, that in many cases differs form each other, the devices could generate their own interactions, and the programmer just needed to aggregate and route the requests and responses. Even in the present reality remoteU¡ can help the developer providing interaction abstractions and allowing generating an interface screen with just a few lines of code. Figure 2 shows the necessary code (in C++) to generate the interface screen example presented in Figure 3. It allows changing the present configuration of two sets of light of a room, the ambient and task lighting.

```
//Create RemoteWidgets object:
RemoteWidgets rw;
//Add Text field:
rw.addText("Id-1", "The system automatically adjusted the ambient "
        "and task lights by default. You may change it now.");
//Add button to turn off ambient lights:
rw.addButton("Turn off ambient lights");
//Add Slider to adjust lamp lights:
vector<string> optionslider;
optionslider.push_back("Choose intensity of lamp lights:"); //title
optionslider.push_back("3"); //default value
optionslider.push_back("1"); //min. value
optionslider.push_back("5"); //max. value
optionslider.push_back("1"); //step value
rw.addSlider(optionslider);
//Add button to close screen:
rw.addButton("Close");
//Get object to send to socket:
RemoteScreen rs = rw.GetRemote();
```

Figure 2 – Example of code to generate an interface screen.

Another good example is in the context of public displays, where it's very common to have mapping applications available for users to search points of interest and get directions to a certain destination. Most of the times this requires having a display with touch screen technology so users can interact and input some query. Besides being more expensive than normal ones, current solutions have other disadvantages: correct physical positioning of the screen and difficulty in sharing with multiple users. Using the mobile phone as an input mechanism solves these drawbacks: remoteU¡ allows the development of complex user interaction with the screens.

RemoteU¡ can easily be integrated with already developed systems, not requiring significant changes in an existing application to extend features like presenting UI's in a mobile device recurring to our middleware.

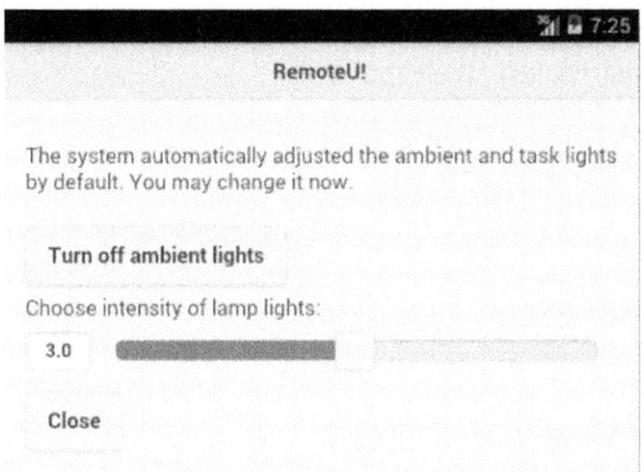

Figure 3 - UI generated on mobile screen.

4. EVALUATION

At the present moment, remoteU¡ is being used as the UI framework for a mobile phone accessory (in the context of the PCAS[1] project) that securely stores user files and controls its access using biometrics. It connects via USB although it could use Bluetooth or Wi-Fi, allowing easily generating necessary interaction screens that are displayed to the users.

Public displays are gaining popularity, and most of them are used only for advertising and information, though users are feeling more interested in the possibility of using them as a resource to their needs. This requires the use of simple interactions, like sending text or selecting between options through their smartphones. In the context of "IoT", remoteU¡ will allow the interaction with a series of objects on the everyday life, for configuration, management or normal operation, even with power or connection constrained devices.

Table 1 - Payload of different types of messages (bytes)

	Request size	Response size
Figure 3. Example	222	86
Single widget (average)	27	58
2 widgets (min/max)	29 / 138	77 / 437
3 widgets (min/max)	48 / 201	91 / 646
10 widgets (min/max)	196 / 642	443 / 2105

[1] www.pcas-project.eu

4.1 Performance metrics

In order to evaluate the efficiency of the system we now present, in table 1, some performance metrics based on the payload of messages to generate interaction screens from the application to the mobile device, and the respective response.

The payloads are minimal, leading to efficient communication independently of the bandwidth and latency of the selected network link.

5. CONCLUSION

The remoteU¡ in conjunction with the programming languages control structures allows the efficient definition of complex interactions with the users. Besides the simple declaration of screens to present, the program logic allows the definition of complex interactions without resorting to event programming, complex resource files or complex communication patterns. This allows the use of this interaction on had-hoc, encounter networks and deployment on low resources devices. Its generality and communication channel agnosticism will allow the use of the same middleware in the interactions with several resources (smartphone accessories, embedded device, "IoT", public advertising) by a common infrastructure. Furthermore its efficient encoding of screen makes it apt to any network link.

The architecture, implementation and API presents satisfies the previously presented requirements: i) allows the reuse of the middleware for multiple applications; ii) implements most available widgets and is usable in most classes of applications; iii) relieves programmers from client-server programming; and iv) is interoperable with the majority of the devices, and communication links.

6. ACKNOWLEDGMENTS

This work was supported by national funds through Fundação para a Ciência e a Tecnologia (FCT) with reference UID/CEC/50021/2013, and by the European Commission through the contract no. 610713 (PCAS).

7. REFERENCES

[1] Asente, P. and Swick, R. X Window System Toolkit: The Complete Programmer's Guide and Specification. Digital Press, 1990.

[2] Cardoso, J. and José, R. PuRe Widgets: A Programming Toolkit for Interactive Public Display Applications. In Proceedings of the 4th ACM SIGCHI symposium on Engineering interactive computing systems, 51-60, 2012.

[3] Cardoso, J. and Barreira, M. A web-based toolkit for remote direct manipulation interaction with public displays via smartphones. In Proceedings of the 11th International Conference on Mobile and Ubiquitous Systems: Computing, 357-358, 2014.

[4] Kovachev, D., Renzel, D., Nicolaescu, P. and Klamma, R. DireWolf - Distributing and Migrating User Interfaces for Widget-based Web Applications. In Proceedings of the 13th International Conference on Web Engineering, 2013.

[5] Oat, E., Francesco, M., and Aura, T. MoCHA: Augmenting Pervasive Displays through Mobile Devices and Web-based Technologies. In The First Workshop on Developing Applications for Pervasive Display Networks, 506-511, 2014.

[6] Richardson, T., Stafford-Fraser, Q., Wood, K. R. and Hopper, A. 1998. Virtual network computing. Internet Computing, vol. 2, no. 1, pp. 33-38, January 1998.

Poster: Use your Senses: A Smooth Multipath TCP WiFi/Mobile Handover

Alexander Frömmgen
Databases and Distributed Systems
TU Darmstadt, Germany
froemmge@dvs.tu-darmstadt.de

Sreeram Sadasivam
Databases and Distributed Systems
TU Darmstadt, Germany
sreeram.sadasivam@stud.tu-darmstadt.de

Sabrina Müller
Communications Engineering Lab
TU Darmstadt, Germany
s.mueller@nt.tu-darmstadt.de

Anja Klein
Communications Engineering Lab
TU Darmstadt, Germany
a.klein@nt.tu-darmstadt.de

Alejandro Buchmann
Databases and Distributed Systems
TU Darmstadt, Germany
buchmann@dvs.tu-darmstadt.de

ABSTRACT

The handover from WiFi to mobile networks is known to lead to TCP connection drops due to changing IP addresses. Multipath TCP (MPTCP), a recent TCP extension, enables a transparent mobile handover by combining subflows on multiple interfaces, such as WiFi and LTE, to one logical connection. MPTCP provides multiple handover modes, which differ in their energy consumption and the performance during the handover. The *Full-MPTCP* mode uses permanently both WiFi and the mobile network, which increases energy consumption. The *Single-Path* mode establishes the mobile network connection after the WiFi connection broke, which leads to a short performance degradation.

In this paper, we argue that this trade-off is not necessary. We propose to use the available (sensor) information to forecast the mobile handover. This allows switching to the Full-MPTCP mode before the WiFi connection breaks, providing both low energy consumption and high performance during the handover. For a first experimental evaluation, we use a declining WiFi link quality to forecast a handover. Our real world measurements show that both low energy consumption and high performance during the handover are possible at the same time.

Categories and Subject Descriptors

C.2.1 [**Computer-Communication Networks**]: Network Architecture and Design—*Wireless Communication*; C.2.5 [**Computer-Communication Networks**]: Local and Wide-Area Networks

MobiCom'15, September 7–11, 2015, Paris, France.
ACM ISBN 978-1-4503-3619-2/15/09.
DOI: http://dx.doi.org/10.1145/2789168.2795171.

Keywords

MPTCP, Vertical Handover, WiFi/LTE

1. INTRODUCTION

The handover of mobile devices from WiFi to mobile networks is known to lead to TCP connection drops due to changing IP addresses. Many approaches, such as Mobile IP [5] and application layer solutions, were proposed, but are not widely used. Multipath TCP (MPTCP) [2] is currently the most promising solution. Apple's natural language user interface *Siri*[1], for example, is known to use MPTCP for mobile handover. MPTCP can use multiple network interfaces simultaneously by combining TCP subflows on these interfaces as one logical connection. Thereby, MPTCP follows the end-to-end principle and does not require changes to the network or the application, i.e., an MPTCP connection appears like a regular TCP connection to the network. Raiciu et al. [6] showed with their Linux kernel implementation that MPTCP is deployable in real mobile networks.

Paasch et al. [4] analyzed the vertical MPTCP handover and proposed three handover modes. 1) The *Full-MPTCP* mode, which uses all possible interfaces and subflows as early as possible. 2) The *Backup* mode, which creates additional connections as early as possible, but only uses them after the initial subflow breaks. 3) The *Single-Path* mode, which creates additional subflows after the initial subflow breaks, leading to a short throughput drop. These modes imply trade-offs regarding the performance during the handover, the energy consumption due to the concurrent usage of multiple interfaces, and the mobile traffic usage.

In this paper, we argue that these trade-offs are not necessary. We propose to use all available (sensor) information on the mobile device to forecast handover situations. A declining WiFi signal strength or additional sensor data can efficiently forecast a breaking WiFi connection. We propose that the mobile device switches from the energy efficient Single-Path mode to the Full-MPTCP mode before the WiFi

[1]See `https://support.apple.com/en-en/HT201373`

connection breaks. As the establishment of the additional subflows requires only a few seconds, it is finished until the WiFi connection breaks, leading to a smooth and efficient handover. This smooth handover combines the very good handover performance of the Full-MPTCP mode with the energy efficiency of the Single-Path mode. In case the WiFi connection does not break and the forecast turns out to be wrong, the system returns to Single-Path mode without any performance degradation for the application. As this can be detected very fast, the unnecessary activation of the additional interface consumes only a small amount of energy. For a first experimental evaluation, we developed an application that forecasts mobile handover based on the WiFi link quality and controls the MPTCP connections accordingly. We show that this smooths the mobile handover, combining high performance and low energy consumption.

The remainder of this paper is structured as follows. Based on a description of the details of our proposed design in Section 2, we provide a first evaluation in Section 3. Finally, in Section 4 we conclude the paper and give an outlook on future work.

2. DESIGN

In order to exploit information available on the mobile device, a forecast decision function is defined which chooses an MPTCP mode based on the observed contextual information. Formally, we define the context space $\mathcal{C}$ of possible context information available at the mobile device. An element $c \in \mathcal{C}$ describes the context information currently observed at the device. As an example, such a context information can be a changing WiFi link quality, a reducing throughput, or an increasing packet drop rate. If, for example, the link quality falls below a threshold for a short period of time, this is an indicator that the WiFi connection may break soon. Other possible context information is based on activity recognition or mobility patterns. A running user, for example, does more likely leave the range of the WiFi access point than a sitting user. Moreover, user preferences can be taken into account by defining the user-preference space $\mathcal{U}$. An example of a user preference $u \in \mathcal{U}$ could be to exclusively use WiFi when almost reaching the traffic volume limit in the mobile network. With an extended application interface, as for example proposed by Schmidt et al. [7], the applications might also express own preferences. Applications with very high bandwidth requirements might, for example, always prefer Full-MPTCP. Based on context information and user preferences, a suitable mode from the set of modes $\mathcal{M} = \{$"Full-MPTCP", "Single-Path"$\}$ should be chosen. This is done by a forecast decision function $f : (\mathcal{U}, \mathcal{C}) \mapsto \mathcal{M}$. Note that we ignore the Backup mode, because an efficient handover forecast leaves no usage scenario for this mode. The Backup mode requires an active mobile interface, but still has a worse performance than Full-MPTCP during the handover.

Observing the true status $s \in \mathcal{S} = \{$"WiFi breaks", "WiFi stable"$\}$ of the WiFi after the forecast decision was taken, we can identify two types of errors. The first error occurs when the mode is switched from Single-Path to Full-MPTCP, even though the WiFi connection does not break. In this case, the (unnecessary) activation of the additional interfaces can be reverted, which causes only a short period of time with an increased energy consumption. The second error occurs when Single-Path mode is maintained and the WiFi connection breaks. In this case, the switching to Full-MPTCP mode happens after the WiFi connection breaks, leading to a performance degradation.

Keeping this in mind, the forecast decision function should be chosen carefully. For this purpose, we propose to use learning methods to constantly improve the forecasting decisions. For example, by observing the true status of the WiFi after the decision was taken and checking if the correct mode was chosen, the forecast decision function could be adapted to increase accuracy. This can be combined with existing WiFi forecasting models, such as Breadcrumbs [3], a predictive mobility model. Breadcrumbs forecasts user locations and therefore connectivity of mobile devices based on past observations and wireless network capabilities.

3. EVALUATION

To evaluate our approach, we first reproduced the results by Paasch et al. [4] to then compare them with our proposed smooth handover. Figure 1 shows our reproduced results for the Full-MPTCP and the Single-Path mode handover during a long running FTP download. The WiFi connection breaks at second 8, leading to a short downtime for the Single-Path mode. The Full-MPTCP mode, which permanently uses the mobile network, has no performance degradation during the handover, but consumes more energy, as both interfaces are always active in parallel.

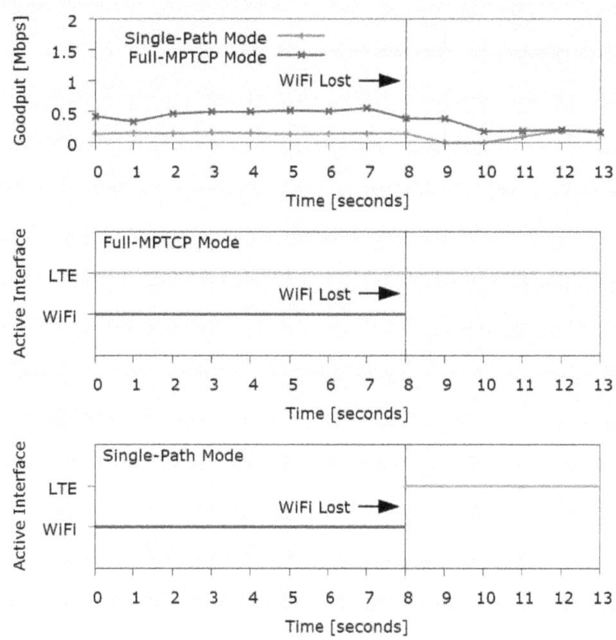

Figure 1: Goodput and active interfaces for the Single-Path and Full-MPTCP handover at second 8 from WiFi to LTE.

For an experimental evaluation of our smooth handover, we chose a scenario as shown in Figure 2. We used a Linux notebook with MPTCP 0.89.2 and Linux Kernel 3.14.22 with both a WiFi and an LTE interface. For the LTE interface, we used a Nexus 5. After connecting to a WiFi access point, we started an FTP download and moved away from the access point, leaving its range. For the handover forecast, we used the link quality as provided by the operating system[2]. The link quality is a unit-less indicator between 0 and 100, which is determined by the operating system and the device driver using signal strength and noise information. We manually tuned the forecast decision function to trigger a handover when the link quality continues to decrease after it is less than 40 for 3 seconds.

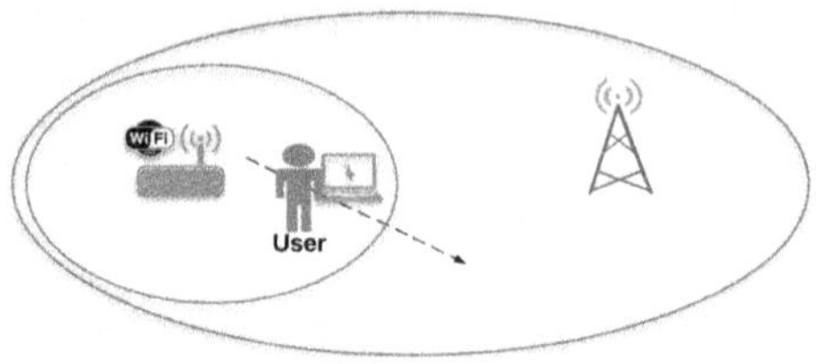

Figure 2: The evaluation scenario with a mobile device leaving the range of a WiFi connection.

Figure 3 shows the WiFi link quality, the total goodput[3] of the MPTCP connection, and the active interfaces during the experiment. At the beginning, the link quality indicates a good connection, which leads to the Single-Path mode. While the user moves away, the link quality decreases. Thus, the forecast function expects a WiFi connection drop and therefore triggers the switch to Full-MPTCP mode at second 7. When the actual WiFi connection is lost at second 15, the mobile connection is already fully established. Thus, our proposed approach allows a smooth handover with only 8 seconds of parallel active interfaces.

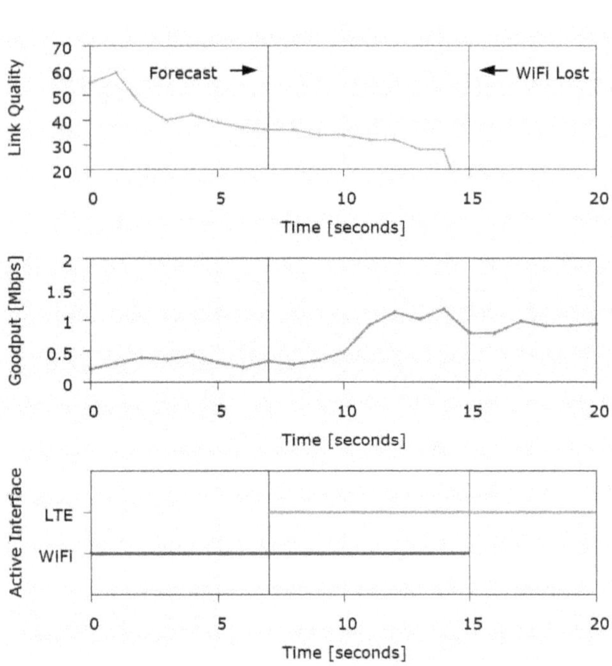

Figure 3: A smooth handover using the WiFi link quality for handover forecast.

[2]Linux provides information about the link quality in *linux/include/linux/wireless.h*

[3]During all our measurement experiments, we found high variances in the LTE performance.

4. CONCLUSION AND OUTLOOK

In this paper, we proposed a smooth MPTCP handover based on the available (sensor) information. We described our design of a forecast decision function, and showed in an experimental evaluation for a first prototype that both minimal energy consumption and high performance during the handover are possible.

For the future, we plan to implement and evaluate the remaining features, such as the integration of learning approaches to automatically calibrate the forecast decision function. Additionally, we will apply our approach to the handover from mobile network to WiFi and between WiFi access points, as recently discussed for MPTCP [1].

Acknowledgments

This work has been funded by the German Research Foundation (DFG) as part of projects A02 and B03 within the Collaborative Research Center (CRC) 1053 – MAKI.

5. REFERENCES

[1] A. Croitoru, D. Niculescu, and C. Raiciu. Towards Wifi Mobility without Fast Handover. In *NSDI 15*. USENIX Association, 2015.

[2] A. Ford, C. Raiciu, M. Handley, and O. Bonaventure. TCP Extensions for Multipath Operation with Multiple Addresses. RFC 6824, 2013.

[3] A. J. Nicholson and B. D. Noble. BreadCrumbs: Forecasting Mobile Connectivity. In *MobiCom*. ACM, 2008.

[4] C. Paasch, G. Detal, F. Duchene, C. Raiciu, and O. Bonaventure. Exploring Mobile/WiFi Handover with Multipath TCP. In *ACM SIGCOMM workshop Cellnet*, 2012.

[5] C. Perkins. IP Mobility Support for IPv4, Revised. RFC 5944, 2010.

[6] C. Raiciu, C. Paasch, S. Barre, A. Ford, M. Honda, F. Duchene, O. Bonaventure, M. Handley, et al. How Hard Can It Be? Designing and Implementing a Deployable Multipath TCP. In *NSDI*, 2012.

[7] P. S. Schmidt, T. Enghardt, R. Khalili, and A. Feldmann. Socket Intents: Leveraging Application Awareness for Multi-access Connectivity. In *CoNEXT*. ACM, 2013.

Poster: Towards Encrypted Query Processing for the Internet of Things

Hossein Shafagh, Anwar Hithnawi, Andreas Dröscher
Department of Computer Science
ETH Zurich, Switzerland
{shafagh, hithnawi, andreasd}@inf.ethz.ch

Simon Duquennoy
SICS Swedish ICT AB
Kista, Sweden
simonduq@sics.se

Wen Hu
School of Computer Science and Engineering
UNSW, Sydney, Australia
wen.hu@unsw.edu.au

ABSTRACT

The *Internet of Things* (IoT) is envisioned to digitize the physical world, resulting in a digital representation of our proximate living space. The possibility of inferring privacy violating information from IoT data necessitates adequate security measures regarding data storage and communication. To address these privacy and security concerns, we introduce our system that stores IoT data securely in the Cloud database while still allowing query processing over the encrypted data. We enable this by encrypting IoT data with a set of cryptographic schemes such as order-preserving and partially homomorphic encryptions. To achieve this on resource-limited devices, our system relies on optimized algorithms that accelerate partial homomorphic and order-preserving encryptions by 1 to 2 orders of magnitude. Our early results show the feasibility of our system on low-power devices. We envision our system as an enabler of secure IoT applications.

Categories and Subject Descriptors

C.2.0 [**Computer-Communication Networks**]: General – Security and Protection

Keywords

Data Security, Internet of Things, System Design, Computing on Encrypted Data

1. INTRODUCTION

IoT devices are physically integrated in our living space, and hence, deal with sensitive and private data that could be misused to infer privacy violating information. End-to-End secure communication is a necessary measure for the secure IoT. However, it protects merely the communication against unauthorized entities (e.g., eavesdropping, and modification attacks) and leaves the data unprotected on the Cloud. Storing data in such form leaves it vulnerable to breaches [8], caused by hackers and curious administrators [1].

MobiCom'15, Sep 07-11 2015, Paris, France
ACM ACM 978-1-4503-3619-2/15/09.
http://dx.doi.org/10.1145/2789168.2795172.

Figure 1: Our system enables protection of IoT data at personal devices, either at IP-enabled IoT devices or at the personal gateway, such as the smartphone. The Cloud database has no access to the encryption keys, but is able to process queries over encrypted data. All keys are derived from a master secret held by the user.

IoT Devices. The asymmetry of available resources in terms of bandwidth, computation, and energy within different entities of the IoT (e.g., constraint IoT devices, mobile devices, and powerful Cloud) necessitates a careful design of security solutions that advocate protection of data at personal devices. As illustrated in Figure 1, we distinguish between two main classes of constrained IoT devices: *a)* IP-enabled, and *b)* short-range wireless devices such as wearables that rely on a personal gateway (e.g., smartphone) for IP communication. Accommodating the logic and cryptographic algorithms for securing IoT data on IoT devices or the personal gateways, brings the challenge of designing an efficient system with regards to the limited resources, yet not compromising security nor quality of experience.

Encrypted Query Processing. An intuitive approach to counter attacks on IoT data is to store data encrypted on the Cloud database, with data en-/decryption performed at the user-side. This, however, is impractical, as it prevents any server-side query processing and results into undesirable application delays. To overcome this limitation, several encrypted query processing approaches [9, 10, 4, 3] have been introduced in the recent years. These approaches utilize cryptographic techniques (e.g., order-preserving encryption and partial homomorphic encryption) that allow computations to be carried out on encrypted data.

CryptDB [9] is one of the first systems that integrates efficient encrypted query processing into database management systems. In CryptDB, the Cloud performs traditional database queries over encrypted data and replies with the encrypted result. This is realized using a *trusted proxy that intercepts the communication and applies en-/decryption* (see Figure 2). CryptDB is designed with web applications in mind and is not suitable for IoT application scenarios, mainly because: *(i)* it employs cryptographic schemes that are prohibitively expensive for constrained devices and *(ii)* it relies on a trusted proxy, which implies no protection between proxy and the application server.

Encrypted Query Processing for the IoT. In this paper, we present our IoT data protection system which securely stores encrypted IoT data on the Cloud database, while allowing for efficient database query processing over encrypted data. In our design, we move away from a mere web application communication paradigm. Instead, we design a secure E2E system that stores encrypted data from personal devices on a Cloud database, and where data protection is executed at the personal device (see Figure 2). Thus, we *dispense the role of a trusted proxy on the path that has access to all keying material.* This allows us to address a stronger threat model, as the keying material does not leave user's personal devices.

To motivate the use case of our system, let us consider the application scenario of a health monitoring device similar to Fitbit Tracker (provided as built-in app on modern smartphones) which logs heart rate, location, and timestamps. The heart rate measurements can be used to infer sensitive information about a person, such as stress, depression, and heart-related diseases. Hence, heart rate information should be protected from untrusted parties. To still allow certain computations, e.g., average over the protected heart rate data, we utilize additive homomorphic encryption. The location is potentially also sensitive. Thus, we apply deterministic encryption, allowing encrypted queries correlating heart rate with location. Finally, the timestamps could be encrypted with order-preserving encryption, to allow searches in specified time-frames.

2. RELATED WORK

Related work to our approach can be grouped into two main categories.

Privacy-Preserving Cryptography. There has been a significant amount of work on cryptographic schemes [7, 12, 2, 3] that could be utilized in privacy-preserving computation. Gentry's work [5] depicts a breakthrough, showing a fully homomorphic encryption (FHE) scheme. Since then, his work has been incrementally enhanced up to 6 orders of magnitudes by the research community [6]. Prior to Gentry's work, the focus was on partial homomorphic encryption, where only one type of computation such as multiplication or addition is supported [3].

Although FHE provides semantic security and supports at the same time arbitrary computations over encrypted data, it is not yet best suited for encrypted query processing. This is due to both its prohibitive cost and the fact that the Cloud must process all existing data in database for queries such as equality check or comparison.

Computation on Encrypted Data. Perrig et al. [4] introduced an efficient search over encrypted text files. This is achieved by deterministically encrypting metadata of files which are themselves encrypted using strong encryption, i.e., probabilistic. Perrig et al.'s efforts paved the way for more advanced systems enabling encrypted query processing [9, 10] (just to mention a few). CryptDB [9], as detailed in §1, realizes the encrypted query processing for web applications by means of a trusted proxy intercepting and modifying the communication before the database. Mylar [10] introduces

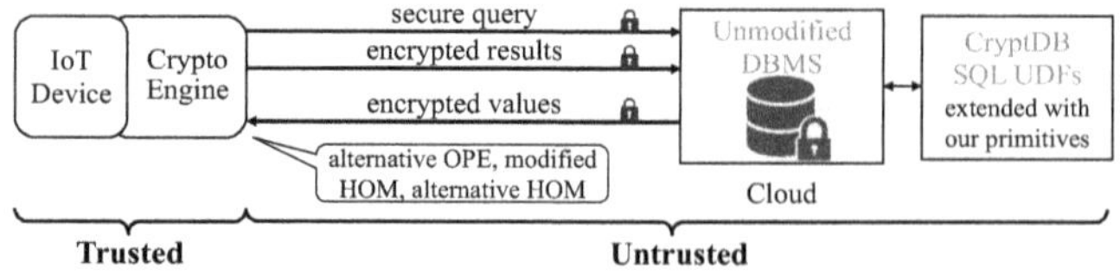

Figure 2: Our system extends CryptDB [9] to secure IoT data. It supersedes a trusted proxy with access to all keys. Instead, data protection is performed at IoT devices or user devices.

a multi-key searchable encryption scheme, exemplified by smartphone apps. Mylar protects the content of the documents and the searched words from the untrusted server.

3. SYSTEM ARCHITECTURE

We consider three main parties in our system: IoT devices, the users, and the Cloud. We embrace the trend in the IoT to store collected data in the Cloud. Hence, our system is suitable for applications which store sensor data in the Cloud for client-side processing. Such applications can either upload the data directly to the Cloud (e.g., smart appliances), or by means of a personal gateway such as the smartphone (e.g., wearables). Our system consists of the following components:

a) Crypto Engine for Constrained Devices. We design and implement the cryptographic algorithms required to protect data on IoT devices with attention to efficient performance, small memory footprint, and reasonable energy consumption. Our targeted constrained device platforms are equipped with similar resources as today's typical IoT devices, such as FitBit (e.g., System-on-Chip ARM Cortex-M family with Bluetooth Low Energy or IEEE 802.15.4).

b) Client-side Library. We exemplify the client's personal gateway with a smartphone. Our library enables secure storage and interaction with the Cloud. It provides the data protection services to local applications and external devices, such as heath monitoring systems. It manages the keying material and performs en-/decryption operations within a reasonable time, so that the user's experience remains unchanged while interacting with the Cloud.

c) User Defined Functions for Databases. In our system, the database remains unchanged and is only extended with new functionality. This is possible with *User Defined Functions* (UDFs). While computing over encrypted data, the corresponding UDF is executed. For instance, the UDF for an ordering-related query (e.g., order by, MAX, MIN) is aware of the order-preserving encryption and computes the result without access to the plaintext values.

Encrypted Data Processing. Utilization of encrypted data processing is dependent on the application scenario and security requirements. One of the main challenges in our system is identifying lightweight cryptographic algorithms. Then in contrast to current approaches [9, 10] which rely on full-fledged machines for cryptographic operations, in our system such operations are performed on constrained IoT or/and end-user devices. Considering the set of encryption schemes to support most of queries over encrypted data, additive homomorphic encryption and order-preserving encryption are the most computation-intensive ones. In our system, we explore alternative lightweight cryptographic

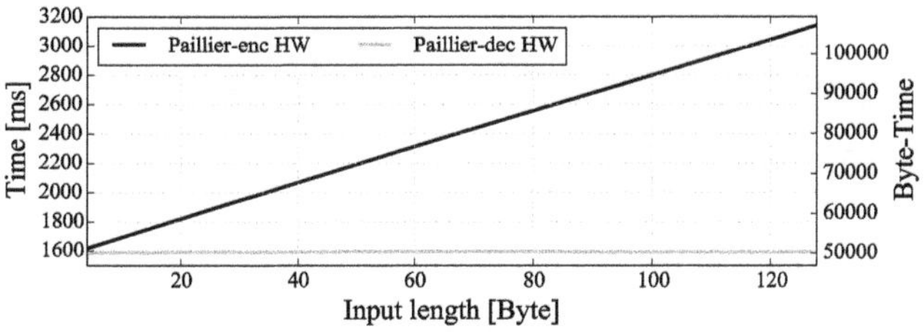

Figure 3: Additive homomorphic encryption by means of Paillier utilizing the cryptographic hardware accelerator (HW) of our IoT device (OpenMote). Paillier's plaintext-size can be as large as the key size, in our case 1024 bit.

algorithms which provide the same level of security, but exhibit significantly lower computation requirements. With the EC-ElGamal and mutable order-preserving encoding (mOPE) [11], we find alternatives for additive homomorphic encryption and order-preserving encryption, respectively. However, before being able to utilize them in our system we have to address two issues: *(i)* deterministic mapping of plaintext values to elliptic curve points for EC-ElGamal, and *(ii)* increased communication overhead of mOPE in favor of lower computations. We address the former with elliptic curve point multiplication ($P = mG$) of the plaintext m with a known elliptic curve point G. For mapping back, a bounded *Elliptic Curve Discrete Logarithmic Problem* (ECDLP) by means of the Baby-Step-Giant-Step algorithm is solved. The latter can be optimized with K-ary trees to reduce the interactions-rounds [11].

Extendibility. In our design, we show the potential and feasibility of encrypted query processing for the IoT. Although we focus on a subset of encryption schemes that support queries that are widely used in IoT data processing, our design can be extended to include more advanced, however carefully optimized, encrypted data processing schemes.

4. INITIAL RESULTS

We are prototyping our system consisting of three main components: *(i)* the IoT component is being implemented for OpenMotes[1], *(ii)* the gateway component for Google Nexus 5, an *(iii)* the Cloud database component is an extended implementation of CryptDB [9].

Our early results of additive homomorphic encryption by means of EC-ElGamal as compared to the Paillier cryptosystem indicate a performance improvement by 1 order of magnitude. As shown in Figure 3, Paillier's encryption takes 1.6 to 3.1 s, depending on the plaintext-size. With EC-ElGamal, we have a constant encryption time of 210 ms, including our plaintext to elliptic curve mapping.

Note the decryption process in EC-ElGamal, specifically due to computation of an ECDLP, is computationally more intensive than the encryption. This is not an issue, since the decryption is performed on the more powerful user device. In our early results of EC-ElGamal, decryption on Google Nexus 5 takes about 190 ms and requires 45 Mbyte of memory. We intend to reduce this value further with an improved implementation of the Baby-Step-Giant-Step algorithm.

[1]OpenMote platform, 32-bit ARM Cortex-M3 microcontroller, 32 MHz CPU, 802.15.4 radio: `www.openmote.com`

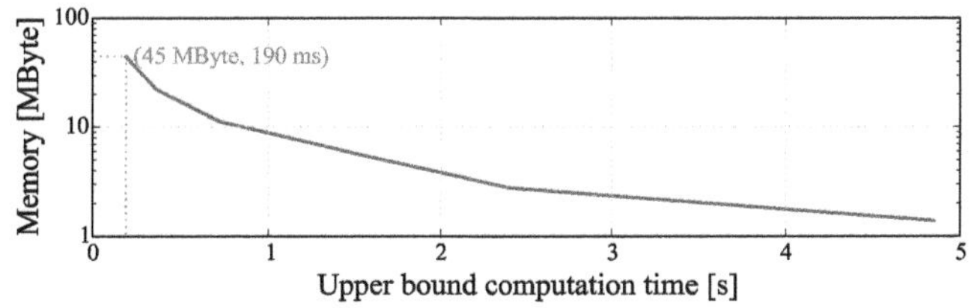

Figure 4: Memory-computation tradeoff in the Baby-Step-Giant-Step algorithm on a Google Nexus 5. Our system stores a pre-computed look-up table of 45 MByte and solves an ECDLP for a 32-bit value in maximum 190 ms.

5. FUTURE WORK

We introduced a secure system that provides strong communication and data security for privacy-preserving IoT applications. Our system leverages and tailors cryptographic primitives that allow computation on encrypted data without disclosing decryption keys to the Cloud. In this paper, we show the feasibly of our system and discuss initial results. We will show the practically and performance of our system through an enhanced prototype implementation and thorough evaluation considering both micro-benchmarking and system performance. We quantify the overhead of our system in terms of energy, computation, and latency. Moreover, we show the benefits of our system with a case-study discussion.

6. REFERENCES

[1] A. Chen. GCreep: Google Engineer Stalked Teens, Spied on Chats, Gawker. www.gawker.com/5637234, 2010.

[2] M. Bellare, A. Boldyreva, and A. O'Neill. Deterministic and Efficiently Searchable Encryption. In *Advances in Cryptology (Crypto)*, 2007.

[3] D. Boneh, C. Gentry, S. Halevi, F. Wang, and D. J. Wu. Private Database Queries Using Somewhat Homomorphic Encryption. In *Applied Cryptography and Network Security (ACNS)*, 2013.

[4] D. X. Song, D. Wagner, and A. Perrig. Practical Techniques for Searches on Encrypted Data. In *IEEE Security and Privacy*, 2000.

[5] C. Gentry. Fully Homomorphic Encryption Using Ideal Lattices. In *Annual ACM Symposium on Theory of Computing (STOC)*, 2009.

[6] C. Gentry, S. Halevi, and N. P. Smart. Homomorphic Evaluation of the AES Circuit. In *CRYPTO*, 2012.

[7] S. Goldwasser, Y. Kalai, R. A. Popa, V. Vaikuntanathan, and N. Zeldovich. Reusable Garbled Circuits and Succinct Functional Encryption. In *Annual ACM Symposium on Theory of Computing (STOC)*, 2013.

[8] Privacy Rights Clearinghouse. Chronology of Data Breaches from 2005 to Present Date. www.privacyrights.org/data-breach.

[9] R. A. Popa, C. M. Redfield, N. Zeldovich, and H. Balakrishnan. CryptDB: Protecting Confidentiality with Encrypted Query Processing. In *ACM SOSP*, 2011.

[10] R. A. Popa, E. Stark, S. Valdez, J. Helfer, N. Zeldovich, and H. Balakrishnan. Building Web Applications on Top of Encrypted Data Using Mylar. In *USENIX NSDI*, 2014.

[11] R. A. Popa, Frank H. Li, and N. Zeldovich. An Ideal-Security Protocol for Order-Preserving Encoding. In *IEEE Symposium on Security and Privacy*, 2013.

[12] A. Shamir. Identity-based Cryptosystems and Signature Schemes. In *Advances in Cryptology (Crypto)*, 1984.

[SRC] Poster: Regression-based Characterization of 802.11ac Indoor Performance

Edgar Costa Molero
ETH Zurich
cedgar@student.ethz.ch

Lito Kriara
Disney Research Zurich
lito@disneyresearch.com

Thomas Gross
ETH Zurich
thomas.gross@inf.ethz.ch

ABSTRACT

We investigate the applicability of IEEE 802.11ac for entertainment low-latency show control systems (to orchestrate free-riding vehicles in a theme-park environment) by experimentally characterizing the indoor throughput and jitter performance of 802.11ac using statistical analysis. 802.11ac is the successor of 802.11n that provides higher throughput by incorporating wider channels, more spatial streams and denser modulation. We show that multiple linear regression provides valuable insight in the influence of 802.11ac's independent features and their combinations on performance, for various links and interference scenarios. Finally, we show that 802.11ac could be used for not only delivering high throughput for multimedia streaming but also supports applications requiring minimal jitter variance in the setup investigated.

Categories and Subject Descriptors

C.2.1 [**Computer-Communication Networks**]: Network Architecture and Design–Wireless communication

General Terms

Experimentation, Measurements, Performance, WLAN

Keywords

802.11ac, Analysis, Characterization, MIMO

1. INTRODUCTION

A recent survey reported that *"by 2016 the amount of mobile devices' traffic, relying on Wireless Local Area Networks (WLANs) for Internet access, will exceed the traffic from wired devices"* [1]. IEEE 802.11ac [2] was introduced to address this increased need in wireless traffic. It has the potential to deliver multi-gigabit per second throughput, by incorporating wider channels, more spatial streams, and a denser modulation than 802.11n.

MobiCom'15, September 07-11, 2015, Paris, France
ACM 978-1-4503-3619-2/15/09.
http://dx.doi.org/10.1145/2789168.2795173.

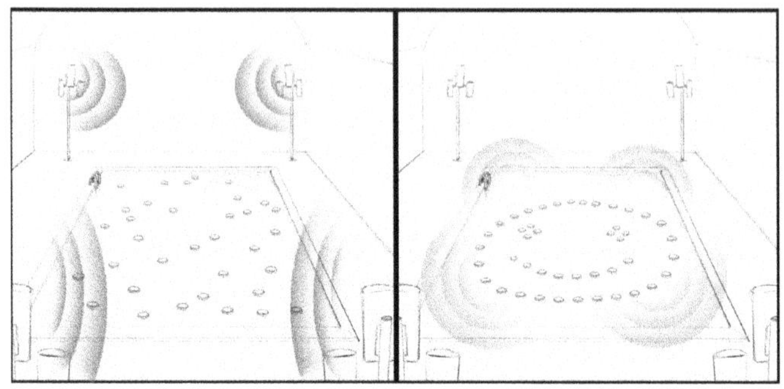

Figure 1: Concept art (© Disney): Future indoor 802.11ac–based show control system with free-riding vehicles.

We report on an investigation of the available 802.11ac features on throughput and jitter performance across a wide range of link qualities, via extensive real–world testbed experimentation. We do that so to determine if 802.11ac is a standard that could possibly support low latency show control systems in the future (Fig. 1). As a first step in this direction, we perform a thorough real–world evaluation and characterization study of the 802.11ac performance in an indoor environment using already available hardware in an 802.11ac office testbed.

Zeng et al. conduct an outdoor characterization of 802.11ac focusing on power consumption and the impact of channel width [3]. In this paper, we present a more thorough evaluation of the standard by considering all available features and their combinational influence on performance.

2. METHODOLOGY

2.1 Testbed setup

We deploy an indoor 802.11ac WLAN testbed, covering a $40 \times 15m^2$ area, as shown in Fig. 2; the blue square indicates the access point, and the red circles represent the clients of the WLAN. Each node is a laptop running Ubuntu with kernel 3.16, the open source ath10k wireless driver [4], and is equipped with a 3×3 Qualcomm Atheros QCA9880 chipset–based mini PCIe. The transmission power is always fixed to the default (i.e., 30 dBm for channels 149-161, and 17 dBm for channels 32-44).

The metrics we use to evaluate the testbed's performance are application level throughput and jitter on the receiver side, measured between a client and access point using the

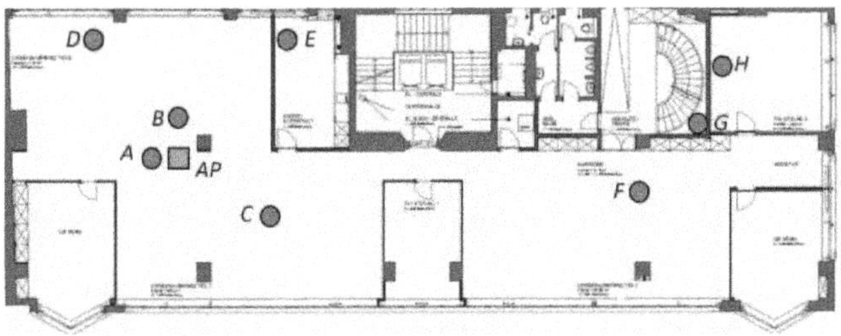

Figure 2: 802.11ac testbed for the throughput and jitter measurements. Blue square: access point, red circle: clients.

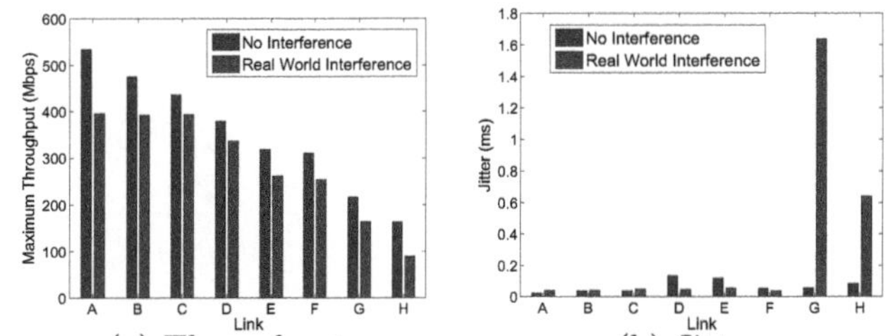

(a) Throughput (b) Jitter

Figure 3: Maximum throughput and corresponding jitter in case of no and real world interference for all links in the testbed.

Link	RSSI	Line of Sight	Quality
A	-10 dBm	Yes	Strong
B	-14 dBm	Yes	Strong
C	-27 dBm	No	Strong
D	-40 dBm	No	Medium
E	-45 dBm	No	Medium
F	-57 dBm	No	Medium
G	-61 dBm	No	Weak
H	-75 dBm	No	Weak

Table 1: Average RSSI values for each link type.

Iperf traffic generator tool [5]. Note that MAC layer packet loss related statistics were not available using the ath10k driver at the time the experiments were conducted. We demonstrate results in "no interference" and "real-world interference" scenarios, with varying channel conditions. For the "no interference" scenario we use during night hours the 5 GHz band and channel 149, where no activity was detected by a spectrum analyzer. For "real-world interference" we use channel 36 in the 5GHz band, where another 9 access points are operating during working hours to account for human interference, too. Table 1 shows the different link characteristics.

We consider all available 802.11ac features in our characterization study, namely channel bonding (CB), spatial streams (SS), guard interval (GI), and the modulation and coding schemes (MCS) index. For channel bonding, we explore the options of 20, 40 and 80 MHz channel width; for spatial streams we vary from one to maximum three streams available in our hardware, and for the MCS index, we explore the ten options as described in the 802.11ac standard. Finally, for the guard interval option there is the long (LGI) or short guard interval (SGI). To sum up, there are 180 combinations for each link/interference type. Given that our testbed has eight nodes, and we consider two interference scenarios, our possible setting number increases to almost 3000 different configurations. Therefore, we explore the use of statistical techniques on this dataset to gain meaningful insights.

2.2 Multiple Linear Regression

Multiple linear regression [6] is an empirical tool in epidemiology, economics and other sciences and is used to search for evidence of causal relationships between parameters and observational data of controlled experiments. We use it to model the relationship between two or more explanatory variables, as well as their influence on a response variable, by fitting a linear equation.

The explanatory variables are 802.11ac features (i.e., CB, SS, GI and MCS), and the response variable is our respective metric (i.e., throughput and jitter). Hence, we can use the coefficients of the linear equation to infer, for example, whether the impact of wider channels is positive or negative on the throughput performance by the sign of the CB coefficient. For normalized coefficients across different links, we can also confirm that a specific feature has a higher impact than another in certain scenarios.

To evaluate whether multiple linear regression is applicable to our data, we examine the significance (*p-value*) of the regression model's F-test. If the *p-value* is lower than an *alpha* threshold, then the model can accurately describe the data. We set the *alpha* threshold to 0.05 (i.e., the model should describe 95% of the data), and we find that indeed the *p-value* is always lower than *alpha*, validating that multiple linear regression can properly fit our data, and therefore our multiple linear regression results can be trusted.

3. EXPERIMENTAL EVALUATION

We follow the methodology described in the previous section for the "no interference" and "real world interference" scenarios. Fig. 3 depicts the maximum throughput (Fig. 3(a)) observed for each link in the testbed (Fig. 2), under both setups of interference, as well as the corresponding jitter observed (Fig. 3(b)). With this kind of visualization we cannot gain much insight on why does an observed change (e.g., between different interference scenarios) happen. Why does jitter increase rapidly for weak links? Are there setting combinations to minimize jitter, but maximize throughput performance?

To answer such questions, we use multiple linear regression on our measurements. Results in Fig. 4 show the impact of single features and their combinations on throughput and jitter performance, under "no" and "real world" interference. Warmer colors (i.e., redder) mean that this feature combination has a higher positive impact on the performance when its value is increased; colder colors indicate negative impact. E.g., red CB means that larger channel width increases throughput performance. On the other hand, colder colors (i.e., bluer) would indicate negative impact and a decrease of throughput for larger channel width. Green shows that the specific feature combination does not have a significant impact on the performance of the metric. Note that for the case of GI, a redder color GI indicates that enabling SGI increases throughput performance.

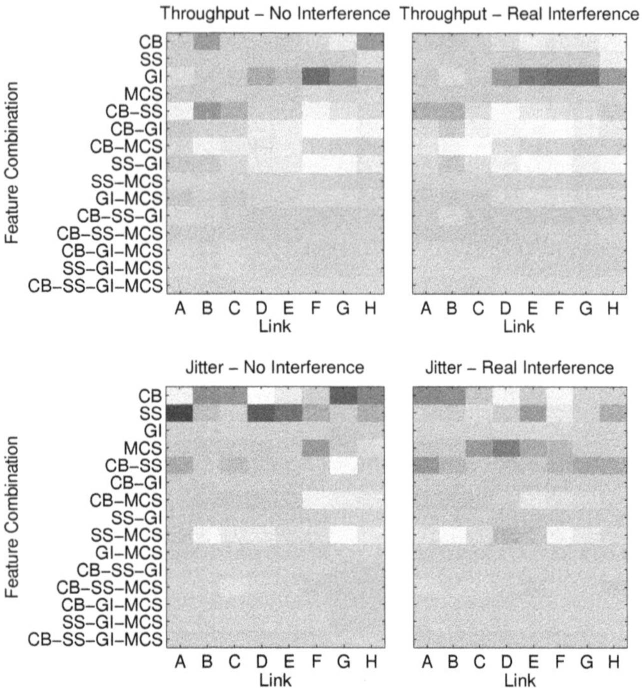

Figure 4: 802.11ac feature combination impact in case of "no" and "real world" interference on throughput and jitter.

Fig 4 shows that jitter performance is more susceptible to changes in parameter settings than throughput (darker colors noticed). Moreover, even though the guard interval is not an important factor for jitter performance, it is the feature with the strongest impact on throughput performance. As expected, enabling the SGI creates even more losses as the link quality decreases, resulting in lower throughput, whereas in an ideal link quality scenario with no interference, GI proves to be increasing throughput performance.

Next, we notice that wider channels result in decreasing throughput performance, because the signal transmission power is divided across a larger number of subcarriers. This setup degrades the link quality of the specific scenario, when the remaining of the settings are set to high values, similar to the 802.11n case [7]. Wider channels have an even higher impact on jitter variance. Better link qualities (i.e., A–E) have an increased jitter with higher channel width, compared to the poorer links (i.e., F–H), because better links have fewer losses, so more delayed packets. We see this changing for the real world interference case, where the losses are so high that most packets do not arrive at all, so delay cannot be measured, explaining the high jitter of link G (Fig. 3).

As far as the SS is concerned, we see that on average more streams deteriorate throughput performance, because the transmission power is divided between the multiple streams, decreasing the range and strength of the signal, and consequently incurring losses. Surprisingly, we see that at the same time, more spatial streams reduce the jitter, because when trying to transmit data to the full capacity of the link, more streams can more efficiently transmit all the data.

Moreover, the MCS index does not look like a dominant factor on throughput performance, suggesting that the correct setting of the previously mentioned features is more crucial for the same MCS setting. However, we see that higher MCS indexes reduce the jitter, in both interference cases. Jitter increases with higher MCS indexes in the case of poor links, similarly to the channel bonding.

We also see that not only single parameter estimation is significant for achieving better performance but also combinations of multiple parameters. Fig. 4 shows the combinations that are more significant and their impact. Is it surprising that even though increasing *only* the channel width or *only* the spatial stream number has a negative impact on throughput, increasing the channel width *and* spatial stream number jointly has a highly positive impact on throughput performance and at the same time decreases jitter, for both interference scenarios. Similarly, we see that jointly increasing the number of SS and MCS index increases the jitter, even though this combination has no significant impact on throughput performance. This is due to the reduced transmission power, when more streams are used. Hence, the link quality is reduced even more, introducing higher jitter.

Finally, we notice that on average the two-way interactions (e.g., CB–SS, CB–GI) increase throughput performance when the settings are higher, whereas increasing the setting of single features has the opposite impact, surprisingly. This observation also supports the argument of jointly adapting all available features would result in higher throughput performance gain, as also shown in [8].

4. CONCLUSION

We performed an extensive experimental characterization of the throughput and jitter variance performance of 802.11ac WLANs. Unlike previous approaches we consider all 802.11ac features in this study. We show that multiple linear regression analysis can provide valuable insight in analyzing network performance measurements, and we validate that jointly adapting feature setting may increase performance. Finally, the results on jitter obtained in this testbed indicate that 802.11ac can be employed not only for delivering high throughput but may also be useful for applications that demand low jitter variance.

5. REFERENCES

[1] Cisco. *Visual Networking Index (VNI), The Zettabyte Era - Trends and Analysis*, 2013.

[2] IEEE 802.11ac. Enhancements for Very High Throughput for Operation in Bands below 6GHz. In *IEEE P802.11ac/D5.0*, 2013.

[3] Y. Zeng et al. A First Look at 802.11ac in Action: Energy Efficiency and Interference Characterization. In *IEEE IFIP Networking*, 2014.

[4] Qualcomm. Ath10k Linux driver.

[5] M. Gates et al. *Iperf version 2.0.0*, 2004.

[6] David Freedman. *Statistical Models: Theory and Practice*. Cambridge University Press, 2005.

[7] L. Kriara et al. Characterization of 802.11n Wireless LAN Performance via Testbed Measurements and Statistical Analysis. In *IEEE SECON*, 2013.

[8] L. Kriara and M. K. Marina. SampleLite: A Hybrid Approach to 802.11n Link Adaptation. *ACM SIGCOMM Comput. Commun. Rev.*, April 2015.

Poster: ParkMaster - Leveraging Edge Computing in Visual Analytics

Giulio Grassi
Sorbonne Universitès, UPMC
Univ Paris 06, CNRS, LIP6
giulio.grassi@lip6.fr

Matteo Sammarco
Sorbonne Universitès, UPMC
Univ Paris 06, CNRS, LIP6
matteo.sammarco@lip6.fr

Paramvir Bahl
Microsoft Research - USA
bahl@microsoft.com

Kyle Jamieson
Dept. of Computer Science,
University College London
k.jamieson@cs.ucl.ac.uk

Giovanni Pau
Sorbonne Universitès, UPMC
Univ Paris 06, CNRS, LIP6;
UCLA
giovanni.pau@lip6.fr

ABSTRACT

In this work we propose ParkMaster, a low-cost crowdsourcing architecture which exploits machine learning techniques and vision algorithms to evaluate parking availability in cities. While the user is normally driving ParkMaster enables off the shelf smartphones to collect information about the presence of parked vehicles by running image recognition techniques on the phones camera video streaming.

The paper describes the design of ParkMaster's architecture and shows the feasibility of deploying such mobile sensor system in nowadays smartphones, in particular focusing on the practicability of running vision algorithms on phones.

Categories and Subject Descriptors

I.4.9 [**Computing Methodologies**]: Image Processing and Computer Vision—*Applications*

Keywords

Cloudlet; Crowdsourcing; Design; Edge Computing; Mobile sensors; Vision Computing

1. INTRODUCTION

Driving in large cities can be stressful sometimes, among traffic jams, road works etc. and even when we reach our destination, the stress is not over: the desperate search for a parking space has still to begun. For instance [9] shows that in a small commercial area in Los Angeles a driver spends on average 3.3 minutes to find a parking spot after reaching the destination, thus adding about 2.5 miles to the trip. Clearly, this is not only a bother to that particular drivers, but it affects everyone: other than creating additional traffic driving around looking for parking, [9] shows that this searches consume about 47,000 gallons of gasoline in one year (by driving 950,000 miles more), producing thus 730 tons of carbon dioxide. Therefore simply by steering the driver to the closest available parking spot one could alleviate traffic congestion and pollution in big cities. While there are several projects which let the user know the availability of parking inside garages [1], more complex is to provide such information for road-side parking spots. Some cities are installing sensors on parking meters to detect cars presence, like San Francisco [2], but these solutions require the deployment of a large infrastructure of sensors connected to the Internet, with a considerable cost. To avoid such expenses, [8] proposes to install ultrasonic sensors on cars (i.e. taxis) to detect empty spots on the road where a driver can park. While this solution seems quite accurate, it still requires the installation of additional hardware on cars, which may slow down the deployment of this solution and certainly increases the cost. Nevertheless, the idea of having the cars themselves to collect data about the parking availability seems promising. Such collection system indeed would have large coverage without the deployment of an additional infrastructure on the road. ParkMaster capitalizes this observation and proposes to solve the parking dilemma with a sensing system deployed on cars at zero cost by using the cameras installed in today's smartphones.

Previous works propose to use image recognition techniques to detect cars' presence in parking lots by using cameras placed on top of buildings or poles [6] [7] [12] [10]. While this approach is feasible for a single parking lot, it's not suitable for road-side parking spaces because it still requires the deployment of an expensive infrastructure on the urban streets.

ParkMaster proposes to exploit the cameras on drivers' smartphones to evaluate the presence or absence of cars on road-side parking spots by using image recognition algorithms running on the driver's smartphone. The data collected by the cars is then uploaded to the cloud, which aggregates and makes this information available to other drivers, like other famous crowdsourcing systems do for information about traffic (i.e. Waze [3]).

MobiCom'15, September 07–11, 2015, Paris, France.
ACM 978-1-4503-3619-2/15/09.
http://dx.doi.org/10.1145/2789168.2795174.

Figure 1: Smartphone on a windshield

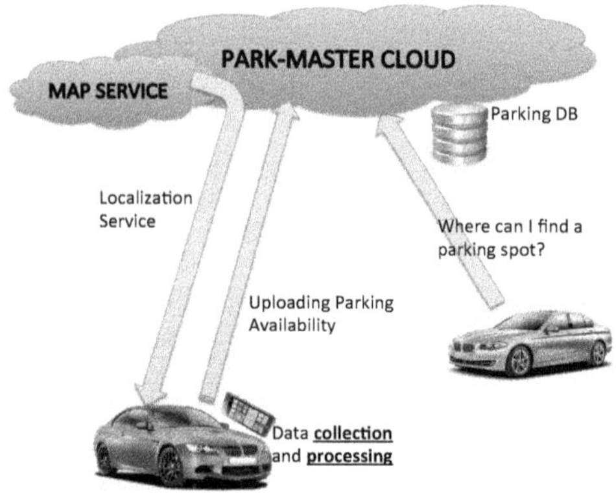

Figure 2: ParkMaster Architecture

2. ARCHITECTURE

While the user is driving, the smartphone placed on the windshield (as in figure 1) processes in real time the video stream of the street, detecting and counting cars on the side of the road. Based on the maximum number of parking spots the road can host (provided by the cloud) and the number of detected cars, the smartphone computes the number of available parking spots and uploads this information to the cloud. The latter collects and processes data from multiple providers and then steers drivers looking for parking towards areas where it's more likely to find a parking spot. The architecture of ParkMaster, depicted in figure 2, has three main players, the cloud, the data provider and the data user.

2.1 ParkMaster Cloud

The ParkMaster cloud offers three services: (1) collecting and processing data from users' smartphones; (2) making the data available to drivers looking for parking and (3) assisting the drivers in their own localization, making GPS data more accurate.

Location Service: When drivers collect information about the parking availability around them, this data is useless if not associated with a specific location (i.e. a road name). The data provided by the GPS sensors in the smartphones is not always accurate, which may lead the user to associate information about the parking availability to the wrong road-segment[1]. To avoid this ParkMaster relies on Google fused location provider [4] to correct the GPS data. The smartphone periodically uploads raw data (GPS, network information, sensor information, etc.) to the Google cloud, which then provides the user with a more accurate location.

Nevertheless, a precise GPS location by itself is not enough. To properly evaluate the number of available parking spots ParkMaster must know the current road-segment. The cloud therefore offers an additional localization service which takes care of the identification of the correct road-segment based on GPS coordinates (using reverse geocoding techniques). For simplicity, the cloud relies on an external service provided by Google Maps Road [5] for the computation.

Moreover, the ParkMaster cloud integrates a digital city map with data about the maximum number of parking spots each road-segment can host[2] and the relative parking regulations and pricing (if any).

Parking Availability Service: Different users may provide the cloud with incongruous information about the parking availability on the same road, due to different sampling time and errors in the data collection. The cloud stores this information and elaborates it, aggregating data and correcting incongruities by leveraging on large samples for the same road coming from different providers. Furthermore, the parking availability changes over time, therefore the cloud, while aggregating samples, gives a larger weight to more recent values.

2.2 Data provider

Information about the parking availability can be provided by any driver with a smartphone (the application runs on an off the shelf smartphone[3]) without any input from the users. The ParkMaster application captures the video stream of the street and processes each frame looking for vehicles on the side of the road. It applies machine learning techniques in order to detect cars, in particular, it uses a cascade classifier [11], which we trained with a set of 1000 images of vehicles. Whenever a car is detected, ParkMaster utilizes advanced algorithms to determine the position of the detected vehicles relative to the user's smartphone and track it among subsequent frames, in order to count all the parked cars only once. Whenever the user drives into a new road-segment, the application asks the cloud about the maximum number of parking spots that specific road-segment can host, counts the number of cars it has detected in that segment, computes the difference and uploads the result to the cloud. By default, to spare bandwidth, the client uploads only the number of available parking spots, thus with a negligible cost in terms of cellular data usage. Nevertheless, whenever the cloud-service receives conflictual information from different data producers it may request some of the frames recorded by the users in order to perform in-cloud advanced visual analytics. The accuracy of the final result - the number of available parking spots - depends not only on the car detection algorithm, but also on the estimation of the maximum number of parking spots a road may host, which depends on the type of parking. Road-side parking indeed can be of two types: slotted or unslotted (figure 3). In the first case spots

[1] A road-segment is the smallest piece of street which connects two intersections

[2] While we have manually built our parking map, we believe that city authorities can easily provide this information

[3] The current implementation runs on Android

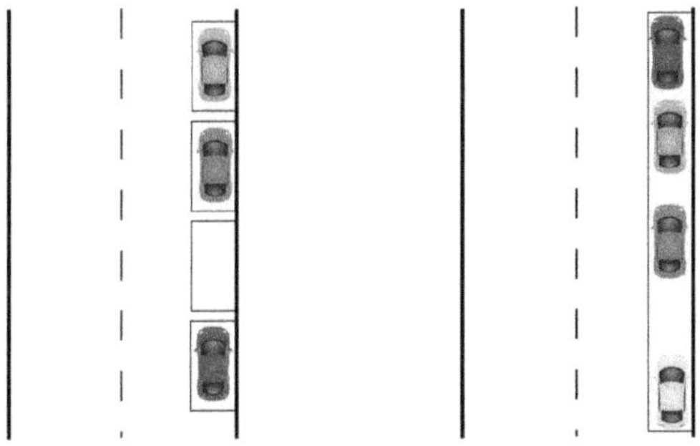

Figure 3: Parking spots: slotted (left) and unslotted (right)

are marked and the maximum number of parked cars the area can host is certain. In the second case the parking area doesn't have any marked space and the maximum number of parked vehicles on the road is only an estimation. While at the moment ParkMaster doesn't take any additional action to cope with the uncertainty of unslotted areas, we are confident that with more sophisticated techniques (i.e. measuring the free space among parked cars) the effects of the estimation error will be negligible in the computation of the parking availability.

2.3 Data user

Drivers may be at the same time data provider and data consumer. In the latter case, the driver sends a request to the cloud specifying the location of interest (i.e. the destination of the trip or the actual position). The cloud then replies with a list of road-segments ids within a specific range from the location of interest and the parking availability for each of these segments. The user's smartphone may display the result on a map in order to steer the driver towards the closest parking spot.

3. PRELIMINARY RESULTS

ParkMaster has been tested on a Samsung Galaxy S4 running Android. Figure 4 shows few frames captured by the smartphone camera and used as input for the car detection algorithm during preliminary experiments: the cascade classifier analyzes each frame looking for cars; in case of a match, it provides a box bounding the detected car (the red rectangle in figure 4).

Preliminary experiments have been run to verify the feasibility of the system: from the accuracy of the detection algorithms to the feasibility of running vision algorithm in the smartphone. While there is still some work to do to increase the accuracy of the car detection process, especially with scarce luminosity, the system seems quite promising. Furthermore, we believe that improving the data aggregation/correction process running on the cloud will further increase the system accuracy.

As one could predict, running ParkMaster on the smartphone causes a high level of energy consumption, mainly due to sensors, processor, camera and display usage. Nevertheless, the power issue can be easily solved plugging the phone to the car charger.

Figure 4: Car detection: frame samples

4. REFERENCES

[1] `http://www.streetlinenetworks.com/`.

[2] `http://sfpark.org/`.

[3] `http://waze.com/`.

[4] `https://developer.android.com/google/play-services/location.html`.

[5] `https://developers.google.com/maps/documentation/roads/`.

[6] T. Fabian. An algorithm for parking lot occupation detection. In *Computer Information Systems and Industrial Management Applications, 2008. CISIM'08. 7th*, pages 165–170. IEEE, 2008.

[7] N. Kaempchen, U. Franke, and R. Ott. Stereo vision based pose estimation of parking lots using 3d vehicle models. In *Intelligent Vehicle Symposium, 2002. IEEE*, volume 2, pages 459–464. IEEE, 2002.

[8] S. Mathur, T. Jin, N. Kasturirangan, J. Chandrasekaran, W. Xue, M. Gruteser, and W. Trappe. Parknet: drive-by sensing of road-side parking statistics. In *Proceedings of the 8th international conference on Mobile systems, applications, and services*, pages 123–136. ACM, 2010.

[9] D. C. Shoup. Cruising for parking. *Transport Policy*, 13(6):479–486, 2006.

[10] N. True. Vacant parking space detection in static images. *University of California, San Diego*, 2007.

[11] P. Viola and M. Jones. Rapid object detection using a boosted cascade of simple features. In *Computer Vision and Pattern Recognition, 2001. CVPR 2001. Proceedings of the 2001 IEEE Computer Society Conference on*, volume 1, pages I–511. IEEE, 2001.

[12] C. Wah. Parking space vacancy monitoring. *Projects in Vision and Learning*, 2009.

Poster: User Location Fingerprinting at Scale

Puneet Jain
Duke University
puneet.jain@duke.edu

Justin Manweiler
IBM Research
jmanweiler@us.ibm.com

Romit Roy Choudhury
UIUC
croy@illinois.edu

ABSTRACT

The goal of this project is to uniquely fingerprint an environment in the visual domain. The fingerprinting should be such that if a user takes a video swipe of the environment with the phone camera, her precise location can be immediately inferred. The problem is challenging because the user is continuously scanning the environment and the opportunity of capturing unique parts is fleeting. A typical environment may consist of repeating visual patterns such as ceiling, floor, wall texture, etc. and a painting hanging on the wall may be the only unique identifier of the location. Our approach to solve this problem is motivated by the ability of human brain in differentiating two similar looking environments by observing subtle differences in them. Our contribution in this work is two fold: (1) summarize global uniqueness of a location in few bits of information to quickly determine whether the current phone camera view contains a unique part, (2) scale this notion of uniqueness to buildings of arbitrary sizes yet delivering near real-time performance. Once fully developed, we believe our approach can apply to accelerate mobile augmented reality and correct indoor localization errors.

Categories and Subject Descriptors

H.3.4 [**Information Storage and Retrieval**]: Systems and Software

General Terms

Algorithms, Design, Experimentation, Performance

Keywords

Continuous Vision, Cloud Offloading, Localization

1. INTRODUCTION

With advances in the mobile computing, camera-based applications are slowly moving from offline processing on a stationary image to real-time processing on continuous video feed. Unfortunately, phone's processing power is limited and network latencies are too high for real-time computation offloading. Therefore, hybrid architectures are gaining popularity: where phone does light-weight processing to avoid resource wastage and the cloud periodically performs heavy-weight computation to deliver high accuracy [3, 4]. The current generation phone cameras are capable of capturing up to 30 frames in a second; therefore offloading decision needs to be made within a few milliseconds. In this project, we are trying to design a system, which can quickly identify user location from a video swipe. Our intuition is that an environment possesses enough visual diversity that most locations can be uniquely identified (without moving) if scanned for a sufficient interval. The intuition is synonymous to functioning of our brain, which helps us in locating ourselves in an already visited environment by identifying unique visual anchors. Harnessing this intuition in a system is hard because the user is continuously moving the camera and a video frame containing unique part may be transient. If the computation on the phone was not a bottleneck, matching every video frame with pre-captured visual data of the environment could have solved the problem. This brings a need of uniqueness summarization scheme, especially in a way that it can be queried efficiently on current generation phones. Note that the summarization doesn't have to be accurate, since periodically, the computation can be offloaded to the cloud to achieve higher confidence.

Motivated by these intuitions, we propose *InstantLoc*: a system capable of identifying user location from a video swipe in the environments of arbitrary sizes. InstantLoc consists of three major components : (1) a Google Project Tango [1] based wardriving app to quickly construct a database of visual features of various parts of the building. A user is required to walk across the building with the InstantLoc tango wardriving app. The app captures and stores colored photographs, depth-map, and the location of the user relative to the start position. (2) cloud cluster to perform the following tasks: (a) process the captured data and construct feature database (b) efficiently answer location based queries emerging from user phones. For database construction, visual features such as keypoints are extracted from the colored photographs and 3D point cloud from the depth-map. Since color and depth cameras are co-located on the device, each keypoint can be mapped to a 3D point in the point cloud. By merging these two information, a mapping between keypoints and corresponding 3D points is constructed. We replicated these mappings on a distributed key-value store for efficient query and retrieval. Note that given plethora of key-value stores available today, selection of the one fitting this problem is important. A keypoint descriptor is a multi-dimensional vector and efficiently answering queries based on them requires complex partitioning of the database. Motivation behind the platform selection and database summarization is discussed in detail in the next section. (3) A phone camera app, which captures and extracts visual features from continuous video frames on the phone. The extracted features are first tested against bloom-filters for rough estimate of uniqueness in the global key-value store. If sufficient evidence is found, selected set of most unique features are uploaded to the cloud and a reverse look-up (from features to 3D point cloud) is performed.

MobiCom'15, September 7–11, 2015, Paris, France.
ACM. ISBN 978-1-4503-3619-2/15/09
http://dx.doi.org/10.1145/2789168.2795175.

The result of lookup operation is a subset of 3D point cloud from where indoor location of the user can be estimated using advance mobile sensing based techniques.

2. SYSTEM DESIGN

In this section, we first introduce existing technologies used in InstantLoc and then expand on their usability in the following components: (1) Wardriving App (2) Client App (3) Server.

HyperDex Primer

Distribute key-value stores are now widely used across various cloud computing applications. These key-value stores often achieve benefits over traditional SQL databases by allowing restrictive set of search primitives e.g., object can be retrieved only based on the key it was inserted. On contrary to this, HyperDex [2] is a distributed key-value store, which provides an efficient querying on secondary attributes or range queries. HyperDex achieves this using the concept of hyperspace hashing where multiple attributes are mapped into a multidimensional hyperspace. For example a traditional SQL table with three columns is mapped into a 3D dimensional space. A region in this hyperspace is stored on a particular server. An object is queried by tessellating the hyperspace into a grid of non-overlapping regions.

We apply this concept of hyperspacing hashing to our multidimensional feature database. In computer vision, a keypoint descriptor is represented by set of fixed length real numbers. These numbers can be considered as attributes of a hypercube. Therefore, storing keypoint descriptors in a HyperDex cluster can enable their efficient lookups.

Project Tango Primer

Project tango is a prototype tablet-like hardware built by Google. Project tango combines 3D motion tracking with depth sensing to enable precise indoor localization and 6-DOF pose estimation. While not ready for widespread use due to limitations in energy, portability, and stability; the following properties of project tango still makes it good fit for the research and wardriving purpose:

Area Learning

Project tango tries to learn visual features (such as the edges, corners) of the area it visits. The concept of area learning is very similar to the concept of visual-SLAM in robotics. It uses learnt features in the past to: (1) correct drift by resetting deadreckoning errors at places seen before (2) localize by orienting and positioning itself with respect to the same place.

Depth Perception

Project tango is among first hardware prototype to use IR depth sensor on a portable hardware. It uses projected IR light to estimate depth based on how the light is shaped by objects in the environment. The depth information is made available to the application layer in the form of XYZ_{ij} point cloud, where (X, Y, Z) represents 3D coordinates of visible points and (i, j) represents its pixel coordinates in raster format.

2.1 Wardriving App

The wardriving app is a project tango app used to collect a series of snapshots consisting of 6-DOF pose of the device (w.r.t. to the start location), RGB image in the view, and a lower resolution depth map of the corresponding view. To wardrive a venue, an user needs to walk across the building – periodically capturing snapshots and uploading them to the cloud server. These snapshots are pre-processed to create mapping between image keypoints and corresponding 3D locations. The number of such mappings inside a building can be exceedingly large, on the order of millions to billions. This process is currently manual but it can be automated using area-covering robots like Roomba in the future.

2.2 Client App

The client app is a camera app, which runs on user's phone and is used to query indoor location. When the client app starts for the first time, the server sends precomputed bloom filters to the phone (explained in the next section). These counting bloom filters encode frequency of database features in a certain floating point hyper-ranges. To query a location, user makes a swipe in the environment. During the swipe, features from the non-blurred frames are extracted and their frequencies on the server database are extracted from the bloom filter. A feature of high frequency implies it is less unique, hence cannot help in disambiguating two locations. Therefore, all extracted frequencies are sorted in the increasing order and a small fraction of less frequent features is uploaded to the server for the location identification.

2.3 Server Implementation

Our server implementation consists of four parts:

Input pre-processing

In the pre-processing step, our goal is to construct image keypoint to 3D point mapping. These mappings need to be extracted from the snapshots uploaded from the wardriving app. We achieve this in the following steps: (1) Each snapshot contains device's rotation and translation with respect to the start of the app. These values are converted to a global coordinate system by starting tango app from a known GPS location and applying respective transformations. (2) From the RGB image in the snapshot, keypoints and descriptors are extracted. A keypoints is typically represented by a pixel value (i, j) (2D image coordinates) and corresponding N length descriptor vector. (3) Using depth map of the snapshot, a pixel (i, j) is also mapped to a 3D point (X, Y, Z) in the world. Note that (X, Y, Z) are initially captured in the device frame of reference, they need to be converted to the world coordinates. (4) Since the project tango depth map resolution is typically lower compared to the RGB image – it is interpolated by applying linear filters. Once done, every keypoint may be mapped to the corresponding 3D point. (5) Since a 3D point may be visible in multiple snapshots, snapshots are merged using iterative point cloud algorithms (ICP) to avoid duplications. (6) All keypoints to unique 3D point mappings are created and stored in the HyperDex cluster.

Bloom Filters

The keypoint to 3D point mappings are combined at a global cloud service with mappings collected from many other buildings. At this point, the database size could range in the size of hundreds of millions to billions. Periodically, an O(n.log(n)) scan on the entire data store is conducted. For each keypoint, we make constant number of range queries (hence O(log(n))) in keypoint descriptor space. The output of each query is a count of the number of keypoints "similar" to the queried keypoint. For our purposes, more similarity is bad – implies a

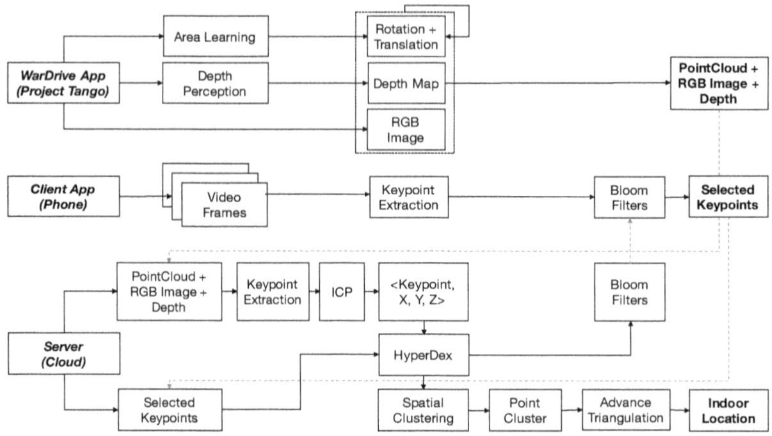

Figure 1: System Overview. Top: wardriving-app. Middle: phone-app. Bottom: Server consisting of HyperDex and vision/pointcloud libraries.

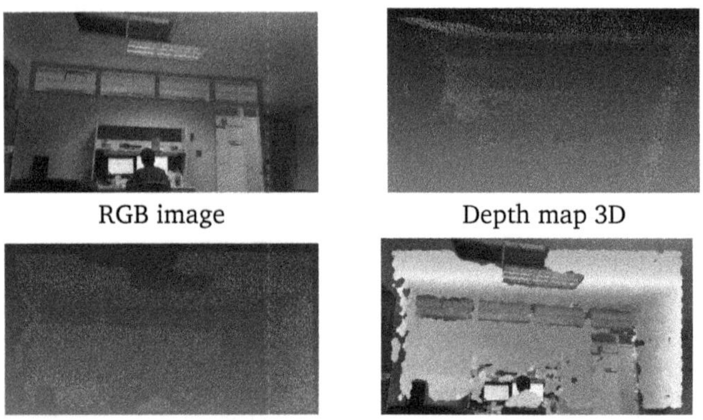

RGB image | Depth map 3D | Depth map 2D projection | Processed depth map on the RGB image

Figure 2: Pre-processing life-cycle of a snapshot on the server

keypoint is less unique, less discriminating. Consider the distribution of such counts and order them in decreasing order. These counts can be divided into sets of quantiles – likely candidates, the 0th, 50th, 75th, 90th, 95th, 99th percentiles. For each quantile, we create a set of bloom filters. Each bloom filter here encodes keypoints that meet a "uniqueness criterion" corresponding to the respective quantile. For example, a keypoint that only appears once would be encoded in every bloom filter. A common keypoint (e.g., the corner of a tile in a repeating pattern) might only appear in the 0th or 50th. All of the bloom filters are pushed to the client app when it starts for the first time and refreshed periodically. Though the global data store is expected to be huge (many TB), the bloom filters can be several orders of magnitude smaller (MB).

Feature Matching

When the user opens client app for the first time, bloom filters are downloaded on the device. An user making a swipe continuously captures image and inertial sensor data such as accelerometer and gyroscope. From the image, keypoints are extracted – typically ranging between 1000-20K. Each keypoint is tested against the bloom filters. This identifies how "rare" each keypoint is, relative to the global data store. Each keypoint is ranked based on it's rarity – selecting the top K most rare points as candidate for uploading on the server (K typically range between 5-50). On the server, We query the global data store with these K selected keypoints, returning N_k 3D points corresponding to each of them (a keypoint may belong to multiple 3D points). This gives us $\sum_k N_k$ 3D points. On these 3D points, spatial clustering such as k-means is applied – leaving us with the largest cluster, discarding others.

Location Estimation using Triangulation

For each of the point in the largest spatial cluster, it's slope from a random origin is computed. If two points were visible in the same frame, the exact angular disparity is known. Otherwise it can be estimated with gyroscope/accelerometer or optical flow. Finally, we use "enhanced" triangulation technique discussed in [5] to triangulate to a single location from arbitrary number of such points. The solution to this optimization provides us exact location of the user.

3. CONCLUSION

Many emerging mobile computing applications are continuous vision based. The primary challenge these applications face is computation partitioning between the phone and cloud. The indoor location information is one metadata that can help these applications in making this decision. In this extended-abstract, we propose a vision based scheme to uniquely fingerprint an environment which can in turn be used to identify user's location from the uploaded visual features. Our approach takes into account that the opportunity to identify location is fleeting and the phones are resource constrained – therefore minimal yet sufficient computation needs to be performed to make the offloading decision. Our work aims to achieve near real-time performance while scaling to buildings of arbitrary sizes. The current work is in preliminary stages but holds promise for the future – may apply to many applications in this area.

4. REFERENCES

[1] Project tango. https://www.google.com/atap/projecttango/, 2014.

[2] R. Escriva, B. Wong, and E. G. Sirer. Hyperdex: A distributed, searchable key-value store. *ACM SIGCOMM Computer Communication Review*, 42(4):25–36, 2012.

[3] P. Jain, J. Manweiler, A. Acharya, and K. Beaty. Focus: clustering crowdsourced videos by line-of-sight. In *SenSys*, page 8. ACM, 2013.

[4] P. Jain, J. Manweiler, and R. Roy Choudhury. Overlay: Practical mobile augmented reality. In *MobiSys*, pages 331–344. ACM, 2015.

[5] J. G. Manweiler, P. Jain, and R. Roy Choudhury. Satellites in our pockets: an object positioning system using smartphones. In *MobiSys*, pages 211–224. ACM, 2012.

Poster: Understanding YouTube QoE in Cellular Networks with YoMoApp - a QoE Monitoring Tool for YouTube Mobile

Florian Wamser (1), Michael Seufert (1), Pedro Casas (2)
Ralf Irmer (3), Phuoc Tran-Gia (1), Raimund Schatz (2)
(1) University of Würzburg, (2) FTW Vienna, (3) Vodafone Research and Development
{florian.wamser|surname}@informatik.uni-wuerzburg.de; {surname}@ftw.at; ralf.irmer@vodafone.com

ABSTRACT

The performance of YouTube in cellular networks is crucial to network operators, who try to find a trade-off between cost-efficient handling of the huge traffic amounts and high perceived end-user Quality of Experience (QoE). In this paper we present YoMoApp (YouTube Performance Monitoring Application), an Android application which passively monitors key performance indicators (KPIs) of YouTube adaptive video streaming on end-user smartphones. The monitored KPIs (i.e., player state/events, re-buffering, and video quality levels) can be used to analyze the QoE of mobile YouTube video sessions. YoMoApp is a valuable tool to assess the performance of cellular networks with respect to YouTube traffic, as well as to develop optimizations and QoE models for mobile HTTP adaptive streaming. We try YoMoApp through real subjective QoE lab tests showing that the tool is accurate to capture the experience of end-users watching YouTube on smartphones.

Categories and Subject Descriptors

C.2 [**Computer-Communication Networks**]: Miscellaneous; C.4 [**Performance of Systems**]: Measurement Techniques

Keywords

QoE; Smartphones; Subjective Lab Tests; Mobile Apps

1. MOTIVATION & METHODOLOGY

YouTube is one of the most popular services in today's Internet. It has more than 1 billion users and every day people watch hundreds of millions of hours of YouTube videos. Half of those YouTube views are done on mobile devices [1]. On the one hand, operators want to handle the huge amount of video traffic as efficiently as possible (high revenue per bit), on the other hand, they want to deliver a high Quality of Experience (QoE) to satisfy their customers. Therefore, it is paramount to cellular operators to understand the performance of their networks wrt YouTube traffic.

MobiCom '15, September 7–11, 2015, Paris, France.
ACM. ISBN 978-1-4503-3619-2/15/09
DOI: http://dx.doi.org/10.1145/2789168.2795176

To measure the network performance in terms of QoE, different approaches are proposed in literature. First, operators can conduct subjective studies and ask the users about the perceived service quality. Subjective studies can directly assess the QoE in terms of mean opinion scores (MOS), but their design and execution is complex and costly. Second, operators can perform active measurements with client devices to probe the network. However, these samples can only provide a rough estimation of the network performance, as they only cover the geo-temporal-span of the active measurements. Finally, passive measurements can be conducted either in the network or at the client device. In-network measurements (e.g., YouQMON [2]) have a more global scope and cover more users, but the resulting QoE has to be estimated from traffic characteristics and/or deep-packet inspection. Moreover, the recent trend towards HTTPS (e.g., YouTube, Vimeo) is about to inhibit its applicability. As a consequence, client side passive measurements are becoming a practical means to QoE-based network performance analysis, with the paramount advantage of having a vantage point next to the end-customer (i.e., on its device).

In this paper we present YoMoApp (YouTube Performance Monitoring Application), a passive measurement application for client side monitoring of YouTube video streaming on mobile Android devices. The application uses the YouTube mobile website and the YouTube HTML5 API to exactly replicate the well-known YouTube service, which employs HTTP adaptive streaming (HAS) technology based on resolution adaptation. However, it additionally monitors and stores multiple Key Performance Indicators (KPIs) of the video streaming via the YouTube API (i.e., player state/events, buffer, and video quality level), which allow to analyze the QoE of adaptive video streaming sessions.

YoMoApp is an accurate and highly valuable tool for passive measurement of YouTube performance in cellular networks, which is becoming highly needed and popular among cellular operators. In addition, the tool can be used to develop novel QoE models for HAS in mobile devices, enabling multiple QoE-based monitoring applications for YouTube traffic, such as dynamic traffic engineering [3], troubleshooting, load balancing and caching, and many more.

2. THE YOMOAPP TOOL

The goal is to monitor application layer KPIs of YouTube that have a high correlation with the actual QoE of mobile app users. According to [4], the main influence parameters of the YouTube QoE are *stallings* and *video quality*. To obtain these parameters, we monitor the buffer filling levels and the resolution of the YouTube videos.

Name	Description
buffered	List of time ranges of the media content that have been buffered
height/ width	Height and width of the video's display area in CSS pixels
played	Object indicating all the ranges of the video that have been played
currentTime	Current video playtime
youtubeId	Object indicating YouTube identifier of the video content
totalVideo-Frames	Total number of frames that would have been displayed if no frames are dropped
dropped-Video-Frames	Total number of frames dropped predecode or dropped because the frame missed its display deadline
corrupted-Video-Frames	Total number of corrupted frames that have been detected
Timestamp	Timestamp of the data query
Name	Pre-defined device name
Session timestamp	Session timestamp to identify the YouTube session.

Figure 1: Screenshot of the app and selected parameters from the HTML5 ⟨*video*⟩ object [6], Media Source Extensions [7], and device, which can be investigated by the app.

YoMo works as follows. The original YouTube app is fully replicated in functionality and design, see Fig. 1. To this end, existing libraries from YouTube are used that are available for YouTube developers. An Android web view browser element is embedded for the YouTube video playback, such that HTML5 video playback is possible, including adaptive streaming according to the MPEG Dynamic Adaptive Streaming over HTTP (DASH) approach [5] of YouTube. Additional functions are added, which ultimately perform the monitoring of the application parameters in the newly created app. The monitoring is done at runtime via JavaScript, which queries the embedded HTML5 ⟨*video*⟩ object. In Fig. 1, the utilized parameters are listed. Note that the obtained parameters can be displayed in YoMoApp for validation (see Fig. 1), but are usually hidden. The measurement methodology in the app follows 4 steps:

Step #1: *HTML Detection* - the YouTube web page is detected and the HTML video player element is identified. YouTube consists of many web pages and elements. Thus, the name and id of the relevant video elements must be determined. The detection is done via the injection of JavaScript code to the running Android WebView browser element of the app. The JavaScript code analyzes the HTML Document Object Model (DOM) tree for the ⟨*video*⟩ element.

Step #2: *Request the Data* - parameters such as current playtime or current available video content are retrieved. This is realized by injecting JavaScript code that requests the application parameters from the detected video player element in Step #1 every second.

Step #3: *Calculation* - from the retrieved parameters, the buffer filling level can be calculated. The parameter *buffered* is subtracted from *currentTime*, which results in the current buffer level. Likewise, the video resolution is obtained based on *height* and *width* of the video player.

Step #4: *Data Transfer* - finally, data is transferred to an external database located in the Internet. Data is compressed and stored as structured objects, and can be transmitted at different time instances: a) when closing the app, b) manually by the user, c) at predetermined intervals, etc. Data is also locally cached, since the connection from the smartphone to the Internet server is often not reliable.

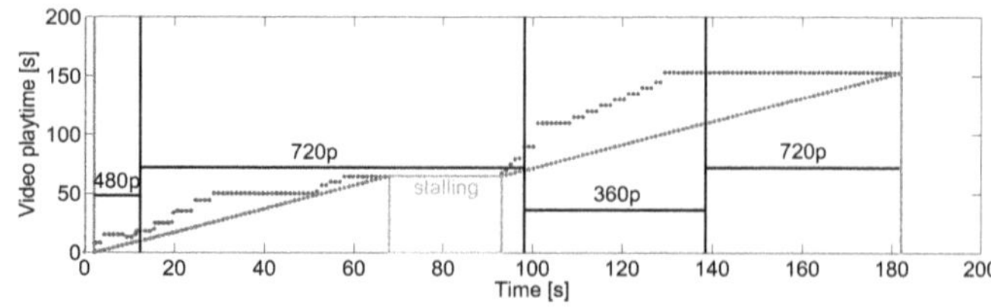

Figure 2: Illustration of monitored parameters for an exemplary video streaming: current video playtime (green) and buffered video playtime (blue). Events are displayed as vertical lines: page load (blue), playback start (green), quality switch (black), playback end (red). Stalling is depicted as orange box. The horizontal black lines indicate the currently played out video quality/resolution.

Fig. 2 shows the data of an exemplary run in their processed form. Postprocessing of the data is recommended because the usage of JavaScript can sometimes introduce inconsistencies and obvious errors, e.g., missed player events, non-equidistant data queries, missing/incorrect values. However, after removing unusable runs and the recovery of missing events (e.g., stalling events can be estimated from buffer filling level), YoMoApp proved to perform accurate measurements on a sufficiently small time scale (~1 s).

3. YOMOAPP IN ACTION

To demonstrate the applicability of YoMoApp to analyze the QoE of YouTube in mobile devices, we conducted a subjective study in which participants watched YouTube videos in smartphones instrumented with the YoMoApp tool and rated the resulting watching experience. To induce different QoE levels, the downlink traffic from YouTube servers to the mobile devices was throttled through an intermediate instrumented router imposing different bandwidth profiles.

3.1 Subjective Study Overview

The subjective study was performed in a dedicated lab for subjective analysis, compliant with the recommendations provided by the QoE subjective studies standards [8]. 52 people participated in the study (29 female, 23 male), the average age was 32 years old, with 40 participants being less than 30 years old.

Android smartphone devices (Samsung Galaxy S4, OS Android 4.4 KitKat) were used in the tests. Devices were connected to the Internet through independent WiFi access points. The downlink traffic was routed through a modified version of the well-known NetEm network emulator to impose different access network bandwidth profiles to the video streaming. Three different bandwidth profiles were used: (i) constant downlink bandwidth: 1 Mbps, 2 Mbps, and 4 Mbps; (ii) fluctuating downlink with variable bandwidth ("var"): downlink bandwidth is periodically increased from 1 Mbps to 3 Mbps for periods of 5 seconds, 3 times per minute. The resulting average downlink bandwidth is 1.5 Mbps; (iii) downlink bandwidth outages ("out"): downlink bandwidth drops from 4 Mbps to 0 Mbps for periods of 10 seconds, twice per minute. In this case, the resulting average downlink bandwidth is 2.7 Mbps.

The specific task imposed to participants was to watch two minute long YouTube adaptive streaming videos using YoMoApp for the five different downlink bandwidth condi-

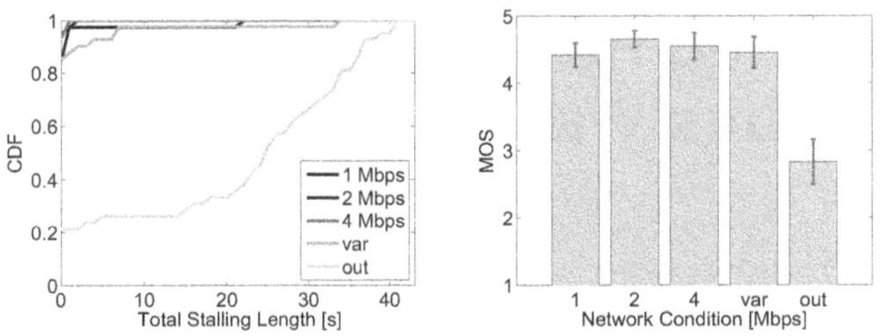

(a) Total stalling time. (b) Impacts of stallings on QoE.

Figure 3: Monitoring of stallings and their impact on QoE.

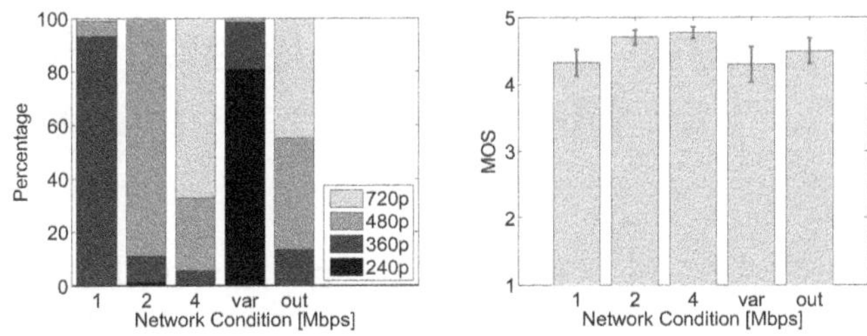

(a) Distribution of quality levels. (b) Video image QoE.

Figure 4: Monitoring of video quality switches and the resulting image QoE.

tions, and rate the resulting watching experience afterwards (i.e., overall experience, impact of initial playback delay and stalling, video image quality, etc.) on continuous ACR MOS scales [8]. The tested videos are available as 4K ultra-HD videos (i.e., 2160p), but the maximum video quality observed in the tests was HD (i.e., 720p) due to the devices' display capabilities (i.e., screen size and resolution).

3.2 Analysis of Stallings

Stalling, i.e., the interruption of playback due to a playout buffer under-run, is considered the worst quality degradation of video streaming [4]. Stalling occurs when the available network bandwidth is lower than the video bit rate. The playout buffer is filled slower by the download than it is emptied by the playback, which will eventually lead to stalling. During a stalling event, the playback is paused until the buffer is filled with a sufficient amount of video data to continue the playback. Authors in [4] found an exponential relationship between stalling parameters and MOS and that users tolerated at most one stalling event of up to three seconds length. Thus, it is important to monitor the stalling during the video playback.

Fig. 3a shows the distribution of the total stalling time for each tested condition. Almost no stalling occurs for the constant bandwidth conditions. For 4 Mbps, 93.48% of the streaming sessions have no stalling, the remaining sessions have less than 1 s of stalling. A maximum of 2 s of stalling was measured for the 2 Mbps condition, with 95.12% of the sessions showing no stalling at all. For the 1 Mbps condition, 85.00% of the streaming sessions do not include stalling. However, one outlier with 22 s stalling was observed. For the variable condition ("var"), stalling occurs in 14.63% of the conditions ranging up to a total stalling time of 34 s. 78.57% of the outage condition ("out") streams contained stalling. The average total stalling time in this condition is 25 s, and the maximum total stalling time is 41 s.

In Fig. 3b, the MOS and 95% confidence intervals of the QoE ratings are presented. Participants were asked to which extend they perceived the interruptions caused by stalling as disturbing. The MOS values for the disturbance of stalling range from 1 (very disturbing) to 5 (not disturbing at all). For 1 Mbps, 2 Mbps, 4 Mbps and variable condition stalling is not considered as disturbing, having MOS scores of at least 4.4. This corresponds to the measured total stalling time, which indicated very short stalling events, if any at all. Only for the outage condition, stalling is perceived as disturbing, having a MOS of 2.83. Again, this corresponds to the frequently long total stalling times measured by YoMoApp.

3.3 Analysis of Quality Switches

HTTP adaptive streaming trades off stalling for video quality. It adapts the downloaded video quality (i.e., video bit rate) to the currently available network conditions, thereby avoiding stalling to the greatest possible extend. In YouTube, this is implemented by adaptively changing the resolution of the streamed video. However, quality switches, i.e., the change of the video bit rate, occur during streaming and can be perceived by the users. In the following, the monitored quality of the video streaming will be investigated.

Fig. 4a shows the percentage of time on each quality level per condition, i.e., the percentage of time which each video resolution was played out during the streaming. In the 1 Mbps condition, all available resolutions were used with the following overall shares: 240p (0.23%), 360p (92.89%), 480p (5.85%), 720p (1.02%). The 2 Mbps condition shows a larger percentage of 480p quality (88.84%), and in the 4 Mbps condition a significant share of 720p quality (67.15%) can be played out. Additionally, the outage condition has similar quality shares to the 4 Mbps conditions, which is not surprising considering that it is a 4 Mbps on/off pattern. The variable condition contains a large percentage of the lowest resolution (240p, 80.86%), which indicates that the YouTube adaptation is very conservative when the network conditions fluctuate considerably.

Fig. 4b shows how the image quality of each condition was rated by the participants (MOS and 95% confidence intervals). It can be observed that the image quality is rated good for all conditions, having a MOS of at least 4.17. This means that resolution adaptation does not have a big impact on the subjectively perceived image quality, which is most probably linked to the small display size of smartphones. Nevertheless, the increasing levels of quality played out for 1 Mbps, 2 Mbps, and 4 Mbps correspond to the increasing image quality ratings by the participants.

4. REFERENCES

[1] [Online]. https://www.youtube.com/yt/press/statistics.html
[2] P. Casas, M. Seufert, and R. Schatz, "YOUQMON: A System for On-line Monitoring of YouTube QoE in Operational 3G Networks," *ACM SIGMETRICS PER*, vol. 41, 2013.
[3] F. Wamser, D. Hock, M. Seufert, B. Staehle, R. Pries, and P. Tran-Gia, "Using Buffered Playtime for QoE-Oriented Resource Management of YouTube Video Streaming," *IEEE Trans. ETT*, vol. 24, 2013.
[4] T. Hoßfeld, R. Schatz, M. Seufert, M. Hirth, T. Zinner, and P. Tran-Gia, "Quantification of YouTube QoE via Crowdsourcing," in *MQoE*, 2011.
[5] ISO/IEC, "23009-1:2012 Information Technology – Dynamic Adaptive Streaming over HTTP (DASH) – Part 1: Media Presentation Description and Segment Formats," 2012.
[6] [Online]. Available: http://developer.mozilla.org/en-US/docs/Web/HTML/Element/video
[7] [Online]. Available: http://dvcs.w3.org/hg/html-media/raw-file/tip/media-source/media-source.html
[8] ITU-T, "Recommendation P.910: Subjective Video Quality Assessment Methods for Multimedia Applications," 2008.

Poster: Continuous and Fine-grained Respiration Volume Monitoring Using Continuous Wave Radar

Phuc Nguyen[1], Xinyu Zhang[2], Ann C. Halbower[3], and Tam Vu[1]
[1]University of Colorado, Denver, [2]University of Wisconsin-Madison,
[3]University of Colorado School of Medicine and Children's Hospital Colorado
{phuc.v.nguyen, tam.vu}@ucdenver.edu,
xyzhang@ece.wisc.edu, ann.halbower@childrenscolorado.org

ABSTRACT

An unobtrusive and continuous estimation of breathing volume could play a vital role in health care, such as for critically ill patients, neonatal ventilation, post-operative monitoring, just to name a few. While radar-based estimation of breathing rate has been discussed in the literature, estimating breathing volume using wireless signal remains relatively intact. With the presence of patient body movement and posture changes, long-term monitoring of breathing volume at fine granularity is even more challenging. In this work, we propose for the first time an autonomous system that monitors a patient's *breathing volume with high resolution*. We discuss the key research components and challenges in realizing the system. We also present an initial system design encompassing a continuous wave radar, motion tracking and control system, and a set of methods to accurately derive breathing volume from the reflected signal and to address challenges caused by body movement and posture changes. Our implementation shows promising results in estimating breathing volume with fine granularity.

Categories and Subject Descriptors

J.3 [**Computer Applications**]: Life and Medical Sciences

General Terms

Design; Human Factors; Algorithms

Keywords

Radar technique; Mobile health; Breathing volume monitoring; Fine-grained estimation.

1. INTRODUCTION

Continuous and fine-grained breathing volume monitoring plays an important role in health care. While abnormality in breathing rate is a good indication of many respiratory diseases such as [5], fine-grain breathing volume information is required in many others. Patients with lower airway diseases such as chronic obstructive pulmonary diseases (COPD), cystic fibrosis, or tuberculosis, for example, could be diagnosed when sudden drops in breathing volume are frequently detected [3]. In many instances, patients with lung disease only show their symptoms during sleep, in which cases long-term monitoring is needed. In another important health care practice, breathing volume of prematurely-born, or preterm, babies is closely and continuously monitored. A decrease of breathing flow and volume must be promptly detected even before it causes oxygen desaturation in order for doctors to give an effective neonatal ventilation intervention. In a recent study on the effects of sleep apnea during pregnancy [1], it has been shown that early detection of the sleep disorder could results in a significantly better pregnancy. However, many patients only start developing apnea for a short period of time. Hence monitoring them non-invasively to get breathing volume and flow limitation is critical. In all above mentioned health care practices, the symptoms can only be detected with an accurate and fine-grained (in time) breathing volume monitoring technique over an extended period of time.

In previous work, breathing rate can be estimated using camera [8], laser [6], or infrared (IR) [4], but these approaches cannot be applied in cases where the subject wears a thick shirt, a jacket or covered by a blanket. To overcome these issues, Doppler-based radar techniques have been investigated to estimate respiration rate while penetrating through clothes or blankets [7, 9, 11, 2]. The concept is to transmit a continuous wave signal (sometimes with modulated frequency), which will bounced back when hits the human chest, and then demodulates it to estimate the chest movements and breathing rate. The respiration rate is usually estimated based on phase shift [7], harmonics distribution [9], distance measured by frequency modulation continuous wave (FMCW) [2, 11]. In contrast, there is not much works done in finding breathing volume. Massagram *et al.* [10] described a calibration technique to estimate the tidal volume relying on peak to peak calibration between reconstructed DC coupled and breathing volume. However, this work has made many impractical assumption about subject's posture and movement between training and testing. For example, it assumes that the human body doesn't move through out the whole estimation process. It also assumes, more importantly, the radar is pointing to the same point on the subject's body through out the monitoring process, from the training phase to the testing phase. Last, but not least important, it can only provide a coarse-grained volume estimation with low accuracy.

Fine-grained and long-term breathing volume estimation is hard due to the following challenges:

- Respiration volume information is buried in the very minor phase shift of the reflected signal. That is in sharp contrast with respiration rate where a simple peak count applied on the phase shift time series might reveal the accurate estimation of the rate. In addition, phase shift is fluctuated as the distance between the radar and subject is changed, or influenced by the imperfection

MobiCom'15, September 07–11, 2015, Paris, France.
ACM 978-1-4503-3619-2/15/09.
DOI: http://dx.doi.org/10.1145/2789168.2795177.

of the hardware circuitry, or the non-linear/abnormal breathing behavior of the subjects.

- A minor non-respiratory movement could cause significant volume estimation error. That movement makes radar beam to new area on human's body, which leads the estimation inaccurate because different areas on the human chest move differently (while they reflect the same breathing volume). Therefore, the radar needs to know exactly which posture the subject is sleeping as well as where the radar is beaming to on subject's body.
- Posture change or body part's movements, *e.g.* subject's arms, also might block the chest movements to be seen by radar. In this case, an alternative area on human chest that isn't blocked should be found to replace the current area.

2. SOLUTIONS AND SYSTEM DESIGN

Basic principle and system overview. Phase shifting of the received signal is considered as the input of our analysis. The principle relationship between the phase $\phi(t)$ and traveling distance $d(t)$ of a wireless signal is formulated by $\phi(t) = 2\pi d(t)/\lambda$, with λ is the wavelength. Hence, by analyzing the phase change of the received signal, distance change between radar and chest surface can be inferred.

We design a system operating with the concepts as in Figure 1, the phase shift captured on receiving signal is converted into the normalized chest position. The chest position is then used to estimate the breathing volume if there is no random body movement presence. If body movement is detected, the system will predict the new posture as well as new cross section area. The radar is then navigated to the new location and direction, where it can see the chest movements clearly. We estimate the posture and cross section area by comparing the features of upcoming and trained signals on both time and frequency domains. The following discussions in this section describe the solutions more in details.

Estimating volume in fine-grained, not the rate. The amplitude of chest position change reflects the level of breathing volume change. The distance between subject's chest and radar might change every breathing cycle this leads to inaccuracy of estimating the actual chest position. To overcome this issue, we delay one breathing cycle to normalize the receiving signal so that the chest position can be inferred correctly. This method removes the effect from the change of distance between human chest and radar. After normalizing the received signal, we then convert the phase shift $\phi(t)$ into the chest position $x(t)$. Let $v_c(t)$, $v_\phi(t)$ be the velocity of chest movement and phase shift, respectively. Then, $v_c(t) \approx v_\phi(t)$. The $x(t)$ is as an integration of $v_c(t)$ over time. We calibrate the chest position $x(t)$ with the breathing volume estimated by ground-truth devices.

We use Bayesian back-propagation neural network technique to find the correlation between chest position and breathing volume. As such relationship lightly repeats every breathing cycle, a network that could take the history information into account for predicting the upcoming value as a good reference. Bayesian interpretation of regularization has been investigated.

Dealing with non-periodic or irregular body movement during sleep. When the subject changes his posture, the system first has to recognize which posture that the user is sleeping. Three common sleeping postures investigated in our system include: soldier, left foetus, right foetus (when the subject sleeps on his back, his left, and his right, respectively). We compare the features of upcoming signal with that of the trained ones to get the current posture's name (class). K-nearest neighbors algorithm (k-NN) technique has been used to estimate the human posture. Nineteen features of the data are considered: min, max, median, variance, range, signal dispersion, asymmetry, peakness, first, second, and third quartiles, inter quartile range, mean crossing rate, absolute area, signal's energy, entropy, dominant frequency ratio, heart range crossing rate, and respiration range crossing rate. Moreover, we also built a rail as in Figure 2 supporting 360° pan, tilt, and slide directions to navigate the radar to proper location.

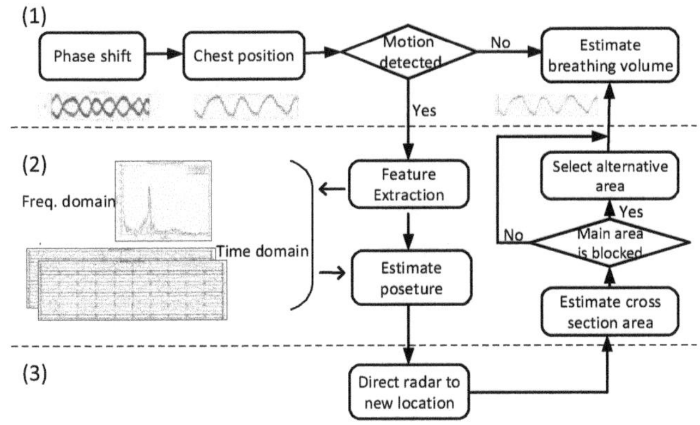

Figure 1: System overview. (1) Breathing estimation without the presence of random body movement. (2) Key components that handle posture change and blocking radar's visibility situations. (3) Motion control system to navigate the radar to the proper location.

Different areas on the chest wall move differently with the same breathing volume changes. We need to distinguish the movements of different areas on human chest, and know exactly where radar is beaming to in order to estimate the breathing volume correctly. To address this, we narrow down the beam-width of radar transmitter so that the size of each referenced area (left rig-cage, right rig-cage, and abdomen) is close to the size of radar cross section. Extracting the features and compares with that of each referenced area, we can know where the wireless signal is hitting on the human chest. In addition, the radar sometimes cannot see the chest movements during sleep because the radar's vision has blocked by human's parts, such as arms. We apply the results of above observation to find the new area on the chest where radar's visibility isn't blocked. Then, the breathing volume is inferred from the movements on new cross section area. We select the left side as the main area because it contains both breathing and heart beat information. The other two alternative areas, which would be used when the main area is blocked, are the right chest and abdomen areas.

3. EXPERIMENT SET UP AND RESULTS

We evaluate the performance of the system on different parameters and environment set up. The radar uses continuous wave technique and operates at frequency 2.4 GHz AC coupled, with the sampling rate is at 1 kHz. The experiment set up is shown in Figure 2.

Training. As breathing volume depends on human's health, height, weight, chest area and so on, the training step must be performed for each subject before starting the monitoring process. The training output include: (a) correlation function between chest position and breathing volume for three postures when radar is located in front of the chest, (b) features of signal received when user in soldier, left foetus, right foetus postures when radar is located in the middle of the rails, (c) features of the signal received when radar is beam to subject's left rig-cage, right rig-cage, and abdomen. Those results are used to estimate the breathing volume, estimate the current posture and cross section area.

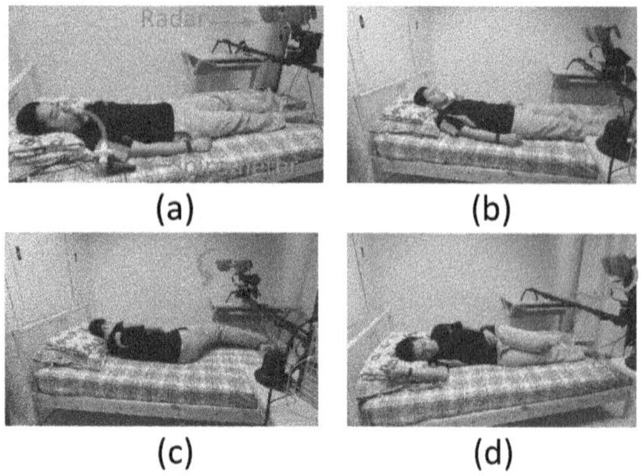

Figure 2: An experiment set up and example execution of our proposed system. The spirometer is used as a ground-truth for training (a). Then, the subject is sleeping on (b) his back, (c) his left and (d) his right side while his breathing activities are monitored by the radar.

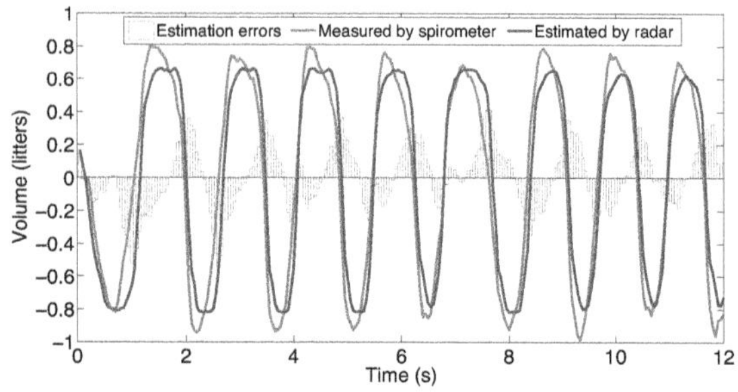

Figure 3: Breathing volume estimated by radar and measured from ground-truth device

Fine-Grained Breathing Monitoring. We use radar to estimate the breathing volume and then compare that with the ground-truth values measured by spirometer. The results area showed in Figure 3. As can been from the figure, the breathing volume and rate are precisely estimated. However, we still need to improve the performance of volume estimation, the errors come from the imperfect relationship between chest movement and breathing volume. This problem would be fixed by improving calibration technique. In addition, Figure 4 shows the results of obtaining respiration volume using our technique, and an approximation based on the breathing rate (assume that breathing volume function has a form $V(t) = Asin\omega t$, $f = \frac{2\pi}{\omega}$ is the breathing rate). Results show that we obtain better results in fine-grained estimation.

Detecting posture. In this experiment, the subject frequently changes his posture and checks the response from the radar. We detect three main postures when the radar is located in front (soldier), on the left side (right foetus) and right side (left foetus) of the human body by comparing the features of receiving signal with the trained ones. We repeat this set up in 50 times for each postures, radar can detect successfully 49/50, 50/50, and 45/50 times when subject sleeps on his back, his right, and his left, respectively. Note that because the system has to collect data as the input for estimation, this process takes at most 20 seconds.

Detecting location of cross section area over human chest. The subject frequently moves his chest in front of the radar so that radar points to three different locations: left rig-cage, right rig-cage, and abdomen randomly. We repeat this set up in 50 times for each location, our radar can detect successfully 41/50, 44/50, and 35/50 times for left rig-cage, right rig-cage, and abdomen cases, respectively. These results can be improved if we continue narrowing

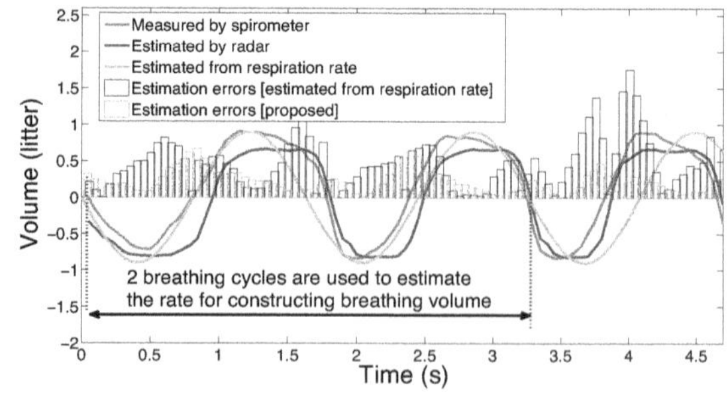

Figure 4: Results of breathing volume estimation using our approach and approximating from breathing rate using sine function. The results are compared with the values measured by ground-truth device (the errors are absolute values).

the beam-width of the radar transmitter because the movements of areas would be captured separately. This process also takes at most 20 seconds.

4. CONCLUSION AND FUTURE WORKS

We have presented an autonomous radar system to monitor breathing volume during sleep. The system is now capable to estimate the breathing volume accurately based on the reflected signal while dealing with random body movements. For the next step of our research, we attempt to optimize the system so that it can be used in practical sleep study. We also want to improve the system's performance in terms of time and accuracy for posture/area detection and breathing volume estimation.

5. REFERENCES

[1] Pregnancy and sleep. http://sleepfoundation.org/sleep-topics/pregnancy-and-sleep.

[2] F. Adib et al. Smart homes that monitor breathing and heart rate. *ACM CHI*, 2015.

[3] R. Balkissoon et al. Chronic obstructive pulmonary disease: a concise review. *The Medical Clinics of North America*, 2011.

[4] L. Boccanfuso and J. O'Kane. Remote measurement of breathing rate in real time using a high precision, single-point infrared temperature sensor. *IEEE BioRob*, 2012.

[5] S. R. Braun. Respiratory rate and pattern. *Clinical Methods: The History, Physical, and Laboratory Examinations*, 1990.

[6] A. Bulanova et al. The analysis of breath air by laser spectroscopy method for diagnosis of COPD. *European Respiratory Journal*, 2014.

[7] A. Droitcour et al. Range correlation and I/Q performance benefits in single-chip silicon doppler radars for noncontact cardiopulmonary monitoring. *IEEE Trans. on Micro. Theory Techn.*, 2004.

[8] Lewis et al. A novel method for extracting respiration rate and relative tidal volume from infrared thermography. *Psychophy.*, 2011.

[9] L. Lu et al. Doppler radar noncontact vital sign monitoring. *Neural Comp., Neural Devices, and Neural Prosthesis*, 2014.

[10] W. Massagram et al. Tidal volume measurement through non-contact doppler radar with dc reconstruction. *IEEE Sensors Journal*, 2013.

[11] R. Nandakumar et al. Contactless sleep apnea detection on smartphones. *ACM Mobisys*, 2015.

Poster: Distributed Voronoi-based Acoustic Source Localization with Wireless Sensor Networks

Xueshu Zheng, Naigao Jin, Lei Wang
Dalian University of Technology
zhengxs90@gmail.com
{ngjin, lei.wang}@dlut.edu.cn

Mathew L. Wymore, Daji Qiao
Iowa State University
{mlwymore, daji}@iastate.edu

ABSTRACT

This paper presents DiVA, a new acoustic source localization scheme that uses an ad-hoc network of microphone sensor nodes to produce an accurate estimate of the source's location. DiVA uses pairwise comparisons of sound detection timestamps between local Voronoi neighbors to identify the node closest to the acoustic source and then estimates the source's location. The scheme improves on the state of the art by effectively dealing with anchor nodes' position error, time stamp measurement error and time synchronization error in real world conditions. Through simulation and experimental evaluations, DiVA is shown to be more robust than existing solutions under different error conditions.

Categories and Subject Descriptors

J.0 [**Computer Applications**]: General

Keywords

Acoustic Source; Localization; Voronoi; Sensor Network

1. INTRODUCTION

The loss of flight MH370 in early 2014, and the failure to date to locate its wreckage, have shown the need for better methods of locating acoustic sources within a large area. An ad-hoc wireless sensor network deployed in the search area could use onboard microphones and a robust localization method to perform this task. A similar network could also be used for applications such as shooter localization [1], if deployed in advance.

This paper presents DiVA, a distributed Voronoi-based [2] acoustic source localization scheme. DiVA is based on the observation that an acoustic source may be roughly localized using only pairwise comparisons of sound detection timestamps of neighboring nodes, and that such comparisons are tolerant to reasonable amounts of error from either node.

DiVA is a unique hybrid solution, which first (1) uses a distributed Voronoi-based range-free method to identify a (small) final region where the source may reside, and then (2) uses a time difference of arrival based (TDOA-based) method to output a precise estimate of the source location by solving a constrained (on the identified final region) optimization formulation. DiVA is completely distributed, quick to converge, and robust to real-world conditions such as node failure, microphone position errors, sound time of arrival (TOA) measurement errors, and clock synchronization errors.

This work is supported by the Haitian Scholar Grant of Dalian University of Technology, NSF China grant under No. 61272524, and the Fundamental Research Funds for the Central Universities under grants No. DUT15QY05 and No. DUT15QY51. Naigao Jin is the corresponding author.

MobiCom'15, September 7-11, 2015, Paris, France.
ACM 978-1-4503-3619-2/15/09.
http://dx.doi.org/10.1145/2789168.2795178.

2. BASELINE APPROACH

DiVA's overall approach is to divide the area covered by the microphone nodes into local Voronoi cells and use pairwise comparisons between neighbors to traverse the diagram to the acoustic source. This is accomplished in four phases. In the initialization phase, nodes determine their local Voronoi neighbors (LVNs), a subset of their neighbors. Then, when a sound is heard, nodes collaborate with their LVNs to identify the node closest to the source of the sound. This node then uses information from its LVNs to narrow down the location to a target subregion. Finally, TDOA estimates are used to produce a final location estimate within the target subregion.

2.1 Phase I - Initialization

To participate in localization, a node must first determine its *Local Voronoi Neighbors* (LVNs) using its local neighbor information and a Voronoi diagram. Specifically, if V_A is the set of A's Voronoi Neighbors (VNs), C_A is the set of A's Communication Neighbor (CNs), and Φ_A is the set of A's LVNs, then $\Phi_A = V_A \cap C_A$.

When a node enters Phase I, it broadcasts a request to discover its CNs and their positions. With this information, the node can determine its set of LVNs by computing its local Voronoi diagram. This set is maintained over time as sensors join and leave. Since nodes in DiVA only track the information of their neighbors, DiVA is highly scalable.

2.2 Phase II - Target Cell Identification

In Phase II, each node that hears a sound matching the target acoustic signature, called a *beep*, designates itself the *leader*, shown in Figure 1(a), of its own *localization instance*, a unique execution of DiVA's localization process. This leader then probes its LVNs in a circular pattern, looking for an LVN closer to ▲, determined by comparing timestamps for the beep. These timestamps are corrected for clock offset between the nodes using a well-known one-hop local time synchronization method [3]. If the leader finds an LVN that is closer to ▲, it resigns leadership and promotes the closer LVN to leader, shown in Figures 1(a) - 1(c). In this way, leadership is passed among the nodes until the node closest to ▲ becomes the leader. This node probes all of its LVNs and finds none closer to ▲, and this node's cell is thus identified as the target cell, as shown in Figure 1(d).

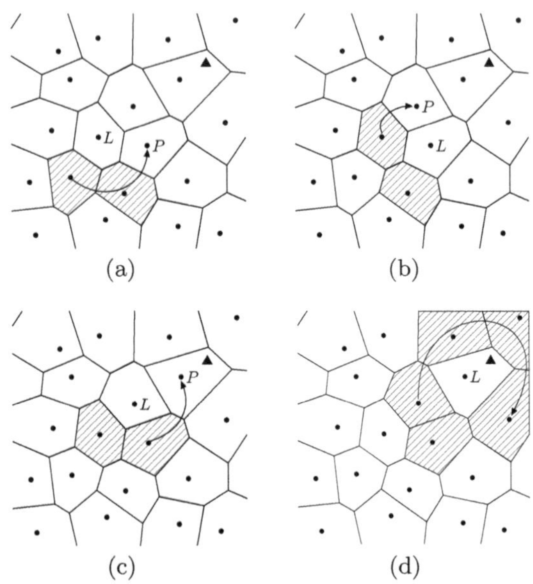

Figure 1: Example of Target Cell Identification.

Phase II is the key to guarantee DiVA's high robustness. In Phase II, DiVA is capable of detouring around nodes that have failed or are reporting excessively high microphone position error or beep measurement error. In these cases, a leader L may not promote P to leader, even though P may be closer to ▲ than L. However, if a second route exists, the leadership will be transferred around P and eventually to the node closest to ▲.

2.3 Phase III - Target Subregion Identification

Let L be the node whose local Voronoi cell was determined to contain ▲ in Phase II. In Phase III, L uses pairwise timestamp comparisons to narrow down the location of ▲ to a *target subregion* of its local Voronoi cell. First, L cuts its cell into subregions by drawing a perpendicular bisector between each pair of its LVNs. Then, for each cut, L determines which side of the cut contains ▲ by comparing the time stamp for the corresponding LVNs. L discards all subregions on the side of the cut without ▲. After slicing and discarding for each pair of LVNs, only the subregion containing ▲ remains.

2.4 Phase IV - Constrained Target Location Estimation

In Phase IV, L produces a final estimate of the target's location. The target subregion R identified in Phase III is trusted to contain ▲, so R is used as a constraint to aid in estimation.

First, L calculates TDOA estimates of the location of ▲ using all combinations of three nodes in $L \cup \Phi_L$, where Φ_L is the set of L's LVNs. The set of TDOA location estimates is denoted as T. L then performs a simple Grubbs' test [4] on these estimates to remove the outliers from T. Let T' denote the set of TDOA estimates remaining after the Grubbs' test. Then the final location estimate $\hat{t}$ is the point in R that minimizes the mean squared error (MSE) for $t_i = (x_i, y_i) \in T'$, as follows:

$$\hat{t} = (x^*, y^*) = \underset{(\hat{x},\hat{y})\in R}{\operatorname{argmin}} \frac{1}{|T'|} \sum_{t_i \in T'} \left[(x_i - \hat{x})^2 + (y_i - \hat{y})^2\right]. \tag{1}$$

Finally, L reports $\hat{t}$ and its MSE to the user. If multiple estimates are reported for a single beep, the user selects the $\hat{t}$ with the lowest MSE as the most likely location of ▲. This ability to filter out false readings is another aspect of DiVA's robustness.

3. PRELIMINARY RESULTS

3.1 Simulation Study

A MATLAB simulation was used to evaluate DiVA in comparison to TOA and TDOA, as well as to gauge the effect of microphone position and beep measurement error on DiVA. The average distance from a node to its nearest neighbor, R, was used to normalize the results. Using a well-known formula, R was calculated for the 2D case as $R \approx 1.58$ m. The speed of sound, v_s, was taken to be 340 m/s. The clock synchronization error for DiVA was assumed to be 44 μs [3].

TOA and TDOA can use any group of three microphones to produce a location estimate. In the simulation, the estimates of all possible groups were calculated and sorted in ascending order by output error. The 40th percentile (denoted as $K = 0.4$) and 80th percentile ($K = 0.8$) measurements were then used in the comparisons with DiVA's average, shown in Figure 2. Figure 2 also shows a reduced version of DiVA that does not include Phase IV. This reduced version of DiVA uses the center of gravity of the target subregion found in Phase III as the location estimate.

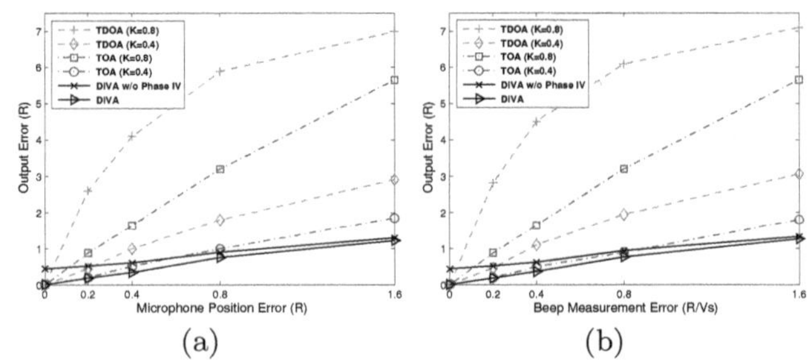

Figure 2: DiVA's output error versus (a) microphone position error and (b) beep measurement error, compared to TOA and TDOA.

The detailed effects of microphone position and beep measurement on DiVA are shown in Figure 3, which shows the cumulative distribution functions (CDFs) for output error at four different levels of microphone position or beep measurement error. Clock synchronization error is held constant at 44 μs. DiVA performs well, almost always producing an output error less than R for position error up to $0.4R$ or measurement error up to $0.4R/v_s$. This means that ▲ is unlikely to be farther from the estimated location than any given node is from its "known" position.

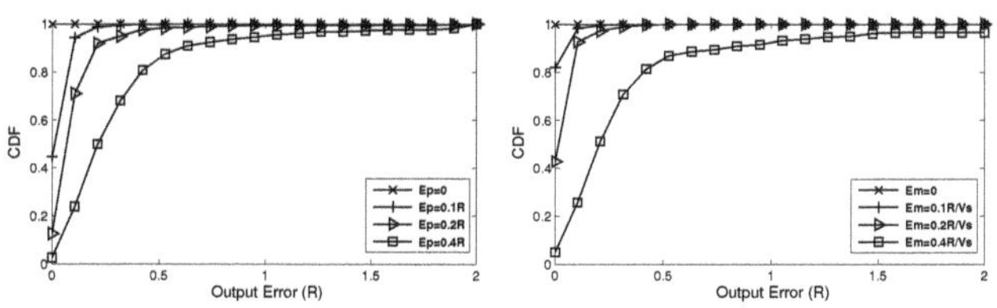

(a) (b)

Figure 3: CDFs of DiVA's output error for various amounts of (a) microphone position error and (b) measurement error.

3.2 Experimental Evaluation

DiVA was implemented using Lenovo T400 laptops as sensor nodes. The audio capturer sampled at 8 KHz, and the audio analyzer used a speech analysis algorithm to verify a beep's signature and timestamp the beep. Both a regular and an irregular deployment of microphone nodes were tested.

3.2.1 Regular Deployment

In the regular deployment, 18 microphone nodes were arranged with $R \approx 1.58$ m, the same R as the simulation environment. Results were obtained for 48 acoustic sources arranged in a grid pattern, with all sources located in the interior of the network to avoid edge effects.

Figure 4(a) shows two CDFs of DiVA's output error for these sources. One CDF is for output error when the full DiVA scheme is used, and the second is for DiVA without Phase IV, in order to highlight the importance of Phase IV in refining the final estimate. The individual tests are shown in Figure 4(b).

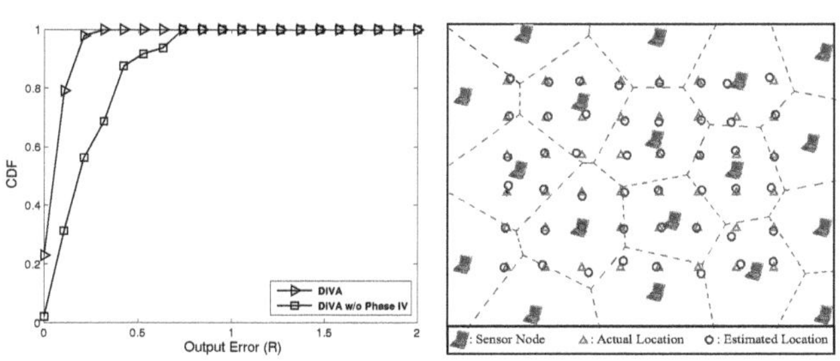

(a) CDF of output error for 48 tests.
(b) Actual (△) and estimated (○) locations.

Figure 4: Experimental results for the regular deployment.

3.2.2 Irregular Deployment

The irregular deployment has a large void in the center, as shown in 5(b). Since some nodes lack LVNs on the side of the void, their local Voronoi cells extend into the void and overlap with each other. DiVA produces multiple location estimates for targets inside the overlapping region; in this case, all the nodes at the edge may produce an estimate. In the experiment, the estimate with the lowest associated MSE in Phase IV was used in the results.

The CDFs for the irregular deployment are shown in Figure 5(a), and the actual and estimated locations are shown in Figure 5(b). The output error is higher in general than the regular deployment case. The full DiVA scheme maintains good performance. Without Phase IV, the error is much higher. Therefore, Phase IV is especially critical for the irregular deployment case.

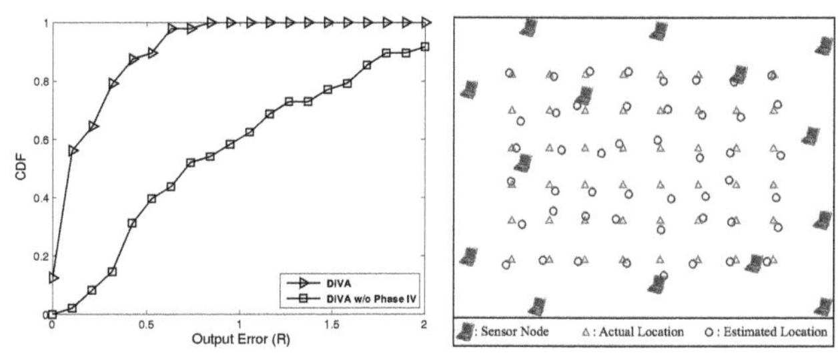

(a) CDF of output error for 48 tests.
(b) Actual (△) and estimated (○) acoustic source locations.

Figure 5: Experimental results for the irregular deployment.

4. FUTURE WORK

This paper presents DiVA, a new acoustic source localization algorithm for wireless sensor networks that uses pairwise comparisons of the sound detection timestamps of neighboring microphone nodes to traverse the Voronoi diagram and find the node closest to the acoustic source, then estimates the source's location using a TDOA-based method. Simulation and experimental results show the ability of DiVA to localize a single beep and demonstrate the robustness of DiVA under real-world challenges such as measurement and position error. We are currently preparing for large-scale experiments and extending DiVA to localize beeps from multiple sources or multiple beeps from one source. Future work includes extending DiVA to 3D space and adapting DiVA to underwater environments.

5. REFERENCES

[1] János Sallai, Ákos Lédeczi, and Péter Völgyesi. Acoustic shooter localization with a minimal number of single-channel wireless sensor nodes. In *ACM SenSys*, 2011.

[2] Franz Aurenhammer. Voronoi diagrams–a survey of a fundamental geometric data structure. *ACM Journal on Computing Surveys*, 23(3), 1991.

[3] Saurabh Ganeriwal, Ram Kumar, and Mani B. Srivastava. Timing-sync protocol for sensor networks. In *ACM SenSys*, SenSys '03, 2003.

[4] Frank E Grubbs. Sample criteria for testing outlying observations. *The Annals of Mathematical Statistics*, pages 27–58, 1950.

Poster: TRIM: A Truthful Incentive Mechanism for Dynamic and Heterogeneous Tasks in Mobile Crowdsensing

Yue Fan, Hailong Sun, Xudong Liu
School of Computer Science and Engineering, Beihang University
Beijing, China 100191
{fanyue,sunhl,liuxd}@act.buaa.edu.cn

ABSTRACT

Stimulating user participation is of paramount importance for mobile crowdsensing applications to obtain high-quality data. Although many incentive mechanisms have been designed, most of them ignore the dynamic arrivals and different sensing requirements of tasks. Thus, the existing mechanisms will fail when being applied to the realistic scenario where tasks are publicized dynamically and heterogeneous with different sensing requirements of locations, time durations and sensing times. In this work, we propose an auction-based truthful mechanism for realistic mobile crowdsensing. Through extensive simulations, we demonstrate that our mechanism can satisfy the desired properties of truthfulness, individual rationality, computational efficiency with both low social cost and low total payment.

Categories and Subject Descriptors

C.2.1 [**Computer-Communication Networks**]: Network Architecture and Design

General Terms

Algorithm, Design, Economics

Keywords

Mobile crowdsensing; Truthful incentive mechanism; Dynamic and heterogeneous tasks

1. INTRODUCTION

Nowadays, smartphones with powerful sensors, such as GPS, camera and digital compass, are increasingly used in everyday life. As a result, mobile crowdsensing has received tremendous attention for collecting various data with people's smartphones. As shown in Fig. 1, a mobile crowdsensing system consists of a *platform*, which locates in the cloud with several servers, and a crowd of randomly arrived *smartphone users*. When the platform needs to collect sensing data, it will dynamically publicize location-aware sensing *tasks* and recruit users to provide sensing services.

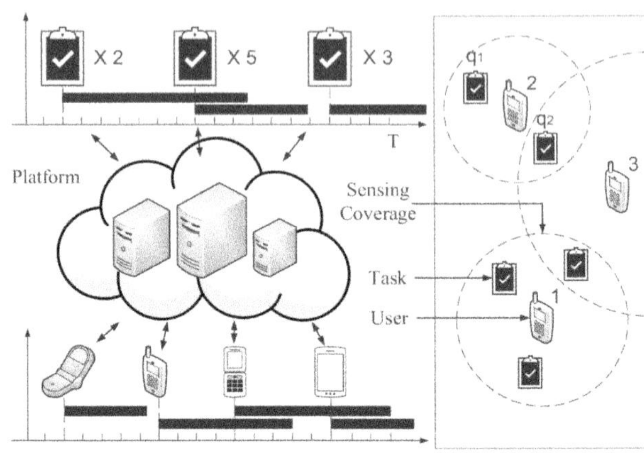

Figure 1: A mobile crowdsensing system with dynamic and heterogeneous tasks

Although many mobile crowdsensing applications rely on volunteer contributions, smartphone users can be reluctant to contribute without any incentive since conducting sensing tasks will consume resources like battery, CPU and memory. Therefore, it is of great importance to stimulate user participation so as to obtain high-quality data. However, simply providing monetary rewards is not feasible because rational users can untruthfully report information of real costs, arrival and departure time, for maximizing their benefits. Thus, several truthful incentive mechanisms have been designed to prevent users' strategic behaviors. Nonetheless, most of the existing mechanisms, such as [1–3], make the impractical assumption that sensing tasks are static in mobile crowdsensing campaign. Though some research efforts [4] [5] have considered dynamic task arrivals, they ignore the diversity of tasks by assuming all tasks need to be processed only once and can be completed within one time slot. In practice, sensing tasks are heterogeneous and usually characterized by different locations, time durations and sensing times, which cannot be dealt with by existing work. In this work, we propose TRIM, an auction-based truthful mechanism, for realistic mobile crowdsensing. Through extensive simulations, we show TRIM meets our design requirements of truthfulness, individual rationality, computational efficiency, and achieves both low social cost and total payment.

MobiCom'15, September 7–11, 2015, Paris, France.
ACM. ISBN 978-1-4503-3619-2/15/09
DOI: http://dx.doi.org/10.1145/2789168.2795179.

2. SYSTEM MODEL AND PROBLEM FORMULATION

As illustrated in Fig. 1, we divide the time into T time slots with the same length. The platform dynamically publicizes a set of tasks $Q = \{q_1, q_2, ..., q_m\}$ and each task q_j has a profile $\sigma(q_j) = \{b_j, e_j, l_j, r_j\}$, including b_j and e_j for the begin and end of its time duration, the location l_j and the sensing times r_j it requires to be sensed. We assume there is a set $N = \{1, 2, ..., n\}$ of smartphone users, and each user i shares the sensing coverage Φ_i with the platform, but keeps his true type unknown to others. User i's true type θ_i consists of his arrival time a_i, departure time d_i and real cost c_i of completing any task within Φ_i, denoted as $\theta_i = \{a_i, d_i, c_i\}$. Then, we use a reverse auction framework to model the interactions between the platform and users. Once a user i arrives at the platform, he will strategically submit a bid $B_i = \left\{\hat{a}_i, \hat{d}_i, \hat{c}_i\right\}$ ($\hat{c}_i \geqslant c_i, \hat{a}_i \geqslant a_i$ and $\hat{d}_i \leqslant d_i$), which can be different from his true type. Upon receiving the bids of users in each time slot, the platform needs to (1) select users into set S and allocate to each selected user one task which has the unexhausted sensing times (2) pay p_i to each selected user i. Each user aims at maximizing his own utility, and the utility of user i is

$$u_i = \begin{cases} p_i - c_i & \text{if } i \in S; \\ 0 & \text{otherwise} \end{cases} \tag{1}$$

The platform expects to minimize the total payment after each sensing task is completed, i.e.,

$$min\ P = \sum_{i \in S} p_i \quad s.t. \quad |S_j| = r_j, \ \forall\ q_j \in Q \tag{2}$$

where S_j denotes the subset of S for performing task q_j. Our objective is to design an incentive mechanism satisfying the following three properties:

- **Truthfulness**: A mechanism is truthful if a user cannot increase his utility by misreporting his true type, no matter what other users report.
- **Individual Rationality**: Each participating user has a non-negative utility.
- **Computational Efficiency**: A mechanism is computationally efficient if it can be executed in polynomial time.

3. TRUTHFUL MECHANISM DESIGN

We propose a truthful incentive mechanism, called TRIM, in this section. As described in Algorithm 1, TRIM mainly solves two problems: *the user selection problem* and *the payment calculation problem*.

The user selection process (lines 5-10) is executed at the beginning of each time slot. We adopt two sets O_t and A_t to denote the online users and the available tasks of the current time slot t, respectively. For meeting sensing times requirements r_j of each available task q_j in its time duration, we divide its time duration into multiple stages and allocate specific stage-sensing-times s_j. As long as the current stage-sensing-times s_j is not exhausted, we will choose the user i whose coverage covers the target task q_j and claimed cost $\hat{c}_i$ is not higher than the current price threshold ρ_j of q_j. After selecting user i, we will increase q_j's completed sensing

Algorithm 1 TRIM

Input: User set N, Sensing task set Q.
Output: set S of selected users, total payment vector $P = (p_1, p_2, \cdots, p_n)$

1: $(S, t, P) \leftarrow (\varnothing, 1, 0)$;
2: **while** $t \leqslant T$ **do**
3: $O' \leftarrow O_t$;
4: **for** each task q_j in A_t **do**
5: **for** each user i in O' **do**
6: **if** q_j is within i's coverage and $\hat{c}_i \leqslant \rho_j$ and $p_i < \rho_j$ and $s'_j < (s_j + |S \cap \{i\}|)$ **then**
7: $s'_j \leftarrow (s'_j + 1 - |S \cap \{i\}|)$; $S \leftarrow S \cup \{i\}$;
8: $p_i \leftarrow \rho_j$; $O' \leftarrow O' \setminus \{i\}$;
9: **end if**
10: **end for**
11: **if** $t = g_j$ **then**
12: $\rho_j \leftarrow$ **GetPriceThreshold**(s_j, Γ_j);
13: $g_j \leftarrow (2 * (g_j - b_j + 1) + b_j - 1)$;
14: $s_j \leftarrow 2 s_j$;
15: **end if**
16: **end for**
17: $t \leftarrow t + 1$
18: **end while**
19: **return** S, P

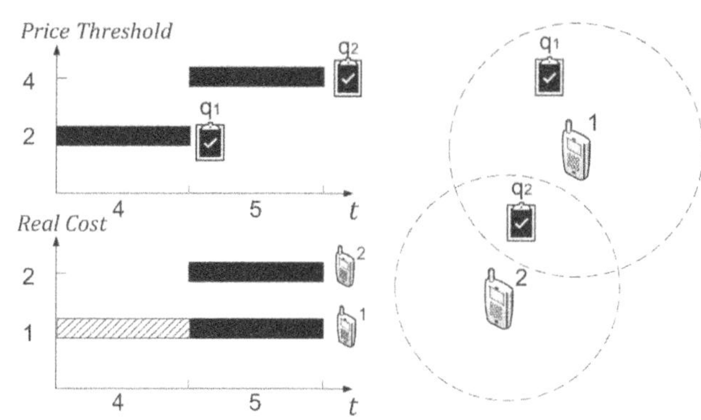

Figure 2: An example illustrating how the simple payment scheme fail in time-truthfulness

times s'_j, add i to the set S and give i an initial payment $p_i = \rho_j$. As shown in lines 11-15, when the time slot is at the end of some stage of q_j (in line 11), threshold ρ_j of task q_j will be updated by calling the **GetPriceThreshold** algorithm, which utilizes the stage-sensing-times s_j and the users sample set Γ_j of the previous stage to compute a new threshold for making future user selection decisions, where Γ_j contains the departed users whose coverage covers q_j (Due to space limit, we omit the details of the algorithm). Then, the stage-sensing-times of q_j is increased and set as the new one for next stage.

Undoubtedly, the simple payment scheme of paying each selected user such an initial payment guarantees the cost-truthfulness, because payment p_i is independent of the claimed cost $\hat{c}_i$. However, this simple payment scheme will fail in time-truthfulness. An example is shown in Fig. 2, when applying the simple payment scheme, user 1 will be selected in the 4th time slot and paid 2, and then user 2 will be selected in the 5th time slot and paid 4. However, user 1 can obtain

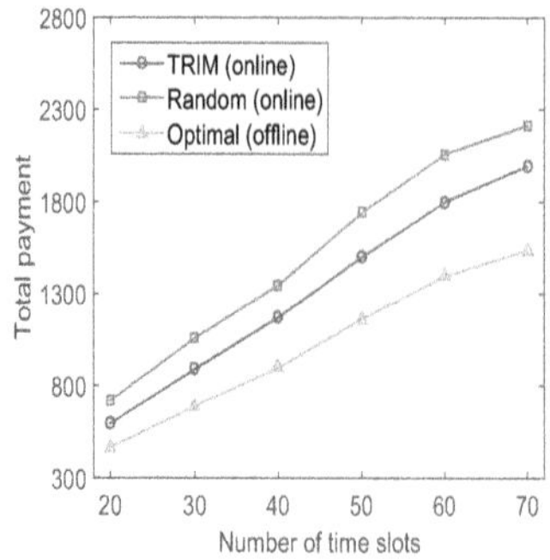

Figure 3: Impact of T on P

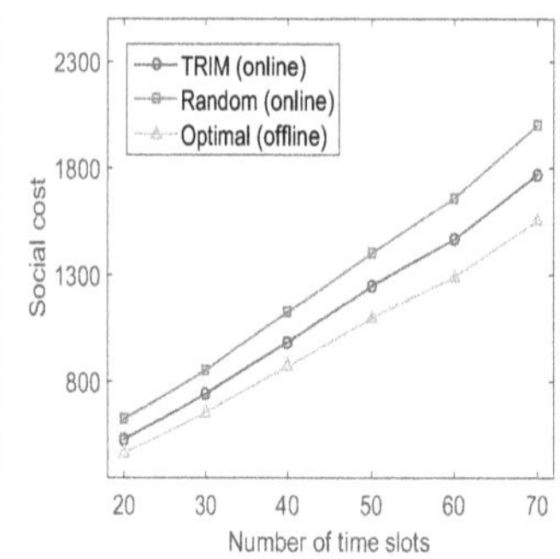

Figure 4: Impact of T on C

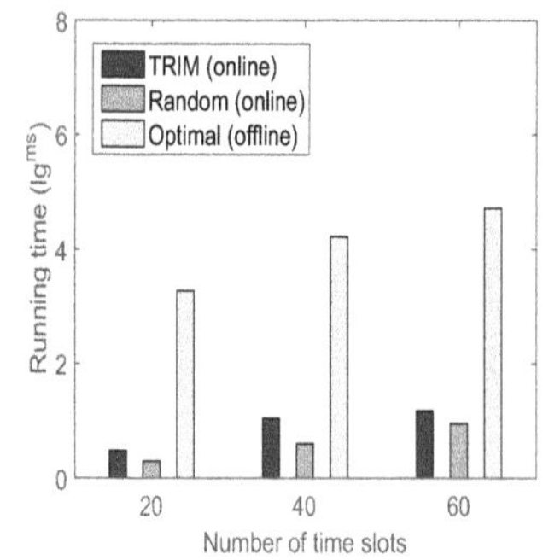

Figure 5: Running time

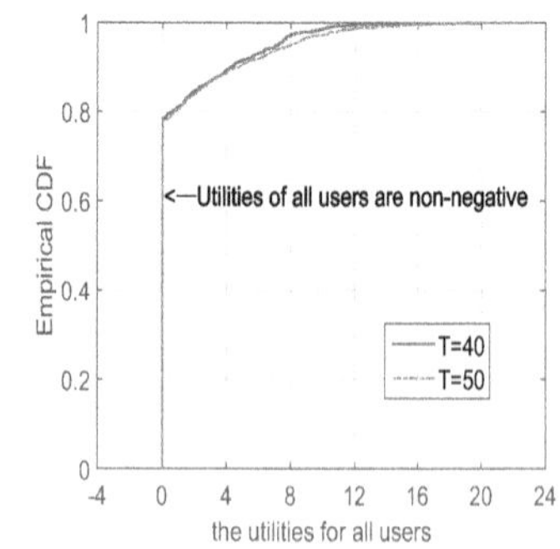

Figure 6: Empirical CDF of utilities

a higher payment of 4 if he misreports a delayed arrival time of 5. Thus, in order to make each user disclose his true type, we improve the simple payment scheme. The main idea of our method is to pay each selected user i the highest payment he can gain from his active time $[a_i, d_i]$. To be specific, in each time slot of the user selection process (lines 5-10), we reconsider those selected and still online users. If such a user i can be selected again and obtain a higher payment due to the increased price threshold of current task q_j, we will update his payment p_i to the higher one and keep the completed sensing times s'_j unchanged. According to the above analysis, we can see that TRIM has a polynomial-time computation complexity of $O(mnT)$, where m, n, T denote the number of tasks, users and time slots respectively.

4. EVALUATION RESULTS

We conduct thorough simulations to evaluate the performance of TRIM. The arrivals of the smartphone users and sensing tasks are generated with Poisson distributions, and the locations of tasks and users are uniformly distributed in a fixed area. We also generate the real cost, active time of each user, the time duration of each task according to uniform distributions.

To show the efficiency of TRIM, we compare TRIM with two benchmarks using four metrics: total payment P, social cost C, running time, and individual rationality. The first benchmark is the offline optimal mechanism which has full knowledge about users' true types, and the second benchmark is the random mechanism which pays users based on an uninformed fixed price threshold of each task. Note that, social cost is the sum of the real costs of all selected users.

Fig. 3 and Fig. 4 show TRIM pays and costs less than the random mechanism does due to its threshold-updating process, but pays and costs a little more than the optimal mechanism does. Since the optimal mechanism making an impractical assumption of knowing all users' future availability in advance, TRIM achieves very low total payment and social cost in reality. As shown in Fig. 5, TRIM spends much shorter time than the optimal mechanism. Fig. 6 shows all users' utilities are non-negative, which demonstrates TRIM satisfies the property of individual rationality.

5. CONCLUSION

In this work, we design a truthful incentive mechanism considering the dynamic arrivals of heterogenous tasks with different sensing requirements that the existing mechanisms ignore. Sufficient simulations are performed, and the results demonstrate that our mechanism satisfies the properties of truthfulness, individual rationality, computational efficiency and achieves both low social cost and low total payment.

6. ACKNOWLEDGMENTS

This work was supported partly by China 973 program (No.2014CB340304, No.2015CB358700), the National Natural Science Foundation of China (No. 61370057), A Foundation for the Author of National Excellent Doctoral Dissertation of PR China (No. 201159), and the Fundamental Research Funds for the Central Universities(No. YWF-15-JSJXY-013).

7. REFERENCES

[1] Dejun Yang, Guoliang Xue, Xi Fang, and Jian Tang. Crowdsourcing to smartphones: incentive mechanism design for mobile phone sensing. In *The 18th Annual International Conference on Mobile Computing and Networking, Mobicom'12, Istanbul, Turkey, August 22-26, 2012*, pages 173–184, 2012.

[2] Zhenni Feng, Yanmin Zhu, Qian Zhang, Lionel M. Ni, and Athanasios V. Vasilakos. TRAC: truthful auction for location-aware collaborative sensing in mobile crowdsourcing. In *2014 IEEE Conference on Computer Communications, INFOCOM 2014, Toronto, Canada, April 27 - May 2, 2014*, pages 1231–1239, 2014.

[3] Dong Zhao, Xiang-Yang Li, and Huadong Ma. How to crowdsource tasks truthfully without sacrificing utility: Online incentive mechanisms with budget constraint. In *2014 IEEE Conference on Computer Communications, INFOCOM 2014, Toronto, Canada, April 27 - May 2, 2014*, pages 1213–1221, 2014.

[4] Yanmin Zhu, Qian Zhang, Hongzi Zhu, Jiadi Yu, Jian Cao, and Lionel M. Ni. Towards truthful mechanisms for mobile crowdsourcing with dynamic smartphones. In *IEEE 34th International Conference on Distributed Computing Systems, ICDCS 2014, Madrid, Spain, June 30 - July 3, 2014*, pages 11–20, 2014.

[5] Yue Fan, Hailong Sun, Yanmin Zhu, Xudong Liu, and Ji Yuan. A truthful online auction for tempo-spatial crowdsourcing tasks. In *2015 IEEE Symposium on Service-Oriented System Engineering, SOSE 2015, San Francisco Bay, USA, March 30 - April 3, 2015.*

Poster: A Multi-Drone Platform for Empowering Drones' Teamwork

Seungho Yoo, Kangho Kim, Jongtack Jung, Albert Y. Chung,
Jiyeon Lee, Suk Kyu Lee, Hyung Kyu Lee, and Hwangnam Kim
School of Electrical Engineering, Korea University
Seoul, Rep. of Korea
{pen0423, mybalam2k, skylover89, aychung, jiyeon524, sklee25, schk00, hnkim}@korea.ac.kr

ABSTRACT

The rapid development of UAV technology has opened up numerous applications. Further, cooperating drones[1] possess a great potential in various areas of applications. Yet, there has not been a platform for a fleet of drones. It is rather difficult to control multiple drones through a single ground control station. In fact, drones need to consistently exchange flight information to maintain the formation of the fleet and follow the commands given from the GCS. Thus, drones need a robust network established among the fleet to provide a fleet control. In this paper, we propose Net-Drone, a multi-drone platform for applications that require cooperation of multiple drones. Net-Drone is equipped with strong network functionalities to provide a control system for a fleet of drones. Through case studies conducted with a prototype implementation, the proposed system is demonstrated. Video of the conducted case study can be found in [5].

Categories and Subject Descriptors

C.2.1 [**Computer-Communication Networks**]: Network Architecture and Design; J.2 [**Computer Applications**]: Physical Sciences and Engineering

General Terms

Design, Implementation, Experimentation, Performance

Keywords

Unmanned Aerial Vehicle (UAV), Drone, Fleet Control

1. INTRODUCTION

With the rise of the unmanned aerial vehicle (UAV), it is common to see UAV related applications nowadays. Even though drone technology has been initiated as a military purpose, it is expanding its usage to both the industry and the academia. Google initiated the Project Loon [2], DHL and Amazon [1] are starting drone delivery system, and numerous researchers are conducting researches related to drone applications. Yet, most of the drone related products, services and projects regard only a single drone, and what a single drone can accomplish is somewhat limited by the physical features. For instance, a multi-rotor can fly only for a short period of time and the payload of most drones is considerably limited. Deploying multiple drones can overcome the hardware limitations, but simultaneous management of multiple drones presents multiple challenges.

Efficiently and effectively coordinating multiple devices to complete a single task is always an important issue in many fields. Further, in case of drones, the numbers can lengthen the time of flight, widen the sensing and communication range, or provide higher accuracy and robustness to a given task. In this paper, we propose Net-Drone, a multi-drone platform where multiple drones work cooperatively to complete a given task. We have designed and implemented the prototype of Net-Drone to ascertain the potential of the proposed platform.

Net-Drone is not just an application for multiple drones, but a platform that can support various applications that require multiple drones. Our proposed platform converts the hassle of planning mission and controlling multiple drones one-by-one into a unified control system where multiple drones are controlled as a single fleet.

2. DESIGN

In this section, we present the description of the Net-Drone. In order to manage a fleet of drones, it is crucial to establish and maintain communication among the drones and with the ground control station (GCS). However, solely equipping an access point (AP) onto a drone is not sufficient. The fleet of drones is not only establishing communication with the GCS, but it needs to collect and share the information of the drones within the fleet for management purposes. Furthermore, with this communication feature, we can further utilize the proposed platform by designing a novel application with the network assistance from the GCS and a fleet of drones. Thus, the communication medium of each drone needs to communicate with the drones within the fleet and the GCS. Based on this networking feature, a drone fleet management platform can control the entire fleet and provide necessary information to the user. With this in mind, we prototype Net-Drone primarily based on the communication within the fleet and establish a communication between the GCS and the fleet for management purpose within the platform. Figure 1 elaborates the architecture of the proposed platform. Net-Drone consists of multiple drones and a GCS, and both are equipped with core modules.

Operation flow. Based on the platform architecture in Figure 1, the operation flow is as follows. The planning of a fleet mission is devised through the GCS. The core modules of the GCS interpret

[1]In this paper, we refer to all types of UAVs as drones.

MobiCom'15, September 7–11, 2015, Paris, France.
ACM. ISBN 978-1-4503-3619-2/15/09
DOI: http://dx.doi.org/10.1145/2789168.2795180.

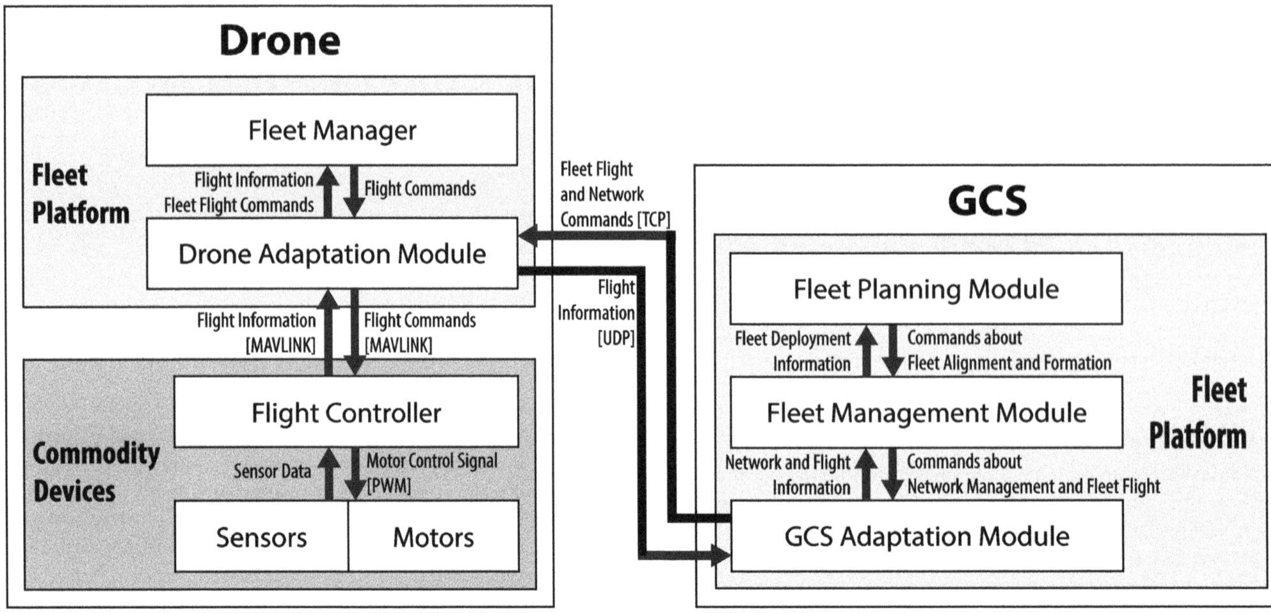

Figure 1: Platform architecture.

the deployment planning into multiple drone tasks. The tasks are sent to each drone either directly or through multi-hop communication function of Net-Drone. Upon task reception, each drone sets its position in the fleet and the destination of the fleet. After deployment, the fleet manager keeps track of its position and continuously sends flight commands to the flight controller. The flight controller flies the drone by managing the motor control signal.

Drone modules. The core module that flies the drone is the flight controller. The flight controller is equipped with sensors that are required for automated flight such as GPS, IMU, and acoustic sensors. Flight information, including various sensor data, is sent to the fleet manager which will be used to create flight commands and other flight information. The flight controller generates motor control signal according to the flight commands.

The fleet manager is the module that processes the high level instructions transmitted from the GCS. High level instructions are converted into flight commands that are sent to the flight controller. The flight commands that the fleet manager transmits are simple locations where the drone needs to be located at. Not only does the fleet manager converts the high level instructions into flight commands, but also maintains the formation of the fleet. According to the flight information received from the flight controller and the neighboring drones via the drone adaptation module, the fleet manager calculates its precise location in the fleet and the distance between the neighboring drones. If the formation of the fleet is distorted or if two drones are located too close to each other, the fleet manager can schedule to move the drone to maintain the shape of the fleet or the distance between the drones.

The drone adaptation module delivers data from one module to another and provides network functions. When a drone receives flight commands from the fleet manager or the GCS, the commands need to be translated into a message that the flight controller can interpret. Net-Drone aims to support various flight controllers and thus requires drone adaptation module to translate commands into a flight controller specific message. The drone adaptation module is also equipped with network functionalities. Since drones tend

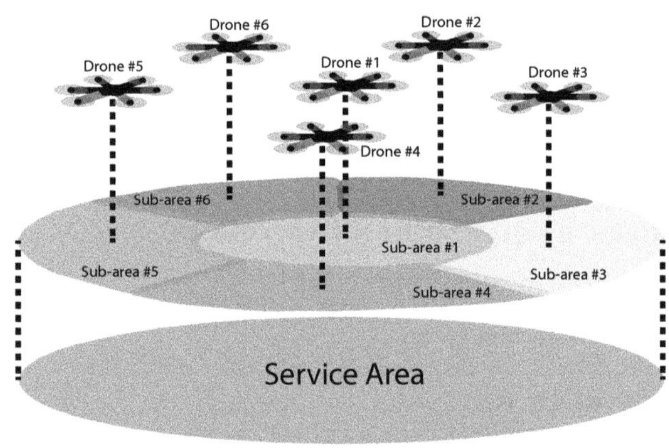

Figure 2: Deployment scenario.

to experience high mobility, non-robust network will result in frequent disconnections and unstable routing. Also for the drones to perform a fleet flight, drones need to consistently exchange flight information. Therefore, a strong network function is crucial for drones to successfully perform a fleet-wise flight. The drone adaptation module enables robust connectivity among the drones and also between the drones and the GCS.

GCS modules. The GCS is the user-interactive management system for Net-Drone. Through GCS, users can set the movement of a fleet as well as the behavior of each drone after deployment. The GCS can connect to multiple drones and send control messages. The GCS adaptation module is equipped with network interfaces, which allows GCS to connect to multiple drones using the multi-hop communication function of Net-Drone.

The mission planning scheme of Net-Drone GCS allows users to easily set service areas for multiple drones. Figure 2 demonstrates the mission planning scheme of the drone fleet. User can set the general service area by interacting with the fleet planning module

Figure 3: Drone prototype and fleet flight using Net-Drone.

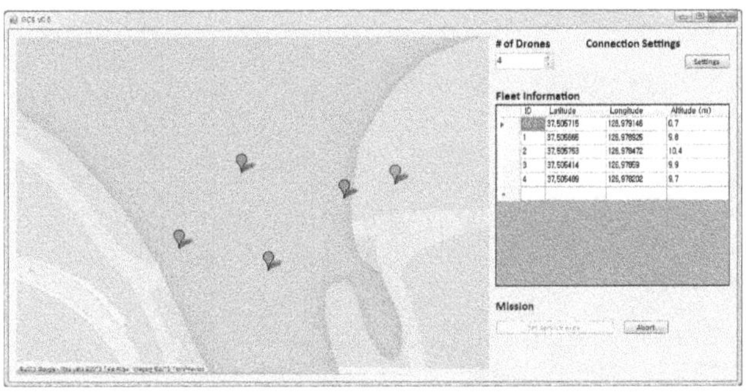

Figure 4: GCS prototype.

of the GCS. The service area information is sent to fleet management module, and the fleet management module divides the area into sub-areas according to the number of drones in the fleet. Each drone in the fleet is assigned to a sub-area which acts as its service area. The GCS adaptation module sends the sub-area information and fleet formation information to each drone, and case specific controls are handled within the drone. Sub-area information and fleet formation information are both critical data, and thus this information is transmitted using TCP to guarantee the delivery of information. On the other hand, the flight information sent from the drones is somewhat less important and the system can tolerate some data loss. Therefore, UDP is used for delivering flight information of drones.

3. IMPLEMENTATION

Based on the architecture design of the proposed platform, we developed and deployed a prototype of Net-Drone. In this section, we describe the details of the implementation and its application scenarios.

Prototype implementation. Figure 3 shows a drone prototype and multiple drones flying as a fleet using Net-Drone. We adopted the Pixhawk autopilot [4] of 3D Robotics for the flight controller, and Odroid U3 of HardKernel for the fleet manager and the drone adaptation module. Pixhawk and Odroid U3 are connected via USB to UART module. MAVROS, installed on the fleet manager, takes the role of translating the MAVLINK messages [3] sent from the flight controller and also the vice versa. Fleet manager runs ROS to provide real-time data to the flight controller. Odroid U3 is equipped with a Network Interface Controller to grant network capability to the drone adaptation module.

Figure 4 shows the implementation of GCS prototype. Our GCS prototype was implemented from scratch with C# language on a Samsung Series 8 Laptop with a 2.5 GHz Intel Core i7 processor. An wireless AP is connected to the GCS to establish connections with the drones.

Applications. We conducted a couple of case studies to show the potential of Net-Drone. For the first case study, we conducted a landscape mapping application. Unlike the traditional landscape mapping using a single drone, we used Net-Drone to control three drones, each equipped with a camera, to perform landscape mapping simultaneous. Using Net-Drone for the landscape mapping application, we were able to successfully map an area with multiple drones.

The second case study is a network service provision application (refer to the video in [5]). Four drones were used in the case study and each drone is equipped with an extra NIC to provide connection with objects other than the drones. With the case study, we were able to confirm that a fleet of drones controlled by Net-Drone is capable of providing a network service over a wide area, which is an application that cannot be accomplished with a single drone.

Other than the two case studies we conducted, Net-Drone can be applied to the following applications: surveillance, cooperative delivery, and efficient sensor data gathering.

4. CONCLUSION AND FUTURE WORK

In this paper, we designed and implemented Net-Drone, a platform for a drone fleet control platform. The fleet based control system is successfully constructed with our design, and applications using it is demonstrated. Net-Drone can widen the application of drones by enabling multiple drones to accomplish missions that were not suited for a single drone. The applications of Net-Drone is not limited to the applications depicted in this paper, but can be further expanded. In our future works, we plan to investigate such applications and provide a more thorough evaluation of Net-Drone.

5. ACKNOWLEDGMENTS

The first four authors of this paper contributed equally and listed in the reverse alphabetical order. This work was supported by Samsung Research Funding Center of Samsung Electronics under Project Number SRFC-IT1401-09.

6. REFERENCES

[1] D. A. P. Dr. Vinay Pandit. A study on amazon prime air for feasibility and profitability– a graphical data analysis. *IOSR Journal of Business and Management*, 16(11-1):06–11, 2014.

[2] S. Katikala. Google project loon. 2014.

[3] L. Meier, J. Camacho, B. Godbolt, J. Goppert, L. Heng, M. Lizarraga, et al. Mavlink: Micro air vehicle communication protocol. *Online]. Tillgänglig.[Hämtad 2014-05-22]*, 2013.

[4] L. Meier, P. Tanskanen, L. Heng, G. H. Lee, F. Fraundorfer, and M. Pollefeys. Pixhawk: A micro aerial vehicle design for autonomous flight using onboard computer vision. *Autonomous Robots*, 33(1-2):21–39, 2012.

[5] S. Yoo, K. Kim, J. Jung, A. Y. Chung, J. Lee, S. K. Lee, H. K. Lee, and H. Kim. A multi-drone platform for empowering drones' teamwork. [Video] Retrieved from `http://youtu.be/lFaWsEmiQvw`, 2015.

Poster: Visible Light Communication in the Dark

Zhao Tian, Andrew T. Campbell, and Xia Zhou
Department of Computer Science, Dartmouth College
{tianzhao, campbell, xia@cs.dartmouth.edu}

ABSTRACT

We present a new visible light communication (VLC) primitive: VLC in the dark, where the communication sustains even when the LED light appears dark. We achieve the goal by reducing the duty cycle of the light source to an extremely low level (0.0019%) such that the illuminance is imperceptible to human eyes and yet can still be sensed by photodiodes to decode data. VLC in the dark consumes much lower energy than the conventional VLC links and thus is appealing for enabling VLC uplink or communication among Internet-of-Things devices with tight energy budget. We build a preliminary prototype to demonstrate its feasibility. Our current single link achieves 190.7 bps data rate with 46.8 μW power consumption at the LED.

Categories and Subject Descriptors

C.2.1 [**Network Architecture and Design**]: Wireless communication

Keywords

Visible light communication; Energy efficiency; Internet of Things

1. INTRODUCTION

Operating on the visible light spectrum, Visible Light Communication (VLC) holds a great potential to mitigate the spectrum crunch problem. All existing designs of VLC links commonly require the lights to be always on — the VLC link ceases when the lights are off. This constraint imposes a fundamental limit on the applicable scenarios of VLC. Furthermore, keeping LED lights on entails a high energy consumption, making VLC less appealing for smart devices with tight energy budget to transmit data.

In this poster, we design and implement *VLC in the dark*, a new VLC primitive that can operate even if the LED lights appear dark. This new primitive enables VLC links to maintain always-on communication, greatly broadening its applicable scenarios and lowering the energy consumption of LED lights. In particular, we achieve VLC in the dark by reducing the duty cycle of the light source to an extremely low level such that it becomes imperceptible (Figure 1) to human eyes. VLC in the dark is inspired by a prior study [1] that discusses the standard for the lights to appear "off" and the required receive power for a target data rate using simulations. Our work differs in that we go beyond the analytical results and simulations, tackle the practical challenges to actually realize this concept, and explore its potential applications. We build a prototype of VLC in the dark using off-the-shelf LEDs, photodiodes, and circuit components. The implementation of the prototype involves deliberate trade-off of system parameters (Section 2) and design of the circuits (Section 3).

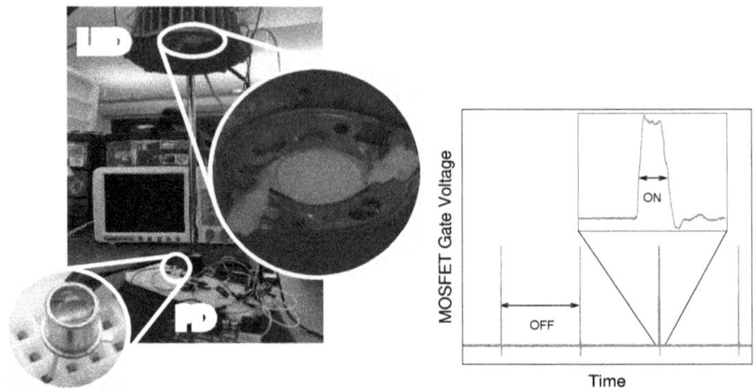

(a) System Overview (b) Pulse Width Modulation

Figure 1: VLC in the dark. (a) A picture of our system. In the picture, the duty cycle of the LED is so small (0.0019%) that the light appears off. (b) Duty cycle $d = t_{ON}/(t_{ON} + t_{OFF})$. With the peak forward current fixed, the illuminance of the LED light is proportional to its duty cycle. The switching frequency $f = 1/(t_{ON} + t_{OFF})$.

VLC in the dark is imperceptible to human eyes and is energy-efficient. In our testbed, the minimum illuminance shift incurred by the LED is 0.09 lx and the LED consumes only 46.8 μW. This new VLC primitive can enable many novel VLC applications. It can be used to build the VLC uplinks for mobile devices. A recent proposal implements VLC uplink using backscatter [5], which reflects the LED light coming from the ceiling. However, this design still requires the lights to be on. VLC in the dark can also enable communication for Internet of things (IoT) devices, through either always-on ceiling-to-device or device-to-device VLC links. VLC in the dark consumes ultra-low energy and is appealing for IoT devices with energy constraints.

2. VLC IN THE DARK: THE DESIGN

We make the LED light appear off by decreasing its flashing duty cycle. We do not completely switch off the light; instead, we reduce

MobiCom'15, September 7–11, 2015, Paris, France.
ACM 978-1-4503-3619-2/15/09.
http://dx.doi.org/10.1145/2789168.2795181.

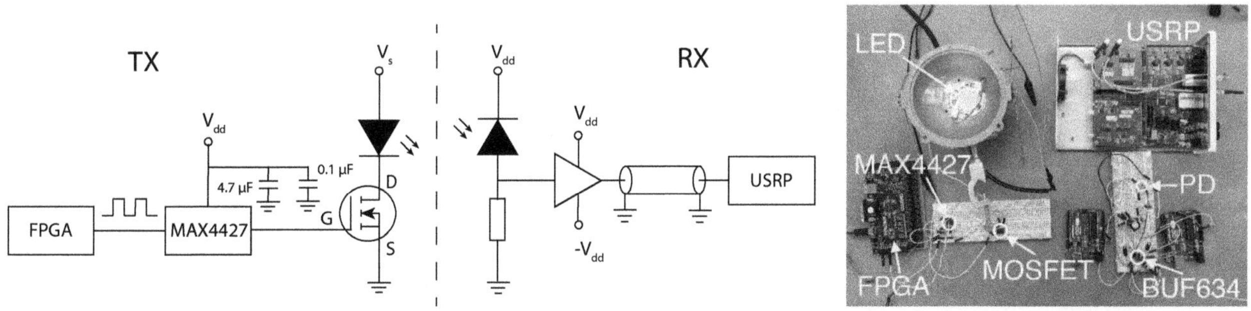

(a) Circuit design (b) Testbed

Figure 2: Implementation of the transmitter and receiver. The LED (Cree CXA2520) is driven by a Xilinx Artix-7 FPGA through a MOSFET (STF5N52U) and a gate driver (MAX4427). The photocurrent generated by the photodiode (Honeywell SD5421) is transformed to voltage signal by a resistor, and the signal is sampled by USRP with an LFRX daughterboard. The voltage follower (BUF634) between the resistor and the USRP is for impedance matching.

its illuminance to a negligible level but still maintain its ability of communication.

For LEDs, the luminous flux, which determines the illuminance, is nearly proportional to the forward current. In practice, the LEDs are not always switched on but periodically on and off. The illuminance is determined by both the peak intensity and duty cycle (Figure 1(b)). We can decrease the LED's illuminance by reducing the peak current flowing through the LED. But this method will curtail the communication distance according to the inverse-square law. So we keep the peak intensity high but reduce the duty cycle:

$$d = \frac{t_{\mathrm{ON}}}{t_{\mathrm{ON}} + t_{\mathrm{OFF}}} = \frac{t_{\mathrm{ON}}}{t_{\mathrm{period}}} .$$

To reduce the duty cycle, we should narrow t_{ON} and widen t_{period}. The configuration of these two parameters is subject to the capacity of the electrical components and human's perception (e.g. flickering effect). The minimal t_{ON} is determined by the turn-on time of the LED as well as the rise- and fall-time limits of the switching circuitry [2]. No matter how small we choose t_{ON}, the communication is always possible as long as the photodiodes are able to sense the pulse. So meanwhile, we should also consider the bandwidth of the receiver photodiodes. We can set t_{ON} to the physical limit of the system. But there is a dilemma when choosing t_{period}. We want t_{period} to be large, in order for the duty cycle to be small. But there are two drawbacks if we set it too large: one is the flickering effect and the other is the low potential data rate. Note that the switching frequency is

$$f = \frac{1}{t_{\mathrm{period}}} .$$

Human eyes can perceive the light flashes if f is too small (120 Hz or 160 Hz according to different studies [6]). Suppose we can encode N bits in each flashing cycle, then the potential data rate is Nf. There is no one fixed choice of t_{period}; it depends on the application scenario. Actually, we can adapt: in the day when the ambient illuminance is high, we can squeeze t_{period} for higher data rate, while at night when there is little ambient light, we can extend t_{period} for lower illuminance.

3. IMPLEMENTATION

In order to facilitate the slim ON pulse, we need deliberate design of the transmitter and receiver circuits (Figure 2(a)). Switching speed is the major concern when we develop the circuit (Figure 2). The high switching speed requires the driver circuit, wiring, and the micro-controller all to be fast.

Conventionally, we use an electrical switch (e.g. MOSFET) to modulate the LED (e.g. PWM) and a micro-controller to drive the gate of MOSFET directly. We need a high current to charge the capacitor at the gate because we want to switch the MOSFET on and off fast. But common micro-controllers are not able to provide such a high current. For example, Arduino Uno can provide up to only 40 mA. So we need to insert a dedicated gate driver between the micro-controller and the MOSFET, which can supply a burst current when switching on and off the MOSFET. The gate driver also acts as a voltage amplifier if the output voltage of the micro-controller cannot reach the threshold voltage of the MOSFET.

Besides the switching speed of the electrical devices, wiring can also hinder the speed of circuit. If the wires are too long and become so-called transmission line [4], the reflection of the signal would occur. The signal can oscillate at the falling edges. The effect is insignificant in low frequency circuit but it occurs during our system implementation as the speed is high enough. So the wires should be kept as short as possible.

We use an FPGA as our micro-controller because it offers the control granularity at the clock-cycle level. We use a Digilent BASYS 3 board equipped with a Xilinx Artix-7 FPGA. The clock cycle of Artix-7 can reach 10 ns. Because the capacity of the Pmod I/O interface on the board is only 24 MHz [3], the minimum pulse width that the FPGA board can achieve is approximately 40 ns. But considering the speed of our driver circuit and the bandwidth of the photodiodes we use, we set t_{ON} as 100 ns in our current testbed. The current bottleneck is the bandwidth of the photodiode ($ 6). We plan to examine high-end photodiodes in our future work to further reduce the pulse width.

At the receiver end, in order to detect the fleeting pulse signal, we need an analog-to-digital convertor (ADC) with a very high sampling rate. In our implementation we use USRP N200, whose sampling rate can reach 100 MS/s. We equip the USRP with an LFRX daughter board, which has a 50-Ω input impedance. Because the resistor that we connect in series with the photodiode is 100 kΩ, we need a unity gain voltage amplifier (a.k.a voltage follower) to transform the impedance, such that the USRP will not load the signal source [7].

4. PRELIMINARY RESULTS

We investigate the relation between the illuminance and the switching period time (Figure 3(a)), which provides us the basis to choose the period in different scenarios. The experiment was conducted at night. We first measured the environment illuminance (I_0) without the LED light source using a light meter (Extech 401036), and then gradually increased t_{period} (with fixed t_{ON}) thus decreasing the duty

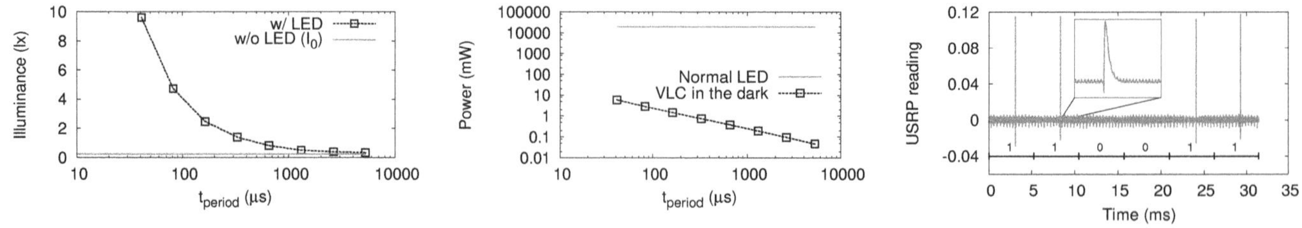

(a) Illuminance vs period time (b) Power vs period time (c) On-Off Keying (OOK)

Figure 3: (a) Illuminance of the LED with fixed t_{ON} (100 ns) but varying t_{period}. The illuminance is measured at night and the environment illuminance (I_0) is 0.25 lx. The distance between the LED and light meter is 15 cm. The increase of the period time causes the illuminance to approach the ambient illuminance. (b) We measure the average forward current using a multimeter and calculate the power by $P = V_s I$. The power of the LED used in common mode is 19.8 W, while the power of the LED used in VLC in the dark is as low as 46.8 μW. (c) On-Off Keying (OOK). The occurrence and absence of peak represent 1 and 0 respectively. The switching frequency is 190.7 Hz, so the potential data rate using OOK is 190.7 bps.

cycle. We can see that the illuminance gradually drops to I_0. The minimum illuminance shift incurred by the LED is only 0.09 lx. For reference, the full moon on a clear night produces about 3 lx of illuminance outside [1]. The same experiment conducted in the day shows that the variation of the ambient illuminance (60–110 lx) due to the movement of the clouds can already exceed the the illuminance of the LED. So the LED light is even harder to perceive in the day.

We measure the power of the LED when using VLC in the dark (same setting as the illuminance measurement) and compare it with the power using in normal mode (Figure 3(b)). The low transmit power does not make VLC in the dark prone to interference. On the one hand, the flashing frequency of potential interference is low, no matter it is natural (sunlight) or artificial (fluorescent or LED lamp). Our experiment shows the sunlight is almost a DC signal, while the frequency of a commercial LED lamp (Cree A19) is only 120 Hz (8 ms period). The intended 100-ns pulse signal can still be reliably detected in the presence of those interferences. Furthermore, a high pass filter can remove those low frequencies. On the other hand, most photodiodes have a limited field of view (FoV), resembling a directional antenna. The receiver gain of signal with an incidence angle exceeding half of the FoV is very small. For SD5421, at 20° incidence angle, the received signal strength is only 10% of that at 0°. In this way, the interference is largely attenuated.

Our transmitter can send bits using On-Off Keying (OOK) modulation, and our receiver can successfully detect the 100-ns pulse emitted by the LED (Figure 3(c)). The potential data rate (without considering the preamble overhead) using OOK is 190.7 bps with a period time of 5.24 ms, the longest t_{period} shown in Figure 3(a).

We also consider the visibility when humans view the light source directly. In the day, with the longest t_{period} mentioned above, the light is invisible. But at night, because human eyes are very sensitive to light, we could always feel the light, with any period time that yields a reasonable data rate and will not lead to flickering.

The threshold duty cycle varies with the LED as well as the ambient light. If the peak intensity of the LED is higher, we should decrease the duty cycle accordingly. If the ambient light becomes brighter, human eyes become more tolerant toward the "dark" LED, thus the threshold duty cycle rises.

5. DISCUSSION AND FUTURE WORK

Boosting the Link Rate. We plan to examine photodiodes with higher bandwidth so that we can further decrease the ON duration. With the same duty cycle, the period time can shrink thus increasing the switching frequency and achieving a higher data rate. We will also implement more sophisticated modulation schemes to improve the data rate. Pulse Position Modulation (PPM) is a good candidate for VLC in the dark. It encodes more bits in one cycle by varying the position of the pulse.

Supporting Distance. Our current prototype has a limited communication distance (15 cm), which is mainly constrained by the sensitivity of the photodiodes. To increase the supporting distance, we plan to test more sensitive photodiodes that are able to sense weaker light signals.

Ambient Light Aware Adaptation. We also plan to study the impact of the system parameters (e.g. ON duration, period time, and modulation scheme) on the system performance (e.g. communication distance, data rate, and reliability). Based on the understanding, we can adapt the LED light's duty cycle and modulation schemes based on the ambient light condition to achieve the best tradefoff between user perception and link data rate.

Potential Applications. We will also implement applications that can leverage this new VLC primitive, e.g., building device-to-device and device-to-ceiling IoT network. VLC in the dark can demonstrate its ability in the Near Field Communication (NFC). For example, thanks to the high directionality of visible light, VLC in the dark can serve as a secure link during contact-less payment.

6. ACKNOWLEDGMENTS

We sincerely thank the reviewers for their insightful feedback. We also thank Kevin Wright (Dartmouth College) for the advice and support on building the hardware prototype. This work is supported in part by the National Science Foundation under grant CNS-1421528.

7. REFERENCES

[1] T. Borogovac, M. B. Rahaim, M. Tuganbayeva, and T. D. Little. "Lights-off" visible light communications. In *Proceedings of 2nd IEEE Globecom 2011 Workshop on Optical Wireless Communications*, pages 797–801. IEEE, 2011.

[2] Cree, Inc. *Pulsed over-current driving of Cree XLamp LEDs: information and cautions.* REV 1B.

[3] Digilent, Inc. *Digilent Pmod interface specification*, November 2011.

[4] R. Gilmore and L. Besser. *Practical RF circuit design for modern wireless systems*, volume 1. Artech House, 2003.

[5] J. Li, A. Liu, G. Shen, L. Li, C. Sun, and F. Zhao. Retro-VLC: Enabling battery-free duplex visible light communication for mobile and iot applications. In *Proceedings of HotMobile'15*.

[6] L. Li, P. Hu, C. Peng, G. Shen, and F. Zhao. Epsilon: A visible light based positioning system. In *Proceedings of NSDI'14)*.

[7] Texas Instruments, Inc. *Amplifiers and bits: an introduction to selecting amplifiers for data converters*, May 2015.

Poster: Scoping Environment to Assist 60 GHz Link Deployment

Sanjib Sur and Xinyu Zhang
sur2@wisc.edu and xyzhang@ece.wisc.edu
University of Wisconsin-Madison

ABSTRACT

Line-of-Sight blockage by human body is a severe challenge to enable robust 60 GHz directional links. Beamsteering is one feasible solution to overcome this problem by electronically steering phased-array beam towards Non-Line-of-Sight. However, effectiveness of beamsteering depends on the link deployment and a lack of assessment of steering effectiveness may render the link completely blacked-out during human blockage. In this poster, we propose a new technique called *BeamScope*, that predicts best possible location for a randomly deployed link in an indoor environment without the need of any explicit war-driving. *BeamScope* first characterizes the environment exploiting measurement from the randomly deployed reference location and then predicts the performance in unobserved locations to suggest a possible re-deployment. The environment characterization is captured through a novel metric and prediction is achieved via how this metric is shared between the reference location and unobserved locations. Our preliminary results show promising accuracy of identifying the best possible alternate location for 60 GHz link to achieve a robust connection during human blockage.

Categories and Subject Descriptors

C.2.1 [**Computer-Communication Networks**]: Network Architecture and Design - Wireless communication

Keywords

60 GHz, millimeter-wave, link deployment

1. INTRODUCTION

Millimeter-wave (mmWave) communication is the emerging frontier for next-generation wireless applications. With multi-Gbps data rate, it is a promising technology to support a new plethora of data-hungry applications such as uncompressed video streaming, cordless computing, wireless projector, instant file synchronization and wireless fiber-to-home access. IEEE standard 802.11ad [1] has proposed MAC/PHY design of 60 GHz mmWave frequency band and has already been adopted in few commercial devices *e.g.* Wilocity radio [2]. Figure 1 shows some of the potential indoor application scenarios at 60 GHz.

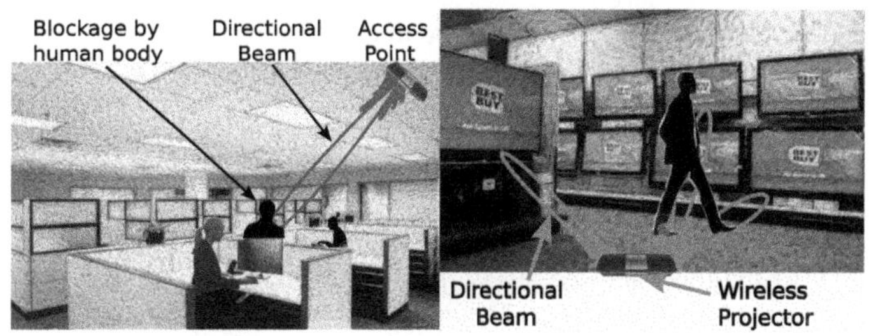

Figure 1: **Concept applications of 60 GHz.** (a) **Enterprise network.** (b) **Wireless Gbps projector.**

However, 60 GHz links are highly vulnerable to propagation loss. The standard proposal recommends using narrow directional beams formed by phased-array antennas to overcome the strong signal attenuation. But, narrow directional beams at 60 GHz are highly susceptible to human blockages that can occur in indoor deployments with reasonable human activity [3]. A phased-array antenna can electronically steer its beam direction, bouncing the signals off opportunistic reflectors, thus detouring any Line-Of-Sight (LOS) obstacle. However, effectiveness of beamsteering depends highly on the environment *e.g.* availability of any secondary reflective paths *etc.* [4], which depends on the placement of the link.

An obvious way to find out the best possible *spot* to deploy a 60 GHz link would be, to war-drive the entire deployment area covering every *nook and cranny* and deploy the link in best possible *spot*. But two problems pertain to the war-driving, (1) *Overhead.* War-driving is tedious and cumbersome process requiring significant effort from network deployer. Even though an automated robot can be used to scour the place, physical *search space* involving possible combinations of node pair locations can be quite large even for a small $10m \times 10m$ indoor room. (2) *Blockage occurrence.* Exhaustive war-driving may specify best possible *spot* in a humanless indoor room, but it does not consider possible blockage occurrences and their patterns. Rather than using tedious war-driving, in this work we propose an environment scoping algorithm that can find the best *spot* to place 60 GHz link from measurements obtain from a single *spot*.

2. DEPLOYMENT ISSUE OF 60 GHZ LINKS

A LOS 60 GHz link can be extremely susceptible to human blockage if there is no secondary path for the link arrangement. Presence of reflective concrete walls, metallic cabinet *etc.* can provide significant opportunities to bounce the signals off from a secondary path in presence of large obstacles like human body in LOS that

MobiCom'15, September 07–11, 2015, Paris, France
Copyright © 2015 ACM 978-1-4503-3619-2/15/09.
http://dx.doi.org/10.1145/2789168.2795182.

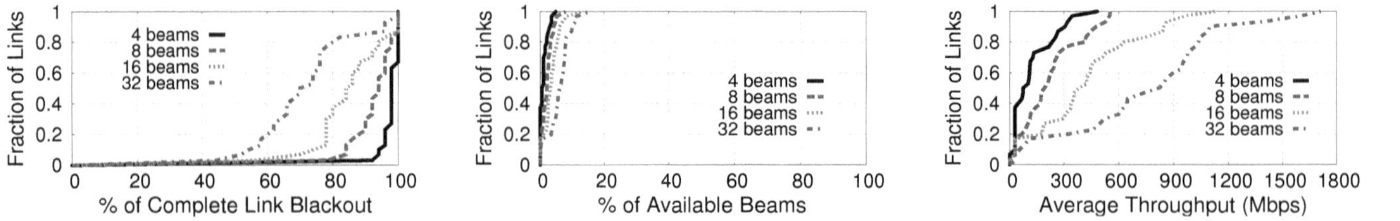

Figure 2: (*a*) **Fraction of complete link blackout.** (*b*) **Fraction of available beams.** (*c*) **Average throughput of best available beam when link is sustained. CDF are plotted across** 30 **different links during blockage.**

penalizes the link by $20 \sim 30$ dB [3,4]. Figure 2 shows the performance disparity during blockage across 30 different links arbitrary deployed in an indoor office environment. We deploy each link randomly in LOS with 5 m. distance between Tx and Rx. For each link, we emulate random blockage scenarios and collect the performance traces of the phase-array beams during blockage. Figure 2(a) shows the fraction of complete link blackouts during blockage duration (*i.e.* no beam can sustain the connection) and we plot the CDF across the 30 links. For nodes having 32 beams, more than 50% of the links showed atleast 70% of time complete link outage during human blockage. The difference between the fraction of time a complete link outage occurred is significant when comparing a randomly vs. best deployed link [1]. For nodes having 4 beams, this difference is only 8% but grows to 56% when the number of phased-array beams is 32. This shows that a carefully deployed link will be able to sustain the connection during human blockage more effectively than a random one. Further, deployment disparity becomes more severe when the number of phased-array beams increases, which necessitate an environment-aware deployment. Figure 2(b) shows the average number of fraction of available beams during blockage across the 30 different links. Although, we found that as the number of phased-array beams increase, more number of beams are available that can sustain connection, but Figure 2(c) again shows strong disparity between a best link vs. a randomly deployed link. For nodes having 4 beams, the difference of average achievable throughput is only 483 Mbps, while this difference grows to 1.7 Gbps when the number of available beam is 32! This further warrant the requirement of a careful 60 GHz link deployment that can not only sustain the connection more effectively but also may drastically improve link layer throughput during blockage.

3. BEAMSCOPE DESIGN

BeamScope exploits the *sparsity* property of 60 GHz link [5] to establish a *spot* performance prediction framework. The framework *determines the quality of unobserved spot's performance in an environment while observing channel information only from a single measurement spot*. *BeamScope*'s key principle lies in extracting the environmental information from a single measurement *spot* and extrapolating that in an unobserved *spot*. The environmental information is characterized in a novel *environment path skeleton* model during measurement. Furthermore, modeling the way an unobserved *spot* shares the *environment path skeleton* with the measured *spot*, *BeamScope* can predict the performance of it. *BeamScope*'s design can be separated into two different stages: first, when user deploys the link in certain physical positions, *BeamScope* scans the environment by electronically steering pairwise Tx-Rx beams and extracts modeling parameters to construct *environment path skeleton*. Next, *BeamScope* applies a spatial transfer function over the *environment path skeleton* to infer how the environment should look like from any other *spots* within the environment.

[1] The link that showed best result out of all 30 links, although it may not be an oracle best link.

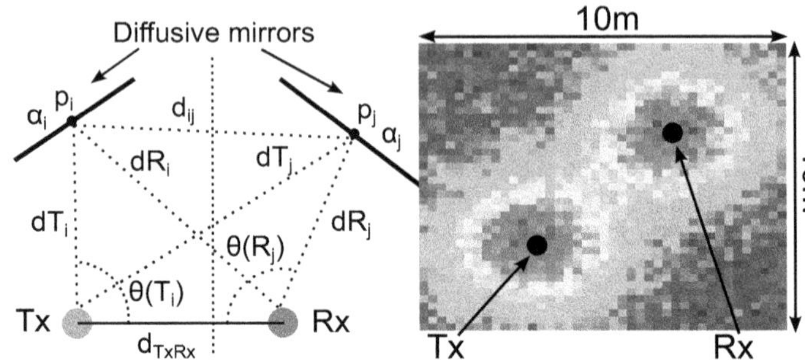

Figure 3: **(a) Environment as a recursive diffusive mirror. (b) Simulated *BeamScope*'s best beam prediction accuracy in spatial region. Reference Tx and Rx placement is shown. Dark color represents higher accuracy.**

The main idea behind environment scoping from single view-point is to extend the aperture of that view-point. *BeamScope* extends the view-point by treating environment as a *recursive diffusive mirror*. The basic idea is simple. When characterizing a part of the environment, use another part of the environment as a diffusive mirror. Figure 3(a) shows an example of characterizing the environment exploiting the recursive mirror concept. Here, while characterizing the object p_i of the environment, we extend the aperture of the receiver Rx by considering object p_j as the diffusive mirror. The receiver Rx's aperture is now extended to fully characterize the object p_i in the environment which includes estimating the distance and the diffusion coefficient. Similarly, while characterizing p_j, p_i is considered as the diffusive mirror.

When the 60 GHz devices are deployed at certain positions, *BeamScope* invokes full beam-scanning procedure (such as in 802.11ad) once to capture the *Channel Impulse Response* (CIR) between each pair of Tx/Rx beams. *BeamScope* then uses matrix $\mathbf{M}$ of $K \times K$ entries to store the CIR of the K received beams from each of the K transmit beam.

When the narrow beam of 60 GHz transmitter incident on an object in the environment, it creates the first signal bounce. This direct bounce is followed by a complex pattern of inter-reflections whose dynamics are governed by the environment geometry and the diffusion property of the material in the environment. At any time instant the receiver observe a projection of the complete set of paths from the environment and this comprises only the paths that are directed towards the receiver and within it receive beam space. Now, lets consider the environment $\mathbb{E}$ comprise of K planar objects $\{p_1, p_2, \ldots, p_K\}$. Let the Euclidean distance vector $\mathbf{dT} = \{dT_1, dT_2, \ldots, dT_K\}$ and $\mathbf{dR} = \{dR_1, dR_2, \ldots, dR_K\}$ denote the distance between the planar object and the transmitter and

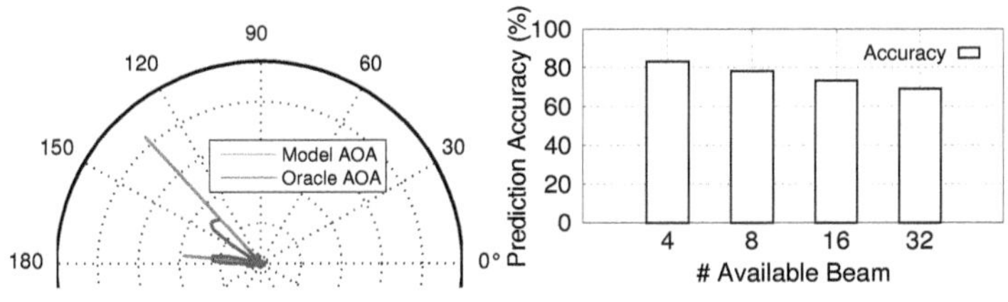

***Figure 4*: (a) Examples of predicting the AOA. (b) *BeamScope*'s best beam prediction accuracy.**

receiver respectively. In addition, let the diffusion coefficient of each planar point is denoted by α_i, which refers to the amount of signal reflected from the point towards direction i. We assume that signals in rest of the directions is uniformly distributed with signal energy is fraction $(1-\alpha_i)$ of the original signal energy. Also, consider $\mathbf{D} = [d_{ij}]$ be the pairwise distance between the planar objects. The *Environment Path Skeleton* is the vector $[\mathbf{dT}, \mathbf{dR}, \alpha]$ comprising of distance of planar object from the transmitter, receiver and the diffusivity. *BeamScope* constructs the *Environment Path Skeleton* using the CIR matrix M. Simply put, each CIR entry m_{ij} in $\mathbf{M}$ contains information about the complete path traversed by the 60 GHz signal which was emitted from a narrow beam at Tx and captured using a narrow beam at Rx. The captured CIR provides with RSS and phase information of signal that interacted and modulated by the environment. To put it concretely, the RSS/phase of the 60 GHz signal transmitted from beam direction T_i and received by beam direction R_j contains information about the distance of Tx from the planar object p_i, the inter-distance between the object p_i and p_j, distance of Rx from p_j and the diffusion coefficient α_i and α_j. Therefore, the amplitude $A(\cdot)$ and phase $\Phi(\cdot)$ of CIR m_{ij} is modeled as,

$$\begin{aligned} A(m_{ij}) &= \frac{\alpha_i \cdot \alpha_j}{dT_i^2 \cdot d_{ij}^2 \cdot dR_j^2} \\ \left(n_{ij} + \frac{\Phi(m_{ij})}{2\pi}\right) \cdot \lambda &= dT_i + d_{ij} + dR_j \end{aligned} \quad (1)$$

In addition, the triangular equality from the Figure 3(a) gives,

$$\begin{aligned} dR_i^2 &= dT_i^2 + d_{TxRx}^2 - 2 \cdot dT_i \cdot d_{TxRx} \cdot cos(\theta(T_i)) \\ dT_j^2 &= dR_j^2 + d_{TxRx}^2 - 2 \cdot dR_j \cdot d_{TxRx} \cdot cos(\theta(R_j)) \end{aligned} \quad (2)$$

We extract the vector $[\mathbf{dT}, \mathbf{dR}, \alpha]$ by jointly solving Equations (1) and (2) for all $i = 1, 2, \ldots, K$ and $j = 1, 2, \ldots, K$.

The *Environment Path Skeleton* captures snapshot of the environment and how a 60 GHz link interacts with it. Therefore, the main step to predict performance in an unobserved *spot* is, to predict how the environment snapshot is supposed to look like from that *spot*. Specifically, we assume that location of the *spot* where we want to predict the performance is known to *BeamScope* system. To simplify the exposition, we assume that we only want to predict unobserved Rx *spot i.e.* Tx is now fixed. Further, the coordinate of the unobserved *spot* is (x_s, y_s) *w.r.t.* the reference coordinate, where the reference coordinate is the position of the Tx. Therefore, predicted *environment path skelenton* from the unobserved *spot* is given by, $[\mathbf{dT}, \mathbf{Tr}_R(\mathbf{dR}), \alpha]$, where $\mathbf{Tr}_R(\cdot)$ denotes the transposition of the distance metric of planar objects from the receiver and calculated using standard coordinate translation method. The translated *Environment Path Skeleton* is converted to the spatial RSS utilizing the Equation (1).

4. EVALUATION

We evaluate feasibility of *BeamScope* by implementing it on a reconfigurable 60 GHz radio platform. We evaluate the feasibility of *BeamScope* of predicting the performance of unobserved from 2 aspects. (1) How accurately *BeamScope* can predict the AOA? (2) What is the accuracy in predicting the performance of best beam?

(1) **Predicting AOA and performance.** We test accuracy of *BeamScope* in predicting the AOA of unobserved *spot* from measurement results obtained from a reference link deployment. We deploy a reference link in an indoor office environment and measure the CIR matrix from Tx-Rx pairwise beamforming. This measurement is used to construct the *Environment Path Skeleton* as per Sec. 3. Further, we move receiver randomly in 8 different *spots*, noted the physical distance from the original receiver *spot* and collect there angular RSS that serve as oracle measurement. The modeled *Environment Path Skeleton* is used to predict the performance in those 8 random *spots* and compared the result *w.r.t.* the oracle measurement. Fig. 4(a) show an example case of predicting the AOA. Further, we compare the prediction accuracy of finding the best beam index in the unobserved *spots* and Fig. 4(b) shows the average accuracy with varying number of available phased-array beams at the receiver side. The accuracy drops as the number of available beams increase.

(2) **Spatial prediction accuracy.** To evaluate the feasibility of *BeamScope* in large-scale, we evaluate the prediction algorithm through simulation. We follow [6] in detail and simulate the interaction of a 60 GHz link in an indoor room (dimension: $10m \times 10m$) with reflective objects deployed randomly. We fixed the reference *spot* of the link and compared the modeled and measured best beam's prediction accuracy. Fig. 3(b) shows the heatmap of the prediction accuracy of finding the best beam in unobserved *spots* using measurement only from the reference link *spot*. This simulation result showcase that the accuracy is poor as we move further away from the reference link. This also suggests the need for collecting measurement from multiple reference *spots* in order to cover the whole indoor area, which we have planned in our future work.

5. CONCLUSION

The poster presents *BeamScope*, a system that scopes the environment to scour best possible location to deploy a 60 GHz link in an indoor environment. *BeamScope* characterizes the environment by capturing sparse path metric. Further, it models the way the metric is shared between unobserved and reference locations and exploits this information to predict the performance in unobserved locations.

6. REFERENCES

[1] IEEE Standards Association, "IEEE Standards 802.11ad-2012: Enhancements for Very High Throughput in the 60 GHz Band," 2012.

[2] "Wilocity 802.11ad Chipset," http://wilocity.com, 2013.

[3] S. Collonge, G. Zaharia, and G. Zein, "Influence of the Human Activity on Wide-Band Characteristics of the 60 GHz Indoor Radio Channel," *IEEE Trans. on Wireless Comm.*, vol. 3, no. 6, 2004.

[4] S. Sur, V. Venkateswaran, X. Zhang, and P. Ramanathan, "60 GHz Indoor Networking through Flexible Beams: A Link-Level Profiling," 2015, proc. of ACM SIGMETRICS.

[5] H. Xu, V. Kukshya, and T. Rappaport, "Spatial and Temporal Characteristics of 60-GHz Indoor Channels," *IEEE Journal on Selected Areas in Communications*, vol. 20, no. 3, 2002.

[6] H. Deng and A. Sayeed, "Mm-Wave MIMO Channel Modeling and User Localization Using Sparse Beamspace Signatures," in *IEEE International Workshop on Signal Processing Advances in Wireless Communications (SPAWC)*, 2014.

Poster: Crowdsourced Location Aware Wi-Fi Access Control

Bingxian Lu, Zhicheng Zeng, Lei Wang
Dalian University of Technology
{bingxian.lu, z.alex.zeng}@gmail.com
lei.wang@dlut.edu.cn

Brian Peck, Daji Qiao
Iowa State University
{bpeck, daji}@iastate.edu

ABSTRACT

In recent years, Wi-Fi has seen extraordinary growth; however, due to the cost, performance and security issues, many Wi-Fi hotspot owners would like to restrict the network access only to individuals inside the physical property. Unfortunately, due to the nature of wireless, this is difficult to accomplish, especially with the off-the-shelf omni-antenna devices. In this work, we develop and implement CLaWa, a Crowdsourced Location Aware Wi-Fi Access Control scheme to address this challenge. Our system is based on observations of differing characteristics of physical layer information across physical boundaries such as walls and corners. CLaWa crowdsources both channel state information (CSI) and received signal strength (RSS) of already validated users to classify future users. We have also selected an appropriate machine learning algorithm for CLaWa. Evaluation results show that CLaWa can identify the boundary around a given area precisely, thus granting network access only to users inside the area while not validating users outside the boundary. Compared to indoor localization schemes, CLaWa is a lightweight solution which does not require expensive localization operations.

Categories and Subject Descriptors

C.2.1 [**Network Architecture and Design**]: Wireless communication

Keywords

Crowd Sourcing, User Validation, IEEE 802.11 WLAN

1. INTRODUCTION

Currently, many businesses and public areas seek to attract customers and patrons by offering Internet access through Wi-Fi Access Points (APs). However, as providing this access is not cheap, a business may wish to restrict Wi-Fi access only to paying customers, or restrict access to customers inside the physical space.

This work is supported by the Haitian Scholar Grant of Dalian University of Technology, and NSF China grant under No. 61272524. Lei Wang is the corresponding author.

MobiCom'15, September 7–11, 2015, Paris, France.
ACM 978-1-4503-3619-2/15/09.
DOI: http://dx.doi.org/10.1145/2789168.2795183.

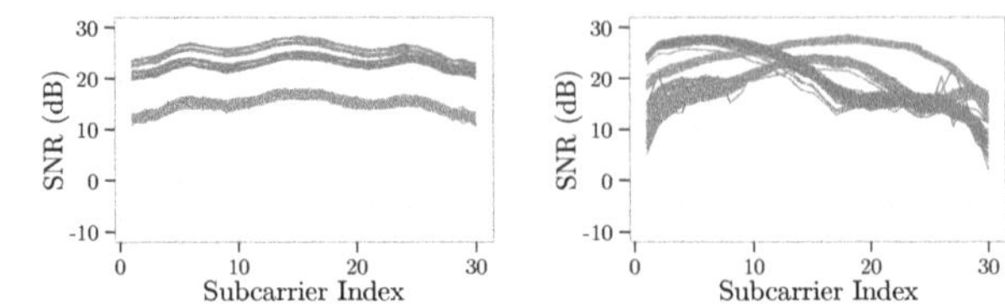

(a) Close to AP (b) Far from AP

Figure 1: CSI Amplitude values at the AP. We observe that close, stationary users result in high correlation coefficients.

According to our observations, CSI variance correlates with multipath effect and movement status. When a user is stationary and close enough to an AP, the corresponding CSI values on different antennae will be similar and stable between frames, as in Figure 1a, where each line in a given color (antenna) represents a single frame.

CLaWa first uses CSI data to determine if a user is in direct proximity of an AP; if so, the user is classified as a valid user. We also collect RSS data from each user to form a fingerprint. As valid users move around the area, we feed their RSS data into a machine learning algorithm, which quickly populates a training set. This crowdsourcing allows CLaWa to quickly identify future valid users. Finally, users that are incorrectly classified as being outside the area (false negatives) could then obtain an access code which would add their device to a whitelist, granting them accesses on future validation attempts.

Different from indoor localization solutions [4] and some works relying on special hardware [3], CLaWa attempts to address a distinct but related problem, while not requiring accurate localization of each user.

Therefore, compared with indoor localization schemes, CLaWa is a lightweight solution which does not require expensive localization operations or supporting devices.

2. SYSTEM DESIGN

2.1 System Overview

The design of CLaWa is outlined in Figure 2. The user's RSS and CSI data is collected and fed into a model which outputs a probability P that the user should be classified

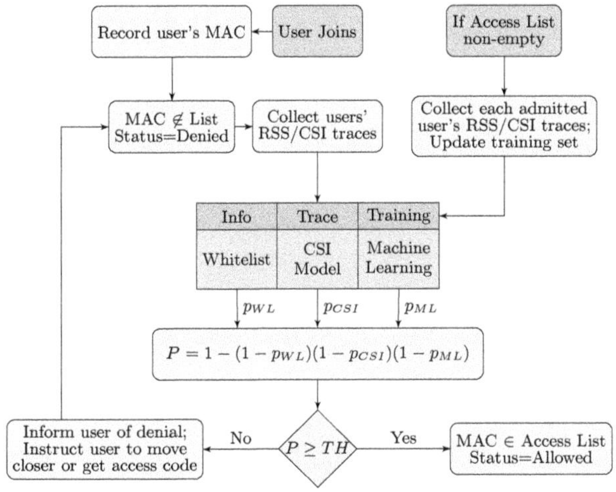

Figure 2: Design Overview

as a valid user. We then compare P to a threshold TH to determine if this user should gain access.

The core of CLaWa is a set of three parallel prediction components, which each determines a probability that a particular user is valid. The results of each component are then combined as:

$$P = 1 - (1 - p_{WL})(1 - p_{CSI})(1 - p_{ML}) \quad (1)$$

where each p is the probability of positive classification for each component.

2.2 Whitelist Component

The Whitelist component simply outputs a binary probability p_{WL} to signify whether or not a user has been added to a whitelist. If a user enters an access code, we know that they are a valid user of the system and should be given access, and thus they are added to a whitelist.

2.3 Channel State Information Component

The CSI component outputs the probability p_{CSI} that a user is in the direct proximity of an AP, and thus in target area. To do this, we use a simple CSI model based on data collected at the AP. Each data point is the received SNR value and is recorded as $H_j^{i,k}$ which represents the j-th frame collected by the i-th antenna on the k-th subcarrier. A group of each SNR value across all subcarriers for one frame j on a single antenna i can be represented as CSI_j^i.

2.3.1 CSI Stability Measurements

Since we wish to capture both the stability of CSI values over time, as well as the similarity of CSI values between antennae, we propose a two step process to determine a CSI stability metric. We first measure the correlation of CSI values between antennae for successive frames using the Pearson correlation coefficient, as in:

$$CSI_{corr}^{a,b} = \frac{\text{cov}(CSI_j^a, CSI_{j+1}^b)}{\sigma_{CSI_j^a} \cdot \sigma_{CSI_{j+1}^b}}, \forall a, b \in \{1, 2, 3\}, \quad (2)$$

where cov is the covariance between successive CSI_j^i readings, and σ is the standard deviation of the respective values. This yields 9 total correlation coefficients, one for every combination of antenna pair. We then use the minimum of these values as our final CSI stability metric for a given frame, as

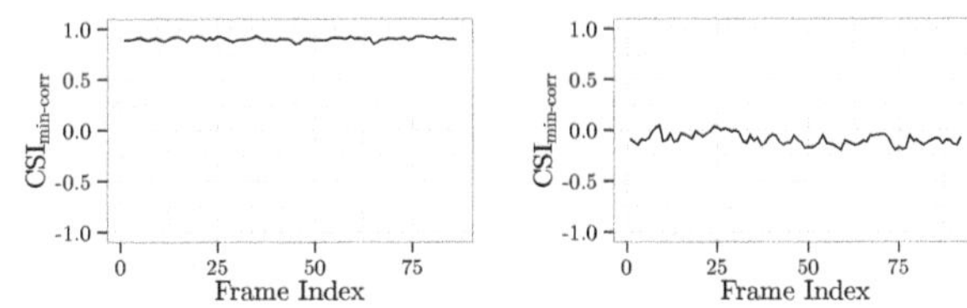

(a) Close to AP (b) Far from AP

Figure 3: $CSI_{min-corr}$ at the AP.

in:

$$CSI_{min-corr} = \min_{\forall a,b \in \{1,2,3\}} (CSI_{corr}^{a,b}). \quad (3)$$

2.3.2 User Recognition

When a user connects to an AP, it will measure its CSI and give a $CSI_{min-corr}$ for each frame according to the above equations. Intuitively, we expect $CSI_{min-corr}$ to be large (close to 1) when the user is near the AP. We count the number of frames with $CSI_{min-corr}$ above the threshold 0.5 and use the ratio of these frames to the total number of frames in a measurement period to determine the likelihood that a user is close to the AP, as in:

$$p_{CSI} = \frac{\sum_{j=1}^{N} [CSI_{min-corr,j} > 0.5]}{N}. \quad (4)$$

We continue the example from Figure 1a, and look at all frames as shown in Figure 3a. In this case, every $CSI_{min-corr,j}$ for every frame is above the threshold, and thus $p_{CSI} = 1$. As seen from Figure 1b, the shapes of the lines are not similar, and thus the $CSI_{min-corr,j}$ values in Figure 3b are low.

2.4 Machine Learning Component

The Machine Learning component outputs a probability p_{ML} that a user is in the target area according to calculations by a machine learning algorithm. We use the One-Class Support Vector Machine (OSVM) [2] algorithm, where our one class is valid users.

CLaWa uses RSS data from valid users to build a training set in real time. When a user device sends out N_{total} frames in a measuring period, and by OSVM there are $N_{outliers}$ frames which are classified into the negative class, then the machine learning component outputs a probability given by

$$p_{ML} = \frac{N_{total} - N_{outliers}}{N_{total}}. \quad (5)$$

3. IMPLEMENTATION

We provide a working implementation of CLaWa in order to fully evaluate our scheme. The CLaWa implementation consists of two complementary components: *CLaWa Access Point and Monitor*, and *CLaWa Server*, as depicted in Figure 4. The AP, along with passive CLaWa monitors, collects RSS and CSI information using a modified `iwlwifi` driver by employing the Linux 802.11n CSI Tool [1]. The server primarily uses `iptables` to control access for connected users.

4. EVALUATION

In the experiment, we use three Lenovo ThinkPad T400 laptops as the AP and monitors shown in Figure 5. Each

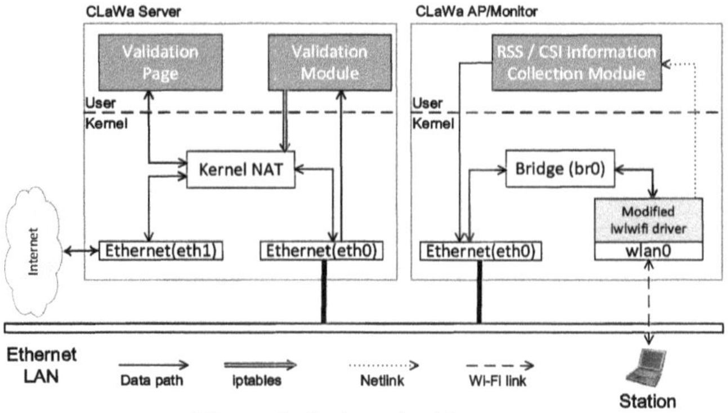

Figure 4: System Architecture

Figure 5: Thinkpad T400 with Intel 5300 NIC

laptop runs a 32-bit Ubuntu Server 10.04 (LTS) operating system, and is configured with the Intel 5300 802.11n wireless network card. We set up a testbed in a $6.5m \times 8m$ laboratory with 8 work cubes and 8 tables. The laboratory has a concrete wall of 0.5 meters, and the door is open throughout the experiments.

We partition up the area into 140 $60cm \times 60cm$ blocks, as shown in Figure 6, with 120 blocks inside the room (top 12 rows above the dotted line), and 20 blocks outside the room (bottom two rows below the dotted line). We show the output of the entire scheme at each block over time in Figure 6. We show the probability of validation at each test block at 0, 10, 20, and 120 minutes. Initially, the CSI model outputs high validation probability near the AP, allowing the entire scheme to output high probability. This effectively bootstraps the system for the Machine Learning component to begin working, which learns of valid locations as users travel around the room over time. As a result, the Machine Learning algorithm, and thus the entire algorithm, output high validation probabilities for an increasing number of blocks. After two hours, nearly the entire room is correctly identified. Additionally, the 20 blocks outside the room always have a very low validation probability. This confirms that CLaWa is able to correctly identify the boundary precisely around the room.

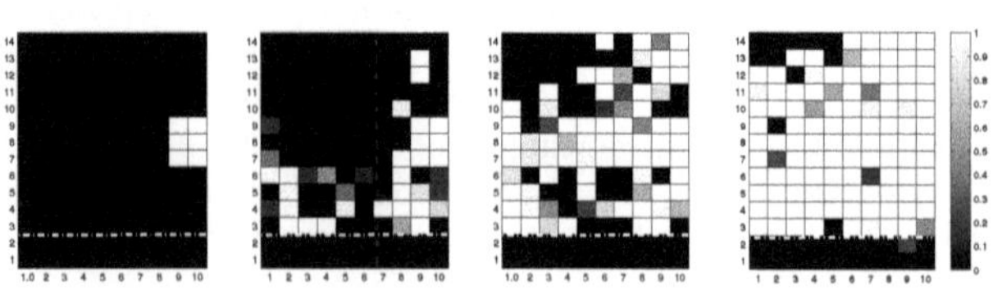

(a) 0 min (b) 10 mins (c) 20 mins (d) 120 mins

Figure 6: Probability P of validation for each test block. Lighter colors signify higher probabilities.

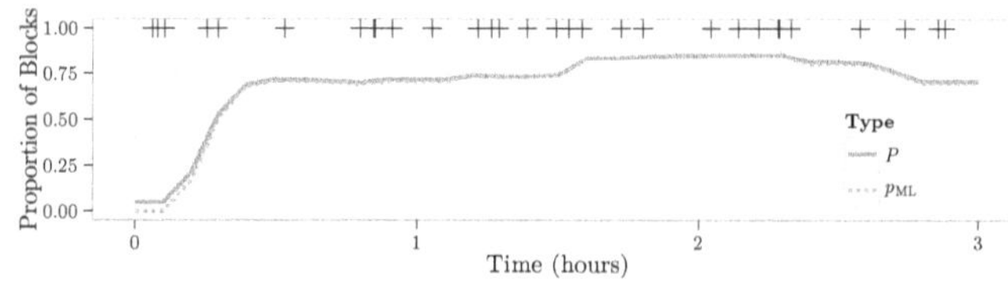

(a) Proportion for both P and p_{ML}. The black ticks represent user arrival times.

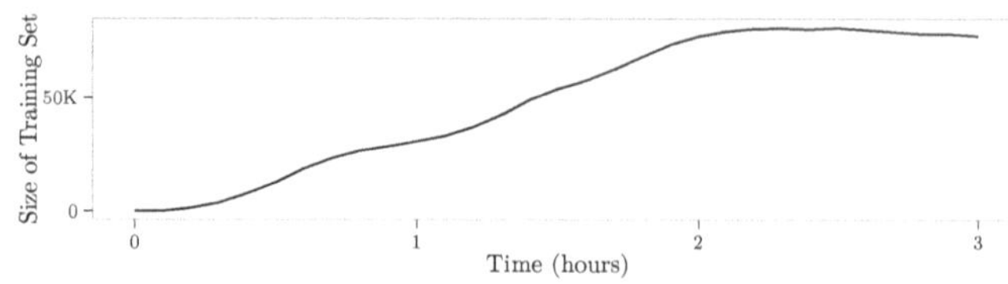

(b) Training Set Size

Figure 7: Result with 30 users in given order.

Given the blocks above, we show the proportion of blocks with $p_{ML} \geq TH$ and $P \geq TH$ in Figure 7a. We also show the size of the training set over time in Figure 7b. In both cases, we see that the blocks with high probability increases along with the size of the training set. Specifically, the proportion increases very rapidly at the beginning of the simulation, as many users are dwelling in new locations. After the initial period, the proportion remains relatively stable until new locations are visited around 1.5 hours. Finally, after about two hours, the proportion stabilizes since the training window W_T is two hours.

5. CONCLUSIONS

We present and implement CLaWa, which enables a location to offer Wi-Fi access to users inside a particular boundary, while preventing users outside the boundary to connect to the network. Specifically, CLaWa first recognizes valid users within direct proximity of the AP by leveraging the rapid de-correlation of CSI between multiple antennae as the distance between the user and the AP increases. Using this data, we then utilize crowdsourcing to build a training set from valid users, based on which we recognize additional valid users over time. As a result, CLaWa is able to successfully recognize valid users, while denying access to invalid users. Future work includes adding better boundary detection for varied settings and environments.

6. REFERENCES

[1] D. Halperin, W. Hu, A. Sheth, and D. Wetherall. Tool Release: Gathering 802.11n traces with channel state information. *ACM SIGCOMM CCR*, 41(1), 2011.

[2] B. Schölkopf, J. C. Platt, J. Shawe-Taylor, A. J. Smola, and R. C. Williamson. Estimating the support of a high-dimensional distribution. *Neural computation*, 13(7):1443–1471, 2001.

[3] A. Sheth, S. Seshan, and D. Wetherall. Geo-fencing: Confining Wi-Fi coverage to physical boundaries. In *Springer Pervasive, LNCS*, volume 5538, 2009.

[4] Z. Yang, Z. Zhou, and Y. Liu. From RSSI to CSI: Indoor localization via channel response. *ACM Computing Surveys (CSUR)*, 46(2), 2013.

Poster: An Insomnia Therapy for Clock Synchronization in Wireless Sensor Networks

Meng Jin[1],Dingyi Fang[1],Xiaojiang Chen* [1],Lin Cai[2],Zhe Yang[3],Zhanyong Tang[1]
[1]Northwest University, Xi'an, China
[2]University of Victoria, BC, Canada
[2]Northwestern Polytechnical University, Xi'an, China
mengj@stumail.nwu.edu.cn,{dyf,xjchen,zytang}@nwu.edu.cn
cai@ece.uvic.ca,zyang@nwpu.edu.cn

ABSTRACT

Intermittent connection of wireless links, caused by low duty-cycle radio operation, harsh working environment, movement of sensor nodes, etc., makes clock synchronization a challenging task. Prior synchronization approaches in wireless sensor networks (WSNs) typically require that nodes exchange time messages frequently with the reference clock, which is difficult in networks with low or intermittent connectivity. This poster presents RobSync, a robust design for clock synchronization in intermittent-connected wireless networks. Having recognized that clock skew is highly correlated to the voltage supply, we use the local voltage information as a reference for clock self-calibration, which helps reduce the frequency of time-stamp exchanges. To prevent a misuse of the voltage information, leading to error accumulation, a re-synchronization interval adjustment design is developed to make a trade-off between accuracy and energy consumption. We present the theory behind RobSync, and provide preliminary results by experiments to compare our approach and the recent approach.

Categories and Subject Descriptors

C.2.1 [**Network Architecture and Design**]: Wireless communication

Keywords

Clock Synchronization; Self-calibration; Interval adjustment

1. INTRODUCTION

Having a synchronized clock, i.e., all nodes having a common notion of time is a fundamental requirement in wireless sensor networks (WSNs), facilitating many technologies such as cooperative transmission, localization, sleep and transmission scheduling, information fusion, etc. However, in WSNs, nodes have their own clocks with different oscillator frequencies. As a result, any two clocks will always have an offset in their tick durations, leading to *clock skew*. Clock skew will gradually cumulate to *clock offset*, i.e. the time difference between two clocks. Therefore, effective synchronization is important for WSNs where tiny clock offset of a few micro-seconds or even less can cause large errors.

Modern synchronization approaches, like RBS[1], TPSN[2], FTSP[3], and many optimizations[4, 5, 6] are able to achieve μs-level accuracy. However, these approaches typically rely on frequent exchanges (e.g., a 150s interval) of their local time messages (*time-stamps*) with high communication cost and sometimes even not feasible. For example, in the low duty-cycle wireless networks[7], the RF module of a node stays active only for a small percentage of time during each duty-cycle period (e.g., 1%), while keeps in low-energy sleep/off mode for the rest of the time (e.g., a 30 minutes sleeping period). Thus frequent time-stamp exchange may be infeasible in such low-duty-cycle wireless networks. Further, frequent communications also introduce significant overhead in terms of bandwidth and energy consumption. The above problems mandate long re-synchronization interval, which may largely harm the synchronization quality.

This poster introduces RobSync, a robust synchronization approach which can deliver decent synchronization accuracy even when the time-stamp messages are not available. RobSync's technology is based on the observation that both clock skew and clock stability is highly correlated to the supply voltage of the node[8]. Leveraging this fact, RobSync enables the nodes to compensate their clock skew by exploiting the local voltage information, so the re-synchronization interval can be substantially prolonged without compromising synchronization accuracy. In addition, we further propose an interval adjustment scheme for duty-cycled clock re-synchronization, which allow a convenient trad-off between accuracy and energy efficiency.

2. CLOCK SKEW VS. SUPPLY VOLTAGE

An important property of clock skew is that it exhibits both long term and short term instabilities. In addition to fabrication and natural component aging, clock skew is also affected by the working conditions such as voltage supply, temperature, etc. The dynamic voltage supply caused by uneven traffic load and rechargeable power supplies (e.g., solar cells and capacitances) fluctuates the clock skew, forcing synchronization approaches to re-synchronization too frequently. Thus, to prolong the re-synchronization interval,

*corresponding author.

MobiCom'15, September 7–11, 2015, Paris, France.
ACM. ISBN 978-1-4503-3619-2/15/09
DOI: http://dx.doi.org/10.1145/2789168.2795184.

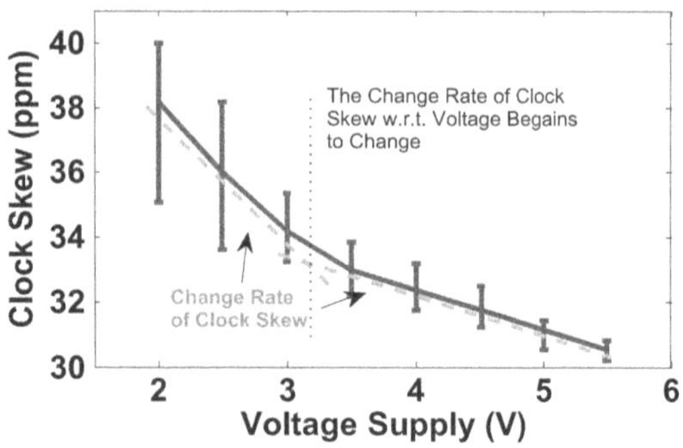

Figure 1: Clock Skew V.S. Supply Voltage

the impact from working condition should be carefully compensated. This paper focuses on compensating the impact of voltage, and to this end we start by investigating how supply voltage affects the clock skew in this section.

To investigate the relationship between clock skew and supply voltage, we conducted an empirical measurement. In the experiment, we measured the frequency of a 32.768 KHz oscillator on the TelosB sensor nodes under different supply voltages with a Lecory oscilloscope. The nodes are powered by a Direct Current Electrical Source (DCES). The supply voltage of node can be changed by varying the DCES.

Figure 1 depicts the clock skew under different supply voltages V. We can observe that, the clock skew increases as expected when the supply voltage decreases. When $V \geqslant 3v$, the change of clock skew is small, stable, and roughly proportional to the supply voltage. When $V < 3v$, the change rate jumps up significantly. Figure 1 also show that variation of clock skew gets serious as supply voltage decreases, and when the supply voltage $V \leqslant 2.5V$, the clock skew exhibits significant variation and becomes hard to predict. Based on the experiment results, we can use a linear model for clock skew vs. voltage if the voltage changes in a small range.

$$\alpha(t_0 + t) = \alpha(t_0) + k \cdot (V(t_0 + t) - V(t_0)), \quad (1)$$

where k is the voltage coefficient (i.e. the change rate of clock skew w.r.t. supply voltage), $\alpha(t)$ and $V(t)$ is the clock skew and the supply voltage at time t. Note that k may vary with time. Thus in RobSync, we need to identify k online based on the time-stamps received in the past.

3. OUR SOLUTION: ROBSYNC

We design RobSync to achieve two goals: 1) prolonging the re-synchronization interval without sacrificing the synchronization accuracy; and 2) adaptively adjusting the re-synchronization period to make a trad-off between accuracy and energy efficiency.

3.1 Two-phase Synchronization

In Figure 2, we illustrate the principle of RobSync which features a two-phase process: 1) *External clock synchronization (ex-sync)*, during which nodes refresh their time information by exchanging time-stamps (blue-filled bars); and 2) *Self-calibration*, during which there is no time-stamp exchange and the clock skew is estimated only based on the voltage information (red-filled bars). As shown in Figure 2, self-calibration can largely mitigate the error accumulation and thus prolong the synchronization period.

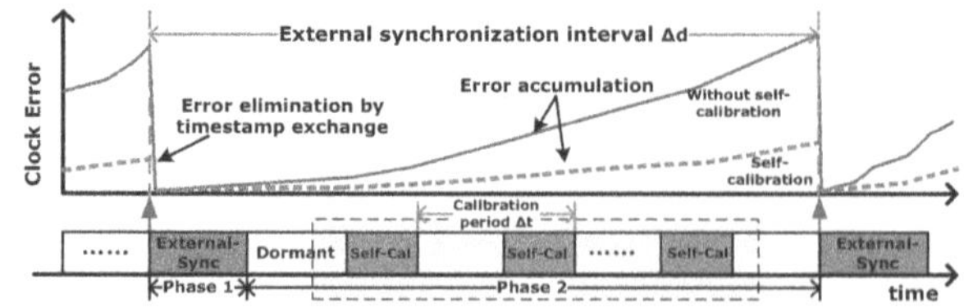

Figure 2: Illustration of two-phase synchronization.

3.1.1 External Clock Synchronization

In each ex-sync phase, the node 1) eliminates the error accumulation during the previous self-calibration phase based on the time-stamps; and 2) calculates the voltage coefficient k for the subsequent self-calibration phase.

Offset and Skew Estimation: In this phase, nodes first exchange time-stamp messages with the reference node to achieve certain time information. Based on such information, nodes can then obtain the clock offset $\theta[n]$ and clock skew $\alpha[n]$ respectively. Such method have been widely adopted in the time-stamp based synchronization schemes [3, 4, 5], and its design detail is omitted here due to space limit.

Voltage Coefficient Estimation: In each ex-sync phase, nodes notes their current voltage levels $V[n]$ and the estimated clock skew $\alpha[n]$ (we term such information as a *data point* (*voltage, skew*)). The voltage coefficient k is further examined: linear regression was used to find the line L best approximating the past W data points (W is the window size) and the voltage coefficient were analyzed. We assume that the voltage coefficient k does not change before the next ex-sync phase, and thus the node can subsequently switch into the self-calibration phase.

3.1.2 Self-Calibration

After acquiring the voltage coefficient k, the node can compensated the clock skew based on the voltage information. During the self-calibration phase, the nodes periodically measure their current supply voltage $V_n(t_i)$. After every measurement, the current clock skew $\alpha_n(t_i)$ can be updated based on $V_n(t_i)$ and $k[n]$ by using Equation (1) as:

$$\alpha_n(t_i) = \alpha[n] + k[n] \cdot (V_n(t_i) - V[n]). \quad (2)$$

After the update in clock skew, the local time can be predicted by using such a new clock skew till the next self-calibration period. Since the voltage supply does not change very quickly, we assume that the clock skew does not change during a calibration period. The clock offset in the (i+1)-th calibration period can be updated as:

$$\theta_n(t_{i+1}) = \theta_n(t_i) + \Delta t \cdot \alpha_n(t_i), \quad (3)$$

where Δt is the calibration period, and we set it as 100s in our current design. If the clock offset exceeds a given threshold (such as half of the granularity of the local clock) , we conduct the compensation to the local clock as:

$$C_n(t_{i+1}) = C_n(t_i) + \hat{\theta}_n(t_{i+1}). \quad (4)$$

Discussion: One may wonder: how to compensate the affect of *other factors* on clock skew, such as temperature? Today's TCXO oscillator can achieve accuracy of $\pm 0.25 \sim \pm 1ppm$ under temperature of $-55°C \sim 85°C$. On the other hand, many smart ideas, such as EACS[9], have been proposed for compensating the effect of temperature, and RobSync is compatible with these designs. Thus RobSync can

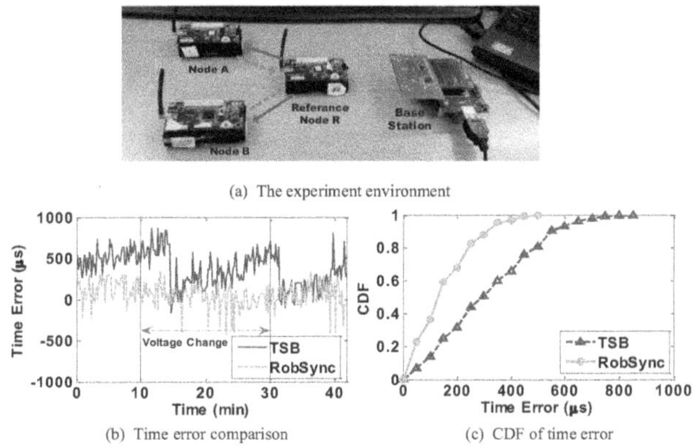

(a) The experiment environment

(b) Time error comparison

(c) CDF of time error

Figure 3: Experimental result.

use these designs as a module to estimate the clock skew when the temperature changes, assuming these factors have independent influence on clock skew.

3.2 Interval Adjustment

There are several trade-offs between self-calibration and ex-sync. Ex-sync has a higher accuracy since the noise introduced by time-stamps is usually at μs level or even smaller[4], while in self-calibration, estimation accuracy is subject to the noise introduced by both the voltage measurement and the dynamic clock skew, which is much higher than that of ex-sync. Nevertheless, in ex-sync a node has to rely on time-stamps exchange, which leads to significant overhead in terms of bandwidth and energy consumption, while in self-calibration the node can rely on its local information.

As discussed in §2, a lower voltage supply leads to a poor clock stability, which seriously affects the synchronization performance of self-calibration phase. Thus to prevent a misuse of the voltage information, which leads to error accumulation, a node should adjust the ex-sync interval according to its current supply voltage and the observed time error during the previous ex-sync interval. Thus the nodes can effectively control the synchronization error, and meanwhile adapt to the working condition.

4. ROBSYNC EXPERIMENTS

We conducted a simple experiment to validate the effectiveness of RobSync using TelosB sensor nodes. As shown in Figure 3(a), we used one node (denoted as R) as the reference, and two other nodes (denoted as A and B) as the slave nodes to synchronize with node R. Node A runs the time-stamp based (TSB) protocol and node B runs RobSync. We set the ex-sync interval of node A as 15min, and the self-calibration interval as 100s. The nodes are powered by DCES and their initial voltage are both 3.0V. We further adjusted the output of DCES to mimic the voltage change caused by uneven traffic load and energy harvesting operation.

The experimental result are shown in Figure 3(b) and (c). We find that as soon as the voltage starts to change, TSB starts to lose accuracy since the change of clock skew caused by voltage change cannot be compensated, while RobSync can keep its accuracy at a very precise level. Figure 3(c) shows the CDF curve of time error for TSB and RobSync. For RobSync, the time error is less than $400\mu s$ for more than 95% of the time. However, for TSB, for almost 20% of the time, the error exceeds $500\mu s$.

5. RELATED WORK

Many intelligent solutions have been proposed to compensate the impact of working condition (e.g., the compensation of voltage[8] and temperature[9]). In those solutions, the correlation between working condition and clock skew is assumed to be invariable, and the clock skew is estimated based on a preset mapping table which is obtained through pre-deployment system profiling. However, this assumption is unrealistic since the correlation may change with time and thus those solutions may suffers a high skew estimation error. In addition, pre-deployment profiling for all nodes involves high labour costs. Therefore, those approaches cannot provide satisfactory synchronization performance for large-scale WSNs that deployed over harsh environments.

Acknowledgments:

This work was supported by the NSFC (61170218, 61272461, 61373177, 61202198), Project National Key Technology R&D Program 2013BAK01B02.

6. REFERENCES

[1] Jeremy Elson, Lewis Girod, and Deborah Estrin. Fine-grained network time synchronization using reference broadcasts. *OSDI*, pages 147–163, 2002.

[2] Saurabh Ganeriwal, Ram Kumar, and Mani B. Srivastava. Timing-sync Protocol for Sensor Networks. In *SenSys*, pages 138–149, 2009.

[3] Miklos Maroti, Branislav Kusy, Gyula Simon, and Akos Ledeczi. The flooding time synchronization protocol. In *Sensys*, pages 39–49, 2004.

[4] Ziguo Zhong, Pengpeng Chen, and Tian He. On-Demand Time Synchronization with Predictable Accuracy. In *Infocom*, pages 2480 – 2488, 2011.

[5] Xuanyu Cao, Feng Yang, Xiaoying Gan, Jing Liu, Liang Qian, Xiaohua Tian, and Xinbing Wang. Joint Estimation of Clock Skew and Offset in Pairwise Broadcast Synchronization Mechanism. *IEEE Transactions on Communications*, 61(6), 2013.

[6] Guotao Zhao, Huadong Ma, Yan Lindsay Sun, and Hong Luo. A Distributed Audio Synchronization Scheme for Wireless Audio Sensor Networks. *Ad Hoc & Sensor Wireless Networks*, 22(3-4):231–257, 2014.

[7] LiangZhang, Qiang Ye, Jie Cheng, Hongbo Jiang, Yake Wang, Rui Zhou, and Peng Zhao. Fault-tolerant Scheduling for Data Collection in Wireless Sensor Networks. In *Globecom*, pages 5567–5571, 2012.

[8] Zhenjiang Li, Wenwei Chen, Mo Li, and Jingsheng Lei. Incorporating Energy Heterogeneity into Sensor Network Time Synchronization. *IEEE Transactions on Parallel and Distributed Systems*, 26(1), 2014.

[9] Zhe Yang, Lin Cai, Yu Liu, and Jianping Pan. Environment-aware clock skew estimation and synchronization for wireless sensor networks. In *Infocom*, pages 1017–1025, 2012.

Research Challenges and Opportunities in a Mobility-centric World

James Kurose*
University of Massachusetts Amherst
US National Science Foundation
kurose@cs.umass.edu, jkurose@nsf.gov

ABSTRACT

The Internet recently passed an historic inflection point, with the number of broadband mobile devices surpassing the number of wired PCs and servers connected to the Internet. Mobility now profoundly affects the architecture, services and applications in both the wireless and wired domains. In this "bottom up" talk, we begin by discussing several specific mobility-related challenges and recent results in areas including mobility measurement (including privacy considerations) and modeling, and context-sensitive services. We then take a broader look at current and future challenges, and conclude by discussing several NSF investments in programs and projects in area of mobile networking.

Categories and Subject Descriptors
C.2 Computer Communication Networks

Keywords
Computer networks, mobility, architecture, measurement, modeling

*Previously to joining the National Science Foundation, this research was supported in part by NSF grants CNS- 1421325, CNS-1040781, and CNS-1345300.

MobiCom'15, September 07-11, 2015, Paris, France
ACM 978-1-4503-3619-2/15/09.
http://dx.doi.org/10.1145/2789168.2790089

SPEAKER BIO

Jim Kurose is a Distinguished Professor of Computer Science at the University of Massachusetts Amherst. He is currently on leave at the US National Science Foundation, where he leads the Directorate of Computer and Information Science and Engineering. His research interests include network protocols and architecture, network measurement, sensor networks, and multimedia networking. He has served as Editor-in-Chief of the *IEEE Transactions on Communications* and was founding Editor-in-Chief of the *IEEE/ACM Transactions on Networking*. He has been Technical Program Co-Chair for *IEEE Infocom*, *ACM SIGCOMM*, *ACM SIGMETRICS* and the *ACM Internet Measurement* Conference. Jim has received a number of research and teaching awards including the IEEE Infocom Award, the ACM Sigcomm Test of Time Award and the IEEE Taylor Booth Education Medal. With Keith Ross, he is the co-author of the textbook, *Computer Networking, a top down approach* (6th edition). He has been a visiting researcher at Technicolor's Paris Research Lab and at the Laboratory for Information, Network and Communication Sciences (LINCS) in Paris.

Recitation: Rehearsing Wireless Packet Reception in Software

Zhenjiang Li, Yaxiong Xie, Mo Li
School of Computer Engineering
Nanyang Technological University
{lzjiang, yxie005, limo}@ntu.edu.sg

Kyle Jamieson
Department of Computer Science
University College London
k.jamieson@cs.ucl.ac.uk

ABSTRACT

This paper presents *Recitation*, the first software system that uses lightweight channel state information (CSI) to accurately predict error-prone bit positions in a packet so that applications atop the wireless physical layer may take the best action during subsequent transmissions. Our key insight is that although Wi-Fi wireless physical layer operations are complex, they are deterministic. This enables us to rehearse physical-layer operations on packet bits before they are transmitted. Based on this rehearsal, we calculate a hidden parameter in the decoding process, called error event probability (EVP). EVP captures fine-grained information about the receiver's convolutional or LDPC decoder, allowing Recitation to derive precise information about the likely fate of every bit in subsequent packets, without any wireless channel training. Recitation is the first system of its kind that is both software-implementable and compatible with the existing 802.11 architecture for both SISO and MIMO settings. We experiment with commodity Atheros 9580 Wi-Fi NICs to demonstrate Recitation's utility with three representative applications in static, mobile, and interference-dominated scenarios. We show that Recitation achieves 33.8% and 16% average throughput gains for bit-rate adaptation and partial packet recovery, respectively, and 6 dB PSNR quality improvement for unequal error protection-based video.

Categories and Subject Descriptors

C.2.1 [**Network Architecture and Design**]: Wireless Communication

Keywords

Wireless; channel state information; packet prediction; EVP; bit rate adaptation; unequal protection

1. INTRODUCTION

To achieve faster speeds in the face of increasing user demand, wireless local and wide area networks now turn to wideband transmission [44, 53]. For example, 802.11ac can now transmit over a full 160 MHz of bandwidth. As a result, different subcarriers now experience different subchannels [2, 30, 34]. Figure 1 illustrates these wide variations in (a) signal-to-noise ratio (SNR) and (b) bit error rate (BER). How do Wi-Fi and other wireless designs cope with this subcarrier diversity? The standard approach comprises two techniques, with the goal of equalizing the BER of all bits in a packet. First, the sender applies error control coding to produce a redundancy-containing stream of *coded bits* from the stream of *data bits* that make up a single packet. Then, the sender interleaves and pseudo-randomly spreads the coded bits over the different subcarriers of the wireless channel, before transmitting them over the air. We illustrate this process in Figure 2. Is this effective? Figure 1(c) shows that often, the answer is unfortunately no: note the visible difference in BER for data bits in different positions of the packet, ranging from 10^{-4} to almost 10^{-2}.

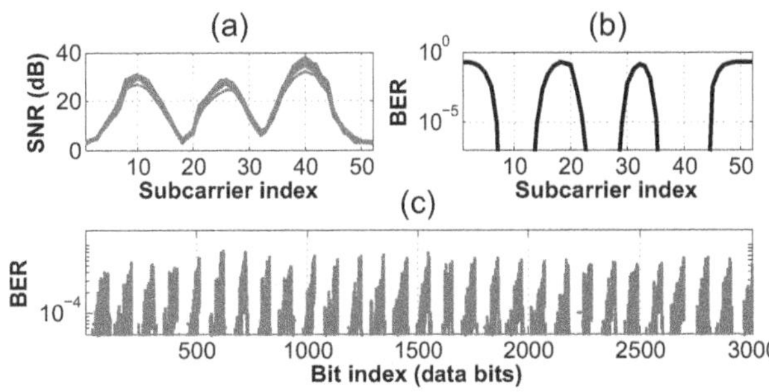

Figure 1: Data from 20 MHz 802.11n wireless channels. **(a)** Signal-to-noise ratio (SNR) across different subcarriers, measured over eight received packets; **(b)** Bit error rates (BERs) across different subcarriers; **(c)** The BER of decoded data bits, by position in the packet.

This forces existing wireless designs like Wi-Fi to take a conservative approach, applying enough coding to drive down BER across the packet so that even the highest BER is less than 10^{-6}. In this work we take a different position, exploring what we could do if we could construct a picture of a future packet like the one in Figure 1(c) simply by hearing the preamble of a recent packet. If we can construct such a picture, a number of possibilities emerge:

1. **Bit-rate adaptation.** Wireless channel quality is dynamic [8, 12, 52], and so senders using fixed bit-rates need to promptly select the rate at which they send information. Senders using rateless codes [11, 36] also benefit by learning when to stop sending rateless coded units.

2. **Partial packet recovery.** Receivers can leverage partially-received packets to improve throughput [14, 21]. More partially-received packets result when the sender selects data rates at or higher than the channel can support. Accurate per-bit BER pre-

MobiCom'15, September 7–11, 2015, Paris, France.
© 2015 ACM. ISBN 978-1-4503-3619-2/15/09...$15.00.
DOI: http://dx.doi.org/10.1145/2789168.2790126.

dictions allow the sender to decide whether the speed gains resulting from such higher data rates outweigh the consequent retransmission overheads.

3. **Unequal error protection.** Packet bits may have differing levels of importance, *e.g.*, key frames versus difference frames in video packets. Important bits are better placed at positions that are less likely to suffer from decoding errors [1, 19, 43].

In order to realize this vision, the wireless system needs to analyze each element of the physical layer design shown in Figure 2, most notably the error-controlling encoder and decoder, and the interleaving and de-interleaving. The missing piece is a way of analyzing how BER measured at each constituent subcarrier impacts the final confidence of each received data bit.

This paper presents *Recitation*, the first system that uses the channel state information (CSI) present in a packet's preamble as input, and based on this information alone, makes highly accurate packet error rate predictions so that a sender may select the best bit rate before the next transmission (Applications 1 and 2). Solely based on CSI data in the header, Recitation can also identify the error-prone bit positions in a packet so that the sender may rearrange packet bits based on application-level importance (Application 3).

To accomplish this, Recitation directly tackles the heretofore unclear relationship between diverse subcarrier SNRs and 802.11 decoding failures. Our key insight is that while the wireless physical layer is highly complex, it is (or can be designed to be) deterministic. This enables us to "rehearse" every operation on future received bits, for more accurate results than previous approaches such as Effective SNR (ESNR) [12] and SoftRate [52], as explained below in §6. We calculate the BER for each coded bit at point (a) in Figure 2 and carefully replay the operation of the decoder. Based on this "rehearsal" of the decoder, we calculate a quantity we term *error event probability* (*EVP*), a hidden parameter in the decoding process. EVP captures the probability of the decoder making a mistake at each step of its operation, thus giving extremely fine-grained decoding information. Based on EVP we then derive confidences of each data bit's correctness at point (b) in Figure 2, without requiring any wireless channel training. We demonstrate this approach in both 802.11's standard convolutional codes, as well as cutting-edge LDPC codes, establishing the generality of our approach.

Contributions. This paper makes following contributions. First, we formulate a novel metric that explicitly and precisely takes error control coding into account in its estimation of which packet data bits are likely to be correct (EVP). Second, we describe the design and implementation of Recitation, a system that integrates EVP with unequal error protection, partial packet recovery, and bit rate adaptation schemes. Third, we implement Recitation on the commodity Atheros chipset and present a comprehensive, testbed-based experimental evaluation that shows EVP's utility in both static and mobile scenarios with background traffic and interference.

Limitations. Recitation accurately calculates per-bit confidences of future packet receptions based on past receptions, and is thus most effective in the case of a channel where packet collisions are not the dominant factor limiting throughput, but in §4 we show promising throughput gains both in networks with typical levels of background traffic, and in interference-dominated networks.

We implement Recitation on commodity Atheros 9580 Wi-Fi network interface cards (NICs), and present experiments that validate the efficacy of the Recitation design. We demonstrate Recitation's utility in the three above applications. For each application, we compare Recitation with state-of-the-art approaches using a trace-driven GNU Radio evaluation. Recitation achieves significant performance improvements: a 33.8% average throughput

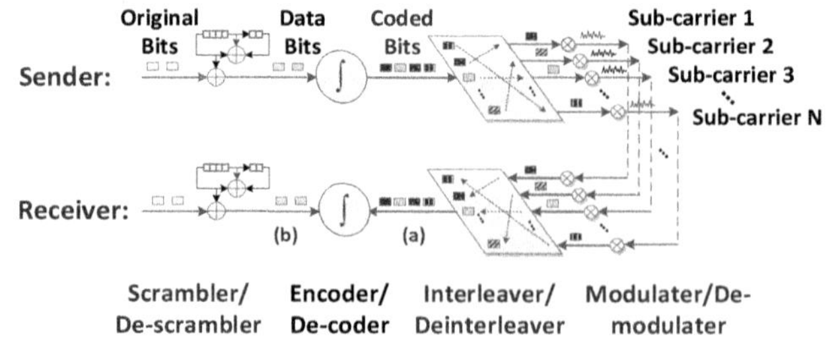

Figure 2: Scrambling, error control coding, spreading, and interleaving in the standard Wi-Fi architecture.

gain over ESNR [12] for bit-rate selection, a 16% average throughput gain over Maranello [14] for partial packet recovery, and 6 dB PSNR video quality improvement over standard approaches for unequal error protection. We also evaluate the amount of computation Recitation requires to show that that it is practical. §4 concludes that Recitation is software-implementable and compatible with the existing 802.11 multiple-input and multiple-output (MIMO) physical layer without hardware modification.

Roadmap. The rest of this paper is structured as follows: §2 presents our design, §3 our implementation, and §4 an experimental evaluation. §5 discusses future extensions to Recitation. §6 surveys related work before §7 concludes.

2. DESIGN

This section outlines the design of Recitation, starting with a primer on the relevant parts of the Wi-Fi physical layer in §2.1. Next we present the design of the EVP metric in Section 2.2, first in principle (§2.2.1), then in the context of Wi-Fi (§2.2.2), and then conclude with refinements that make its computation tractable in practice (§2.2.3).

2.1 Primer: Controlling errors in Wi-Fi

Figure 2 illustrates the 802.11 architecture [17] at a high level. At the sender, a scrambler deterministically whitens the original data bits. An encoder then maps the data bits into a larger number of partly-redundant coded bits. Orthogonal Frequency Division Multiplexing (OFDM) [26] divides the channel bandwidth of 20 or 40 MHz into 64 or 128 312.5 KHz *subcarriers*. The sender then interleaves the coded bits before mapping them to subcarriers and *modulating* them into *symbols*. Each subcarrier conveys independent symbols simultaneously on different frequencies. Together, the combined signal is called an *OFDM symbol*. At the receiver, each received OFDM symbol undergoes the complementary series of operations to recover the original data bits.

2.1.1 Scrambling, interleaving, and modulation

The scrambler performs bit-wise XORs between a pseudo random sequence and the original data bits. At the receiver, the original data bits are recovered by the same operation. As the random number sequence is specified in 802.11 standards [17], knowing the scrambled data bits is tantamount to knowing the original data bits. In the rest of the paper, we focus on the scrambled data bits and refer them to data bits for short, unless explicitly stated otherwise.

After encoding (discussed separately below in §2.1.2), the sender *interleaves* coded bits within each block of B bits in one OFDM symbol, to avoid consecutive coded bits being mapped onto faded subcarriers. The block interleaver uses two known and pseudo-random mappings, also specified by the 802.11 standard. After interleaving, the sender maps the data bits onto OFDM subcarriers for transmission. Due to interleaving, long runs of consecutive coded bit errors are largely avoided. The interleaving, however, only re-allocates the positions of coded bits (their BERs are still diverse). The decoded data bit BERs thus remain diverse, as we can see from Figure 1(c). The periodical BER pattern across data bits is because interleaving is performed in the unit of OFDM symbols, *i.e.*, the operations within each OFDM symbol is the same and these operations are repeated over different symbols.

Although interleaving and modulation are complex, their operations are deterministic. We thus know the subcarrier over which each coded bit travels. Furthermore, subcarriers are narrow-band in 802.11, and so their SNRs can be computed from the CSI. We thus employ narrow-band SNR-BER relationships to calculate the BER of each coded bit (point (a) in Figure 2).

2.1.2 Encoding and decoding

Encoding. *Convolutional coding* is the default error control scheme in 802.11a/g/n/ac. Encoding can be seen as transitions of a state machine between a number of different states. At each step, the encoder inputs one data bit, triggers a state transition, and outputs two coded bits.[1] To illustrate the concepts, we consider in this section the simple ½-rate convolutional code with four states in Figure 3. At state *a*, if the input packet bit is "0", the state machine stays at this state after the ith state transition and outputs two coded bits "00". It will transition to state *c* and output coded bits "11" when the input packet bit is "1". Suppose the incoming data bits were all zeros: then the encoder will remain at state *a* and all the output coded bits would be zero, corresponding to PATH-1 in Figure 3.

Low-Density Parity Check (LDPC) codes are recently appearing in 802.11n/ac [17]. They are block codes where the encoder divides data bits into k-bit data blocks, encoding each data block into n-bits by a matrix computation [31, 41]. The ratio between k and n, *i.e.*, k/n, defines the code rate.

Decoding. At the receiver, the received coded bits may contain errors. The decoder aims to find the most likely decoding result according to different criteria. The convolutional decoder approximates an optimal decoding by computing the number of differing bits, or *Hamming distance*, between the coded bits and the received bits, choosing the path that minimizes this Hamming distance. The best LDPC decoders typically adopt a variety of *belief propagation* (BP), which propagates information in a graph structure containing parity checks, stopping decoding when the propagated information (*beliefs*) satisfy all parity checks, or after a predefined maximum number of iterations.

2.2 Error event probability

A packet decoding fails exactly when excessive errors occur in the received coded bits, *i.e.*, the convolutional decoder selects an incorrect path (*e.g.* PATH-2 in Figure 3) or the LDPC decoder experiences a number of errors exceeding its error correction capability (ECC) in any coded block.[2]

In this event (an *error event*) the decoded data bits also contain errors. We denote the probability that an error event occurs the *error event probability* or EVP in this work. More precisely, EVP_i describes the probability that any faulty path diverges from the correct path in the ith state transition for convolutional codes, which

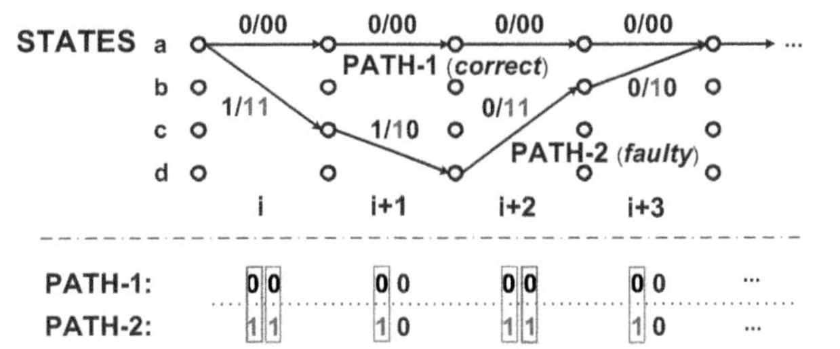

Figure 3: Convolutional coding. 1/11 along a branch means data bit "1" is decoded from the two coded bits "11".

captures the likelihood of a decoding error at data bit i. For LDPC codes, EVP_i describes the probability that an error event occurs within data block i.

2.2.1 EVP calculation in principle

We now explain how to compute EVP for convolutional and LDPC codes, showing that EVP can accurately predict packet error rate (PER) and bit error locations.

Convolutional codes. An incorrect path such as PATH-2 diverges from the correct path PATH-1 at some data bit i, as shown in Figure 3.[3] Since PATH-1 and PATH-2 differ by 6 coded bits, if more than three ($= \lfloor (6-1)/2 \rfloor + 1$) errors occur in the coded bit stream for PATH-1, these errors will result in an incorrect PATH-2 decoding. Therefore, in this example, the probability that the received sequence is decoded as PATH-2 can be calculated by the summation of the probabilities for all $\sum_{k=4}^{6} \binom{6}{k}$ cases. The probability of each case can be further calculated using the coded bit BERs. For instance, the probability in our example that only the first four highlighted bit positions are in error is $\prod_{j \in \mathcal{F}} p_j \cdot \prod_{j \in \overline{\mathcal{F}}} (1 - p_j)$, where p_j is the BER of coded bit j, $\mathcal{F} = \{1,2,3,5\}$, and $\overline{\mathcal{F}} = \{6,7\}$.

PATH-2 is of course just one of many incorrect paths, so EVP_i is the probability that *any* path diverges from the correct path at packet bit i:

$$\text{EVP}_i \;=\; \sum\nolimits_{j \in \mathcal{P}_i} p_{\text{PATH-j}}, \qquad (1)$$

where $\mathcal{P}_i$ is the set of all faulty paths diverging at packet bit i, and $p_{\text{PATH-j}}$ is the probability that the received coded bits are decoded as PATH-j.[4] $\mathcal{P}_i$ contains all possible faulty paths with different Hamming distances and thus grows exponentially in path length. Therefore we need a way of bounding the number of paths Recitation searches.

Faulty paths have *diverging segments* to the correct path, *e.g.*, from state transitions i to $i + 3$ on PATH-2. The longer diverging segment a faulty path has, the more coded bit differences to the correct path, *i.e.*, a larger Hamming distance to the correct path, it tends to have. Error events caused by a faulty path with a longer Hamming distance are thus more unlikely to occur, because a longer Hamming distance requires more coded bit errors to occur together. In a classic paper [51], Viterbi *et al.* analytically derive the probability that an error event is caused by any faulty path with Hamming distance k for our example code of Figure 3.

[1]Other code rates are achieved using the puncturing technique [17] based on the ½ rate.

[2]Since convolutional codes are not block-based, instead processing data bits as a bit stream, the number of coded bit errors they can tolerate depends on the density of those errors [51]. Therefore, in contrast with LDPC codes, convolutional codes have no fixed ECC value, and their decoding performance must be explicitly analyzed.

[3]There may exist other paths that diverge from the correct path in the ith state transition as well, which will also cause error events.

[4]Although we assume the transmitted coded bits are all zeros in Figure 3, the EVP definition in Eq. (1) can generalize to any coded bit sequence by symmetry, as when we focus on the difference between the transmitted and received coded bit sequences for PATH-1 and PATH-2 each "1" bit is an error, but this choice is arbitrary.

Their result shows that 98% of the error events are due to faulty paths with Hamming distance less than eight, suggesting considering only faulty paths whose Hamming distances are less than eight in the EVP calculation.

However, two difficulties arise that preclude a direct application of this analysis: first, the 802.11 specification convolutional code has 64 states instead of the four in Figure 3. Second, the analysis of Viterbi *et al.* assumes uniform coded bit BERs, which is not true in real wireless channels. Below in §2.2.2 we develop empirical approximations that reduce the amount of calculation required to practical levels while adopting the basic principle described above.

Before detailing this empirical calculation, we remind the reader of the two major uses of EVP:

1. Given the EVPs of each packet bit, the packet error rate (PER) can be estimated as $1-\prod_{i=1}^{N}(1-\text{EVP}_i)$, where N is the number of packet bits in a packet.
2. When the wireless channel is wideband, EVP varies within the packet, as we show in §4.1.3, and can identify the error-prone bit positions in the packet.

LDPC codes. Since LDPC codes are block codes, instead of analyzing the probability that each individual error event would occur in Eq. (1), we can rely on ECC to directly calculate EVP_i as:

$$\begin{aligned}\text{EVP}_i &= \text{Prob}\{\text{e}_i > \text{ECC}\},\\ &= \sum\nolimits_{l=\text{EEC}}^{n_i} \sum\nolimits_{\mathcal{F}_l \in \mathbf{F}_l} \prod_{j\in\mathcal{F}_l} p_j \cdot \prod_{j\in\overline{\mathcal{F}_l}} (1-p_j), \quad (2)\end{aligned}$$

where e_i is the number of bit errors in coded block i, n_i is the number of bits in coded block i, p_j is the BER of each coded bit j, $\mathcal{F}_l$ is a set of l coded bit errors, $\overline{\mathcal{F}}_l$ is $\mathcal{F}_l$'s complement, and $\mathbf{F}_l$ is the set of all possible $\mathcal{F}_l$s. The ECC can be calculated either theoretically or empirically: we take the latter approach for 802.11 LDPC codes in §4.1.2.[5]

2.2.2 EVP calculation in 802.11

In this section, we describe a practical algorithm to implement the EVP calculation for convolutional code. Our experiments guide the design of an algorithm to prune the search space of possible paths in Eq. (1) for the 802.11 convolutional code. We collect 10,000 real-world CSI measurements from Atheros 9580 NICs and feed them to an 802.11n specification-compliant transceiver on the GNU Radio, which features coding rates from ½ to ⅚ and modulations from BPSK to 64-QAM. Each CSI measurement reflects an instantaneous measurement of the wireless channel. The sender adapts the data rate with PER ≤ 20% to transmit packets (which may succeed or fail) over each channel realization. We record all data bits and coded bits of each 1,000-byte packet for ground truth, and all received coded bits and decoded data bits.

Error burst length. We first examine the distribution of the diverging segment lengths of faulty paths from the experiment. In fact, this length cannot be directly measured. For example, in Figure 3, the diverging segment length of PATH-2 is 8 coded bits. The length is known only when we can explicitly identify this path. To address this issue, we introduce the concept of *error burst length* to approximate the diverging segment length of a faulty path. We define an *error burst* as a sequence of consecutive coded bits, where the sequence starts and ends both from one coded bit error. In addition, the distance from any other coded bit error outside of the sequence to either the beginning or the end of the sequence should be sufficiently large, *e.g.*, 10 bits. For PATH-2 in Figure 3, the error burst length is seven (from the first coded bit error to the last one). The error burst length is always less or equal to the diverging segment length of a faulty path.

[5]Prior work [9] theoretically derives ECC for a family of simplified regular codes, but for irregular codes in general (*e.g.* the LDPC codes in 802.11), closed-form solutions are unknown.

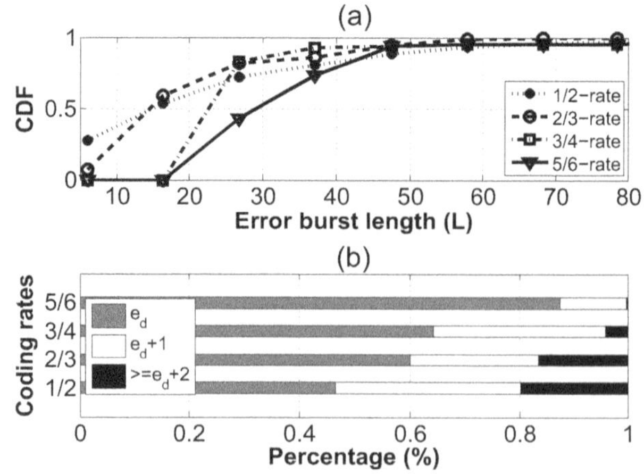

Figure 4: (a) CDF of the error burst length L; **(b)** Distribution of the number of coded bit errors, e, relative to the min. number of errors needed to cause a data bit error e_d.

For each received corrupted packet, we identify the error burst and feed the underlying coded bit error burst to the convolutional decoder to generate the decoded data bit errors. We then remove the data bit errors from the packet and continue searching for error bursts. Figure 4(a) depicts the CDF of the error burst lengths L. In general, L rarely exceeds about 40, and so we conclude that most faulty paths in 802.11 also have short diverging segment lengths. In other words, they have just a few bits differing with the correct path, *i.e.*, low Hamming distances, which is consistent with the conclusion made in §2.2.1 using the simple code.

Number of coded bit errors. A short Hamming distance k also implies that the number of errors in the error burst e is also small, since $\lfloor(k-1)/2\rfloor+1 \le e \le k$. In Figure 4(b), we further investigate the number of coded bit errors contained in error events under different code rates in 802.11. For different code rates, the minimum number of coded bit errors to cause an error event is different, denoted as e_d (although the EEC value for each specific convolutional code is not fixed, this value has a lower bound, represented by e_d [51]), where e_d ranges from five down to two for the 802.11 code rates from ½ to ⅚, respectively. Figure 4(b) shows that error events usually contain e_d or e_d+1 coded bit errors for all the code rates. In particular, e_d and e_d+1 together account for more than 80% of the error events for all four code rates.

Our conclusion is that we only need consider relatively few coded bit errors e that form relatively short bursts of length l in the EVP calculation. Based on the data, we consider only $e = e_d$ and e_d+1, and $l \le L = 40$, 32, 30, and 43 for the code rates from ½ to ⅚, capturing around 80th percentile burst length for each respective code rate. Therefore, these two parameters determined from Figure 4 can help eliminate unlikely cases from the EVP calculation. We will show in §4 that this error burst length reduction can make the computation in Recitation tractable on commodity devices, and achieves substantial performance gains.

Handling different bit error patterns. So far, one more issue remains. In Figure 3, to calculate the probability that the received sequence is decoded as PATH-2, we enumerate all possible cases that result in PATH-2. The reason we can do so is because we know

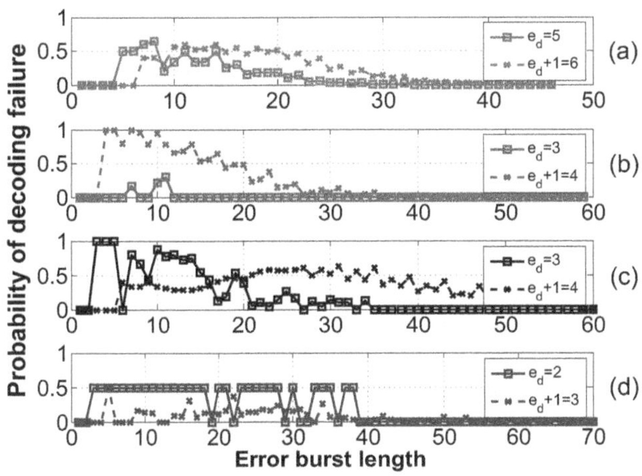

Figure 5: Weights of error combinations with different error numbers and burst lengths for **(a)** 1/2, **(b)** 2/3, **(c)** 3/4, **(d)** 5/6 code rates.

which coded bits on PATH-2 are different from the correct path. In general, when e errors form a l-bit burst, there are $\binom{l-2}{e-2}$ possible error combinations (a burst starts and ends from one coded bit error). For each combination, we need to tell whether it can cause a decoding failure even when we do not know which coded bits the faulty path are different from the correct path. To address this issue, we test all possible error combinations off-line in Figure 5. For each coding rate, Figure 5 provides the probability that an error combination, with e coded bit errors forming a l-bit burst, will cause a decoding failure. When $e = e_d + 1$, we eliminate the redundant combinations that are already calculated when $e = e_d$. We view Figure 5 as a look-up table for Recitation's EVP calculation. We note that the computation of the data in Figure 5 is just an one-time effort, which we have completed offline.

Recitation's EVP calculation. For each data bit i, we put the above ideas together in the following algorithm:

Step 1. Use CSI to compute the BER of each coded bit, p_j and initialize $\text{EVP}_i \leftarrow 0$
Step 2. For each error combination $\mathcal{F}$, update $\text{EVP}_i \leftarrow \text{EVP}_i + w_{e,l} \cdot \prod_{j\in\mathcal{F}} p_j \cdot \prod_{j\notin\mathcal{F}}(1-p_j)$
Step 3. Return EVP_i

EVP_i is initialized as zero and the algorithm updates it when enumerating all possible error combinations, e.g., e coded bit errors form an error burst and the burst length l is no more than L. In Step 2, p_j is the BER of the coded bit j derived from CSI. Each error combination $\mathcal{F}$ indicates the positions of the coded bit errors. The term $\prod_{j\in\mathcal{F}} p_j \cdot \prod_{j\notin\mathcal{F}}(1-p_j)$ gives the probability that this error combination could occur, and the weight $w_{e,l}$ is the probability that this error combination will cause a decoding failure, which is obtained from Figure 5. Recitation then iterates the above EVP calculation for all data bits. As mentioned in §2.2.1, these calculated EVPs can be used to derive the packet error rate (PER) and indicate the error-prone bit positions in the packet.

In 802.11 MIMO transmissions, the sender encodes data bits to coded bits and then distributes them deterministically across different spatial streams. Our design Recitation is thus applicable to these transmission modes as well, with a similar EVP calculation.

Recitation's protocol summary. In Recitation, a sender uses the CSI from the previous transmission to predict the future packet reception under different configurations and then select the best action for the subsequent transmission. The CSI information is obtained by explicit CSI feedback, which is lightweight [12, 38].

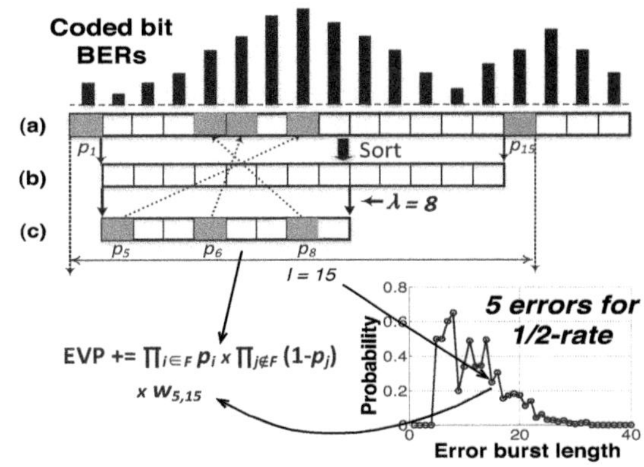

Figure 6: Recitation's error combination pruning technique, where coded bit errors occur at positions $\mathcal{F} = \{1, 5, 6, 8, 15\}$.

2.2.3 *Reducing computational complexity*

The delay with which the sender can compute and act on the EVP metric gates Recitation's efficacy. For example, if we want to select a data rate for a packet using the PER predicted, the EVP computation has to be completed before that packet's transmission. Our experimental investigation with Atheros AR9580 NICs reports typical 2 ms delays for processing a packet of the maximum payload under the 802.11n data rates (*i.e.*, from 6.5 Mbit/s to 65 Mbit/s). It introduces a stringent timing requirement for the EVP computation. Recitation therefore employs two additional techniques to reduce computation complexity of the EVP calculation. We evaluate the algorithm in §2.2.2 in conjunction with the techniques proposed in this section in §4.

Error combination pruning. SNRs and thus the coded bit BERs can be highly diverse for wide-band transmissions (as shown in Figure 7), which makes the probability that each error combination occurs dramatically different. According to our experiments, such a difference can be as high as 10 orders of magnitude. Based on this observation, we only consider the combinations that consist of high coded bit BERs in the EVP calculation. We sort $l-2$ coded bits in the burst (except the first and last bits) according to their coded bit BERs in a decreasing order and only examine the first $\binom{e-2}{\lambda}$ combinations, where $\lambda \le l-1$. Figure 6 shows an example of the error combination pruning with $l = 15$ and $e = 5$. The five marked squares in line (a) of Figure 6 represent one error combination. Line (b) of Figure 6 depicts the sorted sequence (except the first and the last coded bits) in decreasing order according to their coded bit BERs. With $\lambda = 8$ and $e = 5$, we only consider $\binom{8}{3} = 56$ error combinations, instead of $\binom{17}{3} = 680$.

Periodicity of the EVP. The second technique we adopt is to leverage the periodic property of the EVP. We find that the EVPs of exhibit a period length related to the number of coded bits contained in one OFDM symbol. The periodic property exists because the interleaving and modulation operations are deterministic and the wireless channel is stationary for the duration of one frame at normal walking or even driving speeds [50]. The coded bits at the same position of their own OFDM symbols are transmitted over the same subcarrier, experiencing the same channel quality. The BERs of the coded bits are thus periodic, leading to the EVPs of the decoded packet bits having a periodical property. We experimentally verify this phenomenon in §4.1.3. With this observation, we can compute EVPs for the data bits in one period only and reuse them for the following symbols in practice. As the period length in 802.11 is a small integer, by doing so, the computation complicity of Recitation is dramatically reduced and does not increase as the packet length.

3. IMPLEMENTATION

We implement Recitation on Atheros 9580 NICs that work on 802.11n 20 MHz channels with 64 subcarriers. Each 9580 NIC is connected to a Qualcomm System-on-Chip QCA9558 running an embedded Linux system, as shown in Figure 7(b). According to the 802.11 standard, the physical layer calculates CSI upon each correctly received packet when the sounding flag is set. We modify the driver to turn on this flag and let Atheros 9580 chipset export CSI, which causes no additional computation overhead. We also record both correct and corrupted packets at the receiver. Other useful information related to the packet transmission, *e.g.*, RSSI, noise floor, data rate, *et c.* is reported as well. This implementation forms the basis for all results reported in §4.

4. EVALUATION

We present a testbed-based experimental evaluation of Recitation. We begin in §4.1 with microbenchmarks evaluating Recitation's accuracy in predicting PER and error-prone bit positions, and measuring its computational complexity overhead. In §4.2 we present the results of experiments measuring end-to-end application performance. The parameter e, the number of coded bit errors to investigate, equals to e_d and $e_d + 1$, where e_d = 5, 3, 3, and 2 for 1/2, 2/3, 3/4, and 5/6 code rates, respectively. The maximum error burst length is set to 40, 32, 30, and 43 for rates from 1/2 to 5/6, respectively. These parameters have been investigated and determined in §2.2.2. We also implement other approaches used in three applications for the performance comparison.

4.1 Microbenchmarks

Methodology. We deploy Atheros 9580 nodes in our campus as access points (APs). These cover a path from a bus station to a research lab as shown in Figure 7 (a). We deploy another Atheros 9580 node as receiver to connect each AP to 50 random positions. At each position, the AP sends 10,000 UDP packets with 1,000-byte random payloads to the receiver. We iterate the transmissions for all eight rates using between one and three spatial streams. In each run, we fix the data rate and turn off link-layer retransmissions to measure the underlying PER. We thus obtain the PER statistics for all SISO and MIMO rates at each position. Throughout the experiment, the receiver records both correct and corrupted packets, and CSI from each correct packet. We thus obtain the decoding bit error patterns within each packet over lossy links. We then evaluate Recitation by comparing its prediction results with the measurement results.

4.1.1 Frequency selective fading

Our measurements in Figure 7 (a) cover typical 802.11 Wi-Fi environments, *e.g.*, an open-space hall, a parking lot surrounded by cars and stores, an office, etc, with different levels of frequency selective fading. Figure 7 (c) plots the CDF of the maximum subcarrier SNR difference from each CSI measurement. In 20 MHz channels, we observe a difference of at least 2.7 dB, nearly 10 dB for 50% of the links, and a maximum of 22 dB. From Figure 7 (c), we see that 40 MHz channels have even higher subcarrier diversity, from 7.6 dB up to 28 dB. As the trend of the 802.11 development is to further increase the bandwidth, we expect subcarrier diversity will increase in future Wi-Fi standards.

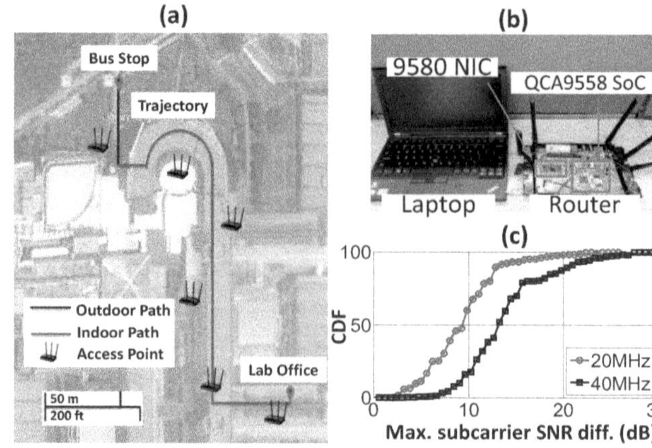

Figure 7: **(a)** Testbed map; **(b)** Atheros 9580 node used in the experiment; **(c)** CDF of the maximum subcarrier SNR difference (dB) in each CSI measurement.

4.1.2 PER prediction

Figure 8(a) and (b) depict the packet error rate (PER) prediction performance Recitation achieves with 802.11n convolutional codes. We also compare against the state-of-the-art approach Effective SNR (ESNR) [12].

802.11n SISO. Figure 8 (a) shows prediction accuracy for 802.11 single-antenna rates.[6] For all the links whose measured PERs fall into one bucket, we calculate the differences between the measured and predicted PERs, and plot the average prediction error as well as the error variance. From the figure, we see that Recitation's predictions are highly accurate in all buckets, with an average prediction error between 0.003 and 0.05, and variance less than 0.01. ESNR makes a prediction error of 0.22 on average. ESNR's inaccuracy arises because the PER versus SNR curve has a narrow transition range, and ESNR is a relatively coarse channel quality indicator whose predictions are more sensitive to uncertainty in the SNR measurement. ESNR thus provides mostly binary information about whether PER is less than a small threshold, *e.g.*, in bucket [0 ~ .01]. As Recitation can utilize all subcarrier SNRs in the EVP calculation, it accurately predicts PER even in the transition range.

802.11n MIMO. Figure 8 (b) depicts the PER prediction performance for 3 × 3 MIMO rates. Similar to Figure 8 (a), we divide the PER transition range into seven buckets. Due to larger throughput gaps between two consecutive MIMO rates, we obtain fewer measurements between 0.06 and 0.3 in the PER transition range. Therefore, the prediction errors are slightly higher than that in Figure 8 (a). Recitation's average prediction error varies between 0.002 and 0.07, while ESNR's average prediction error can be up to 0.34. Similar to SISO rates, ESNR achieves a small PER prediction error in the bucket [0 ~ .01]. In contrast, the average errors Recitation achieves are much smaller in all buckets.

LDPC codes. To evaluate Recitation with LDPC codes, we investigate the EECs of the 802.11 LDPC codes experimentally (different data rates employ different LDPC codes). We implement the 802.11 LDPC encoder/decoder and integrate them in our 802.11n specification-compliant transceiver introduced in §2.2.2. After a

[6]For clarity of presentation, we divide the PER range (0.0 to 0.3) into seven buckets. Most applications, like rate adaptation, partial packet recovery, *etc.*, work within this PER range.

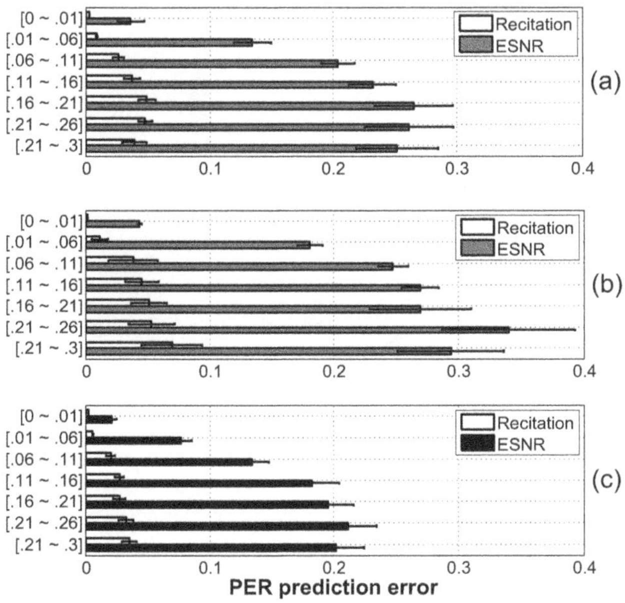

Figure 8: PER prediction comparison. **(a)** Convolutional codes, SISO rates (1 × 1); **(b)** Convolutional codes, MIMO rates (3 × 3); **(c)** LDPC codes, SISO rates (1 × 1).

LDPC encoder encodes a data packet, we manually flip coded bits to introduce coded bit errors. We then feed the *polluted* coded bits into LDPC decoders and repeat this process to evaluate the maximum number of coded bit errors each LDPC code can tolerate.

As the LDPC codes implementation on Atheros 9580 NICs as well as other NICs, like the widely used Intel 5300 NICs in the community, is not available to us, we use an 802.11n simulator to evaluate the PER prediction performance with LDPC codes. We adopt the CSI trace collected in Figure 7 as the ground truth for the channel, and transmit packets over the channel described by the CSIs. We then compare the predicted PER against the measured PER. Figure 8 (c) depicts that Recitation can also achieve an accurate PER prediction using LDPC codes. According to the statistics, the average prediction error varies from 0.002 to 0.035, and the variance is less than 0.01. The accuracy achieved in this figure is higher than that in Figure 8 (a) because simulations introduce less channel uncertainty. Similar to convolutional codes, the ESNR's average prediction error is much higher than Recitation, up to 0.21, and it performs well in the bucket [0 ~ .01] merely.

4.1.3 *Prediction of decoding error locality*

In this section we continue our evaluation of Recitation with convolutional codes on Atheros 9580 nodes. Figure 9 (a) plots the BERs of the data bits in one packet. We measure BER from a randomly-selected link in our test-bed using a $^1/_2$ code rate and QAM-16 modulation. For clarity, we show the BERs of the first 3,000 bits. The BERs of the remaining data bits follow similar patterns. From the figure, we observe (echoing similar observations by Miu *et al.* [33] and Han *et al.* [13]) that the BERs of each data bit are highly different, forming a pattern that has a period length equal to the size of the OFDM symbol. Therefore, we plot the average BER of the data bits in one period in Figure 9 (b), where the x-axis is each bit position in the period and the y-axis is the average BER over all the data bits with the same offset in each individual period. Figure 9 (b) clearly shows that some data bits are more likely to have decoding errors. In Figure 9 (c), we use Recitation to

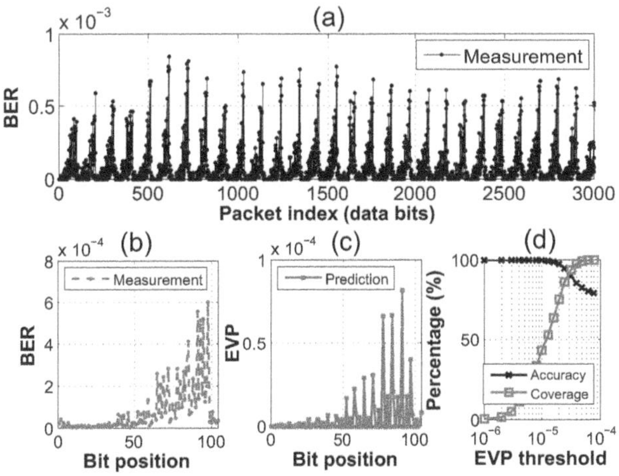

Figure 9: **(a)** BERs of each data bit in a packet; **(b)** Data bit BER in one period; **(c)** Data bit EVP in one period; **(d)** The prediction accuracy of error-prone bit positions.

predict those error-prone positions. The predicted pattern matches the measured one, based on which we can identify all error-prone bit positions in one packet.

Since EVP does not describe the error dependence with other bits (§2.1), the EVP of each bit is smaller than the BER. Thus, to quantify prediction accuracy, we do not conduct a bitwise comparison. Instead, we divide each period into equal ranges, using thresholds to classify each into "safe" and "unsafe" clusters. All data bits in a safe range are considered to be safe and more important bits of a packet can be placed in the safe ranges.

Through our experiment, we find that it is sufficient to divide one period into 4 to 32 ranges for the eight data rates. For all the links with corrupted packets in our experiment, we calculate the range error rates and use an empirical threshold, *e.g.*, 0.04, to classify all the ranges into the "safe" and "unsafe" categories as ground truth. For each range, we then use Recitation to calculate its average EVP and adopt an EVP threshold to evaluate its prediction results. We divide our packet trace into training and testing sets. In the training set, Figure 9 (d) shows when the EVP threshold is small, Recitation can identify only a few safe ranges from the ground truth ("Coverage" in Figure 9 (d)), but identification accuracy is high. As the threshold increases, Recitation identifies more safe ranges but accuracy decreases slightly. We find that the EVP threshold 2.6×10^{-5} achieves a good tradeoff between the accuracy (92%) and the coverage (91%). In the testing set, Recitation achieves a similar performance. The setting is used for the application in §4.2.3.

4.1.4 *Computation and energy overhead*

Computation overhead. While Recitation is accurate in its PER and error-prone bit position predictions, it can be truly useful in practice only if its computational overhead is manageable. To this end, the parameter λ used in the "error combination pruning" technique controls the computation overhead and the EVP accuracy of Recitation. According to the 802.11 timing requirement in §2, an acceptable delay should be less than 0.25 ms such that the predictions for eight different data rates can be completed within two milliseconds. Figure 10 (a) depicts the average delay to predict PER for one PHY configuration when λ varies. When λ varies from 5 to 30, Figure 10 (a) shows that the computational delay of Recitation increases from 0.004 to 0.934 ms. For one such eligible λ

setting, e.g., $\lambda = 18$, Figure 10 (b) breaks down the computational overhead for individual data rates with the average delay at around 0.161 *ms*. The reason that the computation delays for rates 6.5, 13, 26, and 52 Mbit/s are larger is because they use the 1/2 and 2/3 code rates. One OFDM symbol thus contains more coded bits and there are more error combinations to calculate. It introduces much more computations than other three rates 19.5, 39, 58.5, and 65 Mbit/s, which adopts the 3/4 and 5/6 code rates.

In Figure 10(c), we evaluate the PER prediction accuracy under different choices of λ. For each link investigated in Figure 8, we vary λ to obtain different PER predictions and compare them with the measured results. Figure 10 (c) shows that when λ is small, e.g., $\lambda \leq 15$, the prediction error is large, *e.g.*, up to 0.23 on average. When λ is sufficiently large, Recitation achieves high accuracy, *e.g.*, the error decreases to 0.013 when $\lambda = 18$. As λ further increases, the accuracy improvement becomes marginal, while the computation overhead dramatically increases. Based on the results, we select $\lambda = 18$ as a default setting, which was used in both Figures 8 and 9. In Figure 10 (c), we also examine Recitation without the "error combination pruning" approximation. From the figure, we can see its average prediction error is 0.011, showing that this technique introduces a negligible accuracy loss, while reducing computational complexity dramatically.

Energy consumption. We measure the Recitation power consumption on Atheros 9580 nodes using an APPA 72 multimeter, by investigating its energy usage in comparison with the baseline when our design is not used. Since Recitation is a fully software-based system, power consumption mainly stems from CPU computation, which is lightweight. Our measurement shows that the additional power consumption caused by Recitation varies from 601 mW to 685 mW, which is comparable to or even longer than a variety of recent mobile applications [27, 60, 61], indicating that Recitation is energy efficient for mobile platforms. When a mobile device of Recitation communicates with a line-powered AP, the energy efficiency can be further improved: the AP can always compute the optimal configuration using the CSI measurement. For the downlink, the AP uses the optimal configuration to transmit packets; for the uplink, the AP sends the optimal configuration, instead of CSI [57], as feedback to avoid computation on the mobile device.

4.2 Applications

In this section, we demonstrate the utility of the accurate and fine-grained decoding predictions Recitation achieves through three representative applications: bit-rate adaptation, partial packet recovery, and unequal error protection-based video transmission. The first two applications aim to evaluate the accurate PER prediction of Recitation. In particular, the former one focuses on the PER prediction when PER is close to zero and the latter one focuses on the prediction with the PER transition range. The third application targets to evaluate the utility of the fine-grained error-prone bit position prediction. We use extensive trace-driven evaluations to compare against the state-of-the-art approaches.

Evaluation setup. We collect packet transmission and CSI traces in the laboratory (the bottom AP in Figure 7), considering both mobility and non-line-of-sight in the trace collection. We repeat the trace collection twice for 1×1 SISO and 3×3 MIMO settings, respectively. The AP continuously generates UDP packets. For each packet, AP sends out eight copies, iterating for all eight rates. The CSI from the eight copies are approximately the same since CSI is measured from the preamble, which does not depend on the rate. We thus view the transmissions of the eight copies as the ground truth for eight different rates when AP sends one packet over the current channel. During the AP's transmission, a receiver moves in a U-shaped route at a walking speed [15] in the laboratory and collects about 93,000 channel measurements. From CSI indices 0 to 30,000, the receiver moves far away from the AP and there is line-of-sight for most of time. From indices 30,000 to 50,000, the receiver takes a U-turn and traverses through a meeting room. The channel is hence relatively poor and non line-of-sight. In the rest of the CSI trace, the receiver moves towards the sender and there is no line-of-sight for most of time. In addition, the CSI feedback is included and its overhead is factored into the evaluation.

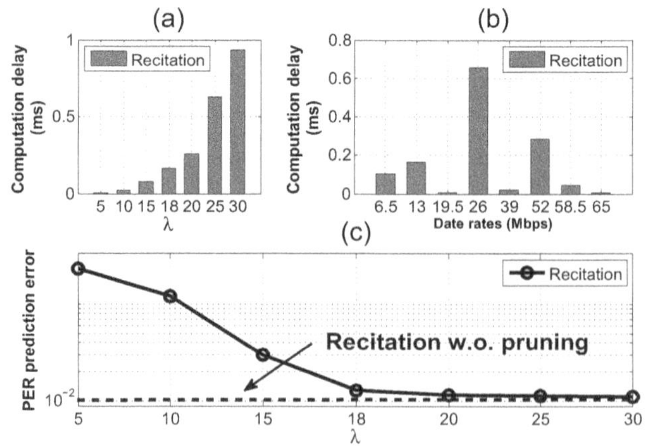

Figure 10: **(a)** Average Recitation computation delay for one rate when λ varies; **(b)** Recitation computation delay breakdown for different rates ($\lambda = 18$); **(c)** PER prediction errors when λ varies.

4.2.1 Wi-Fi rate selection

We evaluate the following bit-rate selection algorithms:

1. **Rect-Rate:** The sender uses the CSI from the receiver feedback to predict PER for each data rate by Recitation, and selects the highest rate with the predicted PER ≤ 0.1.
2. **ESNR:** The rate selection based on the proposed ESNR approach in [12]. ESNR is compared as it reports the best known throughput performance so far. ESNR has shown to outperform other recent approaches, *e.g.*, SoftRate [52]. We do not evaluate each of those individually.
3. **OPT:** An oracle selects the optimal data rate for each transmission, thus performance is an upper bound for all rate selection approaches in the experiment.

Some recent works, *e.g.*, [4, 38], propose to harness the frequency diversity to adapt rates, but they require a substantial redesign of the current 802.11 PHY with customized hardware. Therefore, we do not empirically compare Recitation with them. In this experiment, we feed the CSI trace into each approach. For each CSI, different approaches select different rates to transmit the packet, and the collected ground truth determines the transmission result for a particular scheme. We compare the throughput of each approach, where each reported throughput value is averaged in a window of 200 packets transmitted over 200 consecutive CSIs. Figures 11 and 12 plot average achieved throughput against time windows of 200 CSI readings.

802.11 SISO rates. Due to the inaccuracy of the PER prediction, ESNR selects suboptimal bit rates more frequently than Rect-Rate thus suffering a throughput penalty. Rect-Rate tracks the performance of OPT within 16% on average, while ESNR is only within 29%. Rect-Rate outperforms ESNR by 25.6% on average and 63.8% at most. To analyze the performance achieved by each approach, we characterize the rate selection accuracy of Rect-Rate

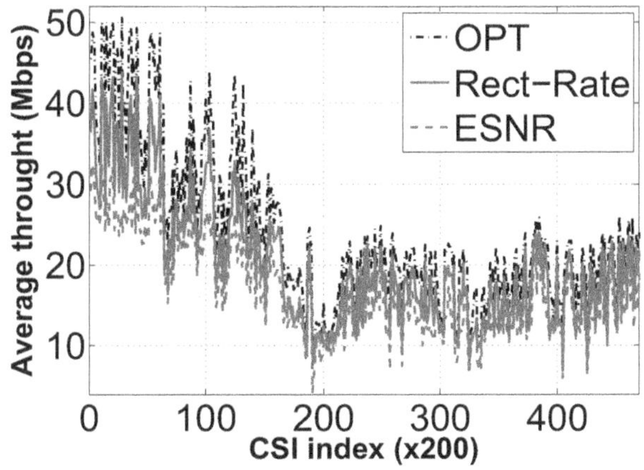

Figure 11: Throughput comparison for 802.11 SISO rates in human-speed mobility.

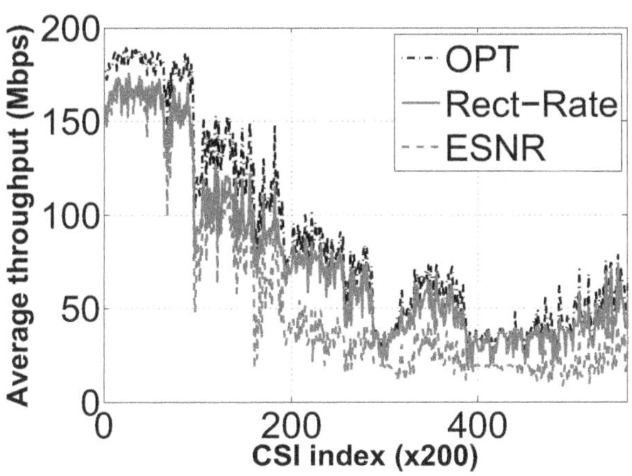

Figure 12: Throughput comparison for 802.11 MIMO rates in human-speed mobility.

and ESNR, with respect to OPT, for each transmitted packet. We classify the transmitted packets into three categories: over-selected, accurate, and under-selected data rates. Rect-Rate selects correct rates for about 70% of packets. The performance gap between Rect-Rate and OPT attributes to the 20% under-selected and 10% over-selected data rates. In comparison, ESNR has nearly half transmissions with under-selected data rates, which primarily limit its throughput.

802.11 MIMO rates. The performance of the two approaches with MIMO rates is similar to that in Figure 11. From the statistics, we find that the Rect-Rate outperforms ESNR by 33.8% on average and up to 78.2% occasionally. Referring to OPT, we observe that the fractions of the accurate data rate selection are 52% and 38% for Rect-Rate and ESNR, respectively. For 80% of transmissions, throughput gaps of Rect-Rate and ESNR (to OPT) are less than 17 Mbit/s and 35 Mbit/s, respectively. In addition, Rect-Rate tracks the performance of OPT within 14.3% on average, while ESNR is only within 34.4%.

Accelerated mobility. To evaluate each approach in different mobile environments, we sample the CSI trace, collected when the receiver moves at a walking speed, to accelerate the mobility of the sender. We sample the trace every c CSIs to form a new trace,

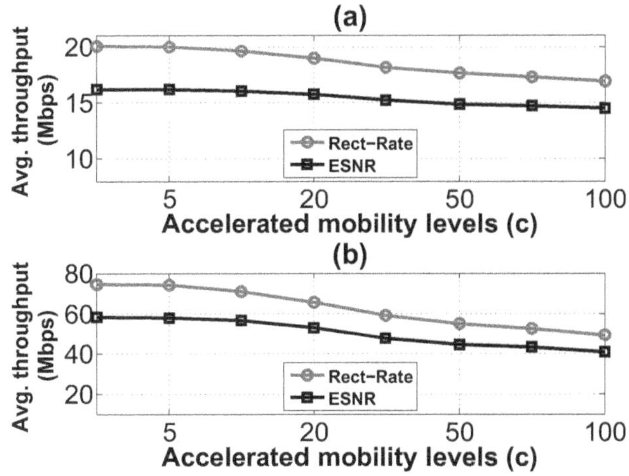

Figure 13: Throughput comparison with faster mobility for 802.11 **(a)** SISO; **(b)** MIMO rates.

which simulates a varying channel that the channel dynamics are accelerated c times. We evaluate the effect of mobility on each approach in Figure 13. Both approaches select the current data rate based on the past CSI measurement. They implicitly rely on the correlation between the current channel quality and the previous one. When the sampling interval c is increased to accelerate channel dynamics, the performance of both approaches decreases. OPT is not affected, and we omit it in Figure 13. But as c varies from one to 100, Rect-Rate can still outperform ESNR for both SISO and MIMO rates. Rect-Rate achieves 21% and 24% average throughput gains for SISO rates in Figure 13 (a) and for MIMO rates in Figure 13 (b), respectively.

Burst errors (interference). To evaluate the performance of each approach against burst errors [18, 25, 37], we repeat the CSI trace collection in the laboratory, but in addition to the background traffic, we introduce an external interferer close to the receiver and a hidden terminal to the sender. The interferer periodically generates interference packets without carrier sense, with an interval between two error bursts of 11-packets' worth of airtime. We vary the error burst duration from two to eight packets in the experiment. To deal with burst errors, the sender will use the next lower rate if CSI feedback is not received after certain packets transmitted [14], which is set at two in our evaluation.

Figure 14(a) illustrates a snapshot of the rate selections of two approaches when the burst duration is five. When burst errors occur, two approaches both gradually decrease their data rates. When such an interference disappears, after one packet gets successfully received by the receiver, the sender can promptly adjust its data rate according to the CSI feedback. The result indicates that the CSI-based rate selection approaches can promptly recover from burst errors. In Figure 14 (b), due to the accurate PER prediction, Rect-Rate outperforms ESNR by 30% on average when the burst error duration varies from two to eight packets.

4.2.2 *Partial packet recovery*

We evaluate the following approaches:

1. **Maranello:** It is the most recent partial packet recovery approach with the best reported performance [14]. It divides a packet into blocks and only retransmits erroneous blocks when the transmission fails.
2. **Rect-Maranello:** Before a packet transmission, Rect-Maranello uses Rect-Rate to select the data rate and further evaluates the

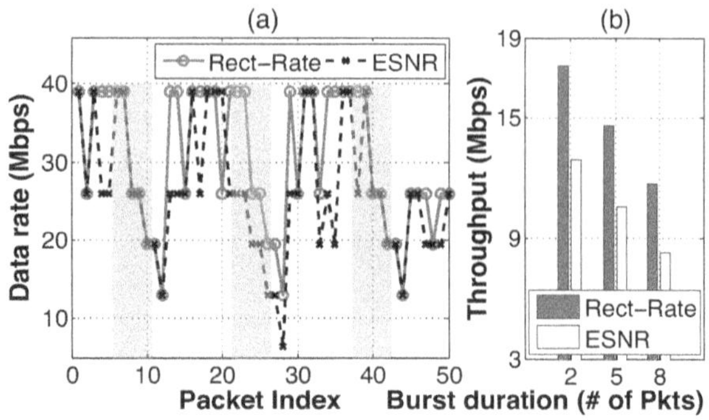

Figure 14: Throughput in presence of burst errors. Shadow area indicates burst errors. **(a)** Rate selection snapshot; **(b)** Average throughput under different burst error durations.

PER of the next higher rate. If this PER is not sufficiently high, *e.g.*, < 0.3, Rect-Maranello transmits the packet with the augmented rate. It degrades to the original Maranello when the transmission fails. The data rate is not increased for retransmissions in the experiment.

3. **Agg-Maranello:** To understand the utility of the accurate PER prediction, we also compare against an aggressive design, Agg-Maranello, that always augments to the next higher data rate to harness more partial packets, suggested by μACK [58]. Similar to Rect-Maranello, the data rate is not increased for retransmissions neither.

We use the CSI trace collected in §4.1. Figure 15 depicts the throughput gains achieved by the three approaches, normalized to the throughput of Rect-Rate (without the data rate augmentation) in §4.2.1. As Rect-Rate can select the highest data rate with a low PER, the throughput gain of Maranello is limited, *e.g.*, 1.1× on average. Maranello has an advantage only when the transmission failure occurs occasionally. For Agg-Maranello, we find that it even performs worse than Rect-Rate in our experiment. It is because when the data rate is increased, the PER of the next rate could be moderate or very high. Without an accurate PER assessment, aggressively increasing the data rate may cause huge transmission overhead, which overwhelms the throughput gain from the higher rate. In our experiment, Agg-Maranello causes a 2% throughput loss. Benefiting from accurate PER prediction, Rect-Maranello can wisely increase the rate to make a full use of the channel bandwidth. According to the statistics, Rect-Maranello outperforms Maranello and Agg-Maranello by 16% and 30% on average, and 50% and 400% at most. Rect-Maranello performs within 5% of OPT. μACK in [58] can also harvest such a throughput gain with the help of extra hardware (additional antennas working on another frequency band). However, Figure 15 shows that without an accurate PER prediction, it is challenging to leverage partial packet recovery to fully utilize the channel bandwidth.

To further analyze the throughput each approach achieves, we find: Rect-Maranello selects correct rates for most packets. For Maranello, 37% of rates could be augmented. For Agg-Maranello, around half of the rates are over-selected.

4.2.3 Unequal bit protection

Packet bits may have different importance, and one of the most representative applications is media streaming [1, 43]. For example, in MPEG-4 video, the packet header is more important than the payload, and I-frames in payload in turn have a higher priority than other frames, *e.g.*, P and B frames. The media player can tolerate

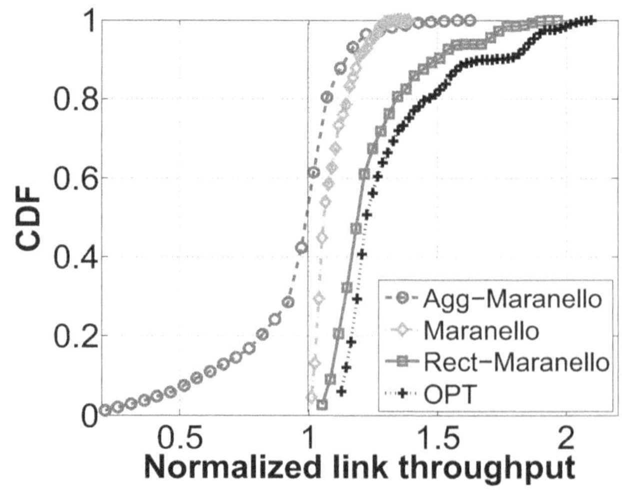

Figure 15: Throughput comparison for partial packet recovery.

decoding errors in these frames, playing the video with a reduced quality. In contrast, when errors occur in I-frames, video quality drops significantly, and when errors occur in the header, the entire packet cannot contribute to the video playback. We evaluate the following approaches for this application:

1. **Rect-Video:** Each packet consists of multiple frames and a fixed-length header. Prior to the packet transmission, sender uses the EVP threshold to identify "safe" ranges in one data bit period introduced in Figure 9 and expand them to the entire packet. In our current design, we provide two safety levels: "safe" and "unsafe", where the EVP threshold used for this classification has been determined in §4.1.3. The packet header and I-frames are given a higher priority than other frames, which are placed in "safe" ranges sequentially. When "safe" ranges are occupied, the remaining bits are sequentially placed in "unsafe" ranges. In our current design, we use only one byte of extra overhead to record the original position of I-frames in the packet for the receiver to recover the original packet.
2. **Stan-Video:** Denotes the existing approach that treats every bit equally in the transmission. We adopt Rect-Rate to select rates for Stan-Video and focus on the performance comparison for the unequal error protection.

We adopt the standard metric, peak signal-to-noise ratio (PSNR), to measure the video quality [1]. PSNR is on the log scale, and a differences above 0.5 dB are visually detectable. When PSNR is above 37 dB, the video quality is considered to be "excellent" and "bad" when PSNR drops below 20 dB [8, 43]. We use the CSI trace collected in § 4.2.1 for evaluation. The sender generates a video streaming to the receiver at 30 frames per second. The video is MPEG-4 encoded and looped until the end of the experiment. In Figure 16, we plot the CDF of PSNRs achieved by the two approaches. We do not distinguish PSNRs that are greater than 40 dB since the video quality is excellent when it is above 37 dB. Similarly, we do not distinguish PSNRs less than 18 dB. From the figure, we see that half the time, the video quality in Rect-Video can be nearly 6 dB higher than Stan-Video, and the improvement can be up to 11 dB at most. The video quality gain of Rect-Video comes from the good protection of the packet header and I-frames.

In Figure 17, we further evaluate two approaches in three typical 802.11 WLANs environments: a open-space academic hall, a large library, and an indoor office, where the frequency selective fading levels increase. Figure 17 shows that Rect-Video outperforms Stan-

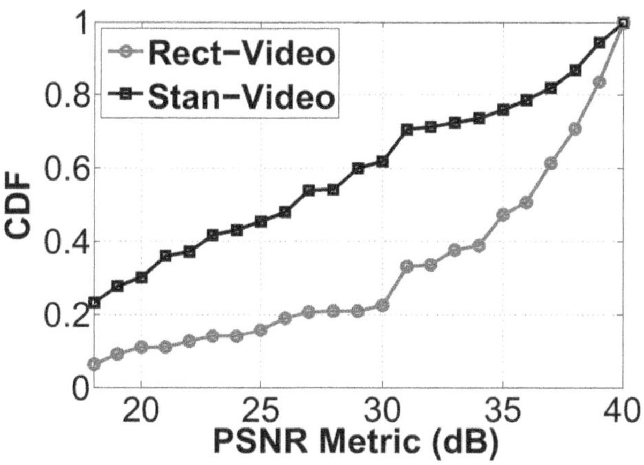

Figure 16: CDF of PSNRs achieved by two approaches.

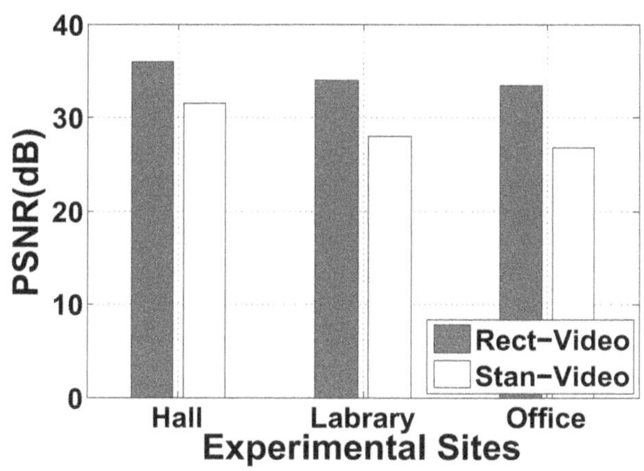

Figure 17: PSNR comparison at different positions.

Video in all three scenarios. The average PSNR gain over Stan-Video is at least 4.5 dB in hall and up to 6.6 dB in office.

5. DISCUSSION

Relationship with BER. One error event in the decoder usually results in a sequence of decoded data bit errors. The consequent "smearing" of probabilities across the data bits causes the BER of one data bit to be raised by errors from prior data bits. Hence, BER does not provide a direct measurement due to the dependence introduced among different packet bits by the encoding, *i.e.*, PER is not equal to $1 - \prod_{i=1}^{N}(1 - p_i)$, where p_i is the BER of each data bit i and N is the total number of packet bits. In contrast, there does exist a PER-EVP relationship (§2.2.1).

Packet prediction rationale. The prediction of packet reception is possible because the channel coherence time, within which the channel quality is relatively stable [10]. 802.11 Wi-Fi is mainly targeted at a static environment or an environment with walking-speed mobility, where the channel coherence time varies from tens of milliseconds to seconds. Since the transmission delay of one wireless packet is about one to two milliseconds, Recitation can confidently predict for future packets in the above environments.

Interfering packets. Recitation focuses on predicting wireless packet reception when packet collisions are not the dominant factor limiting throughput. While Recitation does not predict the effect of interfering packets [47, 48], the sender can promptly adjust its data rate upon receiving the CSI feedback from the receiver when interference disappears (see Figure 14). Hence, Recitation can act quickly against burst errors and achieve experimental gains in the presence of background traffic in unlicensed Wi-Fi spectrum (§4). Joint consideration of Recitation and interfering packets is possible, *e.g.*, exploring the SINR metric.

Scope of Recitation. The design of Recitation focuses on 802.11 WLANs, in which convolutional codes is the default coding scheme and LDPC codes is an emerging alternative. The packet bit processing in commodity Wi-Fi NICs is regulated by 802.11 standards and the sole input of our design is CSI. Recitation is thus generic for different Wi-Fi chipsets.

6. RELATED WORK

Subcarrier aggregation-based techniques. ESNR [12] has the advantage that it can be derived from the CSI in a Wi-Fi packet header and can translate a wideband channel to an equivalent narrow band channel to facilitate the upper-layer analysis. But as we show in §4, ESNR leaves performance on the table due to the approximation of channel quality with a single SNR value. Since the packet error rate (PER) versus SNR relationship has a very narrow transition range, a small inaccuracy in SNR measurement can cause a significant PER prediction error. In addition, ESNR does not provide per-bit BER confidences within each packet, making it unsuitable for our purposes. SoftRate [52] bit rate adaptation similarly aggregates BER across subcarriers in a similar computation to ESNR. Recitation emulates SoftRate's per-bit confidence computation with just the CSI information from the header. Error estimating codes (EEC) [8] adopt an advanced sampling technique to estimate the data bit BER, but only estimate the average packet BER.

Approximate communication. Apex [43] demonstrates the utility of unequal error protection for the purpose of media applications such as video or voice communication that can tolerate loss. While Apex demonstrates convincing experimental gains for video applications, it is designed and implemented only for 16-QAM and higher-order QAM modulations [43, Table 1, Table 2]. Recitation's design, in contrast, works with any QAM modulation. In additional, Recitation does not require any hardware modifications, unlike Apex—it is realizable on commodity Wi-Fi chipsets.

Softcast [19], FlexCast [1], and ParCast [29] recently propose novel joint source-channel coding schemes to deliver video quality that unequally protect video contents. Those works, however, either require additional physical layer information support (SoftPHY [20] in FlexCast) or a completely new physical design (Softcast and ParCast). On the contrary, Recitation enables unequal error protection via the CSI information from the packet header available on commodity Wi-Fi chipsets.

Partial packet recovery. Partial packet recovery approaches such as PPR [21], SOFT [55], Maranello [14], ZipTx [28] and Unite [56] minimize retransmission overhead. They have the advantage when packet collisions are the dominant factor limiting throughput or the channel is extremely lossy even the lowest data rate cannot reliably transmit a packet. Given the data rate selected bit-rate adaptation selects with a low PER, the throughput may still increase when the bit-rate is further augmented, if the throughput gain from the higher data rate outweighs the retransmission overheads. The accurate PER Recitation predicts enables such an assessment to fully utilize the channel.

Bit-rate adaptation. A variety of SNR-based bit-rate adaptation approaches exist, *e.g.* PBAR [16], OAR [42], CHARM [22], BlockRate [49], and Medusa [44]. Due to frequency selective fading,

Zhang *et al.* [59] and Camp *et al.* [6] observe that the SNR measurement needs careful calibration. To overcome the SNR measurement issue, many solutions utilize packet reception statistics, *e.g.*, SampleRate [5], RRAA [54], and MIMO-Rate [35]. Shen *et al.* [46] further studies the rate adaptation in multi-user MIMO networks. [3, 7, 24] focus on the rate adaptation analysis, [23, 39] concentrate on the energy/power control, and [32, 62] explore to correlate the link behaviors to rate adaptation in a target network. Recent studies further propose to adapt data rates by directly measuring coded BER [52] or symbol-level dispersion in AccuRate [45], but require specialized hardware. EEC [8] can adapt rates based on the estimated data bit BER without the hardware modification. Although most of above works are CSI-agnostic, they mainly adapt, instead of selecting, bit rates. The adaptation is less effective when channels change faster and the configuration space is more complex (*e.g.*, MIMO). The most recent approach [12] uses ESNR for the bit-rate selection. Benefiting from an accurate PER prediction, Recitation outperforms the best reported performance for both 802.11 SISO and MIMO rates.

Other physical-layer designs. Bhartia *et al.* [4] proposes a smart interleaver to directly map data bits to different subcarriers based on the bit importance. FARA [38] designs independent modulation and interleaving for each subcarrier to maximize throughput on each subcarrier. Both approaches harness frequency selective fading by substantially redesigning the current 802.11 PHY. However, the hardware-level implementation and transceiver coordination difficulties are the two major hurdles that prohibit them being adopted in practice. Recent rateless codes such as Strider [11] and Spinal [36] can avoid the channel measurement. They however require either a new PHY design [11] or dedicated hardware to accelerate the rateless decoding [36], not applicable to the 802.11 PHY. COLLIE [40] is a system that statistically discriminates between loss due to collision and loss due to a weak received SNR. It is thus complementary to Recitation in much the same way SoftRate is.

7. CONCLUSION

We have described Recitation, a fully software-based system that uses lightweight CSI information from Wi-Fi NICs to make precise predictions about the number and location of bit errors in subsequent packets. It works with 802.11's standard convolutional codes, and recent LDPC codes. We have shown significant performance improvements for three different applications: bit rate adaptation, partial packet recovery, and unequal protection-based video streaming.

Acknowledgments

We would like to thank the anonymous reviewers and shepherd for their useful feedback. This work is supported by Singapore MOE AcRF Tier 2 Grant MOE2012-T2-1-070 and NTU Nanyang Assistant Professorship (NAP) Grant M4080738.020. The research leading to these results has received funding from the European Research Council under the European Union's Seventh Framework Programme (FP/2007-2013) / ERC Grant Agreement no. 279976.

References

[1] S. Aditya and S. Katti. FlexCast: Graceful wireless video streaming. In *Proc. of ACM MobiCom*, 2011.

[2] A. Akella, G. Judd, S. Seshan, and P. Steenkiste. Self-management in chaotic wireless deployments. In *Proc. of ACM MobiCom*, 2005.

[3] M. Y. Arslan, K. Pelechrinis, I. Broustis, S. V. Krishnamurthy, S. Addepalli, and K. Papagiannaki. Auto-configuration of 802.11 n wlans. In *Proc. of ACM CoNEXT*, 2010.

[4] A. Bhartia, Y.-C. Chen, S. Rallapalli, and L. Qiu. Harnessing frequency diversity in Wi-Fi networks. In *Proc. of ACM MobiCom*, 2011.

[5] J. Bicket. Bit-Rate Selection in Wireless Networks. Master's thesis, Massachusetts Inst. of Technology, 2005.

[6] J. Camp and E. Knightly. Modulation rate adaptation in urban and vehicular environments: Cross-layer implementation and experimental evaluation. In *Proc. of ACM MobiCom*, 2008.

[7] P. Chaporkar, A. Proutiere, and B. Radunoviac. Rate adaptation games in wireless LANs: Nash equilibrium and price of anarchy. In *Proc. of IEEE INFOCOM*, 2010.

[8] B. Chen, Z. Zhou, Y. Zhao, and H. Yu. Efficient error estimating coding: Feasibility and applications. In *Proc. of ACM SIGCOMM*, 2010.

[9] S. K. Chilappagari and B. Vasic. Error-correction capability of column-weight-three ldpc codes. *IEEE Transactions on Information Theory*, 2009.

[10] A. Goldsmith. *Wireless communications.* Cambridge university press, 2005.

[11] A. Gudipati and S. Katti. Strider: Automatic rate adaptation and collision handling. In *Proc. of ACM SIGCOMM*, 2011.

[12] D. Halperin, W. Hu, A. Sheth, and D. Wetherall. Predictable 802.11 packet delivery from wireless channel measurements. In *Proc. of ACM SIGCOMM*, 2010.

[13] B. Han, L. Ji, S. Lee, B. Bhattacharjee, and R. R. Miller. Are all bits equal?: experimental study of IEEE 802.11 communication bit errors. *IEEE/ACM Transactions on Networking*, 2012.

[14] B. Han, A. Schulman, F. Gringoli, N. Spring, B. Bhattacharjee, L. Nava, L. Ji, S. Lee, and R. Miller. Maranello: Practical partial packet recovery for 802.11. In *Proc. of USENIX NSDI*, 2010.

[15] J. Han, C. Qian, X. Wang, D. Ma, J. Zhao, P. Zhang, W. Xi, and Z. Jiang. Twins: Device-free object tracking using passive tags. In *Proc. of IEEE INFOCOM*, 2014.

[16] G. Holland, N. Vaidya, and P. Bahl. A rate-adaptive MAC protocol for multi-hop wireless networks. In *Proc. of ACM MobiCom*, 2001.

[17] IEEE Standard for Information Technology—Part 11: Wireless LAN Medium Access Control (MAC) and Physical Layer Specifications, 2012.

[18] K. Jain, J. Padhye, V. N. Padmanabhan, and L. Qiu. Impact of interference on multi-hop wireless network performance. In *Proc. of ACM MobiCom*, 2003.

[19] S. Jakubczak and D. Katabi. A cross-layer design for scalable mobile video. In *Proc. of ACM MobiCom*, 2011.

[20] K. Jamieson. *The SoftPHY Abstraction: from Packets to Symbols in Wireless Network Design.* PhD thesis, MIT, 2008. http://hdl.handle.net/1721.1/41857.

[21] K. Jamieson and H. Balakrishnan. PPR: Partial packet recovery for wireless networks. In *Proc. of ACM SIGCOMM*, 2007.

[22] G. Judd, X. Wang, and P. Steenkiste. Efficient channel-aware rate adaptation in dynamic environments. In *Proc. of ACM MobiSys*, 2008.

[23] M. O. Khan, V. Dave, Y.-C. Chen, O. Jensen, L. Qiu, A. Bhartia, and S. Rallapalli. Model-driven energy-aware rate adaptation. In *Proc. of ACM MobiHoc*, 2013.

[24] R. Kumar, S. Tati, F. De Mello, S. V. Krishnamurthy, and T. L. Porta. Network coding aware rate selection in multi-rate IEEE 802.11. In *Proc. of IEEE ICNP*, 2010.

[25] L. E. Li, R. Alimi, D. Shen, H. Viswanathan, and Y. R. Yang. A general algorithm for interference alignment and cancellation in wireless networks. In *Proc. of IEEE INFOCOM*, 2010.

[26] L. E. Li, K. Tan, Y. Xu, H. Viswanathan, and Y. R. Yang. Remap decoding: Simple retransmission permutation can resolve overlapping channel collisions. In *Proc. of ACM MobiCom*, 2010.

[27] R. LiKamWa, B. Priyantha, M. Philipose, L. Zhong, and P. Bahl. Energy characterization and optimization of image sensing toward continuous mobile vision. In *Proc. of ACM MobiSys*, 2013.

[28] K. C.-J. Lin, N. Kushman, and D. Katabi. Ziptx: Harnessing partial packets in 802.11 networks. In *Proc. of ACM MobiCom*, 2008.

[29] X. L. Liu, W. Hu, Q. Pu, F. Wu, and Y. Zhang. Parcast: Soft video delivery in MIMO-OFDM WLANs. In *Proc. of ACM MobiCom*, 2012.

[30] F. Lu, G. M. Voelker, and A. C. Snoeren. SloMo: Downclocking Wi-Fi communication. In *Proc. of USENIX NSDI*, 2013.

[31] D. J. MacKay. Good error-correcting codes based on very sparse matrices. *IEEE Transactions on Information Theory*, 1999.

[32] M. Mirza, P. Barford, X. Zhu, S. Banerjee, and M. Blodgett. Fingerprinting 802.11 rate adaption algorithms. In *Proc. of IEEE INFOCOM*, 2011.

[33] A. Miu, H. Balakrishnan, and C. E. Koksal. Improving loss resilience with multi-radio diversity in wireless networks. In *Proc. of ACM MobiCom*, 2005.

[34] J. Pang, B. Greenstein, M. Kaminsky, D. McCoy, and S. Seshan. WiFi-Reports: Improving wireless network selection with collaboration. In *Proc. of ACM MobiSys*, 2009.

[35] I. Pefkianakis, Y. Hu, S. H. Wong, H. Yang, and S. Lu. MIMO rate adaptation in 802.11n wireless networks. In *Proc. of ACM MobiCom*, 2010.

[36] J. Perry, P. Iannucci, K. Fleming, H. Balakrishnan, and D. Shah. Spinal codes. In *Proc. of ACM SIGCOMM*, 2012.

[37] L. Qiu, Y. Zhang, F. Wang, M. K. Han, and R. Mahajan. A general model of wireless interference. In *Proc. of ACM MobiCom*, 2007.

[38] H. Rahul, F. Edalat, D. Katabi, and C. G. Sodini. Frequency-aware rate adaptation and MAC protocols. In *Proc. of ACM MobiCom*, 2009.

[39] K. Ramachandran, R. Kokku, H. Zhang, and M. Gruteser. Symphony: synchronous two-phase rate and power control in 802.11 WLANs. In *Proc. of ACM MobiSys*, 2008.

[40] S. Rayanchu, A. Mishra, D. Agrawal, S. Saha, and S. Banerjee. Diagnosing wireless packet losses in 802.11: Separating collision from weak signal. In *Proc. of IEE INFOCOM*, 2008.

[41] T. J. Richardson and R. L. Urbanke. Efficient encoding of low-density parity-check codes. *IEEE Transactions on Information Theory*, 2001.

[42] B. Sadeghi, V. Kanodia, A. Sabharwal, and E. Knightly. Opportunistic media access for multirate ad hoc networks. In *Proc. of ACM MobiCom*, 2002.

[43] S. Sen, S. Gilani, S. Srinath, S. Schmitt, and S. Banerjee. Design and implementation of an "approximate" communication system for wireless media applications. In *Proc. of ACM SIGCOMM*, 2010.

[44] S. Sen, N. K. Madabhushi, and S. Banerjee. Scalable Wi-Fi media delivery through adaptive broadcasts. In *Proc. of USENIX NSDI*, 2010.

[45] S. Sen, N. Santhapuri, R. R. Choudhury, and S. Nelakuditi. AccuRate: Constellation based rate estimation in wireless networks. In *Proc. of USENIX NSDI*, 2010.

[46] W. Shen, Y. Tung, K. Lee, K. C. Lin, S. Gollakota, D. Katabi, and M.-S. Chen. Rate adaptation for 802.11 multiuser MIMO networks. In *Proc. of ACM MobiCom*, 2012.

[47] K. Srinivasan, M. Jain, J. I. Choi, T. Azim, E. S. Kim, P. Levis, and B. Krishnamachari. The κ factor: inferring protocol performance using inter-link reception correlation. In *Proc. of ACM MobiCom*, 2010.

[48] K. Srinivasan, M. A. Kazandjieva, S. Agarwal, and P. Levis. The β-factor: measuring wireless link burstiness. In *Proc. of ACM SenSys*, 2008.

[49] X. Tie, A. Seetharam, A. Venkataramani, D. Ganesan, and D. L. Goeckel. Anticipatory wireless bitrate control for blocks. In *Proc. of ACM CoNEXT*, 2011.

[50] D. Tse and P. Viswanath. *Fundamentals of Wireless Communication*. Cambridge University Press, 2005.

[51] A. J. Viterbi. Convolutional codes and their performance in communication systems. *IEEE Transactions on Communication Technology*, 1971.

[52] M. Vutukuru, H. Balakrishnan, and K. Jamieson. Cross-layer wireless bit rate adaptation. In *Proc. of ACM SIGCOMM*, 2009.

[53] Y. Wang, J. Liu, Y. Chen, M. Gruteser, J. Yang, and H. Liu. E-eyes: Device-free location-oriented activity identification using fine-grained WiFi signatures. In *Proc. of ACM MobiCom*, 2014.

[54] S. H. Wong, H. Yang, S. Lu, and V. Bharghavan. Robust rate adaptation for 802.11 wireless networks. In *Proc. of ACM MobiCom*, 2006.

[55] G. R. Woo, P. Kheradpour, D. Shen, and D. Katabi. Beyond the bits: cooperative packet recovery using physical layer information. In *Proc. of ACM MobiCom*, 2007.

[56] J. Xie, W. Hu, and Z. Zhang. Revisiting partial packet recovery in 802.11 wireless lans. In *Proc. of ACM MobiSys*, 2011.

[57] X. Xie, X. Zhang, and K. Sundaresan. Adaptive feedback compression for MIMO networks. In *Proc. of ACM MobiCom*, 2013.

[58] J. Zhang, H. Shen, K. Tan, R. Chandra, Y. Zhang, and Q. Zhang. Frame retransmissions considered harmful: improving spectrum efficiency using micro-acks. In *Proc. of ACM MobiCom*, 2012.

[59] J. Zhang, K. Tan, J. Zhao, H. Wu, and Y. Zhang. A practical SNR-guided rate adaptation. In *Proc. of IEEE INFOCOM*, 2008.

[60] L. Zhang, X.-Y. Li, W. Huang, K. Liu, S. Zong, X. Jian, P. Feng, T. Jung, and Y. Liu. It starts with igaze: Visual attention driven networking with smart glasses. In *Proc. of ACM MobiCom*, 2014.

[61] X. Zhang and K. G. Shin. E-MiLi: Energy-minimizing idle listening in wireless networks. In *Proc. of ACM MobiCom*, 2011.

[62] X. Zhou, J. Zhao, and G. Yang. Correlation based rate adaptation via insights from incomplete observations in 802.11 networks. In *Proc. of IEEE ICC*, 2007.

Hekaton: Efficient and Practical Large-Scale MIMO

Xiufeng Xie
University of Wisconsin-Madison
xiufeng@ece.wisc.edu

Eugene Chai
NEC Labs America
eugene@nec-labs.com

Xinyu Zhang
University of Wisconsin-Madison
xyzhang@ece.wisc.edu

Karthikeyan Sundaresan
NEC Labs America
karthiks@nec-labs.com

Amir Khojastepour
NEC Labs America
amir@nec-labs.com

Sampath Rangarajan
NEC Labs America
sampath@nec-labs.com

ABSTRACT

Large-scale multiuser MIMO (MU-MIMO) systems have the potential for multi-fold scaling of network capacity. The research community has recognized this theoretical potential and developed architectures [1,2] with large numbers of RF chains. Unfortunately, building the hardware with a large number of RF chains is challenging in practice. CSI data transport and computational overhead of MU-MIMO beamforming can also become prohibitive under large network scale. Furthermore, it is difficult to physically append extra RF chains on existing communication equipments to support such large-scale MU-MIMO architectures.

In this paper, we present Hekaton, a novel large-scale MU-MIMO framework that combines legacy MU-MIMO beamforming with phased-array antennas. The core of Hekaton is a two-level beamforming architecture. First, the phased-array antennas steer spatial beams toward each downlink user to reduce channel correlation and suppress the cross-talk interference in the RF domain (for beamforming gain), then we adopt legacy digital beamforming to eliminate the interference between downlink data streams (for spatial multiplexing gain). In this way, Hekaton realizes a good fraction of potential large-scale MU-MIMO gains even under the limited RF chain number on existing communication equipments.

We evaluate the performance of Hekaton through over-the-air testbed built over the WARPv3 platform and trace-driven emulation. In the evaluations, Hekaton can improve single-cell throughput by up to 2.5× over conventional MU-MIMO with a single antenna per RF chain, while using the same transmit power.

1. INTRODUCTION

Multi-User MIMO (MU-MIMO) systems allow a single transmitter with multiple antennas to serve multiple downlink users (*e.g.*, cellphones) concurrently using the same spectrum resource. Every single antenna is driven by one entire *RF chain* that consists of many PHY hardware components such as the baseband processor, the de/modulator, power amplifier and the ADC/DAC.

Theoretically, we have the potential to scale up the network throughput multiple-folds by increasing the number of RF chains. Several large-scale platforms, such as Argos [1] and BigStation [2], have recognized this potential and successfully demonstrated research platforms with a large number of antennas. These potential gains are critical for 5G cellular network and future WiFi network to meet the sharply increasing throughput demands. Unfortunately, we will encounter difficulties in achieving such gains in practice.

***(i)* Energy-Efficiency (bits-per-Joule).** To scale up the MU-MIMO downlink capacity, we add more RF chains (and thus more antennas) to the base station. However, the rank of the MU-MIMO channel in a particular environment is limited [3], *i.e.*, there is an upperbound for the multiplexing gain, which only depends on the environment, regardless of what kind of equipment is used. When we reach this limit, further increase in the number of antennas (and RF chains) only improves the beamforming gain. The rate of capacity scaling will thus fall behind the increasing rate of energy consumption, and the *energy-efficiency* will decrease. This is evident in MU-MIMO systems with large antenna number N, where serving N users can steeply degrade the performance due to the tightness of the degrees of freedom at the base station. In this case, the maximum downlink capacity is achieved when serving less than N users. This effect has been reported in existing MU-MIMO research works [1, 2, 4], where number of costly RF chains needs to be $1.5\times \sim 2\times$ the downlink user number to guarantee the channel orthogonality between these users.

***(ii)* High Overhead.** The *coordination overhead* of a MU-MIMO system increases linearly with the number of antennas. Before each MU-MIMO downlink beamforming, the base station must send a probe from each of its antennas, in turn, to obtain the channel state information (CSI) between each of its antennas and each user antenna involved in the transmission. Note that current LTE networks are typically Frequency Division Duplexing (FDD) networks. This means that different frequency bands are used for uplink and downlink transmissions. Hence, the implicit feedback [5] mechanisms that are used to reduce CSI feedback overhead cannot be employed here. As we increase the number of RF-chains/antennas on the base station, the overhead due to these measurements can easily overwhelm the capacity gains from having more antennas. Furthermore, the computational overhead of the commonly used Zero-Forcing Beamforming (ZFBF) mechanism can become prohibitive in existing large-scale MU-MIMO systems. Novel beamforming mechanism [1] or hardware design [2] are proposed to address this issue, which, however, deteriorate the backward compatibility.

***(iii)* No Standards Support.** Existing LTE and WiFi standards only support up to 8 MU-MIMO UEs/clients. This is a far cry from the hundreds of users envisioned for large-scale MU-MIMO networks [1]. Support for large-scale MU-MIMO systems is planned for 5G networks, but the 5G standard is not expected to be widely available before the year 2020. Given the complexities involved in upgrading LTE BSs or WiFi APs, it will be difficult to increase the number of RF-chains and antennas on the base station in a non-

MobiCom'15, September 7–11, 2015, Paris, France.
 ISBN 978-1-4503-3619-2/15/09...$15.00.
DOI: http://dx.doi.org/10.1145/2789168.2790116.

standards-compliant manner. In spite of these challenges, it is well-accepted that large-scale MU-MIMO systems offer the best capacity scaling potential for future wireless networks. The key question then is: *can we achieve a good fraction of these gains in existing systems in a standards-compliant manner?*

In this paper, we present Hekaton, a large-scale MU-MIMO framework for indoor environments (*e.g.*, LTE femtocell and WiFi). Hekaton stems from the key insight that performance gains in MU-MIMO networks consist of two components: multiplexing gains and beamforming gains. Multiplexing gains depend on the number of transmitted streams, each of which requires at least one separate RF chain[1]. On the other hand, beamforming gains depend on the number of antennas used to transmit each steam. In conventional MU-MIMO, every single antenna is driven by one entire RF chain, which enforces a tradeoff between multiplexing gain and beamformin gain under the base station's given number of RF chains. Hekaton eliminates this tradeoff by equipping every RF chain on the base station with a phased-array antenna that consists of multiple antenna elements each. As a result, the number of base station antennas is no longer bounded by the number of RF-chains. Hekaton can thus increase the beamforming gains independently of the number of RF chains.

Hekaton addresses the MU-MIMO scalability challenges in the following ways.

***(i)* Scaling up the beamforming gain.** Hekaton increases only the beamforming gains through the addition of phased-array antennas. Note that even though phased-arrays do require an energy source, the power consumed[2] is typically very small [6]. Hence, given the same energy-budget of the base station, Hekaton increases the capacity and thus, the energy efficiency over MU-MIMO under the same number of RF chains.

Furthermore, the multiplexing gain is practically limited by the *rank* of the channel [3]. Any additional RF chains beyond the channel rank can essentially be only used towards improving beamforming gains. Hekaton enables us to increase beamforming gains without unnecessary increase in the number of RF chains beyond the maximum channel rank.

***(ii)* Low coordination overhead.** A by-product of the improved beamforming gain is efficient inter-cell coordination. Hekaton needs only coarse-timescale analog beamforming to steer signal energy away from adjacent cells and maximize the Signal-to-Leakage Ratio (SLR). If Hekaton is not used, inter-cell coordination must occur over the fine-timescales that are used by conventional MU-MIMO-only networks.

Beamforming gains can be obtained using coarse-timescale control while multiplexing gains must be obtained using fine-timescale, frame-by-frame coordination. Inspired by this fact, we advocate a two-level two-time-scale beamforming architecture for Hekaton, which consists of a coarse-grained *analog beamforming* component that is performed by the phased-array antenna, and a *fine-grained* digital MU-MIMO precoding component, implemented by the existing RF-chains.

The per-frame per-antenna CSI measurement overhead is largely due to the multiplexing gains of the system. Hekaton maintains this overhead as it only increases the beamforming gains. The phased-array antenna only needs to be updated on a coarse timescale (*e.g.*, every 200ms in our implementation) and the effort required for each update is small.

[1]The RF chain consists of many PHY hardware components such as the baseband processor, the de/modulator, power amplifier and the ADC/DAC.

[2]The power is used to operate the codebook and program the phase shifters. It does not depend on the transmit power.

***(iii)* Retrofitted solution.** Hekaton extends existing architectures with phased-array antennas along with associated updates to the schedulers (in LTE) and software drivers (in WiFi). No changes to the LTE and WiFi standards, or changes to the wireless transceiver hardware is necessary. Hence, Hekaton is backward compatible with existing wireless infrastructure. For example, the deployment of Hekaton does not require approval from the 3GPP.

However, using phased-arrays in practice raises an important challenge: how does one steer beam of the analog phased-array efficiently? Unlike the case with traditional non-Hekaton MU-MIMO arrays, Hekaton cannot obtain channel information from each antenna element of the phased-array and therefore cannot directly compute the optimal downlink beam pattern from the CSI. Previous uses of phased-array antennas [7] exhaustively probe all possible beam directions and select the one that results in the highest SNR. Unfortunately, the overhead of such an approach scales *exponentially* with the number of phased-array antennas and the size of each antenna array.

Hekaton employs a novel compressive-sensing algorithm to steer the analog phased-array with only a *constant* overhead, regardless of the number of phased-array antennas or the size of each one. The downlink beam is steered towards the angle-of-arrival (AoA) of the strongest signal path from the target user. There are infinitely many possible AoAs over which to search for this direction. Fortunately, in real-world channels, the AoAs that result in strong signal energy at the user are clustered into 3-5 groups, and are thus *sparse*. We exploit this sparsity to select beam directions with a fraction of the overhead of other typical approaches [8]. We note that compressive sensing (CS) has been used previously for AoA measurements [9]. However, such approaches typically require one RF chain per antenna. Our novelty lies in our application of compressive sensing to phased-array antennas that are simply attached to existing RF chains. *This is the key algorithm that now enables phased-array antennas to be used together with existing basestations efficiently and effectively.*

We implemented and evaluated Hekaton on a WARP testbed. Hekaton , with two RF chains, achieves a throughput gain of $2.5\times$ over non-Hekaton MU-MIMO.

We will motivate our design in §2 and describe the key elements of Hekaton in §3. We then cover the design details of Hekaton in §4, §5 and §6. We discuss experimental evaluation in §7 and §8. Additional discussions are in §9 and related work are reviewed in §10. §11 contains the conclusion.

2. BACKGROUND AND MOTIVATION

2.1 MU-MIMO Background

Multi-User MIMO (MU-MIMO) enables one transmitter with multiple antennas to send concurrent data streams to *multiple* users with one or more antennas on each. As a comparison, in *single-user* MIMO (SU-MIMO), all receiving antennas rest on a single device. Assume the MU-MIMO transmitter has N antennas and each MU-MIMO receiver has one antenna, then the *total* number of MU-MIMO receivers M cannot exceed the number of antennas at the transmitter, i.e. $N \geq M$. The multiplexing gain depends on the total number of parallel streams of transmitted data, while the beamforming gain drives the capacity of each stream. In a typical MU-MIMO network, each antenna (on either the transmitter or the receiver) is driven by one RF chain.

2.2 MU-MIMO Capacity Scaling

In MU-MIMO, the increase in multiplexing gain without ensuring channel orthogonality between users may drastically affect the

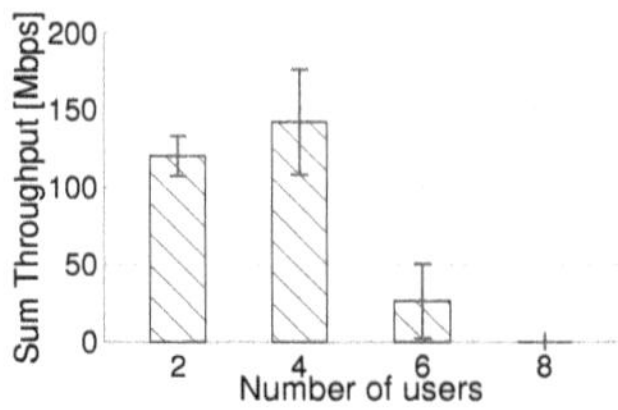

Figure 1: MU-MIMO DL throughput with increasing number of users (fixed 8 transmit antennas, 8 RF chains).

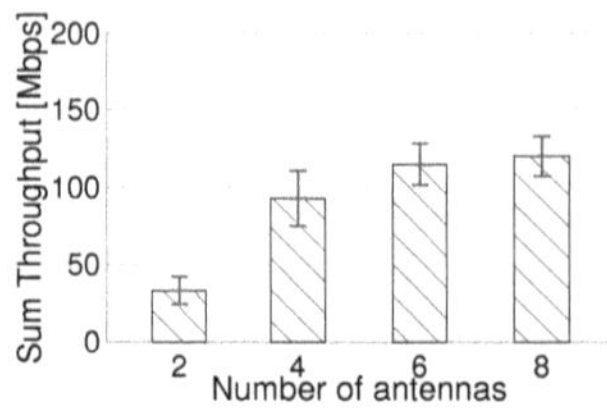

Figure 2: MU-MIMO DL throughput with increasing number of transmit antennas (fixed 2 users, 2 RF chains).

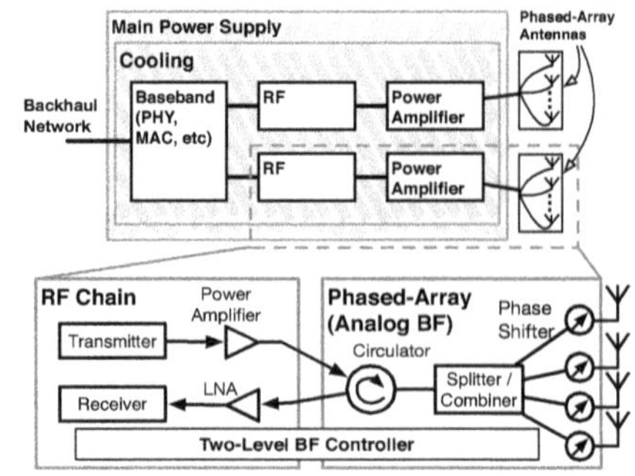

Figure 3: Hekaton basestation architecture.

downlink performance [3]. As an example, Figure 1 shows the total throughput obtained using a MU-MIMO transmitter with eight antennas and a set of single antenna receivers. To obtain these results, we place WARP radios throughout a typical office environment, collect the MU-MIMO SINR, then map the SINR to the downlink throughput using the lookup table from [10]. Details of the MU-MIMO precoder used can be found in Section 7. It is observed that the total throughput increases as we increase the number of receivers from two to four. However, as we further increase the number of of receivers from four to eight, the total throughput actually decreases. Similar observations to Figure 1 have been reported in [2, 4]. Alternatively, we can increase wireless capacity by only increasing the beamforming gains. Figure 2 shows the total throughput with two single-antenna MU-MIMO receivers. As we increase the number of antennas at the transmitter from two to eight, the total network throughput strictly increases. Note that the total transmit power is kept constant as the number of antennas increases. Also, similar observations to Figure 2 have been reported in existing works like [1, 2].

2.3 The Benefits of Beamforming Gain

Our two-level hybrid beamforming architecture introduced in §1 scales up the beamforming gain and the downlink capacity under a given number of RF chains by equipping a phased-array antenna, instead of an omnidirectional antenna, to each RF chain.

Phased-array antennas ensure that more transmit power is projected towards desired downlink users. Hence, phased-arrays increase the channel orthogonality between users. This in turn reduces the condition number of the MU-MIMO channel matrix and improves the overall downlink capacity.

More specifically, users that are spatially correlated when using omnidirectional transmit antennas may no longer be correlated after the channel preconditioning of the phased-array antennas. Thus the system can even support more "usable" downlink streams (when maximizing the downlink capacity) without adding more RF chains. For example, in conventional MU-MIMO with 8 RF chains, serving only 4 users maximizes the downlink capacity as shown in Figure 1. However, if we equip each RF chain with a phased-array antenna, then with the same 8 RF chains, serving 8 downlink users can become the best choice as shown later in our evaluations (Figure 16a).

The two-level beamforming approach brings a multitude of benefits to large-scale networks: *(i) Energy-efficiency:* The additional phased-array antennas improve beamforming gain, with only an insignificant additional power outlay. As a result, with the same number of RF chains and hence the same energy consumed, the downlink capacity can be increased significantly (up to 2.5× in our empirical measurements); *(ii) Low coordination overhead:* Beamforming gains are achieved using the phased-array. Analog beamforming can only steer directional, coarse beams towards the UEs. Hence, it only needs the coarse-timescale, long-term CSI statistics of each UE. Multiplexing gains, on the other hand, must be obtained from the fine-timescale, frame-by-frame CSI information. Hence, by increasing only the beamforming gains, we only require additional coarse-grained control feedback, which incurs very minimal additional coordination overhead; *(iii) Retrofittable:* Phased-array antennas can be easily retrofitted onto existing MU-MIMO BSs, simply by replacing the existing omni-directional/directional antennas.

A Word on Multiplexing Gains. Our focus on beamforming gains does not trivialize the importance of multiplexing gains. Rather, we emphasize the fact that beamforming gains can be achieved *independently* of multiplexing gains, and without any additional energy and with a negligible coordination overhead. Hence, even for large-scale MU-MIMO systems [1, 2] that support a much larger number of RF chains than current LTE BSs, Hekaton can still be retrofitted to those systems to obtain even greater capacity via beamforming gain increases.

3. HEKATON OVERVIEW

3.1 Architecture

The radio of a node in typical wireless networks consists of a baseband component that contains the PHY, MAC and other upper layer protocols, and an RF component that modulates baseband I/Q signals into passband signals. A power amplifier increases the transmit power of these signals before they are transmitted over the channel via the antenna. All these components share the same cooling and power supply [11]. Figure 3 shows an example of a wireless transceiver with two RF chains, where Hekaton replaces the conventional antenna on each RF chain with an analog phased-array antenna.

Analog phased-array antenna. An analog phased-array antenna consists of multiple antenna elements arranged in a fixed, pre-defined pattern. Each antenna element is connected to a single analog phase shifter. Analog passband signals received from the RF chain is split equally amongst these antenna elements.

A set of unique phase shifting values for each antenna element defines a unique signal beam direction. This is known as a *codebook entry*. The set of all codebook entries supported by the phased array are arranged into a *codebook*. The codebook is typically preloaded into the phased array. During normal operations, the phased array switches between codebook entries to change the direction where the transmitted signal energy is focused.

Digital MU-MIMO Precoding. Hekaton is designed to be backward compatible with existing MU-MIMO systems like 802.11ac and LTE. Therefore its digital MU-MIMO precoding component reuses that on existing MU-MIMO systems. It does not require

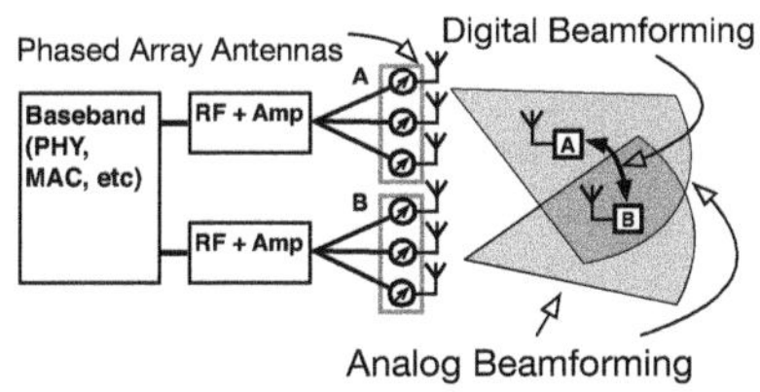

Figure 4: Hekaton operation with two RF chains.

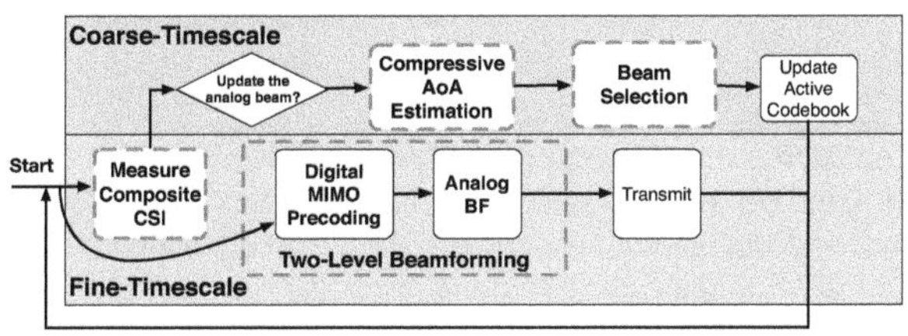

Figure 5: Hekaton two-timescale transmission.

new digital beamforming methods like in [1] to facilitate real-time large scale MU-MIMO.

Two-level beamforming. The core of Hekaton is a two-level beamforming architecture which consists of two main components: a coarse-grained *analog* beamforming enabled by the phased-array antennas, and a fine-grained *digital* MU-MIMO precoding performed by the RF chains.

Figure 4 illustrates the interaction between these two beamforming levels. Hekaton uses analog beamforming to steer signal energy in a coarse-grained fashion. Each phased-array antenna is always assigned to a unique user and it only steers the beam towards its assigned user. Digital MIMO precoding is then used to further reduce the cross-talk between users.

For example, in Figure 4, phased-array antennas A and B serve clients A and B with separate beams. The one-to-one mapping[3] between the phased-array antenna and the user is constructed to maximize the SLR, which is detailed in Section 6.1. However, since the coarse analog beamforming cannot achieve pinpoint focusing of transmitted signals, there will be residual interference between the different user. The digital MU-MIMO precoder is then used to cancel this residual interference between the downlink users.

3.2 Hekaton Operation

The two-level beamforming in Hekaton operates on two different timescales. Figure 5 shows how this two-level scheme works in practice. Each frame transmission follows a fast-timescale process, where the transmitted signal undergoes the two-level beamforming before being transmitted. The beam selection/update of the phased-array antenna occur over a slower, coarse-timescale process. The three-key components of Hekaton are:

1. Composite CSI Measurement. The Hekaton base station cannot access signal information from each of its phased-array antenna elements. Instead, given a codebook entry, the phased-array antenna combines the correspondingly phase-shifted signals from all antenna elements, and returns only this combined CSI signal to the RF chain.

2. Compressive AoA Estimation. The Hekaton base station selects the downlink beam direction (*i.e.*, the codebook entry) corresponding to the angle-of-arrival (AoA) direction with the strongest signals when it hears from the user. It is worth noting that although the channel reciprocity may not hold for an FDD system, the AoA direction of the user should still be similar across different frequencies. In fact there are many AoA-based indoor localization works using different frequency bands [8,12]. Hekaton is compatible with FDD systems as it uses codebook-based analog beamforming (8 beam patterns in our implementation), which creates a wide beam pattern and hence is robust to frequency diversity.

Unfortunately, conventional AoA estimation requires CSI measurement for each antenna element [7–9,12], which is infeasible for a Hekaton base station since it can only obtain composite CSI of all elements in a phased-array. Furthermore, an exhaustive search would require test transmissions over all possible AoAs and is too time-consuming to be practical. In Hekaton, we design a novel algorithm that can efficiently compute the AoA from just four composite CSI measurements. To the best of our knowledge, ours is the first algorithm that achieves a constant AoA measurement overhead, regardless of the number of phased-array antennas.

3. Downlink Beam Selection. Hekaton uses the AoA measurements to determine beam directions that both maximize the signal power at its intended user while minimizing the interference to users in adjacent cells. These beam directions are selected using signal-to-leakage ratio (SLR) as a metric.

We detail these components in §4, §5 and §6. We note that Hekaton can be implemented, via a two-level beamforming controller, as a minor firmware update in the downlink transmitter like a WiFi AP or an LTE eNodeB, without further hardware modifications.

4. COMPOSITE CSI MEASUREMENT

4.1 LTE Support for Composite CSI Measurement

Hekaton can be retrofitted onto existing LTE BSs. It uses three key features in current LTE BSes:

Coordinated MultiPoint (CoMP) synchronization. Each Hekaton-enabled LTE BS must measure the CSI of both its local UEs and UEs in neighbouring cells. Hence, because LTE operates using a TDMA schedule, uplink frames from neighbouring cells must be time-synchronized with those of the local cell. The LTE CoMP support ensures that this synchronization is achieved. Note that Hekaton only relies on CoMP features for inter-cell UE scheduling, and not cooperative transmissions. Hence, Hekaton does not require fast CSI/data exchange between BSes in different cells.

Coordinated scheduling. The LTE specification partitions the spectrum into multiple resource blocks (RBs), with each RB occupying a set of subcarriers for a period of time. Each UE is assigned one or more RBs for uplink transmission. With CoMP, the schedulers of different BSes coordinate to ensure that interfering uplink transmissions from different UEs are assigned non-overlapping RBs. This ensures that Hekaton can obtain a good CSI measurement from each UE.

Sounding Reference Signals (SRS). Hekaton uses the SRS that is transmitted at the end of a UE's frame for CSI measurement. CoMP support allows the BS to limit the bandwidth of the SRS to the RBs assigned by the UE. Hence, Hekaton can obtain CSI measurements from multiple non-interfering UEs concurrently.

4.2 Measuring the Composite CSI

The composite CSI is concurrently measured at all phased-arrays using uplink transmissions. Each transmission from the UE is received by all phased-arrays at the BS, and is used by each phased-array to measure the composite CSI. Figure 6 illustrates an example where Hekaton obtains upstream composite CSI from three separate UEs, A, B and C.

[3]This mapping may be suboptimal, a detailed discussion is in Section 9

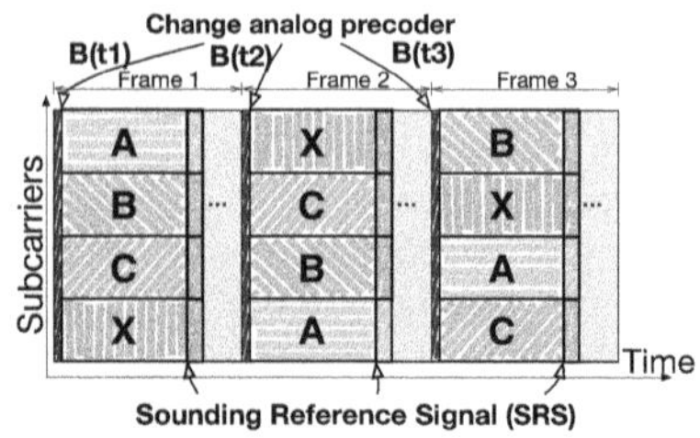

Figure 6: Obtaining the upstream CSI measurements from three UEs, A, B and C. Client X belongs to a neighbouring cell.

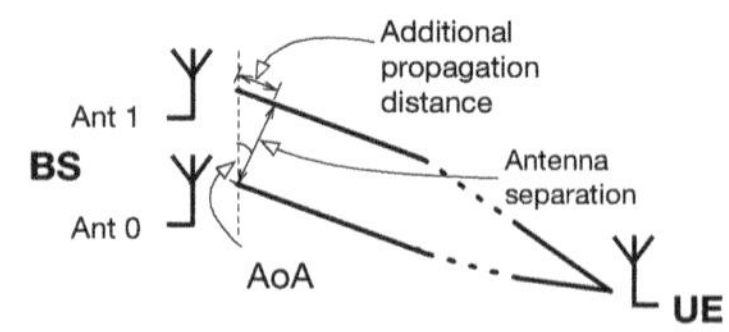

Figure 7: Arrival of a signal from the UE at two antenna elements (Ant1 and Ant2) at the BS.

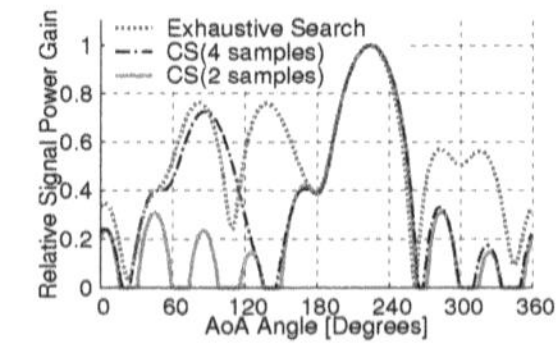

Figure 8: Azimuth signal power distribution estimated with compressive sensing algorithm.

At the first measurement frame, Hekaton randomly selects a codebook entry (corresponding to one beam direction) for each phased-array. The unmodified RF chain receives the combined signal from the phased-arrays, and computes the CSI for UEs A, B and C as per normal. Hekaton retrieves these composite CSI values from the RF chains. This process is repeated two more times, with a different random codebook entry selected for each measurement. At the end of the CSI collection step, Hekaton obtains three distinct composite CSI measurements for UEs A, B and C. Two points are worth noting here: (i) The CSI collection spans three frames. But meanwhile the data frame transmission can continue using the previous CSI since the channel coherence time usually spans multiple frames. (ii) The overhead of beam switching is very low. Modern phased-array antennas [13] can switch between codebook entries in as little as $1.2\mu s$, which is an order of magnitude smaller than the LTE subframe duration of $1ms$.

The above process is also used to measure the CSI to UEs in adjacent cells. With inter-cell time synchronization, Hekaton can also decode the SRS from UEs in adjacent cells, and obtain CSI measurements to them.

5. COMPRESSIVE AOA ESTIMATION

Hekaton employs a novel compressive-sensing based algorithm to estimate the AoA of the uplink probing signal from only a small number of composite CSI measurements. Existing AoA estimation approaches, such as those in [7, 8, 12], incur too large of a probing overhead and cannot be used efficiently in a two-level architecture. Even previous compressive-sensing approaches, such as [9], require per-antenna-element CSI and cannot operate with only the composite CSI.

5.1 What is the Angle-of-Arrival?

Because of multipath propagation, a single transmission from an antenna, even a phased-array one, will travel along multiple paths before arriving at the receiver. Each copy of the signal from the UE, travelling along a different path, arrives at the BS at a particular *angle-of-arrival (AoA)*, and will experience a different amount of attenuation and distortion. We refer to the magnitude of the arriving signal at a particular AoA as its *gain*. A distribution of signal gains, over all possible AoAs of $0 - 2\pi$ radians, is known as the *AoA distribution*. These signal paths are symmetric — a return signal transmitted from the BS to the UE along the same AoA will encounter the same gain.

5.2 How is the AoA Conventionally Estimated?

For the sake of clarity, we describe the conventional AoA estimation process using a Uniform Linear Array (ULA), where antennas are arranged in a line and with equal spacing between them. The extension to circular arrays (Hekaton uses circular arrays) is straightforward.

Consider a single signal path from a UE arriving at a phased-array at the BS. Figure 7 shows an example of this with two antenna elements at the phased-array. Since these two elements are spaced a distance of d apart, the additional propagation distance, travelled by the signal reaching the ith antenna element is

$$\tau_i(\theta) = (i-1)\frac{d \sin\theta}{c} \tag{1}$$

where θ is the AoA and c is the speed of light. Note that for signals originating from UEs that are far away, the signals arriving the phased-array can be assumed to be parallel. The phase difference measured by all antennas is thus given by the column vector

$$\phi(\theta) = [1, e^{j2\pi f_c \tau_2(\theta)}, \ldots, e^{j2\pi f_c \tau_L(\theta)}]^T, \tag{2}$$

where f_c is the carrier frequency of the signal. For a single UE with P multipath signals $s_1, \ldots, s_P$ arriving at the BS, The received signal at the L antenna elements is thus

$$\mathbf{r} = [\phi(\theta_1), \ldots, \phi(\theta_P)][s_1, \ldots, s_P]^T + \mathbf{n} \tag{3}$$

where $\mathbf{n}$ is the channel noise energy.

In order to find the AoA distribution, we first discretize the angular space into D distinct, equally spaced, angles $\{\theta_1, \ldots, \theta_D\}$. We then scan through the discrete angular space of the phased-array and determine the gain at each discrete angle. This scanning process for l^{th} UE at the kth phased-array antenna uses a correlation matrix $\mathbf{\Phi}$. The expression for the AoA distribution is

$$\mathbf{a}_l^k(\theta) = \mathbf{\Phi}\mathbf{r}. \tag{4}$$

5.3 How Does Hekaton Estimate the AoA?

Observe that with a phased-array antenna, because we cannot access each antenna element individually, the correlation procedure is replaced with D separate probes, each using a different row of the matrix $\mathbf{\Phi}$ as the active codebook entry.

Hekaton avoids this overhead by estimating the AoA from the CSI measurements of the channel. Consider, for the sake of simplicity, that Hekaton is estimating the AoA between a single phased-array antenna and the lth UE in the cell. According to antenna theory [14], the measured CSI is related to the AoA distribution via an *Inverse Discrete Space Fourier Transform (IDSFT)*,

$$\mathbf{h}_l = \mathbf{F}^{-1}\,\mathbf{a}_l^k(\theta), \tag{5}$$

where $\mathbf{F}^{-1}$ is the IDSFT matrix and $\mathbf{h}$ is the (non-composite) CSI vector between the BS and the lth UE.

Recall that Hekaton can only obtain the composite CSI, which is dependent on the active codebook entry (i.e. the weights of the phase-shifters). Hence, the actual CSI-AoA relationship that is used by Hekaton is

$$\hat{h}_l = \mathbf{b}^T\mathbf{h}_l = \mathbf{b}^T\mathbf{F}^{-1}\,\mathbf{a}_l^k(\theta), \tag{6}$$

where $\mathbf{b}$ is a vector specifying the weights of each of the phase-shifters, and $(\cdot)^T$ refers to a vector/matrix transpose. $\hat{h}_l$ is the composite CSI between the phased-array antenna and the lth UE.

Unfortunately, the addition of the analog beamforming weights makes the CSI-AoA relation of (6) non-invertible as one can conceive of multiple AoA distributions that can map to the same composite CSI. This is a classic linear algebra problem — $\mathbf{a}_l^k(\theta)$ is a vector of length D and we can recover it precisely if we have D different measurements of $\hat{h}_l$, each taken using a different active codebook entry $\mathbf{b}$.

However, this is not a practical approach since D is typically very large ($D = 360$, in this case). Instead, Hekaton efficiently recovers the AoA distribution by exploiting its *sparsity* property.

5.4 AoA Sparsity

Empirical measurements [15] have shown that the AoA distribution is clustered. In a typical multipath environment, the dominant multipath components (i.e. those with the highest gain) arrive at the receiver from 3-5 distinct directions [15]. The signal gain at other AoAs are small and thus can be ignored as they do not contribute significantly to the fidelity of the received signal.

How is the AoA distribution sparse? If we discretize the angular space into $D = 360$ equally spaced angles, then $P < 5$ dominant signal paths is much smaller than the number of possible AoAs and is thus sparse. The signal gains along paths outside the P dominant ones are low and can be ignored as they do not contribute significantly to the decodability of the signal at the phased-array. The AoA measurement overhead is bounded by the number of multipath clusters. Because the AoA distribution is sparse, we can recover it from only a small, fixed number of composite CSI measurements.

5.5 Compressive AoA Estimation

We have seen how (a) the number of dominant AoA directions is sparse and (b) Hekaton obtains a transformed AoA distribution through CSI measurements. The objective of the compressive AoA estimation algorithm is to recover the AoA distribution $\mathbf{a}_l(\theta)$ from a fixed but small number of composite CSI measurements following (6).

Let $\hat{h}_{s,c}^{(1)}, \ldots, \hat{h}_{s,c}^{(V)}$ be a vector formed by V different composite CSI measurements, each taken with a different codebook entry $\mathbf{b}^{(1)}, \ldots, \mathbf{b}^{(V)}$. We can recover the AoA distribution using compressive sensing [16] via

$$\hat{\mathbf{a}}_l^k(\theta) = \arg\min \|\mathbf{a}_l^k(\theta)\|_1$$
$$\text{s.t. } \hat{h}_{s,c}^{(v)} = \mathbf{b}^{(v)}\mathbf{F}^{-1}\mathbf{a}_l^k(\theta),\ 1 \le v \le V \quad (7)$$

where $\|\cdot\|_1$ denotes the L1-norm.

How many CSI measurements are needed? Empirically, we have found that $V = 4$ is sufficient for recovering $\hat{\mathbf{a}}_{s,c}^k(\theta)$ accurately. This matches the measurements for the number of signal clusters for indoor environments [15]

We emphasize that unlike the naive, brute-force method, Hekaton's AoA estimation overhead is independent of the number of phased-arrays, or the number of antenna elements per phased-array.

5.6 AoA Estimation Example

Figure 8 shows the accuracy of the AoA estimation using the compressed sensing algorithm. We compare the AoA distribution estimated using 2 and 4 composite CSI measurements with a ground-truth distribution obtained using an exhaustive search of all possible AoA directions. Observe that even with only the few samples needed by the compressive-sensing algorithm, we can determine the AoA distribution peak accurately. The angle corresponding to this peak is the direction of the signal cluster from BS that results in the highest signal power gain at the UE.

6. DOWNLINK BEAM SELECTION

Hekaton can directly use a phased-array codebook entry that has a direction closest to the estimated AoA. However, a better approach is to chose a beam direction that maximizes the ratio of the signal energy to the intended UE to the total interfering signal energy to all *unintended UEs*. Give a phased-array antenna, an unintended UE is one that is either a UE in the local cell that is assigned to a different phased-array, or a UE in an adjacent cell. This metric is known as the *signal-to-leakage-power-ratio (SLR)*.

6.1 Selecting the SLR-maximizing Beam

Hekaton first determines the beam pattern between every phased-array antenna and every downstream user that maximizes the SLR. However, recall that each phased-array antenna in Hekaton only directs its beam towards a single user. Hence, Hekaton then assigns each user to the phased-array for which maximum SLR is achieved.

Hekaton uses the AoA distribution to users in both the local and adjacent cells to compute the SLR distribution. Simply put, the SLR distribution to a particular user l from a phased-array antenna k is defined as the element-wise ratio of the AoA distribution to this user, to the sum of all the AoA distributions from this same phased-array to concurrently active users in adjacent cells. Mathematically, this is expressed as

$$\eta_l^k(\theta) = \frac{\mathbf{a}_l^k(\theta)}{\sum_{d \in C_U} \mathbf{a}_d^k(\theta)}, \quad (8)$$

where C_U is the set of unintended. Then we have the beam pattern from the phased-array to the user that maximizes the SLR:

$$\hat{\theta}_l^k = \arg\max_{\theta} \ \eta_l^k(\theta). \quad (9)$$

At this point, Hekaton has the SLR-maximizing beam direction between every phased-array antenna and every user. The next step is to construct a unique mapping between users and phased-array antennas, so that the SLR at the users are maximized. Hekaton uses a greedy algorithm for this.

For each user, Hekaton selects the phased-array antenna that can achieve the highest SLR when directing a beam to that user. Hekaton then pairs the phased-array antenna with that user. This is a one-to-one mapping: no user will be assigned to more than one phased-array antenna, and no phased-array antenna will be assigned more than one user. Hekaton then activates the codebook entry in each phased-array that corresponds to the beam direction which most closely matches its SLR-maximizing direction.

6.2 Downlink Beam Update Interval

The duration of the update interval of the analog beam has an impact on the performance of Hekaton. In environments with high mobility, the downlink beam must be constantly updated to track the user's direction of movement. Hence, a shorter update interval is necessary. Conversely, in a static environment, the beam update interval can be long.

Empirically, we have found that in an indoor office environment with typical mobility, Hekaton can outperform a comparable MU-MIMO transmission with the same number of RF chains if the analog update occurs every 10 frames.

7. IMPLEMENTATION

We prototype our two-level beamforming architecture using the WARPv3 software radio platform. Our prototype implementation of Hekaton uses four WARPv3 boards, each with four antennas. This allows us to evaluate Hekaton in configurations utilizing up to 16 antennas in total (e.g. 4 RF streams each with a 4-antenna phased array). We rely on trace-driven emulations for larger-scale configurations that utilize more than 16 transmit antennas. The set of beams supported by our emulated phased-array is specified in a codebook. We employ another 2 WARPv3 boards to emulate up to 8 single-antenna clients.

Phased-Array Implementation. Hekaton design leverages analog phased-arrays to achieve efficient and practical large-scale MU-MIMO. However, fine-time-grained control over commercial phased-array antennas may require a custom FPGA controller[4]. For the sake of simplicity, we construct digital phased-array antennas using the WARPv3 platform.

The key difference between digital and analog phase-shifting is the phase resolution: digital phase-shifting is limited by the number of bits used to represent the phase angle, while its analog counterpart can shift the beam over a continuous set of angles. Fortunately, in practice, this resolution difference is very small and negligible.

In our implementation, we emulate circular phased arrays of up to eight antenna elements each, with corresponding codebooks of eight different beam patterns [17]. All phased-arrays used in any specific experiment have the same size. We also normalize the transmit power of each emulated phased-array to be equal to that of a single WARP RF chain.

We emulate each digital phased array by arranging up to eight antennas (each connecting to a WARP RF interface) in a circle. The radius of the circle is fixed at half the wavelength of the 2.4GHz carrier [18]. If multiple WARP devices are needed, they are synchronized via CM-MMCX clock modules [19] to eliminate sampling and frequency errors across the entire phased-array.

Phased-Array Codebook Design. The phased-array codebook is implemented using standard techniques [17] to obtain single-lobe beams with dominant directions equally spaced over 2π. The number of codebook entries is equal to the size of the phased-array antenna. All beamforming weights in the codebook are specified to the nearest one degree, so as to closely emulate the performance of real-world phased-arrays. The geometry of the phased array is a circle with radius $N\lambda/16$, where N is the total number of antenna elements in the codebook.

We note that our digital phased array implementation is different from conjugate beamforming. Unlike conjugate beamforming, the codebook only encodes phase, and not amplitude, changes.

Latency and Synchronization. Hekaton is optimized to minimize latency and maintain time/frequency-synchronizatoin across all its antenna elements.

(i) Low-Latency. We develop a C++ WARP software controller to enable simultaneous I/Q transfer between all WARP radios. OpenMP is used to accelerate PHY processing in parallel across multiple CPU cores. As a result, our implementation achieves an inter-frame PHY latency, in a 8×8 MU-MIMO transmission, of merely $23ms$ with an eight-core Intel i7 CPU. This latency is well below the empirical channel coherence time of $300ms$ in our office environment. We can thus perform real-time evaluation of Hekaton's performance under varying channel dynamics and mobility.

We note that the L1-norm minimization step required AoA estimation can take up to $200ms$, which is larger than the frame interval of our implementation. However, this does not impact our evaluations as the beam pattern of each phased-array antenna only needs to be updated asynchronously on a coarse timescale.

[4]The FCI-3710 [13] has a digital interface for use with FPGA controllers

(ii) Phased-Array Calibration. A key feature of phased-array antennas is that the transmit phases at each of its antenna elements is known to the phased-array. However, since we use different WARP radios for each antenna, hardware differences across the radios introduce varying phase-offsets between antennas. Hence, phase calibration mechanism must be applied to these antennas [1] to synchronize the phase of all antenna-elements in a phased array.

We synchronize all antenna-elements to a randomly chosen *primary antenna.* Recall that the exact placement of each antenna is fixed and known in advance. The primary antenna simply transmits an OFDM preamble. Each non-primary antenna uses the received phase information, along with its known physical location, to derive its true phase-offset from the primary antenna. It then compensates for this offset in all subsequent transmissions. This calibration is done for both uplink and downlink. We have empirically determined the phase-offsets between antennas remain unchanged for up to several hours (the duration of our experiments).

(iii) Scheduling. Cellular protocols are synchronous and rely on the presence of a global protocol clock. Since all WARP boards are connected to a central PC, we enforce this protocol clock without additional outside synchronization.

Digital Beamforming. We implement digital beamforming component of Hekaton using a 802.11-based OFDM PHY. The 20 MHz channel bandwidth is divided into 64 subcarriers, including 48 data subcarriers, 4 pilots, 1 DC and 11 guard band subcarriers. QAM-modulated input data symbols are precoded using zero-forcing beamforming (ZFBF).

8. EXPERIMENTAL EVALUATION

In this section, we demonstrate Hekaton's performance based on the aforementioned testbed implementation. Our evaluation answers three major questions: *(i)* Can Hekaton achieve capacity scaling while maintaining energy efficiency by simply increasing the number of passive antennas? *(ii)* Can each component of Hekaton effectively limit the coordination overhead, thus achieving throughput efficiency for large-scale MU-MIMO? *(iii)* Can Hekaton still manage interference in multi-cell networks through its two-level beamforming?

Hekaton is equally applicable to both indoor and outdoor environments. However, the indoor environment presents more challenging wireless channel conditions due to the abundance of multipath reflections. We thus conduct our experiments in a typical office environment (Figure 15) during normal office hours with around $300ms$ channel coherence time.

8.1 Experimental Setup

Hekaton configuration. Unless otherwise indicated, each Hekaton node in our experiments has two RF chains, each connected to an eight-antenna phased-array. Therefore each Hekaton node has two degrees-of-freedom and can serve up to two users concurrently. Trace-driven emulation is used for larger number of users.

Baseline MU-MIMO configuration. In our evaluation, we compare Hekaton with conventional MU-MIMO that has only a single omnidirectional antenna per RF chain. Unless otherwise indicated, the baseline MU-MIMO configuration shares the same user number and RF chain number with the Hekaton configuration. In Section 8.3, we also consider the oracle MU-MIMO configuration that exhaustively searches among all user subsets with all possible cardinalities to maximize the downlink capacity. To ensure a fair comparison, Hekaton and the baseline MU-MIMO configurations share the same center frequency, channel bandwidth and digital precoder specified in Section 7.

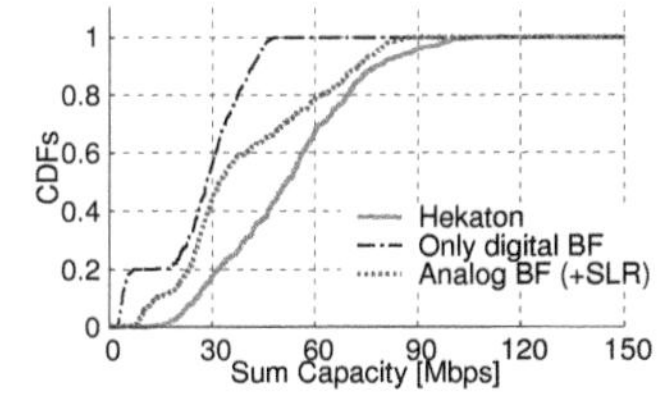

Figure 9: Combining digital and analog beamforming improves the performance.

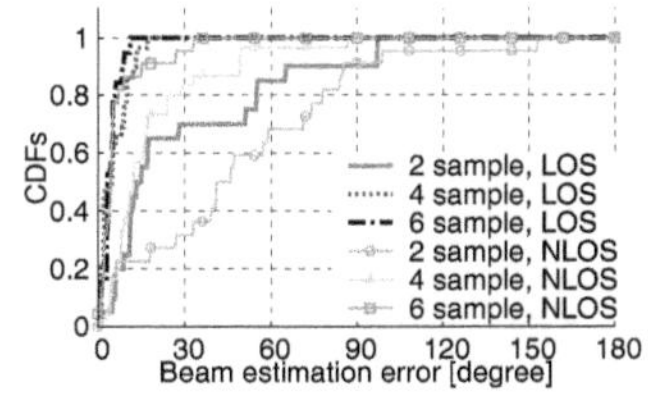

Figure 10: Accuracy of compressive AoA estimation.

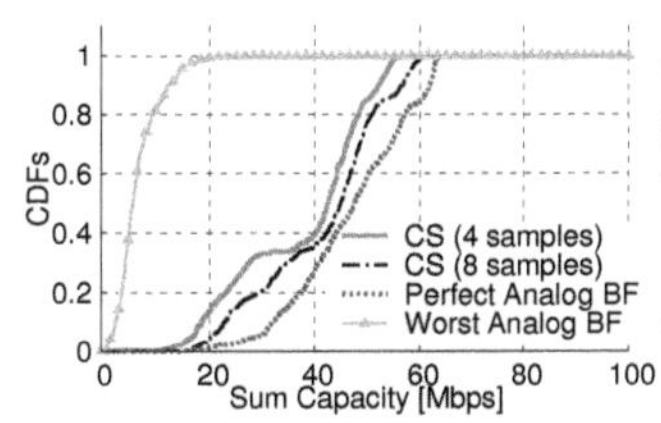

Figure 11: Data rate of AoA-based beamforming.

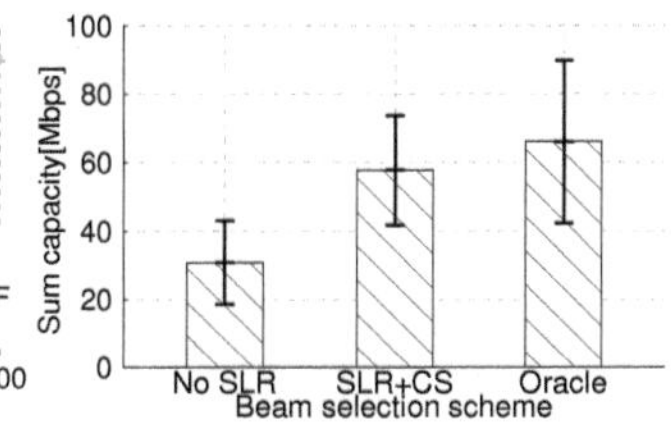

Figure 12: Capacity of SLR based analog beam selection.

Trace-driven emulation setup. Due to the limited number of WARP nodes available, we conduct trace-driven emulation for the scenarios that require more than 6 WARP nodes, *e.g.*, the multi-cell evaluation in Section 8.4. In order to collect these traces, we first note the antenna locations of the virtual phased array of the intended size, as described in §7. We then place the antennas of the physical transmitter on these locations in turn and collect the CSI between that antenna and multiple receivers via over-the-air transmission. The collected channel matrices are finally concatenated to emulate a large-scale multi-antenna transmitter serving the same user group.

During the trace collection, we ensure that the users and the environment are static (with around $300ms$ coherence time using 0.5 as the threshold for channel correlation). The trace collection *w.r.t.* a particular user group takes up to 40 minutes. This long measurement duration will reduce the overall spatial correlation between antennas. However, we note that this will affect both MU-MIMO and Hekaton similarly, and thus will not affect performance comparisons between MU-MIMO and Hekaton.

8.2 Hekaton Micro-Benchmarks

Analog Beamforming vs Digital Precoding. We compare the performance of Hekaton with two alternative architectural choices with the same number of RF chains: *(i) Standalone analog beamforming*: The base station has two 8-antenna phased-arrays, each connected to a separate RF chain. It beamforms to 2 users with minimized SLR but without digital precoding to eliminate the crosstalk; *(ii) Standalone digital precoding*: The base station has 2 omnidirectional antennas, each also connected to a separate RF chain. It employs a zero-forcing beamforming (ZFBF) precoder to serve 2 downlink users. Our Hekaton base station has the same configuration to the standalone analog beamforming except that it also uses digital precoding to eliminate the crosstalk between the two concurrent data streams.

Figure 9 plots the CDFs of the sum downlink capacity under the above three architectures. It shows that Hekaton's median throughput is 66% higher than that of standalone analog beamforming. This is due to the distortion of the spatial beams in practice. Ideally, the two phased arrays can steer their beams towards orthogonal directions. However, multipath reflections indoor will easily distort the beams, resulting in crosstalk interference among different users. Hekaton overcomes this limitation by combining with digital ZFBF precoding to eliminate this residual interference after analog beamforming. On the other hand, compared with standalone digital precoding, the analog beamforming component of Hekaton essentially acts as a preconditioner, which makes the digital channel of the 2 users "seen" by the RF chain more orthogonal and reduces the condition number of the channel matrix. As a result, Hekaton also achieves substantial (median 76%) improvement over standalone digital precoding.

Compressive AoA Estimation. We now evaluate the accuracy of Hekaton's compressive AoA estimation algorithm using a single RF chain and a single eight-antenna phased-array. Note that due to the limited number of antennas in this setup, we can only make use of up to eight composite CSI measurements, thus limiting the number of recoverable multipath clusters to eight. However, this is already sufficient to identify the 3-5 clusters in typical indoor environments [15]. Based on the compressive sensing theory [9], we believe that our results in this evaluation are still valid for larger scale phased array under the same environment. With the eight-antenna phased array connecting to a single RF chain on the base station and one user sending the uplink probing signal, we first estimate the AoA of the strongest incoming signal path based on eight composite CSI measurements, and then study the error incurred when fewer composite CSI measurements is used. This comparison is made under 20 random line-of-sight (LOS) topologies and an equal number of non-line-of-sight (NLOS) channels.

Figure 10 plots the CDF of these AoA estimation errors of the strongest incoming signal path over all users in all topologies. Recall that Hekaton uses four CSI measurements for AoA estimation. We can observe that Hekaton has only around 6° of median error in LOS environment since the signal AoA is dominated by an LOS component. Meanwhile, the NLOS channel results in slightly higher error (median 12°) due to richer multi-path reflections. In both cases (LOS and NLOS), the AoA error should only have a marginal impact to Hekaton's beam selection from the eight-entry circular phased-array codebook (about 45° beam width).

To verify this, we further evaluate the impact of the compressive AoA estimation on Hekaton's beam selection and the resulting network capacity. In this micro-benchmark evaluation, We exclude the influence of the digital MU-MIMO precoder by running a Hekaton base station with only one RF chain connecting to an eight-antenna phased array. This modified Hekaton setup serves only one user. We compare the compressive approach using four or all eight composite CSI measurements with 2 other configurations in the same antenna and RF chain setup: *(i) Perfect analog BF*, which uses conjugate beamforming to steer the beams of each phased-array. Conjugate beamforming is equivalent to having a discrete codebook with infinitely fine resolution in theory (bounded by the hardware in practice), and thereby serves as a performance upper-bound. We emphasize that typical analog phased-array antennas are codebook-based and cannot perform conjugate beamforming; *(ii) Worst analog BF*, which intentionally chooses the worst analog beam pattern that leads to the lowest downlink capacity based on exhaustive search from the codebook, and thus acts as the performance lower bound.

Figure 11 plots the downlink capacity of these configurations, we see that Hekaton's compressive approach with four measurements only causes 5% median capacity loss compared to the one with eight measurements. Both schemes exhibit gains of more than $7\times$ over the worst-analog BF case. They also exhibit between 10% to 30% lower capacity than the perfect analog BF case due to the

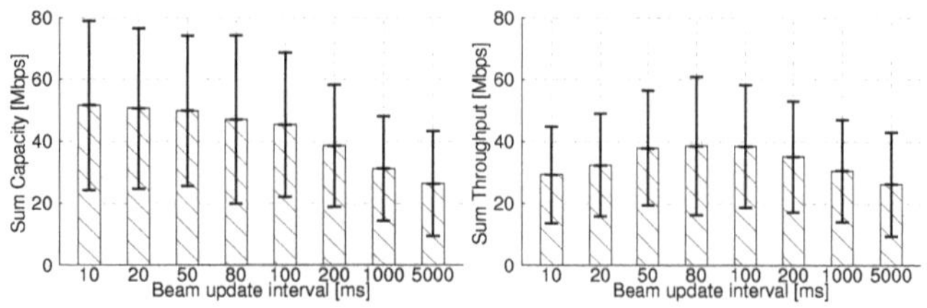

(a) Without probing overhead.

(b) With probing overhead.

Figure 13: The relationship between Hekaton performance and analog beam update interval.

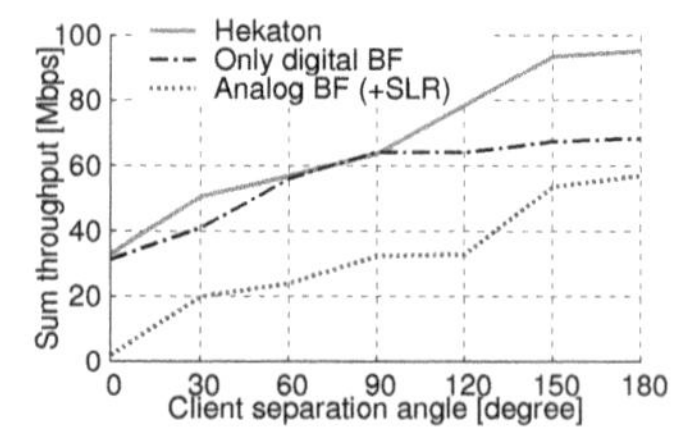

Figure 14: Spatial separation between users affects downlink beamforming.

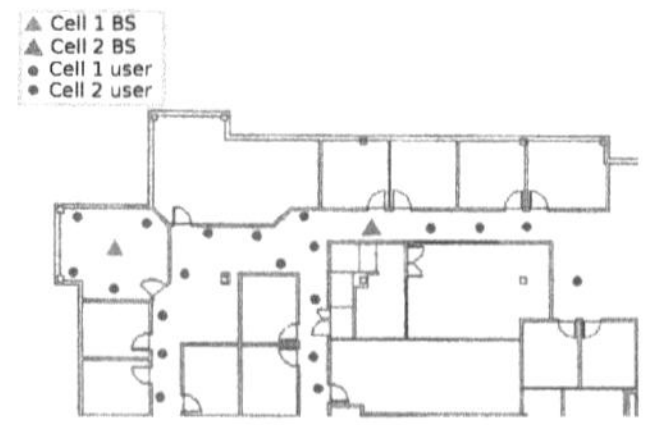

Figure 15: Topology for trace-driven emulation.

discrete codebook they used, but this gap will naturally decrease as the number of antenna elements grows (which results in a codebook of finer resolution).

SLR-Based Beam Selection. Hekaton uses the SLR metric to select downlink beam for each phased array that minimize interference to non-intended users. In this micro-benchmark evaluation, we compare the performance of the SLR-based beam selection to two other configurations: *(i) Peak-AoA-based*, where we only use the peak AoA direction as the beam direction and *(ii) Oracle*, where we select the downlink beam direction assuming full non-composite CSI knowledge at the BS.

We test 30 topologies where a Hekaton base station with two eight-element phased-arrays serves two randomly selected users simultaneously. Figure 12 shows that the capacity under the SLR-based beam selection outperforms that of the AoA-based approach by almost 50% on average. Furthermore, the SLR-based approach achieves only 12% lower capacity than the oracle with optimal beam selection.

Update Interval vs Downlink Throughput. Hekaton must continuously update the beam direction so that it accurately "follows" the motion of mobile users. However, note that during a coarse-timescale beam update procedure (spanning multiple frames), random codebook entries are activated on the phased-array. This results in non-ideal analog beamforming for upstream and downstream transmissions for the duration of the update. Obviously, a non-stop update of the phased-array will have a detrimental impact on the achievable throughput.

We evaluate this trade-off in a dynamic topology where users in the testbed move at walking speed. We use the Hekaton base station with two 8-element phased arrays to serve two LOS users simultaneously. Sum downlink capacity of the two users are evaluated under different beam update intervals. Each experiment lasts for 5 minutes, and the resulting mean capacity is plotted in Figure 13a.

If we ignore the overhead due to beam update and probing, the results follow an expected pattern: the shorter the interval between updates, the higher the throughput, as seen in Figure 13a. However, due to the degraded channel during the analog beam update, we can see from Figure 13b that the best update interval is $80ms$, or once every 80 LTE subframes. Hence, Hekaton updates its active codebook entry every $80ms$.

Impact of Spatial Correlation. Since a Hekaton BS relies on analog beamforming as a first-level separation between concurrently-served users, its effectiveness is naturally affected by spatial separation of the users. We study this performance factor with our Hekaton base station and two downlink users. The Hekaton base station has 2 RF chains, each are connected to a circular phased array with 8 antenna elements. The angular separation between the two users (with respect to the BS) varies from 0 to 180 degrees. For each angular separation, we create 30 different topologies (all the while maintaining the same angular separation between the two users), and plot the mean downlink capacity in Figure 14. For comparison, we also repeat the experiments with standalone analog and digital beamforming.

In general, the performance of Hekaton and standalone analog beamforming keeps increasing with node separation since it becomes easier to form non-overlapping beams pointing towards the users. Standalone digital precoding is relatively less affected by node separation because it operates based on precise CSI information of each user. We also see that Hekaton and standalone digital precoding achieve similar performance under small node separation since the beams from the Hekaton phased-array antennas overlap with each other in this scenario and hence the interference cancellation is mainly left to the digital precoder. Hence, explicitly selecting distant users will improve Hekaton's overall performance.

8.3 Single-Cell Performance

Throughput. We first examine how the throughput of Hekaton and conventional MU-MIMO scales in terms of the number of RF chains and antenna elements. We vary the number of RF chains in both configurations between 2 and 16. The number of users served by both cases is always equal to the number of RF chains used. For a given number of RF chains, we also vary the number of antenna elements in the phased-array connected to each RF chain to between 1 and 8 (1-antenna-per-RF-chain configuration corresponds to conventional MU-MIMO). Trace-driven emulation is used for the configurations where the total number of antennas exceeds the maximum number of 16 antennas supported by our implementation. The traces are collected using the Cell 1 topology in Figure 15 following the methodology detailed in Section 8.1.

Figure 16a shows the average downlink throughput and standard deviation across randomly selected downlink user combinations. We observe two interesting trends from the results.

First, when we only have a single antenna per RF chain, the sum throughput can decrease even if we increase the number of RF chains. For example, the sum throughput in the 16×16 configuration (16 RF-chains serving 16 users) is lower than the 8×8 configuration. This is because the channel orthogonality between users diminishes with increasing user number. We note that real-world MU-MIMO systems do not always operate in such a configuration to avoid this throughput scaling behavior.

Second, for a given number of RF chains, Hekaton scales up the network capacity by increasing the number of antenna elements per RF chain. The phased-array antennas effectively improves the channel orthogonality between users and reduces the channel condition number. Hence, sum throughput of Hekaton in 16×16 consistently outperforms the 8×8 Hekaton configuration.

In the results above, MU-MIMO cannot exploit beamforming gain since its user count is equal to its antenna count. However,

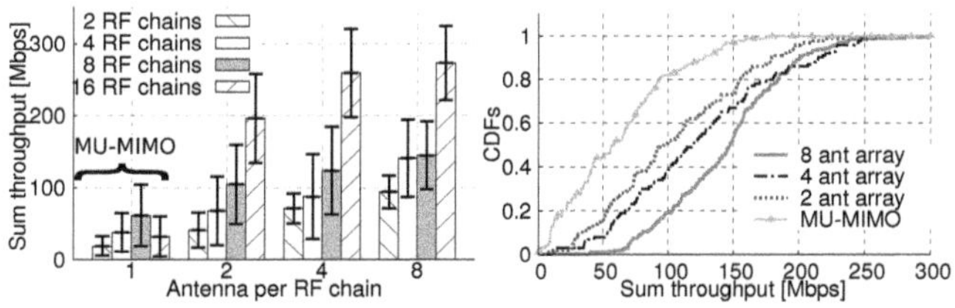

(a) Hekaton capacity scaling in a single cell. (b) Transmitter with 8 RF chains serving 4 users.

Figure 16: Single cell performance comparison.

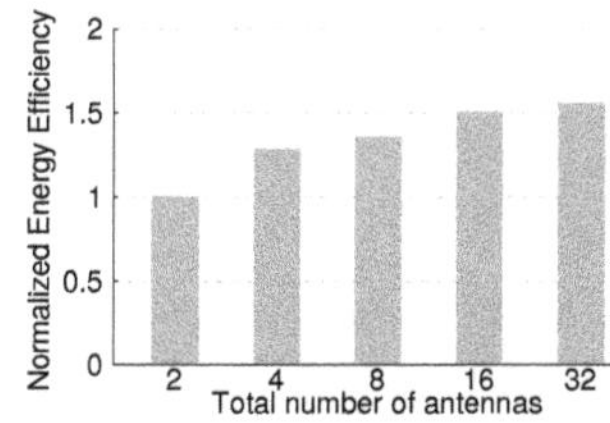

Figure 17: Energy-efficiency over conventional MU-MIMO with the same RF chain number.

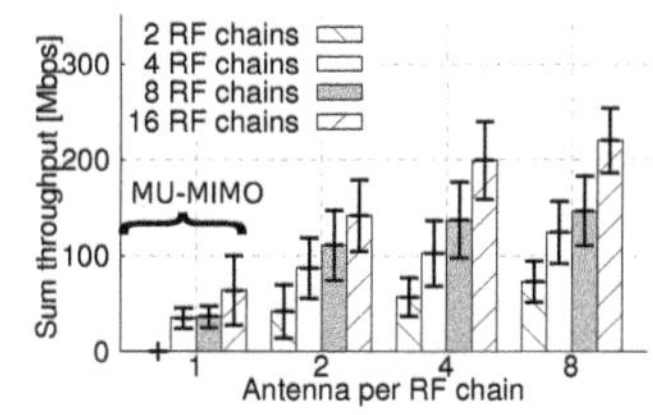

Figure 18: Throughput in 2-cell topologies.

Hekaton still achieves a significant throughput gain over MU-MIMO with fewer users. Here, we use MU-MIMO with 8 RF chains (i.e. 8 antennas) serving 4 users as the baseline. Note that this is the configuration that achieves the highest throughput in Figure 1. We compare MU-MIMO in this configuration against Hekaton with 2 RF chains and 2,4, and 8 antennas in each phased-array.

Figure 16b shows the throughput distribution over all topologies. We see that Hekaton achieves an impressive increase in throughput under the same transmit power — with 8 RF chains and 8-element phased-arrays serving 4 users, Hekaton achieves $2.5\times$ throughput gain over the 8×4 conventional MU-MIMO configuration.

Energy Efficiency. We have already seen that the throughput of Hekaton increases with the size of phased-array. We further demonstrate that the two-level beamforming architecture employed by Hekaton improves energy-efficiency alongside this throughput increase. We benchmark Hekaton with two RF chains and varying phased-array sizes, serving two users. The energy efficiency values (in bits-per-Joule) is normalized using 2×2 MU-MIMO as the baseline. Both Hekaton and the 2×2 MU-MIMO configuration have the same number of RF chains, although Hekaton uses phased arrays with each RF chain while MU-MIMO uses omnidirectional antennas. Note that since the power consumed by the phased array is typically very small, as discussed in Section 1, we assume that the power consumption of both of these configurations are equal. For the sake of clarity, we report results w.r.t. the total number of antennas used. Figure 17 shows this mean normalized energy efficiency. Since Hekaton supports more transmit antennas than conventional MU-MIMO under the same RF chain number thanks to its unique two-level beamforming architecture, we see that its energy-efficiency almost shows a monotonically increasing trend, and the energy efficiency gain is up to $1.67\times$ over conventional MU-MIMO with the same number of RF chains. We expect even greater efficiency gain with larger phased-array antennas.

8.4 Multi-Cell Performance

Hekaton uses two-level beamforming to simplify inter-cell coordination and reduce interference between adjacent cells. In this section, we compare its performance against conventional MU-MIMO in a two-cell network. Due to the large number of antennas required, our evaluation will rely primarily on trace-driven emulation. The locations of these two cells are chosen so induce inter-cell interference, and is shown in Figure 15.

We evaluate the sum throughput across both cells for the BSes with 2-, 4- and 8-RF chains. Hekaton uses phased-array antennas of varying sizes, similar to the configuration used in the single-cell experiments in §8.3. The number of users is always equal to the number of RF chains.

Figure 18 shows that Hekaton achieves significant throughput gain over conventional MU-MIMO. Specifically, due to the strong inter-cell interference, conventional MU-MIMO (1 antenna per RF chain) with only 2 RF chains achieves almost zero throughput. As we increase the multiplexing gains (by increasing the number of RF chains), MU-MIMO throughput increases marginally to a mean of 60 Mbps. On the other hand, as we increase beamforming gains in Hekaton, it can achieve throughput that is up to 300% that of MU-MIMO. Note that the transmit power in both Hekaton and MU-MIMO experiments is identical. Hence, this gain comes from (a) the ability of Hekaton to improve beamforming gain and better focus the signal energy on the intended users, and (b) the ability of Hekaton to direct signal energy *away* from unintended users. Hence, Hekaton can increase the throughput to its intended users, while simultaneously reducing inter-cell interference.

MOS Video Quality	PSNR Range (dB)
Excellent	>37
Good	31-37
Fair	25-31
Poor	20-25
Bad	< 20

Table 1: Mapping between video quality and PSNR.

8.5 Impact of Hekaton on Application Performance

In this section, we combine the PHY layer implementation of Hekaton with application-layer simulation. Without loss of generality, our experiments compare two different large-scale MU-MIMO designs: *(i) Hekaton* BS with two phased-arrays (eight antenna elements each), and *(ii) conventional MU-MIMO*, with 2 RF chains. Both of these networks serve two single-antenna users concurrently.

8.5.1 Hekaton with H.264 Video Streaming

We first implement a H.264 video streaming emulator on top of our Hekaton testbed. The emulator runs at the BS that has two RF chains and transmits different H.264 video streams to two different users simultaneously. Upon receiving and decoding the video stream, each user computes its PSNR and user-perceived Mean Opinion Score (MOS) (the standard measures of video quality). The relationship between the PSNR and video quality [20] is summarized in Table 1. We evaluate both Hekaton and MU-MIMO across 10 different pairs of users using QPSK and 1/2-rate FEC, each test transmits 100 different 40-second videos.

Figure 19a shows the PSNR distribution over all clients and across all video frames (original PSNR of the videos is 48dB). Hekaton achieves *twice* the median PSNR, from 15 to 30dB, when compared to MU-MIMO. Figure 19b shows the corresponding MOS video quality. We see that Hekaton increases the ratio of excellent video streams by up to $10\times$ and reduces the ratio of all lower-quality video frames. With the base station's total transmit power unchanged, Hekaton's performance improvement comes by improv-

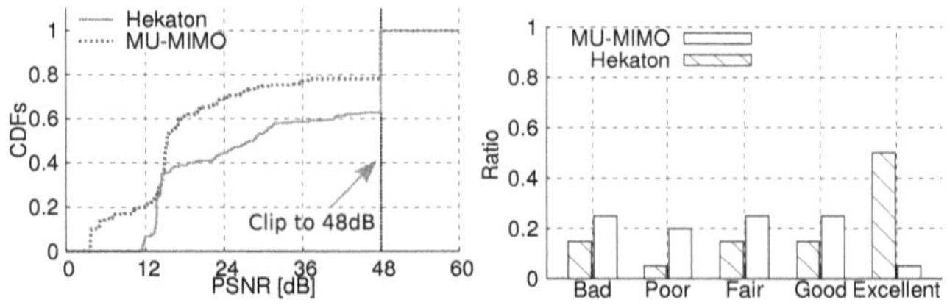

(a) PSNR distribution. (b) Video quality.

Figure 19: Video streaming evaluation.

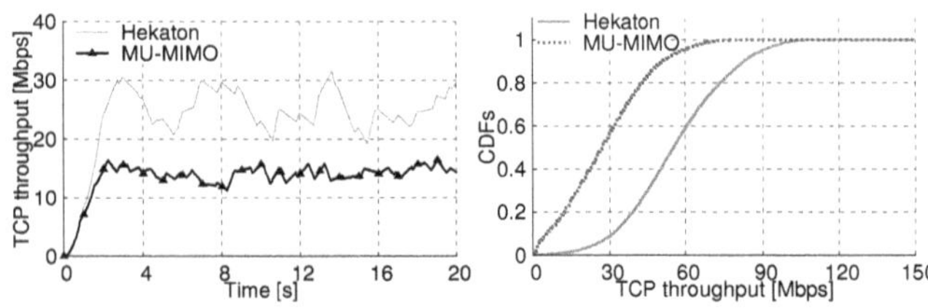

(a) Time domain throughput comparison for one transmission. (b) Throughput CDF comparison.

Figure 20: TCP throughput comparison in an FTP application.

ing the beamforming gain and user channel orthogonality via the phased array.

8.5.2 *Hekaton with FTP File Transfer*

We then emulate the FTP protocol over TCP using PHY channel traces. These traces are obtained by running Hekaton over our testbed with the same antenna and RF chain setup in Section 8.5.1, and extracting the per-packet SNR (and achievable bit-rate) over time. The FTP data is fragmented into 1460-byte frames. The receiver window size, TCP maximum congestion window size, and round-trip delay are set to 200, 100 and 20ms, respectively. We assume the downlink and uplink have symmetrical rate.

Figure 20a shows the time-varying performance of one FTP transfer. We observe that even after taking into account the effects of slow start, signaling overhead, and the AIMD congestion control, Hekaton still outperforms convention MU-MIMO with respect to long-term throughput. Figure 20b further plots the CDF of TCP-flow throughput distributed across 10 pairs of clients. Hekaton improves the median TCP throughput of all TCP flows by more than 2× over conventional MU-MIMO.

9. DISCUSSION

Is Hekaton useful with more users? One may assume that in networks with a large number of users, one will always be able to find users with uncorrelated channels due to the user diversity. Accordingly, the gain (and usefulness) of large-scale MU-MIMO is limited under large user population. However, such an assumption ignores the fact that the CSI measurement overhead needed to locate these uncorrelated users scales *linearly* with the total number of users. This overhead can easily negate any benefit of a larger users selection pool [21]. On the other hand, the additional overhead incurred by Hekaton is independent of the user population.

One- vs Two-Level Beamforming. Instead of increasing the number of RF chains, Hekaton adopts a two-level approach and relies on phased-array antennas to get higher total antenna number and hence lower channel condition number.

A phased-array antenna consists of multiple (*e.g.*, $K > 1$) antenna elements. However, a K-element phased-array antenna is not equivalent to K RF chains, each with an omni-directional antenna. Each antenna element is only equipped with an analog phase shifter that adjusts the phase but not the magnitude of the antenna signal. Hence, phased-array antennas cannot achieve the same beamforming gain or downlink capacity as a group of RF chains (with associated omni-directional antennas) of the same size.

However, increasing the number of MU-MIMO RF chains results in a proportional increase in the energy consumed. We emphasize that increasing the number of RF chains beyond the rank of the channel will only increase the beamforming gain. At this operating point, we can obtain a similar improvement of the beamforming gain with Hekaton, but without the associate increase in energy consumption.

Hekaton is a retrofittable solution that can improve the beamforming gain of existing wireless platforms without additional energy consumption. If backwards-compatibility is not a requirement, other energy-efficient operating points can be achieved by increasing RF chains instead of antenna elements, and employing one-level beamforming instead. We leave such studies to future work.

Beamforming in the 3-D space. In this paper, we use the standard codebook designed for the 2-D space [17], and thus the signal arriving path or AoA is correspondingly estimated in the 2-D space to facilitate the downlink beam selection. We emphasize that our design can also be used to estimate the signal arriving path in the 3-D space if codebook designed for 3-D space is available in the phased-array. There are on-going discussions on the 3-D beamforming in 3GPP. We expect that the knowledge of signal path in the 3-D space will allow us to better target the beams, especially in urban environments, and we leave this to future work.

Optimizing Hekaton. Currently, Hekaton does not exploit the full potential of two-level beamforming architecture because (a) it is limited to fixed number of users and (b) we enforce a one-to-one mapping between each user and phased array to simplify the problem formulation. It is worth noting that MU-MIMO schedulers [22,23] can optimize the users served, and similar approaches can also be applied to Hekaton . However, such extensions will increase the complexity of Hekaton. Given that our suboptimal Hekaton design already shows remarkable performance gains over conventional MU-MIMO, it is not immediately clear if the additional complexity will result in a commensurate performance improvement. We leave an in-depth study of this challenge to future work.

Hekaton with implicit and explicit CSI feedback. When explicit CSI feedback is used for MU-MIMO as in most existing wireless standards like 802.11ac and LTE, Hekaton shows an obvious advantage over existing large-scale MU-MIMO architecture [1,2] due to the much smaller number of RF chains. However, when implicit CSI feedback is used, the probing process Hekaton used to find the SLR-optimal beam direction incurs extra overhead. Fortunately, it is mitigated by the fact that the additional probing overhead in Hekaton is a small constant number. We emphasize that this is not a constant scaling factor, but a constant of four probes due to the indoor signal sparsity [15]. Hence, when taken together with its two-level design, Hekaton is still an efficient, retrofittable design for large-scale MU-MIMO networks.

Hekaton with Mobility. Due to the limitation of our implementation, we only evaluate Hekaton in static environments with around $300ms$ channel coherence time. However, it is worth noting that the novel two-level beamforming architecture of Hekaton may improve the MU-MIMO performance under mobility if supported by proper hardware with sufficient processing capability. Since the analog beamforming component reduces the crosstalk interference between concurrent data streams and only needs to be updated in a coarse time manner, the system becomes more robust to the stale

CSI used in the digital precoder compared to a pure digital beamforming system.

10. RELATED WORK

Large-scale MU-MIMO. Several research platforms, such as Argos [1] and BigStation [2], have demonstrated the significant performance gain that can be achieved by large-scale MU-MIMO systems — Argos with 64 antennas achieves $12.7\times$ the capacity of a single-antenna system; BigStation [2], when using 12 antennas and 9 clients, achieves $6.8\times$ the capacity of a single-antenna-single-client setup. However, these platforms suffer from scalability issues. For example, the authors in [1] acknowledge that suboptimal conjugate beamforming is preferred in larger systems as ZFBF suffers from unacceptable complexity and overhead. In [2], parallel computing is used to reduce the processing time of ZFBF, but the solution requires powerful computing server that is not available in current base stations. Furthermore, when the number of RF chains goes well beyond the channel rank supported by current environment [3], further improving capacity by increasing the number of RF chains may reduce energy efficiency.

In contrast, Hekaton aims to achieve good energy efficiency, low hardware complexity, and affordable computational overhead while enjoying a good fraction of the potential performance gain of a large-scale MU-MIMO system by using phased arrays. We emphasize that Hekaton is designed to enhance the performance of MU-MIMO with the same number of RF chains, this design philosophy does not conflict with existing large-scale MU-MIMO architectures, it is possible to replace omni-directional antennas with phased-array ones in systems like Argos or BigStation to further boost the network performance.

Two-Level Beamforming. While the high-level concept of combining an analog beamformer with a digital RF chain is not new, Hekaton is the first design that efficiently adopts this architecture in a MU-MIMO communications system. ProBeam [7] is a comparable work that integrates a phased-array antenna with a non-MIMO WiMAX basestation. However, the optimal beam is chosen using an exhaustive search of all codebook entries. This overhead scales with the size of the phased-array antenna. Two-level digital beamforming is discussed in [24]. However, since both levels of beamforming are digital, to support a large number of antennas, such a system still requires the same number of RF chains. Two-level beamforming is also prevalent in 60 GHz networks [25,26]. However, exhaustive beam searches are typically employed there too. Faster beam searches, such as those based on simulated annealing [27], can reduce the search time, but the overhead still increases with the size of the phased-array.

Joint optimization schemes [28,29] have also been proposed for two-level beamforming. However, these algorithms require tight integration between the analog phased-array and digital RF chains. This level of integration is not feasible for a solution that is to be backwards compatible with existing BSs.

Two-level beamforming is also employed in other areas such as MIMO radar [30]. However, such systems are purpose-built for object tracking, not communications, and also require tight coordination between the analog and digital RF components.

Coordination Overhead. The distributed coordination scheme in [31] increases throughput through opportunistic use of degrees of freedom. However, it requires precise clock phase and frequency synchronization. Other centralized coordinated multipoint systems [32–36] demonstrate impressive gains from cooperative transmissions across access points, but also comes at the cost of significant synchronization and inter-cell CSI sharing overhead. Such an overhead is impractical for large-scale deployment in real-world cellular networks.

AoA Estimation. ArrayTrack [8] demonstrates a practical method of localizing indoor WiFi clients using MIMO techniques. This approach uses standard AoA estimation techniques, together with multipath smoothing to determine the direction of each client from the BS. However, ArrayTrack cannot be integrated into Hekaton as it requires one RF chain for each antenna. Furthermore, due to multipath effects, the downlink beam direction used by Hekaton is not necessarily the direction of the direct path from the BS to the UE.

PinPoint [12] has a similar goal of localizing wireless clients. However, it relies on the cyclostationary properties of many existing wireless protocols to estimate the AoA. It too, requires that each antenna is connected to a single RF-chain, and thus, cannot be used in Hekaton. The method in [9] is most similar to the technique in Hekaton as it too relies on a compressive-sensing approach to AoA estimation. However, its compressive-sensing method differs from that in Hekaton in one critical aspect: it requires one-antenna-per-RF-chain, and thus is unsuitable for use with phased-array antennas. Recall that we cannot get time-domain signal information directly from each antenna element. Hekaton uses a key relationship between CSI and AoA to extract AoA information from composite CSI data, and thus requires no modifications to the LTE protocol.

11. CONCLUSION

Large-scale MU-MIMO has the potential to introduce multi-fold capacity gains into wireless networks at high spectral efficiency. However, in practice, these gains are plagued by the diminishing user channel orthogonality, high coordination overhead and the lack of support in current standards. In this paper, we designed and evaluated Hekaton, a novel two-level, two-timescale beamforming architecture that brings a sizable fraction of these gains into existing networks in a standards-agnostic form. In our evaluation, Hekaton achieves up to $2.5\times$ capacity gain over conventional MU-MIMO in single-cell networks, without additional energy requirements.

Acknowledgement

We thank the anonymous shepherds for their helpful comments on the paper. This research was supported in part by the NSF under Grant CNS-1318292, CNS-1343363 and CNS-1350039.

12. REFERENCES

[1] C. Shepard, H. Yu, N. Anand, E. Li, T. Marzetta, R. Yang, and L. Zhong, "Argos: Practical Many-Antenna Base Stations," in *Proc. of ACM MobiCom*, 2012.

[2] Q. Yang, X. Li, H. Yao, J. Fang, K. Tan, W. Hu, J. Zhang, and Y. Zhang, "Bigstation: Enabling scalable real-time signal processing in large mu-mimo systems," in *SIGCOMM*, 2013.

[3] D. Tse and P. Viswanath, *Fundamentals of Wireless Communication*. Cambridge University Press, 2005.

[4] E. Aryafar, N. Anand, T. Salonidis, and E. W. Knightly, "Design and Experimental Evaluation of Multi-User Beamforming in Wireless LANs," in *MobiCom*, 2010.

[5] D. Love, R. Heath, V. Lau, D. Gesbert, B. Rao, and M. Andrews, "An overview of limited feedback in wireless communication systems," *IEEE JSAC*, 2008.

[6] S. Jeon, A. Babakhani, and A. Hajimiri, "Integrated phased arrays," in *Advanced Millimeter-Wave Technologies*. John Wiley and Sons, Ltd, 2009, ch. 14.

[7] J. Yoon, K. Sundaresan, M. A. Khojastepour, S. Rangarajan, and S. Banerjee, "Probeam: A practical multicell

beamforming system for ofdma small-cell networks," in *Proc. of ACM MobiHoc*, 2013.

[8] J. Xiong and K. Jamieson, "Arraytrack: A fine-grained indoor location system," in *NSDI*, 2013.

[9] S. Hong and S. Katti, "Cognitive spatial degrees of freedom estimation via compressive sensing," in *CoRoNet*, 2010.

[10] Cisco Systems Inc., "Wireless Mesh Access Points, Design and Deployment Guide," *Release 7.3*, 2012.

[11] O. Arnold, F. Richter, G. Fettweis, and O. Blume, "Power consumption modeling of different base station types in heterogeneous cellular networks," in *Future Network and Mobile Summit*, 2010.

[12] K. Joshi, S. Hong, and S. Katti, "Pinpoint: Localizing interfering radios," in *NSDI*, 2013.

[13] F. Comtech, "Fci-3740 phased array antenna," http://www.fidelity-comtech.com/products/phased-array-antennas.

[14] S. J. Orfanidis, *Electromagnetic Waves and Antennas*, 2014. [Online]. Available: http://eceweb1.rutgers.edu/ orfanidi/ewa/

[15] N. Czink, X. Yin, H. Ozcelik, M. Herdin, E. Bonek, and B. Fleury, "Cluster characteristics in a mimo indoor propagation environment," *Trans. on Wireless Comms*, 2007.

[16] E. Candes, J. Romberg, and T. Tao, "Robust uncertainty principles: exact signal reconstruction from highly incomplete frequency information," *Trans. on Information Theory*, 2006.

[17] W. Feng, Z. Xiao, D. Jin, and L. Zeng, "Circular-antenna-array-based codebook design and training method for 60ghz beamforming," in *IEEE WCNC*, 2013.

[18] R. Vescovo, "Array factor synthesis for circular antenna arrays," in *Antennas and Propagation Society International Symposium*, 1993.

[19] "CM-MMCX Clock module," http://warpproject.org/trac/wiki/HardwareUsersGuides/CM-MMCX.

[20] S. Sen, S. Gilani, S. Srinath, S. Schmitt, and S. Banerjee, "Design and implementation of an "approximate" communication system for wireless media applications," in *SIGCOMM*, 2010.

[21] X. Xie, X. Zhang, and K. Sundaresan, "Adaptive Feedback Compression for MIMO Networks," in *ACM MobiCom*, 2013.

[22] X. Xie, X. Zhang, and E. Chai, "Cross-Cell DoF Distribution: Combating Channel Hardening Effect in Multi-Cell MU-MIMO Networks," in *Proc. of ACM MobiHoc*, 2015.

[23] X. Xie and X. Zhang, "Scalable User Selection for MU-MIMO Networks," in *IEEE INFOCOM*, 2014.

[24] "Two-Layer Linear Processing for Massive MIMO on the TitanMIMO Platform," http://nutaq.com/en/library/whitepaper-news/new-paper-two-layer-linear-processing-massive-mimo-titanmimo-platform.

[25] S. Yoon, T. Jeon, and W. Lee, "Hybrid beam-forming and beam-switching for ofdm based wireless personal area networks," *JSAC*, 2009.

[26] J. Wang, Z. Lan, C.-W. Pyo, T. Baykas, C.-S. Sum, M. A. Rahman, J. Gao, R. Funada, F. Kojima, H. Harada *et al.*, "Beam codebook based beamforming protocol for multi-gbps millimeter-wave wpan systems," *IEEE Journal on Selected Areas in Communications (JSAC)*, 2009.

[27] B. Li, Z. Zhou, H. Zhang, and A. Nallanathan, "Efficient beamforming training for 60-ghz millimeter-wave communications: A novel numerical optimization framework," *IEEE Trans. on Vehicular Tech*, 2014.

[28] J. Nsenga, A. Bourdoux, and F. Horlin, "Mixed analog/digital beamforming for 60 ghz mimo frequency selective channels," in *IEEE ICC*, 2010.

[29] A. Alkhateeb, O. El Ayach, G. Leus, and R. W. Heath, "Hybrid precoding for millimeter wave cellular systems with partial channel knowledge," in *Information Theory and Applications Workshop (ITA), 2013*, 2013.

[30] D. Fuhrmann, J. Browning, and M. Rangaswamy, "Signaling strategies for the hybrid mimo phased-array radar," *Selected Topics in Signal Processing, IEEE Journal of*, 2010.

[31] K. C.-J. Lin, S. Gollakota, and D. Katabi, "Random Access Heterogeneous MIMO Networks," in *ACM SIGCOMM*, 2011.

[32] H. S. Rahul, S. Kumar, and D. Katabi, "Jmb: Scaling wireless capacity with user demands," in *SIGCOMM*, 2012.

[33] H. V. Balan, R. Rogalin, A. Michaloliakos, K. Psounis, and G. Caire, "Achieving High Data Rates in a Distributed MIMO System," in *Proc. of ACM MobiCom*, 2012.

[34] H. Dahrouj and W. Yu, "Coordinated Beamforming for the Multicell Multi-Antenna Wireless System," *IEEE Transactions on Wireless Communications*, vol. 9, no. 5, 2010.

[35] C.-B. Chae, I. Hwang, R. Heath, and V. Tarokh, "Interference Aware Coordinated Beamforming in a Multi-Cell System," *IEEE Transactions on Wireless Communications*, vol. 11, no. 10, 2012.

[36] Y. Noam and A. Goldsmith, "Exploiting Spatial Degrees of Freedom in MIMO Cognitive Radio Systems," in *Proc. of IEEE ICC*, 2012.

FreeBee: Cross-technology Communication via Free Side-channel

Song Min Kim and Tian He

Department of Computer Science and Engineering, University of Minnesota, USA

{ksong, tianhe}@cs.umn.edu

ABSTRACT

This paper presents FreeBee, which enables direct unicast as well as cross-technology/channel broadcast among three popular wireless technologies: WiFi, ZigBee, and Bluetooth. Our design aims to shed the light on the opportunities that cross-technology communication has to offer including, but not limited to, cross-technology interference mitigation and context-aware smart operation. The key concept of FreeBee is to modulate symbol messages by shifting the timing of periodic beacon frames already mandatory for wireless standards without incurring extra traffic. Such a generic cross-technology design consumes zero additional bandwidth, allowing continuous broadcast to safely reach mobile and/or duty-cycled devices. A new *interval multiplexing* technique is proposed to enable concurrent broadcasts from multiple senders or boost the transmission rate of a single sender. Theoretical and experimental exploration reveals that FreeBee offers a reliable symbol delivery under a second and supports mobility of 30mph and low duty-cycle operations of under 5%.

Categories and Subject Descriptors

C.2.1 [**Network Architecture and Design**]: Wireless communications

Keywords

Wireless; Protocol; Cross-technology

1. INTRODUCTION

The unprecedented proliferation of wireless devices in the last decade has been led by multiple wireless technologies, each offering convenience in different aspects of our daily lives. However, wireless technologies are victims of their own success: spectrum sharing among incompatible wireless technologies has led to a severe *wireless coexistence problem* [18, 28, 33, 38, 39, 42].

This paper begins with the recognition that this coexistence is indeed double side: although it may cause inefficiency and unfairness in channel/spectrum utilization, it also provides new opportunities because the standards for individual technologies are specialized and hence possess strengths in different areas that are, often the weaknesses of the others. For example, while WiFi has access to a virtually unlimited amount of information via the Internet, it consumes a considerable amount of power, causing battery problems in mobile devices [10, 16]. Conversely, the ZigBee network often operates as a stand-alone and has limited information, but is extremely energy efficient. Thus, both networks can be enhanced via mutual supplementation, demonstrating the positive side of coexistence.

In this paper, we propose FreeBee, a cross-technology communication framework that is generic and transparent (i.e., no extra traffic). Our design aims to mitigate the detrimental effect of coexistence while exploring the opportunities behind it. As such, FreeBee sheds the light on the opportunities that cross-technology communication has to offer including, but not limited to, cross-technology interference mitigation and context-aware smart operation. Specifically we achieve this via embedding symbol into beacons by shifting their transmission timing. Although the concept of modulating via signal timings is known as PPM (Pulse Position Modulation), legacy PPM supports only communication between homogeneous devices and requires precise pulse timing, which can be hardly satisfied in wireless coexistence environments with mainly contention-based MACs.

Existing cross-technology communication works [14, 40] are technology-specific and require dedicated packets for communication, burdening already-crowded channels with further overhead. In contrast, Freebee utilizes mandatory beacons widely adopted among wireless technologies [5, 35, 36], achieving a generic and free-side-channel design. In summary, our original contribution is three-fold:

- We propose FreeBee, a novel cross-technology communication framework that allows direct communication between heterogeneous senders and receivers. In addition, FreeBee allows heterogeneous devices to receive broadcast simultaneously from a sender with overlapping frequencies (e.g., Bluetooth to WiFi and ZigBee) and support a sender with a wider bandwidth (e.g., WiFi) to reach multiple narrower-band receivers (e.g., WiFi to multi-channel ZigBee).
- FreeBee requires no hardware modification and does not introduce dedicated traffic. Its existence is transparent to legacy wireless systems. Our new *interval multiplexing scheme* supports concurrent transmission and reception of multiple signals.

MobiCom'15, September 7–11, 2015, Paris, France.

DOI: http://dx.doi.org/10.1145/2789168.2790098.

- We present three prototype implementations: WiFi, ZigBee, and Bluetooth. Results suggest that FreeBee offers reliable symbol delivery within less than a second and supports mobility up to 30mph and duty cycle operation of under 5%. We also demonstrate a practical use of FreeBee: Inspecting real WiFi deployment patterns in a shopping mall area, FreeBee was found to save 78.9% of the energy otherwise wasted by the WiFi interface.

The paper is organized as follows. Section 2 presents motivations. The FreeBee design and features are introduced in Sections 3 and 4. Sections 5 and 6 evaluate performance analytically and empirically, followed by a FreeBee application in Section 7. We summarize related work in Section 8 and conclude in Section 9.

2. MOTIVATION

This section demonstrates a wide range of benefits the FreeBee technology has to offer.

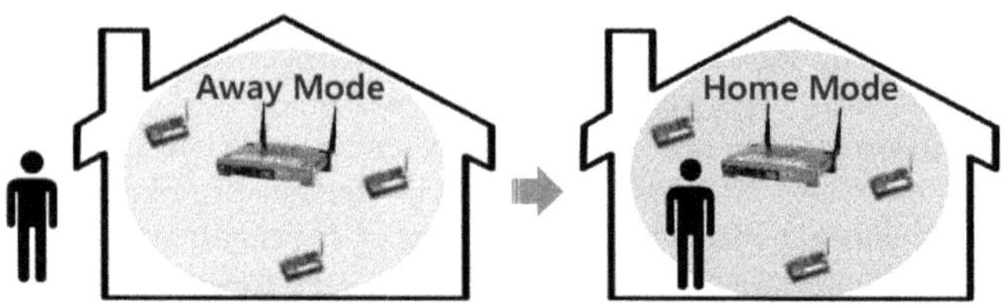

Figure 1: Context-aware home automation

- **Benefit to ZigBee – Smart homes**: FreeBee enables direct sharing of information without assistance from costly (>150 USD) dual-radio gateways that are mostly unavailable in real-life settings. One such type of information is user presence, which is accessible by WiFi AP by observing the nodes associated to it. Sharing this information enables other networks to provide context-aware service. Figure 1 demonstrates the example of a smart home with ZigBee-assisted appliances. Home WiFi AP first determines whether the resident is away or home (i.e., his/her smart phone is associated or not). Using FreeBee, this information is broadcast from the AP to all the ZigBee nodes inside the home to drive them to the appropriate operation mode. For instance, once the resident leaves they turn to "away mode", such as lowering home temperature to an energy-economic value.

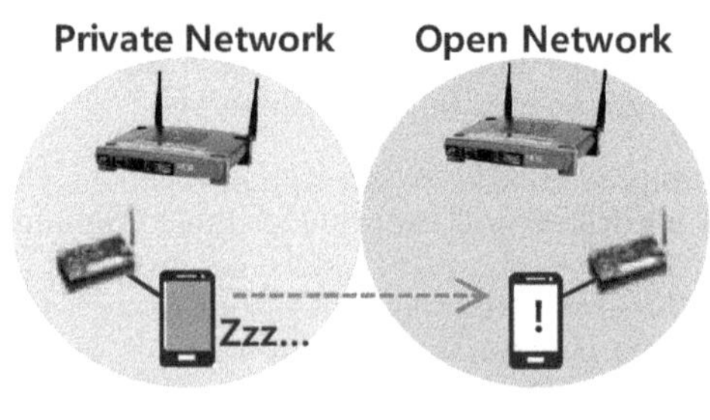

Figure 2: Wake on selective WLAN

- **Benefit to WiFi – Mobile devices**: Operating a WiFi Network Interface Card (NIC) continuously depletes precious energy in portable devices [10, 16]. To tackle this, ZiFi [43] suggests attaching a low-power ZigBee radio to the device to wake up the WiFi NIC whenever it detects the existence of *any* WiFi AP. While this approach can significantly reduce standby energy, we believe that further savings can be achieved.

Nowadays most of metropolitan areas are overloaded with WiFi APs, many of which are private. Thus, it is still a waste of energy to blindly wake up a WiFi NIC when an arbitrary AP shows up, without knowing if it is accessible or not. As shown in Figure 2, we avoid this issue by embedding 1-bit accessibility information (i.e., open/private) into WiFi beacons and allowing the attached low-power radio (Bluetooth or ZigBee) to capture this information through FreeBee. Accordingly, the WiFi NIC can wake up only when it finds an open AP. We refer to this function as *wake on selective WLAN*. We note that this approach can be extended to limiting WiFi wakeup only to discovering an AP that fits the user's interest; for instance, when there is an AP that matches a user-defined SSID.

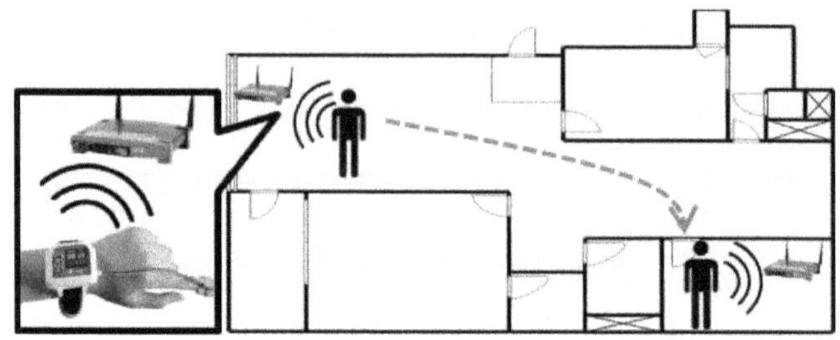

Figure 3: Real-time patient monitoring

- **Benefit to Bluetooth – Health care**: Taking advantage of its low-power operation, Bluetooth technology is widely used in portable medical devices, including glucose and heart monitors [13]. Although FreeBee is not designed to transfer a large volume of medical data, it enables health alerts by embedding urgent information into Bluetooth beacons. The ubiquitous WiFi coverage in most indoor environments today provides a continuous alert service even if patients are away from their Bluetooth-enabled medical station, as shown in Figure 3. This figure also shows that FreeBee can offer the location of the patient via geolocation provided by WiFi AP, allowing accurate and timely medical actions in case of an emergency.

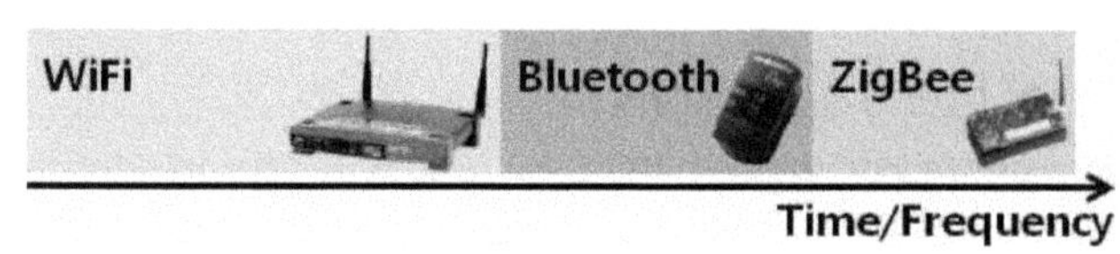

Figure 4: Cross-technology coordination

- **Benefit to all – Channel efficiency**: All WiFi, ZigBee, and Bluetooth networks can benefit from FreeBee via cross-technology channel coordination. As a result of evolving separately without considering each other, channel access schemes in heterogeneous wireless technologies are incompatible, leading to a severe CTI [20, 25, 40, 41]. This cross-technology channel access problem can be addressed by allowing explicit communication among different technologies. As demonstrated in Figure 4, FreeBee essentially allows TDMA or FDMA among heterogeneous wireless platforms, alleviating CTI. For instance, FreeBee realizes mechanisms similar to NAV (Network allocation vector) or RTS/CTS in WiFi for spectrum allocation that is global across technologies.

3. FRAMEWORK DESIGN

This section presents an overview of FreeBee, followed by design specifics such as modulation and demodulation techniques. Without loss of generality, we use communication between WiFi (sender) and ZigBee (receiver) to illustrate the generic design of FreeBee.

3.1 Design Overview

We propose a cross-technology communication framework in which symbols are embedded into the timing of beacon frames. Specifically, we slightly shift the transmission time (advance or delay) of beacon frames, a configurable setting in most WiFi APs deployed today, simply via HTTP protocol. The shift is made in the units of 1.024ms, compliant to the 802.11 standard unit used in beacon scheduling, known as TBTT (Target Beacon Transmission Time) [35]. To ensure a free side-channel operation, FreeBee shifts timing in such a way that the average interval remains the same as the original setting. Thus, the proposed communication framework is not only transparent, but also does not consume additional bandwidth or energy. This unique aspect enables important information to be broadcast continuously, safely reaching mobile and/or duty-cycled ZigBee receivers whose presence or active periods are a priori unknown to the sender.

However, WiFi beacons cannot be directly captured and recognized by ZigBee nodes, due to incompatible PHY layers. Instead, as WiFi coexists with ZigBee on the 2.4GHz ISM band, a ZigBee receiver statically detects the position of the WiFi beacons in the wireless channel, using its RSSI sensing capability. We note that, as a foundational function for MAC techniques including CSMA, RSSI sampling is common among varieties of wireless standards (e.g., Bluetooth).

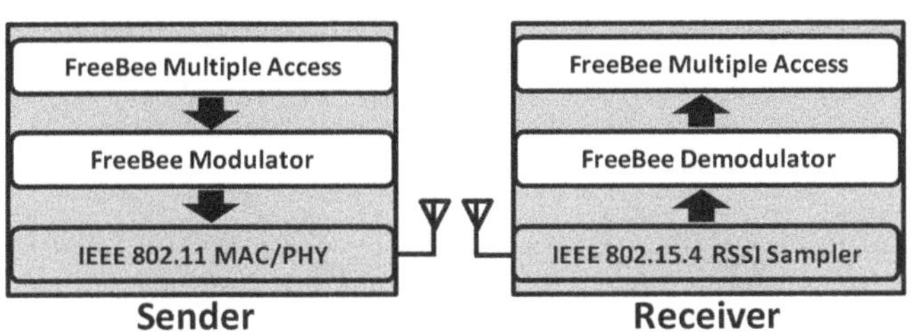

Figure 5: Architecture and scope in white boxes

Figure 5 depicts the overall architecture and the scope of this paper. Our design spans modulation/demodulation techniques, as well as a multiple access scheme for concurrent communications. We note that the WiFi-ZigBee FreeBee design is based on 802.11 and 802.15.4 standards, and our design is compatible with all 802.11 variants (i.e., a/b/g/n) and 802.15.4-compliant nodes (e.g., TelosB and MICAz) and requires no hardware modification. In fact, FreeBee can be adopted to enable communication between any heterogeneous wireless platforms as long as the channel is shared. In the following, we first propose a basic version of FreeBee with the simplest form, followed by elaborated designs that enhance the basic version.

3.2 Basic FreeBee

In this section, we describe the basic version of modulation/demodulation we refer to as *FreeBee*. This design assumes that the unmodulated position of the beacon is found during the initial network setup, which we refer to as the *reference position*. This position can be simply obtained by running FreeBee when the AP is sending beacons in their original timing. Modulated beacon positions found later are compared to the reference position for symbol interpretation (i.e., demodulation).

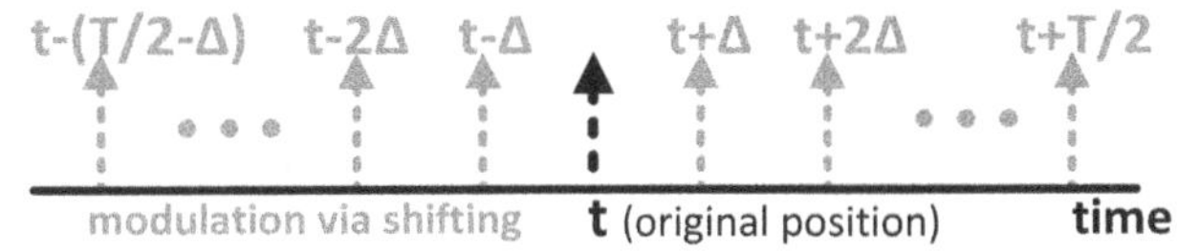

Figure 6: The symbol is embedded by shifting the beacon from its reference position, t, where the degree of shift ranges between $(-T/2, T/2]$.

3.2.1 Modulation

For timely advertisement, the 802.11 standard requires APs to periodically broadcast beacons. FreeBee establishes a free side-channel by embedding symbols within the *transmission timing* of these mandatory packets. Referring to Figure 6, let's consider a beacon whose reference position is at t, where the interval is T. Applying FreeBee, we *shift* the beacon from its reference position in the range of $(-T/2, T/2]$ to indicate the symbol to be delivered. The amount of information that can be embedded is determined by T and the granularity of shift, indicated by Δ in Figure 6. We set Δ as $1.024ms$ following the beacon scheduling granularity as defined by the 802.11 standard (We note that the information amount can easily be increased by adopting smaller Δ). Under this setting the typical T of $102.4ms$, adopted in the majority of legacy WiFi APs, corresponds to 100Δ, indicating that the beacon can be positioned at 100 different time instances. Thus, beacon shift can express $\lfloor log_2 100 \rfloor = 6$ bits.

Due to incompatible PHY layers, the ZigBee receiver is unable to decode the beacons and thus cannot detect the presence of beacons directly. Therefore we statistically locate beacons by their periodic repetition. For instance, to deliver a FreeBee symbol corresponding to $t - \Delta$ in Figure 6, multiple consecutive beacons are shifted for the same amount (i.e., beacons are transmitted at $t+T-\Delta$, $t+2T-\Delta$, and so on). The required number of beacon repetitions per symbol is decided by the channel noise, which is analyzed in detail in later sections. Lastly, we note that the beacon interval still remains at T in the process of FreeBee transmission, indicating free side-channel operation.

3.2.2 Demodulation

Here we describe how FreeBee captures and interprets position-modulated beacons for successful demodulation, especially under channel noise (i.e., other ongoing traffic within the same band). FreeBee demodulation starts from sampling the energy in the channel. This is done by consecutively recording the values obtained from the RSSI register on an 802.15.4-compliant RF chip on the ZigBee node. Upon recording a stream of RSSIs, the captured values are quantized to binaries–0 if below threshold and 1 if above–to indicate clear and busy channels. The threshold is set to be -75dBm following the CCA (Clear Channel Assessment) threshold for the 802.15.4 standard [36]. We note that WiFi also runs CCA, where the threshold is -82dBm [35]. For simplicity, we hereafter will refer to the binary value simply as RSSI. Furthermore, as a RSSI sample in ZigBee is a measurement spanning for $128us$, the sampling rate is set to be $1/128us = 7.8KHz$ to avoid time gaps between samples while keeping the rate at its minimum.

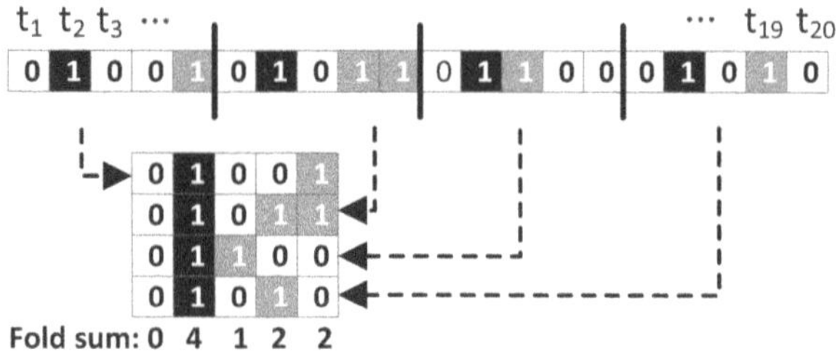

Figure 7: Folding example: series of RSSI samples expressed as boxes. Both black and gray indicate a busy channel where the former is a periodic beacon signal with $\lambda = 5$, while the latter is random noise induced by traffic or interference. White represents an idle channel. By *folding* the series into a matrix with $P = 5$ $(= \lambda)$, the black boxes align column-wise.

We then apply *folding* to the obtained RSSI vector, a signal processing technique that allows detecting periodic signal under noise. We note that this technique was originally introduced in [34] and was recently featured by ZiFi [43] to detect the presence of WiFi AP. Given a sampled RSSI vector, folding by P simply cuts the vector into sub-vectors of equal lengths of P and stacks them to yield a matrix. An example of folding is shown in Figure 7, where a sampled RSSI vector of length 20 is considered. Let the interval of the beacons captured in the vector be T seconds, and the number of samples in T as λ In the example $\lambda = 5$, and upon folding by $P = \lambda$, RSSIs of beacons (in black) align in a column. the column-wise sum is referred to as the *fold sum*, where the column with the highest fold sum indicates the position of the beacon. Note that the fold sums are likely to be smaller in other columns, as they are induced by either random (thus aperiodic) traffic or beacons with different intervals.

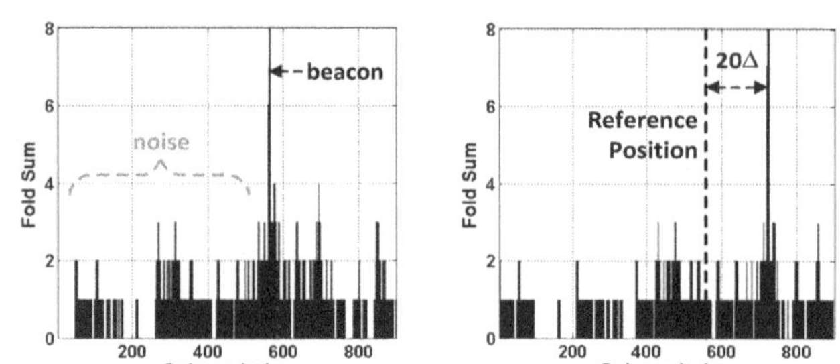

(a) Reference Position (b) Modulated Position

Figure 8: Example of FreeBee demodulation in practice, when $T = 113\Delta = 115.7ms$ and $\lambda = 904$

Figure 8 presents an example of demodulating FreeBee symbol (20Δ) in practice. To sum up, FreeBee demodulation is process of finding the column corresponding to beacon position, which can easily be achieved by folding and simply picking the column with the maximum fold sum. This same process is used to learn the reference position of the beacon during network initialization and to find the modulated position. The difference of the two positions indicates the symbol within. Other harmonic analysis techniques, such as FFT (Fast Fourier Transform) and autocorrelation, do not yield the position (i.e., phase) of the beacon, and hence are not suitable for our purpose.

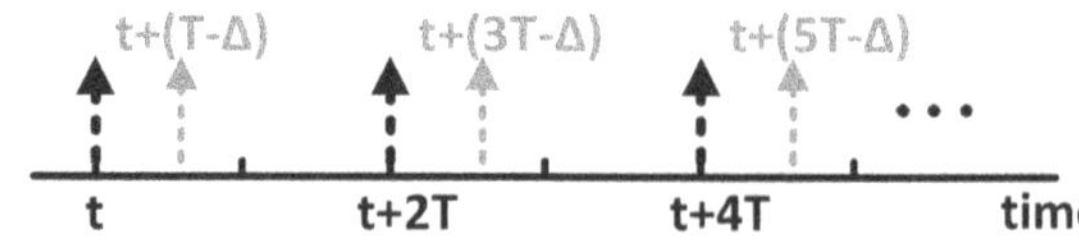

Figure 9: A-FreeBee: the positions of *every other* beacons are shifted (in gray), whereas the degree of shift is Δ in the example.

3.3 Enhanced Feature #1: Asynchrony

The basic FreeBee design embeds the symbol as a beacon time shift from the reference position, a concept that requires learning the position beforehand. We relax this condition to introduce A-FreeBee (Asynchronous FreeBee), freeing our design from any prior knowledge to offer instantaneous communication.

Figure 9 shows Modulation of A-FreeBee. Applying A-FreeBee to beacons with an interval of T, beacons are scheduled to construct two streams of beacons (black and gray) with the same interval of $2T$, where one stream (i.e., gray beacons) is a shifted version of the other (i.e., black beacons). This is achieved by shifting *every other* beacon by the amount that corresponds to the symbol to be delivered. The figure demonstrates a case where the symbol corresponds to Δ, indicating one unit of shift. We note that A-FreeBee is also a free-side-channel, as the average interval between consecutive beacons is still T.

Under A-FreeBee design, the reference position is no longer required; it simply looks for two beacon streams with the same period by folding with $P = 2\lambda$. The embedded symbol is interpreted directly from the phase difference, i.e., *Two* columns with the first and second highest fold sums are found, where the distance between them indicates A-FreeBee symbol. A demodulation example of A-FreeBee is

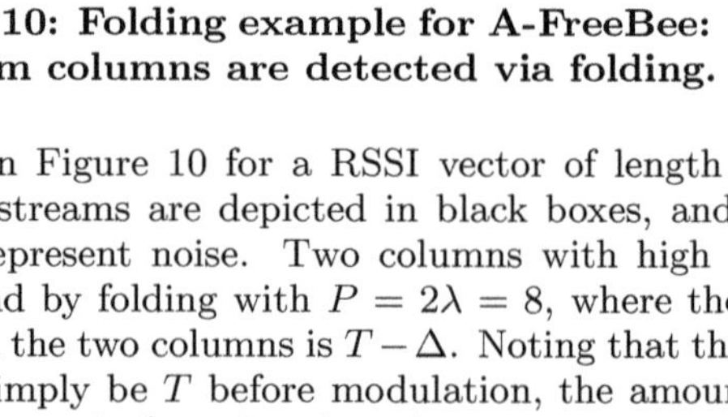

Figure 10: Folding example for A-FreeBee: two high fold sum columns are detected via folding.

shown in Figure 10 for a RSSI vector of length 16. Two beacon streams are depicted in black boxes, and the gray boxes represent noise. Two columns with high fold sums are found by folding with $P = 2\lambda = 8$, where the distance between the two columns is $T - \Delta$. Noting that the distance would simply be T before modulation, the amount of shift (i.e., the symbol) is therefore Δ. Figure 11 below demonstrates A-FreeBee demodulation in practice, where the conveyed symbol is 20Δ.

The asynchronous version features several advantages over the basic FreeBee, including that it (i) requires no synchro-

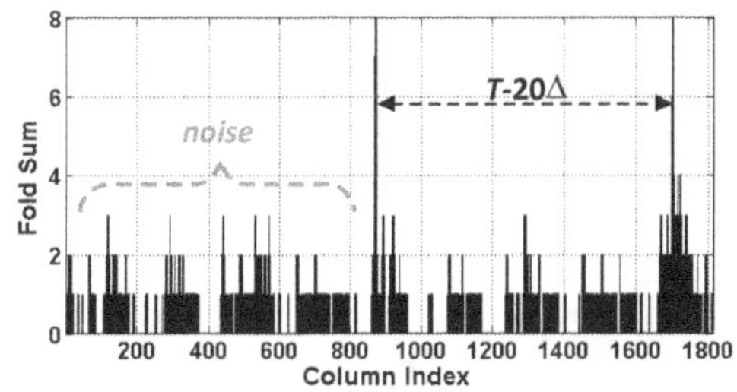

Figure 11: A-FreeBee demodulation ($T = 113\Delta$)

nization, (ii) is robust to clock drifts, and (iii) supports instantaneous communication without prior knowledge. We note that all these improvements come with a trade-off in data rate; A-FreeBee, compared to the basic FreeBee, requires collecting a higher number of beacons to form *two* high fold sums instead of one. The relationship between the performances of FreeBee and A-FreeBee are analyzed both theoretically and empirically in later parts of the paper.

3.4 Enhanced Feature #2: Concurrency

In the face of multiple (A-)FreeBee senders, selecting the same or arbitrary intervals may lead the signals to tangle and cause errors in demodulation. In this section, we address this issue to allow *simultaneous transmissions* of an arbitrary number of (A-)FreeBee symbols such that each of them can be safely demodulated at the receiver.

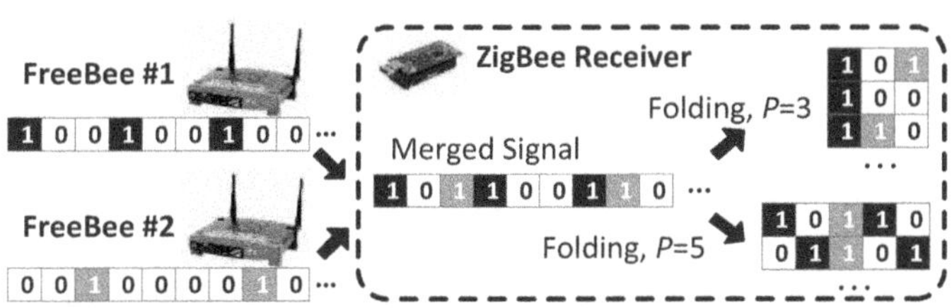

Figure 12: Demodulating interval-mutiplexed FreeBee symbols.

3.4.1 Interval Multiplexing

Recall that, according to the 802.11 standard, beacon intervals are defined in the unit of $\Delta(=1.024ms)$. Let beacon intervals of n neighboring APs be $x_1\Delta$, $x_2\Delta$, ..., $x_n\Delta$. Then, FreeBee allows simultaneous communication of n APs if x_1, x_2, ... x_n are pair-wise co-primes. We refer to this as *interval multiplexing*.

Figure 12 demonstrates a scenario of interval multiplexing/demultiplexing, where two FreeBee senders with intervals $T_1 = 3\Delta$ (in black) and $T_2 = 5\Delta$ (in gray) introduce a vector of merged RSSI signals at a receiver, and this receiver utilizes interval de-multiplexing to demodulate. Specifically, by folding with $P = 3$ and 5 and looking for the column with the highest fold sum, the receiver can detect the position of the beacons as if the other signal does not exist. This is because 3 and 5 are co-primes, and no longer holds when they are not; for example, consider a sampled RSSI vector including beacons with intervals $T_1 = 2\Delta$ and $T_2 = 4\Delta$. When folded by $P = 4$, both beacons will form high fold sums, causing demodulation error. We note that while the figure shows only two senders for clarity, this idea can be extended to n senders as long as the intervals are pairwise co-prime. The rationale behind this scheme is given in the following proposition:

PROPOSITION 3.1. *For FreeBee signals with co-prime intervals, folding for one signal restricts the fold sum of the others to a maximum of 1.*

PROOF. Let $T_1 = x_1\Delta$ and $T_2 = x_2\Delta$ be two beacon intervals where x_1 and x_2 are co-primes. When a sampled RSSI vector containing beacons of interval T_2 is fold by $P = x_1$, beacon repeats in a column every LCM (least common multiple) of x_1 and x_2, which is $x_1 \times x_2$. Since the total length of the sampled RSSI vector is much smaller than $x_1 \times x_2$, beacons with the interval of $x_1\Delta$ cannot be folded into the same column when folded by x_2 (and vice versa), yielding the maximum fold sum of 1. □

The proposition states that the cross-interference between FreeBee signals is effectively suppressed when intervals are co-prime, essentially granting orthogonality between signals for concurrent communication. We note that this holds for both basic FreeBee and A-FreeBee.

In practice, to avoid the overhead in computing for co-prime numbers, we allow APs to select among a set of pre-stored *prime* numbers instead. Moreover, the same interval should not be chosen among neighboring APs, which can be easily achieved in *listen before talk* fashion; they listen to each other to acquire the beacon interval information (i.e., x in $T = x\Delta$) that, according to the 802.11 standard, is recorded within beacons. After storing a set of intervals used by the neighboring APs, an unoccupied prime number is chosen as its interval. Conversely, coordination via wired connection (i.e., WLAN or the Internet) may be preferred, which avoids the hidden terminal problem.

3.4.2 Implicit Addressing Feature of FreeBee

This section discusses the unique addressing scheme used in FreeBee. As a reminder, demodulating each interval-multiplexed FreeBee signals remains the same as the case for a single signal; folding with P yields the corresponding FreeBee signal with P.

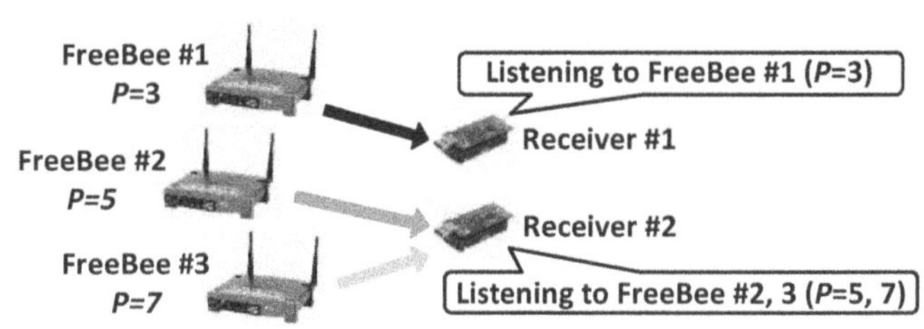

Figure 13: Implicit addressing via interval multiplexing

- **For stationary deployment**: As shown in Figure 13, each interval P is allocated to one freeBee sender, implicitly addressing that sender. Hence a receiver may select a subset of P's that corresponds to the sender(s) of interest.
- **For mobile deployment**: In mobile scenarios, mobile devices are not aware of Ps used by nearby FreeBee enabled devices. We need to fold for all Ps in the prime set to receive from every sender. This is not as computationally heavy as it may sound, as the number of primes, by the prime number theorem [21], is limited to $\frac{x_{max}}{ln(x_{max})} - \frac{x_{min}}{ln(x_{min})}$ when x_{max} and x_{min} are the maximum and minimum values in the prime set. For example, there are 20 primes in the interval range of $x_{min} = 53$ and $x_{max} = 149$.

From a practical point of view, we emphasize that implicit addressing is a unique and effective feature of our design: as each sender is required to select different beacon interval, symbols demodulated with the same P are ensured to be from the same sender. This allows safely constructing a long symbol by appending received symbols. However, this is not the case for all other cross-technology techniques. In Esense [14] and HoWiES [41], a sender ID has to be embedded along with information in order to concatenate separate symbols correctly, leading to a large overhead in such a low-rate cross-technology communication.

4. PRACTICAL ISSUES

In this section, we discuss practical issues and their effects on our design.

• **Channel access delay**: Although beacons are prioritized over data packets and hence queueing delays are negligible [35], they *do* suffer from channel access delays according to CSMA. This is in fact a challenge uniquely imposed on our design, which is different from traditional the PPM environment where all pulses are transmitted at their exact times. Upon long delays, a beacon may fail to contribute to folding. This is precisely why beacon repetitions are needed (e.g., four beacons in Figure 7) for statistical performance guarantee. Our empirical study in Section 6.3 suggests that 5 beacons yield an error of less than 1%.

• **Noise**: Any non-beacon signal occupying the spectrum serves as noise and is a potential source of error. That is, as frequent 1's due to noise fill up the sampled RSSI, there is an increased chance of a large fold sum formed elsewhere to the beacon position, thus inducing demodulation failure. In other words, the performance of our design is enhanced by reducing the noise. This is simply done by taking only the first two RSSI samples for *any* packet including beacons and discarding (i.e., set to 0) the rest. The reason behind this approach is two-fold: (i) As data packets tend to be much longer than beacons, this reduces noise to 1/6 on average in our experiments. (ii) Our empirical analysis indicates that the channel access delays of beacons are mostly (>90%) less than 256us, where a similar result was reported in a recent study [19]. Noting that the duration of a RSSI sample is 128us, this suggests the first two RSSI samples (256us) of beacons maintain a high chance of overlapping (i.e., contributing to fold sum) upon folding.

5. ANALYTICS

In this section, we provide a theoretical analysis of the performance of FreeBee and A-FreeBee.

5.1 SER vs. Sampling Duration

As noted earlier, the symbol error occurs upon demodulation failure, essentially when the fold sum of noise is higher than that of the beacons. For brevity, we defer a detailed SER (Symbol Error Rate) derivation to Appendix 9 and here move directly to the results to demonstrate the impact of three system parameters: (i) T, the beacon interval. (i) ρ, the number of beacon repetitions for statistical demodulation; and (iii) Sampling duration, the sampling time to obtain a symbol, which is $\rho \times T$ for FreeBee and $\rho \times 2T$ for A-FreeBee.

Figures 14(a) and 14(b) show Symbol Error Rate (SER) when default beacon interval is set as $T = 97\Delta = 99.3ms$.

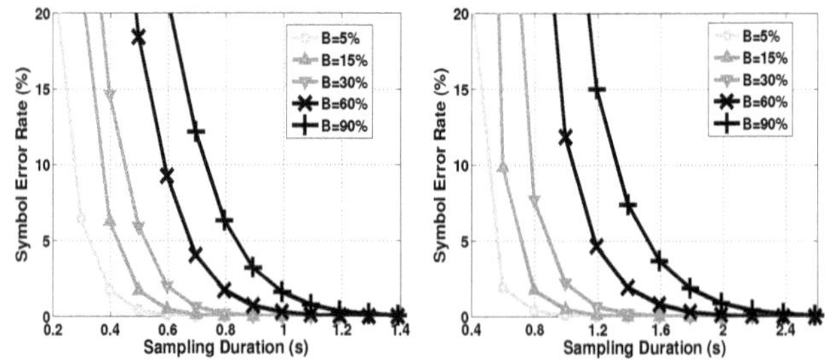

(a) FreeBee (b) A-FreeBee

Figure 14: SER vs. sampling duration ($T = 97\Delta$).

These figures convey three ideas: (i) longer sampling (i.e., higher ρ) lowers SER, as more beacons are utilized to fight against noise; (ii) for a given duration, FreeBee achieves a lower SER than A-FreeBee; and (iii) higher channel occupancy, denoted by B, indicates more noise, thus higher SER. The figures have B up to 90% for completeness of analysis, where $B \leq 30\%$ was observed in our experiment (under the threshold of -75dBm) in a university building with 50+ APs. Similar observations were reported in a recent study from a large-scale open WiFi trace [3, 43]. The figures suggest analytically that FreeBee and A-FreeBee achieve SER<1% for durations of $0.7s$ and $1.2s$ under such condition. We note this analytical result matches well with results from empirical experiments shown in Section 6.3.

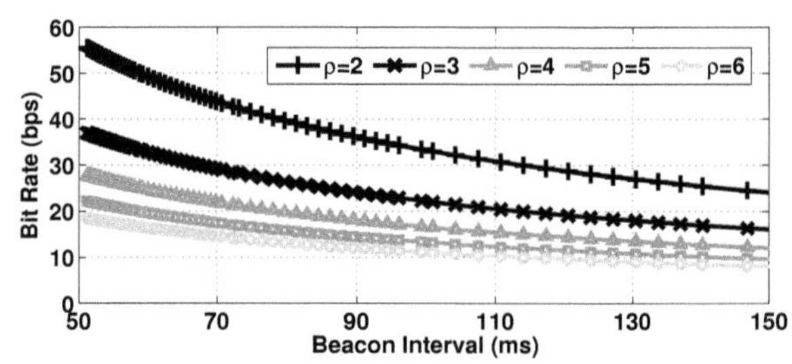

Figure 15: Bit rate vs. T for different ρ.

5.2 Transmission Rate vs. Beacon Interval

Beacon interval, T, is another factor that can affect (A-)FreeBee performance. The impact of beacon interval T can be observed with bit rate R. Intuitively, enlarging the beacon interval has two effects: (i) it offers more space for shift, or equivalently, yields more bits per symbol; and (ii) it requires more time to reach the same ρ. The bit rate for FreeBee can be computed as below:

$$R = \frac{log_2 T/\Delta}{T \times \rho}\ bps \tag{1}$$

Noting that Δ (1.024ms in WiFi) defines the granularity of shift, the numerator in the Equ. 1 implies *bit per symbol*. Figure 15 shows the impact of beacon interval T on R in different scenarios for the range of practical intervals. In A-FreeBee, the rate is cut in half as it takes double sample duration (i.e., $\rho \times 2T$) to convey a same symbol. It is important to note that the rate given here is per sender, without bandwidth consumption (i.e., without incurring extra traffic). Due to interval multiplexing, the aggregated throughput linearly increases according to the number of senders. Furthermore, boosting the throughput of a single sender by adopting additional beacons is also a viable option. Performances under such cases are shown via experimental evaluations in the next section.

6. PERFORMANCE EVALUATION

We show the generality of (A-)FreeBee by evaluations performed across four platforms operating on three different wireless standards: WiFi, ZigBee, and Bluetooth.

(a) WiFi(WARP) (b) WiFi(laptop)

(c) ZigBee (d) Bluetooth

Figure 16: Four evaluation platforms on three different wireless technologies – WiFi, ZigBee, and Bluetooth.

Table 1: Experiment Settings

Communication Direction	Tx Ch.	Tx Power	Rx Ch.	Dist.
WiFi → ZigBee	1,4	13 dBm	11-15	8m
ZigBee → WiFi	11-14	0 dBm	1	1.5m
Bluetooth → WiFi	37-39	4 dBm	4	3m
Bluetooth → ZigBee	37-39	4 dBm	15	3m

6.1 Experiment Settings

The experiment parameters are specified in Table 1, where the detailed settings are as follows.

• **Design generality:** As a generic cross-technology communication framework, our design mechanisms including modulation, demodulation, and interval multiplexing commonly apply to different underlying technologies. This is possible because, according to the standards, (i) beacons are adopted in all three technologies of WiFi, ZigBee, and Bluetooth, (ii) they commonly allow modification of beacon timings, (iii) they reside on overlapping frequencies in the 2.4GHz band and finally, (iv) the light-weight design makes our design feasible even to low-end devices, as demonstrated later in the section.

• **WiFi:** Figures 16(a) and 16(b) show the two WiFi platforms on which our design is implemented: WARP [9] and laptops. The former is a wireless research platform fully integrated with WiFi PHY/MAC layers. As a FPGA-based system allowing real-time operation, the evaluation on WARP enables precise exploration into FreeBee performance. Further implementation on six different laptops with various WiFi NICs from Qualcomm, Realtek, and Intel avoids hardware bias.

Evaluations via laptops utilize `Lorcon2` packet injection library [7] to schedule beacons according to FreeBee, which is a reasonable approach since laptops/PCs running software AP are frequently used in practice [4]. In Table 1, we use WiFi channel 1 (unless otherwise specified) for communication with ZigBee, one of the three most commonly used channels (i.e., 1, 6, and 11), granting generality to our result. We then tune to channel 4, which overlaps with a Bluetooth advertising channel (i.e., 38), for communication with Bluetooth.

• **ZigBee:** We use 30 ZigBee-compliant MICAz nodes (Figure 16(c)) for our experiments. When operating as a receiver, a MICAz node captures RSSI values (at 7.8KHz sampling rate by default) and records them within its 512KB on-board flash. The values are either processed (i.e., demodulated) within the node or flushed to a PC for analysis, depending on experiments. We use channels 11-15, overlapping with WiFi channels 1 and 4, and a Bluetooth advertising channel of 38.

• **Bluetooth:** Our design is implemented on IOGEAR Bluetooth LE USB adapter, a cheap (~12 USD) off-the-shelf product, shown in Figure 16(d). On this device, we utilize `AltBeacon` [1] library running under Linux's BlueZ driver for FreeBee embedding. Specifically, connectable directed advertising was used to generate FreeBee-enabled beacons on all three advertising channels of 37-39, which complies to the standard on Bluetooth beaconing.

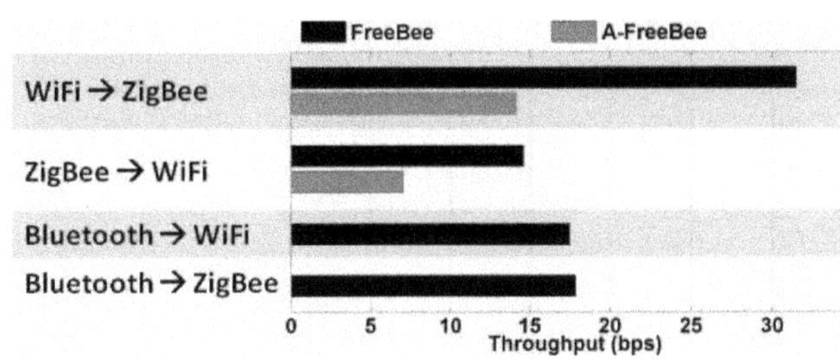

Figure 17: Per-sender throughputs achievable without incurring any extra traffic, evaluated on four different communication channels

6.2 Per-sender Throughput

In this section we demonstrate the data rate achievable per sender, under free side-channel as well as when the channel is fully utilized.

• **Free side-channel throughput:** Figure 17 illustrates per-sender data rate without introducing additional traffic (i.e., free side-channel). The experiment was conducted in a residential area with 20+ APs in proximity. Beacon intervals are set as 99.3, 76.8, and 78.75ms for WiFi, ZigBee, and Bluetooth, respectively, where the rate may easily be enhanced with shorter beacon intervals. The figure demonstrates two ideas: (i) The performance of A-FreeBee is slightly less than half of that of FreeBee, due to doubled sampling duration in A-FreeBee. Longer sampling duration increases the chance of larger fold sum of noise, hence yields higher SER in A-Freebee compared to FreeBee. This agrees with our theoretical analysis in Section 5.1. (ii) Among different communication directions, WiFi to ZigBee exhibits the fastest rate of 31.5bps for FreeBee. The rate drops to

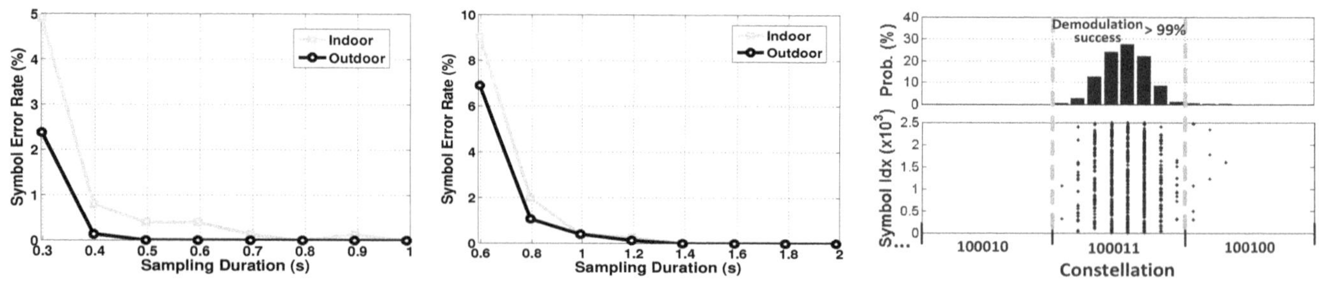

(a) FreeBee (b) A-FreeBee (c) Constellation diagram and distribution

Figure 18: Indoor and outdoor performances of (a)FreeBee and (b)A-FreeBee when $T = 97\Delta = 99.3ms$. Due to less noise outdoors, both FreeBee and A-FreeBee reach SER<1% at $\rho = 4$, whereas indoor environment required $\rho = 5$. (c) shows where the received symbols are positioned when '100011' was sent 2,500 times.

14.6bps for ZigBee to WiFi as the ZigBee standard enforces large unit shift (i.e., Δ=15.36ms), reducing the amount of information embedded in a symbol. While the Bluetooth standard defines a fine-grained beacon shift unit (Δ = 0.625ms), the random backoff ranging up to 10ms affects the performances of Bluetooth to WiFi and ZigBee communications where they show 17.5 and 17.8bps, respectively. While disabling the backoff functionality would increase the throughput significantly, the case is not considered in this paper as it requires modification to the standard (lacks compatibility).

• **Upper bound throughput under ideal conditions:** We demonstrate the effectiveness of our design by comparing the maximum throughput of our design to that of Esense [14], a state-of-art cross-technology communication scheme. Esense, as a WiFi to ZigBee communication technique, conveys data by modulating WiFi packet durations, where its ideal maximum throughput is reported under the ideal condition of interference-free channel that is fully utilized by a single sender. Hence we adopt this setting in evaluating FreeBee. Evaluation parameters also follow the values proposed in Esense; That is, RSSI sampling rate of $32KHz$ (= sampling interval of $30.5us$), inter-frame duration of $90us$, and the maximum WiFi transmission rate of 54Mbps (802.11g).

To obtain the ideal FreeBee performance, we first note that beacons need not be repeatedly transmitted under the interference-free channel. That is, a single beacon frame conveys a symbol where SER=0. When the maximum shift is $x\Delta$, a symbol (i.e., a beacon) embeds $log_2(x+1)bits$, where the time it consumes consists of inter-frame duration, beacon transmission time, and the amount of shift, where the unit of shift may be as small as the sampling interval (i.e., Δ = $30.5us$). When $x = 4$, FreeBee yields the throughput of 10.2Kbps given the beacon length of 100Bytes. Esense, according to its researchers, achieves the throughput of 5.13Kbps under the same setting. This is because Esense requires to use long-length packets (with long air-time) up to 1,500Bytes to enable measurement of WiFi packet durations via a low-end ZigBee node. Meanwhile, FreeBee utilizes short beacons to offer higher channel efficiency.

6.3 Symbol Error Rate

Here we present the reliability of our design in practice by evaluating SER under both indoor and outdoor environments in a residential area. This experiment is based on WiFi(WARP) to ZigBee communication, where more than 2,500 symbols are sent and demodulated for SER computation. The results for FreeBee and A-FreeBee are depicted in Figures 18(a) and 18(b). Both designs reach $SER \leq 0.5\%$ when $\rho = 5$ (i.e., $0.5s$ and $1s$ for FreeBee and A-FreeBee), regardless of the environment. Furthermore, both designs perform better in outdoor environments, due to lower channel occupancy, B.

The lower figure in 18(c) illustrates the constellation, along with the demodulated positions of received symbols, when the 6bit symbol of '100011' is repeatedly sent 2,500 times. Demodulation is successful when a dot resides inside the region marked by gray dotted lines in the constellation. The upper figure in 18(c) shows the distribution of the dots, in which >99% are successfully demodulated.

6.4 Cross-technology/channel Broadcast

This section demonstrates FreeBee's unique capability to *broadcast* to receivers with heterogeneous technologies and channels.

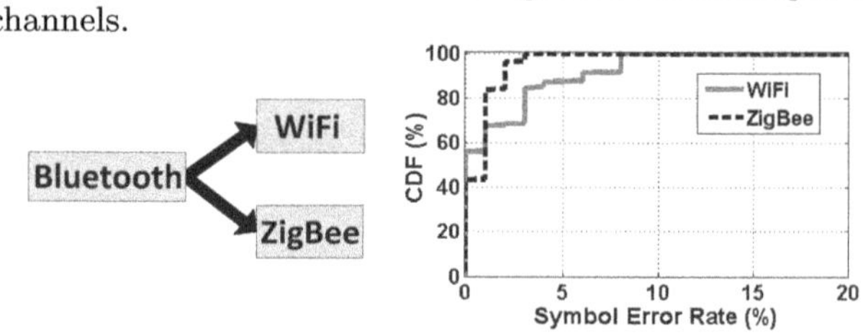

Figure 19: Simultaneous broadcast from Bluetooth to WiFi and ZigBee.

• **Cross-technology broadcast**: Depicted in Figure 19, as a generic communication framework, FreeBee allows broadcast to heterogeneous receivers with overlapping frequencies. Our generic design is effective in practice, since it avoids the complexity associated with technology-specific operation. In the experiment, WiFi and ZigBee were set to channels 4 and 15 to listen to Bluetooth's advertisement channel of 38 simultaneously. In this particular case shown in Figure 19, WiFi receiver, compared to ZigBee, suffers from larger SER. It is due to higher noise, as WiFi channel 4 overlaps with the popular WiFi channels of 1 and 6, while ZigBee channel 15 does not.

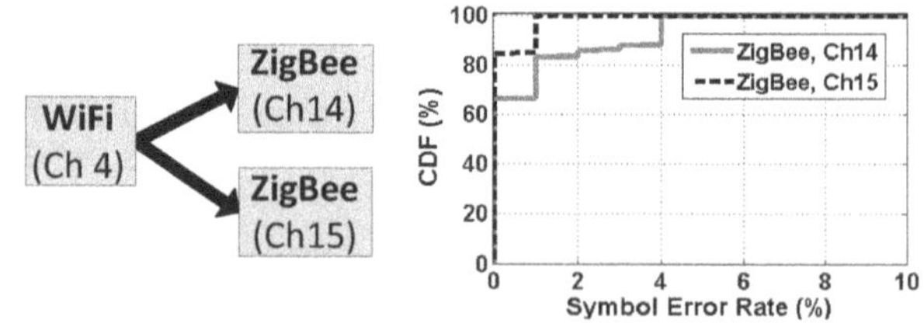

Figure 20: Simultaneous broadcast from WiFi to ZigBees on different channels.

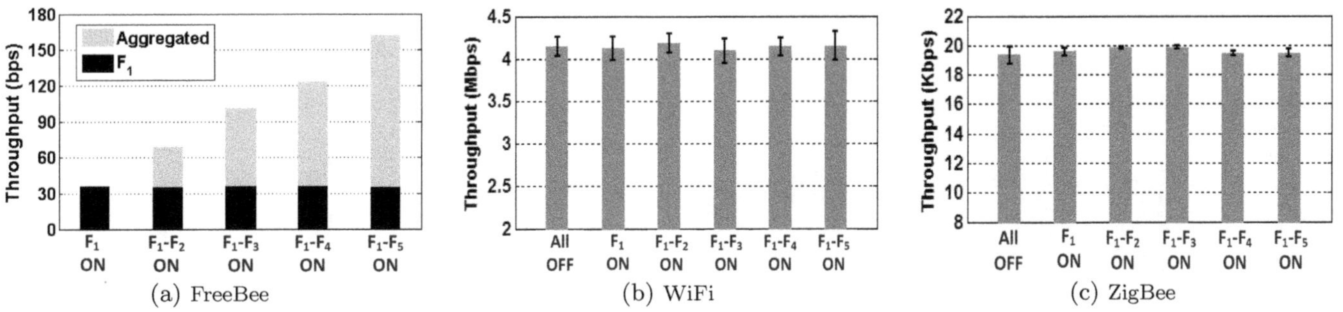

(a) FreeBee (b) WiFi (c) ZigBee

Figure 21: Transparency of FreeBee to (a)concurrent FreeBee signals, (b)WiFi, and (c)ZigBee

• **Cross-channel broadcast**: Figure 20 demonstrates another FreeBee's feature where a sender with wider bandwidth (WiFi) reaches multiple narrower-band receivers (ZigBee) on different channels with a single broadcast. WiFi's bandwidth spans 20MHz while it is only 2MHz for ZigBee. The experiment result in Figure 20 shows that SER on channel 14 is larger than that of channel 15. This is because channel 14 is affected by the noise from the heavily-used WiFi channel 1.

We note cross-technology broadcast and cross-channel broadcast can be combined to support more sophisticated scenarios where multiple heterogeneous senders deliver control symbols (through interval multiplexing) to multiple heterogeneous wireless receivers running under different channels. Such a capability would encourage further research on cross-technology coordination and control.

6.5 Transparency

We deploy five WiFi FreeBee senders, F_1-F_5, with beacon intervals of $\{91.1, 99.3, 103.4, 105.5, 109.6\}$ ms corresponding to $\{89\Delta, 97\Delta, 101\Delta, 103\Delta, 107\Delta\}$. Prime intervals indicate they are interval-multiplexed. Each sender is allowed to operate in FreeBee ON or OFF modes. A sender embeds FreeBee symbols only when it is ON. When OFF, the sender acts as a legacy AP to simply transmit beacons periodically without symbol embedding. Under this setting, we observe the throughput of legacy wireless networks when a single to multiple FreeBee APs are operational, as well as the cross-interference among them. To do so, we first turn only F_1 to ON mode, while leaving all the others OFF. Then, we turn $F_2 - F_5$ to ON one by one every 10 minutes.

• **Transparency between FreeBees**: As the black bar in Figure 21(a) demonstrates, the throughput of F_1 is kept stable at an average of 35.5bps in the face of multiple concurrent FreeBee transmissions. This validates the performance of interval multiplexing in suppressing cross-interference among FreeBee signals. In fact simultaneous transmission helps to linearly increase the aggregated throughput up to 161.8bps, as shown by the gray bar. While the throughput can be enhanced by selecting shorter intervals for $F_1 - F_5$, we select ones close to that of a legacy AP ($102.4ms = 100\Delta$) to limit the channel usage to a similar level.

• **Transparency to legacy networks**: We again turn $F_1 - F_5$ to ON mode one at a time every 10 minutes, during which throughput between a pair of WiFi or ZigBee nodes are measured. The results are demonstrated in Figures 21(b) and 21(c). For WiFi, we use `Iperf` [6] to measure TCP throughput when operating in 802.11g. The WiFi sender was placed beside the FreeBees, 8m away from the WiFi receiver. For ZigBee measurement, sender and receiver were placed 5m apart, where 20byte packets were continuously transmitted at the fastest speed (i.e., with the minimum inter-packet delay). The figures show stable throughputs averaging 4.1Mbps and 19.6Kbps for WiFi and ZigBee, respectively, with small standard deviations. This suggests that both networks are unaffected by the presence of FreeBees, confirming that the free side-channel design successfully keeps FreeBee transparent to legacy networks.

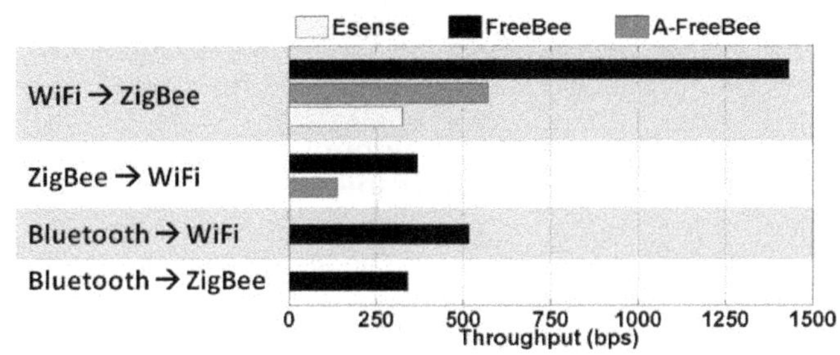

Figure 22: Aggregated throughput via interval multiplexing across multiple senders and/or within a sender. Compared to the state-of-the-art, Esense, FreeBee and A-FreeBee shows 4.3× and 1.8× performance, respectively.

6.6 Aggregated Throughput

This section investigates throughputs achievable via interval multiplexing, under different communication scenarios. Through interval multiplexing our design supports: (i) boosted aggregated throughput via concurrent transmission from multiple senders and (ii) adoption of additional beacons in a single sender to increase the throughput of that sender. We note that (i) and (ii) can be applied simultaneously; that is, multiple senders transmit concurrently while each sender freely adopts additional beacons in case of a need for higher throughput. Figure 22 depicts the throughputs for different communication scenarios, where we compare our design to the state of the art, Esense. According to the authors, when multiple Esense senders are present and the interference from the heterogeneous wireless systems are negligible, Esense achieves the bit rate of 1.63Kbps when a single WiFi packet is used to deliver one symbol, where five consecutive packets are needed per symbol for reliable communication [14]. This yields a throughput of 326bps. Following the same setting, Figure 22 demonstrates the rate achievable when the channel is shared among multiple (A-)FreeBee senders. FreeBee from WiFi to ZigBee shows the highest throughput of 1.4Kbps. The rate drops in other scenarios due to the same reasons discussed in the previous section; that is, a large shift unit in ZigBee and random ac-

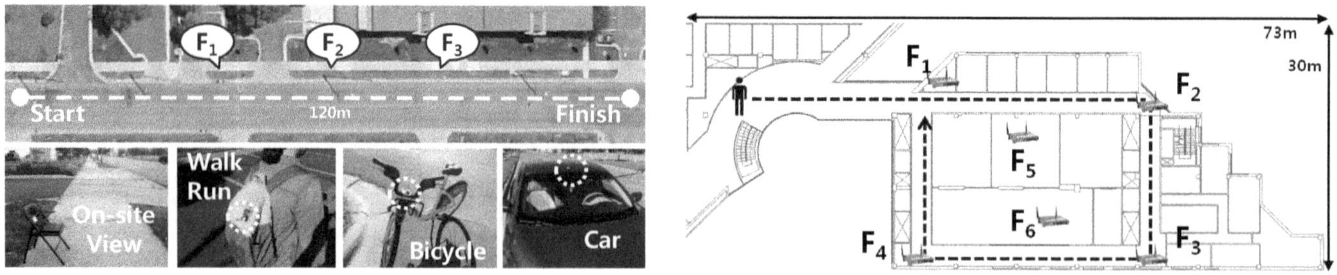

(a) Outdoor (b) Indoor

Figure 23: Mobile scenario evaluation: we experimentally reveal the impact of mobility on FreeBee on both indoor and outdoor scenarios, when the receivers are duty-cycled.

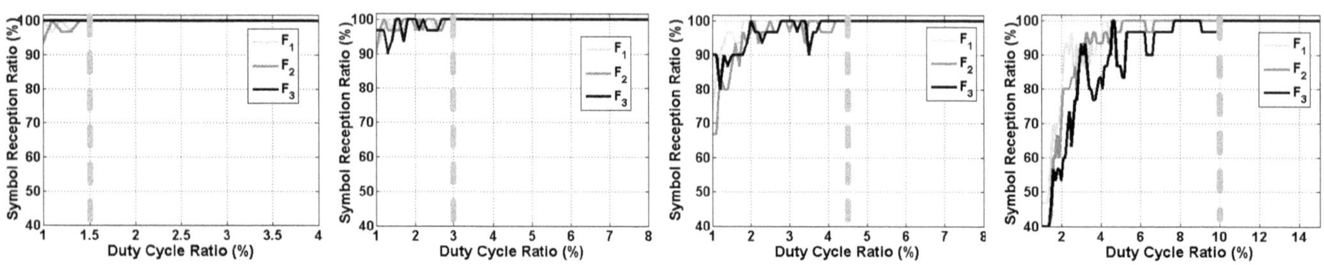

(a) Walk (b) Run (c) Bicycle (d) Car

Figure 24: When walking, running, riding bicycle and car, reception can be ensured with duty cycling of only 1.5%, 3%, 4.5% and 10%, respectively.

cess delay in Bluetooth. It is notable that Bluetooth to WiFi shows higher throughput of 514bps, compared to 349bps in the Bluetooth to ZigBee case. This is because higher sampling rate achievable in WiFi compared to ZigBee (10MHz versus 7.8KHz in our setting) allows precise measurement of the beacon timings and reduces the chance of noise forming a high fold sum.

We note that the results in Figure 22 is achievable under a large number (~hundreds) of concurrent senders, which can be realized by the following two techniques: (i) To allow numerous interval-multiplexed symbols, we choose beacon intervals from a set of numbers whose pair-wise LCM is longer than the length of the sampled RSSI vector. This clearly offers many more adoptable intervals compared to just using primes, while maintaining the effect of the interval multiplexing. (ii) As shown in the previous section, interval-multiplexed FreeBee symbols are transparent to each other under usual volume of concurrent senders (e.g., tens of FreeBee WiFi APs). Here we consider the extreme case of hundreds of senders where we take cross-interference into account. We address this issue of cross-interference by eliminating the beacons from the RSSI vector after they are interpreted. Specifically, we demodulate symbols in the ascending order according to their intervals. After demodulating each symbol, the beacons (i.e., RSSIs) corresponding to that symbol are eliminated (i.e., flipped from 1 to 0 in the RSSI vector). By doing so the cross-interference between symbols are effectively canceled to yield a high throughput. For instance, in WiFi to ZigBee FreeBee, SER is suppressed to be less than 5% when over 400 symbols with intervals between 91.1ms and 2s are concurrently sent.

6.7 Mobility and Duty Cycling

Here we consider a practical scenario of mobile receivers. For instance, this insight offers ideas on the feasibility of A-FreeBee for applications that requires location tracking. Furthermore, we take duty cycle into account where radios are turned off the majority of the time to preserve energy, a technique often adopted in battery-powered ZigBee networks to support long-term operations [11, 32, 24]. We deploy several WiFi A-FreeBee senders (laptop) in a university building and on a street, where the mobile receivers pass by the senders at different speeds: walking, running, on a bicycle, and in a car. It is worth noting that this experiment takes advantage of our free-side channel design, as (A-)FreeBee symbols can be continuously broadcast without occupying the channel, thus reaching mobile and/or duty-cycled receivers whose presence or active periods are unknown a priori.

- **On a street**: In this experiment, we deploy 3 A-FreeBee senders, 20m apart, on a street as shown in Figure 23(a). The figure also shows ZigBee receivers with different degrees of mobility: walking (4.3 mph), running (6.8 mph), on a bicycle (10.8 mph) and in a car (30 mph). Thirty receivers were tested for each speed. Figure 24 informs that A-FreeBee symbols from all the senders can be safely received with duty-cycling of only 1.5%, 3%, 4.5% and 10% when walking, running, cycling and riding in a car, respectively.
- **In a university building**: A total of 6 FreeBee senders are deployed as shown in Figure 23(b) to show the impact of various positions, such as hallways and rooms with closed or open doors. A person walks at a moderate speed of 4.3 mph through the hallway following the arrow in the figure, with a ZigBee receiver tied to his/her backpack. The result after repeating for 30 different receivers is shown in Figure 25. Overall, as indicated by the gray dotted line, duty cycling of 6% ensures reception of A-FreeBee symbols from all the senders. A higher duty cycle ratio is required compared to

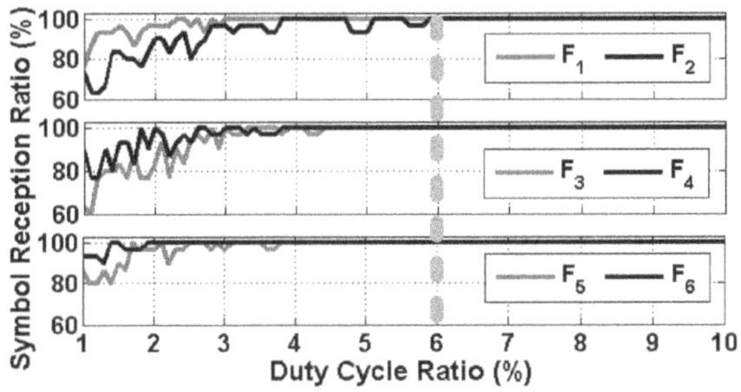

Figure 25: Duty cycling of 6% guarantees reception when walking in a university building.

the 1.5% when walking outside in the previous experiment due to the noisy environment with 50+ legacy WiFi APs deployed.

6.8 Receiver Overhead

In this section we demonstrate light-weight storage and computation/energy overheads of (A-)FreeBee demodulation, making it affordable even to low-end devices (e.g., ZigBee mote) without disrupting the ongoing legacy protocols.

• **Storage**: Let us consider an example case where the sender is a WiFi AP with the beacon interval of $T = 97\Delta = 99.3ms$ (i.e., λ=776) and the receiver is a ZigBee mote. As explained earlier, the receiver samples RSSI every $128us$, where the total number of $\rho \times \lambda$ samples are collected for demodulation. As a RSSI value is represented as a single bit, under $\rho = 5$ FreeBee requires 5×776=3.88Kbits (i.e., 485Bytes) of memory. This takes up less than 1% of the storage offered in popular commodity ZigBee motes of MICAz and TelosB, where they offer 512KBytes and 1MBytes of on-board flash, respectively. Moreover, it is also important to note the followings: First, concurrent demodulation of n interval-multiplexed FreeBee symbols whose intervals are $\lambda_1 < \lambda_2 < ... < \lambda_n$, is achieved by collecting $\rho \times \lambda_n$ samples. Second, it is possible to reduce the memory usage by storing only the timing of transitions (i.e., $0 \leftrightarrow 1$) in RSSI values. Third, A-FreeBee requires to store twice the number of samples compared to the basic FreeBee.

• **Computation/Energy**: The demodulation process can be decomposed into three parts: (i) sampling RSSI, (ii) adding to fold sum, and lastly, (iii) locating the position of the maximum fold sum. (i) and (ii) are repeatedly performed every $128us$, periodically incurring small overheads to perform a fetch and an addition operations. Upon collecting sufficient number (i.e., $\rho \times \lambda$) of samples (iii) takes place in which series of compare operations are executed in search for the maximum of the λ fold sums (2λ for A-FreeBee).

We demonstrate the overhead of the entire steps (i.e., (i)-(iii)) on a off-the-shelf, low-end system – ZigBee-compliant MICAz node. Specifically, we observe the execution time the node spends to process the demodulation. This is accurately measured by triggering a GPIO (general-purpose input/output) pin, whose activity is captured with Tektronix DPO 4054 oscilloscope. It is found that the demodulation of a symbol with an interval of $\lambda = 776$ costs $51.5ms$ of computation time, consuming only $1.2mJ$ of additional energy compared to sleeping. The light overhead allows FreeBee to run on commodity low-end hardwares without disrupting the legacy protocols. Finally, we note that demodulating multiple, interval-multiplexed FreeBee symbols requires more computation/energy where they still remain affordable; For instance, listening to 10 concurrent symbols costs $98.5ms$ of computation, indicating $2.4mJ$ of energy.

7. APP: WAKE ON SELECTIVE WLAN

In battery-powered mobile devices such as smart phones, WiFi NIC continuously scanning the channel for available APs, leading to significant energy drainage. To tackle this issue, recent studies utilize a low-power secondary radio to wake up the WiFi interface only when APs are present, since a WiFi interface consumes $669.9mW$ [2] when it is awake, but it drops to only $10mW$ once it starts to sleep. ZigBee, in contrast, requires only $75mW$ [8], even when active. Among the works in this category, ZiFi [43] is a state-of-the-art solution that offers a simple, infrastructure-free approach to detect APs in proximity with a ZigBee SD card inserted in a smart phone.

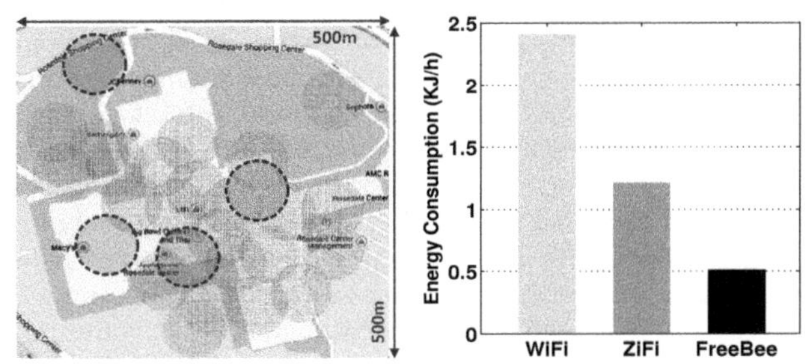

(a) WiFi zones (b) Energy Consumption

Figure 26: In (a), private and open WiFi zones are marked as light gray and dark gray (outlined) circles in a mall area; (b) shows the energy consumption, where FreeBee saves 78.9%.

Although results in [43] are encouraging, we believe that further savings can be achieved with FreeBee. Given that most of APs nowadays are private, blindly waking up the WiFi without knowing if it is accessible or not leads to energy waste. This problem can be easily solved with FreeBee by allowing APs to broadcast binary information indicating if it is an open or a private WiFi. Figure 26(a) illustrates the benefit of this approach by considering a $500 \times 500m^2$ area around a shopping mall. For a realistic evaluation, we observe all private and open WiFi APs currently running in the area[1]. Private WiFi APs are marked as light gray circles and open APs illustrated as outlined circles. The radius of the circles is set as 43.7m, following the value obtained in our experiments. A total of 27 WiFi APs take up 43.2% of the entire area. On the other, hand only 4 open WiFi APs are found, covering only 9.6%.

To ensure a fair comparison, the energy consumption of the ZigBee node is also considered in case of ZiFi and FreeBee. The results in Figure 26(b) indicate that the energy consumption for WiFi, ZiFi, and FreeBee are 2.41KJ/h, 1.21KJ/h, and 0.51KJ/h, respectively. In sum, FreeBee saves 78.9% and 58.2% of the energy required by WiFi and ZiFi, respectively, without sacrificing opportunities for open WiFi access.

[1]Real AP deployment information retrieved from *wigle.net* and *openwifispots.com*.

8. RELATED WORKS

The FreeBee design of embedding information within the beacon timing is inspired by PPM (Pulse Position Modulation), which has been widely studied in the field of optical and UWB (Ultra Wide Band) communications [12, 15, 17, 27, 31, 37]. The extensive research in this area, however, is not applicable to our scenario because they are designed for pulses (which correspond to beacons in our case) that occur at their exact timing and/or can be differentiated from noise via a matched filter. Neither of these conditions is met by the beacons, since they are prone to channel access delays due to CSMA and they are indistinguishable from other traffic for receivers with incompatible PHY layers.

Improvement through cross-platform interaction has been investigated in many recent works [19, 22, 23, 26, 29, 30, 43], while only a handful have focused on cross-platform direct communication, including Esense [14], HoWiES [41], and GSense [40]. Esense establishes communication channels from WiFi to ZigBee by modulating packet lengths to those are unlikely to be used in normal WiFi traffic. HoWiES extends the Esense mechanism to convey data with combinations of WiFi packets, and introduces a simple coding technique. Finally, GSense enables cross-technology communication by prepending a customized preamble to legacy packets containing sequence of pulses in which gaps between them embed the data to be delivered. FreeBee uniquely departs from the above works in a few aspects: (i) the use of the mandatory beacons allows free-side-channel communication, (ii) interval multiplexing allows concurrent communication between multiple senders and receivers with implicit addressing, (iii) does not require modification to the commodity hardware (in contrast to GSense), and (iv) provides the first running prototype showcasing a generic communication capability among three popular wireless technologies.

9. CONCLUSION

In this paper we propose FreeBee, a cross-technology communication framework that aims to take advantage of the coexistence problem by adopting mutual supplementation. Extensive testbed experiments on three popular wireless technologies, WiFi, ZigBee, and Bluetooth, reveal that FreeBee offers reliable symbol delivery within less than a second. Its unique free side-channel design and the utilization of short beacon frames grant high spectrum efficiency and feasibility; FreeBee exhibits 4.3× the rate compared to the state-of-the-art, Esense, and demonstrates strong support for highly mobile (in a car) and extremely duty cycled ($\leq 5\%$) receivers, implying its applicability to a wide range of practical applications. An examination of real WiFi deployment patterns in a shopping mall area finds that FreeBee can save 78.9% of the energy otherwise wasted by the WiFi interface.

APPENDIX: SER DERIVATION

Table 2: Parameters

T	Beacon interval in time
λ	# of RSSI sample in T
ρ	# of repetitions
B	Channel occupancy rate
B_f	Channel occupancy rate after filter
B_b	Probability of beacon fold

From Table 2, recall that beacon repetition ρ is the number of rows in the matrix upon folding. The number of columns after folding is λ and 2λ in FreeBee and A-FreeBee. B is the ratio of 1's in the sampled RSSI vector, reflecting the amount of traffic (i.e., noise) present in the channel. B_f stands for the ratio after taking only first two samples as introduced in Section 4. Due to such filtering, beacon is folded (i.e., contributes to fold sum) only when the delay of the beacon is less than $256us$, where this probability is denoted as B_b.

• **FreeBee**: SER corresponds to the probability where fold sum of noise in *any* of $\lambda - 1$ columns (excluding the one with beacon) is greater than or equal to that of beacon. The probability of a column to have n fold sum follows binomial distribution, $\binom{\rho}{n} B_f^n (1 - B_f)^{\rho-n}$. Let N denote a random variable indicating the *maximum* of the noise fold sums. Then, N is distributed as:

$$Pr(N \leq n) = \left\{ \sum_{i=0}^{n} \binom{\rho}{i} B_f^i (1 - B_f)^{\rho-i} \right\}^{\lambda-1}$$
$$Pr(N = n) = Pr(N \leq n) - Pr(N \leq n - 1)$$

Letting S indicate the fold sum induced by beacons, then it is also binomially distributed:

$$Pr(S = s) = \binom{\rho}{s} B_b^s (1 - B_b)^{\rho-s} \quad (2)$$

where SER can be computed from S and N.

$$SER = Pr(S - N \leq 0) = \sum_{s=0}^{\rho} \sum_{n=s}^{\rho} Pr(S = s) Pr(N = n)$$

• **A-FreeBee**: Symbol error occurs in A-FreeBee when fold sum of noise in any of $2\lambda - 2$ columns (excluding the two with beacon) is greater than or equal to that of either beacon fold sums. Maximum noise fold sum, N, follows below distribution:

$$Pr(N \leq n) = \left\{ \sum_{i=0}^{n} \binom{\rho}{i} B_f^i (1 - B_f)^{\rho-i} \right\}^{2(\lambda-1)}$$
$$Pr(N = n) = Pr(N \leq n) - Pr(N \leq n - 1)$$

The distribution of the beacon fold sum, S, is equivalent to Eq 2 where SER is found from S and N.

$$SER = 1 - \{Pr(S - N > 0)\}^2 = 1 - \left\{ \sum_{n=0}^{\rho-1} \sum_{s=n+1}^{\rho} Pr(S = s) Pr(N = n) \right\}^2$$

In summary, our analysis indicates that SER increases with B (or B_f) and reduces with larger ρ as also shown in Figures 14(a) and 14(b).

ACKNOWLEDGEMENT

This work was supported in part by the National Science Foundation under grants CNS-0845994 and CNS-1444021. We sincerely thank our anonymous shepherd and the reviewers for their valuable comments and feedback.

10. REFERENCES

[1] Altbeacon. http://altbeacon.org/.

[2] Cisco aironet 802.11a/b/g datasheet. http://www.cisco.com.

[3] Crawdad: A community resource for archiving wireless data at dartmouth. http://crawdad.cs.dartmouth.edu/.

[4] Hostapd. http://hostap.epitest.fi/hostapd/.

[5] ios: Understanding ibeacon. http://support.apple.com/kb/HT6048/.

[6] Iperf. https://iperf.fr/.

[7] Lorcon wireless packet injection lib. https://code.google.com/p/lorcon/.

[8] Micaz datasheet. http://www.memsic.com/.

[9] Wireless open-access research platform. http://warpproject.org/trac/.

[10] N. Balasubramanian, A. Balasubramanian, and A. Venkataramani. Energy Consumption in Mobile Phones: A Measurement Study and Implications for Network Applications. In *Proc. ACM IMC*, 2009.

[11] Z. Cao, Y. He, and Y. Liu. L 2: Lazy forwarding in low duty cycle wireless sensor networks. In *INFOCOM*, pages 1323–1331, 2012.

[12] C. Carbonelli and U. Mengali. M-ppm noncoherent receivers for uwb applications. *Wireless Communications, IEEE Transactions on*, 5(8):2285–2294, 2006.

[13] R. Carroll, R. Cnossen, M. Schnell, and D. Simons. Continua: An interoperable personal healthcare ecosystem. *Pervasive Computing, IEEE*, 6(4):90–94, 2007.

[14] K. Chebrolu and A. Dhekne. Esense: communication through energy sensing. In *MOBICOM*, 2009.

[15] A. A. D'Amico, U. Mengali, and E. Arias-de Reyna. Energy-detection uwb receivers with multiple energy measurements. *Wireless Communications, IEEE Transactions on*, 6(7):2652–2659, 2007.

[16] N. Ding, D. Wagner, X. Chen, A. Pathak, Y. C. Hu, and A. Rice. Characterizing and modeling the impact of wireless signal strength on smartphone battery drain. In *ACM SIGMETRICS Performance Evaluation Review*, volume 41, pages 29–40. ACM, 2013.

[17] Z. Ghassemlooy, A. Hayes, N. Seed, and E. Kaluarachchi. Digital pulse interval modulation for optical communications. *Communications Magazine, IEEE*, 36(12):95–99, 1998.

[18] S. Gollakota, F. Adib, D. Katabi, and S. Seshan. Clearing the rf smog: making 802.11n robust to cross-technology interference. In *SIGCOMM*, 2011.

[19] T. Hao, R. Zhou, G. Xing, and M. Mutka. Wizsync: Exploiting wi-fi infrastructure for clock synchronization in wireless sensor networks. In *RTSS*, 2011.

[20] A. C. Hsu, D. S. L. Wei, and C. C. J. Kuo. Coexistence wi-fi MAC design for mitigating interference caused by collocated bluetooth. *IEEE Trans. Computers*, 64(2):342–352, 2015.

[21] A. E. Ingham. *The Distribution of Prime Numbers*. Cambridge University Press, 1932.

[22] T. Jin, G. Noubir, and B. Sheng. Wizi-cloud: Application-transparent dual zigbee-wifi radios for low power internet access. In *INFOCOM*, pages 1593–1601, 2011.

[23] W. Li, Y. Zhu, and T. He. Wibee: Building wifi radio map with zigbee sensor networks. In *INFOCOM*, 2012.

[24] Z. Li, M. Li, and Y. Liu. Towards energy-fairness in asynchronous duty-cycling sensor networks. *TOSN*, 10(3):38, 2014.

[25] C.-J. M. Liang, B. Priyantha, J. Liu, and A. Terzis. Surviving wi-fi interference in low power zigbee networks. In *SenSys*, 2010.

[26] R. Mahindra, H. Viswanathan, K. Sundaresan, M. Y. Arslan, and S. Rangarajan. A practical traffic management system for integrated lte-wifi networks. In *MOBICOM*, pages 189–200, 2014.

[27] R. C. Qiu, H. Liu, and X. Shen. Ultra-wideband for multiple access communications. *Communications Magazine, IEEE*, 43(2):80–87, 2005.

[28] B. Radunovic, R. Chandra, and D. Gunawardena. Weeble: enabling low-power nodes to coexist with high-power nodes in white space networks. In *CoNEXT*, 2011.

[29] S. Sen, T. Zhang, M. M. Buddhikot, S. Banerjee, D. Samardzija, and S. Walker. A dual technology femto cell architecture for robust communication using whitespaces. In *Dynamic Spectrum Access Networks (DYSPAN)*, 2012.

[30] C. Sengul, M. Bakht, A. F. Harris, T. Abdelzaher, and R. H. Kravets. On the feasibility of high-power radios in sensor networks. *SIGMOBILE Mob. Comput. Commun. Rev.*, 12(1):37–39, 2008.

[31] D.-s. Shiu and J. M. Kahn. Differential pulse-position modulation for power-efficient optical communication. *Communications, IEEE Transactions on*, 47(8):1201–1210, 1999.

[32] D. Spenza, M. Magno, S. Basagni, L. Benini, M. Paoli, and C. Petrioli. Beyond Duty Cycling: Wake-up Radio with Selective Awakenings for Long-lived Wireless Sensing Systems. In *INFOCOM*, 2015.

[33] K. Srinivasan, P. Dutta, A. Tavakoli, and P. Levis. An empirical study of low-power wireless. *ACM Transactions on Sensor Networks (TOSN)*, 6(2):16, 2010.

[34] D. Staelin. Fast folding algorithm for detection of periodic pulse trains. *Proceedings of the IEEE*, 57:724 – 725, 1969.

[35] Wireless LAN Working Group. Ieee standard part 11: Wireless lan medium access control (mac) and physical layer (phy) specifications. *IEEE Std 802.11-2012 (Revision of IEEE Std 802.11-2007)*, pages 1–2793, March 2012.

[36] Wireless Personal Area Network (WPAN) Working Group. Ieee standard part 15.4: Low-rate wireless personal area networks (lr-wpans). *IEEE Std 802.15.4-2011 (Revision of IEEE Std 802.15.4-2006)*, pages 1–314, Sept 2011.

[37] J. Wu, H. Xiang, and Z. Tian. Weighted noncoherent receivers for uwb ppm signals. *Communications Letters, IEEE*, 10(9):655–657, 2006.

[38] X. Zhang and K. G. Shin. Enabling coexistence of heterogeneous wireless systems: case for zigbee and wifi. In *MobiHoc*, 2011.

[39] X. Zhang and K. G. Shin. Cooperative carrier signaling: harmonizing coexisting wpan and wlan devices. *Networking, IEEE/ACM Transactions on*, 21(2):426–439, 2013.

[40] X. Zhang and K. G. Shin. Gap sense: Lightweight coordination of heterogeneous wireless devices. In *INFOCOM*, 2013.

[41] Y. Zhang and Q. Li. Howies: A holistic approach to zigbee assisted wifi energy savings in mobile devices. In *INFOCOM*, 2013.

[42] Z. Zhao, X. Wu, X. Zhang, J. Zhao, and X. Li. Zigbee vs wifi: Understanding issues and measuring performances of their coexistence. In *IPCCC*, pages 1–8, 2014.

[43] R. Zhou, Y. Xiong, G. Xing, L. Sun, and J. Ma. Zifi: wireless lan discovery via zigbee interference signatures. In *MOBICOM*, 2010.

Human Sensing Using Visible Light Communication

Tianxing Li, Chuankai An, Zhao Tian, Andrew T. Campbell, and Xia Zhou
Department of Computer Science, Dartmouth College, Hanover, NH
{tianxing, chuankai, tianzhao, campbell, xia}@cs.dartmouth.edu

ABSTRACT

We present LiSense, the first-of-its-kind system that enables both data communication and fine-grained, real-time human skeleton reconstruction using Visible Light Communication (VLC). LiSense uses shadows created by the human body from blocked light and reconstructs 3D human skeleton postures in real time. We overcome two key challenges to realize shadow-based human sensing. First, multiple lights on the ceiling lead to diminished and complex shadow patterns on the floor. We design light beacons enabled by VLC to separate light rays from different light sources and recover the shadow pattern cast by each individual light. Second, we design an efficient inference algorithm to reconstruct user postures using 2D shadow information with a limited resolution collected by photodiodes embedded in the floor. We build a 3 m $\times$ 3 m LiSense testbed using off-the-shelf LEDs and photodiodes. Experiments show that LiSense reconstructs the 3D user skeleton at 60 Hz in real time with 10° mean angular error for five body joints.

Categories and Subject Descriptors

C.2.1 [**Network Architecture and Design**]: Wireless communication

Keywords

Visible light communication; sensing; skeleton reconstruction

1. INTRODUCTION

Light plays a multifaceted role (e.g., illumination, energy source) in our life. Advances on Visible Light Communication (VLC) [30, 59] add a new dimension to the list: data communication. VLC encodes data into light intensity changes at a high frequency imperceptible to human eyes. Unlike conventional RF radio systems that require complex signal processing, VLC uses low-cost, energy-efficient Light Emitting Diodes (LEDs) to transmit data. Any devices equipped with light sensors (photodiodes) can recover data by monitoring light changes. VLC has a number of appealing properties. It reuses existing lighting infrastructure, operates on an unregulated spectrum band with bandwidth 10K times greater than the RF spectrum, and importantly, is secure (i.e., does not penetrate walls, resisting eavesdropping), energy-efficient, and free of electromagnetic interference.

MobiCom'15, September 7–11, 2015, Paris, France.

ISBN 978-1-4503-3619-2/15/09 ...$15.00.
DOI: http://dx.doi.org/10.1145/2789168.2790110.

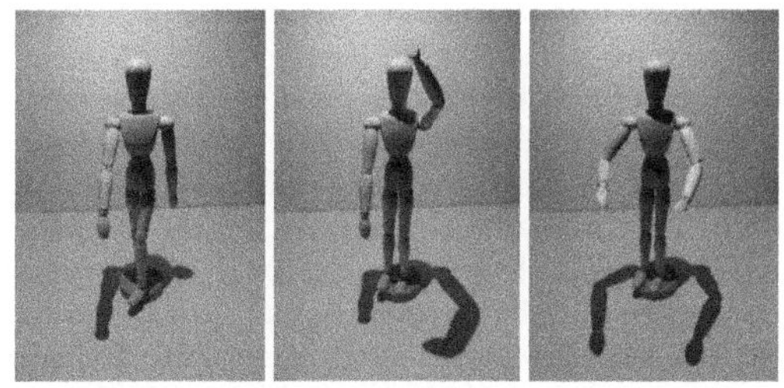

Figure 1: Shadow cast by varying manikin postures under an LED light (CREE XM-L). In this scaled-down table-top testbed, the manikin is 33 cm in height, and the LED light is 22 cm above the manikin.

In this paper, we push the envelope further and ask: *Can light turn into a ubiquitous sensing medium that tracks what we do and senses how we behave?* Envision a smart space (e.g., home, office, gym) that takes the advantage of the ubiquity of light as a medium that integrates data communication and human sensing [71]. Smart devices (e.g., smart glasses, smart watches, smartphones) equipped with photodiodes communicate using VLC. More importantly, light also serves as a passive sensing medium. Users can continuously gesture and interact with appliances and objects in a room (e.g., a wall mounted display, computers, doors, windows, coffee machine), similar to using the Kinect [57] or Wii in front of a TV, but there are no cameras (high-fidelity sensors with privacy concerns) monitoring users, neither any on-body devices or sensors that users have to constantly wear or carry [27, 62], just LED lights on the ceiling and photodiodes on the floor.

The key idea driving light sensing is strikingly simple: shadows. Any opaque object (e.g., human body) obstructs a light beam, resulting in a silhouette behind the object. Because the wavelength of visible light is measured in nanometers, any macroscopic object can completely block the light beam, much more significant than the radio frequencies [16, 50, 65, 70]. The shadow cast on the floor is essentially a two-dimensional projection of the 3D object. As the object moves and changes its shape, different light beams are blocked and the projected shadow changes at light speed – the same principle as the shadow puppet. Thus, by analyzing a continuous stream of shadows cast on the floor, we can infer a user's posture and track her behavior. As a simple illustration, Figure 1 shows the shadow shapes for varying manikin postures under a single light.

We present *LiSense, the first-of-its-kind system that enables fine-grained, real-time user skeleton reconstruction*[1] *at a high frame rate (60 Hz) using visible light communication.* LiSense consists

[1]We define skeleton reconstruction as calculating the vectors of the skeleton body segments in the 3D space.

of VLC-enabled LED lights on the ceiling and low-cost photodiodes on the floor.[2] LiSense aggregates the light intensity data from photodiodes, recovers the shadow cast by individual LED light, and continuously reconstructs a user's skeleton posture in real time. LiSense's ability of performing 3D skeleton reconstruction in real time puts little constraints on the range of gestures and behaviors that LiSense can sense, which sets a key departure from existing work that either targets a limited set of gestures [3, 17, 46] or only tracks user's 2D movements [2, 4, 10]. More importantly, by integrating both data communication and human sensing into the ubiquitous light, LiSense also fundamentally differs from vision-based skeleton tracking systems (e.g., Kinect) that are built solely for the sensing purpose. In addition, these systems rely on cameras to capture high-resolution video frames, which bring privacy concerns as the raw camera data can be leaked to the adversary [52, 64]. While prior vision methods [55, 56] have leveraged shadow to infer human gestures, they work strictly under a single light source and do not apply in a natural indoor setting with multiple light sources.

LiSense overcomes two key challenges to realize shadow-based light sensing: 1) *Shadow Acquisition:* Acquiring shadows using low-cost photodiodes is challenging in practice. In the presence of multiple light sources, light rays from different directions cast a diluted composite shadow, which is more complex than a shadow cast by a single light source. A shadow can also be greatly influenced by ambient light (e.g., sunlight). Both factors limit the ability of photodiodes detecting the light intensity drop inside a shadow. To address this challenge, LiSense leverages the fact that each light is an active transmitter using VLC and designs *light beacons* to separate light rays from individual LEDs and ambient light. Each LED emits light beacons by transmitting (i.e., flashing) at a unique frequency. LiSense transforms the light intensity perceived by each photodiode over time to the frequency domain. By monitoring frequency power changes, LiSense detects whether the photodiode is suddenly blocked from an LED and aggregates the detection results from all photodiodes to recover the *shadow map* cast by each light.

2) *Shadow-based Skeleton Reconstruction:* Shadow maps measured by photodiodes are 2D projections with a limited resolution (constrained by the photodiode density). Such low-resolution, imperfect shadow images pose significant challenges to reconstruct a user's 3D skeleton. Existing computer vision algorithms [11, 19, 21, 24, 42, 66, 51] cannot be directly applied to this problem because they all deal with video frames in a higher resolution and are often augmented with the depth information. LiSense overcomes this challenge by combining shadows cast by light sources in different directions and infers the 3D vectors of key body segments that best match shadow maps. LiSense fine-tunes the inferences using a Kalman filter to take into account movement continuity and to further reduce the skeleton reconstruction errors.

LiSense Testbed. We build a 3 m $\times$ 3 m LiSense testbed (Figure 9), using five commercial LED lights, 324 low-cost, off-the-shelf photodiodes, 29 micro-controllers, and a server. We implement light beacons by programming the micro-controllers that modulate LEDs. We implement blockage detection and 3D skeleton reconstruction algorithms on the server, which generates a stream of shadow maps and continuously tracks user gestures. The reconstruction results are visualized in real time using an animated user skeleton (Figure 11). We test our system with 20 gestures and seven users in diverse settings. Our key findings are as follows:

- LiSense reconstructs a user's 3D skeleton with the average angular error of 10° for five key body joints;
- LiSense generates shadow maps in real time. It is able to produce shadow maps of all LEDs every 11.8 ms, reaching the same level of capturing video frames yet without using cameras;
- LiSense tracks user gestures in real time. It reconstructs the user skeleton within 16 ms based on five shadow maps, thus generating 60 reconstructed postures, each of which consists of the 3D vectors of five key body segments. The reconstructed skeleton is displayed in real time (60 FPS), similar to playing a video at a high frame rate;
- LiSense is robust in diverse ambient light settings (morning, noon, and night) and users with different body sizes and shapes.

Contributions. We make the following contributions:

- We propose for the first time the concept of continuous user skeleton reconstruction based on visible light communication, which enables light to be a medium for both communication and passive human sensing;
- We design algorithms to extract the shadow of each individual light source and reconstruct 3D human skeleton posture continuously using only a stream of low-resolution shadow information;
- We build the first testbed implementing real-time, human skeleton reconstruction based on VLC, using off-the-shelf, low-cost LEDs, photodiodes, and micro-controllers in an indoor environment;
- Using our testbed, we test our system with diverse gestures and demonstrate that it can reconstruct a user skeleton continuously in real time with small reconstruction angular errors.

Our work takes the first step to go beyond conventional radio spectrum and demonstrates the potential of using visible light spectrum for both communication and fine-grained human sensing. We believe that with its unbounded bandwidth, light holds great potential to mitigate the spectrum crunch crisis. By expanding the applications VLC can enable, we hope that our work can trigger new radical thinkings on VLC applications. Our work examines the interplay between wireless networking, computer vision, and HCI, opening the gate to new paradigms of user interaction designs.

2. LIGHT SHADOW EFFECT

Shadow is a common phenomenon we observe everyday. It is easily recognizable under a single light source by unaided human eyes. Our goal is to understand whether off-the-shelf, low-cost photodiodes can reliably detect the light intensity drop in the shadow. If so, we can deploy them on the floor and aggregate their light intensity data to obtain the shadow cast by a human body. In this section, we first study the impact of a blocking object on light propagation using low-cost photodiodes. We then examine the challenges of shadow-based analysis in the presence of multiple lights.

2.1 Experiments on Blocking the Light

Consider a single photodiode on the floor, we hypothesize that if any opaque object stands in the direct path between the point light source and the photodiode, the photodiode will not be able to perceive any light coming from this point light source. Thus, the photodiode observes a light intensity drop compared to the case when there is no object blocking its direct path to the light source.

To confirm our hypothesis, we build a scaled-down table-top testbed (Figure 2) using commercial LED lights (CREE XM-L) and low-cost photodiodes (Honeywell SD3410-001). We set up a single LED chipset as the point light source at 55 cm height and place the photodiode directly below the light. By default we calibrate the photodiode's location using a plumb bob to ensure 0° of light's incidence angle. The photodiode has 90° field of vision (FoV), i.e., it

[2]Engineering photodiodes on the floor sounds labor-intensive today, but it can be eased by smart fabric [1, 45] (see more in § 7).

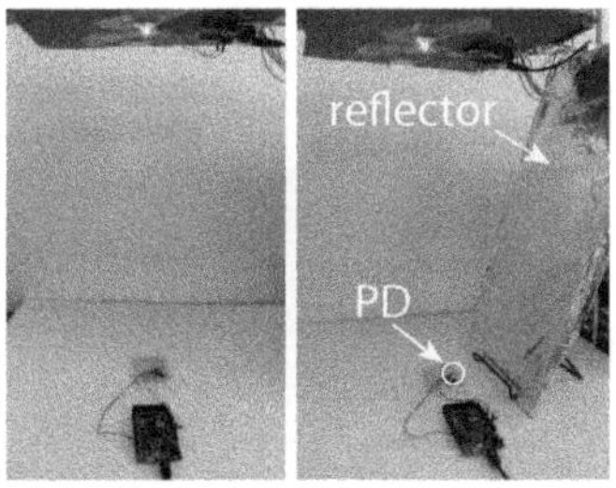

(a) Default setup (left) and setup w/ reflector (right)

(b) LED and photodiode (PD) w/ Arduino boards

Figure 2: Experiment setup with an LED and a photodiode (a), both attached to micro-controllers (b).

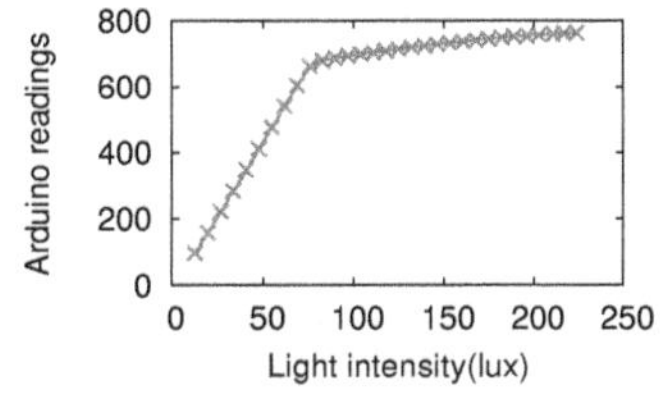

(a) Light intensity vs Arduino reading

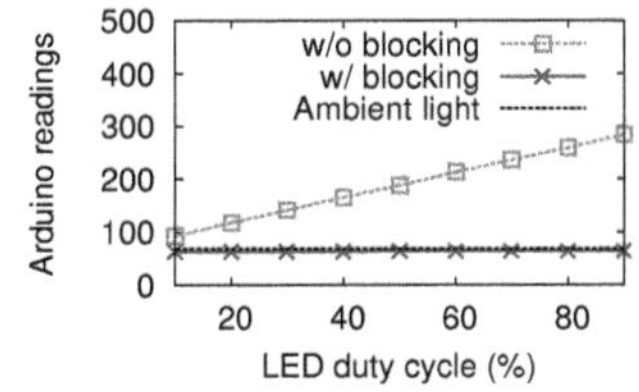

(b) Light source light intensity

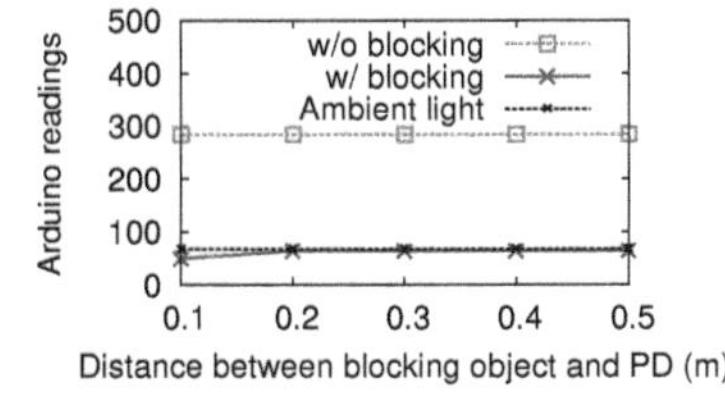

(c) Blocking object distance

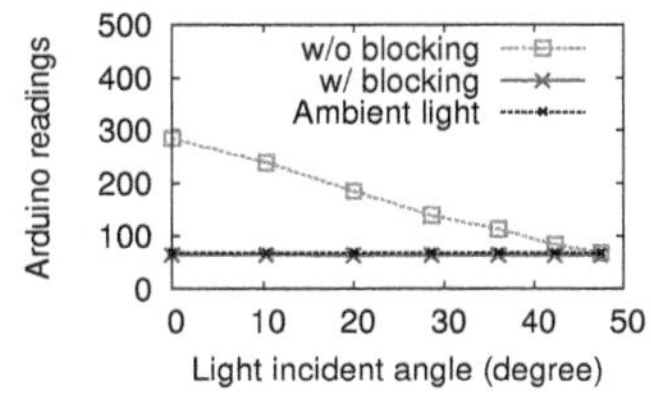

(d) Incident angle

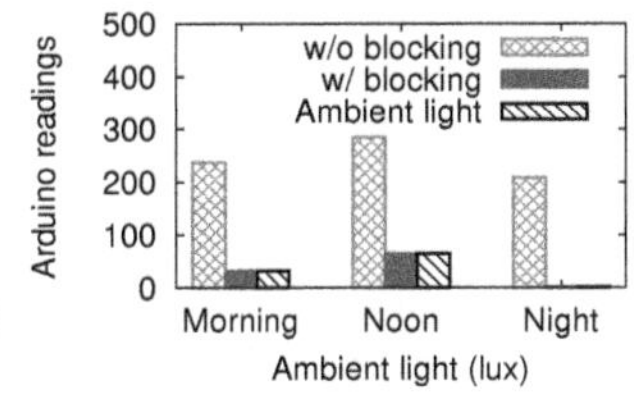

(e) Ambient light

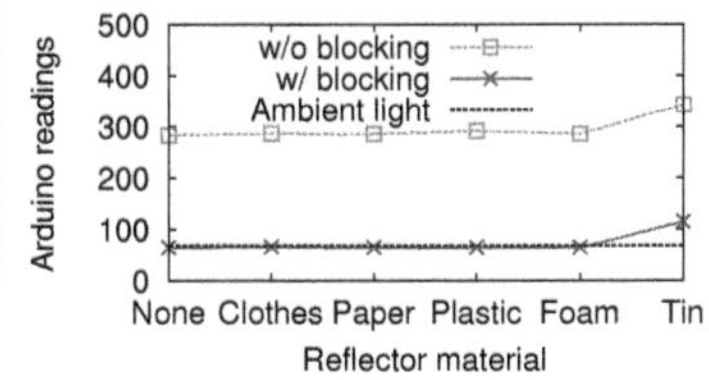

(f) Multi-path

Figure 3: Experiments on blocking the light using our scaled-down table-top testbed. (a) shows that the measured Arduino reading is directly proportional to the perceived light intensity, where the slope decreases after the photodiode enters its saturation range. (b)-(f) show the impact of blockage on the measured Arduino reading under varying settings.

can sense incoming light with incidence angle within 45°. To fetch signal continuously from the photodiode, we cascade the photodiode and a resistor (10 KΩ) and measure the resistor voltage using a micro-controller (Arduino DUE in Figure 2(b)). It maps the measured voltage to an integer between 0 and 1023. Since the photodiode's output current is directly proportional to the perceived light intensity, resistor voltage (thus the Arduino reading) reflects the perceived light intensity. Using a light meter (EXTECH 401036) we have verified that the Arduino reading is directly proportional to the perceived light intensity (Figure 3(a)). To understand the impact of blockage, we place a 10 cm × 10 cm × 2 cm wood plate between the photodiode and the LED, and compare the Arduino readings before and after placing the wood plate[3]. We aim to answer the following key questions:

Q1: Is the shadow dependent on the light intensity of the light source? We first examine how the light source brightness affects the photodiode's sensing data upon blockage. We connect the LED to an Arduino UNO board to vary the LED's duty cycle from 10% to 90% (Figure 2(b)), resulting in light intensities from 5 to 30 lux perceived by the photodiode. For a given duty cycle, we record the average Arduino reading before and after blocking the LED and plot the results in Figure 3(b). We observe that upon blockage, the Arduino's reading reports only the ambient light in all duty cycle settings, meaning that an opaque object completely blocks the light rays regardless of the brightness of the light source.

Q2: Does the distance between the blocking object and the light source matter? Next, we test whether the relative distance between the blocking object and the light source affects the photodiode's sensed light intensity. To do so, we fix the LED's duty cycle to 90%, move the wood plate along the line between the LED and the photodiode, and record the Arduino data at each distance. Figure 3(c) shows that as long as the object stays in the direct path between the LED and the photodiode, the light beam is completely blocked regardless of the relative distance of the blocking object.

Q3: How does the light incidence angle come into play? Because a photodiode has a limited viewing angle and can perceive incoming light only within its FoV, we further examine whether it can detect blockage under varying light incidence angles. We move the photodiode horizontally with 10-cm intervals and record the Arduino's reading before and after blockage. As expected, the perceived light intensity gradually drops as the photodiode moves further away from the LED (Figure 3(d)). More importantly, at all locations (incidence angles), the light beam blockage result in a significant drop in the Arduino's reading. The drop is less significant when the incidence angle approaches half of the photodiode's FoV. This is because the photodiode can barely sense any light coming at its FoV and thus blocking the light beam has a negligible impact.

Q4: What is the impact of ambient light? We also perform our measurements during different time of a day as the ambient light varies. In Figure 3(e), we plot the Arduino reading before and after blockage as the ambient light intensity increases from 2 to 100 lux. In all conditions, we observe a significant drop in the Arduino reading. Because the photodiode senses a combination of the ambient light and the light from the LED, its perceived light intensity increases as the ambient light intensity increases.

Q5: How significant is the light multi-path effect? Would it diminish the shadow? Visible light is diffusive in nature. While a object blocks the direct path between the photodiode and the LED, light rays can bounce off surrounding objects and reach the photodiode from multiple directions. Since the photodiode perceives a combination of light rays coming in all directions, this multipath effect can potentially reduce the light intensity drop caused by blocking the direct path. To examine the impact of the multipath effect, we place a flat board vertically close to the LED to increase the reflected light rays (Figure 2(a), right) and record the Arduino's reading with and without blocking the direct path to the LED. Among all types of material we have tested, the significant drop in the Arduino's reading is consistent (Figure 3(f)). Thus, light in the direct path dominates the perceived light intensity. The tin has the highest light intensity because of its minimal energy loss during reflection.

Overall, our experiment results confirm that opaque objects can effectively block light in diverse settings and the blockage can be detected by low-cost photodiodes under a single point light source.

[3] We also measured the blockage impact using different body parts (e.g., arms, hands) of a manikin and observed similar results.

(a) 2 LEDs (b) 3 LEDs (c) 4 LEDs (d) 5 LEDs (e) Setup w/ PD (f) Sensed light intensity

Figure 4: Shadow cast by multiple LEDs on the table-top testbed (a)-(d). We further measure the light intensity change caused by blockage using off-the-shelf photodiode (e). Light intensity drop caused by blockage is less significant under more LEDs (f).

2.2 Where is My Shadow?

Detecting a shadow is relatively straightforward under a single point light source. However, when there are multiple light sources present, shadow detection becomes much more challenging. This is because light rays from different sources result in a *composite shadow*, which comprises shadow components created and fused by multiple light sources. Figure 4 illustrates the resulting shadow of the manikin as we switch on more LED lights in our table-top testbed. We make two key observations. *First*, the shadow is gradually diluted as more LEDs are switched on. This is because there are more light rays coming from different directions, and hence blocking a beam from one LED does not necessarily block the light beams from other LEDs, leaving a fading shadow. *Second*, the shadow shape becomes more complex under more LEDs as a result of superimposing different shadows cast by individual LEDs. As a result, it becomes harder to infer the manikin's posture based upon the resulting tangled shape pattern.

While visually less noticeable, a shadow is also much harder to detect under these conditions using off-the-shelf photodiodes. In our experiments, we place the photodiode in a shadow region caused by the manikin's posture, gradually switch on more LEDs, and compare the Arduino's reading with and without the manikin's blockage (Figure 4(e)). We observe that as more LEDs are switched on, more light rays coming in different directions hit the shadow region and thus the perceived light intensity level rises. Furthermore, once three or more LED lights are switched on, the photodiode enters the saturation region (Figure 3(a)), thus blocking light rays from a single LED has a negligible impact on the Arduino reading. As a result, detecting shadow using these low-cost photodiodes is very challenging in practice under multiple lights.

In the next two sections, we introduce LiSense, which disambiguates composite shadows using VLC and continuously tracks user posture in real time.

3. DISAMBIGUATING SHADOWS

To disambiguate composite shadows created by multiple lights, LiSense recovers the shadow shape, referred to as the *shadow map*, resulting from each individual light source. Specifically, the shadow map associated with light source L_k is the shadow if only light source L_k is present. We describe this as disambiguating a composite shadow. The key challenge is that each photodiode perceives a combination of light rays coming from different light sources and cannot separate light rays purely based on the perceived light intensity (Figure 5(a)(b)).

To overcome this technical barrier, we leverage the fact that each LED light is an active transmitter using VLC. We instrument each light source to emit a unique *light beacon*, implemented by modulating the light intensity changes at a given frequency. By assigning a different frequency to each light source, we enable photodiodes to differentiate lights from different sources. This allows LiSense to recover the shadow cast by each individual light.

In this section, we first describe our design of light beacons, followed by the mechanism to detect blockage (shadow) and infer shadow maps.

3.1 Separating Light Using Light Beacons

The design of light beacons is driven by the observation that while the perceived light intensity represents the sum of all incoming light rays, these light rays can be separated in the frequency domain if they flash at different frequencies. That is, if we transform a time series of perceived light intensity to the frequency domain using Fast Fourier Transform (FFT), we can observe frequency power peaks at the frequencies at which these light rays flash. Figure 5 shows an example with two LED lights flashing at 2.5 kHz and 1.87 kHz, respectively, in an unsynchronized manner. The light intensity perceived by the photodiode is a combination of these two light pulse waves, and yet FFT can decompose the light mixture and generate peaks at the two flashing frequencies. Thus, a light beacon can be implemented by programming each light source to flash at a unique frequency.

Benefits. Light beacons bring three key benefits when considering blockage detection. *First*, by examining the resulting frequency power peaks after applying FFT, we can separate light rays from different light sources. The frequency power at frequency f_i is approximately directly proportional to the intensity of light rays flashing at f_i. Thus, the changes in power peaks allow the photodiode to determine *which* lights are blocked. *Second*, light beacons also allow us to avoid interference from ambient light sources by applying a high pass filter (HPF). This is because the change of ambient light is random and generates frequency components close to zero in the frequency domain. *Third*, by separating light rays from different sources, we observe a much more significant drop in the frequency power caused by blocking a light, which is the key to achieving robust detection of blockage, especially when the photodiode perceives a weak light intensity because of a long distance or a large incidence angle.

Light Beacon Frequency Selection. Designing robust light beacons, however, is nontrivial, mainly because selecting the flashing frequency for each light source is challenging. Specifically, assume an LED flashes as a pulse wave with a duty cycle of D and flashing frequency of f, the Fourier series expansion of this pulse wave is:

$$f(t) = D + \sum_{n=1}^{\infty} \frac{2}{n\pi} \sin(\pi n D) \cos(2\pi n f t). \quad (1)$$

It indicates that the power emitted by the pulse wave is decomposed into the main frequency power, which is the first AC component when $n = 1$, and an infinite number of harmonics (components

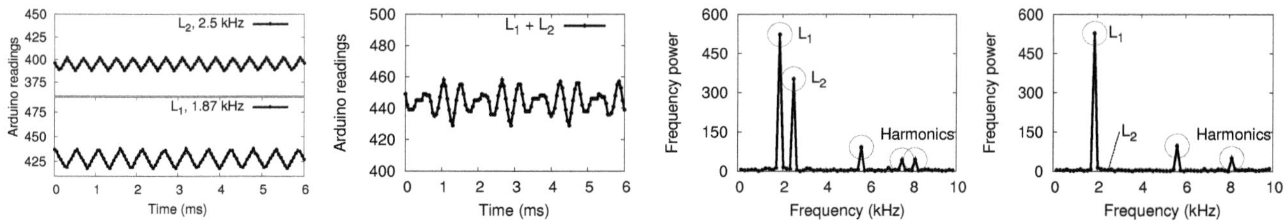

(a) A single LED on (b) Two LEDs on (c) After applying FFT (d) After blocking L_2

Figure 5: Experiments with a photodiode (PD) and two LEDs (L_1 and L_2, 50% duty cycle) that flash at different frequencies. (a)-(b) show the PD's readings when only one LED is on and when both are on. PD perceives a combination of light rays, which however can be separated in the frequency domain after applying FFT (c). The frequency power of the flashing frequency f_i reflects the perceived intensity of light rays flashing at f_i. Thus the power peak at 2.5 kHz disappears after L_2 is blocked (d).

Algorithm 1: Selecting the candidates of flashing frequency for light beacons.

input : 1) R, signal sampling rate; 2) A, the number of FFT points; 3) $f_{flicker}$, the threshold to avoid flickering; 4) $f_{interval}$, the minimal interval between adjacent flashing frequencies

output: $f_{candidate}$, flashing frequency candidates for all LEDs

$f_{candidate} = \{\frac{R}{A} \times \lceil \frac{f_{flicker} \times A}{R} \rceil\}$

for $k \leftarrow \lceil \frac{f_{flicker} \times A}{R} \rceil + 1$ **to** $\frac{A}{2}$ **do**

  $f_k = \frac{R}{A} \times k$

  $valid = true$

  for $f_s \in f_{candidate}$ **do**

    if $(f_s \mod f_k) == 0)$ *OR* $(|f_s - f_k| \leq f_{interval})$ **then**

      $valid = false$

      break

  end

  if $valid$ **then** $f_{candidate} \leftarrow f_k \cup f_{candidate}$

end

with $n > 1$). Hence, an LED light L_i flashing at frequency f_i leads to not only a global power peak (main frequency power) at frequency f_i, but also small local power peaks at all the harmonics frequencies (Figure 5(c)). In other words, if the perceived light intensity from light L_i changes, it will affect not only the main frequency power at f, but also the power peaks at harmonics. To separate out the light rays and avoid interference across lights, we need to ensure that the harmonics do not overlap with the main frequencies of other lights. Tracking all harmonics is infeasible. In our design, we focus on the top-ten harmonics frequency components. This is because the harmonics frequency power drops significantly as n increases. We observe it becomes negligible once $n > 10$.

Furthermore, the flashing frequencies need to satisfy three additional constraints. *First*, since lights are also used for illumination, the flashing frequencies need to be above a threshold $f_{flicker}$ (1 kHz in our implementation) to avoid the flickering problem [32, 36, 48]. *Second*, the highest flashing frequency is limited by the sampling rate of the micro-controller fetching data from photodiodes. The Nyquist Shannon sampling theorem [25] says that it has to be no larger than $R/2$, where R is sampling rate. *Finally*, the adjacent frequencies have to be at least $f_{interval}$ away to ensure robust detection of frequency power peaks. We set $f_{interval}$ = 200 Hz based on a prior study [32]. Algorithm 1 details the procedure to select all candidate flashing frequencies satisfying all the above constraints.

We then assign the candidate flashing frequencies to all LED lights, such that the lights within each photodiode's viewing angle (FoV) flash at different frequencies. Since photodiodes have a limited FoV (90 degrees for Honeywell SD3410-001), each photodiode perceives only a small subset of all lights. Thus we do not need a large number of candidate frequencies to cover all lights and the system can easily scale up to more lights. Supporting denser lights requires more candidate flashing frequencies, which can be achieved by increasing the signal sampling rate R.

Light Beacon Overhead. Light beacons can be seamlessly integrated into existing VLC systems, enabling light to fulfill a dual role of data communication and human sensing. For VLC systems [5, 14, 36, 48] that use Frequency Shift Keying (FSK) to modulate data, all the data packets serve as light beacons, as long as LED lights within the FoV of a photodiode use different flashing frequencies to modulate data. For VLC systems that use other modulation schemes [34, 35], we can instrument each LED light to emit light beacons periodically, in the same way that Wi-Fi access points periodically transmit beacons. For an ADC sampling rate of 20 kHz and modulation window of 128 points, a light beacon lasting for 6.4 ms is sufficient for the photodiode to separate light rays. Thus, the overhead of transmitting light beacons is negligible given that a data packet typically lasts for hundreds of ms based on the IEEE 802.15.7 standard [8].

3.2 Blockage Detection

We detect blockage by transforming the time series of light intensity values of light beacons to the frequency domain and examining the frequency power changes. Specifically, the intensity of light rays from light L_i flashing at frequency f_i is represented by the frequency power of f_i. If an opaque object blocks the direct path from light L_i to a photodiode, the frequency power of f_i changes (Figure 5(d)).

To examine the impact of blockage on the frequency power, we mount five commercial LED lights (Cree CXA25) on an office ceiling (2.65 m in height), attach them to an Arduino UNO board, which modulates the Pulse Width Modulation (PWM) of each light to allow each LED to emit light beacons at a given frequency (Table 1 by running Algorithm 1). We place photodiodes (Figure 2(b)) at 324 locations in a 3 m x 3 m area on the floor. Each photodiode can perceive light rays from all LED lights. We then measure the readings of the Ardunio controllers connected to the photodiodes for 6.4 ms before and after blocking each LED light.

Figure 6 shows the CDF of relative frequency power change. Assume the $P_{ij}(t)$ is the frequency power of f_i (the flashing frequency of the light beacons from light L_i) at time t perceived by the photodiode at location p_j, its relative frequency power change $\Delta P_{ij}(t)$ is defined as:

$$\Delta P_{ij}(t) = |\frac{P_{ij}^{\text{nonBlock}} - P_{ij}(t)}{P_{ij}^{\text{nonBlock}}}|, \quad (2)$$

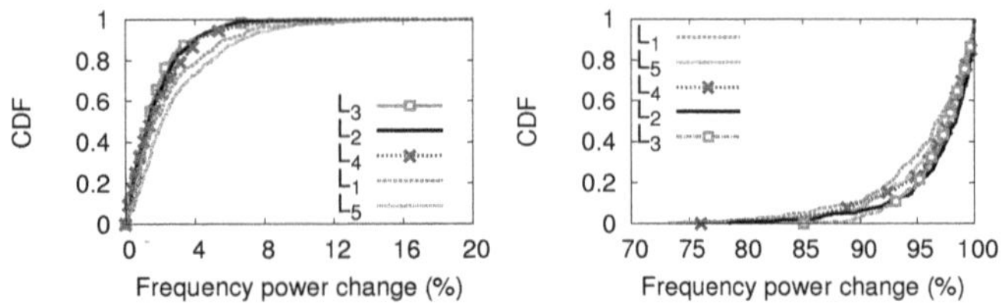

(a) w/o blocking (b) w/ blocking

Figure 6: Relative frequency power changes in the non-blocking (a) and blocking state (b).

where P_{ij}^{nonBlock} is the average of non-blocking frequency power from light L_i at location p_j. Clearly the frequency power change caused by blockage is much more significant (>70%) than that caused by the normal light intensity fluctuation[4] (<20%) in non-blocking state. Therefore, using a threshold τ (60% in our implementation) on the relative frequency power change can effectively detect the occurrence of blockage.

Shadow Map. By aggregating the blockage detection result from all photodiodes, we can recover the shadow map cast by each light L_i. Specifically, assuming N photodiodes on the floor, which can sense K LED lights within their FoVs, we define the shadow map $S_i(t)$ cast by LED light L_i at time t as: $S_i(t) = \{s_{ij}(t)|0 < j \leq N\}$, where $s_{ij}(t)$ indicates whether the direct path from location p_j to light L_i is blocked at time t, i.e., $s_{ij}(t) = 1$ if $\Delta P_{ij}(t) \geq \tau$, and $s_{ij}(t) = 0$ otherwise. Figure 8 shows five example shadow maps obtained from our testbed (§ 5) for a given user posture (Figure 8(a)). Since each shadow map is generated by blocking light rays from a different angle, the combination of the 2D shadow maps can be used to reconstruct the human skeleton in the 3D space.

4. FROM SHADOW MAPS TO POSTURE

Given the set of inferred shadow maps at time t, LiSense next reconstructs the user's 3D skeleton at t, referred to as the user's posture at time t. By continuously inferring the user's posture over time, LiSense recovers the user's gesture, which consists of a sequence of postures. While computer vision literature has studied similar problems on 3D human motion reconstruction, we face two new challenges here. *First*, constrained by the limited photodiode density, shadow maps have limited resolution (18 × 18 pixels in our testbed), far below the resolution of video frames (at least 640 × 480 pixels [40]) used by existing vision techniques [11, 21, 24, 66]. Also shadow maps are imperfect and a small portion of pixels can suffer from blockage detection errors. *Second*, a shadow map is only a two-dimensional projection of the 3D object and lacks the depth information. As shown in our prior experiment (Figure 3(c)), the blockage at a single photodiode is independent of its relative distance to the blocking object. Existing vision techniques [24, 19, 51], however, are typically augmented by the depth input.

To address these challenges, we combine shadow maps cast by LEDs from different perspectives to reconstruct the user's 3D skeleton. Inspired by existing methods on skeleton-based motion capture [20, 41, 58, 67], we design a shadow-based inference algorithm to compute the 3D vectors of the key user body segments. We also take into account the continuity of human movement and apply Kalman filter to iteratively fine-tune the current inference based on the prior inferred posture. Next we first describe the posture inference algorithm, followed by the fine-tuning using Kalman filter.

[4]The light intensity fluctuation in the non-blocking state is attributed to the ADC errors at the Arduino board, the imperfect pulse waves generated by the LED, and the photodiode noise.

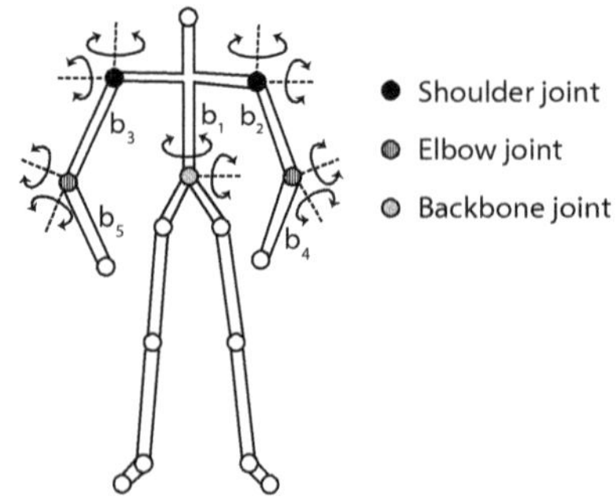

Figure 7: User skeleton model. We track key body segments b_i by rotating the key body joints. Each joint has two degrees of freedom because of human body's physical limit.

4.1 Inferring Posture based on Shadow

Our inference algorithm takes four inputs: 1) inferred shadow maps for all K LEDs ($S_1(t), ..., S_K(t)$) at time t, 2) 3D locations of all LED lights, 3) 3D locations of all N photodiodes, and 4) user's body parameters (e.g., body height, body part size). The algorithm does not require any training to reconstruct the user skeleton. It needs only initial calibration on user's body parameters.

User Skeleton Model. We model the user using a standard human skeleton model [20, 41, 58, 67] shown in Figure 7. We do not target specific pre-defined gestures and each body part can freely rotate under the physical constraints of the human body. We aim to reconstruct the set of 3D vectors B to represent M body segments, denoted by $B = \{b_i|0 < i \leq M\}$. In our implementation, we consider five body segments ($M = 5$): backbone, left and right upper arms, and left and right lower arms. We focus on upper-body segments because of the current testbed setting (see more in § 7). The inference algorithm, however, is applicable for all body segments. The movements of these body segments are controlled by the rotation of five key body joints: backbone joint, left and right shoulder joints, and left and right elbow joints, respectively. We assume that each key body joint has two degrees of freedom for its rotation (Figure 7) because of human body's physical limit. Then the rotation of each body joint can be represented by the actual rotation angles in both degrees. We use coordinate conversion, denoted by $g_m(\cdot)$, to transform a set of body joint rotation angles to the 3D vector of each body segment b_m.

Shadow-based Inference. At the core, our inference algorithm aims to seek the optimal 3D vectors for body segments, so that the resulting human skeleton best matches the shadow map cast by each LED. Leveraging the shadow information, our inference is based on a simple fact: If a photodiode at location p_j is blocked from LED L_i at time t, i.e., $s_{ij}(t) = 1$ in shadow map $S_i(t)$, then the light ray l_{ij} from L_i to p_j is blocked by at least one user body segment, meaning that the minimal perpendicular distance between light ray l_{ij} to all body segments should be smaller than the radius r_i of the body part that the corresponding body segment b_i represents. Therefore, we aggregate the blockage information from all shadow maps. We infer the optimal set of body segments $B^\star$ as the body segments that lead to the minimal summation of perpendicular distances between all blocked light rays and their closest body segments. In the meantime, the body segments should not block any light ray l_{ix} if photodiode p_x is not blocked from LED L_i, i.e., $s_{ix}(t) = 0$. Thus we represent the optimization problem as below:

$$B^\star = \underset{B \in \mathbb{B}'}{\text{argmin}} \sum_{\substack{s_{ij}(t)=1 \\ i\in[1,K], j\in[1,N]}} \min_{b_m \in B} (dist(l_{ij}, b_m) - r_m), \quad (3)$$

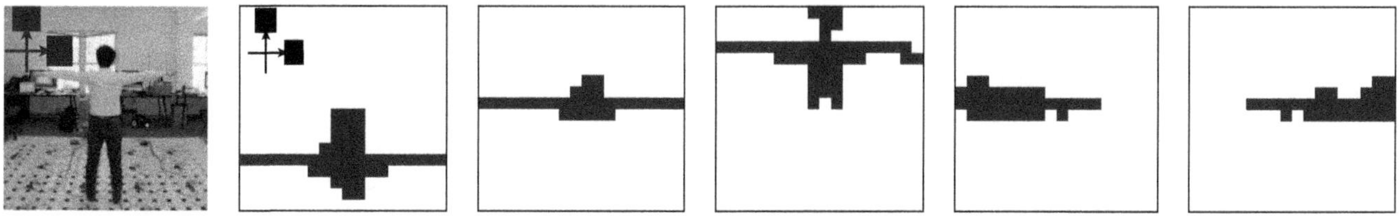

(a) User gesture (b) Inferred shadow maps (18x18 pixels) cast by five LEDs: L_1, L_2, L_3, L_4, and L_5 (Figure 9(a)) respectively.

Figure 8: Shadow maps obtained from LiSense testbed.

where $dist(l_1, l_2)$ calculates the perpendicular distance between two line segments l_1 and l_2, and $\mathbb{B}'$ contains the candidate 3D-vector set B satisfying the below constraint:

$$dist(l_{ix}, b_m) > r_m, \forall b_m \in B, \text{if } s_{ix}(t) = 0, x \in [1, N].$$

We iteratively optimize the objective function (Eq. (3)) for each body segment. The maximum number of iterations is 6 in our current implementation. Given the number of possible movements a body segment can make, the search space for the optimal $B^\star$ is daunting. We speed up the search in two ways. *First*, instead of examining all blocked photodiodes (shadow pixels), we check only the blocked photodiodes on the shadow boundary to reduce the number of blocked light rays needed to process. *Second*, we apply a greedy algorithm to prioritize the search order based on the body part size. We first consider the movement of the largest body part, which is the backbone. To do so, we rotate the backbone joint and search the optimal rotation angles of this joint to match the shadow maps. We then move on to the upper arms by rotating the shoulder joints, and finally the lower arms by rotating the elbow joints. At each step, we apply a greedy algorithm to identify the optimal rotation angles of each joint. In the end, we aggregate the optimal rotation angles of each joint, and apply $g_m(\cdot)$ to convert them to the optimal 3D vectors $B^\star$ of body segments.

4.2 Fine-Tuning Posture Inference

We further fine-tune the inferred vectors of body segments $B^\star$, which can be affected by blockage detection errors (wrong shadow pixels) and the lack of information on body occlusion due to shadow map's low resolution and photodiode's limited viewing angle. The key idea is to leverage the prior inferred posture and smooth the inference result over time. A simple method is to average the rotation angle of each joint within a time window. However, determining the time window size is non-trivial. We observe that the final performance suffers from non-Gaussian noise and occlusion from other body parts.

To overcome the above problems, we apply a Kalman filter to smooth body part movements over time given the movement continuity. We model each body part movement as a stochastic process – it moves at a constant velocity with random perturbations in its trajectory. Let (x_t, y_t, z_t) denote the 3D position of a body segment's end point at time t and dx_t, dy_t, dz_t is the velocity in each dimension respectively, we represent the process as:

$$\begin{pmatrix} x_t \\ y_t \\ z_t \\ dx_t \\ dy_t \\ dz_t \end{pmatrix} = \underbrace{\begin{pmatrix} 1 & 0 & 0 & 1 & 0 & 0 \\ 0 & 1 & 0 & 0 & 1 & 0 \\ 0 & 0 & 1 & 0 & 0 & 1 \\ 0 & 0 & 0 & 1 & 0 & 0 \\ 0 & 0 & 0 & 0 & 1 & 0 \\ 0 & 0 & 0 & 0 & 0 & 1 \end{pmatrix}}_{\text{Physical constrain matrix}} \begin{pmatrix} x_{t-1} \\ y_{t-1} \\ z_{t-1} \\ dx_{t-1} \\ dy_{t-1} \\ dz_{t-1} \end{pmatrix} + \begin{pmatrix} n_x \\ n_y \\ n_z \\ n_{dx} \\ n_{dy} \\ n_{dz} \end{pmatrix},$$

where n_x, n_y, n_z are statistic variables representing the random perturbation in each dimension. Here the physical constraint matrix captures human body movement contiguity. The initial values of (x_t, y_t, z_t) and dx_t, dy_t, dz_t are known, and n_x, n_y, n_z are initialized to zeros. The Kalman filter then iteratively fine-tunes the body part position (x_t, y_t, z_t) and updates the statistic noise. We repeat the fine-tuning for each body segment. In the end, the fine-tuned body segments are visualized on the screen. By estimating the stochastic noise, Kalman filter further reduces the skeleton reconstruction errors and smooths the visualization.

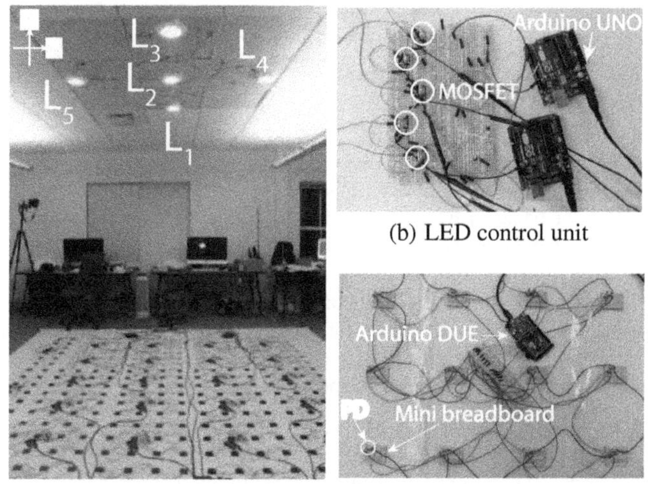

(a) LiSense overview (b) LED control unit (c) 12 photodiodes + Arduino

Figure 9: LiSense testbed.

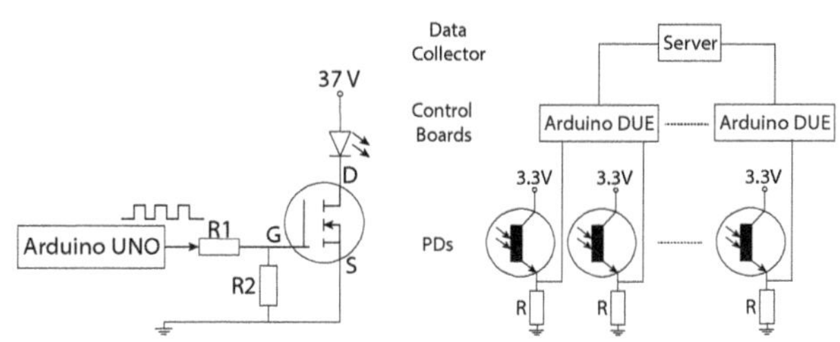

(a) LED control circuit (b) Circuit for photodiodes

Figure 10: The circuit designs for the LED control unit and for connecting photodiodes to micro-controllers.

5. LiSense TESTBED

We build LiSense using five off-the-shelf LED lights (CREE CXA25), 324 low-cost (<\$2 in wholesale) photodiodes (Honeywell SD3410-001) in a 3 m × 3 m area, 29 micro-controllers (Arduino UNO and DUE), and a server (DELL M4600) in a research lab setting (Figure 9), where the ceiling height is 2.65 m. Each LED chipset is equipped with a commercial LED lampshade (CREE T67) and adjacent LED lights are 0.8 m away.

LED Lights. We mount five LED lights on the ceiling. We connect all five LED lights to two Arduino UNO boards using five out-

Table 1: **LED flashing frequency.**

LED light	L_1	L_2	L_3	L_4	L_5
PWM frequency (kHz)	2.5	1.9	2.2	3.4	1.6

Figure 11: The visualized 3D skeleton reconstructed by LiSense for two example postures.

put pins and each output pin connects to a MOSFET driver module (Figure 10(a)). We fix the LED's duty cycle to 50%. We implement light beacons by programming the Arduino boards to modulate the PWM frequency of each light. We run Algorithm 1 to select the flashing frequencies used by light beacons, assuming the ADC sampling rate of 20 kHz and 128-point FFT. Table 1 lists the frequency of each LED light's light beacons. To support different PWM frequency for each light, we drive the LED lights using five independent 37 V DC power adapters.

Photodiodes. We select SD3410-001 photodiodes for two reasons. First, with the FoV of 90°, all photodiodes in the 3 m × 3 m area can sense light rays from all LED lights that are 2.65 m in height. Second, with the rise time of 75 μs, they support the maximal flashing frequency (3.4 kHz) of the LED lights. We cascade a photodiode and a resistor (10 KΩ) on a mini-breadboard (1.4" × 0.4" × 1.8" in size). Figure 10(b) shows the circuit design. The photodiodes are placed with a uniform interval of 16.7 cm. The resulting photodiode density is sufficient for the posture inference algorithm to track common gestures (e.g., hugging, pointing) with a good accuracy. Capturing finer-grained movements (e.g., finger movements) requires denser photodiodes. We will discuss it in § 7.

Micro-controllers. Each Arduino DUE micro-controller is connected to 12 photodiodes (mini-breadboards). It samples analog voltage numbers of the cascaded resistors on the mini-breadboards (Figure 10(b)) and maps the voltage numbers to integers within 0 and 1023. The Arduino DUE supports 300 kHz ADC sampling rate, sufficient for supporting 20 kHz sampling rate per photodiode. We implement Split-radix Real FFT algorithm [13] on the Arduino board, which processes the Arduino readings for each photodiode using 128 FFT points and computes the frequency power of the PWM frequencies used by the LED lights (Table 1). We select Split-radix Real FFT algorithm because of its efficiency. Running complex FFT subroutine on Arduino boards entails prohibitive overhead – it leads to 2x memory redundancy and wastes half of the processing power on the imaginary part of a complex number, which our input data does not contain.

The Arduino DUE board computes five frequency power numbers (Table 1) for each photodiode, aggregates these numbers for 12 connected photodiodes, and sends them to the server. Each frequency power number is rescaled below 128 and represented by a byte. Thus an Arduino DUE sends 60 bytes to the server each time. We connect the 27 Arduino DUE boards to the server using extended USB cables via series 232 ports (115.2 Kbps data rate).

Server. To aggregate data from all Arduino boards, the server considers the first data packet from each Arduino board within a time window (16.7 ms). We implement the blockage detection mechanism (§ 3.2) and posture inference algorithm (§ 4) in C++ on the server. These two algorithms are run in two separate threads in parallel so that a stream of shadow maps are produced continuously while the skeleton reconstruction thread infers the user posture for each set of concurrent (five) shadow maps. A separate visualization thread then displays the reconstruction results in real time by updating an animated user skeleton (Figure 11).

6. LiSense EXPERIMENTS

We conduct experiments using LiSense testbed, focusing on its skeleton reconstruction accuracy and latency for a wide range of gestures. We also seek to understand the inferred shadow maps accuracy and the impact of practical factors including ambient light, user diversity and clothing, as well as LiSense's energy overhead.

Experimental Setup. We initialize LiSense system in two steps. *First*, we measure the frequency power corresponding to the PWM frequency of each LED L_i (Table 1) at each photodiode p_j when no user stands in the testbed, i.e., P_{ij}^{nonBlock} in Eq. (2). *Second*, we calibrate system parameters by instrumenting the user to stand in the middle of the testbed with arms drooping naturally. When the experiment starts, the user performs a free-form gesture for 2–10 seconds. The server continuously fetches data from all Arduino DUE boards, generates shadow maps, infers user posture for each shadow map, records the 3D vector for each of the five key joints on a user body (backbone joint, left shoulder joint, right should joint, left elbow joint, and right elbow joint), and displays the results as an animated user skeleton. As shadow maps come on the fly, the system continuously tracks user posture overtime and is able to generate 60 inference results per second. By default, all experiments are conducted at night in a typical indoor environment.

To obtain the ground truth of user postures, we set up three high-end SLR cameras (Cannon 60D) on tripods (1.2 m in height), located in the front and on the left and right sides of the user. While a user is performing a gesture, the three cameras capture video at 30 FPS from three perspectives. We then manually label the five key joints every five video frames[5] and calculate the 3D vector of each key point by combining concurrent video frames taken by three cameras. To identify concurrent video frames across cameras, we play a background music during the experiment and later seek the identical audio signal pattern across the video frames from different cameras. We cover a photodiode in the testbed corner before the experiment and remove the cover once each experiment begins. We mark the moment when the corner photodiode becomes unblocked as the starting point for both the video clips and testbed inference results. Human labeling has been the standard technique to seek ground truth in computer vision [26, 41]. In the future, we plan to use VICON to gain finer-grained accuracy.

6.1 Skeleton Reconstruction Accuracy

We first examine LiSense's 3D skeleton reconstruction accuracy with a single user (1.73 m body height, 65 kg body weight, right-handed) performing 20 free-form gestures[6]. These gestures span from single-hand movements (e.g., pushing, pointing, circling, waving), to two-hand movements (e.g., driving, hugging, boxing), to more sophisticated movements involving both user's upper torso and hands (e.g., Combo1: raising and flipping arms, Combo2: pointing and then circling). To examine the skeleton reconstruction accuracy, we represent each key joint as a 3D vector and calculate the

[5]To minimize human labeling errors, we attach flashy, bright strips to the user's key joints during experiments so that they are easily recognizable in video frames.

[6]Current test gestures involve only upper-body movements to avoid accidentally damaging photodiodes on the floor. See more in § 7.

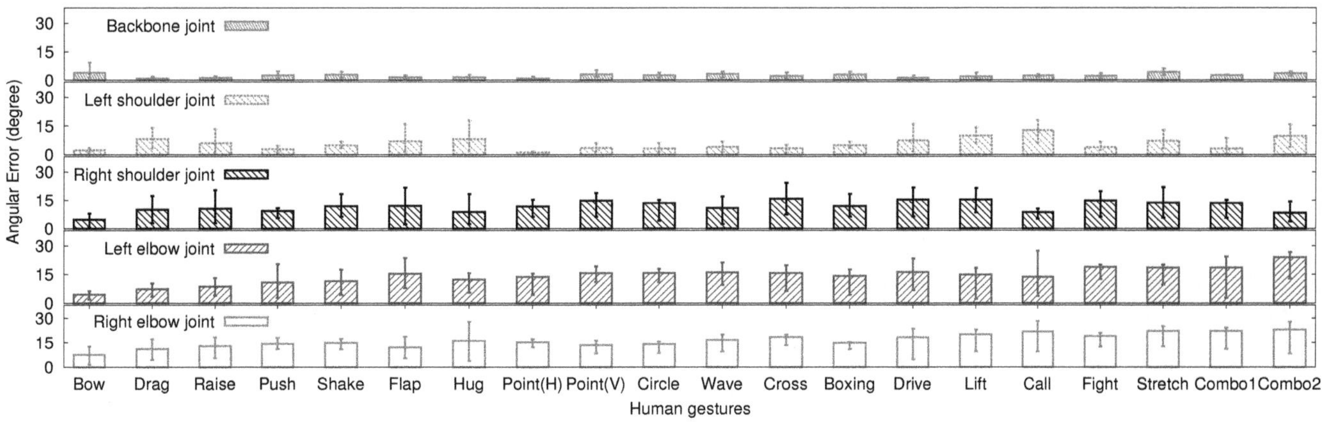

Figure 12: LiSense's skeleton reconstruction accuracy of five key joints on a user body while the user is performing one of the 20 gestures.

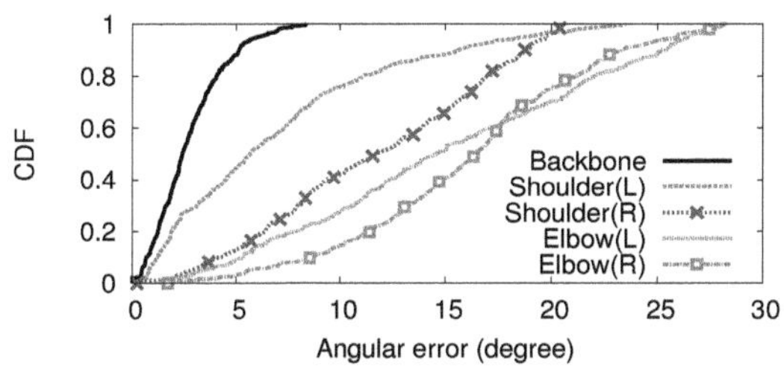

Figure 13: LiSense's skeleton reconstruction accuracy of five key joints on a user body, by aggregating 9292 posture inference results over continuous stream of shadow maps generated by 20 user gestures.

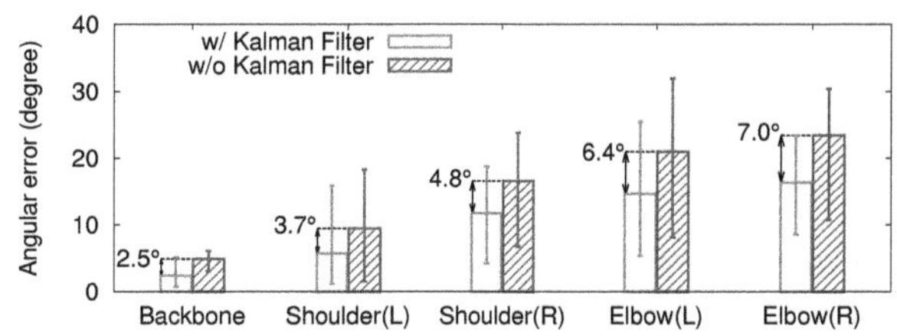

Figure 14: The contribution of the Kalman filter on improving LiSense's reconstruction accuracy. The error bars cover the 90% confidence interval.

absolute angular difference between the inferred and actual vectors for each key joint, referred to as the *3D angular error* of a key joint. This metric has also been widely used by prior work on human motion tracking and skeleton reconstruction [2, 9, 31, 43].

Overall Accuracy. In Figure 12, we plot the mean angular error of each key joint under each test gesture. We also include the error bars covering the 90% confidence interval. Figure 13 further compares the angular errors of the key body joints. Overall, for all gestures, LiSense achieves 10° mean angular error, similar to that of prior gesture tracking systems using RF signals [2, 3]. However, these systems only track a limited set of gestures (e.g., pointing) with a single body part (e.g., arm), while LiSense is capable of reconstructing arbitrary skeleton postures. We recognize that existing vision-based skeleton tracking systems such as Kinect (6.8° – 13.2° angular errors reported in [15]) outperform LiSense in terms of the tracking accuracy. Built upon cameras and depth sensors, these systems are dedicated to skeleton reconstruction and tracking, while LiSense integrates communication and sensing. We will discuss our plan to improve LiSense's accuracy in § 7.

In particular, we observe three key factors that affect LiSense's skeleton reconstruction accuracy under a given photodiode density: *1) Body part size:* LiSense better tracks larger body parts (e.g., backbone joint that corresponds to the user's main body). Because they generate larger shadow than other body parts, their movements lead to more significant differences in shadow maps, allowing our skeleton reconstruction algorithm to infer the 3D vectors more accurately (2° mean angular error). In contrast, reconstructing smaller body parts (e.g., forearms) is more challenging given the limited photodiode density (16° mean angular error). For gestures such as calling, our collected shadow maps do not reflect the shadow change resulted from the forearm movement, because the width of forearm shadow is smaller than the interval between adjacent photodiodes. Therefore the resulting angular errors of shoulder/elbow joints are slightly higher.

2) Movement magnitude: Gestures involving movements at a larger magnitude have smaller angular errors of all key joints, because they lead to more significant change in the shadow maps and are less vulnerable to the occlusion problem. Example gestures include bowing, raising arms, pointing, and dragging. This finding is also exemplified by the results of single-hand gestures (e.g., pushing, pointing, circling). Certain gestures (e.g., stretching) with large movement magnitude have higher angular errors because the shadow exceeds the testbed boundary.

3) Movement speed: High-speed movement can lead to higher angular errors, because LiSense examines the change of the frequency power perceived by each photodiode in a modulation window (6.4 ms). High-speed movement can result into a mixture of blocking and non-blocking states for a single photodiode within a modulation window, which leads to errors in inferred shadow maps and thus larger angular errors. For the same reason, the angular errors of left-side joints are smaller than the right joints for some two-hand gestures (e.g., boxing, fighting), since the right-handed user moves the left hand slightly more slowly. To track faster movements, we can improve the ADC sampling rate and reduce the modulation window size.

Contribution of the Kalman Filter. We further examine the contribution of the Kalman filter (§ 4.2) on reducing the reconstruction error. We analyze all the shadow maps in the experiments and calculate the reconstruction angular error offline without using the Kalman filter for fine-tuning. Figure 14 shows that the fine-tuning reduces the angular error by up to 7 degrees, especially for body parts (e.g., right elbow) with relatively faster movements. The reason is that faster movements lead to more drastic change in the adjacent shadow maps in the time domain. As a result, the raw reconstruction result of LiSense is more vulnerable to bursty errors.

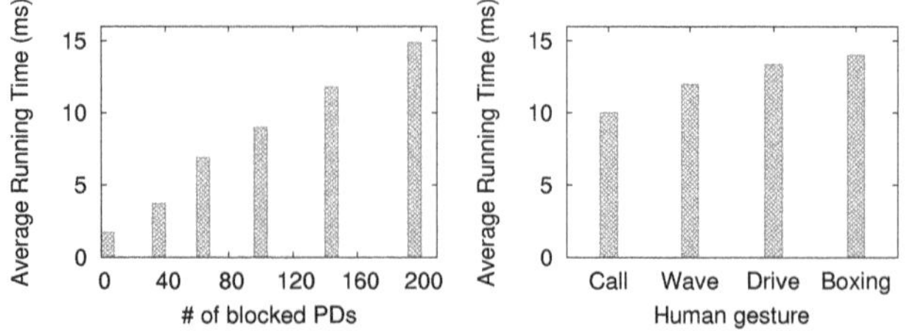

(a) Shadow size (b) Movement speed

Figure 15: The impact of shadow size and movement speed on the running time of user posture inference.

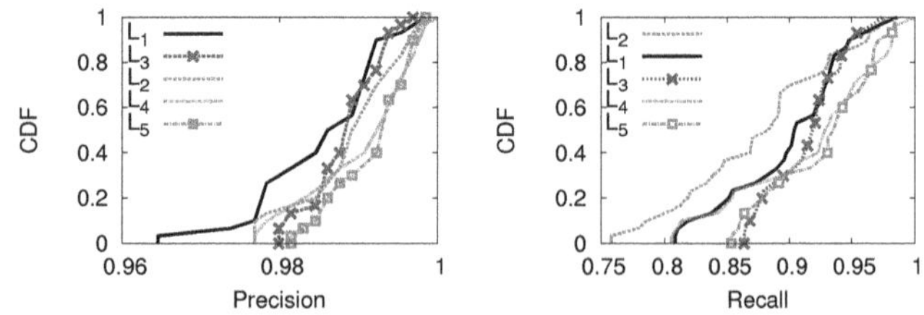

Figure 16: Shadow map accuracy with 30 static user postures.

Table 2: Processing time of generating shadow maps of all LEDs. The blockage detection algorithm (§ 3.2) runs instantaneously on the server and thus is not included.

Step	ADC sampling	FFT	Transmission	OS scheduling
Time (ms)	6.4	1.2	4.2	0.2 – 3.2

The Kalman filter smooths out the movement trajectory by modeling the movement as a stochastic process. It filters out the bursty errors and thus improves the reconstruction accuracy.

6.2 Skeleton Reconstruction Latency

We next examine LiSense's skeleton reconstruction latency, consisting of the duration of acquiring shadow maps of all LEDs and the processing time of inferring the user posture based on a single set of shadow maps. Note that these two steps run in parallel in our implementation (§ 5), thus the skeleton reconstruction latency perceived by the end user only depends on the slower step.

Acquiring Shadow Maps. Acquiring shadow maps of all LEDs has four steps: 1) each Arduino DUE samples photodiode data; 2) the Arduino DUE applies FFT over data collected from each photodiode within a modulation window and computes the frequency power of each LED's PWM frequency; 3) the Arduino sends the frequency power numbers of 12 photodiodes to the server; 4) the server runs the blockage detection scheme, aggregates the detection results of all photodiodes, and generates the five shadow maps.

Table 2 lists the latency of each step running at the Arduino DUE board. Overall, generating all five shadow maps takes 16 ms. Specifically, the ADC sampling (step 1) contributes more than half of the delay. Since the ADC sampling rate for each photodiode is 20 kHz, to support 128-point FFT computation in the second step, it takes 6.4 ms for the Arduino DUE to sample all 12 connected photodiodes. The Split-radix Real FFT algorithm is very efficient and takes only 1.2 ms (step 2). The data transmission (step 3) takes 4.2 ms, where the Arduino DUE sends 60 bytes (5 bytes for each photodiode's frequency power numbers) to the server via the series 232 port. Running the blockage detection scheme (step 4) entails negligible delay thanks to the simplicity of the detection scheme (§ 3.2). The only delay in the final step comes from the OS scheduling. It is because the OS (Ubuntu 14.04) of our server does not have a real-time kernel. With 27 threads collecting data from all Arduino boards, the OS can delay some threads when fetching data from a particular Arduino board. We observe that the OS scheduling delay varies from 0.2 – 3.2 ms.

Inferring User Posture. Two factors affect the latency of inferring a user posture based on five shadow maps, which are the shadow size (i.e., the number of photodiodes inside the shadow) and the movement complexity. *First*, to examine the impact of shadow size, we increase the number of blocked photodiodes by increasing the size of the blocking paperboard and plot the average running time of the posture inference in Figure 15 (a). As expected, it takes longer for the inference algorithm to process shadows in larger sizes. However, for all the shadow sizes in our experiments, the posture inference never takes more than 15 ms. LiSense handles large shadow size well because it minimizes the shadow points to process by considering only shadow's boundary points, rather than all its inner points (§ 4). *Second*, we examine four representative gestures with different moving speed and movement complexity, and compare the inference running time. Figure 15 (b) shows that as the gesture becomes more complex with more moving body parts, it takes longer for the skeleton reconstruction algorithm to identify the best-fit skeleton posture. However, the inference delay never exceeds 15 ms even for complex fast-moving gestures (e.g., boxing).

Overall, the processing time of the above two steps shows that LiSense can produce at least 60 user skeleton postures per second on the fly, the same as playing a video at a high frame rate.

Table 3: Blockage detector error at a photodiode under varying light incidence angle. The detection accuracy starts to drop only when the incidence angle approaches 45°, half of the photodiode's FoV.

Incidence angle (°)	[0,32)	[32,40.8)	[40.8,43.2)	[43.2, 45)
Blockage detection accuracy (%)	100	95 – 100	90 – 95	58 – 90

6.3 Shadow Map Accuracy

Shadow maps are the key intermediate results for LiSense to reconstruct user's skeleton posture. Now we examine the accuracy of inferred shadow maps and seek to understand the performance of the blockage detection scheme (§ 3.2). We obtain the ground truth shadow maps as follows. We first instruct the user to keep a static posture in the middle of the testbed. We then switch on a single LED light by turns, use an SLR camera (Cannon 60D) mounted at 1.8 m height to take a high-resolution (5184 × 3456) photo of the shadow cast on the floor, and repeat the process for all LED lights. Finally we manually label the shadow maps based on the captured photos and use the labeled shadow maps as the ground truth. We test 30 static postures with a single user.

We compare the inferred shadow maps to the ground truth and evaluate the accuracy using two metrics: 1) *precision*: among all photodiodes, the percentage of photodiodes that are correctly identified as being blocked; and 2) *recall*: among all photodiodes that are actually blocked, the percentage of photodiodes that are correctly identified. We plot the results in Figure 16 for all five LED lights. Overall the shadow maps are fairly accurate: 98% precision and 88-94% recall on average. The shadow maps cast by LED light L_2 have slightly lower recall because L_2 is right above the user (Figure 9(a)) and casts smaller shadow than other lights. Thus its recall results are more sensitive to errors.

As we further analyze the cause of the errors in a shadow map, we find that blockage detection errors occur only when the light rays arrive at the boundary of the photodiode's viewing angle (i.e., the light's incidence angle approaches half of the photodiode's FoV),

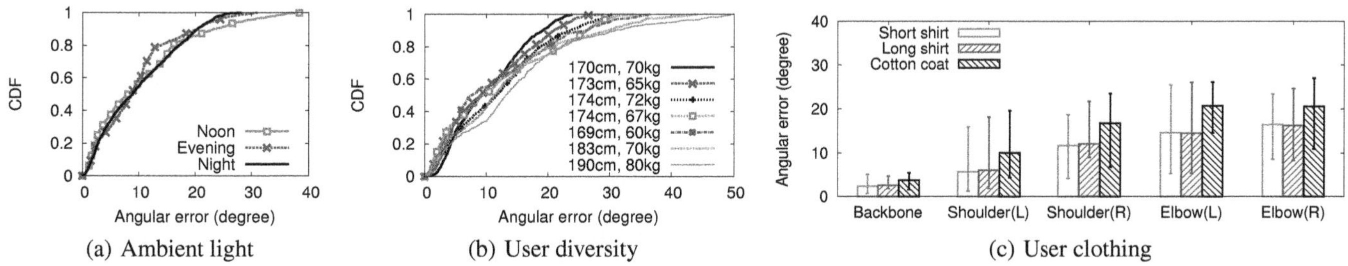

Figure 17: Impact of practical factors on LiSense's skeleton reconstruction accuracy.

as shown in Table 3. This is because as the light's incidence angle approaches the photodiode's FoV, the photodiode is more sensitive to the hardware noise and its response sensitivity drops drastically. As a result, it barely detects the light intensity changes, leading to the blockage detection errors. We expect that shadow map errors will be diminished when using photodiodes with larger FoVs.

6.4 Practical Considerations

Finally we examine the impact of ambient light, user diversity, and user clothing on LiSense's skeleton reconstruction accuracy. We also examine the energy overhead of human sensing in LiSense.

Ambient Light. We conduct experiments in LiSense at different times of a day, where the intensity of natural light varies from 375 lux at noon, 47 lux at evening, to 0 lux at night. We test a single user performing 10 gestures at each time of a day, and plot the angular errors in Figure 17(a). Overall LiSense's performance is stable in all ambient light conditions. The results obtained at noon have a slightly longer tail, because the higher level of ambient light intensity pushes the photodiodes further up into the saturation region (Figure 3(a)). Thus blocking an LED leads to smaller amplitude change in the perceived light signal, resulting into smaller frequency power changes and slightly higher error in inferred shadow maps and skeleton reconstruction results.

User Diversity. We test LiSense with seven users in different body sizes and shapes. The body height varies from 1.69 m to 1.9 m and the body weight ranges from 60 kg to 80 kg. Each user performs 10 gestures at night and Figure 17(b) compares the angular errors across users. The mean angular error is similar ($9°$ – $16°$) across all users, demonstrating LiSense's robustness under diverse users. The taller users have larger tail errors because these users' shadows often exceed the testbed boundary (3 m $\times$ 3 m), especially for gestures with large movement magnitude (e.g., stretching). The incomplete shadows lead to slightly higher errors. We expect these tail errors to disappear once we expand the testbed.

User Clothing. User clothing can also affect LiSense's performance. Consider a user wearing loose clothes, casting a shadow slightly larger than that of the actual user body. This mismatch can confuse LiSense's posture inference algorithm, which is initialized based on the user's body parameters. To examine the impact of user clothing, we repeat the experiments with a single user wearing different types of clothes. We plot the average angular error for each key body joint and the 90% confidence interval in Figure 17(c). We see that bulky or loose clothes (e.g., coat) can decrease the reconstruction accuracy by 6 degrees. In comparison, thin clothes such as short shirts create less interference in the resulting shadow, leading to a higher reconstruction accuracy. To maintain a good reconstruction accuracy under different user clothing, we can adapt user's body parameters to take into account the impact of clothing on the resulting shadow. We plan it for future work.

Energy Overhead. The energy overhead of LiSense comes from acquiring shadow maps from 324 photodiodes and 27 Arduino boards, and running the posture inference algorithm on the server. Our experiments show that acquiring shadow maps consumes 0.4 W atop the 27.4 W idle power of the Arduino boards and photodiodes. The inference algorithm consumes 19 W on our server (DELL M4600 with Ubuntu 14.04) atop the server's idle power. In comparison, the Kinect sensor (Version 2) consumes additional 11 W power for acquiring depth images and the skeleton tracking algorithm consumes 63 W on DELL M4600 with Window 8.1 atop the idle power. Kinect consumes much more power because it needs to capture dense (512 $\times$ 424) depth images and run a heavy classification algorithm on both the CPU and GPU [57].

We can further lower LiSense's energy overhead by reducing its idle power and implementing the inference algorithm on low-power micro-controllers such as Raspberry Pi (2 W). We have successfully migrated LiSense's code to Raspberry Pi. It currently reconstructs the user skeleton at 4 FPS. We plan to further optimize our inference algorithm and reduce the reconstruction latency on Pi.

7. DISCUSSIONS

The initial results from our LiSense testbed are encouraging. But based on our experiences building the LiSense testbed we also recognize several limitations of the existing system and potential applications that motivate future work.

Photodiode Deployment. Deploying hundreds of photodiodes on the floor has been a significant endeavor and learning curve both in terms of the number of man hours to develop such a photodiode floor – connecting 324 photodiodes to 27 micro-controllers – and developing techniques to make our testbed experiments robust and repeatable. We are convinced that the complexity can be eased in the future. Advances in smart fabric [45] will allow us to integrate photodiodes directly into textile. The electrical component in a photodiode is tiny (i.e., 0.5 mm $\times$ 0.5 mm in size) and thus the integration will be feasible in the next few years given the increasing interests in the industry (e.g., Google's Jacquard project [1]). Photodiode-embedded fabric would also allow a much denser deployment of photodiodes – the key to realize reconstructing finer-grained gestures (e.g., finger movements). We also plan to explore the use of photodiodes in wearable devices and in walls to further pursue the vision.

Environmental Factors. Our current testbed is in an open lab space where the test user is the only blocking object. Clearly, this is a simplification of more realistic environments where furniture and other people would block light. We plan to examine settings with other static blocking objects (e.g., sofa, chairs), which can cast their own shadows or block a user's shadow. In this case, we can extract the human gesture by detecting the moving objects in the shadow maps. In the case of multiple users, their shadows would likely overlap, making the reconstruction of individual user skeletons much more challenging. With denser LEDs on the ceiling, LiSense can extract more details on the human gesture by examining the shadows cast from different viewing angles. These shadows help the system differentiate multiple users. We plan to study these realistic settings as part of our future work.

Improving LiSense Accuracy. LiSense's current skeleton reconstruction accuracy is still below that of vision-based skeleton tracking systems (e.g., Kinect), which use both cameras and depth sensors. However, LiSense holds potential to achieve a greater accuracy. First of all, we can leverage learning algorithms such as the decision forest [57] to segment a shadow map into body parts and optimize each body part individually. The segmentation provides additional information on how and whether a body part moves in the 3D space. It refines the inference and helps the algorithm converge more quickly. Furthermore, we plan to examine placing photodiodes on other planes (e.g., walls) in addition to the floor. Combining the light intensity data from multiple planes allows us to obtain shadow information in multiple dimensions and thus boost the skeleton reconstruction accuracy.

Testbed Maintenance. All photodiodes and control circuits are currently exposed in the air. We observe that practical issue can complicate the maintenance of the testbed; for example, dirt and dust harm electrical component – 41 photodiodes have been damaged in 40 days of testing. Our initial approach has limited gestures to upper-body movements to avoid unexpected damage to photodiodes caused by walking over the fairly fragile photodiode flooring. In the near future, we plan to add a cover made of thin, durable plastic glass (e.g., polycarbonate plastic) over the photodiodes floor so users can stand on the "glass floor" allowing us to experiment with a larger, more realistic set of leg movements – further advancing the gestures we can infer with LiSense.

Potential Applications. With the ability of reconstructing the user skeleton in real time at a high frame rate, LiSense enables new interaction designs and facilitates existing applications. Here we discuss three examples. *First*, LiSense allows users to freely control smart devices (e.g., nano-copters, robot vacuum) in the environment at a fine granularity, using only the ubiquitous light, without any cameras or on-body sensors. *Second*, LiSense facilitates the augmented reality (AR) applications by allowing the users to naturally interact with the virtual scene. AR applications can leverage the reconstructed user skeleton posture to adapt its virtual scenes. *Third*, LiSense serves as the basis for building a passive human behavioral and health monitoring system. By aggregating the reconstructed human posture data over time, we can infer higher-level human behavioral patterns (e.g., gait, movement characteristics) and correlate these patterns to the user's health status.

8. RELATED WORK

VLC Physical Layer. The research group led by Nakagawa at Japan pioneered the early work on VLC [29, 30]. They envisioned the integration of VLC with the power-line communication (PLC) to provide ubiquitous Internet access indoors [29], and first studied VLC propagation properties in indoor settings [30]. Since then, active efforts focus on boosting VLC data rate, by either filtering out the yellow light [33], or designing sophisticated modulation schemes (e.g., CSK [49], OFDM [14]), or enabling parallel data streams via MIMO [68]. The fastest VLC system to date has achieved 10Gbps data rate using arrays of specialized micro-LEDs [59, 60]. Advancements on VLC physical layer techniques are encouraging and LiSense can be built atop them by seamlessly integrating light beacons with VLC communication.

VLC Applications. Current VLC applications span from indoor communication [38], indoor localization [28, 32, 36, 69], screen-camera communication [7, 18, 22, 23, 37, 44, 61], vehicular networks [6, 39], LED-to-LED communication [12, 54], underwater communication [53], to in-flight entertainment [47]. Our work broadens VLC use cases and explores the feasibility of using VLC for fine-grained, real-time human sensing, enabling a new paradigm of user interaction. Existing work on VLC indoor localization [28, 32, 36, 69] is similar in the spirit by sensing user location. LiSense differs in that it enables much finer-grained user sensing and tracks a wide range of user's gestures.

Gesture Recognition and Reconstruction. We divide existing work into two categories. The first type of work uses sound waves [17] or RF signals [2, 3, 4, 46, 62, 63] to recognize and track gestures. These systems focus on either classifying a limited set of gestures or activities [4, 17, 46, 63], or tracking the movement of a single body part [2, 3], or requiring on-body sensors [62]. LiSense differs in that it reconstructs the user's skeleton posture in the 3D space in real time. Thus it is capable of tracking any gestures, without requiring the user to wear on-body sensors.

The second type of work [11, 20, 21, 24, 41] uses cameras and/or depth sensors to capture high-resolution video frames and build dedicated sensing systems. They apply computer vision algorithms to track or reconstruct gestures. Overall, these methods typically involve a heavy computation, which limits their achieved frame rates (30 FPS for Kinect). Furthermore, these methods often require an exhaustive training to achieve a reasonable accuracy. The skeleton tracking algorithm [57] used in Kinect relies on hundreds of thousands of training images to build the classifier. Finally, capturing and storing the raw camera data raises privacy concerns since these sensitive data can be leaked to the adversary [52, 64]. In comparison, LiSense integrates sensing and communication. It uses low-resolution shadow maps to reconstruct the user skeleton. The inference algorithm is lightweight and achieves 60 FPS frame rate in our current implementation.

9. CONCLUSION

In this paper, we discussed the design, deployment, and evaluation of LiSense, the first human gesture tracking system purely powered by visible light communication (VLC) – light is used for both human sensing and communication. LiSense uses light beacons to recover the shadow pattern cast by individual light sources. It infers 3D human postures at 60 Hz in real time with mean 10° angular error in 3D skeleton reconstruction. LiSense lies in the intersection of wireless networking, computer vision, and HCI. It enables new VLC applications and new forms of interactions not possible before.

10. ACKNOWLEDGMENTS

We sincerely thank anonymous reviewers for their valuable comments that helped improve the paper. We also thank Guanyang Yu and Xiaole An for their contribution on visualizing the user skeleton, Xing-Dong Yang for the support on Kinect experiments, Will Campbell and DartNets Lab members Fanglin Chen, Peilin Hao, and Rui Wang for their help on our experiments. This work is supported in part by the National Science Foundation under grant CNS-1421528. Any opinions, findings, and conclusions or recommendations expressed in this material are those of the authors and do not necessarily reflect those of the funding agencies or others.

11. REFERENCES

[1] Google Project Jacquard. `https://www.google.com/atap/project-jacquard/`.

[2] ADIB, F., KABELAC, Z., AND KATABI, D. Multi-Person Motion Tracking via RF Body Reflections. In *Proc. of NSDI* (2015).

[3] ADIB, F., KABELAC, Z., KATABI, D., AND MILLER, R. C. 3D Tracking via Body Radio Reflections. In *Proc. of NSDI* (2014).

[4] ADIB, F., AND KATABI, D. See through walls with WiFi! In *Proc. of SIGCOMM* (2013).

[5] AFGANI, M. Z., HAAS, H., ELGALA, H., AND KNIPP, D. Visible light communication using OFDM. In *Proc. of TRIDENTCOM* (2006).

[6] ARAI, S., ET AL. Experimental on hierarchical transmission scheme for visible light communication using LED traffic light and high-speed camera. In *Proc. of VTC* (2007).

[7] ASHOK, A., ET AL. Challenge: Mobile optical networks through visual MIMO. In *Proc. of MobiCom* (2010).

[8] ASSOCIATION, I. S., ET AL. IEEE Std. for Local and metropolitan area networks-Part 15.7: Short-Rang Wireless Optical Communication Using Visible Light. *IEEE Computer Society* (2011).

[9] BEAUDOIN, P., POULIN, P., AND VAN DE PANNE, M. Adapting wavelet compression to human motion capture clips. In *Proc. of GI* (2007).

[10] CHEN, V. C., LI, F., HO, S.-S., AND WECHSLER, H. Analysis of micro-doppler signatures. *IEE Proceedings-Radar, Sonar and Navigation 150*, 4 (2003), 271–276.

[11] CHEUNG, G. K., KANADE, T., BOUGUET, J.-Y., AND HOLLER, M. A real time system for robust 3D voxel reconstruction of human motions. In *Proc. of CVPR* (2000).

[12] DIETZ, P., YERAZUNIS, W., AND LEIGH, D. Very low-cost sensing and communication using bidirectional LEDs. In *Proc. of UbiComp* (2003).

[13] DUHAMEL, P., AND HOLLMANN, H. Split radix FFT algorithm. *Electronics letters 20*, 1 (1984), 14–16.

[14] ELGALA, H., MESLEH, R., HAAS, H., AND PRICOPE, B. OFDM visible light wireless communication based on white LEDs. In *Proc. of VTC* (2007).

[15] FERNANDEZ-BAENA, A., SUSÍN, A., AND LLIGADAS, X. Biomechanical validation of upper-body and lower-body joint movements of kinect motion capture data for rehabilitation treatments. In *Proc. of INCoS* (2012).

[16] GHADDAR, M., TALBI, L., AND DENIDNI, T. Human body modelling for prediction of effect of people on indoor propagation channel. *Electronics Letters 40*, 25 (2004), 1592–1594.

[17] GUPTA, S., MORRIS, D., PATEL, S., AND TAN, D. SoundWave: Using the Doppler effect to sense gestures. In *Proc. of CHI* (2012).

[18] HAO, T., ZHOU, R., AND XING, G. COBRA: Color barcode streaming for smartphone systems. In *Proc. of MobiSys* (2012).

[19] HENRY, P., KRAININ, M., HERBST, E., REN, X., AND FOX, D. RGB-D mapping: Using depth cameras for dense 3D modeling of indoor environments. In *Proc. of ISER* (2010).

[20] HERDA, L., FUA, P., PLANKERS, R., BOULIC, R., AND THALMANN, D. Skeleton-based motion capture for robust reconstruction of human motion. In *Proc. of International Conference on Computer Animation* (2000).

[21] HOWE, N. R., LEVENTON, M. E., AND FREEMAN, W. T. Bayesian Reconstruction of 3D Human Motion from Single-Camera Video. In *Proc. of NIPS* (1999).

[22] HU, W., GU, H., AND PU, Q. LightSync: Unsynchronized visual communication over screen-camera links. In *Proc. of MobiCom* (2013).

[23] HU, W., MAO, J., HUANG, Z., XUE, Y., SHE, J., BIAN, K., AND SHEN, G. Strata: Layered Coding for Scalable Visual Communication. In *Proc. of MobiCom* (2014).

[24] IZADI, S., KIM, D., HILLIGES, O., MOLYNEAUX, D., NEWCOMBE, R., KOHLI, P., SHOTTON, J., HODGES, S., FREEMAN, D., DAVISON, A., ET AL. KinectFusion: real-time 3D reconstruction and interaction using a moving depth camera. In *Proc. of UIST* (2011).

[25] JERRI, A. J. The Shannon sampling theorem–Its various extensions and applications: A tutorial review. *Proc. of the IEEE* (1977).

[26] JHUANG, H., GALL, J., ZUFFI, S., SCHMID, C., AND BLACK, M. J. Towards understanding action recognition. In *Proc. of ICCV* (2013).

[27] KIM, D., HILLIGES, O., IZADI, S., BUTLER, A. D., CHEN, J., OIKONOMIDIS, I., AND OLIVIER, P. Digits: Freehand 3D Interactions Anywhere Using a Wrist-worn Gloveless Sensor. In *Proc. of UIST* (2012).

[28] KIM, H.-S., ET AL. An indoor visible light communication positioning system using a RF carrier allocation technique. *Journal of Lightwave Technology 31*, 1 (2013), 134–144.

[29] KOMINE, T., AND NAKAGAWA, M. Integrated system of white LED visible-light communication and power-line communication. *IEEE Transactions on Consumer Electronics 49*, 1 (2003), 71–79.

[30] KOMINE, T., AND NAKAGAWA, M. Fundamental analysis for visible-light communication system using LED lights. *IEEE Transactions on Consumer Electronics 50*, 1 (2004), 100–107.

[31] KROSSHAUG, T., AND BAHR, R. A model-based image-matching technique for three-dimensional reconstruction of human motion from uncalibrated video sequences. *Journal of biomechanics 38*, 4 (2005), 919–929.

[32] KUO, Y.-S., PANNUTO, P., HSIAO, K.-J., AND DUTTA, P. Luxapose: Indoor positioning with mobile phones and visible light. In *Proc. of MobiCom* (2014).

[33] LE-MINH, H., ET AL. 100-Mb/s NRZ visible light communications using a postequalized white LED. *Photonics Technology Letters, IEEE 21*, 15 (2009), 1063–1065.

[34] LE MINH, H., O'BRIEN, D., FAULKNER, G., ZENG, L., LEE, K., JUNG, D., OH, Y., AND WON, E. T. 100-Mb/s NRZ visible light communications using a postequalized white LED. *Photonics Technology Letters, IEEE 21*, 15 (2009), 1063–1065.

[35] LEE, K., AND PARK, H. Modulations for visible light communications with dimming control. *Photonics Technology Letters, IEEE 23*, 16 (2011), 1136–1138.

[36] LI, L., HU, P., PENG, C., SHEN, G., AND ZHAO, F. Epsilon: A visible light based positioning system. In *Proc. of NSDI* (2014).

[37] LI, T., AN, C., XIAO, X., CAMPBELL, A. T., AND ZHOU, X. Real-Time Screen-Camera Communication Behind Any Scene. In *Proc. of MobiSys* (2015).

[38] LITTLE, T. D. C., ET AL. Using LED lighting for ubiquitous indoor wireless networking. In *Proc. of WiMob* (2008).

[39] LIU, C. B., SADEGHI, B., AND KNIGHTLY, E. W. Enabling vehicular visible light communication (V2LC) networks. In *Proc. of VANET* (2011).

[40] MCKINNEY, J. C., AND HOPKINS, C. D. R. ATSC digital television standard. *Advanced Television System Committee* (1995).

[41] MOESLUND, T. B., HILTON, A., AND KRÜGER, V. A survey of advances in vision-based human motion capture and analysis. *Computer vision and image understanding 104*, 2 (2006), 90–126.

[42] MOHR, R., QUAN, L., AND VEILLON, F. Relative 3D reconstruction using multiple uncalibrated images. *The International Journal of Robotics Research 14*, 6 (1995), 619–632.

[43] MOSCHINI, D., AND FUSIELLO, A. Tracking human motion with multiple cameras using an articulated model. In *Computer Vision/Computer Graphics Collaboration Techniques*. Springer, 2009, pp. 1–12.

[44] PERLI, S. D., AHMED, N., AND KATABI, D. PixNet: Interference-free wireless links using LCD-camera pairs. In *Proc. of MobiCom* (2010).

[45] POST, E. R., ORTH, M., RUSSO, P. R., AND GERSHENFELD, N. E-broidery: Design and fabrication of textile-based computing. *IBM Systems Journal 39*, 3.4 (2000), 840–860.

[46] PU, Q., GUPTA, S., GOLLAKOTA, S., AND PATEL, S. Whole-home gesture recognition using wireless signals. In *Proc. of MobiCom* (2013).

[47] QUINTANA, C., ET AL. Reading lamp-based visible light communication system for in-flight entertainment. *Consumer Electronics, IEEE Transactions on 59*, 1 (2013), 31–37.

[48] RAJAGOPAL, N., LAZIK, P., AND ROWE, A. Visual light landmarks for mobile devices. In *Proc. of IPSN* (2014).

[49] RAJAGOPAL, S., ROBERTS, R., AND LIM, S.-K. IEEE 802.15.7 visible light communication: modulation schemes and dimming support. *Communications Magazine, IEEE 50*, 3 (2012), 72–82.

[50] RYCKAERT, J., DE DONCKER, P., MEYS, R., DE LE HOYE, A., AND DONNAY, S. Channel model for wireless communication around human body. *Electronics Letters 40*, 9 (2004), 543–544.

[51] SAXENA, A., CHUNG, S. H., AND NG, A. Y. 3-D depth reconstruction from a single still image. *International journal of computer vision 76*, 1 (2008), 53–69.

[52] SBÎRLEA, D., BURKE, M. G., GUARNIERI, S., PISTOIA, M., AND SARKAR, V. Automatic detection of inter-application permission leaks in android applications. *IBM Journal of Research and Development 57*, 6 (2013), 10–1.

[53] SCHILL, F., ZIMMER, U. R., AND TRUMPF, J. Visible spectrum optical communication and distance sensing for underwater applications. In *In Proc. of Australasian Conference on Robotics and Automation* (2004).

[54] SCHMID, S., CORBELLINI, G., MANGOLD, S., AND GROSS, T. R. LED-to-LED visible light communication networks. In *Proc. of MobiHoc* (2013).

[55] SEGEN, J., AND KUMAR, S. Shadow gestures: 3D hand pose estimation using a single camera. In *Proc. of CVPR* (1999).

[56] SHOEMAKER, G., TANG, A., AND BOOTH, K. S. Shadow reaching: a new perspective on interaction for large displays. In *Proc. of UIST* (2007).

[57] SHOTTON, J., ET AL. Real-time human pose recognition in parts from single depth images. In *Proc. of CVPR* (2011).

[58] SILAGHI, M.-C., PLÄNKERS, R., BOULIC, R., FUA, P., AND THALMANN, D. Local and global skeleton fitting techniques for optical motion capture. In *Modelling and Motion Capture Techniques for Virtual Environments*. Springer, 1998, pp. 26–40.

[59] TSONEV, D., ET AL. A 3-Gb/s Single-LED OFDM-based Wireless VLC Link Using a Gallium Nitride μLED. *Photonics Technology Letters, IEEE PP*, 99 (2014), 1–1.

[60] WALL, M. 'Li-fi' via LED light bulb data speed breakthrough. BBC News, 2013.

[61] WANG, A., MA, S., HU, C., HUAI, J., PENG, C., AND SHEN, G. Enhancing Reliability to Boost the Throughput over Screen-camera Links. In *Proc. of MobiCom* (2014).

[62] WANG, J., VASISHT, D., AND KATABI, D. RF-IDraw: Virtual Touch Screen in the Air Using RF Signals. In *Proc. of SIGCOMM* (2014).

[63] WANG, Y., LIU, J., CHEN, Y., GRUTESER, M., YANG, J., AND LIU, H. E-eyes: Device-free Location-oriented Activity Identification Using Fine-grained WiFi Signatures. In *Proc. of MobiCom* (2014).

[64] WEINBERG, Z., CHEN, E. Y., JAYARAMAN, P. R., AND JACKSON, C. I still know what you visited last summer: Leaking browsing history via user interaction and side channel attacks. In *Proc. of IEEE Symposium on Security and Privacy* (2011).

[65] WELCH, T., MUSSELMAN, R., EMESSIENE, B., GIFT, P., CHOUDHURY, D., CASSADINE, D., AND YANO, S. The effects of the human body on UWB signal propagation in an indoor environment. *IEEE Journal on Selected Areas in Communications 20*, 9 (2002), 1778–1782.

[66] WHITAKER, R. T. A level-set approach to 3D reconstruction from range data. *International journal of computer vision 29*, 3 (1998), 203–231.

[67] YEUNG, K.-Y., KWOK, T.-H., AND WANG, C. C. Improved Skeleton Tracking by Duplex Kinects: A Practical Approach for Real-Time Applications. *Journal of Computing and Information Science in Engineering 13*, 4 (2013), 041007.

[68] ZENG, L., ET AL. High data rate multiple input multiple output (MIMO) optical wireless communications using white LED lighting. *IEEE Journal on Selected Areas in Communications 27*, 9 (2009), 1654–1662.

[69] ZHANG, W., AND KAVEHRAD, M. Comparison of VLC-based indoor positioning techniques. In *Proc. of SPIE* (2013).

[70] ZHANG, Z., ET AL. I Am the Antenna: Accurate Outdoor AP Location Using Smartphones. In *Proc. of MobiCom* (2011).

[71] ZHOU, X., AND CAMPBELL, A. Visible Light Networking and Sensing. In *Proc. of HotWireless* (2014).

Extending Mobile Interaction Through Near-Field Visible Light Sensing

Chi Zhang, Joshua Tabor, Jialiang Zhang and Xinyu Zhang
{czhang296,jtabor,jzhang625}@wisc.edu, xyzhang@ece.wisc.edu
Department of Electrical and Computer Engineering
University of Wisconsin-Madison

ABSTRACT

Mobile devices are shrinking their form factors for portability, but user-mobile interaction is becoming increasingly challenging. In this paper, we propose a novel system called Okuli to meet this challenge. Okuli is a compact, low-cost system that can augment a mobile device and extend its interaction workspace to any nearby surface area. Okuli piggybacks on visible light communication modules, and uses a low-power LED and two light sensors to locate user's finger within the workspace. It is built on a light propagation/reflection model that achieves around one-centimeter location precision, with zero run-time training overhead. We have prototyped Okuli as an Android peripheral, with a 3D-printed shroud to host the LED and light sensors. Our experiments demonstrate Okuli's accuracy, stability, energy efficiency, as well as its potential in serving virtual keyboard and trackpad applications.

Categories and Subject Descriptors

H.5.2 [**INFORMATION INTERFACES AND PRESENTATION**]: User Interfaces—*Input devices and strategies*

Keywords

Mobile human computer interaction; visible light sensing; visible light channel modeling; wearable computing

1. INTRODUCTION

Touch has been a de facto mode of input for modern mobile devices like smartphones. Despite its popularity, it carries a number of inherent limitations. Interacting with touchscreens can lead to fingers occluding valuable screen real estate, which is especially cumbersome for real-time applications such as gaming. The problem is being exacerbated given a continued trend for ever-smaller devices. For emerging wearable computing devices, *e.g.*, smart watches, touch input becomes virtually infeasible.

Alternative mobile interaction technologies have been explored to unleash user's finger/hand from the screen. RF-IDraw [1] and PhonePoint [2] use RFID or motion sensors to track hand trajectory, creating opportunities for writing in the air. These approaches can achieve sub-meter scale tracking accuracy, but require instrumenting the hand with additional devices. Vision-based input detection systems [3, 4] achieve finer granularity, by projecting a keyboard or trackpad and extracting user's finger movement with image processing. Yet the need for bulky cameras/projectors compromises portability. UbiK and TapSense [5, 6] piggyback on ambient objects' surface to create a virtual trackpad/keyboard, yet their touching and keystroke identification algorithms rely on tedious run-time training.

Inspired by the emerging visible light communication (VLC) technology [7, 8], we propose Okuli, a novel system that moves interaction off the display and into nearby field around a mobile device. Recent VLC systems have demonstrated capabilities to localize active objects instrumented with light sensors [9, 10]. In contrast, Okuli enables a VLC-capable mobile device to sense passive object, in particular, user's single-finger input. The mobile device uses an LED transmitter to project a light beam towards the finger, and uses photodetectors (PDs) to sense the reflected light intensity, thus localizing the finger position. Okuli affords two immediate interactions for small mobile devices: *(i)* A virtual trackpad that tracks a user's finger, enabling hand-writing based input for smart watches or smartphones with a small display area. *(ii)* A ubiquitous text-entry system that locates user's finger click on a virtual keyboard, *e.g.*, one printed on a flat surface or a piece of paper [5].

In contrast to prior fine-grained input sensing systems that learn location-dependent acoustic/RF signal features [5], Okuli adopts a *model-driven* framework for finger positioning, which is free of run-time training overhead. Okuli achieves this based on two empirical principles originating from physical properties of the visible-light channel. *(i)* Unlike the well-known infrared-based proximity sensing technology that detects "beam cutting" activities [11], Okuli harnesses the non-linear propagation/attenuation effect of light signals, enabling a large input canvas and richer localization information than a binary "presence or absence". *(ii)* Unlike acoustic/RF signals, light propagation bears a more deterministic model, yet this also implies more spatial ambiguity. Okuli thus employs two light sensors to discriminate finger locations that reflect similar light intensity.

Despite its simplicity in principle, Okuli faces a number of key challenges in meeting centimeter-level localization granularity in its anticipated application scenarios. In particular, although light attenuation follows well-defined model in free-space, reflection on irregular-shaped finger, together with irregular LED/PD angular gain patterns, incurs substantial uncertainties. To enable robust finger positioning, Okuli *grooms* the light by reshaping the LED/PD's field-of-view (FoV) with a shroud. It then executes a 3-point initial calibration, based on which it models/predicts the expected light intensity perceived by each PD, when the finger is touching an arbitrary location on the canvas. Okuli's light grooming also enables it to accurately detect finger touching/clicking events.

MobiCom'15, September 7–11, 2015, Paris, France.
 ISBN 978-1-4503-3619-2/15/09...$15.00.
DOI: http://dx.doi.org/10.1145/2789168.2790115.

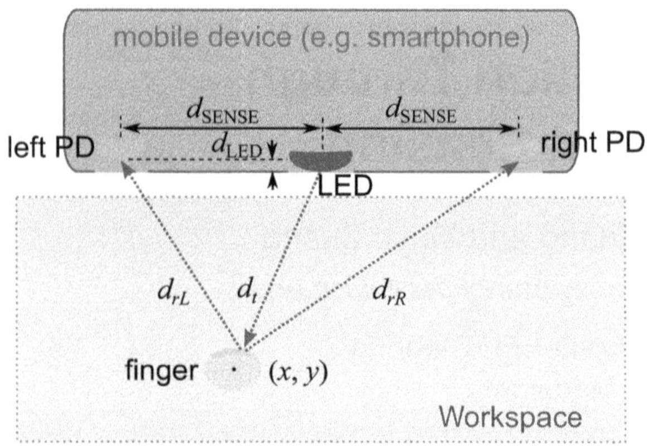

Figure 1: Okuli system architecture.

Uncertainties can also be induced by reflection from irrelevant background objects, and interference from ambient light source. Okuli takes advantage of the flickering capability of VLC transceivers to perform common mode rejection, thus highlighting the finger's impact only. Okuli further leverages flickering to adapt the emitting/sampling rate of LED, thus constraining its energy cost.

We prototype Okuli as a peripheral module to an Android device. The light grooming mechanism is realized via a 3D-printed shroud, which hosts the LED/PDs. We use near-infrared (NIR) LED and PDs in the prototype, whose wavelength is very close to that of visible light, and has identical channel characteristics. The driver circuit for light projection/sensing interfaces with a tablet running virtual keyboard/trackpad applications. All signal processing and localization algorithms run inside the tablet. We expect a product-level implementation can easily embed the LED/PDs on the side of a mobile device, and use part of its body as shroud.

Our experiments on this prototype demonstrate Okuli's great potential in realizing near-field mobile interaction. On a 9cm×7cm region, equivalent to a small trackpad, it can detect and localize random finger positions with a median error of 0.7cm, and 90-percentile error of 1.43cm. It shows consistent precision over different surfaces. Given LEDs/PDs with wider FoV and higher power/sensitivity, Okuli's working region can be further expanded.

We have also prototyped the aforementioned keyboard and trackpad applications on top of Okuli. Our experiments show that handwriting tracked by Okuli achieves a character recognition rate of 90.6%, comparable to that from a tablet. In addition, Okuli realizes a small keyboard within its workspace, with keystroke recognition rate of 90.7%. A field test with multiple users demonstrates that Okuli maintains consistent performance in the presence of different fingers and usage behaviors.

The key contributions of Okuli can be summarized as follows.

(i) Proposing a model-driven framework, facilitated by a light-grooming mechanism, to realize fine-grained finger positioning using visible light signals. The model also enables us to examine salient system properties including spatial ambiguity and dimension scalability.

(ii) Designing mechanisms to eliminate the interference from background reflection and ambient light, and limiting the power consumption of a passive light sensing system.

(iii) Implementing and validating the entire system as a smartphone peripheral with a 3D-printed shroud. Performing case studies of Okuli in trackpad/keyboard applications.

2. Okuli OVERVIEW

System Architecture. Okuli is a low cost passive finger localization system based on visible light sensing. As shown in Figure 1,

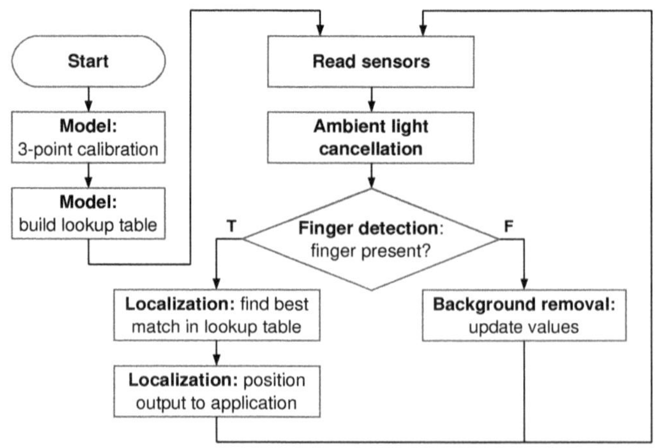

Figure 2: Simplified workflow of Okuli.

Okuli consists of 1 light source and 2 light sensors. The light source is an LED, and sensors are photodetectors (PDs) whose output increases linearly with input light intensity. The LED is centered between the 2 PDs which are typically separated well below 10cm so as to be fitted into the edge of a mobile device. We refer to the straight line between the two PDs as Okuli's *front face*.

Okuli uses the region in front of this line as the *workspace*. The workspace's coordinate system uses the center-point between two PDs as the origin, and its x-axis is parallel to Okuli's front face. Finger position within the workspace is denoted with (x, y). The LED can be placed slightly in front of the front face if desired. In the rest of this paper, we denote the distance between the origin and each PD as d_{SENSE}, and that between the origin and the LED as d_{LED}. The distances between the finger and the LED, left and right PD are denoted by d_t, d_{rL} and d_{rR}, respectively.

Usage conditions. Since Okuli uses a light propagation/reflection model for finger localization, its accuracy highly relies on the accuracy of the modeling parameters. However, Okuli will perform consistently as long as the following conditions are satisfied: *(i)* The reflectivity of user's finger does not change significantly over time. *(ii)* User maintains a relatively consistent usage habit (*e.g.*, same finger), and the hand/wrist does not touch the working surface, just like when using a touchscreen. *(iii)* The workspace stays on the same surface with a consistent reflectivity.

From our user study, we found that these conditions are naturally met in Okuli's targeted application scenarios, and users naturally maintain the consistency needed. When the usage conditions are violated, Okuli requires the user to input 3 anchoring points to recalibrate the modeling parameters (Section 4.3).

Design goals and challenges. Okuli needs to achieve the following goals in order to facilitate mobile interaction:

(i) Fine-grained, model based finger localization: Okuli aims for model-driven localization with around one-centimeter accuracy (around the size of a key on a keyboard), and without a fingerprinting-like training procedure. It needs to account for all factors that can affect the light intensity reflected by the finger into the PDs. These include not only finger-to-PD distance, but also the LED/PDs' angular response, finger reflectivity, *etc.*

(ii) Robustness: Okuli's model should be stable over time. In addition, since Okuli uses visible light to locate the finger, two kinds of visible light sources may interfere our system: (a) Ambient light such as fluorescent lamp and sunlight; (b) Reflection from background object other than the finger. The first type of interference could be easily canceled due to its stability, but the second type imposes challenges since it is "coherent" with the finger reflection and may be dynamic.

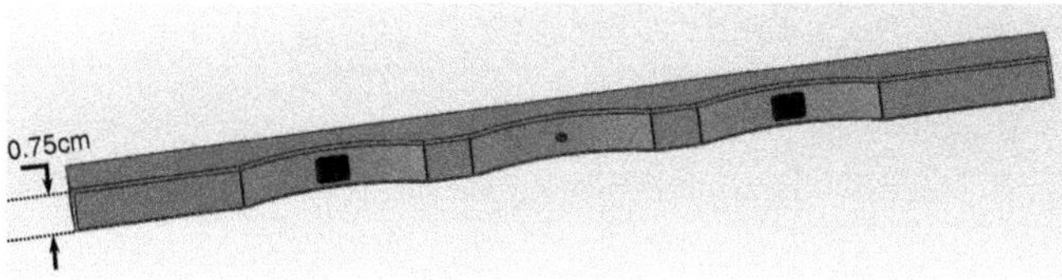

Figure 3: Concept-art of a product version of Okuli, to be fit into the edge of a small mobile device with a thickness around 7.5mm.

(iii) Power consumption and form factor: Okuli should have a relatively low power consumption to be equipped on battery-powered devices. In addition, Okuli should have a small dimension so as to be integrated to small mobile devices such as smartphones and smart watches.

System workflow. To achieve the above goals, Okuli incorporates the following four signal processing modules on top of its hardware substrate: visible light channel modeling and calibration, ambient light cancellation, finger detection and background removal, and finger localization. Figure 2 illustrates a simplified workflow of Okuli.

The *modeling/calibration* module (Section 4) requires the user to conduct a 3-point initial calibration procedure. The calibration sets user specific parameters in the light propagation/reflection model. The model then builds a lookup table that predicts sensor output when the finger is located at an arbitrary point within the workspace.

The *ambient light cancellation* module (Section 5.1) suppresses the interference caused by other light sources. It works by turning the LED on and off and then calculating the difference of sensor outputs, thus eliminating the components contributed by external light sources.

The *finger detection and background removal* module (Section 5.2) first determines whether user's finger is present. Upon detecting the finger, it invokes the finger localization module; Otherwise, it opportunistically updates the estimation of dynamic background values, which result from reflections upon nearby objects such as user's body.

Finally, at run-time, the *finger localization* module (Section 5.3) compares the PDs' outputs with those in the lookup table and determines the most likely location of the finger, *i.e.*, the position that has a predicted sensor output that best matches the measured one.

3. DISCIPLINING THE LIGHT SENSING

3.1 Field-of-View (FOV) Consideration for Visible Light Sensing

Okuli uses a visible light source and dual PDs to locate a finger within its working space. If the light sensing is not carefully controlled, Okuli can become very susceptible to background reflections and ambient light interference. The former can be attributed to reflections from user's hand, arm or other objects close to Okuli. The latter can saturate Okuli's PDs and, if the ambient light is dynamic, can lead to false detections.

To alleviate these problems, Okuli should ideally use PDs with a very wide horizontal FOV and a very narrow vertical FOV. The wide horizontal FOV creates a wide workspace, and the narrow vertical FOV helps reduce background and ambient light interference by limiting the amount of objects capable of reflecting light into Okuli's PDs. By constraining the FOV of the PDs, Okuli only views a small slice of the user's finger, plus a limited amount of interference.

FOV can be shaped through custom-built PDs or lenses, which can be made extremely small and fit comfortably on the side of a smartphone or smart watch. Figure 3 shows an example of how Okuli could look in an actual product-level implementation.

3.2 A 3D Printed Shroud for Light Grooming

Since there exist no PDs with the required FOV characteristics on the market, a shroud is 3D printed to hold the PDs and discipline their FOV. Figure 4 shows a CAD drawing of the shroud. We have printed the shroud on a Dimension Elite 3D printer using ABS thermoplastic painted in black.

The PDs' vertical FOV is limited by the slits on the left and right side of the shroud. The light source, an LED, sits in the center of the shroud and is blocked from the PDs to prevent light-of-sight leakage. The shroud is painted black to prevent complicated reflections and to reduce the impact of ambient light diffusion/interference. It allows the PDs to be mounted in different positions. Such extra flexibility make the prototype larger than what would be necessary in a product version.

Figure 5 and Figure 6 show the horizontal/vertical angular responses of a PD, with and without the shroud. We observe that the shroud grooms the vertical FOV into a super-narrow, non-divergent beam, while forcing the horizontal FOV within 90°. Thus, it achieves the same effect as an ideal PD for Okuli.

We also observe that the shroud helps alleviate the impact of background reflection from the user's hand. As shown in Figure 7, without the shroud, the received light intensity shows large variation with the same finger position but different hand postures. The shroud significantly reduces such variation and enables stable finger-localization.

4. MODELING NEAR-FIELD LIGHT REFLECTION

To achieve localization, Okuli uses a model to estimate the intensity of reflected light when a finger is placed at a specific coordinate within the workspace.

Light emitted by the LED is subject to 4 processes before reaching the PD: emission, propagation, reflection and reception, which correspond to 4 attrition factors: LED's angular response; pathloss between LED, finger and PDs; reflectivity of finger; and finally, PD's angular response. The final light intensity sensed by the PD is a multiplication of the 4 attribution factors. We model the attrition factors in three parts: a *finger response estimator*, a *free-space path loss estimator* and *parameter calibration*, respectively.

For a given finger position (x, y), the *finger response estimator* (Section 4.1) estimates the percentage of light reflected by the finger. The LED and PD are at different angles for different (x, y) coordinates, resulting in different amounts of light being reflected and received.

The *free-space loss estimator* (Section 4.2) estimates the light's attenuation as it traverses the illuminating path and reflecting path.

Finally, the *parameter calibration* mechanism (Section 4.3) acquires hardware and user-specific attrition factors. Through a one-time measurement, it obtains normalized angular responses of the LED and PDs, which vary from advertised ones, and can be changed radically after light grooming. In addition, a constant $C_X (X \in \{L, R\})$ for left/right PD is used to capture other parameters, *e.g.*, the reflectivity of the finger and the coefficients for the real gain of the LED and PD. We emphasize that the calibration procedure only needs to be conducted at factory-production stage, and when Okuli serves a new user or new workspace.

4.1 Finger Response Estimator

Okuli uses a *finger response estimator* to model the amount of light reflected from a user's finger. There are two major factors that

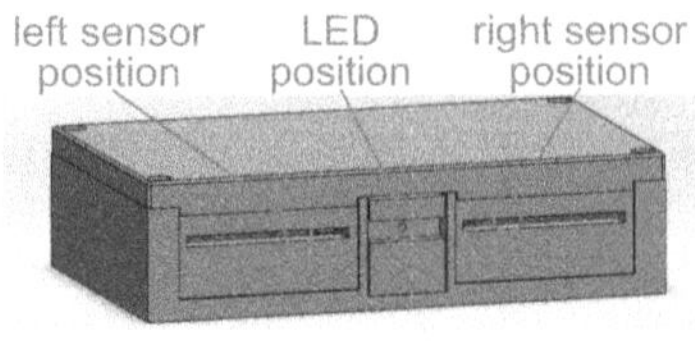

Figure 4: CAD model of the front view of our Okuli prototype. Note only the PDs' slot width (2mm) and depth (3mm) determine the dimension of a product-level implementation.

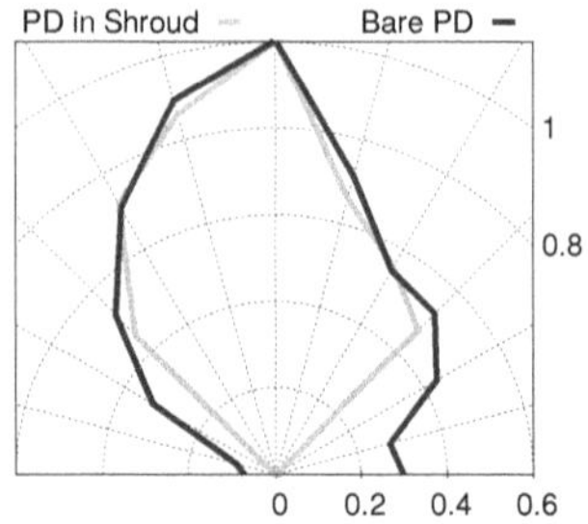

Figure 5: Horizontal angular response of bare PD and PD in shroud.

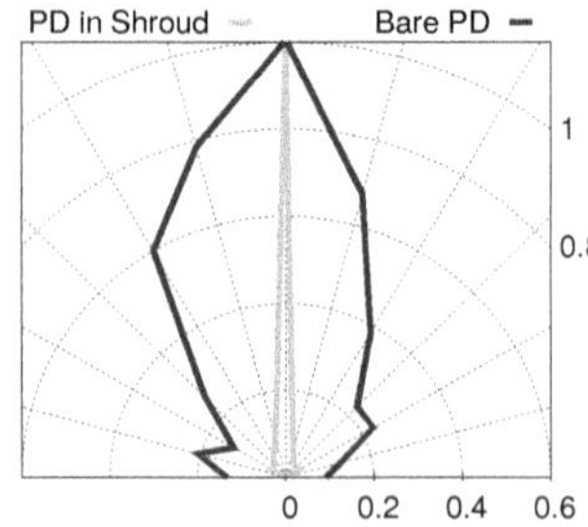

Figure 6: Vertical angular response of bare PD and PD in shroud.

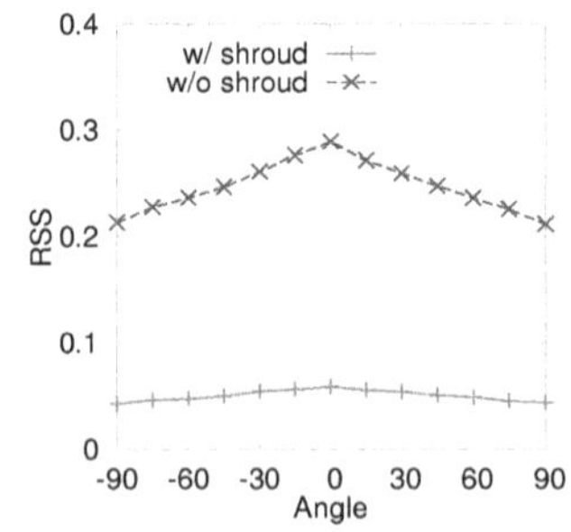

Figure 7: RSS of one PD with user's hand posture in different angles.

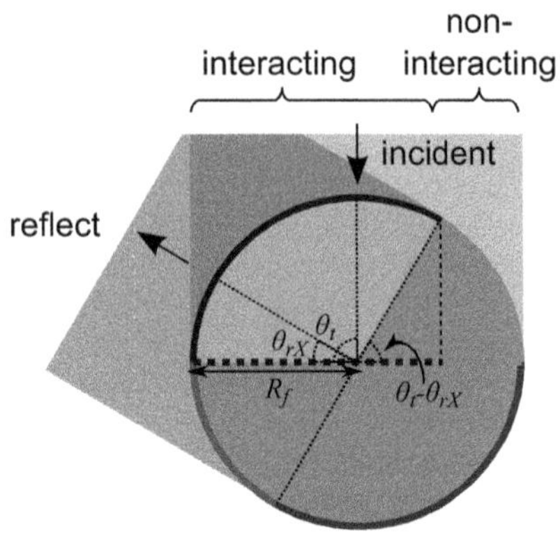

Figure 8: Modeling the *reflection coefficient* of the finger. R_f is the approximate radius of the finger.

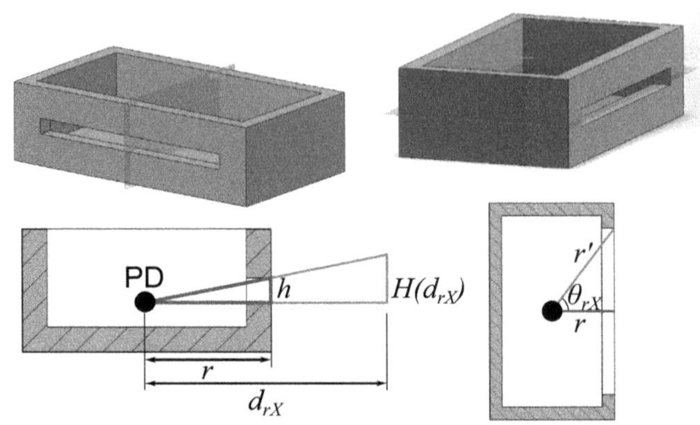

Figure 9: Illustration describing Equation (5). The top of shroud is removed for illustration purpose. To generate the cross-sections at the bottom, the shroud is cut by the red plane.

shape the finger response. First, the finger receives and reflects light in different angles at different locations, which can lead to different overall reflectivity. Second, the distance between user's finger and Okuli's front face determines how much of the finger can be seen by Okuli, and hence how much light is reflected. Accordingly, the finger response estimator comprises two essential coefficients: the *reflection coefficient* and the *visible height coefficient*.

4.1.1 Modeling the Reflection Coefficient

The reflection coefficient models how the finger "bends" incoming light. It can be represented as:

$$C_r \cdot \frac{\textit{Light Reflected towards PD}}{\textit{Light Reflected in All Directions}} \tag{1}$$

where C_r is a user-related constant that represents skin's reflectivity and is calculated during calibration (Section 4.3). The remainder fraction term falls in the range $[0, 1]$, representing the percentage of the light arriving at the finger that is reflected on to the PD.

As illustrated in Figure 8, this fraction term is determined by incident and reflecting angles. It can be modeled using a function $R_X(\theta_t, \theta_{rX})$, where θ_t denotes the angle between the incidental and reflecting light directions, and $\theta_{rX}(X \in \{L, R\})$ the angle between the reflection direction to left/right PD and the horizontal plane (parallel to Okuli's front face). For each finger location (x, y), θ_t can be calculated by simple geometry based on Okuli's setup (Figure 1, where $x_{\mathrm{LED}} = 0$, $y_{\mathrm{LED}} = d_{\mathrm{LED}}$, $x_{\mathrm{PD_X}} = \pm d_{\mathrm{SENSE}}$ and $y_{\mathrm{PD_X}} = 0$):

$$\theta_t = \arctan\left(\frac{y - y_{\mathrm{LED}}}{x - x_{\mathrm{LED}}}\right) \tag{2}$$

Similarly, θ_{rX} can be calculated as:

$$\theta_{rX} = \arctan\left(\frac{y - y_{\mathrm{PD_X}}}{x - x_{\mathrm{PD_X}}}\right) \tag{3}$$

From Figure 8, $R_X(\theta_t, \theta_{rX})$ equals the length of the projection of the incident and reflecting beams (red and blue areas respectively), divided by the total width of the beam received from the LED, which is $2R_f$. Consequently, we have:

$$\begin{aligned} R_X(\theta_t, \theta_{rX}) &= \frac{R_f + R_f \cdot \cos(\theta_t - \theta_{rX})}{2R_f} \\ &= \frac{1}{2}\left[1 + \cos(\theta_t - \theta_{rX})\right] \end{aligned} \tag{4}$$

which only depends on the angle between the incident and reflected beam. Intuitively, the coefficient achieves its maximum when $\theta_t - \theta_{rX} = 0°$ as both the LED and the PD see the whole vertical cross section of the finger, and goes to zero when $\theta_t - \theta_{rX} = 180°$ as the light from the LED is totally blocked by the finger.

4.1.2 Visible Height Coefficient

The *visible height coefficient* estimates the total vertical height visible to both the LED and the PD. Since the LED's vertical FOV is much larger than the one of the shroud and thus relatively unrestricted, the PD's FOV in the shroud is the sole factor in determining this coefficient, which compensates for the fact that more of the user's finger is visible the farther it is away from the PD, so more light can be reflected from the finger towards the PD.

Figure 9 illustrates the derivation of the visible height coefficient. In the bottom left of Figure 9, r represents the distance between the PD and the opening of the shroud, and h is the height of the opening. $d_{rX}(X = \{L, R\})$ denote the distance from the finger to left and right PD, respectively. The inner blue triangle and the outer red triangle are similar, so a simple proportion can model the *visible height coefficient* in terms of d_{rX}, r and h:

$$H(d_{rX}) = \frac{d_{rX} \cdot r}{h} \tag{5}$$

Note that r changes with the angle θ_{rX}: as shown in the bottom right of Figure 9, for a finger position near the edge of the PD's FOV, corresponding $r' = \frac{r}{\cos\theta_{\mathrm{rX}}}$, which changes Equation (5) to be:

$$H(d_{\mathrm{rX}}) = \frac{d_{\mathrm{rX}} \cdot \frac{r}{\cos\theta_{\mathrm{rX}}}}{h} \tag{6}$$

However, since this change only affects the overall angular response of the PD, it will also be accounted for during calibration. So the simpler Equation (5) suffices, *i.e.*, r and h can be considered as constant parameters.

4.1.3 Assumptions in the Finger Response Estimator

We have made two assumptions in the finger response estimator to simply the model. First, the reflection coefficient is accurate only if the finger is relatively round, as the reflection coefficient assumes a circular cross-section. Second, it is assumed that the finger is a good diffuser of light.

To verify the first approximation, we place a finger vertically in front of Okuli, and measure the RSS as the finger rotates. If the finger were a perfectly round, uniform reflector, the RSS would change very little with the rotation. Figure 7 shows how little RSS changes as the user rotates finger (and hand) within $\pm 90°$. In practical usage scenarios, a user will rarely rotate finger beyond this range. So the round-finger assumption can be used without a considerable loss in accuracy.

In addition, the *visible height coefficient* assumes the finger is a diffusive reflector, and hence the visible height grows with distance. If the finger instead creates specular reflection, none of its surface area above the light source would reflect light into the PD, resulting in a constant height. Figure 10 shows the finger part lit by a camera in a dark room. The finger is evenly colored, which testifies to the diffusion effect. Assuming fingers are perfect diffusers adds some small inaccuracies, but it also greatly simplifies the model.

4.2 Free-Space Path Loss Estimator

The second component of Okuli's modeling framework is the *free-space loss estimator*, which estimates the light intensity attenuation due to traveling through free-space. The free-space loss along the illuminating path follows the inverse-square law for visible light propagation [12]. We denote this loss as g_t and the distance between the LED and user's finger as d_t, then we have $g_t = 1/d_t^2$.

On the other hand, we denote the reflection path from the finger to the PD as g_{dX}, $X = L$ and R for left and right PD, respectively. This path involves a more sophisticated model that needs to account for the increasing amount of finger surface area visible to the PD as the finger moves farther. Taking into account this phenomenon along with the finger response estimator and the inverse-square law, we can derive the reflection pathloss as:

$$\begin{aligned} g_{\mathrm{dX}} &= \frac{R(\theta_t, \theta_{\mathrm{rX}}) \cdot H(d_{\mathrm{rX}})}{d_{\mathrm{rX}}^2} \\ &= \frac{\frac{1}{2}[1 + \cos(\theta_t - \theta_{\mathrm{rX}})] \cdot C_r \cdot \frac{d_{\mathrm{rX}} \cdot r}{h}}{d_{\mathrm{rX}}^2} \\ &= \frac{[1 + \cos(\theta_t - \theta_{\mathrm{rX}})] \cdot C_r \cdot r}{2 d_{\mathrm{rX}} \cdot h} \end{aligned} \tag{7}$$

From Equation (7), it is clear that *the reflection pathloss follows an inverse-linear law instead of the common inverse-square law, due to change in the finger's visible height.*

4.3 Model Calibration

Finally, to conduct the model calibration, we first merge hardware-related parameters (*e.g.*, the output power of LED), user-related parameters (*e.g.*, variation in finger reflectivity caused by different skin color), and workspace-related parameters (*e.g.*, surface reflectivity), together into a constant, which we denote as $C_X (X \in \{L, R\})$ for each PD. Also, we denote the signal output of each PD as $\mathrm{RSS}_X (X \in \{L, R\})$, beam shape (angular response) of the LED as $S_{\mathrm{LED}}(\theta_t)$, and angular response of the sensor as $S_{\mathrm{PD_X}}(\theta_{\mathrm{tX}}) (X \in \{L, R\})$. Following our discussion in the beginning of Section 4, the final model can be expressed as:

$$\mathrm{RSS_L} = C_L \cdot g_t \cdot g_{\mathrm{dL}} \cdot S_{\mathrm{PD_L}}(\theta_{\mathrm{rL}}) \cdot S_{\mathrm{LED}}(\theta_t) \tag{8}$$

$$\mathrm{RSS_R} = C_R \cdot g_t \cdot g_{\mathrm{dR}} \cdot S_{\mathrm{PD_R}}(\theta_{\mathrm{rR}}) \cdot S_{\mathrm{LED}}(\theta_t) \tag{9}$$

Equations (8) and (9) involve parameters that need calibration before being used to estimate the expected RSS's at different locations. The calibration follows two stages.

The first stage consists of experimentally determining the angular responses of both the LED (*i.e.*, $S_{\mathrm{LED}}(\theta_t)$) and the PD (*i.e.*, $S_{\mathrm{PD_X}}(\theta_{\mathrm{rX}}), X \in \{L, R\}$) after they are mounted in the shroud. To obtain the LED response, we simply point a PD towards it, rotate the PD along a half-circle while measuring the RSS at different angles. To obtain the PD response, we use LED to do the measurement in a reciprocal way. This is a one-time factory calibration procedure, and is necessary for two reasons: the manufacturer-reported angular response does not match the actual device very well, which can be clearly seen from the irregular response curve of the PD before applying the shroud (Figure 5); also, the shroud significantly changes the responses of both the LED and the PD.

Given the angular responses, we proceed to the second stage. Since we model the reflection light intensity as the transmitted light intensity $S_{\mathrm{LED}}(\theta_t)$ multiplied by a chain of attrition factors, we can extract all the user-related and workspace-related constants and multiply them into a single factor, which is represented in the aforementioned constant C_X. The calibration fits 3 sample inputs from the user in order to obtain the parameter C_X. While the user inputs samples for 3 known anchoring points within the workspace, RSS values are taken from each PD, and the constant C_X is calculated for each point by plugging in the measured RSS values into Equations (8) and (9) to solve for C_X. To avoid biasing the model to recognize one point better than the others, the averaged C_X value across the 3 anchoring points is used. If the user misplaces her finger or otherwise completes calibration incorrectly, a sanity check of the calibration points is done by taking standard deviation of the individual C_X values. If the standard deviation is higher than an empirical threshold, then the user is asked to reinitiate the calibration.

The resulting C_X accounts for the shape and reflectivity of each user's finger, the gain and aging of the LED and PD, and the reflectivity of the surface Okuli is placed on. Therefore, Okuli needs to be recalibrated when placed on a new surface, or used by a different person.

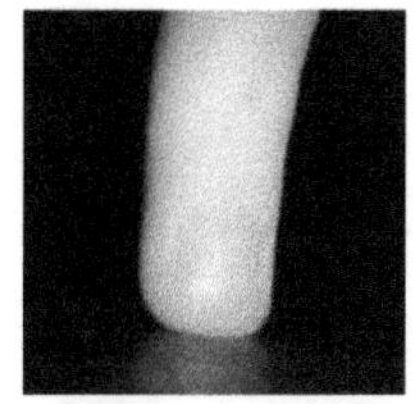

Figure 10: Diffusion of light source on finger as viewed by a camera. We have adjusted the exposure to ensure that the camera is not saturated.

5. FINGER POSITIONING

In this section, we introduce how Okuli incorporates the above model to establish a practical finger localization framework. Specifi-

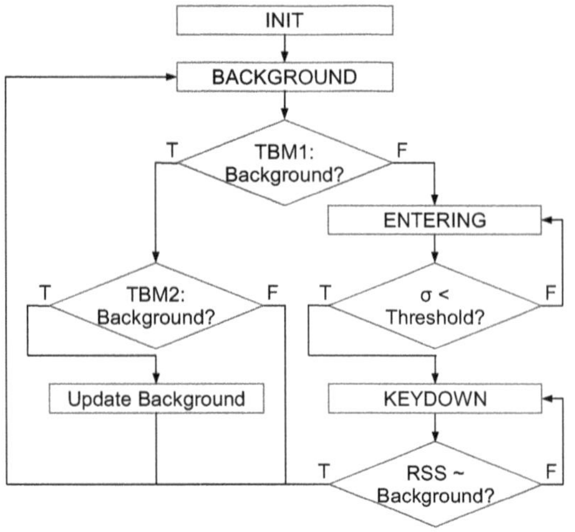

Figure 11: Flow chart for dynamic background removal.

cally, we first describe how Okuli suppresses ambient interferences to obtain the RSS of desired signals, *i.e.*, signals solely due to finger reflection and pertinent to our model. Then, we discuss the localization mechanism, analyze its error tolerance and scalability in larger workspace. Finally, we briefly analyze Okuli's energy efficiency.

5.1 Canceling Ambient Light Interference

In practical usage scenarios, Okuli may be subject to a variety of ambient interferences, which can be broadly classified into ambient light interference and irrelevant background reflection. This section tackles the former.

Okuli uses a simple cancellation mechanism to suppress interference from ambient light sources such as sunlight and indoor fluorescent/LED lights. It modulates the LED's light emission using periodic On-Off-Keying (OOK), with a switching rate of around 30Hz — much higher than the typical variation rate of ambient light sources. During the ON period, Okuli's PD takes one RSS sample that contains both the desired signal and ambient light interference, and subtracts the sample from previous OFF period, which only contains the ambient light intensity. Thus, light intensity contributed by ambient light is removed from the measured value.

We note that the ambient light cancellation mechanism may not work under extreme conditions, such as direct sunlight, where ambient light can easily saturate the ADC. An analog subtracter built with multiplexers and operational amplifiers, which are synchronized with the modulation, might overcome this challenge. We leave the exploration of such schemes for future work.

5.2 Dynamic Background Removal

In addition to ambient light interference, it is also possible that there exist interferences "coherent" to Okuli's modulated light, interferences that are emitted during the on period and dark during the off period. Any secondary sources of reflection other than the target finger can cause such interference. Examples include reflection from user's body parts/clothes, the working surface, people walking by, and even self-interference due to insufficient isolation between the LED and the PD. We colloquially refer to these interferences as *background*.

To remove the background interference, we can assume that the background does not change very quickly (within a few sampling periods of the PD), and Okuli can keep track of the background readings when the finger is absent from the workspace. Then, Okuli can subtract the latest measurement of background interference from the measured RSS values. We call this approach *dynamic background removal* (DBR). The approach requires two essential mechanisms: finger presence detection and background estimation.

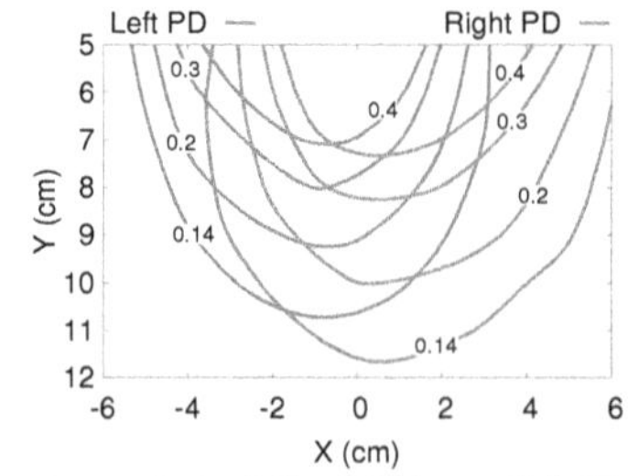

Figure 12: Contour plot of the RSS spatial distribution of the left and right PD at different locations.

Finger presence detection. To realize DBR, we need to identify the presence of finger and classify each RSS reading into 2 cases: foreground and background. We use the Temporal Background Modeling (TBM) in [13] for the classification. The TBM was originally borrowed from computer vision and image processing, to help identify and remove slow-changing background from signal. It uses a Gaussian kernel and a set of parameters to determine how likely a certain sample is the background. For image processing, either a decrease or an increase of values can be considered as a foreground event. However, for Okuli, only an increasing RSS can indicate a finger-presence event in the foreground. Thus, we added an exponential term to the Gaussian kernel in TBM to penalize classifying reducing RSS as foreground.

We design the DBR in conjunction with *finger-touch detection*, as shown in the work flow in Figure 11. It has 4 states: `INIT` (initialization), `BACKGROUND`, `ENTERING` and `KEYDOWN`. During initialization, a circular buffer is filled with a certain amount of samples. In the background state, after each sample update, `TBM1` which favors background assertions is run first. If its output indicates a likely background presence, a second `TBM2`, which is stricter and favors non-background assertions, is executed. If the outcome still indicates high likelihood of background presence, then the background value is updated.

Meanwhile, if `TBM1` indicates a non-background situation, the state will be switched to `ENTERING`. During this state, the finger is supposed to be on its way to touch the working surface, which generates a large standard deviation relative to the mean value. Thereafter, touch occurs, moving the system into the `KEYDOWN` state.

Background estimation. Okuli opportunistically switches back to the `BACKGROUND` state, and updates the background value, whenever the finger leaves the surface. We expect that a finger staying on the working surface for an extended time will be rare. Thus, Okuli should be able to update the background value in a timely way.

5.3 Spatial Ambiguity and System Dimensioning

Eliminating spatial ambiguity. The basic principle of Okuli's localization mechanism is to map a given light intensity measurement into finger location, based on the aforementioned light propagation/reflection model. Note that a single pair of LED/PD is insufficient for location discrimination as there exist many finger spots with the same reflecting light intensity. Okuli eliminates such spatial ambiguity with two PDs.

Figure 12 shows a contour plot of spatial distribution of the RSS, for left and right PD (separated by 2.5 cm), respectively, under an example setup. The contours are generated using the aforementioned model, with parameters calibrated in our real Okuli prototype. We can see that any curve from the left PD has only one intersection with any curve from the right PD. Therefore, *any location* (x, y) *can be mapped to a unique pair of RSS values, and hence, two PDs plus one LED are sufficient to discriminate locations on Okuli's 2-D workspace.* In general, suppose the PDs' angular responses are homogeneous and close to half-circle, it can be proven using simple geometry that this one-to-one mapping strictly holds [14]. Practical angular responses may deviate from half-circle. However, we conjecture that as long as they are convex and homogeneous, spatial ambiguity can be eliminated given two appropriately separated PDs. We leave the proof for the conjecture as future work.

Location matching. To map the measured RSS pair to location, we note that the RSS pair (RSS_L, RSS_R) provided by model (Equations (8) and (9)) does not have a closed form, and hence it is impossible to directly inverse the RSS to location. So we use a *location matching* mechanism instead. We first use the model to compute a look-up table that maps every location spot on 1mm×1mm grid into an RSS pair. At run-time, Okuli can look for the RSS pair that matches closely with its measured one, and then reverse it to a location spot. The error metric for matching can be either Euclidean distance or Manhattan distance.

The foregoing discussion on spatial ambiguity assumes Okuli's model is perfect. In practice, Okuli's location precision depends on the separation between the target location spots, and also the separation between the LED and PD. We now analyze how such dimensioning parameters affect Okuli's performance.

Error tolerance for a given separation between spots. For a given location (x, y), based on Equations (8) and (9), we can obtain the expected RSS of left and right PD, denoted by L_{xy} and R_{xy}. Since all factors in Equations (8) and (9) are multiplicative, we assume the errors in modeling L_{xy} and R_{xy} are multiplicative Gaussian variables with zero mean and variance σ^2. We denote the two variables as N_L and N_R, respectively. Further, we denote L'_{xy} and R'_{xy} as the actual RSS of left and right PD with modeling error for a given finger location (x, y). Then we have

$$L'_{xy} = (1 + N_L)L_{xy} \tag{10}$$

$$R'_{xy} = (1 + N_R)R_{xy} \tag{11}$$

We use normalized Euclidean distance as the modeling error metric, denoted as RSS_e:

$$\begin{aligned} RSS_e &= \sqrt{\frac{(L'_{xy} - L_{xy})^2}{L_{xy}^2} + \frac{(R'_{xy} - R_{xy})^2}{R_{xy}^2}} \\ &= \sqrt{N_L^2 + N_R^2} \end{aligned} \tag{12}$$

If we further assume N_L and N_R are independent, then RSS_e follows Rayleigh distribution with variance σ^2. The kth-percentile p of Rayleigh distribution is known to be [15]:

$$p = \sigma \sqrt{\ln\left[\left(1 - \frac{k}{100}\right)^{-2}\right]} \tag{13}$$

To distinguish two nearby locations (x_1, y_1) and (x_2, y_2) with probability larger than $k\%$, the percentile of modeling error of Okuli should be smaller than the normalized Euclidean distance of RSS between the two locations:

$$p < \sqrt{\frac{(L_{x_2y_2} - L_{x_1y_1})^2}{L_{x_1y_1}^2} + \frac{(R_{x_2y_2} - R_{x_1y_1})^2}{R_{x_1y_1}^2}} \tag{14}$$

Therefore, the Euclidean distance of RSS pairs determines how much modeling error Okuli can tolerate in order to discriminate two locations. We refer to this tolerance level as *error bound.* A larger error bound means Okuli can tolerate larger modeling error, thus achieving higher spatial resolution. The error bound depends on both L_{xy} and R_{xy}, which renders it location-dependent.

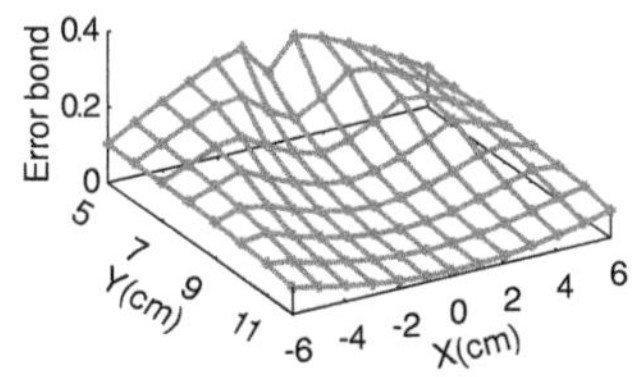

Figure 13: Modeling error bound at different locations.

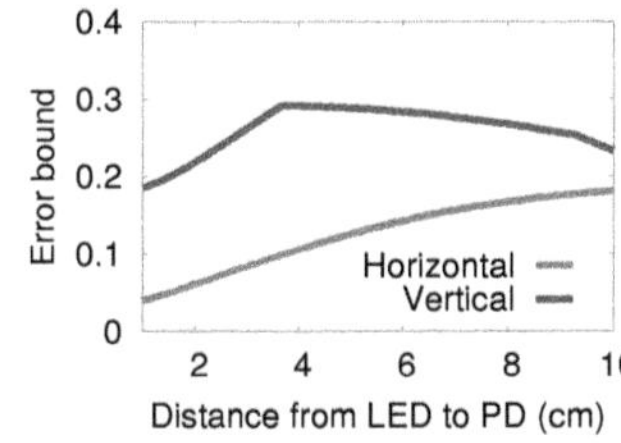

Figure 14: Error tolerance as system dimension varies.

In Figure 13, we plot the location-dependent distribution of error bound (maximum normalized error allowed to maintain 1cm accuracy), where we assume the angular responses of both LED and PDs have the typical cosine shape [12] and the workspace's dimension is consistent with the one used in our prototype. The separation between nearby spots to be localized is set to 1cm, along both horizontal and vertical directions. We observe a minimum error bound of 0.08, corresponding to the right hand side of Equation (14). From Equation (14), we can bound p and subsequently obtain the parameter k in Equation (13). For example, to achieve 90% localization confidence for the most error-prone location spot, the standard derivation of Okuli's modeling error σ should be bounded below 4%.

In practice, the error bound may differ from this analysis due to imperfect LED/PD response. However, the analysis can still be used empirically to determine how resilient Okuli can be for a given separation between target location spots.

System dimensioning. Based on the above analysis, we can numerically obtain *Okuli's localization resolution (i.e., error bound) as a function of the distance between LED and PD* (which affect the L_{xy} and R_{xy}). In Figure 14, we show the relationship between the minimum error bound and distance between LED and PD. The separation between spots is again set to 1cm. We can see the horizontal resolution keeps increasing with the LED-PD distance, *i.e.*, Okuli can tolerate more horizontal location errors with a larger LED-PD distance. This is because a larger distance between LED and PD could generate larger difference of angular response near the center which has the worst horizontal resolution. On the other hand, the vertical resolution has a turning point, since the sum distance from finger to left and right PD achieves maximum there. The vertical resolution is always higher than the horizontal one in practical range of dimensions (LED-PD distance from 1cm to 10cm).

As a result, in practical operating regime, increasing the distance between LED and PD is favorable. For instance, if the distance increases from 4cm to 10cm, the limiting error bound will nearly double, and resolution can be much higher.

5.4 Energy Efficient Light Emission

The power consumption of Okuli comes from three major components: LED, ADC and CPU, with the LED being the most power hungry one. Fortunately, Okuli can tame the LED energy cost using duty-cycling, *i.e.*, controlling the fraction of ON-period as it runs the OOK modulation (Section 5.1).

However, the duty-cycle cannot be arbitrarily reduced. Due to the rising/falling time of LED/PD and the settling time of ADC, a guard interval (GI) is needed between turning on/off the LED and reading RSS measurement from the ADC. The requirement of GI limits the updating frequency as well as the energy efficiency. In our prototype, the GI duration, denoted as t_{GI}, is large and equal to 15ms due to the slow rising/falling time of the PD. By definition of duty cycle, we have $D = t_{\text{on}}/T$, where t_{on} is the duration of LED being turned on and T is the period (total duration of a cycle). Since we want to reduce the duty cycle, t_{on} should be set as short

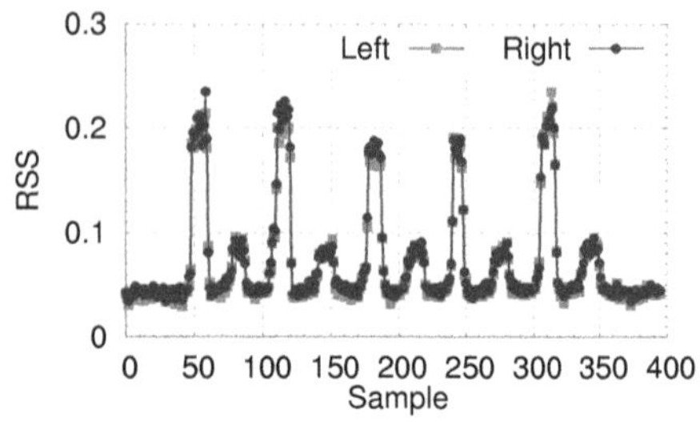

Figure 15: Time domain trace of RSS while alternately clicking a close-by and far-away point (relative to Okuli's front LED).

as possible, which implies $D \leqslant 0.5$ and $t_{\text{on}} = t_{\text{GI}}$ in the best case. Thus,

$$\frac{t_{\text{GI}}}{D} \leq \frac{t_{\text{on}}}{D} = T = \frac{1}{f}, \tag{15}$$

where D is the duty cycle and f is the sampling rate. Hence the minimum duty cycle D equals $t_{\text{GI}} \cdot f$, which is determined by the required GI and sampling rate, and cannot be further reduced.

We can model the system power consumption if we assume the power consumption of LED increases proportionally with duty cycle D and the power consumption of CPU increases proportionally with sampling rate:

$$\begin{aligned} P_{\textit{system}} &= P_{\textit{static}} + P_{\text{LED}} \cdot D + P_{\text{CPU}} \cdot f \\ &= P_{\textit{static}} + P_{\text{LED}} \cdot f \cdot t_{\text{GI}} + P_{\text{CPU}} \cdot f \end{aligned} \tag{16}$$

where $P_{\textit{static}}$ is the static power consumption of the whole system. P_{LED} is the power consumption of LED when transmitting continuously and P_{CPU} is the power consumption of CPU while Okuli runs location update at 1 Hz. We can see a trade-off between sampling rate (*i.e.*, latency) and power consumption. Okuli can leverage this trade-off to adaptively switch to idle mode and wake up when finger is detected by changing the duty cycle. We leave the exploration of this mechanism for future work.

6. MOBILE INTERACTION USING Okuli

6.1 A Virtual Keyboard

We envision a virtual keyboard printed on a flat surface, or a cover that can be unfolded to one side of the Okuli-enabled mobile device. This virtual keyboard is more convenient and durable than a physical keyboard since it does not require any electrical connections or batteries. Finger clicks on the printed keys can be identified by Okuli, and interpreted by mobile applications. This requires us to augment Okuli with *finger-generated keystroke detection* along with *localization*.

Keystroke Detection. Unlike the aforementioned static finger localization, keystroke gestures generate highly dynamic light intensity at run-time — we need to isolate such dynamics from those caused by finger movement across locations. To meet this challenge, we take advantage of the unique time-domain signal features from keystrokes.

Figure 15 plots the RSS perceived by the left/right PDs during various keystroke events. We observe that the keystroke gestures generate a highly consistent pattern of RSS increasing and then sharply decreasing. This is partly due to the light grooming mechanism that constrains light reflection to a small slice of the finger, and partly due to the determinism of light propagation, which suffers relatively less multipath than RF signals [16].

This observation inspires us to use a simple threshold based feature detection algorithm to detect a keystroke event. During the initial 3-point calibration stage, when a user generates a *single keystroke* at the farthest point, the resulting 80-percentile RSS peak is used by Okuli as a barrier for declaring a keystroke. In addition, Okuli only passes peaks lasting more than 100ms in order to filter out spurious interferences.

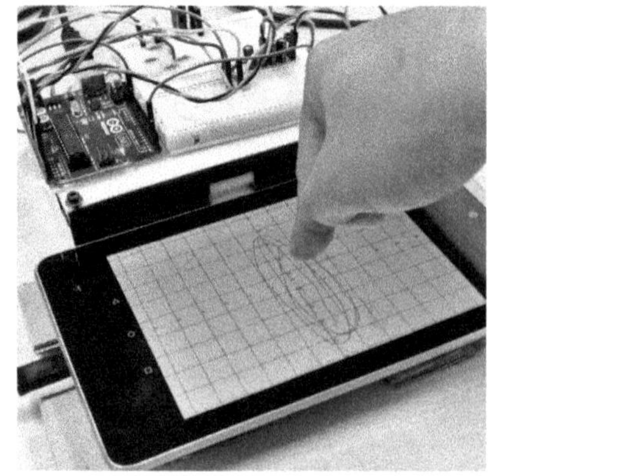

Figure 16: A portrait of Okuli implementation under test.

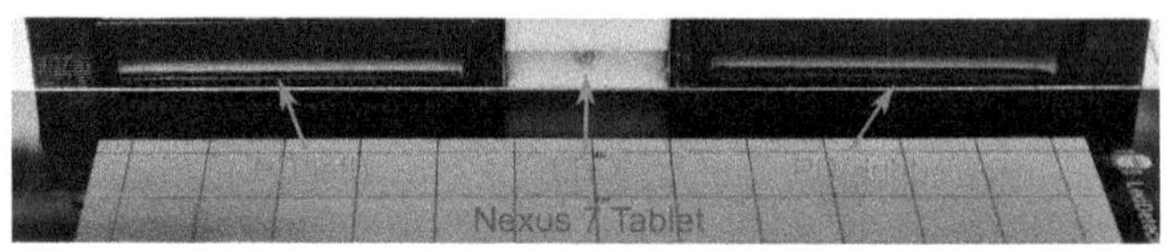

Figure 17: A close-up of Okuli implementation.

Keystroke Localization. Given a keystroke event, Okuli uses a two-step location matching algorithm to localize the key. It first computes the finger location by matching the resulting RSS to the model-predicted RSS of one 1mm×1mm grid on the workspace. It then maps the grid's location to the closest key (around 1cm^2 grid) based on the keyboard's geometrical outline. This approach is empirically proven to have superior performance than directly locating the keys (Section 8.2).

6.2 A Virtual Trackpad

Okuli can be easily extended to provide a trackpad-like experience for mobile interaction around a smartphone, smart watch, *etc.* A full-fledged trackpad entails two primitives: tracking finger movement and detecting clicks (taps).

Okuli extends its model-driven finger localization framework (Section 4) to realize tracking. It first obtains the millimeter-grid location estimation similarly to the keystroke localization. It then uses a simple averaging filter to remove outliers in the localization output. It keeps a moving average of a fixed number of recent localization results and averages their x and y coordinates to produce the final output. This technique removes abrupt jumps from trackpad traces, but also introduces a small delay in trackpad position updates. In our prototype of Okuli, a circular buffer of size 10 is used as the moving average window.

The click detection mechanism is naturally realized as part of the dynamic background removal (Section 5.2).

7. IMPLEMENTING Okuli

An experimental version of Okuli is implemented for research purposes (Figure 16 and Figure 17). It contains two PDs and an LED, a 3D-printed shroud to control the PDs' FOV, an embedded microcontroller to collect ADC samples from the PDs, a Nexus 7 Android tablet to display the output and run the localization algorithm, and a Serial-To-Bluetooth module to send samples from the embedded microcontroller to the Android tablet.

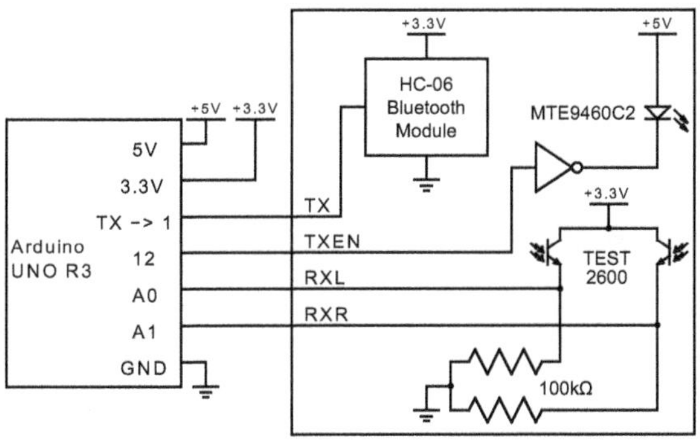

Figure 18: Simplified schematic of the Okuli experimental prototype.

Electronics. A number of factors are considered when choosing the experimental implementation's electronic components. The LED used for the experimental implementation is *MTE9460C2*, which has an FOV of around 120° in both horizontal and vertical directions. To conserve power, it would be better to have an LED custom designed with a narrower (30°) vertical FOV. This would allow a higher percentage of the LED's total light to be concentrated in useful directions and help alleviate multipath interference. The PD used is *TEST2600*, which has an FOV of nearly 120° in axial direction but 60° in the lateral direction. Due to such characteristic of the PD, we place the PDs with their axial direction being horizontal to maximize the FOV. The distance between the PDs is 8.8cm, and LED is slightly in front of the PDs. The shroud isolates the LED and the PDs so the light emitted by LED does not directly come into the PDs. Both the LED and the PDs work in the 950nm near-infrared spectrum, which is very close to visible light.

Okuli also needs a small amount of supporting electronic components. First, it needs a transistor to drive the LED and enable blinking, which is essential for ambient light removal and energy efficiency. Second, Okuli needs to digitize the light received from the PD's. To do this, we use an Arduino UNO with a built-in ADC. The Arduino sends the sampled light intensity values to a Nexus 7 via a Bluetooth interface. Figure 18 shows the schematic corresponding to this setup.

We emphasize that a production version of Okuli can be directly built into a mobile device, evading the Arduino/Bluetooth interface plus discrete circuit components. This will significantly reduce the form-factor and improve the energy-efficiency compared with our prototype.

Applications and UI. We implement the finger localization algorithm and the virtual keyboard/trackpad applications (Section 6) in Android. The Android program runs on a Nexus 7 tablet, which processes light intensity samples, detects touch events, maps the finger location to keystroke or writing trajectory, and displays the results on the screen.

Limitations. Due to limitations with our hardware prototype (discussed in Section 5.4), Okuli can only sample the PDs at 30Hz. Together with the 10-sample smooth filter, this produces a noticeable delay of 0.33 seconds for each localization output. In a production version of Okuli, much faster ADCs and PDs could be used, which would hide this delay and would allow lower-latency position updates.

8. SYSTEM EVALUATION

In this section, we first evaluate Okuli's performance in terms of modeling accuracy, finger-localization accuracy, and system energy efficiency. Then we showcase Okuli's effectiveness when serving virtual keyboard/trackpad applications.

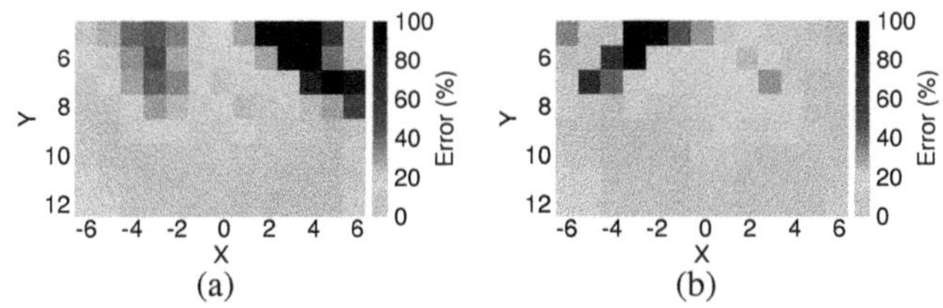

Figure 19: Modeling error within the workspace for (a) left PD and (b) right PD. X coordinate is parallel to the LED-PD line (Okuli's front face) and center-aligned with the LED. Y coordinate denotes the distance from the LED-PD line.

8.1 Microbenchmarks

8.1.1 Accuracy of Modeling Framework

We first evaluate the accuracy of the light propagation/reflection model (Section 4). Specifically, we follow Section 4.3 to perform the hardware and user calibration, and then directly compute the expected light RSS distribution in a 13cm × 8cm workspace, with 1cm × 1cm resolution. We compare this model output with actual RSS measurement when a finger is placed at each 1cm × 1cm spot.

Figure 19 depicts the error map within the workspace. Each grid shows the percentage error of the model *w.r.t.* the spot-by-spot measurement. We observe that the modeling error is location dependent. First, close to the bottom of the workspace, there exists a 9cm × 4cm region with high accuracy (90-percentile error below 10%), for both the left and right PDs. This region can reliably serve trackpad-like applications. In addition, some significant error exists, and are generally on a line pointed from PD/LED towards outside. This kind of radiative error pattern can be caused by errors introduced in angular response calibration. The factory calibration we have done is coarse-grained due to limited resolution of the light sensor we are using. The calibration tends to induce larger error near the outer-edge of the angular response curve where the LED/PD's gain tends to be small and not discernible. We expect such errors to be reduced in a stricter factory calibration for actual products.

Second, the modeling error tend to be slightly larger near the left/right edges, since the edges are further away from the LED/PDs, suffering from insufficient lighting. There also exists a few black spots, which is caused by the edge of our 3D-printed shroud blocking part of the LED signals. A product-level implementation with customized lenses would be able to overcome such imperfectness (Section 3).

Furthermore, note that areas with larger error tend to overlap with areas where the PDs have low angular response. Lower response means lower SNR, which causes larger error. The variation of angular response and propagation loss over space leads to location-dependent SNR and error tolerance (Section 5.3), which in turn explains the location-dependent error distribution.

8.1.2 Accuracy of Finger Localization

As analyzed in Section 5.3, Okuli can tolerate a certain amount of modeling error, as long as it does not confuse the RSS-vector at different locations. To test its localization accuracy, we focus on 100 randomly-picked points (including repeated locations) in a 9cm × 7cm area (including points on the edge) within the workspace. All the points are selected on the 1cm × 1cm grid. The workspace sits on a wood table surface in an office environment with natural background (fluorescent lighting and people walking by occasionally).

We test two different setup: the "manual" case localizes a static finger, while the "auto" case detects a finger touch and then localizes

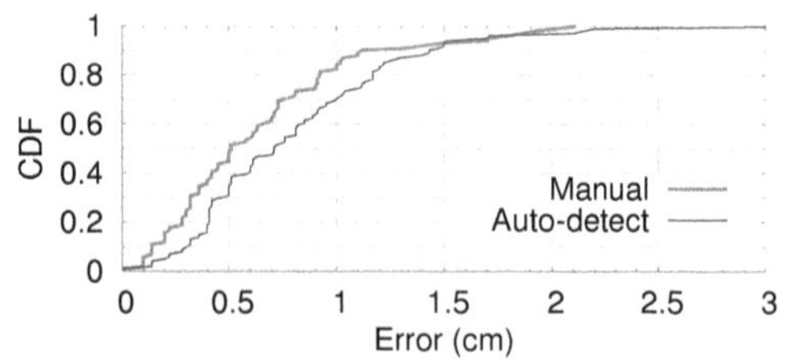

Figure 20: CDF of localization errors.

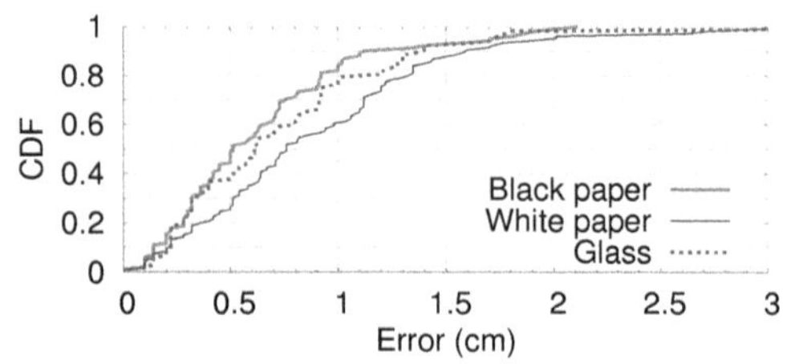

Figure 21: CDF of localization errors on various surfaces.

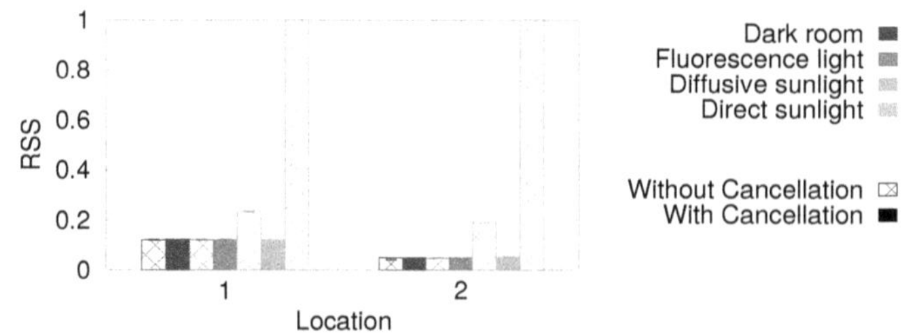

Figure 22: RSS under different lighting condition with and without ambient cancellation.

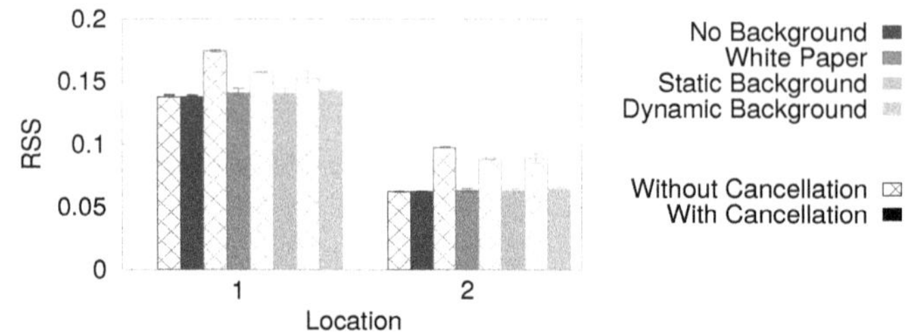

Figure 23: RSS under different background with and without dynamic background removal.

the finger. As shown in Figure 20, for the static finger localization, over 80% points have an error of less than 1cm, and 90% of the error values is below 1.12cm. When the location matching works in conjunction with finger detection, the error increases, because there exist decision errors that make it possible for the finger to become registered before it makes full contact with the surface, or is on its way leaving the surface. This will result in the reading being smaller than desired. Still, 90% of the errors fall below 1.43cm in this case. We have also conducted a closer examination of the spatial error distribution, and found the edge-spots tend to suffer from larger errors, which is consistent with the previous micro-benchmark.

It is also possible to use Okuli on various surfaces. As Figure 21 shows, the CDF of localization error remains relatively consistent on surfaces including black paper, white paper and a mirror-like glass. This corroborates the effectiveness of our model and calibration, which takes surface-specific impact on light reflection into account.

8.1.3 Effectiveness of Interference Suppression

Effectiveness of ambient light cancellation. To evaluate the performance of the ambient light cancellation, we put Okuli under various lighting conditions, and measure the RSS before/after the cancellation while putting finger on a fixed location. As shown in Figure 22, ambient light cancellation works ideally in an indoor environment with fluorescent light sources, whose signal strength is usually weaker or comparable with Okuli's near-field LED light.

To test Okuli under diffusive sunlight, we place it near the window facing towards inside of the building. Despite the strong ambient light interference (shown in case w/o cancellation), Okuli can restore its legitimate RSS after cancellation. The ambient light cancellation stops working under direct sunlight, especially on a sunny day, due to ADC saturation (Section 5.1). The problem may be alleviated by increasing the ADC's dynamic range or using analog cancellation, but this is left for our future work.

Effectiveness of dynamic background removal. To evaluate the performance of dynamic background removal, we arrange 4 different kinds of background: *(i)* very far-away background that can be treated as no background, *(ii)* a white paper standing vertically in front of Okuli, *(iii)* static background with the user himself/herself being the only significant background, and *(iv)* dynamic background with people walking by constantly. We then record the RSS before and after the cancellation. From Figure 23, we can see that although the RSS before cancellation varies significantly, it can be restored to the original level after cancellation. This indicates that our dynamic background cancellation is indeed effective.

Temporal stability of finger localization. It is a common concern for systems requiring initial calibration, that the usable duration of each calibration can be short, due to environmental changes.

To find out whether Okuli can perform consistently throughout a period of time with one calibration, we repeated the prior localization accuracy test twice – immediately after the system is calibrated and 10 days afterwards. As shown in Figure 24, the localization accuracy almost does not change over a long period of time. This is partly due to the determinism of the light propagation channel, and partly due to Okuli's capability to suppress environment dynamics throughput background cancellation.

8.1.4 System Energy Efficiency

To measure the power consumption of Okuli, we disconnect the Bluetooth module (since it is not needed in a product-level implementation), and use the Monsoon Power Monitor [17] to supply the Arduino and the sensor board with 4.5V power. We also use the same power monitor to measure the computational power consumption of our test App running on a Galaxy Nexus phone. In Figure 25, we show the power consumption of LED, CPU and ADC respectively. Consistent with our analysis in Section 5.4, the power consumption of LED dominates, and increases proportionally with the sampling duty-cycle. The CPU power follows a similar trend, but the absolute value is much lower. The ADC consumes a stable power of 35mW. Overall, at Okuli's default duty cycle of 0.5, the total system power consumption is 380mW, comparable to a typical web browsing session on a smartphone's WiFi interface [18].

Given the dominating LED power consumption in Okuli, we envision huge space for making Okuli more energy efficient. According to Equation (15), when the hardware can work with a short GI, it is possible to employ a duty cycle well below 0.5. For instance, if 100Hz sampling rate is desired, and the system can work with 0.5ms GI, then the minimum duty cycle is 0.05, hence the energy consumption can be reduce to around 100mW as predicted by Equation (16). Currently the GI of our system is limited by the hardware prototype which requires us to maintain a high duty cycle of 0.5 and hence relatively higher operating power than ideal.

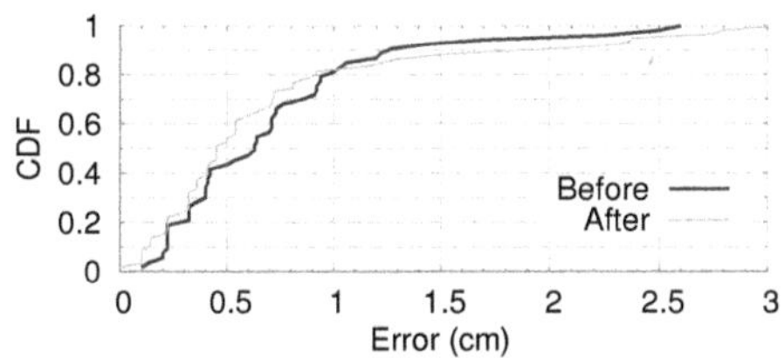

Figure 24: Localization accuracy before and after 10 days without re-calibration.

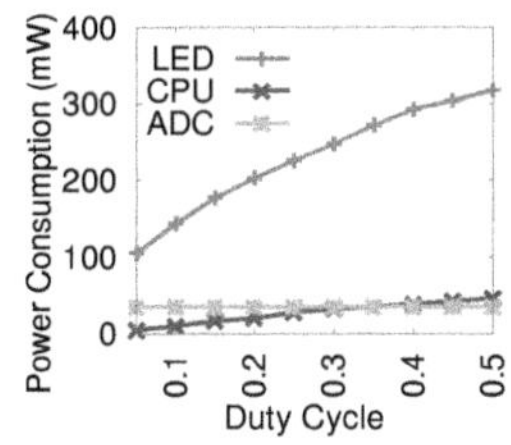

Figure 25: A breakdown of Okuli's power consumption.

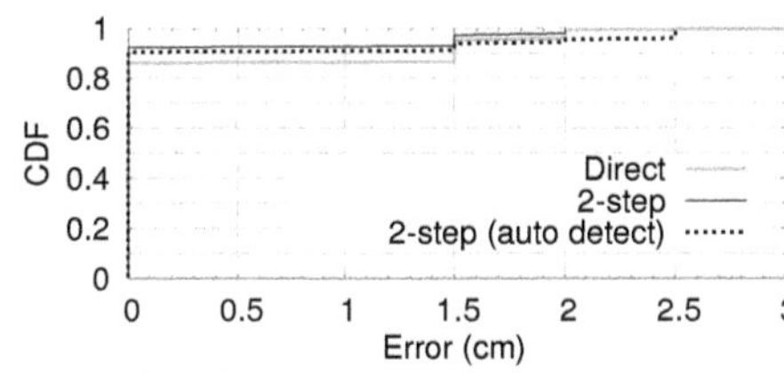

Figure 26: Localization error on a virtual keyboard.

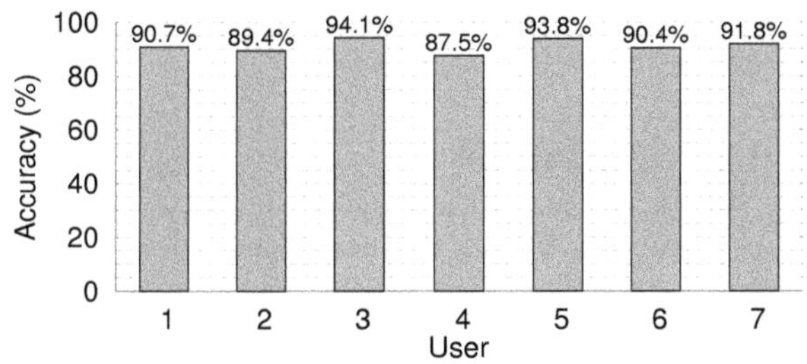

Figure 27: A user study of Okuli's virtual keyboard application.

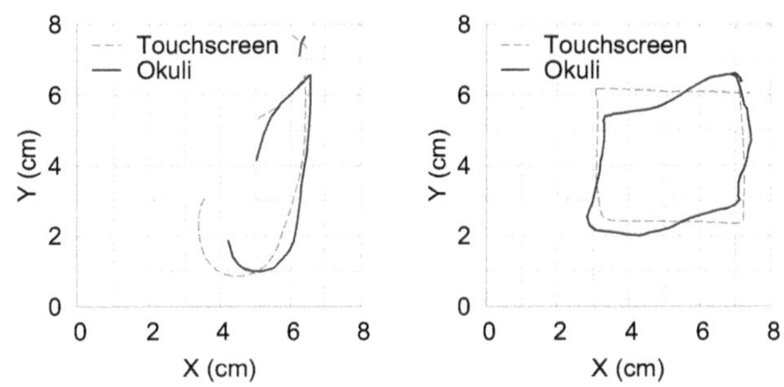

Figure 28: Okuli's virtual trackpad traces (solid) in comparison to touchscreen traces (dashed).

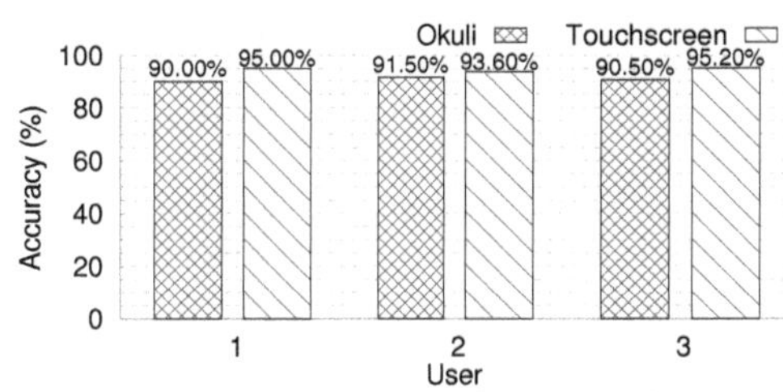

Figure 29: A user study of Okuli's virtual trackpad application.

8.2 Application Tests

Virtual Keyboard. We print 20 rectangular-shaped keys of 2cm width and 1.5cm height on a piece of paper, and use it as the workspace for Okuli's virtual keyboard application. The keys are next to each other and placed together in the center of the working area, arranged in a 4-key-per-row manner, and totaling 5 rows. After calibration, we generate 100 random keystrokes, and the error in distance of the pressed key and detected key is recorded. As shown in Figure 26, over 90% of the keystrokes are detected correctly with 2-step method, while the direct locate method only detects about 86% of the keystrokes correctly.

We also conduct a user survey that covers 7 users with different finger characteristics. Each user repeats the above experiment (20 1cm$\times$1cm keys). The users are told to use the device just like a touchscreen. With 100 random key inputs on the same keyboard, average accuracy is 91.1%, and performance is highly consistent across users (Figure 27).

Virtual Trackpad. We evaluate the virtual trackpad's performance by replaying the user input captured into a handwriting recognition software, MyScript Stylus, to assess the accuracy for possible handwriting input applications. The user runs our virtual trackpad Android app to write on the Nexus 7 tablet, which is simultaneously used as the workspace for Okuli. Figure 28 shows two example writing trajectories.

We also conduct a user study of the trackpad, where each user inputs 100 random Latin characters. The result (Figure 29) demonstrates an overall recognition rate of 90.6%, which is comparable to writing directly on the Nexus 7 tablet (94.5%). The trackpad has a noticeable latency of around 0.5s due to the low-end PD, ADC and microcontroller we are using (Section 7). We expect a full-fledged implementation, integrated with a mobile device, will be able to overcome these limitations.

9. DISCUSSION

Multi-finger input and touch. Currently, Okuli is limited to single-finger localization, which has no ambiguity as long as the two PDs' angular responses are well conditioned (Section 5.3). By using more PDs, Okuli may further improve its resolution and discern multi-finger inputs. It would be interesting to investigate the system dimensioning and resolution as the number of PDs increases. However, this is beyond the scope of our current work.

Full-sized keyboard. Due to the PDs' limited field-of-view, the workspace of our current Okuli implementation cannot cover a full keyboard. However, this limitation can be easily overcome by using better hardware, *i.e.*, LEDs/PDs with wider FOV and higher sensitivity. In addition, since Okuli's localization mechanism is generic and can track fingers in arbitrary location within the working area, more complicated key arrangement other than the dial-pad-like layout is also possible.

System stability and usability. The light grooming mechanism and background suppression has greatly reduced the impact of irrelevant body parts and environment dynamics. Users' inconsistent behavior does affect the accuracy of the model behind Okuli. Fortunately, the range of such uncertainties is quite limited. In particular, we have observed in the user study that users' finger rotation/tilting is usually well below 60° unless intentionally induced. Moreover, Okuli's light grooming mechanism ensures a super-narrow vertical FOV, such that the PD still sees a relatively consistent light intensity even under such behavior dynamics.

Reducing processing latency. As a prototype, the circuit of Okuli is not optimally tuned at this stage. The photo-transistor is slower than a carefully chosen photo-diode, and there is no amplifier or matching circuitry between the sensors (which generate tiny photo-currents) and the microcontroller (which has a large input capacitance). We expect a full-fledged circuitry design can achieve significantly lower latency than what we observed in the prototype.

Impact of sunlight. The current Okuli implementation does not work well under direct sunlight. Sunlight creates very strong interference and easily saturates the sensors, rendering the ambient light cancellation ineffective. Yet, by employing hardware improvements, such as DC removal and high resolution ADC, this issue can be resolved.

10. RELATED WORK

Object location sensing technologies have been extensively explored for the purpose of human-computer/mobile interaction. The object can be human body, limb, hand, or as fine-grained as fingers. The underlying technologies can be classified into active sensing (*w.r.t.* objects instrumented with sensors or transceivers), and passive sensing (*w.r.t.* uninstrumented objects).

Visible light based *active location sensing* techniques have been driven by the emerging trend of visible light communication (VLC). A VLC link piggybacks information by flashing LED lights or an LED screen, which can be demodulated by a light sensor or camera [8, 19, 20]. The light attenuation vs. distance relation is explored in Epsilon [10] to complement motion sensors and locate a mobile VLC receiver. Luxapose [9] leverages multiple ceiling mounted LED lights to triangulate a smartphone, by using the camera and image distortion algorithms. Both systems achieve sub-meter scale location accuracy. Besides visible light, alternative medium of signals and devices have been explored in active sensing, including RFID [1], infrared [21], magnetic field [22] and motion sensors [2]. All these techniques require instrumenting the user with retro-reflective tags, sensors or transceivers.

Passive sensing systems can overcome such limitations. Infrared photoplethysmogram (PPG) tracks pulses or blood volume changes by measuring reflectance or transmittance. Infrared (IR) *proximity sensors* have also found mature applications in modern mobile devices. For example, SideSight [11] captures multi-touch gestures by observing the diverse proximity detection output of an array of 10 IR sensors, placed on the edge of a smartphone. Hoverflow [23] orients the IR sensor array towards the user to cover a large 3D space, allowing for handheld interaction. A similar concept was explored to facilitate gesture input for smart watch [24]. These systems can only sense coarse hand/finger gestures and require intensive training for each input. High-resolution, training-free multi-touch sensing has been demonstrated in ZeroTouch [25], FlexAura [26], *etc.*, which install hundreds of IR sensors around a flat panel or similar interaction space.

Okuli's fundamental design principle departs from these passive IR sensing systems, in that it treats the light propagation channel as a wide-angle diffusive channel, instead of a "laser-beam". Its fundamental approach is *model-driven* — it explicitly models the light intensity attenuation and reflection and can localize a finger within the wide FOV of an LED transmitter, instead of detecting finger "cutting" or proximity. This principle enables Okuli to achieve an unprecedented precision using only a single LED and two light sensors, allowing deployment on the edge of mobile devices of practical size.

Prior art has extensively explored vision based approaches for mobile interaction. Intuitively, by using a high-resolution camera instead of "single-pixel" photodetector, objects can be detected and localized with high precision. For example, hand gestures can be easily recognized via continuous video frame processing [27]. Infrared or near-infrared cameras can detect thermal emission or near-IR reflection from hands/fingers, thus identifying touch/click gestures [28–31]. Higher precision can be achieved via structured infrared-light projection [32], *i.e.*, emitting bar patterns or speckles towards target, and identifying its 3D structure and distance. This approach has been adopted by commercial hand/finger tracking systems like Kinect [33] and Leap Motion [34]. Such vision based systems, however, share many common limitations. As previously mentioned, they typically require a projector and/or multiple cameras, which do not suit very thin form factor devices. Also, cameras incur high energy cost under continuous sensing/processing, and hence they are unsuitable for battery-powered devices. Finally, cameras, especially side-facing ones, can pose threats to privacy if the system is compromised and exploited maliciously.

Passive sensing can be alternatively realized using acoustic sensors [5, 35], electric field sensors [36, 37], *etc.* These signals are relatively less deterministic compared with light, and thus they typically require extensive training before use.

11. CONCLUSION

Light emitters and sensors have been widely used to sense proximity or object presence, with the intuitive rationale of "object cutting light beams". In this paper, we have achieved a more ambitious goal of locating a small object on a 2D plane, with around one-centimeter scale precision, using only one LED emitter and two photodetectors (PDs). Our solution, called Okuli, uses a model-driven approach to localize a finger with minimal user training. We have navigated various design/performance tradeoffs in Okuli, using both analysis and real experiments. We believe Okuli marks an important step in passive object/activity sensing through visible light.

Acknowledgement

We appreciate insightful comments and feedback from the shepherd and the anonymous reviewers. The work reported in this paper is supported in part by the NSF under Grant CNS-1318292, CNS-1343363 and CNS-1350039.

12. REFERENCES

[1] J. Wang, D. Vasisht, and D. Katabi, "RF-IDraw: Virtual Touch Screen in the Air using RF Signals," in *Proc. of ACM SIGCOMM*, 2014.

[2] S. Agrawal, I. Constandache, S. Gaonkar, R. Roy Choudhury, K. Caves, and F. DeRuyter, "Using Mobile Phones to Write in Air," in *Proc. of ACM MobiSys*, 2011.

[3] H. Roeber, J. Bacus, and C. Tomasi, "Typing in Thin Air: The Canesta Projection Keyboard - a New Method of Interaction with Electronic Devices," in *ACM CHI Extended Abstracts*, 2003.

[4] C. Harrison, H. Benko, and A. D. Wilson, "OmniTouch: Wearable Multitouch Interaction Everywhere," in *Proc. of ACM UIST*, 2011.

[5] J. Wang, K. Zhao, X. Zhang, and C. Peng, "Ubiquitous Keyboard for Small Mobile Devices: Harnessing Multipath Fading for Fine-Grained Keystroke Localization," in *Proc. of ACM MobiSys*, 2014.

[6] C. Harrison, J. Schwarz, and S. E. Hudson, "TapSense: Enhancing Finger Interaction on Touch Surfaces," in *Proc. of ACM UIST*, 2011.

[7] H. Elgala, R. Mesleh, and H. Haas, "Indoor Optical Wireless Communication: Potential and State-of-the-Art," *IEEE Communications Magazine*, vol. 49, no. 9, 2011.

[8] S. Rajagopal, R. Roberts, and S.-K. Lim, "IEEE 802.15.7 Visible Light Communication: Modulation Schemes and Dimming Support," *IEEE Communications Magazine*, vol. 50, no. 3, 2012.

[9] Y.-S. Kuo, P. Pannuto, K.-J. Hsiao, and P. Dutta, "Luxapose: Indoor Positioning with Mobile Phones and Visible Light," in *Proc. of ACM MobiCom*, 2014.

[10] L. Li, P. Hu, C. Peng, G. Shen, and F. Zhao, "Epsilon: A Visible Light Based Positioning System," in *Proc. of USENIX NSDI*, 2014.

[11] A. Butler, S. Izadi, and S. Hodges, "SideSight: Multi-Touch Interaction Around Small Devices," in *Proc. of ACM UIST*, 2008.

[12] Z. Ghassemlooy, W. Popoola, and S. Rajbhandari, *Optical Wireless Communications: System and Channel Modelling with MATLAB*. CRC Press, 2012.

[13] A. Edelstein and M. Rabbat, "Background Subtraction for Online Calibration of Baseline RSS in RF Sensing Networks," *Mobile Computing, IEEE Transactions on*, vol. 12, no. 12, pp. 2386–2398, Dec 2013.

[14] W. Cui, Z. Cao, and J. Wei, "Dual-Microphone Source Location Method in 2-D Space," in *Proc. of IEEE International Conference on Acoustics, Speech and Signal Processing (ICASSP)*, 2006.

[15] A. Papoulis and S. U. Pillai, *Probability, random variables, and stochastic processes*. Tata McGraw-Hill Education, 2002.

[16] P. Melgarejo, X. Zhang, P. Ramanathan, and D. Chu, "Leveraging Directional Antenna Capabilities for Fine-grained Gesture Recognition," in *ACM UbiComp*, 2014.

[17] Monsoon Solutions, Inc., "Monsoon Power Monitor," http://www.msoon.com/LabEquipment/PowerMonitor/.

[18] A. Carroll and G. Heiser, "An Analysis of Power Consumption in a Smartphone," in *Proc. of the USENIX Annual Technical Conference*, 2010.

[19] T. Hao, R. Zhou, and G. Xing, "COBRA: Color Barcode Streaming for Smartphone Systems," in *Proc. of ACM MobiSys*, 2012.

[20] S. D. Perli, N. Ahmed, and D. Katabi, "PixNet: Interference-free Wireless Links Using LCD-camera Pairs," in *Proc. of ACM MobiCom*, 2010.

[21] M. Ogata, Y. Sugiura, H. Osawa, and M. Imai, "iRing: Intelligent Ring Using Infrared Reflection," in *Proc. of ACM UIST*, 2012.

[22] C. Harrison and S. E. Hudson, "Abracadabra: Wireless, High-precision, and Unpowered Finger Input for Very Small Mobile Devices," in *Proc. of ACM UIST*, 2009.

[23] S. Kratz and M. Rohs, "Hoverflow: Exploring Around-device Interaction with IR Distance Sensors," in *Proc. of ACM MobileHCI*, 2009.

[24] J. Kim, J. He, K. Lyons, and T. Starner, "The Gesture Watch: A Wireless Contact-free Gesture Based Wrist Interface," in *Proc. of IEEE International Symposium on Wearable Computers (ISWC)*, 2007.

[25] J. Moeller and A. Kerne, "ZeroTouch: An Optical Multi-touch and Free-air Interaction Architecture," in *Proc. of the SIGCHI Conference on Human Factors in Computing Systems (CHI)*, 2012.

[26] S. Liu and F. Guimbretière, "FlexAura: A Flexible Near-Surface Range Sensor," in *Proc. of ACM UIST*, 2012.

[27] J. P. Wachs, M. Kölsch, H. Stern, and Y. Edan, "Vision-based Hand-gesture Applications," *Communications of the ACM*, vol. 54, no. 2, 2011.

[28] A. Sahami Shirazi, Y. Abdelrahman, N. Henze, S. Schneegass, M. Khalilbeigi, and A. Schmidt, "Exploiting Thermal Reflection for Interactive Systems," in *Proc. of SIGCHI Conference on Human Factors in Computing Systems (CHI)*, 2014.

[29] E. Larson, G. Cohn, S. Gupta, X. Ren, B. Harrison, D. Fox, and S. Patel, "HeatWave: Thermal Imaging for Surface User Interaction," in *Proc. of the SIGCHI Conference on Human Factors in Computing Systems (CHI)*, 2011.

[30] P. Mistry and P. Maes, "Mouseless: a computer mouse as small as invisible," in *Adjunct Proceedings of ACM UIST*, 2010.

[31] D. Kim, S. Izadi, J. Dostal, C. Rhemann, C. Keskin, C. Zach, J. Shotton, T. Large, S. Bathiche, M. Niessner, D. A. Butler, S. Fanello, and V. Pradeep, "RetroDepth: 3D Silhouette Sensing for High-precision Input on and Above Physical Surfaces," in *Proc. of ACM Conference on Human Factors in Computing Systems (CHI)*, 2014.

[32] R. Xiao, C. Harrison, K. D. Willis, I. Poupyrev, and S. E. Hudson, "Lumitrack: Low Cost, High Precision, High Speed Tracking with Projected M-sequences," in *Proc. of ACM UIST*, 2013.

[33] Microsoft Corporation, "Kinect for Windows," 2014. [Online]. Available: http://www.microsoft.com/en-us/kinectforwindows/

[34] Leap Motion, Inc., "Leap Motion: Mac & PC Gesture Controller for Game, Design and More," 2013. [Online]. Available: https://www.leapmotion.com/

[35] C. Harrison, D. Tan, and D. Morris, "Skinput: Appropriating the Body As an Input Surface," in *Proc. of SIGCHI Conference on Human Factors in Computing Systems (CHI)*, 2010.

[36] M. Le Goc, S. Taylor, S. Izadi, and C. Keskin, "A Low-cost Transparent Electric Field Sensor for 3D Interaction on Mobile Devices," in *Proc. of ACM Conference on Human Factors in Computing Systems (CHI)*, 2014.

[37] T. Grosse-Puppendahl, S. Herber, R. Wimmer, F. Englert, S. Beck, J. von Wilmsdorff, R. Wichert, and A. Kuijper, "Capacitive Near-field Communication for Ubiquitous Interaction and Perception," in *Proc. of ACM UbiComp*, 2014.

EcoDrive: A Mobile Sensing and Control System for Fuel Efficient Driving

Lei Kang, Bozhao Qi, Dan Janecek and Suman Banerjee
University of Wisconsin-Madison
{lkang, bozhao, suman}@cs.wisc.edu , janecek@wisc.edu

ABSTRACT

This paper introduces EcoDrive, a fuel consumption sensing and control system for modern vehicles, implemented in an embedded platform, to improve fuel efficiency and reduce carbon emissions. EcoDrive senses vehicle dynamics through the standard vehicle On-board diagnostics (OBD) port and models various vehicle forces, i.e., propulsion, drivetrain loss, wind resistance and grade resistance, as functions of instant fuel consumption. By sensing vehicular speed and controlling air/fuel injection rate in real time, EcoDrive can adjust speed carefully to improve fuel efficiency.

We have collected more than 10,000 miles of driving traces from 12 different vehicles to build models of vehicle dynamics. Based on the models, a prototype of EcoDrive is implemented in an off-the-shelf embedded platform. The prototype is installed on a regular vehicle and evaluated through test drives of more than 100 miles across both urban and highway environments. In comparison with human drivers, EcoDrive achieves an average of 20% higher fuel efficiency in urban road segments and 30% higher fuel efficiency on highways.

1. INTRODUCTION

Modern vehicles are the ultimate mobile computing platforms. They are often on the move at significant speeds and are equipped with significant embedded computing systems that control and manage different functions including providing various types of assistance to its driving function [1, 2, 3, 4, 5]. The computational capabilities of automobile systems provide opportunities and challenges to manage and control every aspects of a vehicle's drive. The focus of this work has been in the design of a system to improve the fuel efficiency of a vehicle's drive by sensing, computing, and actuating the acceleration behavior of the vehicle in an autonomous manner, by modeling properties of the vehicle, road conditions, and driving actions. The benefits of such a system can be profound — Morgan Stanley reported that there could be $158 billion in annual savings in the US, if all cars adopted a smoother driving style [6]. With the global push for improving fuel efficiency of vehicles to reduce consumptions and carbon emissions, we believe solution such as ours can be one of many important mechanisms to meet such a goal.

MobiCom'15, September 7–11, 2015, Paris, France.
 ISBN 978-1-4503-3619-2/15/09...$15.00.
DOI: http://dx.doi.org/10.1145/2789168.2790111.

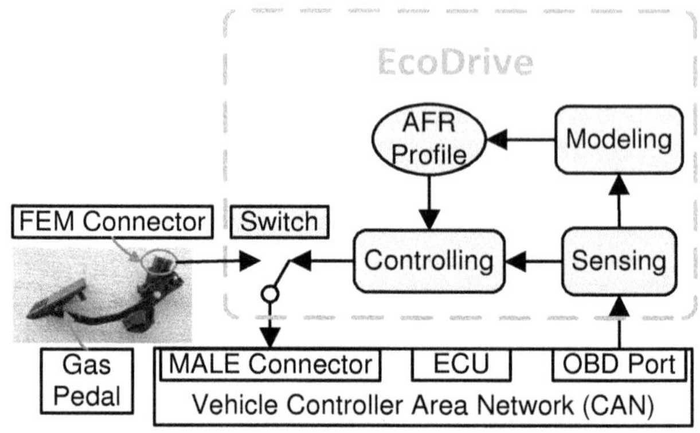

Figure 1: EcoDrive Architecture.

System and Assumptions. This paper introduces EcoDrive, a fuel consumption sensing and control system that improves fuel efficiency and reduces carbon emissions. EcoDrive estimates instant fuel consumptions of different driving behaviors based on sensed vehicle parameters from the On-board diagnostics (OBD) port [7, 8]. It can adjust vehicular speed in real time according to individual vehicle properties and road conditions to achieve higher fuel efficiency measured by Kilometer Per Liter (KPL) [1]. EcoDrive is an independent system that can be installed on or removed from regular vehicles easily. This system controls the vehicle's acceleration and speed to provide a fuel efficient drive on its path. In our work and current implementation, we design this system assuming there is no other factors that would contribute to a choice of acceleration and speed, e.g., other vehicles, pedestrians, etc. or other obstacles in vicinity. Clearly in a practical system, this knowledge would be critical in modifying the acceleration behavior. Currently, we adopt the approach followed by other equivalent systems, such as cruise control [9], which allows the driver to instantly disable cruise control by actively pressing the brake pedal. In an analogous way, in our current implementation, we provide the driver a switch which can be pressed to instantly

[1]KPL refers to the distance travelled per unit volume of fuel consumed. It interchangeable with Mile Per Gallon (MPG), i.e., 1 KPL = 2.35214583 MPG.

disable EcoDrive, if its acceleration behavior is perceived to be unsafe for nearby vehicles or obstacles.

EcoDrive Components. EcoDrive delivers its design via three components including an OBD sensing component, a vehicle dynamics modeling component and an acceleration controlling component. The architecture is illustrated in Fig. 1. The sensing component reads real-time OBD parameters through the OBD port. The modeling component models various vehicle forces as functions of instant fuel consumption and produces a fuel consumption profile, called Air/Fuel Rate (AFR) profile [2]. The controlling component utilizes the AFR profile to calculate fuel efficient driving strategies according to speed limit and road conditions. EcoDrive emulates the gas pedal by sending voltage values to the connector through an Arduino board. The vehicular Electronic Control Unit (ECU) controls air/fuel injection rate according to the voltage inputs.

EcoDrive addresses two main challenges.

a) Model Vehicle Dynamics based on OBD Parameters. EcoDrive uses the OBD parameters delivered by the sensing component to build an AFR profile, which records instant fuel consumptions of various accelerations under different speeds. To this end, EcoDrive models various vehicle forces, including propulsion, drivetrain loss, wind resistance and grade resistance, as functions of instant fuel consumption. First, we model propulsion (or output torque) as a function of engine torque and gear ratio [10, 11]. We use AFR to model engine torque, and use the ratio between RPM and vehicular speed to model gear ratio. Second, we represent drivetrain loss and wind resistance as a function of vehicular speed [12]. The coefficients are estimated from recorded data traces where the car is driving at constant speeds. The basic idea is that the sum of resistances is equal to propulsion when the car is driving at a steady-state speed. Third, we model grade resistance by altitude changes over road segments. The altitudes of the locations are obtained from National Elevation Dataset [13]. Based on the three models, AFR is modeled as a function of speed, acceleration and road conditions.

b) Control Air/Fuel Rate and Vehicular Speed to Improve Fuel Efficiency. EcoDrive controls vehicular speed by emulating gas pedal. It sends the emulated gas pedal position values to the Arduino board which then converts the position values to corresponding output voltages. The output voltages are delivered to the ECU through a 6 Pin Connector. The problem is how to adjust vehicular speeds to travel through a certain distance with the lowest fuel consumption. We solve this problem by using dynamic programming. Each state of the dynamic programming model records the minimum air/fuel cost that allows the car to achieve the current speed at the current location. In this model, speed can only increase and the last state of each speed records the minimum fuel consumption if the car reaches the pre-assigned distance at that speed. We call the speed with minimum fuel consumption the target speed. By backtracking the state matrix from the last state of target speed, EcoDrive can obtain the desired AFR at each speed. EcoDrive adjusts air/fuel injection rate based on real-time sensed vehicular speed. Once the vehicular speed reaches the target speed, EcoDrive enters a cruising state and commands a constant air/fuel injection rate until the car reaches the pre-assigned distance.

[2]AFR refers to the volume of air/fuel cost per unit time.

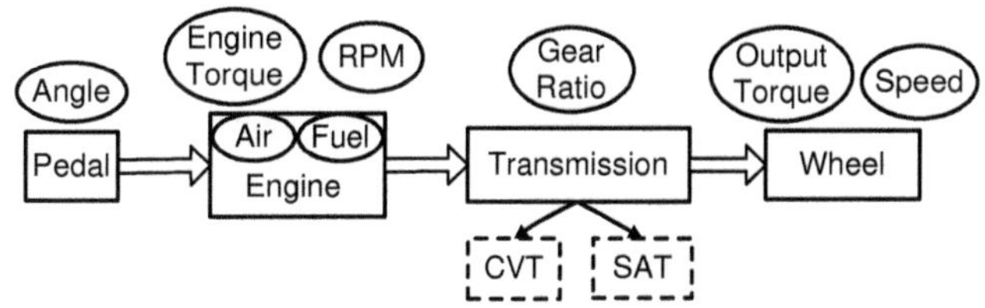

Figure 2: Vehicle Drivetrain.

EcoDrive Prototype. We build a prototype of EcoDrive in an off-the-shelf mobile embedded platform. The prototype is installed and tested on a 2011 Chevrolet Impala. We test EcoDrive on the Impala for more than 100 miles in both urban and highway environments. We evaluate the fuel consumption of EcoDrive and human drivers on different road segments. In urban areas, EcoDrive achieves 10%-40% higher fuel efficiency than four recruited human drivers. On highway, we evaluate EcoDrive on two highway segments with different target speeds. In our user tests, EcoDrive has over 30% improvements compared to different human drivers. In comparison with cruise control, which is more fuel efficient than human drivers in the traces we collected, EcoDrive achieves an average of 10% higher fuel efficiency. We evaluate the performance of EcoDrive on other vehicles by using trace-driven simulation based on the 10,000 miles data collected from 12 different vehicles. We further find that instant fuel economy display on regular vehicles is misleading and cruise control is fuel consuming during speed changes (either requested by user or affected by road conditions).

Contributions. EcoDrive is an independent fuel consumption sensing and control system that can improve fuel efficiency. The system is implemented on an embedded platform that can be easily installed on regular vehicles. We model various vehicle forces as functions of instant fuel consumption and the models are evaluated by utilizing 10,000 miles of driving traces collected from 12 vehicles. EcoDrive is installed on a regular vehicle and evaluated by more than 100 miles of driving in both urban and highway environments, and demonstrated to improve fuel efficiency compared to cruise control system of the vehicle and to human drivers.

2. PRELIMINARY

To illustrate how vehicle system works and how each components are related to different OBD parameters, we present a high-level vehicle system control flow in Fig. 2. Drivers accelerate vehicle by pressing the gas pedal, and then the gas pedal position will be sent to the Electronic Control Unit (ECU). The ECU controls air/fuel injection rate to produce engine torque to drive the vehicle. Transmission is used in this process to transit power from engine to wheel and match engine rotational speed with wheel rotational speed.

2.1 Power Production and Transition

In a car engine, the explosion of compressed fuel and air produces the power to drive a car. The air is injected through an intake port and expelled from an exhaust port. The volume of oxygen in the exhaust air is monitored by fuel trim sensors. Based on fuel trim sensor readings, the

Electronic Control Unit (ECU) calculate the desired fuel injection rate to maintain the ideal air/fuel ratio [3].

The burning of air and fuel mixture triggers the revolution of crankshaft, which carries piston power out of the engine to the transmission. The transmission carries power to wheels. Transmission is also known as gearbox that uses gears and gear trains to provide speed and torque conversion. The transmission reduces the higher engine speed to the slower wheel speed and increases torque in the process of accelerating the vehicle. The transmission converts engine revolutions to driveshaft revolutions, and then to axle revolutions. A Continuously Variable Transmission (CVT) is a transmission that can change seamlessly through an infinite number of effective gear ratios between maximum and minimum values. This contrasts with Step Automatic Transmissions (SAT) that offer a fixed number of gear ratios.

2.2 OBD Parameters

Table 1: Collected OBD Data

Name	PID	Unit
Fuel Level (FL)	2F	%
Mass Air Flow Rate (MAF)	10	g/s
Fuel System Status (FSS)	03	Bitmask
Long Term Fuel Trim (LTFT)	07	%
Short Term Fuel Trim (STFT)	06	%
Vehicular Speed (VS)	0D	km/h
Engine RPM (RPM)	0C	rpm
Accelerator Position (AP)	5A	%

On-board diagnostics (OBD) is an automotive term referring to a vehicle's self-diagnostic and reporting capability. It is the interface between car Controller Area Network (or CAN bus) and external devices, e.g., a OBD scan tool that connects the OBD port and a laptop. Car CAN bus allows vehicular components to communicate with each other. For example, a position value is sent to the Electronic Control Unit (ECU) after human driver press the gas pedal, and the ECU adjusts air/fuel injections according to the position value. Therefore, we can read this position message transmitted over CAN bus from the OBD port.

The data we collected from the OBD port are summarized in Table 1. Fuel Level (FL) of the vehicle is usually measured by a float sensor, which is usually visualized on the fuel gauge in the car [14]. The FL is calculated according to the height of the float. The Fuel System Status (FSS) is used to indicate current engine mode, open loop mode or closed loop mode. In open loop mode, the engine calculate the fuel injection based on the pre-calculated table and there is no feedback to the engine to adjust the fuel injection rate. The engine runs in open loop mode during short warm up time and runs in closed loop mode at most of the time. In closed loop mode, the engine adjusts fuel injection rate based on fuel trims and air flow rate. Mass Air Flow Rate (MAF) is used to measure the air intake rate of the engine, and therefore an effective indicator of instant fuel consumption [15, 16, 17]. Both Long Term Fuel Trim (LTFT) and Short Term Fuel Trim (STFT) are used to adjust the air/fuel rate injected into engine. LTFT changes less frequent than STFT. In this paper, we use AFR as a metric of instant fuel consumption and/or carbon emission.

[3] Air/fuel ratio is a constant value around 14.67, while air/fuel rate is the volume of air/fuel injected per unit time.

Table 2: Vehicles (distance in miles)

No.	Car Model	Urban	Highway
1	Chevrolet Impala 2011	1051	852
2	Nissan Rogue 2011	1198	1063
3	Subaru Forester 2011	651	757
4	Buick LaCrosse 2006	599	649
5	Volkswagen Tiguan 2014	600	347
6	Honda Accord 2013	173	840
7	Toyota Camry 2011	35	338
8	Volkswagen Touareg 2014	21	156
9	Nissan Altima 2014	193	271
10	Nissan Rogue 2011	105	0
11	Subaru Legacy 2015	119	30
12	Mazda CX5 2014	202	89

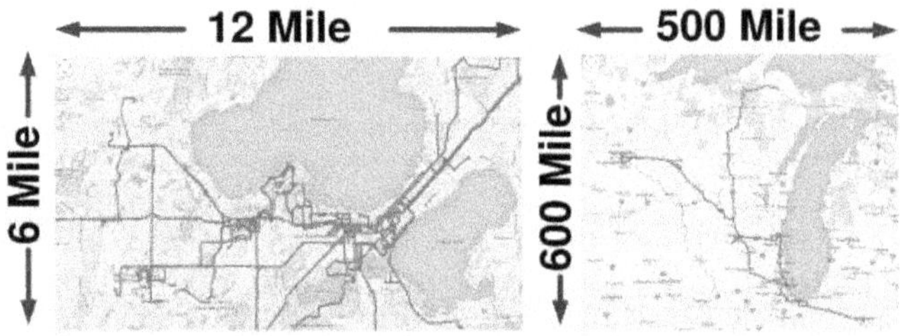

Figure 3: Urban driving data (left) is collected from a US mid-size city. Highway driving data (right) is collected from both local highways and cross-state highways.

$$AFR = C_f * MAF * (1 + LTFT) * (1 + STFT). \quad (1)$$

where C_f is a constant value for unit conversion, e.g., from air flow rate to fuel rate or to carbon emission rate.

Vehicular Speed is measured by the perimeter of the wheel and number of rotations. Accelerator Position is measured by the angle of the gas pedal. It controls the air/fuel rate injected into the Engine. Engine RPM is measured by the rotation speed of the engine motor.

2.3 Dataset

We use a customized Android application to collect OBD and GPS data from different car makes and models. The dataset is summarized in table 2. The transmission of car 2,6,9,10 and 11 is CVT and the rest is SAT. The driving data of car 1-6 is collected over a course of three months, and the rest is collected from random events, e.g., three cross-state highway trips are collected by car 7, 8 and 9, respectively. Here we separate urban driving and highway driving, as urban driving patterns are dominated by frequent accelerations and decelerations while highway driving patterns are dominated by constant speed cruising. The dataset covers car makes from three different countries, urban data over 5,000 miles, highway data across 5 US states and over 5,000 miles, two common types of transmissions. We use the first car to install a prototype of EcoDrive and tested it in both urban and highway environments.

2.4 EcoDrive Architecture

EcoDrive reads real-time OBD parameters through OBD port and controls air/fuel injection rate by emulating the gas pedal. We illustrate the architecture of EcoDrive in Fig. 1. The sensed parameters from OBD port are passed to modeling component to train the models. The modeling component builds an AFR profile to record the instant fuel consumptions of various accelerations at different speeds. Based on pre-calculated driving strategy and real-time sensed vehicular speed, the controlling component controls air/fuel injection rate to adjust vehicular speed by sending the gas pedal position values to the ECU. To emulate the gas pedal, we utilize the drive-by-wire technology, where the gas pedal and throttle are connected by electronic messaging instead of mechanical linkage. It enables the position of gas pedal can be sent as a message to control throttle position. The throttle controls the volume of air flow injected into the engine.

2.5 Applications

EcoDrive is used as an independent system that can be installed on regular vehicles. It can be used as a control system in a way similar to cruise control [9, 18, 19]. In this application, it is used as a EcoDrive mode that a human driver can switch it on or off. Drivers are required to press the brake pedal to turn this mode off to keep safe distance to front car or traffic lights/signs accordingly. This mode can be integrated with intelligent front object or traffic light detection systems [18, 19] to further enhance driving experience. EcoDrive requires two inputs, the speed limit and road length. The speed limit can be specified by human driver or obtained from online database [20]. The road length can be calculated by a navigation software. How to obtain these information is beyond the scope of this paper.

It can also be used as a subsystem of autonomous driving systems [1, 4, 5, 21]. We envision a highly autonomous and intelligent system that all the route information are pre-calculated, e.g., speed limit, traffic conditions and distances of each road segment etc. EcoDrive can be used as a subsystem to predict fuel consumption of possible routes [22] and calculate the optimal driving strategy.

3. VEHICLE DYNAMICS AND FUEL CONSUMPTION

EcoDrive models various forces as functions of instant fuel consumption and produces fuel consumption profile as output. Different from Existing vehicle dynamics models [23], we only use parameters available from OBD instead of assuming the engine parameters are known in advance. We consider several factors that affect car fuel consumption, e.g., engine torque, drivetrain loss, wind resistance and grade resistance. The vehicle force can be modeled as follows.

$$F = F_p - F_l - F_g - F_w. \tag{2}$$

where F_p refers to the propulsion caused by car engine, F_l refers to the drivetrain loss caused by transmission and various gears connecting engine and wheels, F_w refers to the wind resistance, F_g refers to the grade resistance. Since we are only interested in fuel consumption on acceleration and cruise, we exclude the forces caused by brake.

We model the forces in the following steps. First, we use RPM and vehicular speed to model gear ratio and use AFR to model engine torque. Second, the drivetrain loss and wind resistance is modeled as the counterforce of propulsion when the car is driven in constant speeds. Finally, we use driving data extracted from flat road to train the parameters of our propulsion and loss models, and then use the propulsion model to model grade resistance.

3.1 Propulsion Modeling

The propulsion (or output torque) of vehicle is closely related to transmission gear ratios and engine torque [10, 11]. The propulsion produced by vehicle engine can be represented by

$$F_p = a_p * \tau_e * R_G. \tag{3}$$

where τ_e refers to the engine torque, R_G refers to transmission gear ratio and a_p is the coefficient used for unit conversion.

3.1.1 Gear Ratio Modeling

Modern vehicles are usually using automatic transmission and freeing the driver from shifting gears manually. There are mainly two types of transmissions, Step Automatic Transmission (SAT) and Continuously Variable Transmission (CVT). SAT uses discrete transmission gear ratios while CVT has an infinite number of effective transmission gear ratios. Since different transmission types show different properties of gear ratio changes over different speeds, we use gear ratio changes to identify different vehicle transmission types. We estimate gear ratios by using RPM and speeds when the car is driving in constant speeds.

In a SAT vehicle, R_G are discrete values.

$$R_G = R_i = \frac{RPM}{v} \qquad i = 1, ..., n \tag{4}$$

where v represents the vehicular speed and n is the number of gears of a transmission, e.g., $n = 4$ for a 4-speed transmission.

In a CVT vehicle, R_G changes continuously over time and always approach the optimal RPM.

$$R_G = \begin{cases} \frac{RPM_a}{v} & \text{if } v < v_T, \\ R_b & \text{if } v \geq v_T. \end{cases} \tag{5}$$

where RPM_a is the optimal RPM of a given engine, and v_T is the speed threshold. If the vehicular speed is lower than v_T, the engine RPM converges to a constant value RPM_a under different speeds. If the vehicular speed is higher than or equal to v_T, the gear ratio is a constant value R_b.

3.1.2 Engine Torque Modeling

Engine torque is produced by the explosion of air and fuel, therefore, we can use AFR to model engine torque.

$$\tau_e = AFR^{f(v)}. \tag{6}$$

where $f(v)$ is a parameter function that is monotonically increasing with vehicular speed. Based on our empirical

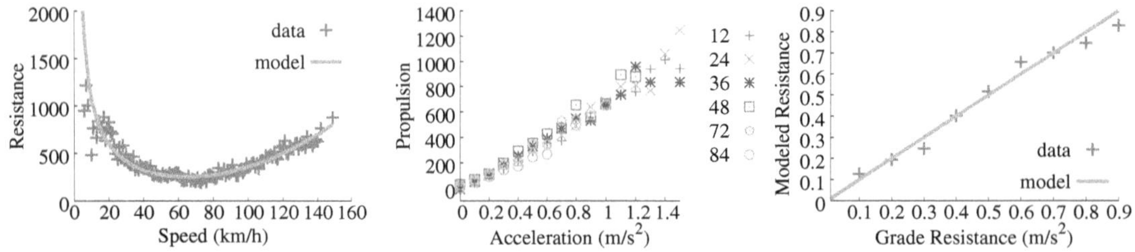

Figure 4: Vehicle Dynamics Modeling. The figures are about drivetrain loss and wind resistance under each speed (left), relation between acceleration and propulsion (minus wind resistance and drivetrain loss) under each speed (middle), modeled grade resistance with groundtruth (right).

observation, it starts from 0.3 at speed 0 and converges to 1 when the speed is larger than $20km/h$.

Therefore, the propulsion of a car on the wheel can be written as

$$F_p = a_p * \tau_e * R_G = a_p \frac{AFR^{f(v)} * RPM}{v}. \tag{7}$$

3.2 Drivetrain Loss and Wind Resistance Modeling

Instead of modeling each loss individually, we model all the power losses as a whole. There are mainly two power losses in automotive systems, drivetrain loss and wind resistance. Drivetrain loss consists of transmission loss and other mechanical system losses. Transmission connects car engine and wheels by various gears and power loss occurs when transmit the power from engine to wheels. We model drivetrain loss in the following form.

$$F_l = \frac{a_l}{v} + b_l * v + c_l. \tag{8}$$

where v is the vehicular speed and the rest are coefficients. The drivetrain loss drops to minimum when the car is driving in moderate speed.

The force from the air drag [12] can be represented by following equation,

$$F_w = 0.5 * \rho_a * c_d * A_a * v^2 = a_w * v^2. \tag{9}$$

where ρ_a is the air mass density, c_d is the air drag coefficient and A_a is the effective area of the vehicle. Since the effective area of vehicle is different from vehicle to vehicle, we model air drag as a function of vehicle speed with unknown coefficient a_w.

After we put drivetrain loss and wind resistance together, the modeled loss and actual loss are shown in the Fig. 4. In low speed, the main loss comes from drivetrain loss due to mechanical frictions. In high speed, the main loss comes from wind resistance due to air compression. After we have drivetrain loss and wind resistance, we use propulsion minus the loss ($F_p - F_l - F_w$) to model the relation between acceleration and propulsion, as shown in the middle of Fig. 4. For accelerations, we use extra MAF instead of raw MAF readings from the OBD port. Raw MAF minus the MAF required to maintain a certain speed is the extra MAF for this speed.

3.3 Grade Resistance Modeling

Different road types, i.e., flat road, uphill and downhill, have significant different impacts on vehicle movements and fuel consumptions. Similar to [12], the grade resistance can be modeled as a combination of forces caused by grade and rolling resistance.

$$F_r = mgc_r \cos\theta. \tag{10}$$

where c_r is the grade resistance coefficient, m is the vehicle mass, g is the gravity of earth , θ is the road grade and v is vehicular speed. The road elevation information is obtained from National Elevation Dataset [13].

3.4 AFR Profile

Vehicle needs different air/fuel injection rate to achieve different accelerations under different speeds. Based on the vehicle dynamics models we built in previous sections, we can build a fuel consumption profile. In this profile, we can lookup the AFR required to accelerate a vehicle with an arbitrary acceleration under any speed. Let $AFR(v,a)$ denotes the air/fuel rate is required to accelerate the vehicle at acceleration a when the vehicle is driving at speed v. The profile can be represented as the following equation.

$$AFR(v,a) = e^{\frac{log(a/R_G)}{f(v)}} + AFR_c(v) \tag{11}$$

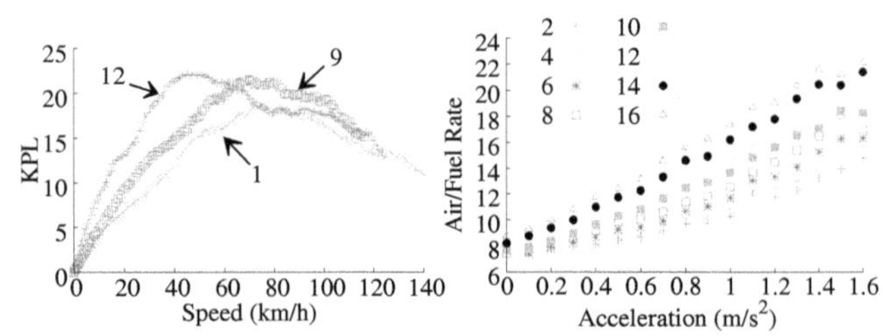

Figure 5: AFR profile.

An illustration of AFR profile of car 1 is shown in the right subfigure of Fig. 5. The profile provides the AFR required to accelerate the car at a certain acceleration under a certain speed. We can infer a lookup table for each $AFR(v,a)$ based on the profile. The left subfigure in Fig. 5 illustrates different vehicles have different speed-KPL matching, which indicates AFR profile needs to be built based on individual vehicles.

4. ACCELERATION CONTROL

EcoDrive controls air/fuel injection rate to control vehicular speed by emulating gas pedal. EocDrive calculates accelerations of each speed and leaves brake decision to drivers or other systems. It needs two inputs, road speed limit and segment length. The speed limit can be set by human drivers or queried from online database [20]. The road segment length can be estimated by human drivers or by a third-party navigation software. Road segment length is not necessary for long distance roads, as the driving strategy will be the same if the distance is longer than a threshold. For example, if the speed limit is $25mph$, the fuel efficient acceleration strategies for $300m$ and $500m$ are the same. In this paper, we assume both speed limit and road segment length are known. The output of EcoDrive is a matrix and each element in the matrix is the minimum fuel consumption when the car arrives at a certain distance with a certain speed. By traversing all the possibilities, EcoDrive is able to find all reasonable driving strategies with different fuel consumption and travel time.

4.1 Problem Statement

Driving pattern can be abstracted as accelerate-cruise-brake. EcoDrive focuses on the accelerate-cruise part and leaves brake decision to human drivers. For example, in a $300m$ road segment with speed limit $25mph$ (or $40km/h$), the EcoDrive accelerates and cruises to $200m$ and the driver uses the rest $100m$ to stop the car as there is a stop sign at the end of the road. Similar to cruise control, we assume there is enough distance to front obstacles for drivers to brake.

EcoDrive needs two key inputs: 1) The length of the road segment, i.e., from current location to the point driver will make a brake, 2) The lower and upper speed limits of the road segment. Such inputs can be given by user or extracted from online databases and navigation softwares. We focus on how to utilize such inputs to calculate fuel efficient strategies. Therefore, the problem that EcoDrive is going to address can be stated as follows: *Given a road segment length with lower and upper speed limits, how to control air/fuel injection rate in real time to achieve the most fuel efficient driving strategy.*

4.2 Driving Strategy by Dynamic Programming

We use dynamic programming to traverse all the possibilities to find all reasonable driving strategies. This is inspired by the fact that the fuel efficiency and travel time are related to the speed and distance. We divided the road segment into smaller equal length road segments. We use v_i and d_k to represent the ith speed and the length of kth segment, respectively. We use $s(i,k)$ to represent the state when the car is driving at speed v_i at the start location of road segment d_k. For any state $s(i,k)$, there are two sets of possible transitions. First, it transits from $s(i,k-1)$, which means that the car is driving in constant speed v_i in last road segment. Second, it transits from $s(i-1,k-1-m)$, which means the car is accelerating from speed v_{i-1} to v_i under acceleration a_j. The lower speed bound is used to eliminate some unreasonable cruising speed, e.g. it is obviously not fuel efficient and reasonable if the car is cruising at 1 km/h.

In the first case, the accumulated fuel consumption is the sum of the fuel consumption used to reach state $s(i,k-1)$ and the cruising fuel consumption from d_{k-1} to d_k.

$$FC_c(i,k) = FC(i,k-1) + AFR(v_i, 0.0) * t_i. \quad (12)$$

where t_i means the time cost when the car is driving through road segment d_{k-1} and $t_i = \frac{d_{k-1}}{v_i - v_{i-1}}$.

In the second case, the accumulated fuel consumption is the sum of the fuel consumption used to reach state $s(i-1,k-1-m)$, the cruising fuel consumption FC_c in part of road segment $k-1-m$, and the acceleration fuel consumption FC_j. The car may start to accelerate at any location in road segment $k-1-m$. The road segment is split into two parts, the car cruises to a point within the road segment $k-1-m$ and then starts to accelerate at acceleration a_j. Therefore, the fuel consumption of this case can be represented as follows.

$$FC_a(i,k) = FC(i,k-1-m) + FC_c + FC_j. \quad (13)$$

where $FC_c = AFR(v_i, 0.0) * t_c$ and t_c is the cruising time cost within road segment $k-1-m$. To calculate t_c, we need to calculate the distance used to accelerate from v_{i-1} to v_i. Before that, we present the acceleration fuel consumption cost as

$$FC_j = AFR(v_{i-1}, a_j) * t_a. \quad (14)$$

The acceleration time is $t_a = \frac{v_i - v_{i-1}}{a_j}$ and the acceleration distance is $d_a = v_{i-1} * t_a + 0.5 * a_j * t_a^2$. The cruising distance is simply $d_c = \sum_{x=k-m-1}^{k-1} d_x - d_a$ and the cruising time is $t_c = \frac{d_c}{v_{i-1}}$.

Therefore, the fuel consumption at the start of state $s(i,k)$ is

$$FC(i,k) = min\{FC_c(i,k), min\{FC_a(i,k)\}\}. \quad (15)$$

After we traverse all the states, the last state of each speed is the minimum fuel consumption when the car is finally cruising in that speed. The most economy driving strategy can be traced back from the state with minimum fuel consumption. Different travel time is used when the car is cruising in different speeds. By using this property, we can find a tradeoff between travel time and fuel consumption.

Assume that we split the road segment into n smaller equal length road segments , there are m different speeds and l different accelerations, the time complexity of the dynamic programming algorithm is $O(n*m*l)$ and the space complexity is $O(n*m)$. In practice, the most road segment length in urban area is less than $1km$ and we set each smaller road segment to be $1m$. The unit of the speed sensed from the OBD port is km/h and the speeds are integers, so we have $0-60$ different speeds in urban area. The acceleration is normally from $0.1m/s^2$ to $1.4m/s^2$. Therefore, the time complexity of the algorithm grows linearly with the total road length.

Different road conditions affect air/fuel rate as the car needs lower (or higher) air/fuel injection rate to achieve the same acceleration in downhill (or uphill) conditions. The air/fuel rate for a specific road segment d_k becomes $AFR(v_i, a_j - a_k)$, where a_k refers to the acceleration/deceleration caused by the kth road segment. The driving strategy can be calculated based on the dynamic programming solution as well.

4.3 Fuel Economy and Travel Time

In general, fuel efficient driving strategies require longer travel time in urban environments. Therefore, there is a trade-off between fuel efficiency and travel time. EcoDrive provides different travel time by selecting different target speed. The higher the target speed, the less the travel time.

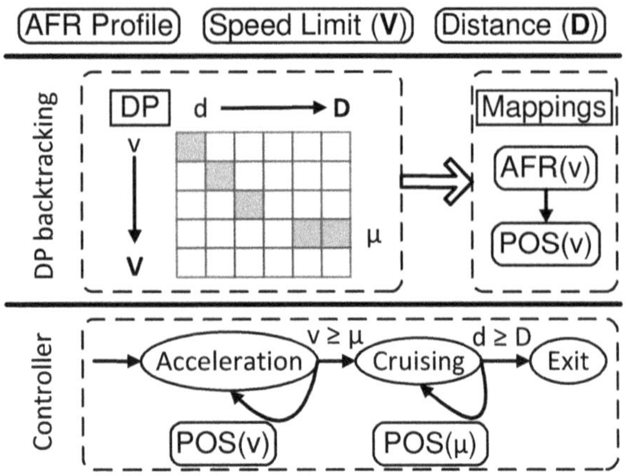

Figure 6: EcoDrive control flow.

The user can select the most fuel efficient driving strategy with fixed target speed, or select desired travel time with corresponding target speed. The selection of target speed also depends on the speed limit, i.e., the target speed should not be higher than the speed limit. The most fuel efficient cruising speed ranges from 30mph to 60mph for different types of vehicles. In urban environments, the most fuel efficient target speed is around the speed limit. However, in short road segments, it is generally more fuel efficient to select a target speed that is lower than speed limit due to extra cost on acceleration.

4.4 Highway Strategy

The most fuel efficient highway speeds range from $40km/h$ to $80km/h$ for the vehicles we observed. Given the highway speed limit ranging from $80km/h$ to $110km/h$ in US, drivers can find a trade-off between fuel efficiency and travel time by selecting different cruising speeds. Generally speaking, constant speed cruising generally has higher KPL than frequent accelerations and decelerations. Therefore, traditional cruise control is considered a good option for economic driving. However, traditional cruise control sticks to one target speed. If the driver manually increases target speed, the car will aggressively approach to the target speed, which will bring extra fuel consumptions. Similarly, when the car is cruising uphill, the road will slow down the car and cruise control will aggressively approach the target speed. In downhill condition, cruise control will reduce air/fuel injection to maintain the target speed. EcoDrive increases speed gradually and utilizes the acceleration caused by downhill to achieve higher KPL.

4.5 Acceleration Controller

We summarize the control flow of EcoDrive in Fig. 6. The AFR profile is calculated offline by the modeling component. Given the travel distance D and speed limit V, EcoDrive uses dynamic programming model to calculate the speed to acceleration mapping of the most economic driving strategy. This process is done by backtracking the last state of target speed μ. The speed to acceleration mapping records the desired acceleration under that speed. This mapping is converted into speed to air/fuel injection rate mapping $AFR(v)$ by querying the AFR profile. The acceleration controller retrieves the air/fuel injection rate based on the mapping and real-time sensed vehicular speed. A air/fuel rate to gas pedal position mapping and a gas pedal position to voltage mapping are calculated in advance. The controller gets the speed to gas pedal position mapping $POS(v)$. Based on the air/fuel injection rate, EcoDrive sends corresponding voltage values to the ECU. In this process, EcoDrive maintains three states, acceleration, cruising and exit. EcoDrive is in acceleration state by default and enters cruising state when sensed OBD speed is not less than target speed. After it enters cruising state, it remains constant air/fuel rate injection. Different from traditional cruising control, EcoDrive may increase/decrease speed in cruising state by adapting to various road conditions. If the car reaches the distance or EcoDrive is turned off by switch of brake, it enters exit state. EcoDrive releases all the resources in exit state and aborts to wait for next inputs.

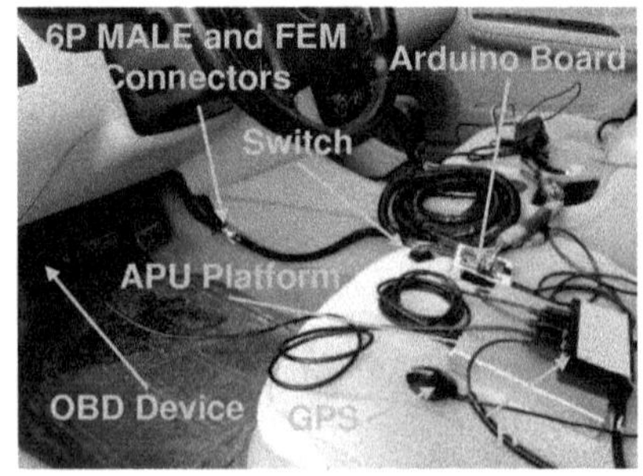

Figure 7: EcoDrive in-vehicle setup.

5. IN-VEHICLE SETUP AND IMPLEMENTATION

We explain the in-vehicle setup and implementation of EcoDrive.

5.1 In-vehicle Setup

The in-vehicle setup of EcoDrive is shown in Fig. 7. EcoDrive uses Arduino Uno microcontroller to emulate gas pedal by delivering signals to the ECU through a 6P FEM Connector. The microcontroller outputs a 16-bit resolution digital pulse-width modulation (PWM) signal which is smoothed out by an RC filter. A 6P MALE Connector is used to read signal outputs from the original gas pedal. A wiring harness and switch button are built that allows the user to switch the signal read by the ECU between the gas pedal and the microcontroller. Therefore, the setup supports two mode, human driving mode and EcoDrive mode. In human driving mode, the gas pedal and air/fuel injection rate is controlled by human driver. In EcoDrive mode, the gas pedal is unusable and air/fuel injection rate is controlled by the system. In EcoDrive mode, The APU platform [24] sends pedal positions to the microcontroller through serial communication and the microcontroller converts the pedal position values into analog voltages outputs. To do this, we construct a mapping between sensor analog voltage outputs and pedal positions. By using the mapping between gas pedal position and air/fuel rate built from driving traces, we can send position values from laptop to the car to control air/fuel injection rate.

5.2 Implementation

We implement EcoDrive data sensing module and air/fuel injection control module in C++. We operate EcoDrive on the Ubuntu 14.04 32bit distribution (with linux kernel version 3.13.0-34-generic), that runs on PC Engines APU platform [24]. APU platform is a mobile embedded platform that is equipped with 1GHz dual core CPU and 4G DDR3 DRAM. EcoDrive uses two threads to query and read OBD messages, respectively. One thread sends OBD query message to the OBD port in every 250ms. Higher frequency OBD query will cause CAN read error. Another thread listens on the OBD port for echo messages and sends voltage control commands to Arduino board. The Arduino board initiates a loop to listen on the USB serial and sets the voltage output of two pins based on received command. The two pins represent the voltage output pins of gas pedal's two position sensors.

6. EVALUATION

Our evaluation consists of four parts, EcoDrive road testing results in both urban and highway environments, vehicle dynamics modeling accuracy, driving data statistics and trace-driven simulation.

6.1 Fuel Efficiency Test Results

6.1.1 Urban

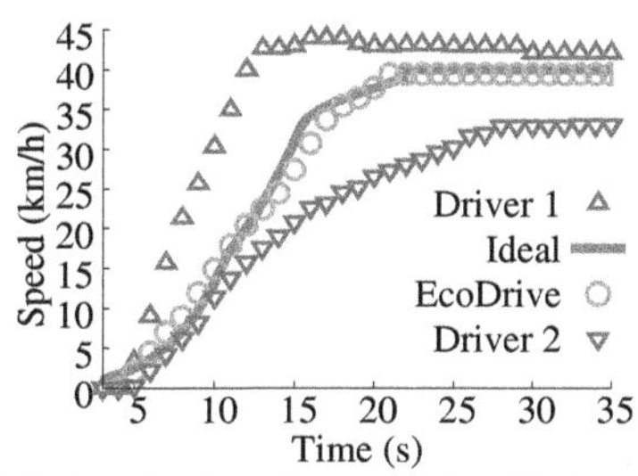

Figure 8: Driving behaviors of EcoDrive and Human Drivers on a 300m length road segment.

In this experiment, we compare EcoDrive with human drivers in urban road segments. EcoDrive uses drive-by-wire technology to control air/fuel injection rate. It accelerates the vehicle by sending gas pedal position values to ECU. EcoDrive provides driver a switch button which can disable EcoDrive immediately. In our evaluation, we did not experience any bugs or out of control situations, but we made our risk management as follows. First, we control the input parameters. i.e., the gas pedal position value, on both the controller and the Arduino board. Second, we can shift the transmission to neutral or park to disconnect the engine and wheel if the engine is out of control due to unexpected gas pedal position input. Third, the brake dominates the gas pedal and we can brake even when the engine is out of control.

Test Drive Example. A EcoDrive prototype test drive and human drive tests are conducted in a 300m length road segment with speed limit of 25mph (or 40km/h). The vehicular speed traces are shown in Fig. 8. The ideal curve is plotted from the traces obtained from dynamic programming model. In our prototype, the air/fuel injection rate is controlled based on sensed speed. The speed may change at any point during the query interval, so that it is challenge

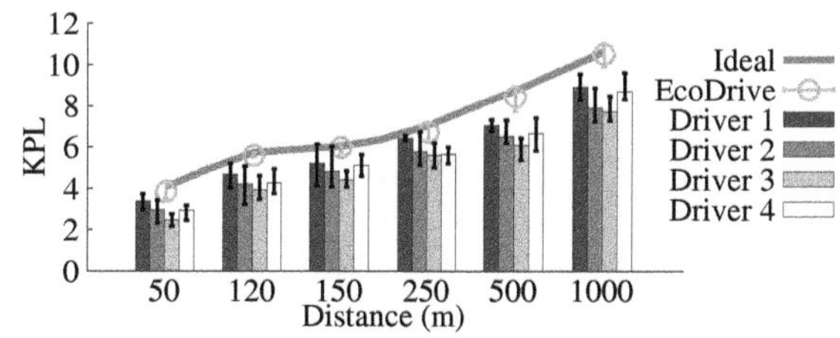

Figure 9: Fuel efficiency comparison between EcoDrive and human drivers on urban road segments.

to control the air/fuel injection rate precisely at each speed. The differences between estimated speed traces and actual speed traces are mainly caused by the impreciseness of speed sensing and road conditions. Some other factors affect the preciseness of vehicular speed control include wind speed and passenger weights etc. Two human drivers are asked to drive on the same road segment. It is shown that the driver 1 is more aggressive by fast accelerations and driver 2 is more conservative by slow accelerations. The driving trace of EcoDrive prototype falls in between. In this comparison, the prototype shows 23% and 19% fuel efficiency improvements than driver 1 and 2, respectively. Driver can reach a fuel efficient speed faster by fast acceleration, but it takes more fuel during the acceleration process. If a driver uses lower accelerations to reduce fuel consumption during acceleration process, overall fuel efficiency will not be increased due to driving in low (less fuel efficient) speeds and longer travel time. EcoDrive chooses the best strategy for economic driving.

Urban Road Segments. We select six different road segments and let EcoDrive drive the car 10 times on each road segment. We recruited four drivers to drive on the same road segments 10 times as well. The speed limit of the $500m$ and $1000m$ road segments is $30mph$ (or $50km/h$) and the that of the $150m$ and $250m$ road segments is $25mph$ (or $40km/h$). There is no speed limit for the $50m$ and $120m$ road segments. The length is the driving length of EcoDrive and the overall road segment length is longer so that drivers have enough time to stop the car. The results are shown in Fig. 9. The ideal fuel consumption is the theoretical fuel consumption that is calculated based on AFR profile and dynamic programming model. The actual fuel consumption of EcoDrive on certain road segment length is very stable. EcoDrive shows 10%-40% fuel efficiency improvement compared to different drivers with different road segment lengths. The fuel efficiency improvement comes from the smooth driving behaviors of EcoDrive. EcoDrive has an average of 20% more travel time than human drivers. EcoDrive can have 5%-10% improvements than human drivers if not sacrificing travel time. The plots of tradeoff between fuel consumption and travel time are omitted due to the space limit.

6.1.2 Highway

In this experiment, we compare EcoDrive with cruise control and human drivers on highway.

Compare to Cruise Control. Fig. 10 plots the different acceleration patterns between cruise control and EcoDrive. Cruise control is a vehicle built-in feature that can keep car driving at a certain speed while human drivers can manually increase or decrease the cruising speed. The cruise control pattern is extracted when the gas pedal position is 0 but the air/fuel injection rate is higher than the idle state

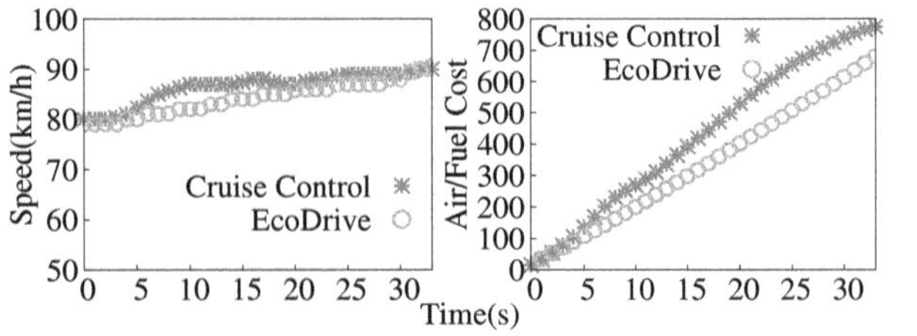

Figure 10: Acceleration comparison between Cruise Control and EcoDrive.

rate. As shown in the figure, cruise control consumes more fuels than EcoDrive due to the aggressive acceleration strategy. The travel distance is similar for both cases, so EcoDrive is more fuel efficient than cruise control. Similarly, driving uphill by using cruise control will consume more fuels as well. When the car is driving uphill, the vehicular speed drops due to grade resistance, so cruise control will aggressively accelerate to the setting speed. In downhill conditions, cruise control will reduce air/fuel injection rate, while accelerating by maintaining the same air/fuel injection rate has higher fuel efficiency.

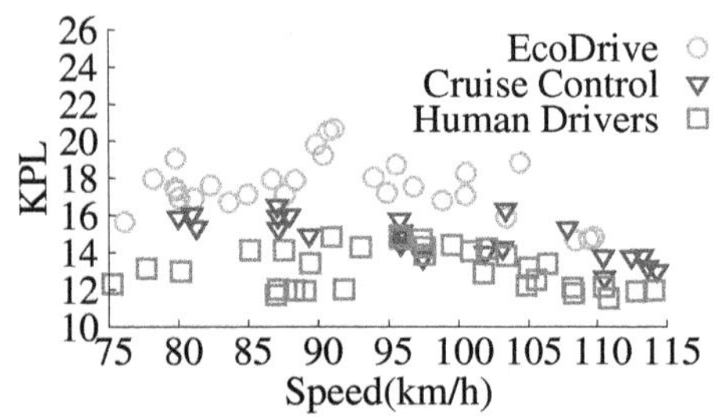

Figure 11: Highway experiments.

Compare to Human Drivers. We evaluate EcoDrive by driving on two highway segments, one is a local highway segment and another is a cross state highway segment. The highway segments are selected based on historical driving traces of car 1. EcoDrive is evaluated by two-way driving in each highway segment, e.g., if EcoDrive enters highway at A and exits at B in one experiment and it will enter at B and exits at A in next experiment. The two-way road testing is used to evaluate EcoDrive in both uphill and downhill conditions. EcoDrive is evaluated between exit 256 and 262 on Madison's West Betline Highway, and between exit 132 and 136 on US 14 Highway.

The cruise control and human driving traces are extracted from historical driving traces collected on the same highway segments. In each driving trace, the car is traveling at a constant speed(it may have some small speed variations). And we calculate the average speed of each trace as the vehicle speed. The results are shown in Fig. 11, where each point represents the KPL of a $2km - 3km$ length road segment. To eliminate the impact of traffic, the traces that have speed decrease due to brake are not included. In this experiment, EcoDrive shows more than 10% fuel efficiency than cruise control and more than 30% fuel efficiency than human drivers on average.

6.1.3 *Travel Time and Fuel Efficiency*

In this experiment, we evaluate the tradeoff between travel time and fuel consumption.

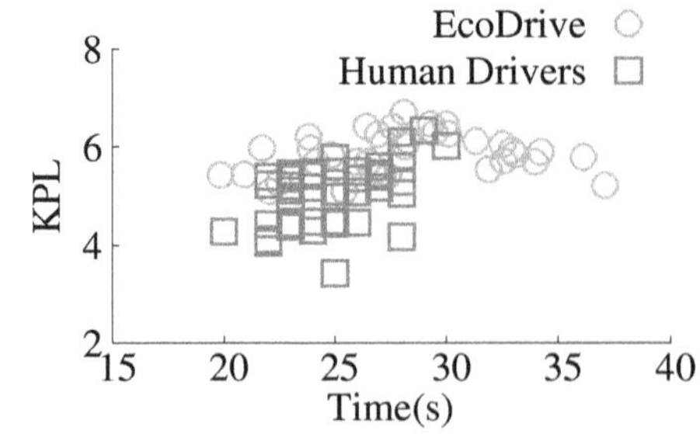

Figure 12: Tradeoff between travel time and fuel consumption on a 250m road segment.

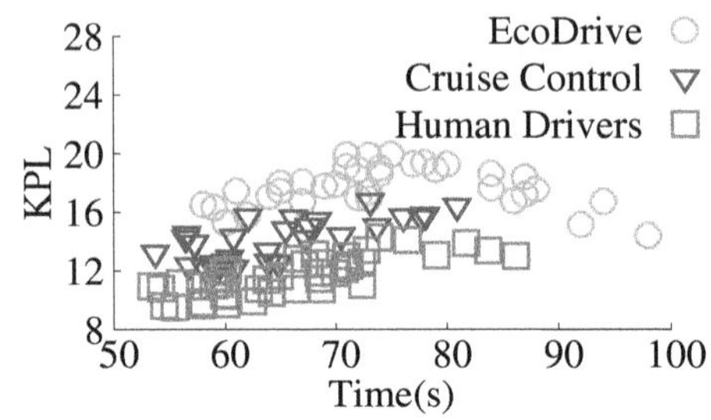

Figure 13: Tradeoff between travel time and fuel consumption on highway.

Urban. The tradefoff between travel time and fuel consumption of EcoDrive on $250m$ road segment is shown in Fig. 12. For EcoDrive, the optimal KPL is around 7 and the travel time is around 28 seconds. On the other hand, the average KPL for human drivers is around 5.5 and the average travel time is around 25 seconds. EcoDrive can achieve a 20% fuel efficiency improvement on average by sacrificing travel time by around 10%. EcoDrive can also improve fuel efficiency under same travel time in most cases.

Highway. Fig. 13 shows the tradeoff between travel time and fuel efficiency on highway. Each highway segment length is around $2km - 3km$. EcoDrive can improve fuel efficiency by more than 30% on average without sacrificing travel time. The gain comes from smooth acceleration and road adaptation. More fuel efficiency can be achieved by cruising at the peak KPL speed, which is around $90km/h$ in this evaluation.

6.2 Modeling Accuracy

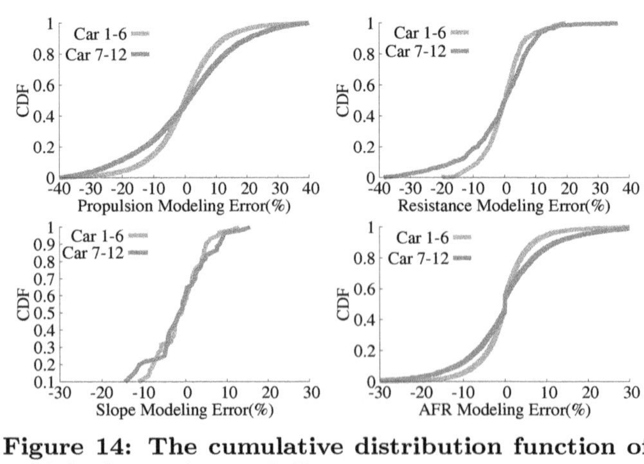

Figure 14: The cumulative distribution function of vehicle dynamics modeling errors.

In this experiment, we evaluate the modeling accuracy of vehicle dynamics models. Different vehicle forces, propulsion, resistance and grade resistance, are evaluated separately. The AFR profile calculation accuracy is evaluated as well. We divide the data into two sets, one set is the training set used to build the model and another set is the testing set for evaluating the model. For each model, we repeat this process and plot the modeling accuracy of various vehicle dynamics models in Fig. 14. From top-left to bottom-right, they are propulsion model evaluation, drivetrain loss and wind resistance model evaluation, grade resistance model evaluation, and AFR profile evaluation.

We use green curves to represent the cars have more than one thousand miles driving traces (Car 1-6) and use red curves to represent the rest (Car 7-12). The green curves show that the fitting errors of more than 95% cases are within ±10%. The red curves show less fitting accuracy due to less miles.

6.3 Driving Data Statistics

6.3.1 Urban Road Segment Length

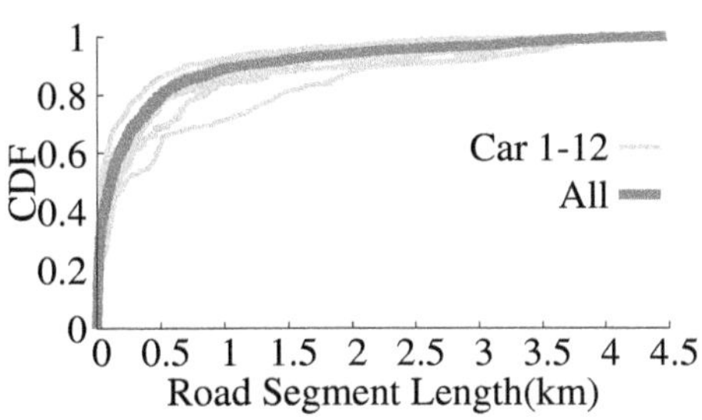

Figure 15: Road segment length in urban area.

We summarize the length of road segments in Fig. 15. A road segment is defined as the distance between two stand/stop locations. A stand/stop location is defined as following: 1) The speed of the car is zero; 2) The car is making a turn. The speed of the car can be easily sensed from the OBD port. We identify turns from GPS data. The driving direction of car can be calculated from two adjacent GPS points. If the accumulated driving direction change are close to 90 degree, then we mark this is a stand/stop location. This rough road segment length statistics give us a guideline for experiments. As shown in the figure, the most of road segments are within 1000m. This indicates that the driving pattern in urban area is primarily accelerate-brake.

6.3.2 Urban Acceleration

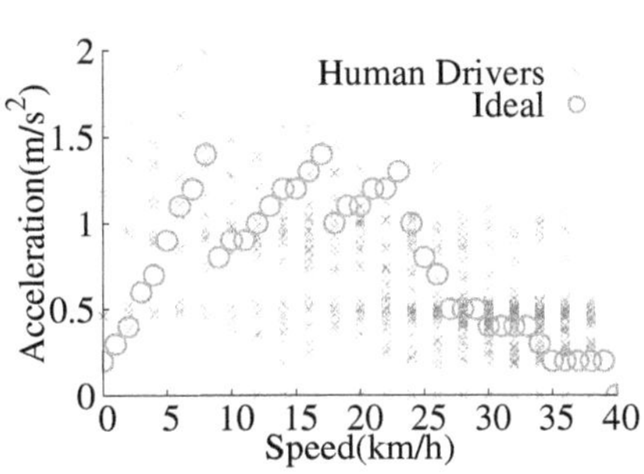

Figure 16: The urban acceleration patterns of different drivers.

Fig. 16 explains the acceleration patterns of car 1 and the ideal acceleration pattern calculated by EcoDrive with equal road length. As shown in the figure, drivers are not aware of the most efficient accelerations of different speeds and not able to drive at a certain speed. They drive either lower than desired accelerations, which will increase fuel consumption due to longer travel time in low KPL speeds, or higher than desired accelerations, which will increase fuel consumption due to extra fuel consumption to achieve the target speed.

6.3.3 Highway Driving Speed

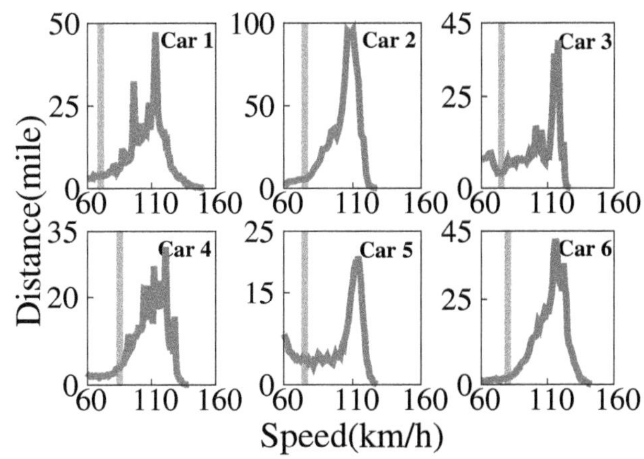

Figure 17: The highway driving speed distributions of car 1-6.

The speed limits of rural highway is $65mph$ ($104.6km/h$) to $70mph$ ($112.6km/h$), and the speed limit of urban highway is $55mph$ ($88.5km/h$). We summarize the highway driving speeds of car 1-6 and illustrate the distribution and best KPL speed in Fig. 17. We observe that most drivers drive above the speed limits with noticeable mileages and much higher than the best KPL speed. This is partially because the drivers are not aware of the much higher fuel consumption in high speeds. Also, slowing down when following a slow car will increase fuel consumption due to power loss when braking. Frequent accelerations and decelerations increase fuel consumption as well.

6.4 Trace-driven Simulation

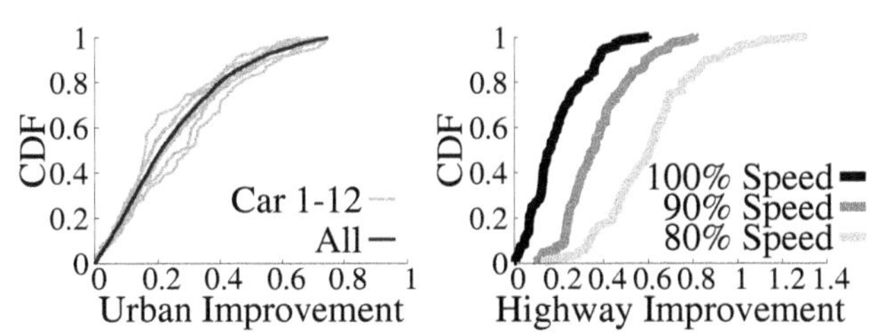

Figure 18: Fuel efficiency improvements by trace-driven simulation.

In this experiment, we evaluate EcoDrive by trace-driven simulations.

Urban. We divide urban trips into variable-length road segments where the vehicular speed is 0 at the start and end of each segment. Each segment is divided into four parts, accelerating part, cruising part, braking part and idle part. Accelerating part ended when the speed does not increase in

5 seconds. Braking part started when the driver release gas pedal at the end of each segment. Cruising part falls between accelerating part and braking part. Idle part follows braking part after the vehicular speed reach 0. The speed limit is calculated based on the average speed of cruising part. We calculate the fuel cost of EcoDrive by replaying acceleration and cruising parts. We use the same braking and idle cost extracted from original traces. We sum up the two costs to calculate the final fuel consumption of EcoDrive. As shown in Fig. 18, EcoDrive can improve a median of 20% fuel efficiency in urban environment. The travel time is reduced by 10%-30% in 20% cases and is increased by less than 25% in 60% cases. The plots of travel time are omitted due to the space limit.

Highway. We divide highway trips into road segments based on deceleration. If the deceleration is larger than a threshold, we separate current segment into one highway segment. The average speed of highway segment is used as target speed for EcoDrive. We replay each highway segment by EcoDrive with three different target speeds, the same target speed, 90% of target speed and 80% of target speed. As shown in Fig. 18, EcoDrive can improve fuel efficiency by more than 20% on average without sacrificing travel time and can improve an average of 40% fuel efficiency by sacrificing 10% travel time on highway.

7. RELATED WORK

7.1 Cruise Control

Cruise control [9] is a system that automatically controls the vehicle to drive in a certain speed. [18] introduces Adaptive Cruise Control (ACC) that adjusts vehicle speed based on distance to cars ahead by using radar. [25] studies the effects of time-gap settings of adaptive cruise control on driving performance in a bus driving simulator. [26] studies a distributed car control system that every car is controlled by adaptive cruise control. [19] develops an intelligent cruise control system for automatic vehicles and verify the effectiveness of the system under emergency situations by simulation. EcoDrive is more fuel efficient than adaptive cruise control in two ways. First, EcoDrive is able to improve fuel efficiency by adjusting speed according to road conditions and vehicle types. Second, EcoDrive tracks the fuel efficiency under different cruising speeds and provides a tradeoff between fuel efficiency and travel time.

7.2 Fuel Efficiency Enhancement

Increasing vehicular fuel efficiency has been a topic of much recent research [22, 17, 27, 28]. GreenGPS [22] requires a fuel map server to record the statistical route fuel usage and calculate the most fuel efficient route for drivers. SignalGuru [17] requires vehicles sharing traffic light information so that drivers can adjust the speed of the vehicle to avoid stops in front of traffic lights. [27] uses an on-board eco-driving device that provides instantaneous fuel economy feedback affects driving behaviors, and consequently fuel economy. [28] evaluates the impacts of a smartphone application on driving behaviors to enhance fuel efficiency. Different from existing approaches that are focusing on advising human drivers to adjust driving behaviors, EcoDrive is designed to assist human drivers. Both [29] and [30] show that some reduction of fuel consumption can be achieved by vehicle-to-vehicle communication.

7.3 Vehicle Dynamics Sensing

Smartphones equipped with various sensors are widely used to sense vehicle dynamics to understand driving behaviors and road conditions. [31] detects aggressive driving behaviors based on accelerometer sensor readings from smartphone. [32] determines driver phone use by comparing the centrifugal force of smartphone with that of a fixed reference sensor during turns. [33] monitors road surface conditions by using accelerometers. [34] detects various road and traffic conditions, e.g., potholes, bumps, braking, and honking, by using various sensors in smartphones. [35] senses speeds from the OBD port to identify aggressive driving behaviors and offer discounts for drivers with good driving habits. However, none of these work models vehicle dynamics as functions of instant fuel consumption.

7.4 Vehicle Force Modeling

[12] models rolling resistance and air drag based on some measurements on the vehicle, e.g., effective areas to model air drag. [36] models vehicle transmission system based on gear sizes. [37] models tire friction based on tire parameters, e.g., radius. [38] presents an electronic system attached on wheel to measure and monitor of the torque transmitted to the wheel of a moving vehicle. [10] models engine torque and horsepower by RPM when the engine is not connected with transmission. Our model uses the parameters available on car CAN bus to find the relations between fuel consumption and vehicle speed changes. Different from existing work, our model does not rely on the detail physics properties of the car, e.g., tire radius and transmission gear size etc.

7.5 Autonomous Driving

There have been major advances in designing and building autonomous vehicle operating systems to realize safer and more convenient vehicles [1, 4, 5, 21]. These work focuses on issues related to object detection and efficient navigation and so forth. CarSpeak [3] is designed as a communication system to share sensory data between autonomous vehicles for obstacle detection. Different from autonomous cars studies, we focus on the design and implementation of fuel-aware acceleration control system that works on existing regular vehicles. We expect that EcoDrive can be integrated with autonomous driving cars, but EcoDrive can also be used independently. Also, EcoDrive can work on existing vehilces with little hardware changes.

8. DISCUSSION

In this section, we discuss some design considerations of EcoDrive.

Hybrid Vehicle (HV) and Electric Vehicle (EV). EcoDrive is designed for gasoline-powered vehicles, but the modeling process and gas pedal emulation can also be applied to HVs and EVs. Currently, the majority of vehicles running on street are still gasoline-powered vehicles. It is important to develop systems like EcoDrive to work on regular vehicles to improve fuel efficiency and limit carbon pollution. The core of EcoDrive is that it can work on regular vehicles with easy and recoverable installation.

Instant Fuel Economy Display. In urban environments, acceleration is not fuel efficient, but accelerating to a higher speed in a careful way can improve fuel efficiency. If the driver refuses to accelerate due to low instant fuel efficiency, the car will drive in low fuel efficient speed and eventually increase fuel consumption. Similarly, releasing gas pedal can increase instant fuel efficiency dramatically, but frequent acceleration and deceleration will consume more fuel than cruising under certain speed. Therefore, instant fuel economy display is misleading and may reduce overall fuel efficiency.

Impact of Traffic and User Experience. EcoDrive controls the vehicle in a way that is similar to cruise control, so the driver should keep a safe distance to front vehicle. Since EcoDrive accelerates the vehicle in various ways according to different road segment lengths, it is more challenging for human drivers to keep safe distance than cruise control in dense traffic scenarios, because drivers need to frequently brake to avoid front-end collision. Therefore, EcoDrive is more suitable for drivers to use in low traffic volume scenarios. However, it is shown from the data we collected that drivers tend to accelerate much more aggressive than the optimal acceleration patterns. In other words, EcoDrive achieves higher fuel efficiency by accelerating slower than most drivers usually do. Also, EcoDrive uses fixed acceleration pattern for fixed road length and speed limit, drivers and passengers can easily get used to the driving style of EcoDrive. Therefore, we expect EcoDrive can be useful in most urban driving scenarios (except traffic hours) and drivers can still feel that the vehicles are under control due to predictable accelerations. We also expect that EcoDrive can tolerate more complex traffic conditions when integrating with front object detection and route planning systems equipped on driverless cars.

Limitations. First, EcoDrive requires the road length as input in short length road segment (e.g., shorter than 200m). Road length can be obtained by navigation softwares, but how to retrieve such information is beyond the scope of this paper. Second, it relies on drivers to brake or switch to disable EcoDrive mode. The operation complexity is acceptable for drivers as proven by cruise control. Third, EcoDrive requires mileage trainings to build an accurate model, i.e., 1000 miles driving data can build a very accurate model as shown in evaluation. Some optimization can be made to reduce training time, e.g., sharing the AFR profile among same vehicle models. Fourth, we did not evaluate EcoDrive by end-to-end scenarios in urban environment, e.g., what are the fuel savings from home to work. There are different traffic volumes and different traffic light schedules among different trips. Therefore, it is challenging to compare EcoDrive with human drivers in such scenarios. Given the fuel improvement in arbitrary length road segments, we believe EcoDrive can improve fuel efficiency in end-to-end scenarios as well.

Each trip can be divided into three parts: acceleration, cruising and braking. Acceleration and cruising consume most of the fuel during a trip. For this work, EcoDrive focuses on the acceleration part and cruising part. There is no direct way to fairly compare two brakes that made by different drivers, or different brakes made by the same driver. Therefore, we did not include the fuel consumption of braking in our evaluation.

There are other factors that affect fuel consumption, e.g., tire pressure, temperature and wind direction etc. A more accurate model can be built by using more vehicle parameters. However, there is no direct way to access some in-vehicle parameters like tire pressure. We advocate that the vehicle manufacturers provide more information through OBD port that can be used to enable more applications. Some other real world parameters, e.g., traffic light schedule, stop sign and wind direction etc., can also be used to improve fuel efficiency. We believe such extra information can be used to improve EcoDrive in broader aspects, the detailed integration methods are out of scope of this paper though.

9. CONCLUSION

This paper introduces EcoDrive, a fuel consumption sensing and control system that assists human driver to drive fuel efficiently. EcoDrive calculates driving strategy based on the properties of individual vehicles and road conditions. To this end, it models vehicle dynamics as functions of instant fuel consumption and calculates acceleration strategies accordingly. We build a prototype of EcoDrive on a mobile embedded platform. The prototype is installed on a regular vehicle and tested for more than 100 miles in both urban and highway environments. In comparison with human drivers, EcoDrive improves fuel efficiency by 10%-40% in urban environments. It has an average of 10% higher fuel efficiency than vehicle built-in cruise control and more than 30% fuel efficiency than human drivers on highway.

10. ACKNOWLEDGMENTS

We would like to acknowledge the anonymous reviewers and our shepherd, whose comments helped bring the paper into its final form. This research project is supported in part by the US National Science Foundation through awards CNS-1405667, CNS-1345293, CHE-1230751, CNS-1343363 and CNS-1525586.

11. REFERENCES

[1] Google driverless car. *http://en.wikipedia.org/wiki/Google_driverless_car.*

[2] Qnx operating system for diverless car by blackberry. *http://www.qnx.com/.*

[3] Swarun Kumar, Lixin Shi, Nabeel Ahmed, Stephanie Gil, Dina Katabi, and Daniela Rus. Carspeak: a content-centric network for autonomous driving. In *Proceedings of the ACM SIGCOMM 2012.*

[4] Chris Urmson, Joshua Anhalt, Drew Bagnell, Christopher Baker, Robert Bittner, MN Clark, John Dolan, Dave Duggins, Tugrul Galatali, Chris Geyer, et al. Autonomous driving in urban environments: Boss and the urban challenge. *Journal of Field Robotics*, 2008.

[5] Todd Litman. Autonomous vehicle implementation predictions. 2013.

[6] Morgan Stanley Research. Autonomous cars: Self-driving the new auto industry paradigm. 2013.

[7] Obd. *http://en.wikipedia.org/wiki/On-board_diagnostics.*

[8] Obd pids. *http://en.wikipedia.org/wiki/OBD-II_PIDs.*

[9] Cruise control, wikipedia. *http://en.wikipedia.org/wiki/Cruise_control.*

[10] Chi-Man Vong, Pak-Kin Wong, and Yi-Ping Li. Prediction of automotive engine power and torque using least squares support vector machines and bayesian inference. *Engineering Applications of Artificial Intelligence*, 19, 2006.

[11] Robert A Giannelli, EK Nam, Kent Helmer, Theodore Younglove, George Scora, and M Barth. Heavy-duty diesel vehicle fuel consumption modeling based on road load and power train parameters. Technical report, SAE Technical Paper, 2005.

[12] Robin Andersson. Online estimation of rolling resistance and air drag for heavy duty vehicles. 2012.

[13] National elevation databases. *http://nationalmap.gov/elevation.html.*

[14] Fuel gauge. *http://auto.howstuffworks.com/fuel-gauge1.htm.*

[15] Adriano Alessandrini, Francesco Filippi, and Fernando Ortenzi. Consumption calculation of vehicles using obd data. 2012.

[16] Min Goo Lee, Yong Kuk Park, Kyung Kwon Jung, and Jun Jae Yoo. Estimation of fuel consumption using in-vehicle parameters. *International Journal of U-& E-Service, Science & Technology*, 4(4), 2011.

[17] Emmanouil Koukoumidis, Li-Shiuan Peh, and Margaret Rose Martonosi. Signalguru: leveraging mobile phones for collaborative traffic signal schedule advisory. In *Proceedings of the 9th international conference on Mobile systems, applications, and services*, pages 127–140. ACM, 2011.

[18] Johan Bengtsson. *Adaptive cruise control and driver modeling.* Department of Automatic Control, Lund Institute of Technology, 2001.

[19] Petros A Ioannou and Cheng-Chih Chien. Autonomous intelligent cruise control. *IEEE Transactions on Vehicular Technology*, 1993.

[20] Wikispeedia, a road speed limit database. *http://en.wikipedia.org/wiki/Wikispeedia.*

[21] Junsung Kim, Ragunathan Raj Rajkumar, and Markus Jochim. Towards dependable autonomous driving vehicles: a system-level approach. *ACM SIGBED Review*, 2013.

[22] Raghu K Ganti, Nam Pham, Hossein Ahmadi, Saurabh Nangia, and Tarek F Abdelzaher. Greengps: a participatory sensing fuel-efficient maps application. In *Proceedings of the 8th international conference on Mobile systems, applications, and services*, pages 151–164. ACM, 2010.

[23] Kerem Koprubasi. *Modeling and control of a hybrid-electric vehicle for drivability and fuel economy improvements.* PhD thesis, The Ohio State University, 2008.

[24] Apu platform. *http://www.pcengines.ch/apu.htm.*

[25] Tsang-Wei Lin, Sheue-Ling Hwang, and Paul A Green. Effects of time-gap settings of adaptive cruise control (acc) on driving performance and subjective acceptance in a bus driving simulator. *Safety science*, 47(5):620–625, 2009.

[26] Sarah M Loos, André Platzer, and Ligia Nistor. Adaptive cruise control: Hybrid, distributed, and now formally verified. In *FM 2011: Formal Methods*, pages 42–56. Springer, 2011.

[27] Kanok Boriboonsomsin, Alexander Vu, and Matthew Barth. Eco-driving: pilot evaluation of driving behavior changes among us drivers. *University of California Transportation Center*, 2010.

[28] Johannes Tulusan, Thorsten Staake, and Elgar Fleisch. Providing eco-driving feedback to corporate car drivers: what impact does a smartphone application have on their fuel efficiency? In *Proceedings of the 2012 ACM Conference on Ubiquitous Computing*, pages 212–215. ACM, 2012.

[29] Dominik Lang, Thomas Stanger, and Luigi del Re. Opportunities on fuel economy utilizing v2v based drive systems. Technical report, SAE Technical Paper, 2013.

[30] Dominik Lang, Roman Schmied, and Luigi Del Re. Prediction of preceding driver behavior for fuel efficient cooperative adaptive cruise control. *SAE International Journal of Engines*, 7(2014-01-0298):14–20, 2014.

[31] Derick A Johnson and Mohan M Trivedi. Driving style recognition using a smartphone as a sensor platform. In *Intelligent Transportation Systems (ITSC), International IEEE Conference on.* IEEE, 2011.

[32] Yan Wang, Jie Yang, Hongbo Liu, Yingying Chen, Marco Gruteser, and Richard P Martin. Sensing vehicle dynamics for determining driver phone use. *ACM Mobisys*, 2013.

[33] Jakob Eriksson, Lewis Girod, Bret Hull, Ryan Newton, Samuel Madden, and Hari Balakrishnan. The Pothole Patrol: Using a Mobile Sensor Network for Road Surface Monitoring. In *MobiSys*, 2008.

[34] Prashanth Mohan, Venkata N. Padmanabhan, and Ramachandran Ramjee. Nericell: Rich monitoring of road and traffic conditions using mobile smartphones. SenSys '08. ACM, 2008.

[35] Progressive. Linking driving behavior to automobile accidents and insurance rates. *Report*, 2012.

[36] R Zanasi, A Visconti, G Sandoni, and R Morselli. Dynamic modeling and control of a car transmission system. In *2001 IEEE/ASME International Conference on Advanced Intelligent Mechatronics*. IEEE, 2001.

[37] C Canudas de Wit and P Tsiotras. Dynamic tire friction models for vehicle traction control. In *Proceedings of the 38th IEEE Conference on Decision and Control*. IEEE, 1999.

[38] Valner Brusamarello, Alexandre Balbinot, Luiz Carlos Gertz, and André CervieÌĄri. Dynamic torque measurement for automotive application. In *Instrumentation and Measurement Technology Conference (I2MTC)*. IEEE, 2010.

Kaleido: You Can Watch It But Cannot Record It

Lan Zhang[1], Cheng Bo[2], Jiahui Hou[3,4], Xiang-Yang Li[1,3]
Yu Wang[2], Kebin Liu[1], Yunhao Liu[1]
[1]School of Software and TNLIST, Tsinghua University, China
[2]Department of Computer Science, University of North Carolina at Charlotte, USA
[3]Department of Computer Science, Illinois Institute of Technology, USA
[4]Department of Computer Science, University of Science and Technology of China, China
{lan, kebin, yunhao}@greenorbs.com, {cbo1,Yu.Wang}@uncc.edu, {jhou11,xli}@cs.iit.edu

ABSTRACT

Recently a number of systems have been developed to implement and improve the visual communication over screen-camera links. In this paper we study an opposite problem: how to prevent unauthorized users from videotaping a video played on a screen, such as in a theater, while do not affect the viewing experience of legitimate audiences. We propose and develop a light-weight hardware-free system, called KALEIDO, that ensures these properties by taking advantage of the limited disparities between the screen-eye channel and the screen-camera channel. KALEIDO does not require any extra hardware and is purely based on re-encoding the original video frame into multiple frames used for displaying. We extensively test our system KALEIDO using a variety of smartphone cameras. Our experiments confirm that KALEIDO preserves the high-quality screen-eye channel while reducing the secondary screen-camera channel quality significantly.

Categories and Subject Descriptors

C.21 [**Network Architecture and Design**]: Network Communications

Keywords

Screen-Camera Communication; Image Privacy; Image Copyright Protection

1. INTRODUCTION

Recently we have witnessed a blooming of electronic visual displays deployed for a variety of purposes (*e.g.*, for news and entertainment, for advertising, for tour guide, or for human-computer interaction) and in a wide range of devices (*e.g.*, phone-screen, tablet, TV, electronic board). The volume of information exchanged between these visual displays and their audiences is tremendous. For example, video playback has contributed to about 80% of the Internet traffic [15]. Researchers recently propose to encode information into the screen-camera side-channel by taking advantage of the extra signal that can be captured by camera but not the human eye. A number of innovative systems have been developed to implement and improve the visual communication over screen-camera links [14, 20, 22–24, 26–28, 35, 44, 45, 50]. In this paper we study a relevant but different problem: how to prevent unauthorized users from videotaping a video played on a (projected) screen (such as in a cinema or a lecture hall) for high-quality redisplay while do not affect the viewing experience of live audiences. While existing techniques try to maximize decodability of screen-camera channel, we seek to maximize the quality degradation of the display-camera channel while retain the quality of the screen-eye channel. A technology developed in this regard will have a lasting effect in protecting the copyright of the video, preventing audiences from taking a high-quality pirated copy of the video (called *pirate video* hereafter in this work). Film piracy causes lost of revenue about $20.5 billion annually according to a recent survey [6], and over 90% of this illegal online content is delivered from these pirate movies [4]. Unauthorized videotaping during the exhibition could cause unwanted information leakage. So, for the purpose of copyright issues, many exhibitions have strict no-camera policies. Moreover, videotaping a presentation or project demonstration could also cause infringement of copyright and even plagiarism.

Copyright protection is becoming increasingly important. With the rapid spread of camera-enabled mobile devices or wearable devices, recording video in a cinema or a lecture hall is extremely easy and hard to detect. Traditionally, to protect the copyright, copyright is first filed for a digital property indicating that it is protected by law and unauthorized usage is illegal. Various technologies have been developed in the industry and research community for conveying this copyright protection information and/or protecting the digital property copyright from being violated. For example, watermarking [16, 48, 49] schemes are often used to claim the ownership of the released digital property, where a watermark is added to the digital property (*e.g.*, images or videos) while broadcasting. Film industry often implements expensive security strategies or equips guards with night vision goggles [4] to prevent film piracy. Unfortunately, these technologies are ineffective in preventing attendees from taking pirate video for later redisplay. Such intellectual property disrespect behavior has sparked new technologies to prevent illegal video recording, such as inserting extra frames to obscure a recording [56], or projecting ultraviolet or infrared light onto the screen so as to wash out recorded picture [5]. Although such recorded videos contain both valuable video and obscure image or shade, the content could still be more likely perceived by human in large extent. In addition, some technologies cannot be adopted in other display devices, *e.g.*, large LCD screens for personnel use. The goal of this work is to develop a *universal* technology that can be used to protect the video displayed in a variety of devices without introducing extra hardware from pirate videotaping using typical mobile devices, such as smartphone or smartglasses.

MobiCom'15, September 7–11, 2015, Paris, France.
© 2015 ACM. ISBN 978-1-4503-3619-2/15/09 ...$15.00.
DOI: http://dx.doi.org/10.1145/2789168.2790106.

In contrast to effective screen-camera communications, achieving such a lofty goal of preventing mobile pirate recording is extremely challenging. The main challenging issue is that we have to ensure a smooth view experience/quality of legitimate live audiences while still preventing a good quality pirate-video recording by the adversary audiences. Notice that the recording schemes of smart devices are typically designed to mimic the basics of how human views the surrounding world. Thus, there is a very small design opportunity for such a transformative technology. In this work, we will first extensively explore the basics of human vision, video encoding, screen display, and video-recording mechanisms. By taking advantage of the limited disparities (*e.g.*, the *spectral and temporal color mixture*, the *flicker* effect and *critical flicker frequency*, and the *rolling shutter* of commonly used digital camera) between human vision and video-recording, we develop KALEIDO, a secure video encoding and displaying system. KALEIDO provides smooth viewing experience for human audience but prevents adversaries from recording a good quality pirate-video using mainstream camera-enabled smart devices. As we do not want to use any extra hardware device in our system, KALEIDO is designed purely based on re-encoding the video for screen-display. Notice that the original video is filmed in $24fps$ or $30fps$ (called *video rate*, whose unit is frame per second) typically, while for ensuring better viewing experience, the *refresh rate* of a display screen could be as large as 240fps. To address such disparity, when being played, each frame of the original video will be duplicated so as to fit the refresh rate of each display system. KALEIDO designs a new scheme to "duplicate" the original frame, which we call it *watch-only video re-encoding*. Instead of directly duplicating the original frame, a sequence of d frames ($d \simeq \frac{\text{refresh rate}}{\text{video rate}}$) for each original frame is carefully produced, such that the visual perception of the newly designed frames is same as the original video frame while there is a significant information loss in the pirate video. We have implemented KALEIDO and conducted a comprehensive evaluation over a variety of common mobile cameras.

Summary of Results: We test KALEIDO over 30 videos of different styles, use both LCD monitor and projectors for displaying watch-only videos, and use a variety of smart devices to videotape the video. We evaluate the video quality of watch-only video and pirate video respectively using both subjective video quality measurement (via extensive survey of 50 audiences) and objective video quality measurement with a number of different metrics (such as PSNR and SSIM). Our experiments confirm that KALEIDO preserves the high-quality screen-eye channel while reducing the secondary screen-camera channel quality significantly. First, the viewing experience of legitimate audience is not affected: over 90% of the surveyed audiences do not see any quality differences between the original video and watch-only video. The average score of the survey is over 4 out of 5, indicating the video quality degradation is almost unnoticeable. Second, the scheme is very effective for preventing pirate videotaping: among surveyed audiences, 96% experience a significant quality drop in the pirate video; and the objective video quality measurement of pirate video also confirms this observation (PSNR dropped over 60%, SSIM dropped over 40%). Notice that, due to various techniques used in reducing the quality of the video, the pirate video actually experiences a larger quality degradation when played in real-time than in each of the frames in the pirate video.

The rest of paper is organized as follows. In Section 2, we briefly review the preliminary knowledge about human vision and coloring, the video encoding, the video display, and the video-taping. In Section 3, we highlight the design space and principles, and the design challenges and opportunities. We then introduce our KALEIDO for generating watch-only video. We report results from our extensive evaluation of KALEIDO in Section 4. We review the related work in Section 6 and conclude the paper in Section 7.

2. BACKGROUND AND PRELIMINARY

In this work, we design a special video type, a *watch-only video*, *i.e.* the video can be displayed on common devices and be watched by human with the same visual quality as the original video, but the pirate version, captured by pirates' mobile cameras, will suffer a severe quality degradation. This is challenging as nowadays mobile devices are equipped with sophisticated cameras which are imitation of the human eye. Before presenting our design, we briefly review the properties of the human eye as the information receiver and the constraints that the display and camera technologies place on the transmission of the light signal.

2.1 Characterizing Human Vision

Human possess a photopic vision system, which is driven by the cone-cells in the retina. When we see the rich light spectra of objects, different light wavelengths stimulate the three kinds of cone-cells of a viewer in different degrees, providing her perception of distinct colors. Color is usually recognized by the viewer with two aspects: (1) *luminance*, which is the indication of the "brightness" of the light; (2) *chromaticity*, which is the property that distinguishes the composition of the light spectra.

Color Description: Various models are designed to quantify human color vision. The commonly used 1931 CIE color spaces are the first defined quantitative links between the physical pure colors (*i.e.*, wavelengths) in the electromagnetic visible spectrum and the physiological perceived colors in human color vision. It converts the spectral power distribution of light into the three tristimulus values X, Y, Z. Here Y determines the illuminance (brightness), and X and Z give chromaticity (hue) at that luminance. The chromaticity values can be presented in a CIE chromatic diagram as illustrated in Fig. 1, where coordinates are defined by $x = \frac{X}{X+Y+Z}$ and $y = \frac{Y}{X+Y+Z}$. The diagram represents all of the colors visible to the average person. In the rest of this paper, we use (x, y, Y) values to describe the chromaticity and illuminance of a specific color.

Spectral Color Additive Rule: The colors along any line-segment between two points can be made by mixing the colors at the end points, which is called the *chromatic additive rule*. Specifically, if we have two colored light C_1 and C_2 with values (x_1, y_1, Y_1) and (x_2, y_2, Y_2), and mix the two colors by shining them *simultaneously*, we obtain the mixed color (x, y, Y) denoted by

$$\begin{cases} (x,y) = \frac{Y_1}{Y_1+Y_2}(x_1,y_1) + \frac{Y_2}{Y_1+Y_2}(x_2,y_2) \\ Y = (Y_1+Y_2)/2 \end{cases} \quad (1)$$

The rule shows that, the chromaticity for the mixed color lies on the line segment joining the individual chromaticities, with the node position on the line segment depending on the *relative brightness* of the two colors being mixed. Clearly, the combination of colors to produce a given perceived color is not unique. For example, the pair C_1C_2, C_3C_4, C_5C_6 in Fig. 1 can each produce the same color C if combined in the right proportions.

Temporal Color Additive Perception: When people watch temporal varying colors, they receive both illuminance change and chromaticity change. When two isoluminant colors alternate at frequencies of $25Hz$ or higher, an observer typically perceives only one fused color, whose chromaticity is determined based on the chromatic additive rule previously discussed. This may also relate to *persistence of vision*, the theory where an afterimage is thought

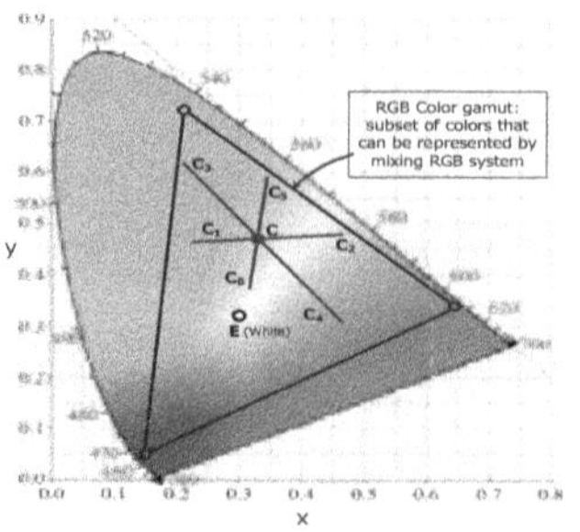

Figure 1: CIE 1931 chromatic diagram and color mixture.

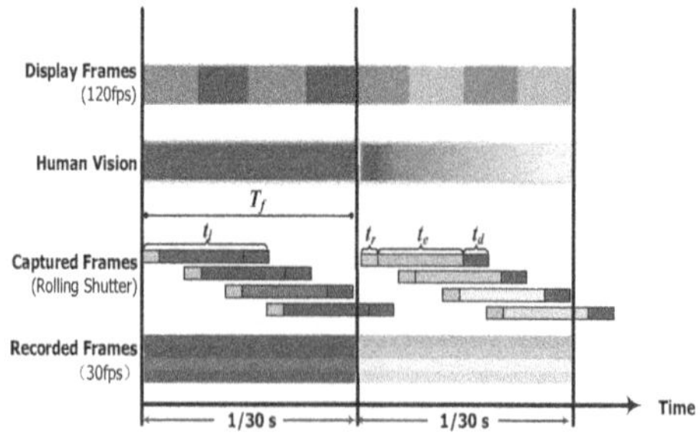

Figure 2: Color perception by human eyes and image capturing by CMOS cameras.

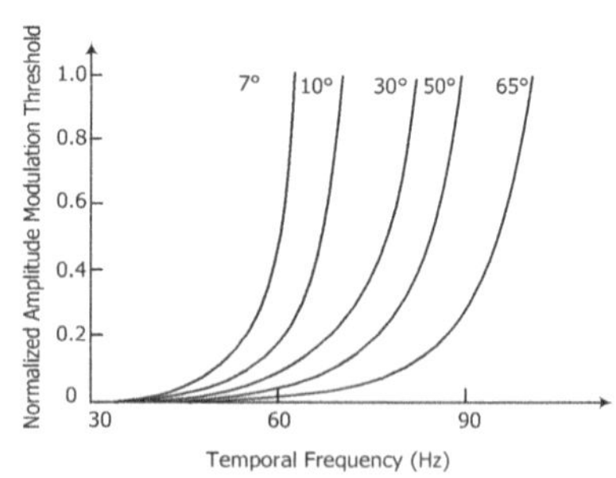

Figure 3: Flicker regression equation for different display field sizes.

to persist for approximately $\frac{1}{16}$ of a second on the retina, which is also believed to be the explanation for motion perception. Fig. 2 illustrates the color fusion result by the human eye. For example, people perceive alternate red and blue as magenta, and alternate red and green as yellow.

Flicker and Critical Flicker Frequency (CFF): Although, human's visual system is very efficient and powerful, its ability to interpret the temporal information presented on video displays is limited. When the change frequency is smaller than eye's *temporal resolution*, called *critical flicker frequency* (CFF), *flicker* happens [8, 25, 32]. Illuminance flicker is a visible illuminance fading between frames displayed on screen when the brightness drop for time intervals sufficiently long to be noticed by the human eye. Chromatic flicker is defined similarly. On the other hand, when the flicker frequency is larger than the CFF threshold, the illuminance flicker stimulus and chromatic flicker stimulus from a sequence of continuous frames are only perceived by human as time-averaged luminance and time-averaged wavelength respectively.

Typically, human eyes can only resolve up to $50Hz$ to *luminance flicker* and $25Hz$ to *chromatic flicker* [25]. Thus our eyes cannot capture fast moving objects and high frequency flickery images [45]. In practice CFF depends on both the spatial and temporal modulation of luminance across the display [18,43]. If the absolute amplitude of the main frequency of the display luminance modulation is greater than a pre-determined frequency-dependent threshold (denoted as $A(f)$) the observers will perceive flicker. Typically

$$A(f) = a \cdot e^{bf} \tag{2}$$

where f is the refresh frequency and a and b are constants that depend on the size of the luminous area. Fig.3 illustrates the equation for different display field sizes where the degree value measures the angle of the smallest cone apexed at eye to cover the display field. Then we have $CFF = \frac{\ln[A(f)/a]}{b}$.

2.2 Video Encoding and Display

Most screens produce a wide range of colors by stimulating the cones of eyes with varying amounts of three primary colors - red, green and blue. The most widely used display devices are LCD monitors and projectors. We cannot display the full range of human color perception with these devices, because the gamut of normal human vision covers the entire CIE diagram while the gamut of an RGB display can be represented as a triangular region within the CIE diagram, with three vertexes are red, green and blue (see Fig. 1).

Video is typically stored in compressed form to reduce the file size, and a number of video file formats were developed. In this work, we will consider a generic video stream consisting of sequential still images, referred to as *frames*. Each frame is a matrix of color pixels. During playing the video, the video stream is decoded and presented by the display system frame by frame. Displaying frames in high frequency (or called *refresh rate*) creates the illusion of moving images because of the phi phenomenon [19]. Modern off-the-shelf LCD monitors and projectors support $120Hz$ refresh rate, and the refresh rate for some game LCD monitors could reach $240Hz$. Since most films are shot in 24 or 30 frame per second, it is common that each original video frame will be repeated several times while being displayed on screen. In KALEIDO, instead of repeating each original video frame directly, we will carefully design these *displayed frames* by changing the color pixel such that the viewing experience of live audiences is not affected and it also prevents high-quality videotaping from third-party cameras.

2.3 Video Recording

When a video is displayed in screen, two communication channels will be investigated: *screen-eye* channel and *screen-camera* channel. The screen-eye channel represents how a human will perceive the displayed video, which has been discussed in Subsection 2.1. Here we will review some important specifics of screen-camera channel, which later we use to design our watch-only video.

Varying Recording Rate: Cameras sense color similarly as the human eye. Each pixel receives light of different wavelength during the exposure time, and fuses them to compute the illuminance and chromaticity values of this pixel. Onboard cameras now could capture high-resolution mega-pixel images at fast frame rate (called *record rate*), which even exceed the perception capability of retina. For example, the record rate of traditional onboard cameras is 24, 30 or $60fps$, while some of latest mobile smartphones, *e.g.*, iPhone 5, iPhone 6 and Samsung Note 4, support up to 120 and $240fps$ in high quality.

Rolling Shutter: CMOS image sensors have become mainstream in onboard cameras for mobile devices, which expose and readout each rows of pixels consecutively [38]. Most of consumer-grade cameras implement such image sensor due to its low energy cost, but this leads to geometric distortion of captured image, called *rolling-shutter effect*. We explain the rolling-shutter mechanism by a simple example as shown in Fig. 2. Assume that, before exposure, each line of a video frame requires duration of t_r second by the camera sensor for resetting the line to query the data. The sensor scans the scene line by line to synthesize the complete image, and for each line, the duration for the sensor exposed to the light is t_e before it takes t_d line scan acquisition time for the driver to dump the data. Then the total acquisition duration (denoted as t_l) for retrieving a line is

$$t_l = t_r + t_e + t_d. \tag{3}$$

Assume the recording rate of a camera is $30fps$, so that the duration for constructing a single frame is $1/30s$, denoted as T_c. Since each frame contains multiple batches of line scans with each line of duration t_l, which are exposed and dumped sequentially and overlapped in parallel, we define *effective light sampling frequency* as the number of lines being captured in one second. Although typical rolling-shutter camera captures an image at its reported frame rate $f_c = \frac{1}{T_c}$, its effective sampling frequency is $f_s = f_c \times n$, where n denotes the actual number of lines in individual images.

Unstable Inter-frame Interval: Generally, the shutter is required to open for a certain duration for sufficient light to complete a single frame, and cameras generate single frame continuously in pre-defined high frequency to record a video. The exposure duration depends on the sensitivity of sensor itself and the actual lighting condition, including the contrast and intensity. Most consumer-graded cameras adjust their frame rate automatically to ensure the frame visual quality for the whole captured video. According to the experiments conducted by [23], some off-the-shelf mobile devices cannot reach nominal frame rate when recording, and the inter-frame time intervals often fluctuate.

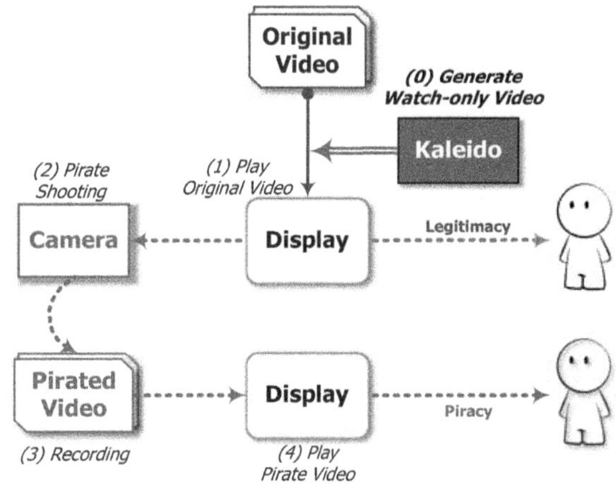

Figure 4: Original display v.s. pirated video display.

3. SYSTEM DESIGN

In this section, we will discuss the design space and principles of KALEIDO, the design challenges and opportunities for implementing KALEIDO, and finally the architecture and our detailed design of watch-only video for KALEIDO.

3.1 Design Space and Principles

We assume that an original video is produced with 24fps or 30fps video rate, and the video will be displayed in some screens with larger refresh rate, say $120fps$. Our goal is to protect the copyrighted video from undesired recording by commercial mobile devices with diversified recording rates, instead of prohibiting the display of the video using mobile devices. The pirate shooting is limited to those using commercial onboard cameras of mobile devices. The professional high-end film cameras are thus excluded. We aim at designing a more radical and effective method to generate a legitimate watch-only version of the videos from the original video. For each original video frame, we will generate a sequence of watch-only frames (precisely $\frac{\text{refresh rate}}{\text{video rate}}$ frames). The watch-only video can be displayed by any off-the-shelf display device. When the watch-only video is displayed normally, viewers will not notice any quality difference from the original one, *e.g.*, without color distortion, artifacts or flicker. But when watching the pirated version recorded by a camera, viewers will suffer a severe intolerable quality degradation.

Leveraging opportunities offered by the limited resolution of human vision system, rolling shutter of the camera and asynchronization between display and camera systems, we propose a system KALEIDO which takes the original video as input and produces a *watch-only* version. As shown in Fig. 4, KALEIDO is an add-on for the current video play system without extra hardware. The piracy procedure typically consists of four steps:

Step 1: the legitimate video is re-encoded and displayed;
Step 2: the pirate shoots the displayed video with a camera;
Step 3: the captured frames are recorded into a video file, which is the pirate version of the original one;
Step 4: the pirate video is displayed for the viewer.

The core of our solution is to re-encode the original video into a *watch-only* one, under the constraint that the viewer's watching experience should be reserved in Step 1; but after the Step 2 and Step 3, the watching experience degradation should be maximized in Step 4.

3.2 Design Challenges and Opportunities

Our basic approaches for causing a quality loss into the viewing experience of the pirated video are to introduce illuminance flicker and chromatic distortion into the re-encoded frames. The most challenging part of KALEIDO is to ensure the encoded flicker and distortion are imperceivable to the legitimate viewers at first, and then become perceivable after a piracy procedure.

To address these challenges, we will reinvestigate the disparity between the human vision system and the camera system. As shown in Fig. 2, the human eye receives light illuminance and chromatic perturbations in a continuous but low-pass manner, while camera captures light as a discontinuous sampling system with a higher temporal resolution. Taking the continuous frame stream as a varying light signal with specific spatial and temporal color distribution, we exploit the information loss and distortion by camera shooting to look for opportunities. Let the refresh rate of display be f_d and frame record rate of camera be f_c. Then the display duration for each frame is $T_d = \frac{1}{f_d}$ and recording window of a recorded frame is $T_c = 1/f_c$. We analyze the following two complementary cases.

Case 1: $f_d > f_c$. (Display rate is larger than record rate)

In this case, there are multiple frames displayed during a single capture time window T_c by the camera. Remember that the rolling shutter effect of camera causes a line's exposure time t_e be less than T_c. In practice t_e could be less than the half of T_c. Hence, for a specific line in the recorded frame, its exposure time is not enough to record the complete light signal during T_c. If the signal is time-invariant, the line doesn't lose any information. That's why we can record a traditional video ($30fps$) displayed on a $120Hz$ screen using a $30fps$ camera, since it repeats each frame four times. If the signal is time-varying (*i.e.*, re-encoded frames from a single original frame are different), then part of the variation cannot be recorded, *i.e.*, the temporal distribution of the recorded signal in the pirate video deviates from the original video frame. Because eye perceives time-averaging chromaticity and illuminance, the temporal variation loss could cause a perceivable distortion. Besides, different lines in the recorded pirate video lose different portions of the temporal variation, which could cause a spatial deformation of each recorded frame. Fig. 2 presents an example, where $f_d = 120Hz$

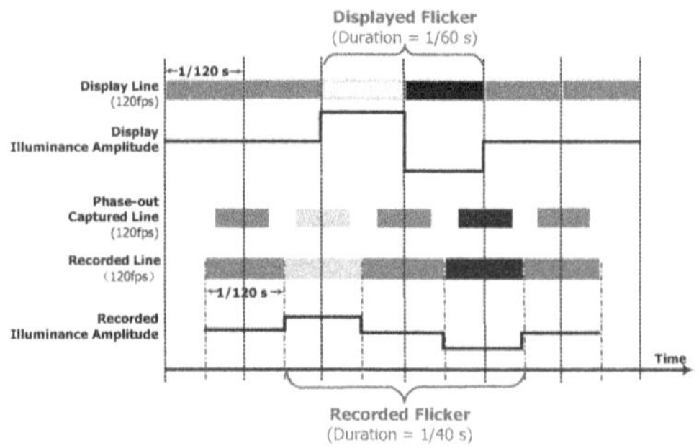

Figure 5: Flicker pollution due to out-phase camera sampling.

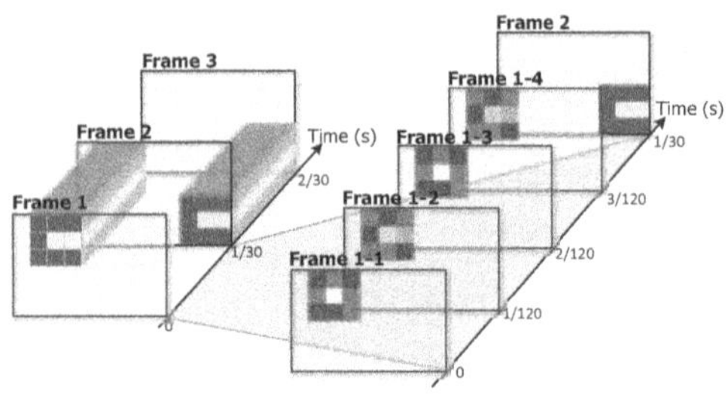

Figure 6: Color decomposition for display frames.

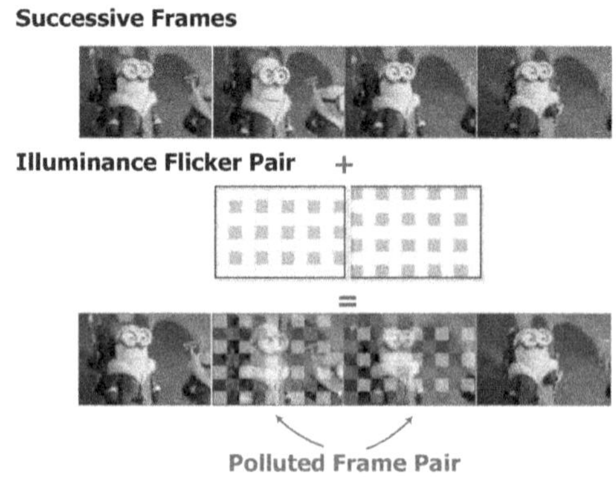

Figure 7: Illuminance frame pollution in display frames.

and $f_c = 30fps$. It is a common setting for commercial display devices and cameras. In this figure, two intervals defined by three vertical lines represent two original video frames. The first row represents four encoded display frames for each of the original video frame. During one capture time window, four frames display alternate colors in this case. The second row denotes the colors to be perceived by the human eye. The human vision perceives one color by fusing them equally. The third row denotes the video capture procedure by camera with rolling shutter effect, while the fourth row denotes the recorded two frames by the camera. Each line of the camera captures only part of the display frames, which results in distorted color fusion results for each line. And the recorded image presents a stripped pattern.

Case 2: $f_d \leq f_c$. (Display rate is less than record rate)

In this case, every displayed frame can be captured by at least one recorded frame. If the display system and camera system are ideally synchronized, then during the exposure time of any line of the recorded frame the light signal is constant (from a single display frame) and the camera can record the displayed light signal with high fidelity. In practical applications, with high probability, the camera is asynchronized with the display, which causes out-phase lines in each recorded frame. As illustrated in Fig. 5, one out-phase line captures light signal from two successive displayed frames. If there is a flicker (two successive darker and lighter frames, or vice versa) at a frequency $f_f = f_d/2$, the perturbation will be captured by $2\frac{f_c}{f_d} + 1$ temporal successive out-phase lines. As a result, the flicker is recorded but its frequency is down-converted to $\frac{2}{2+f_d/f_c} f_f$. In the example of Fig. 5, the flicker frequency is down-converted from 60Hz to 40Hz. With this observation, we have an opportunity to encode invisible noises, whose frequency is larger than CFF, to the original video. After the down-conversion by camera recording, the noise could become visible because its frequency now falls below the CFF.

Additionally, unstable inter-frame intervals of most commercial onboard cameras aggravate the information loss and distortion for both Case 1 and Case 2, hence making the color distortion of recorded frames even worse.

Consequently, during a single capture time window (T_c), rolling shutter effect and unstable intervals could cause a temporal information loss or deviation in the recorded frame if the displayed frames for each original video frame are time-varying. We then propose two techniques to aggravate the temporal information distortion.

Technique 1: Chromatic Frame Decomposition. Since most current videos are $24fps$ or $30fps$, with high refresh rate display devices (*e.g.*, $120Hz$) one video frame can be decomposed into n (*e.g.*, 4 or 5) successive display frames following the temporal chromatic additive rule of human eyes. We propose to decompose one invariant chromatic signal into chromatic flickers, which can be fused by human eye. Fig. 6 shows an example of the color frame decomposition. The chromatic flicker frequency is 60, which is larger than the chromatic CFF. Note that our design is different from the visual cryptography [33], based on the visual effect produced by overlapping multiple transparent slides.

Technique 2: Illuminance Frame Pollution. When there is illuminance fluctuation, human eye works as a low pass filter to eliminate the high-frequency flicker and perceives the averaging illuminance. We propose to add imperceivable illuminance flickers to pollute the frames. As illustrated in Fig. 7, each flicker is a pair of pollution frames. The time averaging illuminance of each pixel from two pollution frames equals 0, which cancels out illuminance change for human eye. But if there is a temporal information distortion in the recorded frames, the flicker cannot be balanced out. Besides, the flicker's frequency is just above the illuminance CFF and its amplitude will be maximized. So if any down-conversion happens, the flicker will become perceivable.

Technique 3: Embrace Spatial Deformation. In company with temporal distortion achieved by chromatic frame decomposition and illuminance pollution, we also design KALEIDO to deform each decomposed frame's shape to prevent image capturing during the video play. Our goal is to make display frames' colors appear as random as possible. Randomizing each display frame's color, while preserving the view experience of legitimate audiences, is possible due to the metamerism. Note that a color can be decomposed to an infinite number of different color pairs. Randomizing different decomposition color pairs will make each display frame like a random noise.

3.3 Kaleido: Watch-Only Video Generation

We are now ready to present KALEIDO by exploiting the main techniques (chromatic frame decomposition, illuminance frame pollution, and spatial deformation) and integrating them to generate watch-only videos.

For simplicity, we consider a $30fps$ video, which consists of N sequential frames $\{V^1, V^2, \cdots, V^N\}$. Each frame V^k is a $R \times C$ matrix, with each pixel's P_{ij}^k color is $C_{ij}^k = (x_{ij}^k, y_{ij}^k, Y_{ij}^k)$. Recall that, (x, y) determines the pixel's chromaticity, *i.e.* coordinates in the CIE diagram, and Y is the illuminance level. In KALEIDO, we focus on an off-the-shelf display device. As a running example to demonstrate our design, we assume that the refresh rate of the display device is $120Hz$. Our scheme can easily be modified to adapt to different refresh rates. We decompose each original frame V^k into 4 display frames (called *sub-frames*) $\{V^{k,1}, V^{k,2}, V^{k,3}, V^{k,4}\}$. Note that all sub-frames have the same duration $1/120s$. To guarantee the flicker frequency greater than CFF and the sub-frames can be fused by human eye, we decompose each frame into two different sub-frames, referred to as fusion pair, and repeat the fusion pair. We then need to determine the $(x_{ij}^{k,l}, y_{ij}^{k,l}, Y_{ij}^{k,l})$ values of each pixel $P_{ij}^{k,l}$ in sub-frames. For $24fps$ video, it can be easily converted to $30fps$ using standard pulldown tools, or each frame can be decomposed to 5 frames, which makes the decomposition more complex, but the principle and techniques are the same.

According to the chromatic additive rule and flicker fusion rule, given the color of a pixel $C = (x, y, Y)$, we need to decompose it to two colors $C_1 = (x_1, y_1, Y_1)$ and $C_2 = (x_2, y_2, Y_2)$, which satisfies

$$\begin{cases} (x, y) & = \alpha(x_1, y_1) + (1-\alpha)(x_2, y_2) \\ Y & = (Y_1 + Y_2)/2, \end{cases} \tag{4}$$

where $\alpha = \frac{Y_1}{Y_1+Y_2}$. Since the mixed chromaticity (x, y) is a weighted average depending on the relative illuminance of the decomposed two colors, we should determine the illuminance of each pixel first. So, based on the pixel illuminance of the original video, KALEIDO firstly determines the illuminance pollution of the sub-frame sequence, which gives the final illuminance level (*i.e.*, Y values) of every pixel. Then the illuminance ratio α is fixed. Secondly, (x_1, y_2) and (x_2, y_2) are selected to (approximately) maximize the temporal distortion and spatial deformation.

3.3.1 Illuminance Frame Pollution

Let the initial illuminance levels of every pixel in sub-frames equal to the illuminance in its original frame, say Y_{ij}^k. Given two successive sub-frames $\{V^{k,1}, V^{k,2}\}$, a pixel pair $P_{ij}^{k,1}$ and $P_{ij}^{k,2}$ have illuminance levels $Y_{ij}^{k,1} = Y_{ij}^{k,2} = Y_{ij}^k$. If we can add an illuminance complementary perturbation $(+\delta, -\delta)$ to the pixel pair, it changes their illuminance levels to $Y_{ij}^{k,1} + \delta$ and $Y_{ij}^{k,2} - \delta$. Then the human eye perceives an average illuminance Y_{ij}^k, which equals the original illuminance level if the refresh frequency is above the CFF. In this way, the added complementary perturbation is imperceivable. However, when there is a temporal information loss (as in Case 1), the perturbation cannot be canceled out; when outphase captures happen (as in Case 2), the perturbation's frequency is down-converted. In those situations, the perturbation becomes perceivable flicker to human.

Based on this rule, we can add imperceivable flicker (either $(+\delta, -\delta)$ or $(-\delta, +\delta)$) to pixel blocks of two successive sub-frames to pollute the displayed video. The values of the amplitude δ and block size should be maximized to aggravate the pollution. Remember that the CFF increases as greater amplitude and larger block size, which could cause the flicker perceivable once CFF $> 60Hz$. For example, the CFF is about $90Hz$ when the block size, together with a viewing distance, resulting a $65°$ angle of view and the normalized amplitude is greater than 0.4 (Fig. 3). So our pollution mechanism chooses the desired CFF as between 50-$55Hz$. Then when the recorded video converts the $60Hz$ flicker down to a lower frequency, *e.g.*, $40Hz$, it will be below the CFF. To obtain a larger space for amplitude modulation, we design the block size as about $10°$ with respect to that human's vertical field of view at about $120°$. Hence, based on Fig. 3, the normalized amplitude of the flicker could be as large as 0.2. For each original frame, we add the block-pattern flicker pair to its second and third sub-frames. Fig. 7 shows an example of illuminance pollution.

3.3.2 Chromatic Frame Decomposition

After the illuminance frame pollution, the illuminance of each pixel in the sub-frames is determined. For a fusion pair, any pair of corresponding pixels have an infinite number of chromaticity combinations to achieve the desired mix color. We propose to choose a set of combinations that will (approximately) maximize the potential color distortion and spatial deformation.

Given a pixel pair P_1 with $C_1 = (x_1, y_1, Y_1)$ and P_2 with $C_2 = (x_2, y_2, Y_2)$ from a fusion pair, to maximize the recorded color distortion, we need to find out the relation between the distortion and the choice of (x_1, y_1) and (x_2, y_2). The correctly fused color is C with coordinate $(x, y) = \alpha(x_1, y_1) + (1-\alpha)(x_2, y_2)$, here $\frac{Y_1}{Y_2} = \frac{\alpha}{1-\alpha}$. Recall that color distortion happens when the camera fails to capture the complete light signal, which causes the recorded illuminance ratio of P_1 and P_2 deviates from the correct ratio. Let the recorded ratio be $\frac{Y_1'}{Y_2'} = \frac{\beta}{1-\beta}$, then we have $\alpha \neq \beta$. The distorted color is C' with $(x', y') = \beta(x_1, y_1) + (1-\beta)(x_2, y_2)$. Then the color distortion is

$$D_c(C, C') = |\alpha - \beta| D_c(C_1, C_2).$$

Here α is determined by the original video and the illuminance pollution, while β is determined by the camera's parameters. This shows that, larger $D_c(C_1, C_2)$ can lead to severe potential color distortion. As a result, when we choose two decomposed colors, we need to maximize the distance between them. Note that, the distance is bound by the range of the RGB triangle in the CIE diagram (as shown in Fig. 1). Three vertexes of the RGB triangle are $R = (0.64, 0.33)$, $G = (0.177, 0.712)$ and $B = (0.15, 0.06)$.

Given the color of the original pixel with color $C = (x, y, Y)$, Y_1 and Y_2 of the decomposed pixels's colors C_1 and C_2 are predetermined. Then determination of (x_1, y_1) and (x_2, y_2) is an optimization problem:

$$\max D_c(C_1, C_2) \quad \text{such that} \tag{5}$$
$$\begin{cases} \frac{D_c(C_1, C)}{D_c(C_2, C)} = \frac{Y_2}{Y_2} \\ \text{both } C_1 \text{ and } C_2 \text{ are within the RGB triangle.} \end{cases}$$

We notice that, the optimal solution must have at least one decomposed color lying on the edge of the RGB triangle. We then propose an algorithm to achieve the optimum with constant time complexity. Our algorithm works as follows. We first divide the RGB triangle into six regions as illustrated in the left figure in Fig.8(a). Then we start to search the local optimum within each region. Within a single region, we find that the optimization objective $D_c(C_1, C)$ changes monotonically (as illustrated in the right figure in Fig.8(a)). Leveraging the monotonicity, one can simply find the optimum in each region using constant computation. We get at most six local optimal solutions. In some regions, there could be no solution. Finally, comparing those six solutions gives us the optimal solution. There is a special case that, three primary colors

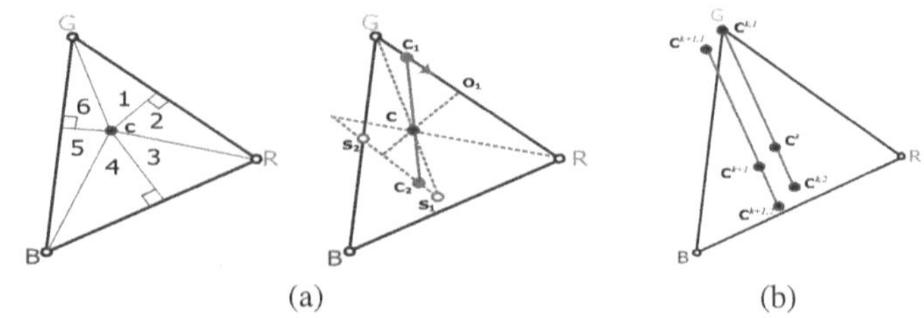

(a) (b)

Figure 8: (a) Color space division and solution search, (b) reducing successive pixel decomposition cost.

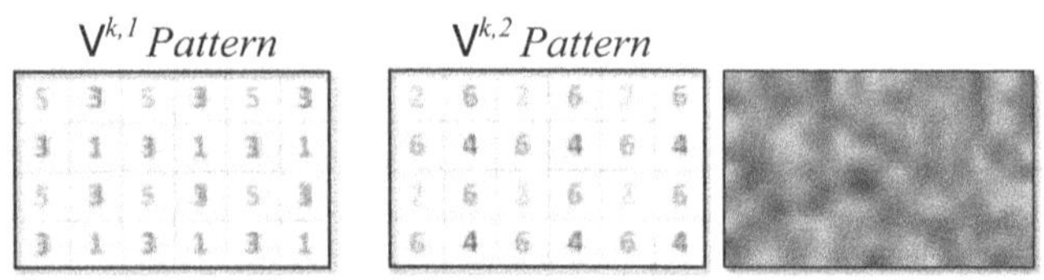

(a) Patterned Color Selection (b) Mixture

Figure 9: Spatial deformation.

(red, green and blue) cannot be decomposed. So the primary color remains the same in sub-frames.

3.3.3 Maximize Spatial Deformation

When determining the decomposed color pair, it is difficult to achieve the tradeoff between maximization of color distortion and spatial deformation. Notice that, unlike visual cryptography, we cannot pick an arbitrary sub-frame and then compute the other sub-frame accordingly s.t. the perceived visual effect is exactly same as the original frame, because the constraints on color additive rule. We propose several simple light-weight methods for achieving a good balance between temporal and spatial quality degradation.

Patterned Color Selection: This is based on the 6 regions divided in Fig. 8, We divide each sub-frame into small grids of certain fixed size. The grid division can be consistent with the illuminance pollution. For one sub-frame of a fusion pair, we assign each grid a region following the left pattern presented in Fig. 9. If a pixel with color C is in a grid labeled Region q, then the decomposed color C_1 will only be searched within the Region q. Thus, the whole sub-frame will have the assigned pattern despite the original shape. The other sub-frame of this fusion pair will use the right pattern in Fig. 9(a) for finding the corresponding color to produce the original color. Fig. 10(b) and (c) illustrate two sub-frames produced for an original frame in Fig. 10(a).

Random Color Selection: For each pixel, we first select a random color, and then compute the corresponding pixel's color in the complement frame. As shown in Fig. 10, although intuitively it will produce a pair of random sub-frames, the actual produced sub-frames still contains a rich shape information. The reason is that the similar color in adjacent pixels may result in similar optimal solution in each region. Fig. 10(d) and (e) show two sub-frames produced.

Mixture of Random and Smoothing: The third method is to use a combination of random choice for each pixel and smoothing among adjacent pixels. First, for each pixel with color C, we randomly select a color C_1 till that there is another color C_2 such that C is produced using color additive rule with C_1 and C_2. Then for each pixel $P^k_{i,j}$, the color of the pixel $P^{k,1}_{i,j}$ in the first sub-frame is an average of the neighboring pixels in this sub-frame. Fig. 9(b) shows an example of chromatic deformation map for the mixture based method. Fig. 10(f) and (g) show two sub-frames produced.

Fig. 10 illustrates the original frame, and a pair of sub-frames produced by these different methods. Note that such randomization and mixture can effectively remove the spatial information in the original frame with different tradeoffs between the viewing experience and anti-piracy ability.

3.3.4 Reducing the Encoding Cost

The computational overhead for decomposing the frames of original video into two successive sub-frames pixel by pixel cannot be neglected, especially for high-definition video with 1920×1080 spatial resolution. Leveraging the inherent property of the video, we improve the method to reduce the decoding overhead. Given a normal $30fps$ video, the color for the pixel P_{ij} in both k and $k+1$ frame are $C^k_{ij} = (x^k_{ij}, y^k_{ij}, Y^k_{ij})$ and $C^{k+1}_{ij} = (x^{k+1}_{ij}, y^{k+1}_{ij}, Y^{k+1}_{ij})$ respectively. Thus the color difference,

$$D_c(C^k_{ij}, C^{k+1}_{ij}) = \sqrt{(x^k_{ij} - x^{k+1}_{ij})^2 + (y^k_{ij} - y^{k+1}_{ij})^2},$$

between the same pixel in two successive original video frames could be considered as the chromatic distance in the color space. To reduce the computational overhead, we define ϵ as the threshold of the color difference, and if the difference is less than ϵ the pixel color in the two sub-frame could be calculated directly from the previous one without conducting the color distortion maximization repeatedly.

We use a two stage method of complementary color pair determination as illustrated in Fig. 8(b): (1) we draw a parallel line segment to the line segment $C^{k,1}_{ij}C^{k,2}_{ij}$ in the previous frame. (2) the illuminance of pixels in the sub-frames are determined after the illuminance frame pollution. Then we shrink the length of the parallel line segment align with the illuminance ratio so that the adjusted line segment is within the RGB triangle, and determine the coordinate of both $(x^{k+1,1}_{ij}, y^{k+1,1}_{ij})$ and $(x^{k+1,2}_{ij}, y^{k+1,2}_{ij})$ with maximized line segment distance between $C^{k+1,1}_{ij}$ and $C^{k+1,2}_{ij}$.

4. EVALUATION

We now evaluate the performance of KALEIDO via experiments. The prototype of KALEIDO is implemented in C++ with OpenCV library. KALEIDO re-encodes the original video stream into high frame rate video stream, and displays it through regular LCD monitors or projectors. We then evaluate the video quality of both watch-only video and pirate video respectively. We generate the watch-only video through the basic methods mentioned in the previous section, and compare the corresponding pirate video captured by multiple cameras with original video clips to determine whether the content of the original video is protected through some standard video quality assessment metrics. As such objective video quality metrics may not directly reflect the subjective viewing experience by human eyes, we also combine both objective and subjective experiments to measure the effectiveness of the pirate video recording prevention.

4.1 Experiment Settings

In our evaluation, we use both LCD monitor and projector as the main display. The 27' LCD monitor (AOC G2770PQU) supports 1920×1080 spatial resolution and up to 144Hz refresh rate, while Acer $D600$ projector supports 1280×720 spatial resolution with 120fps frame rate. During the evaluation, we set the frame rate for both two display devices as 120fps. We simulate the working scenarios of both movie and presentation, and verify whether the

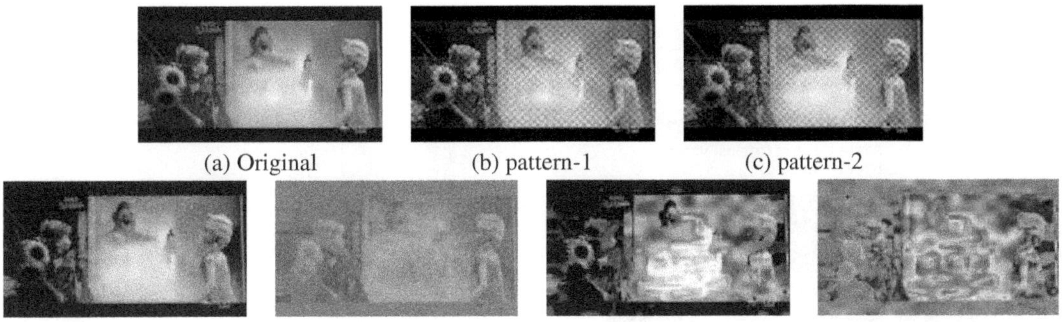

(a) Original (b) pattern-1 (c) pattern-2

(d) random-1 (e) random-2 (f) mixed-1 (g) mixed-2

Figure 10: Encoding the subframes for deforming and hiding the spatial information in the frame.

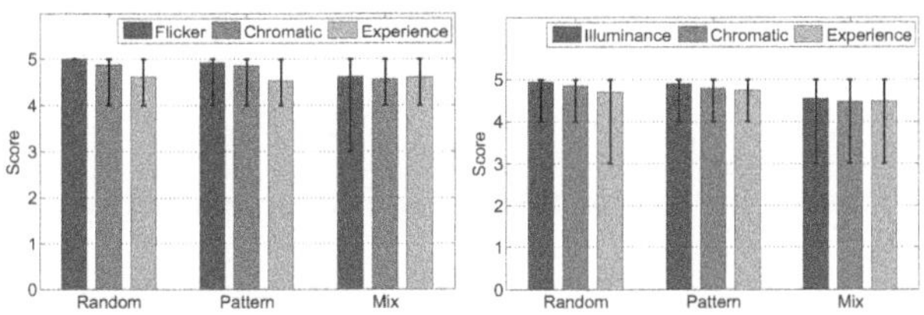

(a) LCD Monitor (b) Projector

Figure 11: Average subjective score.

viewing quality of watch-only video escapes from degradation. On the camcorder side, we use 5 different smartphones (iPhone 5s, iPhone 6, Samsung Note3, Note4 Edge, HTC M8) to capture and record the video projected on the screen.

We also employ a various of video source to examine whether our system could be widely applicable. We select twenty different high-definition (1280×720) video clips with different characteristics on brightness, contrast, and motion. The content of videos are ranged from drama, sports, landscape to animation.

The subjective perception quality of is conducted through users' study. We invite 50 volunteers in aging from 20 to 40 with 31 males and 19 females. All the volunteers have regular visual sensitivity, and one of them is graphic designer with great sensitivity to the video quality.

4.2 Watch-Only Video Quality Assessment

We first evaluate the video quality of the displayed watch-only video. As the original video is re-encoded before displaying, and the content in each frame in the watch-only video is irregular and random, it is difficult to evaluate the quality of the watch-only video objectively by existing standard quality assessment metrics. Thus, we only evaluate its quality by subjective watching experience of volunteers.

In the evaluation, we display both the original video and the watch-only video side by side in two identical display system, and ask them to rate the video quality of the watch-only video by comparing with the original one in three aspects respectively: illuminance level, chromatic correctness, and overall watching experience. Similar to [45], we use score 5 to 1 for each aspect, where 5 indicates the highest quality without any differences in illuminance, chromaticity and the video quality is satisfying; 4 represents the difference being "almost unnoticeable", and 3 to 1 denote "merely noticeable", "evident noticeable", and "strong noticeable or artifact". Since the format of all the selected video clips are high-definition, only scores above 4 indicate the acceptable video quality. We collect the watching experience feedback from all volunteers, and plot the average score in Fig. 11. All the watch-only videos show great smoothness in both projector and LCD monitor, where no jitter is noticed by the audiences. The main subjective difference come from flickers brought by both the illuminance change and the chromatic distortion, which also results in the spacial deformation. The encoding method with random choice of pixel colors provides the best view quality, where the average scores for the first two metrics are both greater than 4.9. 96% volunteers did not even notice they are watch-only video clips. The encoding method with pattern follows with slight drop in performance, because the illuminance and chromatic flicker blocks have larger size than pixels. 92% volunteers did not distinguish them. The encoding method with mixed techniques disturb the original frames mostly, where audiences may experience distortion of both chromaticity and illuminance. Although 38% volunteers noticed that those video clips are re-encoded, but the degradation is acceptable and the average score is above 4.

We also consider other parameters affecting the watching experience, including display devices, different light conditions and different video types. As shown in Fig. 11, LCD monitors have a slightly better performance than projectors, possibly because the projector has a larger display area, which makes illuminance and chromatic flicker easily noticable. Moreover, light condition and video type do not cause significant differences of watching experience.

4.3 Pirated Video Quality Assessment

We then evaluate the performance of our KALEIDO prototype in dealing with piracy camcorder by comparing the pirate video first with the original video clips to present the quality degradation of the pirate watch-only video. However, it is still not easy to determine whether the large amount of quality degradation results from the recording process or the success of frame decomposition. Since multiple factors will lead to quality degradation, and the standard metrics for video quality assessment do not have strong linear correlation to the actual watching experience, it is difficult to compare the definite video quality based on the metric results only. Essentially, the content of the pirate video from regular video is easy to recognize, especially when the recording devices are increasingly powerful. Here we also compare the quality of pirated watch-only video to the pirated video from the original video.

Five smartphones are used to record pirate video, where the capturing rate is $1080p$ in $30fps$ or $60fps$ and $720p$ in $120fps$. The extensive evaluation is conducted in an indoor office with two different light conditions: *nature light condition* representing the p-

Figure 12: The snapshot of pirate videos with different capturing scenarios.

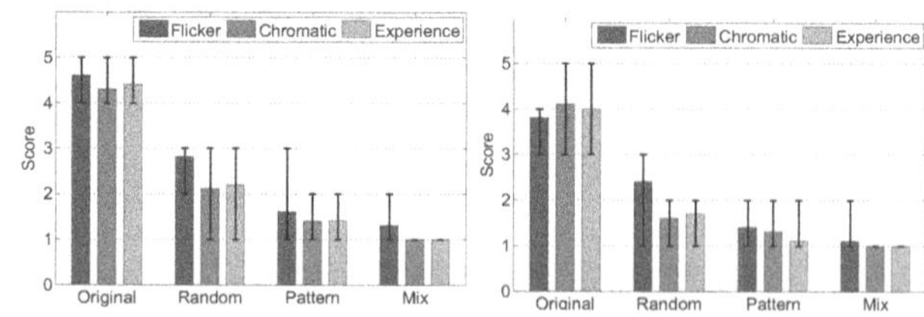

(a) LCD Monitor (b) Projector

Figure 13: Subjective view experiences: pirate original video, pirate watch-only video with various techniques.

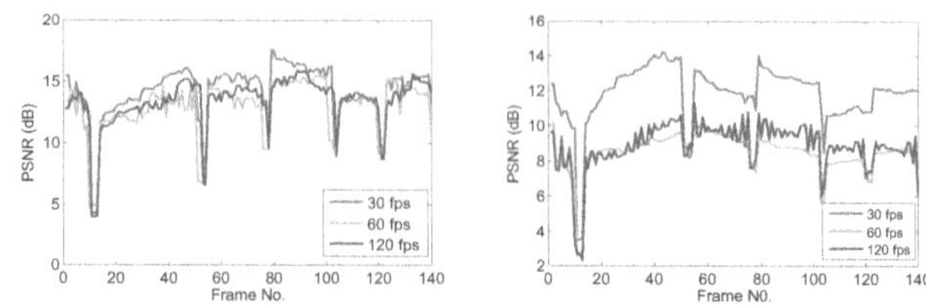

(a) LCD Monitor (b) Projector

Figure 14: PSNR in different recording frame rates.

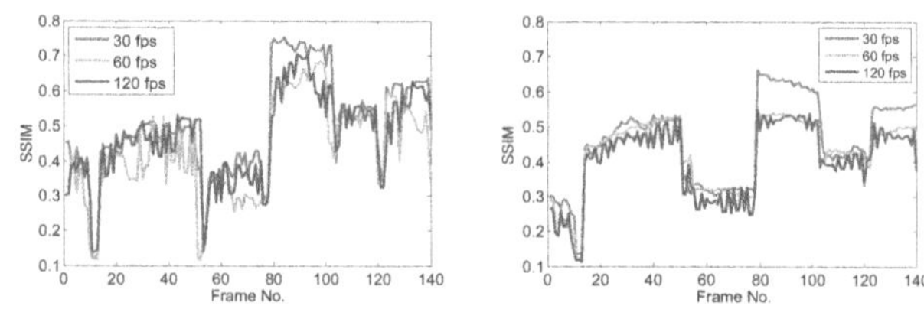

(a) LCD Monitor (b) Projector

Figure 15: SSIM in different recording frame rates.

resentation scenarios and *dark condition* indicating the theater scenarios. The quality of the pirate video will be evaluated both subjectively by watching experience and objectively by standard metrics.

4.3.1 Subjective Viewing Experience

Several facts could affect the pirate video quality, including display device (LCD or projection), camera capture frame rate and light condition. Fig. 12 illustrates the comparison of pirate videos captured using different display devices or fps, where the top-left image is the snapshot of the original video frame. If the pirate video is recorded from the playing of original video, it could still reveal most significant detail of the image, as shown in top-right. When recorded from watch-only video, the content of the frames is difficult to recognize compared with from the original video. For example, the middle two frames come from the watch-only video played in LCD and the last two are displayed by projector. We notice that the pirate video quality degrades with increasing fps, because the flicker frequency down-conversion (as analyzed in Case2 of Section. 3) and more unstable frame interval. Different display devices and light conditions do not cause any significant difference of watching experience. One thing we should keep in mind is that although some of the frames still could be perceived by human eyes, when a sequential of such distorted image frames are played in a regular frame rate, the viewers' viewing experience is significantly affected when playing the pirate video recorded from the watch-only video. Thus, we pay more attention to the overall video quality degradation.

In the subjective assessment, we consider the content of the pirated video, compared to both original video clips and pirated original video clips. We display the original video, pirated video of original video and pirate video of watch-only video side by side in three identical display systems. The rating score for the pirated video is still from 1 to 5 as in previous evaluation. Fig. 13 illustrates the rating for all pirated video clips captured using different display devices (LCD monitor and projector) respectively. The score for pirated original video is about 4, which indicates acceptable quality. Both our watch-only video effectively reduces the quality of the pirate video from the watch-only video in all tested scenarios. 96% volunteers claim the quality degradation is intolerable, and the average rating score is below 2.

4.3.2 Objective Measurement

We use five different standard metrics to measure the quality of the pirated video, including PSNR, SSIM, CD, and Histogram. For objective measurement, we setup the evaluation scenario to the finest where the video is being displayed in the screen with largest brightness and the camera is directly facing the screen so that the whole screen could be captured without trapezoid. The usual pirate videotaping scenario would be worse than this ideal testing scenario. Thus, if the quality of the pirate video in this ideal scenario is intolerable, the pirate video taken in worse conditions will experience more severe quality degradation. Due to the disparity between the frame rate of the original video ($30fps$) and the pirate video, we duplicate the frame of original video to align each frame to the captured frames in the pirate video.

PSNR (Peak-Signal-to-Noise-Ratio) is one of the most basic video quality assessment metrics to measure the quality of lossy video compression so as to provide an approximation to human perception of re-encoded video quality. Fig. 14 plots the real-time PSNR for a random selected video clip in different shooting frame rates. The PSNR usually has a value ranging form 30 to 50dB for medium to high quality video [46]. However, the PSNR values fluctuate in a wide range for all pirate video frames, and the values are always below 18dB, indicating a significant quality degradation.

SSIM [47] is proposed as a method to calculate the similarity between two images. The SSIM gets the best value of 1 for two

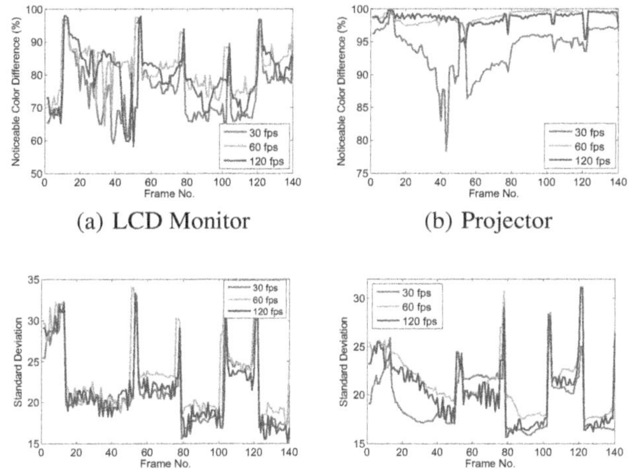

(a) LCD Monitor (b) Projector

(c) LCD Monitor (d) Projector

Figure 16: Color difference in different recording frame rates (proportion and standard deviation).

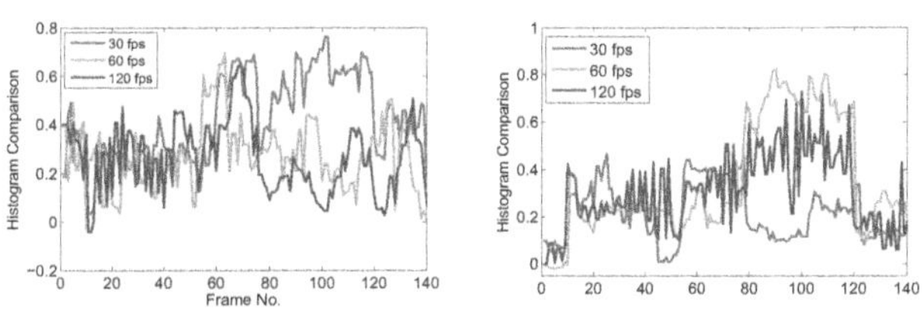

(a) LCD Monitor (b) Projector

Figure 17: Histogram in different recording frame rates.

identical images, and with the quality decrease, the value of SSIM drops accordingly. The value drops below 0.7 when the image contain large distortion, and the content is difficult to recognized clearly [47]. Our evaluation (Fig. 15) shows that the videos have strong structure distortion when captured by camcorder in three different frame rates from 30fps to 120fps. The average SSIM for LCD are 0.4615, 0.4305 and 0.4070 respectively and 0.5053, 0.4339 and 0.4717 for the projector.

Color Difference (CD, or Chromatic Aberrations CA) is another reliable metric to verify the quality of captured video stream, which usually is generated from a failure of lens to focus all colors to the convergence point. Recording a pirate video will definitely generate color difference, and the value of the color difference determines the amplitude of the color distortion. In this case, we adopt ICEDE2000 [31] to calculate the color difference between the pirate video frame and original video frame on each pixel. When the value of ICEDE2000 exceeds 6, the color difference could be noticed clearly. As the amplitude of color difference usually has nonuniform distribution on the frame, it is ineffective to measure the average color distortion. Instead we calculate the proportion of pixels in each frame that has color difference larger than 6, and compute the variance for those pixels. Based on our evaluation (Fig. 16), such proportion is beyond 70% for most of the video frames and the standard deviation for the color difference is over 21.

We also compare the color histogram of the pirate video to the original video, and plot the correlation for different frame rates in two display systems. As shown in Fig. 17, the value of histogram has no obvious correlation to the frame rate, and all the video shows moderate correlation.

We then evaluate the performance of quality degradation in different decomposition methods (pattern based, random, and mixed) (see Fig. 18). Clearly, all our methods distort the color of original frames, which leads to significant quality degradation in all videos.

We extend our comparison of the video quality degradation in two difference light conditions. The watch-only video is displayed by projector, which is used to simulate the theater and presentation scenarios, and we record the video by two most popular mobile phones in two frame rates. As the results shown in Fig. 19, the pirate video contains similar quality degradation in both environments, and when the camcorder captures the video in lower frame rate, the amplitude of quality degradation is lower than high frame rate.

The purpose of the previous experiments is to present the quality degradation of the pirate watch-only video, comparing the original video clips. We now evaluate the same metrics of pirated watch-only video compared with pirated original video (video recorded from playing the original video). As shown in Fig. 20, our results indicate that the pirate watch-only video also has severe quality degradation compared to the pirate original video of non-modified version. Since the pirate original video has already given viewers a unpleasant watching experience, the pirate watch-only video has a much worse quality.

Summary: KALEIDO re-encodes the original video into a watch-only one. The subjective assessment shows that the watch-only video can preserve the viewer's watching experience satisfactorily. And both the subjective and objective evaluation results indicate that the quality of the pirate video from watch-only video is severely degraded in all cases (different combinations of display device, camera fps, video type and light condition) compared to both original video and pirated original video. There is still a room for audience experience optimization, and we will improve it in our future work.

5. DISCUSSION AND OPEN ISSUES

KALEIDO is a first step towards solving piracy problem by generating watch-only videos. While our evaluations demonstrate that KALEIDO is promising, there are some limitations and open problems as discussed below.

System Applicability: In our system design, we leverage the rolling shutter effect to achieve watch-only video against mobile devices. Thus our method may not be working well when facing high-end cameras with global shutter. But, our mechanism could prevent most piracy events caused by current consumer cameras, which is the main focus of this work. On one hand, pirate video captured by personal mobile devices cause great loss to movie industry and severe infringement of copyright. It is easy to prevent high-end professional camcorder from cinema or lecture hall, but it's difficult to forbid attendees to bring personal mobile phones. In MPAA's latest attempt to crack down on piracy, it is pressuring movie theaters to adopt a ban on mobile phones with cameras and certain kinds of eyeglasses, which causes great concern on the security of personal phones and degrades the experience of audiences. On the other hand, the rolling shutter camera dominates the consumer camera market. According to Grand View Research's report about image sensor market [3], by 2013 CMOS image sensors takes 83.8% market share, while CCD image sensors takes only 16.2%. By 2015, CMOS shipments will amount to 3.6 billion units or 97 percent market share, compared to CCD shipments of just 95.2 million, or 3 percent [1]. The majority of CMOS sensors

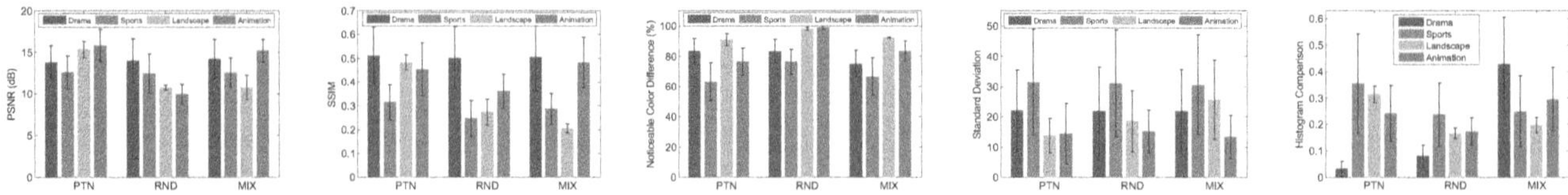

(a) PSNR (b) SSIM (c) CD Proportion (d) CD Std. Dev. (e) Histogram

Figure 18: The quality evaluation for different decomposition methods.

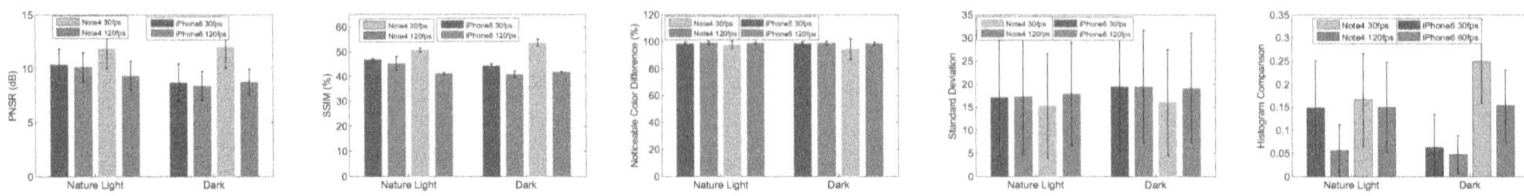

(a) PSNR (b) SSIM (c) CD Proportion (d) CD Std. Dev. (e) Histogram

Figure 19: The video quality assessment in two light conditions.

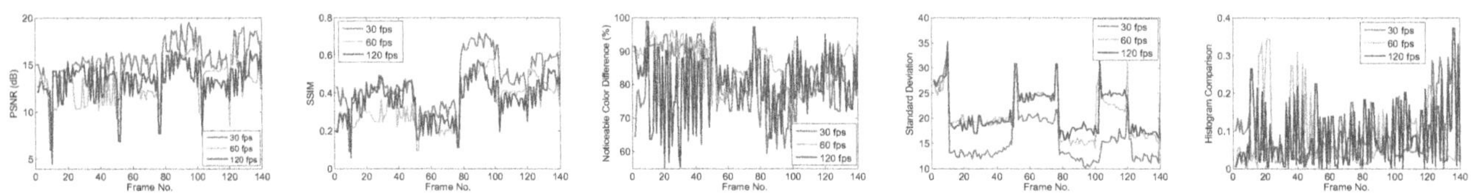

(a) PSNR (b) SSIM (c) CD Proportion (d) CD Std. Dev. (e) Histogram

Figure 20: Comparing pirate video for both original and watch-only.

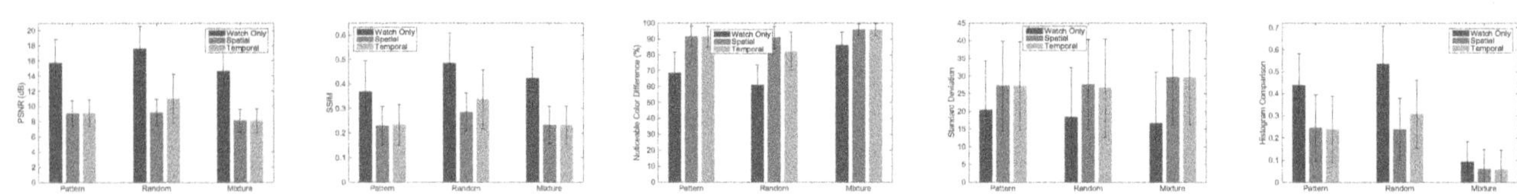

(a) PSNR (b) SSIM (c) CD Proportion (d) CD Std. Dev. (e) Histogram

Figure 21: The video quality comparison after noise removal

found in the consumer market utilize a rolling shutter, while only few expensive high-end CMOS sensor can support global shutter, as the global shutter is hard to accomplish in current CMOS designs. We will explore the solution against high-end cameras in our future work.

Post Processing: Since KALEIDO re-encodes the common video into a watch-only one, one of possible attack to our approach is to remove the noise in the video through post processing. Generally, video denoising methods have two different categories: spatial and temporal. Non-local means are the most common spatial video denoising method, which removes the noise at a pixel through certain operations with neighbors within single video frame, such as gaussian weighted average. Although temporal approaches will reduce the noise between frames through tracking blocks along trajectories defined by motion vector and removing the noise of a pixel by taking a number of same pixels from different frames, it is still not suit our watch-only video. In our method we decompose each frame by chromaticity and illuminance in a random manner, and pollute frame temporally and deform frames spatially. As we have described in Section 3.2 due to the rolling shutter effect and unstable inter-frame intervals, there are information loss and distortion in the recorded frames rather than simple Gaussian white noise, and our techniques maximize such loss and distortion. Therefore, it is still difficult to restore original pixels using incomplete and distorted information. To better present that our method is resistent to existing noise removal techniques, we conduct the attack through two mainstream video denoising method: spatial [13] and temporal [12] noise cancelation process, and plot the results in Fig. 21. In this experiment, we compared all the processed videos to the pirate video of original video with standard metrics as before, and we also put the video quality metrics of the watch-only video as comparison. Obviously, the common post denoising process not only cannot recover the original video, but also deteriorate the video quality compared to the watch-only version in all five basic metrics due to recognizing noise incorrectly. Therefore, KALEIDO is insusceptible to common denoising attack, and guarantees the reliable video privacy preservation.

System Overhead: KALEIDO does not generate watch-only video while playing it, but converts the video off-line and loads processed frames to GPU buffer for playing to optimize the watch experience. We evaluate the computation cost for video conversion using a commercial computer with Intel i7-4790 3.6GHZ CPU and

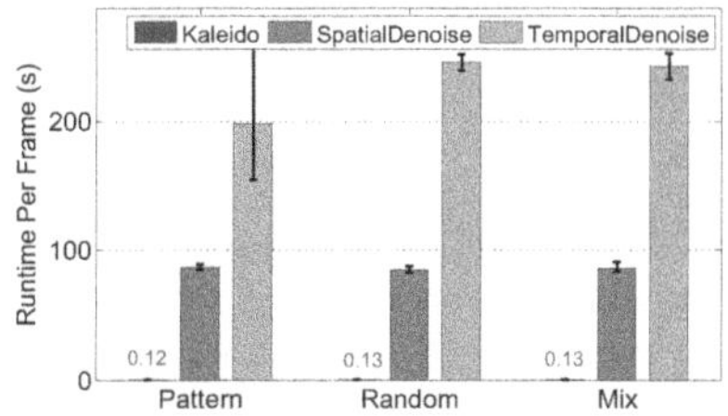

Figure 22: Processing runtime of one video frame for generating watch-only video and denoising. It takes 0.12s for KALEIDO to process one frame.

8G RAM. For software, we employ matrix operations provided OpenCV to achieve optimal performance. As presented in Fig. 22, it takes 0.12s in average to process one 1280×720 video frame, *i.e.*, the process speed is about $8.3fps$. Compared to generating watch-only video, denoising is orders of magnitude slower. Two mainstream video denoising methods cost about 85s and 200s to process one frame separately. For the storage cost, since our method increase the frame rate from $30fps$ to $120fps$, the watch-only video quadruples the file size of the original one.

Watching Experience Degradation: Although KALEIDO can severely reduce the quality of pirate video, we admit that there still has some degradation on watching experience for onsite audiences. Actually, there is a tradeoff between watching experience and piracy prevention. We design our method to maximize the viewing experience and the evaluation results show that the degradation is nearly negligible. There is still a room to improve the viewers' experience, and we will leave this as our future work.

6. RELATED WORK

Screen-Camera Communication: High quality information transmission and decodability maximization [30] are important issues for communication systems. Screen-camera communication systems employ one-way video stream to transmit information [22, 26]. PixNet [35] leverages 2D OFDM to modulate high-throughput 2D barcode frame, and optimizes high-capacity LCDs and camera communication. COBRA [20] achieves real-time phone-to-phone optical streaming by designing a special code layer supporting fast corner detector and blur-resilience technology. VRCodes [50] explores unobtrusive barcode design which is imperceptible to human eyes. Rolling shutter is utilized to simulate high frequency changes of selected color so that only the mixed color is perceived by human eyes. Such idea is also adopted by [23], in addition to address the imperfect frame synchronization. Diversity of cameras will also lead to unsynchronized light-to-camera channel, RollingLight [27] allows a light to deliver information to diverse rolling-shutter cameras while boosting the data rate and the communication reliability. Strata [24] supports wide range of frame capture resolutions and rates so as to deliver information rate correspondingly. Hilight [28, 29] transmit the information by adjusting the hues of the image dynamically. Both InFrame [45] and InFrame++ [44] achieve dual-mode full frame communication between screen and both humans and devices simultaneously. [51] develops an optical communication channel which takes the characteristics of light emittance from the display into account. And [14] proposes a systematic approach to measure the performance of screen-camera communication channel. Our techniques are relevant to screen-camera communication, but also different from it. While existing algorithms try to maximize decodability of screen-camera channel, we seek to maximize the quality degradation of the display-camera channel while retain the quality of the screen-eye channel.

Visual Cryptography: Visual cryptography [33] is a simple but perfectly secure solution for image encryption. Exploiting HVS (Human Visual System) to recognize a secret image from overlapping shares without any additional computation required in traditional cryptography. There are many algorithms to encrypt an image in another image [7, 21, 33, 39]. Rijmen and Preneel [39] propose visual cryptography scheme for color images by expanding each pixel of secret images into a 2×2 block. Hou [21] presents three different methods for visual cryptography of gray-level and color images via exploiting halftone technology and color decomposition. Sozan [7] proposes a different approach by splitting an image into three shares based on three primitive color components.

Image and Video Privacy: Privacy protection is always a broad topic, especially when sharing photos and videos online is becoming increasingly popular [9, 10, 54]. Some efforts have been taken to protect the privacy by concealing a person, blurring faces, masking and mosaicking the selected area of a image [2, 36, 53]. Bo *et al.* [11] proposes a privacy expressing protocol, which requires people to wear a Privacy.Tag to express their privacy desire and the photo sharing services to exert privacy protection by following users' policy expression. By leveraging the sparsity and quality of images to store most significant information in a secret part, P3 [37] extracts and encrypts such small component while preserving the rest in public. Some methods focus on providing privacy preserving image search in a photo database [40, 52]. A number of creative methods [17, 41] were proposed for protecting the privacy of objects in a video. E.g., [34] removes people's facial characteristics from video frame for privacy protection. [42] proposes that denaturing should not only involve content modification but also meta-data modification. [55] designs a protocol to protect portrait privacy when capturing photos. Although existing works could offer privacy protection to the required image/video, they cannot prevent quality pirate video-taping of the displayed video. To the best of our knowledge, our work is the first that allows smooth viewing experience while preventing pirate video-taping.

7. CONCLUSION

In this work we propose a scheme for re-encoding the original video frames such that it can prevent a good quality pirate video-taping of the displayed video using commercial off-the-shelf smart-devices, while do not affect the high-quality viewing experience of live audiences. Our design exploits the subtle disparities between the screen-eye link and the screen-camera link. Extensive evaluations of our implementation demonstrate its effectiveness against pirate video. One remaining work is to improve the encoding efficiency, and reduce the time delay of generating the watch-only video. A more daunting challenge is to design a scheme that can even prevent a good-quality pirate video-taping by high-end professional cameras.

Acknowledgments

This research is partially supported by the National Natural Science Foundation of China under Grant No. 61125202, 61170216, 61228202, 61428203 and CERG-61361166009, and the US National Science Foundation under Grant No. ECCS-1247944, ECCS-1343306, CNS-1319915, CNS-1343355 and CMMI-1436786. We thank all the reviewers and our shepherd for their valuable comments and helpful suggestions.

8. REFERENCES

[1] Cmos image sensors continue march to dominance over ccds. https://technology.ihs.com/389476/cmos-image-sensors-continue-march-to-dominance-over-ccds.

[2] Google street view. http://www.google.com/streetview.

[3] Image sensors market analysis. http://www.grandviewresearch.com/industry-analysis/image-sensors-market.

[4] Pirateeye. http://www.pirateeye.com/.

[5] Preventing movie piracy. http://www.technologyreview.com/news/406063/preventing-movie-piracy/.

[6] Putting a price tag on film piracy. http://blogs.wsj.com/numbers/putting-a-price-tag-on-film-piracy-1228/.

[7] ABDULLA, S. New visual cryptography algorithm for colored image. *arXiv preprint arXiv:1004.4445* (2010).

[8] ANDERSON, S. J., AND BURR, D. C. Spatial and temporal selectivity of the human motion detection system. *Vision research 25*, 8 (1985), 1147–1154.

[9] BADEN, R., BENDER, A., SPRING, N., BHATTACHARJEE, B., AND STARIN, D. Persona: an online social network with user-defined privacy. In *ACM SIGCOMM Computer Communication Review* (2009), vol. 39, ACM, pp. 135–146.

[10] BESMER, A., AND RICHTER LIPFORD, H. Moving beyond untagging: photo privacy in a tagged world. In *Proceedings of the SIGCHI Conference on Human Factors in Computing Systems* (2010), ACM, pp. 1563–1572.

[11] BO, C., SHEN, G., LIU, J., LI, X.-Y., ZHANG, Y., AND ZHAO, F. Privacy.tag: Privacy concern expressed and respected. In *Proceedings of the 12th ACM Conference on Embedded Network Sensor Systems* (2014), USENIX, pp. 163–176.

[12] BUADES, A., COLL, B., AND MOREL, J.-M. Denoising image sequences does not require motion estimation. In *Proceedings of Conference on Advanced Video and Signal Based Surveillance* (2005), IEEE, pp. 70–74.

[13] BUADES, A., COLL, B., AND MOREL, J.-M. A non-local algorithm for image denoising. In *Proceedings of Conference on Computer Vision and Pattern Recognition* (2005), vol. 2, IEEE, pp. 60–65.

[14] CHEN, C., AND MOW, W. H. A systematic scheme for measuring the performance of the display-camera channel. *arXiv preprint arXiv:1501.02528* (2015).

[15] CISCO, I. Cisco visual networking index: Forecast and methodology, 2013–2018. *CISCO White paper* (2014), 2013–2018.

[16] COX, I. J., KILIAN, J., LEIGHTON, T., AND SHAMOON, T. Secure spread spectrum watermarking for images, audio and video. In *International Conference on Image Processing* (1996), vol. 3, IEEE, pp. 243–246.

[17] DUFAUX, F., AND EBRAHIMI, T. Scrambling for privacy protection in video surveillance systems. *IEEE Transactions on Circuits and Systems for Video Technology 18*, 8 (2008), 1168–1174.

[18] FARRELL, F. Fitting physical screen parameters to the human eye. *Vision and visual dysfunction: The man-machine interface. Boca Raton, FL: CRC* (1991).

[19] GILBERT, G. M. Dynamic psychophysics and the phi phenomenon. *Archives of Psychology (Columbia University)* (1939).

[20] HAO, T., ZHOU, R., AND XING, G. Cobra: color barcode streaming for smartphone systems. In *Proceedings of International conference on Mobile systems, applications, and services* (2012), ACM, pp. 85–98.

[21] HOU, Y.-C. Visual cryptography for color images. *Pattern Recognition 36*, 7 (2003), 1619–1629.

[22] HRANILOVIC, S., AND KSCHISCHANG, F. R. A pixelated mimo wireless optical communication system. *IEEE Journal of Selected Topics in Quantum Electronics 12*, 4 (2006), 859–874.

[23] HU, W., GU, H., AND PU, Q. Lightsync: Unsynchronized visual communication over screen-camera links. In *Proceedings of International Conference on Mobile Computing & Networking* (2013), ACM, pp. 15–26.

[24] HU, W., MAO, J., HUANG, Z., XUE, Y., SHE, J., BIAN, K., AND SHEN, G. Strata: layered coding for scalable visual communication. In *Proceedings of International conference on Mobile computing and networking* (2014), ACM, pp. 79–90.

[25] JIANG, Y., ZHOU, K., AND HE, S. Human visual cortex responds to invisible chromatic flicker. *Nature neuroscience 10*, 5 (2007), 657–662.

[26] JO, K., GUPTA, M., NAYAR, S., LIU, D., GU, J., HITOMI, Y., MITSUNAGA, T., YIN, Q., ISO, D., SMITH, B., ET AL. Disco: Displays that communicate. *IEEE Transactions on Pattern Analysis and Machine Intelligence 99* (2013), 1.

[27] LEE, H.-Y., LIN, H.-M., WEI, Y.-L., WU, H.-I., TSAI, H.-M., AND LIN, K. C.-J. Rollinglight: Enabling line-of-sight light-to-camera communications. In *Proceedings of International Conference on Mobile Systems, Applications, and Services* (2015), ACM, pp. 167–180.

[28] LI, T., AN, C., CAMPBELL, A. T., AND ZHOU, X. Hilight: Hiding bits in pixel translucency changes. *ACM SIGMOBILE Mobile Computing and Communications Review 18*, 3 (2015), 62–70.

[29] LI, T., AN, C., XIAO, X., CAMPBELL, A. T., AND ZHOU, X. Real-time screen-camera communication behind any scene. In *Proceedings of International Conference on Mobile Systems, Applications, and Services* (2015), ACM, pp. 197–211.

[30] LI, Z., DU, W., ZHENG, Y., LI, M., AND WU, D. O. From rateless to hopless. In *Proceedings of International Symposium on Mobile Ad Hoc Networking and Computing* (2015), ACM.

[31] LUO, M. R., CUI, G., AND RIGG, B. The development of the cie 2000 colour-difference formula: Ciede2000. *Color Research & Application 26*, 5 (2001), 340–350.

[32] MASON, R. J., SNELGAR, R. S., FOSTER, D. H., HERON, J. R., AND JONES, R. E. Abnormalities of chromatic and luminance critical flicker frequency in multiple sclerosis. *Investigative ophthalmology & visual science 23*, 2 (1982), 246–252.

[33] NAOR, M., AND SHAMIR, A. Visual cryptography. In *Advances in Cryptology - EUROCRYPT'94* (1995), Springer, pp. 1–12.

[34] NEWTON, E. M., SWEENEY, L., AND MALIN, B. Preserving privacy by de-identifying face images. *IEEE Transactions on Knowledge and Data Engineering 17*, 2 (2005), 232–243.

[35] PERLI, S. D., AHMED, N., AND KATABI, D. Pixnet: Lcd-camera pairs as communication links. *ACM SIGCOMM Computer Communication Review 41*, 4 (2011), 451–452.

[36] POLLER, A., STEINEBACH, M., AND LIU, H. Robust image obfuscation for privacy protection in web 2.0 applications. In *IS&T/SPIE Electronic Imaging* (2012), International Society for Optics and Photonics, pp. 830304–830304.

[37] RA, M.-R., GOVINDAN, R., AND ORTEGA, A. P3: Toward privacy-preserving photo sharing. In *Proceedings of Symposium on Networked Systems Design and Implementation* (2013), pp. 515–528.

[38] RAJAGOPAL, N., LAZIK, P., AND ROWE, A. Visual light landmarks for mobile devices. In *Proceedings of international symposium on Information processing in sensor networks* (2014), IEEE Press, pp. 249–260.

[39] RIJMEN, V., AND PRENEEL, B. Efficient colour visual encryption or ąőshared colors of benettonąŕ. *rump session of EUROCRYPT 96* (1996).

[40] SADEGHI, A.-R., SCHNEIDER, T., AND WEHRENBERG, I. Efficient privacy-preserving face recognition. In *Information, Security and Cryptology*. Springer, 2010, pp. 229–244.

[41] SENIOR, A., PANKANTI, S., HAMPAPUR, A., BROWN, L., TIAN, Y.-L., EKIN, A., CONNELL, J., SHU, C. F., AND LU, M. Enabling video privacy through computer vision. *IEEE Security & Privacy 3*, 3 (2005), 50–57.

[42] SIMOENS, P., XIAO, Y., PILLAI, P., CHEN, Z., HA, K., AND SATYANARAYANAN, M. Scalable crowd-sourcing of video from mobile devices. In *Proceeding of international conference on Mobile systems, applications, and services* (2013), ACM, pp. 139–152.

[43] TYLER, C. W., AND HAMER, R. D. Analysis of visual modulation sensitivity. iv. validity of the ferry-porter law. *JOSA A 7*, 4 (1990), 743–758.

[44] WANG, A., LI, Z., PENG, C., SHEN, G., FANG, G., AND ZENG, B. Inframe++: Achieve simultaneous screen-human viewing and hidden screen-camera communication. In *Proceedings of International Conference on Mobile Systems, Applications, and Services* (2015), ACM, pp. 181–195.

[45] WANG, A., PENG, C., ZHANG, O., SHEN, G., AND ZENG, B. Inframe: Multiflexing full-frame visible communication channel for humans and devices. In *Proceedings of Workshop on Hot Topics in Networks* (2014), ACM, p. 23.

[46] WANG, Y. Survey of objective video quality measurements.

[47] WANG, Z., LU, L., AND BOVIK, A. C. Video quality assessment based on structural distortion measurement. *Signal processing: Image communication 19*, 2 (2004), 121–132.

[48] WOLFGANG, R. B., AND DELP, E. J. A watermark for digital images. In *International Conference on Image Processing* (1996), vol. 3, IEEE, pp. 219–222.

[49] WONG, P. W. A public key watermark for image verification and authentication. In *International Conference on Image Processing* (1998), vol. 1, IEEE, pp. 455–459.

[50] WOO, G., LIPPMAN, A., AND RASKAR, R. Vrcodes: Unobtrusive and active visual codes for interaction by exploiting rolling shutter. In *Proceedings of International Symposium on Mixed and Augmented Reality* (2012), IEEE, pp. 59–64.

[51] YUAN, W., WENGROWSKI, E., DANA, K. J., ASHOK, A., GRUTESER, M., AND MANDAYAM, N. Optimal radiometric calibration for camera-display communication. *arXiv preprint arXiv:1501.01744* (2015).

[52] ZHANG, L., JUNG, T., FENG, P., LIU, K., LI, X.-Y., AND LIU, Y. Pic: Enable large-scale privacy preserving content-based image search on cloud. In *Proceedings of the International Conference on Parallel Processing* (2015), IEEE.

[53] ZHANG, L., JUNG, T., LIU, C., DING, X., LI, X.-Y., AND LIU, Y. Pop: Privacy-preserving outsourced photo sharing and searching for mobile devices. In *Proceedings of the International Conference on Distributed Computing Systems* (2015), IEEE.

[54] ZHANG, L., LI, X.-Y., LIU, K., JUNG, T., AND LIU, Y. Message in a sealed bottle: Privacy preserving friending in mobile social networks. In *IEEE Transactions on Mobile Computing* (2014), IEEE.

[55] ZHANG, L., LIU, K., LI, X.-Y., FENG, P., LIU, C., AND LIU, Y. Enable portrait privacy protection in photo capturing and sharing. *arXiv preprint arXiv:1410.6582* (2014).

[56] ZHAO, J., AND MERCIER, G. Transactional video marking system, Mar. 14 2014. US Patent App. 14/214,366.

CAreDroid: Adaptation Framework for Android Context-Aware Applications

Salma Elmalaki
University of California, Los Angeles
selmalaki@ucla.edu

Lucas Wanner
Department of Informatics and Statistics, Federal University of Santa Catarina, Brazil
lucas@lisha.ufsc.br

Mani Srivastava
University of California, Los Angeles
mbs@ucla.edu

ABSTRACT

Context-awareness is the ability of software systems to sense and adapt to their physical environment. Many contemporary mobile applications adapt to changing locations, connectivity states, available computational and energy resources, and proximity to other users and devices. Nevertheless, there is little systematic support for context-awareness in contemporary mobile operating systems. Because of this, application developers must build their own context-awareness adaptation engines, dealing directly with sensors and polluting application code with complex adaptation decisions.

In this paper, we introduce CAreDroid, which is a framework that is designed to decouple the application logic from the complex adaptation decisions in Android context-aware applications. In this framework, developers are required—only—to focus on the application logic by providing a list of methods that are sensitive to certain contexts along with the permissible operating ranges under those contexts. At run time, CAreDroid monitors the context of the physical environment and intercepts calls to sensitive methods, activating only the blocks of code that best fit the current physical context.

CAreDroid is implemented as part of the Android runtime system. By pushing context monitoring and adaptation into the runtime system, CAreDroid eases the development of context-aware applications and increases their efficiency. In particular, case study applications implemented using CAreDroid are shown to have: (1) at least half lines of code fewer and (2) at least 10× more efficient in execution time compared to equivalent context-aware applications that use only standard Android APIs.

Categories and Subject Descriptors

D.4.7 [**OPERATING SYSTEMS**]: Organization and Design—*Real-time systems and embedded systems*

MobiCom'15, September 7–11, 2015, Paris, France.
© 2015 ACM. ISBN 978-1-4503-3619-2/15/09...$15.00.
DOI: http://dx.doi.org/10.1145/2789168.2790108.

General Terms

Design, Performance

Keywords

Context-aware computing, Android, Context-adaptation

1. INTRODUCTION

Computation is becoming increasingly coupled with the physical world. It is now commonplace for mobile applications and systems to adapt their functionality to user location, connectivity status, device orientation, and remaining battery percentage. This ability for software to sense, react, and adapt to the physical environment has been termed *context-awareness* [31].

Context-aware applications typically feature multiple interchangeable methods and sets of parameters, each of which is activated when the system is under a specific set of physical conditions. A music streaming application, for example, may request lower quality streams from a server when using a cellular network radio than when using WiFi. Social network applications may discover and promote interaction between users in close physical proximity. A video encoding application may delay or lower the quality of its processing to save energy when the system is running out of battery.

When implementing context-aware applications, developers typically must probe sensors, derive a context from sensor information, and design an adaptation engine that activates different methods for different contexts. With adequate support from the runtime system, context monitoring could be performed efficiently in the background and adaptation could happen automatically [27]. Application developers would then only be required to implement methods tailored to different contexts. Just as file and socket abstractions help applications handle traditional input, output, and communication; a context-aware runtime system could help applications adapt according to user behavior and physical context.

In this paper we introduce CAreDroid, a framework for Android that makes context-aware applications *easier to develop* and *more efficient* by decoupling functionality, mapping, and monitoring and by integrating context adaptation into the runtime. In CAreDroid, context-aware methods are defined in application source code, the mapping of methods to context is defined in configuration files, and context-monitoring, and method replacement are performed by the runtime system.

Because applications using CAreDroid do not need to monitor and handle changes in context directly, they can be written using significantly fewer lines of code than would be required if only using the standard Android APIs. Because CAreDroid introduces context-monitoring at the system level, it can avoid the indirection overhead of reading sensor data in the application layer, therefore making context-aware applications more efficient.

To allow for transparent switching between polymorphic implementations—which are alternative implementations of the same method that either provide same functionality with different performances or provide alternative functionality for the same method—the CAreDroid framework is integrated as part of the Dalvik Virtual Machine (DVM). In particular, at runtime, CAreDroid intercepts the various sensor flows in order to determine the current context of the phone (where context parameters include energy, network connectivity, location, and user activity). CAreDroid uses this information along with the provided per-application configuration in order to dynamically and transparently trigger adaptations and to find the set of methods that, at any point in time, better suit the device's context.

1.1 Related Work

A context-aware system requires three major elements: (1) a set of mutually replaceable polymorphic methods, (2) a context monitoring system, and (3) an adaptation engine that switches between different methods based on the monitored context. We divide the related work based on the three elements mentioned above.

1.1.1 Developing Context-Dependent Behavior

We can identify three main strategies in developing the context-dependent behaviors as follows.

Code partitioning: Code partitioning for remote execution is based on the idea of cyber-foraging [30] where mobile devices offload some of the work to a remote machine with more resources like a server [23]. The server can then execute the heavy work on behalf of the mobile devices that have scarce energy. The idea of cyber foraging has been addressed in previous work with different aspects. Both Spectra and Chroma [16, 9] do program partitioning and run part of the code on a surrogate server. They both rely on an earlier work called Odyssey [26] that explored the idea of application adaptation based on network bandwidth and CPU load. Puppeteer [15] focusses on adaptation to limited bandwidth by making transcoding. Transcoding is a transformation of data to change the fidelity [26] of the application to save energy.

Reflective techniques: Reflection, originally noted by Smith [32], is a technique that has emerged in computing languages to provide inspection and adaptation of the underlying virtual machine. Reflective techniques have been exploited in mobile computing middleware to address context change. Reflective mechanisms have been used by Capra et al. [11] such that applications acquire information about the context, and then the middleware behavior and the underlined device configuration are tuned accordingly.

Alternate code paths: Alternate code paths or algorithmic choice has been addressed in energy-aware software literature such as Petabricks [5] and Eon [33]. The choice between alternate algorithmic implementations of the same code is done dynamically based on the energy availability. Each code path has different energy consumption in a trade-off with quality or the accuracy of the result. A code path that is chosen by a pre-determined battery life has been explored in [21] in which tasks that have identical functionality are defined by developers. These tasks have different quality of service versus energy usage characteristics for embedded sensors application. In Green [7] a calibration phase is done at the beginning to determine the sampling rate—which eventually affects the accuracy of the result—in order to adapt to the available energy. Algorithmic choice has been further used in software libraries to deliver the best performance based on the hardware configuration [17, 22].

1.1.2 Context Monitoring

Efficient context monitoring has been studied throughly in literature. The work reported in [19, 24] provides frameworks for sensor-rich context monitoring. The main focus of that work is to minimize the energy consumption of the context-monitoring system. To further enhance the energy efficiency, Suman [25] exploits the temporal correlation between contexts in order to infer some context from others without reading the actual sensor measurements. To avoid performance degradation due to minimizing the energy consumption in context monitoring frameworks, the work in [20, 13] focuses on the optimization between continuous context monitoring, energy, latency and accuracy. Moreover, mobile operating systems currently support context monitoring functionalities. For example, the recently added *getMostProbableActivity()* API can be used to return the result of the Android OS activity recognition engine (e.g. biking or walking). Other examples are the Geofencing APIs provided by both Andorid and iOS which allow listening to the entrance and exit events from particular places and therefore allow for location based context applications.

1.1.3 Adaptation Engine

Prior work related to adaptation engines can be classified into two broad categories (i) *application-oriented adaptation engines* and (ii) *operation system-oriented adaptation engines.* The work reported in [10, 35] is a representative work for the first class. In this work, an application specific adaptation engines are designed and implemented with specific focus on energy-aware context adaptation. The work in [6, 34, 12] lies in the second category, where adaptation engines are proposed to perform context-aware OS functionalities such as context-aware memory management, context-aware scheduling, ... etc.

1.2 Paper Contribution

The work reported in this paper can be categorized under the class of *application-oriented adaptation engines.* While there is a rich body of work in designing application-specific adaptation engines, a systematic support for context-awareness is still missing from contemporary mobile operating systems. The work in this paper aims to fill this gap by providing OS support for the adaptation needed by context-aware Android applications.

In this paper we discuss the design and implementation of CAreDroid and present application case studies demonstrating the effectiveness of the system. Technically, we make the following contributions:

- We design CAreDroid, a framework for the implementation of context-aware polymorphic methods and for

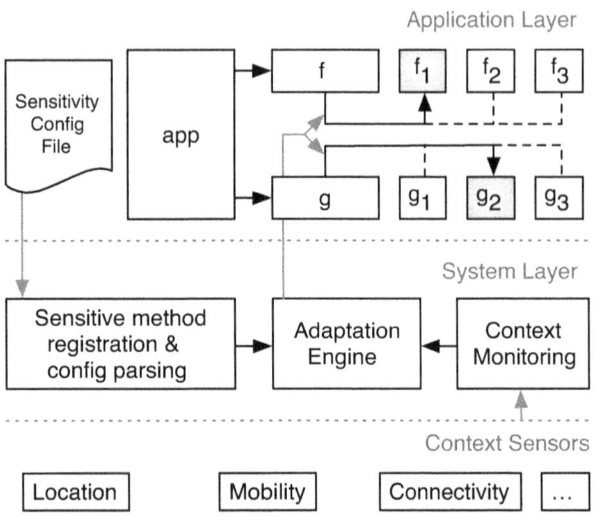

Figure 1: CAreDroid System Architecture. The developer provides a set of polymorphic methods and provides a configuration file describing how these methods shall be called. At runtime, CAreDroid monitors the phone context and adapts the application behavior accordingly.

the definition of application-specific rules used to map methods to contexts (Section 3);

- We extend the Dalvik Virtual Machine in the Android OS to provide adaptation support for context-aware application. The resulting CAreDroid can transparently switch between polymorphic versions of application methods at runtime (Section 5);
- We provide two levels of complexity of the mapping between contexts to methods, (i) a binary criteria (called must fit) and a relaxed criteria (called best fit) (Section 5.2);
- We demonstrate how application developers can leverage CAreDroid to make applications context-aware with minimal disruptions to the standard application development process (Section 6).

The remainder of this paper is organized as follows. Section 2 introduces the system architecture of CAreDroid. Details of CAreDroid including its configuration, monitoring, and context adaptation algorithms are presented in Sections 3, 4, and 5 respectively. Section 6 shows the evaluation and case studies. Finally, we discuss some issues related to the design of CAreDroid and give conclusions in Sections 7 and 8, respectively.

2. SYSTEM ARCHITECTURE

The main objective of CAreDroid is to provide the application developer with support to easily build adaptation in context-aware applications. Hence, from a developer perspective, the design of CAreDroid needs to satisfy the following properties:

1. **Usability:** CAreDroid needs to add minimal overhead on the application developer at development time.
2. **Performance:** The adaptation engined needs to add minimal execution overhead when the application is running.

Motivated by these two design objectives, we designed CAreDroid as discussed in this section. A conceptual overview of the CAreDroid architecture is shown in Figure 1. Applications normally call polymorphic methods f and g. Each method is aliased to one of its versions (f_1 and g_2, respectively, in the example). A sensitivity configuration file, defined on a per-application basis, describes rules that determine under what context each of the polymorphic versions should be used. For each version of a method, sensitivity rules define acceptable ranges of operation for different sensors of system context. Method f_1 could define, for example, two rules stating that WiFi connectivity and battery charging status should be equal to true, while f_2 could define one rule stating that remaining battery capacity should be between 0% and 20%. Rules are assigned priorities that help determine which of the versions should be used when multiple rules are valid.

In the system layer, CAreDroid parses the application configuration file to discover adaptable methods and their rules of operation. A context-monitoring module abstracts the various sensors in the system, and exposes context information to an adaptation engine. When changes in context occur, the adaptation engine changes the aliasing of the adaptable methods according to the sensitivity rules. If more than one version of a method matches the current context, the priorities of the sensitivity rules are used to choose between them. When there are no alternatives of a method that exactly matches the context, CAreDroid chooses the version that most closely conforms to the current state of the device. CAreDroid is organized in three modules:

Context Sensitivity Configuration File

For each context-aware application, a sensitivity configuration file maps methods to contexts. The file is structured as a series of *sensitive methods* and their respective context *sensitivity lists* described in XML format. In keeping with our goal of decreasing development complexity for context-aware applications, the file is a straightforward description of acceptable ranges of operation for each method under different contexts. A detailed description of the CAreDroid configuration file is presented in Section 3.

Context Monitor

CAreDroid has a dedicated module that continuously probes the current phone context. CAreDroid supports both *raw contexts* that can be directly known by reading the state of the hardware (e.g. WiFi connectivity, battery level) as well as higher level *inferred contexts* such as mobility status (e.g., walking, running) that require advanced processing of sensor information. As mentioned in Section 1.1.2, the design of context monitoring systems is a well studied topic. The main work in this paper does *not* focus on efficient implementation of context monitoring system. However, context monitoring is yet an essential part in order to evaluate any adaptation engine. Hence, in Section 4 we describe a simplistic implementation of context monitoring which can be augmented by any of the previous proposed context monitoring algorithms.

Adaptation Engine

In order to choose the correct polymorphic implementation that best suits the current context, CAreDroid uses the data supplied by the developer in the configuration file. Alternative implementations of sensitive methods are connected together through a replacement map that lists all *candidates methods* that can be used for a sensitive call. Whenever more than one candidate implementation fits the current context, CAreDroid uses a conflict resolution mechanism to pick the implementation with the highest priority. Because it frees developers from having to implement adaptation strategies in the application layer, the CAreDroid adaptation engine is the main factor in meeting our goal of decreasing development complexity for context-aware appications. Section 5 shows how context-to-method matching and conflict detection are implemented efficiently to meet our goal of reducing runtime overhead.

3. SENSITIVITY CONFIGURATION FILE

The configuration file is an XML file that is supplied by the application developer. To fit in the Android flow, the configuration file is stored as an asset file packed with the application package file (APK). In this section, we describe the structure of this XML file along with the post-processing steps performed by CAreDroid over this file.

3.1 Configuration File Structure

For each *sensitive method*, the developer provides different polymorphic implementations. Each polymorphic implementation of a method is described by a name, a tag, and a priority. The name corresponds to the method name in source code. The tag associates different implementations of a method with one another. For example, if methods f_1 and f_2 are polymorphic implementations of the same method, then both of them must be associated with the same tag, for example f. Finally the priority for a method helps the system resolve ambiguities when multiple versions of a method satisfy the current context.

For each polymorphic implementation, the developer assigns a *sensitivity list*. This *sensitivity list* is the list of context states for which this polymorphic implementation shall be triggered. In our current implementation of CAreDroid, we focus on four context categories:

- **Battery state:** In this category, we define three contexts which are (1) the remaining battery capacity (0% – 100%) (2) the battery temperature ($-30°$ C – $100°$ C) which is an indicative of high battery load as well as elevated power consumption; and (3) operating battery voltage, which is an indicative of the battery health.
- **Connectivity state:** In this category, we define three contexts: (1) WiFi connection status (On - Off), (2) WiFi link quality (0–70 A/V°), and (3) RSSI Received signal strength indication (0 – 4).
- **Location:** In this category, we consider one context state, which is GPS location. In this state, the developer is allowed to provide the latitude and longitude coordinates of a square area.
- **Mobility state:** In this category, we consider only the current mobility state of the phone holder, which can take one of the following values: still, walking, running and driving.

```
<Method>
  <MethodName>AdjustCameraPowerAware
  </MethodName>
  <priority>1</priority>
  <tag>cameraAdjust</tag>
  <batterycapacity>
    <vstart>0</vstart>
    <vend>25</vend>
  </batterycapacity>
</Method>
<Method>
  <MethodName>AdjustCameraWhileRunning
  </MethodName>
  <priority>2</priority>
  <tag>cameraAdjust</tag>
  <batterycapacity>
    <vstart>20</vstart>
    <vend>100</vend>
  </batterycapacity>
   <mobility>run</mobility>
</Method>
```

Figure 2: Snippet of a CAreDroid configuration file.

3.1.1 Example

To illustrate the construction of the configuration file, we provide a small example in Figure 2. In this example, we have two polymorphic methods for adjusting the camera parameters under different contexts. One method, `AdjustCameraPowerAware`, is designed to save energy. Hence, its `BatteryCapacity` range is from 0% up to 25%, and it can execute whether `wifi` is on or off. The second method is dedicated to adjusting the camera while the user of the device is running. For example, this method should adjust the focus and the scene parameters of the camera to give a better quality image. Accordingly, the `mobility` is assigned to be *run*.

3.2 Configuration File Processing

After the developer supplies the CAreDroid configuration file, several post-processing steps are required at the installation time of the application. In particular, the XML file needs to be parsed, and the extracted information is then used to fill specific data structures. Figure 3 shows how CAreDroid flow extends the normal Android compilation and installation flow. This flow diagram shows the steps needed to post-process the configuration file. Parsing of the configuration file, discovery of sensitive methods, and registration of adaptation parameters with the adaptation engine is implemented in the Dalvik Virtual Machine (DVM), as described in the remainder of this section.

3.2.1 Sensitive Method Discovery

Upon compilation of the Java code, the generated Dalvik Executable File (DEX) contains all compiled bytecodes of methods stacked on top of each other. A call to a method is then accomplished by pointing to the offset of the first instruction inside the DEX file. For example, let us consider a call to the `myObject.foo()` method. The following bytecode:

```
invoke-virtual {v14}, [method@101e]
```

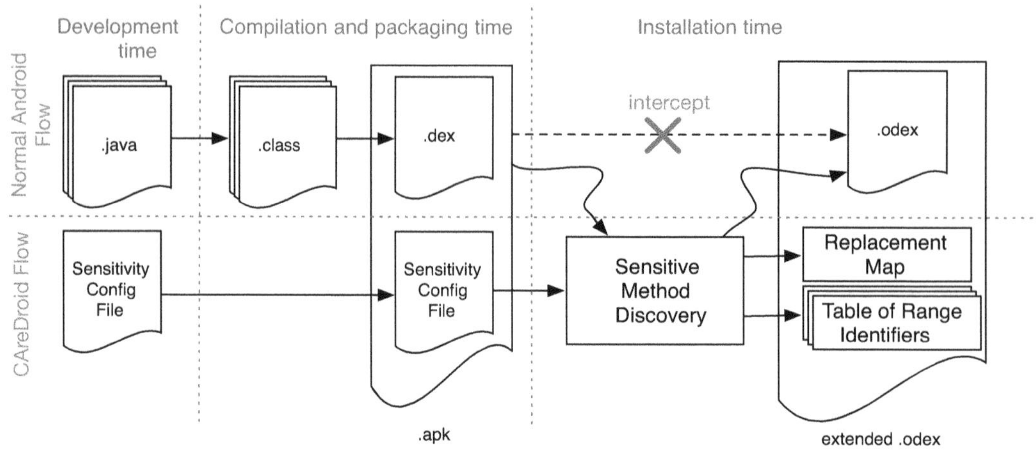

Figure 3: CAreDroid's extended installation flow. CAreDroid intercepts the installation process of the app on the device in order to parse the sensitivity configuration file. The final outcome of this process is two data structures named "Replacement Map" and "Table of Range Identifiers."

is used, where `v14` is the reference to the object instantiated from the class `myObject`, and `0x101e` is the offset of the first instruction in `myObject.foo()` in the DEX file. Note that the textual name of the method (e.g. "foo") is still preserved in the generated DEX file and the association between the method name and the method offset can still be extracted.

The DEX file along with all asset files (including the CAreDroid configuration file) are then packaged in the application package file (APK). When the APK file is installed, Android creates a new virtual machine to host the application. During this process, the Android flow extracts the DEX file and post-processes it in order to generate the Optimized DEX (ODEX) file.

The DEX optimization consists of two main steps. The first step is executed while class loading takes place. During this step, each method is assigned with a local method ID (compared to the global method ID assigned in the DEX). The second step of the DEX optimization process takes place when object references are linked with their classes. In this step, inheritance, polymorphism, method overriding, and method overloading are resolved. In particular, a virtual table is generated for each class. Each resolved method corresponds to an entry in this virtual table. Therefore, each method is now identified with its unique index inside it class virtual table. As a result, the call to the `myObject.foo()` method is further translated into:

```
invoke-virtual-quick {v14}, [000c]
```

where `v14` is the reference to the class object, `myObject`, and `000c` is the index for method `foo` inside that class's virtual table. Note that the association of the method name with its index in the virtual table is no longer preserved in the ODEX file.

Switching between different polymorphic implementations is equivalent to intercepting the operation of the bytecode corresponding to `invoke-virtual-quick` and supplying a different method ID. To perform this operation, CAreDroid must be able to keep track of the method IDs and relate them back to the IDs of different polymorphic implementations. Therefore, CAreDroid modifies the DEX/ODEX build process in Android to add hooks for context-awareness in sensitive method calls. This is accomplished through a *table of range identifiers* and a *replacement map.* This process is shown in Figure 3.

3.2.2 Replacement Map (RM) and Table of Range Identifiers (TRI)

The "Replacement Map" (RM) is a collection of (key, value) pairs defined for each polymorphic method.
The purpose of this map is to link each of the multiple polymorphic alternatives with their *sensitivity lists.* The *key* of this map is a composite key that consists of the pair of class-id and method-id extracted initially from the DEX file. The *value* field of the RM is an array whose length is equal to the number of contexts (mobility, location, battery capacity, etc.). This array specifies the *sensitive* operation range for this method for all different contexts. To facilitate this association, we introduce another data structure called the "Table of Range Identifiers" (TRI).

The TRI consists of multiple *associative arrays.* For each of the context sensors, we create a corresponding associative array. To construct such an array, we extract all the operation ranges provided in the configuration file, and and associate a uniquely generated *operation range identifier* (ORI) to each of the operation ranges. An example for such an associative array for battery capacity is shown in Table 1. Since the ranges of operations can vary from one class to another (based on the developer's intent , as described by the configuration file), we generate a TRI per class per context. The association between the class and the corresponding set of TRIs is made after the optimization of the DEX file process takes place. Once all TRI tables are built, we connect them to the RM by copying the corresponding ORI from the TRI data structure. An example of the RM is shown in Table 1.

At runtime, CAreDroid uses the TRI along with the current context to retrieve all ORIs that satisfy the current context. These ORIs are then used as inputs to the RM to retrieve the corresponding method IDs. If more than one method matches the ORIs, a conflict is discovered and needs to be resolved as described in Section 5.

B-Range	ORI
0→100	1
20→30	2
10→20	3
30→100	4

S-Range	ORI
0→2	1
1→4	2
2→3	3
0→3	4

...

Class ID	Method ID	B	T	V	W	Q	S	M	L
0x01	0x00F	1	2	1	2	4	2	1	4
0x01	0x01E	2	3	4	2	3	3	2	2
0x02	0x02A	2	2	1	0	0	0	2	1
0x02	0x01F	2	2	1	0	0	0	8	3

Table 1: On the left, examples of TRI tables for Battery capacity and Signal strength (RSSI) contexts. Each TRI associates a unique *Operation Range Identifier* (ORI) to each record. For each class, CAreDroid creates TRI for all different contexts. The association between the TRIs and the class is done later, after the optimization of the DEX files takes place. On the right, a Replacement Map that associates each key = (class-id, method-id) with its corresponding ORIs. CAreDroid creates a unique RM for the application. — *legend:* B: Battery Capacity, T: Battery Temperature, V: Battery Voltage, W: WiFi connectivity, S: Signal strength, Q: Signal Quality M: Mobility L: Location.

3.2.3 *ODEX Extension*

After CAreDroid constructs all the TRIs and the RM data structures, the DEX file passes through the normal Android optimization process, resulting in the generation of the ODEX file. Since the optimization process of the DEX file can result in a change in the method IDs, CAreDroid intercepts the process of optimizing the DEX files in order to update the RM, as shown in Table 1.

Finally, we extend the ODEX file structure by adding a reference to the RM data structure, which is generated by the described process. We extend the internal Android *class* data structure in order to associate the corresponding TRIs generated for that particular class. We also extended the internal Android *object* and *method* data structures by adding *sensitivity flags*. These flags are used later by the **CAreDroid Adaptation Engine** to facilitate the method switching.

3.3 Online Change of Context Ranges

While the configuration file needs to be specified by the developer at development time, the sensitive values of some sensitive contexts may not known until the code is running on the phone. For example, an application that changes its behavior whether the user is at *home* or at *work*. The location information (longitude and latitude of home and work) is not known at development time. Accordingly, CAreDroid supports online modification of the values associated with each sensitivity context. This takes place by asking the developer to write a specific file to the file system. CAreDroid parses this file whenever appropriate and re-updates the TOI accordingly. Note, that CAreDroid allows only changing the values associated with each sensitivity list but not the number of sensitive contexts associated to a polymorphic implementation.

4. CAREDROID CONTEXT MONITORING

In this section, we describe how CAreDroid acquires the current context at runtime with less overhead than Android Java APIs. Phone contexts can be numerous, and include raw values (like accelerometer data, GPS longitude and latitude, remaining battery capacity, etc.), or inferred states (like user mobility). While the in contribution of this paper is *not* efficient implementation of a context monitoring system, this is an essential part of any adaptation engine. In this section, we give details on how CAreDroid acquires both raw and inferred phone contexts. The work in this section can be indeed complemented by any of the context monitoring systems that appeared currently in the literature.

4.1 Raw Context Monitoring

Android exposes sensor information to the software stack through a Hardware Abstraction Layer (HAL). The HAL features a set of sensor managers that work as an intermediate layer between the low-level drivers and the high-level applications.

In order to reduce the overhead, we need to bypass the HAL layer and the associated sensor managers. This can be done by snooping on the interface between the HAL and the low-level device drivers through the `sysfs` virtual file system. In particular, each sensor (e.g. accelerometer, battery sensors, and WiFi) device driver exports its data into a set of files located under `/sys/class/`. In our work, we create an internal Dalvik VM thread that continuously reads these files to determine the state of the battery sensors and WiFi availability. The WiFi signal quality and signal strength are monitored via reading `/proc/net/wireless`. Similarly, the GPS location is determined by snooping over the Android Binder that connects the `Android LocationManager` with the GPS hardware driver.

4.2 Inferred Context: Mobility State

Mobility state detection is calculated by processing the raw accelerometer data obtained by the internal VM thread described above. In order to infer the mobility state, we adapt the classification procedure described in [28, 29] to detect whether the user is stationary, walking, or running. This classifier is based on the Geortzel algorithm [18]. Finally, to reduce the computational delay due to running the mobility state classifier, we let the classifier run on a separate DVM internal thread.

5. CAreDroid ADAPTATION ENGINE

The adaptation Engine is the core of CAreDroid. It is where the method replacement happens at runtime. In this section, we explain how CAreDroid extends the execution phase of the Android flow to automatically and transparently switch between methods.

5.1 Dalvik Interpreter Extension

Recall that the developed application is compiled and translated into an ODEX file. Bytecode stored in the ODEX file is then interpreted at runtime. In particular, the Dalvik Virtual Machine (DVM) runtime utilizes two types of interpreters. The first is called the *portable* interpreter, which is

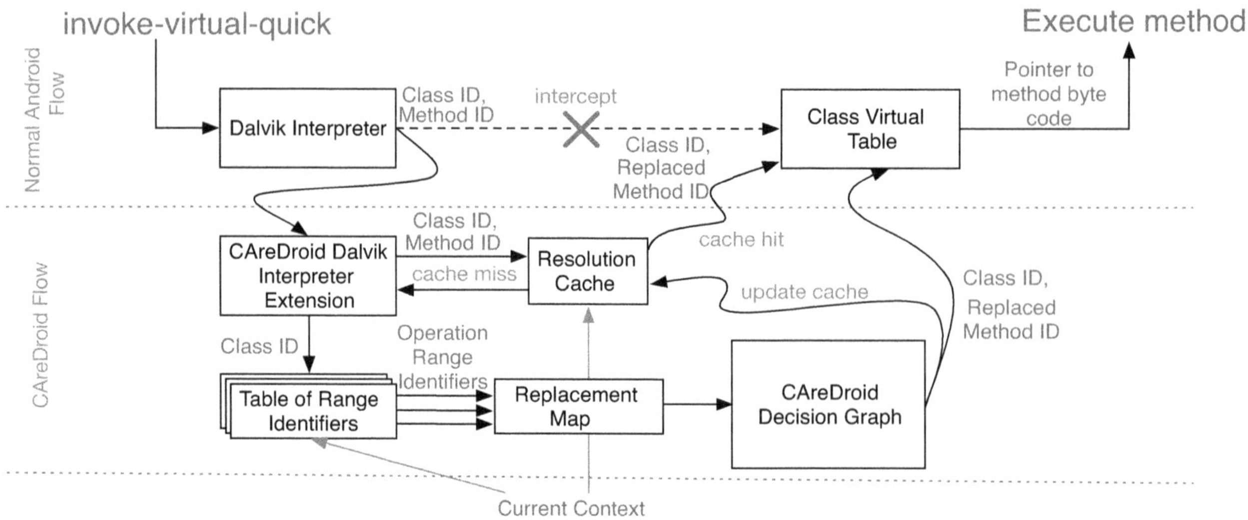

Figure 4: Flow of CAreDroid Adaptation Engine at runtime. The CAreDroid extended interpreter intercepts the execution of the Dalvik opcode *invoke-virtual-quick* to check whether the method invoked is sensitive or not. If the method is sensitive, then the CAreDroid adaptation engine checks the current context and picks the correct polymorphic method. This process is done through leveraging the information in the TRI and RM data structures along with the conflict resolution mechanism implemented using the decision graph. Finally, to speed up the process, CAreDroid uses a resolution cache, which exploits the temporal locality of the context.

implemented in C code and is not specific to a certain platform architecture. The second interpreter is called the *fast* interpreter which is implemented in assembly language and tailored towards a specific platform. The DVM supports switching between the two interpreters at runtime.

In our framework, we extend the *portable* interpreter to support the CAreDroid runtime engine. The extended interpreter checks the current interpreted ODEX bytecode. Whenever the bytecode corresponding to the `invoke-virtual` instruction is detected, CAreDroid intercepts the execution of the interpreter. It then checks the arguments of the `invoke-virtual` instruction — the method ID and the class ID — against the *sensitivity flags* in the extended ODEX file, described in Section 3.2.3. If the *sensitivity flag* is set, then CAreDroid needs to pick the polymorphic method that best fits the current context.

The process of choosing the best polymorphic implementation needs to resolve the conflicts in the user configuration. This is done through the CAreDroid decision graph module (discussed later) along with the TRI and RM data structures. In order to accelerate the process of picking the correct polymorphic implementation, CAreDroid uses a *resolution cache* that exploits the temporal locality of the adaptation decisions. This process is shown in Figure 4 and illustrated in the CAreDroid *decision graph* and the *resolution cache* in the following subsections.

Note that the *portable* interpreter (where CAreDroid is running)has a negative effect on the execution time of the application. To address this issue, we switch between the *fast* interpreter and the *portable* interpreter at runtime. The execution starts normally with the *fast* interpreter and, when the interpreter hits an invocation of a sensitive class, the interpreter switches to the *portable* interpreter and the CAreDroid adaptation process takes place. After executing the sensitive method, the interpreter switches back to the *fast* version.

5.2 Which Polymorphic Implementation to Pick?

In order to choose the correct implementation that best suits the current context, our framework utilizes the data supplied by the developer in the configuration file. Note that it is possible that, for a given context, multiple methods are valid *candidates*, leading to a conflict that needs to be resolved.

5.2.1 Best Fit vs Must Fit

The first step is to choose a set of *candidate* methods. We allow for two policies. In the first policy, *must fit*, a method is considered a valid *candidate* if the current context satisfies *all* the operation ranges for all sensitive contexts. In the second policy, *best fit*, a method is a valid candidate if the current context satisfies *at least one* operation range of the sensitive contexts. The choice of policy is determined by the configuration file.

5.2.2 Decision Graph

We use a Directed Acyclic Graph (DAG) to choose the candidate method. Each level of the graph marks one sensitive context (e.g. battery capacity, mobility state). The sensitive contexts are ordered based on their priority as defined in the configuration file. For each sensitive context, we create nodes for all *operation range identifiers* (ORI)—previously discussed in Section 4— that appear in the *replacement map* (RM) data structure. In other words, to build the decision tree, we traverse the RM horizontally.

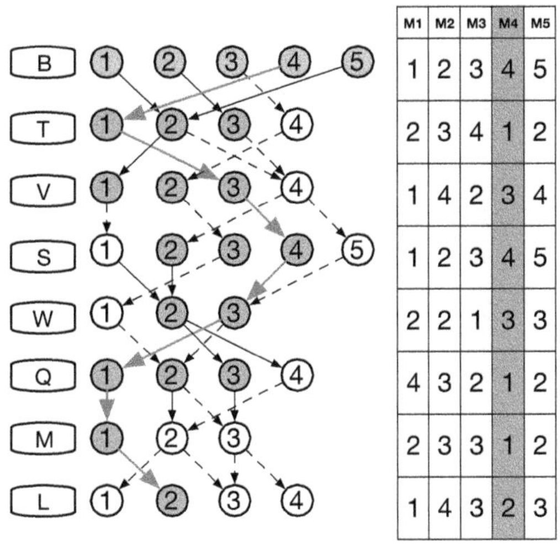

Figure 5: An example of a Replacement Map(RM) (right) and its associated decision graph (left). The nodes at each level correspond to the ORIs in the same level of the associated RM. The edges in the decision graph correspond to the five methods shown in the RM. The shaded nodes correspond to the ORIs that match the current context. The solid arrows correspond to the active paths that match both the RM and the current context. Finally the path marked in green corresponds to the method that satisfies all the ORIs, and therefore this method is the one picked by CAreDroid for execution.

For each row of the RM, we create nodes corresponding to all distinctive ORIs in that row. This process is repeated for all the rows in the RM. An example of an RM and the associated decision graph is shown in Figure 5.

The methods contained in the RM columns dictate the decision graph topology. Accordingly, we traverse the RM vertically and connect the ORIs that correspond to the same method by edges. This is shown for the same example, in Figure 5.

When the phone context is reported, we use the TRIs in order to know which ORIs are active, i.e., which ORIs match the current context. The next step is to use this information to eliminate some choices in the decision graph. For example, in Figure 5, we mark the active ORIs with a gray color and the corresponding active edges with solid arrows.

The final step is to compare the available active paths that start from the top level. In the *must fit* policy, CAreDroid considers only the active paths that connect the first level all the way to the lower level. If no such path exists, then no method replacement is going to take place. On the other hand, the *best fit* policy considers the longest path that starts from first level. Referring to the example in Figure 5, only one active path is passing through all the DAG levels and corresponds to method M4. Therefore, CAreDroid picks this method for execution. The Class ID and Method ID of this method is reported back to the normal Android flow to be executed. If further conflict exits, we use the method priority reported in the configuration file.

Platform	SLOC	% Increase
Non-context aware (Base)	275	-
Context-aware (Pure Java)	606	120%
CAreDroid	275 +78[a]	28.3%

[a]SLOC of the XML Configuration file

Table 2: significant line of code (SLOC) results for case study 1 showing the SLOC for different implementations along with the percentage increase of SLOC relative to the non-context aware implementation.

5.3 Conflict Resolution Cache

While the adaptation strategy for CAreDroid is fairly straightforward, performing it for every individual sensitive method call in the system would incur in an unnecessary overhead. In order to decrease the overhead of the context-to-method resolution mechanism, our framework uses a resolution cache. Our heuristic assumes that the operating point does not change over short time periods. Therefore, if a method is called multiple times within a short amount of time (inside a loop for example), the same polymorphic implementation might be used for all of these calls. The cache is used to store the recently resolved candidates, that is, the recent phone context along the method ID that is chosen for each phone context. Each entry corresponds to the eight values of the phone context along with the method ID for the optimal method. The cache uses a Least Recently Used (LRU) approach to replace entries.

6. EVALUATION

We evaluate CAreDroid with four case studies. In the first one, we focus on assessing two metrics namely, reducing the number of significant lines of code and the execution time of the context-aware application. In the remaining three case studies, we show examples of applications that can benefit from context adaptation using CAreDroid.

All case studies are carried over a Nexus 4 phone running a modified system image for platform 4.2 API 17 [3]. The execution time is obtained using the Android SDK tracer [4]. The size of the original system image for Android 4.2 is 234.368 MB, the modified system image that support CAreDroid is 245.26 MB. Hence, the overhead in the system image is 4.6%.

6.1 Case Study 1: A Simple Application

In this case study, we implement a simple application that has only one sensitive method with three polymorphic implementations. In particular, this simple application implements a numerical solver for linear equations (which is a cornerstone algorithm in many image processing algorithms used to enhance photos before posting them to social media applications). We implement three polymorphic variants of this solver named LUP-decomposition (LU), Cholesky decomposition (CHD), and Conjugate Gradient (CG). These three methods have different memory and computation time characteristics. These mathematical functions are exhaustively used in image processing applications. Each implementation corresponds to a particular tradeoff between performance and computation time. In particular, CHD gives

Platform	Solver	Method time	CPU time (ms): Decision Tree without cache	Decision Tree with cache	Context Monitoring (parallel thread)	Total without cache	Total with cache	Overhead: without cache	with cache
Non-context aware (Base)	LU	8.322	-		-	8.322		-	
	CHD	16.872	-		-	16.872		-	
	CG	13.375	-		-	13.375		-	
Context aware (Pure Java)	LU	8.322	0.227		5.093	13.642		63.92%	
	CHD	16.872	0.776		5.093	25.741		52.56%	
	CG	13.375	0.351		5.093	18.819		40.70%	
CAreDroid (Must Fit)	LU	8.322	0.183	0.030	0.336	8.841	8.688	6.23%	4.39%
	CHD	16.872	0.335	0.031	0.336	17.543	17.239	3.98%	2.17%
	CG	13.375	0.198	0.030	0.336	13.909	13.741	3.99%	2.736%
CAreDroid (Best Fit)	LU	8.322	0.183	0.031	0.336	8.841	8.689	6.23%	4.41%
	CHD	16.872	0.732	0.031	0.336	17.635	17.239	4.522%	2.17%
	CG	13.375	0.489	0.030	0.336	14.2	13.741	6.17%	2.73%

Table 3: Execution time results for case study 1 showing the profiling of different parts for all the three implementations. The overhead is computed relative to the non context-aware implementation. The results show the efficiency of both the must fit and best fit policies. It also shows the performance increase resulting from using the cache.

the most accurate results while suffers from high computation time. On the other extreme, LU gives the least accurate results (compared to CHD and CG) while leads to better computation time. The purpose of this case study is to characterize the performance of CAreDroid while switching between these three polymorphic implementations.

In order to characterize the CAreDroid performance, we generate an arbitrary configuration file that assigns each of the three solvers to different battery and connectivity contexts. We evaluate CAreDroid against a pure Java implementation performing the same functionality. That is, the pure Java application listens to changes in battery and WiFi connectivity using the standard HAL callback mechanism provided by the Android APIs. We implement a *non-context aware* implementation that *magically* knows which polymorphic method shall be called without knowing the context (for the purpose of comparison) and we call it the *base non-context aware.*

6.1.1 Reduction in Significant Line of Code (SLOC)

In this example, using CAreDroid reduces the SLOC for the application by a factor of 2x compared to a Java implementation using standard Android APIs. Table 2 shows the SLOC for each of the implementations.

6.1.2 Reduction in Execution Time

In this test case, we let the 4 different implementations (non context aware, pure Java, must fit and best fit) run over the phone for several hours while collecting profiling information. The profiling information are then averaged out and the result is reported in Table 3. To further investigate the effect of the resolution cache, we run the test with and without the cache functionality to allow for comparison. The results in Table 3 show that CAreDroid reduces the CPU time overhead (compared to the pure Java implementation) by a factor of 12x, on average, while adding a minimal overhead (2.5%–4.4%) compared to the non context-aware case. Furthermore, the resolution cache leads to decreasing the decision tree time by at least an order of magnitude whenever there is no change in the operating point. Finally, with no cache (or alternatively when a cache miss occurs) *best fit* policy adds slightly more overhead compared to the *must fit* policy due to the complexity of the decision graph used by the former. The same order of overhead also appears in the pure Java implementation because of the added code for switching between contexts.

6.1.3 Energy Profiling

Finally, we characterize the energy consumption (and hence the battery life time) due to context monitoring and adaptation. In this experiment, we monitor the voltage and discharging current of the battery during 2.5 hours while running the application under the four platforms (best fit, must fit, pure Java, and non-context aware). The experiment starts at the same battery capacity and at room temperature. We run each experiment three times. In the first one, we deactivate the context switching functionalities and focus only on the energy consumed by the context monitoring. These results are reported in Figure 6(a). In the second run, we run both context monitoring as well as context switching but calling an empty method. The energy measurements are then subtracted from the energy measurements from the previous experiment. The purpose of this experiment is to profile the effect of the decision tree and the context switching mechanism. This is shown in Figure 6(b). Finally, we run the full implementation to get the overall energy consumption of our system and compare it to the non-context aware one.

Overall, the results show that bypassing the HAL layer and performing the context monitoring inside the OS lead to decreasing the energy consumed by a factor of 36%. The results also show a similar decrease of energy consumption due to implementing the context switching inside the OS with a slight difference between the must fit and the best fit switching policies. Also, as seen in Figure 6(c), the energy consumption of pure Java implementation consumes around 69.33% more energy compared to CAreDroid. This energy consumption can be further improved by using energy-aware context monitoring techniques that previously reported in the related work (Section 1.1.2).

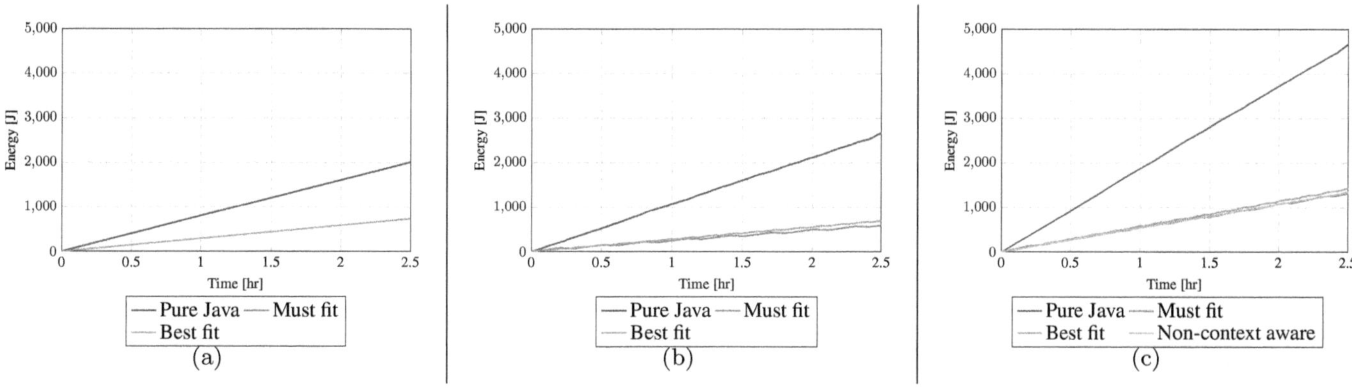

Figure 6: Energy consumption results for case study 1 showing (a) energy used when context monitoring is running alone (b) energy consumed by the context switching subsystem and (c) the total energy consumed. On each case, we plot the energy consumed by the pure Java implementation as well as the must fit and best fit implementations of CAreDroid. The results in (a) show that bypassing the HAL layer and implementing the context monitoring inside the OS allowed CAreDroid to use 36% less energy within the 2.5 hours lapse of the experiment. The results in (b) show that both Must fit and Best fit adaptation significant outperform the pure Java implementation in terms of energy consumed (and hence battery lifetime). The overall results (c) show that CAreDroid consumes only 6.73% energy compared with the non-context aware implementation and provides 69.33% energy saving compared to the pure Java implementation.

6.2 Case Study 2: A Context-Aware Phone Configuration

With increasing reported accidents resulting from texting while driving, we develop an application that changes the phone configuration based on the underlying context of the phone[1]. We manifest the **location**, **mobility state**, and **battery** in this application. In particular, we would like the application to change the phone configuration as follows:

- **Default**: keep the phone in its default configuration.
- **Driving**: (1) disable messaging and email notifications, (2) block certain caller numbers specified by a list (i.e. forward calls from this list to the voice mail) and (3) enable bluetooth (to connect the phone to car speaker).
- **Running**: (1) enable GPS (if not enabled), (2) block certain caller numbers specified by a list, and (3) mute the alarms.
- **At home**: (1) enable WiFi, (2) block certain caller numbers specified by a list, (3) raise the alarm volume, and (4) set ringer volume to normal.
- **At work**: (1) enable WiFi, (2) lower the alarm volume, (3) put the phone in vibrating mode, and (4) block certain list of caller numbers.
- **Power saving**: (1) lower the ringer volume, (2) disable bluetooth (if enabled), and (3) enable the automatic adjustment of screen brightness.

[1]Some applications in the market attempt to control the phone configuration like Tasker [2] and Locale [1] by providing hooks to the user to configure the phone based on certain rules that the user defines. However, these applications have only boolean decision. The rules must be all satisfied in order to change the configuration, while CAreDroid provides more complex formula (the best-fit policy). Moreover, Tasker and Locale do not support all the contexts supported by CAreDroid.

Platform	SLOC	% Increase
Non-context aware (Base)	282	-
Context-aware (Pure Java)	873	201%
CAreDroid	282 +277[a]	98.2%

[a]SLOC of the XML Configuration file

Table 4: Significant lines of code (SLOC) results for case study 2 showing the SLOC for the three implementations along with the percentage increase of SLOC relative to the non-context aware implementation.

Platform	CPU time[a]	Overhead
Non-context aware (Base)	1.942	-
Context aware (Pure Java)	12.14	525.12%
CAreDroid (Best Fit)	2.015	3.76%

[a]CPU Time (ms) = Method time + HAL Callback time + Inferences

Table 5: Execution time results for case study 2 showing the overhead for the different implementations.

For each of these configurations, a polymorphic method is implemented. The objective is to call the correct method based on the context. Similar to the previous case study, we implemented a non-context aware implementation (for the purpose of comparison), a context-aware implementation using the normal Android flow, and a context-aware implementation using CAreDroid.

6.2.1 Reduction in Significant Line of Code (SLOC)

CAreDroid decreases the code complexity (quantified by SLOC) by a factor of 2× (including the SLOC of the XML configuration file) compared to the implementation based on the normal Android flow, as shown in Table 4.

6.2.2 Reduction in Execution Time

In this test case, CAreDroid is configured and the phone is allowed to change between different contexts leading to a change in the application behavior. The time profiling is done across different contexts and the one with maximum CPU overhead is reported in Table 5.

For this case study, the pure Java implementation adds a 525.12% CPU overhead. On the other hand, CAreDroid introduces a minimal overhead of 3.76% compared to the non-context aware implementation. The large overhead of the former can be explained by observing that there are 16 possible cases that need to be handled if the application developer were to implement the same app without using CAreDroid. Needless to say that the developer—without CAreDroid—has to implement all the Android listeners to all contexts as well as provide the high-level inferences of mobility state from the raw data. The small overhead in CAreDroid compared to the pure Java implementations again can be accounted to the fact that all the context-awareness operations (context monitoring and adaptation) are implemented natively inside the operating system.

6.3 Case Study 3: Context-Aware Camera

In this case study, we build a context-aware camera application. The camera adjusts its features parameters based on the phone context. We have five different methods that CAreDroid alternates between. The focus of this study is on making the *focus*, *scene mode* and *flash mode* adaptive to the context. However, this can be extended to handle all the camera features. The five modes are listed as follows:

- **Default**: Configure the focus mode to "default"
- **When runing**: adjust the focus mode to the "continuous picture" mode.
- **When walking**: adjust the scene mode to the "steady photo" mode.
- **When still**: adjust the focus mode to the "fixed" mode".
- **Power saver**: (1) adjust the flash mode to "off", (2) adjust the focus mode to "fixed" mode, and (3) adjust the quality of the picture to "minimum."

Similar to previous case studies, we implemented a polymorphic method for each of these modes and the objective is to call the appropriate method based on the phone context.

Platform	SLOC	% Increase
Non-context aware (Base)	277	-
Context-aware (Pure Java)	782	182%
CAreDroid	277 +133[a]	48%

[a]XML Configuration file

Table 6: Results of the significant line of code (SLOC) for the three implementations of the Smart Camera application used in case study 3. The results shows the SLOC along with the percentage increase relative to the non-context aware implementation.

The test is performed as follows. First a photo is captured while the phone is held in a standstill position using the original *camera* application provided by the phone. Next, the user starts to walk/run while trying to capture the photo for the same object again using the original *camera* application. Finally, the same experiment is done while using the CAreDroid-based *context-aware camera* application.

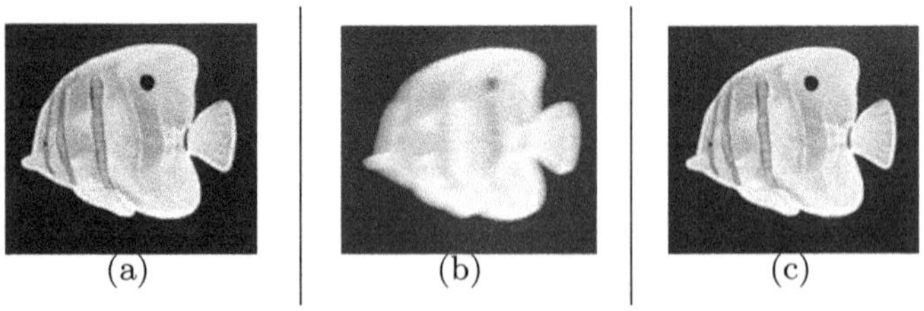

Figure 7: Photos taken by the Smart Camera application developed for case study 3: (a) the photo taken while the phone holder is standing still, (b) the photo taken while the phone holder is walking and no context-awareness is taking place, and (c) photo taken while the phone holder is walking and using the Smart Camera application built on top of CAreDroid.

The results of the implemented application is shown in Figure 7. Figure 7(a) shows the original photo captured from a stand still position. Figure 7(b) shows the captured photo while the phone holder is walking and no context-awareness processing is taking place, and finally, Figure 7(c) shows the captured photo with the user is walking and using the developed context-aware camera with CAreDroid. As with the previous case studies, Table 6 shows the reduction of the overhead in SLOC when the context-aware Camera application is developed using normal Android flow compared to the proposed CAreDroid flow. The table shows a reduction of SLOC by more than a factor of 3×.

7. DISCUSSION

The underlying idea behind CAreDroid is the ability of the system to sense and adapt to variations in the environment and available resources. In this section we discuss some issues that faced us during the design and implementation of CAreDroid.

7.1 Why is CAreDroid implemented inside the OS?

One possible design of CAreDroid was to design it as a library which provided context adaptation functionalities through a set of exposed APIs. Compared to the current design of CAreDroid, the library-based design falls behind in terms of the two design criteria discussed in Section 2 named *Usability* design and *Performance*. From the usability point of view, the library implementation of the adaptation engine forces the developer to issue subsequent calls to the library APIs. Missing calls to the library APIs may result to degradation in the context awareness of the developed application. On the other hand, the current design of CAreDroid makes the application developer completely *oblivious* from the adaptation. He is asked only to provide the adaptation *policy* in the XML configuration file. Afterwards, CAreDroid intercepts the execution of the methods while it is being interpreted by the Dalvik VM and perform the adaptation automatically. From the performance point of view, implementing the context adaptation and monitoring in the low level results into less execution time as proved by the experimental test cases shown in Section 6.

7.2 Privacy

Sensing and understanding the user's context and taking decisions accordingly can lead to various privacy leaks. Android privacy mechanism depends on providing the user with different queries in order to grant permissions to the application to use the sensory data. In our work, CAreDroid ensures that the adaptation policy specified by the developer does not use sensory data that are not permitted by the user. For this end, CAreDroid parses the application's permissions included in the Android *manifest file*[2]. The adaptation engine in CAreDroid uses only permissible contexts as per application permissions.

7.3 Developer Matters

Despite the fact that the adaptation engine decision is obfuscated from the developing phase, in some scenarios—for example when the best fit policy is used—the developer may be interested in retrieving the current operating point. Therefore, CAreDroid addresses this issue by providing an API called "*read_operating_point*()" which can be used to read the current values of different contexts.

7.4 Limitations

The CAreDroid framework described here is not without some limitations:

- Polymorphic methods in CAreDroid must be pure functions, i.e., they cannot perform I/O and cannot change global program states, and their output must depend only on the method arguments. To allow for non-pure functions, the framework would require state-migration procedures between every possible pair of polymorphic methods.
- CAreDroid assumes that an application developer can provide multiple implementations of sensitive methods. Specifying the right constraints is not an easy task and it may be better to suggest the right constraints to the developer during a validation phase of the application. However, this is an open research point and previous work [14, 8] has identified the importance of enforcing the developer to suggest the adaptation policy and not letting the adaptation engine automatically synthesize the adaptation policy.
- CAreDroid also expects the application programmer to be aware of suitable ranges of operations for different sensitive methods. In the future, we intend to explore automated code profilers that could suggest ranges of operation for each of the choices, helping users in defining suitable adaptation configuration files.

7.5 Broader Uses of CAreDroid

CAreDroid supports connectivity context such as Wifi connectivity, signal strength and quality of the signal as well as low level context such as battery temperature. These contexts can be manifested to decide if some intensive computation should be *offloaded* to a server or if an *approximate* computation should be used. In particular, if battery capacity is good (high enough) and there is WiFi connectivity with good strength then CAreDroid can switch to a method that offloads intensive computation to a server and remove the burden of computation from the phone. Hence, the concept of cyber-foraging discussed in Section 1.1.1 can be directly implemented using CAreDroid. Similarly, approximate computation (or algorithmic choice as discussed in Section 1.1.1) can be implemented using CAreDroid by manifesting the temperature context as well as the battery capacity context.

[2]an Android XML file that declares the permissions required by the application

8. CONCLUSION

Context-aware computing is a powerful technique for physically coupled software. It can enhance functionality and improve resource usage of applications by adapting them to context. In this paper, we present CAreDroid, an adaptation framework for context-aware applications in Android. CAreDroid allows applications developers to develop context-aware applications without having to deal directly with context monitoring and context adaptation in the application code. In CAreDroid, multiple versions of methods that are sensitive to context are dynamically and transparently replaced with each other according to application-specific configuration file. By pushing the context monitoring and adaptation functionalities to the Android runtime, CAreDroid is able to provide context-awareness more efficiently and with significantly fewer lines of code compared to current Android development flow. In particular, using different case studies, we show how CAreDroid can be used to develop context-aware applications. Results from these case studies show that CAreDroid reduces the code complexity by at least half while decreasing the computation overhead by at least a factor of 10× compared to non-CAreDroid applications.

Acknolwedgment

This research is funded in part by the National Science Foundation under grant CCF-1029030, by the Center for Excellence for Mobile Sensor Data-to-Knowledge under National Institutes of Health grant #1U54EB020404, and by the U.S. ARL, U.K. Ministry of defense (MoD) under Agreement Number W911NF-06-3-0001. Any opinions, findings and conclusions or recommendations expressed in this material are those of the author(s) and do not necessarily reflect the views of the funding agencies. The U.S. and U.K. Governments are authorized to reproduce and distribute reprints for Government purposes notwithstanding any copyright notation hereon.

9. REFERENCES

[1] Locale for android. http://www.twofortyfouram.com.
[2] Tasker for android. total automation for android. http://tasker.dinglisch.net/index.html.
[3] Android. Android open source project. https://source.android.com.
[4] Android SDK. Profiling with traceview. http://developer.android.com/tools/debugging/.
[5] J. Ansel, C. Chan, Y. L. Wong, M. Olszewski, Q. Zhao, A. Edelman, and S. Amarasinghe. Petabricks: a language and compiler for algorithmic choice. *SIGPLAN Notices*, 44:38–49, June 2009.

[6] K. Ariyapala, M. Conti, and C. Keppitiyagama. Contextos: A context aware operating system for mobile devices. In *Green Computing and Communications (GreenCom), 2013 IEEE and Internet of Things (iThings/CPSCom), IEEE International Conference on and IEEE Cyber, Physical and Social Computing*, pages 976–984, Aug 2013.

[7] W. Baek and T. M. Chilimbi. Green: a framework for supporting energy-conscious programming using controlled approximation. *SIGPLAN Notices*, 45:198–209, June 2010.

[8] G. Bai, L. Gu, T. Feng, Y. Guo, and X. Chen. Context-aware usage control for android. In *Security and Privacy in Communication Networks*, pages 326–343. Springer, 2010.

[9] R. K. Balan, M. Satyanarayanan, S. Y. Park, and T. Okoshi. Tactics-based remote execution for mobile computing. In *Proceedings of the 1st international conference on Mobile systems, applications and services*, pages 273–286. ACM, 2003.

[10] A. Beach, M. Gartrell, X. Xing, R. Han, Q. Lv, S. Mishra, and K. Seada. Fusing mobile, sensor, and social data to fully enable context-aware computing. In *Proceedings of the Eleventh Workshop on Mobile Computing Systems & Applications*, pages 60–65. ACM, 2010.

[11] L. Capra, G. S. Blair, C. Mascolo, W. Emmerich, and P. Grace. Exploiting reflection in mobile computing middleware. *ACM SIGMOBILE Mobile Computing and Communications Review*, 6(4):34–44, Oct. 2002.

[12] D. Chu, A. Kansal, J. Liu, and F. Zhao. Mobile apps: It's time to move up to condos. In *13th Workshop on Hot Topics in Operating Systems (HotOS XIII)*. USENIX, May 2011.

[13] D. Chu, N. D. Lane, T. T.-T. Lai, C. Pang, X. Meng, Q. Guo, F. Li, and F. Zhao. Balancing energy, latency and accuracy for mobile sensor data classification. In *Proceedings of the 9th ACM Conference on Embedded Networked Sensor Systems*, SenSys '11, pages 54–67, New York, NY, USA, 2011. ACM.

[14] M. Conti, B. Crispo, E. Fernandes, and Y. Zhauniarovich. Crêpe: A system for enforcing fine-grained context-related policies on android. *Information Forensics and Security, IEEE Transactions on*, 7(5):1426–1438, 2012.

[15] E. De Lara, D. S. Wallach, and W. Zwaenepoel. Puppeteer: Component-based adaptation for mobile computing. In *USENIX Symposium on Internet Technologies and Systems - USITS*, volume 1, pages 14–14, 2001.

[16] J. Flinn, S. Park, and M. Satyanarayanan. Balancing performance, energy, and quality in pervasive computing. In *Distributed Computing Systems, 2002. Proceedings. 22nd International Conference on*, pages 217–226. IEEE, 2002.

[17] M. Frigo and S. G. Johnson. The design and implementation of FFTW3. *Proceedings of the IEEE*, 93(2):216–231, 2005. Special issue on "Program Generation, Optimization, and Platform Adaptation".

[18] G. Goertzel. An algorithm for the evaluation of finite trigonometric series. *American mathematical monthly*, pages 34–35, 1958.

[19] S. Kang, J. Lee, H. Jang, H. Lee, Y. Lee, S. Park, T. Park, and J. Song. Seemon: Scalable and energy-efficient context monitoring framework for sensor-rich mobile environments. In *Proceedings of the 6th International Conference on Mobile Systems, Applications, and Services*, MobiSys '08, pages 267–280, New York, NY, USA, 2008. ACM.

[20] A. Kansal, S. Saponas, A. B. Brush, K. S. McKinley, T. Mytkowicz, and R. Ziola. The latency, accuracy, and battery (lab) abstraction: Programmer productivity and energy efficiency for continuous mobile context sensing. In *Proceedings of the 2013 ACM SIGPLAN International Conference on Object Oriented Programming Systems Languages & Applications*, OOPSLA '13, pages 661–676, New York, NY, USA, 2013. ACM.

[21] A. Lachenmann, P. J. Marrón, D. Minder, and K. Rothermel. Meeting lifetime goals with energy levels. In *Proceedings of the 5th international conference on Embedded networked sensor systems*, SenSys '07, pages 131–144, New York, NY, USA, 2007. ACM.

[22] X. Li, M. Garzaran, and D. Padua. Optimizing sorting with machine learning algorithms. In *Proceedings of Parallel and Distributed Processing Symposium*, March 2007.

[23] T.-Y. Lin, T.-A. Lin, C.-H. Hsu, and C.-T. King. Context-aware decision engine for mobile cloud offloading. In *Wireless Communications and Networking Conference Workshops (WCNCW), 2013 IEEE*, pages 111–116, April 2013.

[24] H. Lu, J. Yang, Z. Liu, N. D. Lane, T. Choudhury, and A. T. Campbell. The jigsaw continuous sensing engine for mobile phone applications. In *Proceedings of the 8th ACM Conference on Embedded Networked Sensor Systems*, SenSys '10, pages 71–84, New York, NY, USA, 2010. ACM.

[25] S. Nath. Ace: Exploiting correlation for energy-efficient and continuous context sensing. In *Proceedings of the 10th International Conference on Mobile Systems, Applications, and Services*, MobiSys '12, pages 29–42, New York, NY, USA, 2012. ACM.

[26] B. D. Noble, M. Satyanarayanan, D. Narayanan, J. E. Tilton, J. Flinn, and K. R. Walker. Agile application-aware adaptation for mobility. *SIGOPS Oper. Syst. Rev.*, 31(5):276–287, Oct. 1997.

[27] C. Perera, A. Zaslavsky, P. Christen, and D. Georgakopoulos. Context aware computing for the internet of things: A survey. *Communications Surveys Tutorials, IEEE*, 16(1):414–454, First 2014.

[28] S. Reddy, J. Burke, D. Estrin, M. Hansen, and M. Srivastava. Determining transportation mode on mobile phones. In *Wearable Computers, 2008. ISWC 2008. 12th IEEE International Symposium on*, pages 25–28. IEEE, 2008.

[29] J. Ryder, B. Longstaff, S. Reddy, and D. Estrin. Ambulation: A tool for monitoring mobility patterns over time using mobile phones. In *Computational Science and Engineering, 2009. CSE'09. International Conference on*, volume 4, pages 927–931. IEEE, 2009.

[30] M. Satyanarayanan. Pervasive computing: Vision and challenges. *Personal Communications, IEEE*, 8(4):10–17, 2001.

[31] B. Schilit and M. Theimer. Disseminating active map information to mobile hosts. *Network, IEEE*, 8(5):22–32, Sept 1994.

[32] B. C. Smith. *Procedural reflection in programming languages*. PhD thesis, Massachusetts Institute of Technology, 1982.

[33] J. Sorber, A. Kostadinov, M. Garber, M. Brennan, M. D. Corner, and E. D. Berger. Eon: a language and runtime system for perpetual systems. In *Proceedings of the 5th international conference on Embedded networked sensor systems*, SenSys '07, pages 161–174, New York, NY, USA, 2007. ACM.

[34] N. Vallina-Rodriguez and J. Crowcroft. Erdos: Achieving energy savings in mobile os. In *Proceedings of the Sixth International Workshop on MobiArch*, MobiArch '11, pages 37–42, New York, NY, USA, 2011. ACM.

[35] X. Zhao, Y. Guo, Q. Feng, and X. Chen. A system context-aware approach for battery lifetime prediction in smart phones. In *Proceedings of the 2011 ACM Symposium on Applied Computing*, SAC '11, pages 641–646, New York, NY, USA, 2011. ACM.

CIDER: Enabling Robustness-Power Tradeoffs on a Computational Eyeglass

Addison Mayberry   Yamin Tun   Pan Hu   Duncan Smith-Freedman
Deepak Ganesan   Benjamin M. Marlin   Christopher Salthouse
University of Massachusetts, Amherst
Amherst, MA 01003
{amayberr, ytun, panhu, dganesan, marlin}@cs.umass.edu
salthouse@ecs.umass.edu

ABSTRACT

The human eye offers a fascinating window into an individual's health, cognitive attention, and decision making, but we lack the ability to continually measure these parameters in the natural environment. The challenges lie in: a) handling the complexity of continuous high-rate sensing from a camera and processing the image stream to estimate eye parameters, and b) dealing with the wide variability in illumination conditions in the natural environment. This paper explores the power–robustness tradeoffs inherent in the design of a wearable eye tracker, and proposes a novel staged architecture that enables graceful adaptation across the spectrum of real-world illumination. We propose CIDER, a system that operates in a highly optimized low-power mode under indoor settings by using a fast Search-Refine controller to track the eye, but detects when the environment switches to more challenging outdoor sunlight and switches models to operate robustly under this condition. Our design is holistic and tackles a) power consumption in digitizing pixels, estimating pupillary parameters, and illuminating the eye via near-infrared, b) error in estimating pupil center and pupil dilation, and c) model training procedures that involve zero effort from a user. We demonstrate that CIDER can estimate pupil center with error less than two pixels (0.6°), and pupil diameter with error of one pixel (0.22mm). Our end-to-end results show that we can operate at power levels of roughly 7mW at a 4Hz eye tracking rate, or roughly 32mW at rates upwards of 250Hz.

Categories and Subject Descriptors

C.3 [**Special-Purpose and Application-Based Systems**]: Real-time and embedded systems; J.3 [**Life and Medical Sciences**]: Health

Keywords

eye tracking; pupil; neural network; power robustness tradeoff; near-infrared; wearable

MobiCom'15, September 7–11, 2015, Paris, France.

DOI: http://dx.doi.org/10.1145/2789168.2790096.

1. INTRODUCTION

The human eye offers a fascinating window into an individual's personality traits, medical problems, brain abnormalities, behavioral conditions, cognitive attention, and decision making. These characteristics have made it the subject of decades of research by experts in cognition, ophthalmology, neuroscience, epidemiology, behavior, and psychiatry, who have not only enhanced our understanding of how the eye works, but also revealed new ways of diagnosing health concerns. For example, nearly every health condition that affects the brain causes substantial variations in eye movement patterns including ADHD [15], Autism [29], Williams syndrome [30], Schizophrenia [6], Parkinsons [1, 5, 7, 31], Alzheimers disease [26], Depression [8], and others. The eye also reveals a great deal about our current cognitive state, thereby providing surprising benefits for even healthy individuals. In the landmark book "Thinking Fast and Slow" [20], Nobel laureate Daniel Kahneman eloquently describes how an individual's System 2, which is our slow, deliberate, analytical and consciously effortful mode of reasoning, tires after too much cognitive effort, resulting in greater reliance on the unreliable but less effortful System 1, leading to poor decision making (also known as ego depletion). The effects are wide-ranging: judges are more likely to deny parole at the end of the day [12], clinicians have been found to prescribe unnecessary antibiotics [23], soldiers make poor decisions in operational environments [17], people buy more junk food [3], consume more alcohol and cigarettes [4, 10], and so on. How would we detect such cognitive "fatigue?" By looking at the eye and measuring pupil dilation.

Despite the enormous potential for advancing detection of health states and understanding of human decision making by measuring the eye, progress has been stymied by the lack of wearable eye trackers that are integrated into a regular pair of eyeglasses. But the design of a low-power wearable eye tracker is remarkably challenging from the computation, sensing, communication, and aesthetic design perspectives. A real-time eye tracker involves an eye-facing imager sampling at frame rates of tens of Hz (up to 100Hz to detect fine-grained eye movements or saccades) thereby generating megabits of data per second and making communication to a phone extremely power-hungry. As a reference point, the Google Glass lasts only a few hours when streaming from its outward facing camera, while running too hot for comfort [22]. Real-time computation on the eyeglass is also remarkably challenging, particularly given the volume of data and complexity of the image processing techniques. While our focus in this paper is on the computation and power aspects, aesthetic design presents an equally significant challenge since the sensors need to be embedded in an unobtrusive manner within an eyeglass frame.

Several initial efforts have been made to design low-power wearable eye trackers (e.g. iShadow [25], iGaze [39]), but many challenges remain. We tackle two in this work — power and robustness. Power consumption is a major avenue for improvement in eye trackers. The iGaze eye tracker consumes 1.5W, and a more optimized eye tracker, iShadow [25] has a power budget at around 70mW. These numbers are still much higher than typical wearables which only consume a few milliwatts of power, so there is a significant gap that we need to bridge to enable long-term operation of eye trackers on small wearable batteries.

Another major avenue for improvement is robustness. Eye trackers simply do not work outdoors given the variability in outdoor lighting conditions. More generally, achieving robust operation in environments with different illumination conditions is extraordinarily challenging and hasn't been achieved so far by either research prototypes or bulkier commercial products. Some eye trackers such as iShadow and iGaze rely on visible light, but clearly this fails under poorly illuminated conditions. Many commercial eye trackers use near-infrared illumination of the eye, but these do not operate outdoors since they are overwhelmed by ambient infrared light.

Our fundamental contribution is the design of a staged architecture for computational eyeglasses that can trade off between power and robustness to illumination conditions. The principle underlying our architecture is well-known to systems researchers — we optimize heavily for the common case but provide more power-hungry features to deal with the more difficult but uncommon scenarios that occur.

The common case is that a) we spend a substantial fraction of time indoors (homes, shopping malls, etc), and b) we spend 80% of the time fixating on points, during which time the eye moves only a small amount (referred to as microsaccades, which are typically less than 0.4°). We optimize for this regime by using a small amount of near-infrared illumination, a few tens of pixels sampled per estimate, and a few dozen instructions executed per pixel to estimate eye gaze and pupil dilation parameters. The power consumption for the common case is, therefore, only about 7mW — in contrast, iGaze [39] consumes 1.5W (three orders of magnitude difference), and iShadow [25] consumes 70mW (order of magnitude difference).

The question, however, is how to deal with much more antagonistic environments involving outdoor sunlight, shadows, and specular reflection of an onboard illumination source from off the cornea. To tackle this regime, we propose several adaptation methods, where we sacrifice energy-efficiency and switch between the sensing and computational blocks that we activate depending on how much noise and variability we observe. This includes sampling more pixels to get a better estimate of the pupil, performing more computation on the pixels to deal with noise, and using more complex models to estimate eye parameters. These stages of the pipeline consume 20mW, which is more than an order of magnitude higher than the typical power consumption, but these are triggered less than 10% of the time, therefore our overall efficiency does not increase significantly.

One of the interesting auxiliary benefits of our staged processing pipeline is that it can operate at very high frame rates during typical operation. Our optimized pipeline can operate at rates exceeding 100 fps, which is at the the high end of tethered remote eye trackers. This capability is particularly useful for detecting small fine-grained saccadic movements which happen while reading or when fatigued, providing further window into an individual's neural activities. Our algorithm, CIDER (CIrcle Detection of Edges with Reinforcement), is the first wearable eye tracker to achieve such high frame rates.

Our experiments show that

- CIDER can track pupil center with accuracy of roughly 1 pixel (0.3°) and pupil dilation with accuracy of approximately 1 pixel (0.22mm) in indoor lighting conditions.
- CIDER adjusts to indoor and outdoor illumination using an indoor-outdoor NIR detector in conjunction with different models and hardware settings. We show that the pupil center error increases only by a modest amount in outdoor settings (4 pixels or 1.2°).
- We operate end-to-end at a total power budget of 7.5mW when running at 4Hz, which is 10× less than previous state-of-art in this area [25]. Alternatively, we can achieve eye tracking rates of upwards of 250 frames/second by scaling power consumption up to 32mW.

2. DESIGN TRADEOFFS

Robust estimation of eye measures on a computational eyeglass presents a number of technical issues that cut across many aspects of design. In this section, we separate each component of the system and identify the key robustness–power tradeoffs that they present.

Sensing: Continuous operation of a camera is power-hungry. The energy cost of sensing primarily arises from digitization of pixels — while the analog electronics of a CMOS camera has very low power consumption (few milliwatts), digitizing hundreds of pixels per image at high frame rate (upwards of 30fps) consumes orders of magnitude more power, resulting in a power consumption of several tens to hundreds of milliwatts for typical cameras.

To reduce power consumption of such a camera, we would need to throttle the rate at which pixels are digitized. This can be done in one of several ways, including sub-sampling the image, reducing the resolution of the image, or acquiring fewer frames. However, reducing power consumption in this manner can be detrimental to dealing with variations — for example, in the presence of variable illumination or shadows, acquiring more pixels and more frames is better since it provides more contextual information and facilitates more robust de-noising methods.

Computation: Once pixels are acquired from the imagers, we need to process them to estimate eye parameters. The computational demands of continuous high-rate image processing (filtering, feature extraction, and detection) are significant, and require CPUs that have more resources and are more power-hungry than low-power MCU-class processors. One way of addressing this issue is simply to use an MCU with a higher clock rate that can meet the processing requirements. However, as with using a more advanced image sensor, such capability would come with a significant increase in power needs. This tradeoff makes higher-end processors generally infeasible for use with wearables.

If using a more powerful MCU is not an option, the most natural alternative is to trim the computational requirements by using a specialized model. For example, iShadow [25] uses a neural network rather than a typical image processing pipeline, which greatly reduces the amount of computation. However, this often comes at the cost of robustness since such a one-size-fits-all model is not always able to deal with variations in illumination conditions and still achieve high accuracy.

Communication: Can we solve some of the computation issues by offloading it to the phone and cloud? The challenge is dealing

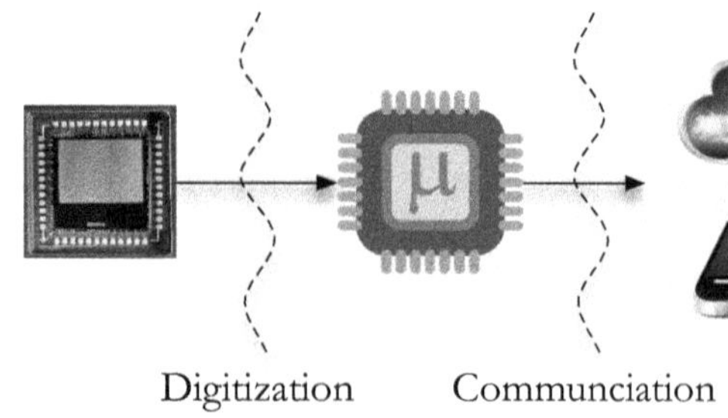

(a) Architecture Challenge

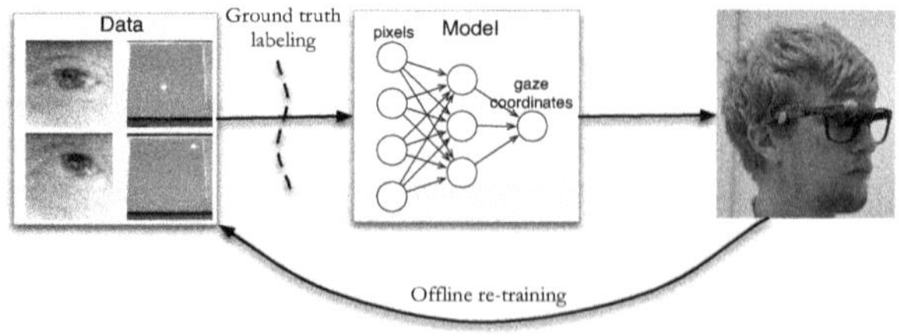

(b) Modeling Challenge

Figure 1: Design challenges. (left) Two major challenges in system design are the power consumed for digitizing pixels from the camera and the power consumed for high-rate communication to a mobile phone. (right) Another major challenge is calibrating the system during online operation without requiring explicit interaction with the user.

with the power-efficiency of radios at high data rates — while radios like BLE, Zigbee, and even WiFi Direct are all relatively low power when used intermittently in a duty-cycled manner, continuous transfer at 30fps from a camera requires always-on radios and increases the power consumption to several tens or hundreds of milliwatts. However, offload has the benefit of being able to leverage vast computational resources to re-train models, adjust parameters, and deal with noise in sensor data, so when judiciously used, it can be effective.

Illumination: One of the key challenges in CIDER is how to deal with the peculiarities of indoor and outdoor lighting to enable robust estimation of eye parameters in both environments. Existing techniques rely either on natural illumination [25, 39] or artificial illumination using a near infrared light source (e.g. [34]). Both techniques have significant advantages and drawbacks. Natural illumination has power savings since typical near-infrared LEDs consume many tens or hundreds of milliwatts during continuous operation. However, this technique is highly sensitive to ambient lighting, and has poor performance when operating in low lighting conditions such as while driving a car at night. In contrast, illuminating the eye via near-infrared (NIR) can provide higher signal to noise ratio, but NIR illumination does not work outdoors since sunlight has significant infrared content, which overwhelms the illumination from the NIR LEDs. Thus, the conditions observed by the IR camera vary significantly, and require more robust methods to process images and extract eye parameters.

Calibrating to new users: An under-explored challenge in designing eye trackers is how to deal with calibration to a new user. The training process is cumbersome and typically performed each time a user wears the device. This was also the case in our prior work [25], where the neural network model is learnt via a calibration procedure requiring the user to look at dots on a computer monitor before wearing the glasses. One question that we ask is whether we can train these systems for a new user with zero-effort i.e. no user involvement whatsoever. Such capability can enable us to train the system without asking the user to alter their normal behavior. This also opens up the possibility to automatically re-train the system when needed, thereby allowing greater flexibility in dealing with robustness issues.

In the following section, we outline a design that provides power efficiency while also creating robustness to variability.

3. CIDER OVERVIEW

At a high level, CIDER uses two different approaches to trade off between robustness and power — the first is a two-stage rapid eye tracking controller, and the second is indoor-outdoor model switching to deal with different illumination conditions and noise. Under typical indoor illumination, CIDER relies on a "Search–Refine" two-stage controller and a small amount of NIR illumination of the eye to estimate eye parameters in a fast, efficient, and accurate manner.

The search stage operates with no prior knowledge of pupil location, and uses a neural network to obtain an estimate of pupil center and size from a sub-sampling of pixels. The refine stage takes an estimate from the search stage, and uses a very fast and accurate procedure to locate and track the eye. When the refine stage loses track of the pupil due to specular reflections or other unpredictable variations, it reverts to the search stage to get another estimate of the eye location. The two stages differ in terms of the amount of sensing required (i.e. number of pixels acquired per frame from the imager) as well as the amount of computation performed to extract eye parameters from the pixels.

In outdoor settings, CIDER turns off NIR illumination (since there is too much ambient infrared), switches to different camera hardware parameters to deal with outdoor lighting, and switches the neural network model to one that is trained for outdoor conditions. We detect indoor vs outdoor conditions using an NIR photodiode that tracks the level of ambient infrared light. In the outdoor mode, CIDER does not use the refine stage and only relies on the neural network to track the eye. We generally find that there is significant variability, which makes it difficult for a more optimized model to operate in a reliable manner.

Overall our pipeline achieves a graceful tradeoff between robustness and power — under typical indoor illumination, CIDER spends most of its time in the fastest and most efficient stage while occasionally using the neural network to provide estimates. In outdoor illumination, CIDER spends all of its time in the slower but more robust neural network stage.

CIDER also addresses robustness issues by designing a model training pipeline that operates with no input from the user. Whenever the eyeglass is fully charged or has good connectivity, a block of images can be communicated to the phone, and a new model trained offline. The enabler is an offline image processing pipeline that generates accurate labels of pupil center and dilation from noisy image data (collected either indoors or outdoors), which makes it possible to learn the neural network models with zero effort from the user.

Finally, CIDER also improves on prior work in that we can simultaneously estimate pupil center and pupil dilation, thereby providing two key measures of the eye in real-time. In principle, CIDER's estimate of pupil center can be used to determine the

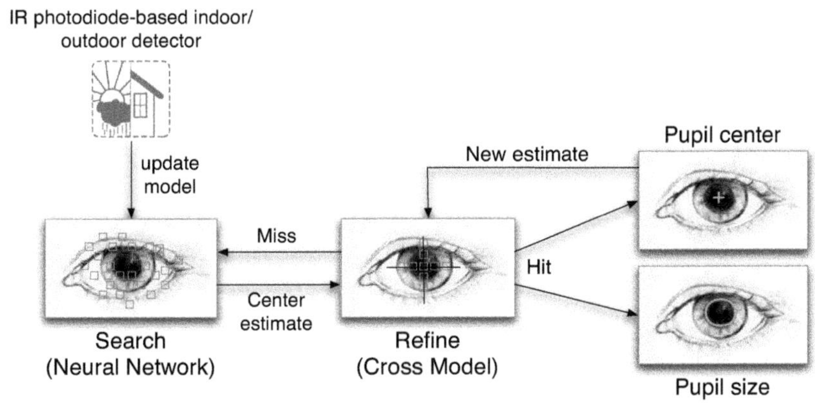

Figure 2: The CIDER pipeline: a) search stage using a neural network to get an initial estimate of pupil location, b) refine stage to zone in on exact pupil center and perform rapid tracking unless the pupil is missed, and c) NIR-photodiode-based detection of indoor/outdoor mode to update neural network model.

gaze direction of the user by leveraging geometric mapping methods from the inward-facing image plane to outward-facing image plane as done in iGaze [39].

4. CIDER DESIGN

In this section, we discuss the details of how CIDER works. We first discuss operation in the indoor case, for which CIDER is highly optimized, and then discuss how we handle the more variable outdoor case.

4.1 Search–Refine Controller

CIDER achieves high speed, high accuracy, and low power by using a rapid switching loop between the search and the refine stage.

Search stage – neural network model: The search stage is an artificial neural network (ANN) prediction model that operates over a subsampled set of pixels, based on the design outlined in [25]. We provide a high-level overview for completeness, and refer the interested reader to [25] for a more thorough overview. The process involves setting up the prediction problem as a neural network where the inputs are the pixel values obtained from the imager, and the output is a predicted (x,y) coordinate pair. The problem is set up as a bi-objective optimization, where one objective is to minimize the set of pixels that need to be sampled to reduce power consumption, and the second objective is to minimize loss in pupil center prediction accuracy. This is achieved using a neural network learning algorithm together with a regularizer that penalizes models that select more pixels. The optimization problem has two terms: a) an error term that captures how well the algorithm predicts gaze coordinates, and b) a penalty term that increases with the number of pixels selected. To promote sparsity i.e. to select a small active pixel set to sample, the algorithm uses a sparsity-inducing ℓ_1 regularization function, which minimizes the number of pixels sampled. The optimization function is solved offline using labeled training data, and the parameters are hard-coded into the eyeglass platform for real-time prediction of the pupil center.

The only major change to the ANN model in [25] for this work is the output target of the model. The goal of the original iShadow work was to predict the gaze location of the subject based on the orientation of their eye in the image. For this work, we instead want to identify the pupil within the eye image and report relevant parameters - center xy-coordinate, and radius of the shape. Since the original ANN model has several desirable properties, including input feature reduction and good accuracy, we chose to use the same model to estimate these parameters. The input to the neural network is still the subsampled pixels, however it is now trained to minimize error over three target values- center x, center y, and radius.

Refine stage – cross-search model: The refine stage is a cross-search model (shown in Figure 3) that leverages the estimate from the neural network to track the center of the pupil and pupil size with minimal sampling overhead. The first step of the cross model is to sample one row and one column of pixels at the estimated location provided by the neural network. There is substantial fixed pattern noise from our camera, so we need to first remove this noise (described in more detail in §5.2). Once the fixed pattern noise has been removed, the pixel values are median filtered and segmented into several regions — Sclera, Iris, Pupil, and Sclera. The segmentation process convolves the pixels with a box filter to detect edges. Since we run the same operations on a column and a row of pixels, we have two chords corresponding to the pupil along the vertical and horizontal axes. We assume that the pupil is a circle for simplicity of computation, and then it is straightforward to compute the center of the circle from the mid-point of the two chords.

Rapid switching between stages: Switching between the two stages works as follows. The ANN executes once, and then hands control over to the cross model to see if it can handle further refinements without requiring the ANN. The cross model is extremely fast, and takes a fraction of the time of the ANN, so it can execute quickly and check if further tracking of the eye can be handled entirely by using the cross model. To determine when to switch back, the cross model performs an internal validity check to see if the results it has obtained are consistent. Specifically, the cross model checks if the two chords (horizontal and vertical) result in a consistent solution. If there is too much error, it falls back to the ANN model. Since the cross model is fast, any misses are quickly handed by the ANN within a short time window, so the time window during which we do not have an estimate of the eye parameters is tiny.

The speed at which the cross model operates means that it is not only refining the estimate from the ANN, but is also tracking the eye. The cross model can operate at frame rates of several hundreds of Hz, which is much faster than the speed at which larger saccades occur. As a result, even if the eyeball is moving, the cross model makes small adjustments each frame, thereby tracking the eye. The

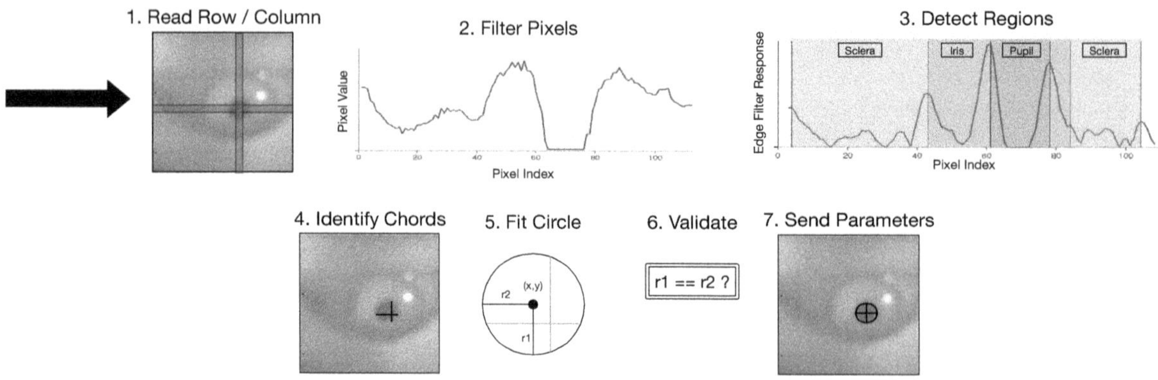

Figure 3: The CIDER cross-search model: 1) a row and column of pixels near the pupil center are sampled, 2) values are median filtered, 3) regions of the eye are detected using edge detection, 4) chords within the pupil are detected, 5) circle is fitted to the chords, 6) consistency check is performed to detect hit or miss, 7) the pupil center and size are estimated.

only occasions when the cross model fails is when there are blinks, specular reflections, shadows, or other artifacts, in which case it switches to the neural network.

Optimizing NIR power consumption: One of the key enablers of the rapid switching controller described above is NIR-based illumination of the eye. Even though indoor lighting can vary significantly, there is virtually zero infrared content in the light emitted by lightbulbs (FL, CFL, LED, etc). This gives us an opportunity to use a small NIR light source to illuminate the eye, and use an NIR-pass filter on the camera to make sure that only the NIR illuminated content is captured. This gives us very controlled lighting conditions despite potential changes in the indoor lighting level.

One issue that we face is that typical NIR LEDs have high power consumption (the one we use consumes 180mW at peak power) — this is small compared to the overall power budget of typical eye trackers that consume watts of power, but it is exorbitant when we are attempting to operate at a few milliwatts of power. Thus, one question that we faced is how to reduce this power consumption.

There are two ways to reduce NIR power consumption — one is to duty-cycle the NIR photodiode, and the other is to reduce the operating voltage of the LED. NIR duty-cycling can be done between frames, therefore the reduction in number of pixels acquired using the cross-search model plays a significant role in the duty-cycling benefits. Reducing the operating voltage of the LED is effective as well — we found that NIR LEDs operate down to about 1.15V, and while reducing the voltage results in increased noise, there is sufficient signal for the neural network to learn a robust mapping. A small downside of this approach is that we lose some efficiency since NIR LEDs are typically most efficient at the high-end of their voltage range, however, this is balanced by the substantial power benefits that can be obtained. The combination of duty-cycling and low voltage operation reduces the NIR power budget by roughly two orders of magnitude, from 180mW to less than a milliwatt.

We note that our use of NIR is very different from methods used by commercial eye trackers. Typical eye trackers use multiple narrow NIR beams, and process the image data to locate these NIR beams, before combining this information with an eye model. However, this process requires several NIR LEDs, more complex geometric methods for estimating eye parameters, and does not generalize to outdoor settings. We operate with just two NIR LEDs, very simple models, and our computational methods continue to work in outdoor settings albeit at higher cost (as we describe below).

4.2 Indoor-Outdoor Model Switching

A second switching mechanism in CIDER is between indoor and outdoor modes of operation. Indoor and outdoor operation are very different for two reasons: a) NIR illumination is useful in indoor settings since it provides a controlled environment for eye tracking, but not for outdoor settings where there is too much ambient IR, and b) camera gain parameters need to be adjusted for outdoor settings and this requires modification of the neural network parameters.

Our idea is to track ambient IR conditions using a separate infrared photodiode that is built into our eyeglass (facing outward rather than inward). We use the IR levels to switch between different camera parameters (gain settings), as well as different neural networks trained for different conditions. This mechanism can be viewed as a camera gain control mechanism that is tightly integrated with the eye parameter estimation pipeline. Typical cameras use automated gain control (AGC) to deal with lighting variations, but a downside is that the pixel values are continually changing depending on the gain parameters. This makes it difficult to run a specialized computational function such as neural network, particularly when subsampling pixels to operate with as few pixels as possible. Rather than continuous adjustments, our method can be viewed as a discrete approach, where we have two models corresponding to specific ambient IR settings, and we switch both the hardware parameters of the camera and the model based on the observed settings.

The switching process itself is extremely simple from the perspective of the firmware, requiring only a few MCU instructions to sample the photodiode at regular intervals. Since lighting conditions can be reasonably expected not to change with high frequency (i.e. more than once every few seconds), this sampling can be done as infrequently as once a second or less. If the MCU detects a significant change in lighting conditions, altering the camera gain parameters also only requires a small handful of instruction cycles. Thus, the overall power and time cost of the switching process is negligible.

This indoor–outdoor model switching can be viewed as a form of power vs robustness adaptation. In indoor settings, we consume more power due to NIR illumination of the eye, but save much more power by reducing the number of pixels sampled and associated computation. In outdoor settings, we shut off the NIR LED and opportunistically leverage ambient IR to save power. We rely on

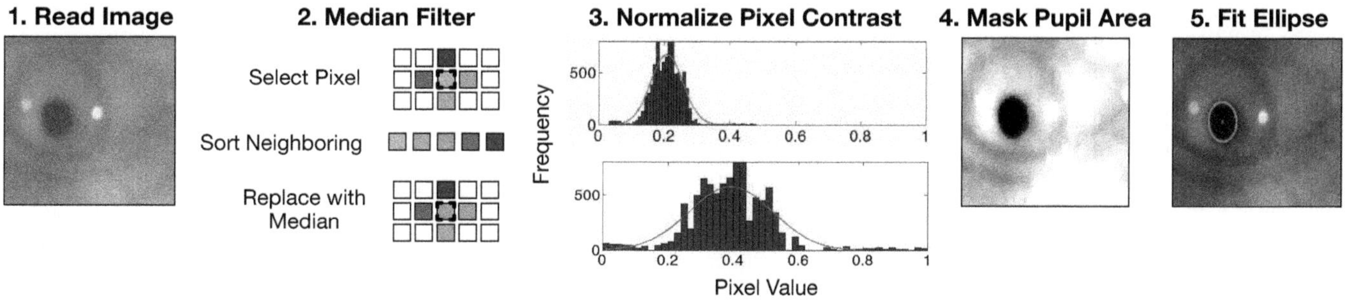

Figure 4: Labeling pipeline with select stages shown

a more complex neural network model, which implies more pixels and more computation, but gain robustness in the process.

4.3 Zero-Effort Model Training

One remaining question in our system is how to train the models for each user. Ideally, we would want such training to be completely automated to minimize burden on the user. This problem often goes unaddressed in existing approaches, most of which are designed to require a period of explicit user participation in order to generate model training data (e.g. [25]). Zero-effort training could greatly increase the likelihood of broader applicability of our system.

The core question in training is how to develop a robust offline method for generating labels from noisy images collected by the camera. The offline procedure that we use for training the neural network is shown in Figure 4. The raw image is processed through a median filtering stage, from which the region corresponding to the eye is extracted. This region is further contrast-adjusted and filtered, and segmented to extract dark regions in the image. In good conditions, only the pupil shows up as a dark region, but we faced two additional challenges.

First, we see specular reflection of the NIR LED from the eye, and when the specular reflection overlaps with the pupil, the dark region can look like a disk, or like a disk with a bite on the side. To address this, we fill holes that we might observe in the segmented shape using standard image-fill techniques that identify distinctive regions of color within a larger area (the pupil) and adjust them using the surrounding pixels. Since the specular reflection is small relative to the size of the pupil, these simple techniques work extremely well in practice. Second, in outdoor conditions, we often see shadows caused by the sun's position relative to the eyeglass frame, and these shadow regions are also picked up by the segmentation block. To isolate the pupil, we look for the roundest segment to detect the pupil.

Given the target pupil location from the above image processing pipeline, we then divide the data into train and test sets and learn the neural network parameters. The new model is then uploaded to the glasses.

5. CIDER SYSTEM

In this section, we describe the main components of our eyeglass system and our implementation of CIDER, and the improvements over other prototypes that have been designed in past work.

5.1 CIDER Platform

Our eyeglass platform has a low-power camera that is mounted in the lower part of the frame facing the eye, as well as an NIR

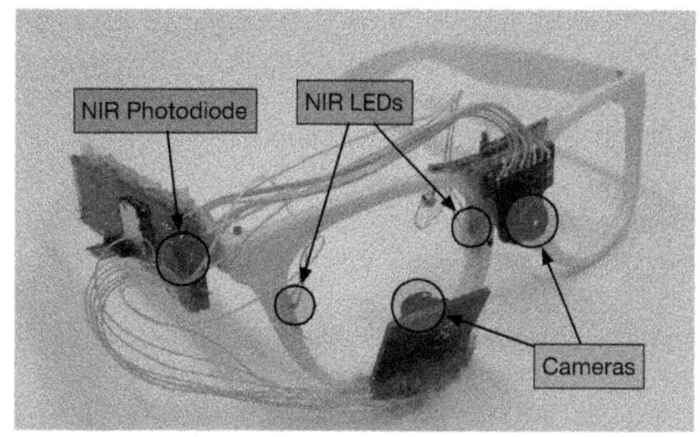

Figure 5: Eyeglass platform

illuminator, as shown in Figure 5. We also have another outward-facing camera, as well as other sensors, but we do not discuss them in detail since they are not pertinent to the methods in this paper. We use the standard optics on the image sensors, which give a 36° field of view. The eye-facing camera has an NIR filter to capture the illuminated eye.

Our platform is similar to iShadow [25], with three key differences. First, we mount the eye-facing camera at the bottom of the frame rather than the top as in iShadow. The difference in how we mount the camera has implications on the tracking accuracy, as well as robustness to different conditions. One major consideration in this decision is that people naturally tend to look down with their eyes much more frequently than they look up. If the camera is mounted in the lower position we observed that, when looking down, the user's pupil is pointed nearly directly at the camera, making detection easier. In addition, when a person looks down for any reason, the upper eyelid naturally lowers a little. This can obscure the eye features when viewed from a higher vantage point (we have observed this in practice). Note that the lower eyelid does not noticeably raise when looking up, so the eye does not become obscured even when viewed from a lower angle. Thus, we concluded that mounting the camera on the lower portion of the frame was a strict improvement over the upper portion.

The second major change from iShadow is that we illuminate the eye with a pair of NIR LEDs shown in Figure 5. The placement point for the LEDs was chosen after careful characterization of what location would provide best illumination while minimizing issues due to specular reflections. Similarly, the choice of NIR LED was made after a rigorous measurement study involving more than a dozen types of NIR LEDs to understand their power-illumination profiles. The third and final difference is that we have an NIR photodiode that detects the level of ambient NIR and allows us to detect indoor conditions vs outdoor conditions.

Our platform is very different from other prototypes such as iGaze [39]. The iGaze device consumes more than a watt, and uses a Raspberry Pi attached to a glasses frame with cameras and sensors. The difference in power between our prototype and iGaze is between two and three orders of magnitude, and virtually every component in our system from algorithm to hardware components is optimized to achieve the power reduction.

Microcontroller: The iShadow platform uses an MCU with an ARM Cortex M3 core [11]. Our implementation of the platform uses an STM32L151 microcontroller, which is manufactured by STMicro Corporation [32] and is an implementation of the Cortex M3 standard. The STM32L1 family emphasizes low power consumption and includes a wide variety of processor sleep modes that are useful for reducing power draw by inserting timed sleep cycles where possible. It also includes several built-in peripherals for handling common communication protocols such as USB, reducing the firmware development burden significantly.

Image sensors: Our hardware framework is built around the Stonyman Vision Chip produced by Centeye, Inc.[9]

The Stonyman camera has a resolution of 112x112 pixels, each of which is characterized by a logarithmic voltage response to lighting conditions. These pixels have a high dynamic range, and more importantly, allow a random-access interface which the Stonyman provides via a register-based control scheme. Besides the extremely low power consumption compared to off-the-shelf cameras (3mW), the main advantage of the imager is that it allows for random access to individual pixel values. This feature allows us to sub-select specific pixels that we need for CIDER, and results in significant reduction in the digitization cost.

Another important characteristic of the Stonyman imager that is the fact that the camera gain parameters are controlled programmatically rather than automatically (i.e. there is no automatic gain control like in other cameras). While this could be viewed as disadvantage, we find the ability to control gain to be beneficial for us in that we can adjust gain parameters and the model parameters in tandem when triggered by the NIR photodiode.

Finally, the Stonyman camera also provides features such as a sleep mode, during which the pixel acquisition circuitry can be powered down. The low-power state has power consumption less than half a microwatt since only a few control registers are running to maintain camera state.

5.2 Handling Camera Noise

We faced several implementation challenges, particularly in how we deal with the camera noise and identify camera gain parameters, which we briefly list in this section

Fixed pattern noise: One of the biggest challenges that we face in designing CIDER is dealing with low-level noise and the way in which the noise is intertwined with the hardware circuitry of the Stonyman camera. For example, one issue was that the fixed pattern noise of the pixels looked different when we were reading pixels along a horizontal line vs along a vertical line for the cross model. We identified that this issue was related to the way in which the pixel readout circuitry is designed on the Stonyman camera. The pixels along each row are daisy-chained to a single readout circuit, therefore, once we started reading out pixels from the beginning of the row, all the pixels along that row were activated. This resulted in varying noise along the row since the pixels at the end of the row had higher magnitude signal and noise. This issue does not occur when sampling pixels along a column since each only one pixel is read from each row. To address this problem, we learned a different fixed pattern noise mask per column and per row through offline calibration, and we subtracted the mask from the measured values to obtain the actual signal.

Gain settings: Another issue that we faced is that the Stonyman camera provides four gain parameters, each of which has roughly 20 settings. This results in a huge search space (20^4) to determine which is the best parameter setting for indoor and outdoor conditions. The search process is largely mechanical but time-consuming since an image has to be captured for each setting, and the values checked to see if it is appropriate. The setting is important, however, since indoor gain values simply do not work outdoors and result in the pixel values saturating. While the settings we identified works well under different outdoor conditions, it may be possible to perform further fine-tuning to specific conditions and get better results than those which we have reported.

6. EVALUATION

We first describe the datasets that we have collected and the evaluation metrics we use and then describe our experimental evaluation.

6.1 Datasets and Ground Truth Labeling

We evaluate CIDER with four datasets that correspond to different environments and dynamics. All data collection experiments involving human subjects received approval from an institutional review board.

- **Indoor-Stable data (fixed pupil, fixed illumination)** We collected data from 16 users, 12 male and 4 female. Each subject performed a video calibration routine where they looked at a high contrast dot moving on a computer monitor for several minutes. This gives us good coverage of eye positions, and allows us to train a good model as well as determine robustness to position of the eye. The illumination was held constant during this period, and subjects' pupils were roughly 5–7 pixels wide in this illumination. We generated approximately 2500 eye images for each user. The subjects involved in the data collection represent a range of ethnic groups with different eye shapes and iris colorations. We refer to this dataset as `indoor-stable`. All subjects in the other datasets were also in the `indoor-stable` dataset.
- **Indoor-Variable data (variable pupil, variable illumination)** We collected this data for 14 users, 10 male and 4 female. We varied the lighting conditions in five discrete levels using a combination of different sets of ceiling lights as well as target spotlights. The subjects pupils dilated between 5–15 pixels during this period, which gives us a fairly large range of pupil dilations that is representative of what one would observe in real-world settings. The screen brightness was kept low enough to not impact dilation much. The above computer-based calibration routine was executed for each setting to obtain data. We refer to this dataset as `indoor-variable`.
- **Outdoor data (uncontrolled illumination)** We collected this data for three users, all male, under outdoor settings. The conditions were generally bright. We obtained several minutes of data from each participant generally gazing at the outside scene under different orientations.
- **Indoor-Outdoor switching data** Our indoor-outdoor data was collected for one user, who walked between indoor and outdoor conditions repeatedly for four iterations, while spending roughly a minute in each environment. This dynamic setting helps us evaluate whether the NIR photodiode-based

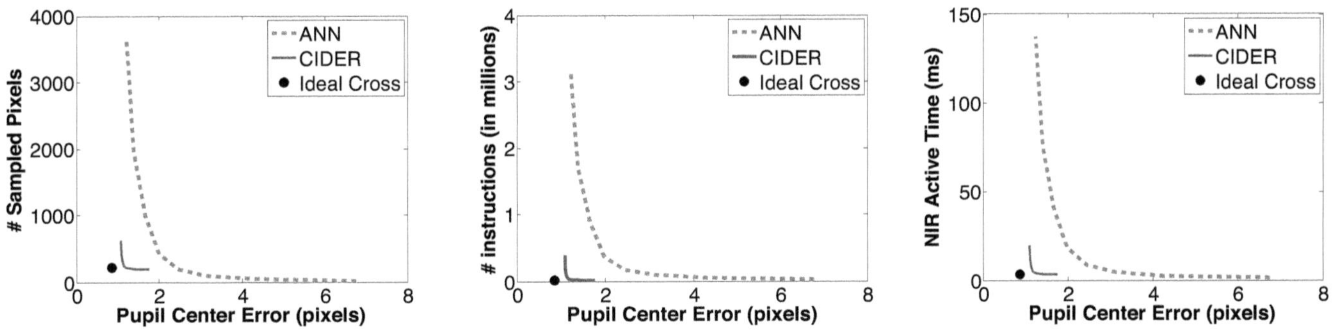

(a) Sensing pixels vs center accuracy

(b) Computation cycles vs center accuracy

(c) NIR time vs center accuracy

Figure 6: Cost vs Accuracy

model switching algorithm works effectively with real scene changes.

Ground truth labeling: All data collected above was labeled for pupil center and pupil size using the process described in §4.3. Once labeled, we trained the neural network to identify the pupil center and radius of the best-fit circle approximating the pupil shape using a standard five-fold cross-validation scheme. We averaged the test set error over the five folds to get an average score. Pupil center error is computed as the L2 (Euclidean) distance between the estimate and the label, pupil size error as the difference between the estimated radius and the label. The errors were averaged over all subjects per model size to get a final set of error estimation accuracies over a range of neural network model sizes.

6.2 Evaluation Metrics

We use several performance métrics to evaluate our system. Since our power numbers are specific to our platform, we provide both a more general metric that could generalize to any platform as well as a more specific metric for our platform given the hardware components that we choose.

Cost metrics: We use three performance metrics to evaluate our system.

- ► **Sensing cost** We measure sensing cost in two ways: a) the number of pixels sub-sampled from the imager, and b) the power consumed for sampling the pixels for the Stonyman camera. The former measure generalizes to any camera that can be sub-sampled, while the latter measure provides a real measurement that includes constant overheads of switching the camera from sleep to active mode, sampling the pixels, and switching back to sleep mode.
- ► **Computation cost** We measure computation cost in two ways as well: a) the number of instructions that need to be executed for each model, and b) the power consumed for executing instructions.
- ► **NIR cost** Similar to the above two metrics, we measure the NIR cost in terms of active time (i.e. time for which the NIR is turned on), as well as the power consumed for our NIR LED with duty-cycling and voltage optimizations described in §2.

Accuracy metrics: We measure accuracy of estimating eye parameters using two metrics

- ► **Pupil center** The accuracy in measuring pupil center is measured in pixels in the image captured by the eye-facing imager. This measure gives us an idea of how far we are from the best-case performance given the sampling granularity of the imager. From an application perspective, the key metric of interest is the degree error in estimating gaze. We estimate that each pixel corresponds to roughly 0.3°, so this gives us a mapping from pupil center error measured in pixels to gaze error. Commercial (tethered) gaze trackers achieve errors of roughly 0.5° [35], which is slightly less than two pixel error on our system.
- ► **Pupil radius** Similar to pupil center, we measure pupil dilation in pixels. Each pixel in in the camera's visual field corresponds to roughly 0.22mm when measured on the pupil, which is similar to the resolution of high-end gaze trackers.

6.3 CIDER Performance

As we have outlined, the search and refine stages of CIDER are intended to maximize estimation accuracy and power efficiency over a range of environmental parameters. Our first set of results evaluates the performance of CIDER by comparing it against the two stages (search and refine) independently. We use the `indoor-stable` data in this evaluation, which gives us an understanding of best case performance under limited dynamics. We compare the following schemes in this evaluation:

1. **Neural network** The neural network model is learnt as described in §4.1 — we vary λ (regularization parameter) to learn various models that have different tradeoffs between accuracy and pixels (which translates to power). This gives us a pareto optimal set of solutions i.e. a set of solutions that shows the tradeoff between the two objectives.

2. **Idealized cross** The idealized cross method is initialized by the pupil center estimated by our offline algorithm. The cross model then estimates the pupil center and pupil size, and we compare the accuracy against ground truth. Clearly, this is an idealized scenario where the cross model should perform very well, but it still helps us understand how well the edge detection and parameter estimation methods work in the best case.

3. **CIDER** The CIDER method is the fast switching technique. Since the CIDER pipeline involves switching between the ANN and cross model, we expect performance to be in-between the above models.

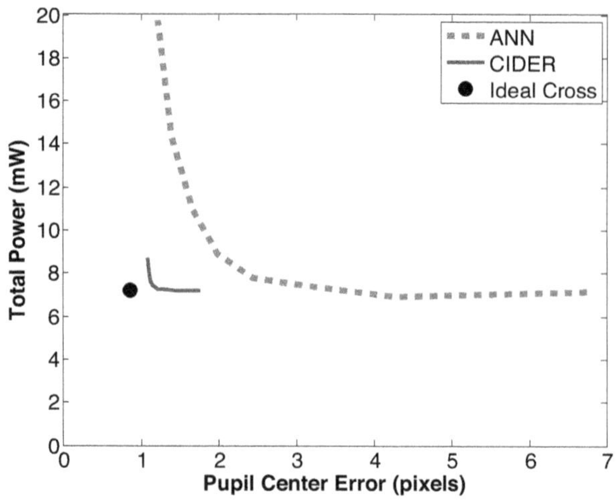

Figure 7: Aggregate power vs accuracy

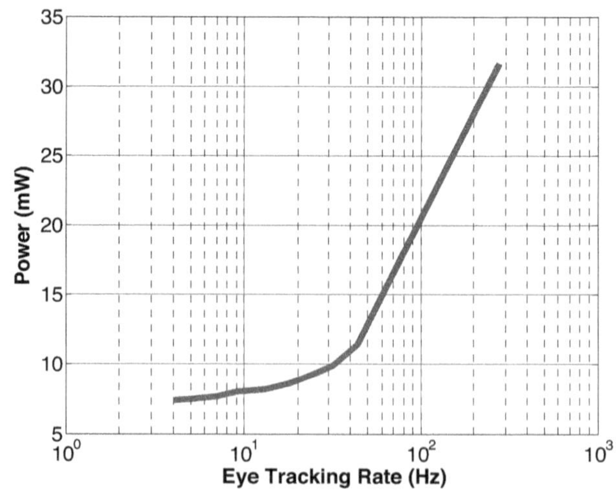

Figure 8: Aggregate power vs eye tracking rate (log scale)

Sensing, computation and NIR cost: Figure 6a shows the curve of sensing cost (in number of pixels sampled) against pupil center estimation error (in number of pixels). The curve is obtained by tuning the neural network regularization parameter, which allows for the generation of a number of network sizes with varying power needs and corresponding accuracy. The result clearly shows that there is a significant gap between any pareto optimal solution that can be obtained for the neural network vs the solution provided by the idealized cross model. CIDER operates between the two but closer to the idealized cross model. This can be explained by the fact that the neural network is triggered only about 10-15% of the time whereas the cross model operates the remaining 85-90% of the time.

The performance difference in terms of computation cost is substantial as well, in fact, even more than in the case of sensing (Figure 6b). The neural network computation is much more involved than the cross model, so there are significantly more operations per pixel. In addition, since the cross model requires fewer pixels, the number of times the computation needs to be performed is also much lower. Thus, the number of instructions that need to be computed for the cross model is orders of magnitude lower than for the neural network.

Finally, the time spent with the NIR LED on is also substantially lower for the idealized cross and CIDER models (Figure 6c). Since the cross model needs very little time to sense, the NIR LED needs to be turned on for a minuscule amount of time for each frame.

Energy savings: We now look at how the benefits in sensing, computation and NIR translate into energy savings on our platform. We measure the average power over a 10 second window of operation using a DAQ running at a 10 kHz sampling rate. To measure power consumption for all three models, we fix the pixel capture + predict rate of the system to 4 Hz by inserting MCU sleep periods as needed. The 4Hz rate is chosen to enable us to measure a sufficiently large range of neural network model sizes to plot the pareto optimal graph.

Figure 7 shows the aggregate power consumption of CIDER and compares against the two other baselines. We see similar trends as we saw earlier in that CIDER operates in between the idealized cross and ANN model with roughly a 3× reduction (compared to neural network models that have low error). The overall power budget for CIDER is roughly 7mW, which is a huge improvement over state-of-art (order of magnitude less power consumption than [25]), and a substantial achievement considering that the system is operating a camera, estimation algorithm, and NIR LED.

One curious feature of the graph is that the baseline for all schemes is shifted by about 6mW. The baseline shift corresponds to constant overheads incurred by our platform, and for configuring various parameters for the camera upon wakeup and shutdown. We suspect that there are various sources of power leakage that contribute significantly to the baseline, but we have not yet been able to fully debug these issues. Looking forward, we expect that some of this constant overhead can be eliminated with a more optimized computational block such as an FPGA rather than a general-purpose MCU.

Power vs tracking rate: Another benefit of CIDER is that it can achieve high tracking rates. We plot the power vs pupil tracking rate in Figure 8, which shows the total system power consumed as the tracking rate is varied. To generate this graph, we used the same model as was used for the measurements in Table 1, and inserted sleep periods of variable length between each single execution of the CIDER pipeline. The measurements were again taken using a DAQ sampling at 10kHz.

Component	Power (4 Hz)	Power (278 Hz)
Camera	7.30 μW	30.8 μW
MCU (digitization)	2.67 mW	11.3 mW
MCU (computation)	4.79 mW	20.2 mW
NIR	8.24 μW	34.8 μW
Overall	7.48 mW	31.6 mW

Table 1: CIDER power breakdown

Table 1 shows a finer-grained breakdown of the power vs tracking rate for each component of CIDER (with a moderately large neural network chosen to use 10% of the pixels). We give two power measurements - one taken at the maximum eye tracking rate possible for this model size, namely, 278 Hz, and one taken at the 4Hz rate used for the rest of the evaluation results. There are several useful observations that can be made from this result. Interestingly, the camera and NIR consume virtually no power compared to other components since they are turned on for a very tiny amount of time. The acquisition consumes a significant amount of power — this is because digitization of the analog signal output from the camera is expensive. One of the major improvements that CIDER provides is reduction of the digitization overhead. The MCU computation is also expensive, however some of this cost could be reduced by using a more optimized computation block such as an FPGA.

Estimation accuracy: The above discussions emphasize power consumption, but it is instructive to look at the absolute accuracies that can be achieved by CIDER. The above results show that CIDER achieves pupil center estimation accuracy within 1.2 pixels. The neural network method cannot achieve such accurate estimation even when consuming considerably more power and resources.

This result may seem surprising at first, since it is natural to expect a more power-hungry technique to have a corresponding increase in performance. The main reason is that the NIR-illuminated eye (indoors) presents very strong edges that are easier to accurately identify using edge detection techniques (the cross model) than using a neural network. So, the accuracies tend to be higher for CIDER even though the power consumption is much lower. This is not the case in the outdoor environment, however, hence the need for the indoor-outdoor switching model. Thus, not only are we able to achieve substantially reduced power consumption, we also do so while simultaneously improving accuracy to within a small amount of the lower bound of what is achievable with our camera.

Model	Pupil Size Error (pixels)
Neural Network	0.50
CIDER	0.85

Table 2: Pupil radius estimation accuracy of CIDER

Table 2 shows the results for pupil size estimation when using only the neural network and when using CIDER. We do not show the entire power-accuracy profile for pupil size since we find that even the smaller ANN models perform well in estimating the pupil size, and there is not much difference in using a larger model. So, we present only the mean performance across all model sizes. We see that the pupil size estimation error is typically less than one pixel, which suggests that both stages can do an excellent job in estimating pupil size. Indeed, we find that the error for CIDER may be over-estimated since we often see that the cross model's estimates are closer to the real value than even ground truth labels.

6.4 CIDER Under Variable Conditions

Having evaluated CIDER under relatively stable conditions, we turn to situations that have more variability. Specifically, we look at three cases: a) variability in the pupil dilation of the user, b) an outdoor setting with variable illumination, and c) the user moving from an indoor to an outdoor setting.

Variable pupil dilation: The results in §6.3 were taken under fixed pupil dilation, so one question is whether the results are robust to varying pupil sizes. Figure 9 compares the pupil center and pupil size estimation errors of CIDER for the 14 users in `indoor-variable`, all of whom are also in the `indoor-stable` dataset. Figure 9a compares the pupil center prediction results for fixed and variable illumination conditions, each as an error CDF, and Figure 9b gives the same comparison for size prediction. The center prediction accuracy under varying pixel sizes is marginally worse than the accuracy under fixed pixel sizes, but the difference is not significant. For the size prediction task, CIDER actually generated slightly better estimates on the variable pupil size dataset. This seems counter-intuitive at first, however, in the `indoor-variable` dataset, the pupil size is generally larger than in `indoor-stable`, as the lighting conditions were darker for most of the experiment.

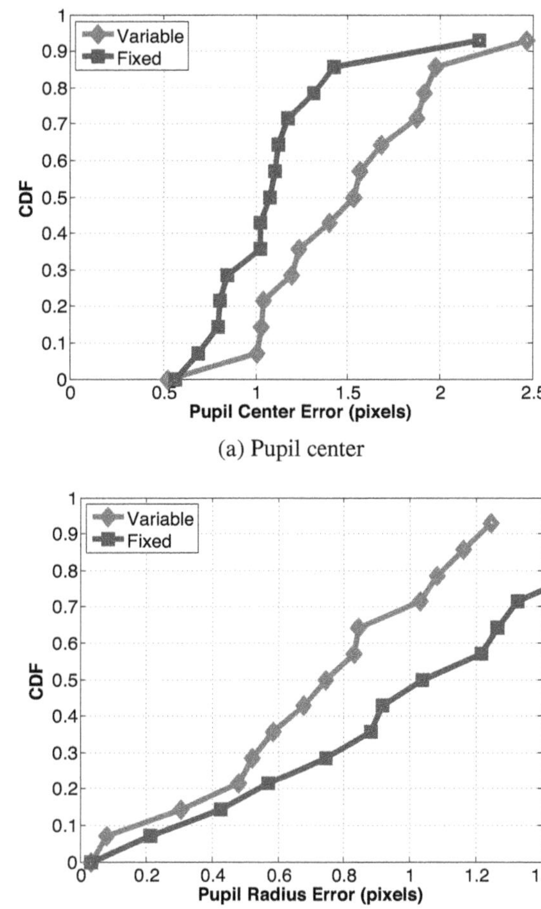

(a) Pupil center

(b) Pupil size

Figure 9: Performance comparison - fixed and variable pupil size

This makes accurate detection of the size slightly easier for both the ANN and the cross model. Overall, we see that performance of CIDER is robust to variation in pupil size.

Outdoor dataset: The outdoor scenario represents another high variability situation for CIDER. The cross model does not work in this situation, so the system relies primarily on the neural network that is trained for outdoor settings. We find that the accuracy with CIDER under outdoor settings is roughly 4 pixels (for moderately sized ANNs). The results are worse than accuracy in indoor settings, but not far off. In fact, the accuracy that we obtain in outdoor settings is better than the results that were obtained in [25] under indoor settings. One of the main reasons for the performance difference is the vastly improved labeling pipeline that we have developed, which allows us to label noisy data quite well.

We get about 1 pixel pupil dilation error, but we find that that this is an over-estimate of the real error for reasons described above. There is about a 1 pixel offset between the radius estimated by the offline labeling algorithm (which performs filtering), and by the cross model. For transparency, we have reported the error as observed, but we think the error is about one pixel smaller than that reported.

Indoor-Outdoor switching: We now look at a situation where a user is moving between an indoor and outdoor environment, and show how well our IR photodiode-based model switching performs. Figure 10 shows the error distribution during the indoor segments

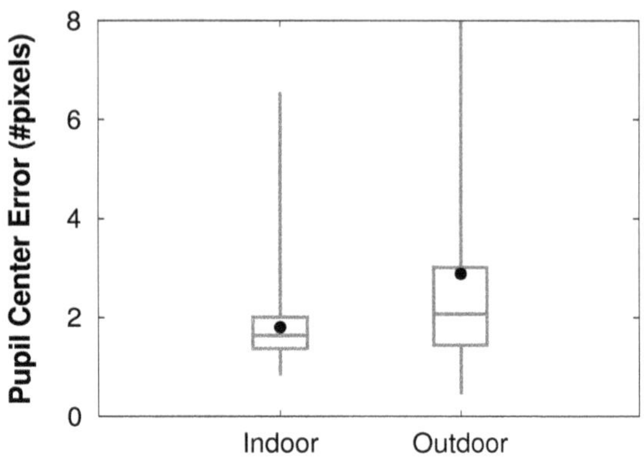

Figure 10: Indoor-Outdoor switching

vs outdoor segments. This is shown as a box plot, where the three lines in the box corresponds to the quartiles (25 percentile, median, and 75 percentile), the whiskers correspond to the max and min, and the dot is the mean. We truncate the max error whisker for the outdoor case since there are some cases where CIDER returns more than 10 pixel error.

We also verified from the traces that the NIR-based switching works effectively, and switches models between the indoor and outdoor modes whenever the user changes environments. As observed in §4.2, the instruction cycle and power cost of the detection and switching process itself is negligible. The error distribution of the predictions is higher for the outdoor case, but it is still relatively low with a mean of less than three pixels. The error when indoors is lower with a mean of less than two pixels.

6.5 CIDER High-Speed Eye Tracking

One of the major benefits of CIDER is the eye tracking speeds that it can achieve. High-speed eye tracking is useful for understanding fast saccadic movements of the eye, which is one of the neural mechanisms for maintaining visibility. For example, one of the interesting use-cases for measuring micro saccades is as a diagnostic test for ADHD [16], and there are other applications of such measurements [24].

However, high speed eye tracking is also very challenging on a wearable device. Commercial high-speed eye trackers achieve several hundred hertz tracking rates (e.g. the Eyelink high-speed eye tracker samples at 500Hz, and the ASL H7-HS can sample at rates up to 360Hz). Of course, these eye trackers are also bulky, tethered for power and connected to a computer for data storage and processing. One interesting question is, how fast CIDER can operate if it is not duty-cycled and is allowed to perform pupil estimation as fast as possible?

To evaluate the maximum speed achievable by CIDER, we run it continuously on our eyeglass without duty-cycling. We measure the rate at which it generates pupil center measures, and find that CIDER achieves frame rates of 250–350 Hz (depending on whether a medium-sized or small ANN is used). These speeds are comparable to the rates achieved by high-speed eye trackers. One caveat is that CIDER is not uniformly sampling since it occasionally uses the ANN. However, the irregularity during the use of ANN can be mitigated by using a smaller ANN model. The power consumption at this frame rate is several tens of milliwatts since the system is operating in always-ON mode. Therefore, many of the optimizations that we used earlier no longer work. However, we don't anticipate that the high-speed mode will be used continuously; rather, this mode may be triggered when appropriate. Overall, we think that the ability to sample at high speed has substantial implications for a wide range of health and cognition applications.

6.6 Accuracy of Labeling

To evaluate the accuracy of the labeling scheme described in §4.3, we hand-labeled 100 eye images from one subject's data. For each image, we selected an elliptical region that visually seemed to best fit the pupil area. We then compared the pupil center and size estimate with those provided by the automatic labeling system for the same frames. The results are given in Table 3. Note that for both measures, the hand-labeling and automatic labeling techniques yield very similar results. The pupil size is slightly higher, but this is most likely due to the fact that the low-resolution images do no provide as sharp of an edge as would be expected with a higher-resolution camera. Thus, the pupil edge appears spread over a one- to two-pixel area, and distinguishing the exact pupil boundary within that region is difficult for a human to do visually.

Feature	Mean Difference (pixels)
Pupil Center	0.853
Pupil Size	1.52

Table 3: Automatic labeling vs hand labeling of pupil

7. RELATED WORK

At a high level, the idea of trading off energy consumption against robustness is present in a plethora of computing systems, but our novelty lies in enabling such tradeoffs by optimizing cost of digitizing pixels while robustly tracking eye parameters. We briefly highlight related efforts that have not already been mentioned in this paper.

Dynamic energy-aware adaptation: At a high level, our work can also be viewed as an instance of runtime energy-aware adaptation. Many techniques can be used to achieve such adaptation, including techniques such as varying application fidelity to achieve desired battery lifetime (e.g. changing the fidelity of a speech recognizer or video playback on a mobile device) [14] and adaptive sampling and communication that leverages spatial and temporal structure in sensor signals [36, 13, 21], among others. Our work is a very specialized instance of such adaptation in the context of eye trackers, and proposes the use of two models that are optimized to extract eye parameters at different costs (cross model and neural network), and techniques for switching between the models based on observed dynamics.

Eye tracking overview: Eye and gaze tracking has been a field of study for several decades [18, 28, 38]. Until recently, gaze tracking had mostly been applied to laboratory settings, where a subject sits facing one or more cameras that record video of their eyes and estimates eye parameters, often with their heads in a chin rest so as to remain motionless.

Algorithms to compute gaze positions fall into three categories: shape-based, appearance-based and hybrid algorithms [18]. The shape-based approach uses features of the eye image to fit an ellipse to the boundary between the pupil and the iris [18]. This approach typically works best with near-infrared (NIR) illumination sources, which make it easier to detect the pupil-iris boundary as previously discussed [28]. The cross-search model used in CIDER falls into this category of algorithm.

Appearance-based gaze tracking algorithms attempt to predict the gaze location directly from the pixels of the eye image without an intermediate geometric representation of the pupil. This approach essentially treats the gaze inference problem as a regression problem where the inputs are the pixels of the eye image and the outputs are the vertical and horizontal components of the point of gaze in the outward facing image plane. Due to the generality of the gaze inference problem when formulated in this way, predictions can be based on essentially any multivariate regression approach. Two prominent approaches used in the gaze tracking literature are multi-layer neural networks [2] and manifold-based regression [33]. The neural-network model used in the iShadow work [25] and adapted for CIDER falls into this category.

Mobile eye tracking devices: Recently, there has been tremendous interest in mobile eye trackers that can track eye parameters "in the wild." Companies such as Tobii and SMI have produced devices which have shown great promise for opening up new avenues of research [27, 37]. However, existing industrial-grade mobile eye tracking devices are predominantly a condensed version of a standard remote tracking system, including carefully calibrated on-board illumination and multiple high-definition cameras. While the engineering required to condense such a complex system to a wearable form-factor (usually in the shape of a standard pair of eyeglasses) is impressive, the power requirements of such systems are inordinately large by wearables standards - the user is required to carry a large battery pack, and even then their average run time is less than four hours. In addition, the devices only perform video recording and storage. Since processing the eye data often means running computations over thousands or hundreds of thousands of high resolution simultaneous image streams, even with a full desktop machine the processing can be a time-intensive task. And finally, the cost of these devices is often in the tens of thousands of dollars, making any kind of large-scale study infeasible to all but the most well-funded organizations.

Another notable device of relevance to our work is iGaze. The goal of iGaze is to detect gaze fixations and determine whether the user is looking at a networking-capable device, and if so, the user can initiate a wireless connection to facilitate some useful exchange of data between the iGaze platform and the device in question. The platform itself is comprised of a head-mounted camera monitoring the eye, very similar to this work, and a Raspberry Pi device carried by the user to do image processing and gaze computation. iGaze's predictive error and power consumption are relatively high compared to our work - they report average gaze error of 5° and average power consumption in excess of 1 W, whereas our error is below 1° and power consumption is 7mW. The high power consumption is presumably due to the use of traditional computer vision algorithms for pupil identification, which incur high cost as they require relatively high-resolution images and do not allow for subsampling.

8. FUTURE WORK

To close, we discuss in this section some avenues of future work that we have not addressed in this paper.

Adaptation to dynamics: While our zero-effort pupil-labeling approach tackles the initial calibration problem, one question that we have not addressed is how to deal with dynamics in eyeglass positioning or the environment. For example, shifts in the position of the glasses relative to the user's eye would increase error in ANN predictions. Similarly, prediction error would also increase if the ambient infrared in outdoor settings is significantly different from the data used in training the ANN model. To address such dynamics, we need approaches to detect in real-time that the existing model is performing less accurately than expected, and dynamically adjust the model, perhaps by leveraging our zero-effort training procedures described in this paper. We are exploring techniques for dynamic re-calibration in ongoing work.

Form-factor: The form-factor of the eyeglass is a particularly important problem to tackle for more widespread use of such devices. The biggest challenge in the design is finding an unobtrusive placement of the cameras while simultaneously achieving good coverage of the eye to enable robust estimation of eye parameters. Even with our current prototype, there were instances where we could not obtain complete coverage of the eye due to differences in face shape and the limited field-of-view of the camera. This problem is exacerbated when the camera needs to be embedded in the eyeglass frame since the positioning of the camera is closer to the eye and more sensitive to changes in placement. One of the questions that we are currently exploring is how to embed the cameras in the eyeglass frame so as to reduce form-factor without sacrificing accuracy.

9. CONCLUSIONS

In summary, this paper describes a new method, CIDER, for estimating eye parameters on a computational eyeglass using a staged architecture that trades off power for robustness. Our architecture uses an optimized detector for the "common case" involving a user being indoors and in limited-noise settings, and tremendously reduces the overall power consumption down to numbers that are within the range of typical wearable devices. CIDER deals with more noise and variable illumination settings by using more computational and sensing heft to filter out noise and deal with variability. Finally, we achieve very high frame rates, which gives us the ability to sense fine-grained eye parameters. Most surprisingly, we enable all of this functionally while operating on a small ARM Cortex M3 micro controller. To see a video demonstration of CIDER, visit [19].

Acknowledgments

The authors thank REU student Jose LaSalle for his contributions in the early stages of the glasses design process and for his assistance in exploring various avenues of hardware improvement. We would like to thank Geoffrey Barrows, of Centeye, Inc. for his continued support with the development and use of the Stonyman cameras. His assistance has relieved significant development burden and made much of this work possible. We also thank anonymous reviewers for their suggestions to improve this work. This research was partially supported by NSF grants #1217606, #1218586, and #1239341, as well as NIH grant #1U54EB020404.

10. REFERENCES

[1] M. B. Aerts, R. A. J. Esselink, W. F. Abdo, F. J. A. Meijer, G. Drost, N. Norgren, M. J. R. Janssen, G. F. Borm, B. R. Bloem, and M. M. Verbeek. Ancillary investigations to diagnose parkinsonism: a prospective clinical study. *J. Neurol.*, Nov 2014.

[2] S. Baluja and D. Pomerleau. Non-intrusive gaze tracking using artificial neural networks. Technical report, Pittsburgh, PA, USA, 1994.

[3] R. Baumeister and J. L. Alquist. Self-regulation as a limited resource: Strength model of control and depletion. *Psychology of self-regulation: Cognitive, affective, and motivational processes*, 11:21–33, 2009.

[4] R. F. Baumeister and T. F. Heatherton. Self-regulation failure: An overview. *Psychological inquiry*, 7(1):1–15, 1996.

[5] H. Bekkering, S. F. Neggers, R. Walker, B. Gleissner, W. H. Dittrich, and C. Kennard. The preparation and execution of saccadic eye and

goal-directed hand movements in patients with Parkinson's disease. *Neuropsychologia*, 39(2):173–83, 2001.

[6] M. S. Bolding, A. C. Lahti, D. White, C. Moore, D. Gurler, T. J. Gawne, and P. D. Gamlin. Vergence eye movements in patients with schizophrenia. *Vision Res.*, 102:64–70, Sep 2014.

[7] C. Bonnet, J. Rusz, M. Megrelishvili, T. Sieger, O. Matoušková, M. Okujava, H. Brožová, T. Nikolai, J. Hanuška, M. Kapianidze, N. Mikeladze, N. Botchorishvili, I. Khatiashvili, M. Janelidze, T. Serranová, O. Fiala, J. Roth, J. Bergquist, R. Jech, S. Rivaud-Péchoux, B. Gaymard, and E. Růžička. Eye movements in ephedrone-induced parkinsonism. *PLoS ONE*, 9(8):e104784, 2014.

[8] N. Carvalho, N. Noiret, P. Vandel, J. Monnin, G. Chopard, and E. Laurent. Saccadic eye movements in depressed elderly patients. *PLoS ONE*, 9(8):e105355, 2014.

[9] `http://www.centeye.com/%20products/current-centeye-vision-chips/`. "Current Centeye Vision Chips", Accessed: 2015-06-24.

[10] P. Christiansen, J. C. Cole, and M. Field. Ego depletion increases ad-lib alcohol consumption: Investigating cognitive mediators and moderators. *Experimental and clinical psychopharmacology*, 20(2):118, 2012.

[11] `http://www.arm.com/products/processors/cortex-m/cortex-m3.php`. "Cortex-M3 Processor - ARM", Accessed: 2015-06-24.

[12] S. Danziger, J. Levav, and L. Avnaim-Pesso. Extraneous factors in judicial decisions. *Proceedings of the National Academy of Sciences*, 108(17):6889–6892, 2011.

[13] A. Deshpande, C. Guestrin, S. R. Madden, J. M. Hellerstein, and W. Hong. Model-driven data acquisition in sensor networks. In *Proceedings of the Thirtieth international conference on Very large data bases-Volume 30*, pages 588–599. VLDB Endowment, 2004.

[14] J. Flinn and M. Satyanarayanan. Energy-aware adaptation for mobile applications. In *ACM SIGOPS Operating Systems Review*, volume 33, pages 186–201. ACM, 1999.

[15] M. Fried, E. Tsitsiashvili, Y. S. Bonneh, A. Sterkin, T. Wygnanski-Jaffe, T. Epstein, and U. Polat. ADHD subjects fail to suppress eye blinks and microsaccades while anticipating visual stimuli but recover with medication. *Vision Res.*, 101:62–72, Aug 2014.

[16] M. Fried, E. Tsitsiashvili, Y. S. Bonneh, A. Sterkin, T. Wygnanski-Jaffe, T. Epstein, and U. Polat. ADHD subjects fail to suppress eye blinks and microsaccades while anticipating visual stimuli but recover with medication. *Vision Res.*, 101:62–72, Aug 2014.

[17] K. E. Friedl, S. J. Grate, S. P. Proctor, J. W. Ness, B. J. Lukey, and R. L. Kane. Army research needs for automated neuropsychological tests: monitoring soldier health and performance status. *Archives of Clinical Neuropsychology*, 22:7–14, 2007.

[18] D. W. Hansen and Q. Ji. In the eye of the beholder: A survey of models for eyes and gaze. *Pattern Analysis and Machine Intelligence, IEEE Transactions on*, 32(3):478–500, 2010.

[19] `http://sensors.cs.umass.edu/projects/eyeglass/`. "iShadow: The Computational Eyeglass", Accessed: 2015-06-24.

[20] D. Kahneman. *Thinking, fast and slow*. Macmillan, 2011.

[21] M. Li, D. Ganesan, and P. Shenoy. Presto: feedback-driven data management in sensor networks. *IEEE/ACM Transactions on Networking (TON)*, 17(4):1256–1269, 2009.

[22] R. LiKamWa, Z. Wang, A. Carroll, F. X. Lin, and L. Zhong. Draining our glass: An energy and heat characterization of google glass. In *Proceedings of 5th Asia-Pacific Workshop on Systems*, APSys '14, 2014.

[23] J. A. Linder, J. N. Doctor, M. W. Friedberg, H. Reyes Nieva, C. Birks, D. Meeker, and C. R. Fox. Time of Day and the Decision to Prescribe Antibiotics. *JAMA Intern Med*, Oct 2014.

[24] S. Martinez-Conde, S. L. Macknik, X. G. Troncoso, and D. H. Hubel. Microsaccades: a neurophysiological analysis. *Trends Neurosci.*, 32(9):463–475, Sep 2009.

[25] A. Mayberry, P. Hu, B. Marlin, C. Salthouse, and D. Ganesan. ishadow: design of a wearable, real-time mobile gaze tracker. In *Proceedings of the 12th annual international conference on Mobile systems, applications, and services*, pages 82–94. ACM, 2014.

[26] R. J. Molitor, P. C. Ko, and B. A. Ally. Eye Movements in Alzheimer's Disease. *J. Alzheimers Dis.*, Sep 2014.

[27] J. D. Morgante, R. Zolfaghari, and S. P. Johnson. A critical test of temporal and spatial accuracy of the tobii t60xl eye tracker. *Infancy*, 17(1):9–32, 2012.

[28] C. Morimoto and M. Mimica. Eye gaze tracking techniques for interactive applications. *Computer Vision and Image Understanding*, 98(1):4–24, 2005.

[29] L. M. Schmitt, E. H. Cook, J. A. Sweeney, and M. W. Mosconi. Saccadic eye movement abnormalities in autism spectrum disorder indicate dysfunctions in cerebellum and brainstem. *Mol Autism*, 5(1):47, 2014.

[30] W. Seiple, R. B. Rosen, and P. M. T. Garcia. Abnormal fixation in individuals with age-related macular degeneration when viewing an image of a face. *Optom Vis Sci*, 90(1):45–56, Jan 2013.

[31] A. Srivastava, R. Sharma, S. K. Sood, G. Shukla, V. Goyal, and M. Behari. Saccadic eye movements in Parkinson's disease. *Indian J Ophthalmol*, 62(5):538–44, May 2014.

[32] `http://www.st.com/stm32`. "STM32 32-bit ARM Cortex MCUs - STMicroelectronics", Accessed: 2015-06-24.

[33] K.-H. Tan, D. Kriegman, and N. Ahuja. Appearance-based eye gaze estimation. In *Proceedings of the Sixth IEEE Workshop on Applications of Computer Vision, 2002.*, pages 191–195, 2002.

[34] `http://www.tobiiglasses.com/`. "Tobii Glasses: Mobile Eye Tracker for real world research," Accessed: 2015-06-24.

[35] `http://www.tobii.com/Global/Analysis/Marketing/Brochures/ProductBrochures/Tobii_X1_Light_Eye_Tracker_Technical_Specifcation_Leaflet.pdf?epslanguage=en`. "Tobii X1: Gaze Precision and Gaze Accuracy", Accessed: 2015-06-24.

[36] R. Willett, A. Martin, and R. Nowak. Backcasting: adaptive sampling for sensor networks. In *Proceedings of the 3rd international symposium on Information processing in sensor networks*, pages 124–133. ACM, 2004.

[37] Z. Ye, Y. Li, A. Fathi, Y. Han, A. Rozga, G. D. Abowd, and J. M. Rehg. Detecting eye contact using wearable eye-tracking glasses. In *Proceedings of the 2012 ACM Conference on Ubiquitous Computing*, pages 699–704. ACM, 2012.

[38] L. Young and D. Sheena. Survey of eye movement recording methods. *Behavior Research Methods*, 7(5):397–429, 1975.

[39] L. Zhang, X.-Y. Li, W. Huang, K. Liu, S. Zong, X. Jian, P. Feng, T. Jung, and Y. Liu. It starts with igaze: Visual attention driven networking with smart glasses. In *Proceedings of the 20th annual international conference on Mobile computing and networking*, pages 91–102. ACM, 2014.

piStream: Physical Layer Informed Adaptive Video Streaming Over LTE

Xiufeng Xie and Xinyu Zhang
University of Wisconsin-Madison
{xiufeng, xyzhang} @ece.wisc.edu

Swarun Kumar
MIT
swarun@mit.edu

Li Erran Li
Fudan University
erranlli@gmail.com

ABSTRACT

Adaptive HTTP video streaming over LTE has been gaining popularity due to LTE's high capacity. Quality of adaptive streaming depends highly on the accuracy of client's estimation of end-to-end network bandwidth, which is challenging due to LTE link dynamics. In this paper, we present piStream, that allows a client to efficiently monitor the LTE basestation's PHY-layer resource allocation, and then map such information to an estimation of available bandwidth. Given the PHY-informed bandwidth estimation, piStream uses a probabilistic algorithm to balance video quality and the risk of stalling, taking into account the burstiness of LTE downlink traffic loads. We conduct a real-time implementation of piStream on a software-radio tethered to an LTE smartphone. Comparison with state-of-the-art adaptive streaming protocols demonstrates that piStream can effectively utilize the LTE bandwidth, achieving high video quality with minimal stalling rate.

Categories and Subject Descriptors

C.2.1 [**Computer-Communication Networks**]: Network Architecture and Design—*Wireless Communications*

General Terms

Algorithms, Design, Theory, Performance

Keywords

LTE; Adaptive Streaming; MPEG-DASH; HTTP

1. INTRODUCTION

Mobile video streaming has witnessed a surge in the past few years, accounting for 70% of the mobile Internet traffic, with a compound annual growth rate of 78% [1]. The LTE cellular services have been massively deployed to match such growing traffic demand, with a peak downlink bitrate of 300 Mbps, almost 10× over 3G. However, user-perceived quality of experience (QoE) remains unsatisfactory. A recent world-wide measurement survey [2] reveals that, even in regions with wide LTE coverage, LTE only increases video quality by 20% over 3G. On the other hand, the average stalling time remains 7.5 to 12.3 seconds for each minute's mobile video playback [2].

MobiCom'15, September 7–11, 2015, Paris, France.

DOI: http://dx.doi.org/10.1145/2789168.2790118.

These two effects are seemingly contradictory: the video streaming application seems to severely underutilize the LTE bandwidth, yet stalling occurs due to bandwidth overestimation. However, based on a microscopic measurement study (Section 2), we identify a single root cause behind: the inability of the streaming application to track the network bandwidth which is affected by downlink traffic dynamics at the basestation.

Our measurement focuses on the popular HTTP based adaptive streaming protocols (collectively called *DASH*) [2]. A DASH client adaptively requests video segments of certain quality (size) from the server, to ensure the best-quality segment can be downloaded in time for playback. Due to high probing cost, a DASH client needs to infer the *current bandwidth* implicitly from the throughput of its video segments. However, the throughput value may largely *underestimate* the bandwidth unless a video segment can saturate the client's end-to-end bandwidth. On the other hand, DASH uses historical bandwidth records to predict future bandwidth, which occasionally leads to *overestimation*, and hence video stalling, as the LTE network condition fluctuates. In either aspect, the DASH client is left to suffer from the worst impact of both underestimation and overestimation of the end-to-end network bandwidth.

To meet the above challenges, we dig for the network bandwidth utilization from the LTE physical layer. The well organized radio resource structure distinguishes LTE from most other wireless communication systems like WiFi or Bluetooth. Given a particular LTE cell and time duration, the total amount of radio resources available for downlink transmission is always known. Moreover, the end-to-end network bandwidth is typically bottlenecked by the access link bandwidth due to the architectural property of cellular networks [3,4]. These unique features bring new opportunities to remedy the bandwidth underutilization problem.

This paper presents piStream, which takes full advantage of the aforementioned features to enhance adaptive video streaming over LTE. piStream is a client-centric video adaptation framework, compatible with the MPEG-DASH standard [5], but tailored for LTE clients. From a high level, piStream enables an LTE client to monitor the cell-wide physical layer resource utilization status and instantaneously map it to the potential network bandwidth.

piStream's resource monitor scheme aims to be accurate, efficient, and deployable on LTE user equipment (UE). A straightforward way to obtain the resource allocation status is to decode the basestation's entire control channel[1] [6,7]. However, this approach falls short of efficiency and scala-

[1]In LTE, UEs within the same cell share frequency/time resources allocated by the basestation in a centralized manner. Per-UE resource assignment is conveyed to each target UE over a dedicated control channel.

bility. It requires each UE to keep monitoring the control channel and decoding the control messages to all other UEs, for which the error detection mechanism specified in current LTE standard cannot take effect (Section 3.1). piStream addresses this challenge by taking advantage of the well organized LTE resource structure. Instead of decoding the downlink control messages dedicated to all other UEs, a UE only needs to inspect the signal energy on LTE radio resources to assess their occupancy.

After acquiring the amount of surplus radio resources at the physical layer, piStream scales up its measured throughput accordingly to obtain an estimation of the potential network bandwidth it can leverage, which is then exposed to the application layer to facilitate video rate adaptation. In this way, piStream overcomes a common limitation of a wide range of DASH protocols that are slow at exploring unused bandwidth [8–10].

From the DASH application perspective, to maximize bandwidth utilization while minimizing video stalling rate, the adaptation logic ideally needs to predict the future bandwidth evolution [11,12], which is challenging for an LTE UE. Instead of forecasting the elusive bandwidth value, piStream takes advantage of the invariant burstiness of traffic patterns in packet switching networks [13,14]. It estimates how likely the aggregated downlink traffic (or resource usage), and hence available bandwidth, is to remain at a similar level as the current one. It then makes a probabilistic decision to maximize video quality while minimizing the risk of stalling.

We validate the piStream design by tethering a software-radio that implements the PHY-informed bandwidth estimation mechanisms, to an LTE smartphone that implements the application-layer video adaptation scheme. Our piStream client prototype can directly play video in real-time from any server that follows the industrial MPEG-DASH standard [5]. We benchmark piStream's performance against a standard DASH player from GPAC[2], and three state-of-the-art DASH schemes that have demonstrated superior performance over commercial DASH players. These schemes include buffer-based adaptation (BBA [9]), optimization-based adaptation using historical throughput (FESTIVE [10]), and TCP-like bandwidth probing (PANDA [15]). Under a variety of experimental settings including time, location and mobility, piStream outperforms all other DASH schemes by achieving higher video quality and lower/comparable video stalling rate. Under typical static indoor environments, piStream achieves around 1.6× video quality (bitrate) gain over the runner-up (BBA) while maintaining a low video stalling rate close to 0%.

To our knowledge, piStream represents the *first* protocol to facilitate LTE adaptive video streaming using PHY-informed bandwidth estimation, which is evaluated via a *real-time* implementation. The specific contributions of piStream can be summarized as follows:

(i) We design a lightweight PHY-layer resource monitor (Section 3.1) and rate scaling mechanism (Section 3.2) that enables an LTE client to efficiently estimate available bandwidth, and facilitate application-layer protocols;

(ii) We propose a video adaptation algorithm that harnesses the PHY-informed bandwidth estimation, while probabilistically balances video quality and stalling rate, taking into account the LTE bandwidth variation (Section 3.3);

(iii) We conduct a real-time implementation of the piStream framework on a software-radio platform tethered to a smartphone (Section 4), and demonstrate its significant performance gains over four state-of-the-art protocols (Section 5).

piStream does not require any changes in existing cellular infrastructure or video streaming servers. Its PHY modules piggyback on the UEs' existing communication hardware, and can potentially be deployed via a firmware upgrade.

2. BACKGROUND AND MOTIVATION

In this section, we first provide a brief background of DASH, and then conduct a measurement study of the challenges in running DASH over the highly dynamic LTE channel.

A primer on DASH. DASH refers to the class of protocols (MPEG-DASH [5], Microsoft Smooth Streaming [16], Apple HLS [17], Adobe HDS [18], *etc.*) that adopt HTTP based adaptive video streaming. A DASH server splits a video into multiple segments with uniform playback time (typically 1 to 10 seconds). Each segment is encoded into multiple copies with discrete encoding bitrate levels and thus different sizes. Before a DASH video session starts, a client obtains an available bitrate map from the server. To download each segment, the client needs to send an HTTP request to the server, and specify the bitrate level it prefers for that segment.

DASH has gained broad interest owing to several salient advantages over the traditional server-controlled video transport protocols [19]. It eases deployment as HTTP video traffic can easily bypass middleboxes and firewalls, and can be supported by commodity web servers and CDNs. The use of stateless servers also simplifies load balancing and fault tolerance. Therefore, DASH is becoming the dominant Internet video streaming technology [2].

The client is fully responsible for executing DASH's adaptation logic, which should choose the video bitrate on a per-segment basis to maximize the Quality of Experience (QoE). An optimal bitrate choice can be made only if the current and future network bandwidth are known. Many existing DASH algorithms attempt to approximate this objective by estimating/predicting available bandwidth [10,12,15], or by balancing the buffer occupancy at a desired level [9]. However, these solutions render unsatisfactory performance in LTE networks as detailed in the following section.

Challenges in estimating the current network bandwidth. Typical DASH protocols [5,8,10] use the throughput observed from each video segment to estimate the available end-to-end network bandwidth. However, such estimations stay blow the bandwidth unless the segment size (and equivalently the video bitrate) is large enough to saturate the network pipeline. This is rarely the case in LTE, which bears large in-network buffers with hundred-millisecond scale end-to-end latency [20]. Therefore using throughput to guide video adaptation often underutilizes the network bandwidth.

To validate this problem in existing DASH protocols, we conduct DASH video streaming tests over Verizon LTE network (more details about our set up are available in Section 4). The DASH server is hosted by Akamai[3] and our

[2]GPAC [8] is a popular (over 3300000 homepage visits during 2014) open-source framework to generate and play DASH video data sets following the MPEG-DASH standard [5].

[3]http://dash.edgesuite.net/akamai/streamroot/050714/Spring_4Ktest.mpd

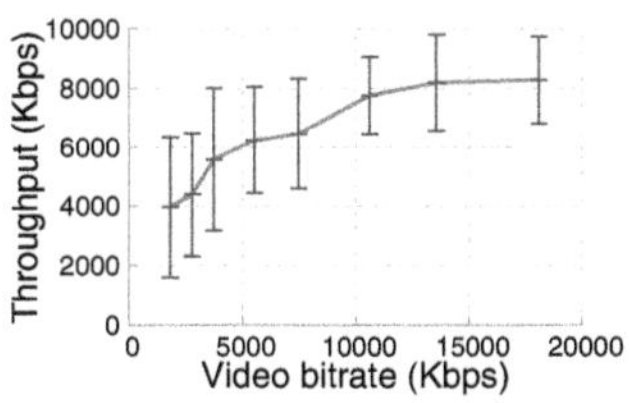

Figure 1: Throughput measurement depends on the traffic demand.

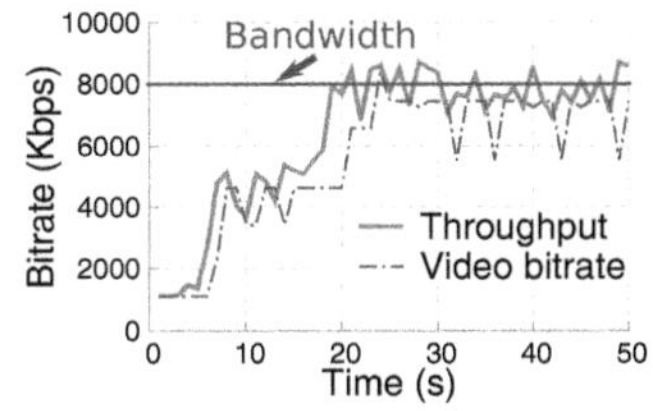

Figure 2: Throughput-based DASH adaptation converges slowly to bandwidth.

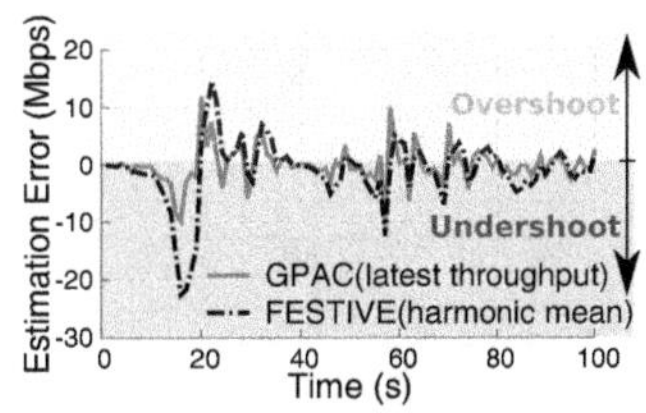

Figure 3: Existing DASH adaptation cannot follow the bandwidth variation.

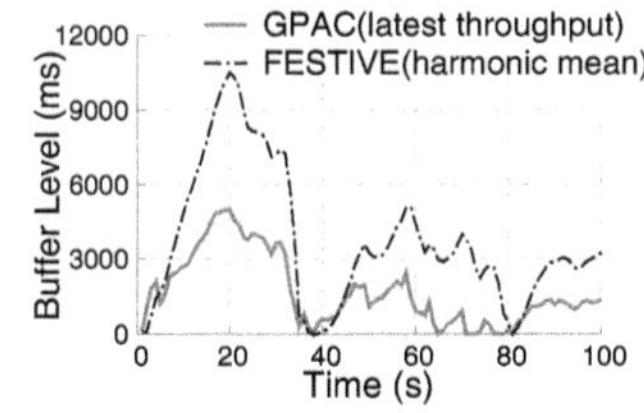

Figure 4: Poor bandwidth predictions drain out client's buffer and cause video stalls.

client is the GPAC player [8]. We run the tests in static environment during late night to ensure a relatively stable bandwidth.

We first disable the DASH adaptation by forcing the client to keep selecting a fixed video bitrate and repeat the tests for all bitrate levels in the server's DASH data set. Figure 1 plots the mean per-segment throughput under each video bitrate level. Error bars represent the *standard deviation* across all segments. As bitrate increases, measured throughput grows until a saturation point where it matches the available bandwidth. As a natural consequence, if the DASH client selects a video segment with low bitrate, it may experience a throughput far below the bandwidth. Using this throughput as bandwidth estimation, it proceeds to select a low video bitrate for next segment. This vicious cycle remains until the client opportunistically experiences a higher throughput owing to end-to-end throughput variation, but it will take a long time to eventually converge to the available bandwidth.

Then we enable the client's DASH adaptation under the same setting. Figure 2 illustrates the slow converging process as discussed above, where the blue curve shows the client's per-segment bitrate decisions and the red curve plots the resulting throughput. Consequently, the client takes around 25 seconds to converge to the bandwidth. Notably, a similar phenomenon has been observed in existing work [12] through trace-driven simulation.

It is worth noting that *(i)* The slow convergence is not caused by TCP. In one test, we manually switch the video bitrate from 1 Mbps to 8 Mbps and TCP (Cubic) only takes a few hundred milliseconds to ramp up; *(ii)* DASH clients usually pick a small *initial* segment size (video bitrate) to reduce the video loading time and build a sufficiently large buffer level to avoid future stalling [21], which exacerbates the slow convergence; *(iii)* LTE bandwidth of a client typically fluctuates more than shown in Figure 2 due to the competing traffic and mobility. In such cases, the slow convergence causes the throughput estimation to keep lagging behind bandwidth, which severely compromises the performance.

One may consider using TCP-like probing mechanism to explore available bandwidth [15]. However, video adaptation runs at segment-level (second-level) in contrast to TCP's packet-level (millisecond) adaptation. DASH cannot afford the frequent probing that pushes the throughput to the limit but causes frequent video stalling, especially for the highly dynamic LTE link. Besides, using very small video segments seems helpful but eventually causes more problems: Due to the large RTT of LTE networks (100 to 300 ms according to [20] and our measurements), the request delay from client to server will incur formidable overhead unless amortized by large segments [10].

Challenges in predicting future bandwidth. An estimation of *current available bandwidth* helps a client choose the best video quality if the bandwidth is relatively stable. Yet clients suffering from link dynamics, *e.g.*, cellular network clients, ideally needs to look ahead to predict *future bandwidth* [12]. To approximate the future bandwidth, most existing DASH protocols can be classified as two categories: *(i)* those using the bandwidth estimation of the latest video segment as the bandwidth prediction for the next segment, *e.g.*, GPAC's player [8]; *(ii)* those using smoothed historical bandwidth (for example, harmonic mean over a time window) as the prediction, *e.g.*, FESTIVE [10]. Such strategies have proven effective in wireline networks, but perform poorly in LTE networks due to frequent bandwidth variations.

We then inspect these two widely used strategies to reveal their ineffectiveness. To isolate the aforementioned bandwidth underestimation problem, we assume current and historical (but not future) bandwidths are known exactly. Specifically, we collect a time series of available LTE bandwidth by measuring a saturated Iperf [22] session, and then perform trace-driven emulation for the above two strategies.

Figure 3 plots the time series of bandwidth prediction error at segment-level granularity. The error falls between -20 Mbps to 10 Mbps, and thus the selected video quality can deviate wildly from the optimal one. When a severe overestimation occurs, even though infrequently, the accumulated video buffer can quickly drain off (Figure 4), resulting in video stalls. The harmonic-mean based prediction causes less video stalling, but at the cost of severe bandwidth underutilization and thus video quality degradation.

3. piStream DESIGN

piStream is a cross-layer framework to address the above challenges for adaptive video streaming over LTE. It incorporates several client-side innovations and remains compatible with any MPEG-DASH servers [5]. piStream consists of three main design components (Figure 5). A *radio resource monitor* (RMon) estimates the amount of unused radio resources by sensing the LTE downlink channel. A *PHY-informed rate scaling* (PIRS) scheme translates the utilization statistics into the current available network bandwidth that can be legitimately exploited. Finally, an *LRD-based video adaptation* (LVA) algorithm estimates how long the current available bandwidth is likely to last, and accordingly selects the bitrate for the next video segment to maximize the QoE.

3.1 Radio Resource Monitor (RMon)

The radio resource monitor (RMon) acts as a PHY-layer daemon in each UE that monitors cell-wide utilization of

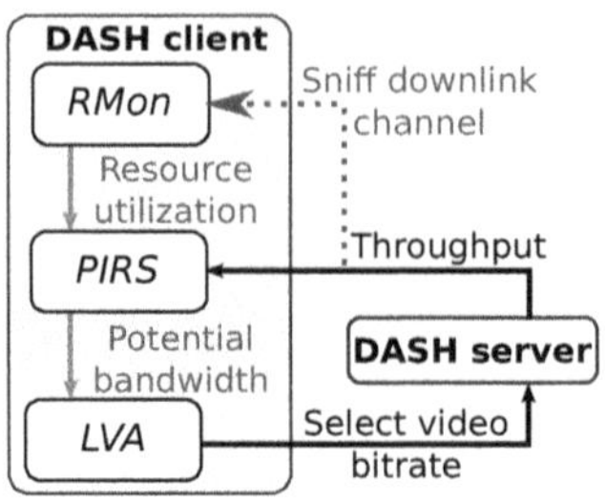

Figure 5: piStream system architecture.

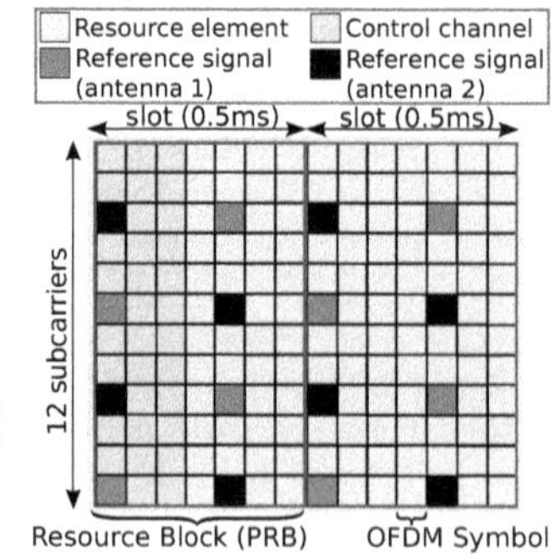

Figure 6: LTE resource allocation example for a two antenna basestation.

radio resources (referred to as Physical Resource Blocks, or PRBs). RMon needs to be highly reliable, yet simple enough to be executable in real-time and easily compatible with current UE's hardware. Below we present the background, challenges and our design to meet these goals.

3.1.1 A Primer on LTE Resource Allocation

LTE downlink channel is divided into fixed time frames, each spanning 10 ms. Each frame is further divided into 10 sub-frames, each spanning 1 ms and containing two slots (Figure 6). The basestation transmits each subframe using OFDM (Orthogonal frequency-division multiplexing), which divides available radio resources into grids in both time and frequency domain. Each grid cell (spanning 15 kHz $\times$ 66.7 μs) is called a *resource element* (RE). A basestation awards radio resources at the granularity of *physical resource block* (PRB) comprising multiple resource elements. Each PRB spans half-a-subframe (*i.e.*, 0.5 ms) in time and 12 OFDM subcarriers (*i.e.*, 180 kHz) in frequency domain.

The basestation dynamically allocates non-overlapping sets of PRBs to different UEs, depending on their channel conditions and traffic demands. The allocation strategy is vendor-specific. However, typical basestations enforce some form of proportional fairness, which ensures a balance between UEs with the best channel quality and those consuming the most resources. The per-UE resource assignment is conveyed to its target UE over a dedicated downlink control channel.

3.1.2 Why Existing LTE Sniffers are Insufficient?

piStream calls for a highly efficient radio resource monitor that is compatible with the UE's hardware. There exist a few platforms that sense the resource allocation by decoding LTE's downlink control channel (Section 3.1.1). Yet none of them meet piStream's design goal.

(i) QXDM [23], a monitor available for UEs with a Qualcomm LTE modem, can only analyze the radio resource utilization of a single UE rather than cell-wide information.

(ii) LTEye [6] can provide cell-wide resource utilization by decoding the downlink control information for all UEs. However, it requires a UE to keep monitoring the downlink control information to all other UEs, which is unspecified in LTE standard and incurs significant modifications to the UE's PHY layer. Besides, the decoding overhead increases with the total number of UEs, hence it is unscalable. Finally, the LTE error detection mechanism[4] does not work

[4]Since the CRC of downlink control information (DCI) is scrambled by each UE's physical layer ID [24] which is transmitted via encrypted upper layer channels and only available

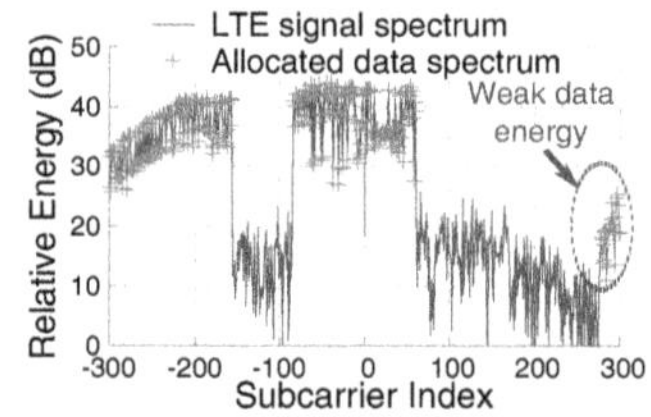

Figure 7: Energy-based resource utilization monitor is feasible but challenging.

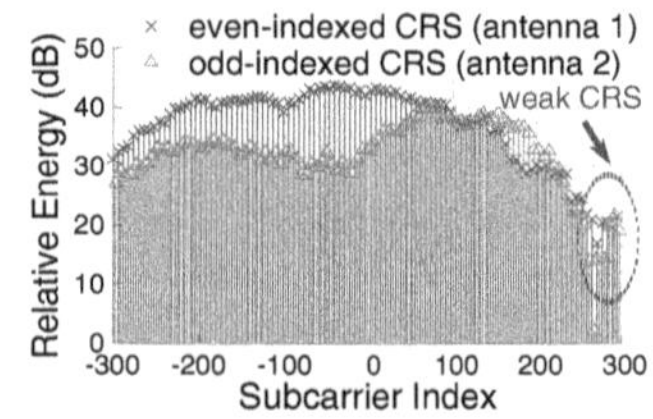

Figure 8: Reference signals can capture frequency selectivity and antenna diversity.

for LTEye since LTE design never considered that a UE will attempt to decode other UE's downlink control information. Thus, LTEye works well only when the wireless channel induces almost zero bit errors and hence the resource allocation can be deciphered without CRC.

(iii) OpenLTE [7] provides a software-radio based LTE downlink demodulator, which has the same problem as LTEye when decoding the resource allocation information.

In summary, to obtain cell-wide resource (PRB) allocation status, decoding the downlink control channels is not a deployable solution as it seems. It is unscalable, entails significant hardware modifications, and its results are unreliable.

3.1.3 Energy-based Radio Resource Monitor

piStream adopts an energy-based spectrum monitor called RMon to assess cell-wide PRB allocation status without decoding the control channel. RMon offers a robust, energy-efficient and readily-deployable solution to expose the PHY-layer downlink resource assignment to a UE.

Despite its conceptual simplicity, the unique features of LTE PHY layer bring several challenges to RMon's design. In particular, frequency selectivity makes it difficult to set up a threshold to examine whether an LTE resource element is allocated. Besides, wide adoption of multi-antenna basestations exacerbates the variation of energy levels across frequency/time, since the antennas may have diverse channel gains to the UE.

Figure 7 showcases these challenges through one OFDM data symbol over a 10MHz LTE downlink channel with 600 usable subcarriers (resource elements). We obtain the ground truth of subcarrier allocation by running the LTEye sniffer [6] intentionally close to the basestation to ensure almost zero bit error in decoding. We see that the energy on allocated subcarriers is generally 20dB higher than the noise floor. However, the energy levels of different subcarriers vary by up to 33 dB, some even falling below the noise floor. According to LTEye's decoded control information, the basestation enforces transmit diversity using 2 antennas around subcarrier index -300 and 0, which causes a wild energy variation (about 15dB).

In the rest of this section, we detail the design of our resource monitor RMon to meet such challenges.

Obtaining per-subcarrier energy-level statistics. The resource monitor RMon can be considered as a simple intercepting module to a standard LTE UE which already performs frequency-time synchronization to the basestation, and runs an FFT on each OFDM symbol to obtain the energy levels across subcarriers. RMon only requires the UE

to the UE itself, a UE cannot legitimately obtain the CRC of other UE's DCI.

to expose such per-subcarrier energy-level statistics. Thus, it does not require any additional communication hardware. Although this is not yet feasible in most current LTE hardware (which usually only exposes total energy as signal strength indicator), we believe the potential of cross-layer design provides compelling reason to enable it. In fact, the Qualcomm QXDM already exposes to each UE its per-subcarrier energy level [23]. In many recent WiFi chipsets, per-subcarrier statistics are already available to higher layers [25,26].

Locating resource elements available for downlink data. When monitoring the resource assigned to downlink data, the control signals and reference signals from the basestation should be excluded. Such signals are scattered across the resource grid (Figure 6). Fortunately, they can be located and then isolated owing to LTE's well defined resource structure.

Specifically, RMon first senses the physical channel width based on the frequency domain spectrum, which can be converted to N_{rb}^{DL}, the total number of physical resource blocks (*PRBs*) available in one LTE time slot. It then locates the OFDM symbols assigned to *control signals* based on the control format indicator (*CFI*) field specifying the location of control symbols. Finally, RMon locates the resource elements allocated to *reference signals*, which are mapped from the physical cell ID (*PCI*) following the LTE specification [24]. The PCI is in turn obtained during the UE-to-basestation synchronization procedure.

RMon is designed to operate well in cases where LTEye fails (Section 3.1.2). It only relies on robust control informations: CFI and PCI are available to all UEs, and are designed to be very robust by using 32 bit code to carry 2 bit information (CFI) or signal correlation techniques (PCI).

Evaluting resource element occupancy. Since not all available resource elements are occupied by actual transmission. RMon employs an energy detector to single out active resource elements. Since the resource elements' energy levels depend on link distance, frequency selectivity, and multi-antenna diversity, it is infeasible to use a constant energy threshold to examine resource element occupancy. To remedy this problem, RMon adopts a dynamic threshold customized for each LTE resource element.

Specifically, to combat the signal variation caused by pathloss and frequency selective fading, we note that for each resource element on subcarrier k and OFDM symbol t, there exist two persistent reference signals within the subcarrier range $[k-2, k+2]$ and symbol range $[t-2, t+2]$. When active, the resource element should have similar energy level as the nearby reference signals owing to channel coherence. As an example, Figure 8 depicts the reference signal energy corresponding to the data signals in Figure 7. We let resource elements in the first half of a subframe refer to the reference signals inside the 1st symbol of this subframe and the 2nd half refer to the 4th symbol. We use t_r to denote the global index of the nearest symbol containing reference signals. Suppose k^+ is the nearest reference signal subcarrier indexed higher than k, and k^- the one indexed lower than k. If k is an even number, we have $k^+ = k+1$ and $k^- = k-2$. Otherwise $k^+ = k+2$ and $k^- = k-1$ [24].

Moreover, for a multi-antenna basestation, the reference signals from different antennas are perfectly separated in frequency domain (Figure 8). Regardless of the basestation's transmission mode[5] (*e.g.*, SISO, transmit diversity, and open-loop MIMO), a subcarrier's energy should be no less than the energy from the transmit antenna with the worst channel gain, which can be approximated by the smallest energy on the two close-by reference signal subcarriers.

Consequently, for each subframe, RMon specifies the energy-detection threshold $\tau(k,t)$ for an LTE resource element (RE) on subcarrier k and in the symbol at time t as:

$$\tau(k,t) = \alpha \min(e(k^+, t_r), e(k^-, t_r)) \qquad (1)$$

where $e(k,t)$ is the measured energy of the RE on subcarrier k in the symbol at time t. Since the RE to inspect at (k,t) and its nearest reference signal REs at (k^+, t_r) and (k^-, t_r) are very close to each other in both time and frequency domain, there will only be slight channel diversity between them, and hence we can use a constant factor $\alpha = 0.8$ in Eq. (1) to safely accommodate such slight channel diverstiy.

Sanity check based on PRB resolution. The OFDM PHY layer naturally allows energy monitoring on each resource element. However, the smallest resource allocation unit in LTE is one PRB, which spans 12 consecutive subcarriers. RMon leverages this structure to further combat variation of subcarrier energy due to narrow band interference, noise, or deep fading. It computes the harmonic mean energy-level within each 12-subcarrier window, and then compares it with the threshold $\tau(k,t)$ to decide whether the PRB is allocated, thus filtering out outlier subcarriers. In this way, we obtain the total number of allocated PRBs.

Output the resource utilization ratio. After all steps above, RMon is ready to compute its output, the resource (PRB) utilization ratio u over a time duration of M subframes, *i.e.*, M ms, by comparing the number of allocated resource elements to the total number of resource elements available for downlink data:

$$u = \frac{N_{alloc}}{2N_{rb}^{DL}M} \qquad (2)$$

where N_{alloc} is the number of allocated PRBs over duration M, N_{rb}^{DL} is the number of PRBs in each $0.5ms$ time slot. Note that a subframe has 2 time slots. Intuitively, M should be small enough to enable responsive online adaptation algorithm. However, a too small M leads to very unstable average PRB utilization since the traffic load and per-subframe resource allocation are sporadic at a small time scale. In piStream, M is default to 200 ms, which can effectively capture the relationship between PRB utilization and traffic load, while remaining responsive to traffic variation.

The PRB utilization output of RMon is then leveraged to enable the PHY-informed rate scaling (PIRS), which is detailed in the following section.

3.2 PHY-Informed Rate Scaling (PIRS)

Given the PRB utilization, instead of using the throughput-based adaptation to underutilize the bandwidth (Section 2), a piStream client can scale up its measured throughput to obtain an estimation of its *potential bandwidth* at this time.

[5]Closed-loop MU-MIMO beamforming is not supported in typical commerical LTE networks yet, and hence we leave the design to handle this particular transmission mode to future work. Even if MU-MIMO frames are used, current piStream UE can at least detect this based on the length of Downlink Control Information (DCI) and then revert to conventional DASH mode.

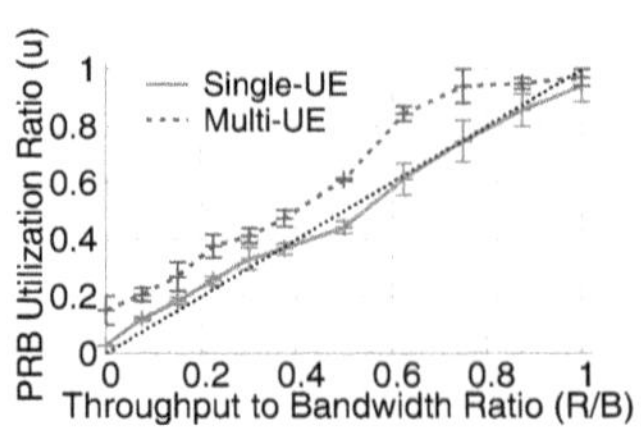

Figure 9: PRB utilization versus bandwidth utilization.

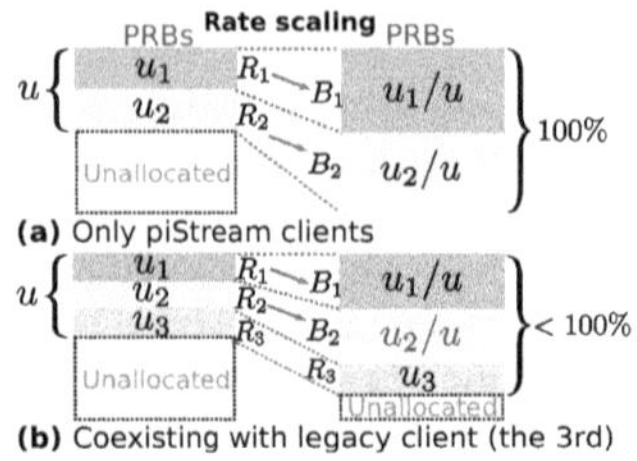

(a) Only piStream clients

(b) Coexisting with legacy client (the 3rd)

Figure 10: PHY-informed rate scaling example.

In this section, we detail the rationale and operations of such a PHY-informed rate scaling (PIRS) mechanism.

Relation between PRB and bandwidth utilization. PIRS builds on a hypothesis that *the PRB utilization of a client grows linearly proportional with throughput until it saturates network bandwidth.* Behind this hypothesis are two observations: *(i)* The end-to-end network bandwidth is bottlenecked by the LTE access link, which has been validated in existing measurement [4]; *(ii)* The access link capacity is determined by the bit-rate and the cell-wide PRB utilization. However, since the basestation already performs rate adaptation to maximize the link bit-rate, the additional bandwidth available should only depends on the available PRBs. Below we validate this observation through experiments.

Our experiment is conducted in late night with relatively stable network condition. We first measure the end-to-end bandwidth (B) similarly to Sec. 2, and then initiate a fixed-rate TCP stream from the server to one UE and record its throughput (R). Meanwhile, we use RMon to measure the cell-wide PRB utilization (u) per 200ms, and compute the harmonic mean over an entire 300s Iperf session. We also inspect a multi-UE test case, where the measurements are collected during busy hours so that our UE coexists with multiple UEs in this commercial LTE network.

Figure 9 shows that the bandwidth utilization R/B almost equals the PRB utilization u for the singe-UE test case. Therefore, *when the downlink is dominated by a single UE, the cell-wide PRB utilization directly reflects the UE's bandwidth utilization.* For the multi-UE case, we see that u tends to be higher than R/B. This is because the PRB utilization comprises the traffic load of not only our target UE, but also other UEs within the same cell. Meanwhile, the target UE's B decreases due to downlink resource sharing. However, a linear relation still holds before u saturates, *i.e.*, *cell-wide PRB utilization increases linearly with a UE's throughput to bandwidth ratio until the utilization approaches 100%.* This essentially validates our hypothesis.

Rate scaling based on PRB utilization. Based on the above observations, we derive the following principle for a UE to scale up its measured throughput to obtain an estimation of its current bandwidth[6]: *Suppose current cell-wide PRB utilization ratio is u, and the UE's current throughput is R, then at least a throughput of R/u can be supported without over-utilizing PRB.* Below we conduct a case-by-case analysis of this principle.

(i) piStream client only (no legacy clients). First, suppose the basestation serves only one client who can thus enjoy all surplus PRBs. Given that the current PRB utilization u supports the client's current throughput R, the maximum achievable throughput when the client is granted all PRBs should equal:

$$B = R/u \tag{3}$$

Now, consider the more complicated cases when there are multiple piStream clients in the network, they will detect the same cell-wide PRB utilization u. Suppose client i is allocated an actual fraction u_i of the total PRBs, then it will scale u_i by $1/u$ accordingly. Even if they happen to scale up their rates at the same time, as shown in Figure 10(a), the resulting PRB utilization will not exceed 100% since $u_i/u + (u - u_i)/u = 1$. Therefore, all piStream clients can improve their rates without overshooting the bandwidth, as illustrated in Figure 10(a).

(ii) piStream client(s) coexisting with conventional client(s). In this case, Figure 9 has shown that the PRB utilization stays above the bandwidth utilization. Hence, a client can still scale up its throughput following Eq. (3) without overshooting its bandwidth. More specifically, suppose piStream client i is allocated a fraction u_i of the total PRBs. After rate scaling, the cell-wide PRB utilization becomes $\sum_i u_i/u + (u - \sum_i u_i) \leq \sum_i u_i/u + (u - \sum_i u_i)/u = 1$. A simple example is illustrated in Figure 10(b). Although in this case the total PRB utilization may be less than 100% after a single rate scaling, it can quickly ramp up to 100% after several successive rate scalings.

For the legacy clients in this scenario, firstly, if their traffic demands do not increase, they will not be affected by piStream at all because piStream clients only attempt to leverage the unused PRBs. Second, if the traffic demand of any legacy client increases after the PRB utilization reaches 100%, the LTE basestation will invoke its proportional fairness scheduler to arbitrate the resource contention. Note that the same problem will happen even in a network with only legacy clients, and hence this is a general issue, not the limitation of our design.

(iii) New client joining after full PRB utilization. If a new client joins the network when the existing ones have exhausted the PRBs, the LTE basestation's proportional fairness scheduler will take effect so that the new client gradually gains more PRBs. When the basestation transfers PRBs to the new client, the cell-wide PRB utilization stays at 100%. Therefore, existing piStream clients will not scale up their rates any more. Furthermore, with a proportionally fair scheduler, the basestation will allocate less resource to them, so the DASH senders serving existing piStream clients will slow down and the saved resources are gradually "transfered" to the new client.

Ultimately, when PRB is fully utilized, the basestation's scheduler will be responsible for *ensuring fairness* among clients based on their link condition. As a client-side mechanism, piStream's rate scaling does not affect the basestation's fair scheduler. However, it does help the clients to quickly reach the full PRB utilization state to use the network resource more effectively.

3.3 LRD-based Video Adaptation (LVA)

Given an estimation of current available bandwidth (the output of PIRS module), a piStream client runs a probabilistic LRD-based video adaptation (LVA) algorithm to select the rate for each next video segment, and balance the tradeoff between video quality and stalling risk.

Theoretical work [12] has shown that DASH performance can improve significantly if *future bandwidth* is known. How-

[6]This paper focuses on the general cases where the LTE link bottlenecks the end-to-end network bandwidth [4]. We leave other corner cases to future work.

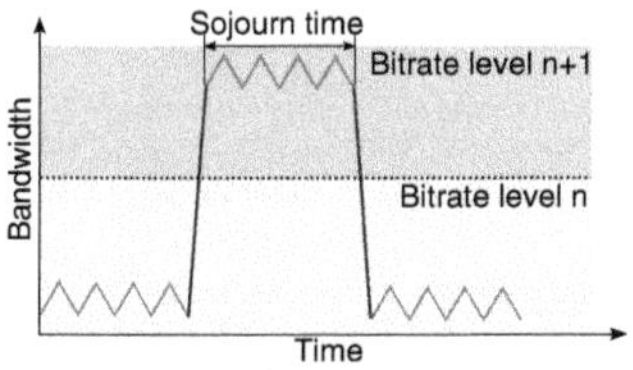

Figure 11: A simple example for the bandwidth sojourn time.

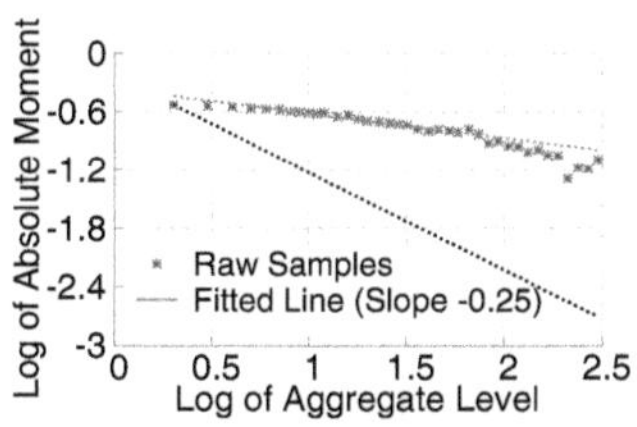

Figure 12: A Hurst parameter 0.75 indicates the long range dependency.

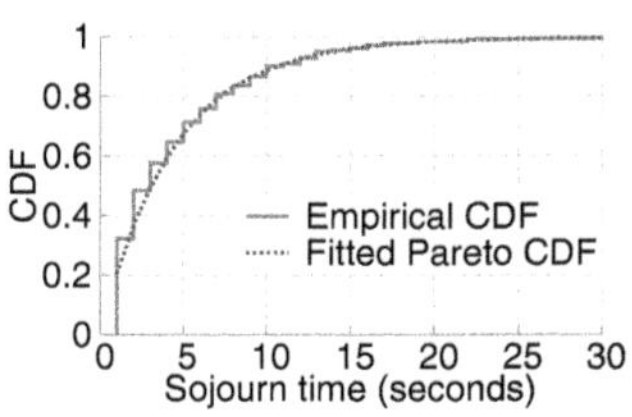

Figure 13: Sojourn time distribution fits a Pareto distribution.

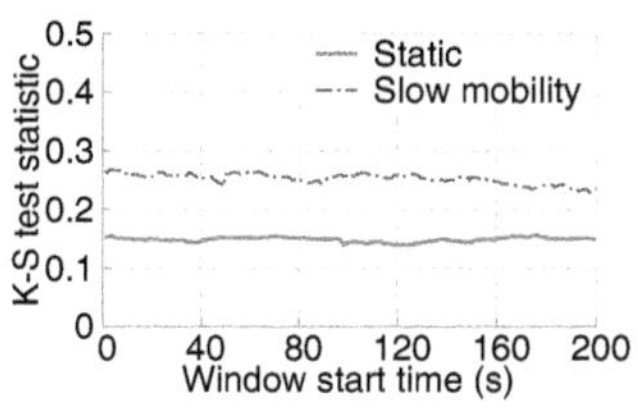

Figure 14: K-S test statistic. (difference between the empirical and the fitted CDF)

ever, the wireless channel fading and random traffic demand make bandwidth prediction very challenging in LTE.

Instead of attempting to predict the exact value of future bandwidth, the piStream client takes advantage of the invariant burstiness, or long-range dependency (LRD) of LTE downlink traffic. Based on a model of its LRD profile, it estimates how long its current bandwidth-level is likely to remain consistent, and then chooses the per-segment video bitrate in a probabilistic way.

Modeling sojourn time of network bandwidth. The LRD property of Internet and local-area network traffic has been well established [13, 14]. The downlink resource sharing and large buffers in LTE intensifies such traffic patterns, which naturally causes the available bandwidth to exhibit LRD. To model LRD, we first define the *sojourn time* T_s as the period between two consecutive bandwidth jumping events, as illustrated in Figure 11. The bandwidth (estimated by the PIRS component) is considered to jump to another level when the highest video bitrate below the bandwidth (*i.e.*, the quantized bandwidth) changes.

The arrival of a sequence of bandwidth variations can be considered as a renewal process, with sojourn time equal to the inter-arrival time. As verified later in this section, the sojourn time distribution is relatively stable and follows a long tail or power law distribution. We use the widely adopted Pareto distribution to model such behavior:

$$\mathbb{P}\{T_s > t\} = \begin{cases} (\frac{\alpha}{t})^{\beta}, & t \geq \alpha \\ 1, & \text{otherwise} \end{cases} \quad (4)$$

where α and β are referred to as the *scale* and *shape* parameter for the Pareto model.

Based on the Pareto model, the piStream client estimates the probability $\boldsymbol{p}(t)$ that its bandwidth will sojourn at current level for one more video segment of duration Δt, conditioned on the observation that it has already been staying at this level for a duration t:

$$\boldsymbol{p}_s(t) = \mathbb{P}(T_s > t + \Delta t | T_s > t) = (\frac{t}{t + \Delta t})^{\beta} \quad (5)$$

We define $\boldsymbol{p}_s(t)$ as the *sojourn probability*. Eq. (5) implies that $\boldsymbol{p}_s(t)$ increases with t. In other words, the UE's bandwidth is more likely to sojourn at its current level if it has been staying there for a longer duration. Note that α disappears in this equation since typical video segment length $\Delta t > \alpha$, and thus we only use the first case in Eq. (4) to compute the conditional probability.

LRD model validation. We first use experiments to verify the LRD pattern of the LTE downlink bandwidth. We collect 5 time series of bandwidth values by running saturated Iperf sessions, each lasting 300 seconds. We use the absolute moment method [27] to estimate the Hurst parameter H for the time sequence of bandwidth. When $0.5 < H < 1$, the sequence has long range dependency, and the degree of long range dependency increases as H gets closer to 1. Figure 12 gives the log-log plot of the absolute moment. The slope of the regression line is $k = -0.25$, and accordingly the Hurst parameter $H = 1 + k = 0.75$ [27], indicating strong long range dependency of the LTE bandwidth.

We further verify the goodness-of-fit for the Pareto model using the same bandwidth time series. To incorporate the impact of mobility, we collect an additional set of bandwidth trace in a car during slow driving with constant speed and direction. To process the time samples of bandwidth, we run a sliding window with size of 60s across all the samples and compute the Pareto fit of the samples in the window. The empirical CDF of bandwidth sojourn time and its Pareto fit in a particular time window under static environment are plotted in Figure 13. We see that more than 40% of the bandwidth level lasts longer than 5 seconds, which leaves enough room for the LVA design to take effect. Moreover, 90% of the bandwidth levels last no more than 10s. Hence, existing DASH design (*e.g.*, FESTIVE [10]) that uses a long smoothing window (typically 20s) may not adapt fast enough to follow this bandwidth variation.

Besides, in Figure 14, we report the Kolmogorov-Smirnov Test (K-S test) statistic $D = \sup_x |F_n(x) - F(x)|$ in each sliding time window, which uses the difference between the empirical CDF $F_n(x)$ and the fitted CDF $F(x)$ to characterize the goodness-of-fit. It is worth noting that a high mobility level may reduce the goodness-of-fit of our model. We will discuss the corresponding design to handle this issue in the end of this section.

From the results we can observe that: *(i)* The K-S test statistics are small, indicating small difference between empirical CDF and fitted CDF. *(ii)* The K-S test statistics are stable in time domain, which suggests the stability of the Pareto model parameters. *(iii)* The goodness-of-fit in high mobile environment is worse than that in static environment due to the bandwidth variations caused by channel fluctuation which are not captured by the Pareto model.

It should be noted that prior work [28] reported Poisson (memoryless) distribution of LTE downlink traffic. However, the experiments only examines short-term, packet-level inter-arrival time distribution, which does not conflict with the bursty traffic pattern at larger time scale observed here[7].

LRD-based adaptation design. The LVA algorithm proceeds as summarized in Algorithm 1 and detailed below.

(i) First, the client periodically (empirically set to 60s) applies a maximum-likelihood regression [29] to recent bandwidth samples to estimate the Pareto parameter β in Eq. (4).

[7]Based on our private correspondence with the authors.

Algorithm 1 LRD-based video adaptation (LVA).

Input: B_n: Bandwidth estimation of the n-th segment
L_{new}: Bitrate level after bandwidth variation
L_{old}: Bitrate level before bandwidth variation
t_0: When last bandwidth variation happened
$Q(\cdot)$: Quantize bandwidth to video bitrate
Output: V_{n+1}: Video bitrate for the next video segment

```
/*Finish downloading the n-th segment at t*/
Update Pareto parameter β using historical bandwidth
if Q(B_n) == L_new then /*Check bandwidth variation*/
    T_s = t − t_0; /*update the sojourn time T_s*/
else
    T_s = 0; t_0 = t; /*reset the sojourn time*/
    /*update the bitrate levels*/
    L_old = L_new; L_new = Q(B_n);
Update bandwidth sojourn probability following Eq. (5)
if rand < p_s then /*Stochastic video bitrate selection*/
    V_{n+1} = L_new; /*switch to the new bitrate level*/
else
    V_{n+1} = L_old; /*stay at the old bitrate level*/
```

(ii) Meanwhile, the *rate scaling module* continuously reports current bandwidth estimation to the adaptation logic. When the bandwidth (quantized to match the video bitrate levels) experiences a jump from L_{old} to L_{new} at time t_0, the client starts to count the sojourn time T_s, the time that the bandwidth has been staying at the new level L_{new}. Based on Eq. (5), the client then computes the bandwidth sojourn probability $\boldsymbol{p}_s(t)$: For the next video segment the network bandwidth will stay at the new level L_{new} with probability $\boldsymbol{p}_s(t)$ or go to any other level with probability $1 - \boldsymbol{p}_s(t)$.

(iii) Finally, the client performs stochastic video bitrate selection based on the sojourn probability $\boldsymbol{p}_s(t)$. With lower sojourn probability, the new bandwidth is less likely to last for the next video segment, hence the client is reluctant to switch to the bitrate matching the new bandwidth. In contrast, higher $\boldsymbol{p}_s(t)$ indicates a possibly more stable bitrate level thus the client is more inclined to switch.

To reduce the impact of a probabilistically wrong decision, LVA performs a sanity check based on the client's current buffer level. When the buffer level is low (we empirically set the threshold to 2000ms), even if a rare mistake can incur intolerable buffer underrun. Thus, the client acts more conservatively and reduces the video bit rate upon every bandwidth decrease it experiences.

Handling mobility. The bandwidth variations caused by channel fluctuations in mobility are unpredictable and not captured in our bandwidth sojourn time model. This leads to reduced goodness-of-fit in mobile environment and thus less accurate adaptation. To handle mobility, we use the accuracy of our model to guide the aggressiveness of the adaptation. More specifically, the client proactively evaluates the level of mobility based on the goodness-of-fit of bandwidth samples in current sliding window. A worse goodness-of-fit indicates higher mobility, which then forces the client to act more conservatively, *i.e.*, the client becomes more likely to reduce the video bitrate upon bandwidth decrease even when the sojourn time model suggests this decrease is temporary.

4. IMPLEMENTATION

We prototype piStream on a cross-layer testbed comprised of a PHY-layer resource monitor and a PHY-aware DASH layer. Figure 15(a) and (b) illustrate the implemented system architecture and the prototype testbed, respectively. Since the Android phone lacks native support for many of the libraries essentially needed to implement piStream and also cannot be directly connected to the USRP, we implement most piStream components on the laptop as shown in Figure 15(b). Note that this does not affect the fidelity of our evaluation because the phone is still the LTE client and all traffic goes through the LTE network.

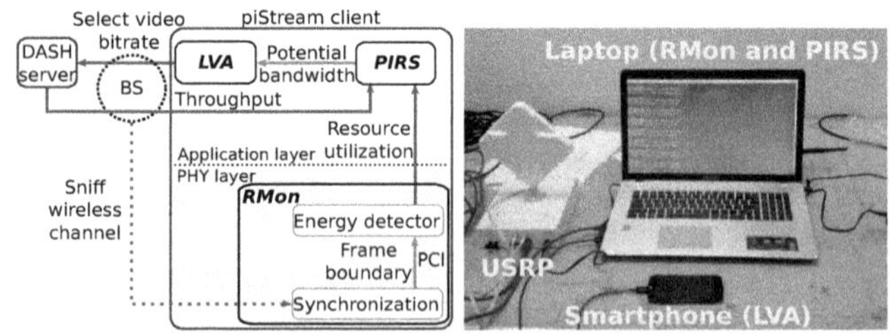

(a) Implemention architecture **(b)** piStream testbed

Figure 15: piStream implementation.

Real-time LTE radio resource monitor (RMon). We implement piStream's *real-time* resource monitor over the USRP N210 software equipped with WBX daughterboard and an antenna covering the 690-960/1710-2620 MHz LTE band. The resource monitor is executed on USRP's PC host as a C module. It processes the LTE downlink signal samples captured by the USRP, and extracts the cell-wide PHY resource allocation information, following the frequency-domain energy-detection algorithm in Section 3.1. The resource (*i.e.*, PRB) allocation statistics are computed over a moving window of 200 ms, and passed on to the upper layers online. Since this 200ms time granularity for PRB utilization output is much smaller than typical video segment length in DASH (2000 ms in our experiments), our implementation can perform DASH adaptation in real time. We average the PRB utilization statistics in each segment duration before performing rate-scaling to its throughput.

Our resource monitor RMon essentially implements major PHY-layer primitives that exist in every UE, plus the customized energy detector in piStream. Specifically, we have implemented the following crucial sub-components following the LTE standard [24]:

(i) Synchronization. The *synchronization* block enables a UE to read the physical cell ID (PCI) of the current cell and identify the downlink frame boundaries.

(ii) Signal energy detection. The *energy-based data signal detector* in RMon realizes fast and robust monitoring of PRB allocation. The frame boundaries provided by the synchronization block are used to determine the starting points of data symbols, so that we can perform FFT to estimate the frequency-domain resource allocation. Meanwhile, as detailed in Section 3.1, the PCI is used to locate the cell-specific reference signals (CRS) and determine the energy detection threshold, which varies following the CRS energy for different PRBs to accommodate the frequency selectivity.

PHY-aware DASH client. We implement piStream's adaptation logic by extending the DASH player from the GPAC [8] project. To interface the extended DASH layer with the RMon module, we tether an LTE smartphone (via USB) and a USRP radio (via Ethernet) to the same laptop PC host. Then we expose the PHY resource utilization statistics to the DASH player by setting up a named pipe between the resource monitor RMon and the DASH player. To

Algorithm name	*BBA*	*FESTIVE*	*PANDA*	*GPAC*	*piStream*
Bandwidth estimation	N/A	Harmonic mean throughput	N/A	Latest throughput	PIRS & LVA
Buffer knowledge	Yes	No	No	No	Yes
PHY information	No	No	No	No	Yes

Table 1: Implemented DASH algorithms.

leverage the PHY resource utilization statistics, we replace the default DASH adaptation logic in GPAC's DASH player with our implementation of the PHY-informed rate scaling (PIRS) and LRD-based video adaptation (LVA) algorithms in piStream.

DASH server. We set up an MPEG-DASH server with high bandwidth (66 Mbps measured with Iperf over a wireline network) on Amazon EC2 using Apache 2. This follows typical scenarios where the LTE downlink, instead of the wireline backbone, acts as the bottleneck for video streaming. The server hosts multiple DASH video data sets with typical $2s$ video segment length.

Benchmark protocols for comparison. To benchmark piStream's performance, we implement state-of-the-art DASH adaptation protocols including BBA [9], FESTIVE [10], and PANDA [15] in the GPAC's DASH player [8] by replacing its default video rate adaptation algorithm which quantizes throughput of the latest segment as the bitrate selection. All implemented algorithms are summarized in Table 1.

(i) BBA denotes a broad class of buffer-based algorithms proposed in [9]. Among these variants, we implement BBA-2, a hybrid algorithm which uses throughput to control video bitrate in the startup phase. After reaching the steady state, the client then maps its current buffer level to the video bitrate selection using a linear function.

(ii) FESTIVE algorithm selects video bitrate based on the harmonic mean of historical throughput measurements. As recommended in [10], our implementation adopts the averaging window over 20 segments and 30 seconds target buffer size. We also implement FESTIVE's stateful bitrate selection, *i.e.*, we delay the switch to bitrate level k by k segments, but decrease the bitrate level immediately if necessary.

(iii) PANDA allows a client to keep increasing its video bitrate to probe the bandwidth until observing a throughput decrease, which is taken as a congestion indicator. Then it reduces video bitrate based on the difference between bitrate and throughput of the last video segment. Our implementation exactly follows the default PANDA parameters in [15], the parameter k controlling the rate reduction speed is set to 0.14, which means slow rate reduction after a congestion.

5. EVALUATION

In this section, we first validate each component in piStream, including the real-time monitor (RMon), PHY-aware bandwidth scaling (PIRS), and LRD-based video adaptation (LVA) (Section 5.1). Then we combine everything together and perform a thorough system-level test under various network conditions (Section 5.2). All experiments (except one with trace-driven emulation in Section 5.1.3) are conducted over real-world Verizon LTE network on channel 13 (746-756MHz) using Samsung Galaxy Nexus smartphones. They also use the same server and DASH data sets specified in Section 4.

The performance evaluation focuses on two major QoE metrics [30]: *(i)* The *average video bitrate* represents video quality. It is defined as the mean video bitrate over all streamed video segments. *(ii)* The *video stall rate* represents playback smoothness. It is defined as the percentage

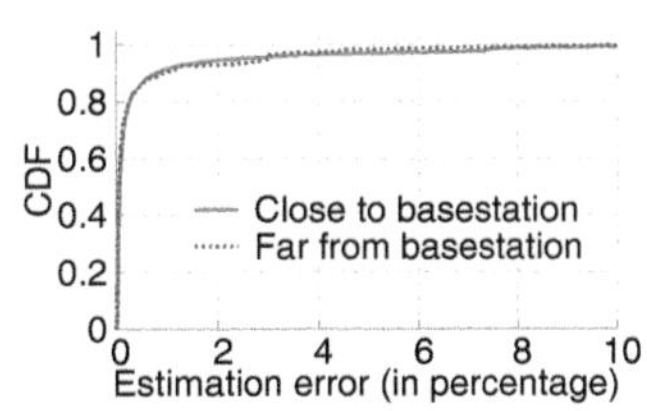

Figure 16: Our resource monitor RMon outputs accurate resource utilization.

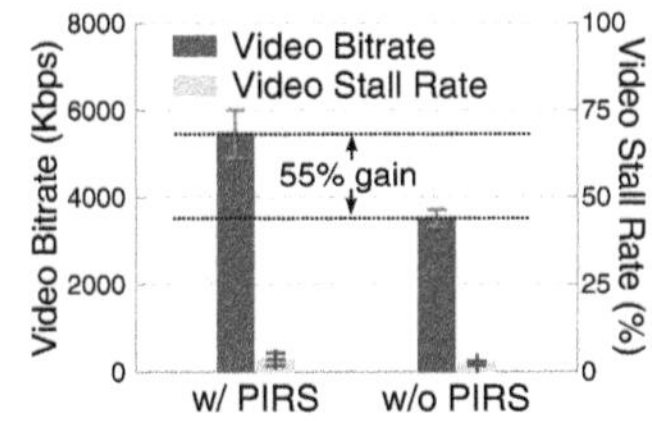

Figure 17: PIRS component alone improves the performance.

of video stalls, *i.e.*, the number of video segments that stall the video divided by the total number of streamed video segments to obtain the video stall rate. We obtain these metrics by logging the bitrate of every video segment and the buffer level on the client testbed in real time.

5.1 Micro-benchmark

5.1.1 Validating the Radio Resource Monitor (RMon)

We first examine how accurate piStream's resource monitor RMon can estimate the PRB utilization statistics. We evaluate the PRB utilization (in percentage) for a single-user video streaming. Meanwhile, we record the bandwidth utilization (in percentage). As discussed in Section 4, LTE downlink channel is usually the bottleneck between server and client. Hence, if RMon is accurate, its PRB utilization output should equal bandwidth utilization for this single user. Estimation error is defined as the difference between PRB utilization and bandwidth utilization. The experiments are performance in static environment during idle hours so that the bandwidth utilization is *w.r.t.* the same bandwidth. We repeat the experiments under two link conditions, created by moving the client close by and far from the basestation while ensuring connectivity. In each case, we compute RMon's estimation error over 200 seconds and plot its CDF.

Figure 16 shows that RMon is highly accurate — it produces the same output as the ground truth for more than 90% of the time. In case it errs, it differs by no more than 10%. In addition, its accuracy is only slightly affected by link condition. Therefore, its PRB statistics can be reliably used by piStream's higher-layer modules. In our system tests (Section 5.2), we will demonstrate the synergistic performance under a variety of conditions including node mobility.

5.1.2 Validating the PHY-informed Rate Scaling (PIRS)

To verify the eventual impact of PHY-informed rate scaling, we evaluate how much performance improvement it can achieve in DASH video steaming. In this experiment, the RMon keeps sniffing the LTE downlink channel during DASH video streaming and reports the PRB utilization to the DASH client periodically. The client then scales up its bandwidth estimation based on the latest PRB utilization and directly sets the quantized bandwidth estimation as the bitrate for the next video segment. To exclude the influence of downlink bandwidth variation, we test a single static client during late night for 10 consecutive runs.

Figure 17 compares the performance of using PIRS or simply the throughput for video bitrate adaptation. We see that PIRS module alone improves the average video quality by 55% at the cost of only 1% increase in the number of video stalls. Therefore, PIRS can effectively overcome the

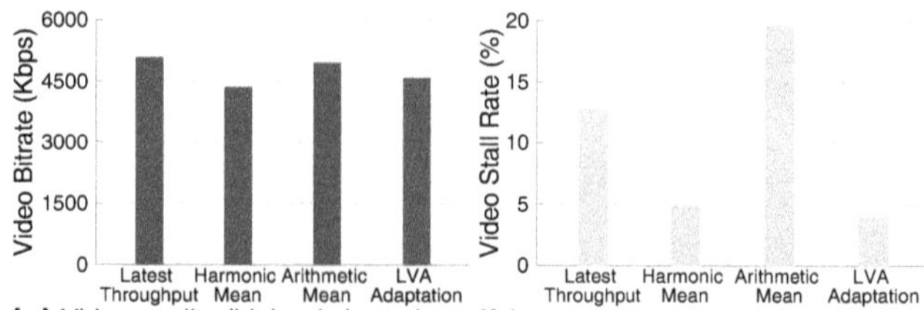

(a) Video quality (higher is better) **(b)** Video stall rate (lower is better)

Figure 18: Trace-driven emulation with perfect knowledge of current & historical (but not future) bandwidth.

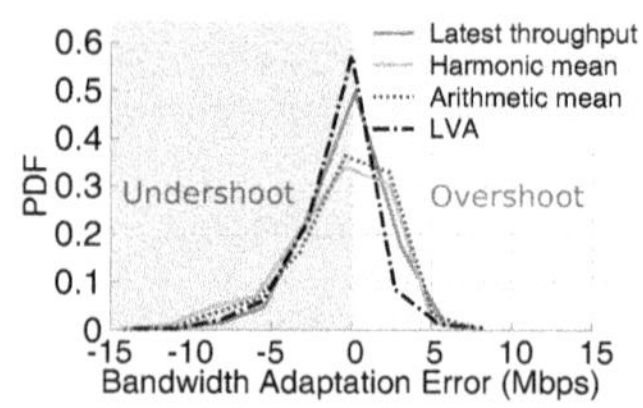

Figure 19: LVA has the lowest overshoot prob.(18% lower than the runner-up)

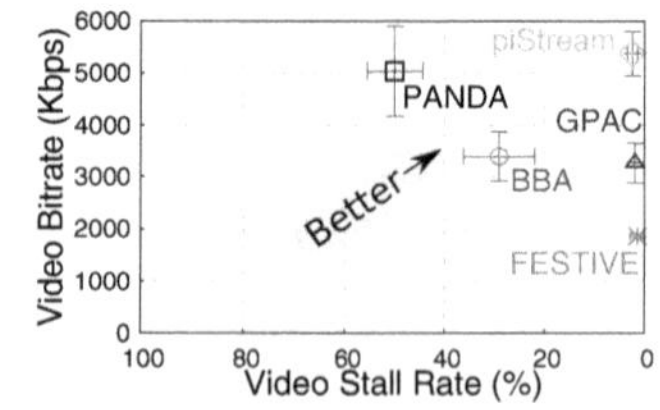

Figure 20: Average video bitrate & video stall ratio for a static client.

slow ramp-up behavior typically seen in throughput-based bandwidth estimators (Section 2).

5.1.3 *Validating the LRD-based Video Adaptation (LVA)*

In this micro-benchmark, we compare LRD-based video adaptation with several widely adopted DASH adaptation algorithms: *(i)* Latest-throughput-base adaptation, which uses bandwidth experienced by the latest video segment as the expected future bandwidth. *(ii)* To handle the bandwidth variation, adaptation based on the smoothed historical bandwidth is also widely used. A straightforward solution is to compute the arithmetic mean. *(iii)* Harmonic mean based bandwidth smoothing has demonstrated superior performance [10] than the arithmetic mean since it is more robust to larger outliers.

We use trace-driven emulation only for this micro-benchmark to isolate the effect of inaccurate bandwidth estimation in other algorithms. Instead of using the C++ implementation as in all other real-world experiments, we implement the algorithms again in MATLAB. The DASH video set used here is the same as that in all other real-world experiments. The transmission time is emulated within MATLAB based on the video segment size and the LTE downlink bandwidth in the collected traces. The traces contain a time series (at second level time granularity) of available LTE downlink bandwidth during busy hours for the target UE, collected by running a saturated Iperf TCP session. All DASH algorithms are run over the same trace. Arithmetic and harmonic mean based adaptation algorithms work on a granularity of 20 segments, as suggested in [10].To investigate video stalls, we compute the buffer level at the client as a time series based on the bitrate selection for each video segment and the bandwidth at that time, where the buffer level may drop to 0 and cause a video stall when the selected bitrate exceeds the bandwidth. Note that among DASH schemes, only piStream can obtain an accurate estimation of the *current available* bandwidth and use it for video bitrate adaptation. Yet for a micro-benchmark comparison of adaptation algorithms, we assume the current bandwidth (not future bandwidth) is known and used by all algorithms.

(i) Video streaming performance of adaptation algorithms. We first compare the video streaming performance of these algorithms. Figure 18 plots the results of this trace-driven emulation. Compared to the latest-throughput-based adaptation, LVA reduces the video stalling rate from 13% to 4%, at the cost of slight video quality loss (9%). Meanwhile, compared to the harmonic mean based adaptation, LVA improves video quality by 5% and the video stall rate by 1%.

(ii) Effectiveness of adaptation algorithms. To further investigate the reason behind the performance improvement, we look into the accuracy of adaptation by comparing the bitrate selection and the actual bandwidth of a video segment. Figure 19 shows that, 57% of the time, our LVA algorithm picks the video bitrate exactly matching the bandwidth, which is the highest among all tested algorithms. Moreover, we also see that the LVA algorithm has less overshoots and undershoots in the adaptation compared to other algorithms.

These results explain what Figure 18 shows. First, the latest-throughput-based adaptation has the highest video bitrate but lots of video stalls since it has more overshoots and less undershoots than other algorithms. LVA algorithm has the smallest video stall rate since it has the highest accuracy in adaptation (the peak at $x = 0$ in Figure 19). Both the harmonic and arithmetic mean based adaptation have low accuracy in adaptation, hence much worse performance.

5.2 System Level Test

We now compare piStream with state-of-the-art DASH adaptation algorithms (Section 4), including GPAC's DASH player [8], BBA [9], FESTIVE [10], and PANDA [15].

5.2.1 *piStream Client in Real-world LTE Network*

We first conduct experiments with a static piStream client playing MPEG-DASH video over populated commercial LTE network. To ensure a practical test environment with sufficient link dynamics, *e.g.*, other clients joining or leaving the network, we perform the experiments in a library with about 100 students inside during the afternoon, where our resource monitor constantly reports around 30% background PRB utilization caused by other LTE clients.

Before the experiments, we first use Iperf to measure the end-to-end bandwidth using wireline network to ensure there are no other bottlenecks between the DASH server and the client. We also use OpenLTE [7] to scan the LTE downlink channel to ensure there is no inter-cell interference. Each of our test lasts around 200 seconds, and we repeat each experiment with 10 runs.

(i) From Figure 20, we see that piStream substantially boosts video quality compared with alternative approaches. In particular, it improves the average video rate by 64% over GPAC, 125% over FESTIVE, 61% over BBA, and comparable to PANDA. This performance boost in video quality is mainly attributed to the PHY-informed bandwidth scaling, which enables the piStream client to select higher video bitrate than other algorithms without exceeding the bandwidth.

Meanwhile, piStream maintains a low video stall rate of close to 0. This implies that the LRD-based video adaptation can minimize the risk of buffer underrun, despite the aggressive video rate selection upon bandwidth scaling. *(ii)* GPAC's DASH player experiences a lower video stall rate compared to the trace-driven simulation (*i.e.*, the latest-value-based adaptation in Figure. 18) where the cur-

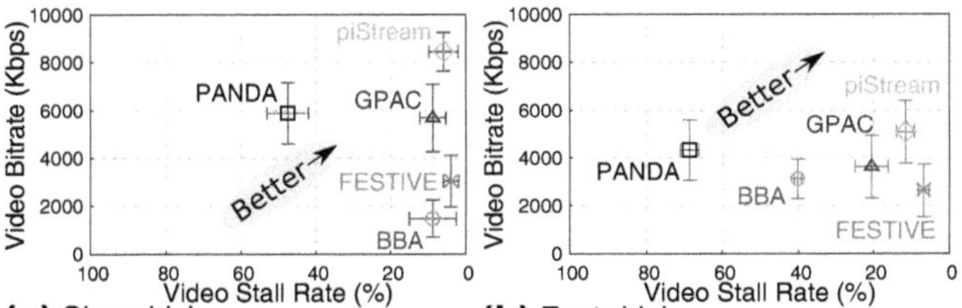

(a) Slow driving **(b)** Fast driving

Figure 21: piStream outperforms other DASH algorithms in mobile environments.

rent downlink bandwidth is assumed to be known. In this real experiment, the GPAC client needs to execute its historical averaging based bandwidth estimation, which tends to be conservative, resulting in less video stalling.

(iii) The FESTIVE algorithm relies on the harmonic mean of the historical throughput to control the video bitrate. Despite its effectiveness in wireline networks [10], the harmonic mean takes a long time to converge. Under the high bandwidth variation of LTE, it results in severe bandwidth underutilization, despite a comparable stalling rate with piStream.

(iv) Surprisingly, the BBA algorithm exhibits an unacceptably high video stall rate (23%). It should ideally mitigate stalling by reducing the video rate whenever it sees a low buffer level. By examining at its adaptation logs, we found that, given a high buffer level, BBA decides on a high video bitrate regardless of the current downlink throughput. Such uninformed aggressive choice tends to drain the buffer off before the high-rate video segment finishes downloading.

(v) The PANDA algorithm is built on a bandwidth probing mechanism and should ideally make more informed decisions. Yet the results show 50% of stalling rate despite its comparable video quality with piStream. We found that PANDA probes the bandwidth until observing a decrease in the downlink throughput, which is taken as an indicator for congestion. However, it may have already overshoot the bandwidth before experiencing such a throughput decrease. Also, its slow end-to-end probing can hardly keep track of the bandwidth in real-time.

In summary, piStream makes the best tradeoff between video quality and stalling rate compared with a wide range of video adaptation protocols that adopt rate-based, buffer-based and probing-based approaches. These adaptation algorithms fall short of agility and precision in the presence of high bandwidth variation in LTE. piStream's PHY-informed design effectively overcomes such limitations.

5.2.2 *Impact of Mobility*

We further evaluate piStream's performance by running it inside a moving vehicle in two outdoor scenarios: *slow-driving* (20 to 25 mph in an urban downtown area) and *fast-driving* (45 to 50 mph in a suburban area). The software-radio running piStream's RMon module is driven by a 120V power-inverter inside the vehicle. To ensure similar effect of mobility to all algorithms, we conduct the experiment by driving through the same route when testing different algorithms. Since our current spectrum monitor design cannot properly handle the hand-off between cells, we need to ensure that the car remains in current cell during the evaluation time. Therefore, we only stream for 100 seconds for each algorithm.

Figure 21(a) and (b) plot the experimental results. First, we see that the performance of all algorithms suffers under higher mobility, which is expected since mobility is known

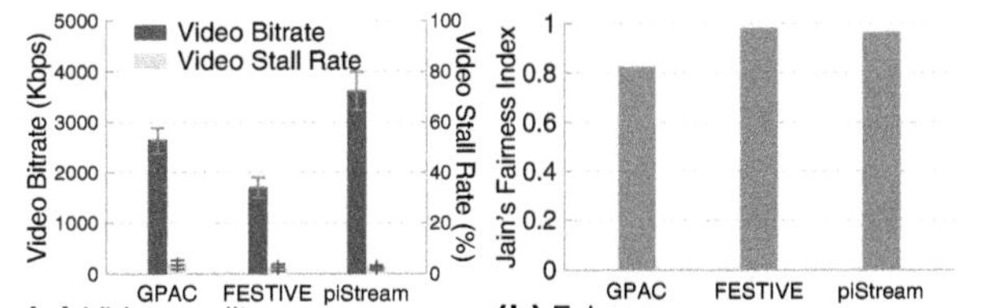

(a) Video quality **(b)** Fairness

Figure 22: Performance with multiple DASH clients.

to worsen the channel condition and bring more bandwidth variations. Notably, the average video rate in the slow driving case is even higher than that in the static indoor environment (Figure. 20). This is because the higher signal strength outdoor can partly offset the negative effect of mobility.

piStream maintains the highest video quality among all tested algorithms and a low video stalling rate. This also implies that the RMon module in piStream is robust and reports accurate PRB utilization ratio even in the high mobility cases. In contrast, we found the control information decoding based method in LTEye [6] easily fails due to high bit errors induced by channel fading. It missed 40% of the downlink PRBs filled with higher energy, and it erroneously detected more than 1000 UEs in 20 seconds within a small cell. This poor performance is caused by the CRC failure, since LTE is designed to only let the UE to decode its own downlink allocation (Sec. 3.1.2).

The performance ranking of other tested algorithms also remains similar as in the static case. These algorithms can not keep track of the high bandwidth variation, and hence the video quality degradation becomes even more pronounced.

5.2.3 *Multiple piStream Clients Coexisting*

Will piStream's bandwidth scaling method cause unfairness when multiple clients coexist? We have provided a negative answer with basic intuitions in Section 3.2. Now we conduct experiments with four clients[8] running piStream concurrently and evaluate the Jain's fairness index. We only compare piStream with GPAC and FESTIVE, since BBA and PANDA keeps an unacceptably high stalling rate.

Figure 22(a) shows that piStream maintains the highest video quality among all users, with comparable/lower stalling rate than other approaches. On average, a piStream client enjoys 42.3% and 108% higher video rate than GPAC and FESTIVE, respectively. More importantly, Figure 22(b) shows a Jain's fairness index of close to 1 among all users. This implies that each piStream client takes a fair share of the available resource when enforcing the bandwidth scaling. Note that GPAC tends to result in low fairness (index around 0.8), with its simple historical throughput based adaptation, whereas FESTIVE has trade video quality for fairness into its adaptation algorithm, *i.e.*, sacrificing many bitrate increase opportunities in its stateful bitrate selection, thus achieving good fairness.

6. RELATED WORK

LTE measurement profiling and application optimization. The study in [31] represents a first measurement of commercial LTE deployment, revealing architecture-

[8]piStream can support many more users than 4, but we believe fairness is meaningful only when all concurrent clients have good QoE (*e.g.*, with stalling rate of below 10%). Therefore we only serve 4 users to trade concurrent user number for QoE.

level properties enabling lower-latency and higher throughput than 3G networks, as well as low-layer configurations (*e.g.*, large in-network queues) that cause high-layer anomaly. Huang *et al.* [32] examined how radio state machine interacts with application traffic in LTE networks, focusing on the end-host energy wastage due to uninformed active radio state maintenance. More recent studies examined the impact of handover [33], traffic burstiness and fair scheduling policies [4] on LTE/HSPA transport-layer. All such measurement/simulation hints to the importance of cross-layer interaction in LTE networks.

Adaptive video streaming protocols. Video streaming applications have kept challenging mobile Internet infrastructure and protocol design. Conventional video streaming relied on propriety services, often on top of UDP [34, 35]. Mobile video services like YouTube used to execute adaptation at server side, often employing simple strategies such as periodically downloading fixed-sized chunks, or downloading an entire video file at once [19]. More recent services are converging to DASH, which allows simply repurposing commodity web infrastructure (*e.g.*, CDN servers) for video streaming. This trend has proliferated many variants of DASH (*e.g.*, Microsoft Smooth Streaming, Apple HTTP Living Streaming, and Netflix). Existing DASH algorithms strive for a balance between high video quality (bitrate) and the risk of buffer underrun. This tradeoff can be deemed as an optimization problem. The key challenge lies in the under-determined "available bandwidth" constraint, which has been approximated using either historical TCP throughput [10, 15], or buffer dynamics [9]. We have shown that piStream essentially overcomes the limitations of these approaches via an informed cross-layer available-bandwidth estimation.

RAN-based throughput guidance. In cellular networks, the Radio Access Network (RAN) performs RRM (Radio Resource Management), all PHY layer details are available at the basestation. This fact inspires RAN-based throughput guidance solutions [36, 37], in which the traffic scheduling algorithm runs on the basestation and controls the end-to-end traffic by sending non-LTE-standard control messages. However, such RAN-based solutions require heavy modifications on the LTE basestation or even the core network [37]. In contrast, our piStream design is UE-oriented, which only requires a firmware upgrade for the UE devices. We believe this makes our design more practical and easier to deploy.

Adapting higher layer protocols to wireless bandwidth variation. Substantial research has been devoted to tailoring TCP for wireless networks. Many wireless TCP protocols proposed to prevent unnecessary TCP congestion reaction caused by lossy wireless links (see [38] for a survey). Modern cellular networks have masked link-level losses through smart retransmission mechanisms like HARQ. However, substantial challenges remain, *e.g.*, highly variable channel condition [39] and bufferbloat [40]. In the end, all these problems can be solved in future if an accurate end-to-end bandwidth estimation is available for the TCP layer.

In wireline networks, end-to-end bandwidth can be estimated by active probing using, *e.g.*, packet pairs and out-of-band parallel TCP connections [41]. However, the approach cannot be readily used in LTE, because the resource allocation at probing time does not represent that of real applications which experience bursty contending traffic, highly variable network conditions, and intermittent queue build-up. In [31], a passive estimation mechanism is deployed at a middlebox between user device and LTE core gateways, but instead of run-time bandwidth, it can only obtain a bandwidth upperbound when sending rate is fast enough to exceed the available bandwidth.

Sprout [28] introduces a stochastic forecast framework to predict future bandwidth of a cellular link based on historical statistics. It assumes each flow is isolated from competitors, and only deals with self-inflicted congestion behavior. Unlike piStream, PROTEUS [42] builds a regression tree to predict future throughput/delay based on historical application-layer statistics. In DASH, since application-layer itself may be trapped on a state with low bandwidth utilization, application-layer history can no longer indicate achievable throughput.

CQIC [43] represents the first work to augment bandwidth estimation in HSPA+ cellular networks using PHY-layer channel quality information (CQI). It estimates PHY-layer bandwidth by multiplying a CQI-based bitrate estimation with the fraction of time a UE is scheduled. Though bearing similar cross-layer design principle, piStream differs from CQIC in three aspects: *(i)* piStream not only inspects historical resource usage, but also explores unused resource; *(ii)* CQIC targets at packet-level congestion control while piStream handles second-level video segments. At this time scale, CQI information is inessential since the impact of short-term channel fading depreciates while long-term fading is directly captured in per-segment throughput; *(iii)* For LTE networks where resources are shared among UEs, CQI alone cannot represent available bandwidth – competing traffic and available resource are equally important, and become the dominating factor for relatively static UEs (Section 2).

7. CONCLUSION

Video streaming is surging to dominate the cellular network traffic today. However, current adaptive video streaming protocols fall short of the expected QoE even under LTE's high bandwidth provisioning. To address the problem, we present piStream, a DASH-compatible adaptive video streaming framework that exposes LTE's PHY layer information to facilitate video rate adaptation. piStream's PHY-informed design enables a more accurate bandwidth estimation and agile video rate adaptation. Extensive experiments on a real-time prototype show that piStream outperforms state-of-the-art video streaming algorithms in both video quality and playback smoothness. Under typical video streaming environments, piStream achieves around 1.6× video quality (bitrate) gain over the runner-up algorithm while maintaining a lower video stalling rate. We believe piStream's PHY-informed design can be applicable to a wider range of LTE applications than what we have explored.

Acknowledgement

We appreciate the anonymous reviewers for their insightful comments. This research was supported in part by the NSF under Grant CNS-1318292, CNS-1343363 and CNS-1350039.

8. REFERENCES

[1] Cisco Systems, Inc., "Cisco Visual Networking Index: Global Mobile Data Traffic Forecast Update, 2012–2017,"

2012. [Online]. Available: http://www.cisco.com/en/US/solutions/collateral/ns341/ns525/ns537/ns705/ns827/white_paper_c11-520862.html

[2] Ctrix, "Mobile Analytics Report," 2014. [Online]. Available: http://www.citrix.com/content/dam/citrix/en_us/documents/products-solutions/citrix-mobile-analytics-report-september-2014.pdf

[3] Y. Zhang, A. Arvidsson, M. Siekkinen, and G. Urvoy-Keller, "Understanding HTTP flow rates in cellular networks," in *IFIP Networking Conference*, 2014.

[4] Y. Xu, Z. Wang, W. Leong, and B. Leong, "An End-to-End Measurement Study of Modern Cellular Data Networks," in *Proc. of Passive and Active Measurement Conference*, 2014.

[5] I. Sodagar, "The MPEG-DASH Standard for Multimedia Streaming Over the Internet," in *IEEE Multimedia*, 2011.

[6] S. Kumar, E. Hamed, D. Katabi, and L. Erran Li, "LTE Radio Analytics Made Easy and Accessible," in *Proc. of ACM SIGCOMM*, 2014.

[7] Ben Wojtowicz, "OpenLTE." [Online]. Available: http://openlte.sourceforge.net/

[8] ENST, "GPAC." [Online]. Available: http://gpac.wp.mines-telecom.fr/

[9] T.-Y. Huang, R. Johari, N. McKeown, M. Trunnell, and M. Watson, "A Buffer-based Approach to Rate Adaptation: Evidence from a Large Video Streaming Service," in *Proc. of ACM SIGCOMM*, 2014.

[10] J. Jiang, V. Sekar, and H. Zhang, "Improving Fairness, Efficiency, and Stability in HTTP-based Adaptive Video Streaming with FESTIVE," in *Proc. of ACM CoNEXT*, 2012.

[11] X. Yin, V. Sekar, and B. Sinopoli, "Toward a Principled Framework to Design Dynamic Adaptive Streaming Algorithms Over HTTP," in *Proc. of ACM HotNets*, 2014.

[12] X. K. Zou, J. Erman, V. Gopalakrishnan, E. Halepovic, R. Jana, X. Jin, J. Rexford, and R. K. Sinha, "Can Accurate Predictions Improve Video Streaming in Cellular Networks?" in *Proc. of ACM HotMobile*, 2015.

[13] W. Leland, M. Taqqu, W. Willinger, and D. Wilson, "On the Self-Similar Nature of Ethernet Traffic," *IEEE/ACM Transactions on Networking*, vol. 2, no. 1, 1994.

[14] M. E. Crovella and A. Bestavros, "Self-similarity in World Wide Web Traffic: Evidence and Possible Causes," in *Proc. of ACM SIGMETRICS*, ser. SIGMETRICS '96, 1996.

[15] Z. Li, X. Zhu, J. Gahm, R. Pan, H. Hu, A. Begen, and D. Oran, "Probe and Adapt: Rate Adaptation for HTTP Video Streaming At Scale," *IEEE Journal on Selected Areas in Communications*, vol. 32, no. 4, 2014.

[16] Microsoft, "Microsoft Smooth Streaming," http://www.iis.net/downloads/microsoft/smooth-streaming.

[17] Apple, "HTTP Live Streaming." [Online]. Available: https://developer.apple.com/streaming

[18] Adobe, "HTTP Dynamic Streaming," http://www.adobe.com/products/hds-dynamic-streaming.html.

[19] M. Hoque, M. Siekkinen, J. Nurminen, and M. Aalto, "Dissecting Mobile Video Services: An Energy Consumption Perspective," in *Proc. of IEEE WoWMoM*, 2013.

[20] N. Becker, A. Rizk, and M. Fidler, "A Measurement Study on the Application-Level Performance of LTE," in *IFIP Networking Conference*, 2014.

[21] A. Gouta, D. Hong, A.-M. Kermarrec, and Y. Lelouedec, "HTTP Adaptive Streaming in Mobile Networks: Characteristics and Caching Opportunities," in *Modeling, Analysis & Simulation of Computer and Telecommunication Systems (MASCOTS)*, 2013.

[22] Lawrence Berkeley National Laboratory, "iperf3." [Online]. Available: http://software.es.net/iperf/

[23] Qualcomm, "QXDM." [Online]. Available: https://www.qualcomm.com/documents/qxdm-professional-qualcomm-extensible-diagnostic-monitor

[24] "LTE; Evolved Universal Terrestrial Radio Access (E-UTRA); Physical channels and modulation," *3GPP TS 36.211 version 12.3.0 Release 12*, 2014.

[25] D. Halperin et. al., "Linux 802.11n CSI Tool." [Online]. Available: http://dhalperi.github.io/linux-80211n-csitool/

[26] S. Sen, B. Radunovic, J. Lee, and K.-H. Kim, "CSpy: Finding the Best Quality Channel Without Probing," in *Proc. of ACM MobiCom*, 2013.

[27] M. S. Taqqu, V. Teverovsky, and W. Willinger, "Estimators for Long-Range Dependence: an Empirical Study," *Fractals*, 1995.

[28] K. Winstein, A. Sivaraman, and H. Balakrishnan, "Stochastic Forecasts Achieve High Throughput and Low Delay over Cellular Networks," in *USENIX NSDI*, 2013.

[29] S. Kotz and S. Nadarajah, *Extreme Value Distributions: Theory and Applications*. London: Imperial College Press, 2000.

[30] O. Oyman and S. Singh, "Quality of experience for HTTP adaptive streaming services," *IEEE Communications Magazine*, vol. 50, no. 4, 2012.

[31] J. Huang, F. Qian, Y. Guo, Y. Zhou, Q. Xu, Z. M. Mao, S. Sen, and O. Spatscheck, "An In-depth Study of LTE: Effect of Network Protocol and Application Behavior on Performance," in *Proc. of ACM SIGCOMM*, 2013.

[32] J. Huang, F. Qian, A. Gerber, Z. M. Mao, S. Sen, and O. Spatscheck, "A close examination of performance and power characteristics of 4g lte networks," in *Proc. of ACM MobiSys*, 2012.

[33] B. Nguyen, A. Banerjee, V. Gopalakrishnan, S. Kasera, S. Lee, A. Shaikh, and J. Van der Merwe, "Towards Understanding TCP Performance on LTE/EPC Mobile Networks," in *Proc. of the Workshop on All Things Cellular (AllThingsCellular)*, 2014.

[34] X. Zhu and R. Pan, "NADA: A Unified Congestion Control Scheme for Low-Latency Interactive Video," in *International Packet Video Workshop (PV)*, 2013.

[35] H. Lundin and S. Holmer and H. Alvestrand, "A Google Congestion Control Algorithm for Real-Time Communication," 2013, internet-Draft (Informational).

[36] Internet Engineering Task Force, "Mobile Throughput Guidance Signaling Protocol." [Online]. Available: https://tools.ietf.org/html/draft-flinck-mobile-throughput-guidance-00

[37] J. Chen, R. Mahindra, M. A. Khojastepour, S. Rangarajan, and M. Chiang, "A Scheduling Framework for Adaptive Video Delivery over Cellular Networks," in *Proc. of ACM MobiCom*, 2013.

[38] H. Balakrishnan, V. N. Padmanabhan, S. Seshan, and R. H. Katz, "A Comparison of Mechanisms for Improving TCP Performance over Wireless Links," in *Proc. of ACM SIGCOMM*, 1996.

[39] M. C. Chan and R. Ramjee, "TCP/IP Performance over 3G Wireless Links with Rate and Delay Variation," in *Proc. of ACM MobiCom*, 2002.

[40] H. Jiang, Y. Wang, K. Lee, and I. Rhee, "Tackling Bufferbloat in 3G/4G Networks," in *Proc. of ACM Internet Measurement Conference (IMC)*, 2012.

[41] M. Jain and C. Dovrolis, "End-to-End Available Bandwidth: Measurement Methodology, Dynamics, and Relation with TCP Throughput," *IEEE/ACM Transactions on Networking*, vol. 11, no. 4, 2003.

[42] Q. Xu, S. Mehrotra, Z. Mao, and J. Li, "PROTEUS: Network Performance Forecast for Real-time, Interactive Mobile Applications," in *Proc. of ACM MobiSys*, 2013.

[43] F. Lu, H. Du, A. Jain, G. M. Voelker, A. C. Snoeren, and A. Terzis, "CQIC: Revisiting Cross-Layer Congestion Control for Cellular Networks," in *Proc. of ACM HotMobile*, 2015.

The Design and Implementation of a Wireless Video Surveillance System

Tan Zhang[†], Aakanksha Chowdhery[‡], Paramvir Bahl[‡], Kyle Jamieson[§], Suman Banerjee[†]
[†]University of Wisconsin-Madison, [‡]Microsoft Research Redmond, [§]University College London
{tzhang, suman}@cs.wisc.edu, {ac, bahl}@microsoft.com, k.jamieson@cs.ucl.ac.uk

ABSTRACT

Internet-enabled cameras pervade daily life, generating a huge amount of data, but most of the video they generate is transmitted over wires and analyzed offline with a human in the loop. The ubiquity of cameras limits the amount of video that can be sent to the cloud, especially on wireless networks where capacity is at a premium. In this paper, we present Vigil, a real-time distributed wireless surveillance system that leverages edge computing to support real-time tracking and surveillance in enterprise campuses, retail stores, and across smart cities. Vigil intelligently partitions video processing between edge computing nodes co-located with cameras and the cloud to save wireless capacity, which can then be dedicated to Wi-Fi hotspots, offsetting their cost. Novel video frame prioritization and traffic scheduling algorithms further optimize Vigil's bandwidth utilization. We have deployed Vigil across three sites in both whitespace and Wi-Fi networks. Depending on the level of activity in the scene, experimental results show that Vigil allows a video surveillance system to support a geographical area of coverage between five and 200 times greater than an approach that simply streams video over the wireless network. For a fixed region of coverage and bandwidth, Vigil outperforms the default equal throughput allocation strategy of Wi-Fi by delivering up to 25% more objects relevant to a user's query.

Categories and Subject Descriptors

C.2.1 [**Network Architecture and Design**]: Distributed networks

Keywords

Edge computing; video surveillance; wireless

1. INTRODUCTION

Video surveillance today has become pervasive: it provides inventory control for today's retail stores, security for corporate and educational campuses, and both security and demand monitoring for roadways and rapid transit networks in smart cities. Furthermore, the trend is expected to increase: according to a recent IDC report as much as 5,800 exabytes of video footage will be stored by the year 2020 [15]. But, while cities such as London and Beijing have close to a million cameras deployed today, the vast majority of them are wired into the physical infrastructure, which incurs massive deployment cost and effort. As a result, the coverage these cameras provide is necessarily limited. Smart video cameras currently on the market such as Dropcam [8] use a passive infrared motion detection sensor to transmit video in response to human or animal movement, but miss potentially notable stationary objects or people in a camera's field of view. We therefore see an opportunity for a surveillance system to radically scale by leveraging a user's query to look deeper into the video feed.

This paper examines the possibility of building a wireless video surveillance network over UHF whitespace and unlicensed Wi-Fi spectrum bands for uploading real-time video feeds to the cloud, similar to today's wired video surveillance systems. The important challenge in realizing such a system is the limited capacity of wireless spectrum, far from sufficient to accommodate many simultaneous high-definition video feeds. The bandwidth usage of Dropcam has already been shown to be several order of magnitude higher than peer-to-peer file-sharing applications [3]. Moreover, wireless networks suffer channel losses that need to be overcome by channel coding and retransmission techniques, introducing overhead that further limits the effective capacity of the network. When wireless capacity lags behind the surveillance cameras' demands, queue lengths increase and the system is forced to degrade application performance.

Our approach begins with an analysis of more than 250 hours of real-world video feeds showing that most of the time there is nothing of interest in a video feed. For example, in one of our deployments in a lounge area, we found that over a period of two weeks, 99.8% of the time a state-of-the-art face detection algorithm finds no faces, obviating the need to use wireless capacity to upload video feed to the cloud. Even watching a scene where many people are present such as a busy corridor during a lunchtime period in an office building, state-of-the-art vision algorithms detect very few faces most of the time. Figure 1 shows a time series of faces detected and a CDF of the face count: 80% of the time the face-detection algorithm finds no faces.

We present *Vigil*, a real-time wireless video surveillance system that leverages edge computing [24] to enable wireless video surveillance to scale to many cameras and expand its region of coverage in a crowded wireless spectrum. Vigil's processing flow begins with a user inputting a *query* into the system, such as locating people or objects of interest, counting the number of people passing in an area of interest, or locating people seen nearby a person of interest. Vigil's edge compute nodes (ECNs) then locally process each camera's video feed with lightweight, stateless vision algorithms such as motion and object detection, resulting in a stream of

MobiCom'15, September 7–11, 2015, Paris, France.
© 2015 ACM. ISBN 978-1-4503-3619-2/15/09 ...$15.00.
DOI: http://dx.doi.org/10.1145/2789168.2790123.

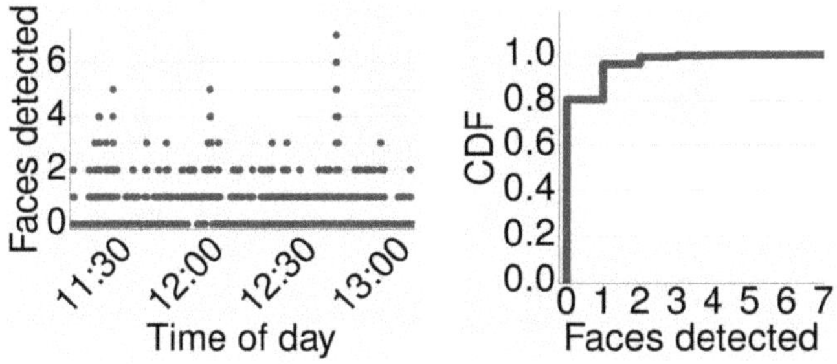

(a) Face count time series **(b)** Face count CDF

Figure 1: Time series and CDF of a count of the number of faces a state-of-the-art vision algorithm detects during a busy period at an office building.

analytic information comprising the indices of significant frames in the raw surveillance video stream. This analytic information triggers the ECNs to upload analytic information, together with significant associated video frames, to the cloud. The ECN also locally stores video footage temporally-close to frames of significance for subsequent retrieval. Later and if needed, Vigil performs a deeper analysis on the video feed (*e.g.* object/face recognition or trajectory synthesis).

Once Vigil has extracted analytic information from cameras' video frames, it has to decide the relative importance of different frames to the query at hand. This allows it to prioritize more important frames over less important frames when wireless capacity is scarce. To quantify frames' relative importance, we propose and evaluate a new metric called *ops* (objects per second) whose objective is to maximize the number of query-specified objects (of interest in the video frame) delivered to the cloud while minimizing the bandwidth required to upload images containing those objects. We also incorporate a priority-based mechanism into Vigil so that queries can incorporate their own logic into the way that Vigil prioritizes traffic, overriding *ops*.

Once Vigil has prioritized frames, a novel traffic scheduling algorithm uploads the frames most relevant to the user's query in reverse-priority order (*i.e.* most-relevant frames first), to ensure efficient utilization of available wireless capacity. This *video content-aware* uploading strategy suppresses a large fraction of unrelated image data, conserving utilization of the scarce wireless medium while simultaneously boosting the responsiveness of the system.

As an additional feature, Vigil scavenges the wireless capacity it conserves to provide public Wi-Fi access. This *hybrid* network design offsets the deployment and maintenance cost of the underlying network infrastructure.

We have deployed Vigil at three sites in two countries under vastly different operational conditions. Two of our deployments are based on TV whitespace networks, and operate in multiple indoor locations and a campus-wide outdoor area. A third deployment is based on a Wi-Fi network and deployed indoors. We compare the performance of Vigil to an "oracle" system running a state-of-the-art vision algorithm on all the frames every camera captures and uploading these frames to the cloud. Depending on the level of activity in a scene, experimental results show that Vigil allows a video surveillance system to support a geographical area of coverage between five and 200 times greater than an approach that simply streams video over the wireless network. For a fixed region of coverage and bandwidth, Vigil outperforms the default equal throughput allocation strategy of Wi-Fi by delivering up to 25% more objects relevant to a user's query.

(a) Object of interest. **(b)** Line of people.

Figure 2: The two Vigil use-cases targeted in this paper.

This paper makes the following contributions:

1. **Edge-computing architecture for wireless video surveillance:** We propose and evaluate a novel architecture for wireless video surveillance that leverages edge computing for a highly scalable, real-time wireless video surveillance system. Our proposed architecture partitions its design between computing elements at the edge of the network and in the cloud.
2. **Camera & frame selection to suppress redundancy:** When multiple cameras looking at the same scene capture different views of an object or person of interest to the user's query, Vigil uploads only the frames that best capture the scene. This collaboration *between* cameras distinguishes Vigil from popular solutions on the market such as Dropcam [8].
3. **Content-aware traffic scheduling:** We propose and experimentally evaluate the *ops* metric, showing that it maximizes utility in the sense of objects per second uploaded to the cloud for person-counting applications and applications that recognize objects. We also incorporate a priority-based scheduling mechanism, showing increased utility for security applications.
4. **Hybrid surveillance-access network:** We introduce a hybrid network architecture where ECNs also provide Wi-Fi network access to recoup the cost of deploying and running the surveillance network.

2. MOTIVATION: USE CASES

Security and counter-terrorism. Across our cities, CCTV cameras are installed in underground transport networks, on buses, and in airports and other public areas. We envisage online, real-time processing of the wireless video feed so that law enforcement and counter-terrorism can track public threats in real-time. For example, in the event of multiple co-ordinated attacks on public transport, the video surveillance network can pick out the face of one perpetrator, scan the database of cloud-stored video for other people the perpetrator was spotted with, and then search for those associated persons in real-time as the attack progresses, directing law-enforcement to the locations of the perpetrator's accomplices for intervention.

Locating people or objects of interest. In many situations, people are interested in locating objects or people of interest, such as an "Amber Alert" in the United States, or an unattended bag of a certain color (Figure 2(a)). An airport might choose to continuously run a query on CCTV footage looking for bags that are not held by any person nearby, flagging up unattended baggage to airport authorities. Traffic monitoring systems use vision-based algorithms to detect and count the number of cars on the highways [4, 22].

Customer queue analytics. In places where customers line up for service, such as coffee shops, supermarkets, or amusement parks, management has an interest in knowing numbers of people waiting in line and the dynamics thereof over the course of a day (Figure 2(b)). Cameras are used to track line length, but face or body

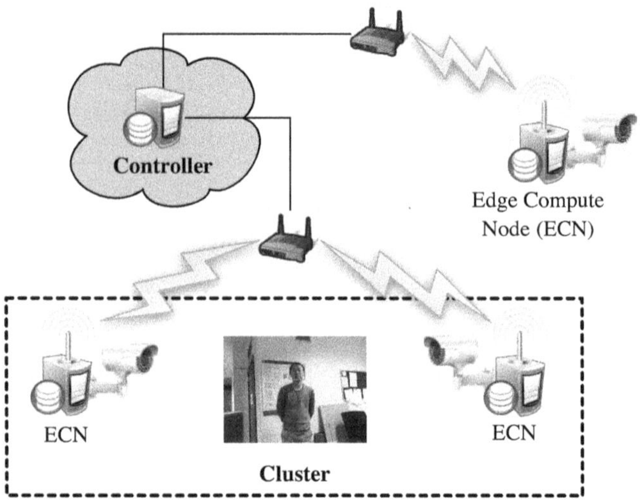

Figure 3: Vigil architecture, in which *Edge computing nodes (ECN)* are connected to camera devices to perform simple vision analytic functions, while uploading a relevant portion of video feed to a *Controller* in the Internet. Cameras monitoring the same areas form a *cluster*.

(a) Camera 1 **(b)** Camera 2 **(c)** Camera 3

Figure 4: Different views on the same scene can reveal more people at favorable angles to the camera, as captured by Camera 1's view of this scene with three people.

counting is challenging, as people strike different poses and turn at different angles to the camera. Consequently, a better design is to deploy an array of cameras surrounding the queuing area. The system then fuses their data together to form a more accurate count of the people in line.

3. DESIGN

Vigil proposes a novel architecture (Contribution 1 in Section 1) that leverages the computing elements at the edge of the network to minimize bandwidth consumption of a wireless video surveillance network without sacrificing surveillance accuracy. Vigil consists of the two major components shown in Figure 3. The *controller* is located in the cloud and receives users' queries, coordinating all the other parts of the system to answer the query. An *edge compute node* (ECN) is a small computing platform (*e.g.*, a laptop or embedded system) that is attached to a camera to bring cloud resources close to the edge of the network.[1] [2] Each ECN receives the video feed from its connected camera, and executes the first, stateless, stages of computation such as face detection or object recognition. It then periodically uploads analytic results to the controller. The ECNs also perform video compression, indexing and maintaining a short-term store of the video frames they capture. ECNs connect to the controller via wireless links operating over TV whitespace or Wi-Fi bands. The controller runs a frame scheduling algorithm, requesting ECNs to only upload a fraction of relevant video frames to conserve wireless bandwidth.

Vigil further utilizes saved wireless bandwidth to provide public network access, by augmenting each ECN with a Wi-Fi access point. The AP forwards users' traffic over the controller to the Internet, thus providing Internet hotspot functionality for nearby users (Contribution 4 of Section 1).

To improve the accuracy of vision analytic functions, we introduce the notion of a *cluster*: a group of camera nodes monitoring a single geographical area with *substantially overlapping* views, as illustrated in Figure 3. Leveraging a cluster of cameras allows us to capture multiple views of objects from different angles and overcome the limitations of the state-of-the-art visions algorithms (Figure 4). These clusters are constructed during a calibration phase based on the covered area of each camera. Vigil effectively fuses the observations from cameras in a cluster to improve surveillance accuracy without significant wireless bandwidth overhead while existing surveillance systems upload video from each camera to the cloud before executing vision analytic functions.

Design goals and scope. The primary goal of our design is to maximize the number of query-specified objects the system returns while minimizing the bandwidth required to upload the images containing these objects. We also limit the scope of our design, noting the following non-goals:

1. Each vision algorithm has a certain accuracy and degree of confidence in the results it returns. Improving the accuracy of vision algorithms is outside this paper's scope.
2. Enough cameras are present and use a high enough resolution and frame rate so that with high probability, the resulting raw video streams capture objects of interest.
3. In a Vigil deployment, cameras are line-powered, so there are no battery-conservation issues.

The next section describes the ECN in detail, followed by a description of how Vigil's controller prioritizes frames to upload within a cluster of ECNs (§3.2, *Intra-cluster processing*), and arbitrates demand across multiple clusters (§3.3, *Inter-cluster traffic shaping*).

3.1 Edge compute node

We begin by describing the stateless image processing functions performed by each ECN. Each Vigil application implements a callback API `frameUtility`, which returns an integer value evaluating the importance of a video frame to that application. Referring to our two use-cases, queue counting application at a coffee shop defines `frameUtility` to be the number of people visible in the frame. The application that locates people or objects of interest defines `frameUtility` to be one if the object of interest is found in the frame, and zero otherwise. When Vigil receives a new query, the query contains a definition of the `frameUtility` function, which is disseminated to all ECNs. Each ECN calls `frameUtility` on every received frame to generate an array of *analytic data* we denote as `utils`. It then uploads these analytic data to the controller.[3] While we focus on person-counting applications to define `frameUtility` in this paper, Vigil can process any queries that can process a vision analytic function at ECN and output a `frameUtility` (for example, an object or a license plate number is present or not).

[1] Note that we use the terms ECN and camera interchangeably in the remainder of the paper.

[2] We discuss the case of connecting multiple cameras to a single ECN in § 7.

[3] As discussed below in Section 3.2.2, an advanced intra-cluster scheduling algorithm also requires ECNs to upload the location of each detected object.

Frame index:	0	1	2	3	4	5	6	7	8	9
`util[1]:`	1	1	3	3	3	3	3	1	1	1
`util[2]:`	1	1	1	1	1	1	1	1	1	1

Figure 5: The intra-cluster frame selection algorithm processes on counts representing the number of objects from each ECN camera in a cluster. This example shows object counts over a certain time epoch from two ECNs.

	0	1	2
`sis:`	(2,3)	(7,1)	(0,1)

Figure 6: Step 2 of the Vigil intra-cluster frame selection algorithm aggregates one camera's beginning frame index and utility into a *selected image sequence* (`sis`) array containing a sequence of (frame index, utility) pairs.

We note here that camera placement, focus, environmental conditions, motion and many other factors can blur objects and faces of interest to the system. Indeed, based on our experience, vision algorithms such as face detection are more likely to fail on blurred images, and so `frameUtility` implicitly factors the image quality into the number of detected objects.[4] We elaborate further on this design choice in Section 7.

Video storage. Each ECN is equipped with some persistent storage devices to retain all the video frames captured close to the time of detected events. This allows Vigil to support "drill-down" queries, which can be answered by uploading additional video data from ECNs to the cloud for more detailed analysis. Consequently, Vigil provides a time window, such as one or two weeks, within which the system retains important video information, as existing wired surveillance systems do.

3.2 Intra-cluster processing

The Vigil controller runs an intra-cluster algorithm to determine the most valuable frames from cameras within a cluster to upload (Contribution 2 in Section 1). The key challenge is to eliminate redundant observations of multiple cameras within a cluster, capturing the same objects, to minimize communication bandwidth without actually exchanging the redundant frames. This section describes our intra-cluster scheduling algorithm in two iterations: a strawman version described next, and its generalization in Section 3.2.2, which proposes a re-identification approach to check if the same objects are captured by cameras in a cluster.

3.2.1 Basic frame-selection algorithm

The basic algorithm selects frames to upload by examining the frame utility array `utils[c]` that each ECN `c` reports to the controller. We show an example of the controller's view of the frame utility arrays for a cluster containing two ECNs in Figure 5: each element of `util` is an object count captured by a ECN during consecutive time slots. The maximum object count is based on the vision analytic function ECN is running (i.e., practically, the vision analytic algorithm will only detect a limited number of faces in a frame, for example). To reduce protocol overhead, our intra-cluster algorithm operates over a certain number of L_e time slots, referred to as an *epoch* in this section. The controller selects a single ECN in each epoch—the selected ECN then uploads a fraction of its frames to the controller determined by inter-cluster traffic shaping (§3.3 on p. 5). The basic version of our scheduling algorithm proceeds in three steps:

Step 1: The controller sums the L_e object counts from each camera across the epoch, selecting the camera c^* with the highest average counts (most information about the scene) in the epoch. In the running example of Figure 5, the algorithm selects Camera 1 for further processing.

Step 2: The second step of the algorithm processes Camera c^*'s counts, finding the frames that begin changes to the scene, and collecting them into a *selected image sequence* array `sis`, as shown in Figure 6. The `sis` array contains pairs of (frame index, utility), sorted by utility, breaking ties in utility by favoring the `sis` element with the longer duration sequence of images.

The frames can only be uploaded at a rate lower than the capacity of the wireless link from the ECN to avoid network congestion and frames from being dropped. To avoid congestion, the controller estimates the link capacity (in bits per second) C available from each ECN by examining the near-term sending rates and the loss rates. The ECN measures a time-averaged packet loss rate L at its wireless link layer, and the physical-layer bit rate R. The ECN then estimates the link capacity as:

$$C = R \cdot (1 - L). \quad (1)$$

Step 3: The final step of the algorithm takes as input the estimated available wireless capacity C, and estimates the number of bits that ECN c^* can upload. We make a simplifying assumption that ECNs within a cluster have similar wireless links to controller because they cover same geographical area of interest. Suppose the size (in bits) of the frames in the `sis` is N_{sis} and the length of the epoch in seconds is T_e. At the end of the epoch, the controller sends a control message to ECN c^* soliciting an upload. If $N_{sis} \leq C \cdot T_e$, the ECN uploads `sis`, along with all the changing frames as indicated in the `sis` after compression. Otherwise, the ECN uploads a fraction of the compressed images in `sis` in the decreasing order of utility. In the example of Figure 6, `sis[0]` has utility of 3, so frame 2 is uploaded first, followed by frame 7 and 0.

We note that this algorithm is an approximation that will lose information when more than one camera in the cluster sees objects that other cameras in the cluster miss. So, we describe a sophisticated intra-cluster algorithm to select the most valuable frames within a cluster.

3.2.2 Sophisticated frame-selection algorithm

Vigil's sophisticated intra-cluster frame-selection algorithm specifically targets cases where one camera in a cluster sees objects that other cameras miss to select more than one ECN to upload images during a time epoch.

This algorithm relies on geometry and known locations of the ECNs to detect redundant viewpoints without actually exchanging the redundant frames. The algorithm first identifies duplicates of the same objects from multiple ECNs in overlapping camera views using object re-identification. It then prioritizes video frames from the cluster, factoring the count of "re-identified" objects into the frame utility metric.

Object re-identification. Object re-identification determines redundant objects reported by multiple ECNs in a cluster with overlapping camera views. By selecting the smallest subset of camera

[4]Blurry frames will result in fewer objects being detected, thus the `frameUtility` metric will characterize blurry frames as less useful. Furthermore, the minimum size required in terms of face pixels is encoded in the face or person detector.

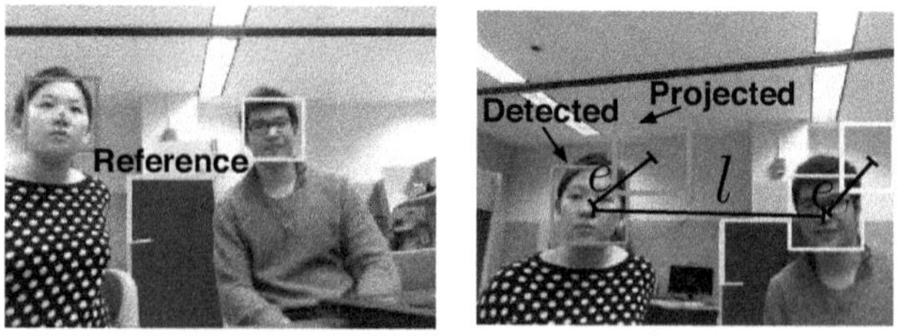

(a) Camera 1 (b) Camera 2

Figure 7: Two cameras simultaneously capture a scene containing the same two faces. To avoid redundant counting, Vigil projects faces from Camera 1 to Camera 2 based on common reference points denoted by the two blue lines labeled "Reference" in Camera 1's view. If projection error does not exceed the distance between the detected faces, re-identification correctly identifies the two views of each face.

Frame index:	0	1	2	3	4	5
objects[1]:	**a**, **b**, c	**a**, **b**, c	b, **d**	b, d	b, **d**, f, g	b, d, **f**, g
objects[2]:	**a**, **b**	**a**, **b**	**d**, e	e	**d**, h, i	**f**, h, i

Frame index:	0	1	2	3	4	5
util[1]:	3	3	2	2	4	4
util[2]:	0	0	1	1	2	2

Figure 8: The advanced intra-cluster frame selection algorithm operating on unique objects after applying the object re-identification algorithm. Each letter denotes an unique object identified by re-identification. The algorithm chooses ECN 1's camera to be the primary camera view, while debiting the object counts reported by ECN 2 by the number of duplicate objects re-identified (in bold).

views to cover the overlapping views, we identify the unique objects across cameras within a cluster. To achieve this, Vigil uses the following lightweight approach [33] called re-identification.

Figure 7 shows an example where two cameras simultaneously detect the faces of two people in their overlapping views. The re-identification algorithm identifies if the detected face instances belong to the same person or not. It first selects common reference points between the camera views, for e.g., the two blue lines in Figure 7.[5] The reference points are then used to project *any* pixel in Camera 1's view onto the plane of Camera 2's view. The detected face instances are identified as the same person when the distance between projected face and the detected face is below a threshold. For e.g., the error e between the projection and the detected face in Figure 7(b) is much smaller than the distance between the two different faces. We set an empirical value to determine the threshold for this projection error e that accounts for any inaccuracy in marking reference points as benchmarked in Section 5.3. The threshold value is set during a calibration stage and can remain useful for a long period of time for static cameras. This re-identification approach has linear complexity in number of cameras because it projects all of the captured scenes to a common plane to calculate inter-object distance.

To integrate the re-identification technique on top of the basic algorithm Section 3.1, each ECN reports the center coordinates of detected faces and the frame utility in the modified `utils` to the

[5]The reference points are manually determined in a camera calibration phase or extracted using algorithms that extract SIFT image features [17].

index:	0	1	2	3	4
sis:	(1, 4, 4)	(1, 0, 3)	(1, 2, 2)	(2, 4, 2)	(2, 2, 1)
	Primary ECN			Complementary ECN	

Figure 9: Step 2 of the advanced intra-cluster algorithm generates a selected image sequence (*sis*) array comprising (camera identifier, frame index, utility) tuples.

controller. The controller then performs re-identification using the analytic data in `utils`. Based on the results of object reidentification, The controller then executes the following sophisticated scheduling algorithm:

Step 1: The controller determines an ECN that has maximal average object counts (thus capturing the most information about the scene) to be the *primary* ECN. It then projects the detected objects from other (*complementary*) camera views onto the primary camera view. For each re-identified object, the controller debits the object count of all the complementary ECNs by one. This produces an updated utility array for each ECN. For example, Figure 8 shows unique object counts captured by two ECNs after applying object re-identification, along with their utility arrays. We choose ECN 1 as the primary camera view, while debiting object counts for ECN 2 by the number of duplicate objects re-identified (marked in bold).

Step 2: The controller determines a selected sequence of frames in the *sis* array for each ECN, which comprises tuples of (ECN identifier, frame index, utility). As illustrated in Figure 9, the modified *sis* array includes the frames captured by the primary ECN with changes in its object count (*i.e.*, frames four, zero, two). It also contains frames captured by the complimentary ECNs when a frame captured by the primary ECN fails to cover all the unique objects. For example, frames four and two of the (complementary) ECN 2 are appended to the *sis* array because they include additional unique objects, *i.e.*, objects h and i in frame four and object e in frame two.

Step 3: The controller consults the estimated wireless capacity C to determine whether all the selected frames in *sis* can be uploaded. If not, it prioritizes the selected images from the primary ECN, in decreasing order of their utility value. It then polls the selected images from all the complementary ECNs, in the order of their debited utility value.

Vigil can handle a large number of objects in a single frame as long as the vision analytic function is capable of doing so. The intra-cluster frame selection falls back to uploading each frame when the number of objects per frame are very large for each camera in the scene.

3.3 Inter-cluster traffic shaping

After determining the priority of frames to be uploaded within a cluster, the Vigil controller needs to coordinate upload bandwidth demand across the clusters that are within a wireless contention domain (*i.e.* served by a single access point). To do so, Vigil uses a novel inter-cluster traffic scheduling algorithm that attempts to allocate upload rates to each cluster that maximizing the number of useful objects per second delivered to the application (Contribution 3 in Section 1).

We describe our algorithm in the context of two application scenarios, i.e., counting applications such as customer queue analytics, and security based applications such as tracking a person or finding a suspicious object. These scenarios are monitored by two clusters of ECNs, which can contend with each other for uploading im-

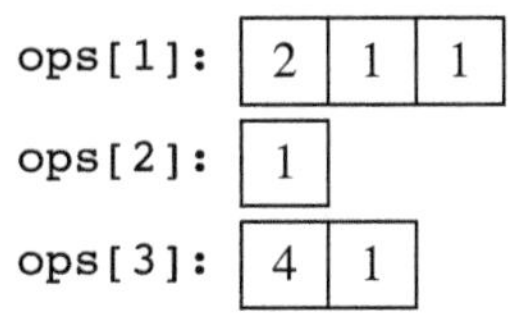

Figure 10: The per-cluster `ops` queues at the controller measure the utility, in operations per second, of sending the respective image sequences from each cluster.

ages. For the application scenarios related to analyzing a queue of customers or locating an object of interest, Vigil allocates rates proportional to the objects detected per second at each camera cluster. In these scenarios, the application can manually intervene when it detects large number of people or objects. For e.g., in a Starbucks coffee shop, the queues with higher person count could be served faster, and at the airport security checkpoints, the queue with highest person count would use more personnel to manage the queue. Following the notation of Section 3.2, we denote wireless capacity from cluster c as C_c. Since different video frames compress at different ratios, ECNs may also upload unequal frame sizes: we denote the size of the compressed frame in ith index of the selected image sequence from cluster c as L_i^c. Based on the these quantities, we calculate the number of useful objects per second (*ops*) for ith index of the selected image sequence of cluster c:

$$\texttt{ops}[\texttt{c}][\texttt{i}] = \frac{\texttt{sis}[\texttt{c}][\texttt{i}].\texttt{utility}}{L_i^c/C_c}. \tag{2}$$

The numerator of the *ops* metric is a count of objects, while the denominator has units of seconds (bits divided by bits per second). The *ops* thus captures how many useful objects per second the frame at ith index of the selected image sequence from cluster c will deliver if it is scheduled for transmission.

Step 1: Every time epoch, each cluster `c` uploads its selected image sequence `sis`, to the controller, which the controller stores in array element `sis[c]`, an array of selected image sequences indexed by cluster number `c`.

Step 2: For each cluster `c` and frame group index `i`, the controller computes `ops[c][i]` using Equation 2. The controller's state now appears as in Figure 10: a per-cluster queue of image sequences' *ops* values.

Step 3: The controller schedules service to different clusters using a variant of deficit round robin (DRR) scheduling [25] to approximate fair queuing [6]. To define terminology and provide context, we now briefly recall the DRR algorithm, in the context of serving Vigil clusters. Each cluster has a *deficit counter*, which represents the amount of information it is allowed to transmit when it is its turn. Vigil-DRR works by considering clusters in round-robin order. The controller adds a fixed amount of credit, called the *quantum*, to each cluster's deficit counter.[6] If the cluster's deficit counter exceeds the size of the packet, then the cluster transmits the packet and the controller decrements the cluster's deficit counter by the size of the transmitted packet.

Our DRR variant uses the reciprocal of *ops* in place of the packet length, for queue weights

$$\texttt{q}[\texttt{c}][\texttt{i}] = \frac{1}{\texttt{ops}[\texttt{c}][\texttt{i}]}, \tag{3}$$

[6]We describe our setting of `quantum` in Section 4.

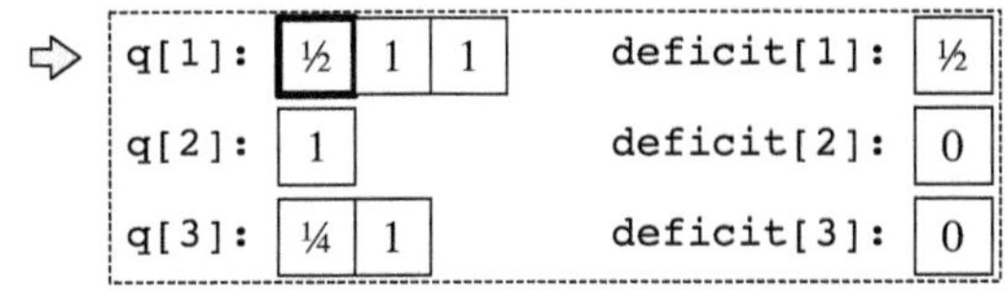

(a) Transmit from `q[1]`.

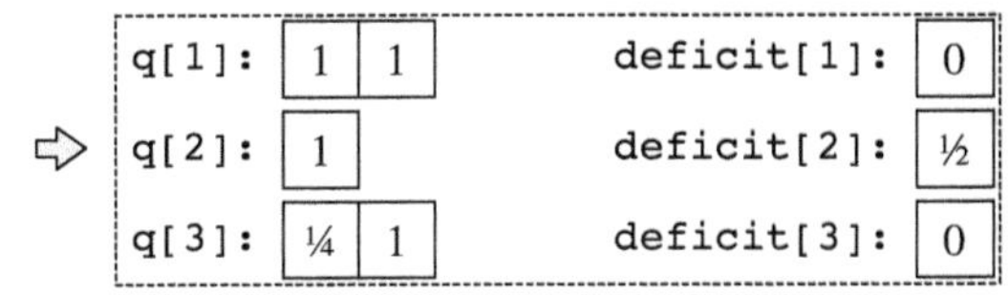

(b) No transmit from `q[2]`, update deficit.

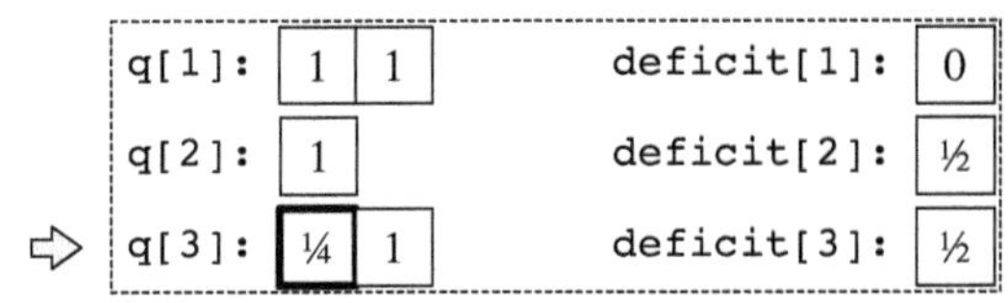

(c) Transmit from `q[3]`.

Figure 11: The Vigil-DRR algorithm operating over three camera clusters with a quantum of ½.

in the case that *ops* is non-zero, and drop the upload in the case that *ops* is zero. Vigil-DRR provides fair air-time to different clusters, each of which may have different wireless throughputs possible to the base station. Vigil-DRR also provides fairness between clusters in terms of the number of seconds per object change (utility). Thus a cluster that can upload a frame containing two object changes compared to a cluster that can upload a frame containing one object change.

Vigil-DRR also maximizes the number of objects per second delivered to the controller. To see this, consider the example of Figure 10 where there are three clusters, with frames at their respective queue heads having *ops* of two, one, and four respectively. If we service the clusters at rates r_1, r_2, and r_3 (bits per second), the number of objects per second uploaded to the controller will be the inner product of the preceding rate vector with the *ops* vector $(2,1,4)$: $\langle (r_1,r_2,r_3),(2,1,4)\rangle = 2\cdot r_1 + 1\cdot r_2 + 4\cdot r_3$. The Cauchy-Schwartz inequality states that we can maximize this inner product (*i.e.*, the number of objects per second uploaded) by choosing (r_1,r_2,r_3) proportional to the *ops* vector. Setting packet length inversely proportional to *ops* in the DRR algorithm accomplishes this, as DRR will schedule packets at rates inversely proportional to the packet length normalized by the wireless throughput.

Figure 11 shows an example of Vigil-DRR in operation over three clusters, with a `quantum` value of ½. Figure 11(a) shows the initial state of all queues. At the first time-step, the algorithm increments the deficit counter of the first queue by `quantum` (½ in this example) and then checks the `q[]` value of the change at the head of the queue. Since it is ½, Vigil-DRR transmits the change and decrements the deficit counter by ½, leaving zero in the deficit counter, as shown in Figure 11(b). At the next time-step, the algorithm increments the deficit counter of the second queue by ½, but the `q[]` value at the head of the second queue is greater than ½, and no transmission occurs, as shown in Figure 11(c). At the final time-step, the algorithm increments `deficit[3]` by ½ and transmits, leaving ¼ in the deficit counter. The algorithm then proceeds similarly in a round-robin fashion.

(a) Site #1 lounge. **(b)** Site #2 office. **(c)** Site #3 lab.

(d) Site #1 outdoor bus stop pilot.

Figure 12: Vigil deployment at three sites.

For certain security-based applications such as intruder detection and tracking a person, the ECN nodes may assign high-priority to the captured frames. We modify the design of Vigil-DRR algorithm similar to MDRR algorithm to allow a high priority queue that allows the frames requesting priority access on the channel to be uploaded immediately overriding the *ops* metric.

4. IMPLEMENTATION

In this section, we describe our implementation of Vigil. With the goal of understanding system performance *in situ*, we have deployed Vigil at three sites. We describe these deployments in the next section, and hardware and software details in Section 4.2 and Section 4.3, respectively.

4.1 Testbed deployments

We deploy a single cluster of Vigil cameras at three sites under vastly different operational conditions.[7] Firstly, we study an outdoor surveillance scenario by deploying a cluster of camera ECN nodes at a shuttle bus stop at Site #1's outdoor campus (Figure 12(d)), where we monitor real-time vision analytic functions such as counting passengers. The ECN nodes in this deployment connect to a controller by long-distance backhaul links over TV whitespaces. Secondly, we study an indoor surveillance scenario in a busy office hallway by deploying a cluster of camera ECN nodes at Site #1, where we monitor the frequency of passers-by. The ECN nodes in this deployment use unlicensed 2.4 GHz Wi-Fi to connect to the controller. Finally, we surveil an open-plan office at Site #2 (Figure 12(b)) and an indoor lab environment at Site #3 (Figure 12(c)), where we monitor working hours and office occupancy. The ECN nodes in these deployments use unlicensed 2.4 GHz Wi-Fi at Site #2 and TV whitespace radios at Site #3 to connect to the controller. The indoor deployments in the three sites have been operational for the last two months, giving us valuable information on traffic patterns.

[7]Privacy of the monitored users is preserved by ensuring that the cameras only capture users who had given prior permission to take part in the study.

4.2 Hardware

This section describes the hardware platform we used to deploy the controller and the ECNs. To implement the ECN nodes, we use laptops running a user-space program to perform image analysis functions on video feeds from the connected cameras. We have used laptops and the Intel Next Unit of Computing (NUC) to prototype our system, but embedded devices (e.g. Gatework routers or NUC) with 500 MHz–1 GHz CPU have enough processing power to run image analysis functions for ECNs. Recent trends in vision are moving toward smart cameras, thereby enabling face recognition, motion detection, and other image analysis tools to be implemented to an increasing extent in hardware [10].

Each laptop is also attached to a Wi-Fi based router to provide public Internet access. Wi-Fi traffic along with vision analytic data are sent over the connected routers to a central controller. Linux-based routers running the OpenWRT operating system upload vision analytic traffic from the ECN nodes to the controller. These router boards control two different types of wireless interface cards for communication in TV whitespaces and the 2.4 GHz ISM band, respectively. In our outdoor deployment, we use TV-band transmitters from Doodle Labs [7] for TV whitespace communications. The radios are configured in a single vacant TV channel at a center frequency of 580 MHz, with a 5 MHz bandwidth.[8] In our indoor deployment, we use off-the-shelf 802.11a/b/g radios operating in the 2.4 GHz band.

We implemented the central controller on a workstation hosting a user-space program that collects ECN traffic for further processing. Both ECN and controller run code implemented in Microsoft Visual Studio on Windows 8.1.

4.3 Software architecture

This section describes the software architecture of the controller and ECNs. The entire software codebase consists of 6,000 lines of C Sharpcode that implements vision analytic algorithms and end-to-end protocols, along with approximately 100 lines of C code for `ath5k` driver modifications.

Virtual networking device: We use the `tun` virtual networking device in OpenVPN [21] software at each camera node. All traffic from Wi-Fi users is directed through this virtual device, which is subsequently captured by our application for traffic shaping, then transmission via the underlying whitespace interface.

MAC layer modifications: We disable the rate adaptation function in the `ath5k` driver, and allow the ECN nodes to control the physical-layer data rate used to send each packet by appending a special bit-rate in the header of each packet to be transmitted. This allows the controller to accurately estimate the wireless capacity C of the link from the ECN node to the controller (equation 1). In our evaluation, we fixed C to isolate the effect of our frame selection algorithms. However, any rate adaptation algorithm can be easily adopted in ECNs to further improve performance.

5. EVALUATION

In this section we evaluate Vigil's performance gains over conventional approaches. Sections 5.1 and 5.2 evaluate the accuracy improvement of Vigil's intra-cluster frame selection (§3.2.1) and inter-cluster traffic shaping (§3.3) components. Section 5.3 presents microbenchmarks that stress-test Vigil's vision and advanced scheduling algorithms (§3.2.2).

[8]Before each experiment, we query a commercial spectrum occupancy database [27] to ensure this channel is vacant.

Frame index:	0	1	2	3	4	5	6	7	8	9
utility:	1	1	2	2	2	2	1	1	3	3
Changes:	1		2				1		3	

Figure 13: Frame utilities and frames where utility changes. Uploading all the frames where utility changes gives 100% accuracy relative to a baseline (*i.e.* human validation, or a vision algorithm working on full M-JPEG camera streams).

For object-counting applications, we measure the accuracy of Vigil as the accuracy of object counts relative to baseline data from running vision algorithms on all frames of the raw video streams of all available cameras. If the system uploads all the frames where the object count changed (*i.e.* the zeroth, second, sixth, and eighth frames, as shown in Figure 13) the system will make no errors relative to baseline and has 100% accuracy. Otherwise the accuracy is the percentage of frames that the system uploads where the object count changed.

5.1 Intra-cluster frame selection

In this section, we evaluate the accuracy of Vigil in a cluster of cameras using intra-cluster frame selection (§3.2).

Methodology. In this experiment, we use video traces collected from a cluster of three cameras at Site #3 in a lab environment. The three cameras log video traces synchronously for a duration of 180 seconds, with about 2,000 image frames. The ECN connected to the camera uploads detected face counts and the controller selects which frames are uploaded from ECNs based on the intra-cluster frame selection algorithm.

We choose the ECN's slot time (§3.1, p. 3) to be 100 milliseconds: this strikes a good tradeoff between the detection errors of vision algorithm and responsiveness in detecting people. We configure the epoch time L_e to be five slots: this choice of epoch length reduces the protocol overhead of sending control messages, while enabling use of the best available camera in detecting people. We experimented with other choices of L_e and found end-to-end performance was not sensitive to this parameter.

We compare the accuracy of intra-cluster frame selection in Vigil to two approaches: a *Round-Robin* approach that cycles through all cameras within a cluster in a round-robin manner to upload frames and a *Single-Camera* approach that arbitrarily selects a single camera to upload frames. Note that all approaches only upload the frames where the count of detected faces changes. We constrain the capacity of wireless link from each ECN to the controller and repeat the experiment five times.

Results. Figure 14 shows the performance gains of Vigil as we increase the per-camera available wireless capacity for video traces collected at low, medium and high activity levels. The bandwidth required at each activity level is summarized in table 1. In Figure 14, the bandwidth required at low activity level (at most 16 Kbit/s) is lower than the available per-camera wireless capacity and therefore, both Vigil and *Round-Robin* achieve more than 90% accuracy, while the single camera suffers because of lack of sufficient coverage. Similar results are observed for medium activity level, except Vigil outperforms other approaches when the available per-camera wireless capacity 50 kbps is lower than the bandwidth required for medium activity level (at most 80 kbps). Finally at high activity level, the bandwidth required is much higher than the available per-camera wireless capacity and we observe 23-30% gains for Vigil compared to *Round-Robin* because Vigil prioritizes those frames across cameras that maximize the accuracy.

Level	# people	Change interval(s)	Bandwidth(Kbps)
Low	1	5–15	4–16
Medium	4	1–2	32–80
High	7	0.2–1	100–400

Table 1: Summary of video traces used to benchmark intra-cluster algorithms in terms of the number of participants, the frequency of change in object counts, and required bandwidth to upload the frames where object count changes.

We gather more insight in to why Vigil results in higher accuracy compared to a round-robin or a single camera approach. Figure 15 illustrates that Vigil's accuracy increases with the number of cameras up to the point where no blind spots are left uncovered. In this example, two cameras provide a significant gain over a single camera approach, but subsequently adding more cameras does not improve performance, because Vigil already prioritizes those frames which maximize accuracy.

5.2 Inter-cluster scheduling

In this section, we evaluate the accuracy of Vigil across multiple clusters of cameras by using the inter-cluster traffic scheduling algorithm (§3.3), examining to what extent the system can maintain accuracy as wireless capacity becomes more and more scarce, and more camera clusters contend on the same wireless bandwidth. We compare the accuracy of Vigil's inter-cluster traffic scheduling algorithm to two approaches: an equal throughput allocation which is a throughput-based fairness policy that gives equal throughput to all the camera clusters such as in the case of Wi-Fi and an equal time based allocation which is a time-based fairness policy. Note that all approaches only upload the frames from the selected image sequence `sis` of each ECN.

Methodology. We simulate a network of clusters of cameras that contend over a shared wireless channel. We vary the wireless capacity of this shared channel from 1 Mbps to 20 Mbps to quantify the ability of inter-cluster frame selection to alleviate congestion on the shared wireless medium. We emulate different activity levels by modeling the arrivals at each camera cluster by a Poisson arrival process to emulate the traffic patterns from our real-world deployments, where an increasing rate λ corresponds to higher activity levels. We assume that each arriving person departs after a constant dwell time. A single image in our experiments is 30 Kbytes, which takes approximately 240 ms to upload at one Mbit/s. We choose a Vigil-DRR `quantum` of 100 (seconds/object) so that Vigil-DRR would transmit a three-object frame without cycling round the clusters. We found that Vigil-DRR is not sensitive to our choice of `quantum`. We simulate the system over a time period of approximately one hour.

We evaluate the accuracy of Vigil-DRR algorithm across multiple clusters of cameras. In these experiments, we simulate a network of ten clusters of cameras that contend over a shared wireless bandwidth where each cluster has two cameras. The number of faces detected at each cluster is modeled by a Poisson arrival process, where the rate of the Poisson arrival process λ is set to 2.5 (objects/second) for low activity level, 5 (objects/second) for medium activity level, and 12.5 (objects/second) for high activity level. Note that while Vigil selects the most relevant frames from two cameras in each cluster based on intra-cluster frame selection, but the equal throughput and equal time approach assume one camera per cluster for fair comparison of traffic scheduling.

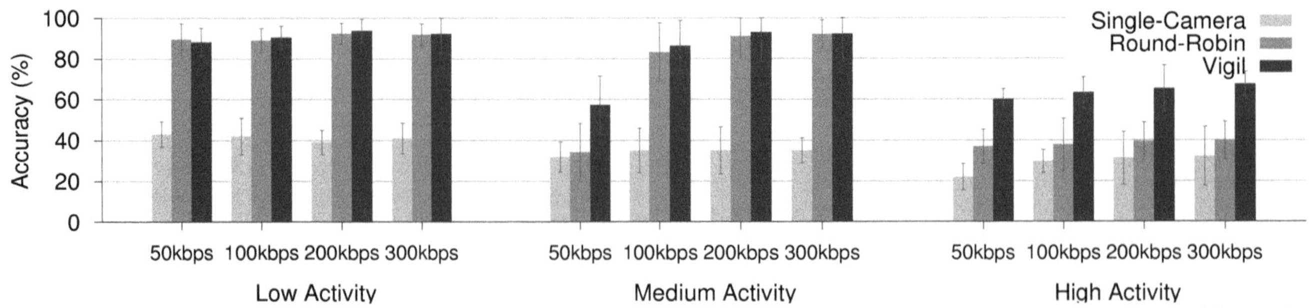

Figure 14: Accuracy of intra-cluster frame-selection in Vigil relative to a single-camera system and a multi-camera system with round-robin scheduling. Error bars show standard deviation of the experiment in varying wireless conditions.

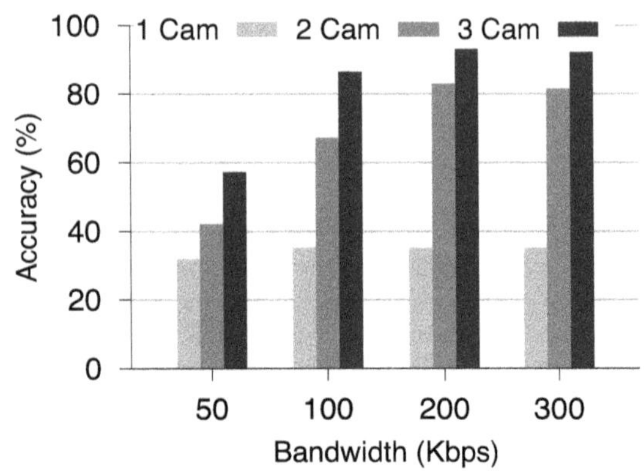

Figure 15: Vigil's accuracy in a single-cluster surveillance network with different number of cameras.

5.2.1 *Equal wireless capacity*

We first consider the scenario where the available wireless capacity is same from each ECN to the controller in ten camera cluster. Figure 16 shows the performance gains of Vigil-DRR as we increase the shared wireless capacity at low, medium and high activity levels. We observe that Vigil-DRR requires more wireless bandwidth to achieve 100% accuracy at higher activity levels. In this example, Vigil-DRR utilizes only 10 Mbit/s at low activity level to achieve 100% accuracy for ten camera clusters, but at high activity level, it achieves only 80% accuracy at bandwidths as high as 20 Mbps. Further, we note that Vigil-DRR significantly outperforms the equal throughput allocation and equal time allocation approach when the shared wireless capacity is not sufficient because it prioritizes the frames with maximum object count, using the *ops* metric. In this example, Vigil-DRR achieves gains of 20-25% over the other two approaches at 5 Mbit/s in low activity level and 10 Mbit/s in medium activity level. Finally, we note that the equal throughput and equal time allocation approaches achieve similar accuracy gains because the available wireless capacity is same from each ECN to the controller.

5.2.2 *Unequal wireless capacity*

Now we consider a scenario where the available wireless capacity from each ECN to the controller varies across ECNs. Figure 17 shows the performance gains of Vigil-DRR when the available wireless capacity from five clusters to ECN is C_1 and from the other five clusters to ECN is C_2 in a network with ten clusters of cameras. We first note that equal throughput allocation approach penalizes the clusters with high wireless capacity C_2 to sacrifice accuracy to ensure all clusters get equal throughputs. On the other hand, equal time allocation approach ensures time-based fairness allowing the clusters with high wireless capacity C_2 to upload more frames than clusters with low capacity C_1. But Vigil-DRR outperforms both these approaches in terms of accuracy for both the clusters with low wireless capacity C_1 and high wireless capacity C_2. Further, the gap in accuracy between the high-capacity and low-capacity clusters is much smaller for Vigil-DRR compared to equal time allocation approach because of maximizing the *ops* metric.

5.3 Vision algorithm microbenchmarks

In this section, we evaluate the two vision algorithms Vigil uses: face detection and a re-identification algorithm to associate faces detected in overlapping camera views.

5.3.1 *Face detection*

This evaluation answers two questions: first, how accurate is the Haar-cascade-classifier-based face detection algorithm used in our system? Second, in terms of that accuracy, what is the impact of various video compression schemes on system bandwidth savings? We compare two state-of-the-art video compression algorithms, M-JPEG and MPEG-4, to determine which fits the design of Vigil best.

Methodology. We use a single camera to record five-minute video traces at two different resolutions. Each trace contains about 7,000 images. Two people arrive and departed randomly in the scene, facing the camera. The distance of the subjects to the camera ranges from two to eight meters. The ground-truth person count is established by visual confirmation. We compress the frames with different state-of-the-art compression algorithms at different levels, and then apply a face detection algorithm on the compressed images to understand the tradeoff of accuracy and bandwidth required.

Results. Figure 18 shows a scatter plot of bandwidth required as the accuracy of the face detection vision algorithm increases. For each video compression algorithm, the accuracy of the face detection increases when it is compressed less because of low information loss. Here Vigil-crop applies M-JPEG compression only on the cropped faces in an image (by replacing the image background with a single RGB color). We observe that Vigil-crop outperforms M-JPEG compression without object cropping by 2–5× in bandwidth savings. It even outperforms the state-of-the-art MPEG-4 algorithm by a factor of two in bandwidth savings for the same accuracy. We therefore choose M-JPEG algorithm with object cropping in Vigil. Further, we note that Vigil allows a wide accuracy and bandwidth tradeoff compared to MPEG-4. This is because MPEG-4 applies delta-based frame compression, which either removes all the details in intermediate frames, or have to keep most of the redundant information.

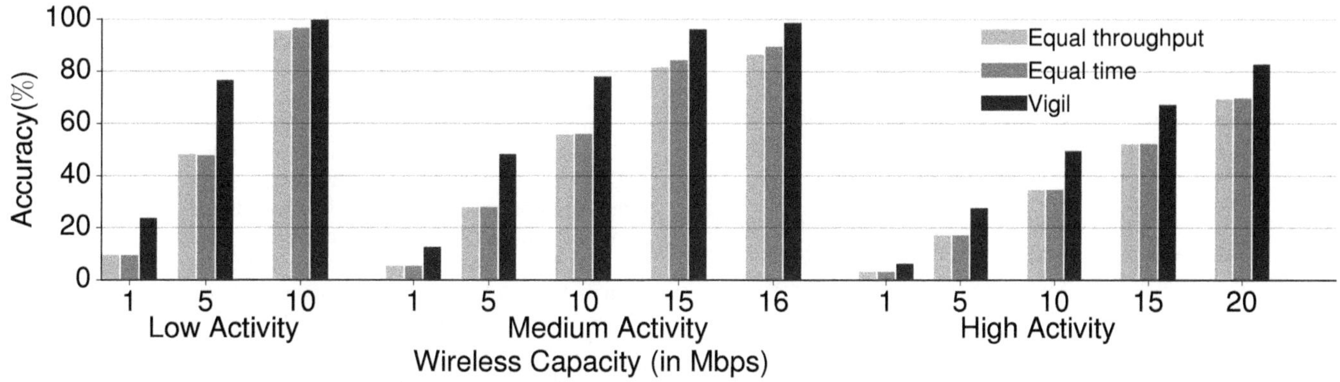

Figure 16: Accuracy of a multi-cluster system as the wireless capacity varies as shown on the x-axis. We compare Vigil with time-based fairness and equal throughput allocation for ten cluster of cameras. Vigil uses two cameras per cluster to select the most relevant frames, but equal throughput and equal time approach assume one camera per cluster for fair comparison.

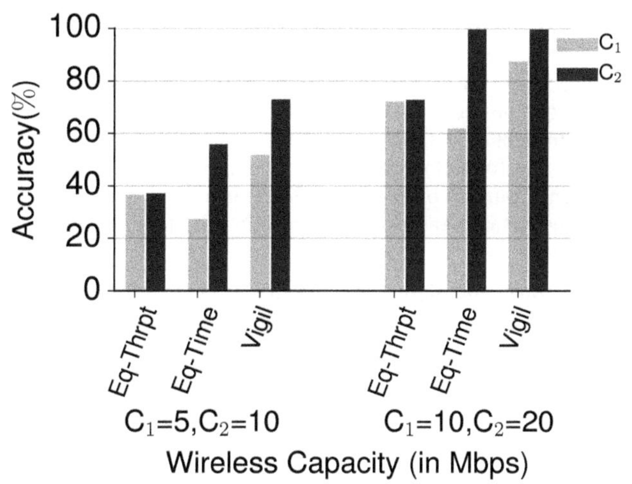

Figure 17: Accuracy of a multi-cluster system with 10 clusters where the wireless capacity of 5 clusters is C_1 and other 5 clusters C_2. Vigil outperforms both equal time-based fairness (Eq-Time) and equal throughput allocation (Eq-Thrpt).

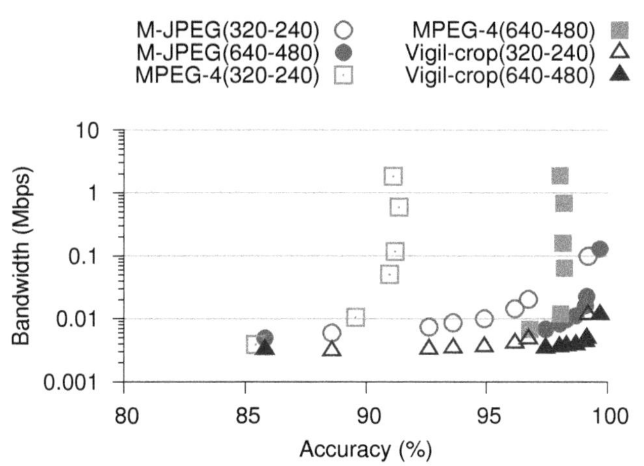

Figure 18: Bandwidth required versus accuracy of the face detection vision algorithm on videos compressed with different video compression algorithms, including our algorithm Vigil-crop that performs M-JPEG on the cropped objects. Only the selected frames in the `sis` array are compressed for this bandwidth calculation.

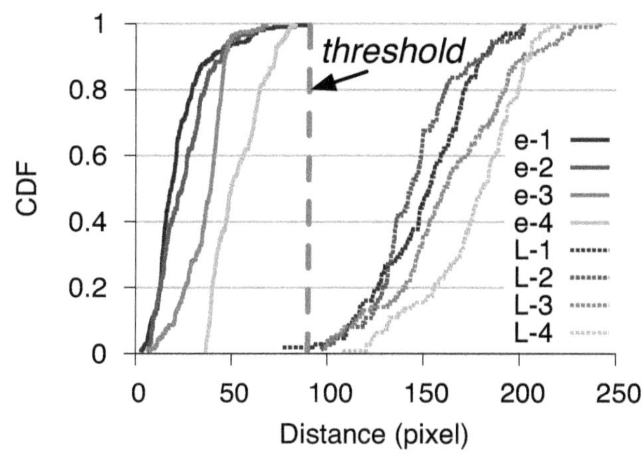

Figure 19: CDF of the distance l between two people's faces and the projection errors e when mapped from one camera view to another (illustrated in Figure 7(b)).

5.3.2 *Object re-identification*

We evaluate the accuracy of the re-identification algorithm described in Section 3.2.2. This section addresses the question of how well Vigil can tag faces in overlapping camera views as to the same person.

Methodology. In this experiment, two cameras synchronously log video traces at four indoor locations, where each trace consists of 300 images with the faces of same two people detected at different locations. The two cameras have a partially overlapping view as illustrated in Figure 7. The re-identification algorithm projects the faces detected at the first camera onto the corresponding images captured by the second camera. It then calculates the distance between the projection and the faces detected at the second camera, which is the projection error e in Figure 7(b). This projection error is then compared to the distance l between the two people's faces detected in the same camera view.

Results. Figure 19 shows the CDF of the projection error e and the distance l between different faces of all the images at each captured location. We observe that the maximum projection error e is 89 pixels at these locations, and is much lower than l for most of the cases. Thus, we use this maximum e as the threshold of associating projected faces in our implementation. (§ 3.2.2), which

Resolution	Face detection	Re-identification	Compression
320 × 240	32ms	2ms	13ms
640 × 480	80ms	2ms	15ms

Table 2: Average processing delay of different vision analytic functions in Vigil using a laptop with a 2.4GHz dual-core CPU.

can lead to >98.1% re-identification accuracy at all the measured locations. The maximum projection error can be obtained by running this experiment as part of the camera calibration process. The threshold value, set during calibration process, is useful for a long period of time for static cameras. Finally, our current algorithm can fail to distinguish unique objects that are densely located (e.g., within <89 pixel). In such a scenario, we may revert back to the basic intra-cluster scheduling by picking the maximum object counts from all the ECNs. Enabling Vigil to dynamically switch between different scheduling algorithms remains as our future work.

Finally, Table 2 summarizes the processing delay of running different vision analytic functions of Vigil on a standard laptop. The latency is measured based on our video traces at two different resolutions. We observe a low latency of <80ms for all the processing functions, which enables Vigil to promptly capture objects in highly dynamic scenes.

5.4 Area coverage

The following back-of-the-envelope calculation shows that Vigil can achieve significant area coverage gains over systems that stream MPEG-4 video. Assuming that we cluster cameras in groups of four covering a 100 sq. ft. area per cluster, each camera covers an amortized 25 sq. ft. area. Assuming an available capacity of 20 Mbit/s, the status quo approach of deploying a camera stream 1 Mbit/s video (a typical MPEG-4 rate) will support 20 cameras, for a total coverage area of 500 sq. ft. But referring to Table 1, we see that the bandwidth a low activity scene actually requires is only on the order of 10 Kbit/s, while a high activity scene requires approximately 200 Kbit/s. So Vigil can function at data rates ranging from 40–800 Kbit/s per cluster, resulting in 500 clusters for low activity and 25 clusters for high activity. Consequently, Vigil covers between 2,500 sq. ft. and 50,000 sq. ft, resulting in a coverage gain of between 5× and 200× over status quo video streaming.

6. RELATED WORK

We delineate Vigil from prior work in the following three categories, i.e., cloud-based video surveillance systems, vision analytic algorithms, and video compression algorithms.

Cloud-based video surveillance systems. Many of "smart" surveillance systems today such as Dropcam [8]) rely on a wired network to upload camera feed to the cloud for vision analysis. A similar architecture has been explored in early research prototypes like IrisNet [9], Bolt [11], and S3 [29] aiming to coordinate camera sensors at a large scale. While existing systems manage to address various scalability challenges in computation and storage, their wired backhauls lead to high deployment cost and low flexibility in providing pervasive surveillance. To address this limitation, Vigil has explored a wireless video surveillance design, while leveraging specific scheduling techniques combined with edge computing technology to conserve wireless bandwidth.

Another line of work [12, 23]) aims to reduce the latency of uploading data to the cloud, by partitioning computation tasks between mobile sensors and the cloud. Odessa [23] supports interactive perception applications by dynamically offloading parts of computation tasks from mobile devices to the cloud. A recent system Gabriel [12] targets a similar class of augmented reality applications based on a cloudlet architecture, which comprises computation devices located at the edge of network to reduce network latency. In contrast to prior systems, Vigil focuses on an orthogonal problem of wireless bandwidth limitation, and tackles it with various scheduling algorithms among multiple ECNs.

Dao *et al.* [5] present a framework that suppresses uploading of redundant images from smartphones based on feature matching algorithms run on thumbnails of candidate images to be uploaded. Hu *et al.* [14] make a case for offload shaping, using image metrics such as focus, blur detection, and similarity of successive frames. These systems, developed in parallel with Vigil, differ from our work because they make uploading decisions solely on image similarity rather than the presence of objects in a user's query. In addition, Vigil advances the state-of-the-art by using re-identification algorithms running on images from multiple simultaneous cameras and schedules the uploads to match the network conditions as well as the dynamics of the scene.

Vision analytic algorithms. A large body of prior work has leveraged vision algorithms for different applications. For example, Gabriel [12] and Glimpse [13] use a Harr Cascade classifier for face detection. CarSafe [32] and WalkSafe [31] use SIFT based object detection algorithms to detect cars and lanes on the road. Finally, InSight [30] aims to detect clothing patterns by applying Wavelets transformation on the distribution of color pixels. Vigil is different from this prior work, and can give additional gains by leveraging these advanced vision algorithms to make better scheduling decisions.

Video compression algorithms. Motion JPEG (M-JPEG) [1] and MPEG-4 (H.264) [2] are two popular techniques for video compression. We choose M-JPEG in Vigil because it offers a wide range of trace between accuracy and image size (§5.3.1). It also allows the controller to decode each image independently, without waiting for other images in the same group to arrive. This effectively reduces the end-to-end latency of surveillance applications in a lossy wireless network.

Generally, video compression techniques are orthogonal to Vigil as they rely on redundancy between frames to compress the video stream. By sending only changes that maximize objects per second delivered to the cloud, Vigil removes that redundancy, reducing the efficacy of change-based video compression. State-of-the-art video compression standards like MPEG-4 and H.264 use object segmentation to identify moving objects in each frame of a video sequence [26] and cross-frame compression to eliminate the redundant image portions, *e.g.*, background scenery.

The re-identification algorithms we study are part of a family of algorithms that measure image similarity. Other algorithms include perceptual hashing techniques that encode image properties onto strings of bits [16, 19].

7. DISCUSSION

In this section we discuss various the design points of Vigil with the full hindsight of the previous sections.

Required compute resources at edge compute node. Recent trends in vision are moving toward smart cameras, thereby enabling face recognition, motion detection, and other vision tools to be implemented to an increasing extent in hardware [10, 20, 28]. Consequently, simple embedded platforms with 500 MHz–1 GHz CPU are sufficient to implement the vision analytic functions at ECNs.

Amount of ECN-local storage. The local storage at ECN retains video frames captured close in time to significant events in the video stream. MPEG-4 video at sufficient resolution for our application (320 × 200 or above) consumes a maximum bit-rate of between 384 and 8,000 Kbit/second (172 to 3,600 Mbytes/hour), depending on the encoding rate. The price of hard drive storage has been rapidly falling over the years, reaching USD 0.03/gigabyte in recent months [18], pricing the local storage between ½ and five US cents per hour for MPEG-4 video. Based on these figures, we expect the incremental cost for including storage for most queries requires less than USD 1.00 per ECN, adding a negligible cost to the overall bill.

Cost of distributed processing. Deploying ECNs together with cameras can inevitably increase the infrastructure cost. However, when wireless capacity is limited, the saved bandwidth by Vigil can be used to forward users' traffic, thereby recouping the cost of ECNs. To further reduce the cost, we envision that multiple cameras can connect to a single ECN to upload vision analytic functions of each connected camera to the controller. But this leads higher contention on the wireless medium between camera nodes, and hence, a more complex design of scheduling algorithms that we plan to address in future work.

Hybrid hotspot functionality. The hybrid camera-hotspot functionality can subsidize the cost of a droplet. With the cost of a camera in the range of USD 5–10, ECNs can become ubiquitous.

Choice of an object count-based metric. In Section 3.1 we motivated the use of an object count-based metric (`frameUtility`) for Vigil. We choose an object count-based metric in our design because it is a good first order approximation to frame value in a vast number of surveillance applications such as object identification and tracking. Also, our design is general enough to support any utility function by letting the controller push the utility function to the edge compute node. Therefore, the definition of utility can be modified based on the specific surveillance function performed by the system.

8. CONCLUSION

We began this work with the goal of investigating the feasibility of building a scalable wireless surveillance system, and to that end we built the Vigil system. In the process of building Vigil, we discovered several interesting design points, introducing the *ops* metric to maximize the number of query-specified objects uploaded to the cloud, and using clusters to add redundancy to camera views of a scene. We built and deployed Vigil in three different locations, and with this deployment experience our conclusion is that a system like Vigil is sufficient for most but not all surveillance use cases, but it is especially good for situations where the scene changes are infrequent. Experimental results show that Vigil allows a video surveillance system to support a geographical area of coverage between five and 200 times greater than an approach that simply streams video over the wireless network. For a fixed region of coverage and bandwidth, Vigil outperforms the default equal throughput allocation strategy of Wi-Fi by delivering up to 25% more objects relevant to a user's query. We are currently pursuing future work to even further increase Vigil's utility.

Acknowledgements

We would like to thank Jie Xiong for his help in deployment and valuable suggestions to improve the quality of our work. We are grateful to the anonymous shepherd and reviewers whose comments helped bring the paper to its final form. The research leading to these results has received funding from the European Research Council under the European Union's Seventh Framework Programme (FP/2007-2013) / ERC Grant Agreement no. 279976. Tan Zhang and Suman Banerjee are supported in part by the US National Science Foundation through awards CNS-1405667, CNS-1345293 and CNS-1343363.

9. REFERENCES

[1] Motion JPEG Video Codec. http: //www.digitalpreservation.gov/formats/fdd/fdd000063.shtml.
[2] MPEG4/H264 Video Coding Standard. http://mpeg.chiariglione.org/standards/mpeg-4.
[3] S. Biswas, J. Bicket, E. Wong, R. Musaloiu-E, A. Bhartia, and D. Aguayo. Large-scale measurements of wireless network behavior. In *ACM SIGCOMM*, 2015.
[4] B. Coifman, D. Beymer, P. McLauchlan, and J. Malik. A real-time computer vision system for vehicle tracking and traffic surveillance. *Elsevier Transportation Research Part C: Emerging Technologies*, 6(4):271 – 288, 1998.
[5] T. Dao, A. K. Roy-Chowdhury, H. V. Madhyastha, S. V. Krishnamurthy, and T. L. Porta. Managing redundant content in bandwidth constrained wireless networks. In *ACM CoNEXT*, 2014.
[6] A. Demers, S. Keshav, and S. Shenker. Analysis and simulation of a fair queueing algorithm. In *ACM SIGCOMM*, 1989.
[7] Doodle Labs. Broadband TV Whitespace Transceiver. http://www.doodlelabs.com/products/radio-transceivers/sub-ghz-range/470-790-mhz-tvws-100.
[8] Dropcam. Dropcam website. https://www.dropcam.com.
[9] P. B. Gibbons, B. Karp, Y. Ke, S. Nath, and S. Seshan. Irisnet: An architecture for a worldwide sensor web. *Pervasive Computing, IEEE*, 2(4):22–33, 2003.
[10] E. Gudis, L. Pullan, D. Berends, K. Kaighn, G. Van der Wal, G. Buchanan, S. Chai, and M. Piacentino. An embedded vision services framework for heterogeneous accelerators. In *Computer Vision and Pattern Recognition Workshops (CVPRW), 2013 IEEE Conference on*, pages 598–603, June 2013.
[11] T. Gupta, R. P. Singh, A. Phanishayee, J. Jung, and R. Mahajan. Bolt: Data management for connected homes. In *NSDI*, 2014.
[12] K. Ha, Z. Chen, W. Hu, W. Richter, P. Pillai, and M. Satyanarayanan. Towards Wearable Cognitive Assistance. In *ACM MobiSys*, 2014.
[13] S. Han, R. Nandakumar, M. Philipose, A. Krishnamurthy, and D. Wetherall. GlimpseData: Towards continuous vision-based personal analytics. In *ACM MobiSys Workshop on Physical Analytics*, 2014.
[14] W. Hu, B. Amos, Z. Chen, K. Ha, W. Richter, P. Pillai, B. Gilbert, J. Harkes, and M. Satyanarayanan. The case for offload shaping. In *HotMobile*, 2015.
[15] IDC. The Digital Universe in 2020: Big Data, Bigger Digital Shadows, and Biggest Growth in the Far East, Dec. 2012. http://www.emc.com/leadership/digital-universe/2012iview/executive-summary-a-universe-of.htm.
[16] S. Kozat, R. Venkatesan, and M. Mihcak. Robust perceptual image hashing via matrix invariants. In *ICIP*, 2004.
[17] D. Lowe. Object recognition from local scale-invariant features, 1999.
[18] mkomo.com. A History of Storage Cost. http://www.mkomo.com/cost-per-gigabyte-update.
[19] V. Monga and B. Evans. Perceptual image hashing via feature points: Performance evaluation and tradeoffs. *IEEE Trans. on Image Processing*, 15(11):3452–3465, 2006.

[20] V. Moshnyaga, K. Hashimoto, and T. Suetsugu. A Hardware Design of Camera-based UserâĂŹs Presence Detector. In *IEEE International conference on Systems, Man and Cybernetics*, 2008.

[21] OpenVPN Technologies. OpenVPN Virtual Networking Device. https://openvpn.net.

[22] B. Płaczek. A real time vehicle detection algorithm for vision-based sensors. In L. Bolc, R. Tadeusiewicz, L. Chmielewski, and K. Wojciechowski, editors, *Computer Vision and Graphics*, volume 6375 of *Lecture Notes in Computer Science*, pages 211–218. Springer Berlin Heidelberg, 2010.

[23] M. Ra, A. Sheth, L. Mummert, P. Pillai, D. Wetherall, and R. Govindan. Odessa: Enabling Interactive Perception Applicaitons on Mobile Devices. In *ACM MobiSys*, 2011.

[24] M. Satyanarayanan, P. Bahl, R. Caceres, and N. Davies. The Case for VM-Based Cloudlets in Mobile Computing. *IEEE Pervasive Computing*, 8(4):14–23, 2009.

[25] M. Shreedhar and G. Varghese. Efficient fair queuing using deficit round robin. In *ACM SIGCOMM*, 1995.

[26] T. Sikora. The MPEG-4 video standard verification model. *IEEE Trans. on Circuits and Systems for Video Technology*, 7:19–31, 1997.

[27] Spectrum Bridge Inc. Spectrum bridge database. http://www.spectrumbridge.com/Home.aspx.

[28] T. Theocharides, G. Link, N. Vijakrishnan, M. Irwin, and W. Wolf. Embedded hardware face detection. In *IEEE Conf. on VLSI Design*, 2004.

[29] Y.-L. Tian, L. Brown, A. Hampapur, M. Lu, A. Senior, and C. Shu. IBM Smart Surveillance System (S3): Event Based Video Surveillance System with an Open and Extensible Framework. *Mach. Vision Appl.*, 19(5-6):315–327, Sept. 2008.

[30] H. Wang, X. Bao, R. R. Choudhury, and S. Nelakuditi. Insight: Recognizing humans without face recognition. In *ACM HotMobile*, 2013.

[31] T. Wang, G. Cardone, A. Corradi, L. Torresani, and A. T. Campbell. WalkSafe: A Pedestrian Safety App for Mobile Phone Users Who Walk and Talk While Crossing Roads. In *ACM HotMobile*, 2012.

[32] C.-W. You, N. D. Lane, F. Chen, R. Wang, Z. Chen, T. J. Bao, M. Montes-de Oca, Y. Cheng, M. Lin, L. Torresani, and A. T. Campbell. CarSafe App: Alerting Drowsy and Distracted Drivers Using Dual Cameras on Smartphones. In *MobiSys*, 2013.

[33] Z. Zhang, A. Scanlon, W. Yin, L. Yu, and P. L. Venetianer. Video surveillance using a multi-camera tracking and fusion system. In *M2SFA2*, 2012.

SAMPLES: Self Adaptive Mining of Persistent LExical Snippets for Classifying Mobile Application Traffic

Hongyi Yao†, Gyan Ranjan‡, Alok Tongaonkar‡, Yong Liao‡ and Z. Morley Mao†
†Department of EECS,
University of Michigan, Ann Arbor, MI, USA.
†{hyyao, zmao}@umich.edu
‡Center for Advanced Data Analytics,
Symantec Corp., Mountain View, CA, USA.
‡{firstname_lastname}@symantec.com

ABSTRACT

We present **SAMPLES**: **S**elf **A**daptive **M**ining of **P**ersistent **LE**xical **S**nippets; a systematic framework for classifying network traffic generated by mobile applications. SAMPLES constructs *conjunctive* rules, in an automated fashion, through a supervised methodology over a set of labeled flows (the *training set*). Each conjunctive rule corresponds to the lexical context, associated with an application identifier found in a *snippet* of the HTTP header, and is defined by: (a) the identifier type, (b) the HTTP header-field it occurs in, and (c) the prefix/suffix surrounding its occurrence. Subsequently, these conjunctive rules undergo an *aggregate-and-validate* step for improving accuracy and determining a priority order. The refined rule-set is then loaded into an application-identification engine where it operates at a per flow granularity, in an *extract-and-lookup* paradigm, to identify the application responsible for a given flow. Thus, SAMPLES can facilitate important network measurement and management tasks — e.g. behavioral profiling [29], application-level firewalls [21,22] etc. — which require a more detailed view of the underlying traffic than that afforded by traditional protocol/port based methods.

We evaluate SAMPLES on a *test set* comprising 15 million flows (approx.) generated by over 700 K applications from the Android, iOS and Nokia market-places. SAMPLES successfully identifies over 90% of these applications with 99% accuracy on an average. This, in spite of the fact that fewer than 2% of the applications are required during the training phase, for each of the three market places. This is a testament to the universality and the scalability of our approach. We, therefore, expect SAMPLES to work with reasonable coverage and accuracy for other mobile platforms — e.g. BlackBerry and Windows Mobile — as well.

Categories and Subject Descriptors

C.2.3 **[Communication Networks]**: Network Operations - Network monitoring.

Keywords

Mobile App Identification; Automated Rule Generation.

MobiCom'15, September 07 - 11, 2015, Paris, France
Copyright 2015 ACM 978-1-4503-3619-2/15/09 ...$15.00
DOI: http://dx.doi.org/10.1145/2789168.2790097.

1. INTRODUCTION

Network operators need clear visibility into the applications running within — and responsible for the traffic in — their networks to perform key network management tasks. These may include network planning and bandwidth provisioning, billing, traffic engineering, deployment of application level firewalls and access control systems. For instance, a network operator might want to prioritize traffic from online meeting applications, block traffic from a given gaming app, or catalog application behavior profiles [29] and usage statistics for users within a given enterprise [21,22]. Such nuanced policy formulation and enforcement requires a granular view of the network traffic that is clearly beyond the scope of traditional protocol/port/volumetric based classification systems [8, 10, 18]; and their primitive DPI (deep-packet-inspection) counterparts [14].

The problem has been further compounded in recent years with the adoption of hand-held devices, such as mobile phones and tablets, as preferred end-hosts for accessing the Internet. Users of such devices often download and install applications, commonly called *mobile apps*, that provide a wide range of functions. A significant number of these applications use the HTTP/HTTPS protocols for communicating with not only their respective content hosting servers, but also a plethora of third party services (e.g. advertisement and analytics). This, coupled with the so called *Bring-Your-Own-Device* (BYOD) to work phenomenon, poses unprecedented challenges for network managers; particularly in an enterprise setting. With the advent of wearable devices (e.g. Apple watch, Google-glass etc.), this trend is expected to continue for the foreseeable future. Needless to say, all this necessitates the design and development of new approaches to tackle a rapidly changing network landscape. Consequently, several recent studies have tried to address the problem of identifying mobile applications in network traffic [11, 19, 23, 27, 29], at a per flow granularity. While interesting in their own right, these solutions are either platform specific [19, 23, 27, 29], and thus limited, or too computationally expensive to attain desired levels of scalability [11]. We discuss each of these in detail later.

In this work, we present **SAMPLES**: **S**elf **A**daptive **M**ining of **P**ersistent **LE**xical **S**nippets; a systematic framework for classifying network traffic generated by mobile applications at a per-flow granularity. In order to do so, SAMPLES relies on the content of the HTTP headers generated by mobile applications. An HTTP header is, in effect, an ensemble of structured fields (cf. Table 1); one or more of which may potentially contain an identifier string — such as the market-place application id or the name of the application — that identifies the app responsible for the flow. Indeed, it is known that mobile applications use such identifiers while communicating with their content host servers as well as third party services (e.g. advertisement and analytics); for a variety of practi-

Field Name	Tag used in this study	Description
Domain host-name	HST	The host-name in a URL [csi.gstatic.com/csi?v=3&s=gmob]
Method	MET	HTTP method [GET, PUT, POST, REST].
User-Agent	AGN	See [4].
Path	URI	Part of URL b/w first / and ? [csi.gstatic.com/csi?v=3&s=gmob).
Query Parameters	PAR	Part of URL after ? [csi.gstatic.com/csi?v=3&s=gmob).
Referrer	REF	A referrer URL, see [4].
Cookies	COO, SCO	Cookie and Set-Cookie, see [4].
Others	ALP, APL_WO, APL_CX, XRW	Non-standard fields.

Table 1: Commonly seen fields in the HTTP flow header of mobile app network traces. For details see [4].

cal reasons [23, 24]. SAMPLES exploits the occurrence of such identifiers, and the lexical context in which they occur, to construct generalized *conjunctive rules* through a supervised methodology as follows: SAMPLES samples a subset of randomly selected applications for each mobile platform (Android, iOS and Nokia). Using a lightweight *crawl-download-execute* infrastructure, it builds a repository of all possible identifier strings — such as *application name*, *application id* etc — by parsing market webpages as well as lexically meaningful contents of the application's executable archive. Next, in an automated execution environment, SAMPLES executes the applications, one at a time, to produce HTTP flows. The flows that contain in their header one or more identifiers of the parent app, are then grouped them into a flowset labeled with the unique application identifier. These flowsets constitute both the *training* as well as the *test* sets for the supervised methodology. Next, for each flow in the training set, SAMPLES characterizes the *lexical context* associated with an identifier string, found in a snippet of the header, in terms of three lexical conjuncts: (a) the identifier type, (b) the HTTP header-field (or payload) it occurs in, and (c) the prefix/suffix that surrounds such occurrences. Clearly, the same *lexical context* may persist across flows produced by multiple applications. This is due, in part, to functional specifications of host services as well as structural idiosyncrasies of third party libraries [23, 30]. It is precisely such persistent lexical contexts that constitute a conjunctive rule in the SAMPLES framework. Once constructed, the rule-sets are loaded into an app identification engine where they operate at a per-flow granularity.

We evaluate SAMPLES using 15 million flows generated by 700 K applications from the Android, iOS and Nokia market-places. SAMPLES successfully identifies over 90% of these applications with 99% accuracy on an average. This, in spite of the fact that the training phase requires fewer than 2% of the applications in the market-place, per platform; a testament to the scalability and generality of our design. Moreover, SAMPLES can achieve processing *goodputs* of 217 Mbps, 40 Mbps and 150 Mbps respectively on the three platforms. Although measured in a controlled laboratory environment, the results bode well from a real-world deployment standpoint. Given that SAMPLES relies on seemingly universal network behavior of mobile apps, we believe that it should extend to other platforms such as Windows Mobile and BlackBerry; as is.

The rest of this paper is organized into the following sections: in §2, we introduce preliminary notations and assumptions, along with the datasets used in the course of this study. Next, in §3, we describe the various types of application identifiers and the lexical context in which they are found in the *snippets* of HTTP headers, followed by a formal definition of what constitutes a *conjunctive rule*. We then outline the design goals for SAMPLES in §4 and the system architecture in §5. Experimental evaluation of SAMPLES from coverage, accuracy and performance standpoints is presented in §6. Finally, in §7, we review relevant studies in literature and conclude the paper with a discussion of potential future work in §8.

```
200 OK
...
Client: 192.168.1.10 Scheme: https
GET
216.115.100.103:443/pe/4d8c5d92/92bcb62d/3
661ec2a/15957/config/prod/config.xml
User-Agent: YahooMobileMessenger/1.0
(Android Messenger; 1.8.4) (grouper; asus; Nexus
7; 4.2.2/JDQ39B)
Host: s.yimg.com
Connection: Keep-Alive
```

Figure 1: Decrypted HTTPS flow header from Yahoo Messenger app on Android platform.

2. PRELIMINARIES AND DATASETS

We now introduce the notations and assumptions of our framework (§2.1), followed by a brief discussion of the datasets used in the course of this study (§2.2).

2.1 Notations and Assumptions

Network flow: A flow $\mathcal{F}$ is defined as a single application layer request-response pair. In particular, all flows considered in this work are HTTP flows. When referring to an HTTP flow, we will use the notational schema for its constituent fields as defined in Table 1.

Identifiable flow/app: We define an HTTP flow as **identifiable** if it contains at least one **identifier** for its parent app in the header (cf. §3.1). Similarly, a mobile application is deemed **identifiable** if it generates at least one identifiable flow during its execution. In our dataset, there are roughly 76.8%, 67.4% and 63.2% identifiable apps for the Android, iOS and Nokia platforms respectively. The rest of the apps either do not exhibit any meaningful network behavior; or simply do not execute in our automated execution environment. However, as shown in §6, this does not hamper the coverage or accuracy of our system in any significant way.

HTTPS and encrypted traffic: HTTPS, in the very general case, is a limitation of our work. We do not deal with the issue of encrypted traffic *in the wild* which, although an interesting and complimentary area of work, is orthogonal to our system [15]. However, in an enterprise deployment scenario, the SAMPLES framework can utilize a *man-in-the-middle* proxy, as described in [21, 22], to gain visibility in the underlying HTTPS traffic. Figure 1 shows a snippet from the header of an HTTPS session between the Yahoo Messenger app installed on an Android device (Nexus 7 phone). The lexical construct of this header is no different from those seen in the case of HTTP (cf. Figure 2). Therefore, in an enterprise set up, the SAMPLES framework extends seamlessly — *as is* — to the HTTPS traffic generated by mobile apps.

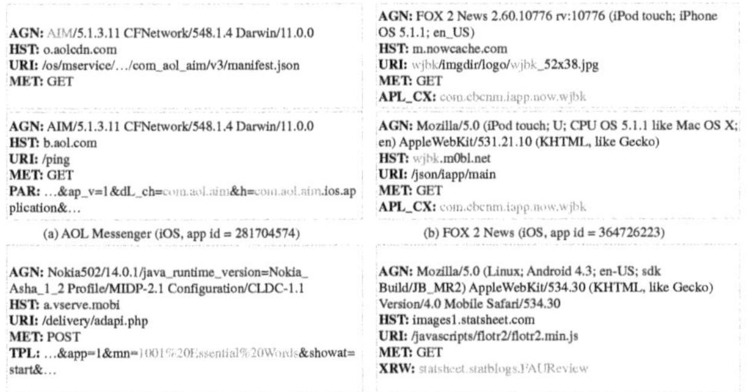

(a) AOL Messenger (iOS, app id = 281704574)
(b) FOX 2 News (iOS, app id = 364726223)
(c) 1001 Essential Words (Nokia, app id = 389585)
(d) FAU Football & Basketball (Android, app id = statsheet.statblogs.FAUReview)

Figure 2: Flow headers: AOL messenger (iOS), Fox 2 News (iOS), 1001 Essential Words (Nokia) and FAU Football and Basketball (Android).

Mobile app executable: We assume that the executable archive for an application (paid or free) can be obtained from the marketplace. This is essential for constructing the identifier sets as well as generating labeled flowsets during the training phase (cf. §5).

2.2 Datasets

App executables, identifiers and labeled flowsets: A set of app executables downloaded from the Google Play (Android), Apple iTunes (iOS) and OVI store (Nokia Symbian) markets. In all, the dataset comprises of over 700 K apps. For each mobile app, we collect the various classes of identifiers (static analysis) as well as network traffic produced by the app (dynamic analysis). The traffic is organized into flowsets at a per app granularity (cf. §5 for details). Each such flowset is labelled and thus constitutes the *ground truth* for our experiments (cf. §6).

Manually generated rulesets: As a baseline for the comprehensiveness of SAMPLES, we leverage three sets of conjunctive rules — respectively for Android, iOS and Nokia platforms — constructed by a team of human experts. These rules were created by manual inspection of HTTP traces. The conjunctive ruleset produced by SAMPLES should be, at the very least, an encompassing superset of these manually generated rule sets.

3. IDENTIFIERS, LEXICAL CONTEXT & CONJUNCTIVE RULES

We introduce the various *identifier types* associated with mobile applications (§3.1) and the *lexical context* in which they are found in the network traffic (§3.2). We then define an *application identification rule* as a conjunction of lexical contexts (§3.3); which forms the intuitive basis for this work.

3.1 Application Identifiers

Simply put, an application identifier is a string label that is uniquely associated with a mobile application. For example, consider the popular game *Angry Birds*. The mobile version of this game has identifiers *com.rovio.angrybirds*, *409807569* and *23158* respectively in the Google Play, Apple iTunes and Nokia OVI store marketplaces[1]. When downloaded from Google Play and Apple iTunes markets, the *apk* and *ipa* files are named *com.rovio.angrybirds.apk* and *409807569.ipa* respectively. In the Nokia OVI Store, the executable archive, a *jad* file, bears the application name instead i.e. *Angry Birds.jad*. Note that the application name — *Angry Birds* — is itself an identifier string, albeit not necessarily unique. Henceforth, we use the terms **app id** and **app name** to respectively mean the market place application identifier and application name for a given app. Both **app id** and **app name** may occur in the network traffic generated by mobile applications (cf. Figure 2).

The app id and app name, however, are not the only identifiers associated with a mobile app. The app executable archive (*apk*, *ipa* and *jad*) contains, amongst other things, a metadata file — *AndroidManifest.xml*, *info.plist* and *Manifest.xml* respectively for the Android, iOS and Nokia platforms — that provides behavioral specifications and access permissions required by the app for proper functioning. This metadata file may also contain other potential identifiers. For example, the *info.plist* file for an iOS app, contains a set of XML-fields (keys); such as **cfbundleidentifier**, **cfbundledisplayname**, **cfbundleexecutable** and **cfbundlename**. For the *Angry Birds* app, they respectively take on the values: **com.rovio.angrybirdsfree**, **Angry Birds**, **AngryBirdsClassicLight** and **Angry Birds Free**. The CFBundle identifiers are specified by application developers for packaging during the app development process. More importantly, some CFBundle identifiers (values) occur in the **User-Agent** (AGN) of the HTTP header. These have been exploited previously for classification tasks [29].

There are several functional reasons why identifiers exist in the HTTP headers. First and foremost, this is a simple, yet effective, mechanism for authentication and access control. Most mobile applications rely on content hosting servers that form the backend for an app enabled service. The hosting servers need to differentiate between different versions of the same app — paid vs. free — while catering content. Similarly, the same application developer may have a suite of applications accessing a common cloud-based content service. Identifiers help keep track of resource usage, userbase and demographics, for each application. This is essential for business objectives. Last but not least, mobile applications often use third party services such as analytics (e.g. Google-Analytics), APIs (e.g. Adobe-Air) and ad-vendors (e.g. Double-Click, iAds, Migital). Such third party services in turn assign additional service specific identifiers to each app for their own record keeping and accounting. Indeed, it is the presence of such service specific identifiers, in the form of key-value pairs in the *manifest* files of Android applications, that is used in [23] for application identification. Our system assumes that most apps use their true identifiers while communicating with their host servers or third party services. This is a reasonable assumption given the aforementioned usefulness of such behavior. If, however, for some reason an app is deliberately adversarial, i.e. obfuscates its identity or puts misleading identifiers in its headers, our system will surely not be able to identify it correctly.

To summarize, a mobile application can have a variety of identifiers, unique or otherwise; and some of these occur in the network traffic generated by the application a subset of which has been alluded to in previous studies [23, 29].

3.2 Identifiers in a Lexical Context

We define the lexical context associated with an identifier string occurring in a given network flow in terms of three contextual clauses — *which*, *where* and *what* — as described below:

1. *Which* identifier type is it?
2. *Where* in the header/payload does it occur?
3. *What* prefix/suffix surrounds its occurrence?

[1]Market-place application identifiers for Android apps usually have a Java package-name format. For iOS, these identifiers are in the form of a 9-digit string, and Nokia OVI store uses a numerical string id.

App Id	Identifier Type	Field Name: Snippet
281704574	cfbundlename/displayname	**AGN:** AIM/5.1.3.11 CFNetwork/548.1.4 Darwin/11.0.0
281935788	cfbundlename/executable	**AGN:** Essentials/1309241730 CFNetwork/609.1.4 Darwin/13.0.0
282935706	cfbundlename/displayname/executable	**AGN:** Bible/4.0.1 CFNetwork/548.0.4 Darwin/11.0.0
		AGN: ^(.+)/[0-9].+ CFNetwork/[0-9].+ Darwin/[0-9].+
364726223	cfbundledisplayname	**AGN:** FOX 2 News 2.60.10776 rv:10776 (iPod touch; iPhone OS 5.1.1...)
372198459	cfbundlename/displayname/executable	**AGN:** Rugby FM 4.3 rv:403 (iPad; iPhone OS 6.0.1; en_US)
371932548	cfbundlename/displayname/executable	**AGN:** Bakodo 3.4 rv:403 (iPad; iPhone OS 6.0.1; en_US)
		AGN: ^(.+)/[0-9].+ rv:*.+ (iP.+; iPhone OS.+; en_US)
364726223	cfbundleidentifier	**APL_CX:** com.cbcnm.iapp.now.wjbk
377749075	cfbundleidentifier	**APL_CX:** com.cbcnm.iapp.now.wfld
386978415	cfbundleidentifier	**APL_CX:** com.cbcnm.iapp.now.kjct
		APL_CX: ^(.*?)$
281704574	cfbundleidentifier	**PAR:** ... **&dL_ch=**com.aol.aim& ...
307840047	cfbundleidentifier	**PAR:** ... **&dL_ch=**com.aol.moviefone& ...
646100661	cfbundleidentifier	**PAR:** ... **&dL_ch=**com.aol.mobile.aolclient& ...
		PAR: **\b dL_ch=**(.*?) \b
380335515	app id	**APL_WO:** ... **&appAdamId=**380335515& ...
382287127	app id	**APL_WO:** ... **&appAdamId=**382287127& ...
382303945	app id	**APL_WO:** ... **&appAdamId=**382303945& ...
		APL_WO: **\b appAdamId=**(\d{9}) \b
286851614	app id	**PAR:** ... **&msid=**286851614& ...
288553125	app id	**PAR:** ... **&msid=**288553125& ...
291826753	app id	**PAR:** ... **&msid=**291826753& ...
		PAR: **\b msid=**(\d{9}) \b

Table 2: Lexical context for different identifier types found in network traffic generated by iOS applications.

For example, consider a pair of flow headers, generated by the *AOL messenger* app (*app id = 281704574*) on the iOS platform (cf. Figure 2(a)). The identifier **AIM**, occurs in both flow headers in the following lexical context: {*Which*: **cfbundlename/ cfbundledisplayname/ cfbundleexecutable**, *Where*: **AGN**, *What*: prefix = ^ (i.e. beginning of the field), suffix = **/5.1.3.11 CFNetwork/548.1.4 Darwin/11.0.0**}. On the other hand, the identifier **com.aol.aim** occurs in two different lexical contexts within the same flow header. First, {*Which*: **cfbundleidentifier**, *Where*: **PAR**, *What*: prefix = **\b dL_ch=**, suffix = **\b**}. And then, {*Which*: **cfbundleidentifier**, *Where*: **PAR**, *What*: prefix = **\b h=**, suffix = **.ios.application\b**} [2]. Other variations can be seen in the remaining flow headers in Figure 2, where identifiers of different types are present in the AGN, HST and URI fields as both *leading* and *non-leading sub-strings* (2(b)), in the TPL field as a value to a key (2(c)) and in the APL_CX and XRW fields as *spanning field values* (2(b), (d)) respectively. In spite of such variations, each one of these occurrences can be represented in the form of the three contextual clauses: *which*, *where* and *what*. Evidently, multiple applications may share one or more generalized lexical contexts for the same identifier type (cf. Table 2). Next, we show how such lexical contexts can be generalized to formulate *conjunctive rules* that help identify mobile applications in network traffic.

[2]The regular expression '**\b**' denotes a *word* boundary.

3.3 From Context to Rules

In its simplest form, an app identification rule is a *conjunction* of a generalized lexical context associated with an identifier type. For instance,

APP-IDENT-RULE 1. ***Extract** FROM **AGN**, **Pattern:^(.+)/[0-9].+ CFNetwork/[0-9].+ Darwin/[0-9].+**, AND **Lookup** IN **{cfbundleexecutable / cfbundlename / cfbundledisplayname}**.*

can be interpreted as the following: if the **User-Agent**(AGN) of a flow matches the pattern in Rule 1, extract the leading sub-string until the first '/'; and then lookup if the sub-string corresponds to a valid {**cfbundleexecutable / cfbundlename / cfbundledisplayname**} for any app (or apps). If found, report the corresponding app (or apps) as the output. In practice, the *lookup* step involves a dictionary (hash) reference. Each identifier type has its own dictionary — built *a priori* through market-place crawling and static analysis of app executable archives (cf. §5 for details) — with identifier strings as keys and the **app id**'s as values. For example, Rule 1 will extract the string **AIM** from flow headers 1 and 2; which then maps to {**cfbundledisplayname**: **AIM** $\rightarrow$ *281704574*} as the output. Observe from Table 2, that similar *extract-and-lookup* conjunctions can be derived for various identifier types occurring in multiple lexical contexts. Moreover, the same lexical context is found across the headers corresponding to multiple applications.

However, before we describe how SAMPLES constructs such conjunctions using a semi-supervised learning approach, we need to add a final contextual dimension to our conjunctive rules, that of a *condition*.

APP-IDENT-RULE 2. ***Extract** FROM **PAR\REF**, **Pattern:\b msid=(\d{9})\b**, AND **Lookup** IN {**app id**}, IF **HST**: **googleads.g.doubleclick.net**.*

The *IF* clause in Rule 2 specifies a condition under which the extraction should be performed. Intuitively, flows directed to and from third-party-services — ad networks, API's, analytics — are likely to have their own specific lexical structure. Therefore, the domain host name provides a good preliminary filter for rules specific to such services. In general, the *IF* clause can be combination of multiple conditions involving more than one field/pattern in the HTTP flow header. Such conditions not only help reduce potential false positives, but also contribute to improved system performance. SAMPLES framework generates such conditions by default, without any additional methodological overheads (cf. §5).

4. IDENTIFICATION & DESIGN GOALS

The set of app identification rules are consumed by an **app identification engine**. For each incoming flow, the app identification engine applies a subset of rules to the flow based on a number of pre-filtering conditions (e.g. host-name / field based pre-filtering) . If a flow matches one of the rules in the rule set, we classify it as **identified**, and report the **app id**; else it is reported as **unidentifed**.

Identification results: The identification result for each flow in the test set can be one of the six possible cases illustrated in Figure 3. We explain each of these below:

1. True positive (unique or fuzzy match): If the extracted app identifier can map either uniquely to its originating app or fuzzily to a few apps including the correct app, we say it is a **unique match** (Figure 3(a) & (b)).

2. False-positive: if the extracted identifier maps to an app id different from the flow's originating app, we say it is an **false positive** (Figure 3(c)).

3. True-negative: if the flow does not contain any known identifier, it is definitely not possible for SAMPLES to identify this flow (Figure 3(d)).

4. False negative (lacking identifier info): if the flows actually contains its originating app's identifier, but we either do not have the correct rule to extract it or cannot find it in the id hash table, it becomes a false-negative (Figure 3(e)).

The reason why we treat both unique and fuzzy match as true-positive is that fuzzy match also helps to reveal the "possible" mobile apps. In fact, these potential apps usually have some common properties. As shown in Figure 3(b), in iOS the cfbundlename *AIM* is used by app *444081514*, *494258199* and *281704574*. All these three apps are AIM Messenger apps developed by different companies. To avoid having fuzzy matching via some generic strings shared by many apps, we can set a threshold to the number of related apps on each identifier and prune the identifier out when the threshold is exceeded. In this case, we can ensure that fuzzy match can also give us useful information about apps in the network.

Design goals: Our goal is to build an efficient rule-based identification system. Specially, we would like to have

1. High coverage: we should be able to find most apps in the network whose flows actually contain app identifier. In other words, the false-negative rate should be small.

2. High accuracy: the identification results should be reliable, i.e. containing as few false-positives as possible.

3. High processing throughput: the system should be able to process flows at high speed.

It is challenging to create a rule set that can achieve all three aforementioned goals. Like any engineering activity, there are trade-offs involved. For example, if we add more "app-specific-rules" (which identify flows from a small set of very specific apps) into the rule set, the coverage can be increased. However, a larger rule set results in longer processing times leading to lower system throughput. In particular, there are bound to be unidentifiable flows that must go through the entire rule set before being regarded as "not identified'. Besides that, if we generate rules with less matching conditions and more general regular expressions, the identification throughput and app coverage may increase. However, the identification results will contain more false-positive; thus being less reliable. Therefore, we should have an effective rule generator that automatically builds rules from training over labeled network flows, via a supervised learning methodology; thereby ensuring good quality and performance.

5. SAMPLES: SYSTEM ARCHITECTURE & OPERATIONAL LIFE CYCLE

In this section, we present the system architecture and the operational life cycle of SAMPLES (cf. Figure 4). SAMPLES comprises of two parts, an offline training system for rule generation and an online app identification engine for traffic classification. Both components can be implemented on commodity hardware. Each subsection describes an individual component along with the underlying intuitions, operational algorithms and the various challenges associated with the sub-tasks that they are designed to handle. Where applicable, we also compare and contrast the three mobile application platforms against each other to bring out the subtle differences between them; particularly those pertinent to the SAMPLES framework.

5.1 The Crawl-Download Infrastructure

SAMPLES comes equipped with a crawl-download infrastructure that periodically samples the three market places for newly released mobile apps: Google Play (Android), Apple iTunes (iOS) and Nokia OVI Store (Symbian)[3]. For the Android and iOS market places, our implementation is essentially the same as that presented in [26]. We deploy a globally distributed infrastructure and crowd-source authentication credentials, to avoid being blocked by the host markets. The task for Nokia platform is more easily managed. Unlike the other two platforms, the Nokia OVI store assigns a numerical **app id** string to the apps; e.g. *app id = 23158* for the *app name = Angry Birds*. The URL is simply `http://store.ovi.com/content/23158`. Given a relatively smaller number of applications in the Nokia market place (roughly 130 K), compared to the Android and iOS market places, it can be spanned quite easily. More importantly, the application executable is accessible by simply appending the tag */download* to the content URL. The download, of course, requires a valid login session.

[3]Needless to say, even though we collect app description web pages for all crawled apps, we only download the executable archives of the *free* ones.

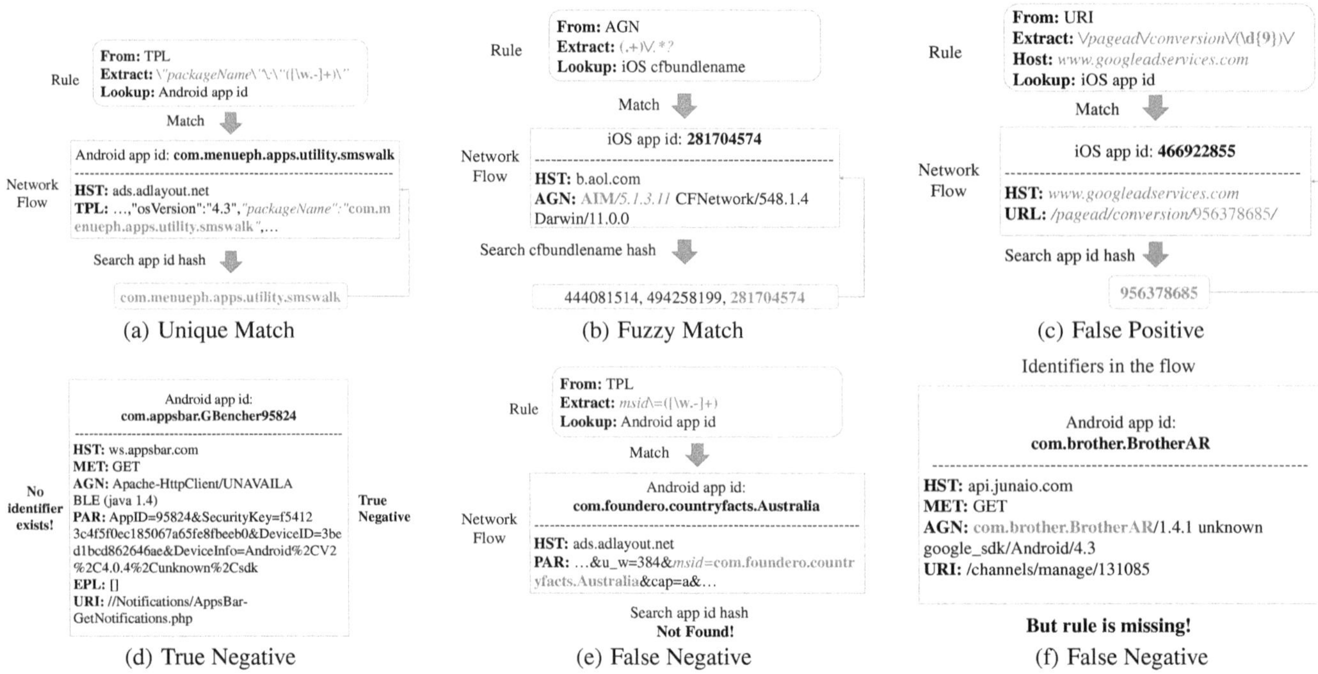

Figure 3: Six kinds of identification results.

The Crawl-Download infrastructure creates two repositories per application platform: (a) an app web page repository (all apps); and (b) an app executable archive repository (free apps). For Android and iOS, these archives are respectively called *apk*'s and *ipa*'s, after their respective extension types. The case for Nokia is a little different where several distinct application executable types (and in fact media files) are found in the market place. Predominant amongst these are Java based executables, called the *jad*'s. Henceforth, all Nokia apps referred to in this work are *jad* apps.

5.2 Identifier Extractor

5.2.1 From application web pages

From the app web pages, we extract the **app id** and the **app name** identifiers. This can be accomplished easily by parsing for static tags in the HTML page. SAMPLES creates two hashes for these two identifier types, on a per platform basis. The hash for identifier type **app id** contains within it the **app id** as key, and a constant 1 as the corresponding value. On the other hand, the hash for **app name** contains the **app name** as the key, and the corresponding **app id** as its value. In the case of key-collision, i.e. more than one app with the same **app name** string, the value field is an array of the corresponding app ids. Clearly, in the matching and look up phase, such a match will qualify as **fuzzy**.

5.2.2 From application executable archive

The app executable archive for a given mobile application contains, amongst other things, the application binary and a metadata file. The metadata file — *AndroidManifest.xml*, *info.plist* and *Manifest.xml* respectively for the Android, iOS and Nokia platforms — is an XML file that provides behavioral specifications and access permissions required by the app for proper functioning. It may also contain a variety of other identifiers in the form of XML fields and their corresponding values (such as the CFBundle identifiers for iOS and those assigned by third party services [23]).

SAMPLES treats the metadata file for each app individually to extract potential application identifiers through a statistical heuristic, thereby obviating the need for manual inspection (as employed by [23]). Using a DOM parser, SAMPLES extracts all XML fields and their corresponding values from the metadata file. Each field name (XML-tag) is considered to be a potential identifier type, and the corresponding value is considered to be a potential identifier string for the app in question. As with the identifier type **app name**, SAMPLES builds a hash for each potential identifier type, with the potential identifier string as key, and the app id as its value. SAMPLES then selects out of these potential identifier types by two criteria.

1. **Universality**: The fraction of apps in the app repository in whose metadata file this potential identifier type (XML field) is found. In other words, the length of the hash divided by the cardinality of the app executable archive repository. Higher the value, more likely the XML field is an identifier type. For instance, the identifier type **app name** is likely to have this fraction is exactly 1 (as all apps have an **app name**).

2. **Uniqueness of values**: The average number of values (i.e. **app ids**) per key in the hash. The lower this number, the greater the likelihood that the XML field is an identifier type. Once again, for the identifier type **app name**, this value is close to 1 (very few apps, if any, share the exact same name for the same platform).

A good example of an identifier type discovered through this statistical sampling is the *pid* XML field found in the manifest files for Nokia apps. As we shall see, even if the identifier extractor errs by selecting an XML field that is not really an identifier type, the impact is mitigated in the dynamic analysis phase where each prospective rule goes through a validation step. This built in checking mechanism helps us prune out extraneous patterns at an early stage.

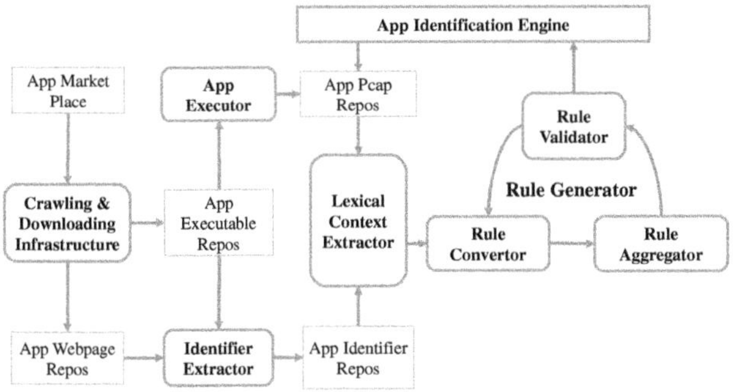

Figure 4: SAMPLES: system architecture and operational life cycle.

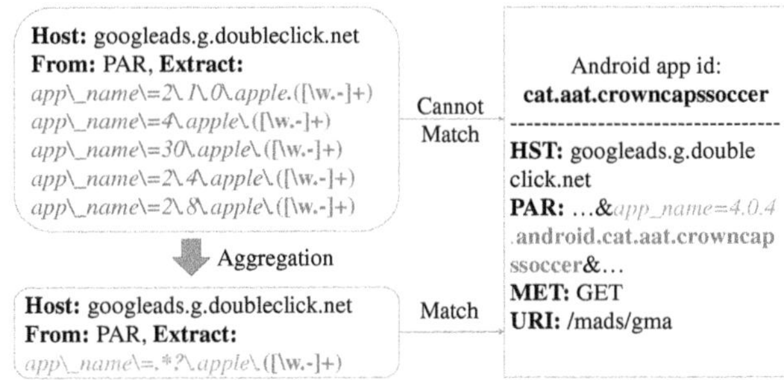

Figure 5: Rule aggregation: EXTRACT clause.

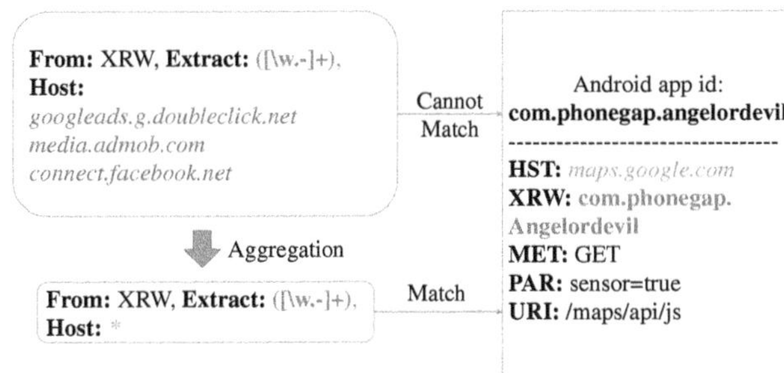

Figure 6: Rule aggregation: IF clause.

5.3 Application Executor

SAMPLES also comes equipped with an app executor which can automatically execute downloaded apps in the emulator or real devices and capture generated HTTP flows. App executor will run each app and generate multiple UI events in order to generate network traffic with more diversity. Then the captured traffic is processed by a deep-packet-inspector (DPI) to extract HTTP flows. For each HTTP flow, We only store the HTTP header and the first 1024 bytes of payload to save storage space.

We can directly control the execution of Android apps by Android automation tools, like monkey-runner [5]. However, there are no similar automation tools for iOS and Nokia platform. So we have to rely on UI automation tools on PC, like AutoIt [2], to control app execution. For Nokia, we could run apps in a emulator and trigger UI events by AutoIt scripts, while for iOS, we have to project the devices' screen to a VNC viewer to export UI and use automation tools due to a lack of emulator support for iOS platform, which is essentially the same infrastructure as presented in [30].

Due to scalability concerns, we do not run a complete and exhaustive app execution to invoke every possible app execution path like [11] requires, which is time-consuming and not scalable. Instead, we allow incomplete app execution to ensure our app executor can scale with large number of apps. In fact, this approach is enough to capture enough useful network flows because we do not rely on a single app to generate all kinds of flows, as rules are common patterns in flows of multiple apps.

5.4 Lexical Context Extractor

First, we perform lexical context extraction on the training flow set. Given a platform, lexical context extraction is performed for each identifier type found in the identifier extractor phase for the apps in the training set for that platform individually. For illustration purposes, we will use the **app id** for the Android platform exclusively for the remainder of this section. The described methodology applies to all other identifier types as well as the other two platforms.

As shown in Figure 2, for a given Android app in the training set, with **app id = statsheet.statblogs.FAUReview**, the lexical extractor searches for the existence of the app id at a per flow basis from the flow set of that app. Once found, it extracts the lexical context with {**Where**: **XRW**, **What**: prefix=^, suffix=**$**, **Which**: **Android app id**}. Note that each **what** clause, which comprises of a prefix and a suffix part, is terminated at either a predefined delimiter set of the given field (e.g. PAR) or the beginning or the end of of that field (e.g. APL_CX or XRW). For standard HTTP fields, the delimiter set is defined in HTTP grammar. For example **&** is the delimiter in URI-query (PAR field). For other non-standard fields, the delimiter set can be automatically inferred from the field value [25].

5.5 Rule Generator

5.5.1 *Create rules from lexical contexts*

As an initial step, we directly convert lexical contexts extracted from training flows into rules by generating regular expression in **Extract** clause and attaching host names, identifier class and other information to the rule. For example, the lexical context {**Where**: **PAR**, **What**: prefix=\b msid=, suffix=**\b**, **Which**: Android app id} will be converted into

APP-IDENT-RULE 3. ***Extract** FROM **PAR**, **msid=([\w.]+)** , AND **Lookup** IN **{Android app id}**, IF HST: **googleads.g.doubleclick.net**.*

Note that instead of simply using ".*" to catch identifier, the characteristic of the identifier class is encoded in the matching pattern. For example, Android app id can contain any number of word, number, underscore and the dot, so the pattern will be **[\w.]+**. And iOS app id is a 9 digit number, so the pattern will be **\d{9}**. This will increase the identification accuracy of the generated rules.

5.5.2 *Aggregate existing rules*

Although rules converted from lexical contexts can directly identify network flows, their matching conditions are usually too strict, thus leading to the following two problems.

Low coverage: as shown in Figure 5, none of those rules in the first rule set can match that network flow. In fact, it is because those rules require to exactly match the version number between "=" and "apple" in PAR field, which is not necessary. Similarly, in Figure 6 we also cannot identify the given flow only because this flow is under a different host. In fact, with a limited training set, we cannot find all possible version numbers and host names. Therefore, it is always possible to miss such flows in the network traffic, which contributes to coverage loss.

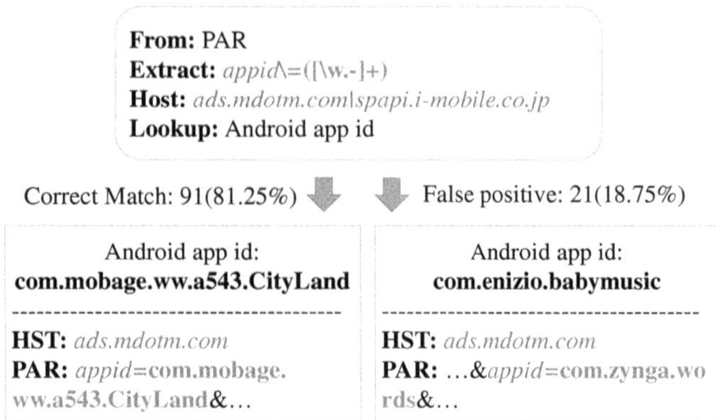

Figure 7: Example of low accuracy rules that should be pruned.

Low throughput: again as shown in Figure 5, we have to go through all 5 "app_name" rules to identify the HTTP flow with such pattern. Therefore, we must spend a longer processing time to find a match, which is not necessary and thus lower the identification throughput.

Obviously, it is the redundant matching conditions that hinder both the coverage and throughput of the rule set. In order to solve this problem, SAMPLES will aggregate and merge similar rules into more general rules to remove redundant matching conditions. Specifically, we can aggregate rules on two clauses:

1. **EXTRACT**(cf Figure 5): To aggregate the EXTRACT clause, we use sequence alignment, a technique which is widely used in bioinformatics area [7], to calculate the similarity between regular expressions. Then we group rules into different clusters based on the alignment sequence. The alignment sequence of two rules contains three parts, MATCH (two tokens are the same), MISMATCH (two tokens are different) and INDEL (one token aligns to a gap in the other rule). In our implementation, we generate new rules by strictly keeping The MATCH and replacing MISMATCH and INDEL with a wildcard **.*?** , as shown in the second rule set in Figure 5.
2. **IF**(cf Figure 6): Here we only take host condition as an example. We first cluster rules with the same FIELD, LOOKUP and EXTRACT conditions together. Then we build a prefix-tree on host names based on their DNS name and generate new rules by keeping the longest common substring between hosts from root to leaf and replacing all the different prefix by a wildcard.

5.5.3 Validate rules

To ensure the quality of generated rule set, SAMPLES will validate each rule by identifying a special flow set, called validation set, whose flows contains source app id as the ground-truth. Then we record the coverage and accuracy of each rule in its identification results. To better explain this process, we generate rule set using 5000 training apps from those three platforms, and plot the validation result of each rule as a point on Figure 8. There are three kinds of rules.

High coverage and high accuracy rules (top right part of Figure 8): these are the rules, out of the constructed rule set, that we want in our rule-based identification engine. Besides that, to improve identification throughput, we assign higher priority to higher coverage rules as they are more likely to be matched first. And if an aggregated rule passes the validation, all the simple rules which generate this rule are also pruned out because their matching range are smaller than the aggregated rule.

Low accuracy rules (bottom part of Figure 8): some rules will generate large ratio of false-positives during identification process,

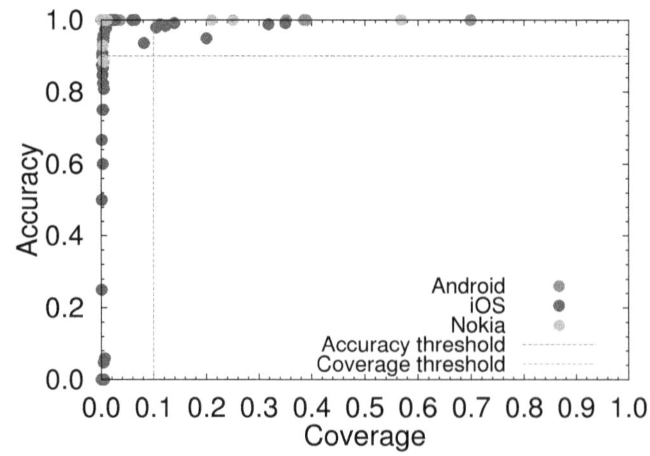

Figure 8: Coverage and accuracy of each individual rule from three platforms (5000 training apps).

which will severely undermine the reliability of identification results. Figure 7 shows such an example, which misclassified 21 apps out of 112 identified apps. Such low accuracy rules could result from aggressive aggregation. For example, if we merge all initial rules into **Extract: .***, then it will definitely cause lots of false positives. However, it is also likely that those rules are affected by app developers, who might fill corresponding HTTP flow with inaccurate app information. For example, the false positive shown in Figure 7 could be caused by a careless developer forgetting to update the corresponding code in his app or an intentional developer who forks several apps with the same ad service identifier. Whatever the reason is, such low accuracy rules will interfere with our identification results and should be pruned out using an **accuracy threshold**.

App-specific/low coverage rules (top-left part of Figure 8): after rule aggregation, there are still some rules which can only match to a small fraction of apps. Some of them can even match to only 1 app, which is therefore named as **app-specific rules**. Such app-specific rules exist mainly because SAMPLES tries to find every occurrence of app identifier in HTTP flows but sometimes those identifiers coincide within an random context that never indicates app identifier for other apps. For example, here is an app-specific Android rule.

APP-IDENT-RULE 4. ***Extract FROM HST, Pattern:www\.(\w.), AND Lookup** IN **{app id}**, IF **HST**: **www.i9suaradio.com.br**.*

It is obvious that this rule does not work for most apps because few apps put its identifier directly in the host name. But it is still generated when SAMPLES finds app *i9suaradio.com.br* generates an HTTP flow with host name *www.i9suaradio.com.br*.

Although most of those rules will eventually either be pruned out after rule validation or does not affect identification results, we still remove them from rule set prior to rule validation for two performance reasons. First, the average app identification rate decreases with the size of rule set, and there is no need to include those rules because they do not contribute any significant app coverage gain. Second, validating all app-specific rules will greatly increase the time overhead on rule validation since the majority of rules are app-specific, as shown in §6.5 Therefore, we purpose two heuristics to prune out those rules. First, any **app-specific rules** will be prune out. Second, if their coverage is lower than a **coverage threshold**, it will be recognized as low coverage rules and be pruned out.

5.6 Application Identification Engine

SAMPLES comes equipped with an app identification engine that performs rule-based identification on network flows. Therefore, SAMPLES can be seamlessly integrated into any middleboxes, like DPI components, firewalls or gateways, that perform traffic classification, without impeding the overall throughput. SAMPLES takes unidentified network flows as input and for each network flow, the app identification engine tries to find a matching rule. Once a match is found, the flow is labeled as **identified**, else it is deemed **not identified**.

Note that the app identification is mainly determined by the rule set. In order to achieve higher coverage, we may add many different rules into the rule set to catch various lexical patterns. However, in the basic implementation we have to run a linear search in the rule set in order to find a match. According to §2.1, since about 35% of flows in network traffic are not identifiable, the average identification time per flow is proportional to the length of rule set. So as the number of rules increases, the processing throughput will gradually drop down and lower the identification engine's performance.

However, as our rules contain many additional matching conditions besides the main **EXTRACT** clause, we could choose a smaller rule set for each incoming flow, thus improving the processing throughput. For example, we can split the whole rule set in different subsets, each of which contains rules matching a particular host name. During identification, we can first calculate the hash value of incoming flow's host name and only use the corresponding subset for rule-based identification. With this optimization, we can make the processing throughput scalable with the number of rule set.

6. EXPERIMENTS

We evaluate SAMPLES on two aspects: rule set quality (app coverage, app accuracy and app identification goodput) and system performance (overhead of rule generation). To generate dataset for training and testing, we run SAMPLES's crawling and downloading infrastructure on Google Play store, iTunes store, and Nokia OVI store and collected $651K$ Android apps, $68K$ iOS apps, and $10K$ Nokia apps, respectively. By executing each downloaded app in software emulators, we captured $13,003K$ Android flows, $478K$ iOS flows and $39K$ Nokia flows. We use flows from $22K$ Android apps, $32K$ iOS apps, and $5K$ Nokia apps as the training set and the rest as the testing set.

6.1 Comprehensiveness of generated rules

We first evaluate the rule set generated from the complete training set for each platform. Table 3 summarizes the number of rules yielded by the engine, and shows a few representative rules for each platform. As one can see, SAMPLES generates many important rules because it finds the general traffic pattern around app identifiers. For example, the #1 Android rule is found by SAMPLES because after Android 2.2 (Froyo), Android webview includes app's package name into `X-Requested-With` field instead of a general "XMLHttpRequest". The #1 iOS rule is discovered since iOS has a guideline that the `User-Agent` field should contain the app identifier [6]. There are also many rules related to various advertisement/analytic services. Those rules are discovered simply because the corresponding services are widely used by mobile apps. If a new service becomes popular in the future, our rule generation engine can also find it by the same analysis.

We also compare the generated rule set with a rule set manually crafted by human analysts to evaluate the comprehensiveness of rules generated by SAMPLES. The manually crafted rule set includes 16 Android rules, 68 iOS rules, and 2 Nokia rules. The rule set generated by SAMPLES has covered 12 of those manually crafted Android rules, 43 of those iOS rules, and all 2 Nokia rules.

6.2 Effectiveness of the generated rules

Here, we evaluate the quality of the conjunctive rule set generated by SAMPLES by verifying whether the rules can correctly identify the apps from in testing set at a per flow granularity. The results are presented in Figure 9 (first column in each plot). One can see that the rules generated by SAMPLES produce highly reliable identification. Over 99% of the flows' originating apps can be correctly identified. Furthermore, the rule set also covers most of identifiable apps in the network. We can identify 74%, 62% and 63% apps on Android, iOS and Nokia test set, respectively. As a comparison, there are only 76.8%, 67.4% and 63.2% apps among those three datasets that is identifiable, respectively. In another word, SAMPLES can identify over 90% of identifiable apps among three platforms

Note that there are still around 2.8% Android apps and 5.4% iOS apps that have app identifier but cannot be identified by our rule set. The reasons are threefold. First, the training data is not comprehensive enough. When executed in emulators in limited amount of time, some apps in the training data do not generate enough flows to exhibit persistent lexical patterns. We believe that this problem can be mitigated if we periodically update the rule set with new training data. Secondly, pruning out low accuracy rules may lead to coverage loss, as shown in Figure 7. However, in most cases it is worthwhile to ensure high accuracy at the cost of minor coverage degradation. Similarly, the removal of app-specific/low coverage rules can lead to coverage loss as well. We will provide more discussion on this issue later in §6.5.

6.3 Identification goodput

Next, we evaluate the system *goodput* in exploiting the generated rule set to identify the originating apps of network traffic. Note that the measured *goodput* should be much lower than the throughput on real network traffic since our dataset has only the HTTP headers and the first 1024 bytes of HTTP payload.

As shown in the first column of Figure 9, SAMPLES's app identification engine can process pure HTTP flows at 87 Mbps. To achieve even higher processing throughput, we can shrink the rule set by adjusting the coverage threshold in validation phase. As shown in Figure 9, when the coverage threshold increases from 0.1% to 1%, the identification goodput of Android rule set increases from 87 Mbps to 217 Mbps, while the coverage drops from 75% to 70%. Similarly, we can achieve at most 40 Mbps and 150 Mbps goodput for iOS and Nokia platform with coverage dropping from 62% to 61% and from 63% to 62.4%, respectively. Obviously, there is a tradeoff between coverage and identification goodput. Having a smaller rule set increases the system identification goodput, at the expense of coverage.

We also notice that the goodput of running iOS rule set is smaller than the goodput of running Android and Nokia rule sets. For example, with 1% coverage threshold, running the iOS rules is 5 times and 3 times slower than running the Android and Nokia rules, respectively. This is mainly due to the characteristic of iOS rules. There are more iOS rules without host matching conditions, and more iOS rules are referring to popular HTTP fields like `User-Agent` that can be found in almost any flow in the test set. Therefore, iOS flows will be checked by more rules. Our experiments show that each iOS flow needs to be checked by at most $3-4$ rules on an average before it can be identified. Similarly, for Android and Nokia platforms the number of rule checks required per flow is $1-2$, on an average.

Pri.	Lookup	Host	From	Extract	Not-Matching
Platform: Android, Number of rules: 51					
1	app id	*	XRW	([\w.]+)	XRWHttpRequest
2	app id	*	PAR,REF	msid\=([\w.]+)	the.nebula
3	app id	googleads.g.doubleclick.net	PAR,REF	app_name\=.*?\.android\.([\w.]+)	
Platform: iOS, Number of rules: 64					
1	cfn,cfe,cfd[4]	*	AGN	(.+)V.*?	Safari, ..., Mail
5	app id	mob.adwhirl.com	EPL	\"key\"\:\"(\d{9})\"	441502580
Platform: Nokia. Number of rules: 12					
1	app name	*.vserv.mobi	EPL,PAR,TPL	mn\=(.+)	
8	app name	www.google-analytics.com	AGN	(.+)V1\.0\..*?	

Table 3: Rules generated by SAMPLES for Android, iOS, and Nokia with 10% accuracy threshold, removing app specific rules and 0.1% coverage threshold. Here cfn, cfe, cfd stand for cfbundlename, cfbundleexecutable, and cfbundledisplayname, respectively.

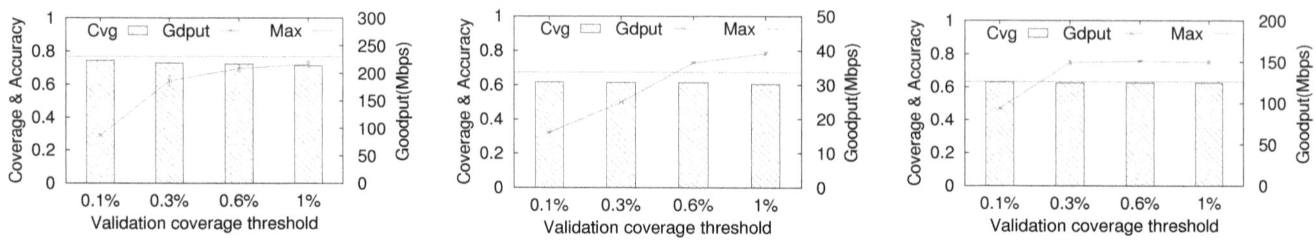

(a) Android (b) iOS (c) Nokia

Figure 9: Quality and performance of rule set built with entire dataset, 10% accuracy threshold and 0.1% coverage threshold. Cov and max stand for the ratio of apps identified by SAMPLES rule set and all identifiable apps in the test set. Gdput stands for identification goodput. Bars and lines are related with coverage and goodput, respectively. Note that the false positive ratios are all less than 1%.

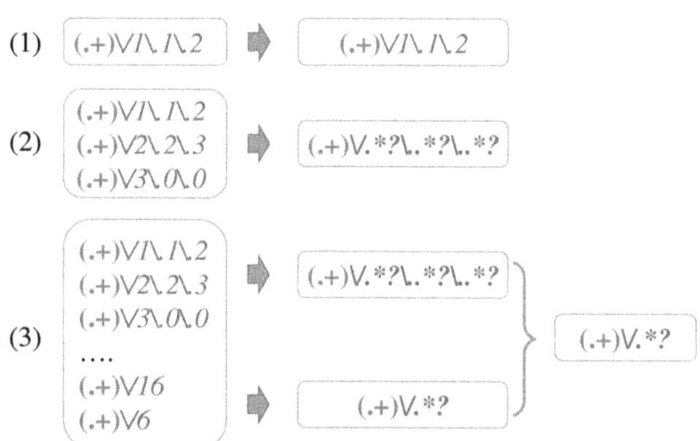

Figure 11: How diversity helps building more essential rules.

6.4 Impact of sampling training sets

We now study the impact of training set size on the coverage and accuracy of SAMPLES. Randomly sampling 200, $1K$, $5K$ and $10K$ apps from each platform's training set [4], we repeat the aforementioned experiments three times. We calculate the app coverage, accuracy, and identification goodput for each experiment. The results are plotted in Figure 10 and it provides us a few interesting insights. We can first confirm that a small sample of apps from market place are enough to build a comprehensive rule set for all three platforms. In fact, even the $10k$ apps represent a mere 1% of the apps in Google Play or iTunes store, both of which have more than 1.3 million apps each [1, 3].

More significantly, for the Android and Nokia platforms, 200 identifiable training apps are enough for building a rule set with similar coverage and accuracy as the one in § 6.1. However, the

[4]For Nokia, we sample at most $5K$ apps because there are only 5, 123 Nokia apps in the training set.

	# covered apps				
	1	2-10	11-100	101-1000	> 1000
Android	7748(79,3%)	1564	379	67	7
iOS	86187(88.7%)	10490	1173	67	0
Nokia	107(72.3%)	31	7	1	2

Table 4: Number of lexical contexts that can cover given number of apps.

app coverage of iOS rule set gradually increases with the number of training apps until there are 5000 training apps. That is mainly because the highest priority rules for identifying Android and Nokia apps are all *simple* rules, like `XRW` rule and `msid` rule for Android and `mn` rule for Nokia. Network flows matching those rules are prevalent in the traffic generated by Android and Nokia apps. Hence, even small number of training apps provide sufficient chance to generate the network flows for SAMPLES to learn those rule. However, the highest priority rules for iOS are usually *complex* rules with pattern ".*?" in their regular expressions. Hence those rules can only be generated by rule aggregation. As shown in Figure 11, we are more likely to build rules with essential pattern as more diverse rules are extracted by more training apps.

6.5 Time overhead of rule set generation

We next evaluate the overhead of generating the rule sets. To that end, we run SAMPLES with 200, $1K$, and $5K$ training apps from all three platform and measure the time consumption of the rule generation phase. We also evaluate how the two optimizations, i.e., *app-specific rule removal* and *coverage threshold*, affect the rule generation time. As shown in Figure 12, without any optimization, the rule generation time increases rapidly with the number of training apps. Besides, the processing time differs largely for apps from different platforms. For example, it takes more than an hour to process 5000 Android apps; processing 5000 iOS apps takes about six hours. The major part of the processing time is due to rule val-

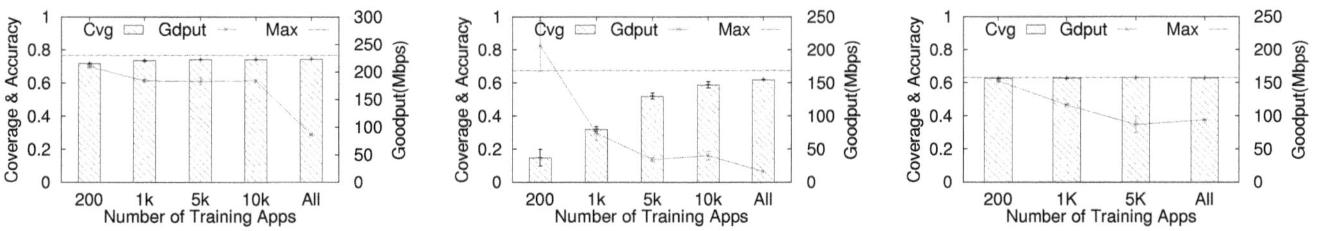

(a) Android (b) iOS (c) Nokia

Figure 10: Impact of sampling training set with 10% accuracy threshold and removing app-specific rules. Cvg and max stand for the ratio of apps identified by SAMPLES rule set and all identifiable apps in the test set. Gdput stands for identification goodput. Bars and lines are related with coverage and goodput, respectively. Note that the false positive ratios are all less than 1%.

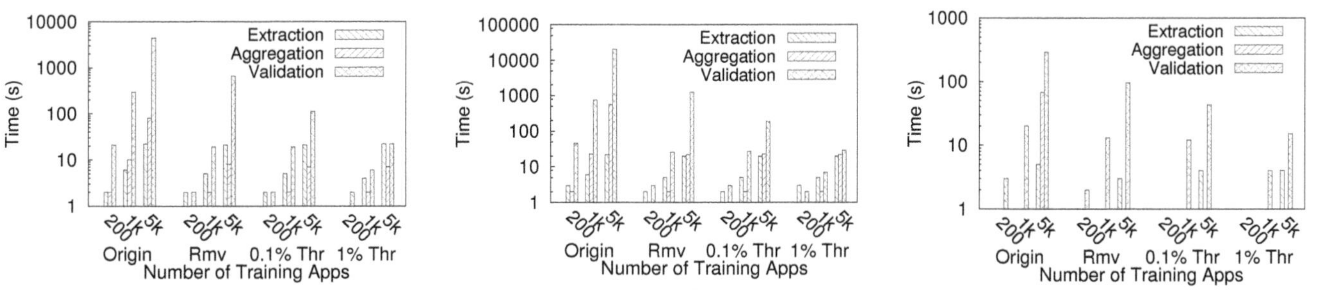

(a) Android (b) iOS (c) Nokia

Figure 12: Time overhead for each rule generation step. Origin means not removing any rules. Rmv means only remove app-specific rules. 0.1% Thr and 1% Thr means removing both app-specific and low coverage rules.

idation, which requires each rule to be validated on the entire validation set. Hence, the computational complexity is $O(M \times N)$, where M is the length of rule set and N is the size of validation set. In general, more rules can be learned from a larger training set. So the validation time increases quadratically with the number of training apps.

Our experiments also demonstrate that each of the two heuristic optimizations can shorten the validation time by one order of magnitude, as plotted in Figure 12. The reduction in rule generation time is mainly due to the removing of those app-specific/low coverage rules in rule generation. As shown in Table 4, more than 70% lexical contexts are app-specific. About 75% of the rest of the lexical contexts can cover only 2-10 apps. These can be considered as low-coverage rules and removed in order to speed up the rule generation. We also evaluate how discarding low coverage rules affects the coverage on the test set. As shown in Figure 13, the coverage of identifying iOS apps is more sensitive to removing of the low coverage rules, especially when there are 1000 training apps. This is because the top coverage rules in Android and Nokia platform are simple rules that can be easily learned, while iOS's top coverage rules are complex rules requiring more training samples to be learned. When there are not enough training samples to generate complex rules, e.g. with only 1000 training apps, the low coverage rules actually contribute to the most of app coverage. With more training apps, e.g. 10000 apps as shown in Figure 10, the impact of those two heuristics to the coverage of identifying iOS apps becomes marginal, and the benefit in saving the rule generation time becomes more significant.

6.6 Comparison with previous works

We now compare SAMPLES with two previous approaches: one based on identifiers associated with advertisement services as proposed in [23] and another on identifiers found in the user-agent field (cf. [29]). The advertisement services based approach obtains specific keys in HTTP headers generated by ad-libraries (e.g. double-click, Migital etc.) as app identifiers. Similarly, the user-agent based approach directly extracts app identifiers from the user-agent field to identify iOS apps. Both approaches are state-of-the-art solutions for mobile app traffic classification. We implement both approaches and use the same test set to evaluate their identification performance. To match the implementation details in [23], we focus on two popular ad services (Google Ads and Smaato) in the ad service approach. For user-agent approach, we manually prune out a list of generic strings as app identifiers, like Safari, iPhone, iOS, etc.

As shown in Figure 14, SAMPLES outperforms both existing approaches on either app coverage (Android) or identification accuracy (iOS). There are mainly two reasons for this. First, both approaches essentially yield a subset of rules that are generated by SAMPLES. Besides the simple key-value pair or user-agent field, SAMPLES generates more sophisticated rules based on other HTTP headers and payload. So the rule set generated by SAMPLES can identify apps whose identifiers appear in several lexical contexts, which explains the coverage gain. Second, the rules generated by SAMPLES are refined by rule validation so they are less prone to generating false positives. Take the User-Agent field as an example. Some strings extracted from this field, like iPhone, Game and Books, are not app identifiers and should be marked as exceptions. In previous work, one has to look for such exceptions by some heuristics, so it is hard to be comprehensive. While in SAMPLES, we can easily get a more complete exceptions set for this rule by providing more training apps. This explains why SAMPLES can achieve lower false-positive ratio on iOS.

To summarize, SAMPLES provides a general, light weight, cross-platform framework, for identifying mobile apps in network traffic with markedly better performance than other competing solutions.

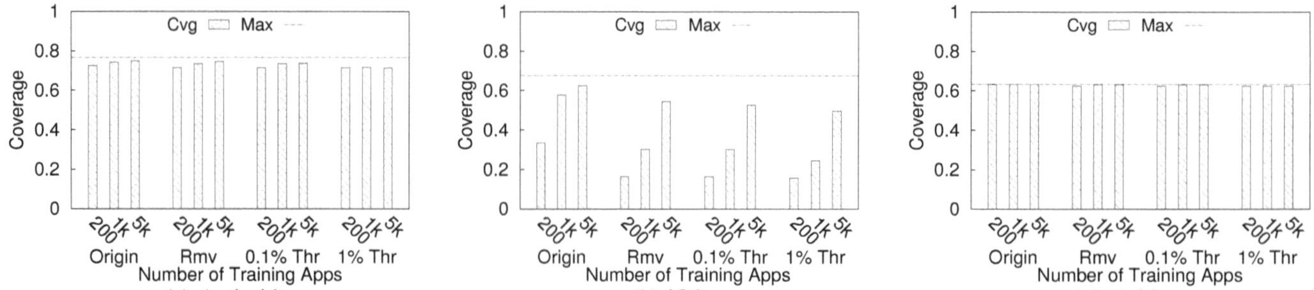

(a) Android (b) iOS (c) Nokia

Figure 13: Two optimization's influence on app coverage. Note that the false positive ratios are always smaller than 1%.

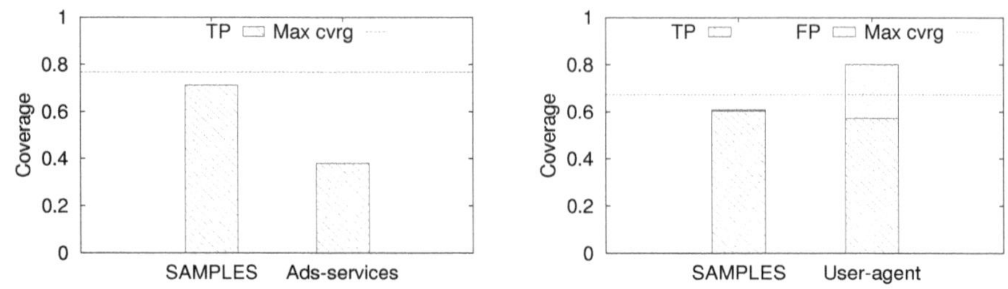

(a) Android (b) iOS

Figure 14: SAMPLES's evaluation results compared with ads services approach for Android [23] and user-agent approach for iOS [29] (Note: the false positive ratios are less than 1% for both methods in (a)).

7. RELATED WORK

Several network management tasks require fine grained traffic classification. Consequently, a number of techniques have been proposed over the years to address this problem; a survey of these may be found in [9, 18]. With the advent of the *mobility-era*, however, the variety of devices and applications has exploded at an unprecedented rate [26], most of which use HTTP (and more recently HTTPS) as a communication protocol. Thus, protocol/port based methods are of little use. The need to identify mobile applications in network traffic, preferably at a per-flow granularity, has therefore been tackled, at least in part, in several recent studies [12, 13, 16, 17, 19, 20, 24, 27]. Alas, most of these techniques are either based on *ad-hoc* heuristics, are too platform specific or computationally too expensive to be of practical use. For instance, in [29], classification and identification of mobile applications at a per flow granularity is limited only to those flows which contain an identifier in the `User-Agent` field of the HTTP header. This happens to be the case for a very small fraction of mobile applications (cf. comparative analysis in §6.6) and mostly for those from the Apple iOS market-place. Similarly, in [23] manual inspection of the *AndroidManifest.xml* is suggested to extract *third-party* assigned identifiers (such as ad-networks). These are then used to build a knowledge base of key-value pairs that can potentially be found in network traffic. Clearly, both solutions lack comprehensiveness and are dependent on manual expertise. To tackle this, some studies suggest active network trace generation [11, 27, 28, 30]. However, the classification methodologies suggested in [27, 28, 30] still require human involvement. A notable exception is NetworkProfiler [11]: a system that generates state machine based signatures, per app, through *exhaustive* execution (i.e. emulating all potential network activity for the app *a priori*). Although automated and comprehensive, this approach is computationally expensive; and hence not scalable. Also, creating one state machine per app implies that each flow needs to be matched exhaustively across the set; rendering live deployment infeasible.

8. CONCLUSION & FUTURE WORK

In this work, we developed **SAMPLES**, a supervised framework for generating conjunctive rules for identifying mobile applications in network traffic at a per-flow granularity. SAMPLES uses a relatively small sample of mobile applications from three prominent platforms (Anrdoid, iOS and Nokia), to extract both the identifiers as well as the lexical context in which they are found in the traffic; which together yield the rule-set. Through experiments over a vast corpus of mobile applications (over 700 K), we have demonstrated the comprehensiveness and applicability of our approach across all three platforms. In particular, the coverage is significantly higher than the other state-of-the-art methodologies from literature. From a system performance standpoint, SAMPLES achieves desirable *goodputs* of 217 Mbps, 40 Mbps, and 150 Mbps respectively for the Android, iOS, and Nokia datasets. Although conducted in a controlled laboratory environment, these results are healthy indicators for a live deployment scenario.

In the immediate future, we intend to expand SAMPLES to include other mobile platforms (such as BlackBerry and Windows Mobile). We expect reasonably similar results — in terms of coverage, accuracy and performance — to those obtained in this work. Also, there is scope for extending the general methodology proposed in this work, that of exploiting lexical contexts around identities, to identify network events (e.g. download, upload, chat etc.) responsible for a given flow. All these we propose for future work.

9. ACKNOWLEDGEMENT

We express our sincerest gratitude towards the anonymous reviewers whose comments helped improve the quality of this work, and our shepherd for guiding us through the revisions. Also, our thanks to Stansilav Miskovic and Ramya Gadiayaram for their help with the data collection activity and preliminary discussions. This research was supported by the National Science Foundation grants CNS-1059372, CNS-1345226 and CNS-0964545, as well as the Narus Fellow Research Program.

10. REFERENCES

[1] App store (ios) - wikipedia, the free encyclopedia. http://en.wikipedia.org/wiki/App_Store_iOS.

[2] Autoit. https://www.autoitscript.com/site/autoit/.

[3] Google play - wikipedia, the free encyclopedia. http://en.wikipedia.org/wiki/Google_Play.

[4] HTTP header fields. http://en.wikipedia.org/wiki/List_of_HTTP_header_fields.

[5] Monkey runner. http://developer.android.com/tools/help/monkeyrunner_concepts.html.

[6] Optimizing web content. https://developer.apple.com/library/mac/documentation/AppleApplications/Reference/SafariWebContent/OptimizingforSafarioniPhone/OptimizingforSafarioniPhone.html.

[7] Sequence alignment. http://en.wikipedia.org/wiki/Sequence_alignment.

[8] J. Caballero, H. Yin, Z. Liang, and D. Song. Polyglot: Automatic extraction of protocol message format using dynamic library analysis. In *Proceedings of 14th ACM Conf. on Computer and Communications Security*, 2007.

[9] A. C. Callado, C. A. Kamienski, G. Szabo, B. P. Gero, J. Kelner, S. F. L. Fernandes, and D. F. H. Sadok. A survey on Internet traffic identification. In *IEEE Communications Surveys and Tutorials*, volume 11, pages 37–52, 2009.

[10] W. Cui, J. Kannan, and H. J. Wang. Discoverer: Automatic protocol reverse engineering from network traces. In *Proceedings of 16th USENIX Security Symposium*, 2007.

[11] S. Dai, A. Tongaonkar, X. Wang, A. Nucci, and D. Song. Networkprofiler: Towards automatic fingerprinting of android apps. In *Proceedings of IEEE Infocom*, 2013.

[12] H. Falaki, D. Lymberopoulos, R. Mahajan, S. Kandula, and D. Estrin. A first look at traffic on smartphones. In *Proceedings of 10th ACM Internet Measurement Conference*, 2010.

[13] M. Grace, W. Zhou, X. Jiang, and A.-R. Sadeghi. Unsafe exposure analysis of mobile in-app advertisements. In *Proceedings of 5th ACM Conference on Security and Privacy in Wireless and Mobile Networks*, 2012.

[14] P. Haffner, S. Sen, O. Spatscheck, and D. Wang. Acas: Automated construction of application signatures. In *Proceedings of 1st ACM SIGCOMM Workshop on Mining Network Data*, 2005.

[15] M. Korczynski and A. Duda. Markov chain fingerprinting to classify encrypted traffic. In *Proceedings of the 33rd IEEE Infocom*, 2014.

[16] I. Leontiadis, C. Efstratiou, M. Picone, and C. Mascolo. Don‘T kill my ads!: Balancing privacy in an ad-supported mobile application market. In *Proceedings of the 12th Workshop on Mobile Computing Systems and Applications*, 2012.

[17] G. Maier, F. Schneider, and A. Feldmann. A first look at mobile hand-held device traffic. In *Proceedings of the International Conf. on Passive and Active Measurement*. Springer-Verlag, 2010.

[18] T. Nguyen and G. Armitage. A survey of techniques for Internet traffic classification using machine learning. In *IEEE Communications Surveys and Tutorials*, volume 10, pages 56–76, 2008.

[19] A. Patro, S. Rayanchu, M. Griepentrog, Y. Ma, and S. Banerjee. Capturing mobile experience in the wild: A tale of two apps. In *Proceedings of the Ninth ACM Conference on Emerging Networking Experiments and Technologies*, CoNEXT ‘13, 2013.

[20] P. Pearce, A. P. Felt, G. Nunez, and D. Wagner. Addroid: Privilege separation for applications and advertisers in android. In *Proceedings of the 7th ACM Symposium on Information, Computer and Communications Security*, ASIACCS ’12, 2012.

[21] A. Sapio, Y. Liao, M. Baldi, G. Ranjan, F. Risso, A. Tongaonkar, R. Torres, and A. Nucci. MAPPER: a mobile application personal policy enforcement router for enterprise networks. In *Proceedings of the European Workshop on Software Defined Networking*, EWSDN ’14, 2014.

[22] A. Sapio, Y. Liao, M. Baldi, G. Ranjan, F. Risso, A. Tongaonkar, R. Torres, and A. Nucci. Per-user policy enforcement on mobile apps through network functions virtualization. In *Proceedings of the 9th ACM workshop on Mobility in the Evolving Internet Architecture*, 2014.

[23] A. Tongaonkar, S. Dai, A. Nucci, and D. Song. Understanding mobile app usage patterns using in-app advertisements. In *Proceedings of the International Conf. on Passive and Active Measurement*, 2013.

[24] N. Vallina-Rodriguez, J. Shah, A. Finamore, Y. Grunenberger, K. Papagiannaki, H. Haddadi, and J. Crowcroft. Breaking for commercials: Characterizing mobile advertising. In *Proceedings of 12th ACM Internet Measurement Conference*, 2012.

[25] R. Vargiya and P. K. Chan. Boundary detection in tokenizing network application payload for anomaly detection. In *https://cs.fit.edu/media/TechnicalReports/cs-2003-21.pdf*, 2003.

[26] N. Viennot, E. Garcia, and J. Nieh. A measurement study of Google Play. In *Proceedings of the ACM SIGMETRICS*, 2014.

[27] X. Wei, L. Gomez, I. Neamtiu, and M. Faloutsos. Profiledroid: Multi-layer profiling of android applications. In *Proceedings of 18th Annual International Conference on Mobile Computing and Networking*, 2012.

[28] Q. Xu, T. Andrews, Y. Liao, S. Miskovic, Z. M. Mao, M. Baldi, and A. Nucci. FLOWR: A Self-Learning System for Classifying Mobile Application Traffic. In *Proceedings of the ACM SIGMETRICS (Poster)*, Austin, Texas, 2014.

[29] Q. Xu, J. Erman, A. Gerber, Z. M. Mao, J. Pang, and S. Venkataraman. Identifying diverse usage behaviors of smartphone apps. In *Proceedings of the ACM Internet Measurement Conference*, 2011.

[30] Q. Xu, Y. Liao, S. Miskovic, Z. M. Mao, M. Baldi, A. Nucci, and T. Andrews. Automatic generation of mobile app signatures from traffic observations. In *Proceedings of the 35th IEEE Infocom*, Hong Kong, China, 2015.

Performance Characterization and Call Reliability Diagnosis Support for Voice over LTE

Yunhan Jack Jia, Qi Alfred Chen, and Z. Morley Mao
University of Michigan
{jackjia, alfchen, zmao}@umich.edu

Jie Hui, Kranthi Sontineni, Alex Yoon, Samson Kwong, Kevin Lau
T-Mobile USA Inc.[1]
{jie.hui, kranthi.sontineni1, alex.yoon4, samson.kwong, kevin.lau}@t-mobile.com

ABSTRACT

To understand VoLTE performance in a commercial deployment, in this paper we conduct the first comprehensive performance characterization of commercially deployed VoLTE, and compare with legacy call and over-the-top (OTT) VoIP call. We confirm that VoLTE excels in most metrics such as audio quality, but its call reliability still lags behind legacy call for all the three major U.S. operators.

We propose an on-device VoLTE problem detection tool, which can capture new types of problems concerning audio quality with high accuracy and minimum overhead, and perform stress testing on VoLTE call's reliability. We discover 3 instances of problems in the early deployment of VoLTE lying in the protocol design and implementation. Although the identified problems are all concerned with the immature LTE coverage in the current deployment, we find that they can cause serious impairment on user experience and are urgent to be solved in the developing stage. For example, one such instance can lead to up to 50-second-long muting problem during a VoLTE call! We perform in-depth cross-layer analysis and find that the causes are rooted in the lack of coordination among protocols designed for different purposes, and invalid assumptions made by protocols used in existing infrastructure when integrated with VoLTE. We summarize learnt lessons and suggest solutions.

Categories and Subject Descriptors

C.2.1 [**Network Architecture and Design**]: Wireless communication; C.4 [**Performance of Systems**]: Measurement techniques, performance attributes

Keywords

VoLTE; VoIP; QoE; Trouble Shooting Cellular Network

[1]The views presented in this paper are as individuals and do not necessarily reflect any position of T-Mobile.

MobiCom'15, September 7–11, 2015, Paris, France.
© 2015 ACM. ISBN 978-1-4503-3619-2/15/09 ...$15.00.
DOI: http://dx.doi.org/10.1145/2789168.2790095.

1. INTRODUCTION

For reasons including improved cost effectiveness, spectrum use, and service quality, wireless operators are actively deploying VoLTE (voice over LTE), to support voice as another application on the data network, similar to over-the-top (OTT) VoIP applications. To ensure high service quality to end users, VoLTE relies on specialized support in both end devices and network architecture [38, 44], as well as dedicated radio resources during the voice call, to achieve an ambitious goal of completely replacing the legacy call in the long term.

VoLTE deployment by U.S. operators is still at an early stage, but it is important to empirically understand its performance from the perspective of mobile end users, especially compared to legacy call and OTT VoIP call. In this paper, we present the first systematic study using a variety of important call performance indicators for the VoLTE service provided by three major U.S. carriers, and also compare VoLTE with legacy 3G call, Skype, and Google Hangouts Voice call using controlled experiment. Our results show that VoLTE is superior in a majority of the metrics: it delivers the best audio quality, much better than legacy 3G call; compared to OTT VoIP call, it consumes 83% less data, 75% less energy, and also has around 40% shorter call setup time.

The major challenge of VoLTE in the early deployment is the inadequate LTE coverage compared with 2G/3G, which affects VoLTE call's reliability under undesired network condition and in the mobility case. To address the challenge in the transition phase, various supporting techniques are adopted by VoLTE service providers to reinforce the reliability (detailed in §2). However, Our study reveals that in the current VoLTE deployment, call reliability is still not competitive with legacy calls. Call failure ratio, including setup failure and unintended call drop, is almost 5× higher (§4.1) than the legacy call, which is a known problem to severely impair user experience [16] and is a common problem seen in all the three major US carriers' network. It is clearly imperative for operators to address the VoLTE call reliability challenges as soon as possible.

Unfortunately, systematically capturing and diagnosing VoLTE problems remains rather challenging, especially for new problems such as audio muting [46]. Current mechanism adopted by carriers to capture them largely depends on user feedback [47], which is not only unreliable, but also insufficient.

In view of these challenges, in this paper, we pursue two directions to identify the root causes of these prevalent VoLTE problems. First, we design and implement a VoLTE problem detection tool (§4.2) to capture audio quality issues of VoLTE with low false positive rate (0.65%) and false negative rate (5%). Second, we use stress testing (§5) to uncover VoLTE problems in controlled settings and diagnose the root causes. Three types of problems of the

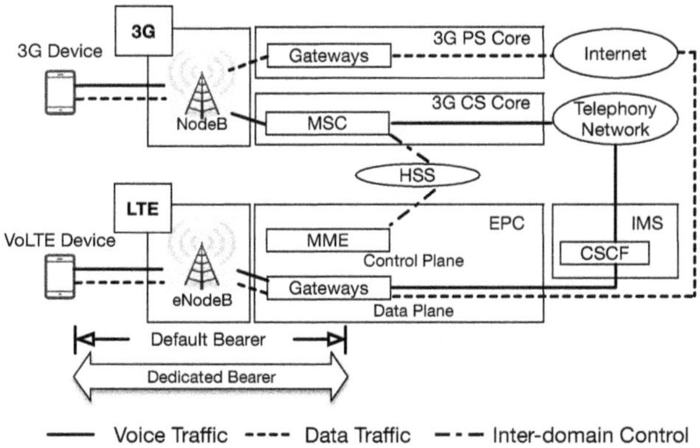

Figure 1: 3G and LTE architecture with VoLTE enabled.

deployed VoLTE service are identified: (1) a lack of coordination between device-originated and network-originated events (§6.1), which leads to consistent VoLTE call setup failure in some cases; (2) incorrectly ordered inter-dependent actions (§6.2), which lead to a high VoLTE call drop rate; (3) a lack of coordination in cross-layer interactions (§6.3), which results in extremely long muting during VoLTE calls. Although we identify that these problems are all temporary in the early deployment, we remind the commity that such problems may always exist as long as we are in a heterogeneous network environment. We summarize learnt lessons in §6 and provide the discussion in §7.

The contributions of this paper can be summarized as:

- We perform the first in-depth systematic study of VoLTE performance in three major U.S. carriers' network, and a comprehensive comparison among VoLTE and related telephony technologies.
- We conduct an extended study of call reliability of VoLTE, together with OTT VoIP and legacy call, and devise a novel online audio quality monitor to discover VoLTE call reliability problems in the production network, which overcomes the challenge of capturing the QoE problems of telephony services in real time.
- We perform stress testing to help identify the root causes for three types of common VoLTE problems, and uncover three instances of lacking coordination within VoLTE related protocols' design and implementation. We perform in-depth cross-layer analysis to deduce the root causes, and suggest potential solutions.

2. BACKGROUND

LTE (Long Term Evolution) is the next generation mobile technology that aims at supporting all services including voice, using a common IP infrastructure without separated voice channels. The architecture of LTE together with the co-existed 3G is shown in Fig. 1. The 3G voice domain, circuit switched (CS) core, transports legacy 3G calls in the same way as a traditional fixed-line telecommunication system. The 4G LTE domain, the packet switched (PS) core, transports data streams between the user and external packet data network such as the Internet via gateways.

2.1 Voice over LTE

VoLTE is technology that allows carriers to transmit voice calls over LTE network and through their IP Multimedia Subsystem (IMS) cores controlled by Call Session Control Functions (CSCF). This means voice calls and data sessions will travel side-by-side over LTE and exchange with Internet through the gateways. During a VoLTE call, VoLTE maintains both control and data sessions. The signaling messages to initiate the call flow over the control plane and use Session Initiation Protocol (SIP) to control the call. Voice packets are encoded with Adaptive Multi-Rate wide band (AMR-WB) codec and are transmitted with RTP protocol over the data plane.

VoLTE is supposed to benefit both carriers and end users. For carriers, VoLTE is expected to be more efficient from both network and spectrum perspective [33], and allows convenient global roaming. For end users, the most noticeable benefit of VoLTE is expected to be the improved voice quality, since it adopts wide band codec, which should make a call clearer than a legacy cell phone call. Furthermore, VoLTE is also expected to have better performance since QoS is guaranteed with dedicated bearer used. As shown in Fig. 1, a bearer is a "pipe line" for transporting data among device, ENodeB, gateways, and other entities. Prior to VoLTE, all the application data is transmitted by a default bearer where QoS is not guaranteed.

Since voice call is the most basic application of a mobile device, users expect VoLTE to provide good audio experience, at least comparable to legacy calls. However, the performance and reliability of VoLTE highly depend on the deployment of the LTE network, which currently is not as ubiquitous as the 2G/3G network. On top of that, to deploy VoLTE, additional complexity added in both the network infrastructure (e.g., IMS) and the process of making a audio call (e.g., CSFB, SRVCC) is very likely to introduce new problems in practice. In view of these challenges, we are motivated to perform the first comprehensive performance characterization of commercially deployed VoLTE, and also diagnose the discovered problems to help carriers improve VoLTE.

2.2 Key Terminology

Legacy call in this paper stands for the 3G/UMTS circuit switch call, which is used before LTE is deployed.

CS fallback (CSFB) is an alternative of VoLTE before the new IMS-based VoLTE architecture is deployed, which redirects a device registered on the LTE network to the 2G/3G network (i.e. fallback) prior to originating or receiving a voice call. After VoLTE is deployed, it is still kept as a standby solution for some carriers: when VoLTE call fails to setup, CSFB will be originated to reestablish the call in CS domain.

Inter Radio Access Technology (RAT) handover stands for a handover between different RAT, which can be either LTE, HSPA+[1], CDMA or other wireless technologies. In this paper, we mainly focus on LTE to HSPA+ handover, which usually happens when leaving LTE coverage, and denote it as *inter-RAT handover* in later sections. By default, an inter-RAT handover will terminate the ongoing VoLTE session if no call continuity technology such as SRVCC (explained below) is supported.

Single Radio Voice Call Continuity (SRVCC) is an advanced LTE functionality that improves inter-RAT handover in terms of VoLTE call continuity. It allows VoLTE call to be seamlessly moved from LTE PS domain to legacy CS voice domain without dropping the call. Differing from CSFB that does handover for call setup process, SRVCC does handover for ongoing VoLTE sessions.

[1]HSPA+ stands for Evolved High-Speed Packet Access. Usually marketed as 4G

3. VOLTE PERFORMANCE CHARACTERIZATION

To validate the performance gain promised by VoLTE in real deployment, in this section, we present our measurement study to characterize VoLTE performance and compare it with its alternative telephony technologies, which are legacy circuit-switched call and OTT VoIP. Note that our focus is on telephony services over cellular network, so other telephony solutions such as Wi-Fi calling [1] are not included.

Table 1 summarizes the results and lists the key performance indicators (KPIs) for a voice call application that are considered in our measurement study, along with their corresponding end-user experience. We cover performance metrics in this section and focus on call reliability metrics in §4.

Experiment setup. We test VoLTE services from three major US carriers, denoted as OP-I, OP-II, and OP-III, which together take 83% of the market share of US. The tesing environment is in good network condition for all the three carriers, which has a LTE Reference Signal Received Power (RSRP) around -95 dBm (5 out of 5 signal strength bars). We also cover the performances in other scenarios, such as undesired network environment and mobility case by simulating network condition and performing drive test.

Based on our measurement results, we find that VoLTE performances of the three carriers are similar in terms of audio quality, network resource requirement, and power efficiency. So in later sections, if not specified, we use OP-I's result to represent VoLTE's general performance and denote as "VoLTE". For comparison, Skype and Hangouts Voice are tested using the same device and data plan as we do for OP-I's VoLTE, and legacy call is also tested in OP-I's network.

Since VoLTE-supported device models vary in different carriers, we use Samsung Galaxy Note 3, LG G3 Vigor, and Samsung Galaxy S5 respectively to test VoLTE of the three carriers. For legacy calls, we use Nexus 5 devices, which doesn't support VoLTE in OP-I's network and will switch back to 3G to complete the legacy CS call. In our experiments the Skype version is 5.0.0 and the Hangouts version is 2.4, which are both the latest versions up to the time we write the paper.

3.1 Audio Quality under Different RSRP

Methodology. To measure the audio quality under different signal strengths, we use a programmable attenuator [27] together with a RF shield box [21] to vary the received RSRP of a mobile device. The RF shield box isolates the devices inside from the over-the-air network signal outside, so that the device can only receive signal from a single antenna connecting the box to the external network. The programmable attenuator is attached to the antenna on the RF box and can attenuate the signal strength of the inside environment within the range of [-95 dBm, -140 dBm].

We use Spirent Nomad HD equipment [45] to calculate the MOS for different applications, which provides us with objective MOS by characterizing the one-way degradation of audio quality. It takes the input audio from microphone on one device, together with the output audio from the earphone jack of another device for comparison, and calculate the MOS based on several metrics including one-way delay and missing frames. The objective MOS given by the equipment is on a 0–5 scale, where 4 and above is regarded as good or excellent quality with imperceptible impairment but below 3 is considered poor quality with annoying impairment [28]. We perform test calls with a 30-minute duration for each application under each RSRP level and the MOS is calculated every 10 seconds. We use uplink MOS to present the result since downlink MOS shows the similar trend according to our experiment.

MOS	OP-II VoLTE	OP-II legacy call
OP-I VoLTE	3.16	3.46
OP-I legacy call	3.28	3.25

Table 2: Median MOS when making calls from device indicated in row to device indicated in column.

Result. Fig. 2 shows the uplink MOS calculated for VoLTE and VoIP applications under different RSRP. Between Skype and VoLTE, Skype has slightly better audio quality over VoLTE in average but larger variance under poor signal strength. We discuss the reason for this in §3.3: Skype tends to use much more bandwidth to ensure a better audio quality. VoLTE and Skype all deliver satisfactory audio quality (mean MOS of 3.8 and above) under reasonably good signal strength levels, while Hangouts Voice lags a little behind. VoLTE demonstrates significant improvement compared with legacy calls, which can only reach 3.3 even in best case.

However, we identify that VoLTE doesn't guarantee superior audio quality all the time considering the lack of cooperation among VoLTE service providers in the current stage of VoLTE deployment. Table 2 shows the mean uplink MOS when making inter-operator calls. Surprisingly, we find that the audio quality of VoLTE call between OP-I and OP-II are even worse than that of the legacy call between them. The cause is that there are two times of transcoding performed by proxies in the network during a VoLTE call between OP-I and OP-II's network [4], which transcode the audio packets to analog and then back to packets, which degrades the audio quality from audio source.

3.2 Audio Quality with Contending Traffic

Methodology. Considering the scenario where applications generate traffic in the background during a voice call session, we are motivated to study the impact of contending traffic on VoLTE and OTT VoIP. We develop a client/server traffic generator with the client running on the testing device, which can control the UDP traffic generating rate of both uplink and downlink. The impact of background traffic on MOS is then measured by tuning the traffic rate during an ongoing call. We only present the uplink result in Fig. 3 since we observe in our experiment that the impact of downlink traffic on downlink MOS is equivalent to the impact of uplink traffic on uplink MOS.

Result. Fig. 3 shows the effect of background upload traffic on audio quality. We confirm that VoLTE won't be affected by background traffic due to its intrinsic dedicated bearer support, which ensures bandwidth isolation between voice and data. The MOS of Skype, on the other hand, degrades quickly to the level of "Annoying impairment" with increasing upload traffic rate, which may be caused by the buffering on the device and in the network.

3.3 Network Resource Consumption

Methodology. We study the network resource consumption of different voice call applications by measuring their throughput when delivering the same speech sample. Considering the bit rate adaptation of the codec, we conduct experiment in good signal strength level and capture the throughput in 3 scenarios that may present in a call session, including silent, speech, and mute, where speech is when the person is talking, silence is when the person is just listening with only background noise, and mute is when the person mutes himself by clicking the mute button during the call. Using Qualcom eXtensible Diagnostic Monitor (QXDM) [39], which can collect radio layer information on the device, we are able to study

§	Figures & Tables	Comparison entities	End user experience	Key performance indicators
3.1	Fig. 2, Table 2	V,S,H,L	Speech quality during a call	Audio quality under various signal strengths
3.2	Fig. 3	V,S,H		Audio quality with contending traffic
3.3	Fig. 4	V,S,H	Data charge [1]	Network resource requirements
3.4	Fig. 5	V,S,H	Smooth audio experience	Jitter, and one-way delay
3.5	Fig. 6	V,S,H,L	Time it takes to start ringing	End-to-end call setup time
3.6	Table 3	V,S,H,L	Battery life	Power efficiency
4.1	Fig. 7	V,S,H,L	Ability to make and maintain phone call	Call reliability

[1] Some carriers charge VoLTE by call durations instead of data usage.

Table 1: Summary of measurement results in §3. **V**, **S**, **H**, and **L** stand for VoLTE, Skype, Hangouts Voice, and Legacy call.

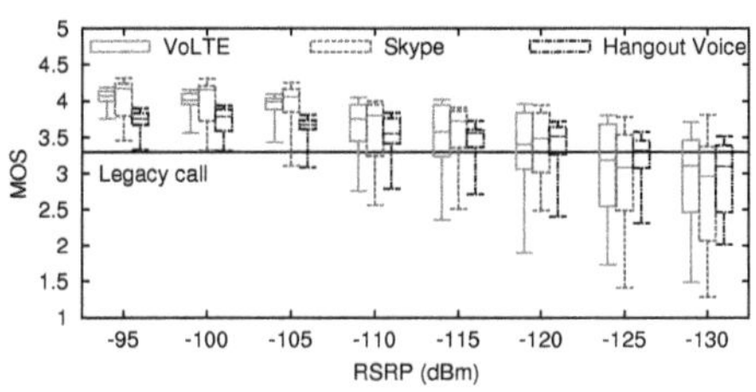

Figure 2: Uplink MOS under variant signal strengths. The dotted line represents the MOS a legacy call achieves in best case.

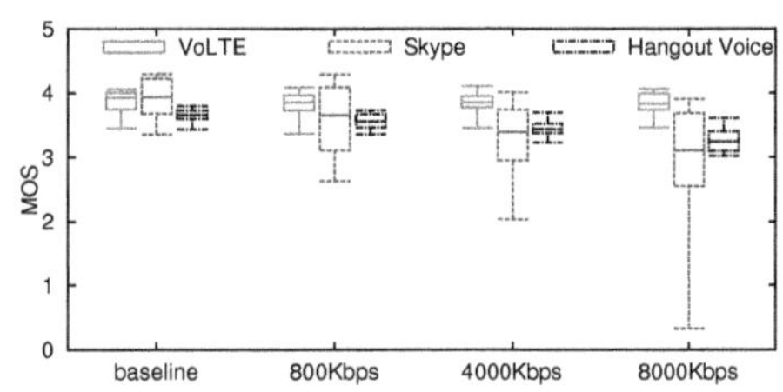

Figure 3: Uplink MOS under different background uploading traffic.X-axis indicates the bit rate the background application generates.

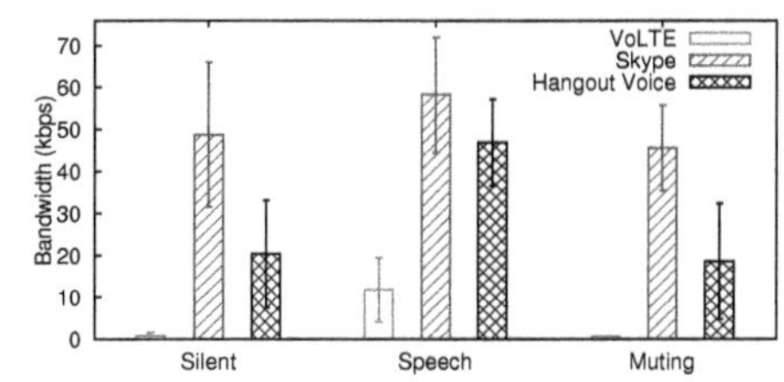

Figure 4: RLC uplink throughput in three scenarios. Silent is when only background noise is presented and muting is when call is intentionally muted.

the radio link control (RLC) layer throughput, which is the aggregation of both audio traffic and control traffic to quantify the total data consumption of different applications.

Result. Fig. 4 shows the throughput comparison results. In normal speech case, VoLTE consumes less network resources by 80% compared with Skype and 75% compared with Hangouts Voice. The difference comes from various factors including some LTE technologies that only available for VoLTE such as discontinuous transmission (DTX) [5] and discontinuous reception (DRX) [15], and the unique codec support [3]. DTX, for example, is a LTE feature, but currently only available for VoLTE, which allows a device to reduce transmission frequency when "no speech" is presented in the conversation. We also observe that AMR-WB codec used by VoLTE only generates minimum Real-time Transport Control Protocol (RTCP) packets to keep link liveness when the call is on hold. These features of VoLTE function together to reduce the transmission rate.

For "Speech" phase, we break down the traffic and examine the throughput of audio packets. In general, Skype generates 3.0× and Hangouts Voice 2.4× audio traffic of VoLTE when transmitting the same audio sample. We also find that VoLTE's rate adaption is more aggressive and efficient in reducing unnecessary transmissions. Compared with the codec adopted by VoIP applications, AMR-WB codec used by VoLTE is more sensitive to the variance of user's voice activity patterns, especially when silence or user-intended muting is presented. In the silence case, AMR-WB is identified to increase its packet generating interval from 20ms to 150ms, which reduces the required network resources significantly.

3.4 Mouth-to-ear Delay and Jitter

As discussed in §2, the difference between VoLTE and OTT VoIP mainly comes from the dedicated bearer. VoLTE is able to use the dedicated bearer that has bit rate guarantee to provide better Quality of Service (QoS), which is 49kbps as observed in our experiment under good signal strength, while the delivery of all other application traffic doesn't have such performance guarantee. Note that ENodeB may decrease the guaranteed bit rate for devices in undesirable network conditions.

Methodology. To validate the QoS guarantee provided by dedicated bearer, we perform VoLTE and OTT VoIP calls under various network conditions and compare the QoS metrics. We use the Spirent Nomad device mentioned in §3.1 to get the accurate *mouth-to-ear delay*, which is defined as the latency between the time when the speaker utters a word and the time when the listener actually hears it [10], containing both the one-way latency in the network and the time spent on encoding and decoding audio packets. We also calculate the packet loss rate and jitter based on the network trace of over 10 hours voice call for each application.

Result. Fig. 5 plots the jitter and mouth-to-ear delay comparison result. VoLTE has 24% less tail jitter and 64% less mean mouth-to-ear delay compared with OTT VoIP. According to the ITU-T standard [29], the 153 ms mean mouth-to-ear delay of VoLTE suggests excellent user satisfactory, while the over 300 ms delay of OTT VoIP indicates some users are not satisfied. In some cases the mouth-to-ear delay of OTT VoIP even exceeds the 400 ms upper bound specified in the standard, which has very negative impact on user experience. Note that the performance gain of VoLTE on the mouth-to-ear delay comes not only from the dedicated bearer, but also from the native codec support in the device firmware [38]. OTT apps adopts user space codec implementation, whereas the embedded VoLTE integrates with low-level audio drivers in the firmware for audio capture and rendering, which is more efficient. In addition, the average packet loss rate of VoLTE among the experiments is 0.009%, which is also clearly better than the 0.03% packet loss rate of Skype and Hangouts Voice.

3.5 User Perceived Call Setup Time

Methodology. We define the *user perceived call setup time* as the time between the caller's click of the "Make phone call" button and the incoming call UI shows on the callee's screen. To support automated measurement of this metric, we use QoE Doctor [18], which integrates UI automation and can be easily adapted to perform automated calls and capture UI updates. We conduct 200 times of call setup experiments for each application in good network condition.

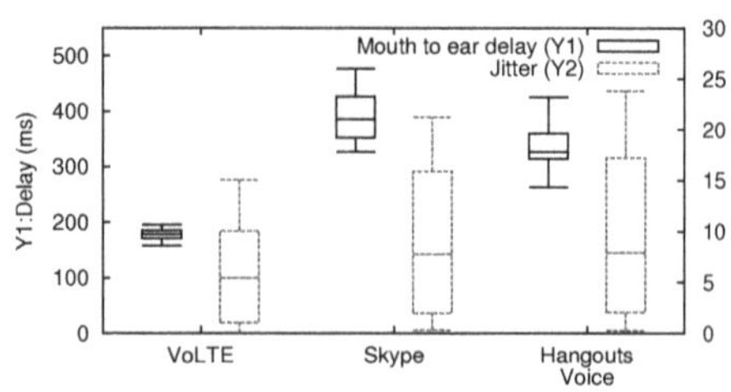

Figure 5: Jitter and mouth-to-ear delay comparison among different applications.

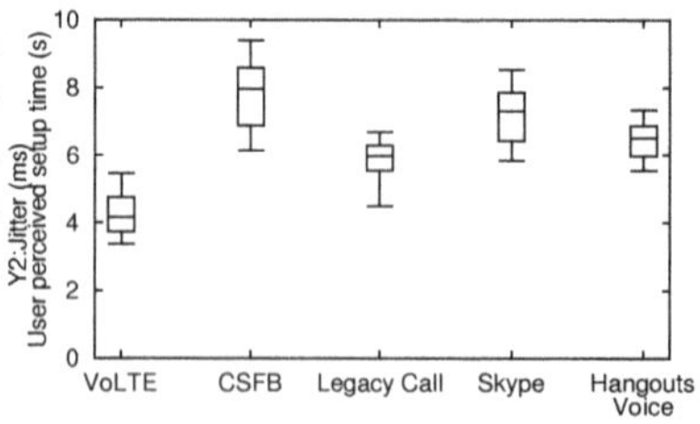

Figure 6: End-to-end call setup time comparison among different applications.

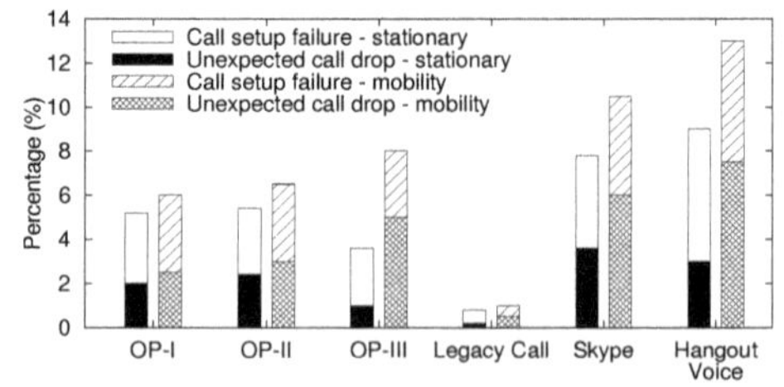

Figure 7: Call reliability comparison among different applications in stationary and mobility experiments.

Description	Mean power (mW)	Std. dev.
Baseline	14.88	134.51
VoLTE	888.74	45.35
Legacy call	511.00	474.98
Skype	2027.06	495.06
Hangouts Voice	2029.53	530.58

Table 3: Power consumption of different applications

Result. Fig. 6 shows that the mean VoLTE call setup time is about 4 s, which is much better than legacy call. In general, VoLTE reduces 48% of user-perceived call setup time compared with CSFB and uses around 40% less time compared to OTT VoIP. The reduced call setup time compared to legacy call and CSFB mainly owes to the simplified IMS based call setup procedure [13].

3.6 Energy Efficiency

VoLTE is expected to have better battery performance compared with OTT VoIP applications when transmitting audio traffic in LTE. According to the technical specifications, the energy benefit mainly comes from these aspects: (1) native codec support reduces the overall CPU computational overhead and power consumption; (2) DTX and DRX reduce the state transitions for transmitting and receiving packets in the silent case; (3) semi-persistent scheduling (SPS)) [32] reduces control channel overhead for VoLTE with radio resource preallocation.

Methodology. We use Monsoon power monitor [26] to calculate the power of different voice call applications. The baseline power is calculated when screen is off and all the background services except mandatory system services are disabled. Each of the result comes from a 10-minute power measurement. Table 3 shows the power consumption comparison result. VoLTE consumes 60% more energy compared with legacy call but uses 75% less energy compared with Skype and OTT VoIP, which conforms with users' expectations.

3.7 Result Summary

Our empirical measurement suggests that VoLTE is a promising technology that integrates the support from both device manufacturer and cellular network providers to deliver excellent audio quality with 83% less bandwidth consumption, around 40% less user-perceived call setup time and 75% less energy consumption compared with OTT VoIP.

4. CALL RELIABILITY STUDY

The ability to make and maintain a phone call is also very critical to good user experience. We conduct both stationary and drive tests to examine and compare the call reliability of all the three operators' VoLTE services, together with OP-I's legacy call and OTT VoIP.

4.1 Call Reliability

We define a "successful call" as one in which the call is successfully established and is maintained for the 1-minute duration of the test, so the call reliability can be measured as the *probability of making a successful call*. We consider two types of failures that lead to an unsuccessful call in our experiment. *Call setup failure* is defined as the call session failing to be established, while *Unintended call drop* is defined as a call drop during an active call session and is not intended by users.

Methodology. For each call application, we perform 500 automatic calls under good signal strength in the stationary reliability test. For mobility case, we conduct drive test on 2 routes, where inter-RAT handover will happen for all the three operators. 100 calls are performed for each call application on each route. We classify the unsuccessful calls according to different failure causes extracted from log analysis and characterize the reliability of different call applications.

Result. Fig. 7 shows the comparison results of call reliability in both stationary and mobility cases. Our experiments show that the reliability of VoLTE and OTT VoIP calls are still not comparable with legacy CS calls, especially in mobility scenario. The root cause is the immature LTE coverage since most of the problems occur when LTE signal strength is low or during the inter-domain switch. Interestingly, we find that the call drop rate of OP-III's VoLTE service significantly increased when moving from stationary test to drive test. We confirm that neither CSFB nor SRVCC are adopted by OP-III, which keeps the simplicity of the LTE network at the risk of a high call drop rate. However, we also notice that even with CSFB and SRVCC adopted, the VoLTE call reliability of OP-I and OP-II is still unsatisfactory. It is crucial to identify the root causes and resolve these reliability problems in the current VoLTE deployment.

4.2 Audio Quality Monitor

However, our call reliability study fails to capture all the VoLTE problems that the end users are experiencing. Some audio experience related problems such as muting and one-way audio [46, 19, 49], cannot be easily detected from log analysis, but have great influence on user experience. To capture such audio experience related problems in real time and understand their impact, we devise a tool called audio quality monitor to detect and report three types of common VoLTE problems with high accuracy.

4.2.1 Audio Problem Detection

Audio quality monitor listens to the phone call state changes and intercepts the incoming audio of a call session to examine the audio quality in real time and report audio problem if detected. Differing from previous work that study performance of real time communication applications using network traffic [24, 25], our approach uses the audio stream output to earphone to study the audio performance. We claim two advantages of our audio stream based analysis. First, network traffic based analysis has accessibility issue on unrooted devices, thus cannot be widely deployed in production network. Even worse, VoLTE audio traffic is transmitted and received in baseband processor [41] and there is no other way to access VoLTE packets than using external tools such as QXDM. Audio stream based analysis overcomes such problem by intercepting the audio channel to get essential information concerning audio quality, which doesn't require root access to the device. Second, audio based approach is closer to real user experience, and can capture some problems that cannot be identified from network trace analysis such as audio decoding failure.

Incoming voice is sampled as byte streams in real time using the Android `AudioRecord` API [11] and we identify audio problems by monitoring the sample buffer. For example, the pattern of a muting problem is defined as consecutive zero buffers presenting in the sampled byte stream and parameters we can configure are the sampling period and the threshold value of reporting a problem. A over-10-second muting is considered intolerable according to the standard [31], we configure the parameters to make the audio quality monitor responsive to muting over 1 second in order to also capture problems such as intermittent audio. This detection algorithm can also distinguish problematic muting from silence, since there are still non-zero bytes received during silent period. To ensure privacy, the audio quality monitor doesn't record any audio and only monitors a sample buffer that flushes frequently.

Using the audio quality monitor, we can capture various telephony audio problems such as muting, intermittent audio and garbled audio besides call setup failure and unintended call drop. We denote these audio related problems as *audio muting* in the rest of this paper, since there is usually short or long periods of muting involved. A context collector is also integrated, which intercepts the `onSignalStrengthChange()` callback function to trace the network environment changes. The collected problematic context information will be uploaded to the server and be analyzed later for diagnosis purpose.

4.2.2 A Useful Diagnostic Tool for Operators

Voice quality measurement through audio stream analysis has been proposed by ITU and has been investigated by some previous work [30, 35, 42]. We present an elegant on-device implementation compared to some existing solutions that are implemented on stand-alone equipment. We claim that the usability of audio quality monitor makes it an efficient diagnostic tool for operators to deploy in their production network. After investigating current problem diagnosis approaches adopted by the three carriers, we find that although some data collection tools are used to help their customer care systems resolve user complaints, the disclosure of many end-user problems still largely relies on user tickets, which are subjective and contain only coarse-grained information. The audio quality monitor overcomes this challenge by providing not only objective problem reports, but also corresponding context information that can assist future diagnosis. Moreover, the capability of reporting problems in the real time also enables remedial actions to be taken by applications to reduce the QoE impairment when encountering problems.

4.2.3 Evaluation

We evaluate the accuracy and overhead of the audio quality monitor in this section. We conduct both a subjective user study and an objective fault injection based evaluation to show the problem detection accuracy. Table 4 shows the summary of the results.

User study evaluation	FP: 0.65%(3/462)	FN: 5%(1/20)
Controlled evaluation	FP: -	FN: 3.7%(37/1000)
Energy consumption	+7% during VoLTE call	
Data usage	1.12 KB on average for each call	

Table 4: Audio quality monitor evaluation result

Tool accuracy: user study. We distribute audio quality monitor to 2 groups of people, ten students from a university and three engineers from one of the operators. With all the participants' consent, we run our app in the background on their personal devices to monitor each call session and upload the results to our server on Google App Engine. For the purpose of evaluation, a feedback window pops up after each call to let the user select whether they have encountered audio muting problem during last call session. Among the 482 calls performed during two weeks, 20 problematic calls are reported by users. Comparing with our detection result, we get the false positive rate as 0.65% (3/462) and the false negative rate as 5% (1/20). After tracking the destination number of the false positive cases, we find that they are all made to some self service numbers, such as airline service, and muting happens when user is interacting with the automatic speech, which will reported by our audio quality monitor, but won't be considered as a problem by users. Since the number of problematic calls is not sufficient to get a convincing false negative rate, we conduct another automated test to evaluate the false negative rate.

Tool accuracy: controlled evaluation. By pressing the "Mute" button during a phone call automatically, we simulate the audio muting problem of adjustable duration to test our detection accuracy. We perform 1000 VoLTE calls with 1-minute call duration and inject 1$\sim$2 seconds muting randomly for each call. Our system is able to detect 96.3% of injected muting issues. After investigation of the false negative cases, we find that the cause is the network type change happening during the muting, which may cause codec changes, or switching between different audio decoder modules. These changes may cause some non-zero bytes appearing in the byte stream during the muting and thus violates our defined pattern of muting problems.

Tool overhead. Comparing the MOS of the VoLTE call with and without audio quality monitor running in the background, we find that audio quality monitor doesn't affect the audio quality. and it only introduces 7% more power consumption during the call session compared with the baseline VoLTE call. Based on our user study data collected for two weeks, the average data consumption of uploading the context information is 1.12 KB for each problematic call.

4.3 Results Summary and Reflection

With the audio quality monitor loaded on the testing devices, we perform a large amount of automated VoLTE call tests in both OP-I and OP-II's network to study VoLTE problems. 3869 VoLTE calls are made in 5 different locations in two cities in US, with durations ranging from 0 to 5 minutes, which is approximately the average wireless call length in US[20]. Fig. 8 shows the occurrence of different types of failures. Note that we also consider failing over to CSFB as a minor problem of VoLTE. CSFB helps reduce VoLTE call setup failure, but will lengthen the call setup time (up to 10 seconds), and may cause temporary out-of-service after the call [52]. The results conform with our expectation that the reliability of a VoLTE call is closely related to the network condition.

We are then motivated to further discover and study these problematic cases under undesirable network conditions. We borrow the idea from "Stress testing" in software engineering, and leverage

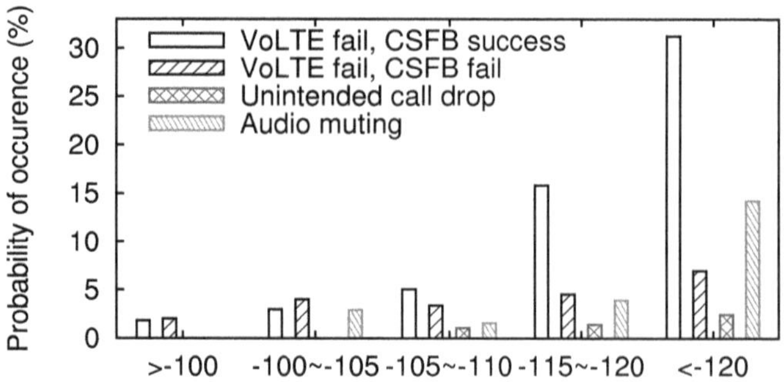

Figure 8: Occurrence of VoLTE problems under different signal strengths. "VoLTE fail, CSFB success" denotes VoLTE fails over to CSFB and establishes the CS call successfully. "VoLTE fail, CSFB fail" denotes the VoLTE call setup failure even with CSFB attempt.

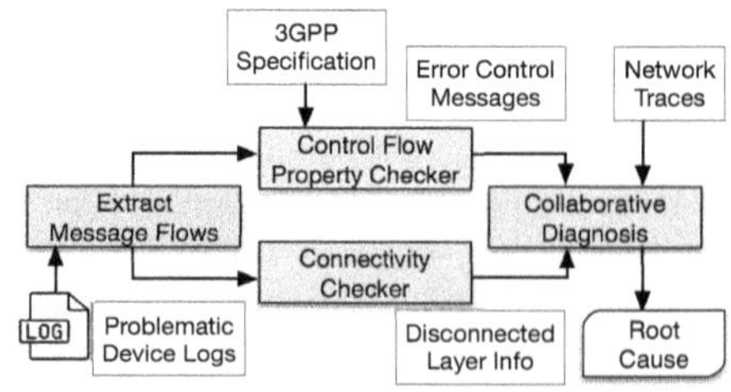

Figure 9: Cross-layer root cause diagnosis flow

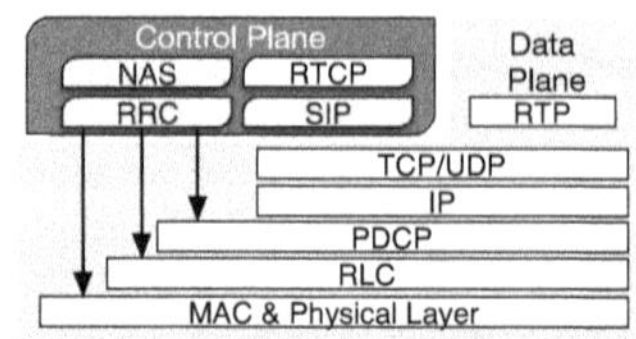

Figure 10: VoLTE control and data plane protocol stack.

fine-grained control of network condition to conduct VoLTE experiments in lab settings. We present our methodology of reproducing and diagnosing these problems in §5.

5. STRESS TESTING AND DIAGNOSIS

We take the stress testing approach to further investigate VoLTE problems in undesirable network conditions. By tuning the network condition worse, we expect more VoLTE problems to be captured by our tool, thus root causes can be identified from the problematic logs. With the help from one of the operators, we gain the control of inter-cell and inter-RAT signal strengths, which enable us to control network events such as inter-cell handover and inter-RAT handover easily in lab settings.

5.1 Stress Testing

The stress testing environment is built upon many equipment that can work together to simulate a given network environment and can give access to different layers' device information, which is hard to obtain before. Besides the previously mentioned RF shield box, antenna and attenuator we used to control the device received signal strength. We further leverage the control of LTE and 4G cells' signal strengths to manipulate various kinds of handover events to simulate the mobility scenario.

We collect QXDM logs, which contain information from chipset, including over-the-air signaling messages and lower layer protocol data units (PDU), `tcpdump` traces, and devices dump state log, which contains SIP messages and debug messages of various system services. These information is not accessible using common methods, but will provide essential information for diagnosing problems on device side and can help troubleshoot problems on network side.

5.2 Cross Layer VoLTE Diagnosis

Previous work [50] proposes a diagnostic approach, that uses model checking to uncover problematic protocol interactions in cellular network. Lesson learned is that problems in cellular network are very likely caused by the interactions between different layers, different entities and different domains. Further motivated by our call reliability measurement and collected problem reports from user study, we take the cross-layer diagnosing approach that investigates both control plane and data plane interactions across multiple layers, and between device and network. We describe the workflow as outlined in Fig. 9.

Extract message flow process takes the massive logs, including QXDM trace and other context information sorted with chronological order as input and output the organized messages flows of each layer. Fig. 10 shows the control plane and data plane protocol stack associated with VoLTE. For control plane traffic, interactions between device and network will be examined in four layers, including RTCP, SIP, Non-Access Stratum (NAS) and Radio Resource Control (RRC). For data plane, flows in another 4 layers, which are RTP, IP, Packet Data Convergence Protocol (PDCP) and Radio Link Control (RLC) will be considered. Data flows and control plane messages will be processed separately later.

Control flow property checker checks the message flows of multiple layers' during a problematic call session, with the intact control flows specified in the 3rd Generation Partnership Project (3GPP) [9] standard. Once violation with specific message in the specification is found, the violation, together with the error messages will be output to the collaborative diagnosis process. For example, network responding with SIP 503 "Server Unavailable" error message to device's SIP 183 "Session Progress" message will be considered as a violation since the SIP 503 error is not supposed to appear after SIP connection has already been established.

Connectivity checker accounts for the data disconnections if occurring during the call session. By calculating the real-time throughput of the four data plane layers, connectivity checker can identify which layer's disconnection causes the audio problem. Observation from the analysis of several instances of problems is that it is not always the case that lower layer's failure causes the upper layer's disconnection, upper layer such as RTP may fail individually due to some control plane problems, thus causing VoLTE service interruption perceived by end users. These layers' connection failures will also be reported to the collaborative diagnosis process.

Collaborative Diagnosis is the core process of the VoLTE diagnosis system. We report the problems to one of the operators, if the problem is not purely caused by device. We then take the corresponding network side logs provided by the operator into analysis, which are captured on base stations, and can be leveraged to verify problems reported from device and diagnose network-originated faults.

5.3 Limitation

Diagnosis process is not fully automated. Among the four processes shown in Fig. 9, checking the control flow property with 3GPP and the collaborative diagnosis still rely heavily on manual inspection. Our current design is the first step towards a highly au-

Symptom	Impact on user experience	Carrier[1]	Potential cause
Unsuccessful call setup	Unable to make any phone call	OP-I OP-II	A lack of coordination in device-network interaction
Unintended call drop	Unable to maintain a phone call	OP-I OP-II	Incorrectly ordered inter-dependent actions
Long Audio muting	Up-to-50-second unrecoverable muting followed with call drop	OP-I OP-II	A lack of coordination in cross-layer interactions

[1] These cases are concerned with system complexity and do not apply to OP-III due to its simpler design choices (e.g., no CSFB and SRVCC support). However, this simplicity leads to other reliability problems as shown in §4.1.

Table 5: Case study overview.

tomated cross-layer diagnostic tool and it will be our future work to build a diagnostic framework to systematically reproduce and diagnose problems.

Checking the control flow property with specifications is non-trivial. A suggested approach is the use of network simulation tools [34, 12]. For example, the Anritsu Signaling Tester [12] implements the protocol stack following the specifications and gives users the control of all the signaling messages. By replaying the traces in the simulated network, violations with the intact flows can be detected automatically.

Discovered root causes may not apply to every instance of problems. Although the symptoms of VoLTE problems we discovered in our stress testing are the same as problems that end users have encountered, there may be various causes rooted in a single symptom. We are working with one of the operators to fix these problems in their network, after which, the impact of the problems we discovered could be quantified.

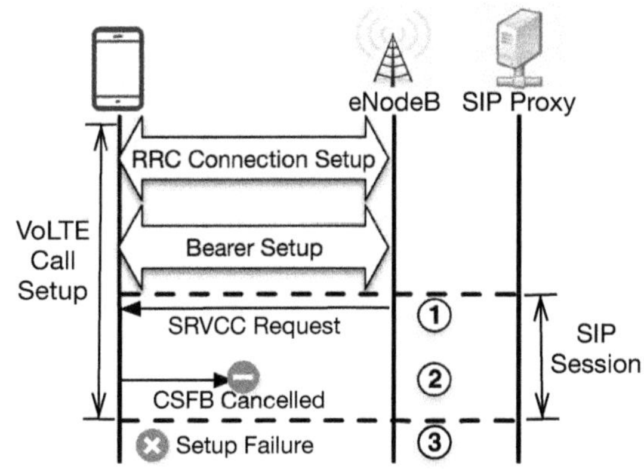

Figure 11: Call setup failure due to untimely SRVCC request.

6. CASE STUDY AND ROOT CAUSES

Table 5 summarizes the uncovered problems in the VoLTE related protocol design and implementation, which contribute to the three most common VoLTE problems affecting users nation wide. Note that the problems related to VoLTE's handoff support don't concern OP-III's VoLTE service since it doesn't have such support. However, simply disabling the handoff support including CSFB and SRVCC is not the panacea, we provide the discussion in §7.

We discuss the uncovered VoLTE problems, deduce the root causes with the help of the diagnosis support, and propose solutions. Since these problems are identified in the telecommunication protocol's design, implementation and configuration, proposed solutions consider all the three entities involved: (1) protocol designers, who develop standard such as RFC and 3GPP; (2) technology vendors, who implement protocols, e.g., Qualcomm and Ericsson; (3) Operators, who configure the products from vendors for deployment.

6.1 A Lack of Coordination in Device-originated and Network-originated Events

Our automated stress testing reports a high call setup failure rate when making VoLTE calls below certain RSRP threshold (-110dBM, 3 out of 5 signal strength bars). From QXDM logs, we observe that VoLTE call setup terminates due to SRVCC failure and CSFB's initiation failure, which is abnormal since CSFB is supposed to redirect the call to CS domain when VoLTE call setup fails.

Problem analysis. Shown in Fig. 11, the call setup failure is caused by problematic interactions between device and network during VoLTE call setup. CSFB is a mobile-originated event and serves as the alternative of VoLTE when LTE condition is not good enough to establish a VoLTE call. We inferred that the trigger for device to originate CSFB is a timer for receiving SIP provisional responses from network during the VoLTE call establishment. Upon expiration, device terminates the VoLTE call setup process and initiates CSFB.

SRVCC, which is a network-originated events, may also be triggered during call setup. Upon receiving measurement report from device, ENodeB may decide to initiate SRVCC if signal strength in a past period of time is considered bad. After the preparation is finished, ENodeB sends SRVCC request to device to handover the ongoing VoLTE session to CS domain (①). Problem occurs when SRVCC request reaches device before CSFB is originated, in which case, device is usually waiting for the SIP timer to expire, in order to initiate CSFB. Device then stops waiting immediately, cancels CSFB process and attempts to do SRVCC since the signaling from network has higher priority (②). However, call will be dropped due to SRVCC failure, since SRVCC works only for established VoLTE sessions, but the call has not yet been set up in this scenario. (③).

Root Cause. From the perspective of protocol design, the cause of such problem is that the specifications [6, 7] fail to coordinate SRVCC and CSFB, which have the same semantics in the call setup context. Since the device-originated CSFB and the network-originated SRVCC both try to switch the call to legacy CS domain during the call setup, it is reasonable to have them coordinated in the specification, so that device can understand the semantics in network-originated request and initiate the handoff process instead of incorrectly releasing the call.

Suggested solutions. We suggest protocol designer to coordinate these two events, which can be done by adding logic to CSFB and SRVCC specification to handle such case that untimely SRVCC request is received during call setup time.

Lessons. Protocol designer should be cautious when designing protocols that involve multiple entities since the interactions among entites may lead to unexpected situations in real time. Adding the logic to handle unexpected events during protocol design is always recommended.

Follow-up. 3GPP Rel-10 introduces a new type of SRVCC called aSRVCC [2], which supports the SRVCC packet-switched to circuit-switched handover to be initiated during the alerting phase of the call setup. It solves the problem by adding the logic on device side to handle the SRVCC request received during the call setup. OP-I has started to require OEM to integrate aSRVCC support and we are expecting to see it implemented on the upcoming series of devices.

6.2 Incorrectly Ordered Inter-dependent Actions

Unintended call drops frequently occur in our stress testing, when signal strength is tuned down to -120dBm (2 out of 5 signal strength bars), which is a common signal strength level in rural area and indoor environment. In normal cases, SRVCC successfully initiates and the call continues in the CS domain. However, abnormal cases are seen that SRVCC fails to initiate due to the device having handed over to the non-LTE domain. From QXDM log, we confirm that it is because the early arrival of inter-RAT handover request that switches device to legacy network. Without SRVCC initiated, such handover results in call drop.

Problem analysis. In a VoLTE call session, ENodeB monitors the measurement reports from device continuously to decide the triggering of several events. SRVCC and inter-RAT handover are two of them that are of interest in this case. SRVCC is designed to be an improvement on the existing inter-RAT handover in terms of keeping the ongoing call after the handover process. It is apparent that SRVCC should be initiated always before the inter-RAT handover to keep the continuity of VoLTE call in undesired LTE network conditions or moving out of the LTE coverage. However, we find that the sequence between such inter-dependent events is not enforced properly, which causes inter-RAT handover request being delivered to the device before SRVCC request. The late-arriving SRVCC request then fails to be served since device is already redirected to the non-LTE network, which leads to call drop after the handover.

Root cause. The problem is reported to one of the operators and they notice that it can be caused by misconfiguration of the threshold values for SRVCC and inter-RAT handover in the ENodeB. When SRVCC is integrated into the network, existing threshold values should be adjusted to guarantee that inter-RAT handover never occurs before SRVCC. However, even after verifying the proper threshold, call drops due to SRVCC failures are still captured, which indicates that incorrectly ordered delivery of the signaling messages still exists. We identify two causes. First, as shown in Fig. 12, upon SRVCC initiation, core network receives request from ENodeB and initiates call continuity procedure with IMS (①). When inter-RAT handover is triggered, ENodeB only needs to wait for core network to complete handover preparation (②). The first instance of the incorrect ordering appears when the response of SRVCC is delayed due to processing and reaches ENodeB later than the inter-RAT handover response (③). Second, incorrectly ordered delivery can also happen due to the unreliable transmission of the signaling channel between device and ENodeB (④), which has been discovered by previous works [50]. In both cases, VoLTE call will drop after handover since SRVCC fails to be initiated to ensure call continuity.

Suggested solution. Thinking out of the scope of the reliability problem of transmission in cellular network, inter-RAT handover is actually redundant for VoLTE call, since SRVCC inherited and improved all its functionalities in VoLTE scenario. We suggest operators to turn off the inter-RAT handover for all VoLTE call sessions, which can be done by disabling inter-RAT handover for all dedicated bearers on ENodeB.

Lessons. When implementing network protocols, it is not reliable to enforce the inter-dependency implicitly by using some configurable values. For example, using the values of signal strength threshold to ensure sequence of events is shown to be not robust in this case. Explicit enforcement of sequence, for example, specifying that event B can only be trigger after event A has been tried, is a recommended solution.

Follow-up. OP-I has turned off the inter-RAT handover for all dedicated bearers in some markets to evaluate its effectiveness in reducing the VoLTE call drop rate. If it turns out to be effective, this change will be applied in a larger scale.

6.3 A Lack of Coordination in Cross-layer Interactions

We discover extremely long VoLTE audio muting problem in our stress testing, when radio link disconnection is injected to an ongoing VoLTE session. We further find out that a merely 3∼4 seconds' radio link disconnection can lead to an up-to-50-second unrecoverable muting followed by call drop. Such long service interruption time may seriously damage user experience.

Problem analysis. Our cross-layer diagnosis discovers the cause rooted in the data plane protocol interactions. VoLTE audio packets are transmitted based on RTP protocol, where RTP timeout is used to determine the ending of a call session if no packets are received for a period of time. The configuration of the RTP timeout refers to the RTCP interval specified in its RFC specification [43], whose minimum value is recommended as *360/bandwidth(kbps)*. We infer the RTP timeout configured in both OP-I and OP-II's network, which are 30 and 45 seconds. They conform with the recommended value since the bit rate of both OP-I and OP-II's AMR-WB codec are fixed to be 12.65 kbps based on our experiments.

However, we find that this long RTP timeout far exceeds the maximum possible lower layers' recovery time in the context of VoLTE, which leads to unnecessarily long service interruption time when radio link problem happens. Fig. 13 shows the cross-layer interaction when radio link problem occurs. Upon radio link disconnection (①), RLC starts retransmitting unacked packets until a *maximum retransmission threshold (maxRetxThreshold)* is exceeded, and a radio link failure event is reported to RRC layer (②). RRC layer then attempts to reestablish the connection, but will stop trying if certain timers expire, when waiting for the network response to the re-establishment request (③). T301 and T311 denote the timeouts of waiting for two types of responses [8] to the RRC re-establishment request. On expiration, device goes to RRC_IDLE state and the radio link failure will never recover in this session. The aggregated recovery time (T) of layers below RTP can be denoted as:

$$T = (t * maxRetxThreshold) * N + min\{T_{301}, T_{311}\} \quad (1)$$

where t denotes the time interval of transmission and can be approximated by a RLC layer RTT, which can be assumed as 100 ms [40]. N denotes the number of RRC connection re-establishment attempts.

The T_{301} and T_{311} timer are all hundreds of milliseconds inferred from our experiments, which means that an over-one-second radio link disconnection during the RRC re-establishment process will cancel the further attempts of recovery ($N = 1$). We further get the $maxRetxThreshold$ value from QXDM logs that it is configured 16 or 32 by different operators. Then the estimated recovery time of radio layers are all within several seconds for both opera-

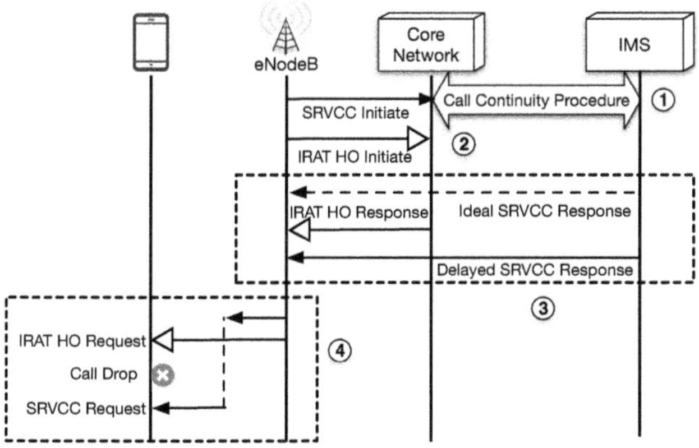

Figure 12: Call drop due to incorrectly ordered messages delivery of SRVCC and inter-RAT handover (IRAT HO).

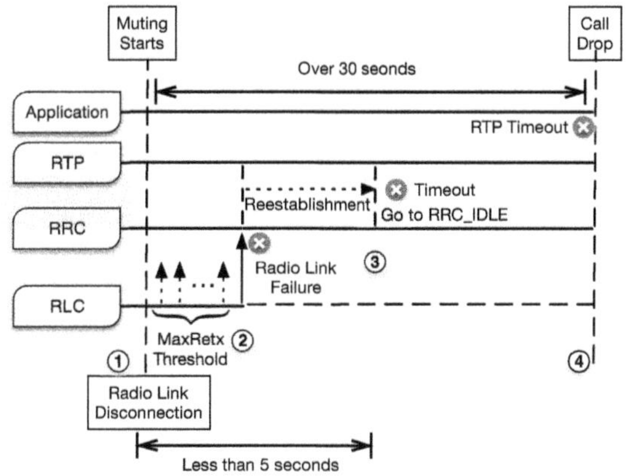

Figure 13: Long audio muting due to lack of coordination among cross-layer timeouts.

tors calculated using the formula (1). The inconsistency between the over-30-second RTP timeout and the several-second recovery time results in the extremely long audio muting.

Root cause. The root cause is identified as the lack of coordination among the design of different specifications. In RTP/RTCP protocol, which is standardized by the Internet Engineering Task Force (IETF), the design principle of the RTCP interval is to limit the portion of control plane traffic over the wire under multiple senders [43]. It doesn't consider the underlying layers' failure recovery mechanism since they are not defined for the use case in the cellular network. The gap between the specifications needs to be bridged if the cross-layer interactions are involved.

This lack of coordination among layers is also considered as an information gap between RTP protocol implemented in the OS and radio layer protocols implemented in the chipset. In the current device implementation of VoLTE stack, radio link events are not passed to the RTP layer, so that upper layer cannot react timely to underlying layers' failures, thus resulting in user experience impairment.

Suggested solution. Since RTP timeout exists both on device and network sides and there are other applications relying on this protocol. It is impractical to simply violate RFC specification to reduce the timeout value. We suggest operators to push OEM to report radio link events such as unrecoverable radio link failure directly to VoLTE call applications, so that reactions, such as sending new service request or dropping the muted call can be taken to reduce service interruption time.

Lessons. When integrating external protocols into an existing protocol stack, it is critical to investigate the difference between the original context and current context before implementing following the specifications. Service providers need to ensure the compatibility of protocols defined for different purposes.

Follow-up. We have worked with OP-I to propose a device-reporting schema to two of the major OEMs in the world, which requires baseband to report radio link information, such as VoLTE signaling message, and RTP statistics to the application in real time during a VoLTE call by broadcasting intents. Currently, parts of the functionalities are implemented on prototype devices and we are expecting the full implementation to evaluate its effectiveness.

7. DISCUSSION

Different choices of implementing VoLTE. As mentioned before, OP-I and OP-II integrate fallback support in their VoLTE service to guarantee a shorter time-to-market, while OP-III didn't launch VoLTE until they thought their LTE network is good enough. In the long-term, the design choice made by OP-III to keep their network simple is preferable. However, it takes high risk of poor service availability during the transition period towards an all-LTE network. For example, the VoLTE call of OP-III is recognized to drop immediately once the LTE RSRP is below a certain threshold, which results in a high call drop rate in mobility scenario as shown in §4.1. Despite the different choices, poor LTE coverage is the major cause behind these problems, so improving their network coverage should be kept as a top priority for operators.

Long-term impact of our work. We admit that the problems we identified are transient, if we assume that all the devices will be in good LTE environment and no fallback support is needed in the future. Since all the three instances of problems are related to the underlying protocols of mobile communication, i.e., 3GPP, we believe that discovering and addressing these problems are important and are complementary to the efforts in improving LTE coverage. Our methodology can also be reused to diagnose problems in other services that support heterogeneous network environment, such as Wi-Fi calling to VoLTE handover.

8. RELATED WORK

Cellular network troubleshooting. There have been quite a few work looking into the protocol design and implementation of cellular network to seek for root causes of end users' problems. Previous work [36, 37, 51] have identified loopholes in the charging system of operators' network, which will cause wrong billing for users' data services. Recent work discover problems lying in the data plane [52] and control plane [50] of cellular network, which causes performance degradation and annoying user experience. Other measurement study (e.g., 4GTest [23] and TailEnder [14]) investigates problems in the interaction between device and network that lead to energy waste. Our work discovers problems in VoLTE, which is a new service not covered by previous studies, but is extremely important since making voice call is the most basic need for mobile users.

Voice call performance analysis. For voice call quality analysis, most of previous studies focus on VoIP service such as Skype. The relationship between Skype's voice streaming efficiency and its forward error correction (FEC) has been measured and tuned for improving user satisfaction [24, 25]. Based on call duration from actual Skype traces, Chen et. al. proposed a model to generate User Satisfaction Index (USI) to quantify the degree of user satisfaction [17]. In comparison, our target is VoLTE, a new carrier-deployed voice call technology intended for replacing legacy calls, which is more challenging due to higher user expectations and additional complexity in network infrastructure discussed in §2.1.

Recently, some VoLTE performance evaluations are reported from both industry and academia [22, 48], which shares the same goal of characterizing VoLTE performance with us. Compared to them, besides QoS metrics, we take a more systematic way to study various QoE metrics such as user-perceived call setup time and call reliability, which have more direct impact on end users' experience. More importantly, we dig deep into the root causes of newly-discovered VoLTE problems and suggested solutions.

9. CONCLUSION

In this paper, we take the first step to quantify the performance of VoLTE, and study its implication on relevant QoE metrics. We also design and implement a on-device VoLTE problem detection tool to examine the impact of these problems on user experience. We perform stress testing based on insights from in-depth call reliability measurement and uncover 3 major VoLTE problems lying in protocol design and implementation, and suggest potential solutions.

10. ACKNOWLEDGEMENTS

We want to thank the anonymous reviews and shepherd for their valuable comments, and would like to acknowledge the support from Yihua Ethan Guo, Yuru Shao, Pete Myron, Abdulshafil Ahmed, Warren McNeel, Philip Hankins, Matthew Harkins, Toaha Ahmad, and QoE Lab team at T-Mobile. Specially, we would like to acknowledge contributions from Suchit Satpathy from operations team at T-Mobile, who grounded us to the practicality of the problems that customers are facing. This research was supported in part by the National Science Foundation under grants CNS-1059372, CNS-1345226, and CNS-1318306.

11. REFERENCES

[1] Wi-Fi Calling. http://www.cisco.com/c/en/us/solutions/collateral/service-provider/service-provider-wi-fi/white-paper-c11-733136.html.

[2] 3GPP. 3GPP aSRVCC Working Item. http://www.3gpp.org/DynaReport/WiCr-500011.htm.

[3] 3GPP. 3GPP.TS129.238 AMR-WB speech codec. http://www.etsi.org/deliver/etsi_ts/126200_126299/126204/12.00.00_60/ts_126204v120000p.pdf.

[4] 3GPP. 3GPP.TS129.238 TrGW. http://www.etsi.org/deliver/etsi_ts/129200_129299/129238/12.04.00_60/ts_129238v120400p.pdf.

[5] 3GPP. 3GPP.TS146 081 DTX for EFR speech traffic channels. http://www.etsi.org/deliver/etsi_ts/129200_129299/129238/12.04.00_60/ts_129238v120400p.pdf.

[6] 3GPP. 3GPP.TS23.216 Single Radio Voice Call Continuity. http://www.etsi.org/deliver/etsi_ts/123200_123299/123216/12.02.00_60/ts_123216v120200p.pdf.

[7] 3GPP. 3GPP.TS23.272 Circuit Switched CS fallback in Evolved Packet System. http://www.etsi.org/deliver/etsi_ts/123200_123299/123272/12.04.00_60/ts_123272v120400p.pdf.

[8] 3GPP. 3GPP.TS24.331 - 7.3 RRC Timers. http://www.etsi.org/deliver/etsi_ts/146000_146099/146081/12.00.00_60/ts_146081v120000p.pdf.

[9] 3GPP. 3rd Generation Partnership Project. http://www.3gpp.org/.

[10] C. Agastya, D. Mechanic, and N. Kothari. Mouth-to-ear latency in popular voip clients. 2009.

[11] Android. Android audiorecord. http://developer.android.com/reference/android/media/AudioRecord.html.

[12] Anritsu. Anritsu signaling tester md8470a. http://www.anritsu.com/en-US/Products-Solutions/Products/MD8470A.aspx.

[13] G. Association. VoLTE Service Description and Implementation Guidlines. http://www.gsma.com/network2020/wp-content/uploads/2014/05/FCM.01-v1.1.pdf.

[14] N. Balasubramanian, A. Balasubramanian, and A. Venkataramani. Energy consumption in mobile phones: a measurement study and implications for network applications. In *Proceedings of the 9th ACM SIGCOMM conference on Internet measurement conference*, pages 280–293. ACM, 2009.

[15] C. S. Bontu and E. Illidge. Drx mechanism for power saving in lte. *Communications Magazine, IEEE*, 47(6):48–55, 2009.

[16] D. Bubley. The big problem for VoLTE. http://disruptivewireless.blogspot.com/2014/02/the-big-problem-for-volte.html.

[17] K.-T. Chen, C.-Y. Huang, P. Huang, and C.-L. Lei. Quantifying skype user satisfaction. In *ACM SIGCOMM Computer Communication Review*, volume 36, pages 399–410. ACM, 2006.

[18] Q. A. Chen, H. Luo, S. Rosen, Z. M. Mao, K. Iyer, J. Hui, K. Sontineni, and K. Lau. Qoe doctor: Diagnosing mobile app qoe with automated ui control and cross-layer analysis. In *Proceedings of the 2014 Conference on Internet Measurement Conference*, pages 151–164. ACM, 2014.

[19] A. S. Communities. People can't hear me on outgoing. https://discussions.apple.com/thread/6800213.

[20] CTIA. Average local mobile wireless call length in the United States from 1987 to 2012 (in minutes). http://www.statista.com/statistics/185828/average-local-mobile-wireless-call-length-in-the-united-states-since-1987/.

[21] R. Electronics. RF Shielded Testing Test Box. http://www.ramayes.com/RF_Shielded_Test_Enclosures.htm.

[22] S. R. Group. An independent benchmark study of AT&T's VoLTE network. http://www.signalsresearch.com/Docs/LTE%20NA%202014%20VoLTE%20Results%20-%20SRG%20Presentation.pdf.

[23] J. Huang, F. Qian, A. Gerber, Z. M. Mao, S. Sen, and O. Spatscheck. A close examination of performance and power characteristics of 4g lte networks. In *Proceedings of*

the 10th international conference on Mobile systems, applications, and services, pages 225–238. ACM, 2012.

[24] T.-Y. Huang, K.-T. Chen, and P. Huang. Tuning skype's redundancy control algorithm for user satisfaction. In *INFOCOM 2009, IEEE*, pages 1179–1187. IEEE, 2009.

[25] T.-Y. Huang, P. Huang, K.-T. Chen, and P.-J. Wang. Could skype be more satisfying? a qoe-centric study of the fec mechanism in an internet-scale voip system. *Network, IEEE*, 24(2):42–48, 2010.

[26] M. S. Inc. Monsoon Power Monitor. https://www.msoon.com/LabEquipment/PowerMonitor/.

[27] J. Industries. JFW Programmable Attenuators. http://www.jfwindustries.com/catalog/Programmable_Attenuators-2-1.html.

[28] ITU-T. Itu-t mean opinion score (mos) terminology. ITU-T P.800.1, 2006.

[29] R. ITU-T and I. Recommend. G. 114. *One-way transmission time*, 18, 2000.

[30] R. ITU-T and I. Recommend. G.720.1 : Generic sound activity detector. 2010.

[31] T. S. ITU-T. E. 855. *Connection integrity objective for the international telephone service*, 1988.

[32] D. Jiang, H. Wang, E. Malkamaki, and E. Tuomaala. Principle and performance of semi-persistent scheduling for voip in lte system. In *Wireless Communications, Networking and Mobile Computing, 2007. WiCom 2007. International Conference on*, pages 2861–2864. IEEE, 2007.

[33] J. Kallio, T. Jalkanen, and J. T. Penttinen. Voice over lte. *The LTE/SAE Deployment Handbook*, pages 157–187, 2012.

[34] LENA. Lte-epc network simulator. http://networks.cttc.es/mobile-networks/software-tools/lena/.

[35] L. Malfait, J. Berger, and M. Kastner. P. 563&# 8212; the itu-t standard for single-ended speech quality assessment. *Audio, Speech, and Language Processing, IEEE Transactions on*, 14(6):1924–1934, 2006.

[36] C. Peng, C.-y. Li, G.-H. Tu, S. Lu, and L. Zhang. Mobile data charging: new attacks and countermeasures. In *Proceedings of the 2012 ACM conference on Computer and communications security*, pages 195–204. ACM, 2012.

[37] C. Peng, G.-h. Tu, C.-y. Li, and S. Lu. Can we pay for what we get in 3g data access? In *Proceedings of the 18th annual international conference on Mobile computing and networking*, pages 113–124. ACM, 2012.

[38] Qualcomm. Qualcomm Announces First Large-Scale Commercial VoLTE Launch in Japan. https://www.qualcomm.com/news/releases/2014/07/08/qualcomm-announces-first-large-scale-commercial-volte-launch-japan.

[39] Qualcomm. Qualcomm eXtensible Diagnostic Monitor. https://www.qualcomm.com/media/documents/files/qxdm-professional-qualcomm-extensible-diagnostic-monitor.pdf.

[40] Qualcomm. Performance evaluation of adaptive rlc pdu size in hspa+ networks. https://www.qualcomm.com/media/documents/files/qualcomm-research-performance-evaluation-of-adaptive-rlc-pdu-size-in-hspa-networks.pdf, 2012.

[41] Qualcomm. Qualcomm chipset powers first successful volte call with srvcc. https://www.qualcomm.com/news/releases/2012/02/02/qualcomm-chipset-powers-first-successful-voip-over-lte-call-single-radio, 2012.

[42] Qualcomm. Spirent audio and vedio testing solution. http://www.spirent.com/Products/ProLab/ProLab-Video-Quality, 2015.

[43] H. Schulzrinne, S. Casner, R. Frederick, and V. Jacobson. Rfc 3550. *RTP: a transport protocol for real-time applications*, 7, 2003.

[44] J. Soininen. Transition scenarios for 3gpp networks. RFC 3574, 2003.

[45] Spirent. Spirent Nomad HD Voice Measurement System. http://www.spirent.com/About-Us/News_Room/Press-Releases/2013/05-21-13_Nomad-HD.

[46] T-Mobile. VoLTE One way or no audio: Samsung Galaxy Note 3. https://support.t-mobile.com/docs/DOC-11793.

[47] I. T-Mobile. Diagnostics metrics collection. https://support.t-mobile.com/docs/DOC-2929, 2011.

[48] M. R. Tabany and C. G. Guy. An End-to-End QoS Performance Evaluation of VoLTE in 4G E-UTRAN-based Wireless Networks. In *the 10th International Conference on Wireless and Mobile Communications*, 2014.

[49] Tektronix. VoLTE Troubleshooting. http://www.tekcomms.com/sites/tekcomms.com/files/VoLTE_Troubleshooting_CCW-30697-2.pdf.

[50] G.-H. Tu, Y. Li, C. Peng, C.-Y. Li, H. Wang, and S. Lu. Control-plane protocol interactions in cellular networks. In *Proceedings of the 2014 ACM conference on SIGCOMM*, pages 223–234. ACM, 2014.

[51] G.-H. Tu, C. Peng, C.-Y. Li, X. Ma, H. Wang, T. Wang, and S. Lu. Accounting for roaming users on mobile data access: Issues and root causes. In *Proceeding of the 11th annual international conference on Mobile systems, applications, and services*, pages 305–318. ACM, 2013.

[52] G.-H. Tu, C. Peng, H. Wang, C.-Y. Li, and S. Lu. How voice calls affect data in operational lte networks. In *Proceedings of the 19th annual international conference on Mobile computing & networking*, pages 87–98. ACM, 2013.

ABSENCE: Usage-based Failure Detection in Mobile Networks

Binh Nguyen[†], Zihui Ge[‡], Jacobus Van der Merwe[†], He Yan[‡], and Jennifer Yates[‡]

[†]School of Computing, University of Utah [‡]AT&T Labs - Research

{binh,kobus}@cs.utah.edu {gezihui,yanhe,jyates}@research.att.com

ABSTRACT

We present our proposed ABSENCE system which detects *service disruptions* in mobile networks using aggregated customer usage data. ABSENCE monitors aggregated customer usage to detect when aggregated usage is lower than expected in a given geographic region (e.g., zip code), across a given customer device type, or for a given service. Such a drop in expected usage is interpreted as a sign of a potential service disruption being experienced in that region / device type / service. ABSENCE effectively deals with users' mobility and scales to detect failures in various mobile services (e.g., voice, data, SMS, MMS, etc). We perform a systematic evaluation of our proposed approach by introducing synthetic failures in measurements obtained from a US operator. We also compare our results with ground truth (real service disruptions) obtained from the mobile operator.

Categories and Subject Descriptors

C.2.3 [**Network Operations**]: Network monitoring, Network management

Keywords

usage-based failure detection; mobile networks; large scale; operational networks

1. INTRODUCTION

The proliferation of sophisticated mobile devices like smart phones, tablets and wearable devices [9] have made them an integral part of today's society. The growth in both the number of mobile devices, the data usage of each device and the types of mobiles devices of course implies an increased reliance and dependence on mobile networks. To address this demand, mobile operators are continuously investing in new mobile networks and technologies. In recognition of the importance of the underlying network, mobile operators are building redundancy into nearly all components of their infrastructure and developing sophisticated systems to monitor the health of their networks and to rapidly respond to any customer impacting events [15].

Despite these efforts, the inherent complexity of mobile networks and their environments (customer devices, applications) may result in service disruptions that go undetected by monitoring the network elements. Hence modern mobile operators adopt the strategy of deploying *service* monitoring, in addition to the *network* monitoring, on the customer service experience. Service monitoring is designed to continuously monitor the end-to-end experience that customers receive from their network-based services. This contrasts with network monitoring, in which the status of individual network elements and links are monitored for failures and impairments (e.g, link losses). Service monitoring is vital as a second line of defense – capturing network, customer device or application issues as well as interaction issues among them which may not be detected by the network/applications/devices themselves. Service monitoring is also crucial to quantifying the service impact of known network problems for prioritizing issue resolution.

Somewhat counter-intuitively, network elements that support the service functions are not always able to alarm on conditions which are in fact service impacting. This may be the result of, for example, software bugs in the network elements' firmware, or in the EMS (element management system) for the network elements, or due to configuration errors. It is possible that, even though all network metrics indicate a healthy network, customers might be experiencing degraded service or a complete service disruption. For example, the deployment of a new service feature or a software upgrade to address a bug, might trigger an unintended side effect (or indeed a new bug) that the monitoring system is not equipped to detect. We define such service disruptions that are not captured by network monitoring as *silent failures*. Furthermore, it is difficult to infer service quality perceived by customers using the status of the network. There is a complicated relationship between the status of the network and the service quality the users experience. For example, because of redundancy mechanisms within the network, a particular network failure does not necessarily imply customer impact. For example, users associated with a failed cell tower could be picked up by neighboring towers as long as they are in the coverage range of the neighboring towers and the neighbors still have enough resources to handle the users' traffic [27].

However, monitoring service performance across a mobile network is extremely challenging. Traditional active monitoring approaches – techniques which send test traffic across the network – simply don't scale, courtesy of the very large number of cell towers (end points) that need to be monitored and the diverse set of services supported by mobile networks. One could alternatively naively imagine looking for service disruptions by looking for drops

MobiCom'15, September 7–11, 2015, Paris, France.
© 2015 ACM. ISBN 978-1-4503-3619-2/15/09...$15.00.
DOI: http://dx.doi.org/10.1145/2789168.2790127.

in traffic volumes on network elements. However, the inherently dynamic nature of a mobile network environment makes it difficult to infer service impact by monitoring individual network elements, e.g., routers or base stations, to distinguish between changes in traffic volume that are simply the result of the normal operation of the network, and changes that are the result of anomalous network behavior.

In this paper we present our work on the ABSENCE system to address the detection of service disruptions in mobile networks in a proactive manner. Our key insight is that service disruptions often impact the traffic consumed by customers, which very likely reflects in customers' usage. This seemingly obvious observation, combined with a suitable mechanism to monitor customer usage, allows ABSENCE to rely on customer usage data to detect the possible presence of service disruptions. Specifically, ABSENCE uses aggregated (e.g., zip code level and handset manufacturer/model level) usage data for different mobile services (e.g., voice call, data, and short message) calculated from anonymized call detail records (CDRs). ABSENCE uses the historical aggregated usage data to predict the expected customer usage for different mobile services at appropriate aggregations of customers, and compares this with real time customer usage data. A deviation from the predicted customer usage is highly likely an indication of a service disruption.

We make the following contributions:

- We present the design of ABSENCE, a novel service disruption detection system for mobile networks that infers service disruptions by monitoring aggregate customer usage. Our design is informed by a data driven exploration of the problem domain using data from an operational mobile network.
- We present a scalable Hadoop-based implementation of our approach which is capable of performing service disruption detection by processing huge volumes of anonymized CDR data (e.g., hundreds of millions of records every hour for mobile data service) in a streaming manner, for all the mobile services associated with an operational mobile network.
- Using data from the same operational mobile network, we perform a systematic data-driven evaluation of our approach by introducing a comprehensive synthetic set of both network and mobile device failure scenarios. Our results show that: (i) Our variable-scale temporal aggregation improves detection by an order of magnitude over fixed interval aggregation. (ii) We achieve overall detection rates of 88%, while we achieve 98% or better detection rates for service disruption that have over 10% usage impact within the corresponding aggregation (e.g., zip code and handset device model).
- We compare our results with ground truth from actual service disruption events and present a number of case studies showing the effectiveness of our approach. For a set of confirmed service disruptions, ABSENCE achieves 100% detection rate.

2. MOTIVATION

In this paper we define a *service disruption* to be a scenario in which customers become unable to utilize the offered service(s) that they would normally utilize. A service disruption can be either due to the network/application fails to complete customers' service requests, or because customers give up making service attempts due to unacceptable service performance. Service disruptions are typically the result of a network, device or application outage or severe performance degradation. The vast majority of service issues are rapidly detected via the network and/or application. However, there are a small number of issues – typically those resulting from complex software bugs – that may remain undetected by the network and/or application.

Given the challenges of scaling active service monitoring techniques, one could imagine instead simply relying on customers to inform a mobile service provider of service disruptions as is performed in other industries, such as the power industry. However, given that individual customer concerns may relate to a large number of underlying causes – individual customer device issues, customer user error or broader service disruptions – identifying a significant service disruption would typically require detecting a pattern in the customer feedback across a number of different customers. This is inherently slow, and thus a highly undesirable approach to detecting service issues. Figure 1a shows an example of customer ticket volume resulting from a service disruption. The figure shows a time series of the number of tickets in the customer care system. The actual event occurred around 16:38 UTC, but was only evident via an increase in customer ticket volumes at 21:00 UTC (i.e., 4.5 hours later), when the number of customer calls rapidly increased. Relying on customer complaints to detect such failures is thus clearly undesirable – customers are simply too slow at calling in for this to be a timely approach for detecting service issues.

Given the relative maturity of network management and operation practices [15], and significant research efforts associated with failure detection [13, 4], network and application interaction [22, 14, 19, 10], mobile network performance [20, 21, 25, 12, 6] and service monitoring [26, 24, 5], the obvious question is: *Why are these service disruptions so difficult to detect?*

Active end to end service monitoring is used extensively across mobile and wireline networks to test service integrity and performance. Active monitoring uses probes placed strategically across the network to send test traffic. However, the major challenge with active monitoring is scale – ideally probes must be deployed so that every combination of service path, customer device type and application is actively tested on an ongoing basis. But this is clearly an unrealistic expectation. There are simply too many different types of customer devices in the market place, a multitude of different applications and a huge geographic environment to probe. In a wireless environment, service performance can vary considerably across a very local region even for customers connected to a common cell site. Thus, even placing a dedicated probe associated with each individual cell site does not provide a comprehensive view of service experience across the entire region associated with that cell site. Thus, active monitoring in a mobile network provides only a sampling of service experience and, depending on the extent of the deployments, will likely not be able to detect all service impairments.

One may alternatively use passive monitoring of customer traffic to detect service impairments. Such monitoring can be performed on traffic aggregates, and thus does not need visibility into individual customer experience. However, service outage detection cannot be achieved by observing customer traffic – by its very nature customer traffic is expected to disappear during an outage. Thus, detecting a service outage using passive monitoring entails looking for an *absence* of expected traffic. Thus, one could natively assume that we could look for drops in load on network elements to identify service outages. However, where in the network to look for such reductions in carried load is an intriguing challenge – traffic is regularly shifting around a mobile network, typically without any service impact. For example, activities such as load balancing or planned maintenance events could cause load changes on network devices, yet has no impact on customers' service experience. Figure 1b shows a load change on an Serving Gateway (SGW) node in an SGW pool during

(a) Customer care tickets indicating a service disruption

(b) Load reduction caused by load balancing

Figure 1: Network events

a load balancing event. Despite the load change on the individual SGW, there was no impact on users. Simply looking at the load of this SGW alone is insufficient to determine customer impact.

While detailed network performance metrics have been defined for mobile networks by 3GPP [3], and are being implemented by equipment vendors, these key performance indicators (KPIs) are not always sufficient to detect user impact either. For example, 3GPP defines *accessibility* as a KPI to measure the probability that a user will be provided with radio access network (RAN) resources (technically with a radio access bearer) on request. This metric can clearly provide insight concerning resource shortages in the radio access network. However, users might still be impacted, even when the RAN accessibility KPI is good, because users that lost radio coverage are not even accounted for in the KPI calculation or when the root cause of the service problems are beyond the RAN (e.g., congestion on a core network element). In other words, service disruption occurs when accessibility is bad, but accessibility being good does not necessarily imply that service is good.

Finally, in order to deliver the end-to-end service successfully, handset device, mobility network and application need to work together seamlessly. Thus the root cause of a service disruption could be well beyond the mobility network. For example, a firmware upgrade on a certain customer device model could result in incompatibility between equipment in the RAN (e.g., a radio network controller (RNC)), and the mobile devices that performed the firmware upgrade, thus resulting in a large number of devices not being able to access the network. Similarly, an update in the delivery protocol of a video streaming application could cause interoperability issues between application and network, which further leads to service disruptions. These types of service disruption are challenging for mobility network operators since there is little evidence of it on the network side.

In this paper, we argue that users' usage, or lack thereof, is a reliable indicator of service outages and severe performance degradations in a mobile network. By monitoring and analyzing users' usage, we are able to detect service disruptions that could be challenging for other event detection mechanisms.

3. APPROACH

With ABSENCE we propose to use historical customer usage data to predict expected usage that should be generated from customers under normal conditions. Any deviation from expected customer usage indicates an anomaly, which might be indicative of a service disruption. While this basic approach conceptually seems to make sense, it is not obvious that the method would be feasible in practice. For example: would customer usage predictions based on usage data be sufficiently accurate to allow anomaly detection? Given the number of mobile devices, the variety of services offered on mobile networks and the complexity of the mobile network infrastructure, is there a level of customer usage aggregation that would provide fidelity of detection fine-grained enough to detect silent failures at a granularity that is practically useful? Given that users in a mobile network are by design using the network while moving around, how should we deal with mobility?

In this section, we present our exploration of these questions using customer usage data from a large mobile network provider. Before describing our exploration we briefly describe the nature of Call Detail Records (CDRs) which, when aggregated, constitute the customer usage data used in ABSENCE.

3.1 Customer usage data

ABSENCE aggregates metrics from Call Detail Records (CDRs) to measure customer usage at different locations and application levels. These aggregates are calculated within ABSENCE using individual, anonymized CDRs. Note that these individual CDRs are only used internally to the system during the aggregation process, and no customer specific data (anonymized or otherwise) is ever exposed to a user of the ABSENCE system. Call Detail Records contain meta data about executed transactions across the mobile network (i.e., phone call, data session, access to voice mail etc.). Each record captures information that is needed for charging and debugging such as a time-stamp of the activity, device specific information (e.g., the international mobile station equipment identity (IMEI)), network related information concerning the activity (e.g., the sector(s) of a cell tower that the device is connected to), the duration of the activity (for voice services) or the volume of data the device downloads/uploads (for data services). Of critical importance for our approach, CDRs are generated in near real time: for Voice service a CDR record is generated right after a call finishes, for Data service a CDR record is generated whenever a PDP context is created and a new CDR record is created every hour if the data connection spans multiple hours. This allows CDRs to be used as a timely indicator of customer activity (or inactivity). Note that CDRs do not contain actual customers' short message, voice call or data content and ABSENCE only uses anonymized CDRs.

3.2 Usage prediction and aggregation size

The primary challenge in calculating aggregate customer usage information is to determine what level of aggregation is most effective to address the problem at hand. In considering the question of accuracy of predicting traffic volumes versus fidelity of anomaly detection, there exists an intuitive tradeoff: At one extreme one might attempt to use the usage data of each individual. While the network usage pattern of an individual user might show fairly predictable patterns, at this granularity a deviation from an expected pattern is clearly not a reliable indication of a service impairment. The user in question might simply have a change in their normal behavior, e.g., going on vacation. At the other extreme, the usage aggregated across all customers in the US is highly predictable. However, at this aggregation level, a service disruption that only impacts a relatively small number of users, e.g., those associated with a particular cell-tower, would not be visible at such a coarse grained data aggregation level. The challenge therefore is to find an aggregation level of usage data that is small enough that it can provide high fidelity of detection, but at the same time large enough to render stable usage patterns to allow for accurate prediction.

For example, Figure 2a and 2b show the amount of voice calls respectively made by a group of 70 and 3020 randomly chosen devices over the course of three weeks. The amount of usage on the smaller group is significantly less that in the larger group and the larger group also shows more stable day-to-day usage pattern between the different weeks.

To understand how the amount of usage affects the tradeoff between the stability of the usage patterns versus the fidelity of detection regardless of device specific, we conduct experiments to predict future usage based on historical usage with different amounts of aggregated data.

Experiment description: We selected a uniform random sampling of users to form different groups (with size ranging from 20 to 150,000 users) for Voice and LTE data service. We assumed that the aggregated service usage follows a weekly seasonal model and we used 16 weeks of data for our training. We constructed a weekly seasonal usage pattern using the additive decomposition technique described in Section 4. The seasonal pattern is the predicted usage for the future usage and the "noise" is the absolute distance between the usage and its seasonal data point. We then used the above seasonal usage pattern to predict another week of usage.

Metric: To quantify the prediction accuracy, we use the normalized noise ratio as the metric. We formally define the noise ratio in Section 4. In short, the noise ratio is the "noise" between the testing data and the training data normalized by the training data. Intuitively, if the usage of an hour deviates too much from the seasonal pattern, the noise of that hour is high and therefore results in a higher normalized noise ratio. We sampled the noise ratio at two regions of a time series (i.e., during the peak usage period 17:00-23:00 UTC and during the low usage period 03:00-11:00 UTC), and plot the noise ratio as a function of usage.

Results: Figure 2c shows the noise ratio as a function of the usage for LTE and voice. Overall, for a sufficient aggregation (i.e., above 1,000 of usage), the usage is quite predictable (i.e., the noise is about 10%). Moreover, the noise ratio is high for a small usage and reduces when the amount of usage increases. This matches the intuition that the usage of an individual user is less predictable than the aggregated usage of a group of users. The figure also suggests that after a certain amount of usage data, the predictability of an aggregation does not increase significantly. This suggests that the size of an aggregation should not be too large for both good predictability and high sensitivity, e.g., if we monitor usage of an entire city as an aggregation, a failure that impact only a single ZIP code area might not cause a significant enough drop on the total usage for a system to detect.

3.3 Practical user aggregation

In this section we consider the question of how groups of users can be selected in practice. While network and service failures can be highly diverse in their impact scope, the mobile network design and operational practice would inherently cause the service failures to be localized to geographically close-by regions and/or user devices with some common hardware or software. For example, rolling out a software upgrade on Radio Network Controllers (RNCs) would typically take place in a few geographical regions, and the upgrade may introduce an unexpected compatibility problem with certain phone models that was not captured by the RNC equipment vendor during lab testing. As another example, a software bug in a packet data network gateway (PGW) may cause the service that the PGW supports (e.g,. visual voice mail) becomes unusable, and all service requests originated from certain geographical regions that are routed toward this PGW are affected. Hence, grouping users geographically and by device hardware and software and tracking usage by different service features would have the best chance of capturing service failures.

Geographical hierarchy: In this grouping method, we utilize the geographical hierarchy in the ZIP-code system to group users. We use the ZIP-code hierarchy for three reasons: (i) the ZIP-code system was designed for efficient postal delivery and therefore each ZIP-code naturally covers a sufficient and relatively equal amount of users, (ii) the ZIP-code hierarchy is geographically driven and the structure of the ZIP-code has geographical meanings, (iii) by utilizing the ZIP-code hierarchy, the system can quickly scale up and down the size of aggregation based on the structure of the ZIP-code. I.e., groups of states, states, large cities etc. Moreover, a ZIP code area is relatively large enough for sufficient usage prediction and small enough to obtain good sensitivity A ZIP code area also often belongs to either an urban or a rural area and therefore users in a same ZIP code often have the same usage pattern. The detailed ZIP-code hierarchy is presented in Figure 3a.

Device type hierarchy: Under each geo-group (i.e, a node in Figure 3a), we divide devices into smaller groups based on operating systems (i.e, Android, IOS, Windows, BlackBerry OS), device make (i.e, Samsung, Apple, Nokia, etc), and device type (i.e, Samsung Galaxy S5, iPhone 4, Nokia Lumia 512, etc). This way the system can monitor not only geographical aggregations (e.g., Salt Lake City) but also specific device types in the area (e.g., all Samsung Galaxy S4 devices in Salt Lake City). As shown in Figure 3b, this device hierarchy can be applied at different levels in the geographical hierarchy.

3.4 Temporal usage aggregation

Recall that in Section 3.2 we found that in order to get good predictability the aggregations being monitored should have a large enough usage. (Figures 2c.) Daily network usage follows a well known diurnal pattern with well established busy and quiet times. During the network quiet time (i.e., after midnight), hourly usage is typically small and might not be sufficient for a good predictability. Figure 3c shows the CDF of hourly voice usage during low usage period (i.e., 03:00 UTC to 11:00 UTC) and peak usage period (i.e., 17:00 UTC to 23:00 UTC) of all ZIP codes. Almost 95% of the hourly usage measurements during low usage period are smaller than 500 which reduces the accuracy of prediction over hourly aggregations. I.e., at the ZIP code level, simply grouping usage into hourly bins results in insufficient usage to obtain a good prediction. In contrast, 48% of the hourly usage measurements during peak period are smaller than 500. Moreover, usage can also be low if, when using the geographical or device aggregation, the chosen aggregation level only has a small number of users (e.g., a ZIP code in a rural area or a ZIP code with a small number of subscribers).

This suggests the utility of grouping multiple hours during low usage period or of small spatial aggregations into a single temporal aggregation. Note that using longer time periods over which to do the usage aggregation would present higher accuracy at the cost of increasing the potential detection time, i.e., when the usage is low this technique increases the likelihood of detecting a failure after several hours while the conventional technique cannot detect it. Based on this observation we employ a *variable scale aggregation* strategy in Section 4 to improve the accuracy of prediction in ABSENCE.

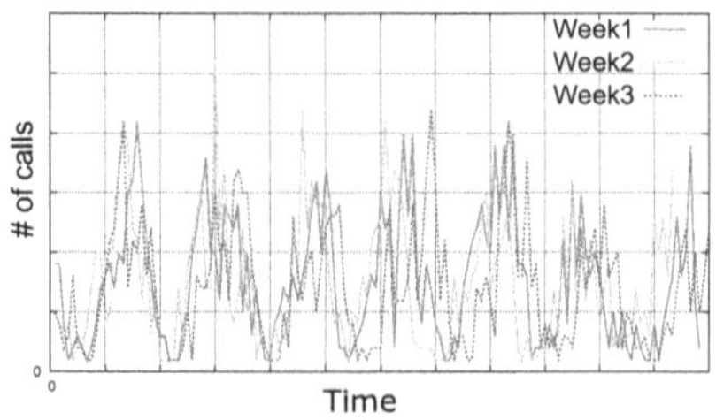

(a) Usage of group of 70 devices

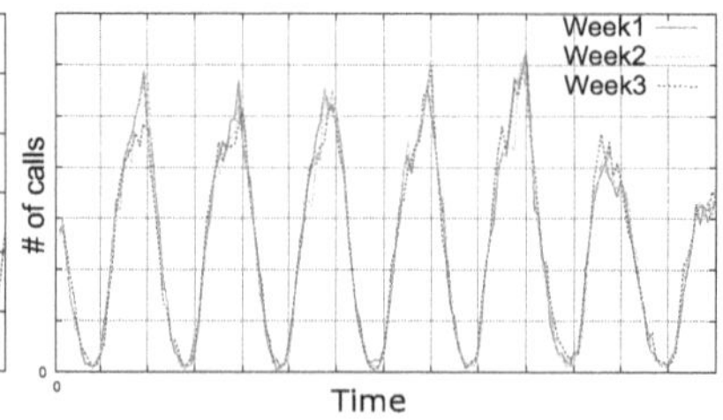

(b) Usage of group of 3020 devices

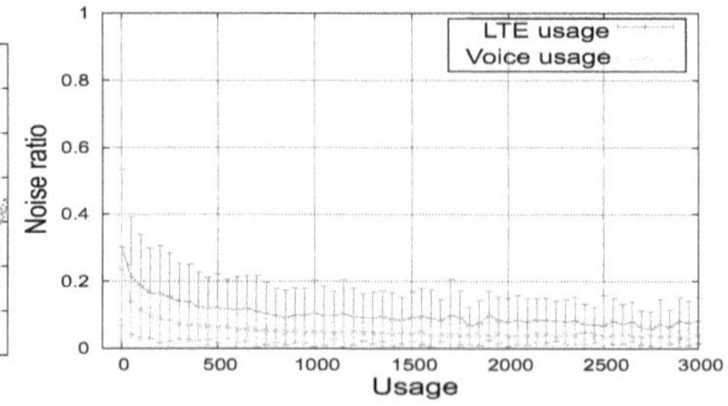

(c) Noise ratio of LTE and voice usage

Figure 2: Usage prediction and noise ratio

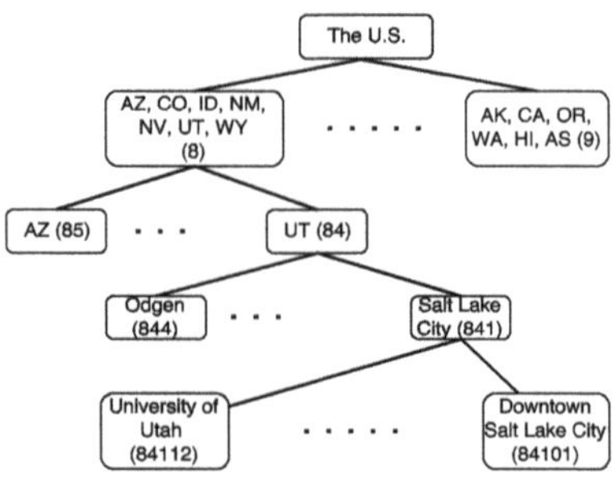

(a) Geographical hierarchy

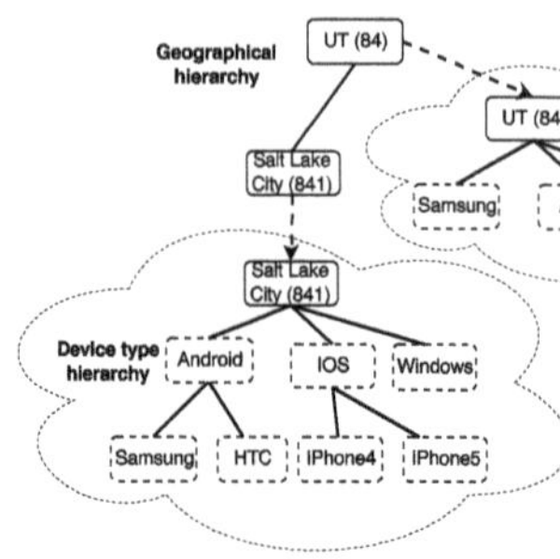

(b) Device hierarchy

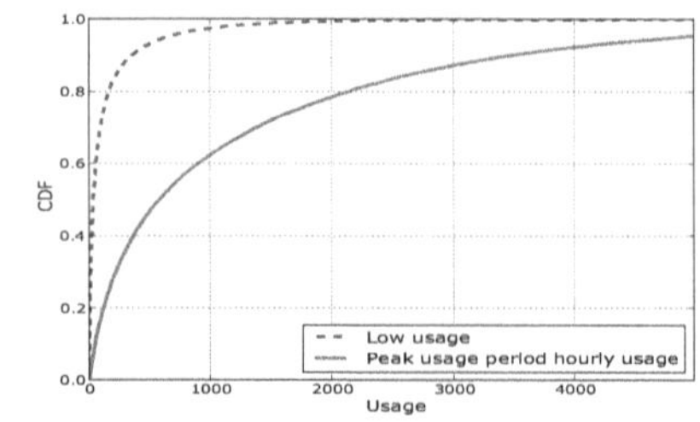

(c) CDF of hourly usage during low usage hours and peak usage hours across ZIP code aggregations

Figure 3: Hierarchies and hourly usage

3.5 Usage aggregation

ABSENCE uses aggregate service usages to detect service disruptions. In order to generate these aggregates, ABSENCE groups individual anonymized CDRs from a set of similar users. In ABSENCE, users are considered similar to each other if their mobile devices are from the same manufacturer/model or from the same zip-code. Aggregation usage from users with the same mobile device manufacturer/model is straight-forward. Due to space constraints, in the section, we only focus on how to group users based on the zip-code that they are in.

The inherent challenge stems from the mobility nature of mobile network users. Thus the set of users in a particular zip-code area, is changing over time. For example, the number of mobile users in a zip-code covering a business or educational campus might vary by thousands, or even tens of thousands, over the course of a day as workers/students arrive for the work day and leave again at the end of the day. In this section we explore mechanisms to deal with this inherent variability in ABSENCE.

Our approach hinges on the observation that for our purposes in ABSENCE, the exact location and mobility patterns of specific users at a particular point in time are not relevant. Rather, we are interested in knowing these properties with sufficient accuracy for a statistically meaningful aggregate of users. Moreover, approximated users' location could be used to localize geographical location of a failure to benefit root cause analysis. Thus, to calculate the zip-code level usage aggregates we simplify the internal operation of our ABSENCE system by simply aggregating over those customers that are typically in the given zip code for that time of day. Thus, within ABSENCE, for each (anonymous) user, we derive a *user zip-code profile* which approximates the user's mobility pattern at zip-code level over time. This user zip-coed profile is derived within ABSENCE using the anonymized CDRs. After calculating an individual user profile, the usage of an user is counted toward *his/her profiled zip-code* regardless of the current zip-code of the user. For example, during summer some students leave their campus for internship, those students' usage will be counted toward their approximated zip-code, i.e., their campus.

Zip-code level profiling: We evaluated a number of strategies to derive the user profiles. We assumed users' mobility pattern follows a daily pattern during weekdays and weekends (i.e., weekends are treated differently). We explored 2 parameters used to approximate users' zip code profile: how many zip-codes in a day a user has and the length of training data used for the approximation. Note that maintaining multiple zip-codes for a user results in more resources required to store the historical data and extract usage in real time. For example, if the user zip-code profile maintains 48 zip-codes for each user (i.e., 24 hours for weekdays and 24 hours for weekends) then there are 48 historical usage measurements for that user and each of them may be grouped differently (recall that ABSENCE groups usage based on user zip-code profile).

Due to space constraints we only describe the *home/work* approach which provided acceptable complexity/accuracy tradeoff and is what we use within ABSENCE. Our experience is that the fine-grained hourly user zip-code estimation does not improve the accuracy yet requires significant more computation. With the home-/work profile approach we make the simplifying assumption that user mobility can be approximated as follows: Depending on the time of day and day of week, a user is typically either at home or at work. Specifically, during week days and working hours, i.e., 9 a.m. to 7 p.m., the user is assumed to be at work. While during weekends and the remaining week day hours, the user is assumed to be at home. Given this assumption, what is required to derive a home/work profile is to determine the user's home and work base station. We make use of historical CDR data over a relatively long period of time, i.e., a couple of months, and simply use the most frequent base stations for the appropriate time (i.e., work or home) to determine the respective base stations for home and work hours. For example, if a user uses a base station most frequently during 9 a.m. to 7 p.m in a month period, his/her work hour zip-code profile will be that base station's zip-code. The home/work profile is clearly quite scalable requiring only two zip-codes (and associated historical information) to be maintained for each user.

Experiment: We evaluated the accuracy of the home/work zip-code level profile. We first derived the users' zip-code profiles as described above using historical CDRs. We varied the amount of the

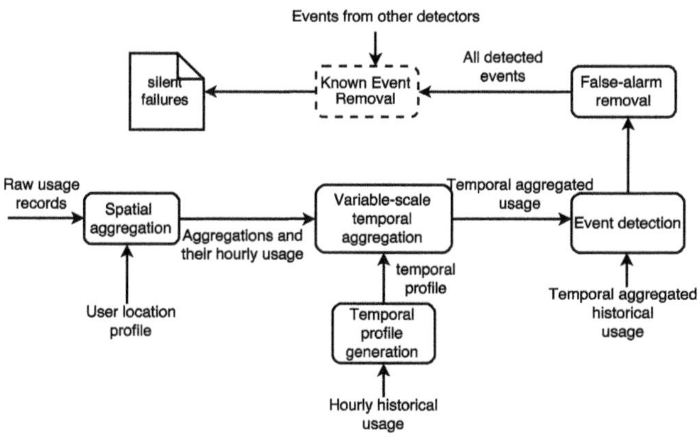

Figure 4: Data processing pipeline of ABSENCE

training data used to evaluate its impact on our approximation by 1,2,4, and 8 weeks. We then used the derived profiles to predict users' zip-code using the same amount of future CDRs. We measured the percentage of users' zip-codes that were correctly predicted (i.e., the hit rate - whether he/she makes calls in the estimated home/work zip-code) using the user profiles.

Results: Table 1 shows the results of this evaluation. As shown the duration of the historical (training) data does not significantly improve the accuracy of the approximation. Given the computational cost to consider this suggests that the home/work zip-code profile, with monthly updating, will be the most suitable for ABSENCE.

	1-week training	2-week training	4-week training	8-week training
Home/work	57.03%	57.92%	58.91%	56.05%

Table 1: Hit rate of zip-code approximations

4. SYSTEM OVERVIEW

In this section we describe ABSENCE and how the data is processed. The logic blocks of the system are shown in Figure 4. From left to the right, "raw usage data" (anonymized call detail records) go through a pipeline, which consists of multiple stages: spatial aggregation, variable-scale temporal aggregation, event detection and false-alarm removal before the detected events are shown to the operators. While we show this step for completeness in Figure 4, our current focus is on developing an effective usage-based detection system and we therefore do not consider this aspect. In Section 8 we do, however, validate ABSENCE against real service disruptions.

Spatial aggregation: We explored the need for spatial aggregation to ensure the accuracy of estimation in Section 3. As we described in Section 3.3, ABSENCE groups users based on their profiled zip-codes (Section 3.5): users that are geographically close are grouped together using their zip-code profile. Users in the same area are often being served by the same set of network elements and therefore likely to be impacted as a group. Moreover, events that impact a group of geolocated users are more likely to be actionable to network operators.

Temporal profile generation: After grouping the users, ABSENCE needs to extract the usage data of the group over time in order to detect abnormal usage for the group. As mentioned in Section 3.4, simply grouping usage into hourly bins is not optimal for usage predictability and anomaly detection. Instead, if the hourly usage is smaller than a predefined threshold (e.g., after midnight or the spatial aggregation is small), ABSENCE groups multiple hours of usage into a single bin in order to satisfy the usage threshold.

To realize this, ABSENCE needs a *temporal profile* for each spatial aggregation to do the grouping. ABSENCE assumes a weekly seasonality for the aggregations, i.e., the usage of an aggregation repeats every week. To generate the temporal profile, ABSENCE first uses hourly historical data to find a regressed weekly time series such that every data point in the regressed weekly time series is the *median* of the historical data points. Note that the historical time series and the regressed weekly time series consist of hourly usages. Having calculated the regressed weekly time series, ABSENCE then runs a greedy algorithm (Algorithm 1) that groups consecutive hours together until the total usage is larger than a predefined threshold (i.e., K in algorithm 1) and repeats this until all the hours in the weekly time series are grouped. If the last temporal bin of a week appears to be too small then it will be combined with the first hours of the following week until the threshold K is satisfied. The output of the algorithm is a *temporal profile* which has each temporal bin is at least the predefined amount of usage. Note that ABSENCE needs to run this training process only once every several months given that the *temporal profile* of the aggregation is usually stable.

Variable-scale temporal aggregation: After obtaining the *temporal profile* for each spatial aggregation, ABSENCE uses the profile and the hourly time series from the spatial aggregation to create a variable-scale time series. The output of the *variable-scale temporal aggregation* is a time series which has multiple temporal granularities and each data point satisfies a predefined usage threshold. This time series is used for *event detection*. We compare this variable-scale approach with the plain hourly temporal aggregation in Section 7.1. Note that ABSENCE currently aggregates usage data on an hourly basis at the finest granularity.[1]

Algorithm 1 Generate temporal profile

Input: Weekly regressed usage time series $T = (t_0, t_1, ..., t_{167})$ for 168 hours in a week, threshold K.
Output: Temporal profile j and $P = (p_0, p_1, ..., p_j)$ as the starting hour of j continuous segments of each profile bin

Initialize: $i \leftarrow 0$, $accumulate\_usage \leftarrow 0$, $j \leftarrow 0$, $tag \leftarrow 0$
while $i < 167$ **do**
  $accumulate\_usage \leftarrow accumulate\_usage + t_i$
  if $\sum(accumulate\_usage) \geq K$ **then**
    $p_j \leftarrow tag$, $accumulate\_usage = 0$, $j \leftarrow j+1$, $tag \leftarrow i$
  end if
  $i \leftarrow i+1$
end while
if $j == 0$ **then**
  return 0, ()
else
  if *accumlate_usage* $== 0$ **then**
    return j, P
  else
    {remainder wrapping around to the beginning of the week}
    $p_0 \leftarrow tag$
    return j, P
  end if
end if

Event detection: After generating the *variable-scale* usage time series of a group, ABSENCE appends the usage with the corresponding *variable-scale* historical usage and feeds the entire time series into a time series decomposition and event detection module that analyzes the time series and outputs abnormal events. Due to the large number of time series that needs to be processed, ABSENCE adopts the additive time series decomposition approach, which is a light-weight time series analysis algorithm and has been found very effective in modeling economic data and recently in network

[1] While an hour might seem long from the perspective of detecting a network outage, it does represent a reasonable tradeoff in the context of network operations scale.

traffic as well [23]. At a high level, the time series decomposition technique de-constructs a given time series into the secular trend component ($\{T_t\}$), the seasonal component ($\{S_t\}$), and the noise component ($\{N_t\}$) [8]. In the additive model, the original time series ($\{V_t\}$) is the summation of these three components.

Figure 5 (b), (c), (d) show the corresponding components for the time series in Figure 5 (a). The general idea of time series decomposition is very simple – with a specified seasonality window W, secular trend can be obtained through smoothing over long term (multiples of W), i.e., by *centered moving average*:

$$T_t = \sum_{i=-W}^{W-1} V_{t+i}/2W$$

Note that to be able to decompose the *variable-scale* time series, the seasonality window W here is set to the number of temporal aggregations of the *temporal profile* generated, i.e., j in Algorithm 1, and W varies for different spatial aggregations.

The seasonal trend can be obtained by averaging the phase value (after removing secular trend) across seasons, i.e., by *seasonal moving average*:

$$S_t = \sum_{i=0}^{K} V_{t-iW} - T_{t-iW}$$

where K is the number of seasonal windows contained in the historical data. And the remainder becomes the noise component:

$$N_t = V_t - T_t - S_t$$

Note that time series decomposition can be applied to analyzing both long range historical data and in a moving window fashion for the recent data (as new data is appended to the time series).

In our approach, we further model the noise components, N_t, at different phases as zero-mean Gaussian variables with different variance, $\sigma^2_{t|W}$, where the phase $t|W$ represents t mod W. We tag the corresponding time series value, V_t, as anomalous (critical value 1.96 at 95% confidence interval) if

$$|N_t/\sigma_{t|W}| > 1.96 \quad (1)$$

This is consistent with classic anomaly detection techniques. We also apply an iterative process such that we remove the anomalous points in the previous iteration from the trends and noise variance computation, which makes our approach robust to bad data/known anomalies.

An example of how the event detection works is shown in Figure 5. The two dips (green dots) in Figure 5 (a) correspond to the two dips in the noise component in Figure 5 (d) (red solid line) and those two dips are smaller than the lower 95% confidence interval of the noise component at the points (blue dashed line). This results in two detected anomalies in the time series.

5. IMPLEMENTATION

Processing the anonymized CDRs is computational intensive (e.g., hundreds of millions of records every hour for data service and tens of millions of records every hour for voice service) and normal serial processing methodologies will not be scalable. Since CDRs can be processed independently, we use a Hadoop Map-Reduce cluster to process the data in parallel to speed up the process.

Running environment: As shown in Figure 6, ABSENCE consists of four components: historical usage retrieval, hourly usage retrieval, time series processing and user location profile retrieval. ABSENCE runs on two environments: usage retrieval is done on a Hadoop cluster and time series processing is done "locally". The

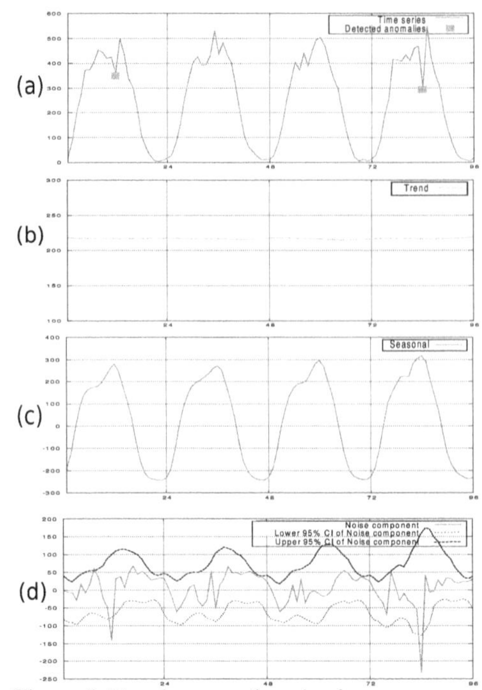

Figure 5: Trend, seasonal, and noise components

Hadoop cluster hosting ABSENCE consists of 100 nodes each with 32 cores CPU and 128GB RAM and runs on a HDFS file system. The local environment is a single node in the Hadoop cluster.

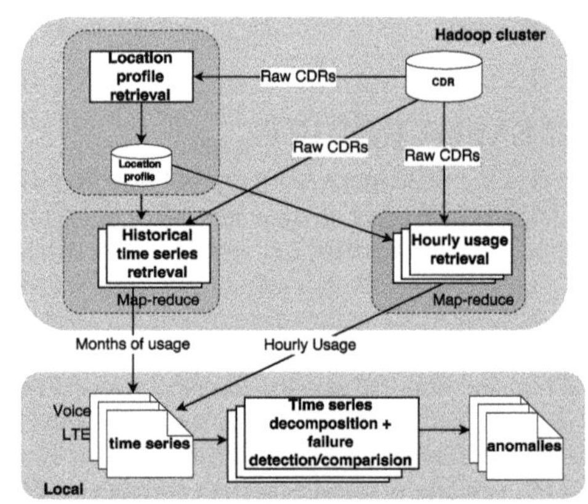

Figure 6: ABSENCE components

Historical/hourly usage retrieval component: We use Apache Pig (pig.apache.org), a platform that offers a high-level language for expressing map-reduce programs, for the usage retrieval components. The hourly usage retrieval component wakes up every hour to extract the usage of the last hour while the historical usage retrieval component is triggered every month to extract the usage of the last months that is used as a historical usage baseline of the coming month. The output of the historical/hourly usage retrieval component is transferred to a local machine for time series processing.

User location profile retrieval: We build the user location profile retrieval using native Hadoop Map-reduce. The location profile retrieval component is triggered every month to construct the latest location profile that is used for the following month. The user location profile is stored on the Hadoop HDFS file system as the usage aggregation components need the information. (Figure 6).

Time series processing component: This component is located locally on a single node in the Hadoop cluster. The component consists of light-weighted modules such as the time decomposition module, the anomaly detection module, false-alarm removal module etc.

6. EVALUATION SETUP

Obtaining ground truth about service disruptions is inherently difficult. (We do, however, evaluate ABSENCE against known service disruptions in Section 8.1.) To allow a systematic evaluation of our approach we introduced synthetic service disruptions into data obtained from a US mobile provider.

6.1 Data overview

We used CDR data collected in a large US mobile network from July 2014 to December 2014 in our evaluation. We used all 6 months worth of data to build up the historical data used in ABSENCE. With 6 months of historical data and the weekly seasonal model, we maintain $6 * 4 = 24$ usage histories for each of the nodes in our geographical hierarchy to use as reference points for anomaly detection in current usage data. This amount of historical usage data is sufficient to maintain acceptable confidence intervals for the time decomposition algorithm. The total amount of data used in our evaluation is 45 TB. The volume of collected CDR data varies from 15-20 GB per hour, depending on user activity, with the monthly volume of 7-8 TB. For the synthetic evaluations presented below, we excluded a week's worth of data from the 6 months data set and used those days as "current usage data" in which the synthetic failures were introduced.

6.2 Synthetic service disruptions

To allow for a systematic evaluation of ABSENCE we emulate service disruptions due to both the network and the device failures. ABSENCE performs service disruption detection by identifying changes in the expected usage data. As such, to emulate both network and device failures, our approach is to *remove* the corresponding data (i.e., data that would disappear if the failure had occurred) from the CDR data for each synthetic scenario.

We mimic *network* failures at the granularity of a base station, i.e., when a base station is down, the service at that base station is lost. In the CDR data, every call record is associated with a list of base stations that served the call, i.e., the "serving list". When we emulate the failure of a base station, we use the serving list to remove call records associated with the base station in question.

We similarly emulate *device* failures by removing all call records associated with the emulated device failure. For example, a firmware bug could affect all devices from one manufacturer after a firmware update and prevent users from making calls even when the network is healthy. To introduce this type of failures, we remove call records with the device make/model associated with the emulated failure.

To introduce different failure scenarios for our evaluation, we combine the basic network and device failures described above with *geographic* information at different granularities and a *severity* factor to be applied. We vary the severity of a failure by failing different numbers of base stations or devices in the chosen aggregation, e.g., 10% of base stations in a ZIP for less severe failures and 100% of base stations in a ZIP for large outages.

6.3 Sensitivity to failure impact

ABSENCE detects anomalies based on variations in the expected normal usage patterns. A key question to answer with our evaluation of this approach is what degree of impact ABSENCE will be able to detect. To answer this question we investigated two factors: (i) failure impact ratio and (ii) absolute impact. Failure impact ratio is defined as the ratio of the total amount of usage reduction during the failure over the total amount of a normal usage, or

$$impact\ ratio = \frac{total\ usage\ reduction}{total\ normal\ usage}.$$

Absolute impact is defined as the total usage reduction during an injected or detected event. For example, if during a 5-hour event, 4,000 out of 5,000 calls were lost, the absolute impact is 4,000 and the impact ratio is 80%. The smaller the impact ratio is, the more challenging it is for an anomaly detection system to identify it. The larger the absolute impact is, the more important it is for operators to pay attention to it. We use both metrics in evaluating ABSENCE regarding the sensitivity and performance in detecting anomalies.

6.4 Failure scenarios

We consider two different geographical aggregation levels: city and ZIP-code area. In term of devices, we consider two popular mobile-device manufacturers namely A and B and two popular mobile-device models, A-1 and B-1. Combinations of the two geographical aggregations and two specific device types allow a variety of test scenarios: city (e.g., all phones in Los Angeles), city+device make (e.g., all A phones in Los Angeles), city + device model (e.g., all A-1 phones in Los Angeles), ZIP code (all phones in ZIP code 07921), ZIP code + device make (e.g., all B phones in ZIP code 07921), etc. To come up with our final failure scenarios we consider three additional attributes: the type of service, the time, duration and the severity of the event (i.e., failure impact ratio).

In order to thoroughly evaluate ABSENCE we generate failure scenarios randomly based on different aspects we want to evaluate. Table 2 shows all aspects and the evaluation values from which we randomly selected to make up our failure scenarios. The table also shows an example scenario for each aspect.

We randomly chose 100 ZIP codes and 10 cities for the geographical aggregations to evaluate. We generated failures with different impacts by varying the amount of failed base stations when generating the failures, i.e., the impact ratio. There are 11 impact ranges each is 5% of impact ratio wide, i.e., [0%-5%], [5%-10%] etc.

We randomly picked 100 failures (i.e., 100 samples) for each impact range, e.g., we picked 100 failures that have [10%-15%] of impact, 100 failures that have [15%-20%] of impact, etc., until all the impact ranges are covered. Note that for each impact range the randomly generated failures should be uniformly distributed across attributes. For example, 100 failures in the (ZIP code + device make) aggregation could happen either to all A devices or B devices and could last for 1,2,3 or 6 hours etc. This way, the set of generated failures should uniformly cover many failure types across attributes and therefore ABSENCE would have a set of diverse failure scenarios to evaluate against.

After generating this "pool" of failure scenarios and using ABSENCE to detect them, we gather the results and break it down into different dimensions based on the aspects in Table 2. In this manner we generated a total of 11,000 synthetic failures across our evaluation space. We present our evaluation results in Section 7.

6.5 Evaluation Metrics

We evaluated ABSENCE using two metrics: detection rate (%) and loss ratio (%). Detection rate is defined as the ratio of correctly detected failures (true positive,TP) over the total amount of introduced failures (true positive,TP + false negative,FN).

$$Detection\ Rate(\%) = \frac{TP}{TP+FN}.$$

Detection rate quantifies how effective ABSENCE is. The higher the detection rate, the more effective ABSENCE.

Aspect	Evaluated values	Example of a failure
Geographical aggregation	100 ZIPs, 10 cities	All devices in L.A. fails
Device make	A, B	All A devices in ZIP 07921 fails
Device model	A-1, B-1	All A-1 devices in L.A. fails
Service	Voice, LTE	All devices in ZIP 07921 can't make calls or can't access the Internet
Start time	quiet period (06:00 UTC), busy period (20:00 UTC)	All devices in ZIP 07921 fails starting from 20:00 UTC
Duration	1, 2, 3, 6, 12 hours for busy; 8,10,12 hours for quiet	Voice service in ZIP 07921 outages for 8 hours starting from 06:00 UTC
Severity impact	0% to 55% of the total usage	A failure that causes 20% reduction of the normal usage in ZIP 07921

Table 2: Aspects and evaluated values of generated failures

Loss ratio is defined as the ratio of the total net-loss *until detection* over the total amount of normal usage during the failure.

$$Loss\ Ratio(\%) = \frac{netloss\ until\ detection}{normal\ usage\ during\ failure}.$$

For example, if the normal usage during a failure is 5,000 and ABSENCE detects the failure when 1,000 calls get dropped then the loss ratio will be 1/5 (20%). In short, for a long lasting failure, the lower the loss ratio means the faster ABSENCE detected the failure.

7. EVALUATION RESULTS

7.1 Variable-scale decomposition

The variable-scale decomposition technique is designed to ensure that ABSENCE uses sufficient usage data to enable accurate detection. To evaluate the effectiveness of this approach we evaluated ABSENCE with and without the variable-scale decomposition technique. We focused our evaluation on ZIP code level aggregations during quiet hours.We introduced failures starting from 03:00 UTC (typically the start of network quiet time) and lasting for 8 hours for voice service. The impact of the failures is in the range of 5% to 100%. We ran the two decomposition techniques (with and without the variable-scale mechanism) over the same set of failures and compare the detection rate of the two.

As shown in Figure 7a, the variable-scale decomposition technique improves the detection rate during the low usage period by *8-10x*, e.g., ABSENCE detected 91% as opposed to 10% of failures that affects more than 2,000 calls in 8 hours respectively with and without the technique.

7.2 Synthetic Failure Evaluation

Overall results. As shown in Table 3 first row, out of 11,000 introduced failures for both Voice and LTE service, ABSENCE was able to detect 9,676 with a detection rate of 88.0%. For failures with an impact larger than 10%, ABSENCE was able to detect 97.7% (8,064 out of 8,254 failures), and for failures that are larger than 20% of impact, ABSENCE detected 99.0% (6,189 out of 6,254 failures).

Table 3 breaks down the detection rate by different aggregations. Overall ABSENCE detected 98% of failures that have more than 10% impact across different aggregations from large aggregations (e.g., city level - all users in LA) to smaller aggregations (e.g., (ZIP code + make) level - all Device A or B devices in a ZIP code). Next, we look into different factors (i.e., failure impact ratio, absolute impact) that affects the detection rate of ABSENCE. With each factor, we also break down the results into different aggregations.

Failure impact ratio and detection rate. We would like to understand the effectiveness of ABSENCE as a function of the severity of failures, i.e., the impact ratio, for different failure scenarios.

(i) Overall results: Figure 7b shows the overall detection rate as a function of the impact ratio of failures across all aggregations and service types. ABSENCE was able to detect 96% of failures that have a 15%-20% of impact across all aggregations, services and device types. For outages (with 50% of impact or more severe), ABSENCE detected 100% of them. For failures that are less severe (i.e., smaller than 10% of impact) ABSENCE detected 20%-67% of them.

(ii) Failures at different aggregation levels: Figure 7c shows ABSENCE's detection rate *for failures with small impact* at different aggregation levels: city, city + device make, city + device model, ZIP code, ZIP code + device make. Overall, for failures with more than 15% of impact, ABSENCE is equally effective across aggregations with a detection rate of 94% or better. This trend continues for failures with higher impact and we omit the results due to space constraints. For failures with lower impact (0%-5% and 5%-10%), ABSENCE's detection rate reduces to between 5% and 80%. For those failures, ABSENCE was slightly more effective for large aggregations such as *city* and *city + device make.*

(iii) Failures happen to different service types: Figure 7d shows ABSENCE's detection rate for failures occurring in LTE and voice services. For failures with more than 15% of impact, ABSENCE's detection rate is high for both voice and LTE (i.e., around 97%). For less severe failures (i.e., less than 15% of impact), ABSENCE detected failures to LTE service slightly better than voice service.

(iv) Failures happen to different mobile device types: Figure 7e shows ABSENCE's detection rate for failures associated with two popular device makes (A and B) and two popular phone models (A-1 and B-1) at city level. ABSENCE detected around 94% of failures with 15%-20% of impact associated with those mobile device makes and models.

(v) Failures break down by duration: Figure 7f shows ABSENCE's detection rate for failures with different durations. Overall ABSENCE is equally sensitive across durations of the failures: it detected about 95% of failures with $15-20\%$ of impact for both short and long-lasting failures. For failures with 0%-10% impact, ABSENCE detected 10%-63% of them.

Absolute impact and detection rate. To understand how effective ABSENCE is in detecting failures ranked by the absolute size, we looked into ABSENCE's detection rate as a function of the absolute impact of the failures. Figure 7g shows that for LTE ABSENCE detected 94% of failures that cause more than 2,000 PDN connections to be dropped at the ZIP code level and 96% of failures at the (ZIP code + device make) level. We omit similar results for voice service because of space constraints.

Loss ratio of detected failures. To understand how quickly ABSENCE can detect long-lasting failures, we obtained the loss ratio (Section 6) of detected failures that last at least 6 hours for all services across different aggregations. We are interested particularly in long-lasting failures because those failures often cause larger impact and early detections mean lower impact.

Figure 7h shows the CDF of the loss ratio of detected failures during quiet hours (i.e., low usage period) and busy hours (i.e., peak usage period). In general, during busy hours 98% of the

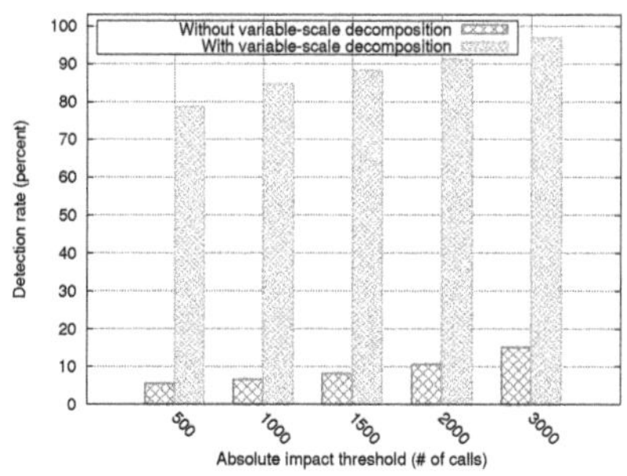

(a) Failure detection during low usage: with and without the variable-scale decomposition

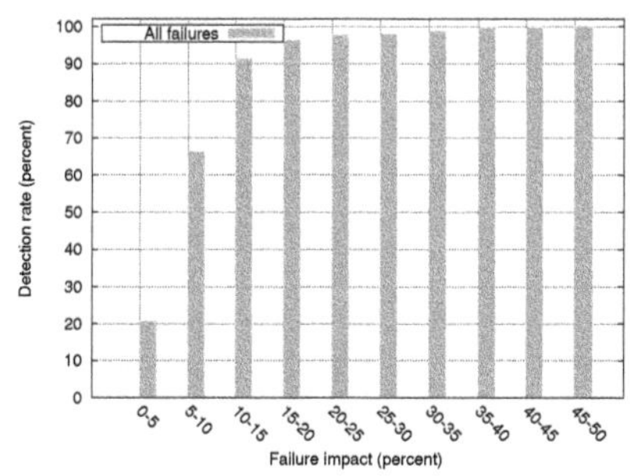

(b) Overall detection rate vs. impact ratio

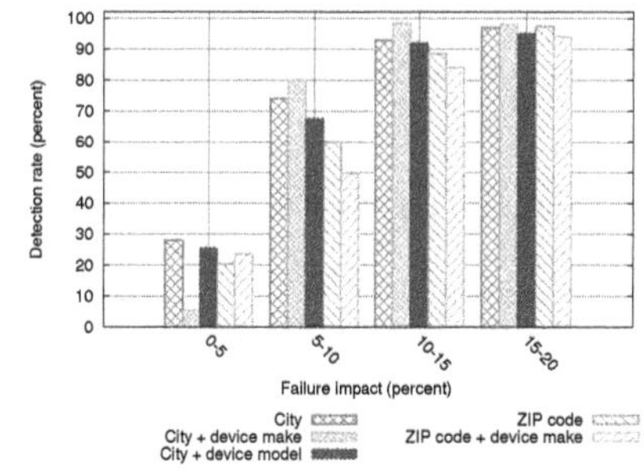

(c) Small failures at different aggregation levels

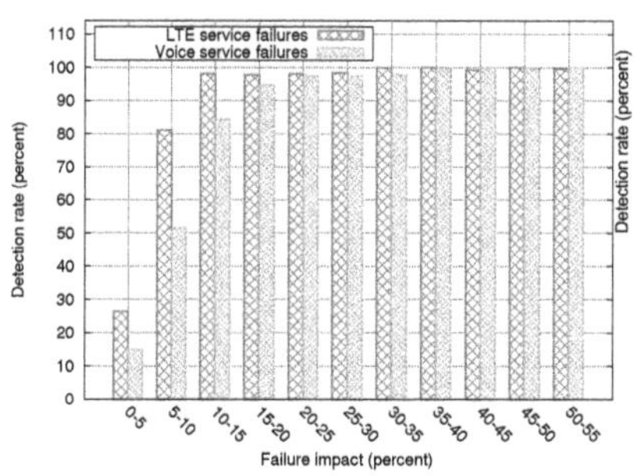

(d) Failures for different service types

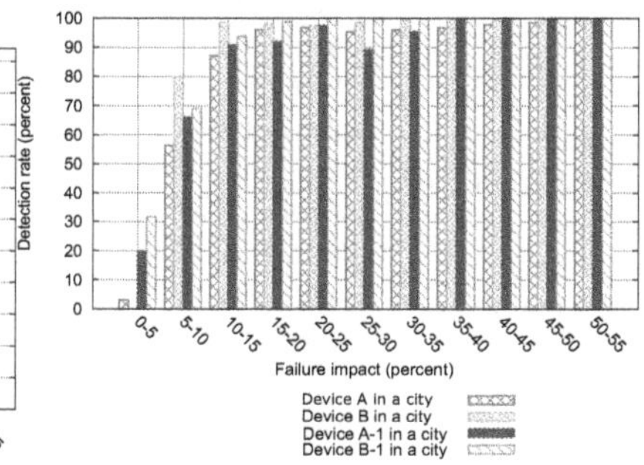

(e) Failures for popular device make/model (city level)

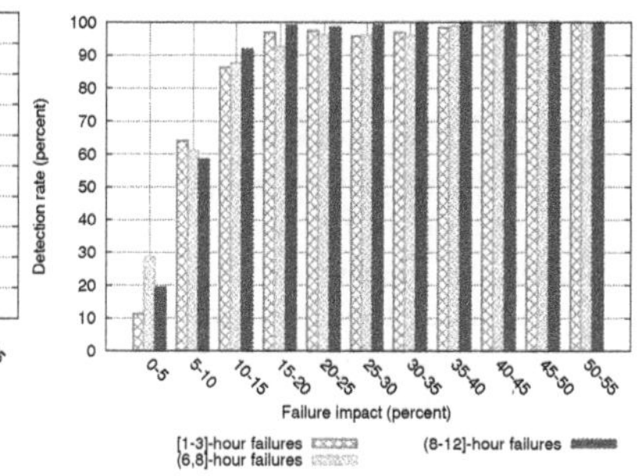

(f) Failure duration

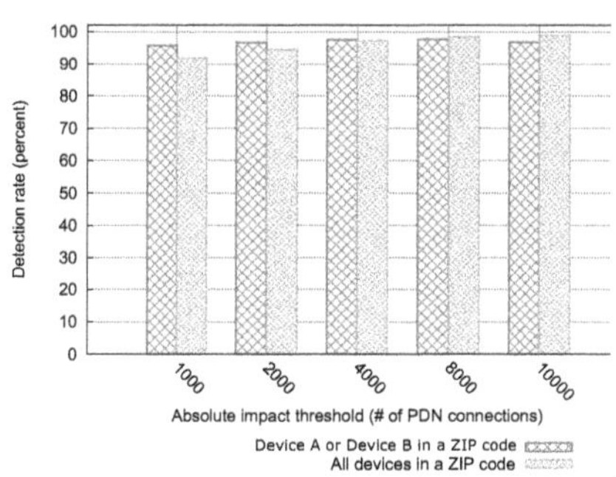

(g) Absolute impact - LTE service

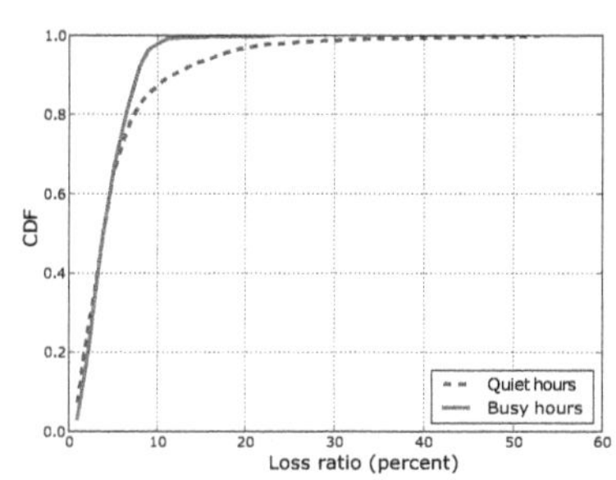

(h) Loss ratio of detected failures that last for at least 6 hours

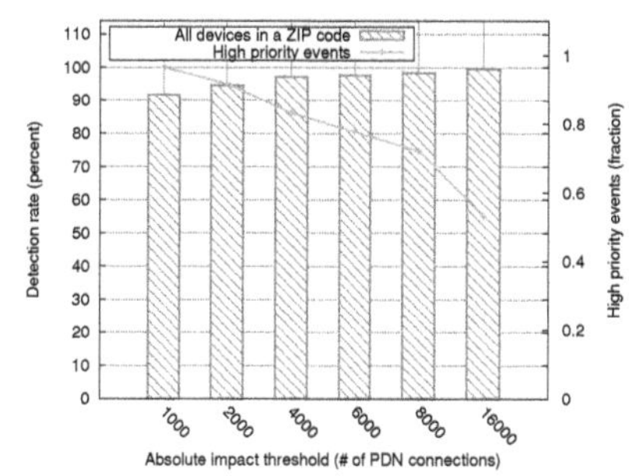

(i) "Cut-off" threshold - LTE service at ZIP code level

Figure 7: Detection rates

Break down	Aggregation	All failures	≥ 10% of impact	≥ 20% of impact
Total	All aggregations	88.0%	97.7%	99.0%
Geographical break down	City	89.6%	98.1%	99.0%
	Zip code	87.5%	97.8%	99.4%
Service break down	Voice	85.2%	96.5%	98.7%
	LTE	90.7%	98.9%	99.3%
Geographical + device break down	City + device make (e.g., A devices in LA)	88.9%	99.0%	99.3%
	City + device model (e.g., A-1 devices in LA)	88.3%	97.3%	98.6%
	ZIP code + device make (e.g, A-1 devices in 07921)	85.5%	96.3%	98.6%

Table 3: Overall results break down by different aggregations

failures were detected when there were less than 10% of the total loss happens (i.e., if the issue is fixed at the detection time, 90% of the usage would be recovered for 98% of the failures). During quiet hours, 90% of the failures were detected when there were less than 10% of loss. Given that the detected failures are at least 6 hours, 10% loss suggests that the failures are mostly detected right after the first hour of the failures.

Impact based event prioritization. Because of resource constraints, in an operational setting providers typically need to prioritize the events that they investigate. Because it is inherently usage based, ABSENCE lends itself to an "operational knob" that operators can tune to distinguish large impact events from the small impact ones, so that they can rapidly respond to more severe conditions. Here we evaluate the tradeoff through such a knob, in the form of a "cut-off" threshold – the threshold above which events are defined as of high priority – between the number of high priority events and the detection rate (rate of high impact events to be included in the high priority list).

Figure 7i shows the detection rate (Y1-axis) and the fraction of synthetic events that are of high priority (Y2-axis) as functions to the threshold for the ZIP code level. We observe that if we only focus on events that have an absolute impact of over 4,000 records, ABSENCE achieves the detection rate of 97% among the 82% of the events.

Implications: Our evaluation of ABSENCE shows that: (i) ABSENCE has a very high detection rate across all scenarios for failures with medium to high impact (i.e., above 15%). (ii) ABSENCE can detect failures relatively quickly (i.e., has a low loss ratio), thus reducing the impact of failures. (iii) Prioritizing events based on the absolute number of missing records provides a simple operational knob that enables operators to tune the number of high priority events generated by ABSENCE. These results suggest the practical feasibility of using ABSENCE to perform service disruption detection at the scale of modern mobile networks.

8. OPERATIONAL VALIDATION

In this section, we validate service impacting events detected in the operational data via ABSENCE with known historical service outages. Specifically, we use events that resulted in anomalous volumes in customer care calls as our known customer impacting network events. Customers can call into customer care centers to report service issues and to discuss other concerns. The vast majority of customer calls relate to individual customer concerns - they may be the result of individual customer device issues or user errors, for example. However, in some situations, these customer calls may be the result of a broader service impacting event. Network, device type or application disruptions can thus result in a spike in the number of customer complaints. These events - spikes in customer care calls - are captured in a database along with their associated underlying network/device/application root cause, and are used here to provide a source of ground truth of service disruptions that we use to compare with those detected by ABSENCE.

We first attempt to validate service disruptions detected by ABSENCE with customer complaint events over a corresponding time period. We then investigate a number of specific use cases in more detail to verify ABSENCE functionality.

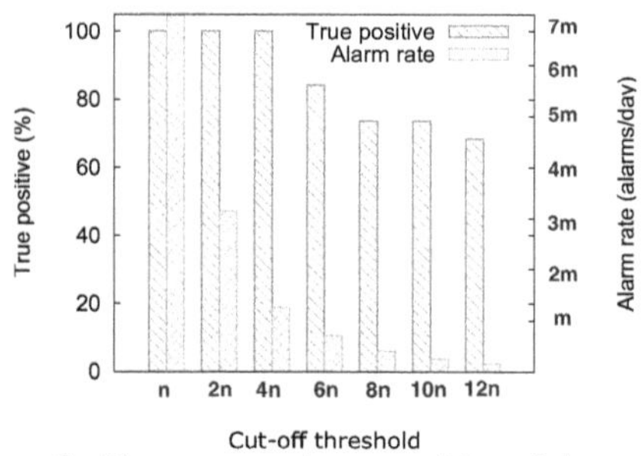

Figure 9: Alarm rate and true positive of ABSENCE

8.1 Comparison with customer complains

From the customer care database, we can extract customer complaint events at a market level, i.e., which market the event is in and the event's start/end time. We obtained a list of a 19 such events from the customer care database that happened to Voice and LTE data services. Operations had confirmed that each of these was a true service disruption. We then attempted to detect these with ABSENCE using CDR aggregates for the corresponding dates.

We ran ABSENCE to get a list of detected events at the ZIP code level and compared the detected events with the 19 customer complaint events mentioned above. Customer complaint events were aggregated at the market level (i.e., a market typically consists of several geographically close cities), while we were detecting events at the ZIP code level. As a result, before performing the comparison, we mapped the ZIP code of ABSENCE detected events to the corresponding market. We considered a *match* between an event detected by ABSENCE and a customer complaint event if the two events are spatially and temporally matching. Using this approach, ABSENCE was able to detect *all* 19 customer complaint events. We noted that ABSENCE also detected possible service disruptions that are not included in the customer care database. Due to lack of ground truth available in this study, it is challenging to investigate these further.

8.2 Alarm rate and true positive rate

ABSENCE detected events that are not included in the customer care database. Due to lack of ground truth it is challenging to determine whether those events are false positives. However, to make ABSENCE practical, the number of events per day (i.e., alarm rate) should be reasonable for an operations team to handle while the true positive rate should be maintained. To adjust the alarm rate, ABSENCE uses different cut-off thresholds (i.e., amount of usage impacted per hour) to filter out events with relatively small impact, i.e., if the impact of an event is smaller than a certain threshold, the event will not trigger an alarm. We used the 19 events in the customer database as the ground truth for the true positive rate and varied the cut-off threshold to observe the alarm rate of ABSENCE. Figure 9 shows the alarm rate and the true positive rate as a function of the cut-off thresholds. As we can see, both the alarm rate and the true positive decrease as the cut-off threshold increases. To protect proprietary information, we show the alarm rate and the cut-off threshold as relative numbers. If ABSENCE only triggers alarms for events which impact greater than $4n$ calls/PDN connections per hour, then the operations team will need to investigate around m such events per day and ABSENCE detects all of the 19 events above (i.e., 100% true positive). We confirmed that m is manageable by Operators and thus ABSENCE is practical in an operational environment.

8.3 Use cases

In this section we explore a number of specific use cases where ABSENCE was able to detect anomalies that also showed up in the customer care database. In this section, ABSENCE used $4n$ as the cut-off threshold for the number of calls or PDN connection per hour.

(i) Voice service in a large metropolitan area:

This failure was on the voice service in several ZIP codes of a large metropolitan area. Users in these areas were not able to receive calls from landline devices. The event started at 16:00 UTC on a given Tuesday according to the customer ticket data. Figure 8a shows the time series in UTC of the historical usage data for voice services of one of the affected ZIP codes (dashed line) for previous Tuesdays and the abnormal usage on the date of the service disruption (red solid line). ABSENCE was able to detect an anomalous event at 16:00 UTC (red point) as the usage falls significantly outside of the range of the normal historical usages.

(ii) Voice service in a large metropolitan area:

This failure was on the voice service in several ZIP code areas in another large metropolitan area. The failure was first evident in customer ticket volume at 12:00 UTC on a Friday according to the customer complaints and the reports by the operator. Figure 8b shows the historical usage (dashed lines) of previous Fridays and the usage of the day that the failure occurred (red solid line) for one of the affected ZIP code areas. As we can see, there are drops in the usage on the day of the failure and ABSENCE can detect the anomaly at 14:00 UTC (red point) – two hours after it commenced.

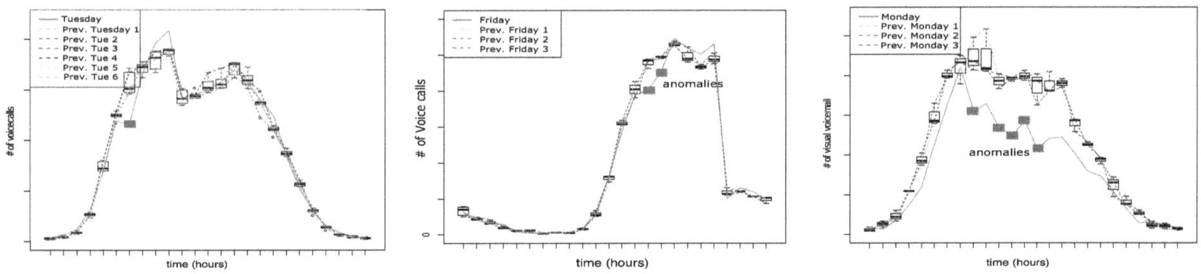

(a) Voice service anomaly: metro area 1 (b) Voice service anomaly: metro area 2 (c) Voicemail service anomaly

Figure 8: Use cases

Note that the sudden drop later in the day is due to the change in the number of users in the area according to the change of the zip-code profile.

(iii) Voice mail:

In this use case the failure happens to a much larger area (i.e, all ZIP codes in a large metropolitan area). This failure started around 18:00 UTC on a Monday and was associated with one of the operator's Voicemail services - a data service that is available to only a subset of user devices. This use case is an example of the failure of a particular service that impacted only particular device types within a given area. ABSENCE detected a series of anomalies happening to devices in the metropolitan area commencing at 18:00 UTC (when the failure itself commenced) (Figure 8c solid red line).

9. DISCUSSIONS

Special events: Special events and holidays may affect users' usage and mobility pattern, which can be challenging for a passive monitoring approach. For example, people make less calls on holidays, or during a sport event. Correlated usage reduction in large scale can cause ABSENCE to generate false positives. If users' service consumption does not change but their mobility pattern changes (e.g., gathering at a stadium and use the phones as normal), ABSENCE will not generate false positives because the location profile will handle this and their usages are counted toward the profile location regardless of where they are.

Metrics to use: ABSENCE uses number of calls and number of PDN connections as the metric for detecting service disruptions. Those two metrics could quantify users' experience in most cases, e.g., if a base station fails and users could not attach or make calls/create PDN connections. Potentially, there are other metrics that could be used such as duration of calls or number of Bytes downloaded/uploaded. These metrics would capture other types of failures. For example, a failure at the routing system in the network may cause voice calls to be routed to voice mail instead of reaching the callee. In this case the total duration of calls would be a better indicator of a potential service impairment worthy of investigation.

New services in Data network: Network operators may introduce new data services such as Wi-Fi offload. Such new services may affect the usage captured in the CDRs, as load is (deliberately) reduced. Since ABSENCE uses multiple months of historical usage as the baseline, if Wi-Fi offload skews the usage, the baseline will be rebuilt. After a sufficiently long period of training (typically 3-4 weeks if a weekly seasonal model is used), the new baseline will include the Wi-Fi offload and ABSENCE will be able to operate in the new environment.

10. RELATED WORK

There are quite a lot related work in the area of service disruption detection including both commercial systems such as Keynote [2] and Gomez [1] and various efforts by the research community [16, 11, 30, 28]. All of them share two limitations. First, their effectiveness are typically limited by the coverage of deployed probes. Second, they all need to inject unnecessary probing traffic to the system, which could affect legitimate users. In the contrast, ABSENCE detects service disruptions in a non-intrusive (passive) manner by purely depending on the existing traffic from real users.

Our work also relates to various mobile network performance studies. For example measurements from mobile devices have been used to study the performance of mobile networks [20]. Several studies have investigated protocol level performance aspects of mobile networks [14, 22, 19]. While these detailed performance aspects of mobile networks are related to our work, ABSENCE is a network management tool dealing with the operational health of a mobile network. As such ABSENCE is most related to various network operations tools [29, 17, 24, 26, 18]. A framework for network anomalies based on a principal component analysis approach has been proposed in [29]. A performance troubleshooting tool [17] and a service quality assessment mechanism [24] for IPTV networks have been developed. Service anomaly detection [26] and troubleshooting tools [18] have been developed for ISP networks. In contrast ABSENCE is focused on service disruption detection in mobile networks and deal with the specific mobility and scalability challenges of that environment. Production tools such as [7] is installed on user devices to collect users' service experience yet they are not available on most Samsung and iPhone popular models due to privacy issues. ABSENCE in contrast works for all device models without installing any software on the device.

11. CONCLUSION

We presented our work on ABSENCE, a service disruption detection system for mobile networks. ABSENCE makes use of customer usage data, in the form of aggregated and anonymized call detail records, to derive historical usage patterns for groups of customers. Appropriate selection of these groups results in stable and accurate predictions of usage patterns, allowing ABSENCE to detect deviations as possible service disruptions. We presented a data driven exploration of the design space. We performed a systematic evaluation of ABSENCE by introducing synthetic failures in data from an operational mobile network and compared ABSENCE's detection results with known ground truth events from the mobile network. ABSENCE is currently operating in a pre-production environment. Our future plans include integration of ABSENCE with the operator's production environment and fine tuning the parameters to improve the accuracy and utility of our approach in an operational setting.

12. ACKNOWLEDGMENTS

We would like to thank our anonymous reviewers and shepherd for their valuable comments. This research was supported in part by the National Science Foundation under grants 1305384 and 1302688.

13. REFERENCES

[1] Gomez, inc. website. `http://www.gomez.com/`.

[2] Keynote systems, inc. website. `http://www.keynote.com/`.

[3] 3GPP. Telecommunication management; Key Performance Indicators (KPI) for Evolved Universal Terrestrial Radio Access Network (E-UTRAN): Definitions. `http://www.3gpp.org/DynaReport/32450.htm`.

[4] AHUJA, S., RAMASUBRAMANIAN, S., AND KRUNZ, M. SRLG Failure Localization in All-Optical Networks Using Monitoring Cycles and Paths. In *INFOCOM 2008. The 27th Conference on Computer Communications. IEEE* (April 2008), pp. –.

[5] AMRUTKAR, C., HILTUNEN, M., JIM, T., JOSHI, K., SPATSCHECK, O., TRAYNOR, P., AND VENKATARAMAN, S. Why is my smartphone slow? on the fly diagnosis of underperformance on the mobile internet. In *Dependable Systems and Networks (DSN), 2013 43rd Annual IEEE/IFIP International Conference on* (June 2013), pp. 1–8.

[6] BOOKER, G., TORRES, J., GUIKEMA, S., SPRINTSON, A., AND BRUMBELOW, K. Estimating cellular network performance during hurricanes. *Reliability Engineering & System Safety 95*, 4 (2010), 337–344.

[7] CARRIERIQ. Carrier IQ, Inc. `http://www.carrieriq.com`.

[8] CHATFIELD, C. *The analysis of time series: an introduction*. CRC press, 2004.

[9] CISCO SYSTEMS. Cisco Visual Networking Index: Global Mobile Data Traffic Forecast Update, 2014-2019. *White Paper, February* (2015).

[10] DONG, W., GE, Z., AND LEE, S. 3G Meets the Internet: Understanding the performance of hierarchical routing in 3G networks. In *Teletraffic Congress (ITC), 2011 23rd International* (Sept 2011), pp. 15–22.

[11] FEAMSTER, N., ANDERSEN, D., BALAKRISHNAN, H., AND KAASHOEK, M. Measuring the effects of internet path faults on reactive routing. In *Proceedings of the 2003 ACM SIGMETRICS international conference on Measurement and modeling of computer systems* (2003), ACM, p. 137.

[12] GEMBER, A., AKELLA, A., PANG, J., VARSHAVSKY, A., AND CACERES, R. Obtaining in-context measurements of cellular network performance. In *Proceedings of the 2012 ACM conference on Internet measurement conference* (2012), ACM, pp. 287–300.

[13] GOYAL, M., RAMAKRISHNAN, K., AND CHI FENG, W. Achieving faster failure detection in OSPF networks. In *Communications, 2003. ICC '03. IEEE International Conference on* (May 2003), vol. 1, pp. 296–300 vol.1.

[14] HUANG, J., QIAN, F., GUO, Y., ZHOU, Y., XU, Q., MAO, Z. M., SEN, S., AND SPATSCHECK, O. An in-depth study of LTE: effect of network protocol and application behavior on performance. In *Proceedings of the ACM SIGCOMM 2013 conference on SIGCOMM* (2013), ACM, pp. 363–374.

[15] KALMANEK, C. R., MISRA, S., AND YANG, Y. R. *Guide to reliable internet services and applications*. Springer, 2010.

[16] KOMPELLA, R., YATES, J., GREENBERG, A., AND SNOEREN, A. Detection and Localization of Network Black Holes. In *INFOCOM 2007. 26th IEEE International Conference on Computer Communications. IEEE* (May 2007), pp. 2180–2188.

[17] MAHIMKAR, A., GE, Z., SHAIKH, A., WANG, J., YATES, J., ZHANG, Y., AND ZHAO, Q. Towards Automated Performance Diagnosis in a Large IPTV Network. In *Proceedings of the ACM SIGCOMM 2009 Conference on Data Communication* (New York, NY, USA, 2009), SIGCOMM '09, ACM, pp. 231–242.

[18] MAHIMKAR, A., YATES, J., ZHANG, Y., SHAIKH, A., WANG, J., GE, Z., AND EE, C. T. Troubleshooting chronic conditions in large IP networks. In *Proceedings of the 2008 ACM CoNEXT Conference* (2008), ACM, p. 2.

[19] NGUYEN, B., BANERJEE, A., GOPALAKRISHNAN, V., KASERA, S., LEE, S., SHAIKH, A., AND VAN DER MERWE, J. Towards understanding TCP performance on LTE/EPC mobile networks. In *Proceedings of the 4th workshop on All things cellular: operations, applications, & challenges* (2014), ACM, pp. 41–46.

[20] NIKRAVESH, A., CHOFFNES, D. R., KATZ-BASSETT, E., MAO, Z. M., AND WELSH, M. Mobile Network Performance from User Devices: A Longitudinal, Multidimensional Analysis. In *Passive and Active Measurement* (2014), Springer, pp. 12–22.

[21] NIKRAVESH, A., CHOFFNES, D. R., KATZ-BASSETT, E., MAO, Z. M., AND WELSH, M. Mobile network performance from user devices: A longitudinal, multidimensional analysis. In *Passive and Active Measurement* (2014), Springer, pp. 12–22.

[22] QIAN, F., SEN, S., AND SPATSCHECK, O. Silent TCP connection closure for cellular networks. In *CoNEXT* (2013), pp. 211–216.

[23] ROUGHAN, M., GREENBERG, A., KALMANEK, C., RUMSEWICZ, M., YATES, J., AND ZHANG, Y. Experience in measuring Internet backbone traffic variability: Models, metrics, measurements and meaning. In *Proceedings of the International Teletraffic Congress (ITC-18)* (2003).

[24] SONG, H. H., GE, Z., MAHIMKAR, A., WANG, J., YATES, J., ZHANG, Y., BASSO, A., AND CHEN, M. Q-score: Proactive Service Quality Assessment in a Large IPTV System. In *Proceedings of the 2011 ACM SIGCOMM Conference on Internet Measurement Conference* (2011), IMC '11, ACM.

[25] XU, Y., WANG, Z., LEONG, W. K., AND LEONG, B. An end-to-end measurement study of modern cellular data networks. In *Passive and Active Measurement* (2014), Springer, pp. 34–45.

[26] YAN, H., FLAVEL, A., GE, Z., GERBER, A., MASSEY, D., PAPADOPOULOS, C., SHAH, H., AND YATES, J. Argus: End-to-end service anomaly detection and localization from an ISP's point of view. In *INFOCOM* (2012), IEEE.

[27] YAN, H., GE, Z., OSINSKI, M., AND YATES, J. When Cell Towers Fail: Quantifying the Customer Impact. `http://www.research.att.com/articles/featured_stories/2013_03/201306_tower-outage-analyzer.html`.

[28] ZHANG, M., ZHANG, C., PAI, V., PETERSON, L., AND WANG, R. PlanetSeer: Internet path failure monitoring and characterization in wide-area services. In *Proc. USENIX OSDI* (2004).

[29] ZHANG, Y., GE, Z., GREENBERG, A., AND ROUGHAN, M. Network Anomography. In *Proceedings of the 5th ACM SIGCOMM Conference on Internet Measurement* (Berkeley, CA, USA, 2005), IMC '05, USENIX Association, pp. 30–30.

[30] ZHANG, Y., MAO, Z., AND ZHANG, M. Effective diagnosis of routing disruptions from end systems. In *Proceedings of USENIX NSDI*, vol. 8.

Experience: Rethinking RRC State Machine Optimization in Light of Recent Advancements

Theodore Stoner
University of Cincinnati
theodore.stoner@uc.edu

Xuetao Wei*
University of Cincinnati
xuetao.wei@uc.edu

Joseph Knight
University of Cincinnati
joseph.knight@uc.edu

Lei Guo
Northeastern University
guolei@ise.neu.edu.cn

ABSTRACT

Broadband mobile networks utilize a radio resource control (RRC) state machine to allocate scarce radio resources. Current implementations introduce high latencies and cross-layer degradation. Recently, the RRC enhancements, continuous packet connectivity (CPC) and the enhanced forward access channel (Enhanced FACH), have emerged in UMTS. We study the availability and performance of these enhancements on a network serving a market with a population in the millions. Our experience in the wild shows these enhancements offer significant reductions in latency, mobile device energy consumption, and improved end user experience. We develop new over-the-air measurements that resolve existing limitations in measuring RRC parameters. We find CPC provides significant benefits with minimal resource costs, prompting us to rethink past optimization strategies. We examine the cross-layer performance of CPC and Enhanced FACH, concluding that CPC provides reductions in mobile device energy consumption for many applications. While the performance increase of HS-FACH is substantial, cross-layer performance is limited by the legacy uplink random access channel (RACH), and we conclude full support of Enhanced FACH is necessary to benefit most applications. Given that UMTS growth will exceed LTE for several more years and the greater worldwide deployment of UMTS, our quantitative results should be of great interest to network operators adding capacity to these networks. Finally, these results provide new insights for application developers wishing to optimize performance with these RRC enhancements.

Categories and Subject Descriptors

C.2.1 [**Network Architecture and Design**]: Wireless communication; C.4 [**Performance of Systems**]: measurement techniques, performance attributes

*Prof. Xuetao Wei is the corresponding author of this paper.

MobiCom'15, September 7–11, 2015, Paris, France.
 ISBN 978-1-4503-3619-2/15/09 ...$15.00.
DOI: http://dx.doi.org/10.1145/2789168.2790105.

Keywords

UMTS; RRC state machine; radio resource optimization

1. INTRODUCTION

The UMTS and LTE RRC state machine implementations play an important role in determining mobile application performance [30]. The purpose of the RRC state machine is to efficiently allocate network radio resources among a multitude of mobile devices. An additional goal is to minimize the utilization of energy intensive resources on the mobile device. The RRC state machine places wireless devices into one of several defined states that determine the amount of control, mobility management, and radio resources allocated. State changes incur a high cost, with delays up to several seconds. Minimizing state changes in the packet flow is required for good performance. A competing requirement is minimizing use of the resource intensive DCH state.

The impact of the RRC state machine on application performance has been studied in detail for CDMA, UMTS, and LTE networks [24,30,32]. Huang *et al.* [21] find TCP performance is affected by the longer delays and delay variability present in mobile wireless networks. TCP typically utilizes less than 50% of the available network bandwidth. Multiple studies investigate the impact of the RRC state machine implementation on device energy consumption. Tail time has been identified as a large contributor to poor power efficiency [20, 27]. While much is now understood about root cause, effective solutions remain elusive.

Existing RRC optimization methods have proved inadequate to resolve the issue, causing many current applications to experience unnecessary latency or excessive energy consumption. Currently, optimization requires trading off energy consumption for reduced performance by either shortening or extending state tail times. Qian *et al.* [27] found that optimization of RRC parameters for any specific class of traffic negatively impacts the majority of other traffic types. These limitations were found to be inherent in the state machine design.

As a solution, the industry organization that sets the technical specifications for LTE and UMTS mobile networks (3GPP) included RRC state machine enhancements in 3GPP Release 7 and 3GPP Release 8. Release 7 introduced *CPC* and *Enhanced FACH*. CPC allows HSPA users in the DCH state to operate without a dedicated control channel and utilizes discontinuous transmission and discontinuous reception. This results in reduced mobile device energy consumption and increased system capacity. Enhanced FACH defines use of the high speed downlink shared channel (HS-DSCH) for the FACH state (HS-FACH). 3GPP Release 8 further improves Enhanced FACH with a shared enhanced uplink channel (EUL-FACH) and DRX for the FACH state (E-FACH DRX).

While the recent growth of LTE subscribers is impressive, we note that increasing the capacity and performance of UMTS networks remains a priority for 3GPP participants. Over the next few years, global subscriber growth for UMTS / HSPA is forecast to exceed that of LTE. In 2019, UMTS subscriptions are forecast to exceed LTE subscriptions by 2.9 Billion [9, 11]. To address these needs, 3GPP has introduced numerous UMTS / HSPA enhancements [8, 10], many of which are implemented as software upgrades. The need for operators to quantitatively assess these enhancements and decide which features to implement motivates our research of recent UMTS state machine improvements.

The key contributions of our paper are as follows:

- **The first measurement of UMTS RRC state machine enhancements in the wild.** We study an operational network serving a large metropolitan area with a population in the millions. We measure the availability of devices supporting the 3GPP Release 7 and 8 optional features. From our measurement study, we found that only a subset of the features are well supported. Specifically 14% of the devices support CPC, 4.5% support HS-FACH, while EUL-FACH and E-FACH DRX were not supported.

- **A new measurement method for assessing the performance of CPC** (§4.1). We use an RF spectrum analyzer to monitor the RF envelope of mobile device transmissions. This provides accurate identification of when a mobile device utilizes CPC DTX with millisecond granularity.

- **A detailed study of UMTS RRC state machine enhancements: CPC and Enhanced FACH** (§4 and §5). We find that CPC reduces device energy consumption during DCH tail time by 25%. This improvement in energy efficiency allows network operators to extend DCH tail times, improving application performance. Enhanced FACH measurements reveal that lack of EUL-FACH support severely limits the potential benefits of this technology. The existing uplink channel for FACH (RACH) is a low bandwidth channel and exhibits high latency. Even with these limitations, we found devices supporting Enhanced FACH reduced 200 byte ping round trip times (RTT) by 26%. We also find that the HS-FACH channel reduces latency of control signaling messages.

- **Analysis of the enhanced RRC state machine performance with popular mobile applications** (§6). We found that for audio and video streaming applications, CPC DTX is active up to 90% of the time during track downloads. This reduces energy consumption by 23%. For a popular social media application, we find that background transfers use the DCH state 13.7% of the time and the energy consumption is reduced by 21% in the DCH state. We also find that HS-FACH offers only limited improvements to the popular applications we studied, but with full implementation of Enhanced FACH, there is potential for improved FACH performance.

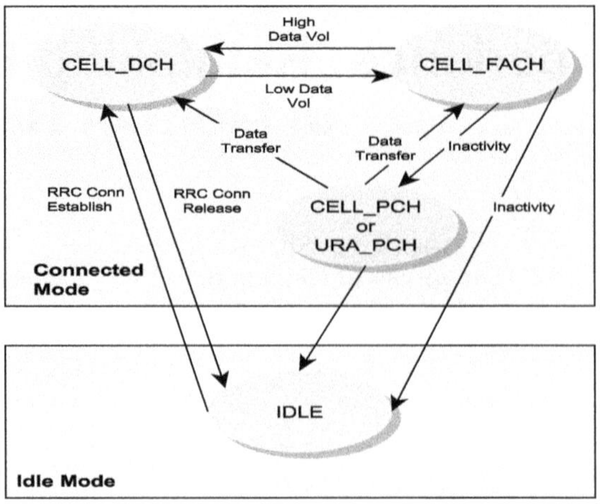

Figure 1: The UMTS RRC state diagram.

Summary: we learned that current RRC state machine enhancements narrow the performance gap between UMTS and LTE. We identified that pre-standard implementations of Fast Dormancy circumvent these enhancements. Further, Release 7 Enhanced FACH is limited in performance by reliance on the legacy RACH channel. Release 8 EUL-FACH is required for an effective Enhanced FACH implementation. Finally, we note FACH requires further improvements to provide needed capacity for developing Machine to Machine and Internet of Things applications.

2. BACKGROUND

Mobile wireless networks use an RRC state machine to allocate shared radio resources and minimize mobile device energy consumption. RRC state machines are implemented in GPRS, EVDO, UMTS, and LTE Networks [25].

We begin by reviewing the UMTS implementation. The state machine is shown in Figure 1. The basic RRC state machine consists of three states: IDLE, DCH, and FACH. These states are maintained simultaneously by the mobile device and the Radio Network Controller (RNC). The RNC provides control functions and radio resource management for the cellular base stations (NodeBs). A basic description of each state is given [19]:

- **IDLE** minimizes the use of network resources and device energy; only occasional monitoring of the network Broadcast channel (BCH), Paging channel (PCH), and Pilot channel (CPICH) are performed in this state.

- **FACH** requires an RRC connection to the RNC and minimizes use of radio resources by utilizing a slow speed shared channel with a bandwidth limited to aproximately 32 kbps. FACH has lower device energy consumption than DCH, and FACH to DCH promotions require less signaling overhead than IDLE to DCH promotions.

- **DCH** utilizes dedicated radio resources and provides a high bandwidth transport channel, however radio energy consumption is high.

3GPP Enhancement	Short Name	Release
Cont. Packet Conn.	CPC	7
Enhanced FACH	HS-FACH	7
	EUL-FACH	8
	E-FACH DRX	8

Table 1: Summary of RRC Enhancements.

Prior work covers operation of the RRC state machine [13, 24, 26, 27]. Optimization requires trading off state promotion delays and signaling load with increased energy consumption and radio resource utilization. Maximizing use of the IDLE state minimizes device energy consumption and radio resource usage. The benefits provided in the IDLE state are at the cost of increased state promotions and demotions. State promotions from IDLE incur signalling load, and delays, in the order of several seconds. In many networks, the optional PCH state is used as an intermediate state between IDLE and the other states to improve performance. When the amount of data in the mobile device or RNC transmit buffers exceeds a defined threshold, a state promotion to DCH is triggered [24]. State demotions from DCH to FACH are triggered when link throughput is below a defined threshold for a specified time. State demotion from FACH to IDLE is triggered by inactivity on the uplink and downlink [19].

3. MEASUREMENT METHODOLOGY

In this section, we first introduce the details of the CPC and Enhanced FACH features shown in Table 1. The RRC enhancements are optional features. Therefore, we determine which features are widely available across the target network. The target network is comprised of 3 RNCs, controlling approximately 280 wireless base stations (NodeBs). The network serves an area with a population in the millions. All of our experiments were conducted over a 5 month period commencing in May 2014. We protect end user privacy by only collecting statistical metadata and signaling messages, without subscriber identifying information.

In section (§3.2), we present the measurement study used to identify mobile devices supporting CPC and Enhanced FACH. As a result of our study, we find that only the Release 7 capabilities (CPC, HS-FACH) are well supported. Regarding the Release 8 features, we note implementation work beginning in late 2012 [17], and note several recent announcements of their availability [18,29,31]. Using our data and these announcements, we infer that mobile devices supporting all four features are just now entering the market place. Consequently, our experiments are limited to CPC and HS-FACH.

3.1 RRC State Machine Enhancements

We now describe the RRC enhancements introduced in 3GPP Release 7 and 8 [4, 5], which are shown in Table 1. CPC defines DTX and DRX capabilities for the DCH state physical channels. CPC capable mobile devices utilize discontinuous transmission in the uplink. On the network under study, CPC utilizes a 20 sub-frame DTX cycle, with a burst of typically one or two subframes every 20 subframes [2,8]. An HSPA subframe is 2 ms and the 20 subframe DTX cycle appears as transmit pulses every 40 ms.

The benefits of CPC are best realized if the DCH tail time is increased to minimize the number of state demotions and promotion between bursts of user data. Our tests show that DCH tail times can be extended significantly with only modest increases in radio resource consumption and no additional energy consumption. Another capability of CPC is DRX. DRX allows the mobile device receiver to power off when there is no downlink data. When using DRX, the mobile device no longer monitors the down link high speed shared control channels (HS-SCCH). Alternatively, it monitors the HS-DSCH directly and uses a specific DRX pattern and transport format to identify down link data. This mode of operation is comparable to the micro sleep capability of LTE [20].

The next RRC enhancements we consider are the HS-FACH and EUL-FACH features. The FACH RRC state uses common or shared channels, eliminating dedicated radio resource assignments for each mobile device connected to the network. FACH provides an uplink and downlink transport channel for mobile devices transmitting small amounts of data, such as periodic heartbeat messages or screen clicks. Energy consumption in the FACH state is lower than the standard DCH state, and by using shared resources FACH provides network connectivity and capacity for a larger number of devices than DCH. Research on the current FACH implementation shows poor performance, as FACH is unable to carry significant data volumes [27]. Rosen et al. [30] show that FACH buffers are set to trigger state promotions for packets as small as 200 bytes. This limits FACH traffic to low values, triggering frequent FACH to DCH state changes with high signaling delays.

In contrast, HS-FACH utilizes the HS-DSCH transport channel, which is the same channel used for HSPA downlink in the DCH state. HS-FACH supports a maximum bit rate of 1 Mbps nearly 30 times the rate provided by the existing R99 downlink FACH channel. The higher bandwidth allows for faster promotion to DCH [15].

3GPP Release 8 further improves FACH with DRX and EUL-FACH. E-FACH DRX lowers energy consumption, allowing mobiles to remain in FACH for extended periods. To support extended FACH connection times, new FACH tail timers are specified for use with E-FACH DRX [7]. The EUL-FACH feature provides a set of common enhanced uplink channels (EDCHs) that are shared among supporting mobile devices. The EDCH transport channel provides much greater bandwidth, and unlike the RACH channel, the mobile device can transmit consecutive protocol data units (PDUs). RACH, however, limits each transmission to one PDU. After each PDU transmission on RACH, the mobile device must repeat the channel access procedure, which greatly limits FACH performance.

3.2 CPC and Enhanced FACH Support

While CPC and Enhanced FACH have been defined in the 3GPP standards for some time, they have been introduced rather slowly [6]. To determine adoption of the CPC and Enhanced FACH features, we monitor the number of RRC Connection Complete Messages sent over the network from May to September 2014. The RRC Connection Setup Complete message includes information elements identifying support for the features [7]. In Figure 2, we find that CPC and HS-FACH capable devices represent over 10,000 mobile devices. Conversely, we found limited support for E-FACH DRX and EUL-FACH. These features were supported on less than 0.5% of mobile devices. As a consequence, mea-

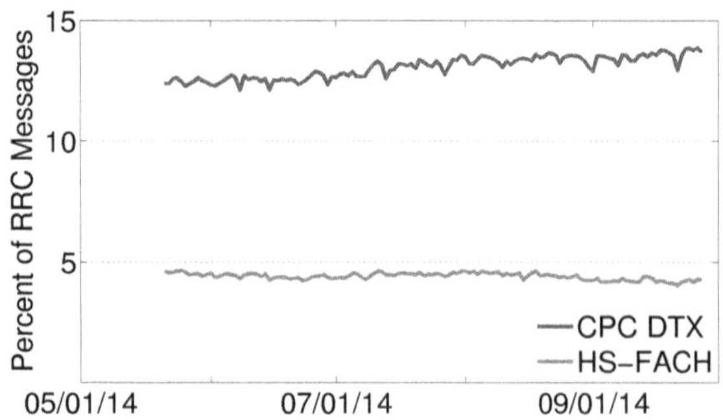

Figure 2: CPC DTX and HS-FACH support.

surements for these features were not conducted. Further, we observed an increase in low end smartphones supporting CPC, but not HS-FACH, while observing high end smartphones were starting to support 3GPP Release 8 features. Based on multiple supplier announcements, regarding full support HS-FACH and EUL-FACH, we expect the small decline in HS-FACH to reverse [18, 29, 31].

Next, we present our method for measuring CPC (§4) along with data from experiments on extending DCH tail time (§4.2).

4. CPC AND DCH PERFORMANCE

Identifying CPC DTX operation requires monitoring the transmitted RF envelope simultaneously with device energy consumption. By correlating these measurement, we accurately model the reduction in energy consumption. After identifying CPC energy savings, new values for the DCH tail timers are determined. In section (§4.2), we implement revised DCH tail timers on two RNCs in the network representing 65% of the cells, and measure the subsequent effect on RRC state changes and radio resource utilization.

4.1 CPC Power Reduction Measurements

CPC improves performance by minimizing the energy consumption of DCH. A major industry chipset company reported that CPC reduces the RF modem energy consumption 30% to 40% [29]. To measure these benefits, we develop a new measurement method that identifies state transitions and when CPC DTX is active. The measurements were made using an Alcatel One Touch 995S smart-phone running Andriod 4.0.4 (Ice Cream Sandwich). This phone supports HS-FACH and CPC, but does not support EUL-FACH nor E-FACH DRX.

In prior work, researchers have relied on mobile device power measurements to identify RRC state transitions and state machine parameters [20, 26, 27, 33]. In practice, there is a large amount of noise on the power measurements. This requires making multiple measurements and averaging results to clearly identify RRC states.

CPC complicates RRC state identification as it increases power measurement noise. After running multiple experiments, we were not able to clearly identify when CPC was active in the DCH state. To solve this problem, we develop a new measurement method. Our method monitors over-the-air transmissions from the mobile device. We use an Agilent 4402B spectrum analyzer for over-the-air measure-

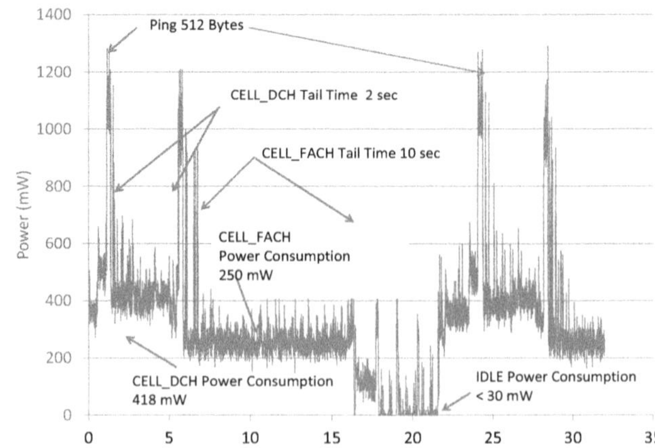

Figure 3: State transitions with noisy power measurements.

ments. The spectrum analyzer is configured in zero span mode. In this mode, the analyzer acts as a fixed tuned receiver measuring received signal power from a test antenna [22]. The test antenna is tightly coupled to the mobile so that the received signal is measured between -40 and -50 dBm.

Without CPC, the mobile device transmits continuously when in DCH. Whenever DTX is active, the device transmits a specific DTX pattern that causes the transmitter to pulse at the rate of the DTX cycle. These pulses occurred every 40ms and allowed clear identification of CPC DTX. To measure power reductions, the over-the-air measurements were synchronized with the battery current measurements.

IDLE mode baseline measurements are conducted with the phone screen, Bluetooth, WiFi, camera, and GPS accessories turned off. This leaves the cellular RF modem as the primary consumer of battery power. The energy consumption measured with all radio interfaces off established the baseline measurement. The energy consumption baseline is 25.7 mW. This is the same power measured in the IDLE state, allowing clear identification of this state.

CPC power measurements. Power measurements were then made with CPC disabled and enabled. In Figure 3, the measurement noise and the current spikes present create an ambiguity in identifying state changes. To overcome this, our additional measurement of received RF power is overlaid onto the battery current measurements. RF power measurements provide a graph of the received signal strength, which we refer to as the *RF envelope*. Transitions in the RF envelope identify the transition from one RRC state to the next.

To correlate RF power measurements with battery current measurements, we used the method described earlier. Shown in Figure 4 is the trace of two 512 byte pings sent 23 seconds apart. The time interval is set to allow for the state promotion delays, state demotion delays, DCH tail time, and FACH tail time to complete before the next ping is initiated. The red trace is triggered by the rising edge of the RF envelope. The rising edge corresponds to the mobile device's first access attempt on the RACH channel. A spike in battery current (blue trace) is observed when transmission of user data occurs. This spike is 1.2 seconds after the mobile starts transmitting, and the delay is caused by the state promotion from IDLE to DCH. There is then a 2

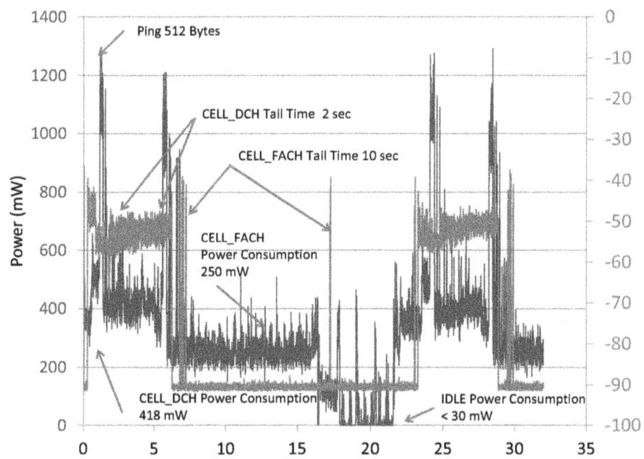

Figure 4: State transitions with RF envelope.

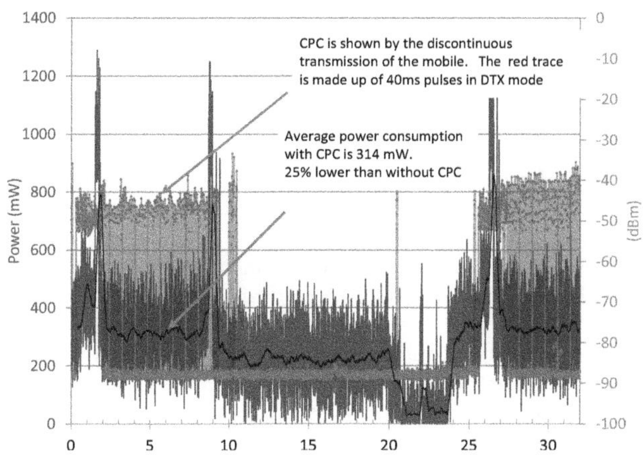

Figure 5: CPC DTX RF envelope.

second DCH tail, where no user data is transmitted. Another spike in battery current is observed just as the mobile device transitions from DCH to FACH. After the DCH to FACH demotion delay, there is 10 seconds of FACH tail then a short TX burst as the mobile device returns to IDLE. The measurements were then repeated with CPC.

The RF envelope clearly identifies the CPC DTX mode. The effects of CPC DTX are seen in Figure 5. During the DCH tail, the pulsed RF envelope of DTX is easily identified. The RF envelope allows for unambiguous identification of when DTX is active and accurate measurement of energy consumption.

DCH tail energy consumption with CPC averages 314 mW and achieves a 25% reduction in power. Our complete results are shown in Table 2, along with measurements reported in prior studies [27,33].

4.2 Extending DCH Tail Time

In this section, we measure the impact on network capacity of increasing DCH tail time by analyzing the consumption of two key radio resources, NodeB TX power and RRC connections. We note, some operators may prioritize increasing mobile device battery life and will not increase existing DCH tail times. The priority for other operators is reducing latency, excess state transitions, and subsequent signaling load. The performance trade offs between longer

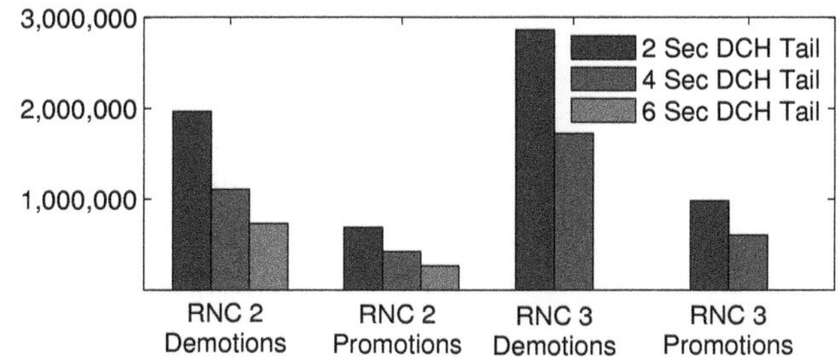

Figure 6: State change improvements.

DCH tail time, decreased battery life, and increased radio resource consumption are well documented in the literature [14,23,24,32]. However, the impact on radio resources of increased tail times has only been discussed analytically. Our experiments provide a set of quantitative results from an operational network.

We extend DCH tail time from 2 to 4 seconds in the first measurement run. The tail time was extended on two different RNCs and the number of state promotions and demotions measured over a period of two weeks. A second run for RNC 2 is made with DCH tail extended to 6 seconds. The increase in DCH tail time results in a 44% and 40% reduction in demotions for RNC 2 and RNC 3 respectively. The number of promotions from FACH to DCH is also reduced by 39% for RNC 2 and RNC 3.

Longer DCH tail times require increased radio resources to maintain the dedicated connections with the NodeB. As we increase DCH tail time, we observe the effect on DCH connections, FACH connections, and Node B TX power. In Figure 7, we measure the 24 hour summation of hourly average DCH and FACH connections. As expected, there is an increase in DCH connections 10% on RNC 2 and 13% on RNC 3 for the 4 s DCH tail. RNC 2 increases an additional 12% for the 6 s DCH tail.

A decrease in FACH connections occurs as DCH tail time increases. There are two possible causes for the reduction in FACH connections, first the longer DCH tail will cause a portion of packet flows to remain in DCH rather than transition to FACH and back to DCH when the flow resumed. This occurs when the gap in the flow t_1 is such that $\alpha_1 < t_1 < \alpha_2$. Where t_1 is the interpacket time, and α_1, α_2 are the original and extended DCH tail times. We also note, in some cases Fast Dormancy was a contributor to decreases in FACH connections. Fast Dormancy is a capability that terminates RRC connections using mobile device control [16]. When the RRC connection is terminated, the mobile device bypasses FACH and returns directly to IDLE or in some network implementations PCH. The timer used to terminate the connection is dependent on the mobile device. When the timer t_f is such that $\alpha_1 < t_f < \alpha_2$, then DCH demotions bypass FACH, reducing FACH connections, where α_1 and α_2 are the original and extended DCH tail times.

Next we examine NodeB TX power. The increased number of DCH connections observed potentially increases the NodeB TX power. To determine this impact, data was collected from two different network RNCs on TX power utilization. Power measurement were collected 2 weeks prior and 2 weeks after the implementation of longer DCH tail times. Transmit power utilization was averaged for all effected cells and the CDF of this usage is presented in Fig-

RRC State	Alcatel 995	Alcatel 995 with CPC	TyTN*	Nexus One*	HTC Dream**
DCH	418 mW	314 mW	800 mW	600 mW	570 mW
FACH	248 mW	224 mW	460 mW	450 mW	401 mW
IDLE	30 mW	32 mW	0	0	10 mW

*Reported in [27], ** Reported in [33]

Table 2: Summary of mobile device power measurements.

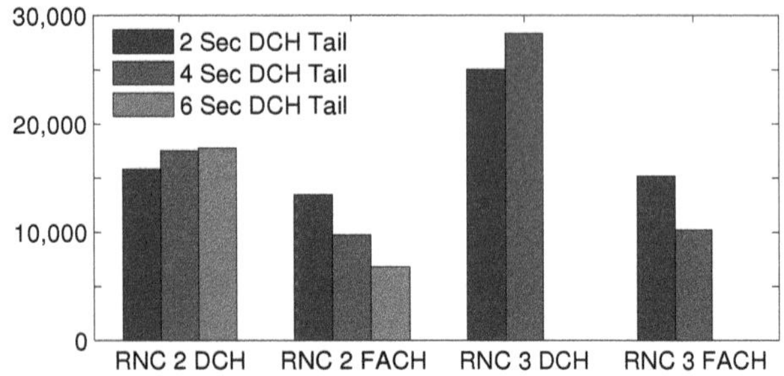

Figure 7: FACH and DCH connections.

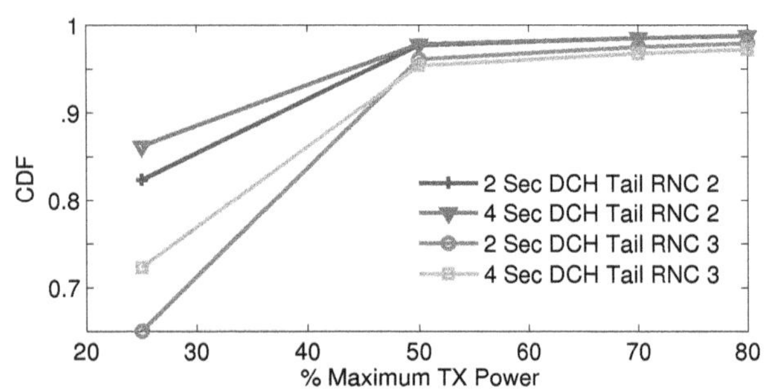

Figure 8: TX Power Resource Utilization.

ure 8. The lower probabilities correspond to higher TX power use. The probability that TX power is less than 25% of maximum actually increases for both RNCs despite the increase number of DCH connections. By examining overall trends in network traffic, we observe the small decreases in NodeB TX power were due to small changes in network traffic, and there is no measurable increase in power from the longer DCH tail.

The NodeB TX power increase is small and we conclude that the longer DCH tail has a negligible effect on overall consumption of available transmission power. Overall, significant reductions in promotions and demotions along with the subsequent delays were obtained with limited increases in the use of other radio resources.

5. ENHANCED FACH

In this section, we assess the performance of the feature HS-FACH. As noted, the majority of mobile devices supporting Enhanced FACH implement only the HS-FACH downlink capability and not the corresponding EUL-FACH uplink enhancement.

5.1 HS-FACH

To measure HS-FACH performance a simple ping test was performed, a packet size of 200 bytes was chosen, as packet sizes larger than 256 bytes trigger a promotion from FACH to DCH. Figure 9 shows the measurement results. Average ping round trip times (RTT) decreased from 600 ms to 440 ms, an improvement of 26%. While significant, the improvement in FACH is much less than expected. It is believed that the RTTs are dominated by the slower RACH channel and the power ramping procedure that is used to access the RACH channel. RACH uses a contention based access method and open loop power control that requires the mobile device to send an identifying preamble at a power level estimated from the received signal strength of the serving base station [1, 19]. If the mobile device does not receive a response, it ramps up the power and sends the preamble again. This continues until the mobile device receives a response. The process must be repeated for each transmission over the RACH channel and greatly limits the possible throughput of this channel, consequently limiting performance in the HS-FACH state.

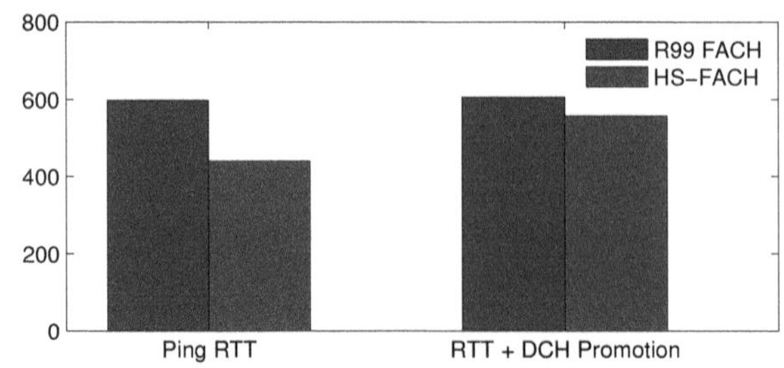

Figure 9: HS-FACH RTT.

HS-FACH improves promotion times from FACH to DCH. The HS-FACH channel allows for faster transmission of signaling messages and corresponding reductions in promotion times. To measure the improvement, RTT measurements were made for 300 byte pings. The 300 byte packet size triggers a promotion from FACH to DCH. Data for several hundred runs were conducted using both FACH and HS-FACH on the same mobile device. The results in Figure 9 show a 48 ms reduction in average RTT times, which is attributed to the reduction in promotion time from FACH to DCH.

In order to obtain an additional assessment of the throughput and performance capability of HS-FACH, throughput on the HS-FACH channel was measured using statistical counters present in the RNC. These counters are samples of the HS-FACH throughput made every 100 ms. If the channel throughput is 0 kbps, the sample is discarded. The samples are then averaged providing a measure of HS-FACH throughput on an hourly basis. Unfortunately, statistical counters for the conventional R99 FACH channel were not available. This necessitated using other throughput measurements. For comparison, the same average throughput data was collected for the 64 kbps DCH channel.

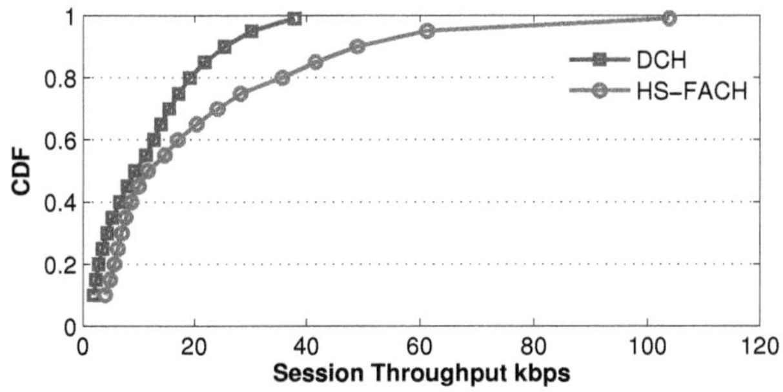

Figure 10: HS-FACH vs. R99 DCH throughput.

The 64 kbps DCH channel has twice the bandwidth of the traditional FACH channel and is a dedicated channel not shared among multiple users. The 64 kbps DCH provides much higher performance than is available on the traditional FACH channel. Statistical data for several days was collected for both channels, and their distributions are shown in Figure 10. HS-FACH consistently provides better throughput than the 64 kbps DCH channel, with the 50th percentile HS-FACH speeds exceeding 11.6 kbps as opposed to 9.3 kpbs for 64 kbps DCH. These results indicate that HS-FACH performance over FACH is qualitatively substantial. As a result, we conclude that HS-FACH provides a significant increase in downlink FACH channel performance. However, the lack of support for the EUL-FACH channel limits mobile application benefits.

5.2 Fast Dormancy and FACH interactions

Fast Dormancy is a mobile device capability introduced to reduce DCH tail energy. Device manufactures introduced this capability outside the 3GPP standardization process, creating unanticipated problems [16]. When invoked, the Fast Dormancy procedure demotes a mobile device in DCH directly to the IDLE state. This bypasses both the FACH and PCH states.

Bypassing the PCH state circumvents it benefits. The PCH state retains the RRC connection with a mobile device and reduces the promotion delay to the DCH state. PCH has low energy requirements similar to IDLE. To correct this problem, 3GPP Release 8 includes an improved Fast Dormancy procedure that transitions the mobile device from DCH to any lower power state IDLE, PCH, or FACH [7, 16]. The new procedure includes an additional information element, "UE Requested PS Data session end", sent by the mobile device when invoking Fast Dormancy. When received, the network moves the mobile device to one of the more battery efficient states; FACH, PCH, or IDLE. The state selected is configured by the network operator.

6. APPLICATION CASE STUDIES

Understanding the benefits of CPC and HS-FACH on application performance motivates us to conduct a series of case studies. For our analysis, we use a widely available application performance optimizer, ARO [12]. From our results, we conclude streaming applications that remain in DCH for extended periods of time use significantly less power with CPC. The benefits of HS-FACH were mixed. The bandwidth of current VoIP applications, such as Skype, are higher than what can be reasonably be met by the Enhanced FACH channels, however VoIP applications with bandwidths of 32 kbps or less should be able to utilize HS-FACH, increasing network capacity and reducing device energy consumption.

6.1 Streaming Media Applications

Pandora is a popular audio streaming application widely used on mobile devices. Both CPC and HS-FACH potentially offer improvements in radio resources utilization. The ARO application analyzes packet flow dynamics to allow tuning of network parameters for the desired behavior. ARO analysis provides a graphical display of the packet flow dynamics including RRC state. Figure 11 shows the dynamics of a captured Pandora session.

Analysis of the captured traces reveal that audio content is received in chunks of 8000 bytes spaced at one second intervals. With overhead the downlink throughput is less than 72 kbps when averaged over several seconds, well within the bandwidth of the HS-FACH channel. However, the dynamics of each chunk include a high bandwidth initial burst that quickly exceeds the downlink RLC buffer threshold, triggering a promotion to DCH. This leads us to conclude that track downloads will quickly up switch to DCH and remain there, and it is not practical for audio streaming applications of this class to use the HS-FACH channel.

The analysis reveals CPC is quite beneficial in minimizing energy consumption. There is minimal uplink traffic during track download. For this flow, the mobile device is transmitting only TCP ACKs and no data payload. Consequently, CPC switches from continuous transmission to DTX immediately after the mobile device's TX buffer is emptied. Without CPC, the transmitter is powered continuously for the duration of the track download. Examination of the uplink flow dynamics shows that the TX is idle more than 90% of the time during the track download. As a result, CPC reduces device energy consumption by 94mW during track download, corresponding to a power reduction of 22%.

YouTube shares similarities with the Pandora application, we observed the same chunk download dynamics that were present for Pandora. Using the 640x360 video format for our downloads, the average bit rate for YouTube content was 1 Mbps, and data was downloaded in blocks of 65,536 bytes. The block size was very consistent, with negligible variance. The blocks were downloaded at 484 ms intervals. The download time per block averaged 82 ms, which shows that the TX is idle 82% of the time, reducing device energy consumption 85 mW during track download.

6.2 Voice over IP

Common voice over IP (VoIP) applications consist of a UDP packet flow with small payloads. Packet loss, delay, and jitter are the first order determinants of application performance. Skype is a popular VoIP, video chat, and messaging application for personal computers and mobile devices. We limit our examination of this application to the VoIP functions. We examined the packet flow of this application with ARO to understand the dynamics of the flow and how the application interacts with CPC and HS-FACH.

Packet flow analysis. On the mobile device downlink, UDP packets with average payload of 104 bytes are received at a rate of 50 packets per second, or one packet per 20 ms. This constitutes an audio stream with a bit rate of 42 kbps.

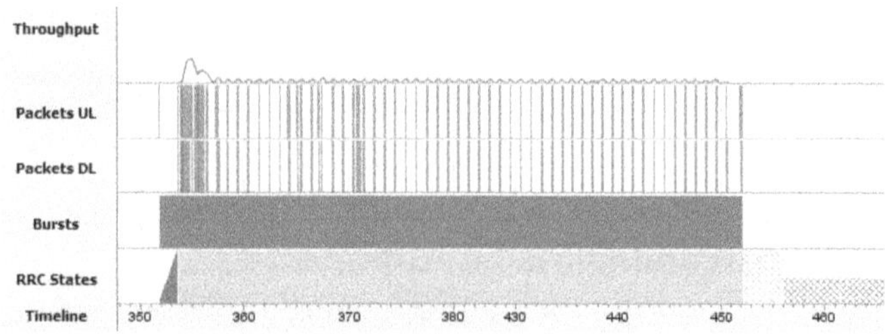

Figure 11: Pandora packet flow analysis with ARO.

The packet payload and bit rate for the uplink were 73 bytes and 30 kbps respectively, however no audio was transmitted on the uplink. The uplink data rate did not change when using an open microphone with background noise or a muted microphone. The packet rate on uplink was also 50 packets per second.

CPC and HS-FACH do not benefit the VoIP packet flow. Based on the packet flow dynamics of Skype, we conclude that CPC will not benefit this application, as the CPC DTX cycle is based on a 20 subframe or 40 ms period, and the packet rate used by Skype precludes use of the CPC DTX cycle. We also note that the application consumes additional power by sending an uplink stream of significant bandwidth, even during periods of silence or with a muted microphone. The inter-packet timing of this stream exceeds the capability of RACH, precluding the possibility of the mobile device utilizing HS-FACH. Optimization of the stream would provide substantial benefits in bandwidth and energy reduction for this application.

6.3 Social Media

We studied the packet flow dynamics of the popular social media application Facebook. While running in the background, Facebook intermittently exchanges information in small to medium sized bursts. In our data set, 46% of the bursts were less than 1 kB, and these small bursts consume substantial energy during the DCH and FACH tail times. Both CPC and Enhanced FACH provide alternative solutions for the handling of small bursts.

DCH was active for 13.7% of the time during our traces. For most of the time in DCH, no data was transmitted and CPC was active. For our traces, CPC is active greater than 82% of the time while in DCH, and reduces radio energy consumption 21%. We also observe that the small transfers are within the capability of the Enhanced FACH state. The enhanced FACH state lowers energy consumption even further than CPC. However, for the FACH channel to be of benefit, the RRC state machine would need to be configured so that promotions from IDLE to DCH first transition to FACH. On many networks including the target network, promotions are from IDLE to DCH and do not pass through the FACH state. Based on the limitation of HS-FACH and its reliance on the RACH channel for uplink, we do not recommend implementing an RRC state machine that would use FACH as an intermediate state for promotions from IDLE or PCH. Consequently, we conclude that performance gains with HS-FACH alone are limited, and the full implementation of Enhanced FACH including EUL-FACH is required to further improve the performance of typical social media applications.

7. RELATED WORK

Perala *et al.* showed significant variations in timer values and the inability to accurately predict state machine operation without network measurements [24]. RRC state machine parameters are often measured by monitoring mobile device battery current [13,20,21,26,27,33]. These measurements are plagued by noise. Our contributions provide a new measurement method, greatly improving identification of RRC states and modes such as CPC DTX.

Energy consumption is studied in [23,32] using simulation and then developing analytical expressions for application in network design. Chua *et al.* [14] uses simulations to identify optimum state machine timing for web browsing. Rosen *et al.* [30] provides a comprehensive study of promotion and demotion delays, showing that in specific circumstances, these delays can be long and create additional degradation of user experience. Researchers have also shown that periodic transfers, inefficient content prefetching, random bursts triggered by user actions, and other common application behaviors use radio network resources inefficiently [25–27]. They created software tools that allow developers to analyze application performance and previously hidden cross-layer interactions [12]. By applying similar techniques, our work shows that recent RRC enhancements address past limitations. Additional timers and RRC parameters are introduced allowing energy efficient mobile devices to remain in high performance states for extended periods of time. Further, we observe prior techniques used to minimize mobile device power can interfere with these improvements [16]. Finally, we note that further RRC state machine enhancements are planned [3,28], and the techniques we develop in this paper are useful for optimization and implementation.

8. CONCLUSIONS

In this paper, we have characterized the performance of recently available RRC state machine enhancements in the wild. Our results show that CPC provides significant reduction in device energy consumption, particularly for streaming applications. CPC reduced energy consumption by 25% during the DCH tail. Based on the measured energy savings, we conclude extending the DCH tail time is generally beneficial, offering improved application performance. We also find that the HS-FACH channel has greatly improved bandwidth. However, limited support of the EUL-FACH uplink channel greatly limits the improvements that can be realized for many of the applications we tested. Our work provides further insight into how new RRC state machine enhancements interact with applications and require developers and operators to update their optimization tools and strategies accordingly.

Acknowledgements

We would like to thank our anonymous reviewers and shepherd for their valuable comments. This work was supported in part by funds from the University of Cincinnati CECH, as well as NSFC (No. 61471109), National Program for Support of Top-Notch Young Professionals and Fundamental Research Funds for the Central Universities (N140405005). The views and conclusions contained in this document are those of the authors and should not be interpreted as representing the official policies, either expressed or implied, of the respective funding agencies.

9. REFERENCES

[1] 3GPP. *Technical Specification, 25.14 V11.10.0, UMTS Physical Layer Procedures.*

[2] 3GPP. *Technical Report, 25.903 V9.0.0,Continuous connectivity for packet data users*, December 2009.

[3] 3GPP. *RP-111321: Further Enhancements to CELL_FACH, TSG-RAN Meeting #53*, September 2011.

[4] 3GPP. *Overview of 3GPP Release 7 V0.9.16*, January 2012.

[5] 3GPP. *Overview of 3GPP Release 8 V0.3.3*, September 2014.

[6] 3GPP. *Specification status report*, July 2014.

[7] 3GPP. *Technical Specification, 25.331 V10.15.0,UMTS Radio Resource Control (RRC) Protocol specification*, March 2014.

[8] 4G Americas. *The Evolution of HSPA: The 3GPP standards progress for fast mobile broadband using HSPA+*, October 2011.

[9] 4G Americas. *4G Mobile Broadband Evolution: 3GPP Release 11 and Release 12 and Beyond*, February 2014.

[10] 4G Americas. *Understanding 3GPP Release 12: Standards for HSPA+ and LTE Enhancements*, February 2015.

[11] 4G Americas / Rysavy Research. *Mobile Broadband Explosion: The 3GPP Wireless Evolution*, August 2013.

[12] AT&T. Application resource optimizer (ARO). `http://developer.att.com/application-resource-optimizer`.

[13] A. Aucinas, M. Almeida, Y. Grunenberger, and J. Crowcroft. Rilanalyzer: a comprehensive 3g monitor on your phone. In *ACM IMC*, 2013.

[14] M. Chuah, W. Luo, and X. Zhang. Impacts of inactivity timer values on umts system capacity. In *IEEE WCNC*, 2002.

[15] E. Dahlman, S. Parkvall, J. Skold, and P. Beming. *3G evolution: HSPA and LTE for mobile broadband.* Academic press, 2010.

[16] F. Dormancy. Fast dormancy best practices. *GSM association, network efficiency task force*, 2010.

[17] Ericsson. Ericsson shows new features that improve smart phone experience. `http://www.ericsson.com/news/121205-features-that-improve-smartphone-experience`, December 2012.

[18] Ericsson. 3G smartphones - optimizing user experience and network efficiency, February 2015.

[19] H. Holma and A. Toskala. *WCDMA for UMTS: HSPA Evolution and LTE.* John Wiley & Sons, 2010.

[20] J. Huang, F. Qian, A. Gerber, Z. M. Mao, S. Sen, and O. Spatscheck. A close examination of performance and power characteristics of 4g lte networks. In *ACM MobiSys*, 2012.

[21] J. Huang, F. Qian, Y. Guo, Y. Zhou, Q. Xu, Z. M. Mao, S. Sen, and O. Spatscheck. An in-depth study of lte: effect of network protocol and application behavior on performance. In *ACM SIGCOMM*, 2013.

[22] Keysight Technologies. *Application Note 150: Spectrum Analysis Basics*, August 2014.

[23] C.-C. Lee, J.-H. Yeh, and J.-C. Chen. Impact of inactivity timer on energy consumption in wcdma and cdma2000. In *IEEE Wireless Telecommunications Symposium*, 2004.

[24] P. H. Perala, A. Barbuzzi, G. Boggia, and K. Pentikousis. Theory and practice of rrc state transitions in umts networks. In *IEEE GLOBECOM Workshops*, 2009.

[25] F. Qian, Z. Wang, Y. Gao, J. Huang, A. Gerber, Z. Mao, S. Sen, and O. Spatscheck. Periodic transfers in mobile applications: network-wide origin, impact, and optimization. In *ACM WWW*, 2012.

[26] F. Qian, Z. Wang, A. Gerber, Z. Mao, S. Sen, and O. Spatscheck. Profiling resource usage for mobile applications: a cross-layer approach. In *ACM MobiSys*, 2011.

[27] F. Qian, Z. Wang, A. Gerber, Z. M. Mao, S. Sen, and O. Spatscheck. Characterizing radio resource allocation for 3g networks. In *ACM IMC*, 2010.

[28] Qualcomm. *RP-112852: UE energy consumption and signaling reduction in CELL_FACH, TSG-RAN Meeting #74*. 3GPP, May 2011.

[29] Qualcomm. CPC and enhanced FACH. `https://www.qualcomm.com/invention/research/projects/hspa-advanced/cpc-enhanced-fach`, May 2014.

[30] S. Rosen, H. Luo, Q. A. Chen, Z. M. Mao, J. Hui, A. Drake, and K. Lau. Discovering fine-grained rrc state dynamics and performance impacts in cellular networks. In *ACM Mobicom*, 2014.

[31] N. Solutions and Networks. Enhanced cell_fach raises operator revenue generating potential, October 2014.

[32] J.-H. Yeh, J.-C. Chen, and C.-C. Lee. Comparative analysis of energy-saving techniques in 3gpp and 3gpp2 systems. *IEEE Transactions on Vehicular Technology*, pages 432–448, 2009.

[33] L. Zhang, B. Tiwana, Z. Qian, Z. Wang, R. P. Dick, Z. M. Mao, and L. Yang. Accurate online power estimation and automatic battery behavior based power model generation for smartphones. In *IEEE CODES+ISSS*, 2010.

European Research Towards 5G

Rémy Bayou
European Commission, Brussels, Belgium
Remy.BAYOU@ec.europa.eu

ABSTRACT

The next generation of wireless networks, the 'fifth generation" or 5G, will have to cope with impressive new challenges. It includes a traffic expected to grow by up to 1000, an extremely low latency, the connection of cars, robots, smart cities, with billions of machines talking to each other and their sensors, new use of spectrum, new architectures and so on. The EU has committed €700 million of public funding over seven years to boost the research in 5G communications and a first wave of about 20 projects started this summer. The talk will address the scientific research challenges to develop 5G networks, the technology building blocks new projects are dealing with, notably as regards the Radio Access Network and the novel mobile architectures.

Categories and Subject Descriptors

C.2.1 [Computer-Communication Networks]: Network Architecture and Design— *Network communications; Wireless communication.* H.0 [Information System]: General

Keywords

5G; Mobile networks; Internet of Things; Radio access, Cellular networks

BIO

Rémy Bayou is Research and Innovation programme and policy Officer for network technologies in DG Connect, European Commission. This year he coordinated the selection of research projects for 5G networks for a budget of €135 million. In the last years he has been active in defining and managing European Commission research funding in the fields of Mobile Communication and Future Internet. He was before head of the Telecom department in the French Defense Directorate for Research and Technology. He graduated from ENSTA and Telecom Paris Tech.

MobiCom '15, September 7–11, 2015, Paris, France.
ACM 978-1-4503-3619-2/15/09.
DOI: http://dx.doi.org/10.1145/2789168.2802127

See Through Walls with COTS RFID System!

Lei Yang*, Qiongzheng Lin*, Xiangyang Li*†‡, Tianci Liu*, Yunhao Liu*

*School of Software, Tsinghua University, China
† Department of Computer Science and Technology, Tsinghua University, China
‡Department of Computer Science, Illinois Institute of Technology, USA

young@tagsys.org, qiongzheng@tagsys.org, xli@cs.iit.edu, tian@tagsys.org, yunhao@greenorbs.com

ABSTRACT

Through-wall tracking has gained a lot of attentions in civilian applications recently. Many applications would benefit from such device-free tracking, *e.g.* elderly people surveillance, intruder detection, gaming, *etc.* In this work, we present a system, named *Tadar*, for tracking moving objects without instrumenting them using COTS RFID readers and tags. It works even through walls and behind closed doors. It aims to enable a *see-through-wall* technology that is *low-cost*, *compact*, and accessible to *civilian* purpose. In traditional RFID systems, tags modulate their IDs on the backscatter signals, which is vulnerable to the interferences from the ambient reflections. Unlike past work, which considers such vulnerability as detrimental, our design exploits it to detect surrounding objects even through walls. Specifically, we attach a group of RFID tags on the outer wall and logically convert them into an antenna array, receiving the signals reflected off moving objects. This paper introduces two main innovations. First, it shows how to eliminate the flash (*e.g.* the stronger reflections off walls) and extract the reflections from the backscatter signals. Second, it shows how to track the moving object based on HMM (Hidden Markov Model) and its reflections. To the best of our knowledge, we are the first to implement a through-wall tracking using the COTS RFID systems. Empirical measurements with a prototype show that Tadar can detect objects behind $5''$ hollow wall and $8''$ concrete wall, and achieve median tracking errors of $7.8cm$ and $20cm$ in the X and Y dimensions.

Categories and Subject Descriptors

C.2 [**Computer Systems Organization**]: Computer Communications Networks

Keywords

RFID, See-through walls, Tracking, Tadar

MobiCom'15, September 7–11, 2015, Paris, France.
© 2015 ACM. ISBN 978-1-4503-3619-2/15/09âĂę$15.00
DOI: http://dx.doi.org/10.1145/2789168.2790100.

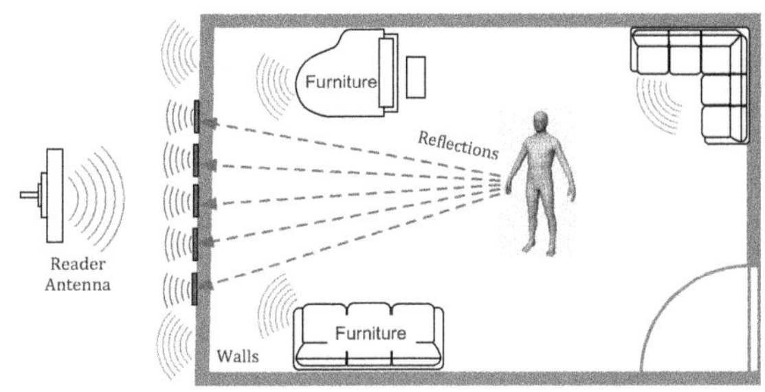

Figure 1: Through-wall tracking of moving object. Tadar logically transforms the tags attached on the outer wall into an antenna array receiving the reflections off the human behind the wall.

1. INTRODUCTION

Motion tracking and localization systems have received a lot of attentions recently. A number of innovative systems using different technologies are developed for improving the accuracy and robustness, *e.g.*, [1–4]. However, these systems typically require the objects to carry an RF device in order to be identified and localized. This paper explores the potential of using COTS RFID systems to build a system that can capture the motion of mobile object behind a wall and in closed rooms without tagging it. Such system is able to provide life-saving benefits for emergency responders, police and military personnel arriving at dangerous situations by letting them know the locations of people inside a building without instrumenting the people in advance. Many other applications would also benefit from this system, such as elderly, people surveillance, intruder detection, and so on.

The concept underlying through-wall tracking is to emit RF signals to a closed room facing with a non-metallic wall. The signal traverses through the wall, reflects off objects and humans, and returns back, imprinted with a glimpse of what is inside a closed-room. Through-wall tracking has been extensively studied in radar community, which mainly employs ultra-wideband and MIMO radar technique [5, 6] to detect moving objects behind a wall. Their devices are almost inaccessible to non-military purpose due to ultra-widebandwith, voracious power consumption, and unaffordable. For example, a typical radar device consumes $2 \sim 4$ GHz bandwidth [5, 7, 8]. The price of the through-war radar sold online is about $80,000$ US dollars [9]. Even worse, the through-wall radar systems in the market are usually prohibited from selling to civilians in most countries in the world. To address these issues, recently several breakthrough systems [10–15] are developed for seeing through the walls with WiFi. However, these past systems still need either customized devices (*e.g.* USRP), specialized signals (*e.g.* FMCW), or additional receivers inside the room.

In this work, we turn our attentions to a mature technology, RFID. RFID is evolving as a major technology enabler for identifying and tracking objects all around the world. The reason for this widespread deployment is the simplicity of tags, which enables very low lost at high volumes. One of the benefits of RFID systems is that it can identify objects without needs of line-of-sight (LOS) owing to the multi-path effect. The challenging question is "Can RFID systems enable us to identify and track objects through walls?". At the first instinct, it seems like an impossible mission because the backscatter signals off tags are too weak (typically at -55 dBm) to traverse a wall (with $\sim$ 18 dB attenuation) or even a thick glass (with $\sim$ 3 dB attenuation) [16].

It is well known that RFID systems adopt an asymmetric architecture in order to reduce the complexity and costs of tags. Such design has three important features. First, the reader is able to provide 30 dBm transmitting signals and connected to higher-gain directional antennas. Such strong signals are sufficient for two-way traversal through a wall. Second, the tag has no transceiver and modulates its ID on the backscatter signals through changing the impedance on its antenna. Its modulation is vulnerable to the interference from ambient reflections [16]. Unlike past approaches [1, 17], which consider this vulnerability as detrimental, we exploit it as an opportunity to monitor the surrounding objects. Third, the RFID technology, stemming from the radar, has strong ability to resolve very weak signals from the background. Inspired by these these features, we redefine RFID system to extend our senses. We leverage the reader to supply RF signals lighting up objects and treat tags as the antennas receiving reflections. To illustrate Tadar's approach, Fig. 1 shows a toy example. We attach an array of tags on the outer wall and use a reader to read them. The signal propagation between reader and tags is kept in line-of-sight. Apart from tags, the transmitting signals from reader are also reflected off other objects like walls, furnitures and mobile objects. These reflections plus the original signals from reader provide a combined signal to each tag for their modulations. As a result, the backscatter signal that carries tag' ID implicitly contains the reflections off human. If we can extract the human's reflections from the backscatter signals, his locations would be pinpointed.

Transforming this high-level idea into a practical system, however, requires addressing multiple challenges. First, it is quite challenging to separate a *weaker* signal (reflections off object) from another weak signal (backscattered signal). In particular, this task should be accomplished using the COTS RFID reader, which does not support any low-level signal access or modifications. The second challenge stems from '*Flash Effect*' (see [11]) that the signal power after traversing the wall twice (in and out of the room) is reduced by three to five orders of magnitude, such that the reflections off objects inside the room will be drown in the reflections off the wall itself (call *flash*). Third, the inherent diversity of devices and objects would introduce many unknown impacts on the magnitude attenuations and phase rotations, leading to *unpredictable* tracking errors.

To address these issues, we present *Tadar* for tracking moving object through walls and behind closed doors using COTS RFID readers and tags. Our objective is to enable a *see-through-wall* technology that is *low-cost*, *compact*, and accessible for *civilian* purpose. We propose two main techniques to address the aforementioned challenging issues. First, Tadar views each read of tag as one channel estimation and recovers the signal with RSS and phase reported by reader. Since the wireless signals linearly combine over the medium, Tadar eliminates the flash by subtracting the signals learned when the room is empty. It also separates the reflections from the backscatter signals by dividing the signal learned in LOS propagation (see §5). Second, Tadar models the object's motions using Hidden Markov Model (HMM), which considers the object's locations as hidden states and its reflections as observations. Then it uses Viterbi decoding to recover the object's trajectory (see §6).

Summary of results: We build a prototype of Tadar using one Impinj Reader and 45 Alien tags, and evaluate it in two office buildings (see §7). Our main results are as follows:

• Tadar can detect object moving behind $8''$ concrete walls, $5''$ hollow walls, and $1.5''$ wooden doors.

• Tadar can achieve detecting ranges of $4m$ and $6m$ on average respectively when pointing at a closed room with $8''$ concrete walls and $5''$ hollow walls supported by steely frames.

• Tadar can track the moving object in a closed room with median errors of $7.8cm$ and $20cm$ in X and Y dimensions when monitoring the room from one side, offering about $3\times$, $3.5\times$ and $1.3\times$ improvement compared with NRES [18], TagTrack [19] and Wision [20].

• Tadar can correctly decode 93% gestures in our application study where 5 volunteers encode the messages through his/her movements.

Contributions: In contrast to the state-of-the-art work, Tadar introduces a low-cost solution to the through-wall tracking of moving objects, enabling civilians to use this technology. Tadar is the first to introduce through-wall tracking using RFID systems by transforming a group of tags attached on the wall into a receiving antenna array. It demonstrates a working system implemented purely based on COTS devices and made accessible to the general public.

The rest of the paper is organized as follows. We review the related work in §2 and the technical background in §3. The main design is overviewed in §4. The technique details of reflection extraction and object tracking are respectively elaborated in §5 and §6. The implementation is described in §7and the system is evaluated in §8. We also conduct an application study in §9. Lastly, we conclude our work in §11.

2. RELATED WORK

In this section, we briefly review the related literature in see-through-wall technology.

See through walls with radar. Through-wall imaging or tracking has gained attentions for a decade, especially in radar community [5, 6, 8, 21–25]. The past systems eliminate the flash effect and localize the moving object by estimating the time of flight of signals. Specifically, the pulse reflected off the wall arrives earlier in time than that reflected off moving object behind it. To differentiate such slight time difference ($< 1ns$), the systems would transmit a linear frequency chirp at cost of ultra-wide bandwidth of the order of 2 GHz [21]. The products developed in the industry [26, 27] also require multiple GHz bandwidth. Adib *et al.* track user's 3D motion or heartbeat [24, 25]. These works utilize the FMCW signals (sweeping from 5.46-7.25 GHz) to estimate the time-of-flight, so it is actually UWB based. UWB would continuously occupy a wide band and may impose interference on other devices that share the same frequency. Tadar employs the COTS RFID devices communicate in 50 KHz narrow band channels [28], overcoming the need of UWB.

See through walls with Wi-Fi. Some efforts proposed recently attempt to break the limitations of UWB systems and exploit the potentials of using Wi-Fi for through-wall technologies [10, 11, 14, 20, 24, 25]. Chetty *et al.* [10] propose to deploy the transmitter and a reference receiver in the room, which cooperates with other re-

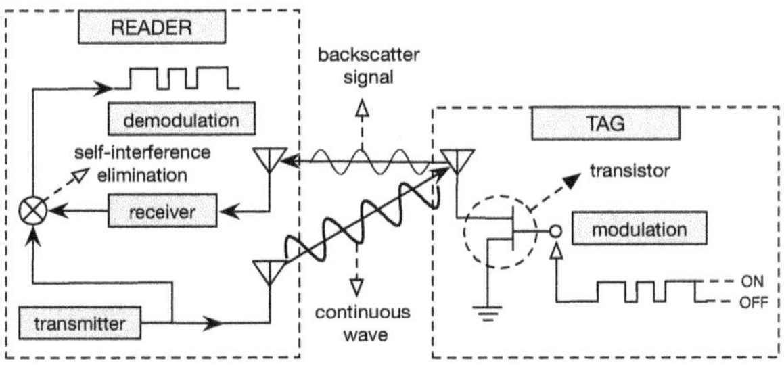

Figure 2: Block diagram of backscatter communication used in UHF RFID system. The tag modulates its ID on the backscatter signal using ON-OFF keying through changing the impedance on its antenna.

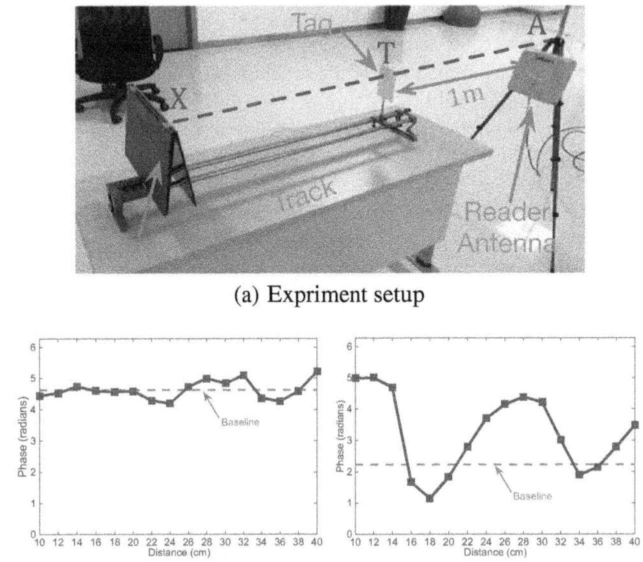

(a) Expriment setup

(b) Indirect impact

(c) Direct impact

Figure 3: Empirical studies on measured RF phase. (a) The default setup of our experiments. (b) The indirect impact on backscatter signals. (c) The direct impact on backscatter signals.

ceivers outside to see objects in the room. This method is limited by its deployment. Adib *et al.* introduce a system, called Wi-Vi, that borrows the MIMO interference nulling to eliminate the flash effect [11]. It creatively treats the motion of a human body as an antenna array and tracks the resulting RF beam. Our work differs from Wi-Vi in that Wi-Vi focuses on the relative motions of human (*e.g.* walking direction) while Tadar aims to exactly recover object's trajectory. Huang *et al.* explore the feasibility of achieving computational imaging using Wi-Fi signals. Their system works without obstruction [20]. Depatla *et al.* proposed a see-through imaging based on WiFi measurements with unmanned vechicles [29,30]. In contrast, Tadar does not need any customized devices or specialized signals and really operates at the narrowband.

See through walls with WSN. Some past works in radio tomography employ networks or hundred sensors to track a person even if he/she does not carry any wireless device. They can be categorized into following groups, *link-based* and *location-based.* (1) *Link-based schemes* measure the RSSI for each of the resulting n^2 links among n sensor nodes, and attribute the variation of RSSI on a link to a human crossing that link [31–36]. Wilson and Patwari find that the changes in RSSI due to human motion can be modeled by the skew-Laplace distribution [31]. Kleisouris *et al.* exploit channel diversities to enhance motion detection accuracy [33]. Nannuru *et al.* develop a measurement model for multi-target tracking using RF tomography, applied for tracking up to three targets [36]. (2) *Location-based schemes* are also known as the radio fingerprint, which is a popular approach for RF-based localization [37–39]. Zhang *et al.* firstly collect a radio map when the subject presents in a few predetermined locations, and then map the test location to one of these trained locations [37]. Moustafa extends RASS to a much large-scaled deployment [38]. Xu *et al.* employ camera to trigger recalibration and update the radio signal data to improve the localization accuracy [39]. These two groups mainly focus on the metric of RSSI, which is not a stable location indicator in RFID systems.

3. UNDERSTANDING REFLECTIONS

In this section, we firstly introduce the technical background of RFID system, and then conduct a series of empirical studies on the backscatter communications.

3.1 Technical Background

Passive RFID system communicates using a backscatter radio link, as shown in Fig. 2. The reader supplies a Continuous Wave (CW) signal, a periodic signal that persists indefinitely without changing its amplitude, frequency or phase, for tags. An RFID reader communicating with a passive tag must operate in full-duplex mode, in the sense that it must supply CW for the tag to backscatter while listening to the tag response at the same time. The tag with no battery equipped, purely harvests energy from the reader's signal. A simple way to understand backscatter radio is as follows [16]. The current flowing on reader's transmitting antenna leads to a voltage induced on the tag's antenna. This induced current also leads to radiation, producing a signal that can be detected: a *backscattered signal.* The tag modulates its ID on the backscatter signal using ON-OFF keying through changing the impedance on its antenna to transmit a '1' bit and remaining in its initial silent state for '0' bit. Referring to [40] published by the ImpinJ, a reader might employ open-loop estimation techniques such a preamble correlation or closed-loop estimation for acquiring and/or tracking *carrier phase and RSS.* For simplicity and saving cost, most of modern RFID readers use one single antenna both for transmitting and receiving.

3.2 Empirical Studies

We conduct empirical studies to better understand the characteristics of backscatter communications, using a COTS ImpinJ reader and an Alien tag. The experiment setup is shown in Fig. 3(a). By default, the reader antenna A, tag T and reflector X are deployed in a straight line. The tag attached on a plastic card, locates between the reader and the reflector. The reader and tag are deployed with $1m$ apart from each other. We horizontally move the reflector (*i.e.* the notebook) to observe how its reflections take impacts on the phase values of the backscatter signal [1]. In an ideal environment, there are two basic channels, forward channel ($A \rightarrow T$) and backward channel ($T \rightarrow A$), between the reader and tag. In our scenario, however, there emerge two additional signal propa-

[1]The phase is chosen as our metric due to its high resolution and sensitivity to reflections [1].

gations, $A \to X \to A$ and $A \to X \to T$, due to the existence of reflector. We categorize the impacts of these two propagations into two types based on whether the reflections *directly* or *indirectly* affect on the tag's backscatter signal.

• *Indirect impact:* The transmitting signal arrives at X and is reflected back to A (*i.e.* $A \to X \to A$). As a result, the reflection mixes with the tag's backscatter signal at reader end, which may *indirectly* affect the identification of the backscatter signal.

• *Direct impact:* The transmitting signal reflected to T (*i.e.* $A \to X \to T$) adds up with the original signal through forward channel (*i.e.* $A \to T$), producing a combined signal at tag end. Since the tag uses this combined signal to modulate its ID, the received backscatter signal contains a *direct* impact from this propagation.

HYPOTHESIS 1. *The indirect impact of reflections off surrounding objects can be negligible.*

We firstly focus on the indirect impact incurred by the reflections propagated from $A \to X \to A$. To isolate the indirect impact, we prevent the reflections from traversing to the tag by placing an RF absorber (with approximately 35 dB attenuation) between the tag and the reflector. The reflector is much larger than the absorber, so there are still many reflections getting back to the reader antenna. We move the reflector to adjust the distance to tag between $10cm$ and $40cm$. The phase measurements are repeated 100 times for a particular distance. The final phase values reported by the reader are illustrated in Fig. 3(b). The dotted line indicates the baseline, *i.e.* the phase value measured when removing the reflector but keeping the absorber. Supperisingly, the figure suggests that the phase value vibrates around the baseline with a very small deviation (< 1 radians) [2] no matter what distance is adjusted. In other words, the impact of propagation from $A \to X \to A$ is reduced to be minimal.

Why the indirect impacts are removed? The RFID systems are *originally* designed for identification. Its main task is to resolve the weak backscatter signal from the CW and environment noise. The reflection from $A \to X \to A$ is a kind of *self-interference* because it does not carry backscatter preamble and highly correlates to the original CW that the reader emits. It can be easily removed by learning the environment before interrogating tag. Removing the self-interference is a standard procedure in RFID reader [2, 16] (see Fig. 2), and also becomes an important metric to evaluate the reader's performance. Any modern COTS RFID reader has the strong ability to eliminate the self-interference, so the indirect impact can be negligible in practice.

HYPOTHESIS 2. *The backscatter signals are vulnerable to the direct impact of the reflections off surrounding objects.*

This hypothesis is our foundation of leveraging tag to sense the reflections off surrounding objects. In this experiment, we remove the RF absorber and re-collect the phase values. The results are plotted in Fig. 3(c). In contrast to the last experiment, the phase value periodically changes as the distance increases. Apparently, the backscatter signals are vulnerable to the direct impact. The tag modulates its ID using the combined signal (through $A \to T$ and $A \to X \to T$). The received backscatter signal contains a standard preamble so the reader would not filter it. Intuitively, the phase non-linearly changes and gradually approaches to the baseline as the distance increases. This is because the direct impact from $A \to X \to T$ gradually weakens as the distance increases, resulting in the signal through $A \to T$ gradually dominates the backscatter signal. We will quantitatively model the reflections in §5.

[2]The vibrations are mainly caused by the thermal noise [1].

4. TADAR OVERVIEW

Tadar is a fine-grained UHF RFID through-wall tracking system that can locate and track moving object including human, and can provide a resolution on the order of a few to tens of centimeters, much smaller than read range of reader.

System Scope. Ultra-low cost UHF tags (5-10 cents each) become the preferred choice of many industry applications. Following the common practices, we concentrate on the UHF tags. We assume that tags are well-positioned so their locations are all known. We also assume that the surveillance region is confined within a limited space. Today's UHF RFID has an operating range of around $10m$. Thus, the assumption is acceptable and can be effectively satisfied by UHF RFID systems. To avoid the tag collisions, the reader adopts TDMA fashion to read them and discard the collided signals [17]. Thus, the effects among tags are negligible. Our systems works in the application layer of reader with the reported RSS and phase values. Our system is general and can capture any mobile objects like robot or drone.

Problem Definition. Suppose n tags, $\{T_1, T_2, \ldots, T_n\}$, are attached on the outer wall. We use the term T_i to denote the ith tag as well as its coordinate. One reader antenna, denoted as A, is employed to light up the objects and read tags. The signals propagated between reader and tags are always kept in LOS. During the surveillance, the geometric relationships between tags remain unchanged. The reader is configured to continously and cyclically read tags, which resembles to using a camera to continously take snapshots of the room. One *read frame* is finished after n tags are all read once. Each frame contains n tags' RSS and phase values reported by a COTS RFID reader. *Our problem is to recovery the trajectory of the moving object behind walls and closed doors given a sequence of read frames.*

Solution Sketch. At a high level, Tadar decomposes the problem into two subproblems.

• *Extracting reflections*: Since Tadar uses the reflections off the moving object for tracking, the first subproblem is how to extract the reflections while eliminating the flash effect. This subproblem is addressed in §5.

• *Tracking objects*: The second subproblem that Tadar addresses in §6 is how to recover the mobile object's trajectory using the extracted reflections.

The next two sections elaborate on these two subproblems, providing the technical details.

5. EXTRACTING REFLECTIONS

In order to distinguish the signals reflected off moving object, off static objects like wall and furniture, and off tags, we respectively call these signals *reflections*, *flash*, and *backscatter signals*. The problem of extracting reflections off objects behind walls is exacerbated by two issues.

First, the signal power after traversing the wall twice (in and out of the room) is reduced by three to five orders of magnitude [11, 16]. The wall is much larger than the object of interest and has a higher reflection coefficient, leading to stronger reflections than that off objects behind the wall. It is like placing a mirror in front of a camera that reflects the camera's flash and prevents it from capturing objects in the scene, which is called *flash effect* [11].

Second, previous through-wall systems all directly receive the reflections through the real antennas connected to the transceiver. In contrast, Tadar logically converts the RFID tags attached on the wall to a virtual antenna array receiving the reflections. These virtual antennas are *wirelessly* connected to the reader and carry the reflections through the backscatter signals. Thus, an additional step

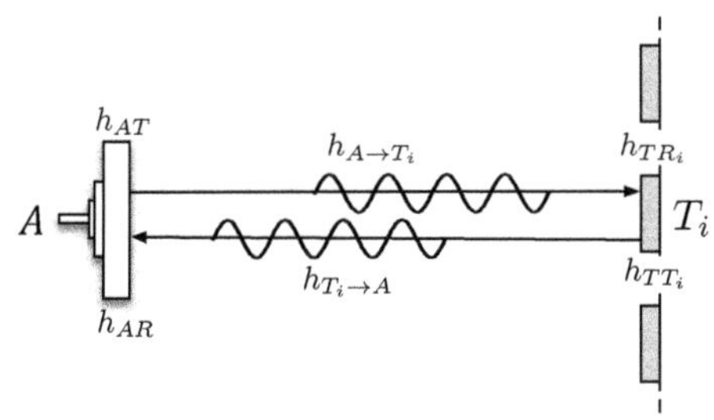

Figure 4: Signal propagation without reflections. There are two basic channels between the reader and the tag.

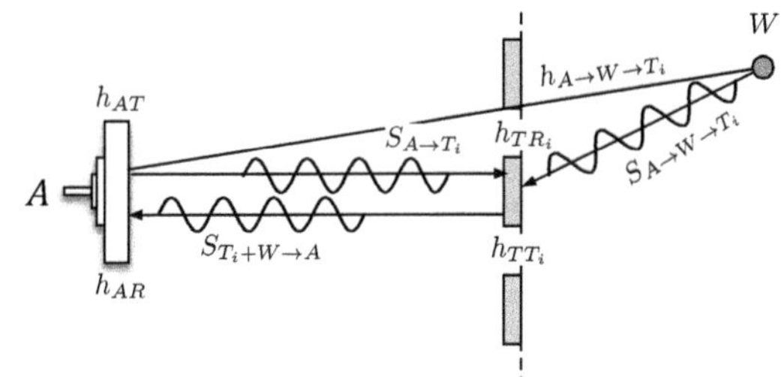

Figure 5: Signal propagation with flash. We treat the flash off wall and other static objects as if they were from a virtual reflection point W.

is required to separate the reflections off the moving object from the backscatter signals reflected by the tags. This is an extremely challenging task as the backscatter signal is already very weak .

To address the above challenges, we start by modeling the backscatter signals through LOS propagation. We then show how to eliminate the flash and derive the reflections from the backscatter signals. Lastly, we sketch the whole algorithm.

5.1 Modeling the Backscatter

A wireless signal is typically represented as a stream of complex numbers. The transmitter modulates the bits into complex symbols to transmit a packet over the wireless channel. The received signal is also represented as a stream of complex symbols. Generally, if the transmitted symbol is denoted as S, then the received symbol S' can be approximated as

$$S' = h \cdot S \tag{1}$$

where $h = \alpha e^{\mathbf{J}\delta}$ is also a complex number, called channel parameter, and α and δ are referred to as *channel attenuation* and its *phase rotation*. The channel can be well approximated by a linear time-variant system. If Alice and Bob concurrently transmit, their signals add up and the received signal can be represented as

$$S' = S'_A + S'_B \tag{2}$$

where $S'_A = h_A S_A$ and $S'_B = h_B S_B$ refer to Alice's and Bob's signals after traversing their corresponding channels to the receiver. These two general features in wireless communications are also hold in backscatter links.

Now we consider the simple scenario that the signal propagates through the LOS between reader and tags without any surrounding objects (*e.g.* no reflections and flash.). In this situation, there are only two basic channels between reader A and each tag T_i: forward channel ($A \to T_i$) and backward channel ($T_i \to A$), as shown in Fig. 4. Let $h_{A\to T_i}$ and $h_{T_i\to A}$ be the parameters of these two basic channels. In an ideal channel model, the channel parameter is defined as follows [16]:

$$h_{A\to T_i} = h_{T_i\to A} = \frac{1}{(d_{A\to T_i})^2} \cdot e^{\mathbf{J}\theta_{A\to T_i}} \tag{3}$$

where the term $\mathbf{J}$ denotes the imaginary number and the term $e^{\mathbf{J}\theta}$ represents a complex exponential signal. The $d_{A\to T_i}$ is the Euclidean distance between A and T_i. The $\theta_{A\to T_i}$ is the phase shift over the distance $d_{A\to T_i}$, which can be calculated for channel wavelength λ as follows.

$$\theta_{A\to T_i} = 2\pi \frac{d_{A\to T_i}}{\lambda} \bmod 2\pi \tag{4}$$

Apparently, $d_{A\to T_i} = d_{T_i\to A}$ and $h_{A\to T_i} = h_{T_i\to A}$ due to the geometric symmetry.

However, the real signal propagations always do not conform to the ideal model due to many factors such as gains of transmitter and receiver, reflectivity, impedance, *etc.* These factors may all introduce additional magnitude attenuations and phase shifts. We abstract their impacts as four unknown parameters, h_{AT}, h_{AR} and h_{TT_i}, h_{TR_i}, respectively denoting the impacts from RFID reader A's transmitter, RFID reader A's receiver and tag T_i's transmitter, tag T_i's receiver. Notice that (1) These four parameters are unknown in practice and vary over tags and readers. (2) A tag in fact does not have obvious transceiver [16]. We use h_{TT_i} and h_{TR_i} to denote its internal reflection characteristics for uniform mathematical expression. Let S_0 be the transmitting signal from the reader. With regard to the above additional impacts, the real signal propagations of forward and backward channels can be represented as follows.

$$\begin{cases} S_{A\to T_i} = h_{TR_i} h_{A\to T_i} h_{AT} S_0 \\ S_{T_i\to A} = h_{AR} h_{T_i\to A} h_{TT_i} S_{A\to T_i} \end{cases} \tag{5}$$

where $S_{A\to T_i}$ is the signal received by T_i and $S_{T_i\to A}$ is the backscatter signal received by A. Merging these two equations, we have

$$S_{T_i\to A} = h_{AR} h_{T_i\to A} h_{TT_i} h_{TR_i} h_{A\to T_i} h_{AT} S_0 \tag{6}$$

How to estimate the received signal? Tadar views each read of tag as one channel estimation. Suppose $\tilde{a}_{T_i\to A}$ and $\tilde{\theta}_{T_i\to A}$ are the magnitude and phase values about T_i reported by the reader, then $S_{T_i\to A}$ can be estimated by

$$S_{T_i\to A} \approx \tilde{a}_{T_i\to A} e^{\mathbf{J}\tilde{\theta}_{T_i\to A}} \tag{7}$$

The estimated $S_{T_i\to A}$ is useful to recover the reflections from the combined backscatter signal later. Note that the reader reports the RSS in unit of dBm instead of watts so we should take a unit conversion between RSS and magnitude. For example, suppose we received $(RSS_{T_i\to A}, \theta_{T_i\to A})$, the magnitude of the backscattered signal can be estimated as follows:

$$a_{T_i\to A} = 10^{\sqrt{\frac{RSS_{T_i\to A}}{1000}}} \tag{8}$$

In spite of involvement of physical-layer information, Tadar only uses the common parameters reported by COTS reader without any modification on hardware or firmware.

5.2 Eliminating the Flash

To eliminate the impact of flash, we firstly consider the scenario that the tags are attached on the outer wall and no object of interest moves inside the room. The transmitting signals are reflected

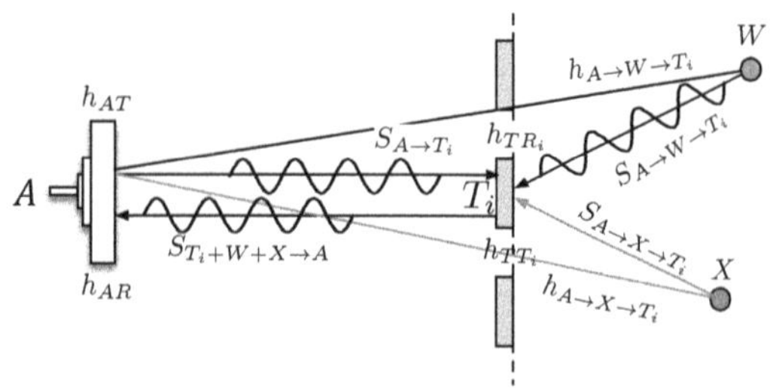

Figure 6: The signal propagation with flash and reflections. The flash and reflections off the moving object X add up at the tag end.

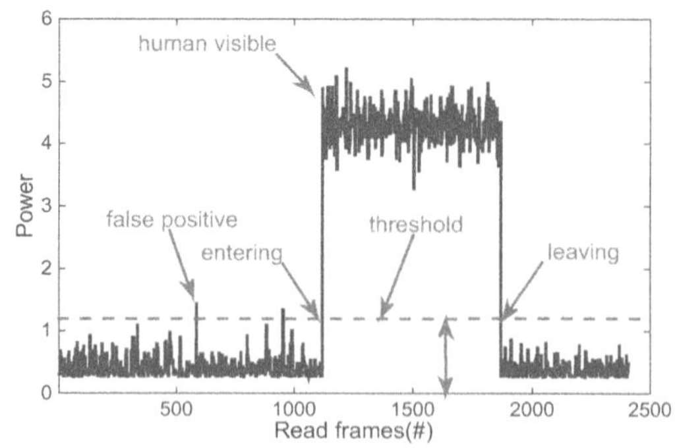

Figure 7: The power of signal difference. The sampled results are shown every $200ms$ for visual clarity.

off the wall and other static objects like chairs. The key idea underlying Tadar is to treat these reflections as if they were from a virtual reflection point W due to the principle of linear superimposing of signals. As Fig. 15(a) shows, there is an additional signal (*i.e.* flash), denoted as $S_{A\to W\to T_i}$ traveling from $A \to W \to T_i$ for each tag besides the two basic channels. The $S_{A\to W\to T_i}$ and $S_{A\to T_i}$ concurrently arrive at the tag end and linearly add up with each other. Both of them are the continuous wave originated from the reader. The tag T_i uses this combined signal to modulate its ID and backscatters it to A. Then the final backscatter signal from T_i, denoted as $S_{T_i+W\to A}$, is also a combined signal and can be expressed as follows.

$$S_{T_i+W\to A} = h_{AR}h_{T_i\to A}h_{TT_i}(S_{A\to T_i} + S_{A\to W\to T_i}) \quad (9)$$

Second, we consider the scenario that a moving object X appears in the room as shown in Fig. 6. There exists a third signal propagating from $A \to X \to T_i$. We denote the corresponding signal as $S_{A\to X\to T_i}$. Similarly, the three signals linearly add up at tag T_i, resulting in a more complex combined backscatter signal, denoted as $S_{T_i+W+X\to A}$, given by:

$$S_{T_i+W+X\to A} = \\ h_{AR}h_{T_i\to A}h_{TT_i}(S_{A\to T_i} + S_{A\to W\to T_i} + S_{A\to X\to T_i}) \quad (10)$$

Likewise, $S_{T_i+W\to A}$ and $S_{T_i+W+X\to A}$ can be estimated using the measured magnitude and phase values. To eliminate the flash, we use Eqn. (10) to subtract Eqn. (9). As a result, we have

$$S_{T_i+W+X\to A} - S_{T_i+W\to A} = h_{AR}h_{T_i\to A}h_{TT_i}S_{A\to X\to T_i} \quad (11)$$

In this way, the flash (*i.e.* $S_{A\to W\to T_i}$) is removed in the above equation. Hence, the flash is eliminated by the end of this step. Notice if no object moves, *i.e.* $S_{A\to X\to T_i} = 0$, then the signal difference approximately equals 0. Thus, we can also use the two signals' difference to determine whether moving object appears or disapears in the room, introducing the following hypothesis.

HYPOTHESIS 3. *In the case of absence (or presence) of moving object, the tags will suggest a signal difference lower (or higher) than a threshold. Thus, if the tags suggest the signal difference is lower (or higher) than a threshold, it indicates the absence (or presence) of moving object.*

An experiment is conducted to verify this hypothesis. We keep the room empty and then let a person move into it. Fig. 7 shows that the signal difference firstly maintains in a very low level (< 1.0), and then sharply increase by 4× due to the person's reflections. The difference returns back a normal level after the person leaves. Notice that there may occur a small number of discrete false positives shown in the figure. To deal with this issue, we borrow the idea of background subtraction in computer vision [41] which is used for foreground segmentation. The main idea behind is to automatically learn and maintain a representation of the background using Gaussian model. When a new frame incomes, it classifies whether a moving object emerges or leaves. It aggregates the determination results of multiple successive frames to filter the false positives.

5.3 Deriving the Reflection

As Eqn. (11) shows, the signal difference implicitly contains the reflections off the moving object (*i.e.* $S_{A\to X\to T_i}$). On the other hand, the reflection can be further modeled as follows:

$$S_{A\to X\to T_i} = h_{TR_i}h_X h_{A\to X\to T_i}h_{AT}S_O \quad (12)$$

where two new parameters, h_X and $h_{A\to X\to T_i}$, are introduced. The h_X indicates the influence caused by the object, varying over its materials. The $h_{A\to X\to T_i}$ is the compound parameter of channel $A \to X \to T_i$, which equals

$$h_{A\to X\to T_i} = \frac{e^{\mathbf{J}(\theta_{A\to X}+\theta_{X\to T_i})}}{(d_{A\to X} + d_{X\to T_i})^2} \quad (13)$$

It is the parameter that presents a clue about the moving object's location, which will be employed to track moving object in §6. Next, we concentrate on introducing how to derive $h_{A\to X\to T_i}$ from the signal difference. Substituting Eqn. (12) into Eqn (11), we have

$$S_{T_i+W+X\to A} - S_{T_i+W\to A} = \\ h_{AR}h_{T_i\to A}h_{TT_i}\underbrace{h_{TR_i}h_X h_{A\to X\to T_i}h_{AT}S_O}_{S_{A\to X\to T_i}} \quad (14)$$

In order to eliminate the unknown parameters, we divide Eqn. (14) by Eqn. (6) as follows.

$$\frac{S_{T_i+W+X\to A} - S_{T_i+W\to A}}{S_{T_i\to A}} = \frac{h_X h_{A\to X\to T_i}}{h_{A\to T_i}} \quad (15)$$

Interesting, all unknown parameters (*i.e.* h_{AR}, h_{AT}, h_{TT_i}, h_{TR_i}) relevant to the devices are removed. More importantly, the transmitting signal S_O are also removed so our tracking results are irrelevant to the transmitting signal. It introduces two benefits: First, we do not have to know the transmitting continuous wave, which actually depends on the internal implementation of reader and varies over the manufactures. Second, we can design a higher-gain antenna boosting the power (see §7) to increase the SNR of reflections, rather than worry about this behavior's influence on the tracking results.

Consequently, the parameter $h_{A\to X\to T_i}$ can be derived as follows.

$$h_{A\to X\to T_i} = \frac{(S_{T_i+W+X\to A} - S_{T_i+W\to A})h_{A\to T_i}}{S_{T_i\to A}} \times \frac{1}{h_X} \quad (16)$$

In this equation, $S_{T_i+W+X\to A}$, $S_{T_i+W\to A}$ and $S_{T_i\to A}$ can be estimated using the reported magnitude and phase values. Meanwhile, $h_{A\to T_i}$ is the parameter of ideal forward channel, which can be calculated using Eqn. (3). Note that all of these values are complex numbers. Let $\hat{h}_{A\to X\to T_i}$ be the estimated result, namely

$$\begin{aligned}\hat{h}_{A\to X\to T_i} &= \frac{(S_{T_i+W+X\to A} - S_{T_i+W\to A})h_{A\to T_i}}{S_{T_i\to A}} \\ &= \hat{a}_{A\to X\to T_i} e^{\mathbf{J}\hat{\theta}_{A\to X\to T_i}} \quad (17)\end{aligned}$$

and $h_X = a_X e^{\mathbf{J}\theta_X}$. Then $h_{A\to X\to T_i}$ can be expressed as follows.

$$h_{A\to X\to T_i} \approx \frac{\hat{a}_{A\to X\to T_i}}{a_X} e^{\mathbf{J}(\hat{\theta}_{A\to X\to T_i} - \theta_X)} \quad (18)$$

Unfortunately, h_X is still an unknown variable that cannot be removed in practice. We will discuss h_X in §6.

5.4 Putting Things Together

The discussion so far focuses on how to extract the reflections off the moving object. Now we put all the pieces together and sketch the algorithm as follows.

Step 1: Tadar learns the basic backscatter signal $S_{T_i\to A}$ through LOS propagation for each tag before attaching tags on the wall.

Step 2: Tadar learns the backscatter signal $S_{T_i+W\to A}$ that involves flash after attaching tags on the wall.

Step 3: Tadar measures the backscatter signal $S_{T_i+W+X}[t]$ at read frame t. It starts to monitor moving object by detecting the signal difference $|S_{T_i+W+X}[t] - S_{T_i+W}|$. If new object emerges, it estimates $\hat{h}_{A\to X\to T_i}$ using Eqn. (17) and delivers it to the next component (see §6).

The virtue of Tadar lies in its graceful and compact calculation only using the results reported by a COTS reader collected in three steps, despite the involvement of very complex mathematical derivation, physical-layer information and various unknown variables.

Another thing worth-noting is that RFID reader adopts TDMA fashion to successively identify each tag to avoid tag collisions,. The collided signals would be discarded. Since our algorithm performs in the application layer of reader, Tadar does not need to worry about the mutual interferences among tags. The question is how can we guarantee the object stays in the same position when reading these n tags? The modern COTS, *e.g.* ImpibJ R420, uses a variety of high performance features making it to read more than 1000+ tags per second [42]. Then we can perform $40 \sim 50$ frames per second. Such high-speed frame rate allows us to monitor the region very fast. It is similar to continuously capture the snapshot of surveillance region using a high-speed camera. Therefore, we have a good reason to assume that the object approximately stays in the same position during a read frame.

6. TRACKING MOBILE OBJECT

There are two main tracking methods employed in most of prior through-wall systems or tracking systems. The first method steers an antenna array's beam to determine the direction of maximum energy. The direction corresponds to the signal's spatial angle of arrival (AoA) [2, 11]. The second method estimates the time of flight by transmitting a specialized signal (*e.g.* pulse or FMCW) and measuring the delay between the transmitted pulse and its received echo [24]. Both of them require the customized device or specialized signals to infer the object's location, which cannot be implemented by the ability-limited RFID tags. Alternatively, Tadar adopts a Hidden Markov Model (HMM) to track the mobile object. In this section, we firstly review the HMM and Viterbi decoding, and then discuss how to apply it into in tracking problem.

6.1 Hidden Markov Model

Consider a HMM whose latent Markovian state X is in one of N discrete states $\{x_1, x_2, \ldots, x_N\}$. Let the actual state at time t be denoted by $X[t]$. The transition matrix

$$\mathcal{A} = \{x_i \mapsto x_j : i, j = 1, 2, \ldots N\} \quad (19)$$

defines the state transition probabilities where $x_i \mapsto x_j = \Pr(X[t+1] = x_j \mid X[t] = x_i)$. The Markov chain is assumed to be stationary, so $x_i \mapsto x_j$ is independent of t. Let the discrete observation space be set $\{y_1, y_2, \ldots, y_M\}$ with the cardinality of M. Let $Y[t]$ be the observation symbol at time t. The observation matrix

$$\mathcal{B} = \{x_i \mapsto y_k : i = 1, 2, \ldots N; k = 1, 2, \ldots, M\} \quad (20)$$

defines the emission probability where $x_i \mapsto y_k = \Pr(Y[t] = y_k \mid X[t] = x_i)$. The initial state distribution is given by

$$\Pi = \{\alpha_1, \alpha_2 \ldots, \alpha_M\} \quad (21)$$

where $\alpha_i = \Pr(X[0] = x_i)$. The HMM is used to solve three kinds of problems. Here we concern the most famous one that given HMM models $\{\mathcal{A}, \mathcal{B}, \Pi\}$ and a sequence of observations, $\{Y[1] \to Y[2] \to \cdots \to Y[t]\}$, to find an optimal state sequence for the underlying Markov process. This problem can be resolved by the Viterbi decoding.

6.2 Tracking Object via HMM

Inspired by HMM, Tadar treats the object's location as the hidden states and the reflections off the moving object as the observations. Then, our tracking problem is transformed to finding the maximum likelihood sequence of positions it traversed given a sequence of reflections. The crucial task is how to represent our problem in form of HMM (*i.e.* $(\mathcal{A}, \mathcal{B}, \Pi)$). Below we describe the modeling process.

Hidden State and Transition Probability. Tadar divides the whole surveillance room into N grids at cm-level. The hidden states are these N divided grids. We assume that the object's movement during two consecutive frames is within a wavelength (*i.e.* its speed $\leq 34m/s$). Suppose the object locates at x_i currently, it may stay at x_i or move to next grid x_j with the constraint of $d_{x_i\to x_j} \leq \lambda$. We do not make any assumptions about the motion behavior, and use uniform transition probability between adjacent steps.

DEFINITION 1 (TRANSITION PROBABILITY). *Given state x_i and x_j, the transition probability $x_i \mapsto x_j$ is defined as follows.*

$$x_i \mapsto x_j = \begin{cases} 1/|\{x_k : d_{x_i\to x_k} \leq \lambda\}| & \text{if } d_{x_i\to x_j} \leq \lambda. \\ 0 & \text{otherwise.} \end{cases}$$

where $k = \{1, \ldots, N\}$ and $|\cdot|$ is the cardinality. The grids in $\{x_k : d_{x_i\to x_k} \leq \lambda\}$ are called as the x_i's neighbors, which are reachable within λ from x_i.

Two points are worth-noting. First, x_i's neighbors include itself because the object may remain at grid x_i. Second, the grids near to

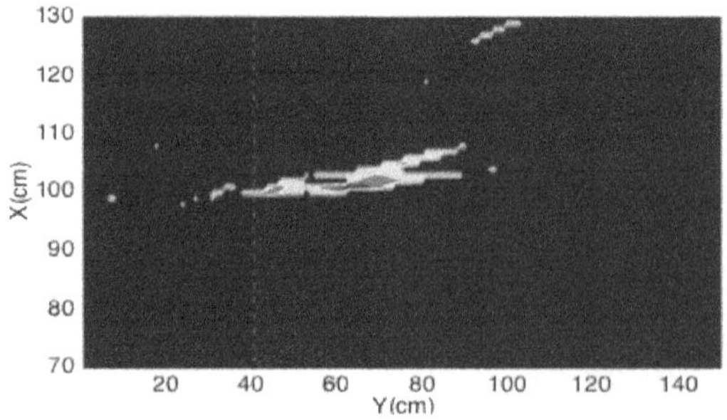

Figure 8: The distribution of emission probability. The object locates at grid $(70, 100)$.

Figure 9: Antenna array beams. Each pair of tags produces a hyperbola.

that in edges of surveillance region have less neighbors than those grids in the center.

Initial State Distribution. We also do not make any assumption about the object's initial location (*i.e.* it may emerge at anywhere), so $\alpha_i = 1/N$. In practice, if the door is the only way that the person enters the room, we should adjust the grids near to the door with higher probabilities.

Observation and Emission Probability. The transmitting signals are scattered to one or more paths after reflected due to the none uniformities of object's surface. Thus, the reflections off the object can be received by multiple tags in the array. On the frame t incomes, the observation $Y[t]$ is a vector including n reflections from n tags. The observation $Y[t]$ can be formalized as follows.

$$Y[t] = [h_{A\to X[t]\to T_1}, \dots, h_{A\to X[t]\to T_n}] \tag{22}$$

where $h_{A\to X[t]\to T_i}$ is the reflection extracted from tag T_i's backscatter signal. The emission probability for a given state presents the probability of seeing the object locates at the grid conditioned on the reflections. Correctly modeling the emission probability is a crucial task for trajectory estimation. We adopt the phase value as the metric to depict emission probability. Due to thermal noise, the measured phase value $\tilde{\theta}_{A\to X[t]\to T_i}$ is a random variable following a Gaussian model. Namely,

$$\tilde{\theta}_{A\to X[t]\to T_i} \sim \mathcal{N}(\theta_{A\to X[t]\to T_i}, \sigma)$$

where $\theta_{A\to X[t]\to T_i}$ is the expectation (*i.e.* $E(\tilde{\theta}_{A\to X[t]\to T_i}) = \theta_{A\to X[t]\to T_i}$), and σ is the standard deviation. The object is supposed to located at $X[t]$ so the expectation in theory should equal to

$$E(\tilde{\theta}_{A\to X[t]\to T_i}) = \theta_{A\to X[t]} + \theta_{X[t]\to T_i} \tag{23}$$

Unfortunately, we can only estimate $\hat{\theta}_{A\to X[t]\to T_i}$ rather than $\tilde{\theta}_{A\to X[t]\to T_i}$ in practice due to the unknown variable θ_X, as shown in Eqn. (18). Their relationships are shown as follows:

$$\tilde{\theta}_{A\to X[t]\to T_i} = \hat{\theta}_{A\to X[t]\to T_i} - \theta_X \tag{24}$$

The fact is that θ_X is common term over different tags (because all reflections come from the same object). We select one of them (*e.g.* T_j) as a reference and compute the phase difference, denoted as $\Delta\tilde{\theta}_{i,j}$, as follows.

$$\begin{aligned} \Delta\tilde{\theta}_{i,j} &= \tilde{\theta}_{A\to X[t]\to T_i} - \tilde{\theta}_{A\to X[t]\to T_j} \\ &= (\hat{\theta}_{A\to X[t]\to T_i} - \theta_X) - (\hat{\theta}_{A\to X[t]\to T_j} - \theta_X) \\ &= \hat{\theta}_{A\to X[t]\to T_i} - \hat{\theta}_{A\to X[t]\to T_j} \end{aligned} \tag{25}$$

Obviously, the unknown variable θ_X is removed from the above equation, so phase difference $\Delta\tilde{\theta}_{i,j}$ can be estimated using Eqn. (17).

Since the mean of the difference of two random variables equals the difference of their expectations, the expectation of$E(\Delta\tilde{\theta}_{i,j})$ is given by

$$\begin{aligned} E(\Delta\tilde{\theta}_{i,j}) &= E(\tilde{\theta}_{A\to X[t]\to T_i}) - E(\tilde{\theta}_{A\to X[t]\to T_j}) \\ &= (\theta_{A\to X[t]} + \theta_{X[t]\to T_i}) - (\theta_{A\to X[t]} + \theta_{X[t]\to T_j}) \\ &= \theta_{X[t]\to T_i} - \theta_{X[t]\to T_j} \end{aligned} \tag{26}$$

The variance of the difference of two random variables is the sum of their variances. Thus, $\text{Var}(\Delta\tilde{\theta}_{i,j}) = \sqrt{2}\sigma$. The standard deviation is irrelevant to object's location but depends on the reader's transceiver. It can be trained in advance. Totally, we have

$$\Delta\tilde{\theta}_{i,j} \sim \mathcal{N}\left(E(\Delta\tilde{\theta}_{i,j}), \sqrt{2}\sigma\right) \tag{27}$$

Then the emission probability is defined as follows.

DEFINITION 2 (EMISSION PROBABILITY). *The emission probability governs the distribution of the observations when the object locates at $X[t]$, which is defined as follows:*

$$\begin{aligned} X[t] \mapsto Y[t] &= \Pr\left([h_{A\to X[t]\to T_1}, \dots, h_{A\to X[t]\to T_N}] \mid X[t]\right) \\ &= \frac{1}{N}\sum_{i=1}^{N} F(\Delta\tilde{\theta}_{i,j}; E(\Delta\tilde{\theta}_{i,j}), \sqrt{2}\sigma) \end{aligned}$$

where $F(X; \mu, \sigma)$ is the cumulative probability function of Gaussian distribution $\mathcal{N}(\mu, \sigma)$.

One important reason using HMM and Viterbi decoding for our tracking is that they can reduce the computations for each step considering the principle of moving continuity in time-domain. It is not necessary to search the whole surveillance region every read frame. Fig. 8 shows the distribution of emission probability from one of our experiments where the tag array is deployed in the negative direction of Y-axis. We observe that the the emission probability achieves the highest probability at the ground truth and diffuses to its neighbors as expected.

6.3 Further Discussion

It is known that the phase value repeats every a wavelength. How can we ensure the $X[t] \mapsto Y[t]$ archives the maximum when visiting the correct grid $X[t]$ given the observation $Y[t]$? Suppose θ_i and θ_j, $\theta_i, \theta_j \in [0, 2\pi]$, are the phases of reflections off object X received by tag T_i and T_j. The distances and the received signal phases have the following relations due to the phase rotation:

$$\begin{cases} \theta_i = \frac{2\pi}{\lambda} d_{A\to X\to T_i} \mod 2\pi \\ \theta_j = \frac{2\pi}{\lambda} d_{A\to X\to T_j} \mod 2\pi \end{cases} \tag{28}$$

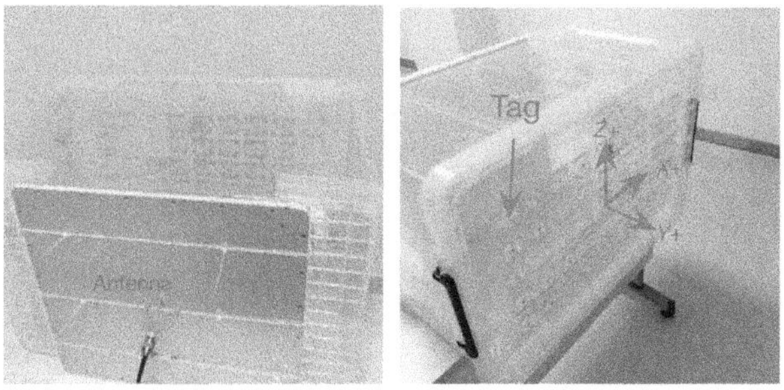

(a) Antenna (b) Tag array

Figure 10: Tadar's setup. A plastic box is used to facilitate our tests. (a) An antenna is fixed on the bottom. (b) A group of tags are attached on its top.

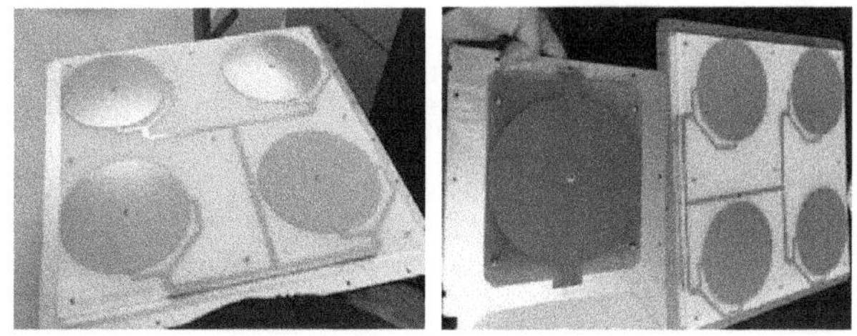

(a) 12dBi (b) 8dBi

Figure 11: Antenna design. We design a high-gain directional antenna with 12dBi to boost power. (a) The 12dBi antenna with four patches. (b) The comparisons of our antenna with 8dBi antenna employed in logistics.

Hence, the phase difference, $\Delta\theta_{i,j} = \theta_i - \theta_j$, between the received signals at the two tags relates to the difference in their distances from the object, $\Delta d_{i,j} = d_{A\to X\to T_i} - d_{A\to X\to T_j}$, as follows.

$$\Delta d_{i,j} = \lambda(\frac{\Delta\theta_{i,j}}{2\pi} + k) \tag{29}$$

where k can be any integer in $[-\frac{D}{\lambda} - \frac{\Delta\theta_{i,j}}{2\pi}, -\frac{D}{\lambda} + \frac{\Delta\theta_{i,j}}{2\pi}]$ and D is the distance between two tags. In our scenario, the $k = 0$ or 1 because all tags are deployed within one wavelength. Thus, the phase difference $\Delta\theta_{i,j}$ used in emission probability is equivalent to the distance difference $\Delta d_{i,j}$ in essence.

$$\begin{aligned} \Delta d_{i,j} &= d_{A\to X\to T_i} - d_{A\to X\to T_j} \\ &= (d_{A\to X} + d_{X\to T_i}) - (d_{A\to X} + d_{X\to T_j}) \\ &= d_{X\to T_i} - d_{X\to T_j} \end{aligned}$$

The above equation is a standard equation representing one hyperbola that focuses on T_i and T_j. Thus, the emission probability actually indicates how the assumed location (*i.e.* the hidden state) matches the $n-1$ hyperbolas. The phase ambiguity is removed by multiple hyperbolas. Fig. 9 shows the 4 hyperbolas including 8 branches produced by the 4 phase differences where the third tag is chosen as the reference. All these curves intersect on the ground truth.

7. IMPLEMENTATION

We build a prototype of Tadar using the COTS RFID reader and tags. Fig. 10 shows the main setup of our devices. We use a plastic box to maintain the geometric relationships between reader antenna and tags instead of attaching them on wall for convenience, because we would move the array to different buildings with a same setting. In details, we deploy the reader antenna on the bottom and attach 5×9 tags on the top. The box's dimension is $61 \times 43 \times 33cm^3$. Tags are separated by $5cm$.

RFID: We adopt one ImpinJ Speedway modeled R420 reader [43] without any hardware or firmware modification. The reader is compatible with EPC Gen2 standard [28]. The whole RFID system operates in the 920 $\sim$ 926 MHz band. We use the Alien tags modeled "2 × 2" (2.25 × $2.25cm^2$) [44], which are widely used in supply chain applications. Each of them costs 5 cents.

Boosting power: The reflections off the wall are 30 $\sim$ 40 dB above the that off moving objects. Even eliminating the flash effect, we can hardly discern the reflections due to human because it is too weak and immersed in the receiver's hardware noise. To boost the power, we build an antenna with 4 patches, as shown in Fig. 11(a). The antenna has a directional gain of 12 dBi, a 3 dB beam width of 40°. Fig. 11(b) shows the comparisons between the antenna with the ordinary antenna with 8 dBi. Our antenna is composed of a couple of two-layer boards (boards with two copper layers and one substrate layer) that are physically connected to each other by plastic screws.

Experiment setup: Majority of our experiments are performed at our conference rooms in one office building. The conference room is $7 \times 4m^2$. There are one big table ($4 \times 0.75m^2$), twelve chairs, one white board, *etc.* The interior walls of the building are $5''$ hollow walls supported by steel frames with sheet rock on top. To discuss the effect of building materials, we also conduct some experiments in a second building with $8''$ concrete walls. To seize the ground truth, we command an iRobot Create robot with a $12''$ Lenovo notebook as the reflector to move along a programed trajectory. We also invite 5 human subjects with different heights and builds for the application study. Each experiment is repeated for many times and the average value is reported only. The coordinate system is shown in Fig. 10(b) that the origin locates at the center of the tag array and the signal is emitted to positive direction of Y-axis.

8. EVALUATION

In this section, we evaluate Tadar from aspects of reflection acquisition, diversity elimination and object tracking.

8.1 Reflection Acquisition

First, we would like to automate the thresholds for the presence of moving objects. To this end, we investigate the SNRs in different scenarios. The SNR is defined as power ratio of signals acquired in presence to absence of moving objects in the room. The reflections with very weak SNR will be overwhelmed by the noise. In this experiment, we place the object at a distance of $3m$ away from the wall. We choose three typical kinds of materials: $0.98''$ glass, $1.5''$ wood door and $5''$ hollow wall to measure their SNRs. The results in form of CDFs are plotted in Fig. 12. Each CDF contains more than 2000 samples with presence of moving objects. The average SNRs detected are 10.61, 4.69 and 7.01. As expected, the thicker and denser the obstructing material, the harder it is for Tadar to capture reflections from behind it. However, the power level is 4× higher than that of noise even in the worst case.

Second, we evaluate Tadar's detection range considering four different building materials including $5''$ hollow wall (C2), $1.5''$ wood door (C3), $0.98''$ glass (C4), and $8''$ concrete (C5). We

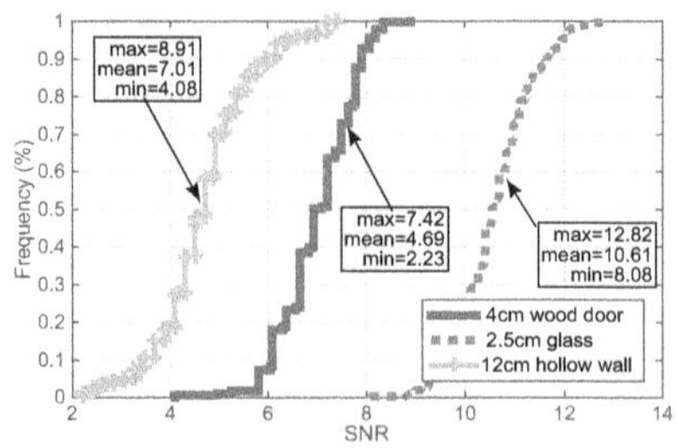

Figure 12: SNR Comparisons

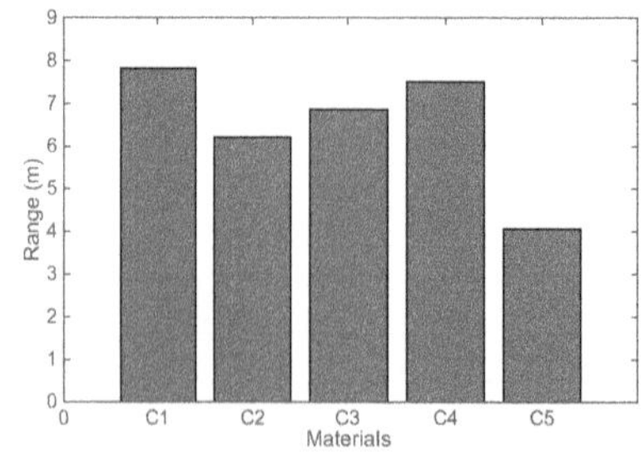

Figure 13: Detecting Range

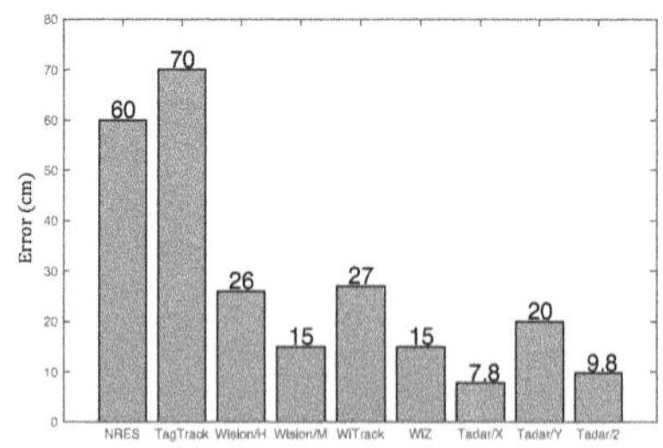

Figure 14: Tracking Accuracy

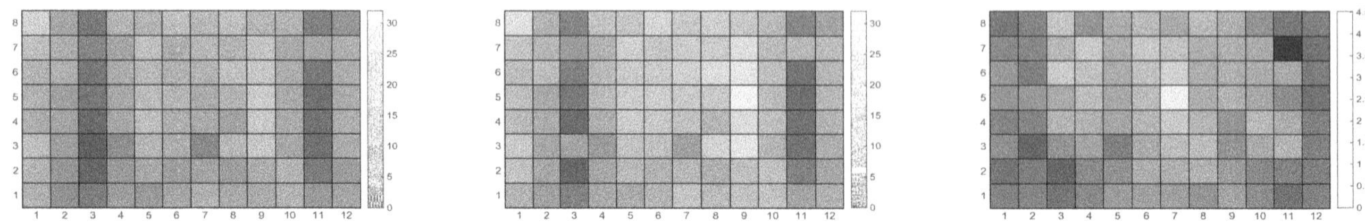

(a) $|S_{T_i \to A}|$ (b) $|S_{T_i + X \to A}|$ (c) $|\hat{h}_{T_i + X \to A}|$

Figure 15: Magnitude distribution based on tag array. The array includes 12×8 tags. Each grid denotes a result collected from the corresponding tag. (a) The signal collected with an empty room. (b) The signal collected when an iPhone 6 Plus is placed in front of the wall. (c) The separated reflections.

also perform experiments in free space (C1) with no obstruction between tag and the object. The range is the maximum distance that Tadar can detect the object. The results are shown in Fig. 13, which are consistent with the comparisons of SNRs. Specifically, Tadar can detect the object with a range of $7.6m$ in free space, and achieve a median range of $6m$, $6.77m$, $7.5m$ and $4.12m$ in other four different buildings materials. RFID system working at $800 \sim 900$ MHz UHF has a bit weaker penetrability compared with the UWB technologies. After all, RFID system is not designed for see-through-wall originally. However, the benefits of Tadar are obvious in that it is low-cost, compact and without needs of specialized signals or customized devices.

Summary. The above two experiments show that Tadar has good behaviors in acquisition of reflections. There are three main reasons for this feature. First, the RFID technology originates from the radar so the RFID devices have the strong ability to resolve the weak signals and remove the self-interference [45]. This feature helps Tadar well suppress the environmental and thermal noise. Second, Tadar utilizes the continuous wave transmitted from the reader to light up the objects. The CW is very stable because it does not carry any information, which facilitates the removal of flash using the learned signals. Third, the tag has no hardware filters for saving cost such that it is hypersensitive to 'interferences', enabling us to capture the weak reflections off surrounding objects.

8.2 Diversity Elimination

Third, we would like to know whether the unknown parameters related to devices are well removed from the results. To visually understand this issue, let us consider a simple setup with 12×8 tags attached on the wall. Fig. 15(a) plots the magnitudes of signals backscattered from these 96 tags with an empty room. A grid in the figure denotes a tag's result. The antenna is deployed at the center. In the ideal wireless model, the magnitude values would descend from center to edges because the magnitude goes as the inverse twice power of the distance (see Eqn. 3). However, the distribution is out of order due to the affects from those unknown parameters (h_{AT_i}, h_{AR}, h_{TT_i}, and h_{TR_i}). Then we place an iPhone 6 Plus in front of the wall with a distance of $1m$. Fig. 15(b) again plots the magnitudes collected from those tags. In total, several grids are lightly brightened (thus large RSS values) because their signals are strengthened by the reflections. However, the results are still too ambiguous to pinpoint the iPhone. Fig. 15(c) plots the magnitude of $\hat{h}_{A \to X \to T_i}$. The result shows quite in agreement with the ideal wireless model. We can even point out the area the phone locates as the tags under the phone have higher values. Specifically, the tag right below the phone has the maximum value. This example demonstrates that $\hat{h}_{A \to X \to T_i}$ indeed well eliminates the impacts from the unknown diversities.

8.3 Object Tracking

Fourth, we investigate Tadar's tracking accuracy compared with other five methods. In the experiments, we let the robot move along a predefined track and then use the HMM and reflections to estimate its trajectory. The accuracy is calculated using the difference of the estimated trajectory and the ground truth. The comparisons are shown in Fig. 14.

NRES: NRES [18] deploys a large number of WSN nodes around the room, and tracks humans in building using changes in the signal strength incurred by the human's motions. It obtains a median tracking error of $60cm$.

TagTrack: TagTrack [19] is the similar attempt using RFID signals to passively localize the objects. It deploys the tags around the objects and employs the RSS changes as the tracking indicator. It improves the result by introducing classification technique, and achieves a median error distance of $70cm$. However, TagTrack is not a see-through-wall technology because the backscatter signals cannot traverse through a wall.

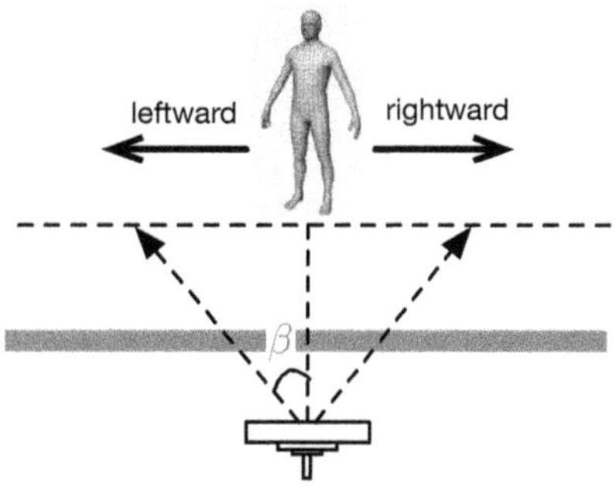

Figure 16: Encoding gesture

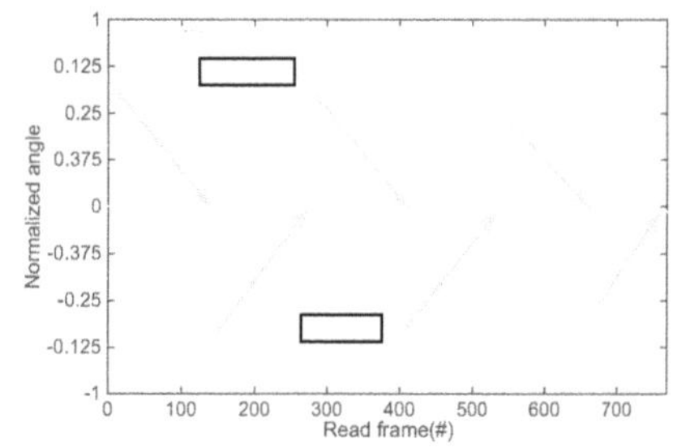

Figure 17: Decoding gesture

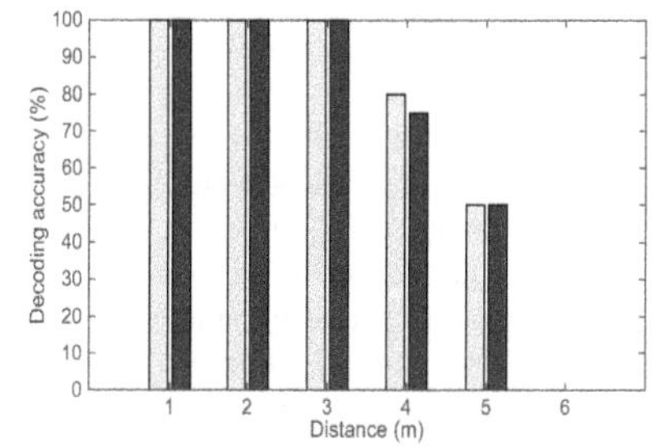

Figure 18: Gesture Accuracy

Wision: Wision [20] leverages the multi-path propagations to perform object imaging using two-dimensional antenna arrays. Wision localizes static humans (Wison/H) with a median accuracy of $26cm$ and metallic objects (Wison/M), like MacBook and HP desktop, with a median of $15cm$. Wision suffers from the effects from objects' materials, which is removed in Tadar by comparing with the reference tag. Note that Wision is also not a see-through-wall method.

WiTrack and **WiZ**: WiTrack [24] is a system that localizes the user's motion in three-dimensional space from the radio signals reflected off his/her body. It localizes the center of a human body to within a median of $27cm$. WiZ [25] is an incremental work extending WiTrack to multi-person and obtains a median of $15cm$. Both WiTrack and WiZ needs a customized hardware to transmit a well-designed radio signal (*e.g.* FMCW) for estimating the traveling time. WiZ generate a signal that sweeps $5.46 \sim 7.25$ GHz, so both of them, strictly speaking, are UWB based methods.

Tadar: Tadar's tracking errors are exhibited in two dimensions. It can achieve a median of tracking error of $7.8cm$ and $20cm$ at X and Y dimensions. It outperforms the existing none-UWB technologies by $3\times$, $3.5\times$ and $1.3\times$ compared with NRES, TagTrack and Wision, and performs as well as WiTrack and WiZ[3]. Why the results show such a dramatic difference in two dimensions? Reviewing Fig. 9, we see that all hyperbolas of emission probability are towards X-axis because all tags are deployed on one side of the surveillance region only. This incurs a lower discernibility at Y-axis. To coverage the results along Y-axis, we could attach two arrays of tags on two sides of the room. In this way, the combined error can be further reduced to a median of $9.8cm$.

Summary: Totally, Tadar improves the see-through and tracking technology from three main aspects. First, Tadar well eliminates all uncertain variables (*e.g.* device diversity, reflectivity differences *etc*) in calculations. Second, the low cost of RFID tags allows us to deploy a large number of tags to acquire reflections, which helps improve the accuracy. Specifically, the cost of each antenna, used in Wision and WiTrack, is able to purchase $40 \sim 50$ RFID tags, while Wision needs to consume 64 antennas (the same price as the sum of 3200 tags). Third, the deployment of Tadar is easier and more compact than other methods, facilitating its application in various domains.

8.4 Cost Comparisons

One of the virtues of the Tadar is low cost. Lastly, we investigate the cost comparisons with other through-wall technologies.

[3]There is a setup difference between WiTrack/WiZ and Tadar. WiTrack/WiZ perfroms the experiments through 6-inch wall while Tadar is with 5-inch wall. This is because thickness standard in China is a little different from that of USA.

Military radar. Through-wall imaging and tracking in radar community is very mature. We search the military-level through-wall radars in Alibaba and find the prices of radar devices are ranged between $80,000 \sim 90,000$ US dollars, $40\times$ as much as ours on average. Apparently, our solution is very low-cost compared with the military radar. In addition, the through-wall radar systems in the market are usually prohibited from selling to civilians in most countries in the world. Our system targets to civilian purpose with COTS devices, which is totally legal in any country. This benefit cannot be offered by the military radar.

Wi-Fi based methods. Wi-Fi based through-wall technologeis need a set of software-defined radio like USRP or WARP to emit customized signals [11, 24, 25]. The total price of USRP including antennas is more than 2000 US dollars, a little higher than ours. However, we must claim that our solution totally employs the COTS devices with industry-level design and encapsulation, which can be deployed without any modification on the hardware. The tracking algorithms can run at normal PC computer. With regard to the price and convenience, we insist our solution is prior to the Wi-Fi based.

WSN based methods. Some past work in radio tomography employs hundred sensors to track a person passively. No matter the approach is linked-based or location-based, they need deploy a large number of nodes around the room to enable the links cover the entire region. Unlike our approach that deploys the tags in one side, the need cover the room from various angles. So their approach is limited by the room arrangement. With regard to the price, 200 nodes costs about 10,000 US dollars, $5\times$ as much as ours.

Summary: We adopt a powerful reader, ImpinJ R420, to build our prototype. The reader costs about $2,000$ US dollars. At first blush, it is not cheap enough. This is because this reader is specially designed for logistics and transportation. There is a very costly industrial computer, serving as a stable HTTP/TCP server, inside the reader to fulfill offline surveillance. In our scenario, we can construct a simpler and cheaper reader only using the reader chip (like Indy RS2000). There is a large space to reduce the system cost. For example, the ThingMagic reader does not embed industrial computer. Its price is around 700 dollars, which is much lower than that of the R420. We will consider the way to further reduce the cost in our future work. Even considering the cost of the current prototype, the low cost is still a major advantage of our solution prior to other methods.

9. APPLICATION STUDY

One of the most popular applications in research community recently is to communicate commands or short message to a system by tracking human's movements or gestures, *e.g.* [11, 46–48]. We also investigate this application using Tadar.

Gesture encoding and decoding. Tadar is more sensitive to the X-axis so we employ the rightward (X+) or leftward (X-) movement for gesture encoding. We adopt the Manchester-like encoding as proposed in Wi-Vi [11]: a '0' bit is a step leftward followed by a step rightward; a '1' bit is a step rightward followed by a step leftward, as shown in Fig. 16. This modulation is very simple so that a human finds it easy to perform them and compose them. To support such gesture encoding, Tadar firstly locates the human and then calculates the angle β, defined as the angle related to the vertical line. For example, Fig. 17 shows a sequence of angles detected when a subject repeatedly walks rightward and leftward. The angle equals zero when he locates at the vertical line, and becomes negative when across the vertical line to right. The main reason that we use angle for encoding instead of his absolute positions is that the human may be not know where he is. The input of this application is the angle sequence. Tadar applies two matched filters: one for the step leftward and one for the step rightward. Note that the human can change his direction at anywhere without need of coming back to the vertical line.

Evaluation. We evaluate Tadar's ability to decode the bits associated with the gesture. All the experiments are conducted in our conference room. In each experiment, we ask a volunteer to randomly stand at the conference room, and perform the two gestures. He walks in a way that he finds comfortable. Total 5 subjects take part in experiments. The experiments are repeated with various range from $1 \sim 6m$. Fig. 18 plots the fraction of experiments that the gestures are exactly decoded. We observe that Tadar can successfully decode the gestures at all distances within $3m$. The percentage falls to 75% when the distance increases to the $4m$. The decoding accuracy of Wi-Vi [11] is better than that of Tadar when the distance is longer than $4m$. However, Wi-Vi cannot exactly pinpoint his location.

10. LIMITATIONS

Tadar marks an important contribution by enabling device-free mobile object tracking. It, however, still has some limitations that are left for future work.

Direction-dependent: Both the RFID tags and reader antenna are directional, so the whole system is also direction-dependent. Current prototype distributes tags in a fairly large area to enable them to capture different perspectives of the mobile objects in the scene. Our future research may advance at both hardware and algorithmic to reduce the dependence of direction allowing for the tags to be stacked within a smaller area.

Learning environment: A second limitation stems from the fact the Tadar needs to train the channel parameters of empty room in advance to eliminate the flash effects. Not all situations, especially in the case of emergency, allow the user to learn the environment ahead. Our future research may address this issue by detecting the differences of two consecutive frames.

Tracking one object: Our algorithm design presented in this paper can track only one mobile object at any point in time. When there are multiple objects present in the scene, the reflections off multiple objects would overlapped together. This limitation is not fundamental to the design of Tadar and can be addressed as the research evolves. For example, considering the case of K moving objects, we can model the HMM state using a K-dimensional vector. Each element in the vector indicates each object's location. Correspondingly, the observations are modeled as the combined signal of K reflections. The optimized state conforming to all observations is the current objects' location distributions.

Beyond FCC power limits: In order to discern the weak reflections off human, we boost the power using a 12 dBi antenna. Considering 30 dBm transmission power, it would result in 42 dBm EIRP (Equivalent Isotropically Radiated Power) which is 6 dBm more than the FCC limit. To conform the FCC limit, Tadar would be confined to detect the objects with high-reflective metallic surface.

Although there is scope for many improvements, we believe that Tadar inspires us from another different perspective to advance the through-wall technology and other various aspects [49, 50].

11. CONCLUSION

In this work, we present Tadar for tracking moving objects without instrumenting them using COTS RFID readers and tags. It works even through walls and behind closed rooms. A key innovation is to logically transform a group of tags into an antenna array receiving the reflections from surrounding objects. We believe that it will open up a wide range of exciting opportunities bridging our physical world and the cyber world.

ACKNOWLEDGMENT

The research is supported by NSF China Major Program 61190110. The research of Lei Yang is supported by China Postdoctoral Science Foundation funded project under NO. 2015M570100. The research of Xiangyang Li is supported by NSF ECCS-1247944, NSF ECCS-1343306, NSF CMMI 1436786, National Natural Science Foundation of China under Grant No. 61170216 and No. 61228202. We thank all the reviewers and shepherds for their valuable comments and helpful suggestions.

12. REFERENCES

[1] Lei Yang, Yekui Chen, Xiang-Yang Li, Chaowei Xiao, Mo Li, and Yunhao Liu. Tagoram: real-time tracking of mobile rfid tags to high precision using cots devices. In *Proc. ACM MOBICOM*, 2014.

[2] Jue Wang and Dina Katabi. Dude, where's my card?: Rfid positioning that works with multipath and non-line of sight. In *Proc. of ACM SIGCOMM*, 2013.

[3] Jue Wang, Deepak Vasisht, and Dina Katabi. Rf-idraw: virtual touch screen in the air using rf signals. In *Proc. of ACM SIGCOMM*, 2014.

[4] Jie Xiong and Kyle Jamieson. Arraytrack: A fine-grained indoor location system. In *Proc. of USENIX NSDI*, 2013.

[5] Tyler S Ralston, Gregory L Charvat, and John E Peabody. Real-time through-wall imaging using an ultrawideband multiple-input multiple-output (mimo) phased array radar system. In *Proc. of IEEE ARRAY*, 2010.

[6] Gregory L Charvat, Leo C Kempel, Edward J Rothwell, Christopher M Coleman, and E Mokole. An ultrawideband (uwb) switched-antenna-array radar imaging system. In *Proc. of IEEE ARRAY*, 2010.

[7] Seeing through walls-MIT's Lincoln Laboratory. http://www.youtube.com/watch?v=H5xmo7iJ7KA.

[8] Yunqiang Yang and Aly E Fathy. See-through-wall imaging using ultra wideband short-pulse radar system. In *IEEE Symposium on Antennas and Propagation Society*, volume 3, pages 334–337, 2005.

[9] Through-wall Radar. http://www.alibaba.com/product-detail/Rescue-tool-Through-wall-radar-Prism_60010869781.html.

[10] Kevin Chetty, Graeme E Smith, and Karl Woodbridge. Through-the-wall sensing of personnel using passive bistatic

wifi radar at standoff distances. *IEEE Transactions on Geoscience and Remote Sensing*, 50(4):1218–1226, 2012.

[11] Fadel Adib and Dina Katabi. See through walls with wifi! In *Proc. of ACM SIGCOMM*, 2013.

[12] WiSee. `http://wisee.cs.washington.edu/`.

[13] Qifan Pu, Sidhant Gupta, Shyamnath Gollakota, and Shwetak Patel. Whole-home gesture recognition using wireless signals. In *Proc. of ACM MOBICOM*, 2013.

[14] Saandeep Depatla, Lucas Buckland, and Yasamin Mostofi. X-ray vision with only wifi power measurements using rytov wave models. *IEEE Transactions on Vehicular Technology*, 2015.

[15] X-Ray Vision. `https://www.youtube.com/watch?v=iF1fY3bPAt0&t=11`.

[16] Daniel M Dobkin. *The RF in RFID: UHF RFID in Practice*. Newnes, 2012.

[17] Lei Yang, Jinsong Han, Yong Qi, Cheng Wang, Tao Gu, and Yunhao Liu. Season: Shelving interference and joint identification in large-scale rfid systems. In *Proc. of IEEE INFOCOM*, 2011.

[18] Yang Zhao, Neal Patwari, Jeff M Phillips, and Suresh Venkatasubramanian. Radio tomographic imaging and tracking of stationary and moving people via kernel distance. In *Proc. of ACM IPSN*, 2013.

[19] Wenjie Ruan, Lina Yao, Quan Z Sheng, Nickolas JG Falkner, and Xue Li. Tagtrack: device-free localization and tracking using passive rfid tags. In *Proc. of Ubiquitous*, 2014.

[20] Donny Huang, Rajalakshmi Nandakumar, and Shyamnath Gollakota. Feasibility and limits of wi-fi imaging. In *Proc. of ACM SenSys*, 2014.

[21] Gregory L Charvat, Leo C Kempel, Edward J Rothwell, Christopher M Coleman, and E Mokole. A through-dielectric radar imaging system. *IEEE Transactions on Antennas and Propagation*, 58(8), 2010.

[22] Fauzia Ahmad, Yimin Zhang, and Moeness G Amin. Three-dimensional wideband beamforming for imaging through a single wall. *IEEE Geoscience and Remote Sensing Letters*, 5(2):176–179, 2008.

[23] Qiong Huang, Lele Qu, Bingheng Wu, and Guangyou Fang. Uwb through-wall imaging based on compressive sensing. *IEEE Transactions on Geoscience and Remote Sensing*, 48(3):1408–1415, 2010.

[24] Fadel Adib, Zach Kabelac, Dina Katabi, and Robert C Miller. 3d tracking via body radio reflections. In *Proc. of USENIX NSDI*, volume 14, 2013.

[25] Fadel Adib, Zachary Kabelac, and Dina Katabi. Multi-person motion tracking via rf body reflections. In *Proc. of USENIX NSDI*, 2015.

[26] Radar Vision, Time Domain Corporation. `http://www.timedomain.com`.

[27] LawrenceLivermore, National Laboratory. `https://www.llnl.gov`.

[28] EPC Gen2, EPCglobal. `www.gs1.org/epcglobal`.

[29] Saandeep Depatla, Lucas Buckland, and Yasamin Mostofi. X-ray vision with only wifi power measurements using rytov wave models. *IEEE Transactions on Vehicular Technology*, 64(4):1376–1387, 2015.

[30] Y. Mostofi. Cooperative Wireless-Based Obstacle/Object Mapping and See-Through Capabilities in Robotic Networks. *IEEE Transactions on Mobile Computing*, 12(5):817–829, May 2013.

[31] Joey Wilson and Neal Patwari. A fade-level skew-laplace signal strength model for device-free localization with wireless networks. *IEEE Transactions on Mobile Computing*, 11(6):947–958, 2012.

[32] Kristen Woyach, Daniele Puccinelli, and Martin Haenggi. Sensorless sensing in wireless networks: Implementation and measurements. pages 1–8. in Proc. of IEEE WIOPT, 2006.

[33] Konstantinos Kleisouris, Bernhard Firner, Richard Howard, Yanyong Zhang, and Richard P Martin. Detecting intra-room mobility with signal strength descriptors. In *Proc. of ACM MobiHoc*, 2010.

[34] Debraj De, Wen-Zhan Song, Mingsen Xu, Cheng-Liang Wang, Diane Cook, and Xiaoming Huo. Findinghumo: Real-time tracking of motion trajectories from anonymous binary sensing in smart environments. In *Proc. of IEEE ICDCS*, 2012.

[35] Frederic Thouin, Santosh Nannuru, and Mark Coates. Multi-target tracking for measurement models with additive contributions. In *IEEE FUSION*, 2011.

[36] Santosh Nannuru, Yunpeng Li, Yan Zeng, Mark Coates, and Bo Yang. Radio-frequency tomography for passive indoor multitarget tracking. *IEEE Transactions on Mobile Computing*, 12(12):2322–2333, 2013.

[37] Dian Zhang, Yunhuai Liu, Xiaonan Guo, and Lionel M Ni. Rass: A real-time, accurate, and scalable system for tracking transceiver-free objects. *IEEE Transactions on Parallel and Distributed Systems*, 24(5):996–1008, 2013.

[38] Moustafa Seifeldin and Moustafa Youssef. A deterministic large-scale device-free passive localization system for wireless environments. In *Proc. of ACM ICPETRAE*, 2010.

[39] Chenren Xu, Mingchen Gao, Bernhard Firner, Yanyong Zhang, Richard Howard, and Jun Li. Towards robust device-free passive localization through automatic camera-assisted recalibration. In *Proc. of ACM SenSys*, 2012.

[40] EPCglobal. Low level reader protocol (llrp). 2010.

[41] W. Hu, T. Tan, L. Wang, and S. Maybank. A survey on visual surveillance of object motion and behaviors. *IEEE Transactions on Systems, Man, and Cybernetics*, 2004.

[42] Speedway installation and operations guide.

[43] Impinj, Inc. `http://www.impinj.com/`.

[44] Alien Tags. `http://www.alientechnology.com/tags/2x2/`.

[45] Jeremy Landt. The history of rfid. *Potentials, IEEE*, 24(4):8–11, 2005.

[46] Joey Wilson and Neal Patwari. See-through walls: Motion tracking using variance-based radio tomography networks. *IEEEE Transactions on Mobile Computing*, 10(5):612–621, 2011.

[47] Herbert Bay, Andreas Ess, Tinne Tuytelaars, and Luc Van Gool. Speeded-up robust features (surf). *Computer vision and image understanding*, 110(3):346–359, 2008.

[48] Bryce Kellogg, Vamsi Talla, and Shyamnath Gollakota. Bringing gesture recognition to all devices. In *Proc. of USENIX NSDI*, 2014.

[49] Zhenjiang Li, Mo Li, Jiliang Wang, and Zhichao Cao. Ubiquitous data collection for mobile users in wireless sensor networks. In *Proceedings IEEE INFOCOM*, pages 2246–2254, 2011.

[50] Zhenjiang Li, Wan Du, Yuanqing Zheng, Mo Li, and Dapeng Wu. From rateless to hopless. In *Proceedings of ACM MobiHoc*, pages 2246–2254, 2011.

Come and Be Served: Parallel Decoding for COTS RFID Tags

Jiajue Ou, Mo Li
School of Computer Engineering
Nanyang Technological University
{jou1,limo}@ntu.edu.sg

Yuanqing Zheng
Department of Computing
The Hong Kong Polytechnic University
csyqzheng@comp.polyu.edu.hk

ABSTRACT

Current commodity RFID systems incur high communication overhead due to severe tag-to-tag collisions. Although some recent works have been proposed to support parallel decoding for concurrent tag transmissions, they require accurate channel measurements, tight tag synchronization, or modifications to standard RFID tag operations. In this paper, we present *BiGroup*, a novel RFID communication paradigm that allows the reader to decode the collision from multiple COTS (commodity-off-the-shelf) RFID tags in one communication round. In *BiGroup*, COTS tags can directly join ongoing communication sessions and get decoded in parallel. The collision resolution intelligence is solely put at the reader side. To this end, *BiGroup* examines the tag collisions at RFID physical layer from constellation domain as well as time domain, exploits the under-utilized channel capacity due to low tag transmission rate, and leverages tag diversities. We implement *BiGroup* with USRP N210 software radio that is able to read and decode multiple concurrent transmissions from COTS passive tags. Our experimental study gives encouraging results that *BiGroup* greatly improves RFID communication efficiency, i.e., 11× performance improvement compared to the alternative decoding scheme for COTS tags and 6× gain in time efficiency when applied to EPC C1G2 tag identification.

Categories and Subject Descriptors

C2.1[Network Architecture and Design]: Wireless communication

Keywords

RFID systems; physical layer; parallel decoding

1. INTRODUCTION

RFID (Radio Frequency IDentification) technology has been extensively used in various applications, such as warehouse inventory [8, 40, 41], object tracking [25–27, 32, 35], human-computer interaction [7, 33], powerless sensing [6, 38], etc. Existing RFID communication standards like EPCglobal C1G2 [1] employ slotted aloha channel access and sequentially read tags at random time slots. The communication efficiency in current RFID systems remains low for two main reasons. (1) Concurrent transmissions of more than one COTS tags would collide and none of the transmission can be decoded. (2) RFID tags send data at low data rates (e.g., 16 kbps for backscatter link frequency of 64 kHz and Miller 4 coding [1])) using on-off keying that cannot fully utilize the channel capacity even when the wireless channel quality is high.

To improve the communication efficiency, recent works [3, 12, 31] explore the possibility of letting RFID tags transmit in parallel and separating the collided transmissions at the reader. These prior designs, however, require substantial modifications to COTS tags to enable collision resolution. For example, Buzz [31] needs to instrument tags to avoid inter-slot interference and perform channel measurements. BST [12] explicitly coordinates tag transmissions and misaligns tag signal edges to separate their signals. Some other designs [23, 24] require coding mechanisms (e.g., CDMA, rateless codes [11]) adopted on RFID tags to facilitate collision recovery. As a result, existing parallel decoding approaches cannot fully support standardized COTS tags in widely deployed RFID systems. While several billions of COTS RFID tags with globalized standards are already in use worldwide, these recently proposed schemes can hardly benefit them.

In this work, we consider an ideal parallel decoding scheme that is able to decode packet collisions from COTS tags. We ask the question: *Can we enable "come and be served" parallel transmissions without any extension to COTS RFID tags?* The design goal is twofold: (1) we aim to enable parallel tag transmissions without the need of any modification to the COTS tags; (2) we aim to support COTS tags to join on-going communication sessions without specific coordination. The "come and be served" design does not tamper C1G2 logics on COTS tags and can provide direct benefits within the C1G2 framework. For example, the tag identification procedure of C1G2 requires individual RFID tags to send RN16 for channel contention. A collision occurs when multiple tags send RN16 in the same slot and the slot is wasted. "Come and be served" parallel decoding allows the reader to acquire RN16 codes of multiple tags from the collision and thus improves identification efficiency. According to our experimental results (which we will detail in Section 4), parallel decoding of merely 2 – 5 tags suffices to improve the tag identification time efficiency by 6×. For another example, the READ command in C1G2 comes after tag identification and reads data from one tag at a time. With "come and be served" design, the READ command can be extended to concurrently read data from multiple tags. The READ sessions from different tags do not need to be synchronized. Later transmissions can ride on on-going sessions. The throughput can be easily multiplied.

This paper presents *BiGroup* (Bipartite Grouping), that instantly decodes concurrent transmissions of COTS tags, by purely extend-

MobiCom'15, September 7–11, 2015, Paris, France.
© 2015 ACM. ISBN 978-1-4503-3619-2/15/09 ...$15.00.
DOI: http://dx.doi.org/10.1145/2789168.2790101.

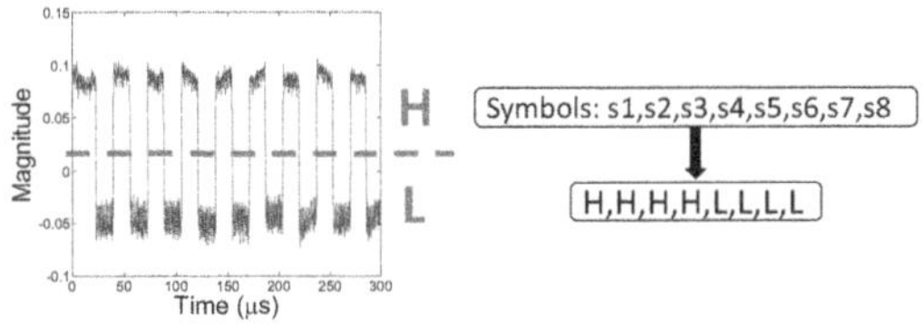

(a) Decoding one tag transmission based on signal magnitude.

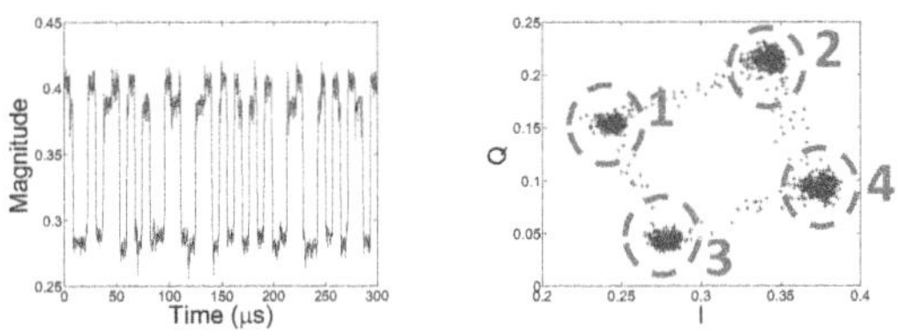

(b) The combined signal magnitude when two tags collide (Left), and the complex physical symbols on the I-Q plane (Right).

Figure 1: Decoding tag signals from single and multiple concurrent transmissions.

ing the decoding intelligence at the RFID reader. Unlike existing approaches, *BiGroup* examines collided tag transmissions at both time domain (time series signal transitions) and constellation domain (complex symbols on constellation plane). Regulated by standard RFID coding schemes, e.g., FM0 or Miller coding, RFID tags flip their reflection states at bit boundaries in backscatter transmission, which results in transitions of the combined signals in the time domain. *BiGroup* iteratively extracts the sequence of each tag's signal transitions in the time domain, and connects with the physical symbol clusters in the constellation domain. As one tag only alternates between reflecting or absorbing states, all clusters can be bipartitely grouped into two according to that tag. We can thus produce a bipartite grouping for each tag involved in the transmission, and the state transitions between the two groups give the transmitted data of that tag.

We implement *BiGroup* on a USRP N210 based RFID reader that concurrently reads different models of COTS tags as well as programmable RFID tags. To the best of our knowledge, *BiGroup* is the first practical design that is able to provide accurate parallel decoding for COTS RFID tags within the C1G2 framework. In particular, compared with source separation methods in [28], *BiGroup* improves the success rate by $11\times$ on average for decoding the collisions of 3 – 5 C1G2 passive tags. Our experimental results also demonstrate huge performance gain over existing schemes for non-COTS tags. The decoding capacity of *BiGroup* is affected by the channel quality and limited when the number of colliding tags increases. Nevertheless, our experimental case study demonstrates that concurrently decoding a small number of tags can already significantly improve the efficiency of some standard EPC C1G2 operations.

In the rest of the paper, we describe the background and motivation of our design in Section 2. We present the design details in Section 3. We evaluate *BiGroup* and present experimental results in Section 4. We detail related work in Section 5 and conclude the paper in Section 6.

2. BACKGROUND AND MOTIVATION

A passive RFID tag encodes its data by reflecting or absorbing incident carrier waves, resulting in two possible states: "High (H)" and "Low (L)". The nth tag's two alternative states are denoted by,

$$S_n = H_n \ or \ L_n \tag{1}$$

which exhibit two distinct signal magnitudes when received at an RFID reader as shown in Figure 1(a). The reader can thus decode the data using a magnitude threshold.

When multiple tags transmit simultaneously, their signals add up at the receiver. One collision state is a combination of all the tags' signal states. The possible collision states of N tags are denoted by,

$$S_{col} = [S_1, S_2, ..., S_N], \tag{2}$$

$[.]$ means all combinations of $S_m = H_m$ and L_m, $m = 1, 2, ...N$. In the example of the collision from two tags, the four collision states are denoted as "HH", "HL", "LH" and "LL", respectively.

In commodity RFID systems, the reader solely examines the received signal magnitudes. As a result, the reader cannot distinguish different collision states when multiple tags transmit at the same time. For example, Figure 1(b) presents the combined signal magnitude detected at a commodity reader when two tags transmit simultaneously. The reader cannot determine the threshold to detect the states of either individual tag. When we plot the received physical symbols in the In-phase and Quadrature (I-Q) coordinates, however, we see that the symbols form four separable clusters, each representing one collision state. Thus, if we can associate each cluster to a specific collision state ("HH", "HL", "LH", or "LL"), the collision can be recovered. Generalized to N tags, the decoding goal is to identify the collision state S_{col}, which is to derive in each collision state whether the separate tag transmission state $S_m = H_m$ or L_m for $m = 1, 2, \ldots, N$.

A variety of approaches have been proposed in view of above observation to decode concurrent transmissions. Buzz [31] first coordinates tags to measure their channel coefficients. Assuming that the collided signal of multiple tags is linear composition of individual signals, Buzz recovers the transmitted signal of each tag with channel measurement. In Buzz, the RFID tags apply rateless codes to encode transmitted data. Other coding mechanisms like [24] can also be used on tags to facilitate collision resolution.

In a recent approach BST [12], tags transmit with allocated initial offsets and data rates in order to create misaligned signal edges. During backscattering, tags monitor whether their signal edges overlap and adjust offsets and data rates. For bootstrapping decoding and correcting decoding errors, tags need to insert known bits called "sentinel" bits at specific intervals in data packets. These demanded tag operations are not supported by standard COTS tags.

Although existing approaches allow parallel decoding for RFID tags programmed with specific logics, they do not meet the "come and be served" requirement and cannot support decoding COTS tags of standard operating logics. The reasons are as follows. First, in order to bootstrap collision recovery, many works require controlled channel measurement (e.g., using preambles [3, 16, 39] or coordinated transmissions [31, 34]) to understand channel coefficients of individual tags. The channel measurement requires non-standard coordination that is not supported by COTS tags. Extra communication and coordination overhead also brings down the efficiency. Second, many designs [3, 4, 16, 31] rely on precise tag synchronization so collided tag signals can align with each other. In practice, however, due to manufacturing diversities, COTS tags have non-identical clocks and respond asynchronously with distinct bit durations. Third, many works require non-standard operations from RFID tags apart from those defined in COTS tags (e.g, adaptive transmission offsets and data rates [12], extra "sentinel" bits

[12], specific tag coding [24, 31], etc.). Affording those operations on ASIC chips for COTS tags remains elusive.

Unlike existing works, *BiGroup* is designed to work with COTS tags. *BiGroup* does not require channel measurement, tag transmission synchronization, or any special operation at tag side. The COTS tags simply follow the standardized response logics when interrogated by the reader. A basic observation is that when the constellation plane is examined, regardless of where the physical symbol clusters are located (which is determined by the channel coefficients), as long as the clusters can be divided into two groups corresponding to the two transmission states ("H" or "L") of one tag, we can decode the data transmitted from that tag. We call it bipartite grouping. For the example case shown in Figure 1(b), we can decode one tag by separating symbols from the group consisting of cluster 1, 2 and symbols from the other group consisting of cluster 3, 4. The other tag can be decoded with the group of cluster 1, 3 and the group of cluster 2, 4.

In the general case of N tags, symbol clusters can similarly be grouped for each tag (e.g., tag n) as follows,

$$\begin{aligned} H_{n,col} &= [S_1, S_2, ...H_n..., S_N] \\ L_{n,col} &= [S_1, S_2, ...L_n..., S_N]. \end{aligned} \tag{3}$$

As more tags collide, however, it becomes increasingly difficult to accurately group the clusters with respect to each tag. *BiGroup* examines time domain tag state transitions to address the problem. Regulated by standard RFID coding schemes, e.g., FM0 or Miller coding, each tag transits between the reflecting and absorbing states at bit boundaries during its backscatter transmission. As such, at the bit boundaries of tag n, the reader knows that tag n would definitely transit from one of the collision states in $H_{n,col}$ to one in $L_{n,col}$, or vice versa. *BiGroup* carries such state transitions into the constellation domain and can thus identify symbol clusters belonging to either $H_{n,col}$ or $L_{n,col}$. As more state transitions are detected along with the time, *BiGroup* is able to eventually bipartitely group all clusters into two, that corresponds to $H_{n,col}$ and $L_{n,col}$. The data from tag n can thus be recovered from the temporal transitions between the two groups.

Designing and implementing *BiGroup* in practice entails substantial challenges. Without coordinated responses from COTS tags, it is challenging to identify state transitions of individual tags. The problem becomes more difficult if we cannot expect any prior knowledge of channel coefficients or linear dependency among collision states. At the same time, the design of *BiGroup* has to be efficiently implemented so the computational overhead imposed by operations like symbol clustering, boundary extraction, etc. can be properly accommodated. We detail the design and implementation of *BiGroup* in the next section.

3. DESIGN

In this section, we first describe the symbol clustering method. We then introduce the design considerations and the principle of *BiGroup*. After that, we give implementation details of *BiGroup* in practice.

3.1 Symbol Clustering

One signal sample received at physical layer is represented as one complex symbol on the I-Q plane. Due to noises and interferences, received symbols of the same collision state are dispersed and scattered around a centroid position, forming a cluster. Before performing bipartite grouping for these clusters, we need to first identify the number of clusters and the symbols belonging to each of those clusters. We use the density based clustering algorithm which obviates the need for cluster number. To reduce the input size for faster clustering, *BiGroup* aggregates received symbols into grids (which are much fewer than symbols) and cluster those grids.

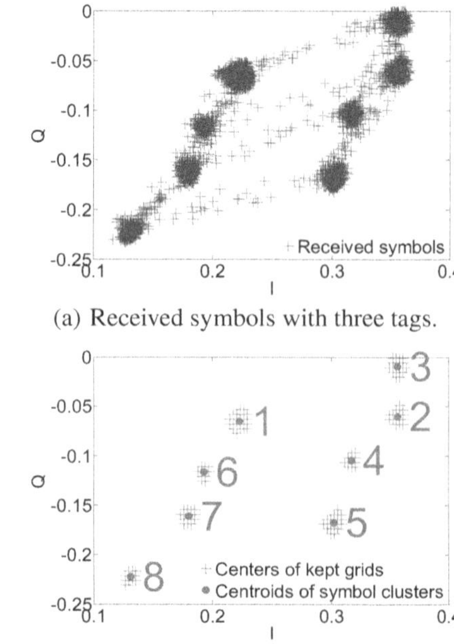

(a) Received symbols with three tags.

(b) Grids after filtering and cluster centroids.

Figure 2: Symbol clustering.

BiGroup divides the constellation plane into grids and denotes all the symbols confined within a grid using the grid center. The grid size can be adapted according to the background noise level. After a reader sends the QUERY command, tags remain absorbing states until they harvest sufficient amount of energy. During the charging stage, the cluster of received symbols corresponds to the all "L" collision state. These symbols can be averaged to derive the cluster centroid and the symbol dispersions can be measured to derive the background noise level. We thereafter set the grid size as 1/3 of the noise level. We filter out the grids with small number of symbols and feed the centroids of the remaining grids into the density based clustering algorithm (DBSCAN [9] in our implementation), which outputs the final symbol clusters. Figure 2 gives an example where 3 tags transmit to the reader concurrently. The received symbol samples are plotted in Figure 2(a). The kept grids and output cluster centroids are depicted in Figure 2(b). After that, each symbol will be marked by the label of its cluster. The received sequence of physical symbols can then be transformed into a sequence of cluster labels for later decoding.

3.2 Bipartite Grouping using Linear Dependency?

Now we have the symbol clusters and each symbol is associated with one cluster. One possible approach to bipartitely group the clusters is to leverage the linear dependency among clusters. Theoretically when two complex signals collide, they add up linearly at the receiver. In the same way, when two tags backscatter the radio signal concurrently, the collided signal is the linear combination of these tags' channel coefficients. Thus we can observe the linear dependency among different collision states (i.e., symbols clusters). One example is shown in Figure 3(a), where

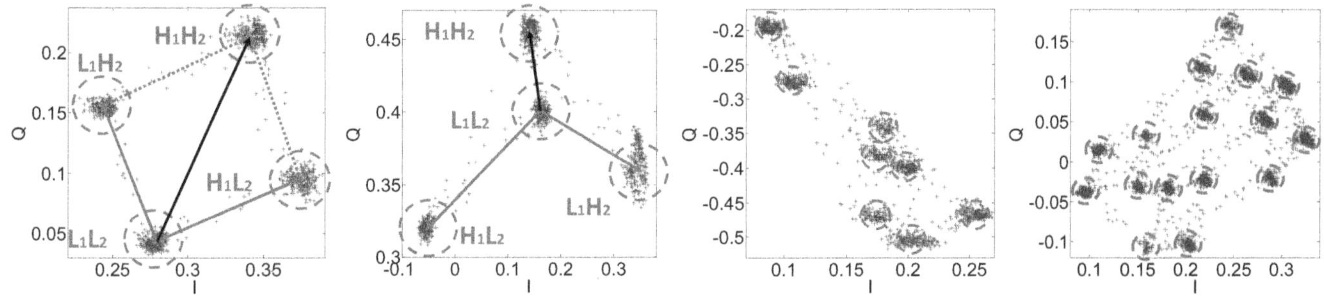

(a) Two tags with linear dependency. (b) Two tags with non-linear dependency. (c) Three tags with non-linear dependency. (d) Four tags with non-linear dependency.

Figure 3: Collision symbol clusters may exhibit non-linear dependency when multiple tags respond.

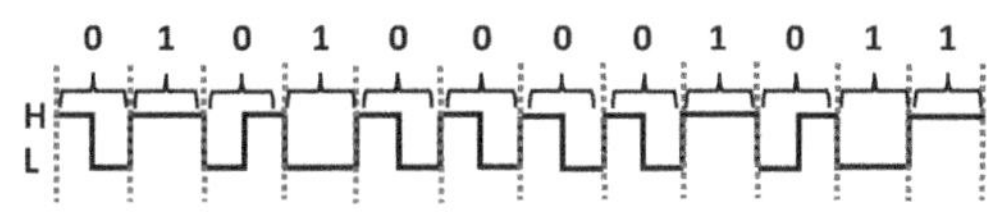

(a) FM0 coding. Tags flip reflections states at bit boundaries represented by dashed lines.

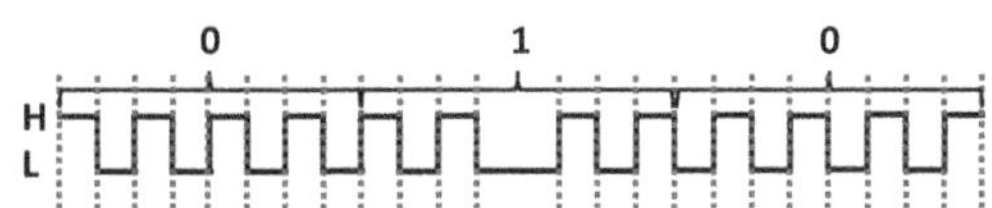

(b) Miller coding ($M = 4$). Similar periodic state changing patterns are observed. Dashed lines represent state flipping locations.

Figure 4: RFID coding property.

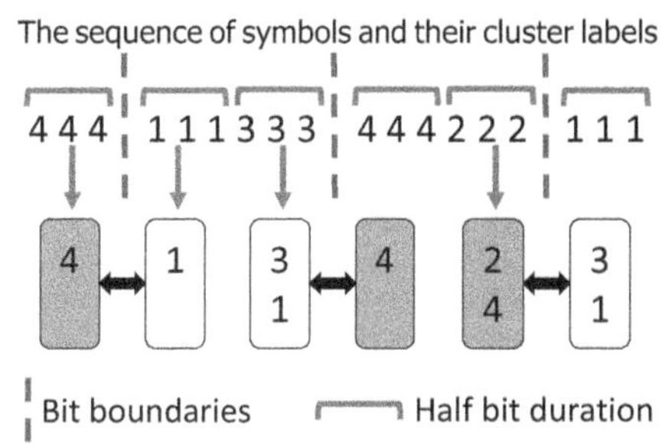

Figure 5: An illustrative example of bipartite grouping.

symbol vector "$L_1L_2 \rightarrow H_1H_2$" (illustrated with the black arrow) is approximately the linear addition of two vectors "$(L_1L_2 \rightarrow H_1L_2)$ + $(L_1L_2 \rightarrow L_1H_2)$" (illustrated with red arrows). The four cluster centroids roughly create a parallelogram. The group of clusters "H_1H_2" and "H_1L_2" are shifted from the group of clusters "L_1H_2" and "L_1L_2". The difference between the former two and latter two is the state of tag 1, meaning that they belong to opposite groups in bipartite grouping for tag 1. In a similar way, clusters "L_1H_2", "H_1H_2" and clusters "L_1L_2", "H_1L_2" are separated in terms of tag 2's state. In this case, we can leverage the linear addition property to do bipartite grouping. Same as other collision recovery methods [28, 31], such a bipartite grouping approach assumes the linear dependency among symbol clusters.

In practice, however, we also observe cases like Figure 3(b). We see that the vector '$L_1L_2 \rightarrow H_1H_2$" deviates from the linear addition of two vectors "$(L_1L_2 \rightarrow H_1L_2)$ + $(L_1L_2 \rightarrow L_1H_2)$". Such non-linear dependency is probably due to the change of tags' channel conditions by nearby tags. We hypothesize that when a tag backscatters alone, the reflected signal is mainly from the reader's carrier wave, but when multiple tags coexist, tags may backscatter the backscattered signals from nearby tags [21], that results in the non-linear dependency in the combined signals received at the reader. According to our measurement, the non-linear dependency becomes more obvious as more tags coexist as shown in Figure 3(c) and Figure 3(d) where 3 and 4 tags collide, respectively. Similar non-linear dependency has been reported in previous studies [12] as well. We note that the non-linear dependency is affected by various factors, e.g., the proximity and positions of tags, the data contents, etc., which are not under control of the RFID reader [12, 42]. In view of that, *BiGroup* has to perform bipartite grouping without assuming the linear dependency property.

3.3 *BiGroup* in Principle

In this section, we describe our key observations and the principle of *BiGroup*.

Data agnostic state flipping. COTS tags use standardized FM0 or Miller coding to encode data and the coding scheme in each communication round is specified by the reader [1]. They have a predictable state flipping pattern regardless of the transmitted data bits. We take FM0 coding (bi-phase space) for example. The bit-0 has an additional mid-bit phase inversion while bit-1 does not flip the phase as Figure 4(a) details. Nevertheless, FM0 inverts the phase at every bit boundary, so in the time domain we may always observe state transitions at bit boundaries independent of the data contents. The bit boundaries are dash lined in Figure 4(a). Similar deterministic state transitions can also be observed in Miller coding schemes as Figure 4(b) depicts. We note that such state transitions are compulsory for all CIG2 COTS tags so the RFID reader is able to track the backscatter frequencies. For brevity, we will later use FM0 codes as a vehicle to describe our method. Our approach can be generalized with slight modifications to handle Miller codes as well[1].

Overview of bipartite grouping. The bit boundaries identified for tag i divide the symbol clusters into two groups, corresponding to the "H" and "L" states of tag i. Since the state of the tag must flip at bit boundaries, we have the knowledge that the state before a bit boundary and state after the boundary must belong to the oppo-

[1]In Miller codes, the signal state flips with a fixed period proportional to the bit duration and with a small number of exceptions (less than 1/10). Majority voting technique in *BiGroup* tolerates such exceptions.

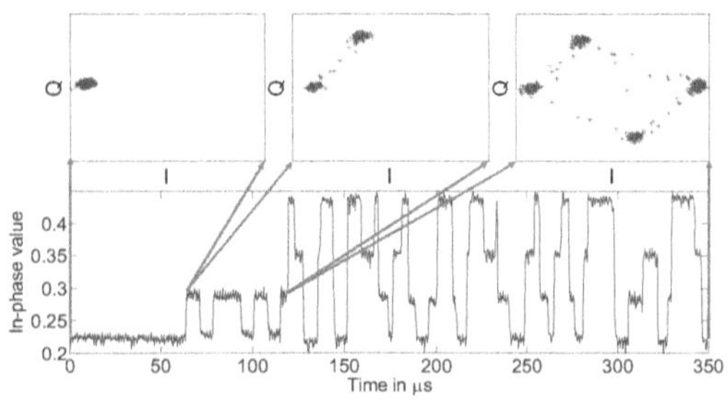

Figure 6: Tags join the transmission at different time.

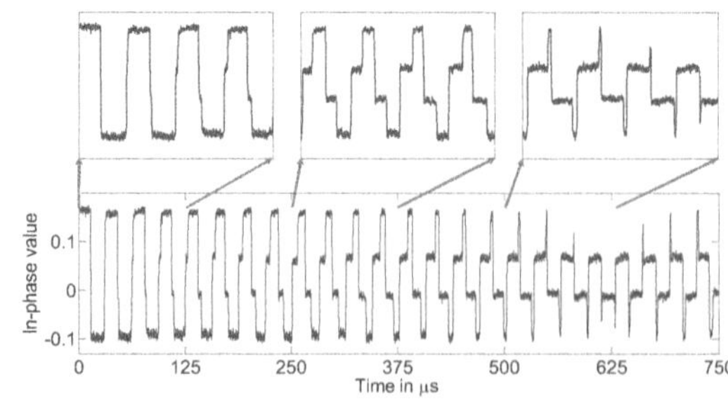

Figure 7: Two tags' signals misalign with each other due to different bit durations.

site groups, i.e., $H_{i,col}$ and $L_{i,col}$. Connecting to the constellation domain, the corresponding symbols (and their cluster labels) can thus be divided as well. As more bit boundaries of tag i are examined, more information can be accumulated on which clusters belong to opposite groups. All the clusters will eventually be bipartitely grouped.

Figure 5 illustrates the process using an example. The bit boundaries of tag i are identified and mapped onto the sequence of symbols and the associated sequence of cluster labels. According to the first bit boundary, cluster 4 and 1 are put in opposite groups. Then according to the second bit boundary, cluster 3 and 4 are put in opposite groups. Similarly, at the third bit boundary, cluster 2 is put in a group opposed to cluster 1's group. As we have already identified the cluster representing all "L" state when all tags are being charged, the group containing that cluster should be $L_{i,col}$, and the other group should be $H_{i,col}$. Note that the success of bipartite grouping does not rely on full detection of all bit boundaries. The process completes once an adequate number of bit boundaries are identified that allows all clusters to be distinguished. The process also tolerates inaccurate bit boundary detection, which we will detail in the next section.

3.4 *BiGroup* in Practice

To obtain the bipartite groups of each tag, we need to accurately extract bit boundaries for each individual tag and deal with imprecise bit boundaries with background noise. We first describe the tag-to-tag unsynchronization. We leverage such tag diversities to extract bit boundaries. We then present the method of bipartite grouping.

Unsynchronized tag signals. In practice, tag responses from different tags are usually unsynchronized for two reasons: different response delays and different bit durations.

Different tags have different response delays. A tag responds to a reader's QUERY with a delay. The length of the delay is largely determined by the tag's clock rate, power charging rate and strength of incident radio power. Due to manufacturing and tag location diversities, tags generally respond to the reader's QUERY with different initial offsets as illustrated in Figure 6. In the figure, we see that the first tag responds at around $60\mu s$ while the second joins the concurrent transmission at around $120\mu s$. The three I-Q planes plot the snapshots of physical symbols received when no tag, one tag, and two tags respond, respectively.

Different tags have different bit durations. A bit duration refers to the time period of transmitting one data bit, which refers to the gap between two closest dashed lines for FM0 in Figure 4(a). RFID tags use digital clocks to control the backscatter link frequency. Due to the clock diversity, the bit durations are not identical for different tags [13, 37]. Commodity RFID readers can tolerate the link frequency variations by tracking bit boundaries when one tag responds. Figure 7 plots the collided signal when two tags simultaneously transmit the same alternating data sequences. We see that two signals which initially align with each other gradually misalign due to different bit durations.

When tags collide, due to unsynchronized starting time and different bit durations, their signals do not always align with each other. Since tags' starting time and bit durations are not known in advance, it is hard to figure out how signals may collide with each other. Thus, previous schemes [4, 31] generally consider the unsynchronization harmful and try to avoid the inter-bit interference among tags with explicit coordination. Unlike previous schemes, we leverage such misalignment properties of RFID tags to identify bit boundaries for individual tags respectively.

Extracting bit boundaries. COTS tags need to invert their states at each bit boundary to allow the RFID reader to recover and track backscatter link frequencies. As a result, when we examine the clusters in an I-Q plane as we receive physical symbols, we observe that the symbols transit from one cluster to another at bit boundaries.

We first detect all the cluster transitions due to state transitions of the RFID tags. After the symbol clustering, the sequence of symbols is transformed to a sequence of cluster labels. Based on the sequence of cluster labels, we identify cluster transitions in the sequence. We may detect each cluster transition by detecting the symbol which has a different cluster label from the preceding symbol. In practical implementation, instead of detecting cluster changes of individual symbols, we detect the cluster changes of f symbols with the same cluster label to f symbols with different clusters as a cluster transition so as to enhance detection robustness.

The detected cluster transitions involve two parts: compulsory transitions at bit boundaries and occasional transitions in bit durations (e.g., the state flip in the middle of the duration of bit "0"). We need to extract bit boundaries by mapping those compulsory cluster transitions to each tag's bit boundaries in time series.

We denote the time points that the bit boundaries of N collision tags fall at as $T = \bigcup_{i=1}^{N} T_i$, where $T_i = \{t_{i,k} | 1 \leq k \leq L\}$ represents L bit boundaries due to state transitions of tag i. We note that L is determined by the packet size and is known in advance to the RFID reader. As the tags respond simultaneously, the bit boundaries are interleaved and mixed together. Fortunately, because of the unsynchronization among tags, the bit boundaries of colliding tags do not completely coincide with each other. We incorporate the tag response delay and bit duration and describe the bit boundaries of tag i (i.e., T_i) as follows

$$T_i = \{a_i + kb_i | 1 \leq k \leq L\}, \tag{4}$$

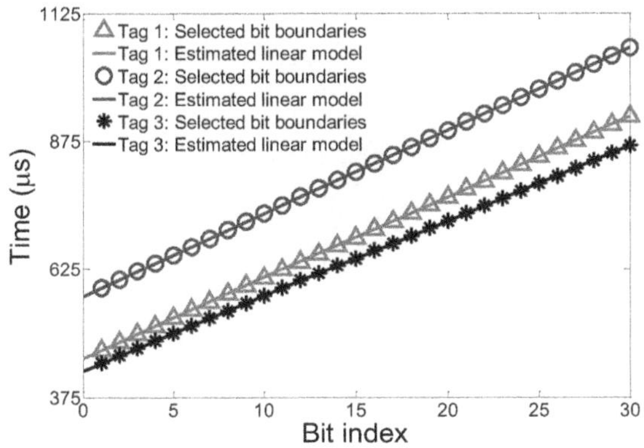

Figure 8: An illustrative example of identifying bit boundaries for three tags. The slope of a line represents the bit duration.

Algorithm 1 Majority voting in bipartite grouping

1: **INPUT**: vote for each cluster pair, e.g. V_{ij} for cluster i and cluster j
2: **OUTPUT**: classification of clusters for one certain tag
3: **PROCEDURE**:
4: Initialization:
5:   Find $\hat{i}, \hat{j}$ s.t. $V_{\hat{i}\hat{j}} = \max\{V_{ij}\}$
6:   group 1← cluster $\hat{i}$
7:   group 2← cluster $\hat{j}$
8: **repeat**
9:   **for** each cluster s that has not been grouped
10:     **for** $k = 1, 2$
11:       $W_{sk} = \text{mean}\{V_{sk_1}, V_{sk_2}, V_{sk_3}...\}$, for cluster $k_i \in$ group k
12:     **end for**
13:   **end for**
14:   Find $\hat{s}, \hat{k}$ s.t. $W_{\hat{s}\hat{k}} = \max\{W_{sk}\}$
15:   group $(3 - \hat{k})$← cluster $\hat{s}$ //Put cluster $\hat{s}$ into group $\hat{k}$
16: **until** all the clusters have been grouped

where a_i and b_i denote the starting transmission time and bit duration of tag i, and thus $a_i + kb_i$ represents the location of the kth bit boundary of tag i.

At first glance, we may determine a_i and b_i, and extract the bit boundaries of T_i with linear regression by optimizing a_i and b_i to minimize the residual errors as follows

$$\min_{\hat{a_i}, \hat{b_i}} \sum_k \{||\hat{a_i} + k\hat{b_i} - t_{i,k}||^2\}, \ k = 1, 2, 3, ..., L. \tag{5}$$

However, since the bit boundaries of different tags ($T_m, m = 1, 2, 3, ..N$) are mixed within detected cluster transitions and are unknown, we cannot trivially optimize a_i and b_i to extract T_i for tag i.

To solve the problem, we search over the possible ranges for a_i and b_i to fit L bit boundaries of T. For each candidate pair of a_i and b_i, specifically, we find the set of cluster transitions that minimizes the residual error. At the same time, we denote the corresponding achieved minimum residual error as R_i and the identified L bit boundaries as T_i, for each candidate pair respectively. We then find the pair of $\hat{a_i}$ and $\hat{b_i}$ and corresponding $\hat{T_i}$ that has the smallest $\hat{R_i}$ among all the R_is. After extracting $\hat{T_i}$ for tag i and decoding tag i, *BiGroup* removes both compulsory and occasional cluster transitions caused by tag i from the detected cluster transitions and iterates to extract bit boundaries for more tags. This iteration ends when there are not enough cluster transitions left.

Figure 8 plots one segment of the identified bit boundaries as well as their linear models for 3 tags. Taking tag 1 for example, the red marks represent the identified bit boundaries for tag 1 (i.e., T_1). The estimated linear model for tag 1 is depicted as the red line ($y = a_1 + xb_1$). We see that the identified bit boundaries fit well with the the linear model, indicating a very small residual error for tag 1. Similarly, our method extracts T_2 and T_3 for tag 2 and 3, respectively. Those identified bit boundaries for different tags will be used in determining bipartite grouping.

The search ranges for a_i and b_i can be determined in the following way. When tag i joins the transmission, its state switches from "L_i" to "H_i", resulting in new collision states and thus new symbol clusters in the I-Q plane (as the example in Figure 6 suggests). Therefore, we select each cluster's first a few transitions as the search range for a_i and let the fitting algorithm to search for the valid starting points. As the fitting algorithm is to find bit boundaries simply used for bipartite grouping not decoding, as long as a_i is one of the valid bit boundaries of tag i, the detected bit boundaries can be used to bootstrap bipartite grouping. The search range of bit duration b_i is set according to the possible link frequency ranges specified in C1G2 standard [1].

Bipartite grouping. After extracting bit boundaries for a tag, we determine bipartite grouping for the tag according to the principle introduced in Section 3.3. In practice, burst noise may result in wrong cluster labels and small fluctuations of the bit duration may cause shifted bit boundaries. Therefore, direct bipartite grouping may mistakenly separate some cluster pairs of the same group to opposite groups, that results in decoding errors. We apply a majority voting algorithm to improve bipartite grouping robustness.

For one tag, we first count the number of each cluster pair's occurrences on opposite sides of the tag's corresponding bit boundaries as the vote of this cluster pair. The vote of one cluster pair is denoted by $V_{i,j}$ for cluster i and j, $i \leq j$. For example, if there are a samples that belong to cluster i on one side of a bit boundary (within half duration), and b samples that belong to cluster j on the other side of the bit boundary (within half bit duration), we increase $V_{i,j}$ by $a \cdot b$.

We present the pseudocode of bipartite grouping for each tag in Algorithm 1. The algorithm initializes the classification with the cluster pair of the highest votes (line 4-7), i.e., if $V_{\hat{i}\hat{j}}$ has the largest value among all the votes, cluster $\hat{i}$ and cluster $\hat{j}$ are assigned to opposite groups. The remaining clusters are iteratively assigned to the two groups (line 8-16). In one iteration, for each ungrouped cluster s, we calculate the vote of cluster s and existing bipartite group k ($k = 1$ *and* 2) as a whole, denoted by W_{sk}. W_{sk} is the average value of $\{V_{sk_1}, V_{sk_2}, V_{sk_3}...\}$, where clusters $k_1, k_2, k_3...$ are already assigned to group k. Then we find the highest value of W_{sk}, denoted by $W_{\hat{s}\hat{k}}$. If $\hat{k} = 1$, cluster $\hat{s}$ will be assigned to group 2, otherwise, cluster $\hat{s}$ will be assigned to group 1. The process iterates until all the clusters are put into one of the two groups.

In the end, the cluster group with the known all "L" state is identified as "L" group, and the opposite group is identified as "H" group. The received symbol sequence, with the knowledge of which cluster a symbol belongs to, is thus turned into a sequence of "H" and "L" states for each individual tag, and input to the conventional single tag decoder.

3.5 Put It Together

Figure 9 illustrates the key workflow of *BiGroup*, which comprises the following three main steps:

Symbol clustering. *BiGroup* first clusters the physical symbols in the I-Q plane. Each symbol is classified into one cluster and marked by the corresponding cluster label. The received symbol

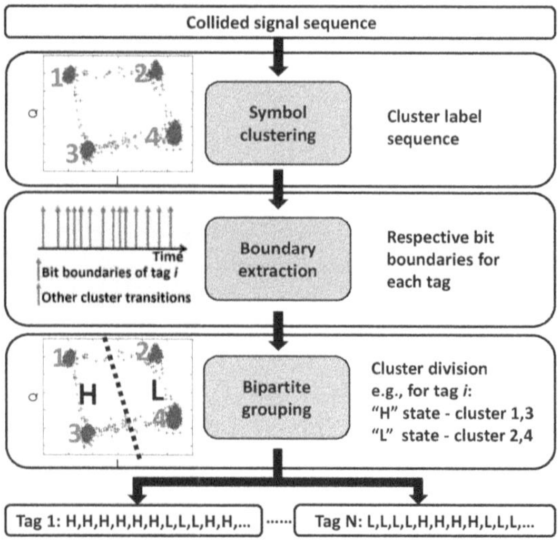

Figure 9: Workflow of *BiGroup*.

sequence is thus converted into a sequence of cluster labels for further processing.

Bit boundary extraction. *BiGroup* detects the time points of symbol transitions among clusters. *BiGroup* then extracts bit boundaries from cluster transitions and map to time series bit boundaries of different tags respectively.

Bipartite grouping. For each tag, *BiGroup* then divides the symbol clusters into bipartite groups of "H" state and "L" state. By examining the "H" or "L" states in the sequence of cluster labels, *BiGroup* outputs a sequence of binary states that represents the transmitted signal of that tag. Different tags have different bipartite groups and thus give different binary sequences. A conventional single tag decoder can then be applied on the binary sequence to decode the data of each tag.

3.6 Discussion

Computation overhead and time. The computation overhead of *BiGroup* mainly lies on symbol clustering and the time series search of bit boundaries. The symbol clustering algorithm used in *BiGroup* is performed on aggregated grids and its computation overhead is $O(k \log k)$, where k is the number of grids. The number of grids is influenced by the cluster dispersion and the size of a grid. Given cluster dispersion, a smaller grid size means higher resolution, but in the mean time results in more grids, thus higher computation overhead. To strike a balance between resolution and overhead, we set the side length of a grid as 1/3 of the cluster dispersion, and the number of grids is around 200. The computation overhead of time series search is $O(n^2p^2 \log(np))$, where n is the number of colliding tags and p is the number of packet bits used in searching. The above procedure does not have to apply to the whole packet, as it suffices to inspect part of the packet bits to obtain the bipartite grouping result (100 bits per packet in our experiments). Our current implementation of *BiGroup* is based on USRP N210 connected to a general PC equipped with 3.2GHz CPU and 16G memory, and the algorithm takes hundreds of μs to decode one collided packet. The computation time can be easily brought down by hardware implementation in the radio.

Decoding capacity and the gain. The decoding capacity of *BiGroup* is inevitably limited when the number of colliding tags increases. The channel quality essentially limits the resolution in symbol clustering. Ideally, received symbols of different collision

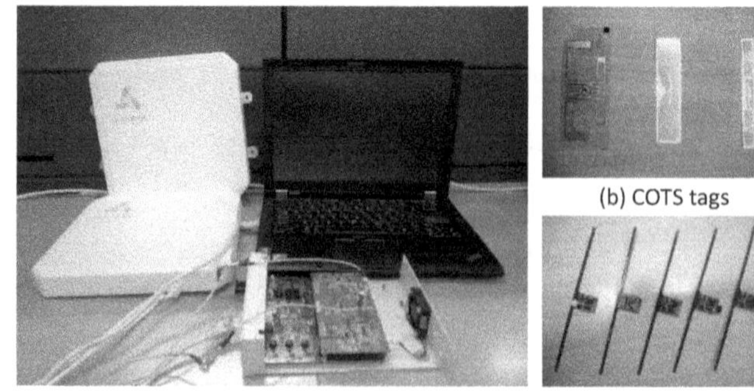

(a) Software defined reader (b) COTS tags (c) Programmable tags

Figure 10: The Open RFID testbed.

states will fall at different positions on the I-Q plane and can always be separated. As SNR decreases or tag number increases, symbol clusters may overlap with each other, making symbol clustering more difficult and error prone. In our experiments, the throughput improvement from *BiGroup* peaks when 4 – 5 tags transmit simultaneously (more details in Section 4). Nevertheless, such decoding capacity can already significantly improve the efficiency of some standard EPC C1G2 operations. In these operations, the maximum number of colliding tags in most transmission slots can be easily controlled by methods such as frame slotted ALOHA access protocol. Take tag identification - the most widely used operation as an example. The reader sends a QUERY command and each tag contends for the channel by responding a random RN16 packet at a randomly selected time slot within the frame. The reader ACKs the RN16 it hears and the corresponding tag of the particular RN16 responds its EPC (tag ID). The conventional reader can only retrieve the RN16 code from a slot with single tag response, and thus has very low efficiency, i.e., with the optimized frame setting more than 63% of the slots are collided and thus wasted. With *BiGroup*, the reader is able to retrieve RN16 from colliding slots (up to 5 concurrent transmissions in our experiment) and thus less than 12% of the slots are wasted. Our experimental study shows that with the help of *BiGroup*, around 6× speedup can be achieved for C1G2 tag identification. Detailed results are presented in Section 4.

Impact of channel variation. In *BiGroup*, received symbols of different states are discriminated according to their clustering on I-Q plane. Channel variation may change the positions of received symbols and thus the cluster distribution. The transmission time of a typical RFID uplink packet, however, is as short as a few milliseconds, which is usually within channel coherence time. The *BiGroup* clustering algorithm naturally tolerates some level of channel variation, which is determined by the Euclidean distances among cluster centroids. In future work, we may explore the possibility of splitting one transmission into multiple time windows during decoding to address significant channel variations.

4. IMPLEMENTATION AND EVALUATION

We implement *BiGroup* on top of our Open RFID Lab (ORL) [2] with the USRP N210 software defined radio (SDR) to read various COTS RFID tags and programmable tags. Figure 10 depicts the testbed. The SDR reader is connected to two USRP RFX900 daughterboards and operates in the 900MHz band. The SDR reader samples physical layer signals at 4MHz. The COTS tags follow the *de facto* EPCglobal C1G2 protocol [1]. The SDR reader interrogates different types of COTS tags (AD-833, ALN-9740 'G', and ALN-9640 Squiggle tags from left to right in Figure 10(b)). We

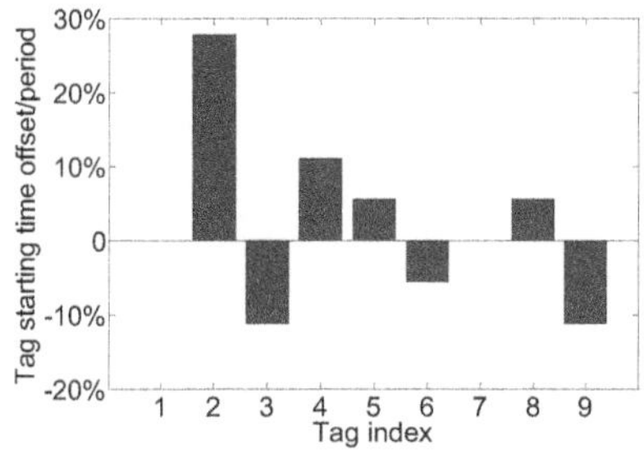

(a) Response starting time offset with respect to Tag 1.

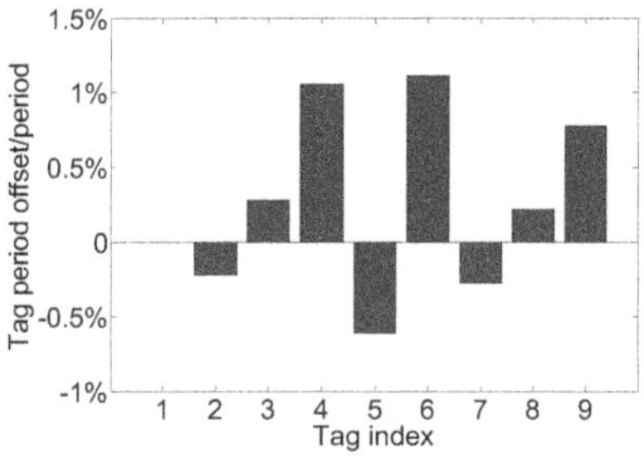

(b) Bit duration offset for each bit with respect to Tag 1.

Figure 11: Response starting time and bit duration of 9 COTS tags.

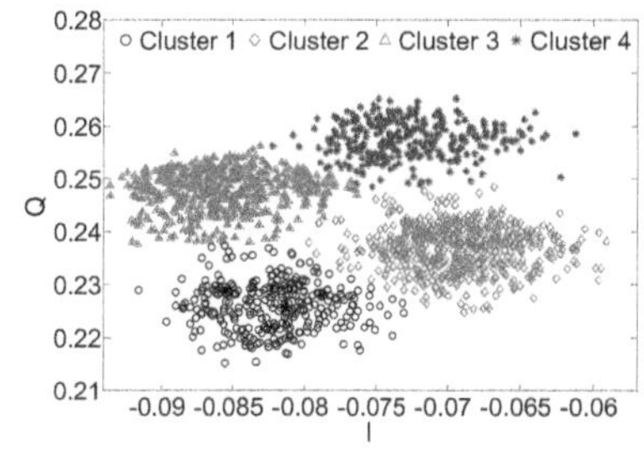

(a) When two tags collide the physical samples exhibit four different clusters.

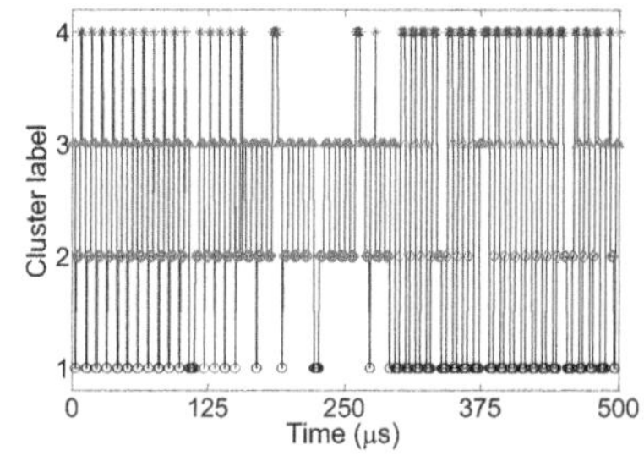

(b) Received samples transit among the four symbol clusters.

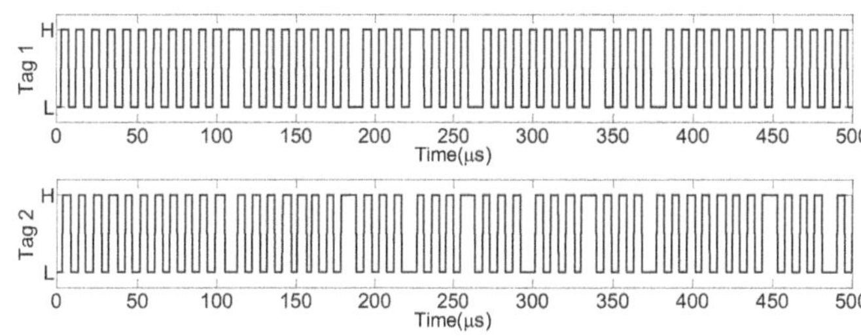

(c) Separated reflection states for the two tags.

Figure 12: Decoding two COTS tags using *BiGroup*.

also test with programmable RFIDs (WISP tags in Figure 10(c)) which implement the same commodity protocol. The reader sends QUERY commands and specifies the frame length f to be 1 by setting the contention parameter Q to 0 ($f = 2^Q$) [1]. Receiving such commands, the tags respond concurrently with RN16 packets, each consisting of a preamble followed by a 16-bit random payload. The RN16 packets are encoded with either the FM0 or Miller encoding scheme as specified by the reader in the QUERY commands. The backscatter link frequency (BLF) is specified as 100kHz.

We evaluate *BiGroup* in comparison with the following RFID concurrent transmission schemes.

- **LA (linear addition) based decoding scheme:** The approach [28] recovers tag collisions assuming that tags' channel coefficients remain static in different collision states. It assumes the linear dependency among cluster centroids to determine collision states and consequently does not perform well in practical scenarios. We compare the performance of *BiGroup* and the LA scheme in decoding the programmable tags.

- **Buzz:** Buzz [31] requires tight synchronization among tags so that the bit alignment can be guaranteed for successful decoding. The channel coefficient of each tag is individually measured, assuming that the channel coefficients would linearly combine at the reader during concurrent transmissions. As a result, Buzz cannot decode COTS tags within C1G2 framework. We compare *BiGroup* with Buzz in trace-driven simulations of decoding ideally synchronized tags. The maximum data rate of Buzz is specified the same as *BiGroup*.

- **BST:** In BST [12], the response delay and the bit duration of each tag are pre-assigned by the reader. BST does not conform to C1G2 standard either. We compare *BiGroup* with BST in trace-driven simulations. We tune parameters of BST (e.g., its signal edge detection threshold, "sentinel" bits, etc.) and report its optimum performance.

4.1 Decoding COTS Tags

Characterizing COTS tag unsynchronization. We first experiment with the ALN-9640 Squiggle COTS tags. We randomly choose 9 tags of the same batch (labeled as tag $1-9$) and measure their response delays and bit durations. We plot the measured ratio of starting time offset and bit duration offset in Figure 11(a) and Figure 11(b), respectively. We see that different tags have different response delays and bit durations, which result in bit misalignment and non-overlapped state transition boundaries. In particular, the response delay offset and the bit duration offset (normalized by period) can be up to 30% and 1% for each bit, respectively. We also observe similar tag diversities among other tag batches. Although the misalignment due to tag diversities was generally considered harmful in previous schemes [4, 31], *BiGroup* leverages such inherent properties to detect bit boundaries and bootstrap bipartite grouping.

Decoding COTS tags. We experiment with COTS tags and illustrate the process of *BiGroup* decoding. Figure 12 presents an example of decoding 2 colliding tags. *BiGroup* first clusters the received samples on the I-Q plane into 4 clusters labeled in different

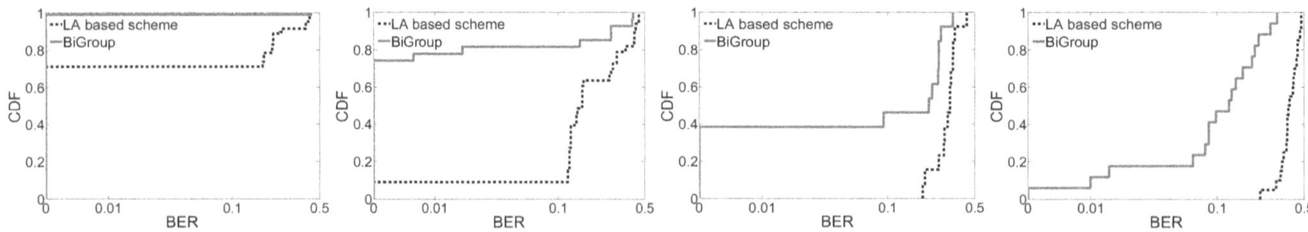

(a) Two tags. (b) Three tags. (c) Four tags. (d) Five tags.

Figure 13: CDF for BERs of different schemes with different numbers of colliding tags.

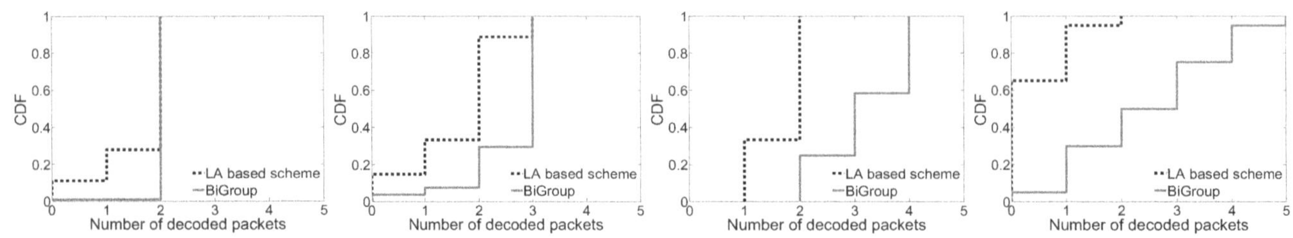

(a) Two tags. (b) Three tags. (c) Four tags. (d) Five tags.

Figure 14: CDF for successfully decoded packets of different schemes with different numbers of colliding tags.

colors as Figure 12(a) depicts. Each cluster represents one collision state. To better understand cluster transitions in time domain, we plot in Figure 12(b) the cluster label of each symbol sample during a time period of $500\mu s$.

By combining the observed time domain state transitions and state flippings at bit boundaries, *BiGroup* performs bipartite grouping. As a result, cluster 3 and 4 represent "H" state of tag 1, and cluster 1 and 2 represent its "L" state, respectively. Similarly, *BiGroup* decodes tag 2 by grouping cluster 2 and 4 which represent state "H", and cluster 1 and 3 which represent state "L", respectively. In Figure 12(c), we see that *BiGroup* separates the individual signals for the two tags from the collision. After the separation, each stream of "H" and "L" states can be decoded to bits by a conventional threshold-based decoder.

In our experiment, *BiGroup* is able to decode all RN16 packets replied from COTS tags to the QUERY command. One RN16 packet includes a predefined 22-bit Miller preamble, followed by a random 16-bit data payload which was instantaneously generated at the tag. While we have no ground truth to assess the decoded random data payloads, our experiment shows that *BiGroup* can correctly recover the fixed 22-bit Miller preambles in most cases.

4.2 Decoding C1G2 Programmable Tags

For more detailed evaluation of *BiGroup* decoding performance, we experiment with programmable passive RFID tags that implement the commodity C1G2 protocol [1]. In particular, we generate random bits offline and load them into WISP tags (Figure 10(c)) as RN16 data payloads that serve as ground truths.

We compare the performance of *BiGroup* and LA based decoding scheme [28] in decoding the WISP tags. We experiment with 2 – 5 tags which respond concurrently to QUERY commands. We repeat the experiment with varied number of tags for 500 times. For each measurement, we vary the channel conditions by manually placing the tags in different locations. The experiment is carried out both during the daytime with people moving around as well as in the relatively stable settings. We evaluate two performance metrics: the BER (Bit Error Rate) and the number of successfully decoded packets. We measure the BER to evaluate the collision recovery capability. We also measure the number of successfully decoded packets in each concurrent transmission to evaluate the goodput.

BER. Figure 13 plots the CDFs of BERs for different numbers of colliding tags. In case of collisions, a recovery scheme may decode and output one or more packets. We compare each output packet with the transmitted packets and record the minimum BER. The BER of undecoded packet is set to 0.5. We measure the average BERs of all packets and report this average.

In Figure 13, we see that *BiGroup* greatly outperforms the LA based decoding scheme. When three tags transmit concurrently, more than 70% of collisions have 0 bit errors in *BiGroup*, while less than 10% have 0 bit errors in the LA based scheme. Around 40% of cases have 0 bit errors in *BiGroup* when four tags transmit concurrently, and around 20% have an average BER below 0.05 in *BiGroup* when five tags transmit concurrently. In contrast, the lowest average BERs when four and five tags collide for the LA based scheme are much higher (>0.1 BERs for all collisions). *BiGroup* achieves much lower BERs compared with the LA based scheme, because *BiGroup* tolerates the variation of channel coefficients and does not assume the linear dependency of signal combinations in practice.

Number of successfully decoding. Figure 14 plots the CDFs of successfully decoded packets of *BiGroup* and the LA based scheme in each collision.

We see that *BiGroup* significantly outperforms the LA based scheme, especially with more colliding tags. When two tags collide, *BiGroup* decodes both for 99% of collisions, while the LA based scheme decodes the two tags in only 70%. When three tags collide, *BiGroup* decodes all three tags in around 71% of cases, and two tags in around 22%, while the LA based scheme decodes the same number of tags in only 11% and 55%, respectively. When four tags collide, *BiGroup* decodes all four tags in around 42% of collisions, three tags in around 33%, and two tags in around 25%, while the LA based scheme is only able to decode at most two tags (in around 62%). When five tags collide, *BiGroup* decodes all five

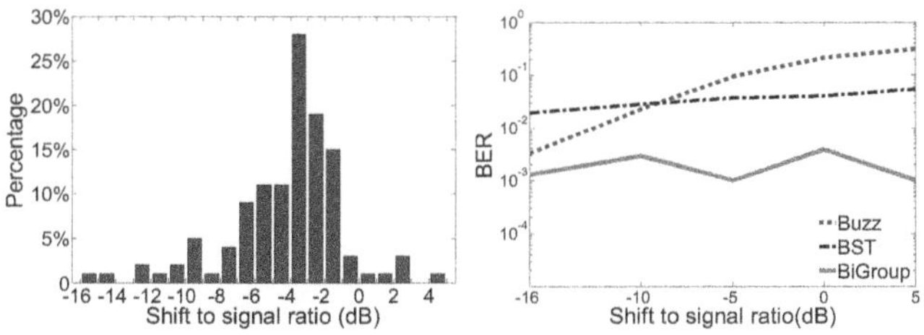

(a) Shift to signal ratio (SSR) distribution. (b) BER of different schemes with varied SSR.

Figure 15: SSR and its influence to bit error rates.

		SNR=10dB	SNR=20dB	SNR=30dB
Two tags	Buzz	90.6	98.7	99.0
	BST	84.3	104.8	105.8
	BiGroup	91.8	125.8	128.0
Three tags	Buzz	119.4	143.0	145.0
	BST	92.5	148.6	155.1
	BiGroup	113.8	180.8	192.0
Four tags	Buzz	140.2	178.7	184.2
	BST	103.5	166.0	196.2
	BiGroup	137.6	224.8	256.0
Five tags	Buzz	155.9	203.8	213.3
	BST	125.4	172.5	245.3
	BiGroup	162.4	236.3	320.0

Table 1: Goodput of different schemes (kbps).

tags in around 5% of collisions, four tags in around 20%, and three tags in around 25%, while the LA scheme is only able to decode at most two tags (in less than 5%). For more than 60% cases in the LA based scheme for five tags, no packets can be successfully decoded. Overall, for the concurrent transmissions of more than two tags, *BiGroup* is able to successfully decode 11× more concurrent transmissions than the LA scheme.

4.3 Trace-driven Evaluation for Non-standard Tags

We perform the trace-driven evaluation to compare *BiGroup* with Buzz and BST. The collision decoding performance is mainly influenced by the following factors: the noise level and the level of cluster non-linear dependency influenced by channel coefficients.

To investigate channel coefficient distributions in practice, we first characterise the backscatter channel of multiple tags using the SDR testbed. In particular, the WISP tags are programmed to backscatter known preambles and payloads, so we can directly identify the states of all the tags in each symbol cluster. We measure how the centroids of the collided symbol clusters are shifted away from the linear combinations of individually backscattered symbols. We quantify based on such shift to signal ratio (SSR) the non-linear dependency, which is the ratio of the shift of cluster centroid to the average signal strength. Figure 15(a) plots the distribution of measured SSRs in all experiments. We expect a small SSR (e.g., -16dB) if the non-linear dependency is weak, and a big SSR (e.g., 0dB) if the non-linear dependency is strong. According to our measurements, we see that SSR ranges from -16dB to 5dB, with majority of SSRs (>70%) concentrated in the range from -6dB to -2dB.

Performance comparison. We then let the SDR reader QUERY the programmed tags and record the traces of backscattered signals in 1000 rounds. Following the protocol specifications of Buzz and BST, we synthesize the collected signals of up to five tags and test the performance of different protocols. We take into consideration the non-linear dependency and incorporate the SSR in the tests.

In Figure 15(b), we display BERs of different decoding schemes with varied SSRs for concurrent transmissions of four tags. We fix the SNR to 24dB. The result suggests that the performance of Buzz is highly related to the SSR. The BER of Buzz significantly increases from 10^{-3} to 0.5 when the SSR changes from -16dB to 5dB. In contrast, the BERs of BST and *BiGroup* remain comparatively stable across different SSRs. *BiGroup* consistently outperforms BST by one order of magnitude.

We further compare the decoding schemes with different number of colliding tags and under different SNRs and plot the results in Figure 16. SSR is fixed at -4dB. Comparing *BiGroup* and Buzz, we see that Buzz cannot achieve low BER even with high SNRs (e.g., 25 – 35dB), while the BER of *BiGroup* decreases with higher SNRs and reaches 0 when the SNR is around 25dB. Comparing Figure 16 (a) – (d), we find that the lowest BER of Buzz increases as the number of tags increases, suggesting more severe performance degradation due to stronger non-linear dependency with more tags. We notice that Buzz has a slightly lower BER than *BiGroup* at low SNRs (e.g., 5 – 20dB), where the noise level is too high for *BiGroup*'s clustering algorithm. The BER provided by Buzz in such cases (e.g., 0.1 for four tags), however, cannot support reliable transmissions.

BiGroup also consistently provides better performance compared with BST. A 3 – 4dB SNR gain is achieved by *BiGroup* for low BER situations. The reason is that BST measures the distance between consecutive symbols to detect a signal edge (bit value transition). Due to noises, such signal edges may not be accurately captured. *BiGroup* only requires majority of the bit boundaries to be identified for the purposes of bipartite grouping, while each misdetected signal edge in BST may cause bit error(s). *BiGroup* is inherently more robust to noises.

In Table 1, we present the goodput of different schemes in different channel conditions. We calculate the goodput from the correctly decoded information bits over the total communication time. The data transmission rate of each tag is 64 kbps. We observe that *BiGroup*'s gain over Buzz and BST in goodput is even larger than the gain in BER. Unlike *BiGroup* which requires zero communication overhead, Buzz spends extra time in identification and channel measurement, and BST transmits extra "sentinel" bits and needs to retransmit when signal edges overlap. *BiGroup* provides up to 1.4× and 1.5× goodput gain over BST and Buzz, respectively.

4.4 *BiGroup* for EPC Tag Identification

We study how *BiGroup* may benefit the EPC tag identification by decoding RN16 parallel transmissions. We use the SDR reader to QUERY 8 C1G2 passive tags. The frame length is set to 4. In an arbitrary collision slot, *BiGroup* tries to recover at least one RN16 packet out of the collision and then the corresponding tag is ACKed for identification. The read rate is calculated as the average number of identified tags in one second. According to the experimental results, the read rate of the enhanced EPC using *BiGroup* is around 11.6 tags/second, while the read rate of the conventional EPC is 3.7 tags/second. Note that we conduct experiments with the USRP/GnuRadio testbed which has a lower read rate than most commercial readers due to the communication delay between the USRP device and the PC. Nevertheless, we see 3× performance improvement when *BiGroup* is applied in the reader to enhance the EPC procedure. Higher performance gain is expected if *BiGroup* is implemented in hardware of commercial readers.

We now investigate the performance gain with a larger number of tags. In this simulation, the reader is capable of decoding RN16

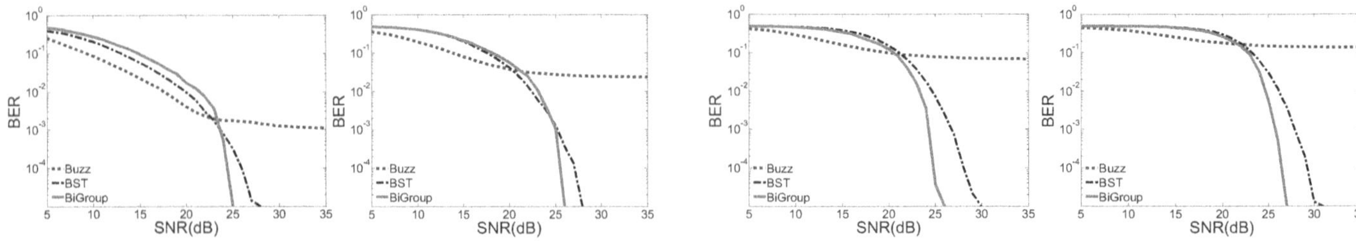

(a) Two tags. (b) Three tags. (c) Four tags. (d) Five tags.

Figure 16: BER of different decoding schemes across a range of channel conditions.

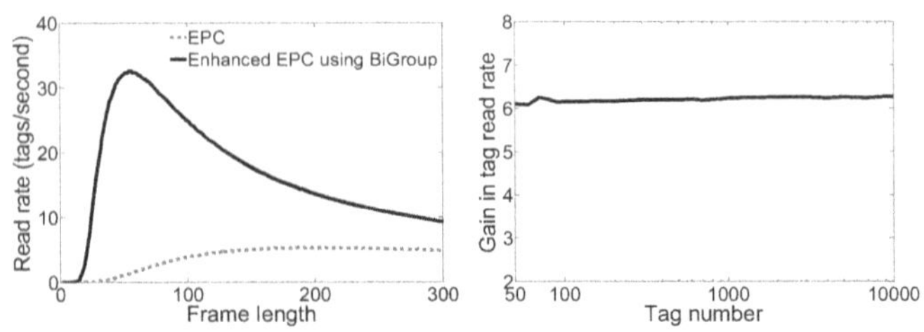

(a) Read rate for varied frame lengths (200 tags). (b) Performance gain provided by *BiGroup* for different numbers of tags.

Figure 17: *BiGroup* speeds up EPC tag identification.

collisions of up to five tags and subsequently ACK these colliding tags. We use the time traces measured in our SDR testbed to calculate read rate. We first plot in Figure 17(a) the read rate of EPC identification with and without *BiGroup* for 200 tags (frame length from 0 to 300). We observe that the enhanced EPC using *BiGroup* achieves a maximum read rate of 32.6 tags/second, when frame length is 55. On the other hand, the maximum read rate of conventional EPC is only 5.2 tags/second, when frame length is 200. The performance gain in maximum achievable tag read rate by using *BiGroup* in EPC identification is thus 6.3× for 200 tags. We further plot in Figure 17(b) the gain in tag read rate for varied tag numbers from 50 – 10000. The result demonstrates that consistent 6× to 6.5× gain is achieved by *BiGroup* for a large scale of RFID tags.

5. RELATED WORK

A variety of approaches have been proposed to enable multiple access in RFID communications. Existing commodity RFID systems typically adopt the frame slotted aloha scheme [1] or the tree-based arbitration [17, 29]. Besides the TDMA based approaches, FDMA/SDMA/CDMA based approaches [19, 20, 23, 36] have also been explored to avoid concurrent tag transmissions in the same collision domain, which incurs high coordination overhead.

Recent works improve communication efficiency by supporting concurrent backscatter transmissions. Buzz [31] identifies all tags and decodes tag collisions bit by bit. It assumes the linear combination of reflecting tags' channel coefficients independent of coexisting tags. Buzz also requires the bit-level synchronization among tags as well as channel measurements which are not supported by COTS tags. The linear addition based scheme proposed in [28] also assumes the linear dependency among symbol clusters to map symbol clusters to collision states. Some designs [3, 4, 16] require the knowledge of channel coefficients (e.g. using predefined preambles) and stringent tag synchronization to recover collisions of up to two concurrent tags. The scheme [10] theoretically explores to extract tags with strong signals by correlating with known preambles. A most recent work BST [12] detects signal edges when distances between consecutive symbols exceed a predefined threshold and separates signal edges of multiple tags. BST, however, requires the tags to transmit with assigned initial offsets and bit durations and insert known bits at specific intervals in data packets, all of which are not supported by COTS tags. Some other works assign orthogonal codes to RN16 packets [14, 18] to recover collisions, which are application specific and non-standard. Unlike all these works, *BiGroup* aims to recover collisions without modifying COTS tags and provide general decoding benefits within EPC C1G2 framework. To the best of our knowledge, *BiGroup* is the first effort made to target such a goal.

Some other recent works explore using higher order modulation schemes to improve single tag transmission rate [5, 30], which provides another way of improving RFID communication throughput. Nevertheless, higher order modulations require more complex tag circuits, higher power supply, and are not compatible with existing EPC standards.

It is demonstrated that battery-free devices (similar to COTS tags) can harvest energy and communicate by backscattering ambient RF signals from TV, cellular [21], and WiFi stations [15]. Moreover, backscatter networks can benefit from multi-antenna designs [24], advanced coding mechanisms [24] and full-duplex communications [22]. *BiGroup* is motivated to enable concurrent transmissions for backscatter devices and orthogonal to those works.

6. CONCLUSION

BiGroup enables parallel transmissions and decoding without any extension to COTS RFID tags. To achieve this, *BiGroup* exploits the RFID upper-layer communication patterns and leverages bipartite grouping to substantially improve the performance of physical layer collision recovery. *BiGroup* does not require modifications to C1G2 logics on COTS tags, channel measurements, or stringent time synchronization. We experiment on the software defined testbed and the results show that *BiGroup* significantly improves performance of COTS RFID systems in comparison with other alternative schemes and directly benefits the C1G2 framework. Future work includes further study on scalability of our scheme as well as hardware speedup for better time efficiency.

7. ACKNOWLEDGEMENTS

We would like to thank anonymous shepherd and reviewers for their constructive feedback and suggestions. This work is supported by Singapore MOE AcRF Tier 1 grant MOE2013-T1-002-005, and Nanyang Assistant Professorship (NAP) grant M4080-738.020 of NTU. This work is also supported in part by Hong Kong ECS (PolyU 252053/15E).

References

[1] EPCglobal Inc. EPCglobal Class 1 Generation 2 V. 1.2.0, www.gs1.org/gsmp/kc/epcglobal/uhfc1g2.

[2] Open RFID Lab (ORL), http://pdcc.ntu.edu.sg/wands/ORL/.

[3] C. Angerer, R. Langwieser, and M. Rupp. RFID Reader Receivers for Physical Layer Collision Recovery. *Communications, IEEE Transactions on*, 58(12), 2010.

[4] A. Bletsas, J. Kimionis, A. Dimitriou, and G. Karystinos. Single-Antenna Coherent Detection of Collided FM0 RFID Signals. *Communications, IEEE Transactions on*, 60(3), 2012.

[5] C. Boyer and S. Roy. Coded QAM Backscatter Modulation for RFID. *Communications, IEEE Transactions on*, 60(7), 2012.

[6] M. Buettner, B. Greenstein, and D. Wetherall. Dewdrop: An Energy-aware Runtime for Computational RFID. In *USENIX NSDI*, 2011.

[7] M. Buettner, R. Prasad, M. Philipose, and D. Wetherall. Recognizing Daily Activities with RFID-based Sensors. In *ACM UbiComp*, 2009.

[8] Q. Dong, A. Shukla, V. Shrivastava, D. Agrawal, S. Banerjee, and K. Kar. Load Balancing in Large-Scale RFID Systems. In *IEEE INFOCOM*, 2007.

[9] M. Ester, H. peter Kriegel, J. S, and X. Xu. A Density-based Algorithm for Discovering Clusters in Large Spatial Databases with Noise. AAAI Press, 1996.

[10] K. Fyhn, R. Jacobsen, P. Popovski, A. Scaglione, and T. Larsen. Multipacket Reception of Passive UHF RFID Tags: A Communication Theoretic Approach. *Signal Processing, IEEE Transactions on*, 59(9), 2011.

[11] A. Gudipati and S. Katti. Strider: Automatic Rate Adaptation and Collision Handling. In *ACM SIGCOMM*, 2011.

[12] P. Hu, P. Zhang, and D. Ganesan. Leveraging Interleaved Signal Edges for Concurrent Backscatter. In *ACM HotWireless*, 2014.

[13] S. Jana and S. K. Kasera. On Fast and Accurate Detection of Unauthorized Wireless Access Points Using Clock Skews. In *ACM MobiCom*, 2008.

[14] L. Kang, K. Wu, J. Zhang, H. Tan, and L. Ni. DDC: A Novel Scheme to Directly Decode the Collisions in UHF RFID Systems. *Parallel and Distributed Systems, IEEE Transactions on*, 23(2), 2012.

[15] B. Kellogg, A. Parks, S. Gollakota, J. R. Smith, and D. Wetherall. Wi-fi Backscatter: Internet Connectivity for RF-powered Devices. In *ACM SIGCOMM*, 2014.

[16] R. Khasgiwale, R. Adyanthaya, and D. Engels. Extracting Information From Tag Collisions. In *IEEE RFID*, 2009.

[17] S. H. Kim and P. Park. An Efficient Tree-Based Tag Anti-Collision Protocol for RFID Systems. *Communications Letters, IEEE*, 11(5), 2007.

[18] L. Kong, L. He, Y. Gu, M.-Y. Wu, and T. He. A Parallel Identification Protocol for RFID systems. In *IEEE INFOCOM*, 2014.

[19] T. Li, M. K. Han, A. Bhartia, L. Qiu, E. Rozner, Y. Zhang, and B. Zarikoff. CRMA: Collision-resistant Multiple Access. In *ACM MobiCom*, 2011.

[20] H.-C. Liu and J.-P. Ciou. Performance Analysis of Multi-Carrier RFID Systems. In *SPECTS*, 2009.

[21] V. Liu, A. Parks, V. Talla, S. Gollakota, D. Wetherall, and J. R. Smith. Ambient Backscatter: Wireless Communication out of Thin Air. In *ACM SIGCOMM*, 2013.

[22] V. Liu, V. Talla, and S. Gollakota. Enabling Instantaneous Feedback with Full-duplex Backscatter. In *ACM MobiCom*, 2014.

[23] C. Mutti and C. Floerkemeier. CDMA-based RFID Systems in Dense Scenarios: Concepts and Challenges. In *IEEE RFID*, 2008.

[24] A. N. Parks, A. Liu, S. Gollakota, and J. R. Smith. Turbocharging Ambient Backscatter Communication. In *ACM SIGCOMM*, 2014.

[25] S. Rallapalli, L. Qiu, Y. Zhang, and Y.-C. Chen. Exploiting Temporal Stability and Low-rank Structure for Localization in Mobile Networks. In *ACM MobiCom*, 2010.

[26] L. Shangguan, Z. Li, Z. Yang, M. Li, and Y. Liu. OTrack: Order Tracking for Luggage in Mobile RFID Systems. In *IEEE INFOCOM*, 2013.

[27] L. Shangguan, Z. Yang, A. X. Liu, Z. Zhou, and Y. Liu. Relative Localization of RFID Tags Using Spatial-temporal Phase Profiling. In *USENIX NSDI*, 2015.

[28] D. Shen, G. Woo, D. Reed, A. Lippman, and J. Wang. Separation of Multiple Passive RFID Signals Using Software Defined Radio. In *IEEE RFID*, 2009.

[29] D.-H. Shih, P.-L. Sun, D. C. Yen, and S.-M. Huang. Taxonomy and Survey of RFID Anti-collision Protocols. *Computer Communications*, 29(11), 2006.

[30] S. Thomas and M. Reynolds. A 96 Mbit/sec, 15.5 pJ/bit 16-QAM Modulator for UHF Backscatter Communication. In *IEEE RFID*, 2012.

[31] J. Wang, H. Hassanieh, D. Katabi, and P. Indyk. Efficient and Reliable Low-power Backscatter Networks. In *ACM SIGCOMM*, 2012.

[32] J. Wang and D. Katabi. Dude, Where's My Card?: RFID Positioning That Works with Multipath and Non-line of Sight. In *ACM SIGCOMM*, 2013.

[33] J. Wang, D. Vasisht, and D. Katabi. RF-IDraw: Virtual Touch Screen in the Air Using RF Signals. In *ACM SIGCOMM*, 2014.

[34] Y. Wang, J. Liu, Y. Chen, M. Gruteser, J. Yang, and H. Liu. E-eyes: Device-free Location-oriented Activity Identification Using Fine-grained WiFi Signatures. In *ACM MobiCom*, 2014.

[35] L. Yang, Y. Chen, X.-Y. Li, C. Xiao, M. Li, and Y. Liu. Tagoram: Real-time Tracking of Mobile RFID Tags to High Precision Using COTS Devices. In *ACM MobiCom*, 2014.

[36] J. Yu, K. Liu, and G. Yan. A Novel RFID Anti-Collision Algorithm Based on SDMA. In *IEEE WiCOM*, 2008.

[37] D. Zanetti, B. Danev, and S. Capkun. Physical-layer Identification of UHF RFID Tags. In *ACM MobiCom*, 2010.

[38] P. Zhang, P. Hu, V. Pasikanti, and D. Ganesan. EkhoNet: High Speed Ultra Low-power Backscatter for Next Generation Sensors. In *ACM MobiCom*, 2014.

[39] X. Zhang and K. G. Shin. E-MiLi: Energy-minimizing Idle Listening in Wireless Networks. In *ACM MobiCom*, 2011.

[40] Y. Zheng and M. Li. PET: Probabilistic Estimating Tree for Large-Scale RFID Estimation. *IEEE Transactions on Mobile Computing*, 11(11), 2012.

[41] Y. Zheng and M. Li. Fast Tag Searching Protocol for Large-scale RFID Systems. *IEEE/ACM Trans. Netw.*, 21(3), 2013.

[42] X. Zhou, Z. Zhang, Y. Zhu, Y. Li, S. Kumar, A. Vahdat, B. Y. Zhao, and H. Zheng. Mirror Mirror on the Ceiling: Flexible Wireless Links for Data Centers. In *ACM SIGCOMM*, 2012.

Last-Mile Navigation Using Smartphones

Yuanchao Shu[*†], Kang G. Shin[†], Tian He[‡], Jiming Chen[*]

[*] Zhejiang University, Hangzhou, China
[†] The University of Michigan, Ann Arbor, USA
[‡] University of Minnesota, USA

ABSTRACT

Although GPS has become a standard component of smartphones, providing accurate navigation during the last portion of a trip remains an important but unsolved problem. Despite extensive research on localization, the limited resolution of a map imposes restrictions on the navigation engine in both indoor and outdoor environments. To bridge the gap between the end position obtained from legacy navigation services and the real destination, we propose FOLLOWME, a "last-mile" navigation system to enable plug-and-play navigation in indoor and semi-outdoor environments. FOLLOWME exploits the ubiquitous, stable geomagnetic field and natural walking patterns to navigate the users to the same destination taken by an earlier traveler. Unlike existing localization and navigation systems, FOLLOWME is infrastructure-free, energy-efficient and cost-saving. We implemented FOLLOWME on smartphones, and evaluated it in a four-story campus building with a testing area of $2000m^2$. Our experimental results with 5 users show that 95% of spatial errors during navigation were 2m or less with at least 50% energy savings over a benchmark system.

Categories and Subject Descriptors

C.3 [**Special-purpose And Application-based Systems**]: Real-time and embedded systems; H.5.2 [**Information Interfaces And Presentation**]: User Interfaces—*User-centered design*

General Terms

Design; Experimentation; Performance

Keywords

Navigation; Smartphone; Plug-and-Play System; Sensory Data

1. INTRODUCTION

Location-relevant services and applications have been studied extensively within the mobile computing community over the past several years. Most researchers have focused on the localization of devices/users. To date, with the help of space satellites, meter-level positioning accuracy can be achieved in outdoor environments (e.g., using GPS, GLONASS, etc.), and numerous approaches have been proposed to localize users in indoor environments [1–7].

Accurate localization, map information and path planning algorithms make real-time navigation a reality, but most research efforts on navigation have been designed for path planning and optimization, given starting and destination locations and wide-area map information. Due to the lack of micro-map information, however, navigation cannot always be successful, especially for the last portion of a trip. For example, Google Map is able to navigate users to a building (more specifically, an entrance of the building) from a location tens of miles away, but fails to find a feasible path to the final destination, e.g., a meeting room inside the building. We call this imperfection the *last-mile* navigation problem.[1]

The main reason for this problem is the incomplete map information, causing incorrect inference on existence and reachability of an exact destination. Technically, most navigation services can guide a user only to a place that is connected by at least one indexed path, such as a trunk road. If the end location is not in the map database (even if it is accessible in real world), navigation systems cannot connect the coordinates of two locations.

Despite the extensive efforts made on indoor localization, few of the resulting solutions have been deployed because of their labor-intensive (hence time-consuming) bootstrapping, especially for indoor map construction. Although multiple model-based [5, 8] and crowdsourcing [6, 9, 10] techniques have been proposed, the need for precise building structure information and a sustainable incentive crowdsourcing mechanism limits their applicability [11]. Even if deployed, indoor localization systems may face an onerous calibration process (for those radio-based fingerprint systems) and need to deploy path-planning algorithms to enable online navigation services. For example, Apple iBeacon can perform localization (*not* navigation) only in the vicinity of pre-deployed iBeacon devices, whereas Path Advisor [12] only provides offline navigation paths with given start and end locations.

To meet the ever-growing demand for navigation, we propose a new lightweight, plug-and-play, last-mile navigation system, called FOLLOWME, to bridge the gap between the user's final destination and the end location provided by current navigation services. The main idea of FOLLOWME is to use "scent" or "crumbs" left behind by previous travelers (a.k.a. leaders). In FOLLOWME, A leader records sensory data with his/her smartphone during the last-mile trip. The location specific features extracted from the sensory data are combined with the leader's walking patterns (e.g., steps, turns, going upstairs/downstairs) to build a reference trace. In

[1] The *last mile* was originally used in the field of communications to refer to the final leg of communications connectivity to retail customers. The last mile is often the speed bottleneck in communication networks.

MobiCom'15, September 7–11, 2015, Paris, France.
© 2015 ACM. ISBN 978-1-4503-3619-2/15/09 ...$15.00.
DOI: http://dx.doi.org/10.1145/2789168.2790099.

the design of FOLLOWME, we adopt the use of the ubiquitous geomagnetic field, which is locally disturbed in indoor and semi-outdoor environments (i.e., close to a building or in a semi-open building, as in a metropolitan area populated with tall buildings) [13–16]. We also consider how to incorporate other location-specific signals including FM and GSM in Section 8.

During the navigation phase, the follower will first arrive at the same starting location (e.g., a building entrance) as at least one leader using legacy navigation services (e.g., Google Maps). From then on, FOLLOWME installed in the follower's smartphone will compare and synchronize current sensor readings with the reference (i.e., the leader's) trace and guides the user, in real time, from the starting location to the final destination. This way, irrespective of incomplete map information, FOLLOWME is able to navigate users[2] to any point of interest (PoI) as long as it has been visited earlier by a leader. For example, a meeting coordinator can provide the attendees with the data trace from the building entrances to the meeting room. Vendors and restaurant owners can collect data traces on their own from several entrances of a shopping mall to their stores and then share them with the public on the cloud to entice customers. The leader and the follower can also be the same person. For example, one can record a trace from a parking spot to the airport terminal and use it for reverse navigation back to one's car after a multi-day trip.

Unlike other leader–follower navigation systems [17–19], FOLLOWME relies neither on an infrastructure (e.g., maps, WiFi APs) nor any additional hardware (e.g., beacons, landmarks). In addition, FOLLOWME exploits people's natural walking patterns, thus minimizing constraints imposed on users.

This paper makes the following three main contributions:

- We identify the last-mile navigation problem and propose an infrastructure-free solution using only sensors on commodity smartphones;
- We devise a novel online magnetic-field-based, step-constrained trace synchronization technique for walking progress estimation and navigation; and
- We implement FOLLOWME on Android smartphones and evaluate it in a four-story campus building with 5 participants. 95% of spatial errors during navigation within 2m is achieved with at least 50% energy savings over a benchmark system.

The remainder of this paper is organized as follows. We first provide motivation for a new indoor navigation system like FOLLOWME in Section 2. We then present the architecture of FOLLOWME in Section 3 and detailed illustrations in Section 4 and Section 5. Section 6 describes the implementation of a prototype system, and Section 7 presents an in-depth evaluation of FOLLOWME. Several practical issues and related work are discussed in Section 8 and Section 9, respectively. Finally, we conclude the paper in Section 10.

2. MOTIVATION

Given that various sensors and methods have been studied or proposed for navigation, why is another navigation system like FOLLOWME necessary? We justify the need for FOLLOWME by answering a few natural questions as follows.

- *Is GPS good enough for navigation?* In most outdoor scenarios, the answer is yes. However, as stated in the Introduction, GPS-like satellite systems offer high positioning accuracy, but the map's insufficiency limits their potential to explore the last-mile navigation and impairs the user experience. GPS also consumes lots of power, suffers from the urban canyon effect, and has poor coverage in indoor environments.
- *Are guide maps sufficient for navigation in an indoor environment?* Guide maps are helpful for indoor navigation, but they are not always handy. Users also need to fully understand the guide map, pinpoint the starting point and the destination, plan a route, and remember the route. This imposes additional burden on the users, especially on the elderly or children. Thus, FOLLOWME is complementary to the guide map with minimal learning cost to users.
- *Is indoor localization helpful?* Yes, but localization is not the same as navigation. Most indoor localization systems (ILSes) are built based on full knowledge of a floor map. In essence, insufficient incentives for map construction and time-consuming bootstrapping hinder their deployment and acceptance. Moreover, in many cases, a complicated and large ILS is an overkill for navigation needs. In other words, users have to bear the additional cost of the entire map construction, even they only need guidance along a single path. Therefore, a lightweight and plug-and-play navigation system such as FOLLOWME is necessary to fill the gap between high navigation demands and limited ILSes deployments.

[2]We use followers and users interchangeably throughout the paper.

3. SYSTEM OVERVIEW

This section provides an overview of FOLLOWME, first presenting the system architecture in Section 3.1 and then a navigation example in Section 3.2 to illustrate how FOLLOWME operates.

3.1 System Architecture

FOLLOWME consists of a trace-collection module and a navigation module, both of which exploit multiple sensors in a smartphone, such as accelerometer, gyroscope, magnetometer, barometer, etc. Figure 1 shows the overall architecture of FOLLOWME.

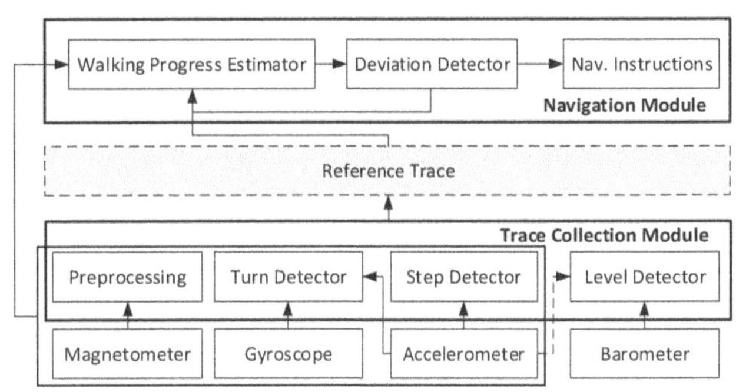

Figure 1: Architecture of FOLLOWME.

Trace-Collection Module: This module works during the leader's walking trip to generate the reference trace. The leader activates the module when s/he starts walking. During the leader's entire walking period, FOLLOWME records the readings of the magnetometer, accelerometer, gyroscope, and barometer. The module then launches a series of signal processing, including magnetic data preprocessing (Section 5.2), step recognition (Section 6.1), turn and level-change detection (Section 6.2 and Section 6.3), and generates a reference trace after the leader's arrival at the destination. The reference trace contains timestamped preprocessed geomagnetic data as well as steps, turns and level changes extracted from different sensors.

Note that we can also leverage combinations of sensors other than those listed in Figure 1 for walking pattern recognition. For example, together with a barometer, an accelerometer can help detect whether or not the user is climbing stairs [20]. Due to space limitation, here we focus on the design of the navigation module and briefly mention the implementation of recognition and detection algorithms in Section 6.

Navigation Module: This module takes the reference trace as an input and helps the followers navigate from the starting location to the same destination as the leader. Typical starting locations are those where GPS/Google Map stops provision of precise navigation, such as the end of a road or the entrance of a building. Like the trace-collection module, it contains a mag-processor and step detector that process the data from magnetometer and accelerometer, respectively, during the follower's walking trip. All the input data are sent to the walking progress estimator (Section 5.2), which estimates the portion the user has walked relative to the entire reference trace. Based on the estimation results, a deviation detector determines whether or not the follower is off course. If not, the navigation module provides navigation directions (i.e., turn, go up/down stairs) on the smartphone screen to guide the user to the destination, or reversely guides the user back to the correct trace and then to the destination.

3.2 A Navigation Example

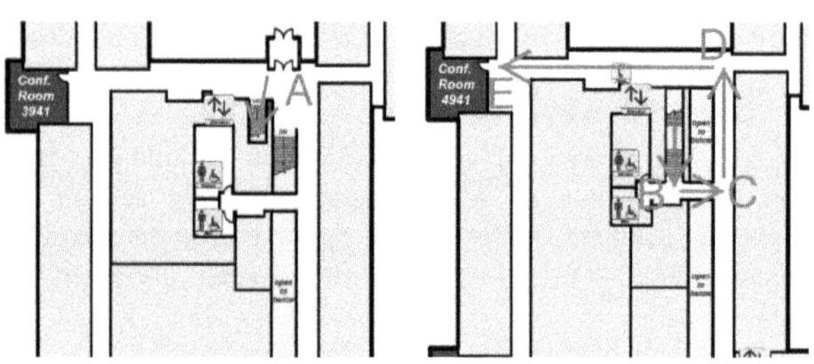

(a) The 3rd floor. (b) The 4th floor.

Figure 2: An indoor navigation example.

For example, suppose a meeting will be held in Room 4941 on the fourth floor of our Department building, and U_a is the coordinator of this meeting. Before the meeting, U_a walks from the building entrance (location A on the third floor) to the conference room as the red arrowed line shows. During the leader's walk, the trace-collection module records the geomagnetic data along the route and identifies walking features (i.e., 1 flight of stairs and 3 left turns). Later, a meeting participant (follower) U_b, who has received the reference trace from U_a, arrives at the same entrance. From that point on, the navigation module will estimate U_b's location relative to the reference trace (i.e., walking progress) in real time and guide U_b to Room 4941. The walking progress estimation is made by matching geomagnetic observations of U_b to those from the reference trace. Based on the estimation result, a "go upstairs" icon will appear first, followed by a "left turn" icon when U_b is approaching locations B, C and D. Once U_b reaches location E, FOLLOWME generates a notification and terminates the navigation process.

Figure 3 shows how the navigation module works in the time domain. Suppose U_a takes t_1 seconds to arrive at position B

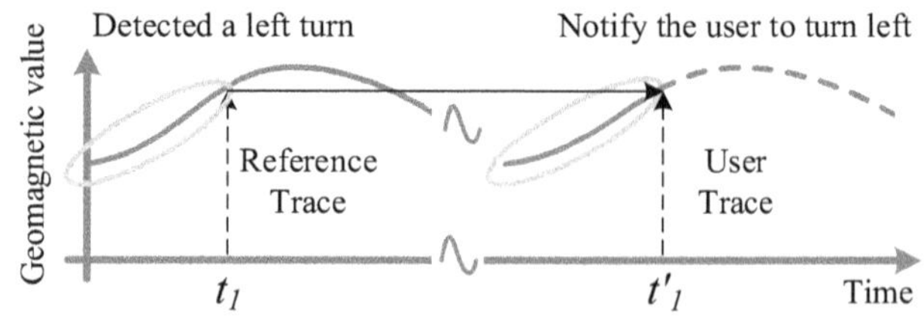

Figure 3: Illustration of the walking progress estimation.

on the path and makes a left turn during the trace collection. In the navigation phase, based on the similarity of geomagnetic observations (in both ellipses), the navigation module infers that U_b reaches B at time t_1', and hence instructs U_b to turn left. In Section 4, we first introduce the reference trace construction and then elaborate on the navigation module in Section 5.

3.3 Assumptions and Limitations

As illustrated with the above example, FOLLOWME has a very different operational model from most existing navigation systems. Instead of enabling generic navigation, FOLLOWME is built as a plug-and-play system for dedicated working scenarios, which inevitably introduces several limitations. First, the user cannot be navigated without a reference trace with the same origin and destination. This may in turn cause a scalability problem as the number of possible routes inside a building could be very large. In this part of the paper, we first focus on the design of FOLLOWME, and discuss the scalability issue in Section 8.2. Second, due to the unavailability of map information, the user, if deviated from the reference route, has to return to the route while using FOLLOWME. Even though it is annoying in certain circumstances, the novelty of this mechanism is to enable navigation without expensive map building and localization. In addition, FOLLOWME has some other specific requirements, e.g., the algorithm requires that the difference between the number of steps taken by the leader and the follower be relatively stable. In situations where such constraints are not met, the performance and accuracy of FOLLOWME is likely to be adversely affected. This is described in more detail in Section 5.2. In Section 8, we will discuss future potential improvements based on our evaluation results.

4. REFERENCE-TRACE CONSTRUCTION

We now describe the reference-trace construction and then introduce the geomagnetic data processing and real-time navigation in Section 5. Section 6 will detail the design of algorithms for step recognition as well as turn and level-change detection.

Table 1: Data format of the reference trace

Geomagnetic data	$m =< t_i, m_i^x, m_i^y, m_i^z >$
Step data	$s =< t_i, s_i >, s_i = 1, 2, 3, \ldots$
Turn data	$tr =< t_i, tr_i >, tr_i =$ turn degrees
Level change data	$l =< t_i, l_i >, l_i = \{up, down\}$

During the leader's walking, the trace-collection module automatically builds the reference trace by (i) recording geomagnetic readings, which are tuples of timestamps and magnetic values; (ii) detecting steps, turns and level-changes based on readings of the accelerometer, gyroscope and barometer; (iii) outputting all detection results (time-stamps, turn directions, etc.) and geomagnetic readings to a file upon leader's arrival at the destination. The data format of the reference trace is summarized in Table 1. Each reference trace is labeled with a (starting point, destination) pair (e.g., from Entrance A to Room 4941). Once the reference trace is generated, the leader can share it on the cloud for future navigation purposes. In the current FOLLOWME implementation, we send the trace file directly to the followers, but it can be deployed as a cloud service in future.

Note that there could be certain detection delays during use of FOLLOWME. For example, a peak detection algorithm will incur a step detection delay; turns can only be recognized after the user completes each turn and the response time of level-change detection is subject to the user's climbing speed of the staircase. However, since each step and turn lasts for a short time and the level-change detection works only in the trace-collection module, these delays affect the navigation performance insignificantly, which is confirmed by our experimental study.

5. REAL-TIME NAVIGATION

Since followers will likely walk at different speeds from the leader, and may even stop en route from time to time, the key challenge in FOLLOWME is to estimate their walking progress. In the navigation phase, the walking progress estimator synchronizes each follower's walking to the reference trace by matching their geomagnetic observations. Based on the estimation results, real-time guidance (i.e., advance notices of turns and level-changes) and an estimated walking time are also provided on the smartphone screen. Section 5.3 further discusses on how FOLLOWME recovers when the user goes off the trail.

5.1 Preliminaries of the Geomagnetic Field

Below we discuss the identified properties of magnetic fields before presenting a walking progress estimation algorithm.

Locally Disturbed Yet Stable Magnetic Field: Due to its global availability and stability, the geomagnetic field is used in several indoor localization systems [13–15, 21–23]. Most of them exploit magnetic field anomalies caused by the local disturbances of ferromagnetic building materials, and localize users/devices based on a pre-established fingerprint map.

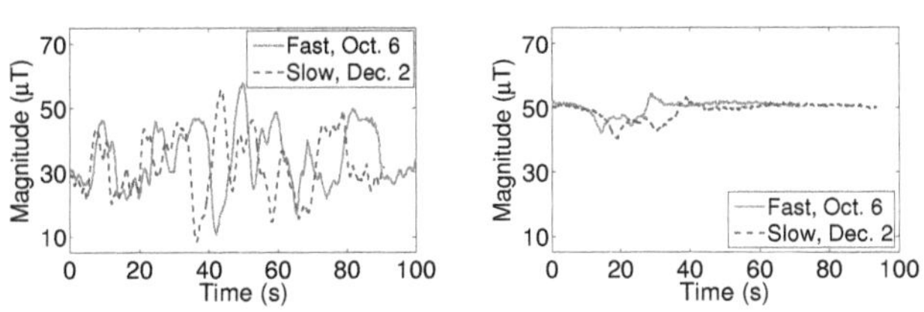

(a) Collected during walk on an indoor corridor.

(b) Collected during walk on an outdoor walking trail. The user passes a building 5m away between 10s and 40s.

Figure 4: Geomagnetic traces collected during walking.

Figure 4 shows 4 magnetic traces in both indoor and outdoor environments. The traces in each figure were collected during walks along the same path on different dates nearly two months apart. Figure 4 shows that anomalies of the geomagnetic field caused by building construction materials exist in both indoor and outdoor environments and that the magnetic field and the local disturbances are very stable over time as the construction layout remains unchanged. In addition, the impact of mobile objects on the magnetic field is very limited. See [13, 24–27] for more detail. These local disturbances, stability over time and robustness make the magnetic field a good candidate for trace synchronization in FOLLOWME.

Note that although the magnetic field is directional and 3D magnetic signals are measured by magnetometer, it is difficult to fully leverage magnetic field readings on three axes, as the frame of reference of the magnetometer may not always align with the global coordinate system. Ensuring that alignment would require either accurately tracking the device's attitude (i.e., orientation or posture) at all times or to constrain the device usage at some fixed attitude (e.g., hand-held horizontally with Y-axis towards heading direction). The former is difficult due to sensor drift and the latter greatly affects users' experiences. Therefore, only the magnitude of the magnetic signal may be used in practice.

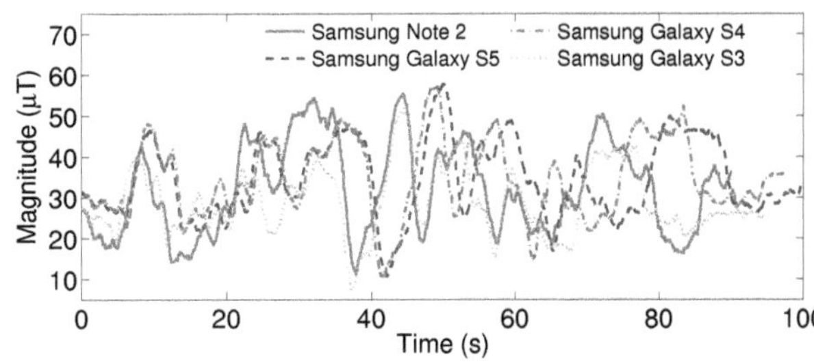

(a) Device diversity

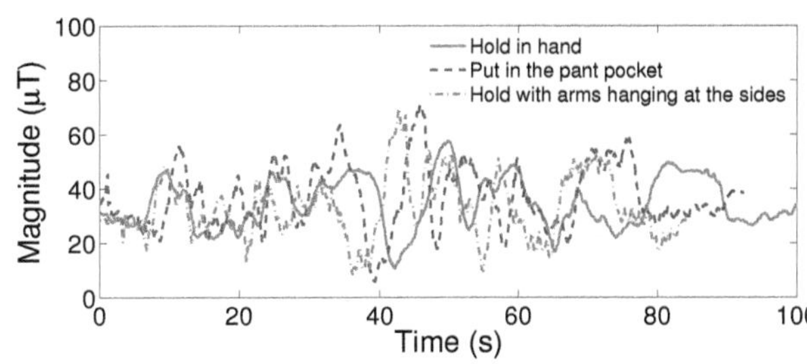

(b) Usage diversity

Figure 5: Challenges of using the geomagnetic field.

Outdoor Low Discernibility and Biased Measurements Due to Device and Usage Diversities: Despite its favorable properties, use of the magnetic field poses several challenges. First, the magnetic field is less interfered in outdoor space than indoor space. For example, in Figure 4(b), outdoor magnetic distortions can only be observed when the user passes by buildings. To handle this problem, FOLLOWME uses a simplified IODetector [16] (only using the magnetism detector) to differentiate outdoor open areas from indoor/semi-outdoor spaces. In indoor or semi-outdoor environments, FOLLOWME leverages a novel step-constrained trace synchronization approach for navigation, while in outdoor open spaces where accurate directions can be obtained by a compass, it uses legacy inertial-sensor-based tracking (i.e., dead reckoning) [1]. Since the majority of last-mile navigation problems occur in indoor/semi-outdoor environments, we will focus on the magnetic-field-based, step-constrained trace synchronization.

The second challenge is the biased magnetic field measurements caused by device and usage diversities. In other words, different devices will show different readings for the same magnetic field. This is verified in Figure 5(a), showing the magnitude of the collected magnetic signals along the same path using different smartphones. Even for the same device (Galaxy S5), the resulting signal varies from the device's height (as shown in Figure 5(b)). However, the trend (i.e., shape) of the measured magnetic field remains consistent across devices and usages, providing opportunities for navigation.

5.2 Walking Progress Estimation

To provide real-time navigation instructions (i.e., for turns, stair-climbing) and estimate the remaining walking time, we need to know how far the follower has walked relative to the length of the reference trace. For this, we devise a step-constrained trace synchronization algorithm based on *Dynamic Time Warping* (DTW). The algorithm matches magnetometer readings from the follower's phone to the pre-loaded magnetic field data from the reference trace.

DTW is a class of algorithms proposed to align and measure the similarity between two time series. Specifically, DTW matches each sample in one time series to one or more samples in another ordered sequence using dynamic programming. The objective of DTW can be stated as: *Given two time series* $S_a = S_a[i], i = 1, \ldots, L_a$ *and* $S_b = S_b[i], i = 1, \ldots, L_b$*, DTW aims to find a monotonic mapping function* $f : I[1, L_a] \to I[1, L_b]$ *between* S_a *and* S_b *so as to minimize* $\sum_{i=1}^{L_a} (S_a[i] - S_b[f(i)])^2$ *where* $I[1, L_a]$ *is the integers from 1 to* L_a*.*

Despite its wide usage, DTW cannot be directly applied to synchronize the user and the reference traces for three reasons. First, DTW works offline on two given time series. However, in FOLLOWME, the length of the user trace continuously increases during his walk. Second, DTW maintains a two-dimensional warping cost matrix of which the size is a quadratic function of the number of samples. This incurs an unacceptably high computational overhead on the smartphone, especially when the walking distance gets longer. Third, DTW compares two sequences based on their absolute values. Due to the device and usage diversities, the observations of biased magnetic fields have negative effects on the matching results. Due to the lack of a full picture of the user trace (especially at the beginning of the walk), simple mean-removal techniques cannot solve the problem.

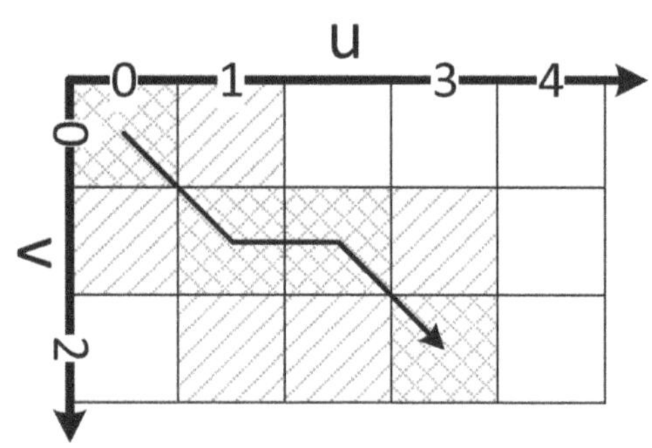

Figure 6: Updating the warping cost matrix in the step-constrained trace synchronization.

To exploit the advantages of the magnetic field and deal with the above problems, FOLLOWME proposes a step-constrained trace synchronization algorithm. The algorithm has three main characteristics. First, to deal with device heterogeneity and usage diversity, we filter out the high-frequency components of the magnetic field sensing and then utilize the differential magnetic field information that is independent of the absolute values. Second, to reduce the computation overhead, we set a global path constraint in DTW based on the step-detection results. This way, the algorithm runs in linearithmic time and we need to maintain similarity scores only within a certain range of the warping cost matrix, which is also memory-efficient. Third, to obtain a better matching result, we adaptively change the search band in the warping cost matrix according to the similarities among traces.

Let us consider Figure 6 as an example to illustrate the matching process. Figure 6 shows a 3×5 warping cost matrix. Entry (i, j) in the matrix indicates the similarity between the $(i-1)$-th sample in the reference trace v and the $(j-1)$-th sample in the user trace u. In this example we maintain a search band with only a fixed width of 2, hence setting the path constraint coefficient $c = 2$. At the beginning of the process, we compute values of the first $c^2 = 4$ entries on the northwest corner and set the pointer of the matrix $p = (p_v, p_u)$ to $(1, 1)$. Then, we find the entry with the minimal value among all entries that are within the distance of $c = 2$ to the pointer on both p_v-th row and p_u-th column. For example, we find the entry $(1, 1)$ is smaller than both $(1, 0)$ and $(0, 1)$ entries. Therefore, both p_v and p_u increase from 1 to 2 and $(1, 2)$, $(2, 1)$ and $(2, 2)$ entries are being calculated. Now, we find the entry $(1, 2)$ contains the smallest value among $(2, 1)$, $(2, 2)$ and $(1, 2)$ entries. Hence, in the next iteration, only p_u increases (i.e., the pointer moves to the right entry $(2, 3)$) and we update $(2, 3)$ and $(1, 3)$ entries.

In this example, all calculated entries are shaded in grey, and the mapped results are also labeled. For example, $f(u_3) = v_2$. This way, we synchronize the walks of the leader and the follower, and can further provide real-time turning and stair climbing instructions when the follower approaches a crossing or stairs or elevators.

Note that in this example, we move the matrix pointer p based only on matching results. A step constraint is also used in our algorithm. The rationale behind the step-constraint is simple: *the difference between the number of steps taken by the leader and the follower within a small given physical distance should be bounded.* For example, for a 5-meter walk, it is unlikely that the difference of steps taken by two users is as large as 10. Hence, in the algorithm, if $f(u_i) = v_m$ and $f(u_j) = v_n$, we first get the number of steps s'^v taken by the leader between t_m^v and t_n^v, and compare it with the number of steps s'^u taken by the follower between t_i^u and t_j^u. Since samples (u_i, v_m) and (u_j, v_n) should be taken at nearby physical positions (if not the same), the difference between s'^u and s'^v should be bounded. Therefore, if the difference is larger than a predefined threshold, we move the pointer horizontally/vertically in the next iteration.

Algorithm 1 and 2 illustrate the detailed step-constrained online trace synchronization algorithm. At first, Algorithm 1 imports reference trace v and preprocesses the magnetic field trace m^v. The function $MagPreprocess$ computes the magnitude, smooths the data through a low-pass filter and calculates the difference between neighboring magnitude values. The matching continues running before the user reaches the destination (lines 5–28). In the main loop, if a new column was calculated ($p_u^{inc} == true$) in the previous iteration, the algorithm calculates and outputs the matching result uv, and then reads a new sample (lines 8–12). Between line 14 and 27, the algorithm calculates a partial row or column of the warping cost matrix D (i.e., compare magnetic field values and compute similarities). The computation is based on standard DTW recursion formula (line 18 and line 25), restricted to using only the entries which have already been computed. The search band is updated in each iteration according to the function $DirInc$.

Input : reference trace $v = \{t^v, m^v, s^v, tr^v, l^v\}$
Output: uv where $uv_i = j$ indicates the i-th sample in u maps to the j-th sample in v

$p_u = 0, p_v = 0, p_u^{inc} = true$;
for *each sample* $m_i^v \in m^v$ **do**
  m_i^{vp} = `MagPreprocess` (m_i^v);
end
while $p_v \leq size(v)$ **do**
  if p_u^{inc} **then**
    $uv_i = \arg\min D[k][p_u], k \in [p_v - c, p_v]$;
    for *each observation* u_i **do**
      get a_i^u, m_i^u;
      s_i^u = `StepDetection` (a^u);
      m_i^{up} = `MagPreprocess` (m_i^u);
    end
  end
  if `DirInc` *(p_u, p_v) != IncColumn* **then**
    $p_v + +$;
    $p_u^{inc} = false$;
    for $j = p_u - c; j \leq p_u; j + +$ **do**
      $D[p_v][j] = \min(D[p_v - 1][j - 1], D[p_v - 1][j], D[p_v][j - 1]) + (m_{p_u}^{up} - m_{p_v}^{vp})^2$;
    end
  end
  if `DirInc` *(p_u, p_v) != IncRow* **then**
    $p_u + +$;
    $p_u^{inc} = true$;
    for $j = p_u - c; j \leq p_u; j + +$ **do**
      $D[j][p_u] = \min(D[j - 1][p_u - 1], D[j - 1][p_u], D[j][p_u - 1]) + (m_{p_u}^{up} - m_{p_v}^{vp})^2$;
    end
  end
end

Algorithm 1: Magnetic-field-based trace synchronization

1 **Function** *DirInc(p_u, p_v)*
2   **if** $i \leq cIni$ **then**
3   **return** *IncBoth*;
4   **end**
5   given $uv_i = k$, calculate
6   $vSteps = s_k^v - s_{k'}^v$ where $t_k^v - t_{k'}^v = t_w$;
7   $uSteps = s_i^u - s_{i'}^u$ where $uv_{i'} = k'$;
8   **if** $vSteps + StepBound \leq uSteps$ **then**
9   **return** *IncRow*;
10   **end**
11   **if** $vSteps - StepBound \geq uSteps$ **then**
12   **return** *IncColumn*;
13   **end**
14   $(m, n) = \arg\min(D[x][y])$ where $x = p_v, y \in [p_u - c + 1, p_u]$ or $y = p_u, x \in [p_v - c + 1, p_v]$;
15   **if** $m < p_v$ **then**
16   **return** *IncColumn*;
17   **end**
18   **if** $n < p_u$ **then**
19   **return** *IncRow*;
20   **else**
21   **return** *IncBoth*;
22   **end**
23 **end**

Algorithm 2: Trace synchronization function

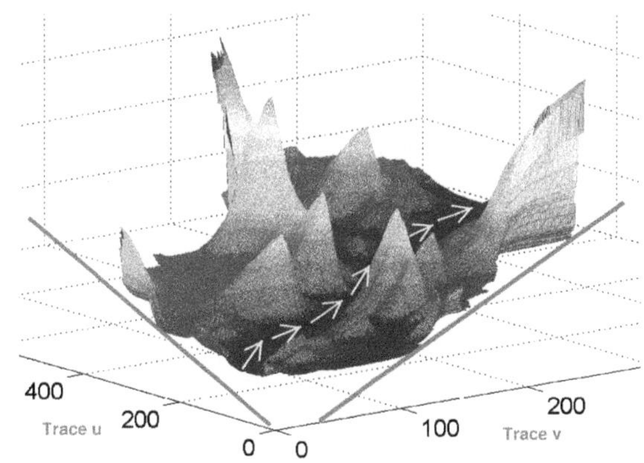

Figure 7: 3D plot of a warping cost matrix.

To determine the forward direction, function $DirInc$ in Algorithm 2 first checks the step conditions between line 8 and 13. Specifically, given the current pointer location (p_v, p_u), we first extract the last t_w-second walk and the corresponding number of steps taken by the leader. Based on the synchronization results between traces u and v, we than identify the time taken by the follower to complete this distance. Finally, we compare the numbers of steps taken by the leader and the follower (line 8–13). If $vSteps$ is much less than $uSteps$, the row number increases (line 9); if $uSteps$ is much less than $vSteps$, the column number increases (line 12). If the step condition is satisfied, the algorithm sets the forward direction based on the position of the minimal similarity scores (lines 14–22). If the local minimal cost is achieved at $D[p_v][p_u]$, both the row and the column numbers increase. If it is on the p_v-th row, the row number increases, else the column number increases. In the current implementation of FOLLOWME, we empirically set $t_w = 2$ and $StepBound = 3$.

Figure 7 shows a snapshot of the warping cost matrix during the execution of Algorithm 1. The valley in the center of this figure (the arrows) is the optimal warping path. We can see that the algorithm dynamically changes the search band and calculates entries only within a certain range of the band (i.e., between the two red lines). To quantify the computational overhead, we ran the algorithm offline on a PC and Galaxy S5 using traces with different lengths and record the running time in Table 2. The linear relation between the trace length and the running time proves the effectiveness of the algorithm.

Table 2: Computation time (s)

# of samples	1000	2000	3000	4000	5000
PC	1.28	4.17	6.96	9.83	12.51
Smartphone	8.21	12.85	18.12	23.29	27.96

5.3 Deviation Detection

In spite of advance notice of turns and level-changes provided by FOLLOWME, users might still accidentally miss a turn or go off the user's trace on purpose (e.g., to see something interesting along the way). To handle this problem, we design a deviation detector in FOLLOWME which performs the following tasks. First, it automatically detects if the user goes off the trail. When happens, it notifies the user to make a U-turn and navigates him back to the correct path. Specifically, FOLLOWME replays (in the reverse direction) turning or stair climbing actions the user took on the smartphone screen. When to display these instructions is computed by the walking progress estimator, which synchronizes the geomagnetic observations before and after the U-turn. Note that the reverse navigation component can also be used to guide the user back to a previously visited place. Since the reverse navigation works the same as the normal forward navigation, in what follows we will focus on deviation detection.

We detect deviations by tracking similarities of geomagnetic observations from the reference and the user traces. The rationale behind this is simple: different paths possess distinct patterns of geomagnetic intensity. To this end, FOLLOWME keeps monitoring the warping cost matrix D during the trip and uses the median absolute deviation (MAD), which is a robust measure of the variability of a univariate sample of quantitative data, to quantify the increase of DTW distance.

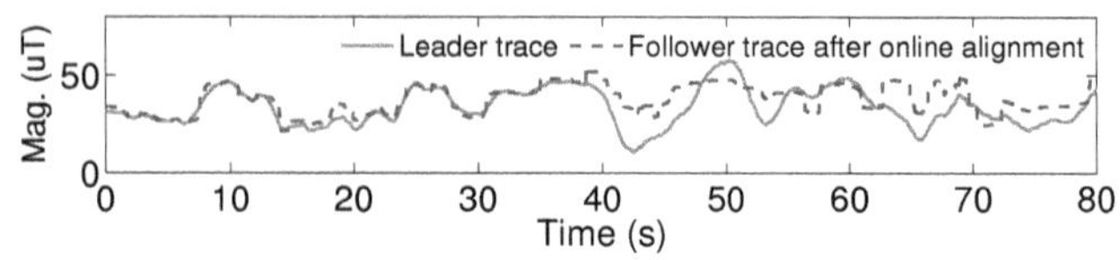

(a) Original traces after alignment

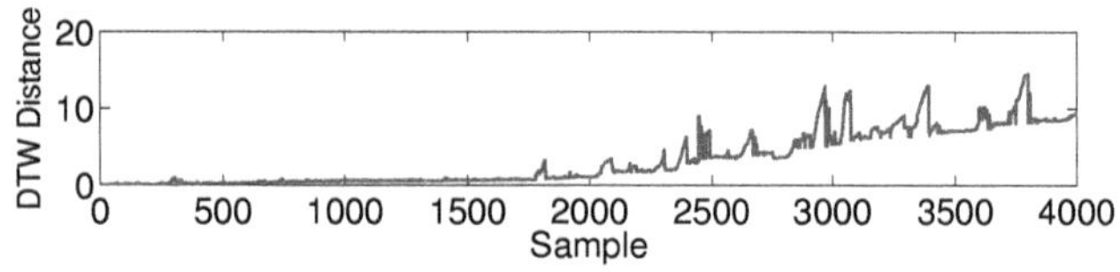

(b) DTW distance

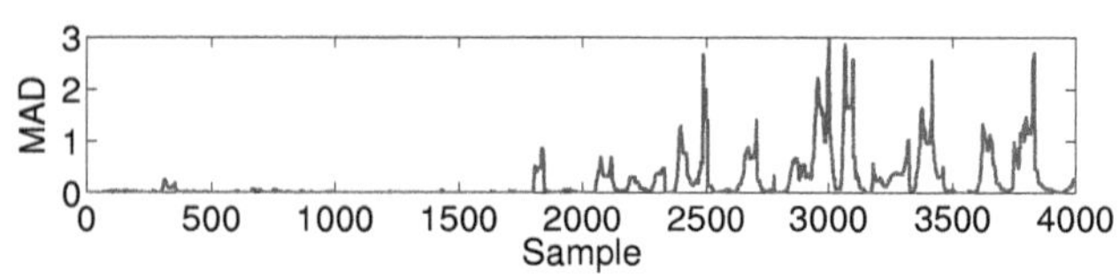

(c) MAD of the DTW distance

Figure 8: Deviation detection.

Take Figure 8 as an example. The user deviated from the correct path after walking for 35 seconds. From Figure 8(a), we can clearly see the difference between the two traces even after time warping. Further, in Figure 8(b), the DTW distance is shown to increase significantly after 1800 samples (i.e., 35 seconds with a sampling frequency of 50Hz). Based on DTW distance, MAD is calculated using a window of 50 samples (Figure 8(c)). Deviation is detected if the cumulative MAD within a certain period grows above a certain threshold. In the current implementation of FOLLOWME, we set the length of this period to 5 seconds and the threshold to the cumulative MAD within a prior neighboring time window.

6. IMPLEMENTATION

To illustrate the application of FOLLOWME, we build a reference system on the Android platform and implement both the trace-collection module and the navigation module. In this section, we first briefly describe the implementation of step, turn, and level-change detections, and then introduce the implementation of online navigation in Section 6.4. Note that other motion-detection techniques can also be leveraged in FOLLOWME.

6.1 Step Detection

Step information of both the leader and the follower is used in the walking progress estimator (in Section 5.2) to navigate users. FOLLOWME recognizes user steps based on the accelerometer readings. Since the maximum amplitudes along all 3 axes of the accelerometer occur when the heel strikes the ground [28], we devise a peak recognition algorithm to detect these strikes/steps. To make the step detection independent of the phone's orientation, only the magnitude of the 3-axis acceleration reading (i.e., $a = \sqrt{(a_x^2 + a_y^2 + a_z^2)}$) is considered.

The signal magnitudes first pass through a smoothing filter in the preprocessing step. To extract better the low-band step component, a low-pass filter is then applied to filter out high-frequency accelerations caused by the phone's random movement. The low-band component of the acceleration magnitude is calculated online using the following first-order difference equation:

$$a_i^l = a_{i-1}^l + \alpha \times (a_i - a_{i-1}^l) \tag{1}$$

where a_i is the i-th original acceleration magnitude and a_i^l is the value after passing through the low-pass filter. The default value of α is set to 0.25.

After the low-pass filter, a peak recognition algorithm with a sliding window is used to detect peaks in the filtered data. Specifically, a_i^l is recognized as a peak (i.e., a user step) if it is larger than all samples located in the range of $[t(i) - t_w/2, t(i) + t_w/2]$. Since the user step frequency is in general lower than 3Hz, the window size t_w in the current implementation is set to $0.3s$.

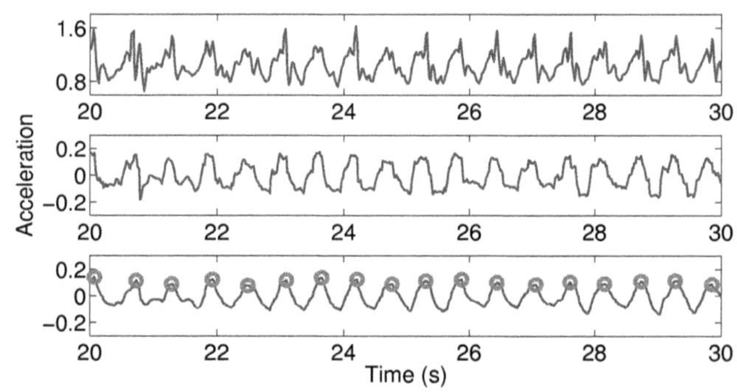

(a) Hold smartphone horizontally.

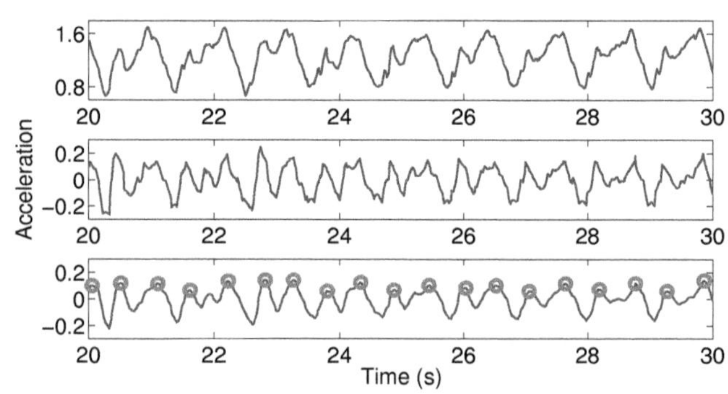

(b) Hold smartphone in hands.

Figure 9: Data processing for step detection.

Figure 9 shows processed acceleration signals. In both figures, the first row displays the original acceleration output from the smartphone, and the smoothed acceleration data and the corresponding low-band component are shown in the second and third rows, respectively. Recognized peaks are highlighted in the third row in red dots. In Figure 9 our step detection algorithm is shown to perform well even when the user swings his arm with the phone in hand.

6.2 Turn Detection

In outdoor environment, turn information can be extracted from the electronic compass. However, due to ferromagnetic interference, reliable direction output cannot be obtained from the compass in indoor environments. Thus, in indoor environments, we detect turns by jointly considering signals from the accelerometer and the gyroscope to exploit their relative strengths: gyroscope readings can be integrated to produce angle estimates that are reliable over a short term, whereas the accelerometer suffering from random vibrations can be trusted over a long term to provide attitude estimation.

Turn detection is achieved based on the fact that the rotation axis of the body during a turn is always directed toward the center of the Earth (i.e., in the direction of gravity). In other words, users as well as smartphones always rotate around the Z-axis of the local vertical, local horizontal (LVLH) frame. Since the gyroscope measures the angular velocities of rotation on each axis of the smartphone's body frame, we first determine the attitude of the smartphone using the value of gravity on 3 axes of the accelerometer on the phone's body frame, and then transform the angular velocity from the body frame to the LVLH frame to determine turns.

In FOLLOWME, we adopt a rotation matrix to describe the orientation of the smartphone from the LVLH frame to its body frame.[3] Detailed derivations of frame transformation are omitted due to space limitation. Note that due to the lack of reliable compass reading, the phone's attitude is confined to a conical surface in the LVLH frame and cannot be uniquely identified. However, without the need for the yaw angle ψ, we are still able to detect turns because the rotation always happens about the Z-axis in the LVLH frame. In addition, to avoid the Gimbal Lock problem [30], we need to be cautious about the rotation sequence of three axes. As turn detection is independent of Z-axis, a simple solution is to exchange the X-axis and Y-axis (i.e., change from the right-hand coordinate system to the left-handed coordinate system) if the gravity acceleration factor on X-axis is larger than that on Y-axis. Once the smartphone attitude is obtained, we transform the angular velocity and compute the amount of rotation via integration.

6.3 Level-Change Detection

Due to its low power and excellent relative accuracy [20, 31], a barometer is adopted in FOLLOWME for level-change detection. Figure 10 shows a barometer trace collected during a user's walk from the third floor to the second and then climbing up to the fourth floor. We also record the timestamps when the user starts walking on the stairs and arrives at a new level as the level-change ground truth. In this figure, we can clearly see the increase/decrease of the atmospheric pressure when the altitude changes.

In FOLLOWME, we devise a two-pass bi-directional searching algorithm to detect level-changes. In this algorithm, we first smooth each atmospheric pressure data p_n by averaging all samples within the previous 4 seconds (as the dark curve in Figure 10). The algorithm then traces back to find the maximal difference

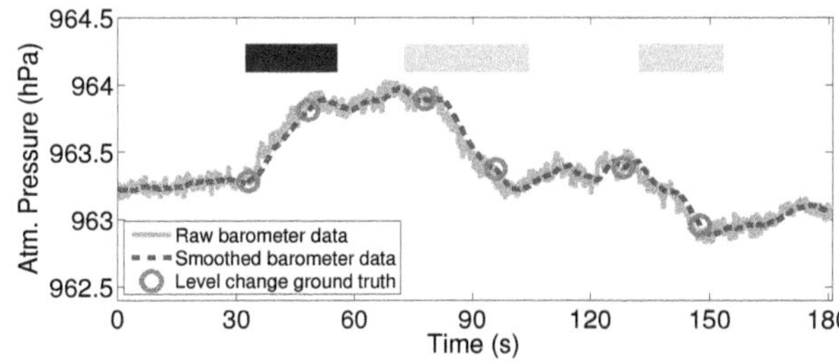

Figure 10: Data processing for level change detection.

between p_n and samples collected within the last T_0 seconds. If a gap $|p_n - p_m|$, indicating a level change, is greater than the threshold p_{tr}, we conduct a forward search afterwards to determine the altitude-changing period.[4] The algorithm outputs a value r_l that indicates whether the altitude increases/decrease ($r_l = -1/1$) or not ($r_l = 0$). Particularly, if less than 5 steps are taken by the user during the level-change period, we record an elevator up/down. A sample detection result of level changes is shown above the curves in Figure 10. In this figure, the dark (blue) area refers to the duration when the user is walking downstairs, and the light (yellow) area indicates walking on an upward staircase. From this figure, we find the detected stair walking periods fit the ground truth well. More on detection performance will be provided in Section 7.

6.4 Navigation Module

We implement FOLLOWME on a Samsung Galaxy S5 running Android (version 4.4.2). In both the reference trace-collection mode and the navigation mode, FOLLOWME runs two threads: one for sensory data collection (using callback function *onSensorChanged*()) and the other to take care of the signal processing asynchronously. We down-sample the sensor data at 50Hz to reduce the computation overhead of the smartphone. The reference trace is saved to the internal storage shared between these two modes. For the walking progress estimator, we set the path constraint coefficient $c = 600$ and $cIni = 200$.

Figure 11 shows the FOLLOWME GUI where navigation instructions are provided: after loading the reference trace and pressing the start button, turning instructions are updated on the right of the screen (the turn icon) during user walk. The follower is allowed to walk at different speeds and even stop anytime during the walk. If the follower is required to walk up/down stairs, a staircase icon shows up on the left of the screen.

7. EVALUATION

We have conducted experiments in a 4-story campus building with the testing area of $2000m^2$. A snapshot of the experimental environment can be seen in Figure 12. Figure 18 also shows preliminary evaluation results of FOLLOWME in semi-outdoor and outdoor open spaces.

Five users participated in our evaluation of the performance of detection of steps, turns, level-changes, and navigation, including trace-synchronization accuracy, timeliness of navigation instructions and deviation-detection performance. To evaluate the performance of navigation, 10 different reference traces were generated by randomly selected users who held their phones

[3]Other techniques such as quaternion rotations can also be leveraged to determine the phone's attitude [29].

[4]The resolution of vertical distance changes depends on the threshold value p_{tr}. In our current implementation, we empirically set $p_{tr} = 0.3$.

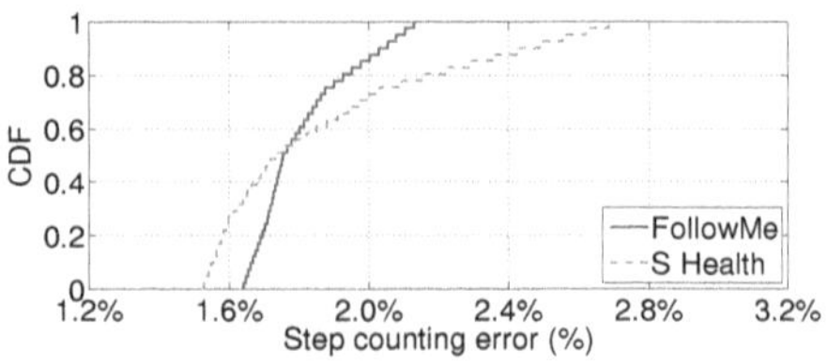

Figure 13: Performance of step detection.

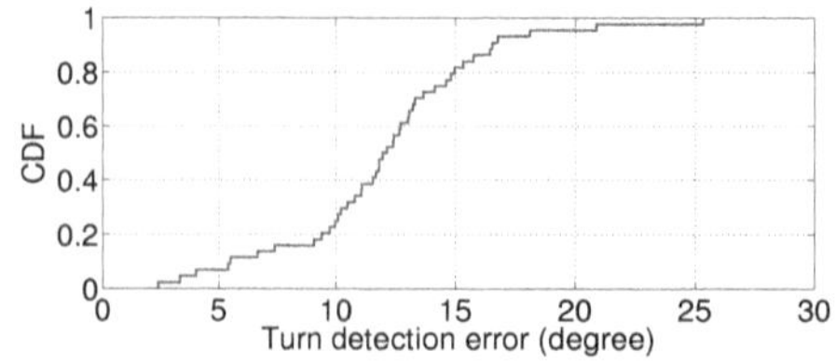

Figure 14: Performance of turn detection.

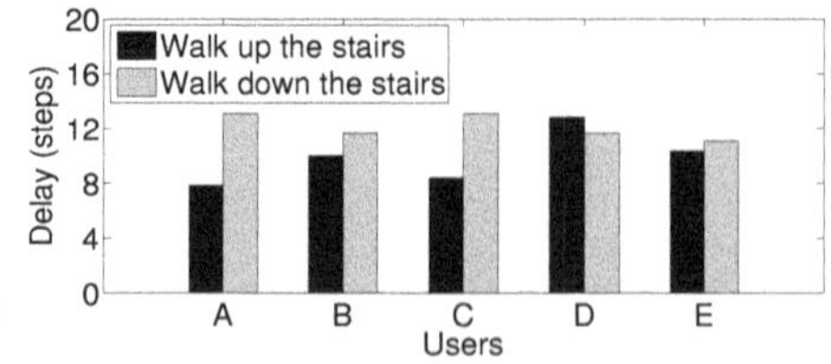

Figure 15: Delay of level-change detection.

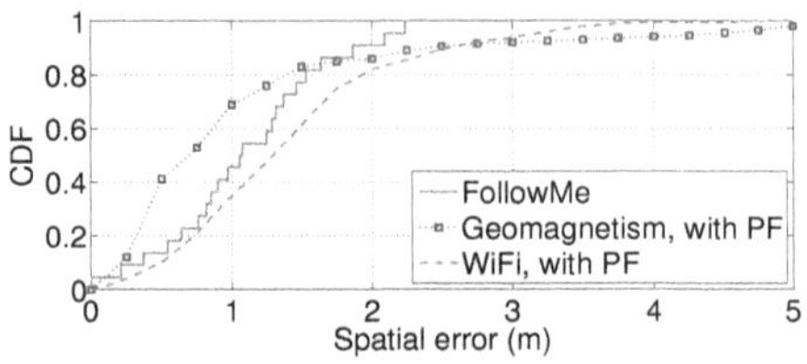

Figure 16: CDF of spatial error in navigation.

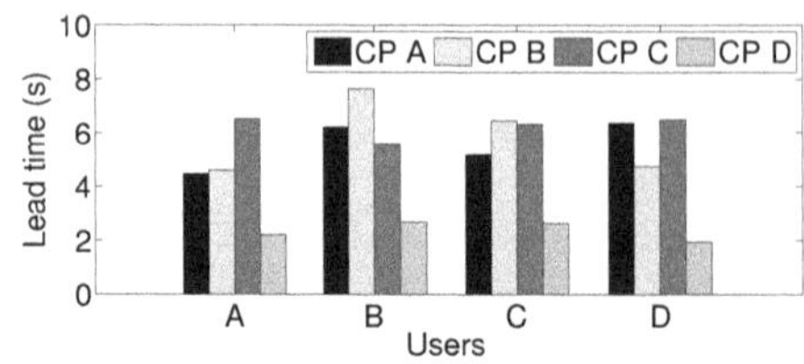

Figure 17: Lead time of navigation instructions at different checkpoints.

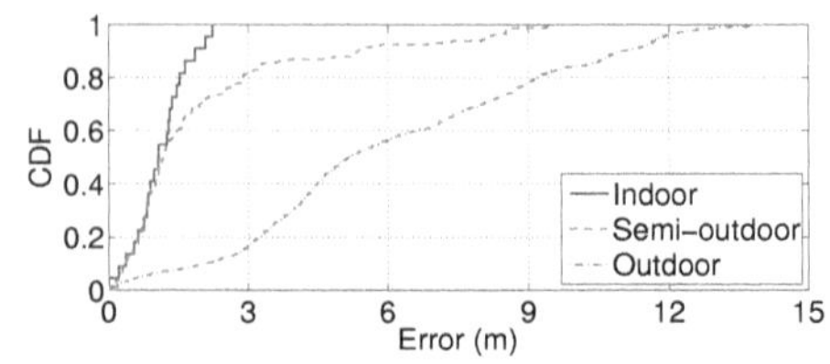

Figure 18: Tracking error of the walking progress estimator.

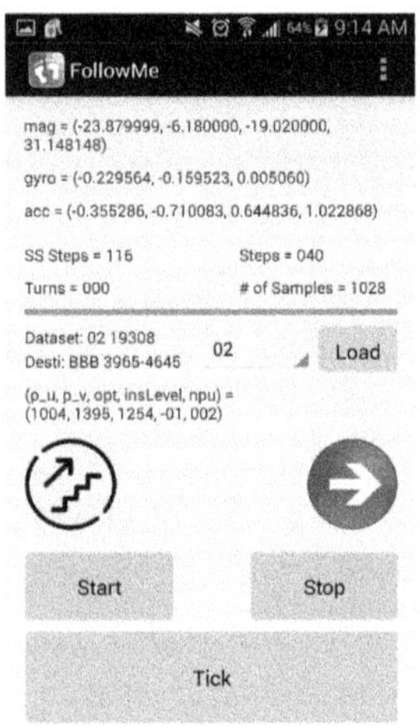

Figure 11: A snapshot of FOLLOWME.

Figure 12: A snapshot of the experimental environment.

in front of their bodies. However, we did not impose any constraints on the phone's orientation (e.g., holding the phone horizontally or vertically) during trace collection and navigation. Although FOLLOWME does not perform level-change detection in the navigation mode, we recorded data from the barometer, accelerometer, and gyroscope, and ran detection algorithms offline for the purpose of evaluation.

7.1 Accuracy of Detection of Steps, Turns, and Level-Changes

We first evaluate the performance of step, turn, and level-change detection.

The step-counting errors are shown in Figure 13. We also compare the error of the pedometer in S Health, a built-in fitness application in Galaxy S5. The figure shows that FOLLOWME achieves comparable step-counting to S Health. The error of FOLLOWME is below 2.2% which indicates the step-counting error per 100 steps is less than 3 steps. In the navigation module of FOLLOWME, such a small error can be compensated for by matching the geomagnetic field features.

The turn-detection results are plotted in Figure 14. Specifically, we obtained the ground-truth angles of turns on each test path using the floor plan, and compared them with the turns detected by the trace collection module. From Figure 14, we find that the turn-detection component achieves a 90 percentile accuracy of 15°. This error is caused by two factors. First, the actual angle of the user's turn may not be identical to that of the path. Second, the accelerometer and gyroscope are susceptible to perturbation which can also lower accuracies.

Our experiments show 100% accuracy in detecting level-changes. To examine another detection performance metric, Figure 15 plots the delay in detecting level-changes. Due to subtle pressure changes, detection of level-changes took more time than both step and turn detections. For example, the average delay of detecting walking downstairs is 12 seconds. Since the level-change detection works in the trace-collection module, the relative large delay has little influence on the navigation performance.

7.2 Navigation Performance

Let us consider the real-time navigation performance. We first recorded the ground truth locations of the leader at different times in the trace-collection process. During the follower's walk, FOLLOWME compared the instantaneous magnetic field measurements and the data collected by the leader to estimate the follower's relative position. This way, we can measure the offset between the follower's true locations and the locations obtained by the matching algorithm. For the purpose of comparison, we also implemented tracking algorithms using the geomagnetic field or WiFi as benchmarks [21]. Both approaches take a fingerprint map and the floor plan as inputs, and use particle filtering (PF) to continuously estimate the device's location. Step and turn detection algorithms in FOLLOWME are also leveraged for particle movement and weight updating.

Figure 16 plots the spatial errors of navigation systems. This figure shows that the spatial errors are less than 2.5m in FOLLOWME. Compared to benchmarks, we find that FOLLOWME outperforms the WiFi-based tracking and achieves a comparable 80 percentile tracking accuracy with the geomagnetic-based algorithm. In addition, the maximal spatial error of FOLLOWME is smaller than both of the other two approaches. This is because the one-dimensional trace synchronization intrinsically limits the search space, thus reducing the estimation error.

Figure 17 examines further the timeliness of navigation instructions and plots the lead time of the instructions at different checkpoints (i.e., crossings and staircases). We find that most navigation instructions are provided 4 seconds ahead of the action. However, for the checkpoint (CP) D, the average lead time of the notification is around 2 seconds, since it is close to a previous turn.

We also conducted experiments in semi-outdoor and outdoor open spaces to evaluate the navigation performance of FOLLOWME. Figure 18 plots the CDF of spatial error in all three environments. FOLLOWME is shown to perform best in indoor environments, where 95% of the absolute spatial errors are less than 2m. However, in outdoor open spaces, only 50% of the errors are within the range of 5m and the error can be as large as 14m. This is due mainly to the unobservable geomagnetic anomalies in outdoor open space.

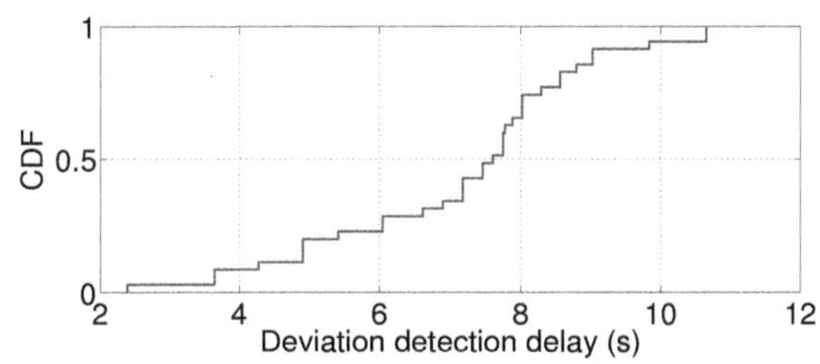

Figure 19: Delay of deviation detection.

We now consider the performance of deviation detection. Specifically, Figure 19 shows the CDF of detection delay. Figure 19 shows that all deviations were successfully detected in 11 seconds. In fact, in 60% of cases, it took 7–9 seconds for FOLLOWME to discover a divergence.

7.3 Energy Consumption

We now evaluate the energy consumption of FOLLOWME. To measure power consumption, we use a Monsoon Power Monitor as a power supply for the smartphone and tracks both current and voltage. During the experiment, we turned off all background applications as well as extra hardware components, such as WiFi, GPS, etc.

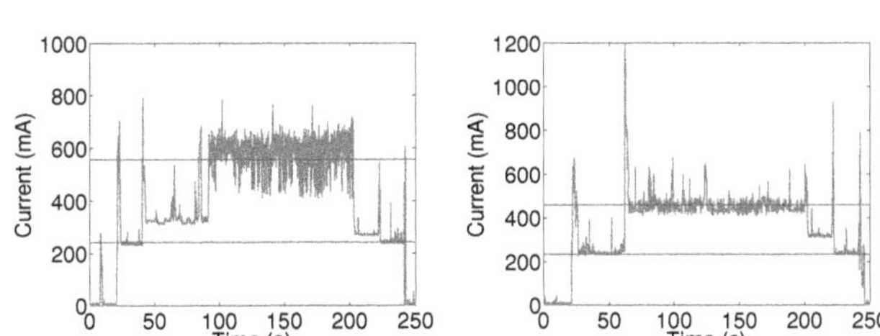

(a) Current measurement of navigation. (b) Current measurement of trace collection.

Figure 20: Power consumption of FOLLOWME.

Runtime current measurements of FOLLOWME are plotted in Figure 20. In Figure 20(a), the smartphone is in sleep mode during the period from 0 to 20s. FOLLOWME began to run at 40s and loaded the reference trace at around 65s. The navigation module started at 90s and continued running until 200s. FOLLOWME was turned off at 220s. In the trace-collection phase, the module started running at 60s and stopped at 200s, as shown in Figure 20(b).

We compared the energy consumption of FOLLOWME and Travi-Navi, a vision-based leader–follower indoor navigation system [19]. As different smartphones (Samsung Galaxy S4 vs. Galaxy S2) are used in two tests, we exclude the energy cost of Android core services, and focused only on incremental energy consumption (i.e., the range between blue lines) when both navigation systems began to run.

Figure 20 shows that the runtime currents of FOLLOWME are 303.4mA and 224.6mA in navigation and trace-collection phases, respectively. According to the data provided in [19], FOLLOWME achieved energy savings of nearly 50% (224.6mA vs. 433.4mA) in the trace-collection phase and of 15% (303.4mA vs. 349.5mA) in the navigation phase. This is because FOLLOWME did not use energy-hungry sensors, such as WiFi and the camera, but instead the lightweight step-constrained trace synchronization algorithm. FOLLOWME can also offload the data preprocessing to co-processors to further reduce energy consumption, which is part of our future work.

8. DISCUSSION AND FUTURE WORK

Although FOLLOWME provides good navigation performance, there is room for further enhancements. Discussed below are several practical issues and limitations of the experiments that warrant further investigation.

8.1 Limitations of the Experiments

Despite the various encouraging results reported in Section 7, the evaluation of FOLLOWME is still preliminary. First, we have not thoroughly assessed the impact of temporal and device diversities on navigation accuracy. Although the step-constrained trace synchronization algorithm plays an active role in walking progress estimation with inconsistent walking speeds, it has not been evaluated systematically for a large group of users (e.g., between the elderly and children) and different combinations of parameters (e.g., t_w and $StepBound$ in Algorithm 2).

In addition, we have not fully tested FOLLOWME in less defined indoor spaces where navigation becomes more challenging. For example, simple instructions, such as left/right turns, may not be enough for successful navigation in a large open indoor space. Users may also have to make a detour if obstacles temporarily block a path. The first problem can be solved as the turn-detection algorithm recognizes turns of different angles, and displays the corresponding arrows on the screen. It imposes the additional constraints on the user (e.g., the smartphone should be held horizontally in hand). For the latter case, we can make the trace synchronization and deviation detection algorithms tolerate transient deviations. Once the user walks back to the correct path (e.g., within 10 seconds), the navigation module automatically discards the detour part, and continues to synchronize the observed sensory data with the reference trace. The design of a detailed algorithm for this is part of our future work.

8.2 Open Issues Related to Reference Traces

We summarize some open problems related to the reference trace, which plays a key role in FOLLOWME.

8.2.1 *Scalability*

As mentioned in Section 3.3, FOLLOWME is designed as a plug-and-play system which meets the need for individuals' navigation.

However, we need to design a more efficient way to store reference traces when they are large in number and size. For example, we can divide traces and store only one copy of common segments of different traces in the database. This way, FOLLOWME is able to create new traces from scratch by concatenating segments. Besides, how to combine traces collected at different locations to help create an indoor fingerprint map is also an interesting subject to pursue.

8.2.2 *Quality Control*

In current design of FOLLOWME, each reference trace is built based on a single user's walking trace. However, no mechanism has been provided to guarantee the quality of the reference traces. A reference trace which is averaged over multiple runs will help improve the navigation performance, although merging traces with time-varying walking speeds is non-trivial.

8.2.3 *Information Privacy*

If users are allowed to share reference traces offline in an uncontrolled manner, FOLLOWME may pose a risk of privacy leakage to the users and third-party organizations. For example, some companies might not want anyone to share any information about their floor plans or indoor sensory data. Therefore, how to build a safeguard to preserve information privacy is an interesting issue to explore.

8.3 Mixed Modality with Additional Location-Specific Features

We exploited the geomagnetic field to synchronize the reference trace and the follower's trace. While enjoying the pervasiveness and stability of geomagnetic field, FOLLOWME faces several ensuing problems. For example, the weak geomagnetic disturbances impair the usability of FOLLOWME in outdoor open spaces. In future, we would like to incorporate more location-specific signals and build a mixed modality for walking progress estimation. For example, we can jointly consider the geomagnetic intensity and GSM/FM signal strength and synchronize multiple traces. In indoor environments, opportunistically-sensed WiFi can also be fused with geomagnetic signals. Even for a given specific type of location feature, we can synchronize multiple traces that have the same destination, thus automatically determining the user's starting point according to their similarities.

9. RELATED WORK

Navigation and localization have been extensively studied in the area of robotics. By fusing odometer outputs with IMU sensing results, robots can compute travel distances, perform accurate localization, and navigate themselves to the desired destination based on the map information. In several robotic systems, additional sensing techniques using laser [32], infrared [33], and camera [34] are also used for ranging and navigation purposes. However, humans' locomotion is much more complicated. The limited sensing capabilities and energy buffer of smartphones also add difficulties to both localization and navigation.

Numerous localization techniques using smartphones have been proposed in the area of mobile computing [1, 3, 5–7, 9, 35–39]. They can be broadly categorized as (i) infrastructure-based localization such as using GPS, cellular and WiFi signals, or (ii) infrastructure-independent localization such as Dead Reckoning (i.e., IMU-tracking). Each of these two types of localization has its own advantages and disadvantages. GPS can provide accurate positioning in outdoor open spaces but encounters fading signals in indoor environments, whereas Dead Reckoning suffers from cumulative errors and is affected by the smartphone's usage. Despite extensive explorations of integrating these approaches, the lack of map information makes the last-mile navigation a difficult problem. In FOLLOWME, we exploit ideas from these techniques (e.g., using IMU to detect steps, turns) as well as several recently-proposed smartphone services [28, 29] to build a lightweight, plug-and-play, last-mile navigation system.

Geomagnetic field anomalies are used for localization and navigation of both robots and smartphones. In [40], the authors leverage observations of the ambient magnetic field for indoor localization, but they can handle only simple straight pathways. Glanzer *et al.* [41] introduced a pedestrian navigation system with human motion recognition, although a pre-established magnetic field map is equipped to correct the severe disturbance of indoor direction sensing. Magnetic signatures were leveraged in [23] to identify locations and rooms. Although mobile phones are used to measure magnetic field intensity, the system relies on pillars and offers only room-level positioning accuracy. Grand *et al.* [22] proposed a lightweight magnetic map construction method and used an online particle filter to estimate the location of a handheld device. Similarly, a particle-filtering-based engine was designed in [21] to localize and track users with a given geomagnetic fingerprint map. In general, these techniques require special hardware [13, 24–27] or dense samples of magnetic data to build a fingerprint map with high training overhead [13, 21, 23, 42]. In contrast, FOLLOWME utilizes the features of geomagnetic field without customized hardware and avoids the time-consuming map construction process.

The leader–follower model has been adopted in several existing navigation systems [17–19, 43]. In [18] and [43], researchers used customized devices of magnetic sensing to navigate blind people and autonomous vehicles. In [17], an electronic escort system was proposed by using crowd encounters information and dead-reckoning techniques, but it requires pre-deployed audio beacons, which impairs its usability. Travi-Navi [19], a vision-guided navigation system, enables a user to easily bootstrap and deploy indoor navigation services without building the entire localization system. FOLLOWME is very different from Travi-Navi in several aspects. First, Travi-Navi uses compute-intensive particle filtering as the navigation engine. Unlike multiple indoor tracking systems proposed to use particle filtering, floor plan (e.g., information of walls) is no longer available to the system and hence cannot help expedite the convergence of particles. The free movement of particles in a two-dimensional space intrinsically introduces difficulties in navigation. To alleviate this problem, Travi-Navi uses WiFi AP information and has to continuously estimate the walking stride length. However, the former is known to be time-varying whereas the latter can be only roughly calculated even with a known user's height. On the contrary, FOLLOWME is a lightweight system that performs matching in a one-dimensional space based on accurate step detection and ubiquitous geomagnetic field. Second, FOLLOWME minimizes the constraints imposed on users by providing wider usage (i.e., in multi-level buildings, semi-outdoors). On the other hand, guiders in Travi-Navi need to hold the smartphone vertically and steadily during walking to achieve a better image quality, and the followers' intelligence is implicitly exploited for image recognition.

10. CONCLUSION

In this paper, we present FOLLOWME, a lightweight, plug-and-play, last-mile navigation system. It guides users by providing the "scent" left behind by leaders or previous travelers. In particular, it introduces a novel online magnetic-filed-based trace synchronization scheme for estimating the user's walking progress.

FOLLOWME also recognizes natural walking patterns to help reduce the computational overhead and to navigate subsequent users. We have implemented FOLLOWME on Android smartphones, evaluated it in a four-story campus building. 95% of FOLLOWME's spatial errors were found to be 2m or less during navigation and FOLLOWME saves at least 50% of energy consumption compared to a benchmark system.

Acknowledgment

This work was done during Yuanchao's visit to the University of Michigan, which is supported in part by 973 Program under grant 2015CB352503 and scholarship funded by China Scholarship Council. We thank the anonymous reviewers and the shepherd for their constructive comments and support.

References

[1] Fan Li, Chunshui Zhao, Guanzhong Ding, Jian Gong, Chenxing Liu, and Feng Zhao. A Reliable and Accurate Indoor Localization Method Using Phone Inertial Sensors. In *ACM UbiComp*, 2012.

[2] Moustafa Youssef and Ashok K. Agrawala. The Horus WLAN Location Determination System. In *ACM MobiSys*, 2005.

[3] Paramvir Bahl and Venkata N. Padmanabhan. RADAR: An In-Building RF-Based User Location and Tracking System. In *IEEE INFOCOM*, 2000.

[4] Sungro Yoon, Kyunghan Lee, and Injong Rhee. FM-based Indoor Localization via Automatic Fingerprint DB Construction and Matching. In *ACM MobiSys*, 2013.

[5] Krishna Chintalapudi, Anand Padmanabha Iyer, and Venkata N. Padmanabhan. Indoor Localization without the Pain. In *ACM MobiCom*, 2010.

[6] Anshul Rai, Krishna Kant Chintalapudi, Venkata N. Padmanabhan, and Rijurekha Sen. Zee: Zero-effort Crowdsourcing for Indoor Localization. In *ACM MobiCom*, 2012.

[7] Jie Xiong and Kyle Jamieson. ArrayTrack: A Fine-Grained Indoor Location System. In *USENIX NSDI*, 2013.

[8] Daniel Turner, Stefan Savage, and Alex C. Snoeren. On the Empirical Performance of Self-calibrating WiFi Location Systems. In *ACM LCN*, pages 76–84, 2011.

[9] Zheng Yang, Chenshu Wu, and Yunhao Liu. Locating in Fingerprint Space: Wireless Indoor Localization with Little Human Intervention. In *ACM MobiCom*, 2012.

[10] Guobin Shen, Zhuo Chen, Peichao Zhang, Thomas Moscibroda, and Yongguang Zhang. Walkie-Markie: Indoor Pathway Mapping Made Easy. In *USENIX NSDI*, 2013.

[11] Liqun Li, Guobin Shen, Chunshui Zhao, Thomas Moscibroda, Jyh-Han Lin, and Feng Zhao. Experiencing and Handling the Diversity in Data Density and Environmental Locality in an Indoor Positioning Service. In *ACM MobiCom*, 2014.

[12] HKUST. Path Advisor. http://pathadvisor.ust.hk/.

[13] Jaewoo Chung, Matt Donahoe, Chris Schmandt, Ig-Jae Kim, Pedram Razavai, and Micaela Wiseman. Indoor Location Sensing Using Geo-magnetism. In *ACM MobiSys*, 2011.

[14] Binghao Li, Thomas Gallagher, Andrew G Dempster, and Chris Rizos. How Feasible Is the Use of Magnetic Field Alone for Indoor Positioning? In *IPIN*, 2012.

[15] Xiaofan Jiang, Chieh-Jan Mike Liang, Kaifei Chen, Ben Zhang, Jeff Hsu, Jie Liu, Bin Cao, and Feng Zhao. Design and Evaluation of a Wireless Magnetic-based Proximity Detection Platform for Indoor Applications. In *ACM IPSN*, 2012.

[16] Pengfei Zhou, Yuanqing Zheng, Zhenjiang Li, Mo Li, and Guobin Shen. IODetector: A Generic Service for Indoor Outdoor Detection. In *ACM SenSys*, 2012.

[17] Ionut Constandache, Xuan Bao, Martin Azizyan, and Romit Roy Choudhury. Did You See Bob?: Human Localization Using Mobile Phones. In *ACM MobiCom*, 2010.

[18] Timothy H. Riehle, Shane M. Anderson, Patrick A. Lichter, Nicholas A. Giudice, Suneel I. Sheikh, Robert J. Knuesel, Daniel T. Kollmann, and Daniel S. Hedin. Indoor Magnetic Navigation for the Blind. In *IEEE EMBC*, 2012.

[19] Yuanqing Zheng, Guobin Shen, Liqun Li, Chunshui Zhao, Mo Li, and Feng Zhao. Travi-Navi: Self-deployable Indoor Navigation System. In *ACM MobiCom*, 2014.

[20] Kartik Muralidharan, Azeem Javed Khan, Archan Misra, Rajesh Krishna Balan, and Sharad Agarwal. Barometric Phone Sensors – More Hype than Hope! In *ACM HotMobile*, 2014.

[21] Yuanchao Shu, Cheng Bo, Guobin Shen, Chunshui Zhao, Liqun Li, and Feng Zhao. Magicol: Indoor Localization Using Pervasive Magnetic Field and Opportunistic WiFi Sensing. *IEEE Journal on Selected Areas in Communications*, 33(7):1443–1457, July 2015.

[22] E. Le Grand and S. Thrun. 3-axis Magnetic Field Mapping and Fusion for Indoor Localization. In *IEEE Multisensor Fusion and Integration for Intelligent Systems (MFI)*, 2012.

[23] B. Gozick, K.P. Subbu, R. Dantu, and T. Maeshiro. Magnetic Maps for Indoor Navigation. *IEEE Transactions on Instrumentation and Measurement*, 60(12):3883–3891, 2011.

[24] Sam Ann Rahok, Yoshihito Shikanai, and Koichi Ozaki. Trajectory Tracking Using Environmental Magnetic Field for Outdoor Autonomous Mobile Robots. In *IEEE/RSJ IROS*, 2010.

[25] S. Suksakulchai, S. Thongchai, D. M. Wilkes, and K. Kawamura. Mobile Robot Localization Using an Electronic Compass for Corridor Environment. In *IEEE ICSMC*, 2000.

[26] I. Vallivaara, J. Haverinen, A. Kemppainen, and J Roning. Simultaneous Localization and Mapping Using Ambient Magnetic Field. In *IEEE Multisensor Fusion and Integration for Intelligent Systems (MFI)*, 2010.

[27] S.A. Rahok and O. Koichi. Odometry Correction with Localization Based on Landmarkless Magnetic Map for Navigation System of Indoor Mobile Robot. In *International Conference on Autonomous Robots and Agents (ICARA)*, 2009.

[28] Nirupam Roy, He Wang, and Romit Roy Choudhury. I am a Smartphone and I Can Tell My User's Walking Direction. In *ACM MobiSys*, 2014.

[29] Pengfei Zhou, Mo Li, and Guobin Shen. Use It Free: Instantly Knowing Your Phone Attitude. In *ACM MobiCom*, 2014.

[30] Wikipedia. Gimbal Lock. http://en.wikipedia.org/wiki/Gimbal_lock.

[31] Kartik Sankaran, Minhui Zhu, Xiang Fa Guo, Akkihebbal L. Ananda, Mun Choon Chan, and Li-Shiuan Peh. Using Mobile Phone Barometer for Low-power Transportation Context Detection. In *ACM SenSys*, 2014.

[32] Shung Han Cho and Sangjin Hong. Map Based Indoor Robot Navigation and Localization Using Laser Range Finder. In *ICARCV*, 2010.

[33] A. M. Flynn. Combining Sonar and Infrared Sensors for Mobile Robot Navigation. *Int. J. Rob. Res.*, 7(6):54–64, December 1988.

[34] Francisco Bonin-Font, Alberto Ortiz, and Gabriel Oliver. Visual Navigation for Mobile Robots: A Survey. *Journal of Intelligent and Robotic Systems*, 53(3):263–296, 2008.

[35] Yin Chen, Dimitrios Lymberopoulos, Jie Liu, and Bodhi Priyantha. FM-based Indoor Localization. In *ACM MobiSys*, 2012.

[36] Jeongyeup Paek, Kyu-Han Kim, Jatinder Pal Singh, and Ramesh Govindan. Energy-efficient Positioning for Smartphones Using Cell-ID Sequence Matching. In *ACM MobiSys*, 2011.

[37] Ionut Constandache, Romit Roy Choudhury, and Injong Rhee. Towards Mobile Phone Localization without War-Driving. In *IEEE INFOCOM*, 2010.

[38] Qiang Xu, Alexandre Gerber, Zhuoqing Morley Mao, and Jeffrey Pang. Acculoc: Practical Localization of Performance Measurements in 3G Networks. In *ACM MobiSys*, 2011.

[39] Yuanchao Shu, P. Coue, Yinghua Huang, Jiaqi Zhang, Peng Cheng, and Jiming Chen. Demo: G-Loc: Indoor Localization Leveraging Gradient-based Fingerprint Map. In *IEEE INFOCOM*, 2014.

[40] Janne Haverinen and Anssi Kemppainen. A Global Self-localization Technique Utilizing Local Anomalies of the Ambient Magnetic Field. In *IEEE ICRA*, 2009.

[41] G. Glanzer and U. Walder. Self-contained Indoor Pedestrian Navigation by Means of Human Motion Analysis and Magnetic Field Mapping. In *Workshop on Positioning Navigation and Communication (WPNC)*, 2010.

[42] M. Angermann, M. Frassl, M. Doniec, B.J. Julian, and P. Robertson. Characterization of the Indoor Magnetic Field for Applications in Localization and Mapping. In *IEEE IPIN*, 2012.

[43] W. Storms, J. Shockley, and J. Raquet. Magnetic Field Navigation in an Indoor Environment. In *IEEE UPINLBS*, 2010.

EchoTag: Accurate Infrastructure-Free Indoor Location Tagging with Smartphones

Yu-Chih Tung and Kang G. Shin
The University of Michigan
Email: {yctung,kgshin}@umich.edu

ABSTRACT

We propose a novel mobile system, called EchoTag, that enables phones to tag and remember indoor locations without requiring any additional sensors or pre-installed infrastructure. The main idea behind EchoTag is to *actively* generate acoustic signatures by transmitting a sound signal with a phone's speakers and sensing its reflections with the phone's microphones. This *active* sensing provides finer-grained control of the collected signatures than the widely-used passive sensing. For example, because the sensing signal is controlled by EchoTag, it can be intentionally chosen to enrich the sensed signatures and remove noises from useless reflections. Extensive experiments show that EchoTag distinguishes 11 tags at 1cm resolution with 98% accuracy and maintains 90% accuracy even a week after its training. With this accurate location tagging, one can realize many interesting applications, such as automatically turning on the silent mode of a phone when it is placed at a pre-defined location/area near the bed or streaming favorite songs to speakers if it is placed near a home entertainment system. Most participants of our usability study agree on the usefulness of EchoTag's potential applications and the adequacy of its sensing accuracy for supporting these applications.

Categories and Subject Descriptors

H.3.4 [**Information Storage and Retrieval**]: Systems and Software

General Terms

Design, Measurement, Performance, Algorithms

Keywords

Localization, Sound, Fingerprinting, Mobile Phones

1. INTRODUCTION

Imagine one day, the silent mode of a phone is automatically activated in order to avoid disturbing a user's sleep when the phone is placed near the bed. Likewise, favorite songs are streamed to speakers whenever the phone is placed near a stereo or a predefined timer/reminder is set if the phone is near a medicine cabinet. This kind of applications is known as context-aware computing or indoor geofencing which provides a natural combination of function and physical location. However, such a function–location combination is still not pervasive because smartphones are not yet able to sense locations accurately enough without assistance of additional sensors or pre-installed infrastructure.

MobiCom'15, September 7–11, 2015, Paris, France.
 ISBN 978-1-4503-3619-2/15/09...$15.00.
DOI: http://dx.doi.org/10.1145/2789168.2790102.

(a) Auto silent mode (b) Auto music (c) Auto timer

Figure 1—Candidate applications of EchoTag. Silent mode is automatically activated when the phone is placed on a drawn box, named *(echo) tag*, near the bed. Favorite songs are streamed to speakers or a predefined timer is automatically set when the phone is placed at other nearby tags.

Existing localization systems are unable to provide this type of functionality for two reasons. First, they usually rely on *passively* recorded WiFi, FM, or background acoustic signals, and can only achieve about room- or meter-level accuracy. Nevertheless, the above-mentioned applications need more accurate location sensing, e.g., both streaming music and setting silent mode might take place in the same room or even on the same table as shown in Fig. 1. Second, more accurate (i.e., with error of a few cm) location sensing with light recording or acoustic beacons requires a pre-installed infrastructure. The cost of such an infrastructure and the ensuing laborious calibrations make its realization expensive or difficult, especially for personal use.

In this paper, we propose a novel location tagging system, called EchoTag, which enables phones to tag and remember indoor locations with finer than 1cm resolution and without requiring any additional sensors or pre-installed infrastructure. The main idea behind EchoTag is to *actively* render acoustic signatures by using phone speakers to transmit sound and phone microphones to sense its reflections. This *active* sensing provides finer-grained control of the collected signatures than the commonly-used passive sensing. For example, EchoTag emits sound signals with different delays at the right channel to enrich the feature space for sensing nearby locations, and exploits the synchronization between the sender and the receiver as an anchor to remove interferences/reflections from objects outside the target area/locations. Moreover, this active sensing relies only on built-in sensors available in commodity phones, thus facilitating its deployment. Note that EchoTag is not designed to replace any localization system since it can only remember the locations where it had been placed before, rather than identifying arbitrary indoor locations. However, this fine-grained location sensing for remembering location tags can enable many important/useful applications that have not yet been feasible due to large location sensing errors or the absence of pre-installed infrastructure.

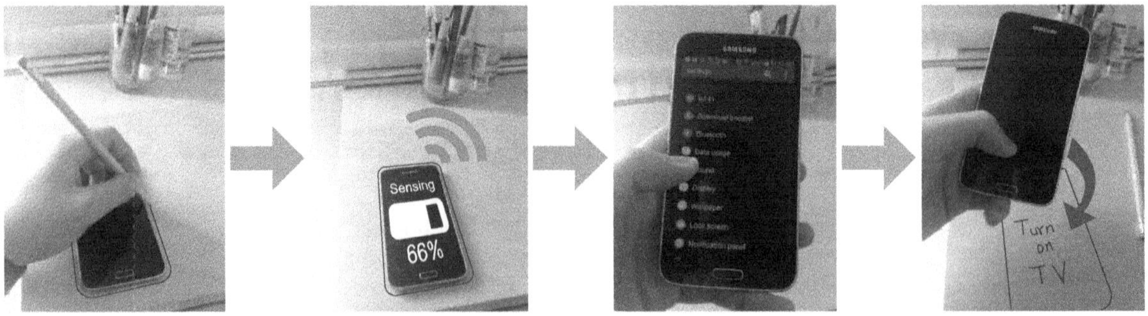

(a) Draw (echo) tags (b) Sense acoustic signatures (c) Select mapped applications (d) Replay recorded tags

Figure 2—Four steps of using `EchoTag`. The user first draws the contour of target locations/areas with a pencil, then commands the phone to sense the environment. After sensing the environment, a combination of applications and functions to be performed at this location is selected. Finally, the user automatically activates the selected applications/functions by simply placing his phone back within the contoured area. The contoured areas are thus called *(echo) tags*.

Fig. 2 demonstrates a 4-step process to set up and use EchoTag. The first step is to place the phone at the target location and draw the contour of the phone with a pencil. This contour is used as a marker for users to remember the target location, which is called an *(echo) tag*. (Tags can also be drawn on papers pasted on target locations.) Then, EchoTag generates and records the surrounding signatures of this target location. The next step is to select the applications/functions being combined and associated with this tagged location. Finally, users can easily activate the combined applications/functions by placing their phones back in the drawn tags. In summary, EchoTag embeds an invisible trigger at physical locations that the phone remembers what to do automatically.

We have implemented EchoTag as a background service in Android and evaluated the performance by using Galaxy S5 and other mobile devices. Our experimental evaluation shows that commodity phones equipped with EchoTag distinguish 11 tags with 98% accuracy even when tags are only 1cm apart from each other and achieves 90% accuracy based on the trace collected a week ago. Since EchoTag only utilizes existing sensors in commodity phones, it can be easily implemented and deployed in other mobile platforms. For example, we also implemented and evaluated EchoTag on iOS (with traces classified in Matlab) but omitted the results due to space limitation. Our usability study of 32 participants also shows that more than 90% of participants think the sensing accuracy and prediction delay of EchoTag are useful in real life. Moreover, about 70% of the participants agree that the potential applications in Fig. 1 can save time and provide convenience in finding and activating expected functions.

This paper makes the following four contributions:

- The first indoor location tagging achieving 1cm resolution by using commodity phones;
- Demonstration of the ability of active sensing to enrich the feature space and remove interferences;
- Implementation of EchoTag in Android without any additional sensors and/or pre-installed infrastructure; and
- Evaluation of EchoTag, showing more than 90% accuracy even a week after locations were tagged.

The remainder of this paper is organized as follows. Section 2 discusses the related work in indoor location sensing. Section 3 provides an overview of EchoTag. Sections 4–6 describe the design of acoustic signature and classifiers. The implementation details are provided in Section 7, and the performance of EchoTag and its real-world usability are evaluated in Sections 8 and 9, respectively. We discuss future directions in Section 10 and conclude the paper in Section 11.

System	Resolution	Infrastructure	Signature
SurroundSense [3]	room-level	No	Fusion
Batphone [25]	room-level	No	Sound
RoomSense [23]	300cm	No	Sound
Radar [4]	400cm	Existing	WiFi
Horus [30]	200cm	Existing	WiFi
Geo [8]	100cm	No	Geomagnetism
FM [7]	30cm	Existing	FM
Luxapose [15]	10cm	Additional	Light
Cricket [22]	10cm	Additional	Sound/WiFi
Guoguo [17]	6–25cm	Additional	Sound
EchoTag	**1cm**	**No**	**Sound**

Table 1—Existing indoor location sensing systems.

2. RELATED WORK

Indoor localization is a plausible entry to location tagging. The existing localization systems are summarized in Table 1. The most popular methods used for indoor localization, such as Radar [4] and Horus [30], sense locations based on WiFi-signal degradation. Their main attractiveness is the reliance on widely-deployed WiFi, hence requiring a minimal deployment effort. However, severe multipath fading of WiFi signals makes WiFi-signature-based localization achieve only room-level accuracy. To overcome the instability of WiFi signatures and increase the accuracy of indoor localization, researchers have also explored other sources of signatures. For example, the authors of [8] adopted the readings of geo-magnetism which varies with location due to the disturbance of steel structure of buildings. FM radio is also adopted to increase the sensing accuracy of WiFi-based localization [7]. Batphone [25] determines the room locations by sensing the background acoustic noise. Unfortunately, even with these improvements, localization systems relying on passive sensing of the environment can only achieve meter-level resolution. Moreover, passively sensing the environment suffers greatly when the environment changes. For example, as shown in [25], the signature of background acoustic noise changes dramatically when the climate control (HVAC) system was shut off for maintenance, and WiFi RSSI is known to change significantly when the transmit power control in an Access Point is enabled [7].

As shown in Table 1, a few systems, such as Luxapose [15], Cricket [22] and Guoguo [17], provide indoor localization with a few cm resolution, thus enabling accurate location tagging. However, these fine-grained localization systems can only be realized with the help from a pre-installed infrastructure. For example, Luxapose requires replacement of ceiling lamps by programmed LED and Guoguo & Cricket require customized WiFi/acoustic beacons around the building. Even if the cost of each additional sensor might be affordable, the aggregated cost and the laborious calibration required for this deployment are still too high to be attractive/feasible for real-world deployment. Even with the pre-installed infrastructure, the localization error is still around 10cm. The localization error can be reduced further by using antenna or microphone arrays [10, 29], but these advanced sensors are not available in commodity phones. In contrast, EchoTag achieves location sensing with 1cm resolution without any pre-installed infrastructure or additional advanced sensors. Location tagging can also be realized by deploying NFC tags [2], but EchoTag makes this functionality realizable in all commodity phones — such as HTC butterfly, the latest Xiaomi 4, and iOS phones[1] — that are commonly equipped with microphones and speakers, but not NFC chips. Note that EchoTag is *not* designed to replace any localization system since it can only remember the locations where it had been placed before, rather than identifying arbitrary indoor locations like [15, 17, 22]. However, as the results shown in this paper and the feedbacks from the participants of our usability study, this fine-grained location sensing for remembering tags can be used to enable many important/useful applications that have not been feasible before, due to large location sensing errors or lack of installed infrastructure.

EchoTag senses locations based on acoustic signatures. Acoustic signals have been studied widely since they are readily available in commodity phones. For example, SurroundSense [3] and Audi-teur [18] classify user behaviors based on background noise. Skinput [12], TapSense [11] and SufaceLink [9] provide new commuter–human interactions based on acoustic reflections from human skin, fingertip, or contacted surface. UbiK [28] provides a input method with acoustic signatures in response to touching different positions on a table. All of these use similar acoustic signatures (e.g., resonances) as in EchoTag, but EchoTag is the first to use it for accurate indoor location tagging. Additional novelties of EchoTag include its *active* generation of acoustic signatures and enrichment of signatures by emitting sound signals with different delays.

The closest to EchoTag are Touch & Active [19], Symbolic Object Localization [14], and RoomSense [23], all of which also actively generate acoustic signals and record their signatures but for different purposes. Touch & Active [19] uses the same multipath signature to identify how the user touches an object equipped with piezo speakers and microphones. Commodity phones were mentioned as a potential interface for Touch & Active, but no evaluation was provided. The authors of [14] use sound absorption by the touched surface as a feature to identify symbolic locations of a phone — i.e., in a pocket, on a wood surface or a sofa — which is unable to detect nearby locations on the same surface. RoomSense [23] also uses the sound reflections from environments to identify different rooms. However, since only the compressed analytical feature (e.g., Mel Frequency Cepstral Coefficient) is used, its sensing resolution is larger than $9m^2$, thus becoming unable to distinguish nearby tags. In this paper, we implement a novel accurate location tagging system based on actively generated acoustic signatures via built-in phone sensors.

[1] Apple locks iPhone 6 NFC to Apple Pay:
http://www.cnet.com/news/apple-locks-down-iphone-6-nfc-to-apple-pay/

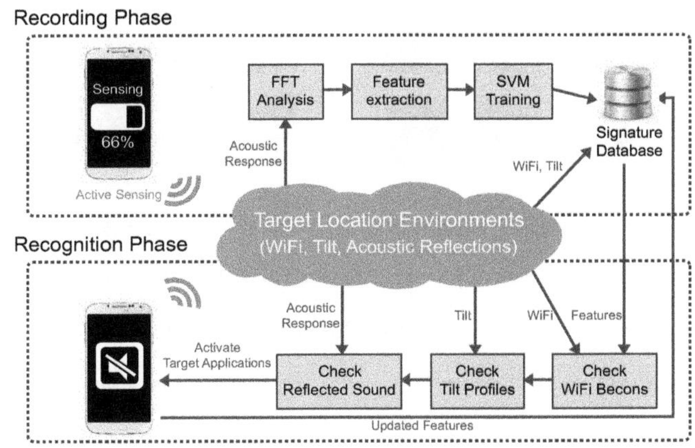

Figure 3—System overview. Locations are sensed based on acoustic reflections while the tilt/WiFi readings are used to determine the time to trigger acoustic sensing, thus reducing the energy consumption of the sensing process.

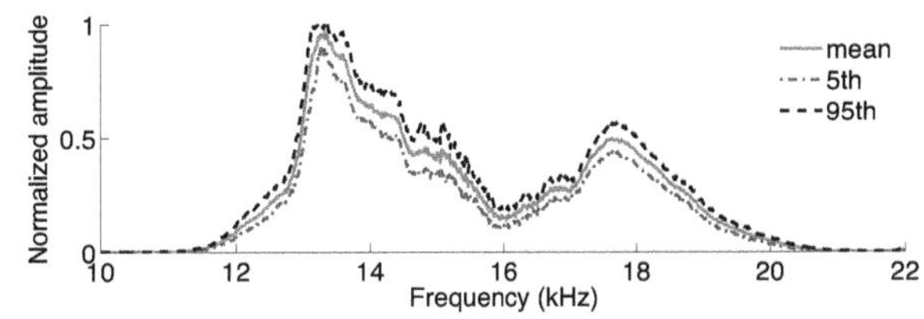

Figure 4—An example of acoustic signatures. The received attenuation of a flat frequency sweep is uneven over different frequencies. The result is an average of 100 trials over 1 minute.

3. SYSTEM OVERVIEW

Fig. 3 gives an overview of EchoTag which is composed of recording and recognition phases. In the recording phase, multiple short sequences of sound signals will be emitted from the phone speakers. Each sequence is repeated a few times with different delays between left and right channels to enrich the received signatures as we will discuss in the following sections. The reading of built-in inertial sensors is also recorded for further optimization. After recording the signature, the selected target application/function and the collected signatures are processed and saved in the device's storage. In the recognition phase, the phone will continuously check if the WiFi SSID and the tilt of the phone match the collected signatures. If the tilt and WiFi readings are similar to one of the recorded target locations, then the same acoustic sensing process is executed again to collect signatures. This new collected signature is compared with the previous records in the database using a support vector machine (SVM). If the results match, the target application/function will be automatically activated.

4. ACOUSTIC SIGNATURE

EchoTag differentiates locations based on their acoustic signatures, characterized by uneven attenuations occurring at different frequencies as shown in Fig. 4. Note that EchoTag does not examine the uneven attenuations in the background noise but those in the sound emitted from the phone itself. For example, as shown in Fig. 4, the recorded responses of a frequency sweep from 11kHz to 22kHz are not flat but have several significant degradations at certain frequencies. The characteristics of this signature at different locations can be observed in Fig. 5 where the phone is moved 10cm away from its original location. In what follows, we will un-

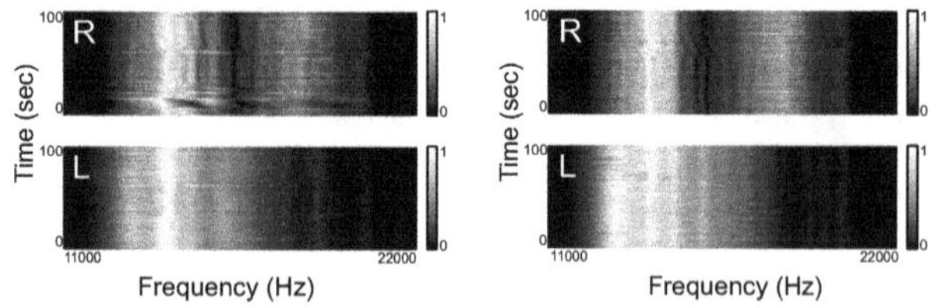

(a) Location A (b) Location B

Figure 5—Frequency responses at nearby locations. Responses varies with location (i.e., the distribution of light and dark vertical lines) and this is used as a feature for accurate location tagging.

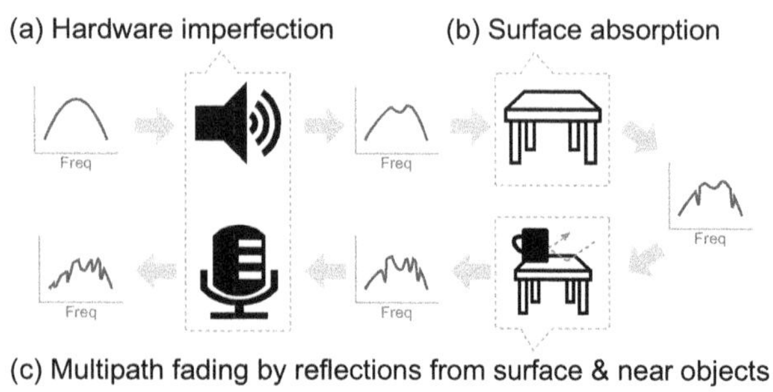

Figure 6—Causes of uneven attenuation. During the recording of emitted sound, hardware imperfection of microphones/speakers, absorption of touched surface materials and multipath reflections from nearby objects incur different degradations at different frequencies. Only the degradation caused by multipath reflections is a valid signature for sensing locations even in the same surface.

earth the causes of this phenomenon and describe how to exploit this feature for EchoTag's accurate location tagging.

4.1 Causes of Uneven Attenuation

There are three main causes of this uneven attenuation: (a) hardware imperfection, (b) surface's absorption of signal, and (c) multipath fading caused by reflection. As shown in Fig. 6, when sound is emitted from speakers, hardware imperfections make the signal louder at some frequencies and weaker at other frequencies. These imperfections have been identified and used as a signature to track people's smartphones for the purpose of censorship [31]. After the emitted sound reaches the surface touched by the phone, the surface material absorbs the signal at some frequencies. Different materials have different absorption properties, thus differentiating the surface on which the phone is placed [14]. Then, when the sound is reflected by the touched surface and the surrounding objects, the combination of multiple reflections make received signals constructive at some frequencies while destructive at other frequencies. This phenomenon is akin to multipath (frequency-selective) fading in wireless transmissions. For example, if the reflection of an object arrives at microphones t milliseconds later than the reflection from the touched surface, then the signal component at $10^3/2t$ Hz frequency of both reflections will have opposite phases, thus weakening their combined signal. This multipath property of sound has been shown and utilized as a way to implement a ubiquitous keyboard interface [28]. When reflections reach the phone's microphone, they will also degrade due to imperfect microphone hardware design.

For the purpose of accurate location tagging, EchoTag relies on the multipath fading of sound among the properties mentioned above as this is the only valid signature that varies with location even on the same surface. In what follows, we will introduce the challenges of extracting this feature and describe how EchoTag meets them.

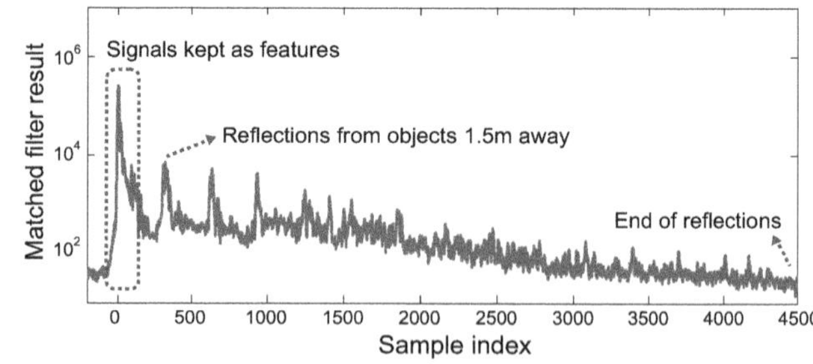

Figure 7—Characteristics of reflections. A matched filter is used to identify the reflections of a 100-sample chirp. Only first 200 samples after the largest peak are kept as a feature in EchoTag, excluding reflections from objects farther than 86cm away.

4.2 Sound Selection

The selection of parameters for the emitted sound is critical for EchoTag to extract valid multipath signatures. According to the guideline of Android platforms,[2] 44.1kHz is the most widely supported sample rate for Android phones, so the highest frequency that can be sensed is about 22kHz. Studies have shown that humans can hear signals of frequency up to 20kHz [21]. It is thus desirable to make the emitted sound inaudible (to avoid annoyance) by sensing 20 to 22kHz. But from our preliminary experiments on commodity phones, we found that the signal responses in this high-frequency range are not strong enough to support accurate indoor location tagging due to the imperfect hardware design that causes significant degradation of signal strength in this high-frequency range. Based on the experiments in [16], certain phones' microphones receive signals with 30dB less strength at 22kHz. This phenomenon is even worse if the degradation of speakers is accounted for. Thus, we choose the chirp (i.e., frequency sweep) from 11kHz to 22kHz to sense locations. The frequency response below 11kHz is not used since it contains mostly background noise of human activities [25]. Even though this selection makes the sensing of EchoTag audible to humans, the impact of this selection is minimal because EchoTag triggers acoustic sensing very infrequently, i.e., only when the tilt and the WiFi readings match its database as shown in Fig. 3. Moreover, the annoyance caused by sensing with audible sounds is mitigated by reducing the sound volume (e.g., to 5% of the maximum volume) without degrading sensing accuracy. None of the 32 participants in our usability study considered the EchoTag's emitted sound annoying and 7 of them didn't even notice the existence of emitted sound until they were asked to answer related questions in the post-use survey.

We must also consider the length of the emitted sound, which is correlated with the signal-to-noise-ratio (SNR) of received signals. The longer the sound of a frequency sweep, the more energy at each frequency is collected. However, a long duration of emitted sound introduces a serious problem to the functionality of EchoTag because reflections from far-away objects are collected during this long duration of sensing. Fig. 7 shows the received signal passed by a matched filter, where the peaks indicate received copies of the emitted sound. The first and largest peak in this figure represents the sound directly traveled from the phone's speakers to its microphones and the subsequent peaks represent the reception of environmental reflections. As the purpose of EchoTag is to remember a specific location for future use, it is unnecessary to collect signatures of reflections from far-away objects since those objects are likely to move/change. For example, the object 1.5m away shown in Fig. 7 might be the reflection from the body of a friend

[2] http://developer.android.com/reference/android/media/AudioRecord.html

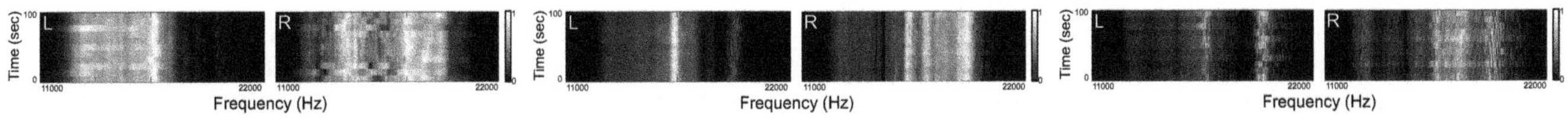

(a) 100% volume (b) 5% volume (c) 1% volume

Figure 8—Frequency responses at different volumes. Responses of full volume are saturated by sound directly transmitted from speakers while responses at 1% of the maximum volume are too weak to pick up valid features.

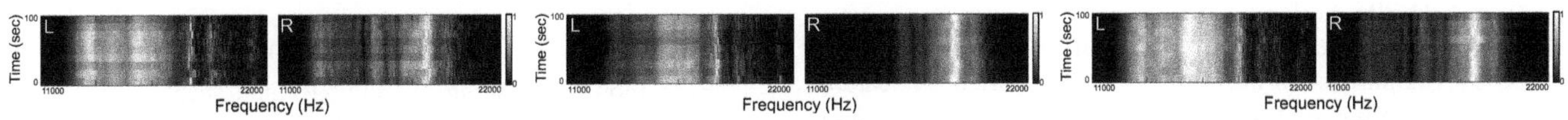

(a) 0 sample delay (b) 1 sample delay (c) 2 samples delay

Figure 9—Frequency responses with delay at the right channel. When the emitted sound is intentionally delayed at the right channel, different portions of features are strengthened, which helps enrich the feature space for sensing locations.

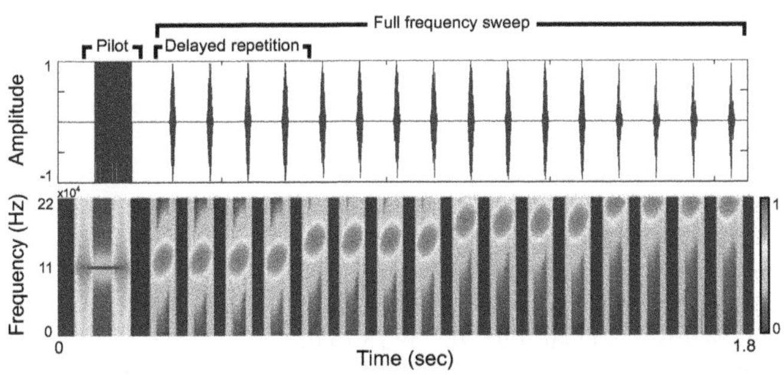

Figure 10—Selected sound signals at EchoTag. The leading pilot is used for time synchronization between speakers and microphones. The following chirps (repeated 4 times each) cover the frequency sweep from 11 to 22kHz. (This figure is scaled for visualization.)

sitting next to the user, and he might move away when EchoTag is triggered to sense locations. One way to mitigate this problem is to truncate the signals generated by the reflections from far-away objects. EchoTag uses 100-sample short signals for sensing and collects only the 200 samples of received signals after the largest peak passes through the matched filter. That is, the sensing range of EchoTag is roughly confined to 1m since the sound of speed is 338m/s and the chosen sample rate is 44.1kHz. The sensing range is actually shown to be shorter than this calculated value since the signals reflected from nearby objects are inherently stronger than those from far-away objects. Our results also confirm that this setting can meet most real-life scenarios in terms of accurate location tagging. One thing to note is that the entire frequency sweep is divided into four smaller 100-sample segments rather than one 100-sample chirp covering the 11–22kHz range. This selection reduces the sample duration (also the sensing range), but keeps enough energy at each frequency for the purpose of sensing locations.

The last parameter in selecting the emitted sound is the time to wait for playing the next chirp after sending a chirp. This parameter is related to the sensing speed of EchoTag. The larger this parameter, the longer the time EchoTag needs for single location sensing. On the other hand, a short wait time causes detection errors since the received signals might accidentally include the reflections of the previously emitted chirp. For example, if EchoTag triggers the next chirp within the 500-th sample shown in Fig. 7, the peaks (i.e., reflections) near the 400-th sample will be added as a noise to the received signals associated with the sensing of the next chirp. From our earlier field study to identify the surrounding objects via sound reflections, we found the speakers and microphones on Galaxy S4 and S5 are able to capture the reflections from objects even 5m away. This phenomenon can also be found in Fig. 7; there is residual energy even after the 1500-th sample. Thus, the interval between two chirps in EchoTag is set to 4500 samples, making its signal sensing time of the entire frequency sweep equal to $4(200+4500)/44100 \cong 0.42$ second.

An example of sensing signals is shown in Fig. 10, where a 500-sample pilot is added before the frequency sweep. This pilot is used for synchronization between speakers and microphones because the operating system delays are not consistent in commodity phones. The way EchoTag synchronizes a microphone and a speaker is similar to the sample counting process in BeepBeep [20]. In the current version of EchoTag, this pilot is set as a 11,025Hz tone, which can be improved further by pulse compression [16, 24], but according to our test results, it doesn't make any noticeable difference. Another 10000 samples follow the pilot before the chirp signals are played. Note that 4 chirps in the same frequency range are played consecutively before changing to the next frequency range. This repetition is used to enrich the acoustic feature space as described in the following sections. Current setting of EchoTag makes the total sensing time of EchoTag near 2–3 seconds. After testing EchoTag, most participants of our usability study were satisfied with this latency in sensing locations. Note that in the training phase of EchoTag, each trace is collected with 4 cycles of the above-mentioned frequency sweep to eliminate transient noises, consuming about 10 seconds to collect.

4.3 Volume Control

The volume of an emitted sound plays a critical role in extracting valid signatures from multipath fading. As shown in Fig. 8, when the volume of emitted sound is full (i.e., 100%), a large portion of the feature space is saturated by the sound emitted directly from the phones' speakers. Moreover, emitting sound in full volume makes the sensing process more annoying to the users since EchoTag uses audible frequency ranges. On the other hand, if only 1% of full volume is used to emit sound, the reflections are too weak to be picked up by phones' microphones. Based on our preliminary experiments, setting the phone volume at 5% is found optimal for Galaxy S5. Even though this setting varies from one phone type to another, calibration is needed only once to find the optimal setting.

4.4 Acoustic Signature Enrichment

The goal of EchoTag is to enable accurate location sensing with fine resolution, but according to our experimental results, one shot of the frequency sweep between 11 and 22kHz can distinguish 1cm apart objects with only 75% accuracy. One way to enrich the feature space is repeating the emitted sound which can be used to eliminate the interference caused by transient background noise. Instead of only repeating the emitted sound, EchoTag also adds delay of emitted sound in the right channel at each repetition. This intentional delay at the right channel is designed for two purposes. First, when there are stereo speakers in the phone, such as HTC M8 and Sony Z3, this intentional delay yields an effect similar to beamforming in wireless transmission, which helps us focus on the response in one specific direction at each repetition. We validated this feature to enrich the collected signatures by HTC M8's two front-faced speakers. A similar concept was also adopted in acoustic imaging [13], but `EchoTag` doesn't need calibration among speakers because the purpose of this delay is used to enrich the feature space rather than pointing to a pre-defined target direction. Second, the intentional delay also helps strengthen features at certain frequencies even when there is only one speaker in the phone. The effects of this delay at the right channel are shown in Fig. 9, where different portions of features are *highlighted* with different delays. Based on the results in Section 8, 4 repetitions with 1 sample delay at the right channel improve `EchoTag`'s sensing accuracy from 75% to 98% in sensing 11 tags, each of which is 1cm apart from its neighboring tags. This way to enrich the acoustic signature space is a unique feature of `EchoTag`, as it *actively* emits sound to sense the environment, rather than passively collecting existing features.

4.5 Modeling of Sensing Resolution

Suppose two (drawn) tags are at distance d from each other, the sensing signal wavelength is λ, and the angle from one of the nearby objects toward these two tags is θ. The difference of the reflection's travel distance from this object to the two tagged locations is $\delta = 2d * cos\ \theta$. Since the sensing signal wavelength is λ, a change, $\delta > \lambda/2$, in any reflection's travel distance will cause the summation of all acoustic reflections to vary from constructive to destructive combing (or vice versa), thus resulting in a significant change in the acoustic signature. So, if θ of all nearby objects is not close to 0 (which is also rare in the real world), tags separated by more than $\lambda/4$ are to be distinguished by their acoustic signatures. Based on this model, the current setting of `EchoTag` is capable of identifying tags with a 1cm resolution. Our evaluation also validates this property as shown in the following sections. However, this fine resolution also implies that users should place their phones close enough to the trained location for collecting valid signatures; this is also the reason why `EchoTag` requires "drawn" tags to remind users where to place their phones. In our usability study, most users didn't have any difficulty in placing phones back at the trained locations with this resolution to activate the tagged functionality of `EchoTag`. The limitations and future direction of this resolution setting will be discussed further in Section 10.

5. CLASSIFIER

Several classifiers, such as k-nearest neighbors (KNN) and support vector machine (SVM), have been tried for location sensing based on acoustic signatures. Our experimental results show that one-against-all SVM [27] performs best in classifying locations. For example, in the experiment of sensing eleven 1cm apart tags based on the training data collected 30min earlier, 98% accuracy can be achieved by SVM while only 65% test data can be correctly classified via KNN with the Euclidean distance and $k = 5$. We believe this inaccuracy is caused by the small training data size and nonlinear nature of acoustics signatures. For example, a 5mm position change might cause more significant feature changes (in the frequency domain measured by the Euclidean distance) than a 10mm position change since the acoustic signatures capture the superposition of all reflections.

In the one-against-all SVM, n classifiers are trained if there are n tags to sense. A location is classified as the tag k if the k-th classifier outputs the highest prediction probability for that tag. In our test with 2-fold cross validation, the linear kernel achieves the optimal performance. As the results shown in Section 8, the difference of prediction probability between the classifiers trained at the target location and the other locations is greater than 0.5 in most cases, which is adequate for `EchoTag` to distinguish locations using acoustic signatures.

6. PERFORMANCE OPTIMIZATION

Even though activating microphones and speakers is shown to be more economical than image or WiFi sensing [5], the cost of continuously collecting acoustic signals is still non-negligible and unnecessary. Our measurements with Monsoon Power Monitor [1] on Galaxy S5 show that acoustic sensing consumes 800mW. Moreover, due to the constraints in existing phone microphones, the signals we used are still audible, especially for the pieces of frequency sweep close to 10kHz. The strength of acoustic signal is reduced greatly by lowering the volume, but its continuous use still annoys the users and consumes energy. We have therefore performed further optimizations by avoiding unnecessary acoustic sensing to reduce the power consumption and user annoyance. For example, in terms of `EchoTag`'s functionality, it is useless to sense the environment via acoustic signals when the user keeps the phone in his pocket while walking. This situation can be easily detected by reading inertial sensors. As shown in Fig. 3, `EchoTag` first checks the status of the surrounding WiFi to ensure that the phone is located in the same target room. Then, the inertial sensor data, such as the accelerometer readings, are used to check if the phone is placed with the same angle as recorded in the database. If both the WiFi status and the inertial readings match the recorded data, one shot of acoustic sensing will be activated to collect the surrounding acoustic signature. The next round of acoustic sensing can be executed only when `EchoTag` finds the phones moved and the recorded WiFi beacons and inertial readings match. Note that WiFi sensing in `EchoTag` incurs minimal overhead, since it only needs connected WiFi SSID, which can be directly retrieved from the data already scanned by Android itself via WifiManager. In the current implementation of `EchoTag`, tilt monitoring only consumes additional 73mW in the background and the power usage of WiFi is negligible since `EchoTag` uses only the (already) scanned results. We will later evaluate the false trigger rate of this design.

7. IMPLEMENTATION

We implemented `EchoTag` as an Android background service. Since `EchoTag` relies only on sensors commonly available in smartphones, it can be readily implemented on other platforms like iOS or Windows. Acquisitions of active acoustic signatures, tilts, and WiFi signals are implemented with Android API while the classifier relying on LIBSVM [6] is written in C layered by Java Native Interface (JNI). The function to trigger applications, such as setting silent mode or playing music, is implemented via Android Intent class. A prototype of `EchoTag` is also implemented in iOS with classifiers trained in Matlab. In our current implementation, one round of acoustic sensing (including SVM processing) takes about 4 seconds. Most participants in our usability study are satisfied with the current setting.

8. PERFORMANCE EVALUATION

We have conducted a series of experiments to evaluate the performance of `EchoTag` using Galaxy S5 for two representative scenarios shown in Fig. 11. Certain experiments are also repeated on Galaxy S4/Note3, and iPhone4/5s, but the results are omitted due to space limitation. The first test environment is a lab/office and

(a) Lab/office (b) Home

Figure 11—Experiments scenarios. Red circles represent the target location to draw (echo) tags.

the second is a two-floor home. The red circles in Fig. 11 represent the test locations to draw tags. Both scenarios represent real-world settings since people usually work or live in either of these two environments. In the lab/office environment, traces were collected while lab members were chatting and passing through the test locations. During the experiment, an active user kept on working (changing the laptop position and having lunch) on the same table. There are two residents living in the home environment, and one of them is unaware of the purpose of our experiments. The residents behave normally, cooking in the kitchen, watching TV, and cleaning rooms. Thus, our evaluation results that include the interference due to human activities should be representative of real-life usage of `EchoTag`.

In the lab/office environment, three tag systems shown in Fig. 12 are used to evaluate the *sensing resolution* which is defined as the minimum necessary separation between two tags. The first system is composed of three tags 10cm apart: A, B, and C, as shown in Fig. 12(a). This setting is used to evaluate the basic resolution to support applications of `EchoTag` (e.g., automatically setting phones to silent mode). The second and third systems include 11 tags which are 1cm (30°) apart from each other as shown in Fig. 12(b) (Fig. 12(c)); this is used to evaluate the maximum sensing resolution of `EchoTag`. In the home environment, 10 locations are selected as shown in Fig. 11(b). At each location, we marked two tags, A and B, similar to the setting in Fig. 12(a).

In both scenarios, traces are collected at different sampling frequencies and time spans, generating three datasets: 1) 30min, 2) 1day, and 3) 1week. In the 30min dataset, traces are collected every 5 minutes for 30 minutes, which is used to evaluate the baseline performance of `EchoTag` without considering the environment changes over a long term. The 1day dataset is composed of traces collected every 30 minutes during 10am – 10pm in a day. The purpose of this dataset is to evaluate the performance changes of `EchoTag` in a single day, which is important for certain applications, such as the silent-mode tag near the bed where the users place their phones every night. The last 1week dataset is collected over a week, which is used to prove the consistency of active acoustic signatures over a one-week period. In the lab/office environment, the 1week dataset is sampled during 9:00am – 9:00pm every day while the 1week dataset in the home environment is tested at 11:00pm.

We believe these experiments can validate the effectiveness of `EchoTag` in real world. Larger-scale experiments including more users and spanning longer periods are part of our future plan after deploying `EchoTag`.

8.1 Accuracy and Resolution

Sensing resolution in `EchoTag` is defined as the minimum necessary distance/degree between tags, which is an important metric since it is related to the number of tags that can exist in the same environment. On the other hand, the sensing accuracy at a location is defined as the percentage of correct predictions at that location, whereas the overall accuracy is defined as the average of accuracy at all locations. In the lab/office environment of 30min dataset, the average sensing accuracy under all settings is higher than 98%. Orientation changes can be detected by `EchoTag` since the microphones/speakers are not placed in the middle of the phone, and hence the relative position changes when the phone is rotated. `EchoTag` can also distinguish 20 tags in a home environment with 95% accuracy. The resulting confusion matrix is shown in Fig. 13(a). This evaluation based on the 30min dataset validates that `EchoTag` can achieve a sensing resolution of 1cm and at least 30°. Without using any infrastructure, this sensing resolution is the finest among existing methods to differentiate locations. Our measurements show that WiFi RSSI or background acoustic noise can only distinguish the 20 tags at home with 30% accuracy.

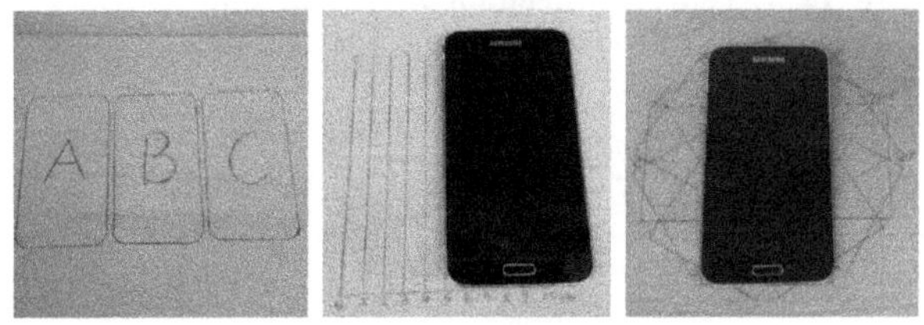

(a) ABC tags (b) 1cm tags (c) 30° tags

Figure 12—Tag systems. The first tag system consists of disjoint (echo) tags while the second and third tag systems are composed of overlapped tags 1cm or 30° apart.

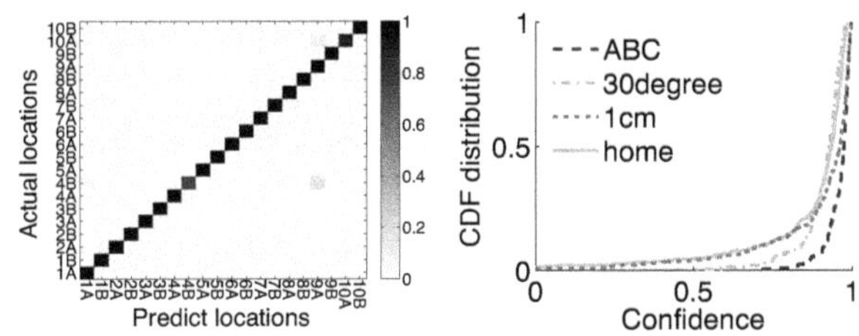

(a) Confusion matrix in home (b) Confidence distributions

Figure 13—Result of 30min dataset. *Confidence* is defined as the prediction probability at the target location minus the largest prediction probability at the other locations.

8.2 Uniqueness and Confidence of Acoustic Signature

To measure the uniqueness of acoustic signature, we define a metric called *confidence* as the prediction probability of the classifier trained at the target location minus the largest prediction probability of classifiers at other locations. A high confidence means high feature uniqueness among locations since SVM gets less confused among locations. A prediction is wrong whenever the confidence is less than 0 because SVM will choose another location with the highest prediction probability as the answer. Fig. 13(b) shows the confidence distribution of 30min dataset in all environments. ABC tags get the highest confidence since the tags are separated by more than 10cm and only 3 tags are considered. However, even 20 tags are set at home or tags in office are separated by only 1cm (overlapped), acoustic signatures are still distinct enough to differ-

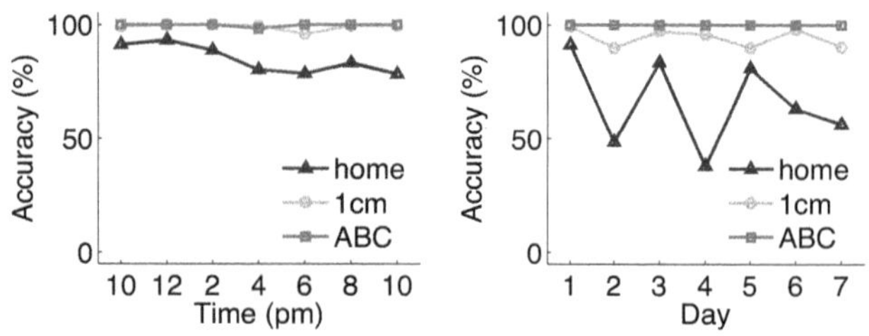

(a) 1day dataset (b) 1week dataset

Figure 14—Accuracy variation over time/day. Prediction is based on 6 traces collected during the first hour/day.

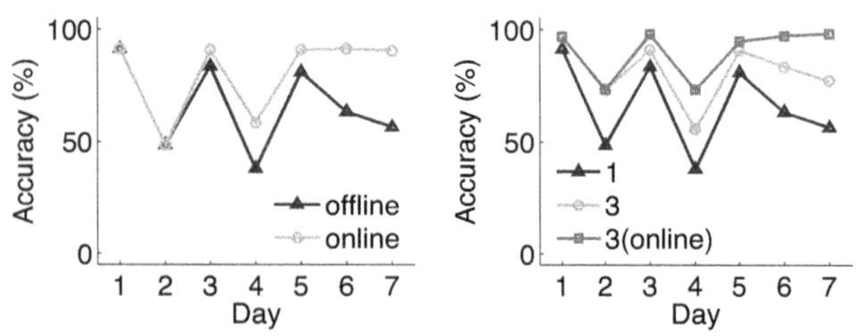

(a) Online SVM (b) Multiple candidates

Figure 15—Performance of online SVM and providing multiple candidates in the 1week home dataset. Online SVM classifiers are updated using the traces collected in previous days while the traces collected on the same day are excluded.

entiate 90% of cases with confidence greater than 0.5. This example demonstrates that the uniqueness of active acoustic signature is good enough to support the function of `EchoTag`.

8.3 False Positives

The above-mentioned accuracy represents the true positive rate to differentiate locations. To prevent `EchoTag` from falsely classifying locations without tags as tagged ones, two more traces are recorded on the same surface but 10cm away from each tag. These traces are used to build an additional *No Tag* SVM classifier which determines if the sensed traces belong to one of tagged locations or not. We set 0.5 as the threshold that any sensed location is classified as *No Tag* when the prediction probability of this classifier is greater than 0.5. In the 30min dataset of home environment, the probability to classify random locations without tags as tagged locations (i.e., false positive rate) is only 3%, and this setting only causes a 1% false negative rate. We conducted another test by deploying the ABC tags on three users' office desks for three days. The users carry their phones as usual but are asked not to place their phones inside the drawn tags. In this test, merely 22 acoustic sensings are triggered per day and only 5% of them are falsely classified as being placed at tags with online-updated classifiers. This rate can be reduced further by fusing other signatures which is part of our future work. We also implemented a manual mode (without any false trigger) in which users can press the home button to manually activate acoustic sensing. This manual mode is a reasonable design choice since it is similar to the way Apple Siri or Google Search is triggered.

8.4 Temporal Variation

The purpose of this evaluation is to test how active acoustic signatures change over time. This is an important metric since `EchoTag` is designed to be able to remember the location at least for a certain period of time. To evaluate this, the average accuracy among tags of 1day and 1week datasets based on the first 6 traces collected in the first hour or day is shown in Fig. 14. As shown in Fig. 14(a),

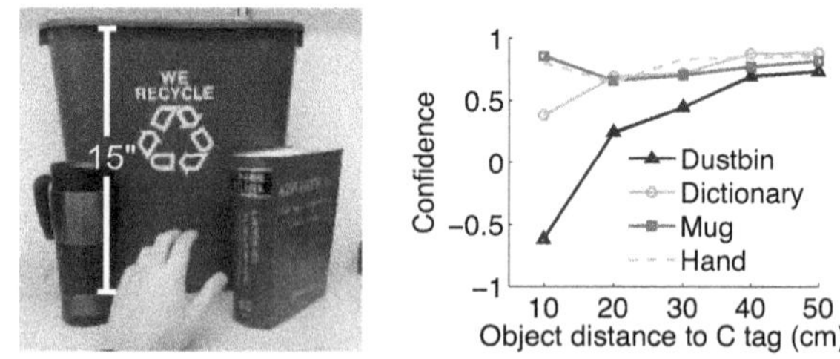

(a) Addition of objects (b) Prediction confidence

Figure 16—Test of environmental changes. `EchoTag` gets less confident when the size of an added object is larger and its position is closer to the test locations.

the decay of active acoustic signatures in one day is not significant. In the lab/office environment, the accuracy drops only by 5% in predicting the traces collected 12 hours later. Even one week later, the average accuracy of `EchoTag` in the lab/office environment is still higher than 90%. However, as shown in Fig. 14, the average accuracy of traces collected in the home environment drops by 15% after 12 hours and the traces collected a week later achieve only 56% accuracy. This phenomenon is caused by a series of environment changes at certain locations. For example, the accuracy drops mainly at 4 locations: (1) drawer, (4) kitchen, (9) desk, and (10) near the bed, which suffer environment changes due to human activities like cooking in the kitchen or taking objects out of drawers. When the above-mentioned objects are excluded from dataset, `EchoTag` can sense the remaining 12 tags at 6 locations with 82% accuracy even a week later. This result suggests where to put tags is critical to `EchoTag`'s performance. When we consider the tags in the kitchen as an example, if the tags are not placed at the original location near the cooker and stove but on one of the shelves, the acoustic signatures decay as slowly as at other locations. Providing guidelines for where to put tags is part of our future work.

Sensing accuracy over a long term can be improved further in two ways. The first is to use online SVM training. We simulated online SVM by retraining the offline SVM classifiers with the traces collected before the test day (i.e., excluding the same day test data). The cost of retraining classifiers can be further optimized by online SVM [26]. As the results shown in Fig. 15(a), with online training, the average accuracy for the home environment in one week can be increased to 91.5% during the last three days. This online training is possible in real world because we assume users will provide feedback, such as selecting the right application/functions when a wrong prediction is made or suspending wrongly-triggered applications. By monitoring this user reaction after each prediction, online training data can be collected during the normal use of `EchoTag`. Moreover, in our experiments, only 8.5% of error predictions need this user interaction.

Another way to improve the sensing accuracy over a long term is to provide more than one predicted candidate for users. The candidates in `EchoTag` are provided based on the prediction probability for each classifier. As shown in Fig. 15(b), when the first three predicted candidates are provided, the accuracy during the last day based only on the first day trace is increased to 77%. Moreover, providing 3 candidates with online SVM training boosts the accuracy of `EchoTag` to 98% during the last day. Evaluating the overhead of users' interactions with online training feedback and multiple candidates is part of our future work.

8.5 Environmental Disturbances

Similar to the signature decay due to significant environmental changes in the kitchen, we investigate the performance of `EchoTag`

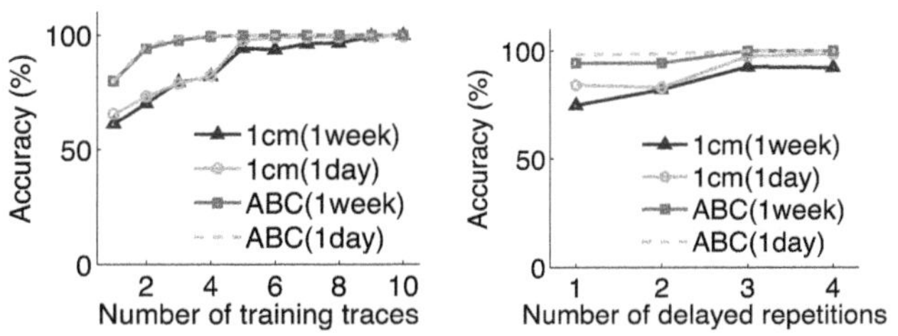

(a) Training traces (b) Delayed repetitions

Figure 17—Impact of acoustic feature space. Accuracy is higher than 95% when 5 traces with 4 delayed repetitions are collected.

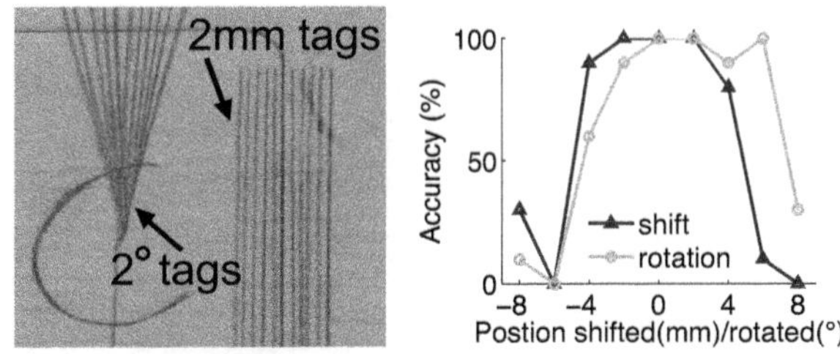

(a) Testbed (b) Accuracy of C tag

Figure 18—Tolerance test. Additional tags separated by 2(mm/°) are placed inside the C tag. Test data at C are collected with errors ranging from -8 to 8(mm/°) for knowing the tolerance of EchoTag. Dataset of ABC and 1cm tags are combined, so the accuracy shown is the prediction among 14 locations.

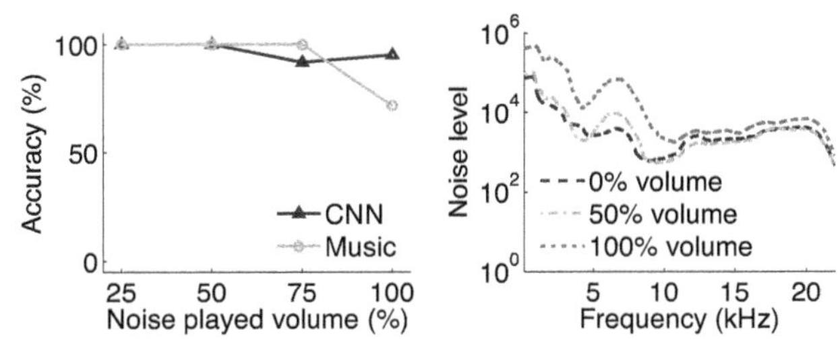

(a) Accuracy at different noise (b) Noise profile of CNN news

Figure 19—Impact of background noise. Predefined noises (i.e., music and CNN news) are played by Macbook Air with different volumes. EchoTag is able to provide effective prediction even when the noise is played at 75% of the full volume.

when objects near a tagged location are different from those during the training. Fig. 16(a) shows 4 selected objects: 1) dustbin, 2) dictionary, 3) mug, and 4) human hands. We add these objects sequentially near the ABC tags and vary their distance to the C tag. The corresponding prediction confidence is used to measure the change of EchoTag's performance. As shown in Fig. 16(b), human hands and small objects like a mug cause little disturbance to EchoTag even when those objects are only 10cm away from the test locations. Medium-size objects like a thick dictionary degrade EchoTag's confidence to 0.38 when it is close to the test locations, but most predictions still remain correct. Placing large objects like a 15" high dustbin around the test locations change the acoustic signatures significantly since it generates lots of strong acoustic reflections. Most predictions are wrong (i.e., confidence < 0) when the dustbin is placed 10cm away from the test locations. It is also the reason why the accuracy in the kitchen degrades after the position of a large cooker is changed. However, this large environment change is less common in real life. For example, users may change their mugs or hands frequently but less likely to move large objects on their office desk.

When a large environmental change occurs, EchoTag needs to retrain its classifier to account for this change. One interesting finding from our 1week trace is that the prediction accuracy in the home environment increased back to 90% after three day classifier online updates. This demonstrates that with enough training data, EchoTag is able to keep only *invariant* features. In future we plan to derive a guideline for setting up tags and providing online feedback when EchoTag finds more training necessary for certain locations. Another interesting finding is that the (dis) appearance of human causes only limited effect on EchoTag because human body is prone to absorb sound signals rather than reflect them. During experiments, a human body (the tester) continuously changed his relative position to the test locations, but no significant performance degradation was observed in spite of the large human body.

8.6 Acoustic Feature Space

Here we discuss the effect of the feature space selected for sensing locations. We first examine accuracy with different training data sizes. The training data size is relevant to the usability of EchoTag since it represents the time required for users to set tags and the number of features necessary to remember a single location. As shown in Fig. 17(a), in the lab/office scenario, 2–4 traces are able to distinguish rough locations and only 5 traces can achieve 95% accuracy with 1cm resolution. Considering the tradeoff between training overhead and sensing accuracy, the current version of EchoTag sets the size of training data at a single location to 4. In our usability study, these 4 traces at each tag can be collected in 58 seconds on average. We also received a comment from one survey participant that the training process and delay of EchoTag are acceptable since the entire procedure is similar to that of setting up Apple TouchID. Based on our informal experiments with 5 participants on iPhone5s, setting up Apple TouchID required 11–13 training traces with different finger placements, taking about 1 minute. See Section 9 for details of the users' other reactions on this training set size.

Next, we study the benefit of our delayed repetitions for sensing locations. The sensing accuracy based on 5 traces with different numbers of delayed repetitions is plotted in Fig. 17(b). As shown in this figure, without help of delayed repetitions to enrich acoustic signatures, the accuracy for the 1cm dataset over a week is only 75% while it can be boosted to 91% when 4 delayed repetitions are used. This way of enriching the feature space is only available in active acoustic sensing since we have the full control of emitted/collected signals. We also find similar effectiveness of this delayed repetitions on phones with stereo speakers like HTC M8, but these results are omitted due to space limitation. The current version of EchoTag uses 4 delayed repetitions.

8.7 Tolerance Range

Since the phone might not be placed exactly at the same locations as it had been trained, it is important to know the maximum tolerance range of EchoTag and if users can handle the tolerance well. To evaluate the maximum tolerance of EchoTag, additional fine-grained tags are drawn inside the C tag as shown in Fig. 18(a). These fine-grained tags are separated by 2(mm/°). Test data of these inside tags are collected with additional errors (i.e., between ±8mm/°), and a prediction is made by the first 4 traces of 30min dataset in the lab/office environment. In the training phase, ABC and 1cm datasets are combined so the prediction is made for sensing 14 locations. The accuracy of the C tag when test data is collected with additional errors is plotted in Fig. 18(b) where the maximum tolerance range of EchoTag is about ±4mm and ±4°. The

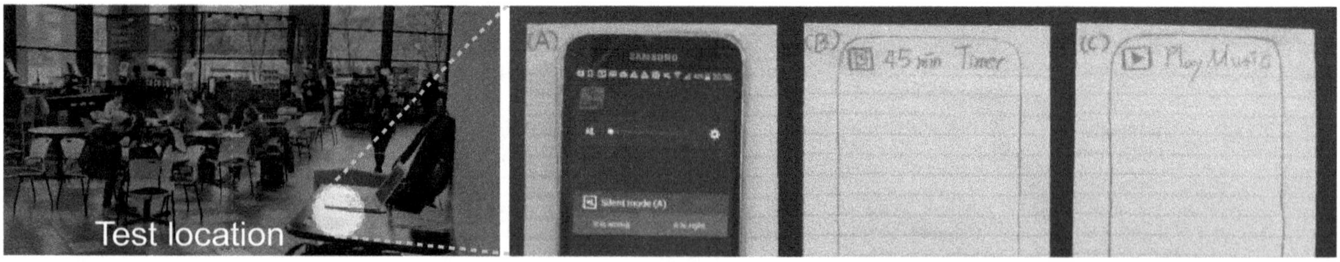

Figure 20—Usability study environments. The test location is selected near the a cafe at a student center. Tags are drawn at memo pads since the table is black. Passers by and students studying in this area are randomly selected to test `EchoTag`.

reason why accuracy with different degree errors is not centered at 0° might be the measurement errors in collecting the training data (i.e., the training data is also collected with a few degree errors). This result also matches our resolution test, where `EchoTag` can provide 1cm resolution since features of tags separated by 8mm vary significantly. With the help of drawn tags, this tolerance range is good enough to allow users to put their phones back at the tags for triggering `EchoTag`. Our usability study of 32 participants validates this hypothesis since most of them think it is easy to place phones on the tags. We will discuss how to enhance the user experience with this limitation of tolerance range in Section 10.

8.8 Noise Robustness

The last issue of `EchoTag` to address is its ability to sense locations in a noisy environment. Basically, the results discussed thus far were obtained in real-life scenarios where traces were collected in the presence of noises from TV, people chatting, and air condition fans. To further test the robustness against noises, we collected traces in a lab/office environment when a laptop was placed 30cm away from tags on the same surface. This laptop is set to either play a song ("I'm yours – Jason Marz") or a clip of CNN news with different volumes. The traces of ABC and the 1cm dataset are combined to make prediction for 14 locations. The results of this experiment are shown in Fig. 19. As shown in Fig. 19(a), `EchoTag` can tolerate the music noise with 75% volume and can perform normally even with noise from CNN news with 100% volume. In our measurements, the intensity of noise from the music with 75% volume and CNN news with 100% volume is about 11*dB* higher than the office background noise. Even though `EchoTag` is unable to work accurately (i.e., only 71% among 14 locations) when the music was played with 100% volume, this is not a typical operation scenario of `EchoTag` since it incurs 17*dB* higher noise.

`EchoTag` is robust to most real-world noises mainly because it relies on signatures actively generated by itself, rather than passively collected from background. That is, as the noise profile of CNN news shown in Fig. 19(b), most noise from human speaking occurs in frequencies less than 10kHz while `EchoTag` uses higher frequencies to sense locations. This phenomenon is also consistent with the results shown in [25]. The current setting of `EchoTag` is already resilient to the noise in our usual environment. Our usability study done at a noisy location near a cafe also validates the robustness against noise. Incorporating other sources of signatures that are free from acoustic noise is part of our future work.

9. USABILITY STUDY

In this section, we explore how real users of `EchoTag` perceive its performance. For example, we would like to answer a question like "can users easily place phones on drawn tags?" To evaluate the usability of `EchoTag`, 32 (9 female and 23 male) participants were recruited at our university students' activity center. The test location was the table near a cafe as shown in Fig. 20. Participants are

Questions	Disagree	No option	Agree
Sensing accuracy is useful	1	0	31
Sensing noise is acceptable	0	3	29
Sensing delay is acceptable	1	6	25
Placing phones inside (echo)tags is easy	0	3	29
`EchoTag` can help me remember turning on silent mode when going to sleep	2	5	25
`EchoTag` can help me remember setting the timer for taking washed clothes	5	3	24
`EchoTag` can save my time in activating apps under specific scenarios	1	0	31

Table 2—Usability survey results of 32 participants.

randomly selected from those passing by this area. All participants didn't know `EchoTag` and its developers, but all have experience in using smart phones (11 Androids, 19 iPhones, and 2 others). Most participants are university students of age 20–29 while 6 of them are not. We first introduced the functionality of `EchoTag` to users and its three representative applications as shown in Section 1. Then, three tags (i.e., turning on silent mode, setting a 45min timer, and playing music) were deployed at the table. Since the table surface is black and is the university's property, we drew the tags on sheets of 5×6 paper which were then attached on the table. Our survey results also validate that drawing tags on attached papers will not affect the accuracy of `EchoTag`. After users were informed of the purpose of `EchoTag`, we asked them to put phones on the tags and `EchoTag` is triggered automatically to make its prediction on attached applications. The participants were asked to first put phones inside the tag for measuring prediction accuracy, and then slightly move the phones away from the tags until a wrong prediction is made for testing the tolerance range of `EchoTag`. After trying the functionality of `EchoTag` with the tags we trained, the participants were asked to train their own tags. This process helps users "sense" the amount of effort to set up and use `EchoTag`, indicating the average user training time. The participants then filled out the survey forms. Each study lasted 15–20 min.

The main results of this usability study are summarized in Table 2. 31 of 32 participants think the sensing accuracy of `EchoTag` is adequate for its intended applications. During this study, three users experienced a bug in our app. In these cases, we restarted the whole survey process and asked the participants to try `EchoTag` again. The average accuracy including these three buggy traces were 87%, while the results excluding these three cases were 92%. One thing to note is that even those three users experienced the low sensing accuracy during the first trial, still think the overall detection accuracy of `EchoTag` is acceptable and useful. Moreover, 25 of the participants think the prediction delay is acceptable for the purpose of `EchoTag`. In another question to learn their expectation of `EchoTag`, only 2 of users hope to have the sensing delay less than 1 second and 12 users hope the sensing delay can be shortened to about 2 seconds.

Based on participants' experience in placing phones on tags, 29 of them think it is easy to do. Five participants put their phones too far away from the drawn tags during the first trial, but they were able to place their phones on the tags after they were told of it. Only one participant made a comment that he expected a larger tolerance range. Actually, there is an inherent tradeoff between the tolerance range and the training overhead. For example, a very long training sequence that moves phones at all possible locations near the drawn tags can increase the tolerance range, but with a significant overhead in the training phase. In the current version of EchoTag, 4 repetitions are used in the training phase to collect signatures at a single location. Between two consecutive repetitions, the phones need to be taken away from, and then placed back on tags for sensing valid signatures. On average, users need 58 seconds to finish the whole training phase for a tag. 8 participants expected less than 2 training repetitions at each location, while 17 of participants think the 4 repetitions setting is reasonable since it is only one-time training. Considering this trade-off between accuracy, tolerance, and training overhead, the existing setting of EchoTag satisfies most scenarios and users.

According to the survey related to potential scenarios based on EchoTag, 25 participants agree the silent mode tag can help them remember setting phones to stay quiet during sleep, and 24 of them agree the auto-timer scenario can help them take clothes out of a washing machine. These results indicate that the users see benefits from EchoTag in remembering things to do in specific situations since the functionality of EchoTag provides natural connections between the locations and things-to-do. Moreover, 31 participants also think the automation of triggered applications can save time in finding and launching desired applications.

10. DISCUSSION AND LIMITATIONS

The purpose of EchoTag is to provide a novel way of accurately tagging locations. With the realization of this functionality, we believe many advanced applications can be realized. Most participants in our usability study agree with the scenarios we considered, and they also provide other possible uses of EchoTag.

10.1 Potential Applications

Similar to those applications mentioned so far, participants also suggest use of an auto-set timer during cooking or auto-set silent mode in an office environment. These applications can be classified into two categories based on the resulting benefits: 1) helping users remember things, and 2) saving time for users in finding and launching desired applications. For example, applications like auto-set silent mode do not save a significant amount of time since pressing a phone's power button can also set up silent mode manually. However, this function turns out to receive most support from the participants because it is easy to forget setting silent mode before going to bed everyday. Instead of doing it manually, a natural combination of a location (i.e., a tag near bed) and target applications/functions (i.e., silent mode) helps users remember them more easily. Other suggested applications like automatically turning off lights or activating a special app for monitoring the sleep behavior are also in this category. On the other hand, the applications like automatically playing favorite songs (movies) on speakers (TV) help users find the expected applications/functions with less time due to the hint of tagged locations. For example, we received a feedback saying that EchoTag can be used to set up Google Map and activate the car mode when a tag is placed inside the car (e.g., an iPhone stand). Actually, this task can be easily remembered whenever the user gets into his car, but it is time-consuming to find and enable these applications. In this scenario, the natural combination of locations and applications can help users *filter* out unnecessary information and save their time in triggering the desired applications.

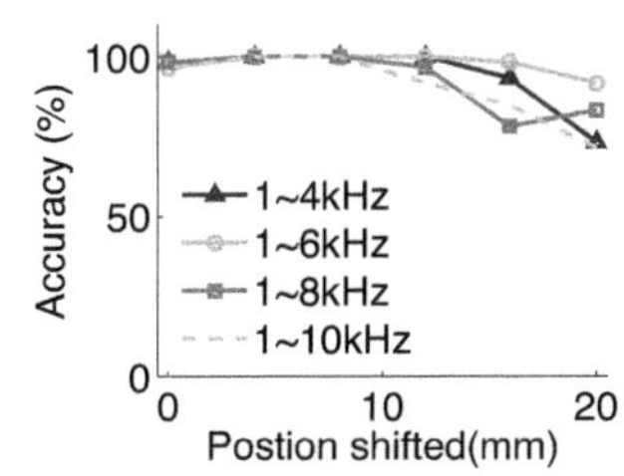

(a) Tolerance in lower frequency

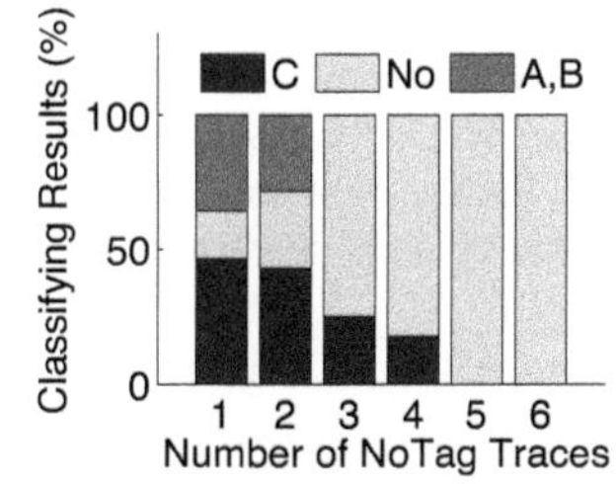

(b) NoTag SVM classifiers

Figure 21—Extension of tolerance range. The tolerance range can be extended by sensing tags with lower-frequency signals. Building 'NoTag' classifiers can also prevent EchoTag from incorrect classification of misplacements.

10.2 Limitation of Tolerance Range

As shown in Section 8, the merit of EchoTag's fine resolution comes with the limitation that the tolerance range of current setting is about 0.4cm. Even though most participants in our user study were able to place phones at the tagged locations accurately after they were instructed on how to use EchoTag, this fine resolution and its limited tolerance range may not be needed for certain applications and cause unintended prediction errors when the phone is not placed correctly. To meet such applications needs, one can take the following two approaches.

First, we can enlarge the tolerance range of EchoTag (while decreasing its sensing resolution). Based on the mathematical model in Section 4.5, we can lower the sensing frequency to extend the tolerance range. For example, setting the highest sensing frequency to 6kHz can increase the tolerance range from 0.4cm to about 1.4cm. This increase of tolerance range is plotted in Fig. 21(a), showing that lower-frequency signals are better in identifying tags with large placement errors. However, lowering sensing frequency will increase the audibility of sensing signal and decrease the feature space. For example, sensing with 1$\sim$4kHz lowers overall accuracy because the collected signature is not enough to be distinguished from others. Studying the tradeoff between tolerance range and other concerns is part of our future work.

Second, instead of trying hard to classify misplacements as trained tags, EchoTag can simply opt to report "There is no tag" once the location is out of the tag's tolerance range. We choose to use the same 'NoTag SVM' classifier as introduced in Section 8.3, which is built from traces in the same surface but at least 0.4cm away from the tags. That is, EchoTag identified locations as "There is no tag" if the trace gets the prediction probability of NoTag classifier which is greater than 0.3 and also larger than the prediction probability of other classifiers. With this method, if the user places his phone outside of the operation range of EchoTag, the message of "There is no tag" (rather than identifying a wrong tag and then triggering a wrong function) will tell the user he needs to place the phone more precisely to activate the tagged function. The result of the same experiment of identifying C tag with traces collected 0.4cm away from the trained location is shown in Fig. 21(b). Without the help of 'NoTag' classifier, 50% of those misplaced traces around the C tag were classified as wrong tags, i.e., as A and B. However, with enough NoTag training traces, EchoTag can identify the misplacements with a high probability, thus not triggering functions attached to wrong tags. Note that NoTag SVM with 6 training traces in this experiment only causes 1% false negatives when the trace is collected at the right location (within the tolerance range), which also matches the result reported in Section 8.3.

11. CONCLUSION

We have proposed and implemented `EchoTag`, a novel indoor location tagging based only on built-in sensors available in commodity phones. `EchoTag` is designed to be able to remember indoor locations with 1cm resolution, enabling the realization of many new applications. The main idea of `EchoTag` is to *actively* sense the environments via acoustic signatures. With the help of active sensing, a fine-grained control of collected signatures can be achieved for either enriching the feature space or removing environmental interferences. Our evaluation in different environments validates the capability of `EchoTag` to meet the users' need. In future, we would like collect larger datasets after deploying `EchoTag`.

ACKNOWLEDGEMENTS

The authors would like to thank Kassem Fawaz, Arun Ganesan, Huan Feng, Dongyao Chen, Yuanchao Shu, Tsung-Han Lin, Lung-Pan Cheng, Yu-Ting Hsu, Chun-Hung Hsiao, Ye-Sheng Kuo, the anonymous reviewers and the shepherd for constructive comments on the earlier versions of this paper.

12. REFERENCES

[1] Monsoon Power Monitor. `http://www.msoon.com/LabEquipment/PowerMonitor/`.

[2] Near Field Communication. `http://www.nfc-forum.org`.

[3] AZIZYAN, M., CONSTANDACHE, I., AND ROY CHOUDHURY, R. Surroundsense: Mobile phone localization via ambience fingerprinting. In *Proceedings of ACM MobiCom '09*, pp. 261–272.

[4] BAHL, P., AND PADMANABHAN, V. Radar: an in-building RF-based user location and tracking system. In *Proceedings of IEEE INFOCOM '00*, pp. 775–784 vol.2.

[5] BEN ABDESSLEM, F., PHILLIPS, A., AND HENDERSON, T. Less is more: Energy-efficient mobile sensing with senseless. In *Proceedings of the ACM MobiHeld '09*, pp. 61–62.

[6] CHANG, C.-C., AND LIN, C.-J. LIBSVM: A library for support vector machines. *ACM Transactions on Intelligent Systems and Technology 2* (2011), 27:1–27:27. Software available at `http://www.csie.ntu.edu.tw/~cjlin/libsvm`.

[7] CHEN, Y., LYMBEROPOULOS, D., LIU, J., AND PRIYANTHA, B. FM-based indoor localization. In *Proceedings of ACM MobiSys '12*, pp. 169–182.

[8] CHUNG, J., DONAHOE, M., SCHMANDT, C., KIM, I.-J., RAZAVAI, P., AND WISEMAN, M. Indoor location sensing using geo-magnetism. In *Proceedings of ACM MobiSys '11*, pp. 141–154.

[9] GOEL, M., LEE, B., ISLAM AUMI, M. T., PATEL, S., BORRIELLO, G., HIBINO, S., AND BEGOLE, B. Surfacelink: Using inertial and acoustic sensing to enable multi-device interaction on a surface. In *Proceedings of ACM CHI '14*, pp. 1387–1396.

[10] GUSTAFSSON, T., RAO, B., AND TRIVEDI, M. Source localization in reverberant environments: modeling and statistical analysis. *Speech and Audio Processing, IEEE Transactions on* (2003), 791–803.

[11] HARRISON, C., SCHWARZ, J., AND HUDSON, S. E. Tapsense: Enhancing finger interaction on touch surfaces. In *Proceedings of ACM UIST '11*, pp. 627–636.

[12] HARRISON, C., TAN, D., AND MORRIS, D. Skinput: Appropriating the body as an input surface. In *Proceedings of ACM CHI '10*, pp. 453–462.

[13] IZQUIERDO-FUENTE, A., DEL VAL, L., JIMÉNEZ, M. I., AND VILLACORTA, J. J. Performance evaluation of a biometric system based on acoustic images. In *Sensors 2011*, vol. 11, Molecular Diversity Preservation International, pp. 9499–9519.

[14] KUNZE, K., AND LUKOWICZ, P. Symbolic object localization through active sampling of acceleration and sound signatures. In *Proceedings of UbiComp '07*, pp. 163–180.

[15] KUO, Y.-S., PANNUTO, P., HSIAO, K.-J., AND DUTTA, P. Luxapose: Indoor positioning with mobile phones and visible light. In *Proceedings of ACM MobiCom '14*, pp. 447–458.

[16] LAZIK, P., AND ROWE, A. Indoor pseudo-ranging of mobile devices using ultrasonic chirps. In *Proceedings of ACM SenSys '12*, pp. 391–392.

[17] LIU, K., LIU, X., AND LI, X. Guoguo: Enabling fine-grained indoor localization via smartphone. In *Proceeding of ACM MobiSys '13*, pp. 235–248.

[18] NIRJON, S., DICKERSON, R. F., ASARE, P., LI, Q., HONG, D., STANKOVIC, J. A., HU, P., SHEN, G., AND JIANG, X. Auditeur: A mobile-cloud service platform for acoustic event detection on smartphones. In *Proceeding of ACM MobiSys '13*, pp. 403–416.

[19] ONO, M., SHIZUKI, B., AND TANAKA, J. Touch & activate: Adding interactivity to existing objects using active acoustic sensing. In *Proceedings of ACM UIST '13*, pp. 31–40.

[20] PENG, C., SHEN, G., ZHANG, Y., LI, Y., AND TAN, K. Beepbeep: A high accuracy acoustic ranging system using cots mobile devices. In *Proceedings of ACM SenSys '07*, pp. 1–14.

[21] PLACK, C. J. The sense of hearing. Lawrence Erlbaum Associates, Inc.

[22] PRIYANTHA, N. B., CHAKRABORTY, A., AND BALAKRISHNAN, H. The cricket location-support system. In *Proceedings of ACM MobiCom '00*, pp. 32–43.

[23] ROSSI, M., SEITER, J., AMFT, O., BUCHMEIER, S., AND TRÖSTER, G. Roomsense: An indoor positioning system for smartphones using active sound probing. In *Proceedings of the 4th Augmented Human International Conference* (2013), pp. 89–95.

[24] SALEMIAN, S., JAMSHIHI, M., AND RAFIEE, A. Radar pulse compression techniques. In *Proceedings of WSEAS AEE'05*, pp. 203–209.

[25] TARZIA, S. P., DINDA, P. A., DICK, R. P., AND MEMIK, G. Indoor localization without infrastructure using the acoustic background spectrum. In *Proceedings of ACM MobiSys '11*, pp. 155–168.

[26] TAX, D., AND LASKOV, P. Online svm learning: from classification to data description and back. In *IEEE Neural Networks for Signal Processing, 2003*, pp. 499–508.

[27] VAPNIK, V. N. *Statistical Learning Theory*. Wiley-Interscience, 1998.

[28] WANG, J., ZHAO, K., ZHANG, X., AND PENG, C. Ubiquitous keyboard for small mobile devices: Harnessing multipath fading for fine-grained keystroke localization. In *Proceedings of ACM MobiSys '14*, pp. 14–27.

[29] XIONG, J., AND JAMIESON, K. Towards fine-grained radio-based indoor location. In *Proceedings of ACM HotMobile '12*, pp. 13:1–13:6.

[30] YOUSSEF, M., AND AGRAWALA, A. The horus wlan location determination system. In *Proceedings of ACM MobiSys '05*, pp. 205–218.

[31] ZHOU, Z., DIAO, W., LIU, X., AND ZHANG, K. Acoustic fingerprinting revisited: Generate stable device id stealthily with inaudible sound. In *Proceedings of ACM CCS '14*, pp. 429–440.

ToneTrack: Leveraging Frequency-Agile Radios for Time-Based Indoor Wireless Localization

Jie Xiong
University College London
j.xiong@cs.ucl.ac.uk

Karthikeyan Sundaresan
NEC Laboratories America
karthiks@nec-labs.com

Kyle Jamieson
University College London
k.jamieson@cs.ucl.ac.uk

Abstract

Indoor localization of mobile devices and tags has received much attention recently, with encouraging fine-grained localization results available with enough line-of-sight coverage and hardware infrastructure. Some of the most promising techniques analyze the time-of-arrival of incoming signals, but the limited bandwidth available to most wireless transmissions fundamentally constrains their resolution. Frequency-agile wireless networks utilize bandwidths of varying sizes and locations in a wireless band to efficiently share the wireless medium between users. ToneTrack is an indoor location system that achieves sub-meter accuracy with minimal hardware and antennas, by leveraging frequency-agile wireless networks to increase the effective bandwidth. Our novel signal combination algorithm combines time-of-arrival data from different transmissions as a mobile device hops across different channels, approaching time resolutions previously not possible with a single narrowband channel. ToneTrack's novel channel combination and spectrum identification algorithms together with the triangle inequality scheme yield superior results even in non-line-of-sight scenarios with one to two walls separating client and APs and also in the case where the direct path from mobile client to an AP is completely blocked. We implement ToneTrack on the WARP hardware radio platform and use six of them served as APs to localize Wi-Fi clients in an indoor testbed over one floor of an office building. Experimental results show that ToneTrack can achieve a median 90 cm accuracy when 20 MHz bandwidth APs overhear three packets from adjacent channels.

Categories and Subject Descriptors

C.2.1 [**Computer-Communication Networks**]: Network Architecture and Design—*Wireless communication*

Keywords

Indoor Wireless Location; Time (Difference) of Arrival (ToA/TDoA); Channel Combination; CSI Combination; Bandwidth Increment; MUSIC Spectrum Identification; Time Synchronization; Distributed MIMO; Triangle Inequality

MobiCom'15, September 7–11, 2015, Paris, France.
ACM 978-1-4503-3619-2/15/09.
http://dx.doi.org/10.1145/2789168.2790125.

Physical layer	Bandwidth	Raw resolution
802.11a/g Wi-Fi	20 MHz	15 m
802.11n Wi-Fi	40	7.5
802.11ac Wi-Fi	< 160	> 1.9
Ultra-wideband	> 500	< 60 cm

Table 1: Popular physical layers used in localization, their frequency bandwidth, and the raw sample spatial resolution each offers—the distance light travels between sampling instants at that bandwidth: Raw resolution = Speed of light / Bandwidth.

1. INTRODUCTION

Recently, indoor wireless localization systems have broken the meter accuracy barrier both for Wi-Fi devices [18, 58, 59] and RFID tags [52, 53, 62], but to achieve these results, require some combination of many access points (APs) and antennas, very long antenna arrays, and/or an RF environment without too many obstacles blocking client-AP lines of sight.

While recent systems have broken the meter accuracy barrier with angle-of-arrival (AoA) and other types of signal processing analysis, time-of-arrival (ToA) analysis promises to improve accuracy even further. ToA has a particular challenge, however, as shown in Table 1: for a typical 802.11a/g Wi-Fi channel with only 20 MHz bandwidth, the signal is sampled once every 50 nanoseconds, during which the signal travels a full 15 meters. As the next rows of the table show, later 802.11n/ac standards enhance this resolution, but still achieve just 1.9 meters of raw sample resolution. Super-resolution spectral signal processing algorithms such as MUSIC [25, 41] and matrix-pencil [39] can enhance this raw sample resolution by an approximate factor of $2\times$, but still achieve an accuracy proportional to the raw sample spatial resolution shown in Table 1, limiting the utility of ToA analysis. Even ultra-wideband (UWB) systems that sample at a rate of 500 MHz and up achieve just 60 cm raw spatial resolution. Focusing on ToA analysis, this paper questions whether we can do better.

The opportunity we leverage in this work is that tomorrow's wireless networks will make adaptive and opportunistic use of a large variety of frequency bandwidths, ranging from narrow 5 MHz channels intended for the exclusive use of one mobile user at a time, to expansive 160 MHz channels shared between users with CSMA. Indeed, the use of narrow frequency-bandwidth channels is now commonplace: Wi-Fi [6, 9, 46] and cellular systems divide the wireless medium into fine-grained time-frequency blocks, conferring many benefits such as reducing fixed-airtime MAC overheads, increasing signal-to-noise ratio (SNR), and allowing for channel assignment algorithms to optimize throughput for many users. Furthermore, the use of wide-bandwidth channels has also emerged.

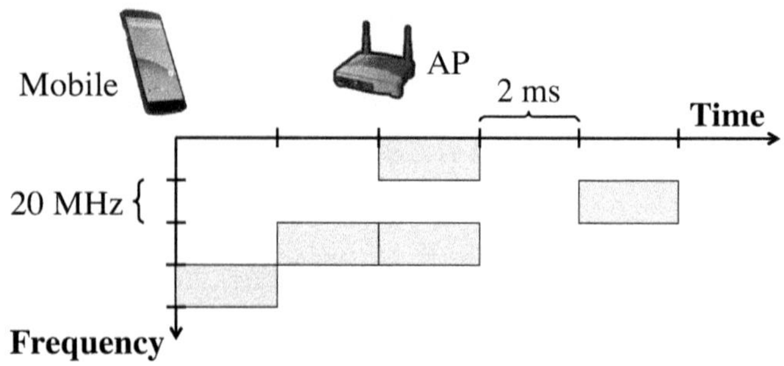

Figure 1: A Wi-Fi mobile hops across 80 MHz of bandwidth in 10 ms in order to avoid other competing Wi-Fi users and in-band interference. Cellular LTE mobiles use a similar strategy for similar reasons. ToneTrack leverages in-band frequency hopping to improve indoor localization accuracy.

The 802.11ac standard [16] specifies transmission bandwidths from 20 to 160 MHz, even allowing two non-contiguous 80 MHz channels to be aggregated together as one 160 MHz channel. Dynamic Frequency Selection (DFS) in the 5.250–5.725 MHz band lets Wi-Fi radios hop channels to avoid any nearby military radar.

In this paper, we present *ToneTrack*, an indoor localization system that leverages frequency-agile wireless networks to enhance the accuracy of indoor localization. ToneTrack measures the ToA of a client's transmission at pairs of APs in the network. In order to do this, it analyzes the correlation between incoming signals on different subcarriers as MUSIC does, but in the frequency domain. This allows ToneTrack to achieve higher time-of-arrival accuracy than simply looking at the sample index of packet detection or channel impulse response. But as noted above, even with super-resolution MUSIC scheme, frequency bandwidth still limits the resolution that ToA algorithms can achieve.

To increase the bandwidth available for time-based localization, ToneTrack contributes a novel signal combination scheme that combines data from a device as it hops across different channels in a frequency band, as shown in Figure 1.[1] The result is that ToneTrack can achieve gains in time resolution that are proportional to the number of channels hopped across when transmitting within a channel coherence time.

After extracting a ToA profile of the mobile device's signal from each AP, ToneTrack analyzes each profile individually. Even when multipath reflections arrive too close in time to the direct path and super-resolution schemes reach their resolution limits, failing to resolve all the paths correctly, ToneTrack is still able to identify the useful data therein, retrieving relatively accurate information despite inaccuracy in the overall ToA profile. Here novel peak classification algorithms identify the accurate direct-path peak in the time-of-arrival profile and retain it for further processing.

Lastly, ToneTrack compares TDoA readings across pairs of APs in the network in order to estimate and refine the mobile client's location. Most prior indoor localization work cope with multipath reflections when both reflection paths and direct path exist. The direct path signal may get attenuated but does exist. However, the direct path signal sometimes gets 100% blocked which is even more challenging. ToneTrack employs the classical triangle inequality property to identify the APs with whose direct path is completely blocked, improving accuracy in this most challenging situation. Then clustering, outlier rejection, and averaging complete the processing chain, yielding the location estimate from a mobile client's transmission. ToneTrack does not require any offline training: preamble data from one to three packets suffice, making the approach amenable to real-time tracking.

Contributions. To summarize, ToneTrack contributes the following novel design elements:

1. A frequency (tone) combining algorithm that allows a ToA/TDoA method to increase the bandwidth it may utilize for finer accuracy without increasing the radio's sampling rate (§2.3).
2. Retrieve useful information from the inaccurate ToA spectrum profile even when the super-resolution scheme reaches the resolution limit (§2.4).
3. A triangle inequality-based method together with outlier rejection scheme for identifying and discarding the AP to which a client's line of sight transmission is completely blocked (§2.5).

Roadmap. The rest of this paper begins with our system design (§2) and implementation (§3). Our evaluation (§4) in an indoor 20×25 meter office testbed demonstrates a 90 cm median localization accuracy with four APs, each equipped with one antenna and overhearing three packets transmitted at adjacent channels with 20 MHz bandwidth. We survey related work in the area in Section 5 before concluding (§6).

2. DESIGN

This section presents the design of ToneTrack, starting with a system description (§2.1) before delving into ToneTrack's constituent parts: super-resolution ToA processing (§2.2), channel combination (§2.3), spectrum identification (§2.4), and multi-AP data fusion (§2.5).

2.1 System design

ToneTrack is designed as a passive system that listens to mobile clients' transmissions at nearby APs. Thus the system requires no additional wireless channel overhead for deployment in a production wireless local-area network. Figure 2 shows the high-level system design: upon hearing multiple packet transmissions on different channels from a mobile device, an AP forwards the packets to the backend server over a backhaul wired network, appended with timestamps. Then, once the backend server receives this data within a channel coherence time, it passes them to the channel combination step described in Section 2.3 to generate a high-resolution time of arrival profile. Next, novel algorithms determine whether the resulting ToA profile is in fact accurate, or alternately, contains an accurate part useful for localization, even when the overall ToA profile is inaccurate (§2.4). After that, the ToneTrack controller combines the ToA information collected at pairs of APs into TDoA estimates. In Figure 2, the hyperbolic curve labeled "AP 1/2" denotes the possible loci of the mobile based on AP 1 and AP 2's TDoA and the hyperbolic curve labeled "AP 1/3" denotes the possible loci of the mobile based on AP 1 and AP 3's TDoA. Finally, the server processes the TDoA estimates across pairs of APs using geometrical reasoning (triangle inequality), clustering and outlier rejection schemes (§2.5), yielding a final location estimate.

2.2 ToA estimation

Once a client's transmission arrives at an AP, ToneTrack measures the time of arrival (*ToA*) of a client's transmission at one AP: this section describes this process in detail.

2.2.1 *Primer: MUSIC in the frequency domain*

We begin with the classical MUSIC algorithm [25, 41], which models the multipath indoor radio propagation channel $h(t)$ as the sum

[1]Hopping between channels within a frequency band allows deployment with just a single kind of antenna.

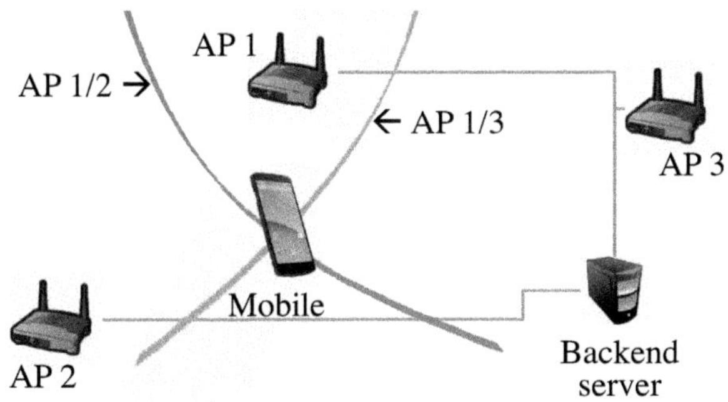

Figure 2: *High-level design of ToneTrack.* APs overhear a packet transmission from a mobile and pass the packets to the backend server to run a time-of-arrival (ToA) estimation algorithm, combining the resulting hyperbolic loci (labeled in the figure with their originating AP pairs) for a location estimate.

of D attenuated and delayed impulse responses:

$$h(t) = \sum_{k=1}^{D} \alpha_k \delta(t - \tau_k). \tag{1}$$

Here α_k and τ_k are the complex attenuation and propagation delay of the kth path. For simplicity, in this section we describe ToneTrack's operation over one Wi-Fi channel. Later sections generalize to multiple Wi-Fi channels.

Processing starts with the per-subcarrier channel response of Equation 1 in the frequency domain:

$$\mathbf{H}[f_n] = \sum_{k=1}^{D} \alpha_k e^{-j2\pi(f_0+n\Delta f)\tau_k}. \tag{2}$$

Here, f_n and Δf are the carrier frequency and the size of subcarrier bandwidth, respectively. We estimate $\mathbf{H}[f_n]$ by taking the DFT of the received 64-sample 802.11 long training symbol and dividing, per-subcarrier, by the known transmitted long training symbol. We denote this estimate as $\hat{\mathbf{H}}[f_n]$. In 802.11a/g, 52 out of 64 subcarriers contain preamble information; we employ all of them in the processing that follows. The *subcarrier correlation matrix* $\mathbf{R_{HH}}$ then measures phase changes between different subcarriers:

$$\mathbf{R_{HH}} = E\{\hat{\mathbf{H}}[f_n]\hat{\mathbf{H}}^*[f_n]\}, \tag{3}$$

where the expectation is calculated across multiple OFDM symbols (spaced in time).

Suppose D copies (direct path and reelection paths) of a transmission $s_1, \ldots, s_D$ arrive at the AP's antenna at D respective times $t_1, \ldots, t_D$, and further suppose the OFDM symbol of the transmission contains M subcarriers ($M > D$) so all copies of the transmission can be captured. Eigenanalysis of the subcarrier correlation matrix $\mathbf{R_{HH}}$ at the AP then results in M eigenvalues associated respectively with M eigenvectors $\mathbf{E} = [\mathbf{e}_1\ \mathbf{e}_2\ \cdots\ \mathbf{e}_M]$. If we sort the eigenvalues in non-decreasing order, the smallest $M - D$ eigenvalues tend to correspond to background noise while the next D eigenvalues tend to correspond to the D incoming copies of the mobile's transmission. Based on this process, the corresponding eigenvectors in $\mathbf{E}$ are classified as noise subspace and signal subspace:

$$\mathbf{E} = \left[\overbrace{e_1 \ldots e_{M-D}}^{\mathbf{E}_N}\ \overbrace{e_{M-D+1} \cdots e_M}^{\mathbf{E}_S}\right] \tag{4}$$

We refer to $\mathbf{E}_N$ as the *noise subspace* and $\mathbf{E}_S$ as the *signal subspace*. We define a *time steering vector* $\mathbf{a}(\tau)$ that represents the channel's

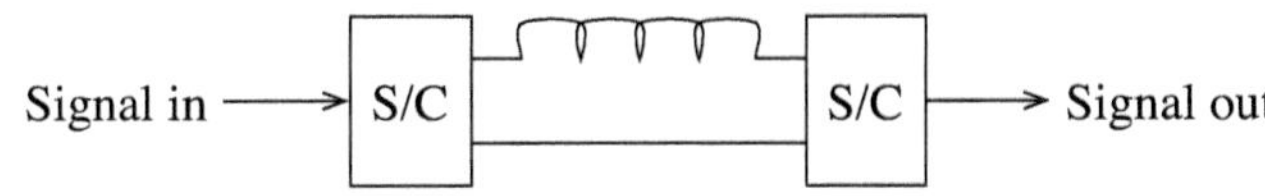

Figure 3: A simple two-tap channel emulator: An RF splitter-combiner ("S/C") splits an incoming signals into two branches: one travels over the longer (upper) cabled path, the other travels over the shorter (lower) cabled path. This network models an idealized wireless channel with two paths (one direct path and one reflection path), of varying differential path length.

response to a signal arriving at time τ:

$$\mathbf{a}(\tau) = \begin{bmatrix} 1 \\ \exp(-j2\pi\tau\Delta f) \\ \vdots \\ \exp(-j2(M-1)\pi\tau\Delta f) \end{bmatrix} \tag{5}$$

The *time steering vector* $\mathbf{a}(\tau)$ is in the signal subspace and is orthogonal to the noise subspace when τ exactly coincides with each time of arrival of the signal. The *MUSIC ToA spectrum* then measures the distance (in a vector space defined by the array correlation matrix above) between the time steering vector and the noise subspace, as τ varies, thus estimating the time arrival of multiple signals with a granularity of our own choosing:

$$P(\tau) = \frac{1}{\mathbf{a}(\tau)^H \mathbf{E}_N \mathbf{E}_N^H \mathbf{a}(\tau)}. \tag{6}$$

With the steering vector and noise subspace vector in the denominator, $P(\tau)$ generates peaks when the steering vector is orthogonal to the noise subspace vector which happens when τ coincides with the time of arrivals of the incoming signals.

Limitations of MUSIC's super-resolution capability. MUSIC is informally known as a *super-resolution* algorithm. The τ variable in Equation 6 can vary in steps of our own choosing smaller than the sampling period shown in Table 1. But this does not imply MUSIC is able to resolve multipaths with arbitrarily small time delay differences. The frequency bandwidth of the received transmission and background noise imposes a resolution limit independent of τ's step size chosen.

To probe this limit in a controlled experimental setting, we use the simple channel emulation setup shown in Figure 3. An RF splitter-combiner first splits a wired signal into two equal components, one of which travels over a longer cabled path than the other. A second RF splitter-combiner then combines the two signals together, where they are received and processed with MUSIC algorithm. We use different cable lengths[2] to control the relative path lengths, and attenuators to control the respective path signal strengths to the same level.

Decreasing the path length difference from 13.5 m (44 ft.) gradually to 2.7 m (8.8 ft.) results in the MUSIC pseudospectra shown in Figure 4. We see from the figure that MUSIC is able to resolve both paths quite accurately when their lengths are sufficiently different, but once the path length difference between the two signals is decreased to around six meters (20 ft.), MUSIC is not able to generate accurate pseudospectra anymore: its two spectrum peaks half-merge in Figure 4 (c) and (d), moving away from ground-truth. When we further decrease the path length difference, the two peaks fully merge into one peak in Figure 4 (e).

[2]Because of lower transmission speed in cable, we translate cable length to equivalent air propagation distance. (The delay of a 1.8 m RG-58 cable is equivalent to 2.7 m propagation delay in the air).

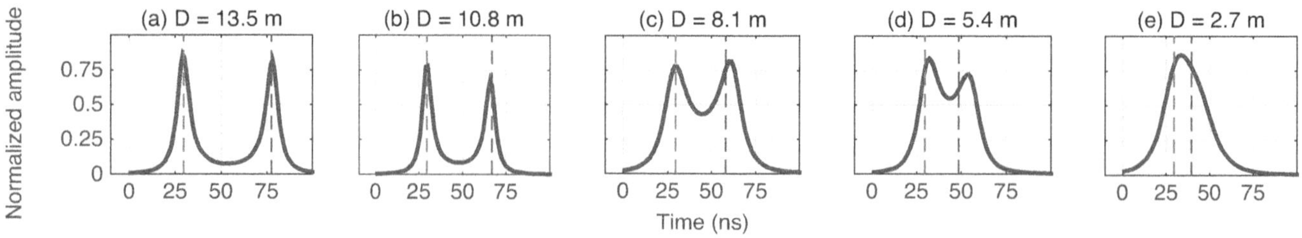

Figure 4: *MUSIC's resolution limit.* At 20 MHz bandwidth, MUSIC loses the ability to resolve two paths with a length difference of less than about six meters (20 ft). We denote the two ground-truth path lengths with dotted vertical lines.

2.3 Channel combination

To overcome the limitations of MUSIC's super-resolution capability noted above in Section 2.2.1, ToneTrack leverages the frequency agility of upcoming Wi-Fi, LTE, and white-space radios as they hop between different frequencies in short periods of time. Note that if frequency hopping happens within a channel coherence time, the ToA spectra generated are very similar, but each is a low-resolution picture of the ToA. The basic idea of ToneTrack's channel combination technique is to combine multiple frequency-agile transmissions from the client to form a virtual wider bandwidth transmission, without increasing the sampling rate. Since the effective *array aperture* of MUSIC's ToA estimate is proportional to the number of subcarriers measured (*i.e.*, the bandwidth), time resolution ought to scale linearly with bandwidth. However, naïvely concatenating data from two channels does not work: we need to align them in both time and frequency domain in order for the combined data to yield a better resolution in the ToA spectrum plot.

Alignment in time domain. While standard packet detection algorithms [40] can synchronize to sample level at typical baseband sampling rates, ToneTrack requires sub-sample level time alignment of the two overheard signals for combination.

Since the data are recorded at the same radio at different times, there are different fractional (sub-sample) time delays introduced to each set of data. In order to combine data, we need to remove this random time difference. As these two groups of data are recorded within a small time interval, the relative amplitudes of the peaks on the spectra are stable. We apply standard fractional interpolation methods [22] to align the two signals based on their respective ToA spectra. Sub-sample interpolation of the raw data in the time domain causes the whole ToA spectrum to move in time. One sample shift is corresponding to a spectrum movement of 50 ns at 20 MHz. We measure the time difference (in ns) of the largest peak position on each of the two spectra. We then align the two sets of data in the time domain, matching the two largest peaks to the same position by a corresponding sub-sample interpolation of the raw data. As demonstrated in Figure 5 (b1) and (b2), with a single signal, time domain alignment equalizes the slopes of the two groups of sub-carrier phases.

To see why this is the case, consider a measurement of phase in the frequency domain. Looking across subcarriers of separation Δ_f, the time-shifting property of the DFT

$$H[k]e^{2\pi j\tau_0 k/N} \xleftrightarrow{\mathscr{F}} h[(n-\tau_0)_N] \tag{7}$$

tells us that if there is only one signal, phase at the AP changes linearly across subcarriers as $2\pi\Delta_f\tau_0/N$ where the slope of the phase is proportional to propagation time τ_0.

Alignment in frequency domain. Unfortunately, concatenating even time-aligned data from adjacent channels fails again, yielding completely inaccurate and noisy ToA spectra. We need to estimate

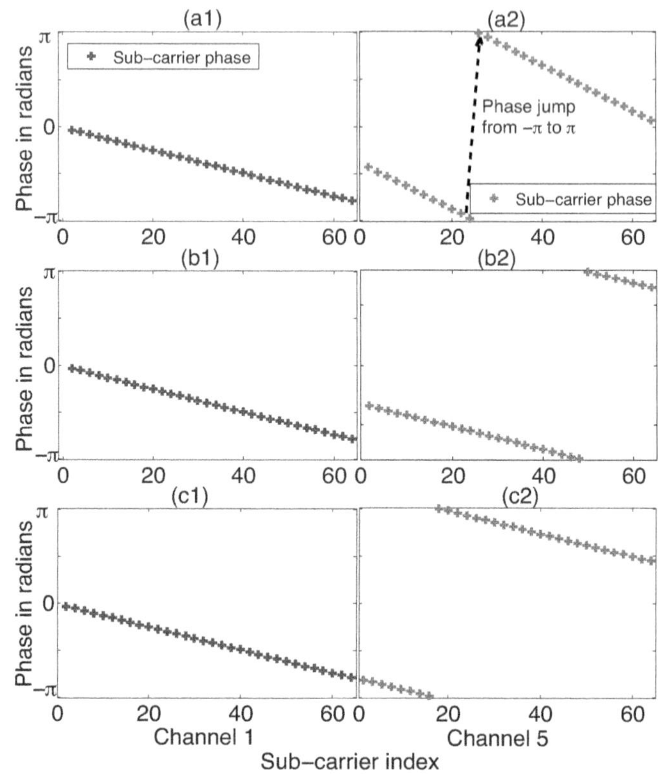

Figure 5: *ToneTrack's channel combination scheme.* Time domain alignment equalizes the slope of the phase in the frequency domain between channels, as shown in *(b1)* and *(b2)*. Subsequent frequency domain alignment removes the phase offset and enables successful concatenation of data as shown in *(c1)* and *(c2)*.

the phase of the sub-carrier just after the last sub-carrier of the first channel. Then we align the phase of the first sub-carrier of the second channel to the estimated one by subtracting the phase offset. This concept is demonstrated in Figure 5 (c1) and (c2) with data from two channels fully aligned in both time and frequency domains. With this step, the two groups of channel response data can now be concatenated to yield better resolution than any one alone. We form a larger virtual bandwidth without increasing the radio's sampling rate. When multipaths are present, the phase change becomes highly non-linear since it is the superposition of many paths of varying magnitude and phase. Our insight is that since this superposition remains continuous across channels in phase, ToneTrack can still align the two groups of data by matching the phase of the last sub-carriers in the first group of data to the first sub-carrier in the second group of data. With the scheme described here, we are

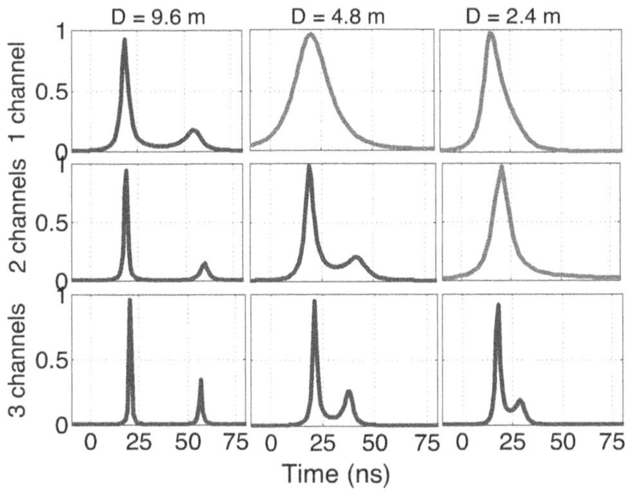

Figure 6: ToneTrack's channel combination scheme effectively increases the resolution capability of MUSIC, as tested by varying the path length difference d in our two-tap channel emulator. Red curves denote ToA spectra where peaks have problematically merged and MUSIC is not able to resolve them correctly.

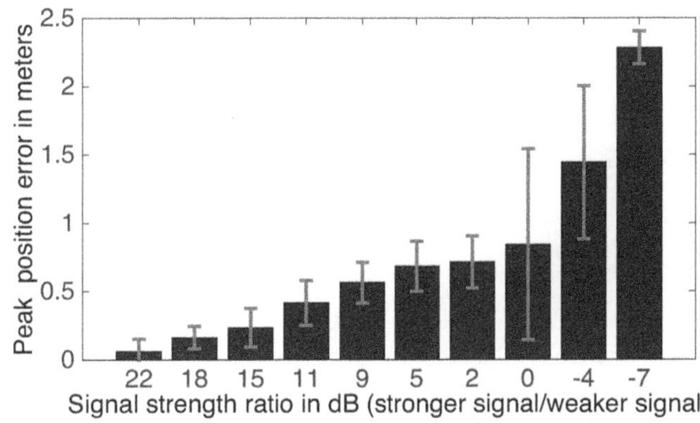

Figure 7: Peak position error when two peaks merged into one, as a function of the relative strength of the two peaks.

able to concatenate multiple groups of data from adjacent channels seamlessly to perform like one single larger bandwidth channel.

2.3.1 *Channel combining microbenchmark*

We demonstrate the effectiveness of ToneTrack's channel combination with the microbenchmark results shown in Figure 6. In the first row, with one single 20 MHz channel, ToneTrack fails to resolve both signals when the path difference D between the signals decreases to 4.8 meters (15.8 feet). With the channel combination scheme applied with two channels, ToneTrack successfully resolves both two signals at $D = 4.8$ meters but fails to resolve when the difference decreases to 2.4 m. With three channels, ToneTrack is able to resolve two signals separated by only a 2.4 m (7.9 feet) path length difference. Our end-to-end localization results in Section 4.2 leverage this channel combining algorithm to markedly improve ToneTrack's accuracy level. The channel combination process at each AP is fully independent of the data fusion process later in Section 2.5 across multiple APs.

There is no limit on the number of channels can be employed for combination in ToneTrack. Our current implementation is based on 2.4 GHz and thus we employ channels 1, 5 and 9 for experiments. The spectrum range available in 2.4 GHz for Wi-Fi is small. We may include channel 11 to further add 10 MHz to the combination. The spectrum range in 5 GHz is much larger and more channels can be combined for higher accuracy.

2.3.2 *Overlapping and non-adjacent channels*

In the case of overlapping channels that may result when the mobile changes its center frequency by an amount less than the bandwidth of its transmissions, it is clear that ToneTrack's channel combining technique generalizes by averaging the channel information in the tones the two transmissions have in common. Then the two overlapping channels can be converted into two equivalent adjacent channels in terms of localization with the overlapping part removed from one channel.

We briefly discuss how our scheme can be generalized to sets of channels that are non-adjacent. The steering vector needs to be modified to reflect the different subcarrier separation between non-adjacent channels. This has the drawback of multiplying the number of peaks in the ToA spectrum, in a way analogous to the grating lobes problem RF-IDraw solves for AoA spectra [53]. Frequency domain alignment is challenging as it's not easy to estimate the correct amount of offset as the phase change is non-linear with strong multipaths. We leave the design and evaluation of non-adjacent channel combination in ToA as future work.

2.4 Spectrum identification

We now describe the processing ToneTrack performs on the ToA profile computed in §2.2 and §2.3 to determine whether the spectrum is accurate and if not, whether we can still retrieve relatively accurate direct-path information from the spectrum. We term this processing *spectrum identification*. As noted in Section 2.2, when the lengths of a line-of-sight path and a reflected path are too close to each other, MUSIC is unable to resolve the two signals correctly in the time domain on the pseudospectrum. This leads to either inaccurate pseudospectrum peak positions or multiple peaks merge. However, ToneTrack leverages the insight that we can sometimes still retrieve useful and relative accurate information from these *inaccurate* pseudospectra.

2.4.1 *Merged-signal peaks*

We first observe that when the two paths' peaks merge into one as shown in Figure 6, as long as the first (direct) path signal is stronger, the error in the peak position is still small. We use the simple two-tap channel emulator of Figure 3 to quantify this experimentally. In Figure 7, we vary the relative signal strength between the direct path and a reflection path 2.7 meters longer, starting from +22 dB (*i.e.*, direct path 22 dB stronger than reflection path) down to -7 dB (*i.e.*, reflection path 7 dB stronger than reflection path). The results in Figure 7 show that the error is well under one meter as long as the direct-path signal is stronger. The error increases significantly when the reflection path is stronger, up to 2.3 meters.

After we identify a merged peak, we measure the *skew direction* of the peak as shown in Figure 8 by finding the peak position and the two midpoints at which the peak amplitude falls by half (this is also known as the -3 *dB beamwidth*). By comparing the distance of the peak position to the two 3 dB beamwidth midpoints, we measure the direction of the peak's skew: a peak position falling to the right of the -3 dB beamwidth's midpoint as shown in Figure 8 (a) indicates that the first peak, which corresponds to the direct path, has merged into a later peak (which corresponds to a reflection path). ToneTrack identifies this merged peak as inaccurate and thus useless. The blue plot shows a spectrum skewing earlier in time (merged towards the direct-path peak). In this case

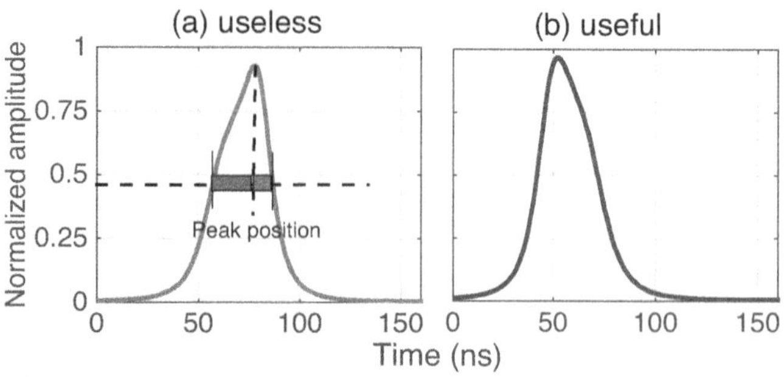

Figure 8: Merged-signal peaks. ToneTrack classifies useful spectra by the skew direction (earlier or later) of a merged peak: *(a)* the first (direct path) peak has merged into a later (reflection path) peak, or *(b)* a later (reflection path) peak has merged into the first (direct path) peak.

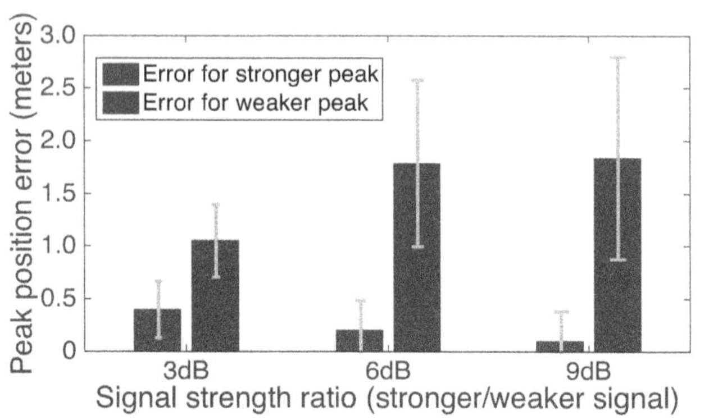

Figure 9: Peak error (translated from time to meters) for separated peaks in the simple two-tap channel emulator, when the direct path and the first-arriving reflection path are separated but arrive too close in time for MUSIC to accurately resolve.

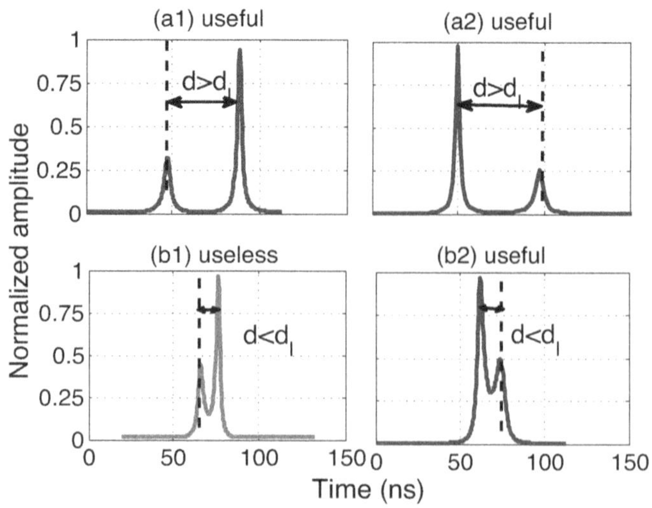

Figure 10: The peak separation d is greater than the resolution limit d_l, both (a1) and (a2) are kept. If the d is smaller than d_l, ToneTrack identifies useful ToA spectra by comparing their respective amplitudes and (b1) is discarded.

the peak has a reasonably small error, and can thus still be kept for localization even it's a peak merged with two signals.

2.4.2 *Single-signal peaks*

If the two peaks are separated by more than the MUSIC resolution limit[3] as shown in Figure 10 (a1) and (a2), then MUSIC can accurately estimate their respective positions, and we feed the position of the first, direct-path peak to the next processing stage. But if the two peak positions are separated by less than the resolution limit as shown in Figure 10 (b1) and (b2), they fall into the zone that MUSIC is not able to resolve accurately.

Often, the direct path and reflection path signals have differing amplitudes. We anecdotally observe that even when the two peaks are too close for MUSIC to resolve, the larger peak on the pseudospectrum corresponding to the stronger signal is still quite accurate compared to the smaller peak. We validate this observation empirically in the simple two-tap channel emulator of Figure 3 with the following microbenchmark. We fix the path length difference between the direct-path and reflection-path signals to be 5.4 m (18 ft), then adjust the relative signal strength between the direct and reflection paths from 3 dB to 9 dB and show the peak position error in Figure 9. We see clearly that when the direct path signal is stronger, although MUSIC is not able to resolve both of them correctly, the error of the direct-path peak is quite small (less than 0.5 m). On the other hand, the smaller reflection path peak has a much larger error, so we can still extract relatively accurate information from the MUSIC spectrum in these scenarios as we only care the direct-path peak. Referring to Figure 10 (b1) and (b2), when the separated peaks are closer than the resolution limit, ToneTrack compares the relative amplitudes of the two. If the amplitude of the first peak is greater than the second peak as in (b2), ToneTrack marks the ToA spectrum as useful; otherwise it discards the ToA spectrum such as in (b1). Referring again to the signals with a 3 dB difference in Figure 9, this bounds the error due to the presence of the second peak to well below one meter.

2.4.3 *Classifying peaks as merged or single-signal*

To apply the above spectrum identification technique, ToneTrack needs to estimate whether a certain peak arises from a single path or is the result of the respective peaks of multiple arrivals merging together in the ToA spectrum. Prior theoretical work [1] has shown that the beamwidth of the MUSIC spectrum is inversely proportional to the square root of SNR and the bandwidth of the signal. Consequently, within the SNR range ToneTrack operates at, a single-signal peak will be thinner compared to a merged peak, even if the merged peak originates from two closely-spaced signals. For example, the difference is apparent when we compare the red merged peaks in Figure 6 with blue peaks. ToneTrack thus measures the peak's -3 dB beamwidth $W_{-3\text{ dB}}$ and compares it with a threshold value W_t to make the decision:

$$W_{-3\text{ dB}} > W_t : \text{Merged peak.}$$
$$W_{-3\text{ dB}} \leq W_t : \text{Single peak.}$$

Using microbenchmarks measuring the impact of SNR and the path difference of the two signals on W_t, we experimentally determine the best value for W_t in Section 4.3, and show that it produces good end-to-end performance in our indoor testbed in Section 4.2.

2.4.4 *Algorithm* (Spectrum Identification)

As the preceding microbenchmarks show, useful and accurate information can still be retrieved even when MUSIC fails to resolve all the signals correctly, as long as information about the direct path peak is relatively accurate. In this section we summarize ToneTrack's *spectrum identification* algorithm, which comprises the pro-

[3]We experimentally verified that at 20 MHz at medium-high SNRs, this resolution limit is stable and measured to be around 6 m.

cessing ToneTrack performs on each (possibly channel-combined, *cf.* §2.3) ToA spectrum from a single AP before passing that ToA spectrum on to the multi-AP data fusion step described next in Section 2.5.

Step 1. Isolate the first two peaks on the ToA spectrum as input to the algorithm. If the two peak positions are separated by greater than the resolution limit, then the first peak contains accurate direct-path distance information, so ToneTrack retains the spectrum and proceed to Step 3. Otherwise, the two peak positions are separated by a distance less than resolution limit (which MUSIC is not able to resolve accurately) so we proceed to Step 2:

Step 2. Compare the relative amplitudes of the two peaks. From the microbenchmarks, we know that as long as the direct path signal is stronger than the reflection path signal, the direct-path peak position will be more accurate. So ToneTrack retains the spectrum if and only if the first peak's amplitude exceeds the second's.

Step 3. Check whether the first peak is a single-signal peak or a merged peak (§2.4.3). ToneTrack retains the spectrum and the algorithm terminates in this step if the peak is a single-signal peak. Otherwise, we proceed to Step 4:

Step 4. Check the direction of the peak's skew (§2.4.1). ToneTrack retains the spectrum if and only if the peak is merged towards the direct path (left side).

After the above steps, only the useful peak remains. At this point ToneTrack sends the ToA spectrum to the multi-AP data fusion step described next.

2.5 Multi-AP data fusion

In this final stage of processing, ToneTrack converts measured ToAs from each AP into distance differences between pairs of APs, using these distance differences to estimate the mobile's location. Occasionally, the direct-path signal may be totally blocked, with only reflection signals detectable at the AP. We propose the following two methods to handle this very challenging scenario.

2.5.1 *Triangle inequality*

As shown in Figure 11(a), when both APs are able to resolve the direct-path signals from the mobile client, the distance estimates to AP 1 and AP 2 (d_1 and d_2, respectively), fit the following triangle inequality property:

$$d_1 + a_{12} \geq d_2, \quad (8)$$

where a_{12} is the distance between APs 1 and 2, which is known. However, when the direct path to AP 2 is completely blocked and only one or more reflection paths exist, as shown in Figure 11(b), the resulting distance estimates may violate this triangle inequality, *i.e.*, $d_1 + a_{12} < d_2$. Whenever we detect such a violation of the triangle inequality, we tag the violating AP (AP 2 in this example) as having its direct path completely blocked, and exclude it from further processing in the chain. We note that it is also possible that when the direct path to AP 2 is blocked, the triangle inequality may not necessarily be violated, and so while this test is conservative in the APs it excludes (thus aiding performance), it is not comprehensive in the elimination of direct path blockage scenarios. With more group of APs, the chance of detection of the blocked APs is higher. Also this scheme may fail when multiple APs are 100% blocked. However, the chance that multiple APs are blocked at the same time is quite low as the APs are usually placed at different locations, and our end-to-end evaluation suffers from these effects as and when they happen in practice. We note here that this method

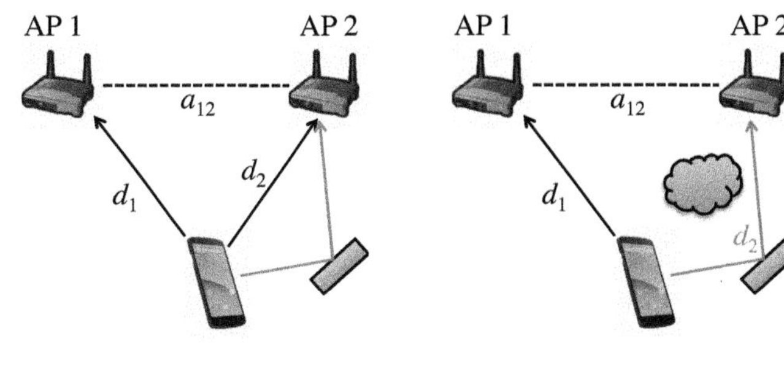

(a) No △ violation. **(b)** △ violation.

Figure 11: The classical triangle inequality can identify APs whose direct path to the client must be blocked.

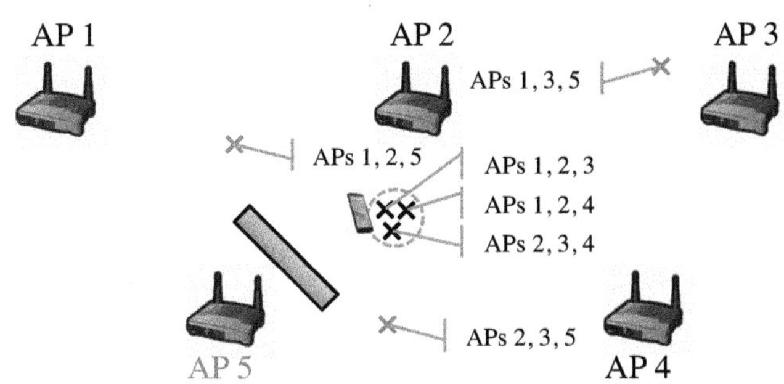

Figure 12: Employing clustering and outlier rejection to remove non-accurate estimates.

has very recently been applied to ToA-based ultrasound positioning [54] and we would like to apply this method to TDoA-based Wi-Fi localization in ToneTrack.

2.5.2 *Clustering and outlier rejection*

Clustering and outlier rejection further reduce the error caused by a complete blockage of the direct path signal and errors from other sources. This is based on the fact that the direct path signals of multiple APs will localize the clients close to the true source location, while reflection path signal will localize the client at random locations. As shown in Figure 12, APs 1, 2, 3 and 4 all have direct path signals while AP 5 has direct path signal blocked. Its estimates with any three APs from {1, 2, 3 and 4} will be around the true location of the mobile. A location estimate from involving AP 5 will be far away from the true location, and can be detected and removed. We can even detect the AP with direct path totally blocked. Note that we need at least four APs whose direct paths are not blocked in order to detect the blocked AP. When the number of available APs is large, the number of combinations ToneTrack needs to check can be very large. One solution to this problem is to remove some APs with small signal strength and only keep the rest for outlier rejection purposes.

2.5.3 *Final location estimation*

As noted above in Section 2.1, each pair of APs yields one TDoA estimate in the shape of a hyperbolic arc. Thus three APs are able to localize the client at the intersection of two hyperbolas.[4] Both closed form solutions and iterative algorithms can be found in [5, 31, 42]. We leverage a closed form solution in 2-D space similar to prior work [31]. With any group of three APs, we have one intersection from two hyperbolas. If we have more than four APs,

[4]If there is no intersection, we discard data from that triplet of APs.

we apply the scheme described in Section 2.5.1 and Section 2.5.2 to detect the 100% blocked AP and remove it from localization. Then we average the location estimates with all combination of three APs. When only four APs exist, the scheme described in Section 2.5.2 can not be applied. We then adopt a simple clustering algorithm to choose a group of three estimates which yields the minimum sum of distances and average them.

From ToA to TDoA. ToneTrack is based on time-difference-of-arrival (TDoA) between the mobile transmission's arrival at each pair of APs. In order to compute TDoA, ToneTrack relies on a time-synchronization mechanism between APs. This is achieved by either a wireless protocol such as SourceSync, which can achieve 5 -10 ns (95th percentile) synchronization error at a typical wireless SNR ratio of 20 dB [36], or the Ethernet-based Precision Time Protocol standardized as IEEE 1588, which Broadcom has shown can provide a five nanosecond time synchronization error [4]. Other schemes include time-synchronization with light [26] and the use of distributed antenna system (DAS) [61] to bypass this time synchronization problem.

The computational load of ToneTrack is mainly a matrix multiplication of size 64 x 64. We note that with channels combined together, the matrix size is increased linearly. When there are many channels, we recommend selecting one sub-carrier out of every N adjacent sub-carriers evenly to reduce the matrix size. When there are many APs, the number of combinations for outlier rejection scheme is large which impedes ToneTrack's real-time objective. We thus only keep a limited number of APs based on the signal strengths as higher SNR presents us more accurate spectrum.

3. IMPLEMENTATION

ToneTrack is implemented on the Rice WARP platform [38] with WARPLab version 7.3. We employ a small part of the preamble of a packet which is the most robust part for our localization. For the long training symbol (LTS) in the preamble, only the middle 52 out of 64 sub-carriers are actually used. With the original LTS, only 52/64 $\times$ 20 MHz = 16.25 MHz bandwidth would be used for localization. In order to use all subcarriers, we build one symbol very similar to the LTS in 802.11 but with all the 64 subcarriers occupied. We attach this symbol just after the original LTS, incurring less than 0.1% overhead in a 1500-byte packet.

We employ five WARPs, one as the transmitter (client) and four as the receivers (APs). The carrier frequency offsets between the WARP transmitter and receivers are measured in the range of serval hundreds to several thousands of Hertz. It is much smaller than the sub-carrier size (312.5 kHz) and hence has very little effect on the ToA spectrum. So a carrier frequency offset (CFO) between mobile and AP, and pairs of APs is not a problem for ToneTrack. Each WARP kit is also attached with the FMC-RF-2X245 module to enable four radios on each board as shown in Figure 13. We connect the antennas to the WARPs with low loss LMR-400 coaxial cables. All the data recorded at the APs are retrieved through Ethernet connections between the WARPs and the server. Our super-resolution MUSIC, spectrum identification (SI), triangle inequality (TI) and clustering schemes are implemented on the server side.

AP Calibration. Due to the nonlinearity of the receiver front end across each subcarrier, we need to calibrate the channel frequency response in terms of both amplitude and phase. Note that this calibration is a one-time effort for one power-on-off cycle of the WARP. We describe our calibration steps briefly here. First, we connect the radio of the transmitter to the radio of the receiver with an RF cable. Then, we calculate the channel frequency response for each sub-carrier and calibrate the phases across each subcarrier into exact linear relationship with the right slope. The slope can be calculated as $2\pi\Delta ft$, where Δf is the sub-carrier size and t is the signal propagation time which can be calculated carefully by measuring the length of the cable attached between the transmitter and the receiver, adding a correction for the small extra path length caused by the splitter and the internal circuitry of the WARP radios. We also calibrate the amplitude of the frequency response across each subcarrier to be equal. After calibration, we are able to achieve a very sharp time of arrival spectrum close to a line with only one signal transmitted through cables. This front-end linear calibration can be restricted only to ToneTrack processing. The calibration does not factor into the transmit waveform either. The calibration coefficients are calculated as phases and amplitudes for each sub-carrier and we only apply them when ToneTrack processing is called.

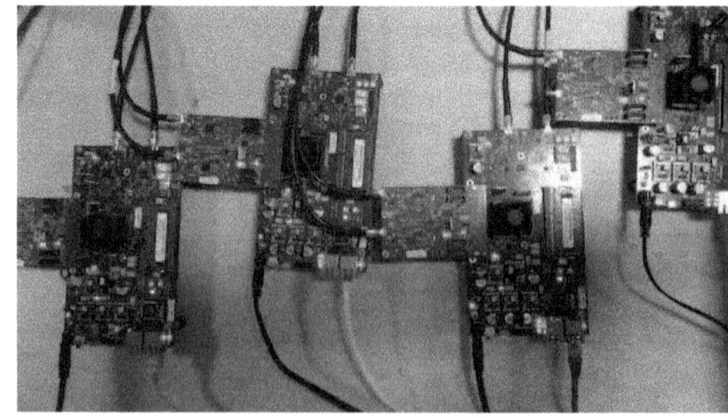

Figure 13: Each AP is a latest WARP v3 Kit with FMC-RF-2X245 module to enable 4 radios. Antennas are placed at the dedicated AP positions with low loss LMR-400 cables.

4. EVALUATION

To show how well ToneTrack performs in real indoor environment, we present the results from the testbed described in Section 3. First we present our evaluation methodology. Then we show our main results in Section 4.2 which answer the following:

1. What is the overall end-to-end performance with channel combination (§4.2)?
2. How much is spectrum identification scheme helping ToneTrack (§4.2.2)?
3. How does our triangle inequality scheme perform in identifying the APs with direct path totally blocked (§4.2.3)?
4. Will increasing numbers of APs improve performance (§4.2.4)?
5. What is the performance of ToneTrack with different levels of time synchronization errors between APs (§4.2.5)?

After we present our main results, we justify our choice of W_t in Section 4.3.

4.1 Experimental methodology

For our experiments, three radios on each AP is utilized to receive signals at channels 1, 5 and 9 respectively. The three radios are connected to a single antenna with combiners. The transmitter either hops across frequencies with one radio, transmitting on three channels sequentially or transmits simultaneously on all three channels with three radios. At each AP position, we collect both data traces from frequency hopping and traces from simultaneous transmissions at multiple channels. They don't have obvious performance difference. Our results presented here include all the traces.

We place the APs in a 25 $\times$ 20 m office, denoting them with numbers shown in Figure 14. We place clients at 40 randomly-chosen locations denoting their positions as red dots on the floor plan. 12 clients are not in the same room as the APs, with at least

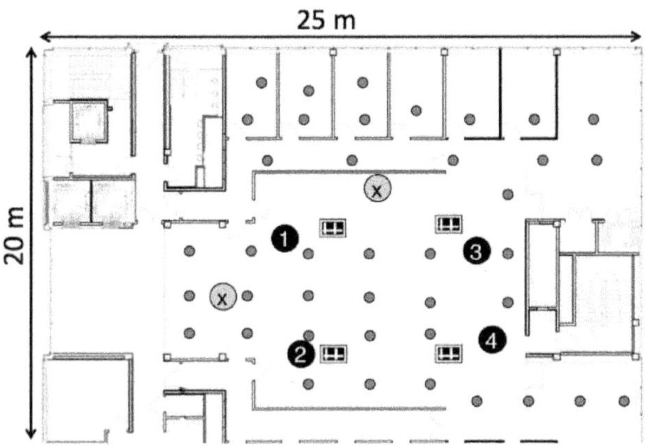

Figure 14: The indoor office environment testbed used for our experiments. The four APs used in our experiments are marked as black numbers while the client locations are marked as red dots.

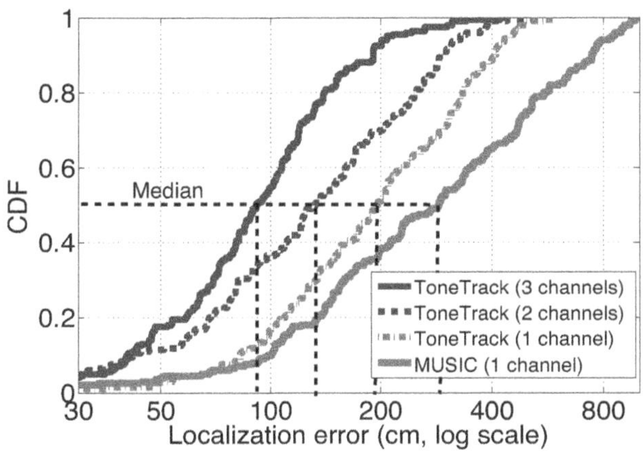

Figure 15: ToneTrack's overall localization performance with different numbers of channels and four APs.

one to two walls in between. Please note that, we only employ four APs for our main evaluation except in Section 4.2.4 where we evaluate the performance with varying number of APs.

4.2 End-to-end localization accuracy

We show the end-to-end performance evaluation of ToneTrack in this section.

4.2.1 Overall performance

The overall performance of ToneTrack is shown in Figure 15. With only three 20 MHz channels, we are able to achieve 0.9 m median accuracy in a typical office environment with strong multipaths. The median accuracies of two and one channel are 1.3 m and 1.9 m respectively, significantly better than the naïve resolution. With three channels, the 90% accuracy is around 2 m. The red curve is the CDF plot for super-resolution MUSIC without any of our proposed schemes. So even with just one channel, we are able to reduce the median localization error by 40% compared to the state-of-the-art super-resolution scheme. With our channel combination schemes applied, we further reduce the median error to below one meter which is a significant improvement with only 20 MHz channels. Also the long tail of MUSIC curve is removed in ToneTrack. We demonstrate the effectiveness of channel combination in 2.4 GHz band here with three channels. More channels can be utilized for combination at 5 GHz and 60 GHz bands which means even finer accuracy level can be achieved. We believe with the channel combination scheme proposed in ToneTrack, it's possible to achieve localization accuracy close to UWB systems.

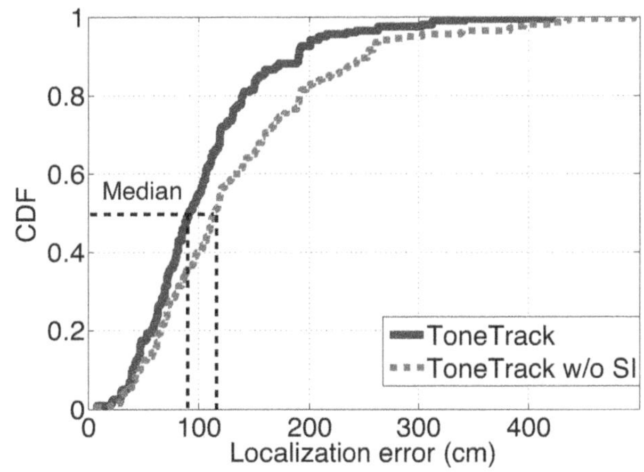

Figure 16: Isolating the effect of the spectrum identification (SI) scheme with three channels. Four APs are used in this experiment.

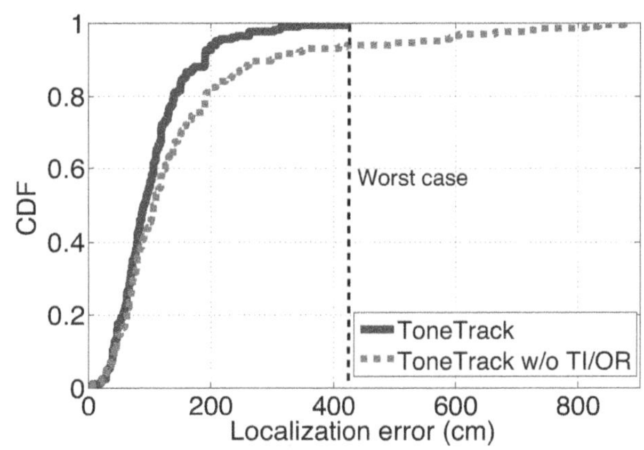

Figure 17: The effect of triangle inequality (TI) and clustering schemes.

4.2.2 Benefit of Spectrum Identification

We now isolate and show the effect of spectrum identification (SI) scheme in Figure 16. With the spectrum identification scheme, the median accuracy is improved from 116 cm to 90 cm. We can see that the spectrum identification scheme is effective in improving the performance by identifying the more accurate part of the spectrum for localization. However, we do note that when we only have three APs, we may not able to apply this scheme because discarding the inaccurate spectrum reduces the number of APs below three which is the minimum requirement for TDoA localization. However, due to the popularity of WiFi in enterprises and universities, this is not an issue as most of the time many APs can be overheard in range. We also note that this spectrum identification scheme is more effective in the environment with stronger multipaths which makes it a suitable candidate for indoor localization.

4.2.3 Impact of TI and clustering

We now remove the triangle inequality (TI) and clustering schemes to see how the performance of ToneTrack is degraded. We can see from Figure 17 that without these schemes, we have a long tail

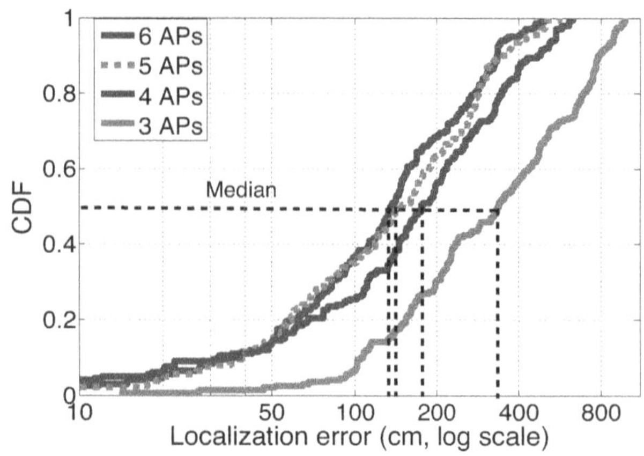

Figure 18: ToneTrack's performance with varying number of APs. Only one channel is used in this experiment.

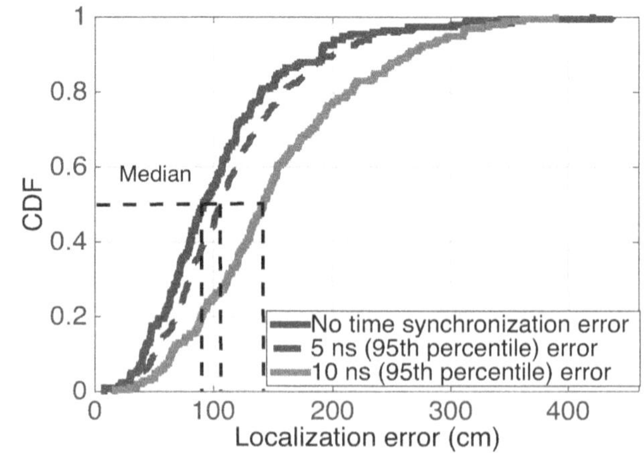

Figure 19: ToneTrack's performance with 5 ns and 10 ns (95th percentile) inter-AP time-synchronization error.

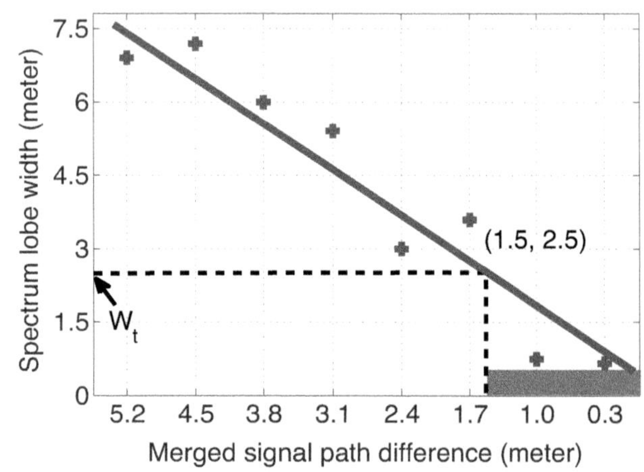

Figure 20: The merged peak width decreases when the signal path difference decreases (21 dB SNR).

on the CDF. These two schemes are effective in identifying those 'bad' APs (APs with direct path 100% blocked) and estimates with large errors. These 'bad' APs usually cause a big error because only the reflection paths exist and they localize the client to random positions. The direct-path blockage issue is more severe than multipaths. We can still try to differentiate the direct path and multipaths if both exist. With direct path 100% blocked, unless we can identify the AP and remove it from localization, it always causes a large error which significantly degrades the performance.

4.2.4 Number of APs

We evaluate the effect of varying number of APs on ToneTrack in this section with two more APs added at positions marked in Figure 14. In order to localize a client, we need a minimum number of three APs to have at least two hyperbolas to intersect. With only three APs, all the schemes proposed are not applied because we don't have any extra AP. From the results in Figure 18, we can see a clear gap between the CDF of three APs and four APs. With more APs added, the performance increases slightly. We believe the best solution is to identify the optimal group of APs rather than include more random APs for localization. In ToneTrack, we are able to detect the 'bad' APs whose direct path is 100% blocked and remove them. However, it's still challenging to tell which group of APs presents the best localization performance. A safe solution is to include more APs for ToneTrack. We leave the best group of APs selection problem open as our future work.

4.2.5 Impact of synchronization error

In our testbed, we fully synchronize all the APs. In a distributed MIMO system, there are still time synchronization errors between APs, leading to a performance degradation of ToneTrack. In order to evaluate the performance of ToneTrack with time synchronization error, we borrow the time synchronization error data from SourceSync [36] and incorporate them into our time estimates. Then we employ the new TDoA estimates to localize the clients. We can see in Figure 19, with 5 ns and 10 ns (95th percentile[5]) time synchronization error, ToneTrack still performs quite well, achieving a median localization accuracy of 1.05 m and 1.4 m respectively with three channels. We expect this time synchronization error to be further reduced in the future to have an even less effect on ToneTrack's localization performance.

4.3 Microbenchmark: Choosing W_t

We justify our choice for the spectrum lobe width threshold W_t to differentiate the single peak and merged peak here. When more than two signals are merged or the signals are in the medium and low SNR regions, the width of the merged lobe is much larger. We show the most challenging scenario in Figure 20 where only two signals are merged and they are in the high SNR region (21 dB). With two signals in the high SNR region, the lobe width is the thinnest among the merged lobes. We show that even under these conditions, we can still choose a constant threshold value safely for a particular bandwidth with very little performance degradation. From Figure 20, we can see that the width of the merged peak is large as long as the path difference between the two signals are above 1.7 m. If we choose the threshold as 2.5 m[6] to differentiate a single and merged peak, we make mistakes only when the path difference of the two signals is below 1.5 m. Note that the merged peak position is always between the true peak positions of the two signals. When the path difference is as small as below 1.5 m, the deviation of the merged peak position from the true direct path peak position is also small. So mis-identification of the merged peak as single peak in this scenario has little effect in the performance.

[5]Note that 5 ns and 10 ns are the 95th percentile values, which mean the average values are significantly smaller.

[6]Note that we measure the spectrum lobe width in distance converted from time at the speed of light.

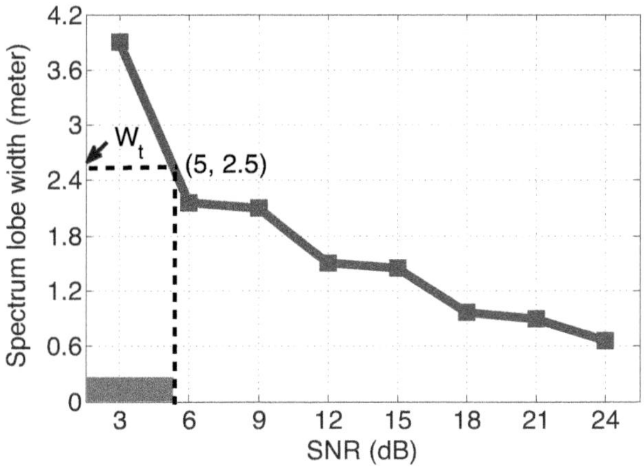

Figure 21: The lobe width of a single signal's ToA spectrum decreases when SNR increases. The lobe width increases dramatically when SNR goes below 6 dB. The red region denotes a range where ToneTrack classifies a single signal peak as a merged peak, but note the extremely low SNR.

From Figure 21, we can see clearly that the lobe width of a single signal remains well below 2.5 m as long as the SNR is above 6 dB. ToneTrack makes mistakes only in the very low SNR region (below 6 dB). In this SNR region, the accuracy level of the spectrum is anyway low and ToneTrack relies more on other APs to localize the client. So the effect of making mistakes on an inaccurate spectrum is also small. It's also noted that with many APs around, it's unlikely all the APs have low SNRs with respect to a client. We plan to adapt this threshold with varying SNR values in our future work. However, a single threshold is performing pretty well as explained.

5. RELATED WORK

Related work on indoor localization broadly groups into the following categories:

Ultrasonic and infrared based. Much early work has employed ultrasonic and infrared infrastructure. Cricket [35] employs a combination of radio and ultrasound, while Bat [14, 56] and Badge [55] leverage infrared sensors in badges carried by users.

RSSI and CSI signatures. Early work also targeted building a database of RSSI signatures at nearby APs, as RADAR [2, 3], Horus [65], and WiGEM [13] do. A slight departure from conventional approaches, Modellet [24] makes the case for a hybrid model combining fingerprint-based and model-driven localization approaches to handle data diversity and density in large scale deployments. In addition to coarser RSSI information, later work has leveraged finer channel state information (CSI). PinLoc [45] generates RF signatures to differentiate spots to within one meter, while CSITE [17] identifies attackers forging Wi-Fi management frames.

PHY-based. This newer line of work leverages various physical-layer signal processing techniques to improve accuracy. For RFID, Pinit [52] leverages antenna motion to create a synthetic aperture radar that is used to localize RFID tags, RF-Compass [51] employs RFIDs located on a robot to localize a given object and hence automatically navigate towards it, and RF-IDraw [53] traces RFID trajectories by intelligently combining various pairs of antenna spacings to yield a high degree of resolution. LTEye [20] localizes LTE clients from their uplink signal transmissions using synthetic aperture radar. Ubicarse [19] takes this one step further by making the smartphone emulate a synthetic aperture radar through user induced motion. Centaur [32] fuses RF and acoustic based ranging using a Bayesian inference framework to enable indoor localization with higher accuracy.

A recent independent work appearing in the literature with ToneTrack, Splicer [57] employs a similar idea of combining CSI information from multiple channels. While Splicer combines CSI information for a more accurate power delay profile, ToneTrack uses the combined CSI to further increase the resolution of super-resolution MUSIC for more accurate localization, integrating the CSI combination process with super-resolution time-of-arrival estimation.

AoA-based techniques. ArrayTrack [59] employs a large antenna array at the AP coupled with AoA signal processing techniques to provide fine-grained indoor localization, and the most promising approaches to indoor localization involve analyzing the signals clients send jointly: both in the spatial domain, analyzing the AoA of the signal, and in the time domain, analyzing the ToA of the signal [11, 12, 29, 44], and it is known that the two offer synergistic accuracy benefits. PinPoint [18] proposes AoA processing with cyclo-stationary analysis, and Phaser [12] combines AoA with time-of-arrival analysis. Cupid [44] reduces reflection path ambiguities by using information from smartphone's inertial sensors and human mobility. Niculescu *et al.* use mechanically-steered antennas in ad-hoc and AP networks [33].

ToneTrack falls in the category of PHY-based localization techniques, sharing some signal processing concepts with AoA-based techniques above. Since it is based on TDoA, it complements PHY- and AoA-based techniques.

ToA/TDoA/UWB-based techniques. Li and Pahlavan [25] propose using MUSIC in the frequency domain for ToA estimation. JADE [48, 49] jointly estimates angle and delay of all the arriving multipath signals. Synchronicity [60] uses MUSIC super-resolution techniques in a similar TDoA system design, but its performance is limited by radio bandwidth. Ultra-wideband radios, which have been commercialized [47], can discern sub-nanosecond time-of-flight, but performance decreases in the presence of multipath propagation and direct path blockage [10], and practical UWB radios use low data rates and power due to government regulator rules.

Compared to the above ToA and TDoA techniques, ToneTrack increases the localization granularity through a novel approach of leveraging frequency hopping to combine signals, thereby aggregating the resolution across multiple discrete channels available in a band, while not requiring a specialized ultrawideband radio.

Inertial and magnetic sensor-driven. Liu *et al.* [27] combine Wi-Fi fingerprinting with acoustic ranging between smartphone users to increase accuracy. SAIL [30] leverages fine-grained CSI information coupled with inertial dead reckoning on smartphones to enable localization with a single AP. Guoguo [28] deploys an acoustic ranging infrastructure, where the innovation is at the APs that are designed to send out acoustic beacons for ranging. Zee [37] and LiFS [63] leverage crowdsourcing and inertial dead reckoning to eliminate the calibration that RSSI fingerprinting requires. Unloc [50] uses internal landmarks with specific RF signatures to recalibrate dead reckoning schemes. SpinLoc [43] leverages the human body's attenuation of Wi-Fi signals when users spin around to estimate bearing to nearby APs.

GPS-enabled techniques. EZ [8] employs genetic algorithms to triangulate users between Wi-Fi APs coupling this with sporadic GPS fixes. COIN-GPS [34] uses GPS directly with the help of a high gain directional antenna at the GPS receiver front-end, coupled with cloud processing to analyze longer GPS signals.

FM radio-based techniques. Another line of work leverages FM radio for indoor localization owing to its lower frequency and hence better robustness to penetration, multipath and distance of transmission. Chen *et al.* [7] leverage FM for indoor radio fingerprinting with infrastructure support, combining it with Wi-Fi. ACMI [64] uses overheard radio signals to build its fingerprinting database without even infrastructure support.

Visible light-based approaches. Epsilon [15, 23] employs visible light modulation from smart LEDs coupled with custom light sensor receivers for localization. Luxapose [21] uses off-the-shelf cameras as receivers coupled with image processing techniques. Travi-Navi [66] proposes a user-bootstrapped indoor navigation system, where followers navigate using a guider's imaging capabilities and sensor readings.

6. CONCLUSION

We have presented the design, implementation, and evaluation of ToneTrack, a TDoA-based indoor localization system that leverages the channel switches that agile radios make to increase the available bandwidth for time-based localization methods, resulting in a 90 centimeter localization accuracy across an entire office floor from four APs overhearing just three packets transmitted over three adjacent 20 MHz bandwidth channels. We have proposed a novel spectrum identification scheme to retrieve useful information from a ToA profile that is mostly inaccurate. Our proposed triangle inequality and clustering schemes also help to remove the APs when a direct path is totally blocked. ToneTrack thus pushes the envelope of localization systems in terms of their accuracy, hardware requirements, and responsiveness.

Acknowledgements

The research leading to these results has received funding from the European Research Council under the EU's Seventh Framework Programme (FP/2007-2013)/ ERC Grant Agreement no. 279976. Jie Xiong is supported by a Google European Doctoral Fellowship in Wireless Networking. We are grateful to the anonymous shepherd and reviewers whose comments helped bring the paper to its final form.

References

[1] A. Amar and A. Weiss. Fundamental resolution limits of closely spaced random signals. *IET Radar and Sonar Navigation*, 2(3):170–179, 2008.

[2] P. Bahl and V. Padmanabhan. RADAR: An in-building RF-based user location and tracking system. In *Infocom*, 2000.

[3] P. Bahl, V. Padmanabhan, and A. Balachandran. Enhancements to the RADAR user location and tracking system. Technical Report MSR-TR-2000-12, Microsoft Research, 2000.

[4] Broadcom Inc. White Paper: Ethernet time synchronization. http://www.broadcom.com/collateral/wp/StrataXGSIV-WP100-R.pdf.

[5] Y. Chan and K. Ho. A simple and efficient estimator for hyperbolic location. *IEEE Trans. on Signal Processing*, 42(8), 1994.

[6] R. Chandra, R. Mahajan, T. Moscibroda, R. Raghavendra, and P. Bahl. A case for adapting channel width in wireless networks. In *SIGCOMM*, 2008.

[7] Y. Chen, D. Lymberopoulos, J. Liu, and B. Priyantha. FM-based indoor localization. In *MobiSys*, 2012.

[8] K. Chintalapudi, A. Iyer, and V. Padmanabhan. Indoor localization without the pain. In *MobiCom*, 2010.

[9] K. Chintalapudi, B. Radunovic, V. Balan, M. Buettener, S. Yerramalli, V. Navda, and R. Ramjee. WiFi-NC: Wi-Fi over narrow channels. In *NSDI*, 2012.

[10] D. Dardari, A. Conti, U. Ferner, A. Giorgetti, and M. Win. Ranging with ultrawide bandwidth signals in multipath environments. *Proc. of the IEEE*, 97(2):404–426, Feb. 2009.

[11] G. Ding, Z. Tan, L. Zhang, Z. Zhang, and J. Zhang. Hybrid ToA/AoA cooperative localization in non-line-of-sight environments. In *VTC*, 2012.

[12] J. Gjengset, J. Xiong, G. McPhilips, and K. Jamieson. Phaser: Enabling phased array signal processing on commodity Wi-Fi access points. In *MobiCom*, 2014.

[13] A. Goswami, L. Ortiz, and S. Das. WiGEM: A learning-based approach for indoor localization. In *CoNEXT*, 2011.

[14] R. Harle and A. Hopper. Deploying and evaluating a location-aware system. In *MobiSys*, 2005.

[15] P. Hu, L. Li, C. Peng, G. Shen, and F. Zhao. Pharos: Enable physical analytics through visible light based indoor localization. In *HotNets*, 2013.

[16] IEEE Standard for Information Technology, Part 11: Wireless LAN Medium Access Control (MAC) and Physical Layer (PHY) Specifications, Amendment 4: Enhancements for Very High Throughput for Operation in Bands below 6 GHz (IEEE Std 802.11ac-2013).

[17] Z. Jiang, J. Zhao, X. Li, J. Han, and W. Xi. Rejecting the Attack: Source Authentication for Wi-Fi Management Frames using CSI Information. In *Infocom*, 2013.

[18] K. Joshi, S. Hong, and S. Katti. PinPoint: Localizing Interfering Radios. In *NSDI*, 2013.

[19] S. Kumar, S. Gil, D. Katabi, and D. Rus. Accurate indoor localization with zero start-up cost. In *MobiCom*, 2014.

[20] S. Kumar, E. Hamed, D. Katabi, and L. E. Li. LTE radio analytics made easy and accessible. In *SIGCOMM*, 2014.

[21] Y.-S. Kuo, P. Pannuto, K.-J. Hsiao, and P. Dutta. Luxapose: Indoor positioning with mobile phones and visible light. In *MobiCom*, 2014.

[22] T. Laakso, V. Valimaki, M. Karjalainen, and U. Laine. Splitting the unit delay. IEEE *Sig. Proc. Mag.*, 13(1):30–60, 1996.

[23] L. Li, P. Hu, G. Shen, C. Peng, and F. Zhao. Epsilon: A visible light based positioning system. In *NSDI*, 2014.

[24] L. Li, G. Shen, C. Zhao, T. Moscibroda, J.-H. Lin, and F. Zhao. Experiencing and handling the diversity in data density and environmental locality in an indoor positioning service. In *MobiCom*, 2014.

[25] X. Li and K. Pahlavan. Super-resolution ToA estimation with diversity for indoor geolocation. *IEEE Trans. on Wireless Comms.*, 3(1), 2004.

[26] Z. Li, W. Chen, C. Li, M. Li, X. Li, and Y. Liu. Flight: Clock calibration using fluorescent lighting. In *ACM MobiCom*, 2012.

[27] H. Liu, Y. Gan, J. Yang, S. Sidhom, Y. Wang, Y. Chen, and F. Ye. Push the limit of Wi-Fi based localization for smartphones. In *MobiCom*, 2012.

[28] K. Liu, X. Liu, and X. Li. Guoguo: Enabling fine-grained indoor localization via smartphone. In *MobiSys*, 2013.

[29] Y. Luo and C. Law. Indoor positioning using UWB-IR signals in the presence of dense multipath with path

overlapping. *IEEE Trans. on Wireless Communications*, 11(10):3734–3743, Oct. 2012.
[30] A. Mariakakis, S. Sen, J. Lee, and K.-H. Kim. SAIL: Single access point-based indoor localization. In *MobiSys*, 2014.
[31] G. Mellen et al. Closed-form solution for determining emitter location using time difference of arrival measurements. *IEEE Trans. on Aerospace and Electronic Systems*, 39(3), 2003.
[32] R. Nandakumar, K. Chintalapudi, and V. Padmanabhan. Centaur: Locating devices in an office environment. In *MobiCom*, 2012.
[33] D. Niculescu and B. Nath. Ad-hoc positioning system (APS) using AoA. In *Infocom*, 2003.
[34] S. Nirjon, J. Liu, G. DeJean, B. Priyantha, Y. Jin, and T. Hart. COIN-GPS: Indoor localization from direct GPS receiving. In *MobiSys*, 2014.
[35] N. Priyantha, A. Chakraborty, and H. Balakrishnan. The Cricket location-support system. In *MobiCom*, 2000.
[36] H. Rahul, H. Hassanieh, and D. Katabi. SourceSync: A distributed wireless architecture for exploiting sender diversity. In *SIGCOMM*, 2010.
[37] A. Rai, K. Chintalapudi, V. Padmanabhan, and R. Sen. Zee: Zero-effort crowdsourcing for indoor localization. In *MobiCom*, 2012.
[38] Rice Univ. Wireless Open Access Research Platform (WARP). http://warpproject.org.
[39] T. Sarkar and O. Pereira. Using the matrix pencil method to estimate the parameters of a sum of complex exponentials. *IEEE Antenna and Propagation Magazine*, 37(1), 1995.
[40] T. Schmidl and D. Cox. Robust Frequency and Timing Synchroniation for OFDM. *IEEE Trans. on Communications*, 45(12):1613–1621, Dec. 1997.
[41] R. Schmidt. Multiple emitter location and signal parameter estimation. *IEEE Trans. on Antennas and Propagation*, AP-34(3):276–80, 1986.
[42] R. Schmidt. Least squares range difference location. *IEEE Trans. on Aerospace and Electronic Systems*, 32(1):234–242, 1996.
[43] S. Sen, R. Choudhury, and S. Nelakuditi. SpinLoc: Spin once to know your location. In *HotMobile*, 2012.
[44] S. Sen, J. Lee, K. Kim, and P. Congdon. Avoiding multipath to revive inbuilding Wi-Fi localization. In *MobiSys*, 2013.
[45] S. Sen, B. Radunovic, R. R. Choudhury, and T. Minka. You are now facing the Mona Lisa: Spot localization using phy layer information. In *MobiSys*, 2012.
[46] K. Tan, J. Fang, Y. Zhang, S. Chen, L. Shi, J. Zhang, and Y. Zhang. Fine-grained channel access in wireless LAN. In *SIGCOMM*, 2010.
[47] Time domain, inc. http://www.timedomain.com.
[48] M. Vanderveen, B. Ng, C. Papadias, and A. Paulraj. Joint angle and delay estimation (JADE) for signals in multipath environments. In *Asilomar Conf. on Signals, Systems, and Computers*, 1996.
[49] M. Vanderveen, C. Papadias, and A. Paulraj. Joint angle and delay estimation (JADE) for multipath signals arriving at an antenna array. *IEEE Communications L.*, 1(1):12–14, Jan. 1997.
[50] H. Wang, S. Sen, A. Elgohary, M. Farid, M. Youssef, and R. Choudhury. No need to war drive: Unsupervised indoor localization. In *MobiSys*, 2012.
[51] J. Wang, F. Adib, R. Knepper, D. Katabi, and D. Rus. RF-Compass: Robot object manipulation using RFIDs. In *MobiCom*, 2013.
[52] J. Wang and D. Katabi. Dude, where's my card? RFID positioning that works with multipath and non-line of sight. In *SIGCOMM*, 2013.
[53] J. Wang, D. Vasisht, and D. Katabi. RF-IDraw: Virtual touch screen in the air using RF signals. In *SIGCOMM*, 2014.
[54] Y. Wang and L. Song. An algorithmic and systematic approach for improving robustness of ToA-based localization. In *IEEE Conf. on High Performance Computing and Communications, Embedded, and Ubiquitous Computing*, 2013.
[55] R. Want, A. Hopper, V. Falcao, and J. Gibbons. The active badge location system. *ACM Trans. on Information Systems*, 10(1):91–102, Jan. 1992.
[56] A. Ward, A. Jones, and A. Hopper. A new location technique for the active office. *IEEE Personal Communications*, 4(5):42–47, Oct. 1997.
[57] Y. Xie, Z. Li, and M. Li. Precise power delay profiling with commodity Wi-Fi. In *ACM MobiCom*, 2015.
[58] J. Xiong and K. Jamieson. Towards fine-grained radio-based indoor location. In *HotMobile*, 2012.
[59] J. Xiong and K. Jamieson. ArrayTrack: A fine-grained indoor location system. In *NSDI*, 2013.
[60] J. Xiong, K. Jamieson, and K. Sundaresan. Synchronicity: Pushing the envelope of fine-grained localization with Distributed MIMO. In *HotWireless*, 2014.
[61] J. Xiong, K. Sundaresan, K. Jamieson, M. A. Khojastepour, and S. Rangarajan. Midas: Empowering 802.11ac networks with multiple-input distributed antenna systems. In *ACM CoNEXT*, 2014.
[62] L. Yang, Y. Chen, X.-Y. Li, C. Xiao, M. Li, and Y. Liu. Tagoram: Real-time tracking of mobile RFID tags to high precision using COTS devices. In *ACM MobiCom*, 2014.
[63] Z. Yang, C. Wu, and Y. Liu. Locating in fingerprint space: Wireless indoor localization with little human intervention. In *MobiCom*, 2012.
[64] S. Yoon, K. Lee, and I. Rhee. FM-based indoor localization via automatic fingerprint DB construction and matching. In *MobiSys*, 2013.
[65] M. Youssef and A. Agrawala. The Horus WLAN location determination system. In *MobiSys*, 2005.
[66] Y. Zheng, G. Shen, L. Li, C. Zhao, M. Li, and F. Zhao. Travi-Navi: Self-deployable indoor navigation system. In *MobiCom*, 2014.

Big Data, IoT, ...
Buzz Words For Academia Or Reality For Industry?

Rui Aguiar
Universidade de Aveiro
DETI-Instituto de Telecomunicações
Portugal
ruilaa@ua.pt

Nora Benhabiles
CEA
EIT Health KIC
France
nora.benhabiles@cea.fr

Tobias Pfeiffer
Preferred Networks
Japan
tgp@preferred.jp

Pablo Rodriguez
Telefonica
Spain
pablo.rodriguezrodriguez@telefonica.com

Harish Viswanathan
Alcatel Lucent Bell Labs
USA
harish.viswanathan@alcatel-lucent.com

Jia Wang
AT&T
USA
jiawang@research.att.com

Hui Zang
Huawei
USA
hui.zang@huawei.com

ABSTRACT
The concepts of Big Data have became intertwined with those of the Internet of Things, creating mental pictures of a fully connected, all-encompassing, cyber-physical world, where each and every object will contribute with information to a "fully aware" society. Academic works are presenting this as the natural evolution for our current technologies. The panel looks at these promises from the hard perspective of reality: what is being done, how much it cost, what needs to be developed, and what can be expected in the near and mid-term.

Categories and Subject Descriptors
C.2.1 [**Network Architecture and Design**]: Network Architecture and Design – wireless networks

H.3.4 [**Information Storage and Retrieval**]: Information Storage and Retrieval - Systems and Software

General Terms
Design, Economics, Security, Standardization

Keywords
Big Data; IoT; Industry-applications

MobiCom'15, September 7–11, 2015, Paris, France
ACM 978-1-4503-3619-2/15/09.
http://dx.doi.org/10.1145/2789168.2802150.

1. INTRODUCTION
The development of sensor networks, coupled with increasingly low power sensors and actuators, has led to the creation of scenarios where the physical reality is being measured and reported at rates which can be considered as continuous for practical purposes. All these devices, these "things", are supposedly exchanging all relevant information, acting as a mediator layer between the assessment of physical reality and the user. This Internet of Things allows the user to see its environment according to his/her specific preferences, with examples like "the fridge is warning that you are out of milk".

Such a level of knowledge, of understanding, is only possible by the developments on automated intelligence. All the data presented by the sensors, must go through a huge set of actions, like synthesis, inference filtering, scoping, or clustering. With the need of intelligent processing for many sensors, it is of no surprise that techniques of Big Data become involved in this process.

It is thus natural that, as concepts, Big Data and IoT have been variously (re-)interpreted and studied extensively in academia, at least in the last decade, with very diverse proposals. For industry, however, these concepts have increasingly become the reality. Data have emerged everywhere, and big data analytics often holds key to business opportunities. Devices of all sorts have also flourished, paving way for a full-connected world. Not surprisingly, the two concepts have become intertwined in some sectors, as more "things" are connected to the Internet, each generating data continuously. This panel is intended to bring together various industry sectors and academia to discuss where we stand and how coupled can these concepts become now and in the mid-term.

2. QUESTIONS TO CONSIDER

We try to shine some light on the point where we are in the intersection of these two concepts, what can be achieved in industry at this stage, and what is already felt as needed. Research questions that are not yet answered will be highlighted, and the challenges on how to transfer existing theoretical work into our society. The questions tackled will consist of two different tracks: where we stand, and where we expect to go.

2.1 Where we stand

Looking into current industry, it is important to look at our status. Several different aspects will be addressed.

- Is there already a global IoT industry? Can we consider that we have reached a maturity stage that any application vendor can deploy an "intelligent connectivity" on its consumer devices? Are standards (both communication and electronics) at such a stage that smooth interoperation is to be expected?
- Are we prepared for the communication and processing needs for this Internet of Things? Do we have adequate architectures for processing data at the required rates, and do we have communication architectures which are adequate for the traffic patterns expected in IoT? Are standards up to these challenges? Do we have "intelligence processors" for our IoT world?
- Do we have an "Internet of Things" or an "Internet of Rich Things"? Can we replace existing physical devices with cost-effective IoT-enable alternatives? Is it possible to show social benefits (economic, environment, safety) for pushing for such a conversion?
- Are there vertical sectors where this widespread usage is now easier to perform than others? Which areas are now intrinsically dependent of the merger of Big Data and IoT?
- Do we have a sustainable industry at this stage? What kind of actors are emerging? Are legacy players (operating system manufacturers, telecom operators, search engines, distribution companies) taking over all new business functions, or can we see independent SMEs increasingly relevant?

2.2 Where do we expect to go

The second line of discussion inside the panel will look into the future, and how our society will react to (and impact) this revolution.

- What challenges do we perceive for the future? Are these mostly technical or fundamentally of economical nature? Do we envisage scalable techniques for data processing? Are communications able to cope with how many sensors?
- What power limitations do we envisage? Do we see realizable power budgets for the sensors? Do we need novel (self) power techniques? Are we requiring an increasingly large piece of world power?
- Will markets be transformed by Big Data usage over widely deployed IoT? For an aging society, do we seen IoT as a piece on elderly care? Can we trust these techniques for health applications, or are they limited to active aging?
- Legal issues are clear? How can these impair worldwide developments? How can we have a global framework for data acquisition, storage and processing, with all the different ethical, cultural and legal frameworks across the world? Will ownership of data and information become as important as ownership of the device? Are there privacy issues to consider? Will the user accept such an intrusive society? Can we expect technology to help in these matters?
- How can we establish a proper market for the whole connected society? Can the user remain in control of its information (and its devices)? Is the IoT society ownerless? Will value pass from data to algorithms?
- What does industry need from academia? Cost reductions or technology performance developments?

mZig: Enabling Multi-Packet Reception in ZigBee

Linghe Kong[1,2]
[1]McGill University, Canada
[2]Shanghai Jiao Tong University, China
linghe.kong@mail.mcgill.ca

Xue Liu
McGill University, Canada
xueliu@cs.mcgill.ca

ABSTRACT

This paper presents mZig, a novel physical layer design that enables a receiver to simultaneously decode multiple packets from different transmitters in ZigBee. As a low-power and low-cost wireless protocol, the promising ZigBee has been widely used in sensor networks, cyber-physical systems, and smart buildings. Since ZigBee based networks usually adopt tree or cluster topology, the convergecast scenarios are common in which multiple transmitters need to send packets to one receiver. For example, in a smart home, all appliances report data to one control plane via ZigBee. However, concurrent transmissions in convergecast lead to the severe collision problem. The conventional ZigBee avoids collisions using backoff time, which introduces additional time overhead. Advanced methods resolve collisions instead of avoidance, in which the state-of-the-art ZigZag resolves one m-packet collision requiring m retransmissions. We propose mZig to resolve one m-packet collision by this collision itself, so the theoretical throughput is improved m-fold. Leveraging the unique features in ZigBee's physical layer including its chip rate, half-sine pulse shaping and O-QPSK modulation, mZig subtly decomposes multiple packets from one collision in baseband signal processing. The practical factors of noise, multipath, and frequency offset are taken into account in mZig design. We implement mZig on USRPs and establish a seven-node testbed. Experiment results demonstrate that mZig can receive up to four concurrent packets in our testbed. The throughput of mZig is 4.5x of the conventional ZigBee and 3.2x of ZigZag in the convergecast with four or more transmitters.

Categories and Subject Descriptors

C.2.1 [**Computer-Communications Networks**]: Network Architecture and Design—*Wireless communication*

General Terms

Design, Experimentation, Performance

1. INTRODUCTION

Based on IEEE 802.15.4, ZigBee [2] is a competitive wireless technology that has draw extensive interests by academia and industry. Different from high-power and high-bitrate WiFi [50] or 4G/5G [29], ZigBee focuses on the field of low-power, low-cost, and low-bitrate communications, which has been widely used in sensor networks [41, 51], cyber-physical systems [48], and smart buildings [38]. In 2013, the new version ZigBee, ZigBee Smart Energy V2 [3], was published. The number of smart devices equipped with ZigBee communication modules is poised to increase dramatically.

ZigBee based networks usually adopt tree or cluster topology [19, 26], in which multiple transmitters (TXs) need to send packets to one receiver (RX), known as convergecast [13, 42]. The convergecast is fundamental for plenty of applications. For example, in a smart home, hundreds of sensors and appliances report data to one control plane via a ZigBee [38]. Some other convergecast examples in recent studies include: data collection [20], neighbor discovery [8], ACK for multicast [9], and link correlation estimation [41].

In such convergecast scenarios, there exist severe collisions due to multiple concurrent transmissions. In ZigBee products, carrier sense multiple access (CSMA) [31, 35] is the conventional solution to avoid collisions, which exploits backoff time to divide transmissions into different time slots. The main drawback of CSMA is to introduce additional time overhead. Moreover, CSMA fails to avoid collisions in the case of hidden terminals [40]. The advanced methods such as interference cancellation [17] and constructive interference [10] resolve collisions instead of avoiding them. In the collision resolution category, the state-of-the-art method is ZigZag, which leverages time offsets among collisions to separate multiple packets. Nevertheless, to separate an m-packet collision, ZigZag requires m retransmissions to form collisions with different offsets. Thus, the upper bound of ZigZag's throughput is equal to that of one-TX one-RX communication without collisions.

To further improve the throughput and address the collision problem better in convergecast, we propose mZig to enable multi-packet reception (MPR) in ZigBee. The goal of mZig is to decompose m concurrent packets from one collision directly. Hence, the theoretical throughput of mZig is m-fold than the current best ZigZag. It is very challenging to achieve this amazing result in practice. The secret of mZig is from the physical layer of ZigBee.

In the physical layer, ZigBee shows three unique features on its chip, where one chip is the smallest unit carrying information in ZigBee's baseband signal. (i) Every chip is oversampled by multiple samples, because the sampling rate of off-the-shelf ADCs is much higher than the chip rate. (ii) The waveform of a chip is known, because ZigBee adopts half-sine pulse shaping on every chip. (iii) The amplitude of every chip is nearly the same in one packet, because O-QPSK modulates chips by different phase but not amplitude. These features provide opportunities to develop mZig.

To see how mZig works, consider the convergecast scenario

MobiCom'15, September 07 - 11, 2015, Paris, France
©2015 ACM. ISBN 978-1-4503-3619-2/15/09... $15.00
DOI: http://dx.doi.org/10.1145/2789168.2790104

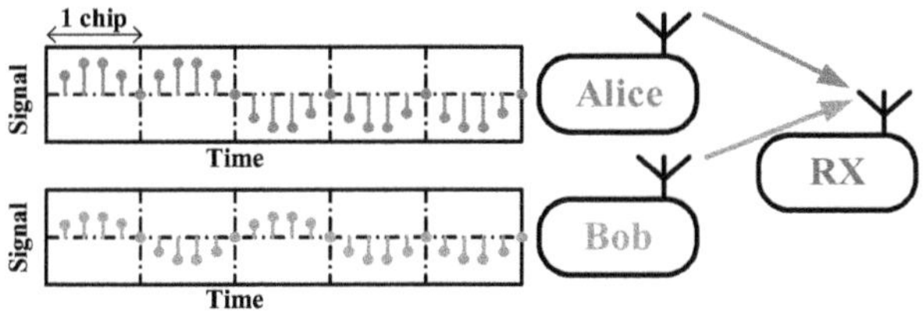

Figure 1: A convergecast scenario.

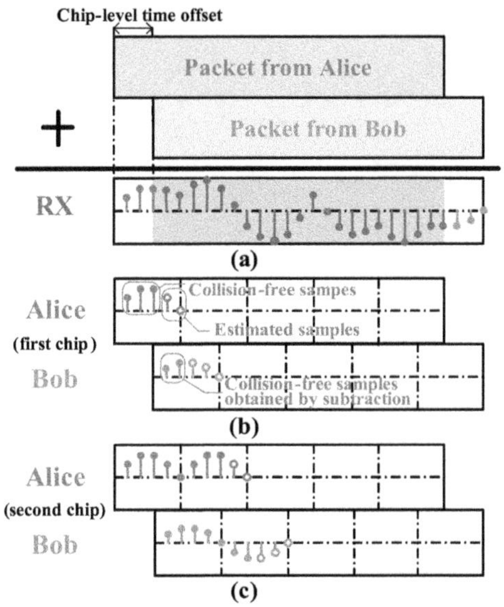

Figure 2: An example of decomposing a two-packet collision with chip-level time offset.

in Fig. 1, where Alice and Bob send packets simultaneously to RX, causing a collision. Alice sends five chips '11000' and Bob sends '10100', respectively. According to ZigBee, a chip '1' is a positive half-sine shaping, and a chip '0' is a negative half-sine. In this example, every chip has five samples. The baseband signals of these two packets are shown in Fig. 1.

When two packets arrive at RX with chip-level time offset, mZig decomposes two packets leveraging the features of oversampling and known shaping. An example of collided packet at RX is shown in Fig. 2(a), where two packets cannot be distinguished because their baseband signals are overlapped. When the time offset can be detected, we find the first three samples are collision-free. Using these three samples and the known half-sine shaping, we can estimate the next two samples and form the first chip of Alice as shown in Fig. 2(b). Then, we subtract this estimated chip from the collided packet. Another two collision-free samples are obtained, which can be used to estimate the first chip for Bob. Repeating the operations of subtraction and estimation as shown in Fig. 2(c), mZig decomposes the collided packet into two packets chip-by-chip.

When two packets arrive at RX synchronously, mZig decomposes packets leveraging the amplitude difference. The collided packet is shown in Fig. 3, where all chips are overlapped without time offset, so the above method using collision-free samples cannot be applied. If there is only one TX, the received signal will have two amplitude levels for chip '1' and '0', respectively. Furthermore, if there are m TXs, there will be 2^m levels of amplitude combinations. In Fig. 3, four different amplitude levels can be counted, so we can estimate that there are two packets in this collision. Denote these four amplitude levels by L_i, where $L_1 > L_2 > L_3 > L_4$.

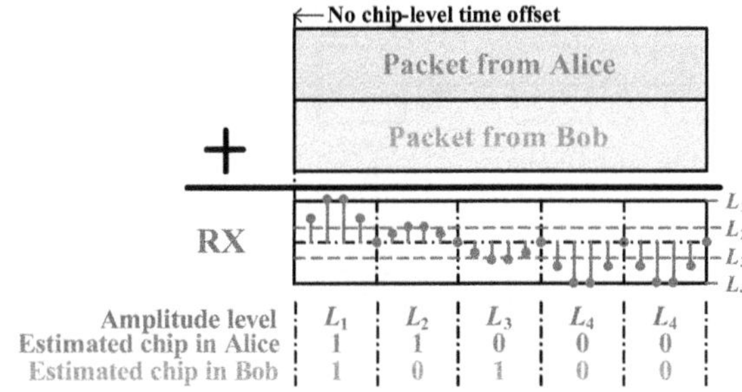

Figure 3: An example of decomposing a two-packet collision without chip-level time offset.

In addition, denote the amplitudes of Alice and Bob by α and β, respectively. Assume $\alpha > \beta$, we can build a mapping relationship that $L_1 = \alpha + \beta$, $L_2 = \alpha - \beta$, $L_3 = -\alpha + \beta$, and $L_4 = -\alpha - \beta$. Based on such relationships, every chip can be decomposed by its amplitude. For example, the third chip at RX reaches L_3, so the third chip for Alice is '0' and the third chip for Bob is '1' according to $L_3 = -\alpha + \beta$.

The main contributions of this paper are as follows:

- We design mZig, a novel physical layer technique on receiver to enable multi-packet reception in ZigBee. The core design of mZig leverages the unique features of ZigBee to decompose multiple packets from one collision chip-by-chip. To enhance the performance of mZig, we carefully address a series of practical issues including noise, multipath, and frequency offset. We theoretically derive the maximal value of m as $\lfloor \frac{S}{2 \times C} \rfloor$, where m is the number of concurrent transmissions, S is the sampling rate, and C is the chip rate.
- We implement mZig on USRPs, and build a seven-node testbed. Experiment results demonstrate that mZig can receive up to four concurrent transmissions with low bit error using 32Msps sampling rate. The throughput of mZig achieves 4.5x of the conventional ZigBee and 3.2x of ZigZag in the convergecast with four or more transmitters. More simulations are conducted to reveal the impacts of chip-level time offset, noises, multipath, and frequency offset, which are uncontrollable parameters in experiments. In simulation, we also transplants mZig on Bluetooth Low Energy (BLE), another key protocol in low-power communications.

The proposed mZig can decompose multi-packet collision without additional requirements such as synchronization or packet length. However, mZig is not omni-directional. For example, it fails when low SNR. In such a case, since the design of mZig is orthogonal to existing collision resolution techniques such as SIC [32], ZigZag [15], and full duplex [21], they can work complementarily for addressing collisions.

2. PRELIMINARY

Since mZig is a physical layer design, we firstly review the physical layer of conventional ZigBee in this section. Then, we summarize the unique features of ZigBee, which provide the opportunity to develop mZig.

2.1 Physical Layer of conventional ZigBee

The ZigBee standard [2] specifies its operation in 2.4GHz (worldwide), 915MHz (America) and 868MHz (Europe) ISM bands. This paper focuses on the most widely used 2.4GHz ZigBee. Sixteen channels are allocated to ZigBee in this band, where the bandwidth of each channel is 2MHz. The bit rate is 250kbps. The block diagram of physical layer in conventional ZigBee is illustrated in Fig. 4, including one

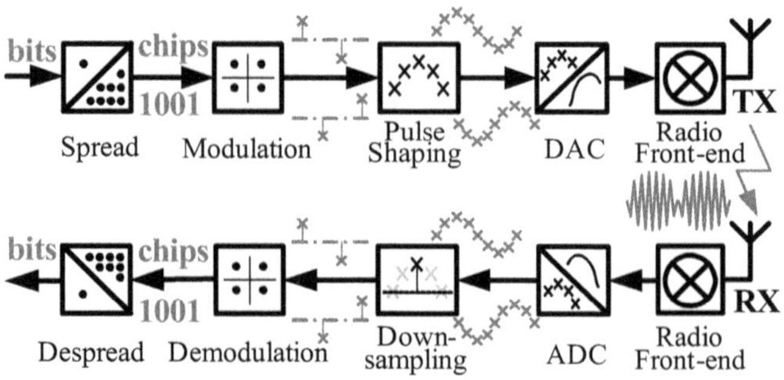

Figure 4: The block diagram of physical layer in conventional ZigBee.

Table 1: Bit to chip spreading

Bits: $b_0b_1b_2b_3$	Chips: $c_0c_1c_2\cdots c_{31}$
0000	11011001110000110101001000101110
1000	11101101100111000011010100100010
0100	00101110110110011100001101010010
⋮	⋮
1111	11001001011000000111011110111000

transmitter (TX) and one receiver (RX).

In the physical layer, a TX sends a packet through five steps: spread, modulation, pulse shaping, digital-analog conversion (DAC), and radio front-end.

First, ZigBee spreads bits into chips by direct-sequence spread spectrum (DSSS). According to the given bit-to-chip spreading relationship as shown in Tab. 1, every four bits are spread to the specified 32 chips. A chip is the smallest unit carrying information in ZigBee. The chip rate is $C =$ 2Mchip/s, which is equal to the bandwidth.

Second, ZigBee modulates chips onto I-Q phases using offset quadrature phase-shift keying (O-QPSK). As shown in Fig. 5, the chips $c_0, c_2, \cdots$ are modulated onto I phase and the chips $c_1, c_3, \cdots$ are modulated onto Q phase one-by-one. The chip rate of each phase is $C/2 =$ 1Mchip/s. Hence, the duration of each chip is $\frac{1\text{s}}{1\text{Mchip/s}} = 1\mu\text{s}$. The 'O' in O-QPSK expresses that a half chip time offset, *i.e.*, $1\mu\text{s}/2 = 0.5\mu\text{s}$, exists between I phase and Q phase.

Third, ZigBee adopts the half-sine pulse shaping to shape a chip into baseband samples. These samples form a digital waveform. A chip '1' is shaped to a positive half-sine and a chip '0' is shaped to a negative half-sine as shown in Fig. 6. The duration of a chip's waveform keeps 1μs. In one packet, the amplitudes of all chips are the same, which depends on the selected transmission power.

Fourth, DAC converts the digital baseband waveform into the analog baseband waveform.

Fifth, the radio front-end up-converts the baseband waveform to 2.4GHz carrier and sends it out.

The physical layer of RX is nearly the inverse of TX as shown in Fig. 4. To receive a packet, the RX down-converts the received signal to an analog baseband waveform, converts the analog waveform to a digital one, down-samples and demodulates the digital waveform into chips, and despreads chips into bits. For ease of understanding, we only draw the major modules of RX in Fig. 4. More detailed RX modules such as phase tracking can refer to [2].

2.2 Features of ZigBee Chips

From the conventional ZigBee, we observe that there are three unique features in the chips.

• **Oversampling**. Since the sampling rate of recent analog-

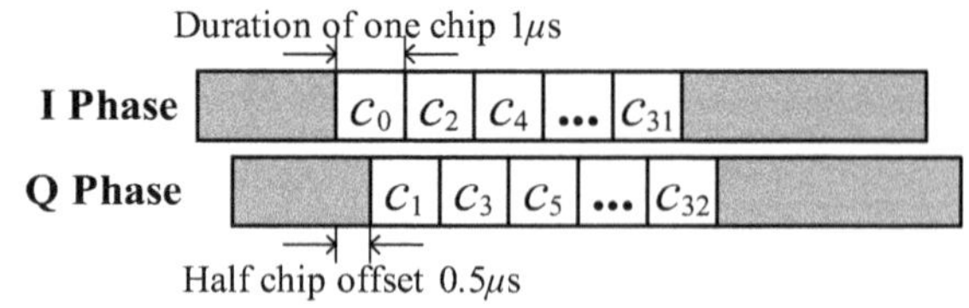

Figure 5: O-QPSK modulation.

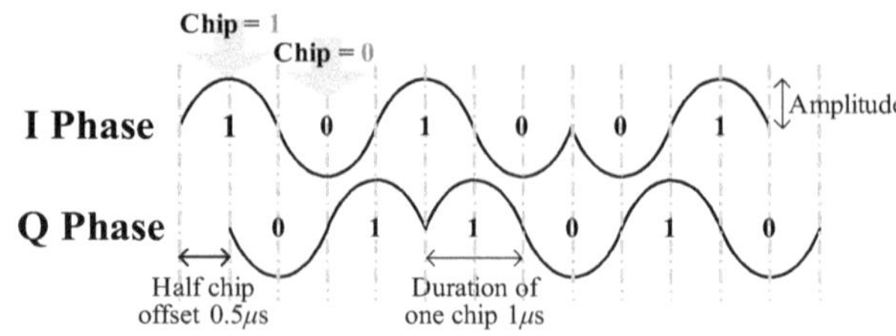

Figure 6: Half-sine pulse shaping.

digital conversions (ADCs) is usually higher than ZigBee's chip rate, a chip at RX is sampled by multiple samples. For instance, USRP B210 [1] has a 61.44Msps ADC, so every chip has no less than $\lfloor \frac{61.44\text{Msps}}{1\text{Mchip/s}} \rfloor = 61$ samples.

• **Known shaping**. As all chips are shaped by half-sine at TX, the shapes of received chips are known. Although these chips are interfered by noises in wireless channels, their basic shapes are maintained.

• **Uniform amplitude**. Unlike ASK or QAM [5], which operates the modulation by different levels of amplitude, ZigBee adopts O-QPSK modulation at TX. As a result, the amplitudes of all chips in one packet are equivalent.

In the following, we will show how to leverage these features to design mZig.

3. CORE DESIGN OF MZIG

The multi-packet collision primer is presented in this section, and collisions are classified into two categories: collisions with or without chip-level time offset. Then, the core designs of mZig are introduced to resolve the collisions in these two categories respectively.

3.1 Multi-Packet Collision Primer

A wireless signal is typically represented as discrete complex values in baseband [37]. As introduced in §2.1, chips in ZigBee are shaped to be a sequence of samples in baseband. Denote $X[n]$ to be the complex value of the n-th baseband sample at TX. The received signal can also be represented as a sequence of samples spaced by the sampling interval $\Delta = 1/S$, where S is the sample rate. If the transmitted sample is $X[n]$, the received sample is formulated by

$$Y[n] = HX[n] + W[n], \tag{1}$$

where $H = he^{\gamma}$ is the channel parameter, whose magnitude h refers to the channel attenuation and its angle γ is a phase shift depending on the distance between the TX and the RX, and $W[n]$ is the noise.

If two TXs Alice and Bob transmit concurrently, the signals of their packets are added up in air. Then, the received sample can be expressed as:

$$Y[n] = H_A X_A[n] + H_B X_B[n] + W[n], \tag{2}$$

where H_A and H_B are the channel parameters of Alice and Bob, respectively. $X_A[n]$ and $X_B[n]$ are the transmitted samples of Alice and Bob.

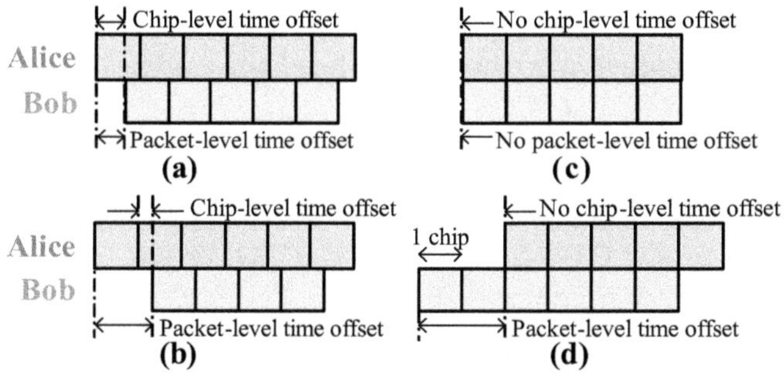

Figure 7: Examples of collisions with or without chip-level time offset.

In the one-TX one-RX case, since the channel parameter H can be estimated [45], the RX is able to resolve $X[n]$ using the received $Y[n]$ and the given Eq. (1), as long as the signal-to-noise ratio (SNR) is large enough. Thus, the transmitted packet is successfully decoded.

In contrast, in the two-TX one-RX case, though H_A, H_B, and $Y[n]$ are known in Eq. (2), two unknown variables $X_A[n]$ and $X_B[n]$ cannot be resolved simultaneously with only one equation. Hence, conventional wireless systems cannot deal with multi-packet collision. To resolve $X_A[n]$ and $X_B[n]$, it is necessary to explore other available information.

3.2 Two Categories of Multi-Packet Collision

In this paper, collisions are classified into two categories according to the chip-level time offset (CTO) among multiple packets in a collision. In the rest part of §3, §4 and §5, we use the two-packet collision (instead of multi-packet) and only the I phase baseband samples (instead of I-Q phases) as examples to explain the mZig design easily.

• **Collision with chip-level time offset**. A collision in this category shows that any chip in packet Alice does not align with any chip in packet Bob. Mathematically, a chip-level time offset exists when

$$\tau_{AB} = |T_{AB}| \textbf{ mod } \frac{1}{C} \neq 0, \tag{3}$$

where τ_{AB} is the chip-level time offset, $|T_{AB}|$ is the packet-level time offset between Alice and Bob in a collision, **mod** is the modulus operator, and $1/C$ is the duration of a chip. Some examples of collisions w/ CTO are shown in Fig. 7(a)(b).

• **Collision without chip-level time offset**. A collision in this category is that the overlapped chips between Alice and Bob are aligned. Such a collision can be judged by

$$\tau_{AB} = |T_{AB}| \textbf{ mod } \frac{1}{C} = 0. \tag{4}$$

Some examples of collisions w/o CTO are shown in Fig. 7(c)(d). In particular, even two packets have a packet-level time offset, it is possible that they have no chip-level time offset as shown in Fig. 7(d).

3.3 CrossIC Design

Cross Interference Cancellation (CrossIC) is one core design in mZig, which leverages the unique features of 'oversampling' and 'known shaping' to decompose multiple packets in a collision with chip-level time offset. The basic idea of CrossIC is to use collision-free samples and known shaping to estimate next some samples within a chip duration.

Denote λ to be the number of samples in one chip, where $\lambda = S/(C/2)$, where $C/2$ is the chip rate of I phase. Since CTO τ_{AB} is able to be detected (refer to §4.1), the number of samples k in CTO can be calculated by $k = \lfloor \tau_{AB} S \rfloor$, τ_{AB} is the duration of CTO and S is the sampling rate. When two packets are detected in one collision, we denote A and B as the packets from Alice and Bob, respectively. As the analysis in §3.1, two unknown variable $X_A[n]$ and $X_B[n]$ cannot be resolved simultaneously in Eq. (2) with only one known sample $Y[n]$. In order to decompose $X_A[n]$ and $X_B[n]$, CrossIC is to introduce the shaping relationship as a new information, which leverages k collision-free samples $X_A[n-1], X_A[n-2], \cdots, X_A[n-k]$ to estimate $X_A[n]$. Then, $X_B[n]$ in Eq. (2) is able to be calculated.

Based on the oversampling and the known shaping features, multiple samples forming a half-sine pulse shaping can be represented by

$$\begin{aligned} H_A X_A[i] &= c\, \alpha \sin(\pi f t), \\ &= c\, \alpha \sin(\pi f \Delta(i - n + k + 1)), \end{aligned} \tag{5}$$

where $H_A X_A[i]$ is the value of i-th sample, c is the sign indicator (+1 for chip '1' and -1 for chip '0'), α is the amplitude of a chip in packet A, $\sin(\pi f t)$ presents the half-sine waveform, $f = C/2 = 1$Mchip/s is the chip rate of I phase, t is the duration of one chip whose range is $0 \leq t \leq 1\mu$s, $t = \Delta(i - n + k + 1)$ bridges t to the i-th sample, Δ is the time interval between two samples, and $(i-n+k+1)$ aligns the i-th sample to the range $0 \leq t \leq 1\mu$s.

CrossIC decomposes a collision chip-by-chip in a cross manner, *i.e.*, one chip for Alice, then one chip for Bob. For every chip, CrossIC have two steps: extraction and estimation. Using the example in Fig. 2, we explain how CrossIC works in detail.

• Extraction A: extract k collision-free samples in the first chip of A. When the packet-level time offset T_{AB} is detected, the chip-level time offset is $\tau_{AB} = T_{AB} \textbf{mod} \frac{1}{C}$. Thus, the number of collision-free samples $k = \lfloor \tau_{AB} S \rfloor$ can be calculated. In Fig. 2(b), k=3 collision-free samples are extracted.

• Estimation A: use k collision-free samples to estimate the next $(\lambda - k)$ samples in the first chip of A. We discuss this estimation step in two cases.

Case I ($\tau_{AB} = |T_{AB}| \neq 0$): When the chip-level time offset is equal to the packet-level time offset as shown in Fig. 7(a), there is no pre-knowledge of α. Hence, in Eq. (5), two variables c and α are unknown. The extracted collision-free samples are used to not only judge c but also estimate α. Given k collision-free samples, c is determined by

$$c = \begin{cases} 1, & \text{if} \sum_{i=n-k}^{n-1} H_A X_A[i] > 0; \\ -1, & \text{if} \sum_{i=n-k}^{n-1} H_A X_A[i] < 0. \end{cases} \tag{6}$$

When the sum of k samples is larger than 0, this chip is '1' and the waveform is a positive half-sine, so $c = 1$. Otherwise, the chip is '0' with a negative half-sine, so $c = -1$.

Only having c is inadequate to decompose the next chips. The value of α is required to be known as well. Substituting any collision-free sample into Eq. (5), we obtain one result of α. However, because collision-free samples suffer from noise in wireless channels, k different values of α are obtained by k collision-free samples. To approach the real value, we adopt the average value $\widetilde{\alpha}$ as the estimated result:

$$\widetilde{\alpha} = \frac{\sum_{i=n-k}^{n-1} H_A X_A[i]}{c \sum_{i=n-k}^{n-1} \sin(\pi f \Delta(i - n + k + 1))}. \tag{7}$$

Substituting c and $\widetilde{\alpha}$ into Eq. (5), we can calculate the values of next $(\lambda - k)$ samples of A such as $X_A[n], X_A[n+1], \cdots, X_A[n+\lambda-k-1]$. In Fig. 2(b), $(\lambda - k) = 2$ samples of the first chip for Alice are estimated.

Case II ($\tau_{AB} \neq 0$ and $\tau_{AB} < |T_{AB}|$): When the chip-level time offset is not equal to the packet-level time offset as shown in Fig. 7(b), there are some collision-free chips at the beginning of packet. The solution for Case II is simpler than Case I, because α can be measured from the collision-free chips directly. With k collision-free samples, we just need to determine c by Eq. (6). And the next $(\lambda - k)$ samples of A can be estimated as the same method in Case I.

- Extraction B: extract $(\lambda - k)$ collision-free samples in the first chip of B. When the $(\lambda - k)$ samples $H_A X_A[i]$ ($i = n, n+1, \cdots, n+\lambda-k-1$) are estimated, the $(\lambda - k)$ samples $H_B X_B[i]$ can be calculated by $Y[i] - H_A X_A[i]$, (we ignore noise W in this section and will discuss it in §4.2). Then, these subtracted samples $H_B X_B[i]$ become collision-free. In Fig. 2(b), $(\lambda - k) = 2$ samples of Bob are collision-free after the substraction.
- Estimation B: use $(\lambda - k)$ collision-free samples to estimate the next k samples in the first chip of B. Similarly, the estimation B step is similar to the estimation A, where the explicit equations are as follows.

$$H_B X_B[i] = c\, \beta \sin(\pi f \Delta(i - n + 1)). \tag{8}$$

$$c = \begin{cases} 1, & \text{if} \sum_{i=n}^{n+\lambda-k-1} H_B X_B[i] > 0; \\ -1, & \text{if} \sum_{i=n}^{n+\lambda-k-1} H_B X_B[i] < 0. \end{cases} \tag{9}$$

$$\widetilde{\beta} = \frac{\sum_{i=n}^{n+\lambda-k-1} H_B X_B[i]}{c \sum_{i=n}^{n+\lambda-k-1} \sin(\pi f \Delta(i - n + 1))}. \tag{10}$$

After the estimation by above three equations, the values of next k samples of B can be calculated. In Fig. 2(b), $k = 2$ samples of the first chip for Bob are estimated.

Repeating the extraction and the estimation iteratively as shown in Fig. 2(c), mZig decomposes the collided packet into two packets A and B chip-by-chip.

The estimation errors of $\widetilde{\alpha}$ and $\widetilde{\beta}$ depend on the signal-noise ratio (SNR). Assume the average noise on every sample is $\overline{W}$. In the conventional ZigBee, the SNR of Alice's chip is

$$\frac{\text{Signal}}{\text{Noise}} = \frac{\sum_{i=1}^{\lambda} \alpha \sin(\pi f \Delta i)}{\overline{W}\lambda}. \tag{11}$$

In CrossIC, the SNRs of Alice's chip and Bob's chip are

$$\frac{\sum_{i=1}^{k} \alpha \sin(\pi f \Delta i)}{\overline{W}k} \quad \text{and} \quad \frac{\sum_{i=k+1}^{\lambda} \beta \sin(\pi f \Delta i)}{\overline{W}(\lambda - k)}, \tag{12}$$

respectively. Compared with ZigBee, the SNRs for chip estimation in CrossIC are a little reduced, which will slightly increase the estimation errors. More impacts of SNRs will be shown in simulation §8.2.

Furthermore, the backward CrossIC is able to operate from the last chip to the first one for a collided packet. In Fig.7(a), we find that there is not only a CTO at the first chip but also a CTO at the last chip. Hence, the decomposition by CrossIC on two directions is symmetric. One more decomposed result is obtained by the backward CrossIC, which is a double check to reduce the estimation errors.

3.4 AmpCoD Design

Amplitude Combination based Decomposition (AmpCoD) is another core design in mZig, which leverages the unique feature of 'uniform amplitude' to decompose packets in a collision w/o CTO. Since there is no CTO, CrossIC fails to work due to no collision-free samples. To this end, AmpCoD is proposed to leverage the different amplitude combinations to decompose every collided chip into two original chips.

Table 2: Four amplitude combinations in a two-packet collision without chip-level time offset.

Alice	chip='1'	'1'	'0'	'0'
Bob	chip='1'	'0'	'1'	'0'
Amplitude	$\alpha+\beta$	$\alpha-\beta$	$-\alpha+\beta$	$-\alpha-\beta$

Consider if only Alice transmits her packet, each received chip at RX is a half-sine waveform with the amplitude either α when chip='1' or $-\alpha$ when chip='0'. If only Bob transmits his packet, the amplitude is either β or $-\beta$. When they transmit concurrently, their signals are added up in air. In the scenario of two-packet collision w/o CTO, their amplitudes form $2^2 = 4$ combinations as listed in Tab. 2. AmpCoD requires that the amplitude difference exists between two packets, *i.e.*, $|\alpha - \beta| > \max(\epsilon, \overline{W})$, where ϵ is the amplitude unit of ADC (*e.g.*, the amplitude unit of an 8-bit ADC is $(\alpha + \beta)/2^8$.) and $\overline{W}$ is the average noise.

AmpCoD also have two steps: amplitude statistic and chip identification. Using the example in Fig. 3, we explain how AmpCoD works in detail.

- Amplitude statistic: count the number of different amplitude levels, estimate the number of packets, and build the relationship between amplitudes. We discuss this statistic step in two cases.

Case III ($\tau_{AB} = |T_{AB}| = 0$): When neither the chip-level nor the packet-level has any time offset as shown in Fig. 7(c), the waveform of a collided chip is still half-sine and there is no pre-knowledge of α or β. AmpCoD needs to count the number of different amplitudes of all chips in the collided packet. If four different levels can be found in the statistics, AmpCoD can determine that the collision is a two-packet collision. Denote these four levels by $L_1, \cdots, L_4$, where $L_1 > L_2 > L_3 > L_4$. Without loss of generality, we assume $\alpha > \beta$. Using Tab. 2, AmpCoD can build a mapping relationship between Ls and amplitude combinations

$$\begin{cases} L_1 = \alpha + \beta; & L_3 = -\alpha + \beta; \\ L_2 = \alpha - \beta; & L_4 = -\alpha - \beta. \end{cases} \tag{13}$$

Case IV ($\tau_{AB} = 0$ and $|T_{AB}| \neq 0$): When a collision has no CTO but has packet-level time offset as shown in Fig. 7(d), α or/and β can be obtained from the collision-free chips. For example, in Fig. 7(d), α can be obtained from the last chip and β can be obtained from the first two chips. In this case, the procedures including the counting of different levels and the estimation of the number of collided packets can be skipped. Then, the mapping relationship in Eq. (13) can be built by known α and β directly.

- Chip identification: identify every chip in the collided packet to be multiple chips according to the built relationship. When a chip's level approaches L_i, both case III and case IV identify this chip using Eq. (13). For example, the amplitude of the fifth chip in Fig. 3 approaches L_4, this chip can be decomposed to be a chip '0' for Alice because of $-\alpha$ and a chip '0' for Bob because of $-\beta$.

4. DESIGN ENHANCEMENT FOR MZIG

With only the core design in §3, mZig cannot provide a satisfactory performance because several practical issues

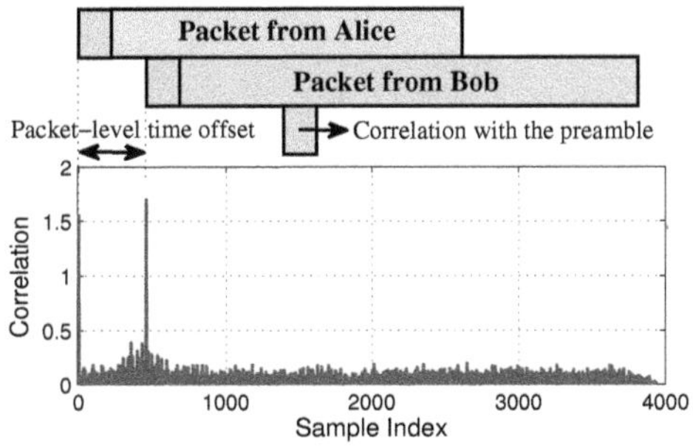

Figure 8: Time offset detection for collision

largely affect the decomposition, such as noise, multipath, and frequency offset. This section presents the design enhancement for mZig in order to mitigate these effects.

4.1 Time Offset Detection

Collision detection and time offset detection are required in practical mZig.

To detect a collision with packet-level time offset, we adopt the similar method in [15]. Any ZigBee packet starts with a preamble including 32 bits of '0's [2]. A collision can be detected by this known preamble using correlation calculation. The known preamble has $L = 32 \times \frac{32}{4} \times \lambda = 256\lambda$ samples, where $\frac{32}{4}$ is the redundancy of bit-to-chip spreading, and λ is the number of samples in a chip. Align these L samples with the first L received samples and compute their correlation. Then, shift the alignment to the next sample and re-compute. Repeat this process until the end of the packet. The correlation result is near zero except when the preamble is perfectly aligned with the beginning of one certain packet. An example of the correlation result for a two-packet collision is shown in Fig. 8. A two-packet collision is detected if there are two spikes in the result. One spike is at the beginning of the collided packet, and the position of the second spike indicates the start of the second packet. Hence, the packet-level time offset $|T_{AB}|$ is detected by the distance between two spikes. Then, the chip-level time offset τ_{AB} can be calculated by Eq. (4). In addition, an m-packet collision is detected if there are m spikes in the result.

To detect a collision without packet-level time offset, we propose a detection method, namely $\underline{2^m}$ $\underline{\text{A}}$mplitude $\underline{\text{L}}$evels (2MAL). When a two-packet collision with $T_{AB} = 0$, the first 256 chips have two levels of amplitudes (*i.e.*, $\alpha + \beta$ and $-\alpha - \beta$) because they have the same 32-bit '0's preamble. In addition, it is possible that there are some collision-free chips in the end of the packet. These collision-free chips can be detected by having two levels of amplitudes, where these two amplitudes are in the range of preamble's two amplitudes because either $|\alpha|$ or $|\beta|$ is $< |\alpha + \beta|$. However, in the other chips, four levels of amplitudes can be found as discussion in Tab. 2. Hence, 2MAL works as follows: if two-level amplitudes are counted in the first 256 chips and 2^m-level amplitudes are counted in the collided chips, an m-packet collision is detected without packet-level time offset.

4.2 Anti-Noise Design

Noises are inevitable in real wireless channels. In order to reduce the negative effect of noises, we propose the anti-noise design to enhance the performance of mZig.

Because the noises are time-varying (*e.g.*, the common noise model follows the Gaussian distribution $W \sim \mathcal{N}(0, \sigma^2)$),

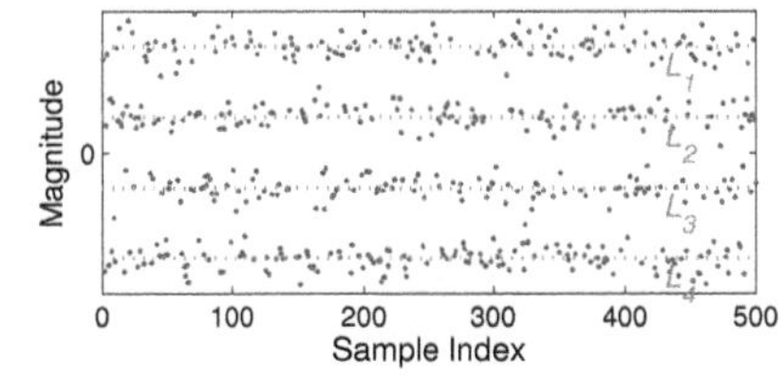

Figure 9: Measured amplitudes of samples.

the effects of noises on every chip are different. The anti-noise design leverages the concept of average noises $\overline{W}$, so the effect of noises on different chips trends to the same.

In CrossIC, the estimation of α (or β) is chip-independent. Thus, the estimated $\widetilde{\alpha}$ of every chip is different when noises $W[n]$s exist. However, the original αs should be the same due to the uniform amplitude feature. After all $\widetilde{\alpha}$s are obtained by CrossIC, the anti-noise design averages all $\widetilde{\alpha}$s to be an $\overline{\alpha}$, in which the noises $W[n]$s are also averaged to be a $\overline{W}$. The effect of noises can be largely reduced by taking $\overline{\alpha}$ as the known amplitude and re-operating CrossIC.

In AmpCoD and 2MAL, the determination of L in the amplitude statistic step is also affected by noises. For example, a original sample should be L_1 but the measured sample is $L_1 + W[n]$. The measured samples of amplitudes in a collision w/o CTO are shown in Fig. 9. The anti-noise design in AmpCoD and 2MAL also resorts to the average concept in order to reduce the effect of noises in α and β estimations. There are four steps in the anti-noise design. (i) Use the channel estimation [18] to get a rough $\overline{W}$. (ii) Use a typical classification method (*e.g.*, SVM [6]) with parameter $\overline{W}$ to classify samples and get the number of amplitude levels. (iii) If the number of amplitude levels is a power of 2^m, an m-packet collision is detected. (iv) Average all amplitudes belonging to one level to get the estimated amplitude of this level as shown in Fig. 9. In addition, the relationship between levels can be used to assist the determination. For example, in Eq. (13), $L_1 = -L_4$ and $L_2 = -L_3$.

4.3 Multipath Filter

In conventional one-TX one-RX ZigBee communications, since the chip rate is low, 2Mchip/s, the multipath effect is not severe (much smaller than WiFi, whose bandwidth is 20MHz). Thus, the redundancy of bit-to-chip spreading is adequate to against multipath. However, in the multi-TX one-RX convergecast scenario, multiple transmissions suffer from different multipath effects and their resultant effect is severe on accurate decomposition. As a result, we design a multipath filter method to reduce the multipath effect.

This method also resorts to the result of channel estimation [18]. The mutlipath feature of any channel between one certain TX to RX can be modeled by a sequences of impulse responses. For example, the multipath feature between Alice and RX is shown in Fig. 10. When a chip '1' is determined, its multipath effect can be calculated by the chip's waveform convolving with the impulse responses as shown in Fig. 10. Assume the channel estimations of Alice-to-RX and Bob-to-RX are known, whenever a chip is estimated, (i) match the amplitude to the channel estimation result in order to know which channel this chip belongs to, (ii) calculate the multipath effect by convolution, and (iii) reduce the estimated multipath effect of this chip from the collided packet. The multipath filter operates as a plug-in step in CrossIC/AmpCoD chip-by-chip during the decomposition.

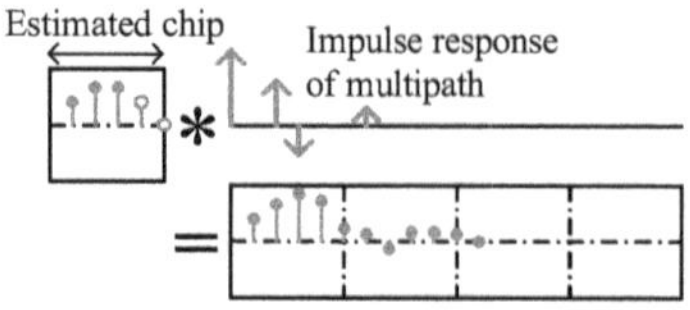

Figure 10: Multipath filter.

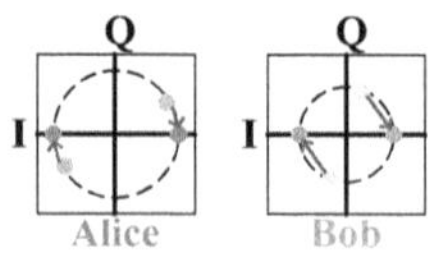

Figure 11: Frequency offset compensation.

4.4 Frequency Offset Compensation

A frequency offset always exists between two commercial radios. Such an offset causes a linear displacement in the phase of the received signal. Typically, a RX estimates the frequency offset by phase tracking and then compensates for it. The frequency offset can be tracked using any prior collision-free packet [15, 34].

In the one-TX one-RX scenario, the compensation of frequency offset is directly applied on the received packet at RX. However, in the convergecast scenario, *e.g.*, two-TX and one-RX, the conventional method fails because the frequency offsets of Alice-to-RX and Bob-to-RX are different. Mathematically,

$$Y[n] = H_A X_A[n] e^{j2\pi n \delta_A \Delta} + H_B X_B[n] e^{j2\pi n \delta_B \Delta} + W[n], \tag{14}$$

where δ_A and δ_B are the frequency offsets of Alice-to-RX and Bob-to-RX, respectively. Our solution compensates the frequency offset in a chip-by-chip manner. In CrossIC, there are two existing steps for every chip: extraction and estimation. With the compensation, the number of steps is extended to three. The new second step is to compensate the frequency offset on the extracted samples. For example, the frequency offsets of Alice and Bob are tracked as shown in Fig. 11. After the step of Extraction A in §3.3, the new second step compensates the tracked offset (Alice-to-RX) on the collision-free samples. The step of Estimation A operates then. Similarly, decomposing a chip for Bob follows the steps: Extraction B, Compensation B, and Estimation B.

5. MZIG ANALYSIS

This section analyzes the capability of mZig, the scope of mZig, and the transplant of mZig to Bluetooth.

5.1 Beyond Two-Packet Collision

The proposed mZig is easy to extend from two-packet collision to m-packet collision. We use three-packet collision as an example. More concurrent transmissions can adopt the same extension method.

The correlation method proposed in §4.1 can detect m-packet collision w/ CTO by m spikes. If there are three spikes detected, a three-packet collision w/ CTO are determined. Using these three spikes, the packet-level time offsets T_{AB}, T_{BC}, T_{CA} can be calculated. Thus, the CTOs τ_{AB}, τ_{BC}, τ_{CA} are also available. Assume that the samples in τ_{AB} are collision-free at the beginning of the collision. CrossIC (§3.3) operates as: extract these samples, and the first chip of Alice is estimated. Then, extract the samples in τ_{BC}, the first chip of Bob can be estimated. At last, extract the samples in τ_{CA}, the first chip of Carol can be estimated. Iteratively operate the extraction and estimation chip-by-chip, a three-packet collision w/ CTO can be decomposed.

The 2MAL method in §4.1 can detect m-packet collision w/o CTO by 2^m amplitude levels. For example, if there are eight different amplitude levels detected by 2MAL, a three-packet collision w/o CTO can be determined. Denote the eight levels by $L_1, L_2 \cdots, L_8$. Assume that $L_1 > L_2 > \cdots > L_8$ and $\alpha > \beta > \zeta > 0$, where ζ is the chip amplitude of the third TX Carol. With the top-2 levels $L_1 = \alpha + \beta + \zeta$ and $L_2 = \alpha + \beta - \zeta$, we have $\zeta = (L_1 - L_2)/2$. Similarly, with L_1 and $L3$, the value of β is determined. With known L_1, β and ζ, we can determine α. Then, the mapping relationship between the amplitude levels and chips can be built. One mapping example is listed in Tab. 3. Based on this table, chips can be decomposed by AmpCoD (§3.4).

Table 3: Eight amplitude levels in a three-packet collision without chip-level time offset.

Alice	'1'	'1'	'1'	'1'	'0'	'0'	'0'	'0'
Bob	'1'	'1'	'0'	'0'	'1'	'1'	'0'	'0'
Carol	'1'	'0'	'1'	'0'	'1'	'0'	'1'	'0'
Level	L_1	L_2	L_3	L_4	L_5	L_6	L_7	L_8

The hybrid m-packet collision is also possible. For example, in a three-packet collision, packets A and B have a CTO while packets A and C have no CTO. In such a case, CrossIC is firstly adopted to decompose the overlapped signal into two group: B and AC, while AC is considered as one packet here because they have no CTO. After B is decomposed out, packets A and C can be decomposed by AmpCoD.

5.2 Error Propagation

Up to now, we have described the system assuming correct decoding. In practice, the estimation of one certain chip may be error. For example, a chip '1' is falsely estimated to be '0'. If a chip error occurs during decomposition, it may affect later chips because of the iterative decomposition manner. Using the analysis in ZigZag [15], we have the result that the error propagation in mZig dies exponentially fast as ZigZag. More error propagation analysis in iterative decoding method can refer to SigSag [36]. We will show the impact of error propagation in performance evaluation §7.2.

5.3 Scope

The proposed mZig adopts a best effort design. In the absence of collisions, mZig acts like the conventional ZigBee. However, when collisions occur, mZig attempts to decompose and decode them.

The theoretical upper bound of concurrent transmission in mZig is $M = \max(m) = \lfloor \frac{S}{2 \times C} \rfloor$, where C is the chip rate, and 2 indicates that at least two collision-free samples are needed to estimate one chip. Using only one collision-free sample may result in estimation failure because Eq. (5) cannot be successfully resolved if $X_A[i] = 0$. However, when there are two successive samples, the half-sine pulse shaping can guarantee that at least one sample is nonzero. From the theoretical upper bound, we observe that the capability of mZig is mainly determined by the sampling rate of the ADC in wireless device. The practical concurrent capability is smaller than the theoretical one due to noises and estimation errors. We will show the experimental results in §7.2.

Most collision patterns are able to be addressed by mZig. Nevertheless, mZig is not omni-directional. For example, AmpCoD fails when any two packets have the same amplitude, in which the levels of amplitude combinations $(\alpha - \beta)$ and $(-\alpha + \beta)$ cannot be distinguished. However, the mZig design is orthogonal to other collision resolution techniques. If the failure of mZig occurs, other alternative techniques can be triggered to resolve the collision.

The proposed mZig is a customized technique for ZigBee, which leverages ZigBee's features in physical layer. mZig

Table 4: **Comparison of physical layer features between Bluetooth Low Energy (BLE) and ZigBee.**

	BLE	ZigBee
Required features for mZig		
Oversampling	Yes, 1Msymbol/s	Yes, 2Mchip/s
Know shaping	Yes, Gaussian	Yes, Half-sine
Uniform amplitude	Yes, GFSK	Yes, O-QPSK
Other physical layer features		
Baseband unit	Symbol	Chip
Bitrate	1Mbps	250kbps
Spreading technique	FHSS	DSSS

cannot be applied in WiFi because their physical layer features are totally different. For example, WiFi adopts the raised cosine pulse shaping (inter-symbol interferences exist in this shaping method, so the chip waveform is not independent) and the QAM modulation (multiple levels of amplitudes in one packet). However, mZig is able to extend to other wireless protocol, which have the similar features.

5.4 Transplant of mZig in Bluetooth

Bluetooth Low Energy (BLE) [4] is another key protocol focusing on the field of low-power communications. The core design of mZig can be easily transplanted to BLE, because BLE has the similar physical layer features as ZigBee. In Tab. 4, we compare the physical layer features between BLE and ZigBee. We find that (i) BLE has the oversampling feature, because its symbol rate is 1Msymbol/s, where symbol is the smallest unit carrying information in BLE's baseband. If an off-the-shelf ADC has 61.44Msps, the samples of a symbol is more than 60. (ii) BLE has the known shaping feature. Based on the Gaussian pulse shaping, the waveform of every symbol in BLE is known and the Gaussian shaping is symbol-independent. (iii) BLE has the uniform amplitude feature. Since BLE adopts GFSK modulation, which modulates samples by frequency but not amplitude, the amplitudes of symbols in one packet are the same.

Several other physical layer features are different between BLE and ZigBee, so the enhancement designs for BLE are different from ZigBee. Since this paper mainly focuses on ZigBee, we do not implement mZig in BLE. However, we simulate the performance of mZig in BLE in §8.2.

6. IMPLEMENTATION

We implement mZig on USRP and build a seven-node testbed. This section presents the details of implementation including the physical (PHY) layer, the media access control (MAC) layer, and the prototype.

6.1 Physical Layer Development

TX side: mZig requires no change on the PHY of TXs. Hence, any TX in our prototype adopts the conventional PHY of ZigBee as shown in Fig. 4.

RX side: mZig requires some lightweight changes on the PHY of RX, including a new decomposition module, namely Decomposition module for mZig (DmZig), and M parallel decoding lines as shown in Fig. 12.

The functionality of DmZig is to decompose the received baseband samples of a collision into m sequences of collision-free samples. The flow chart of DmZig module is illustrated in Fig. 13. The main procedure of DmZig is as follows. (i) DmZig detects whether there is a collision in the baseband samples using the correlation and the 2MAL methods (§4.1). If there is no collision, this sequence of collision-free samples

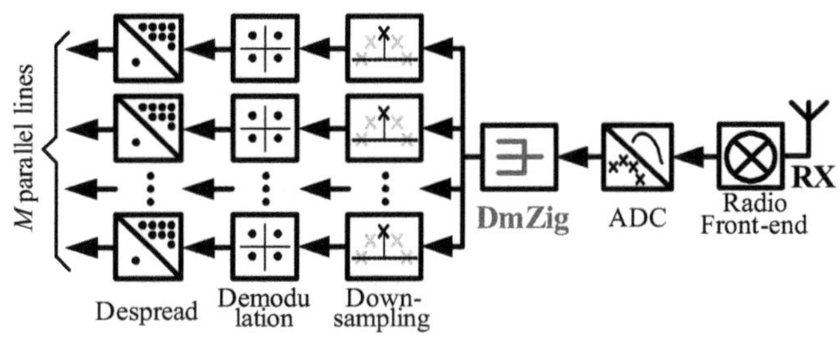

Figure 12: Physical layer of an RX with mZig.

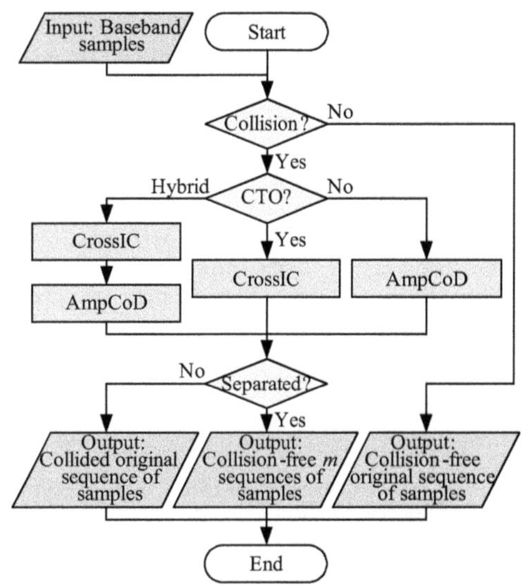

Figure 13: Flow chart in DmZig module.

are output directly. If a collision is detected, DmZig needs to know how many concurrent packets, *i.e.*, m, in this collision and the collision type of these m packets. (ii) The correlation and the 2MAL methods (§4.1) are used to detect the collision type. If the collision is detected w/o CTO, AmpCoD (§3.4) is adopted to decompose the samples. If the collision is detected w/ CTO, CrossIC (§3.3) is adopted. If a hybrid collision (§5.1) is detected, samples are decomposed by CrossIC and AmpCoD in a serial manner. (iii) There are three kinds of outputs in DmZig as shown in Fig. 12. If there is no collision, the output is the original baseband samples, and one decoding line can deal with them; if the collision can be decomposed into m sequences, the output is m sequences of samples, and m decoding lines can deal with them; if the collision can be detected but cannot be decomposed, the output includes a flag of 'collision' and the original samples, then the other alternative collision resolution techniques [15, 17] will be triggered.

With the core and the enhancement designs together, the full version of CrossIC implemented in PHY includes:

- Collision-free samples extraction (§3.3),
- Frequency offset compensation (§4.4),
- Chip estimation (§3.3),
- Multipath filter (§4.3).

Above four steps are iteratively operated. After operating these four steps from the first to the last chip, CrossIC needs to do the anti-noise method (§4.2) and repeats above four steps again for reducing the effect of noises. In addition, the backward CrossIC (§3.3) is used for double check in the end.

The full version of AmpCoD includes:

- Amplitude statistic (§3.4),
- Anti-noise design (§4.2),

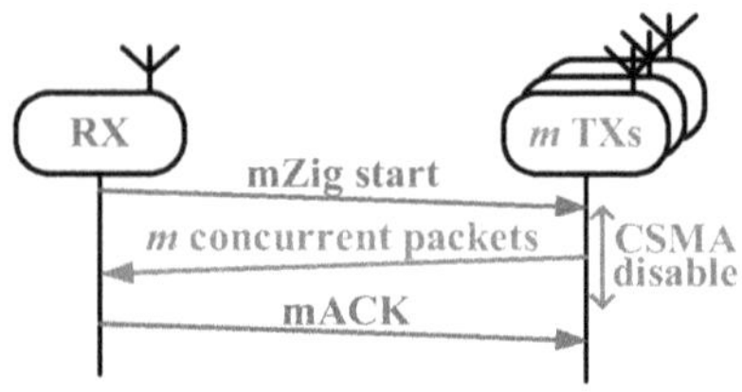

Figure 14: A basic MAC for mZig

• Chip identification (§3.4).

The functionality of M parallel decoding lines is to decode m sequences of collision-free samples (output of DmZig module) into bits in a parallel manner, so that the time consumption on decoding is reduced and the MPR is achieved. Since the number of concurrent transmissions m is not known a priori, we set the value of M is equal to the theoretical upper bound of m, where $M = \max(m) = \lfloor \frac{S}{2 \times C} \rfloor$. When the D-mZig module outputs m sequences of collision-free samples, m (where $m \leq M$) decoding lines are activated and decode m sequences respectively. The implementation complexity of M decoding lines is light, which is just M copies of the conventional decoding line.

6.2 Media Access Control Development

Although MAC design is not our focus in this paper, a basic MAC is still needed to be developed. The conventional MAC cannot be directly applied to mZig due to two problems: (i) The conventional MAC includes CSMA/CA. With CSMA/CA, multiple TXs cannot transmit concurrently. (ii) The conventional MAC includes the acknowledgement (ACK), which is sent by RX to TX for confirming the successful packet reception. But the conventional ACK is not suitable for the multi-TX one-RX convergecast.

A basic MAC for mZig is developed in our implementation, which is shown in Fig. 14, including three steps.

• The RX broadcasts an 'mZig start' message to inform that $\widetilde{M}$ TXs can transmit concurrently in the following time window, where the duration of window is given by this RX, and $\widetilde{M}$ is a number given by the customized scheduler.

• When TXs receive the 'mZig start' message, they disable their CSMA/CA and send packets during the window. CSMA/CA is re-opened after the window time is expired.

• When the window time is expired, the RX stops to receive packets, and sends an ACK to all TXs. This ACK for mZig is named mACK, which include ACKs for $\widetilde{M}$ TXs with all successfully received packets during the window.

In particular, we design an online scheduler built-in the MAC to give an estimated $\widetilde{M}$, where $\widetilde{M}$ is the practical capability of concurrent transmissions. If m TXs send packets concurrently and $m > \widetilde{M}$, mZig fails to decompose the collisions. In order to deal with the $m > \widetilde{M}$ cases, we design this scheduler to assign only $\widetilde{M}$ TXs can transmit in the following window. However, the value of $\widetilde{M}$ is not fixed, because it is varying according to the dynamic environment. This scheduler estimates the value of $\widetilde{M}$ in an online manner according to the bit error rate (BER) of all decoded packets. When BER$<< \xi$, $\widetilde{M}$ is increased; when BER $> \xi$, $\widetilde{M}$ is reduced; when BER$\leq \xi$ but not too far, $\widetilde{M}$ maintains its current value. In our experiment, we set $\xi = 10^{-3}$, which is a common setting in wireless communication to determine the successful reception of a packet. We set BER$<< \xi$ as BER$< 10^{-4}$. The initial $\widetilde{M}$ is set as the theoretical M.

Figure 15: Testbed

The other required functionalities such as phase tracking and channel estimation are the same as the typical ZigBee.

6.3 Prototype Development

We develop the prototype of mZig as follows.

Hardware: The hardware includes one USRP X310, six USRP B210s, and six iRobots. We develop mZig RX in USRP X310, which is a fixed but powerful software defined radio (SDR) device. USRP X310 is linked to a desktop. We develop mZig TXs in USRP B210s, which are portable SDRs, and power supplied by USB 3.0 port. USRP B210s are linked to laptops. Six iRobots can randomly move in a plane with speed less than 0.4m/s. These iRobots carry the laptops and USRP B210s to test not only static but also the dynamic channel effects on mZig in our experiment. Partial hardware devices are shown in Fig. 15.

We select USRP as mZig RX because of its high sampling-rate ADC. Some commercial ZigBee devices such as TelosB adopt 4Msps sampling rate, which are inadequate to operate CrossIC in mZig. On the other hand, both USRP and TelosB can serve as mZig TXs. In this work, we select USRPs as TXs so that the transmission samples can be logged at TX sides for chip-level comparison.

Software: GnuRadio is the software for developing mZig.

Testbed: Our testbed includes seven mZig nodes in a general office, whose area is 7.5×6.8m^2. Six TXs and one RX build a convergecast topology.

7. EXPERIMENT

Using the seven-node testbed, we conduct experiments to verify the feasibility of mZig and evaluate its performance.

7.1 Experiment Setting

Configuration:

• Sampling rate. The default sampling rate is set S=32Msps, which is 16x of the chip rate.

• Transmission power. We set Tx_Gain to be 70 in GnuRadio, so the transmission power is 0dB (USRP B210 is a uncalibrated device on its output power, so this setting is just 'near' 0dB according to the specification [1]), where 0dB (1mW) is the default TX power conditioned by ZigBee standard. With such a power setting, the RX can receive any TX's transmission in our 7.5×6.8m^2 office space.

• Channel selection. In an office environment, there are some WiFi and Bluetooth radios in 2.4GHz band. To avoid the effect of coexistence [11, 47, 50], we select the Channel 26 in our mZig experiment, which is a non-overlapping channel with WiFi. In addition, Bluetooth [4] adopts FHSS technology. Its working frequency quickly hops 1600 times per second. There is only one time channel overlap in 79 times. A comparative study [33] reveals that Bluetooth does not disturb ZigBee in most instances.

• Packet length. Each transmitting packet consists of a 32-bit preamble and a random payload of 200, 400, 600, 800,

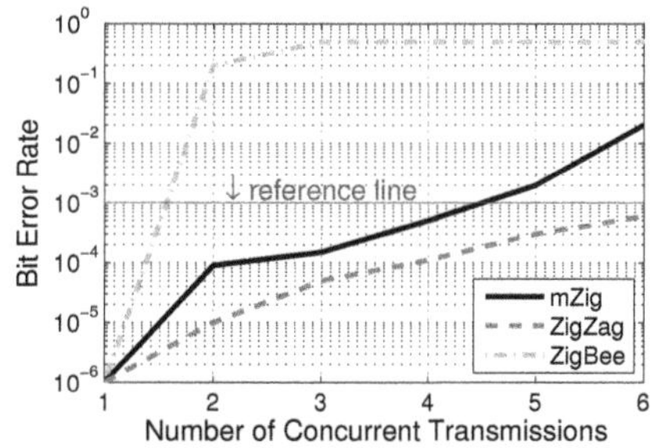

Figure 16: Comparison of different schemes on BER.

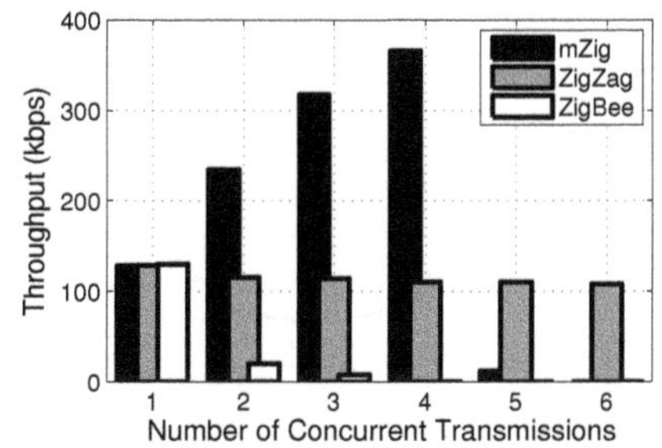

Figure 17: Comparison of schemes on throughput (without MAC).

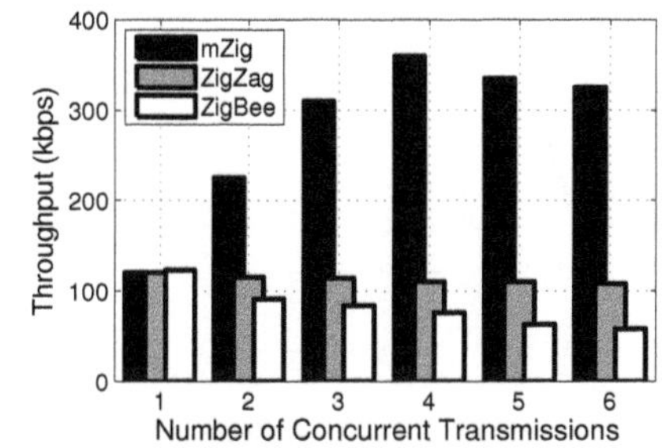

Figure 18: Comparison of schemes on throughput (with MAC).

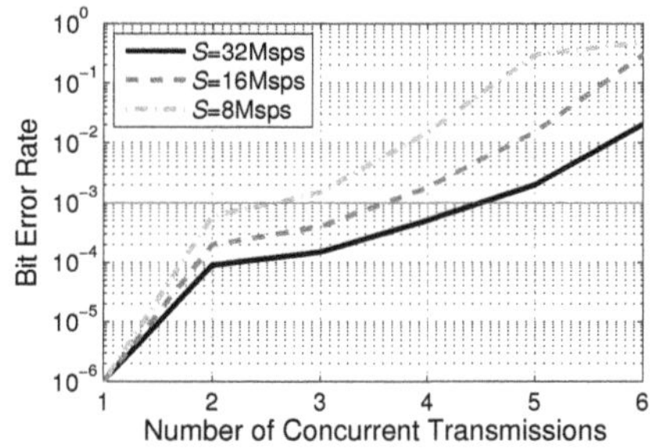

Figure 19: Impact of sampling rate

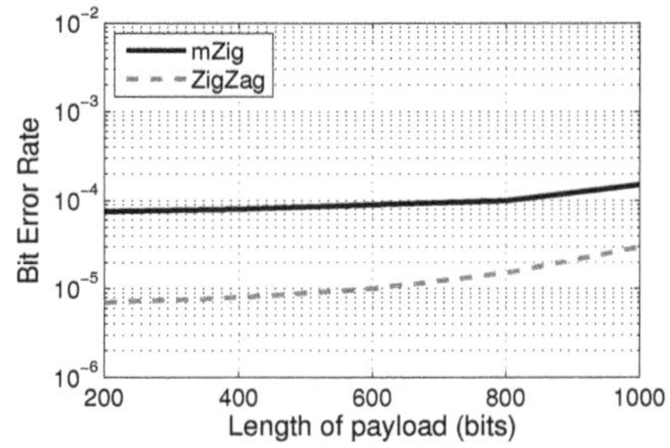

Figure 20: Impact of packet length.

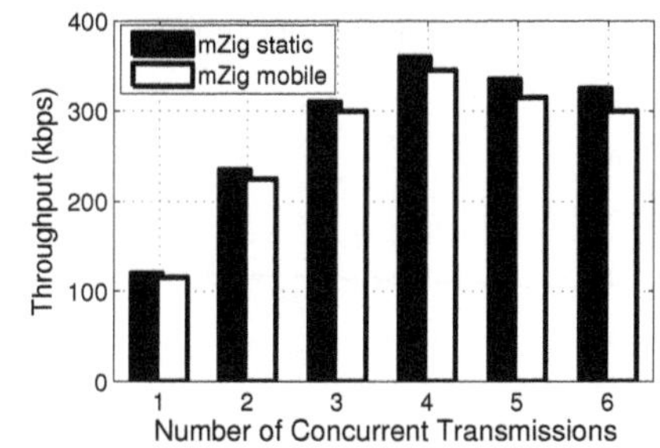

Figure 21: Impact of mobility.

Table 5: Probabilities of different collisions.

m TXs	w/ CTO	w/o CTO	hybrid	collision-free
2	93.4%	5.9%	0%	0.7%
3	82.3%	0.4%	17.2%	0.1%
4	65.7%	0%	34.3%	0%
5	50.3%	0%	49.7%	0%
6	35.8%	0%	64.2%	0%

or 1000 bits, which satisfies the payload length requirement of ZigBee, whose limitation is no more than 1064 bits.

Compared schemes:

- mZig: is the proposed design in this paper.
- ZigZag [15]: is the state-of-the-art design for collision resolution, which is also the closest work to our mZig. ZigZag resolves an m-packet collision using m collided packets.
- ZigBee [2]: is the conventional ZigBee protocol. ZigBee exploits CSMA/CA in its MAC to avoid collisions. ACK and retransmission mechanisms are used to guarantee the successful packet reception.

Metrics:

- Bit Error Rate (BER): is the rate of incorrect bits to all transmitted bits. We consider a packet to be correctly received if its BER is less than 10^{-3}. This setting is in accordance with typical wireless design [15].
- Throughput: is the average received bits in one second. A higher throughput indicates that more data can be received in unit time and more TXs are allowed to transmit concurrently. The throughput is the key metric to express the advantage of mZig.

7.2 Experiment Result

First, the probability statistics of different collisions in our experiments are shown in Tab. 5. We observe that most collisions are w/ CTO and hybrid. Thus, both CrossIC and AmpCoD in mZig are important to tackle different types of collisions. Moreover, the performance of CrossIC is the bottleneck of M, because most collisions have CTOs.

To verify the feasibility of mZig, we start the experiment with a varying number of TXs m from 1 to 6. In this experiment, MACs are disabled (neither scheduling in mZig nor CSMA in ZigBee) to show the decoding capability of PHYs only. Fig.16 compares BERs of three schemes with varying m. The conventional ZigBee cannot decode collisions. When m becomes 2, its BER increases to more than 2×10^{-1}. Since CrossIC in mZig leverages collision-free samples to estimate chips, more TXs lead to fewer available collision-free samples. Hence, the effect of noises on mZig increases with m. When $m \geq 5$, mZig's BER is larger than the reference line 10^{-3}. **This experiment demonstrates that the feasibility of mZig and its MPR capacity in this experimental environment is $m = 4$.** The BER of ZigZag also increases with m, but its trend is smoother than mZig. This result shows that its decoding capacity is over than 6 TXs. Although ZigZag is better than mZig on BER, mZig is better than ZigZag on throughput.

Fig.17 shows the throughput of three schemes, where MACs are still disabled. TXs transmit packets with a random interval between 1 to 4ms. When m=1, three schemes achieve a similar throughput, which is about 129kbps (smaller than the bitrate 250kbps due to channel estimation, interval, and so on). mZig largely improves the throughput with m due to its MPR capability. When $m = 2, 3, 4$, its throughput achieves 235, 318, 366kbps, respectively. However, mZig's PHY cannot decompose $\geq$5-packet collision, so throughput drops sharply when $m = 5$. ZigZag requires retransmissions to build m collided packets, and then m TX's packets can be resolved. Its throughput nearly keeps a constant with a little decrease with m. ZigBee's PHY cannot resolve collisions, so when $m \geq 2$, it nearly has no throughput.

Fig.18 also shows the throughput of three schemes, but MACs are enabled. For mZig, the throughput of m from 1 to 4 has only small change (about 121kbps) because of ACKs. However, when $m = 5$ and 6, the throughput is soared up to 330kbps. This result reveals the advantage of the scheduler, which learns the RX's MPR capability $\widetilde{M}$=4, and schedules 4 concurrent transmissions in every window. *i.e.*, even there are 5 TXs, only 4 TXs are assigned to transmit. Thus, the

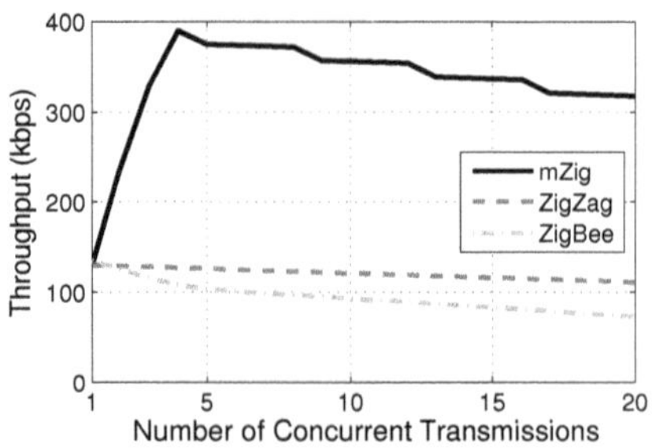

Figure 22: Throughput simulation.

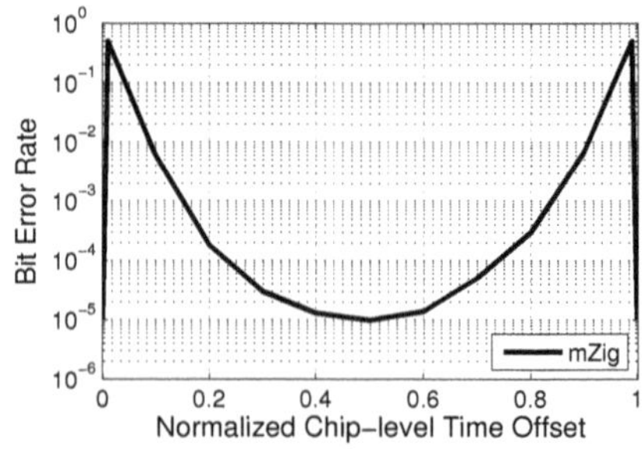

Figure 23: Impact of CTO.

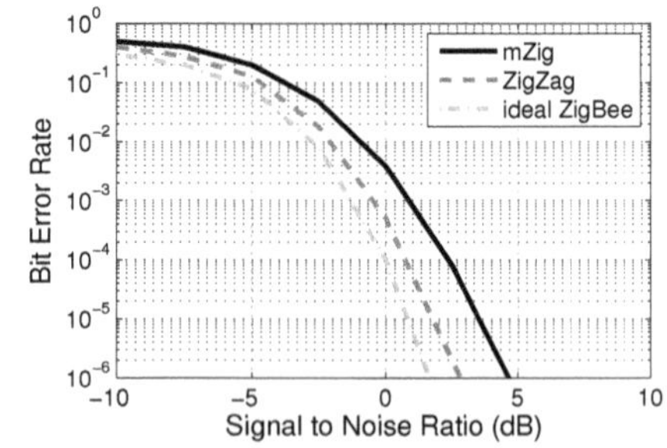

Figure 24: Impact of SNR.

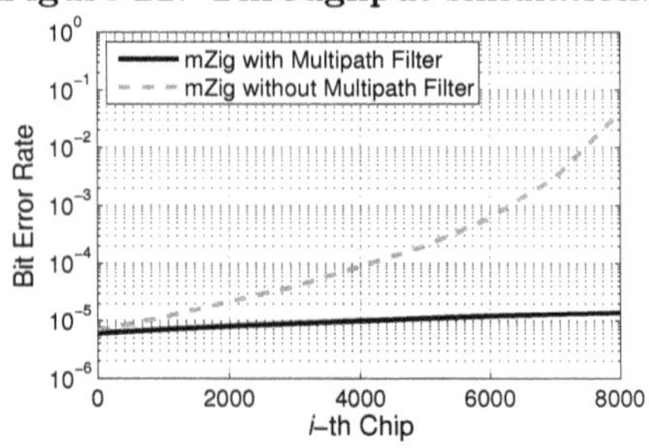

Figure 25: Impact of multipath.

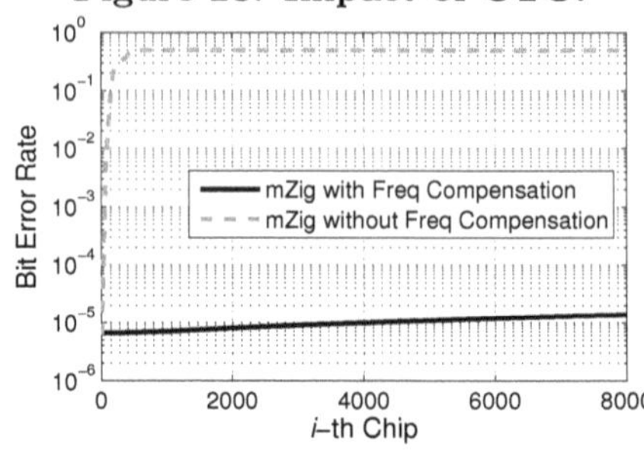

Figure 26: Impact of freq. offset.

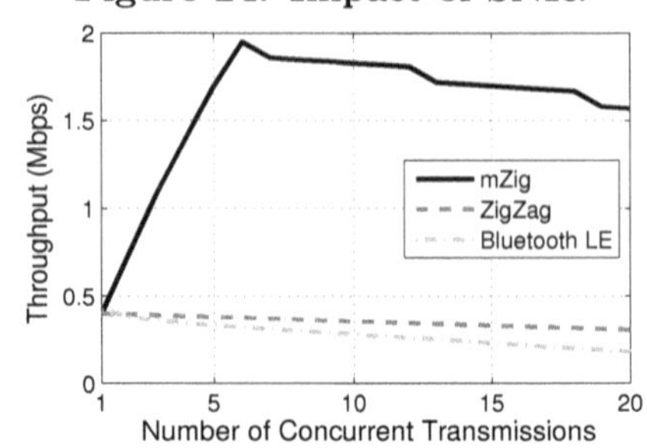

Figure 27: BLE simulation.

throughput of $m = 5$ and 6 is close to $m = 4$. A little decrease is caused by the scheduling overhead. ZigZag also changes slightly compared with Fig.17. Since MAC of ZigBee leverages CSMA to avoid collisions, only one TX can transmit packet in one time slot. We set the MAC parameters according to the ZigBee standard [2], *e.g.*, the maximal backoff is 4 and the ACK waiting duration is set as 120 symbol period. Fig.18 shows that there is some throughput in ZigBee, but it is still smaller than ZigZag. ZigBee's performance decreases with m because more TXs lead to more backoff. **This experiment demonstrates that the throughput is improved up to 3.2x by mZig compared with the state-of-the-art ZigZag, 4.5x compared with the conventional ZigBee.**

To understand the impacts of some practical factors on mZig, we conduct the following experiments.

Fig.19 mines the relation between the sampling rate and the BER in mZig. A larger sampling rate indicates more samples in one chip. *e.g.*, every chip has $\lambda = 16$ samples at 32Msps sampling rate, but $\lambda = 2$ at 4Msps. In addition, more TXs lead to smaller number of collision-free samples. For example, when $m = 2$, 32Msps has average $k = 16/2 = 8$ collision-free samples. But 4Msps has only $k = 0.5$, which is inadequate to decompose collisions w/ CTO. Fig.19 shows that the BER of mZig is gradually improved with the growth of sampling rate. When S=32Msps, the theoretical maximal $M = \lfloor 32M/(2 \times 2M) \rfloor = 8$. However, since the noises in office environment, the practical maximal $\widetilde{M} = 4$, where its BER is still smaller than 10^{-3}. When S=16Msps, $\widetilde{M} = 3$.

Fig. 20 shows the impact of different packet length, where the concurrent transmissions is set as m=2. The payload is varied from 200 to 1000 bits. We observe that BERs of both ZigZag and mZig slightly increase with the payload, which indicates that both schemes have error propagation problem, but not severe due to the limited packet length.

Fig. 21 shows the impact of mobility in mZig. Two cases are compared. In the static case, seven nodes are fixed and form a star topology, where six TXs have the same distance to the RX. In the mobile case, six iRobots randomly move in the office carrying laptops and USRPs. The speed of iRobots is set as 0.2m/s. The result in Fig. 21 is a long-term average. We find that in the mobile case, the throughput is a little lower than the static one. The reason is that the mobility increases the BER. In addition, some links are occasionally weak due to mobility.

8. SIMULATION

In the experiments, several parameters are uncontrollable, such as chip-level time offsets, noises, multipath, and frequency offset. In order to understand the impacts of these parameters, we conduct extensive simulations.

8.1 Simulation Setting

Our simulations inherit most settings from our experiments. Moreover, we amend several settings including: (i) 20 TXs and one RX form a convergecast scenario. (ii) A packet arrives at the RX with a random time point. So all collision types can be evaluated and the number of collision-free samples k is also a random number. (iii) The noise is set as a 3dBm AWGN. Three paths are set in our multipath model, where the power rate is 0.7:0.2:0.1. The frequency offset is a random angle.

8.2 Simulation Result

Our experiment performs based on a seven-node testbed. To investigate the throughput of mZig in a denser scenario, this simulation conducts based on 20 TXs and one-RX. Fig. 22 demonstrates (i) the experimental and the simulated throughput are similar. (ii) mZig can maintain the throughput at 300kbps when $m > 4$. Similarly, ZigZag and ZigBee also maintain their performance on throughput as the trends of constant with a little decrease.

Fig. 23 shows the impact of chip-level time offset. In this simulation, m is set to be 2. The X-axis presents the normalized time offset to the duration of one chip. Fig. 23 indicates that the best BER is achieved when the chip-level time offset is half of a chip duration. In this case, any chip is identified by the same number of collision-free samples. If a chip has λ=16 samples, when m=2, the maximal collision-free samples for both Alice and Bob is its average 16/2=8.

Fig. 24 shows the BER comparison of different schemes in different SNRs when m=2. Since ZigBee has no capability to address even a two-packet collision, its BER is not plotted in this figure. Instead, we plot a reference, which is the BER of ideal ZigBee decoding a collision-free packet. In Fig. 24, ZigZag achieves the similar BER of reference. Since mZig may estimate a certain chip with very few samples depending on the CTO, the impact of SNR on its estimation is large. Hence, the BER of mZig is not good as the other two, but still within the range of 3dB.

Fig. 25 shows the impact of multipath when $m = 2$. The X-axis presents the first chip to the 8000-th chip (1000 bits are spread to 8000 chips). Since mZig operates iteratively from the first to the last chip, without the multipath filter, the value of BER gradually increases. On the contrary, with the multipath filter, a low BER is maintained. This result demonstrates the functionality of our multipath filter.

Fig. 26 shows the impact of frequency offset when $m = 2$. Without the frequency offset compensation, chips cannot be estimated correctly. For example, the BER becomes larger than 10^{-3} when just decomposing to the 4-th chip, and then quickly soars to 50%. However, with the compensation, mZig keeps a low BER. This result demonstrates the functionality of our frequency offset compensation for mZig.

In the last simulation shown in Fig. 27, we transplant mZig in Bluetooth low energy (BLE). This simulation demonstrates the feasibility of mZig in BLE. We observe that mZig achieves the throughput of 1.9Mbps when $m = 6$, which is 5.4x of BLE, and 4.7x of ZigZag. The trends of the curves and the improvement ratio for BLE are similar to the results for ZigBee in Fig. 22.

9. RELATED WORK

Convergecast cannot bypass the collision problem, which attracts extensive studies to tackle this problem from different directions. We classify them into two categories.

Collision avoidance: The conventional ZigBee adopts CSMA [14, 35] to address collisions, which avoids collisions by random backoff time and retransmission. This method fails in some scenarios such as hidden terminals. Field tests [7] show that over 10% packet loss due to collisions in WLAN. In addition, the backoff time mechanism increases the delay by scheduling transmissions into different time slots. Even some recent scheduling studies [28] aim to reduce the time consumption, the theoretical upper bound of this approach is m time slots to transmit m packets.

RTS-CTS [46] is the supplement for CSMA/CA, which addresses the hidden terminal problem by handshake. However, the handshake introduces additional overheads. Experiments [22] show that RTS-CTS significantly reduces the overall throughput. Thus, common wireless devices disable RTS-CTS by default.

Different from the collision avoidance by backoff or handshake, mZig decomposes the collisions directly. So the delay is removed and the throughput is increased.

Collision resolution: Advanced researches advocate to resolve collisions for realizing MPR.

Capture effect [25] separates collisions by requiring significant power difference among multiple packets. But this requirement cannot be guaranteed due to no prior control.

Successive interference cancellation (SIC) [17, 30, 32] resolves collisions by distinct powers or pre-coded signatures. Similar to capture effect, SIC also demands prior scheduling and known users. Thus, most SICs are designed for cellular networks [30], which have the base stations to do the scheduling. SIC has another major limitation: TXs have to operate at a data rate much lower than the maximal one.

Network coding [44], analog network coding [23], XORs [24], interference alignment [16] and full duplex [21] decode collisions by subtracting some known packets from the collided packet. These techniques are not suitable for convergecast, where packets from different TXs are unknown a priori.

PIP [27] presents a customized code to achieve parallel communications. Buzz [39] and virtual full duplex [49] exploits compressive sensing to recover concurrent transmissions from collisions. The computational overhead of these methods is high, which may increase the transmission delay.

Constructive interference [10, 12, 43] is used to receive multiple synchronized transmissions of a same packet. Although constructive interference increases the transmission reliability and reduces the power consumption in ZigBee, its major limitation is that all packets must have the same content. Hence, it is not appropriate for the convergecast, where multiple TXs send different packets.

ZigZag [15] is the most related work to this paper. If a two-packets collision occurs, ZigZag demands two TXs retransmit packets to form another collision. Then, ZigZag separates two original packets in virtue of the different time offsets in two collisions. In this way, ZigZag requires m collided packets to decode m-packet collision. Theoretically, mZig improves the throughput m-fold than ZigZag because only one collided packet is adequate to realize MPR in mZig.

In comparison, mZig decomposes a collision based on the physical layer features of ZigBee and the collision itself, while requiring no pre-coding, priori control, known packets or retransmissions. Besides, mZig is lightweight on implementation and computation. Furthermore, mZig can work with other collision resolution techniques such as ZigZag, XORs, and full duplex complementarily.

10. CONCLUSION

This paper presents mZig, a physical layer design to enable multi-packet reception in ZigBee. Leveraging the physical layer features of ZigBee, mZig decomposes multiple packets from a collision chip-by-chip. Our core contribution is a novel MPR technique customized for ZigBee. Through both theoretical analysis and performance evaluation, we show that mZig embraces the collision, receives the concurrent transmissions, and increases the throughput in convergecast.

We believe mZig has wider implications for wireless design than explored in this paper. For example, mZig PHY motivates a more aggressive MAC in ZigBee to increase throughput by exploiting concurrent transmissions. Moreover, mZig can be extended to other PSK and FSK based wireless networks such as cellular, satellite, and GPS systems.

Acknowledgements

This research was supported in part by the NSERC Discovery Grant 341823, NSERC Collaborative Research and Development Grant CRDPJ418713, Canada Foundation for Innovation (CFI)'s John R. Evans Leaders Fund 23090, NSFC Grant 61303202, and China Postdoctoral Science Foundation Grant 2014M560334.

11. REFERENCES

[1] USRP B210 data sheet. https://www.ettus.com/content/files/b200-b210_spec_sheet.pdf.

[2] ZigBee specification. http://www.zigbee.org.

[3] ZigBee smart energy profile 2 application protocol standard. http://www.zigbee.org/Standards/ZigBeeSmartEnergy/SmartEnergyProfile2.aspx, 2013.

[4] Bluetooth specification. https://www.bluetooth.org/en-us/specification/adopted-specifications, 2014.

[5] M. T. Abuelma'atti. New ASK/FSK/PSK/QAM wave generator using multiple-output operational transconductance amplifiers. *IEEE Transactions on Circuits and Systems*, 48(4):487–490, 2001.

[6] C.-C. Chang and C.-J. Lin. LIBSVM: a library for support vector machines. *ACM Transactions on Intelligent Systems and Technology*, 2(3):27, 2011.

[7] Y. Cheng, J. Bellardo, P. Benkö, A. Snoeren, G. Voelker, and S. Savage. Jigsaw: solving the puzzle of enterprise 802.11 analysis. In *ACM SIGCOMM*, 2006.

[8] R. Cohen and B. Kapchits. Continuous neighbor discovery in asynchronous sensor networks. *IEEE/ACM Transactions on Networking*, 19(1):69–79, 2011.

[9] J. Crowcroft and K. Paliwoda. A multicast transport protocol. In *ACM SIGCOMM Computer Communication Review*, volume 18, pages 247–256, 1988.

[10] M. Doddavenkatappa, M. C. Chan, and B. Leong. Splash: Fast data dissemination with constructive interference in wireless sensor networks. In *USENIX NSDI*, 2013.

[11] J. Fang, K. Tan, Y. Zhang, S. Chen, L. Shi, J. Zhang, Y. Zhang, and Z. Tan. Fine-grained channel access in wireless LAN. *IEEE/ACM Transactions on Networking*, 21(3):772 – 787, 2013.

[12] F. Ferrari, M. Zimmerling, L. Thiele, and O. Saukh. Efficient network flooding and time synchronization with glossy. In *ACM IPSN*, 2011.

[13] L. Fu, Y. Qin, X. Wang, and X. Liu. Throughput and delay analysis for convergecast with MIMO in wireless networks. *IEEE Transactions on Parallel and Distributed Systems*, 23(4):768–775, 2012.

[14] M. Garetto, T. Salonidis, and E. Knightly. Modeling per-flow throughput and capturing starvation in CSMA multi-hop wireless networks. *IEEE/ACM Transactions on Networking*, 16(4):864–877, 2008.

[15] S. Gollakota and D. Katabi. Zigzag decoding: combating hidden terminals in wireless networks. In *ACM SIGCOMM*, 2008.

[16] S. Gollakota, S. D. Perli, and D. Katabi. Interference alignment and cancellation. *ACM SIGCOMM Computer Communication Review*, 39(4):159–170, 2009.

[17] D. Halperin, T. Anderson, and D. Wetherall. Taking the sting out of carrier sense: interference cancellation for wireless LANs. In *ACM MOBICOM*, 2008.

[18] J. Haupt, W. U. Bajwa, G. Raz, and R. Nowak. Toeplitz compressed sensing matrices with applications to sparse channel estimation. *IEEE Transactions on Information Theory*, 56(11):5862–5875, 2010.

[19] Y.-K. Huang, A.-C. Pang, P.-C. Hsiu, W. Zhuang, and P. Liu. Distributed throughput optimization for ZigBee cluster-tree networks. *IEEE Transactions on Parallel and Distributed Systems*, 23(3):513–520, 2012.

[20] O. D. Incel, A. Ghosh, B. Krishnamachari, and K. Chintalapudi. Fast data collection in tree-based wireless sensor networks. *IEEE Transactions on Mobile Computing*, 11(1):86–99, 2012.

[21] M. Jain, J. I. Choi, T. Kim, D. Bharadia, S. Seth, K. Srinivasan, P. Levis, S. Katti, and P. Sinha. Practical, real-time, full duplex wireless. In *ACM MOBICOM*, 2011.

[22] G. Judd and P. Steenkiste. Using emulation to understand and improve wireless networks and applications. In *USENIX NSDI*, 2005.

[23] S. Katti, S. Gollakota, and D. Katabi. Embracing wireless interference: analog network coding. In *ACM SIGCOMM*, 2007.

[24] S. Katti, H. Rahul, W. Hu, D. Katabi, M. Médard, and J. Crowcroft. XORs in the air: practical wireless network coding. In *ACM SIGCOMM*, 2006.

[25] J. Kim and J. Lee. Capture effects of wireless CSMA/CA protocols in rayleigh and shadow fading channels. *IEEE Transactions on Vehicular Technology*, 48(4):1277–1286, 1999.

[26] T. Kim, S. H. Kim, J. Yang, S.-e. Yoo, and D. Kim. Neighbor table based shortcut tree routing in ZigBee wireless networks. *IEEE Transactions on Parallel and Distributed Systems*, 25(3), 2014.

[27] L. Kong, L. He, Y. Gu, M. Y. Wu, and T. He. A parallel identification protocol for RFID systems. In *IEEE INFOCOM*, 2014.

[28] J. Kwak, C.-H. Lee, and D. Y. Eun. A high-order markov chain based scheduling algorithm for low delay in csma networks. In *IEEE INFOCOM*, 2014.

[29] N. Nikaein, M. K. Marina, S. Manickam, A. Dawson, R. Knopp, and C. Bonnet. Openairinterface: A flexible platform for 5g research. *ACM SIGCOMM Computer Communication Review*, 44(5):33–38, 2014.

[30] P. Patel and J. Holtzman. Analysis of a simple successive interference cancellation scheme in a DS/CDMA system. *IEEE Journal on Selected Areas in Communications*, 12(5):796–807, 1994.

[31] S. Sen, R. Roy Choudhury, and S. Nelakuditi. CSMA/CN: Carrier sense multiple access with collision notification. In *ACM MOBICOM*, 2010.

[32] S. Sen, N. Santhapuri, R. R. Choudhury, and S. Nelakuditi. Successive interference cancellation: Carving out mac layer opportunities. *IEEE Transactions on Mobile Computing*, 12(2):346–357, 2013.

[33] A. Sikora and V. F. Groza. Coexistence of IEEE 802.15.4 with other systems in the 2.4 GHz-ISM-Band. In *IEEE IMTC*, 2005.

[34] P. Stoica and O. Besson. Training sequence design for frequency offset and frequency-selective channel estimation. *IEEE Transactions on Communications*, 51(11):1910–1917, 2003.

[35] Y. Tay, K. Jamieson, and H. Balakrishnan.

Collision-minimizing CSMA and its applications to wireless sensor networks. *IEEE Journal on Selected Areas in Communications*, 22(6):1048–1057, 2004.

[36] A. Tehrani, A. Dimakis, and M. Neely. Sigsag: Iterative detection through soft message-passing. In *IEEE INFOCOM*, 2011.

[37] D. Tse and P. Viswanath. *Fundamentals of wireless communication.* Cambridge university press, 2005.

[38] H. Y. Tung, K. F. Tsang, K. T. Chui, H. C. Tung, H. R. Chi, G. P. Hancke, and K. F. Man. The generic design of a high-traffic advanced metering infrastructure using ZigBee. *IEEE Transactions on Industrial Informatics*, 10(1):836–844, 2014.

[39] J. Wang, H. Hassanieh, D. Katabi, and P. Indyk. Efficient and reliable low-power backscatter networks. *ACM SIGCOMM Computer Communication Review*, 42(4):61–72, 2012.

[40] L. Wang, K. Wu, and M. Hamdi. Combating hidden and exposed terminal problems in wireless networks. *IEEE Transactions on Wireless Communications*, 11(11):4204–4213, 2012.

[41] S. Wang, S. M. Kim, Y. Liu, G. Tan, and T. He. Corlayer: A transparent link correlation layer for energy efficient broadcast. In *ACM MOBICOM*, 2013.

[42] X. Wang, L. Fu, X. Tian, Y. Bei, Q. Peng, X. Gan, H. Yu, and J. Liu. Converge cast: on the capacity and delay tradeoffs. *IEEE Transactions on Mobile Computing*, 11(6):970–982, 2012.

[43] Y. Wang, Y. Liu, Y. He, X. Y. Li, and D. Cheng. Disco: Improving packet delivery via deliberate synchronized constructive interference. *IEEE Transactions on Parallel and Distributed Systems*, 26(3):713 – 723, 2015.

[44] Q. Xiang, H. Zhang, J. Wang, G. Xing, S. Lin, and X. Liu. On optimal diversity in network-coding-based routing in wireless networks. In *IEEE INFOCOM*, 2015.

[45] X. Xie, M. Peng, B. Zhao, W. Wang, and Y. Hua. Maximum a posteriori based channel estimation strategy for two-way relaying channels. *IEEE Transactions on Wireless Communications*, 13(1):450–463, 2014.

[46] K. Xu, M. Gerla, and S. Bae. Effectiveness of RTS/CTS handshake in IEEE 802.11 based ad hoc networks. *Elsevier Ad Hoc Networks*, 1(1):107–123, 2003.

[47] Y. Yan, P. Yang, X. Li, Y. Tao, L. Zhang, and L. You. Zimo: Building cross-technology MIMO to harmonize ZigBee smog with WiFi flash without intervention. In *ACM MOBICOM*, 2013.

[48] P. Yi, A. Iwayemi, and C. Zhou. Developing ZigBee deployment guideline under WiFi interference for smart grid applications. *IEEE Transactions on Smart Grid*, 2(1):110–120, 2011.

[49] L. Zhang and D. Guo. Virtual full duplex wireless broadcasting via compressed sensing. *IEEE/ACM Transactions on Networking*, 22(5):1659 – 1671, 2014.

[50] X. Zhang and K. G. Shin. Enabling coexistence of heterogeneous wireless systems: case for zigbee and wifi. In *ACM MobiHoc*, 2011.

[51] X. Zheng, Z. Cao, J. Wang, Y. He, and Y. Liu. ZiSense: towards interference resilient duty cycling in wireless sensor networks. In *ACM SenSys*, 2014.

AirExpress: Enabling Seamless In-band Wireless Multi-hop Transmission

Bo Chen, Yue Qiao, Ouyang Zhang and Kannan Srinivasan
Department of Computer Science and Engineering
The Ohio State University, Columbus, OH 43210
{chebo, qiaoyu, kannan}@cse.ohio-state.edu, zhang.4746@osu.edu

ABSTRACT

This paper describes the design and implementation of AirExpress, a system that enables in-band wireless cut-through transmission. Unlike wired cut-through, wireless cut-through can reduce latency and improve throughput performance of the network at the same time. In AirExpress, all the forwarders along the cut-through path forward the signal they received immediately without decoding. The hierarchical structure of AirExpress enables its interference cancellation ability to handle all kinds of interference among the radios. Novel MAC and routing algorithms based on cut-through transmission are also proposed to support the realization of AirExpress in multi-hop mesh networks.

AirExpress is implemented on an NI-based SDR platform. Through experiments in the 2.4GHz ISM band, we show a throughput gain of up to 3.4 times with a 4-hop AirExpress system. Trace driven evaluation of AirExpress on the NS3 platform shows an average throughput gain of 2.85 for AirExpress over optimal TDMA.

Categories and Subject Descriptors

C.2.1 [**Network Architecture and Design**]: Wireless communication

Keywords

Full Duplex; Wireless Networks; Cut-through Transmission

1. INTRODUCTION

Cut-through routing is a strategy in which every router (or switch) in a path between a source and a destination forwards a packet before fully decoding it. This is a technique that is currently possible in Ethernet transmission [1]. Clearly, the end-to-end delay will significantly reduce when cut-through is employed in a wired network. In the history of wireless cut-through, people used to explore the latency gains using control mechanisms to enable cut-through routing using different frequencies [12]. Some similar works [9,14] got inspired by existing wireline network. They imported the pipeline philosophy from chip architecture and highlighted the importance of ad hoc networks when deployed with existing WLANs. Realizing in-band cut-through in wireless networks, however, is challenging in many ways as we will discuss later. However, wireless cut-through not only improves delay performance but also improves end-to-end throughput.

Figure 1(a) shows a path between source A and destination D in a multi-hop wireless network. When traditional routing is used and A is transmitting packets to B, C cannot transmit to D. Thus only one of the three hops can be active. When cut-through is enabled, however, nodes A, B, C and D, can all be simultaneously active. Thus the end-to-end throughput can be increased by up to three times. This shows that wireless cut-through routing can improve delay performance and throughput of the network.

One of the main requirements for in-band wireless cut-through is that a node (e.g., node B in Figure 1) should be able to forward while it is still receiving. Thus a node should be able to support full duplex operation. However, full duplex alone is insufficient to enable cut-through. In the same figure, when C forwards a packet, C's transmission affects B's reception. We refer to this interference as *forwarder interference(FI)*. This additional interference also needs to be handled while realizing cut-through.

Forwarder interference cancellation is still not enough to realize cut-through. There will be intra-flow interference from nodes more than one-hop away. This *cross-hop interference(CHI)* also needs to be addressed in order to realize cut-through routing.

Another challenge is the cancellation overhead. Overall, we have self interference, forwarder interference and cross-hop interference to deal with. One nice feature of these three types of interference is that they are due to transmissions of symbols that we intend to receive. However, the interference channels are different for these different types of interference. For example, self interference is between a transmitting and a receiving antenna within a node, while forwarder interference is from the next node's transmitting antenna. The channels need to be measured before we can address these interference sources. Thus measuring these channels at every single node along the path itself could be a big overhead. Furthermore, any measured channel is only valid for a short duration (or coherence time), which is typically of the order of a few hundred milliseconds. Thus the measurement needs to be repeated frequently. Overall, the channel measurement overhead, if not handled carefully,

MobiCom'15, September 7–11, 2015, Paris, France.
© 2015 ACM. ISBN 978-1-4503-3619-2/15/09...$15.00.
DOI: http://dx.doi.org/10.1145/2789168.2790114.

could deteriorate the end-to-end throughput and delay gains in the cut-through implementation.

Furthermore, in order to activate a cut-through path, all the nodes along that path need to be available. A node may be unavailable because it is already participating in another cut-through flow or has an active node in its neighborhood. Thus we need a medium access control (MAC) and routing protocol suite that can dynamically handle cases where the entire path is not available. Otherwise, waiting for the whole path to become free itself could affect the end-to-end delay of a packet. Finally, since every node is simply forwarding a packet without decoding it, noise accumulates along hops in one transmission. If the cut-through path is very long, then the accumulated noise could deteriorate the throughput so that it is even below what is achievable by traditional routing.

This paper addresses these challenges and implements a fully functional wireless cut-through system AirExpress. Our system has the following features:

- Inside each radio AirExpress presents a unified cancellation module that handles all three sources of interference such that the channel training for all interference can happen simultaneously. Along the path, AirExpress forms a Hierarchical Cancellation Structure to protect cut-through transmission from interference saturation.
- It presents MAC and routing protocols needed to support cut-through.
- It presents extensive measurements and trace-driven simulation results to show the viability of wireless cut-through.

Overall, to our knowledge, AirExpress is the first prototype to demonstrate in-band wireless cut-through. A recent work [4] simply argued that wireless cut-through may be realizable. But it did not develop a fully working prototype and address cross-hop interference. Furthermore, it did not present MAC and routing schemes needed to realize cut-through routing either.

2. THE PROBLEM AND MOTIVATION

The cut-through transmission is promising as it increases network performance. With the existing full-duplex techniques, two-hop cut-through transmission is already realized. The relay radio can perform self interference cancellation which follows the design in [3]. This paper, however, focuses on a general wireless cut-through transmission problem. Extending beyond two-hop cut-through, the interference experienced at a node is not confined simply to **Self Interference**(SI). Thus, how to **deal with the additional interference** introduced into the network is the key challenge in the realization of cut-through transmission. This section elaborates the challenges and insights behind our solution – AirExpress.

2.1 Interference in Cut-through Transmission

Let us first look at the case of an ideal three-hop cut-through transmission, as shown in Figure1(a). In this example, A is in the transmitting mode while D is in the receiving mode. B and C in between are the forwarders which relay the signal. We assume that there is no signal outlet other than the three links A-B, B-C and C-D, i.e., there is no interference between A and C, B and D.

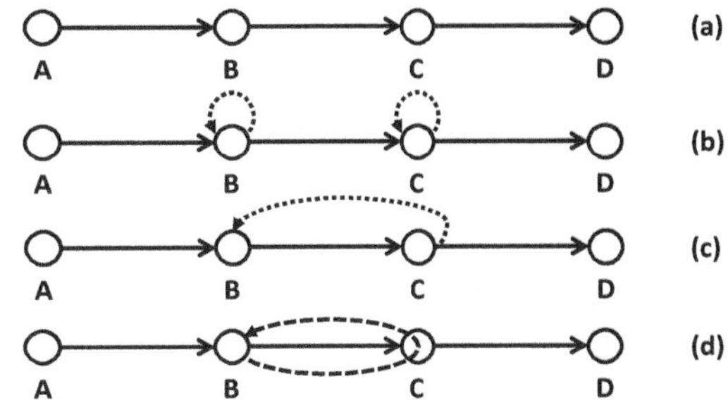

Figure 1: A 3-hop cut-through path. Node A wishes to send packets to D through B and C who are the forwarders. (b)(SI) and (c)(FI) together present the interference components in the ideal cut-through case. (d) illustrates the forwarding channel for the FI at B. Any node in the network will treat the signal from the afterwards nodes as a black box.

2.1.1 *Problem*

There are three interference streams in the network as illustrated in Figure 1(b) and (c). Cut-through transmission can fail because of any one of the three sources of interference. Among the three interference streams, two are the self interference within B and C separately. They can be removed with the assistance of the full-duplex capability enabled for these two radios. The problem reduces to cancelling the interference from C to B. This type of interference will be noted as **Forwarder Interference**(FI) as it comes from the next hop forwarder.

The nice property of the FI is that the forwarders (C) are sending the symbols that the previous nodes (B) along the path have already seen. In other words, the interfering symbols are known.

One obvious way to realize cut-through is to let every node along the cut-through path forward the previous packet while it is receiving the current one. We refer to this method as **Decode-and-Forward** (D&F) cut-through as the forwarders decode the data before forwarding to the next radios. There are many techniques in the literature supporting D&F [2, 6, 8, 13]. Thus forwarder interference cancellation for D&F can follow the existing techniques. However, D&F has the following drawbacks. First, as packets need to be decoded before transmitted, the latency reduction because of cut-through disappears. Secondly, the throughput benefit would be limited if the cut-through path is used only for a few packets. Consider an extreme case where only one packet needs to be delivered. Then the packet needs to go through one hop after another. The throughput performance would be the same as traditional transmission. Last but not least, the efficiency of the interference cancellation relies on the dissimilarities of the samples in different packets since radios usually use correlation to detect and locate interference. When two similar packets are transmitted one after the other, the cancellation module is expected to treat the (new) data as interference also. Thus D&F's performance would be a function of traffic. Thus, we need to seek for some other ways to deal with the interference.

2.1.2 *Intuition*

The intuition in AirExpress is that each forwarder tries to measure the channel and model the interference before the transmission so that the *FI* component can be anticipated before the reception of the forwarder interference signal. With a simple subtraction, the useful data can be recovered from *FI*. Since in this way, data will be directly forwarded without being decoded, it can be treated as a method realizing **Amplify-and-Forward** (A&F) cut-through.

The channel that AirExpress needs to measure so as to cancel *FI* encompasses three entities: (i) the wireless channel from B to C, (ii) the amplification circuitry within C, and (iii) the wireless channel back from C to B. This is also shown in Figure 1(d). Sec.3.1 shows the structure of AirExpress forwarders. Specifically, we discuss the cumulative estimation of the three entities in the path, referred collectively as the forwarding channel. Then *FI* component can be predicted based on the signal output of the same radio.

2.2 More Interference in Practical Cut-through Transmission

The ideal channel condition discussed in the above subsection follows the binary interference model assumption: links either interfere with each other or not at all. However, in real scenarios, any two links can interfere with each other. We take a 4-hop cut-through as an example to show how complicated the observed interference is when all links are considered. Consider the topology in Figure 2(a), A is the transmitter, E is the final receiver, and B, C, D in between are the forwarders in order.

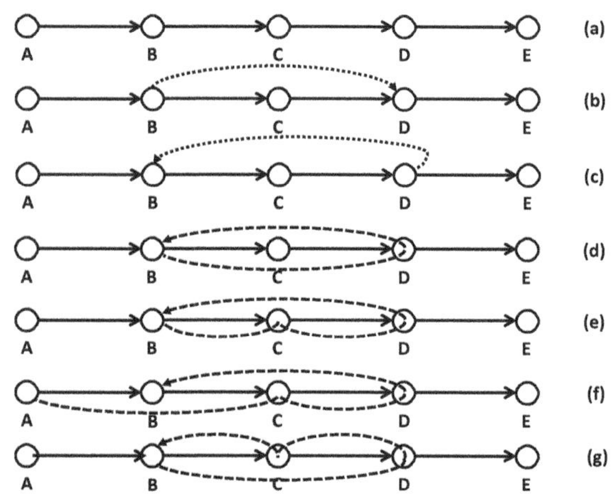

Figure 2: A 4-hop cut-through path. A wishes to send packets to E through B, C and D. Interference in (b) presents the *CHI* from B to D while the one in (c) shows the *CHI* from D to B. (d)(e)(f) are three different signal streams which contribute to the *CHI* from D to B. (g) shows a signal stream of *CHI* path from C to B.

2.2.1 Problem

In traditional routing, if the intra-flow interference is severe, one link can be disabled. However, for the cut-through system, such a setting is contradictory to the idea of enabling the links simultaneously. A working cut-through system should be able to support the successful transmission irrespective of the interference pattern. We refer to the interference introduced by the radios more than one hop away as **cross-hop interference**(*CHI*). Dealing with *CHI* is a significant challenge for wireless cut-through realization.

A straightforward approach could be modelling the channels for all the *CHI* and applying the cancellation following *FI* cancellation modules. However, two limitations render this approach impractical.

- Not all the constituent channels of *CHI* can be modelled. The reason *FI* cancellation works is based on the fact that the signal of *FI* is correlated with the output signal from the same radio so that *FI* can be predicted. However, this does not hold for all the interference components, like the one shown in Figure 2(b). We can see that even the existence of the *CHI* from B to D does not rely on the transmitted signal from D. Thus, the interference is not causal with respect to the transmitted signal from D. Therefore there is no way this *CHI* can be predicted.
- The composite *CHI* is very complicated. Let us consider the *CHI* from D to B as shown in Figure 2(c). There are multiple traces contributing to this *CHI*. Figures. 2(d)&(e) show two traces orginating from B. Since the trace could involve any of the relay nodes within the cut-through, it is expected that the number of traces grows exponentially with the number of forwarders in cut-through transmission. In addition to that, some components observed by B are not causal either. An example of such a trace is shown in Figure 2(f). Moreover, Figure 2(g) shows a case adjacent interference(C→B) also contains *CHI*.

2.2.2 Intuition

As at least the cancellation for some *CHI* is impossible, can we just randomly remove/cancel several *CHI* traces and leave the residual interference as noise? The answer is no. If we do that, it turns out in a short time all the radios would saturate. The reason for this consequence is that *CHI* is bidirectional. As shown in Figure2, there is *CHI* following the transmission direction(from left to right) while some *CHI* in the opposite direction(from right to left). If the interference streams form a loop within the cut-through path, there exists at least one channel condition under which the signal power will keep accumulating until all the radios are saturated. Thus, to validate the cut-through transmission, *CHI* cancellation needs to cut enough signal paths so that the interference streams within the cut-through transmission is loop-free.

To achieve this goal, interference cancellation in AirExpress is designed to follow a **Hierarchical Cancellation Structure**, in which a forwarder judges its descendant forwarders as a black box and cancels all the signals originating from its transmitter, retransmitted within the black box and received by its receiver. Specifically, in the 4-hop example shown in Figure 2, cancellation block in node C cancels the signal originating from C, forwarded by D and received back at C while node B cancels the signal originating from B, retransmitted by C and/or D and received back at B. Combined with the forwarder cancellation block design in AirExpress forwarding channels are modelled to capture this effect as shown in Figure 3. Two insights show that this design satisfies the cut-through *CHI* cancellation requirement: (i) All the *CHI* cancellations happening in our Hierarchical Structure are causal. This is simply due to the fact all the *CHI* components are originating from the radio's transmitter. (ii) This design structure guarantees loop-free property of interference streams. This is because, with any potential interference loop, there is one node at which all the other involved forwarders are the descendants and .thus, the interference signal stream will stop at this node and not loop forward further.

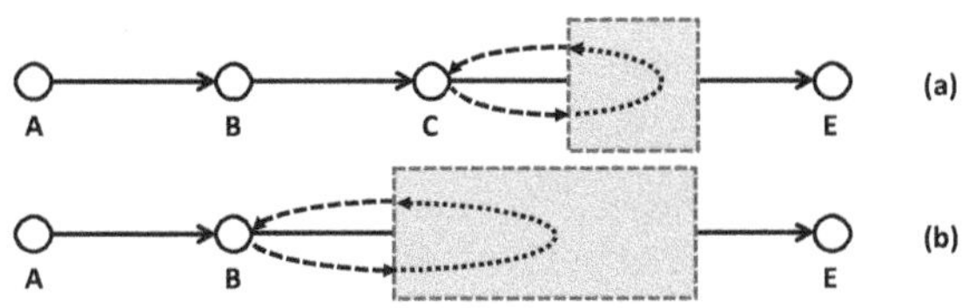

Figure 3: Hierarchical Cancellation Structure for a 4-hop cut-through example. (a) shows the forwarding channel for node C. (b) shows the forwarding channel for node B.

The remaining *CHI* components which can not be cancelled stay within the system. However, they are all copies of the original signal and thus, can be treated as multipath profile. For a n-hop cut-through system ($sr_1r_2 \cdots r_{n-1}e$, where s is the start transmitter, e is the end receiver while $r_1r_2 \cdots r_{n-1}$ are the n-1 relay radios), the longest path would involve $\frac{n(n-1)}{2}+1$ hops[1]. Thus it is quite critical to reduce the latency within each forwarder. Within each forwarder, 10ns latency for *SI* analog cancellation module and 50ns latency for ADC and DAC is unavoidable. For the digital cancellation (for *SI*, *FI* and *CHI*), we utilize the causal nature of the FIR filter to provide a 0 latency forwarding within the digital domain. This feature is also adopted in the Fast-Forward [3] work. In a WiFi OFDM system, CP(cyclic prefix) duration is 800ns and multipath duration exceeds this time limit will introduce inter-symbol interference. Thus, in WiFi settings, theoretically 5-hop cut-through is the setting with highest supported hops. However, if we can change the OFDM configuration or apply AirExpress in other applications, like LTE, cut-through transmission with more hops is also achievable.

3. REALIZING CUT-THROUGH TRANSMISSION

In general, a cut-through path involves a source node, a destination and a sequence of forwarders. The source node transmits the signal, while the destination node tries to decode the signal. Forwarders forward the signal in sequence. The source and destination nodes run as regular wireless radios capable of encoding and decoding messages. The interference component varies with the position of forwarders. Originally, to deal with varying interference components, different forwarders should be designed according to its position within the cut-through path. However, with the hierarchical cancellation structure already introduced in the previous section, the interference cancellation requirement is reduced to the causal interference from the descendent forwarders respective to the radio position within the cut-through path. In the rest of this section, we will first focus on the design of one forwarder radio in AirExpress and then, present AirExpress protocol realizing the cut-through transmission.

[1] $sr_{n-1}r_{n-2} \cdots r_1r_{n-1}r_{n-2} \cdots r_2 \cdots\cdots r_{n-1}r_{n-2}r_{n-1}e$ is the path

3.1 Forwarder Structure

Figure 4(a) illustrates the high-level block diagram of a forwarder node. As shown in the figure, in the forwarding mode, a node only uses the digital-to-analog-converter (DAC), analog-to-digital-converter (ADC) and radio frequency (RF) parts of its radio physical layer. The only processing for data stream a node does in the digital domain is interference cancellation, and then amplification of the received signal. It bypasses all of the other traditional physical layer data processing such as decoding and error correction.

The forwarder is built on a wireless full-duplex radio: As we show in the diagram, both the RF cancellation and digital cancellation of *SI* are also there. The *FI* and *CHI* cancellation modules are additions to the typical wireless full-duplex radio. Three signal characteristics enable us to implement a forwarder node with this design.

First, the interference is causal to the transmitted signal from the forwarder. This point has been illustrated in Sec. 2. Secondly, the power of *FI* and *CHI* is comparable to the regular received signal as they all come from the neighbouring radios: the two signals are within the resolution of analog to digital converter (ADC). This is different from self interference which is many orders larger than the received signal from a different radio. Thus digital cancellation is enough to meet the cancellation requirement in most of the cases. Thirdly, the received signal after interference cancellation is directly amplified and sent to the transmitter side for forwarding. This operation takes fixed time. Note that this forwarded data signal will be observed as *FI* or *CHI* at its ascendant. This means that the timing of the interference is usually small and predictable.

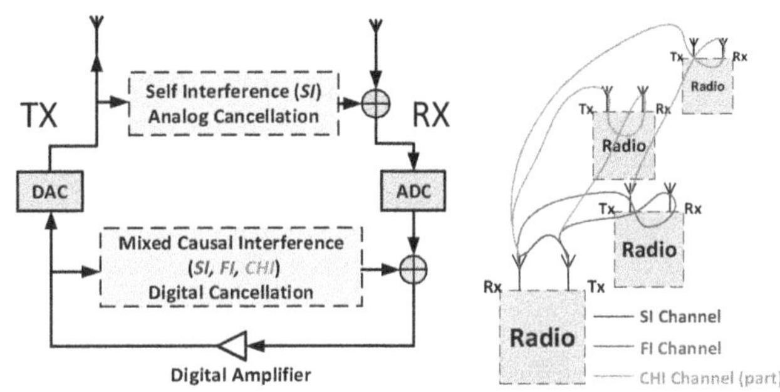

(a) (b)

Figure 4: (a) Overall block diagram of a forwarder in AirExpress. (b) Illustration of the interference received at each receiver.

As the channel is predictable, the forwarding channel has a lot of similarities as the self-interference channel. Thus the forwarder cancellation module in the system can be designed following the structure of digital cancellation in self-interference cancellation.

The digital amplification can be set to any value and it will not affect the cancellation performance. In AirExpress the amplification is adjusted according to the signal power from ancestor radio to maintain a constant output power at each forwarder node.

Is Frequency Offset an Issue for the Interference Cancellation?

It is widely known that any two wireless nodes will have a frequency offset: the notion of 2.4GHz could be different as the crystals used to generate these frequencies have imperfections [6]. A frequency offset between two nodes, if uncorrected, will rotate the phase of a signal continuously over time [11]. This continually changing phase can make channel estimation between two nodes extremely difficult: Even if the channel is relatively stable over time, the rotating phase will affect these estimates. To solve this problem, it is common to use a known sequence as a preamble for every packet. A receiver uses this preamble to estimate the frequency offset so that it can correct the consequent phase rotation.

Note that the digital cancellation for self interference (in full-duplex radios) does not have this problem. This is because the transmit and receive radios belong to the same node and so there is no frequency offset. The *FI* and *CHI* in AirExpress, however, are introduced by other nodes -the descendent forwarders. Therefore, in Figure 4(b), any two radios will have a frequency offset. Does this imply that a frequency offset correction mechanism is required at all the radios in the network? The answer is ***no***. Actually, the interference channel defined in AirExpress is a ***frequency offset free*** channel, even though there is frequency offset among multiple nodes.

To see why the interference channel is frequency offset free, let us first look at the signal between two forwarders. Assume forwarder B is the descendent of forwarder A. Center frequencies at A and B are f_A and f_B, respectively and $f_A \neq f_B$. Thus the signal received in forwarder B is affected by frequency offset $f_B - f_A$. Since nodes in AirExpress do not decode packets, the frequency offset is not corrected. Therefore, Node B directly forwards the signal with the frequency offset. As it goes through the channel B to A, an additional frequency offset $f_A - f_B$ is applied to the signal when it is received by Node A. Thus the two frequency offsets cancel out with each other and the *FI*/*CHI* signal received in node A is frequency offset free. The same argument can be applied to the stream going through three or more forwarders. Assume signal starts with A and comes back to A after going through $B_1, B_2, \cdots, B_k$, the frequency offset of the interference can be expected as $f(B_1)-f(A)+\sum_{i=1}^{k-1}(f(B_{i+1})-f(B_i))+(f(A)-f(B_k)=0$. Thus all the interference is *frequency offset free*. It makes the *FI* and *CHI* cancellation robust to frequency offsets found in distributed radios.

3.2 AirExpress Protocol

So far, we have discussed the physical modules within each node to realize cut-through. However, each node still needs to know its role as a forwarder and the signal it requires to forward. To achieve this, AirExpress relies on the cooperation among all the nodes involved in the transmission. How to control the forwarders and process the cut-through transmission cooperatively is still a problem. In this subsection, the details for the process of AirExpress will be presented. We assume in this section the transmitter S has the data, knows the cut-through destination D and is aware of the order of all the k forwarders $R_1, R_2, \cdots, R_k$ in between. A routing algorithm to obtain this information will be presented in Sec. 4.3. Another preparation we need is that in the network, each node needs to generate a PN sequence according to its address[2] and assume the PN sequence for the node with ID X is PN_X. Also, we assume a pre-reserved PN sequence, PN_{AE}, which is reserved as AirExpress indicator and known to the whole network.

To support the transmission along an AirExpress path, three tasks need to be accomplished:

1. Member Notification. Transmitter S is the only node being aware of the cut-through plan before the transmission. It needs to notify the other radios for their roles within the AirExpress system. It is hard because radios cross multi-broadcasting domains and thus, multiple wireless messages are needed. A comprehensive and efficient notification process is quite important.
2. Channel training. The cancellation module within each forwarder needs to be tuned so that it can cover the cancellation of all the intended interference signal.
3. Forwarder Release. When the transmission is going on, all the forwarders blindly forwards the signal without decoding. When the transmission is done, forwarders need to be aware of the situation and stop forwarding data.

3.2.1 Before Transmission: Notification & Training

The first two tasks need to be done before the transmission. To decrease the overhead of these tasks, AirExpress processes them jointly. For member notification, AirExpress tries to notify the forwarders one after another, following the order of cut-through path so that all the radios will be notified. Although the feasibility of the intended interference cancellation has been proved by our Hierarchical Cancellation Structure, channel training is still not trivial as the number of potential interference paths defined in the structure is still exponential with respect to the number of radios. To achieve this goal, AirExpress extends the 'hierarchical' feature from cancellation design to implement our channel estimation protocol. The forwarders start only when all the descendant forwarders are already operating in forwarding mode while the ancestors are silent. The running of the process can be separated into two phases:

Sequence of Notification: First of all, the source node sends the combined PN sequences of PN_{AE} and all the nodes in the path: $PN_{AE}PN_{R_1}PN_{R_2}\cdots PN_{R_k}PN_D$. When R_1 detects PN_{AE} followed by its PN sequence PN_{R_1}, it will transmit the sequence excluding its own PN sequence as $PN_{AE}PN_{R_2}PN_{R_3}\cdots PN_{R_k}PN_D$. The following forwarders will perform the same process: whenever anyone detects the occurrence of PN_{AE} plus its own PN sequence, it joins the path. In this way, the nodes in the route sequentially join the AirExpress system. At the same time, each forwarder also records the PN sequence of the next hop. For instance, R_1 records PN_{R_2} and R_k records PN_D. In this way, all the forwarders are aware of PN sequence of the next hop radio, which will be used in the next phase. Thus we introduce PN_{AE} to ensure we retain the notification in order of the participating forwarder nodes in spite of cross-hop interference. Under the scenario without PN_{AE}, forwarders would just join the transmission based on the reception of its own PN sequence. It is highly possible that more than one radio detect their PN sequences for the same transmission. In this way, the order information of the forwarders is lost.

[2]PN sequence, Pseudo Random Sequence has already been widely used in recent years [2,10]. It is a predefined sequence of information. A receiver is able to detect this sequence by using correlation. The advantage of PN sequence is that it can be detected even under interference and its duration is short which leads to a small control overhead.

Backward Training: At the beginning of this phase, all the forwarders are already aware of their relative positions in the cut-through path through the knowledge of next-hop PN sequence(based on the recording process illustrated in the previous phase). For channel training, D broadcasts its PN sequence first. When R_k captures this information (D is R_k's next hop), it starts transmitting its training sequence and measures the parameters for *SI* RF cancellation and the digital cancellation parameters for *SI*, *FI* and *CHI* interference streams. When the training is done, this forwarder will set the digital gain according to the received signal power level (from the PN sequence in the previous phase) so that its output power is maximized. Afterwards, the forwarder sends out its PN_{R_k} as an indicator to trigger its previous radio (transmitter or forwarder) and immediately switches to forwarding mode and then begins forwarding. R_{k-1} follows the same procedure to do the training and notify the previous radio. In the end, when S detects PN_{R_1}, it knows the training process is done and all the forwarders are forwarding their received signal.

Throughout these two back and forth phases, whenever a forwarder tries to measure the interference channel, all its descendant forwarders are in forwarding mode while its ancestor forwarders are waiting for the trigger signal. Thus, it satisfies our requirement for hierarchical channel training.

3.2.2 *After Transmission: Forwarder Release*

After the data transmission is complete, the source node S has to release all the nodes involved in forwarding. To do this, S just sends PN_{R_1}. When R_1 detects its PN sequence, it stops forwarding and sends out PN_{R_2}. The same process repeats sequentially at all the forwarders until D receives PN_D as an indication of the end of the current AirExpress session.

AirExpress SNR Implications

It is straightforward that the channel of an AirExpress path is limited by the worst channel in its path. The reason is that there is no error correction module inside the forwarders. So, the physical layer throughput cannot exceed this lower bound. In addition to that, when signal is forwarded, the noise is also forwarded. So the cut-through path also accumulates noise. On the other side, when all the forwarders transmit the signal, they can be treated as multipath components. As long as CP (cyclic prefix) in an OFDM system is able to cover the duration of multipath component, the power from different multipath will also accumulate in the final receiver. In this way, it alleviates noise accumulation in AirExpress.

4. MEDIUM ACCESS CONTROL AND ROUTING

Now that the PHY capability for wireless cut-through transmission is realized, we can enable the cut-through transmission in a network. However, the underlying carrier sensing module in traditional MAC cannot perform the collision avoidance or even detection for cut-through transmission. Thus to enable multiple simultaneous transmissions in the network, a cut-through friendly MAC algorithm is needed. In addition to that, the traditional routing algorithms for mesh network were not designed with consideration of cut-through capability. So, we need to revisit the routing layer as well. In this section, MAC and routing layer algorithms supporting AirExpress capability will be presented.

4.1 Medium Access Control (MAC)

Traditional carrier sensing in wireless radio can only detect the transmission within the broadcast domain of that radio. AirExpress extends beyond a single broadcast domain. Thus cut-through requires carrier sensing beyond a single broadcast domain. A naive solution is to have each participating AirExpress node sense the channel and piggyback this information down to its ancestor nodes. However, this introduces intolerable latency. We achieve this by skipping this step altogether. The transmitter just acts as if the channels are free. The forwarders themselves will cut the length of the cut-through transmission in-between if they can detect transmission around themselves. This means that an n-hop AirExpress could end up to be a k-hop if the (k+1)th forwarder can not forward the signal. The AirExpress MAC protocol is shown in Algorithm. 1.

The major steps of the algorithm following the protocol are described in Sec. 3.2. The carrier sensing modifications are integrated. Nodes will transmit or react to forwarding requests only when channel is free (Line 4). Here, we add a Δt to the carrier sensing to prevent the sequence notification phase, as discussed in the previous section, from generating a false busy channel trigger. When this scenario happens at the next hop forwarder/destination, the current radio can immediately detect collision if it fails to detect the expected PN_{AE}(Line 14,29). When it happens at the transmitter, transmission is aborted(Line 16). For forwarder, the current radio will turn to be the destination for this AirExpress path(Line 31). The last modification to the AirExpress protocol is that the destination will transmit an additional PN_{AE} to trigger the process in the previous forwarder (Line 41).

4.2 Virtual Hop

It seems that combining the source, destination and all the forwarder nodes in between into a single cut-through path is the right way to deploy cut-through in a mesh network. However, through the analysis in previous sections, several realistic situations have already been shown to limit its performance:

(1) Worst link bottleneck: Cut-through routing does not take full advantage of the diversity of the link quality in a path. Since no intermediate node can modify the received symbols, the source needs to pick the transmission rate suitable for the bottleneck link along the path. This is the data rate at which all the links in that path will operate. It means that every link will carry the packets at a data rate supported by the bottleneck link even if the other links are far superior. In traditional routing, however, a packet can be transmitted at higher data rates on other links and sent at a low rate on the bottleneck. This frees up the medium sooner around (superior) links than around the bottleneck allowing other flows to start early.

(2) Noise accumulation: With cut-through, more number of links are enabled simultaneously. Therefore, throughput is improved compared to traditional routing. However, since every node in cut-through needs to forward without decoding, noise accumulates in every hop. This leads to deteriorating SNR as the packet traverses towards the des-

Algorithm 1: AirExpress Protocol

1 **Input:**
2 1. Global PN sequence PN_{AE}. Unique PN sequence PN_{this} for current Radio.
3 2. For a specific transmission request at transmitter S: Its own PN sequence PN_S. PN sequences of forwarders/destination for the next AirExpress path PN_{R_1}, $PN_{R_2} \cdots PN_{R_k}$, RN_D.

4 *Initial State*:
5 **while** *Carrier Sense(Δt)* **do**
  `// Operate when channel is free`
6   **if** *Detect* $PN_{AE}PN_{R_{this}}$ **then**
7   **goto** *Forward State.*
8   **else if** *New Transmission Request* **then**
9   **goto** *Transmit State.*
10   **endif**
11 **endwhile**

12 *Transmit State*:
13 Transmit($PN_{AE}PN_{R_1}PN_{R_2}\cdots PN_{R_k}RN_D$)
14 WaitingFor(PN_{AE})
15 **if** *Timeout* **then**
16   **goto** *Initial State.*`// Abort transmission`
17 **else**
18   WaitingFor(PN_{R_1})`// Training Done`
19   Transmit(Data)`// Data Transmission`
20   Transmit(PN_{R_1})`// Channel Release`
21   **goto** *Initial State.*
22 **endif**

23 *Forward State*:
24 **if** *No signal after* PN_{this} **then**
25   **goto** *Receive State.*`// Destination Node`
26 **endif**
27 Calculate digital gain based on PN sequence Power.
28 Transmit($PN_{AE}PN_{this+1}PN_{this+2}\cdots PN_{R_k}PN_D$)
29 WaitingFor(PN_{AE})
30 **if** *Timeout* **then**
31   **goto** *Receive State.*
  `// Timeout, forwarder turn to be receiver`
32 **else**
33   WaitingFor($PN_{R_{this+1}}$)`// Descendent Training Done`
34   Train for cancellation channel and start forwarding.
35   Transmit(PN_{this})`// Trigger Ancestor Training`
36   WaitingFor(PN_{this})`// End of Data`
37   Transmit(PN_{this+1})`// Channel Release`
38   **goto** *Initial State.*
39 **endif**

40 *Receive State*:
41 Transmit($PN_{AE}PN_{this}$)`// Trigger Channel Measure`
42 Receive(Data) & WaitingFor(PN_{this})`// End of Data`
43 **goto** *Initial State.*

tination. If the deterioration is significant, then it can lead to a throughput even lower than traditional routing. Additionally, an erroneous packet is dropped at an intermediate switch in traditional routing. While in cut-through, errors go undetected until a packet is decoded by its destination. The propagation of errors wastes network resources.

(3) Latency limitation: It has been shown in Sec.2.2.2, the duration of multipath grows quadratically with the number of hops. Although an OFDM system can tolerate multipath effect if the FFT and CP length can be configured. For any fixed setting, there is always an upper bound.

It seems that, in a real scenario, cut-through routing over a long path is not efficient. To resolve this limitation, we introduce the concept of virtual hop. Traditionally, one hop refers to a transmission from one node to its neighbouring node. Comparatively speaking, a virtual hop represents a transmission from one node to a node several hops away. Within a virtual hop, AirExpress is carried out. Thus between a source and a destination, there could be multiple virtual hops. We refer to such a cut-through routing structure as *virtual hop* structure.

By limiting the number of hops in AirExpress, virtual hop mitigates the bottleneck effect and error propagation problem and provides an upper bound for the multipath duration of the system. At the same time throughput improvement is still significant.

4.3 Routing Algorithm

Current routing table in the mesh network tells only the next hop receiver. However, AirExpress protocol requires the transmitter to know the path before the transmission (Line 3, Algo. 1). Thus it is important to come up with a routing algorithm to support AirExpress protocol. In addition to that, the cut-through capability has changed the throughput for a certain route. For example, a simple routing scheme considering the minimum number of hops as the metric to determine the routing is inapplicable for AirExpress transmissions, since there is no fundamental difference between 1, 2 or 3 hops - it is a single virtual hop. In this subsection, we will present a routing protocol based on AirExpress PHY, which provides the routing algorithm to minimize the latency between the source and the destination when employing AirExpress. As the delay between the source and the destination reflects the time during which data stays within a network, it is a good index of the efficiency of the network resource utilization. Thus it should increase the overall network throughput performance.

Consider a mesh network with allowed virtual hop transmission of up to k hops. Our routing algorithm in the following subsection will show how it maintains and updates the routing table so that it would support AirExpress PHY and MAC. For any radio in the network and a given destination node, this routing table provides the list of forwarders and destination of the next virtual hop. Our computation is based on one approximation that the cut-through channel is equivalent to the worst channel within the path.

Routing Table Structure: Let us consider the routing table in the radio R. Usually for a certain destination, routing table will provide one path (or trace). This is also true for our routing algorithm. However, in our routing table, multiple traces are recorded for the same destination. If the data is originated from R itself, then one path is sufficient. However, R could also be a forwarder in an AirExpress path. When R is a forwarder, the trace to the destination depends on the SNR at R from its ancestor. The following example illustrates this point.

Assume there are two routes X and Y from a radio to the same destination. X consists of only one virtual hop and takes $200\mu s$ to directly deliver a 1000 bytes packet to the destination while Y takes two virtual hops with $75\mu s$ each. To deliver data direct from this radio, Y is a better choice. However, when the radio is a forwarder and the channel to its ancestor is bad, delivering the packet alone in that link takes $200\mu s$. Combining this link with the first virtual hop in X and Y, X still takes $200\mu s$ while Y takes 275 μs. Thus X is the better route in this case.

Therefore any path which could potentially outperform all others based on the possible ancestors' channel conditions will be recorded. The paths are recorded in the format as shown in Figure 5. For any path X, $X.i$, $X.d1$, $X.d2$ and $X.list$ are used to denote the items in the format shown in the figure. For any two paths X and Y, if X strictly outperforms Y (X performs better than Y under any ancestors' channel conditions), Y will be removed. We denote this as $X \geqslant Y$. Under our assumption that cut-through channel is equivalent to the worst channel within the path, it is not hard to get the sufficient and necessary condition as follows:

$$\begin{cases} Y.d2 \geqslant (X.d1 + X.d2) & : X.i > Y.i \\ (Y.d1 + Y.d2) \geqslant (X.d1 + X.d2) & \\ \&\&\ Y.d2 \geqslant X.d2 & : X.i = Y.i \\ (Y.d1 \geqslant X.d1\ \&\&\ Y.d2 \geqslant X.d2) & \\ ||\ Y.d2 \geqslant (X.d1 + X.d2) & : X.i < Y.i \end{cases}$$

Directly from the definition, the transition property *strict outperform* also holds as $X \geqslant Y\ \&\&\ X \geqslant Z \Rightarrow X \geqslant Z$.

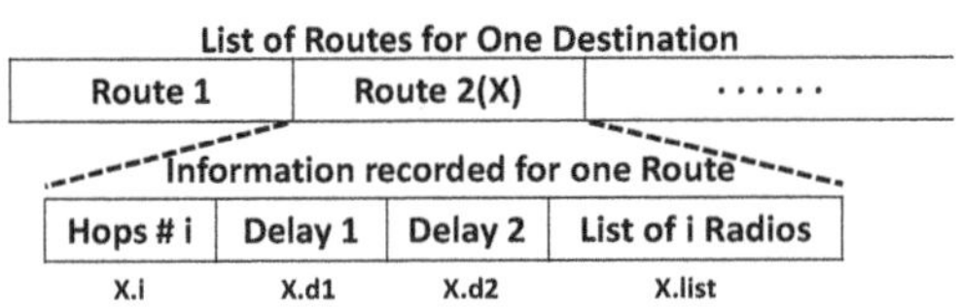

Figure 5: Recording for one destination within the Routing table. It contains a list of traces. For each trace, it records the number of hops within the next virtual hop (i), time to transmit unit size packet in the virtual hop (Delay 1), time to transmit unit size packet to the destination after next virtual hop (Delay 2) and the trace for next virtual hop(List of Radios).

Trace Output: When radio R has the data to transmit, it will search for the trace X in the routing table list that minimizes $X.d1 + X.d2$.

Distributed Routing Table Update: First of all, radios can update their routing table based on new channel measurements. And they periodically broadcast their routing tables to their neighbours. Radios can also update their routing tables based on the neighbours' routing table. Assume radio R receives the routing table from its neighbour R_{nei}, for any route X in R_{nei}, R could generate two potential traces Y_1 and Y_2 based on X and the time d to transmit a unit size packet to R_{nei}. Y_1 treats R_{nei} as the destination for next virtual hop and thus ($Y_1.i$, $Y_1.d1$, $Y_1.d2$, $Y_1.list$) = (1,d,$X.d1 + X.d2$,RR_{nei}). Y_2 treats R_{nei} as the first forwarder in the next virtual hop and thus ($Y_2.i$, $Y_2.d1$, $Y_2.d2$, $Y_2.list$) = ($X.i+1$, $max(d, X.d1)$, $X.d2$, $R_{nei}X.list$). Of course, if $X.i + 1 > k$ the second item will be directly ignored since it violates the virtual hop setting. These new traces will be added to the routing table if no existing traces *strictly outperform* them and all the traces they *strictly outperform* will be removed.

Initialization: When the routing table is generated the first time, all the radios just broadcast their routing table for enough rounds until the routing tables become stable for most of the radios. Since it only needs to be done once, the overhead can be amortized during the running of the system.

5. IMPLEMENTATION

5.1 Hardware Platform

We have built a prototype of AirExpress on the NI-based SDR platform. Each radio has one RF chain and NI PXIe-1082, an RTOS-based controller. The transceiver RF chain consists of NI-5791 (RF frontend and data converter module) and NI PXIe-7965R (Xilinx Virtex-5 FPGA) for baseband processing. The ADC and DAC of each transceiver chain sample at 130 MSps. The ADC/DAC resolution is 14-bit. Our full duplex implementation follows the design in [7]. Transmit and receive antennas are 15cm apart. Together with the Balun cancellation circuit and preconditioning block to cancel the non-linear signal, our RF module supports 68dB self-interference cancellation over 20MHz band. The digital module for self interference alone can provide another 42dB cancellation. With the combination of both the RF and the digital modules, our full-duplex system supports 110dB cancellation. The details of our implementation and performance is presented in our previous work [5].

5.2 Implementation Details

All the radios can transmit and receive OFDM signal with QPSK, QAM16 and QAM64 constellations and convolutional codes with coding rate 1/2, 2/3 and 3/4. Each radio is preassigned a unique PN sequence and a global PN sequence. Two correlation blocks are implemented on the FPGA for the detection of these two PN sequences. Radios support transmission of 20MHz band and operate on the 2.4GHz. Output power of the radio varies from -20dBm to 20dBm.

There is one harware limitation on our AirExpress implementation: NI-5791 introduces $0.5\mu s$ latency in both transmitting and receiving trace. Thus the lower bound of the latency introduced in one forwarder in our implementation is $1\mu s$. As we know the radio latency varies from platform to platform. For instance, WARP only introduces a delay up to 50ns as shown in [3]. So the latency performance is not the fundamental limitation for the deployment of AirExpress. However, to realize AirExpress in the current platform, the communication system needs to tolerate a $1\mu s$ latency. Therefore we keep the same ratio (1/4) for the CP length of the OFDM system, while the FFT size of OFDM system is set to 512. Thus theoretically, the CP is able to tolerate multipath latency up to $6.4\mu s$. To model the channel for *SI*, *FI*, *CHI*, our digital FIR filter is implemented with a duration of 5 μs so that most of the signal can be covered. In this way the physical layer throughput supported by the system matches the setting in WiFi.

Our implementation of AirExpress is deployed on 5 such radios, with which we can show the working of a 4-hop AirExpress system.

6. EVALUATION

6.1 Micro-benchmark

6.1.1 Forwarder Interference Cancellation

We have shown that the *SI* cancellation in digital domain is 40+dB (see results in [5]). In this experiment, we evaluate the *FI* cancellation performance. To study the capability of *FI* cancellation in AirExpress , we use two AirExpress

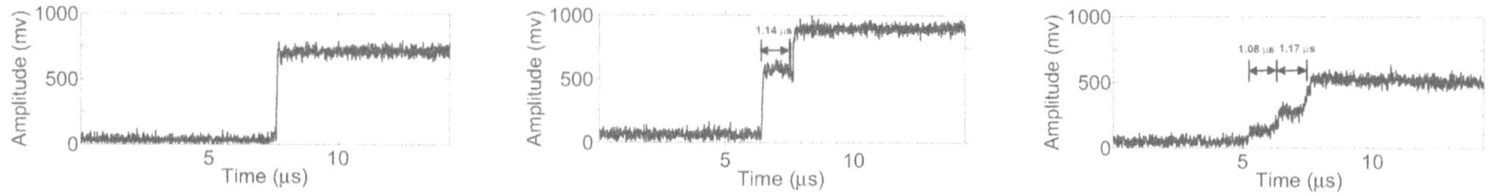

(a) 1 hop (b) 2 hops (c) 3 hops

Figure 6: Power of the received sine wave in 1-hop(a), 2-hop(b) and 3-hop(c) AirExpress system. The multi-path component can be seen as discrete steps.

radios. In the first step, the first radio trains for self interference and then switches to the forwarding mode. In the second step, we turn on the second radio and let it train for the interference from the first radio and perform the interference cancellation. We vary the distance between these two radios so that the power of *FI* changes. Both radios are transmitting with power 0dBm. The experiment is conducted in a relatively quiet environment and we measure the cancellation performance over a 100-ms duration after the *FI* channel measurement.

The *FI* cancellation performance is shown in Figure 7. We can see that our digital cancellation module can cancel around 36dB interference, which is much better than the existing correlation based cancellation [2,8]. In addition we can see that the *FI* from a radio beyond 4 meters is canceled to the noise floor in our system.

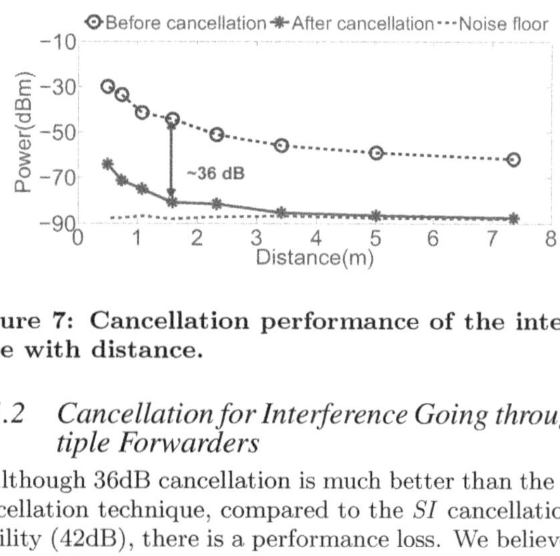

Figure 7: Cancellation performance of the interference with distance.

6.1.2 *Cancellation for Interference Going through Multiple Forwarders*

Although 36dB cancellation is much better than the other cancellation technique, compared to the *SI* cancellation capability (42dB), there is a performance loss. We believe this is due to the clock drift in different radios. So it is natural to wonder whether the clock drift will affect the cancellation performance further when multiple forwarders are involved. To answer this question, we measure the cancellation performance of the forwarding interference which travels through the most number of forwarders in a multi-forwarder setting. To isolate interference caused by intermediate forwarders, we use multiple center frequencies. For example, to evaluate the interference through two forwarders we use three radios A, B and C. Radio A transmits at f_1 and receives at f_3 while radio B transmits at f_2 and receives at f_1, and radio C transmits at f_3 and receives at f_2. A transmits a signal, and B and C are forwarders. We implement *FI* cancellation on A. Therefore, at A, we can measure *FI* cancellation of the interference forwarded through B and C.

Motivated by the previous experiment, we place all the radio close to each other to get the worst case *FI* cancellation performance. The performance is shown in Figure 9. The cancellation stays stable irrespective to the number of radios. Surprisingly, from 1 hop to 4 hops, on average, performance only drops by 3 dB. Given the fact that interference power decreases as the interference stream goes through more radios, the cancellation requirement also decreases with more radios involved. Therefore it is expected the interference stream going through multiple forwarders will eventually be entirely removed.

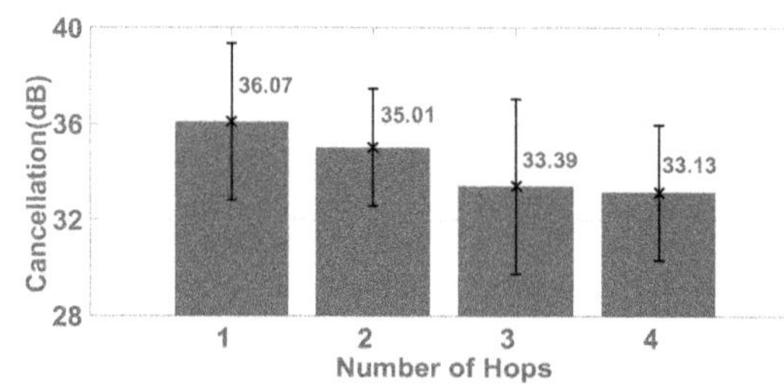

Figure 9: Cancellation performance of the interference going through multiple radios.

6.1.3 *Multi-path Profile*

To illustrate the multi-path profile in AirExpress system, in this experiment, we first transmit a narrowband sine wave of duration 0.2ms after the training. With 1-hop to 3-hop AirExpress setting, we can see the difference in the power of the received signal in Figure 12(b). The small steps before the received sine wave shown in the figure are caused by the cross hop interference. We can see that each step lasts for around $1\mu s$, which is mainly due to the latency introduced by each forwarder.

6.1.4 *Effect of External Interference*

As shown in our MAC protocol 4.1, the transmission in the AirExpress has already taken into account the carrier sensing result. So that multiple transmissions can happen simultaneously in the network. However, collision avoidance is not always perfect. At the same time, WiFi channels are also experiencing interference from other technologies, like Zigbee signal or cordless microphones. What happens when external interference happens after the carrier sensing period of AirExpress is the case we want to discover. To illustrate the scenario, we articulate the collision in the following way. We will transmit 10 packets in a roll periodically and carrier sensing is done every cycle. Thus the 10 packets in a roll can be seen as a continues running AirExpress transmission.

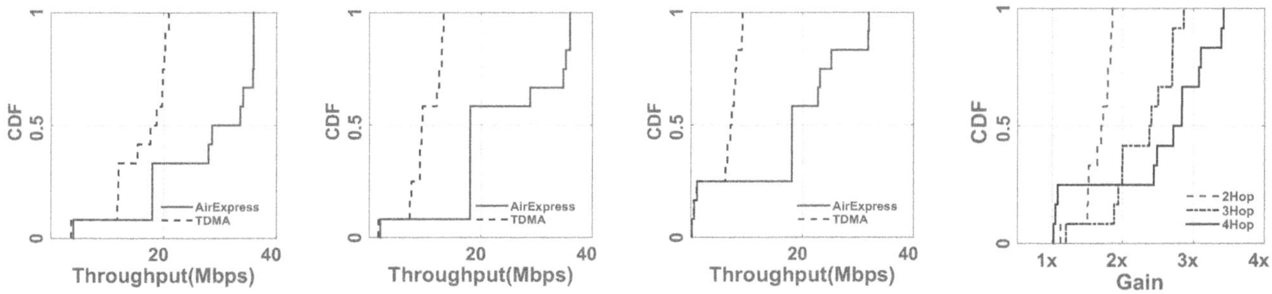

(a) 2 hops (b) 3 hops (c) 4 hops (d) AirExpress over TDMA

Figure 8: Figure (a),(b) and(c) depict the throughput of AirExpress and TDMA respectively with 2-hop, 3-hop and 4-hop routes. Figure (d) depicts the throughput gain of AirExpress over TDMA with 2-hop, 3-hop and 4-hop routes.

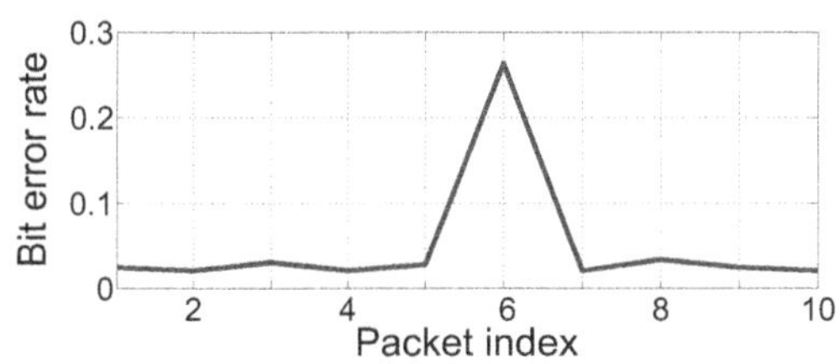

Figure 10: Bit error rate for ten continuous packets. An external packet is introduced as interference aligned with the 6th packet.

We externally introduce an interference packet synchronized with the 6th packet in each cycle. And such cycle is repeated for 100 transmissions. The average bit error rate for all the 10 packets is shown in Figure 10

It is expected packets 1 to 5 are not affected by the interference as shown in the Figure 10. The good phenomena is although Packet 6 can not be recovered due to collision, the interference does not affect the ongoing transmission when the collision signal stops. This is quite important for the AirExpress design. If we can pack multiple packets together after one channel measurement, the mac overhead can be easily amortized.

6.2 System Evaluation

We evaluate the throughput performance of AirExpress via experiments in an indoor setting. 20 locations are chosen as shown in Figure 11 for nodes' placement. For several source-destination pairs picked from the 20 locations, we choose the multi-hop traces which maximize the throughput in TDMA setting. For the same source-destination pair, we apply AirExpress on the same trace to perform cut-through transmission. Rate adaptation is not implemented in the system. To demonstrate the system performance, we calculate the throughput by comparing the performance of transmission under each date rate. To be more specific, for each transmission (AirExpress or single hop transmission in TDMA setting), we deliver 500 packets with different physical layer rates (1/2QPSK, 2/3QPSK, 1/2QAM16, 2/3QAM16, 1/2QAM64, 3/4QAM64). The one that maximizes throughput is chosen as the date rate for that transmission. All the carrier sensing overhead is ignored for the demonstration of throughput comparison. The result is shown in Figure 8.

Figure 11: Floor plan for the system evaluation. AirExpress radios are placed in these 20 possible locations.

The throughput result for TDMA is calculated based on the assumption of a perfect scheduler that could assign different time to different hops to maximize its throughput performance. Even without considering the contention overhead of the TDMA scheduling, we can see the improvement of AirExpress is significant. For the 2-hop case in Figure 8(a), AirExpress increases the throughput by 164% and it provides a median gain of 1.71. In 3-hop scenario as shown in Figure 8(b), AirExpress improves the network throughput by 227% and provides a median gain of 2.39. In the 4-hop case, the throughput improvement is 246% as shown in Figure 8(c) and the median gain is 2.75. We can see in all figures, several cases show limited performance gain of AirExpress. This is usually in the scenario where one link in the trace is relatively bad. As the worst channel in the path dominates the throughput performance in both AirExpress and TDMA cases, it is expected their performance is similar.

6.3 AirExpress in Large Mesh Network

To evaluate AirExpress in a large mesh network, especially to evaluate the routing performance, we use NS3 to do the simulation. In the experiment, we randomly place

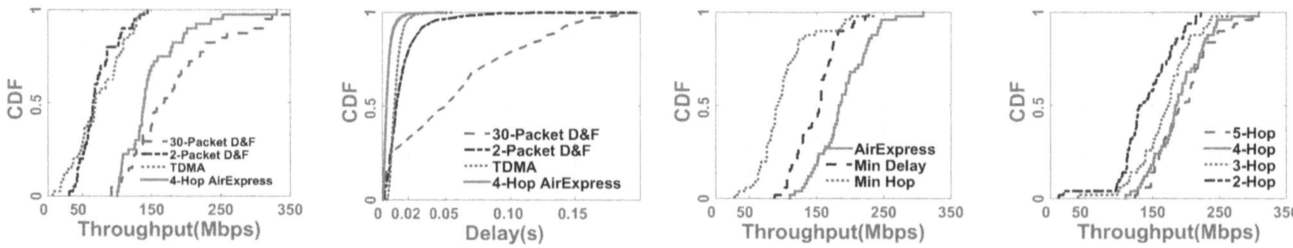

(a) Throughput (b) Delay Performance (c) Different Routing (d) Virtual Hop Size

Figure 12: Performance comparison in NS3 simulation. (a)(b)show the general throughput and delay performance among TDMA and 4-hop AirExpress and *D&F* schemes. For *D&F* we illustrate the performance when 2/30 packets are combined in one set transmission. (c) shows the performance of 4-hop AirExpress working with different routing scheme. (d) shows the performance of AirExpress with different virtual hop settings.

100 nodes in a 1000m×1000m field. All the radios are operating on output power 20dBm. Among these 100 nodes, we randomly pick source-destination pairs to generate traffic. Measurements of the cancellation performance from experiment are fed into the network. As shown in Figure 7 and Figure 9, the cancellation is not perfect. There is residual interference after interference cancellation and the residual interference is related to the channel condition. We take this into account and feeds the measurement from our experiment into the simulator.

To evaluate the performance of AirExpress, in addition to the AirExpress protocol, we implement two more schemes – an omniscient TDMA scheme and a perfect *D&F* scheme. In the TDMA setting, a central controller is assumed to be aware of the global information. It can coordinate the transmission among all the potential links with zero mac overhead. The carrier sensing and contention overhead are all removed. In the *D&F* setting, we assume a *D&F* scheme capable of canceling out all the *FI* and *CHI* components perfectly.

For the routing choices, besides AirExpress routing described in section 4.3, we implement another two routing schemes: the minimum hop scheme and minimum delay scheme. Minimum hop scheme always finds the path with the minimal number of hops, in which each hop is guaranteed to be a link with SNR higher than a basic threshold. Minimum delay scheme grants the routes, through which if a packet is transmitted one hop after another, the transmission time is minimized. The supported virtual hop size ranges from 2 to 5.

6.3.1 AirExpress vs TDMA and D&F

We compare the throughput and delay performance among TDMA, *D&F* and AirExpress. We generate 100 sets of topology and within each topology we generate 10 traffic requests. Routing for TDMA setting is based on the minimum delay routing. AirExpress is operating in the 4-hop virtual hop configuration with corresponding AirExpress routing scheme. *D&F* uses the same routing scheme as AirExpress. There are two configurations of *D&F*: 2-packet *D&F* and 30-packet *D&F*. The number of packets here denotes the number of packets in one batch of transmission.

The CDF of the experiment performance is plotted in Figure 12, in which Figure 12(a) shows the throughput performance while Figure 12(b) illustrates the delay performance. Compared with TDMA scheme, the improvement of AirExpress is clear. AirExpress outperforms TDMA by 2.85 in the throughput performance. At the same time, the latency is reduced by three times comparing to TDMA.

The performance of *D&F* is quite bad through our emulation. The 2-packet *D&F* throughput performance is comparable to TDMA, while its latency is higher than TDMA scheme. 30-packet *D&F* shows its potential in the throughput performance. It outperforms AirExpress by 20 percentage in average. However the latency trade-off is also quite severe. To deliver one packet from source to destination, it takes 15 times more delay comparing to AirExpress and 5 times more delay than the TDMA. Partial reason for the bad performance of *D&F* is that the routing scheme does not match the *D&F* protocol. However, the policy of *D&F* itself hides the fundamental reason. When the number of packets in a batch is small, there is not much improvement of the throughput. At the same time, the time a *D&F* path reserved is proportional to the hop numbers. Thus there are less simultaneous transmissions in the network. The aggregation of these two facts ends up in a worse performance even comparing to TDMA. When the number of packets in the batch increases, the latency performance is extremely high, because packets can only be resolved when all the packets in one batch arrive at the destination.

6.3.2 Routing Algorithm in AirExpress

To illustrate the importance of a matching routing algorithm in presence of the cut-through capability, in this experiment, we compare the throughput performance of 4-hop cut-through in different routing schemes. To make minimum hop or minimum delay routing work with AirExpress, we grant nodes the ability to get the route and the ability to stop at any of the middle forwarders just like the function in AirExpressrouting protocol. Figure 12(c) shows the comparison among their performance. AirExpress routing outperforms minimum hop by 1.88 times and increases the throughput by 1.26 compared to minimum delay.

6.3.3 Virtual Hop Size in AirExpress

When we vary the maximum number of hops in a virtual hop in AirExpress, the network throughput varies as shown in Figure 12(d). We can see that more than four hops within a virtual hop will not further increase the network performance.

This observation somehow matches the expectation. It is true that with more hops involved, more transmissions can be processed together. However the equivalent channel of the AirExpress path becomes worse. The improvement of the cut-through transmission disappears at some point. We believe the optimal virtual hop size is a somehow a topology and flow demand related statistic.

7. RELATED WORK

Cut-through routing is mainly a wired networking concept. In wired cut-through routing, packets are routed after the header of the packet is decoded so that latency is reduced. Along with the delay reduction, cut-through routing also reduces the necessity of storing packets which requires additional resources.

In the history of wireless cut-through, people used to explore the latency gain and the control mechanism to enable cut-through routing using different frequencies [12]. Some similar works [9, 14] got inspired by existing wireline network. They respectively imported the pipeline philosophy from chip architecture and highlighted the importance of ad hoc networks when deployed with existing WLANS.

After the introduction of wireless in-band full-duplex techniques in recent year, literature starts to explore the opportunity of cut-through transmission within channels of the same center frequency. [3] looks at the the opportunity to filter the signal at the forwarder so that in a 2-hop cut-through trace, the signal could constructively add up at the receiver so that the coverage range of WiFi could be extended. The main focus of [3] – constructive signal adding up could potentially improve the performance of the AirExpress transmission in the two-hop setting. However it requires all the transmitters to be aware of the channel information among the radios. [4] shows the possibility of in-band cut-through transmission for more than three hops. But, it treats all the *CI* components as interference, and thus the performance will be quite bad in the real world deployment

AirExpress, however, is the first system realizing 2+ hop in-band cut-through transmission in a practical channel setting. It considers and deals with cross-hop interference. Also efficient MAC and routing algorithms in a mesh network supporting AirExpress are presented.

8. CONCLUSION AND FUTURE

In this paper, we realize the first fully functional in-band wireless cut-through system AirExpress. AirExpress is able to deal with self interference, forwarder interference and cross-hop interference efficiently altogether at the same time. A MAC protocol of AirExpress supporting its running and carrier sensing in the multiple broadcast domains is provided. A routing algorithm adapted to AirExpress PHY and MAC properties is also presented.

We believe with the cut-through capability enabled, the fundamental description of transmission pattern in wireless ad hoc network is challenged. Although AirExpress's protocol going back to the circuit-switched networking looks like a step back in the networking technology evolution, actually it is a big step forward. Our previous belief in the packet-switched networking in the wireless communication area reduces the spacial reuse opportunities. Enabling more transmissions in the same space is just the fundamental resource AirExpress seeks to take advantage of. Although it is true that current AirExpress system has several remaining issues for the real world realization, like how to do the dynamic data rate selection, its potential in the performance improvement from the network perspective will surely drive us to the future realization.

Acknowledgments

We would like to thank our anonymous shepherd and reviewers for their comments and suggestions to improve our paper. The work reported in this paper was supported in part by the NSF under Grant CNS 1254032.

9. REFERENCES

[1] Cut-Through and Store-and-Forward Ethernet Switching for Low-Latency Environments. http://www.cisco.com/c/en/us/products/collateral/switches/nexus-5020-switch/white_paper_c11-465436.html.

[2] Bansal, T., Chen, B., Sinha, P., and Srinivasan, K. Symphony: Cooperative Packet Recovery over the Wired Backbone in Enterprise WLANs. In *ACM MOBICOM* (2013).

[3] Bharadia, D., and Katti, S. Fastforward: Fast and constructive full duplex relays. In *ACM SIGCOMM* (2014).

[4] Chen, B., Tummala, G. K., Qiao, Y., and Srinivasan, K. In-band wireless cut-through: Is it possible? In *ACM HotWireless* (2014).

[5] Chen, B., Yenamandra, V., and Srinivasan, K. Flexradio: Fully flexible radios and networks. In *USENIX NSDI* (2015).

[6] Gollakota, S., and Katabi, D. Zigzag decoding: Combating hidden terminals in wireless networks. In *ACM SIGCOMM* (2008).

[7] Jain, M., Choi, J. I., Kim, T., Bharadia, D., Seth, S., Srinivasan, K., Levis, P., Katti, S., and Sinha, P. Practical, real-time, full duplex wireless. In *ACM MOBICOM* (2011).

[8] Katti, S., Gollakota, S., and Katabi, D. Embracing wireless interference: Analog network coding. In *ACM SIGCOMM* (2007).

[9] Lee, S., Banerjee, S., and Bhattacharjee, B. The case for a multi-hop wireless local area network. In *IEEE INFOCOM* (2004).

[10] Magistretti, E., Gurewitz, O., and Knightly, E. 802.11 ec: Collision Avoidance Without Control Messages. In *Proc. of ACM MOBICOM* (2012).

[11] Rahul, H., Kumar, S., and Katabi, D. JMB: Scaling Wireless Capacity with User Demands. In *ACM SIGCOMM* (2012).

[12] Ramanathan, R. Challenges: A radically new architecture for next generation mobile ad hoc networks. In *ACM MOBICOM* (2005).

[13] Tan, K., Liu, H., Fang, J., Wang, W., Zhang, J., Chen, M., and Voelker, G. M. Sam: Enabling practical spatial multiple access in wireless lan. In *ACM MOBICOM* (2009).

[14] Velayutham, A., Sundaresan, K., and Sivakumar, R. Non-pipelined relay improves throughput performance of wireless ad-hoc networks. In *IEEE INFOCOM* (2005).

Control Channel Design for Many-Antenna MU-MIMO

Clayton Shepard, Abeer Javed, and Lin Zhong
Department of Electrical and Computer Engineering
Rice University, Houston, TX
{cws, abeer.javed, lzhong}@rice.edu

ABSTRACT

Many-antenna MU-MIMO faces a critical, previously unaddressed challenge: it lacks a practical control channel. At the heart of this challenge is that the potential range of MU-MIMO beamforming systems scales with up to the square of the number of base-station antennas once they have channel state information (CSI), whereas the range of traditional control channel operations remains constant since they take place before or during CSI acquisition. This range gap between no-CSI and CSI modes presents a critical challenge to the efficiency and feasibility of many-antenna base stations, as their operational range is limited to the no-CSI mode.

We present a novel control channel design for many-antenna MU-MIMO, *Faros*, that allows the number of base-station antennas to scale up to 100s in practice. *Faros* leverages a combination of open-loop beamforming and coding gains to bridge the range gap between the CSI and no-CSI modes. Not only does *Faros* provide an elegant and efficient control channel for many-antenna MU-MIMO, but on a more fundamental level it exposes flexible, fine-grained, control over space, time, and code resources, which enables previously impossible optimizations. We implement our design on the Argos many-antenna base station and evaluate its performance in bridging the range gap, synchronization, and paging. With 108 antennas, *Faros* can provide over 40 dB of gain, which enables it to function reliably at over 250 meters outdoors with less than 100 μW of transmit power per antenna, 10 mW total, at 2.4 GHz.

1. INTRODUCTION

Many-antenna MU-MIMO is a rapidly growing research field, which has recently shown promise of commercialization [1, 2]. However, there are still many system challenges facing the creation of practical many-antenna base stations. Perhaps the most critical issue is the lack of an efficient and reliable control channel in current architectures. This channel is required for basic network operations such as time-frequency synchronization, association, channel state information (CSI) collection, random access, and paging, which take place *before* a MIMO channel is established. Today, wireless systems realize the control channel using a single high-power antenna, or simple diversity schemes, but these methods rapidly become very inefficient as the number of base-station antennas (M) increases.

MobiCom'15, September 7–11, 2015, Paris, France.
© 2015 ACM. ISBN 978-1-4503-3619-2/15/09...$15.00.
DOI: http://dx.doi.org/10.1145/2789168.2790120.

All MIMO base stations have two modes: the *no-CSI mode* that takes place before the base station knows the CSI for the active users, and the *CSI mode* that provides a much more efficient MIMO channel. In order for the base station to collect CSI, it must establish time-frequency synchronization with the users and receive uplink pilots from them; furthermore, once a user becomes inactive, the base station must be able to notify the user of an incoming transmission, i.e. page the user, prompting it to send a pilot. All of these operations are part of the control channel, which is traditionally sent entirely over the no-CSI mode.

In MIMO systems the CSI mode has a gain of up to M^2 higher than the no-CSI mode (see §3). When M is small, as in current systems, one can easily overcome this gain gap by simply using a lower modulation rate or a coding gain in the no-CSI mode. However, as M increases, this gap quickly becomes large and problematic. In existing systems *all* control channel operations are performed in the no-CSI mode and sent omnidirectionally to the entire coverage area. Thus, the base station's operational range is limited by the no-CSI mode, which is significantly shorter than that of the CSI mode. One naïve solution is to use higher transmission power in the no-CSI mode. This will lead to more expensive hardware, e.g., power amplifier, possible violation of FCC regulations, and increased inter-cell interference.

We present *Faros*,[1] a novel control channel design that addresses the above gain gap for base stations or access points with multiple antennas. *Faros* leverages two key insights. (*i*) First, *as much of the control channel as possible should be sent over the CSI mode.* We find that the only control channel operations that must use the no-CSI mode are time-frequency synchronization, association, CSI collection, paging, and random access, which are required to establish the CSI mode. By implementing the remaining control channel operations over the CSI mode, we substantially increase their efficiency, as well as avoid the aforementioned gain gap. (*ii*) Our second key insight is that *synchronization and association are not time-critical.* That is, synchronization is valid for 100s of ms and association only happens once; thus by reducing the frequency of synchronization *Faros* is able to substantially reduce the channel overhead of these operations in the no-CSI mode, at the cost of slightly increased association latency at the cell edges.

Guided by these insights, *Faros* leverages open-loop beamforming and coding gains to ensure that many-antenna base stations can achieve their full potential range (see §4 and §5). Through open-loop beamforming, *Faros* is able to use the full diversity, power, and beamforming gains from all of the antennas on the base station, which enables it to

[1] $\Phi\acute{\alpha}\rho o\sigma$, or *Faros*, means "beacon" or "lighthouse" in Greek. The rotation of a lighthouse's strong beam of light is analogous to the beamsweeping employed by *Faros*.

scale with M, the number of base-station antennas. Because open-loop beamforming is never as performant as its MU-MIMO counterpart, closed-loop beamforming, *Faros* employs coding gains to further increase the range and to ensure that synchronization and paging are reliable even at the cell edges. To be as efficient as possible, *Faros* only performs these essential tasks and communication outside of the CSI mode, which offers much higher spectral capacity. Specifically, *Faros* uses open-loop beamforming to sweep extra-long synchronization sequences across the coverage area. This synchronization sequence not only enables users to establish time-frequency synchronization with the base station, but also encodes the base-station ID, and optionally user IDs for paging. *Faros* can dynamically configure important parameters, such as the beam patterns, sweep rate, and sequence length, to match the required gain for full coverage of the desired area. Furthermore, by increasing open-loop beamforming and coding gains in no-CSI mode while reducing the modulation rate or number of users served in CSI mode, *Faros* can be used to extend the range of the base station in remote areas.

We implement *Faros* on Argos, a many-antenna MU-MIMO base station over a 2.4 GHz channel, with 108 antennas (see §6) and evaluate the real-world performance and overhead of the implementation (see §7). Measurements show that our implementation provides over a 40 dB gain compared to traditional control channel operations. Anecdotally, this enables us to provide reliable synchronization to mobile users at over 250 meters with less than 100 μW of power per base-station antenna, or 10 mW of total power, using only standard low-gain 3 dBi omnidirectional antennas. Our design facilitates collecting high resolution channel measurements in highly mobile environments, with less than 0.5% channel overhead. To reduce the overhead of paging delay, we additionally implement a simple paging scheme that leverages the users last known location for directing the paging signal, which reduces paging delay by 400%.

In designing and implementing *Faros*, we do not invent any new physical layer techniques. Rather, *Faros* contributes a novel synthesis of known methods, such as beamforming, coding, and synchronization, to achieve a very practical and flexible control channel that bridges the gain gap with extremely low overhead. To the best of our knowledge, *Faros* is the first reported control channel design for many-antenna MU-MIMO that can effectively bridge the gain gap.

2. BACKGROUND

2.1 Beamforming and MU-MIMO

Beamforming utilizes multiple antennas transmitting at the same frequency to realize directional transmission. Constructive and destructive interference of the signals from multiple antennas causes the signal strength received to vary spatially, leading to a *beam pattern*. This beam pattern can be altered by changing the beamforming *weights* applied to each antenna, effectively altering the amplitude and phase of the signal sent from that antenna. *Open-loop* beamforming uses precomputed beamforming weights (beamweights), such as DFT weights [3], to steer the beam in a desired spatial direction, without knowledge of the users' locations. *Closed-loop* or *adaptive* beamforming employs channel state information (CSI) to calculate the beamweights that maximize the signal strength at intended users and minimize the interference at unintended ones.

Multi-user multiple-input multiple-output (MU-MIMO) base stations leverage multiple antennas, each with its own radio, to serve multiple users simultaneously on the same time-frequency-code resource, typically through closed-loop beamforming. For simplicity, we use the term antenna to include both the radio and antenna. It is well-known that the spectral and energy efficiency of MU-MIMO systems grow with the number of base-station antennas (M) and the number of concurrent users (K), given $M \geq K$.

Many-antenna MU-MIMO: In light of this, several strong theoretical analyses have advocated a very large number of base-station antennas [4–6], commonly referred as *massive* MIMO and widely considered one of the few candidate technologies for 5G cellular networks [1, 7, 8]. We use the term *many-antenna* to refer to base stations that have many more antennas than users, but are not necessarily "massive". There have been a number of real-world many-antenna prototypes recently reported, including [2,9–14], as well as efforts towards commercialization and standardization [1,15]. The succinct background of many-antenna MU-MIMO relevant to this work is: (*i*) Efficient massive channel estimation requires uplink pilots that are used to infer the downlink CSI via TDD reciprocity. (*ii*) Since channel estimates are only ephemerally accurate, downlink beamforming must happen immediately after channel estimation. As a result, an efficient many-antenna MU-MIMO transmission frame structure needs four parts, as depicted by Figure 2.

2.2 Control Channel

In wireless systems, the control channel performs operations required to setup data communication. This includes synchronization, gain control, association, timing advance, random access, paging, setting modulation rates, gain control, scheduling and more. Additionally, in MIMO systems, the control channel must coordinate the collection of CSI across many antennas from multiple users efficiently. This paper focus on the control channel operations required to establish the MIMO channel, which are *synchronization*, *association*, *CSI collection*, *random access*, and *paging*, as *Faros* performs the remaining control channel operations over the more efficient MIMO channel using existing techniques.

Synchronization: Since nodes in wireless networks do not share oscillators, their time-frequency reference is subject to drift. Thus all high-performance digital wireless communication schemes require tight time-frequency synchronization. In existing systems users establish time-frequency synchronization in four steps: (*i*) First, they auto-correlate the received signal with itself for frame detection and coarse timing. (*ii*) Then, they perform automatic gain control (AGC) to ensure the received signal is within their ADC's dynamic range. (*iii*) Next, they perform a cross-correlation with a pre-known sequence to achieve fine-grained time synchronization. (*iv*) Finally, they leverage the distortion within the known signal, i.e. phase shift, to recover the frequency offset and establish frequency synchronization.

For example, in 802.11 the user continuously performs an auto-correlation to detect the short training sequence (STS) at the start of a packet, which triggers AGC, then performs a cross-correlation on the following LTS for time synchronization. Similarly, in LTE, the user continuously performs an auto-correlation to detect the cyclic prefix of each symbol, then performs a cross-correlation on the PSS and SSS for time synchronization. Typically reference symbols are transmitted throughout the frame in order to maintain this synchronization, as well as compensate for other channel effects. For example, 802.11 dedicates four subcarriers to pilots, and LTE sends reference symbols in a checkerboard-like pattern that are close enough together in time and frequency to continuously correct for drift.

Association: Before a user can transmit or receive data, it must first identify the nearby base stations, select one, then connect to it. To facilitate this association procedure, base stations typically transmit a unique identifier, often called a *beacon*, at a regular interval. Users scan for base stations, often over multiple frequencies, then choose one to associate with based on specific criteria, such as signal strength and authorization. The user then contacts the base station, usually leveraging the same mechanism as random access, to request and coordinate access, e.g., authorization, encryption, and scheduling.

CSI Collection: To obtain CSI, the transmitter sends a pre-known sequence, called a *pilot*, which the receiver uses to compute this amplitude and phase shift for each subcarrier. However, this requires time-frequency synchronization, as without time synchronization the receiver would not reliably know where the pilot starts, and without frequency synchronization there would be inter-subcarrier interference that causes inaccurate channel estimation.

Traditional MU-MIMO systems employ explicit CSI estimation: the base station sends pilots from each of its antennas, the users estimate the CSI to each antenna, then send this CSI estimation back to the base-station. In CSMA systems, such as 802.11, this CSI collection is performed at the beginning of every frame, whereas in scheduled systems, such as LTE, this is performed continuously using reference symbols from each base-station antenna. These techniques do not scale well as the number of antennas and users increase, thus emerging many-antenna systems typically employ implicit CSI estimation: each user sends an uplink pilot which the base station receives on every antenna, which provides uplink CSI, then leverages reciprocal calibration to estimate the downlink CSI based on the uplink CSI [9,16–19].

Paging and Random Access: Additionally, the control channel handles notifying users when they have incoming data, called *paging*, and coordinating users to randomly access the network when they have outgoing data. Both of these operations must take place before CSI is acquired, as the user has to be paged in order to know it needs to send pilots, or, for random access, it must be able to notify the base station that it has outgoing data so the base station knows to estimate the channel.

3. GAIN GAP EXPLAINED

Multi-antenna base stations operate in two modes: either with CSI or without CSI. With CSI the base station can achieve a gain of M^2 relative to the *peak-power of a single antenna*, whereas without CSI the base station only has a gain of 1 for some control channel operations, illustrated in Figure 1. Furthermore, while the channel is reciprocal for uplink and downlink transmissions, the transceiver hardware is not, which subsequently creates a second gain gap between uplink and downlink modes. In this section, we take a closer look at these gain gaps, taking in to account real-world constraints and hardware.

Mode	CSI	no-CSI	Gap
Uplink	$M \times P_U$	P_U	$\boldsymbol{M}$
Downlink	$M^2 \times P_{BS}/K$	P_{BS}	$\boldsymbol{M^2/K}$
Gap	$K \cdot P_U/M/P_{BS}$	P_U/P_{BS}	

Table 1: Gain gaps between no-CSI and CSI modes. M is the number of base-station antennas; K the number of concurrently served users; P_U the transmission power of a user antenna; P_{BS} that of a base-station antenna.

Table 1 summarizes the analytical results for all modes of operation: no-CSI vs. CSI and downlink vs. uplink assuming an M antenna base station serving K single-antenna users. Each base-station antenna has a transmit power of P_{BS} and each user antenna has a transmit power of P_U. While many theoretical analyses use a total transmit power budget, real systems are constrained by a peak transmit power *per antenna*. For simplicity we assume the average channel and antenna gains are normalized to 1, since they are constant across all modes, and include any non-reciprocal hardware effects, such as the gains from the low-noise amplifiers (LNAs) in the appropriate P, e.g., P_U includes the gain from the base station's LNAs.

We note the above M^2 gain gap is a point of contention, particularly among theoreticians, as they typically assume a total power budget, which reduces this gain to M. In a real system antennas are peak-power constrained so this would require a single antenna to be provisioned with a much higher total transmit power, which can be impractical. Regardless, there is still at least a gain gap of M, and we analyze both situations in our experiments in §7.

3.1 Without CSI

To the best of our knowledge there is no existing scheme which performs better than a single antenna for the no-CSI mode control channel operations of synchronization and channel estimation. Thus the no-CSI mode has a gain of 1, which becomes P_{BS} and P_U for downlink and uplink, respectively, as shown in Table 1. The gain of an M antenna base station in its no-CSI mode is dependent on what operation it is performing. For CSI collection, there is a fundamental gain limitation of 1 because CSI consists of only information about the link between one antenna and another antenna. Therefore, signals received at other antennas do not contain information about that link's CSI. On the other hand, this theoretical limitation doesn't exist for synchronization, as the desired signal can be sent from all the base-station antennas, which is exploited in our design.

While there are no-CSI mode techniques which achieve a theoretic gain of M, these methods are either impractical, or, in fact, reduce the performance of time-frequency synchronization. One naïve technique would be to use an RF combiner to merge the power output of the M base-station antennas to a single antenna. Not only is this difficult and expensive to implement in hardware, as it requires perfect phase matching to avoid feedback in to the antennas, and complex wiring, but it also loses the diversity gain of the M antennas; in essence this is just using a single high-power transmitter, i.e., it is no longer an $M \times K$ system. Despite these drawbacks, we include this scheme for comparison in our experimental analysis. Another method, which is currently used in multi-antenna systems, such as 802.11n and 802.11ac, is cyclic delay diversity (CDD), which cyclicly rotates the symbols by different amounts of time from each antenna [20]. CDD spreads the power output of all M antennas

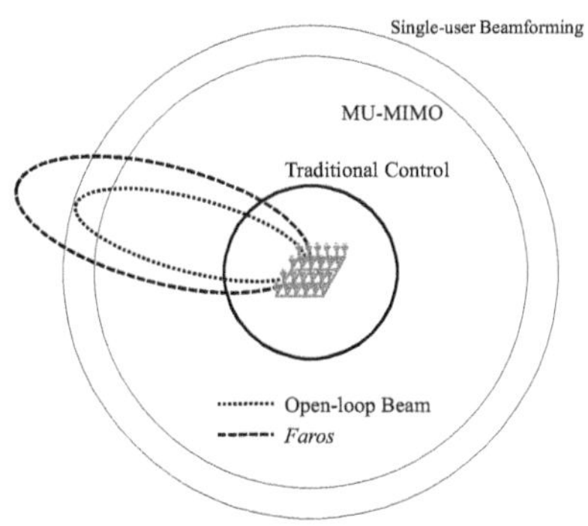

Figure 1: The downlink gain gap. Note that while the figure depicts omnidirectionality, the gap is equivalent for directional antennas.

spatially, and can be thought of as arbitrarily beamforming on different subcarriers. This causes time-domain distortion, which substantially degrades the performance of existing synchronization techniques, and, even worse, this performance degrades rapidly as more antennas are added [20]. Finally, both of these naïve schemes only help in the downlink, and do not provide any gain in the uplink.

3.2 With CSI

The potential power gain of an $M \times K$ MU-MIMO system with CSI, in both uplink and downlink, is well known to be $P \cdot M$, where P is the transmission power [21]. Leveraging CSI, the base station can direct radiation towards, or listen to radiation from, the intended K users using beams with an approximate width of $1/M$, which provides a spatial power gain of M. In the downlink, the base station transmits power from all M antennas, but has to split the power among K users, thus providing a per-link power of $P_{BS} \cdot M/K$, assuming equal power allocation among the users. In the uplink, the base station receives power from each user on all M antennas, thus providing a power of P_U. This renders a total gain of $M^2 \cdot P_{BS}/K$ and $M \cdot P_U$, respectively, as shown in Table 1. Note that a MU-MIMO base station capable of serving K users likely will not always serve K users simultaneously; with a single user the gap increases to a full M^2.

4. FAROS GAIN MATCHING

With the gain gaps above, we next present the design of *Faros* in two parts: (*i*) mechanisms to bridge the gain gaps (this section), and (*ii*) the control channel system design that overcomes the limitations of these mechanisms (§5).

To bridge the gain gap of the no-CSI and CSI modes in the downlink, *Faros* combines open-loop beamforming with a coding gain. It sweeps open-loop beams carrying orthogonal sequences, which enable the *synchronization* and *paging* operations. In the uplink, *Faros* exploits the natural per-antenna asymmetric transmit power and employs an additional coding gain to enable *CSI collection* and *random access* operations. By encoding a base-station ID in the downlink synchronization sequence and exploiting the random access operation, *Faros* facilitates the *association* operation.

4.1 Open-Loop Beamforming

Faros employs open-loop beamforming to exploit the power and diversity of all antennas on the base station. The combined power of the antennas provides a gain of M, and the beamforming provides another gain of M, for a total gain of $O(M^2)$. However, this beamforming gain does not come for free, as it focuses the radiated power on $1/M$ of the antennas' coverage area, thus *Faros* must sweep beams to provide complete coverage. Leveraging our key insight that *association* and *synchronization* are delay-tolerant, *Faros* employs open-loop beamforming for these operations *without* impacting user-perceived performance or creating significant channel overhead.

While there are many MIMO and diversity schemes that exploit the gains from multiple antennas, only open-loop beamforming is effective for time-frequency synchronization, as it provides the full potential combined power and directivity gain from all of the available antennas without causing time-domain distortion. Furthermore, open-loop beamforming has four practical benefits in a real-world MU-MIMO system: (*i*) the increased received power allows the user to employ cheaper RF components, e.g., the LNA, (*ii*) the increased directivity and lower total power reduce the interference to adjacent cells, (*iii*) it does not require any additional hardware or computation, as the beamforming precoders are already required on the base station for MU-MIMO, and (*iv*) it allows the coverage area to be finely tuned.

4.1.1 Beamsweeping

To overcome the spatial selectivity of open-loop beamforming, *Faros* employs *beamsweeping* that transmits a signal, s, in different spatial directions using beamforming. Fundamentally, beamsweeping trades off increased spatial coverage with additional time overhead. Guided by our second key insight that some control channel operations are delay-tolerant, we leverage beamsweeping for synchronization, and to help facilitate association.

Each beam is defined by a $M \times 1$ vector, $\mathbf{b_n}$, thus an N length sweep pattern can be defined by a $M \times N$ matrix, $\mathbf{B}$, composed of $\mathbf{b_1}, \mathbf{b_2}, ..., \mathbf{b_n}$. The M-antenna base station transmits an entire sweep pattern in N time-slots, as the transmission in a given time-slot n and given base station antenna m is simply: $s \cdot B_{m,n}$. Thus, if each beam is sent contiguously, then beamsweeping takes N times longer than a single omnidirectional transmission of the same sequence. Because *Faros* sends a beam at the beginning of each frame, an entire beamsweep takes $N \cdot F$, where F is the frame duration, as further described in §5.6, and shown in Table 2.

Complete Spatial Coverage: If $\mathbf{B}$ forms an orthogonal basis, i.e., it consists of $N = M$ orthogonal or pseudo-orthogonal beams, then it provides complete spatial coverage. Any complete M-dimensional basis used for beamsweeping will provide complete coverage of the CSI space, since, by definition, the CSI of any user can be represented by a linear combination of the basis. This ensures that for any given point in the coverage area at least one beam in B will not have a perfect null.

It is important to note that as M increases, the probability that a user detects a given beam is reduced, since the energy is more spatially selective. However, the probability that a user will detect at least one beam in the sweep pattern increases, as, given a complete orthogonal basis, at least one beam is pointed towards the user, and that beam has a higher EIRP since it is narrower.

Techniques and Range: *Faros* can leverage many beamforming techniques with compelling tradeoffs for specific implementations. Without detailed information about the environment and precise calibration, any orthogonal basis with low peak to average power ratio (PAPR) works well for open-loop beamforming. While a complete basis guarantees spatial coverage, it does not guarantee a strong signal. Since it is statistically impossible that every user will have an open-loop beam pointed directly at them, the gain of beamsweeping is reduced by an inaccuracy factor of a, to M^2/a. As such, an overcomplete **B**, i.e. $N > M$, can provide extended coverage by statistically reducing a. Otherwise, given careful consideration of the propagation environment and antenna placement, as well as hardware calibration, techniques such as DFT open-loop beamforming can be tuned to provide the desired coverage area. For our implementation we choose Hadamard beamforming weights, as further described in §6.

4.2 Coding Gain

The use of open-loop beamsweeping will reduce the gain gap between no-CSI and CSI modes. To close the remaining gap, *Faros* additionally employs a variable coding gain in both the downlink and uplink. In theory, a coding gain is achieved by sending a signal over a longer period of time, thus, the total received power, integrated over time, increases linearly as the duration increases. However, this gain comes at a cost of increasing the channel usage overhead linearly as well. Coding gains are ideal for tuning the gains to match between modes because they are easily adjustable and thus can be used to dynamically fine-tune the gain vs. overhead tradeoff.

While Table 1 analyzes the gain gap in terms of SINR, not all parts of the frame have the same SINR requirements. For example, data transfer can benefit from a higher SINR by altering the modulation and coding scheme. Higher-ordered modulation requires a higher SINR to be successfully decoded, thus it can be thought of as a negative coding gain in the CSI mode. For instance, in 802.11 OFDM BPSK modulation requires 15 dB SINR, whereas 64-QAM requires 31 dB [22]. In contrast, the detection threshold for a length 128 Kasami sequence is roughly -5 dB [23]. This effectively further reduces the gain gap between the CSI mode, which is used for tranmitting data, and no-CSI mode, but how much is dependent on actual data modulation rate. By leveraging a dynamic coding gain, the range and overhead of *Faros* can be tuned to the specific needs of each deployment.

Downlink Coding Method: In the downlink, *Faros* transmits variable length orthogonal synchronization sequences to encode the base-station ID and paging information, while simultaneously providing synchronization and achieving a gain, C_{down}, proportional to the length of the sequence. Orthogonal sequences are extensively used in wireless systems; an overview of them can be found in [24]. Since these downlink sequences need to be detected *prior* to synchronization, they must have low streaming auto-correlations, both with themselves and the other sequences in the orthogonal set. That is, since the sequences must be detectable without knowledge of when they start, the receiver must perform a full correlation at every sample, thus a time-shift of the sequences must produce a low correlation; otherwise it could cause an erroneous detection.

Uplink Coding Method: In the uplink, the *Faros* base station assigns orthogonal pilot slots to active users, and reserves dedicated slots for association and random access, as shown in Figure 2(b). These pilot slots are variable length to enable a coding gain based on users' channel quality, e.g., users on the cell edges will use longer pilots to increase the accuracy of their channel estimate.

By orthogonalizing pilots in frequency *Faros* is able to increase the accuracy of the channel estimates, and provide an uplink gain of at least K. Frequency orthogonalization (OFDMA) enables all the users to transmit simultaneously, which increases the instantaneous power received at the base station by a factor of K. To collect complete CSI for every frequency, users are further time orthogonalized, as shown in Figure 2b. As such, the total power received for a given user, integrated over time, also increases by a factor of K. Theoretically, to obtain accurate CSI each user must send a pilot for at least a duration of the inverse of the frequency coherence every coherence time interval. However, by scheduling users with poor channel quality to send even longer than required by the frequency coherence interval, *Faros* increases the coding gain, C_{up}; this ensures high-quality channel measurements across the entire cell and fully closes the gain gap.

For association and random access, users send orthogonal synchronization sequences on dedicated time-frequency blocks during the training phase. This allows the users to still achieve a coding gain, while simultaneously enabling collision avoidance and timing-advance estimation, as further discussed in §5.4.

4.3 Combined Gain

Faros employs a combination of open-loop beamforming and coding gain to close the gain gap, as depicted in Figure 1. Beamsweeping provides the majority of downlink gain by focusing the full power of the base station on a small portion of the coverage area; it achieves a gain of M^2/a, where a is the beamforming inaccuracy. In the downlink *Faros* reduces the gap between no-CSI and CSI gains from M^2/K to $M^2/K/(C_{down} \cdot M^2/a) = a/(C_{down} \cdot K)$, thus the coding gain should be tuned so that $C_{down} \approx a/K$.

In the uplink *Faros* leverages OFDMA and coding to achieve a gain of $C_{up} \cdot K$ in the no-CSI mode. This reduces the no-CSI to CSI gap from M to $M/(K \cdot C_{up})$, which suggests C_{up} should be roughly M/K to close the gap.

However, once a proper downlink coding gain, C_{down}, is applied, combined with beamsweeping, the *Faros* no-CSI downlink gain is M^2/K. In contrast, the no-CSI uplink gain is only $(C_{up} \cdot K \cdot P_U)$, which leads to a new gain gap. To mitigate this gap, in *Faros* the *total* transmission power of the base station and user need to be roughly the same, e.g. $O(P_U) \approx O(M \cdot P_{BS})$; this is typical of existing bidirectional communication systems, though macro cells can have as high as a 10 to 18 dB difference. This reduces the gap from $(C_{up} \cdot K \cdot P_U)/(M^2/K \cdot P_{BS})$ to $(C_{up} \cdot K^2)/M$, and suggests that the uplink coding gain should be tuned to approximately M/K^2, along with any residual discrepancy between P_U and P_{BS}, to finish closing the gap.

Comparing the C_{up} needed for the no-CSI vs. CSI, M/K, and uplink vs. downlink, M/K^2, we see there is a residual gap of K. Since the range of the base station is limited by the downlink mode, C_{up} should be selected to match the uplink-downlink gap, then the residual gain of K in the CSI uplink can be used to reduce transmission power or increase modulation rate. Notably, this full coding gain is only required at cell edges, where *Faros* uses extra-long pilots.

It is important to realize that when compared to existing systems, for a given coverage area *Faros reduces* the required per-antenna transmission power of the base station by M^2 and of the user by K.

5. FAROS CONTROL CHANNEL DESIGN

We next describe the design of *Faros* control channel design and how it realizes synchronization, association, CSI collection, random access, and paging.

5.1 Synchronization

Faros achieves both time and frequency synchronization by beamsweeping carefully designed, extended-length, sequences from the base station to the user.

5.1.1 Time Synchronization

With *Faros*, users perform a streaming cross-correlation on received samples to detect the synchronization sequence sent from the base station. That is, it computes the correlation of the received signal R with the sequence S, $\sum_{i=1}^{n}(R_{t-i} \cdot S_i^*)$, at every sample. This produces a peak at the single sample when R and S are aligned in time.

While this is the same concept employed by existing systems, *Faros* faces two new challenges: (*i*) *Faros* needs to detect multiple synchronization sequences simultaneously since it uses both beacon and paging sequences for synchronization, which are sent simultaneously on separate beams. (*ii*) *Faros* needs to perform time synchronization *without* coarse timing information or automatic gain control (AGC). As discussed in §2.2, existing solutions leverage coarse frame detection and AGC to achieve fine-grain time synchronization; however, these techniques are inefficient or even impossible for *Faros* to employ in the no-CSI mode. This is because *Faros*' beamsweeps and MU-MIMO downlink are highly spatially selective and, as a result, users receive every synchronization sequence with highly varying power. While *Faros* could precede every synchronization sequence with a training sequence to facilitate coarse frame detection and AGC, similar to the STS in 802.11, this training sequence would have to have significantly increased length to overcome the gain gap. Moreover, the gains set by this sequence would only be valid for a single beam, making it highly inefficient.

Faros addresses these two challenges with three techniques. First, it employs two full-precision correlators. Existing implementations, such as [25,26], perform only 1-bit and 3-bit correlations, respectively, and only detect a single pre-set sequence. While this approach is computationally efficient, it does not work well without gain control, and performs poorly when trying to distinguish different sequences. By performing two parallel full-precision correlations, e.g. 12-bit for WARPv3, *Faros* is able to reliably detect synchronization sequences with highly varying signal strengths, as well as reliably distinguish paging and beacon synchronization sequences that are sent simultaneously.

Second, since performing AGC on every sequence is inefficient, *Faros* employs *transmit* gain control. That is, since *Faros* beamsweeps the sequence, a user receives every sequence with a substantially different signal strength. Therefore, the users can simply wait for a sequence in the sweep that is within their dynamic range. If they don't detect any sequences, e.g. before discovering any base stations, the users slowly vary their receive gain settings until they detect sequences. After synchronization is established the users listen to all of the subsequent synchronization sequences and adjust their gain accordingly. Notably, *Faros* performs uplink gain control identically to LTE [27], using feedback, and fine-grain downlink gain control is performed at the beginning of each downlink phase, as depicted by Figure 2.

Finally, *Faros* dynamically sets detection threshold by combining the running average of the correlator output and a spike detector. This is because without traditional AGC, the single-sample correlation peak varies drastically in magnitude. The average correlator output provides the average input power, but is additionally scaled by the power of the correlation sequence so that different sequences can be detected without adjusting the threshold. The spike detector simply raises the threshold exponentially when there is a short burst of power, thus avoiding erroneous false-positives. Existing techniques, such as [25,26], employ a static threshold for peak detection, as they leverage AGC to consistently set the magnitude of the digital samples, and thus peak. Other reported correlator designs, e.g., [23], use the input power to set the detection threshold, however we found this approach by itself to be inadequate for *Faros*. This approach is susceptible to false-positives from power spikes without retrospective processing, and does not automatically adapt the threshold to sequences with different PAPRs.

5.1.2 Frequency Synchronization

To determine the carrier frequency offset (CFO), the user calculates the phase drift in the downlink synchronization sequence. This sequence consists two repetitions of the same sub-sequence; since the drift from CFO is constant, corresponding received samples in each repetition have the same phase offset. That is, for an n length sequence repeated twice to give the synchronization sequence S, $\theta(S_i, S_{i+n}) = \theta(S_j, S_{j+n})$, where θ is the phase difference between the complex samples. This is because S_i and S_{i+n} are the same symbol, thus in the absence of CFO $\theta(S_i, S_{i+n}) = 0$; with CFO there is a phase drift that is proportional to time n, which is thus constant across all i: $\theta(S_i, S_{i+n}) = drift(n)$. Thus, we can use the following equation to compute CFO:

$$CFO = \frac{1}{2\pi \cdot n} \sum_{i=1}^{n} \theta(S_i, S_{i+n}) \qquad (1)$$

Notably, in hardware the division by 2π is not actually performed, since the CFO is multiplied by 2π when generating the correcting complex sinusoid. Thus by selecting n to be a power of 2, the division becomes a trivial bitshift. In the presence of noise, longer sequences become more reliable, as the noise is filtered out by the averaging operation. While there are other techniques to compute CFO, such as the conjugate method adopted by LTE [27], *Faros* employs this technique since it enables two synchronization sequences to be simultaneously without affecting CFO recovery. Since both sequences have sub-sequences that repeat twice, the combined signal also repeats twice and can still be used to accurately calculate CFO.

To avoid frequency distortion in multipath environments, typically a cyclic prefix is prepended to the synchronization sequence. However, this cyclic prefix makes time synchronization less robust, as it can cause false positives in the correlator, since it aligns with a subset of the sequence. To avoid this, we use a cyclic *postfix*, then delay the CFO calculation accordingly, i.e., the sum in equation 1 starts at the length of the cyclic postfix. Note that this does not affect the correlator performance, as it operates in the time-domain.

5.2 Association Procedure

Faros enables association by: (*i*) encoding a unique base-station identifier in the beamswept synchronization sequence,

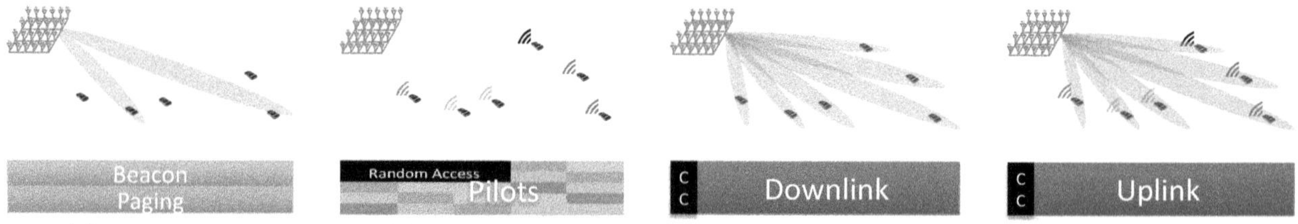

(a) Beamsweep (b) CSI collection (c) Downlink data (d) Uplink data

Figure 2: An example *Faros* frame structure. First, in (a), the base station beamsweeps a beacon that provides the users with time-frequency synchronization and the base-station ID. If a user needs to be paged, the base station will simultaneously beam a paging sequence towards that user. Next, in (b), users send orthogonal uplink pilots in scheduled slots. Users that require random access or association send an uplink pilot in the one of the reserved slots. Finally, in (c) and (d), the base station leverages the acquired CSI to provide downlink and uplink data connectivity, as well as any remaining control channel information, over the efficient MU-MIMO link.

i.e. the *beacon*, (*ii*) having users scan for these beacons to *select a base station*, and (*iii*) providing a *'soft' association* mechanism that allows users to quickly obtain more information about the base station over a MIMO link. We next elaborate on each of these steps.

Beacons: In *Faros*, every base station beamsweeps a synchronization sequence that encodes a locally unique identifier, called a beacon, as shown in Figure 2(a) and discussed in §4.2. This enables users to simultaneously synchronize with a base station, as well as identify it. For the sake of brevity, we assume that the base stations are coordinated so that they each have locally unique identifiers and can ensure that their beacons do not overlap in time, which prevents random access collisions and reduces pilot contamination. While there are straightforward techniques for achieving this coordination, e.g., through the backhaul or via a user, that discussion is outside the scope of this paper.

Base Station Selection: Before associating, a user listens for at least one entire sweep interval, perhaps on multiple frequencies, to determine the IDs of all nearby base stations, as well as the average power of the beacons from each base station. Since the beacon is beamformed, its received power does not indicate the actual channel quality between the user and the base station. Thus it is important for the user to listen to beacons for an entire sweep interval to obtain a rough estimate of the signal strength from each base station, but the true SINR and channel quality, cannot be accurately determined until after association due to the beamforming inaccuracy described in §4.1. Furthermore, the unique identifier contained in the beacon does not convey any additional information, such as authentication, encryption, and a human-readable identifier (e.g. an SSID). Therefore, the user may soft-associate to multiple base stations in order to search for the best match.

Soft-Association: Since *Faros* beacons only contain a unique identifier, we additionally provide a mechanism called *soft-association* which enables users to gather more information over the CSI mode. Traditional control channel designs broadcast information about the base station in their beacons. For example, 802.11 beacons include the BSSID, SSID, modulation rate, encryption information, and more. This information is essential for users to determine if they want to, or even can, connect to the base station. Moreover, the users need to be able to judge their channel quality to the base station, which can only be done in CSI mode.

Guided by our first key insight, that as much control information as possible should be sent over the more efficient MU-MIMO channel, *Faros* provides soft-association to enable users to quickly establish a MIMO link with the base station to efficiently exchange control channel information. To perform a soft-association, users must first synchronize with the base station by successfully decoding a beacon, then send a pilot in one of the slots reserved for random access, as discussed below. Once the base station successfully receives the pilot it has CSI for that user, which it leverages to open a MIMO link and convey the remaining control channel information. If the user proceeds with a full association, based on authorization, link quality, etc., the base station schedules the user dedicated pilot slots and a unique paging sequence to maintain the link. Otherwise, the user continues to scan for and soft-associate to other base stations.

5.3 Collecting CSI

After each beacon, all active users send uplink pilots in their scheduled slots which the base station leverages to collect CSI. It is best to think of the CSI collection phase as a number of time-frequency-code resource slots that can be arbitrarily assigned to users, with some resource slots dedicated to random access, including association requests and paging responses. Users which send reference signals in a given resource element gain spatial resource elements in the corresponding time and frequency coherence interval for both the uplink and downlink phases. That is, any given reference symbol provides an estimation that is valid both for the coherence time interval, as well as a wider frequency coherence interval. As noted in §4.2, *Faros* assigns longer pilot slots to users that have worse channels in order to improve CSI accuracy.

5.4 Random Access

Faros facilitates random access by reserving pilot slots at the beginning of each channel estimation phase, as shown by Figure 2(b). To initiate a connection users simply send an uplink pilot in one of these pilot slots. For the user to send in the correct pilot slots, without interfering with other users, it must have successfully received a beacon, and thus established synchronization. The base station uses this pilot to estimate the user's channel, as well as timing advance, and create a highly efficient MU-MIMO link to the user. As guided by our first key insight, this link is then used to convey all remaining control channel information, including modulation rates and pilot scheduling, as well as maintain/improve synchronization.

LTE already provides a compelling random access solution which fits well within the *Faros* design, with the exception that *Faros* allows for longer length sequences to be employed to finely tune the gain gap. Thus, due to space constraints, we defer to [28] to fully describe the LTE random access

Var	Description	Overhead	Description
L	Sequence Length	C	Channel Utilization
B	Bandwidth	D_A	Association Delay
F	Frame Duration	D_R	Random Access Delay
N	# of beams		

$$C = \frac{L/B}{F} \quad D_A = \frac{N \cdot F}{2} \quad D_R = \frac{F}{2}$$

L	B	F	N	C	D_A	D_R
128	$20MHz$	$15ms$	100	0.043%	750 ms	7.5 ms
128	$40MHz$	$1ms$	100	0.32%	50 ms	0.5 ms
256	$20MHz$	$10ms$	100	0.128%	500 ms	5 ms
256	$20MHz$	$5ms$	500	0.256%	1250 ms	2.5 ms
512	$40MHz$	$2ms$	1000	0.64%	1000 ms	1 ms
1024	$80MHz$	$1ms$	4000	1.28%	2000 ms	0.5 ms

Table 2: Analysis of *Faros*' beacon overhead. *Top:* Variable descriptions. *Middle:* Equations used for analysis. *Bottom:* Expected value of the worst-case overheads of the simplest version of *Faros* given various realistic system parameters.

scheme, including collision detection and avoidance, as well as timing advance, which we employ in *Faros*.

5.5 Paging

Faros enables many-antenna base stations to reliably and *quickly* page users across their entire coverage area. To accomplish this *Faros* applies the beamsweeping and coding gains described in §4; unfortunately, unlike synchronization and association, paging is not delay tolerant. Thus *Faros* leverages the users last known location to substantially reduce the delay from beamsweeping.

Upon association, the base station assigns each user a unique paging sequence. This paging sequence is constructed and transmitted almost identically to the beacon. That is, it is chosen from the same codebook as the beacon to ensure orthogonality, as well as repeated twice to facilitate time-frequency synchronization. To page a user the *Faros* base station beamsweeps their unique paging sequence with the beacon at the beginning of each frame, but on a separate beam, as shown in Figure 2(a). This additional spatial separation between the beacon and paging sequence helps improve the detection of either, as it reduces the inter-sequence interference. To detect the paging sequence, users perform the same synchronization correlation used for the beacon, described in §5.1. Successful detection similarly provides the user with synchronization, however in the case of a paging sequence the user immediately sends an uplink pilot in the dedicated random access pilot slot. This allows the base station to estimate CSI and begin MIMO communication.

One key challenge facing *Faros* is that while association and synchronization are not time-sensitive, the delay from beamsweeping is likely unacceptable for paging, e.g., up to 2 s in Table 2. To solve this challenge, *Faros leverages knowledge of the user's prior location to guide the beamsweep*, even in our naïve implementation this sped up paging by 400%, as demonstrated in §7.3. Note that leveraging the users last known location can only improve expected paging delay, as the sweep continues until the user is paged.

Link Maintenance: Additionally, or alternatively, users will periodically send a random access request to the base station. This serves the multi-purpose of maintaining the association, checking for missed page requests, and updating the users' last known location at the base station to assist with efficient paging and inter-base station handovers.

Figure 3: Our prototype, Argos. *Left:* 80-antenna array in an anechoic chamber. *Top Right:* 104-antenna array in an indoor environment. *Bottom Right:* ArgosMobile user devices.

5.6 Overhead Analysis

By design, *Faros* has a small, if not negligible, overhead. This overhead can be measured by four metrics: (*i*) total channel overhead, (*ii*) association delay, (*iii*) random access delay, and (*iv*) paging delay. Table 2 provides the equations for determining these overheads, then provide example values for reasonable system configurations. For this analysis we assume that frames are sent continuously, with the beacon at the beginning of each frame similar to a scheduled MAC. Since the expected paging delay is dependent on the paging scheme, we discuss its real-world performance using a naïve scheme in §7.3, however it is upper-bounded by the association delay as that is how long it takes to perform a full beam-sweep.

It is important to note that active users *do not* need to receive valid beacons to maintain synchronization, as it is maintained in the CSI downlink control phase. Inactive, but associated users can also maintain synchronization by listening for beacons and paging signals. We note that the duration that time-frequency synchronization is valid depends on the accuracy of the oscillators, frame design, e.g., cyclic prefix, as well as fluctuations in temperature. Given the typical accuracy of oscillators in WiFi and LTE devices, and according to our measurements, the synchronization is usually valid for 100s of ms, but this can be determined on a per-system basis [29]. As such, beacons are only needed for association, and thus the sweep interval can be adjusted accordingly. We also find these overheads are very easy to tune by changing the system parameters. Note that per Table 2, *Faros* can support thousands of antennas with less than 2% overhead, at the cost of slightly increased association delay at the cell edges.

6. IMPLEMENTATION

We implement *Faros* on ArgosV2 [30], a prototype of many-antenna MU-MIMO base station that consists of an array of 27 WARP boards [26], driving 108 antennas, and 5 battery powered WARP-based ArgosMobiles that can be controlled wirelessly through a WiFi bridge, as shown in Figure 3. Both the implementations of *Faros* and Argos can support many times more antennas and users; the reported implementation is only limited by the number of WARP boards available to us. To the best of our knowledge, this is the largest many-antenna MU-MIMO base station with publicly reported results.

Our implementation of *Faros* serves as the basis of Argos' realtime design, and involves development across all layers of the Argos architecture. To enable realtime operation we designed multiple custom Xilinx System Generator IP cores for both the base station and mobile nodes' Virtex 6 FPGA. The most computationally complex IP core we developed for the mobile nodes is the streaming correlator. The correlator enables realtime detection of beacon and paging codes simultaneously, can be dynamically reprogrammed with different sequences, and supports multiple rates and lengths. For the base station our most significant IP core is the MU-MIMO precoder, which we modified to support beamsweeping, as well as selecting and sending multiple paging sequences simultaneously on different beams. While System Generator IP cores are built with a graphical model and do not directly have lines of code, we use the Xilinx xBlock scripting language to dynamically build a significant portion of them, which constitutes over 4,000 lines of code. These IP cores are integrated with peripherals and other IP cores, including a Microblaze soft-core that is programmed with over 1,000 lines of embedded C.

We implement two versions of the central controller, one in Matlab, and one in Python, both of which are over 2,000 lines of code. The Matlab version facilitates flexible non-realtime experiments with rapid analysis, whereas the Python version supports realtime operation, including fully mobile channel estimation with a time resolution up to 200 μs. Our implementation of *Faros* is extremely versatile; it can be compiled to support detecting any code length, given adequate FPGA resources, and can support any beamforming technique by simply reloading the beamsweep buffers with the corresponding precomputed $\mathbf{B}$.

Open-loop beamsweeping: Our implementation uses Hadamard beamweights [31] for beamsweeping for the following reasons. First, they use a minimal number of weights to provide a complete, perfectly orthogonal, basis; this enables a full diversity gain and provides complete spatial coverage with the minimal amount of overhead. Second, they have a perfect peak-to-average power ratio (PAPR) of 1, which allows the antennas to use their full potential transmit power. Finally, calculating Hadamard beamweights does not require any knowledge of the antenna aperture or environment, enabling rapid deployment without calibration or environmental considerations.

Coding: The implementation uses Kasami sequences for the downlink coding. Kasami sequences [32] provide very good detection performance and have low, bounded, streaming correlation both with themselves and the other orthogonal sequences. This allows them to be reliably detected *without* time synchronization, as a streaming correlation on other sequences could produce peaks, and thus false positives, which is important since they are used for time synchronization. Moreover, they provide a large number of orthogonal sequences, e.g., 4096 for a length 256 Kasami sequence, which enables co-located users and base stations to be uniquely identified.

The implementation uses Zadoff-Chu sequences [33, 34] for the uplink channel estimation coding for the following reasons: First, they have a constant amplitude and thus have a perfect PAPR. Second, they can be used to detect multiple users' random access request simultaneously, along

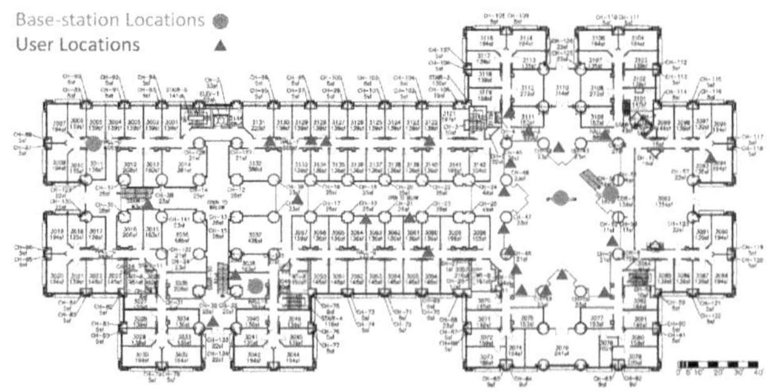

Figure 4: Floorplan depicting example locations of indoor measurements. Both the users and base station locations spanned three floors of elevation.

with each users' path delay to estimate timing advance, with small computational overhead. This is very similar to LTE's random access preamble [27]. However, in our design we allow variable length sequences in order to match gain requirements, as well as use the sequence for CSI estimation.

Thresholding and Variability: *Faros* leverages a realtime streaming time-domain correlator for the beacon, paging, and synchronization, which creates a very strong single-sample peak when the correct sequence is detected. As such, the performance range and accuracy is highly dependent on the detection *threshold.* This threshold is well understood theoretically with regard to false-positive and false-negative performance, and as such we defer to [23] for a more thorough analysis. Since we do not perform gain control for the beacon or paging code we must set this threshold dynamically based on the input power, as well as increase it during power surges to avoid false-positives. This dynamic threshold in *Faros* can be scaled by a constant via software; for the experiments we set the threshold somewhat aggressively so that it is close to impossible to receive a false positive, as we didn't across the 100,000s of synchronization sequences we sent during our experimentation. This threshold could be further optimized to increase range, particularly with mechanisms to deal with false positives.

7. REAL-WORLD PERFORMANCE

We evaluate the performance of *Faros* in bridging the gain gap in real-world topologies. We examine the fully functioning system, and evaluate its performance regarding synchronization, beacons, and paging in diverse environments. Our results demonstrate that *Faros* can extend the no-CSI mode range by over 40 dB when compared to traditional control channels. Furthermore, we find that leveraging knowledge of the users previous location can improve paging delay by 400%, and that *Faros* can reliably correct CFO of over 10 kHz. We first describe our experimental setup, then look at how each of the components performs individually.

7.1 Experimental Setup

We test the performance of the reported *Faros* implementation in 100 discrete user locations at varying distances from the base station in indoor environments and an anechoic chamber, using five ArgosMobiles simultaneously. Additionally, we perform an outdoor range and mobility test, presented in§7.2.1.

Antenna Configurations: Due to hardware availability, and to test the performance of different antennas, we employed *Faros* with three separate antenna configurations: (*i*) In the anechoic chamber with 80 directional 6 dBi patch an-

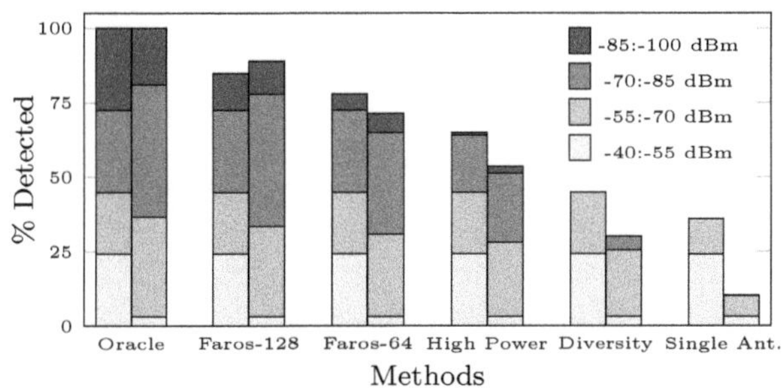

Figure 5: Beacon detection performance across all 32 anechoic chamber (left) and 68 indoor (right) experiment locations. *Oracle* denotes an oracle that detects every beacon sent.

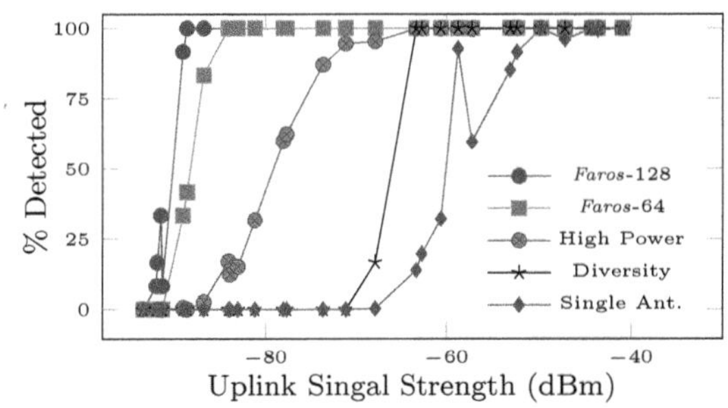

Figure 6: Beacon detection performance vs. uplink RSSI (range) for *Faros* in an anechoic chamber. *Faros* outperforms traditional by over 40 dB. Number indicates beacon length.

tennas, (*ii*) indoors and outdoors with 104 omnidirectional 3 dBi monopole antennas, and (*iii*) indoors with 108 of the same omnidirectional antennas. In all configurations the users also leveraged the 3 dBi omnidirectional antennas.

Power Settings: In the downlink we use a power of approximately -12 dBm per antenna and in the uplink we use 10 dBm. This downlink power is chosen since it results in a ~10 mW total power and an EIRP of up to 1 W, which is the FCC limit. Our prototype is capable of over 10 W total power, and EIRPs exceeding 1 kW, which is only appropriate in licensed bands. For high-power single antenna mode we use the approximate combined power of all of the base station antennas, which is 8 dBm.

Environments and Range: As Figures 5 and 6 depict, we selected locations at increasing distances until the beacons couldn't be detected, providing a fairly uniform selection of signal strengths. In indoor locations this required spacing the users at up to 80 m away, across 3 floors of elevation, as illustrated by the sample of locations presented in Figure 4; in outdoor line-of-sight locations it was over 250 m away. For the anechoic chamber experiments users were spaced up to 15 m away from the base station, and we used variable attenuators with up to 60 dB of suppression to simulate increased distance.

Measurement: At each location we test the *Faros* control channel system over a 20 MHz bandwidth at 2.4 GHz and analyze the performance with regard to the accurate detection of the beacon, paging signal, and uplink pilot, which demonstrate *Faros*' performance in no-CSI mode. As a control, we additionally send an unbeamformed beacon and paging signal from each base-station antenna, i.e. a "beamsweep" using the identity matrix, in both low and high-power modes using a 64 length code to compare the performance with traditional single antenna systems and the naïve high-power solution. While *Faros* is capable of running in realtime, we briefly pause after every beam in order to collect performance statistics from the nodes, such as successful detections, false positives, and received signal strength indicators (RSSIs). Because of this measurement delay, these experiments were conducted without mobility, in relatively stationary channels. We use these results to analyze the performance of *Faros*' beacon, paging, and CSI collection vs. traditional methods, which we present below. Additionally we setup a controlled experiment to test the performance of our CFO estimator, presented in §7.4.

7.2 Beacon Performance

Figures 5 and 6 show the probability of successfully receiving the base station's beacon, i.e., the synchronization sequence encoded with the base-station ID, with various configuration parameters. We compare single-antenna transmission, both high power (*High Power*) and low power (*Single Ant.*), diversity, and *Faros* using code lengths of 64 and 128. In the single antenna diversity mode (*Diversity*) the base station rotates which antenna is transmitting, thus exploiting the full diversity of the array; this is equivalent to *Faros* using the identity matrix for beamsweeping.

The figures sort the results based on the average uplink CSI signal strength across all base-station antennas for the given location, which is an approximation of distance and a fair metric for coverage area. We note that downlink RSSI is not a good metric, since it varies per-beam. Distance is not a good metric since scatterers can significantly alter signal strength. Clearly, changing uplink transmission power will simply shift the same plot either left or right, which indicates how code length and both uplink and downlink transmission powers should be balanced in a real system.

The results across all locations are shown in Figure 5, with separate bars for the 36 anechoic chamber locations and 64 indoor, including 104- and 108-antenna, locations. We see that indoor locations *Faros* is able to reliably serve over 8.8 times more locations than the traditional control channel, and 1.6 times more than a single high power antenna. Even when users have over a -70 dBm average RSSI to the base station, they miss almost 25% of the beacons sent with the high-power single-antenna scheme. This is due to multipath; in some locations, even fairly close, two paths will destructively interfere and create a null, which is not easily overcome with additional signal strength. While the diversity scheme performs better than the single antenna, it is still unable to reliably receive many beacons where users have lower than -70 dBm uplink RSSI. This illustrates the necessity of *Faros*, which leverages both the power and diversity of the entire array, in many-antenna MU-MIMO systems.

The results from the anechoic chamber are shown in Figure 6. Since there is no multipath in the anechoic chamber, the detection rate of each technique is very closely related to RSSI, thus these results accurately demonstrate the relative performance of each technique. We find that *Faros* is able to outperform a single-antenna scheme by over 40 dB, and the high-power scheme by 20 dB.

7.2.1 Range and Mobility Performance

To demonstrate the realtime capability of *Faros*, as well as test its range and mobility performance, we performed an outdoor experiment where we ran *Faros* at full speed. Unfortunately, the previous tests required us to pause the experiments after every beacon or paging signal was trans-

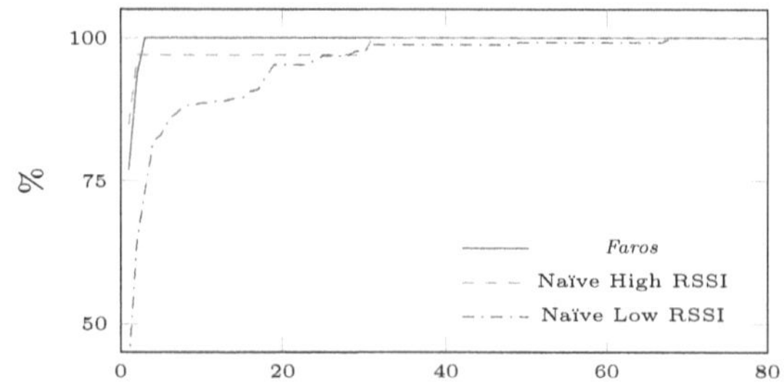

Figure 7: Cumulative distribution functions of paging delay. The naïve method does not use location data to sweep. *Faros* improves mean paging delay by 400% at low RSSIs.

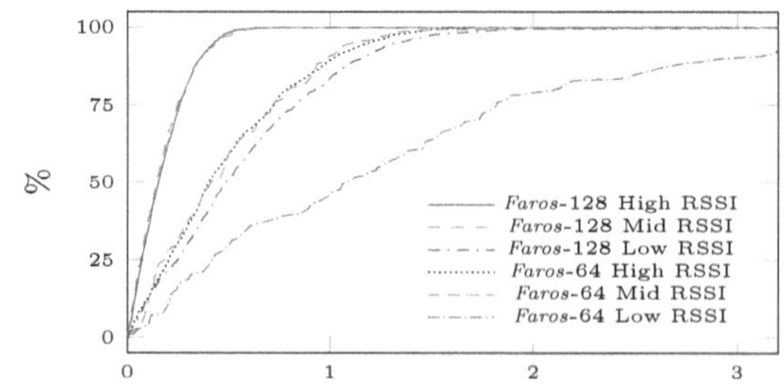

Figure 8: Cumulative distribution functions of CFO estimation error with various sequence lengths and RSSIs. *Faros* provides frequency synchronization within 800 Hz at up to -75 dBm.

mitted and collect measurements, which prevented realtime operation. For this experiment we had the base station continuously beamsweep the beacon at a frame rate of one beam per 10 ms, then had users move away from the base station at a walking pace. In line-of-sight the users performed reliably, and concurrently, at over 250 meters at multiple angles from the base station, and only began to lose reliability the users had to move behind buildings due to space constraints.

7.3 Paging Performance

To demonstrate *Faros*' ability to leverage location information to accelerate paging, we tested a simple scheme which guided the paging sweep based on the intended user's last location. These experiments were performed on the 108-antenna base station configuration in the last 44 locations. In the prior locations we had employed RSSI to guide the sweep, but realized that due to multipath distortion this was not the best detection performance metric, since the time-domain correlation essentially filters individual paths. Instead, we paged mobiles based on each beam's detectability, which is determined by the correlation magnitude to threshold ratio.

We find that *Faros* was able to successfully page 94% of users by the second frame, compared to only 70% without leveraging the user location, as shown in Figure 7. When users are near the base station they receive the majority of the beams in a sweep, and thus optimizing based on their location does not provide much benefit, as shown by the low RSSI plot. However, we still see the paging delay reduced from an average of 4.8 frames to 1.2 frames, an improvement of 4 fold, and a worst-case improvement of 68 frames to 3 frames. This system is very naïve, and is intended to demonstrate *Faros*' ability to leverage spatial information to drastically improve the performance of the control channel without additional overhead.

7.4 CFO Correction Performance

While successful detection of a beacon or paging sequence inherently provides time-frequency synchronization, to more accurately test the accuracy of our realtime CFO correction we setup a more controlled experiment. We shared a reference clock between the base station and user, effectively removing CFO, and placed the user at 0.5 m from the the base station. Then we *induced* a controlled CFO in our beacon sequence by multiplying it with a complex sinusoid ranging from -10 kHz to 10 kHz. To measure the performance vs. coding gain and SNR, we sent beacons of length 64 and 128, as well as used attenuators on the base station to reduce the transmission power from -12 dBm to -42 dBm. These attenuations resulted in the user receiving roughly -60 dBm (*High*), -75 dBm (*Mid*), and -90 dBm (*Low*) RSSIs. We present the cumulative distribution of the error magnitude of our CFO estimates in Figure 8. For clarity, these results are derived from a single estimation, however multiple estimates can be employed to reduce the error by an order of magnitude, as shown in [29].

We find that with mid and high RSSI *Faros* is always able to correct CFO within 0.8 kHz using a 128-length beacon, and within 1.3 kHz using a 64-length beacon. This estimation error is sufficient to not restrict the capacity of an LTE system, [35]. In the low RSSI regime we see that the 64-length beacon begins to perform poorly, and is only able to correct 80% of the beacons to within 2 kHz error. In contrast, the 128-length beacon with low RSSI is performs similarly to the high RSSI 64-length, which indicates extending the beacon length could further reduce CFO estimation error. The amount of induced CFO did not affect accuracy, and thus is not shown separately.

8. DISCUSSION

Broader use of Faros: Our original goal for *Faros* is to provide a very efficient control channel for many-antenna base stations. More fundamentally however, it represents an interesting paradigm that provides fine-grained control over time, code, and spatial resources, enabling previously impossible optimizations both within a single base station, and across the network. *Faros* allows base stations to leverage existing information, such as users' last known location, traffic patterns, and environmental properties to intelligently optimize timing, coding gains, and spatial coverage. Moreover these same properties can be used to further extend the range of the cell in sparse networks, restrict coverage area, carefully tune interference, or dynamically incorporate more antennas to increase the capacity of a given base station.

MAC and standards: So far we have intentionally avoided discussing the MAC, as the conceptual *Faros* design is MAC-agnostic. The primary requirement of *Faros* is a short regularly scheduled downlink phase in order to perform the beamsweep and paging; and both scheduled and CSMA MACs have this. However, we do not intend *Faros* to be a plug-n-play solution for either LTE or 802.11: both standards must be revised to integrate *Faros*. Applying *Faros* to a scheduled MAC is more intuitive, and likely more efficient: the phases depicted in Figure 2 simply have to continuously repeat, though not necessarily in that order. Schemes to adapt *Faros* to CSMA are also fairly straightforward and we provide one example below.

Design sketch of Faros in 802.11: In an 802.11-like CSMA MAC, the beacon would need to be replaced by the beamformed *Faros* beacon immediately followed by the CSI collection phase, including the dedicated random access and association slots. Since 802.11 typically supports only a small number of users with relatively low mobility, each user could have a dedicated CSI slot, which they use at every beacon interval when they are active. The AP can page inactive users during the beacon phase, making them become active, or, if the channel is idle, the AP could page users asynchronously, prompting them to send a pilot immediately. Since these mechanisms allow the AP to maintain accurate CSI for the users, the downlink phase is straightforward: when the channel is idle the AP simply sends a MU-MIMO transmission to the intended users. Uplink MU-MIMO is difficult to efficiently coordinate in CSMA, which, combined with typical asymmetric data requirements, is why current 802.11 standards do not support uplink MU-MIMO. However, one naïve solution would be to allow the users to indicate an uplink request during the CSI collection phase. The AP could then respond with a "clear-to-send" to selected users over the MU-MIMO channel. Of course, to reduce latency users would not have to wait for the beacon to send a single-user uplink packet.

9. RELATED WORK

To the best of our knowledge, *Faros* is the first reported control channel design that effectively addresses the gain gap between the CSI and no-CSI modes for many-antenna MU-MIMO systems. Nevertheless, various previous works are related to *Faros* in terms of both problem and solution. The challenge of control channel design for many-antenna MU-MIMO is well-known. The authors of [5] suggest utilizing space-time block coding for the control channel, but do not address the gain gap or suggest a design. The authors of [36] discuss control channel operation from a purely theoretical and feasibility perspective, which is complementary to our work. However, its assumption that "the only reasonable transmit strategy is to spread the power omnidirectionally" is questionable: *Faros* beamforms the control and provides a working counter-example. It also assumes that the total base-station power can be sent omnidirectionally in the first place, e.g., there is no peak-power per antenna constraint, which is incorrect for real systems, as discussed in §3. Another recent work from Samsung mentions the control channel briefly, but suggests the solution is to carefully create a wide open-loop beam using all of the antenna elements [11]. This approach requires careful calibration of the antenna elements, is environment and deployment specific, and, more importantly, does not completely serve the full potential coverage area of the base station.

802.11ad suffers from a related gain gap and employs a beamsweeping mechanism to initiate communication. Because 802.11ad does not employ MU-MIMO but phased arrays, its gain gap is fundamentally different and scales with less than M. Moreover, the contiguous Sector Level Sweep (SLS) that 802.11ad performs for synchronization and discovery is naïve, unscalable, and highly inefficient. An 802.11ad SLS with 128 elements can take over 1.5 ms [37], whereas a comparable *Faros* beacon would take less than 150 ns. This indicates that 802.11ad and other mm-wave technology could benefit substantially by incorporating design principles from *Faros*, particularly as they adopt MU-MIMO.

Faros' use of Kasami sequences to send a small portion of the control channel information is inspired by 802.11ec [23], which uses time-domain BPSK modulated Kasami sequences to encode control information in the preamble of 802.11 packets. However, *Faros* addresses an entirely different problem, the gain gap in many-antenna MU-MIMO, and as such, it employs different techniques and contributes an entire from-scratch control channel design. Other recent works, such as [38], have also used similar sequences for other purposes including control messages and power reduction.

Like most modern digital wireless systems, *Faros*' synchronization is based on the seminal works in [39, 40]. More recently, some research has focused on over-the-air time-frequency synchronization in distributed antenna systems, including [41, 42]. However, these works deal with the distributed antennas, not between the distributed system and users. As such, they do not address the synchronization range gap that emerges with multiple antennas on a single base station, or the challenge of paging in such a system. Since these distributed systems require backhaul, this synchronization can also similarly be solved with CPRI, [43], or PTP and SyncE, as employed by CERN's WhiteRabbit [44].

Open-loop beamforming techniques have been thoroughly researched. While we do not advocate for a specific technique in this work, our experiments leveraged Hadamard matrices for the beamweights; recent work in [31] covers the performance of Hadamard beamforming more thoroughly. Fourier transform based beamforming is a classic technique, however we note that it requires precise antenna calibration in order to be effective, as discussed in [9, 16–19].

10. CONCLUDING REMARKS

In this work we present the design, implementation, and experimental validation of *Faros*, a fundamental re-design of the wireless control channel in many-antenna MU-MIMO systems. By holistically considering the practical design constraints of many-antenna base stations, we are able to achieve a flexible design which improves the range, or transmission efficiency, by over 40 dB on a 108 antenna base station with negligible overhead. On a more fundamental level, *Faros* provides flexible optimzation of space, time, code, and frequency resources, enabling it to scale from a few antennas up to 1000s of antennas. Not only does *Faros* drastically improve the performance of basic control channel operations by leveraging MU-MIMO as much as possible, but it also utilizes spatial information to make paging operations as quick and efficient as possible. *Faros* unlocks the full potential of real-world many-antenna MU-MIMO, and brings it one significant step closer to real-world adoption.

Acknowledgements

This work was funded in part by NSF grants MRI 1126478, NeTS 1218700, EARS 1444056, and CRI 1405937. Clayton Shepard was supported by an NDSEG fellowship. We thank Hang Yu, Eugenio Magistretti, Ashutosh Sabharwal, and Nathan Zuege for their input, support, and help. We appreciate the support of the Xilinx University Program, and NASA, JSC for the use of their Antenna Test Facility. We thank the reviewers and shepherd for their constructive input; we especially thank Reviewer B for correcting a mistake in our original uplink gain gap analysis.

REFERENCES

[1] Samsung takes first 5G steps. http://www.computerworld.com/article/2497385/data-center/samsung-takes-first-5g-steps-with-advanced-antenna.html.

[2] Steve Perlman and Antonio Forenza. pCell: Wireless reinvented. http://www.rearden.com/artemis/An-Introduction-to-pCell-White-Paper-150224.pdf, 2014.

[3] P. Rudnick. Digital Beamforming in the Frequency Domain. *Acoustical Society of America Journal*, 46:1089, 1969.

[4] F. Rusek, D. Persson, B. K. Lau, E. G. Larsson, T. L. Marzetta, O. Edfors, and F. Tufvesson. Scaling up MIMO: Opportunities and challenges with very large arrays. *IEEE Signal Processing Magazine*, 30(1):40–60, 2013.

[5] E. Larsson, O. Edfors, F. Tufvesson, and T. L. Marzetta. Massive MIMO for next generation wireless systems. *IEEE Communications Magazine*, 52(2):186–195, 2014.

[6] L. Lu, G. Y. Li, A. L. Swindlehurst, A. Ashikhmin, and R. Zhang. An overview of massive MIMO: Benefits and challenges. *IEEE Journal on Selected Topics in Signal Processing*, 8(5):742–758, October 2014.

[7] F. Boccardi, R. W. Heath, A. Lozano, T. L. Marzetta, and P. Popovski. Five disruptive technology directions for 5G. *IEEE Communications Magazine*, 52(2):74–80, February 2014.

[8] J. G. Andrews, S. Buzzi, W. Choi, S. V. Hanly, A. Lozano, A. C. K. Soong, and J. C. Zhang. What will 5G be? *IEEE Journal on Selected Areas in Communications*, 32(6):1065–1082, June 2014.

[9] C. Shepard, H. Yu, N. Anand, E. Li, T. Marzetta, R. Yang, and L. Zhong. Argos: Practical many-antenna base stations. In *Proc. ACM MobiCom*, 2012.

[10] Qing Yang, Xiaoxiao Li, Hongyi Yao, Ji Fang, Kun Tan, Wenjun Hu, Jiansong Zhang, and Yongguang Zhang. BigStation: Enabling scalable real-time signal processing in large MU-MIMO systems. In *Proc. ACM SIGCOMM*, 2013.

[11] Yang Li, Yan Xm, Mian Dong, Gary Xu, Jianzhong Charlie Zhang, Younsun Kim, and Juho Lee. Implementation of full-dimensional MIMO (FD-MIMO) in LTE. In *Proc. IEEE Asilomar Conference*, pages 998–1003, 2013.

[12] Joao Vieira, Steffen Malkowsky, Karl Nieman, Zachary Miers, Nikhil Kundargi, Liang Liu, Ian Wong, Viktor Owall, Ove Edfors, and Fredrik Tufvesson. A flexible 100-antenna testbed for massive MIMO. In *IEEE GLOBECOM Wrkshp. Massive MIMO: from theory to practice*, 2014.

[13] Nutaq. TitanMIMO. http://nutaq.com/en/products/titanmimo.

[14] Xilinx. Xilinx and BEEcube announce highly scalable prototyping platform for 5G massive MIMO antenna systems. http://press.xilinx.com/2015-02-25-Xilinx-and-BEEcube-Announce-Highly-Scalable-Prototyping-Platform-for-5G-Massive-MIMO-Antenna-Systems.

[15] 3GPP. Study on elevation beamforming/full-dimension (FD) MIMO for LTE. http://www.3gpp.org/ftp/tsg_ran/tsg_ran/TSGR_65/Docs/RP-141644.zip.

[16] Per Zetterberg. Experimental investigation of TDD reciprocity-based zero-forcing transmit precoding. *EURASIP Journal on Advances in Signal Processing*, 2011:5, 2011.

[17] Ryan Rogalin, Ozgun Y. Bursalioglu, Haralabos C. Papadopoulos, Giuseppe Caire, Andreas F. Molisch, Antonios Michaloliakos, Horia Vlad Balan, and Konstantinos Psounis. Scalable synchronization and reciprocity calibration for distributed multiuser MIMO. *IEEE Transactions on Wireless Communications*, pages 1815–1831, 2014.

[18] Kentaro Nishimori, Keizo Cho, Yasushi Takatori, and Toshikazu Hori. Automatic calibration method using transmitting signals of an adaptive array for TDD systems. *IEEE Transactions on Vehicular Technology*, 50(6):1636–1640, 2001.

[19] K. Nishimori, T. Hiraguri, T. Ogawa, and H. Yamada. Throughput performance on IEEE 802.11ac based massive MIMO considering calibration errors. In *Intl. Symp. Antennas and Propagation (ISAP)*, Dec 2014.

[20] Eldad Perahia and Robert Stacey. *Next Generation Wireless LANs: 802.11 n and 802.11 ac*. Cambridge university press, 2013.

[21] David Tse and Pramod Viswanath. *Fundamentals of Wireless Communication*. Cambridge University Press, 2005.

[22] Cisco Systems, Inc. *Cisco Wireless Mesh Access Points, Design and Deployment Guide, Release 7.3.* 2012.

[23] Eugenio Magistretti, Omer Gurewitz, and Edward W Knightly. 802.11ec: collision avoidance without control messages. In *Proc. ACM MobiCom*, 2012.

[24] Farooq Khan. *LTE for 4G mobile broadband: air interface technologies and performance*. Cambridge University Press, 2009.

[25] C. Dick and F. Harris. FPGA implementation of an OFDM PHY. In *Proc. IEEE Asilomar Conference*, November 2003.

[26] Rice University Wireless Open Access Research Platform. warp.rice.edu.

[27] Farooq Khan. *LTE for 4G mobile broadband: air interface technologies and performance*. Cambridge University Press, 2009.

[28] Almamy Touray. LTE: Random access. http://www.lmk.lnt.de/fileadmin/Lehre/Seminar09/Ausarbeitungen/Ausarbeitung_Touray.pdf, 2009.

[29] P. Murphy and A. Sabharwal. Design, implementation, and characterization of a cooperative communications system. *IEEE Transactions on Vehicular Technology*, 60(6):2534–2544, July 2011.

[30] Clayton Shepard, Hang Yu, and Lin Zhong. ArgosV2: A flexible many-antenna research platform. In *Extended Demonstration Abstract in Proc. ACM MobiCom*, 2013.

[31] Young Gil Kim and N.C. Beaulieu. On MIMO beamforming systems using quantized feedback. *IEEE Transactions on Communications*, 58(3):820–827, March 2010.

[32] Dilip V Sarwate and Michael B Pursley. Crosscorrelation properties of pseudorandom and related sequences. *Proceedings of the IEEE*, 68(5):593–619, 1980.

[33] Robert L Frank. Polyphase codes with good nonperiodic correlation properties. *IEEE Transactions on Information Theory*, 9(1):43–45, 1963.

[34] David Chu. Polyphase codes with good periodic correlation properties (corresp.). *IEEE Transactions on information theory*, pages 531–532, 1972.

[35] Qi Wang, Christian Mehlfuhrer, and Markus Rupp. Carrier frequency synchronization in the downlink of 3gpp lte. In *IEEE Int. Synp. Personal Indoor and Mobile Radio Communications (PIMRC)*, pages 939–944, 2010.

[36] Marcus Karlsson and Erik G Larsson. On the operation of massive mimo with and without transmitter csi. In *IEEE Int. Wrkshp. Signal Processing Advances in Wireless Communications (SPAWC)*, pages 1–5, 2014.

[37] Thomas Nitsche, Adriana B Flores, Edward W Knightly, and Joerg Widmer. Steering with eyes closed: mm-wave beam steering without in-band measurement. In *Proc. IEEE INFOCOM*, 2015.

[38] Xinyu Zhang and Kang G Shin. E-Mili: energy-minimizing idle listening in wireless networks. *IEEE Transactions on Mobile Computing*, 11(9):1441–1454, 2012.

[39] Timothy M Schmidl and Donald C Cox. Robust frequency and timing synchronization for OFDM. *IEEE Transactions on Communications*, 45(12):1613–1621, 1997.

[40] Fredrik Tufvesson, Ove Edfors, and Mike Faulkner. Time and frequency synchronization for OFDM using PN-sequence preambles. In *Proc. IEEE VTC*, volume 4, pages 2203–2207, 1999.

[41] Hariharan Rahul, Swarun Kumar, and Dina Katabi. JMB: scaling wireless capacity with user demands. In *Proc. ACM SIGCOMM*, 2012.

[42] H.V. Balan, R. Rogalin, A. Michaloliakos, K. Psounis, and G. Caire. AirSync: Enabling distributed multiuser MIMO with full spatial multiplexing. *IEEE/ACM Transactions on Networking*, 21(6):1681–1695, Dec 2013.

[43] Common public radio interface. http://www.cpri.info/spec.html.

[44] Javier Serrano, M Lipinski, T Wlostowski, E Gousiou, Erik van der Bij, M Cattin, and G Daniluk. The white rabbit project. http://www.ohwr.org/projects/white-rabbit, 2013.

QuickSync: Improving Synchronization Efficiency for Mobile Cloud Storage Services

Yong Cui
Department of Computer Science and Technology
Tsinghua University
Beijing, China
cuiyong@tsinghua.edu.cn

Zeqi Lai
Department of Computer Science and Technology
Tsinghua University
Beijing, China
laizq13@mails.tsinghua.edu.cn

Xin Wang
Department of Electrical and Computer Engineering
Stony Brook University
Stony Brook, New York, USA
xwang@ece.sunysb.edu

Ningwei Dai
Department of Computer Science and Technology
Tsinghua University
Beijing, China
lemondnw@gmail.com

Congcong Miao
Department of Computer Science and Technology
Tsinghua University
Beijing, China
mccmiao@163.com

ABSTRACT

Mobile cloud storage services have gained phenomenal success in recent few years. In this paper, we identify, analyze and address the synchronization (*sync*) inefficiency problem of modern mobile cloud storage services. Our measurement results demonstrate that existing commercial sync services fail to make full use of available bandwidth, and generate a large amount of unnecessary sync traffic in certain circumstance even though the incremental sync is implemented. These issues are caused by the inherent limitations of the sync protocol and the distributed architecture. Based on our findings, we propose QuickSync, a system with three novel techniques to improve the sync efficiency for mobile cloud storage services, and build the system on two commercial sync services. Our experimental results using representative workloads show that QuickSync is able to reduce up to 52.9% sync time in our experiment settings.

Categories and Subject Descriptors: C.4 [Performance of Systems]

Keywords: Mobile Cloud Storage, Measurement, Performance.

1. INTRODUCTION

Cloud storage services, such as Dropbox [13], OneDrive [4] (used to be SkyDrive) and GoogleDrive [2], are expanding their mobile market by enabling users to conveniently synchronize files across multiple mobile devices (laptops, tablets or smartphones) and back up data. These services are gaining tremendous popularity in recent years, and have attracted a huge number of users.

As a primary technique for cloud storage services, data synchronization (sync) enables the client to automatically update local file changes to the remote cloud through network communications. *Synchronization efficiency* is determined by the speed of updating the change of client files to the cloud, and considered as one of the most important performance metrics for cloud storage services. Changes on local devices are expected to be quickly synchronized to the cloud and then other devices with low traffic overhead.

However, efficient sync of data is more challenging for mobile cloud storage services as the client often suffers higher delay and loss caused by the mobility and varying channel conditions. The sync process may also be interrupted due to the intermittent connections. Therefore, the sync efficiency of popular services is still far from being satisfactory, and in certain circumstances, the sync time may be much longer than expected. As commercial storage services are mostly closed source with data encrypted, their designs and operational processes remain unclear to the public. It is important but a big challenge to identify the performance bottlenecks and address the issues accordingly.

The aim of this paper is to identify and address the sync inefficiency problem of modern mobile cloud storage systems. Our work consists of three major components: 1) identifying the performance bottlenecks based on the measurement of the sync operations of popular commercial cloud storage services in the wireless environment, 2) providing detailed analysis on the problems identified, and 3) proposing a new mobile cloud storage service framework which integrates a few techniques to enable efficient sync operations in mobile cloud storage services.

We first measure the sync performance of the most popular commercial cloud storage services in wireless networks (§3). Our measurement results show that the sync protocol used by these services is indeed inefficient. Specifically, the sync protocol can not fully utilize the available bandwidth in high RTT environment or when synchronizing multiple small files. Furthermore, although some services, e.g. Drop-

MobiCom'15, September 7–11, 2015, Paris, France.

DOI: http://dx.doi.org/10.1145/2789168.2790094.

Capabilities	Windows				Android			
	Dropbox	Google Drive	OneDrive	Seafile	Dropbox	Google Drive	OneDrive	Seafile
Chunking	4 MB	8 MB	var.	var.	4 MB	260 KB	1 MB	×
Bundling	√	×	×	×	×	×	×	×
Deduplication	√	×	×	√	√	×	×	×
Delta encoding	√	×	×	×	×	×	×	×
Data compression	√	√	×	×	×	×	×	×

Table 1: Capability implementation of four popular cloud storage services. The var. refers to variable chunk size.

box, have implemented incremental sync to reduce traffic size [11, 17], this technique is not valid in all scenarios. We observe that a document editing process may result in sync traffic 10 times that of the modification.

We further conduct in-depth analysis of the trace data and also apply decryption to find the root cause of the inefficiency identified in the sync protocol (§4). Our studies indicate that the inherent limitations of the sync protocol and the distributed architecture are two major factors that cause the inefficiency. Specifically, effective deduplication to reduce redundant data transmissions does not always contribute to the sync efficiency. The distributed nature of storage services poses a challenge to the practical implementation of the delta encoding algorithm, and the failure in the incremental sync may lead to a large traffic overhead. The iterative sync scheme suffers from low throughput when there is a need to synchronize a set of files and when the network is slow.

Based on our observation and analysis, we propose QuickSync, a system with three novel techniques to improve the sync efficiency for mobile cloud storage services (§5). To reduce the sync time, we introduce *Network-aware Chunker* to adaptively select the proper deduplication strategy based on real-time network conditions. To reduce sync traffic overhead, we propose *Redundancy Eliminator* to correctly perform delta encoding between two similar chunks located in the original and modified files at any time during the sync process. We also design *Batched Syncer* to improve the network utilization of sync protocol and reduce the overhead when resuming the sync from an interruption.

We build our QuickSync system on Dropbox, currently the most popular cloud storage services, and Seafile [5], an popular open source personal cloud system (§6). Collectively, these techniques achieve significant improvement in the sync latency for cloud storage services. Evaluation results (§7) show that the QuickSync system is able to significantly improve sync efficiency, reducing up to 51.8% sync time in representative sync scenarios with our experiment settings. To the best of our knowledge, we are the first to study the sync efficiency problem for mobile cloud storage services.

2. BACKGROUND

Before analyzing the sync inefficiency issues, we first give a brief overview of the typical architecture of cloud storage services and the key capabilities that are often implemented for speeding up data transmissions.

Architecture: A typical architecture of cloud storage services includes three major components [10]: the *client*, the *control server* and the *data storage server*. The file system on the server side has an abstraction different from that of the client. Metadata (including the hashes, modified time etc.) and contents (often split into chunks) of user files are separated and stored in the control and data storage servers respectively. The key operation of the cloud storage services is *data sync*, which automatically maps the changes in users' local file system to the cloud via a series of network communications. During the sync process, metadata are exchanged with the control server through the *metadata information flow*, while the contents are transferred via the *data storage flow*. In a practical implementation, the control server and the data storage server may be deployed in different locations. For example, Dropbox builds its data storage server on Amazon EC2 and S3. Another important flow, namely *notification flow*, pushes notifications to the client once changes from other devices are updated to the cloud.

Key capabilities: Cloud storage services can be equipped with several capabilities to optimize the storage usage and speed up data transmissions: *1) chunking* (i.e., splitting a content into a certain size data unit), *2) bundling* (i.e., the transmission of multiple small chunks as a single chunk), *3) deduplication* (i.e., avoiding the retransmission of content already available in the cloud), *4) delta-encoding* (i.e., only transmitting the modified portion of a file) and *5) compression*. Previous work [11] shows how the capabilities have been implemented on the desktop client. We further follow the methods in [11] to analyze the capabilities that have been implemented on the mobile client. Table 1 summarizes the capabilities of each service on multiple platforms, with the test client being the newest released version before March 1, 2015. In the following sections, we will show that these capabilities also make a strong side impact on the sync efficiency.

3. SYNCHRONIZATION INEFFICIENCY

As discussed previously, sync efficiency indicates how fast client can update changes to the cloud. In this section, we conduct a series of experiments to investigate the sync inefficiency issue existing in four most popular commercial cloud storage service systems in wireless/mobile environments. We will further analyze the observations and explain the root cause in Section 4.

3.1 Low DER Not Equal to Efficiency

To evaluate the effectiveness of deduplication in reducing the original transmission data size, the metric *Deduplication Efficiency Ratio* (DER) is defined as the ratio of the *deduplicated file size* to the *original file size*. Intuitively, lower DER means more redundancy can be identified and the total sync time can be reduced. However, our experiment indicates that lower DER *may not* alway make sync efficient.

As only Dropbox and Seafile incorporate the deduplication function, to study the relationship between the sync time and DER, we use `Wireshark` to measure the packet level trace of the two services in a controlled WiFi environment. We use `tc` to tune the RTT for each service according to the typical RTT values in wireless/cellular networks [8]. We only perform measurement on the Windows platform

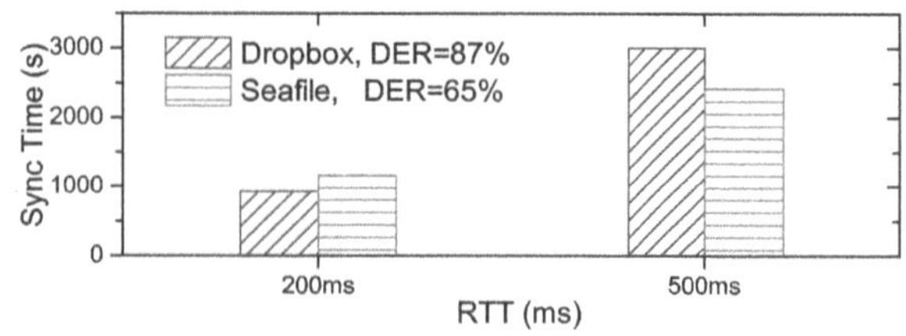

Figure 1: Lower DER does not always make efficient.

because most services did not implement the deduplication on the Android platform. We collect about 500MB user data from a Dropbox user and upload these fresh data via the tested services. From the trace captured we can get the sync time and calculate the DER as a ratio of the transmission traffic size and the original traffic size.

Figure 1 shows that the DER for Dropbox and Seafile are 87% and 65% respectively under each RTT setting. Intuitively, a higher DER would take more time for sync. However, when the RTT is 200ms, it costs more time for Seafile to complete the sync as compared to Dropbox.

3.2 Failure of Incremental Sync

To reduce the network traffic for synchronizing changes, some services such as Dropbox leverage the delta encoding algorithm (e.g. rsync [24]) to achieve *incremental sync* instead of *full-file sync*. However, next we will show that the incremental sync *is not* always available, and the client software may synchronize much more data than expected. We use the metric *Traffic Utilization Overhead (TUO)* [17], defined as the ratio of *generated traffic size* to *expected traffic size*, to evaluate how much additional traffic is incurred. We conduct two sets of experiments to find out when the claimed incremental sync mechanism fails.

In experiment 1, we perform three types of basic operation in typical real-world usage patterns: *flip bits*, *insert* and *delete* over continuous w bytes at the head, end or random position of the test file, and see how much sync traffic will be generated when the given operation is performed. Thereby, we have $TUO = \frac{SyncTrafficSize}{w}$. Since 10KB is the recommended default window size in the original delta encoding algorithm [24], we vary w from 10KB to 5MB to ensure that the modification size is larger than the minimum delta that can be detected. To avoid the possible interaction between two consecutive operations, the next operation is performed after the previous one is completed. Operation in each case is performed 10 times to get the average result. Because Seafile, GoogleDrive and OneDrive have not implemented the incremental sync, they upload the whole file upon the modification, and are expected to have a large amount of traffic even for a slight modification. Thus in this section our studies focus on Dropbox.

Figure 2 displays our results. Interestingly, the three types of operation result in totally different traffic size for Dropbox. For the flip operation, in most cases the TUO is close to 1. Even when the modification window is 10KB, the TUO is less than 1.75, indicating that incremental sync works well for flip operations in any position. The sync traffic of insert operation is closely related to the position of the modification. The TUO is close to 1 when inserting is performed at the end of the file, but the generated traffic is much higher than expected when an insertion is made at the head or a random position. Specifically, inserting 3MB data at the

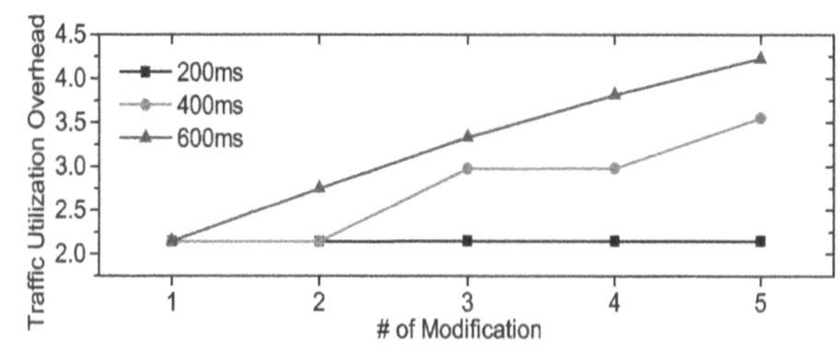

Figure 3: TUO of synchronizing modification in the middle of sync process.

head or random position of a 40MB file results in nearly 40MB sync traffic, which is close to the full file sync mechanism. The TUO results for the delete operation are similar to the insert operation. Differently, deleting at the end of the file generates small sync traffic (TUO is close to zero). However deleting at the head or random position leads to larger sync traffic, especially for a large file, e.g. 40MB (TUO is larger than 10). Another interesting finding is that for both insert and delete operations in Dropbox, the TUO drops to a very low value when the modification window w is 4MB, where the TUO is close to 1 for the insert operation and close to 0 for the delete operation.

In experiment 1 all operations are performed on synchronized files (both the metadata and contents are completely updated to the cloud). In experiment 2, we investigate the sync traffic of performing modification on being synchronized files, i.e., the files in the middle of the transmissions to the cloud. We first create a 4MB fresh file in the sync folder, and perform the same flip operation as that in experiment 1 at a random position with the modification window $w = 512KB$ in every 20s. Note that the TUO of such an operation is close to 1 in the experiment 1, and in the experiment 2, the flip operation is performed *immediately* after file is created while the sync process has not completed. Such a behavior is common for an application such as MS-word or VMware which creates fresh temp files and periodically modify them at runtime. We vary the number of modifications to measure the traffic size. We also use `tc` to involve additional RTT to see the traffic under different network conditions.

Figure 3 shows the sync traffic for periodic flip on 4MB file with various RTT. Interestingly, for all cases the TUO is larger than 2, indicating that at least 8MB data are synchronized. Moreover, we observe that the TUO is affected by the RTT. When the RTT is 600ms, surprisingly the TUO raises with the increase of the modification times. The sync traffic researches up to 28MB, 448% of the new content size when the modifications are performed five times.

In summary, our measurement results show that the incremental sync does not work well in all cases. Specifically, for insert and delete operations at certain positions, the generated traffic size is much larger than the expected size. Moreover, the incremental sync mechanism may fail on the being synchronized files, causing undesired traffic overhead.

3.3 Bandwidth Inefficiency

Sync throughput is another critical metric that reflects the sync efficiency. The sync protocol relies on TCP and its performance is affected by network factors such as RTT or packet loss. Because of different system implementations, it is unreasonable to evaluate how the underlying bandwidth of

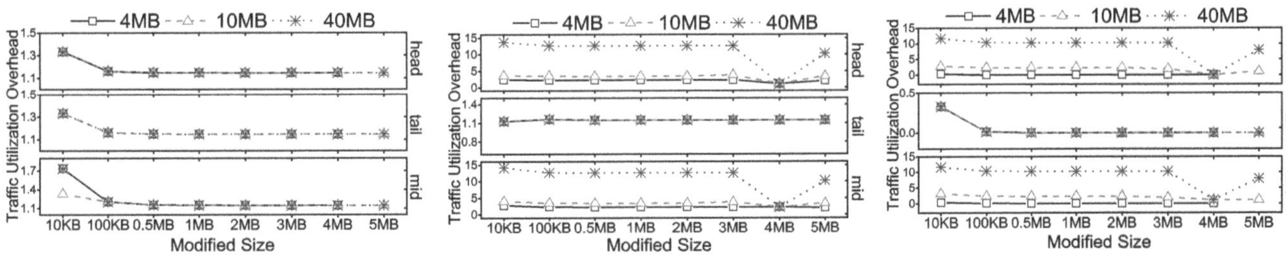

(a) flip (b) insert (c) delete

Figure 2: Traffic utilization overhead of Dropbox generated by a set of modifications.

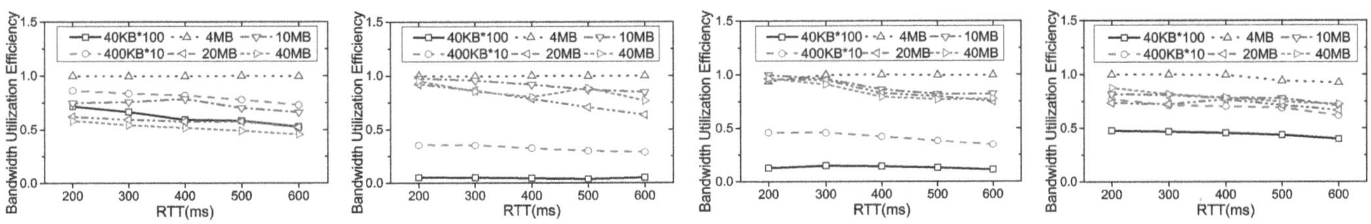

(a) Dropbox (b) GoogleDrive (c) OneDrive (d) Seafile

Figure 4: Bandwidth utilization efficiency of 4 cloud storage services in various network conditions

a storage service is used by directly measuring the throughput or latency [11]. To characterize the network usage of sync protocol, we introduce a novel metric, *Bandwidth Utilization Efficiency (BUE)* to characterize the network usage of sync protocol. We define BUE as the ratio of the *practical measured throughput* to the *theoretical TCP bandwidth*. The latter indicates the available bandwidth in steady state and can be estimated by $\frac{Segment\_size*cwnd}{RTT}$, where *cwnd* is the observed average congestion window size during the transmission. Compared with the throughput, BUE better reveals the essential bandwidth utilization capability of cloud storage services.

To investigate how the sync protocol utilizes the underlying network bandwidth, we conduct experiments over Dropbox, GoogleDrive, OneDrive and Seafile with their Windows and Android clients running in Wi-Fi and cellular networks (UMTS) respectively. We create a set of highly compressed files (to exclude the effect of compression) with various total sizes in the sync folder and measure the packet-level trace using `Wireshark` and `tcpdump`. We compute the *theoretical TCP bandwidth* based on real-time observed RTT and *cwnd* to get BUE. In Wi-Fi networks, we use `tc` to tune the RTT, simulating various network conditions. In cellular networks we change the position to tune the RTT. Each test is performed 10 times to calculate the average result.

The BUE is measured for all services in WiFi networks with different RTT, as shown in Figure 4. For each service, the BUE of synchronizing 4MB file is close to 1. The traffic size of syncing 40KB*100 files is close to that of 4MB file, but we observe that the BUE slumps significantly when synchronizing multiple files. This degradation is more serious for GoogleDrive and OneDrive, with their BUE dropping under 20% when syncing 40KB*100 files. For all services, BUE decreases for large files such as 20MB or 40MB and when RTT increases. The degradation of BUE indicates that the sync protocol cannot efficiently utilize the underlying available bandwidth. The decrease of BUE for large RTT indicates that the sync protocol can not well adapt to a slow network. Results in cellular networks are similar and be omitted due to the page limit.

4. ROOT CAUSE ANALYSIS

Our observations have demonstrated that cloud storage services suffer sync inefficiency problems. In this section, we analyze the sync protocol and explain the root cause for previous inefficiency observations.

4.1 Pinning Down the Sync Protocol

To understand the reasons of sync inefficiency, it is difficult to directly analyze the sync protocol of commercial services such as Dropbox, as they are close source and most of the network traffic is encrypted. In our work, we exploit both measurement and decryption to understand the sync protocol. Specifically, we first analyze the network traces of all services studied in Section 3 to show the general sync process, and then we hijack the encrypted traffic of Dropbox so that we can understand the details of the sync protocol.

Commonality analysis: Although all tested services encrypt their sync traffic and we are unable to directly obtain the protocol details, we still can get some high-level knowledge of the protocol by analyzing the packet-level network traces. Our analyses on the traces in Section 3 indicate that the sync processes of all services in various platforms commonly have three key stages: *1) sync preparation stage*, the client first exchanges data with the control server; *2) data sync stage*, the client sends data to, or retrieves data from the data storage server. In case that the chunking scheme is implemented, data chunks are sequentially stored or retrieved with a "pause" in between, and the next chunk will not be transferred until the previous one is acknowledged by the receiver; *3) sync finish stage*, the client communicates with the control server again to conclude its sync process.

In-depth analysis: The Dropbox client is written in Python. To decrypt the traffic and obtain the details of the sync protocol, we leverage the approach in [15] to hijack the SSL socket by DynamoRIO [1]. Although we only decrypt the Dropbox protocol, combining the commonality analysis we believe the other three services may follow a sync protocol similar to that of Dropbox.

Figure 5 shows a typical Dropbox sync workflow when uploading a new file. In the *sync preparation stage*, the file is first split and indexed locally, and the *block list* which includes all identifiers of chunks is sent to the control server in the *commit_batch*. Chunks existing in the cloud can be identified through hash-based checking and only new chunks will be uploaded. Next in the *data-synchronization stage*, the client communicates with the storage server directly. The client synchronizes data iteratively, and in each round of iteration several chunks will be sent. At the end of one round of iteration, the client updates the metadata through the *list* message to inform the server a batch of chunks have been successfully synchronized, and the server sends an *OK* message in response. Finally in the *sync-finish stage*, the client communicates with the control server again to ensure that all chunks are updated by the *commit_batch*, and refresh the metadata.

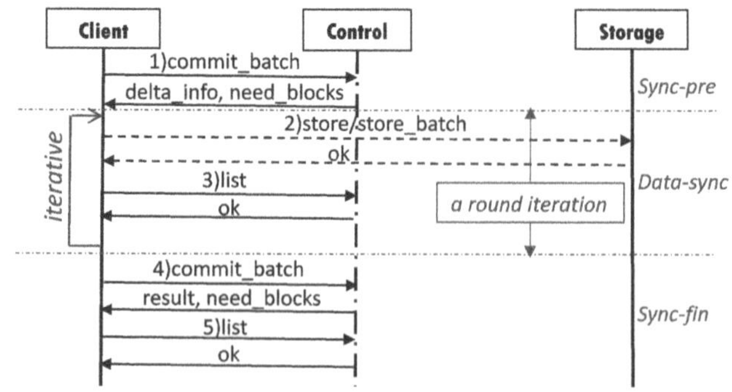

Figure 5: A typical sync process of Dropbox

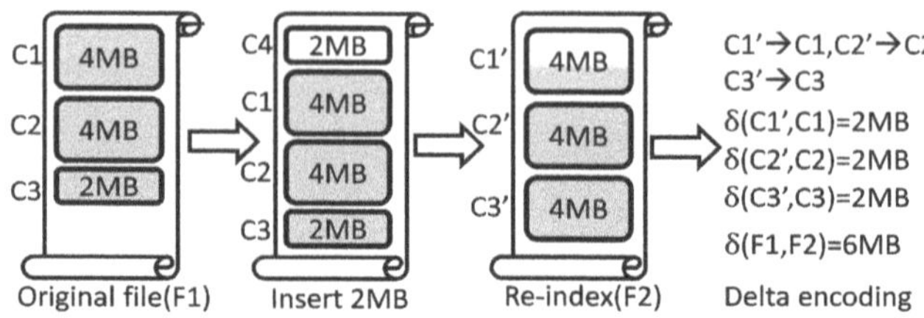

Figure 6: An example to explain why the incremental sync fails in Dropbox.

4.2 Why Less Data Cost More Time

Generally, to identify the redundancy in the sync process, the client splits data into chunks and calculates their hashes to find the redundancy. However, chunking with a large number of hashing operations is computationally extensive, and the time cost and effectiveness of deduplication are strongly impacted by the chunking method. Fixed-size chunking used by Dropbox is simple and fast, but is less effective in deduplication. Content defined chunking [20] used by Seafile is more complex and computation extensive, but can identify a larger amount of redundancy. In our experiment in Section 3.1, when RTT is 200ms, Seafile uses the content defined chunking to achieve 65% DER. Although the available bandwidth is sufficient, the complex chunking method takes too much time hence its total sync time is larger than Dropbox. However, when the RTT is 500ms and the bandwidth is limited, lower DER leads to lower sync time by significantly reducing the transmission time. The key insight from this observation is that it is helpful to dynamically select the appropriate chunking method according to the channel condition.

4.3 Why the Traffic Overhead Increases

Although delta encoding is a mature and effective method, it is not implemented in all cloud storage services. One possible reason is that most delta encoding algorithms work at the granularity of file, while to save the storage space thus reducing the cost, files are often split into chunks to manage for cloud storage services. Naively piecing together all chunks to reconstruct the whole file to achieve incremental sync would waste massive intra-cluster bandwidth.

Instead, Dropbox implements delta encoding at the chunk granularity. From the decrypted traffic we find that each chunk has a "parent" attribute to map it to another similar chunks, and delta encoding is adopted between the two chunks. Figure 6 shows how Dropbox performs delta encoding at the granularity of chunk when inserting 2MB data at the head of a 10MB file. When the file is modified, the client follows the fixed-size chunking method to split and re-index the file. After re-indexing, the chunks without hash change are not processed further, so the TUO results of 4MB window size in Figure 2 are all close to 1. Otherwise, a map is built based on the relative locations of the original and modified versions, and delta encoding is executed between mapped chunk. Thus the delta of C1' and C1 is 2MB and the total delta is 6MB, 3 times of the insertion size. Therefore, now we can clearly understand our observations in Figure 2. Inserting 3MB data at the head of 40MB file causes nearly 40MB total sync traffic, because after the re-indexing, all chunks are mapped to different parents. In this case, the incremental sync fails to only update the changed content.

As discussed in Section 4.1, the metadata is updated after contents are successfully uploaded. Therefore, for a chunk in the middle of sync, if it is modified before sync finishes, the chunk can not be used for delta encoding. In the experiment 2 in Section 3.2, when the modification happens at the beginning time of the sync process, the client has to upload both the original and modified versions and thus the TUO is at least 2. Moreover, in the case that RTT=600ms, every modification is performed during the uploading process, and each modified version has to be uploaded entirely.

4.4 Why the Bandwidth Utilization Decreases

Iteration is a key characteristic of the data sync, but may significantly reduce the bandwidth utilization. There are several reasons. First, when synchronizing a lot of chunks smaller than the maximum chunk size, as the client has to wait for an acknowledgement from the server before transferring the next chunk, the sequential acknowledgement limits the bandwidth usage, especially when sending a number of small files and RTT is high.

Second, although Dropbox incorporates bundling to bundle small chunks into a bigger one (up to 4MB) to mitigate the problem, we can still see the throughput slumps between two iterations when synchronizing large files (e.g. 40MB). Different from other storage services, when transferring multiple big chunks at 4MB, Dropbox opens up to 4 concurrent TCP connections during the sync process. At the beginning of a new iteration, the client assigns new chunks for different connections. If one connection has transferred the assigned chunk and received the acknowledgement, it will not immediately start to send the next chunk. Only after the other three connections have finished transmissions, the new chunks are assigned. During the iterations, because of the idle waiting of several connections the throughput reduces significantly.

Moreover, we observe that for GoogleDrive, it opens several new TCP connections, each taking one iteration to transfer one chunk. For instance, it totally creates 100 storage flows in 100 iterations to synchronize 100 small files. Such a mechanism would incur additional overhead for opening a new SSL connection and extend the slow start period, leading to significant throughput degradation thus reduced BUE.

5. SYSTEM DESIGN

Improving the sync efficiency in wireless networks is important for mobile cloud storage services. In light of various issues that result in sync inefficiency, we propose QuickSync, a novel system which concurrently exploits a set of techniques over current mobile cloud storage services to improve the sync efficiency.

5.1 System Overview

To efficiently complete a sync process, our QuickSync system introduces three key components: the Network-aware Chunker (§5.2), the Redundancy Eliminator (§5.3), and the Batched Syncer (§5.4). The basic functions of the three components can be summarized as follows: *1) identifying redundant data through a network-aware deduplication technique; 2) reducing the sync traffic by wisely executing delta encoding between two "similar" chunks;* and *3) adopting a delayed-batched acknowledgement to improve the bandwidth utilization.*

Figure 7 shows the basic architecture of QuickSync. The sync process begins upon detecting a change in the sync folder (e.g. add or modify a file). First, the Network-aware Chunker splits an input file through content defined chunking with the chunk size determined based on the network condition. Metadata and contents are then delivered to the Redundancy Eliminator, where redundant chunks are removed and delta encoding is executed between similar chunks to reduce the sync traffic for modification operations. A database is applied to store metadata of local files. Finally the Batched Syncer leverages a delay-batched acknowledgement mechanism to synchronize all data chunks continuously to the cloud and conclude the sync process. Like other cloud storage systems, QuickSync separates the control server for metadata management from the storage server for data storage. Metadata and file contents are transferred by meta flow and content flow respectively. Next we describe the detailed design for each component.

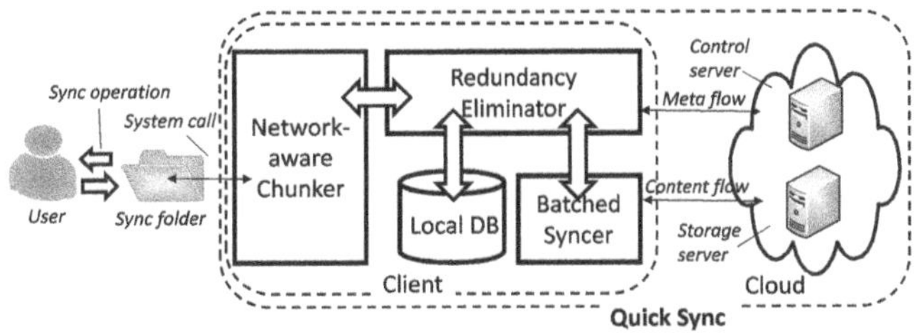

Figure 7: System overview.

5.2 Network-aware Chunker

To improve the sync efficiency, our first step is to identify the redundant data before the sync process. Although deduplication is often applied to reduce the data redundancy for storage in general cloud systems, extending existing deduplication techniques for personal cloud storage services faces two new challenges. First, previous deduplication techniques mostly focus on saving the storage space [28], improving the efficiency for large-scale remote backup [22, 14], or only optimizing the downlink object delivery [6]. These strategies are difficult to apply for personal cloud storage because they often involve huge overhead and require an important property named "stream-informed" [28] not included for personal scenario. Second, a deduplication scheme with aggressive chunking will incur high computational cost for mobile devices, which may degrade the performance under good network conditions (Section 3.1).

Generally, the chunking granularity is closely related to the computation overhead and the effectiveness of deduplication. A more aggressive chunking scheme with very small chunk size may allow for more effective deduplication, but would involve higher total computation overhead to identify the duplicated data over a large number of chunks, and vice versa. All previous deduplication systems use a static chunking strategy with a fixed average chunk size. Deriving from the basic idea of Dynamic Adaptive Streaming over HTTP (DASH), the basic procedure of our approach is to adaptively select an appropriate deduplication scheme according to the real-time network conditions to reduce the total sync time. Intuitively, in slow networks, since the bandwidth is limited, we select aggressive chunking strategy to identify more redundancy and reduce the transmission time. When the bandwidth is sufficient, we prefer larger chunks because of its lower computation overhead. Specifically, our approach consists of two key strategies as we will introduce below.

5.2.1 Network-aware Chunk Size Selection

The chunking method in our system is based on the content defined chunking (CDC), which introduces *cut-points* to split an input file into chunks based on contents. When the number of operations for insertion, deletion or recording is small, the set of representative hashes for chunks remain mostly the same, this method helps to improve the deduplication efficiency. Moreover, as the average chunk size can be changed to adapt the computational overhead and thus the effectiveness of deduplication, we can select an appropriate chunk size to trade off between computational time and deduplication effectiveness to reduce the total sync time.

To achieve multi-level chunking based on different sizes, both the client and server of QuickSync store *a list of chunking strategies*, along with their *deduplication capacity, average chunk size* and *computation cost.* Selecting strategy i means to split the input data into chunks with average size S_i by content defined chunking. At the beginning of a sync process, a client first collects current TCP-level information and follow the method in [21] to estimate the available bandwidth by $Available\_BW = \frac{Segment\_size*cwnd}{RTT}$, where both the `RTT` and `cwnd` can be observed in the persistent notifi-

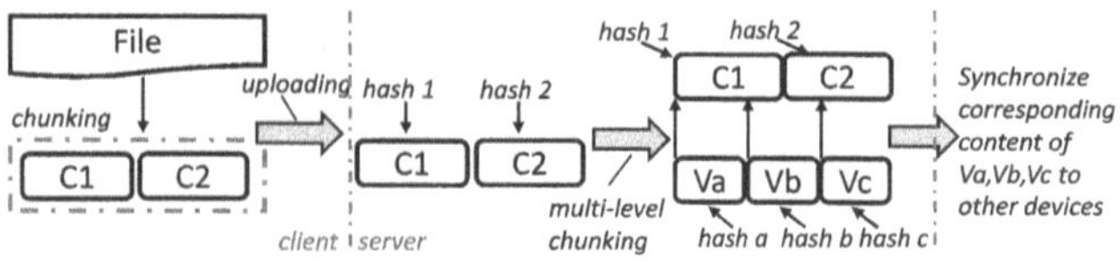

Figure 8: Virtual Chunks in the server.

cation flow. Assume the data size for sync is C bytes, the client will select the chunking strategy i based on the following estimation to minimize the total sync latency:

$$i = \arg\min_{i \in S}\{T_i * C + \frac{(1-\beta_i) * C + Meta\_Size_i}{Available\_BW}\} \quad (1)$$

where T_i (seconds per byte) and β_i are the corresponding computation time and deduplication ratio of the strategy i respectively. $Meta\_Size_i$ is the size of the metadata of the strategy with chunk size S_i. In runtime, a client selects the chunking strategy that provides the minimum sync latency corresponding to its network condition.

5.2.2 *Virtual Chunks in the Server*

When synchronizing data from the server to devices, the server needs to fetch the chunk content in the storage according to the metadata given by the client. In order to respond to different chunking requirements of the client, the server needs to store the hashes under different strategies. However, it would cost a large amount of storage space if simply executing all chunking strategies in the list and storing all their corresponding metadata and chunks.

To support multi-granularity deduplication, we propose the concept of *Virtual Chunk* that only stores the offset and length which can be used to generate the pointers to the content instead of multiple copies of contents. In an uploading process, after receiving all chunks of a file, the server forms the file according to its metadata. It then conducts all other strategies in the *chunking strategy list* to resplit the file and generate metadata under various strategies. Instead of storing several copies of the same file processed by multiple strategies, the server keeps the Virtual Chunk points to the corresponding chunk in the original file. When the server needs to synchronize data to a client, the server first finds the corresponding chunk through the given metadata. If the chunk found is a virtual one, the server fetches the corresponding content based on the offset and length of the chunk recorded. For all Virtual Chunks generated by a chunking strategy, we add a *vblock list*, which includes all hashes of these Virtual Chunks to the metadata. As a result, the offset of a chunk can be implicitly stored as the sum of all previous chunk sizes in the *vblock list.* Therefore, each Virtual Chunk size only needs to store the length of its corresponding recorded chunk.

Figure 8 shows an example. Like all other commercial systems, QuickSync does not transfer contents between two clients directly. A file is split into two chunks and uploaded to the server. Then the server takes other strategies to get three Virtual Chunks that point to the real contents. When the server needs to update or send the Virtual Chunks, it fetches the content from the storage based on its pointer.

5.3 Redundancy Eliminator

The Redundancy Eliminator is designed to eliminate the redundant sync traffic. Ideally, only the modified parts of the file need to be synchronized to the server through a technique such as delta encoding. However the effective function of delta encoding has two requirements. First, the map of the new to the old version must be identified as the input for encoding. Second, the two versions for encoding must be "similar", otherwise executing the delta encoding will not provide any benefit but only involves additional computation overhead. As discussed in the previous section, in the current cloud storage systems, because all files are stored as independent chunks distributedly, the delta encoding algorithm is executed between pairs of chunks in the modified and the original file. Therefore, with the fixed-size chunking, modification on file may lead to a map between two "un-similar" chunks. Moreover, a chunk in the middle of the uploading process cannot be compared to enable delta encoding. We employ two techniques to alleviate the above problems.

5.3.1 *Sketch-based Mapping*

In QuickSync, once changes are detected and the modified files are split into chunks, two similar chunks in the original and the modified files are mapped in two steps. We first compare the hashes of the new chunks with those of the original file to identify the unchanged chunks that do not need to be updated. Further, for the chunks without a hash match in the original version, we leverage a technique named *sketch* to estimate the similarity of chunks in the two versions. We only build a map between two similar chunks in the new and old versions to perform delta-encoding. The chunks without either a hash or sketch match are treated as "different" chunks and will be transferred directly. We get the sketch by identifying "features" [22] of a chunk that would not likely change when there are small data variations. As one typical approach, a rolling hash function can be applied over all overlapping small data regions, and we choose the maximal hash value seen as one feature. We generate multiple features of the same chunk using different hash functions. Chunks that have one or more features in common are likely to be very similar, but small changes to the data are unlikely to perturb the maximal values. To better represent a chunk, we get the sketch of the chunk by calculating the XOR of four different features.

5.3.2 *Buffering Uncompleted Chunks*

To take advantage of the chunks in the air for delta encoding, we introduce two in-memory queues to buffer the uncomplete chunks that have been processed by the Network-aware Chunker. The *uploading queue* temporarily stores all chunks waiting to be uploaded via network communication, with each chunk recorded with three parts: the data content, the hash value and the sketch of it. New chunks from the Chunker are pushed into this queue and popped up if they have been completely uploaded. We can thus build a map between a new chunk and the one found in the uploading queue.

To handle modification operations, we create an *updating queue* to buffer a chunk that finds a sketch match with another chunk either in the server or the local uploading queue. Each chunk in the updating queue is tagged with the hash of its matched chunk. Chunks are inserted into updating queue if a sketch match is found and popped up when delta encoding for two similar chunks is completed.

Upon file modifications and the triggering of sync, files are first split into chunks by the Network-aware Chunker. Then the Redundancy Eliminator executes the two-step mapping process. The chunk without a sketch or hash match is treated as a new chunk and inserted into the uploading queue directly, while the ones found with sketch match are bundled by the Eliminator along with their hashes and put in the updating queue. An independent updating process is designed to continuously fetch chunk from the updating queue, and then calculate the delta between the mapped chunks. The delta will be inserted into the uploading queue. All data in the uploading queue are synchronized to the server by the Batched Syncer.

5.4 Batched Syncer

As discussed in the previous section, the per-chunk sequential acknowledgement from the application layer and the TCP slow start are the main factors that decrease the bandwidth utilization, especially for the sync of multiple chunks. To improve the sync efficiency, we design the Batched Syncer with two key techniques to improve the bandwidth utilization.

5.4.1 Batched Transmission

Cloud storage services leverage the app-layer acknowledgement to maintain the chunk state. As a benefit, upon a connection interruption, a client only needs to upload the un-acknowledged chunks to resume the sync. Dropbox simply bundles small chunks into a large chunk to reduce the acknowledgement overhead. Although this helps improve the sync throughput, when there is a broken connection, the Dropbox client has to retransmit all small chunks if the bundled one is not acknowledged.

Our first basic technique is to defer the app-layer acknowledgement to the end of the sync process, and actively check the un-acknowledged chunks upon the connection interruption. This method on the one hand reduces the overhead due to multiple acknowledgements for different chunks and also avoids the idle waiting for the acknowledgement between two chunk transmissions, and on the other hand avoids the need of retransmitting many chunks upon a connection interruption. The check will be triggered under two conditions. First, the check will be initiated when the client captures a network exception, usually caused by the process shut down or the connection loss at the local side. Second, the failure of the sync process can be also caused by interruption in the network that cannot be easily detected by the local devices. Therefore we design a timer for the sync process. If the sync process gets stuck for a long time and timeout, the Syncer will actively terminate the current connection and check the control server for the missing chunks.

During the transmission, the Syncer continuously sends chunks in the uploading queue of the Redundancy Eliminator. If the connection is interrupted by network exceptions or the sync gets stuck for a period of time, the client connects to the control server to query the un-acknowledged chunks, and then uploads them after the content flow is reestablished.

5.4.2 Reusing Existing Network Connections

The second technique is to reuse the existing network connections rather than making new ones in storing files. While it may be easy and natural to make a new network connection for each chunk, the handshake overhead for establishing a new connection is not negligible, and creating many new connections also extends the period in the slow start state especially for small chunks. The Batched Syncer reuses the storage connection to transfer multiple chunks, avoiding the overhead of duplicate TCP/SSL handshakes. Moreover, cloud storage services maintain a persistent notification flow for capturing changes elsewhere. Hence we reuse the notification flow for both requesting notification and sending file data to reduce the handshake overhead and the impact of slow start. Specifically, both the request and data are transferred over HTTP(S), so we use the `Content-Type` field in the HTTP header to distinguish them in the same TCP connection.

6. SYSTEM IMPLEMENTATION

To evaluate the performance of our proposed schemes, we build the QuickSync system over both Dropbox and Seafile platforms.

6.1 Implementation over Dropbox

Since both the client and server of Dropbox are totally close source, we are unable to directly implement our techniques with the released Dropbox software. Although Dropbox provides APIs to allow user program to synchronize data with the Dropbox server, different from the client software, the APIs are RESTful and operate at the full file level. We are unable to get the hash value, or directly implement delta-encoding algorithm via the APIs.

To address this problem, we leverage a proxy in Amazon EC2 which is close to the Dropbox server to emulate the control server behavior. The proxy is designed to generate the Virtual Chunks, maintain the map of file to the chunk list and hash the chunk to sketch. During a sync process, user data are first uploaded to the proxy, and then the proxy updates the metadata in the database and stores the data to the Dropbox server via the APIs. Since the data storage server of Dropbox is built on Amazon EC2, the throughput between our proxy and Dropbox is sufficient and not the bottleneck.

To make our Network-aware Chunker efficient and adjustable, we use the SAMPLEBYTE [6] as our basic chunking method. Like other content defined chunking methods, the sample period p set in SAMPLEBYTE also determines both the computation overhead and deduplication ratio. We leverage the adjustable property of p to generate a suite of chunking strategies with various deduplication capacity and computation overhead, including the chunk-based deduplication with the average chunk size set to 4MB, 1MB, 512KB and 128KB. Each Virtual Chunk contains a 2-byte field for chunk length.

We use `librsync` [3] to implement delta encoding. We use a tar-like method to bundle all data chunks in sync process, and a client communicates with our proxy at the beginning of a sync process to notify the offset and length of each chunk in the sync flow. The timer of our Syncer is set to 60s. We write the QuickSync client and proxy in around 2000 lines of Java codes. To achieve efficiency, we design two processes to handle chunking and transmission tasks respectively in the client. The client is implemented in Galaxy Nexus with a 1.2GHz Dual Core CPU, 1GB memory and the proxy is built on an Amazon EC2 server with a 2.8GHz Quad Core CPU and 4GB memory.

6.2 Implementation over Seafile

Although we introduce a proxy between the client and the Dropbox server, due to the lack of full access of data on the server, this implementation suffers from the performance penalty. For instance, to perform delta encoding, the proxy should first fetch the entire chunk from the Dropbox server, update its content and finally store it back to Dropbox. Even though the bandwidth between the proxy and the Dropbox server is sufficient, such an implementation would inevitably involve additional latency during the sync process.

In order to show the gain in the sync efficiency when our system is fully implemented and can directly operate over the data, we further implement QuickSync with Seafile, an open source cloud storage project. The implementation is similar to that with use of Dropbox but without the need of a proxy. We only need to directly modify both the client and server side source codes to implement our system. Because only the client software on Linux is open source, we implement the modified client in a laptop with a 2.6GHz Intel Quad Core CPU and 4GB memory. and build the server on a machine with a 3.3GHz Intel Octal Core CPU, 16GB memory. We believe our QuickSync can also be implemented in the similar way on other mobile platforms.

7. PERFORMANCE EVALUATION

To evaluate the performance of our schemes, we first investigate the throughput improvement of using the Network-aware Chunker, and then show that the Redundancy Eliminator is able to effectively reduce the sync traffic. We further evaluate the capability of the Batched Syncer in improving the bandwidth utilization efficiency. Finally, we study the overall improvement of the sync efficiency using real-world workloads. In each case, we compare the performances of the original Seafile and Dropbox clients with those when the two service frameworks are improved with QuickSync.

7.1 Impact of the Network-aware Chunker

We first evaluate how the Network-aware Chunker improves the throughput under various network conditions. We collect about 200GB data from 10 cloud storage services users, and randomly pick about 50GB as the data set for uploading. The rest about 150GB data are pre-stored in the server for deduplication purpose. We repeat the sync process under various RTT to measure the the sync speed, defined as the ratio of the original data size to the total sync time, and the average CPU usage of both the client and server. The minimal RTT from our testbed to the Seafile and Dropbox server is 30ms and 200ms respectively.

Figure 9 shows the results. When the RTT is very low (30ms), since the bandwidth is sufficient, the client selects the un-aggressive chunking strategy with low computation overhead to split files, and the sync speed outperforms the original one by 12%. As the RTT increases, the sync speed decreases, but our implementations can still achieve higher total sync speed by taking advantage of the aggressive chunking strategies to eliminate more redundancy and thus reduce the transmission time. Overall, our implementations can dynamically select an appropriate chunking strategy for deduplication, which leads up to about 31% increase of the sync speed under various network conditions.

We plot the CPU usages of QuickSync client and server in Figure 10. Since the original systems do not change their chunking strategies based on network conditions, we also plot their constant CPU usages as the baseline. As RTT increases, the CPU usages for both the client and server of QuickSync increase, as more aggressive chunking strategy is applied to reduce the redundant data. The CPU usage for Seafile is lower because of more powerful hardware. The CPU usage of client reaches up to 12.3% and 42.7% in two implementations respectively which is still within the acceptable range.

7.2 Impact of the Redundancy Eliminator

Next we evaluate the sync traffic reduction of using our Redundancy Eliminator with the average chunk size set to 1MB to exclude the impact of adaptive chunking. We conduct the same set of experiments for modify operation as shown in Figure 2, and measure the sync traffic size to calculate their TUO.

In Figure 11, for both flip and insert operations, the TUO of our mechanism for all files in any position is close to 1, indicating that our implementation only synchronize the modified content to server. Note that the TUO results for flip or insert operation on small files ($\leq 100KB$) have reached 1.3. The additional traffic is due to the basic overhead of delta encoding. The TUO results for delete operation are close to 0 because the client does not need to upload the delta besides performing the delta encoding. The results of Dropbox modification are similar and omitted due to the page limit.

Furthermore, to evaluate the traffic reduction for synchronizing changes of file whose corresponding chunks are on their way to the server, we conduct the same set of experiments as those in Figure 3. The TUO results in each case are close to 1, showing that our scheme only needs to synchronize the new contents under arbitrary number of modifications and any RTT, because the in-memory uploading queue buffers files in the middle of transmissions to facilitate delta encoding.

7.3 Impact of the Batched Syncer

7.3.1 *Improvement of BUE*

To examine the performance of the Batched Syncer in improving the bandwidth utilization, we set the average chunk size to 1MB to exclude the impact of adaptive chunking. In Section 3.3, we observe that cloud storage services suffer low BUE, especially when synchronizing a lot of small files. We conduct the same set of experiments with use of our proposed schemes.

Figure 12 shows the level of BUE improvement under different network conditions. Our mechanism can improve up to 61% the bandwidth utilization efficiency for synchronizing a batch of chunks by reducing the acknowledgement overhead. The improvement is more obvious in high RTT environment where the throughput often experiences big reduction especially when the acknowledgements are frequent.

7.3.2 *Overhead for Exception Recovery*

The per chunk acknowledgement is designed to reduce the recovery overhead when the sync process is unexpected interrupted. In our Batched Syncer, the client will not wait for an acknowledgement for every chunk. Now we examine whether this design will cause much more traffic overhead for exception recovery. We upload a set of files with different sizes, and close the TCP connection when half of the file has been uploaded. After the restart of the program, the client

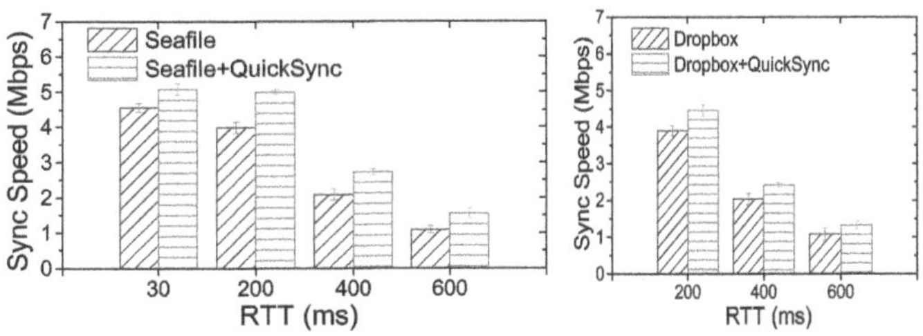

(a) Seafile (b) Dropbox

Figure 9: Speed improved by Network-aware Chunker.

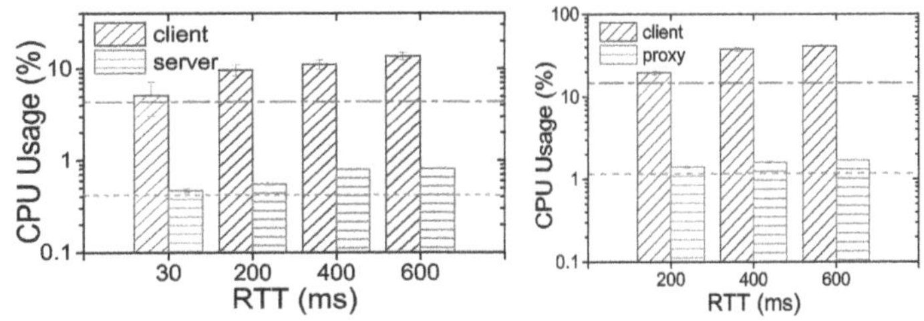

(a) Seafile+QuickSync (b) Dropbox+QuickSync

Figure 10: CPU overhead of Network-aware Chunker

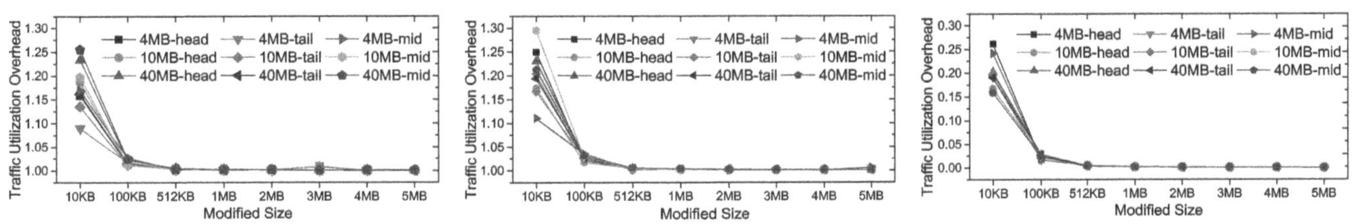

(a) flip (b) insert (c) delete

Figure 11: Traffic utilization overhead reduction of Seafile modification.

will create new connection to finish the sync. We record the total sync traffic and calculate the TUO in Figure 13. Our results show that in each case, the TUO of QuickSync is close to 1, and the highest TUO is only about 1.5, indicating that our implementations will not cause very high overhead for exception recovery. In our design, before resuming the sync, the client communicates with the server first to check the chunks that are not received and need to be transferred.

7.4 Performance of the Integrated System

We assess the overall performance of our implementation using a series of representative workloads for cloud storage services on Windows or Android. Each workload combines a set of file operations, including creation, modification or deletion, which will trigger corresponding events in the local file system. The performance results are shown in Table 2.

We first generate the workloads on Windows platform based on Seafile and its modification. The QuickSync Paper workload is resulted from uploading the files of this paper, and the Seafile Source generates load by storing all the source codes of the Seafile. Both types of workload contain a lot of small files and do not contain file modification or deletion. Although the traffic size reduction for the two workloads are small (7.5% and 8.9%), our implementation reduces the total sync time by 35.1% and 51.8% respectively. The reduction is mainly caused by bundling the small files to improve the bandwidth utilization, as the Seafile Source contains 1259 independent files. The Document Editing workload on Windows is generated when we naturally edit a PowerPoint file in the sync folder from 3MB to 5MB within 40min. We capture many creation and deletion events because during the editing process, temporary files whose sizes are close to that of the original .ppt file are created and deleted. Changes are automatically synchronized. Our solution significantly reduces the traffic size, as QuickSync can execute delta encoding on the temporary files in the middle of the sync process to reduce the traffic. The Data Backup workload on Windows is a typical usage for large data backup. This workload contains 37655 files, with various file types (e.g. PDF or video) and sizes (from 1KB to 179MB). Our QuickSync achieves 37.4% sync time reduction by eliminating the redundancy and reducing the acknowledgement overhead to improve the bandwidth utilization.

We also play the workload on Android platform. The Document Editing workload on Android is similar to the editing workload generated in the above experiment but contains fewer modifications. Our implementation reduces 41.4% of the total sync time. The Photo Sharing is a common workload for mobile phones. Although the photos are often in the encoded format and hard to be deduplicated, our implementation can still achieve 24.1% time saving through the batched transmission scheme. The System Backup workload is generated to back up all the app binaries and their data in a phone via a slow 3G network. As our implementation adaptively selects aggressive chunking strategy to eliminate larger amount of the backup traffic and bundles chunks to improve the bandwidth utilization, 52.9% sync time saving is achieved.

7.5 Server-side Storage Overhead

QuickSync leverages content defined chunking with smaller chunk size and dynamically selects an appropriate deduplication scheme based on real-time network conditions to improve the sync efficiency. Compared with other cloud storage systems using larger fixed-size chunk, our methods may add the metadata overhead on the server side. Now we analyze the impact that our design may have on a Dropbox-like system.

Using the method in Section 4.1, we first measure and analyze the sync flow of uploading a set of files via Dropbox. The metadata of Dropbox contains a number of fields to describe a file, such as modified time, revision number, file path and a list of chunk hashes. The dynamical chunking

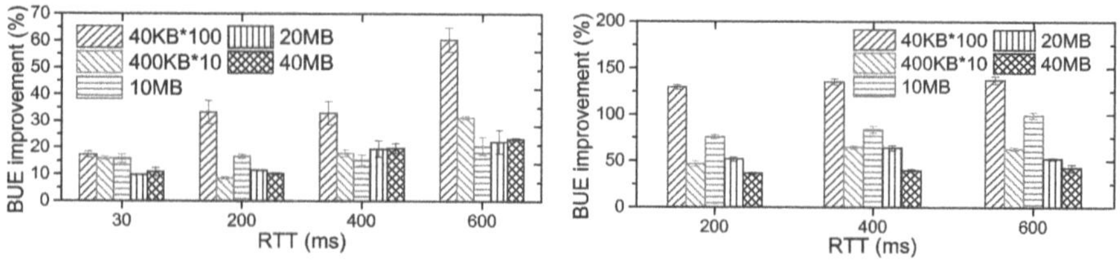

Figure 12: BUE improvement.

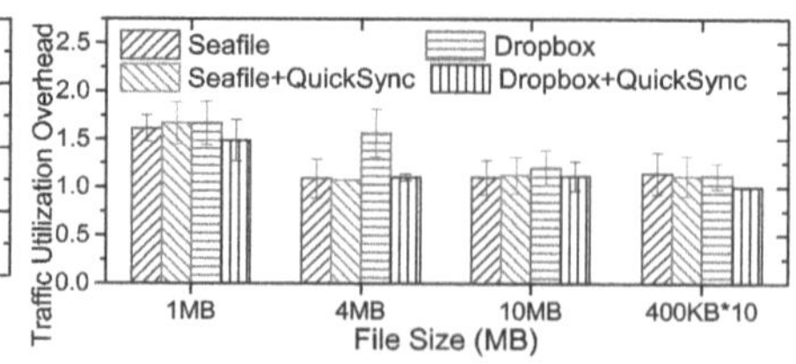

Figure 13: Recovery overhead.

Workload (Platform)	# of Events (C/M/D)	Traffic Size (Origin/Ours/Reduction%)	Sync Time (Origin/Ours/Reduction%)
QuickSync Paper (W)	74/0/0	4.67MB/4.32MB/7.4%	27.6s/17.9s/35.1%
Seafile Source (W)	1259/0/0	15.6MB/14.2MB/8.9%	264.1s/127.3s/51.8%
Document Editing (W)	12/74/7	64.3MB/12.7MB/80.3%	592.0s/317.3s/46.4%
Data Backup (W)	37655/0/0	2GB/1.4GB/30.6%	68.7m/43.1m/37.4%
Document Editing (A)	1/4/0	4.1MB/1.5MB/63.4%	24.4s/14.3s/41.4%
Photo Sharing (A)	11/0/0	21.1MB/20.7MB/1.9%	71.9s/54.6s/24.1%
System Backup (A)	66/0/0	206.2MB/117.9MB/42.8%	612.3s/288.7s/52.9%

Table 2: Practical performance evaluation for QuickSync using a series of real world representative workloads. W: Windows platform. A: Android platform. Event C: Creation. Event M: Modification. Event D: Deletion.

Data set	Hash (byte)	% in Metadata	% in Overall Sync Traffic
1 MB	43[1]	2%	0.004%
10×100 KB	430	13%	0.037%
10 MB	129	7%	0.001%
10×1 MB	430	11%	0.004%

Table 3: The volume of chunk hash and its occupancy in metadata and overall sync traffic of Dropbox.

scheme in QuickSync mainly increases the volume of hashes in the metadata and will not affect other fields. Table 3 shows the size of hashes and its occupancy in the metadata and the total sync traffic of Dropbox. We find that hashes occupy a very small fraction in the metadata and the overall sync traffic.

Further, we analyze and estimate the additional storage overhead incurred by QuickSync. If we only consider the hash values in metadata and use the SHA-1 hashing for each chunk, the storage overhead of a 4MB file in Dropbox is the sum of contents and metadata, i.e. (4MB+20B). The additional storage overhead of QuickSync is caused by two factors: 1) the additional hashes incurred by multi-level chunking (Section 5.2.1) and 2) the storage of Virtual Chunks (Section 5.2.2). Because our implementation of QuickSync uses 4MB, 1MB, 512KB and 128KB chunking, the hash size of a 4MB in QuickSync is 20B*(1+4+8+32)=900B. Moreover, a 4MB file has at most (4+8+32)=44 Virtual Chunks and the rest one contains the real contents. Since a Virtual Chunk occupies a 2-byte field for the chunk length, the maximal cost of Virtual Chunks is (2B*44)=88B. Therefore the total storage cost of a 4MB file in QuickSync is (4MB+988B). In summary, QuickSync adds 968B additional storage cost, which is only 0.02% of the overall storage cost. Consider that in practice the hash values are only a very small fraction of the overall storage cost, QuickSync may not incur much storage overhead on the server side.

[1]The chunk hash is salted in practice.

8. RELATED WORK

Measurement study. Recently a large number of measurement research efforts have been conducted on cloud storage services [16, 12, 11, 17, 19]. CloudCmp [16] measures the elastic computing, persistent storage, and networking services for four major cloud providers. Focusing on personal cloud, Drago *et al.* give a large scale measurement for Dropbox [12], and then compare the system capabilities for five popular cloud storage services in [11]. However, all these previous studies only focus on the desktop services, and all of them are based on black-box measurement. Li *et al.* give the experimental study of the sync traffic, demonstrating that considerable portion of the data sync traffic is wasteful [17]. Our work steps closer to reveal the root cause of inefficiency problem from the protocol view, and we are the first to study the sync efficiency problem in wireless networks.

System design. There are also many studies about the system design for cloud storage services [26, 25, 9]. However they are mostly focusing on enterprise backup instead of personal cloud. Li *et al.* propose an adaptive sync defer (ASD) mechanism, which adaptively tunes its sync deferment to follow the latest data update [18]. The bundling idea of our Batched Syncer is similar to ASD, but ASD will incur much more recovery overhead when the sync is interrupted. Moreover, as a middleware solution, ASD can not avoid the incremental sync failure described in Section 3.2. ViewBox [27] is designed to detect corrupt data through the data check sum and ensure the consistency by adopting view-based synchronization. It is complemented with our QuickSync system.

CDC and delta encoding. QuickSync leverages some existing techniques, such as content defined chunking (CDC) [20, 28, 22, 14, 5, 6, 23, 7] and delta encoding [24]. Rather than directly using these schemes, the aim of QuickSync is to design best strategies to adjust and improve these techniques for better supporting mobile cloud storage services. In all previous systems using CDC, both the client and server use the fixed average chunk size. In contrast, QuickSync utilizes CDC addressing for a unique purpose, adaptively selecting the optimized average chunking size to achieve the sync efficiency. Delta encoding is also not a new idea but it poses big challenge when implemented with the cloud storage system where files are split into chunks and stored distributedly. The techniques in Redundancy Eliminator address the limitation and wisely use delta encoding to reduce the sync traffic overhead.

9. CONCLUSION

Despite their near-ubiquity, mobile cloud storage services fail to efficiently synchronize data in certain circumstance. In this paper, we first study four popular cloud storage services to identify their sync inefficiency issues in wireless networks. We then conduct in-depth analysis to give the root causes of the identified problems concurrently exploiting trace study and data decryption. To address the inefficiency issues, we propose QuickSync, a system with three novel techniques. We further implement QuickSync to support sync with Dropbox and Seafile. Our extensive evaluations demonstrate that QuickSync can effectively save the sync time and reduce significant traffic overhead for representative sync workloads.

10. ACKNOWLEDGMENTS

We sincerely thank Matt Welsh for shepherding our paper, as well as the anonymous reviewers for their valuable comments and feedback. This research was supported by National Natural Science Foundation of China (no. 61120106008 and no. 61422206), National High Technology Development 863 Program of China (no.2013AA010401). The research of Wang is supported by NSF 1408247 and NSF 1247924.

11. REFERENCES

[1] Dynamorio. http://dynamorio.org.
[2] Googledrive. http://www.google.com/drive/index.html.
[3] librsync. http://librsync.sourceforge.net/.
[4] Onedrive. https://onedrive.live.com.
[5] Seafile source code. https://github.com/haiwen/seafile.
[6] B. Agarwal, A. Akella, A. Anand, A. Balachandran, P. Chitnis, C. Muthukrishnan, R. Ramjee, and G. Varghese. Endre: An end-system redundancy elimination service for enterprises. In *NSDI*, pages 419–432. USENIX, 2010.
[7] A. Anand, A. Gupta, A. Akella, S. Seshan, and S. Shenker. Packet caches on routers: the implications of universal redundant traffic elimination. In *SIGCOMM*. ACM, 2008.
[8] A. Balasubramanian, R. Mahajan, and A. Venkataramani. Augmenting mobile 3g using wifi. In *MobiSys*, pages 209–222. ACM, 2010.
[9] B. Calder, J. Wang, A. Ogus, N. Nilakantan, A. Skjolsvold, S. McKelvie, Y. Xu, S. Srivastav, J. Wu, H. Simitci, et al. Windows azure storage: a highly available cloud storage service with strong consistency. In *SOSP*, pages 143–157. ACM, 2011.
[10] Y. Cui, Z. Lai, and N. Dai. A first look at mobile cloud storage services: Architecture, experimentation and challenge. http://www.4over6.edu.cn/others/technical_report.pdf.
[11] I. Drago, E. Bocchi, M. Mellia, H. Slatman, and A. Pras. Benchmarking personal cloud storage. In *IMC*, pages 205–212. ACM, 2013.
[12] I. Drago, M. Mellia, M. M Munafo, A. Sperotto, R. Sadre, and A. Pras. Inside dropbox: understanding personal cloud storage services. In *IMC*, pages 481–494. ACM, 2012.
[13] Dropbox. https://www.dropbox.com.
[14] Y. Hua, X. Liu, and D. Feng. Neptune: Efficient remote communication services for cloud backups. In *INFOCOM*. IEEE, 2014.
[15] D. Kholia and P. Wegrzyn. Looking inside the (drop) box. In *7th USENIX Workshop on Offensive Technologies (WOOT), Washington, DC, USA*, pages 1–7, 2013.
[16] A. Li, X. Yang, S. Kandula, and M. Zhang. Cloudcmp: comparing public cloud providers. In *IMC*, pages 1–14. ACM, 2010.
[17] Z. Li, C. Jin, T. Xu, C. Wilson, Y. Liu, L. Cheng, Y. Liu, Y. Dai, and Z.-L. Zhang. Towards network-level efficiency for cloud storage services. In *IMC*. ACM, 2014.
[18] Z. Li, C. Wilson, Z. Jiang, Y. Liu, B. Y. Zhao, C. Jin, Z.-L. Zhang, and Y. Dai. Efficient batched synchronization in dropbox-like cloud storage services. In *Middleware 2013*, pages 307–327. Springer, 2013.
[19] T. Mager, E. Biersack, and P. Michiardi. A measurement study of the wuala on-line storage service. In *Peer-to-Peer Computing (P2P), 2012 IEEE 12th International Conference on*, pages 237–248. IEEE, 2012.
[20] A. Muthitacharoen, B. Chen, and D. Mazieres. A low-bandwidth network file system. In *SIGOPS*. ACM, 2001.
[21] S.-H. Shen and A. Akella. An information-aware qoe-centric mobile video cache. In *MobiCom*, pages 401–412. ACM, 2013.
[22] P. Shilane, M. Huang, G. Wallace, and W. Hsu. Wan-optimized replication of backup datasets using stream-informed delta compression. *TOS*, 8(4):13, 2012.
[23] N. T. Spring and D. Wetherall. A protocol-independent technique for eliminating redundant network traffic. *SIGCOMM*, 2000.
[24] A. Tridgell, P. Mackerras, et al. The rsync algorithm, 1996.
[25] M. Vrable, S. Savage, and G. M. Voelker. Cumulus: Filesystem backup to the cloud. *TOS*, 5(4):14, 2009.
[26] M. Vrable, S. Savage, and G. M. Voelker. Bluesky: a cloud-backed file system for the enterprise. In *FAST*, page 19. USENIX, 2012.
[27] Y. Zhang, C. Dragga, A. C. Arpaci-Dusseau, and R. H. Arpaci-Dusseau. Viewbox: integrating local file systems with cloud storage services. In *FAST*, pages 119–132. USENIX, 2014.
[28] B. Zhu, K. Li, and R. H. Patterson. Avoiding the disk bottleneck in the data domain deduplication file system. In *FAST*, volume 8, pages 1–14. USENIX, 2008.

FlexiWeb: Network-Aware Compaction for Accelerating Mobile Web Transfers

Shailendra Singh
University of California, Riverside
singhs@cs.ucr.edu

Harsha V. Madhyastha
University of Michigan
harshavm@umich.edu

Srikanth V. Krishnamurthy
University of California, Riverside
krish@cs.ucr.edu

Ramesh Govindan
University of Southern California
ramesh@usc.edu

***Abstract*—**To reduce page load times and bandwidth usage for mobile web browsing, middleboxes that compress page content are commonly used today. Unfortunately, this can hurt performance in many cases; via an extensive measurement study, we show that using middleboxes to facilitate compression results in up to 28% degradation in page load times when the client enjoys excellent wireless link conditions. We find that benefits from compression are primarily realized under bad network conditions. Guided by our study, we design and implement FlexiWeb, a framework that determines both *when* to use a middlebox and *how* to use it, based on the client's network conditions. First, FlexiWeb selectively fetches objects on a web page either directly from the source or via a middlebox, rather than fetching all objects via the middlebox. Second, instead of simply performing lossless compression of all content, FlexiWeb performs network-aware compression of images by selecting from among a range of content transformations. We implement and evaluate a prototype of FlexiWeb using Google's open source Chromium mobile browser and our implementation of a modified version of Google's open source compression proxy. Our extensive experiments show that, across a range of scenarios, FlexiWeb reduces page load times for mobile clients by 35–42% compared to the status quo.

Categories and Subject Descriptors

C.4 [**PERFORMANCE OF SYSTEMS**]: Performance attributes; Measurement techniques; C.2.2 [**Network Protocols**]: Applications

Keywords

Cellular Network, Mobile Web Browsing, Compression Proxy, Middle Box

MobiCom'15, September 7–11, 2015, Paris, France.

DOI: http://dx.doi.org/10.1145/2789168.2790128.

1 Introduction

The ill-effects of slow websites, especially when browsing using a cellular network, are well-documented. Recent surveys suggest that two-thirds of users encounter slow websites every week [1], and that 49% of such users abandon a site or switch to a competitor upon experiencing large delays [1]. To address this, several systems augment mobile web browsing with support from middleboxes or proxies in the cloud (e.g., [2], [3], [4], [5], [6], [7]); many of these systems are widely used today, such as Opera Mini [5], Amazon Silk [6] and Chrome beta [7]. These cloud-supported mobile browsing options can potentially reduce download times, device energy consumption, and data usage costs.

Network conditions should dictate whether or not a middlebox should be used for performing content compression: The aforementioned middleboxes primarily compress content to be delivered to wireless clients based on the common belief that compression reduces the volume of bytes downloaded, and thus, improves performance. Unfortunately, this is not always the case. As our first contribution, we conduct an extensive measurement study which shows that, when network conditions are good, there could in fact be an *increase* in page load times (by as much as 28%) due to the use of middleboxes (we refer to this as `Proxy Assisted` browsing). The problem especially occurs if the web page to be downloaded only contains small objects (no high quality images or large scripts). The primary reason for this degradation is that diverting content to a middlebox causes additional delays due to longer routes and/or processing at the middlebox; these delays offset the gains achieved due to compression in some cases, and thus, worsen page load times. On the other hand, when network conditions are bad, `Proxy Assisted` browsing decreases page load times compared to `Conventional` browsing by 32%. This suggests that the decision on whether or not to use middlebox support for mobile web transfers must be made based on (i) network conditions and (ii) object sizes.

Content transformations ought to be network-aware: Today, most middleboxes for the mobile web apply the same compression to all content. Insufficient compaction could potentially lead to large page load times when network conditions are poor. If users and web providers are willing to compromise on content quality for better page load times, one could enable middleboxes to perform different degrees of content compaction based on network conditions. Specifically, this is possible in the case of images if the network conditions are bad. For example, when the quality of the client's network connection is very poor, the middlebox could even take extreme steps, such as transform a color image to a gray scale version, to ensure reasonable load times.

Challenges: Realizing the above vision towards network-aware, dynamic usage of a middlebox for accelerating mobile web transfers is associated with two primary challenges: (1) For every object, the decision as to whether to fetch it directly or via the proxy depends on the object's size, but that is typically known only after fetching the object. Issuing a HTTP HEAD request just to query the webserver hosting the object for its size will add significant overhead. (2) The extent to which any particular object on a page should be compressed depends on the sizes of other objects on the page. However, given how the process of loading a web page works, the objects on a web page are only revealed iteratively as the page load proceeds.

Design and implementation of FlexiWeb: As our primary contribution, we design and prototype the FlexiWeb framework, which addresses the above challenges, towards providing dynamic, network-aware middlebox support for the mobile web. FlexiWeb has a novel design that encompasses three key elements. First, it uses an empirically derived model that determines, given an object's size and the network conditions, whether the object should be fetched via a proxy[1] or not. Second, FlexiWeb incorporates a classifier that predicts an object's size, based primarily on features derived from the object's URL. Third, FlexiWeb performs network-aware data compaction at the proxy, wherein appropriate transformations are applied to images based on the bandwidth available between the client and the proxy; other objects (e.g., Javascripts) are compressed as in conventional middleboxes. For this, FlexiWeb uses an online algorithm that selects near-optimal compaction levels while attempting to keep page load times within a latency target dictated by user tolerance (shown to be 2–5 seconds by user studies [8]). We cast this algorithm as a utility maximization subject to latency constraints.

Flexibility: While performing content transformation, it is important to ensure that web browsing sessions do ensure a good Quality-of-Experience (QoE). While transformations reduce delays, they must still cater to a user's or a web provider's requirements in terms of quality (e.g., a user may not want gray scale transformations). Hence, we allow users or web providers to set a minimum quality limit either via browser settings or via metadata embedded in a web page's HTML; this sets the maximum allowable compression allowed on each object in a web page.

Evaluations: Finally, we perform extensive evaluations of FlexiWeb both via in-house emulations and real-world experiments using AT&T and T-Mobile's 4G networks in both static and mobile settings. Our experiments demonstrate that FlexiWeb reduces page load times by up to 35–42% as compared to both `Proxy Assisted` and `Conventional` mobile web browsing.

2 To proxy or not to proxy

We begin with a measurement study to understand the implications of using a middlebox for compressing mobile web content. We first describe our setup for the measurements and then discuss the results.

Client side setup: We set up multiple rooted mobile devices (HTC One phones with Android 4.3) running the open source web browser, Chromium, for Android. A Python program controls the browser via Chromedriver using RemoteWebDriver. All experiments are performed with a cold browser cache. We use "page load times" as the primary metric to capture performance. The page load time is defined as the time it takes for the browser to download and process all the objects associated with a web page. Most browsers fire a Javascript event (onLoad()) when the page is loaded. Chrome's remote debugging interface provides us the time taken to download each object in a web page.

[1]We use the terms proxy and middlebox interchangeably.

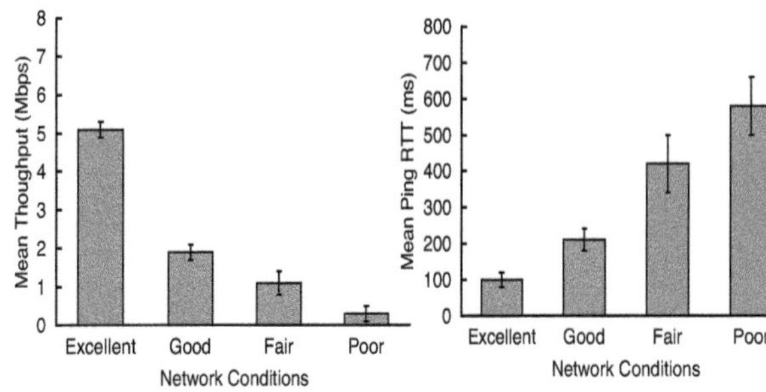

(a) (b)

Figure 1 (a) Average values of (a) Throughput (b) RTT between the client and the proxy server in different cellular network conditions

Network Conditions	RTT(ms)	Throughput(Mbps)	Loss Rate(%)
Excellent	100	5	0.006
Good	200	2	0.006
Fair	400	1	0.04
Poor	600	0.3	0.1

Table 1 Network Conditions (Note that MAC layer retransmissions limit error rates even under poor conditions [9])

Server side setup: To ensure that a phone retrieved the same content each time it fetched a particular URL (in repeated experiments), we captured Alexa's top 500 websites (we believe these represent typically downloaded web pages) and replayed the content using the Web Page Replay tool [10]. All content was cached on our Web Page Replay server. Our server has 16 CPU cores and 64 GB of memory and is hosted on our campus network.

Network conditions: We operate over the 4G networks of two major US cellular providers, AT&T and T-Mobile. To examine the influence of different network conditions, for each provider, we carefully choose four locations where the RTT and throughput values were similar to those listed in Table 1. We choose these locations after monitoring the network conditions by running a long term (2 day) experiment to ensure the stability of the conditions (they stayed more or less the same) as shown in Figures 1a and 1b.

Data collection: For each page downloaded, we record the browser-reported page load time, as well as the load time for each individual resource on the page. In addition, we run `tcpdump` on the phone to capture a trace of all network traffic during the page load. In each run, we first load a page by downloading the resources on a page directly from the webservers hosting them, and then via a compression proxy, back-to-back. We perform 10 trials for each experiment.

Today's compression proxies can increase mobile web page load times: First we perform experiments over both AT&T and T-Mobile's networks, with currently deployed commercial compression proxies. Google's Chrome mobile browser comes with the `Proxy assist` option. Upon enabling this, the browser redirects all the requests to Google's compression proxy. Using this feature, we perform experiments with a *live version* (clients download the webpages directly from the source web sites as opposed to downloading a replay from our web server) of Alexa's top 500 websites.

Figure 2a shows the percentage gain in performance in different network conditions, when using Google's proxy in comparison to

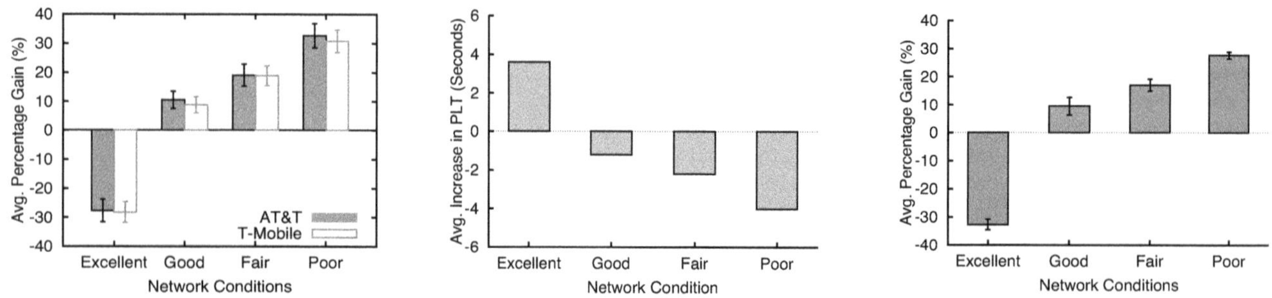

(a) (b) (c)

Figure 2 (a) Gains from using a commercial compression proxy (Google compression proxy) in downloading Alexa's top 500 web pages under different client network conditions. Gains are measured in comparison to a `Conventional` browser. (b) Average increase in Page Load Time (PLT) in seconds from using a commercial compression proxy (Google compression proxy) in comparison to a `Conventional` browser.(c) Gains from using a `Proxy Assisted` browser (using our own proxy) in downloading Alexa's top 500 web pages under different network conditions. Gains are measured in comparison to a `Conventional` browser.

a `Conventional` browser (where all content is retrieved from the source). We see that the use of the proxy provides an average gain of about 32% in bad network conditions. In excellent network conditions, the `Conventional` browser (no proxy) outperforms the `Proxy assisted` browser by about 28%. Figure 2b shows the average gain in page load times in seconds. We see that the proxy can increase the page load time by ≈ 4 seconds. According to prior studies [11] a 1 second delay could potentially result in a nett loss of 2.5 million dollars in sales for an e-commence website. It is also seen that a 4 second delay can cause up to 25% increase in page abandonment. These results clearly demonstrate that the use of a proxy can significantly hurt performance when network conditions are excellent; however, as conditions degrade, compression at a proxy can provide significant benefits.

An in-depth study: To get a further understanding of the implications of using a compression proxy, we set up our own proxy (to emulate the behavior of Google's proxy) and conduct more in depth studies.

Compression proxy setup: We set up the compression proxy on Amazon EC2 to have a controlled environment. The proxy is located in northern California, relatively close to the geographical region of the client. We use Google's open-source compression proxy module called PageSpeed, which we setup as a forward proxy [12]. We use the optimization strategies [13] recommended for reducing page load times. These include combining and minifying JavaScript (JS) and Cascading Style Sheets (CSS) files, inlining small resources, and others. We configure PageSpeed to dynamically optimize images by removing unused metadata, resizing images to specified dimensions, and re-encoding images to the WebP format (which requires fewer bytes than other popular formats such as JPEG and PNG).

Figure 2c presents the average gain in page load time with the compression proxy as compared to `Conventional` browsing (or direct downloads). We see that the results are very consistent with what was observed with the real-world compression proxies.

The question that we then seek to answer is: *"why does performance degrade in excellent network conditions due to the use of a proxy?"* Via a careful study, we find that this is primarily due to penalties associated with loading content via a compression proxy: (i) circuitous routing between the client and web servers via the middlebox, and/or (ii) processing delays at the middlebox.

Penalties due to route stretch: Zarifis et al [9] provide a detailed analysis of path inflation in mobile networks and suggest that factors that primarily contribute to the path inflation are diversions due to (i) ingress points and (ii) peering points. With regards to the former factor, the device's carrier network may not have ingress points to the Internet in the device's area. With regards to the latter, the carrier network may connect with a web service provider at a peering point or Internet exchange point (IXP), which may be at a location distant from both the mobile device and the web provider.

An analysis of our traceroute data indicates that, in the presence of a proxy, traversal of multiple peering points (because of three different networks viz., the carrier network, the network hosting the proxy and the network hosting the web server, instead of two) is likely to lead to longer paths. Indeed, we observed that end-to-end routes in some cases were inflated by up to 8 hops due to the use of the proxy, which resulted in increases in RTTs by up to 45ms.

For example, when we fetched cnn.com without using the proxy, from a location in Southern California, the request for object `http://i.cdn.turner.com/cnn/.e/img/4.0/logos/city_of_tomorrow_bw.png` traversed through AT&T's core mobile network to a CDN (content distribution network) server which was geographically proximate to the client (near Los Angeles). We also found that ingress points for AT&T's mobile core network were in the same geographical location. When fetching the same object via the compression proxy, the request went to the proxy server located in northern California and the request for the object was forwarded to the CDN located near the proxy server (northern California). We observe a similar effect when fetching the same object via Google's compression proxy; the request was sent to Google's compression proxy located in northern California while the closest CDN server was in region Southern California (Los Angeles).

We wish to point out here that the cellular providers also deploy (transparent) proxies in their core network. According to [14] however, only Sprint performs any form of content rewriting. Other providers (T-Mobile, ATT and Verizon) primarily perform delayed handshaking, connection persistence and redirection using such a transparent proxy.

Penalties due to processing overhead: We find that the processing overhead to convert an image to WebP format (the image transformation performed by Google's compression proxy) ranges from 10ms to 30ms per image, depending on the image's size; if a web page contains a large number of objects, the total processing delay can be significant. In general, when compared to JPEG, the encoding speed for WebP is $\approx 10X$ slower (and the decoding is $\approx 1.4X$ slower) but it does provide $\approx$ a 30% gain in terms of a size re-

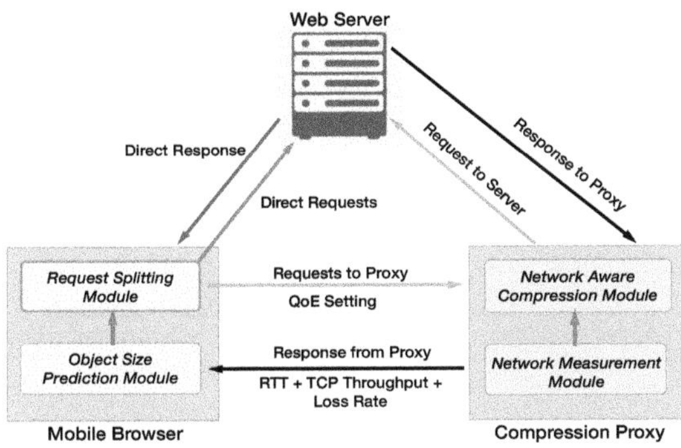

Figure 4 Overview of FlexiWeb's architecture

duction, on average [15]. A commercial proxy can reduce the processing times by using advanced caching techniques (to amortize processing costs across users) but websites are increasingly personalizing their content, e.g., amazon.com shows different items to different users based on their browsing patterns. This, in turn, results in the fetching of different objects for different users.

Impact of object size: To summarize, our evaluations indicate that neither the `Conventional` nor `Proxy Assisted` approach is the winner in all scenarios (in terms of network conditions). To further understand the implications of using `Proxy assisted` browsers, we next analyze the data collected for both types of browsing to understand the impact of network conditions on load times for objects of different sizes. We partition objects into 7 bins: 0–1 KB, 1–3 KB, 3–6 KB, 6–10 KB, 10–20 KB, 20–40 KB, and $\geq$ 40 KB. In Figure 3, we compare the average load times computed over all objects in each category, with both browsing strategies in different network conditions. We see that when the conditions are good, using the proxy is only beneficial for objects larger than 30 KB. This suggests that the delays due to indirection via the proxy outweigh the benefits of data compaction for small objects. As network conditions degrade, fetching compressed objects via the proxy improves object download times as compared to fetching them uncompressed directly from the source. In the extreme case, we see that the proxy's compression enables better download times for objects of all sizes in poor network conditions.

Takeaways: In summary, our measurement studies suggest the following. In very good/excellent network conditions, it is best if only larger sized objects (> 30 KB) are diverted to a compaction middlebox during a web page download. Under fair to poor network conditions, one should retrieve all content indirectly via the middlebox. While FlexiWeb addresses other key challenges as well, these takeaways form the basis for middlebox usage in our framework.

3 Design of FlexiWeb

In this section, we describe the design of the FlexiWeb framework. As discussed earlier, FlexiWeb seeks to reduce page load times while browsing the web on mobile devices. The key property of FlexiWeb is that it is adaptive and achieves its goal under all network conditions.

Overview: To improve the performance vs. experience tradeoff on the mobile web, our over-arching goal is to enable mobile clients to dynamically select which resources on a web page to download via a proxy and to enable the proxy to determine how it should transform every resource that it relays. This goal imposes three logical challenges:

- How can a client account for the characteristics of the objects on a page and its network conditions to determine what to fetch directly from the source web servers and which objects to fetch via the proxy?
- Since the determination of whether to fetch an object via the proxy or not depends on the object's size, how can we predict an object's size before fetching it?
- To ensure that all objects on a page are delivered to a client within a target load time, the manner in which the proxy transforms any particular object on a page must depend on the sizes of other objects on the page. How can the proxy do so, given that all the objects on a page are only revealed iteratively during the page load process?

Our architecture of FlexiWeb towards tackling these challenges is shown in Figure 4. The *Network Measurement component* at the proxy measures the network's characteristics via a series of measurements. The measurements made by FlexiWeb do not consume excessive resources on the client side in terms of bandwidth or energy. These measurements are then fed back to the mobile browser. The mobile browser contains an *Object size prediction module* which estimates object sizes in a web page that it seeks to download. This module essentially uses (i) measured distributions to determine what objects (in terms of sizes) to fetch via the proxy after transformation, and what objects to fetch directly from the source and (ii) an incremental learning algorithm to predict object sizes. The *Request splitting module* then fetches each object, either directly from a web server or via the proxy; large objects are always fetched via the proxy, while the decision on "from where to fetch a small object?" is made based on network conditions (this part of FlexiWeb uses the inferences from our measurements in Section 2).

The *Network Aware Compression module* at the proxy fetches the objects from their sources. Note here that different objects could be potentially fetched from different web servers (e.g., ads may be fetched from a different domain than the one in which the web page being fetched is hosted). Since not all objects are fetched simultaneously, the proxy has to decide on the level of compression (transformation) to be performed on each object as it is fetched, with the objective of trying to keep the total page load time within a target. The proxy meets this goal by using a novel algorithm to dynamically choose the compression level for each object (images specifically) prior to sending it to the mobile client. Specifically, it performs an online optimization to determine object transformations that allow the download to fit within a target budget page load time; it reverts to a minimal transformation (maximum compression) when the optimization formulation is infeasible.

Handling Videos: Videos in a webpage are downloaded as an image (snapshot from the video) when a page is loaded by the browser. If a user clicks on the play button of the video it starts downloading/streaming the video from a server. Video streaming is not considered to be part of the webpage download [16] and hence, we do not address videos explicitly in this work.

In the rest of this section, we elaborate on the different functionalities of FlexiWeb.

3.1 Splitting requests

Current proxy-assisted browsers either fetch all or none of the objects in a web page, via a middlebox. However, as seen earlier, this model can hurt page load times when network conditions are excellent. To minimize the page load times given the conditions, FlexiWeb seeks to identify which objects should be diverted to the proxy and which ones should not. Based on our measurements in Section 2, we create a mapping between how objects should be re-

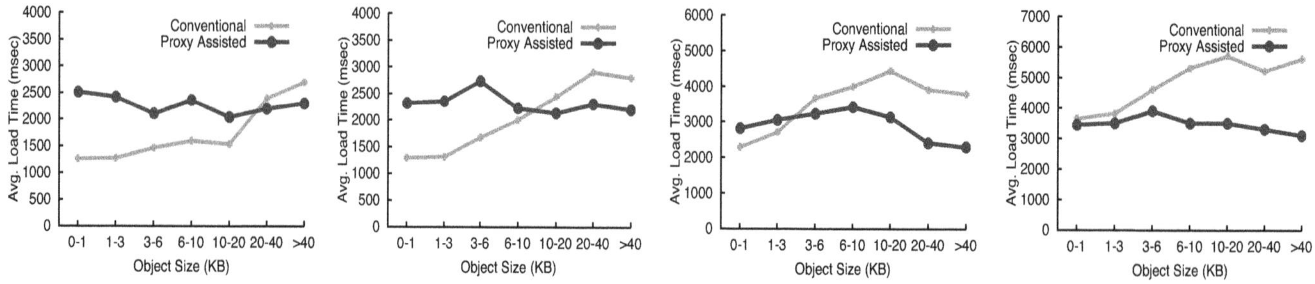

(a) (b) (c) (d)

Figure 3 Download times of objects under various network conditions (a) Network: Excellent (b) Network: Good (c) Network: Fair (d) Network: Poor

Network Condition	0–1 KB	1–3 KB	3–6 KB	6–10 KB	10–20 KB	20–40 KB	≥ 40 KB
Excellent	Direct	Direct	Direct	Direct	Direct	Proxy	Proxy
Good	Direct	Direct	Direct	Direct	Proxy	Proxy	Proxy
Fair	Direct	Direct	Proxy	Proxy	Proxy	Proxy	Proxy
Poor	Proxy	Proxy	Proxy	Proxy	Proxy	Proxy	Proxy

Table 2 Mapping that dictates when to fetch an object directly from the source server and when to fetch it via the proxy

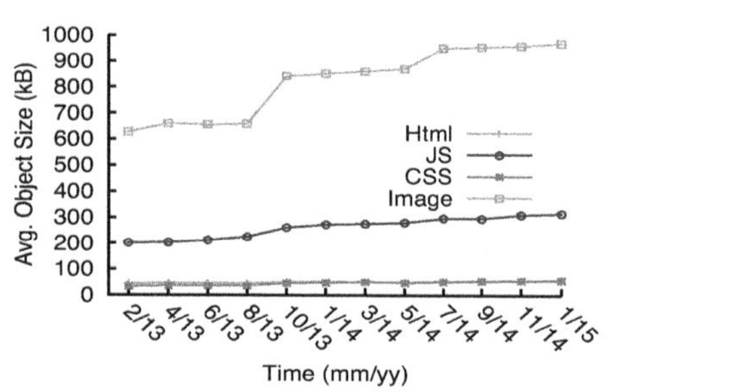

Figure 5 Average object size of top 4000 Alexa web pages over last 2 years

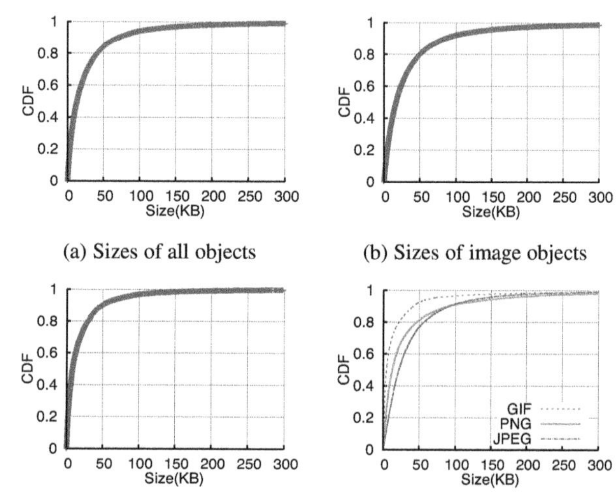

(a) Sizes of all objects

(b) Sizes of image objects

(c) Sizes of CSS, JS, and HTML objects

(d) Sizes of different types of images

Figure 6 Characteristics of top 4000 Alexa Web pages.

trieved based on their sizes and current network conditions; Table 2 depicts this mapping. The *Request Splitting Module* uses this mapping to dynamically send the request for an object either directly to the web server or to the proxy.

Dynamically selecting how to fetch an object based on its size is challenging because any object's size is not readily available to the client. After fetching the main HTML file (e.g., index.html) of a web page, current browsers parse the file to determine the next object that is to be fetched in order to render the web page. At this point, the browser only knows the object's URL; the object size information is yet unknown. While the browser could try to determine an object's size by issuing a HTTP HEAD request [17] to the web server hosting the object, this would add significant overhead since it imposes an additional round trip of wide-area communication for every object.

3.2 Predicting object sizes

To predict the size of an object given only its URL, we rely on learning and applying a predictive classifier. Based on the objects that it fetches over time the proxy continually builds this classifier, and periodically sends its prediction model to the client. The data from Alexa's top 4000 web pages gathered by http archive [16], shows that the average size of web page objects changes only once every few months (as shown in Figure 5). Thus, it suffices that the update frequency of the prediction model is set to (say) every few months.

Training the model: To construct a prediction model, a dataset to train the model is required. The middlebox records the URLs of the objects that it fetches and their corresponding sizes, and it feeds this information as input to a machine learning algorithm to predict the sizes of objects not seen thus far. Figure 6(a) depicts the distribution of object sizes in such a sample dataset, which comprises all objects seen on Alexa's top 4000 websites. We see that over 80% of objects are smaller than 50 KB. This is also true in the case of images (Figure 6(b)). Figure 6(c) shows that objects with text content (JavaScript, HTML, and CSS) are even smaller. We find that images are one of the biggest contributors to large web page sizes, and hence, we looked at the distribution of the sizes of different image types. Figure 6(d) shows that GIF images are much smaller in size than PNGs and JPEGs.

Rather than attempt to predict the precise size of every object, which is likely an impossible task, we leverage the fact that we only need to map every object to one of the bins in Table 2. Therefore, the problem at hand is to accurately predict the size range given an object's URL.

Extracting features: To perform this classification of object URLs to size ranges, we extract various features from every URL. First, we extract a "bag of words" [18] from the host name in the URL. For example, the host name in the URL `http://i.cdn.turner.com/cnn/.e/img/3.0/global/icons/gallery_icon2.png` yields the following bag of words: {i, cdn, turner, com}. In addition to features extracted from the host name, we include features from the URN and the type of content. Hence, the feature set for the above URL would be domain = {i, cdn, turner, com}, urn = {cnn, .e, img, 3.0, global, icons, gallery_icon2.png} and type = png.

Classifier: The problem of classifying a URL into one of the size ranges is a multi-class classification problem, i.e., it is a classification task with more than two classes. Many multi-class classification algorithms make the assumption that each sample is assigned to one and only one label; in our case, this means that an object's URL can only be "classified" into one size range.

The random forest learning algorithm [19], which is known to perform well for multi-class classification problems can be utilized at the proxy for our purposes. It uses multiple decision trees and the final decision is made based on an aggregation of different decision outcomes from the individual trees. The main parameters of the random forest algorithm are the maximum depth of each (individual) tree, the maximum number of trees, and the maximum number of features used to train the model; details can be found in [19].

Execution: In summary, the object size prediction component of FlexiWeb executes as follows. First, the proxy labels every URL in the training dataset by assigning each object to the appropriate class based on its size. Next, the proxy uses the random forest learning algorithm to generate a classifier model based on the extracted features from the labeled dataset. The client browser then uses this model to predict the size of the object associated with each request, and subsequently (in conjunction with network condition assessments), it makes a decision on whether to retrieve the object via the proxy or directly from the source.

3.3 Assessing Network Conditions

An assessment of network conditions by the *Network measurement module* at the proxy serves two purposes. First, it enables the *Request splitting module* at the client to determine whether to retrieve each object from the source directly or via the proxy. Second, it also enables the proxy to make an informed decision on the extent to which it should compress each object. To assess network conditions, the *Network measurement module* at the proxy tracks the RTT, the loss rate, and the TCP throughput to the client.

A simple way to accurately estimate network conditions is to perform measurements in the background; the client and the proxy would exchange packets periodically to infer network conditions. However, such an approach will be prohibitive in terms of bandwidth and energy overheads on the client side. In FlexiWeb, to enable accurate estimation of the average RTT and throughput, the client browser always downloads the main HTML file for every web page via the proxy. The main HTML file is typically sufficiently large for the purposes of FlexiWeb's estimation of network conditions, since the HTML's transfer requires the transmission of tens of packets. This also solves the issue of cold start, when the client browser is sending a page request for the first time.

From the HTML's transfer, the *Network measurement module* obtains a sequence of RTT samples, and uses the median sample value to estimate the RTT to the client; we borrow this approach from [20]. Since web page loads last only tens of seconds, these RTT measurements suffice in predicting subsequent data transfer delays to the specific client.

The proxy sends this "network condition report" back to the client in the object response headers of the requests; this enables the client to determine the network conditions (excellent, good, fair or poor as in Table 1) and how to fetch other objects on the web page (using Table 2).

3.4 Network Aware Compression

Current practices: Current proxy-assisted browsers transform content in a pre-determined manner. For example, scripts, CSS files, and other text-based content are minified and zipped before they are sent to the mobile client [21]. On the other hand, proxies convert images to a fixed image format with a fixed compression ratio [13]. For example, Google compression proxy's recommended setting is to transform images to Google's *WebP* image format with a pre-defined quality; WebP is known to have much better performance in comparison to other image formats (e.g., the average WebP file size is 25–34% smaller compared to the JPEG file size with equivalent image quality).

Problem formulation: In contrast to the status quo, we seek to adaptively transform any web page's content in a manner that enables us to deliver the page within the user's attention span, irrespective of the client's network conditions; a user's attention span has been shown to be in the 2 to 5 second range previously [8].

To deliver a web page's content within the user's attention span, in this work, we focus only on *adaptively* transforming images on the page. Since images make up around 65% of the bytes on the average web page [16], transformation of images (to either significantly compressed versions or lower qualities) can significantly reduce page load times. Text and Javascript are compressed as with traditional proxy assisted browsers (to static extents). The adaptive transformation of images is based on assessed network conditions. If network conditions are good very little compression is invoked; on the other hand, if conditions are poor, higher levels of compression (including a lowering of the image quality) are in play. Our focus here is primarily to achieve the right balance between page load time and user experience. Reducing the download time of an image by applying an appropriate transformation is important, but at the same time, quality or utility of the transformed image is also important. To achieve the right balance, we associate each transformed version of an image with a cost and a utility.

Cost: We define the cost of a transformation as the time taken to download the transformed image from the proxy to the client. Since TCP throughput can be modeled as $\frac{MSS}{RTT \times \sqrt{p}}$ [22] (where MSS is the maximum segment size, RTT is the round-trip time between the proxy and the client, and P is the packet loss rate), we compute the download time for an image of size S bytes as $\frac{S \times RTT \times \sqrt{P}}{MSS}$; the proxy measures the RTT and loss rate using the technique described earlier. Here, the size S corresponds to the *transformed size* of the image. Thus, the higher the degree of compression due to the transformation, the lower will be the cost.

Utility: We use the Peak signal-to-noise ratio (PSNR) as the utility resulting from a transformation. PSNR is the most widely used metric to quantify the quality or utility of images. It essentially captures the relative quality between two images and is defined as:

$$PSNR = 10log\left(\frac{MAX^2}{MSE}\right),$$

where MAX is the maximum possible pixel value (defined next) and MSE is the mean-squared error given by:

$$MSE = \frac{1}{mn}\sum_{i=0}^{m-1}\sum_{j=0}^{n-1}[I(i,j) - K(i,j)]^2.$$

In the above, the two images are of size $m \times n$ and $I(i,j)$ and $K(i,j)$ are the pixel values in the two images at position (i,j). The pixel values essentially reflect the intensity level in each pixel; thus, if the intensity is represented using 8 bits, then MAX will be 255. For color images (with three RGB values per pixel), note that the MSE is the average over all RGB values. With higher levels of compression or transformation, MSE increases and thus, PSNR decreases.

The proxy calculates the PSNR (utility) with each transformation with respect to the original image. Clearly, the more aggressive the transformation, the lower will be the utility of the image.

Cost vs. utility trade-off: As evident from the above discussion, a higher degree of compression reduces both utility and cost; an attempt to either decrease cost or increase utility adversely affects the other. Thus, though FlexiWeb should ideally maximize utility and minimize cost, both objectives cannot be realized simultaneously. Instead, it seeks to do the best it can in reducing cost and increasing utility as follows.

For tractability, we consider a limited number of transformation choices, and the proxy chooses from one of these options depending on network conditions. The set of transformations range from high utility and high cost to low utility and low cost: WebP with 85% quality, WebP with 65% quality, WebP with 45% quality, WebP with 25% quality, WebP with 5% quality, and a gray scale version of the image. As one might expect, the lowest quality image (gray scale) has the least associated cost but also offers the least utility; the highest quality image provides the highest utility but also incurs the highest cost.

Processing times: In the above discussion, we characterize the cost associated with a transformation to be the time taken to download that specific transformed version of an image. In reality, there is an additional cost due to processing the image. We find that regardless of which transformation we perform on each specific object, the processing delay does not change by much. We perform all of the transformations on 1000 images from Alexa's top 500 webpages and we find that the processing times are almost identical; in the worst case, the difference in processing time is about 8 % for a very few objects (we omit results due to space constraints). Thus, the processing cost does not influence the choice of transformation and is hence ignored here.

Compressing objects based on network conditions: Utilizing the cost vs. utility characterization of web content as above, we cast the proxy's task of performing network aware compression as follows.

Suppose that the client needs to download a total of N images in sequence over the duration of a web page download, and that it has a total page load time budget of B seconds (within which the page should be ideally downloaded). For every image object i, let us assume that the proxy can apply M_i different transformations. The question then is "which transformation should the proxy apply on each image ?" The overall goal here is to maximize the sum of utilities (i.e., PSNR values) of all the selected versions for the N images, subject to the constraints that (i) exactly one version for each requested image must be selected, and (ii) the total cost of all the selected versions must be within budget B (within the desired page download time). Note that maximizing the sum of the PSNR (chosen as the utility) values corresponds to a minimization of the sum of expected distortion over the images in the web page; the lower this value, the better the quality of the downloaded content and thus, user experience.

The above optimization can be formulated as follows:

$$maximize_{x_{ij} \in \{0,1\}} \quad \sum_{i=1}^{N} \sum_{j=1}^{M_i} u_{ij} x_{ij} \qquad (1)$$

$$\text{subject to} \quad \sum_{j=1}^{M_i} x_{ij} = 1, \forall i$$

$$\sum_{i=1}^{N} \sum_{j=1}^{M_i} c_{ij} x_{ij} \leq B,$$

Here, the indicator variable x_{ij} is 1 if version j of image i is selected, and 0 otherwise. u_{ij} and c_{ij} are the utility and cost, respectively, associated with version j of image i.

The transformation selection problem as formulated in Equation 1 maps to the Multi-Choice Knapsack Problem (MCKP). The time budget is the size of the knapsack, and the goal is to fill in objects (images) such that the total utility of the objects in the knapsack is maximized. However, in our case, a client's requests for objects are made online, i.e., the middlebox does not have a priori knowledge of future image requests since the objects are dynamically fetched. Thus, we need an online algorithm for solving the MCKP problem.

The online MCKP problem is well studied. Competitive online algorithms have been proposed [23] with the relaxed constraint $\sum_{j=1}^{M} x_{ij} \leq 1$ for all i, i.e., the algorithm need not to choose a version for each image (image can also be discarded). We modify the relaxed online MCKP algorithm designed by Zhou et al. [23] for solving our problem. Specifically, (i) we do not allow for the discarding of images and (ii) we modify the time budget dynamically to account for time spent either due to transfer of other content (e.g., compressed Javascripts or text) or inactivity due to waiting for objects. However, these uncertainties can cause us to exceed the original target time budget. Thus, our modified goal is to try and stay within the budget, but if we are to exceed it, to do so to the minimum extent possible.

Now, the online transformation selection problem 1 can be transformed into the following relaxed problem with the inequality constraints shown; if an online algorithm for the relaxed problem has competitive ratio C (the performance of the algorithm w.r.t the optimal), then, so does the original problem in Equation 1.

$$maximize_{x_{ij} \in \{0,1\}} \quad \sum_{i=1}^{N} \sum_{j=1}^{M_i} u'_{ij} x_{ij} \qquad (2)$$

$$\text{subject to} \quad \sum_{j=1}^{M_i} x_{ij} = 1, \forall i$$

$$\sum_{i=1}^{N} \sum_{j=1}^{M_i} c'_{ij} x_{ij} \leq B,$$

In the above formulation, the key idea is to subtract the utility and cost of the cheapest transformation of each image from other transformations of the same image, and use these *modified* utilities u' and costs c' as the new representations associated with the corresponding transformations. If the relaxed problem does not choose a transformation, in our case we default to the cheapest transformation. The reader is referred to [24] for the proof of the above claim.

The algorithm provides a competitive ratio of $log(\frac{U'}{L'})+1$, where the utility to cost ratio of the transformations are upper and lower

Algorithm 1 Online selection of best image transformations

1: **Initialize:** $b = 0$, Q (QoE level)
2: **Event:** Image i requested at time t_i
3: **if** $Q \leftarrow auto$ **then**
4: $\quad M_i \leftarrow M_i$
5: **else**
6: $\quad$ **if** $Q \in \{1, 2, 3, 4, 5\}$ **then**
7: $\quad\quad M_i \leftarrow M_i - Q$, by removing the lower Q transformations
8: $\quad$ **end if**
9: **end if**
10: **for** $j = 1 \rightarrow M_i$ **do**
11: $\quad u'_{ij} \leftarrow u_{ij} - u_{i1}$
12: $\quad c'_{ij} \leftarrow c_{ij} - ci1$
13: **end for**
14: $transformations \leftarrow \{j|\frac{u'_{ij}}{c'_{ij}} \geq \phi(b, B)\}$
15: **if** $transformations$ is not empty **then**
16: $\quad J \leftarrow \arg\max_j\{u'_{ij}|j \in transformations\}$
17: $\quad$ **if** $b + c'_{ij} \leq B$ **then**
18: $\quad\quad selectedTransform \leftarrow J$
19: $\quad$ **else**
20: $\quad\quad selectedTransform \leftarrow 1$
21: $\quad$ **end if**
22: **else**
23: $\quad selectedTransform \leftarrow 1$
24: **end if**
25: Deliver transformation $selectedTransform$
26: **if** time $t_i \geq b$ **then**
27: $\quad b \leftarrow t_i + c'_{i,selectedTransform}$
28: **else**
29: $\quad b \leftarrow b + c'_{i,selectedTransform}$
30: **end if**

bounded by U' and L', respectively. Zhou et al. also assume that all transformed versions are much smaller in size than the knapsack, which is true of objects on a web page (each image is transferred in a time $<< B$).

Algorithm 1 presents our approach to modifying and using Zhou et al.'s solution to our problem of selecting the appropriate transformations of images at the FlexiWeb proxy. The intuition behind the algorithm is as follows. We only want to pick image transformations that have a sufficiently high utility to cost ratio, i.e., ones that satisfy a certain efficiency threshold. As we spend more budget, this threshold should increase (in other words, the cost for transferring objects later in the page load should decrease). This efficiency threshold is captured by a function $\phi(b(t), B) = (\frac{U}{L})^{\frac{b(t)}{B}} \frac{L}{e}$, where $b(t)$ is the amount of the budget spent at time t.[2] $\phi(b(t), B)$ increases with $\frac{b(t)}{B}$, the fraction of the knapsack filled at time t. Therefore, as time progresses, fewer transformations satisfy the efficiency condition.

Referring to Algorithm 1, the proxy first initializes the current usage b to 0. Then, the transformations $u_{ij} \longrightarrow u'_{ij}$ and $c_{ij} \longrightarrow c'_{ij}$, are performed. The proxy then considers the set of transformations that have a utility-to-cost ratio that is higher than $\phi(b, B)$. It chooses the transformation that has the maximum utility and fits within the budget; otherwise (i.e., if none fit within the budget), it chooses the cheapest transformation. At the end of each step (i.e., after an image is transformed and sent to the client), the proxy updates b with the cost of the selected transformation. The current budget usage is updated after the selection of a transformation. In case of inactive time periods (because of waiting for objects) an increase in knapsack usage is applied (lines 19-22 in Algorithm 1).

[2]We perform a one time estimation of U and L offline, using a training set of images.

Whenever static compression is applied to objects such as JS, CSS etc., we again apply an increase in knapsack usage (as with inactivity periods). If the target budget is exceeded, then the middlebox simply performs the cheapest transformation on each image, prior to sending it to the client. Note here that we simply subtract an object's cost from the budget, despite the client fetching multiple objects on a page in parallel, because we consider bandwidth to be the bottleneck between the client and the proxy.

QoE vs. page load latency: While transforming content, it is important to ensure that web browsing has a good, associated Quality-of-Experience (QoE). While transformations reduce delays, they must still cater to a user's or a web provider's requirements in terms of quality (e.g., a user may not want gray scale transformations). Hence, users or web providers can set a minimum quality limit either via browser settings or via metadata embedded in a web page's HTML; this sets the maximum allowable compression level (QoE level) allowed on each object in a web page. The QoE level is set to an auto mode by default. In this mode, all possible (M_i) transformations are considered (when applying Algorithm 1). Instead of the auto mode, the user or the provider can specify a QoE level from 1 to 5. If QoE level 1 is chosen, Algorithm 1 can use $M_i - 1$ transformations; the the lowest quality transformation is left out. If a QoE level of 5 is chosen, Algorithm 1 can only apply a single transformation, viz., the one that performs the minimum compression and retains the highest quality (WebP with 85% quality). Note that the higher the level of QoE chosen, the larger could be the deviation (increase) with respect to a desired page load time. At this time, FlexiWeb chooses the higher of the QoE levels specified by the user and the provider.

4 Implementation and Setup

In this section, we first describe our implementation; subsequently we elaborate on our experimental setup.

4.1 Implementation of FlexiWeb

Client side implementation: We modify Google's Chromium 38.0.2125.50, an open source Android browser to implement the client side modules of FlexiWeb. Specifically, we make changes to the $url\_request$ module in Chromium to 1) determine whether or not to go through the proxy, for each object, and 2) to predict the size of any object based on its URL. We also modify Chromium to store network measurements in the browser cache after retrieving them from the HTTP request response header sent by the proxy. For each web page, the request for the main HTML file always goes through the compression proxy; this allows the proxy to gather accurate network condition estimates (RTT and throughput). These estimates are returned to the client in a custom field in the HTTP response (sent by the proxy). The estimates stay valid for 15 seconds, and if no object is fetched via the proxy by then, the client sends the immediately following request via the proxy. Based on an object's size and the current network conditions (stored in the browser), our modified version of Chromium chooses between retrieving the object via a proxy or directly from the source.

Proxy side implementation: We configure the compression proxy with 4GB memory and 2.40 GHz Intel Core 2 CPU, running Ubuntu 12.04. It is implemented using Google's mod_pagespeed-1.8.31.4 module running on top of an Apache 2.2 web server. TCP CUBIC is used. The Apache web server runs in the forward proxy mode. All the requests pass through mod_pagespeed module before content is compressed. We implement the passive RTT, throughput and loss rate estimation scheme described in [22] as a kernel module; the estimated values are exposed using the Linux socket interface, to other programs and modules. Specifically, these values are used by the network aware compression module to calculate the cost of a transformation. We implement the network-aware compression module by modifying the mod_pagespeed's image transformation module to invoke network-aware compression (using Algorithm 1) instead of static compression. To report the network conditions to the client, we implement an Apache module to control and modify the HTTP response headers. This Apache module reads the current RTT, loss rate and throughput values and adds them to every out going response to the client using the previously discussed custom header field.

4.2 Experimental Setup

Scenarios for evaluation: We have three different scenarios in which we evaluate FlexiWeb.

Controlled settings: To reduce variability and control network conditions, we tethered our client phone to a laptop using a USB connection and applied traffic shaping to the tethered connection using Dummynet [25]. We emulated a 4G network with an uplink bandwidth of 1 Mbps [26] and with varying downlink bandwidths shown in Table 1.

An automated script was used to change the values of the link bandwidth, the loss rate and RTT for every test case.

Static clients on cellular networks: To evaluate FlexiWeb on real cellular networks, we use AT&T and T-Mobile's 4G network connections. To create different network conditions we run experiments at the same locations that we used to gather our measurements in Section 2. Due to space constraints, we only present results from AT & T's network except in some sample cases.

Mobile scenarios: Finally, we also evaluate FlexiWeb in mobile scenarios. We choose around 20 paths in two US metropolitan areas in two states with a mix of local streets and Interstate highways. Our speeds on interstate highways were around 65 miles per hour while on city streets our speeds were 30-40 miles per hour. We omit the exact details of the paths to preserve anonymity.

Web pages requested: We use the top 500 web sites visited by mobile users to run our tests (the top Alexa sites). These have a good mix of news websites, online shopping and auction sites as well as professionally developed websites of large corporations. These websites contain anywhere from 5 to 323 objects. The objects in these sites were spread across 3 to 84 domains. Each web site had HTML pages, Javascript objects, CSS and images. Due to experimentation constraints (time), the experimental results reported for mobile scenarios are only using the top 50 web pages.

Execution: We setup 2 rooted mobile devices (HTC One phones with Android 4.3) running Chromium (with our modifications) for Android. We generated a random order in which to visit the web sites and used that same order across all experiments. The period between website requests was set to 60 seconds both to allow for websites to load completely, and to reflect a nominal think time that users typically indulge in between requests. If the web page took a much shorter time to load, the system was idle until the 60 second window elapsed. We used the "page load time" as the primary metric of performance. We alternated our test runs between "Direct", "Compression Proxy" and "FlexiWeb" to ensure that temporal factors did not affect our results. With Direct, requests are directly sent to the source web server. With Compression proxy, all the requests are sent to a proxy with static compression settings where images are transformed to WebP with a quality of 75% (this is what is done with commercial proxies today [27] to achieve some compression without compromising the quality significantly). We ran each experiment multiple times at different times during the day.

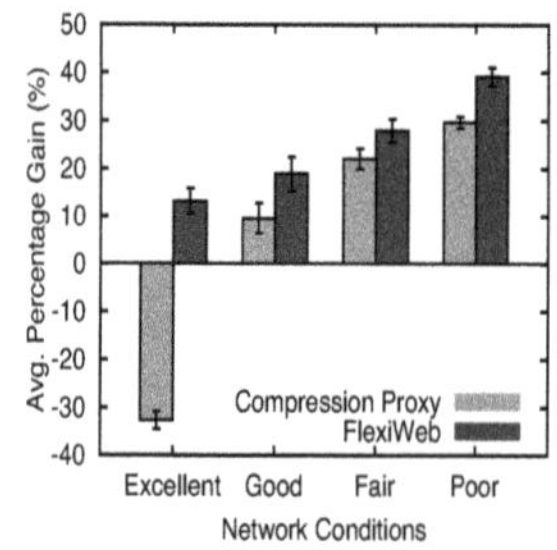

(a)

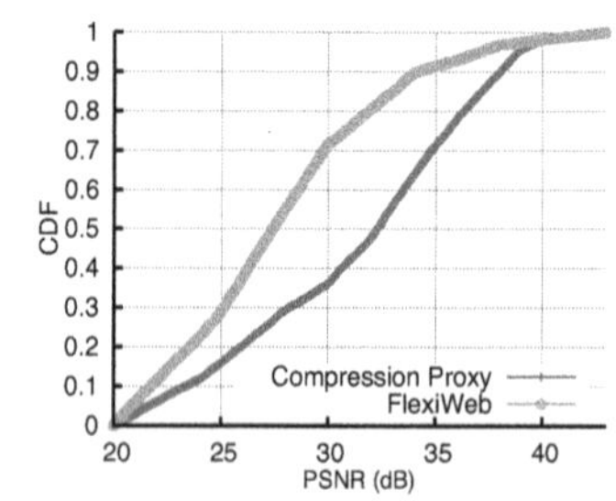

(b)

Figure 7 : (a) Performance gains with FlexiWeb (b) PSNR of transformed images

5 Evaluation of FlexiWeb

We evaluate FlexiWeb extensively, in each of the scenarios described in Section 4, and discuss the results below.

Performance of FlexiWeb in controlled settings: We first evaluate FlexiWeb in the controlled network settings listed in Table 1. We calculate the percentage gains relative to the direct scheme (no proxy) for both (i) FlexiWeb and (ii) compression proxy based browsing. Figure 7a shows the average percentage gains in page load times under different network conditions. The results, shown in Figure 7a, indicate that the compression proxy degrades the performance in terms of page load times, by up to 32% as compared to direct browsing in excellent network conditions (also seen earlier). As network conditions degrade, the compression proxy outperforms direct browsing; in all other settings the reduction in object sizes (from compression) outweigh the latency overheads of longer routes and processing. We see that FlexiWeb outperforms compression proxy based browsing by up to 45% in excellent network conditions. FlexiWeb significantly gains from sending requests for small objects directly to the web server; it thereby avoids the latency overheads incurred in retrieving such objects via the proxy. FlexiWeb still downloads the large objects via the proxy, but after performing network-aware compression (large objects benefit from compression). As network conditions deteriorate, the performance gains with FlexiWeb in comparison to compression proxy based browsing diminish (only about 10 %). This is because the gains due to compression now increase and almost all objects are now retrieved via the proxy; FlexiWeb outperforms the compression based proxy here, mainly due to network-aware compression.

Next, we present the PSNR values of the transformed images with FlexiWeb and the traditional compression proxy. Figure 7b shows that the average degradation of PSNR using FlexiWeb is only $\approx$ 4 dB in comparison to compression proxy; this is in spite of FlexiWeb performing more aggressive compression during poor network conditions.

How does FlexiWeb provide performance gains?: Next, we examine the gains from the two main functions performed by FlexiWeb i.e., request splitting and network-aware compression. We analyze the web page download traces and separate the objects into those retrieved directly from the source web server and those via the proxy. We measure the gain with respect to each object's load time due to each function, in comparison to the load time of the object when fetched directly from the server. We then calculate the average gain across all objects fetched, with respect to each function. From Figure 8a, we see that in excellent and good network conditions the gains are primarily due to objects being fetched directly from the source web server; in excellent conditions, almost 70% of the gains are due to this. As network conditions degrade

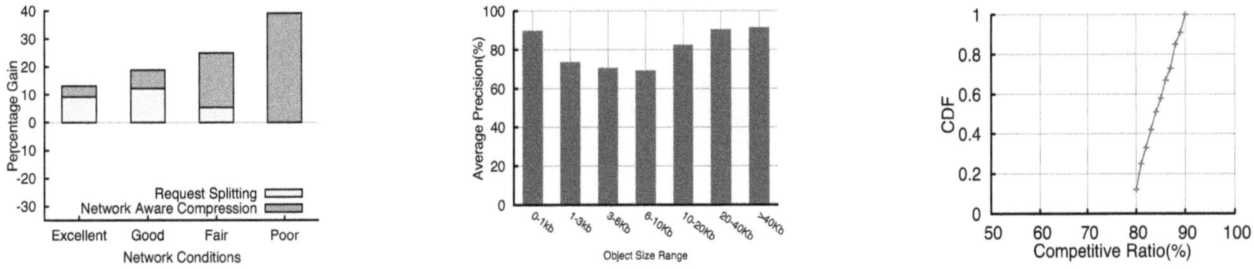

(a) (b) (c)

Figure 8 : (a) Impact of request splitting and network aware compression on FlexiWeb's gains (b) Precision in predicting object sizes (c) Competitive analysis of online MCKP

the number of objects fetched via the proxy increases and the gains due to network-aware compression dominate. Since in poor network conditions, FlexiWeb fetches all objects via the proxy, all the gains are due to network-aware compression.

Accuracy of object size predictions: Next, we evaluate the accuracy with which FlexiWeb predicts the size of objects. We use the data collected at the proxy as described in Section 3. We use the 10 fold cross validation method [28]. We divide our dataset into two parts: a training set that contains 30% of the dataset, and a test set that contains the remaining 70%. We train our model using the training set and later perform prediction on the remainder (70 %) of the data which was held out. For the purposes of evaluation, we use the *precision criterion* [29], which determines the fraction of records that are correctly classified from among those that that are grouped under a classification. Specifically,

$$Precision(\%) = \left(\frac{TruePositive}{TruePositive + FalsePositive}\right) \times 100.$$

Figure 8b shows that the accuracy of predicting the size of objects based on the URL text is quite high. We can predict objects of size 0 to 1 KB and objects larger than 20 KB with more than 90% accuracy. We can predict other object sizes with at least 70% accuracy. Note that an inaccurate prediction simply causes FlexiWeb to fetch the object sub-optimally (directly instead of via the proxy or vice versa). Thus, while it slightly causes a degradation in FlexiWeb's performance, it does not disrupt the web browsing process. Note here that our prediction has high accuracy because we only seek to predict "the" range into which an object's size falls, and not the object's precise size.

Quantifying the sub-optimality of network-aware compression: For network-aware compression, we use the modified online MCKP algorithm shown in Algorithm 1. To illustrate the difficulty of the online transformation selection problem, consider an end user with a time budget of 5 seconds to download a page. Let the download of version j of image i be represented by a utility-cost pair (u_{ij}, c_{ij}), where u_{ij} is the utility (e.g., PSNR or negative distortion) and c_{ij} is the cost. Suppose the first image has two possible versions with utility-cost pairs (1,1), (2,2), and the second image also has two versions with utility-cost pairs (2,1),(4,2). If the user requests for both the images sequentially, then the optimal (offline) solution is to choose the stream (1,1) followed by (4, 2). This gives a total utility of 5 with a total cost of 3. However, an online transformation selection algorithm must first choose a stream from $(1,1),(2,2)$, without knowledge of the subsequent request. Our online MCKP algorithm is likely to choose the transformation (2, 2) followed by (2, 1), resulting in sub-optimal utility.

Here, we seek to quantify the sub optimality of Algorithm 1. We select 100 web pages from the Alexa's top 500 web pages with varied number and sizes of the objects. We first download the pages using a modified version of MCKP, called OPT-MCKP. OPT-MCKP [30] is an offline version of MCKP, where the object requests are known in advance. With this information OPT-MCKP can always choose the right transformation. We repeat the same experiment using our ON-MCKP algorithm (Algorithm 1) . A popular way to evaluate online algorithms is using what is called the "Competitive Ratio" [31]. The competitive ratio of an online algorithm for an optimization problem is simply the ratio between the cost of the solution found by the algorithm and the cost of an optimal solution. Figure 8c shows the CDFs of Competitive ratio (converted to percentage) across the 100 pages; we see that 80% of the time, the page load times with ON-MCKP are within 10%-20% of that with OPT-MCKP.

Number of objects and web pages downloaded within a time budget: Next we evaluate FlexiWeb in terms of number of objects retrieved within a specified time budget of 5 seconds. We compare the number of requests satisfied by FlexiWeb in comparison with conventional compression proxy based browsing. Figure 9a depicts the CDF of the percentage of additional objects retrieved by FlexiWeb as compared to conventional compression proxy based browsing; we see that FlexiWeb fetches 17% more objects on average, within the same time budget. FlexiWeb achieves this by fetching small objects directly from the web server in excellent and good network conditions; the decrease in per-object download times allow the downloading of more objects within the page load time budget. Even in bad network conditions FlexiWeb fetches 1-2% more objects on an average than conventional compression proxy based browsing, but mainly due to network aware compression. An increase in number of additional fetched objects also translates to an increase in the number of web pages downloaded in the target budget. Figure 9b shows the CDF of page down load times of web pages using regular compression proxy and FlexiWeb. We see that FlexiWeb can download about 19% more web pages on average, within a target budget of 5 seconds.

Evaluations on AT &T and T-Mobile's networks: We evaluate FlexiWeb on real cellular networks to show that the gains seen in controlled settings also exist in real cases. From Figure 9c and 9d we see that FlexiWeb outperforms conventional compression proxy based browsing in excellent network conditions (by up to 38% with T-Mobile and 37 % with AT & T) In poor conditions it out performs the latter by up to 6% with T-Mobile and 2 % with AT & T. The gains are in between for other network conditions.

Scenarios with mobility: Next, we seek to evaluate FlexiWeb in scenarios where a passenger accesses web pages while in a mov-

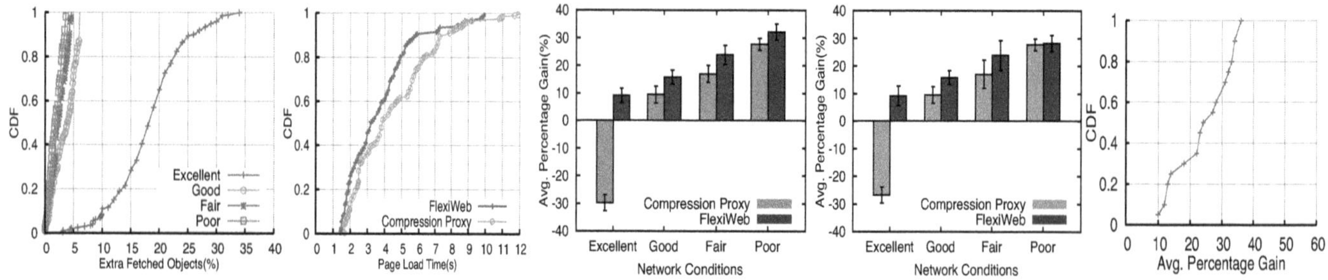

(a) (b) (c) (d) (e)

Figure 9 : (a) Percentage of extra fetched objects in a time budget of 5 seconds (b) Gains in page load times (c) Performance of FlexiWeb on T-Mobile's network (d) Performance of FlexiWeb on AT&T's network (e) Gains with FlexiWeb in mobile settings

ing car. We choose 20 different paths to capture typical scenarios: (i) driving on a highway at high speeds and (ii) driving around in a city at moderate speeds. We used two mobile devices (both HTC One phones) connected to two laptops via USB, one downloading web pages via a conventional compression proxy while the other does so using FlexiWeb. We choose to download Alexa's top 50 web pages for this experiment. Both the devices are connected to AT & T's network. In addition to page load times we also keep track of signal strengths at both the devices. We start the experiments on both the phones at almost the same time to avoid variations in network conditions. We measure the average percentage gains with FlexiWeb while downloading all the web pages. In Figure 9e, we plot the CDF of this average percentage gain over all the webpages downloaded on the different paths; we see that 80% of the time, FlexiWeb provides an average percentage gain of 34 % over compression proxy based browsing, in terms of page load times. In 20% of the cases, it only provides 14% gains. Upon closer inspection, we found that some paths were experiencing excellent to good signal strength throughout while others were experiencing low signal strengths much more often than good signal strengths. It is well known that excellent/good signal strength is highly correlated with good network conditions (low RTT and loss rates, high throughputs) while the opposite is true with low/poor signal strength [32]. In excellent/good network conditions FlexiWeb significantly outperformed conventional compression proxy based browsing (since FlexiWeb retrieved most objects in the web pages directly and only few large objects via the proxy). On paths where network conditions were bad, both the conventional compression proxy based browser and FlexiWeb, fetched almost all objects via the proxy. FlexiWeb outperformed conventional compression proxy based browsing because of its network-aware compression module.

6 Related Work

Measurement studies: There is prior work on characterizing the properties of web pages, and protocols that impact mobile web browsing. The study in [33] shows that optimization of compute intensive tasks at proxies only offers marginal gains. In [34], the complexity of web sites is studied via browser-based active measurements. Other studies have evaluated the benefits of existing mechanisms for improving mobile web performance. Erman et al. [35] showed that SPDY [36], a recently proposed alternative to HTTP, does not clearly outperform HTTP over cellular networks. They identify the disharmony between TCP and cellular networks as the underlying cause. Similarly, Sivakumar et al. [37] showed that proxy-assisted thin client browsers, such as Amazon Silk [6], do not provide clear benefits in terms of page load time and energy. None of these efforts study the implications of using `Proxy Assisted` mobile web browsing in different network conditions, as we do here.

Client-based solutions: Client-side solutions have been proposed to improve mobile web performance. WebSieve [38] generates mobile-friendly websites from the original desktop versions. Zoomm [39] speeds up web page loads by parallelizing the execution of dynamic components of any web page. Adrenaline [40] parallelizes the fetching of web pages by decomposing existing web pages on the fly into loosely coupled mini pages, and loading mini pages in parallel via separate processes.

User studies: Lymberopoulos et al.'s user study [41] shows that mobile web browsing exhibits a strong spatio-temporal signature, different for every user. Based on this study, they propose a machine learning based model to accurately predict future web accesses for a user, and they use this prediction to prefetch content in a timely manner. Wang et al. [42] show that caching and prefetching provide very limited benefits for mobile web browsing, but speculative loading can decrease page load times by up to 20%.

Unlike FlexiWeb, none of the above approaches consider modifying web clients to dynamically select when to use proxies for data compaction.

Proxy-based solutions: Due to the computation and bandwidth limitations on mobile devices, researchers have proposed to offload various types of functionality from client devices to proxies. For example, Zhao et al. [3] offload execution of dynamic content to the proxy, while Cho et al. [43] propose the delegation of DNS lookups and TCP connection establishment to the proxy. Chava et al. [44] try to reduce the usage cost incurred by the end-user by computing a cost quota for each web request, and having a proxy adapt the web page accordingly. The cost quota for each web request is dynamically calculated based on the pricing plan of the user and her current data usage levels. Recently, Google [13] and Nokia [45] have incorporated data compression proxies in their mobile web browsers; these proxies (hosted in data centers) are expected to reduce cellular data usage and speed up mobile web browsing. Wang et al. [2] propose a framework that allows the execution of "any" portion of the page load process in the cloud (unlike browsers such as Opera Mini that only allow fixed parts to be executed in the cloud).

None of these proxy-based solutions are network-aware. While some of the proprietary solutions are not documented, to our knowledge, all existing systems always fetch content via the proxy, unlike FlexiWeb; further, they apply the same content compression irrespective of network conditions.

7 Conclusions

In this paper, we argue based on an in-depth measurement study that always using cloud-based middleboxes to assist mobile browsing can be detrimental to performance in terms of web page download times. Our measurements reveal that the middlebox should be used only when network conditions are bad; otherwise, most objects in the web page should be directly fetched from the source web server. Based on this observation we build FlexiWeb, a framework that supports network-aware middlebox usage. In addition, FlexiWeb also performs dynamic network-aware compression to provide further performance gains. We demonstrate via extensive experiments that FlexiWeb outperforms conventional compression proxy based browsing by decreasing page load times by as much as 42 %, on average.

8 Acknowledgments

This work was sponsored by the Army Research Laboratory and was accomplished under Cooperative Agreement Number W911NF- 09-2-0053. The views and conclusions contained in this document are those of the authors and should not be interpreted as representing the official policies, either expressed or implied, of the Army Research Laboratory or the U.S. Government. The U.S. Government is authorized to reproduce and distribute reprints for Government purposes notwithstanding any copyright notation here on. We would like to thank our anonymous shepherd, for her/his constructive comments and guidance through the camera ready submission process.

9 References

[1] [Online]. Available: http://bit.ly/1sgDfJ1

[2] X. S. Wang, H. Shen, and D. Wetherall, "Accelerating the mobile web with selective offloading," in *Proceedings of the Second ACM SIGCOMM Workshop on Mobile Cloud Computing*, ser. MCC '13. New York, NY, USA: ACM, 2013, pp. 45–50. [Online]. Available: http://doi.acm.org/10.1145/2491266.2491275

[3] B. Zhao, B. C. Tak, and G. Cao, "Reducing the delay and power consumption of web browsing on smartphones in 3g networks," in *Distributed Computing Systems (ICDCS), 2011 31st International Conference on*, 2011.

[4] K. Matsudaira, "Making the mobile web faster," *Commun. ACM*, 2013.

[5] [Online]. Available: http://www.opera.com/turbo

[6] [Online]. Available: http://docs.aws.amazon.com/silk/latest/developerguide/split-arch.html

[7] [Online]. Available: https://developers.google.com/chrome/mobile/docs/data-compression

[8] J. Nielsen, *Usability Engineering*. Morgan Kaufmann, 1993.

[9] K. Zarifis, T. Flach, S. Nori, D. Choffnes, R. Govindan, E. Katz-Bassett, Z. M. Mao, and M. Welsh, "Diagnosing Path Inflation of Mobile Client Traffic," in *Passive and Active Measurement Conference (PAM '14)*, March 2014.

[10] [Online]. Available: http://info.iet.unipi.it/~luigi/dummynet/

[11] [Online]. Available: https://blog.kissmetrics.com/loading-time/?wide=1

[12] [Online]. Available: https://httpd.apache.org/docs/2.0/mod/mod_proxy.html#forwardreverse

[13] [Online]. Available: https://developers.google.com/speed/articles/spdy-for-mobile

[14] X. Xu, Y. Jiang, T. Flach, E. Katz-Bassett, D. Choffnes, and R. Govindan, "Investigating transparent web proxies in cellular networks," in *Technical report 14-944, University of Southern California*. USC, 2014.

[15] [Online]. Available: https://www.igvita.com/2013/03/07/faster-smaller-and-more-beautiful-web-with-webp/

[16] [Online]. Available: http://httparchive.org

[17] [Online]. Available: http://www.w3.org/Protocols/rfc2616/rfc2616-sec9.html

[18] T. M. Mitchell, *Machine Learning*. McGraw-Hill, Inc., 1997.

[19] R. A. Berk, *Statistical Learning from a Regression Perspective*. Springer, 2008.

[20] J. MOGUL and L. BRAKMO, *Method for dynamically adjusting multimedia content of a web page by a server in accordance to network path characteristics between client and server*. U.S. Patent 6,243,761, 2001.

[21] [Online]. Available: https://developers.google.com/web/fundamentals/performance/optimizing-content-efficiency/optimize-encoding-and-transfer

[22] M. Mathis, J. Semke, J. Mahdavi, and T. Ott, "The macroscopic behavior of the tcp congestion avoidance algorithm," *SIGCOMM Comput. Commun. Rev.*, 1997.

[23] Y. Zhou, D. Chakrabarty, and R. M. Lukose, "Budget constrained bidding in keyword auctions and online knapsack problems," in *Proceedings of the 17th International Conference on World Wide Web, WWW 2008, Beijing, China, April 21-25, 2008*, 2008.

[24] A. G. Jiasi Chen and M. Chiang, "Qava: Quota aware video adaptation technical report," Department of Electrical Engineering Princeton University, Princeton NJ, USA, Tech. Rep., 2012.

[25] [Online]. Available: http://info.iet.unipi.it/~luigi/dummynet/

[26] J. Huang, F. Qian, A. Gerber, Z. M. Mao, S. Sen, and O. Spatscheck, "A close examination of performance and power characteristics of 4g lte networks," in *Proceedings of the 10th International Conference on Mobile Systems, Applications, and Services*, ser. MobiSys '12. ACM, 2012.

[27] [Online]. Available: https://developers.google.com/speed/pagespeed/module/install

[28] [Online]. Available: http://scikit-learn.org/stable/modules/cross_validation.html

[29] D. M. W. Powers, "Evaluation: From Precision, Recall and F-Factor to ROC, Informedness, Markedness & Correlation," Tech. Rep., 2007.

[30] H. Kellerer, U. Pferschy, and D. Pisinger, *Knapsack Problems*. Springer, Berlin, Germany, 2004.

[31] S. M. LaValle, *Planning Algorithms*, 2006.

[32] Q. Xiao, K. Xu, D. Wang, L. Li, and Y. Zhong, "Concise paper: Tcp performance over mobile networks in high-speed mobility scenarios," *IEEE ICNP*, 2014.

[33] Z. Wang, F. X. Lin, L. Zhong, and M. Chishtie, "Why are web browsers slow on smartphones?" in *Proceedings of the 12th Workshop on Mobile Computing Systems and Applications*, ser. HotMobile '11. New York, NY, USA: ACM, 2011. [Online]. Available: http://doi.acm.org/10.1145/2184489.2184508

[34] M. Butkiewicz, H. V. Madhyastha, and V. Sekar, "Understanding website complexity: Measurements, metrics, and implications," in *Proceedings of the 2011 ACM SIGCOMM Conference on Internet Measurement Conference*, ser. IMC '11. New York, NY, USA: ACM, 2011, pp. 313–328. [Online]. Available: http://doi.acm.org/10.1145/2068816.2068846

[35] J. Erman, V. Gopalakrishnan, R. Jana, and K. K. Ramakrishnan, "Towards a spdy'ier mobile web?" in *Proceedings of the Ninth ACM Conference on Emerging Networking Experiments and Technologies*, ser. CoNEXT '13. New York, NY, USA: ACM, 2013, pp. 303–314. [Online]. Available: http://doi.acm.org/10.1145/2535372.2535399

[36] [Online]. Available: http://www.chromium.org/spdy/spdy-whitepaper

[37] A. Sivakumar, V. Gopalakrishnan, S. Lee, S. G. Rao, S. Sen, and O. Spatscheck, "Cloud is not a silver bullet: a case study of cloud-based mobile browsing," in *15th Workshop on Mobile Computing Systems and Applications, HotMobile '14, Santa Barbara, CA, USA, February 26-27, 2014*, 2014.

[38] M. Butkiewicz, Z. Wu, S. Li, P. Murali, V. Hristidis, H. V. Madhyastha, and V. Sekar, "Enabling the transition to the mobile web with websieve," in *Proceedings of the 14th Workshop on Mobile Computing Systems and Applications*, ser. HotMobile '13. ACM, 2013. [Online]. Available: http://doi.acm.org/10.1145/2444776.2444795

[39] C. Cascaval, S. Fowler, P. Montesinos-Ortego, W. Piekarski, M. Reshadi, B. Robatmili, M. Weber, and V. Bhavsar, "Zoomm: A parallel web browser engine for multicore mobile devices," in *Proceedings of the 18th ACM SIGPLAN Symposium on Principles and Practice of Parallel Programming*, ser. PPoPP '13. New York,

NY, USA: ACM, 2013, pp. 271–280. [Online]. Available: http://doi.acm.org/10.1145/2442516.2442543

[40] H. Mai, S. Tang, S. T. King, C. Cascaval, and P. Montesinos, “A case for parallelizing web pages,” in *Proceedings of the 4th USENIX Conference on Hot Topics in Parallelism*, ser. HotPar'12. Berkeley, CA, USA: USENIX Association, 2012, pp. 2–2. [Online]. Available: http://dl.acm.org/citation.cfm?id=2342788.2342790

[41] D. Lymberopoulos, O. Riva, K. Strauss, A. Mittal, and A. Ntoulas, “Pocketweb: Instant web browsing for mobile devices,” in *Proceedings of the Seventeenth International Conference on Architectural Support for Programming Languages and Operating Systems*, ser. ASPLOS XVII. New York, NY, USA: ACM, 2012, pp. 1–12. [Online]. Available: http://doi.acm.org/10.1145/2150976.2150978

[42] Z. Wang, F. X. Lin, L. Zhong, and M. Chishtie, “How far can client-only solutions go for mobile browser speed?” in *Proceedings of the 21st International Conference on World Wide Web*, ser. WWW '12. New York, NY, USA: ACM, 2012, pp. 31–40. [Online]. Available: http://doi.acm.org/10.1145/2187836.2187842

[43] J. Cho, J. Jeong, and E. Seo, “Twob: A two-tier web browser architecture optimized for mobile network,” in *Proceedings of the 10th International Conference on Advances in Mobile Computing & Multimedia*, ser. MoMM '12. New York, NY, USA: ACM, 2012, pp. 267–270. [Online]. Available: http://doi.acm.org/10.1145/2428955.2429006

[44] S. Chava, R. Ennaji, J. Chen, and L. Subramanian, “Cost-aware mobile web browsing,” *Pervasive Computing, IEEE*, vol. 11, no. 3, pp. 34–42, 2012.

[45] [Online]. Available: http://developer.nokia.com/Develop/Series_40/Nokia_Browser_for_Series_40/

Author Index

Aguiar, Ana 168
Aguiar, Rui 550
Ali, Kamran 90
An, Chuankai 331
Anttila, Tuikku 236
Baerts, Matthieu 230
Bahl, Paramvir 173, 257, 426
Banerjee, Suman 358, 426
Baron, Loïc 199
Barros, João 168
Bayou, Rémy 486
Benhabiles, Nora 550
Bo, Cheng 372
Bonaventure, Olivier 230
Bonnet, Christian 193
Boubekeur, Fadwa 199
Braun, Torsten 193
Buchmann, Alejandro 248
Bui, Duc Hoang 14
Bujari, Armir 212
Cai, Lin 287
Calcada, Tania 168
Campbell, Andrew T. 278, 331
Capdevielle, Veronique 233
Carvalho, Miguel Almeida 245
Casas, Pedro 263
Chae, Chan-Byoung 201
Chai, Eugene 304
Chan, Justin 227
Chang, Liqiong 242
Chaurasia, Avinash 196
Chen, Bo 566
Chen, Chung Shue 233
Chen, Jiming 512
Chen, Qi Alfred 452
Chen, Xiaojiang .. 40, 221, 242, 287
Chen, Yingying 142
Chowdhery, Aakanksha 426
Chung, Albert Y. 275
Condeixa, Tiago 168
Costa Molero, Edgar 254
Crowcroft, Jon 182
Cui, Yong 592
Dai, Ningwei 592
De Coninck, Quentin 230
Ding, Aaron Yi 182
Ding, Ning 40
Dou, Yanzhi 218
Droescher, Andreas 251
Duquennoy, Simon 251
Eckford, Andrew 201
Elmalaki, Salma 386
Fan, Yue 272
Fang, Dingyi 221, 242, 287
Farsad, Nariman 201
Fdida, Serge 173, 199
Ferrari, Alan 215
Flinck, Hannu 182
Foremski, Paweł 190
Friedman, Timur 199
Frömmgen, Alexander 248
Gallais, Antoine 207
Ganesan, Deepak 400
Gauthier, Lionel 193
Ge, Zihui 464
Giordano, Silvia 215
Giustiniano, Domenico 180
Gjoka, Minas 170
Gnawali, Omprakash 180
Govindan, Ramesh 604
Gowda, Mahanth 210
Grapinet, Gilles 1
Grassi, Giulio 173, 257
Grochla, Krzysztof 190
Gross, Thomas 254
Gruteser, Marco 142
Guimarães, Diogo 168
Guo, Lei 477
Gupta, Maruti 40
Haddad, Majed 233
Halbower, Ann C. 266
Hänninen, Tuomo 188
Harter, Gaetan 176
He, Songtao 27, 185
He, Tian 317, 512
Herculea, Dalia-Georgiana 233
Hesmans, Benjamin 230
Hithnawi, Anwar 251
Hoque, Mohammad A. 236, 239
Hou, Jiahui 372
Hu, Pan 400
Hu, Wen 251
Hu, Yu Charlie 40
Hui, Jie 452
Irmer, Ralf 263
Jain, Puneet 260
Jamieson, Kyle .. 257, 291, 426, 537
Janecek, Dan 358
Javed, Abeer 578
Jia, Yunhan Jack 452
Jiang, Hongbo 221
Jin, Meng 287
Jin, Naigao 269
Jindal, Abhilash 40
Jung, Jongtack 275
Kabelac, Zachary 2
Kaltenberger, Florian 193
Kang, Lei 358
Kar, Gorkem 142
Katabi, Dina 2
Khojastepour, Amir 304
Kim, Hwangnam 275
Kim, Hyosu 14
Kim, Kangho 275
Kim, Kyu-Han 77
Kim, Na-Rae 201
Kim, Song Min 317

Klacza, Radomir 199
Klein, Anja 248
Knight, Joseph 477
Knopp, Raymond 193
Kong, Linghe 552
Koo, Bonhong 201
Koutsonikolas, Dimitrios 77
Kriara, Lito 254
Krishnamurthy, Srikanth V. 604
Kumar, Swarun 413
Kurose, James 290
Kurose, Nina 199
Kwong, Samson 452
Lagerspetz, Eemil 239
Lai, Ted Tsung-Te 156
Lai, Zeqi 592
Langhoff, Simon 170
Lau, Kevin 452
Le, Anh 170
Lee, Changmin 201
Lee, Hyung Kyu 275
Lee, Jiyeon 275
Lee, Suk Kyu 275
Li, Li Erran 413
Li, Mo 53, 291, 500
Li, Tianxing 331
Li, Xiangyang 487
Li, Xiang-Yang 372
Li, Zhenjiang 53, 291
Liao, Yong 439
Lin, Qiongzheng 487
Ling, Kang 65
Liu, Alex X. 65, 90
Liu, Chen 221, 242
Liu, Jian 142
Liu, Kebin 372
Liu, Tianci 487
Liu, Xudong 272
Liu, Xue 552
Liu, Yanhe 182
Liu, Yunhao 372, 487
Liu, Yunxin 14, 27, 185
Lu, Bingxian 284
Lu, Sanglu 65
Madhyastha, Harsha V. 604
Mainland, Geoffrey 210
Maity, Mukulika 196
Mäkeläinen, Marko 188
Manweiler, Justin 260
Mao, Z. Morley 439, 452
Markopoulou, Athina 170
Marlin, Benjamin M. 400
Masood, Wasif 204
Mayberry, Addison 400
Miao, Congcong 592
Mikhaylov, Konstantin 188
Mineraud, Julien 239
Müller, Sabrina 248
Nguyen, Binh 464, 266
Nie, Weike 221
Nikaein, Navid 193
Noël, Thomas 207
Nussbaum, Dominique 193
Ou, Jiajue 500
Paatelma, Anton 188
Palazzi, Claudio Enrico 212
Papadopoulos, Georgios Z. 207
Pau, Giovanni 173, 257
Peck, Brian 284
Perreault, David 2
Pesavento, Davide 173
Petäjäjärvi, Juha 188
Pfeiffer, Tobias 550
Pichon, Dominique 193
Pissard-Gibollet, Roger 176
Pozza, Matteo 212
Puccinelli, Daniele 215
Qi, Bozhao 358
Qiao, Daji 269, 284
Qiao, Yue 566
Radunović, Božidar 210
Rahman, Mohammed Yasin 199
Raman, Bhaskaran 196
Rangarajan, Sampath 304
Ranjan, Gyan 439
Rodriguez, Pablo 550
Roy Choudhury, Romit 155, 260
Saarikoski, Kasperi 239
Sadasivam, Sreeram 248
Saint-Marcel, Frederic 176
Salthouse, Christopher 400
Sammarco, Matteo 257
Santos, Pedro M. 168
Sargento, Susana 168
Schatz, Raimund 263
Schiller, Eryk 193
Schmidt, Jorge F. 204
Schreiner, Guillaume 176, 207
Schröder, Yannic 224
Scognamiglio, Ciro 199
Sen, Souvik 77
Seufert, Michael 263
Shafagh, Hossein 251
Shahzad, Muhammad 65, 90
Shepard, Clayton 578
Shi, Lixin 2
Shin, Insik 14
Shin, Kang G. 512, 525
Shu, Yuanchao 512
Shuba, Anastasia 170
Silva, João Nuno 245
Singh, Shailendra 604
Smith-Freedman, Duncan 400
Sontinei, Kranthi 452
Srinivasan, Kannan 566
Srivastava, Mani 386
Srivastava, Rachit 196
Stewart, Gordon 210
Stoner, Theodore 477
Sun, Hailong 272
Sun, Li 77
Sundaresan, Karthikeyan .. 304, 537
Sur, Sanjib 281
Tabor, Joshua 345
Tang, Zhany 221
Tang, Zhanyong 242, 287

Tarkoma, Sasu 182, 236, 239
Tian, Zhao 278, 331
Tongaonkar, Alok 439
Tran-Gia, Phuoc 263
Tun, Yamin 400
Tung, Yu-Chih 525
Van der Merwe, Jacobus 464
Vandaele, Julien 176
Vannithamby, Rath 40
Varmarken, Janus 170
Viswanathan, Harish 550
von Zengen, Georg 224
Vu, Tam 266
Vutukuru, Mythili 196
Vytiniotis, Dimitrios 210
Wamser, Florian 263
Wang, He 155
Wang, Jia 550
Wang, Ju 221, 242
Wang, Lei 269, 284
Wang, Qing 180
Wang, Shu 130
Wang, Wei 65, 90
Wang, Xin 592
Wang, Yan 142
Wang, Yu 372
Wanner, Lucas 386
Wei, Teng 117, 130
Wei, Xuetao 477
Wolf, Lars 224
Wymore, Mathew L. 269
Xie, Xiufeng 304, 413
Xie, Yaxiong 53, 291
Xing, Tianzhang 242
Xiong, Jie 537
Yan, He 464
Yang, Jie 142
Yang, Lei 487
Yang, Yaling 218
Yang, Zhe 287
Yao, Hongyi 439
Yates, Jennifer 464
Yilmaz, H. Birkan 201
Yin, Shengrong 180
Yoo, Seungho 275
Yoon, Alex 452
Zang, Hui 550
Zeng, Kexiong (Curtis) 218
Zeng, Zhicheng 284
Zhang, Chi 345
Zhang, Jialiang 345
Zhang, Lan 372
Zhang, Ouyang 566
Zhang, Tan 426
Zhang, Xinyu 117, 130, 266, 281, 304, 345, 413
Zhao, Ben Y. 103
Zhao, Feng 14
Zheng, Changxi 227
Zheng, Haitao 103
Zheng, Xueshu 269
Zheng, Yuanqing 500
Zhong, Lin 578
Zhou, Anfu 130
Zhou, Hucheng 27, 185
Zhou, Xia 227, 278, 331
Zhu, Yanzi 103
Zhu, Yibo 103

www.ingramcontent.com/pod-product-compliance
Ingram Content Group UK Ltd.
Pitfield, Milton Keynes, MK11 3LW, UK
UKHW051417290926
15471UKWH00009B/1658